THE
WESTERN
FELLS

A PICTORIAL GUIDE TO THE LAKELAND FELLS

50TH ANNIVERSARY EDITION

being an illustrated account
of a study and exploration
of the mountains in the
English Lake District
by
A Wainwright

BOOK SEVEN
THE WESTERN FELLS

Frances Lincoln Limited
4 Torriano Mews
Torriano Avenue
London NW5 2RZ
www.franceslincoln.com

Originally published by
Westmorland Gazette, Kendal, 1966

First published by Frances Lincoln 2003

50th Anniversary Edition with re-originated artwork
published by Frances Lincoln 2005

Copyright © The Estate of A. Wainwright 1966

All rights reserved. Without limiting the rights under
copyright reserved above, no part of this publication may
be reproduced, stored in or introduced into a retrieval
system, or transmitted, in any form or by any means
(electronic, mechanical, photocopying, or otherwise),
without either prior permission in writing from the
publisher or a licence permitting restricted copying.
In the United Kingdom such licences are issued by
the Copyright Licensing Agency, Saffron House,
6-10 Kirby Street, London EC1N 8TS.

Printed and bound in China

A CIP catalogue record for this book
is available from the British Library.

ISBN 978 0 7112 2460 5

18 17 16 15 14 13 12

50TH ANNIVERSARY EDITION
PUBLISHED BY
FRANCES LINCOLN, LONDON

THE PICTORIAL GUIDES

Book One: The Eastern Fells, 1955
Book Two: The Far Eastern Fells, 1957
Book Three: The Central Fells, 1958
Book Four: The Southern Fells, 1960
Book Five: The Northern Fells, 1962
Book Six: The North Western Fells, 1964
Book Seven: The Western Fells, 1966

PUBLISHER'S NOTE

This 50th Anniversary edition of the Pictorial Guides to the Lakeland Fells is newly reproduced from the handwritten pages created in the 1950s and 1960s by A. Wainwright. The descriptions of the walks were correct, to the best of the author's knowledge, at the time of first publication and they are reproduced here without amendment. However, footpaths, cairns and other waymarks described here are no longer all as they were fifty years ago and walkers are advised to check with an up-to-date map when planning a walk.

Fellwalking has increased dramatically since the Pictorial Guides were first published. Some popular routes have become eroded, making good footwear and great care all the more necessary for walkers. The vital points about fellwalking, as A. Wainwright himself wrote on many occasions, are to use common sense and to remember to watch where you are putting your feet.

A programme of revision of the Pictorial Guides is under way and revised editions of each of them will be published over the next few years.

BOOK SEVEN
is dedicated to
ALL WHO HAVE HELPED ME

sometimes with advice, sometimes with information, sometimes with no more than a friendly nod or smile. They are too many to be named, and indeed some are unknown, anonymous fellow-walkers who pass the time of day and are gone. I must, however, thank my wife, for not standing in my way, and a few special friends who would not ask for identification here, for making the way easier for me to travel. It has been a long and lonely way, but I have trodden it increasingly aware of the goodwill and encouragement of many kind people, most of whom I shall never meet. And now, after thirteen years, I have come to the end of it and my final task, a difficult one, is to find words adequate to express my appreciation to everybody who has helped. The least I can do, and the most I can do, is to acknowledge my debt by this dedication.

Wasdale Head

INTRODUCTION

Classification and Definition

Any division of the Lakeland fells into geographical districts must necessarily be arbitrary, just as the location of the outer boundaries of Lakeland must always be a matter of opinion. Any attempt to define internal or external boundaries is certain to invite criticism, and he who takes it upon himself to say where Lakeland starts and finishes, or, for example, where the Central Fells merge into the Southern Fells and *which* fells *are* the Central Fells and which the Southern and *why* they need be so classified, must not expect his pronouncements to be generally accepted.

Yet for present purposes some plan of classification and definition must be used. County and parochial boundaries are no help, nor is the recently-defined area of the Lakeland National Park, for this book is concerned only with the high ground.

First, the external boundaries. Straight lines linking the extremities of the outlying lakes enclose all the higher fells very conveniently. There are a few fells of lesser height to the north and east, however, that are typically Lakeland in character and cannot properly be omitted: these are brought in, somewhat untidily, by extending the lines in those areas. Thus:

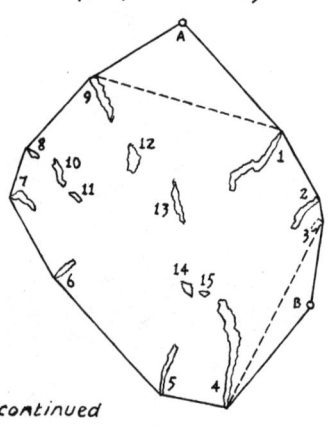

1 : *Ullswater*
2 : *Hawes Water*
3 : proposed *Swindale Res.*
4 : *Windermere*
5 : *Coniston Water*
6 : *Wast Water*
7 : *Ennerdale Water*
8 : *Loweswater*
9 : *Bassenthwaite Lake*
10 : *Crummock Water*
11 : *Buttermere*
12 : *Derwent Water*
13 : *Thirlmere*
14 : *Grasmere*
15 : *Rydal Water*
A : *Caldbeck*
B : *Longsleddale* (church)

continued

INTRODUCTION

Classification and Definition

continued
    The complete Guide is planned to include all the fells in the area enclosed by the straight lines of the diagram. This is an undertaking quite beyond the compass of a single volume, and it is necessary, therefore, to divide the area into convenient sections, making the fullest use of natural boundaries (lakes, valleys and low passes) so that each district is, as far as possible, self-contained and independent of the rest.

This division gives seven areas, each with a well-defined group of fells, and each will be the subject of a separate volume

1 : The Eastern Fells
2 : The Far Eastern Fells
3 : The Central Fells
4 : The Southern Fells
5 : The Northern Fells
6 : The North-western Fells
7 : The Western Fells

INTRODUCTION

Notes on the Illustrations

THE MAPS............... Many excellent books have been written about Lakeland, but the best literature of all for the walker is that published by the Director General of Ordnance Survey, the 1" map for companionship and guidance on expeditions, the 2½" map for exploration both on the fells and by the fireside. These admirable maps are remarkably accurate topographically but there is a crying need for a revision of the paths on the hills: several walkers' tracks that have come into use during the past few decades, some of them now broad highways, are not shown at all; other paths still shown on the maps have fallen into neglect and can no longer be traced on the ground.

The popular Bartholomew 1" map is a beautiful picture, fit for a frame, but this too is unreliable for paths; indeed here the defect is much more serious, for routes are indicated where no paths ever existed, nor ever could — the cartographer has preferred to take precipices in his stride rather than deflect his graceful curves over easy ground.

Hence the justification for the maps in this book: they have the one merit (of importance to walkers) of being dependable as regards delineation of *paths*. They are intended as supplements to the Ordnance Survey maps, certainly not as substitutes.

THE VIEWS............... Various devices have been used to illustrate the views from the summits of the fells. The full panorama in the form of an outline drawing is most satisfactory generally, and this method has been adopted for the main viewpoints.

THE DIAGRAMS OF ASCENTS............... The routes of ascent of the higher fells are depicted by diagrams that do not pretend to strict accuracy: they are neither plans nor elevations; in fact there is deliberate distortion in order to show detail clearly: usually they are represented as viewed from imaginary 'space-stations.' But it is hoped they will be useful and interesting.

THE DRAWINGS....... The drawings at least are honest attempts to reproduce what the eye sees: they illustrate features of interest and also serve the dual purpose of breaking up the text and balancing the layout of the pages, and of filling up awkward blank spaces, like this:

Thirlmere

THE
WESTERN
FELLS

If Lakeland can be thought of as being circular in plan, the Western Fells may be described as being contained within a wide sector, the apex driving deep into the heart of the district at Sty Head and the boundaries running therefrom northwest along the valley of the Cocker, jewelled by the lovely lakes of Buttermere and Crummock Water, and southwest along Wasdale towards the sea.

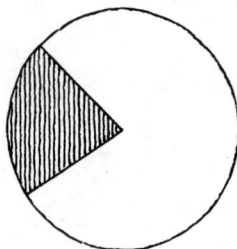

If Lakeland can be thought of as a wheel, the Western Fells may be likened, simply yet appropriately, to two spokes (the Pillar and High Stile ranges) radiating from a central hub (Great Gable), with Ennerdale between the spokes and the two valleys of the Cocker and Wasdale bordering them.

In this area is a wide diversity of scenery. The section nearest to and including the hub is entirely mountainous, crowded with fine peaks although none quite attain 3000 feet. Here is the hoary old favourite, Great Gable, and the magnificent Pillar, the fascinating Haystacks and the exhilarating spine of the High Stile ridge: a rugged territory of volcanic rock and syenite. Further west the slopes are smooth and rounded, characteristic of the underlying slate; towards the arc of the circle they decline into low grassy foothills and rolling sheep pastures, a splendid walking country but comparatively unexciting and unfrequented.

Valley and lake scenery is of the very best vintage, excepting Ennerdale, where natural beauty has been sacrificed to material gain, an irretrievable mistake. There is water extraction from some of the lakes, a process carried out by the responsible authorities unobtrusively and with due regard to amenities.

There are no centres of population within the area, and only hamlets and small villages around the perimeter; most of them cater for visitors but accommodation is necessarily restricted.

Buttermere and Wasdale Head in particular are popular resorts.

The Western Boundary

The western boundary of the area described in this book is fairly well defined by the fells themselves, although lesser hills continue into the industrial belt of West Cumberland. This arbitrary boundary coincides, in places, with that of the Lake District National Park but is generally within it.

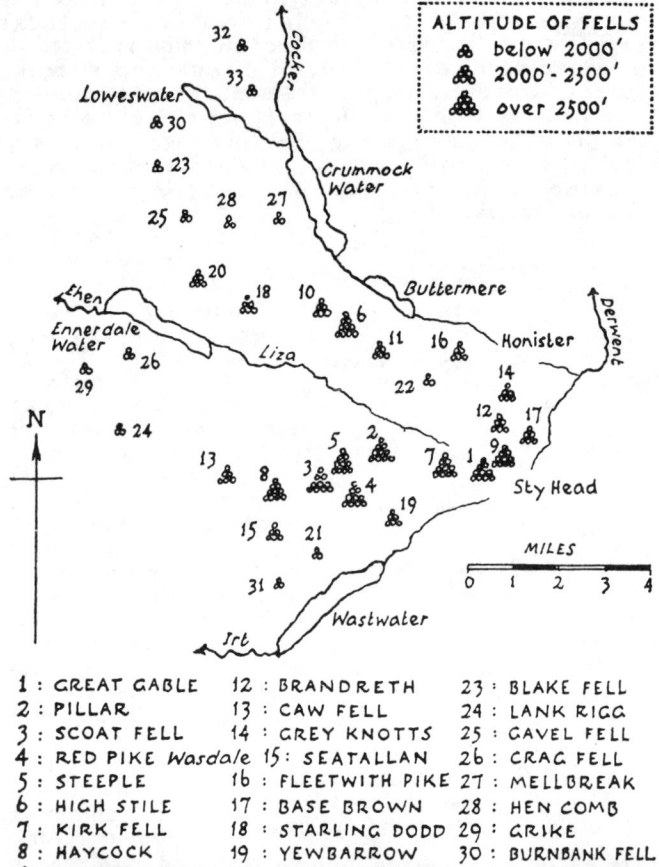

THE WESTERN FELLS

Reference to map opposite

in the order of their appearance in this book

over 2500' / 2000-2500' / below 2000'			Altitude in feet
17	..	BASE BROWN	.. 2120
23	..	BLAKE FELL	.. 1878
12	..	BRANDRETH	.. 2344
31	..	BUCKBARROW	.. 1410
30	..	BURNBANK FELL	.. 1580
13	..	CAW FELL	.. 2288
26	..	CRAG FELL	.. 1710
32	..	FELLBARROW	.. 1363
16	..	FLEETWITH PIKE	.. 2126
25	..	GAVEL FELL	.. 1720
20	..	GREAT BORNE	.. 2019
1	..	GREAT GABLE	.. 2949
9	..	GREEN GABLE	.. 2603
14	..	GREY KNOTTS	.. 2287
29	..	GRIKE	.. 1596
8	..	HAYCOCK	.. 2618
22	..	HAYSTACKS	.. 1900
28	..	HEN COMB	.. 1661
11	..	HIGH CRAG	.. 2443
6	..	HIGH STILE	.. 2644
7	..	KIRK FELL	.. 2630
24	..	LANK RIGG	.. 1775
33	..	LOW FELL	.. 1360
27	..	MELLBREAK	.. 1676
21	..	MIDDLE FELL	.. 1908
2	..	PILLAR	.. 2927
10	..	RED PIKE Buttermere	.. 2479
4	..	RED PIKE Wasdale	.. 2707
3	..	SCOAT FELL	.. 2760
15	..	SEATALLAN	.. 2266
18	..	STARLING DODD	.. 2085
5	..	STEEPLE	.. 2687
19	..	YEWBARROW	.. 2058

9 11 13
33

Each fell is the subject of a separate chapter

Base Brown 2120'

from the Borrowdale Yews

Base Brown 2

NATURAL FEATURES

Base Brown marks the end of roads and farmsteads, of woods and green pastures, as one proceeds into the upper recesses of Borrowdale. It marks the beginning of wildness and desolation. It is the first of the rough and rugged heights extending to and around Wasdale, and introduces its hinterland excellently, being itself of striking appearance, gaunt, steep-sided, a pyramid of tumbled boulders and scree, a desert abandoned to nature. It is a cornerstone, walkers' paths to Sty Head curving around its base below sixteen hundred feet of chaotic fellside scarred by gully and crag and strewn with the natural debris of ages; a stark declivity. The opposite slope, although also rimmed and pitted with rocks, is much shorter, being halted by the hanging glacial valley of Gillercomb. Only along the narrow crest of the fell are walkers likely to venture, and but rarely even here, for the ridge rising from Borrowdale is defended by bristly crags; the continuation beyond the summit, however, to a grassy neck of land linking with Green Gable and overlooking Sty Head on one side and Gillercomb on the other, is much easier, and a new popular path (Seathwaite direct to Great Gable) comes into the scene at this point. Base Brown belongs to Borrowdale exclusively, and its streams, attractively broken by waterfalls and cascades, feed the youthful Derwent only.

Taylorgill Force

Sour Milk Gill

Base Brown 3

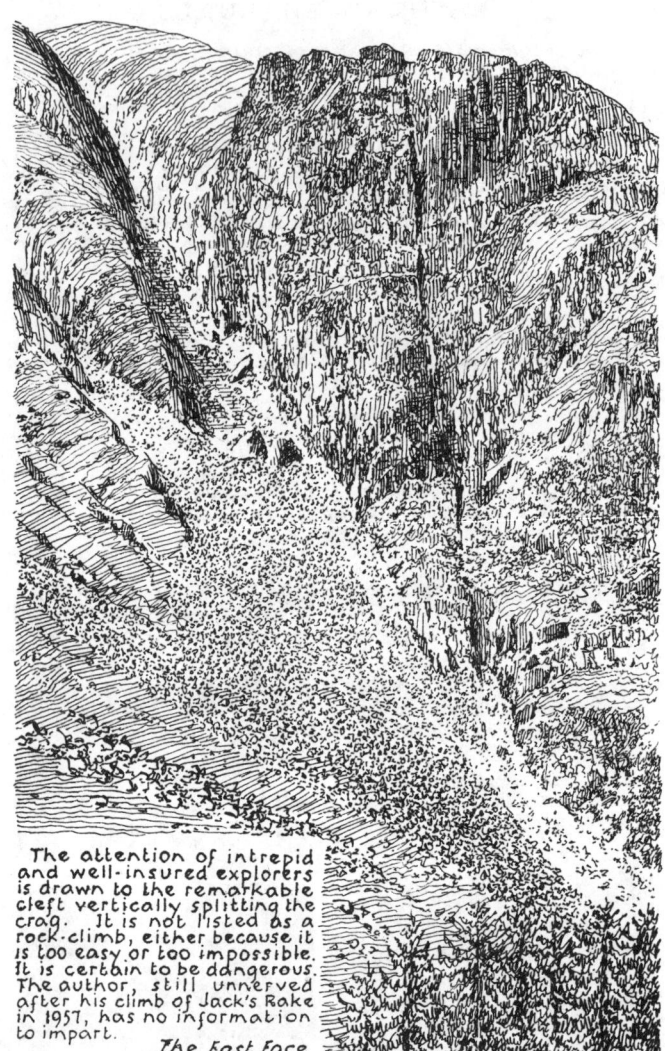

The attention of intrepid and well-insured explorers is drawn to the remarkable cleft vertically splitting the crag. It is not listed as a rock-climb, either because it is too easy or too impossible. It is certain to be dangerous. The author, still unnerved after his climb of Jack's Rake in 1957, has no information to impart.

The East Face above Taylor Gill

Base Brown 4

Hanging Stone

The Hanging Stone is repeatedly featured conspicuously in successive editions of the Ordnance Survey maps, where its name is given as much prominence as that of the fell itself, although its precise location is never pinpointed. The Stone occupies a startling position balanced on the rim of a crag, apparently half its bulk being unsupported and overhanging the void, but it is smaller than one is led to expect (a few tons only) and the special distinction given to it on the O.S. maps is not really merited.

looking steeply upwards

People with bad coughs should keep out of the line of fall

Sixty yards further up the ridge a large rounded boulder has come to rest on a number of small ones.

Fallen Stone

Immediately below the crag is a tremendous mass of rock that must at some time have fallen from it, although silting now gives it the appearance of a natural outcrop. It has been badly fractured in the fall, and identifiable fragments from it can be found lower down the slope.

Near the top end of the rock several large boulders have tumbled together, forming caves and foxholes.

Base Brown 5

MAP

The paths through Gillercomb and Taylor Gill are recognised by the Ordnance Survey for the first time in their 1963 Edition of the one-inch Tourist Map.

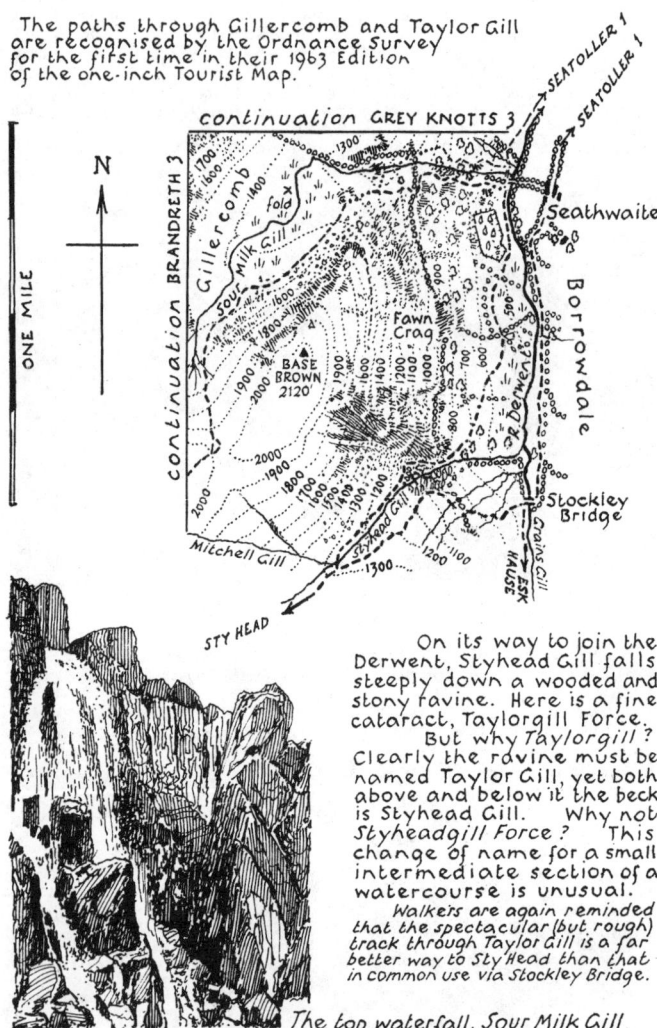

On its way to join the Derwent, Styhead Gill falls steeply down a wooded and stony ravine. Here is a fine cataract, Taylorgill Force.

But why *Taylorgill*? Clearly the ravine must be named Taylor Gill, yet both above and below it the beck is Styhead Gill. Why not *Styheadgill Force*? This change of name for a small intermediate section of a watercourse is unusual.

Walkers are again reminded that the spectacular (but rough) track through Taylor Gill is a far better way to Sty Head than that in common use via Stockley Bridge.

The top waterfall, Sour Milk Gill.

Base Brown 6

ASCENT FROM SEATHWAITE
1750 feet of ascent : 1½ miles

BASE BROWN

When the direct route comes fully into view its appearance is hostile. Those walkers who do not like the look of it may still reach the summit without trouble by continuing along the Green Gable path to the col at 2000 feet, an easy stroll on grass then leading to the top.

Gillercomb

× fold

Direct Route:
Leave the Green Gable path where it becomes quite level and turn left uphill past the big boulder to the base of the crag directly below the Hanging Stone. A distinct path here is followed round the corner to the left, where the top of the crag may be gained up a grass slope and the broken ridge ascended without difficulty.
Or continue further along the path, climbing a steep bilberry slope to the depression.

hurdle

R. Derwent

STOCKLEY BRIDGE ¾ — lane — ROAD — SEATOLLER 1¼

Seathwaite

Seathwaite Slabs —
a training ground for novice rockclimbers, conveniently sited five minutes from Seathwaite.

Start under the arch of the farm buildings. The footbridge over the Derwent was provided as a war memorial by the Ramblers Association.

There is a path on each side of Sour Milk Gill. The usual one is on the left and involves some simple rock-scrambling. The other path is easier, but calls for a fording of the stream, difficult if in spate: the best place is 50 yards above the cross-wall.

Base Brown 7

THE SUMMIT

The summit is out of character, being a broad grassy expanse with no suggestion of the rough craggy slopes that support it. A sprinkling of boulders and some low outcrops do their best to relieve the monotony.

DESCENTS: The eastern slope is excessively steep in all parts, and, above Taylor Gill, positively dangerous. The north-west side overlooking Gillercomb is precipitous.

For Borrowdale the easiest way off, and the best in mist, is to proceed down the gentle slope south-west, there joining the Green Gable - Seathwaite path as it turns to descend into Gillercomb. The direct route of ascent may be reversed in clear weather, but it is advisable NOT to persist in following the ridge to its extremity, which is a 40-foot vertical cliff; instead, turn to the right at the depression down a bilberry slope until a distinct horizontal path is reached (ignore two sheep-tracks crossed earlier) and go along this path, left, to the area of boulders below the 40-foot crag, where a way may be made downhill to the Green Gable - Seathwaite path clearly seen 200 yards below.

If Wasdale is the objective, get Styhead Tarn in view and make a beeline for it, crossing Mitchell Gill; an easy stroll.

RIDGE ROUTE

To GREEN GABLE, 2603': 1 mile: SW
Depression at 1990': 620 feet of ascent

Interest quickens as the walk proceeds. Soon after leaving the summit south-west the distinct path coming up from Gillercomb is seen in the depression ahead; this is joined and followed up the opposite slope, which becomes stony, to the main watershed and the broad path from Honister 300 yards short of the top of Green Gable.

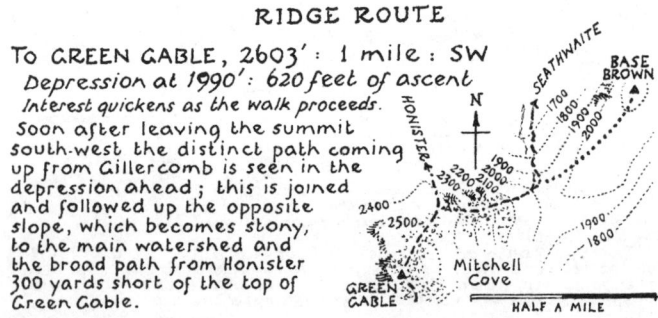

Base Brown 8

THE VIEW

Higher fells on three sides restrict the open view to the section between north and east, where the village of Rosthwaite and much of Borrowdale are also seen. South is the mountain wall of the Scafells in close detail. West, Pillar and Scoat Fell make an unexpected appearance over Gillercomb Head.

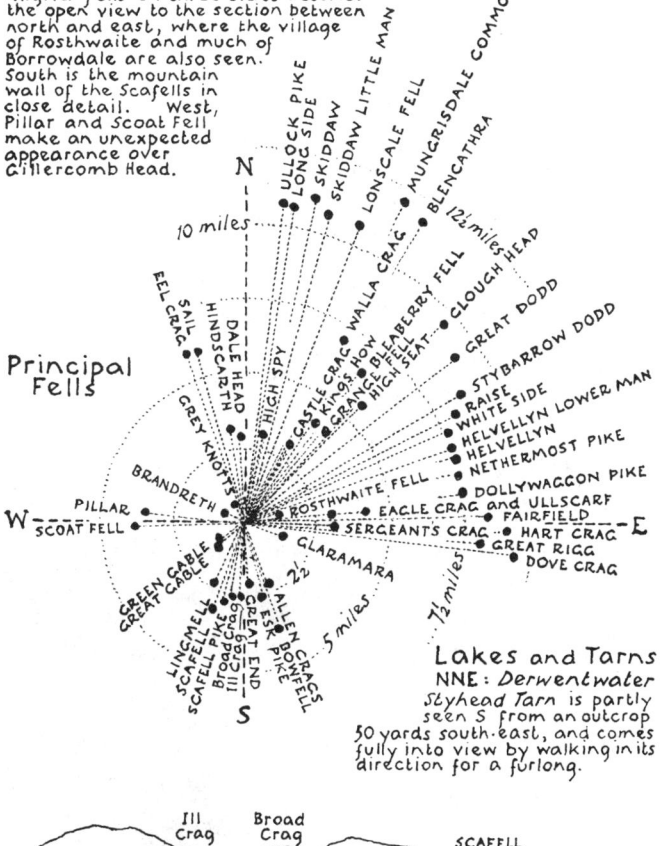

looking south

Lakes and Tarns

NNE: Derwentwater
Styhead Tarn is partly seen S from an outcrop 50 yards south-east, and comes fully into view by walking in its direction for a furlong.

In good lighting conditions this view south to the Scafells calls for a photograph, but before releasing the shutter walk towards the scene until Styhead Tarn appears fully in the middle distance and gives relief to the sombre background. Then do it.

Blake Fell 1878'

Blake Fell 2

NATURAL FEATURES

Blake Fell (locally known simply as Blake) is the highest of the Loweswater uplands, overtopping the others considerably and asserting this superiority by a distinctive final upthrust that makes it prominent in views of the group. A long high shoulder, Carling Knott, extends towards Loweswater, hiding the main summit from that valley, but on the opposite western flank, facing industrial Cumberland, a scree-covered declivity drops immediately from the summit-cairn to the hollow of Cogra Moss and encircling arms comprise many subsidiary tops, of which the chief is the shapely peak of Knock Murton. This side of the fell has for long been commissioned to the service of man : here, up to fifty years ago, were extensive iron-ore mines and a railway to serve them; Cogra Moss has been dammed to make a reservoir, and now the Forestry Commission have moved in and already planted the first trees in a project likely to alter the landscape completely. The fell, by reason of its fringe situation, gives the feeling of belonging more to West Cumberland than to the Lake District; more to Lamplugh, where everybody knows it, than to Loweswater, where Mellbreak is favourite. Its waters mainly feed the Derwent

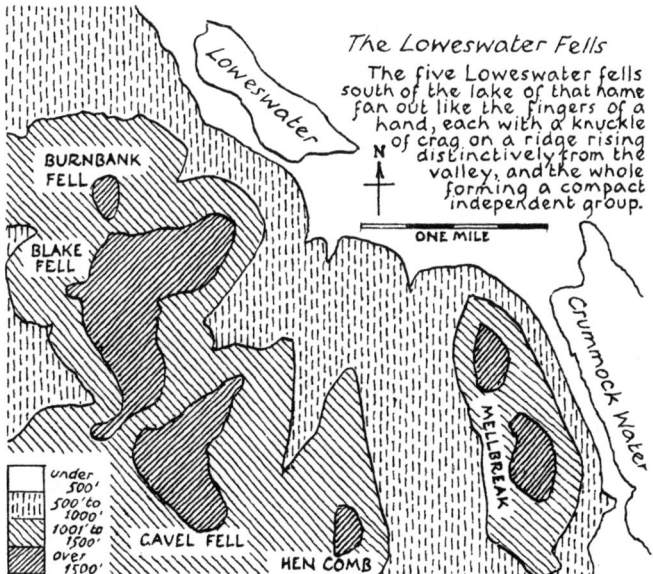

The Loweswater Fells

The five Loweswater fells south of the lake of that name fan out like the fingers of a hand, each with a knuckle of crag on a ridge rising distinctively from the valley, and the whole forming a compact independent group.

Blake Fell 3

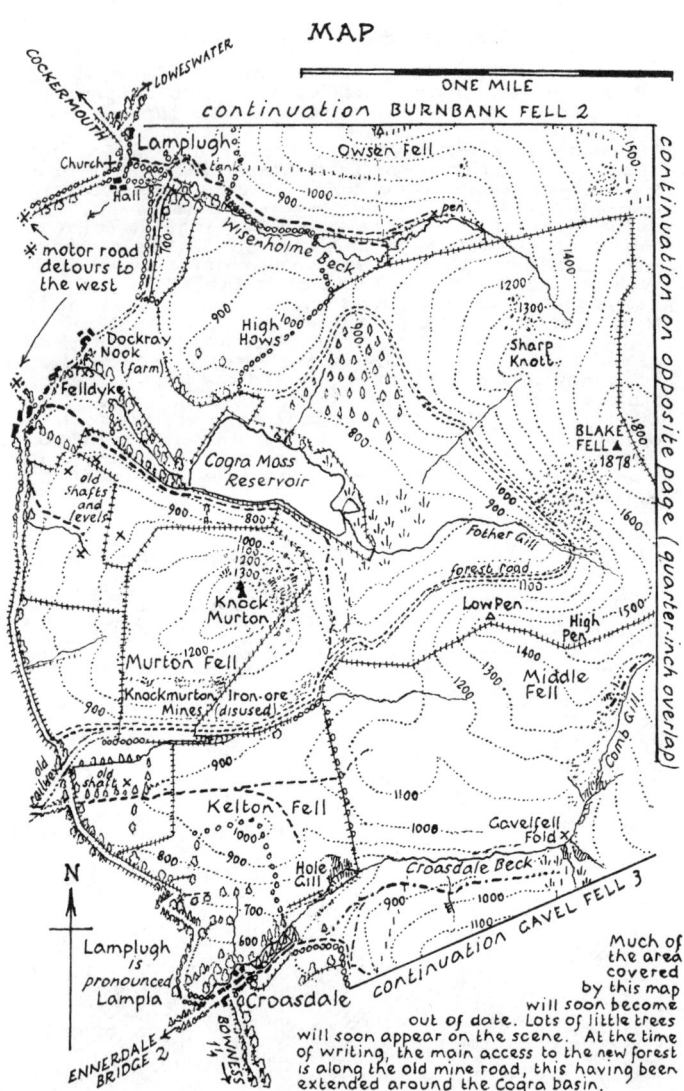

Blake Fell 4

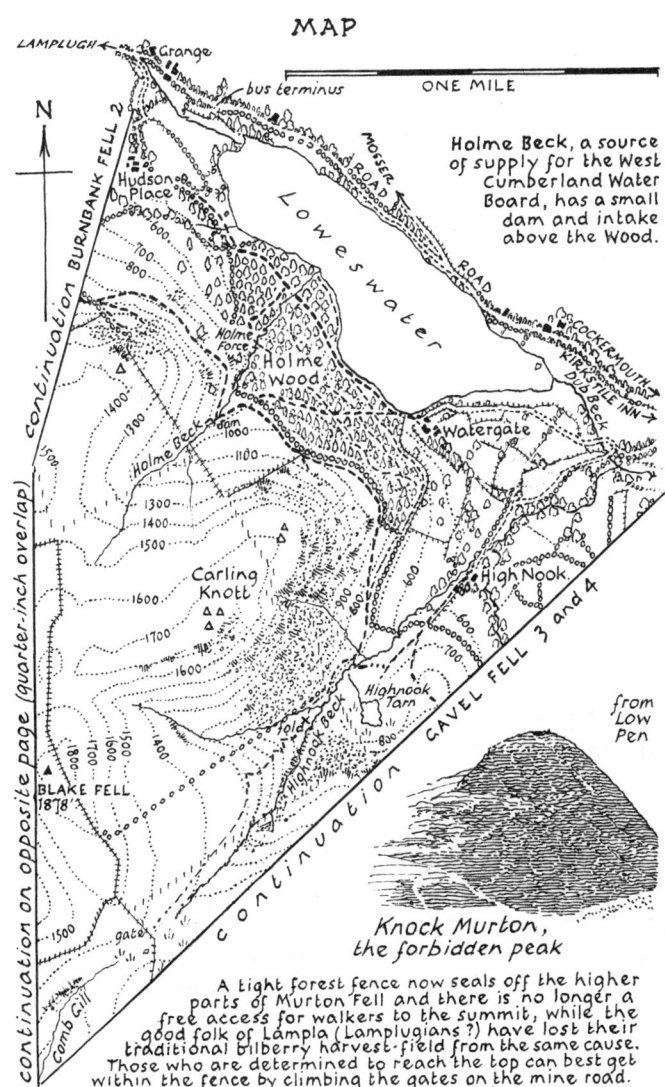

MAP

ONE MILE

Holme Beck, a source of supply for the West Cumberland Water Board, has a small dam and intake above the Wood.

Knock Murton, the forbidden peak

A tight forest fence now seals off the higher parts of Murton Fell and there is no longer a free access for walkers to the summit, while the good folk of Lampla (Lamplugians?) have lost their traditional bilberry harvest-field from the same cause. Those who are determined to reach the top can best get within the fence by climbing the gates on the mine road.

Blake Fell 5

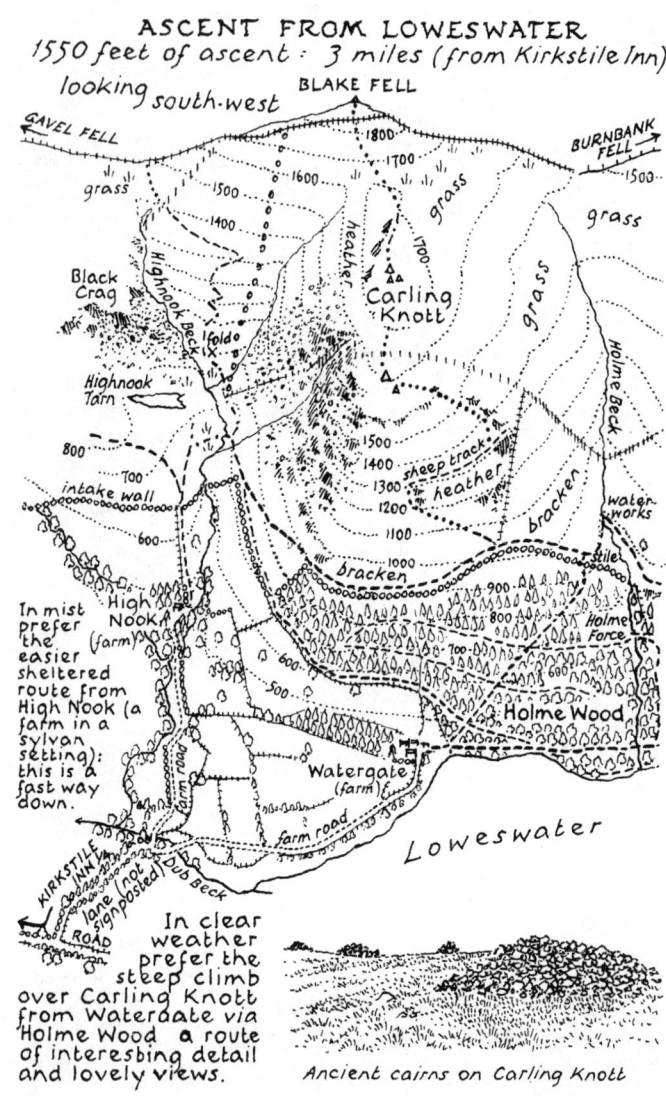

Ancient cairns on Carling Knott

Blake Fell 6

ASCENT FROM LAMPLUGH
1400 feet of ascent : 3¼ miles

looking east-south-east

A: road to LOWESWATER
B: road to COCKERMOUTH

From the west the approach by Cogra Moss has always been the best, even in the days of unimpeded access, and at present it is not only still the best but the only route provided with a stile in the new forest fence.

At the head of the reservoir turn up by a thin track to the col; then follow the fence along the ridge around the hollow to the summit.

A road to service the forest-to-be has already been cut, and planting on the fellsides has commenced. In a few years' time the scenery here will be changed drastically, and the ascent from the west will be mainly a forest walk.

At the col the route crosses the newly-made forest road coming up from the disused iron mine on the south side of Knock Murton. At present, this is the only access for vehicles into the new forest. It is not available to private cars.

The reservoir is not a natural lake, having been formed by damming the outflow from Cogra Moss, once a marsh.

Starting from Lamplugh Church, there is obviously a more direct way along the valley of Wisenholme Beck, but even if a walkers' route is permitted there the Cogra Moss approach should be chosen for its greater interest.

Reach Felldyke from Lamplugh via the back lane passing Dockray Nook.

Blake Fell 7

THE SUMMIT

The summit is well defined by rising ground on all sides, and the large cairn merely emphasises the obvious. It is a fine airy place, overtopping everything around: the highest point of the Loweswater fells.

But a great humiliation has recently befallen it. It stands no less proudly, but man has seen fit to place a shackle around it, a shackle in the shape of a new unclimbable wire-mesh fence, denying to sheep their inherited right to graze the sweet grasses amongst the stones, and denying to fellwalkers their inherited right to visit the cairn. The fence marks the boundaries of the land newly-acquired by the Forestry Commission, but was it really necessary to indicate ownership with such precision? Nobody is likely to question the title deeds, and surely it is not intended to plant trees right over the summit, 1800 feet up and fully exposed to western gales? Could not the higher parts of the fell have been left with free access? If not, if possession must be demonstrated so visibly on the ground, could not the fence have been provided with simple stepstiles — two are needed, one to link with Carling Knott, the other with Gavel Fell. Dammit, if a man wants to climb a hill, any hill, he should be allowed to do so without being forced to commit a trespass. Why make the innocent feel guilty?

DESCENTS: For Lamplugh, reverse the line of ascent via Cogra Moss, keeping within the fence. For Loweswater, it is first necessary to climb the unclimbable fence (it is easier to do this when reaching it from above than from below); then follow the ridge over Carling Knott in clear weather, or, in mist, go down the easy tongue west of Highnook Beck.

Summit cairns on Knock Murton

Blake Fell 8

THE VIEW

The view inland, comprising a splendid array of mountains, is excellent; seawards, it extends uninterrupted far across West Cumberland to the Scottish hills.

Principal Fells

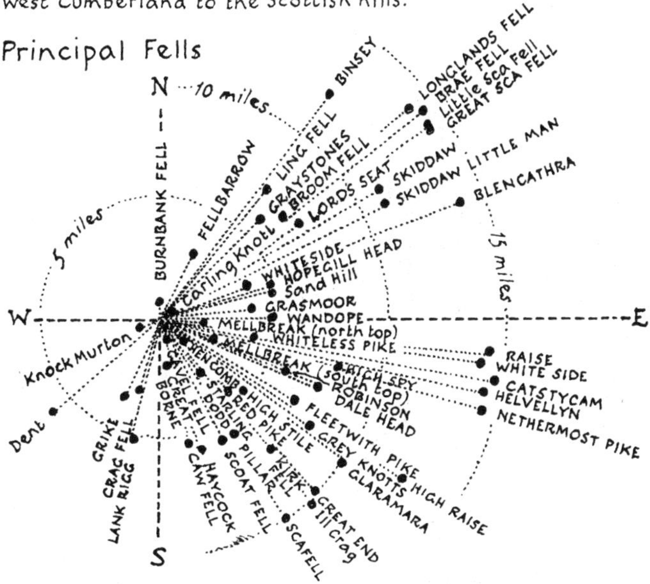

Fells visible (clockwise from N): BINSEY, LONGLANDS FELL, BRAE FELL, Little Sca Fell, GREAT SCA FELL, LING FELL, GRAYSTONES, BROOM FELL, LORDS SEAT, SKIDDAW, SKIDDAW LITTLE MAN, BLENCATHRA, FELLBARROW, Darling Knott, WHITESIDE, HOPEGILL HEAD, Sand Hill, GRASMOOR, WANDOPE, MELLBREAK (north top), WHITELESS PIKE, RAISE, WHITE SIDE, CATSTYCAM, HELVELLYN, NETHERMOST PIKE, MELLBREAK (south top), HIGH STILE, ROBINSON, DALE HEAD, FLEETWITH PIKE, GREY KNOTTS, HIGH RAISE, GREAT END, Ill Crag, SCAFELL, GREAT GABLE, KIRK FELL, PILLAR, SCOAT FELL, HAYCOCK, CAW FELL, CRAG FELL, LANK RIGG, GRIKE, BURNBANK FELL, Knock Murton, Dent.

N — 10 miles; 5 miles; 15 miles

Lakes and Tarns

E : Crummock Water
SE : Buttermere
SSW : Ennerdale Water
SW : Meadley Reservoir
W : Cogra Moss Reservoir
NW : Mockerkin Tarn

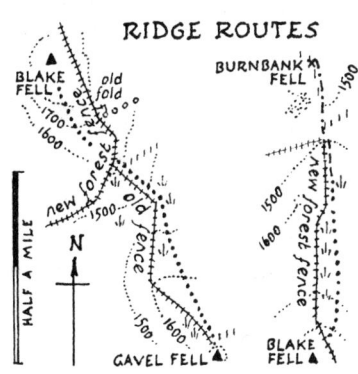

RIDGE ROUTES

TO GAVEL FELL, 1720':
1 mile : SSE
Depression at 1465'
270 feet of ascent

TO BURNBANK FELL, 1580':
1 mile : N, then NNW
Depression at 1470'
150 feet of ascent

On both routes the only difficulty is the new fence.

Brandreth 2344'

from Base Brown

- Gatesgarth
  Honister Pass

Black Sail
• Y.H. ▲ GREY KNOTTS
BRANDRETH ▲ • Seathwaite

▲ GREEN GABLE
▲ GREAT GABLE

MILES
0   1   2   3

Brandreth 2

NATURAL FEATURES

Brandreth is an intermediate height on the broad tilted ridge, almost a tableland, rising gently from the back of Honister Crag and culminating in Great Gable. Its summit is little higher than the general level of the plateau and has nothing of particular interest; indeed, the path along the ridge takes a wide sweep to avoid it, preferring to maintain an easy contour rather than go up-and-down over the top. Brandreth's one claim to distinction is based on its superb view of the High Stile range flanked by the valleys of Ennerdale and Buttermere, a magnificent prospect; but this is a view as well seen from the west slope, around which the path curves, as from the top. This western slope is broad and sprawling, part of it declining to Ennerdale and part re-shaping into the undulating summit of Haystacks; in sharp contrast, the eastern is abruptly cut away in cliffs falling into the great upland basin of Gillercomb. On this side any attempt to determine the boundaries separating this and the adjoining fells of Grey Knotts and Green Gable must be purely arbitrary, the long craggy wall of Gillercomb Head extending the length of all three, but without any dividing watercourses; an unusual arrangement.

Of the fells on this watershed between Windy Gap and Honister, Brandreth is geographically the most important, being the only one to feed three distinct river systems — Derwent, Liza and Cocker.

The Honister-Windy Gap watershed

1: GREY KNOTTS
2: BRANDRETH
3: GREEN GABLE

looking south

Brandreth 3

MAP

The map is extended to the north to include the old quarry tramway, by which the approach from Honister Pass or Gatesgarth is usually made.

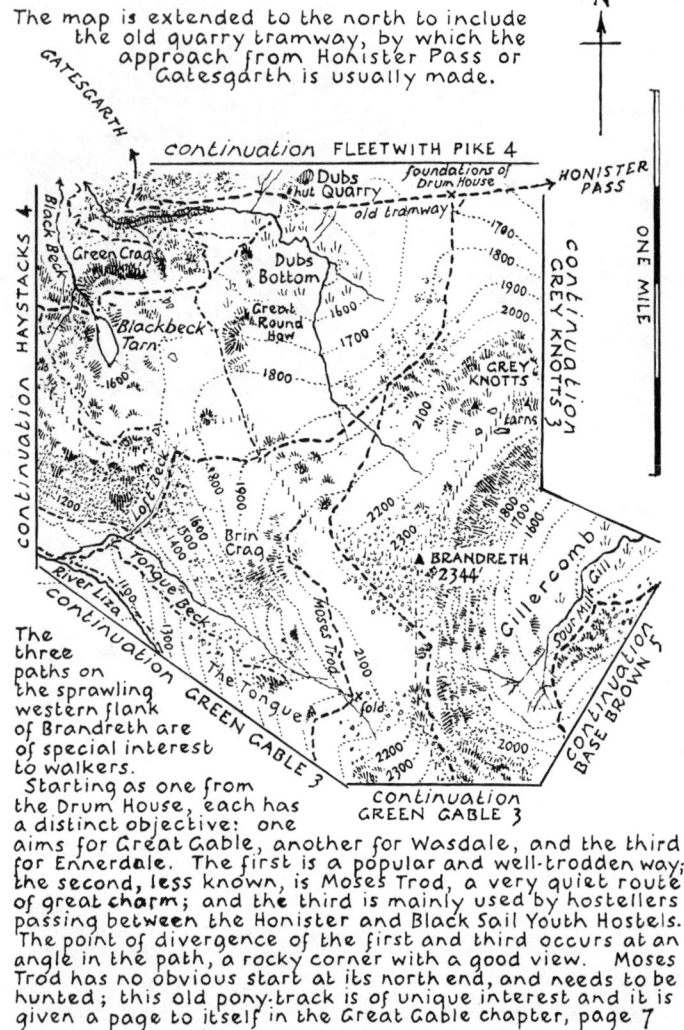

The three paths on the sprawling western flank of Brandreth are of special interest to walkers.

Starting as one from the Drum House, each has a distinct objective: one aims for Great Gable, another for Wasdale, and the third for Ennerdale. The first is a popular and well-trodden way; the second, less known, is Moses Trod, a very quiet route of great charm; and the third is mainly used by hostellers passing between the Honister and Black Sail Youth Hostels. The point of divergence of the first and third occurs at an angle in the path, a rocky corner with a good view. Moses Trod has no obvious start at its north end, and needs to be hunted; this old pony-track is of unique interest and it is given a page to itself in the Great Gable chapter, page 7

Brandreth 4

ASCENT FROM HONISTER PASS
1150 feet of ascent : 2 miles

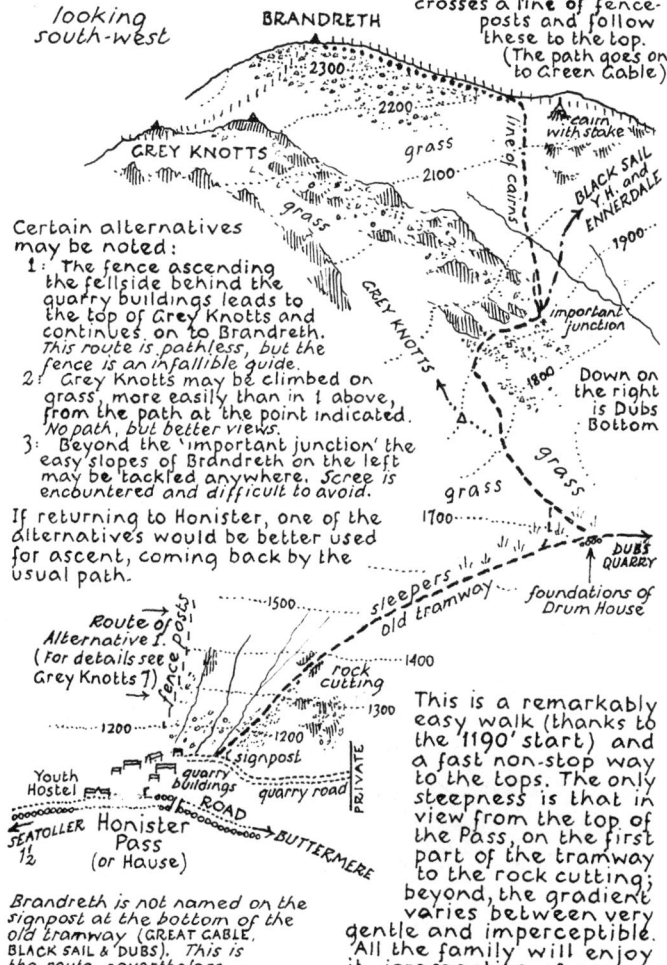

looking south-west

BRANDRETH

Leave the path where it crosses a line of fence-posts and follow these to the top. (The path goes on to Green Gable)

GREY KNOTTS

line of cairns

cairn with stake

grass

BLACK SAIL Y.H. and ENNERDALE

grass

GREY KNOTTS

important junction

Down on the right is Dubs Bottom

Certain alternatives may be noted:
1: The fence ascending the fellside behind the quarry buildings leads to the top of Grey Knotts and continues on to Brandreth. *This route is pathless, but the fence is an infallible guide.*
2: Grey Knotts may be climbed on grass, more easily than in 1 above, from the path at the point indicated. *No path, but better views.*
3: Beyond the 'important junction' the easy slopes of Brandreth on the left may be tackled anywhere. *Scree is encountered and difficult to avoid.*

If returning to Honister, one of the alternatives would be better used for ascent, coming back by the usual path.

grass

DUBS QUARRY

sleepers old tramway

foundations of Drum House

Route of Alternative 1. (For details see Grey Knotts 7)

fence posts

rock cutting

Youth Hostel

quarry buildings

signpost

quarry road

PRIVATE

SEATOLLER 1½

Honister Pass (or Hause)

ROAD → BUTTERMERE

Brandreth is not named on the signpost at the bottom of the old tramway (GREAT GABLE, BLACK SAIL & DUBS). This is the route, nevertheless.

This is a remarkably easy walk (thanks to the '1190' start) and a fast non-stop way to the tops. The only steepness is that in view from the top of the Pass, on the first part of the tramway to the rock cutting; beyond, the gradient varies between very gentle and imperceptible. All the family will enjoy it, irrespective of age.

Brandreth 5

ASCENT FROM GATESGARTH
2,000 feet of ascent : 3 miles

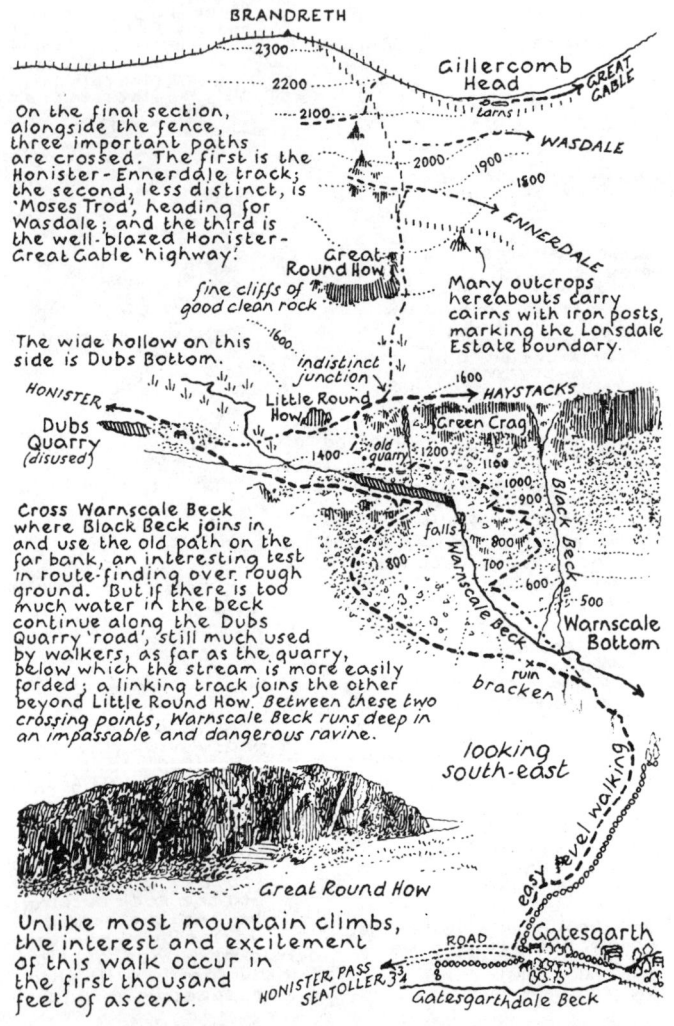

BRANDRETH — Gillercomb Head — GREAT GABLE — tarns — WASDALE — ENNERDALE

On the final section, alongside the fence, three important paths are crossed. The first is the Honister-Ennerdale track; the second, less distinct, is 'Moses Trod', heading for Wasdale; and the third is the well-blazed Honister-Great Gable 'highway'.

Great Round How — fine cliffs of good clean rock

Many outcrops hereabouts carry cairns with iron posts, marking the Lonsdale Estate boundary.

The wide hollow on this side is Dubs Bottom.

HONISTER — Dubs Quarry (disused) — indistinct junction — Little Round How — old quarry — HAYSTACKS — Green Crag — Black Beck — falls — Warnscale Beck — Warnscale Bottom — ruin — bracken

Cross Warnscale Beck where Black Beck joins in, and use the old path on the far bank, an interesting test in route-finding over rough ground. But if there is too much water in the beck continue along the Dubs Quarry 'road', still much used by walkers, as far as the quarry, below which the stream is more easily forded; a linking track joins the other beyond Little Round How. Between these two crossing points, Warnscale Beck runs deep in an impassable and dangerous ravine.

looking south-east

easy level walking

Great Round How

Unlike most mountain climbs, the interest and excitement of this walk occur in the first thousand feet of ascent.

ROAD — Gatesgarth — HONISTER PASS SEATOLLER 3½ — Gatesgarthdale Beck

Brandreth 6

ASCENT FROM ENNERDALE
(BLACK SAIL YOUTH HOSTEL)
1400 feet of ascent : 1¾ miles

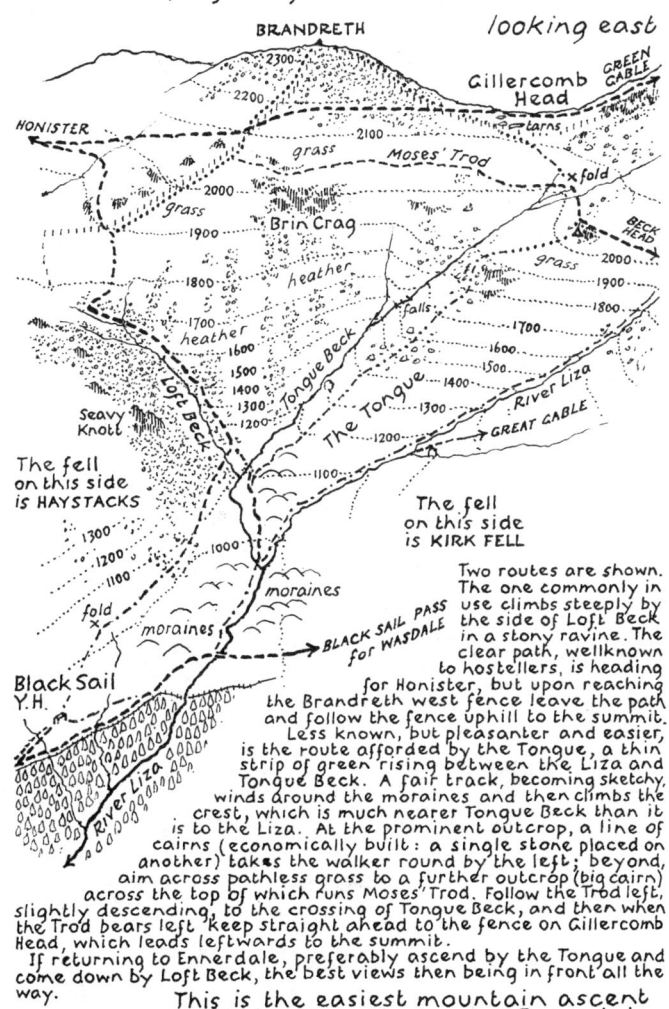

looking east

Two routes are shown. The one commonly in use climbs steeply by the side of Loft Beck in a stony ravine. The clear path, well known to hostellers, is heading for Honister, but upon reaching the Brandreth west fence leave the path and follow the fence uphill to the summit.

Less known, but pleasanter and easier, is the route afforded by the Tongue, a thin strip of green rising between the Liza and Tongue Beck. A fair track, becoming sketchy, winds around the moraines and then climbs the crest, which is much nearer Tongue Beck than it is to the Liza. At the prominent outcrop, a line of cairns (economically built : a single stone placed on another) takes the walker round by the left; beyond, aim across pathless grass to a further outcrop (big cairn) across the top of which runs Moses' Trod. Follow the Trod left, slightly descending, to the crossing of Tongue Beck, and then when the Trod bears left keep straight ahead to the fence on Gillercomb Head, which leads leftwards to the summit.

If returning to Ennerdale, preferably ascend by the Tongue and come down by Loft Beck, the best views then being in front all the way.

This is the easiest mountain ascent available from the head of Ennerdale

Brandreth 7

ASCENT FROM SEATHWAITE
2000 feet of ascent : 2 miles

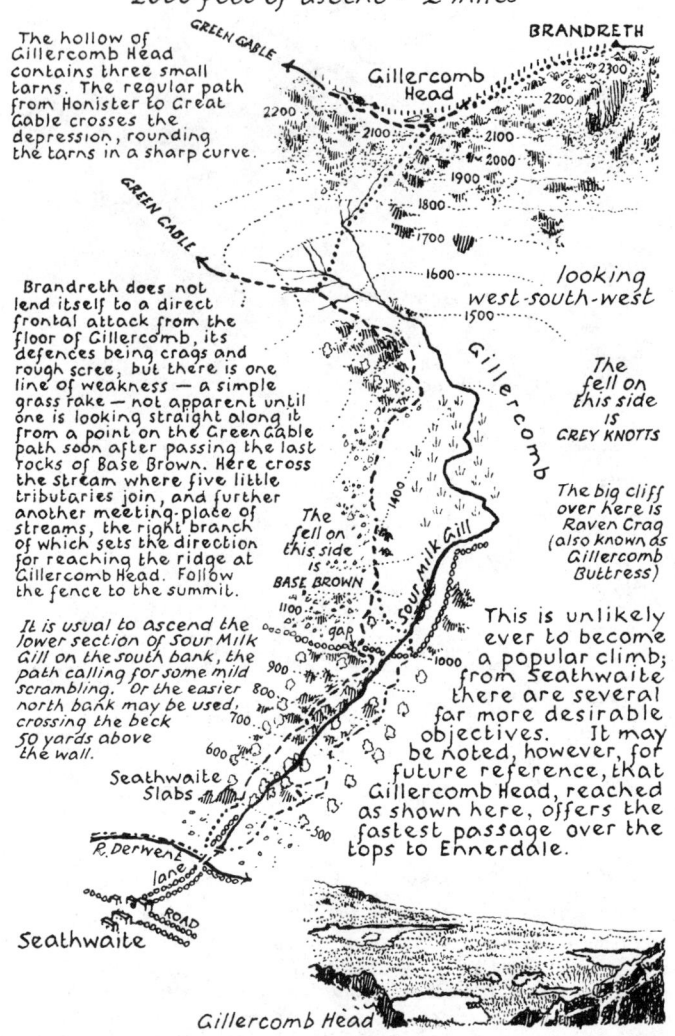

The hollow of Gillercomb Head contains three small tarns. The regular path from Honister to Great Gable crosses the depression, rounding the tarns in a sharp curve.

BRANDRETH
GREEN GABLE
Gillercomb Head
GREEN GABLE

looking west-south-west

Brandreth does not lend itself to a direct frontal attack from the floor of Gillercomb, its defences being crags and rough scree, but there is one line of weakness — a simple grass rake — not apparent until one is looking straight along it from a point on the Green Gable path soon after passing the last rocks of Base Brown. Here cross the stream where five little tributaries join, and further another meeting-place of streams, the right branch of which sets the direction for reaching the ridge at Gillercomb Head. Follow the fence to the summit.

The fell on this side is GREY KNOTTS

The big cliff over here is Raven Crag (also known as Gillercomb Buttress)

Gillercomb
Sour Milk Gill

The fell on this side is BASE BROWN

gap

It is usual to ascend the lower section of Sour Milk Gill on the south bank, the path calling for some mild scrambling. Or the easier north bank may be used, crossing the beck 50 yards above the wall.

This is unlikely ever to become a popular climb; from Seathwaite there are several far more desirable objectives. It may be noted, however, for future reference, that Gillercomb Head, reached as shown here, offers the fastest passage over the tops to Ennerdale.

Seathwaite Slabs

R. Derwent
lane
ROAD
Seathwaite

Gillercomb Head

Brandreth 8

THE SUMMIT

looking to Green Gable and Great Gable

The summit is a bare and cheerless place, a desert of stones with nothing of interest. The cairn is sited at a meeting of fences, and is adorned with a Lonsdale boundary post.

DESCENTS: For HONISTER PASS direct, the line of fenceposts heading north-east across Grey Knotts is a perfect guide; keep on north-east at a junction of fences; no path. If a path is preferred, go down by the western fence for a quarter-mile to join a broad cairned path and turn to the right along it for Honister via the Drum House. For BUTTERMERE via Warnscale, use this route but turn left at the Drum House. For ENNERDALE, continue along the western fence beyond the first path for another quarter-mile (ignoring a thin track crossing midway) and turn left downhill along a fair path with cairns. For BORROWDALE, descend by the south fence until the Honister-Gable 'highway' is met and go left along it to the nearby depression of Gillercomb Head, where there are three tarns. Leave the ridge here to go left down a grass slope into Gillercomb and cross the beck to join the Sour Milk Gill path for Seathwaite.

RIDGE ROUTES

To GREY KNOTTS, 2287': ½ mile: NE
Depression at 2250': 50 feet of ascent
    Follow the fence north-east and arrival on Grey Knotts is inevitable.

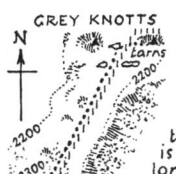

To GREEN GABLE, 2603': 1 mile: S
Depression (Gillercomb Head) at 2160': 450 feet of ascent
    Follow the fence south to join the Honister-Great Gable path, which is distinct and well-cairned on the long climb to the top of Green Gable.

BRANDRETH — ONE MILE — GREEN GABLE

Brandreth 9

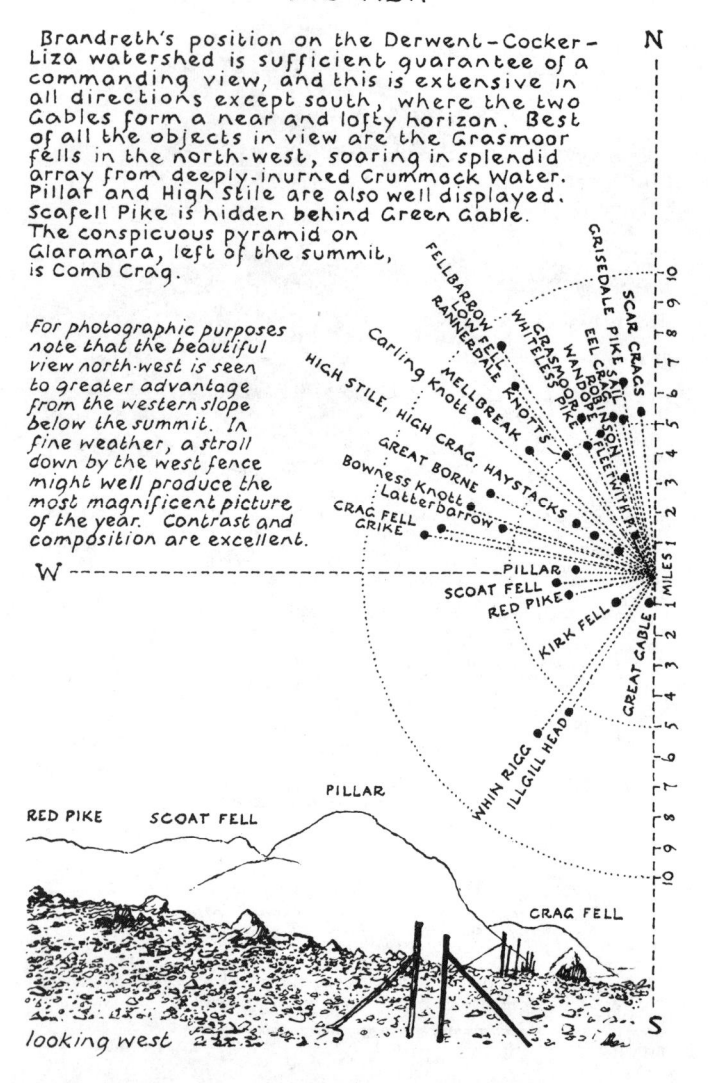

THE VIEW

Brandreth's position on the Derwent-Cocker-Liza watershed is sufficient guarantee of a commanding view, and this is extensive in all directions except south, where the two Gables form a near and lofty horizon. Best of all the objects in view are the Grasmoor fells in the north-west, soaring in splendid array from deeply-inurned Crummock Water. Pillar and High Stile are also well displayed. Scafell Pike is hidden behind Green Gable. The conspicuous pyramid on Glaramara, left of the summit, is Comb Crag.

For photographic purposes note that the beautiful view north-west is seen to greater advantage from the western slope below the summit. In fine weather, a stroll down by the west fence might well produce the most magnificent picture of the year. Contrast and composition are excellent.

looking west

Brandreth 10

THE VIEW

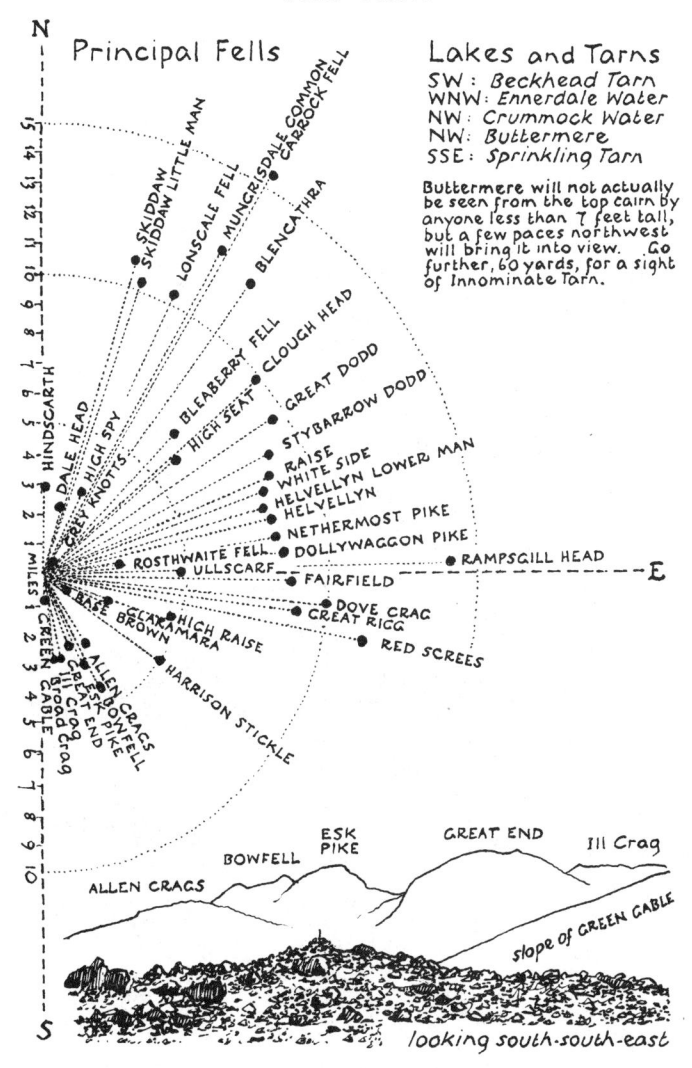

Principal Fells

- SKIDDAW
- SKIDDAW LITTLE MAN
- LONSCALE FELL
- MUNGRISDALE COMMON
- CARROCK FELL
- BLENCATHRA
- BLEABERRY FELL
- HIGH SEAT
- CLOUGH HEAD
- GREAT DODD
- STYBARROW DODD
- RAISE
- WHITE SIDE
- HELVELLYN LOWER MAN
- HELVELLYN
- NETHERMOST PIKE
- DOLLYWAGGON PIKE
- ROSTHWAITE FELL
- ULLSCARF
- FAIRFIELD
- RAMPSGILL HEAD — E
- DOVE CRAG
- GREAT RIGG
- RED SCREES
- HINDSCARTH
- DALE HEAD
- HIGH SPY
- GREY KNOTTS
- BASE BROWN
- HIGH RAISE
- (PAVEY ARK)
- HARRISON STICKLE
- ALLEN CRAGS
- GLARAMARA
- GREAT END
- ESK PIKE
- BROAD CRAG
- GREEN GABLE

Lakes and Tarns
SW: *Beckhead Tarn*
WNW: *Ennerdale Water*
NW: *Crummock Water*
NW: *Buttermere*
SSE: *Sprinkling Tarn*

Buttermere will not actually be seen from the top cairn by anyone less than 7 feet tall, but a few paces northwest will bring it into view. Go further, 60 yards, for a sight of Innominate Tarn.

ALLEN CRAGS — BOWFELL — ESK PIKE — GREAT END — Ill Crag

slope of GREEN GABLE

looking south-south-east

Buckbarrow

1410' approx

from Harrow Head

```
      Wasdale Head
      ▲ SEATALLAN  ●
MIDDLE ▲    Bowderdale
 FELL       ●
      ▲ BUCKBARROW
        ● Greendale

   ● Strands
         MILES
   0   1   2   3   4
```

Buckbarrow faces the famous Screes across Wastwater and being itself a steep and stony declivity bears some resemblance, if only in miniature. From the road along its base, Buckbarrow seems to be a separate fell, but the name has reference merely to the half-mile rock escarpment, beyond which a grassy plateau is succeeded by a featureless slope rising easily to the top of Buckbarrow's parent fell, Seatallan.

Buckbarrow 2

MAP

ONE MILE

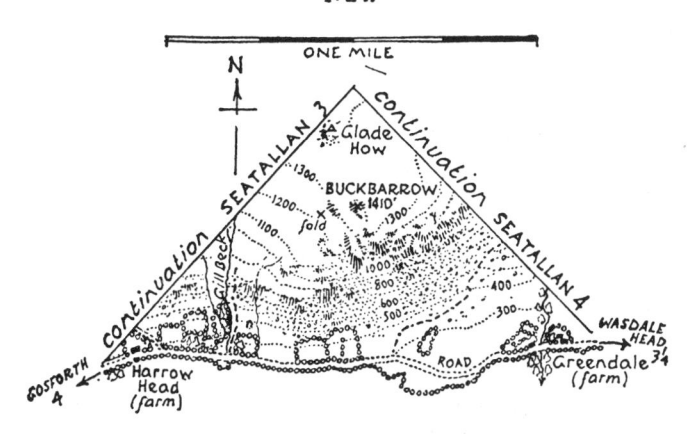

continuation SEATALLAN 3 — continuation SEATALLAN 4

Glade How
BUCKBARROW 1410'
fold
Gill Beck
Harrow Head (farm)
ROAD
Greendale (farm)
GOSFORTH 4
WASDALE HEAD

ASCENT FROM WASDALE
(HARROW HEAD)

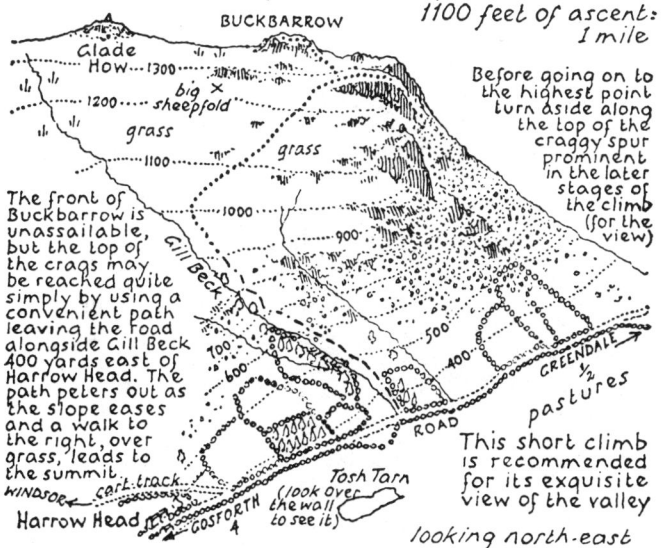

1100 feet of ascent: 1 mile

BUCKBARROW
Glade How
big sheepfold
grass
grass
Gill Beck

Before going on to the highest point turn aside along the top of the craggy spur prominent in the later stages of the climb (for the view)

The front of Buckbarrow is unassailable, but the top of the crags may be reached quite simply by using a convenient path leaving the road alongside Gill Beck 400 yards east of Harrow Head. The path peters out as the slope eases and a walk to the right, over grass, leads to the summit

WINDSOR
Harrow Head
cart track
GOSFORTH 4
Tosh Tarn (look over the wall to see it)
ROAD
GREENDALE ½
pastures

This short climb is recommended for its exquisite view of the valley

looking north-east

Buckbarrow 3

THE SUMMIT

Calder Hall Atomic Power Station →

The highest point in the vicinity of the escarpment is a rocky mound behind the edge of the crags, overlooking the grassy basin below Seatallan. It has no cairn and is undistinguished as a viewpoint in comparison with several less-elevated places along the top of the cliffs. A quarter of a mile west of north is the prominent cairn on Glade How.

DESCENTS: The route recommended for ascent is also the best way down, but if an alternative is wanted it may be found (in clear weather) by skirting the head of Tongues Gills at 1250' to join the path from Greendale Tarn down to the road.

The cairn on Glade How

SCAFELL PIKE ↓

A perched and split boulder (obviously split after perching, probably by frost or lightning)

Buckbarrow from Greendale

Buckbarrow 4

THE VIEW

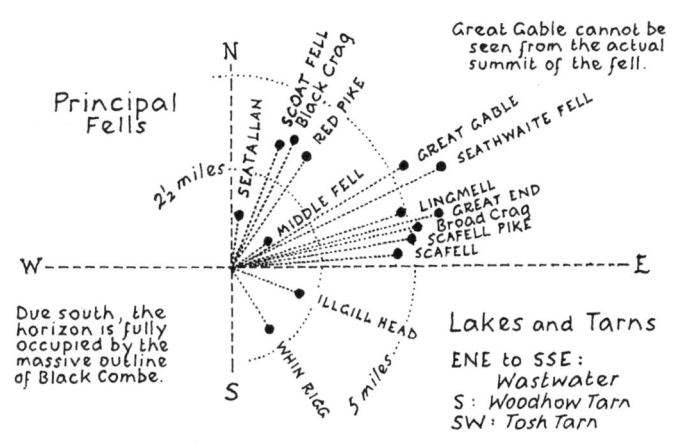

Principal Fells

Great Gable cannot be seen from the actual summit of the fell.

(compass diagram with principal fells labelled: SEATALLAN, SCOAT FELL, Black Crag, RED PIKE, MIDDLE FELL, GREAT GABLE, SEATHWAITE FELL, LINGMELL, GREAT END, Broad Crag, SCAFELL PIKE, SCAFELL, ILLGILL HEAD, WHIN RIGG; 2½ miles, 5 miles)

Due south, the horizon is fully occupied by the massive outline of Black Combe.

Lakes and Tarns
ENE to SSE: Wastwater
S: Woodhow Tarn
SW: Tosh Tarn

It happens frequently that a view from a point below the top of a fell is more attractive than that from the summit, but only rarely that it is more extensive. On Buckbarrow, the best view is obtained from the end of the rocky spur prominently seen in the ascent, this being much finer than that from the summit and actually covering a wider range. Nothing more can be seen from the summit, and a good deal less. The diagrams on this page are based on the end of the spur overlooking Wasdale. The Screes are directly opposite, Wastwater is seen full length and the head of the valley is magnificently closed in by the Scafells.

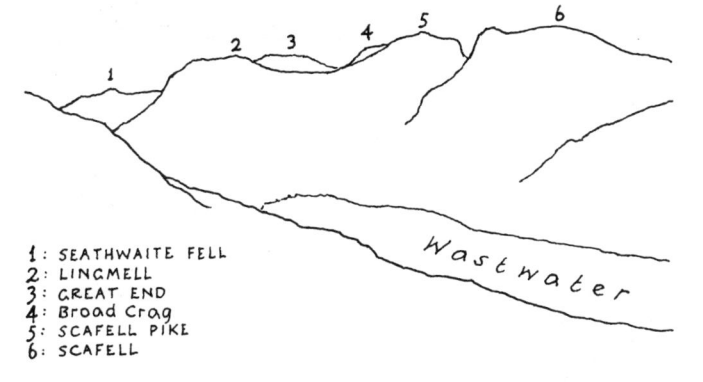

1: SEATHWAITE FELL
2: LINGMELL
3: GREAT END
4: Broad Crag
5: SCAFELL PIKE
6: SCAFELL

The Scafells, from Buckbarrow

Burnbank Fell

1580'
approx.

from Waterend

West of Loweswater the high ground of Lakeland gives place to the undulating rural countryside of the quiet Marron valley, and the last height of all is the grassy dome of Burnbank Fell, a cornerstone, a beginning and an end. This is a dull hill, with little to suggest the grandeur of the mountain masses piled inland from it and nothing to divert the attention of a passing traveller. Helped by Holme Wood the northern slope makes a colourful background to Loweswater and has a fine terrace path (not well enough known) contouring high above the lake with charming views, but the sprawling west flank going down to Lamplugh over a lesser height, Owsen Fell, is a moorland lacking interest.

- Mockerkin
- Loweswater
- Lamplugh
- ▲ BURNBANK FELL
- ▲ BLAKE FELL

MILES
0 1 2 3 4

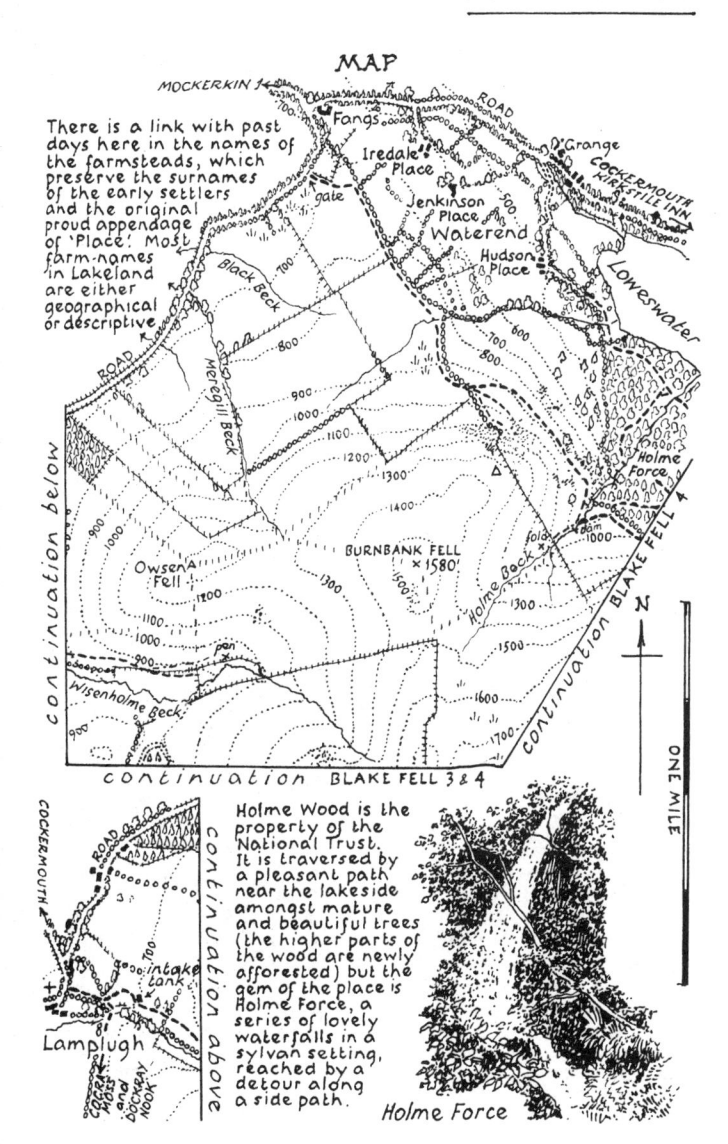

# Burnbank Fell 2

MAP

There is a link with past days here in the names of the farmsteads, which preserve the surnames of the early settlers and the original proud appendage of 'Place'. Most farm-names in Lakeland are either geographical or descriptive.

Holme Wood is the property of the National Trust. It is traversed by a pleasant path near the lakeside amongst mature and beautiful trees (the higher parts of the wood are newly afforested) but the gem of the place is Holme Force, a series of lovely waterfalls in a sylvan setting, reached by a detour along a side path.

Holme Force

Burnbank Fell 3

ASCENT FROM WATEREND
1250 feet of ascent : 2¾ miles

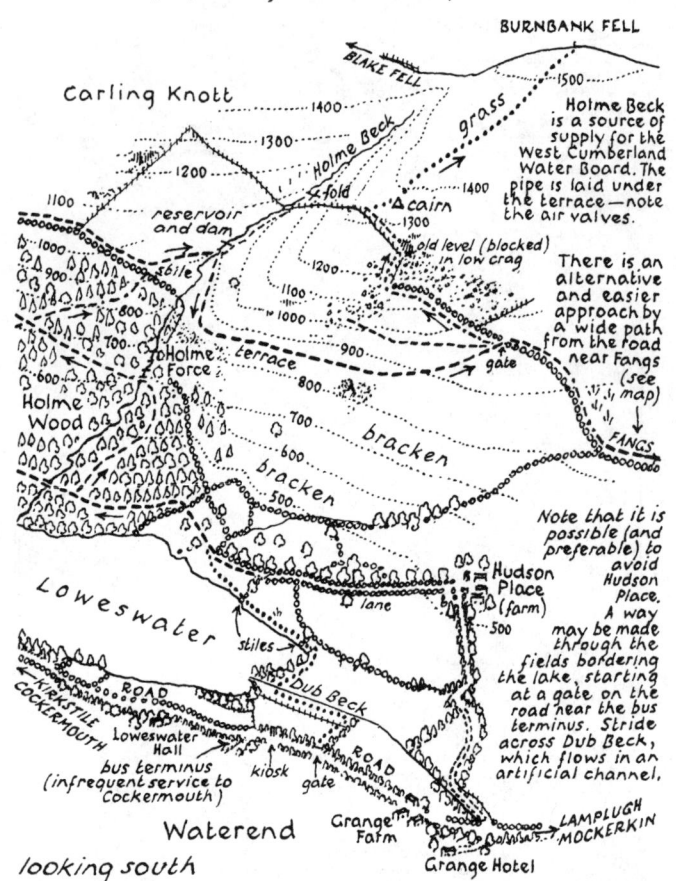

looking south

Holme Beck is a source of supply for the West Cumberland Water Board. The pipe is laid under the terrace — note the air valves.

There is an alternative and easier approach by a wide path from the road near Fangs (see map)

Note that it is possible (and preferable) to avoid Hudson Place. A way may be made through the fields bordering the lake, starting at a gate on the road near the bus terminus. Stride across Dub Beck, which flows in an artificial channel.

This is a dull climb if done straight up the slope, but it can be made interesting and attractive by including in the itinerary a visit to the delightful Holme Force and a stroll along the terrace path. The route recommended is arrowed on the diagram. If views only are the object of the walk there is no point in going on beyond the cairn.

Burnbank Fell 4

ASCENT FROM LAMPLUGH
1000 feet of ascent : 1¾ miles

Without being in any way exciting or even exhilarating, this pleasant ramble among the smooth fells west of Loweswater by an approach 'from behind' will be found restful and peaceful, and when the summit is reached — there ahead, in glorious array, is the real Lakeland!

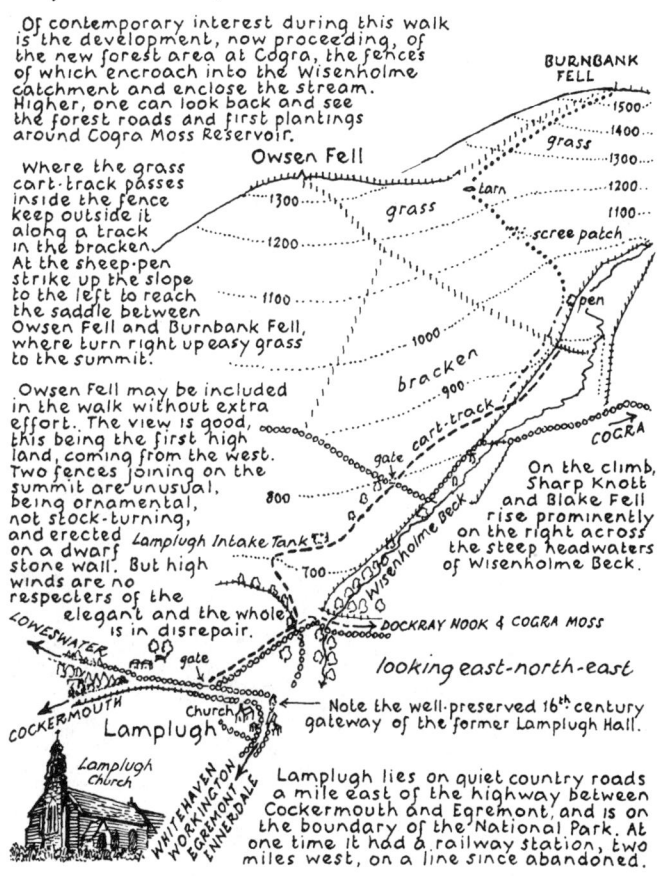

Of contemporary interest during this walk is the development, now proceeding, of the new forest area at Cogra, the fences of which encroach into the Wisenholme catchment and enclose the stream. Higher, one can look back and see the forest roads and first plantings around Cogra Moss Reservoir.

Where the grass cart-track passes inside the fence keep outside it along a track in the bracken. At the sheep-pen strike up the slope to the left to reach the saddle between Owsen Fell and Burnbank Fell, where turn right up easy grass to the summit.

Owsen Fell may be included in the walk without extra effort. The view is good, this being the first high land, coming from the west. Two fences joining on the summit are unusual, being ornamental, not stock-turning, and erected on a dwarf stone wall. But high winds are no respecters of the elegant and the whole is in disrepair.

On the climb, Sharp Knott and Blake Fell rise prominently on the right across the steep headwaters of Wisenholme Beck.

looking east-north-east

Note the well-preserved 16th century gateway of the former Lamplugh Hall.

Lamplugh lies on quiet country roads a mile east of the highway between Cockermouth and Egremont, and is on the boundary of the National Park. At one time it had a railway station, two miles west, on a line since abandoned.

Burnbank Fell 5

THE SUMMIT

The summit is best described as the gently rounded dome of an upland prairie, and there is little else to say about it. Items of interest are absent. There is no cairn. A solitary straining post, which is almost the last visible evidence of an old fence, indicates the highest point (which is nothing like a point).

DESCENTS: The fell may be descended with ease in almost every direction. *For Loweswater* aim northeast for the only cairn on the fell (not seen from the top and sited inconspicuously, yet of some antiquity); below this the slope becomes rough and steeper in the vicinity of old quarries, but after crossing a fence the broad 'terrace' path is joined and a way made down to Hudson Place, or to Watergate through Holme Wood. *For Lamplugh*, rolling grasslands lead over Owsen Fell and down to the Loweswater road, but descend south-westerly to join the pleasant cart-track coming out of the valley of Wisenholme Beck.

BLAKE FELL

"....the only cairn on the fell."

GRASMOOR
WANDOPE
WHITELESS PIKE
Sand Hill
Coledale Hause
WHITESIDE
Lanthwaite
Crummock Water
Loweswater

Burnbank Fell 6

THE VIEW

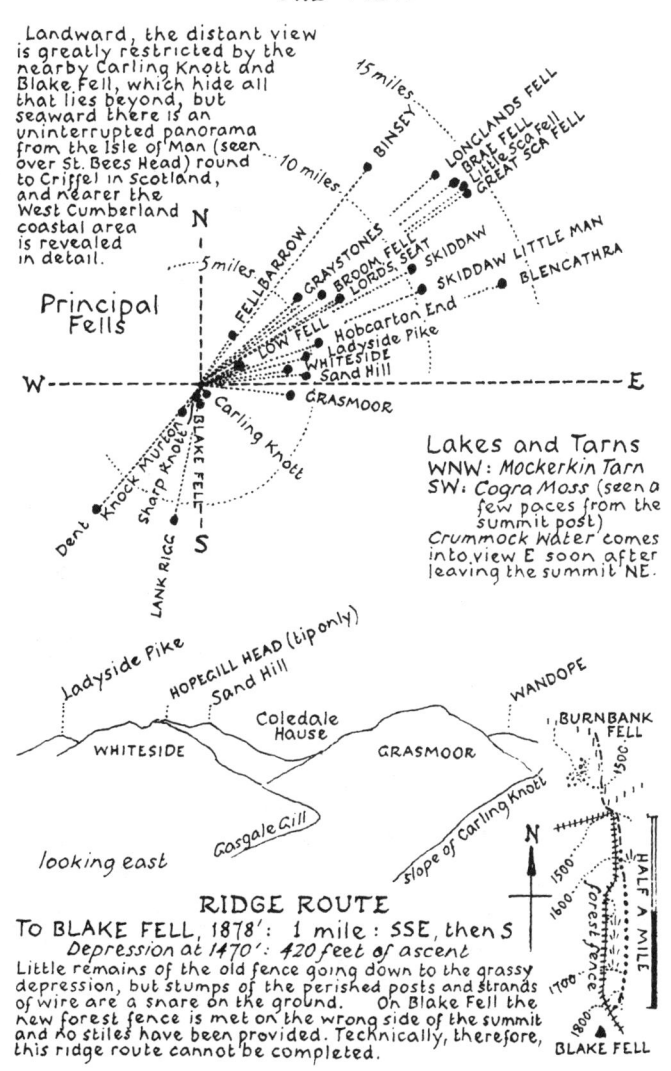

Landward, the distant view is greatly restricted by the nearby Carling Knott and Blake Fell, which hide all that lies beyond, but seaward there is an uninterrupted panorama from the Isle of Man (seen over St. Bees Head) round to Criffel in Scotland, and nearer the West Cumberland coastal area is revealed in detail.

Principal Fells

(Diagram with bearings showing: FELLBARROW, BINSEY, CRAYSTONES, BROOM FELL, LORDS SEAT, LONGLANDS FELL, GRAF FELL, LITTLE SCA FELL, GREAT SCA FELL, SKIDDAW, SKIDDAW LITTLE MAN, BLENCATHRA, LOW FELL, Hobcarton End, Ladyside Pike, WHITESIDE, Sand Hill, GRASMOOR, Carling Knott, BLAKE FELL, Knock Murton, Sharp Knott, Dent, LANK RIGG — with range circles at 5 miles, 10 miles, 15 miles)

Lakes and Tarns
WNW: Mockerkin Tarn
SW: Cogra Moss (seen a few paces from the summit post)
Crummock Water comes into view E soon after leaving the summit NE.

(Panorama looking east showing: Ladyside Pike, HOPEGILL HEAD (tip only), Sand Hill, WHITESIDE, Coledale Hause, GRASMOOR, WANDOPE, BURNBANK FELL, Gasgale Gill, slope of Carling Knott)

looking east

RIDGE ROUTE
TO BLAKE FELL, 1878': 1 mile : SSE, then S
Depression at 1470': 420 feet of ascent

Little remains of the old fence going down to the grassy depression, but stumps of the perished posts and strands of wire are a snare on the ground. On Blake Fell the new forest fence is met on the wrong side of the summit and no stiles have been provided. Technically, therefore, this ridge route cannot be completed.

(Route map showing BURNBANK FELL to BLAKE FELL, HALF A MILE, forest fence, contours 1500, 1600, 1700, 1800)

Caw Fell

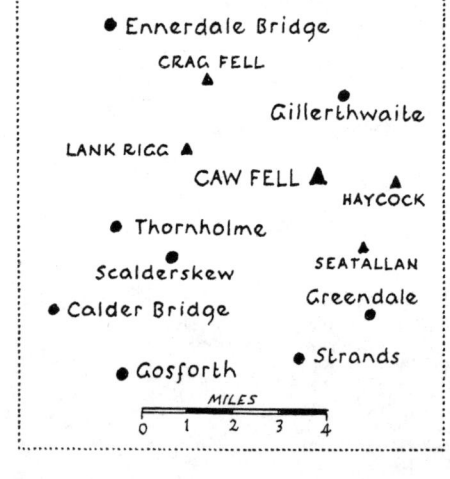

2288'

```
              • Ennerdale Bridge
                    CRAG FELL
                       ▲
                                  Gillerthwaite
                                      •
    LANK RIGG ▲
                  CAW FELL ▲         ▲
                                    HAYCOCK
         • Thornholme
                                  ▲
             Scalderskew        SEATALLAN
                                Greendale
      • Calder Bridge             •

             • Gosforth    • Strands
                      MILES
                   0  1  2  3  4
```

Caw Fell, like many of us who lack a good shape and attractive features, objects to having his picture taken and is not at all co-operative as a subject for illustration. From no point of view does the fell look like anything other than a broadly-buttressed sprawling uncorseted graceless lump with a vast flattened summit similarly devoid of a single distinguishing landmark.

In the drawing above, of Caw Fell as seen from Lank Rigg, the great scoop in the western ridge shows prominently. The highest point of the fell occurs above the dark shadow, top left, here seen overtopped by Haycock.

Caw Fell 2

NATURAL FEATURES

The magnificent group of mountains between Wasdale and Ennerdale, topped by Pillar and including several other redoubtable peaks, is as rugged and craggy as any in the district, exhibiting steep and precipitous slopes to north and east, where they overlook deep valleys. To south and west, however, this upland area is of entirely different character, declining much more gradually, in easy stages. Mountain gives way to moorland, and the rocky nature of the terrain smooths into wide pastures, slow in descent from the tops and therefore more amiable in gradient; the streams follow long and gentler courses but thread their way through gathering grounds so vast that they quickly assume the proportions of rivers. These are the sheepwalks of Copeland Forest, of Stockdale Moor and of Kinniside Common, rolling grasslands linking the untamed heights with the cultivated valleys — a region uninhabited and unfrequented in this day and age, yet at one time, from evidences that still remain to be seen, the home of primitive man.

Caw Fell occupies much of this territory. It has many unnamed summits, many ridges and many streams. Its ten square miles contain much geographical detail of interest rather than importance, for all its waters ultimately mingle in the Irish Sea off the Seascale coast although to get there they flow in all directions of the compass.

There is not much here to attract walkers whose liking is for rough ground and airy ridges; there is little to excite the senses, nothing of beautiful or dramatic effect. Yet here one can stride out for hour after hour in undisturbed solitude and enjoy invigorating exercise amongst scenery that has not changed since the world began. Only when the lower ground is reached does one become mindful again of the twentieth century: here, spreading like a dark cloak from the valleys are plantations of conifers alongside the ancient settlements of the first Britons.

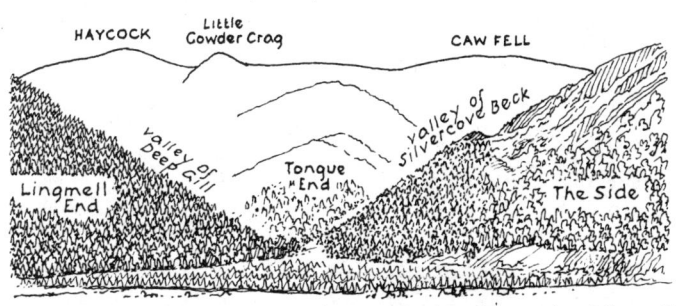

The top of Caw Fell can be seen from a short section only of the walk up Ennerdale, near the first footbridge, where, across the valley, Deep Gill has carved a great opening in the fellside.

Caw Fell 3

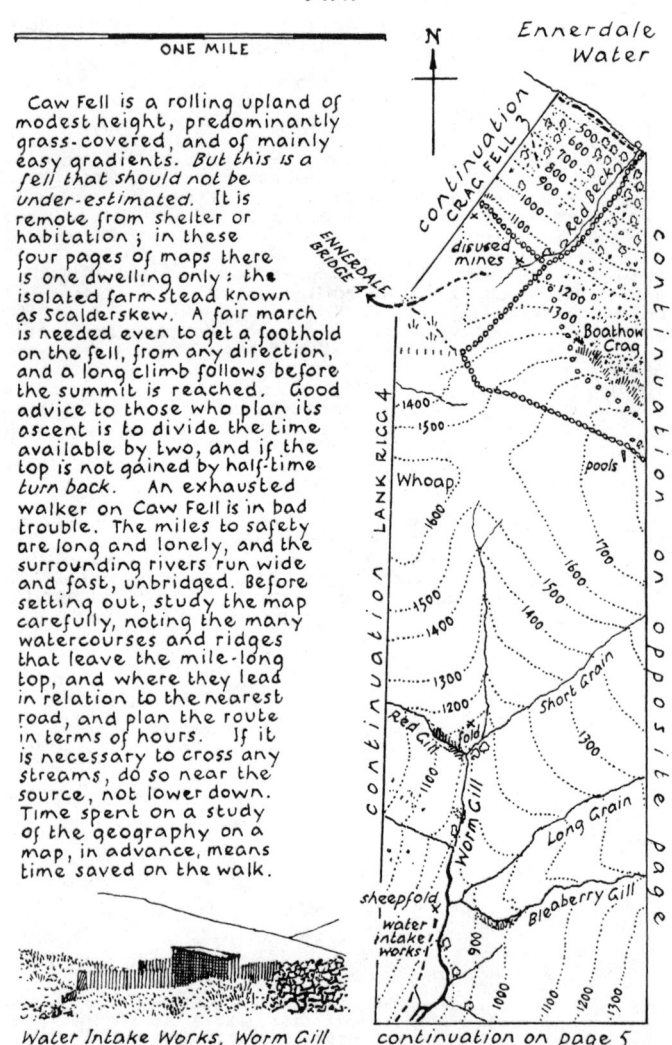

MAP

Caw Fell is a rolling upland of modest height, predominantly grass-covered, and of mainly easy gradients. *But this is a fell that should not be under-estimated.* It is remote from shelter or habitation; in these four pages of maps there is one dwelling only: the isolated farmstead known as Scalderskew. A fair march is needed even to get a foothold on the fell, from any direction, and a long climb follows before the summit is reached. Good advice to those who plan its ascent is to divide the time available by two, and if the top is not gained by half-time turn back. An exhausted walker on Caw Fell is in bad trouble. The miles to safety are long and lonely, and the surrounding rivers run wide and fast, unbridged. Before setting out, study the map carefully, noting the many watercourses and ridges that leave the mile-long top, and where they lead in relation to the nearest road, and plan the route in terms of hours. If it is necessary to cross any streams, do so near the source, not lower down. Time spent on a study of the geography on a map, in advance, means time saved on the walk.

Water Intake Works, Worm Gill

continuation on page 5

MAP

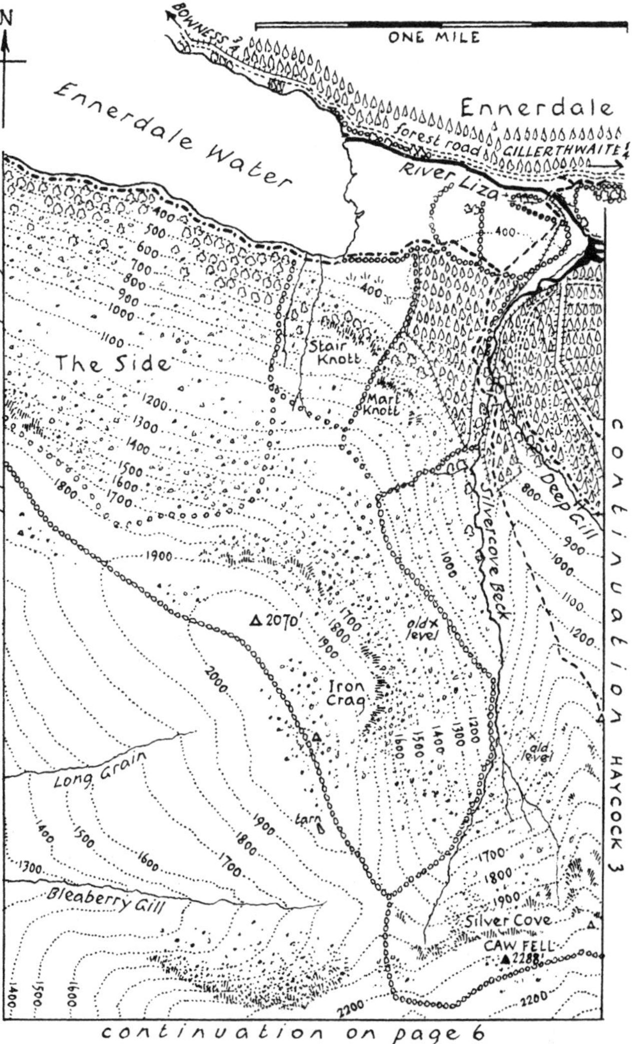

continuation on opposite page

continuation HAYCOCK 3

continuation on page 6

Caw Fell 5

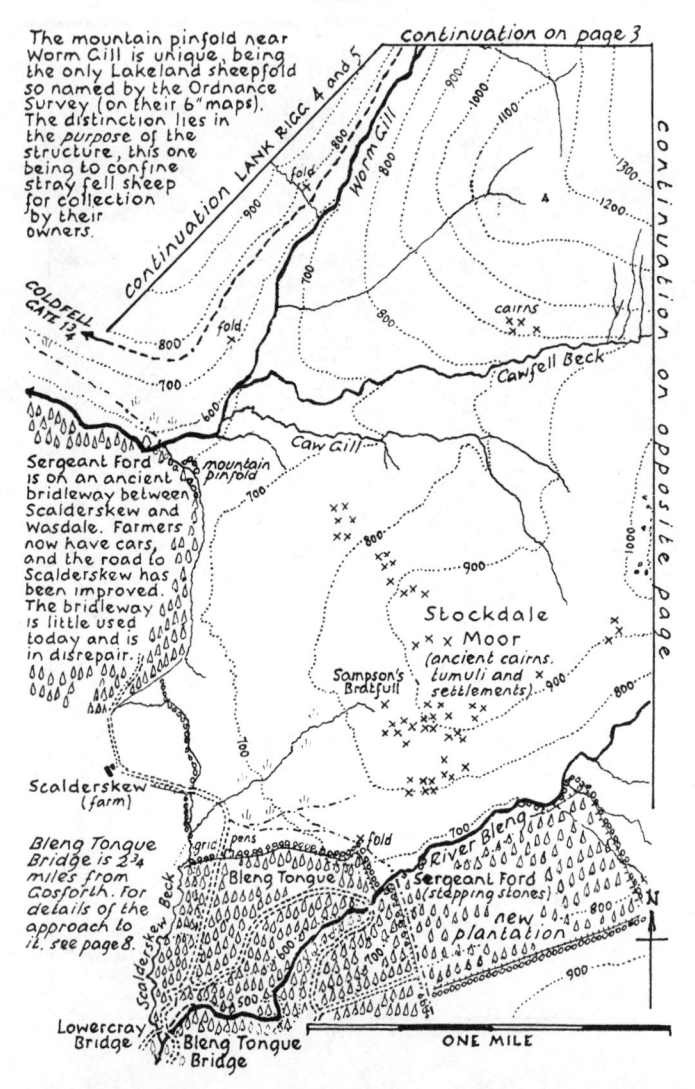

MAP

The mountain pinfold near Worm Gill is unique, being the only Lakeland sheepfold so named by the Ordnance Survey (on their 6" maps). The distinction lies in the *purpose* of the structure, this one being to confine stray fell sheep for collection by their owners.

continuation LANK RIGG 4 and 5

continuation on page 3

continuation on opposite page

COLDFELL GATE 14

fold

Worm Gill

cairns ××

Cawfell Beck

Caw Gill

Sergeant Ford is on an ancient bridleway between Scalderskew and Wasdale. Farmers now have cars, and the road to Scalderskew has been improved. The bridleway is little used today and is in disrepair.

mountain pinfold

Stockdale × Moor (ancient cairns, tumuli and × settlements)

Sampson's Bratfull

Scalderskew (farm)

Bleng Tongue Bridge is 2¼ miles from Gosforth. For details of the approach to it, see page 8.

agric pens

fold

Bleng Tongue

River Bleng

Sergeant Ford (stepping stones)

new plantation

N

Scalderskew Beck

Lowercray Bridge

Bleng Tongue Bridge

ONE MILE

Caw Fell 6

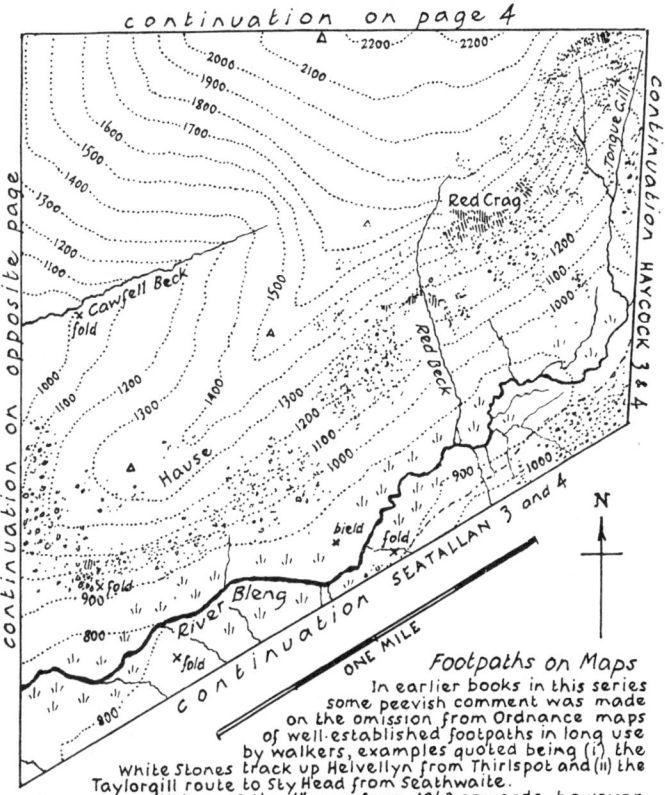

MAP

Footpaths on Maps

In earlier books in this series some peevish comment was made on the omission from Ordnance maps of well-established footpaths in long use by walkers, examples quoted being (i) the White Stones track up Helvellyn from Thirlspot and (ii) the Taylorgill route to Sty Head from Seathwaite.

In revised editions of the 1" map from 1963 onwards, however, footpaths galore appear for the first time; but, unfortunately, many of them are not visible on the ground: in other words, footpaths are now shown that do not exist, although a right of way is not disputed. For example, without going beyond the environs of Caw Fell, (a) there is no path visible along the north bank of Long Grain; (b) nor on the north bank of the Bleng above Sergeant Ford; (c) nor, continuously, to the ridge from Tongue End; and (d) the paths on the adjacent Tewit How are fictional. Rights of way are all very well, but they cannot be seen and they do not help and guide feet over rough ground.

In this matter of indicating footpaths on maps, most walkers will agree that errors of commission are even worse than errors of omission: it is better for one's peace of mind to find a distinct path one does not expect than to fail to find a path one is told to expect.

Caw Fell 7

A tumulus

The Antiquities of Stockdale Moor

In the uncultivated areas of the Lake District, many evidences remain of the former existence of primitive habitations and settlements, and these are usually to be found on open moorlands around the 900'-1200' contours at the upper fringe of the early forests, lying between the swampy valleys, as they would then be, and the inhospitable mountains. These evidences are very profuse in the area of Stockdale Moor and on the nearby slopes of Town Bank (Lank Rigg) and Seatallan. Here are to be seen the walled enclosures, hut circles, cairns, clearance-heaps, barrows and tumuli of a pre-historic community, with traces of cultivation terraces. This is a great field of exploration for the archaeologist, and much work has been done and recorded, notably in the Transactions of the local Cumberland and Westmorland Antiquarian and Archaeological Society.

Walkers should not visit the area, however, expecting to see a pageant of the past unfold before their eyes. Knowledge and imagination are necessary to recognise and understand the remains. A person both uninformed and unobservant may tramp across Stockdale Moor and notice nothing to distinguish his surroundings from those of any other boulder-strewn upland. Indeed, except for the purposes of a study of the subject, a special visit to the area cannot really be recommended: the scenery is drab and desolate, there is no quick run-off for water on the flattish ground and consequently most of it is marsh; on a wet day the moor is downright depressing.

A cairn

A name that arouses interest on the map of Stockdale Moor is *Sampson's Bratfull*, a concentration of stones dropped from the apron of a giant as he strode across the moor. So legend has it, but learned sources prefer the opinion that this is the site of a tumulus or barrow (a burial place), giving its measurements as 35 yards long and 12 yards wide tapering to the west end.

An enclosure

Caw Fell 8

ASCENT FROM BLENGDALE
2100 feet of ascent : 5½ miles (7½ from Gosforth)

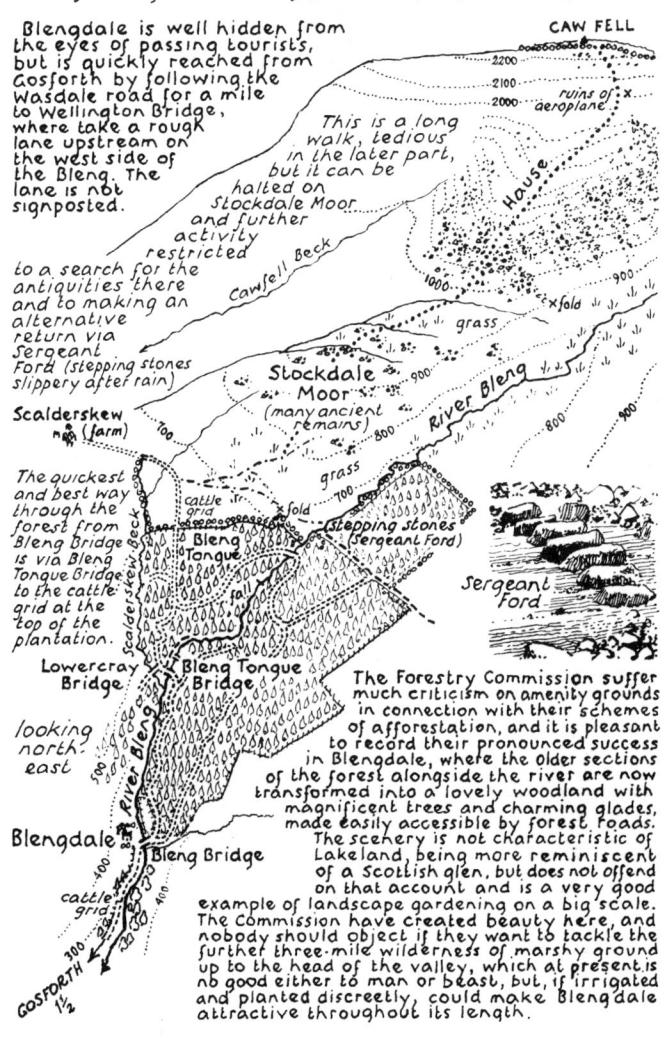

Blengdale is well hidden from the eyes of passing tourists, but is quickly reached from Gosforth by following the Wasdale road for a mile to Wellington Bridge, where take a rough lane upstream on the west side of the Bleng. The lane is not signposted.

CAW FELL

ruins of aeroplane

This is a long walk, tedious in the later part, but it can be halted on Stockdale Moor and further activity restricted to a search for the antiquities there and to making an alternative return via Sergeant Ford (stepping stones slippery after rain)

House

Cawfell Beck

x fold

grass

Stockdale Moor (many ancient remains)

River Bleng

Scalderskew (farm)

The quickest and best way through the forest from Bleng Bridge is via Bleng Tongue Bridge to the cattle grid at the top of the plantation.

cattle grid

fold

Bleng Tongue

stepping stones (Sergeant Ford)

grass

fall

Sergeant Ford

Lowercray Bridge

Bleng Tongue Bridge

looking north-east

Scalderskew Beck

River Bleng

Blengdale

Bleng Bridge

cattle grid

GOSFORTH 1½

The Forestry Commission suffer much criticism on amenity grounds in connection with their schemes of afforestation, and it is pleasant to record their pronounced success in Blengdale, where the older sections of the forest alongside the river are now transformed into a lovely woodland with magnificent trees and charming glades, made easily accessible by forest roads. The scenery is not characteristic of Lakeland, being more reminiscent of a Scottish glen, but does not offend on that account and is a very good example of landscape gardening on a big scale. The Commission have created beauty here, and nobody should object if they want to tackle the further three-mile wilderness of marshy ground up to the head of the valley, which at present is no good either to man or beast, but, if irrigated and planted discreetly, could make Blengdale attractive throughout its length.

Caw Fell 9

ASCENT FROM KINNISIDE STONE CIRCLE
1850 feet of ascent : 6 miles

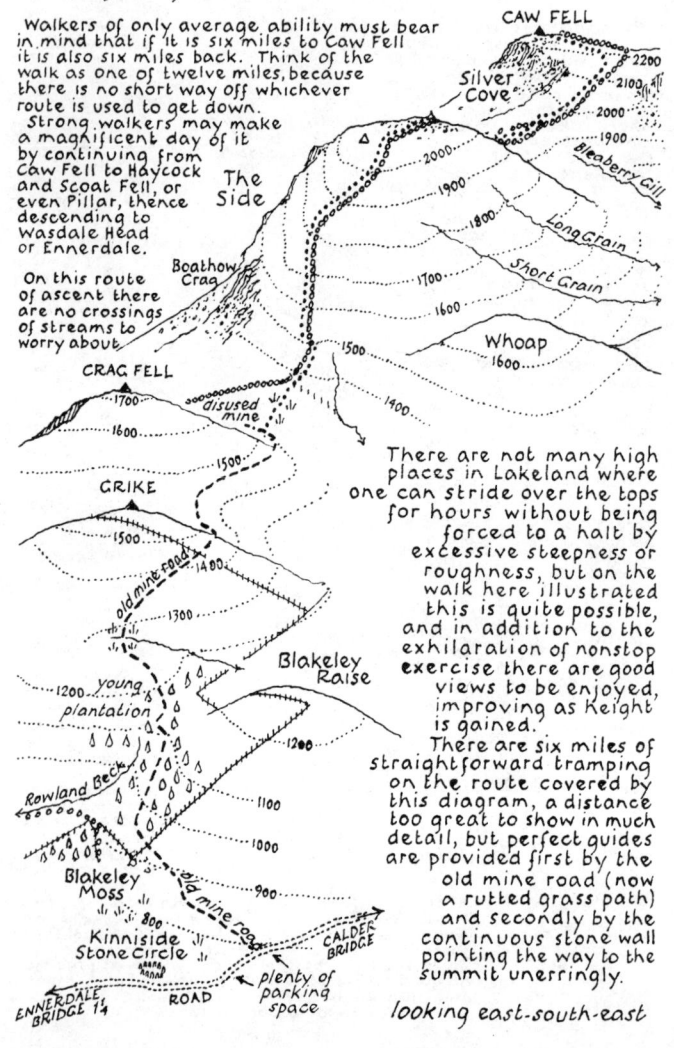

Walkers of only average ability must bear in mind that if it is six miles to Caw Fell it is also six miles back. Think of the walk as one of twelve miles, because there is no short way off whichever route is used to get down.

Strong walkers may make a magnificent day of it by continuing from Caw Fell to Haycock and Scoat Fell, or even Pillar, thence descending to Wasdale Head or Ennerdale.

On this route of ascent there are no crossings of streams to worry about.

There are not many high places in Lakeland where one can stride over the tops for hours without being forced to a halt by excessive steepness or roughness, but on the walk here illustrated this is quite possible, and in addition to the exhilaration of nonstop exercise there are good views to be enjoyed, improving as height is gained.

There are six miles of straightforward tramping on the route covered by this diagram, a distance too great to show in much detail, but perfect guides are provided first by the old mine road (now a rutted grass path) and secondly by the continuous stone wall pointing the way to the summit unerringly.

looking east-south-east

Caw Fell 10

ASCENT FROM ENNERDALE
(LOW GILLERTHWAITE)
1950 feet of ascent : 2¾ miles

Little Gowder Crag ← HAYCOCK   CAW FELL

Great Cove   Silver Cove

This is not only the shortest way from valley-level to the summit of Caw Fell, but the best. The river and woodland and gorge scenery in the vicinity of the confluence of Deep Gill and Silvercove Beck is charming, the more so because the spot is known to very few and rarely visited; indeed, the side opening in which it is situated, being across the valley from the Ennerdale highway, may escape the notice altogether, of travellers thereon. The footbridge over the Liza has recently been replaced and is not the precarious adventure it once was, but the public path leading onto Tongue End from the flatlands of the valley is now obscured by new plantations and in danger of becoming lost in a jungle of young trees. Stiles have been provided in the new forest fences but unless the route is kept in use it will soon be a write-off.

Deep Gill

Silvercove Beck

heather

heather

Tongue End
falls

This route is especially worth noting as a different approach to the main ridge, for the Pillar group. Permitted ways out of the floor of Ennerdale are few and far between since afforestation: this is the easiest route for gradients and certainly the most beautiful.

← new plantation — trees planted too near to the path. An axe or machete will soon be necessary here.

← single-plank bridge

← new plantation — an open avenue has been left in the trees as a pathway, but is being choked by tall bracken.

Woundell Beck

SOUTH SHORE OF ENNERDALE WATER

forest road

for additional notes on this route see Haycock 7

LOW GILLERTHWAITE

bracken

Perhaps the Whitehaven Rambling Club would kindly be responsible for keeping this trail blazed? 20 pairs of boots twice a year would do it.

looking SOUTH

Char Dub (River Liza)
valley road → BOWNESS POINT 2

Caw Fell 11

THE SUMMIT

The highest of the several tops in the territory of Caw Fell is immediately above Silver Cove, at 2288', on an unattractive stony plateau bisected by the substantial wall (part of the 'Ennerdale fence') that runs for miles hereabouts along the south Ennerdale watershed and is a depressing ornament in fair weather but a reliable friend in foul. Sharp eyes will discern fragments of an aeroplane on both sides of the wall west of the summit cairn; otherwise there are no items of interest and very little to warrant a prolonged halt.

DESCENTS: For the head of Ennerdale Water, reverse the route of ascent over Tongue End in preference to a more direct course alongside Silvercove Beck; for the foot of the lake the wall running over the northwest ridge can be followed to its end at the lakeside path; avoid an intermediate line down The Side, which is very rough. For Gosforth and Nether Wasdale use the southwest ridge (the Hause) to reach Blengdale, but if, in mist, this route cannot be located, it is reassuring to know that all ways off down the western slopes are free from hazard.

RIDGE ROUTES

To HAYCOCK, 2618': 1 mile : E, then SE
450 feet of ascent : Depression at 2210'
An interesting move to rougher country
There is no danger of going astray, however bad the weather, the wall leading directly to the top of Haycock over ground at first grassy but becoming very stony. Little Gowder Crag is an interesting feature en route.

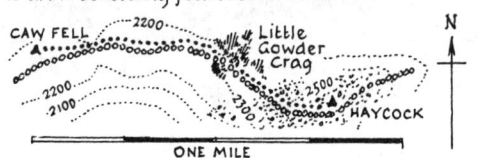

The boundary wall is interrupted by the low crags of Little Gowder Crag.

To CRAG FELL, 1710': 3½ miles : W, then NNW, NW and NNW
550 feet of ascent : Depressions at 1900' and 1325'
Too far unless heading thereafter for Ennerdale Bridge
This is a long but simple walk over easy ground, with navigation merely a matter of following a wall to the marshy depression at the end of the northwest ridge, of which Crag Fell, now directly ahead, is really a continuation.
For a diagram of this route, see Crag Fell 5 and 6.

Caw Fell 12

THE VIEW

Caw Fell is sufficiently removed from the dominant heights of the Pillar group to permit a fairly good all-round view; it is not, however, particularly attractive in any direction.

The wall across the top obstructs the panorama and those fells named in the diagram south of Scafell can only be seen by looking over it, all the others being visible from the cairn.

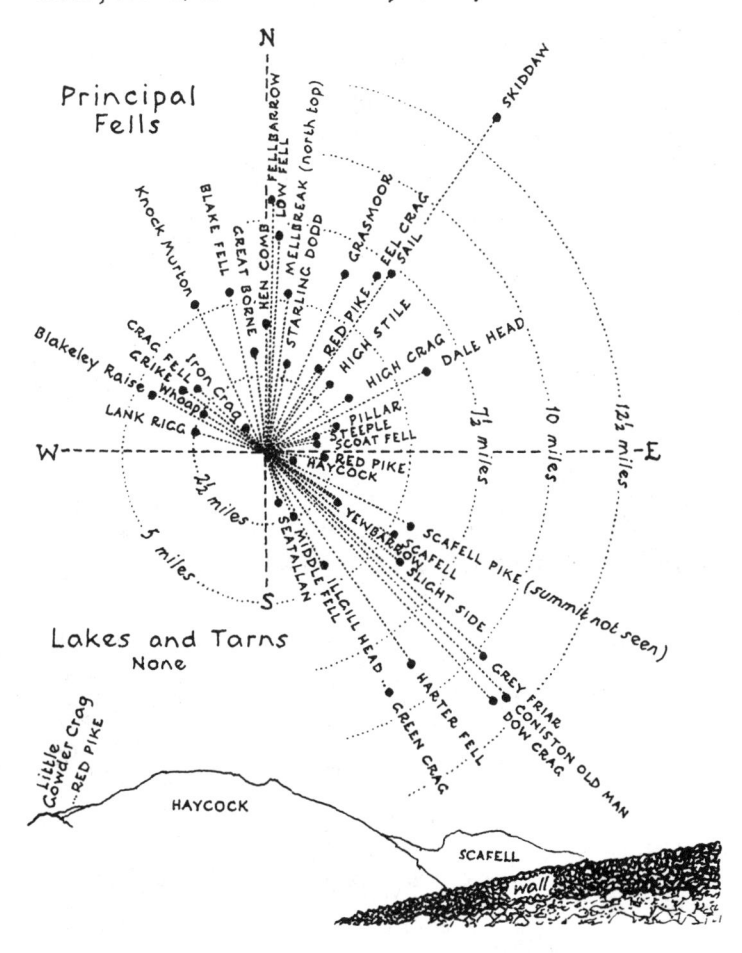

Principal Fells

N — FELLBARROW, LOW FELL, HEN COMB, MELLBREAK (north top), STARLING DODD, GRASMOOR, FEL CRAG, SAIL, SKIDDAW, RED PIKE, HIGH STILE, HIGH CRAG, DALE HEAD, GREAT BORNE, BLAKE FELL, Knock Murton, IRON CRAG, CRAG FELL, GRIKE, WHOAP, Blakeley Raise, LANK RIGG, PILLAR, STEEPLE, SCOAT FELL, RED PIKE, HAYCOCK, SEATALLAN, ILLGILL HEAD, MIDDLE FELL, YEWBARROW, SCAFELL, SLIGHT SIDE, SCAFELL PIKE (summit not seen), GREY FRIAR, CONISTON OLD MAN, DOW CRAG, HARTER FELL, GREEN CRAG

Distances: 2½ miles, 5 miles, 7½ miles, 10 miles, 12½ miles

Lakes and Tarns
None

Little Gowder Crag — RED PIKE — HAYCOCK — SCAFELL — wall

Crag Fell

1710' approx.

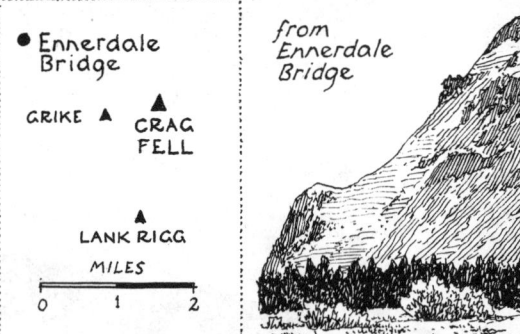

from Bowness Point

from Ennerdale Bridge

- Ennerdale Bridge
- ▲ GRIKE
- ▲ CRAG FELL
- ▲ LANK RIGG

MILES
0   1   2

Crag Fell 2

NATURAL FEATURES

Crag Fell is a fine, abrupt height, prominently in view on the approach to Ennerdale from the west, its configuration being such that it may easily be, and often is, mistaken for Pillar by those who have not studied their maps sufficiently, the illusion being strengthened by the conspicuous excrescence of rock on its north slope, which, seen in profile, might, at a glance, be thought to be the famous Pillar Rock. This comparison is a compliment to Crag Fell because Pillar is in fact a greater mountain by far and its Rock much more impressive than anything Crag Fell can show. Yet the north face of Crag Fell, falling sheer into Ennerdale Water, is an arresting sight; it is the dull hinterland of of smooth grassy slopes around the source of the River Calder that detracts from all round merit. In the rocky headland of Anglers' Crag, jutting into the lake; in the curious pinnacles of Revelin Crag, above; and not least in the tremendous ravine of Ben Gill, are centred the attractions of Crag Fell, and all face north. Elsewhere is moorland with nothing of interest but the few decayed remains of the former Cragfell Iron Ore Mines.

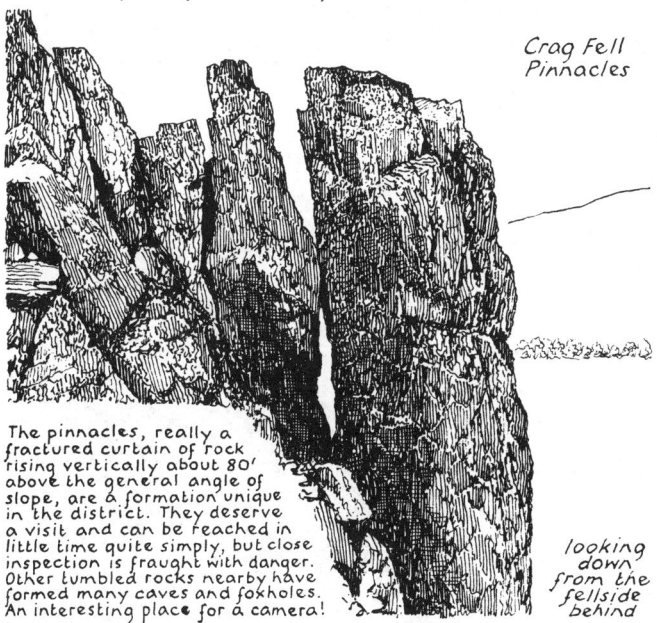

Crag Fell Pinnacles

The pinnacles, really a fractured curtain of rock rising vertically about 80' above the general angle of slope, are a formation unique in the district. They deserve a visit and can be reached in little time quite simply, but close inspection is fraught with danger. Other tumbled rocks nearby have formed many caves and foxholes. An interesting place for a camera!

looking down from the fellside behind

Crag Fell 3

MAP

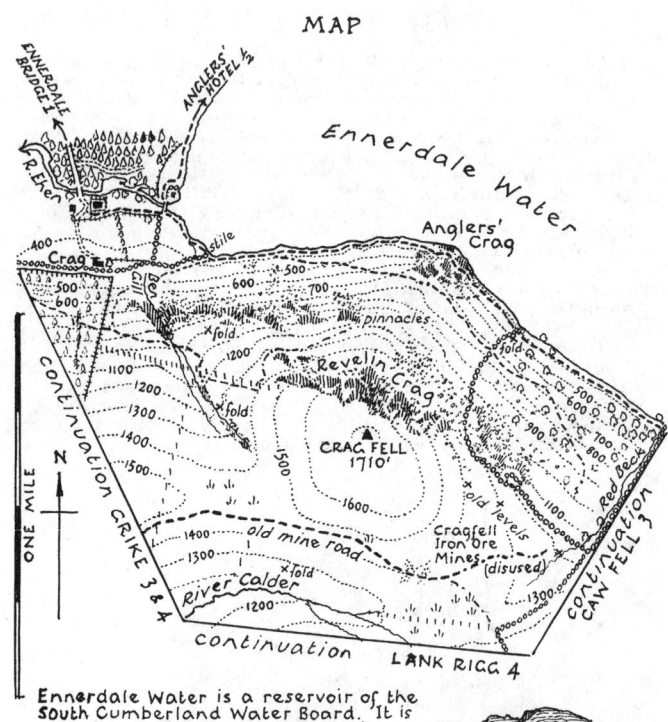

Ennerdale Water is a reservoir of the South Cumberland Water Board. It is proposed to increase storage capacity by raising the level of the lake. This will mean changes to the map at the outflow, but access will continue to be provided to the shore path, which will not be materially affected.

Anglers' Crag
(also known as Angling Crag)

The lakeside path below Anglers' Crag was formerly regarded as dangerous, and walkers were recommended to take the longer route over the top. The passage of many boots, however, has smoothed out the difficulties, and today it is no more than a simple, rather rough, walk.

Crag Fell 4

ASCENT FROM ENNERDALE BRIDGE
1350 feet of ascent : 2½ miles

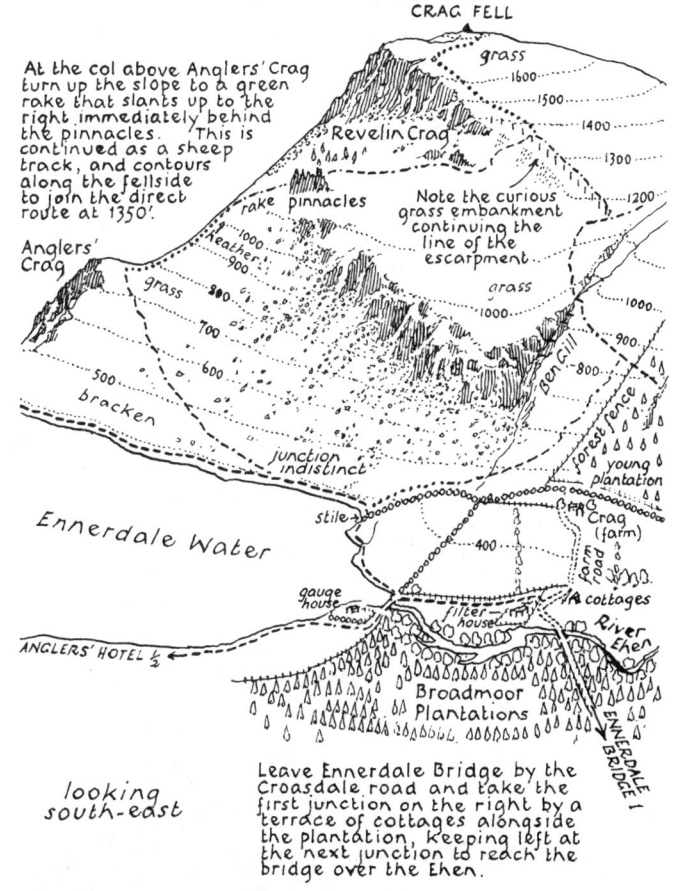

At the col above Anglers' Crag turn up the slope to a green rake that slants up to the right immediately behind the pinnacles. This is continued as a sheep track, and contours along the fellside to join the direct route at 1350'.

Note the curious grass embankment continuing the line of the escarpment.

looking south-east

Leave Ennerdale Bridge by the Croasdale road and take the first junction on the right by a terrace of cottages alongside the plantation, keeping left at the next junction to reach the bridge over the Ehen.

The direct, and usual, route is shown on the right of the diagram, but a suggested new start is indicated to avoid the new plantation above Crag farm through which the original path passed.
If it is desired to visit the pinnacles, take the route on the left of the diagram.

Crag Fell 5

RIDGE ROUTES

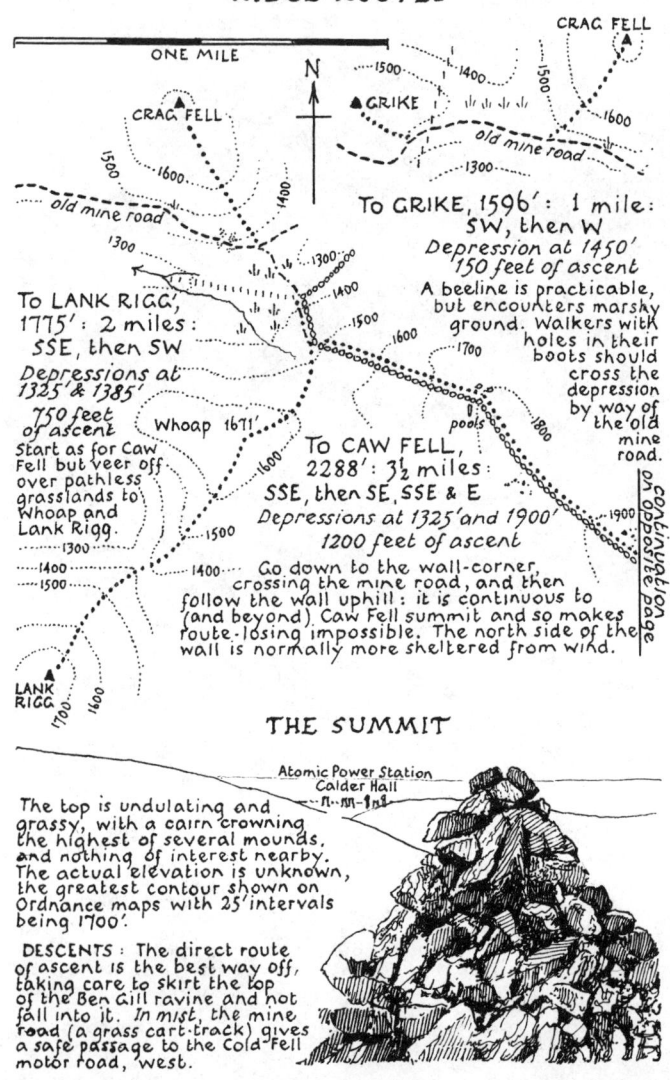

ONE MILE

CRAG FELL

GRIKE

CRAG FELL

old mine road

**TO GRIKE, 1596': 1 mile:
SW, then W**
Depression at 1450'
150 feet of ascent
A beeline is practicable, but encounters marshy ground. Walkers with holes in their boots should cross the depression by way of the old mine road.

old mine road

**TO LANK RIGG, 1775': 2 miles:
SSE, then SW**
Depressions at 1325' & 1385'
750 feet of ascent
Start as for Caw Fell but veer off over pathless grasslands to Whoap and Lank Rigg.

Whoap 1671'

**TO CAW FELL, 2288': 3½ miles:
SSE, then SE, SSE & E**
Depressions at 1325' and 1900'
1200 feet of ascent
Go down to the wall-corner, crossing the mine road, and then follow the wall uphill: it is continuous to (and beyond) Caw Fell summit and so makes route-losing impossible. The north side of the wall is normally more sheltered from wind.

pools

continuation on opposite page

LANK RIGG

THE SUMMIT

Atomic Power Station
Calder Hall

The top is undulating and grassy, with a cairn crowning the highest of several mounds, and nothing of interest nearby. The actual elevation is unknown, the greatest contour shown on Ordnance maps with 25' intervals being 1700'.

DESCENTS: The direct route of ascent is the best way off, taking care to skirt the top of the Ben Gill ravine and not fall into it. In mist, the mine road (a grass cart-track) gives a safe passage to the Cold Fell motor road, west.

Crag Fell 6

THE VIEW

Principal Fells

Lakes and Tarns
E: Ennerdale Water

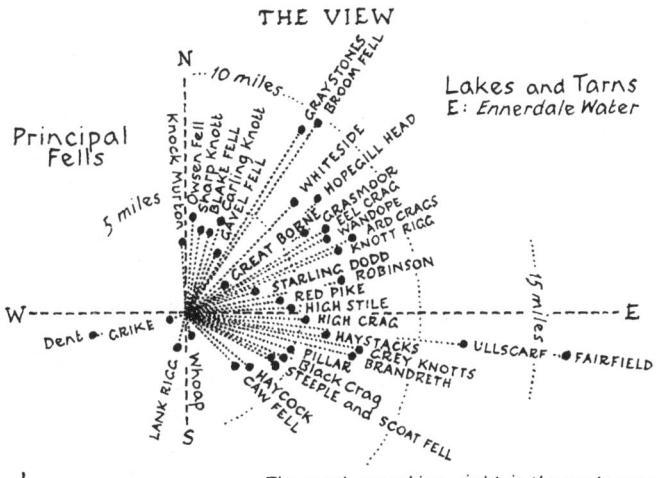

(Fells labelled on the diagram: Graystones, Broom Fell, Knock Murton, Owsen Fell, Sharp Knott, Blake Fell, Gavel Fell Knott, Whiteside, Hopegill Head, Great Borne, Grasmoor, Eel Crag, Wandope, Ard Crags, Knott Rigg, Starling Dodd, Red Pike, Robinson, High Stile, High Crag, Haystacks, Crey Knotts, Brandreth, Pillar, Black Crag, Steeple and Scoat Fell, Haycock, Caw Fell, Lank Rigg, Whoap, Dent, Grike, Ullscarf, Fairfield)

10 miles, 5 miles, 15 miles

RIDGE ROUTE continued

This walk to Caw Fell is easy, but distance and time should be considered carefully in advance.

Caw Fell is in the heart of lonely and inhospitable fells, and a long way from shelter and accommodation. It is extensive, and in mist, if sight of the wall is lost, there may be difficulty in taking bearings on the indefinite top.

Before setting out for Caw Fell there should be a well-thought-out plan for getting off it.

The most arresting sight is the grotesque collection of towers and minarets of the Calder Hall Atomic Power Station strangely tormenting the land horizon southwest; it is seen along the valley of the Calder, with the sea beyond, in a frame of serene fells. The contrast is striking: a modern toy and the timeless hills! A pleasanter prospect is the green strath of Gillerthwaite, but even here, man, learning nothing from nature, has let loose his fancy ideas of tree-planting and done his damnedest to ruin the scene.

The view inland is generally confined to the mountains in the vicinity but seawards the panorama is very extensive.

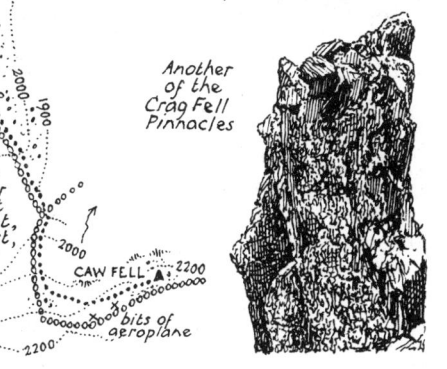

Another of the Crag Fell Pinnacles

CAW FELL ▲ 2200

bits of aeroplane

Fellbarrow   1363'

*from the slopes of
Burnbank Fell
above Waterend*

Waterend, a scattered hamlet, is really mis-named. Here is the extremity of the lake of Loweswater, true, but this is the head (the beginning) of the lake, not the foot, which is properly the end, the exit, the place of outflow.

Fellbarrow 2

NATURAL FEATURES

The Vale of Lorton is sheltered on the west by a low range of grassy rounded hills uncharacteristic of Lakeland and not really part of it, this despite having southern roots in Loweswater amid scenery that is wholly typical of the district. The range has several tops of approximately the same height, none of them distinctive because the undulations are shallow, but the northern half builds up on all sides to the massive flattened dome of Fellbarrow.

The extensive slopes of grass, which serve as a vast sheep pasture, decline gradually westwards to quiet Mosser, northwards to Brandlingill and eastwards to the valley of the Cocker, all farming country. The scenery is pleasant but unexciting. The underlying rock is slate, and rarely exposed to view below its smooth green covering. There are traces of an old plantation in a basin on the east, of which a few straggly trees remain, and a still-flourishing wood on the side of the abrupt headland of Dodd nearby.

Southwards, rounded humps succeed each other with little loss of height before a more distinctive shape resolves itself from the rolling acres. This is Low Fell and beyond is Loweswater.

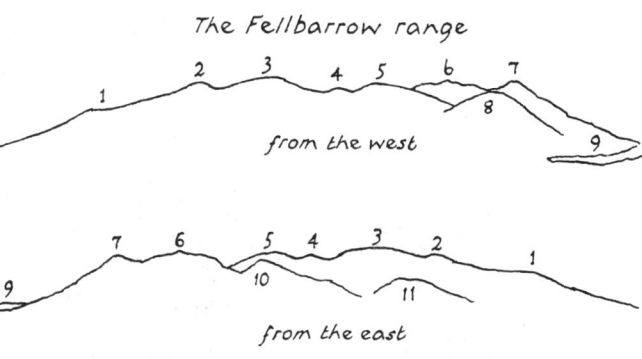

The Fellbarrow range

from the west

from the east

```
1: Whin Fell    2: Hatteringill Head
3: Fellbarrow   4: Smithy Fell
5: Sourfoot Fell 6: Low Fell, north top
7: Low Fell, main top  8: Darling Fell
9: Loweswater  10: Watching Crag  11: Dodd
```

The traverse of the Fellbarrow range on a clear sunny day is one of the most rewarding of the simpler fellwalks, although not often undertaken. Its particular merit, apart from the easy going, is the beautiful view of the Buttermere-Crummock valley, which is seen to perfection.

To enjoy it fully, walk the range from north to south.

Fellbarrow 3

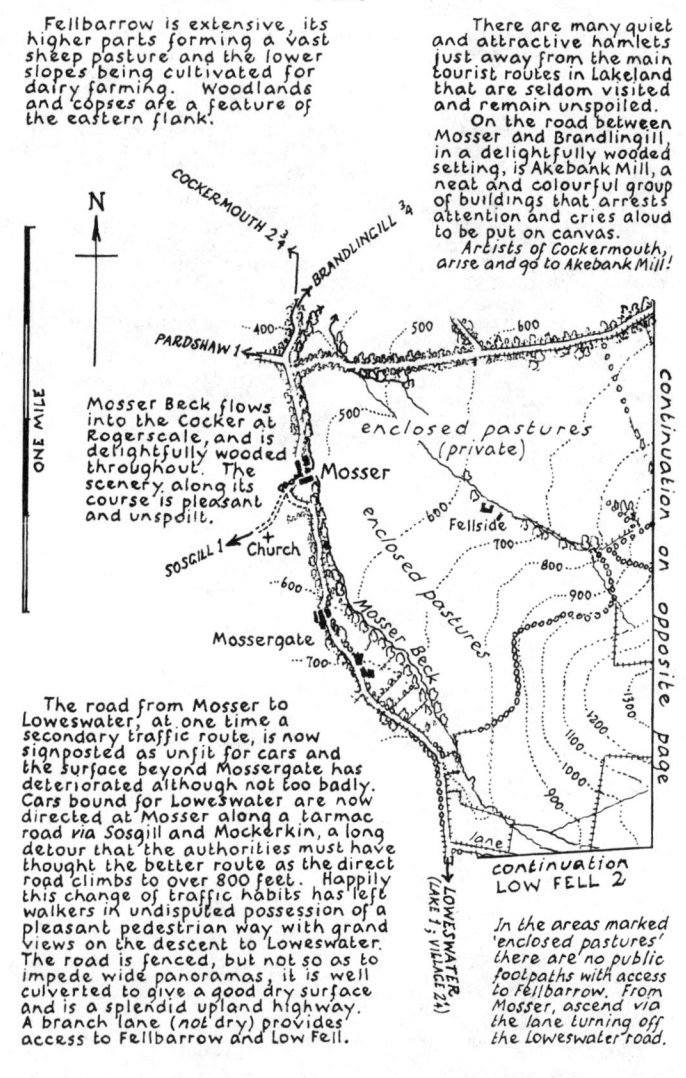

MAP

Fellbarrow is extensive, its higher parts forming a vast sheep pasture and the lower slopes being cultivated for dairy farming. Woodlands and copses are a feature of the eastern flank.

There are many quiet and attractive hamlets just away from the main tourist routes in Lakeland that are seldom visited and remain unspoiled.

On the road between Mosser and Brandlingill, in a delightfully wooded setting, is Akebank Mill, a neat and colourful group of buildings that arrests attention and cries aloud to be put on canvas.

Artists of Cockermouth, arise and go to Akebank Mill!

Mosser Beck flows into the Cocker at Rogerscale, and is delightfully wooded throughout. The scenery along its course is pleasant and unspoilt.

The road from Mosser to Loweswater, at one time a secondary traffic route, is now signposted as unfit for cars and the surface beyond Mossergate has deteriorated although not too badly. Cars bound for Loweswater are now directed at Mosser along a tarmac road via Sosgill and Mockerkin, a long detour that the authorities must have thought the better route as the direct road climbs to over 800 feet. Happily this change of traffic habits has left walkers in undisputed possession of a pleasant pedestrian way with grand views on the descent to Loweswater. The road is fenced, but not so as to impede wide panoramas, it is well culverted to give a good dry surface and is a splendid upland highway. A branch lane (not dry) provides access to Fellbarrow and Low Fell.

In the areas marked 'enclosed pastures' there are no public footpaths with access to Fellbarrow. From Mosser, ascend via the lane turning off the Loweswater road.

Fellbarrow 4

MAP

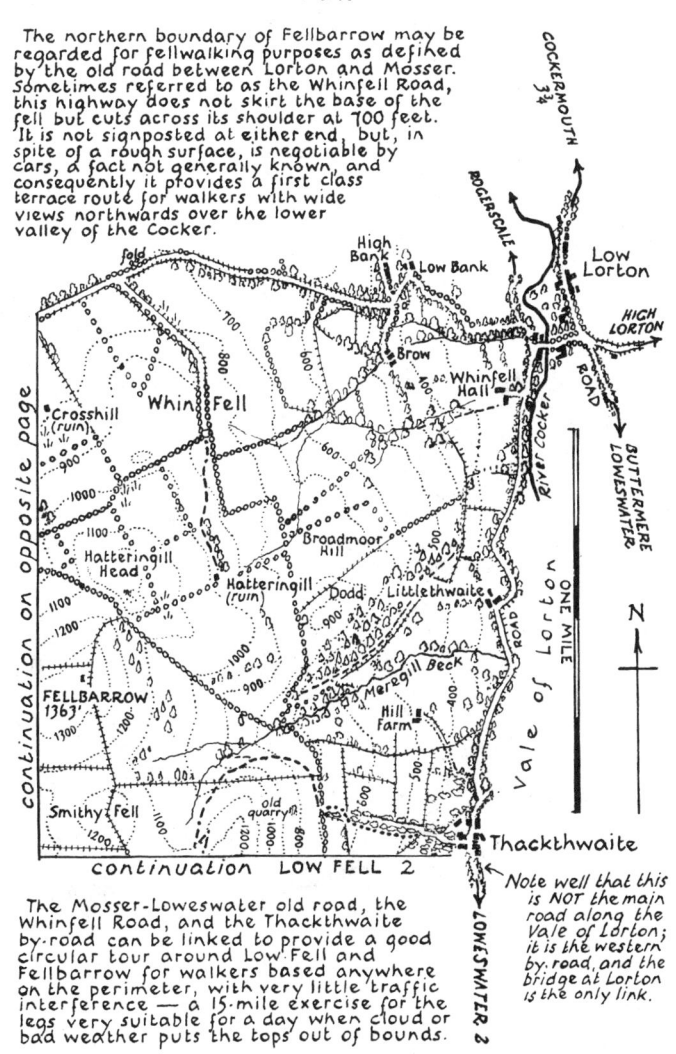

The northern boundary of Fellbarrow may be regarded for fellwalking purposes as defined by the old road between Lorton and Mosser. Sometimes referred to as the Whinfell Road, this highway does not skirt the base of the fell but cuts across its shoulder at 700 feet. It is not signposted at either end, but, in spite of a rough surface, is negotiable by cars, a fact not generally known, and consequently it provides a first class terrace route for walkers with wide views northwards over the lower valley of the Cocker.

The Mosser-Loweswater old road, the Whinfell Road, and the Thackthwaite by-road can be linked to provide a good circular tour around Low Fell and Fellbarrow for walkers based anywhere on the perimeter, with very little traffic interference — a 15-mile exercise for the legs very suitable for a day when cloud or bad weather puts the tops out of bounds.

Note well that this is NOT the main road along the Vale of Lorton; it is the western by-road, and the bridge at Lorton is the only link.

Fellbarrow 5

ASCENT FROM LOW LORTON
1200 feet of ascent : 3 miles

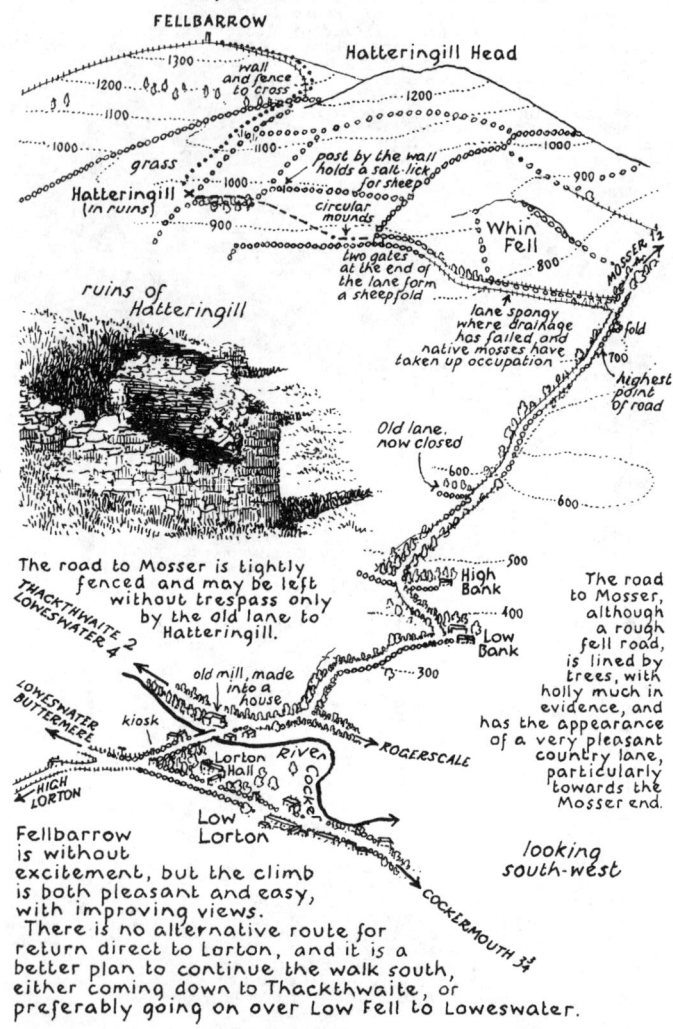

FELLBARROW

Hatteringill Head

wall and fence to cross

post by the wall holds a salt-lick for sheep

grass

Hatteringill (in ruins)

circular mounds

Whin Fell

two gates at the end of the lane form a sheepfold

MOSSER 1½

lane spongy where drainage has failed and native mosses have taken up occupation

fold

highest point of road

ruins of Hatteringill

Old lane, now closed

The road to Mosser is tightly fenced and may be left without trespass only by the old lane to Hatteringill.

THACKTHWAITE 2
LOWESWATER 4

High Bank

Low Bank

old mill, made into a house

kiosk

LOWESWATER
BUTTERMERE

HIGH LORTON

Lorton Hall

River Cocker

ROGERSCALE

Low Lorton

Fellbarrow is without excitement, but the climb is both pleasant and easy, with improving views.
There is no alternative route for return direct to Lorton, and it is a better plan to continue the walk south, either coming down to Thackthwaite, or preferably going on over Low Fell to Loweswater.

The road to Mosser, although a rough fell road, is lined by trees, with holly much in evidence, and has the appearance of a very pleasant country lane, particularly towards the Mosser end.

looking south-west

COCKERMOUTH 5½

Fellbarrow 6

ASCENT FROM THACKTHWAITE
ROUTE A: 1000 feet of ascent : 1¼ miles
ROUTE B: 1150 feet of ascent : 2 miles

On Route B the last two fence-gates are locked and must be climbed.

Watching Crag — Sourfoot Fell — Smithy Fell — FELLBARROW

This swampy hollow is the site of a former plantation, now almost denuded of trees.

ROUTE B: The walk may be extended and improved by following the drove road to the fence crossing its summit, where a short detour left leads to Watching Crag, a superb viewpoint, after which Fellbarrow may be reached along the ridge.

looking south-west

Above the wall an excellent drove-road winds round the shoulder of the fell, gaining height gradually.

ROUTE A (direct) leaves the drove-road on the curve and makes a beeline for the top of Fellbarrow, directly ahead.

Thackthwaite

Leave the hamlet by the lane opposite the telephone kiosk.

This lane has seen better days. At one time it must have been a delightful tree-lined avenue linking the hamlet with the open fell. The lane is still attractive at the start, like a wooded dell, but after 200 yards, at a corner, it becomes overgrown and is barricaded. At this point it is permissible to use the gate on the left and continue upwards in the field alongside. At the fence ahead cross to the other (north) side to reach the gate in the intake wall — and fasten it securely after using it.

Thackthwaite, midway between Loweswater and Low Lorton on a quiet by-road and peacefully carrying on its rural activities undisturbed by tourists, is a good place to leave this road for the ascent of Fellbarrow; in fact, here is the only obvious right of way leading off the four miles of the road. The climb is simple and the views excellent if Watching Crag is visited.

Fellbarrow 7

THE SUMMIT

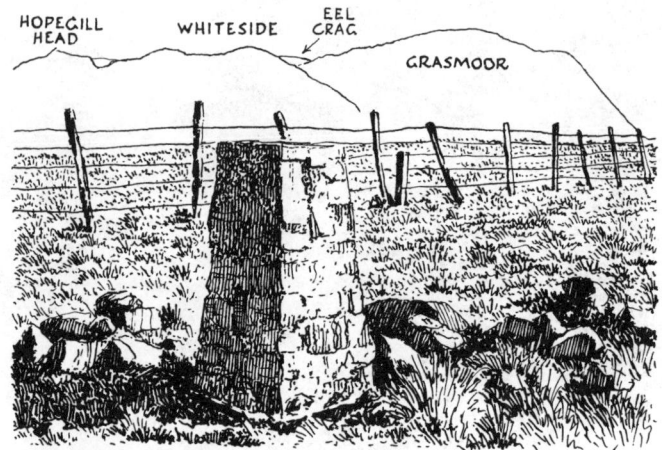

HOPEGILL HEAD — WHITESIDE — EEL CRAG — GRASMOOR

Everything there is to see on the summit can be seen at a glance: a rounded swell of grass crossed by a wire fence, crowned with an Ordnance Survey column (S.5229) and littered with a few untidy stones that may be surplus building material brought up by the surveyors, or ruins of a former cairn. Note, 60 yards west, a collection of stones arranged in a ring: it has no special significance and no history.

DESCENTS: Reverse the routes of ascent, or risk entanglement in barbed fences.

RIDGE ROUTE

TO LOW FELL, 1360': 1½ miles : S
several depressions
400 feet of ascent

An easy walk towards beautiful scenery. Follow the watershed, taking all bumps (and fences) as they appear. Easy going on grass throughout. Lovely views unfold.

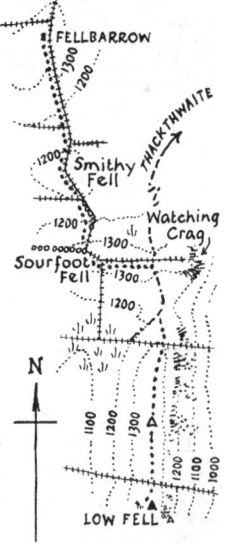

ONE MILE

Fellbarrow 8

THE VIEW

As the diagram suggests, Fellbarrow stands on the fringe of the high country, and to north and west there is a wide and uninterrupted view of the coastal plain of Workington and district and across the Solway Firth to the Scottish hills, a scene predominantly rural but with some obvious evidences of urban development and industry. More of Lakeland is visible than the fell's low elevation of 1363' would lead one to expect. Southeast the skyline is crowded with peaks (this view is much better from the neighbouring Low Fell) and the best thing is the lofty ridge of the Hopegill Head range across the Vale of Lorton backed by Grasmoor.

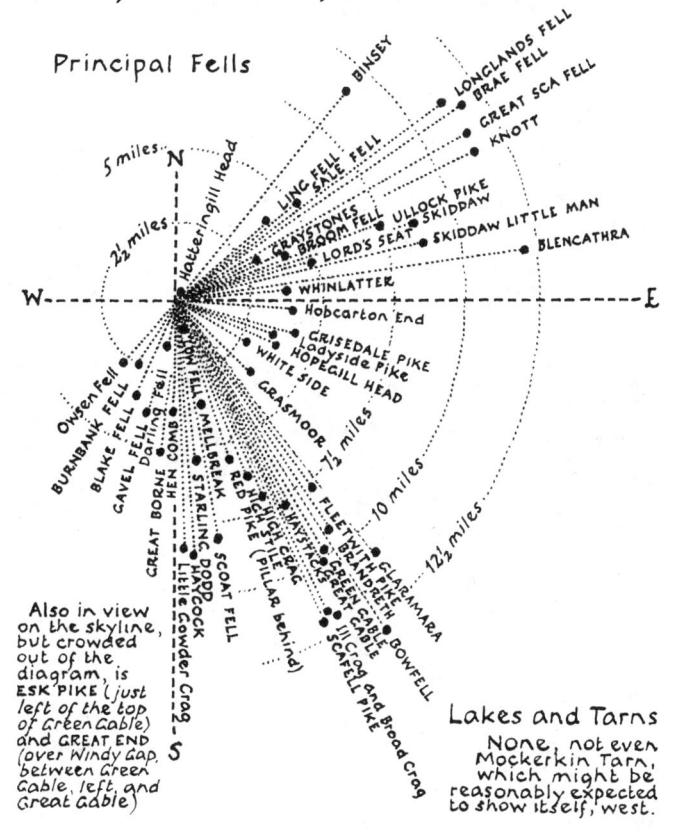

Principal Fells

(diagram of bearings to surrounding fells, with distance rings at 5 miles, 7½ miles, 10 miles, 12½ miles, and 22 miles; compass points N, E, S, W)

Fells labelled: Hatteringill Head, BINSEY, LING FELL, SALE FELL, LONGLANDS FELL, BRAE FELL, GREAT SCA FELL, KNOTT, BROOM FELL, GRAYSTONES, ULLOCK PIKE, LORD'S SEAT, SKIDDAW, SKIDDAW LITTLE MAN, BLENCATHRA, WHINLATTER, Hobcarton End, GRISEDALE PIKE, Ladyside Pike, HOPEGILL HEAD, WHITE SIDE, GRASMOOR, Owsen Fell, BURNBANK FELL, BLAKE FELL, GAVEL FELL, Darling Fell, HEN COMB, LOW FELL, MELLBREAK, STARLING DODD, RED PIKE, HAYCOCK, SCOAT FELL, LITTLE DODD, Little Gowder Crag, GREAT BORNE, FLEETWITH PIKE, HIGH CRAG, HIGH STILE, KIRK FELL, GREEN GABLE, GREAT GABLE, BOWFELL, GLARAMARA, JIL CRAG and Broad Crag, SCAFELL PIKE, RED PIKE (PILLAR behind)

Also in view on the skyline, but crowded out of the diagram, is ESK PIKE (just left of the top of Green Gable) and GREAT END (over Windy Gap, between Green Gable, left, and Great Gable)

Lakes and Tarns

NONE, not even Mockerkin Tarn, which might be reasonably expected to show itself, west.

Fleetwith Pike 2126'

from Gatesgarth

- Buttermere
- Gatesgarth
- ▲ DALE HEAD
- ▲ FLEETWITH PIKE
- Seatoller
- Honister Pass

MILES
0 1 2 3

Fleetwith Pike 2

NATURAL FEATURES

Honister Crag is a landmark of renown, well known to Lakeland's visitors and as familiar to those who journey on wheels as to those who travel on foot. This precipice towers dramatically above the road between Borrowdale and Buttermere, a savage wall of rock and heather strewn with natural debris and spoil from the quarry-workings high on the cliff, a place without beauty, a place to daunt the eye and creep the flesh. This huge barrier extends for two miles northwest from the top of Honister Pass, but becomes less intimidating as Gatesgarth is approached.

looking west

1 : The summit
2 : Honister Crag
3 : Honister Pass
4 : Gatesgarthdale Beck

The fell of which Honister Crag is so striking a part is Fleetwith, and its summit, overlooking Buttermere, is Fleetwith Pike, not so well known by name or shape as its illustrious subsidiary but nevertheless associated in the minds of many visitors with a conspicuous white memorial cross on its lower slopes. A smaller company of people, with better discrimination, relate the fell to a supremely beautiful view and a soaring ridge and a wild hollow rimmed by crags: the first is of the three lakes in the Buttermere valley, the second shoots into the sky like an arrow from the fields of Gatesgarth, and the third, Warnscale Bottom, is a natural amphitheatre of impressive proportions. These are the things that identify Fleetwith in the mind of the fellwalker.

looking south-east

1 : The summit
2 : Honister Crag
3 : Northwest ridge
4 : Gatesgarthdale Beck
5 : Warnscale Beck
6 : Warnscale Bottom

The downward slope of the summit, away from and behind the cliffs of Honister, is gently inclined to the upland marsh of Dubs Bottom, beyond which a broad moor rises gradually to Great Gable, the dominating influence hereabouts, of which Fleetwith Pike may be described, geographically, as the northern terminus.

All the Fleetwith streams are headwaters of the River Cocker and flow northwest into Buttermere, the green colour of the water of the lake being attributed to the slate dust carried down by them from the quarries.

Fleetwith Pike 3

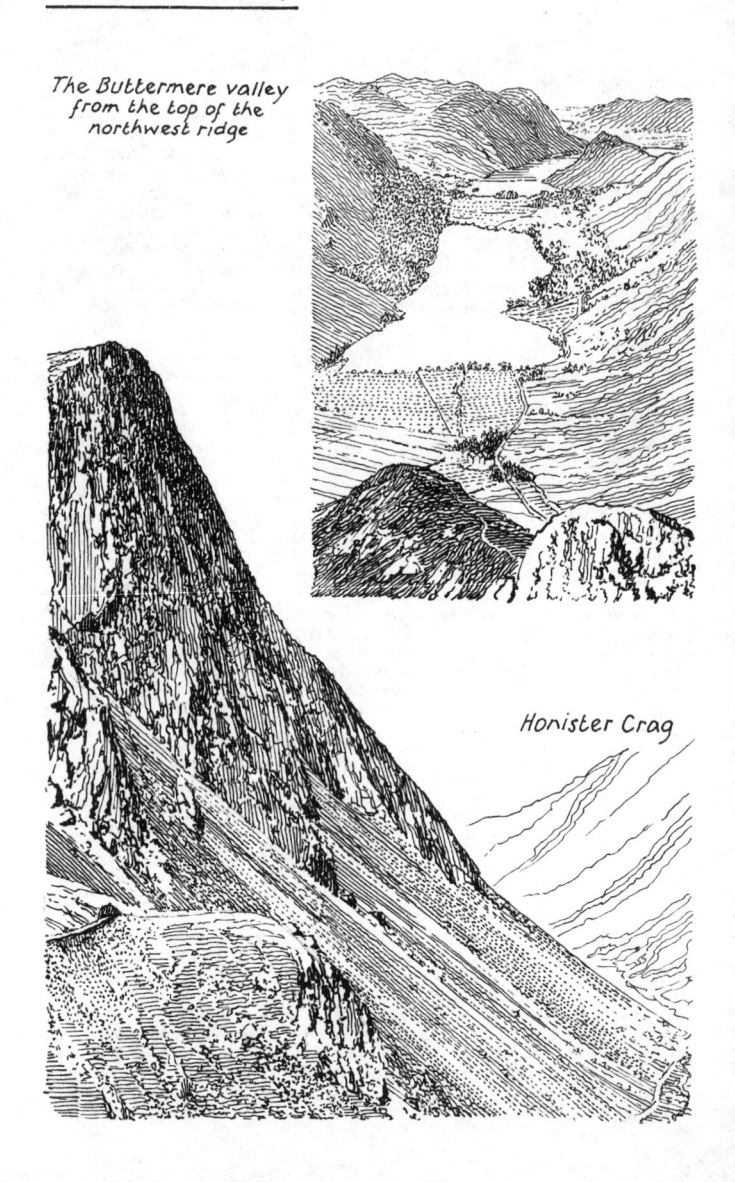

The Buttermere valley from the top of the northwest ridge

Honister Crag

Fleetwith Pike 4

MAP

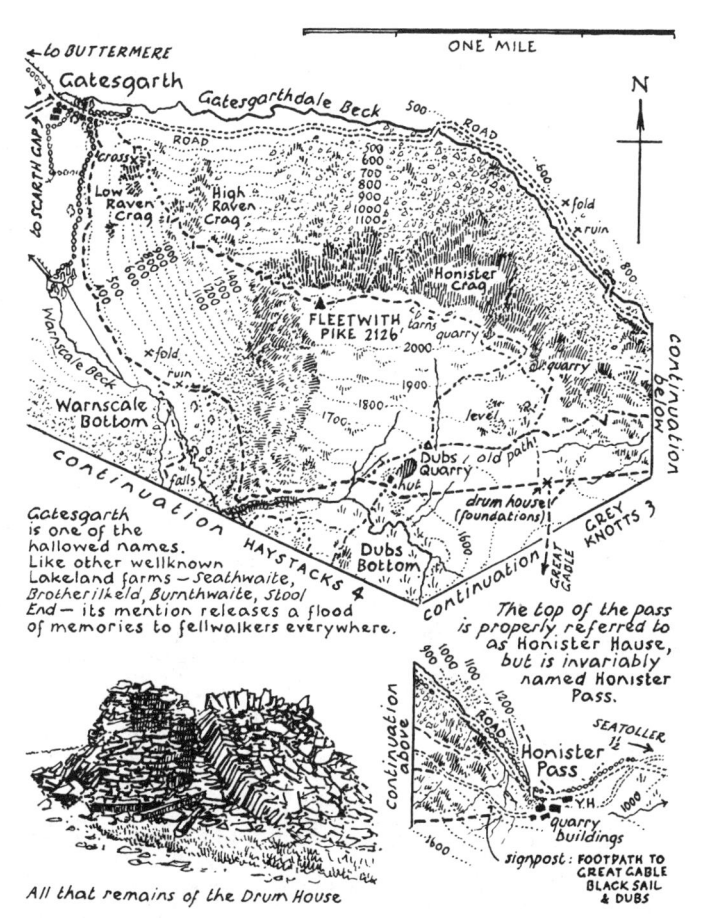

Gatesgarth is one of the hallowed names. Like other wellknown Lakeland farms — Seathwaite, Brotherilkeld, Burnthwaite, Stool End — its mention releases a flood of memories to fellwalkers everywhere.

All that remains of the Drum House

The top of the pass is properly referred to as Honister Hause, but is invariably named Honister Pass.

The path between the quarry buildings on Honister Pass and Dubs Quarry is the straightest mile in Lakeland. Originally it was the permanent way for trucks conveying stone, the winding gear being accommodated in the Drum House at the highest point on the line. Since abandonment of the tramway the track of the rails has been adopted as a path (the rails have been removed, but some sleepers remain) with the blessing of the quarry management, who have signposted it for walkers.

Fleetwith Pike 5

ASCENT FROM HONISTER PASS
1000 feet of ascent : 1¼ miles

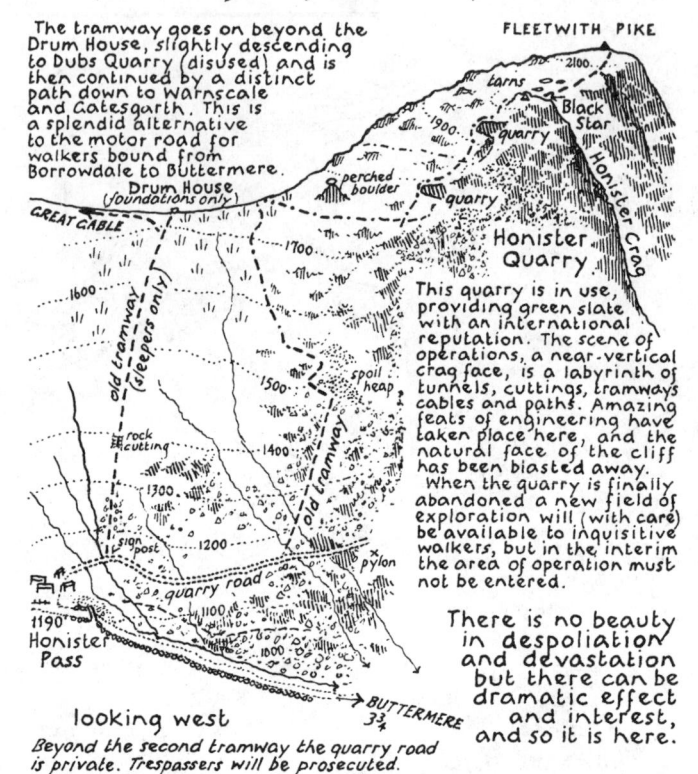

The tramway goes on beyond the Drum House, slightly descending to Dubs Quarry (disused) and is then continued by a distinct path down to Warnscale and Gatesgarth. This is a splendid alternative to the motor road for walkers bound from Borrowdale to Buttermere.

FLEETWITH PIKE

Honister Crag

Honister Quarry

This quarry is in use, providing green slate with an international reputation. The scene of operations, a near-vertical crag face, is a labyrinth of tunnels, cuttings, tramways, cables and paths. Amazing feats of engineering have taken place here, and the natural face of the cliff has been blasted away.

When the quarry is finally abandoned a new field of exploration will (with care) be available to inquisitive walkers, but in the interim the area of operation must not be entered.

looking west

There is no beauty in despoliation and devastation but there can be dramatic effect and interest, and so it is here.

Beyond the second tramway the quarry road is private. Trespassers will be prosecuted.

The old tramway to the Drum House, long out of commission, has been adopted as a path and is in popular use. It leaves the quarry road beyond the cutting sheds and is signposted FOOTPATH TO GREAT GABLE, BLACK SAIL & DUBS. Less known is another abandoned tramway rising from the quarry road 300 yards further on. The original footpath used to ascend alongside and at the head of this tramway it can be clearly seen and may be followed across the shoulder of the fell to Dubs Quarry. Rarely used now, it gives a more interesting approach to Fleetwith Pike from the top of the Pass. When opposite the Drum House, note a perched boulder on a low crag and pass to the right of this (old path, indistinct at first on wet ground) to the edge of the crags. A thin track climbs up the edge, skirting two quarries and becoming clearer on the final easy half-mile to the summit-cairn. The top of Honister Crag (Black Star) occurs just beyond the second of these two quarries.

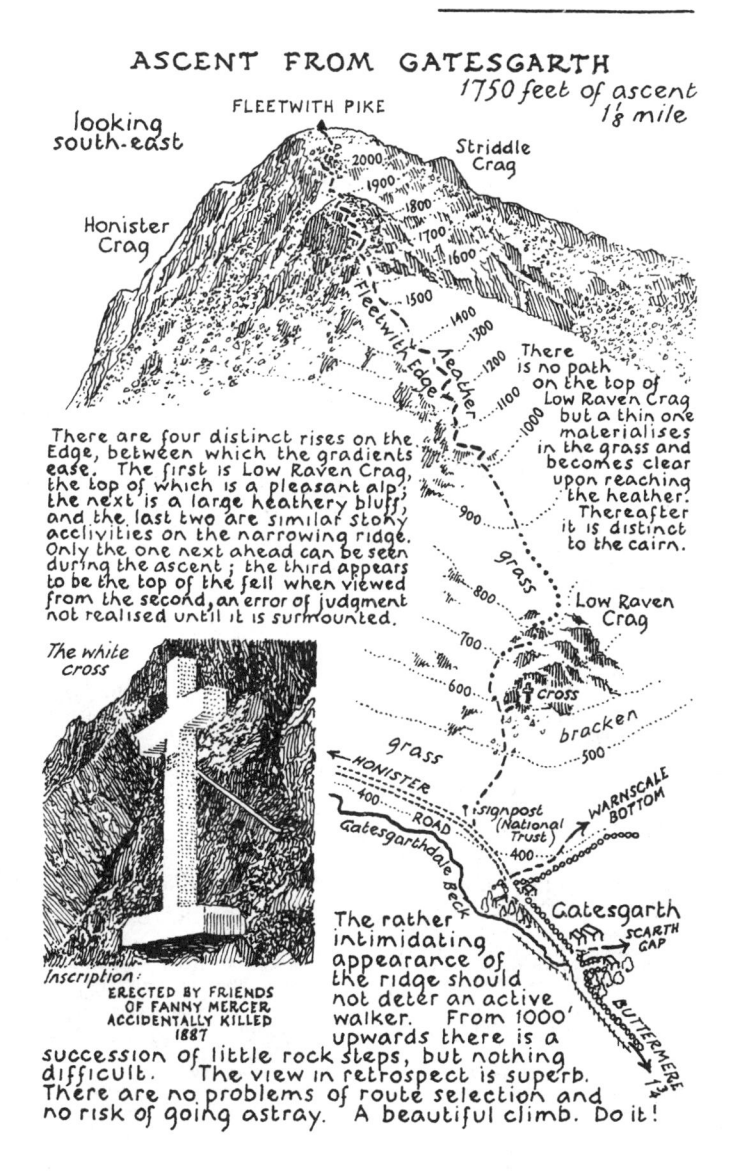

Fleetwith Pike 6

ASCENT FROM GATESGARTH
1750 feet of ascent
1⅛ mile

looking south-east

FLEETWITH PIKE
Striddle Crag
Honister Crag
Fleetwith Edge
heather

There are four distinct rises on the Edge, between which the gradients ease. The first is Low Raven Crag, the top of which is a pleasant alp; the next is a large heathery bluff; and the last two are similar stony acclivities on the narrowing ridge. Only the one next ahead can be seen during the ascent; the third appears to be the top of the fell when viewed from the second, an error of judgment not realised until it is surmounted.

There is no path on the top of Low Raven Crag but a thin one materialises in the grass and becomes clear upon reaching the heather. Thereafter it is distinct to the cairn.

grass
Low Raven Crag
cross
bracken
grass
HONISTER ROAD
Gatesgarthdale Beck
signpost (National Trust)
WARNSCALE BOTTOM
Gatesgarth
SCARTH GAP
BUTTERMERE

The white cross

Inscription:
ERECTED BY FRIENDS
OF FANNY MERCER
ACCIDENTALLY KILLED
1887

The rather intimidating appearance of the ridge should not deter an active walker. From 1000' upwards there is a succession of little rock steps, but nothing difficult. The view in retrospect is superb. There are no problems of route selection and no risk of going astray. A beautiful climb. Do it!

Fleetwith Pike 7

THE SUMMIT

HIGH CRAG   HIGH STILE   RED PIKE

Standing by the cairn, little is seen to suggest that there is a fearful downfall only a few score paces to the north, and the craggy southwest declivities contributing to Warnscale's barren and stony wilderness are similarly unsuspected although quite close. Indeed the environs are pleasant, with grass and heathery patches stretching into the distance amongst rocky outcrops and a fine company of greater hills all around. Eastwards along the top there is little change in altitude to an uprising a third of a mile away: this is the summit of Honister Crag.

DESCENTS: The northwest ridge is a splendid way down to the road at Gatesgarth, but it is necessary to proceed slowly in several places and to keep strictly to the track — there is a reason for every zigzag. The route is safe in mist, but care is then needed near the foot of the ridge, where there is no track and Low Raven Crag forms a precipice. Remember the cause of the white cross and incline to the right (on grass) when the first rocks appear.

Under ice or snow the ridge is a different proposition, and it may be safer then to go down via Dubs Quarry and the path therefrom.

For Honister Pass (top) the route of ascent may be reversed, but in bad weather wander southeast until the unmissable Drum House path is struck, and follow it eastwards to the Pass.

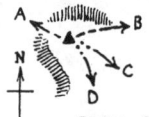

A: to Gatesgarth
B: to Honister Pass (top) direct
C: to Drum House
D: to Dubs Quarry

PLAN OF SUMMIT

RIDGE ROUTES

The neighbouring heights on the same upland mass are Haystacks and Grey Knotts, but connecting ridges are absent, the journey to either being across open country. For Grey Knotts aim first for the Drum House (which is in sight) and for Haystacks aim first for Dubs Quarry (which is not), taking up the ascent from there as indicated in the chapters on those two fells.

Fleetwith Pike 8

THE VIEW

Most visitors to the cairn will consider the prospect along the Buttermere valley the best thing in view, and this is certainly remarkably fine, and exclusive to Fleetwith Pike (it is even better 100 yards down the north-west ridge).

Yet, predominantly, mountains occupy the scene. The Grasmoor fells, the High Stile and Dale Head groups, Great Gable and Pillar are all seen at close range, the latter two appearing as giants.

Principal Fells

(diagram of fells radiating from viewpoint, labelled with compass directions N, W, S and distances 5 miles, 7½ miles, 10 miles)

Fells labelled include: ULLOCK PIKE, LONG SIDE, SKIDDAW, SCAR CRAGS, CAUSEY PIKE, EEL CRAGS, WANDOPE, ROBINSON, HINDSCARTH, FELLBARROW, WHITELESS, GRASMOOR, HIGH SNOCKRIGG, DALE HEAD, LOW FELL, RANNERDALE KNOTTS, MELLBREAK, BURNBANK FELL, BLAKE FELL, HEN COMB, GAVEL FELL, RED PIKE, HIGH STILE, HIGH CRAG, PILLAR, HAYSTACKS, YEWBARROW, WHIN RIGG, KIRK FELL, BRANDRETH, GREEN GABLE, GREAT GABLE, ESK PIKE, BOWFELL, SCAFELL, GREAT END, GREY KNOTTS, GLARAMARA, ROSTHWAITE FELL, HIGH RAISE, ULLSCARF, HIGH STREET, FAIRFIELD, STYBARROW DODD, RAISE, WHITE SIDE, HELVELLYN LOWER MAN, HELVELLYN, NETHERMOST PIKE, DOLLYWAGGON PIKE

(panorama sketch labelled): BRANDRETH, GREAT END, GREEN GABLE, GREAT GABLE, Beck Head, LINGMELL, SCAFELL, KIRK FELL

looking south

Lakes and Tarns
SSW: Blackbeck Tarn
SW: Innominate Tarn
NW: Loweswater
NW: Crummock Water (2 sections)
NW: Buttermere

Great Round How

Green Crag

Gavel Fell 1720'

from the terrace path below Carling Knott

Loweswater ●
▲ BLAKE FELL
▲ GAVEL FELL
● HEN COMB
● Croasdale

MILES
0 1 2 3

High Nook Farm

Gavel Fell 2

NATURAL FEATURES

Gavel Fell is the central and second highest of the five Loweswater fells south of the lake, having Blake Fell on the west and Hen Comb on the east. It rises as a well-defined ridge between Highnook Beck and Whiteoak Beck but becomes sprawling towards the summit, which is a wide grassy tableland of no particular interest and lacking a distinctive outline. Along the top is the Derwent-Ehen watershed; much of the rain that falls here, however, prefers to linger indefinitely in marshy ground and peaty pools by the side of the boundary fence, the remainder being taken down to the Loweswater valley in the two becks named above, or to Ennerdale by way of Croasdale Beck and Gill Beck. This latter watercourse rises near Floutern Tarn Pass, where there is a crossing between Ennerdale and Buttermere, and for two miles the path lies along the side of Banna Fell, a subsidiary of Gavel Fell south of the summit with some claim to independence. On this side, too, is the curious little crest of Floutern Cop overlooking Floutern Tarn.

All the Loweswater fells have a foundation of slate and the smooth grass slopes characteristic of the type. Less characteristic is the tarn nestling in a hollow of Gavel Fell's north flank, for tarns more usually favour the harder volcanic rock. Since Gavel Fell also has a stake in Floutern Tarn it is doubly distinguished and twice blessed.

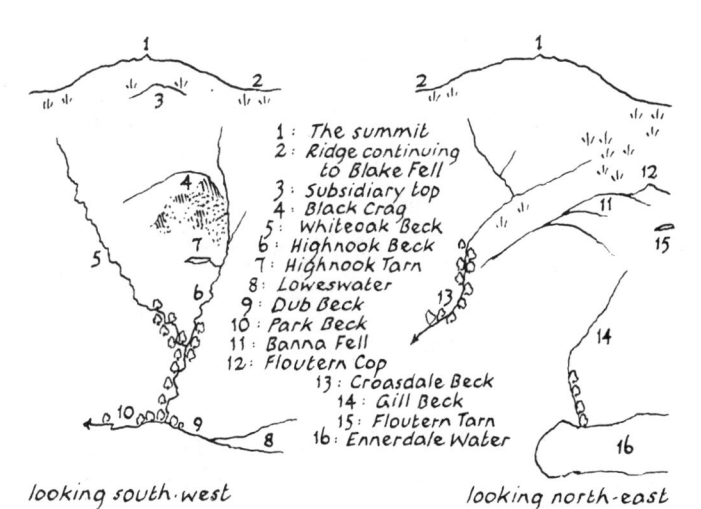

1 : The summit
2 : Ridge continuing to Blake Fell
3 : Subsidiary top
4 : Black Crag
5 : Whiteoak Beck
6 : Highnook Beck
7 : Highnook Tarn
8 : Loweswater
9 : Dub Beck
10 : Park Beck
11 : Banna Fell
12 : Floutern Cop
13 : Croasdale Beck
14 : Gill Beck
15 : Floutern Tarn
16 : Ennerdale Water

looking south-west   *looking north-east*

Gavel Fell 3

MAP

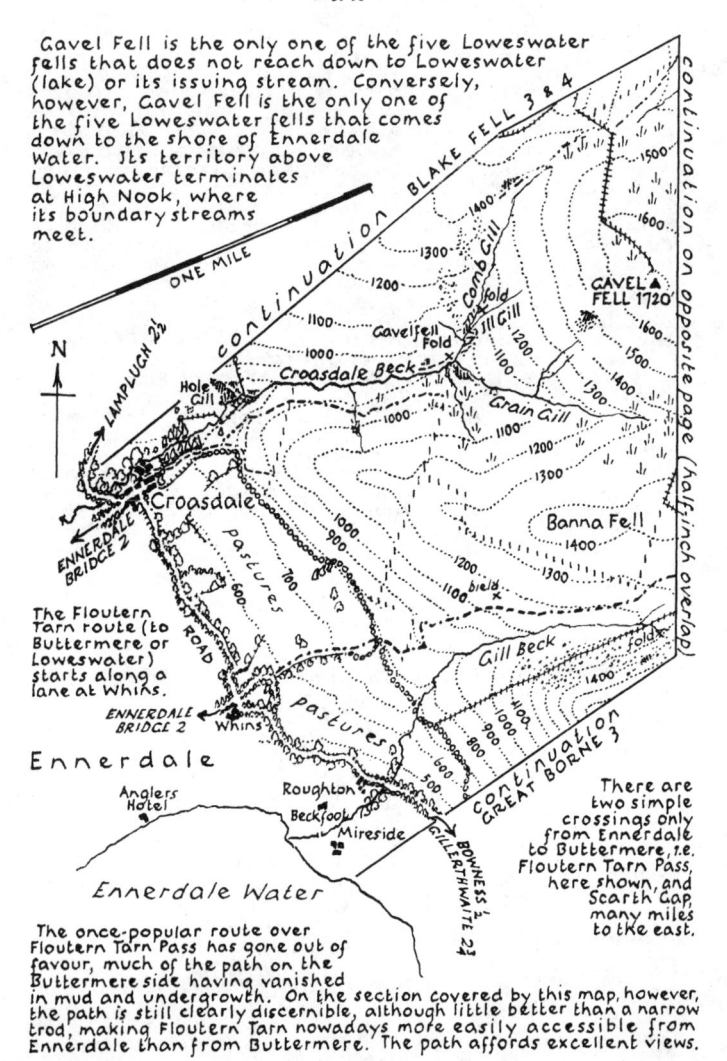

Gavel Fell is the only one of the five Loweswater fells that does not reach down to Loweswater (lake) or its issuing stream. Conversely, however, Gavel Fell is the only one of the five Loweswater fells that comes down to the shore of Ennerdale Water. Its territory above Loweswater terminates at High Nook, where its boundary streams meet.

The Floutern Tarn route (to Buttermere or Loweswater) starts along a lane at Whins.

There are two simple crossings only from Ennerdale to Buttermere, i.e. Floutern Tarn Pass, here shown, and Scarth Gap, many miles to the east.

The once-popular route over Floutern Tarn Pass has gone out of favour, much of the path on the Buttermere side having vanished in mud and undergrowth. On the section covered by this map, however, the path is still clearly discernible, although little better than a narrow trod, making Floutern Tarn nowadays more easily accessible from Ennerdale than from Buttermere. The path affords excellent views.

Gavel Fell 4

MAP

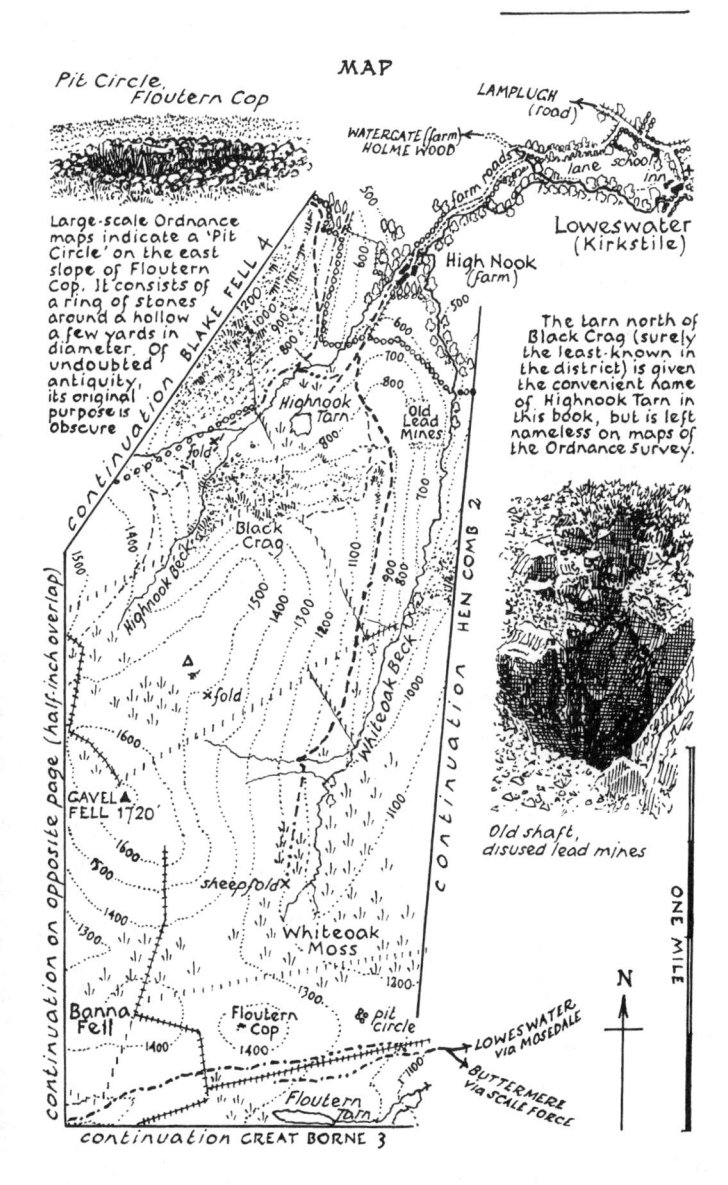

Pit Circle, Floutern Cop

Large-scale Ordnance maps indicate a 'Pit Circle' on the east slope of Floutern Cop. It consists of a ring of stones around a hollow a few yards in diameter. Of undoubted antiquity, its original purpose is obscure.

The tarn north of Black Crag (surely the least-known in the district) is given the convenient name of Highnook Tarn in this book, but is left nameless on maps of the Ordnance Survey.

Old shaft, disused lead mines

ONE MILE

N

Gavel Fell 5

ASCENT FROM LOWESWATER
1400 feet of ascent : 3 miles

Leave the drove road where it descends slightly and turns into the Whiteoak valley. A thin trod winds up to the top of Black Crag. Then the route is pathless. Pleasant dry walking leads over undulations to a cairn (which, in mist, might wrongly be thought to be the top). A marshy depression intervenes between this cairn and the summit.

Gavel Fell, set well back and lacking in shapeliness, is not an obvious objective for a climb, yet it has clearly-defined boundaries, a direct ridge, and good views. This ascent is a fair example of the easy, unexciting climbing available from Loweswater.

looking south-west

In the shady hollow where Dub Beck is crossed, the lane divides into two farm roads (gated). Car parking in the fields is politely discouraged by notices, rightly. There is peace and quietness here.

High Nook is a farm enclosed by beautifully wooded becks and embowered in lovely trees. The situation is truly Arcadian. At the farm use the facing gate to gain a rising grass path to the intake wall.

Dub Beck — (issuing from Loweswater lake)

This pleasant approach is typical of the shy charm of the Loweswater countryside. All is very rural and unspoilt. Here is an Old English scene of honeysuckle and wild roses.

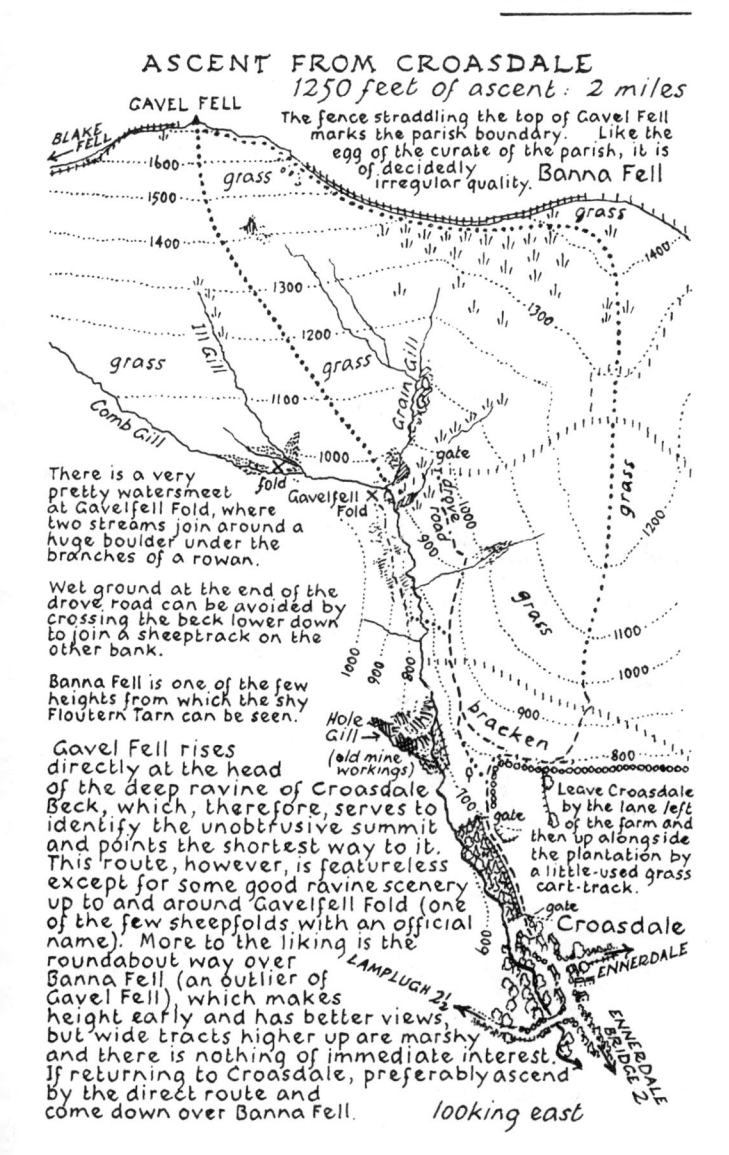

Gavel Fell 6

ASCENT FROM CROASDALE
1250 feet of ascent : 2 miles

The fence straddling the top of Gavel Fell marks the parish boundary. Like the egg of the curate of the parish, it is of decidedly irregular quality. Banna Fell

There is a very pretty watersmeet at Gavelfell Fold, where two streams join around a huge boulder under the branches of a rowan.

Wet ground at the end of the drove road can be avoided by crossing the beck lower down to join a sheeptrack on the other bank.

Banna Fell is one of the few heights from which the shy Floutern Tarn can be seen.

Gavel Fell rises directly at the head of the deep ravine of Croasdale Beck, which, therefore, serves to identify the unobtrusive summit and points the shortest way to it. This route, however, is featureless except for some good ravine scenery up to and around Gavelfell Fold (one of the few sheepfolds with an official name). More to the liking is the roundabout way over Banna Fell (an outlier of Gavel Fell) which makes height early and has better views, but wide tracts higher up are marshy and there is nothing of immediate interest. If returning to Croasdale, preferably ascend by the direct route and come down over Banna Fell.

Leave Croasdale by the lane left of the farm and then up alongside the plantation by a little-used grass cart-track.

looking east

Gavel Fell 7

THE SUMMIT

(panorama labels: SKIDDAW, WHITESIDE, HOPEGILL HEAD, CRISEDALE PIKE, Sand Hill, GRASMOOR, EEL CRAG)

(foreground labels: Lanthwaite, MELLBREAK)

The summit is broad and gently undulating, but there is no difficulty in locating the highest point, which is decorated with a large cairn near the point where the fence, a wreck of its former self, suddenly gives up the ghost altogether. It is obvious that this cairn is the result of much labour, (for loose stones are at a premium on the all-grassy top), by an ardent member of the ancient company of Cairnbuilders Anonymous. It is a particularly tidy cairn, probably little disturbed since erection.

DESCENTS : Descents may be made in any direction after consulting the map. No terrors will be met, even in mist; no discomfort will be suffered except wet feet. The driest plan (for Loweswater) is to go down east to the drove-road near Whiteoak Beck, which leads pleasantly to High Nook.

The subsidiary top

A third of a mile north-east from the summit, across a marshy depression, with peat-hags, is an abrupt rise surmounted by a small cairn, marking the beginning of the Loweswater ridge in descent; this is a landmark on the ascent by that route. 1570' is its approximate elevation.

Gavel Fell 8

THE VIEW

The interest lies mainly in the eastern arc, where a goodly array of mountains is available for inspection, although they are not seen at their best except for the Grasmoor group.
Seawards, too, the prospect is disappointing, being interrupted by the neighbouring Blake Fell, a much superior viewpoint.

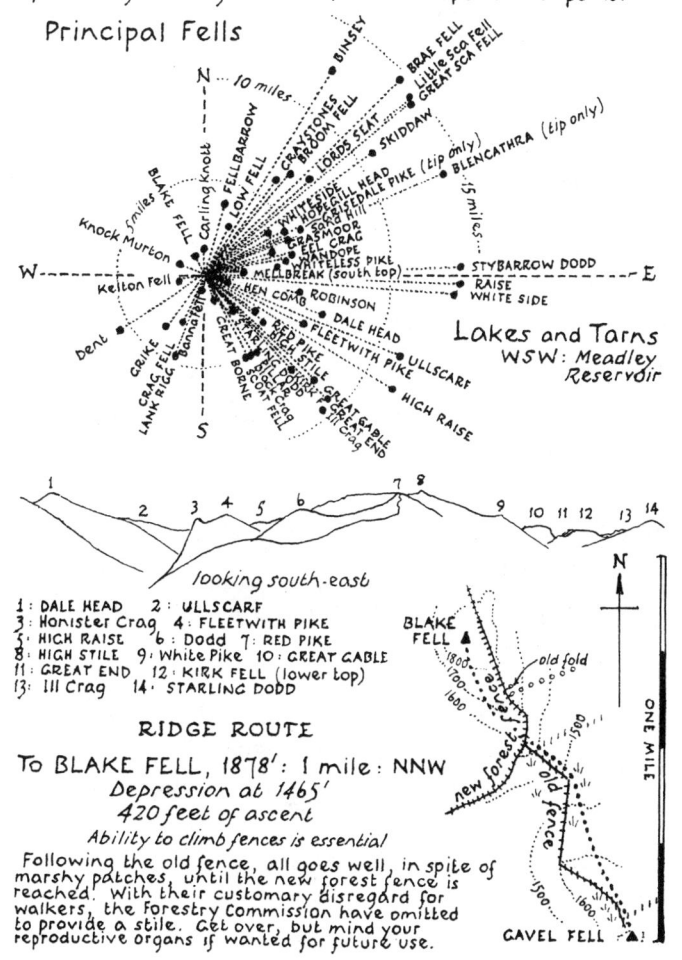

Principal Fells

Lakes and Tarns
WSW: Meadley Reservoir

looking south-east

1: DALE HEAD 2: ULLSCARF
3: Honister Crag 4: FLEETWITH PIKE
5: HIGH RAISE 6: Dodd 7: RED PIKE
8: HIGH STILE 9: White Pike 10: GREAT GABLE
11: GREAT END 12: KIRK FELL (lower top)
13: Ill Crag 14: STARLING DODD

RIDGE ROUTE

To BLAKE FELL, 1878': 1 mile: NNW
Depression at 1465'
420 feet of ascent
Ability to climb fences is essential

Following the old fence, all goes well, in spite of marshy patches, until the new forest fence is reached. With their customary disregard for walkers, the Forestry Commission have omitted to provide a stile. Get over, but mind your reproductive organs if wanted for future use.

Great Borne
also known as Herdus
2019'

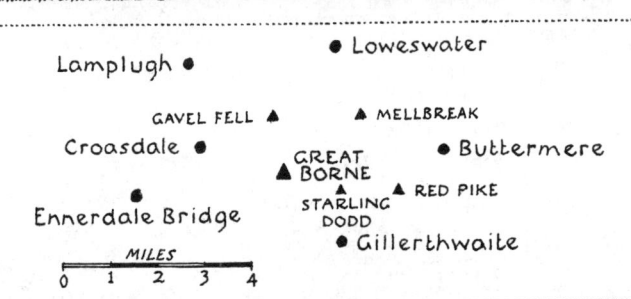

from Mosedale

Great Borne 2

NATURAL FEATURES

Great Borne is the name of the summit of the fell locally and correctly known as Herdus, an abbreviated version of the former name of Herdhouse. The fell is a familiar sight to West Cumbrians: from Ennerdale Water it rises as a massive buttress to the High Stile ridge. It is not prominent in views from other directions, however, and is not frequented by walkers.

Along its northern base, where it towers imposingly above the shy Floutern Tarn, there is a crossing of the high ground between Buttermere and Ennerdale: this is the once-popular but no-longer-popular Floutern Pass, the route having been partly submerged in the quagmire of Mosedale Head.

Facing Ennerdale the slope is steep and rough, having the name of Herdus Scaw, or Scar, and has little appeal, but on this side there is a gem of mountain architecture on a small scale in Bowness Knotts, which can be climbed by a short indirect scramble and commands a fine view of the valley but impresses most when the evening sun lights up it's colourful rocks and screes. On the lower Ennerdale flanks the Forestry Commission's evergreens encroach rather patchily, there being areas of infertility.

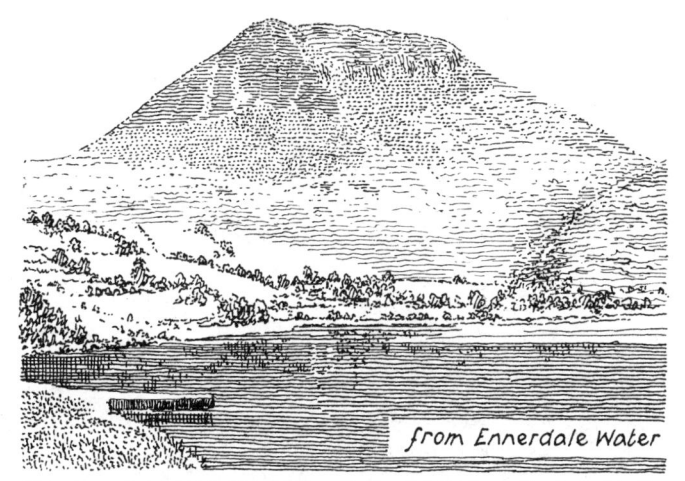

from Ennerdale Water

The viewpoint of this illustration is the lakeside path alongside the Anglers Hotel, which is uniquely situated at the water's edge. When the proposals of the South Cumberland Water Board to raise the level of the lake are implemented, the hotel will be demolished and a new one erected on a higher site. The pleasant pedestrian causeway along the lakeside to Bowness and the fringe of trees will also be sacrificed.

Great Borne 3

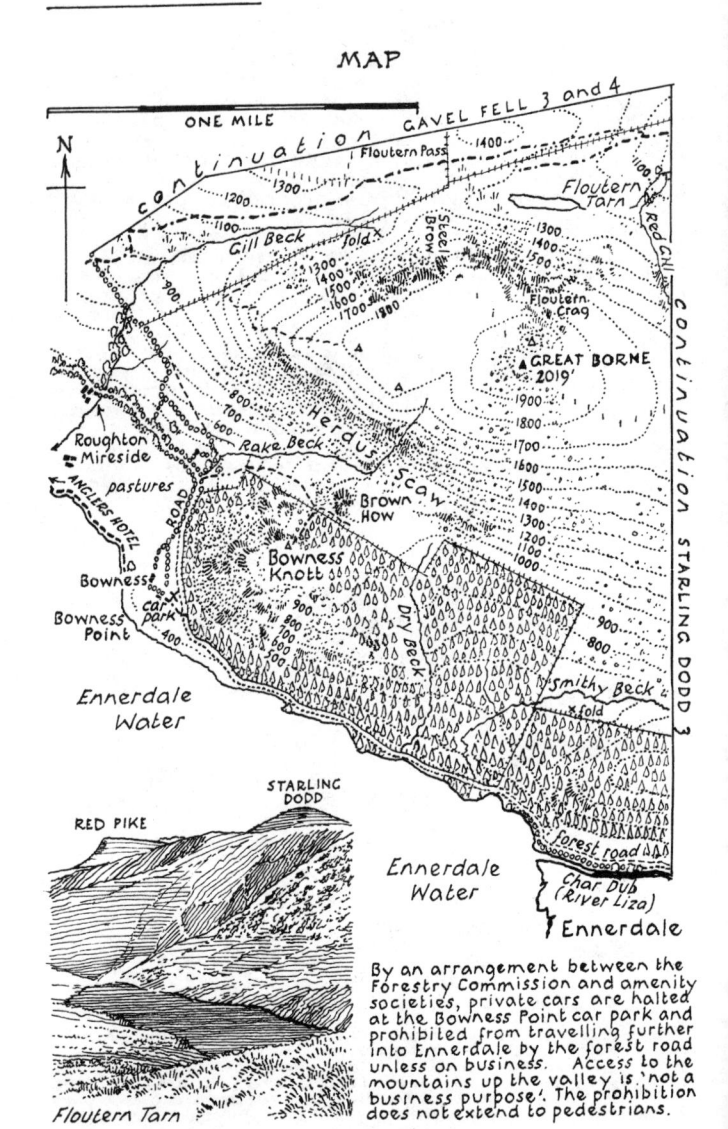

MAP

By an arrangement between the Forestry Commission and amenity societies, private cars are halted at the Bowness Point car park and prohibited from travelling further into Ennerdale by the forest road unless on business. Access to the mountains up the valley is 'not a business purpose'. The prohibition does not extend to pedestrians.

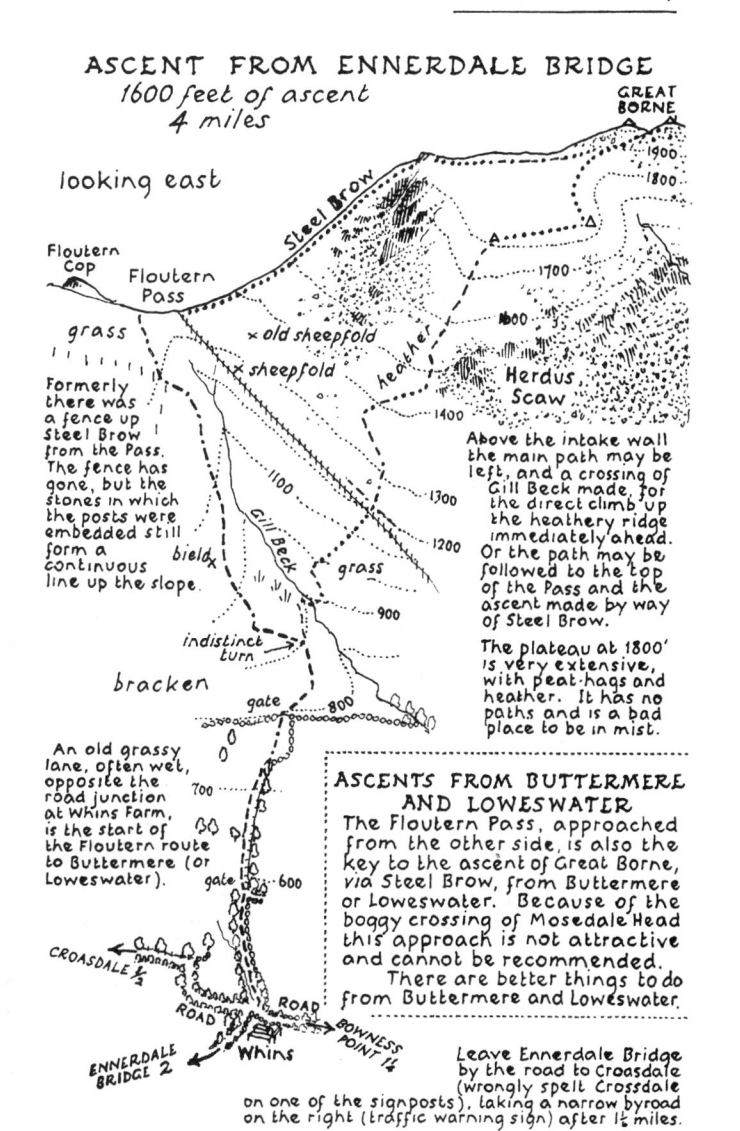

Great Borne 4

ASCENT FROM ENNERDALE BRIDGE
1600 feet of ascent
4 miles

looking east

GREAT BORNE

1900
1800

Floutern Cop
Floutern Pass
Steel Brow
grass
× old sheepfold
× sheepfold
heather
1700
1600
Herdus Scaw
1400

Formerly there was a fence up Steel Brow from the Pass. The fence has gone, but the stones in which the posts were embedded still form a continuous line up the slope.

bield ×
Gill Beck
1100
1200
1300
grass
900

Above the intake wall the main path may be left, and a crossing of Gill Beck made, for the direct climb up the heathery ridge immediately ahead. Or the path may be followed to the top of the Pass and the ascent made by way of Steel Brow.

The plateau at 1800' is very extensive, with peat-hags and heather. It has no paths and is a bad place to be in mist.

indistinct turn
bracken
gate
800
700

An old grassy lane, often wet, opposite the road junction at Whins Farm, is the start of the Floutern route to Buttermere (or Loweswater).

gate
600

CROASDALE ½
ROAD
ENNERDALE BRIDGE 2
Whins
ROAD
BOWNESS POINT 1½

ASCENTS FROM BUTTERMERE AND LOWESWATER

The Floutern Pass, approached from the other side, is also the key to the ascent of Great Borne, via Steel Brow, from Buttermere or Loweswater. Because of the boggy crossing of Mosedale Head this approach is not attractive and cannot be recommended.
There are better things to do from Buttermere and Loweswater.

Leave Ennerdale Bridge by the road to Croasdale (wrongly spelt Crossdale on one of the signposts), taking a narrow byroad on the right (traffic warning sign) after 1½ miles.

Great Borne 5

THE SUMMIT

above (left): the big cairn on the north top
above: the column on the south top

There are two separate tops, divided by a shallow 'valley' along which are the remains of a former fence. The north top, directly above Floutern Crag, carries a large cairn — a landmark for miles — but the south top, slightly higher, is the one chosen by the Ordnance Survey for the site of a triangulation column, and here too is a substantial wind-shelter. The summit is grassy, with embedded stones, and there are evidences of excavations to provide the materials for the column and shelter.

DESCENTS: Leave by way of the shallow valley between the two tops. There should be no difficulty in clear weather, but if going down direct to Floutern Pass descend *exactly* in line with the fence seen crossing the pass below: it is easy to start down a false ridge and be stopped by crags. In mist, make a wide curve east to north on easy ground, descending into Mosedale Head beyond Red Gill.

Bowness Knott

The sands are fast running out for those who would climb Bowness Knott to enjoy its fine full-length view of Ennerdale. Plantations have recently encroached on the summit and unless walkers keep a trail blazed through an abomination of forest trees the highest point of the fell will be inaccessible in a few years.

From the public car park at Bowness the fell already looks inaccessible, not because of foreign trees but native screes, this western face being an untrodden chaos of steep crags and talus slopes above a fringe of roadside trees. But easy access to the top is provided by the bracken slope away to the left. At 900 feet the fence is crossed where stones piled alongside assist the high step necessary to get over it.

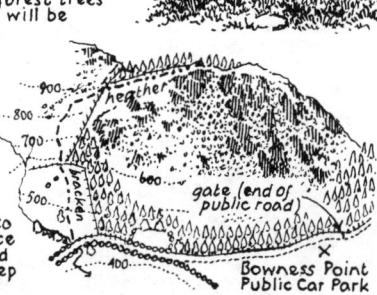

Great Borne 6

THE VIEW

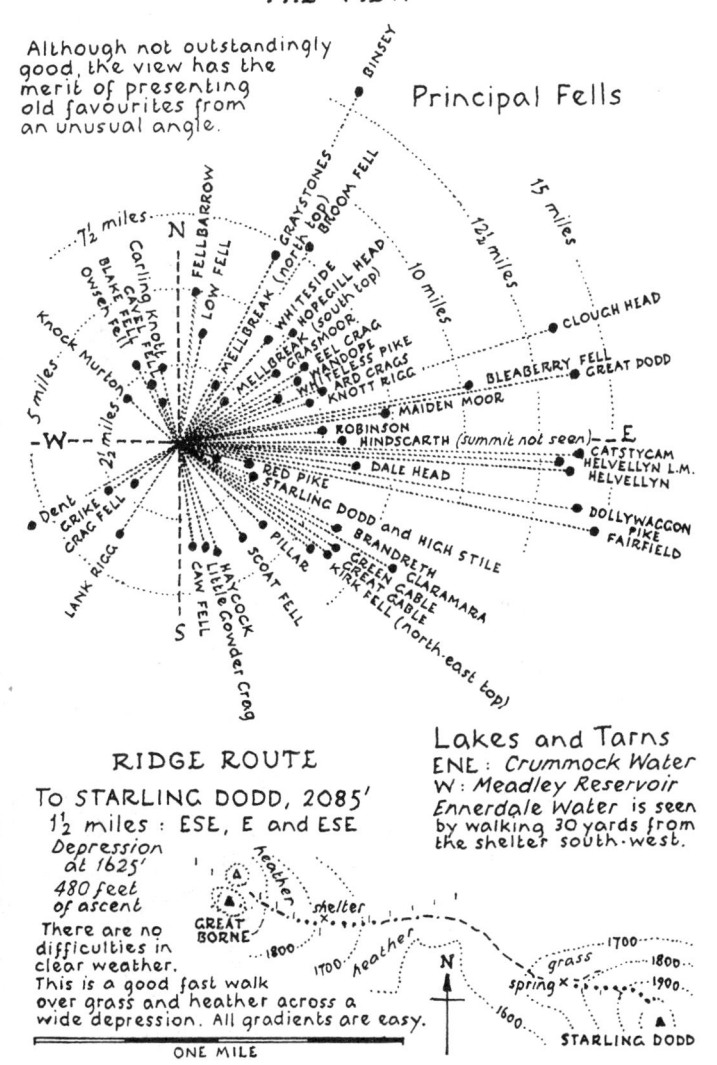

Although not outstandingly good, the view has the merit of presenting old favourites from an unusual angle.

Principal Fells

(panorama diagram with distance rings at 2½, 5, 7½, 10, 12½, and 15 miles; fells labelled clockwise:)

- BINSEY
- GRAYSTONES
- BROOM FELL
- LOW FELL
- FELLBARROW
- Carling Knott
- CAYET FELL
- BLAKE FELL
- Owen Fell
- Knock Murton
- MELLBREAK (north top)
- WHITESIDE
- HOPEGILL HEAD
- MELLBREAK (south top)
- GRASMOOR
- EEL CRAG
- WHITELESS PIKE
- ARD CRAGS
- KNOTT RIGG
- CLOUGH HEAD
- BLEABERRY FELL
- GREAT DODD
- MAIDEN MOOR
- ROBINSON
- HINDSCARTH (summit not seen)
- CATSTYCAM
- HELVELLYN L.M.
- HELVELLYN
- DALE HEAD
- Dent
- CRIKE
- CRAG FELL
- RED PIKE
- STARLING DODD and HIGH STILE
- DOLLYWAGGON PIKE
- FAIRFIELD
- LANK RIGG
- BRANDRETH
- GREEN CLARAMARA
- GREEN GABLE
- GREAT GABLE
- KIRK FELL (north-east top)
- HAYCOCK
- Little Gowder Crag
- PILLAR
- SCOAT FELL
- CAW FELL

RIDGE ROUTE

TO STARLING DODD, 2085'
1½ miles : ESE, E and ESE
Depression at 1625'
480 feet of ascent

There are no difficulties in clear weather. This is a good fast walk over grass and heather across a wide depression. All gradients are easy.

ONE MILE

Lakes and Tarns
ENE: *Crummock Water*
W: *Meadley Reservoir*
Ennerdale Water is seen by walking 30 yards from the shelter south-west.

(route map showing GREAT BORNE with shelter, heather at 1700–1800 ft, spring, grass, and STARLING DODD at 1900 ft)

Great Gable 2949'

from Wastwater

Great Gable 2

NATURAL FEATURES

Great Gable is a favourite of all fellwalkers, and first favourite with many. Right from the start of one's apprenticeship in the hills, the name appeals magically. It is a good name for a mountain, strong, challenging, compelling, starkly descriptive, suggesting the pyramid associated with the shape of mountains since early childhood. People are attracted to it because of the name. There is satisfaction in having achieved the ascent and satisfaction in announcing the fact to others. The name has status, and confers status... Yes, the name is good, simple yet subtly clever. If Great Gable were known only as Wasdale Fell fewer persons would climb it.

continued

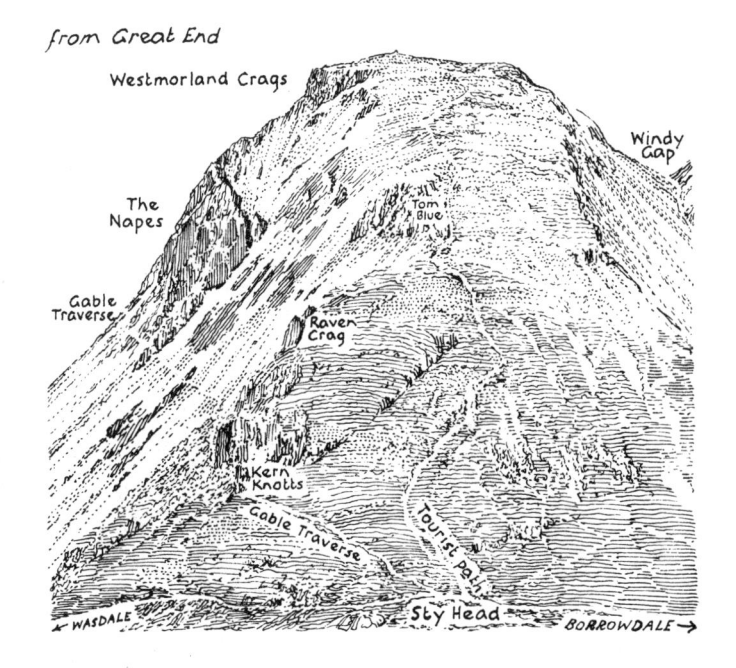

from Great End

Westmorland Crags
Windy Gap
The Napes
Tom Blue
Gable Traverse
Raven Crag
Kern Knotts
Gable Traverse
Tourist path
← WASDALE
Sty Head
BORROWDALE →

Great Gable 3

NATURAL FEATURES
continued

In appearance, too, Great Gable has the same appealing attributes. The name fits well. This mountain is strong yet not sturdy, masculine yet graceful. It is the undisputed overlord of the group of hills to which it belongs, and its superior height is emphasised tremendously by the deep gulf separating it from the Scafells and allowing an impressive view that reveals the whole of its half-mile altitude as an unremitting and unbroken pyramid: this is the aspect of the fell that earned the name. From east and west the slender tapering of the summit as seen from the south is not in evidence, the top appearing as a massive square-cut dome. From the north, where the build-up of height is more gradual, the skyline is a symmetrical arc.

continued

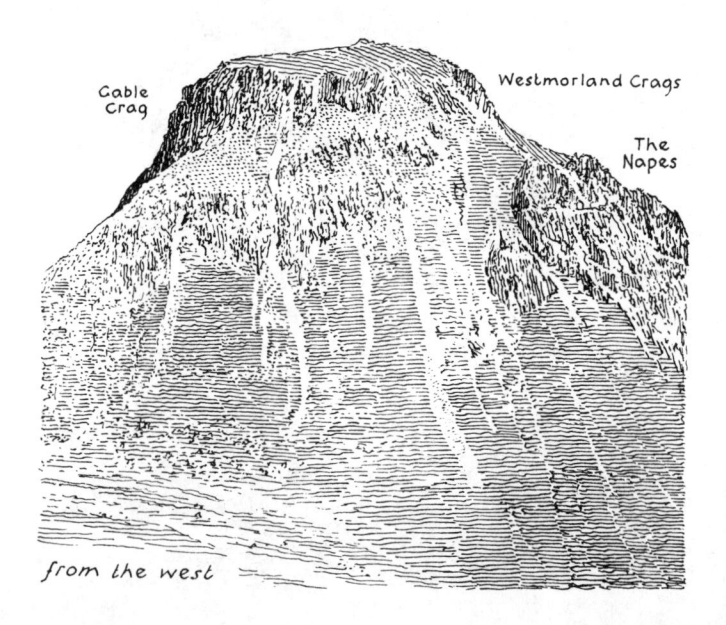

Gable Crag

Westmorland Crags

The Napes

from the west

Great Gable 4

NATURAL FEATURES

continued

Great Gable is a desert of stones. Vegetation is scanty, feeding few sheep. Petrified rivers of scree scar the southern slopes, from which stand out the bony ribs of the Napes ridges; the whole fell on this side is a sterile wilderness, dry and arid and dusty. The north face is a shadowed precipice, Gable Crag. Slopes to east and west are rough and stony. In some lights, especially in the afterglow of sunset, Great Gable is truly a beautiful mountain, but it is never a pretty one.

The view from the top is far-reaching, but not quite in balance because of the nearness of the Scafells, which, however, are seen magnificently. The aerial aspect of Wasdale is often described as the finest view in the district, a claim that more witnesses will accept than will dispute.

continued

from the north

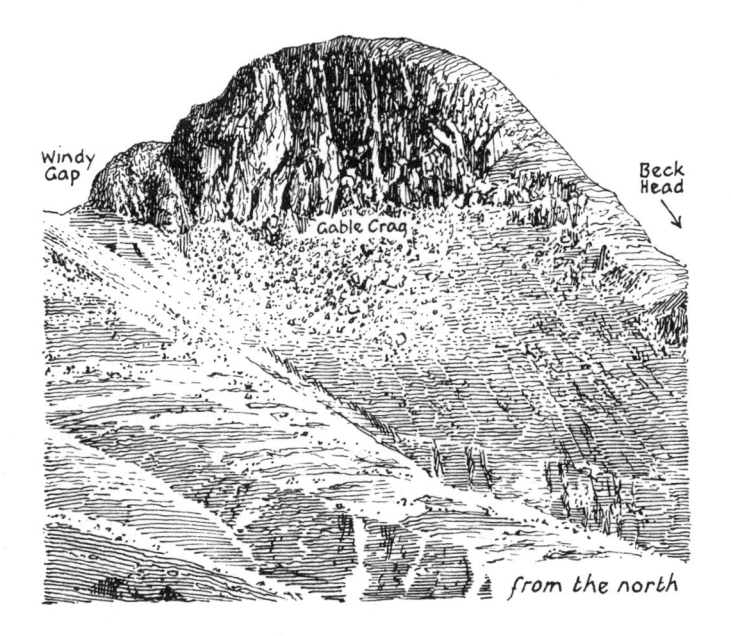

Great Gable 5

NATURAL FEATURES
continued

The failing of Great Gable is that it holds few mysteries, all its wares being openly displayed. The explorer, the man who likes to look around corners and discover secrets and intimacies, may be disappointed, not on a first visit, which cannot fail to be interesting, but on subsequent occasions. There are no cavernous recesses, no hidden tarns, no combes, no hanging valleys, no waterfalls, no streams other than those forming the boundaries.

Yet walkers tread its familiar tracks again and again, almost as a ritual, and climbers queue to scale its familiar rocks. The truth is, Great Gable casts a spell. It starts as an honourable adversary and becomes a friend. The choice of its summit as a war memorial is testimony to the affection and respect felt for this grand old mountain.

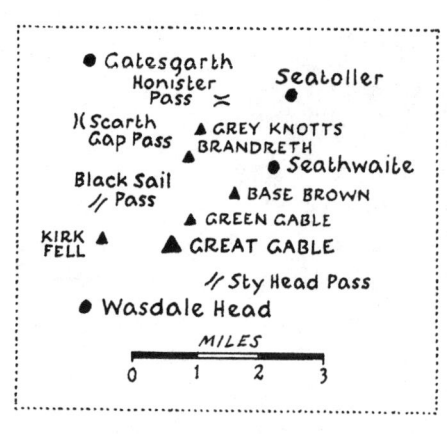

```
● Gatesgarth
  Honister        Seatoller
    Pass         ×
)(Scarth     ▲ GREY KNOTTS
Gap Pass    BRANDRETH
              ▲         ● Seathwaite
Black Sail
// Pass      ▲ BASE BROWN
             ▲ GREEN GABLE
KIRK
FELL ▲       ▲ GREAT GABLE
                 // Sty Head Pass
● Wasdale Head
         MILES
       0   1   2   3
```

Dry Tarn

This is a tarn that Nature fashioned and forgot. It is invariably bone-dry although mossy stones indicate the former presence of water. Dry Tarn is almost unknown, yet is within sight of the main path up Great Gable from Sty Head, being situated at 2100 feet on a grass shelf: it is more likely to be seen when descending.

This is Great Gable's only tarn.

Great Gable 6

MAP

Crags and other features are shown in greater detail, and named, on the larger-scale maps and diagrams appearing elsewhere in this chapter.

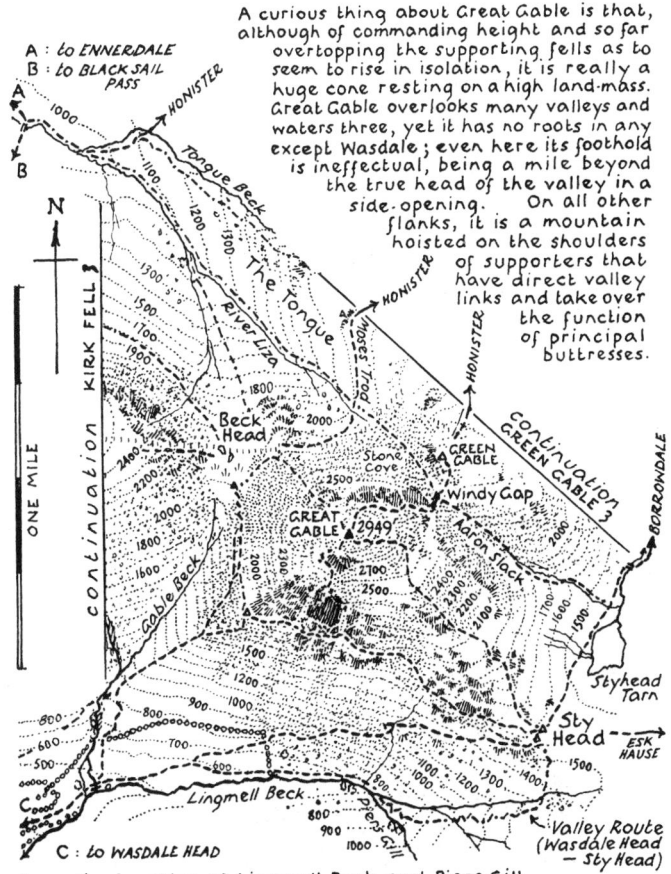

A: to ENNERDALE
B: to BLACK SAIL PASS

A curious thing about Great Gable is that, although of commanding height and so far overtopping the supporting fells as to seem to rise in isolation, it is really a huge cone resting on a high land-mass. Great Gable overlooks many valleys and waters three, yet it has no roots in any except Wasdale; even here its foothold is ineffectual, being a mile beyond the true head of the valley in a side-opening. On all other flanks, it is a mountain hoisted on the shoulders of supporters that have direct valley links and take over the function of principal buttresses.

C: to WASDALE HEAD

From the junction of Lingmell Beck and Piers Gill the summit is two-thirds of a mile north in lateral distance and the difference in altitude is 2,200 feet, a gradient of 1 in 1½. This is the longest slope in the district of such continuous and concentrated steepness.

Great Gable 7

Moses' Trod

In the years before the construction of the gravitation tramways to convey slate from Dubs and the upper Honister quarries, when man-handled sledges were the only means of negotiating the steep slopes to the road below, it was more convenient to transport supplies destined for South Cumberland and the port of Ravenglass by packhorse directly across the high fells to Wasdale, a practice followed until the primitive highway through Honister Pass was improved for wheeled traffic. This high-level route, cleverly planned to avoid steep gradients and rough places, can still be traced almost entirely although it has had no commercial use since about 1850. Because of the past history and legend connected with it the early tourists in the district were well aware of its existence, and the path is kept in being today by discerning walkers who appreciate the easy contours, fast travel, glorious scenery and superb views.

In places, the original line of the path is in doubt. The earlier Ordnance Survey maps indicated a wide divergence from the present footpath in the vicinity of Dubs Beck, but this may have been a rare error of cartography, for there are now no signs of it and it would have involved an obviously unnecessary descent and re-ascent. Traces are also missing on both sides of the Brandreth fence, but beyond the way is clear to the west ridge of Great Gable above Beck Head, where again the path is indistinct for a short distance until it starts the descent to Wasdale Head.

xxxxx : line of original path, according to Ordnance maps.

ooooooo : suggested links between present walkers' path and Moses' Trod. (In mist, the second (2) is better)

SCALE OF MAP:
Three inches = one mile

N

Unaccountably the greater part of the centuries-old Moses' Trod (i.e. from Brandreth almost to Wasdale Head) was omitted from O' maps until 1963!

continued on next page

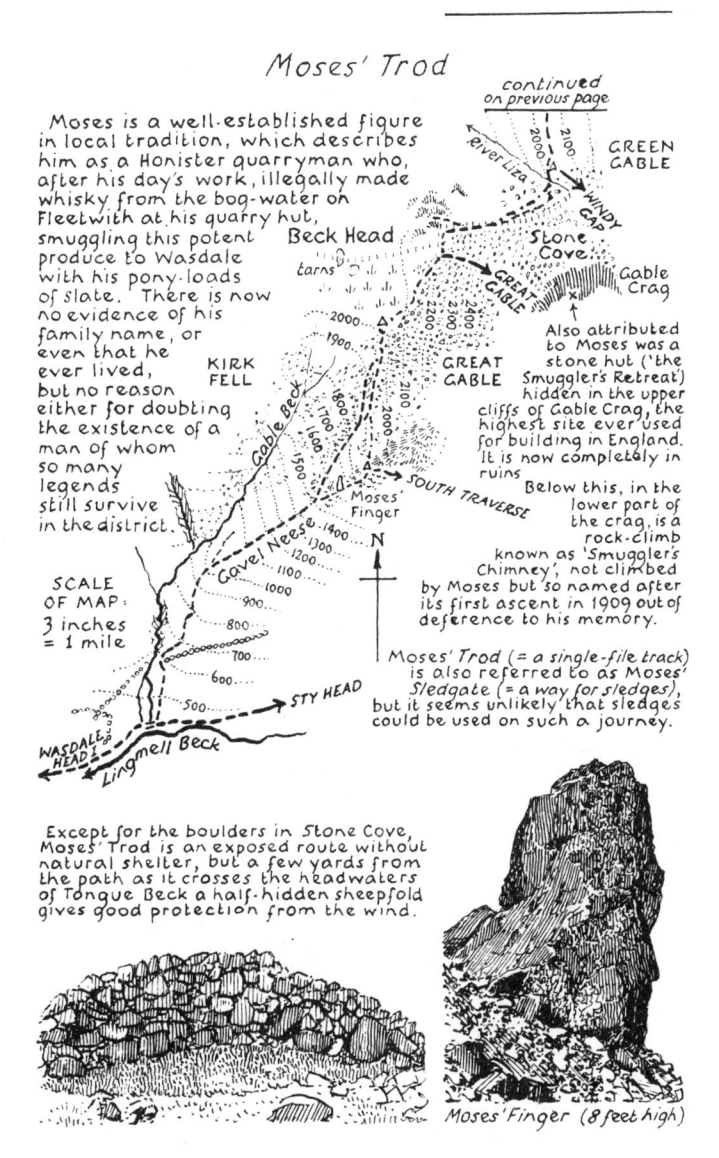

Great Gable 8

Moses' Trod

Moses is a well-established figure in local tradition, which describes him as a Honister quarryman who, after his day's work, illegally made whisky from the bog-water on Fleetwith at his quarry hut, smuggling this potent produce to Wasdale with his pony-loads of slate. There is now no evidence of his family name, or even that he ever lived, but no reason either for doubting the existence of a man of whom so many legends still survive in the district.

SCALE OF MAP:
3 inches = 1 mile

continued on previous page

GREEN GABLE
river Liza
WINDY GAP
Beck Head tarns
Stone Cove
Gable Crag
KIRK FELL
GREAT GABLE
Gable Beck
SOUTH TRAVERSE
Moses Finger
Gavel Neese
N
STY HEAD
WASDALE HEAD
Lingmell Beck

Also attributed to Moses was a stone hut ('the Smuggler's Retreat') hidden in the upper cliffs of Gable Crag, the highest site ever used for building in England. It is now completely in ruins.

Below this, in the lower part of the crag, is a rock-climb known as 'Smuggler's Chimney', not climbed by Moses but so named after its first ascent in 1909 out of deference to his memory.

Moses' Trod (= a single-file track) is also referred to as Moses' Sledgate (= a way for sledges), but it seems unlikely that sledges could be used on such a journey.

Except for the boulders in Stone Cove, Moses' Trod is an exposed route without natural shelter, but a few yards from the path as it crosses the headwaters of Tongue Beck a half-hidden sheepfold gives good protection from the wind.

Moses' Finger (8 feet high)

Great Gable 9

The Gable Girdle
(linking the South Traverse and the North Traverse)

Originally a track for a privileged few (i.e. the early rock-climbers) the South Traverse, rising across the flank of Great Gable from Sty Head, has now become a much-fancied way for lesser fry (i.e. modern hikers). The North Traverse passes immediately below the base of Gable Crag, and although still largely the province of climbers is equally accessible to walkers. The two traverses can be linked on the west by tracks over the scree above Beck Head; to the east the North Traverse is continued by the regular path down Aaron Slack to Sty Head. It is thus possible for walkers to make a full circuit of the mountain through interesting territory with fairly distinct tracks underfoot the whole way.

This is the finest mountain walk in the district that does not aim to reach a summit.

It is not level going: the route lies between 1500' and 2500', with many ups and downs. There are rough places to negotiate and nasty scree to cross and climb, but no dangers or difficulties. It is a doddle compared with, say, Jack's Rake or even Lord's Rake. Here one never has the feeling that the end is nigh.

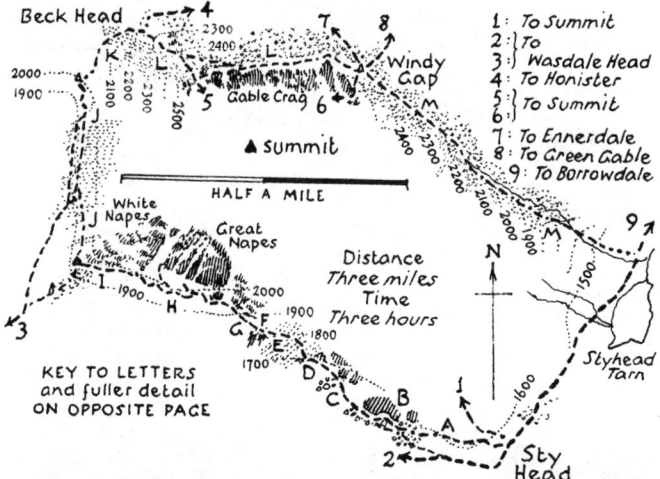

```
1: To Summit
2:  } To
3:  } Wasdale Head
4: To Honister
5:  } To Summit
6:
7: To Ennerdale
8: To Green Gable
9: To Borrowdale
```

Distance Three miles
Time Three hours

KEY TO LETTERS
and fuller detail
ON OPPOSITE PAGE

Boots, not shoes, should be worn,
and they must have soles with a firm grip, or there will be trouble on the boulders. There are few sections where the splendid views may be admired while walking: always *stop* to look around. The route is almost sheep-free, and dogs may be taken. So may small children, who are natural scramblers, and well-behaved women — but nagging wives should be left to paddle their feet in Styhead Tarn. The journey demands and deserves concentration.

Great Gable 10

The Gable Girdle

The South Traverse leaves Sty Head near the stretcher box, by a distinct stony path slanting left of the direct route up the mountain. There has been a big change here in the last twenty years. At one time, when the Traverse was the exclusive preserve of climbers, the commencement at Sty Head was deliberately kept obscure, so that walkers bound for the summit direct would not be beguiled along a false trail. But now the start is clearer than the start of the direct route, and many walkers enter upon it in the belief that it will lead them to the top of the mountain. It won't, not without a lot of effort.

KEY TO THE MAP ON THE OPPOSITE PAGE:
Sty Head to Kern Knotts:
  A: Undulating path over grassy alps to bouldery depression and stony rise to the base of the crag.
  B: Huge boulders to be negotiated along the base of the crag. [A simpler variation passes below these boulders (good shelter here) and climbs roughly up the far side]

Kern Knotts to Great Hell Gate:
  C: Horizontal track over boulders leads to easier ground. A small hollow is skirted (boulders again) after which there is a short rise to a rocky corner.
  D: A cave on the right provides a trickle of water (the last until Aaron Slack). A short scramble up rocky steps follows.
  E: An easy rising path on scree.
  F: The head of two gullies is crossed on rocky slabs.
  G: Easy rising path to Great Hell Gate (a scree shoot). Tophet Wall in view ahead.

Great Hell Gate to Little Hell Gate:
  H: A section of some confusion, resolved by referring to the next page following.

Little Hell Gate to Beck Head:
  I: The scree-shoot of Little Hell Gate is crossed and a track picked up opposite: this trends downwards to a cairn at the angle of the south and west faces. Here endeth the South Traverse. [A scree-path goes down to Wasdale Head at this point]
  J: Around the grassy corner a thin trod contours the west slope and joins a clear track rising to Beck Head (cairn on a boulder).

Beck Head to Windy Gap:
  K: Skirt the marshy ground ahead to a slanting scree-path rising to the angle of the north and west faces. [Moses' Trod goes off to the left here by a small pool]
  L: The steep loose scree of the north-west ridge is climbed for 100 yds. Watch closely for two cairns forming a 'gateway' (illustrated on page 27). Here commenceth the North Traverse. A track runs along the base of Gable Crag, descending to round the lowest buttress and then rising across scree to Windy Gap.

Windy Gap to Sty Head:
  M: A popular tourist path descends Aaron Slack to Styhead Tarn, where, if women are found paddling their feet, a greeting may be unwise.

High Kern Knotts

The water-hole (D)

Great Gable 11

The Great Napes

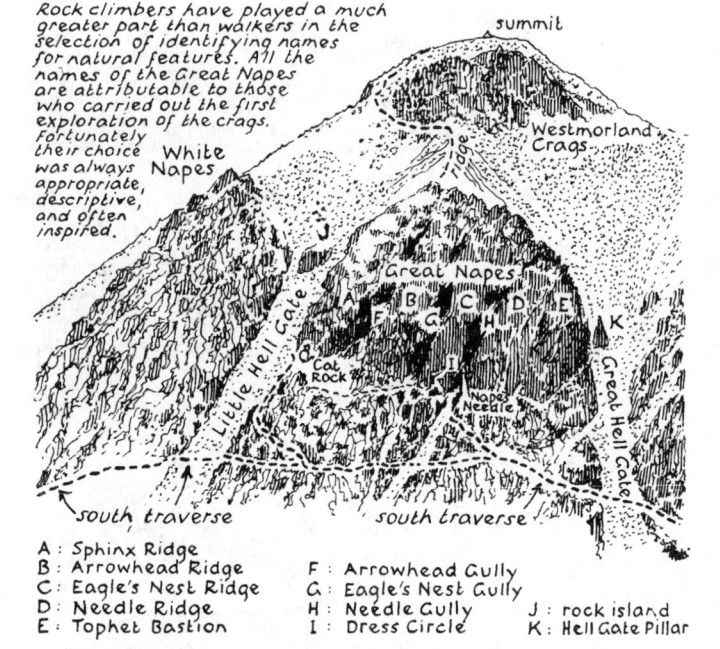

Rock climbers have played a much greater part than walkers in the selection of identifying names for natural features. All the names of the Great Napes are attributable to those who carried out the first exploration of the crags. Fortunately their choice was always appropriate, descriptive, and often inspired.

A: Sphinx Ridge
B: Arrowhead Ridge
C: Eagle's Nest Ridge
D: Needle Ridge
E: Tophet Bastion
F: Arrowhead Gully
G: Eagle's Nest Gully
H: Needle Gully
I: Dress Circle
J: rock island
K: Hell Gate Pillar

The Great Napes is a rocky excrescence high on the southern flank of Great Gable. Unlike most crags, which buttress and merge into the general slope of a mountain, the Great Napes rises like a castle above its surroundings so that there is not only a front wall of rock but side walls and a back wall too. This elevated mass is cut into by gullies to form four ridges, three of slender proportions and the fourth, and most easterly, broadly based and of substantial girth. The steepest rock occurs in the eastern part, the ground generally becoming more broken to the west. The front of the ridges, facing Wasdale, springs up almost vertically, but the gradient eases after the initial steepness to give grassy ledges in the higher reaches; the gullies, too, lose their sharp definition towards the top. Gradually the upper extremities of the Napes rise to a common apex, and here, at this point only, the Napes is undefended and a simple, grassy, and quite delightful ridge links with the main body of the fell. Here a climber may walk off the Napes and a walker may enter, with care, upon the easier upper heights. From the link ridge wide channels of scree pour down both sides of the Napes, thus defining the area clearly.

Across the westerly scree-channel the rocky tower of the White Napes emphasises the angle of the south and west faces of the mountain but has no notable crags and little of interest.

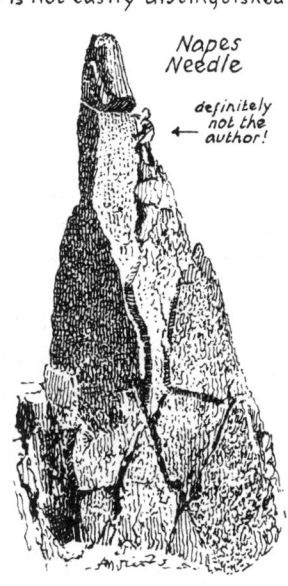

Great Gable 12

The Great Napes

continued

The South Traverse reaches its highest elevation in the section of about 250 yards between the two Hell Gates and beneath the Great Napes, but it does not venture to the base of the wall of crags, preferring an easier passage 50-80 yards lower down the slope, where it maintains a horizontal course on the 2000' contour. The intervening ground is steep and rocky, especially in the vicinity of the Needle, and its exploration calls for care. The Needle is in full view from the Traverse but does not seem its usual self (as usually seen in illustrations) and on a dull day is not easily distinguished from its background of rock. To visit it, take the rising branch-path from the Traverse into Needle Gully, and go up this to the base of the pinnacle; a scrambling track *opposite* climbs up to a ledge known as the Dress Circle, the traditional balcony for watching the ascent of the Needle. From this ledge a higher traverse can be made along the base of the crags, going below the Cat Rock into Little Hell Gate, but there is a tricky section initially and this is no walk for dogs, small children, well behaved women and the like.

Midway between the two Hell Gates Needle Gully and a branch gully, full of scree, cut across the South Traverse, which otherwise hereabouts is mainly a matter of rounding little buttresses. Another bifurcation leads off to Little Hell Gate at a higher level, near the Cat Rock. If proceeding west (i.e. from Sty Head) the two rising branch-paths may be followed by mistake without realising that the Traverse has been left, they being the more distinct, a circumstance that does not arise when proceeding east.

ROUTES TO THE SUMMIT FROM THE SOUTH TRAVERSE

It is no uncommon thing for walkers to venture upon the South Traverse, from Sty Head, in the fond hope that it will lead them in due course to the summit of Great Gable. This hope is dashed when the Napes is reached, for here the path becomes uncertain and the rocks are an impassable obstacle. The clue to further ascent is provided when it is remembered that 'gate' is a local word for 'way' and that the Napes is bounded by the two Hell Gates. Either of these will conduct the walker safely upwards, but both are chutes for loose stones and steep and arduous to climb. (In Little Hell Gate it is possible, with care, to scramble off the scree onto Sphinx Ridge at several points). The two routes converge at the little ridge below Westmorland Crags, which are rounded on the left by a good track that winds up to the summit plateau.

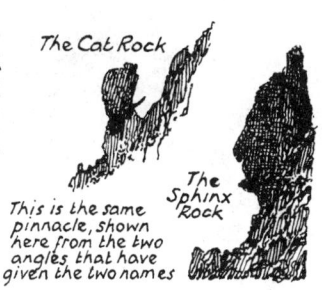

Napes Needle

← definitely not the author!

The Cat Rock

The Sphinx Rock

This is the same pinnacle, shown here from the two angles that have given the two names

Great Gable 13

The Great Napes

left:
Tophet Bastion, as seen from the South Traverse on the approach from Sty Head.
　The scree of Great Hell Gate runs down to the bottom left.

below:
looking steeply down on Tophet Bastion and the upper wall of the Napes, with the scree of Great Hell Gate running down to the left, from Westmorland Cairn.

Great Gable 14

The Great Napes

looking upwards from just above the South Traverse

- Eagle's Nest Gully
- Eagle's Nest Ridge (lower part known as Abbey Buttress)
- Needle Gully
- Needle Ridge
- Napes Needle

looking up Little Hell Gate
- rock island
- Westmorland Crags

looking up Great Hell Gate
- Tophet Bastion
- Hell Gate Pillar

Great Gable 15

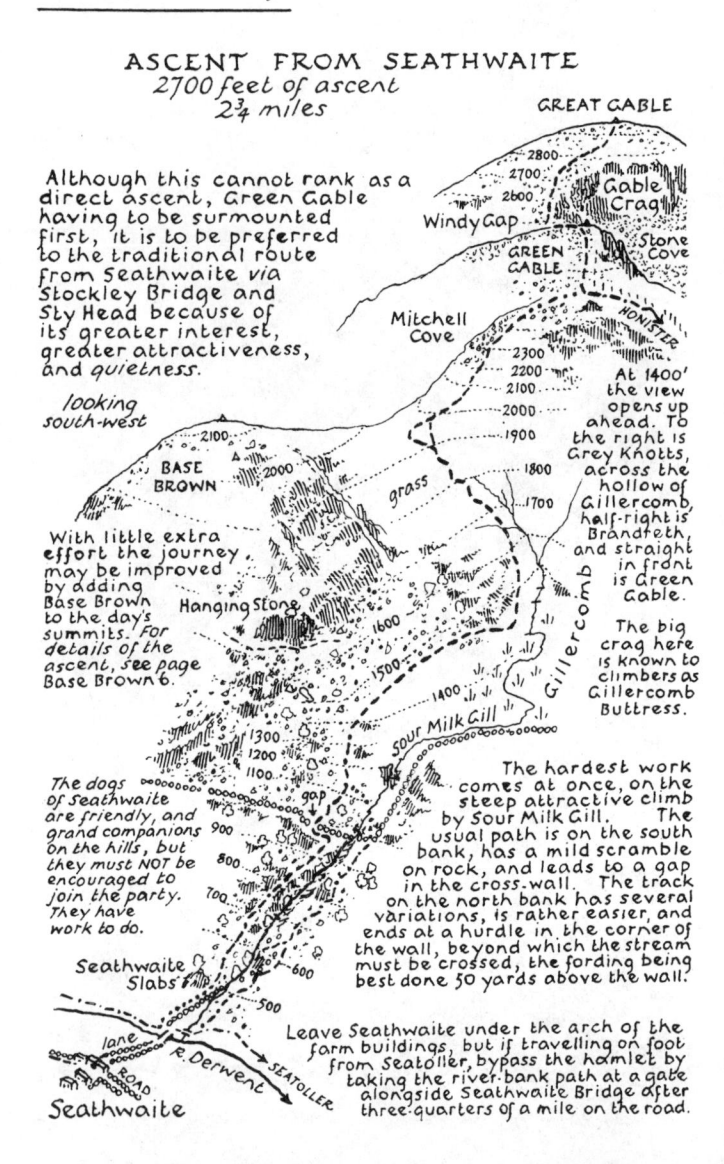

ASCENT FROM SEATHWAITE
2700 feet of ascent
2¾ miles

GREAT GABLE

Although this cannot rank as a direct ascent, Green Gable having to be surmounted first, it is to be preferred to the traditional route from Seathwaite via Stockley Bridge and Sty Head because of its greater interest, greater attractiveness, and quietness.

looking south-west

BASE BROWN

With little extra effort the journey may be improved by adding Base Brown to the day's summits. For details of the ascent, see page Base Brown 6.

Gable Crag
Windy Gap
Stone Cove
GREEN GABLE
Mitchell Cove
HONISTER

At 1400' the view opens up ahead. To the right is Grey Knotts, across the hollow of Gillercomb, half-right is Brandreth, and straight in front is Green Gable.

The big crag here is known to climbers as Gillercomb Buttress.

Hanging Stone
Gillercomb
Sour Milk Gill

The dogs of Seathwaite are friendly, and grand companions on the hills, but they must NOT be encouraged to join the party. They have work to do.

The hardest work comes at once, on the steep attractive climb by Sour Milk Gill. The usual path is on the south bank, has a mild scramble on rock, and leads to a gap in the cross-wall. The track on the north bank has several variations, is rather easier, and ends at a hurdle in the corner of the wall, beyond which the stream must be crossed, the fording being best done 50 yards above the wall.

Seathwaite Slabs
lane
R. Derwent
SEATOLLER
ROAD
Seathwaite

Leave Seathwaite under the arch of the farm buildings, but if travelling on foot from Seatoller, bypass the hamlet by taking the river-bank path at a gate alongside Seathwaite Bridge after three-quarters of a mile on the road.

Great Gable 16

ASCENT FROM STY HEAD
1350 feet of ascent : 1 mile
(from Wasdale Head: 2750 feet : ¾ miles
from Seathwaite: 2600 feet : 3¼ miles)

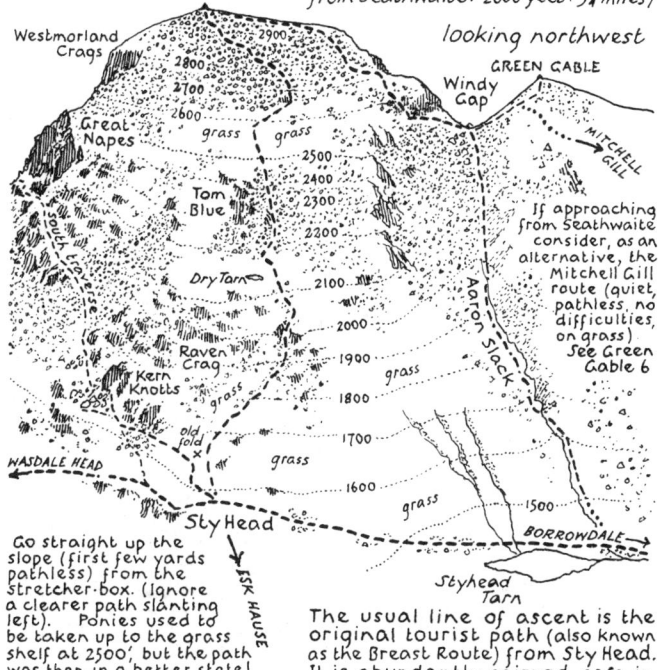

looking northwest

If approaching from Seathwaite consider, as an alternative, the Mitchell Gill route (quiet, pathless, no difficulties, on grass) See Green Gable 6

Go straight up the slope (first few yards pathless) from the stretcher-box. (Ignore a clearer path slanting left). Ponies used to be taken up to the grass shelf at 2500, but the path was then in a better state!

The usual line of ascent is the original tourist path (also known as the Breast Route) from Sty Head. It is abundantly cairned, safe in mist, but very bad underfoot (loose scree) on the steep rise by Tom Blue, where clumsy walkers have utterly ruined the path. The Aaron Slack route gives a rather firmer footing.

There are good walkers and bad walkers, and the difference between them has nothing to do with performances in mileage or speed. The difference lies in the way they put their feet down.
A good walker is a *tidy* walker. He moves quietly, places his feet where his eyes tell him to, on beaten tracks treads firmly, avoids loose stones on steep ground, disturbs nothing. He is, by habit, an improver of paths.
A bad walker is a *clumsy* walker. He moves noisily, disturbs the surface and even the foundations of paths by kicking up loose stones, tramples the verges until they disintegrate into debris. He is, by habit, a maker of bad tracks and a spoiler of good ones.
A good walker's special joy is zigzags, which he follows faithfully. A bad walker's special joy is in shortcutting and destroying zigzags.
All fellwalking accidents are the result of clumsiness.

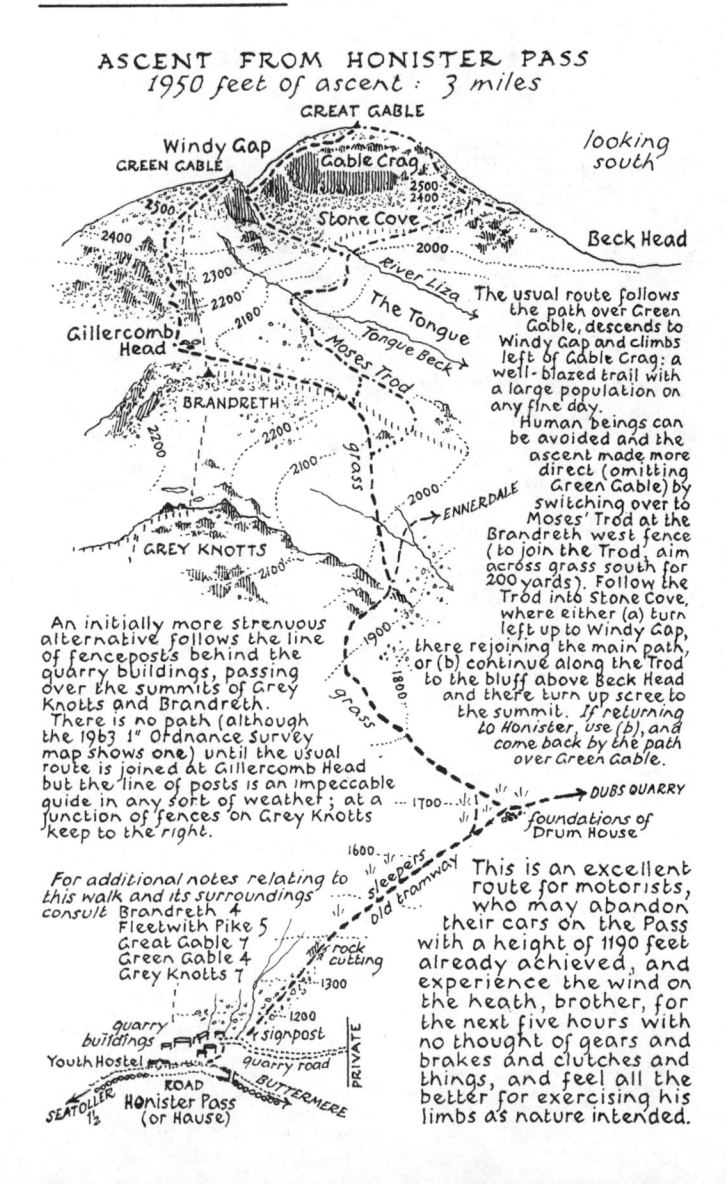

Great Gable 17

ASCENT FROM HONISTER PASS
1950 feet of ascent : 3 miles

looking south

The usual route follows the path over Green Gable, descends to Windy Gap and climbs left of Gable Crag: a well-blazed trail with a large population on any fine day.

Human beings can be avoided and the ascent made more direct (omitting Green Gable) by switching over to Moses' Trod at the Brandreth west fence (to join the Trod, aim across grass south for 200 yards). Follow the Trod into Stone Cove, where either (a) turn left up to Windy Gap, there rejoining the main path, or (b) continue along the Trod to the bluff above Beck Head and there turn up scree to the summit. If returning to Honister, use (b), and come back by the path over Green Gable.

An initially more strenuous alternative follows the line of fenceposts behind the quarry buildings, passing over the summits of Grey Knotts and Brandreth.
There is no path (although the 1963 1" Ordnance Survey map shows one) until the usual route is joined at Gillercomb Head but the line of posts is an impeccable guide in any sort of weather; at a junction of fences on Grey Knotts keep to the right.

For additional notes relating to this walk and its surroundings consult Brandreth 4
Fleetwith Pike 5
Great Gable 7
Green Gable 4
Grey Knotts 7

This is an excellent route for motorists, who may abandon their cars on the Pass with a height of 1190 feet already achieved, and experience the wind on the heath, brother, for the next five hours with no thought of gears and brakes and clutches and things, and feel all the better for exercising his limbs as nature intended.

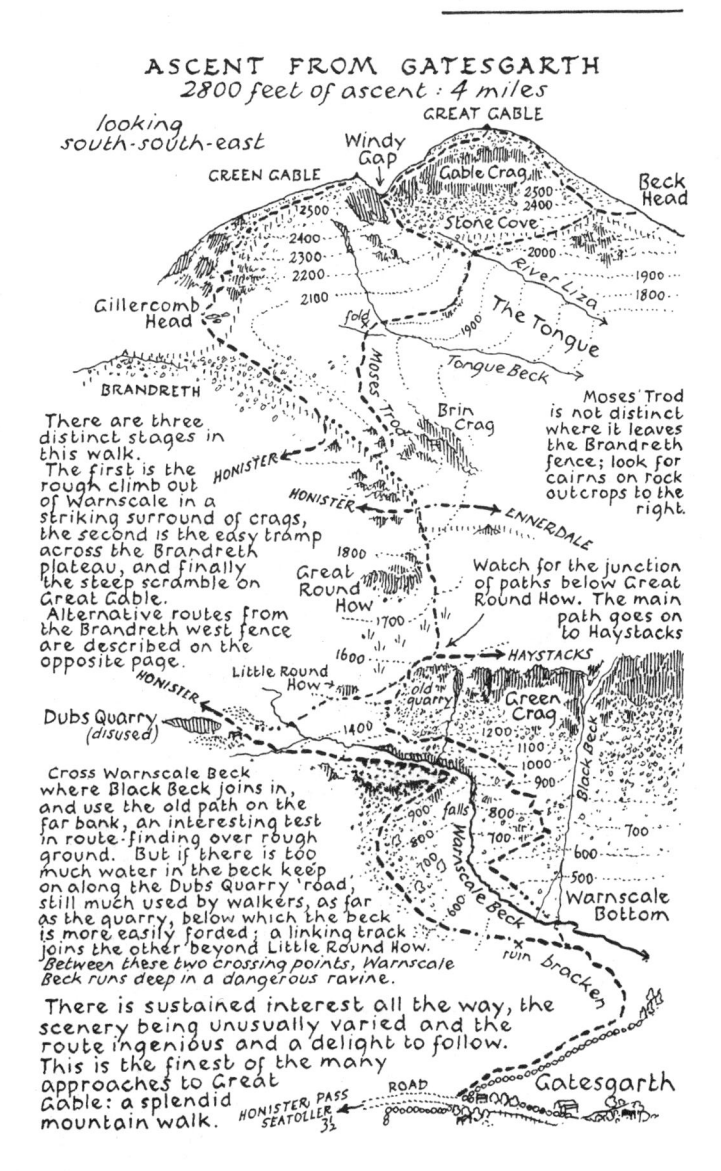

Great Gable 18

ASCENT FROM GATESGARTH
2800 feet of ascent : 4 miles

looking south-south-east

GREAT GABLE — Windy Gap — Gable Crag — Beck Head — GREEN GABLE — Stone Cove — River Liza — The Tongue — Gillercomb Head — Tongue Beck — BRANDRETH — Brin Crag — Moses' Trod — HONISTER — ENNERDALE — Great Round How — HAYSTACKS — Little Round How — old quarry — Green Crag — HONISTER — Dubs Quarry (disused) — falls — Warnscale Beck — Black Beck — Warnscale Bottom — ruin — bracken — HONISTER PASS / SEATOLLER — ROAD — Gatesgarth

There are three distinct stages in this walk.
The first is the rough climb out of Warnscale in a striking surround of crags, the second is the easy tramp across the Brandreth plateau, and finally the steep scramble on Great Gable.
Alternative routes from the Brandreth west fence are described on the opposite page.

Moses' Trod is not distinct where it leaves the Brandreth fence; look for cairns on rock outcrops to the right.

Watch for the junction of paths below Great Round How. The main path goes on to Haystacks.

Cross Warnscale Beck where Black Beck joins in, and use the old path on the far bank, an interesting test in route-finding over rough ground. But if there is too much water in the beck keep on along the Dubs Quarry 'road', still much used by walkers, as far as the quarry, below which the beck is more easily forded; a linking track joins the other beyond Little Round How. Between these two crossing points, Warnscale Beck runs deep in a dangerous ravine.

There is sustained interest all the way, the scenery being unusually varied and the route ingenious and a delight to follow. This is the finest of the many approaches to Great Gable: a splendid mountain walk.

Great Gable 19

ASCENT FROM ENNERDALE
(BLACK SAIL YOUTH HOSTEL)
2000 feet of ascent : 2¼ miles

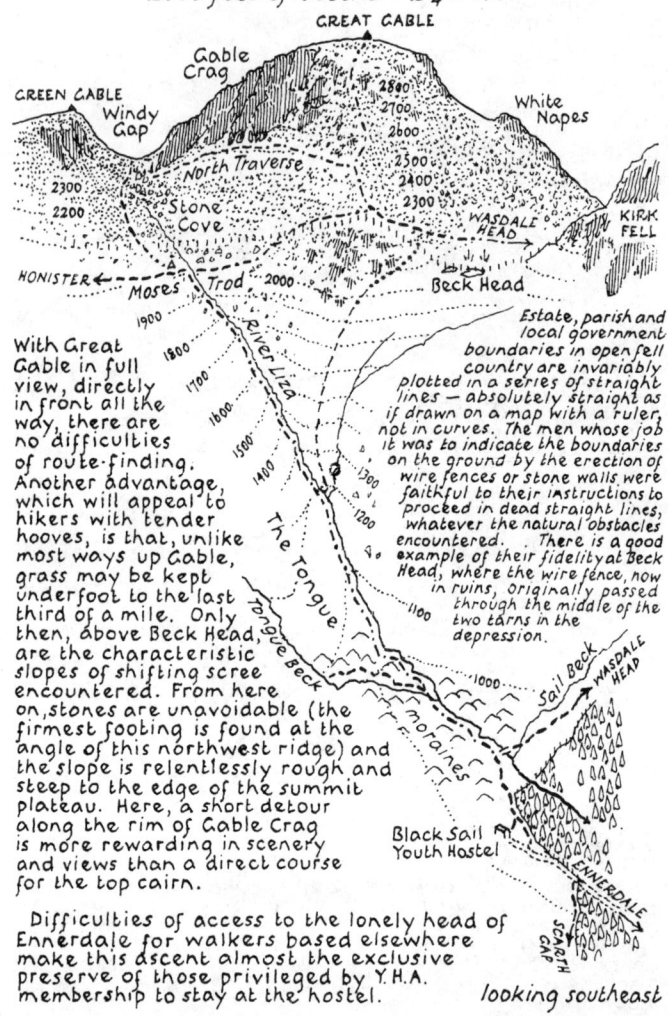

With Great Gable in full view, directly in front all the way, there are no difficulties of route-finding. Another advantage, which will appeal to hikers with tender hooves, is that, unlike most ways up Gable, grass may be kept underfoot to the last third of a mile. Only then, above Beck Head, are the characteristic slopes of shifting scree encountered. From here on, stones are unavoidable (the firmest footing is found at the angle of this northwest ridge) and the slope is relentlessly rough and steep to the edge of the summit plateau. Here, a short detour along the rim of Gable Crag is more rewarding in scenery and views than a direct course for the top cairn.

Difficulties of access to the lonely head of Ennerdale for walkers based elsewhere make this ascent almost the exclusive preserve of those privileged by Y.H.A. membership to stay at the hostel.

Estate, parish and local government boundaries in open fell country are invariably plotted in a series of straight lines — absolutely straight as if drawn on a map with a ruler, not in curves. The men whose job it was to indicate the boundaries on the ground by the erection of wire fences or stone walls were faithful to their instructions to proceed in dead straight lines, whatever the natural obstacles encountered. There is a good example of their fidelity at Beck Head, where the wire fence, now in ruins, originally passed through the middle of the two tarns in the depression.

looking southeast

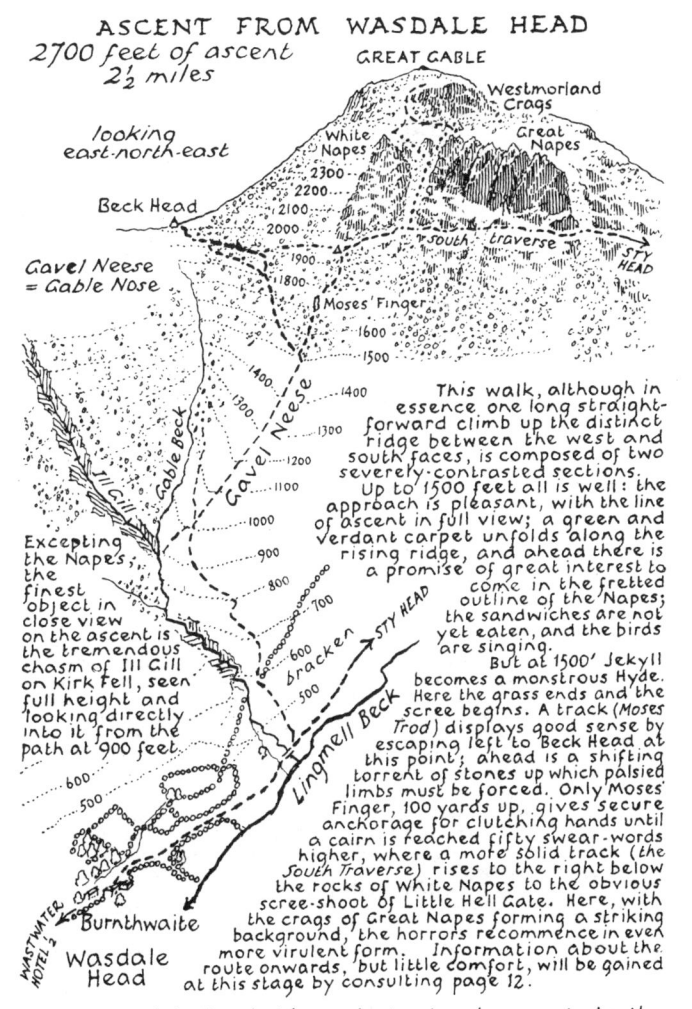

Great Gable 20

ASCENT FROM WASDALE HEAD
2700 feet of ascent
2½ miles

looking east-north-east

GREAT GABLE
Westmorland Crags
White Napes
Great Napes
Beck Head
Gavel Neese = Gable Nose
Moses' Finger
south traverse
STY HEAD

Excepting the Napes, the finest object in close view on the ascent is the tremendous chasm of Ill Gill on Kirk Fell, seen full height and looking directly into it from the path at 900 feet.

Gable Beck
Ill Gill
Gavel Neese
bracken
STY HEAD
Lingmell Beck

WASTWATER HOTEL
Burnthwaite
Wasdale Head

This walk, although in essence one long straightforward climb up the distinct ridge between the west and south faces, is composed of two severely-contrasted sections. Up to 1500 feet all is well: the approach is pleasant, with the line of ascent in full view; a green and verdant carpet unfolds along the rising ridge, and ahead there is a promise of great interest to come in the fretted outline of the Napes; the sandwiches are not yet eaten, and the birds are singing.

But at 1500' Jekyll becomes a monstrous Hyde. Here the grass ends and the scree begins. A track (Moses Trod) displays good sense by escaping left to Beck Head at this point; ahead is a shifting torrent of stones up which palsied limbs must be forced. Only Moses' Finger, 100 yards up, gives secure anchorage for clutching hands until a cairn is reached fifty swear-words higher, where a more solid track (the South Traverse) rises to the right below the rocks of White Napes to the obvious scree-shoot of Little Hell Gate. Here, with the crags of Great Napes forming a striking background, the horrors recommence in even more virulent form. Information about the route onwards, but little comfort, will be gained at this stage by consulting page 12.

From Wasdale Head this route is clearly seen to be the most direct way to the summit. It is also the most strenuous. (Its conquest is more wisely announced at supper, afterwards, than at breakfast, in advance).

Great Gable 21

THE SUMMIT

Great Gable's summit is held in special respect by the older generation of fellwalkers, because here, set in the rocks that bear the top cairn, is the bronze War Memorial tablet of the Fell and Rock Climbing Club, dedicated in 1924, and ever since the inspiring scene of an annual Remembrance Service in November. It is a fitting place to pay homage to men who once loved to walk on these hills and gave their lives defending the right of others to enjoy the same happy freedom, for the ultimate crest of Gable is truly characteristic of the best of mountain Lakeland: a rugged crown of rock and boulders and stones in chaotic profusion, a desert without life, a harsh and desolate peak thrust high in the sky above the profound depths all around.

Gable, tough and strong all through its height, has here made a final gesture by providing an outcrop of rock even in its last inches, so that one must climb to touch the cairn (which, being hallowed as a shrine by fellwalkers everywhere, let no man tear asunder lest a thousand curses accompany his guilty flight!). On three sides the slopes fall away immediately, but to the north there extends a small plateau, with a little vegetation, before the summit collapses in the sheer plunge of Gable Crag. The rim of this precipice, and also the top of Westmorland Crags to the south, should be visited for their superlative views.

There are few days in the year when no visitors arrive on the summit. Snow and ice and severe gales may defy those who aspire to reach it in winter, but in the summer months there is a constant parade of perspiring pedestrians across the top from early morning to late evening.

To many fellwalkers this untidy bit of ground is Mecca.

continued

Great Gable 22

THE SUMMIT

continued

DESCENTS : All ways off the summit are paved with loose stones and continue so for most of the descent. Allied to roughness is steepness, particularly on the Wasdale side, and care is needed to avoid involuntary slips. In places, where scree-runners have bared the underlying ground, surfaces are slippery and unpleasant. Never descend Gable in a mad rush!

In fine weather there should be no trouble in distinguishing the various cairned routes; in mist their direction is identified by the memorial tablet, which faces north overlooking the path to Windy Gap. Not all cairns can be relied upon; some are not route-markers but indicators of viewpoints and rock-climbs. Generally, however, the principal traffic routes are well-blazed by boots.

In bad conditions the safest line is down the breast of the mountain to Sty Head. Care is needed in locating the descent to Beck Head, which keeps closely to the angle of the north and west faces and does not follow any of the inviting scree-runs on the west side, which end in fields of boulders. Caution is also advised in attempting direct descents of the Wasdale face if the topography of the Napes is not already familiar.

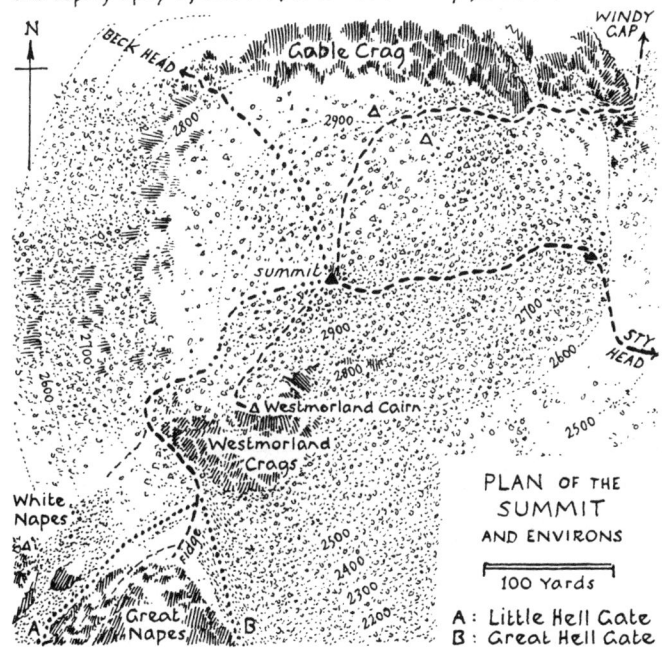

PLAN OF THE SUMMIT AND ENVIRONS

100 Yards

A: Little Hell Gate
B: Great Hell Gate

Great Gable 23

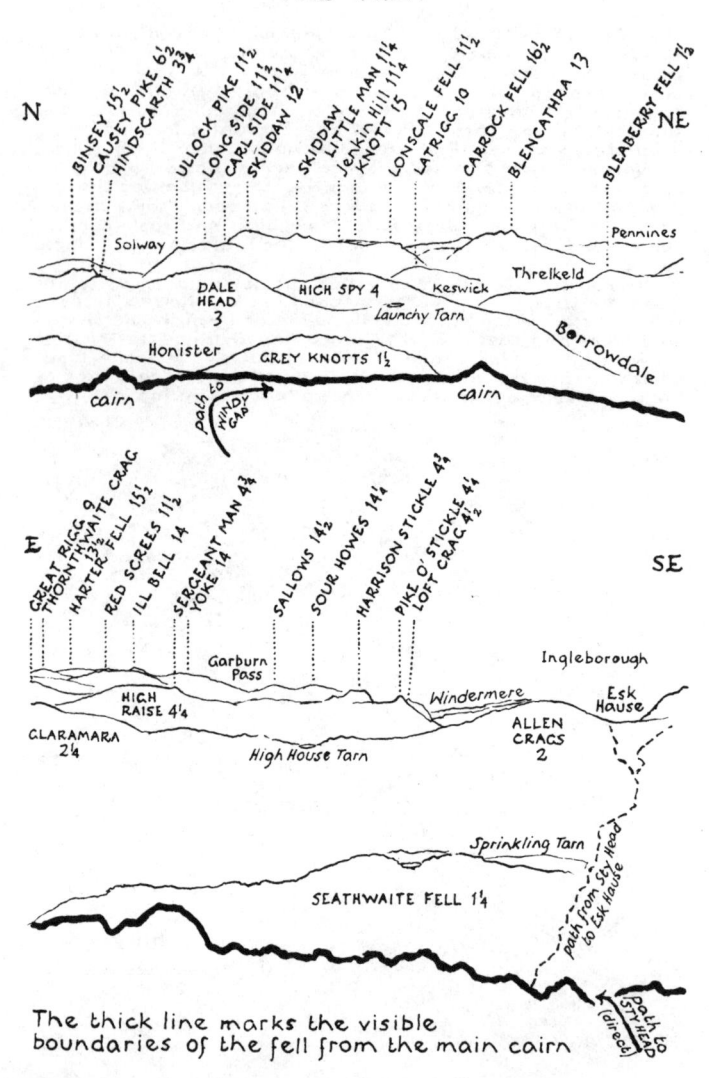

THE VIEW

N — BINSEY 15½, CAUSEY PIKE 6½, HINDSCARTH 3¾, ULLOCK PIKE 11½, LONG SIDE 11½, CARL SIDE 11¾, SKIDDAW 12, SKIDDAW LITTLE MAN 11¼, JENKIN HILL 11¾, LONSCALE FELL 11½, LATRIGG 10, CARROCK FELL 16½, BLENCATHRA 13, BLEABERRY FELL 7½ — NE

Solway, Pennines, DALE HEAD 3, HIGH SPY 4, Keskwick, Threlkeld, Launchy Tarn, Honister, GREY KNOTTS 1½, Borrowdale

cairn — path to WINDY GAP — cairn

E — GREAT RIGG 9, THORNTHWAITE CRAG 13½, HARTER FELL 15½, RED SCREES 11½, ILL BELL 14, SERGEANT MAN 4¾, YOKE 14, SALLOWS 14½, SOUR HOWES 14¼, HARRISON STICKLE 4¾, PIKE O' STICKLE 4¼, LOFT CRAG 4½ — SE

Garburn Pass, Ingleborough, Windermere, Esk Hause, CLARAMARA 2¼, HIGH RAISE 4¼, High House Tarn, ALLEN CRAGS 2

Sprinkling Tarn, SEATHWAITE FELL 1¼, path from Sty Head to Esk Hause, path to STY HEAD (direct)

The thick line marks the visible boundaries of the fell from the main cairn

Great Gable 24

THE VIEW

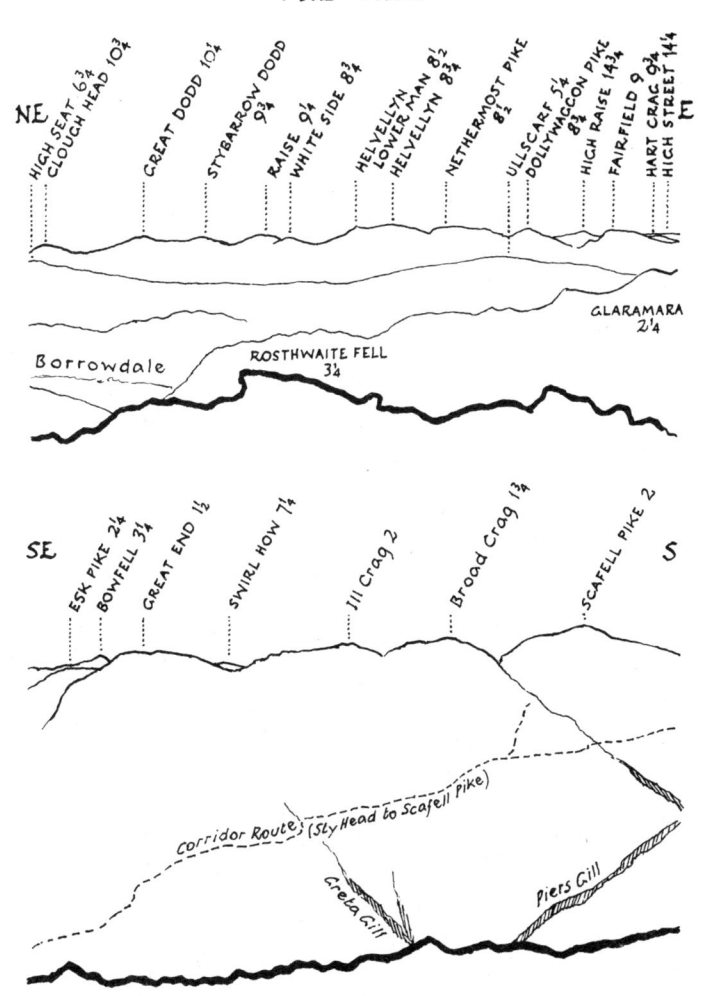

NE — HIGH SEAT 6¾ / CLOUGH HEAD 10¾ / GREAT DODD 10¼ / STYBARROW DODD 9¾ / RAISE 9¼ / WHITE SIDE 8¾ / HELVELLYN LOWER MAN 8½ / HELVELLYN 8¾ / NETHERMOST PIKE 8½ / ULLSCARF 5¼ / DOLLYWAGGON PIKE 8½ / HIGH RAISE 14¼ / FAIRFIELD 9 / HART CRAG 9¼ / HIGH STREET 14¼ — E

GLARAMARA 2¼

Borrowdale — ROSTHWAITE FELL 3¼

SE — ESK PIKE 2¼ / BOWFELL 3¼ / GREAT END 1½ / SWIRL HOW 7¼ / ILL CRAG 2 / BROAD CRAG 1¾ / SCAFELL PIKE 2 — S

Corridor Route (Sty Head to Scafell Pike)

Greta Gill

Piers Gill

The figures accompanying the names of fells indicate distances in miles

Great Gable 25

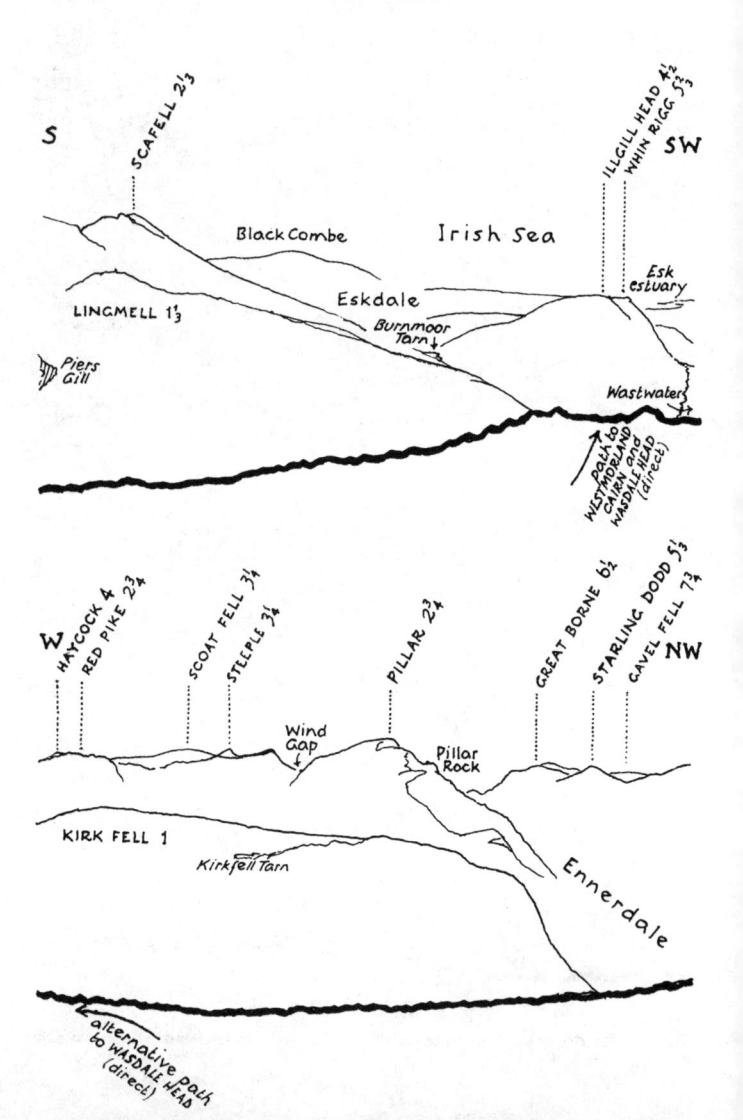

THE VIEW

S — SCAFELL 2½, Black Combe, Irish Sea, ILLGILL HEAD 4½, WHIN RIGG 5⅓ — SW

LINGMELL 1⅓, Eskdale, Esk estuary, Burnmoor Tarn, Wastwater

Piers Gill

Path to WASTDALE HEAD CAIRN and WASDALE HEAD (direct)

W — HAYCOCK 4, RED PIKE 2¾, SCOAT FELL 3¼, STEEPLE 3¼, PILLAR 2¾, GREAT BORNE 6½, STARLING DODD 5⅓, GAVEL FELL 7¼ — NW

Wind Gap, Pillar Rock

KIRK FELL 1, Kirkfell Tarn, Ennerdale

alternative path to WASDALE HEAD (direct)

Great Gable 26

THE VIEW

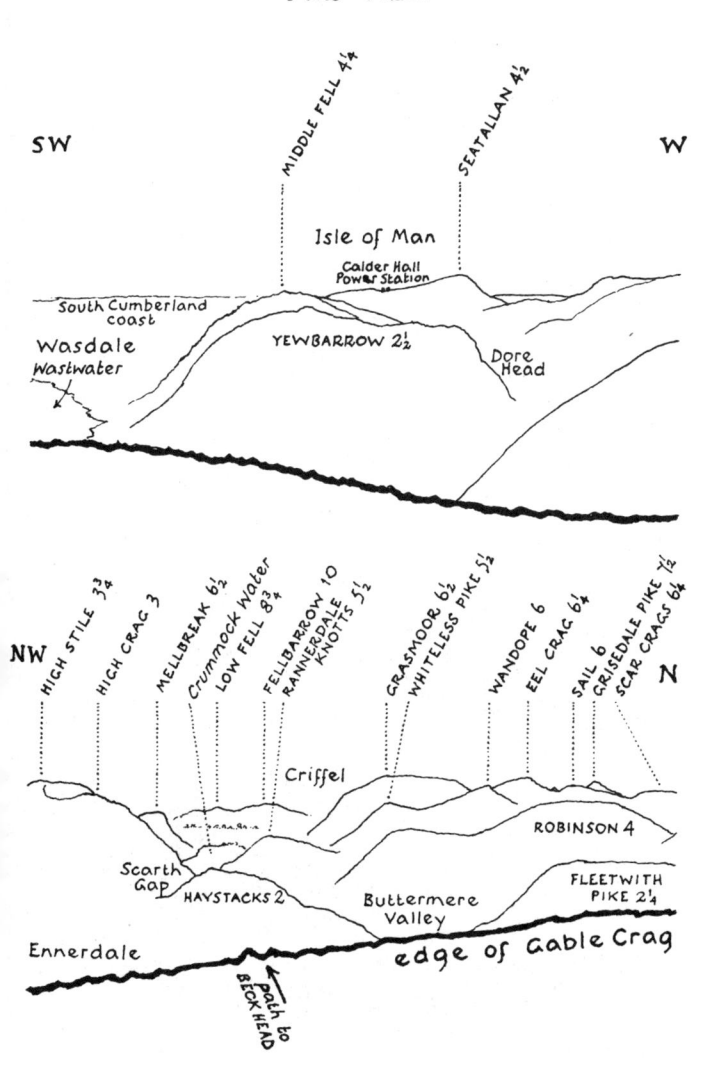

SW — MIDDLE FELL 4¼ — SEATALLAN 4½ — W

Isle of Man
Calder Hall Power Station
South Cumberland coast
YEWBARROW 2½
Wasdale Wastwater
Dore Head

NW — HIGH STILE 3¾ — HIGH CRAG 3 — MELLBREAK 6½ — Crummock Water — LOW FELL 8¾ — FELLBARROW 10 — RANNERDALE KNOTTS 5½ — GRASMOOR 6½ — WHITELESS PIKE 5½ — WANDOPE 6 — EEL CRAG 6¼ — SAIL 6 — GRISEDALE PIKE 7½ — SCAR CRAGS 6¼ — N

Criffel
ROBINSON 4
Scarth Gap
HAYSTACKS 2
Buttermere Valley
FLEETWITH PIKE 2¼
Ennerdale
edge of Gable Crag
path to BECK HEAD

Great Gable 27

RIDGE ROUTES

To GREEN GABLE, 2603': NNE, then E and NNE : ½ mile
  Depression (Windy Gap) at 2460'
    150 feet of ascent
      Rough and stony all the way

The best that can be said for the path is that it is clearly defined throughout, which is as well, there being unseen precipices in the vicinity. One section, where Gable Crag is rounded to reach Windy Gap, is particularly objectionable and needs care on smooth rocky steps.

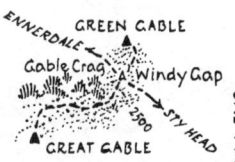

To KIRK FELL, 2630': NW, then W and SW : 1½ miles
  Depression (Beck Head) at 2040'   700 feet of ascent.

A passing from the sublime to the less sublime, better done the other way.

Pick a way carefully down the north-west ridge, avoiding false trails that lead only to boulder slopes and keeping generally near the angle of the ridge, where the footing is firmest. When a line of fence posts is joined, the remainder of the route is assured, the posts leading across the depression of Beck Head, up the steep facing slope of Rib End, and visiting first the lower and then the top summit of Kirk Fell across a wide grassy plateau.

A place to remember.......

Some quite ordinary patches of fellside have extraordinary significance when they indicate important route junctions occurring in rough terrain and not clearly defined by paths on the ground. The best example is the upper exit of Lords Rake on Scafell, and there are many others.

Illustrated here is the place where the North Traverse leaves the northwest ridge to cross below Gable Crag to Windy Gap.

Pass between the two cairns and the track comes into view

Great Gable 28

Westmorland Cairn

Erected in 1876 by two brothers of the name of Westmorland to mark what they considered to be the finest mountain viewpoint in the district, this soundly-built and tidy cairn is wellknown to climbers and walkers alike, and has always been respected. The cairn has maintained its original form throughout the years quite remarkably; apart from visitors who like to add a pebble, it has suffered neither from the weather nor from human despoilers. It stands on the extreme brink of the south face, above steep crags, and overlooks Wasdale. Rocky platforms around make the place ideal for a halt after climbing Great Gable. The cairn is not in sight from the summit but is soon reached by walking 150 yards across the stony top in the direction of Wastwater.

Green Gable 2603'

Gatesgarth
Seatoller
Honister Pass
Seathwaite
▲ GREEN GABLE
▲ GREAT GABLE
• Wasdale Head
MILES

from Great End

Green Gable 2

NATURAL FEATURES

A thousand people, or more, reach the summit-cairn of Green Gable every year, yet it is probably true to say that no visitor to Lakeland ever announced at breakfast that this fell was his day's objective; and, if he did, his listeners would assume a slip of the tongue: of course he must mean Great Gable. The two Gables are joined like Siamese twins, but they are not likenesses of each other. Great Gable is the mighty mountain that every walker wants to climb; Green Gable is a stepping stone to it but otherwise of no account. All eyes are fixed on Great Gable; Green Gable is merely something met en route. So think most folk who pass from one to the other.

But Green Gable is not at all insignificant. At 2603' its altitude, by Lakeland standards, is considerable. A sharp peaked summit, more delicately wrought than Great Gable's, adds distinction. Rock-climbers' crags adorn its western fringe. Important paths reach it on all sides. Unsought though the top may be, nevertheless it is much-used and well-known through the accident of its position. There are two main slopes, one going down to Sty Head Gill, the other gaining a slender footing in Ennerdale.

It is a crowning misfortune for Green Gable, however, that the volcanic upheaval ages ago stopped upheaving at a moment when this fell was in a position completely subservient to a massive neighbour, and so fashioned the summit that it is forever destined to look up into the pillared crags of Great Gable as a suppliant before a temple. It is because of the inferiority induced by Big Brother that Green Gable cannot ever expect to be recognised as a fine mountain in its own right.

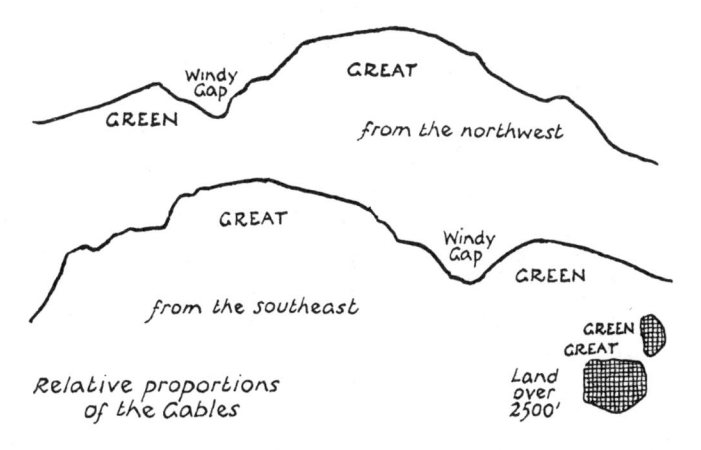

Relative proportions of the Gables

Green Gable 3

MAP

Greengable Crags

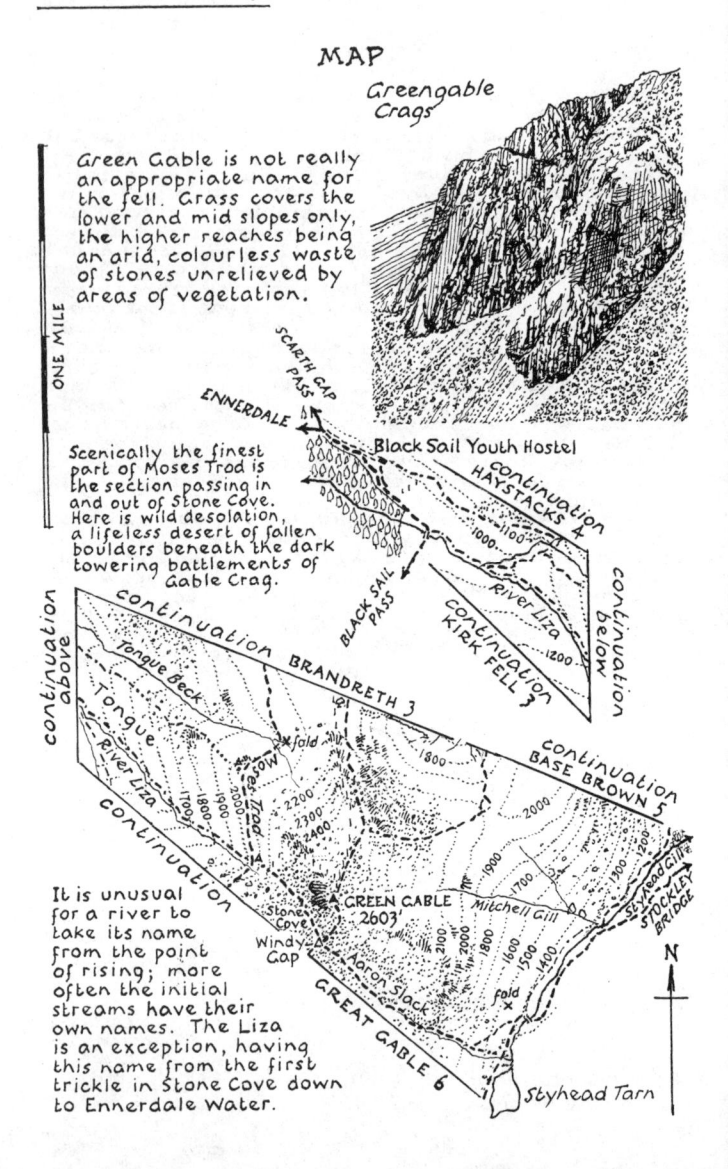

Green Gable is not really an appropriate name for the fell. Grass covers the lower and mid slopes only, the higher reaches being an arid, colourless waste of stones unrelieved by areas of vegetation.

ONE MILE

Scenically the finest part of Moses Trod is the section passing in and out of Stone Cove. Here is wild desolation, a lifeless desert of fallen boulders beneath the dark towering battlements of Gable Crag.

SCARTH GAP PASS
ENNERDALE
Black Sail Youth Hostel
continuation HAYSTACKS 4
BLACK SAIL PASS
River Liza
continuation KIRK FELL 7
continuation below

continuation above
continuation BRANDRETH 3
Tongue Beck
Tongue
River Liza
fold
continuation BASE BROWN 5
continuation
Stone Cove
GREEN GABLE 2603'
Mitchell Gill
STOCKLEY BRIDGE
Styhead Gill
Windy Gap
Aaron Slack
GREAT GABLE 6
fold
N

It is unusual for a river to take its name from the point of rising; more often the initial streams have their own names. The Liza is an exception, having this name from the first trickle in Stone Cove down to Ennerdale Water.

Styhead Tarn

Green Gable 4

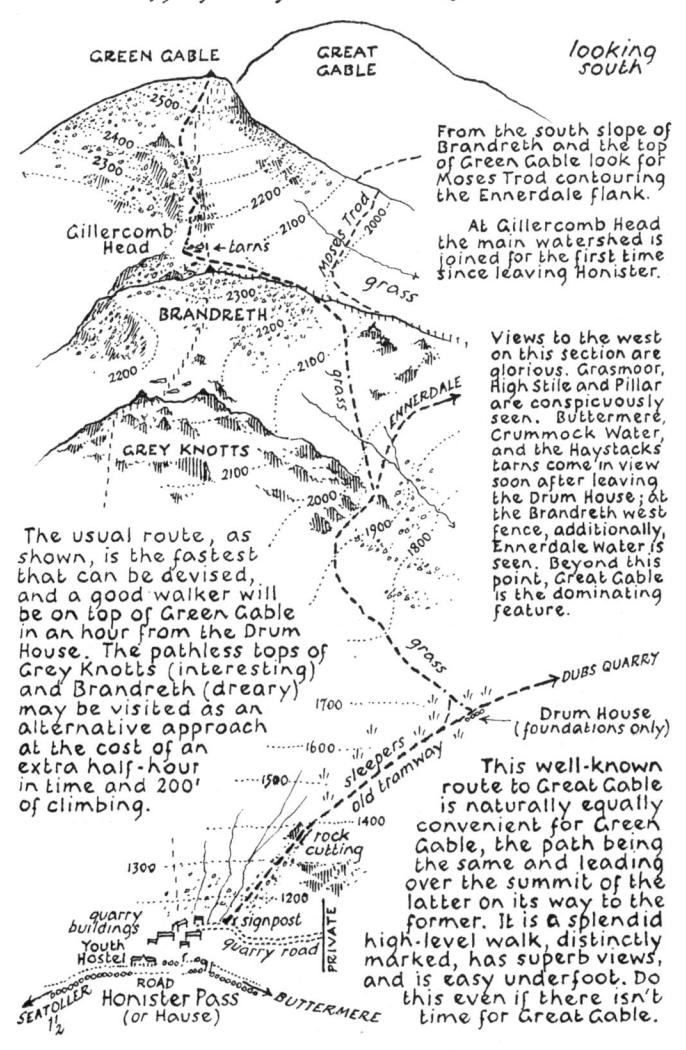

ASCENT FROM HONISTER PASS
1550 feet of ascent : 2½ miles

looking south

From the south slope of Brandreth and the top of Green Gable look for Moses Trod contouring the Ennerdale flank.

At Gillercomb Head the main watershed is joined for the first time since leaving Honister.

Views to the west on this section are glorious. Grasmoor, High Stile and Pillar are conspicuously seen. Buttermere, Crummock Water, and the Haystacks tarns come in view soon after leaving the Drum House; at the Brandreth west fence, additionally, Ennerdale Water is seen. Beyond this point, Great Gable is the dominating feature.

The usual route, as shown, is the fastest that can be devised, and a good walker will be on top of Green Gable in an hour from the Drum House. The pathless tops of Grey Knotts (interesting) and Brandreth (dreary) may be visited as an alternative approach at the cost of an extra half-hour in time and 200' of climbing.

This well-known route to Great Gable is naturally equally convenient for Green Gable, the path being the same and leading over the summit of the latter on its way to the former. It is a splendid high-level walk, distinctly marked, has superb views, and is easy underfoot. Do this even if there isn't time for Great Gable.

Green Gable 5

ASCENT FROM SEATHWAITE
2250 feet of ascent : 2¼ miles

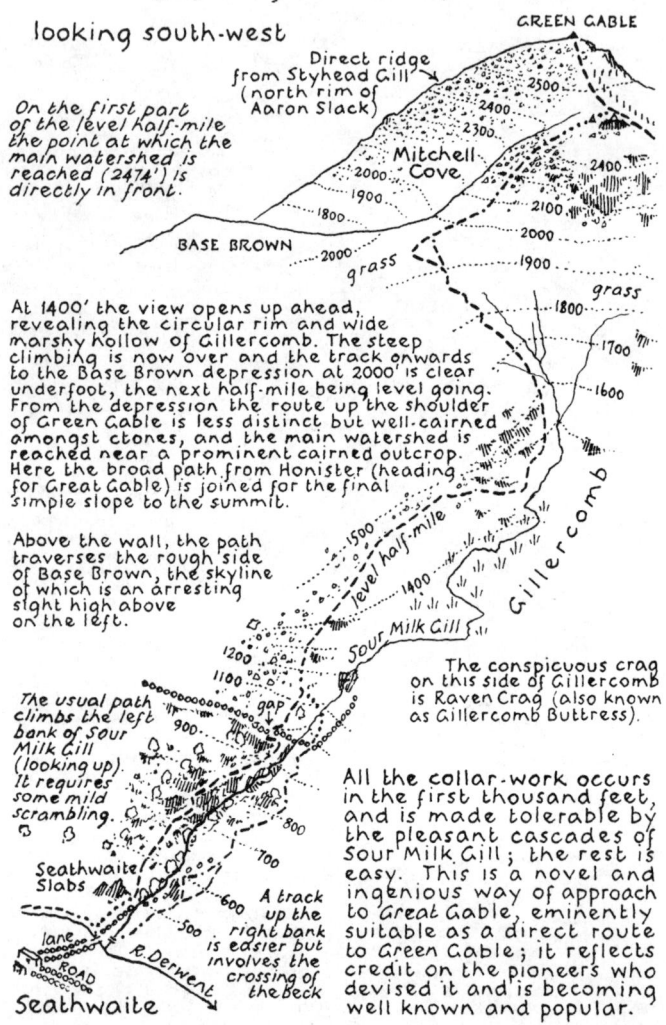

looking south-west

On the first part of the level half-mile the point at which the main watershed is reached (2474') is directly in front.

Direct ridge from Styhead Gill (north rim of Aaron Slack)

GREEN GABLE

Mitchell Cove

BASE BROWN

grass

grass

At 1400' the view opens up ahead, revealing the circular rim and wide marshy hollow of Gillercomb. The steep climbing is now over and the track onwards to the Base Brown depression at 2000' is clear underfoot, the next half-mile being level going. From the depression the route up the shoulder of Green Gable is less distinct but well-cairned amongst stones, and the main watershed is reached near a prominent cairned outcrop. Here the broad path from Honister (heading for Great Gable) is joined for the final simple slope to the summit.

Above the wall, the path traverses the rough side of Base Brown, the skyline of which is an arresting sight high above on the left.

level half-mile

Sour Milk Gill

Gillercomb

The conspicuous crag on this side of Gillercomb is Raven Crag (also known as Gillercomb Buttress).

The usual path climbs the left bank of Sour Milk Gill (looking up). It requires some mild scrambling.

Seathwaite Slabs

lane
ROAD
Seathwaite

R. Derwent

A track up the right bank is easier but involves the crossing of the beck

All the collar-work occurs in the first thousand feet, and is made tolerable by the pleasant cascades of Sour Milk Gill; the rest is easy. This is a novel and ingenious way of approach to Great Gable, eminently suitable as a direct route to Green Gable; it reflects credit on the pioneers who devised it and is becoming well known and popular.

Green Gable 6

ASCENT FROM STYHEAD GILL
1200 feet of ascent : ¾ mile

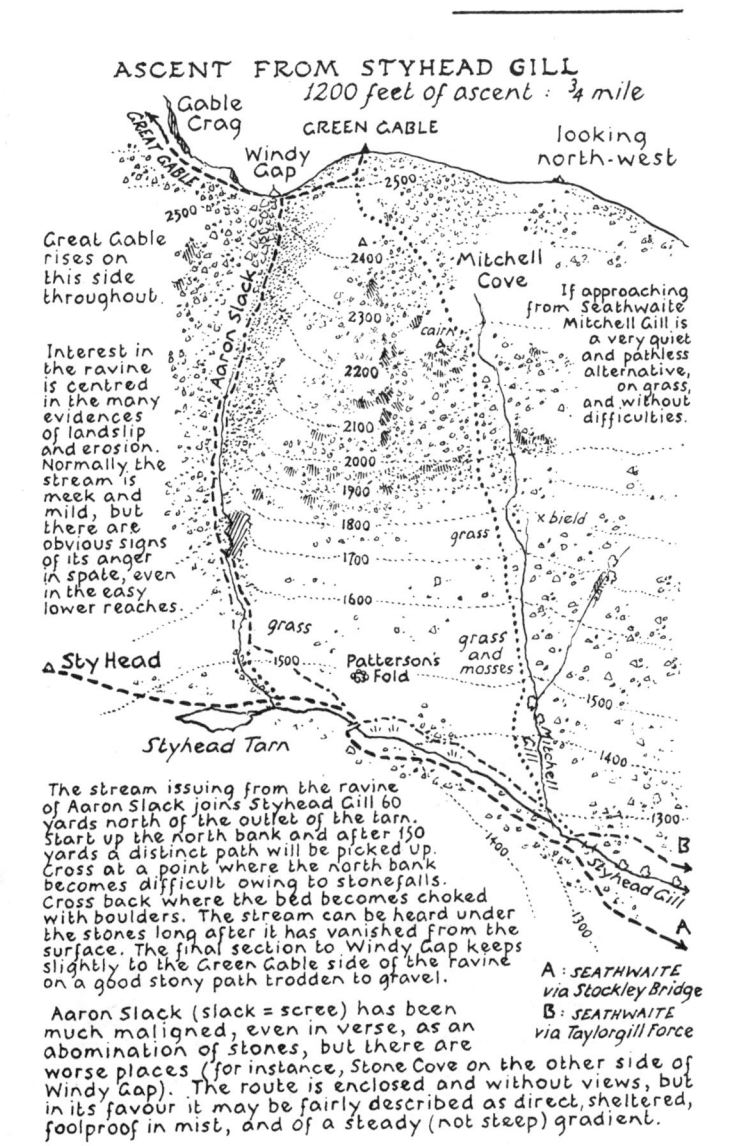

looking north-west

Gable Crag — GREEN GABLE — Windy Gap — GREAT GABLE

Great Gable rises on this side throughout.

Interest in the ravine is centred in the many evidences of landslip and erosion. Normally the stream is meek and mild, but there are obvious signs of its anger in spate, even in the easy lower reaches.

Aaron Slack

Mitchell Cove

If approaching from Seathwaite Mitchell Gill is a very quiet and pathless alternative, on grass, and without difficulties.

cairn

x bield

grass

Sty Head

Patterson's Fold

grass and mosses

Mitchell Gill

Styhead Tarn

Styhead Gill

A: SEATHWAITE via Stockley Bridge
B: SEATHWAITE via Taylorgill Force

The stream issuing from the ravine of Aaron Slack joins Styhead Gill 60 yards north of the outlet of the tarn. Start up the north bank and after 150 yards a distinct path will be picked up. Cross at a point where the north bank becomes difficult owing to stonefalls. Cross back where the bed becomes choked with boulders. The stream can be heard under the stones long after it has vanished from the surface. The final section to Windy Gap keeps slightly to the Green Gable side of the ravine on a good stony path trodden to gravel.

Aaron Slack (slack = scree) has been much maligned, even in verse, as an abomination of stones, but there are worse places (for instance, Stone Cove on the other side of Windy Gap). The route is enclosed and without views, but in its favour it may be fairly described as direct, sheltered, foolproof in mist, and of a steady (not steep) gradient.

Green Gable 7

ASCENT FROM ENNERDALE
(BLACK SAIL YOUTH HOSTEL)
1650 feet of ascent : 2¼ miles

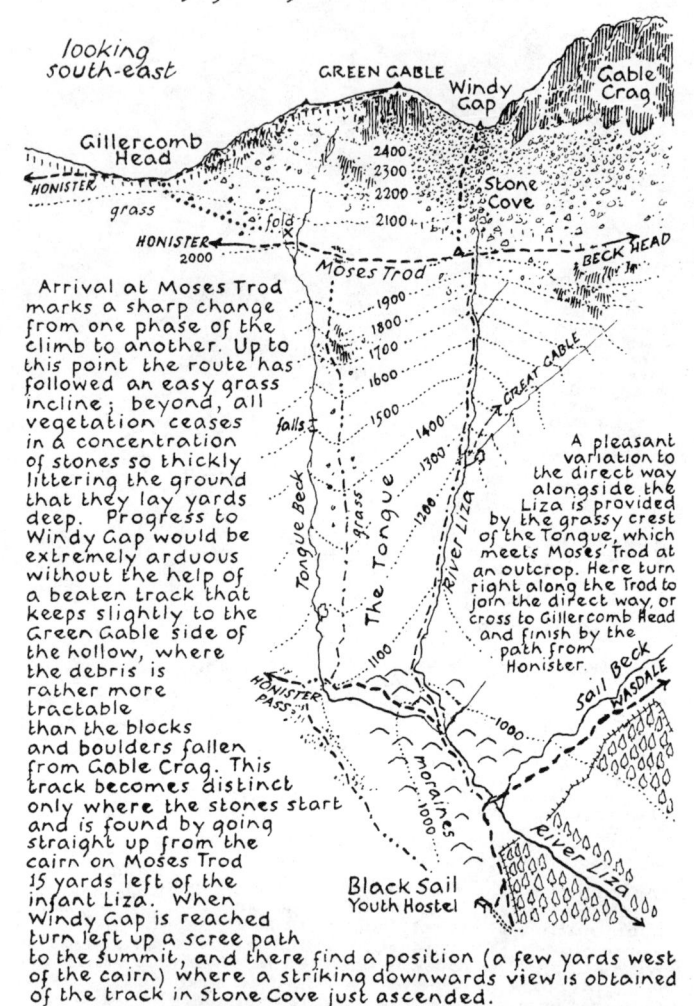

looking south-east

Arrival at Moses Trod marks a sharp change from one phase of the climb to another. Up to this point the route has followed an easy grass incline; beyond, all vegetation ceases in a concentration of stones so thickly littering the ground that they lay yards deep. Progress to Windy Gap would be extremely arduous without the help of a beaten track that keeps slightly to the Green Gable side of the hollow, where the debris is rather more tractable than the blocks and boulders fallen from Gable Crag. This track becomes distinct only where the stones start and is found by going straight up from the cairn on Moses Trod 15 yards left of the infant Liza. When Windy Gap is reached turn left up a scree path to the summit, and there find a position (a few yards west of the cairn) where a striking downwards view is obtained of the track in Stone Cove just ascended.

A pleasant variation to the direct way alongside the Liza is provided by the grassy crest of the Tongue, which meets Moses Trod at an outcrop. Here turn right along the Trod to join the direct way, or cross to Gillercomb Head and finish by the path from Honister.

Green Gable 8

THE SUMMIT

It is a pity that most visitors to the summit are in a hurry to get off it, for the narrow strip of rough ground between the cairn and the rim of the western crags is a fine perch to study the massive architecture of Gable Crag and the deep pit of stones below it: this is a tremendous scene. A wide gravelly path crosses the top, which is uncomplicated, making a sharp angle at the cairn. There are windshelters.

DESCENTS: Honister can be reached at a fast exhilarating pace by the good cairned path northwards via the Drum House (where turn left for Buttermere, right for Borrowdale). The Gillercomb route to Seathwaite is the best direct way down to Borrowdale in clear weather. The Windy Gap and Aaron Slack descent for Sty Head is not recommended as a way down except in mist, when it is very safe; this route is the best for Wasdale, however. For Ennerdale it is palpably necessary first to go down to Windy Gap to avoid crags, there turning to the right on a scree path.

RIDGE ROUTES

TO BRANDRETH, 2344': NE, then N: 1 mile
Depression (Gillercomb Head) at 2160'
200 feet of ascent

Use the Honister path until, after rounding the three tarns of Gillercomb Head, it swings left to cross a line of fence-posts. Here go straight up.

TO GREAT GABLE, 2949'
SE, then SW: ½ mile
Depression (Windy Gap) at 2460'
500 feet of ascent
Follow everybody else.

HALF A MILE

Green Gable 9

THE VIEW

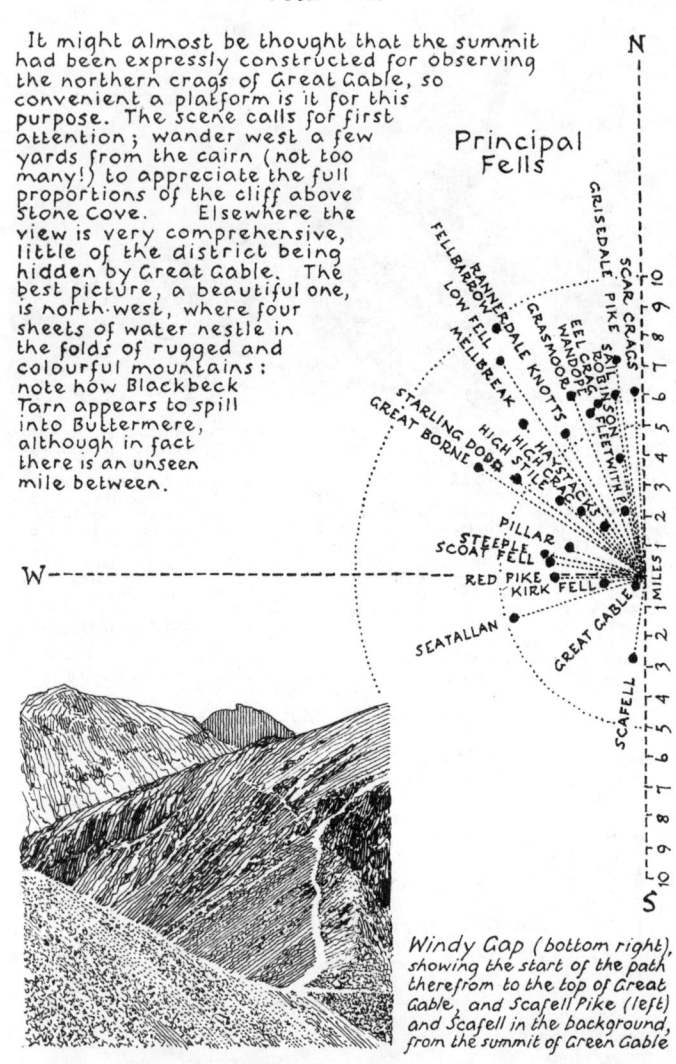

It might almost be thought that the summit had been expressly constructed for observing the northern crags of Great Gable, so convenient a platform is it for this purpose. The scene calls for first attention; wander west a few yards from the cairn (not too many!) to appreciate the full proportions of the cliff above Stone Cove. Elsewhere the view is very comprehensive, little of the district being hidden by Great Gable. The best picture, a beautiful one, is north-west, where four sheets of water nestle in the folds of rugged and colourful mountains: note how Blackbeck Tarn appears to spill into Buttermere, although in fact there is an unseen mile between.

Principal Fells

Windy Gap (bottom right), showing the start of the path therefrom to the top of Great Gable, and Scafell Pike (left) and Scafell in the background, from the summit of Green Gable

Green Gable 10

THE VIEW

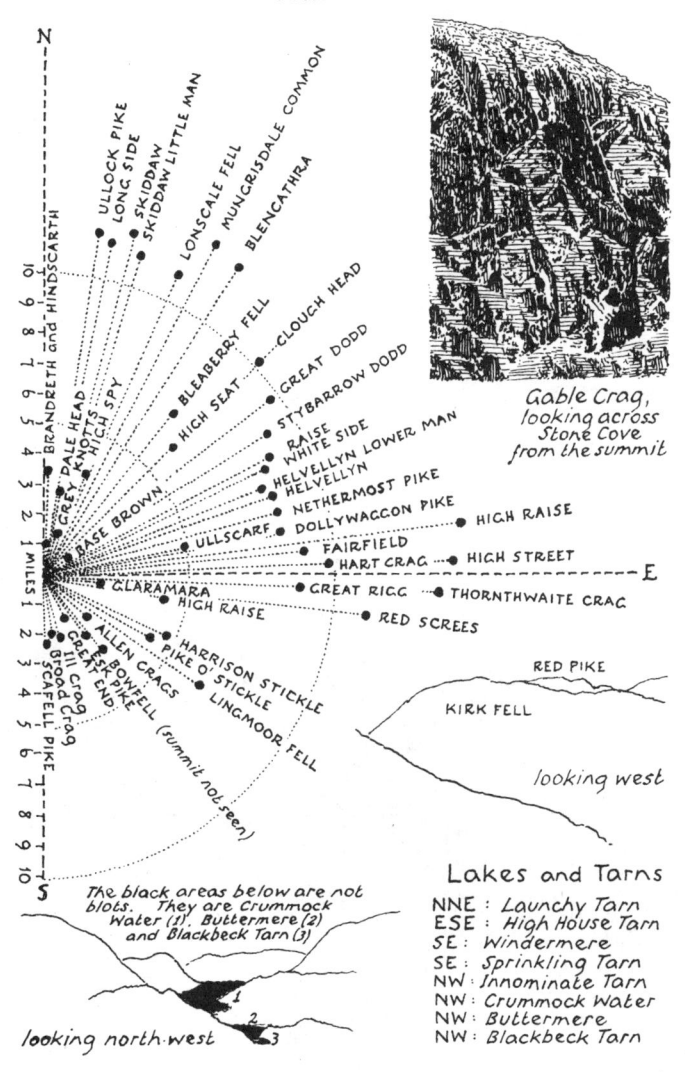

Gable Crag, looking across Stone Cove from the summit

looking west

RED PIKE
KIRK FELL

The black areas below are not blots. They are Crummock Water (1), Buttermere (2) and Blackbeck Tarn (3).

looking north west

Lakes and Tarns

NNE : Launchy Tarn
ESE : High House Tarn
SE : Windermere
SE : Sprinkling Tarn
NW : Innominate Tarn
NW : Crummock Water
NW : Buttermere
NW : Blackbeck Tarn

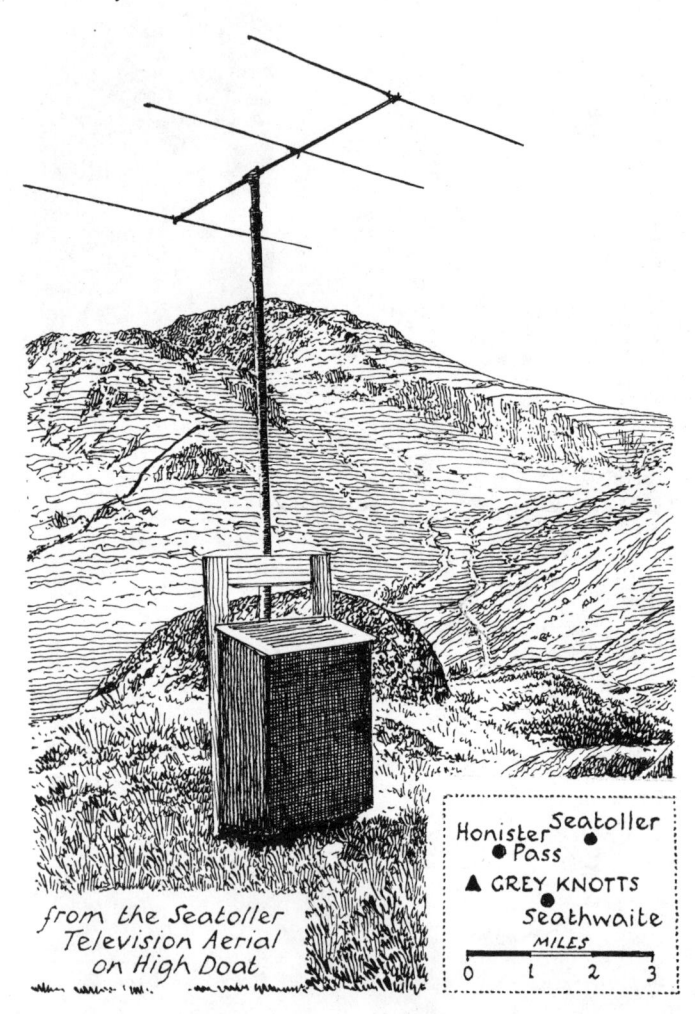

Grey Knotts 2287'

from the Seatoller
Television Aerial
on High Doat

Honister • Seatoller
Pass
▲ GREY KNOTTS
• Seathwaite
MILES
0 1 2 3

Grey Knotts 2

NATURAL FEATURES

Grey Knotts has an interesting situation, rising as a long narrow wedge between upper Borrowdale and an entrant valley half-concealed on the west that carries the motor-road over Honister to Buttermere. So thin is this wedge of high ground that, at the dreary and desolate summit of Honister Pass, sylvan Seathwaite in Borrowdale is still only a straight mile distant.

The ridge of Grey Knotts starts to rise at once, quite steeply, from the woods of Seatoller, levels out at mid height, and finally climbs roughly amongst crags to a broad summit decorated with rock-turrets and tarns. The Honister side of the ridge is plainly unattractive, the Borrowdale side pleasant and interesting, having several notable features: chiefly, high up, the massive buttress of Raven Crag and the scarped hanging valley of Gillercomb. Unique in Lakeland, a once-famous wad or plumbago mine pierces deeply into the Borrowdale flank above Seathwaite. Here, too, is yet another Sour Milk Gill, a leaping white cascade, and not far away is the location of the celebrated 'fraternal four', the Borrowdale Yews written of by Wordsworth and the only individual trees named on maps of Lakeland.

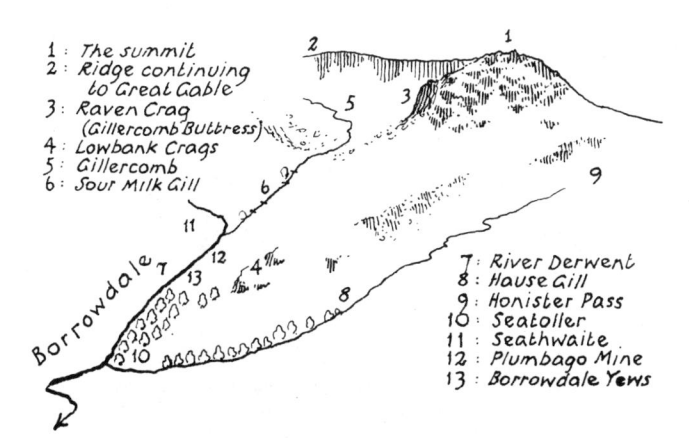

1 : The summit
2 : Ridge continuing to Great Gable
3 : Raven Crag (Gillercomb Buttress)
4 : Lowbank Crags
5 : Gillercomb
6 : Sour Milk Gill
7 : River Derwent
8 : Hause Gill
9 : Honister Pass
10 : Seatoller
11 : Seathwaite
12 : Plumbago Mine
13 : Borrowdale Yews

Grey Knotts is geographically the first stepping-stone to Great Gable from the north (although not commonly used as such), the connection being a high ridge that runs over the two intermediate summits of Brandreth and Green Gable. The western slope descends easily to halt in the marshes of Dubs Bottom and is redeemed from dreariness only by the fine views it commands.

Grey Knotts 3

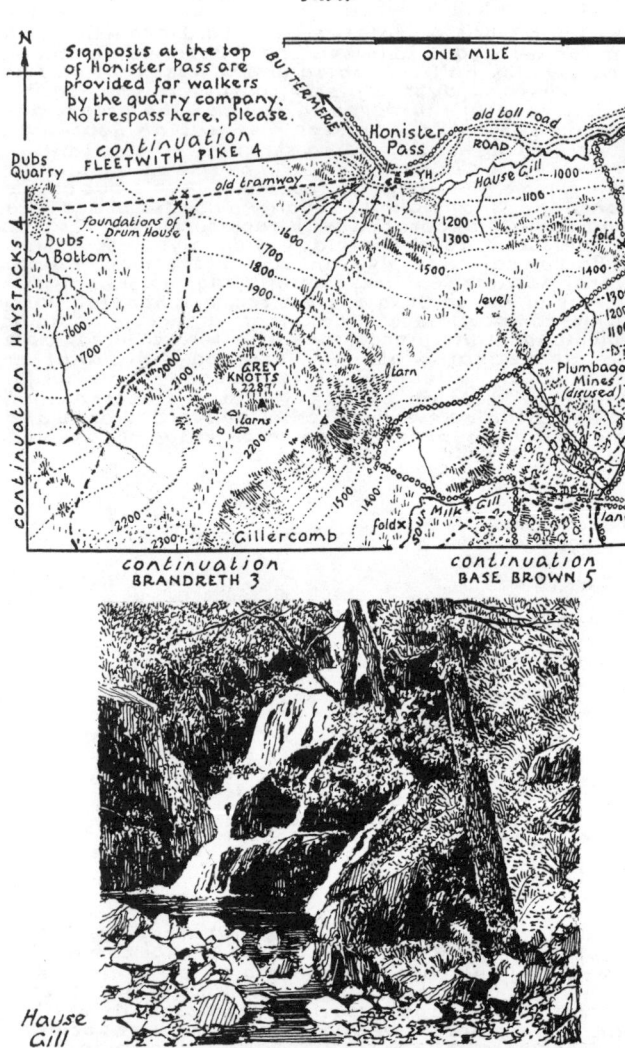

MAP

Signposts at the top of Honister Pass are provided for walkers by the quarry company. No trespass here, please.

Hause Gill

Grey Knotts 4

MAP

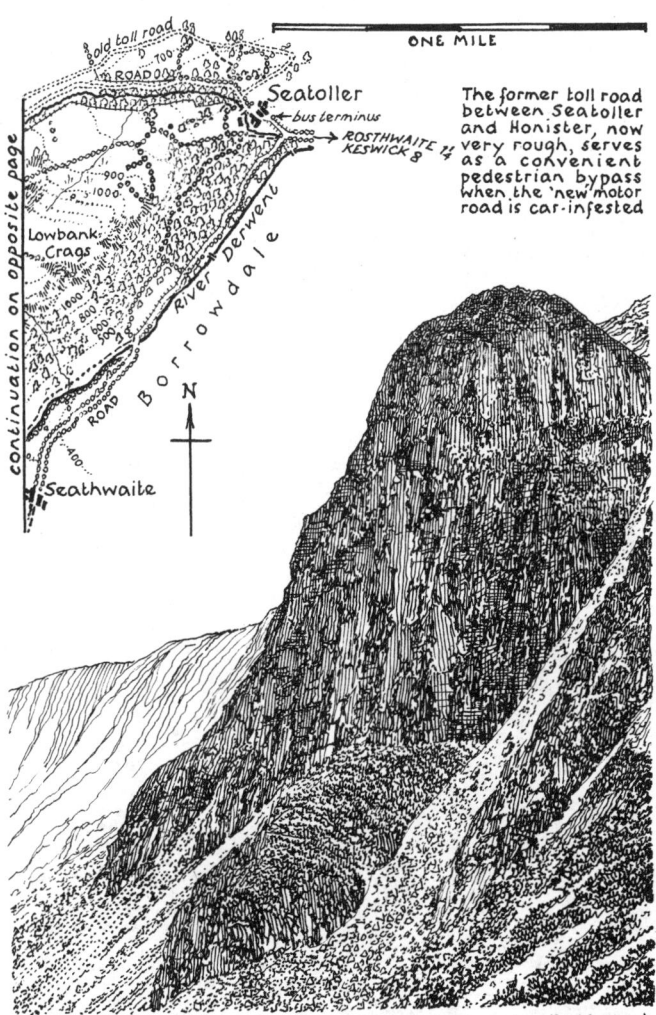

The former toll road between Seatoller and Honister, now very rough, serves as a convenient pedestrian bypass when the new motor road is car-infested

Seatoller — bus terminus
→ ROSTHWAITE 1¾ KESWICK 8
Lowbank Crags
River Derwent
Borrowdale
Seathwaite
continuation on opposite page

Raven Crag (known to climbers as Gillercombe Buttress)

Grey Knotts 5

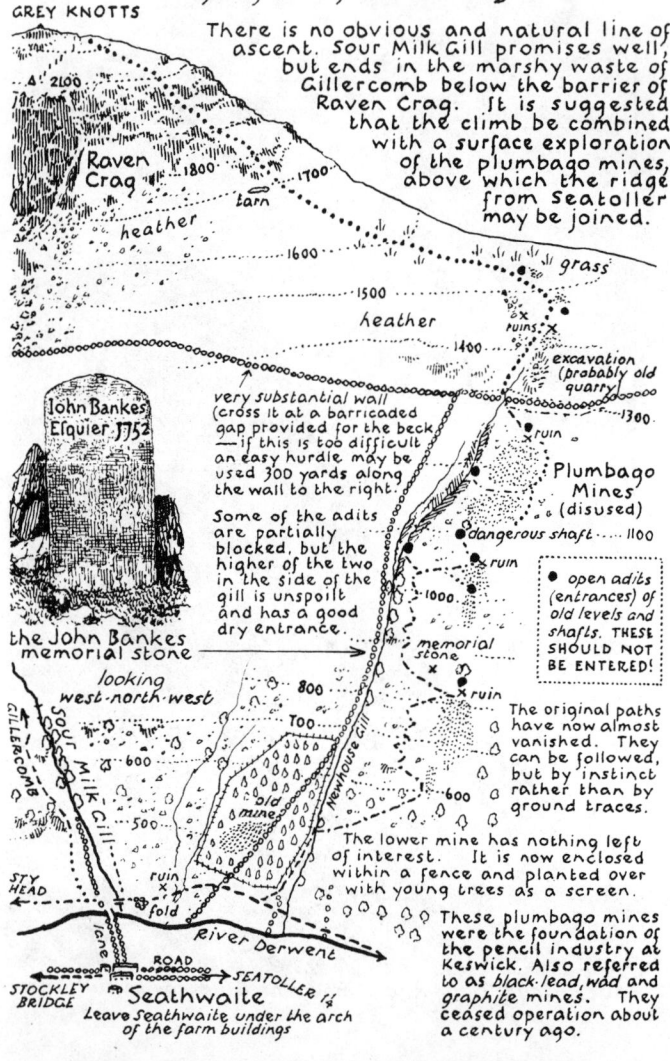

ASCENT FROM SEATHWAITE
1900 feet of ascent : 1½ miles

There is no obvious and natural line of ascent. Sour Milk Gill promises well, but ends in the marshy waste of Gillercomb below the barrier of Raven Crag. It is suggested that the climb be combined with a surface exploration of the plumbago mines, above which the ridge from Seatoller may be joined.

GREY KNOTTS
Raven Crag
heather
tarn
grass
heather
ruins
excavation (probably old quarry)
ruin

Plumbago Mines (disused)

• dangerous shaft 1100
ruin

● open adits (entrances) of old levels and shafts. THESE SHOULD NOT BE ENTERED!

very substantial wall (cross it at a barricaded gap provided for the beck — if this is too difficult an easy hurdle may be used 300 yards along the wall to the right.

Some of the adits are partially blocked, but the higher of the two in the side of the gill is unspoilt and has a good dry entrance.

John Bankes Esquier 1752

the John Bankes memorial stone

looking west-north-west

memorial stone
ruin

The original paths have now almost vanished. They can be followed, but by instinct rather than by ground traces.

old mine
Newhouse Gill
Sour Milk Gill
GILLERCOMB

STY HEAD
ruin
fold
River Derwent
lane
ROAD
STOCKLEY BRIDGE — SEATOLLER 1¼
Seathwaite
Leave Seathwaite under the arch of the farm buildings

The lower mine has nothing left of interest. It is now enclosed within a fence and planted over with young trees as a screen.

These plumbago mines were the foundation of the pencil industry at Keswick. Also referred to as *black-lead, wad* and *graphite mines*. They ceased operation about a century ago.

Grey Knotts 6

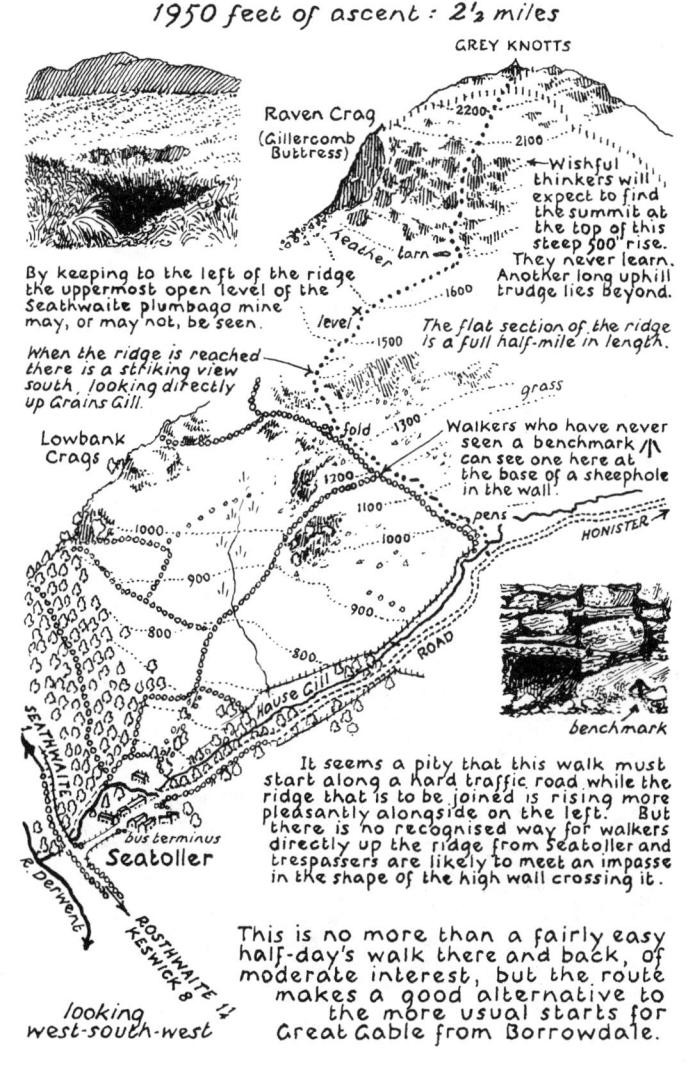

ASCENT FROM SEATOLLER
1950 feet of ascent : 2½ miles

GREY KNOTTS

Raven Crag
(Gillercomb Buttress)

← Wishful thinkers will expect to find the summit at the top of this steep 500' rise. They never learn. Another long uphill trudge lies beyond.

By keeping to the left of the ridge the uppermost open level of the Seathwaite plumbago mine may, or may not, be seen.

The flat section of the ridge is a full half-mile in length.

When the ridge is reached there is a striking view south, looking directly up Grains Gill.

Lowbank Crags

Walkers who have never seen a benchmark /|\ can see one here at the base of a sheephole in the wall.

HONISTER →

House Gill ROAD

benchmark

SEATHWAITE
bus terminus
Seatoller
R. Derwent
ROSTHWAITE
KESWICK 8

It seems a pity that this walk must start along a hard traffic road while the ridge that is to be joined is rising more pleasantly alongside on the left. But there is no recognised way for walkers directly up the ridge from Seatoller and trespassers are likely to meet an impasse in the shape of the high wall crossing it.

This is no more than a fairly easy half-day's walk there and back, of moderate interest, but the route makes a good alternative to the more usual starts for Great Gable from Borrowdale.

looking west-south-west

Grey Knotts 7

ASCENT FROM HONISTER PASS
1150 feet of ascent : 1 mile

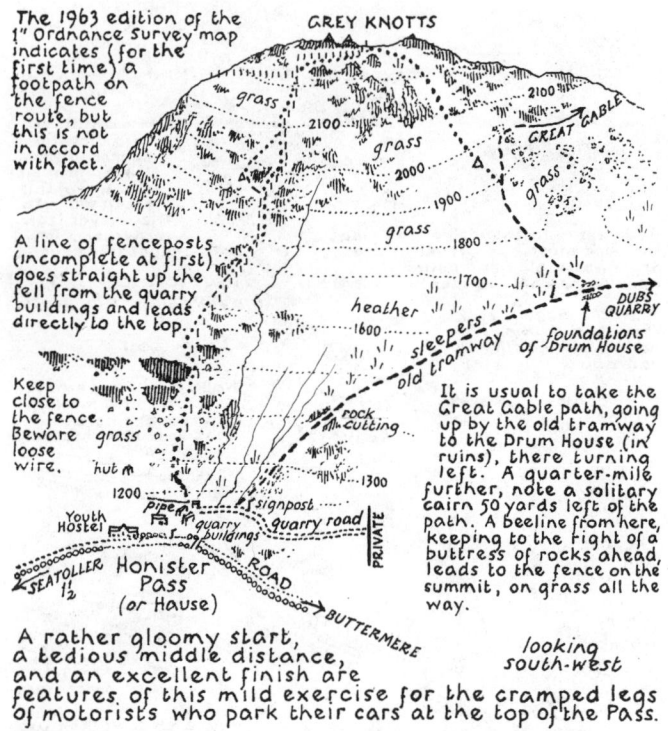

The 1963 edition of the 1" Ordnance Survey map indicates (for the first time) a footpath on the fence route, but this is not in accord with fact.

A line of fenceposts (incomplete at first) goes straight up the fell from the quarry buildings and leads directly to the top.

Keep close to the fence. Beware loose wire.

It is usual to take the Great Gable path, going up by the old tramway to the Drum House (in ruins), there turning left. A quarter-mile further, note a solitary cairn 50 yards left of the path. A beeline from here, keeping to the right of a buttress of rocks ahead, leads to the fence on the summit, on grass all the way.

A rather gloomy start, a tedious middle distance, and an excellent finish are features of this mild exercise for the cramped legs of motorists who park their cars at the top of the Pass.

looking south-west

The rock cutting

The skyline of Grey Knotts from the Drum House

Grey Knotts 8

THE SUMMIT

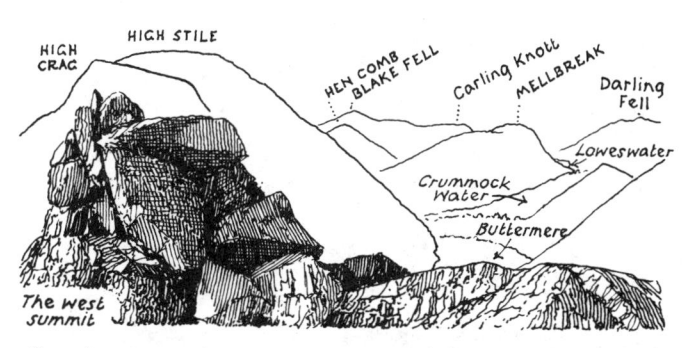

The west summit

Grey tors of rock, most of them bearing cairns and looking much alike, and several small sheets of water, make the top of the fell very attractive, but in mist this would be a most confusing place were it not crossed by a line of fence-posts from which it is possible to take direction. Two tors compete for the distinction of being the highest: the survey station at 2287' is within the angle of the fence and the other summit is 180 yards west and apparently at the same elevation or within inches of it.

DESCENTS: If the fence is being followed east from the angle, it is essential to watch for the junction of the Honister fence — the other branch, still going east, heads for sudden death over the edge of Gillercomb Buttress. For Seatoller, strike a course midway between the two fences, picking a way down among low crags to the level ridge below, and when a wall is reached it is preferable to follow it left to the Honister road. The easiest way off the summit is via the grass slope to the Gable-Honister path.

The west summit from the east summit

The east summit, looking to Glaramara

PLAN OF SUMMIT
100 yards

The name 'Grey Knotts' is apt, and appropriate to the scenery of the top. But it clearly refers only to the summit, this being yet another example of a summit-name commonly but quite wrongly adopted for the whole fell from the roots up. Compare 'Great Gable', another descriptive name, which obviously applies to the mountain in its entirety, the summit having no separate name.

Grey Knotts 9

THE VIEW

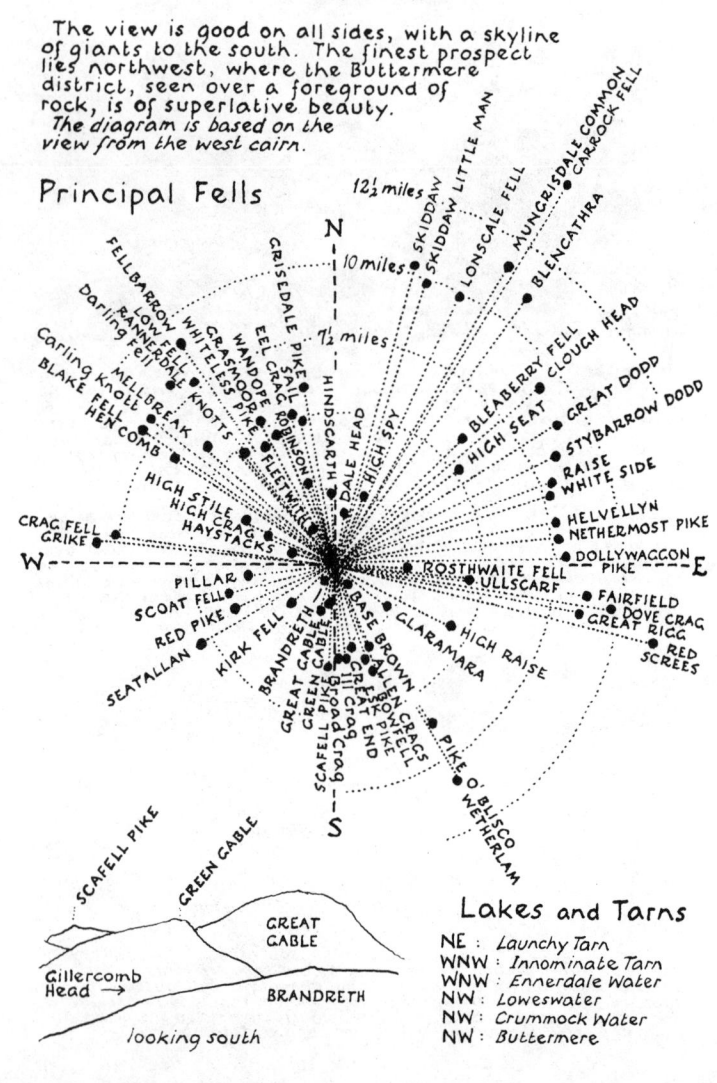

The view is good on all sides, with a skyline of giants to the south. The finest prospect lies northwest, where the Buttermere district, seen over a foreground of rock, is of superlative beauty.

The diagram is based on the view from the west cairn.

Principal Fells

12½ miles · 10 miles · 7½ miles

N — Skiddaw, Skiddaw Little Man, Lonscale Fell, Mungrisdale Common, Carrock Fell, Blencathra, Bleaberry Fell, Clough Head, High Seat, Great Dodd, Stybarrow Dodd, Raise, White Side, Helvellyn, Nethermost Pike, Dollywaggon Pike, Fairfield, Dove Crag, Great Rigg, Red Screes

Fellbarrow, Lowfell, Rannerdale, Darling Fell, Mellbreak, Carling Knott, Blake Fell, Hen Comb, Whiteless, Grasmoore, Grisedale Pike, Eel Crag, Sail, Wandope, Knotts, Robinson, Fleetwith, Dale Head, Hindscarth, High Spy

High Stile, High Crags, Haystacks

W — Crag Fell, Grike, Pillar, Scoat Fell, Red Pike, Seatallan — Rosthwaite Fell, Ullscarf — E

Kirk Fell, Brandreth, Great Gable, Green Gable, Base Brown, Glaramara, High Raise

Scafell Pike, Broad Crag, Great End, Allen Crags, Lingmell, Esk Pike, Bowfell, Pike o' Blisco, Wetherlam

S

looking south — Scafell Pike, Green Gable, Gillercomb Head →, Great Gable, Brandreth

Lakes and Tarns

NE : *Launchy Tarn*
WNW : *Innominate Tarn*
WNW : *Ennerdale Water*
NW : *Loweswater*
NW : *Crummock Water*
NW : *Buttermere*

Grey Knotts 10

RIDGE ROUTE

To BRANDRETH, 2344': ½ mile: SW
Depression at 2250': 100 feet of ascent

Only those of unusual talent could go astray on this simple walk, the line of fenceposts being a sure pointer to the top of Brandreth. Some interest may be added by a detour leftwards to look down into Gillercomb.

ONE MILE

Gillercomb and Raven Crag

Crike 1596'

from Lanefoot

← cows sitting down (explanatory note)

Ennerdale Bridge
● Cleator Moor
CRIKE ▲ CRAG FELL ▲

MILES
0 1 2 3 4

from Kinniside Stone Circle

Grike 2

NATURAL FEATURES

Grike is the beginning of Lakeland from the west. Approaching from Whitehaven an industrial belt has first to be crossed to Cleator Moor, after which follows an attractive undulating countryside watered by the Ehen, until, quite sharply, Grike and Crag Fell dominate the view ahead, with a glimpse of greater fells beyond closing in the valley of Ennerdale.

Grike, smooth and grassy for the most part, is not a typical forerunner, although the north side overlooking the valley is seamed and scarred with huge ravines, and only its position makes the fell interesting. It is a good viewpoint, and the summit boasts a massive cairn that can be seen for miles around. The indefinite top forms a watershed, the southern slopes draining into the Calder, which, curiously, shares the same estuary near Sellafield as the Ehen coming round from the north.

Grike is undergoing a transformation. The Forestry Commission, denied further activity in the central areas of the district after making such a mess of Ennerdale, are acquiring more land along the western fringe, where they are less subject to public outcry, and Grike, like Murton Fell and Blake Fell, is now festooned with new fences and decorated with little trees that will grow into big ones, all looking exactly the same, trees without character. In twenty years another fox sanctuary will have been created, the landscape will have been drastically altered, and the pages of this guidebook dealing with Grike will be obsolete. Come to think of it, so will the author, God rest his soul.

the Kinniside Stone Circle

looking north-east

Knock Murton — BLAKE FELL — GAVEL FELL — HOPEGILL HEAD — GRASMOOR

It is a remarkable fact that the Kinniside Stone Circle, although a wellknown ancient monument, is omitted from Ordnance Survey maps. The explanation seems to be that at the time of the first, and early subsequent, surveys, the Kinniside Stone Circle was non-existent, all twelve stones having long before been taken by local farmers for use as gateposts and building materials. But forty years ago a grand job of restoration was accomplished by an enterprising working party, to whom great credit is due. Having cleaned out and measured the sockets in the ground in which the stones were originally set, they searched for — and located — the original twelve, recovered them all, and completely restored the site. Today the circle is exactly as it was when first laid out, thousands of years ago, waiting to surprise the next Ordnance Survey team. *Note for survivors of the working party: one stone is loose.*

Grike 3

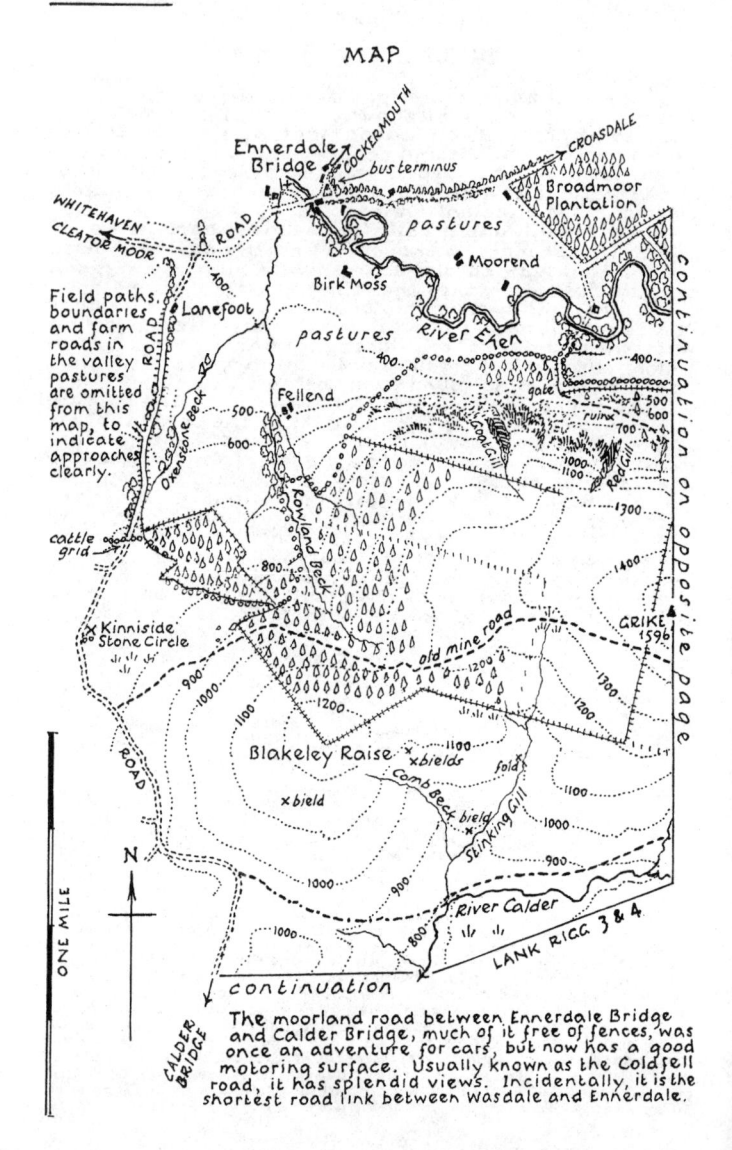

MAP

The moorland road between Ennerdale Bridge and Calder Bridge, much of it free of fences, was once an adventure for cars, but now has a good motoring surface. Usually known as the Coldfell road, it has splendid views. Incidentally, it is the shortest road link between Wasdale and Ennerdale.

Grike 4

ASCENT FROM KINNISIDE STONE CIRCLE
850 feet of ascent : 2 miles

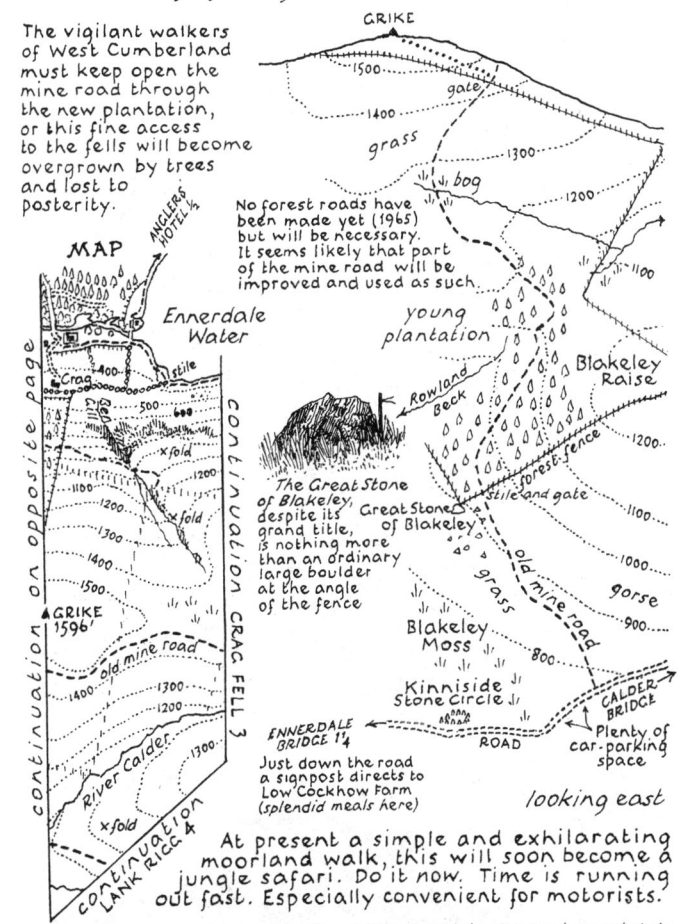

The vigilant walkers of West Cumberland must keep open the mine road through the new plantation, or this fine access to the fells will become overgrown by trees and lost to posterity.

No forest roads have been made yet (1965) but will be necessary. It seems likely that part of the mine road will be improved and used as such.

GRIKE
gate
grass
bog
young plantation
Rowland Beck
Blakeley Raise
forest fence
stile and gate
The Great Stone of Blakeley, despite its grand title, is nothing more than an ordinary large boulder at the angle of the fence
Great Stone of Blakeley
old mine road
grass
gorse
Blakeley Moss
Kinniside Stone Circle
CALDER BRIDGE
Plenty of car-parking space
ROAD
looking east

MAP
ANGLERS HOTEL
Ennerdale Water
stile
Crag
x fold
x fold
▲ GRIKE 1596'
old mine road
River Calder
x fold
continuation on opposite page
CONTINUATION CRAG FELL 3
CONTINUATION LANK RIGG 2
ENNERDALE BRIDGE 1¼
Just down the road a signpost directs to Low Cockhow Farm (splendid meals here)

At present a simple and exhilarating moorland walk, this will soon become a jungle safari. Do it now. Time is running out fast. Especially convenient for motorists.

The Coldfell road is reputedly of Roman origin. It runs immediately alongside the Kinniside Stone Circle, reputedly of pre-Roman origin. Is this interesting evidence that the Romans treated ancient monuments with respect? The stones would obviously make handy paving blocks, but were not violated — until centuries later, when Cumbrian natives, more civilised and less scrupulous, saw a good use for them.

Grike 5

ASCENT FROM ENNERDALE BRIDGE
1250 feet of ascent : 2½ miles

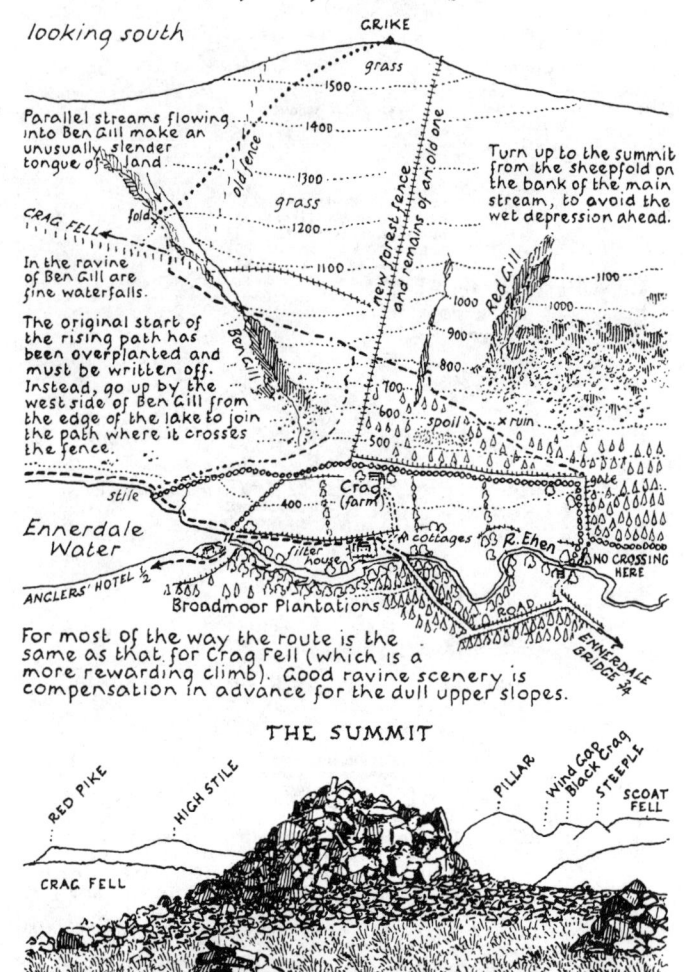

looking south

Parallel streams flowing into Ben Gill make an unusually slender tongue of land.

In the ravine of Ben Gill are fine waterfalls.

The original start of the rising path has been overplanted and must be written off. Instead, go up by the west side of Ben Gill from the edge of the lake to join the path where it crosses the fence.

Turn up to the summit from the sheepfold on the bank of the main stream, to avoid the wet depression ahead.

For most of the way the route is the same as that for Crag Fell (which is a more rewarding climb). Good ravine scenery is compensation in advance for the dull upper slopes.

THE SUMMIT

continued

Crike 6

THE SUMMIT
continued

The summit is remarkable for its massive cairn and two baby ones, cairn-building here being an easy task thanks to a rash of stones on the highest part of the fell, an eruption quite out of character: all around is uninterrupted grass. Because of this big cairn, which is prominently seen over long distances, the top is locally spoken of not as Crike but as the Stone Man. Diligent search will not reveal anything else of interest, but it may be noted, with apprehension, that a new forest fence crosses the western shoulder, replacing a dilapidated boundary fence, very close to the summit.

DESCENTS: The best views are obtained by aiming north-east (not north, where there are crags) to descend by the west bank of Ben Gill, keeping well out of the ravine, and so reach the outflow of Ennerdale Water. The descent by the mine road, soon located south of the summit, is a fast walk and the best way down in mist; on reaching tarmac, turn right along it for Ennerdale Bridge.

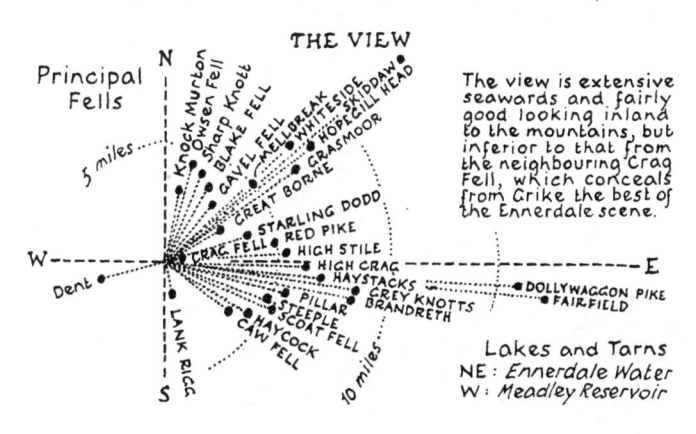

THE VIEW

Principal Fells

(diagram of fells radiating from Crike: Knock Murton, Owsen Fell, Sharp Knott, Gavel Fell, Blake Fell, Mellbreak, Whiteside, Skiddaw, Hopegill Head, Great Borne, Grasmoor, Starling Dodd, Red Pike, Crag Fell, High Stile, High Crag, Haystacks, Dollywaggon Pike, Fairfield, Pillar, Grey Knotts, Brandreth, Steeple, Scoat Fell, Haycock, Caw Fell, Lank Rigg, Dent; scale 5 miles, 10 miles)

The view is extensive seawards and fairly good looking inland to the mountains, but inferior to that from the neighbouring Crag Fell, which conceals from Crike the best of the Ennerdale scene.

Lakes and Tarns
NE: Ennerdale Water
W: Meadley Reservoir

RIDGE ROUTE

To CRAG FELL, 1710':
1 mile : E, then NE
Depression at 1450'
260 feet of ascent
An easy stroll

A beeline may be taken, with a good chance of getting wet feet in the depression, a circumstance that can be avoided by making use of the mine road to pass from one to the other.

(map showing Crike and Crag Fell with contours 1300–1600 and old mine road)

ONE MILE

Haycock

2618'

from Winscale Hows, Seatallan

Haycock 2

NATURAL FEATURES

Haycock rises in a massive dome on the Wasdale and Ennerdale watershed, and its comparative neglect by walkers must be ascribed more to its remote position on the fringe of the dreary and unattractive moors of Kinniside and Copeland than to its own shortcomings, which are few. The fell, indeed, has all the qualities of ruggedness and cragginess characteristic of the Wasdale mountains, and the approaches to it have charm of surroundings not usually associated with such rough terrain. Despite its considerable height, however, Haycock is not rooted in valleys, being instead hoisted on the shoulders of supporting fells of lesser altitude but greater extensiveness. Pleasant streams flow north to Ennerdale and to Wasdale southwards, but the biggest waterway leaving the fell, a great natural channel, is that occupied by the River Bleng, southwest. Seen from this latter direction, Haycock is a giant in stature, completely dominating the head of the valley and unchallenged by other peaks. Here, at least, it is supreme; it cannot be neglected.

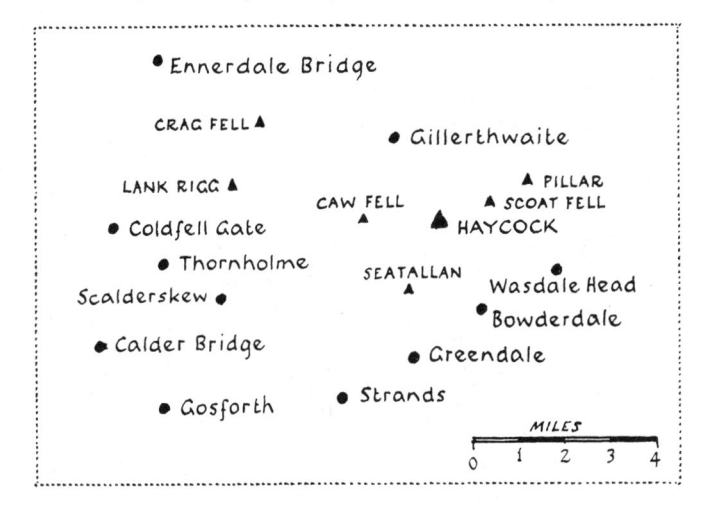

Haycock 3

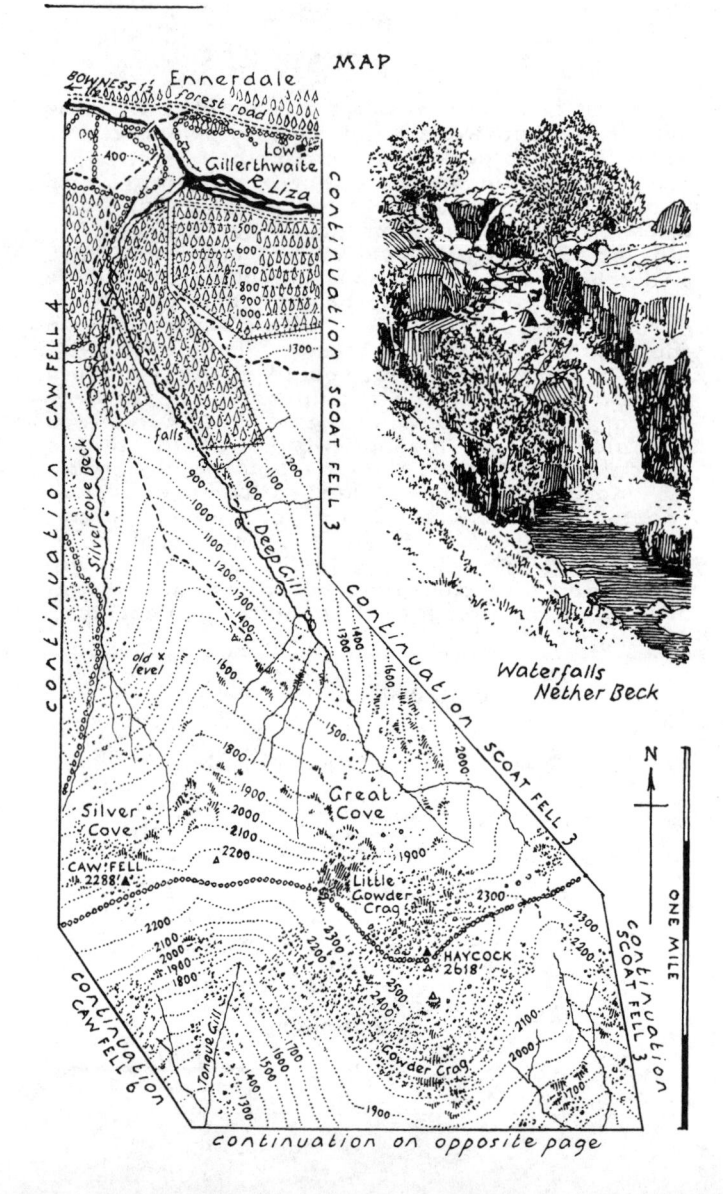

MAP

Waterfalls
Nether Beck

Haycock 4

MAP

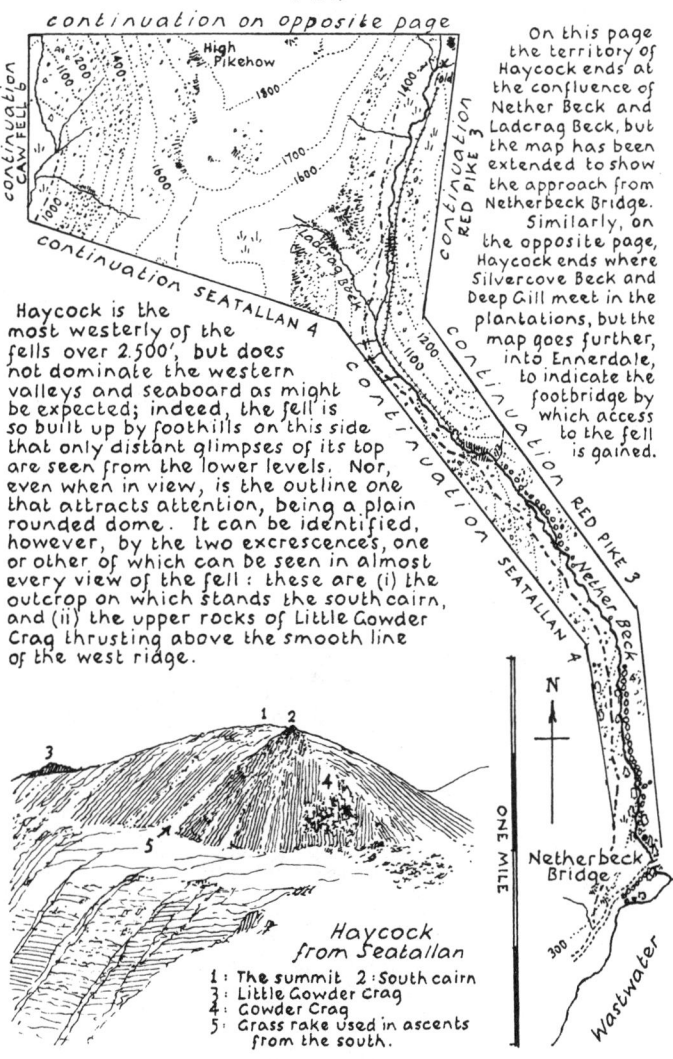

continuation on opposite page

On this page the territory of Haycock ends at the confluence of Nether Beck and Ladcrag Beck, but the map has been extended to show the approach from Netherbeck Bridge.
Similarly, on the opposite page, Haycock ends where Silvercove Beck and Deep Gill meet in the plantations, but the map goes further, into Ennerdale, to indicate the footbridge by which access to the fell is gained.

Haycock is the most westerly of the fells over 2,500′, but does not dominate the western valleys and seaboard as might be expected; indeed, the fell is so built up by foothills on this side that only distant glimpses of its top are seen from the lower levels. Nor, even when in view, is the outline one that attracts attention, being a plain rounded dome. It can be identified, however, by the two excrescences, one or other of which can be seen in almost every view of the fell: these are (i) the outcrop on which stands the south cairn, and (ii) the upper rocks of Little Gowder Crag thrusting above the smooth line of the west ridge.

Haycock from Seatallan

1: The summit 2: South cairn
3: Little Gowder Crag
4: Gowder Crag
5: Grass rake used in ascents from the south.

Haycock 5

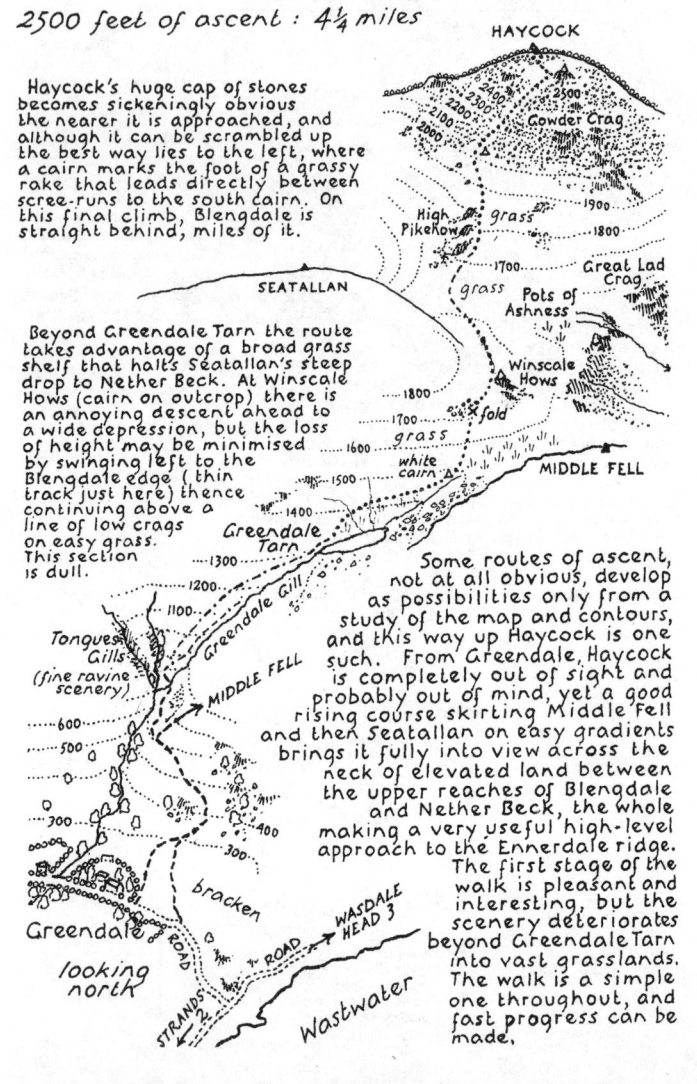

ASCENT FROM WASDALE
(GREENDALE)

2500 feet of ascent : 4¼ miles

Haycock's huge cap of stones becomes sickeningly obvious the nearer it is approached, and although it can be scrambled up the best way lies to the left, where a cairn marks the foot of a grassy rake that leads directly between scree-runs to the south cairn. On this final climb, Blengdale is straight behind, miles of it.

Beyond Greendale Tarn the route takes advantage of a broad grass shelf that halts Seatallan's steep drop to Nether Beck. At Winscale Hows (cairn on outcrop) there is an annoying descent ahead to a wide depression, but the loss of height may be minimised by swinging left to the Blengdale edge (thin track just here) thence continuing above a line of low crags on easy grass. This section is dull.

Some routes of ascent, not at all obvious, develop as possibilities only from a study of the map and contours, and this way up Haycock is one such. From Greendale, Haycock is completely out of sight and probably out of mind, yet a good rising course skirting Middle Fell and then Seatallan on easy gradients brings it fully into view across the neck of elevated land between the upper reaches of Blengdale and Nether Beck, the whole making a very useful high-level approach to the Ennerdale ridge.

The first stage of the walk is pleasant and interesting, but the scenery deteriorates beyond Greendale Tarn into vast grasslands. The walk is a simple one throughout, and fast progress can be made.

Haycock 6

ASCENT FROM WASDALE
(NETHERBECK BRIDGE)
2400 feet of ascent : 4 miles

A fair path proceeds along the west side of Nether Beck. It leaves the road a quarter-mile from Netherbeck Bridge (not very distinctly) but may be joined direct from the bridge by slanting across to it, over open ground, half left.

RED PIKE rises on this side

Two routes are shown beyond Ladcrag Beck. It is usual, and more simple, to continue up the valley and aim for the depression on the ridge ahead (to the right of Haycock), turning up alongside the wall to the summit. But if returning down the valley afterwards variety may be added to the later stages of the climb by going up instead by Ladcrag Beck to the plateau above and then finishing by the rake mentioned on the page opposite. If both routes are so employed, use B for ascent and A for coming down. In mist use A only, in both directions.

looking north-north-west

Haycock 7

ASCENT FROM ENNERDALE
(LOW GILLERTHWAITE)
2300 feet of ascent : 3 miles

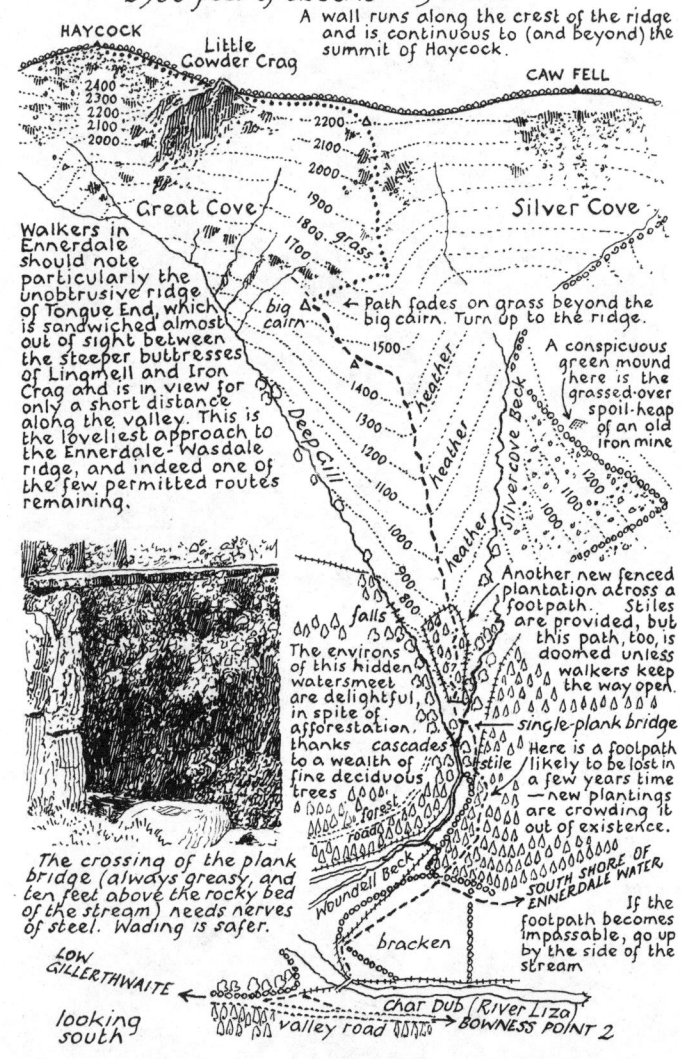

A wall runs along the crest of the ridge and is continuous to (and beyond) the summit of Haycock.

HAYCOCK — Little Gowder Crag — CAW FELL

Great Cove — Silver Cove

Walkers in Ennerdale should note particularly the unobtrusive ridge of Tongue End, which is sandwiched almost out of sight between the steeper buttresses of Lingmell and Iron Crag and is in view for only a short distance along the valley. This is the loveliest approach to the Ennerdale-Wasdale ridge, and indeed one of the few permitted routes remaining.

big cairn ← Path fades on grass beyond the big cairn. Turn up to the ridge.

A conspicuous green mound here is the grassed-over spoil-heap of an old iron mine

Deep Gill — heather — Silvercove Beck

Another new fenced plantation across a footpath. Stiles are provided, but this path, too, is doomed unless walkers keep the way open.

falls — single-plank bridge

The environs of this hidden watersmeet are delightful, in spite of afforestation, thanks cascades to a wealth of fine deciduous trees

stile — Here is a footpath likely to be lost in a few years time — new plantings are crowding it out of existence.

forest road — Wourdell Beck

SOUTH SHORE OF ENNERDALE WATER

The crossing of the plank bridge (always greasy, and ten feet above the rocky bed of the stream) needs nerves of steel. Wading is safer.

bracken

If the footpath becomes impassable, go up by the side of the stream

← LOW GILLERTHWAITE

looking south

valley road — Char Dub (River Liza) → BOWNESS POINT 2

Haycock 8

THE SUMMIT

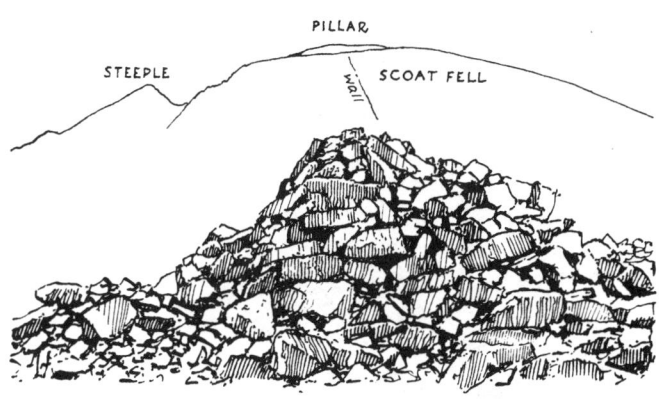

There are two summit cairns, one on each side of the sturdy stone wall running over the top of the fell, that on the north side having slightly the greater elevation and the other one offering some shelter against the elements. The top is stony everywhere and without paths: it is usual not to stray far from the wall. 150 yards south is another cairn, prominent on an outcrop of rock and commanding a better view of the Wasdale scene.

DESCENTS:

For Wasdale, the quickest route lies alongside the wall to the east depression, there turning right (path for a few yards only) down an easy grass slope. Keep to the right of an incipient stream. Nether Beck is joined on its way down from Scoat Tarn, and from this point onwards a path, at first indistinct, can be followed to the Wasdale road at Netherbeck Bridge. This is a simple and straightforward way off the fell, the best for a party that has already had enough for one day, and the safest route in mist, but the time required for it should not be under-estimated.

For Ennerdale, follow the north side of the wall north-west over Little Gowder Crag and on the grass beyond turn down an indefinite ridge that soon becomes more pronounced, and, when heather is reached, provides a good track down Tongue End into the new plantations, gaining the valley road across the footbridge a few fields east of the head of Ennerdale Water.

The second (slightly lower) summit cairn. On the far side is a wind shelter.

Haycock 9

THE VIEW

Although the view of Lakeland tends to deteriorate on the long decline to the west from Pillar, that from the summit of Haycock is still remarkably good in all directions. The full length of the Scafell range is seen, but, curiously, only the uppermost feet of Pillar and Great Gable are visible above the intervening heights of Scoat Fell and Red Pike.

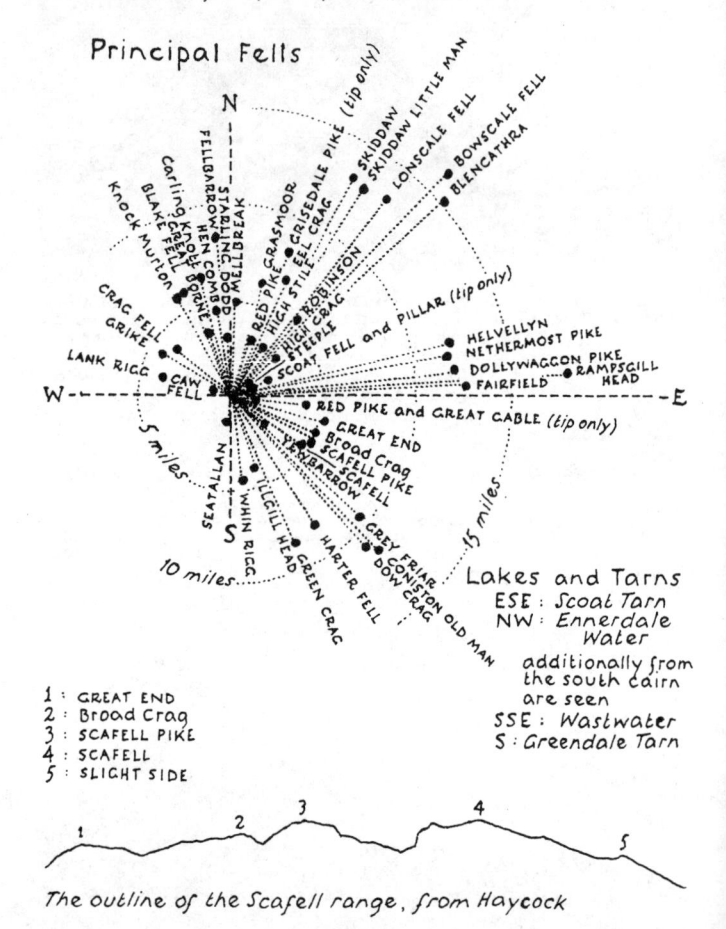

Principal Fells

(compass diagram of surrounding fells, with radial distance rings at 5 miles, 10 miles, 15 miles)

Labels around the diagram include:
- N: FELLBARROW, STARLING DODD, HEN COMB, MELLBREAK, RED PIKE, GRASMOOR, GRISEDALE PIKE, SKIDDAW LITTLE MAN, SKIDDAW (tip only), LONSCALE FELL, BOWSCALE FELL, BLENCATHRA
- Carling Knott, BLAKE FELL, Knock Murton, HIGH STILE, LEE CRAG, HIGH CRAG, ROBINSON
- CRAG FELL, GRIKE, STEEPLE, SCOAT FELL and PILLAR (tip only), HELVELLYN, NETHERMOST PIKE, DOLLYWAGGON PIKE, FAIRFIELD, RAMPSGILL HEAD
- LANK RIGG, CAW FELL — W — — E — RED PIKE and GREAT GABLE (tip only)
- GREAT END, Broad Crag, SCAFELL PIKE, SCAFELL, YEWBARROW
- SEATALLAN, MIDDLE FELL, NINDLE RIGG, YOADCASTLE HEAD, GREY FRIAR, CONISTON OLD MAN
- S: HARTER FELL, GREEN CRAG, DOW CRAG

Lakes and Tarns
ESE: *Scoat Tarn*
NW: *Ennerdale Water*

additionally from the south cairn are seen

SSE: *Wastwater*
S: *Greendale Tarn*

1 : GREAT END
2 : Broad Crag
3 : SCAFELL PIKE
4 : SCAFELL
5 : SLIGHT SIDE

The outline of the Scafell range, from Haycock

Haycock 10

RIDGE ROUTES

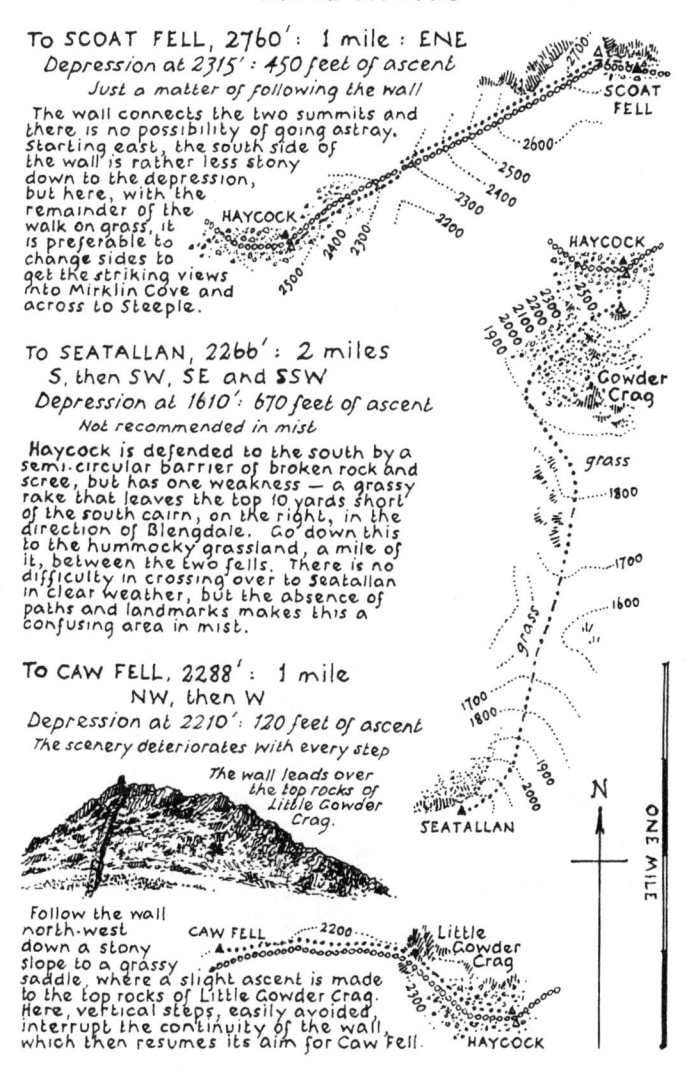

To SCOAT FELL, 2760': 1 mile : ENE
Depression at 2315': 450 feet of ascent

Just a matter of following the wall

The wall connects the two summits and there is no possibility of going astray. Starting east, the south side of the wall is rather less stony down to the depression, but here, with the remainder of the walk on grass, it is preferable to change sides to get the striking views into Mirklin Cove and across to Steeple.

To SEATALLAN, 2266': 2 miles
S, then SW, SE and SSW
Depression at 1610': 670 feet of ascent

Not recommended in mist

Haycock is defended to the south by a semi-circular barrier of broken rock and scree, but has one weakness — a grassy rake that leaves the top 10 yards short of the south cairn, on the right, in the direction of Blengdale. Go down this to the hummocky grassland, a mile of it, between the two fells. There is no difficulty in crossing over to Seatallan in clear weather, but the absence of paths and landmarks makes this a confusing area in mist.

To CAW FELL, 2288': 1 mile
NW, then W
Depression at 2210': 120 feet of ascent

The scenery deteriorates with every step

The wall leads over the top rocks of Little Gowder Crag.

Follow the wall north-west down a stony slope to a grassy saddle, where a slight ascent is made to the top rocks of Little Gowder Crag. Here, vertical steps, easily avoided, interrupt the continuity of the wall, which then resumes its aim for Caw Fell.

Haystacks

1900' approx.

properly
Hay Stacks
(two words)
as on
Ordnance maps

from Gamlin End, High Crag

Gatesgarth ●
HIGH ▲
CRAG
HAYSTACKS
▲
Black ● Sail Y.H.
MILES
0   1   2

Haystacks 2

NATURAL FEATURES

Haystacks stands unabashed and unashamed in the midst of a circle of much loftier fells, like a shaggy terrier in the company of foxhounds, some of them known internationally, but not one of this distinguished group of mountains around Ennerdale and Buttermere can show a greater variety and a more fascinating arrangement of interesting features. Here are sharp peaks in profusion, tarns with islands and tarns without islands, crags, screes, rocks for climbing and rocks not for climbing, heather tracts, marshes, serpentine trails, tarns with streams and tarns with no streams. All these, with a background of magnificent landscapes, await every visitor to Haystacks but they will be appreciated most by those who go there to linger and explore. It is a place of surprises around corners, and there are many corners. For a man trying to get a persistent worry out of his mind, the top of Haystacks is a wonderful cure.

The fell rises between the deep hollow of Warnscale Bottom near Gatesgarth, and Ennerdale: between a valley familiar to summer motorists and a valley reached only on foot. It is bounded on the west by Scarth Gap, a pass linking the two. The Buttermere aspect is the better known, although this side is often dark in shadow and seen only as a silhouette against the sky: here, above Warnscale, is a great wall of crags. The Ennerdale flank, open to the sun, is friendlier but steep and rough nevertheless.

Eastwards, beyond the tangle of tors and outcrops forming the boundary of Haystacks on this side, a broad grass slope rises easily and unattractively to Brandreth on the edge of the Borrowdale watershed; beyond is Derwent country.

> The spelling of Haystacks as one word is a personal preference of the author (and others), and probably arises from a belief that the name originated from the resemblance of the scattered tors on the summit to stacks of hay in a field. If this were so, the one word *Haystacks* would be correct (as it is in *Haycock*).
> But learned authorities state that the name derives from the Icelandic 'stack', meaning 'a columnar rock', and that the true interpretation is *High Rocks*. This is logical and appropriate. *High Rocks* is a name of two words and would be wrongly written as *Highrocks*.

The summit tarn

Haystacks 3

Big Stack,
looking east from a point near the path to the summit from Scarth Gap.

In the picture below Big Stack appears on the extreme right.

The north crags,
looking west from the slopes of Green Crag.

The path is seen skirting the cliff on the left.

Haystacks 4

MAP

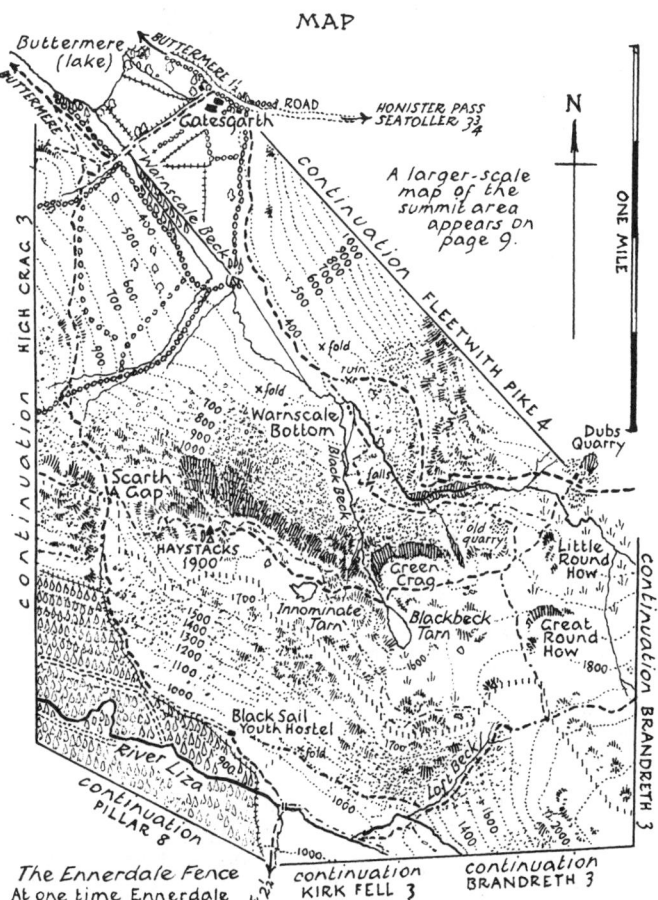

The Ennerdale Fence

At one time Ennerdale was enclosed by a fence nearly twenty miles in length, running along both watersheds and around the head of the valley. The fence was mainly of post and wire and only the posts now survive, with omissions, but part of the southern boundary was furnished with a stone wall, which is still in fair condition. In general, the line of the fence followed parish boundaries but on Haystacks there is considerable deviation. Here the series of cairns built around iron stakes (erected to mark the boundary of the Lonsdale estate) coincides with the parish boundary, but the fence keeps well to the south of this line.

Haystacks 5

ASCENT FROM GATESGARTH
1550 feet of ascent : 1¾ miles

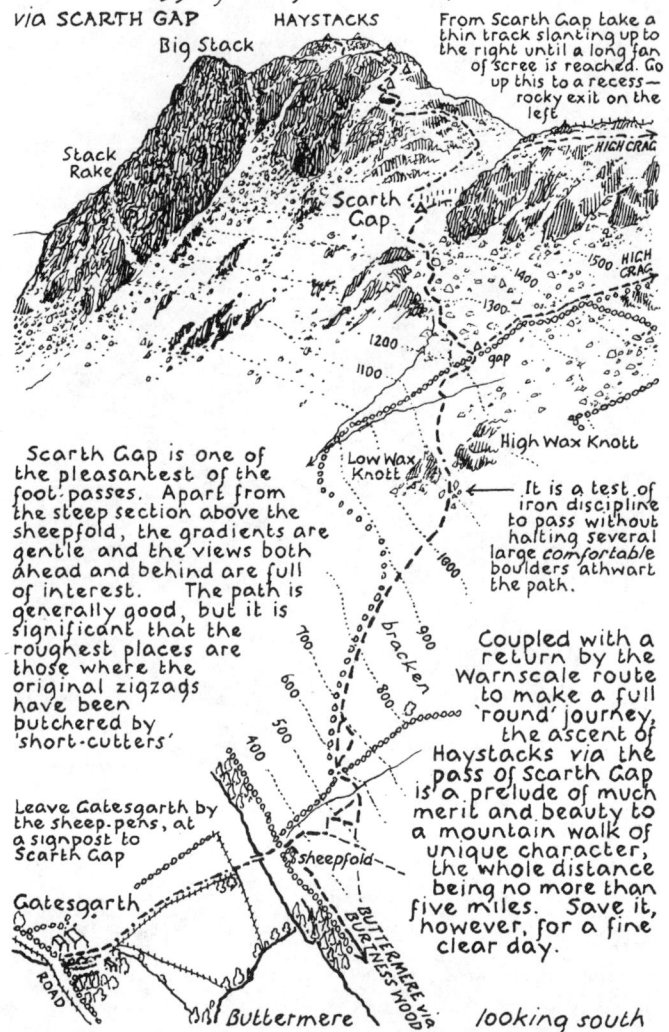

via SCARTH GAP

Big Stack — HAYSTACKS — Stack Rake — Scarth Gap — HIGH CRAG — Low Wax Knott — High Wax Knott — gap — bracken — sheepfold — Gatesgarth — ROAD — Buttermere — BUTTERMERE via BURTNESS WOOD

From Scarth Gap take a thin track slanting up to the right until a long fan of scree is reached. Go up this to a recess — rocky exit on the left

Scarth Gap is one of the pleasantest of the foot-passes. Apart from the steep section above the sheepfold, the gradients are gentle and the views both ahead and behind are full of interest. The path is generally good, but it is significant that the roughest places are those where the original zigzags have been butchered by 'short-cutters'

← It is a test of iron discipline to pass without halting several large *comfortable* boulders athwart the path.

Coupled with a return by the Warnscale route to make a full 'round' journey, the ascent of Haystacks via the pass of Scarth Gap is a prelude of much merit and beauty to a mountain walk of unique character, the whole distance being no more than five miles. Save it, however, for a fine clear day.

Leave Gatesgarth by the sheep-pens, at a signpost to Scarth Gap

looking south

Haystacks 6

ASCENT FROM GATESGARTH
via WARNSCALE
1600 feet of ascent : 2¾ miles

HAYSTACKS

A : Slack Gill
B : Warn Gill
C : The Y Gully
D : Toreador Gully
E : Green Crag Gully
F : Little Round How
G : Great Round How
H : Blackbeck Tarn
I : Innominate Tarn

looking south

Cross the stream near the confluence (easier said than done). Try a little higher where it runs in two channels.

Gatesgarth used to be served by buses, but isn't now.

Two paths climb out of Warnscale Bottom. On the left, in a great loop, rises a wellknown quarry road (this is an excellent route to Honister). On the right, across the beck, is an old 'made' path, originally serving a quarry: this is now little used but is still well-cairned, and it provides a fascinating stairway of zigs and zags over rough ground with impressive views of the wall of crags above; this is the path to take. (It is possible to scramble up the only breach in the crags, alongside Black Beck, but this is not recommended.)
The grassy upland is reached directly opposite Great Round How, the path at this point being joined by another from Dubs Quarry. Full of variety and interesting situations, it swings right, passing Blackbeck and Innominate Tarns, to the top of the fell. Or, before reaching Innominate Tarn, a track on the right may be taken: this skirts the rim of the crags and crowds more thrills into the walk.

HONISTER PASS
SEATOLLER 3¾ ← ROAD Gatesgarthdale Beck BUTTERMERE 1½

For sustained interest, impressive crag scenery, beautiful views, and a most delightful arrangement of tarns and rocky peaks, this short mountain excursion ranks with the very best.

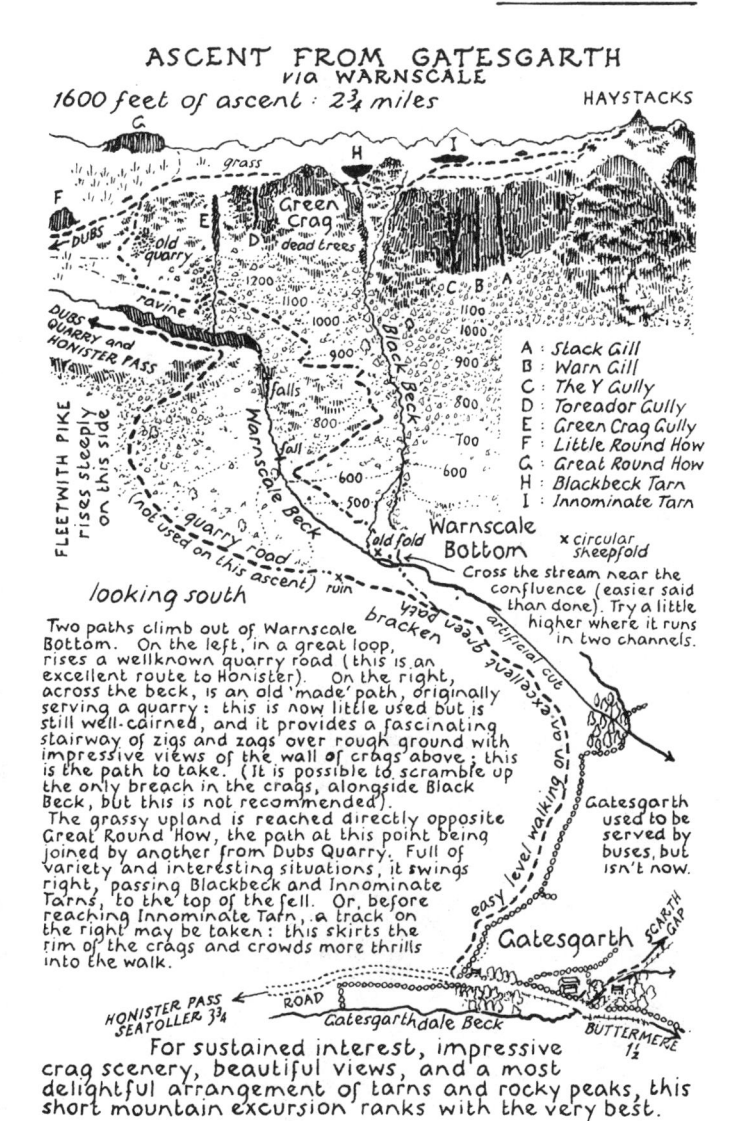

Haystacks 7

ASCENT FROM HONISTER PASS
1050 feet of ascent : 2¼ miles

A note of explanation is required.   This ascent-route does not conform to the usual pattern, being more in the nature of an upland cross-country walk than a mountain climb: there are two pronounced descents before foot is set on Haystacks. The wide variety of scene and the fascinating intricacies of the path are justification for the inclusion of the route in this book.

If returning to Honister, note the path to Brandreth just below Innominate Tarn. By using this until it joins the Great Gable path and then swinging left around Dubs Bottom, the Drum House can be regained without extra effort or time.

After traversing the back of Green Crag the path drops to the outlet of Blackbeck Tarn, rising stonily therefrom with a profound abyss on the right. This section is the highlight of the walk. An alternative way to the top, turning off opposite the Brandreth junction, follows closely the edge of the crags.

From the hut at Dubs Quarry leave the path and go down to the stream, crossing it (somehow) where its silent meanderings through the Dubs marshes assume a noisy urgency.

From the top of Honister Pass Haystacks is nowhere in sight, and even when it comes into view, after crossing the shoulder of Fleetwith Pike at the Drum House, it is insignificant against the towering background of Pillar, being little higher in altitude and seemingly remote across the wide depression of Dubs Bottom. But, although the route here described is not a natural approach, the elevation of Honister Pass, its car-parking facilities, and the unerring pointer of the tramway make access to Haystacks particularly convenient from this point.

Haystacks 8

ASCENT FROM ENNERDALE
(BLACK SAIL YOUTH HOSTEL)

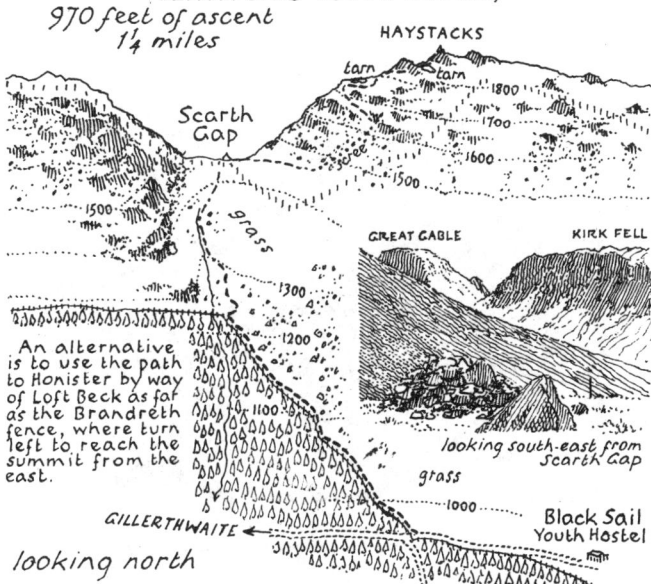

970 feet of ascent
1¼ miles

looking north

An alternative is to use the path to Honister by way of Loft Beck as far as the Brandreth fence, where turn left to reach the summit from the east.

looking south-east from Scarth Gap

This route is likely to be of interest only to youth hostellers staying at the magnificently situated Black Sail Hut. Other mortals, denied this privilege, cannot conveniently use Ennerdale Head as a starting point for mountain ascents.

formerly a shepherd's hut,......

Black Sail Youth Hostel

Haystacks 9

THE SUMMIT

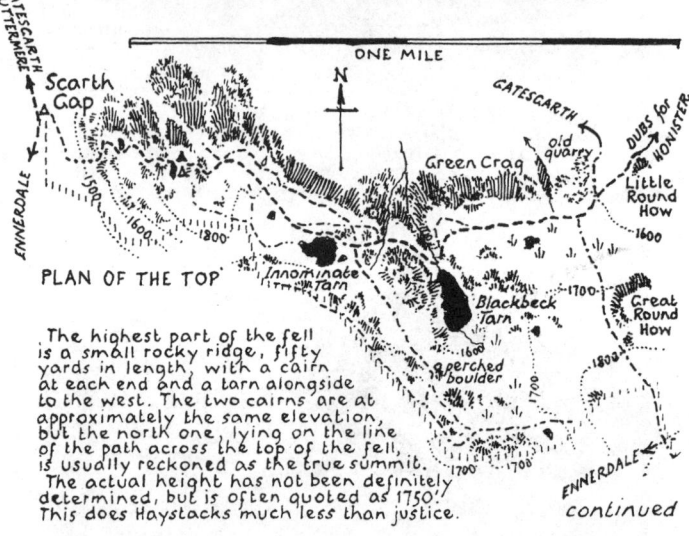

PLAN OF THE TOP

The highest part of the fell is a small rocky ridge, fifty yards in length, with a cairn at each end and a tarn alongside to the west. The two cairns are at approximately the same elevation, but the north one, lying on the line of the path across the top of the fell, is usually reckoned as the true summit. The actual height has not been definitely determined, but is often quoted as 1750'. This does Haystacks much less than justice.

continued

Haystacks 10

THE SUMMIT
continued

Haystacks fails to qualify for inclusion in the author's "best half-dozen" only because of inferior height, a deficiency in vertical measurement. Another thousand feet would have made all the difference.

But for beauty, variety and interesting detail, for sheer fascination and unique individuality, the summit-area of Haystacks is supreme. This is in fact the best fell-top of all — a place of great charm and fairyland attractiveness. Seen from a distance, these qualities are not suspected: indeed, on the contrary, the appearance of Haystacks is almost repellent when viewed from the higher surrounding peaks: black are its bones and black is its flesh. With its thick covering of heather it is dark and sombre even when the sun sparkles the waters of its many tarns, gloomy and mysterious even under a blue sky. There are fierce crags and rough screes and outcrops that will be grittier still when the author's ashes are scattered here.

Yet the combination of features, of tarn and tor, of cliff and cove, the labyrinth of corners and recesses, the maze of old sheepwalks and paths, form a design, or a lack of design, of singular appeal and absorbing interest. One can forget even a raging toothache on Haystacks.

perched boulder on a rock platform

Note the profile in shadow. Some women have faces like that.

On a first visit, learn thoroughly the details of the mile-long main path across the top, a magnificent traverse, because this serves as the best introduction to the geography of the fell.

Having memorised this, several interesting deviations may be made: the parallel alternative above the rim of the north face, the scramble onto Big Stack, the 'cross-country' route around the basin of Blackbeck Tarn, the walk alongside the fence, and so on.

typical summit tors

DESCENTS: Leave the top of Haystacks only by a recognisable route. It is possible to make rough descents in the vicinity (left bank) of Black Beck and Green Crag gully, but more advisable to regard the whole of the north edge as highly dangerous. The only advice that can be given to a novice lost on Haystacks in mist is that he should kneel down and pray for safe deliverance.

Haystacks 11

THE VIEW

This is not a case of distance lending enchantment to the view, because apart from a glimpse of Skiddaw above the Robinson-Hindscarth depression and a slice of the Helvellyn range over Honister, the scene is predominantly one of high mountains within a five-mile radius. And really good they look — the enchantment is close at hand. Set in a tight surround, they are seen in revealing detail: a rewarding study deserving leisurely appreciation.

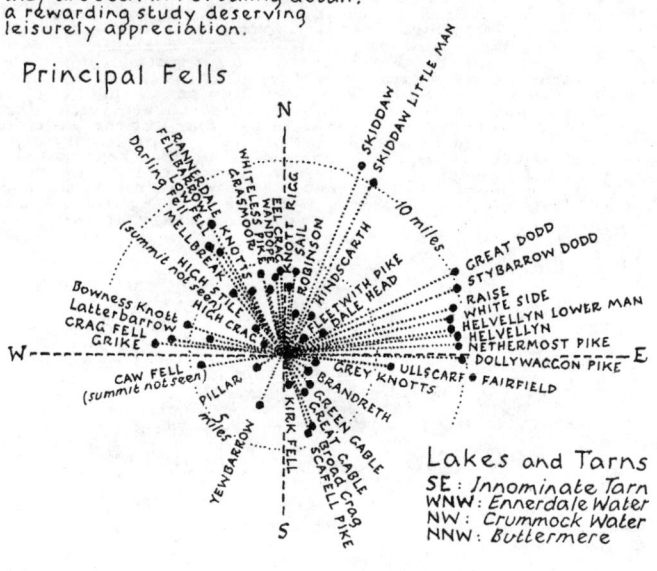

Principal Fells

Lakes and Tarns
SE: *Innominate Tarn*
WNW: *Ennerdale Water*
NW: *Crummock Water*
NNW: *Buttermere*

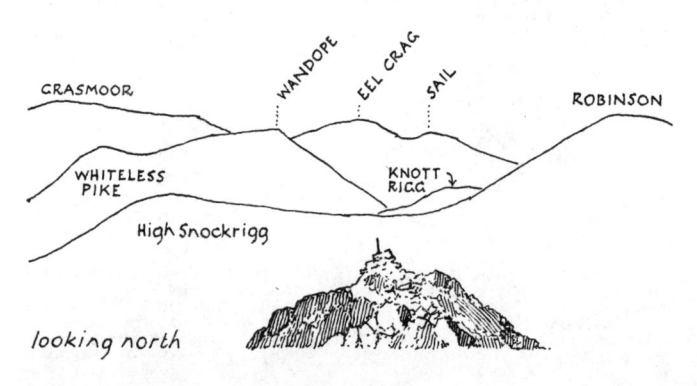

looking north

Haystacks 12

RIDGE ROUTES

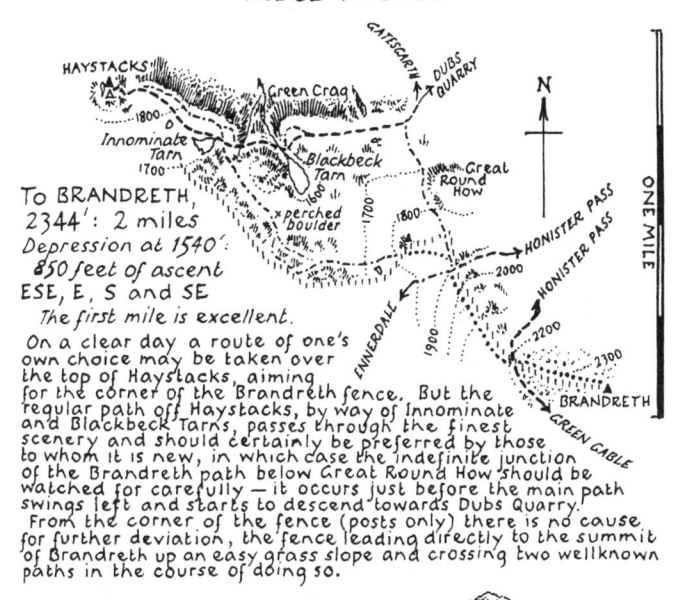

To BRANDRETH, 2344': 2 miles
Depression at 1540'
850 feet of ascent
ESE, E, S and SE

The first mile is excellent.

On a clear day a route of one's own choice may be taken over the top of Haystacks, aiming for the corner of the Brandreth fence. But the regular path off Haystacks, by way of Innominate and Blackbeck Tarns, passes through the finest scenery and should certainly be preferred by those to whom it is new, in which case the indefinite junction of the Brandreth path below Great Round How should be watched for carefully — it occurs just before the main path swings left and starts to descend towards Dubs Quarry.

From the corner of the fence (posts only) there is no cause for further deviation, the fence leading directly to the summit of Brandreth up an easy grass slope and crossing two wellknown paths in the course of doing so.

To HIGH CRAG, 2443'
1¼ miles: W, then NW
Depression at 1425' (Scarth Gap)
1100 feet of ascent

A fine walk in spite of scree

Follow faithfully the thin track trending west from the summit, a delightful game of ins and outs and ups and downs although the scree to which it leads is less pleasant: at the foot slant right to Scarth Gap. More scree is encountered across the pass on the climb to Seat; then a good ridge follows to the final tower of High Crag: this deteriorates badly into slippery scree on the later stages of the ascent.

High Crag, from Scarth Gap

Hen Comb 1661'

from Mosedale

Following the general pattern of the Loweswater Fells, Hen Comb rises as a long ridge from the valley to a round summit set well back. It is a grassy fell, almost entirely, with a rocky knuckle, Little Dodd, midway on the ridge, and there is very little of interest on the flanks apart from slight traces of former mining activity. The main mass of the fell rises on three sides from a desolate moorland with extensive tracts of marsh that serve as a moat and effectively discourage a close acquaintance. It is the sort of fell sometimes climbed, but rarely twice. It is unfortunate in having Mellbreak as a neighbour.

Hen Comb 2

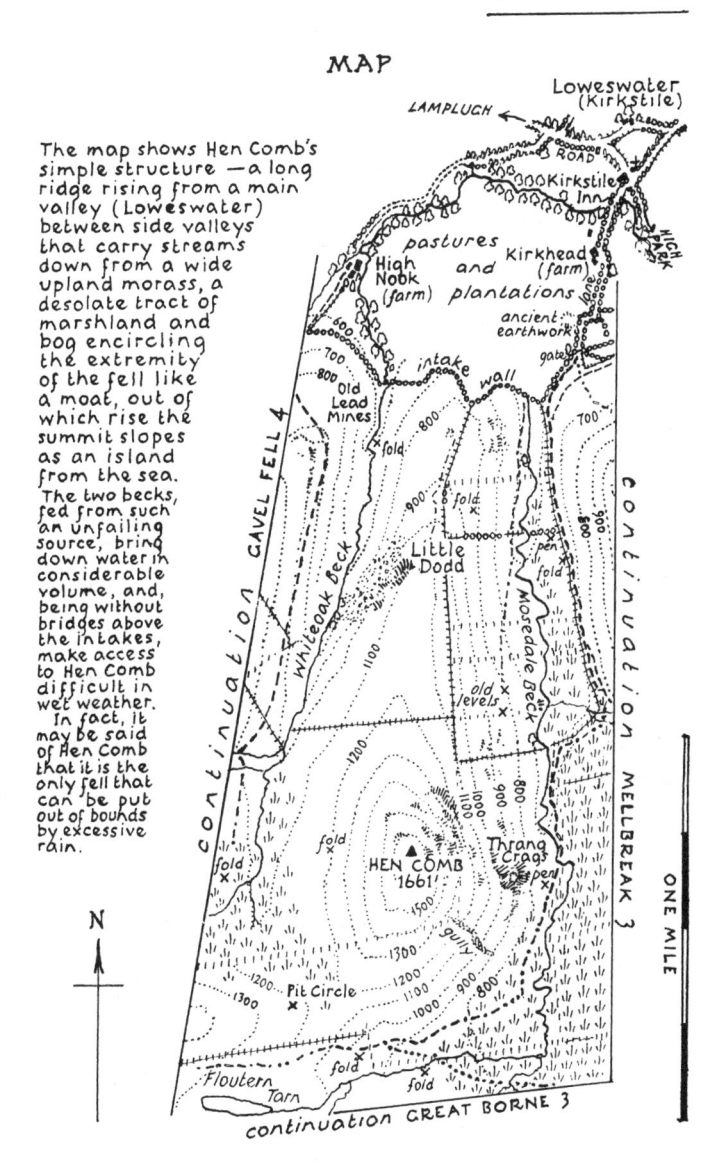

MAP

The map shows Hen Comb's simple structure — a long ridge rising from a main valley (Loweswater) between side valleys that carry streams down from a wide upland morass, a desolate tract of marshland and bog encircling the extremity of the fell like a moat, out of which rise the summit slopes as an island from the sea. The two becks, fed from such an unfailing source, bring down water in considerable volume, and, being without bridges above the intakes, make access to Hen Comb difficult in wet weather.

In fact, it may be said of Hen Comb that it is the only fell that can be put out of bounds by excessive rain.

Hen Comb 3

ASCENT FROM LOWESWATER
1300 feet of ascent : 2½ miles

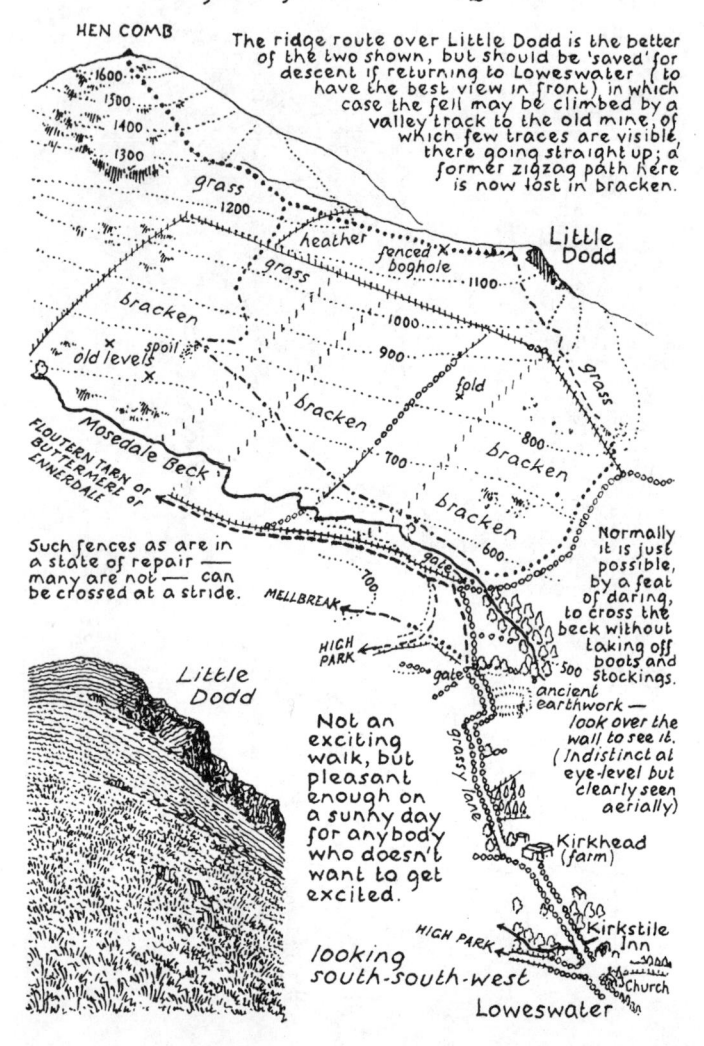

The ridge route over Little Dodd is the better of the two shown, but should be 'saved' for descent if returning to Loweswater (to have the best view in front) in which case the fell may be climbed by a valley track to the old mine, of which few traces are visible, there going straight up; a former zigzag path here is now lost in bracken.

Such fences as are in a state of repair — many are not — can be crossed at a stride.

Normally it is just possible, by a feat of daring, to cross the beck without taking off boots and stockings.

ancient earthwork — look over the wall to see it. (Indistinct at eye-level but clearly seen aerially)

Not an exciting walk, but pleasant enough on a sunny day for anybody who doesn't want to get excited.

looking south-south-west

Little Dodd

Hen Comb 4

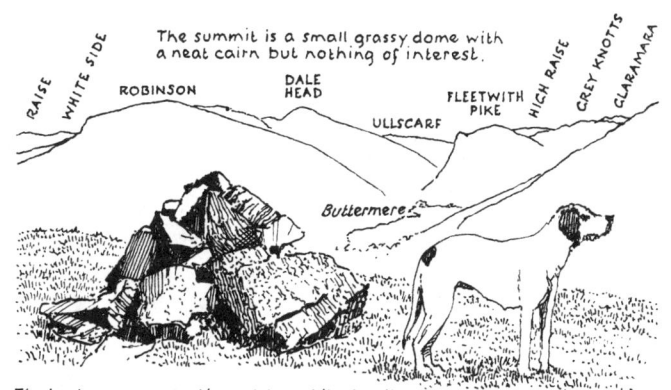

THE SUMMIT

The summit is a small grassy dome with a neat cairn but nothing of interest.

The bystander, patiently waiting while details are noted but eager to be off, is Barmaid of the Melbreak Foxhounds.

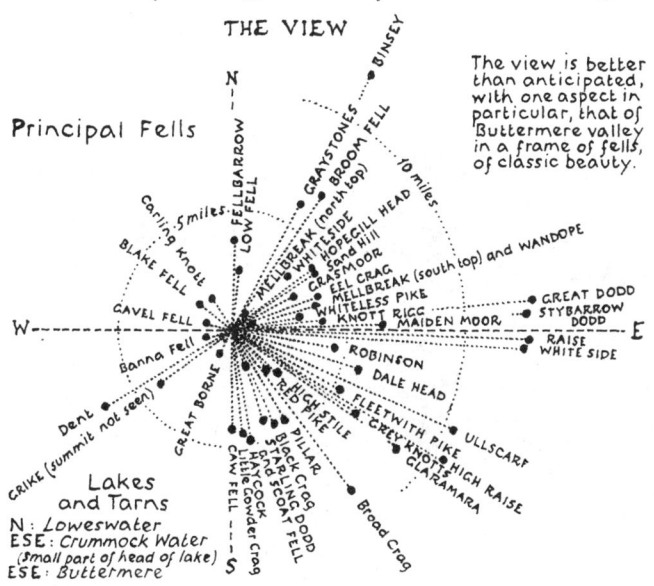

THE VIEW

The view is better than anticipated, with one aspect in particular, that of Buttermere valley in a frame of fells, of classic beauty.

Principal Fells

Lakes and Tarns
N: Loweswater
ESE: Crummock Water (small part of head of lake)
ESE: Buttermere

RIDGE ROUTES: There are no ridges connecting with other fells.

High Crag 2443'

from Haystacks

High Crag 2

NATURAL FEATURES

High Crag is the least known of the three linked peaks of the High Stile range towering above the Buttermere valley and is the lowest in elevation, but it concedes nothing in grandeur and ruggedness to the other two, High Stile and Red Pike, its formidable northern buttress being the finest object in the group. To the west of this buttress lies deeply inurned the stony rock-girt hollow of Burtness (or Birkness) Comb, a favourite climbing ground, with High Stile soaring beyond, the two summits being connected by a narrow ridge overlooking the Comb. Eastwards are vast scree runs, where few men venture; the continuation of the ridge on this side is at first unpleasantly stony until an easier slope of grass leads down to a depression beyond which the ridge re-asserts itself as a distinctive crest and then falls abruptly in crags and scree to the top of Scarth Gap Pass. The fell's aspect from Buttermere is exceedingly impressive, giving an air of complete inaccessibility, but the opposite flank falling to Ennerdale's new forests lacks distinctive features although everywhere rough. The summit commands a glorious view of mountainous country, a deserved reward for it is neither easily attained nor easily left, its defence of battlemented crags and hostile stones being breached only by the narrow ridge connecting with High Stile, a mountain with difficulties of its own. Indeed, if it were not for this ridge (which goes on to and beyond Red Pike) the summits of both would be almost unattainable by the ordinary pedestrian. With the help of the ridge they should certainly be visited, the scenery being of the highest order and the situations exciting.

High Crag from the north-east ridge of High Stile

High Crag 3

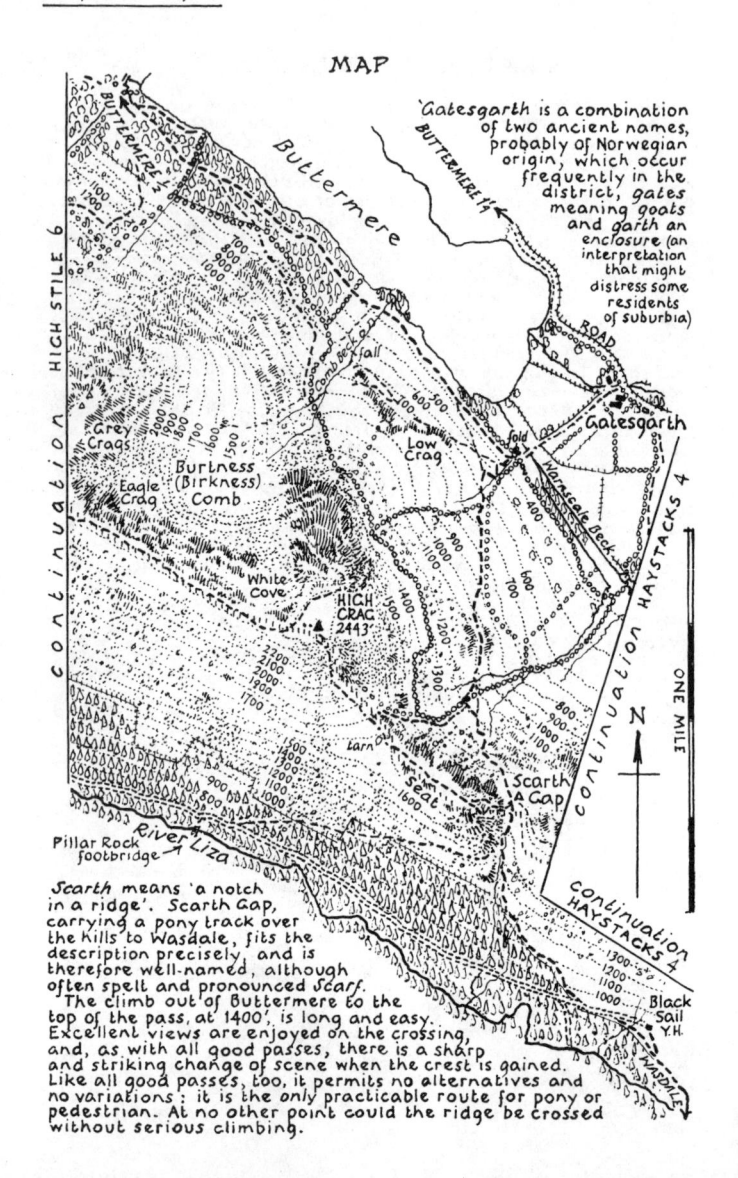

MAP

'Gatesgarth' is a combination of two ancient names, probably of Norwegian origin, which occur frequently in the district, *gates* meaning goats and *garth* an enclosure (an interpretation that might distress some residents of suburbia)

Scarth means 'a notch in a ridge'. Scarth Gap, carrying a pony track over the hills to Wasdale, fits the description precisely, and is therefore well-named, although often spelt and pronounced *Scarf*.

The climb out of Buttermere to the top of the pass, at 1400', is long and easy. Excellent views are enjoyed on the crossing, and, as with all good passes, there is a sharp and striking change of scene when the crest is gained. Like all good passes, too, it permits no alternatives and no variations: it is the only practicable route for pony or pedestrian. At no other point could the ridge be crossed without serious climbing.

High Crag 4

ASCENT FROM ENNERDALE
(BLACK SAIL YOUTH HOSTEL)
1500 feet of ascent : 1¼ miles

Gamlin End looks unpromising when viewed from below and more so when one is engaged upon it. A track of giant footmarks, with the fence now on the right, goes straight up the grass until no more grass can be found, but only loose slippery scree. Manoeuvres to avoid this nasty section are in vain, but it can be surmounted by frantic efforts and the firmer ground of the summit gained just above.

big boulder (with fence post embedded) is known as the Marble Stone (6" O.S. map)

Scarth Gap from the head of Ennerdale is the easiest of passes, the difference in altitude being only 400 feet, and the path, at first skirting a plantation, is clear.
At the top of the pass, however, where the boundary fence is joined, conditions change for the worse, the stiff pull to the subsidiary ridge known as Seat being over loose scree; towards the top the fence posts take a bolder line across craggy ground. The crest of this ridge is pleasant, with a fair track that keeps mainly to the north side and soon reaches a grassy hollow with two small tarns, Gamlin End now appearing directly ahead.

looking north

GILLERTHWAITE 3 (cart track)

Ennerdale

This route will be of use only to sojourners at the Youth Hostel, all other bases being too remote (although hardy travellers from Wasdale to Buttermere could include it as a variation finish from Scarth Gap).
It is the recognised (in fact, the only) way of gaining the High Stile ridge from the head of Ennerdale; and if this ridge is traversed throughout its length to Red Pike, finally descending to Buttermere, a splendid walk will have been enjoyed.

High Crag 5

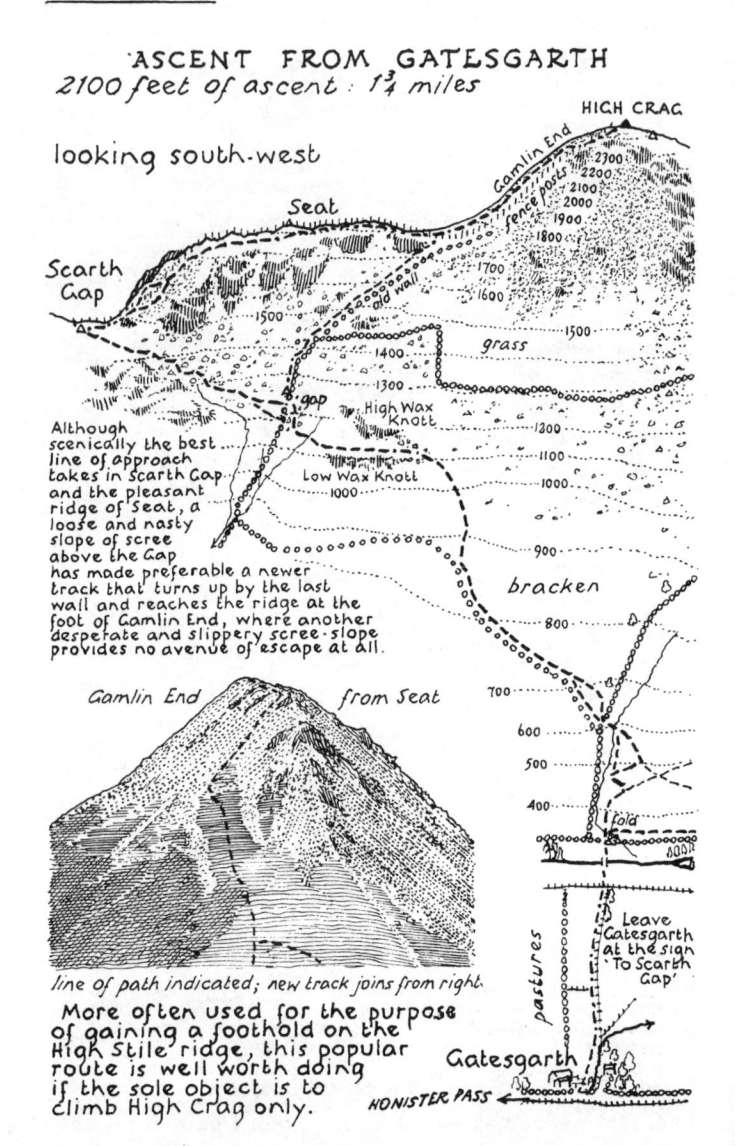

ASCENT FROM GATESGARTH
2100 feet of ascent : 1¼ miles

looking south-west

HIGH CRAG

Gamlin End
fence posts
2200
2100
2000
1900
1800
1700
1600
1500

Seat

Scarth Gap

old wall

1500
1400
1300

grass

gap

High Wax Knott

1200
1100

Low Wax Knott
1000

1000
900

bracken

800

700
600
500
400

fold

Although scenically the best line of approach takes in Scarth Gap and the pleasant ridge of Seat, a loose and nasty slope of scree above the Gap has made preferable a newer track that turns up by the last wall and reaches the ridge at the foot of Gamlin End, where another desperate and slippery scree-slope provides no avenue of escape at all.

Gamlin End from Seat

line of path indicated; new track joins from right.

More often used for the purpose of gaining a foothold on the High Stile ridge, this popular route is well worth doing if the sole object is to climb High Crag only.

pastures

Leave Gatesgarth at the sign 'To Scarth Gap'

Gatesgarth

← HONISTER PASS

High Crag 6

ASCENT FROM BUTTERMERE
(DIRECT)

2100 feet of ascent
2½ miles

Leave the Comb at an outcrop on the left, go straight up through a rock gateway and ascend to the left of the Buttress until the rock wall ceases and a scramble up a green slope leads to a track across the north top. Stones hidden by vegetation make the climb arduous.

If the climbers' track is missed, retrieve the position by following Comb Beck upstream.

The route may be used with equal facility from Gatesgarth by direct path to the Comb (see High Stile 8)

This route is NOT advised for descent

This being a serious essay in mountaineering, it is appropriate to take the rock-climbers' track into the Comb (which is not generally known). It leaves the broad path in Burtness Wood as a green forest ride (not obvious) 120 yards beyond the wall in the wood and reaches a stile to gain the open fell.

Ordinary pedestrians, having already been warned (page 2) that direct access to High Crag is virtually impossible, are here provided with a route that, if safely accomplished, will establish their right to be classed as better than ordinary.

The northern buttress is a thousand feet high, all of it craggy or of excessive steepness, but rising across it from the scree of the Comb is a curious slanting gangway free from obstacles that will lead an enterprising scrambler to the easier ground of the summit. This breach in the impregnability of the buttress is clearly in view from Buttermere village. The gangway is a safe route, but steep and sensational. Probably more than 50% of those who try it will live to tell a stirring tale of valour in high places. The casualties must accept the fact that they were only ordinary after all.

This surprising and uncharacteristic weakness in the mountain's defences must be given a name. The only topographical feature in the immediate vicinity of the gangway already named is Sheepbone Buttress, which forms part of the right wall. Sheepbone Rake is therefore suggested.

High Crag 7

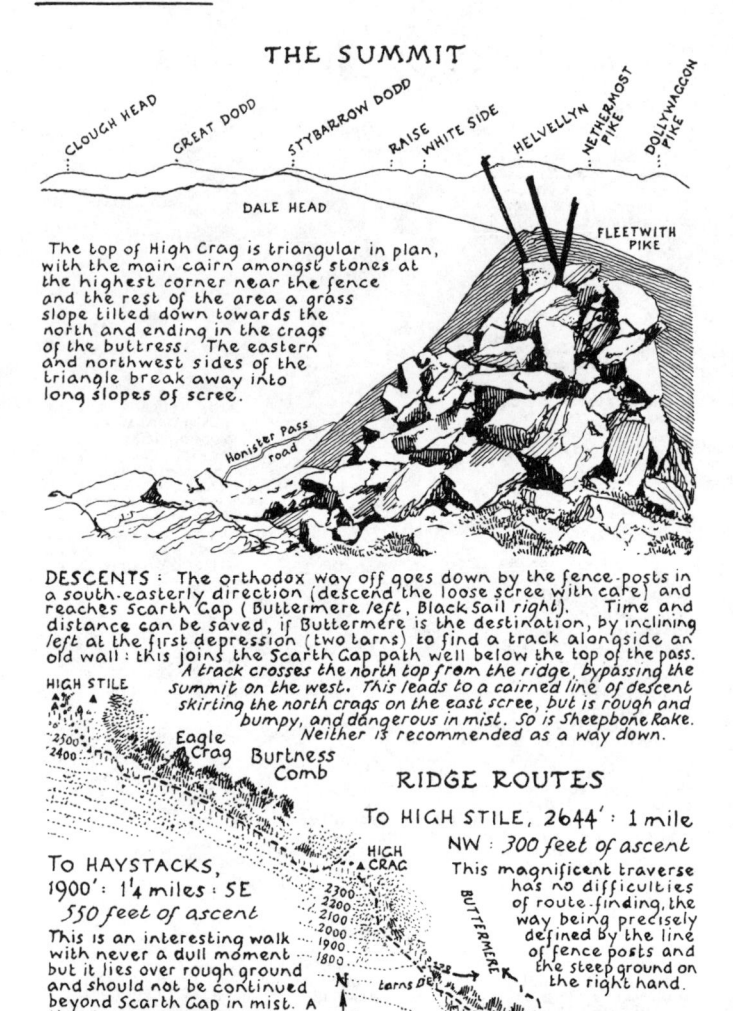

THE SUMMIT

CLOUGH HEAD — GREAT DODD — STYBARROW DODD — RAISE — WHITE SIDE — HELVELLYN — NETHERMOST PIKE — DOLLYWAGGON PIKE

DALE HEAD

FLEETWITH PIKE

The top of High Crag is triangular in plan, with the main cairn amongst stones at the highest corner near the fence and the rest of the area a grass slope tilted down towards the north and ending in the crags of the buttress. The eastern and northwest sides of the triangle break away into long slopes of scree.

Honister Pass road

DESCENTS: The orthodox way off goes down by the fence-posts in a south-easterly direction (descend the loose scree with care) and reaches Scarth Gap (Buttermere left, Black Sail right). Time and distance can be saved, if Buttermere is the destination, by inclining left at the first depression (two tarns) to find a track alongside an old wall: this joins the Scarth Gap path well below the top of the pass.
A track crosses the north top from the ridge, bypassing the summit on the west. This leads to a cairned line of descent skirting the north crags on the east scree, but is rough and bumpy, and dangerous in mist. So is Sheepbone Rake. Neither is recommended as a way down.

HIGH STILE
Eagle Crag Burtness Comb

RIDGE ROUTES

TO HIGH STILE, 2644': 1 mile
NW: 300 feet of ascent

This magnificent traverse has no difficulties of route-finding, the way being precisely defined by the line of fence posts and the steep ground on the right hand.

TO HAYSTACKS, 1900': 1¼ miles: SE
550 feet of ascent

This is an interesting walk with never a dull moment but it lies over rough ground and should not be continued beyond Scarth Gap in mist. A thin track slants to the right from the pass and ascends a scree-run to gain height on Haystacks.

ONE MILE

High Crag 8

THE VIEW

The view is less comprehensive than that from High Stile, but the outlook towards the heart of the district is even better. Wander north a little for some good camera shots not apparent from the top cairn.

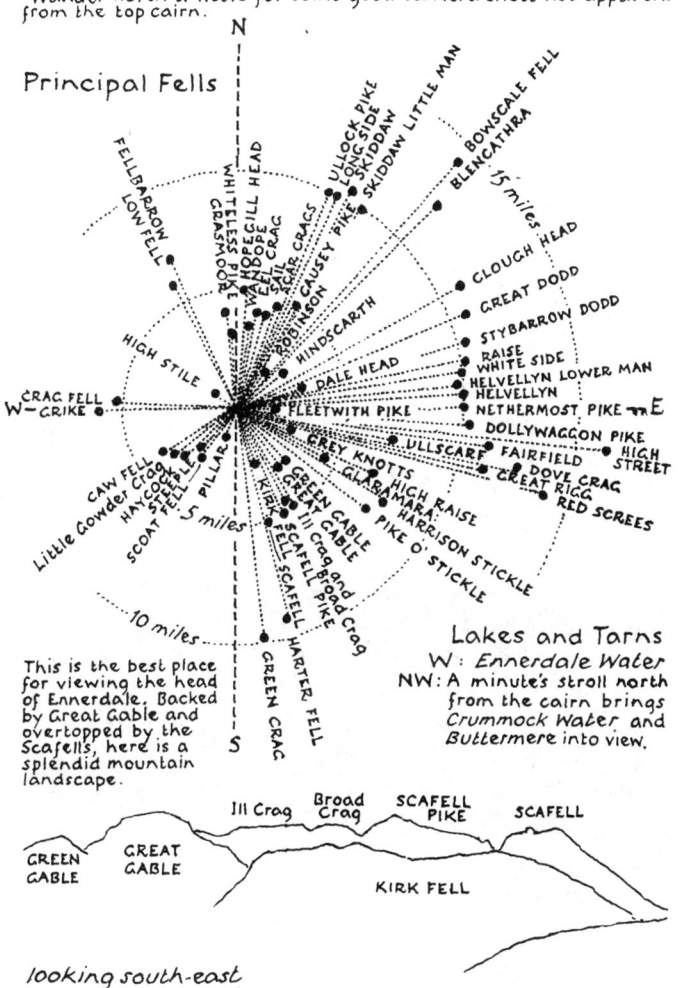

Principal Fells

(panoramic diagram with fells labelled:)

FELLBARROW, LOW FELL, WHITELESS PIKE, GRASSMOOR, WANDOPE, HOPEGILL HEAD, SAIL, EEL CRAGS, SCAR CRAGS, CAUSEY PIKE, ULLOCK PIKE, LONG SIDE, SKIDDAW, SKIDDAW LITTLE MAN, BOWSCALE FELL, BLENCATHRA, ROBINSON, HINDSCARTH, CLOUGH HEAD, GREAT DODD, DALE HEAD, STYBARROW DODD, RAISE, WHITE SIDE, HELVELLYN LOWER MAN, HIGH STILE, HELVELLYN, CRAG FELL, GRIKE, FLEETWITH PIKE, NETHERMOST PIKE, DOLLYWAGGON PIKE, FAIRFIELD, DOVE CRAG, HIGH STREET, CAW FELL, ULLSCARF, GREY KNOTTS, HIGH RAISE, GREAT RIGG, RED SCREES, LITTLE GOWDER CRAG, HAYCOCK, STEEPLE, PILLAR, GLARAMARA, HARRISON STICKLE, SCOAT FELL, KIRK FELL, GREEN GABLE, SCAFELL, GREEN GABLE, SCAFELL PIKE, Crag and Ill Crag, Broad Crag, PIKE O' STICKLE, HARTER FELL, GREEN CRAG

circles marked: 5 miles, 10 miles, 15 miles

N / S / E marked on compass lines.

This is the best place for viewing the head of Ennerdale. Backed by Great Gable and overtopped by the Scafells, here is a splendid mountain landscape.

Lakes and Tarns

W: *Ennerdale Water*
NW: A minute's stroll north from the cairn brings *Crummock Water* and *Buttermere* into view.

(skyline sketch labelled:) GREEN GABLE, GREAT GABLE, Ill Crag, Broad Crag, SCAFELL PIKE, SCAFELL, KIRK FELL

looking south-east

High Stile 2644'

from Buttermere

High Stile 2

from Gatesgarth

Buttermere •
RED PIKE ▲   Gatesgarth •
HIGH STILE ▲   HIGH CRAG ▲
• Gillerthwaite
Scarth Gap ✕
Black Sail Y.H. •

MILES
0   1   2   3

High Stile 3

NATURAL FEATURES

The Buttermere valley is robbed of winter sunshine by a rugged mountain wall exceeding two thousand feet in height and of unusual steepness, its serrated skyline seeming almost to threaten the green fields and dark lake and homesteads far below in its shadow. No mountain range in Lakeland is more dramatically impressive than this, no other more spectacularly sculptured, no other more worth climbing and exploring. Here the scenery assumes truly Alpine characteristics, yet without sacrifice of the intimate charms, the romantic atmosphere, found in Lakeland and nowhere else. From the level strath of the valley the wall rises steeply at once, initially through forests, above which, without respite, buttresses spring upwards from the bare fellside to lose themselves high above in the battlemented crags of the long summit ridge. Three summits rise from this ridge, a trinity of challenging peaks, and of these the central one is the loftiest and grandest.
This is High Stile.

1: High Stile   2: Red Pike
3: High Crag
4: Burtness Comb
5: Bleaberry Comb
6: Ling Comb
7: Burtness Wood
8: Buttermere
9: Crummock Water

looking south

The range is magnificently carved to a simple design on a massive scale. Each of the three summits sends down to the valley a broad buttress, steep, rough, untrodden. To the north of each buttress natural forces ages ago eroded a great hollow, leaving a rim of broken crags. A stream cascades from each hollow. A tarn lies in the central recess like a jewel.
    This is superb architecture.

High Stile 4

NATURAL FEATURES

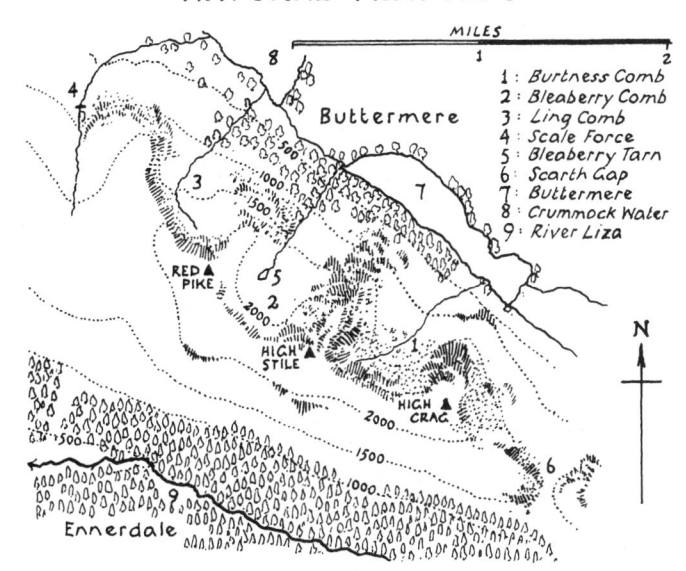

1 : Burtness Comb
2 : Bleaberry Comb
3 : Ling Comb
4 : Scale Force
5 : Bleaberry Tarn
6 : Scarth Gap
7 : Buttermere
8 : Crummock Water
9 : River Liza

Most mountains have a good side and a not-so-good side, and High Stile and its lesser companions, Red Pike and High Crag, conform to the rule. The Buttermere side of the ridge is tremendously exciting and darkly mysterious, compelling attention, but the other flank, by comparison, is plain and dull, without secrets, falling to the new forests of Ennerdale steeply but lacking attractive adornment; for here the contours do not twist and leap about, they run evenly in straight lines. Ennerdale, repeating the Buttermere design, concentrates its finest features on the southern wall of the valley.

North-flowing streams from the High Stile range contribute to the Cocker river system, so reaching the sea at Workington, but the sparser drainage southwards joins the River Ehen* on its remarkable journey from Great Gable to the sea at Sellafield — remarkable because of its obvious hesitation before taking the final plunge.

*nee Liza

High Stile 5

*Chapel Crags
from
Bleaberry Tarn*

*Dale Head
and
Fleetwith Pike
from
Grey Crags,
northeast spur*

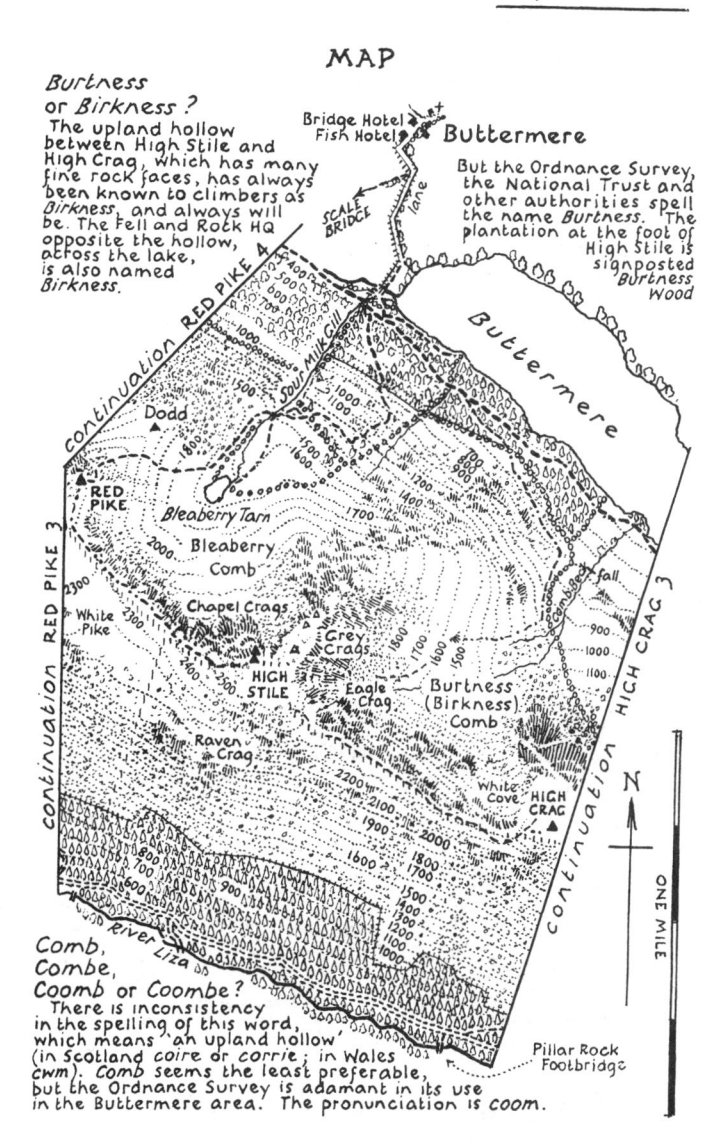

High Stile 6

MAP

Burtness or Birkness?

The upland hollow between High Stile and High Crag, which has many fine rock faces, has always been known to climbers as *Birkness*, and always will be. The Fell and Rock HQ opposite the hollow, across the lake, is also named *Birkness*.

But the Ordnance Survey, the National Trust and other authorities spell the name *Burtness*. The plantation at the foot of High Stile is signposted *Burtness Wood*.

Comb, Combe, Coomb or Coombe?

There is inconsistency in the spelling of this word, which means 'an upland hollow' (in Scotland *coire* or *corrie*; in Wales *cwm*). *Comb* seems the least preferable, but the Ordnance Survey is adamant in its use in the Buttermere area. The pronunciation is *coom*.

High Stile 7

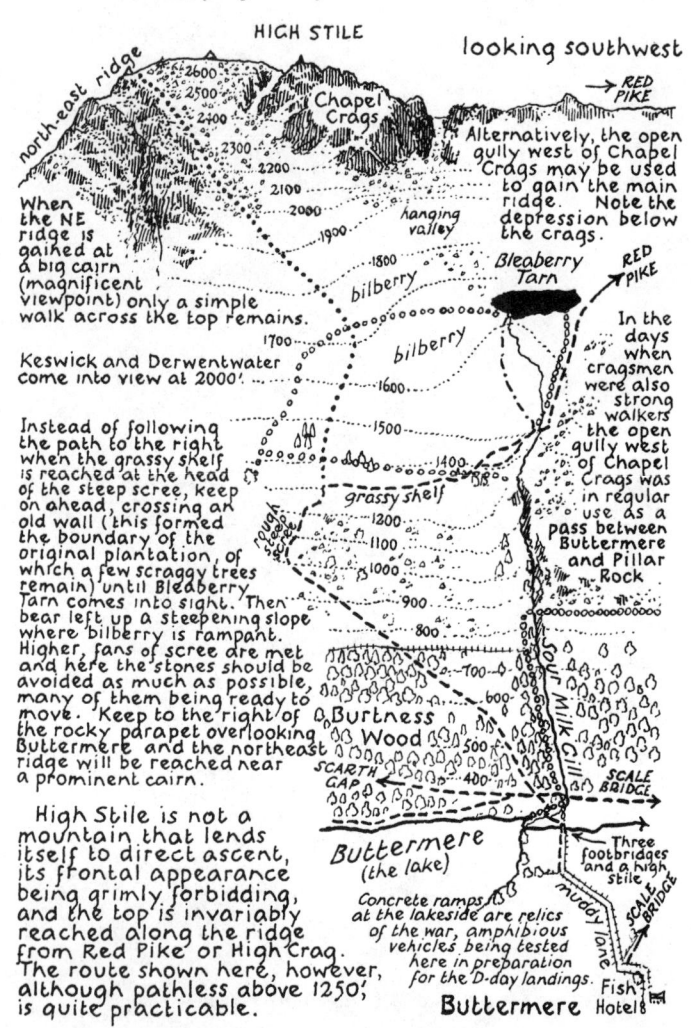

ASCENT FROM BUTTERMERE
2350 feet of ascent : 2¼ miles

HIGH STILE

looking southwest

→ RED PIKE

north-east ridge

Chapel Crags

hanging valley

bilberry

bilberry

Bleaberry Tarn

RED PIKE

Alternatively, the open gully west of Chapel Crags may be used to gain the main ridge. Note the depression below the crags.

When the NE ridge is gained at a big cairn (magnificent viewpoint) only a simple walk across the top remains.

Keswick and Derwentwater come into view at 2000'.

In the days when cragsmen were also strong walkers the open gully west of Chapel Crags was in regular use as a pass between Buttermere and Pillar Rock.

Instead of following the path to the right when the grassy shelf is reached at the head of the steep scree, keep on ahead, crossing an old wall (this formed the boundary of the original plantation, of which a few scraggy trees remain) until Bleaberry Tarn comes into sight. Then bear left up a steepening slope where bilberry is rampant. Higher, fans of scree are met and here the stones should be avoided as much as possible, many of them being ready to move. Keep to the right of the rocky parapet overlooking Buttermere and the northeast ridge will be reached near a prominent cairn.

grassy shelf

Burtness Wood

SCARTH GAP

Sour Milk Gill

SCALE BRIDGE

Buttermere (the lake)

Three footbridges and a stile

Concrete ramps at the lakeside are relics of the war, amphibious vehicles being tested here in preparation for the 'D-day landings.

muddy lane

SCALE BRIDGE

Fish Hotel

Buttermere

High Stile is not a mountain that lends itself to direct ascent, its frontal appearance being grimly forbidding, and the top is invariably reached along the ridge from Red Pike or High Crag. The route shown here, however, although pathless above 1250', is quite practicable.

High Stile 8

ASCENT FROM GATESGARTH
2300 feet of ascent · 2 miles

looking west

HIGH STILE

Grey Crags

← HIGH CRAG

north east ridge

The north-east ridge is decidedly rough, consisting of successive turrets of rock surrounded by boulders, which cannot be avoided (some are balanced precariously: handle with care). There are no insuperable barriers, however, and an agile scrambler will have no difficulty in reaching the top.

Burtness (Birkness) Comb

heather

Use the climbers' track (cairns) into the Comb for a quarter-mile above the wall, then turn up to the right, preferring a grass slope to heather. There follows a long incline to the foot of the north-east ridge, where the fun starts.

The north-east ridge does not start to look really impressive until one sets foot on it. Quite the most imposing object on the walk thus far is the tremendous buttress of High Crag on the other side of the Comb

grass

bracken

fall

SCARTH GAP

Low Crag

bracken

BUTTERMERE

This line of ascent may be used conveniently from Buttermere village. Take the broad rising cart-track through Burtness Wood to reach the junction (point A on the edge of the diagram) 120 yards beyond a cross-wall and a stream.

Buttermere

Gatesgarth

← HONISTER

→ BUTTERMERE (VILLAGE) 1½

This is the only feasible direct route (it is usual to proceed via High Crag). Expect some moments of unhappiness on the steep northeast ridge

High Stile 9

ASCENT FROM ENNERDALE
(HIGH GILLERTHWAITE)
2200 feet of ascent : 2½ miles

Access to the Ennerdale slopes of High Stile is completely barred by fenced forests, and the only public right of way up the fellside is a narrow strip of unplanted ground further to the west provided for the ascent of Red Pike. This route may also be adopted for High Stile, following the top fence south-east when it is reached at 2400'; up to this point the route is identical with that for Red Pike and suffers from the same demerits and disabilities. A diagram is given on page Red Pike 9, and there is no point in repeating it.

Let's have some pictures of Burtness Comb instead.

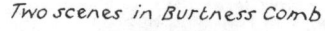

Two scenes in Burtness Comb

left : looking across the Comb to Eagle Crag from Sheepbone Rake.
right : looking up the Comb to Eagle Crag.

Burtness Comb has no tarn, and cannot compete with Bleaberry Comb in popular favour. Yet it is the finer of the two, as cragsmen have long realised, and is a grand place to spend a quiet day.

Unlike most mountain hollows its floor is bone-dry and even the beck is partly subterranean; it is notable for a rich July harvest of bilberries, which grow in lush carpets among the tumbled boulders.

High Stile 10

THE SUMMIT

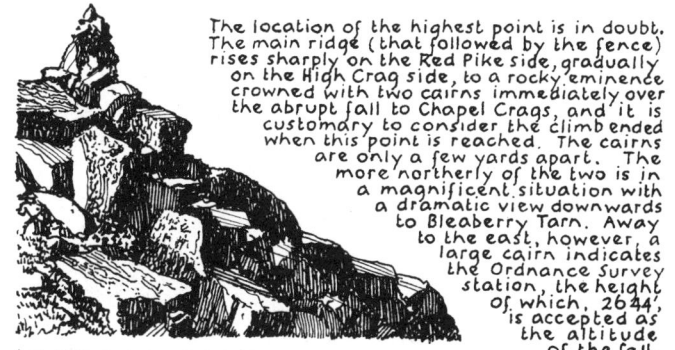

The location of the highest point is in doubt. The main ridge (that followed by the fence) rises sharply on the Red Pike side, gradually on the High Crag side, to a rocky eminence crowned with two cairns immediately over the abrupt fall to Chapel Crags, and it is customary to consider the climb ended when this point is reached. The cairns are only a few yards apart. The more northerly of the two is in a magnificent situation with a dramatic view downwards to Bleaberry Tarn. Away to the east, however, a large cairn indicates the Ordnance Survey station, the height of which, 2644', is accepted as the altitude of the fell, but this cairn, situated where the northeast spur takes shape before narrowing to the northeast ridge, does not seem to be quite so elevated as the two first mentioned, perhaps because the latter occupy a more pronounced rise, nor are the environs so attractive. Just north of this large cairn, a smaller one marks the highest point of the northeast spur. Without measuring instruments it is not possible to say definitely where the highest inches are, and better not to worry about it but to enjoy the sublime surroundings instead.

Stones and boulders litter the top everywhere, and, as all visitors prefer to pick their own way amongst these obstacles, no clear path has been formed.

DESCENTS: A woe-begone series of fence-posts, shorn of all connecting strands, pursues an erratic course across the stony top, and now serves a purpose not originally intended: that of guiding woe-begone walkers to zones of safety. Followed east, the posts lead over High Crag to Scarth Gap; west, to Red Pike, and these are the best ways off. The routes of ascent (pages 7 and 8) from Buttermere and Gatesgarth are not recommended for descent, but Ennerdale (page 9) is a good, fast route.

In emergency, the gully between the ridge-top and the northeast spur may be resorted to — it is a rough and steep but safe descent to Bleaberry Tarn, for Buttermere

PLAN OF SUMMIT

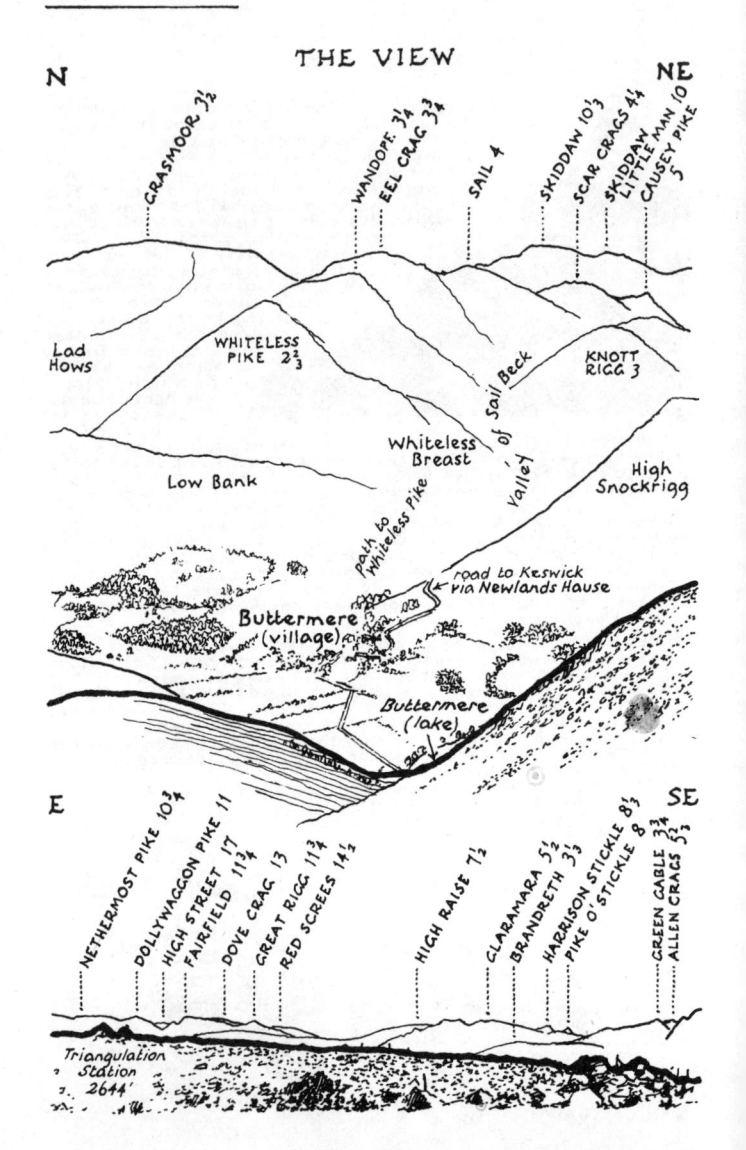

High Stile 11

THE VIEW

N — CRASMOOR 7½, WANDOPE 3¼, EEL CRAG 3¾, SAIL 4, SKIDDAW 10½, SCAR CRAGS 4½, SKIDDAW LITTLE MAN 10, CAUSEY PIKE 5 — NE

Lad Hows
WHITELESS PIKE 2⅔
Valley of Sail Beck
KNOTT RIGG 3
Whiteless Breast
Low Bank
High Snockrigg

path to Whiteless Pike
road to Keswick via Newlands Hause
Buttermere (village)
Buttermere (lake)

E — NETHERMOST PIKE 10¾, DOLLYWAGGON PIKE 11, HIGH STREET 17, FAIRFIELD 11¾, DOVE CRAG 13, GREAT RIGG 11¾, RED SCREES 14½, HIGH RAISE 7½, GLARAMARA 5½, BRANDRETH 3⅓, HARRISON STICKLE 8⅓, PIKE O'STICKLE 8, GREEN GABLE 3¾, ALLEN CRAGS 5⅓ — SE

Triangulation Station 2644'

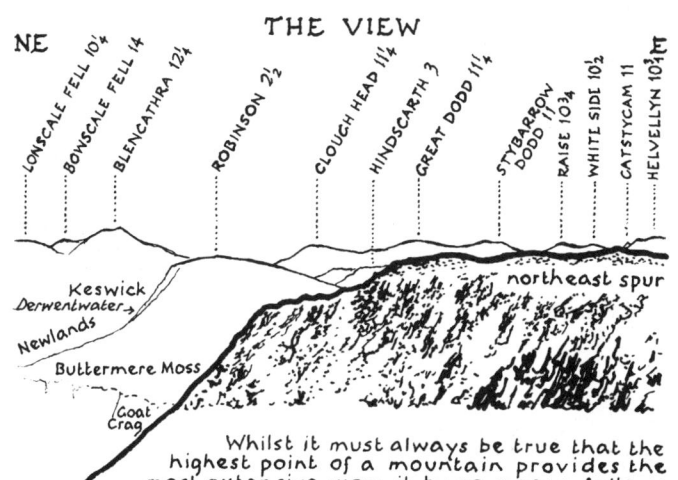

High Stile 12

THE VIEW

NE

LONSCALE FELL 10¼
BOWSCALE FELL 14
BLENCATHRA 12¼
ROBINSON 2½
CLOUGH HEAD 11¼
HINDSCARTH 3
GREAT DODD 11¼
STYBARROW DODD 11
RAISE 10¾
WHITE SIDE 10½
CATSTYCAM 11
HELVELLYN 10¾

Keswick
Derwentwater
Newlands
Buttermere Moss
Goat Crag

northeast spur

Whilst it must always be true that the highest point of a mountain provides the most extensive view it by no means follows that it must therefore be the best station for surveying the surrounding landscape, nor even that it must be most prominently seen in views of the mountain from other heights in the vicinity. On the map of Lakeland there are several instances where the triangulation stations of the Ordnance Survey are sited some distance away from the actual summit.

On High Stile the highest point appears to occur on the main ridge coming up from Red Pike, and this elevation has been selected for the panorama here given, but the Ordnance Survey station is a furlong to the east and not quite on the highest point of the northeast spur, which, in the view above, cuts into the horizon between White Side and Catstycam.

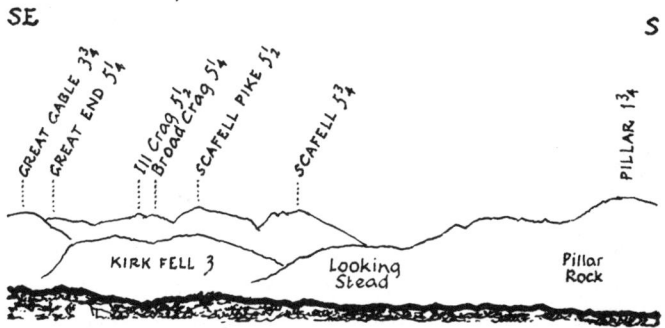

SE   S

GREAT GABLE 3¾
GREAT END 5¼
ILL CRAG 5¼
BROAD CRAG 5¼
SCAFELL PIKE 5½
SCAFELL 5¾
PILLAR 1¾

KIRK FELL 3
Looking Stead
Pillar Rock

High Stile 13

THE VIEW

S — SW
SCOAT FELL 2¼   HAYCOCK 3
Black Crag
cairn

SW — W
CAW FELL 3¼
LANK RIGG 5
Dent 8¼
CRAG FELL 4½
Ennerdale Water
Latterbarrow 2¼

W — NW
Bowness Knott 3½
White Pike
GREAT BORNE 3
STARLING DODD 1¾
Knock Murton 5⅓
GAVEL FELL 4
BLAKE FELL 4¾
RED PIKE ⅔

The figures accompanying the names of fells are distances in miles
The thick line marks the visible boundaries of the fell from the viewpoint

In clear weather, the Isle of Man appears over Lank Rigg, Scotland and the Solway Firth above Crummock Water, and the Irish Sea extends across the western horizon.

High Stile 14

THE VIEW

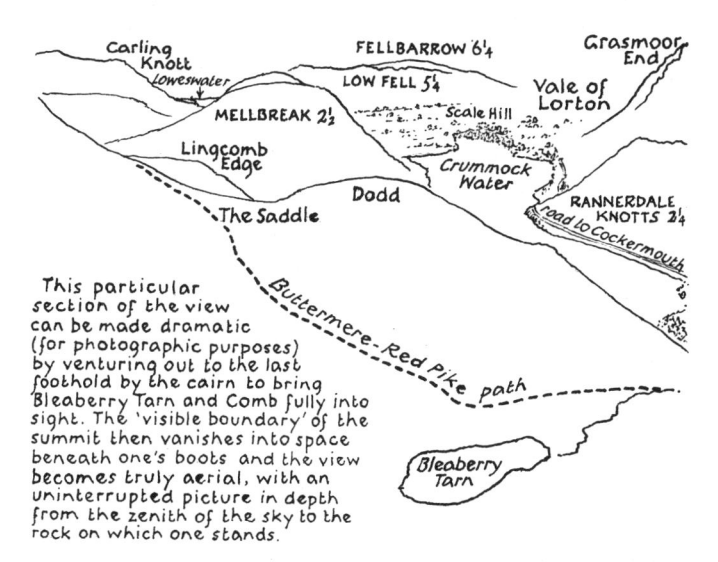

NW — N

Carling Knott, Lowesmater, MELLBREAK 2½, Lingcomb Edge, The Saddle, FELLBARROW 6¼, LOW FELL 5¼, Scale Hill, Dodd, Crummock Water, Grasmoor End, Vale of Lorton, RANNERDALE KNOTTS 2¼, road to Cockermouth, Buttermere–Red Pike path, Bleaberry Tarn

This particular section of the view can be made dramatic (for photographic purposes) by venturing out to the last foothold by the cairn to bring Bleaberry Tarn and Comb fully into sight. The 'visible boundary' of the summit then vanishes into space beneath one's boots and the view becomes truly aerial, with an uninterrupted picture in depth from the zenith of the sky to the rock on which one stands.

High Stile 15

RIDGE ROUTE

TO RED PIKE, 2479': ¾ mile : NW
Depression at 2300': 200 feet of ascent
Very easy walking after initial roughness.

A track of sorts leads down the bouldery side of High Stile, but beyond the gaping mouth of the Chapel Crags gully soon vanishes in a stretch of excellent turf. Follow the edge of Bleaberry Comb in good weather, but in mist don't lose sight of the fence posts, which are continuous on to Red Pike but skirt the actual summit: turn right for the top beyond the first rocks.

ONE MILE

Red Pike from High Stile

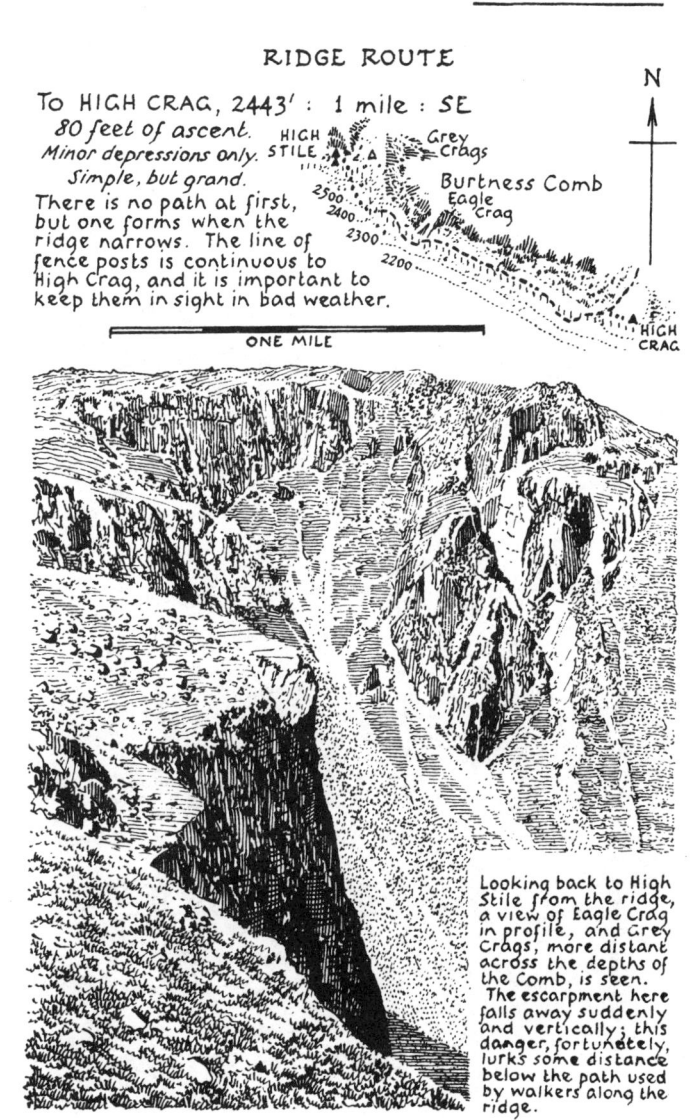

High Stile 16

RIDGE ROUTE

To HIGH CRAG, 2443': 1 mile : SE
80 feet of ascent.
Minor depressions only.
Simple, but grand.

There is no path at first, but one forms when the ridge narrows. The line of fence posts is continuous to High Crag, and it is important to keep them in sight in bad weather.

Looking back to High Stile from the ridge, a view of Eagle Crag in profile, and Grey Crags, more distant across the depths of the Comb, is seen.
The escarpment here falls away suddenly and vertically; this danger, fortunately, lurks some distance below the path used by walkers along the ridge.

Kirk Fell 2630'

from Green Gable

Kirk Fell 2

NATURAL FEATURES

Kirk Fell is the patron fell of Wasdale Head, a distinction little recognised. To most visitors in this grandest of all daleheads, Great Gable so catches the eye that Kirk Fell, next to it, is hardly looked at; and even the other two fells enclosing the valley, Lingmell and Yewbarrow, win more glances. Kirk Fell, although bulking large in the scene, is in fact plain and unattractive, a vast wall of bracken and grass, every yard of it much like the rest. Everybody's camera points to Great Gable, nobody's to Kirk Fell. But look at the map. The streams coming down each side of Kirk Fell, Lingmell Beck and Mosedale Beck, are long in meeting: for a mile or more at valley level they enclose a flat tongue of land at the foot of Kirk Fell. Every building in the little hamlet of Wasdale Head — cottages, farmhouses, church and hotel, and all the valley pastures, lie in the lap of Kirk Fell on this flat extension between the two streams. The fell takes its name from the church. Kirk Fell accommodates the community of Wasdale Head, but the footings in the valley of Great Gable and Lingmell and Yewbarrow are barren.

Bland the southern aspect may be, but the dark north face is very different. Here, shadowed cliffs seam the upper slopes in a long escarpment, a playground for climbers, above rough declivities that go down to the Liza in Ennerdale. Linking with Great Gable is the depression of Beck Head to the east; westwards is a counterpart in Black Sail Pass, linking with Pillar. And between is a broad undulating top, with tarns, the ruins of a wire fence, and twin summits: on the whole a rather disappointing ornamentation, a poor crown for so massive a plinth.

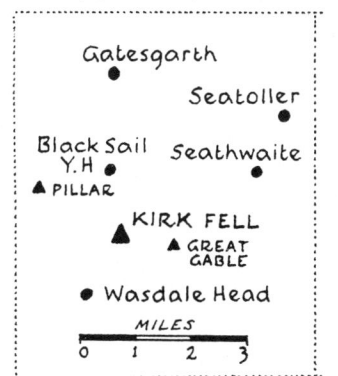

Kirk Fell 3

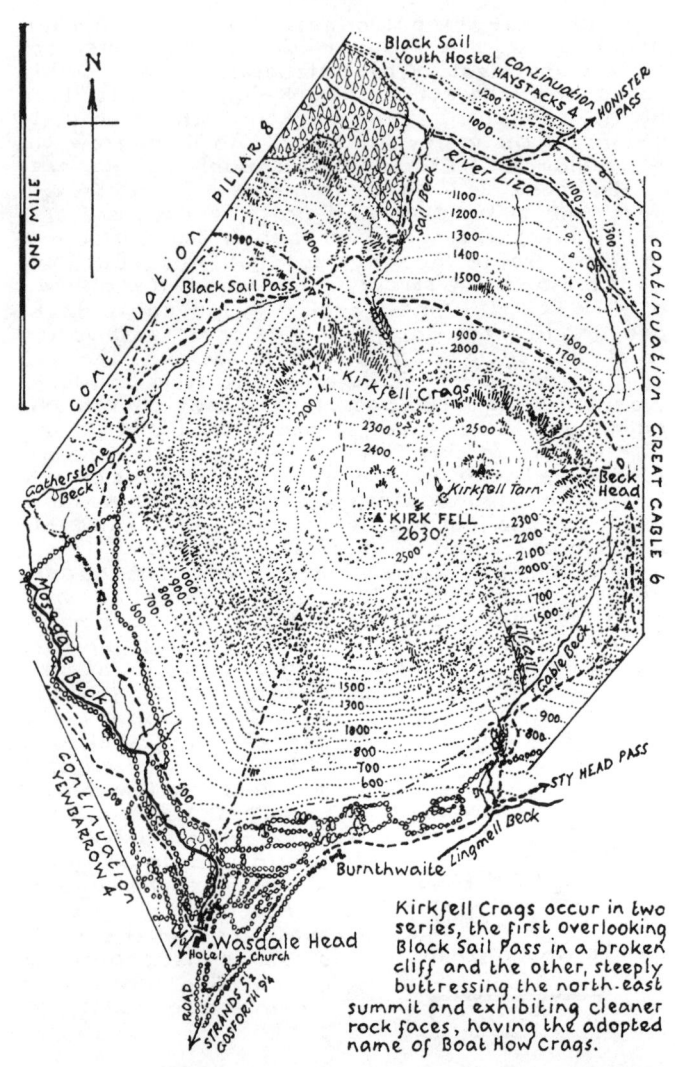

MAP

Kirkfell Crags occur in two series, the first overlooking Black Sail Pass in a broken cliff and the other, steeply buttressing the north-east summit and exhibiting cleaner rock faces, having the adopted name of Boat How Crags.

Kirk Fell 4

ASCENT FROM WASDALE HEAD
2330 feet of ascent : 1¼ miles

A straight line is the shortest distance between two points. This route is the straightest and therefore the most direct ascent in Lakeland. It is also the steepest — a relentless and unremitting treadmill, a turf-clutching crawl, not a walk. There are only three opportunities of standing upright, three heaven-sent bits of horizontal, before the slope eases into the summit plateau. Apart from steepness, there are no difficulties or hazards of any sort.

KIRK FELL

natural dykes

third halting place (small delectable grass ridge at the top of the scree)

Highnose Head — second halting place (crest of steep grass slope)

Back buttons cannot stand the strain, and wearers of braces are well advised to profit from a sad experience of the author on this climb and take a belt as reserve support.

Looking backwards (between one's legs) there is a superb upside-down view of Wasdale Head

first halting place (top of small crag)

Two alternative routes are available and more generally used. Either (a) proceed to the top of Black Sail Pass, thence climbing the north ridge, or (b) go up to Beck Head and ascend Rib End. In both cases the top of the fell is reached after an interesting scramble on a stony track alongside the watershed fence.

BLACK SAIL PASS

looking north

Wasdale Head — Row Head — Hotel

Leave Wasdale Head by the Black Sail path, starting through the yard of Row Head, up the lane from the hotel.

Kirk Fell 5

ASCENT FROM ENNERDALE
(BLACK SAIL YOUTH HOSTEL)

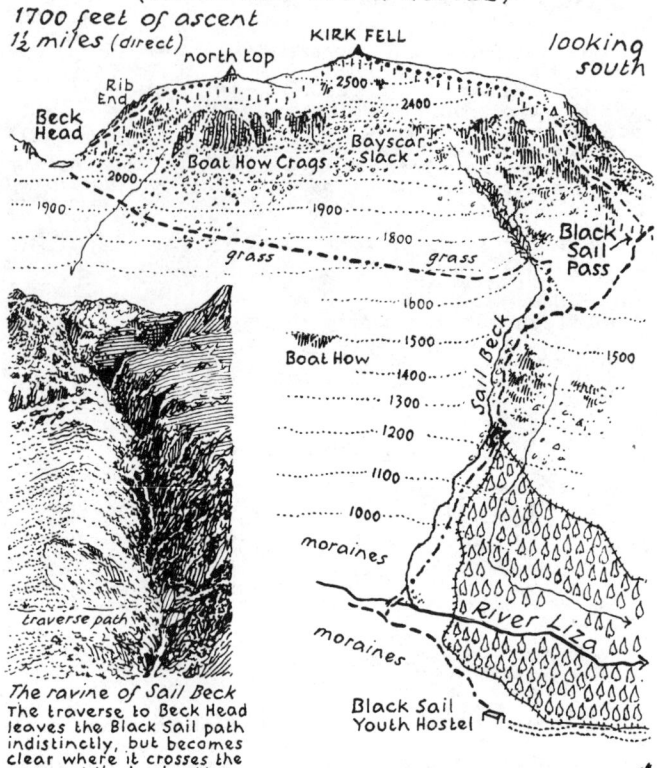

1700 feet of ascent
1½ miles (direct)

looking south

KIRK FELL
north top

Rib End
Beck Head
Boat How Crags
Bayscar Slack
Black Sail Pass
grass
Boat How
Sail Beck
moraines
River Liza
moraines
Black Sail Youth Hostel

The ravine of Sail Beck
The traverse to Beck Head leaves the Black Sail path indistinctly, but becomes clear where it crosses the ravine at the big boulders.

The *best* route is via Black Sail Pass and the fenced ridge going up therefrom. The *easiest* route, free of crags, is by Bayscar Slack (avoid the boulder-fields). The *most interesting* route, passing beneath Boat How Crags, is along the traverse and up from Beck Head via Rib End.

Boat How Crags

Kirk Fell 6

THE SUMMIT

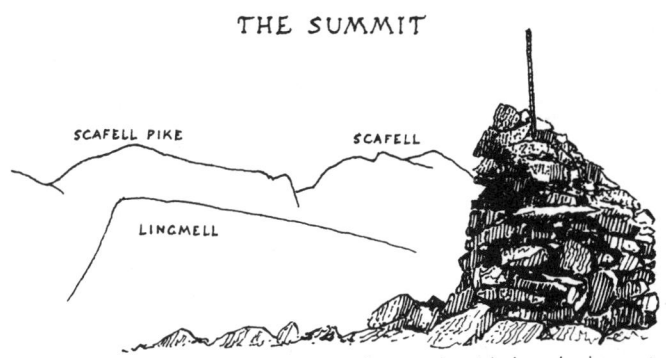

Kirk Fell has two separate tops, the higher being at the head of the Wasdale slope in an area of stones. Here is the main cairn, which is combined with a windshelter. The fence, which otherwise follows the water-shed strictly, rather oddly does not quite visit the highest point at 2630'. The other top, north east, is appreciably lower, the cairn here surmounting a rocky outcrop. In a hollow between the two summits are two unattractive tarns, named as one, Kirkfell Tarn.

Some maps record the height of the fell as 2631'.

DESCENTS: The top of the fell is usually left with the guidance of the fence, which, after a long crossing of the summit plateau, goes down northwards to Black Sail Pass; or, eastwards, over the lesser summit and down Rib End to Beck Head. Either route may be used for Wasdale Head or Ennerdale and both descend roughly on distinct stony tracks amongst crags although the top of the fell is pathless. For Wasdale Head direct, wander south, where a line of cairns leads down to a small and dainty grass ridge (it is important to find this). Below starts the very steep and straight descent, stony at first. Grass is reached at 2000', and from this point onwards a badly-shod walker will suffer many slips and spills, none fatal, and it is not a bad plan to continue in bare or stockinged feet, which give a better grip than boots.

The north east summit

Kirk Fell 7

THE VIEW

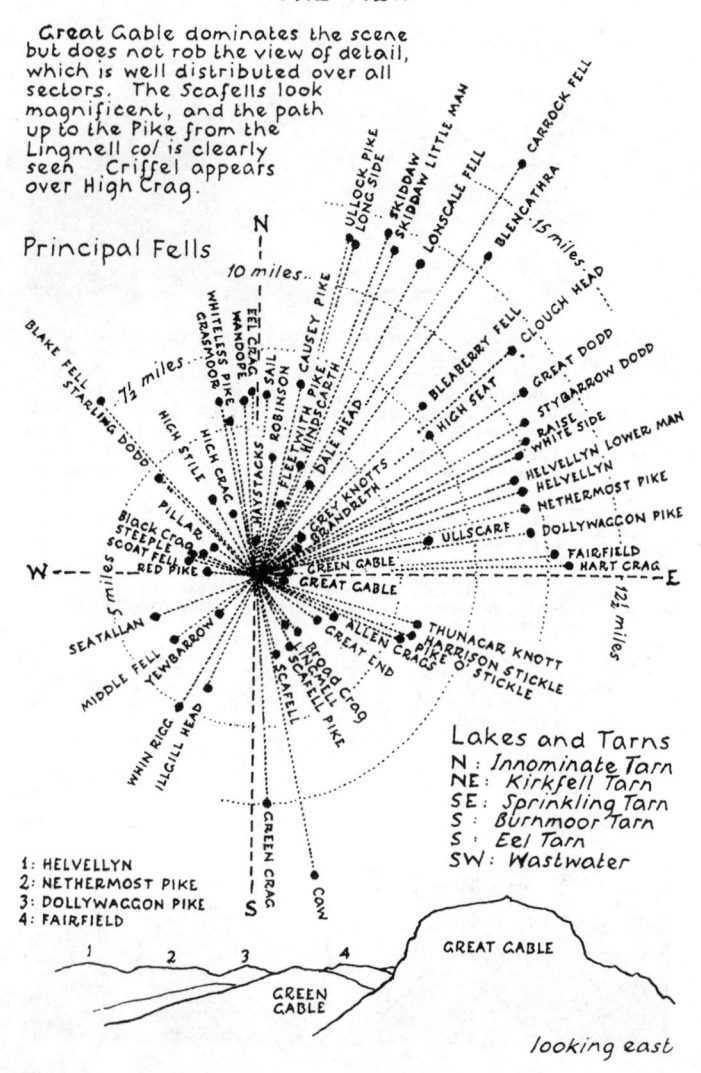

Great Gable dominates the scene but does not rob the view of detail, which is well distributed over all sectors. The Scafells look magnificent, and the path up to the Pike from the Lingmell col is clearly seen. Criffel appears over High Crag.

Principal Fells

Lakes and Tarns
N : Innominate Tarn
NE : Kirkfell Tarn
SE : Sprinkling Tarn
S : Burnmoor Tarn
S : Eel Tarn
SW : Wastwater

1: HELVELLYN
2: NETHERMOST PIKE
3: DOLLYWAGGON PIKE
4: FAIRFIELD

looking east

Kirk Fell 8

RIDGE ROUTES

To PILLAR, 2927': 2½ miles: NW, then N and WNW
Depression at 1800' (Black Sail Pass)
1150 feet of ascent

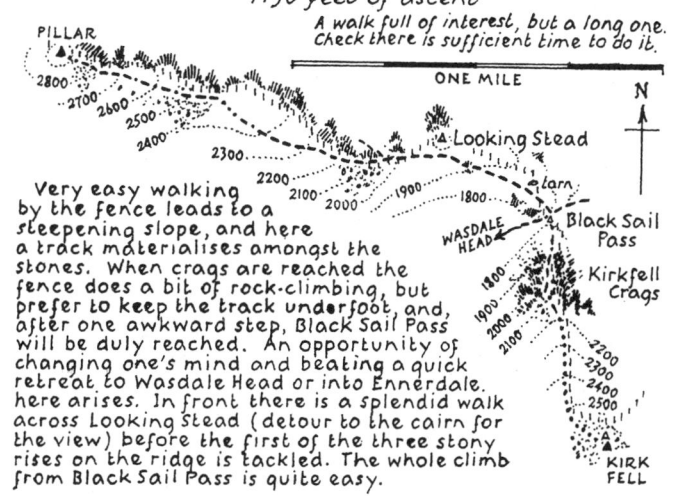

A walk full of interest, but a long one. Check there is sufficient time to do it.

Very easy walking by the fence leads to a steepening slope, and here a track materialises amongst the stones. When crags are reached the fence does a bit of rock-climbing, but prefer to keep the track underfoot, and, after one awkward step, Black Sail Pass will be duly reached. An opportunity of changing one's mind and beating a quick retreat to Wasdale Head or into Ennerdale here arises. In front there is a splendid walk across Looking Stead (detour to the cairn for the view) before the first of the three stony rises on the ridge is tackled. The whole climb from Black Sail Pass is quite easy.

To GREAT GABLE, 2949': 1⅓ miles: NE, then E and SE
Depression at 2040' (Beck Head): 990 feet of ascent.

Rough going, but well worth the effort.

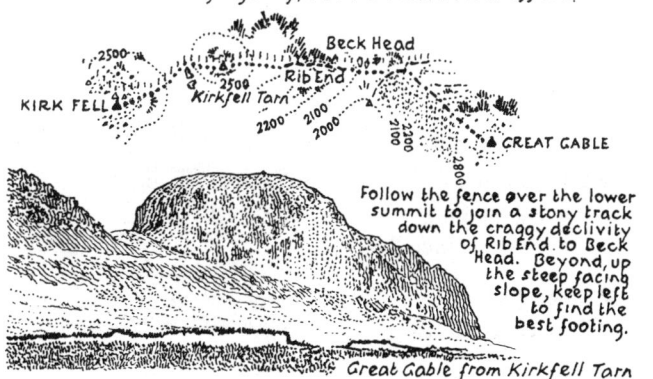

Follow the fence over the lower summit to join a stony track down the craggy declivity of Rib End to Beck Head. Beyond, up the steep facing slope, keep left to find the best footing.

Great Gable from Kirkfell Tarn

Lank Rigg 1775'

from Friar Moor near Coldfell Gate

- Ennerdale Bridge
- GRIKE ▲   ▲ CRAG FELL
- ▲ LANK RIGG
- CAW FELL ▲
- Coldfell Gate
- Thornholme
- Scalderskew
- Calder Bridge

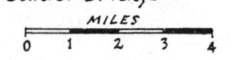

MILES
0 1 2 3 4

Water Intake Works Worm Gill

Lank Rigg 2

NATURAL FEATURES

Ridgewalkers on the more frequented western fells will occasionally notice the isolated summit of Lank Rigg appearing on the skyline and almost certainly will need to refer to a map to determine its identity, for this is a fell most visitors have never heard of and few know sufficiently well to recognise on sight. The map will confirm further that Lank Rigg is an outsider, beyond the accepted limits of Lakeland, too remote to bother about. If Pillar and High Stile haven't yet been climbed, there is admittedly no case to be made out for this humble fell, but walkers already familiar with the district might well devote a day to this lonely outpost of Kinniside; they will do so with especial advantage if of an enquiring turn of mind for things ancient. A column on the summit shows that the Ordnance men have a regard for the place. And Lank Rigg is, after all, within the Lake District National Park boundary.

The fell has wide sprawling slopes and is extensive. It calls for a full day's expedition even if the problem of reaching its environs can be overcome by car or helicopter, for it is distant from tourist centres. To walk all round it, having got there, is a rough tramp of ten miles. Meeting another human is outside the realms of possibility! Die here, unaccompanied, and your disappearance from society is likely to remain an unsolved mystery.

Lank Rigg is bounded by two streams that quickly assume the proportions of rivers. One of them, the Calder, has the name of river from birth; the other, Worm Gill, even though tapped for water supplies, is a fast-flowing torrent that has carved a wide course through the hills.

Some prehistoric remains suggest that the fell was probably better known in ages past. More recent, but still many centuries old, is a pack-horse bridge spanning a ravine of the Calder, a thing of beauty.

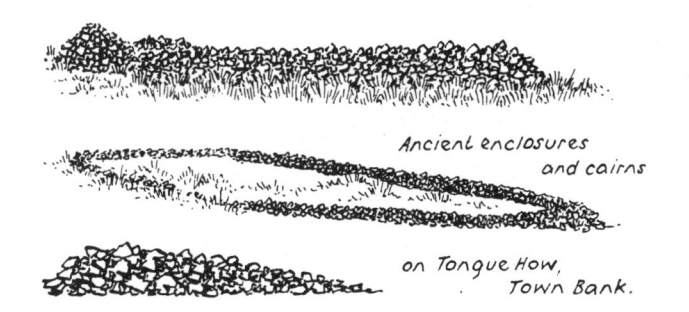

Ancient enclosures and cairns

on Tongue How, Town Bank.

Lank Rigg 3

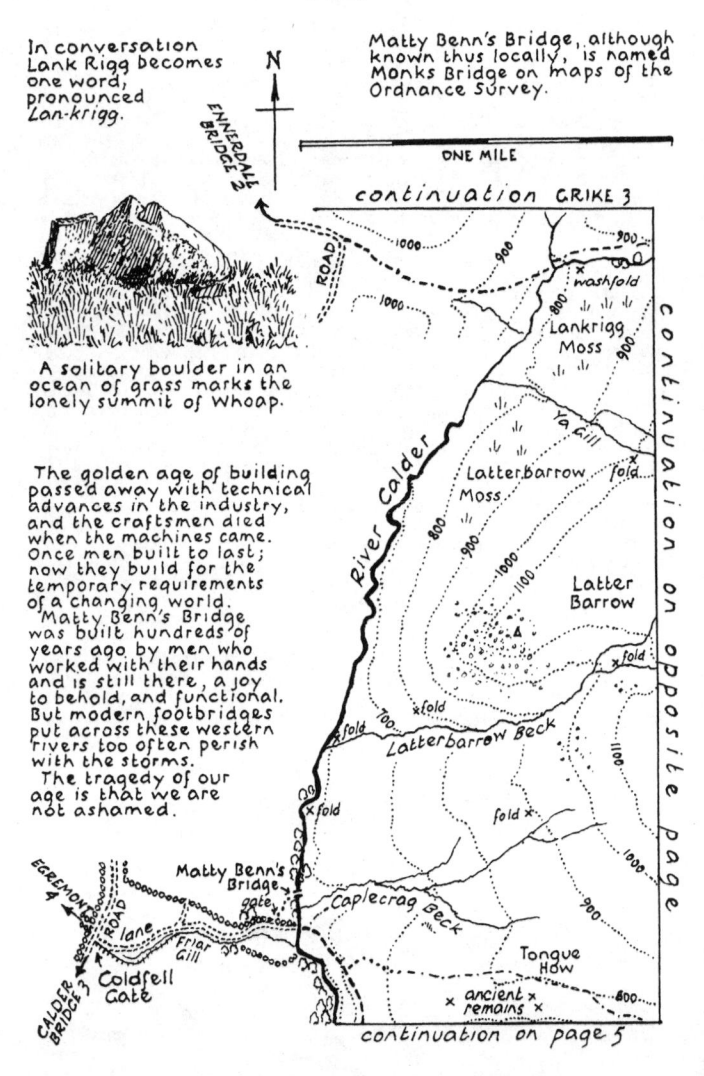

MAP

In conversation Lank Rigg becomes one word, pronounced Lan-krigg.

Matty Benn's Bridge, although known thus locally, is named Monks Bridge on maps of the Ordnance Survey.

ONE MILE

continuation GRIKE 3

A solitary boulder in an ocean of grass marks the lonely summit of Whoap.

The golden age of building passed away with technical advances in the industry, and the craftsmen died when the machines came. Once men built to last; now they build for the temporary requirements of a changing world.
 Matty Benn's Bridge was built hundreds of years ago by men who worked with their hands and is still there, a joy to behold, and functional. But modern footbridges put across these western rivers too often perish with the storms.
 The tragedy of our age is that we are not ashamed.

continuation on opposite page

continuation on page 5

Lank Rigg 4

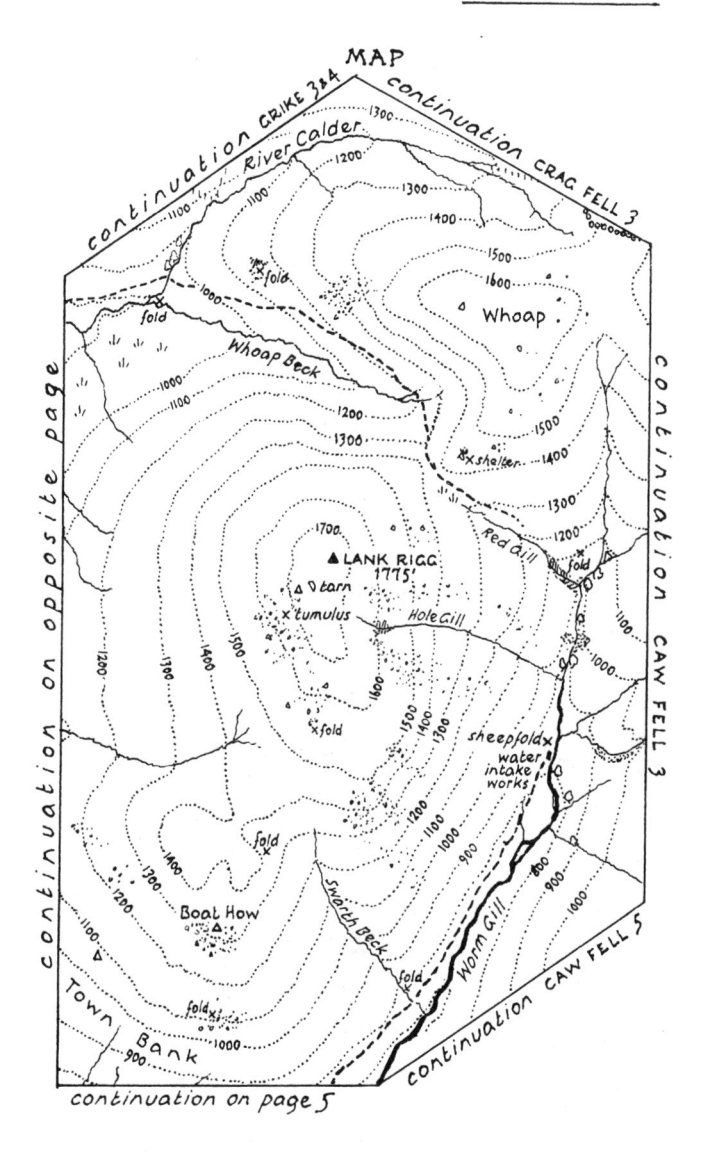

MAP

Lank Rigg 5

MAP
continuation on pages 3 and 4

The path across Town Bank to the intake (which accompanies the water pipe) has become overgrown with rushes and is wet. In places it is now difficult to follow.

Matty Benn's Bridge

The valley of the River Calder near Thornholme

Lank Rigg 6

ASCENT FROM THE COLDFELL ROAD
1400 feet of ascent : 2½ miles

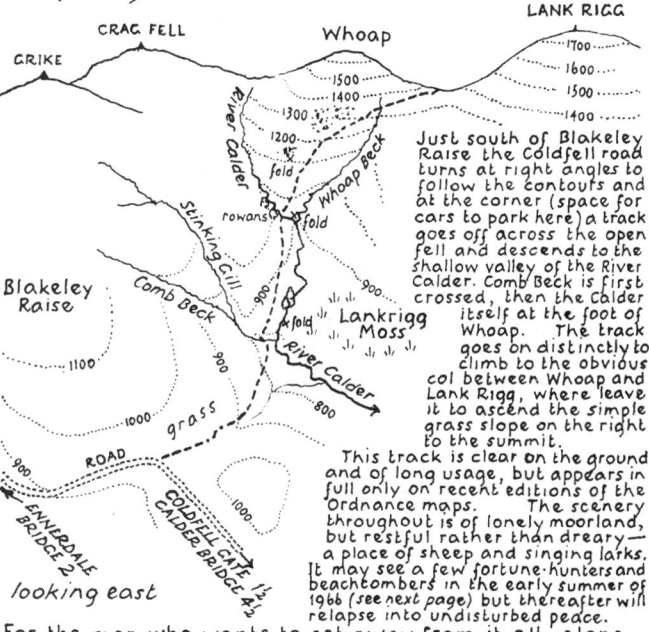

looking east

Just south of Blakeley Raise the Coldfell road turns at right angles to follow the contours and at the corner (space for cars to park here) a track goes off across the open fell and descends to the shallow valley of the River Calder. Comb Beck is first crossed, then the Calder itself at the foot of Whoap. The track goes on distinctly to climb to the obvious col between Whoap and Lank Rigg, where leave it to ascend the simple grass slope on the right to the summit.

This track is clear on the ground and of long usage, but appears in full only on recent editions of the Ordnance maps. The scenery throughout is of lonely moorland, but restful rather than dreary — a place of sheep and singing larks. It may see a few fortune-hunters and beachcombers in the early summer of 1966 (see next page) but thereafter will relapse into undisturbed peace.

For the man who wants to get away from it all, alone.

ASCENT FROM COLDFELL GATE

Rather less conveniently, a footing may be gained on Lank Rigg from Coldfell Gate (3 miles from Calder Bridge; 4¼ from Ennerdale Bridge, on the Coldfell road). Here a lane goes down to ford the Calder, and upstream 120 yards of this point, reached from a gate in the field-wall, is Matty Benn's Bridge, which must be visited even if the ford can be forded, which it cannot be dryshod. Across the river rise the long gentle slopes of Lank Rigg and they may be tackled anywhere, but the most interesting plan is to go via Tongue How and Boat How, both of which have many ancient remains in the vicinity. The summit is a mile north of Boat How.

ASCENT FROM CALDER BRIDGE

When there was a footbridge across Worm Gill just short of its confluence with the Calder at Thornholme, a very pleasant approach could be made from Calder Bridge, visiting the Abbey on the way, but at the time of writing the footbridge is gone, and the stream at this point is 15 yards wide and awkward to wade; in spate, it would be dangerous to attempt a crossing. On the other side an easy slope rises to Tongue How.

Lank Rigg 7

THE SUMMIT

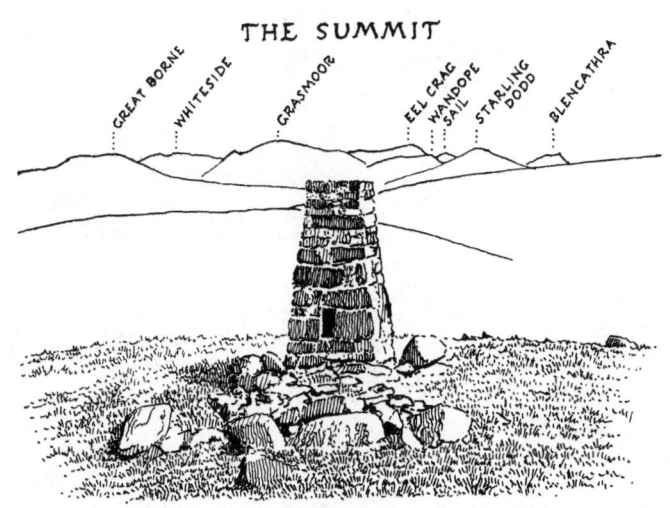

Peaks labeled left to right: GREAT BORNE, WHITESIDE, GRASMOOR, EEL CRAG, WANDOPE, SAIL, STARLING DODD, BLENCATHRA

The highest point on the grassy summit is indicated by a column of the Ordnance Survey, S 3647. Southwest across the flat top is a small tarn and beyond this a rough outcrop and cairn from which is seen, further southwest, a large tumulus of antiquarian interest.

Buried Treasure on Lank Rigg

The only exciting experience in the lonely life of the Ordnance column occurred on a gloriously sunny day in April 1965, when it was a mute and astonished witness to an unparalleled act of generosity. In an uncharacteristic mood of magnanimity which he has since regretted, the author decided on this summit to share his hard-won royalties with one of his faithful readers, and placed a two-shilling piece under a flat stone: it awaits the first person to read this note and act upon it. There is no cause to turn the whole top over as though pigs have been at it — the stone is four feet from the column. If the treasure cannot be found at this distance it can be assumed that a fortunate pilgrim has already passed this way rejoicing. The finder may be sufficiently pleased to write in c/o the publishers and confirm his claim by stating the year of the coin's issue. If nobody does so before the end of 1966 the author will go back and retrieve it for the purchase of fish and chips. It was a reckless thing to do, anyway.

Ancient and Modern —
Tumulus on Lank Rigg
and atomic power
station at
Calder Hall

Lank Rigg 8

THE VIEW

Except for an unexpected appearance by Blencathra, the scene inland to the mountains is unremarkable, and it is the villages and towns of West Cumberland, seen as on a map, that provide most interest.

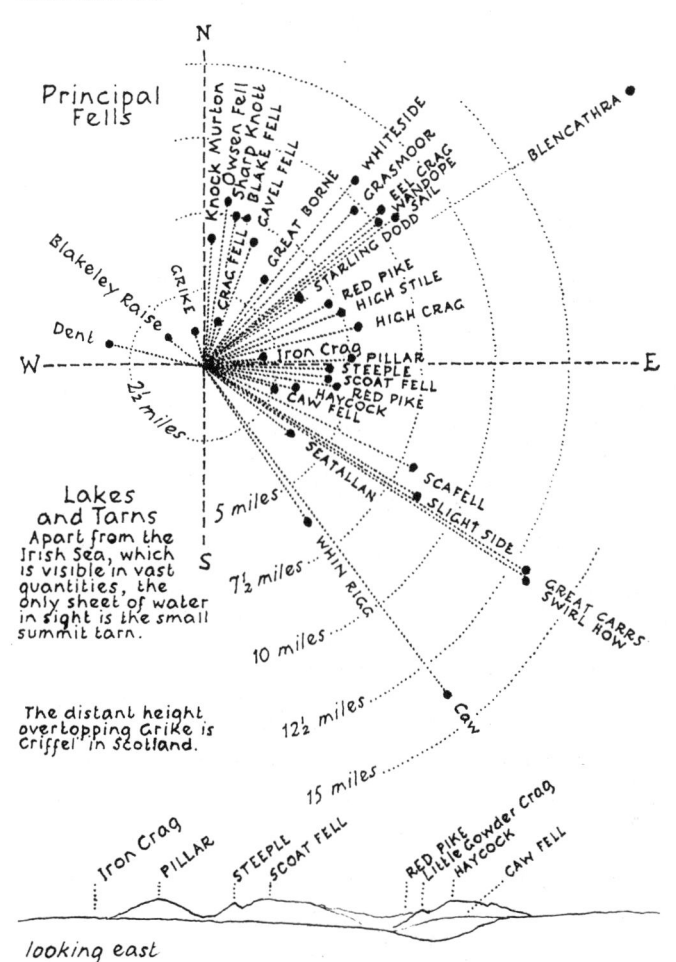

Principal Fells

Knock Murton, Owsen Fell, Sharp Knoll, Blake Fell, Gavel Fell, Crag Fell, Great Borne, Whiteside, Grasmoor, Eel Crag, Wandope, Dodd, Grisedale Pike, Starling Dodd, Red Pike, High Stile, High Crag, Blencathra, Blakeley Raise, Grike, Dent, Iron Crag, Pillar, Steeple, Scoat Fell, Red Pike, Haycock, Caw Fell, Seatallan, Scafell, Slight Side, Whin Rigg, Great Carrs, Swirl How, Caw

2½ miles, 5 miles, 7½ miles, 10 miles, 12½ miles, 15 miles

Lakes and Tarns

Apart from the Irish Sea, which is visible in vast quantities, the only sheet of water in sight is the small summit tarn.

The distant height overtopping Grike is Criffel in Scotland.

looking east — Iron Crag, Pillar, Steeple, Scoat Fell, Red Pike, Lillie Gowder Crag, Haycock, Caw Fell

Low Fell

1360'
approx.

from Lanthwaite Hill

The lesser heights and foothills of Lakeland, especially those on the fringe, are too much neglected in favour of the greater mountains, yet many of these unsought and unfashionable little hills are completely charming. In this category is Low Fell, north of Loweswater and west of the Vale of Lorton. It has many tops, uniformly around 1350 feet, rising from a ridge. The most southerly eminence has the main cairn and a perfectly composed view of mountain and lake scenery, a connoisseur's piece.

Low Fell and Fellbarrow together form a separate range, a final upthrust of land between Lakeland and the sea. The underlying rock is slate, and the hills exhibit smooth rounded slopes in conformity to pattern; but they deny conformity to the lake of Loweswater, forcing its issuing stream, by a freak of contours, to flow inland, away from the sea, in compliance with the inexorable natural law that water always obeys.

▲ FELLBARROW
● Thackthwaite
▲ LOW FELL
Loweswater
●

MILES
0   1   2

Low Fell 2

MAP

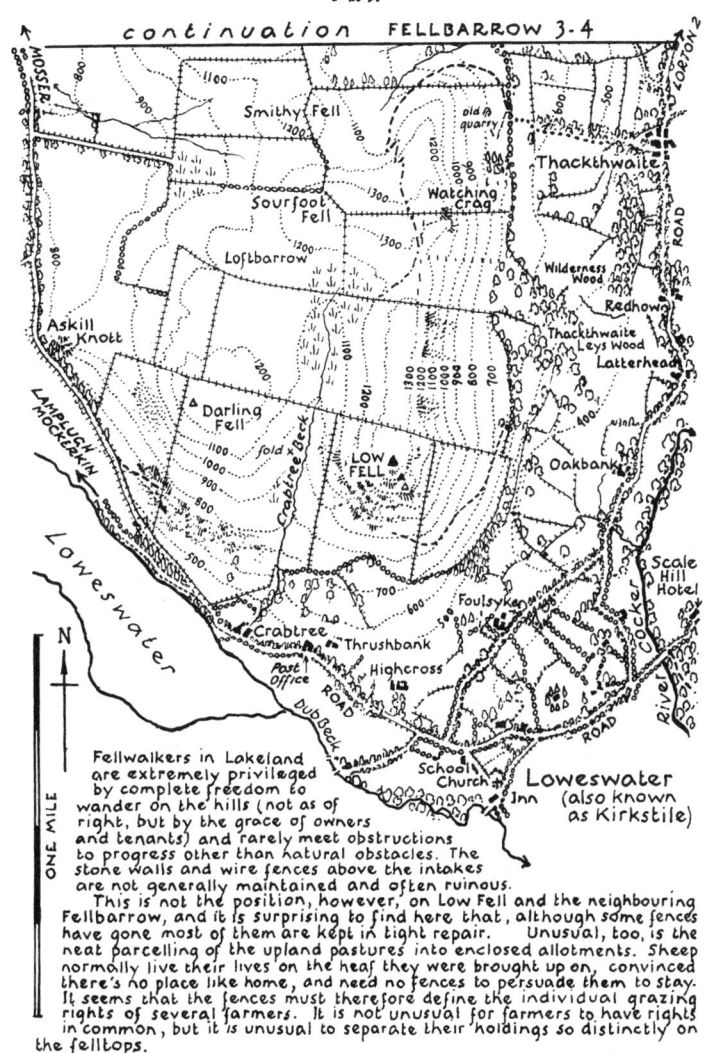

continuation FELLBARROW 3-4

Fellwalkers in Lakeland are extremely privileged by complete freedom to wander on the hills (not as of right, but by the grace of owners and tenants) and rarely meet obstructions to progress other than natural obstacles. The stone walls and wire fences above the intakes are not generally maintained and often ruinous.

This is not the position, however, on Low Fell and the neighbouring Fellbarrow, and it is surprising to find here that, although some fences have gone most of them are kept in tight repair.   Unusual, too, is the neat parcelling of the upland pastures into enclosed allotments. Sheep normally live their lives on the heaf they were brought up on, convinced there's no place like home, and need no fences to persuade them to stay. It seems that the fences must therefore define the individual grazing rights of several farmers. It is not unusual for farmers to have rights in common, but it is unusual to separate their holdings so distinctly on the felltops.

Low Fell 3

ASCENT FROM LOWESWATER
1050 feet of ascent : 2 miles (direct route)
1350 feet of ascent : 3 miles (via Darling Fell)

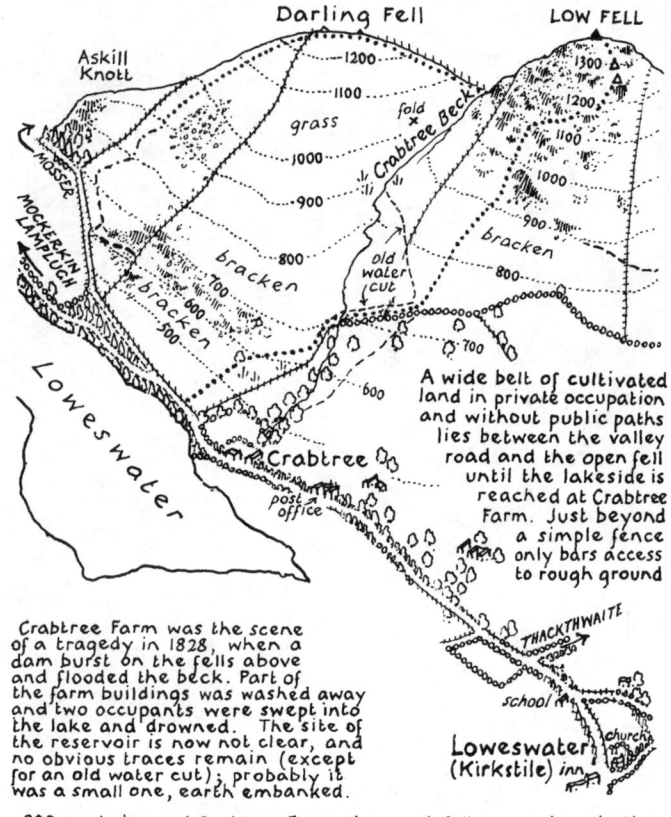

A wide belt of cultivated land in private occupation and without public paths lies between the valley road and the open fell until the lakeside is reached at Crabtree Farm. Just beyond a simple fence only bars access to rough ground

Crabtree Farm was the scene of a tragedy in 1828, when a dam burst on the fells above and flooded the beck. Part of the farm buildings was washed away and two occupants were swept into the lake and drowned. The site of the reservoir is now not clear, and no obvious traces remain (except for an old water cut); probably it was a small one, earth embanked.

200 yards beyond Crabtree Farm the rough fell comes down to the roadside and a direct course may be made from here, through the bracken at first, and finally dodging the outcrops. (A way up from the farmhouse to the intake wall should be regarded as private).
To include Darling Fell in the walk go on up the Mosser lane for a half mile, leaving it at a gate recessed on the right; climb round in an arc to avoid scree ahead. A line of fence posts links Darling Fell and Low Fell, the intervening depression being considerable.

Wait for a bright clear day.   Don't forget the camera.

Low Fell 4

ASCENT FROM THACKTHWAITE
1250 feet of ascent : 2 miles

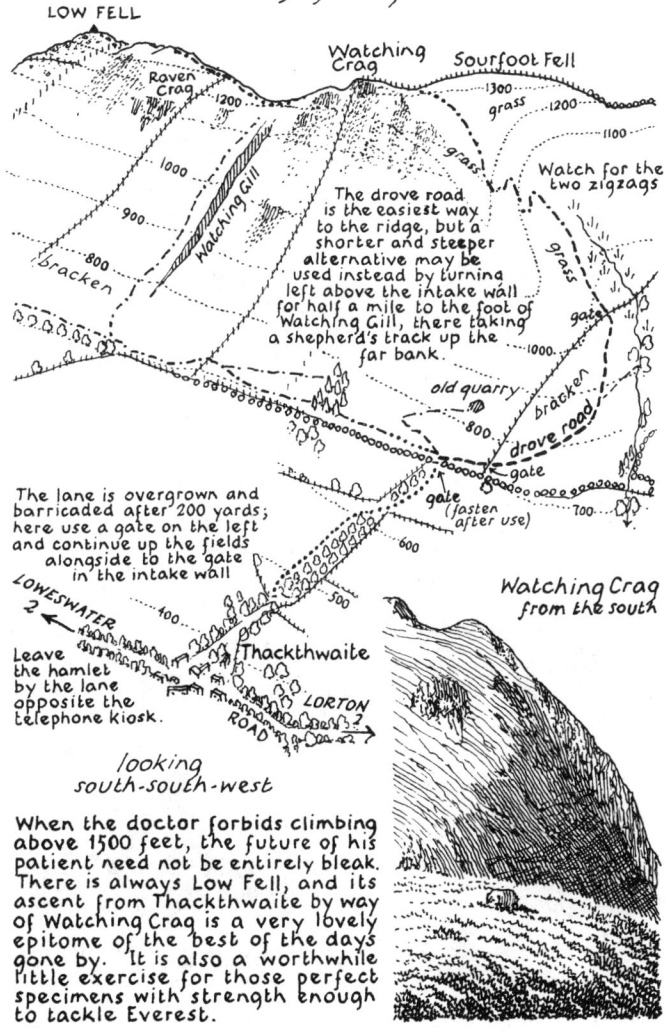

looking south-south-west

LOW FELL
Raven Crag
Watching Crag
Sourfoot Fell
Watching Gill
bracken

The drove road is the easiest way to the ridge, but a shorter and steeper alternative may be used instead by turning left above the intake wall for half a mile to the foot of Watching Gill, there taking a shepherd's track up the far bank.

Watch for the two zigzags

grass
old quarry
drove road
gate
gate (fasten after use)

The lane is overgrown and barricaded after 200 yards; here use a gate on the left and continue up the fields alongside to the gate in the intake wall

LOWESWATER 2
Thackthwaite
LORTON ROAD

Leave the hamlet by the lane opposite the telephone kiosk.

Watching Crag from the south

When the doctor forbids climbing above 1500 feet, the future of his patient need not be entirely bleak. There is always Low Fell, and its ascent from Thackthwaite by way of Watching Crag is a very lovely epitome of the best of the days gone by. It is also a worthwhile little exercise for those perfect specimens with strength enough to tackle Everest.

Low Fell 5

THE SUMMIT

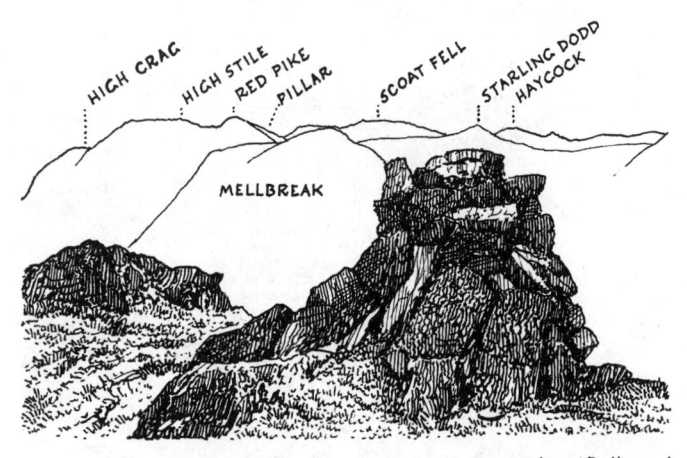

(labelled skyline: HIGH CRAG, HIGH STILE, RED PIKE, PILLAR, SCOAT FELL, STARLING DODD, HAYCOCK, MELLBREAK)

There are no benchmarks on the main ridge of Low Fell, and exact heights have not been measured. The biggest cairn is on the southern eminence, on rough ground, but the smooth north top appears to be slightly higher. The 2½" Ordnance map shows 1350' contours at both places, and if these are accurately plotted there must be heights approaching 1375' within them. Perhaps it is wrongly assumed that the column at 1363' on the more massive Fellbarrow is the highest point on the range, and Low Fell may be given less than justice by an estimated elevation of 1360'. Two cairns 100 and 120 yards southeast of the main cairn indicate better viewpoints for the Loweswater valley.

DESCENTS: No paths leave the top but there is no difficulty in picking a way down the south face to the intake wall; the several outcrops and low crags above 1000' are scattered and easily avoided. Follow the wall to the right, cross Crabtree Beck and go down by the fence to the road.

Cairn on the north top

Cairn on Darling Fell

(sketch labelled: GRASMOOR, LOW FELL (south top))

The highest point on Darling Fell, at 1282', is a triangulation station a few yards from the fence coming up from the Mosser lane. It is marked by a broken stake and has no cairn.

Low Fell 6

THE VIEW

Southeast the view is of classical beauty, an inspired and inspiring vision of loveliness that has escaped the publicity of picture postcards and poets' sonnets, a scene of lakes and mountains arranged to perfection. The grouping of fells above Mosedale is also attractively presented, with Pillar an unexpected absentee, only a small section of its western shoulder being seen behind Red Pike. Grasmoor is a tremendous object.
Westwards is the sea.

Principal Fells

The diagram is based on the view from the south top.

Lakes and Tarns

SE: *Buttermere*
SE: *Crummock Water*
SW: *Loweswater*

Darling Fell is a better viewpoint for Loweswater

SSW: *Highnook Tarn*

RIDGE ROUTE

To FELLBARROW, 1363': 1½ miles. N
See Fellbarrow 7 for map and notes.

This simple walk is better enjoyed in reverse, from north to south.

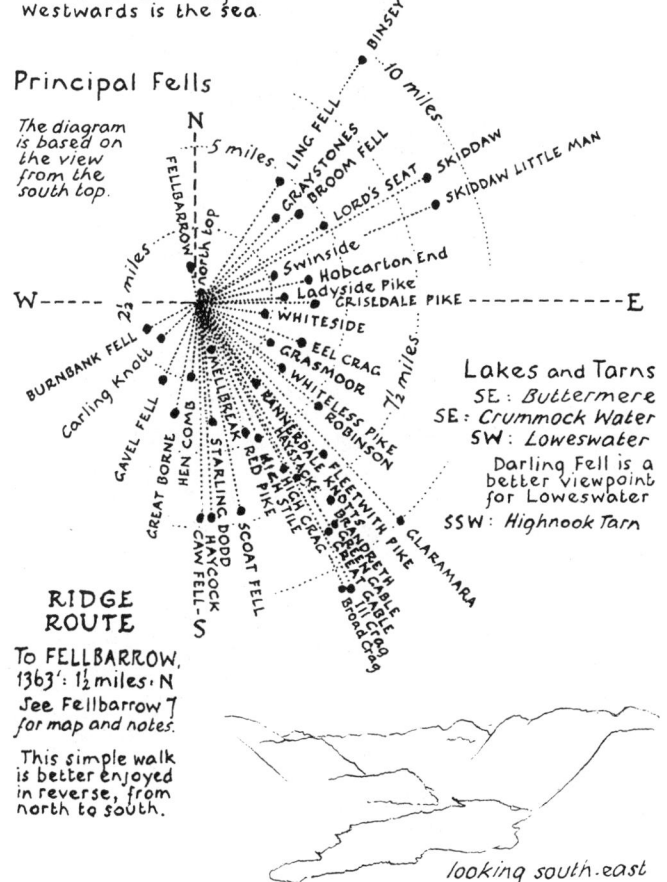

looking south-east

Mellbreak 1676'

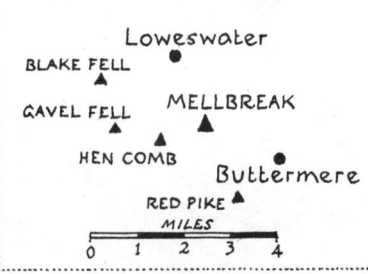

from Kirkhead

Map:
- Loweswater
- BLAKE FELL
- GAVEL FELL
- MELLBREAK
- HEN COMB
- Buttermere
- RED PIKE
- MILES 0 1 2 3 4

In West Cumberland, where Mellbreak is a household word (largely through long association with the Mellbreak Foxhounds (spelt with one 'l')) the fell is highly esteemed, and there have always been people ready to assert that it is the finest of all. This is carrying local patriotism too far, but nevertheless it is a grand hill in a beautiful situation with a character all its own and an arresting outline not repeated in the district.
There is only one Mellbreak.

Mellbreak 2

NATURAL FEATURES

There is, of course, a natural affinity between mountains and lakes; they have developed side by side in the making of the earth. Often there is a special association between a particular mountain and a particular lake, so that, in calling the one to mind the other comes inevitably to mind also: they belong together. The best example of this is provided by Wastwater and the Screes, and perhaps next best is the combination of Mellbreak and Crummock Water, essential partners in a successful scenery enterprise, depending on each other for effectiveness. Crummock Water's eastern shore, below Grasmoor, is gay with life and colour — trees, pastures, farms, cattle, traffic, tents and people — but it is the view across the lake, where the water laps the sterile base of Mellbreak far beneath the mountain's dark escarpment, where loneliness, solitude and silence prevail, that makes the scene unforgettable.

Mellbreak, seen thus, is a grim sight, the austere effect often heightened by shadow, and a much closer examination is needed to reveal the intimate detail of crag and gully and scree, the steep declivities cushioned in heather, the hidden corners and recesses, the soaring ravens of Raven Crag. From Kirkstile, at the northern foot, the gable of the fell assumes the arresting outline of a towering pyramid, suggesting a narrow crest, but the top widens into a considerable plateau having two summits of almost equal height separated by a broad saddle. Symmetry and simplicity are the architectural *motifs*, and the steep flank above Crummock Water has its counterpart to the west descending to the dreariest and wettest of Lakeland's many Mosedales. Thus the severance from other fells is complete. Mellbreak is isolated, independent of other high ground, aloof.

Its one allegiance is to Crummock Water.

from Scalehill Bridge

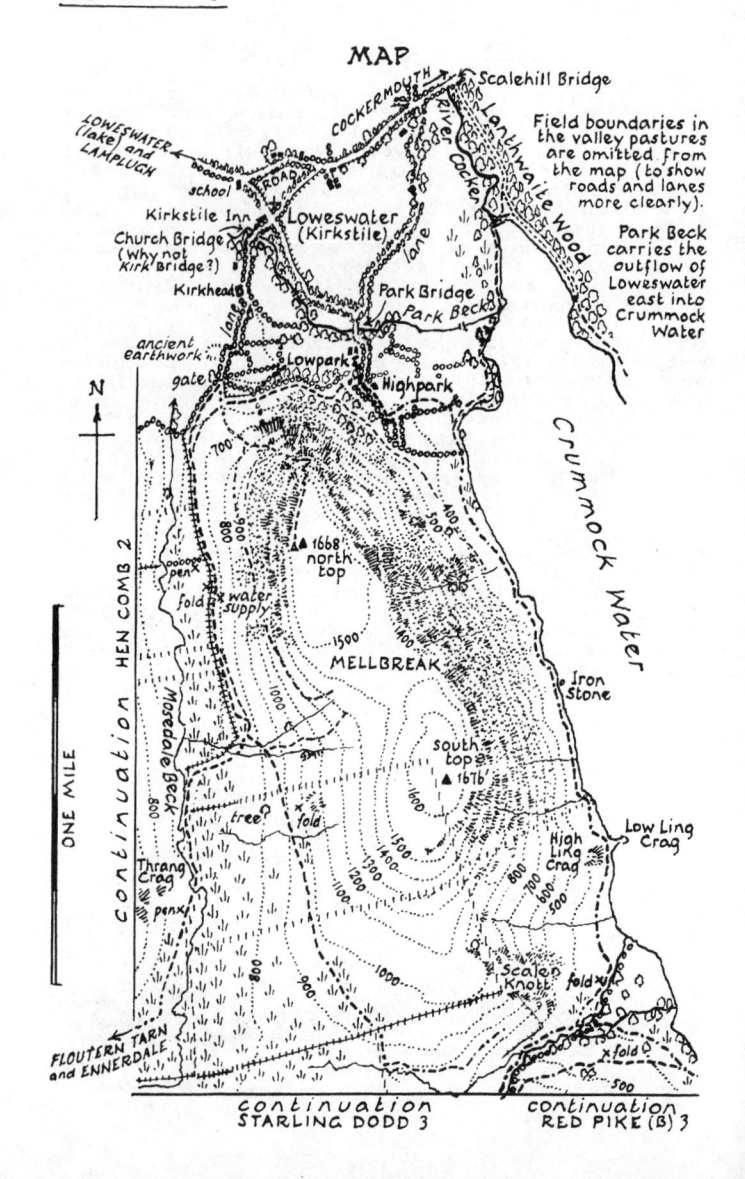

Mellbreak 3

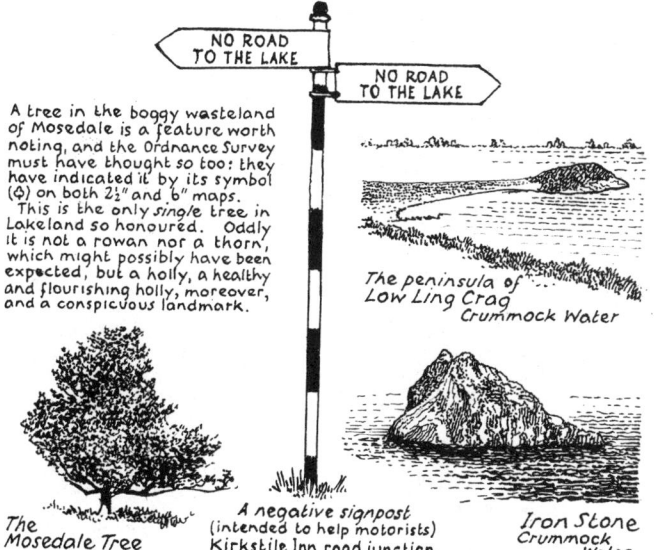

# Mellbreak 4

"....a lovely peep around a corner...."
(direct ascent from Loweswater)

A tree in the boggy wasteland of Mosedale is a feature worth noting, and the Ordnance Survey must have thought so too: they have indicated it by its symbol (♣) on both 2½" and 6" maps.
  This is the only *single* tree in Lakeland so honoured. Oddly it is not a rowan nor a thorn, which might possibly have been expected, but a holly, a healthy and flourishing holly, moreover, and a conspicuous landmark.

NO ROAD TO THE LAKE

NO ROAD TO THE LAKE

The peninsula of
Low Ling Crag
Crummock Water

The Mosedale Tree

A negative signpost
(intended to help motorists)
Kirkstile Inn road junction

Iron Stone
Crummock Water

Mellbreak 5

ASCENT (to the north top) FROM LOWESWATER
1300 feet of ascent : 1¼ miles

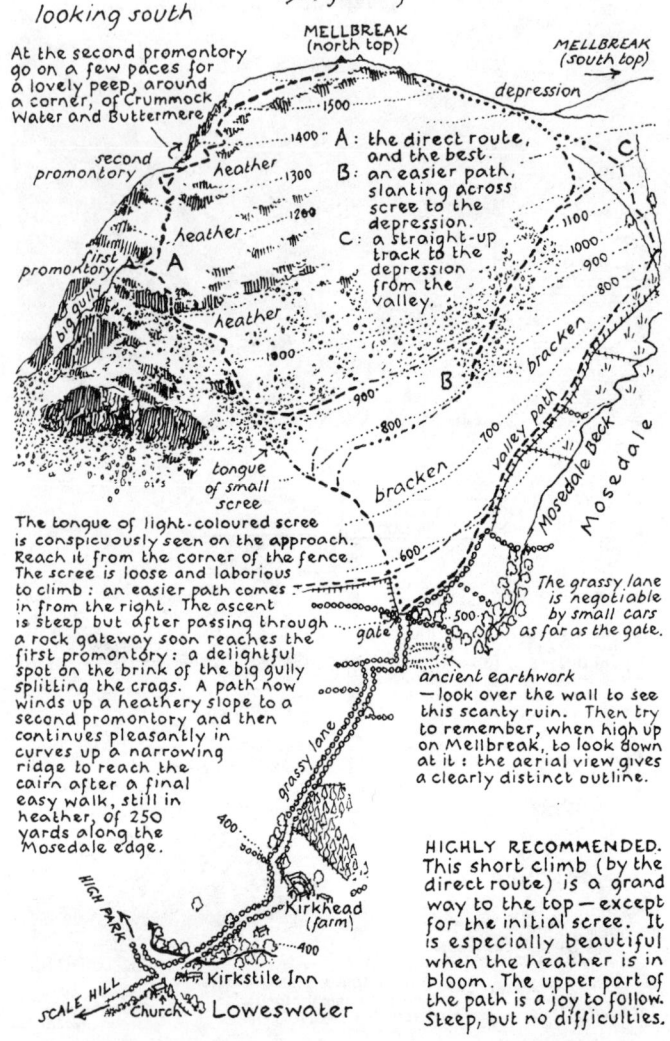

looking south

MELLBREAK (north top)

MELLBREAK (south top)

depression

At the second promontory go on a few paces for a lovely peep, around a corner, of Crummock Water and Buttermere

second promontory

heather

first promontory

big gully

heather

heather

heather

A: the direct route, and the best.
B: an easier path, slanting across scree to the depression.
C: a straight-up track to the depression from the valley.

bracken

tongue of small scree

bracken

valley path

Mosedale Beck

Mosedale

The tongue of light-coloured scree is conspicuously seen on the approach. Reach it from the corner of the fence. The scree is loose and laborious to climb: an easier path comes in from the right. The ascent is steep but after passing through a rock gateway soon reaches the first promontory: a delightful spot on the brink of the big gully splitting the crags. A path now winds up a heathery slope to a second promontory and then continues pleasantly in curves up a narrowing ridge to reach the cairn after a final easy walk, still in heather, of 250 yards along the Mosedale edge.

gate

The grassy lane is negotiable by small cars as far as the gate.

ancient earthwork — look over the wall to see this scanty ruin. Then try to remember, when high up on Mellbreak, to look down at it: the aerial view gives a clearly distinct outline.

grassy lane

HIGH PARK

Kirkhead (farm)

SCALE HILL

Church

Kirkstile Inn

Loweswater

HIGHLY RECOMMENDED. This short climb (by the direct route) is a grand way to the top — except for the initial scree. It is especially beautiful when the heather is in bloom. The upper part of the path is a joy to follow. Steep, but no difficulties.

Mellbreak 6

ASCENT FROM CRUMMOCK WATER
1350 feet of ascent : ¾ mile (to the north top).
1450 feet of ascent : 1 mile (to the south top)

The only merit in this steep line of ascent is the remarkable rock scenery of the short section of the route below the upper crag. A rising grass rake at the base of the crag provides a narrow passage and from this gangway four rocky pillars form a broken parapet and fall as aretes towards the lake. Apart from this, the route has little to commend it.

Do NOT attempt a slanting route to the Rake from Green Wood. Knee-deep heather and steepness make this a bad crossing. Go up the open screeslope further along.

Pillar Rake, lower section, from the north. (route indicated)

looking southwest

Pillar Rake, looking back at the first two pillars (route indicated)

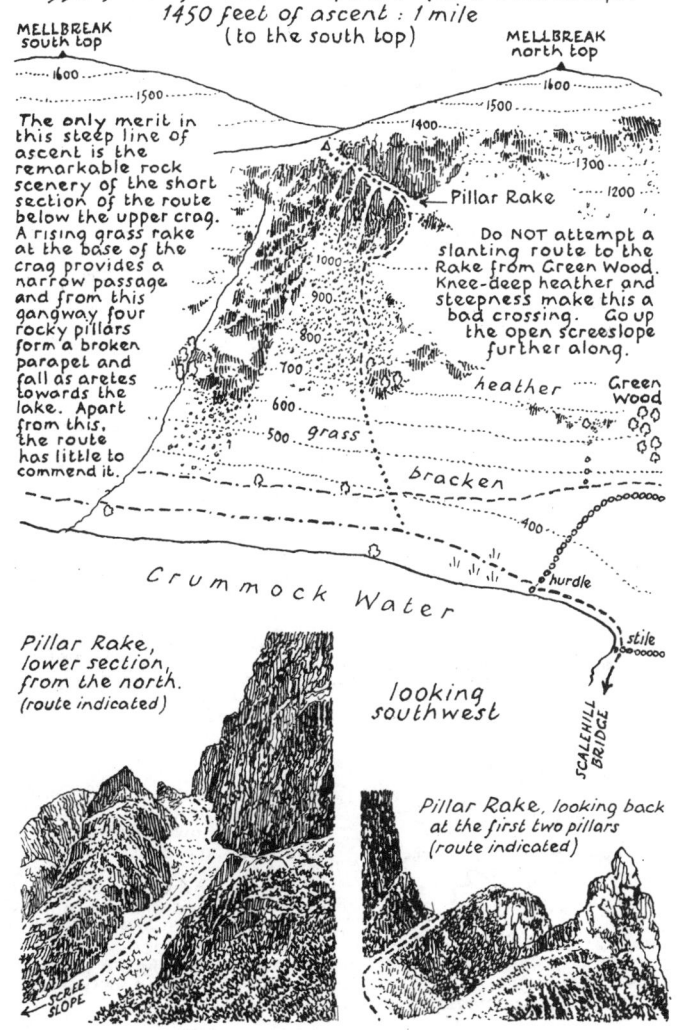

Mellbreak 7

ASCENT (to the south top) FROM BUTTERMERE
1300 feet of ascent : 2½ miles

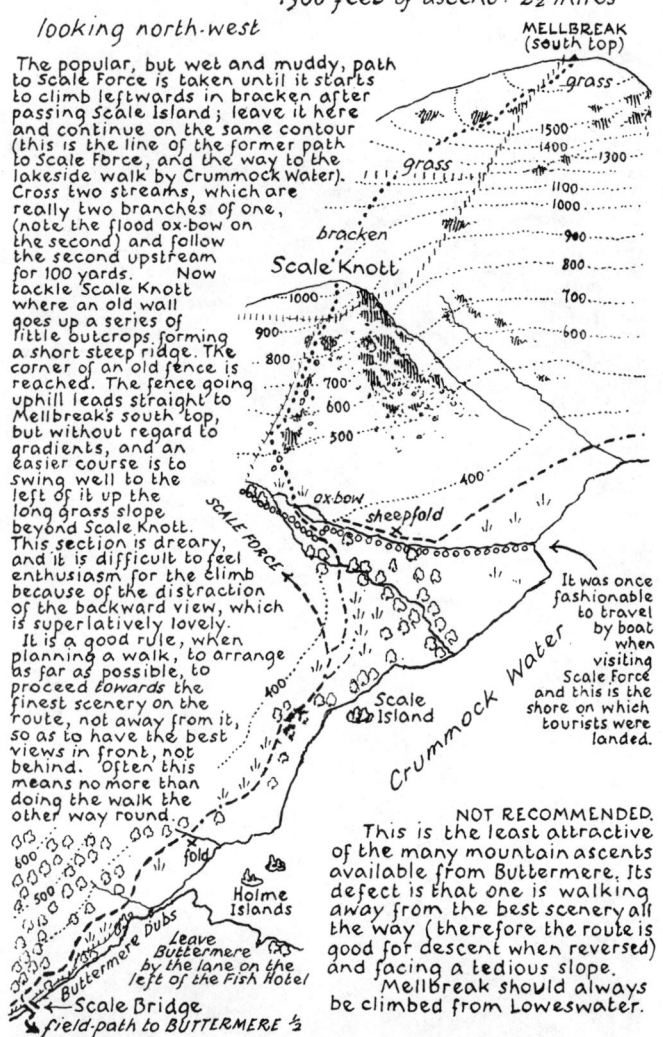

looking north-west

The popular, but wet and muddy, path to Scale Force is taken until it starts to climb leftwards in bracken after passing Scale Island; leave it here and continue on the same contour (this is the line of the former path to Scale Force, and the way to the lakeside walk by Crummock Water). Cross two streams, which are really two branches of one, (note the flood ox-bow on the second) and follow the second upstream for 100 yards. Now tackle Scale Knott where an old wall goes up a series of little outcrops, forming a short steep ridge. The corner of an old fence is reached. The fence going uphill leads straight to Mellbreak's south top, but without regard to gradients, and an easier course is to swing well to the left of it up the long grass slope beyond Scale Knott. This section is dreary, and it is difficult to feel enthusiasm for the climb because of the distraction of the backward view, which is superlatively lovely.

It is a good rule, when planning a walk, to arrange as far as possible, to proceed *towards* the finest scenery on the route, not away from it, so as to have the best views in front, not behind. Often this means no more than doing the walk the other way round.

It was once fashionable to travel by boat when visiting Scale Force and this is the shore on which tourists were landed.

NOT RECOMMENDED.
This is the least attractive of the many mountain ascents available from Buttermere. Its defect is that one is walking away from the best scenery all the way (therefore the route is good for descent when reversed) and facing a tedious slope.

Mellbreak should always be climbed from Loweswater.

Mellbreak 8

THE SUMMIT

1: FLEETWITH PIKE
2: GLARAMARA
3: GREY KNOTTS
4: BRANDRETH
5: GREEN GABLE
6: GREAT GABLE
7: HAYSTACKS

south-east from the north top

Mellbreak has two distinct summits, two-thirds of a mile apart and separated by a pronounced depression. The more attractive of the two is the heathery north top, measured by the Ordnance Survey as 1668 feet above sea level; the duller grassy south top is credited with 1676 feet. Nobody would have complained if the measurements had been reversed, by some rare error, for it is the lower north top, crowning a splendid tower of rock, that captures the fancy, not the other. The width and extent of the top of the fell between the two summits comes as a surprise — the narrow ridge promised by distant views of the fell is an illusion. An odd thing about both summits is that the cairn on each is not quite on the highest ground: this is particularly obvious on the south top.

DESCENTS: It is usual to descend into Mosedale from the west edge of the depression, there being a choice of tracks. From the south top, for Buttermere, the fence down to Scale Knott is a good guide that should not be ignored in mist; keep to the right of it. For Loweswater, from the north top, the routes from the depression into Mosedale are safest unless the direct route is already familiar and the weather clear: in mist, there is a very bad trap at the head of the big gully where a cairn on the promontory suggests a way down that can only lead to disaster; in fact the true path turns down left a few paces short of this cairn. On no account should a descent down the eastern flank to Crummock Water be attempted, except by Pillar Rake, and then only if the route is already known and the weather is clear.

RIDGE ROUTES

Mellbreak is itself a ridge, like the keel of an overturned boat (collapsed in the middle). It has no links with other fells.

west from the south top

Mellbreak 9

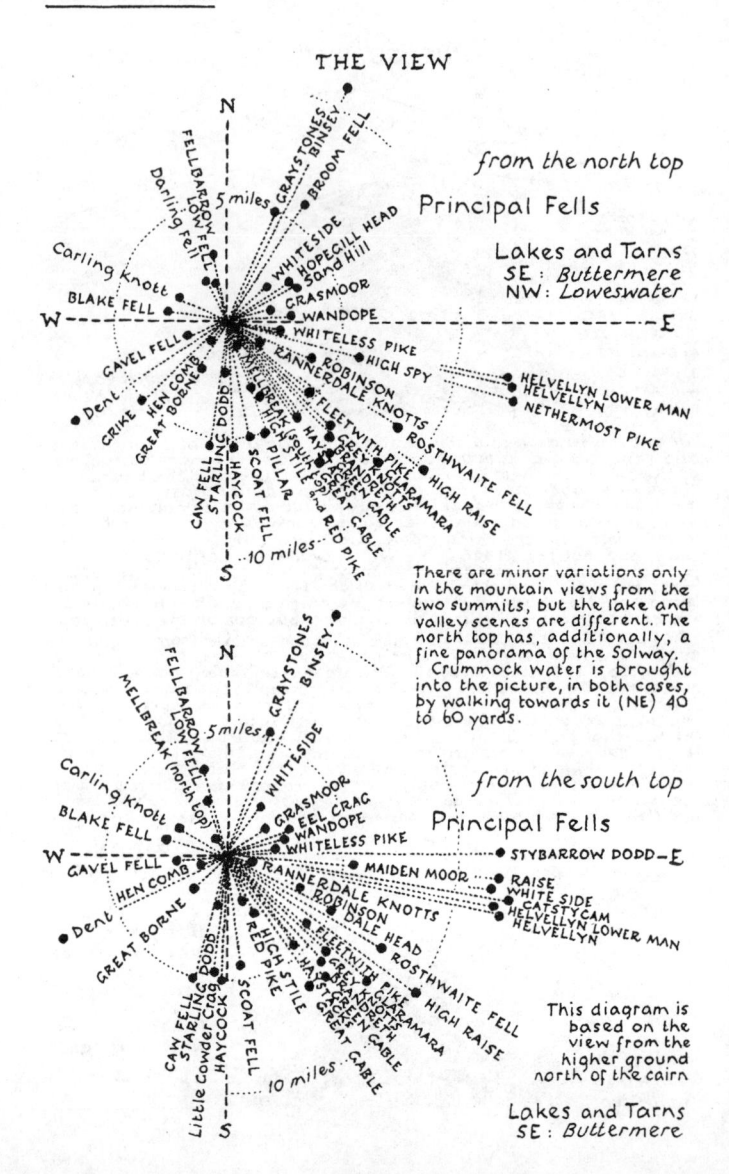

THE VIEW

from the north top

Principal Fells

Lakes and Tarns
SE: *Buttermere*
NW: *Loweswater*

There are minor variations only in the mountain views from the two summits, but the lake and valley scenes are different. The north top has, additionally, a fine panorama of the Solway.
Crummock Water is brought into the picture, in both cases, by walking towards it (NE) 40 to 60 yards.

from the south top

Principal Fells

This diagram is based on the view from the higher ground north of the cairn.

Lakes and Tarns
SE: *Buttermere*

Mellbreak 10

Grasmoor from the north top

*Rannerdale from the south top
(Whiteless Pike, left background)*

Middle Fell

1908'

from Wastwater

Wasdale Head
▲ SEATALLAN ●
MIDDLE ▲ ● Bowderdale
FELL
▲ BUCKBARROW
● Greendale

● Strands

MILES
0 1 2 3 4

Middle Fell 2

NATURAL FEATURES

Many of the lesser fells of Lakeland make up for their lack of height by an aggressive fierceness of expression that seems more appropriate to greater mountains and by an intimidating ruggedness and wildness of terrain that makes their ascent rather more formidable than their size and altitude would suggest. Middle Fell, overlooking Wastwater, comes into this category. Tier above tier of hostile crags, steep slopes overrun by tumbled boulders, vegetation masking pitfalls and crevices: these are the features that rule out, at a glance, any possibility of a simple climb either from the lakeside or from Nether Beck at its eastern base, these being the two aspects that face the traveller along the valley. Nor, if one ventures up by Greendale Gill, on the west, does the scene relent, although a route here presents itself. It is only on the short side of the fell, where there is a high saddle connecting with Seatallan, that a weakness in the fell's armour becomes apparent and the climb to the cairn is comfortable. As a viewpoint for the Wasdale fells, the summit is magnificently placed, and it is fitting that a reward such as this should be earned only by effort.

Waterfalls, Nether Beck

Middle Fell from the headwaters of Nether Beck

Middle Fell 3

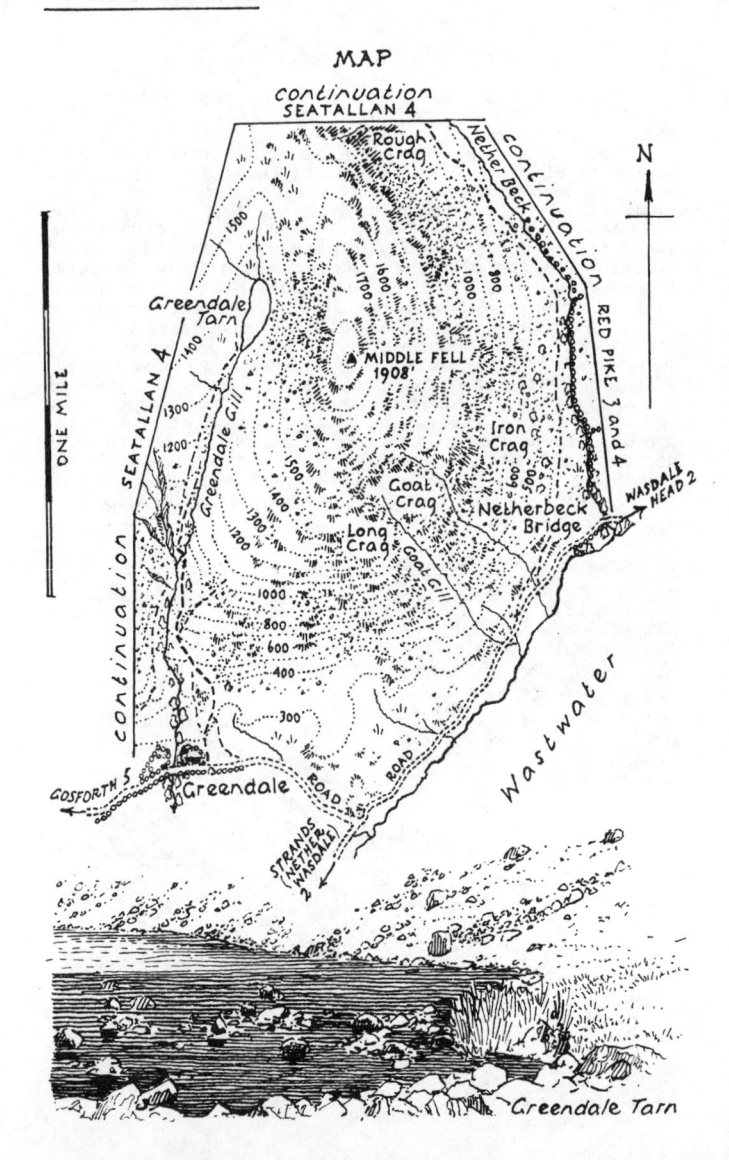

MAP

Greendale Tarn

Middle Fell 4

ASCENT FROM WASDALE
(GREENDALE)
1650 feet of ascent : 1½ miles

Watch for the bifurcation at 700': the uphill branch to the right (which is taken) is an offshoot of the original path for Greendale Tarn. The summit track ascends a green slope first, then a patch of boulders with the help of cairns, but soon fades away. But the gradient is now easy, all the rock outcrops may be avoided, and after a simple climb that will seem longer than expected the summit cairn is reached on the Wasdale edge of a small plateau.

MIDDLE FELL

GREENDALE TARN

Tongues Gills

Greendale Gill

wide green path

old path

fine yew

bracken

Tongues Gills

Cascades, Tongues Gills

GOSFORTH 5

Greendale

ROAD

WASDALE HEAD 3

STRANDS 2

looking north

With free car-parking on the roadside verges, Middle Fell is another 'motorists' mountain and a convenient objective for family parties, *but not in mist.*

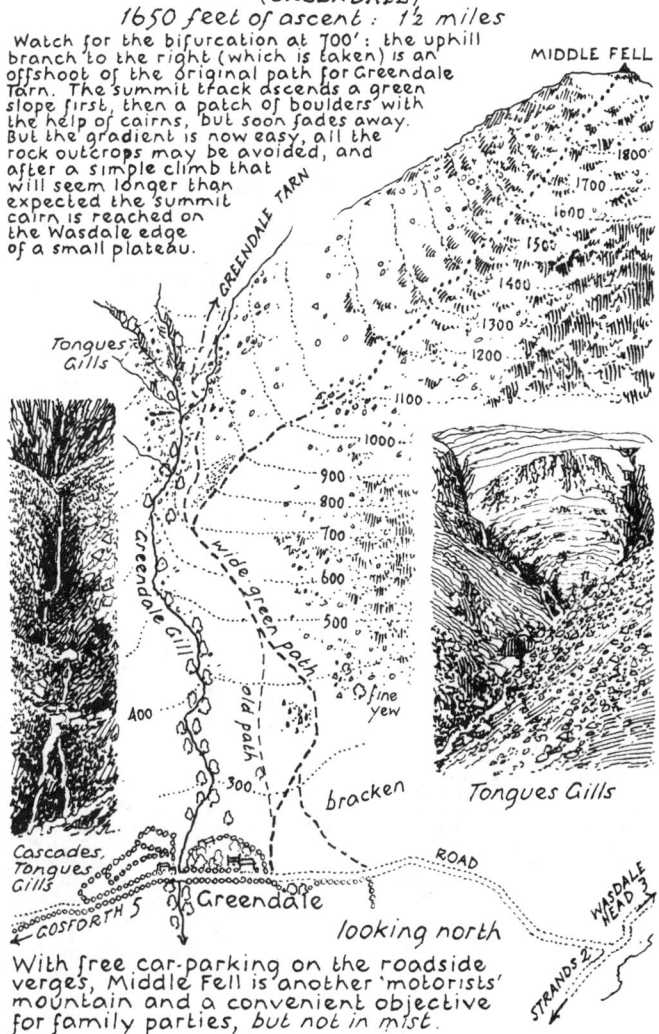

Middle Fell 5

THE SUMMIT

The summit-cairn crowns a small rocky mound on the Wasdale edge of a grassy depression on the top of the fell, and although it is a splendid vantage point there is little in the immediate vicinity to suggest the rocky nature of the slopes just below.

DESCENTS: In clear weather, easy descents may be made to join the path going down to Greendale south-west, or north to the marshy flats above Greendale Tarn; in other directions lies trouble. Keep to grass, skirting innumerable low crags. *In mist use only the south-west route: the slope is gentle (bear right if steep ground is encountered) and longer than expected (nearly a mile) before the path on the east side of Greendale Gill is joined.*

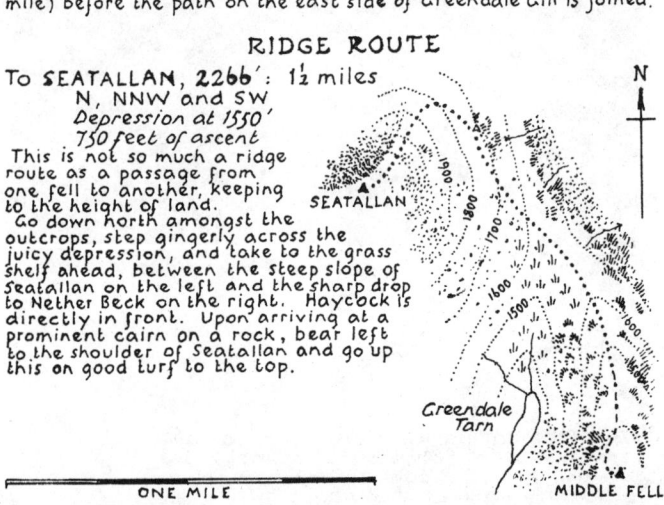

RIDGE ROUTE

To SEATALLAN, 2266': 1½ miles
N, NNW and SW
Depression at 1550'
750 feet of ascent

This is not so much a ridge route as a passage from one fell to another, keeping to the height of land.

Go down north amongst the outcrops, step gingerly across the juicy depression, and take to the grass shelf ahead, between the steep slope of Seatallan on the left and the sharp drop to Nether Beck on the right. Haycock is directly in front. Upon arriving at a prominent cairn on a rock, bear left to the shoulder of Seatallan and go up this on good turf to the top.

ONE MILE

Middle Fell 6

THE VIEW

The most extensive views are not necessarily the finest, and here, from Middle Fell, is a charmer restricted in distance by the Wasdale mountains, which, however, compensate for the deficiency by their own striking appearance. Wastwater is seen full length, backed by the Screes, and, beyond, Black Combe fills up the horizon southward.

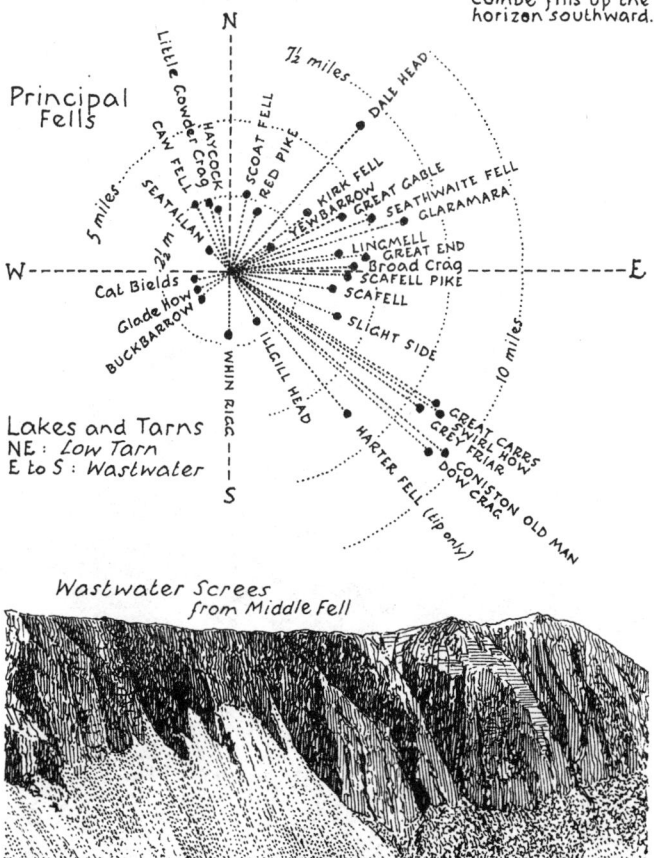

Principal Fells:
Little Gowder Crag, Caw Fell, Haycock, Scoat Fell, Red Pike, Dale Head, Kirk Fell, Yewbarrow, Great Gable, Seathwaite Fell, Glaramara, Seatallan, Lingmell, Great End, Broad Crag, Scafell Pike, Cat Bields, Scafell, Glade How, Slight Side, Buckbarrow, Whin Rigg, Illgill Head, Great Carrs, Swirl How, Grey Friar, Harter Fell (tip only), Dow Crag, Coniston Old Man

7½ miles, 5 miles, 2½, 10 miles

Lakes and Tarns
NE: Low Tarn
E to S: Wastwater

Wastwater Screes from Middle Fell

Pillar 2927'

from Brin Crag, Brandreth

Pillar 2

NATURAL FEATURES

Great Gable, Pillar and Steeple are the three mountain names on Lakeland maps most likely to fire the imagination of youthful adventurers planning a first tour of the district, inspiring exciting visions of slim, near-vertical pinnacles towering grandly into the sky.

Great Gable lives up to its name, especially if climbed from Wasdale; Pillar has a fine bold outline but is nothing like a pillar; Steeple is closely overlooked by a higher flat-topped fell and not effectively seen.

Pillar, in fact, far from being a spire of slender proportions, is a rugged mass broadly based on half the length of Ennerdale, a series of craggy buttresses supporting the ridge high above this wild north face; and the summit itself, far from being pointed, is wide and flat. The name of the fell therefore clearly derives from a conspicuous feature on the north face directly below the top, the most handsome crag in Lakeland, originally known as the Pillar Stone and now as Pillar Rock. The Rock, despite a remote and lonely situation, had a well-established local notoriety and fame long before tourists called wider attention to it, and an object of such unique appearance simply had to be given a descriptive name, although, at the time, one was not yet needed to identify the mountain of which it formed part. *The Pillar* was an inspiration of shepherds. Men of letters could not have chosen better.

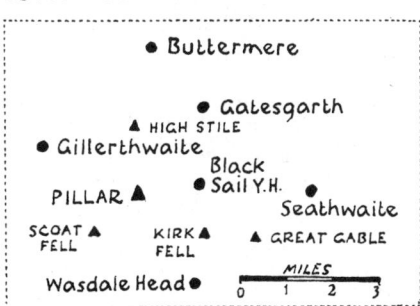

The north face of the fell has a formidable aspect. Crags and shadowed hollows, scree and tumbled boulders, form a wild, chaotic scene, a setting worthy of a fine mountain.

continued

Pillar 3

NATURAL FEATURES
continued

Pillar is the highest mountain west of Great Gable, from which it is sufficiently removed in distance to exhibit distinctive slopes on all sides. It dominates the sunset area of Lakeland superbly, springing out of the valleys of Mosedale and Ennerdale, steeply on the one side and dramatically on the other, as befits the overlord of the western scene. A narrow neck of land connects with a chain of other grand fells to the south, and a depression forms the east boundary and is crossed by Black Sail Pass at 1800', but elsewhere the full height of the fell from valley level is displayed. Some of the streams flow west via Ennerdale Water and some south via Wast Water, but their fate, discharge into the Irish Sea from the coast near Seascale, is the same, only a few miles separating the two outlets.

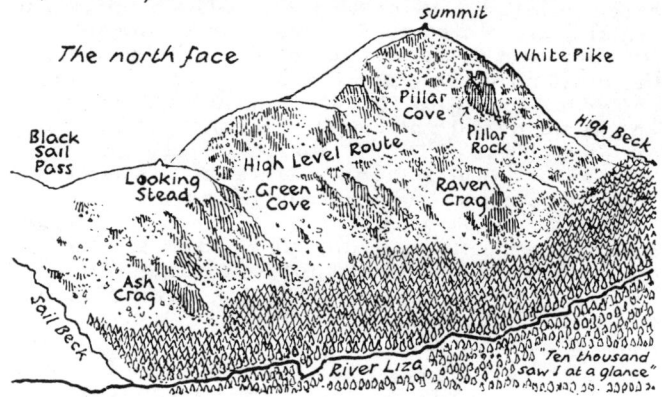

The north face — summit, White Pike, Pillar Cove, Pillar Rock, High Beck, Black Sail Pass, Looking Stead, High Level Route, Green Cove, Raven Crag, Ash Crag, Sail Beck, River Liza, "Ten thousand saw I at a glance"

Afforestation in Ennerdale has cloaked the lower slopes on this side in a dark and funereal shroud of foreign trees, an intrusion that nobody who knew Ennerdale of old can ever forgive, the former charm of the valley having been destroyed thereby. We condemn vandalism and sanction this mess! Far better the old desolation of boulder and bog when a man could see the sky, than this new desolation of regimented timber shutting out the light of day. It is an offence to the eyes to see Pillar's once-colourful fellside now hobbled in such a dowdy and ill-suited skirt, just as it is to see a noble animal caught in a trap. Yet, such is the majesty and power of this fine mountain that it can shrug off the insults and indignities, and its summit soars no less proudly above. It is the admirers of this grand pile who feel the hurt.

Pillar 4

A Pillar Rock portfolio

from the east

Pillar 5

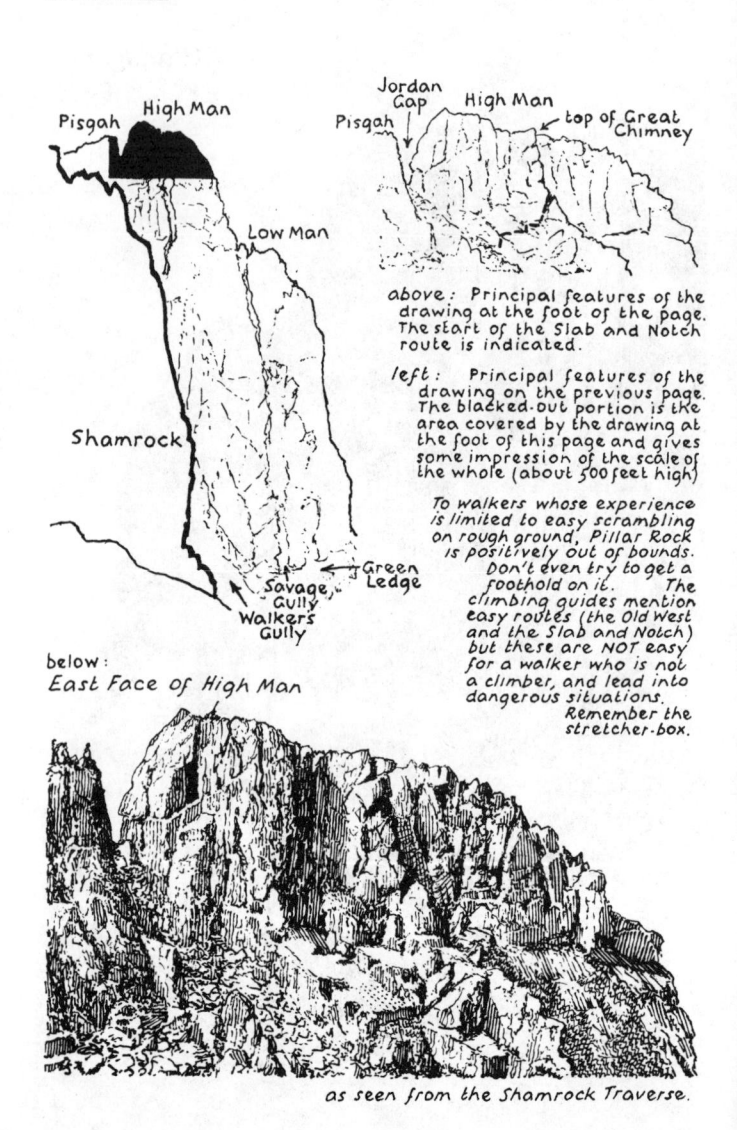

above: Principal features of the drawing at the foot of the page. The start of the Slab and Notch route is indicated.

left: Principal features of the drawing on the previous page. The blacked-out portion is the area covered by the drawing at the foot of this page and gives some impression of the scale of the whole (about 500 feet high)

To walkers whose experience is limited to easy scrambling on rough ground, Pillar Rock is positively out of bounds.
 Don't even try to get a foothold on it. The climbing guides mention easy routes (the Old West and the Slab and Notch) but these are NOT easy for a walker who is not a climber, and lead into dangerous situations.
 Remember the stretcher-box.

below:
East Face of High Man

as seen from the Shamrock Traverse.

Pillar 6

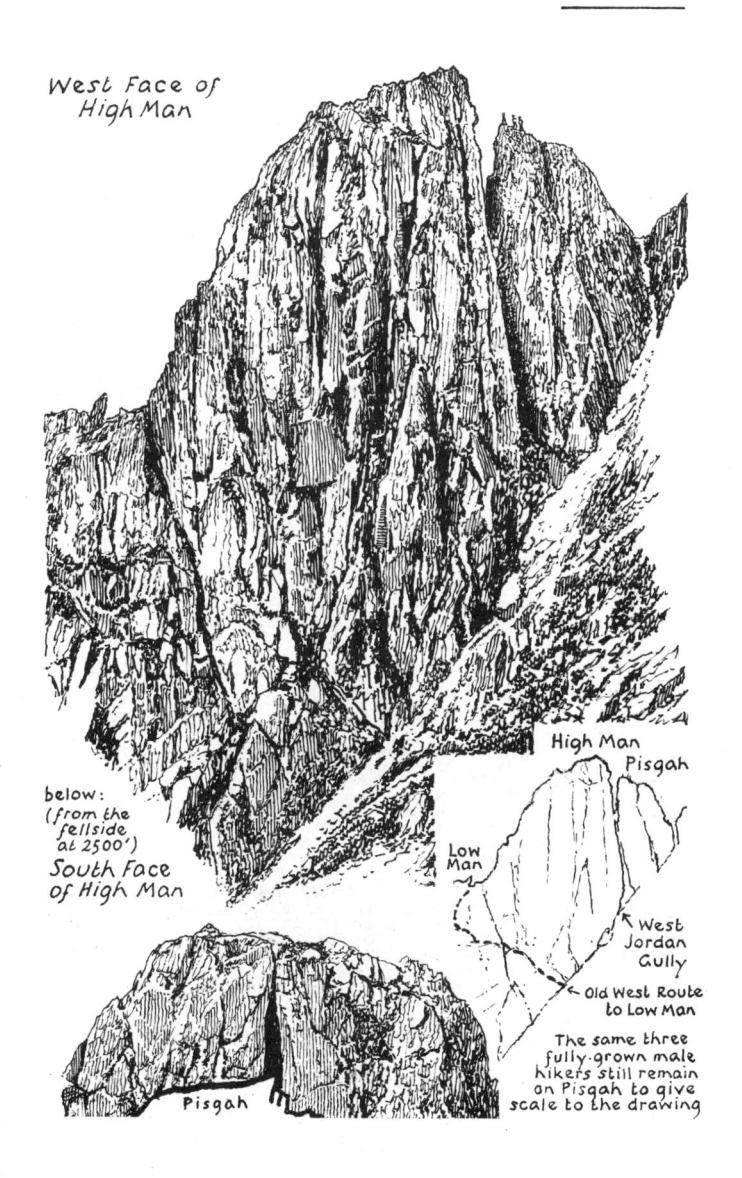

West Face of
High Man

below:
(from the
fellside
at 2500')
South Face
of High Man

Pisgah

High Man
Pisgah
Low Man
← West Jordan Gully
← Old West Route to Low Man

The same three fully-grown male hikers still remain on Pisgah to give scale to the drawing

Pillar 7

MAP

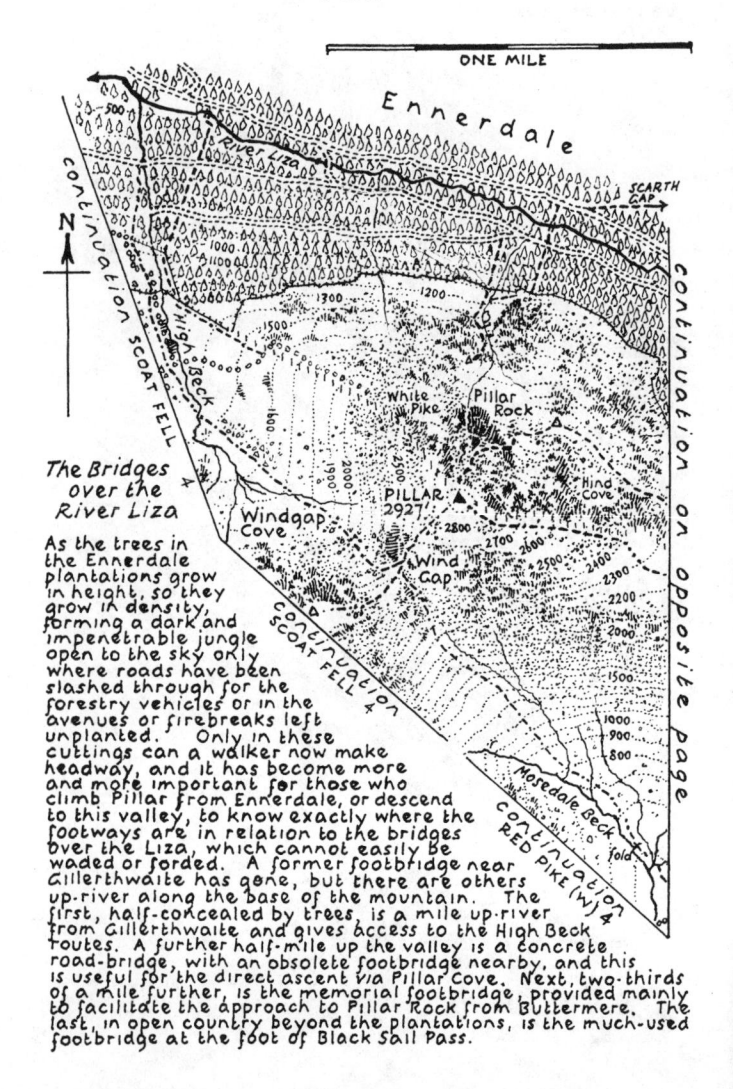

⟵ ONE MILE ⟶

The Bridges over the River Liza

As the trees in the Ennerdale plantations grow in height, so they grow in density, forming a dark and impenetrable jungle open to the sky only where roads have been slashed through for the forestry vehicles or in the avenues or firebreaks left unplanted. Only in these cuttings can a walker now make headway, and it has become more and more important for those who climb Pillar from Ennerdale, or descend to this valley, to know exactly where the footways are in relation to the bridges over the Liza, which cannot easily be waded or forded. A former footbridge near Gillerthwaite has gone, but there are others up-river along the base of the mountain. The first, half-concealed by trees, is a mile up-river from Gillerthwaite and gives access to the High Beck routes. A further half-mile up the valley is a concrete road-bridge, with an obsolete footbridge nearby, and this is useful for the direct ascent via Pillar Cove. Next, two-thirds of a mile further, is the memorial footbridge, provided mainly to facilitate the approach to Pillar Rock from Buttermere. The last, in open country beyond the plantations, is the much-used footbridge at the foot of Black Sail Pass.

Pillar 8

MAP

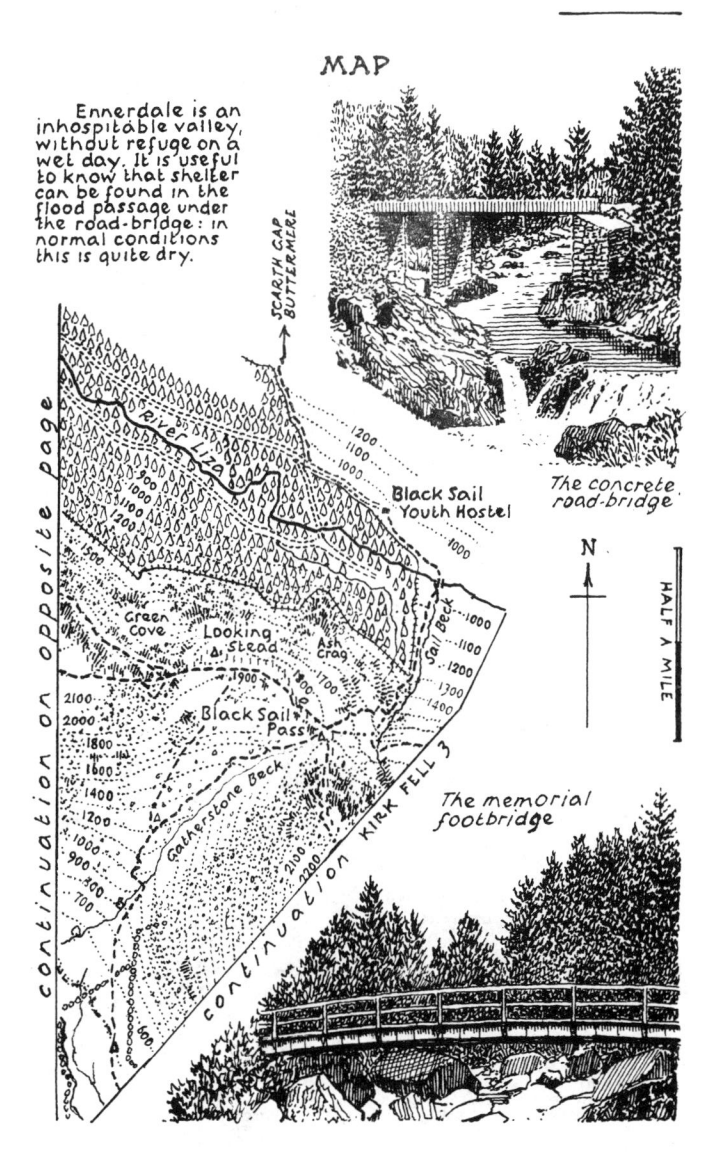

Ennerdale is an inhospitable valley, without refuge on a wet day. It is useful to know that shelter can be found in the flood passage under the road-bridge: in normal conditions this is quite dry.

The concrete road-bridge

The memorial footbridge

Pillar 9

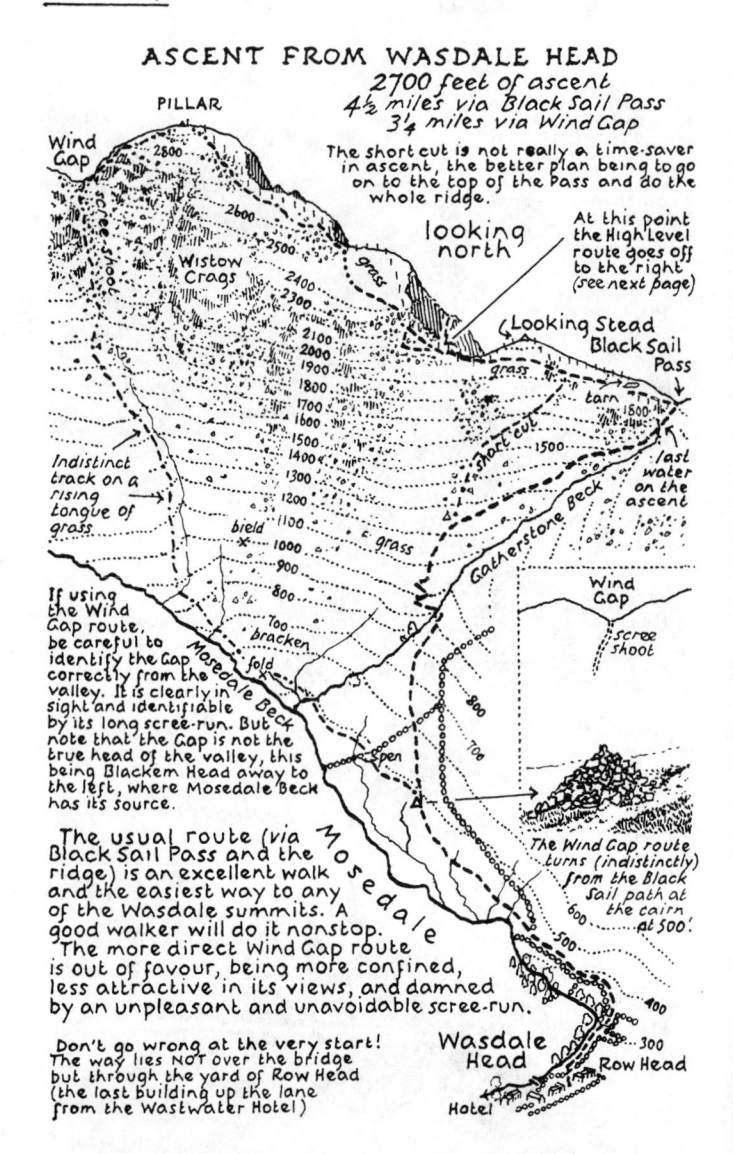

ASCENT FROM WASDALE HEAD
2700 feet of ascent
4½ miles via Black Sail Pass
3¼ miles via Wind Gap

The short cut is not really a time-saver in ascent, the better plan being to go on to the top of the Pass and do the whole ridge.

looking north

PILLAR
Wind Gap
Wistow Crags
Indistinct track on a rising tongue of grass
bield
Looking Stead
Black Sail Pass
tarn
short cut
last water on the ascent
Gatherstone Beck

Wind Gap
scree shoot

If using the Wind Gap route, be careful to identify the Gap correctly from the valley. It is clearly in sight and identifiable by its long scree-run. But note that the Gap is not the true head of the valley, this being Blackem Head away to the left, where Mosedale Beck has its source.

too bracken
fold
Mosedale Beck

The Wind Gap route turns (indistinctly) from the Black Sail path at the cairn at 500'.

The usual route (via Black Sail Pass and the ridge) is an excellent walk and the easiest way to any of the Wasdale summits. A good walker will do it nonstop.
The more direct Wind Gap route is out of favour, being more confined, less attractive in its views, and damned by an unpleasant and unavoidable scree-run.

Don't go wrong at the very start! The way lies NOT over the bridge but through the yard of Row Head (the last building up the lane from the Wastwater Hotel)

Wasdale Head
Row Head
Hotel

Pillar 10

ASCENT FROM ENNERDALE
(BLACK SAIL YOUTH HOSTEL)
2000 feet of ascent : 2¾ miles
(2100 feet, 3 miles by High Level Route)

PILLAR

Originally the High Level Route had an awkward start. A new variation avoids the difficulty.

Pillar Rock

Great Doup

stretcher box

Hind Cove

grass

Green Cove

Robinson's Cairn

High Level Route

The main ridge, from Black Sail Pass to the summit, is a pleasant walk without difficulty, three stony rises being succeeded by splendid turf. A line of iron posts accompanies the ridge but the path, in many places, deviates to the left.
The High Level route is a traverse across the fellside (aiming for Pillar Rock), not a way to the summit, although the two can be connected (see next page). This is a fine pedestrian way, highly recommended, rough but not difficult.

← detail →

Looking Stead

WASDALE HEAD direct route

tarn

WASDALE HEAD

Black Sail Pass

There is a gate at the top of the pass but only a fanatical purist would think of using it.

The path avoids the actual top of Looking Stead, but walkers should not. It is an excellent viewpoint for a survey, both of the High Level route and of Ennerdale.

Main ridge:
1: zigzag path
2: direct path
High Level route:
3: original start
4: new variation
Main ridge
5: from Black Sail

Ash Crag

River Liza

Sail Beck

Black Sail Y.H.

moraines

Sojourners at the hostel are fortunate in having Pillar on their doorstep, and can enjoy one of the best days of their young lives by climbing it.

looking west

Pillar 11

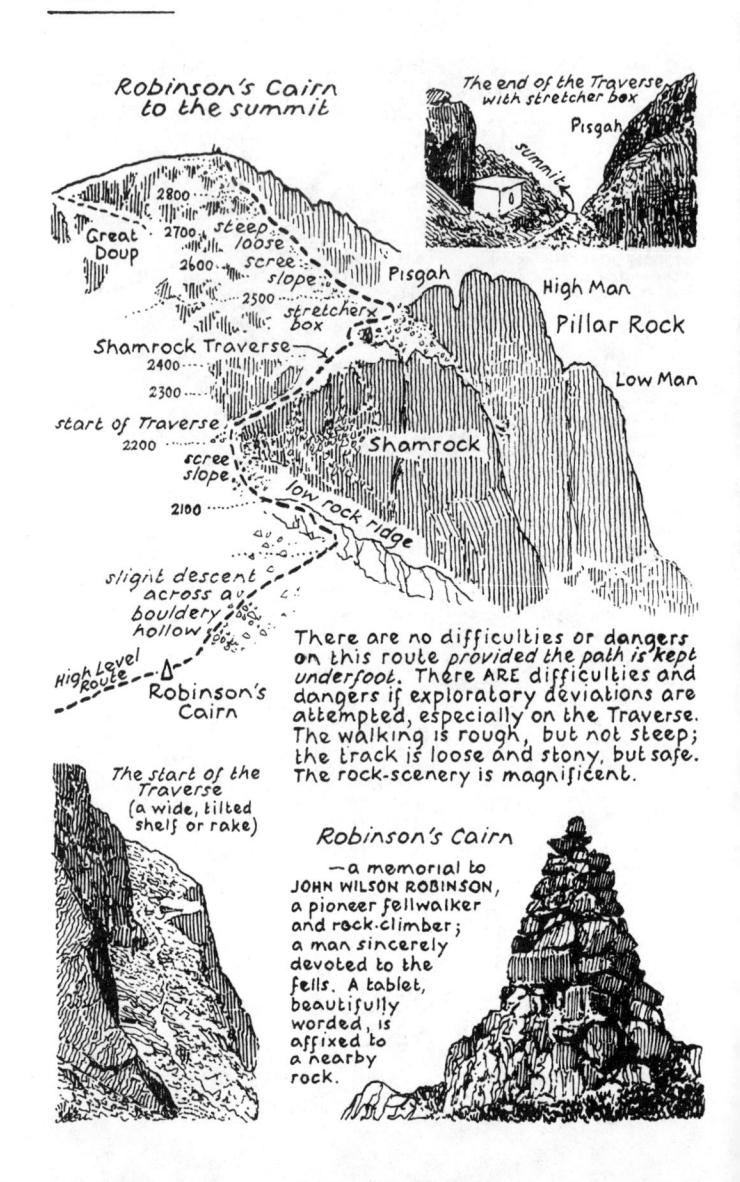

Robinson's Cairn to the summit

The end of the Traverse with stretcher box
Pisgah
summit

2800
Great Doup
2700
steep loose scree slope
2600
2500
Pisgah
stretcher box
High Man
Shamrock Traverse
Pillar Rock
2400
2300
Low Man
start of Traverse
2200
scree slope
Shamrock
2100
low rock ridge

slight descent across a bouldery hollow

High Level Route
Robinson's Cairn

There are no difficulties or dangers on this route *provided the path is kept underfoot*. There ARE difficulties and dangers if exploratory deviations are attempted, especially on the Traverse. The walking is rough, but not steep; the track is loose and stony, but safe. The rock-scenery is magnificent.

The start of the Traverse (a wide, tilted shelf or rake)

Robinson's Cairn

—a memorial to JOHN WILSON ROBINSON, a pioneer fellwalker and rock-climber; a man sincerely devoted to the fells. A tablet, beautifully worded, is affixed to a nearby rock.

Pillar 12

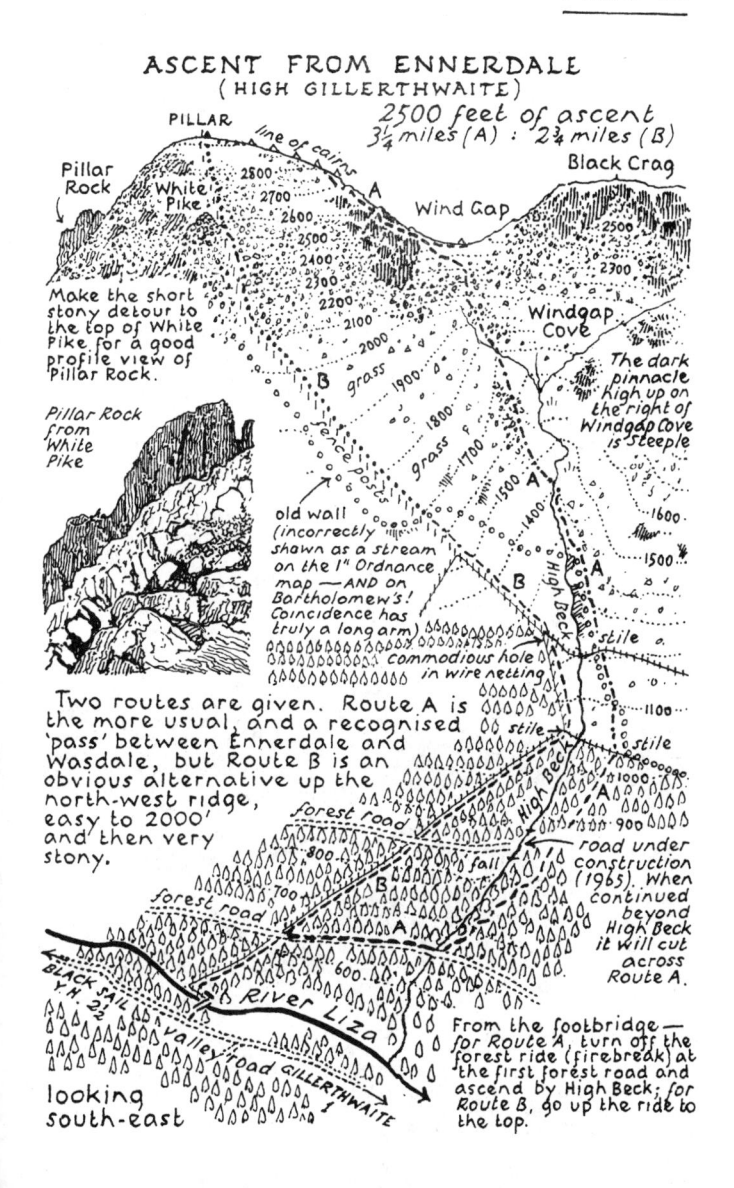

ASCENT FROM ENNERDALE
(HIGH GILLERTHWAITE)
2500 feet of ascent
3¼ miles (A) : 2¾ miles (B)

PILLAR — Pillar Rock — White Pike — 2800 — 2700 — 2600 — 2500 — 2400 — 2300 — 2200 — 2100 — 2000 — line of cairns — A — Wind Gap — Black Crag — 2500 — 2300

Make the short stony detour to the top of White Pike for a good profile view of Pillar Rock.

Windgap Cove

The dark pinnacle high up on the right of Windgap Cove is steeple

B — grass — 1900 — 1800 — grass — 1700 — 1600 — 1500 — A — 1400 — 1500

Pillar Rock from White Pike

old wall (incorrectly shown as a stream on the 1" Ordnance map — AND on Bartholomew's! Coincidence has truly a long arm)

High Beck — B — stile — commodious hole in wire netting — 1100 — stile — stile — 1000 — 900

Two routes are given. Route A is the more usual, and a recognised 'pass' between Ennerdale and Wasdale, but Route B is an obvious alternative up the north-west ridge, easy to 2000' and then very stony.

forest road — 800 — fall — 700 — forest road — B — A — 600

road under construction (1965). When continued beyond High Beck it will cut across Route A.

BLACK SAIL Y.H. 2½ — valley road GILLERTHWAITE

River Liza

looking south-east

From the footbridge — for Route A, turn off the forest ride (firebreak) at the first forest road and ascend by High Beck; for Route B, go up the ride to the top.

Pillar 13

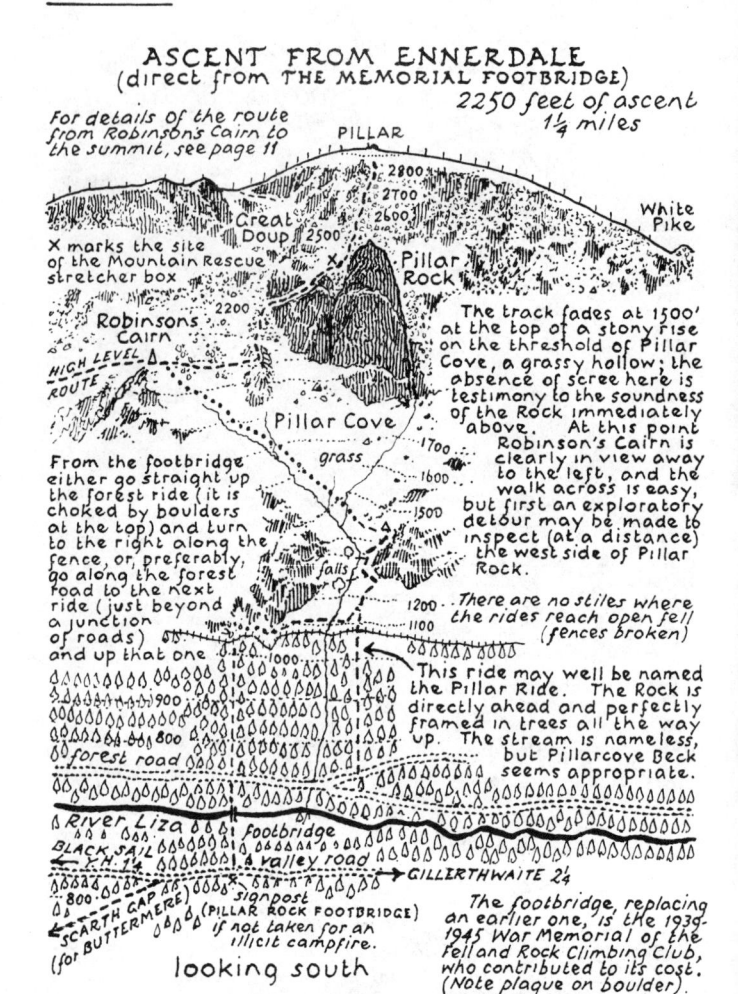

ASCENT FROM ENNERDALE
(direct from THE MEMORIAL FOOTBRIDGE)

2250 feet of ascent
1¼ miles

For details of the route from Robinson's Cairn to the summit, see page 11

PILLAR
2800
2700
2600
White Pike
Great Doup 2500
Pillar Rock
X marks the site of the Mountain Rescue stretcher box
2200
Robinson's Cairn
HIGH LEVEL ROUTE
Pillar Cove
grass
1700
1600
1500
falls
1200
1100
1000
900
800
forest road
River Liza
footbridge
BLACK SAIL
F.H. 14
valley road → GILLERTHWAITE 2½
800
SCARTH GAP
(for BUTTERMERE)
signpost
(PILLAR ROCK FOOTBRIDGE)
if not taken for an illicit campfire.

The track fades at 1500' at the top of a stony rise on the threshold of Pillar Cove, a grassy hollow; the absence of scree here is testimony to the soundness of the Rock immediately above. At this point Robinson's Cairn is clearly in view away to the left, and the walk across is easy, but first an exploratory detour may be made to inspect (at a distance) the west side of Pillar Rock.

From the footbridge either go straight up the forest ride (it is choked by boulders at the top) and turn to the right along the fence, or, preferably, go along the forest road to the next ride (just beyond a junction of roads) and up that one

There are no stiles where the rides reach open fell (fences broken)

This ride may well be named the Pillar Ride. The Rock is directly ahead and perfectly framed in trees all the way up. The stream is nameless, but Pillarcove Beck seems appropriate.

The footbridge, replacing an earlier one, is the 1939-1945 War Memorial of the Fell and Rock Climbing Club, who contributed to its cost. (Note plaque on boulder).

looking south

A steep and rough, but romantic and adventurous climb in magnificent surroundings: the finest way up the mountain. Pillar Rock grips the attention throughout. Unfortunately the route is somewhat remote from tourist centres, but strong walkers can do it from Buttermere via Scarth Gap.

Pillar 14

ASCENT FROM BUTTERMERE

Most walkers when planning to climb a mountain aim to avoid any downhill section between their starting-point and the summit, and if the intermediate descent is considerable the extra effort of regaining lost height may rule out the attempt altogether. A good example is Great Gable from Langdale, where the descent from Esk Hause to Sty Head is a loss of height of 700 feet and a double loss of this amount if returning to Langdale. Plus the 3000' of effective ascent, this is too much for the average walker. Distance is of less consequence. The same applies to ascent of Pillar from Buttermere. This is a glorious walk, full of interest, but it cannot be done without first climbing the High Stile range (at Scarth Gap) and then descending into Ennerdale before setting foot on Pillar. If returning to Buttermere, Ennerdale and the High Stile range will have to be crossed again towards the end of an exhausting day. There is no sadder sight than a Buttermere-bound pedestrian crossing Scarth Gap on his hands and knees as the shadows of evening steal o'er the scene. The route is therefore recommended for strong walkers only.

The most thrilling line of ascent of Pillar is by way of the memorial footbridge, this being very conveniently situated for the Buttermere approach ('the bridge was, in fact, provided to give access to Pillar from this direction). A slanting route down to the footbridge leaves the Scarth Gap path some 150 yards on the Ennerdale side of the pass. The bifurcation is not clear, but the track goes off to the right above the plantation, becoming distinct and crossing the fences by three stiles. The climb from the bridge is described on the opposite page. A less arduous route of ascent is to keep to the Scarth Gap path into Ennerdale and climb out of the valley by Black Sail Pass to its top, where follow the ridge on the right — but this easier way had better be reserved for the return when energy is flagging.

To find the slanting path from Scarth Gap look for the rocky knoll, with tree (illustrated) and turn right on grass above it

Via the footbridge : 3550 feet of ascent : 5¼ miles
Via Black Sail Pass : 3250 feet of ascent : 6¼ miles

Pillar Rock, from the north

The Pillar Ride

Pillar 15

THE SUMMIT

As in the case of many fells of rugged appearance, the summit is one of the smoothest places on Pillar, and one may perambulate within a 50-yard radius of the cairn without being aware of the declivities on all sides. There are stones, but grass predominates. The number of erections, including two wind-shelters and a survey column, testifies to the importance of the summit in the esteem of fellwalkers and map-makers.

DESCENTS:

To Wasdale Head: In fair weather or foul, there is one royal road down to Wasdale Head, and that is by the eastern ridge to join Black Sail Pass on its journey thereto. The views are superb, and the walking is so easy for the most part that they can be enjoyed while on the move. There should be no difficulty in following the path in mist — only in one cairned section is it indistinct — but the fence-posts are there in any event as a guide to the top of the Pass. Ten minutes can be saved by the short cut going down from the side of Looking Stead. The route into Mosedale via Wind Gap is much less satisfactory, and no quicker although shorter. Another way into Mosedale sometimes used is the obvious scree-gully opening off the ridge opposite the head of Great Doup, but why suffer the torture of a half-mile of loose stones when the ridge is so much easier and pleasanter?

To Ennerdale: If bound for Black Sail Hostel, follow the eastern ridge to the pass, and there turn left on a clear path. If bound for Gillerthwaite or places west, follow the fence-posts northwest for White Pike and its ridge, which has a rough section of boulders below the Pike; but in stormy weather prefer the route joining High Beck from Wind Gap.

To Buttermere: In clear weather, the direct route climbing up out of Ennerdale may be reversed; at the forest road beyond the memorial footbridge walk up the valley for 120 yards, then taking a slanting path through the plantation on the left to Scarth Gap. In bad conditions, it is safer to go round by Black Sail Pass.

To any of the above destinations via Robinson's Cairn

Leave the summit at the north wind-shelter. Pillar Rock comes into view at once, and a rough loose track slithers down to the point where the first of its buttresses (Pisgah) rises from the fellside. Here turn right, by the stretcher-box (an excellent landmark) and along the Traverse to easy ground and the Cairn. On no account descend the hollow below the stretcher-box: this narrows to a dangerous funnel of stones and a sheer drop into a gully. (This is known as Walker's Gully, NOT because it is a gully for walkers, but because a man of this name fell to his death here).

PLAN OF THE SUMMIT
100 YARDS

Pillar Rock as seen from the north shelter

Pillar 16

RIDGE ROUTES

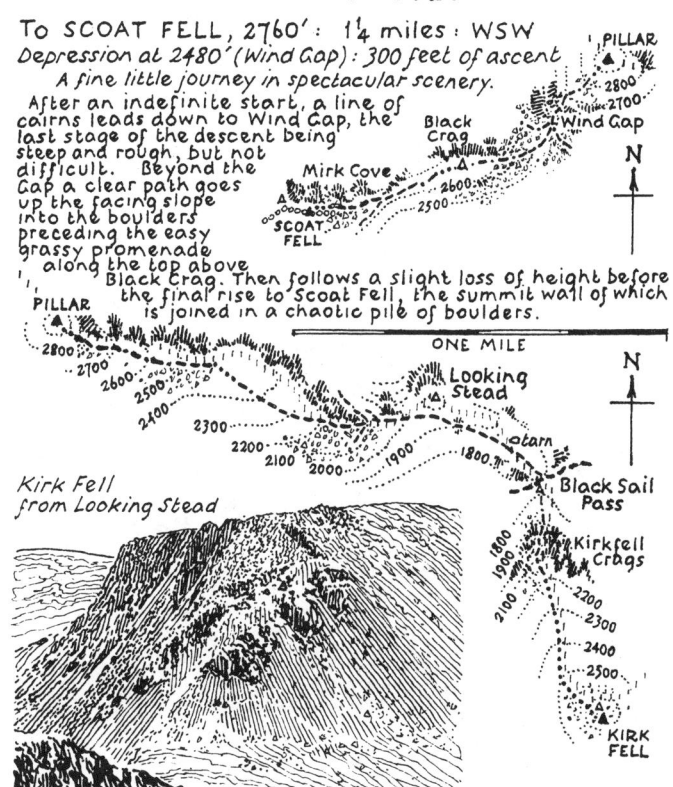

TO SCOAT FELL, 2760': 1¼ miles: WSW
Depression at 2480' (Wind Gap): 300 feet of ascent
A fine little journey in spectacular scenery.

After an indefinite start, a line of cairns leads down to Wind Gap, the last stage of the descent being steep and rough, but not difficult. Beyond the Gap a clear path goes up the facing slope into the boulders preceding the easy grassy promenade along the top above Black Crag. Then follows a slight loss of height before the final rise to Scoat Fell, the summit wall of which is joined in a chaotic pile of boulders.

Kirk Fell from Looking Stead

TO KIRK FELL, 2630': 2½ miles: ESE, then S
Depression at 1800' (Black Sail Pass): 850 feet of ascent
Excellent views, both near and far; a good walk

The Ennerdale fence (what is left of it) links the two tops, and the route never ventures far from it. The eastern ridge of Pillar offers a speedy descent, the path being clear except on one grassy section, which is, however, well cairned. At the Pass, the crags of Kirk Fell look ferocious and hostile, but a thin track goes off bravely to tackle them and can be relied upon to lead to the dull top of Kirk Fell after providing a minor excitement where a high rock step needs to be surmounted.

Pillar 17

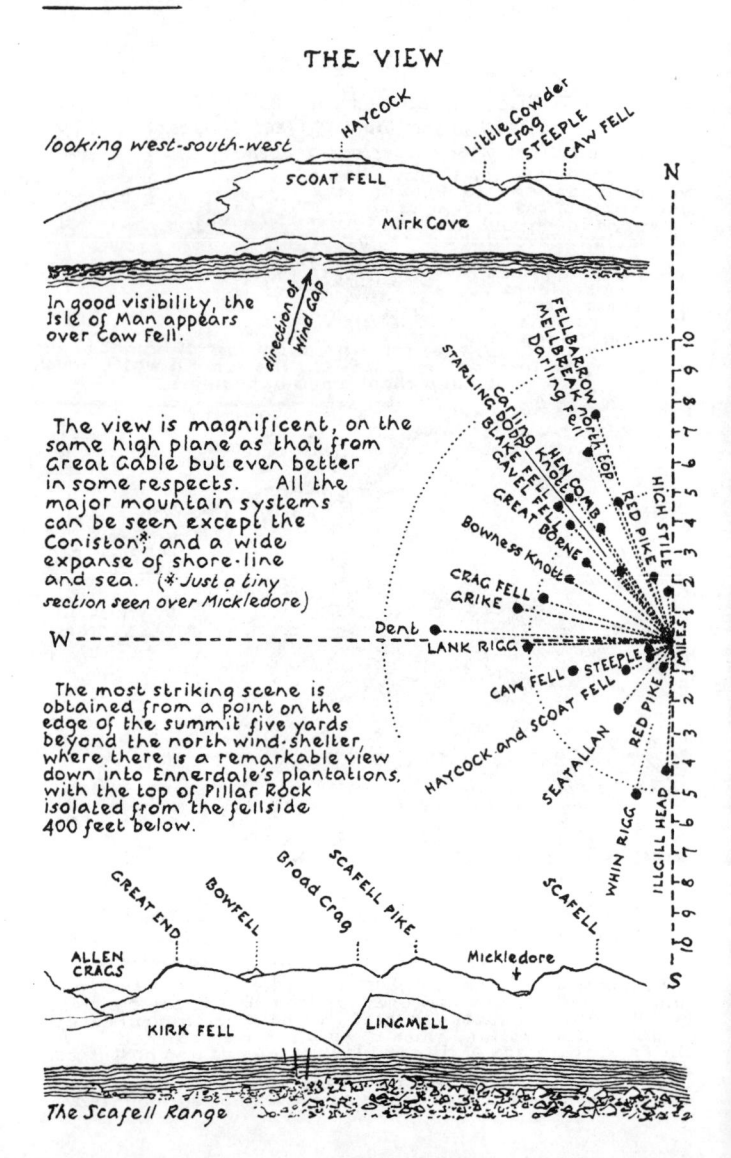

THE VIEW

looking west-south-west

HAYCOCK, Little Cowder Crag, STEEPLE, CAW FELL, SCOAT FELL, Mirk Cove

In good visibility, the Isle of Man appears over Caw Fell.

direction of Wind Gap

The view is magnificent, on the same high plane as that from Great Gable but even better in some respects.   All the major mountain systems can be seen except the Coniston,* and a wide expanse of shore-line and sea.   (*Just a tiny section seen over Mickledore)

W — — — — — — — — — —

The most striking scene is obtained from a point on the edge of the summit five yards beyond the north wind-shelter, where there is a remarkable view down into Ennerdale's plantations, with the top of Pillar Rock isolated from the fellside 400 feet below.

N

FELLBARROW, MELLBREAK North top, Darling Fell, STARLING DODD, CALLING DODD, HEN COMB, BLAKE FELL, GAVEL FELL, GREAT BORNE, HIGH STILE, Bowness Knotts, RED PIKE, CRAG FELL, GRIKE, Dent, LANK RIGG, CAW FELL, STEEPLE, HAYCOCK and SCOAT FELL, RED PIKE, SEATALLAN, WHIN RIGG, ILLGILL HEAD

S

GREAT END, BOWFELL, Broad Crag, SCAFELL PIKE, SCAFELL, ALLEN CRAGS, KIRK FELL, LINGMELL, Mickledore

The Scafell Range

Pillar 18

THE VIEW

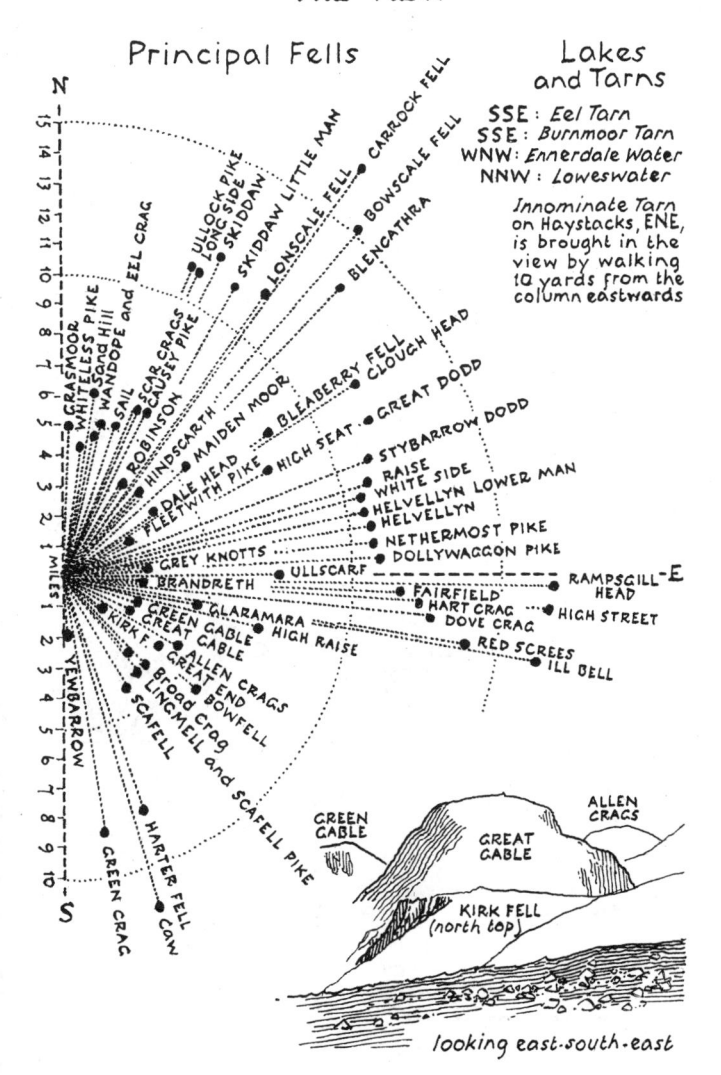

Principal Fells

Lakes and Tarns

SSE: *Eel Tarn*
SSE: *Burnmoor Tarn*
WNW: *Ennerdale Water*
NNW: *Loweswater*

Innominate Tarn on Haystacks, ENE, is brought in the view by walking 10 yards from the column eastwards

N

- ULLOCK PIKE
- LONG SIDE
- SKIDDAW
- SKIDDAW LITTLE MAN
- LONSCALE FELL
- CARROCK FELL
- BOWSCALE FELL
- BLENCATHRA
- GRASMOOR
- WHITELESS PIKE
- WANDOPE and EEL CRAG
- SAIL
- SCAR CRAGS
- CAUSEY PIKE
- ROBINSON
- HINDSCARTH
- DALE HEAD
- MAIDEN MOOR
- BLEABERRY FELL
- CLOUGH HEAD
- FLEETWITH PIKE
- HIGH SEAT
- GREAT DODD
- STYBARROW DODD
- RAISE
- WHITE SIDE
- HELVELLYN LOWER MAN
- HELVELLYN
- NETHERMOST PIKE
- GREY KNOTTS
- ULLSCARF
- DOLLYWAGGON PIKE
- BRANDRETH
- FAIRFIELD
- RAMPSGILL HEAD — E
- GLARAMARA
- HART CRAG
- HIGH STREET
- GREEN GABLE
- HIGH RAISE
- DOVE CRAG
- KIRK F.
- GREAT GABLE
- ALLEN CRAGS
- RED SCREES
- GREAT END
- ILL BELL
- BROAD CRAG
- BOWFELL
- LINGMELL
- SCAFELL
- SCAFELL and SCAFELL PIKE
- YEWBARROW
- HARTER FELL
- CAW
- GREEN CRAG

S

MILES 1–10

looking east-south-east

GREEN GABLE — GREAT GABLE — ALLEN CRAGS — KIRK FELL (north top)

Red Pike
(Buttermere)

2479'

from Crummock Water

The duplication of place-names is a source of confusion and error. In the Lake District there are dozens of Raven Crags and Black Crags, many Dodds, six Mosedales, two Seathwaites, three Sour Milk Gills, and several other instances of name-repetition in different areas.

Amongst the major fells, there are two High Raises, two High Pikes and two Harter Fells — all fortunately well dispersed in widely-separated localities. But two Red Pikes, only three miles apart, require distinct identification. It is usual to refer to the one dealt with in this chapter, which the name aptly fits, as the Buttermere Red Pike, and the other, which is higher and bulkier, but for which the name is less suited, as the Wasdale Red Pike.

Red Pike (B) 2

NATURAL FEATURES

The most-trodden mountain track out of Buttermere, a ladder of stones, leads to the summit of Red Pike (which itself cannot be seen from the village), and indeed this is the only tourist path permitted by the extremely steep and rough fellside on the south, overlooking the valley. Red Pike is deservedly a popular climb: the way to it is both interesting and beautiful, the summit is a graceful cone without complications, the cairn being set exactly at the head of the path; and the view is excellent. Less imposing than its near neighbour, High Stile, Red Pike is nevertheless a greater favourite with visitors (which is unjustifiable on merit).

Following the general pattern of the mountains in the High Stile series, Red Pike sends out a stony buttress to the north-east, but unlike its fellows this one succeeds a depression, the Saddle, and then rises to a subsidiary, Dodd, before plunging down to the valley, the final slope being pleasantly wooded and featuring the attraction everybody remembers Buttermere by — the long cascade of Sour Milk Gill. Westwards, Red Pike extends a curving arm trending north to Crummock, and within it nestles the heathery hollow of Ling Comb; outside its curve the fell creases into a watercourse, and here is another of Red Pike's star attractions, Lakeland's highest waterfall, Scale Force. East of the buttress, shared with High Stile, is the hanging valley of Bleaberry Comb and a secluded tarn, thought to occupy the crater of a dead volcano. To the south the fell slopes steeply down, without incident, to Ennerdale.

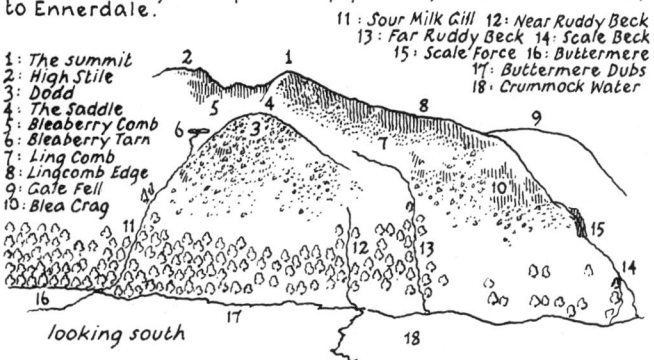

1: The summit
2: High Stile
3: Dodd
4: The Saddle
5: Bleaberry Comb
6: Bleaberry Tarn
7: Ling Comb
8: Lingcomb Edge
9: Gale Fell
10: Blea Crag
11: Sour Milk Gill
12: Near Ruddy Beck
13: Far Ruddy Beck
14: Scale Beck
15: Scale Force
16: Buttermere
17: Buttermere Dubs
18: Crummock Water

looking south

Syenite in the rock and subsoil of the fell produces the rich red colouring that has given Red Pike its name and this is particularly marked in places where surface disturbance has occurred (the stony track by the side of Scale Force is a good example), remaining brilliant until weathering results in a more sombre ruddiness.

Red Pike (B) 3

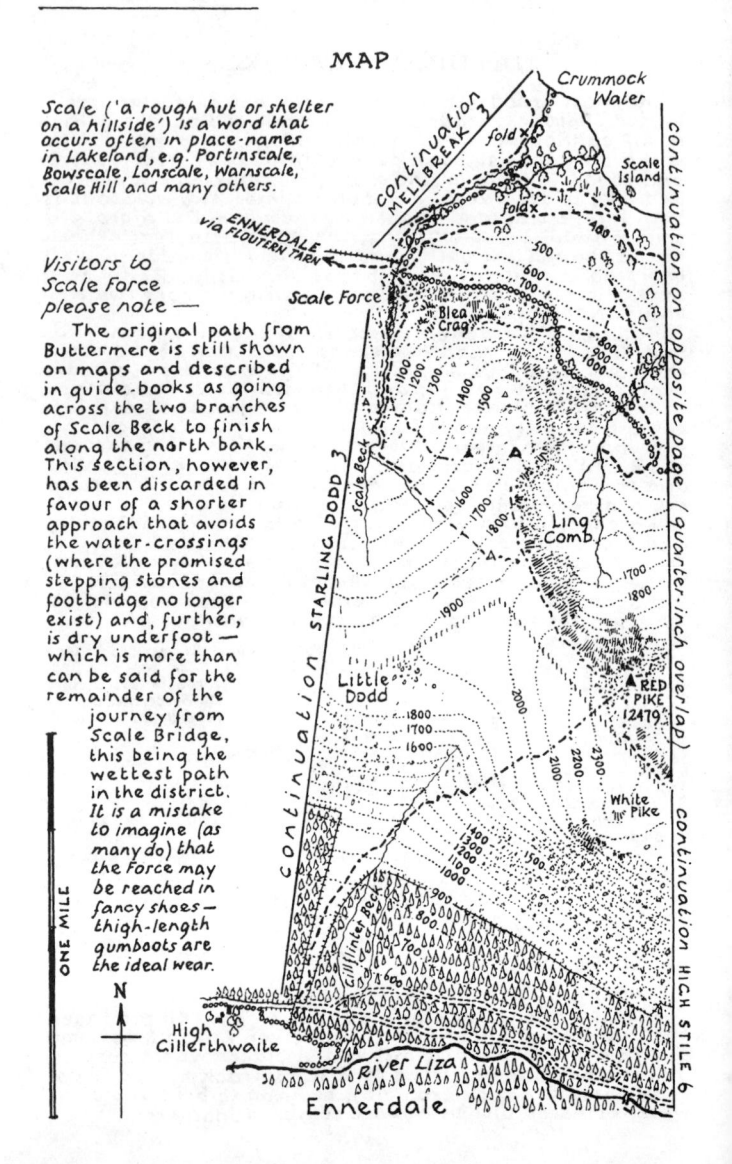

MAP

Scale ('a rough hut or shelter on a hillside') is a word that occurs often in place-names in Lakeland, e.g. Portinscale, Bowscale, Lonscale, Warnscale, Scale Hill and many others.

Visitors to Scale Force please note —

The original path from Buttermere is still shown on maps and described in guide-books as going across the two branches of Scale Beck to finish along the north bank. This section, however, has been discarded in favour of a shorter approach that avoids the water-crossings (where the promised stepping stones and footbridge no longer exist) and, further, is dry underfoot — which is more than can be said for the remainder of the journey from Scale Bridge, this being the wettest path in the district. It is a mistake to imagine (as many do) that the Force may be reached in fancy shoes — thigh-length gumboots are the ideal wear.

Red Pike (B) 4

MAP

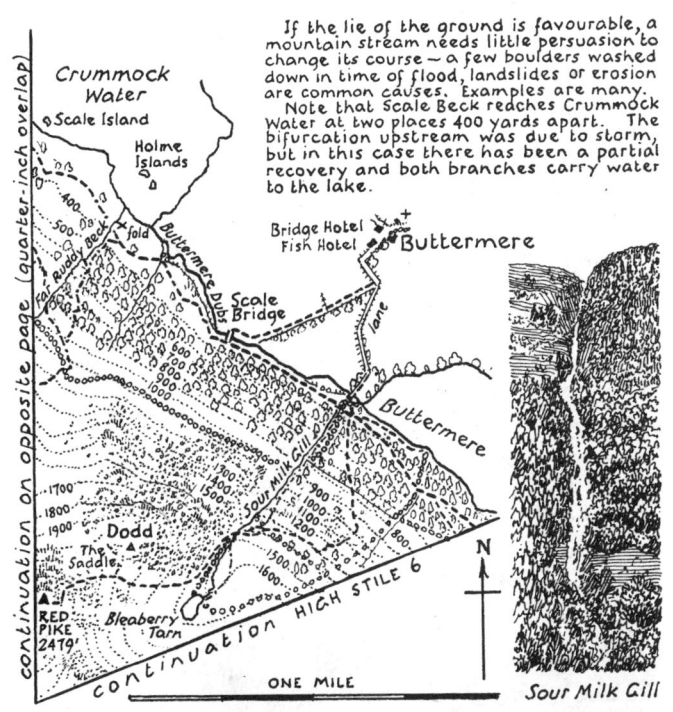

If the lie of the ground is favourable, a mountain stream needs little persuasion to change its course — a few boulders washed down in time of flood, landslides or erosion are common causes. Examples are many.

Note that Scale Beck reaches Crummock Water at two places 400 yards apart. The bifurcation upstream was due to storm, but in this case there has been a partial recovery and both branches carry water to the lake.

Sour Milk Gill

Scale Bridge

Red Pike (B) 5

ASCENT FROM BUTTERMERE
via BLEABERRY TARN
2150 feet of ascent : 1¾ miles

RIDGE TO HIGH STILE

Chapel Crags

RED PIKE

The Saddle

Dodd often hides Red Pike, and is mistaken for it, in views from the valley. The summit of Red Pike cannot be seen from Buttermere village.

At Bleaberry Tarn, Red Pike is seen to be aptly named, the screes below the top having a distinctly ruddy colour.

Bleaberry Tarn

the path fords the stream here, but if it is desired to visit the tarn keep on with the stream on the right.

The line of the route is excellent, affording superb views; a better one could not be devised. BUT the path itself is everywhere very stony (except on the grassy shelf midway) and becoming worse annually. It is clear from the undisturbed ground nearby that the stones have been brought to the surface by the tread of many feet. The stones are loose and ready to slide, making care especially necessary when descending.

bilberry
grassy shelf

Burtness Wood

SCARTH GAP

Sourmilk Gill

SCALE BRIDGE

The variation start, climbing alongside Sourmilk Gill from its foot, is scarcely worth considering. The way up, amongst trees and boulders, is steep and rough, greasy and spidery. But the cascades are beautiful!

Buttermere Dubs

Three footbridges and a lofty stile give access to the Wood

Buttermere (the lake)

unsurfaced lane, always muddy, but much used by visitors

looking south-west

SCALE BRIDGE

Fish Hotel

Buttermere

Buttermere is surrounded by fine mountains, but the challenge of Red Pike predominates and, as the state of the path testifies, it is a very popular objective by the route here shown, this being the most obvious and direct way to the top.

Red Pike (B) 6

ASCENT FROM BUTTERMERE
via FAR RUDDY BECK

2150 feet of ascent
2¼ miles

RED PIKE

The Saddle

Dodd

Lingcomb Edge

looking south-west

a simple cairn

heather

Ling Comb

heather

The shepherd's track ends at the stream. Here turn up left through heather (dense; no path; hard work), keeping the valley in sight to enjoy the fine view of Crummock Water. Aim for the Saddle.

heather

shepherds track

The two Ruddy Becks are named from their red stones. Identify the Far one by its sheepfold. The track uphill through the wood is not distinct, but it can be followed by trial and error.

Waterfall. Far Ruddy Beck

Near Ruddy Beck

Far Ruddy Beck

fall

fold

SCALE FORCE

BUTTERMERE (LAKE)

Buttermere Dubs

Scale Bridge

Crummock Water

sign — field path — gate — lane — Fish Hotel

Buttermere

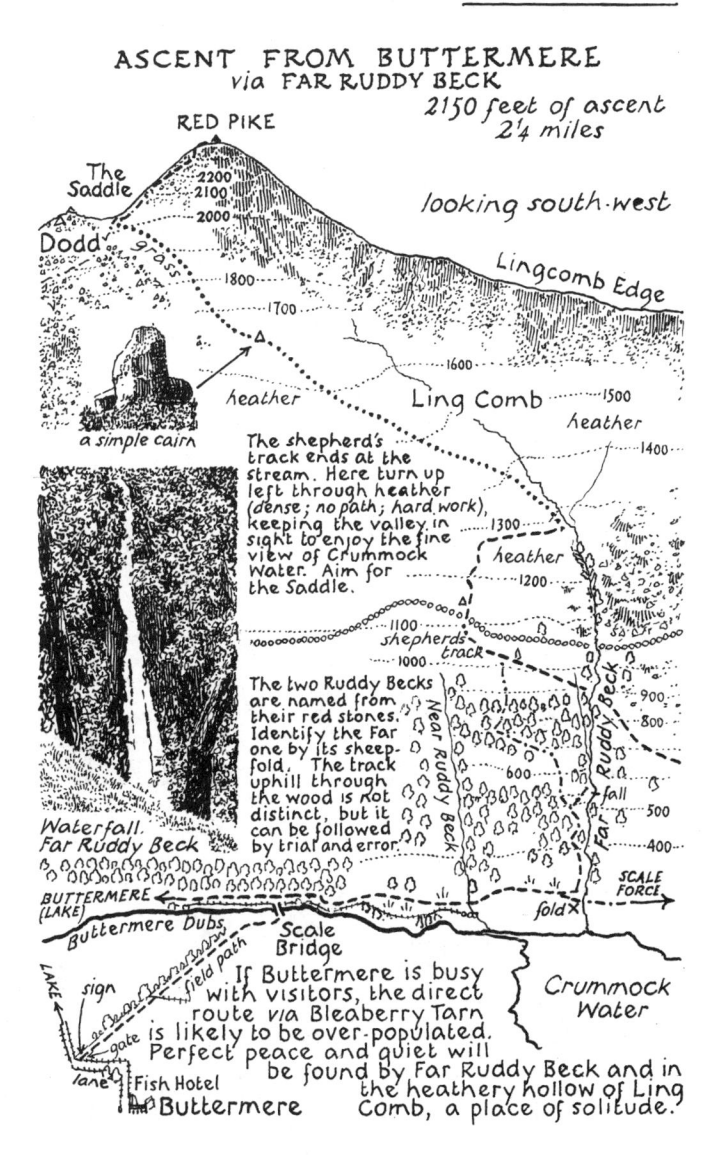

If Buttermere is busy with visitors, the direct route via Bleaberry Tarn is likely to be over-populated. Perfect peace and quiet will be found by Far Ruddy Beck and in the heathery hollow of Ling Comb, a place of solitude.

Red Pike (B) 7

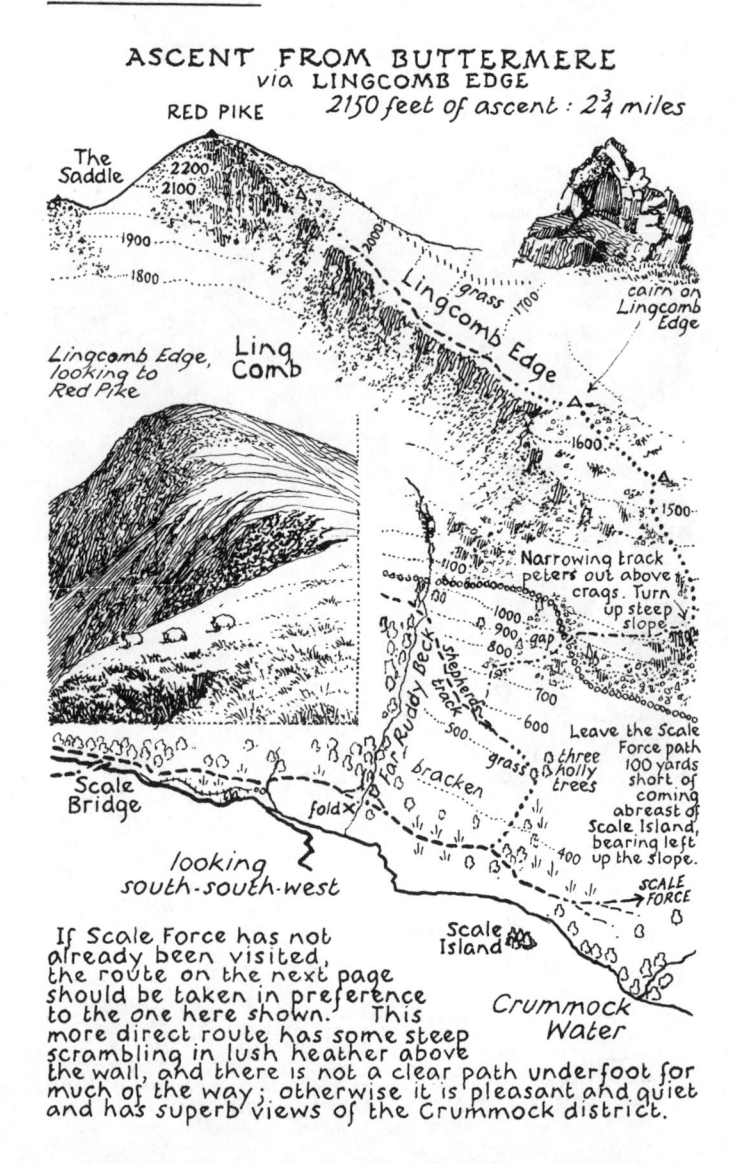

ASCENT FROM BUTTERMERE
via LINGCOMB EDGE
2150 feet of ascent : 2¾ miles

RED PIKE
The Saddle
2200
2100
1900
1800
2000
Lingcomb Edge
grass
1700
cairn on Lingcomb Edge

Lingcomb Edge, looking to Red Pike

Ling Comb

1600
1500

Narrowing track peters out above crags. Turn up steep slope

1100
1000
900 gap
800
shepherds track
700
600
three holly trees

Leave the Scale Force path 100 yards short of coming abreast of Scale Island, bearing left up the slope.

Far Ruddy Beck
500
grass
bracken
400

Scale Bridge
fold ×

looking south-south-west

SCALE FORCE

Scale Island

Crummock Water

If Scale Force has not already been visited, the route on the next page should be taken in preference to the one here shown.   This more direct route has some steep scrambling in lush heather above the wall, and there is not a clear path underfoot for much of the way; otherwise it is pleasant and quiet and has superb views of the Crummock district.

Red Pike (B) 8

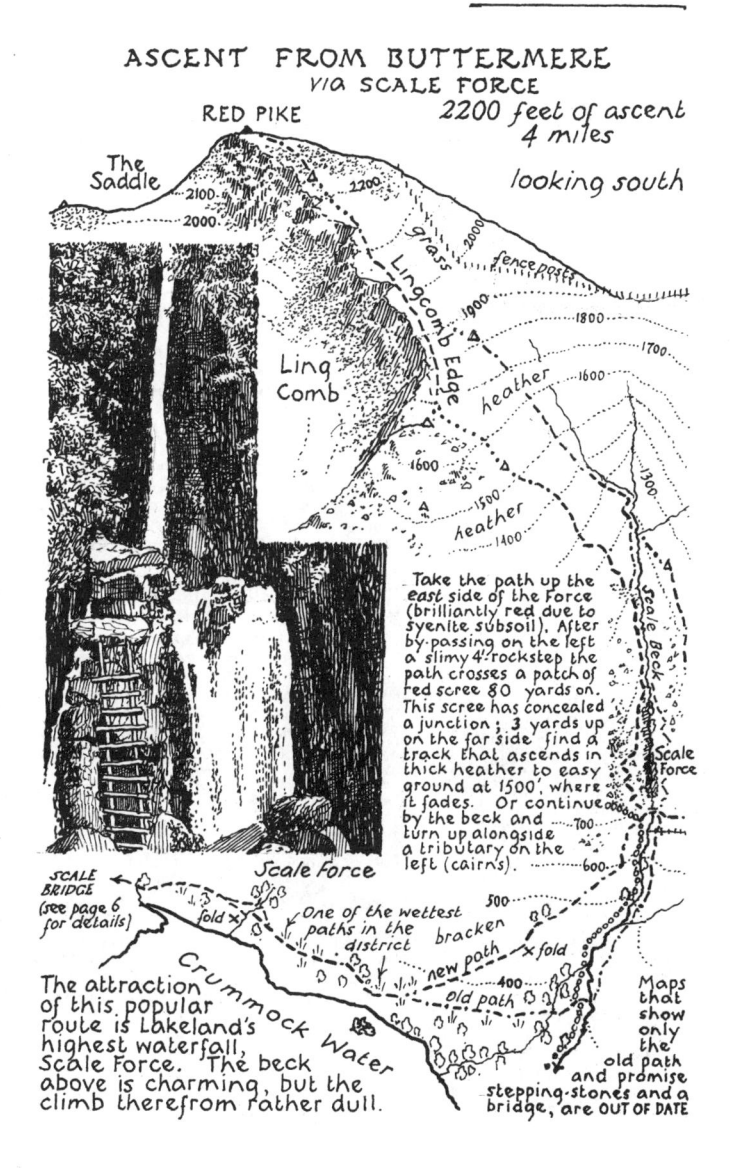

ASCENT FROM BUTTERMERE
VIA SCALE FORCE

2200 feet of ascent
4 miles

looking south

RED PIKE
The Saddle
Ling Comb
Lingcomb Edge
grass
fence posts
heather
heather
Scale Beck
Scale Force

Take the path up the east side of the Force (brilliantly red due to syenite subsoil). After by-passing on the left a slimy 4' rockstep the path crosses a patch of red scree 80 yards on. This scree has concealed a junction; 3 yards up on the far side find a track that ascends in thick heather to easy ground at 1500', where it fades. Or continue by the beck and turn up alongside a tributary on the left (cairns).

Scale Force

SCALE BRIDGE (see page 6 for details)

fold x

One of the wettest paths in the district

bracken
new path
x fold
old path

Crummock Water

The attraction of this popular route is Lakeland's highest waterfall, Scale Force. The beck above is charming, but the climb therefrom rather dull.

Maps that show only the old path and promise stepping-stones and a bridge, are OUT OF DATE

Red Pike (B) 9

ASCENT FROM ENNERDALE
(HIGH GILLERTHWAITE)

2000 feet of ascent
1¼ miles

RED PIKE

looking north-east

HIGH STILE →

old fence

line of cairns

grass   grass

Little Dodd

The fell on this side is STARLING DODD

Cross the beck where it runs in two channels

bracken

bracken

Gillerthwaite Beck

Private cars are not allowed to enter the valley beyond Bowness

old fold
sheep pen

← BOWNESS 2½

BLACK SAIL Y.H. 3 →

High Gillerthwaite

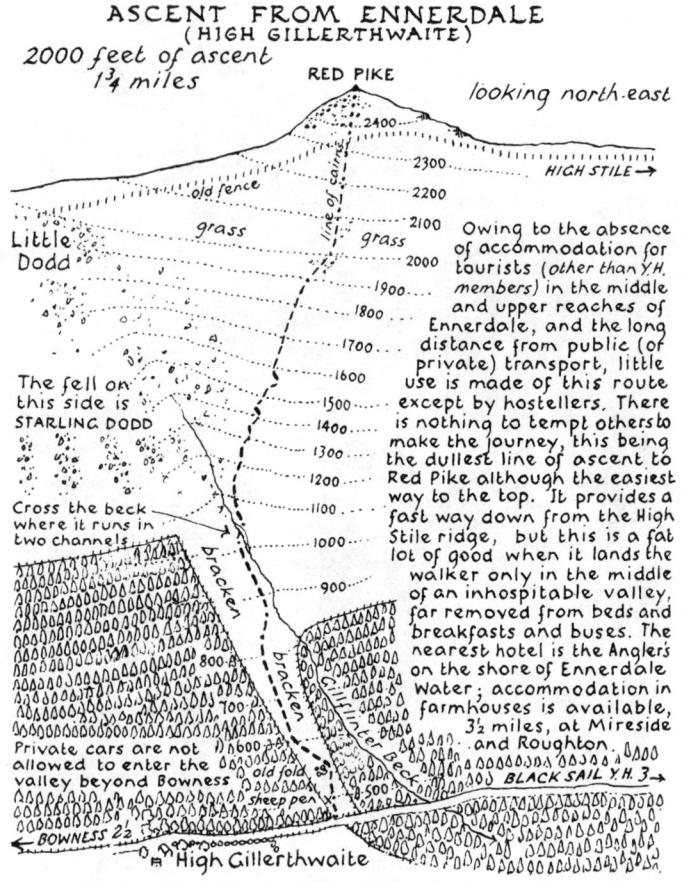

Owing to the absence of accommodation for tourists (other than Y.H. members) in the middle and upper reaches of Ennerdale, and the long distance from public (or private) transport, little use is made of this route except by hostellers. There is nothing to tempt others to make the journey, this being the dullest line of ascent to Red Pike although the easiest way to the top. It provides a fast way down from the High Stile ridge, but this is a fat lot of good when it lands the walker only in the middle of an inhospitable valley, far removed from beds and breakfasts and buses. The nearest hotel is the Anglers on the shore of Ennerdale Water; accommodation in farmhouses is available, 3½ miles, at Mireside and Roughton.

In the six-mile length of Ennerdale between Bowness and Black Sail Youth Hostel there is only one break in the dense plantations on the north side of the rough valley road. This is a narrow strip of unplanted ground between forest fences rising from the road 350 yards east of High Gillerthwaite. It is the only avenue by which sheep may be brought down from the fells and the only public access to Red Pike. The path is cairned and easy to follow, mainly on grass, but tedious and unexciting, interest being restricted to the retrospective view of the Pillar group across the valley.

Red Pike (B) 10

THE SUMMIT

The summit projects from the main mass of the fell, boldly, like a promontory from a cliff-face, having a steep fall on three sides, a flat top, and a gentle decline to a grassy plateau southwards, which is crossed by a boundary fence above the Ennerdale slope. The cairn, a big heap of stones, occupies the abrupt corner of the promontory directly at the head of the Buttermere path. The top is grassy, with an intermingling of small outcrops and stony patches.

DESCENTS: The top is welltrodden but not formed into definite tracks. Two lines of guide-cairns lead away southwards, to Gillerthwaite and to High Stile; if, in mist, doubt arises in selection, error will be revealed when the fence is reached, the High Stile route turning left in company with it, the Gillerthwaite crossing it. The Scale Force line of descent is obvious in clear weather, but a path may not be found until Scale Beck is joined: in mist, this route is better left alone. Most descents will be to Buttermere direct by way of Bleaberry Tarn, and the path will be found almost immediately from the cairn, having an initial zigzag, right then left, before becoming and continuing distinct (and very stony) down to the valley.

The summit, from Bleaberry Tarn

High Stile in the background

Red Pike (B) 11

THE VIEW

Lakes and Tarns
- NE: Derwentwater
- E: Buttermere
- E: Bleaberry Tarn (seen a few paces east of the cairn)
- W: Ennerdale Water
- W: Reservoir near Dent
- NW: Loweswater
- N: Crummock Water

Red Pike's view is notable for the number of lakes that can be seen, *really seen* and not merely glimpsed; their prominence adds an unusual beauty to the scene.

Despite High Stile's impending bulk the mountain view is quite satisfying, the Grasmoor group, seen from tip to toe, being very conspicuous.

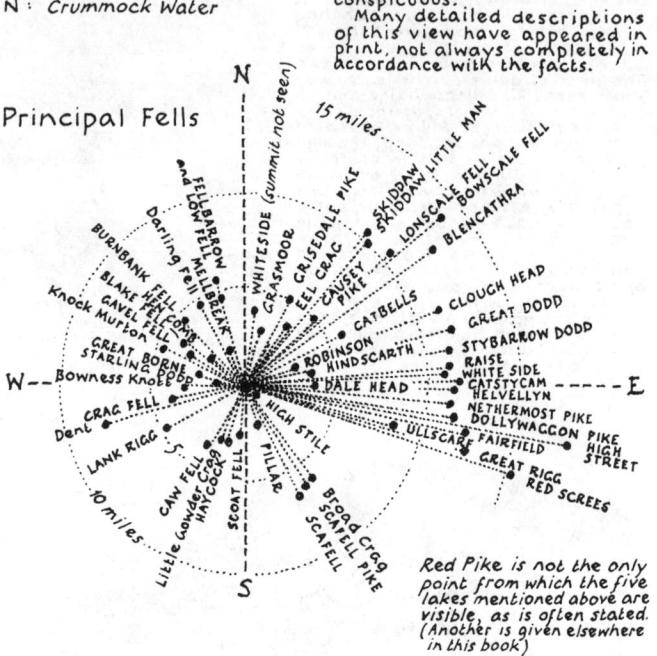

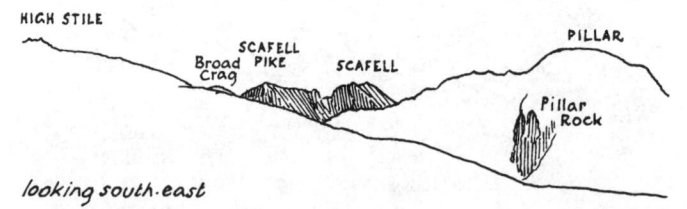

Many detailed descriptions of this view have appeared in print, not always completely in accordance with the facts.

Principal Fells

(compass diagram showing fells in all directions, with 10 miles and 15 miles range rings)

N — Fellbarrow and Lowfell, Darling Fell, Mellbreak, Whiteside (summit not seen), Grasmoor, Eel Crag, Crisedale Pike, Causey Pike, Skiddaw Little Man, Skiddaw, Lonscale Fell, Bowscale Fell, Blencathra

Burnbank Fell, Blake Fell, Gavel Fell, Knock Murton, Catbells, Clough Head, Great Dodd

W — Great Borne, Starling Dodd, Bowness Knott, Robinson, Hindscarth, Dale Head, Stybarrow Dodd, Raise, White Side, Catstycam, Helvellyn — E

Crag Fell, Dent, High Stile, Nethermost Pike, Dollywaggon Pike, Ullscarf, Fairfield, High Street

Lank Rigg, Caw Fell, Haycock, Scoat Fell, Pillar, Broad Crag, Scafell Pike, Scafell, Great Rigg, Red Screes

Little Gowder Crag

S

Red Pike is not the only point from which the five lakes mentioned above are visible, as is often stated. (Another is given elsewhere in this book)

(profile sketch)

HIGH STILE — Broad Crag, SCAFELL PIKE, SCAFELL — PILLAR, Pillar Rock

looking south-east

Red Pike (B) 12

RIDGE ROUTES

To HIGH STILE, 2644': ¾ mile: S, then SE and E.
Depression at 2300'
350 feet of ascent

Very easy, becoming rough finally

A line of marker cairns heads south to the old fence, which may be followed across excellent turf to the stony rise of High Stile, but in clear weather keep to the edge of the escarpment to get the best views; watch in particular for the striking aspect of Chapel Crags from the head of the scree-gully alongside.

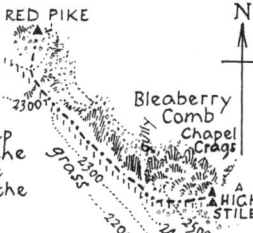

ONE MILE

The ridge to High Stile

Chapel Crags — head of Chapel Crags gully

To STARLING DODD, 2085': 1¼ miles: W, then WNW.
Depressions at 1880' and 1850'.
240 feet of ascent

Little of interest

Surveyed from Red Pike, this route obviously is a long trudge over grass with no excitements. So it proves. As the start of a high-level way down to Ennerdale it is better.

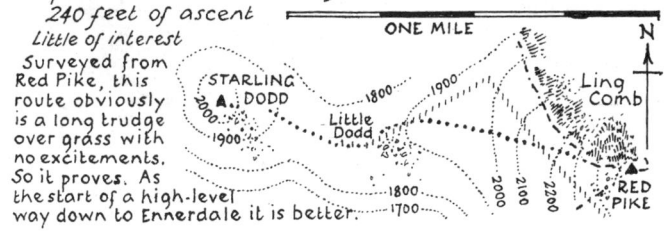

Red Pike
(Wasdale)

2707'

from Over Beck

from Black Crag

▲ PILLAR
▲ SCOAT FELL
▲ HAYCOCK ▲ RED PIKE
● Wasdale Head
▲ YEWBARROW
● Overbeck Bridge

MILES
0 1 2 3 4

Red Pike (W) 2

NATURAL FEATURES

There are several Mosedales, and the best-known of them, and the best, is the one branching from Wasdale Head. The circuit of the ridges around this side-valley is a succession of exciting situations and fine vantage points in rugged surroundings, and a highlight greatly enjoyed on this splendid expedition is the traverse along the crest of the mile-long escarpment of Red Pike, its top cairn dramatically poised on the brink of a wild cataract of crags forming the eastern face: this is a grim declivity falling 2000 feet to the valley, a place for adventurers or explorers perhaps but it carries no walkers' paths.   In contrast the western slopes decline more gradually over an extensive area jewelled by Scoat Tarn and Low Tarn, before coming down roughly to Nether Beck. North, Red Pike abuts closely against Scoat Fell, and the southern boundary is formed by Over Beck.   Red Pike claims a short water frontage on Wastwater in the narrow strip of cultivated land lying between the outlets of Nether Beck and Over Beck, and only here, in the pastures and trees of Bowderdale, does the fell's fierce expression relent a little; only here does its dourness break into a pleasant smile. Just here, by the water's edge, is an oasis of sylvan beauty quite uncharacteristic of the fell towering behind, which, everywhere else, exemplifies the utter wildness and desolation of true mountain country.

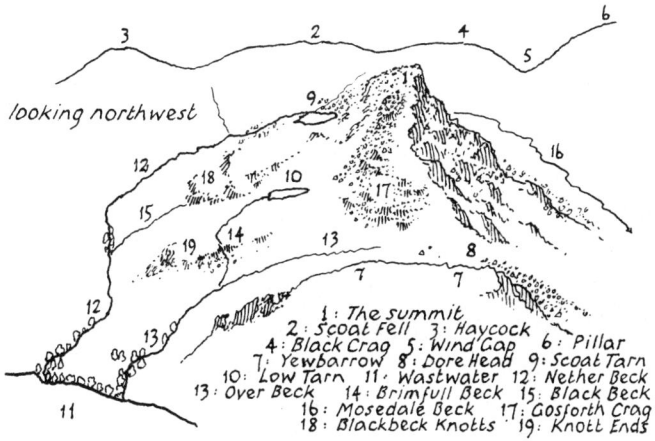

looking northwest

1: The summit
2: Scoat Fell 3: Haycock
4: Black Crag 5: Wind Gap 6: Pillar
7: Yewbarrow 8: Dore Head 9: Scoat Tarn
10: Low Tarn 11: Wastwater 12: Nether Beck
13: Over Beck 14: Brimfull Beck 15: Black Beck
16: Mosedale Beck 17: Gosforth Crag
18: Blackbeck Knotts 19: Knott Ends

For a century there has been confusion between this Red Pike and its namesake overlooking Buttermere. Confusion is worse confounded by their proximity, the summits being only three miles apart. To make a distinction, it is usual to refer to the subject of this chapter as the Wasdale Red Pike.

Red Pike (W) 3

MAP

continuation SCOAT FELL 4

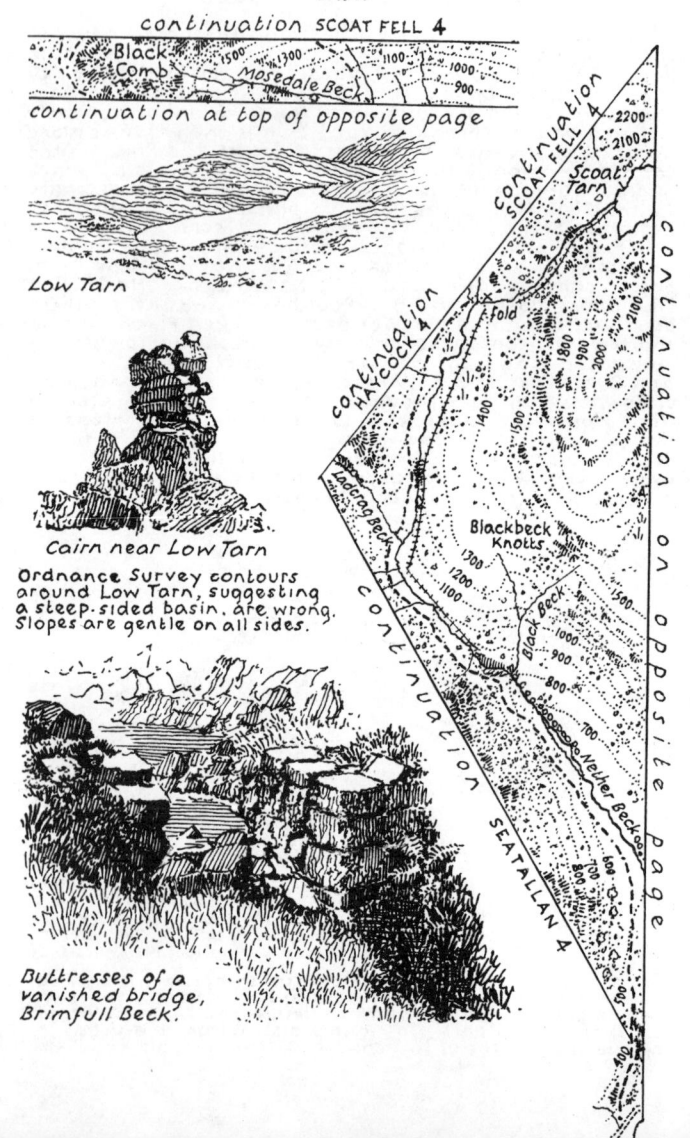

continuation at top of opposite page

Low Tarn

Cairn near Low Tarn

Ordnance Survey contours around Low Tarn, suggesting a steep-sided basin, are wrong. Slopes are gentle on all sides.

Buttresses of a vanished bridge, Brimfull Beck.

continuation SCOAT FELL 4

continuation HAYCOCK 4

continuation SEATALLAN 4

continuation on opposite page

Scoat Tarn

Fold

Blackbeck Knotts

Ladcrag Beck

Black Beck

Nether Beck

Red Pike (W) 4

MAP
continuation at top of opposite page

Red Pike (W) 5

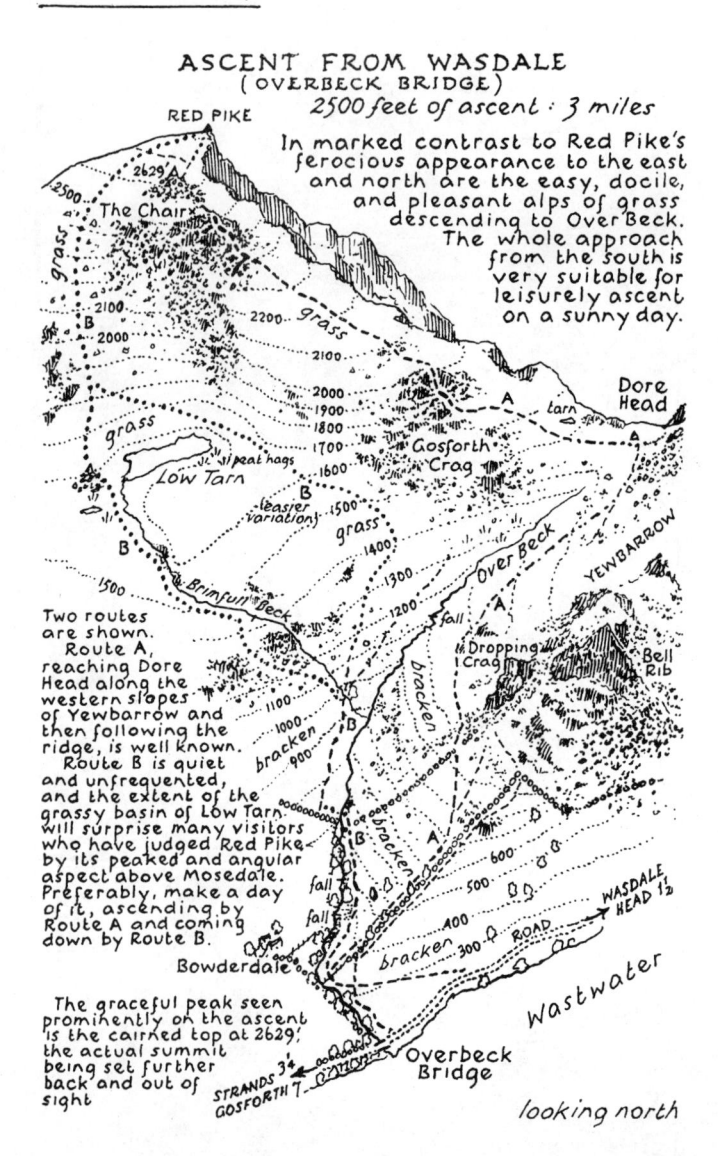

ASCENT FROM WASDALE
(OVERBECK BRIDGE)
2500 feet of ascent : 3 miles

In marked contrast to Red Pike's ferocious appearance to the east and north are the easy, docile, and pleasant alps of grass descending to Over Beck. The whole approach from the south is very suitable for leisurely ascent on a sunny day.

Two routes are shown.
Route A, reaching Dore Head along the western slopes of Yewbarrow and then following the ridge, is well known.
Route B is quiet and unfrequented, and the extent of the grassy basin of Low Tarn will surprise many visitors who have judged Red Pike by its peaked and angular aspect above Mosedale. Preferably, make a day of it, ascending by Route A and coming down by Route B.

The graceful peak seen prominently on the ascent is the cairned top at 2629'; the actual summit being set further back and out of sight.

looking north

Red Pike (W) 6

ASCENT FROM WASDALE HEAD
2450 feet of ascent : 2½ miles

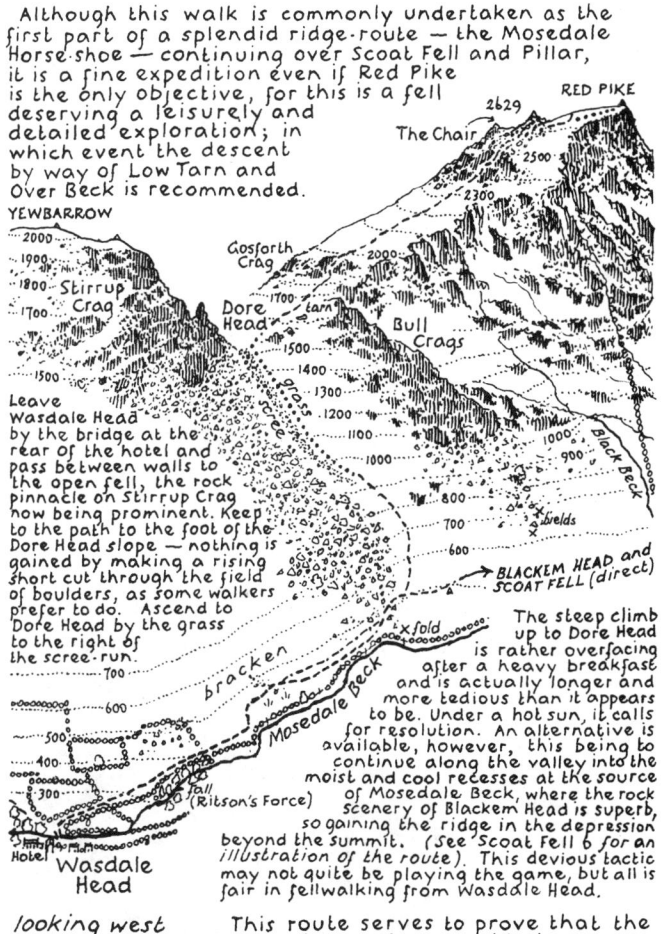

Although this walk is commonly undertaken as the first part of a splendid ridge-route — the Mosedale Horse-shoe — continuing over Scoat Fell and Pillar, it is a fine expedition even if Red Pike is the only objective, for this is a fell deserving a leisurely and detailed exploration; in which event the descent by way of Low Tarn and Over Beck is recommended.

Leave Wasdale Head by the bridge at the rear of the hotel and pass between walls to the open fell, the rock pinnacle on Stirrup Crag now being prominent. Keep to the path to the foot of the Dore Head slope — nothing is gained by making a rising short cut through the field of boulders, as some walkers prefer to do. Ascend to Dore Head by the grass to the right of the scree-run.

The steep climb up to Dore Head is rather overfacing after a heavy breakfast and is actually longer and more tedious than it appears to be. Under a hot sun, it calls for resolution. An alternative is available, however, this being to continue along the valley into the moist and cool recesses at the source of Mosedale Beck, where the rock scenery of Blackem Head is superb, so gaining the ridge in the depression beyond the summit. (See Scoat Fell 6 for an illustration of the route). This devious tactic may not quite be playing the game, but all is fair in fellwalking from Wasdale Head.

looking west   This route serves to prove that the Scafells and Great Gable have not a monopoly of the best walks around Wasdale Head. The ridge of Red Pike is excellent, lovely turf alternating with a few simple scrambles on pleasant rock.

Red Pike (W) 7

THE SUMMIT

Cairn at 2707'

The highest cairn, at 2707', is dramatically sited on the very brink of the Mosedale precipice and is so much on the edge of space that it cannot be walked round. It is a place to avoid in high wind. Yet the opposite western slope rises to the cairn in a gentle incline, carpeted with lovely turf. The transition in a matter of a few feet is a shock to the senses.

500 yards south is a larger cairn set amongst stones on an elevated plateau. This is point 2629', a typical mountain top in appearance and often regarded as the real summit.

DESCENTS: The descent from 2707' (but not from 2629') south to Overbeck Bridge via Low Tarn is, surprisingly, one of the easiest in the district; on grass throughout and gently graded, but there is no path. In mist, aim for Dore Head, keeping the escarpment on the left, and the cairned track will be picked up after passing the 2629' top; at Dore Head go left down the scree or the grass bank alongside, for Wasdale Head, or turn right for Overbeck Bridge. An interesting alternative is to descend from the col northwards to Scoat Tarn and Nether Beck. *Do not attempt the Blackem Head route into Mosedale unless it has been prospected in ascent.*

Cairn at 2629'

Red Pike (W) 8

THE SUMMIT

continued

The Chair

A summit feature that often escapes attention nowadays is an outcrop of rock that has been converted into a comfortable seat by the erection of a back rest and side arms of stones. This is The Chair, and a century ago was so well known that people spoke of climbing The Chair as today they speak of climbing Red Pike. It occupies a vantage point on the edge of the stony plateau of the south summit, overlooking Wastwater, and is 120 yards south of the 2629' cairn. It is within 20 yards of the Dore Head track and prominently in view therefrom but may be mistaken at a glance for a cairn. It has survived the storms of many years remarkably well, but is not proof against vandals. Please respect it.

On the ascent from Overbeck Bridge it is The Chair that is so conspicuously in view, apparently on the highest point, and not the summit cairn as may be thought.

Quite unaccountably, the ridge path prefers to skirt the highest cairn instead of visiting it.

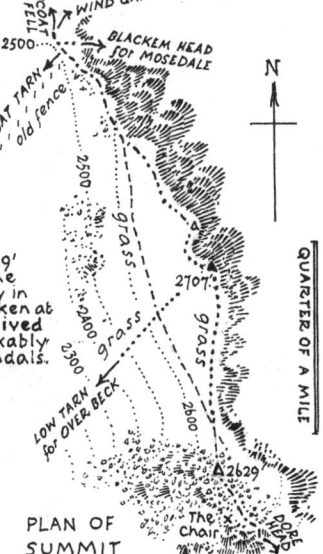

PLAN OF SUMMIT

Red Pike (W) 9

THE VIEW

The view is good only in parts. Scoat Fell and Pillar, nearby and higher, shut out the distance northwards and have little attraction. The Scafell range, seen full length and in true perspective, is the best feature. There is a striking aerial view of Black Comb, which will impress those who have come up by this route.

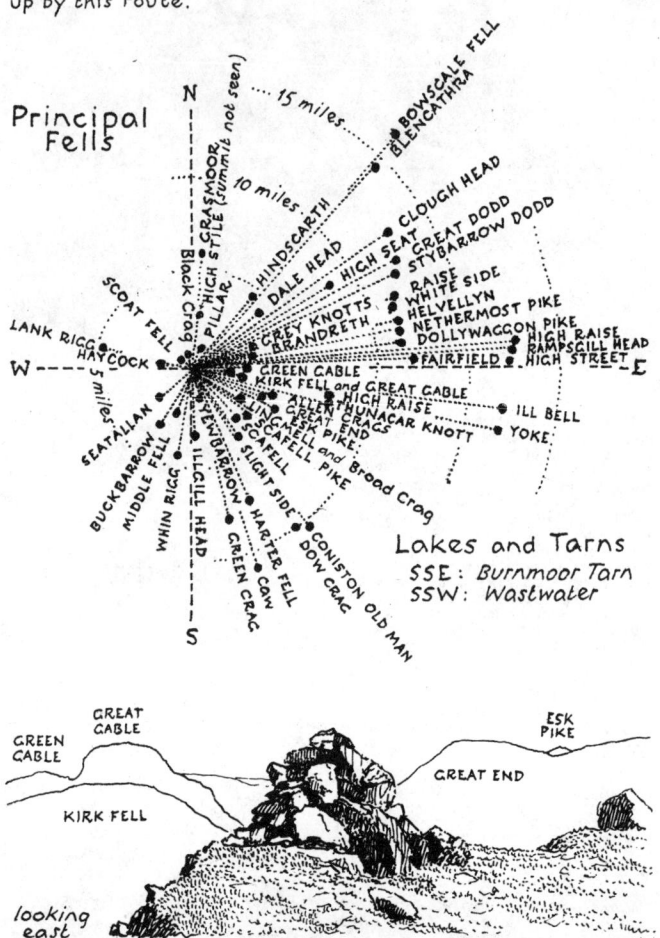

Principal Fells

N — 15 miles: BOWSCALE FELL, BLENCATHRA
10 miles: HINDSCARTH, PILLAR, HIGH STILE, GRASMOOR (summit not seen)
DALE HEAD, HIGH SEAT, CLOUGH HEAD, GREAT DODD, STYBARROW DODD
GREY KNOTTS, GRANDRETH, RAISE, WHITE SIDE, HELVELLYN, NETHERMOST PIKE, DOLLYWAGGON PIKE, HIGH RAISE, RAMPSGILL HEAD
Black Crag, GREEN GABLE, FAIRFIELD, HIGH STREET — E
SCOAT FELL, KIRK FELL and GREAT GABLE, HIGH RAISE, ILL BELL
LANK RIGG, HAYCOCK, ALLEN CRAGS, THUNACAR KNOTT, YOKE
W — 5 miles — GREAT END, ESK PIKE, Broad Crag
SEATALLAN, BUCKBARROW, YEWBARROW, SCAFELL PIKE
MIDDLE FELL, WHIN RIGG, ILLGILL HEAD, SLIGHT SIDE, HARTER FELL, GREEN CRAG, DOW CRAG, CONISTON OLD MAN, CAW
S

Lakes and Tarns
SSE: Burnmoor Tarn
SSW: Wastwater

looking east

GREEN GABLE — GREAT GABLE — KIRK FELL — GREAT END — ESK PIKE

Red Pike (W) 10

RIDGE ROUTES

To SCOAT FELL, 2760' : ¾ mile : NNW
Depression at 2500' : 270 feet of ascent

A dull climb, but brief.

Follow the escarpment north to the depression, then go straight up the opposite slope, ignoring paths trending to the right. Bear left to avoid a rough area of boulders at the east end of the summit wall. Cross the wall (on which the cairn stands) to obtain fine views of Steeple across Mirk Cove.

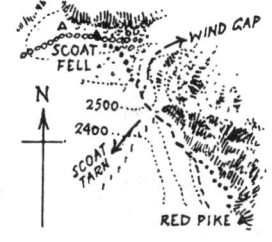

ONE MILE

To YEWBARROW, 2058' : 1¾ miles : S, SE and SSW
Depression at 1520' : 680 feet of ascent

A pleasant descent followed by an arduous scramble

Down to Dore Head at 1520' everything is just fine. The south summit will have been crossed, the Chair will have been found and sat upon, two rough rocky declivities will have been negotiated without much difficulty and a good speed maintained down the easy grass slopes. But, at Dore Head, Yewbarrow looks really hostile. Steep scree and grass lead up to a barrier of rock (Stirrup Crag) that looks impassable, but grimly-determined pedestrians can force a way up a series of cracks following evidences of the sufferings of those who have gone before. After 40 yards of toil there is sudden relief as grass is met again, and easy walking across a wide depression and up the opposite slope leads to the summit. Anxiety then shifts to the job of getting off safely... which is another story in another chapter.

If there are no witnesses about to tell of their shame, timid walkers may avoid Stirrup Crag entirely by taking the Overbeck path from Dore Head for quarter of a mile until beyond the boulders, then slanting up grass to the depression on Yewbarrow (route indicated on map above).

Stirrup Crag and Dore Head, as seen from the slopes of Red Pike

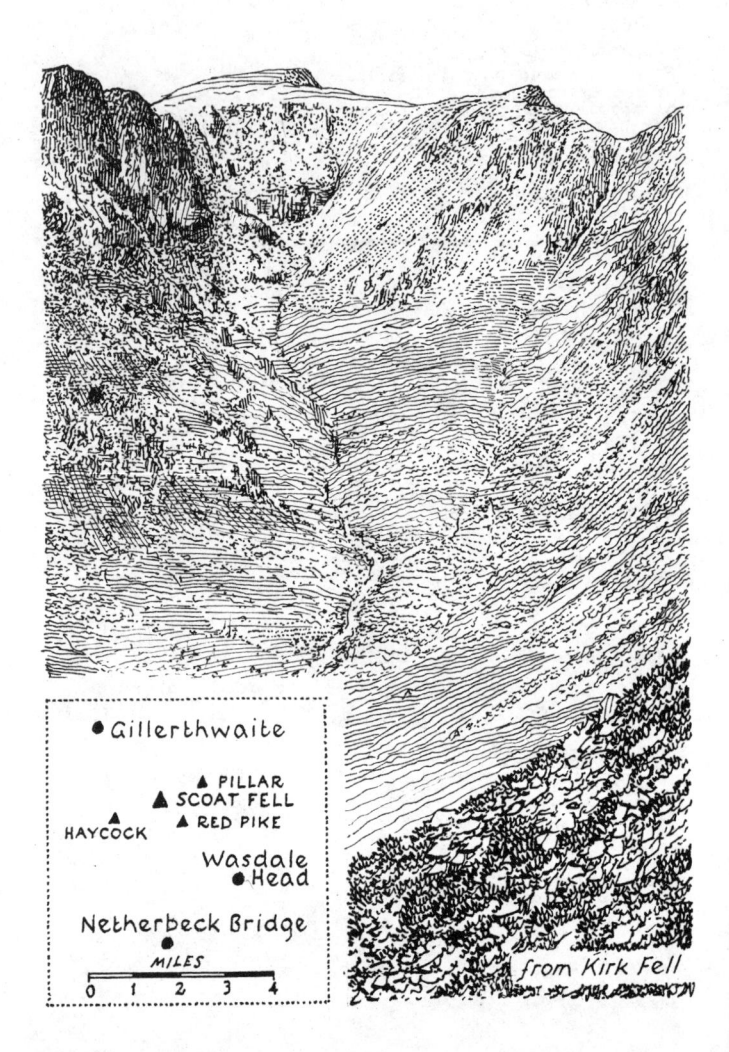

Scoat Fell 2760'

- Gillerthwaite
- ▲ PILLAR
- ▲ SCOAT FELL
- ▲ HAYCOCK
- ▲ RED PIKE
- Wasdale Head
- Netherbeck Bridge

MILES
0 1 2 3 4

from Kirk Fell

Scoat Fell 2

NATURAL FEATURES

Although often climbed from Wasdale as a part of the 'Mosedale Horse-shoe', Scoat Fell has no fan club and few devotees, for the long plateau forming the top compares unfavourably with the more shapely summits of other fells even easier of access from Wasdale Head; and, moreover, a massive stone wall following the watershed impedes freedom of view and freedom of movement: the top of a mountain is never improved by man's handiwork, only a simple cairn being acceptable.

Yet Scoat Fell triumphs over its disabilities, and provides magnificent mountain scenery on all sides. The mile-long escarpment facing Ennerdale, between Wind Gap and Mirklin Cove, is tremendously exciting, wild and desolate terrain, interrupted only by a thin arete linking with Steeple, a subsidiary pinnacle of remarkable proportions towering gracefully across the void. All along here is scenery of high quality.

The fell descends broadly to Ennerdale in grass and heather slopes between Deep Gill and High Beck, and is afforested below 1200 feet; on the Wasdale side, where Red Pike soon obstructs the descent, the upper reaches of Nether Beck and Mosedale Beck form the boundaries.

Scoat Tarn is shared with Red Pike, but two lesser sheets of water, Tewit Tarn (which is shrinking) and Moss Dub, a valley pool now hidden in the Ennerdale forest, are within the territory of Scoat Fell exclusively.

Steeple (left) and Scoat Fell,
looking across Mirklin Cove

Scoat Fell 3

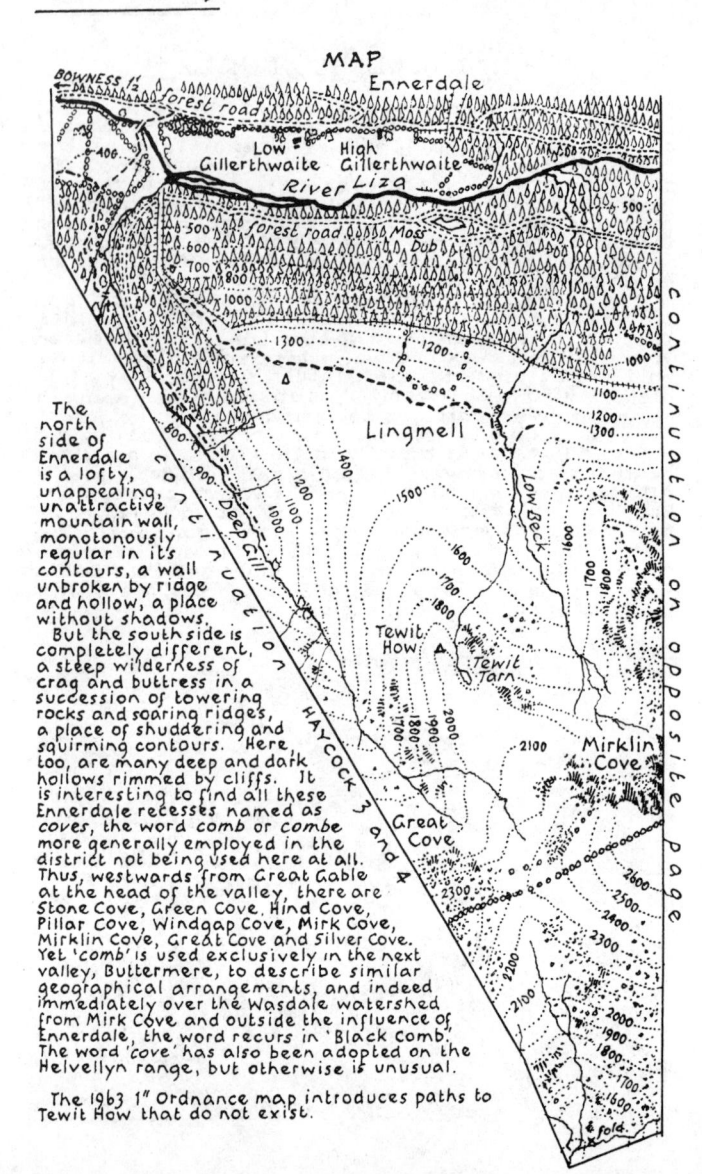

MAP

The north side of Ennerdale is a lofty, unappealing, unattractive mountain wall, monotonously regular in it's contours, a wall unbroken by ridge and hollow, a place without shadows.

But the south side is completely different, a steep wilderness of crag and buttress in a succession of towering rocks and soaring ridges, a place of shuddering and squirming contours. Here, too, are many deep and dark hollows rimmed by cliffs. It is interesting to find all these Ennerdale recesses named as *coves*, the word *comb* or *combe* more generally employed in the district not being used here at all. Thus, westwards from Great Gable at the head of the valley, there are Stone Cove, Green Cove, Hind Cove, Pillar Cove, Windgap Cove, Mirk Cove, Mirklin Cove, Great Cove and Silver Cove. Yet 'comb' is used exclusively in the next valley, Buttermere, to describe similar geographical arrangements, and indeed immediately over the Wasdale watershed from Mirk Cove and outside the influence of Ennerdale, the word recurs in 'Black Comb.' The word 'cove' has also been adopted on the Helvellyn range, but otherwise is unusual.

The 1963 1" Ordnance map introduces paths to Tewit How that do not exist.

… Scoat Fell 4

MAP

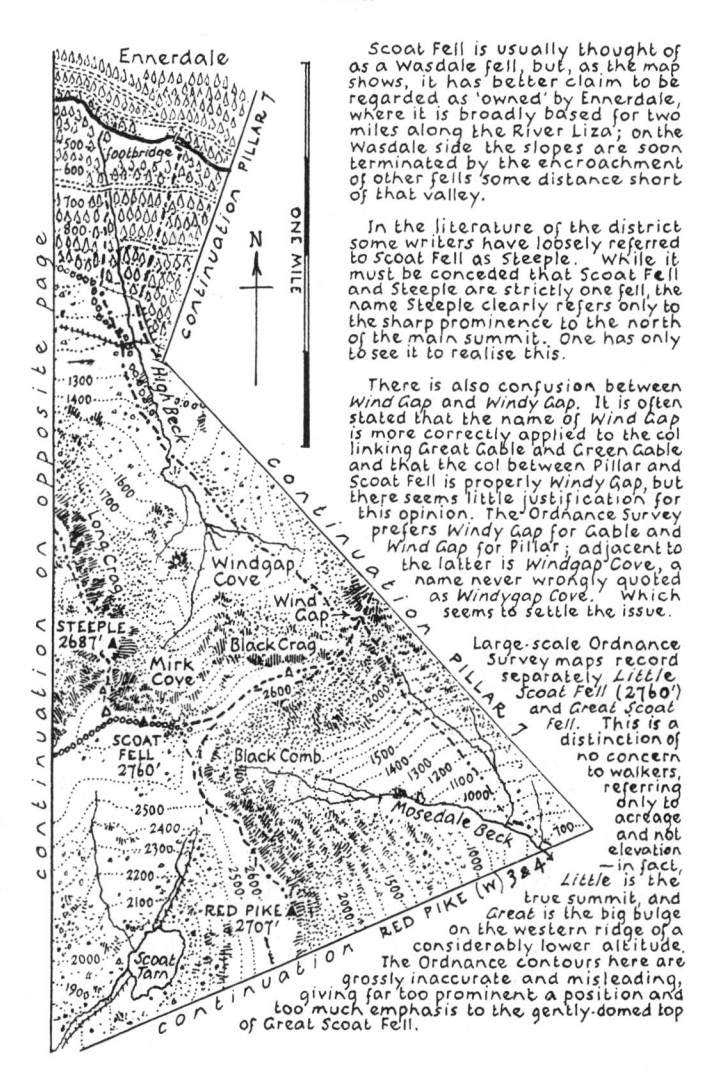

Scoat Fell is usually thought of as a Wasdale fell, but, as the map shows, it has better claim to be regarded as 'owned' by Ennerdale, where it is broadly based for two miles along the River Liza; on the Wasdale side the slopes are soon terminated by the encroachment of other fells some distance short of that valley.

In the literature of the district some writers have loosely referred to Scoat Fell as Steeple. While it must be conceded that Scoat Fell and Steeple are strictly one fell, the name Steeple clearly refers only to the sharp prominence to the north of the main summit. One has only to see it to realise this.

There is also confusion between *Wind Gap* and *Windy Gap*. It is often stated that the name of *Wind Gap* is more correctly applied to the col linking Great Gable and Green Gable and that the col between Pillar and Scoat Fell is properly *Windy Gap*, but there seems little justification for this opinion. The Ordnance Survey prefers *Windy Gap* for Gable and *Wind Gap* for Pillar; adjacent to the latter is *Windgap Cove*, a name never wrongly quoted as *Windygap Cove*. Which seems to settle the issue.

Large-scale Ordnance Survey maps record separately *Little Scoat Fell* (2760') and *Great Scoat Fell*. This is a distinction of no concern to walkers, referring only to acreage and not elevation — in fact, *Little* is the true summit, and *Great* is the big bulge on the western ridge of a considerably lower altitude. The Ordnance contours here are grossly inaccurate and misleading, giving far too prominent a position and too much emphasis to the gently-domed top of Great Scoat Fell.

Scoat Fell 5

ASCENT FROM WASDALE
(NETHERBECK BRIDGE)
2550 feet of ascent : 4¼ miles

looking north

HAYCOCK — SCOAT FELL

Route A is normally used in the ascent of Haycock, but is also convenient for Scoat Fell (best views on the far side of the wall). But Route B is better because of the visit to Scoat Tarn, a gem in a wild setting.

split boulder, Scoat Tarn

A fair path proceeds along the west side of Nether Beck to 1400', where the routes diverge. This path leaves the road a quarter-mile from Netherbeck Bridge but may be joined direct from the bridge by slanting across to it.

On Route B: looking back to Scoat Tarn from 2400'

Netherbeck Bridge

Wastwater

STRANDS 2¼
GOSFORTH 6½

WASDALE HEAD 2

This is the easiest line of approach to Scoat Fell from any direction, there being no steep gradients. The biggest attraction en route is Scoat Tarn, the grandest of the western tarns, and itself sufficient to justify the walk.

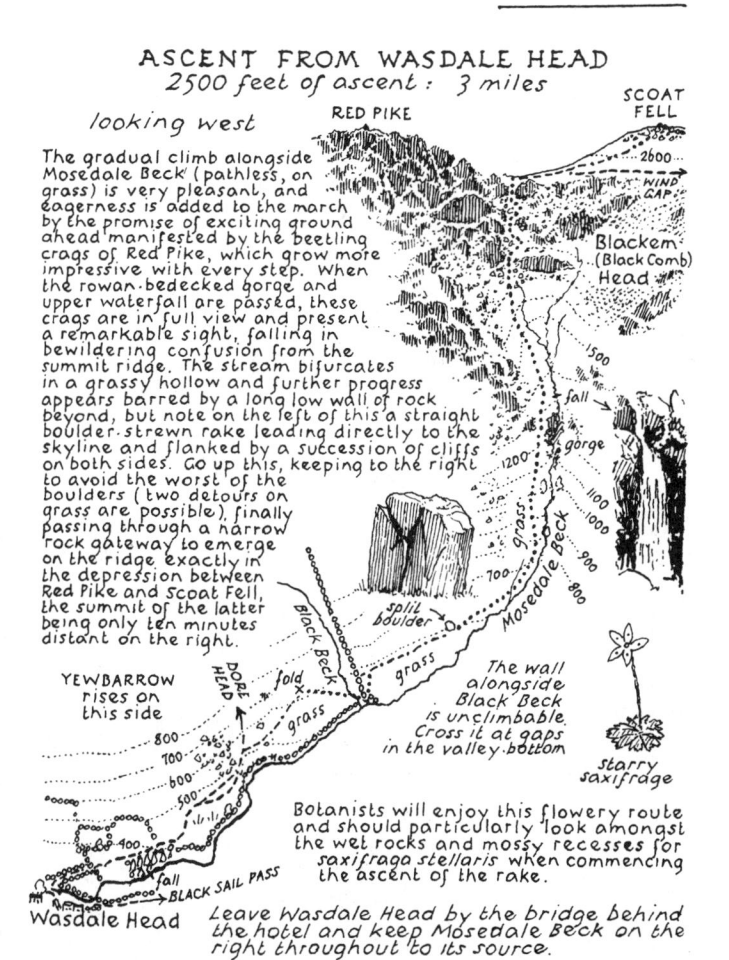

Scoat Fell 6

ASCENT FROM WASDALE HEAD
2500 feet of ascent : 3 miles

looking west

RED PIKE

SCOAT FELL

2600

WIND GAP

Blackem (Black Comb) Head

The gradual climb alongside Mosedale Beck (pathless, on grass) is very pleasant, and eagerness is added to the march by the promise of exciting ground ahead manifested by the beetling crags of Red Pike, which grow more impressive with every step. When the rowan-bedecked gorge and upper waterfall are passed, these crags are in full view and present a remarkable sight, falling in bewildering confusion from the summit ridge. The stream bifurcates in a grassy hollow and further progress appears barred by a long low wall of rock beyond, but note on the left of this a straight boulder-strewn rake leading directly to the skyline and flanked by a succession of cliffs on both sides. Go up this, keeping to the right to avoid the worst of the boulders (two detours on grass are possible), finally passing through a narrow rock gateway to emerge on the ridge exactly in the depression between Red Pike and Scoat Fell, the summit of the latter being only ten minutes distant on the right.

1500
fall
1200
gorge
1100
1000
900
800
Mosedale Beck
grass
split boulder
700

YEWBARROW rises on this side

Black Beck
DORE HEAD
fold
grass
800
700
600
500
400

The wall alongside Black Beck is unclimbable. Cross it at gaps in the valley bottom.

starry saxifrage

Botanists will enjoy this flowery route and should particularly look amongst the wet rocks and mossy recesses for *saxifraga stellaris* when commencing the ascent of the rake.

fall BLACK SAIL PASS

Wasdale Head

Leave Wasdale Head by the bridge behind the hotel and keep Mosedale Beck on the right throughout to its source.

Scoat Fell is usually reached from Wasdale Head via Dore Head and Red Pike, or via Pillar, i.e. as part of a ridge-walk, but illustrated here is a direct way, little-known and unfrequented, that climbs out of Mosedale through the magnificent rock scenery of Blackem Head and provides a route onto the ridge much more exciting than the usual tedious ascents of Dore Head and Wind Gap.

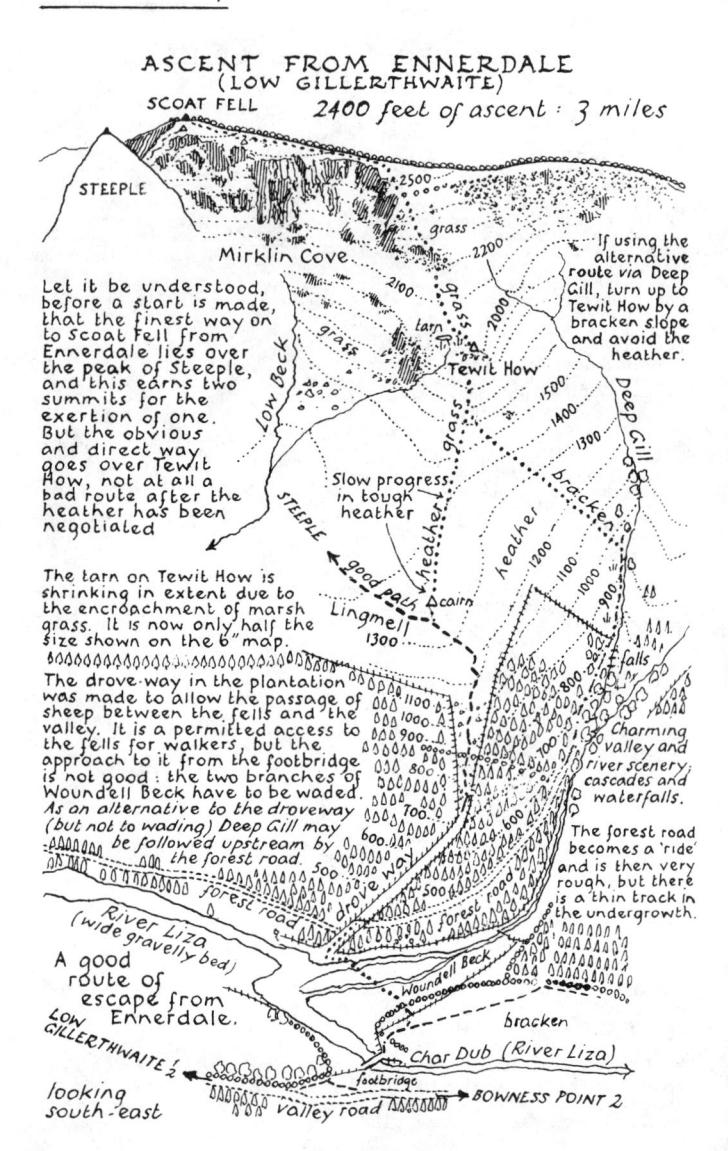

Scoat Fell 7

ASCENT FROM ENNERDALE
(LOW GILLERTHWAITE)
2400 feet of ascent : 3 miles

SCOAT FELL
STEEPLE
Mirklin Cove

If using the alternative route via Deep Gill, turn up to Tewit How by a bracken slope and avoid the heather.

Let it be understood, before a start is made, that the finest way on to Scoat Fell from Ennerdale lies over the peak of Steeple, and this earns two summits for the exertion of one. But the obvious and direct way goes over Tewit How, not at all a bad route after the heather has been negotiated

Tewit How
Slow progress in tough heather
good path
cairn
Lingmell 1300

The tarn on Tewit How is shrinking in extent due to the encroachment of marsh grass. It is now only half the size shown on the 6" map.

The drove-way in the plantation was made to allow the passage of sheep between the fells and the valley. It is a permitted access to the fells for walkers, but the approach to it from the footbridge is not good: the two branches of Woundell Beck have to be waded. As an alternative to the droveway (but not to wading) Deep Gill may be followed upstream by the forest road.

Charming valley and river scenery; cascades and waterfalls

The forest road becomes a 'ride' and is then very rough, but there is a thin track in the undergrowth.

River Liza (wide gravelly bed)

A good route of escape from Ennerdale.

LOW GILLERTHWAITE ½
looking south-east

forest road
drove way
forest road
Woundell Beck
bracken
Char Dub (River Liza)
footbridge → BOWNESS POINT 2
valley road

Scoat Fell 8

THE SUMMIT

Walkers who insist on summit cairns being sited precisely on the highest part of a summit have suffered a frustration here, for the exact spot representing the maximum altitude of Scoat Fell is fully occupied by a very solid wall. Not to be thwarted, however, our purists have had the enterprise to build a cairn on the top of the wall at this point, and so erected an edifice unique in Lakeland. But less meticulous visitors will generally accept as the summit the prominent cairn on open ground near the angle of the wall, where the cliffs of Mirk Cove terminate in a gentle slope leading to the Steeple arete: this is a few feet lower.

HAYCOCK
Great Scoat Fell
wall

The top of the fell, stony in places, is an easy parade in the proximity of the wall but one is always conscious of the profound abyss of the northern coves close at hand and the gullies biting deeply into the edge of the plateau. Striking views are obtained by keeping along the rim of the cliffs and by following some of the headlands until they drop into space.

DESCENTS: *For Ennerdale*, in clear weather, the Steeple ridge is best, followed by High Beck, which leads down to a footbridge over the Liza, but *in mist* prefer a route (there is no path) over Tewit How or by Deep Gill, turning down the easy slope beyond Mirklin Cove. *For Wasdale*, the Red Pike ridge is the finest route if it can be seen, but *in mist* accompany the wall WSW to the Haycock col, where a grass slope *left* descends to Nether Beck, which can be followed by an improving path on the west bank down to the road at Netherbeck Bridge.

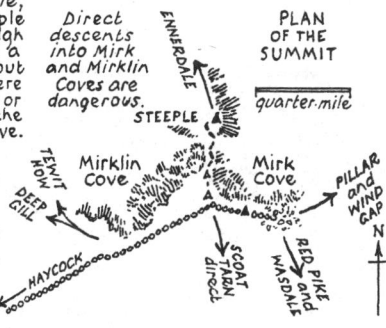

Direct descents into Mirk and Mirklin Coves are dangerous.

PLAN OF THE SUMMIT

quarter-mile

ENNERDALE
STEEPLE
TEWIT HOW / DEEP GILL
Mirklin Cove
Mirk Cove
PILLAR and WIND GAP
HAYCOCK
SCOAT TARN direct
RED PIKE and WASDALE
N

Scoat Fell 9

THE VIEW

Only Pillar of the nearer fells overtops Scoat Fell and although it takes a big slice out of the distance there is enough left to see to occupy the attention for a long time on a clear day. The summit wall is an obstruction, preventing a comprehensive view in all directions.

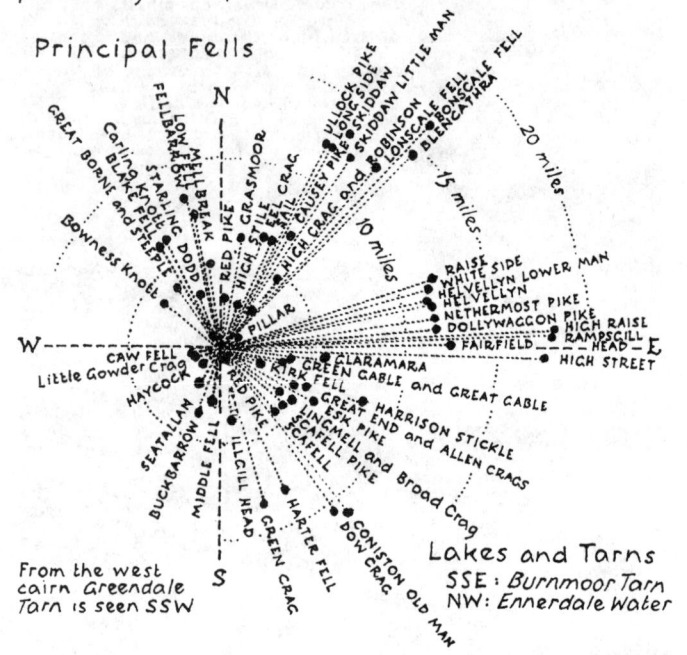

Principal Fells

(Panoramic diagram of principal fells visible from Scoat Fell, with distance rings at 10, 15, and 20 miles, centred on the summit with radial sight-lines labelled with fell names.)

Fells labelled (approximately clockwise from N):
ULLOCK PIKE, LONGSIDE, SKIDDAW LITTLE MAN, SKIDDAW, ROBINSON, LONSCALE FELL, BONSCALE FELL, BLENCATHRA, RAISE, WHITE SIDE, HELVELLYN LOWER MAN, HELVELLYN, NETHERMOST PIKE, DOLLYWAGGON PIKE, HIGH RAISE, FAIRFIELD, RAMPSGILL HEAD, HIGH STREET, CLARAMARA, GREEN GABLE and GREAT GABLE, HARRISON STICKLE, GREAT END and ALLEN CRAGS, ESK PIKE, BOWFELL, LINGMELL and Broad Crag, SCAFELL PIKE, SCAFELL, CONISTON OLD MAN, BOW CRAG, GREEN CRAG, HARTER FELL, ILLGILL HEAD, GREEN FELL, MIDDLE FELL, BUCKBARROW, SEATALLAN, HAYCOCK, Little Gowder Crag, CAW FELL, PILLAR, RED PIKE, HIGH CRAG, HIGH STILE, RED PIKE, GRASMOOR, HIGH CAUSEY PIKE, MELLBREAK, FELLBARROW, LOW FELL, STARLING DODD, Carling Knott, BLAKE FELL, GREAT BORNE and STEEPLE, Bowness Knott

From the west cairn Greendale Tarn is seen SSW

Lakes and Tarns
SSE: *Burnmoor Tarn*
NW: *Ennerdale Water*

Some readers have written to claim that they have identified fells additional to those named on the diagrams of views in these books. This may well be so. The diagrams, as stated, show only the *principal* fells in view. Generally, in the case of a summit of low altitude, the list will be complete, but where a view is extensive, or where several fells appear in a tight group, it becomes impossible to indicate every one in the limited space available and a selection must be made: in such circumstances lower intermediate heights may be excluded to give preference to those forming the skyline; or, again, where only a very small section of a fell can be seen, and then only in favourable conditions, it may be omitted rather than cause confusion, possibly, by including it. With regard to tarns, often these are indistinguishable from their surroundings, especially when of only slightly less elevation, and in many cases will be noticed only when illuminated by sunlight. (Which will account for any omissions of tarns in these views, for the author's wanderings have not always been accompanied by sunshine!)

Scoat Fell 10

RIDGE ROUTES

A pre-requisite of a good mountain, from a walkers' point of view, is that its summit should be the place of convergence of ridges from all directions, and Scoat Fell, which certainly is a good mountain, measures up to this requirement. Its four ridges all lead to the tops of other fells and provide splendid walks in exciting surroundings.

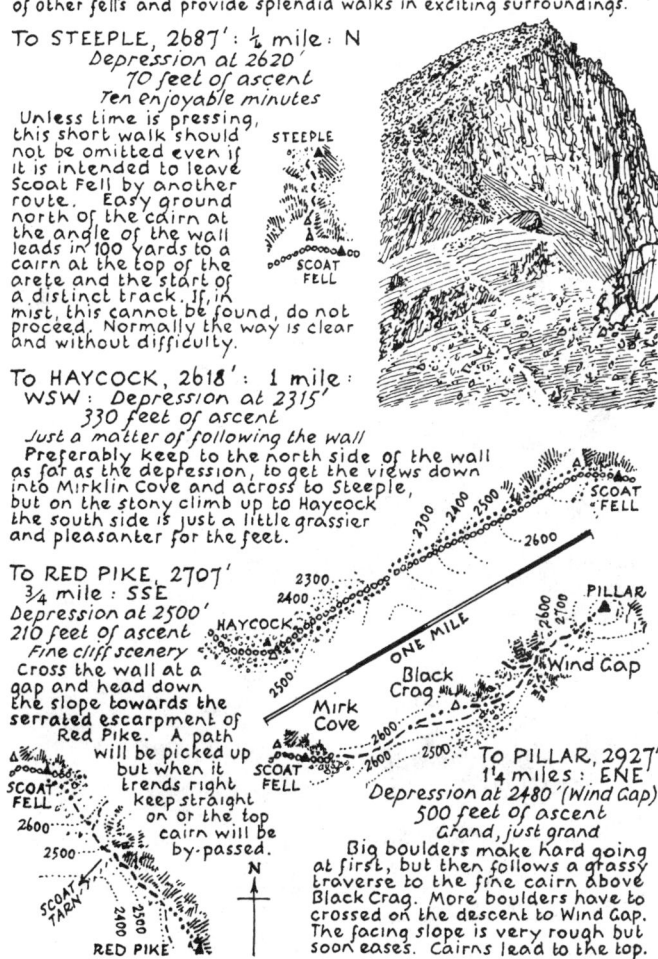

To STEEPLE, 2687': ¼ mile : N
Depression at 2620'
70 feet of ascent
Ten enjoyable minutes

Unless time is pressing, this short walk should not be omitted even if it is intended to leave Scoat Fell by another route. Easy ground north of the cairn at the angle of the wall leads in 100 yards to a cairn at the top of the arete and the start of a distinct track. If in mist, this cannot be found, do not proceed. Normally the way is clear and without difficulty.

To HAYCOCK, 2618': 1 mile : WSW :
Depression at 2315'
330 feet of ascent
Just a matter of following the wall

Preferably keep to the north side of the wall as far as the depression, to get the views down into Mirklin Cove and across to Steeple, but on the stony climb up to Haycock the south side is just a little grassier and pleasanter for the feet.

To RED PIKE, 2707'
¾ mile : SSE
Depression at 2500'
210 feet of ascent
Fine cliff scenery

Cross the wall at a gap and head down the slope towards the serrated escarpment of Red Pike. A path will be picked up but when it trends right keep straight on or the top cairn will be by-passed.

To PILLAR, 2927'
1¼ miles : ENE
Depression at 2480' (Wind Gap)
500 feet of ascent
Grand, just grand

Big boulders make hard going at first, but then follows a grassy traverse to the fine cairn above Black Crag. More boulders have to crossed on the descent to Wind Gap. The facing slope is very rough but soon eases. Cairns lead to the top.

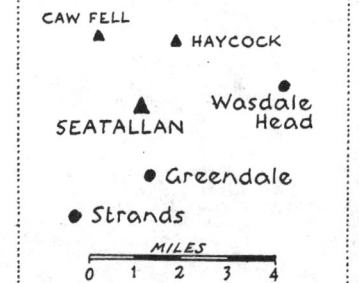

Seatallan 2266'

CAW FELL
▲ HAYCOCK
▲ SEATALLAN   ● Wasdale Head
● Greendale
● Strands

MILES
0 1 2 3 4

from below Scoat Tarn

Seatallan 2

NATURAL FEATURES

When the organisers of a recent mountain race selected the top of Seatallan as a check-point, some of the contestants confessed that they had never before heard of the fell, and it is probably true to say that the name is not generally known to walkers who have not yet based their activities on Wasdale Head.

Seatallan, formerly known as Seat Allan, forms a steep western wall to the quiet valley of Nether Beck for much of its length, exhibiting thereto a rocky slope above which the summit rises in easier gradients to a graceful cone. Northwards, the curve of the skyline, after a sharp initial fall, sweeps up to the more bulky Haycock; southwards are the two subsidiary heights of Middle Fell and Buckbarrow, both craggy, arresting the decline of the ground to Wastwater. In line with Middle Fell from the summit, hidden in an upland combe, is Greendale Tarn.

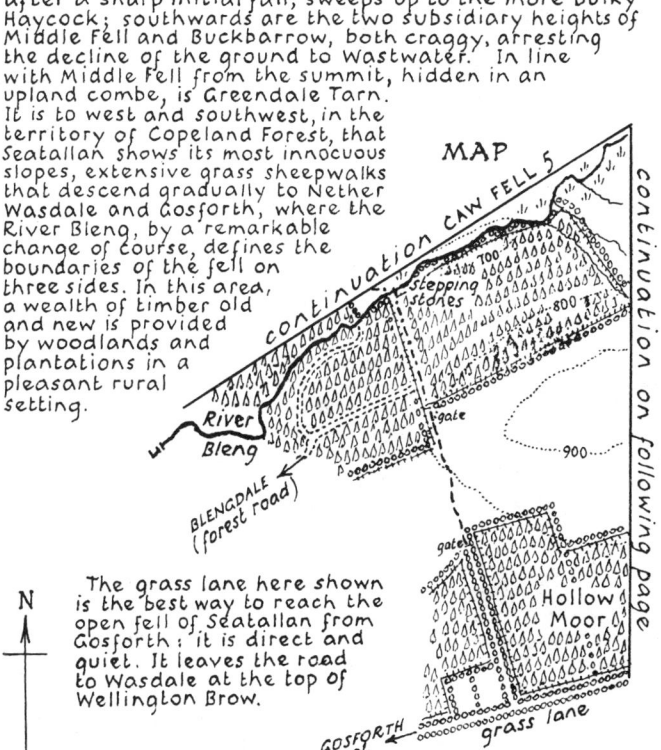

It is to west and southwest, in the territory of Copeland Forest, that Seatallan shows its most innocuous slopes, extensive grass sheepwalks that descend gradually to Nether Wasdale and Gosforth, where the River Bleng, by a remarkable change of course, defines the boundaries of the fell on three sides. In this area, a wealth of timber old and new is provided by woodlands and plantations in a pleasant rural setting.

The grass lane here shown is the best way to reach the open fell of Seatallan from Gosforth: it is direct and quiet. It leaves the road to Wasdale at the top of Wellington Brow.

ONE MILE

Seatallan 3

MAP

ONE MILE

continuation HAYCOCK 4

N ↑

As in other areas lacking in prominent natural features, quite unremarkable objects on Seatallan are given names: Tod Hole, Buck Stone, Gray Crag, etc. These would not get a mention where detail is more crowded, as on Scafell.

continuation CAW FELL 6

continuation on previous page

continuation on opposite page

River Bleng
× bield
fold
Raven Crag
Swinsty Beck
Stare Beck × fold
old cairns ××
× folds
× fold
Tod Hole
Cat Bields
Buck Stone
× bield
Kid Beck
drove road
× fold
Glade How
Gray Crag
fold ×
Hollow Moor
Wash Dub
Windsor (Youth Hostel)
cat track
Harrow Head
GOSFORTH 4
ROAD

In the Blengdale area the Ordnance Survey use the name 'Sheep Shelter' instead of 'Bield' on their 6" maps, this preference being unusual.

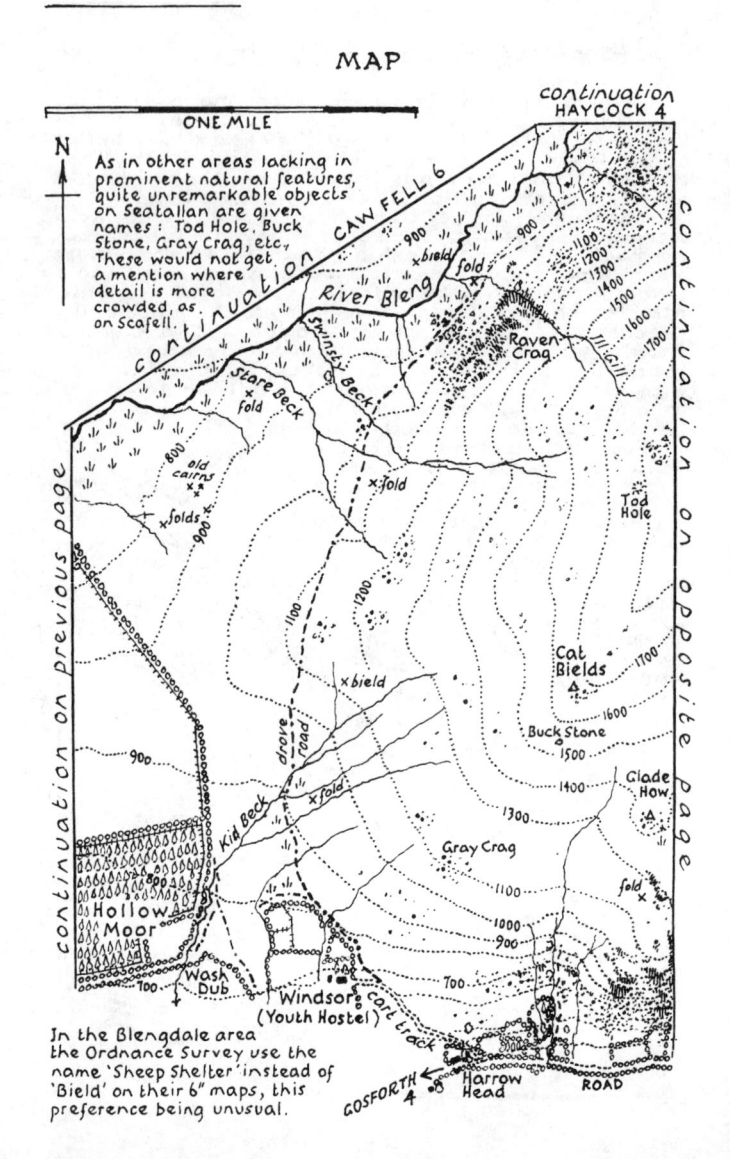

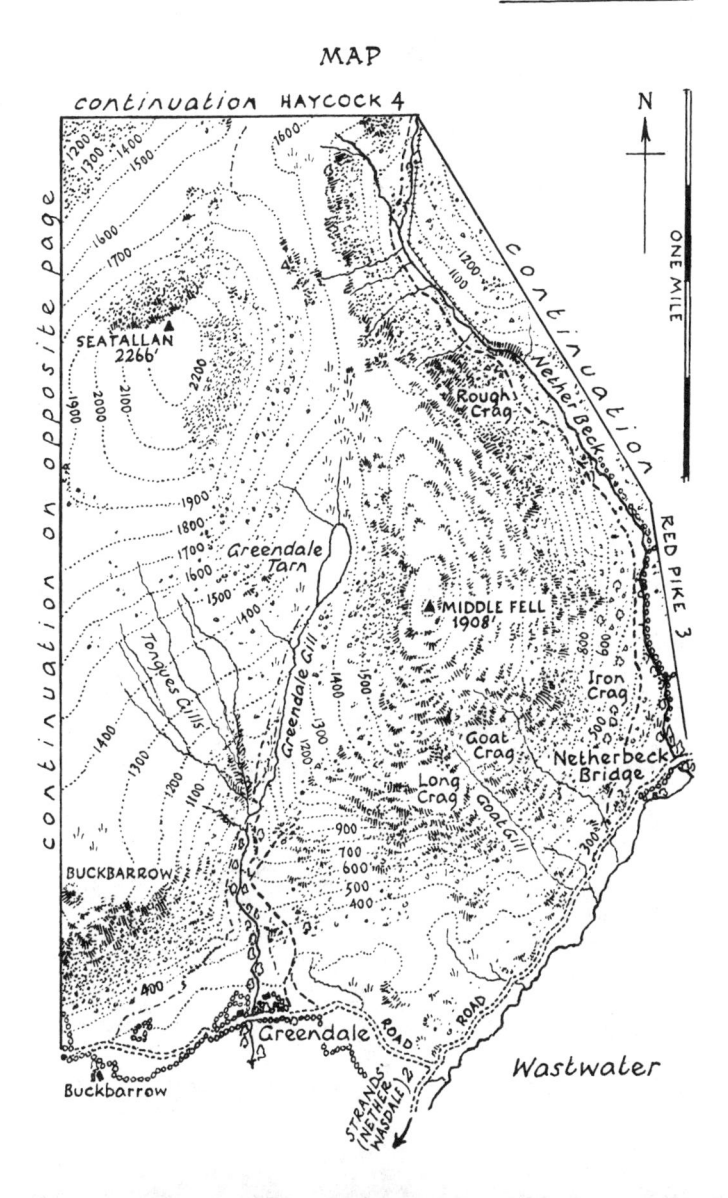

Seatallan 4

MAP

Seatallan 5

ASCENT FROM NETHER WASDALE

2150 feet of ascent
4 miles from Strands
(4½ via Buckbarrow)

Cairn on Cat Bields

GREAT GABLE

SEATALLAN

looking north

Note that the south-west ridge route passes separate shelters for (i) sheep, (ii) foxes (iii) wild cats, and (iv) man.

Two routes are shown, converging at Cat Bields. The south-west ridge above Windsor may be joined from the drove road, but is wide and indefinite and dreary in its lower parts. Interest can be added to the ascent by including a visit to the rocky top of Buckbarrow, which has better views, thereafter reaching Cat Bields via Glade How.

Seatallan 6

ASCENT FROM WASDALE
(GREENDALE)
2050' of ascent : 2 miles

(NETHERBECK BRIDGE)
2100' of ascent : 3 miles

looking north

The walk up the fell to Tongues Gills is delightful, and the grim scenery of the gills (unseen from the road) is a great surprise.

Instead of proceeding thence as far as Greendale Tarn, which is unattractive, avoid its marshy surroundings by turning up the slope of Seatallan, keeping left to avoid the summit screes.

A fair path, with cairns, ascends the valley of Nether Beck. The first easy escape from the craggy confines of the valley is provided by a grass slope alongside Ladcrag Beck, at the top of which turn left for Seatallan (back towards Wastwater), the fell ahead being Haycock.

The start of the path from the road is indistinct, but it may be joined direct from the bridge.

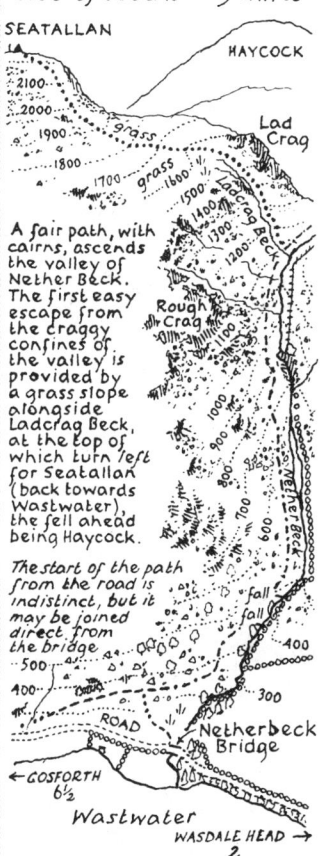

looking north-west

Nether Beck occupies a quiet valley with pretty waterfalls, and the walk alongside is easy and pleasant. In contrast, the climb out of the valley to the top of Seatallan, on grass, will be found tedious.

Seatallan 7

THE SUMMIT

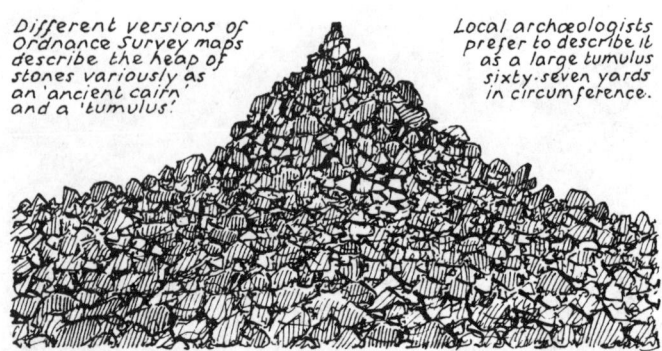

Different versions of Ordnance Survey maps describe the heap of stones variously as an 'ancient cairn' and a 'tumulus'.

Local archaeologists prefer to describe it as a large tumulus sixty-seven yards in circumference.

Stones galore, all in a great heap on a felltop predominantly of soft turf, is an unnatural phenomenon that greets all visitors to Seatallan's summit. Cairns are not a fashion introduced by walkers. Shepherds built cairns as landmarks for their own guidance in bad weather long before people climbed hills for pleasure. And long before the shepherds the first primitive dwellers in the district built cairns in and around their settlements and over their burial places. The big cairn on Seatallan is attributed to the early British inhabitants and may well be thousands of years old. Nearby, on the grass, is a modern erection: S. 5762 — an Ordnance Survey column. The top of the fell is otherwise featureless. A landslip on the north side has left a fringe of crags and aretes, providing a natural quarry from which the stones of the 'tumulus' were probably obtained.

DESCENTS: Routes of ascent may be reversed, but, in mist, Buckbarrow is better left severely alone.

RIDGE ROUTE

To HAYCOCK, 2618': 2 miles : NNE
Depression at 1610'
1050 feet of ascent

Easy grass leads down to and across the depression. A doubt arises as Gowder Crag is approached, but it is not formidable and a scramble over steep scree may be made frontally, or a grassy rake around to the left may be preferred.

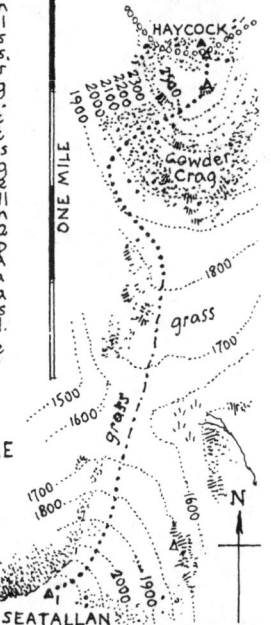

Seatallan 8

THE VIEW

As a viewpoint Seatallan does not rank highly. From Haycock round to Scafell a mountain barrier hides most of the district, only the Coniston fells being well seen at a distance. West and south, however, there is a full and uninterrupted panorama of the coastline and the Black Combe hinterland.

Principal Fells

(compass diagram showing fells radiating from centre point, with 5 miles and 10 miles range circles)

N — Little Cowder Crag, 10 miles, SCOAT FELL, Black Crag, HAYCOCK, PILLAR, RED PIKE, KIRK FELL, GREY KNOTTS, GREEN GABLE, GREAT GABLE, GLARAMARA, HIGH RAISE, GREAT END, LINGMELL, Broad Crag, SCAFELL PIKE, SCAFELL, SLIGHT SIDE, GREAT CARRS, SWIRL HOW, GREY FRIAR, HARTER FELL, CONISTON OLD MAN, DOW CRAG, CAW, GREEN CRAG, GILL HEAD, WHIN RIGG, CAW FELL, LANK RIGG, Dent

W — — — E

S

Lakes and Tarns

None from the cairn, but a short walk NE brings Low Tarn and Scoat Tarn into view directly ahead and a section of Wastwater can be seen to the right.

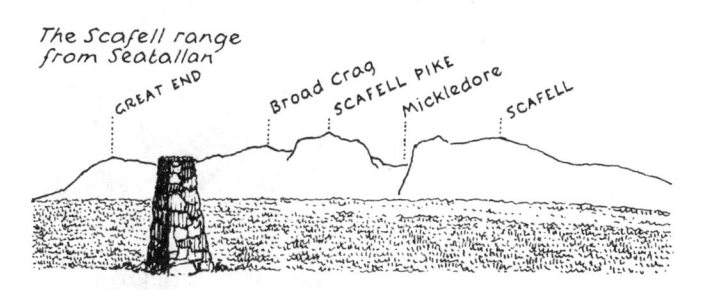

The Scafell range from Seatallan

GREAT END, Broad Crag, SCAFELL PIKE, Mickledore, SCAFELL

A special feature is the symmetrical appearance of Scafell Pike, the shape of which is better emphasised from this viewpoint than from any other. The summit is seen midway above the steep twin flanking profiles of Dropping Crag and Pikes Crag.

Starling Dodd 2085'

from Ennerdale

GREAT BORNE ▲
Buttermere ●
STARLING DODD ▲
▲ RED PIKE
● Gillerthwaite

MILES
0 1 2 3 4

Starling Dodd 2

NATURAL FEATURES

Starling Dodd, between Buttermere and Ennerdale, is one of those unobtrusive and unassuming fells that are rarely mentioned in literature or in conversation, that never really make an impact on mind or memory, that most visitors to the district know vaguely, from a study of maps, without ever wanting to know well. Its neat rounded summit surveys exciting landscapes but remains shyly aloof as though aware of its own limited contribution to the scenery.

The fell closely overlooks Ennerdale, having on this side a steep but featureless slope, the lower part being densely planted and without public access. Its best aspect is to the north, where the extensive plateau of Gale Fell, just below the summit, breaks suddenly into a rough drop to the desolate headwaters and marshes of Mosedale Beck. Gale Fell is bounded by Scale Beck, a place of popular resort in its lower course where Scale Force, Lakeland's highest waterfall, makes its thrilling leap in a deeply-enclosed ravine.

Starling Dodd is a point on a loosely-defined ridge, which runs west to Great Borne before dropping sharply to Ennerdale Water and east to Red Pike and the superb traverse of High Stile. It is seldom conspicuously seen in views from the valleys, being prominent only on the walk into Mosedale from Loweswater, directly in front.

Red Gill, Mosedale

Starling Dodd from High Beck, Ennerdale

Starling Dodd 3

MAP

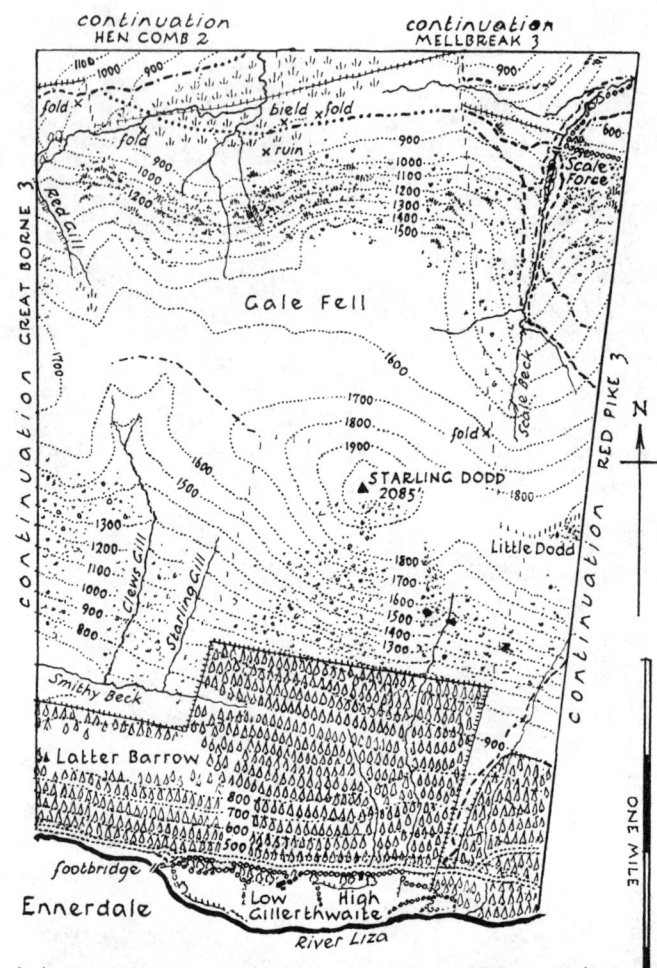

It is now almost impossible to trace on the ground the original line of the Floutern Pass route coming up from Crummock Water, although the Ordnance maps persist in recording it; the present route crosses the foot of Scale Force. Similarly, footpaths shown along the ridge of Starling Dodd should be treated with reserve.

Starling Dodd 4

ASCENT FROM LOWESWATER
1700 feet of ascent : 4½ miles

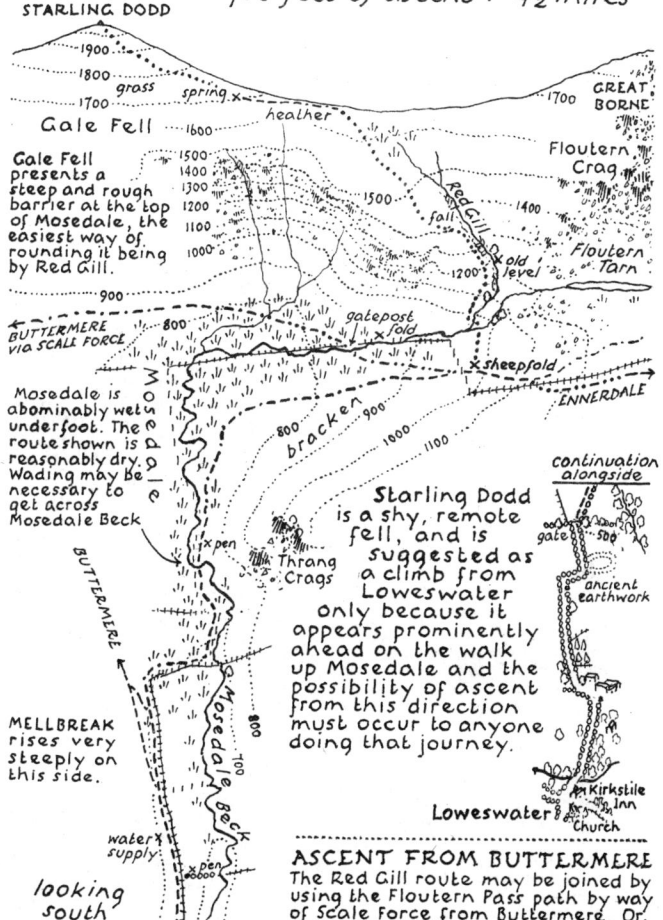

STARLING DODD

GREAT BORNE

Gale Fell

Gale Fell presents a steep and rough barrier at the top of Mosedale, the easiest way of rounding it being by Red Gill.

Floutern Crag

Floutern Tarn

BUTTERMERE VIA SCALE FORCE

ENNERDALE

Mosedale is abominably wet underfoot. The route shown is a reasonably dry. Wading may be necessary to get across Mosedale Beck

BUTTERMERE

Thrang Crags

Starling Dodd is a shy, remote fell, and is suggested as a climb from Loweswater only because it appears prominently ahead on the walk up Mosedale and the possibility of ascent from this direction must occur to anyone doing that journey.

MELLBREAK rises very steeply on this side.

continuation alongside

gate

ancient earthwork

Kirkstile Inn
Loweswater Church

looking south

water supply

continuation alongside

ASCENT FROM BUTTERMERE
The Red Gill route may be joined by using the Floutern Pass path by way of Scale Force from Buttermere. Or, shorter, from the Force climb Scale Beck to its source and bear right.

ASCENT FROM ENNERDALE
Direct access from Ennerdale may now be regarded as prohibited, the lower slopes being entirely planted and fenced for forestry purposes.

Starling Dodd 5

THE SUMMIT

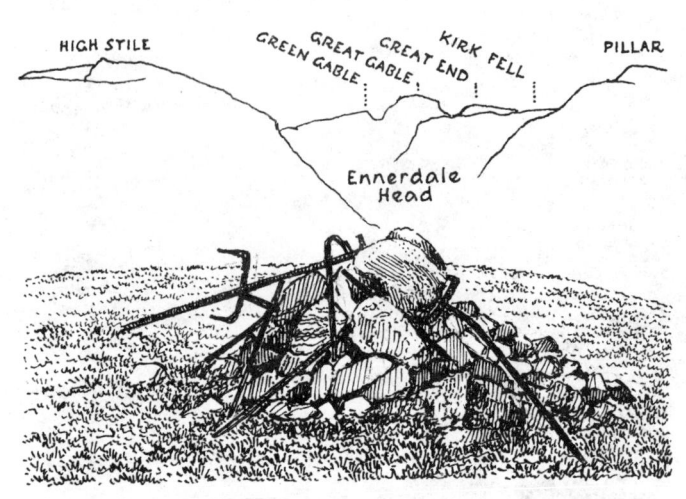

Skyline labels: HIGH STILE — GREEN GABLE — GREAT GABLE — GREAT END — KIRK FELL — PILLAR — Ennerdale Head

On the way to the top there are slight traces of a former fence, and one wonders what has happened to the iron posts, which usually survive long after the wires have gone. Upon arrival at the summit the question is partly answered, for several of them now reinforce the cairn. The top is smooth and grassy, with a little gravel, and except for the cairn, is quite featureless.

DESCENTS: *For Buttermere*, descend north-east, joining the path from Red Pike alongside Scale Beck. *For Loweswater*, reverse the route of ascent via Red Gill (see previous page). *For Ennerdale Bridge*, traverse Great Borne in clear weather, but in mist go down by Red Gill to join the Floutern Tarn route. *For Ennerdale (Gillerthwaite or Black Sail)* contour Little Dodd to join the permitted path through the forest from Red Pike.

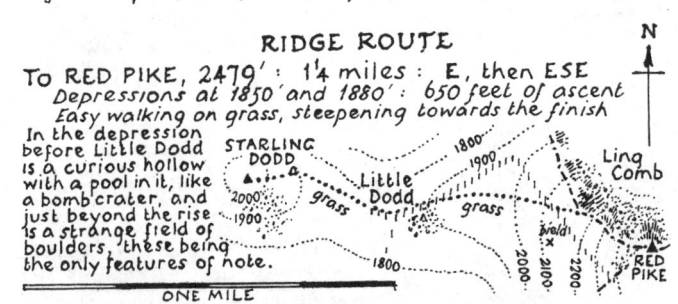

RIDGE ROUTE

TO RED PIKE, 2479' : 1¼ miles : E, then ESE
 Depressions at 1850' and 1880' : 650 feet of ascent
 Easy walking on grass, steepening towards the finish

In the depression before Little Dodd is a curious hollow with a pool in it, like a bomb crater, and just beyond the rise is a strange field of boulders, these being the only features of note.

ONE MILE

Starling Dodd 6

THE VIEW

The best feature of a moderate view is Ennerdale Water, strikingly seen in its entirety except for a small part hidden behind the intervening Bowness Knott.   Of the mountain array, Pillar and Company are the most impressive and, if not in too deep shadow, this is an excellent place to study the topography of the group.

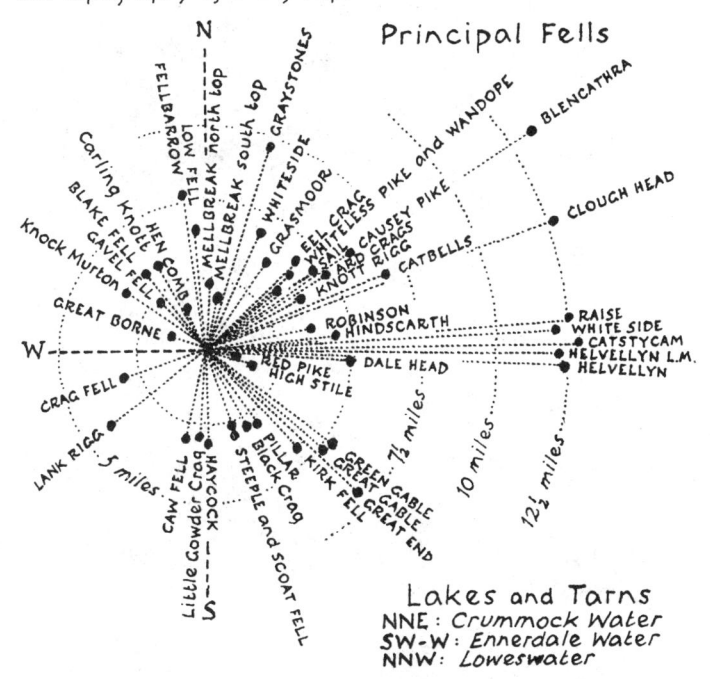

Principal Fells

(diagram showing bearings to surrounding fells, including:)

N: Mellbreak north top, Low Fell, Fellbarrow, Mellbreak south top, Graystones, Whiteside, Grasmoor, Hen Comb, Carling Knott, Blake Fell, Gavel Fell, Knock Murton, Great Borne, Ell Crag, Grisedale Pike, Scar Crags Causey Pike, Lord's Seat, Knott Rigg, Catbells, Blencathra, Clough Head, Robinson, Hindscarth, Dale Head, Raise, White Side, Catstycam, Helvellyn L.M., Helvellyn, Crag Fell, Red Pike, High Stile, Lank Rigg, Caw Fell, Haycock, Little Gowder Crag, Steeple, Black Crag, Pillar, Kirk Fell, Green Gable, Great Gable, Great End, Scoat Fell

Distances: 5 miles, 7½ miles, 10 miles, 12½ miles

Lakes and Tarns
NNE: *Crummock Water*
SW-W: *Ennerdale Water*
NNW: *Loweswater*

RIDGE ROUTE

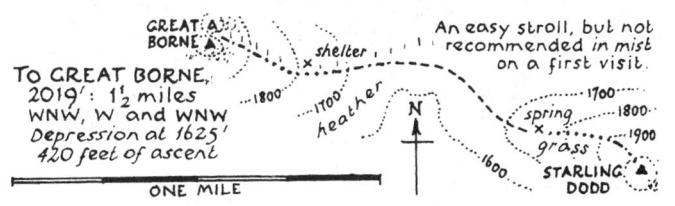

TO GREAT BORNE,
2019′: 1½ miles
WNW, W and WNW
Depression at 1625′
420 feet of ascent

An easy stroll, but not recommended in mist on a first visit.

GREAT BORNE ▲ — shelter × — heather — spring × — grass — STARLING DODD ▲

ONE MILE

Steeple 2687'

from Windgap Cove

- Gillerthwaite

STEEPLE ▲   ▲ PILLAR
         ▲ SCOAT FELL
▲   ▲ RED PIKE
HAYCOCK
              Wasdale
              • Head

Netherbeck Bridge
MILES
0 1 2 3 4

Steeple 2

NATURAL FEATURES

The unknown man who first named this fell was blessed both with inspiration and imagination. Few mountains given descriptive names have fared better. *Steeple* is a magnificent choice. Seen on a map, it commands the eye and quickens the pulse; seen in reality, it does the same. The climbing of Steeple is a feat to announce with pride in a letter to the old folks at home, who can safely be relied upon to invest the writer with undeserved heroism. Fancy our Fred having climbed a steeple!

This fell, however, is no slender spire. A cross-section of the summit-ridge is not like this ∧ but this ⟋. It is a fine pointed peak nevertheless, one of the best. If the west face was as steep as the east and the south ridge as long as the north, Steeple would provide a great climb. What spoils it is its close attachment to the bulkier Scoat Fell, to which it is linked by a short arete and which is not only higher but completely dominant.

Steeple in fact is no more than an excrescence on the side of Scoat Fell, and only its remarkable proportions have earned it a separate identity. The east crags in particular, forming a half-mile escarpment above Windgap Cove, give a fine airiness to the summit and to the rocky spine of the ridge climbing out of Ennerdale to reach it. This is first-rate mountain country. The short drop west to Mirklin Cove is less fearsome, but rough. Boundary streams Low Beck and High Beck both flow into the Liza, so that Steeple is wholly a fell of Ennerdale.

The north ridge

Steeple 3

summit

Scoat Fell

The upper part of the north ridge

Steeple, as seen from Scoat Fell across Mirk Cove

Steeple 4

MAP

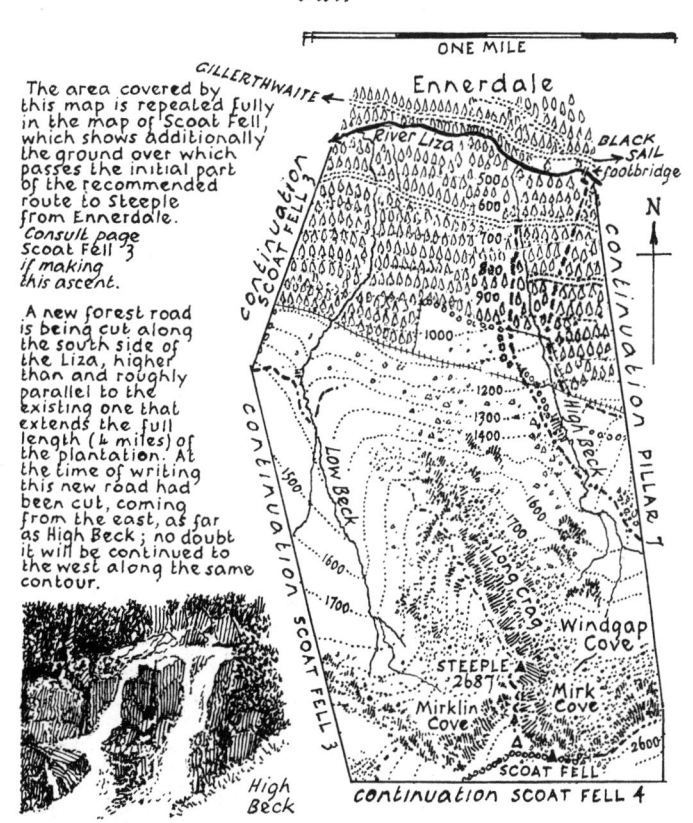

The area covered by this map is repeated fully in the map of Scoat Fell, which shows additionally the ground over which passes the initial part of the recommended route to Steeple from Ennerdale. Consult page Scoat Fell 3 if making this ascent.

A new forest road is being cut along the south side of the Liza, higher than and roughly parallel to the existing one that extends the full length (4 miles) of the plantation. At the time of writing this new road had been cut, coming from the east, as far as High Beck; no doubt it will be continued to the west along the same contour.

Low Beck and High Beck are joyful streams on the last half-mile of their descent to join the River Liza, leaping and tumbling in lovely cascades down the fern-clad ravines they have carved out of the fellside. But they have few visitors, and less since the growing plantations gradually hid them from the sight of travellers in the valley and muted their merry music. Except where the forest roads cross their courses (on concrete bridges that have not the beauty bridges should have) they can neither be properly seen nor easily reached, nor is it possible to follow their banks. A canopy of foreign trees is dimming their sparkle, and they are taking on the sombreness of their new environment.

Things are not what they used to be, in Ennerdale. They never will be, ever again.

Steeple 5

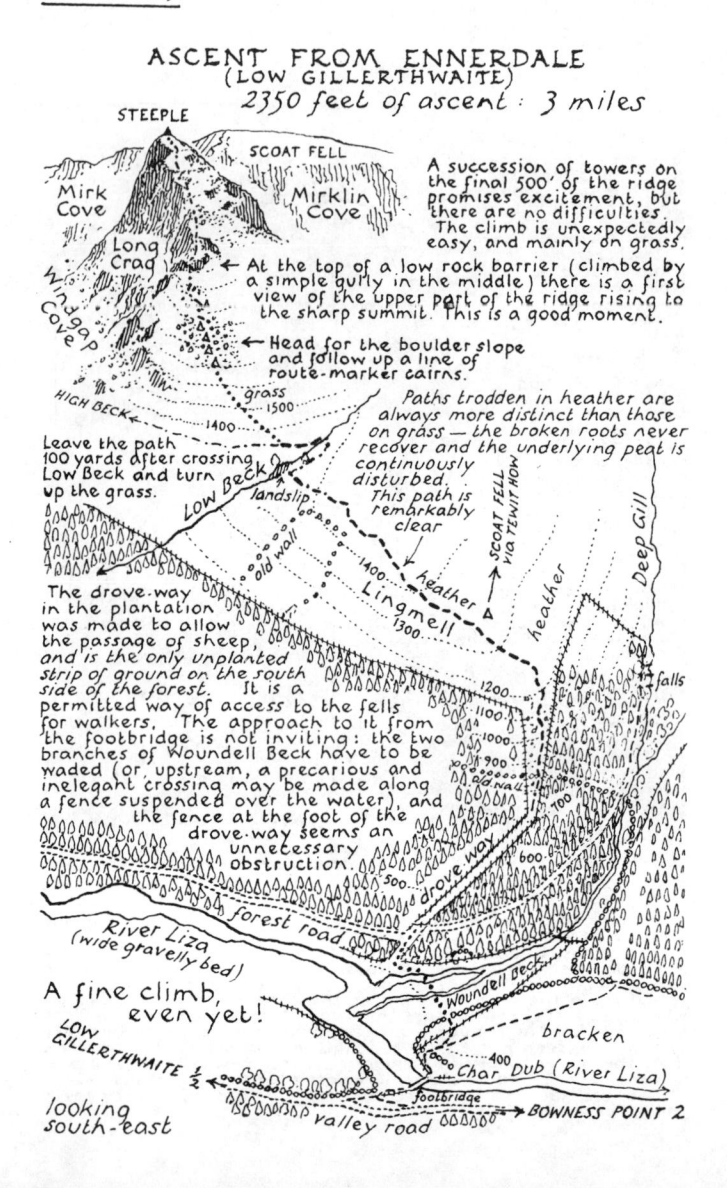

ASCENT FROM ENNERDALE
(LOW GILLERTHWAITE)
2350 feet of ascent : 3 miles

STEEPLE

SCOAT FELL

Mirk Cove

Mirklin Cove

Long Crag

Windgap Cove

A succession of towers on the final 500' of the ridge promises excitement, but there are no difficulties. The climb is unexpectedly easy, and mainly on grass.

← At the top of a low rock barrier (climbed by a simple gully in the middle) there is a first view of the upper part of the ridge rising to the sharp summit. This is a good moment.

← Head for the boulder slope and follow up a line of route-marker cairns.

HIGH BECK

grass 1500

1400

Leave the path 100 yards after crossing Low Beck and turn up the grass.

Low Beck

landslip

old wall

Paths trodden in heather are always more distinct than those on grass — the broken roots never recover and the underlying peat is continuously disturbed.

This path is remarkably clear

SCOAT FELL VIA TEWIT HOW

heather

Lingmell 1300

1400

Deep Gill

heather

1200

falls

1100

1000

The drove-way in the plantation was made to allow the passage of sheep, and is the only unplanted strip of ground on the south side of the forest. It is a permitted way of access to the fells for walkers. The approach to it from the footbridge is not inviting: the two branches of Woundell Beck have to be waded (or, upstream, a precarious and inelegant crossing may be made along a fence suspended over the water), and the fence at the foot of the drove-way seems an unnecessary obstruction.

900

800

700

600

drove way

500

forest road

River Liza (wide gravelly bed)

A fine climb, even yet!

LOW GILLERTHWAITE ½

Woundell Beck

bracken

400 Char Dub (River Liza)

footbridge → BOWNESS POINT 2

looking south-east

valley road

Steeple 6

THE SUMMIT

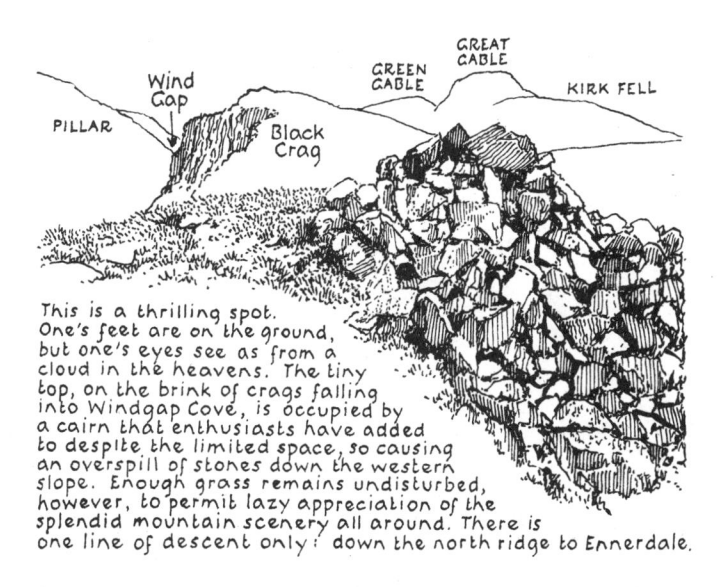

Labels on panorama: PILLAR, Wind Gap, Black Crag, GREEN GABLE, GREAT GABLE, KIRK FELL

This is a thrilling spot. One's feet are on the ground, but one's eyes see as from a cloud in the heavens. The tiny top, on the brink of crags falling into Windgap Cove, is occupied by a cairn that enthusiasts have added to despite the limited space, so causing an overspill of stones down the western slope. Enough grass remains undisturbed, however, to permit lazy appreciation of the splendid mountain scenery all around. There is one line of descent only: down the north ridge to Ennerdale.

RIDGE ROUTE

To SCOAT FELL, 2760': ¼ mile
S, but start W
Depression at 2620'
140 feet of ascent
Every step is a joy.

The arete leading on to Scoat Fell is in clear view, with a path winding up it, from the summit of Steeple, but the col below it cannot be reached by a beeline; instead, first go a few paces to the west and pick up a distinct track that swings round to the col.

The arete is easy, safe in mist, finely situated, and ends on the flat top, the cairn being directly ahead (100 yards).

STEEPLE

SCOAT FELL

QUARTER-MILE

Steeple 7

THE VIEW

Although the view is greatly circumscribed by the loftier and impending masses of Scoat Fell and Pillar, there is to be seen more than Steeple's subservient position on the north side of the watershed would lead one to expect. West and north the scene is uninterrupted and there is a good sweep of mountainous country to be seen eastwards. The view of Ennerdale, where the lake is displayed almost entirely, is excellent, but visitors are likely to be impressed most of all by the craggy hollows of Mirk and Mirklin Coves nearby.

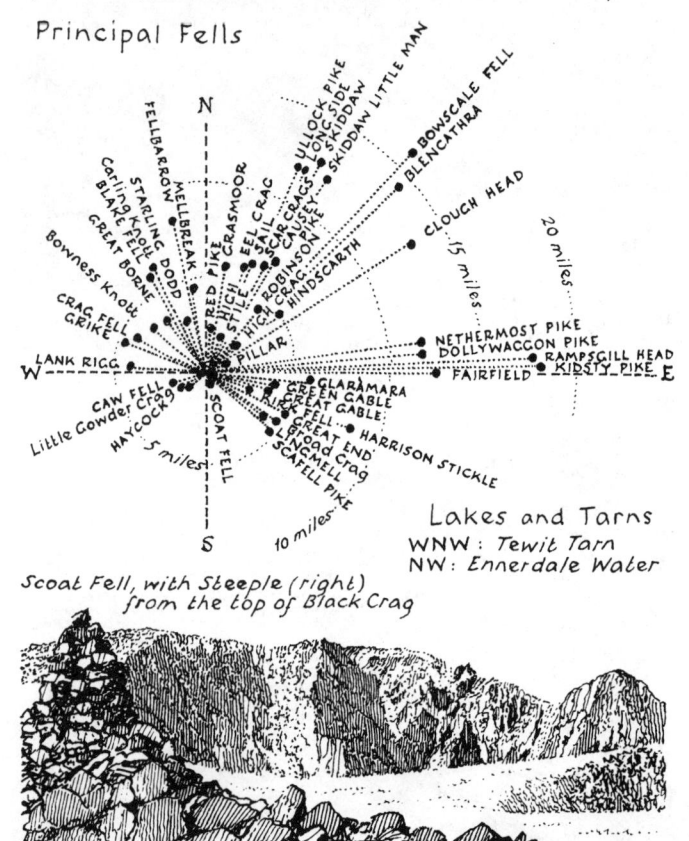

Principal Fells

Lakes and Tarns
WNW: Tewit Tarn
NW: Ennerdale Water

Scoat Fell, with Steeple (right) from the top of Black Crag

Steeple 8

Steeple, east face, from Black Crag

Yewbarrow 2058'

from Netherbeck Bridge

RED PIKE ▲
YEWBARROW ▲ Wasdale
            ● Head
  ▲ MIDDLE FELL
     ● Bowderdale
   MILES
 0 1 2 3 4

Yewbarrow 2

NATURAL FEATURES

Many mountains have been described as having the shape of the inverted hull of a boat, but none of them more fittingly than Yewbarrow, which extends along the west side of Wasdale for two miles as a high and narrow ridge, the prow and the stern coming sharply down to valley level with many barnacled incrustations. These latter roughnesses make the long summit rather difficult of attainment from either end, while the steep sides also deter ascent, so that Yewbarrow is not often climbed although it is a centre-piece of magnificent fell country and commands thrilling views. Nor is the ridge itself without incident, one feature in particular, Great Door, being a remarkable cleft where the crest narrows at the top of the craggy declivity above Wastwater.

Yewbarrow's western side is well defined by Over Beck, which comes down from Dore Head, the col linking the fell with Red Pike and the Pillar group. At one time, Dore Head had the reputation of providing the best scree-run in the district on its northern side, descending to Mosedale, but generations of booted scree-runners have scraped the passage clean in places and left it dangerously slippery.

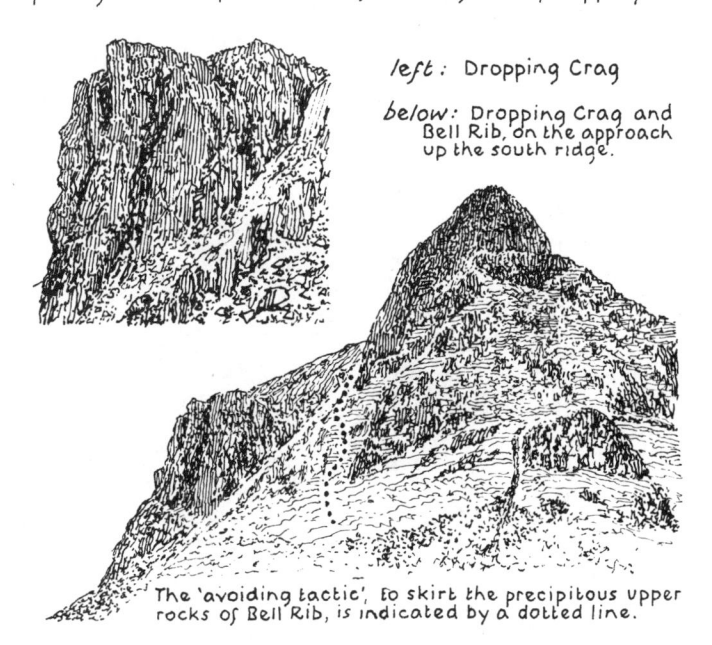

left: Dropping Crag

below: Dropping Crag and Bell Rib, on the approach up the south ridge.

The 'avoiding tactic', to skirt the precipitous upper rocks of Bell Rib, is indicated by a dotted line.

Yewbarrow 3

above:

Great Door, as it is seen on the descent of the south ridge. The line of escape from this *impasse* is indicated (→)

The South Ridge

right: Just before reaching Great Door on the descent, a similar cleft is met which might be mistaken for it; this, however, is rounded without difficulty.

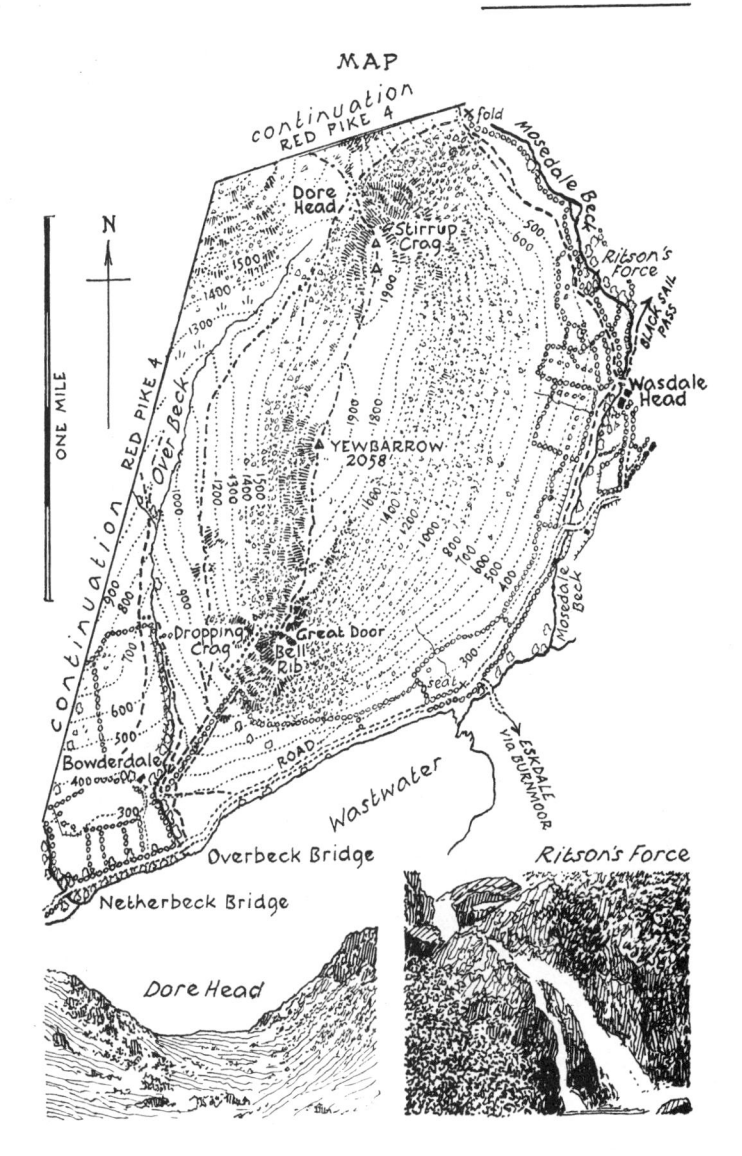

Yewbarrow 4

MAP

ONE MILE

Dore Head
Stirrup Crag
YEWBARROW 2058
Mosedale Beck
Ritson's Force
BLACK SAIL PASS
Wasdale Head
continuation RED PIKE 4
Over Beck
Dropping Crag
Bell Rib
Great Door
Mosedale Beck
seat
ESKDALE via BURNMOOR
Bowderdale
ROAD
Wastwater
Overbeck Bridge
Netherbeck Bridge

Dore Head

Ritson's Force

Yewbarrow 5

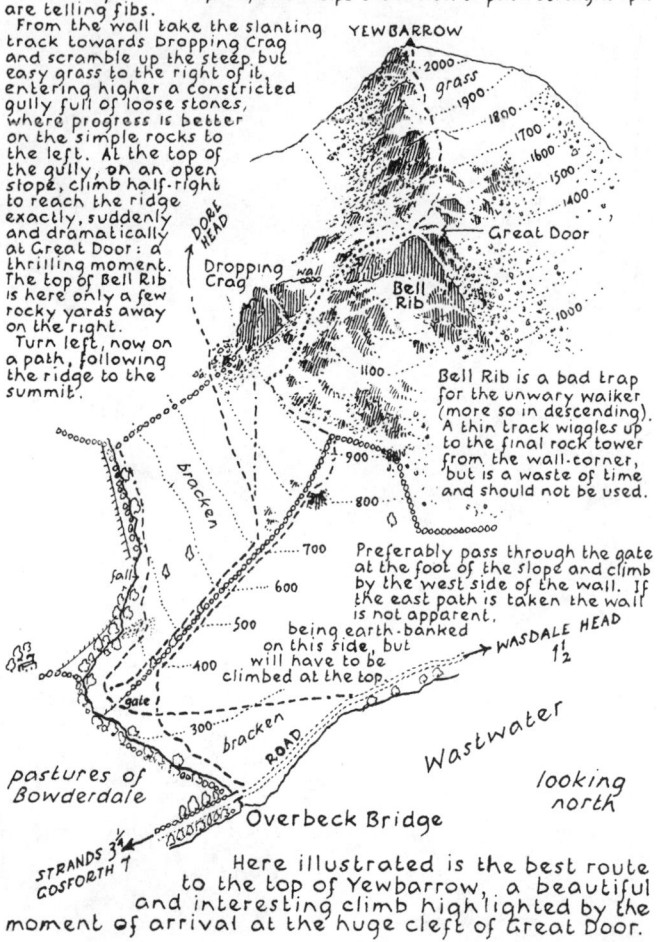

ASCENT FROM WASDALE
(OVERBECK BRIDGE)
1900 feet of ascent : 1½ miles

Very prominent in the early stages of the ascent is the towering pinnacle of Bell Rib, directly astride the ridge. Bell Rib cannot be climbed by a non-expert, and maps that show a path straight up it are telling fibs.

From the wall take the slanting track towards Dropping Crag and scramble up the steep but easy grass to the right of it, entering higher a constricted gully full of loose stones, where progress is better on the simple rocks to the left. At the top of the gully, on an open slope, climb half-right to reach the ridge exactly, suddenly and dramatically at Great Door: a thrilling moment. The top of Bell Rib is here only a few rocky yards away on the right.

Turn left, now on a path, following the ridge to the summit.

Bell Rib is a bad trap for the unwary walker (more so in descending). A thin track wiggles up to the final rock tower from the wall-corner, but is a waste of time and should not be used.

Preferably pass through the gate at the foot of the slope and climb by the west side of the wall. If the east path is taken the wall is not apparent, being earth-banked on this side, but will have to be climbed at the top.

Here illustrated is the best route to the top of Yewbarrow, a beautiful and interesting climb highlighted by the moment of arrival at the huge cleft of Great Door.

Yewbarrow 6

ASCENT FROM WASDALE HEAD
1900 feet of ascent : 2½ miles

Start the climb to Dore Head from the path at the foot of the slope below it; short cuts across the boulders are not rewarding. Keep to the grass on the right of the scree-run.

From Dore Head, Stirrup Crag looks very formidable, and the upper band of rock unassailable, but getting up it is nothing more than a strenuous exercise in elementary gymnastics and unusual postures. The way lies within the confines of rocky cracks and chimneys, and there is no sense of danger or indecent exposure.

Follow the trail of blood left by the author, or, if the elements have removed this evidence of his sufferings, the debris of dentures, bootsoles, etc., left by other pilgrims, and step happily onto the pleasant top. Between this point and the summit of the fell is a wide depression.

Those of faint heart may avoid Stirrup Crag entirely by proceeding from Dore Head towards Over Beck, turning up a grass slope to the depression when the boulders cease. For such, the author bled in vain.

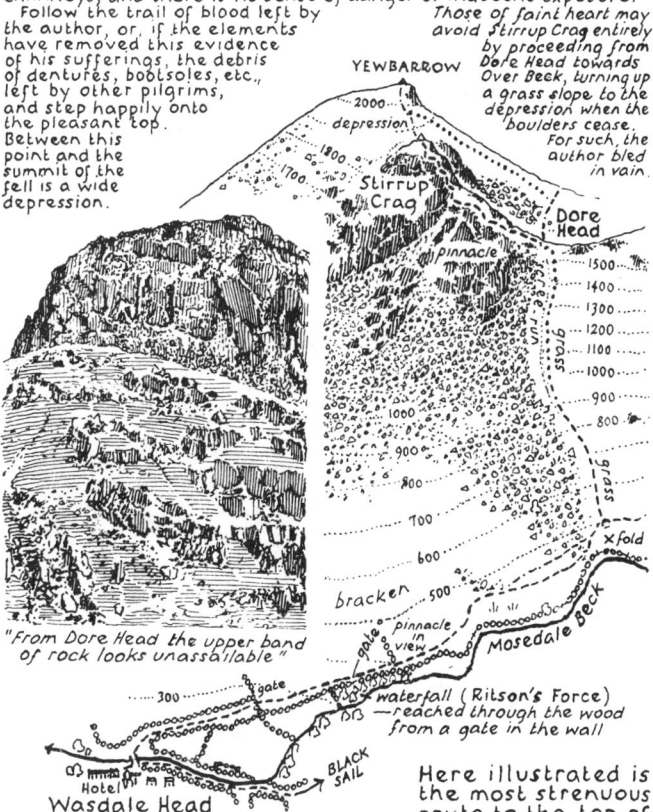

"From Dore Head the upper band of rock looks unassailable"

looking south-west

Here illustrated is the most strenuous route to the top of Yewbarrow, a tiring plod up to Dore Head being followed by an energetic scramble up a rocky rampart.

Yewbarrow 7

THE SUMMIT

KIRK FELL — GREAT GABLE — HELVELLYN — GLARAMARA

After the agonies and perils of the ascent it is an anticlimax to find the summit a peaceful and placid sheep pasture, an elevated field, with the cairn crowning a grassy mound on the west edge.

DESCENTS: The usual descents by way of the ridge, north or south, encounter rock and need care. The south ridge, at first easy, narrows to the width of the path at Great Door in exciting surroundings. The natural continuation of the ridge lies up the facing rocks onto the top of Bell Rib, but do NOT venture into this bad trap; instead, at this point, turn down the slope ON THE RIGHT into a short rocky gully where loose stones are a menace and skirt the lower buttresses of Bell Rib to regain the ridge at a wall, whence an easy slope leads down to Overbeck Bridge. The north ridge route crosses a depression, rises to the cairned top of Stirrup Crag, and then drops steeply and sharply down a series of rocky cracks in the crag for a few desperate minutes: a bad passage, but neither dangerous nor difficult if care is taken. If all goes well, Dore Head, immediately below, is then soon reached at the top of the scree-run into Mosedale. Those who do not fancy steep rocks can avoid Stirrup Crag entirely by slanting down left from the depression; in bad conditions, this is the best way off the fell. It may be noted, too, that a descent may be made direct to Wasdale Head from the summit cairn: the slope is rough and tedious, but safe.

The use of the Bottom in Mountaineering.

A fellwalker's best asset is a pair of strong legs; next best is a tough and rubbery bottom. In ascent this appendage is, of course, useless, but when descending steep grass or rocks such as are met on the ridge of Yewbarrow the posterior is a valuable agent of friction, a sheet-anchor with superb resistance to the pull of gravity.

RIDGE ROUTE
TO RED PIKE, 2707'

1¾ miles: NNE, NW and N
Depression at 1520'
1350 feet of ascent

Reach Dore Head over Stirrup Crag or by the variation, as described above; then follow the fair track up the opposite slope. An excellent journey.

HALF A MILE

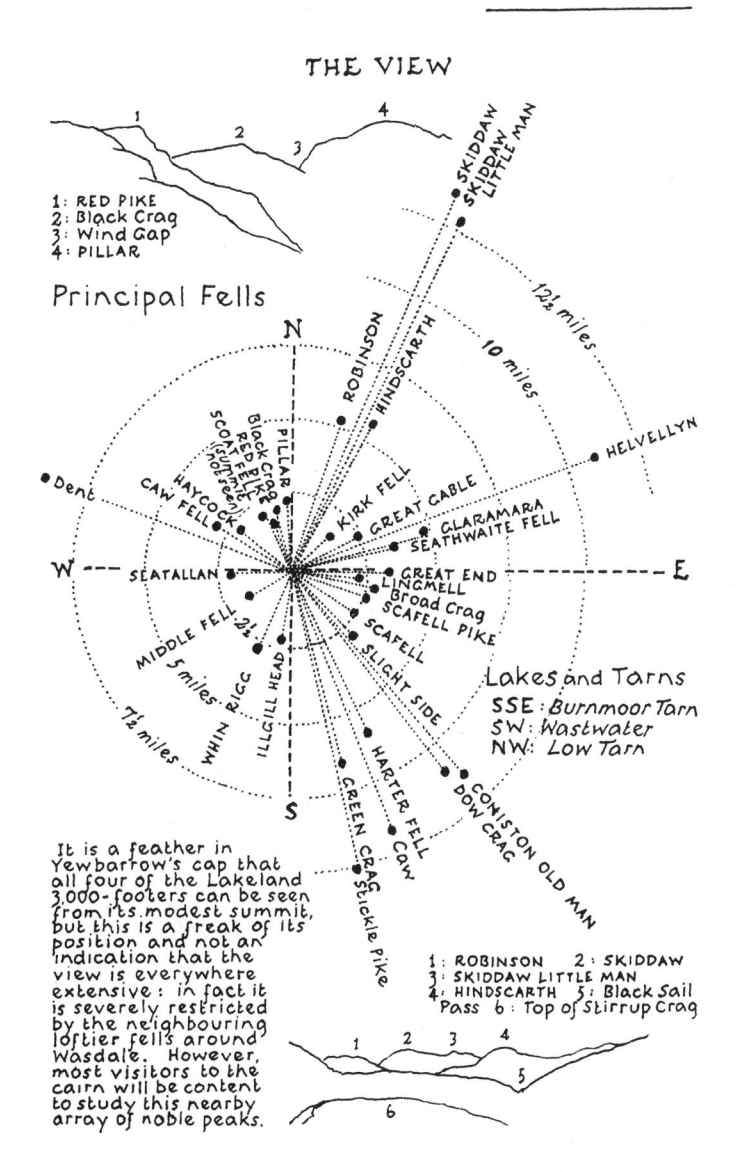

Yewbarrow 8

THE VIEW

1: RED PIKE
2: Black Crag
3: Wind Gap
4: PILLAR

Principal Fells

Lakes and Tarns
SSE: Burnmoor Tarn
SW: Wastwater
NW: Low Tarn

It is a feather in Yewbarrow's cap that all four of the Lakeland 3,000-footers can be seen from its modest summit, but this is a freak of its position and not an indication that the view is everywhere extensive: in fact it is severely restricted by the neighbouring loftier fells around Wasdale. However, most visitors to the cairn will be content to study this nearby array of noble peaks.

1: ROBINSON 2: SKIDDAW
3: SKIDDAW LITTLE MAN
4: HINDSCARTH 5: Black Sail Pass 6: Top of Stirrup Crag

Yewbarrow 9

from Gatherstone Head

THE WESTERN FELLS
*Some Personal notes
in conclusion*

When I came down from Starling Dodd on the 10th of September 1965 I had just succeeded in obtaining a complete view from the summit before the mist descended, after laying patient siege to it through several wet weekends, and in so doing I had concluded the field-work for my last book with only one week left before the end of the summer bus service put the fell out of reach. Thus a 13-year plan was finished one week ahead of schedule. Happy? Yes, I was happy, as anyone must be who comes to the end of a long road ahead of the clock. Sorry? Yes, I was sorry, as anyone must be who comes to the end of a long road he has enjoyed travelling. Relieved? Yes, I was relieved, because a broken leg during these years would have meant a broken heart, too.

    I think I must concede that the scenery of the western half of Lakeland (dropping a vertical through High Raise in the Central Fells) is, on the whole, better than the eastern, although it has nothing more beautiful than the head of Ullswater. This is not to say that the fellwalking is better: it is more exciting and exacting but the Helvellyn and High Street ranges in the east are supreme for the man who likes to stride out over the tops all day. Those who prefer to follow narrow ridges from summit to summit are best catered for in the west. The southern half, too, is generally finer than the northern, so that the highlights of the district are to be found mainly in the southwestern sector, from the Duddon to Whinlatter. But it is all delectable country..... One advantage I found in roaming around the Western Fells is that they are still free from the type of visitor who has spoiled Langdale and Keswick and other places easier of access. Wasdale Head and Buttermere are beginning to suffer from tourist invasion, but on the tops one can still wander in solitude and enjoy the freedom characteristic of the whole district before somebody invented the motor car.

I promised to give my opinion of the six best fells. I should not have used the word 'best', which suggests that some are not as good as others. I think they are all good. The finest, however, must have the attributes of mountains, i.e., height, a commanding appearance, a good view, steepness and ruggedness: qualities that are most pronounced in the volcanic area of the south-western sector. I now give, after much biting of finger-nails, what I consider to be the finest half-dozen:

Be quick, turn over

SCAFELL PIKE
BOWFELL
PILLAR
GREAT GABLE
BLENCATHRA
CRINKLE CRAGS

These are not necessarily the six fells I like best. It grieves me to have to omit Haystacks (most of all), Langdale Pikes, Place Fell, Carrock Fell and some others simply because they do not measure up in altitude to the grander mountains. There will be surprise at the omission of Scafell, the crags of which provide the finest sight in Lakeland, but too much of this fell is lacking in interest. It would be seventh if there were seven in the list. Contrary to general opinion (which would favour Great Gable), the grandest of the lot is Scafell Pike. Of the six, all are of volcanic rock with the exception of Blencathra.

The six best summits (attributes: a small neat peak of naked rock with a good view) I consider to be

DOW CRAG, Coniston
HARTER FELL, Eskdale
HELM CRAG, Grasmere
EAGLE CRAG, Langstrath
SLIGHT SIDE, Scafell
STEEPLE, Ennerdale

All these, except Steeple, are accessible only by scrambling on rock. The top inches of Helm Crag are hardest to reach.

The six best places for a fellwalker to be (other than summits) because of their exciting situations, and which can be reached without danger, are

- STRIDING EDGE, Helvellyn
- First col, LORD'S RAKE, Scafell
- MICKLEDORE, Scafell
- SHARP EDGE, Blencathra
- SOUTH TRAVERSE, Great Gable
- SHAMROCK TRAVERSE, Pillar

Of course I haven't forgotten Jack's Rake on Pavey Ark. I never could. But this is a place only for men with hair on their chests. I am sorry to omit Great Slab and Climbers Traverse on Bowfell.

The finest ridge-walks are, I think,

- THE FAIRFIELD HORSESHOE (Ambleside)
- THE HIGH STREET RANGE (Garburn-Moor Divock)
- THE MOSEDALE HORSESHOE (Wasdale Head)
- CAUSEY PIKE – WHITELESS PIKE
- GRISEDALE PIKE – WHITESIDE
- ESK HAUSE – WRYNOSE PASS, via Bowfell
- THE ESKDALE HORSESHOE (Slight Side-Bowfell)
- THE HELVELLYN RANGE (Grisedale Pass-Threlkeld)
- THE HIGH STILE RIDGE, with Haystacks
- CATBELLS – DALE HEAD – HINDSCARTH – SCOPE END
- THE CONISTON ROUND (Old Man-Wetherlam)

(not in order of merit)

In my introductory remarks to Book One I described my task in compiling these books as a labour of love. So it has been. These have been the best years for me, the golden years. I have had a full reward in a thousand happy days on the fells. But, unexpectedly, it has been a profitable venture for me in terms of money, bringing me a small fortune, simply through the continued support of the many kind readers who have both bought and recommended the books. It is money I have not spent and do not want. One surely does not wish to be paid in cash for writing a love-letter! There is, or soon will be, enough to build and equip an Animal Welfare Centre in Kendal, and the Westmorland Branch of the R.S.P.C.A. have accepted for this purpose a gift which is really donated by the readers of these books. Every true fellwalker develops a liking and compassion for birds and animals, the solitary walker especially for they are his only companions, and it seems to me appropriate that this windfall should be used to provide a refuge in Lakeland where ailing and distressed creatures can be brought for care and attention. I thought you would like to know this. You have provided the bricks.

If Starling Dodd had been the last walk of all for me, and this the last book, I should now be desolate indeed, like a lover who has lost his loved one, and the future would have the bleakness of death. I have long known this and anticipated it, and sought desperately in my mind for some new avenue along which I could continue to express my devotion to Lakeland within the talents available to me. I am in better case than the lover who has lost his loved one, for my beloved is still there and faithful, and if there were to be a separation the defection would be mine. But why need this be the last book? Within a year I shall be retired from work (on account of old age!), but I can still walk, still draw, still write; and love itself is never pensioned off ..... So there must be other books ..... In this series I have crowded details of the fells into some 2000 pages, but as much as I have included has been omitted through lack of space. I would like now, in a more leisurely fashion, to continue acquaintance with the fells, and, out of consideration for my white hairs, explore the valleys and daleheads more. What I have in mind is A LAKELAND SKETCHBOOK, which, all being well, could be the start of a new series that would aim to show the best of Lakeland in pictures and, by indicating the changes taking place in the district, in valley and on fell, serve to supplement the present series of guidebooks. I also have a good title for another book: FELL WANDERER, and might do this first if I can think of something to write about — personal experiences on the fells perhaps — not, definitely not, an autobiography (as if I dare! Let me keep my friends!). In between times I am pledged to do A PICTORIAL GUIDE TO THE PENNINE WAY, and have had four collaborators, four good men and true, sweating their guts out during the past year to provide a mass of detail and resolve certain doubts and generally smooth my own journey subsequently. This will be a unique book the way I plan it: you will start it at the bottom of the last page and you will read upwards and forwards to the top of the first, which is something that even the Chinese never thought of doing. It will seem logical, however, when you see it, and there is no question of your having to stand on your head.

Regretfully, I reject suggestions of a Book Eight: 'The Outlying Fells.'

.... So this is farewell to the present series of books.

The fleeting hour of life of those who love the hills is quickly spent, but the hills are eternal. Always there will be the lonely ridge, the dancing beck, the silent forest; always there will be the exhilaration of the summits. These are for the seeking, and those who seek and find while there is yet time will be blessed both in mind and body.

I wish you all many happy days on the fells in the years ahead.

There will be fair winds and foul, days of sun and days of rain. But enjoy them all.

Good walking! And don't forget — watch where you are putting your feet.

AW.

Christmas, 1965.

SIGN REFERENCES
(signs used in the maps and diagrams)

Good footpath
(sufficiently distinct to be followed in mist)

Intermittent footpath
(difficult to follow in mist)

Route recommended but no path
(if recommended one way only, arrow indicates direction)

Wall   Broken wall

Fence   Broken fence

Marshy ground   Trees

Crags   Boulders

Stream or River
(arrow indicates direction of flow)

Waterfall   Bridge

Buildings   Unenclosed road

Contours (at 100' intervals)   1900 1800 1700

Summit-cairn ▲   Other (prominent) cairns △

SIGN REFERENCES
(signs used in the maps and diagrams)

Good footpath
(sufficiently distinct to be followed in mist)

Intermittent footpath
(difficult to follow in mist)

Route recommended but no path
(if recommended one way only, arrow indicates direction)

Wall **Broken wall**

Fence **Broken fence**

Marshy ground **Trees**

Crags **Boulders**

Stream or River
(arrow indicates direction of flow)

Waterfall **Bridge**

Buildings **Unenclosed road**

Contours (at 100' intervals) 1900 1800 1700

Summit-cairn ▲ **Other** (prominent) **cairns** ∆

THE
EASTERN
FELLS

A PICTORIAL GUIDE
TO THE
LAKELAND FELLS
50TH ANNIVERSARY EDITION

being an illustrated account
of a study and exploration
of the mountains in the
English Lake District

by

A Wainwright

BOOK ONE
THE EASTERN FELLS

Frances Lincoln Limited
4 Torriano Mews
Torriano Avenue
London NW5 2RZ
www.franceslincoln.com

Originally published by Henry Marshall, Kentmere, 1955

First published by Frances Lincoln 2003

50th Anniversary Edition with re-originated artwork
published by Frances Lincoln 2005

Copyright © The Estate of A. Wainwright 1955

All rights reserved. Without limiting the rights under
copyright reserved above, no part of this publication may
be reproduced, stored in or introduced into a retrieval
system, or transmitted, in any form or by any means
(electronic, mechanical, photocopying, or otherwise),
without either prior permission in writing from the
publisher or a licence permitting restricted copying.
In the United Kingdom such licences are issued by
the Copyright Licensing Agency, Saffron House,
6-10 Kirby Street, London EC1N 8TS.

Printed and bound in China

A CIP catalogue record for this book
is available from the British Library.

ISBN 978 0 7112 2454 4

18 17 16 15 14 13 12 11

50TH ANNIVERSARY EDITION
PUBLISHED BY
FRANCES LINCOLN, LONDON

THE PICTORIAL GUIDES

Book One: The Eastern Fells, 1955
Book Two: The Far Eastern Fells, 1957
Book Three: The Central Fells, 1958
Book Four: The Southern Fells, 1960
Book Five: The Northern Fells, 1962
Book Six: The North Western Fells, 1964
Book Seven: The Western Fells, 1966

PUBLISHER'S NOTE

This 50th Anniversary edition of the Pictorial Guides to the Lakeland Fells is newly reproduced from the handwritten pages created in the 1950s and 1960s by A. Wainwright. The descriptions of the walks were correct, to the best of the author's knowledge, at the time of first publication and they are reproduced here without amendment. However, footpaths, cairns and other waymarks described here are no longer all as they were fifty years ago and walkers are advised to check with an up-to-date map when planning a walk.

Fellwalking has increased dramatically since the Pictorial Guides were first published. Some popular routes have become eroded, making good footwear and great care all the more necessary for walkers. The vital points about fellwalking, as A. Wainwright himself wrote on many occasions, are to use common sense and to remember to watch where you are putting your feet.

A programme of revision of the Pictorial Guides is under way and revised editions of each of them will be published over the next few years.

BOOK ONE

is dedicated to

THE MEN OF THE ORDNANCE SURVEY

whose maps of Lakeland
have given me much pleasure
both on the fells
and by my fireside

INTRODUCTION

INTRODUCTION

Surely there is no other place in this whole wonderful world quite like Lakeland ...no other so exquisitely lovely, no other so charming, no other that calls so insistently across a gulf of distance. All who truly love Lakeland are exiles when away from it.

Here, in small space, is the wonderland of childhood's dreams, lingering far beyond childhood through the span of a man's life: its enchantment grows with passing years and quiet eventide is enriched by the haunting sweetness of dear memories, memories that remain evergreen through the flight of time, that refresh and sustain in the darker days. How many, these memories...........the moment of wakening, and the sudden joyful realisation that this is to be another day of freedom on the hills........ the dawn chorus of bird-song........ the delicate lacework of birches against the sky ...... morning sun drawing aside the veils of mist; black-stockinged lambs, in springtime, amongst the daffodils......... silver cascades dancing and leaping down bracken steeps..... autumn colours ....a red fox running over snow....... the silence of lonely hills...... storm and tempest in the high places, and the unexpected glimpses of valleys dappled in sunlight far beneath the swirling clouds............. rain, and the intimate shelter of lichened walls......... fierce winds on the heights and soft breezes that are no more than gentle caresses...........a sheepdog watching its master

INTRODUCTION

.... the snow and ice and freezing stillnesses of midwinter: a white world, rosy-pink as the sun goes down....... the supreme moment when the top cairn comes into sight at last, only minutes away, after the long climb........ the small ragged sheep that brave the blizzards......... the symphonies of murmuring streams, unending, with never a discord ......curling smoke from the chimneys of the farm down below amongst the trees, where the day shall end......oil-lamps in flagged kitchens, huge fires in huge fireplaces, huge suppers...........glittering moonlight on placid waters...... stars above dark peaks..... the tranquillity that comes before sleep, when thoughts are of the day that is gone and the day that is to come......... All these memories, and so many more, breathing anew the rare quality and magical atmosphere of Lakeland .... memories that belong to Lakeland, and could not belong in the same way to any other place.............. memories that enslave the mind forever.

Many are they who have fallen under the spell of Lakeland, and many are they who have been moved to tell of their affection, in story and verse and picture and song.

This book is one man's way of expressing his devotion to Lakeland's friendly hills. It was conceived, and is born, after many years of inarticulate worshipping at their shrines.

It is, in very truth, a love-letter.

INTRODUCTION

Classification and Definition

Any division of the Lakeland fells into geographical districts must necessarily be arbitrary, just as the location of the outer boundaries of Lakeland must always be a matter of opinion. Any attempt to define internal or external boundaries is certain to invite criticism, and he who takes it upon himself to say where Lakeland starts and finishes, or, for example, where the Central Fells merge into the Southern Fells and *which* fells are the Central Fells and which the Southern and *why* they need be so classified, must not expect his pronouncements to be generally accepted.

Yet for present purposes some plan of classification and definition must be used. County and parochial boundaries are no help, nor is the recently-defined area of the Lakeland National Park, for this book is concerned only with the high ground.

First, the external boundaries. Straight lines linking the extremities of the outlying lakes enclose all the higher fells very conveniently. There are a few fells of lesser height to the north and east, however, that are typically Lakeland in character and cannot properly be omitted: these are brought in, somewhat untidily, by extending the lines in those areas. Thus:

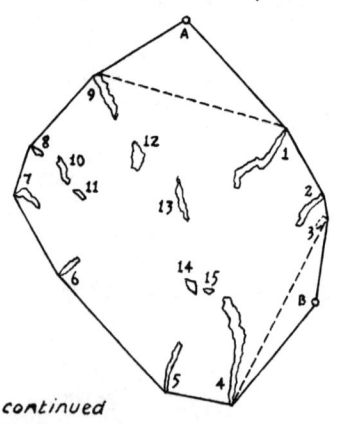

1 : *Ullswater*
2 : *Hawes Water*
3 : proposed *Swindale Res!*
4 : *Windermere*
5 : *Coniston Water*
6 : *Wast Water*
7 : *Ennerdale Water*
8 : *Loweswater*
9 : *Bassenthwaite Lake*
10 : *Crummock Water*
11 : *Buttermere*
12 : *Derwent Water*
13 : *Thirlmere*
14 : *Grasmere*
15 : *Rydal Water*
A : Caldbeck
B : Longsleddale (church)

continued

INTRODUCTION

Classification and Definition
continued

The complete Guide is planned to include all the fells in the area enclosed by the straight lines of the diagram. This is an undertaking quite beyond the compass of a single volume, and it is necessary, therefore, to divide the area into convenient sections, making the fullest use of natural boundaries (lakes, valleys and low passes) so that each district is, as far as possible, self-contained and independent of the rest.

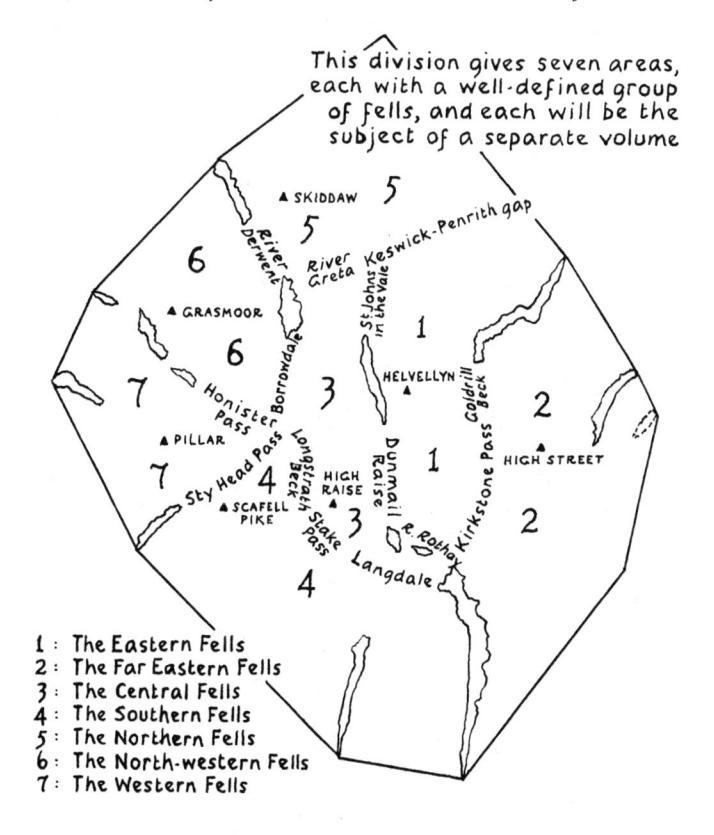

This division gives seven areas, each with a well-defined group of fells, and each will be the subject of a separate volume

1 : The Eastern Fells
2 : The Far Eastern Fells
3 : The Central Fells
4 : The Southern Fells
5 : The Northern Fells
6 : The North-western Fells
7 : The Western Fells

INTRODUCTION

Notes on the Illustrations

THE MAPS.................. Many excellent books have been written about Lakeland, but the best literature of all for the walker is that published by the Director General of Ordnance Survey, the 1" map for companionship and guidance on expeditions, the 2½" map for exploration both on the fells and by the fireside. These admirable maps are remarkably accurate topographically but there is a crying need for a revision of the paths on the hills: several walkers' tracks that have come into use during the past few decades, some of them now broad highways, are not shown at all; other paths still shown on the maps have fallen into neglect and can no longer be traced on the ground.

The popular Bartholomew 1" map is a beautiful picture, fit for a frame, but this too is unreliable for paths; indeed here the defect is much more serious, for routes are indicated where no paths ever existed, nor ever could — the cartographer has preferred to take precipices in his stride rather than deflect his graceful curves over easy ground.

Hence the justification for the maps in this book: they have the one merit (of importance to walkers) of being dependable as regards delineation of *paths*. They are intended as supplements to the Ordnance Survey maps, certainly not as substitutes.

THE VIEWS............... Various devices have been used to illustrate the views from the summits of the fells. The full panorama in the form of an outline drawing is most satisfactory generally, and this method has been adopted for the main viewpoints.

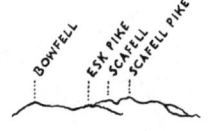

THE DIAGRAMS OF ASCENTS.................... The routes of ascent of the higher fells are depicted by diagrams that do not pretend to strict accuracy: they are neither plans nor elevations; in fact there is deliberate distortion in order to show detail clearly: usually they are represented as viewed from imaginary 'space-stations'. But it is hoped they will be useful and interesting.

THE DRAWINGS....... The drawings at least are honest attempts to reproduce what the eye sees: they illustrate features of interest and also serve the dual purpose of breaking up the text and balancing the layout of the pages, and of filling up awkward blank spaces, like this:

Thirlmere

THE
EASTERN
FELLS

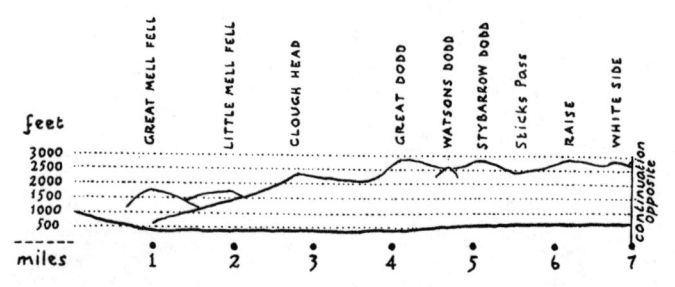

In the area of the Eastern Fells the greatest single mass of high ground in Lakeland is concentrated. It takes the form of a tremendous barrier running north and south, consistently high and steep throughout its length, mainly having an altitude between 2500'-3000', in two places only falling below 2000', and rising above 3000' on Helvellyn. In general the western slopes are steep, smooth and grassy and the eastern slopes are broken and craggy, but at the northern extremity the reverse obtains. The fells in this area may conveniently be classed in two groups divided by Grisedale Pass: in the south is the Fairfield group, pleasingly arrayed and with deep valleys cutting into the mass on both flanks; north is the bigger but less interesting Helvellyn range, with no valleys in the high western wall but several on the eastern side running down to Ullswater.

The geographical boundaries of the area are distinct. In shape it is a long inverted triangle, covering about fifty square miles of territory, based on Ambleside. The western boundary is formed by the deep trough of Dunmail Raise and Thirlmere, a great rift of which the principal road across the district takes advantage;

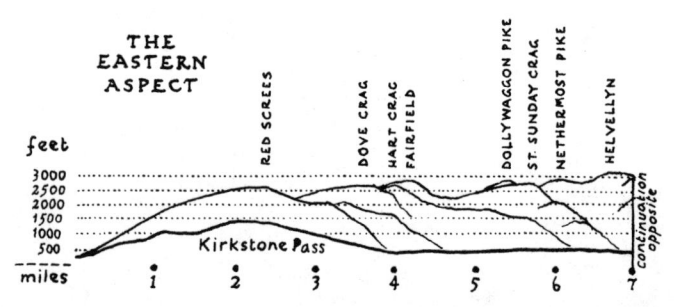

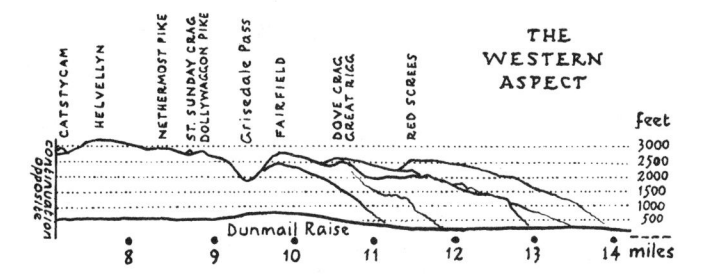

THE WESTERN ASPECT

elevation profile showing peaks: CATSTYCAM, HELVELLYN, NETHERMOST PIKE, ST. SUNDAY CRAG, DOLLYWAGGON PIKE, Grisedale Pass, FAIRFIELD, DOVE CRAG, GREAT RIGG, RED SCREES — with Dunmail Raise marked, miles 8 to 14

the eastern boundary is the trench of Kirkstone Pass and Ullswater, and the northern is the broad Keswick to Penrith gap. These boundaries are very satisfactory, enclosing all the dependencies of Helvellyn and Fairfield, and they are particularly convenient for the purposes of a separate guidebook because they are not crossed, normally, during the course of a day's fell-walk. Only at Kirkstone is there a link with fells outside the area but even here the breach is very pronounced.

This is an area easily accessible and (excepting the fells north of Sticks Pass) much frequented by walkers. It has in Helvellyn the most-often-climbed mountain in Lakeland and in Grisedale Pass one of the best-known footpaths.

Ambleside and Grasmere are favourite resorts for those who frequent these fells, but, because the most dramatic features are invariably presented to the east, the quiet and beautiful Patterdale valley is far superior as a base for their exploration: the eastern approaches are more interesting, the surroundings more charming and the views more rewarding; furthermore, from Patterdale any part of the main ridge may be visited in a normal day's expedition.

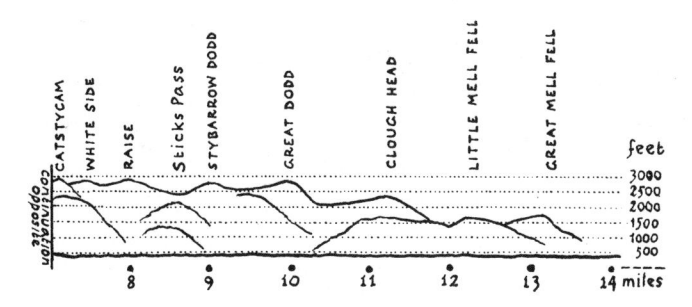

elevation profile showing peaks: CATSTYCAM, WHITE SIDE, RAISE, Sticks Pass, STYBARROW DODD, GREAT DODD, CLOUGH HEAD, LITTLE MELL FELL, GREAT MELL FELL — miles 8 to 14

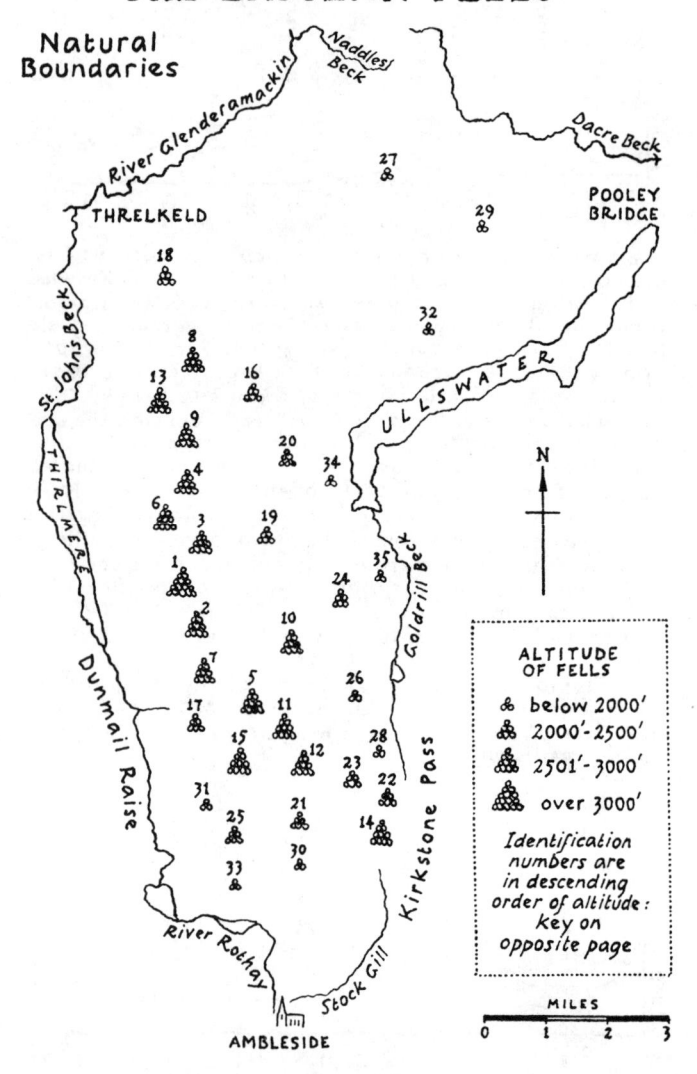

THE EASTERN FELLS
Natural Boundaries

Altitude of Fells
- ♣ below 2000'
- ♣ 2000'–2500'
- ♣ 2501'–3000'
- ♣ over 3000'

Identification numbers are in descending order of altitude: key on opposite page

THE EASTERN FELLS

in the order of their appearance in this book

Reference to map opposite			Altitude in feet
over 3000' / 2501'-3000' / 2001'-2500' / below 2000'			
35	..	ARNISON CRAG	1424
19	..	BIRKHOUSE MOOR	2350
24	..	BIRKS	2040
3	..	CATSTYCAM	2917
18	..	CLOUGH HEAD	2381
7	..	DOLLYWAGGON PIKE	2810
12	..	DOVE CRAG	2603
5	..	FAIRFIELD	2863
34	..	GLENRIDDING DODD	1425
32	..	GOWBARROW FELL	1579
8	..	GREAT DODD	2807
27	..	GREAT MELL FELL	1760
15	..	GREAT RIGG	2513
11	..	HART CRAG	2698
16	..	HART SIDE	2481
26	..	HARTSOP ABOVE HOW	1870
1	..	HELVELLYN	3118
25	..	HERON PIKE	2003
28	..	HIGH HARTSOP DODD	1702
21	..	HIGH PIKE	2155
23	..	LITTLE HART CRAG	2091
29	..	LITTLE MELL FELL	1657
30	..	LOW PIKE	1657
22	..	MIDDLE DODD	2106
33	..	NAB SCAR	1450
2	..	NETHERMOST PIKE	2920
4	..	RAISE	2889
14	..	RED SCREES	2541
10	..	SAINT SUNDAY CRAG	2756
17	..	SEAT SANDAL	2415
20	..	SHEFFIELD PIKE	2232
31	..	STONE ARTHUR	1652
9	..	STYBARROW DODD	2770
13	..	WATSONS DODD	2584
6	..	WHITE SIDE	2832

1 14 10 10
35

Each fell is the subject of a separate chapter

Arnison Crag 1424'

from Keldas

Glenridding

Patterdale

ARNISON CRAG ▲

BIRKS ▲

S? SUNDAY CRAG ▲

MILES
0 1 2

The rough fellside curving out of Deepdale and bounding the highway to Patterdale village has an attractive rocky crown, often visited for the fine view it offers of the head of Ullswater. This is Arnison Crag, a low hill with a summit worthy of a mountain. It is a dependency of S? Sunday Crag, forming the lesser of the two prongs which constitute the north-east spur of that grand fell; Birks is the other. It starts as a grass shelf east of Cold Cove and then takes the shape of a curving ridge of no particular interest except for the sudden upthrust of its craggy summit.

Arnison Crag 2

MAP

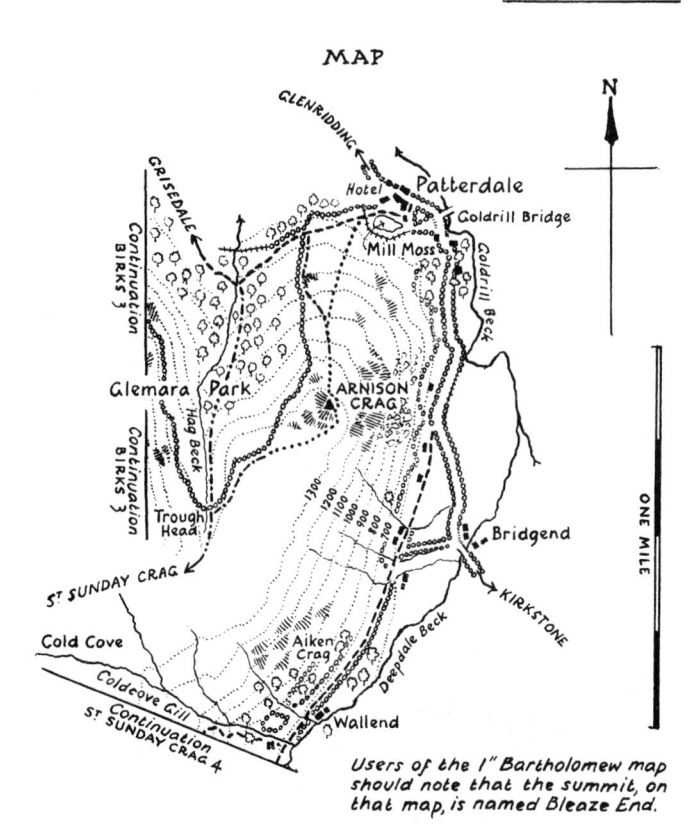

Users of the 1" Bartholomew map should note that the summit, on that map, is named Bleaze End.

ASCENT FROM PATTERDALE

The ascent is invariably made from the village of Patterdale. Behind the cluster of buildings is Mill Moss (once a pleasant tarn, now a refuse tip) and, after picking a way through the foothills of old tin cans and motor tyres which are much in evidence here, the climb may be started from the wire fence, inclining right to the ridge. In summer, however, high bracken hinders progress and it is easier to keep to the path as far as the wall enclosing Glemara Park and then follow the wall up, slanting across to the ridge above the first crag. The summit is finally attained after a steep scramble. *Although a short and easy walk, the ascent may lead to difficulties in mist and should then not be attempted.*

Arnison Crag 3

THE SUMMIT

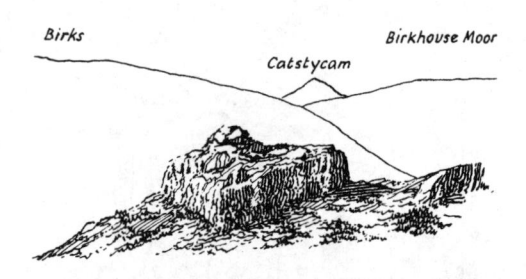

Birks — Catstycam — Birkhouse Moor

The summit is a rock platform, inaccessible to the walker on the west side and attained from other directions only by breaches in a low wall of crag defending it. A rock gateway (seen from the road near Hartsop as a clean-cut notch on the skyline) separates this platform from another at a slightly lower elevation which has the principal cairn and overlooks the approach from Patterdale.

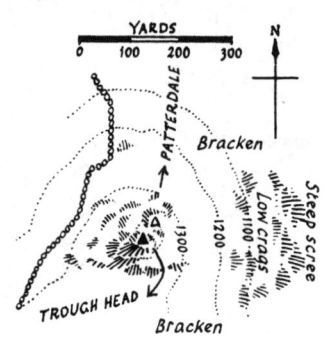

The lower cairn

The summit from the south

DESCENTS: The ridge should be followed down, for Patterdale. 'Short cuts' are likely to encounter rougher ground. A longer alternative follows the wall to Trough Head, where a very awkward stepstile gives access to the wooded Glemara Park and pleasant paths which lead back to Patterdale — pleasant, at any rate, until arrival at the environs of Mill Moss.

In mist, make a wide detour to the wall and follow it down northwards.

Arnison Crag 4

THE VIEW

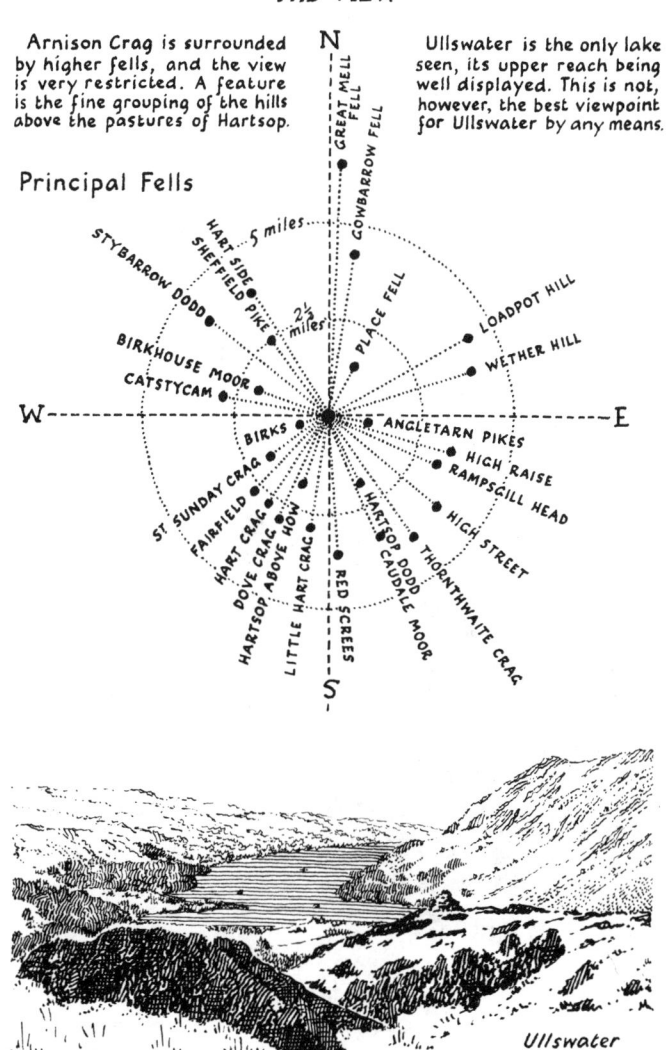

Arnison Crag is surrounded by higher fells, and the view is very restricted. A feature is the fine grouping of the hills above the pastures of Hartsop.

Ullswater is the only lake seen, its upper reach being well displayed. This is not, however, the best viewpoint for Ullswater by any means.

Principal Fells

Ullswater

Birkhouse Moor

2350' approx.

from Lanty's Tarn

RAISE ▲   • Glenridding
          ▲ BIRKHOUSE MOOR
          • Patterdale
▲
HELVELLYN

▲ FAIRFIELD

MILES
0 1 2 3 4

Birkhouse Moor 2

NATURAL FEATURES

The east ridge of Helvellyn starts as a narrow rock arete, known to all walkers as *Striding Edge*, and then gradually widens into the broad sprawling mass of Birkhouse Moor. A long grassy promenade is the main characteristic of the top, but the southern slopes soon steepen to form a natural wall for Grisedale for two miles; this flank is traversed by one of the most popular paths in the district. Northwards, Red Tarn Beck and Glenridding Beck form its boundaries; there are crags on this side, mainly concentrated around the only defined ridge descending from the summit, north-east. The name 'moor' is well suited to this fell, the top particularly being grassy and dull; below, eastwards, there are patches of heather, and in this direction the fell ends abruptly and craggily above Ullswater, the lower slopes being beautifully wooded.

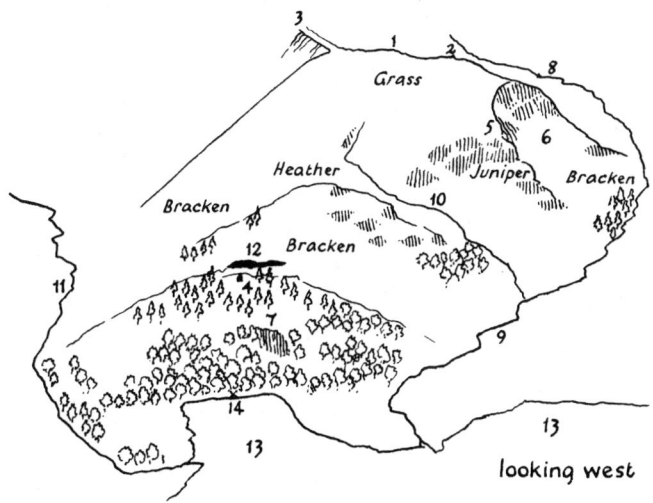

looking west

1 : The highest point
2 : The cairn at 2318'
3 : Ridge continuing to Helvellyn
4 : Keldas
5 : The north-east ridge
6 : Blea Cove
7 : Raven Crag
8 : Red Tarn Beck
9 : Glenridding Beck
10 : Mires Beck
11 : Grisedale Beck
12 : Lanty's Tarn
13 : Ullswater
14 : St. Patrick's Well

Birkhouse Moor 3

MAP

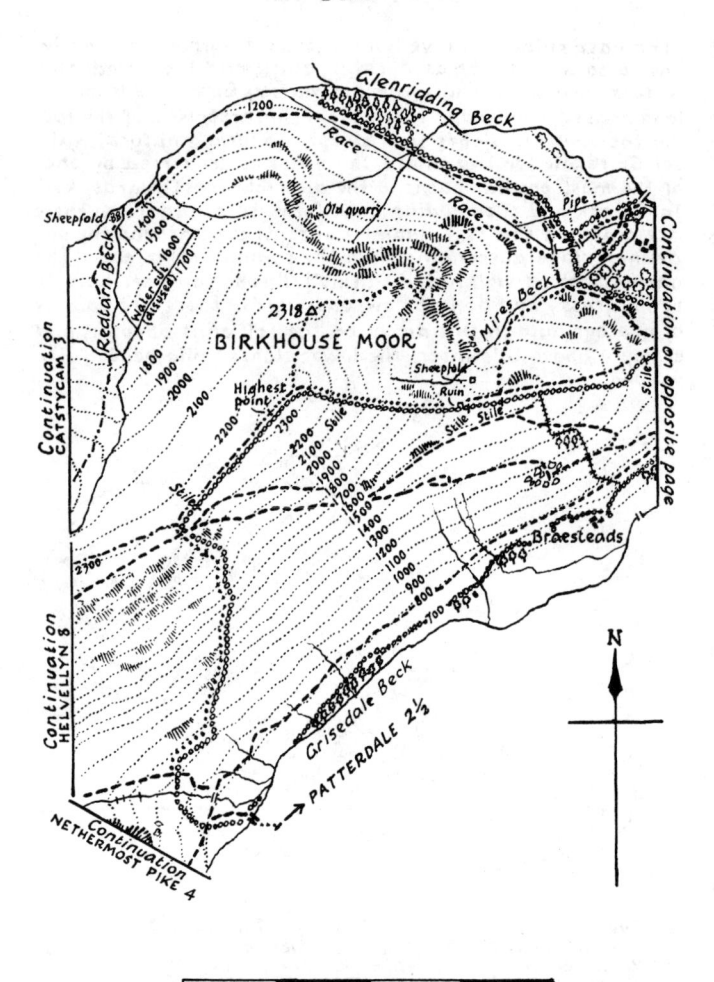

Birkhouse Moor 4

MAP

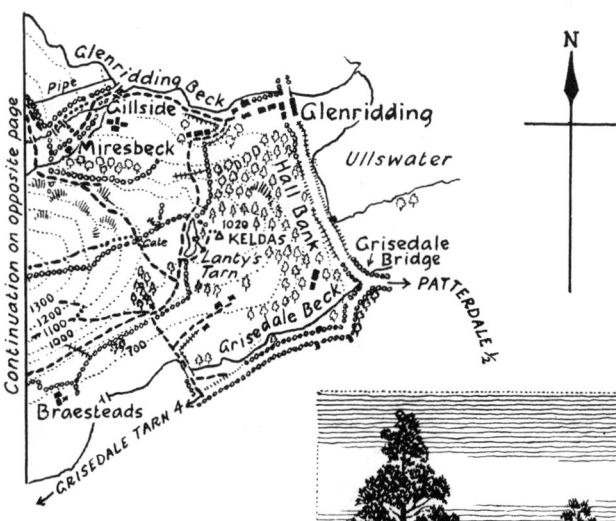

KELDAS

Birkhouse Moor falls away to the east in bracken-clad slopes, but its extremity is an abrupt wooded height overlooking the upper reach of Ullswater. This height has no name on official maps; locally it is referred to as Keldas. The pines here are a joy to behold, framing very beautiful views of the nearby lake and fells. The cairn on its summit is accessible from Lanty's Tarn, but the eastern face is very steep and craggy. Artists and photographers will vote Keldas the loveliest and most delightful place amongst the eastern fells.

Ullswater from Keldas

Birkhouse Moor 5

ASCENT FROM GRISEDALE
1900 feet of ascent : 3½ miles from Patterdale village

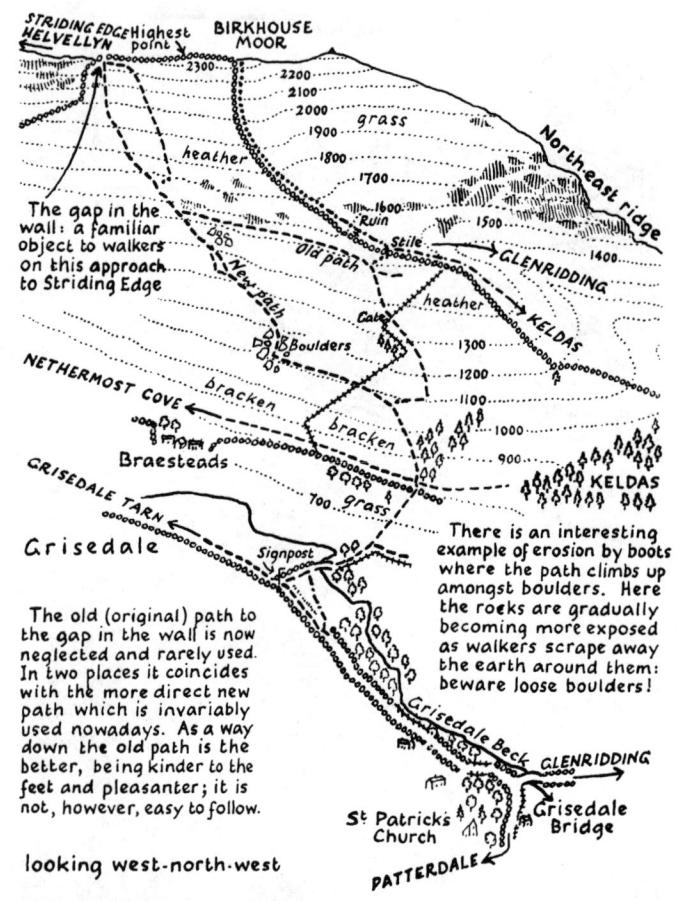

The gap in the wall: a familiar object to walkers on this approach to Striding Edge

The old (original) path to the gap in the wall is now neglected and rarely used. In two places it coincides with the more direct new path which is invariably used nowadays. As a way down the old path is the better, being kinder to the feet and pleasanter; it is not, however, easy to follow.

looking west-north-west

There is an interesting example of erosion by boots where the path climbs up amongst boulders. Here the rocks are gradually becoming more exposed as walkers scrape away the earth around them: beware loose boulders!

Birkhouse Moor may most easily be ascended by using the well-defined Patterdale-Striding Edge path climbing across its flank. The splendid views of Grisedale are the chief merit of this route, which is safe in bad conditions.

Birkhouse Moor 6

ASCENT FROM GLENRIDDING
1900 feet of ascent : 2 miles

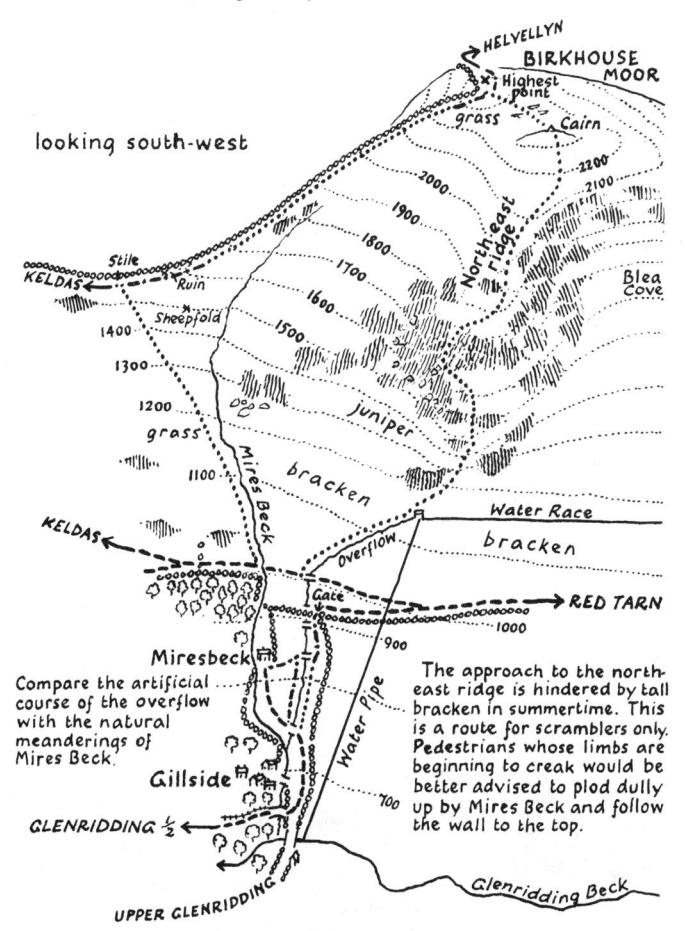

looking south-west

Compare the artificial course of the overflow with the natural meanderings of Mires Beck.

The approach to the north-east ridge is hindered by tall bracken in summertime. This is a route for scramblers only. Pedestrians whose limbs are beginning to creak would be better advised to plod dully up by Mires Beck and follow the wall to the top.

The north-east ridge offers a mild adventure and is a test in route-finding amongst low crags. It is the best way up, with a beautiful view in retrospect, but in bad weather the Mires Beck route is preferable, and safer.

Birkhouse Moor 7

THE SUMMIT

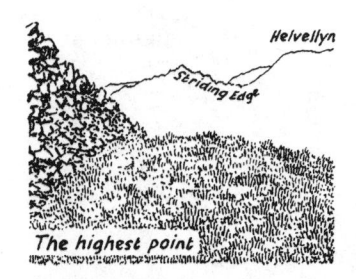

The highest point

The cairn at 2318'

The top can be reached easily and quickly from the popular Striding Edge path, but the detour is not really worth making. A few small tarns relieve the monotony of the grassy expanse, but generally the summit is without interest. A cairn indicates what appears to be the natural summit, but the prominent wall actually passes over higher ground.

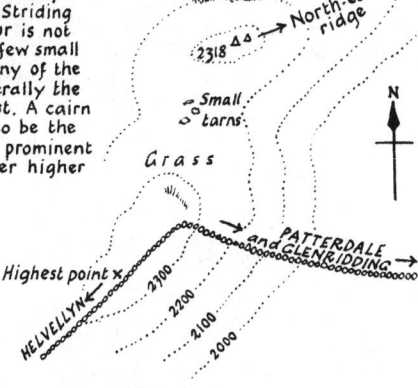

The summit of Keldas

DESCENTS: The descent is best made by following the wall east to the saddle above Mires Beck: here turn left for Glenridding, or (for Patterdale) cross the wall at the stile to join a path going down to the right. The north-east ridge is not suitable for descent.

‖ In bad weather conditions follow the wall east as far as Keldas. Avoid the east and north faces.

Birkhouse Moor 8

THE VIEW

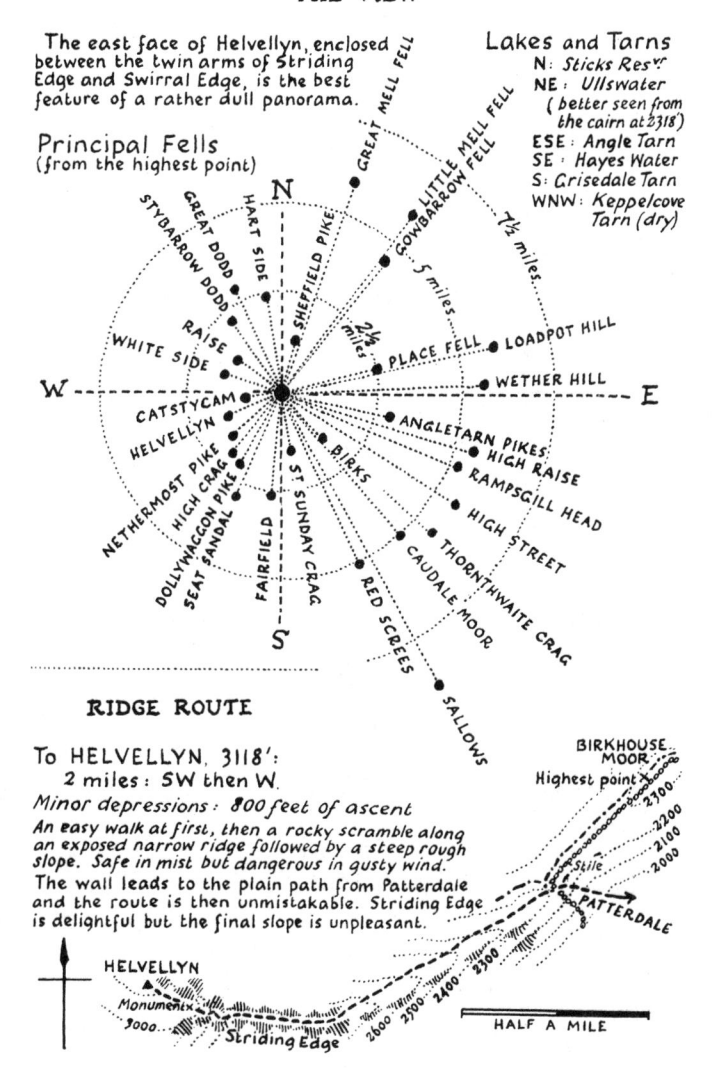

The east face of Helvellyn, enclosed between the twin arms of Striding Edge and Swirral Edge, is the best feature of a rather dull panorama.

Principal Fells
(from the highest point)

N: STYBARROW DODD, GREAT DODD, HART SIDE, SHEFFIELD PIKE, GREAT MELL FELL, LITTLE MELL FELL, GOWBARROW FELL, RAISE, WHITE SIDE, CATSTYCAM, HELVELLYN, NETHERMOST PIKE, HIGH CRAG, DOLLYWAGGON PIKE, SEAT SANDAL, FAIRFIELD, ST SUNDAY CRAG, BIRKS, RED SCREES, CAUDALE MOOR, SALLOWS, THORNTHWAITE CRAG, HIGH STREET, RAMPSGILL HEAD, HIGH RAISE, ANGLETARN PIKES, WETHER HILL, PLACE FELL, LOADPOT HILL

2½ miles, 5 miles, 7½ miles

Lakes and Tarns
N: Sticks Res^r
NE: Ullswater (better seen from the cairn at 2318)
ESE: Angle Tarn
SE: Hayes Water
S: Grisedale Tarn
WNW: Keppelcove Tarn (dry)

RIDGE ROUTE

To HELVELLYN, 3118':
2 miles : SW then W.
Minor depressions : 800 feet of ascent

An easy walk at first, then a rocky scramble along an exposed narrow ridge followed by a steep rough slope. Safe in mist but dangerous in gusty wind. The wall leads to the plain path from Patterdale and the route is then unmistakable. Striding Edge is delightful but the final slope is unpleasant.

HELVELLYN
Monument
3000
Striding Edge
2600 2500 2400 2300

BIRKHOUSE MOOR
Highest point
2700 2600 2500
2400 2300 2200 2100 2000
Stile
PATTERDALE

HALF A MILE

Birks 2040'

from Ullswater

The north-east shoulder of St Sunday Crag falls sharply to a depression beyond which a grassy undulating spur, featureless and wide, continues with little change in elevation towards Ullswater before finally plunging down to the valley through the enclosure of Glemara Park. Although this spur lacks a distinctive summit it is sufficiently well-defined to deserve a separate name; but, being an unromantic and uninteresting fell, it has earned for itself nothing better than the prosaic and unassuming title of Birks. It is rarely visited as the sole objective of an expedition, but walkers descending the ridge from St Sunday Crag often take it in their stride.

Birks 2

NATURAL FEATURES

Above the 1900' contour Birks is a half-mile's easy grass promenade and there is nothing here to suggest that there are formidable crags below on both sides. Yet the Grisedale flank has a continuous line of cliffs and round to the east are several tiers of rock above the lower wooded slopes of Glemara Park. Beyond the hollow of Trough Head, where rises Birks' only stream of note, is a curving ridge which culminates in the rocky pyramid of Arnison Crag; both this lower ridge and Birks itself, together forming a high wedge of rough ground between Grisedale and Deepdale, are dependencies of S⁺ Sunday Crag, Birks especially being dominated by this fine mountain.

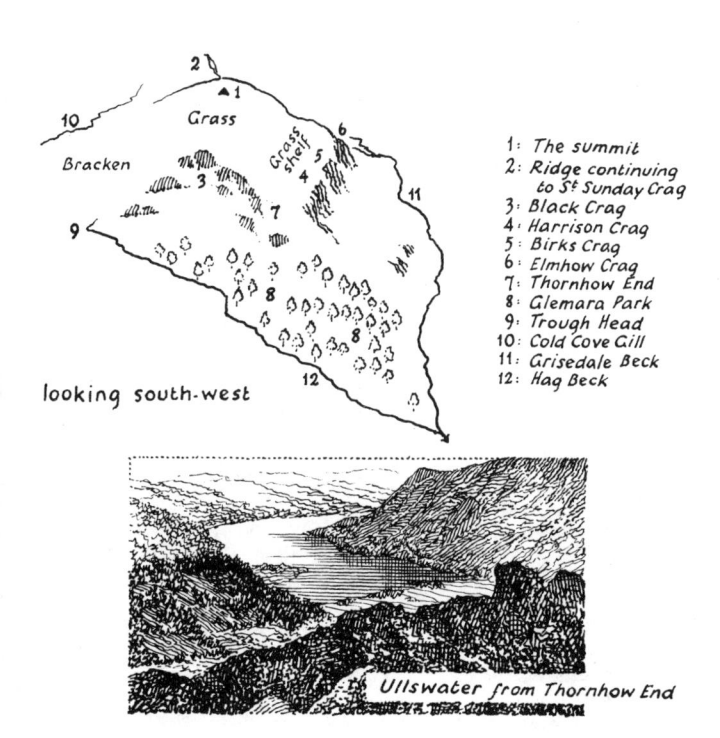

1: The summit
2: Ridge continuing to S⁺ Sunday Crag
3: Black Crag
4: Harrison Crag
5: Birks Crag
6: Elmhow Crag
7: Thornhow End
8: Glemara Park
9: Trough Head
10: Cold Cove Gill
11: Grisedale Beck
12: Hag Beck

looking south-west

Ullswater from Thornhow End

Birks 3

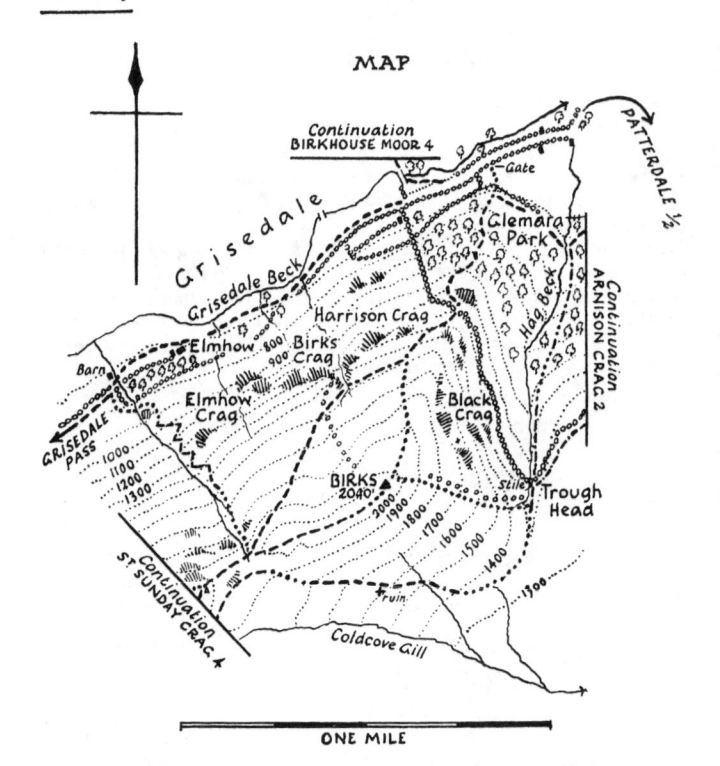

MAP

Place Fell from Glemara Park

Birks 4

ASCENTS FROM PATTERDALE
1600 feet of ascent : 2½ miles (1¾ by short variations)

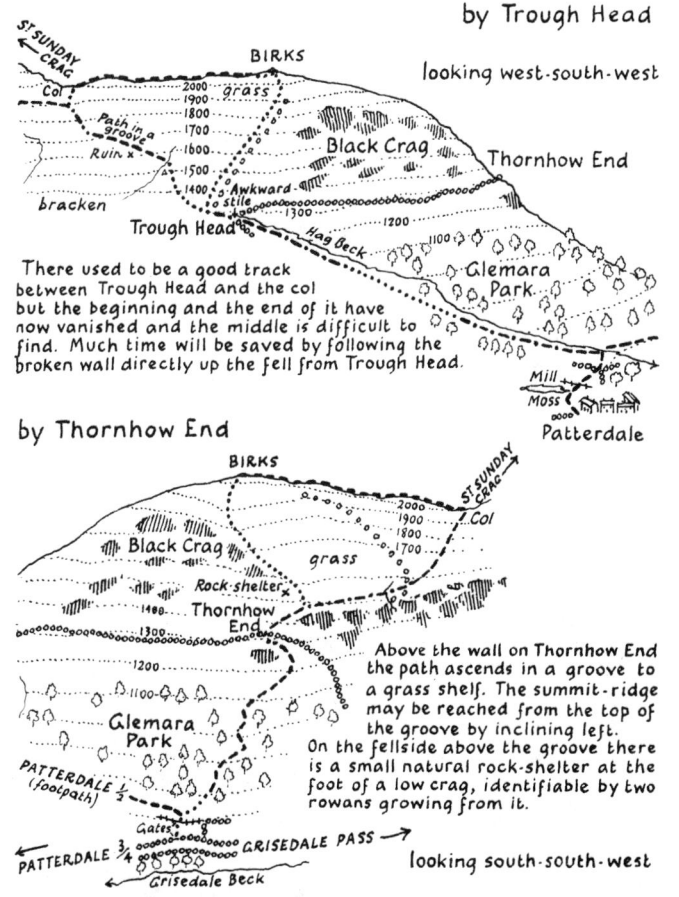

by Trough Head

looking west-south-west

There used to be a good track between Trough Head and the col but the beginning and the end of it have now vanished and the middle is difficult to find. Much time will be saved by following the broken wall directly up the fell from Trough Head.

by Thornhow End

Above the wall on Thornhow End the path ascends in a groove to a grass shelf. The summit-ridge may be reached from the top of the groove by inclining left.
On the fellside above the groove there is a small natural rock-shelter at the foot of a low crag, identifiable by two rowans growing from it.

looking south-south-west

The Thornhow End path is very attractive, with glorious views, but it is steep. The Trough Head route is without a path in places and is uninteresting. There is no pleasure, and some danger, in climbing Birks in misty conditions.

Birks 5

THE SUMMIT

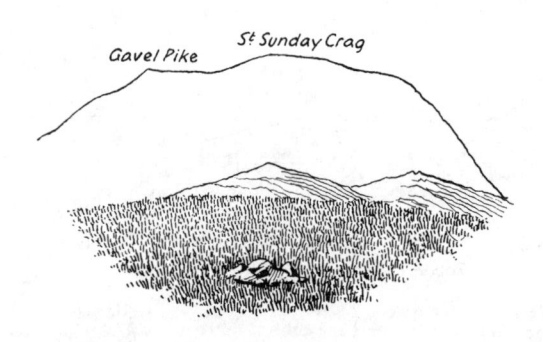

Gavel Pike   St Sunday Crag

The summit has no interesting features. The Ordnance Survey one-inch map promises a beacon on the highest point, but all that can be found is an insignificant mound of stones almost obscured by grass. A more considerable heap of bigger stones further along the ridge appears to be a collapsed edifice of some kind.

There is a narrow track along the crest but none on the actual summit.

DESCENTS: The finest way down (because of the view of Ullswater) is by the ridge to the north, inclining left to the path on the grass shelf below to avoid steep rough ground at the end of the ridge.

▌ *In bad weather conditions*, search eastwards for the top of the broken wall and follow it down to Trough Head.

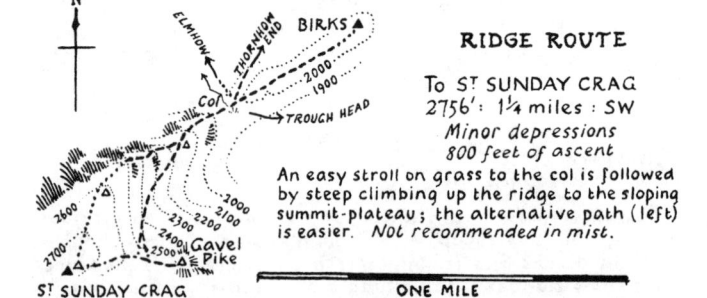

RIDGE ROUTE

To St SUNDAY CRAG
2756′ : 1¼ miles : SW
Minor depressions
800 feet of ascent

An easy stroll on grass to the col is followed by steep climbing up the ridge to the sloping summit-plateau; the alternative path (left) is easier. *Not recommended in mist.*

ONE MILE

Birks 6

THE VIEW

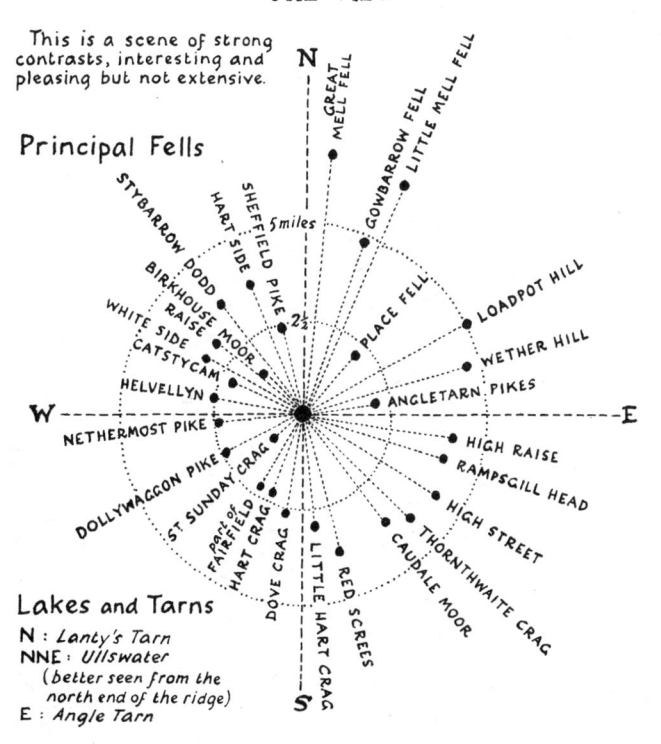

This is a scene of strong contrasts, interesting and pleasing but not extensive.

Principal Fells

(N) GREAT MELL FELL
GOWBARROW FELL
LITTLE MELL FELL
SHEFFIELD PIKE
HART SIDE
STYBARROW DODD
BIRKHOUSE MOOR
RAISE
WHITE SIDE
CATSTYCAM
HELVELLYN
PLACE FELL
LOADPOT HILL
WETHER HILL
ANGLETARN PIKES
HIGH RAISE
RAMPSGILL HEAD
HIGH STREET
THORNTHWAITE CRAG
CAUDALE MOOR
NETHERMOST PIKE
DOLLYWAGGON PIKE
ST SUNDAY CRAG
Part of FAIRFIELD
HART CRAG
DOVE CRAG
LITTLE HART CRAG
RED SCREES

5 miles
2½

Lakes and Tarns

N : Lanty's Tarn
NNE : Ullswater
(better seen from the north end of the ridge)
E : Angle Tarn

Ullswater

Catstycam 2917'

sometimes called
Catchedicam

from Glenridding Beck

RAISE
Glenridding
CATSTYCAM
Patterdale
HELVELLYN

MILES
0 1 2 3 4

Catstycam 2

NATURAL FEATURES

If Catstycam stood alone, remote from its fellows, it would be one of the finest peaks in Lakeland. It has nearly, but not quite, the perfect mountain form, with true simplicity in its soaring lines, and a small pointed top, a real summit, that falls away sharply on all sides. From Birkhouse Moor especially it has the appearance of a symmetrical pyramid; and from the upper valley of Glenridding it towers into the sky most impressively. But when seen from other directions it is too obviously dominated by Helvellyn and although its sharp peaked top identifies it unmistakably in every view in which it appears, clearly it is no more than the abrupt terminus of a short spur of the higher mountain, to which it is connected by a fine rock ridge, Swirral Edge. Its best feature is the tremendous shattered face it presents to the valley to the north, riven by a great scree gully. The steep slopes are nearly dry, but there is marshy ground around the base; the waters from Catstycam drain into Red Tarn Beck and Glenridding Beck.

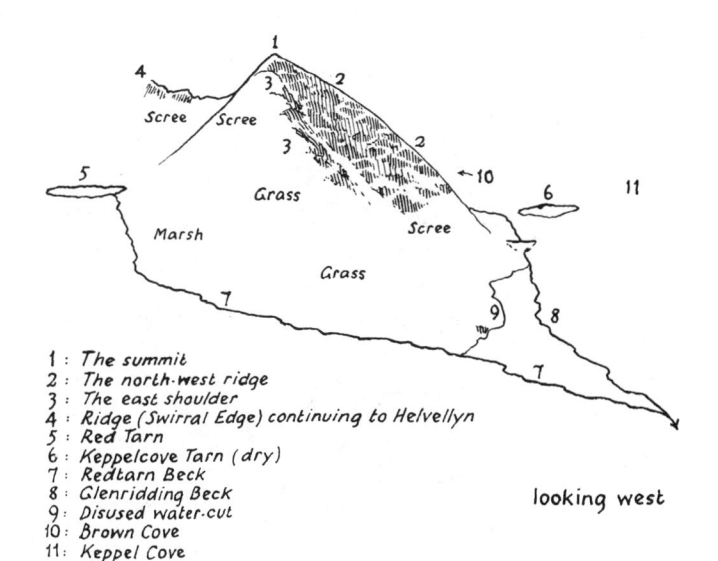

1 : *The summit*
2 : *The north-west ridge*
3 : *The east shoulder*
4 : *Ridge (Swirral Edge) continuing to Helvellyn*
5 : *Red Tarn*
6 : *Keppelcove Tarn (dry)*
7 : *Redtarn Beck*
8 : *Glenridding Beck*
9 : *Disused water-cut*
10: *Brown Cove*
11: *Keppel Cove*

looking west

Catstycam 3

MAP

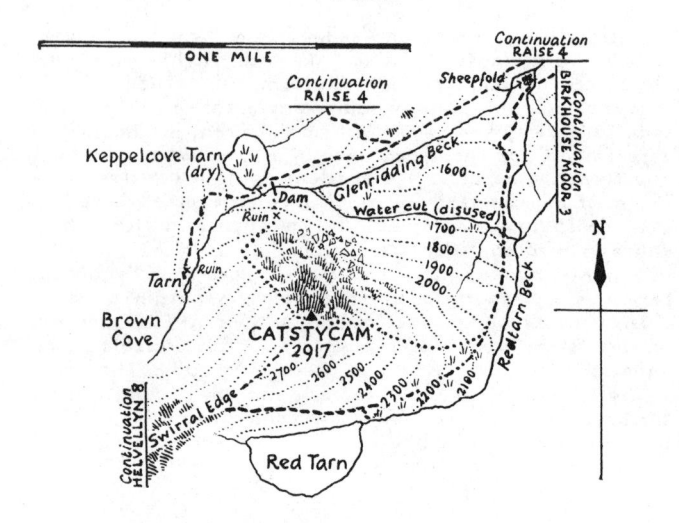

Helvellyn and Swirral Edge

Catstycam 4

ASCENT FROM GLENRIDDING
2500 feet of ascent : 4 miles from Glenridding village

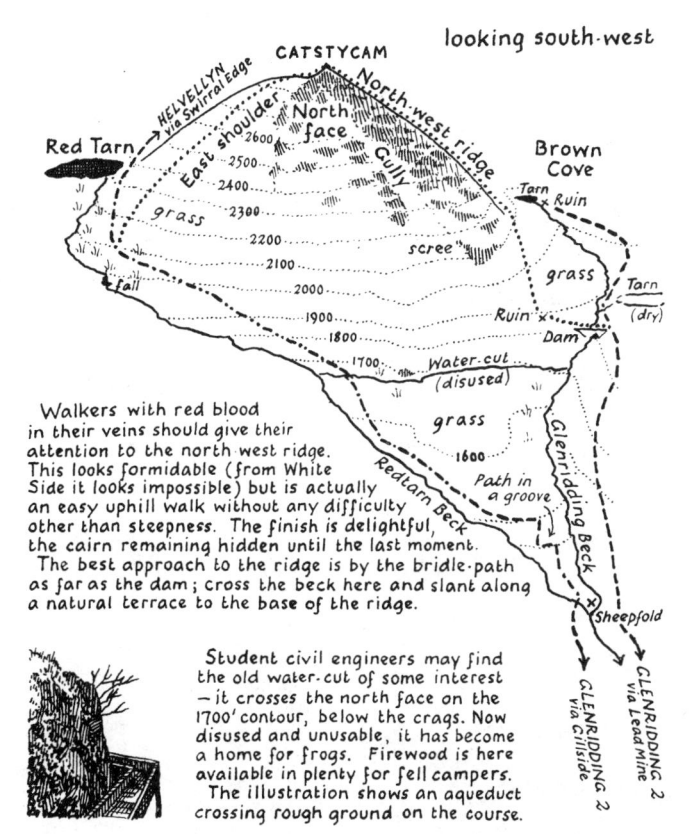

looking south-west

Walkers with red blood in their veins should give their attention to the north west ridge. This looks formidable (from White Side it looks impossible) but is actually an easy uphill walk without any difficulty other than steepness. The finish is delightful, the cairn remaining hidden until the last moment.
The best approach to the ridge is by the bridle-path as far as the dam; cross the beck here and slant along a natural terrace to the base of the ridge.

Student civil engineers may find the old water-cut of some interest — it crosses the north face on the 1700' contour, below the crags. Now disused and unusable, it has become a home for frogs. Firewood is here available in plenty for fell campers.
The illustration shows an aqueduct crossing rough ground on the course.

Of the two routes shown, that by Redtarn Beck and the east shoulder is easy, on grass all the way. The north-west ridge is steep and stony but a good airy climb in its later stages, giving a fine sense of achievement when the summit is gained. Catstycam should be avoided in bad weather.

Catstycam 5

THE SUMMIT

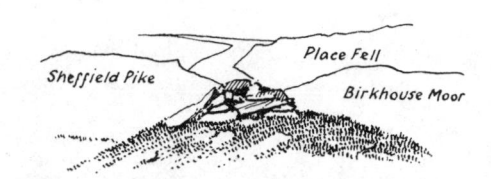

Catstycam is a true peak, and its small shapely summit is the finest in the eastern fells; if it were rock and not mainly grass it would be the finest in the district. Here the highest point is not in doubt!

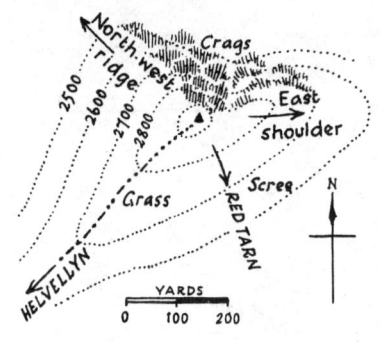

DESCENTS: The quickest and easiest descent is by the east shoulder to Glenridding. The north-west ridge is easy but too steep for comfort. For Patterdale, incline right from the east shoulder and cross Redtarn Beck high up, to join the Striding Edge path.

In bad conditions use the east shoulder, keeping right rather than left in mist, to Redtarn Beck and so down to Glenridding.

KEPPELCOVE TARN
AND ITS ENVIRONS
— *a study in devastation*

Keppelcove Tarn is now a marsh. Formerly it served as a reservoir for the Glenridding lead mine. In October 1927, following a cloudburst, flooded waters burst the banks of the tarn, carved out a new ravine, and caused great damage. The dam was breached later, in 1931, and has never been repaired.

Catstycam 6

The North-west Ridge, from White Side

Catstycam 7

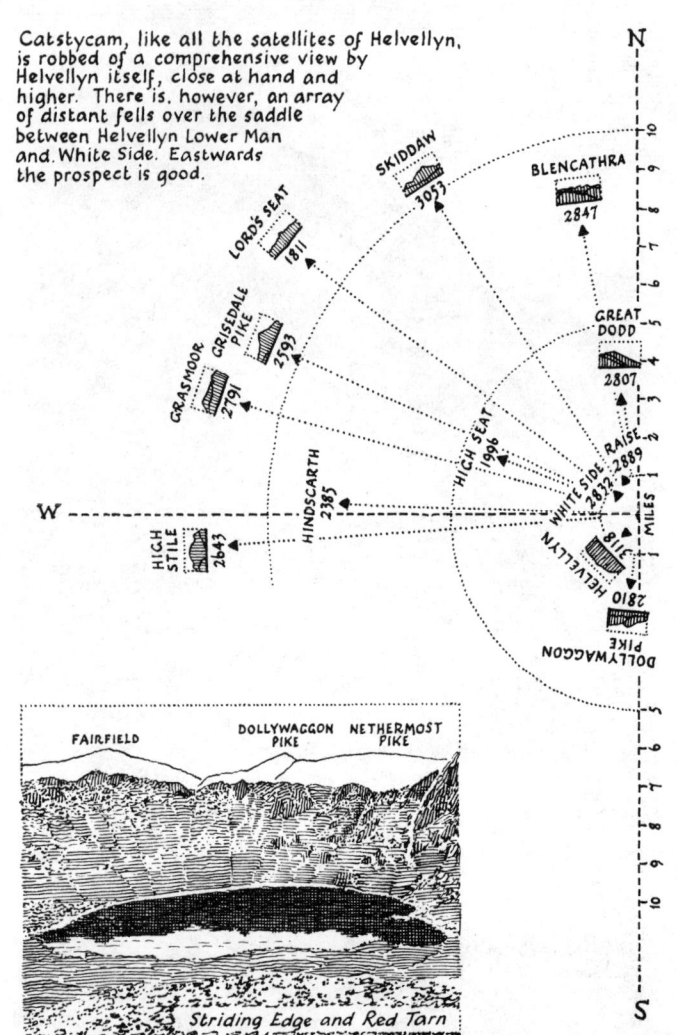

THE VIEW

Catstycam, like all the satellites of Helvellyn, is robbed of a comprehensive view by Helvellyn itself, close at hand and higher. There is, however, an array of distant fells over the saddle between Helvellyn Lower Man and White Side. Eastwards the prospect is good.

Striding Edge and Red Tarn

Catstycam 8

THE VIEW

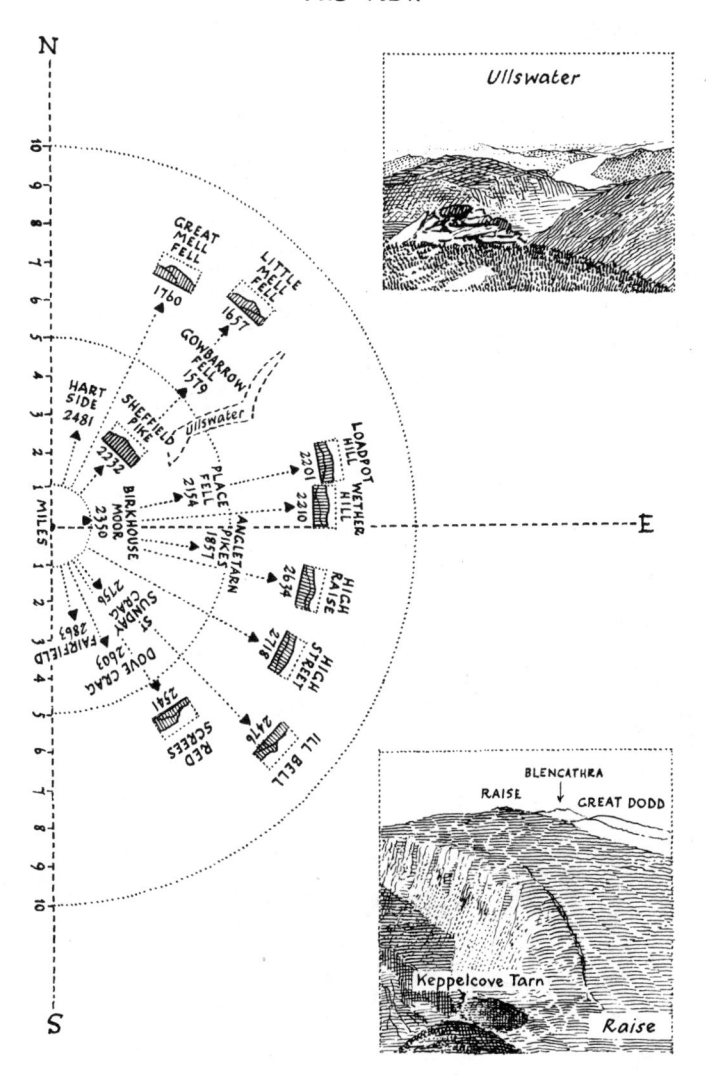

Ullswater

GREAT MELL FELL 1760
LITTLE MELL FELL 1657
GOWBARROW FELL 1579
HART SIDE 2481
SHEFFIELD PIKE 2232
Ullswater
LOADPOT HILL 2201
WETHER HILL 2210
BIRKHOUSE MOOR 2350
PLACE FELL 2154
ANGLETARN PIKES 1857
HIGH RAISE 2634
ST SUNDAY CRAG 2756
FAIRFIELD 2863
DOVE CRAG 2603
HIGH STREET 2718
RED SCREES 2541
ILL BELL 2476

RAISE BLENCATHRA GREAT DODD
Keppelcove Tarn
Raise

Clough Head 2381'

from High Rigg

- Threlkeld

Wanthwaite
▲ CLOUGH HEAD

▲ GREAT DODD

- Legburthwaite

MILES
0 1 2 3

From Kirkstone Pass the massive main ridge of the Fairfield and Helvellyn fells runs north, mile after mile, throughout maintaining a consistently high and a remarkably uniform altitude, and with a dozen distinct summits over 2500'. At its northern extremity the ground falls away swiftly to the deep valley of the Glenderamackin, and the last outpost of the ridge, although not so elevated as the summits to the south, occupies a commanding site: this is Clough Head.

Clough Head 2

NATURAL FEATURES

Contrary to the usual pattern of the Helvellyn fells, of which it is the most northerly member, Clough Head displays its crags to the west and grassy slopes to the east. These crags form a steep, continuous, mile-long wall above St John's-in-the-Vale, with one breach only where a walker may safely venture; they are riven by deep gullies, one of which (Sandbed Gill) is the rockiest and roughest watercourse in the Helvellyn range. After initial steep scree, the northern slopes descend gently to the wide valley of the Glenderamackin at Threlkeld. Clough Head is an interesting fell, not only for walkers and explorers but for the ornithologist and botanist, the geologist and antiquarian also; while the merely curious traveller may content himself by puzzling out why and for what purpose Fisher's wife trod so persistently that remarkable path to Jim's Fold.

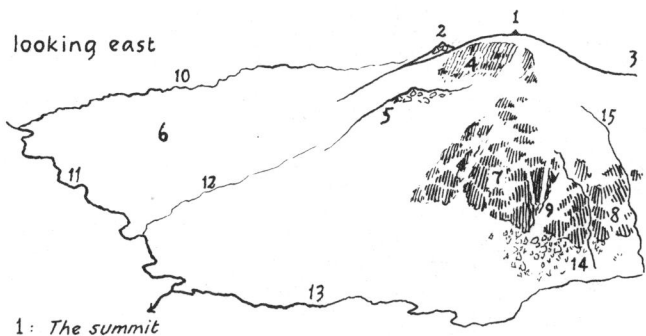

looking east

1: The summit
2: White Pike
3: Ridge continuing to Great Dodd
4: Red Screes
5: Threlkeld Knotts
6: Threlkeld Common
7: Wanthwaite Crags
8: Bram Crag
9: Fisher's Wife's Rake
10: Mosedale Beck
11: River Glenderamackin
12: Birkett Beck
13: St John's Beck
14: Sandbed Gill
15: Beckthorns Gill

Wanthwaite Crags

Clough Head 3

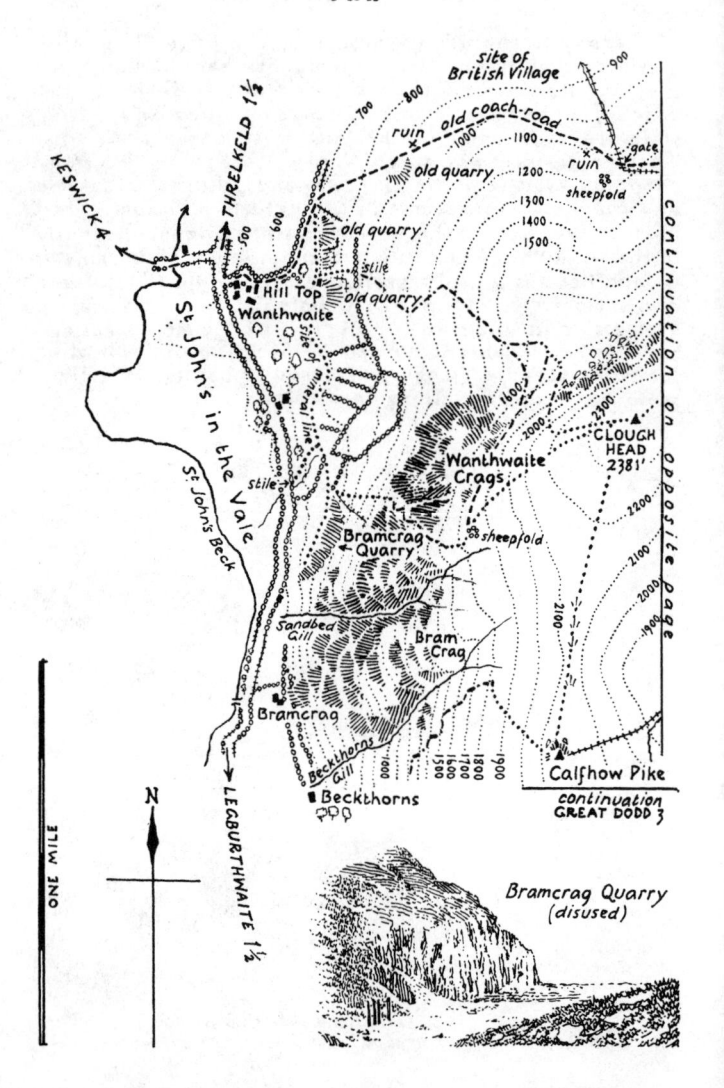

MAP

Clough Head 4

MAP

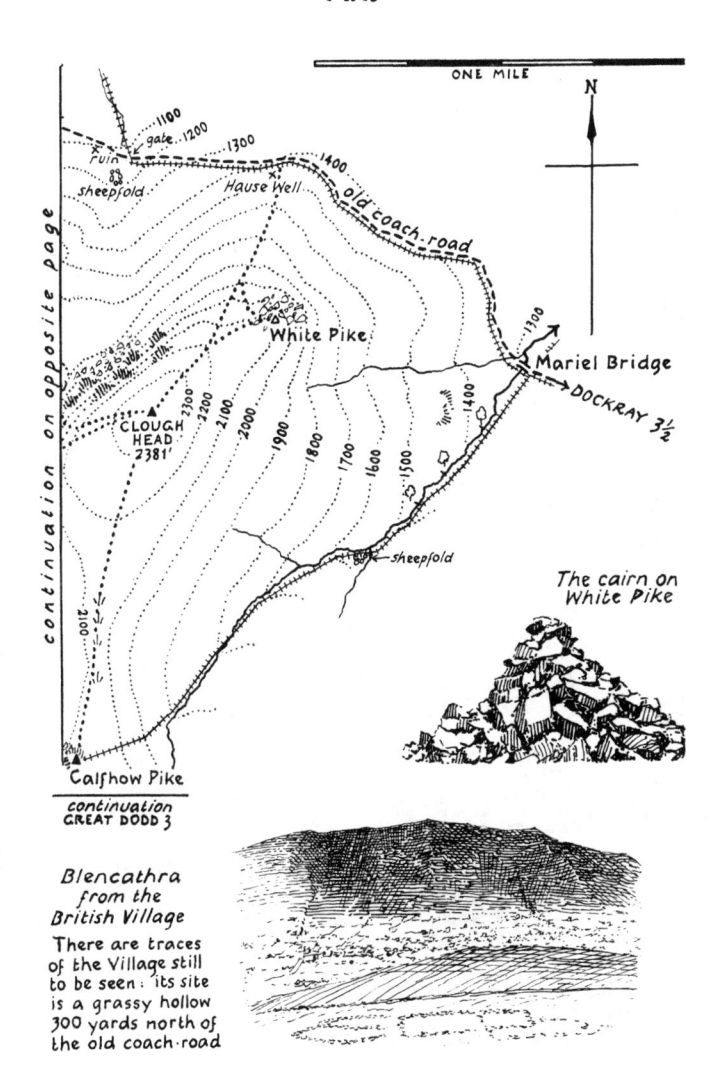

The cairn on White Pike

Blencathra from the British Village

There are traces of the Village still to be seen: its site is a grassy hollow 300 yards north of the old coach road

Clough Head 5

ASCENT FROM WANTHWAITE
1900 feet of ascent : 2 miles ; 3 by way of Hause Well

'Wanthwaite' is pronounced 'Wanthet'
and 'Lowthwaite' 'Lowthet'

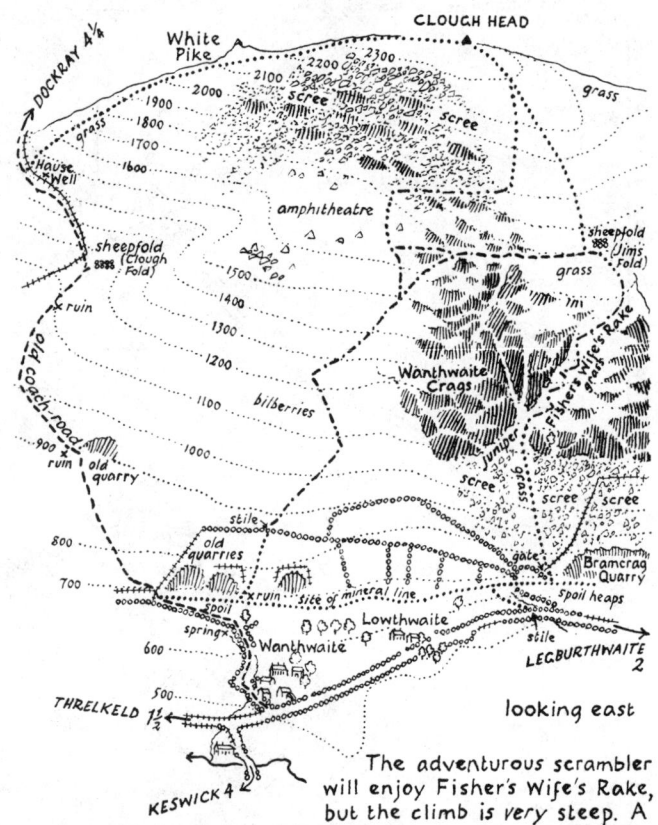

The adventurous scrambler will enjoy Fisher's Wife's Rake, but the climb is *very* steep. A much easier route is by the grass slope above Hause Well. The intermediate route ends with a choice of paths, one a 'sporting' high-level crossing of the crags to Jim's Fold.

looking east

Clough Head 6

THE SUMMIT

The top of the fell is a pleasant grassy sward, adorned with a small wall-shelter and an Ordnance Survey column.

Skiddaw

DESCENTS: Fisher's Wife's Rake is difficult to locate from above and in any case is too steep to provide a comfortable way down. The high-level path from Jim's Fold is an interesting route to the easier ground below the crags. Easiest of all is the grass slope to the old coach-road at Hause Well.

In bad weather conditions Clough Head is a dangerous place. All steep ground should be avoided and the descent made down the easy grass slope north-north-east to the old coach-road. A descent by Fisher's Wife's Rake should not be contemplated and the natural funnel of Sandbed Gill should be strictly left alone

Two oddities on Clough Head

Unlike most Lakeland springs, which rise from grass, HAUSE WELL issues from a crevice in rocks. It is not easy to locate — its situation is near the fence bounding the old coach-road.

SANDBED GILL, a considerable stream in its rocky gorge, has an empty bed at valley-level.

Clough Head 7

RIDGE ROUTE

To GREAT DODD, 2807': 2 miles
SSW then SE and E
Depression at 2100'
720 feet of ascent
An easy walk on grass

This walk would be completely devoid of interest but for an odd outcrop midway, a welcome oasis of rock in a desert of grass — this is Calfhow Pike. Beyond, the long uphill trudge seems longer than it is, and longer still on a hot day.

Calfhow Pike

Blencathra from Clough Head

Clough Head 8

THE VIEW

Clough Head is sufficiently isolated to afford an uninterrupted prospect in every direction except south-east. A special feature, rare in views from the heights of the Helvellyn range, is the nice combination of valley and mountain scenery. This is an excellent viewpoint, the skyline between south and west being especially striking.

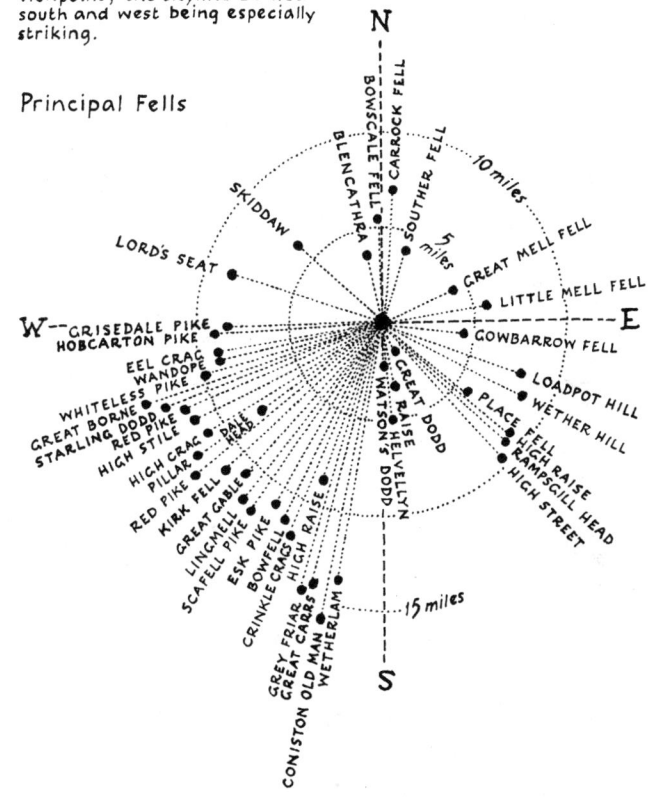

Principal Fells

N
BOWSCALE FELL
CARROCK FELL
BLENCATHRA
SOUTHER FELL
10 miles
SKIDDAW
5 miles
GREAT MELL FELL
LORD'S SEAT
LITTLE MELL FELL
W — GRISEDALE PIKE — E
HOBCARTON PIKE
GOWBARROW FELL
EEL CRAG
WANDOPE
LOADPOT HILL
WHITELESS PIKE
WETHER HILL
GREAT BORNE
STARLING DODD
GREAT DODD
PLACE FELL
RED PIKE
RAISE
HIGH RAISE
HIGH STILE
HELVELLYN
RAMPSGILL HEAD
HIGH CRAG
DALE HEAD
WATSON'S DODD
HIGH STREET
PILLAR
RED PIKE
KIRK FELL
GREAT GABLE
LINGMELL
SCAFELL PIKE
ESK PIKE
BOWFELL
CRINKLE CRAGS
HIGH RAISE
GREY FRIAR
GREAT CARRS
15 miles
CONISTON OLD MAN
WETHERLAM
S

Lakes and Tarns
SW: Thirlmere
W: Derwent Water
WNW: Tewet Tarn
WNW: Bassenthwaite Lake

Dollywaggon Pike 2810'

from Deepdale Hause

Patterdale
▲ HELVELLYN
Wythburn
● DOLLYWAGGON PIKE
▲ FAIRFIELD

Grasmere
MILES
0 1 2 3 4 5

Dollywaggon Pike 2

NATURAL FEATURES

Like most of the high fells south of the Sticks Pass, Dollywaggon Pike exhibits a marked contrast in its western and eastern aspects. To the west, uninteresting grass slopes descend to Dunmail Raise almost unrelieved by rock and scarred only by the wide stony track gouged across the breast of the fell by the boots of generations of pilgrims to Helvellyn. But the eastern side is a desolation of crag and boulder and scree: here are silent recesses rarely visited by walkers but well worth a detailed exploration.

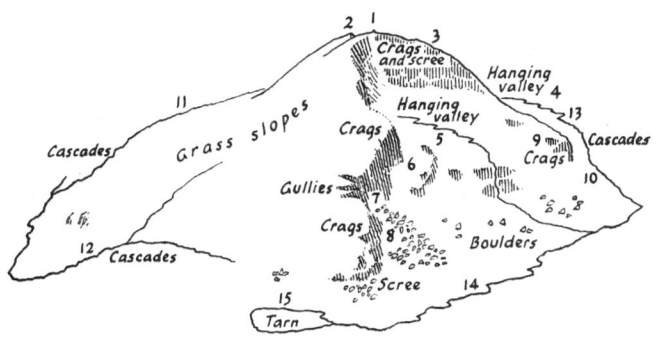

looking north-west

1. The summit of Dollywaggon Pike
2. Ridge continuing to Nethermost Pike
3. The Tongue
4. Ruthwaite Cove
5. Cock Cove
6. Falcon Crag (or Dollywaggon Crag)
7. The three gullies of Tarn Crag
8. Tarn Crag
9. Spout Crag
10. Caves (artificial)
11. Birkside Gill
12. Raise Beck
13. Ruthwaite Beck
14. Grisedale Beck
15. Grisedale Tarn

Falcon Crag

The figure 10 also indicates the position of RUTHWAITE LODGE (built in 1854 as a shooting lodge, but now a climbers' hut)

Dollywaggon Pike 3

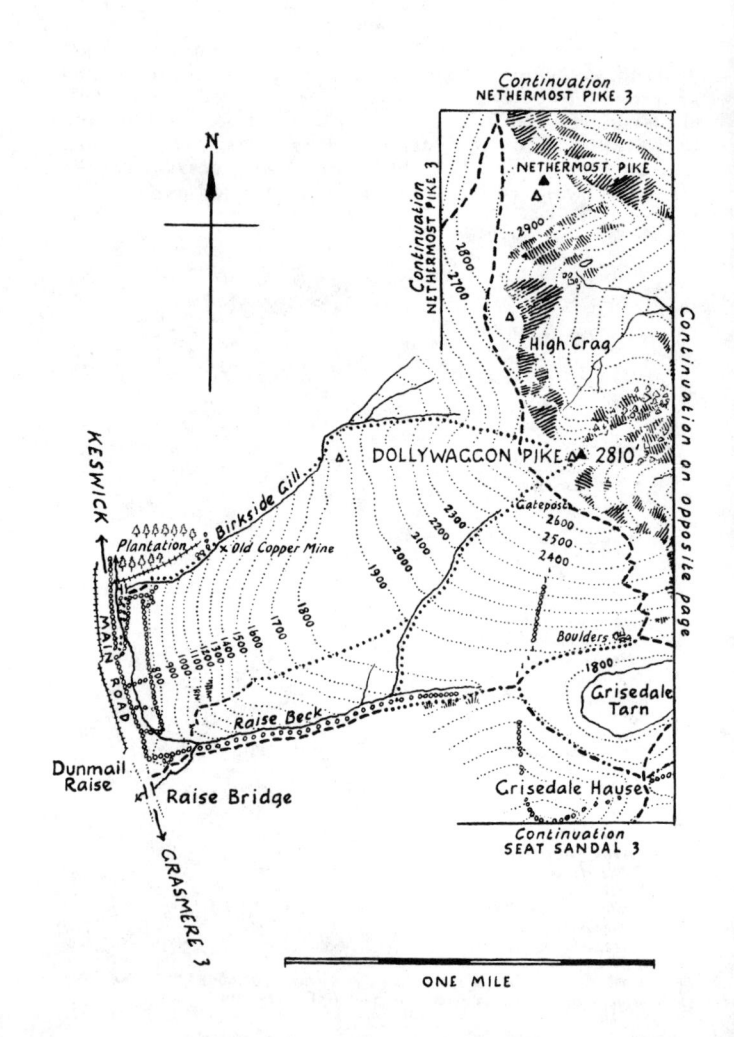

MAP

Dollywaggon Pike 4

MAP

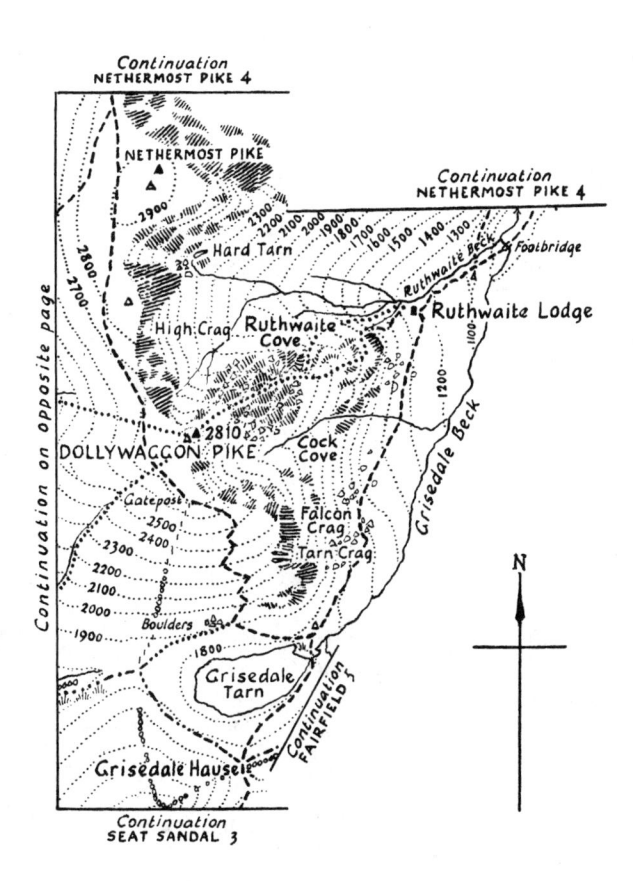

Dollywaggon Pike 5

ASCENT FROM GRASMERE
2700 feet of ascent : 5 miles from Grasmere Church

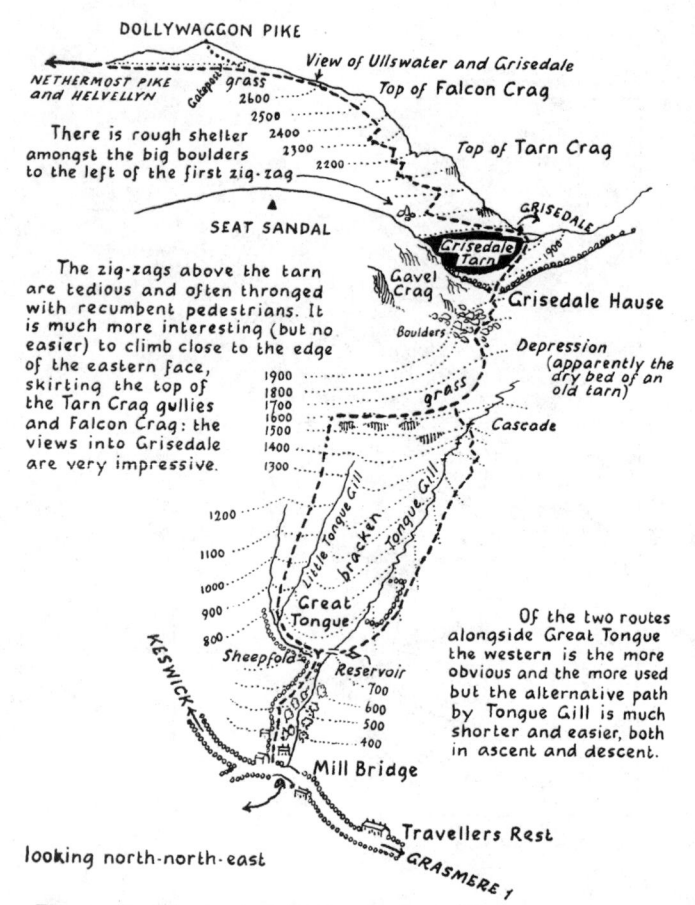

DOLLYWAGGON PIKE

View of Ullswater and Grisedale

NETHERMOST PIKE AND HELVELLYN

Top of Falcon Crag

Top of Tarn Crag

There is rough shelter amongst the big boulders to the left of the first zig-zag

SEAT SANDAL

Grisedale Tarn

GRISEDALE

Gavel Crag

Grisedale Hause

The zig-zags above the tarn are tedious and often thronged with recumbent pedestrians. It is much more interesting (but no easier) to climb close to the edge of the eastern face, skirting the top of the Tarn Crag gullies and Falcon Crag: the views into Grisedale are very impressive.

Boulders

Depression (apparently the dry bed of an old tarn)

Cascade

Little Tongue Gill

Tongue Gill

bracken

Great Tongue

KESWICK

Sheepfold

Reservoir

Of the two routes alongside Great Tongue the western is the more obvious and the more used but the alternative path by Tongue Gill is much shorter and easier, both in ascent and descent.

Mill Bridge

Travellers Rest

GRASMERE 1

looking north-north-east

The route illustrated is the much-trodden path, almost a highway in places, from Grasmere to Helvellyn. It climbs the breast of Dollywaggon Pike and passes slightly below its summit, which is easily attained by a short detour.

Dollywaggon Pike 6

ASCENT FROM DUNMAIL RAISE
2100 feet of ascent : 2 miles

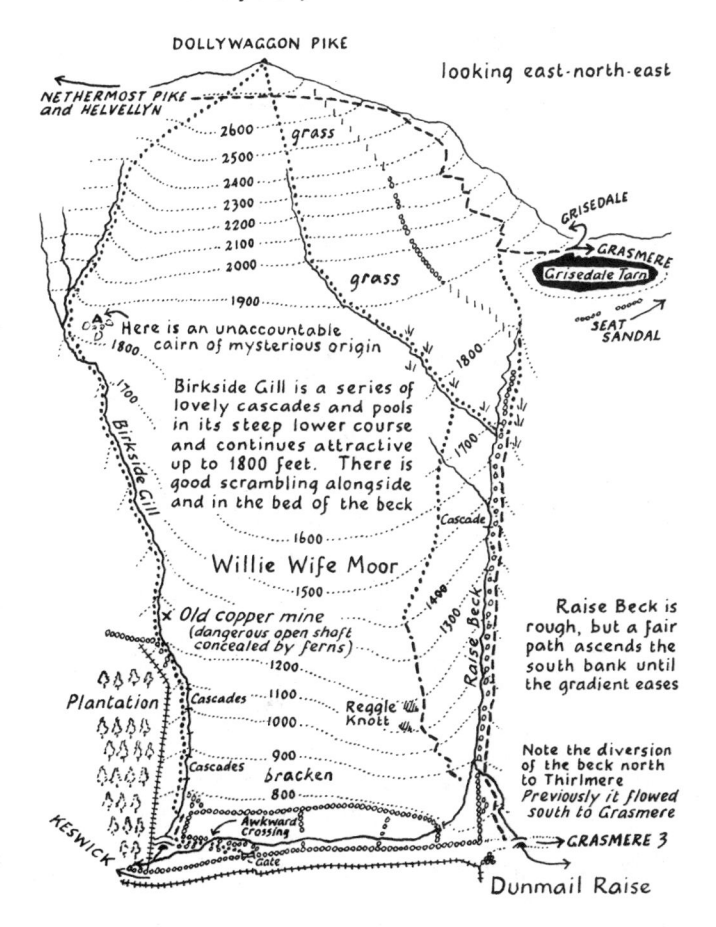

DOLLYWAGGON PIKE

looking east-north-east

← NETHERMOST PIKE and HELVELLYN

grass

GRISEDALE →
→ GRASMERE
Grisedale Tarn

grass

→ SEAT SANDAL

Here is an unaccountable cairn of mysterious origin

Birkside Gill is a series of lovely cascades and pools in its steep lower course and continues attractive up to 1800 feet. There is good scrambling alongside and in the bed of the beck

Birkside Gill

Willie Wife Moor

Raise Beck is rough, but a fair path ascends the south bank until the gradient eases

× Old copper mine (dangerous open shaft concealed by ferns)

Plantation
Cascades
Reggle Knott
Cascades
bracken

Raise Beck

Note the diversion of the beck north to Thirlmere. Previously it flowed south to Grasmere

← KESWICK
Awkward Crossing
Gate
→ GRASMERE 3

Dunmail Raise

The western slopes offer a short and direct route from the main road but are monotonously grassy and of greater interest to sheep than to walkers. Preferably one of the two becks should be followed up, especially on a hot day.

Dollywaggon Pike 7

ASCENT FROM GRISEDALE
2400 feet of ascent : 5 miles from Patterdale village

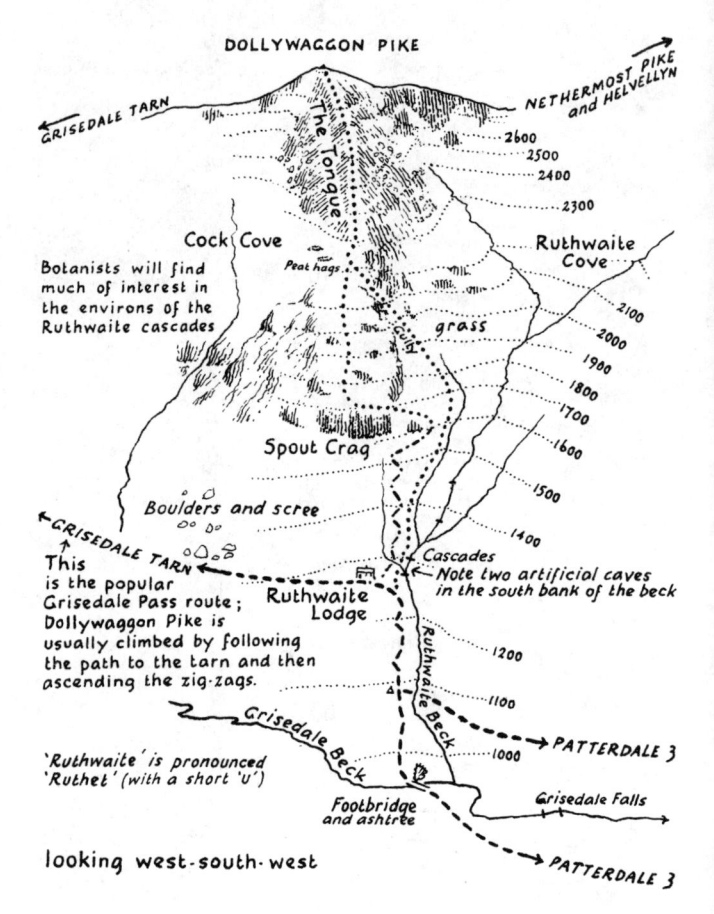

DOLLYWAGGON PIKE

←GRISEDALE TARN

NETHERMOST PIKE and HELVELLYN→

The Tongue

2600
2500
2400
2300

Cock Cove

Peat hags

Ruthwaite Cove

Botanists will find much of interest in the environs of the Ruthwaite cascades

grass

2100
2000
1900
1800
1700
1600
1500
1400

Spout Crag

Boulders and scree

←GRISEDALE TARN

Cascades

Note two artificial caves in the south bank of the beck

This is the popular Grisedale Pass route; Dollywaggon Pike is usually climbed by following the path to the tarn and then ascending the zig-zags.

Ruthwaite Lodge

Ruthwaite Beck

1200
1100

'Ruthwaite' is pronounced 'Ruthet' (with a short 'u')

Grisedale Beck

1000

PATTERDALE 3→

Footbridge and ashtree

Grisedale Falls

looking west-south-west

PATTERDALE 3→

This is much the most interesting and exhilarating way to the summit, but it is relatively unknown and rarely used. The finish up the narrow Tongue is excellent. *This route should not be attempted in bad weather conditions.*

Dollywaggon Pike 8

THE SUMMIT

The summit is a small grassy dome, narrowing to the east. The big cairn is 30 yards west of the highest point.

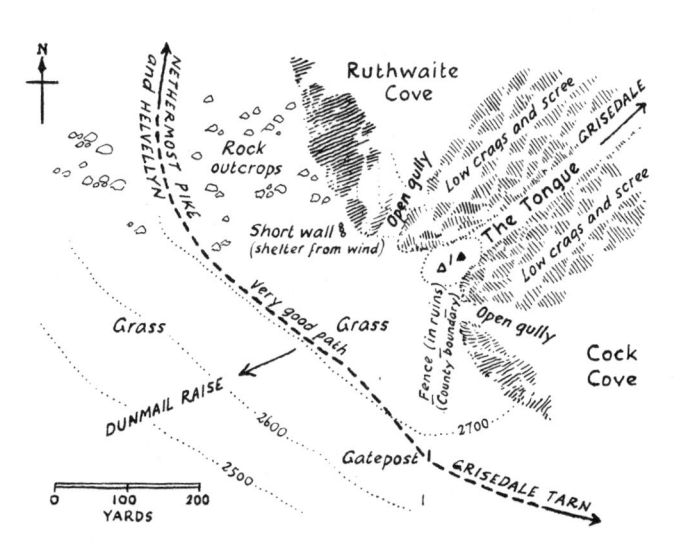

Crinkle Crags Bowfell Scafell Pike

DESCENTS: The quickest and easiest way off is the direct descent to Dunmail Raise, but Birkside Gill should be avoided. The Tongue route should not be attempted, nor descents made into Cock Cove or Ruthwaite Cove, *in mist*: this side of the fell is extremely rough.
|||| *In bad weather conditions*, the safest descent is to Grisedale Tarn by the zig-zag path, for either Grasmere or Patterdale.

Dollywaggon Pike 9

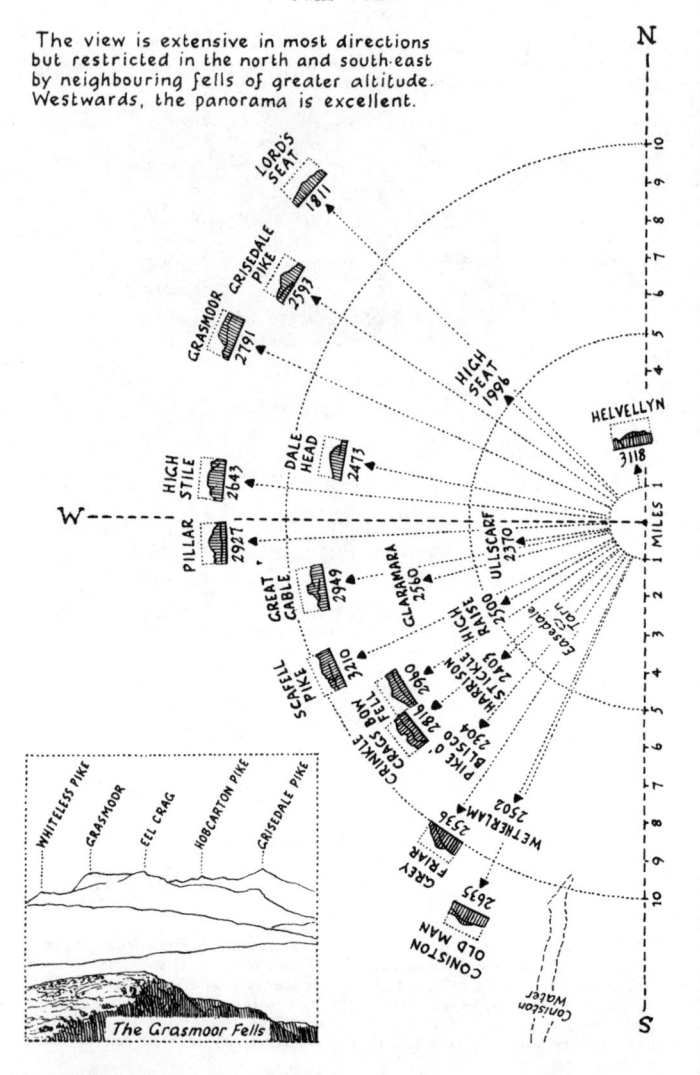

THE VIEW

The view is extensive in most directions but restricted in the north and south-east by neighbouring fells of greater altitude. Westwards, the panorama is excellent.

Peaks shown on the panorama (clockwise from north):
- LORD'S SEAT 1811
- GRISEDALE PIKE 2593
- GRASMOOR 2791
- HIGH SEAT 1996
- HELVELLYN 3118
- DALE HEAD 2473
- HIGH STILE 2643
- PILLAR 2927
- GREAT GABLE 2949
- GLARAMARA 2560
- ULLSCARF 2370
- RAISE 2500
- HIGH STYLE 2403
- HARRISON STICKLE 2403
- SCAFELL PIKE 3210
- CRINKLE CRAGS 2816
- BOW FELL 2960
- PIKE O' BLISCO 2304
- WETHERLAM 2502
- GREY FRIAR 2536
- CONISTON OLD MAN 2635
- Coniston Water
- Easedale Tarn

The Grasmoor Fells (inset panorama):
WHITELESS PIKE — GRASMOOR — EEL CRAG — HOBCARTON PIKE — GRISEDALE PIKE

Dollywaggon Pike 10

THE VIEW

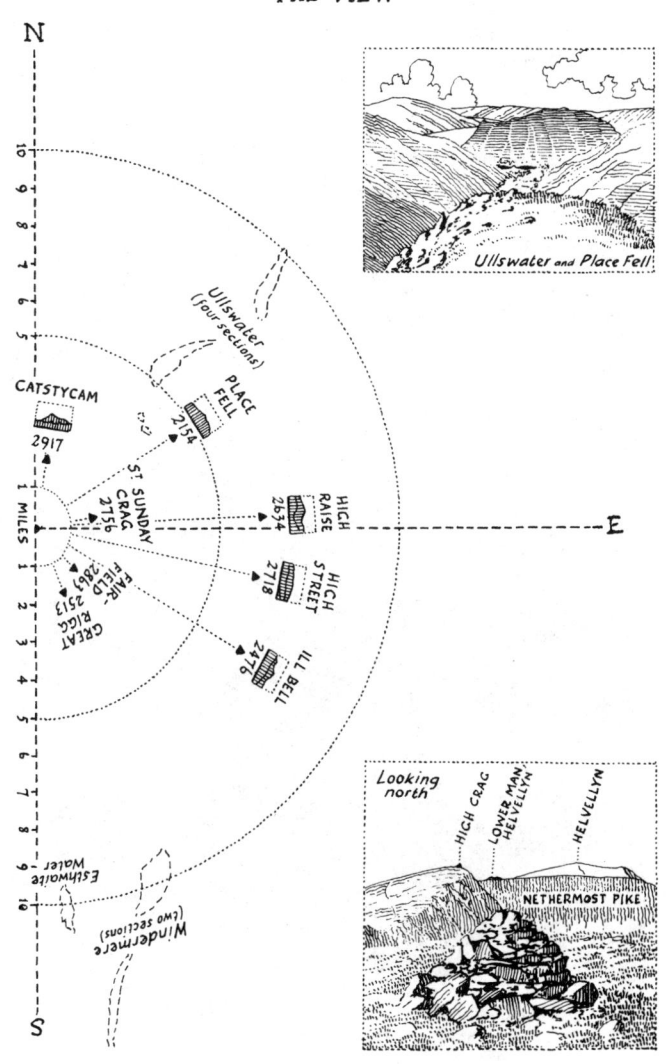

Ullswater and Place Fell

Looking north — HIGH CRAG, LOWER MAN HELVELLYN, HELVELLYN, NETHERMOST PIKE

CATSTYCAM 2917
PLACE FELL 2154
ST SUNDAY CRAG 2756
HIGH RAISE 2634
FAIRFIELD 2863
GREAT RIGG 2513
HIGH STREET 2718
ILL BELL 2476

Ullswater (four sections)
Windermere (two sections)
Esthwaite Water

Dollywaggon Pike 11

Cave and Cascades, Ruthwaite

Dollywaggon Pike 12

RIDGE ROUTES

To NETHERMOST PIKE, 2920': 1 mile : NW then N.
Depression at 2700'
220 feet of ascent

An easy walk with fine views. Safe in mist if the path is followed closely.

An excellent path links Dollywaggon Pike and Nethermost Pike, skirting their actual summits to the west. A more interesting route (no path) lies along the edge of the crags overlooking Ruthwaite Cove.

To SEAT SANDAL, 2415'
1¼ miles : S

Depression at 1850'
600 feet of ascent

A steep but easy descent followed by a dull climb. The depression is marshy. Safe but unpleasant in mist.

Seat Sandal is the next fell to the south, but the direct route to it can hardly be called a ridge. There is no path, but the way is indicated by broken fences and walls.

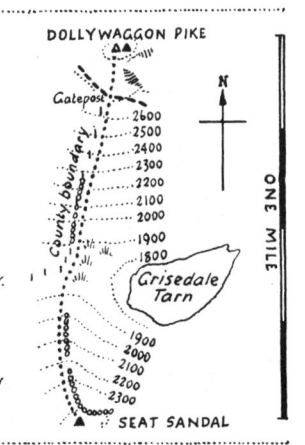

The Tarn Crag gullies

Dove Crag 2603'

from Dovedale

Patterdale •

Hartsop •

▲ FAIRFIELD

DOVE ▲ CRAG

RED SCREES ▲

• Grasmere

Ambleside
•
MILES
0 1 2 3 4

The lofty height that towers so magnificently over Dovedale is indebted for its name to a very impressive vertical wall of rock on its north-east flank: the crag was named first and the summit of the parent fell above, which officially is considered unworthy of any title and is nameless on the Ordnance Survey maps, has adopted it by common consent.

Dove Crag 2

NATURAL FEATURES

Dove Crag is a mountain of sharp contrasts. To the east, its finest aspect, it presents a scarred and rugged face, a face full of character and interest. Here, in small compass, is a tangle of rough country, a maze of steep cliffs, gloomy hollows and curious foothills gnarled like the knuckles of a clenched fist, with the charming valley of Dovedale below and the main crag frowning down over all. Very different is its appearance from other directions. A high ridge runs south, with featureless grass slopes flowing down from it to the valleys of Rydale and Scandale. The fell is a vertebra of the Fairfield spine and is connected to the next height in the system, Hart Crag, by a lofty depression.

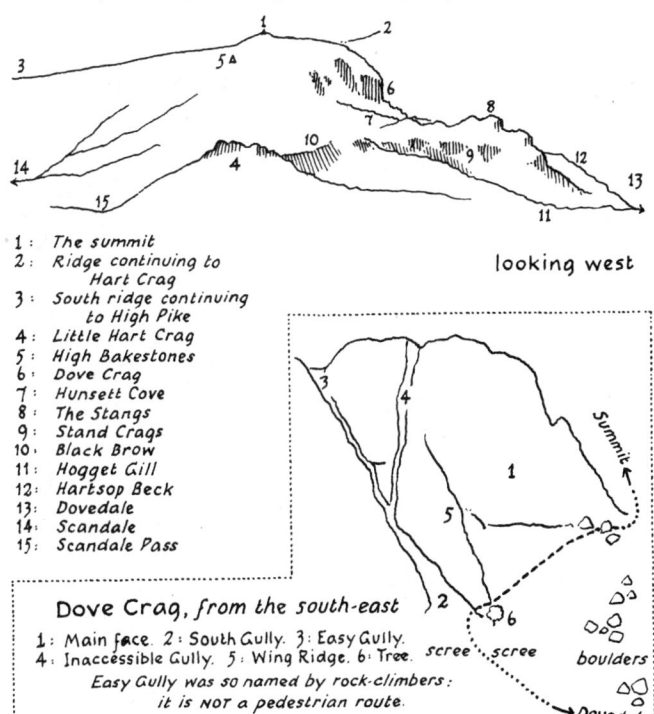

looking west

1 : The summit
2 : Ridge continuing to Hart Crag
3 : South ridge continuing to High Pike
4 : Little Hart Crag
5 : High Bakestones
6 : Dove Crag
7 : Hunsett Cove
8 : The Stangs
9 : Stand Crags
10 : Black Brow
11 : Hogget Gill
12 : Hartsop Beck
13 : Dovedale
14 : Scandale
15 : Scandale Pass

Dove Crag, from the south-east
1 : Main face. 2 : South Gully. 3 : Easy Gully.
4 : Inaccessible Gully. 5 : Wing Ridge. 6 : Tree.
Easy Gully was so named by rock-climbers: it is NOT a pedestrian route.

Dove Crag 3

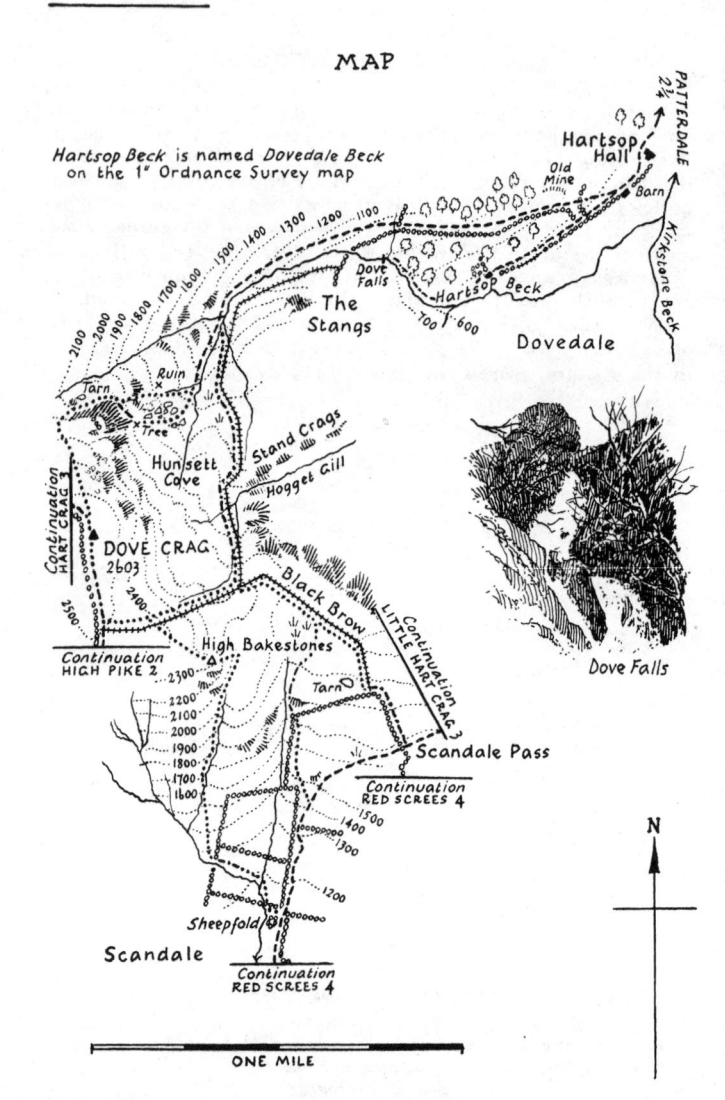

MAP

Hartsop Beck is named Dovedale Beck on the 1" Ordnance Survey map

Dove Falls

ONE MILE

N

Dove Crag 4

ASCENT FROM PATTERDALE
2,200 feet of ascent: 5 miles from Patterdale village

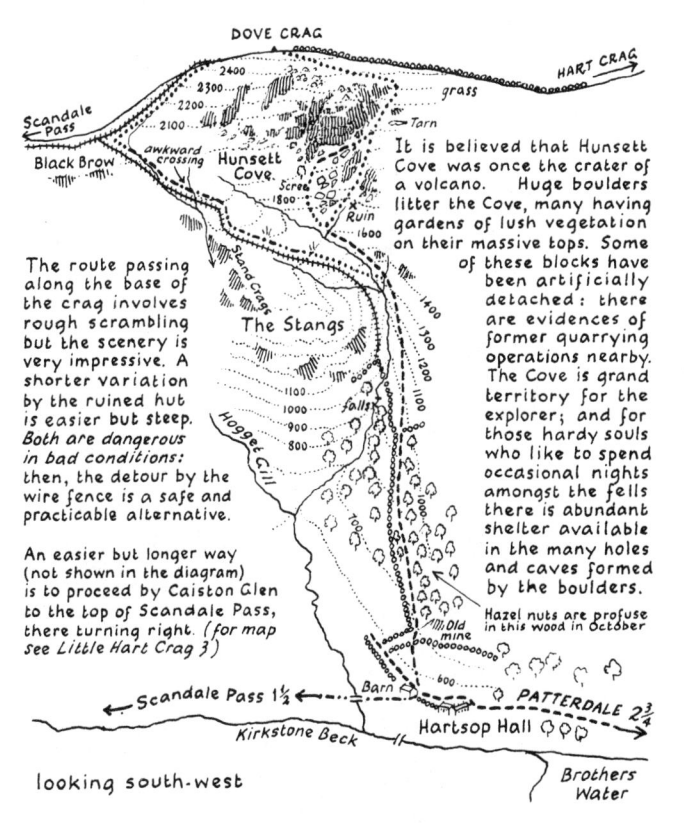

(map annotations:)
DOVE CRAG — HART CRAG — grass — Tarn — Scandale Pass — Black Brow — awkward crossing — Hunsett Cove — Scree — Ruin — Sand Crag — The Stangs — Hogget Gill — falls — Old mine — Barn — Kirkstone Beck — Hartsop Hall — Brothers Water — Scandale Pass 1½ — PATTERDALE 2¾

It is believed that Hunsett Cove was once the crater of a volcano. Huge boulders litter the Cove, many having gardens of lush vegetation on their massive tops. Some of these blocks have been artificially detached: there are evidences of former quarrying operations nearby. The Cove is grand territory for the explorer; and for those hardy souls who like to spend occasional nights amongst the fells there is abundant shelter available in the many holes and caves formed by the boulders.

Hazel nuts are profuse in this wood in October

The route passing along the base of the crag involves rough scrambling but the scenery is very impressive. A shorter variation by the ruined hut is easier but steep. Both are dangerous in bad conditions: then, the detour by the wire fence is a safe and practicable alternative.

An easier but longer way (not shown in the diagram) is to proceed by Caiston Glen to the top of Scandale Pass, there turning right. (for map see Little Hart Crag 3)

looking south-west

Dove Crag is most often ascended from Ambleside on the popular tour of the 'Fairfield Horseshoe' — but the climb from Patterdale, by Dovedale, is far superior: it gives a much more interesting and intimate approach, the sharp transition from the soft loveliness of the valley to the desolation above being very impressive.

Dove Crag 5

ASCENT FROM AMBLESIDE
2500 feet of ascent : 5 miles

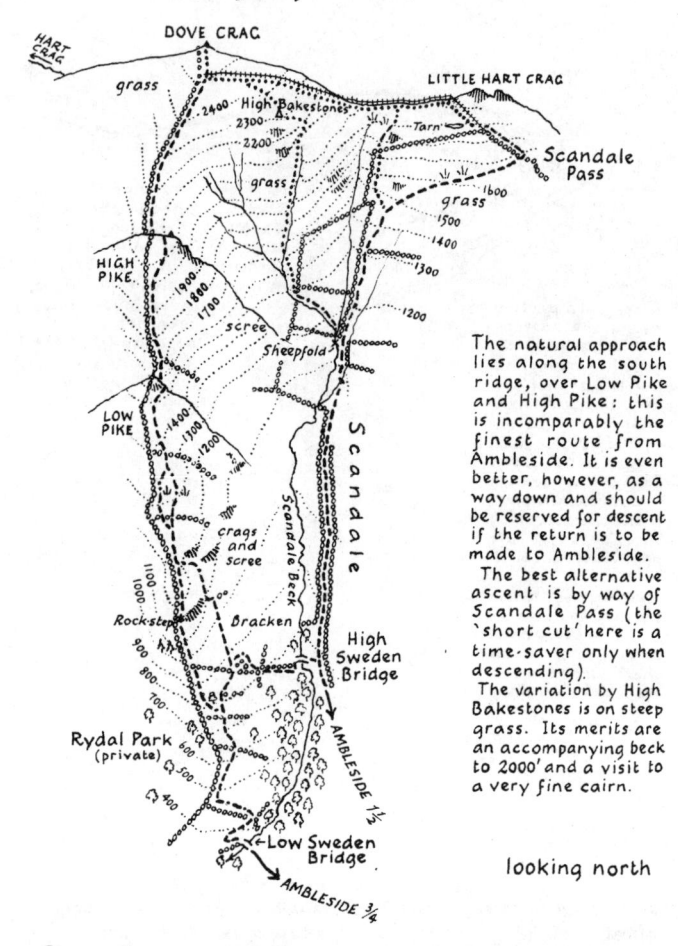

The natural approach lies along the south ridge, over Low Pike and High Pike: this is incomparably the finest route from Ambleside. It is even better, however, as a way down and should be reserved for descent if the return is to be made to Ambleside.

The best alternative ascent is by way of Scandale Pass (the 'short cut' here is a time-saver only when descending).

The variation by High Bakestones is on steep grass. Its merits are an accompanying beck to 2000' and a visit to a very fine cairn.

looking north

Dove Crag cannot be seen from Ambleside, but rising from the fields north of the town is its clearly-defined south ridge, offering an obvious staircase to the summit.

Dove Crag 6

THE SUMMIT

The actual top of the fell is a small rock platform crowned by a cairn, twenty yards east of the crumbling wall crossing the broad summit-plateau. It is of little distinction and there is nothing of interest in the immediate surroundings.

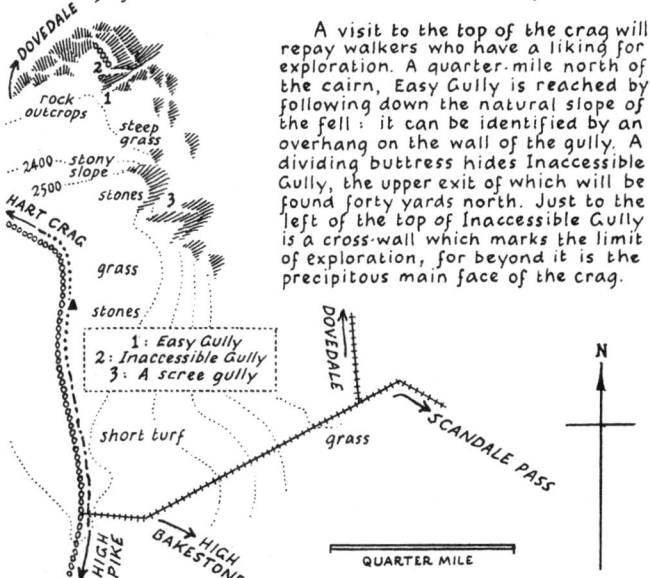

A visit to the top of the crag will repay walkers who have a liking for exploration. A quarter-mile north of the cairn, Easy Gully is reached by following down the natural slope of the fell: it can be identified by an overhang on the wall of the gully. A dividing buttress hides Inaccessible Gully, the upper exit of which will be found forty yards north. Just to the left of the top of Inaccessible Gully is a cross-wall which marks the limit of exploration, for beyond it is the precipitous main face of the crag.

1: Easy Gully
2: Inaccessible Gully
3: A scree gully

DESCENTS: All routes of ascent may be reversed for descent but the way down into Dovedale by the base of the crag is very rough. The High Bakestones route to Scandale is not recommended. *In mist*, whether bound for Ambleside or Patterdale, the wall should be followed south, soon turning left along the fence for Patterdale via Dovedale or Scandale Pass. *Direct descents to Dovedale from the summit must not be attempted.*

Dove Crag 7

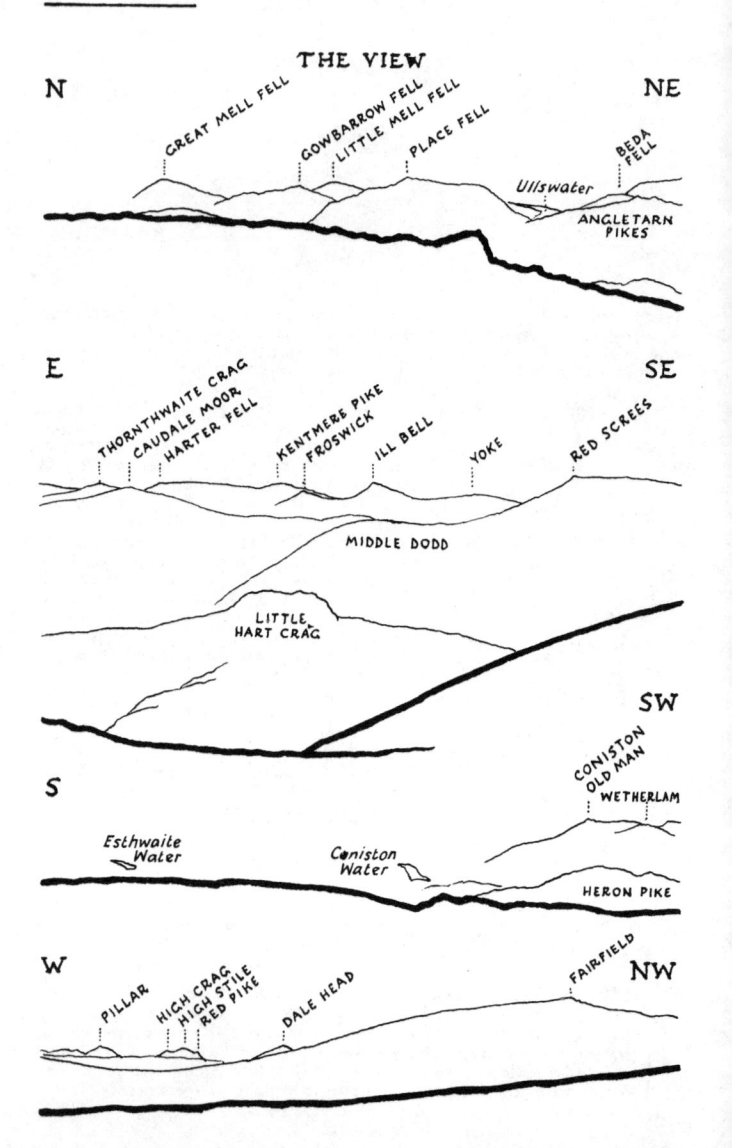

THE VIEW

N — **NE**
- Great Mell Fell
- Gowbarrow Fell
- Little Mell Fell
- Place Fell
- Beda Fell
- Ullswater
- Angletarn Pikes

E — **SE**
- Thornthwaite Crag
- Caudale Moor
- Harter Fell
- Kentmere Pike
- Froswick
- Ill Bell
- Yoke
- Red Screes
- Middle Dodd
- Little Hart Crag

SW
- Coniston Old Man
- Wetherlam

S
- Esthwaite Water
- Coniston Water
- Heron Pike

W — **NW**
- Pillar
- High Crag
- High Stile
- Red Pike
- Dale Head
- Fairfield

Dove Crag 8

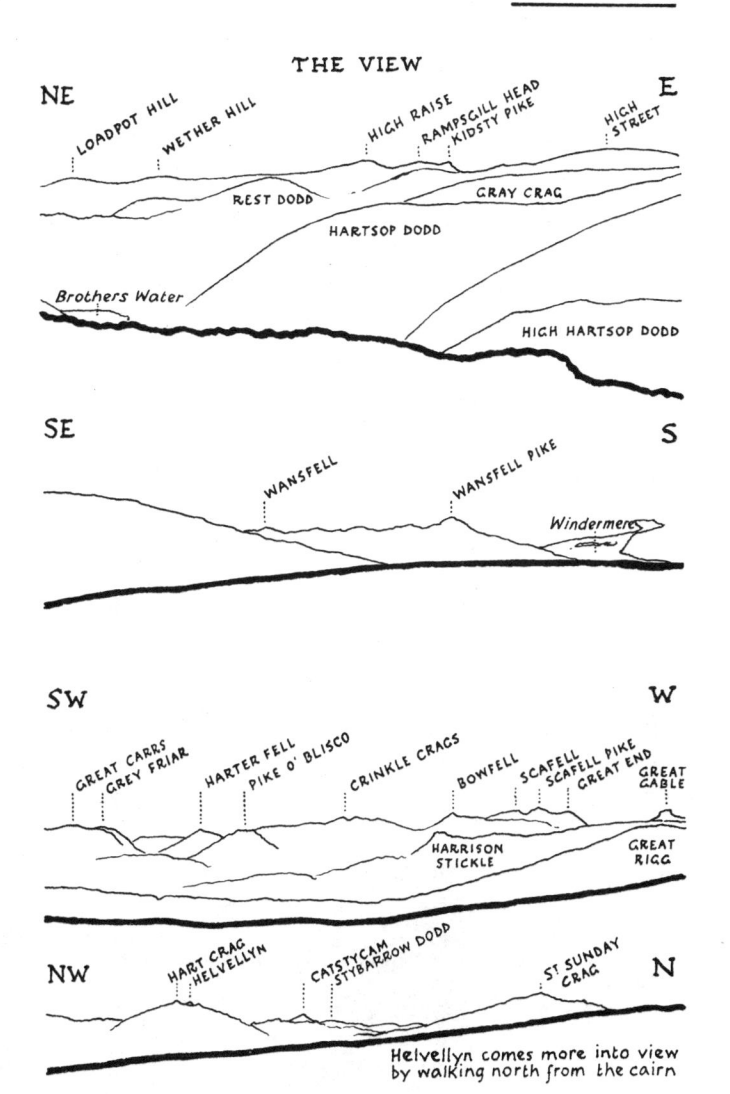

THE VIEW

NE — Loadpot Hill, Wether Hill, Rest Dodd, High Raise, Rampsgill Head, Kidsty Pike, Hartsop Dodd, Gray Crag, High Street — **E**

Brothers Water, High Hartsop Dodd

SE — Wansfell, Wansfell Pike, Windermere — **S**

SW — Great Carrs, Grey Friar, Harter Fell, Pike o' Blisco, Crinkle Crags, Bowfell, Scafell, Scafell Pike, Great End, Great Gable, Harrison Stickle, Great Rigg — **W**

NW — Hart Crag, Helvellyn, Catstycam, Stybarrow Dodd, St Sunday Crag — **N**

Helvellyn comes more into view by walking north from the cairn

Dove Crag 9

RIDGE ROUTES

To HART CRAG, 2698': ¾ mile : NW
Depression at 2350'
350 feet of ascent

An easy walk. Hart Crag is not safe in mist.
A faint grass path accompanies the wall to the depression; beyond, the wall ends at a cluster of rocks. A track, plain at first, goes steeply up the stony breast of Hart Crag and becomes indistinct on the grass at the top.

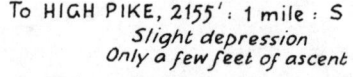

To HIGH PIKE, 2155': 1 mile : S
Slight depression
Only a few feet of ascent

One of the easiest miles in Lakeland; grass all the way. Perfectly safe in mist.
Follow the wall south; an intermittent path keeps a few yards to the left of it.

To LITTLE HART CRAG 2091': 1¼ miles
S then ENE and SE
Minor depressions
200 feet of ascent

Rough grass; may be marshy in places. Little Hart Crag is dangerous in bad conditions.
Follow first the wall south and then the wire fence: it approaches within 200 yards of the summit before turning down towards Scandale Pass.

The cairn on High Bakestones

This beautifully-built 8' column, commanding a view of Scandale, is one of the finest specimens on these hills. It is more than a cairn. It is a work of art and a lasting memorial to its builder.

Dove Crag 10

Dovedale, from the top of Easy Gully

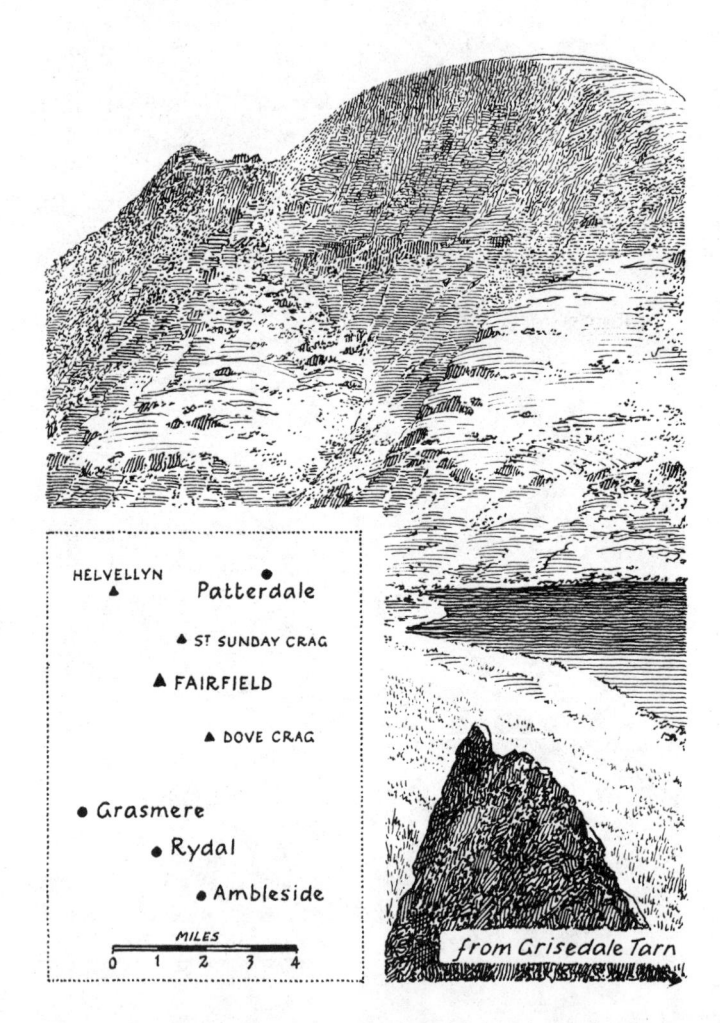

Fairfield 2863'

from Grisedale Tarn

Fairfield 2

NATURAL FEATURES

The rough triangle formed by Grisedale Pass, the Rothay valley and Scandale Pass, with the village of Patterdale as its apex, contains within its area a bulky mountain-system with five distinct summits over 2500'. High ridges link these summits; there are also subsidiary ridges and spurs of lesser altitude, massive rocky buttresses, gloomy coves and fine daleheads. The whole mass constitutes a single geographical unit and the main summit is Fairfield, a grand mountain with grand satellites in support. No group of fells in the district exhibits a more striking contrast in appearance when surveyed from opposite sides than this lofty Fairfield group. From the south it appears as a great horseshoe of grassy slopes below a consistently high skyline, simple in design and impressive in altitude, but lacking those dramatic qualities that appeal most to the lover of hills. But on the north side the Fairfield range is magnificent: here are dark precipices, long fans of scree, abrupt crags, desolate combes and deep valleys: a tangle of rough country, small in extent but full of interest, and well worth exploration. This grimmer side of the Fairfield group can only be visited conveniently from the Patterdale area. Fairfield turns its broad back to the south, to Rydal and Grasmere, and climbers from this direction get only the merest glimpse of its best features; many visitors to the summit, indeed, return unsuspecting, and remember Fairfield and its neighbours as mountains of grass. The few who know the head of Deepdale and the recesses of Dovedale, intimately, have a very different impression.

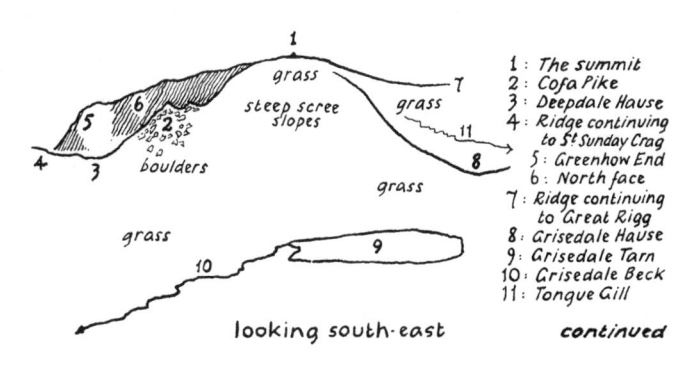

1 : *The summit*
2 : *Cofa Pike*
3 : *Deepdale Hause*
4 : *Ridge continuing to St Sunday Crag*
5 : *Greenhow End*
6 : *North face*
7 : *Ridge continuing to Great Rigg*
8 : *Grisedale Hause*
9 : *Grisedale Tarn*
10 : *Grisedale Beck*
11 : *Tongue Gill*

looking south-east

continued

Fairfield 3

NATURAL FEATURES
continued

Three ridges leave the top of Fairfield: one goes south over Great Rigg to end abruptly at Nab Scar above Rydal Water; another, the spine of the Fairfield system, keeps a high level to Dove Crag, traversing Hart Crag on the way, and the third, and best, runs north inclining east over the splintered crest of Cofa Pike and on to St Sunday Crag. On the west flank only is there no descending ridge: here an ill-defined gable-end falls steeply to Grisedale Hause.

The southern and western slopes are simple, the northern and eastern complicated and far more interesting. Here a mile-long face of alternating rock and scree towers high above the barren hollow of Deepdale. Crags abound: most impressive is the precipitous cliff of Greenhow End, scarped on three sides and thrusting far into the valley, and a wall of even steeper rock, with Scrubby Crag prominent, bounds Link Cove to the east.

Fairfield claims Deepdale Beck, Rydal Beck and the main branch of Tongue Gill as its streams, but is only one of many contributors to Grisedale Beck. It is without a tarn of its own, forming one side only of the green basin containing Grisedale Tarn.

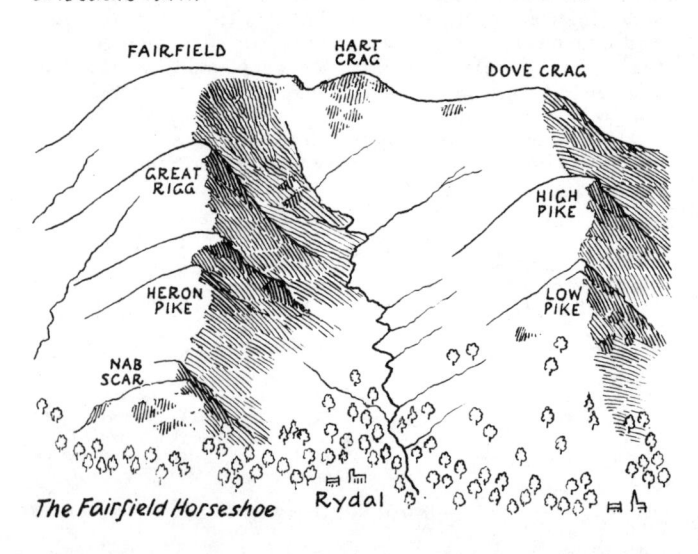

The Fairfield Horseshoe

Fairfield 4

Cofa Pike and the north-east ridge

Greenhow End

Scrubby Crag

The Crags of Fairfield

Black Crag, Rydal Head

Fairfield 5

MAP

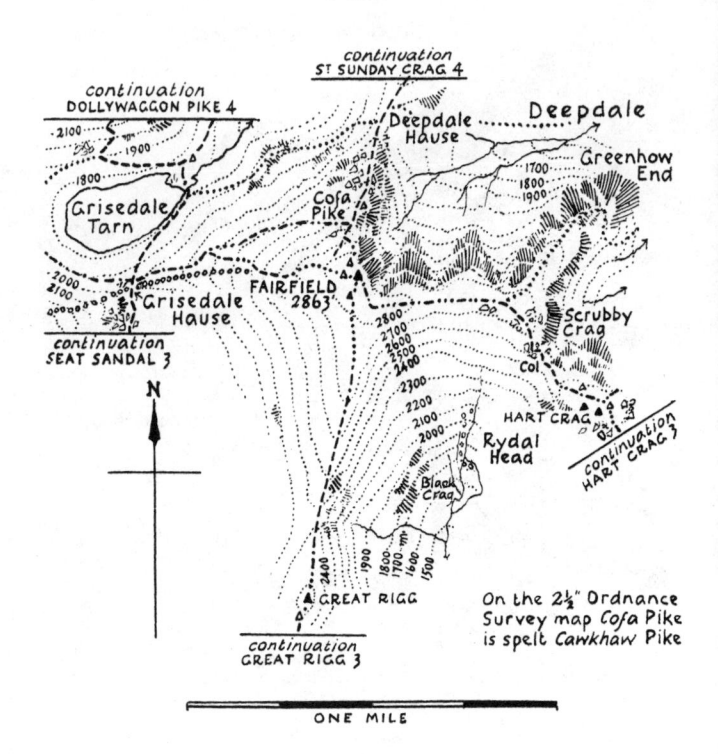

On the 2½" Ordnance Survey map *Cofa Pike* is spelt *Cawkhaw* Pike

ONE MILE

Rocks on Cofa Pike

Fairfield 6

ASCENT FROM GRASMERE
2650 feet of ascent : 4¼ miles from Grasmere Church

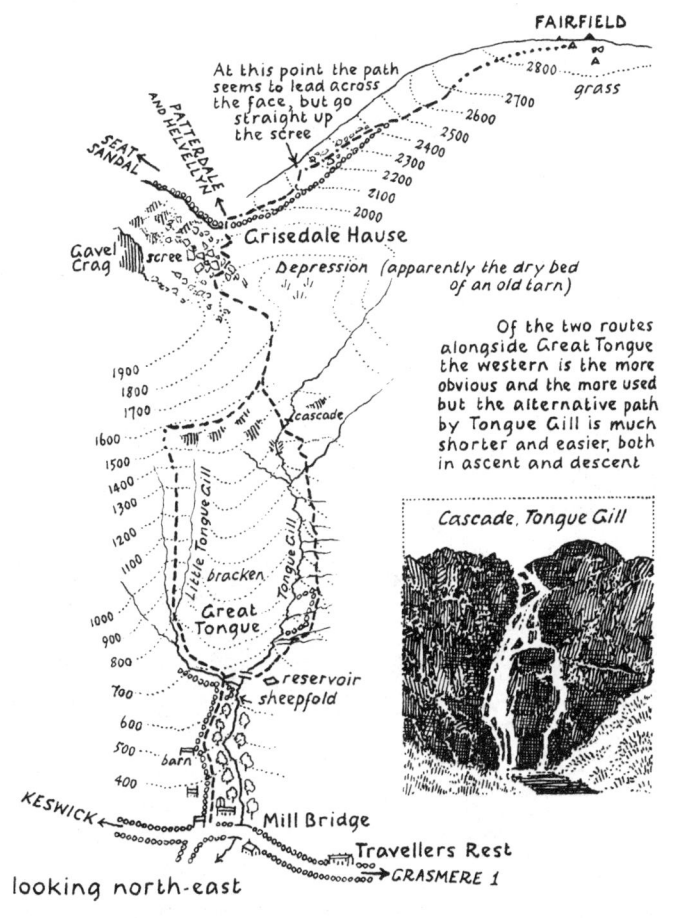

FAIRFIELD

At this point the path seems to lead across the face, but go straight up the scree

grass

SEAT SANDAL ← PATTERDALE AND HELVELLYN

Gavel Crag — scree

Grisedale Hause

Depression (apparently the dry bed of an old tarn)

Of the two routes alongside Great Tongue the western is the more obvious and the more used but the alternative path by Tongue Gill is much shorter and easier, both in ascent and descent

cascade

Little Tongue Gill

Tongue Gill

bracken

Great Tongue

Cascade, Tongue Gill

reservoir
sheepfold

barn

KESWICK ← Mill Bridge — Travellers Rest → GRASMERE 1

looking north-east

The path to Grisedale Hause, by either side of the Tongue, is distinct but above the Hause it is not so well marked. Tongue Gill is an interesting approach but the last 1000' of climbing is dull. The top of Fairfield is confusing in mist.

Fairfield 7

ASCENT FROM PATTERDALE
2400 feet of ascent : 5½ miles

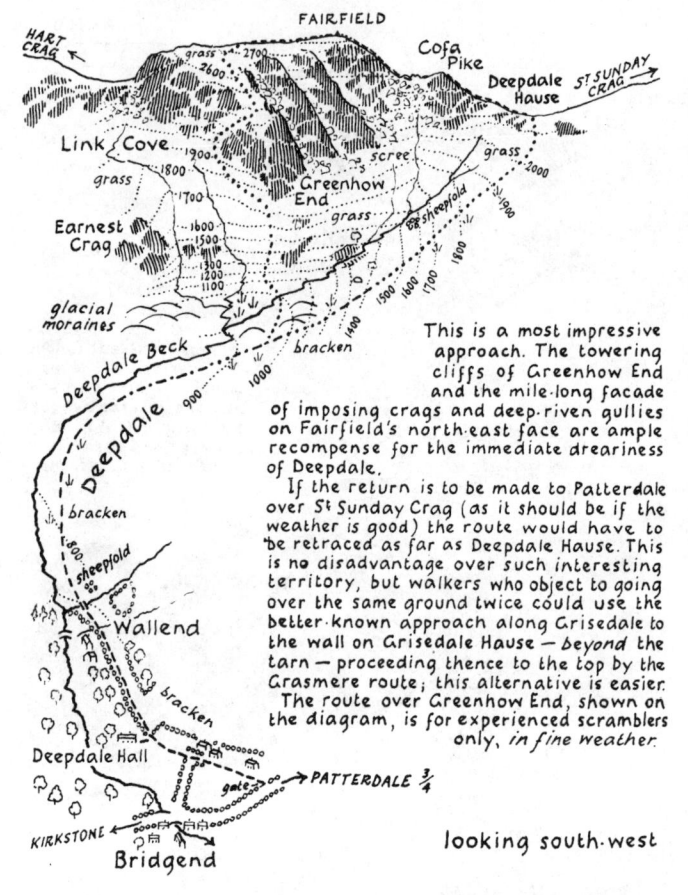

looking south-west

This is a most impressive approach. The towering cliffs of Greenhow End and the mile-long facade of imposing crags and deep-riven gullies on Fairfield's north-east face are ample recompense for the immediate dreariness of Deepdale.

If the return is to be made to Patterdale over St Sunday Crag (as it should be if the weather is good) the route would have to be retraced as far as Deepdale Hause. This is no disadvantage over such interesting territory, but walkers who object to going over the same ground twice could use the better-known approach along Grisedale to the wall on Grisedale Hause — *beyond the tarn* — proceeding thence to the top by the Grasmere route; this alternative is easier.

The route over Greenhow End, shown on the diagram, is for experienced scramblers only, *in fine weather*.

The gradual revelation of the savage northern face of Fairfield as the view up Deepdale unfolds gives a high quality to this route. Deepdale itself is desolate, but has interesting evidences of glacial action; Link Cove is one of the finest examples of a hanging valley.

Fairfield 8

The head of Deepdale

The cliffs of Fairfield, from Greenhow End

Fairfield 9

THE SUMMIT

The summit of Fairfield is an extensive grassy plateau. The absence of distinguishing natural features makes it, in mist, particularly confusing, and the abundance of cairns is then a hindrance rather than a help. The actual top is flat and its surface is too rough to bear the imprint of paths, and the one definable point is a tumbledown windbreak of stones, built as a short wall and offering shelter only to persons of imagination. Thirty yards in front of the shelter is the principal and largest cairn, standing almost on the rim of the steep north face.
Mention should be made of the excellent turf on this wide top: weary feet will judge it delightful.

DESCENTS: Too many cairns are worse than too few, and it is unfortunate that the tops of the buttresses of the north face are unnecessarily adorned with piles of stones, snares in mist for strangers to the fell, who may think they indicate ways off the summit. So they do — sudden ways off. There is no trouble in clear weather in identifying the various routes of descent, the best of which lies over Cofa Pike and St Sunday Crag to Patterdale: an exhilarating and beautiful walk.

In mist, note that none of the usual routes descend over steep ground and that a cairn does not necessarily indicate a path. With care, all routes are quite practicable, but the safest way off, in bad weather and whatever the destination, is westwards to Grisedale Tarn, following a line of cairns until a path appears. (It doesn't matter much about finding a path if the walker is sure he is going either west or south, or between these points, but he who wanders northward courts disaster)

Fairfield 10

THE SUMMIT

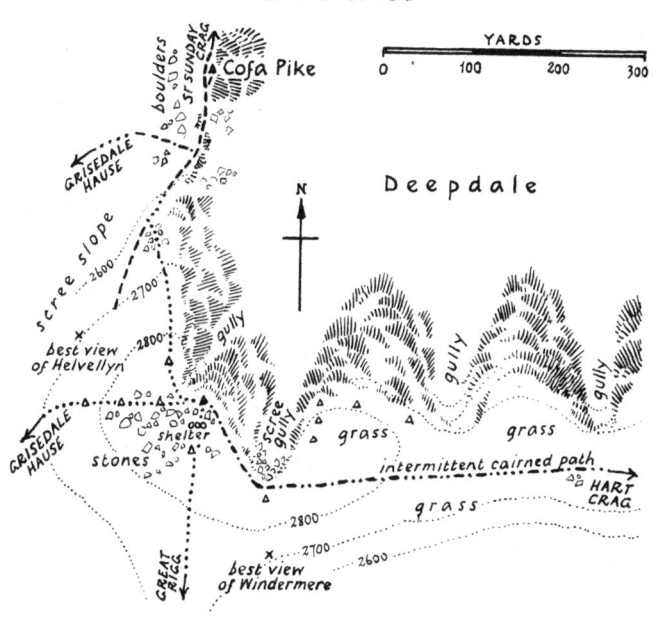

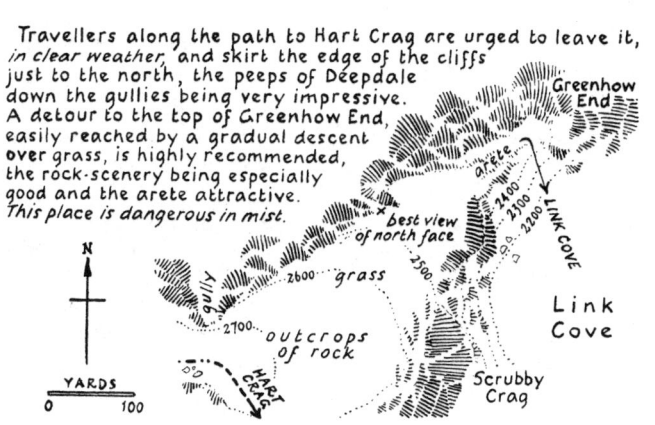

Travellers along the path to Hart Crag are urged to leave it, *in clear weather,* and skirt the edge of the cliffs just to the north, the peeps of Deepdale down the gullies being very impressive. A detour to the top of Greenhow End, easily reached by a gradual descent over grass, is highly recommended, the rock-scenery being especially good and the arete attractive. *This place is dangerous in mist.*

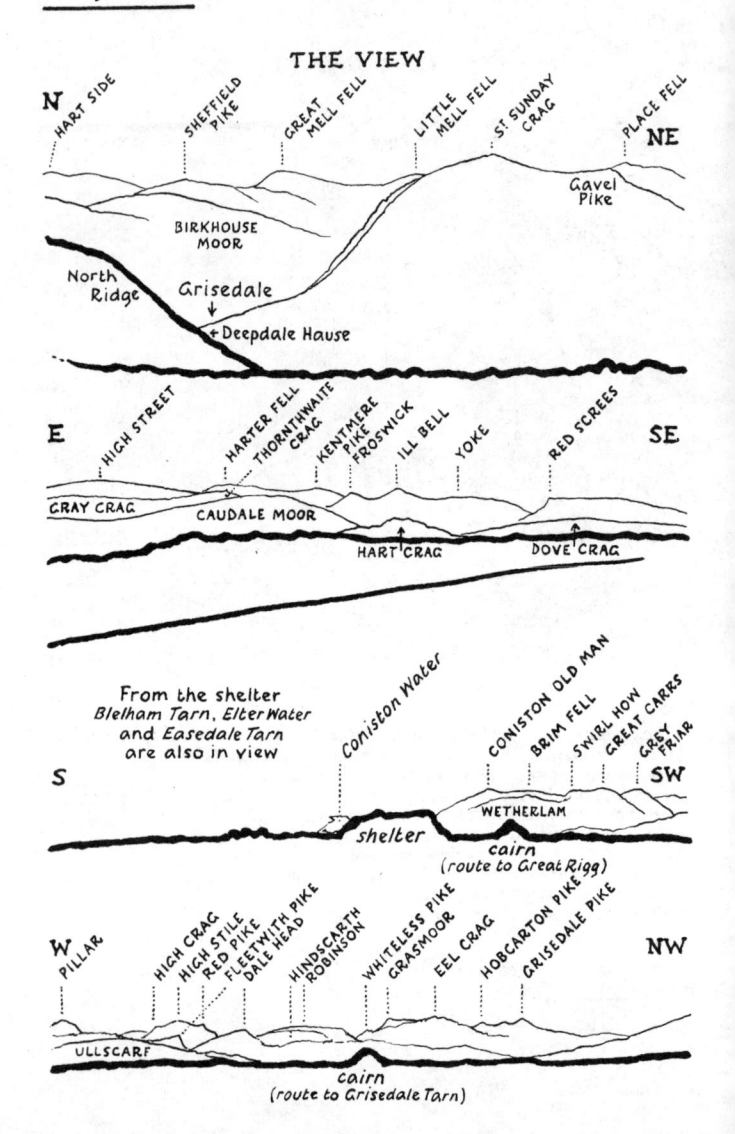

Fairfield 11

THE VIEW

N — HART SIDE — SHEFFIELD PIKE — GREAT MELL FELL — LITTLE MELL FELL — ST SUNDAY CRAG — PLACE FELL — NE

Gavel Pike
BIRKHOUSE MOOR
North Ridge — Grisedale
+ Deepdale Hause

E — HIGH STREET — HARTER FELL — THORNTHWAITE CRAG — KENTMERE PIKE — FROSWICK — ILL BELL — YOKE — RED SCREES — SE

GRAY CRAG — CAUDALE MOOR
HART CRAG — DOVE CRAG

From the shelter *Blelham Tarn*, *Elter Water* and *Easedale Tarn* are also in view

Coniston Water

S — CONISTON OLD MAN — BRIM FELL — SWIRL HOW — GREAT CARRS — GREY FRIAR — SW

WETHERLAM
shelter
cairn (route to Great Rigg)

W — PILLAR — HIGH CRAG — HIGH STILE — RED PIKE — FLEETWITH PIKE — DALE HEAD — HINDSCARTH — ROBINSON — WHITELESS PIKE — GRASMOOR — EEL CRAG — HOBCARTON PIKE — GRISEDALE PIKE — NW

ULLSCARF
cairn (route to Grisedale Tarn)

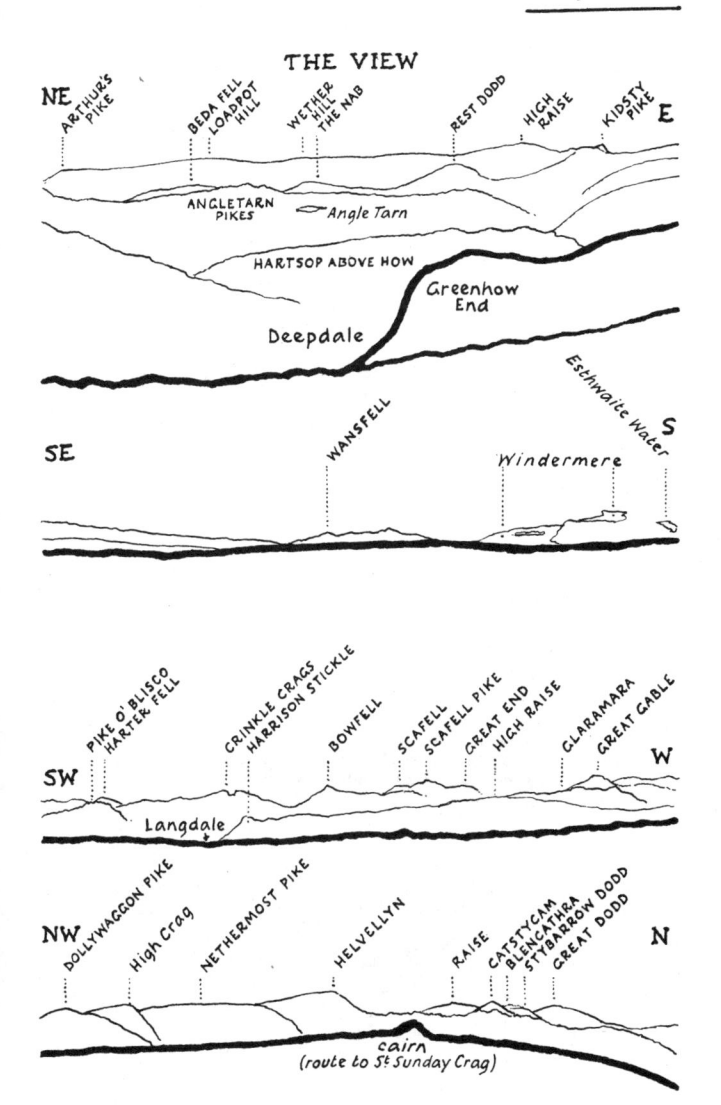

Fairfield 12

THE VIEW

Fairfield 13

RIDGE ROUTES

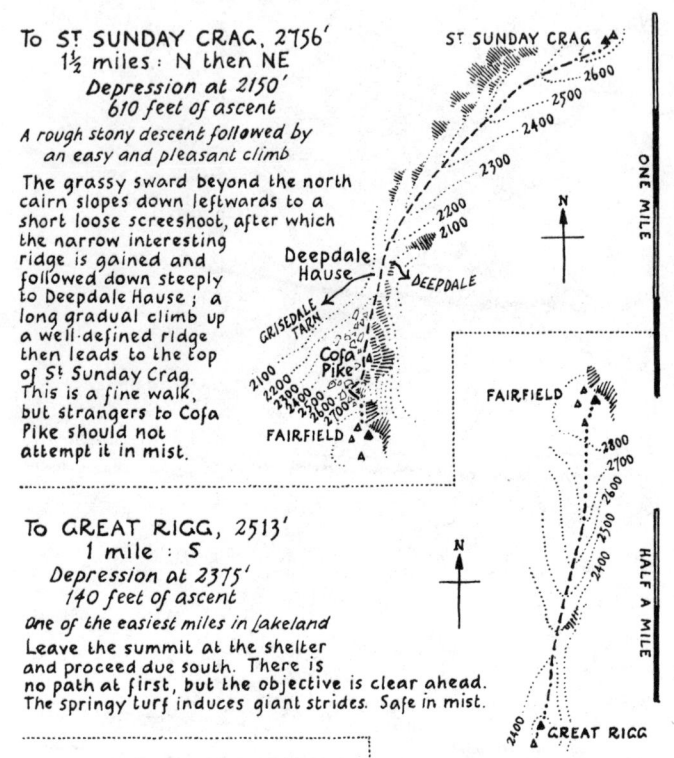

To ST SUNDAY CRAG, 2756'
1½ miles : N then NE
Depression at 2150'
610 feet of ascent
A rough stony descent followed by an easy and pleasant climb

The grassy sward beyond the north cairn slopes down leftwards to a short loose screeshoot, after which the narrow interesting ridge is gained and followed down steeply to Deepdale Hause; a long gradual climb up a well-defined ridge then leads to the top of St Sunday Crag. This is a fine walk, but strangers to Cofa Pike should not attempt it in mist.

To GREAT RIGG, 2513'
1 mile : S
Depression at 2375'
140 feet of ascent
One of the easiest miles in Lakeland

Leave the summit at the shelter and proceed due south. There is no path at first, but the objective is clear ahead. The springy turf induces giant strides. Safe in mist.

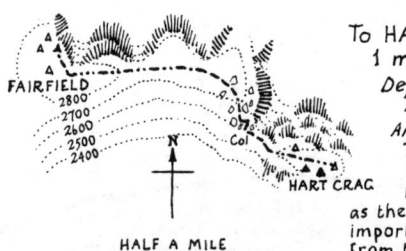

To HART CRAG, 2698'
1 mile : E then SE
Depression at 2550'
150 feet of ascent
An easy, interesting walk.

The path across the broad top of Fairfield is cairned but indistinct; it improves as the col is approached. It is important, in mist, not to stray from the path: danger lurks!

Fairfield 14

The north face of Fairfield

Glenridding Dodd

1425'
approx.

*from Ullswater
(Sheffield Pike behind)*

Fashions change. When people climbed hills only for the sake of the views, the heathery summit of Glenridding Dodd must have been more frequented than it is today, for once-popular paths of ascent are now overgrown and neglected. It occupies a grand position overlooking the upper reach of Ullswater. It is the end, topographically, of the eastern shoulder of Stybarrow Dodd.

Glenridding Dodd 2

MAP

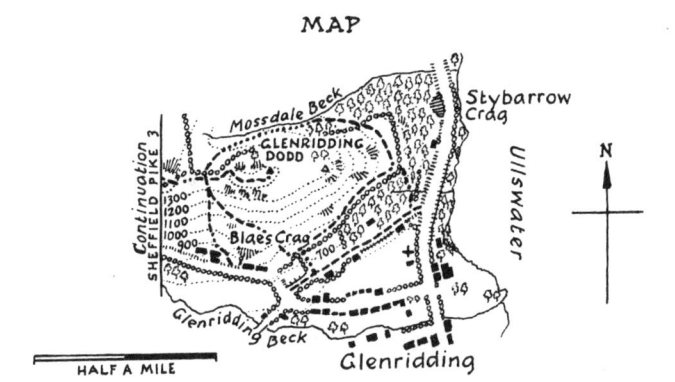

ASCENT FROM GLENRIDDING
1000 feet of ascent

The Dodd is so conveniently situated and offers so delightful a view that it might be expected that walkers would have blazed a wide path to the top. Such is not the case, however, and it is not at all easy to find a route that does not involve a minor trespass. The upper slopes are largely defended by woodlands and a wall which frustrated tourists have broken in places. The most straightforward route climbs steeply by the left (west) of Blaes Crag (see diagram, *Sheffield Pike 4*); the most pleasant traverses the fell above the wall and ascends by Mossdale Beck. The path *through* the woods to the wall, shown on the map, is overgrown and difficult to follow when the bracken is high.

THE SUMMIT

On a sunny day in August the summit is a delectable place. It is richly clothed with heather, and larches almost reach the top on the north side. Many cairns adorn the hummocky summit, the main one overlooking Glenridding village.

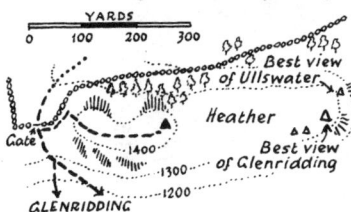

Stybarrow Crag

Glenridding Dodd 3

THE VIEW

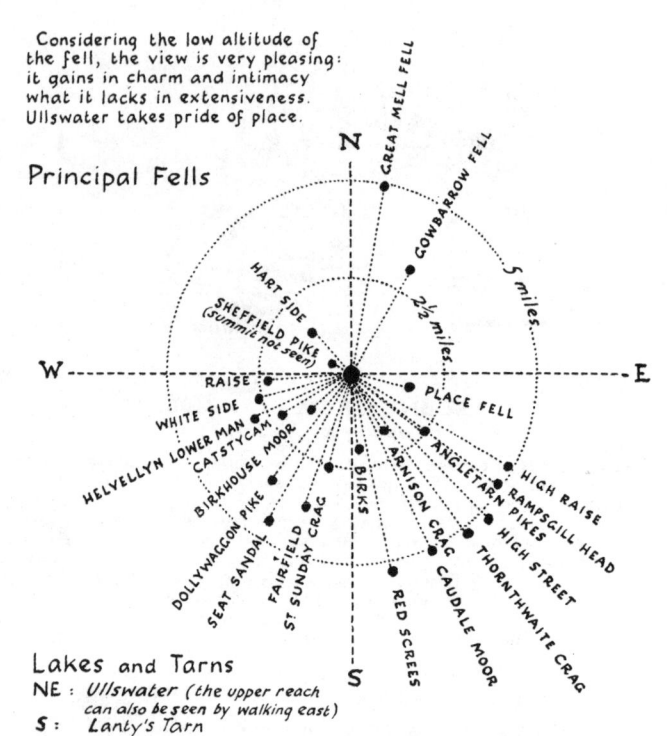

Considering the low altitude of the fell, the view is very pleasing: it gains in charm and intimacy what it lacks in extensiveness. Ullswater takes pride of place.

Principal Fells

N — GREAT MELL FELL
GOWBARROW FELL
HART SIDE
SHEFFIELD PIKE (summit not seen)
2½ miles
5 miles
W — RAISE
WHITE SIDE
HELVELLYN LOWER MAN
CATSTYCAM
BIRKHOUSE MOOR
DOLLYWAGGON PIKE
SEAT SANDAL
FAIRFIELD
ST SUNDAY CRAG
BIRKS
ARNISON CRAG
RED SCREES
CAUDALE MOOR
THORNTHWAITE CRAG
HIGH STREET
RAMPSGILL HEAD
HIGH RAISE
ANGLETARN PIKES
PLACE FELL — E
S

Lakes and Tarns
NE : *Ullswater* (the upper reach can also be seen by walking east)
S : *Lanty's Tarn*

looking down on Glenridding

Glenridding Dodd 4

Ullswater and Birk Fell

Gowbarrow Fell   1579'

from Brown Hills

▲ GREAT MELL FELL
Pooley Bridge •
LITTLE MELL FELL ▲
• Watermillock
▲ GOWBARROW FELL
• Dockray

• Glenridding

MILES
0 1 2 3 4

Gowbarrow Fell 2

NATURAL FEATURES

Gowbarrow Fell is one of the best known of Lakeland's lesser heights, much of it being National Trust property and a favourite playground and picnic-place. It is not the fell itself that brings the crowds, however, and its summit is lonely enough: the great attraction is Aira Force, on the beck forming its western boundary. The fell springs from a mass of high dreary ground in the north and takes the shape of a broad wedge, tapering as it falls to Ullswater, the middle reach of which is its south-eastern boundary throughout. The delightful lower slopes here are beautifully wooded, but low crags and bracken in abundance make them rather difficult of access except where they are traversed by the many pleasant green paths which add so much to Gowbarrow's charms.

The Head of Ullswater from Green Hill

Gowbarrow Fell 3

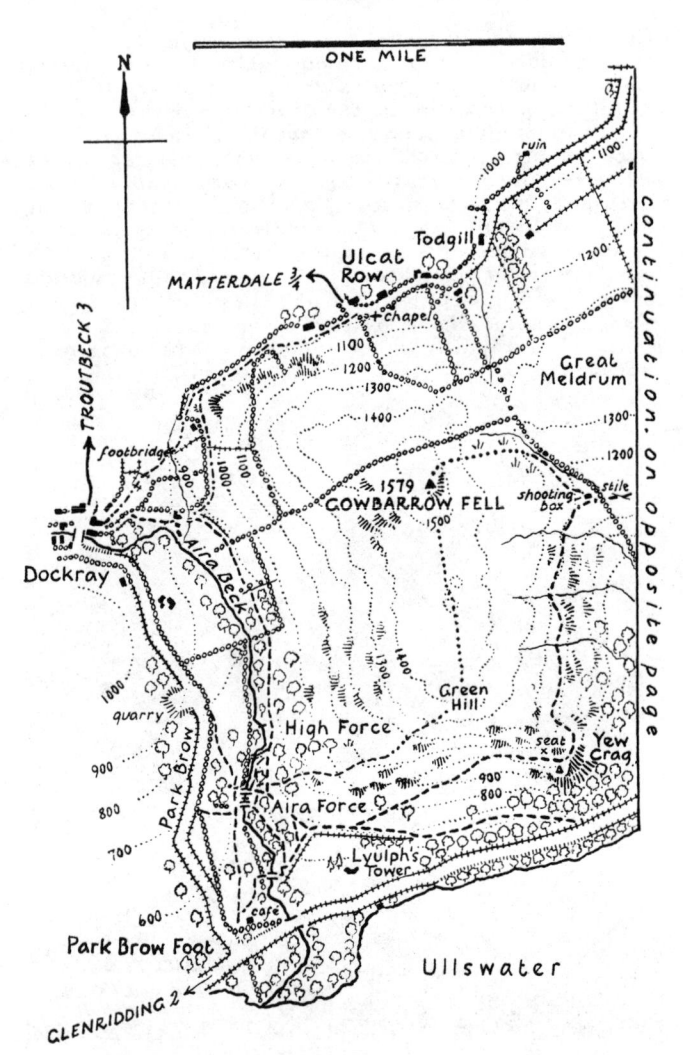

MAP

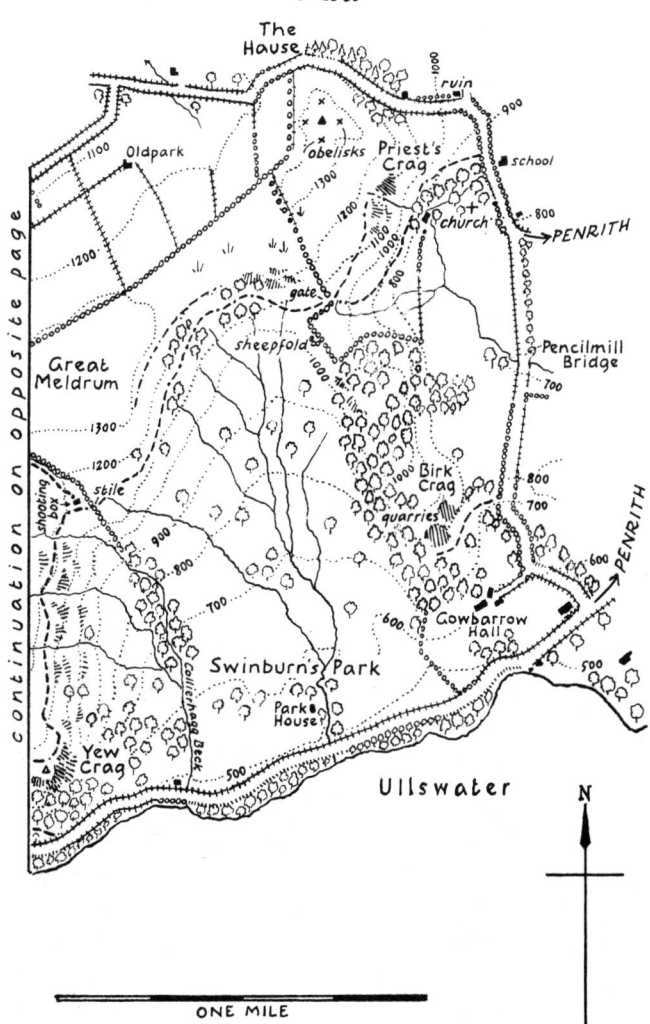

Gowbarrow Fell 4

MAP

Cowbarrow Fell 5

Aira Force

Waterfalls, Aira Beck

High Force

Gowbarrow Fell 6

Place Fell and Ullswater from Gowbarrow Park

ASCENTS

From Park Brow Foot (the usual starting-place for the climb) a path can be seen rising across the fellside behind Lyulph's Tower to the cairn above Yew Crag: this is the best way to the summit. The path, always interesting, continues to the shooting-box (there is shelter here) and then goes upstream to be lost in marshes with the summit-cairn plainly in sight a quarter-mile distant. (The shooting-box may be reached also by a pleasant but overgrown path that starts behind Watermillock Church). A shorter route from Park Brow Foot goes up the shoulder above Aira Force, but the path comes to an early end. The ascent from Dockray direct (by following up the wall) is much less attractive.

Cairn above Yew Crag   *Yew Crag*   *The Shooting-box*

Gowbarrow Fell 7

THE SUMMIT

Great Mell Fell

Flowers, heather and bilberries bloom on the pleasant little ridge where stands the summit-cairn, but the neighbourhood is drab. This ridge is fringed on the side facing Ullswater by a wall of short broken crags and there are other outcrops nearby.

DESCENTS: The best way off the fell is over the undulating top to Green Hill, descending from there to Aira Force. If the bracken is high, it is worth while to search for the path.

In mist, join the wall north of the cairn, turning left for Dockray, right for the shooting box (for either Watermillock or Park Brow Foot).

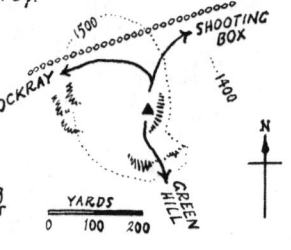

NOTE: Although the altitude of the summit is commonly accepted as 1579', the 2½" Ordnance Survey map (but not the 1") shows a 1600' contour, probably in error.

The summit-ridge

Gowbarrow Fell 8

THE VIEW

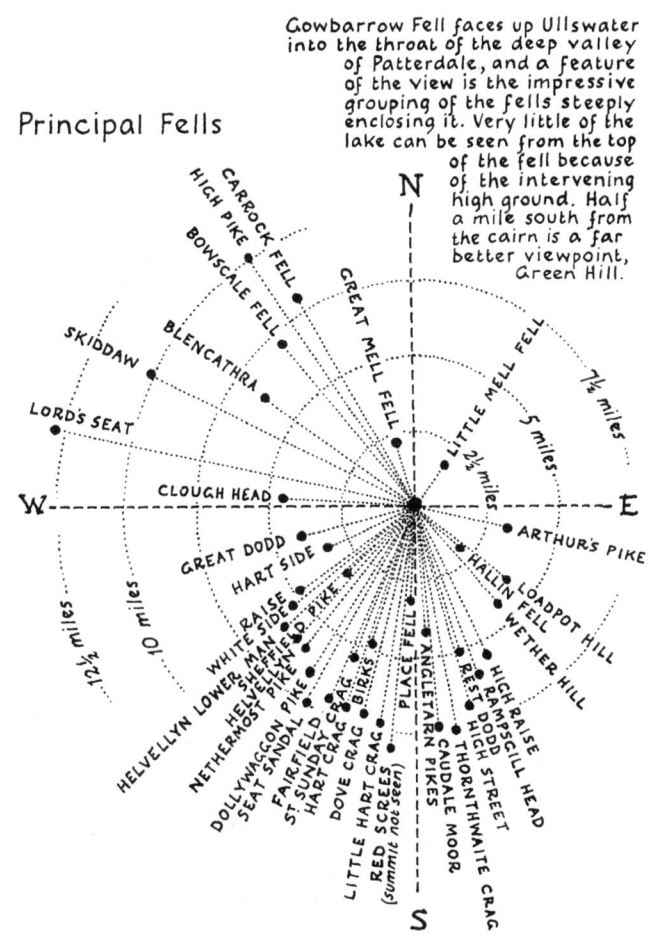

Gowbarrow Fell faces up Ullswater into the throat of the deep valley of Patterdale, and a feature of the view is the impressive grouping of the fells steeply enclosing it. Very little of the lake can be seen from the top of the fell because of the intervening high ground. Half a mile south from the cairn is a far better viewpoint, Green Hill.

Principal Fells

N

CARROCK FELL
HIGH PIKE
BOWSCALE FELL
BLENCATHRA
GREAT MELL FELL
SKIDDAW
LITTLE MELL FELL
LORD'S SEAT
7½ miles
5 miles
2½ miles

W — CLOUGH HEAD — *E*

ARTHUR'S PIKE
GREAT DODD
HART SIDE
LOADPOT HILL
HALLIN FELL
WETHER HILL
WHITE RAISE
HELVELLYN LOWER MAN
SHEFFIELD PIKE
HELVELLYN
NETHERMOST PIKE
HIGH RAISE
DOLLYWAGGON PIKE
RAMPSGILL HEAD
SEAT SANDAL
REST DODD
FAIRFIELD
HIGH STREET
ST. SUNDAY CRAG
HART CRAG
THORNTHWAITE CRAG
DOVE CRAG
PLACE FELL
CAUDALE MOOR
BIRKS
ANGLETARN PIKES
LITTLE HART CRAG
RED SCREES
(summit not seen)

10 miles
12½ miles

S

Lakes and Tarns

ENE : Ullswater — *the lower reach only. The more attractive upper reaches come into view by walking across the top to Green Hill, where the lake is seen most impressively.*

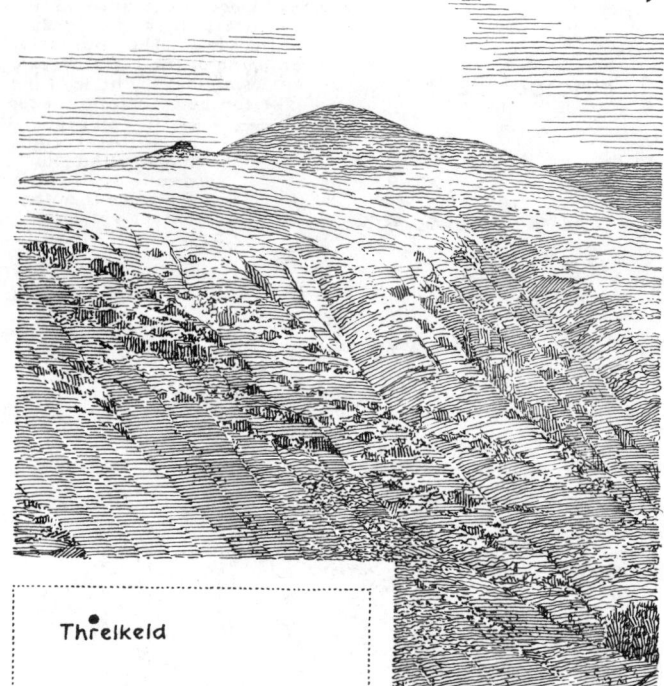

Great Dodd 2807'

from High Rigg

Threlkeld

▲ CLOUGH HEAD
　　　　　　　Dockray
Fornside
　　　▲ GREAT DODD
Legburthwaite
　　　▲ STYBARROW DODD

▲ RAISE
　　Glenridding

▲ HELVELLYN

MILES
0 1 2 3 4

Great Dodd 2

NATURAL FEATURES

Great Dodd, well named, is the most extensive of the fells in the Helvellyn range. To the north-east, its long sprawling slopes fall away gradually in an undulating wilderness of grass to the old coach-road; beyond is a wide expanse of uncultivated marshland, not at all characteristic of Lakeland and of no appeal to walkers. North and south, high ground continues the line of the main ridge, but steepening slopes reach valley-level on both east and west flanks. Grass is everywhere: it offers easy and pleasant tramping but no excitements. Rocks are few and far between: there is a broken line of cliffs, Wolf Crags, overlooking the coach road, and the rough breast of High Brow above Dowthwaitehead breaks out in a series of steep crags (a favourite haunt of buzzards), while there are sundry small outcrops on both east and west flanks well below the summit.

Two of Great Dodd's streams are harnessed to provide water supplies: on the west side, Mill Gill, which has a fine ravine, is diverted to Manchester *via* Thirlmere; on the east, Aira Beck's famous waterfalls are robbed of their full glory to supply rural districts in Cumberland. Mosedale Beck and Trout Beck drain the dreary wastes to the north.

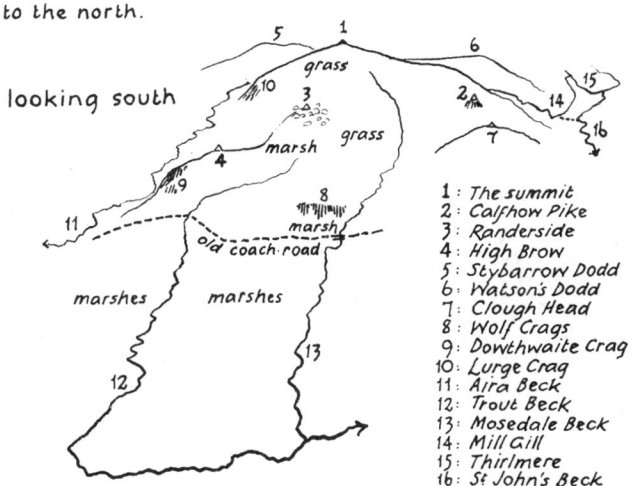

looking south

1 : *The summit*
2 : *Calfhow Pike*
3 : *Randerside*
4 : *High Brow*
5 : *Stybarrow Dodd*
6 : *Watson's Dodd*
7 : *Clough Head*
8 : *Wolf Crags*
9 : *Dowthwaite Crag*
10 : *Lurge Crag*
11 : *Aira Beck*
12 : *Trout Beck*
13 : *Mosedale Beck*
14 : *Mill Gill*
15 : *Thirlmere*
16 : *St John's Beck*

Great Dodd 3

MAP

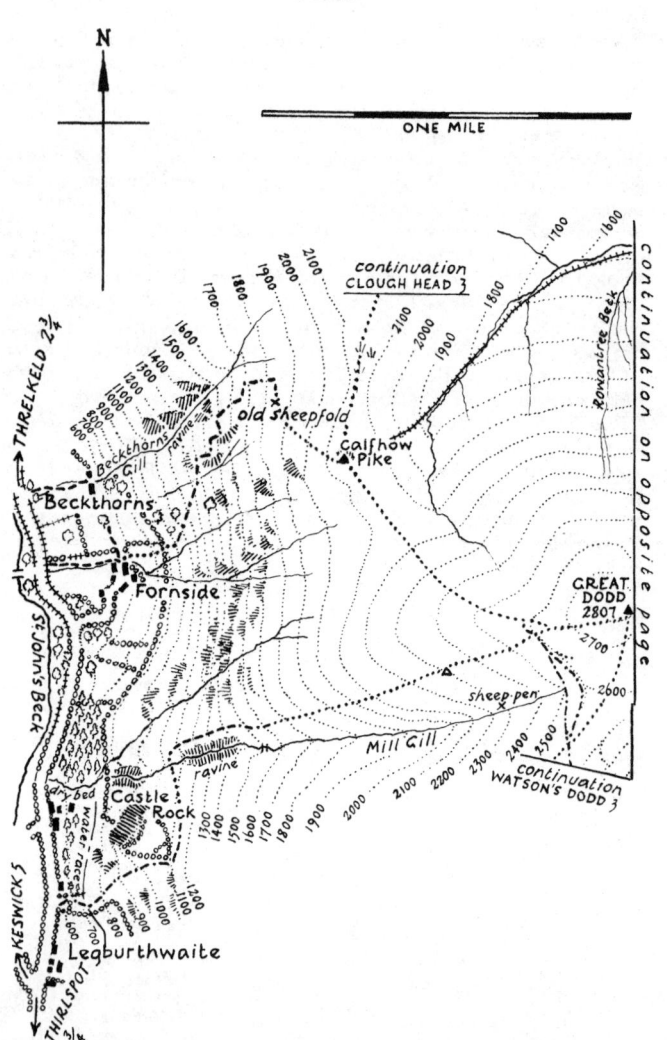

Great Dodd 4

MAP

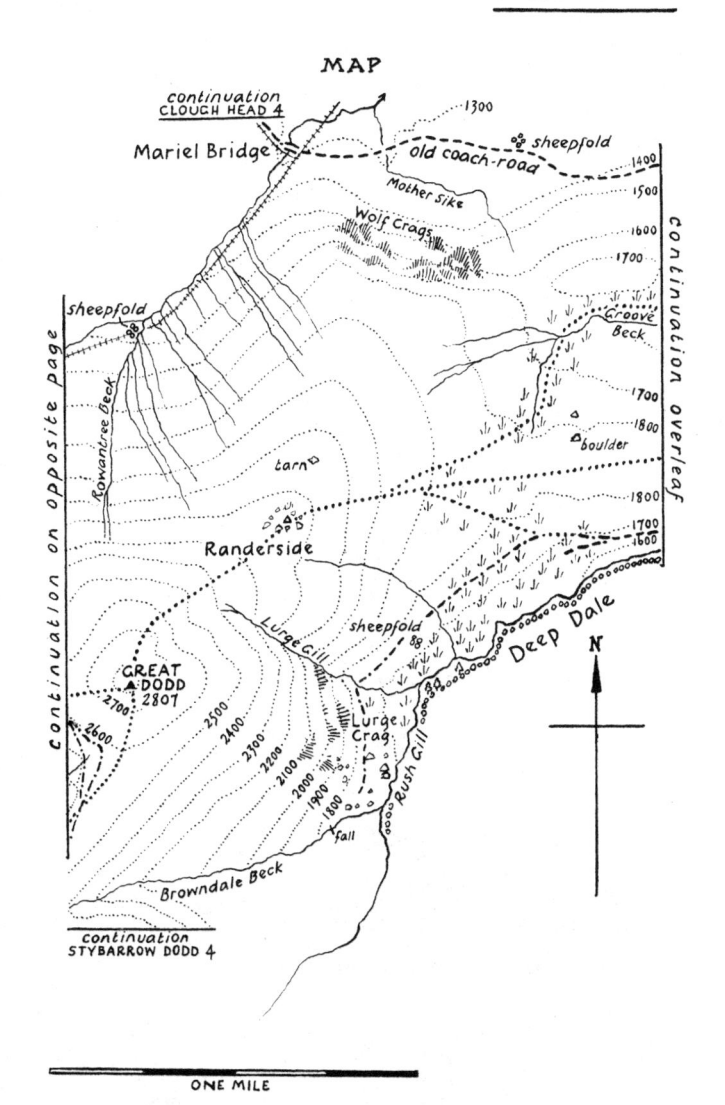

Great Dodd 5

MAP

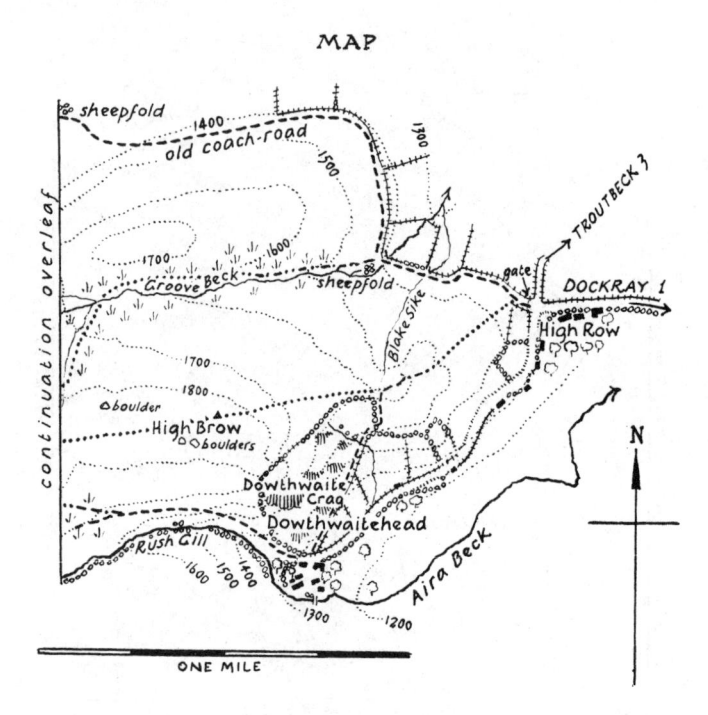

ONE MILE

Wolf Crags

Great Dodd 6

ASCENT FROM DOCKRAY
2000 feet of ascent : 4¼ miles

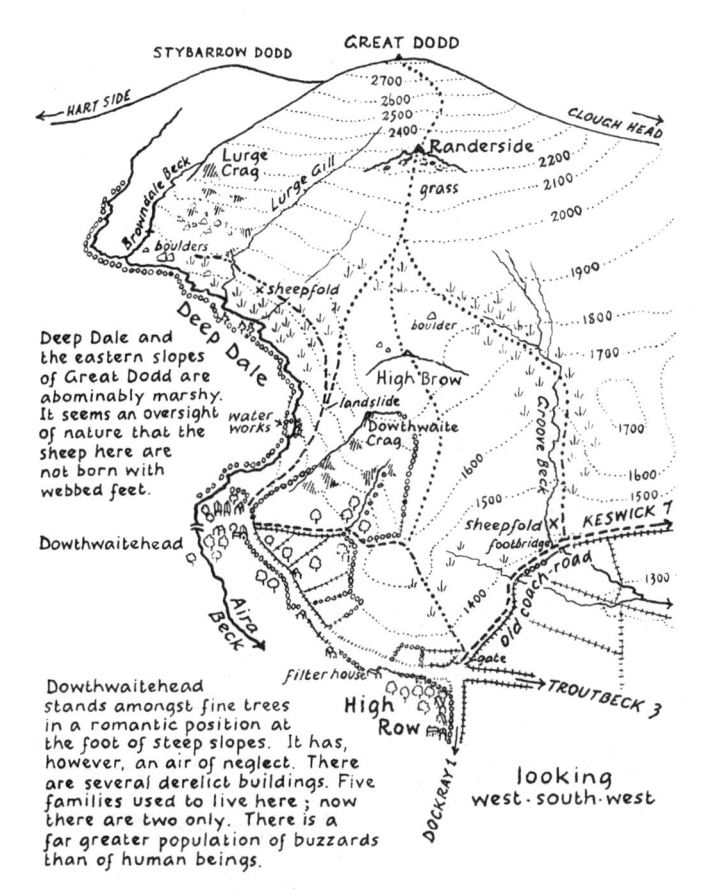

Deep Dale and the eastern slopes of Great Dodd are abominably marshy. It seems an oversight of nature that the sheep here are not born with webbed feet.

Dowthwaitehead stands amongst fine trees in a romantic position at the foot of steep slopes. It has, however, an air of neglect. There are several derelict buildings. Five families used to live here; now there are two only. There is a far greater population of buzzards than of human beings.

looking west-south-west

The ascent of Great Dodd via Groove Beck is one of the easiest climbs in Lakeland, the gradients being very gentle throughout, but otherwise it is without merit. All routes from Dockray are uninspiring and dreary, and most unpleasant in wet weather.

Great Dodd 7

ASCENT FROM FORNSIDE
2300 feet of ascent : 2½ miles

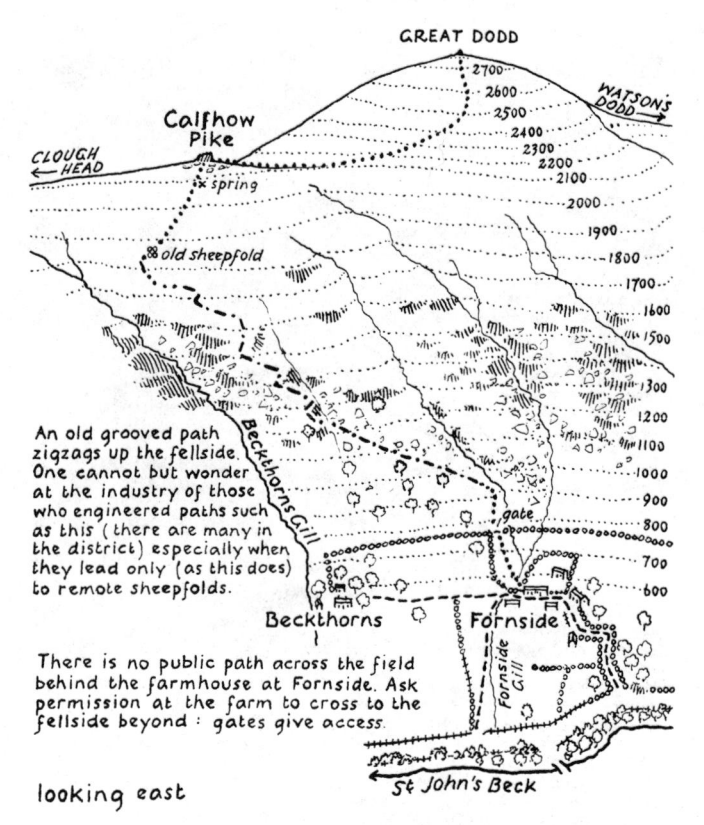

GREAT DODD

WATSON'S DODD

Calfhow Pike

CLOUGH HEAD ←

spring

old sheepfold

Beckthorns Gill

gate

An old grooved path zigzags up the fellside. One cannot but wonder at the industry of those who engineered paths such as this (there are many in the district) especially when they lead only (as this does) to remote sheepfolds.

Beckthorns   Fornside

Fornside Gill

There is no public path across the field behind the farmhouse at Fornside. Ask permission at the farm to cross to the fellside beyond: gates give access.

St John's Beck

looking east

This route is very rarely used. It is steep as far as the sheepfold, but there is recompense in the lovely view of the valley above Fornside. Thereafter it is monotonously grassy, with only the oddity of Calfhow Pike to relieve the tedium of progress.

Great Dodd 8

ASCENT FROM LEGBURTHWAITE
2300 feet of ascent : 2¼ miles

Users of Bartholomew's map should note that Legburthwaite is not indicated thereon

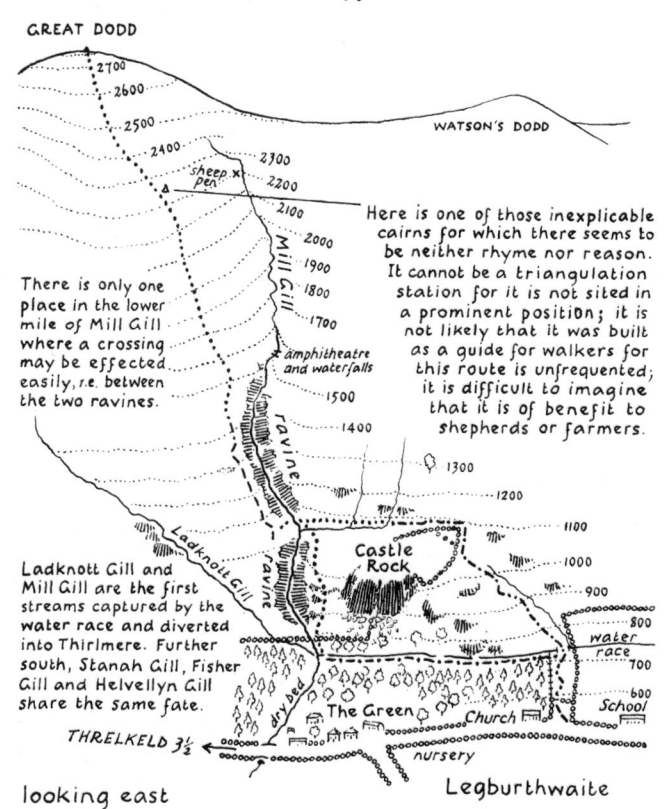

Here is one of those inexplicable cairns for which there seems to be neither rhyme nor reason. It cannot be a triangulation station for it is not sited in a prominent position; it is not likely that it was built as a guide for walkers for this route is unfrequented; it is difficult to imagine that it is of benefit to shepherds or farmers.

There is only one place in the lower mile of Mill Gill where a crossing may be effected easily, r.e. between the two ravines.

Ladknott Gill and Mill Gill are the first streams captured by the water race and diverted into Thirlmere. Further south, Stanah Gill, Fisher Gill and Helvellyn Gill share the same fate.

looking east

Legburthwaite

The first part of this route is pleasant enough; it is interesting also if combined with an exploration of the environs of Castle Rock, but after crossing the attractive Mill Gill it develops into a trudge up a long grass slope : the gradient is easy.

Great Dodd 9

THE SUMMIT

The builders of the cairn must have felt twinges of conscience during their task: they selected as its site a most convenient rash of stones, ignoring the highest point a hundred yards distant, where all is grass except for a naked stone thrusting through the turf, its superior altitude unrecognised. The cairn is hollowed to provide shelter from the west wind. The summit is otherwise featureless.

DESCENTS: Grassy slopes fall away gently on all sides. Distances are greater than they seem hereabouts, but progress is rapid. There are no paths from the summit, but in clear weather all routes are easily determined.

In mist, direction may be taken from the shelter in the cairn, which faces east.

There is no danger in leaving the top even in the thickest weather, but care must be taken to avoid descending into the inhospitable valley of Deep Dale by mistake.

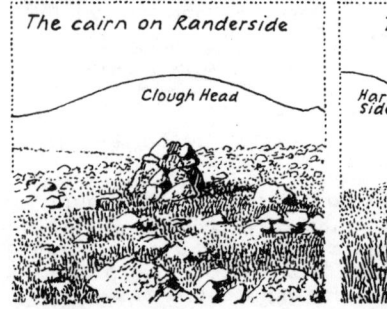

The cairn on Randerside

The cairn on High Brow

Great Dodd 10

RIDGE ROUTES

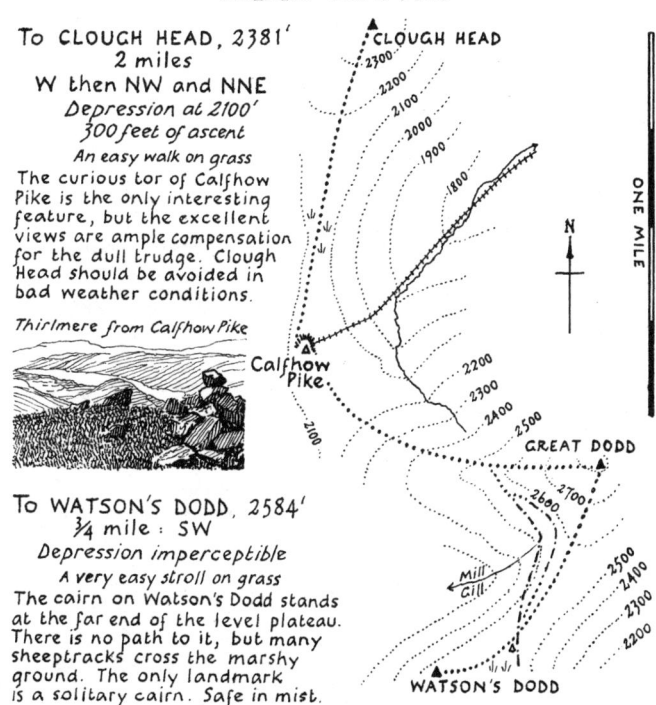

To CLOUGH HEAD, 2381'
2 miles
W then NW and NNE
Depression at 2100'
300 feet of ascent

An easy walk on grass

The curious tor of Calfhow Pike is the only interesting feature, but the excellent views are ample compensation for the dull trudge. Clough Head should be avoided in bad weather conditions.

Thirlmere from Calfhow Pike

To WATSON'S DODD, 2584'
¾ mile : SW
Depression imperceptible

A very easy stroll on grass

The cairn on Watson's Dodd stands at the far end of the level plateau. There is no path to it, but many sheeptracks cross the marshy ground. The only landmark is a solitary cairn. Safe in mist.

Dowthwaitehead

Great Dodd 11

THE VIEW

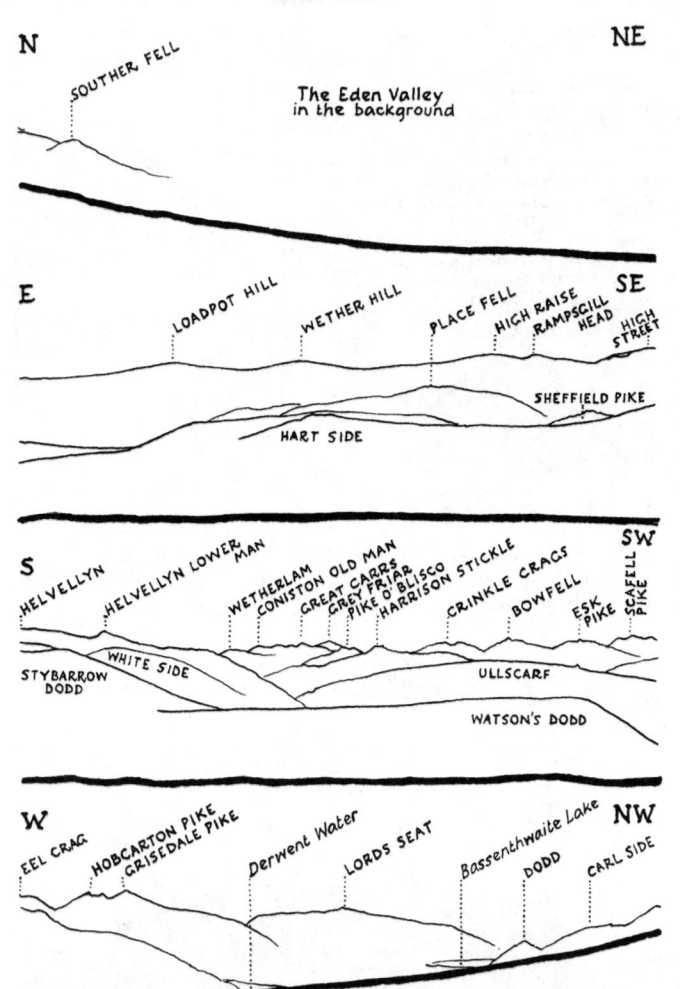

N — SOUTHER FELL

The Eden Valley in the background

NE

E — LOADPOT HILL, WETHER HILL, PLACE FELL, HIGH RAISE, RAMPSGILL HEAD, HIGH STREET **SE**
SHEFFIELD PIKE
HART SIDE

S — HELVELLYN, HELVELLYN LOWER MAN, WETHERLAM, CONISTON OLD MAN, GREAT CARRS, GREY FRIAR, PIKE O' BLISCO, HARRISON STICKLE, CRINKLE CRAGS, BOWFELL, ESK PIKE, SCAFELL PIKE **SW**
STYBARROW DODD, WHITE SIDE
ULLSCARF
WATSON'S DODD

W — EEL CRAG, HOBCARTON PIKE, GRISEDALE PIKE, Derwent Water, LORDS SEAT, Bassenthwaite Lake, DODD, CARL SIDE **NW**

Great Dodd 12

THE VIEW

NE — GREAT MELL FELL — The Pennines in the background — LITTLE MELL FELL — GOWBARROW FELL — **E**

Ullswater

Randerside — High Brow

SE — THORNTHWAITE CRAG, FROSWICK CRAG, ILL BELL, CAUDALE MOOR — RED SCREES, ST SUNDAY CRAG, DOVE CRAG, HART CRAG — FAIRFIELD — CATSTYCAM — RAISE — **S**

Green Side — STYBARROW DODD

SW — LINGMELL, GREAT GABLE, KIRK FELL, RED PIKE, PILLAR — DALE HEAD, HIGH CRAG, HIGH STILE, RED PIKE, ROBINSON — GREAT BORNE, MELLBREAK, WHITELESS PIKE, GRASMOOR — **W**

HIGH SEAT — BLEABERRY FELL

Thirlmere

NW — SKIDDAW — BLENCATHRA — HIGH PIKE — BOWSCALE FELL — CARROCK FELL — **N**

NOTES: This is the view from the cairn, not from the higher ground to the north.
Thirlmere, Derwent Water and Bassenthwaite Lake cannot actually be seen from the cairn, but come into view a few yards to the west.

Great Mell Fell 1760'

from Great Meldrum

```
Troutbeck   Penruddock
   •           •
GREAT ▲ MELL FELL
           ▲ LITTLE
             MELL
             FELL
Matterdale End
   •           ▲ GOWBARROW
                 FELL
Dockray
   •
       MILES
   0   1   2   3   4
```

Great Mell Fell is a prominent object on the Penrith approach to Lakeland. With its lesser twin, Little Mell Fell, it forms the portals to the Helvellyn range on this side. Its round 'inverted pudding-basin' shape does not promise much for the walker and it is rarely climbed. On closer acquaintance, however, it is rather more enjoyable than its appearance suggests, because of the presence of fine woodlands on the lower slopes; indeed, pines and larches persist almost to the summit. (But closer acquaintance is frowned upon by the military authorities, who stake a claim here)

Great Mell Fell 2

NATURAL FEATURES

Great Mell Fell rises sharply from a wide expanse of desolate marshland to the north and west, territory not at all typical of Lakeland, the fell itself being much more fertile and colourful than its surroundings. Its rich red soil carries a wealth of timber, the eastern slopes especially being beautifully wooded. Bleached skeletons of trees near the top of the fell indicate that at one time it was more fully clothed; many of those that yet survive are battered by the prevailing wind into grotesque shapes.

MAP

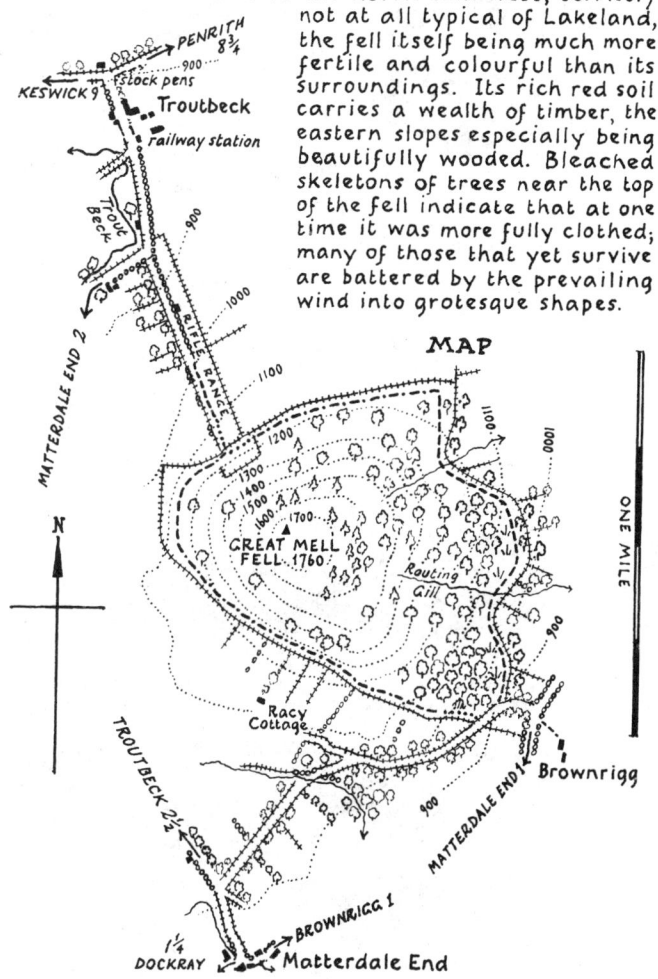

Great Mell Fell 3

ASCENTS

DANGER W.D. RANGE KEEP OUT

Above the 1100' contour, roughly, the fell is enclosed within a fence. Access may be gained at Troutbeck (along a muddy lane) and at two gates at the southeastern corner. Each entrance is guarded by red danger signs. Prudent pedestrians will heed the warning and take no further interest in this page. What follows is therefore exclusively for the walker who (a) holds his life cheaply, or (b) reacts to such signs as a bull to a red rag.

A fair path makes a circuit of the fell inside the fence and it may be left anywhere for the climb to the top, the south slope being easiest if a route is selected clear of trees and bracken. The path itself gives a pleasant walk all the way round, but is excessively wet on the eastern side and, in places, overgrown by bracken. Beware flying ammunition, of course.

THE SUMMIT

Tough grass, interspersed with heather, covers the level top. A decayed tree-trunk, appropriately, indicates the highest point, and there are a few unexpected and unhappy stones, looking quite out of their element.

DESCENTS: A way down to the path may be made in any direction but note that the lower east slope is marshy and overgrown. Firing squads, if on duty, are more likely to be met on the north side.

the highest tree

Great Mell Fell 4

THE VIEW

The highlight of the view is Blencathra undoubtedly, the noble proportions of this fine mountain being seen to great advantage. Otherwise the panorama is uneven, with a wide expanse of the Eden Valley, an impressive grouping of fells southwards, and a vista of the Grasmoor range in the west.

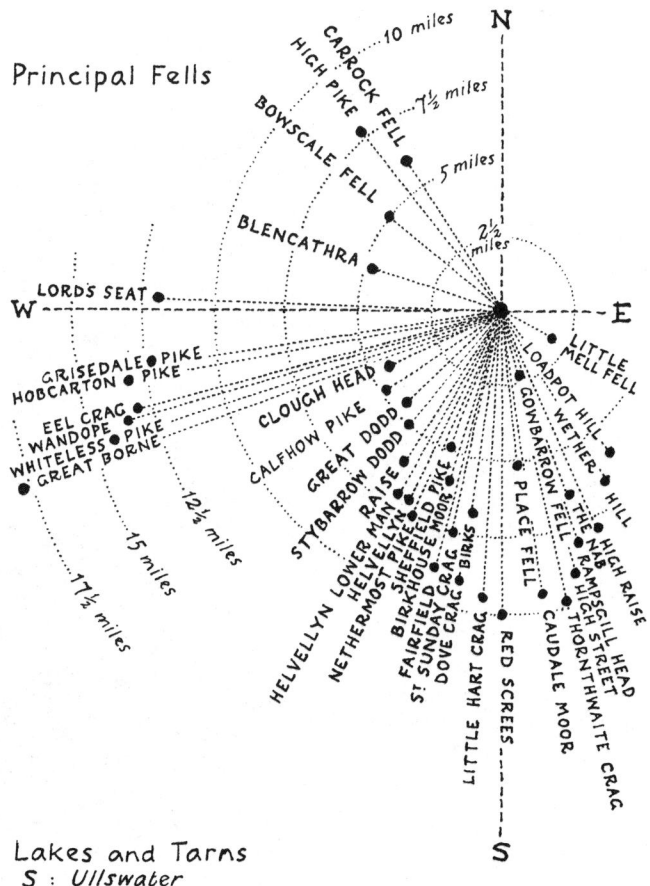

Principal Fells

N — 10 miles — CARROCK FELL
7½ miles — HIGH PIKE
5 miles — BOWSCALE FELL
2½ miles — BLENCATHRA
W — LORD'S SEAT — E
GRISEDALE PIKE
HOBCARTON PIKE
EEL CRAG
WANDOPE
WHITELESS PIKE
GREAT BORNE
CLOUGH HEAD
CALFHOW PIKE
GREAT DODD
STYBARROW DODD
RAISE
HELVELLYN LOWER MAN
HELVELLYN
NETHERMOST PIKE
SHEFFIELD PIKE
BIRKHOUSE MOOR
ST SUNDAY CRAG
FAIRFIELD
DOVE CRAG
BIRKS
LITTLE HART CRAG
RED SCREES
CAUDALE MOOR
PLACE FELL
GOWBARROW FELL
THORNTHWAITE CRAG
HIGH STREET
THE NAB
RAMPSGILL HEAD
HIGH RAISE
WETHER HILL
LOADPOT HILL
LITTLE MELL FELL
12½ miles
15 miles
17½ miles
S

Lakes and Tarns
S : *Ullswater*
(a disappointing view, only a very small section being visible)

Great Rigg

2513'

▲ FAIRFIELD
▲ GREAT RIGG
▲ STONE ARTHUR
▲ HERON PIKE
• Grasmere ▲ NAB SCAR
• Rydal

Ambleside •

MILES
0 1 2 3 4

from Grasmere

Great Rigg 2

NATURAL FEATURES

Great Rigg has no topographical secrets or surprises. It is a plain, straightforward, uninteresting fell on the southern spur of Fairfield, with gentle declivities linking the summit to the continuing ridge on either side. East, stony slopes fall abruptly to Rydal Beck; ruined crags rise from wastes of scree. To the west the fellside is mainly grassy but there are occasional rocks low down on this flank, above Tongue Gill. From the ridge south of the summit a descending shoulder strikes off in the direction of Grasmere; this has a rocky terminus with the name of Stone Arthur. Between the shoulder and the ridge is a deep, narrow trough which carries Greenhead Gill, Great Rigg's only stream of note, down to the River Rothay.

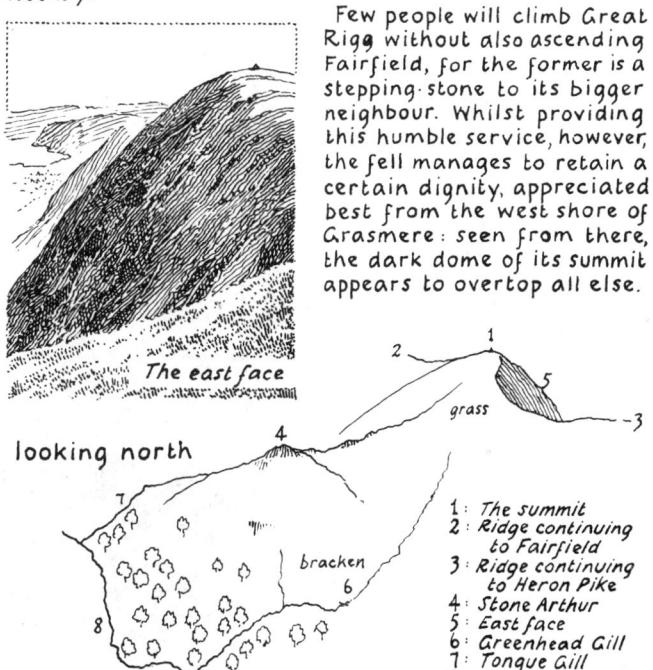

Few people will climb Great Rigg without also ascending Fairfield, for the former is a stepping-stone to its bigger neighbour. Whilst providing this humble service, however, the fell manages to retain a certain dignity, appreciated best from the west shore of Grasmere: seen from there, the dark dome of its summit appears to overtop all else.

The east face

looking north

1 : The summit
2 : Ridge continuing to Fairfield
3 : Ridge continuing to Heron Pike
4 : Stone Arthur
5 : East face
6 : Greenhead Gill
7 : Tongue Gill
8 : River Rothay

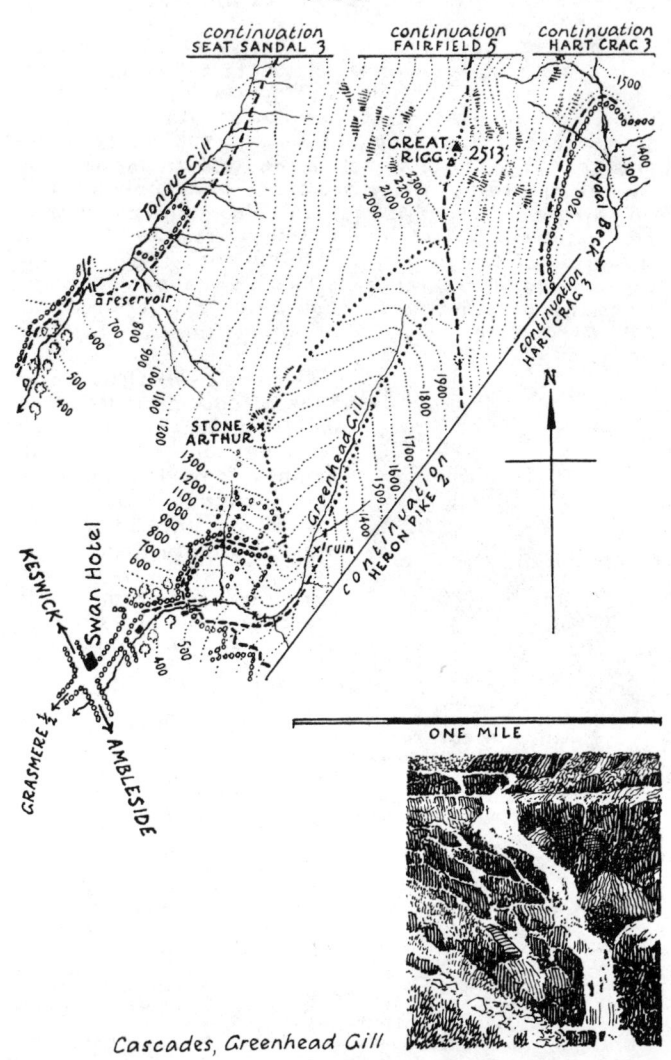

Great Rigg 3

MAP

continuation SEAT SANDAL 3
continuation FAIRFIELD 5
continuation HART CRAG 3

GREAT RIGG 2513

Tongue Gill

reservoir

STONE ARTHUR

Greenhead Gill

Rydal Beck

continuation HART CRAG 3

continuation HERON PIKE 2

ruin

Swan Hotel

KESWICK
GRASMERE ¼
AMBLESIDE

N

ONE MILE

Cascades, Greenhead Gill

Great Rigg 4

ASCENT FROM GRASMERE
2300 feet of ascent : 3 miles

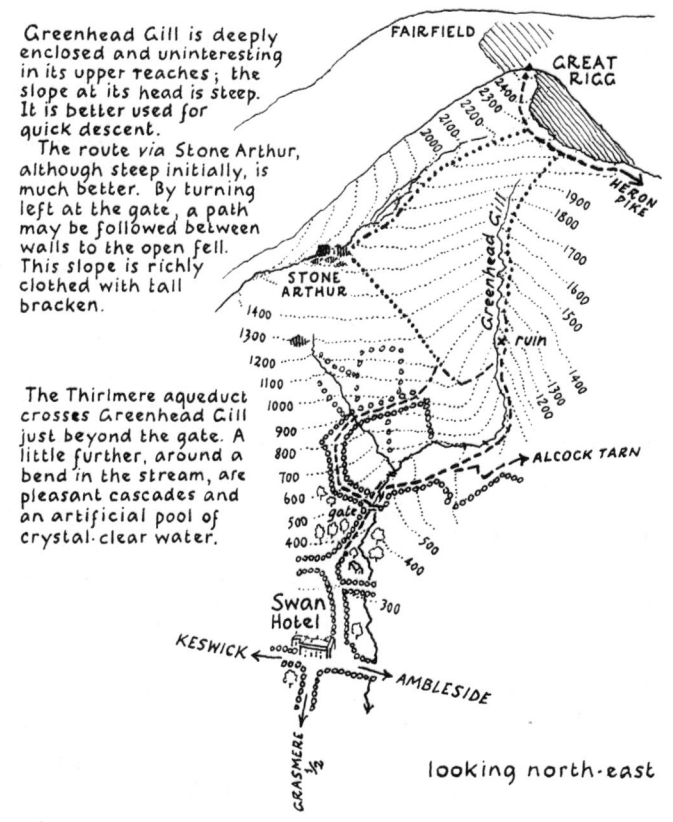

Greenhead Gill is deeply enclosed and uninteresting in its upper reaches; the slope at its head is steep. It is better used for quick descent.

The route via Stone Arthur, although steep initially, is much better. By turning left at the gate, a path may be followed between walls to the open fell. This slope is richly clothed with tall bracken.

The Thirlmere aqueduct crosses Greenhead Gill just beyond the gate. A little further, around a bend in the stream, are pleasant cascades and an artificial pool of crystal-clear water.

looking north-east

Great Rigg is more often visited on the tour of the Fairfield Horseshoe, but it may be ascended directly from Grasmere by the routes illustrated, that by Stone Arthur being the more interesting.

Great Rigg 5

THE SUMMIT

Helvellyn — Fairfield

The summit is comprehended at a glance. A well-constructed symmetrical cairn occupies the highest point and another is 60 yards south, where the ridge steepens on its descent to Heron Pike. The top is a carpet of excellent turf which many a cricket-ground would welcome

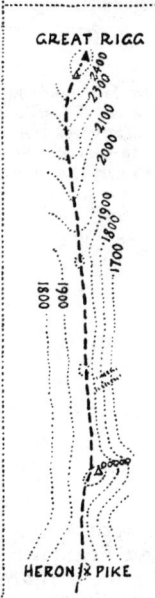

RIDGE ROUTES

To FAIRFIELD, 2863' : 1 mile : N
Depression at 2375' : 500 feet of ascent
An easy climb, needing care in mist

A fair path, on grass, crosses the depression but peters out as the summit is approached. Strangers to Fairfield should avoid it in mist.

To HERON PIKE, 2003' : 1½ miles SSW, then S
Minor depressions : 150 feet of ascent

A very easy high-level walk. Heron Pike is the *second* prominent rise on the ridge.

To STONE ARTHUR, 1652'
1¼ miles : SSW then SW
Downhill all the way

Follow the wide grass shoulder branching from the main ridge. No path. Not quite safe in mist.

Great Rigg 6

THE VIEW

The panorama is interesting and varied, a special feature being the large number of lakes and tarns in view. To the west, the mountain skyline is fine and there is an impressive vista of the Helvellyn group above the deep notch of Grisedale Hause

Principal Fells

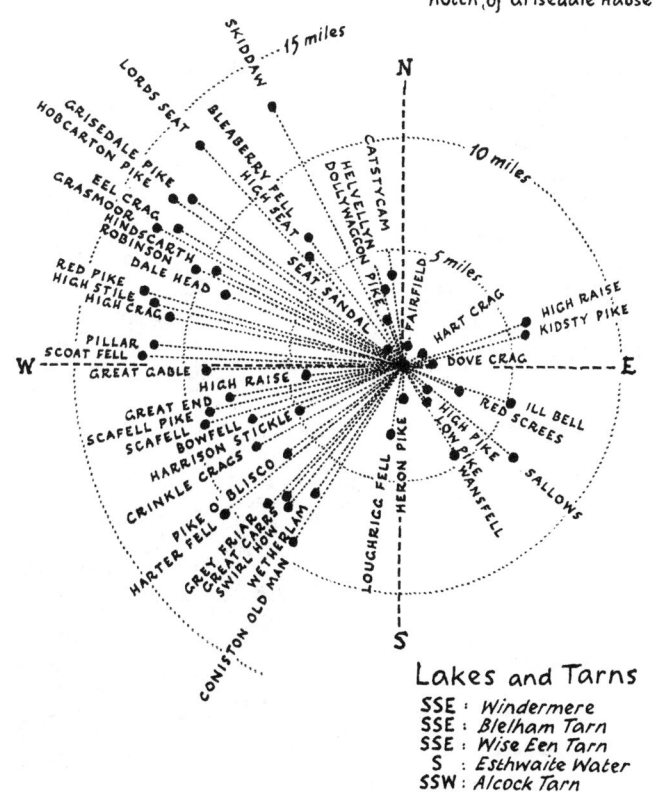

(compass diagram with fells labelled radially)

SKIDDAW — 15 miles
LORDS SEAT
GRISEDALE PIKE
HOBCARTON PIKE
BLEABERRY FELL
EEL CRAG
HIGH SEAT
GRASMOOR
CATSTYCAM
HINDSCARTH
HELVELLYN
ROBINSON
DOLLYWAGGON PIKE
DALE HEAD
SEAT SANDAL
RED PIKE
FAIRFIELD — 10 miles
HIGH STILE
HART CRAG
HIGH CRAG
HIGH RAISE
KIDSTY PIKE
PILLAR — 5 miles
SCOAT FELL
DOVE CRAG
GREAT GABLE
ILL BELL
HIGH RAISE
RED SCREES
GREAT END
HIGH PIKE
SCAFELL PIKE
LOW PIKE
SCAFELL
SALLOWS
BOWFELL
WANSFELL
HARRISON STICKLE
CRINKLE CRAGS
PIKE O' BLISCO
HERON PIKE
HARTER FELL
LOUGHRIGG FELL
GREY FRIAR
GREAT CARRS
SWIRL HOW
WETHERLAM
CONISTON OLD MAN

Lakes and Tarns

SSE : Windermere
SSE : Blelham Tarn
SSE : Wise Een Tarn
S   : Esthwaite Water
SSW : Alcock Tarn
SSW : Elterwater
SSW : Coniston Water
SSW : Grasmere
WSW : Easedale Tarn
NNW : Grisedale Tarn

Hart Crag
2698'

from Dovedale

Patterdale •

Hartsop •

FAIRFIELD ▲
HART ▲ CRAG
DOVE CRAG ▲

RED SCREES ▲

• Grasmere

• Rydal
Ambleside

MILES
0 1 2 3 4

Hart Crag 2

NATURAL FEATURES

Midway along the high-level traverse between Fairfield and Dove Crag is the rough top of Hart Crag, occupying a strategic position overlooking three valleys. To the north-east, Hart Crag follows usual mountain structure by sending out a long declining ridge, which forms a high barrier between desolate Deepdale and delectable Dovedale. North, a wall of crags defends the summit above the wild hollow of Link Cove, a hanging valley encompassed by cliffs: this is its finest aspect by far. South-west, after an initial fringe of broken crags, long stony slopes fall very steeply to Rydal Head. Although bounded by streams, Hart Crag itself is quite curiously deficient in water-courses.

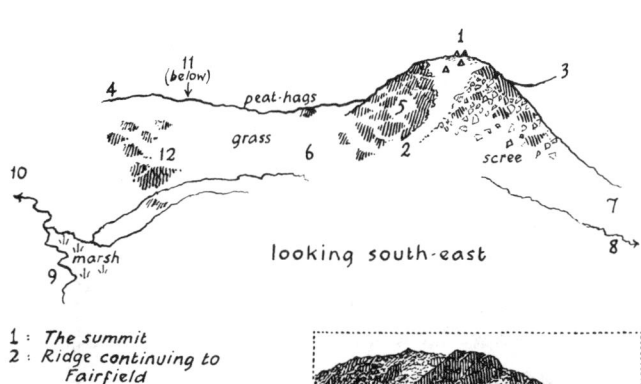

looking south-east

1 : The summit
2 : Ridge continuing to Fairfield
3 : Ridge continuing to Dove Crag
4 : Ridge continuing to Hartsop above How
5 : The north face
6 : Link Cove
7 : Rydal Head
8 : Rydal Beck
9 : Deepdale Beck
10 : Deepdale
11 : Dovedale
12 : Earnest Crag

The summit from the northeast

Hart Crag 3

MAP

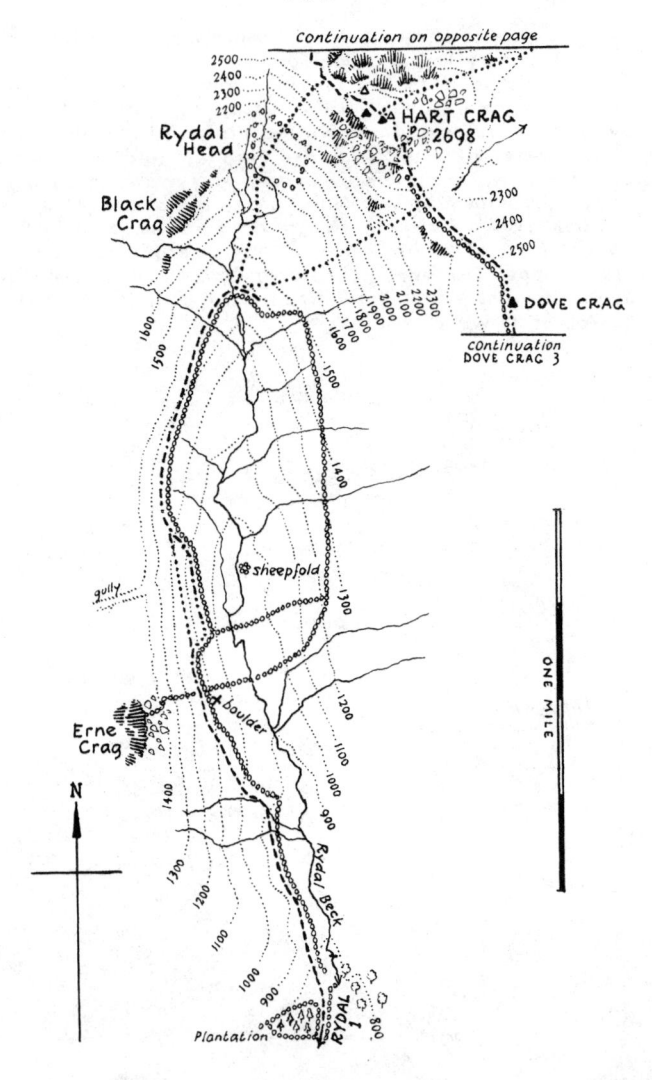

Hart Crag 4

MAP

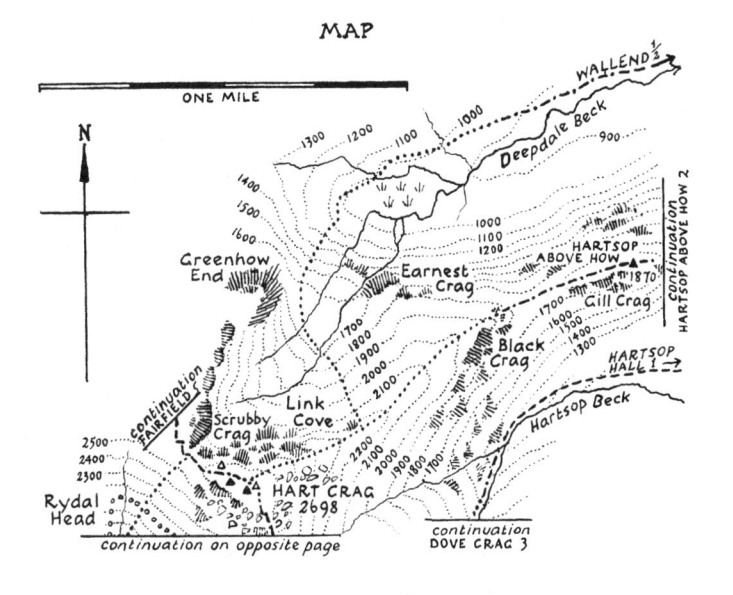

The north face

Hart Crag 5

ASCENT FROM RYDAL
2,600 feet of ascent : 4½ miles

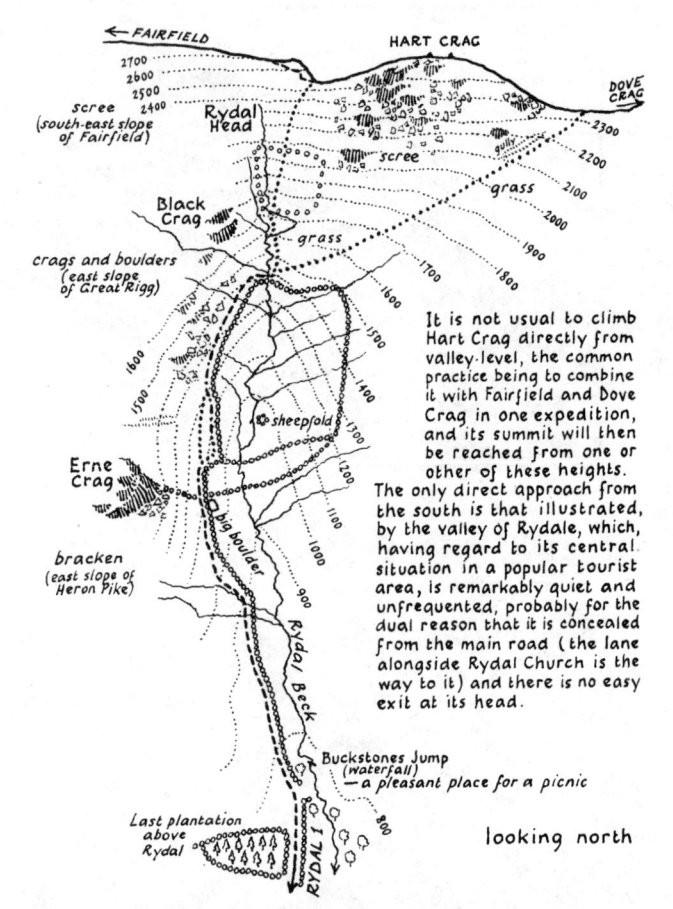

looking north

It is not usual to climb Hart Crag directly from valley-level, the common practice being to combine it with Fairfield and Dove Crag in one expedition, and its summit will then be reached from one or other of these heights. The only direct approach from the south is that illustrated, by the valley of Rydale, which, having regard to its central situation in a popular tourist area, is remarkably quiet and unfrequented, probably for the dual reason that it is concealed from the main road (the lane alongside Rydal Church is the way to it) and there is no easy exit at its head.

The approach by the Rydal Valley (Rydale) is attractive and interesting, but the climb out of it is very steep. The valley lies entirely within the circuit of the 'Fairfield Horseshoe' and is deeply enclosed.

Hart Crag 6

ASCENT FROM PATTERDALE
2,300 feet of ascent : 4½ miles from Patterdale village

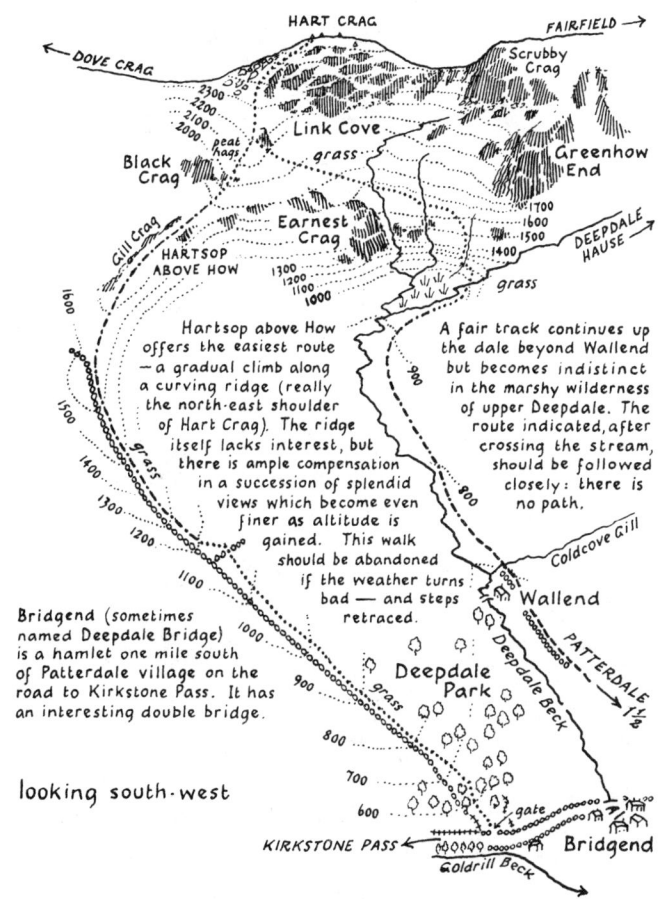

looking south-west

Hartsop above How offers the easiest route — a gradual climb along a curving ridge (really the north-east shoulder of Hart Crag). The ridge itself lacks interest, but there is ample compensation in a succession of splendid views which become even finer as altitude is gained. This walk should be abandoned if the weather turns bad — and steps retraced.

A fair track continues up the dale beyond Wallend but becomes indistinct in the marshy wilderness of upper Deepdale. The route indicated, after crossing the stream, should be followed closely: there is no path.

Bridgend (sometimes named Deepdale Bridge) is a hamlet one mile south of Patterdale village on the road to Kirkstone Pass. It has an interesting double bridge.

The ascent from Patterdale is far superior to that from the south. The Link Cove route especially is an interesting climb through the inner sanctuary of Hart Crag, the scene being impressive, *but it is quite unsuitable in bad weather*.

Hart Crag 7

THE SUMMIT

The summit area is relatively small, its level top being about 120 yards long and having a cairn at each end. Two other cairns indicate viewpoints. The top is stony but a strip of grass running lengthwise across it to the north of the main cairns offers an easy traverse

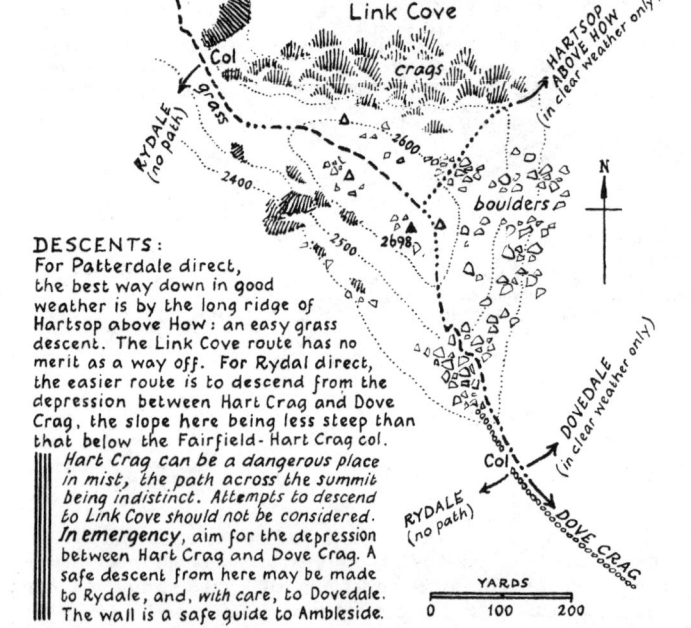

FAIRFIELD

Link Cove

Col

grass

crags

HARTSOP ABOVE HOW (in clear weather only)

RYDALE (no path)

2600

2400

2500

2698

boulders

N

DESCENTS:
For Patterdale direct, the best way down in good weather is by the long ridge of Hartsop above How: an easy grass descent. The Link Cove route has no merit as a way off. For Rydal direct, the easier route is to descend from the depression between Hart Crag and Dove Crag, the slope here being less steep than that below the Fairfield–Hart Crag col.

> Hart Crag can be a dangerous place in mist, the path across the summit being indistinct. Attempts to descend to Link Cove should not be considered. *In emergency*, aim for the depression between Hart Crag and Dove Crag. A safe descent from here may be made to Rydale, and, with care, to Dovedale. The wall is a safe guide to Ambleside.

Col

DOVEDALE (in clear weather only)

RYDALE (no path)

DOVE CRAG

YARDS
0   100   200

Hart Crag 8

THE VIEW

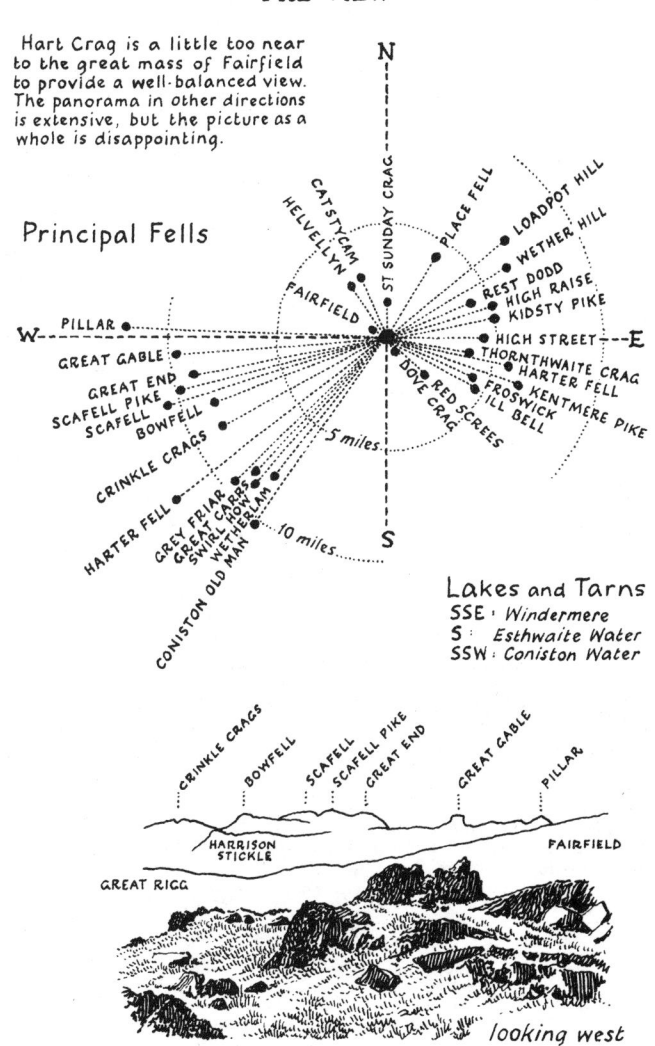

Hart Crag is a little too near to the great mass of Fairfield to provide a well-balanced view. The panorama in other directions is extensive, but the picture as a whole is disappointing.

Principal Fells

- N
- CATSTYCAM
- HELVELLYN
- ST SUNDAY CRAG
- FAIRFIELD
- PLACE FELL
- LOADPOT HILL
- WETHER HILL
- REST DODD
- HIGH RAISE
- KIDSTY PIKE
- W — PILLAR
- GREAT GABLE
- GREAT END
- SCAFELL PIKE
- SCAFELL
- BOWFELL
- HIGH STREET — E
- THORNTHWAITE CRAG
- HARTER FELL
- RED SCREES
- FROSWICK
- KENTMERE PIKE
- DOVE CRAG
- ILL BELL
- CRINKLE CRAGS
- 5 miles
- HARTER FELL
- GREY FRIAR
- GREAT CARRS
- SWIRL HOW
- WETHERLAM
- CONISTON OLD MAN
- 10 miles
- S

Lakes and Tarns

SSE : Windermere
S : Esthwaite Water
SSW : Coniston Water

looking west

CRINKLE CRAGS — BOWFELL — SCAFELL — SCAFELL PIKE — GREAT END — GREAT GABLE — PILLAR
HARRISON STICKLE — FAIRFIELD
GREAT RIGG

Hart Crag 9

RIDGE ROUTES

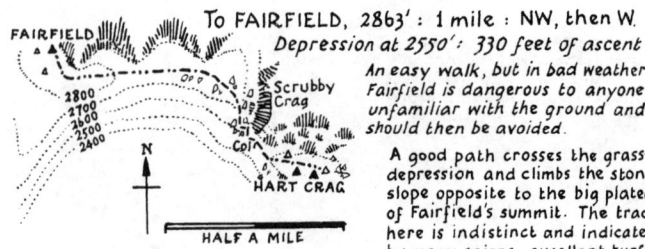

To FAIRFIELD, 2863': 1 mile : NW, then W.
Depression at 2550': 330 feet of ascent

An easy walk, but in bad weather Fairfield is dangerous to anyone unfamiliar with the ground and should then be avoided.

A good path crosses the grassy depression and climbs the stony slope opposite to the big plateau of Fairfield's summit. The track here is indistinct and indicated by many cairns; excellent turf.

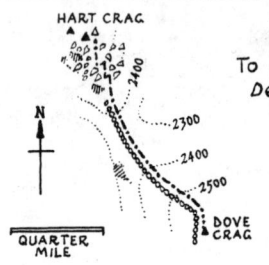

To DOVE CRAG, 2603': ¾ mile : SE.
Depression at 2350': 260 feet of ascent

An easy walk. Dove Crag is safe in mist, but care is then necessary in leaving Hart Crag.

An indistinct path, at first over grass and then, more clearly, among stones goes south from the eastern cairn to the wall at the depression. This wall continues over the summit of Dove Crag.

To HARTSOP ABOVE HOW, 1870': 1½ miles : ENE
Depression at 1775': 150 feet of ascent

An easy walk. In mist the correct way off Hart Crag is not easy to find (there is no path) and this walk should not then be attempted.

Leave the summit near the main cairn, going down a patch of grass and crossing a band of scree before inclining slightly right down a shallow stony gully. Then work left to the ridge, which is broad and grassy, with many undulations and peat-hags. It narrows on the final rise.

Note that this ridge may be safely left *only* between Black Crag and Gill Crag (by descending right, to Dovedale)

Hart Crag 10

from the east ridge, St Sunday Crag

Hart Side 2481'

from Dockray

Hart Side 2

NATURAL FEATURES

The main watershed at Stybarrow Dodd sends out a long spur to the east which curves north from the subsidiary height of Green Side and continues at an elevated level until it is poised high above Ullswater before descending in wide slopes to the open country around Dockray. The principal height on this spur is Hart Side, which with its many satellites on the declining ridge forms the southern wall of the long valley of Deep Dale throughout its sinuous course, its opposite boundary being the short deep trench of Glencoyne. The upper slopes of this bulky mass are unattractive in themselves, but, in strong contrast, the steep flank overlooking Ullswater is beautifully wooded, while the views of the lake from the Brown Hills, midway along the ridge, are of high quality.

Hart Side is rarely visited. Its smooth slopes, grass and marsh intermingling, seem very very remote from industry, but there are evidences that men laboured on these lonely heights a long time ago, and even now the minerals far below its surface are being won by the enterprising miners of Glenridding.

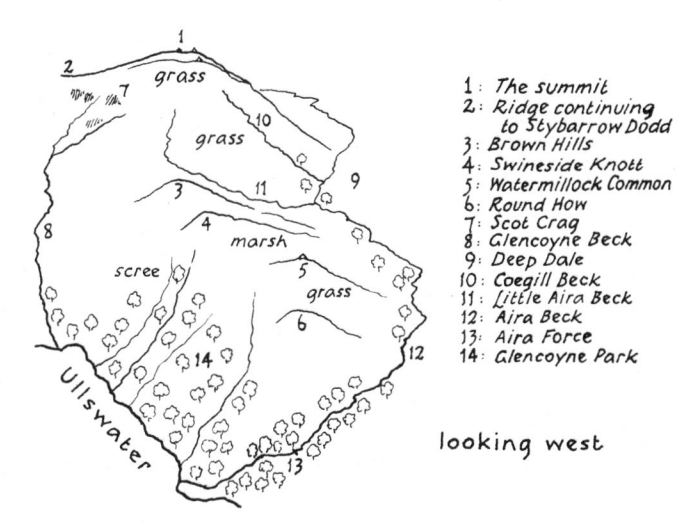

1: The summit
2: Ridge continuing to Stybarrow Dodd
3: Brown Hills
4: Swineside Knott
5: Watermillock Common
6: Round How
7: Scot Crag
8: Glencoyne Beck
9: Deep Dale
10: Coegill Beck
11: Little Aira Beck
12: Aira Beck
13: Aira Force
14: Glencoyne Park

looking west

Hart Side 3

MAP

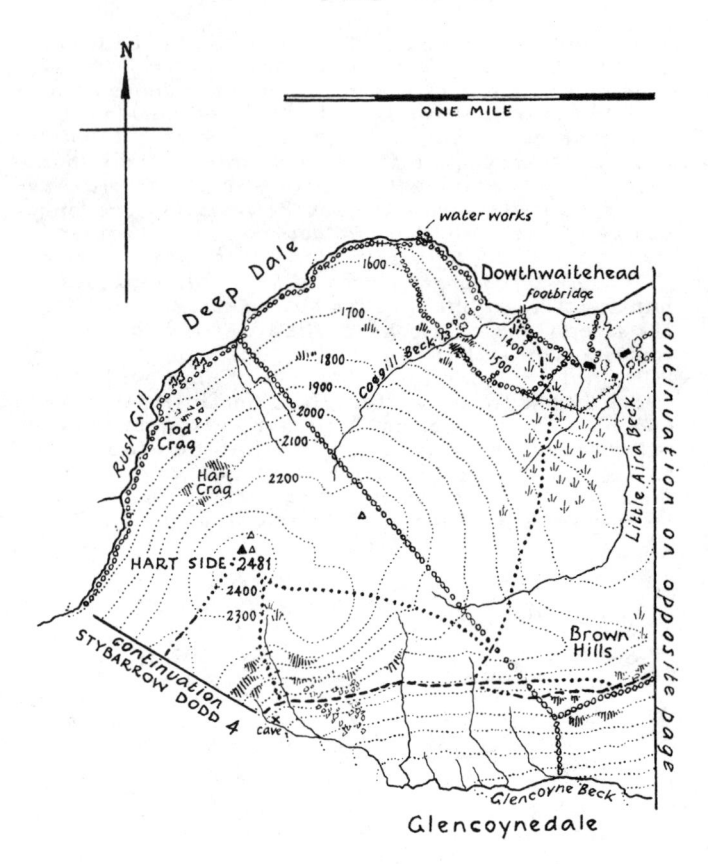

According to the Ordnance Survey and Bartholomew's maps, the representation of a footpath thereon is no evidence of a right of way. Nor, unfortunately, is it evidence that a footpath now exists at all! Some of the paths marked on those maps in the district of Hart Side were made originally by miners on their way to or from work at the Glenridding lead mine, but the miners now use them no more: they have become overgrown and cannot, in many places, be traced.

Hart Side 4

MAP

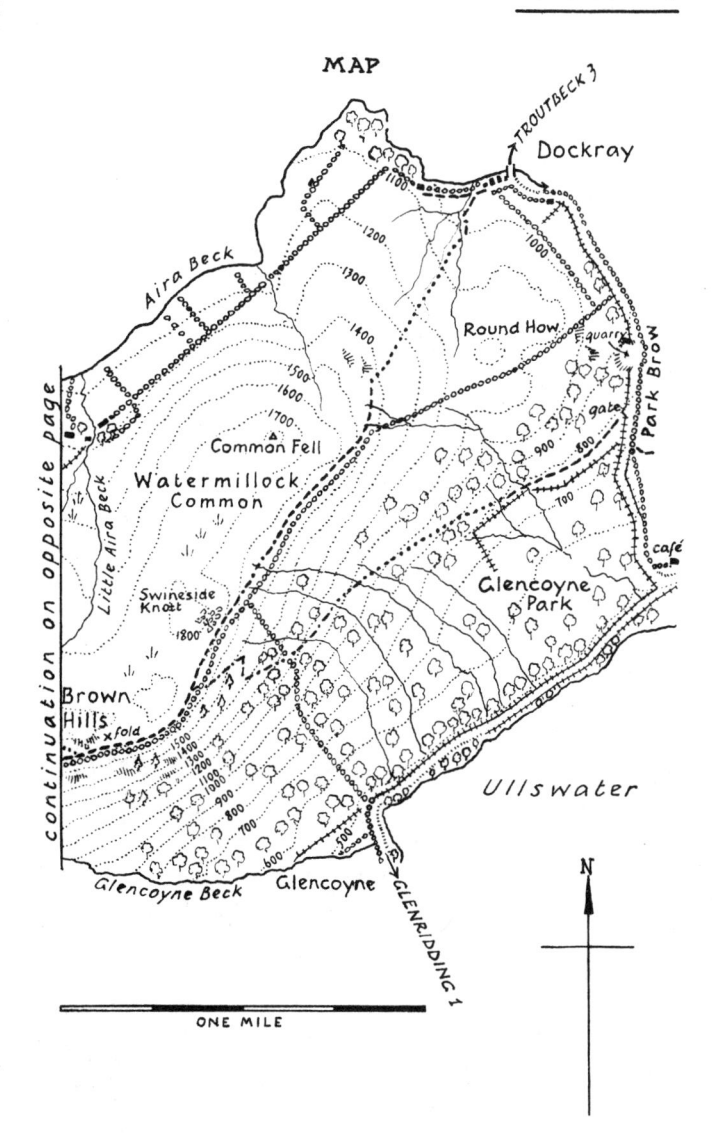

Hart Side 5

ASCENT FROM DOCKRAY
1600 feet of ascent : 4 miles

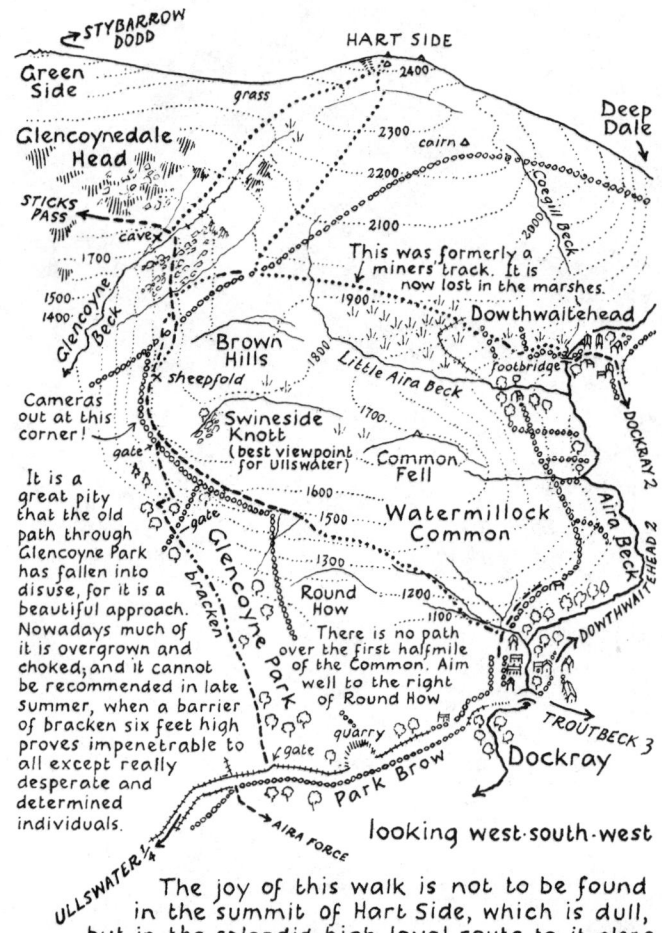

looking west-south-west

It is a great pity that the old path through Glencoyne Park has fallen into disuse, for it is a beautiful approach. Nowadays much of it is overgrown and choked; and it cannot be recommended in late summer, when a barrier of bracken six feet high proves impenetrable to all except really desperate and determined individuals.

Cameras out at this corner!

This was formerly a miners' track. It is now lost in the marshes.

There is no path over the first halfmile of the Common. Aim well to the right of Round How

The joy of this walk is not to be found in the summit of Hart Side, which is dull, but in the splendid high-level route to it along the Brown Hills, which excels in views of Ullswater. The alternative shown deserves no consideration.

Hart Side 6

THE SUMMIT

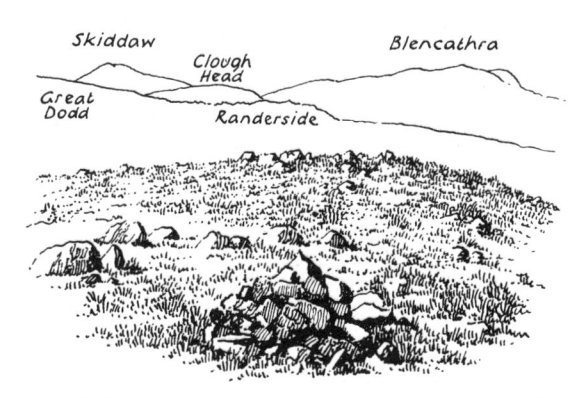

Skiddaw — Clough Head — Blencathra — Great Dodd — Randerside

The summit has nothing extraordinary to show in natural forms, being grassy with a few outcropping boulders. Yet this is a top that cannot be confused with any other, for here man has not contented himself merely with building a few cairns but has really got to work with pick and spade, and excavated a most remarkable ditch, rather like the Vallum of the Roman Wall. As the project was abandoned, the reason for the prodigious effort is not clear. An excavation below the summit, intended as the site of a building, was similarly abandoned. Probably these were workings for the Glenridding lead mine, as is a cave in Glencoynedale Head, near the miners' path: here a warning notice — "Danger. Keep Out." — relieves the duly grateful guide-book writer of the task of exploring its fearsome interior.

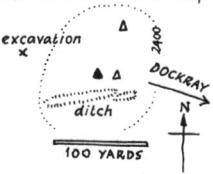

The ditch on the summit

The cave

DESCENTS: Descents will usually be either to Dockray or Glencoyne Walk ESE, over a minor rise, to the wall running across the fell. Follow the wall down, joining the miners' path (at a gap) for Dockray. For Glencoyne, continue by the wall down into the valley. These are the best routes in mist.

Hart Side 7

RIDGE ROUTE

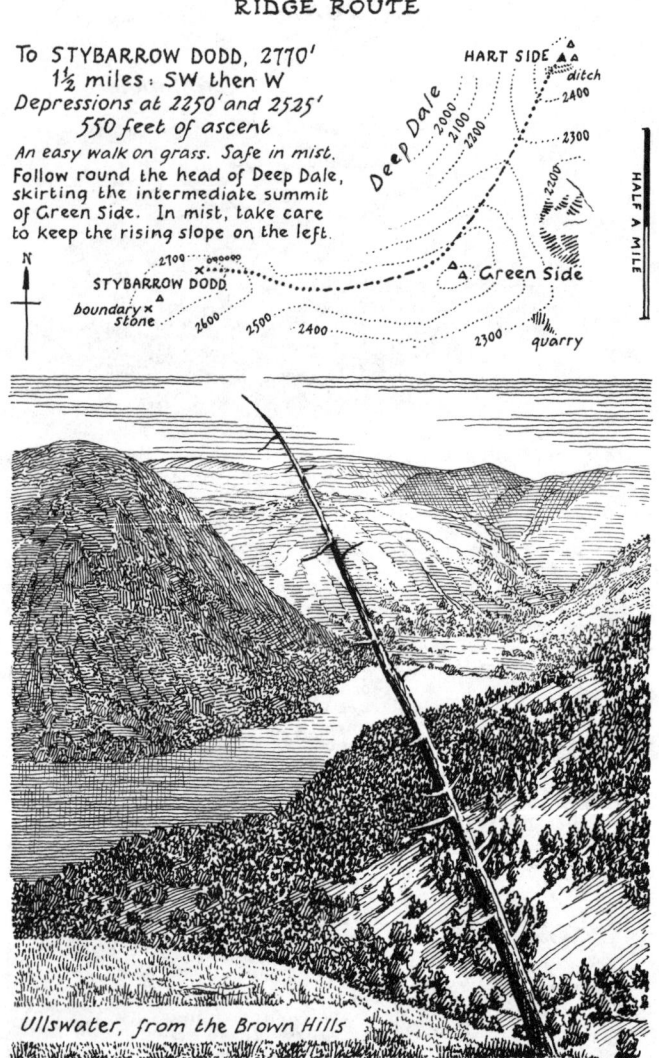

To STYBARROW DODD, 2770'
1½ miles : SW then W
Depressions at 2250' and 2525'
550 feet of ascent

An easy walk on grass. Safe in mist.
Follow round the head of Deep Dale,
skirting the intermediate summit
of Green Side. In mist, take care
to keep the rising slope on the left.

Ullswater, from the Brown Hills

Hart Side 8

THE VIEW

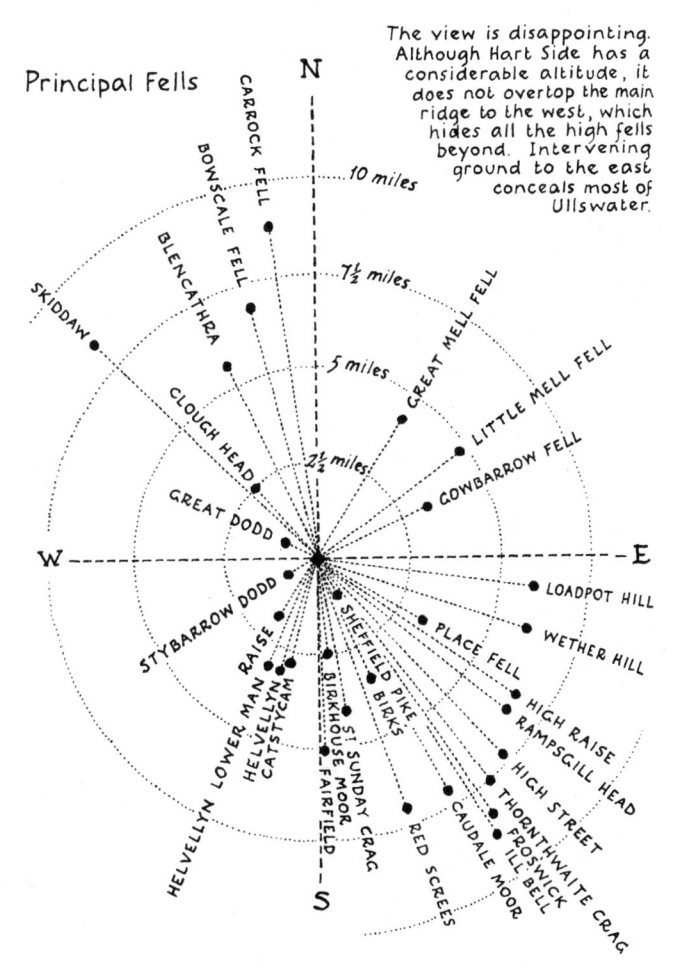

Principal Fells

The view is disappointing. Although Hart Side has a considerable altitude, it does not overtop the main ridge to the west, which hides all the high fells beyond. Intervening ground to the east conceals most of Ullswater.

10 miles
7½ miles
5 miles
2½ miles

N — CARROCK FELL, BOWSCALE FELL, BLENCATHRA, SKIDDAW, CLOUGH HEAD, GREAT MELL FELL, LITTLE MELL FELL, GREAT DODD, GOWBARROW FELL

W — E — LOADPOT HILL, WETHER HILL

STYBARROW DODD, RAISE, HELVELLYN LOWER MAN, HELVELLYN, CATSTYCAM, BIRKHOUSE MOOR, FAIRFIELD, ST SUNDAY CRAG, BIRKS, SHEFFIELD PIKE, PLACE FELL, HIGH RAISE, RAMPSGILL HEAD, HIGH STREET, THORNTHWAITE CRAG, FROSWICK, ILL BELL, CAUDALE MOOR, RED SCREES

S

Lakes and Tarns
ENE : Ullswater

Hartsop above How 1870'

from Hunsett Cove

Patterdale ●

ST SUNDAY
CRAG ▲   Hartsop ●
FAIRFIELD ▲   ▲ HARTSOP
              ABOVE HOW
HART CRAG ▲
           ● DOVE CRAG

MILES
0   1   2   3

The long curving northeast ridge of Hart Crag rises to a separate summit midway, and this summit is generally referred to as Hartsop above How by guidebook writers and mapmakers. Sometimes the three words in the name are hyphenated, sometimes not. Probably the first two should be, but not the last two: the word 'How' is common, meaning a low hill, and the distinctive title of this particular How is 'Hartsop-above', indicating its geographical relationship to the hamlet in the valley below. Most natives of Deepdale, however, know it not by this name, with or without hyphens, but they all know Gill Crag, which fringes the summit, and this would seem to be a more satisfactory name for the fell. But one cannot so wantonly ignore the authority of the guidebooks and maps; and the name Hartsop above How, without hyphens (in the belief that an error of omission is a less sin than an error of commission) will be used here in support of the Director General of Ordnance Survey.

Hartsop above How 2

NATURAL FEATURES

Hartsop above How is a simple ridge (really a part of Hart Crag) curving like a sickle to enclose the valley of Deepdale on the south and east. Only in the vicinity of the summit is it at all narrow, but both flanks are steep throughout most of its three-mile length, the slopes above Dovedale being especially rough. There are several crags on the fell, the most imposing being Black Crag above the rough hollow of Hunsett Cove; also prominent are the grey rocks of Dovedale Slabs (looking as pleasant and attractive as steep rocks can look) below the eastern end of the summit, and, on the Deepdale side, the gloomy cliff of Earnest Crag (looking as unpleasant and unattractive as steep rocks can look). The slopes above Brothers Water are well-wooded over an extensive area, and Deepdale Park also has some fine trees.

Hartsop above How 3

ASCENT FROM PATTERDALE
1400 feet of ascent : 3 miles from Patterdale village

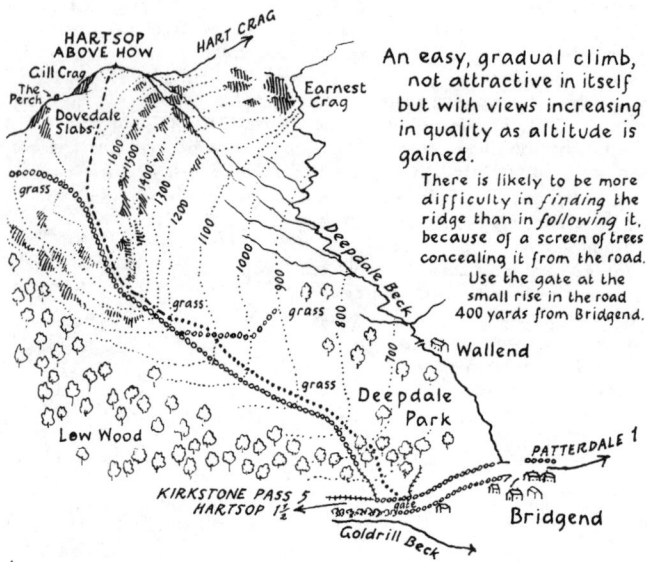

looking south-west

An easy, gradual climb, not attractive in itself but with views increasing in quality as altitude is gained.

There is likely to be more difficulty in *finding* the ridge than in *following* it, because of a screen of trees concealing it from the road. Use the gate at the small rise in the road 400 yards from Bridgend.

THE SUMMIT

The highest point is a grassy knoll adjoining the top of a cleft splitting Gill Crag, but the usually accepted summit is 200 yards northeast and bears a small cairn.

DESCENTS : The easiest way down *in any conditions* is by the ridge to the road. Direct descents, either to Deepdale or Dovedale, are too rough.

Hartsop above How 4

THE VIEW

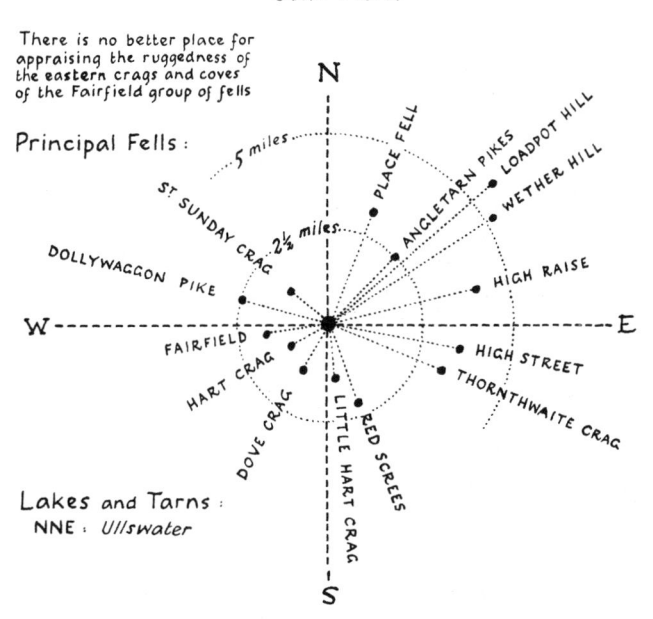

There is no better place for appraising the ruggedness of the eastern crags and coves of the Fairfield group of fells

Principal Fells:

- St SUNDAY CRAG
- DOLLYWAGGON PIKE
- FAIRFIELD
- HART CRAG
- DOVE CRAG
- LITTLE HART CRAG
- RED SCREES
- THORNTHWAITE CRAG
- HIGH STREET
- HIGH RAISE
- WETHER HILL
- LOADPOT HILL
- ANGLETARN PIKES
- PLACE FELL

Lakes and Tarns:
NNE: Ullswater

RIDGE ROUTE

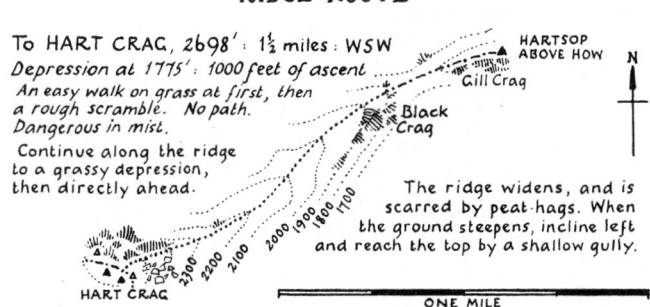

To HART CRAG, 2698′: 1½ miles: WSW
Depression at 1775′: 1000 feet of ascent
An easy walk on grass at first, then a rough scramble. No path. Dangerous in mist.

Continue along the ridge to a grassy depression, then directly ahead.

The ridge widens, and is scarred by peat-hags. When the ground steepens, incline left and reach the top by a shallow gully.

HARTSOP ABOVE HOW
Gill Crag
Black Crag
HART CRAG

ONE MILE

Helvellyn 3118'

from the south-west ridge of S‡ Sunday Crag

Helvellyn 2

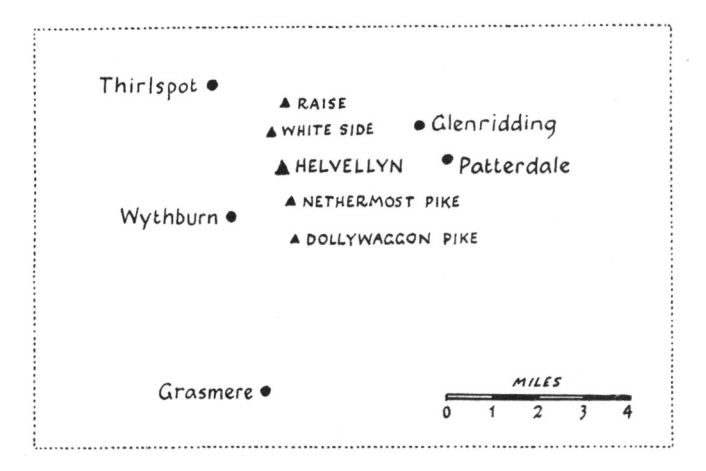

```
Thirlspot •
          ▲ RAISE
          ▲ WHITE SIDE    • Glenridding
          ▲ HELVELLYN     • Patterdale
          ▲ NETHERMOST PIKE
Wythburn •
          ▲ DOLLYWAGGON PIKE



                                    MILES
Grasmere •                    0   1   2   3   4
```

Legend and poetry, a lovely name and a lofty altitude combine to encompass Helvellyn in an aura of romance; and thousands of pilgrims, aided by its easy accessibility, are attracted to its summit every year. There is no doubt that Helvellyn is climbed more often than any other mountain in Lakeland, and, more than any other, it is the objective and ambition of the tourist who does not normally climb; moreover, the easy paths leading up the western flanks make it particularly suitable for sunrise expeditions, and, in a snowy winter, its sweeping slopes afford great sport to the ski parties who congregate on these white expanses. There are few days in any year when no visitor calls at the wall-shelter on the summit to eat his sandwiches. It is a great pity that Helvellyn is usually ascended by its western routes, for this side is unattractive and lacking in interest. From the east, however, the approach is quite exciting, with the reward of an extensive panorama as a sudden and dramatic climax when the top is gained; only to the traveller from this direction does Helvellyn display its true character and reveal its secrets. There is some quality about Helvellyn which endears it in the memory of most people who have stood on its breezy top; although it can be a grim place indeed on a wild night, it is, as a rule, a very friendly giant. If it did not inspire affection would its devotees return to it so often?

Helvellyn 3

NATURAL FEATURES

The Helvellyn Range — looking north

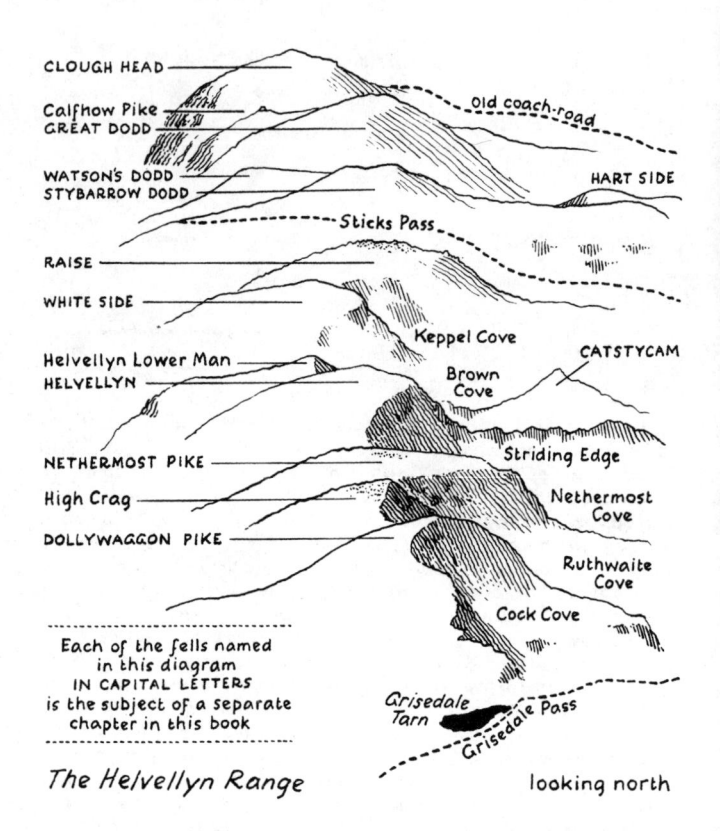

Each of the fells named in this diagram IN CAPITAL LETTERS is the subject of a separate chapter in this book

Labels on diagram:
- CLOUGH HEAD
- Calfhow Pike
- GREAT DODD
- Old coach-road
- WATSON'S DODD
- STYBARROW DODD
- HART SIDE
- Sticks Pass
- RAISE
- WHITE SIDE
- Keppel Cove
- CATSTYCAM
- Helvellyn Lower Man
- HELVELLYN
- Brown Cove
- Striding Edge
- NETHERMOST PIKE
- High Crag
- Nethermost Cove
- DOLLYWAGGON PIKE
- Ruthwaite Cove
- Cock Cove
- Grisedale Tarn
- Grisedale Pass

The altitude of these fells and the main connecting ridges is consistently above 2500 feet from Dollywaggon Pike (2810') to Great Dodd (2807') except for the depression of Sticks Pass, which is slightly below. This is the greatest area of high fells in Lakeland, and the traverse of the complete range from south to north (the better way) is a challenge to all active walkers. (As a preliminary canter, strong men will include the Fairfield group, starting at Kirkstone Pass and reaching Grisedale Tarn over the tops of Red Screes, Little Hart Crag, Dove Crag, Hart Crag and Fairfield)

Helvellyn 4

NATURAL FEATURES

The Helvellyn range is extremely massive, forming a tremendous natural barrier from north to south between the deep troughs of the Thirlmere and Ullswater valleys. The many fells in this vast upland area are each given a separate chapter in this book, and the following notes relate only to Helvellyn itself, with its main summit at 3118' (the third highest in Lakeland) and a subsidiary at 3033'.

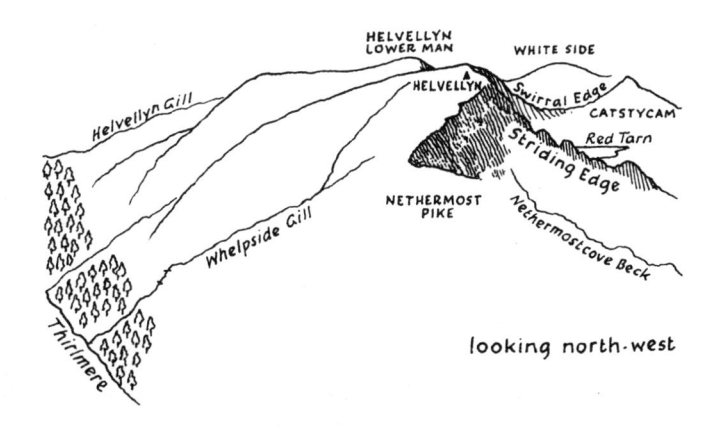

looking north-west

Helvellyn is a high point on a high ridge and therefore is substantially buttressed by neighbouring heights, the connecting depressions, north and south, being relatively slight. Westwards, however, after a gentle incline from the summit the slope quickens and finally plunges steeply down to Thirlmere, the total fall in height being nearly half a mile in a lateral distance of little more than one mile. This great mountain wall below the upper slopes is of simple design, consisting of two broad buttresses each bounded by swift-flowing streams and scarred by broken crags and occasional scree gullies. The base of the slope is densely planted with conifers.

continued

Helvellyn 5

NATURAL FEATURES
continued

The smooth slopes curving up from the west break abruptly along the ridge, where, in complete contrast, a shattered cliff of crag and scree falls away precipitously eastwards: here are the most dramatic scenes Helvellyn has to offer. From the edge of the declivity on the summit Red Tarn is seen directly below, enclosed between the bony arms of Swirral Edge on the left and Striding Edge on the right. Swirral Edge terminates in the grassy cone of Catstycam, a graceful peak, but Striding Edge is all bare rock, a succession of jagged fangs ending in a black tower. The Edges are bounded by deep rough hollows, silent and very lonely. Beyond the Edges is the bulky mass of Birkhouse Moor, Helvellyn's long east shoulder, a high wedge separating Grisedale and Glenridding and descending to the lovely shores of Ullswater.

Striding Edge

Early writers regarded Striding Edge as a place of terror; contemporary writers, following a modern fashion, are inclined to dismiss it as of little account. In fact, Striding Edge is the finest ridge there is in Lakeland, for walkers — its traverse is always an exhilarating adventure in fair weather or foul, and it can be made easy or difficult according to choice. The danger of accident is present only when a high wind is blowing or when the rocks are iced: in a mist on a calm day, the Edge is a really fascinating place.

Helvellyn 6

Swirral Edge

Helvellyn from Red Tarn

Helvellyn 7

MAP

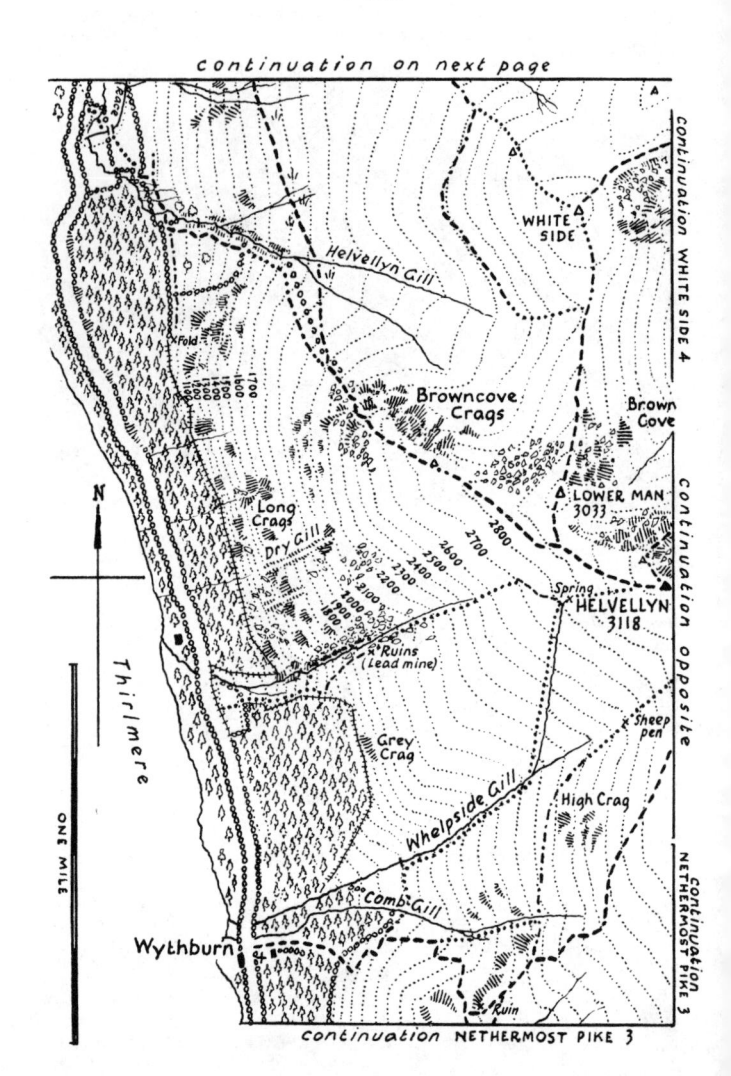

Helvellyn 8

MAP

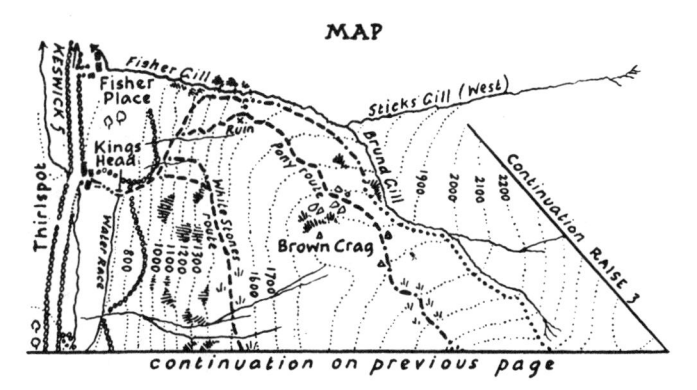

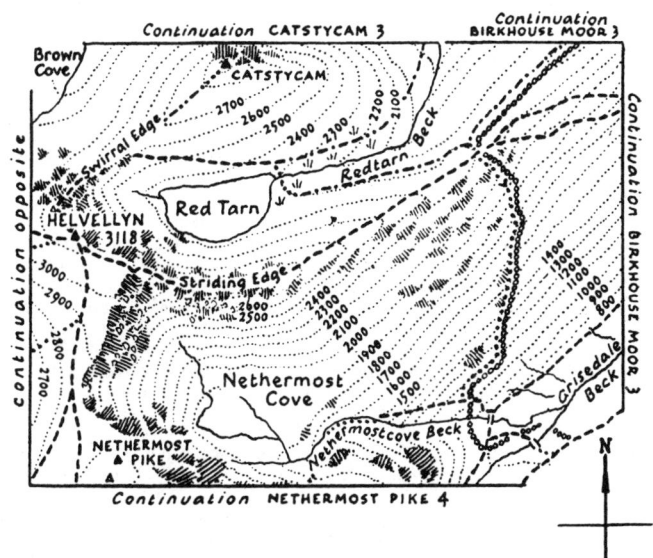

Helvellyn 9

THE WESTERN APPROACHES

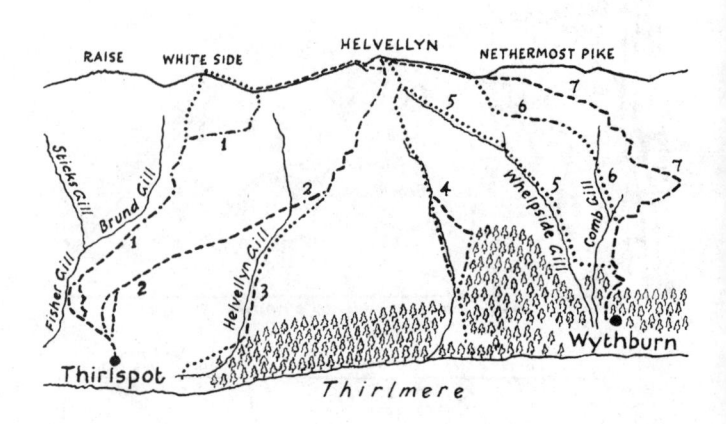

1 : **The old pony-route** : The original, longest and easiest route. The path is now becoming intermittent owing to disuse. This is the route indicated on the Ordnance Survey and Bartholomew's maps, but it is unnecessary to pass over the summit of White Side.

2 : **The 'White Stones' route** : The usual and popular way up from Thirlspot, originally marked by whitewashed stones (now a dim grey). Steep initially and midway, and marshy in places. Inexplicably this path, although long in use, is not shown on the published maps.

3 : **via Helvellyn Gill** : A more pleasant start to Route 2, but it is unremittingly steep for 2,000 feet. Dry underfoot. The correct start from the road is doubtful, and possibly involves a mild trespass: aim for the bridge in the field (over the water-race) and the plantation wall.

4 : **via the old lead mine** : The shortest way to the top from the road, taking advantage of a breach in the plantation. Very steep and rough for 2,200 feet. This is *not* a recognised route, and is not attractive. Solitary walkers with weak ankles should avoid it.

5 : **via Whelpside Gill** : A good route on a hot day, with water close almost to the summit. Rough scrambling in the gill. No path.

6 : **via Comb Gill** : A route of escape from the crowds on the popular Birk Side path. Steep up by the gill, but generally easy walking most of the way, on grass. No path, but a shepherd's track is helpful if it can be found.

7 : **The 'Wythburn' route, via Birk Side** : One of the most popular ways up Helvellyn, and the usual route from Wythburn. Good path throughout. Steep for the first mile, then much easier. This is the route indicated on the published maps.

These routes are illustrated on pages 11 and 12 following

Helvellyn 10

THE WESTERN APPROACHES

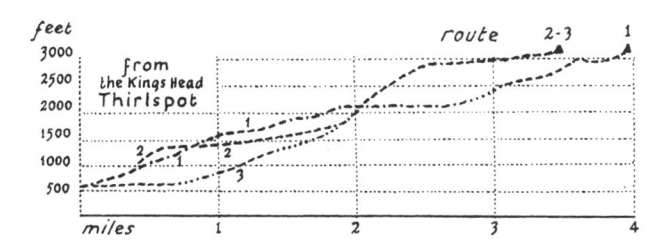

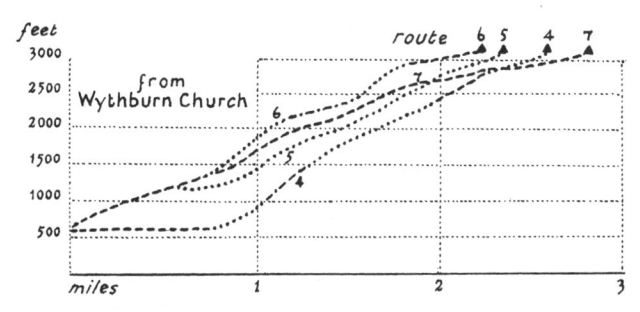

from the Kings Head Thirlspot — route 2·3, 1

from Wythburn Church — route 6, 5, 4, 7

In mist:

Route 1 is very difficult to follow.

Route 2 is fairly clear, but the divergences from Route 1 at 900' and 1000' are not distinct.

Route 3 is safe but is not easy to locate.

Route 4 is safe but seems even rougher in mist.

Route 5 is safe if the gill is kept alongside.

Route 6 is better avoided.

Route 7 is the best of all, the path being distinct throughout its length.

Helvellyn Gill

Whelpside Gill

Helvellyn 11

ASCENT FROM THIRLSPOT
2600 feet of ascent : 3½ - 4 miles

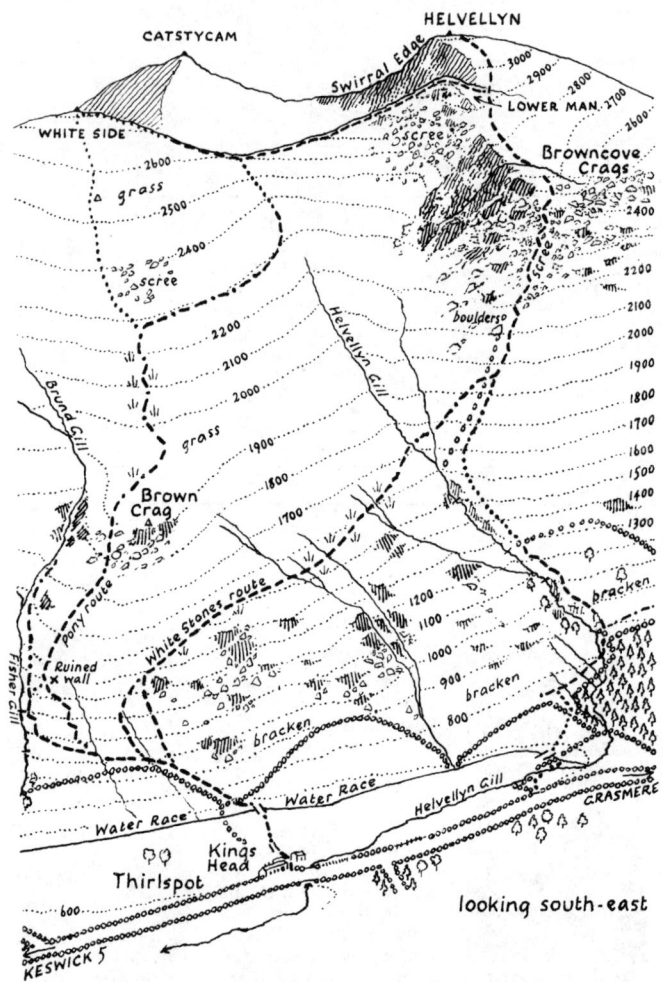

looking south-east

See Helvellyn 9 for details of the routes illustrated

Helvellyn 12

ASCENT FROM WYTHBURN
2550 feet of ascent : 2¼-2¾ miles

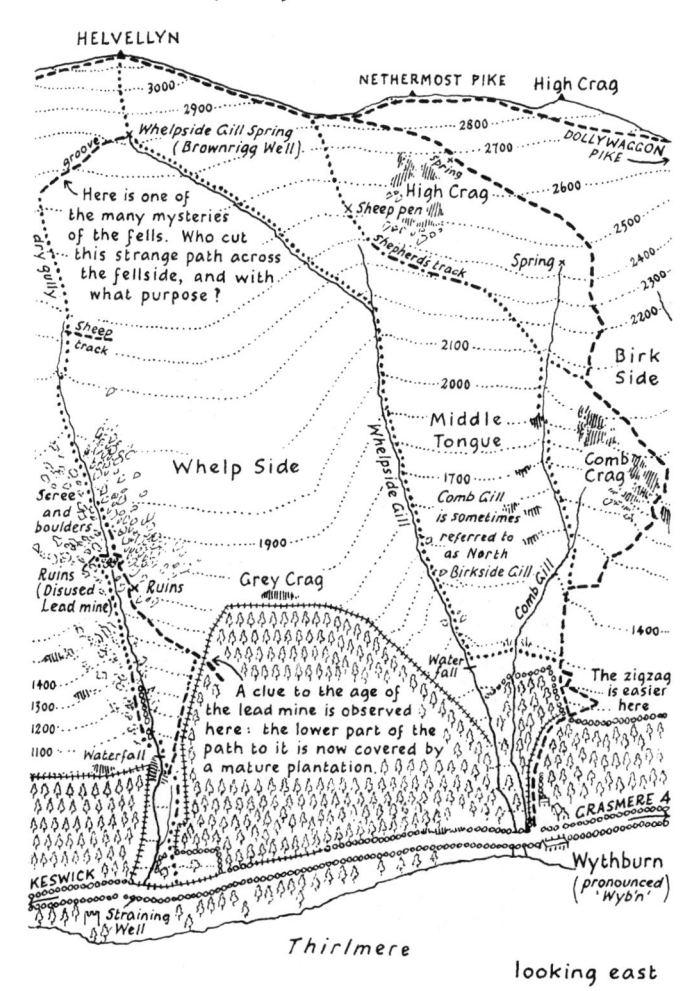

HELVELLYN

NETHERMOST PIKE   High Crag

Whelpside Gill Spring (Brownrigg Well)

DOLLYWAGGON PIKE

High Crag

Sheep pen

Shepherds track

Spring

← Here is one of the many mysteries of the fells. Who cut this strange path across the fellside, and with what purpose?

dry gully

Sheep track

Birk Side

Whelp Side

Middle Tongue

Whelpside Gill

Comb Crag

Scree and boulders

Grey Crag

Comb Gill is sometimes referred to as North Birkside Gill

Comb Gill

Ruins (Disused Lead mine)

× Ruins

A clue to the age of the lead mine is observed here: the lower part of the path to it is now covered by a mature plantation.

Waterfall

The zigzag is easier here

GRASMERE 4

Waterfall

Wythburn (pronounced 'Wyb'n')

KESWICK

Straining Well

Thirlmere

looking east

See Helvellyn 9 for details of the routes illustrated

Helvellyn 13

THE EASTERN APPROACHES

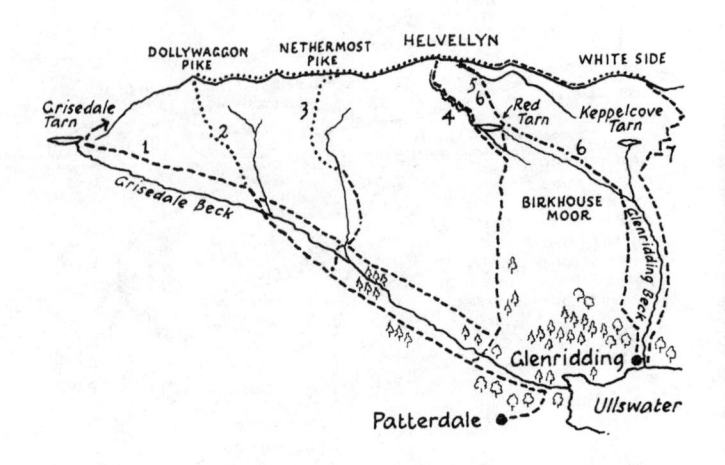

1 : *via Grisedale Tarn* : A long easy walk on a good path, with only one steep section. An interesting and pleasant route, which can be improved by following the edge of the escarpment between Dollywaggon Pike and the summit, instead of the path.

2 : *via Ruthwaite Cove and Dollywaggon Pike* : A very fine route for the more adventurous walker, cutting off a big corner of Route 1 — but the variation is steep and pathless.

3 : *via Nethermost Cove and Nethermost Pike* : A twin to Route 2, with a steep enjoyable scramble. Not for novices.

4 : *via Striding Edge* : The best way of all, well known, popular, and often densely populated in summer. The big attraction is an airy rock ridge, very fine indeed. Good path throughout.

5 : *via Red Tarn and Swirral Edge, from Patterdale* : An easier variation finish to Route 4, marshy by Red Tarn, ending in a good scramble up a steep rock staircase.

6 : *via Red Tarn and Swirral Edge, from Glenridding* : An easy walk, marshy in places, finishing with a good scramble up a steep rock staircase. Path intermittent but not difficult to follow.

7 : *The old pony-route via Keppel Cove* : The original route from Glenridding, now little-frequented but still quite distinct. A long but easy and interesting walk.

Routes 4 to 7 are illustrated on pages 15 and 16 following. For routes 1, 2 and 3, the diagrams on Dollywaggon Pike 5 and 7 and Nethermost Pike 6 respectively, will be helpful.

Helvellyn 14

THE EASTERN APPROACHES

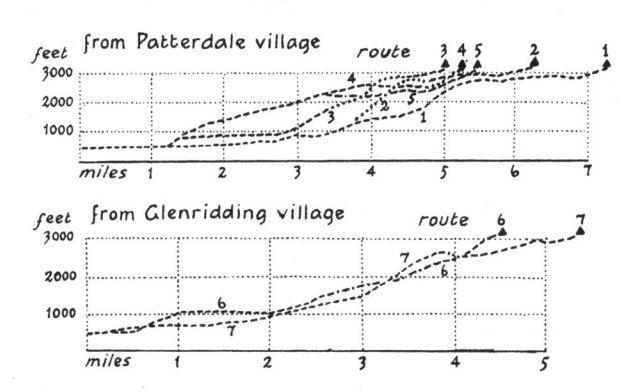

from Patterdale village   route 3 4 5   2   1

from Glenridding village   route 6   7

In mist:

Route 1 is easy to follow every inch of the way.
Routes 2 and 3 should be avoided absolutely.
Route 4 is safe for anyone already familiar with it.
Route 5 is safe, but there will be uncertainty near Red Tarn.
Route 6 is safe if Redtarn Beck is kept alongside to the tarn.
Route 7 is distinct except on the short south slope of White Side.

The summit, from Striding Edge

Helvellyn 15

ASCENT FROM PATTERDALE
2700 feet of ascent : 5 miles

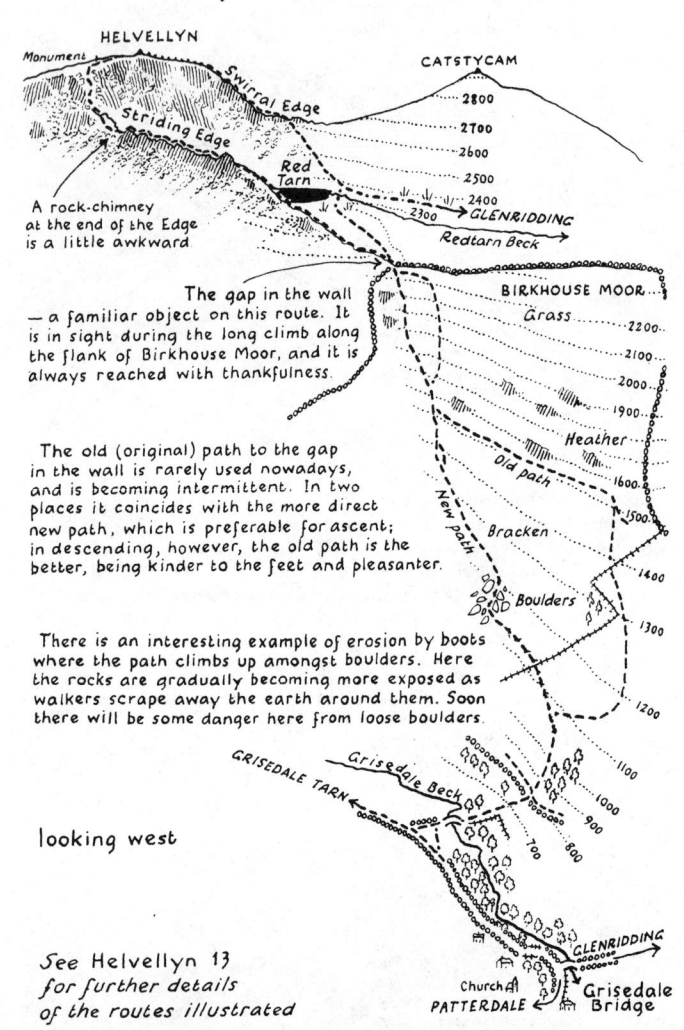

HELVELLYN
Monument
Swirral Edge
Striding Edge
CATSTYCAM
Red Tarn
GLENRIDDING
Redtarn Beck

A rock-chimney at the end of the Edge is a little awkward

BIRKHOUSE MOOR
Grass
Heather
Old path
New path
Bracken
Boulders

The gap in the wall — a familiar object on this route. It is in sight during the long climb along the flank of Birkhouse Moor, and it is always reached with thankfulness.

The old (original) path to the gap in the wall is rarely used nowadays, and is becoming intermittent. In two places it coincides with the more direct new path, which is preferable for ascent; in descending, however, the old path is the better, being kinder to the feet and pleasanter.

There is an interesting example of erosion by boots where the path climbs up amongst boulders. Here the rocks are gradually becoming more exposed as walkers scrape away the earth around them. Soon there will be some danger here from loose boulders.

GRISEDALE TARN ← Grisedale Beck
GLENRIDDING
Church
PATTERDALE ← Grisedale Bridge

looking west

See Helvellyn 13 for further details of the routes illustrated

Helvellyn 16

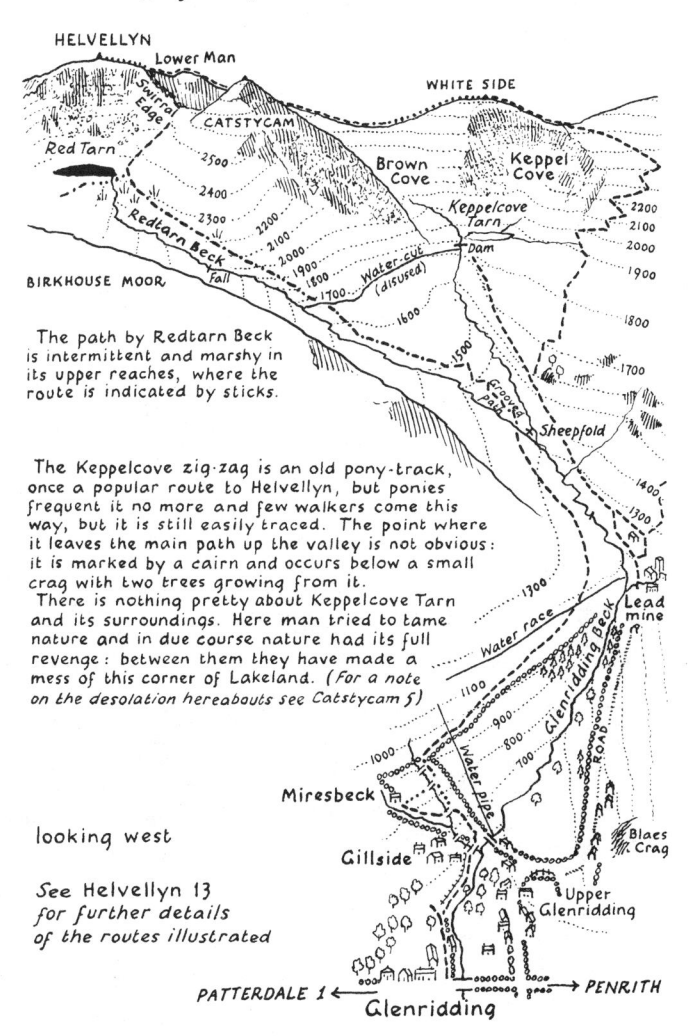

ASCENT FROM GLENRIDDING
2750 feet of ascent : 4½ or 5½ miles

The path by Redtarn Beck is intermittent and marshy in its upper reaches, where the route is indicated by sticks.

The Keppelcove zig-zag is an old pony-track, once a popular route to Helvellyn, but ponies frequent it no more and few walkers come this way, but it is still easily traced. The point where it leaves the main path up the valley is not obvious: it is marked by a cairn and occurs below a small crag with two trees growing from it.
There is nothing pretty about Keppelcove Tarn and its surroundings. Here man tried to tame nature and in due course nature had its full revenge: between them they have made a mess of this corner of Lakeland. (For a note on the desolation hereabouts see Catstycam 5)

looking west

See Helvellyn 13 for further details of the routes illustrated

PATTERDALE 1 ← Glenridding → PENRITH

Helvellyn 17

ASCENT FROM GRASMERE
3050 feet of ascent : 6½ miles from Grasmere Church

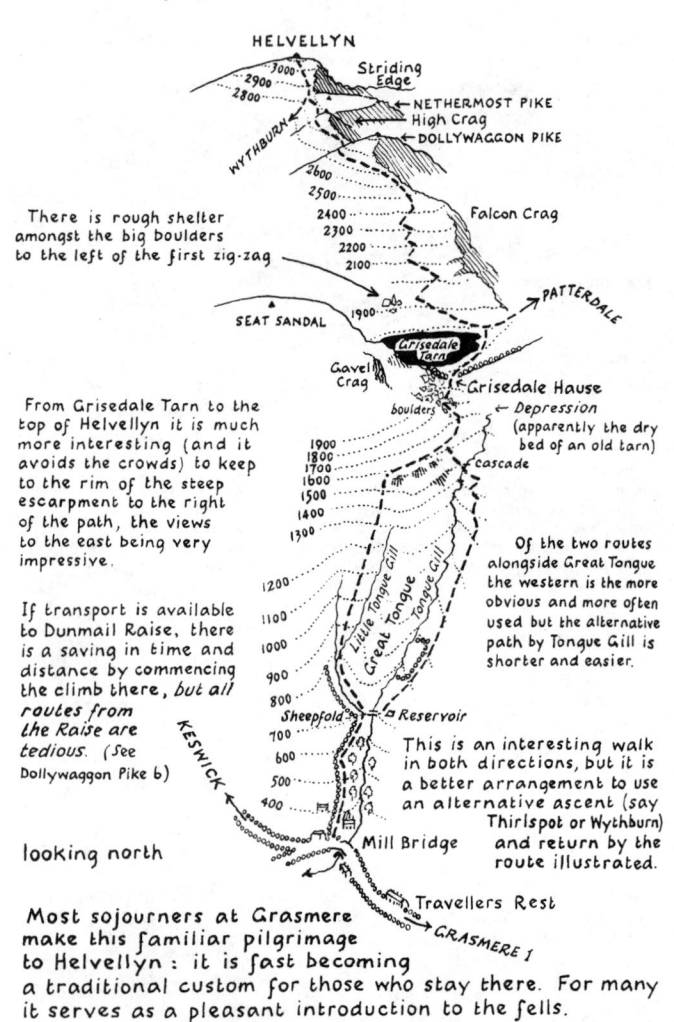

HELVELLYN

Striding Edge

NETHERMOST PIKE
High Crag
DOLLYWAGGON PIKE

WYTHBURN

Falcon Crag

There is rough shelter amongst the big boulders to the left of the first zig-zag

SEAT SANDAL

PATTERDALE

Grisedale Tarn

Gavel Crag

Grisedale Hause

boulders ← Depression (apparently the dry bed of an old tarn)

From Grisedale Tarn to the top of Helvellyn it is much more interesting (and it avoids the crowds) to keep to the rim of the steep escarpment to the right of the path, the views to the east being very impressive.

cascade

Little Tongue Gill
Great Tongue Gill

Of the two routes alongside Great Tongue the western is the more obvious and more often used but the alternative path by Tongue Gill is shorter and easier.

If transport is available to Dunmail Raise, there is a saving in time and distance by commencing the climb there, *but all routes from the Raise are tedious.* (See Dollywaggon Pike 6)

Sheepfold   Reservoir

KESWICK

Mill Bridge

This is an interesting walk in both directions, but it is a better arrangement to use an alternative ascent (say Thirlspot or Wythburn) and return by the route illustrated.

looking north

Travellers Rest
GRASMERE 1

Most sojourners at Grasmere make this familiar pilgrimage to Helvellyn : it is fast becoming a traditional custom for those who stay there. For many it serves as a pleasant introduction to the fells.

Helvellyn 18

Helvellyn Lower Man

looking northwest

Helvellyn Lower Man, half a mile northwest of the principal top, occupies a key position on the main ridge, which here changes its direction subtly and unobtrusively. Walkers intending to follow the ridge north may easily go astray hereabouts. The wide path from Helvellyn skirts the Lower Man and continues clearly along a broad spur which appears to be the main ridge, but is not (*this is the direct way to Thirlspot, not indicated on Bartholomews' and Ordnance Survey maps*); while, being indistinct, the bifurcation to the Lower Man may not be noticed, *will* not in mist.

Summit of Lower Man — HELVELLYN

Browncove Crags
Oddly named because Brown Cove is on the other side of the ridge.

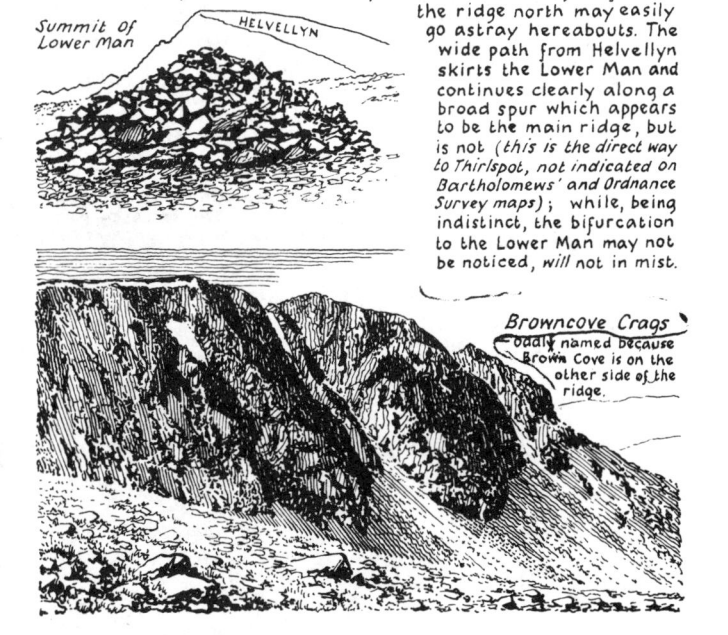

Helvellyn 19

THE SUMMIT

It might be expected that the summit of so popular a mountain would be crowned with a cairn the size of a house, instead of which the only adornment is a small and insignificant heap of stones that commands no respect at all, untidily thrown together on the mound forming the highest point. It is a disappointment to have no cairn to recline against, and as there is no natural seat anywhere on the top visitors inevitably drift into the nearby wall-shelter and there rest ankle-deep in the debris of countless packed lunches. The summit is covered in shale and is lacking in natural features, a deficiency which man has attempted to remedy by erecting thereon, as well as the shelter, a triangulation column and two monuments. And until many walkers learn better manners there is a crying need for an incinerator also, to dispose of the decaying heaps of litter they leave behind to greet those who follow.

The paths across the summit are wide and so well-trodden as to appear almost metalled: they are unnecessarily and amply cairned.

The dull surroundings are relieved by the exciting view down the escarpment to Red Tarn and Striding Edge below.

Helvellyn 20

DESCENTS

Descents should not be attempted in the areas shaded.

In general, the eastern slopes are craggy high up and grassy below, but the western slopes are grassy high up and craggy below.

STICKS PASS Faint path: keep to contour

RAISE No path

GLENRIDDING Good grass path zig-zags down to the valley: watch for the first 'zig', which is indistinct

Keppel Cove

▲ WHITE SIDE

THIRLSPOT No path but one will be reached initially at 2300 contour

GLENRIDDING No path down steep slope; keep left to avoid scree

Brown Cove

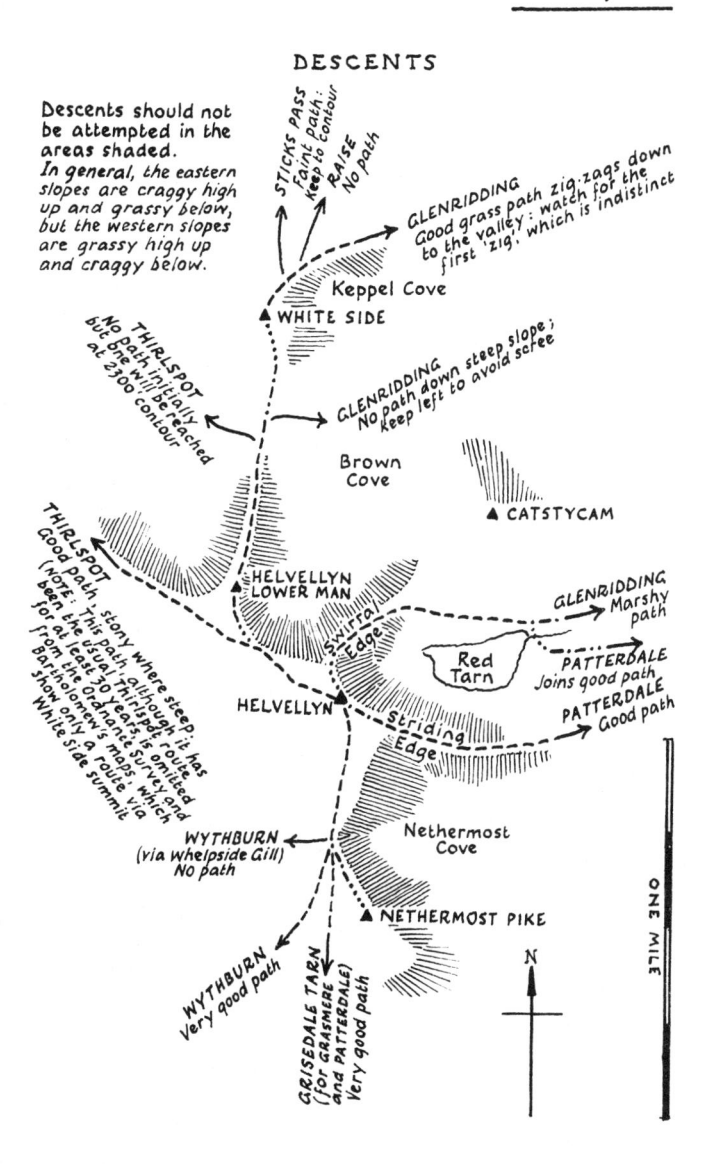

▲ CATSTYCAM

▲ HELVELLYN LOWER MAN

THIRLSPOT Good path (NOTE: Where steep it is stony. This path, although it has been the usual Thirlspot route for at least 50 years and from the Ordnance Survey and Bartholomew's maps show only a route via White Side summit)

Swirral Edge

GLENRIDDING Marshy path

Red Tarn

PATTERDALE Joins good path

▲ HELVELLYN

Striding Edge

PATTERDALE Good path

WYTHBURN (via Whelpside Gill) No path

Nethermost Cove

▲ NETHERMOST PIKE

WYTHBURN Very good path

GRISEDALE TARN (for Grasmere and Patterdale) Very good path

N ↑

ONE MILE

Helvellyn 21

RIDGE ROUTES

To HELVELLYN LOWER MAN, 3033' : ½ mile : NW
Depression at 2975': 60 feet of ascent
A simple stroll, safe in mist.

Take the Thirlspot path, forking right below the cone of Lower Man. Or, better, follow the edge of the escarpment all the way.

NOTE : Helvellyn Lower Man stands at the point where the main ridge makes an abrupt and unexpected right-angled turn. Its summit must be traversed for White Side, Sticks Pass or Glenridding.

....

To CATSTYCAM, 2917' : 1 mile : NW (200 yards), then NE
Depression at 2600': 320 feet of ascent
A splendid walk with a fine rock scramble. Safe in mist; dangerous in ice and snow.

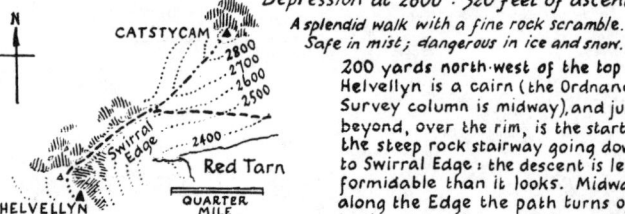

200 yards north-west of the top of Helvellyn is a cairn (the Ordnance Survey column is midway), and just beyond, over the rim, is the start of the steep rock stairway going down to Swirral Edge : the descent is less formidable than it looks. Midway along the Edge the path turns off to the right : here continue ahead up the grass slope to the summit.

....

The Monuments of Helvellyn

The Gough Memorial

Erected 1890 on the edge of the summit above the path to Striding Edge.

This small stone tablet, 40 yards S of the shelter, commemorates the landing of an aeroplane in 1926. (Playful pedestrians may have hidden it with stones)

The Dixon Memorial 1858

Situated on a platform of rock on Striding Edge overlooking Nethermost Cove (often not noticed)

Helvellyn 22

RIDGE ROUTES

To BIRKHOUSE MOOR, 2350': 2 miles : ESE then NE
Minor depressions only : 100 feet of ascent

An unpleasant descent on loose scree, followed by an exhilarating scramble along a narrow rock ridge and an easy walk. Dangerous in snow and ice; care necessary in gusty wind; safe in mist.

Turn down the scree for Striding Edge 30 yards beyond the monument. The Edge begins with a 20' chimney, well furnished with holds : this is the only difficulty. From the rock tower at the far end the path slants across the slope but it is pleasanter to follow the crest.

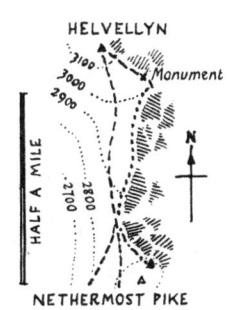

To NETHERMOST PIKE, 2920'
3/4 mile : S then SE
Depression at 2840': 80 feet of ascent
A very easy walk. Safe in mist.

A broad path leads south to the depression. Here note, *in mist*, that the first few yards of the fork on to Nethermost Pike are not clear: the main path goes on to Wythburn and the unwary walker will go with it. A detour from the track across the flat top of Nethermost Pike is necessary to visit the summit-cairn.

In clear weather a more interesting route follows the edge of the escarpment, the views being very impressive.

Whelpside Gill Spring
(Brownrigg Well)

Few visitors to Helvellyn know of this spring (the source of Whelpside Gill), which offers unfailing supplies of icy water. To find it, walk 500 yards south of west from the top in the direction of Pillar.

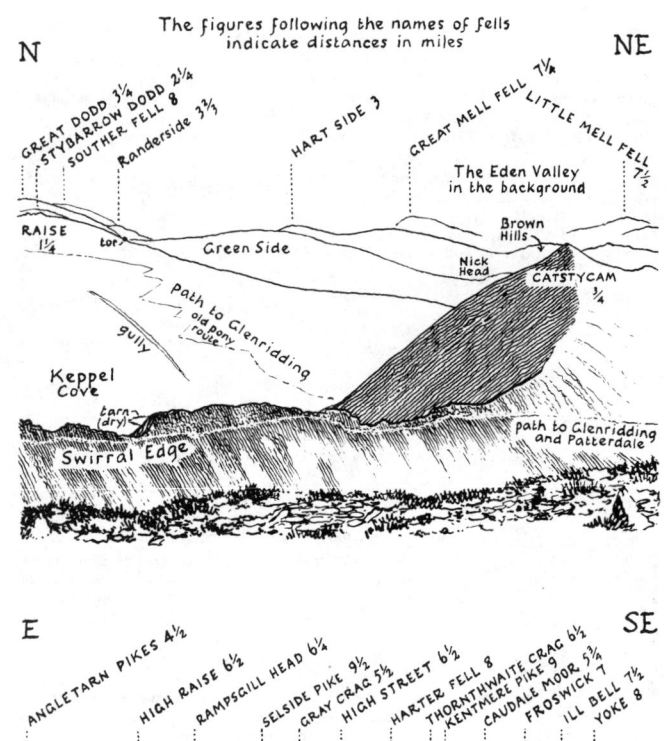

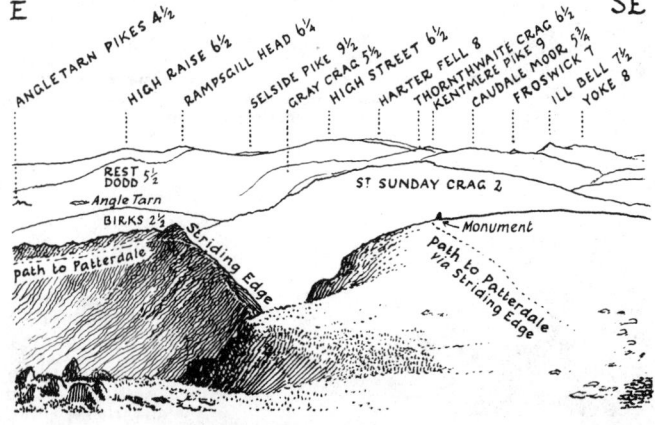

Helvellyn 23

THE VIEW

The figures following the names of fells indicate distances in miles

N   **NE**

- GREAT DODD 3¼
- STYBARROW DODD 2½
- SOUTHER FELL 8
- Randerside 3⅓
- HART SIDE 3
- GREAT MELL FELL 7⅛
- LITTLE MELL FELL 7½
- The Eden Valley in the background
- RAISE 1¼
- tor?
- Green Side
- Brown Hills
- Nick Head
- CATSTYCAM ¾
- Path to Glenridding
- old pony route
- gully
- Keppel Cove
- tarn (dry)
- Swirral Edge
- path to Glenridding and Patterdale

E   **SE**

- ANGLETARN PIKES 4½
- HIGH RAISE 6½
- RAMPSGILL HEAD 6¼
- SELSIDE PIKE 9½
- GRAY CRAG 5½
- HIGH STREET 6½
- HARTER FELL 8
- THORNTHWAITE CRAG 6½
- KENTMERE PIKE 9
- CAUDALE MOOR 5¾
- FROSWICK 7
- ILL BELL 7½
- YOKE 8
- REST DODD 5½
- Angle Tarn
- BIRKS 2⅓
- ST SUNDAY CRAG 2
- Striding Edge
- Monument
- Path to Patterdale
- path to Patterdale via Striding Edge

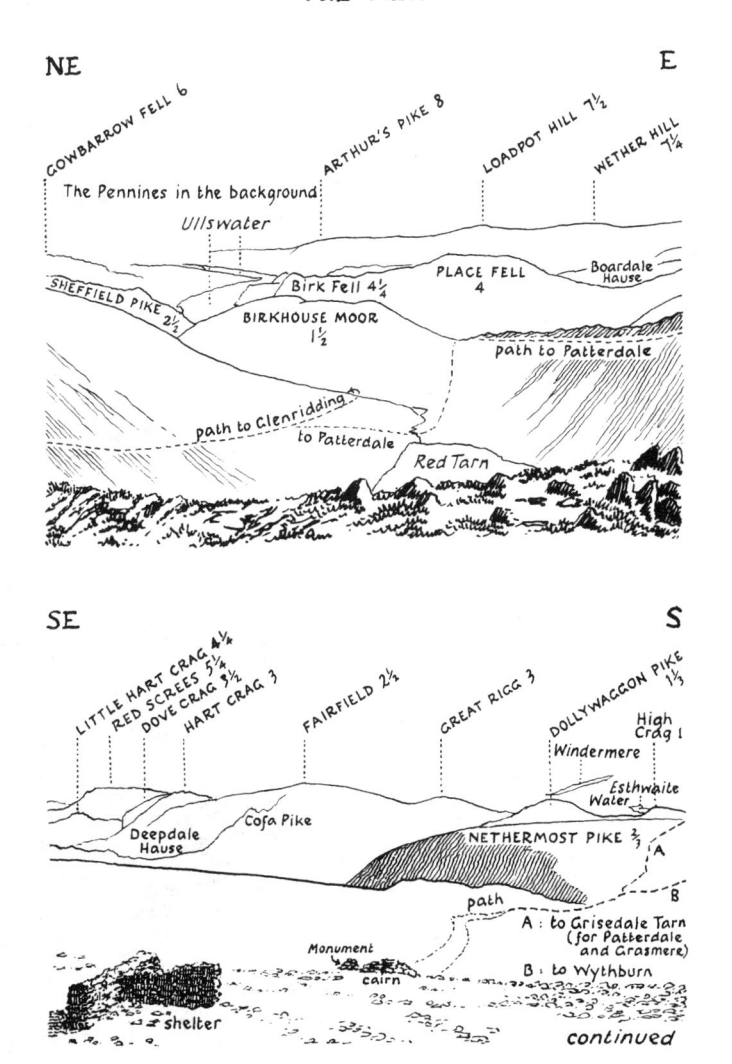

Helvellyn 24

THE VIEW

NE — **E**

- COWBARROW FELL 6
- The Pennines in the background
- Ullswater
- ARTHUR'S PIKE 8
- LOADPOT HILL 7½
- WETHER HILL 7¼
- SHEFFIELD PIKE 2½
- Birk Fell 4¼
- PLACE FELL 4
- Boardale Hause
- BIRKHOUSE MOOR 1½
- path to Patterdale
- path to Glenridding
- to Patterdale
- Red Tarn

SE — **S**

- LITTLE HART CRAG 4¼
- RED SCREES 5¼
- DOVE CRAG 3½
- HART CRAG 3
- FAIRFIELD 2½
- GREAT RIGG 3
- DOLLYWAGGON PIKE 1⅓
- High Crag 1
- Windermere
- Esthwaite Water
- Deepdale Hause
- Cofa Pike
- NETHERMOST PIKE ⅔
- path
- A: to Grisedale Tarn (for Patterdale and Grasmere)
- B: to Wythburn
- Monument
- cairn
- shelter

continued

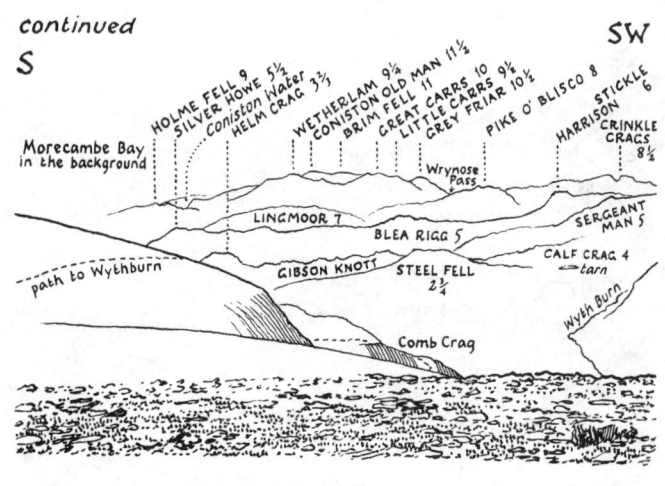

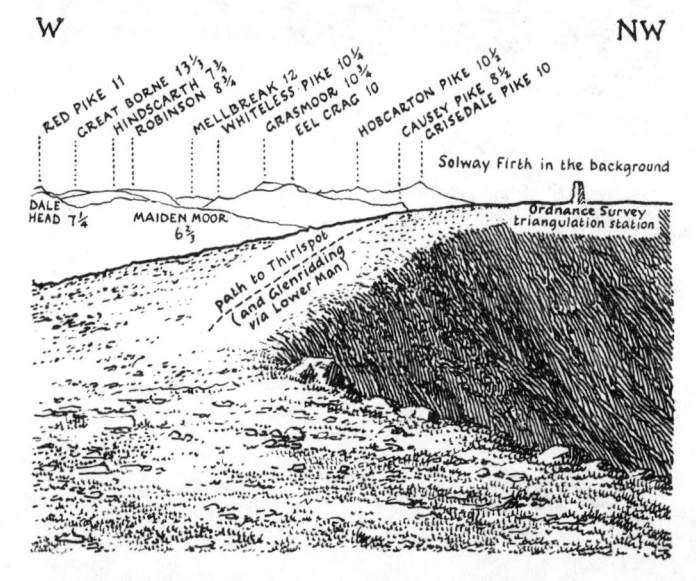

Helvellyn 25

THE VIEW

continued

S — **SW**

- HOLME FELL 9
- SILVER HOWE 5½
- Coniston Water 3⅓
- HELM CRAG 3⅓
- WETHERLAM 9½
- CONISTON OLD MAN 11½
- BRIM FELL 11
- GREAT CARRS 10
- LITTLE CARRS 9½
- GREY FRIAR 10½
- PIKE O' BLISCO 8
- HARRISON STICKLE 6
- CRINKLE CRAGS 8½

Morecambe Bay in the background

Wrynose Pass

LINGMOOR 7
BLEA RIGG 5
SERGEANT MAN 5

path to Wythburn

GIBSON KNOTT
STEEL FELL 2¾
CALF CRAG 4
tarn

Comb Crag

Wyth Burn

W — **NW**

- RED PIKE 11
- GREAT BORNE 13⅓
- HINDSCARTH 7¾
- ROBINSON 8¾
- MELLBREAK 12
- WHITELESS PIKE 10¾
- GRASMOOR 10¾
- EEL CRAG 10
- HOBCARTON PIKE 10½
- CAUSEY PIKE 8¾
- GRISEDALE PIKE 10

DALE HEAD 7¼
MAIDEN MOOR 6⅔

Solway Firth in the background

Ordnance Survey triangulation station

path to Thirlspot (and Glenridding via Lower Man)

Helvellyn 26

THE VIEW

SW — BOWFELL 8, HIGH RAISE 5, ESK PIKE 8¾, SCAFELL PIKE 9, SCAFELL 9¾, GREAT END 8½, LINGMELL 8¼, GLARAMARA 6½, Esk Hause, ULLSCARF 3⅔, YEWBARROW 11, GREAT GABLE 8⅔, GREEN GABLE 8¾, KIRK FELL 9¼, Sty Head, BRANDRETH 8, RED PIKE 11¼, SCOAT FELL 11¼, PILLAR 10⅔, Honister Pass, Borrowdale, HIGH CRAG 10, FLEETWITH PIKE 8½, HIGH STILE 10½ — **W**

Blea Tarn

Direction of Whelpside Gill Spring

NW — Bassenthwaite Lake and Helvellyn Lower Man can be seen from this edge, LONGSIDE 10, CARL SIDE 9⅔, SKIDDAW 10, LONSCALE FELL 8, GREAT CALVA 10½, WHITE SIDE, WATSONS DODD, Calfhow Pike, BLENCATHRA 8, CLOUGH HEAD 4½, BOWSCALE FELL 9½, RAISE, path to Glenridding — **N**

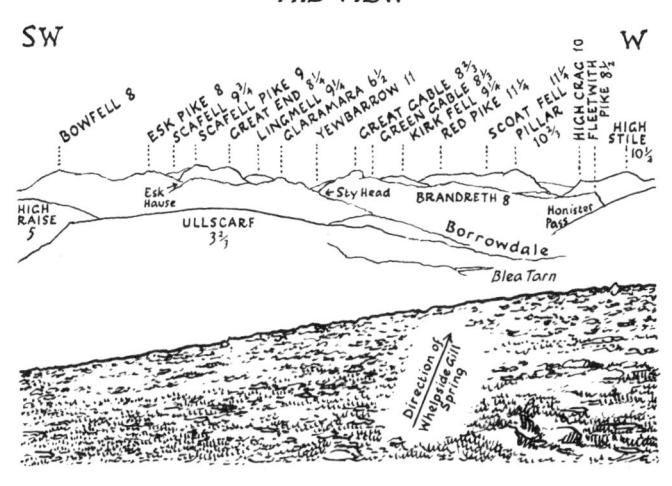

Keppel Cove

Swirral Edge

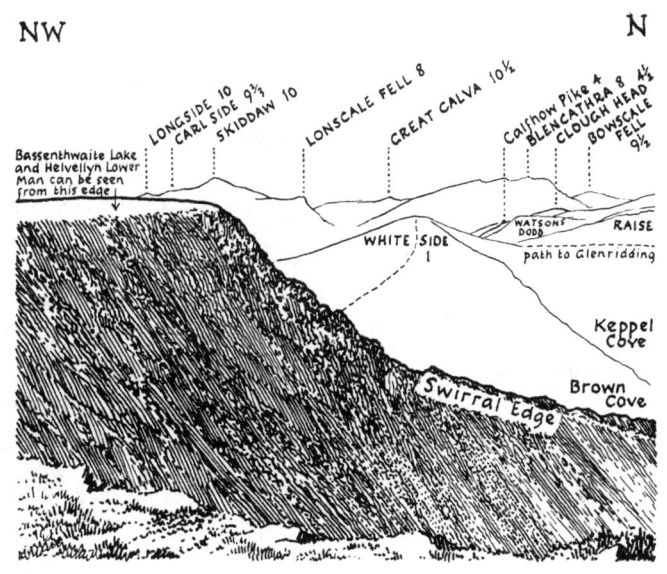

Brown Cove

Heron Pike 2003'

from Grasmere

▲ FAIRFIELD

▲ GREAT RIGG

▲ STONE ARTHUR

▲ HERON PIKE

• Grasmere ▲ NAB SCAR
  • Rydal

Ambleside •

MILES
0 1 2 3 4

Heron Pike is a grassy mound on the long southern ridge of Fairfield. From no direction does it look like a pike or peak nor will herons be found there. It is a viewpoint of some merit but otherwise is of little interest. It is climbed not, as a rule, for any attraction of its own, but because it happens to lie on a popular route to Fairfield. The ridge beyond it undulates with little change of altitude before rising sharply to Great Rigg, and this hinterland of Heron Pike is generally referred to as Rydal Fell: for convenience it will be described in this chapter as a part of Heron Pike.

Heron Pike 2

NATURAL FEATURES

Heron Pike is the watershed between Rydale and the short Greenhead valley. Grass predominates on its slopes but there is much bracken on the Rydale flank and rock outcrops on both. Its streams are small and flow into the Rothay. A dreary sheet of water named Alcock Tarn, once a reservoir, occupies a shelf above Grasmere; here are many low crags. A nameless summit on the ridge to the north of Heron Pike has a steep east face, which at one point falls away abruptly in a formidable wall of rock, Erne Crag (or Earing Crag), and, further north, the fellside is cleft from top to bottom by a straight stony gully, beyond which the ground becomes rough as Great Rigg is approached. In contrast, the western slopes adjoining Great Rigg are entirely grassy.

Erne Crag

MAP

Heron Pike 3

ASCENTS

Usually the summit of Heron Pike is visited only incidentally on the way to or from Fairfield, but it may be recommended as the objective of an easy and remunerative half-day's walk from Grasmere (via Alcock Tarn, to which there are three fair paths) or from Rydal (climbing Nab Scar en route). Gully-addicts will rejoice to learn that a long straight gully, full of shifting scree but with no difficulty other than steepness, falls from the ridge half a mile north of the summit, directly above the sheepfold in mid-Rydale beyond Erne Crag: this offers a scramble they (and they alone) will enjoy, but not even the most avid of them would find any pleasure in *descending* by this route.

THE SUMMIT

The summit is by a little outcrop of rock, distinguished by quartz. All else is grass. There is no cairn and nothing of interest except the view. The nameless north summit is better: at least it has a wall and a cairn and a few rocks suitable for backrests.

DESCENTS: Any route of ascent (except the gully) may be used for descent. A quick way off to Rydal, in a season when the bracken is short, is by Blind Cove. *In mist*, keep *strictly* to the path going south to Nab Scar and Rydal.

RIDGE ROUTES

To GREAT RIGG, 2513'
1½ miles : N then NNE
Minor depressions
550 feet of ascent
A pleasant high-level traverse

A good path undulates over grass and finally climbs the cone ahead. Safe in mist.

To NAB SCAR, 1450'
⅔ mile : S
Downhill all the way
A very easy descent

The path, on grass, forks at a cairn. Either branch may be taken — they soon join. Safe in mist.

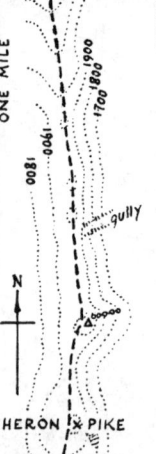

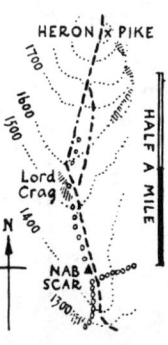

Heron Pike 4

THE VIEW

The smallness of the summit gives depth to the views, which are particularly rich in lakes and tarns. Nearby are the fells of the Fairfield Horseshoe, but the best of the mountain scene is formed by the finely-grouped Coniston and Langdale fells with Scafell Pike overtopping all.

Principal Fells

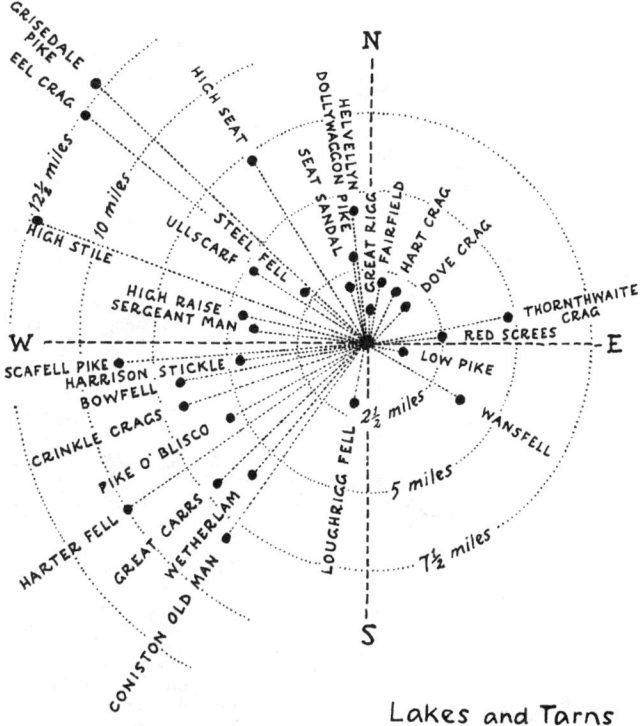

- GRISEDALE PIKE
- EEL CRAG
- 12½ miles
- HIGH SEAT
- 10 miles
- HIGH STILE
- ULLSCARF
- STEEL FELL
- HELVELLYN
- DOLLYWAGGON PIKE
- SEAT SANDAL
- GREAT RIGG
- FAIRFIELD
- HART CRAG
- DOVE CRAG
- THORNTHWAITE CRAG
- HIGH RAISE
- SERGEANT MAN
- RED SCREES
- SCAFELL PIKE
- HARRISON STICKLE
- BOWFELL
- LOW PIKE
- CRINKLE CRAGS
- 2½ miles
- WANSFELL
- PIKE O' BLISCO
- 5 miles
- HARTER FELL
- GREAT CARRS
- WETHERLAM
- LOUGHRIGG FELL
- 7½ miles
- CONISTON OLD MAN

Lakes and Tarns

    SSE : Windermere
      S : Blelham Tarn
      S : Wise Een Tarn
      S : Esthwaite Water
    SSW : Coniston Water
    SSW : Elterwater
      W : Easedale Tarn

High Hartsop Dodd 1702'

from Hartsop Beck

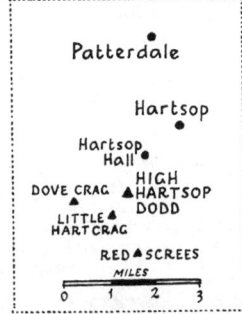

High Hartsop Dodd, seen from the valley near Brothers Water, has the appearance of an isolated mountain with a peaked summit and steep sides, a very shapely pyramid rising from green fields. But in fact it is merely the termination of a spur of a higher fell, Little Hart Crag, which it partly hides from view, and its uninteresting grassy summit has little distinction, though it is always greeted with enthusiasm by walkers who attain it direct from the valley, for the upper slopes above the sparsely-wooded lower flanks are excessively steep. A high ascending ridge links the Dodd with the rough top of Little Hart Crag.

High Hartsop Dodd 2

MAP

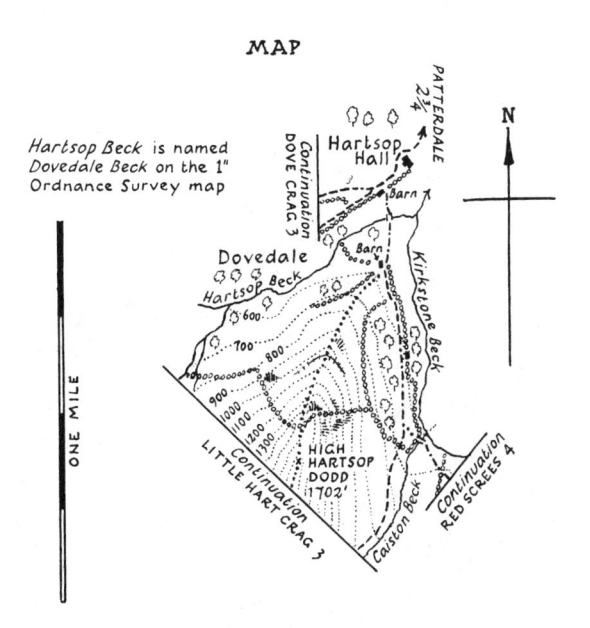

Hartsop Beck is named Dovedale Beck on the 1" Ordnance Survey map

ASCENT FROM HARTSOP HALL
1200 feet of ascent

High Hartsop Dodd may be climbed direct from the barn at its foot — note here the symmetry between the pitch of the roof of the barn as it is approached across the boulder-dotted pastures from Hartsop Hall, and the sides of the pyramid of the Dodd behind — but the steepness of the grass slope, especially as the top wall is neared, makes the ascent laborious. It is really much better first to ascend Little Hart Crag (preferably by way of Dovedale) and to return to the valley over the top of the Dodd.

THE SUMMIT

There is no cairn to indicate the highest point — all is grass — and indeed it is not easy to say which is the summit; but it is assumed to be the top of the *first*

> This unassuming fell had its brief period of glory in 1948 when it won headlines in the newspapers by the efforts of rescuers to save two terriers trapped in a hole on the steep Caiston flank.

rise above the wall. ***In descending, in mist***, remember that the wall does not cross the ridge at right-angles, but at a tangent. Do NOT follow the wall down: on both flanks it leads to crags.

High Hartsop Dodd 3

Dove Crag and Hogget Gill, from High Hartsop Dodd

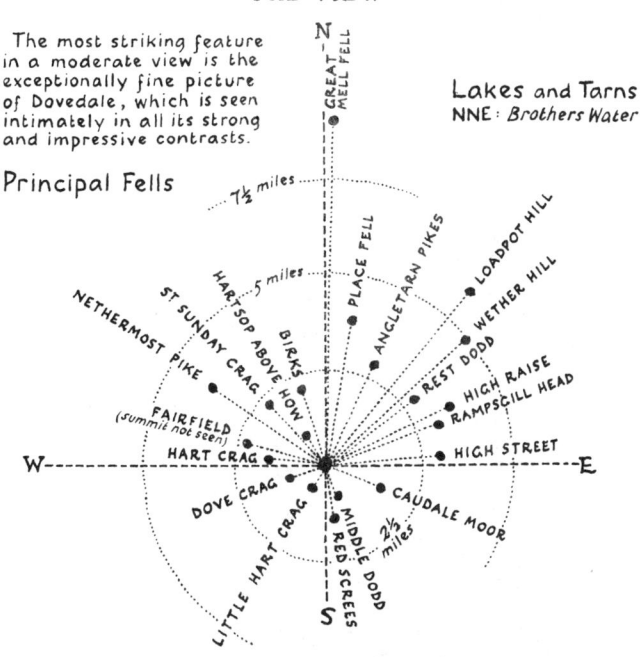

High Hartsop Dodd 4

THE VIEW

The most striking feature in a moderate view is the exceptionally fine picture of Dovedale, which is seen intimately in all its strong and impressive contrasts.

Lakes and Tarns
NNE: *Brothers Water*

Principal Fells

N: GREAT MELL FELL
NNE: PLACE FELL
NE: ANGLETARN PIKES, LOADPOT HILL
ENE: WETHER HILL, REST DODD
E: HIGH RAISE, RAMPSGILL HEAD, HIGH STREET
ESE: CAUDALE MOOR
SE: MIDDLE DODD, RED SCREES
S: LITTLE HART CRAG
SSW: DOVE CRAG
W: HART CRAG, FAIRFIELD (summit not seen)
WNW: NETHERMOST PIKE, ST SUNDAY CRAG, HARTSOP ABOVE HOW, BIRKS

Brothers Water

High Pike

2155'

sometimes referred to as
Scandale Fell

from High Sweden Bridge

▲ DOVE CRAG

▲ HIGH PIKE

▲ LOW PIKE

● Rydal

● Ambleside

MILES
0   1   2   3

Everest enthusiasts will liken the two pronounced rises on the long southern spur of Dove Crag to the 'first and second steps' on the famous north-east ridge (but imagination would indeed have to be vivid to see in the grassy dome of Dove Crag any resemblance to the icy pyramid of that highest of all peaks!). The first rise is Low Pike, the second is High Pike. The latter, with its cairn perched on the brink of a shattered cliff, is the most imposing object seen from Scandale which lies far below.

Some authorities refer to High Pike as Scandale Fell, but the latter name is more properly applied in a general way to the whole of the high ground enclosing Scandale Bottom to north and west.

High Pike 2

NATURAL FEATURES

Viewed from the south, High Pike has the appearance of an isolated peak; viewed from the parallel ridges to east and west, it is seen in its true proportions as merely the flat top of a rise in Dove Crag's long southern ridge; viewed from the north, it is entirely insignificant. High Pike, therefore, cannot be regarded as having enough qualifications to make it a mountain in its own right. Its level top, however, marks a **definite** change in the character of the ridge, which is narrow and rocky below and broad and grassy above. The western flank of High Pike descends to Rydale in uninteresting slopes relieved by occasional outcrops of rock; the eastern face is much rougher and steeper, with an ill-defined stony shoulder going down into Scandale.

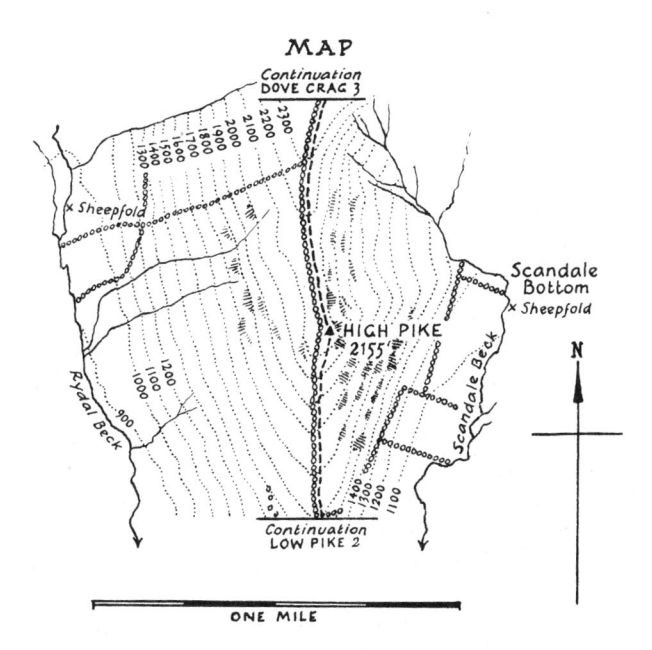

MAP

ONE MILE

NOTE: On Bartholomews 1" Map the summit is shown as 'Scandale Fell'

High Pike 3

ASCENT FROM AMBLESIDE
2000 feet of ascent : 4 miles

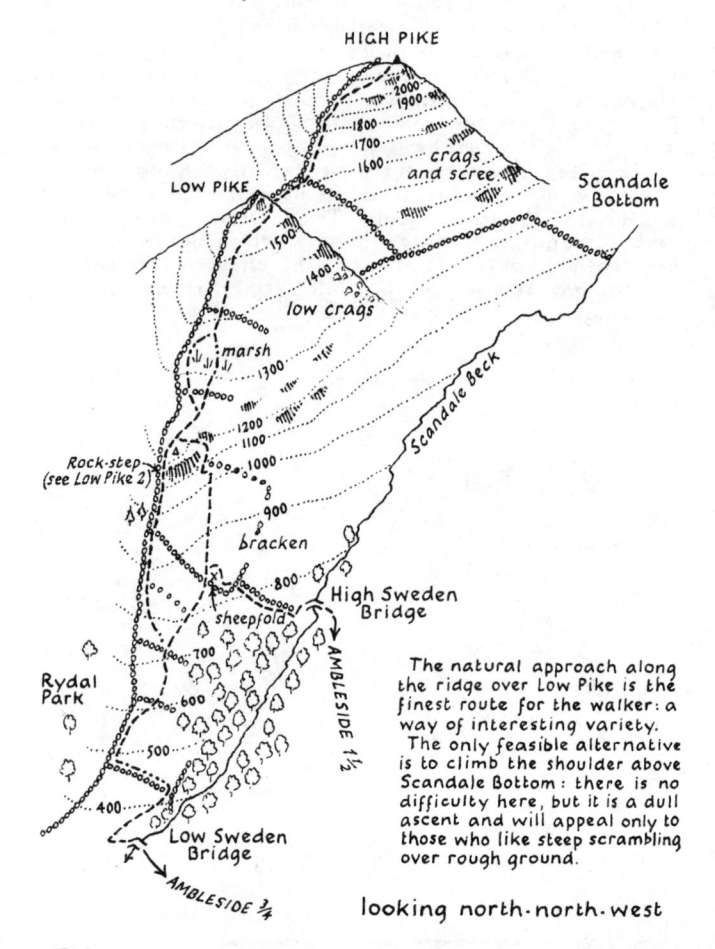

looking north-north-west

The natural approach along the ridge over Low Pike is the finest route for the walker: a way of interesting variety. The only feasible alternative is to climb the shoulder above Scandale Bottom: there is no difficulty here, but it is a dull ascent and will appeal only to those who like steep scrambling over rough ground.

This route, commonly used as the initial stage of the 'Fairfield Horseshoe', provides a pleasant walk along a good ridge. The lower approaches are very attractive.

High Pike 4

THE SUMMIT

The summit is a flat grassy promenade with a cairn standing at the northern end on the edge of a decaying crag, overlooking Scandale. A high wall runs along the top.

DESCENTS: The ridge-path should always be used when leaving the top: nothing but discomfort is to be gained by attempting a direct descent to east or west.
In bad weather conditions, a safe descent may be made to Ambleside by following the ridge over Low Pike, keeping to the path, or, if the path is lost, to the wall. A journey to Patterdale need not be abandoned in the event of bad weather on High Pike: the safe conclusion of the walk is ensured if the wall is followed north to a wire fence, which leads down grassy slopes to Dovedale or, alternatively, to Scandale Pass.

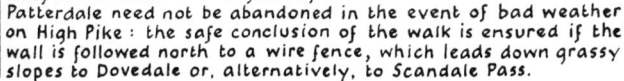

The wall

A traveller along the ridge cannot help but notice the wall: it accompanies him all the way and its intimacy becomes a nuisance. However, it is well worthy of notice, particularly on the steepest rises south of the summit, where the method and style of construction, in persevering horizontal courses despite the difficulties of the ground, compel admiration: it should be remembered, too, that all the stone had to be found on the fell and cut to shape on the site. Witness here a dying art!

High Pike 5

RIDGE ROUTES

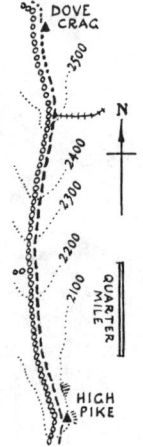

To DOVE CRAG, 2603' : 1 mile : N.
Slight depression: 470 feet of ascent

An easy, gradual climb on grass. Perfectly safe in mist. Follow the wall north; an intermittent path keeps a few yards to the right of it. The cairn does not come into sight until a wire fence is reached.

To LOW PIKE, 1657' : ⅔ mile : S.
Depression at 1575'
100 feet of ascent

An easy walk downhill on a rough but distinct path. Safe in mist.

The path keeps to the left of the wall and skirts the base of the top pyramid of Low Pike, the summit being attained by a short steep scramble.

from Scandale

High Pike 6

THE VIEW

The ridge-wall obstructs the view westwards from the cairn but is worth surmounting for the prospect of the Central Fells, which is good. In other directions, neighbouring higher fells hide the distance, but much of the High Street range is seen over the Scandale Pass.

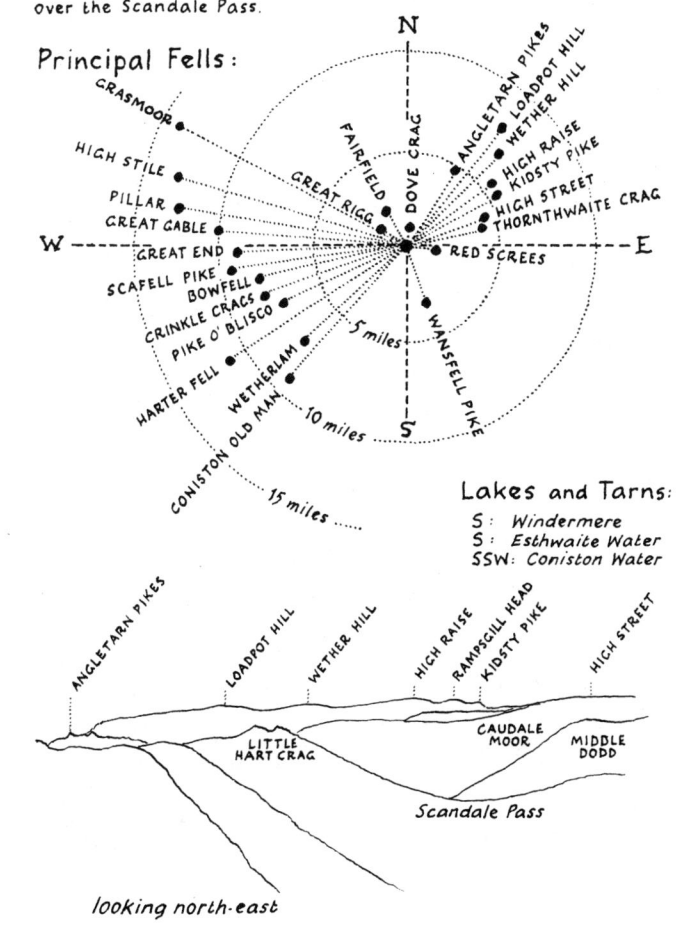

Principal Fells:

GRASMOOR
HIGH STILE
PILLAR
GREAT GABLE
GREAT END
SCAFELL PIKE
BOWFELL
CRINKLE CRAGS
PIKE O' BLISCO
HARTER FELL
WETHERLAM
CONISTON OLD MAN

FAIRFIELD
GREAT RIGG
DOVE CRAG
ANGLETARN PIKES
LOADPOT HILL
WETHER HILL
HIGH RAISE
KIDSTY PIKE
HIGH STREET
THORNTHWAITE CRAG
RED SCREES
WANSFELL PIKE

5 miles
10 miles
15 miles

Lakes and Tarns:

S: *Windermere*
S: *Esthwaite Water*
SSW: *Coniston Water*

ANGLETARN PIKES — LOADPOT HILL — WETHER HILL — HIGH RAISE — RAMPSGILL HEAD — KIDSTY PIKE — HIGH STREET

LITTLE HART CRAG — CAUDALE MOOR — MIDDLE DODD

Scandale Pass

looking north-east

Little Hart Crag 2091'

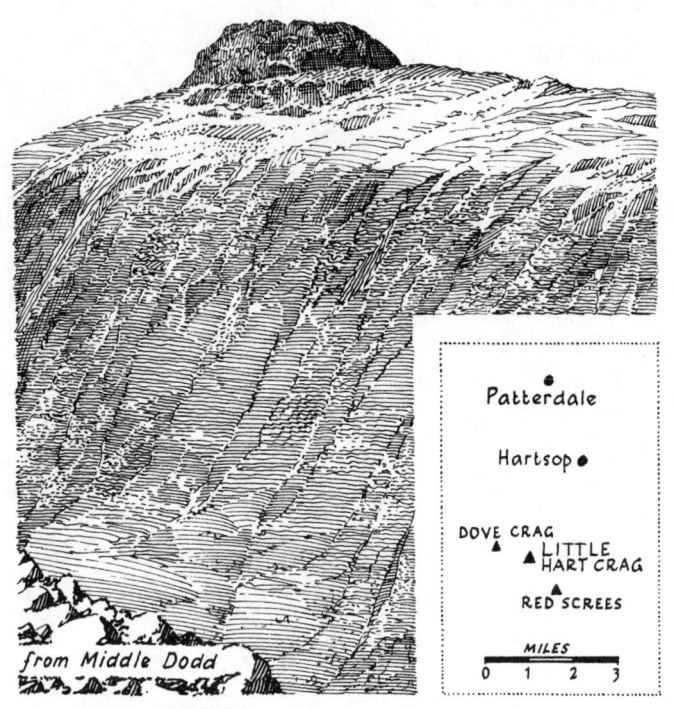

from Middle Dodd

Little Hart Crag is the sentinel of Scandale Pass, four miles north of Ambleside, and takes its duty of guarding the Pass very seriously and proudly. It has the appearance, in fact, of a crouching watchdog, facing Scandale and missing nothing of the happenings there, while its spine curves down to the fields of Hartsop; the path from one place to the other climbs over its shoulder just beneath the hoary head and beetling brows.

It is really a very junior member in a company of grand hills and quite overshadowed by Red Screes and Dove Crag; but it has individuality and an interesting double summit which commands delightful views of Scandale and Dovedale.

Little Hart Crag 2

NATURAL FEATURES

Little Hart Crag descends in uninteresting slopes of grass and bracken to Scandale in the south; it is connected in the west to Dove Crag by the broad marshy depression of Bakestones Moss; south-east is the lower depression of Scandale Pass and the vast soaring flank of Red Screes. North-east is a narrow spur running at a high elevation before plunging sharply to the valley at Hartsop: this

The summit, from the south

is High Hartsop Dodd, and its steep-sided pyramidal form, seen from Brothers Water, gives it the appearance of being a separate height. Just below the summit, west, is a long wall of impressive crags, Black Brow. The eastern slopes, falling to Caiston Glen, are rough and unattractive.

Hartsop, from the summit

Little Hart Crag 3

MAP

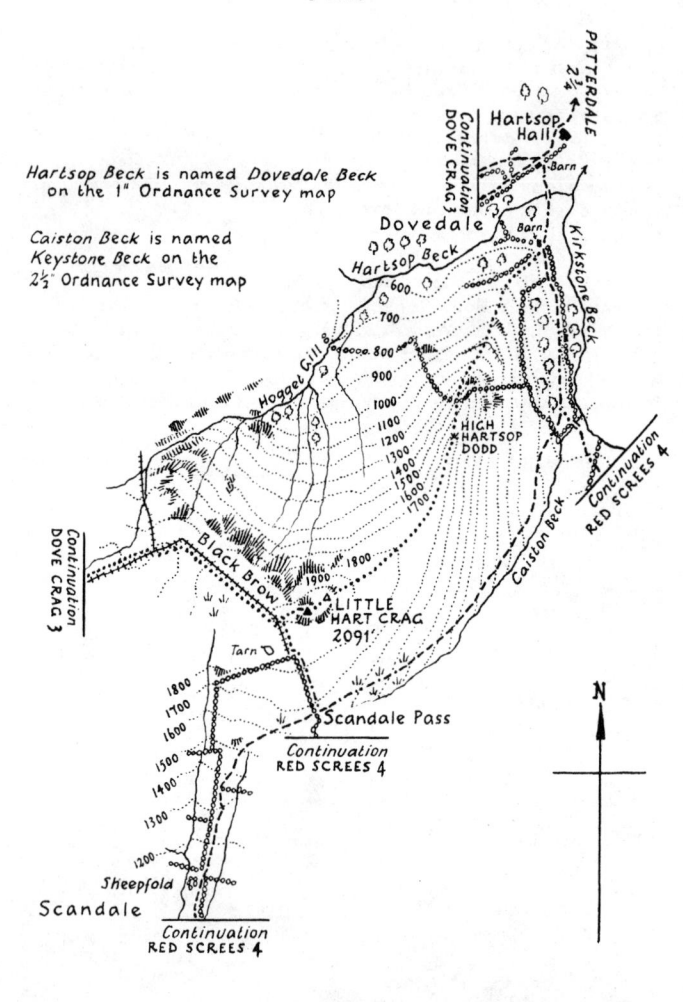

Hartsop Beck is named Dovedale Beck on the 1" Ordnance Survey map

Caiston Beck is named Keystone Beck on the 2½" Ordnance Survey map

ONE MILE

Little Hart Crag 4

ASCENT FROM PATTERDALE
1,700 feet of ascent : 5 miles from Patterdale village

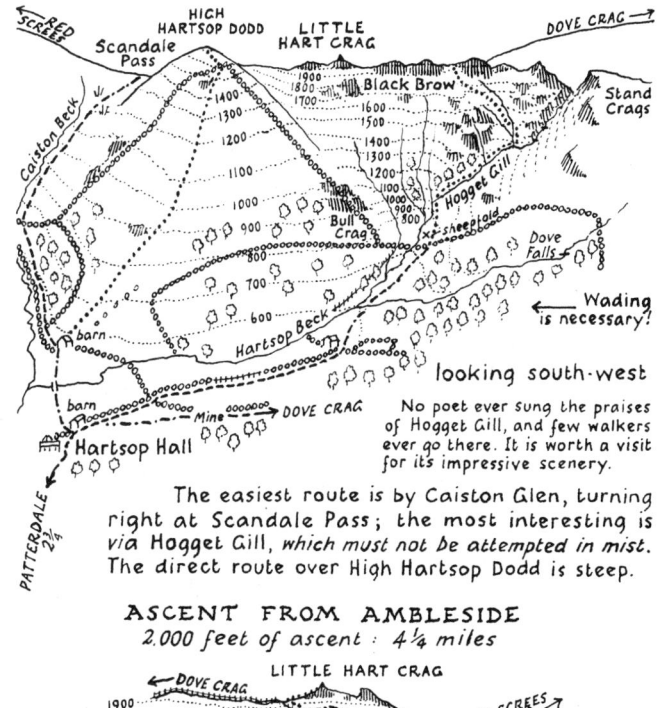

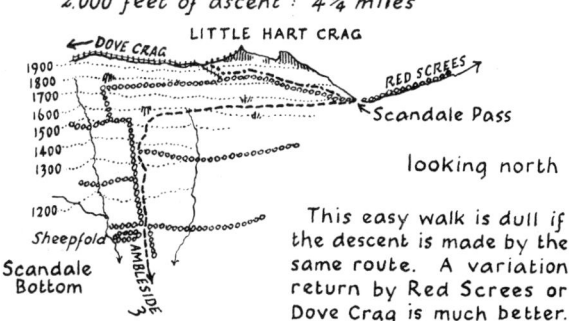

looking south-west

No poet ever sung the praises of Hogget Gill, and few walkers ever go there. It is worth a visit for its impressive scenery.

The easiest route is by Caiston Glen, turning right at Scandale Pass; the most interesting is via Hogget Gill, *which must not be attempted in mist.* The direct route over High Hartsop Dodd is steep.

ASCENT FROM AMBLESIDE
2,000 feet of ascent : 4¼ miles

looking north

This easy walk is dull if the descent is made by the same route. A variation return by Red Screes or Dove Crag is much better.

Little Hart Crag 5

THE SUMMIT

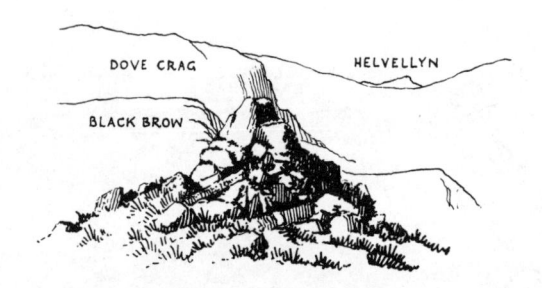

There are two well-defined tops. The higher is that nearer to Dove Crag; it is surmounted by a cairn perched on the extreme edge of a rocky platform. The lower summit, to the north-east, is less conspicuous, but is easily identified in mist by markings of quartz in the stones near the insignificant cairn: this cairn is the key to the ridge going down to High Hartsop Dodd.   Both summits are buttressed to the south by sheer walls of black rock.

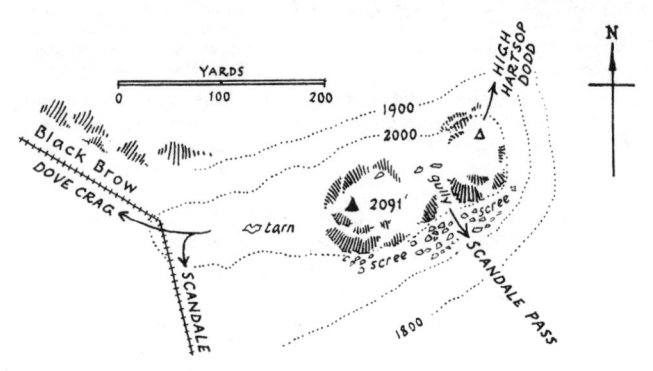

DESCENTS: The descent to Patterdale is best made directly by the grassy ridge over High Hartsop Dodd, the last 1000 feet down to the valley being steep. Scandale, for Ambleside, may be reached by cutting off a corner at the top of the pass.
In mist, the summit is confusing and dangerous. The safest way off is west to the wire fence, following this down south to Scandale Pass for either Patterdale or Ambleside. Descents to Caiston Glen or Dovedale direct should not be attempted.

Little Hart Crag 6

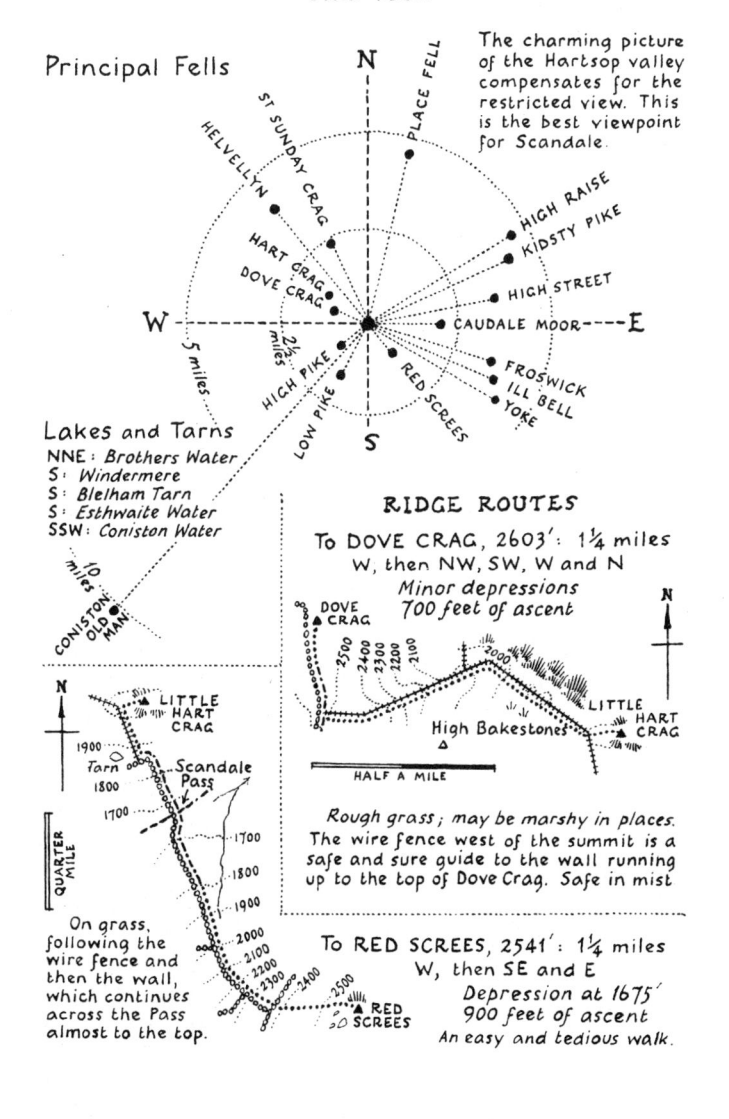

THE VIEW

Principal Fells

The charming picture of the Hartsop valley compensates for the restricted view. This is the best viewpoint for Scandale.

N: PLACE FELL
NNW: ST SUNDAY CRAG
NW: HELVELLYN
NW: HART CRAG
W: DOVE CRAG
NE: HIGH RAISE
NE: KIDSTY PIKE
ENE: HIGH STREET
E: CAUDALE MOOR
SW: HIGH PIKE
SSW: LOW PIKE
S: RED SCREES
ESE: FROSWICK
SE: ILL BELL
SSE: YOKE

Lakes and Tarns

NNE: Brothers Water
S: Windermere
S: Blelham Tarn
S: Esthwaite Water
SSW: Coniston Water
SSW: Coniston Old Man (10 miles)

RIDGE ROUTES

To DOVE CRAG, 2603': 1¼ miles

W, then NW, SW, W and N
Minor depressions
700 feet of ascent

High Bakestones

Rough grass; may be marshy in places. The wire fence west of the summit is a safe and sure guide to the wall running up to the top of Dove Crag. Safe in mist.

To RED SCREES, 2541': 1¼ miles

W, then SE and E
Depression at 1675'
900 feet of ascent
An easy and tedious walk.

On grass, following the wire fence and then the wall, which continues across the Pass almost to the top.

Scandale Pass

Little Mell Fell 1657'

from Gowbarrow Fell

Little Mell Fell barely merits inclusion in this book. It *is* a fell — its name says so — but it is not the stuff of which the true fells are made. It rises on the verge of Lakeland but its characteristics are alien to Lakeland. It stands in isolation, not in the company of others. Its substance looks more akin to the sandstones of the nearby valley of Eden; its patchwork clothing, gorse and ling prominent, is unusual on the other fells; its hedges of stunted, windblown, unhappy trees and tumbledown fences are unsatisfactory substitutes for friendly stone walls. It is ringed by a quiet and pleasant countryside of green pastures and lush hedgerows, and one is as likely to meet a cow as a sheep on its slopes. There is good in all, however, and its heathery top is a fine place for viewing the (greater) merits of other fells.

Little Mell Fell 2

NATURAL FEATURES

Little Mell Fell is an outlier of the Helvellyn range and the last Lakeland fell in the north-east before the high country falls away to the wide plain stretching to the distant Border. It is an uninspiring, unattractive, bare and rounded hump — the sublime touch that made a wonderland of the district overlooked Little Mell — and few walkers halt their hurried entrance into the sanctuary to climb and explore it. In truth, there is little to explore. As though conscious of its failings it tries to aspire to normal mountain structure by throwing out two ridges, but the effort is weak and not convincing. One feels sorry for Little Mell Fell, as for all who are neglected and forlorn, but at least it is beloved of birds and animals and it is one of the few fells that grouse select for their habitat, and not even the great Helvellyn itself can make such a claim!

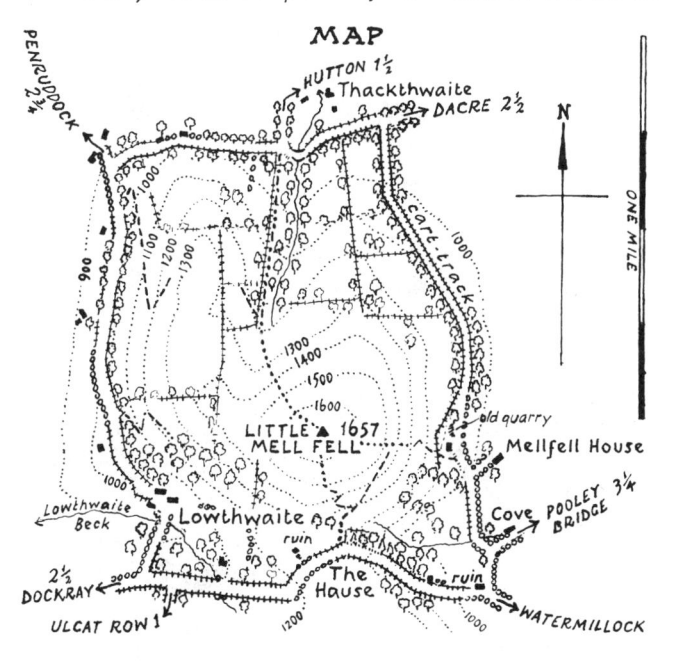

MAP

Little Mell Fell 3

ASCENTS

The fell is almost entirely enclosed within fences and hedges but access may be gained at several places — from the Hause, from the cart-track just above Mellfell House, from the bridge near Thackthwaite, and by a green track from the road to the west — somewhat furtively, for there will be a doubt lurking in the mind of the climber as to whether he is committing an act of trespass.

It is difficult to plan a mountaineering expedition within a single square mile of territory, and probably it is best to climb straight up and down from the Hause and get the job done without frills: half an hour is sufficient from here. A better approach for the purist lies along the wooded hollow above the charming bridge near Thackthwaite: on this route the view is reserved as a last-minute surprise and comes as a reward for a dull climb.

THE SUMMIT

Unexpectedly there are some stones on the summit: these have been scraped together and formed into a low wall that may have been intended as a shelter or a shooting hide. An Ordnance Survey column is nearby. Heather covers the top.

DESCENTS: Descents may safely be made in any direction, in any weather, without the remotest risk of accident by falling over a crag; frisky bullocks are the only obstacles to be feared. The Hause, to which descents will be made usually, is not visible from the summit but comes into sight below by walking south, in the direction of Hallin Fell: beware rabbit-holes obscured by bracken on this slope.

Great Mell Fell from Little Mell Fell

Little Mell Fell 4

THE VIEW

The diagram illustrates effectively the isolated situation of Little Mell Fell on the fringe of mountain country. One half of the view is of Lakeland, the other half of lowlands stretching away to the Pennines and the Border across the lovely Vale of Eden.

This is one of the few good viewpoints for appreciating the shy beauty of Martindale. Gowbarrow Fell hides most of Ullswater, only the unexciting lower reach of the lake being in sight.

Principal Fells

- CARROCK FELL — 12½ miles
- HIGH PIKE — 10 miles
- BOWSCALE FELL — 7½ miles
- GREAT MELL FELL — 5 miles
- 2½ miles
- 15 miles
- SKIDDAW
- BLENCATHRA
- LORD'S SEAT
- GRISEDALE PIKE
- HOBCARTON PIKE
- CLOUGH HEAD
- GREAT DODD
- STYBARROW DODD
- HART SIDE
- RAISE
- HELVELLYN LOWER MAN
- HELVELLYN
- NETHERMOST PIKE
- DOLLYWAGGON PIKE
- SEAT SANDAL
- FAIRFIELD
- ST SUNDAY CRAG
- HART CRAG
- DOVE CRAG
- GOWBARROW FELL
- PLACE FELL
- RED SCREES
- ANGLETARN PIKES
- CAUDALE MOOR
- THORNTHWAITE CRAG
- GRAY CRAG
- HIGH STREET
- RAMPSGILL HEAD
- THE NAB
- REST DODD
- HALLIN FELL
- HIGH RAISE
- WETHER HILL
- LOADPOT HILL
- ARTHUR'S PIKE

W — E
N
S

Lakes and Tarns
SE : *Ullswater*

Low Pike 1657'

from Rydal Beck

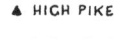

▲ HIGH PIKE
▲ LOW PIKE

● Rydal
　● Ambleside

MILES
0　1　2　3

Low Pike is well seen from the streets of Ambleside as the first prominent peak on the high ridge running northwards. The gradient along the crest of the ridge is slight, but Low Pike, halfway along, is sufficiently elevated above the deep valleys of Scandale, east, and Rydale, west, to give an impression of loftiness which exaggerates its modest altitude. There is a good deal of rock on the fell with several tiers of low crag. Low Pike is the objective in the fell-races at the annual sports meetings in Rydal Park.

Low Pike 2

MAP

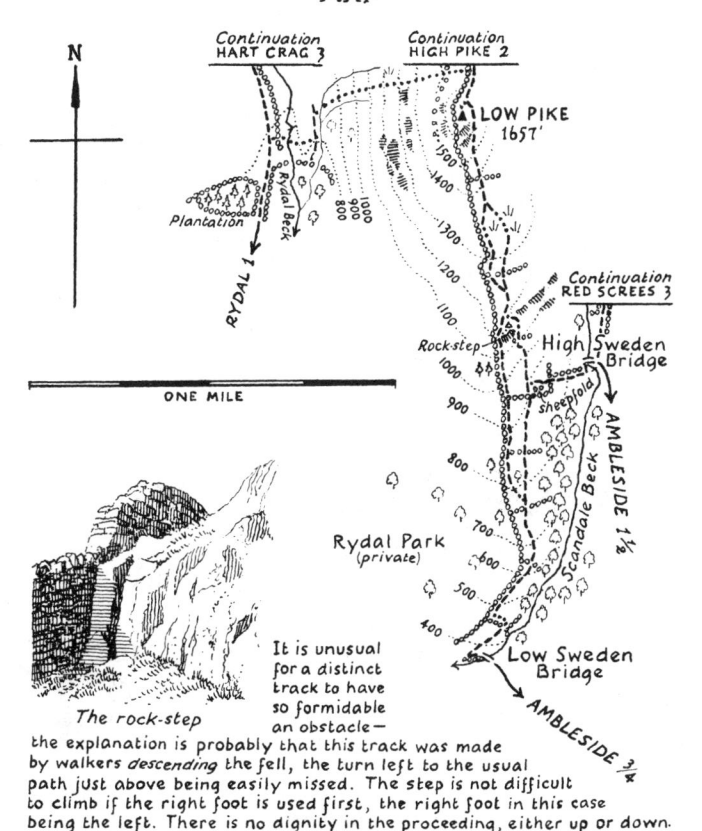

The rock-step

It is unusual for a distinct track to have so formidable an obstacle — the explanation is probably that this track was made by walkers *descending* the fell, the turn left to the usual path just above being easily missed. The step is not difficult to climb if the right foot is used first, the right foot in this case being the left. There is no dignity in the proceeding, either up or down.

ASCENTS

Low Pike is invariably climbed from Ambleside, usually on the way to the high fells beyond; it is, however, an excellent objective for a short walk from that town. The approach, by any of the variations, from the pleasant woods and pastures to the bleak craggy ridge is very attractive. The wall along the watershed detracts from the merits of this enjoyable walk.

The climb from Rydal Beck is tedious; there is no path. Aged pedestrians should note two hazards on this route: the crossing of the beck first, and the scaling of the ridge-wall finally.

Low Pike 3

THE SUMMIT

The summit is an abrupt rocky peak, a place of grey boulders and small grassy platforms in the shadow of a substantial stone wall. Some of the rocks near the summit are big enough to afford simple practice in climbing. There is no cairn nor room for one: the wall occupies the highest inches.

DESCENTS: The way to Ambleside would be obvious even if there was no path. The point of divergence at 1200' is not clear: if the wall is followed beware the rock-step, which appears unexpectedly.

For Rydal, reverse the route of ascent.

In mist, all descents should be made to Ambleside, keeping strictly to the path, or, if the path be lost, to the wall. There are crags at the 1200' level.

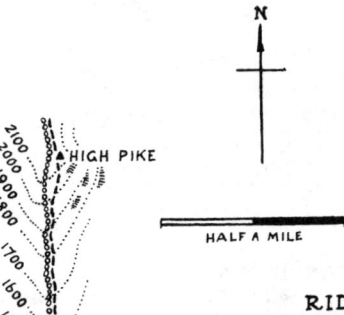

N

HALF A MILE

RIDGE ROUTE

To HIGH PIKE, 2155': ⅔ mile: N.
Depression at 1575': 600 feet of ascent.
A straightforward walk, safe in mist.
A distinct path follows the wall, climbing steadily most of the way amongst rocks.

Low Pike 4

THE VIEW

All the attractiveness of the scene is centred between south and west, where the Coniston and Langdale fells rise grandly from a lowland of lakes.

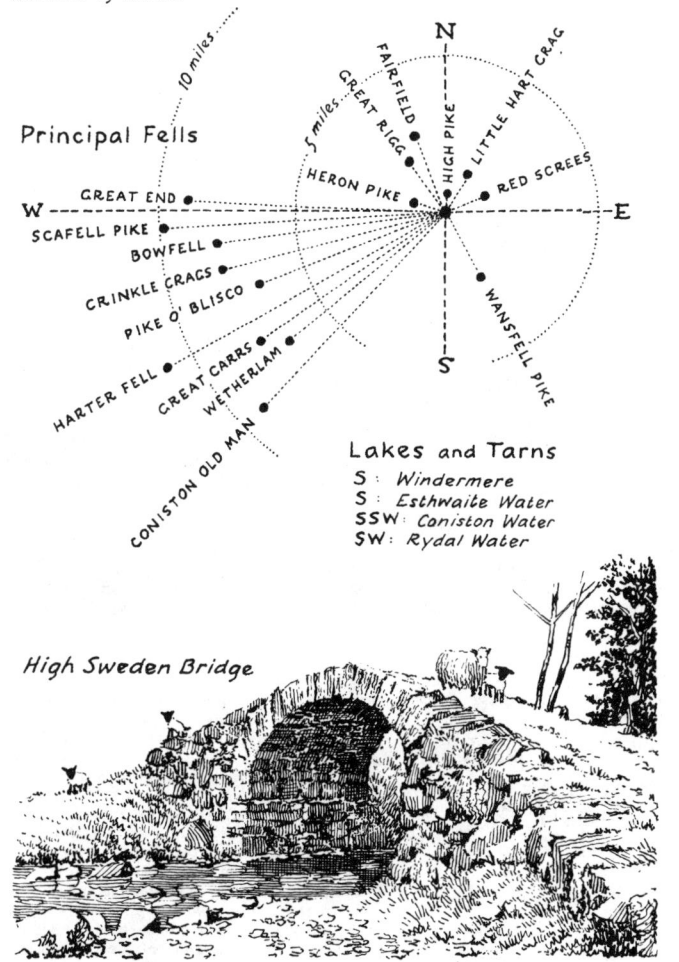

Principal Fells

- GREAT END
- SCAFELL PIKE
- BOWFELL
- CRINKLE CRAGS
- PIKE O' BLISCO
- HARTER FELL
- GREAT CARRS
- WETHERLAM
- CONISTON OLD MAN
- HERON PIKE
- GREAT RIGG
- FAIRFIELD
- HIGH PIKE
- LITTLE HART CRAG
- RED SCREES
- WANSFELL PIKE

10 miles
5 miles

Lakes and Tarns

S : *Windermere*
S : *Esthwaite Water*
SSW : *Coniston Water*
SW : *Rydal Water*

High Sweden Bridge

Middle Dodd 2106'

from Caiston Glen

To the traveller starting the long climb up to Kirkstone Pass from Brothers Water the most striking object in a fine array of mountain scenery is the steep pyramid ahead: it towers high above the road like a gigantic upturned boat, its keel touching the sky, its sides barnacled and hoary. This pyramid is Middle Dodd, the middle one of three dodds which rise from the pastures of Hartsop, all exhibiting the same characteristics. When seen from higher ground in the vicinity, however, Middle Dodd loses its regal appearance (as do the other two); its summit then is obviously nothing more than a halt in the long northern spur of Red Screes.

Middle Dodd 2

MAP

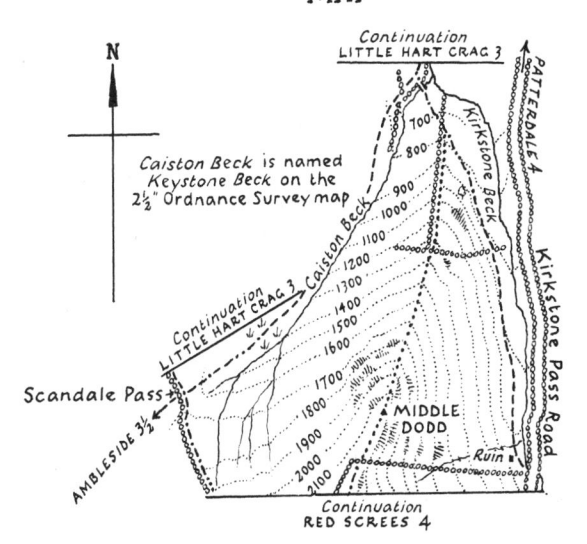

Caiston Beck is named Keystone Beck on the 2½" Ordnance Survey map

ONE MILE

ASCENT FROM HARTSOP HALL
1650 feet of ascent

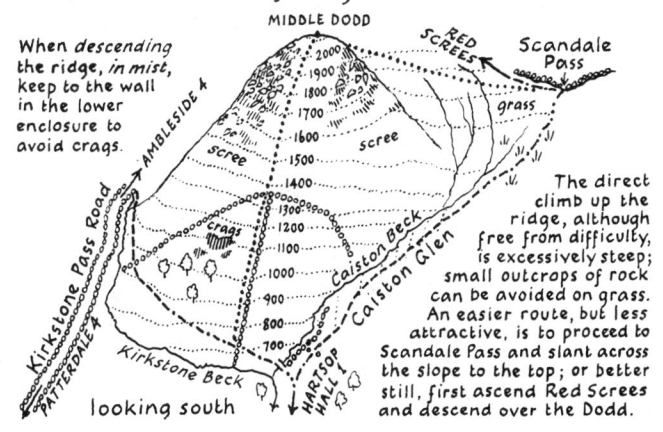

When *descending* the ridge, *in mist*, keep to the wall in the lower enclosure to avoid crags.

The direct climb up the ridge, although free from difficulty, is excessively steep; small outcrops of rock can be avoided on grass. An easier route, but less attractive, is to proceed to Scandale Pass and slant across the slope to the top; or better still, first ascend Red Screes and descend over the Dodd.

looking south

Middle Dodd 3

THE SUMMIT

HELVELLYN — DOVE CRAG — HART CRAG — St SUNDAY CRAG — LITTLE HART CRAG — HARTSOP ABOVE HOW

The top of Middle Dodd is a rather narrow grassy promenade. Its true altitude is slightly more than the 2106' attributed to it, for the ground immediately behind the rocky promontory which serves as the triangulation point rises gently to a knoll some twenty feet higher — here is the summit-cairn — before falling imperceptibly to the saddle linking Middle Dodd to Red Screes.

Near the cairn is a series of curious depressions like a line of sinkholes in limestone country, but as the rock here is volcanic the probability is that they are old earthworks; the detached boulders strewn about in them seem to suggest artificial excavation. Walkers who are neither archæologists nor geologists will see in the depressions only a refuge from the wind.

RED SCREES

Middle Dodd with Red Screes behind from High Hartsop Dodd

Middle Dodd 4

THE VIEW

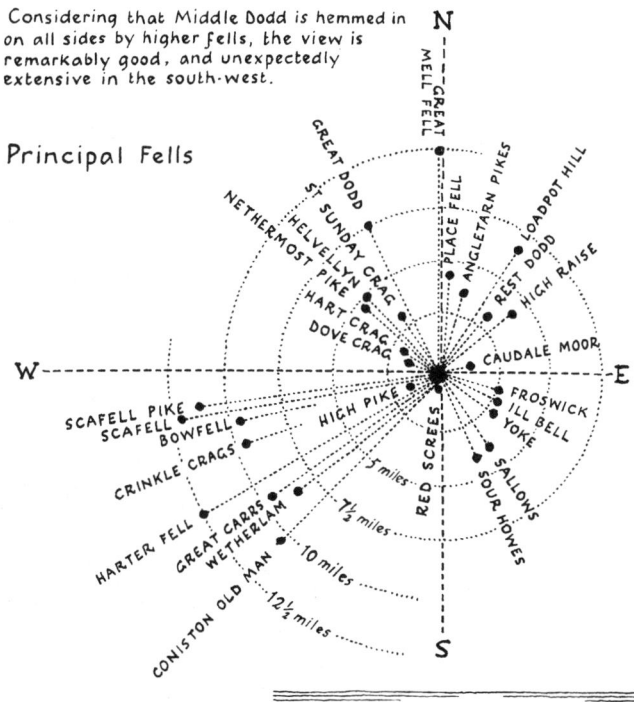

Considering that Middle Dodd is hemmed in on all sides by higher fells, the view is remarkably good, and unexpectedly extensive in the south-west.

Principal Fells

(compass diagram showing fells in directions from Middle Dodd)

- N: GREAT MELL FELL
- GREAT DODD
- ST SUNDAY CRAG
- HELVELLYN
- NETHERMOST PIKE
- HART CRAG
- DOVE CRAG
- PLACE FELL
- ANGLETARN PIKES
- REST DODD
- LOADPOT HILL
- HIGH RAISE
- CAUDALE MOOR
- FROSWICK
- ILL BELL
- YOKE
- SALLOWS
- SOUR HOWES
- RED SCREES
- HIGH PIKE
- SCAFELL PIKE
- SCAFELL
- BOWFELL
- CRINKLE CRAGS
- HARTER FELL
- GREAT CARRS
- WETHERLAM
- CONISTON OLD MAN

Distance rings: 5 miles, 7½ miles, 10 miles, 12½ miles

Lakes and Tarns

- N: *Ullswater*
- N: *Brothers Water*
- SW: *Greenburn Tarn*
  (below Great Carrs)

looking north

Nab Scar

1450' approx.

from Rydal Water

▲ FAIRFIELD
▲ GREAT RIGG
▲ STONE ARTHUR
▲ HERON PIKE
• Grasmere ▲ NAB SCAR
• Rydal

Ambleside •

MILES
0 1 2 3 4

Nab Scar 2

NATURAL FEATURES

Nab Scar is well known. Its associations with the Lake Poets who came to dwell at the foot of its steep wooded slopes have invested it with romance, and its commanding position overlooking Rydal Water brings it to the notice of the many visitors to that charming lake. It is a fine abrupt height, with a rough, craggy south face; on the flanks are easier slopes. Elevated ground continues beyond the summit and rises gently to Heron Pike. Nab Scar is not a separate fell, but is merely the butt of the long southern ridge of Fairfield.

MAP

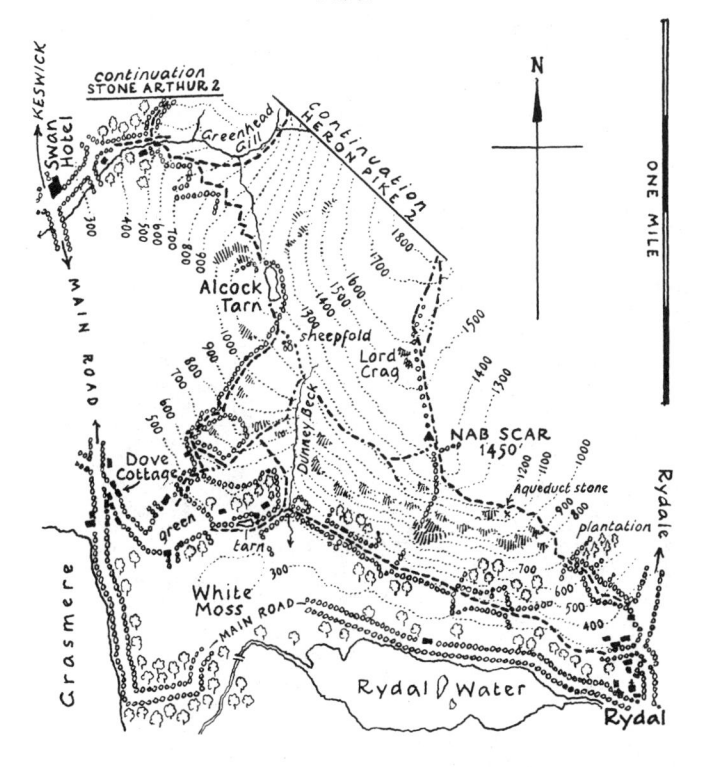

Nab Scar 3

ASCENTS

The popular ascent is from Rydal, a charming climb along a good path, steep in its middle reaches; this is the beginning of the 'Fairfield Horseshoe' when it is walked clockwise. The path from Grasmere is much less used and is not easy to trace in its later stages but this is of no consequence in clear weather.

THE SUMMIT

Strictly, Nab Scar is the name of the craggy south face, not of the fell rising above it, but its recognised summit is a tall edifice of stones built well back from the edge of the cliffs, near a crumbled wall that runs north towards Heron Pike. Hereabouts the immediate surroundings are uninteresting, the redeeming feature being the fine view.

Nab Scar has a subterranean watercourse: below its surface the Thirlmere aqueduct runs through a tunnel. The scars of this operation are nearly gone, but evidence of the existence of the tunnel remains alongside the Rydal path, above the steepest part: here may be found a block of stone a yard square set in the ground; it bears no inscription but marks the position of the tunnel directly beneath.

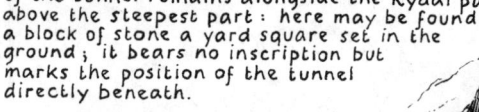

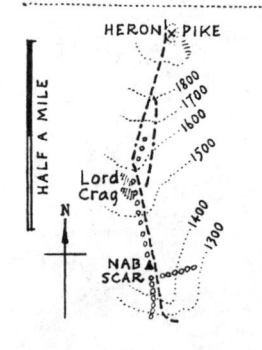

RIDGE ROUTE

TO HERON PIKE, 2003': ⅔ mile: N
570 feet of ascent
An easy climb on grass
A plain path accompanies the old wall. When it forks, either track may be taken

Nab Scar 4

THE VIEW

This is an 'unbalanced' view, most of it being exceptionally dull, the rest exceptionally charming. Lakes and tarns are a very special feature of the delightful prospect to south and west and the grouping of the Coniston and Langdale fells is quite attractive.

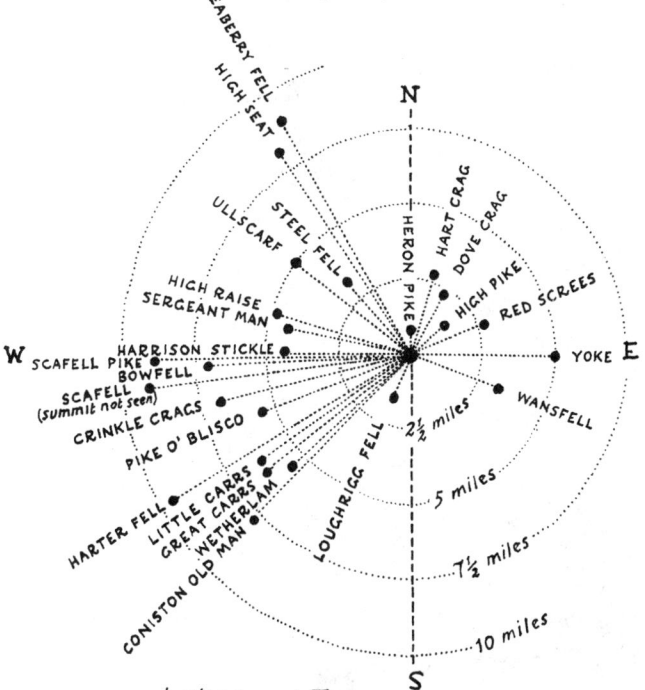

Principal Fells

- BLEABERRY FELL
- HIGH SEAT
- ULLSCARF
- STEEL FELL
- HART CRAG
- DOVE CRAG
- HIGH RAISE
- SERGEANT MAN
- HERON PIKE
- HIGH PIKE
- RED SCREES
- SCAFELL PIKE
- HARRISON STICKLE
- BOWFELL
- YOKE
- SCAFELL (summit not seen)
- WANSFELL
- CRINKLE CRAGS
- PIKE O' BLISCO
- HARTER FELL
- LITTLE CARRS
- GREAT CARRS
- WETHERLAM
- LOUGHRIGG FELL
- CONISTON OLD MAN

2½ miles, 5 miles, 7½ miles, 10 miles

Lakes and Tarns

- SSE : *Windermere*
- S : *Blelham Tarn*
- S : *Esthwaite Water*
- SSW : *Coniston Water*
- SW : *Elterwater*
- WSW : *Grasmere*
- WNW : *Easedale Tarn*
- NW : *Alcock Tarn*

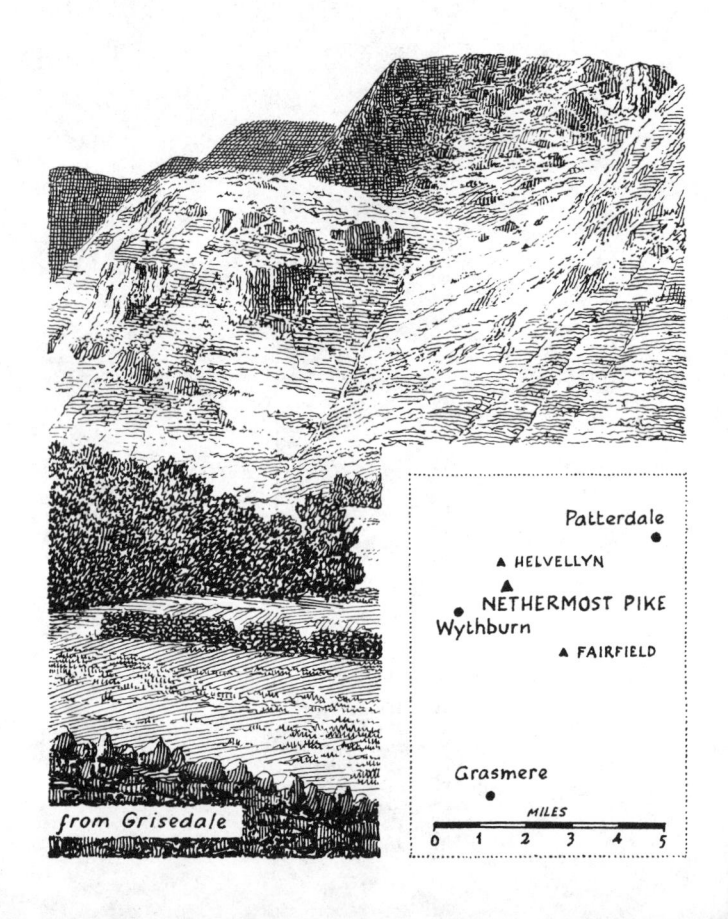

Nethermost Pike 2920'

from Grisedale

Patterdale
▲ HELVELLYN
▲ NETHERMOST PIKE
Wythburn
▲ FAIRFIELD

Grasmere

MILES
0 1 2 3 4 5

Nethermost Pike 2

NATURAL FEATURES

Thousands of people cross the flat top of Nethermost Pike every year, and thousands more toil up its western slope. Yet their diaries record "climbed Helvellyn today." For Helvellyn is the great magnet that draws the crowds to Nethermost Pike: the latter is climbed incidentally, almost unknowingly, only because it is an obstacle in the route to its bigger neighbour. The grassy west slope trodden by the multitudes is of little interest, but the fell should not be judged accordingly: it is made of sterner stuff. From the east, Nethermost Pike is magnificent, hardly less so than Helvellyn and seeming more so because of its impressive surroundings. On this side a narrow rocky ridge bounded by forbidding crags falls steeply between twin hollows, deeply recessed, in a wild and lonely setting; here is solitude, for here few men walk. Here, too, is a gem of a tarn.

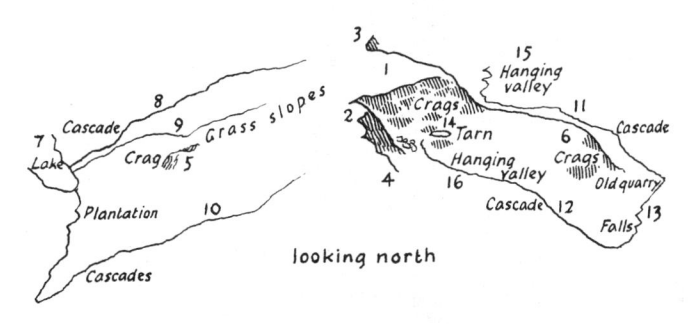

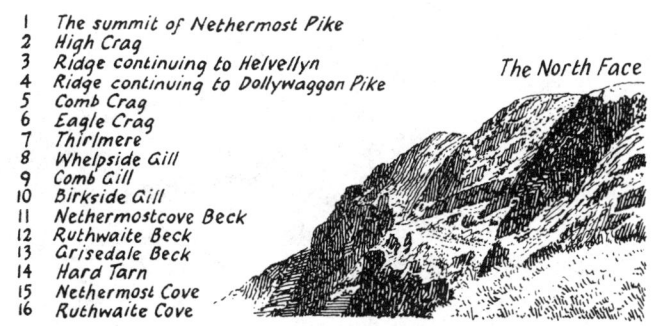

looking north

1 The summit of Nethermost Pike
2 High Crag
3 Ridge continuing to Helvellyn
4 Ridge continuing to Dollywaggon Pike
5 Comb Crag
6 Eagle Crag
7 Thirlmere
8 Whelpside Gill
9 Comb Gill
10 Birkside Gill
11 Nethermostcove Beck
12 Ruthwaite Beck
13 Grisedale Beck
14 Hard Tarn
15 Nethermost Cove
16 Ruthwaite Cove

The North Face

Nethermost Pike 3

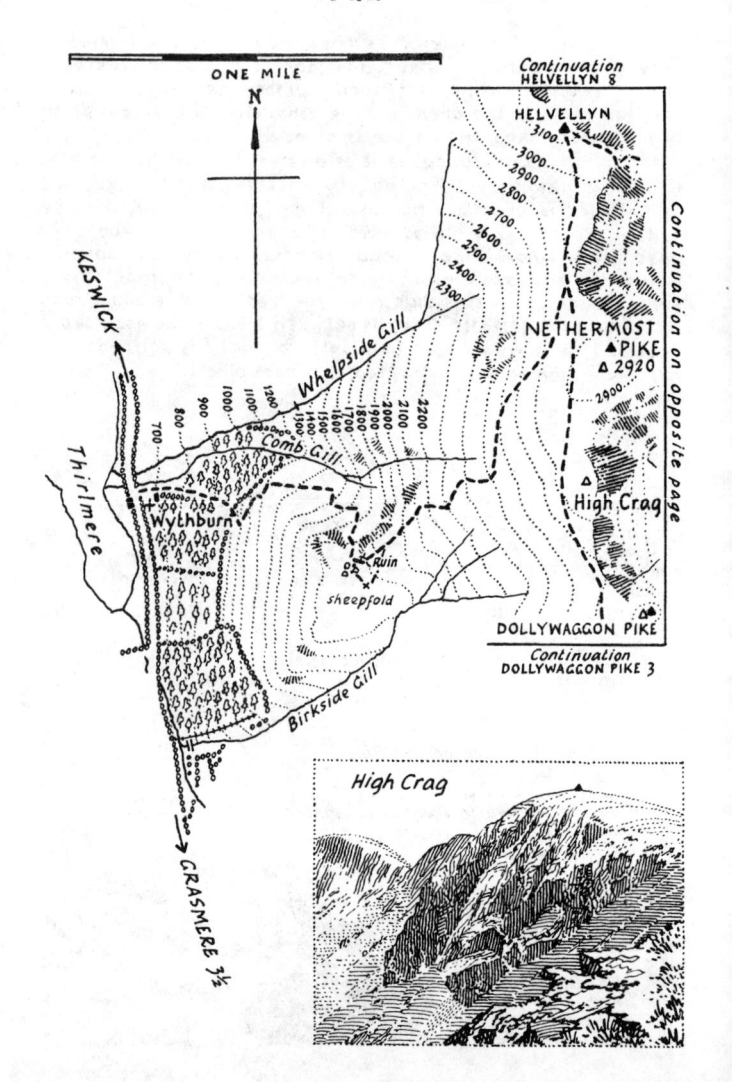

MAP

Nethermost Pike 4

MAP

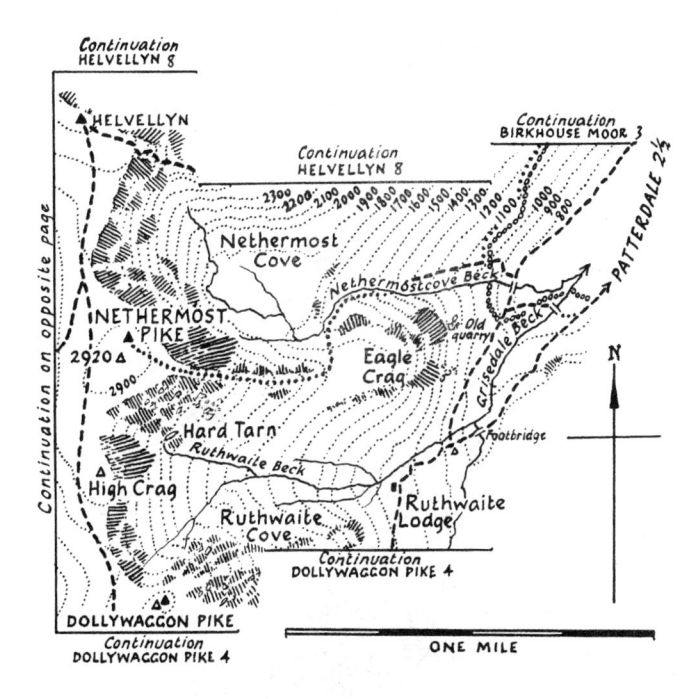

Hard Tarn

Nethermost Pike 5

ASCENT FROM WYTHBURN
2400 feet of ascent : 2 miles

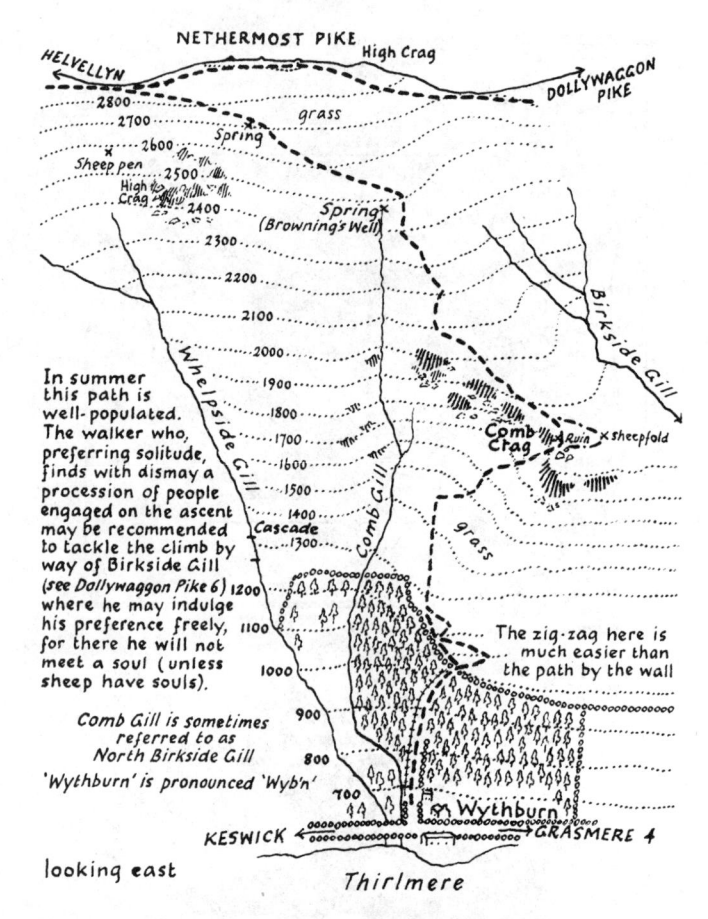

looking east

In summer this path is well-populated. The walker who, preferring solitude, finds with dismay a procession of people engaged on the ascent may be recommended to tackle the climb by way of Birkside Gill (see *Dollywaggon Pike 6*) where he may indulge his preference freely, for there he will not meet a soul (unless sheep have souls).

Comb Gill is sometimes referred to as North Birkside Gill

'Wythburn' is pronounced 'Wyb'n'

The zig-zag here is much easier than the path by the wall

The popular path to Helvellyn from Wythburn climbs steeply up the side of Nethermost Pike, almost reaching its summit before turning off to the higher fell: the top is attained by a short detour. The path is very distinct.

Nethermost Pike 6

ASCENT FROM GRISEDALE
2500 feet of ascent: 5 miles from Patterdale village

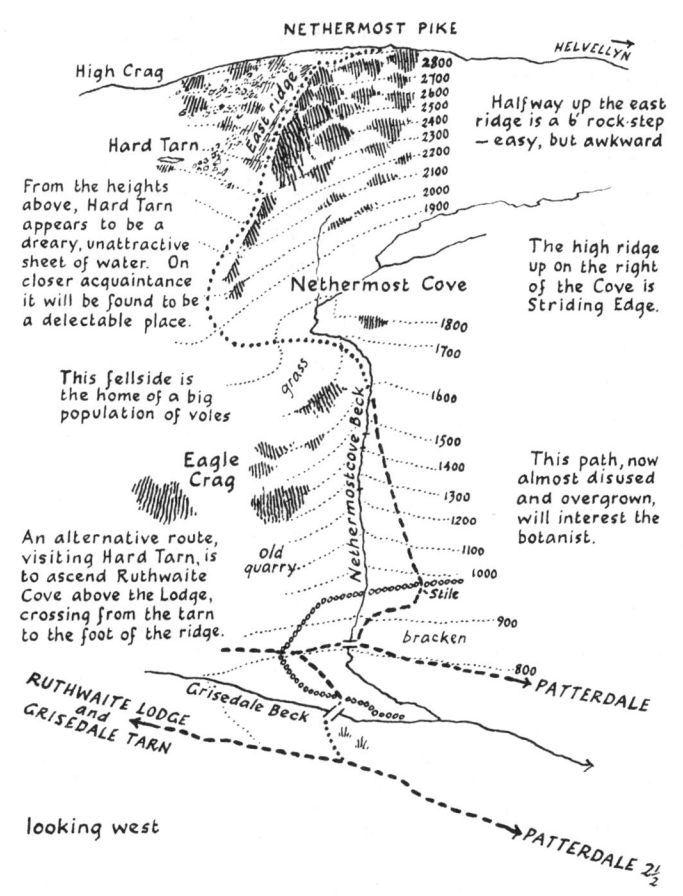

NETHERMOST PIKE — HELVELLYN

High Crag

Hard Tarn

Halfway up the east ridge is a 6' rock step — easy, but awkward

From the heights above, Hard Tarn appears to be a dreary, unattractive sheet of water. On closer acquaintance it will be found to be a delectable place.

Nethermost Cove

The high ridge up on the right of the Cove is Striding Edge.

This fellside is the home of a big population of voles

Eagle Crag

Nethermostcove Beck

This path, now almost disused and overgrown, will interest the botanist.

An alternative route, visiting Hard Tarn, is to ascend Ruthwaite Cove above the Lodge, crossing from the tarn to the foot of the ridge.

old quarry

Stile

bracken

RUTHWAITE LODGE and GRISEDALE TARN

Grisedale Beck

PATTERDALE

looking west

PATTERDALE 2½

This is a first-class route for scramblers, but staid walkers should avoid it and proceed via Grisedale Tarn. The east ridge is steep and exciting, finishing with an arête like a miniature Striding Edge. *This route should not be attempted in bad weather conditions.*

Nethermost Pike 7

THE SUMMIT

The summit is of considerable extent and so remarkably flat that it is not easy to understand why the name 'Pike' was given to the fell (the top of the east ridge, however, has the appearance of a peak when seen from mid-Grisedale). It is mainly grassy — a field on top of a mountain — with thin flakes of rock around the cairn.

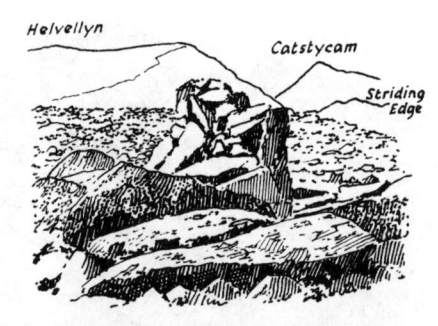

The broad top is level, and it is difficult to locate the highest point exactly, but the cairn illustrated appears to be slightly higher than the small ruined circular wall 100 yards southwest, which has evidences of the former boundary fence and is often regarded as the top of the fell.

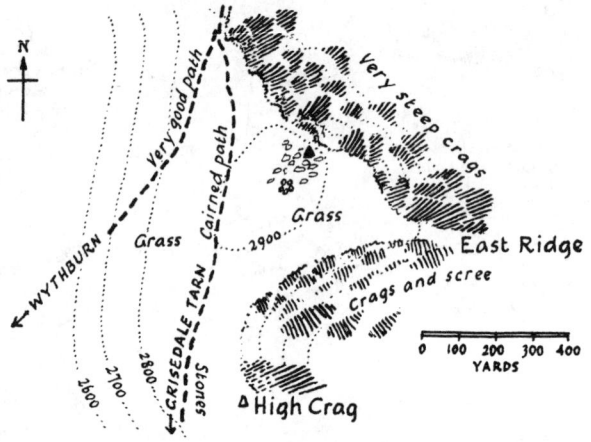

DESCENTS: A cairned path crosses the top but does not visit the actual summit. This path may be followed south to Grisedale Tarn for Grasmere or Patterdale. For Wythburn, cross this path to another running lower along the fellside. The east ridge is a quick way down to Patterdale, but is for experienced walkers only.

In bad weather conditions, leave the summit by one of the two paths mentioned: these are quite safe — the east ridge is not.

Nethermost Pike 8

RIDGE ROUTES

To HELVELLYN, 3118' : ¾ mile : NW then N.

Depression at 2840' : 280 feet of ascent

An easy walk on a broad path, safe in mist.

The path west of the cairn on Nethermost Pike continues north to Helvellyn, developing into a wide uninteresting highway. It is far better, in clear weather, to avoid the path and follow the edge of the cliffs, the views of Nethermost Cove and Striding Edge being very impressive.

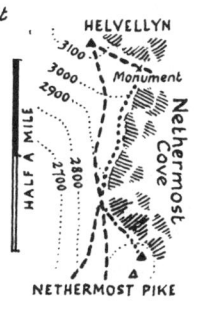

To DOLLYWAGGON PIKE, 2810' 1 mile : S then SE

Depression at 2700' : 120 feet of ascent

A very easy walk, safe in mist

The path west of the cairn on Nethermost Pike continues south, skirting High Crag. It crosses the breast of Dollywaggon Pike, the summit of which is gained by a short detour. (An inexperienced walker should not attempt the detour in mist). A more interesting route, in clear weather, is to follow the edge of the cliffs overlooking Hard Tarn and Ruthwaite Cove, the rock-scenery being impressive.

Cascades in Birkside Gill

Nethermost Pike 9

THE VIEW

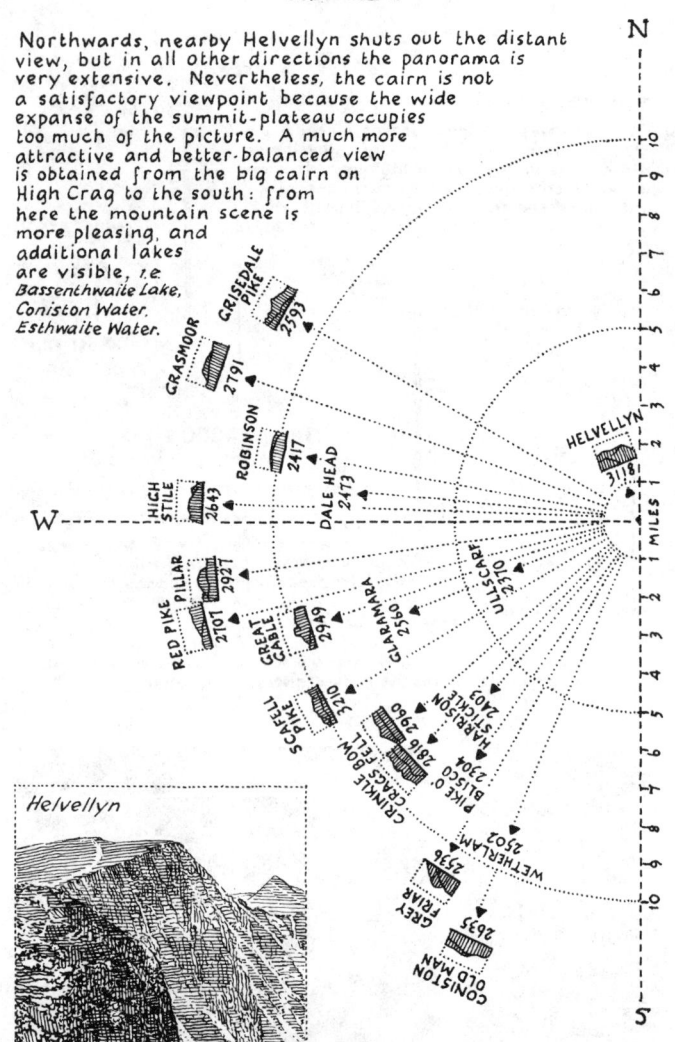

Northwards, nearby Helvellyn shuts out the distant view, but in all other directions the panorama is very extensive. Nevertheless, the cairn is not a satisfactory viewpoint because the wide expanse of the summit-plateau occupies too much of the picture. A much more attractive and better-balanced view is obtained from the big cairn on High Crag to the south: from here the mountain scene is more pleasing, and additional lakes are visible, i.e. *Bassenthwaite Lake, Coniston Water, Esthwaite Water.*

GRISEDALE PIKE 2593
GRASMOOR 2791
ROBINSON 2417
HIGH STILE 2643
DALE HEAD 2473
HELVELLYN 3118
RED PIKE 2707
PILLAR 2927
GREAT GABLE 2949
GLARAMARA 2560
ULLSCARF 2370
SCAFELL PIKE 3210
CRINKLE CRAGS 2816
BOWFELL 2960
PIKE O' BLISCO 2304
HARRISON STICKLE 2403
WETHERLAM 2502
GREY FRIAR 2536
CONISTON OLD MAN 2635

Helvellyn

Nethermost Pike 10

THE VIEW

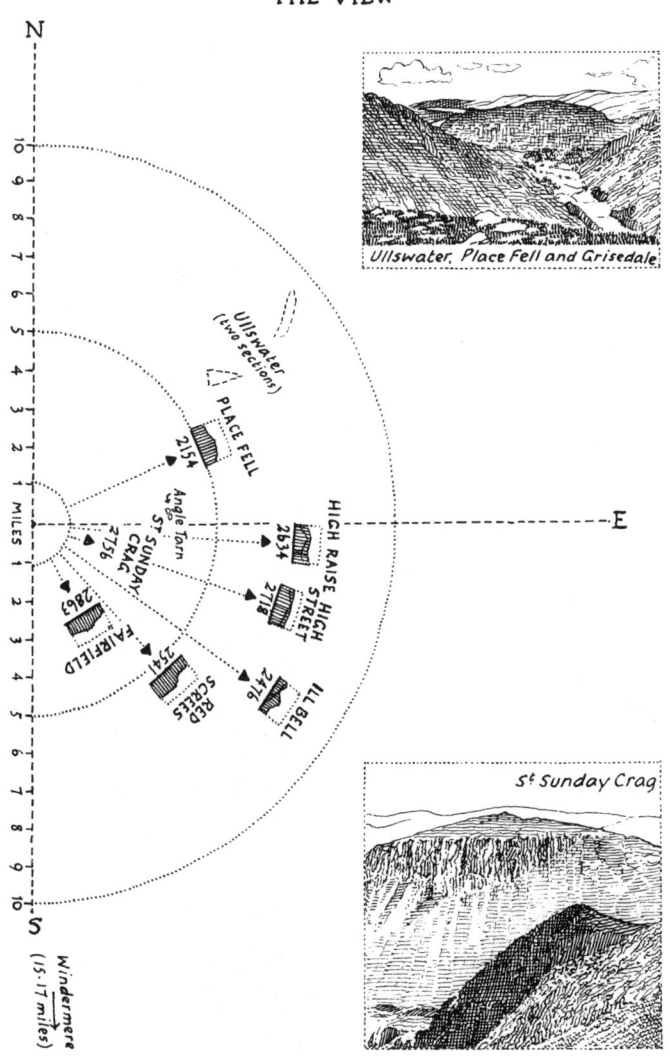

Ullswater, Place Fell and Grisedale

St Sunday Crag

N — 10,9,8,7,6,5,4,3,2,1 MILES

Ullswater (two sections)

PLACE FELL 2154

Angle Tarn

ST SUNDAY CRAG 2756

HIGH RAISE 2634

HIGH STREET 2718

FAIRFIELD 2863

RED SCREES 2541

ILL BELL 2476

S — 10,9,8,7,6,5,4,3,2,1

Windermere (15-17 miles)

E

Raise 2889'

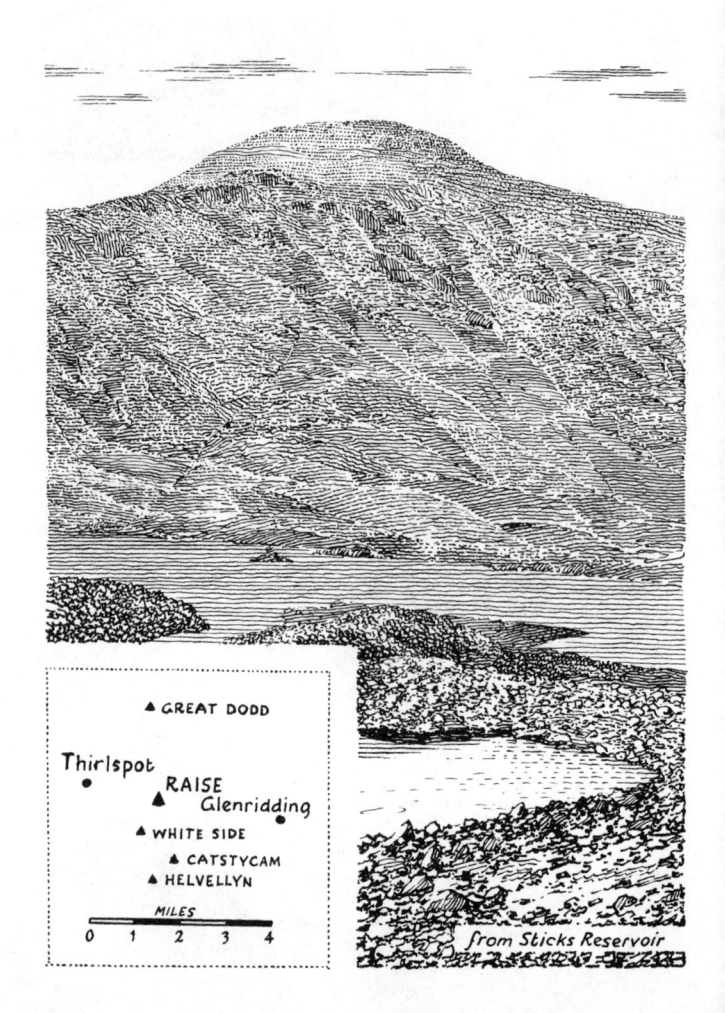

▲ GREAT DODD

Thirlspot
●
RAISE ▲ Glenridding
▲ WHITE SIDE
▲ CATSTYCAM
▲ HELVELLYN

MILES
0 1 2 3 4

from Sticks Reservoir

Raise 2

NATURAL FEATURES

Raise deserves a special cheer. It is the only summit in the Helvellyn range adorned with a crown of rough rocks — and they make a welcome change from the dull monotony of the green expanses around Sticks Pass. But in general the fell conforms to the usual Helvellyn pattern, the western slopes being grassy and the eastern slopes more scarred. It further differs from its fellows on the main ridge, however, in that its western slopes do not reach down to the valley: they are sandwiched between the more extensive, sprawling flanks of Stybarrow Dodd and White Side and are crowded out completely at the 1600' contour.

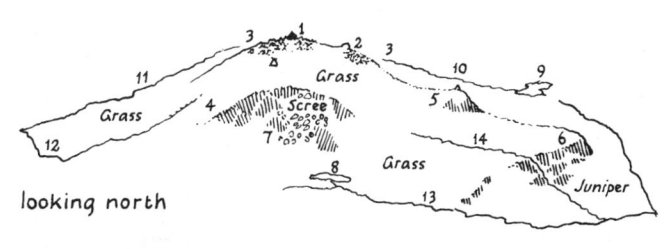

looking north

1 : The summit
2 : Rock tor
3 : Sticks Pass
4 : Ridge continuing to White Side
5 : Stang
6 : Stang End
7 : Keppel Cove
8 : Keppelcove Tarn (dry)
9 : Sticks Reservoir
10 : Sticks Gill (East)
11 : Sticks Gill (West)
12 : Brund Gill
13 : Glenridding Beck
14 : Rowten Beck

The Rock Tor

This small outcrop rises from a slope of lichened scree. It is not remarkable in itself, but stands out so prominently that it forms a ready means of identifying Raise in all views where the east slope is seen in profile.

Raise 3

MAP

ONE MILE

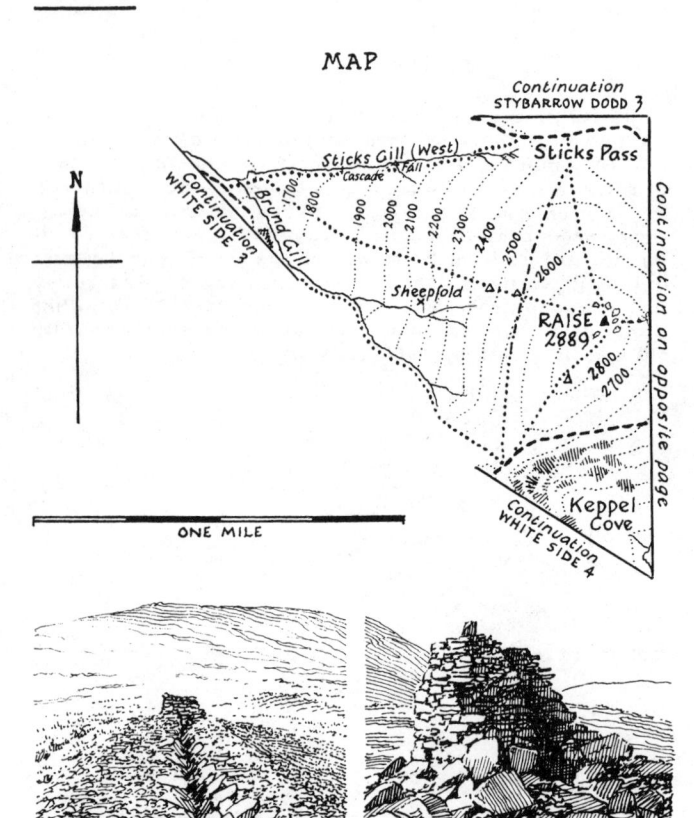

The lower eastern slopes of Raise are pock-marked with the scars of industry. The illustrations above show the now-disused and derelict chimney and stone aqueduct which formerly served the Glenridding lead mine. Only a small portion of the aqueduct remains intact (see picture on left) but it is sufficient to indicate the skill of the masons who built it and to make one envy their pride in the job, and be glad they are not here to see the ruins.

Raise 4

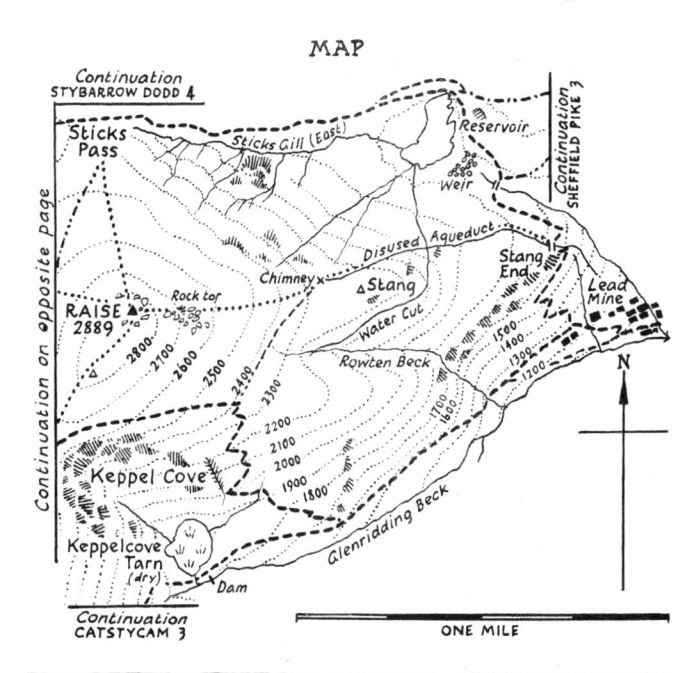

MAP

Glenridding and Ullswater, from Stang End

Raise 5

ASCENTS FROM STANAH AND THIRLSPOT
2400 feet of ascent : 2½ miles

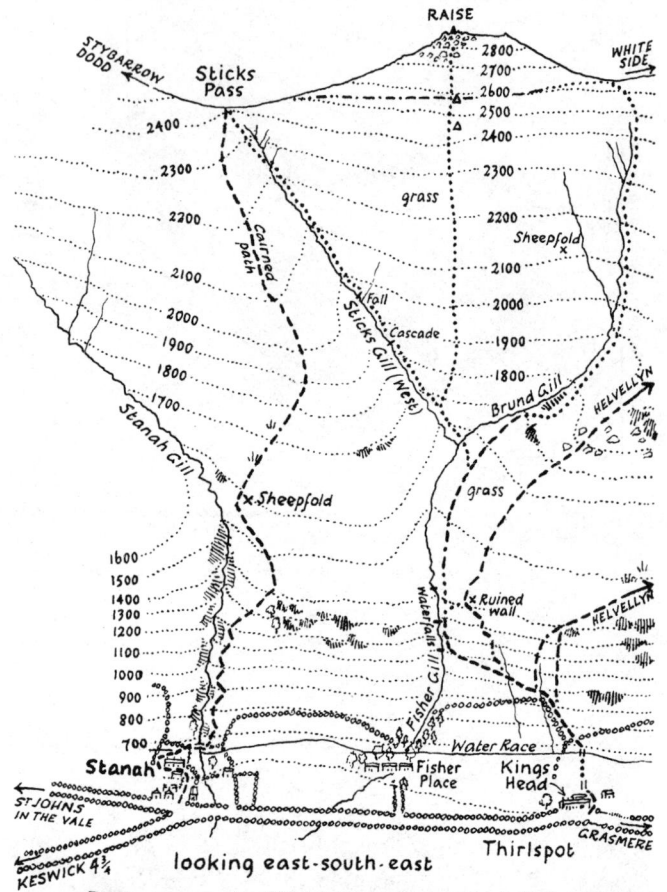

looking east-south-east

Raise overlooks Sticks Pass, from which it is climbed very easily; the path from Stanah to the top of the pass is therefore a convenient route of ascent. Routes from Thirlspot are more direct but lack paths much of the way. All the western approaches are grassy and rather dull.

Raise 6

ASCENT FROM GLENRIDDING
2500 feet of ascent : 4 miles from Glenridding village

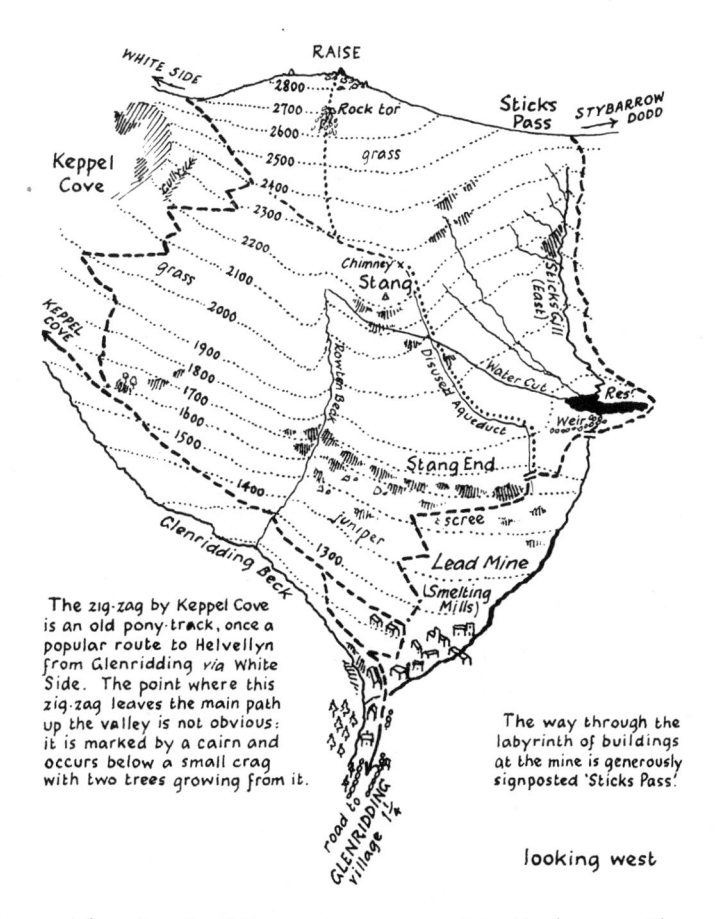

The zig-zag by Keppel Cove is an old pony-track, once a popular route to Helvellyn from Glenridding via White Side. The point where this zig-zag leaves the main path up the valley is not obvious: it is marked by a cairn and occurs below a small crag with two trees growing from it.

The way through the labyrinth of buildings at the mine is generously signposted 'Sticks Pass!'

looking west

All routes from the east are marred by the inescapable evidences of the lead mine. The Keppel Cove route is easy, and gives impressive views of Catstycam. The approach by Sticks Pass is dull, that by the old aqueduct rather better.

Raise 7

THE SUMMIT

The summit is a level grassy plateau, capped at its higher end by an outcrop of very rough gnarled stones. Alongside the main cairn is an iron estate-boundary post. Smaller cairns on nearby rocks indicate other viewpoints. There are no paths.

DESCENTS: In good weather all routes of ascent are suitable also for descent. The quickest way to Thirlspot is down the western slope, joining a path by Fisher Gill. For Glenridding, the route by the old aqueduct is quickest; if the zig-zag by Keppel Cove is preferred, a big corner may be saved initially by descending to it south-east from the summit.
In bad conditions, head for the *top of Sticks Pass*, north, whatever the destination.
In mist, note that the boundary post is on the south-west side of the cairn.

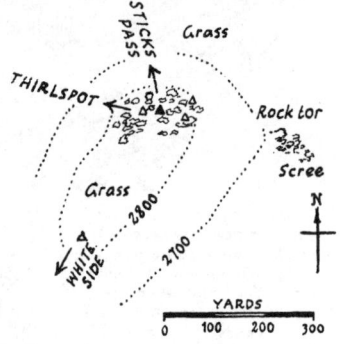

The summit of Stang

Raise 8

RIDGE ROUTES

To STYBARROW DODD, 2770' : 1 mile : N, then NE
Depression at 2420' (Sticks Pass)
350 feet of ascent

Grass all the way after initial stones. Easy.
No path, but safe in mist.

Cross Sticks Pass at its highest point, by a small tarn, and continue up the steepening slope opposite. The boundary stone reached first is usually accepted as the top of the Dodd, but there is higher ground beyond.

To WHITE SIDE, 2832' : ¾ mile : SW
Depression at 2650'. 200 feet of ascent.

Easy walking on grass. No path to the depression but safe in mist.

Cross the summit-plateau to the south-west cairn and descend therefrom to the good path coming up on the left: it climbs easily to the top of White Side.

This slope is a favourite with skiers and, on snowy winter days, presents an animated scene: a ski-lift operates.

Raise from Sticks Pass

Raise 9

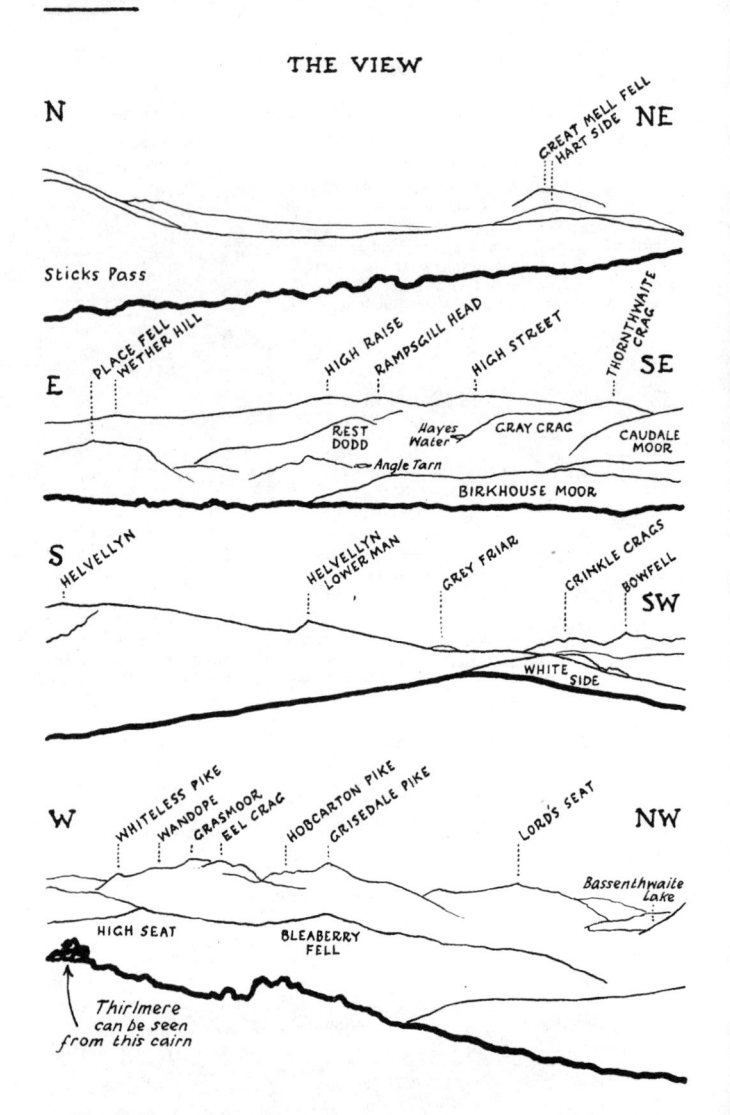

THE VIEW

N — NE
- GREAT MELL FELL
- HART SIDE

Sticks Pass

E — SE
- PLACE FELL
- WETHER HILL
- HIGH RAISE
- RAMPSGILL HEAD
- HIGH STREET
- THORNTHWAITE CRAG
- REST DODD
- Hayes Water
- Angle Tarn
- CRAY CRAG
- CAUDALE MOOR
- BIRKHOUSE MOOR

S — SW
- HELVELLYN
- HELVELLYN LOWER MAN
- GREY FRIAR
- CRINKLE CRAGS
- BOWFELL
- WHITE SIDE

W — NW
- WHITELESS PIKE
- WANDOPE
- GRASMOOR
- EEL CRAG
- HOBCARTON PIKE
- GRISEDALE PIKE
- LORD'S SEAT
- Bassenthwaite Lake
- HIGH SEAT
- BLEABERRY FELL

Thirlmere can be seen from this cairn

Raise 10

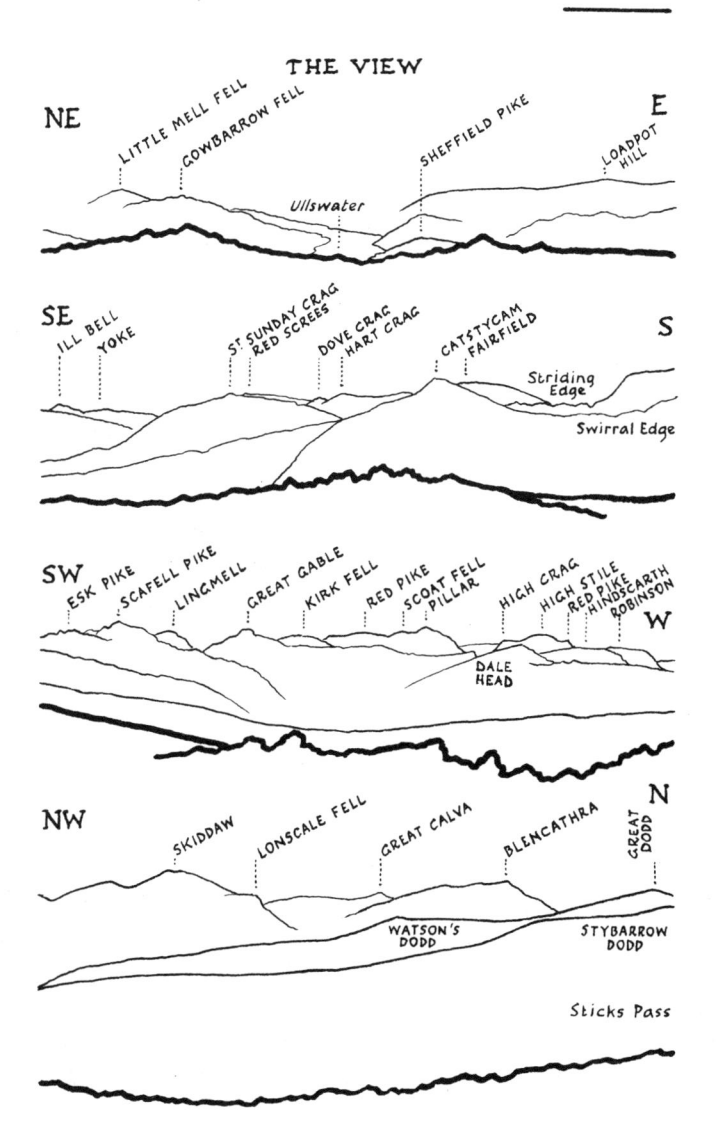

THE VIEW

NE — LITTLE MELL FELL, COWBARROW FELL, Ullswater, SHEFFIELD PIKE, LOADPOT HILL — **E**

SE — ILL BELL, YOKE, ST SUNDAY CRAG, RED SCREES, DOVE CRAG, HART CRAG, CATSTYCAM, FAIRFIELD, Striding Edge, Swirral Edge — **S**

SW — ESK PIKE, SCAFELL PIKE, LINGMELL, GREAT GABLE, KIRK FELL, RED PIKE, SCOAT FELL, PILLAR, DALE HEAD, HIGH CRAG, HIGH STILE, RED PIKE, HINDSCARTH, ROBINSON — **W**

NW — SKIDDAW, LONSCALE FELL, GREAT CALVA, BLENCATHRA, GREAT DODD, WATSON'S DODD, STYBARROW DODD — **N**

Sticks Pass

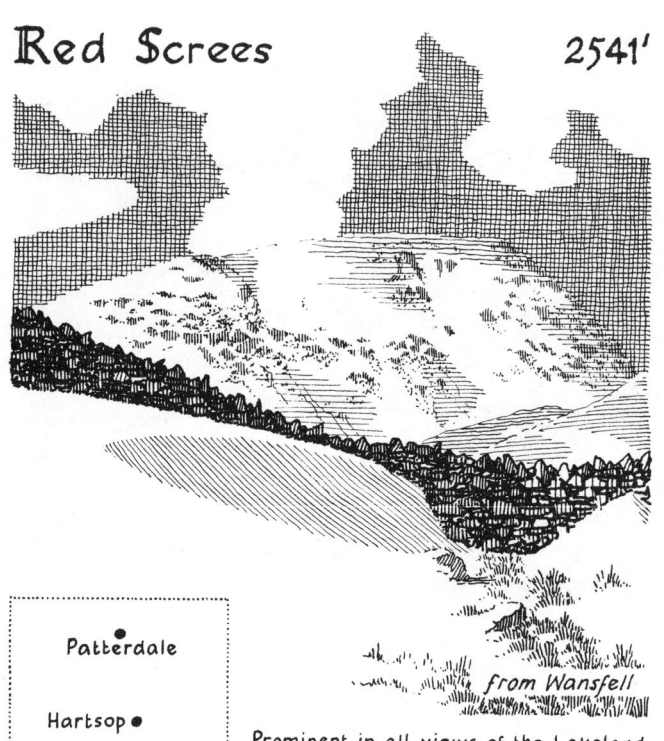

Red Screes 2541'

from Wansfell

- Patterdale
- Hartsop
- ▲ DOVE CRAG
- ▲ RED SCREES
- ● Ambleside

MILES
0 1 2 3

Prominent in all views of the Lakeland fells from the lesser heights of South Westmorland is the high whale-backed mass of Red Screes, rising in a graceful curve from the head of Windermere and descending abruptly at its northern end. Some maps append the name 'Kilnshaw Chimney' to the summit, but Red Screes is its name by popular choice — and Red Screes it should be because of the colour and character of its eastern face. It is a friendly accommodating hill, holding no terrors for those who climb to its summit by the usual easy routes and being very conveniently situated for sojourners at Ambleside; moreover, it offers a reward of excellent views.

Red Screes 2

NATURAL FEATURES

All travellers along the Kirkstone Pass are familiar with Red Screes, for it is the biggest thing to be seen there: for four miles it forms the western wall of the pass. In general structure it is a long broad ridge of considerable bulk. The southern slopes are at an easy gradient, with rock outcrops in abundance and a quarry which produces beautiful green stone; in places the rough ground steepens into crags. The shorter north ridge, after a gradual descent to the lesser height of Middle Dodd, plunges steeply to the fields of High Hartsop. The western slopes are of no particular interest and the pride of Red Screes is undoubtedly its eastern face, where natural forces have eroded two combes which carve deeply into the mountain on both flanks of a wide buttress: runs of fine red scree pour down these hollows. This side of the fell has many crags and tumbled boulders, one of which gave the pass its name; high up is Kilnshaw Chimney, which is hardly as significant as the maps would imply, being only a narrow gully choked with scree.

Red Screes, although in the midst of high country, contrives to appear more isolated from its fellows than any other of the eastern fells. It is independent and is unsupported, not buttressed by its neighbours: to this extent, it may be said to have the purest mountain form among the eastern fells.

Of the many streams which have their birth on Red Screes, the best-known is Stock Ghyll, flowing south and breaking in lovely waterfalls on its way to join the Rothay; on the west, innumerable watercourses feed Scandale Beck; northwards, Kirkstone Beck and Caiston Beck carry its waters to Ullswater.

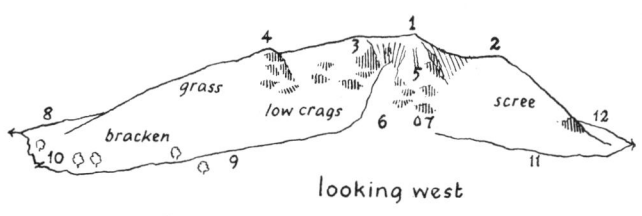

looking west

1: The summit
2: Middle Dodd
3: Raven Crag
4: Snarker Pike
5: Kilnshaw Chimney
6: Kirkstone Pass
7: The Kirk Stone
8: Scandale Beck
9: Stock Ghyll
10: Stock Ghyll Force
11: Kirkstone Beck
12: Caiston Beck

Red Screes 3

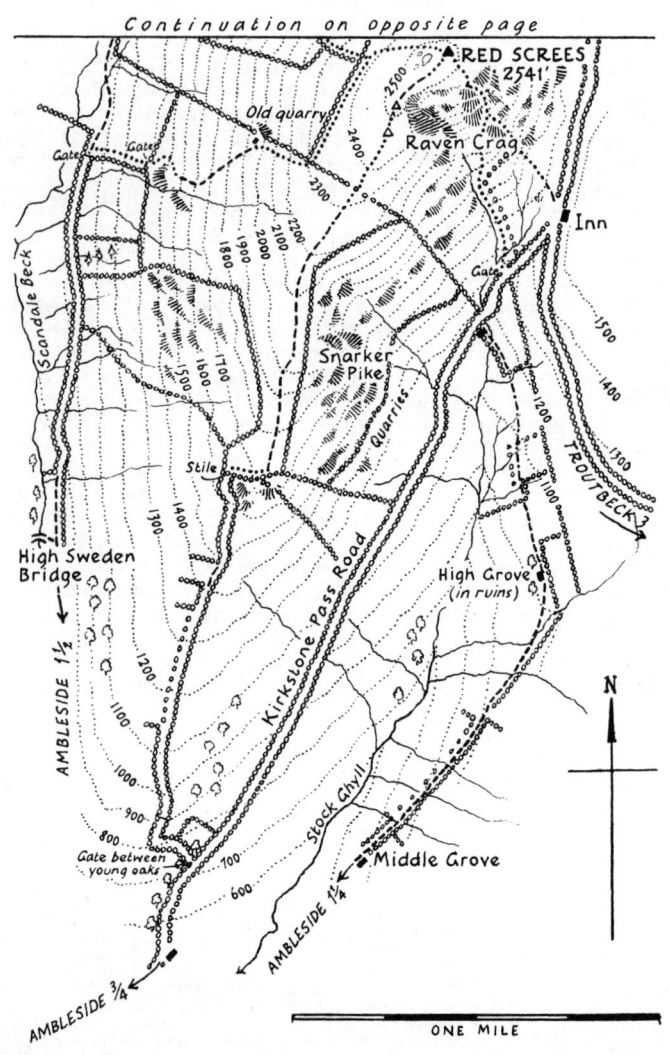

MAP

Continuation on opposite page

Red Screes 4

MAP

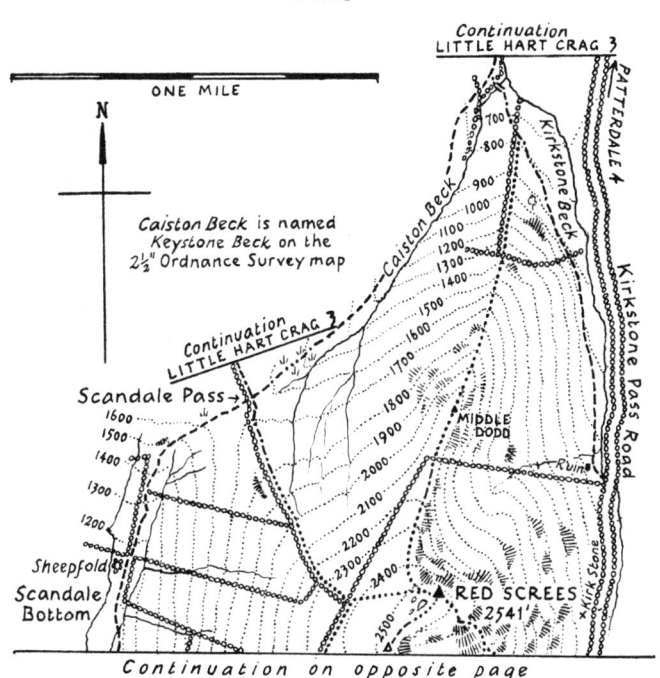

Caiston Beck is named Keystone Beck on the 2½" Ordnance Survey map

Continuation LITTLE HART CRAG 3

PATTERDALE 4

Kirkstone Beck

Caiston Beck

Continuation LITTLE HART CRAG 3

Scandale Pass →

MIDDLE DODD

Ruin

Kirk Sc...

Kirkstone Pass Road

Sheepfold
Scandale Bottom

▲ RED SCREES 2541

Continuation on opposite page

The Kirk Stone

This fallen boulder stands about sixty yards to the left (west) of the road at the top of the steep descent to the north. It is a prominent object on the way up the pass from Brothers Water, having the appearance of a ridged church-tower.

But the 2½" Ordnance Survey map suggests that the Kirk Stone is on the opposite side of the road: there are certainly many larger boulders here but none resembling a church.

Red Screes 5

ASCENT FROM AMBLESIDE
2400 feet of ascent : 4 or 5 miles

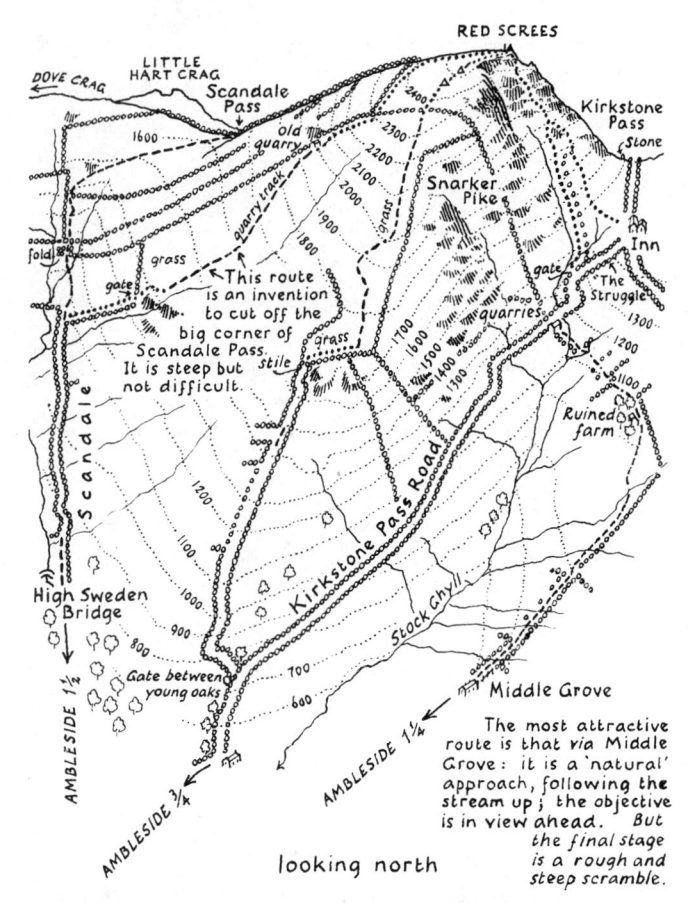

This route is an invention to cut off the big corner of Scandale Pass. It is steep but not difficult.

looking north

The most attractive route is that via Middle Grove: it is a 'natural' approach, following the stream up; the objective is in view ahead. But the final stage is a rough and steep scramble.

Of the routes shown, two only are commonly in use: the direct ridge route (which is better in descending) and the longer Scandale Pass route (the safest in bad weather). The best 'round tour' is to ascend by Middle Grove and return by descending the ridge.

Red Screes 6

ASCENT FROM PATTERDALE
2200 feet of ascent : 6½ miles from Patterdale village

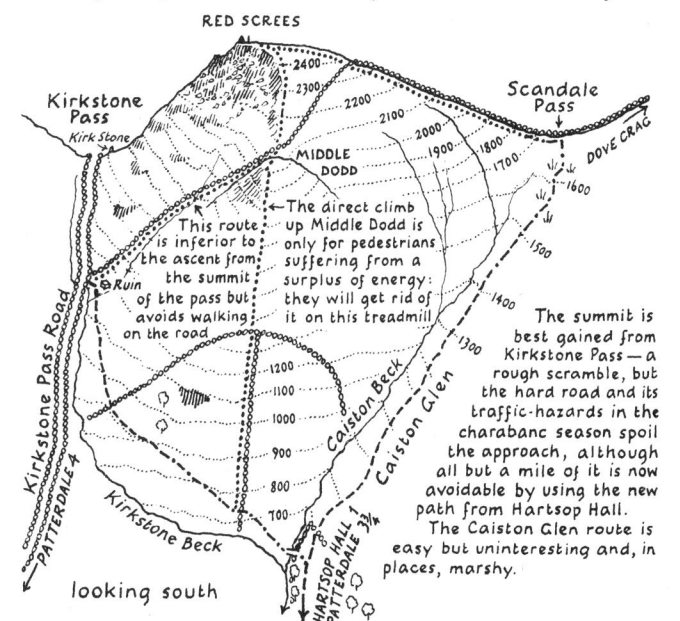

RED SCREES

Kirkstone Pass
Kirk Stone

Scandale Pass

DOVE CRAG

MIDDLE DODD

This route is inferior to the ascent from the summit of the pass but avoids walking on the road

← The direct climb up Middle Dodd is only for pedestrians suffering from a surplus of energy: they will get rid of it on this treadmill

Ruin

Kirkstone Pass Road

PATTERDALE 4

Kirkstone Beck

Caiston Beck

Caiston Glen

The summit is best gained from Kirkstone Pass — a rough scramble, but the hard road and its traffic-hazards in the charabanc season spoil the approach, although all but a mile of it is now avoidable by using the new path from Hartsop Hall.
The Caiston Glen route is easy but uninteresting and, in places, marshy.

looking south

HARTSOP HALL
PATTERDALE 3½

The approach from Patterdale is very fine, but a little road-walking, both going and returning, robs the journey of some of its charm; alternatives along the valley can be found, however. The popular route is by Caiston Glen.

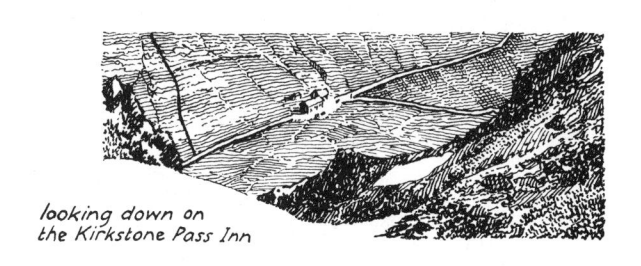

looking down on the Kirkstone Pass Inn

Red Screes 7

THE SUMMIT

The summit is a large grassy plateau, having three principal cairns widely spaced and differing little in altitude. There is no mistaking the highest, a huge mound of stones situated at the extreme corner of the plateau: a dramatic site, for here the ground seems to collapse at one's feet and plunge steeply down to the winding road far below. An Ordnance Survey column stands alongside, and twenty yards west is a small tarn with a few satellite ponds nearby. Below and east of the highest cairn is a prominent cluster of rocks worth visiting: it is a good vantage point and a pleasant place to eat sandwiches if the top is crowded, but it is well to tread cautiously here: beware crag!

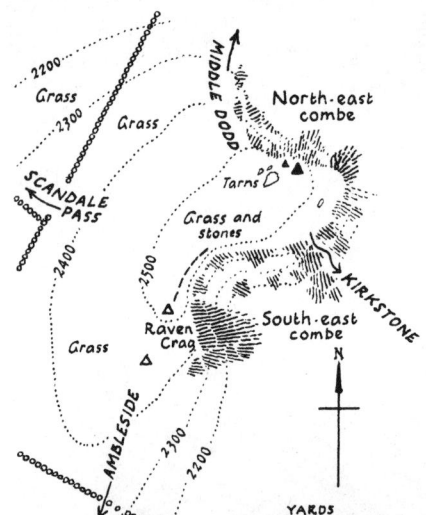

DESCENTS: The best way down to Ambleside is by the south ridge — it is so easy a saunter that the hands need be taken from the pockets only once, to negotiate a stile. Also easy, but longer, is the Scandale Pass route. The direct descent to Kirkstone is rough, too rough to be enjoyable.

For Patterdale, the way over Middle Dodd is excellent, but steep. The Caiston Glen path is easy, but descents to Kirkstone are not recommended, except for the *very* thirsty.

In bad weather, the safest course of all is to aim for the top of Scandale Pass — for either Ambleside or Patterdale.

Red Screes 8

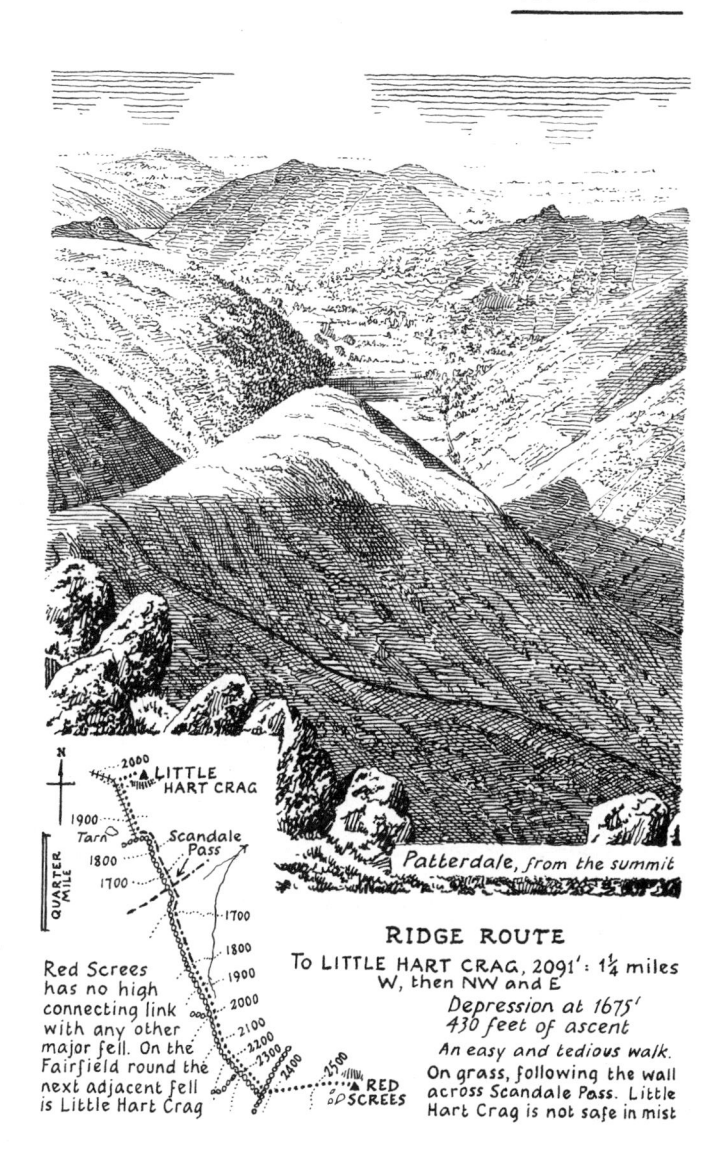

Patterdale, from the summit

RIDGE ROUTE
To LITTLE HART CRAG, 2091': 1¼ miles
W, then NW and E

Depression at 1675'
430 feet of ascent

*An easy and tedious walk.
On grass, following the wall
across Scandale Pass. Little
Hart Crag is not safe in mist*

Red Screes has no high connecting link with any other major fell. On the Fairfield round the next adjacent fell is Little Hart Crag

Red Screes 9

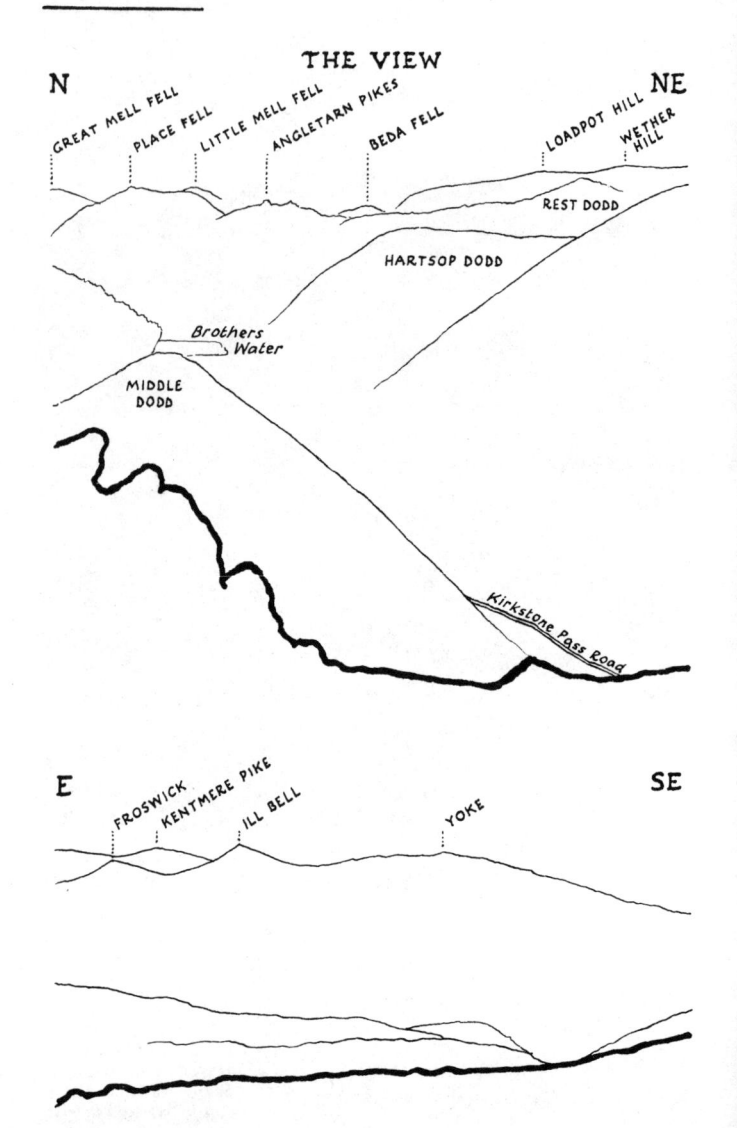

THE VIEW

N — Great Mell Fell, Place Fell, Little Mell Fell, Angletarn Pikes, Beda Fell, Loadpot Hill, Wether Hill — NE

Rest Dodd
Hartsop Dodd
Brothers Water
Middle Dodd
Kirkstone Pass Road

E — Froswick, Kentmere Pike, Ill Bell, Yoke — SE

Red Screes 10

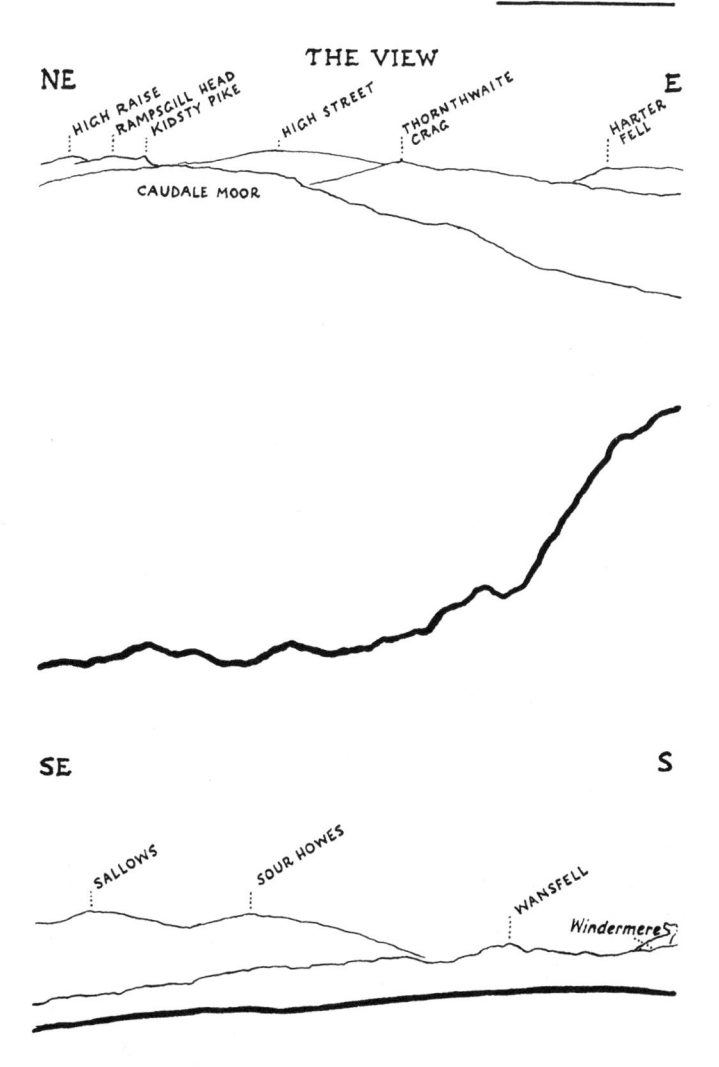

THE VIEW

NE — HIGH RAISE, RAMPSGILL HEAD, KIDSTY PIKE, HIGH STREET, THORNTHWAITE CRAG, HARTER FELL — **E**

CAUDALE MOOR

SE — SALLOWS, SOUR HOWES, WANSFELL, Windermere — **S**

continued

Red Screes 11

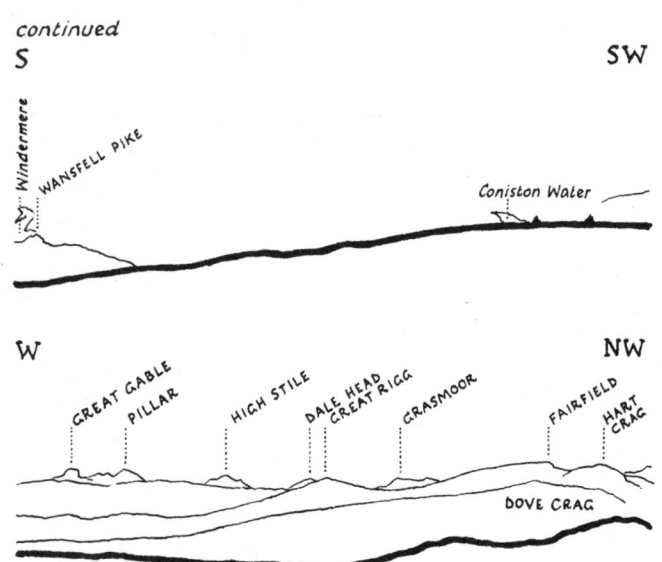

THE VIEW

continued

S — **SW**

Windermere, WANSFELL PIKE, Coniston Water

W — **NW**

GREAT GABLE, PILLAR, HIGH STILE, DALE HEAD, GREAT RIGG, GRASMOOR, FAIRFIELD, HART CRAG, DOVE CRAG

The south-east combe

The north-east combe

Red Screes 12

THE VIEW

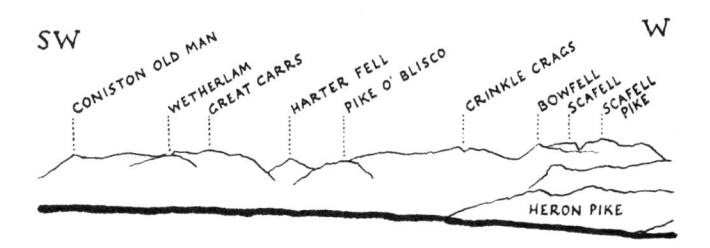

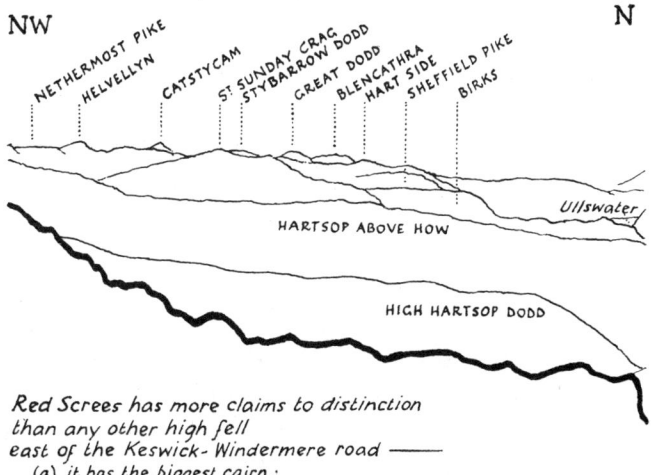

SW — CONISTON OLD MAN, WETHERLAM, GREAT CARRS, HARTER FELL, PIKE O' BLISCO, CRINKLE CRAGS, BOWFELL, SCAFELL, SCAFELL PIKE — W

HERON PIKE

NW — NETHERMOST PIKE, HELVELLYN, CATSTYCAM, ST SUNDAY CRAG, STYBARROW DODD, GREAT DODD, BLENCATHRA, HART SIDE, SHEFFIELD PIKE, BIRKS — N

Ullswater

HARTSOP ABOVE HOW

HIGH HARTSOP DODD

Red Screes has more claims to distinction than any other high fell east of the Keswick-Windermere road —

(a) it has the biggest cairn;
(b) it has the greatest mileage of stone walls;
(c) it has one of the highest sheets of permanent standing water, and, in springtime, the highest resident population of tadpoles;
(d) it has the purest mountain form;
(e) it has the reddest screes and the greenest stone;
(f) it has one of the finest views (but not the most extensive nor the most beautiful) and <u>the</u> finest of the High Street range;
(g) it has the easiest way down;
(h) it offers alcoholic beverages at 1480';
(i) it gives birth to the stream with the most beautiful waterfalls.

[Some of these statements are expressions of opinion; others, especially (h), are hard facts]

Saint Sunday Crag 2756'

from Ullswater

Glenridding
Patterdale
▲ HELVELLYN
ST SUNDAY CRAG ▲
Hartsop
▲ FAIRFIELD

MILES
0 1 2 3 4

St Sunday Crag 2

NATURAL FEATURES

The slender soaring lines of St Sunday Crag and its aloof height and steepness endow this fine mountain with special distinction. It stands on a triangular base and its sides rise with such regularity that all its contours assume the same shape, as does the final summit-plateau. Ridges ascend from the corners of the triangle to the top of the fell, the one best-defined naturally rising from the sharpest angle: this is the south-west ridge connecting with Fairfield at Deepdale Hause. A shorter rougher ridge runs down northeast to Birks. Due east of the top is a subsidiary peak, Gavel Pike, from which a broadening ridge falls to Deepdale. A fringe of crags, nearly a mile in length, overtops the Grisedale face, which drops nearly 2000 feet in height in a lateral distance of half-a-mile: in Lakeland, only Great Gable can show greater concentrated steepness over a similar fall in altitude. The south-east face is also steep but less impressive, and the easy slopes to the north-east break into foothills before dropping abruptly to valley-level in Patterdale: these slopes are the gathering grounds of Coldcove Gill, the main stream.

Every walker who aspires to high places and looks up at the remote summit of St Sunday Crag will experience an urge to go forth and climb up to it, for its challenge is very strong. Its rewards are equally generous, and altogether this is a noble fell. Saint Sunday must surely look down on his memorial with profound gratification.

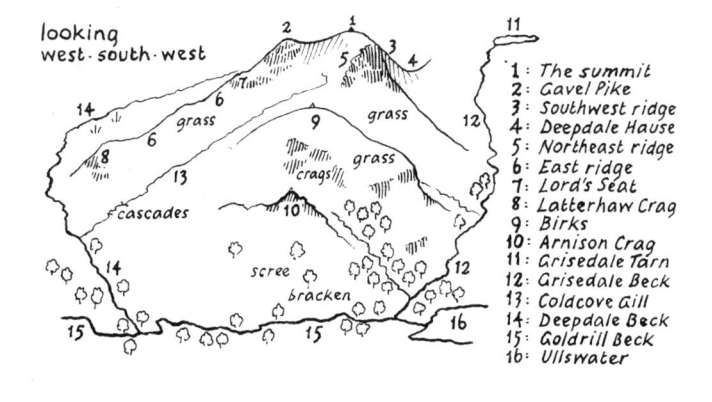

looking west-south-west

1: The summit
2: Gavel Pike
3: Southwest ridge
4: Deepdale Hause
5: Northeast ridge
6: East ridge
7: Lord's Seat
8: Latterhaw Crag
9: Birks
10: Arnison Crag
11: Grisedale Tarn
12: Grisedale Beck
13: Coldcove Gill
14: Deepdale Beck
15: Goldrill Beck
16: Ullswater

St Sunday Crag 3

NATURAL FEATURES

St Sunday Crag has an imposing appearance from whatever direction it is seen, an attribute rare in mountains. From Ullswater and from Grisedale its outline is very familiar; less well known (because less often seen) is its fine eastern aspect.

The East Ridge, from Dubhow

There is a glimpse, often unnoticed, of the lofty east ridge soaring high above Deepdale, from the roadway near Bridgend. A much better view is obtained from Dubhow, nearby on the old cart-track across the valley.

Cascades, Coldcove Gill

Summit of Gavel Pike

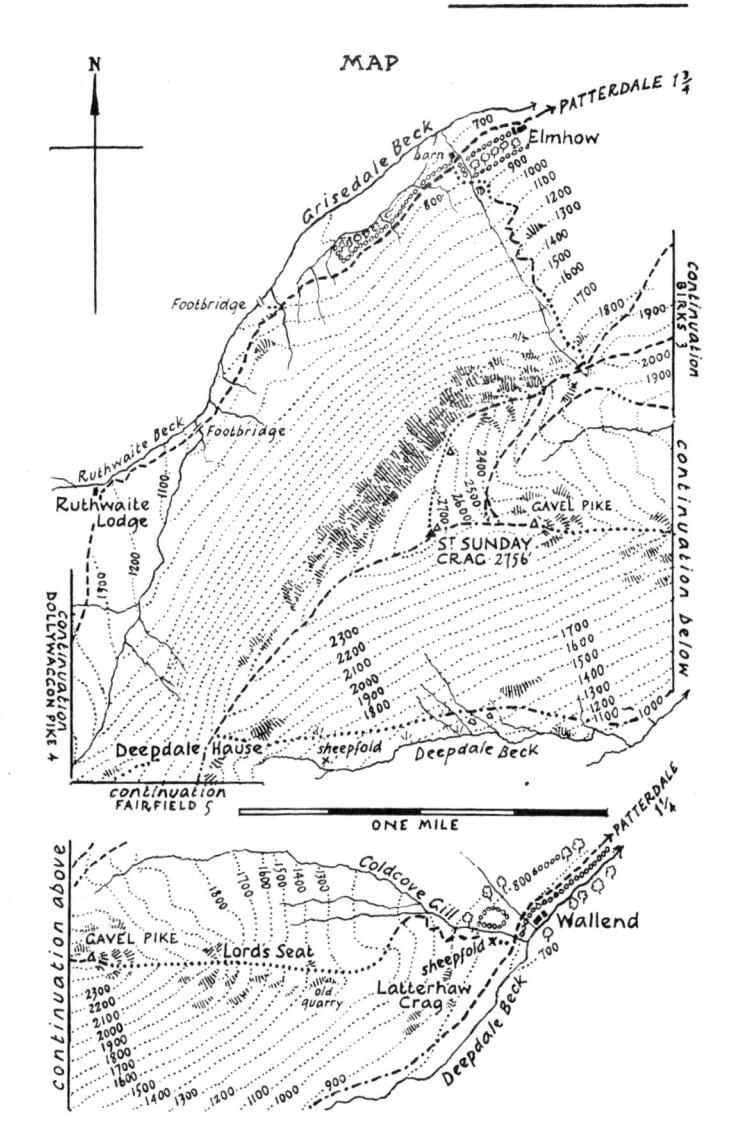

St Sunday Crag 4

MAP

St Sunday Crag 5

ASCENT FROM PATTERDALE
2300 feet of ascent : 3 miles (4 by East Ridge)

looking south-west

The *easiest* route (not depicted) follows Deepdale to its head at Deepdale Hause, then ascends the southwest ridge. Apart from a short sharp pull on to the Hause there is no steep climbing. There are intimate views of the crags of Fairfield

The popular route is *via* Thornhow End and the western flank of Birks (in clear weather it is better to proceed over the top of Birks). The Trough Head route is easier but dull. The east ridge is an interesting alternative and technically the best line of ascent.

St Sunday Crag 6

ASCENT FROM GRISEDALE TARN
1000 feet of ascent : 1¾ miles

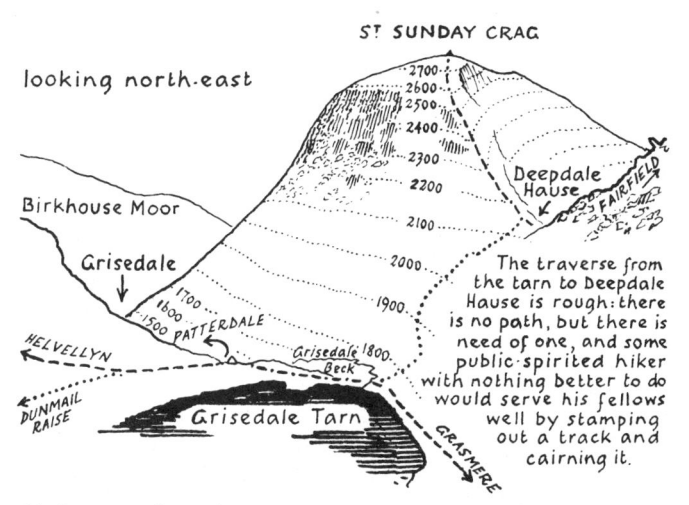

looking north-east

St Sunday Crag is commonly and correctly regarded as the preserve of Patterdale, yet it is interesting to note that the summit is less than three miles from the Keswick-Ambleside road at Dunmail Raise: it may be ascended easily and quickly from here. And from Grasmere via Tongue Gill. In either case, the first objective is Grisedale Tarn.

The traverse from the tarn to Deepdale Hause is rough: there is no path, but there is need of one, and some public-spirited hiker with nothing better to do would serve his fellows well by stamping out a track and cairning it.

St Sunday Crag from Grisedale Tarn

St Sunday Crag 7

THE SUMMIT

The summit hardly lives up to the promise of the ridges: it is merely a slight stony mound set on the edge of a plateau — a pleasant place of mosses and lichens and grey rocks, but quite unexciting. Two cairns adorn the top, and there is also a well-built column of stones a quarter of a mile away across the plateau to the north.

Gavel Pike has a much more attractive summit than the main fell: here are bilberries and heather and natural armchairs among the rocks of the tiny peaked top, and splendid views to enjoy. A delectable place for (packed) lunch!

DESCENTS: The royal way down to Patterdale is by the northeast ridge, traversing the flank of Birks and descending the steep woodland of Glemara Park — a delightful walk with charming views. Other routes are very inferior. For Grisedale Tarn, use the southwest ridge to Deepdale Hause, thence slanting over rough ground to the tarn, which is in view.

In bad conditions, the danger lies in the long line of crags on the Grisedale face, this fortunately being preceded by steep ground which serves as a warning. For Patterdale, the path from the saddle is safest. To find Deepdale Hause in mist, leave the top with the two cairns in line behind.

St Sunday Crag 8

Ullswater from the north-east ridge

St Sunday Crag 9

RIDGE ROUTES

To FAIRFIELD, 2863': 1½ miles : SW then S
Depression at 2150': 750 feet of ascent
A simple descent followed by rough scrambling

A very pleasant stroll down the south-west ridge, on grass, leads to the depression of Deepdale Hause. From here, Cofa Pike looks quite formidable, but a plain path climbs steeply up the stony slope to the interesting crest of the Pike. A loose scree slope is then climbed to the grassy shoulder above and the summit-cairn is just beyond. *In mist, Fairfield is a dangerous place to strangers.*

To BIRKS, 2040': 1¼ miles : NE
Minor depressions : 50 feet of ascent
An easy walk with delightful views

Cross the tilted summit-plateau to the north cairn; beyond, the north-east ridge goes down to a col, whence a level grassy path leads on to Birks.

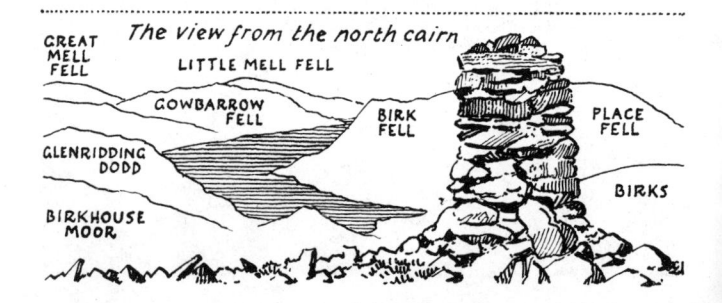

The view from the north cairn

GREAT MELL FELL
LITTLE MELL FELL
GOWBARROW FELL
BIRK FELL
PLACE FELL
GLENRIDDING DODD
BIRKHOUSE MOOR
BIRKS

St Sunday Crag 10

THE VIEW

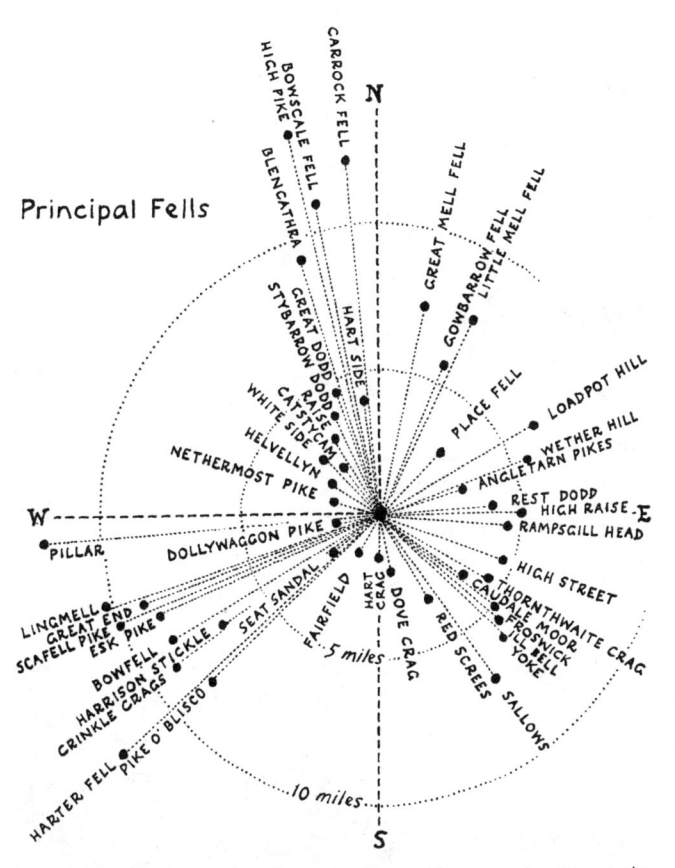

Principal Fells

Fells shown on radial diagram:
CARROCK FELL, BOWSCALE FELL, HIGH PIKE, BLENCATHRA, GREAT CALVA, STYBARROW DODD, HART SIDE, GREAT MELL FELL, LITTLE MELL FELL, GOWBARROW FELL, RAISE, CATSTYCAM, WHITE SIDE, HELVELLYN, PLACE FELL, LOADPOT HILL, WETHER HILL, ANGLETARN PIKES, NETHERMOST PIKE, REST DODD, HIGH RAISE, RAMPSGILL HEAD, PILLAR, DOLLYWAGGON PIKE, HIGH STREET, THORNTHWAITE CRAG, CAUDALE MOOR, HART CRAG, DOVE CRAG, FROSWICK, ILL BELL, LINGMELL, GREAT END, SCAFELL PIKE, ESK PIKE, FAIRFIELD, RED SCREES, YOKE, BOWFELL, HARRISON STICKLE, SEAT SANDAL, CRINKLE CRAGS, SALLOWS, HARTER FELL, PIKE O'BLISCO

5 miles / 10 miles range rings; compass points N, E, S, W

The walker who reaches the summit eagerly expecting to see the classic view of Ullswater from St Sunday Crag will be disappointed — he must go to the bristly rocks at the top of the north-east ridge for that. The lake makes a beautiful picture also from the saddle leading to Gavel Pike. Helvellyn is a fine study in mountain structure, and the best aspect of Fairfield is seen, but these two fells restrict the view. The High Street range, however, is well seen.

Lakes and Tarns
NE : *Ullswater*
E : *Angle Tarn*

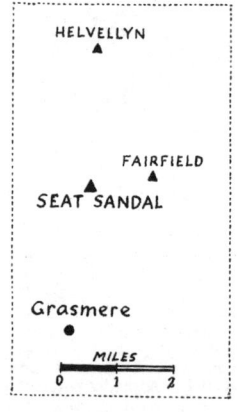

Seat Sandal 2415'

from Grasmere

Cascade, Raise Beck

HELVELLYN

FAIRFIELD
SEAT SANDAL

Grasmere

MILES
0   1   2

Seat Sandal 2

NATURAL FEATURES

Prominent in the Grasmere landscape is the lofty outline of Seat Sandal, soaring gracefully from Dunmail Raise to the flat-topped summit and then suddenly falling away in a steep plunge eastwards. This view reveals its character well: the western flanks are smooth curves of grass and bracken, but the eastern face is a rough slope of shattered cliff and tumbled rock and loose scree from which rises abruptly an overhanging crag. Seat Sandal is a simple straightforward fell, uninteresting except as a viewpoint, with no dramatic effects, no hidden surprises. Geographically it belongs to Fairfield, to which it is connected by a low ridge crossed by the Grisedale Pass.

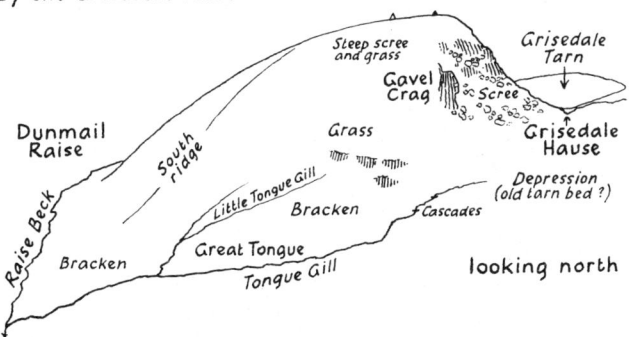

looking north

Seat Sandal has one distinction: its waters reach the sea at more widely divergent points than those of any other Lakeland fell. This has been so since the diversion of Raise Beck to feed Thirlmere. (Dollywaggon Pike shares this distinction only when Raise Beck is flowing south at Dunmail Raise)

1 : Raise Beck —
to Thirlmere and (that which escapes being sent back south over Dunmail to Manchester) via Derwentwater to the sea at Workington.
2 : Raise Beck and Tongue Gill —
to Grasmere, Windermere and Morecambe Bay.
3 : Grisedale Beck —
to Ullswater and the Solway Firth.

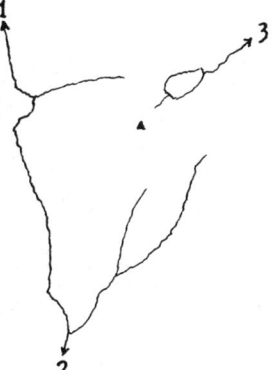

Seat Sandal 3

MAP

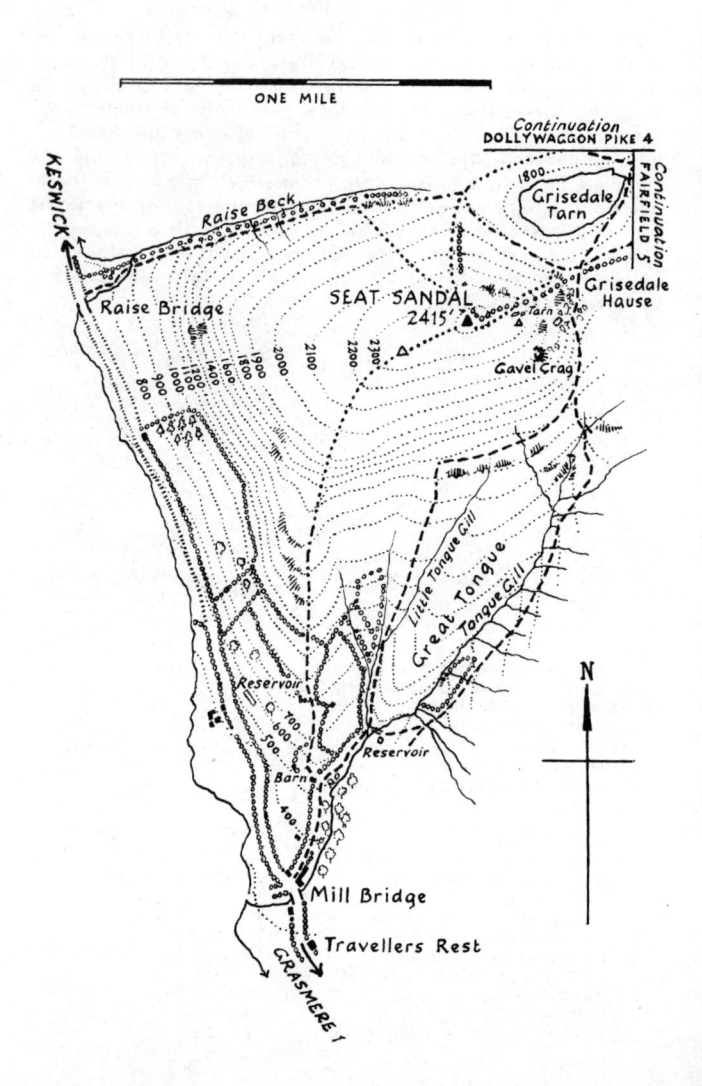

Seat Sandal 4

ASCENT FROM GRASMERE
2200 feet of ascent: 3½ miles from Grasmere Church

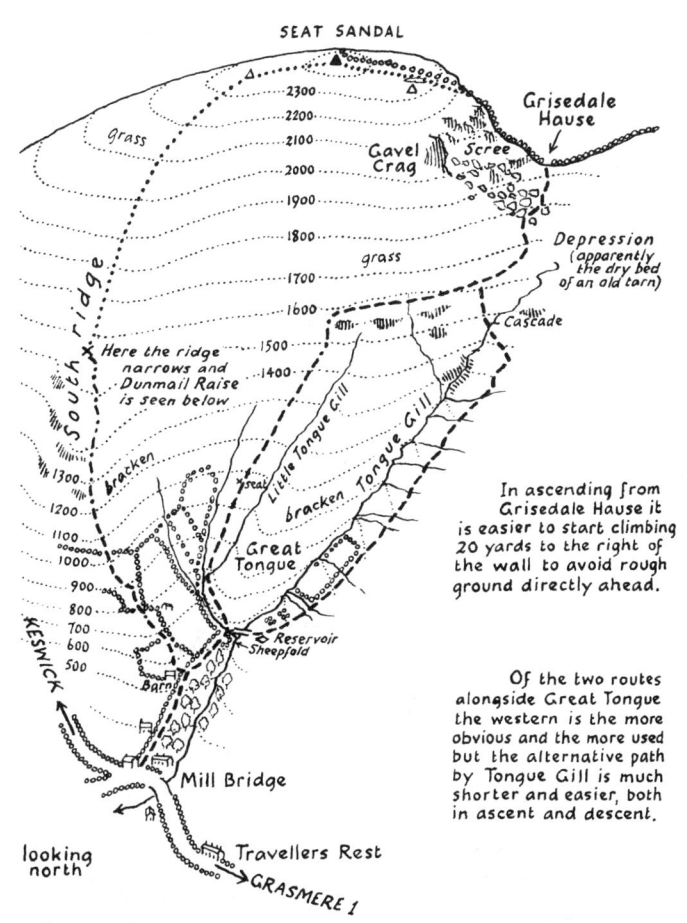

In ascending from Grisedale Hause it is easier to start climbing 20 yards to the right of the wall to avoid rough ground directly ahead.

Of the two routes alongside Great Tongue the western is the more obvious and the more used but the alternative path by Tongue Gill is much shorter and easier, both in ascent and descent.

The path to Grisedale Hause, by either side of the Tongue, is distinct, but there is no track above the Hause or on the upper part of the south ridge. If returning to Grasmere, it is better to ascend by the Hause and descend by the ridge.

Seat Sandal 5

ASCENT FROM DUNMAIL RAISE
1700 feet of ascent : 1½ miles

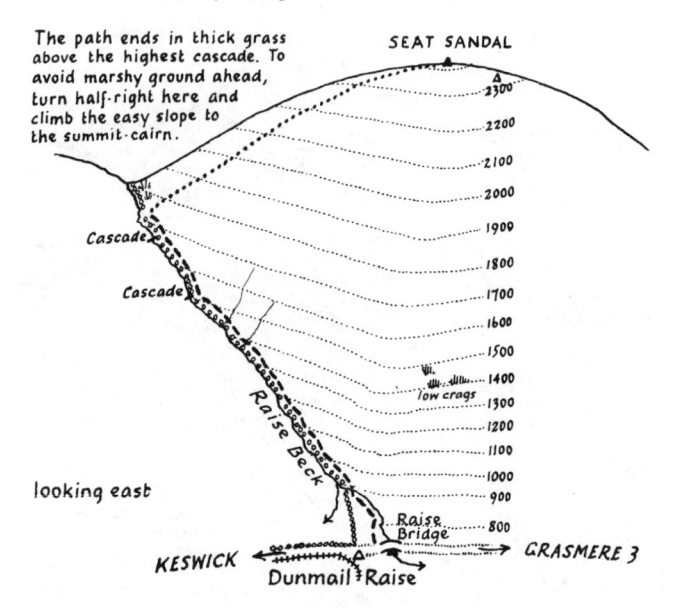

The path ends in thick grass above the highest cascade. To avoid marshy ground ahead, turn half-right here and climb the easy slope to the summit-cairn.

SEAT SANDAL

Cascade
Cascade

Raise Beck

looking east

Raise Bridge

KESWICK ← Dunmail Raise → GRASMERE 3

low crags

Seat Sandal is very easily climbed from Raise Bridge. The direct route by the shoulder is not recommended: it is preferable to commence the ascent by using the rough path alongside the beck. This is a quick way up.

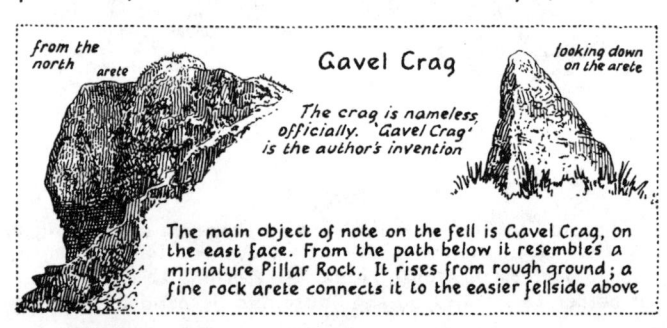

Gavel Crag

from the north arete

looking down on the arete

The crag is nameless, officially. 'Gavel Crag' is the author's invention

The main object of note on the fell is Gavel Crag, on the east face. From the path below it resembles a miniature Pillar Rock. It rises from rough ground; a fine rock arete connects it to the easier fellside above

Seat Sandal 6

THE SUMMIT

St Sunday Crag — Cofa Pike — Fairfield

The summit is a flat grassy plateau with small stony outcrops. A broken wall crosses the top. The main cairn stands 30 yards west of the wall; two other cairns indicate alternative viewpoints.

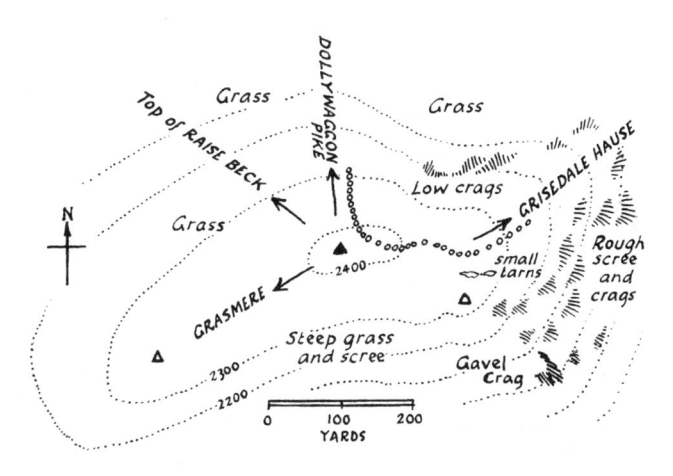

DESCENTS: The best way off the summit, in clear weather, is by the south ridge to Grasmere, the views being excellent and the gradient exactly right — this is one of the quickest descents in the district. All routes are safe in good conditions. *There are no paths on the summit.* The east face is steep, and should be avoided.

In bad weather conditions, the safest descent is to Grisedale Hause (by the wall) where good paths lead to Grasmere and Patterdale.

Seat Sandal 7

THE VIEW

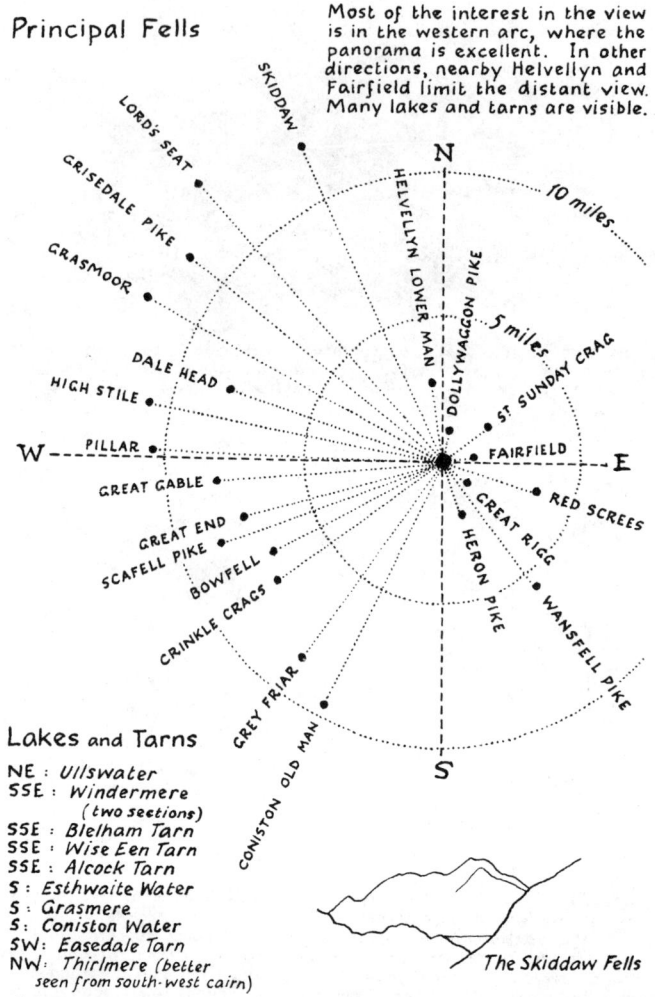

Principal Fells

Most of the interest in the view is in the western arc, where the panorama is excellent. In other directions, nearby Helvellyn and Fairfield limit the distant view. Many lakes and tarns are visible.

Fells shown on compass diagram (clockwise from N): SKIDDAW, HELVELLYN LOWER MAN, DOLLYWAGGON PIKE, ST SUNDAY CRAG, FAIRFIELD, RED SCREES, GREAT RIGG, WANSFELL PIKE, HERON PIKE, GREY FRIAR, CONISTON OLD MAN, CRINKLE CRAGS, BOWFELL, SCAFELL PIKE, GREAT END, GREAT GABLE, PILLAR, HIGH STILE, DALE HEAD, GRASMOOR, GRISEDALE PIKE, LORD'S SEAT.

Distance rings: 5 miles, 10 miles.

Lakes and Tarns

- NE : *Ullswater*
- SSE : *Windermere* (two sections)
- SSE : *Blelham Tarn*
- SSE : *Wise Een Tarn*
- SSE : *Alcock Tarn*
- S : *Esthwaite Water*
- S : *Grasmere*
- S : *Coniston Water*
- SW : *Easedale Tarn*
- NW : *Thirlmere* (better seen from south-west cairn)

The Skiddaw Fells

Grisedale Tarn is seen by walking NE 150 yards from the summit-cairn.

Seat Sandal 8

RIDGE ROUTES

To FAIRFIELD, 2863': 1⅓ miles : E then NE and E
Depression at 1929' : 950 feet of ascent

A rough descent followed by a steep continuous climb. The top of Fairfield is confusing and dangerous in mist to anyone who is not familiar with it, but there is no difficulty in clear weather.

The wall is a guide down to Grisedale Hause: the last part of the descent is rough but there is easier ground just to the left. The wall continues up the shoulder of Fairfield to 2400' and gives up the struggle but the determined walker toils on along a fair path. The final part of the climb, much easier but without a path, follows a line of cairns across grass to the stony top.

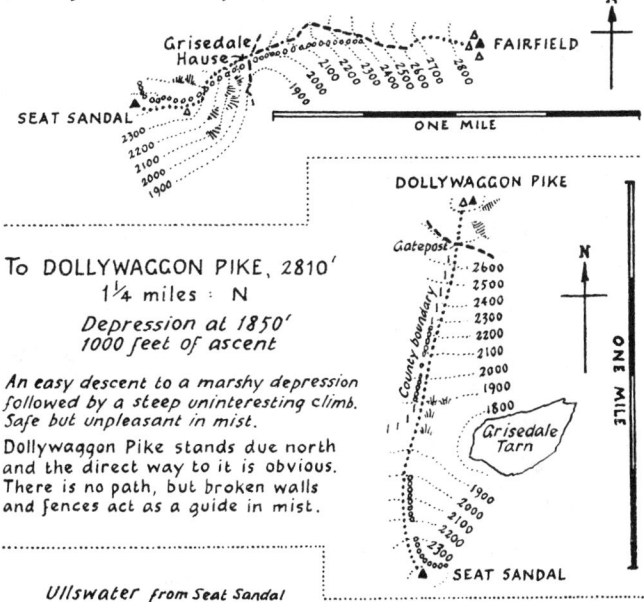

To DOLLYWAGGON PIKE, 2810'
1¼ miles : N
Depression at 1850'
1000 feet of ascent

An easy descent to a marshy depression followed by a steep uninteresting climb. Safe but unpleasant in mist.

Dollywaggon Pike stands due north and the direct way to it is obvious. There is no path, but broken walls and fences act as a guide in mist.

Ullswater from Seat Sandal

Sheffield Pike 2232'

from Glenridding

Sheffield Pike 2

NATURAL FEATURES

Stybarrow Dodd, on the main Helvellyn watershed, has a long eastern shoulder falling in stages to the shore of Ullswater. Midway, the shoulder rises to a distinct and isolated summit: this is Sheffield Pike, which assumes the characteristics of a separate fell. It soars abruptly between the valleys of Glenridding and Glencoyne and it presents to each a continuous fringe of steep crags. The eastern aspect is pleasing, with rock and heather and an occasional rowan mingling above well-wooded slopes, but westwards the fell is drab and, in the environs of a vast lead mine, hideously scarred and downright ugly. Its rich mineral deposits have, paradoxically, caused its ruin: it has been robbed not only of its lead but of its appeal and attractiveness to walkers.

looking north-west

Heron Pike, from the east

Sheffield Pike 3

MAP

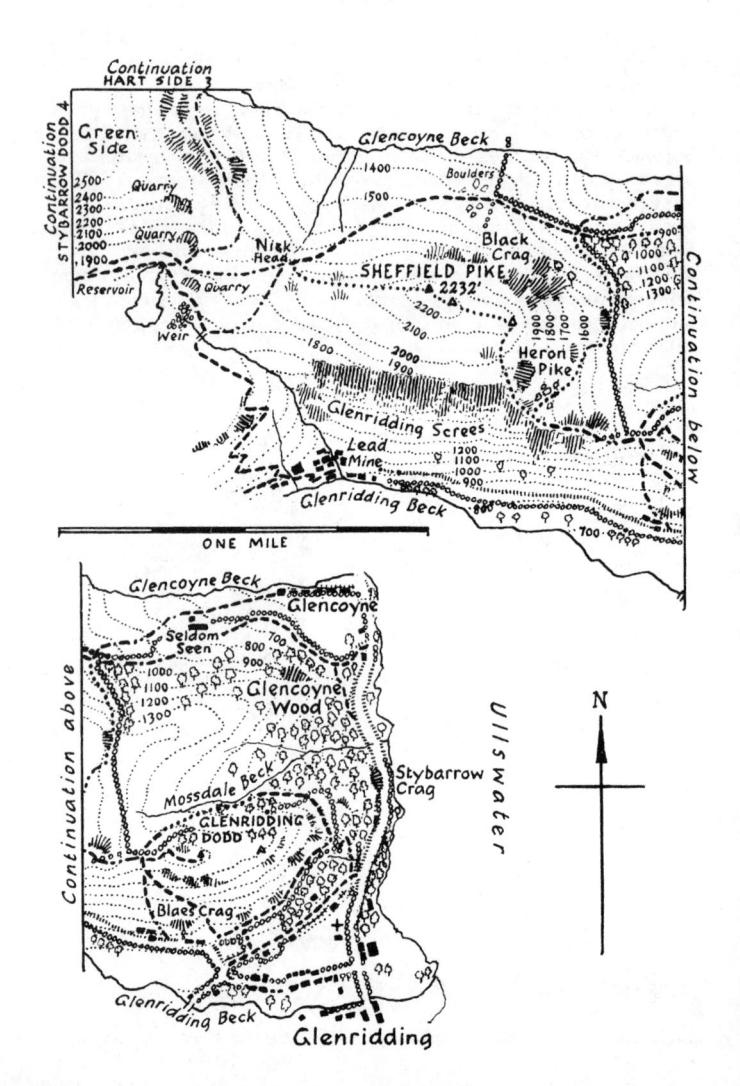

Sheffield Pike 4

ASCENT FROM GLENRIDDING
1800 feet of ascent: 2 (or 3¼) miles

The evidences of industrialism are rampant in mid-Glenridding. The pleasantest way up Sheffield Pike is from Glencoyne (see next page)

Sheffield Pike should not be climbed in mist

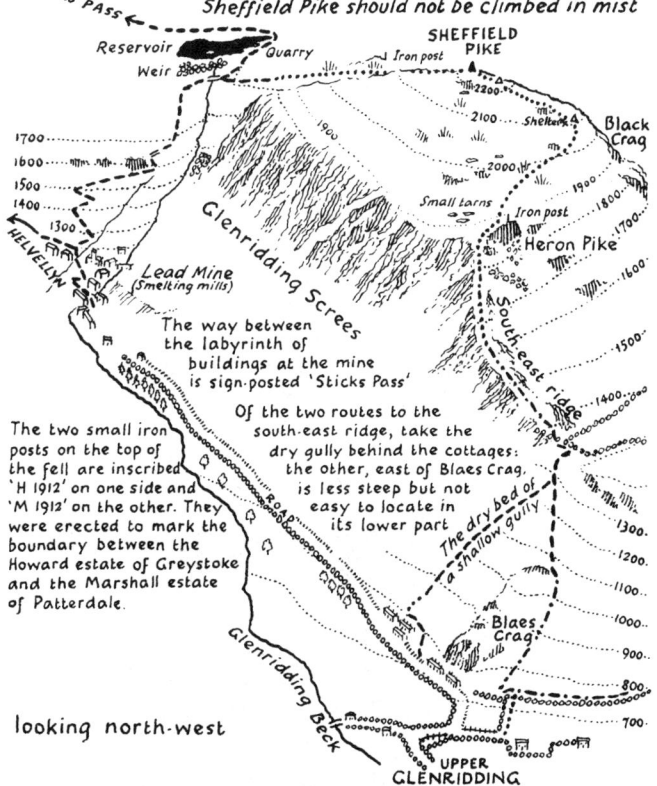

looking north-west

Of the two routes illustrated, the climb up the ridge is much to be preferred, but it is steep and rough. The path zig-zagging above the smelting mills is longer and easier — but much less inspiring and not at all exhilarating.

Sheffield Pike 5

ASCENT FROM GLENCOYNE
1800 feet of ascent : 2½ miles

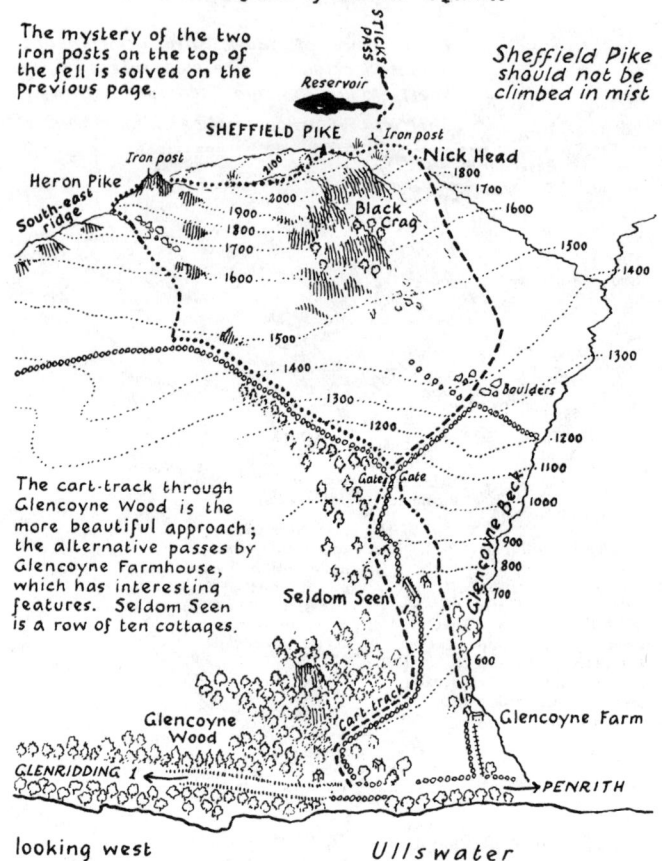

The mystery of the two iron posts on the top of the fell is solved on the previous page.

Sheffield Pike should not be climbed in mist

The cart-track through Glencoyne Wood is the more beautiful approach; the alternative passes by Glencoyne Farmhouse, which has interesting features. Seldom Seen is a row of ten cottages.

looking west — Ullswater

It is usual to follow the path to Nick Head and there turn east to the summit: this is the easiest of all ways on to the fell. Far more attractive, however, is a route traversing below Heron Pike to the top of the south-east ridge, the walking being easy and the views excellent: this is one of the pleasantest short climbs in Lakeland.

Sheffield Pike 6

THE SUMMIT

Even on a sunny summer day the top of the fell seems a dismal, cheerless place; the vicinity of the cairn above Black Crag, and the top of Heron Pike, where there is heather, are both nicer.
There are many slight undulations and craggy outcrops. Marshy ground occurs in several places and there are many small tarns.

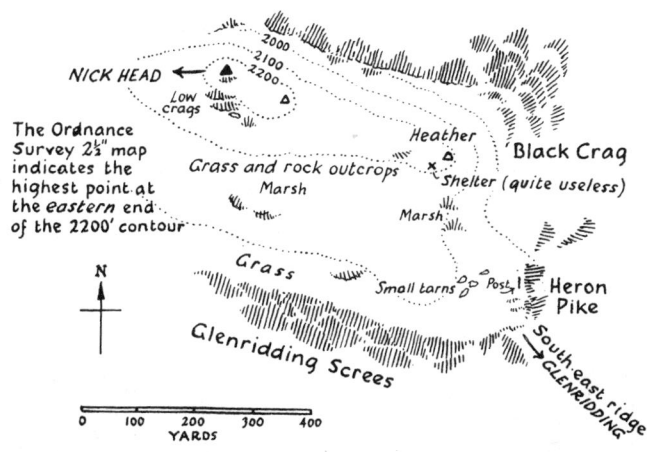

The Ordnance Survey 2½" map indicates the highest point at the *eastern* end of the 2200' contour

DESCENTS: Any of the routes of ascent may be reversed in clear weather, the south-east ridge being incomparably the best. Some care is necessary in getting off Heron Pike on to the ridge. *There are no paths on the summit*, which has crags on all sides except westwards.
In bad weather conditions, the only safe way is due west to Nick Head (very gradual descent, boggy in places), from there preferably following the good path down to Glencoyne.

Sheffield Pike 7

THE VIEW

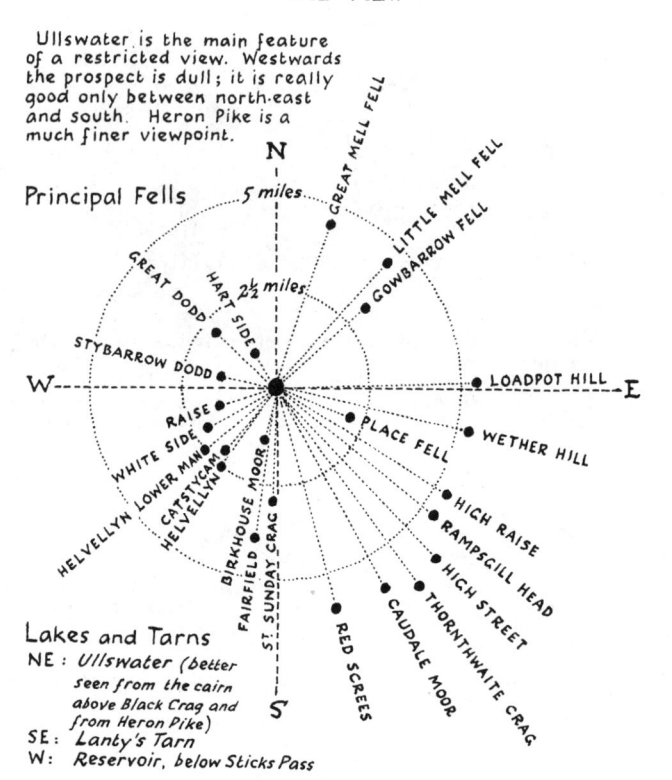

Ullswater is the main feature of a restricted view. Westwards the prospect is dull; it is really good only between north-east and south. Heron Pike is a much finer viewpoint.

Principal Fells

(circular diagram showing fells at distances of 2½ miles and 5 miles from centre)

- N: Great Mell Fell
- Little Mell Fell
- Gowbarrow Fell
- Great Dodd
- Hart Side
- Stybarrow Dodd
- W: (west axis)
- Loadpot Hill — E
- Raise
- Place Fell
- Wether Hill
- White Side
- Helvellyn Lower Man
- Catstycam
- Helvellyn
- High Raise
- Birkhouse Moor
- Fairfield
- Rampsgill Head
- St. Sunday Crag
- High Street
- Thornthwaite Crag
- Caudale Moor
- Red Screes
- S

Lakes and Tarns

- **NE**: Ullswater (better seen from the cairn above Black Crag and from Heron Pike)
- **SE**: Lanty's Tarn
- **W**: Reservoir, below Sticks Pass

Black Crag

Heron Pike

Sheffield Pike 8

RIDGE ROUTES

To STYBARROW DODD, 2770': 2 miles: W then NW and W.
Depression at 1925': 1000 feet of ascent
A simple walk with a long climb on grass midway. No path.

An easy descent westwards, boggy in places, leads to Nick Head. Cross the indistinct paths here and climb the long grassy slope ahead to the cairn on Green Side. Stybarrow Dodd is then in view in front, across a shallow depression. *This route is not recommended in bad conditions.*

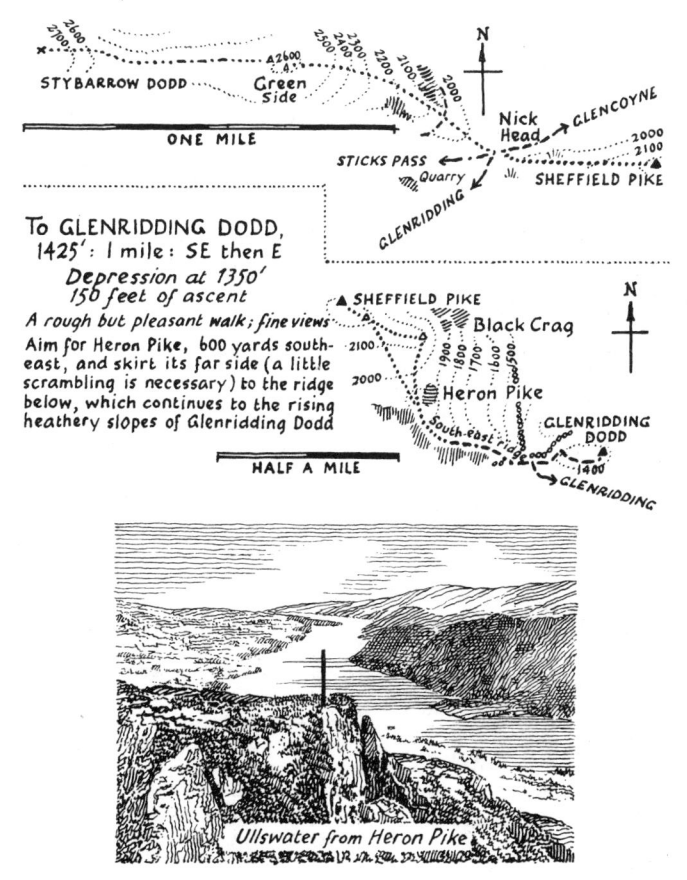

To GLENRIDDING DODD,
1425': 1 mile: SE then E
Depression at 1350'
150 feet of ascent
A rough but pleasant walk; fine views

Aim for Heron Pike, 600 yards south-east, and skirt its far side (a little scrambling is necessary) to the ridge below, which continues to the rising heathery slopes of Glenridding Dodd

Ullswater from Heron Pike

Stone Arthur 1652'

sometimes referred to as Arthur's Chair

from Grasmere

▲ FAIRFIELD

▲ GREAT RIGG

▲ STONE ARTHUR

▲ HERON PIKE

● Grasmere ▲ NAB SCAR

● Rydal

Ambleside ●

MILES
0 1 2 3 4

Without its prominent tor of steep rock, Stone Arthur would probably never have been given a name for it is merely the abrupt end of a spur of Great Rigg although it has the appearance of a separate fell when seen from Grasmere. The outcrop occurs where the gradual decline of the spur becomes pronounced and here are the short walls of rock, like a ruined castle, that give Stone Arthur its one touch of distinction.

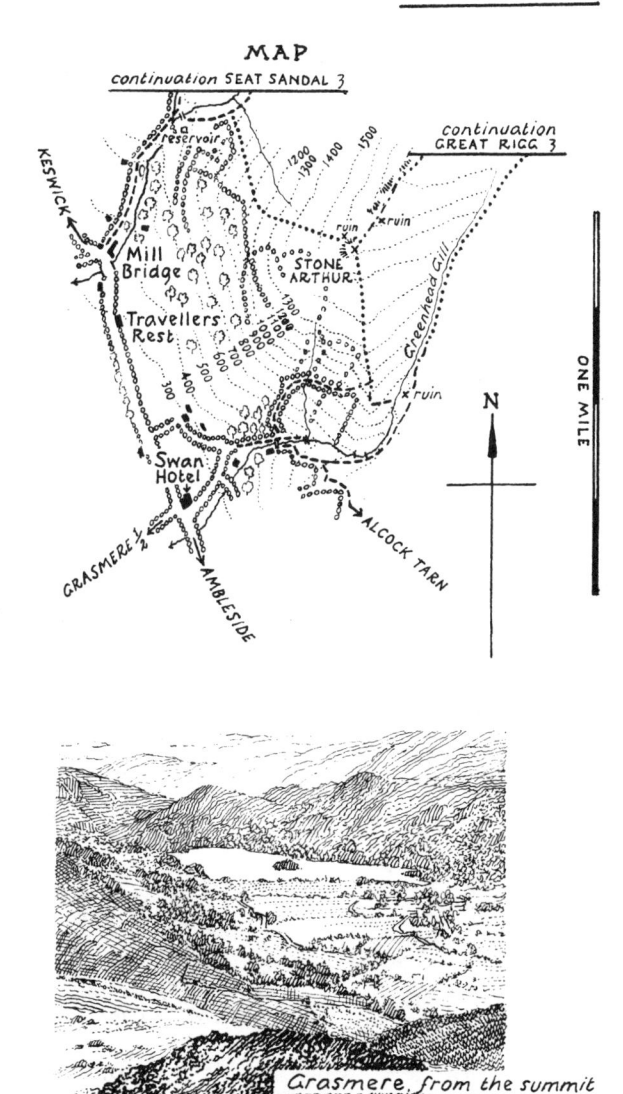

Stone Arthur 2

MAP

Grasmere, from the summit

Stone Arthur 3

THE VIEW

The gem of the view is Easedale Tarn in its wild setting among colourful fells with a towering background culminating in Scafell Pike. The vale of Grasmere, below, is also attractive. The southern ridge of Fairfield occupies the whole horizon to the east, uninterestingly.

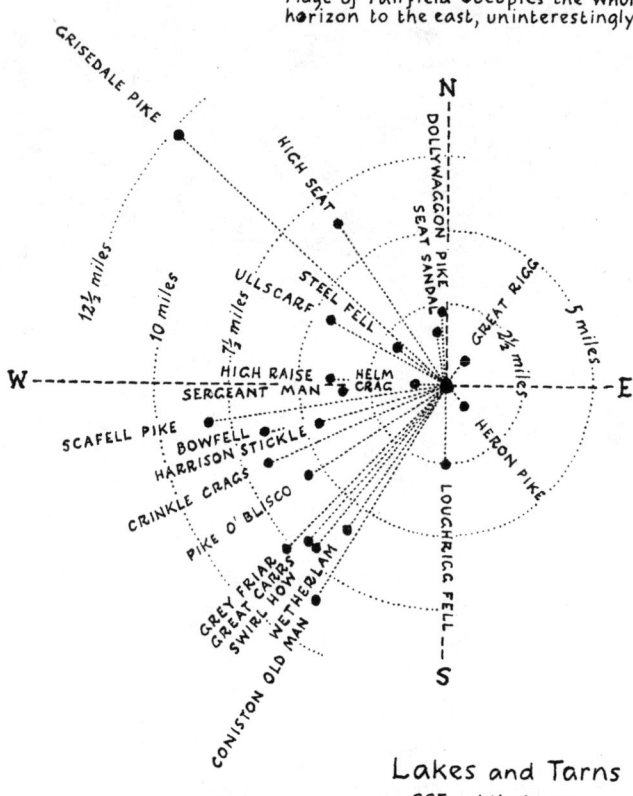

Principal Fells

- GRISEDALE PIKE
- HIGH SEAT
- DOLLYWAGGON PIKE
- SEAT SANDAL
- ULLSCARF
- STEEL FELL
- GREAT RIGG
- HIGH RAISE
- HELM CRAG
- SERGEANT MAN
- HERON PIKE
- SCAFELL PIKE
- BOWFELL
- HARRISON STICKLE
- CRINKLE CRAGS
- PIKE O' BLISCO
- LOUGHRIGG FELL
- GREY FRIAR
- GREAT CARRS
- SWIRL HOW
- WETHERLAM
- CONISTON OLD MAN

12½ miles, 10 miles, 7½ miles, 5 miles, 2½ miles

Lakes and Tarns

SSE : Windermere
SSE : Alcock Tarn
S   : Esthwaite Water
SSW : Coniston Water
SSW : Grasmere
WSW : Easedale Tarn

Stone Arthur 4

ASCENT FROM GRASMERE

Use the lane alongside the Swan Hotel: the *second* turning on the right leads to a track alongside Greenhead Gill. At the gate turn left: an overgrown path winds round the steep slope ahead between walls. When the open fell is reached incline left to the prominent rocky summit.

THE SUMMIT

from the west

The break in the continuity of the fall along the shoulder is so slight that it is not easy to define the summit exactly; there is no cairn. The height 1652', a survey triangulation point, may well be a big embedded boulder on the highest part of the rocky extremity. The small crags around the summit offer practice for embryo climbers whose main concern is not to drop too far if they fall.

DESCENTS : To find the Grasmere path, aim directly for Alcock Tarn. *In mist,* any way down is safe after the initial crags are left behind, but unless the path can be found the thick bracken will prove an abomination.

RIDGE ROUTE

TO GREAT RIGG, 2513'
1¼ miles : NE then N
 Easy climbing all the way
Follow the shoulder upwards;
when it widens and becomes
altogether grassy incline right
to the ridge. Safe in mist.

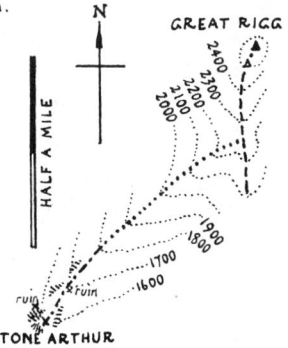

Stybarrow Dodd

2770' approx.

from Brown Crag

Stybarrow Dodd 2

NATURAL FEATURES

Stybarrow Dodd is the first of the group of fells north of the Sticks Pass and it sets the pattern for them all: sweeping grassy slopes, easy walking for the traveller who likes to count his miles but rather wearisome for those who prefer to see rock in the landscape. Rock is so rare that the slightest roughnesses get undeserved identification on most maps, either by distinctive name or extravagant hachures: thus Deepdale Crag is hardly more than a short stony slope. Stybarrow Dodd sends out a long eastern spur that rises to a minor height, Green Side (which, incidentally, gives its name to the lead mine in nearby Glenridding) before falling steeply to Glencoyne; on Green Side there are both crags and dangerous quarries, now disused.

Stybarrow Dodd's one proud distinction is that on its slopes it carries the well-known path over Sticks Pass throughout most of its length. Far more people ascend the slopes of Stybarrow Dodd than reach its summit!

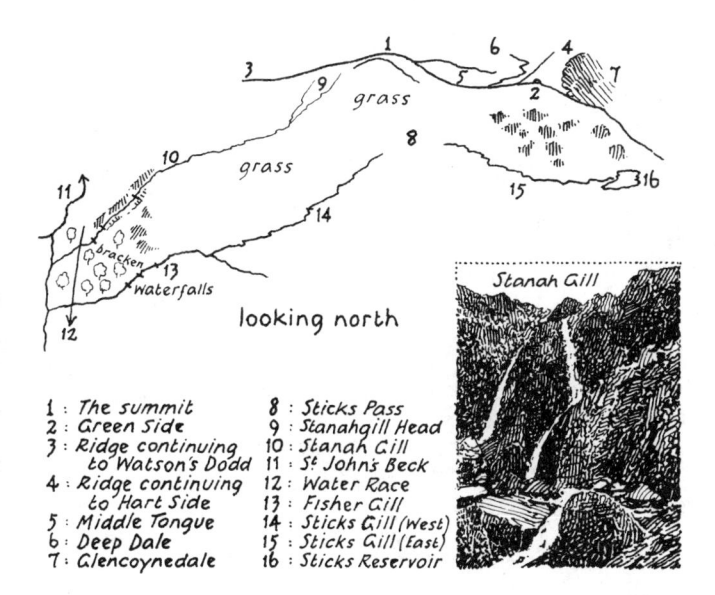

looking north

Stanah Gill

1 : The summit
2 : Green Side
3 : Ridge continuing to Watson's Dodd
4 : Ridge continuing to Hart Side
5 : Middle Tongue
6 : Deep Dale
7 : Glencoynedale
8 : Sticks Pass
9 : Stanahgill Head
10 : Stanah Gill
11 : St John's Beck
12 : Water Race
13 : Fisher Gill
14 : Sticks Gill (West)
15 : Sticks Gill (East)
16 : Sticks Reservoir

Stybarrow Dodd 3

MAP

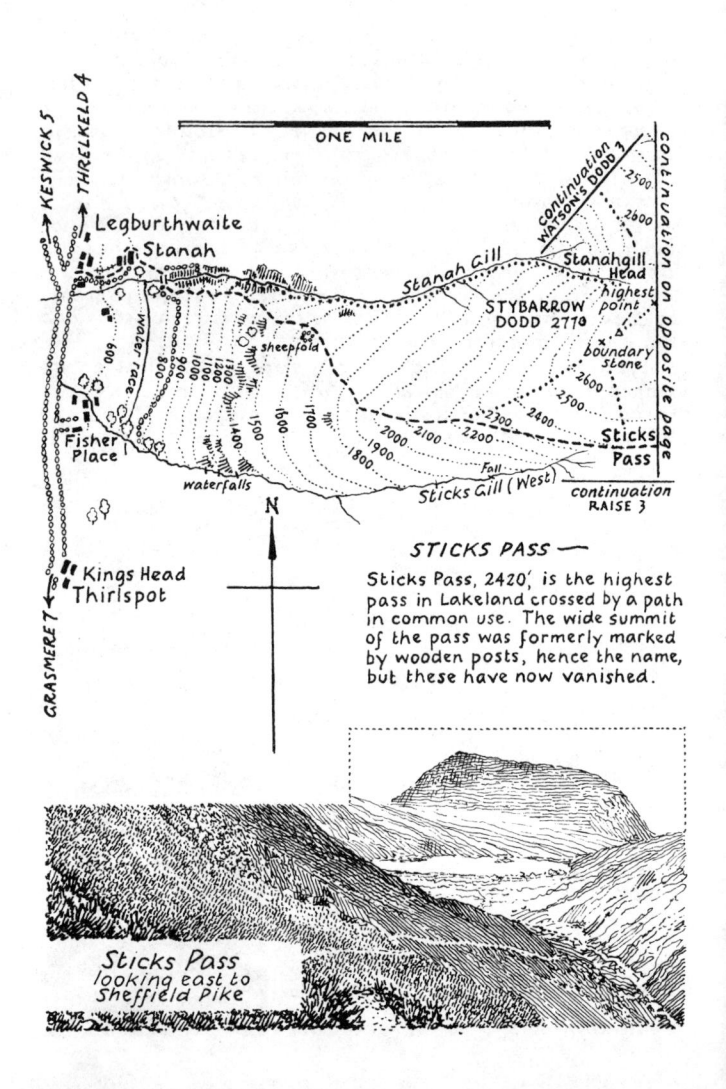

STICKS PASS —

Sticks Pass, 2420', is the highest pass in Lakeland crossed by a path in common use. The wide summit of the pass was formerly marked by wooden posts, hence the name, but these have now vanished.

Sticks Pass looking east to Sheffield Pike

Stybarrow Dodd 4

MAP

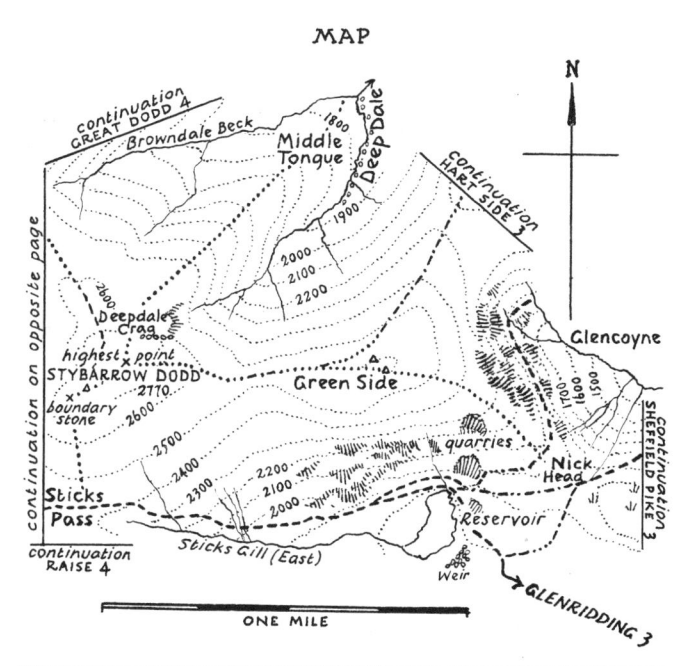

Ullswater from the east slope of Green Side

Stybarrow Dodd 5

ASCENT FROM STANAH
2300 feet of ascent : 2½ miles

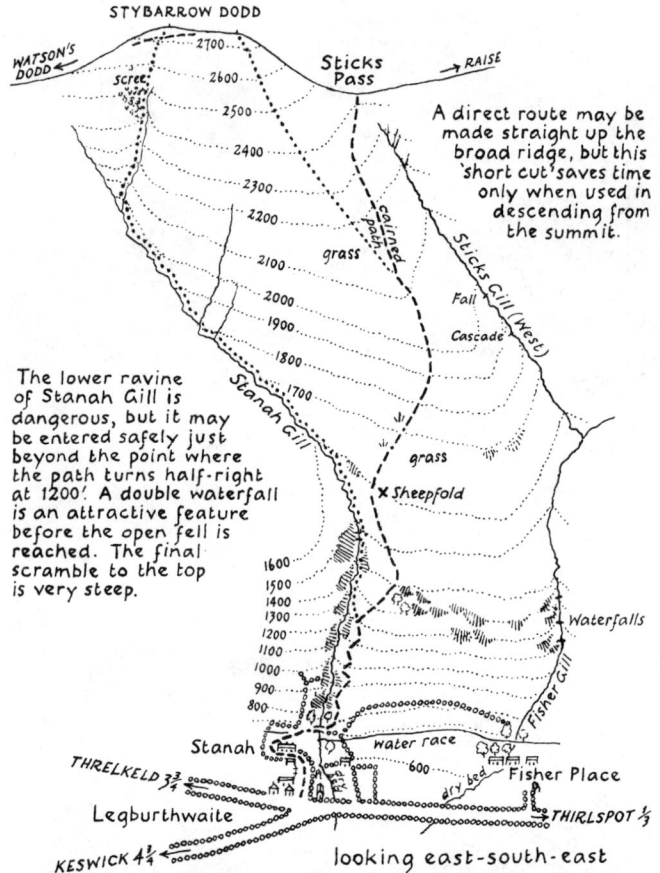

map annotations:

STYBARROW DODD

WATSON'S DODD ← 2700, 2600, scree, 2500, 2400, 2300, 2200, 2100, 2000, 1900, 1800, 1700 — Sticks Pass → RAISE

cairned path · grass · Sticks Gill (West) · Fall, Cascade

A direct route may be made straight up the broad ridge, but this 'short cut' saves time only when used in descending from the summit.

Stanah Gill

grass · × Sheepfold

The lower ravine of Stanah Gill is dangerous, but it may be entered safely just beyond the point where the path turns half-right at 1200'. A double waterfall is an attractive feature before the open fell is reached. The final scramble to the top is very steep.

1600, 1500, 1400, 1300, 1200, 1100, 1000, 900, 800 · Waterfalls · Fisher Gill

Stanah · water race · 600 · Fisher Place

THRELKELD 3¾

Legburthwaite · dry bed · THIRLSPOT ⅓

KESWICK 4¼

looking east-south-east

Conveniently, the path to Sticks Pass climbs the slopes of Stybarrow Dodd, the summit being easily gained from the top of the pass. Stanah Gill is a rough alternative, affording some relief from the dull grassiness of the path.

Stybarrow Dodd 6

ASCENT FROM DOCKRAY
1900 feet of ascent : 5½ miles

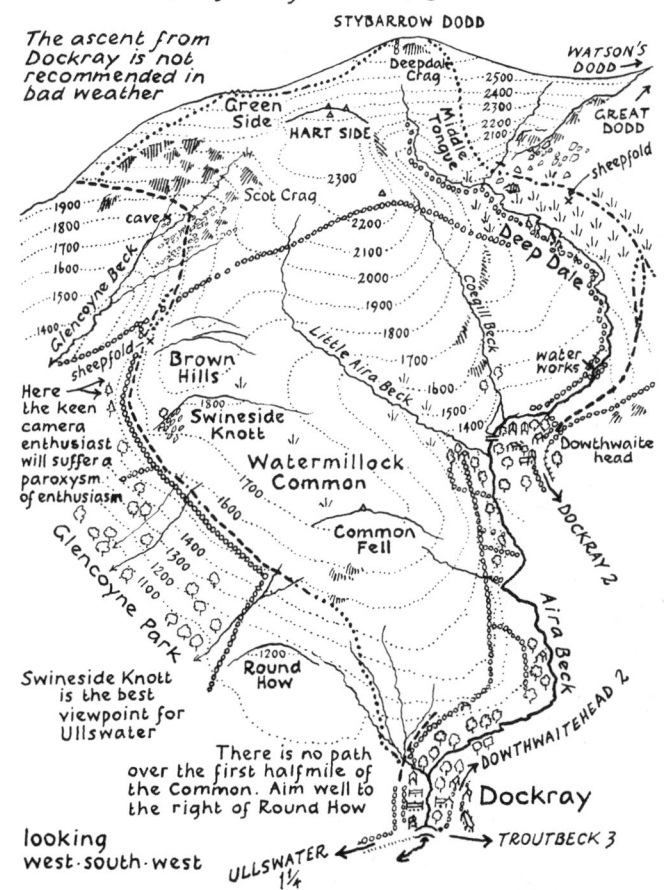

The ascent from Dockray is not recommended in bad weather

STYBARROW DODD — WATSON'S DODD — GREAT DODD — Deepdale Crag — Green Side — HART SIDE — Middle Tongue — Scot Crag — Deep Dale — sheepfold — cave — Glencoyne Beck — Little Aira Beck — Coegill Beck — water works — Brown Hills — Swineside Knott — Watermillock Common — Dowthwaite head — DOCKRAY 2 — Glencoyne Park — Common Fell — Aira Beck — Round How — DOWTHWAITEHEAD 2 — Dockray — ULLSWATER 1¼ — TROUTBECK 3

Here the keen camera enthusiast will suffer a paroxysm of enthusiasm

Swineside Knott is the best viewpoint for Ullswater

There is no path over the first half mile of the Common. Aim well to the right of Round How

looking west-south-west

There is all the difference in the world between the two routes depicted. The direct way by Deep Dale is dreary and depressing; that by the Brown Hills is (after a dull start) a splendid high-level route, excelling in its views of Ullswater below.

Stybarrow Dodd 7

THE SUMMIT

The summit, all grass, is quite devoid of interest, and the walker may care to spend his few minutes' rest by first determining the highest point of the Dodd and then estimating its altitude. The usually-accepted top is the upright slate slab at the south-western end, (2756'), but there is higher ground 300 yards north-east, indicated by a very loose (at the time of writing!) estate-boundary iron post. That it *is* higher is easily proved: from here, the slate slab at 2756' is seen to cover a part of Esk Pike, 9½ miles away, at about 2400'; therefore the view is *downward*. Q.E.D.

The altitude of the highest point can be roughly decided mathematically. It will be noted that the summit of Raise (2889', 7 furlongs) is directly below the summit of Helvellyn (3080' say, 18 furlongs). The walker didn't climb up here to do sums, and is not likely to challenge the statement that the altitude may, from the data, be calculated at 2770' approximately.

The Ordnance Survey maps are so wonderfully accurate that it needs confidence to suggest that an error has been made in the contouring of the 2½" map, which wrongly shows contours rising to 2825'. The 1" map is correct.

DESCENTS: All ways off are obvious in clear weather. Think twice before dropping down into Deep Dale. *In bad conditions aim south for Sticks Pass.*

RIDGE ROUTE

To RAISE, 2889': 1 mile: SW then S
Depression at 2420' (Sticks Pass)
470 feet of ascent
An easy walk, mostly on grass. Safe in mist.

From the boundary stone, descend south to cross Sticks Pass at its highest point. The long facing slope of Raise becomes stony towards the summit.

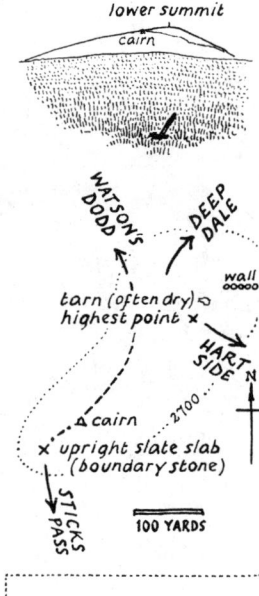

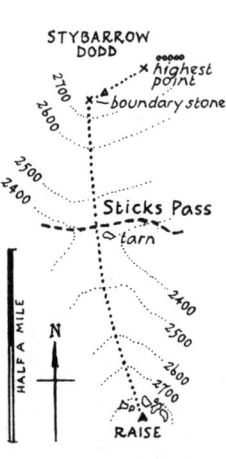

Stybarrow Dodd 8

RIDGE ROUTES

To WATSON'S DODD, 2584': ⅔ mile : NW
Depression slight · Ascent negligible

A very easy stroll. Safe in mist.
A boundary stone and a small tarn
are the only features. A faint path
crosses the depression but does not
lead to the summit cairn, which is
easily reached by inclining left,
slightly ascending across the flat
plateau. Beware marshy ground.

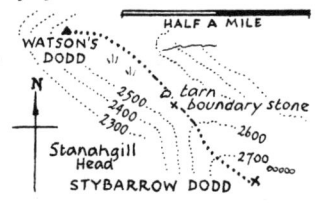

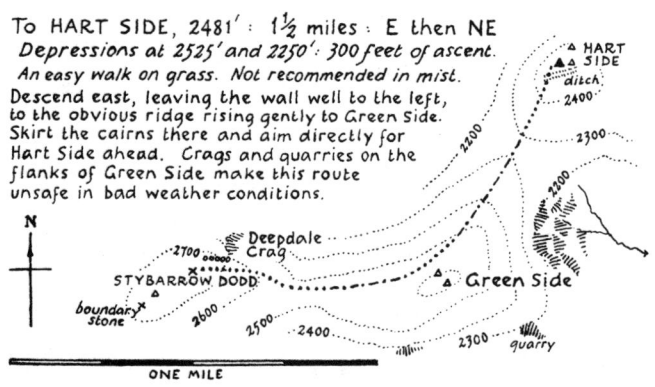

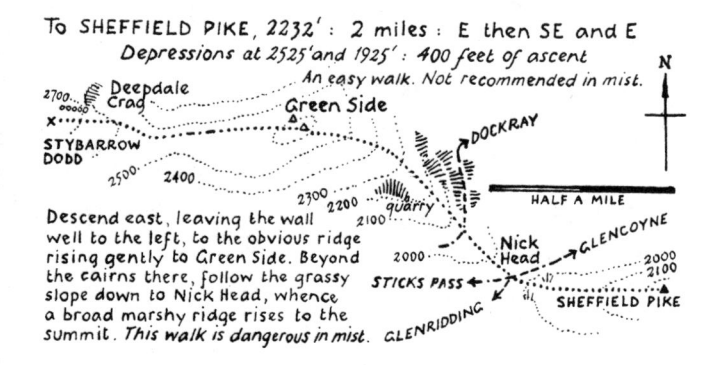

To HART SIDE, 2481': 1½ miles : E then NE
Depressions at 2525' and 2250': 300 feet of ascent.

An easy walk on grass. Not recommended in mist.
Descend east, leaving the wall well to the left,
to the obvious ridge rising gently to Green Side.
Skirt the cairns there and aim directly for
Hart Side ahead. Crags and quarries on the
flanks of Green Side make this route
unsafe in bad weather conditions.

To SHEFFIELD PIKE, 2232': 2 miles : E then SE and E
Depressions at 2525' and 1925': 400 feet of ascent

An easy walk. Not recommended in mist.

Descend east, leaving the wall
well to the left, to the obvious ridge
rising gently to Green Side. Beyond
the cairns there, follow the grassy
slope down to Nick Head, whence
a broad marshy ridge rises to the
summit. This walk is dangerous in mist.

Stybarrow Dodd 9

THE VIEW

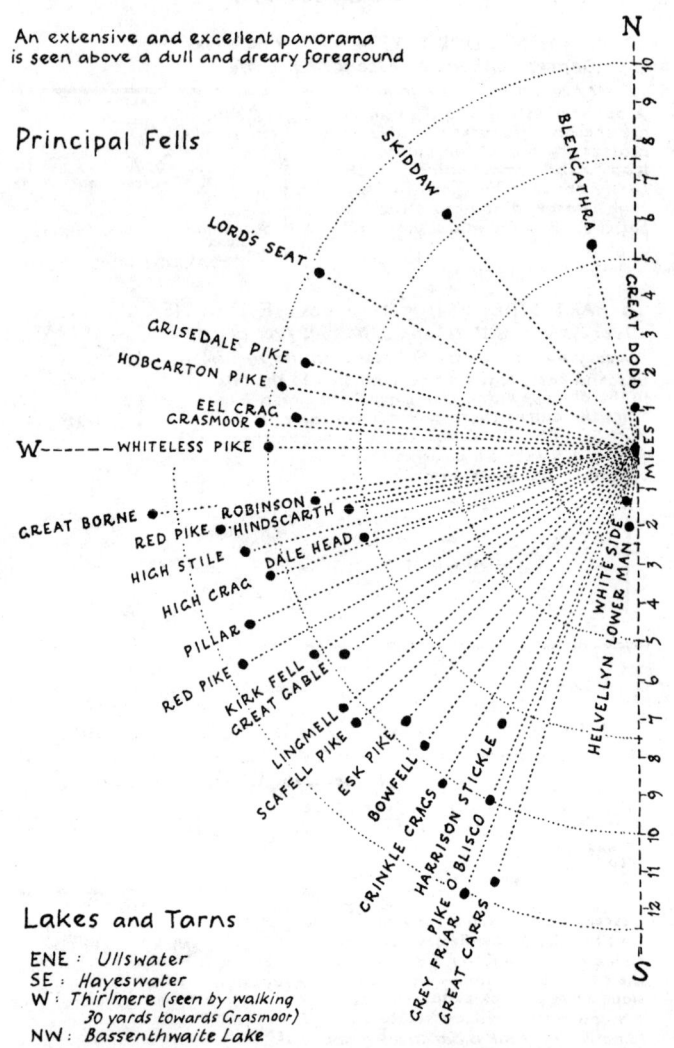

An extensive and excellent panorama is seen above a dull and dreary foreground

Principal Fells

- SKIDDAW
- BLENCATHRA
- LORD'S SEAT
- GREAT DODD
- GRISEDALE PIKE
- HOBCARTON PIKE
- EEL CRAG
- GRASMOOR
- WHITELESS PIKE
- GREAT BORNE
- RED PIKE
- ROBINSON
- HINDSCARTH
- HIGH STILE
- DALE HEAD
- HIGH CRAG
- PILLAR
- RED PIKE
- KIRK FELL
- GREAT GABLE
- HELVELLYN LOWER MAN
- WHITE SIDE
- LINGMELL
- SCAFELL PIKE
- ESK PIKE
- BOWFELL
- CRINKLE CRAGS
- HARRISON STICKLE
- PIKE O' BLISCO
- GREY FRIAR
- GREAT CARRS

Lakes and Tarns

ENE: Ullswater
SE: Hayeswater
W: Thirlmere (seen by walking 30 yards towards Grasmoor)
NW: Bassenthwaite Lake

Stybarrow Dodd 10

THE VIEW

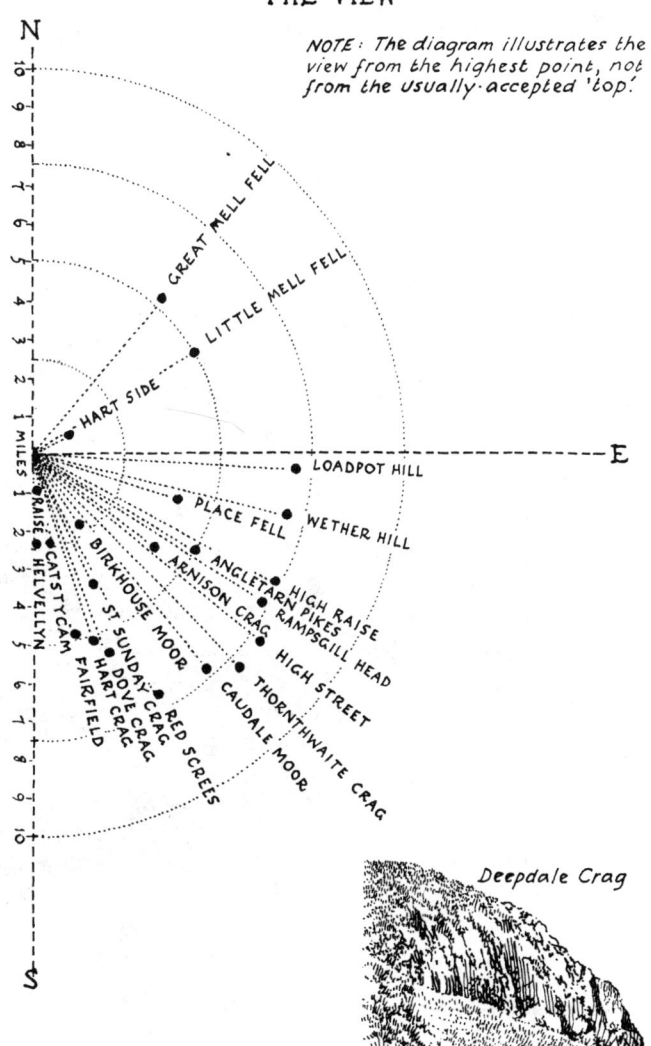

NOTE: The diagram illustrates the view from the highest point, not from the usually-accepted 'top'.

Deepdale Crag

Watson's Dodd 2584'

from Smaithwaite

- ▲ GREAT DODD
- ▲ WATSON'S DODD
- • Legburthwaite
- • Thirlspot

- ▲ HELVELLYN

MILES
0 1 2 3 4

Watson's Dodd 2

NATURAL FEATURES

Whoever Mr Watson may have been, it is a very odd Dodd that has been selected to perpetuate his name. A separate fell it is undoubtedly, with boundaries unusually sharply defined on north and south by deep ravines, but although it conforms to normal mountain structure on three sides — west, north and south — it has no eastern flanks at all: the slope going down east to Deep Dale from the summit-plateau is bisected by a stream that clearly divides Great Dodd and Stybarrow Dodd, and Watson's Dodd cannot stake a claim to any land on this side. In other respects the fell is normal, taking the form of a steepsided ridge, mainly grass with a fringe of crag. With Great Dodd it shares ownership of a very fine ravine, the little-known Mill Gill, but its especial pride and joy is the Castle Rock of Triermain, an imposing and familiar object overlooking the Vale of St John.

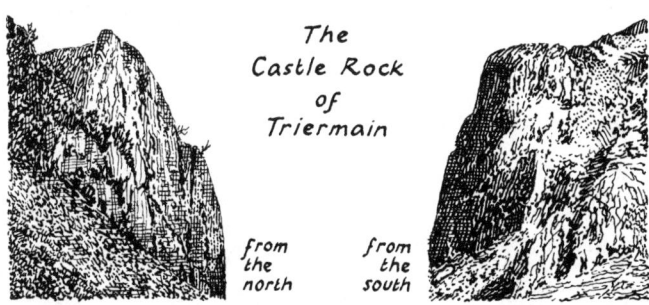

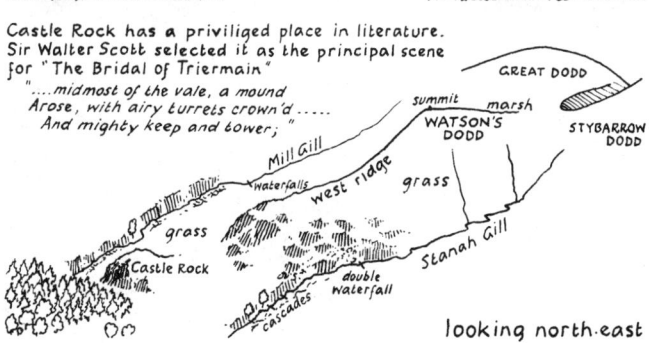

The Castle Rock of Triermain

from the north

from the south

Castle Rock has a privileged place in literature. Sir Walter Scott selected it as the principal scene for "The Bridal of Triermain"

"....midmost of the vale, a mound
Arose, with airy turrets crown'd.....
And mighty keep and tower;"

looking north-east

Watson's Dodd 3

MAP

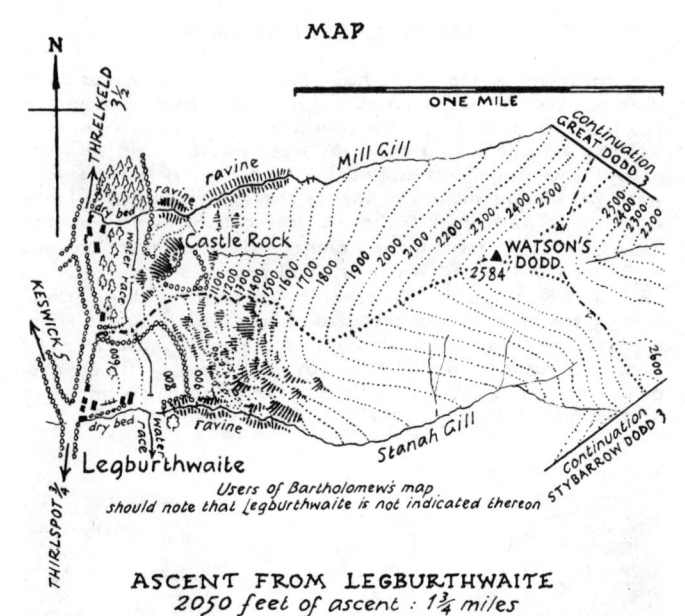

Users of Bartholomew's map should note that Legburthwaite is not indicated thereon

ASCENT FROM LEGBURTHWAITE
2050 feet of ascent : 1¾ miles

A detour may be made below Castle Rock by following the water race (here scenically attractive) crossing amphitheatre and waterfalls it by a plank, climbing a wall and steeply scrambling by the gill to join the ridge-route higher.

This ascent promises well, but deteriorates into a trudge

looking east

Watson's Dodd 4

THE SUMMIT

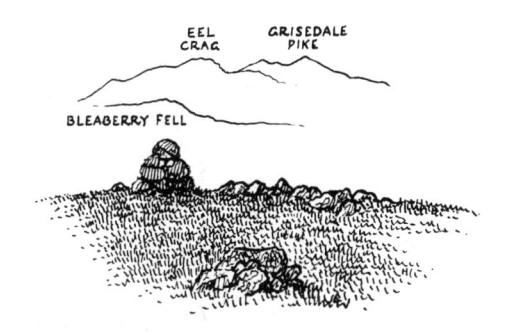

A few big stones adorn the highest point, at the western end of the flat triangular top, and they look strangely alien just there in the universal grassiness of the surroundings, as though they had been carried there. (Maybe Mr. Watson undertook this task: if so, it is fitting that the fell should bear his name!). There is a suggestion of history in these hoary stones.

DESCENTS : The quickest way down to civilisation is by the west ridge, which commences immediately below the cairn. After half a mile, when the ground becomes rough, incline right to avoid crags ahead and aim for the south corner of the wall behind Castle Rock ; an old path in a groove leads down to it and continues to the valley. *In mist*, use the same route : the ridge is fairly well defined, but if in doubt incline right rather than left. Avoid getting into Mill Gill or Stanah Gill, both of which are dangerous.

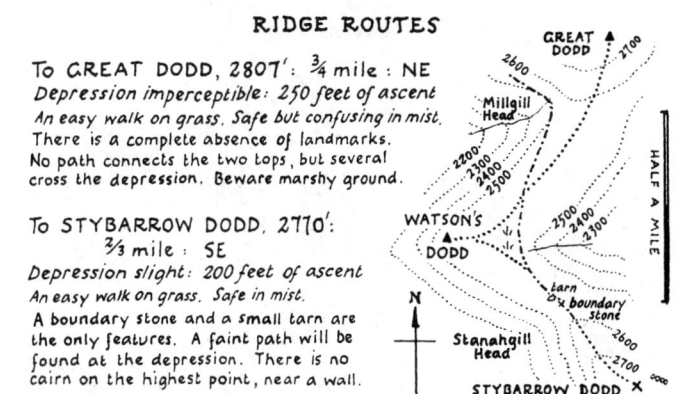

RIDGE ROUTES

To GREAT DODD, 2807': ¾ mile : NE
Depression imperceptible: 250 feet of ascent
An easy walk on grass. Safe but confusing in mist.
There is a complete absence of landmarks.
No path connects the two tops, but several
cross the depression. Beware marshy ground.

To STYBARROW DODD, 2770':
⅔ mile : SE
Depression slight: 200 feet of ascent
An easy walk on grass. Safe in mist.
A boundary stone and a small tarn are
the only features. A faint path will be
found at the depression. There is no
cairn on the highest point, near a wall.

Watson's Dodd 5

Castle Rock and Mill Gill

Watson's Dodd 6

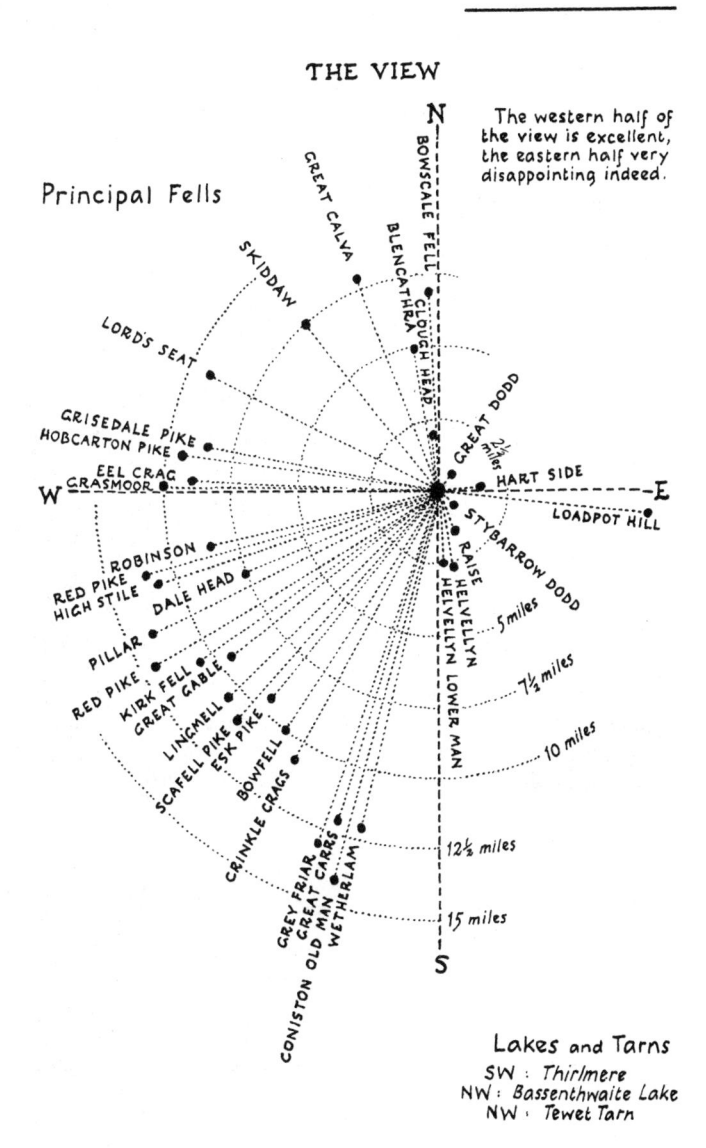

THE VIEW

The western half of the view is excellent, the eastern half very disappointing indeed.

Principal Fells

- BOWSCALE FELL
- GREAT CALVA
- BLENCATHRA
- CLOUGH HEAD
- SKIDDAW
- LORD'S SEAT
- GREAT DODD
- GRISEDALE PIKE
- HOBCARTON PIKE
- HART SIDE
- EEL CRAG
- GRASMOOR
- LOADPOT HILL
- STYBARROW DODD
- ROBINSON
- RAISE
- RED PIKE
- HELVELLYN
- HIGH STILE
- DALE HEAD
- HELVELLYN LOWER MAN
- PILLAR
- RED PIKE
- KIRK FELL
- GREAT GABLE
- LINGMELL
- SCAFELL PIKE
- ESK PIKE
- BOWFELL
- CRINKLE CRAGS
- GREY FRIAR
- GREAT CARRS
- WETHERLAM
- CONISTON OLD MAN

2½ miles
5 miles
7½ miles
10 miles
12½ miles
15 miles

Lakes and Tarns

SW : Thirlmere
NW : Bassenthwaite Lake
NW : Tewet Tarn

White Side 2832'

— a name of convenience.
The summit is strictly nameless,
White Side being the west slope
below the top (probably so-called
from splashes of quartz on many
of the stones).

from Catstycam

White Side 2

NATURAL FEATURES

Although White Side presents an intimidating wall of low crags to travellers on the road at Thirlspot its upper slopes on this western side are docile enough, being wholly of grass at easy gradients: two paths to Helvellyn cross this flank. Very different is the eastern face, which falls sharply and steeply in crag and scree to the silent recesses of the wild upper Glenridding valley.

The summit is no more than a big grassy mound on the high ridge running northwards from Helvellyn and it rises only slightly above the general level of the ridge.

Skiers and sheep share a high regard for White Side.

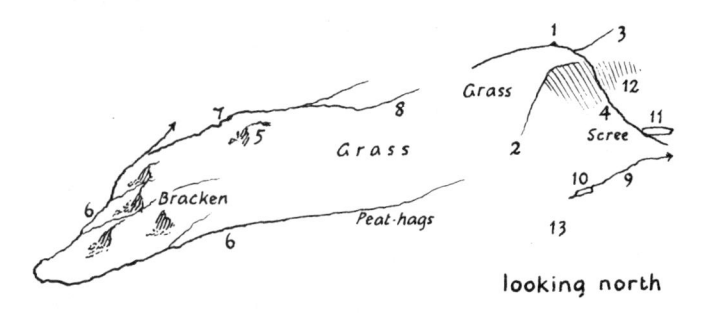

looking north

1: The summit
2: Ridge continuing to Helvellyn Lower Man
3: Ridge continuing to Raise
4: The east ridge
5: Brown Crag
6: Helvellyn Gill
7: Fisher Gill
8: Brund Gill
9: Glenridding Beck
10: Tarn in Brown Cove
11: Keppelcove Tarn (dry)
12: Keppel Cove
13: Brown Cove

Rock pinnacle, Brown Crag

The habit of the west-flowing streams of White Side is interesting. It seems natural that they should feed Thirlmere, but a strip of higher ground alongside the lake turns them north into the outflow, St John's Beck. This perversity of nature has been corrected by the Manchester engineers, who have constructed a water race along the base of the fell to collect the water and divert it south into Thirlmere.

White Side 3

MAP

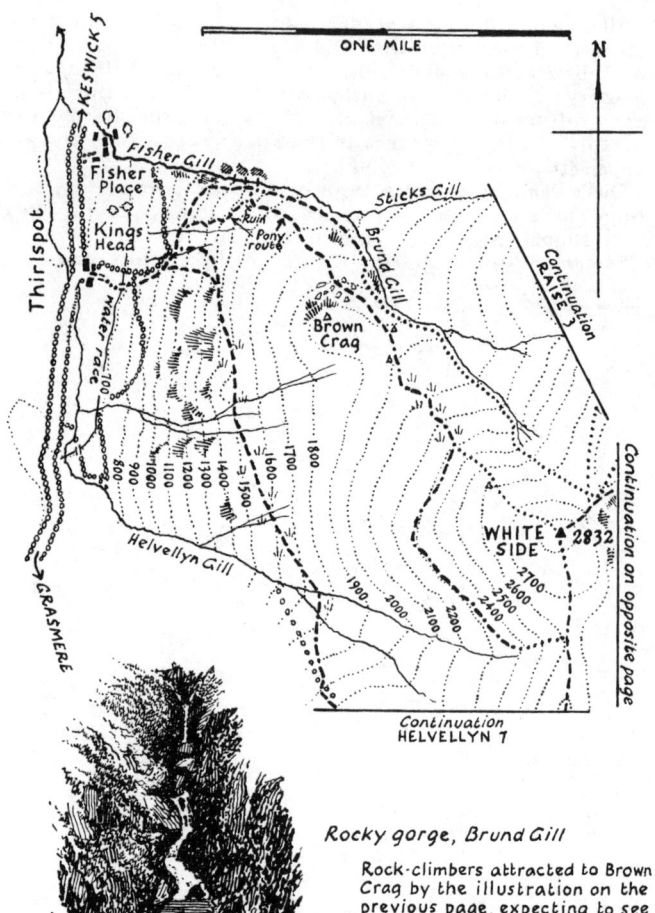

Rocky gorge, Brund Gill

Rock-climbers attracted to Brown Crag by the illustration on the previous page, expecting to see another Napes Needle, will turn away in disgust upon finding it only a few feet high. They may console themselves by trying to climb the nearby gorge in Brund Gill without getting wet.

White Side 4

Waterfalls in Fisher Gill

MAP

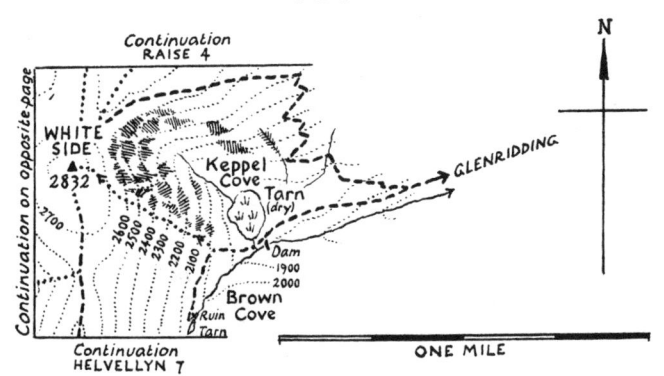

White Side 5

ASCENT FROM THIRLSPOT
2300 feet of ascent : 2½ miles

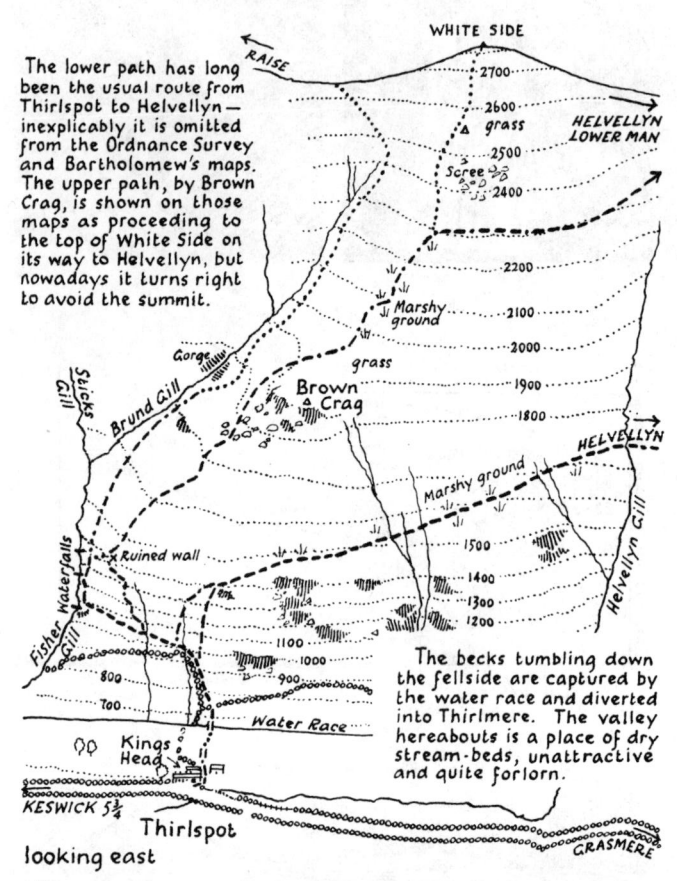

The lower path has long been the usual route from Thirlspot to Helvellyn — inexplicably it is omitted from the Ordnance Survey and Bartholomew's maps. The upper path, by Brown Crag, is shown on those maps as proceeding to the top of White Side on its way to Helvellyn, but nowadays it turns right to avoid the summit.

The becks tumbling down the fellside are captured by the water race and diverted into Thirlmere. The valley hereabouts is a place of dry stream-beds, unattractive and quite forlorn.

looking east

Two paths cross the western flank of White Side above Thirlspot. They lead to Helvellyn, but the upper one is conveniently placed for the ascent of White Side: it is an easy climb on grass after initial steepness.

White Side 6

ASCENT FROM GLENRIDDING
2400 feet of ascent : 4 miles from Glenridding village

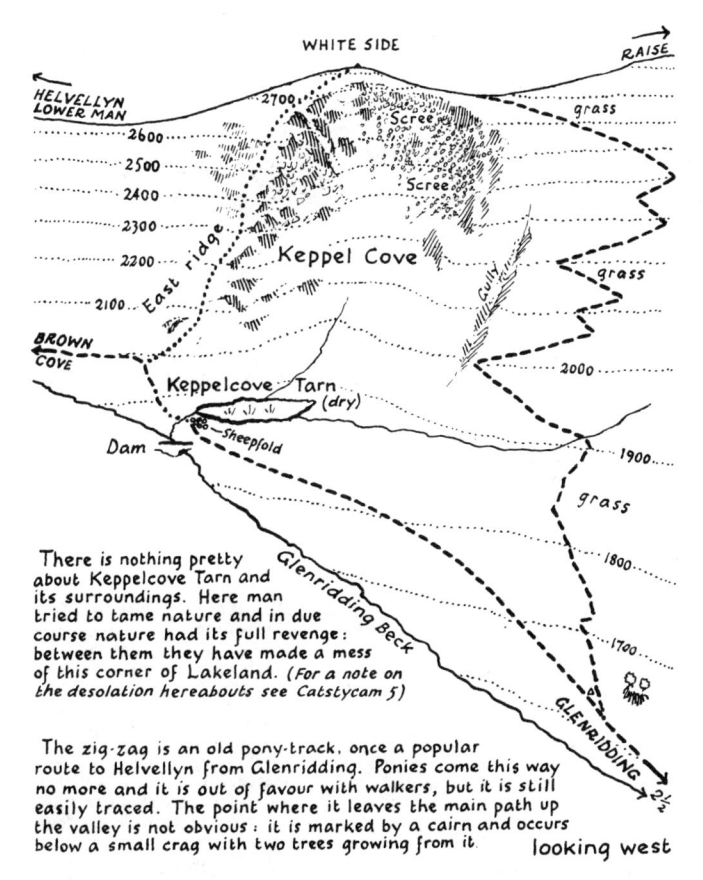

There is nothing pretty about Keppelcove Tarn and its surroundings. Here man tried to tame nature and in due course nature had its full revenge: between them they have made a mess of this corner of Lakeland. *(For a note on the desolation hereabouts see Catstycam 5)*

The zig-zag is an old pony-track, once a popular route to Helvellyn from Glenridding. Ponies come this way no more and it is out of favour with walkers, but it is still easily traced. The point where it leaves the main path up the valley is not obvious: it is marked by a cairn and occurs below a small crag with two trees growing from it.

looking west

There are few high fells more easily climbed than White Side if the zig-zag path from Glenridding is used. The other route shown, by the east ridge, is very different; it is pathless, steep and stony, but not difficult.

White Side 7

THE SUMMIT

The top of White Side is marked by a large cairn set in a wide expanse of excellent turf, with grassy slopes descending gently on all sides, although north-eastwards the ground falls away sharply around the rim of Keppel Cove.

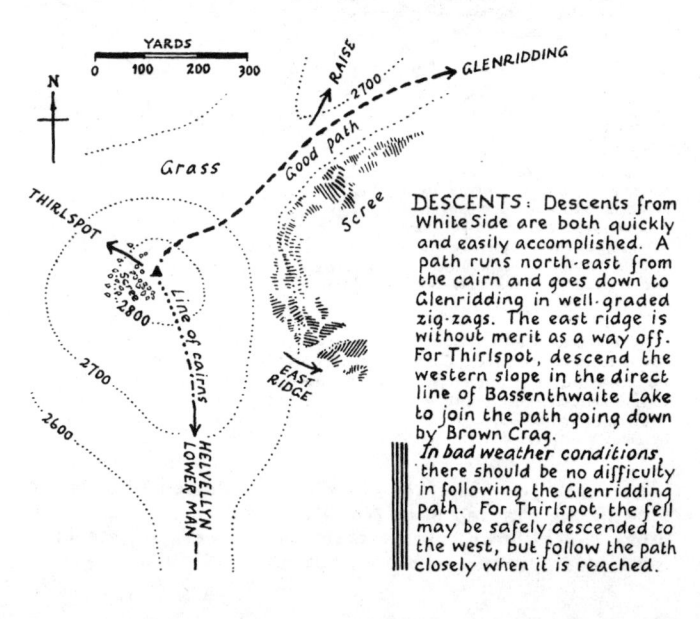

DESCENTS: Descents from White Side are both quickly and easily accomplished. A path runs north-east from the cairn and goes down to Glenridding in well-graded zig-zags. The east ridge is without merit as a way off. For Thirlspot, descend the western slope in the direct line of Bassenthwaite Lake to join the path going down by Brown Crag.

In bad weather conditions, there should be no difficulty in following the Glenridding path. For Thirlspot, the fell may be safely descended to the west, but follow the path closely when it is reached.

White Side 8

THE VIEW

Helvellyn shuts out the distant scene southwards, but in all other directions the panorama is very good, especially to the west. The best picture is provided by Skiddaw, with Bassenthwaite Lake at its foot.

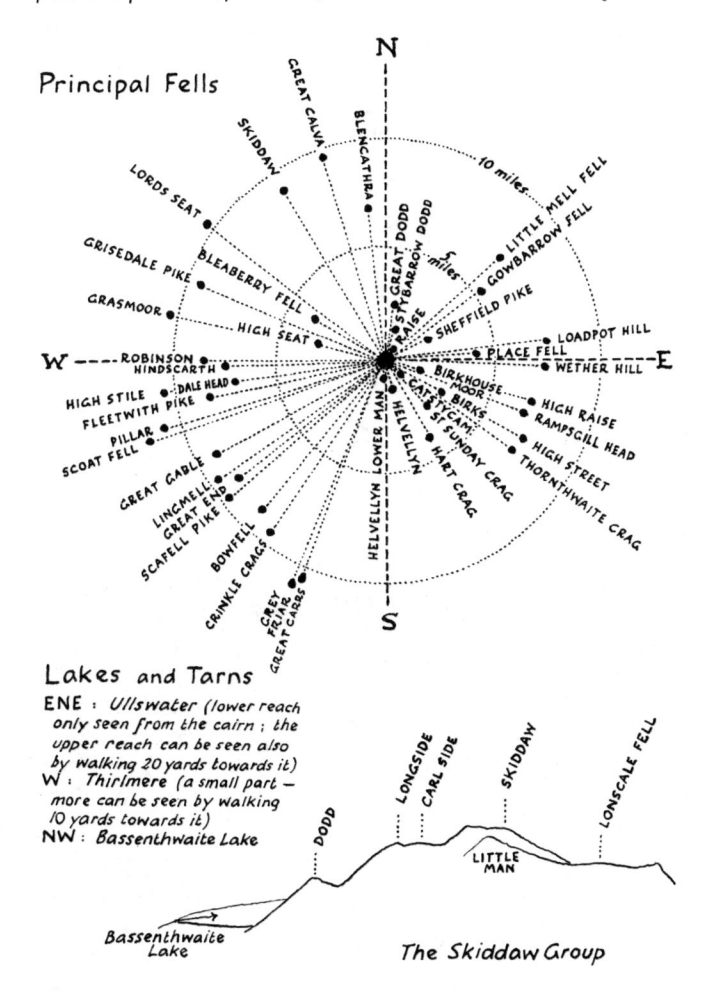

Principal Fells

Lakes and Tarns

ENE : *Ullswater (lower reach only seen from the cairn ; the upper reach can be seen also by walking 20 yards towards it)*
W : *Thirlmere (a small part — more can be seen by walking 10 yards towards it)*
NW : *Bassenthwaite Lake*

The Skiddaw Group

White Side 9

RIDGE ROUTES

To HELVELLYN LOWER MAN, 3033': 1 mile: S
Depression at 2600'
450 feet of ascent

A grassy descent and a long stony climb.
Easy. Safe in mist.

Follow the line of cairns: a fair path materialises at the depression and it continues distinctly up the long ridge ahead, becoming very loose and stony.

To RAISE, 2889'
¾ mile: NE
Depression at 2650'
250 feet of ascent

Easy walking on grass.
Safe in mist.

A good path leads down to the depression (and continues down into Glenridding). Strike up the broad shoulder from the depression — there is no path — and after reaching a cairn cross the level plateau to the stony summit.

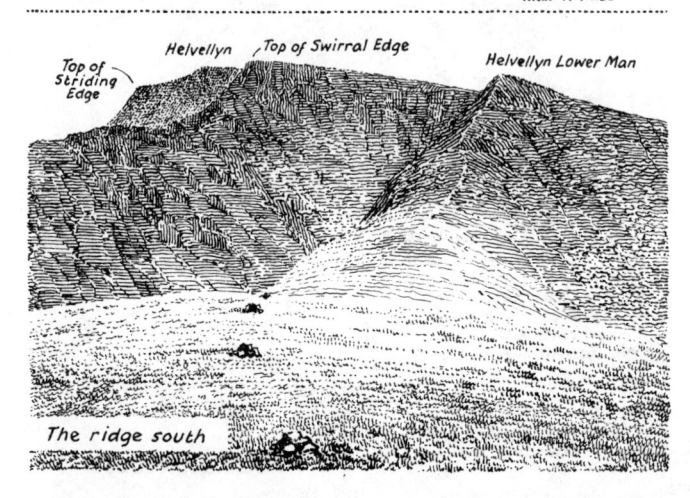

The ridge south

White Side 10

The East Ridge
(In the foreground, the burst banks of Keppelcove Tarn)

THE EASTERN FELLS
Some Personal Notes in conclusion

I suppose it might be said, to add impressiveness to the whole thing, that this book has been twenty years in the making, for it is so long, and more, since I first came from a smoky mill-town (forgive me, Blackburn!) and beheld, from Orrest Head, a scene of great loveliness, a fascinating paradise, Lakeland's mountains and trees and water. That was the first time I had looked upon beauty, or imagined it, even. Afterwards I went often, whenever I could, and always my eyes were lifted to the hills. I was to find then, and it has been so ever since, a spiritual and physical satisfaction in climbing mountains — and a tranquil mind upon reaching their summits, as though I had escaped from the disappointments and unkindnesses of life and emerged above them into a new world, a better world.

But that is by the way. In those early Lakeland days I served my apprenticeship faithfully, learning all the time. At first, the hills were frightening, moody giants, and I a timid Gulliver, but very gradually through the years we became acquaintances and much later firm friends.

In due course I came to live within sight of the hills, and I was well content. If I could not be climbing, I was happy to sit idly and dream of them, serenely. Then came a restlessness and the feeling that it was not enough to take their gifts and do nothing in return. I must dedicate something of myself, the best part of me, to them. I started to write about them, and to draw pictures of them. Doing these things, I found they were still giving and I still receiving, for a great pleasure filled me when I was so engaged — I had found a new way of escape to them and from all else less worth while.

Thus it comes about that I have written this book. Not for material gain, welcome though that would be (you see I have not escaped entirely!); not for the benefit of my contemporaries, though if it brings them also to the hills I shall be well pleased; certainly not for posterity, about which I can work up no enthusiasm at all. No, this book has been written, carefully and with infinite patience, for my own pleasure and because it has seemed to bring the hills to my own fireside. If it has merit, it is because the hills have merit.

I started the book determined that everything in it should be perfect, with the consequence that I spent the first six months filling wastepaper baskets. Only then did I accept what I should have known and acknowledged from the start — that nothing created by man is perfect, or can hope to be; and having thus consoled and cheered my hurt conceit I got along like a house on fire. So let me be the first to say it: this book is full of imperfections. But let me dare also to say that (apart from many minor blemishes of which I am already deeply conscious and have no wish to be reminded) it is free from inaccuracies.

The group of fells I have named the Eastern Fells are old favourites, not quite as exciting as the Scafell heights, perhaps, but enjoyable territory for the walker. They are most conveniently climbed from the west, which is a pity, for the finest approaches are from the Patterdale valley to the east. The walking is easy for the most part; very easy along the main watershed. The coves below the summits eastwards are a feature of these hills: rarely visited, they are very impressive in their craggy surroundings. Exploration also reveals many interesting evidences of old and abandoned industries — quarries, mines, aqueducts, disused paths. Somebody should write a geographical history of these enterprises before all records are lost.

Some of my experiences during many solitary wanderings while collecting information for this book would be worth the telling, but I preserve the memories for the time when I can no longer climb. One, however, returns insistently to mind...... I remember a sunny day in the wilderness of Ruthwaite Cove: I lay idly on the warm rocks alongside Hard Tarn, with desolation everywhere but in my heart, where was peace. The air was still; there was no sound, and nothing in view but the shattered confusion of rocks all around. I might have been the last man in a dead world. A tiny splash drew my gaze to the crystal-clear depths of the tarn .... a newt was swimming there, just beneath the surface. I watched it for a long time. And I fell to wondering........

wondering about it, and its mission as it circled the smooth waters, and the purpose of its life — and mine. A trivial thing to remember, maybe, yet I do. I often think of that small creature, a speck of life in the immensity of desolation in which it had its being.

It is a remarkable thing, now that I come to think of it, that I still set forth for a day on the hills with the eagerness I felt when they were new to me. So it is that I have thoroughly enjoyed my walks whilst this book has been in preparation, much more so because I have walked with a purpose. Yet recently my gaze has been wandering more and more from the path, and away to the fells east of Kirkstone — my next area of exploration.

So, although I take my leave of the Eastern Fells with very real regret, as one parts from good friends, I look forward to equally happy days on the Far Eastern Fells. When this last sentence is written Book One will be finished, and in the same moment Book Two will take its place in my thoughts.

Christmas, 1954   AW.

SIGN REFERENCES
(signs used in the maps and diagrams)

Good footpath `-------`
(sufficiently distinct to be followed in mist)

Intermittent footpath `-·-·-·-·-`
(difficult to follow in mist)

Route recommended but no path `→········→····`
(if recommended one way only, arrow indicates direction)

Wall ∞∞∞∞∞∞∞   **Broken wall** ∘∘∘∘∘∘∘∘∘∘

Fence ++++++++   **Broken fence** ''''''''''''

Marshy ground ⋎⋎⋎⋎   **Trees** 🌳🌳🌳

Crags ⛰⛰⛰   **Boulders** ⋄⋄⋄⋄

Stream or River ～～～→
(arrow indicates direction of flow)

Waterfall ～⩊～   **Bridge** ～⋈～

Buildings ▪▫▪   **Unenclosed road** ::::::::::

Contours (at 100' intervals)
  1900
  1800
  1700

Summit-cairn ▲   **Other** (prominent) **cairns** △

THE
FAR EASTERN
FELLS

A PICTORIAL GUIDE
TO THE
LAKELAND FELLS
50TH ANNIVERSARY EDITION

being an illustrated account
of a study and exploration
of the mountains in the
English Lake District

by

A Wainwright

BOOK TWO
THE FAR EASTERN FELLS

Frances Lincoln Limited
4 Torriano Mews
Torriano Avenue
London NW5 2RZ
www.franceslincoln.com

Originally published by Henry Marshall, Kentmere, 1957

First published by Frances Lincoln 2003

50th Anniversary Edition with re-originated artwork
published by Frances Lincoln 2005

Copyright © The Estate of A. Wainwright 1957

All rights reserved. Without limiting the rights under
copyright reserved above, no part of this publication may
be reproduced, stored in or introduced into a retrieval
system, or transmitted, in any form or by any means
(electronic, mechanical, photocopying, or otherwise),
without either prior permission in writing from the
publisher or a licence permitting restricted copying.
In the United Kingdom such licences are issued by
the Copyright Licensing Agency, Saffron House,
6-10 Kirby Street, London EC1N 8TS.

Printed and bound in China

A CIP catalogue record for this book
is available from the British Library.

ISBN 978 0 7112 2455 1

18 17 16 15 14 13 12

50TH ANNIVERSARY EDITION
PUBLISHED BY
FRANCES LINCOLN, LONDON

THE PICTORIAL GUIDES

Book One: The Eastern Fells, 1955
Book Two: The Far Eastern Fells, 1957
Book Three: The Central Fells, 1958
Book Four: The Southern Fells, 1960
Book Five: The Northern Fells, 1962
Book Six: The North Western Fells, 1964
Book Seven: The Western Fells, 1966

PUBLISHER'S NOTE

This 50th Anniversary edition of the Pictorial Guides to the Lakeland Fells is newly reproduced from the handwritten pages created in the 1950s and 1960s by A. Wainwright. The descriptions of the walks were correct, to the best of the author's knowledge, at the time of first publication and they are reproduced here without amendment. However, footpaths, cairns and other waymarks described here are no longer all as they were fifty years ago and walkers are advised to check with an up-to-date map when planning a walk.

Fellwalking has increased dramatically since the Pictorial Guides were first published. Some popular routes have become eroded, making good footwear and great care all the more necessary for walkers. The vital points about fellwalking, as A. Wainwright himself wrote on many occasions, are to use common sense and to remember to watch where you are putting your feet.

A programme of revision of the Pictorial Guides is under way and revised editions of each of them will be published over the next few years.

BOOK TWO

is dedicated to
the memory of

THE MEN WHO BUILT THE STONE WALLS,

which have endured
the storms of centuries
and remain to this day as monuments to
enterprise, perseverance and hard work

INTRODUCTION

Classification and Definition

Any division of the Lakeland fells into geographical districts must necessarily be arbitrary, just as the location of the outer boundaries of Lakeland must always be a matter of opinion. Any attempt to define internal or external boundaries is certain to invite criticism, and he who takes it upon himself to say where Lakeland starts and finishes, or, for example, where the Central Fells merge into the Southern Fells and *which* fells are the Central Fells and which the Southern and *why* they need be so classified, must not expect his pronouncements to be generally accepted.

Yet for present purposes some plan of classification and definition must be used. County and parochial boundaries are no help, nor is the recently-defined area of the Lakeland National Park, for this book is concerned only with the high ground.

First, the external boundaries. Straight lines linking the extremities of the outlying lakes enclose all the higher fells very conveniently. There are a few fells of lesser height to the north and east, however, that are typically Lakeland in character and cannot properly be omitted: these are brought in, somewhat untidily, by extending the lines in those areas. Thus:

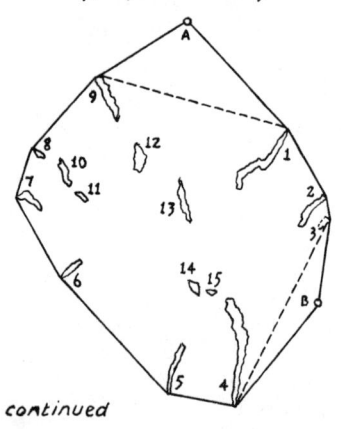

1 : *Ullswater*
2 : *Hawes Water*
3 : proposed *Swindale Res!*
4 : *Windermere*
5 : *Coniston Water*
6 : *Wast Water*
7 : *Ennerdale Water*
8 : *Loweswater*
9 : *Bassenthwaite Lake*
10 : *Crummock Water*
11 : *Buttermere*
12 : *Derwent Water*
13 : *Thirlmere*
14 : *Grasmere*
15 : *Rydal Water*
A : Caldbeck
B : Longsleddale (church)

continued

INTRODUCTION

Classification and Definition
continued

The complete Guide is planned to include all the fells in the area enclosed by the straight lines of the diagram. This is an undertaking quite beyond the compass of a single volume, and it is necessary, therefore, to divide the area into convenient sections, making the fullest use of natural boundaries (lakes, valleys and low passes) so that each district is, as far as possible, self-contained and independent of the rest.

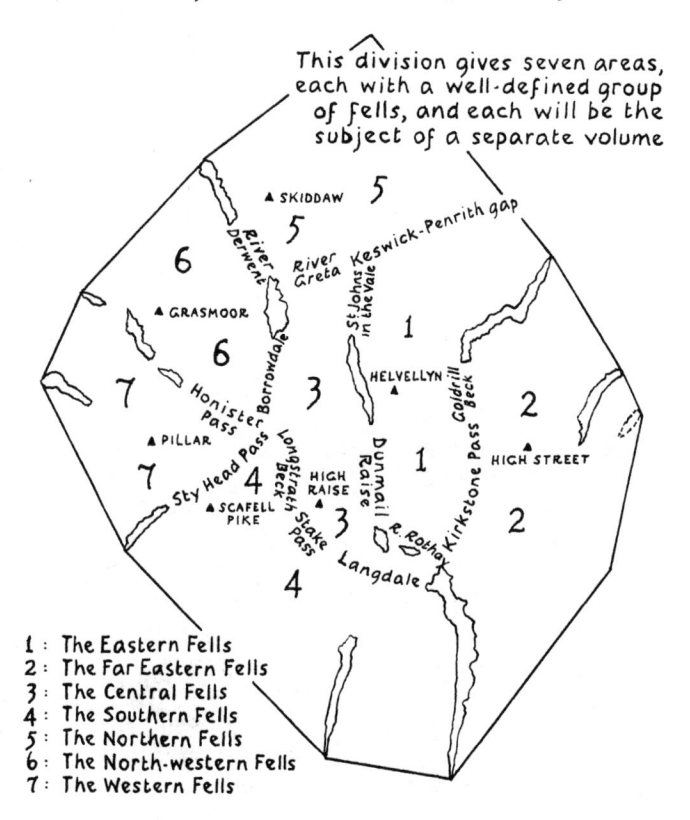

This division gives seven areas, each with a well-defined group of fells, and each will be the subject of a separate volume

1 : The Eastern Fells
2 : The Far Eastern Fells
3 : The Central Fells
4 : The Southern Fells
5 : The Northern Fells
6 : The North-western Fells
7 : The Western Fells

INTRODUCTION

Notes on the Illustrations

THE MAPS................... Many excellent books have been written about Lakeland, but the best literature of all for the walker is that published by the Director General of Ordnance Survey, the 1" map for companionship and guidance on expeditions, the 2½" map for exploration both on the fells and by the fireside. These admirable maps are remarkably accurate topographically but there is a crying need for a revision of the paths on the hills: several walkers' tracks that have come into use during the past few decades, some of them now broad highways, are not shown at all; other paths still shown on the maps have fallen into neglect and can no longer be traced on the ground.

The popular Bartholomew 1" map is a beautiful picture, fit for a frame, but this too is unreliable for paths; indeed here the defect is much more serious, for routes are indicated where no paths ever existed, nor ever could — the cartographer has preferred to take precipices in his stride rather than deflect his graceful curves over easy ground.

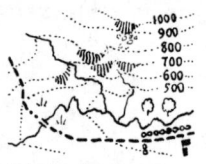

Hence the justification for the maps in this book: they have the one merit (of importance to walkers) of being dependable as regards delineation of *paths*. They are intended as supplements to the Ordnance Survey maps, certainly not as substitutes.

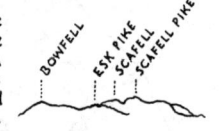

THE VIEWS................. Various devices have been used to illustrate the views from the summits of the fells. The full panorama in the form of an outline drawing is most satisfactory generally, and this method has been adopted for the main viewpoints.

THE DIAGRAMS OF ASCENTS.................... The routes of ascent of the higher fells are depicted by diagrams that do not pretend to strict accuracy: they are neither plans nor elevations; in fact there is deliberate distortion in order to show detail clearly: usually they are represented as viewed from imaginary 'space-stations.' But it is hoped they will be useful and interesting.

THE DRAWINGS....... The drawings at least are honest attempts to reproduce what the eye sees: they illustrate features of interest and also serve the dual purpose of breaking up the text and balancing the layout of the pages, and of filling up awkward blank spaces, like this:

Thirlmere

THE
FAR EASTERN
FELLS

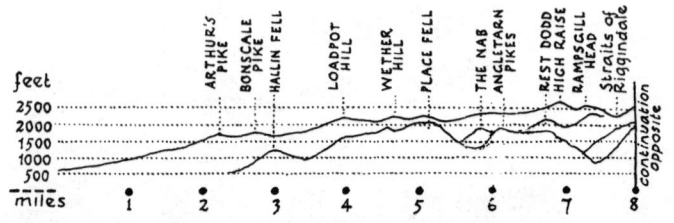

[Elevation profile labels: ARTHUR'S PIKE, BONSCALE PIKE, HALLIN FELL, LOADPOT HILL, WETHER HILL, PLACE FELL, THE NAB, ANGLETARN PIKES, REST DODD, HIGH RAISE, RAMPSGILL HEAD, Straits of Riggindale — continuation opposite]

The Far Eastern Fells rise to the east of Kirkstone Pass and the Patterdale valley, which together form a natural western boundary to the group. To north and south these fells run down to low country, and it is on the east side that difficulty arises in fixing a demarcation line, for here high ground continues, to merge ultimately into the Pennines. Nevertheless, it is possible to adopt a satisfactory boundary, not so much by a selection of obvious natural features as by observation of the characteristics of the fells in this area. Lakeland's fells have a charm that is unique: they are romantic in atmosphere, dramatic in appearance, colourful, craggy, with swift-running sparkling streams and tumbled lichened boulders — and the walker along this eastern fringe constantly finds himself passing from the exciting beauty that is typically Lakeland to the quieter and more sombre attractiveness that is typically Pennine. Broadly, this 'œsthetic' boundary runs along the eastern watersheds of Longsleddale, Mosedale and Swindale.

The group has a main spine running through it, due north and south, that keeps consistently above 2000' over a distance of eight miles and culminates midway in the greatest of these fells, High Street. From this central point there is a general decline in altitude

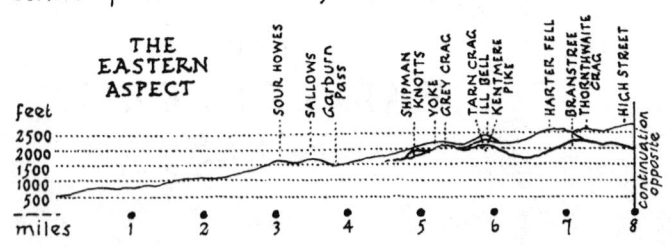

THE EASTERN ASPECT

[Elevation profile labels: SOUR HOWES, SALLOWS, Garburn Pass, SHIPMAN KNOTTS, YOKE, GREY CRAG, TARN CRAG, ILL BELL, KENTMERE PIKE, HARTER FELL, BRANSTREE, THORNTHWAITE CRAG, HIGH STREET — continuation opposite]

THE WESTERN ASPECT

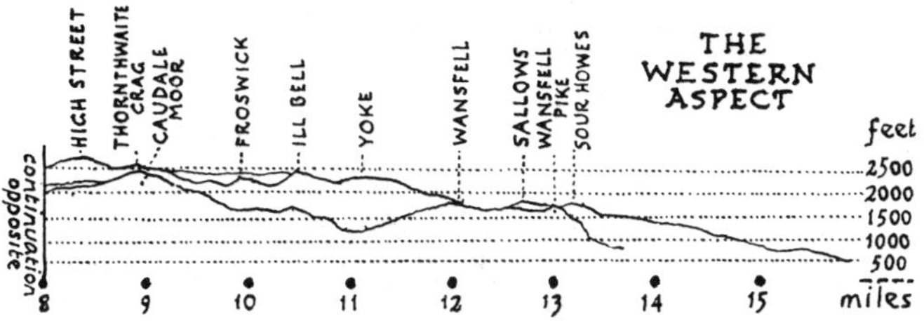
HIGH STREET
THORNTHWAITE CRAG
CAUDALE MOOR
FROSWICK
ILL BELL
YOKE
WANSFELL
SALLOWS
WANSFELL PIKE
SOUR HOWES
feet
2500
2000
1500
1000
500
continuation opposite
8
9
10
11
12
13
14
15
miles

towards the boundaries of the group in all directions but it is not to be inferred that all ridges radiate from High Street: on the contrary, it is the pivot of a complicated system of parallel and lateral ridges separated by deep valleys that contributes greatly to the attractiveness of these fells east of Kirkstone.

The relative inaccessibility of many of the heights (due to a decided lack of tourist accommodation in the valleys) can be the only reason why they remain lonely and unfrequented by visitors, for in the high quality of the scenery and the excellence of the walks they rank with the best. In one respect, indeed, they are supreme, for their extensive and uplifting views across to the distant Pennines are a delight not to be found elsewhere in the district. Solitary walkers will enjoy the area immensely, but they must tread circumspectly and avoid accident. Mountain-camps and bivouacs offer the best means of exploration; for the walker who prefers a bed, Mardale Head used to be the best centre but now has no hospitality nearer than the Haweswater Hotel (which is badly sited for travellers on foot) and the Patterdale valley is most convenient as a base. The area will be appreciated best, however, if occasional nights can be arranged at Howtown, Haweswater, Kentmere and Troutbeck.

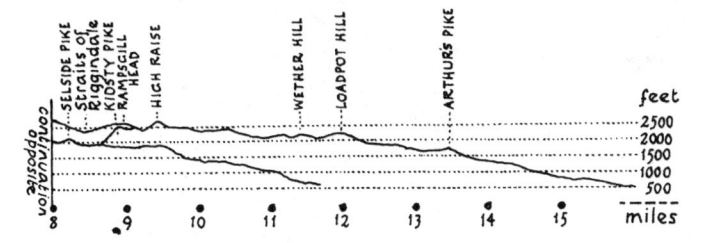

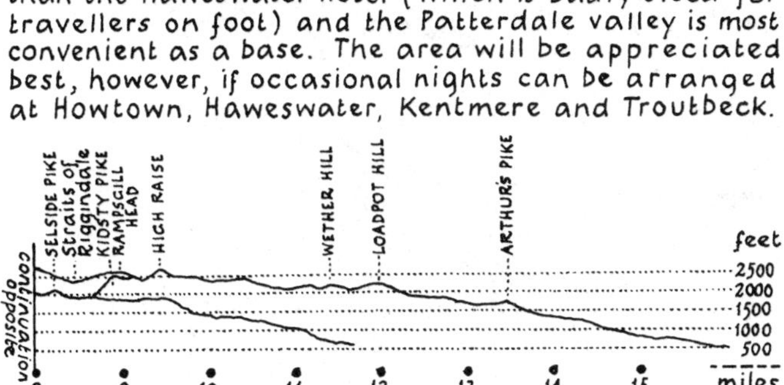
SELSIDE PIKE
Straits of Riggindale
KIDSTY PIKE
RAMPSGILL HEAD
HIGH RAISE
WETHER HILL
LOADPOT HILL
ARTHUR'S PIKE
feet
2500
2000
1500
1000
500
continuation opposite
8
9
10
11
12
13
14
15
miles

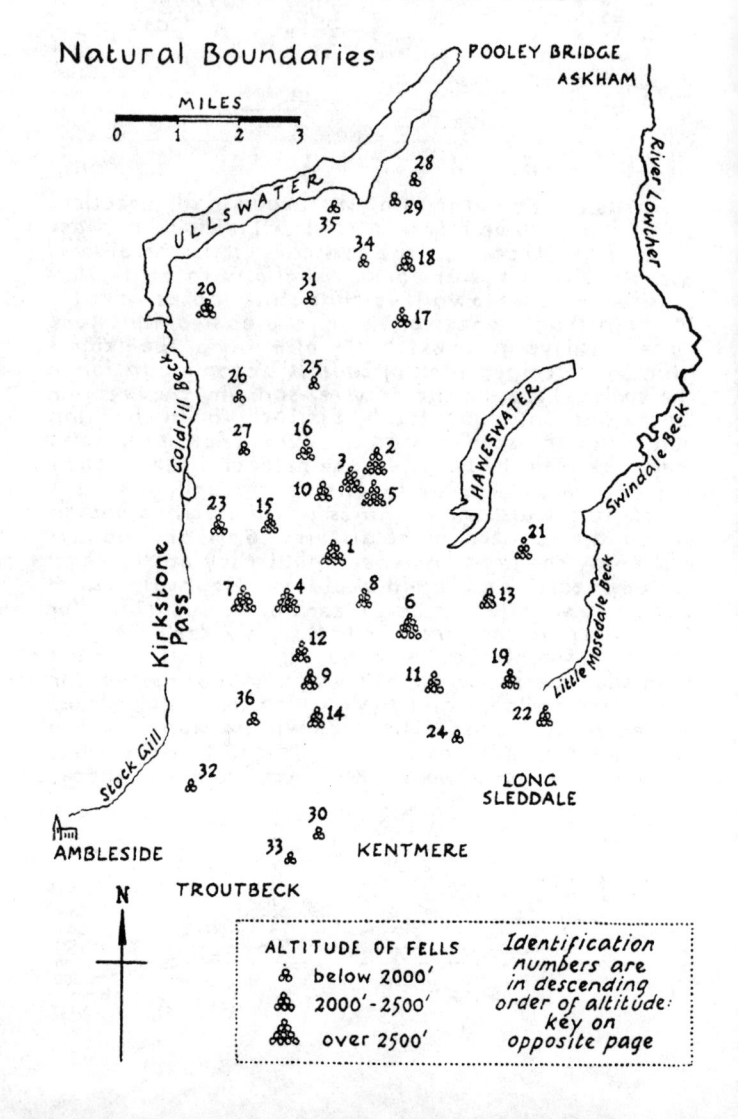

THE FAR EASTERN FELLS

Natural Boundaries

ALTITUDE OF FELLS
- below 2000'
- 2000'-2500'
- over 2500'

Identification numbers are in descending order of altitude; key on opposite page

THE FAR EASTERN FELLS

Reference to map opposite
over 2500 / 2000-2500 / below 2000

in the order of
their appearance
in this book

Altitude in feet

26	..	ANGLETARN PIKES	1857
28	..	ARTHUR'S PIKE	1747
31	..	BEDA FELL	1664
29	..	BONSCALE PIKE	1718
13	..	BRANSTREE	2333
27	..	BROCK CRAGS	1842
7	..	CAUDALE MOOR	2502
12	..	FROSWICK	2359
15	..	GRAY CRAG	2286
22	..	GREY CRAG	2093
35	..	HALLIN FELL	1271
6	..	HARTER FELL	2539
23	..	HARTSOP DODD	2018
2	..	HIGH RAISE	2634
1	..	HIGH STREET	2718
9	..	ILL BELL	2476
11	..	KENTMERE PIKE	2397
5	..	KIDSTY PIKE	2560
10	..	THE KNOTT	2423
18	..	LOADPOT HILL	2201
8	..	MARDALE ILL BELL	2496
25	..	THE NAB	1887
20	..	PLACE FELL	2154
3	..	RAMPSGILL HEAD	2581
16	..	REST DODD	2278
30	..	SALLOWS	1691
21	..	SELSIDE PIKE	2142
24	..	SHIPMAN KNOTTS	1926
33	..	SOUR HOWES	1568
34	..	STEEL KNOTTS	1414
19	..	TARN CRAG	2176
4	..	THORNTHWAITE CRAG	2569
36	..	TROUTBECK TONGUE	1191
32	..	WANSFELL	1597
17	..	WETHER HILL	2210
14	..	YOKE	2309

7 16 13
36

Each fell is the subject
of a separate chapter

Angletarn Pikes 1857'

from Brothers Water

Howtown •

▲ PLACE FELL
• Patterdale
▲ ANGLETARN PIKES
• Hartsop

HIGH STREET ▲

MILES
0 1 2 3 4

Angletarn Pikes 2

NATURAL FEATURES

The distinctive double summit of Angletarn Pikes is a familiar feature high above the Patterdale valley: the two sharp peaks arrest attention from a distance and are no less imposing on close acquaintance, being attainable only by rock-scrambling, easy or difficult according to choice of route. The western flank of the fell drops steeply in slopes of bracken to the pleasant strath of the Goldrill Beck; on this side Dubhow Crag and Fall Crag are prominent. More precipitous is the eastern face overlooking the quiet deer sanctuary of Bannerdale, where the great bastion of Heck Crag is a formidable object rarely seen by walkers. The fell is a part of a broad curving ridge that comes down from the High Street watershed and continues to Boardale Hause, beyond which Place Fell terminates it abruptly.

The crowning glory of the Pikes, however, is the tarn from which they are named, cradled in a hollow just below the summit. Its indented shore and islets are features unusual in mountain tarns, and it has for long, and deservedly, been a special attraction for visitors to Patterdale. The charms of Angle Tarn, at all seasons of the year, are manifold: in scenic values it ranks amongst the best of Lakeland tarns.

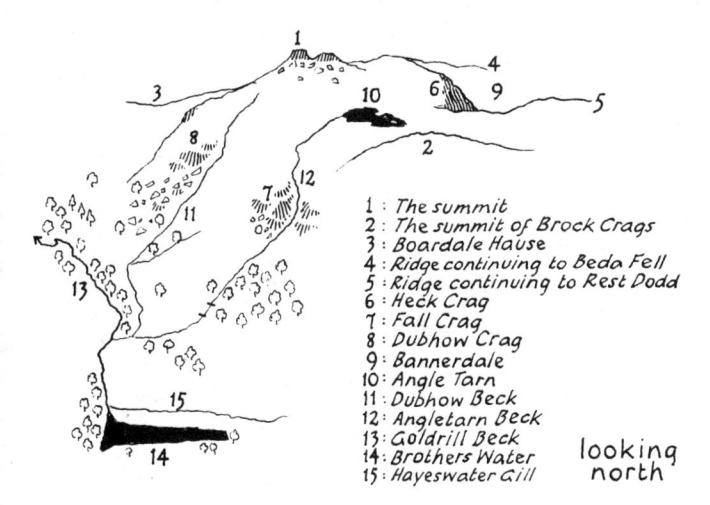

1 : The summit
2 : The summit of Brock Crags
3 : Boardale Hause
4 : Ridge continuing to Beda Fell
5 : Ridge continuing to Rest Dodd
6 : Heck Crag
7 : Fall Crag
8 : Dubhow Crag
9 : Bannerdale
10 : Angle Tarn
11 : Dubhow Beck
12 : Angletarn Beck
13 : Goldrill Beck
14 : Brothers Water
15 : Hayeswater Gill

looking north

Angletarn Pikes 3

Red Screes and Brothers Water from the top of Dubhow Beck

Heck Crag from the Patterdale-Martindale path

Angletarn Pikes 4

MAP

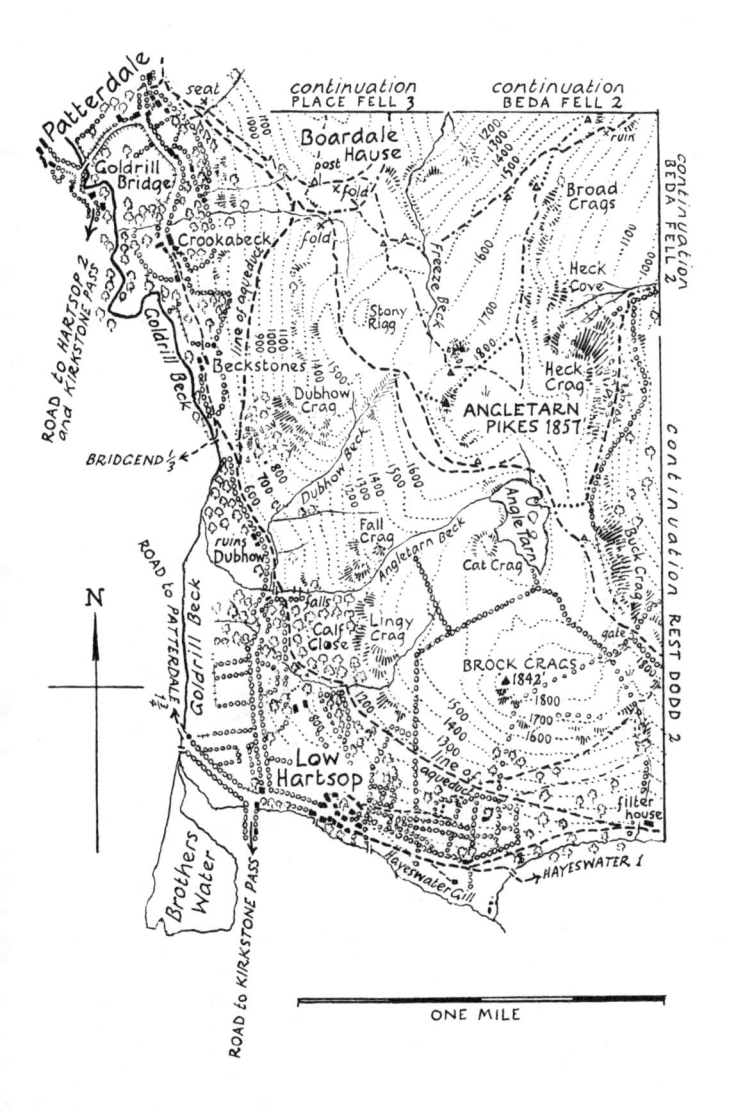

Angletarn Pikes 5

ASCENT FROM PATTERDALE
1400 feet of ascent : 1¾ miles
Note that this is the initial part of the route to High Street

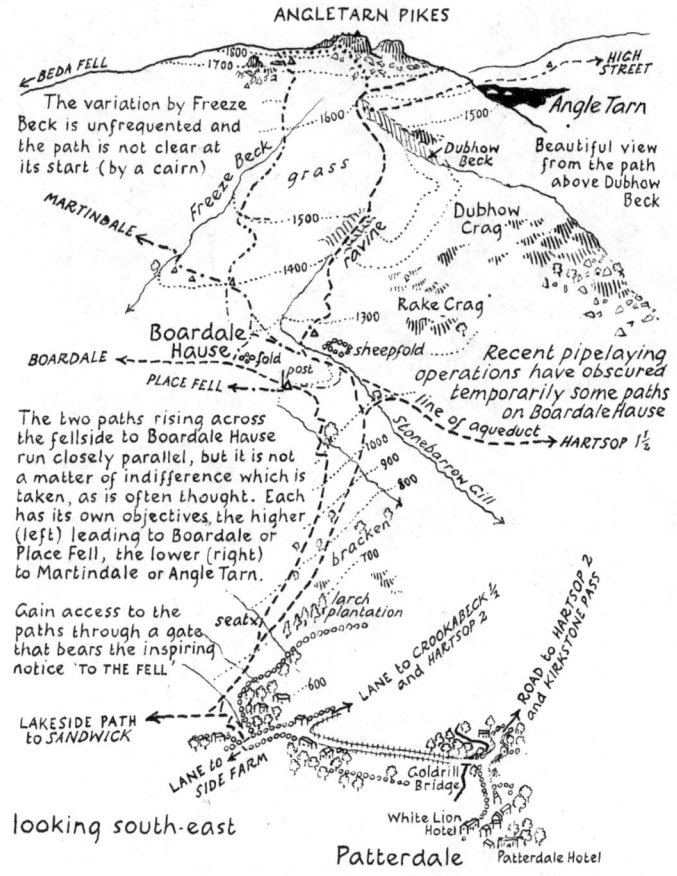

looking south-east

ANGLETARN PIKES

←BEDA FELL — HIGH STREET→

Angle Tarn

The variation by Freeze Beck is unfrequented and the path is not clear at its start (by a cairn)

Beautiful view from the path above Dubhow Beck

←MARTINDALE

Dubhow Beck
Dubhow Crag
Rake Crag

←BOARDALE
Boardale Hause
←PLACE FELL
sheepfold

Recent pipelaying operations have obscured temporarily some paths on Boardale Hause

line of aqueduct — HARTSOP 1½→

The two paths rising across the fellside to Boardale Hause run closely parallel, but it is not a matter of indifference which is taken, as is often thought. Each has its own objectives, the higher (left) leading to Boardale or Place Fell, the lower (right) to Martindale or Angle Tarn.

Stonebarrow Gill
bracken
larch plantation
seat

Gain access to the paths through a gate that bears the inspiring notice 'TO THE FELL'

←LAKESIDE PATH to SANDWICK

LANE to SIDE FARM
LANE to CROOKABECK ½ and HARTSOP 2
ROAD to HARTSOP 2 and KIRKSTONE PASS

Goldrill Bridge
White Lion Hotel
Patterdale
Patterdale Hotel

This delightful walk should be in the itinerary of all who stay at Patterdale; the climb is pleasant and the views excellent. Combined with a detour to Angle Tarn, it is an easy half-day's excursion.

Angletarn Pikes 6

ASCENT FROM MARTINDALE
1300 feet of ascent : 3½ miles from Martindale Old Church

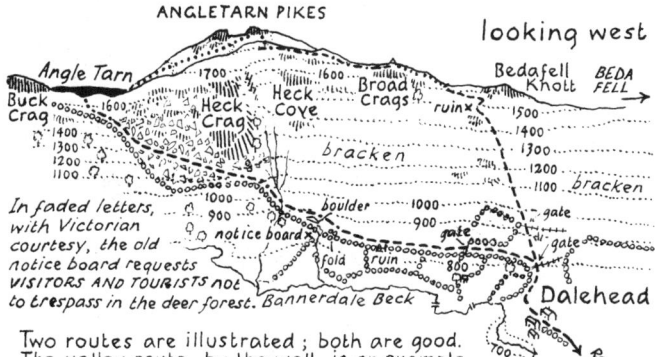

In faded letters, with Victorian courtesy, the old notice board requests VISITORS AND TOURISTS not to trespass in the deer forest.

Dalehead farmhouse is interesting architecturally

Two routes are illustrated; both are good.
The valley route, by the wall, is an example of a beautiful and interesting footway falling from favour simply because few now know of it. It ascends the secluded and unfrequented valley of Bannerdale, passes below Heck Crag by a sporting path on steep scree and crosses a low saddle to Angle Tarn, which comes into view suddenly and dramatically: the highlight of the walk. An easy climb (right) leads to the top.
The more direct way makes use of the path to Patterdale, but turns left when the ridge is gained and keeps to the Bannerdale edge until the summit is close on the right.
If the return is to be made to Martindale, use the valley route for the ascent (because of the sudden revelation of Angle Tarn, a surprise worth planning) and the ridge route for descent.

THE SUMMIT

The north (main) summit   *Angle Tarn, from the south summit*

Twin upthrusts of rock, 200 yards apart, give individuality to this unusual summit; the northerly is the higher. Otherwise the top is generally grassy, with an extensive peat bog in a depression.
DESCENTS : Routes of ascent may be reversed. (Note that, to find the Bannerdale valley-path, it is necessary first to descend to Angle Tarn and there cross the low saddle on the left at a boulder opposite the peninsula). In mist, there is comfort in knowing that the path for Patterdale is only 100 yards distant down the west slope.

Angletarn Pikes 7

THE VIEW

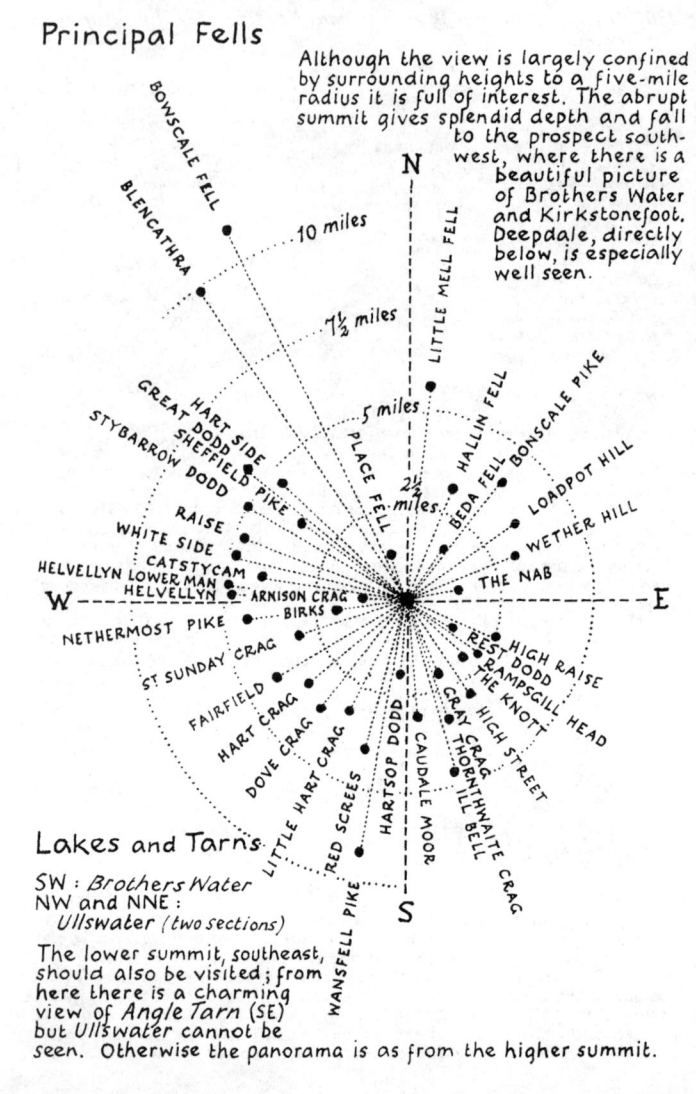

Principal Fells

Although the view is largely confined by surrounding heights to a five-mile radius it is full of interest. The abrupt summit gives splendid depth and fall to the prospect south-west, where there is a beautiful picture of Brothers Water and Kirkstonefoot. Deepdale, directly below, is especially well seen.

Fells shown on diagram (clockwise from N): BOWSCALE FELL, BLENCATHRA, HART SIDE, GREAT DODD, STYBARROW DODD, SHEFFIELD PIKE, RAISE, WHITE SIDE, CATSTYCAM, HELVELLYN LOWER MAN, HELVELLYN, NETHERMOST PIKE, ARNISON CRAG, BIRKS, ST SUNDAY CRAG, FAIRFIELD, HART CRAG, DOVE CRAG, LITTLE HART CRAG, RED SCREES, HARTSOP DODD, CAUDALE MOOR, WANSFELL PIKE, ILL BELL, THORNTHWAITE CRAG, HIGH STREET, GRAY CRAG, THE KNOTT, RAMPSGILL HEAD, HIGH RAISE, REST DODD, THE NAB, WETHER HILL, LOADPOT HILL, BONSCALE PIKE, HALLIN FELL, BEDA FELL, PLACE FELL, LITTLE MELL FELL

Distance rings: 2½ miles, 5 miles, 7½ miles, 10 miles

Lakes and Tarns

SW: *Brothers Water*
NW and NNE: *Ullswater* (two sections)

The lower summit, southeast, should also be visited; from here there is a charming view of *Angle Tarn* (SE) but *Ullswater* cannot be seen. Otherwise the panorama is as from the higher summit.

Angletarn Pikes 8

RIDGE ROUTES

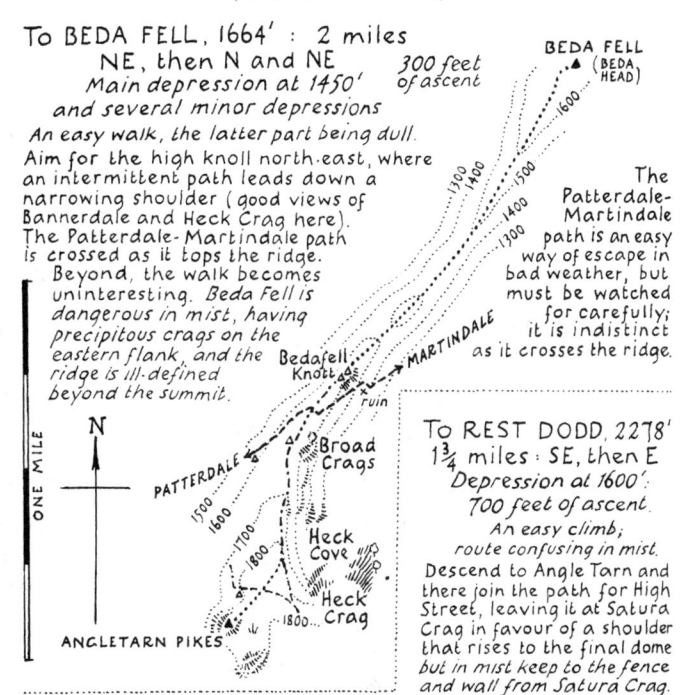

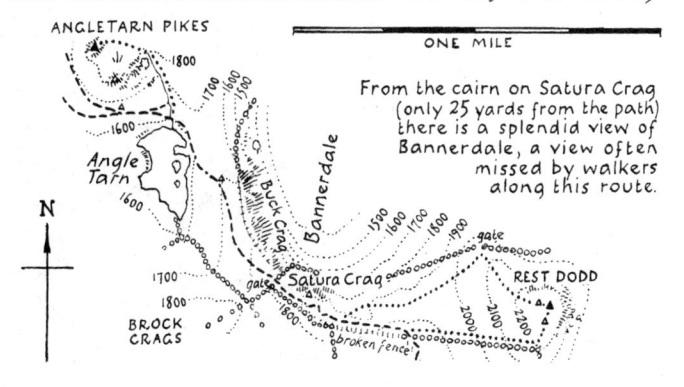

To BEDA FELL, 1664': 2 miles
NE, then N and NE   300 feet of ascent
Main depression at 1450'
and several minor depressions

An easy walk, the latter part being dull.

Aim for the high knoll north-east, where an intermittent path leads down a narrowing shoulder (good views of Bannerdale and Heck Crag here). The Patterdale-Martindale path is crossed as it tops the ridge. Beyond, the walk becomes uninteresting. Beda Fell is dangerous in mist, having precipitous crags on the eastern flank, and the ridge is ill-defined beyond the summit.

The Patterdale-Martindale path is an easy way of escape in bad weather, but must be watched for carefully; it is indistinct as it crosses the ridge.

To REST DODD, 2278'
1¾ miles: SE, then E
Depression at 1600':
700 feet of ascent.

An easy climb; route confusing in mist.

Descend to Angle Tarn and there join the path for High Street, leaving it at Satura Crag in favour of a shoulder that rises to the final dome but in mist keep to the fence and wall from Satura Crag.

From the cairn on Satura Crag (only 25 yards from the path) there is a splendid view of Bannerdale, a view often missed by walkers along this route.

Arthur's Pike 1747'

- Pooley Bridge
- Askham
- ▲ ARTHUR'S PIKE
- Howtown
- ▲ LOADPOT HILL

MILES
0 1 2 3 4

from the Howtown road

Arthur's Pike 2

NATURAL FEATURES

Arthur's Pike is the northerly termination of the long High Street range, and, like the northerly termination of the parallel Helvellyn range, it contrasts with the usual Lakeland fell-structure by exhibiting its crags to the afternoon sun; the northern and eastern slopes, which are commonly roughest, are without rock. The steep flank falling to Ullswater has several faces of crag below the summit-rim, and, especially around the vicinity of Swarthbeck Gill, which forms the southern boundary of the fell, acres of tumbled boulders testify to the roughness of the impending cliffs and the power of the beck in flood. Above the crags, there is little to excite, and the summit merges without much change in elevation into the broad expanses of Loadpot Hill. The gradual northern slope is clothed with heather.

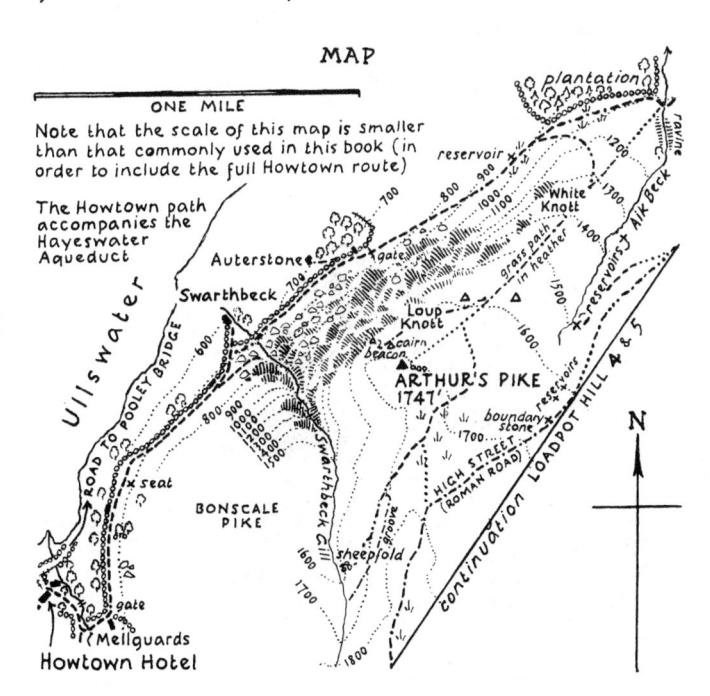

MAP

ONE MILE

Note that the scale of this map is smaller than that commonly used in this book (in order to include the full Howtown route)

The Howtown path accompanies the Hayeswater Aqueduct

Arthur's Pike 3

Ullswater, from the Howtown path

ASCENTS

Arthur's Pike looks particularly forbidding from the Howtown path, by which it is usually climbed, and the timid walker who doubts the wisdom of proceeding will be reassured to discover that the ascent is not only not intimidating but surprisingly easy and everywhere pleasant, *if the route shown on the map is followed.* The obvious and direct alternative by the Swarthbeck ravine is anything but obvious and direct when attempted, and nervous pedestrians should keep away from it.

For the approaches from Askham, Helton and Pooley Bridge, the chapter on Loadpot Hill should be consulted.

THE SUMMIT

Above the edge of the steep Ullswater flank, grassy undulations culminate in a conical knoll crowned by a large cairn; nearby is a shelter (from wind) in a short wall. There are no paths on the top, but an indefinite cairned track skirts the precipice, on the brink of which is a collapsed beacon; and on the eastern side is a fairly good path that goes nowhere in particular in either direction and is of little use to the walker. The beacon cannot be seen from the summit-cairn; it stands 250 yards distant in the direction of Blencathra.

Arthur's Pike 4

THE VIEW

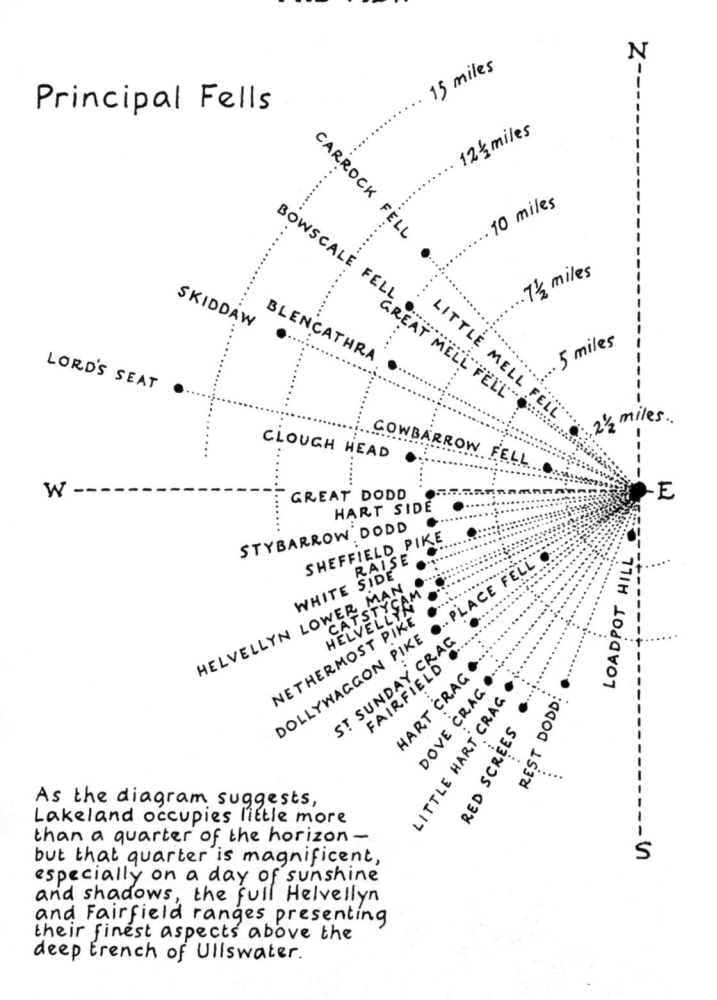

Principal Fells

Distances shown: 2½ miles, 5 miles, 7½ miles, 10 miles, 12½ miles, 15 miles

Fells labelled (roughly N to S):
- CARROCK FELL
- BOWSCALE FELL
- SKIDDAW
- BLENCATHRA
- GREAT MELL FELL
- LITTLE MELL FELL
- LORD'S SEAT
- COWBARROW FELL
- CLOUGH HEAD
- GREAT DODD
- HART SIDE
- STYBARROW DODD
- SHEFFIELD PIKE
- RAISE
- WHITE SIDE
- HELVELLYN LOWER MAN
- CATSTYCAM
- HELVELLYN
- NETHERMOST PIKE
- PLACE FELL
- DOLLYWAGGON PIKE
- ST SUNDAY CRAG
- FAIRFIELD
- HART CRAG
- DOVE CRAG
- LITTLE HART CRAG
- RED SCREES
- REST DODD
- LOADPOT HILL

As the diagram suggests, Lakeland occupies little more than a quarter of the horizon — but that quarter is magnificent, especially on a day of sunshine and shadows, the full Helvellyn and Fairfield ranges presenting their finest aspects above the deep trench of Ullswater.

Lakes and Tarns
W to N: Ullswater (two sections: middle and lower reaches)
Ullswater is better seen from the beacon: an impressive sight.

Arthur's Pike 5

RIDGE ROUTES

To LOADPOT HILL, 2201': 2¼ miles
S. then SSW, SSE and finally N
Minor depressions : 500 feet of ascent
A dull, easy walk, not recommended in mist

Aim for the low hill due south, crossing a good path on the way, and join there the old High Street, which is now indistinct in places and at its best only a series of ruts in the grass, often marshy. When the dome of Loadpot Hill is reached, the path becomes an ascending groove, easy to follow; it turns away downhill just short of the ruins of Lowther House, where turn north to the summit cairn, which encloses a boundary stone. *This is not a walk for a wet day, and the whole of this moorland is a nightmare in mist.*

To BONSCALE PIKE, 1718'
1 mile: S. then SSW and NW
Depression at 1575'
150 feet of ascent
A simple walk which should not be attempted in mist.

Join the good path running east of the summit and follow it south to a sheepfold in the depression between the two Pikes. Cross the beck and slant over grassy slopes to the right. *Swarthbeck Gill is dangerous below the fold.*

Ullswater, from the beacon

Arthur's Pike 6

Swarthbeck Gill

Swarthbeck Gill, if it were but more accessible, would be one of the showplaces of the district. Here, between towering rockwalls, are beautiful cataracts, but, alas, they are out of the reach of the average explorer. The ferny, tree-clad lower gorge, however, may (and should) be visited. The prudent venture no further!

Beda Fell

summit named Beda Head

1664'

from Hallin Fell

Beda Fell is the long north-east ridge of Angletarn Pikes, narrowing as it descends; but midway it asserts itself, broadens considerably and rises to a definite summit, Beda Head, which is the geographical centre of the quiet, enchanting, exquisitely beautiful area known affectionately as "Martind'l." Beyond this top the descent continues over the rocky spine of Winter Crag to valley-level at Sandwick on Ullswater. The fell, although mainly grassy, with bracken, has a most impressive east face, broken into three great tiers of crag. It is bounded by deep valleys, Boardale, Bannerdale and Howe Grain, whose combined waters meet at its northern tip.

```
              Howtown
               •
  PLACE       BEDA
  FELL ▲      ▲ FELL

 • Patterdale
      ▲ ANGLETARN
        PIKES
         MILES
   0   1   2   3   4
```

Beda Fell 2

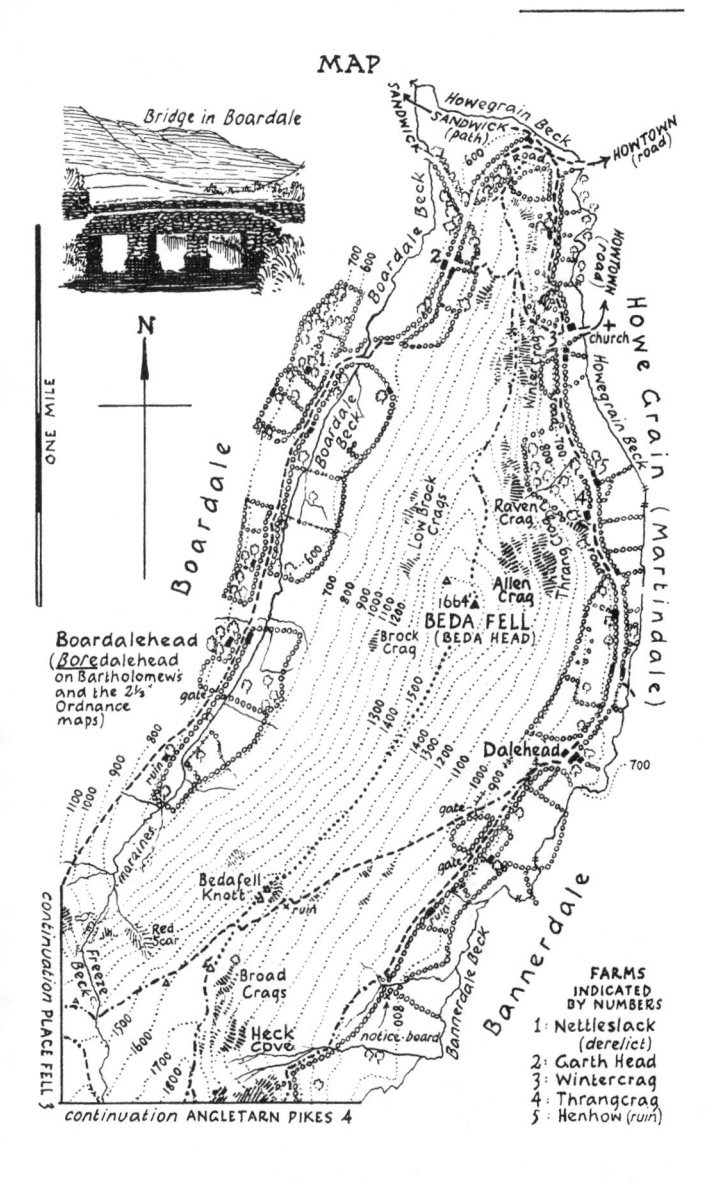

MAP

Bridge in Boardale

N — ONE MILE

Boardale
Boardale Beck
Sandwick (path)
Howegrain Beck
Howtown (road)
church
Howegrain Beck
Howe Grain (Martindale)
Low Brock Crags
Raven Crag
Allen Crag
1664 ▲ BEDA FELL (BEDA HEAD)
Brock Crag
Boardalehead (*Bore*dalehead on Bartholomews and the 2½" Ordnance maps)
gate
Dalehead
Bannerdale Beck
Bannerdale
moraines
ruin
Freeze Beck
Bedafell Knott
Red Scar
ruin
Broad Crags
Heck Cove
notice-board
continuation PLACE FELL 3
continuation ANGLETARN PIKES 4

FARMS INDICATED BY NUMBERS
1: Nettleslack (derelict)
2: Garth Head
3: Wintercrag
4: Thrangcrag
5: Henhow (ruin)

Beda Fell 3

ASCENTS FROM MARTINDALE AND BOARDALE
1100 feet of ascent : 1¾ miles

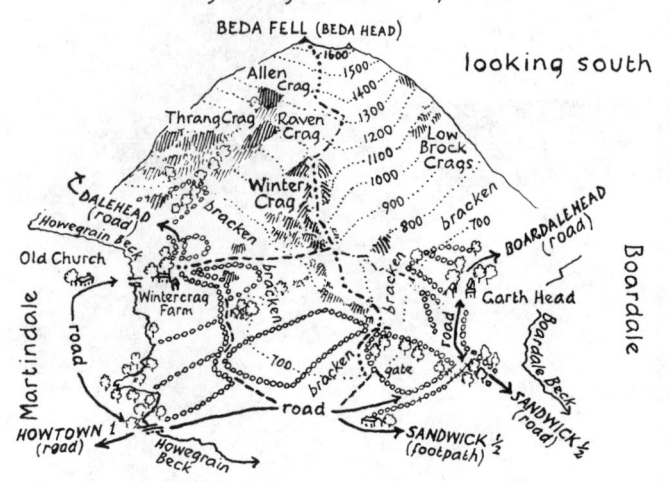

looking south

The fell is best climbed along its north ridge, over the serrated crest of Winter Crag. The ridge may be gained directly at its extremity from the unenclosed road curving round its tip (in high summer, this route involves a tussle with bracken) or by the short paths from Wintercrag Farm and Garth Head. The ridge of Winter Crag is very enjoyable, but the final slope is dreary, although it may be improved by keeping well to the left to look down the crags into Martindale.

DESCENTS: Use the routes of ascent for returning, unless an extension of the walk is desired, in which case the ridge may be continued south-west as far as the Patterdale-Martindale path and a descent made along it.

| *In mist*, exceeding care is necessary to avoid getting entangled among the crags on the east (Martindale) flank, Allen Crag especially being dangerous. In such conditions, it is advisable to descend from the lower cairn, 150 yards northwest, keeping always to the ridge

THE SUMMIT

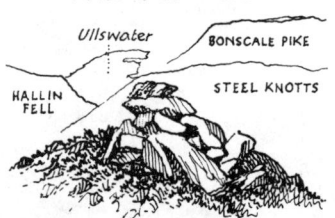

The highest point, Beda Head, is an uninteresting mound set upon undulating grassy slopes. Infinitely more exciting and attractive is the rocky top of Winter Crag along the ridge.

Beda Fell 4

THE VIEW

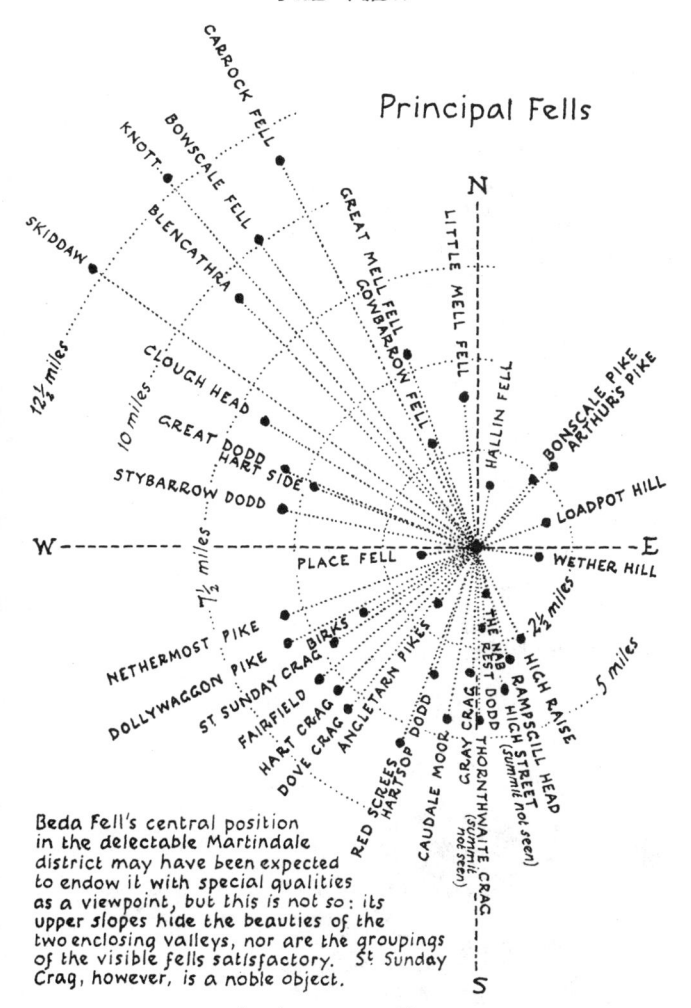

Principal Fells

Fells labelled on the diagram (clockwise from NW):
CARROCK FELL, KNOTT, BOWSCALE FELL, SKIDDAW (12½ miles), BLENCATHRA, GREAT MELL FELL, COWBARROW FELL, LITTLE MELL FELL, CLOUGH HEAD (10 miles), GREAT DODD, HART SIDE, STYBARROW DODD, HALLIN FELL, BONSCALE PIKE, ARTHURS PIKE, LOADPOT HILL, PLACE FELL, WETHER HILL (2½ miles), NETHERMOST PIKE (7½ miles), DOLLYWAGGON PIKE, ST SUNDAY CRAG, BIRKS, FAIRFIELD, HART CRAG, DOVE CRAG, ANGLETARN PIKES, THE NAB, REST DODD, RAMPSGILL HEAD, HIGH RAISE (5 miles), HIGH STREET (summit not seen), BRACK CRAGS, GRAY CRAG, THORNTHWAITE CRAG (summit not seen), RED SCREES, HARTSOP DODD, CAUDALE MOOR

N — E — S — W (compass points marked)

Beda Fell's central position in the delectable Martindale district may have been expected to endow it with special qualities as a viewpoint, but it is not so: its upper slopes hide the beauties of the two enclosing valleys, nor are the groupings of the visible fells satisfactory. St. Sunday Crag, however, is a noble object.

Lakes and Tarns

N to NE: *Ullswater* (two sections, divided by *Hallin Fell*)

Beda Fell 5

RIDGE ROUTE

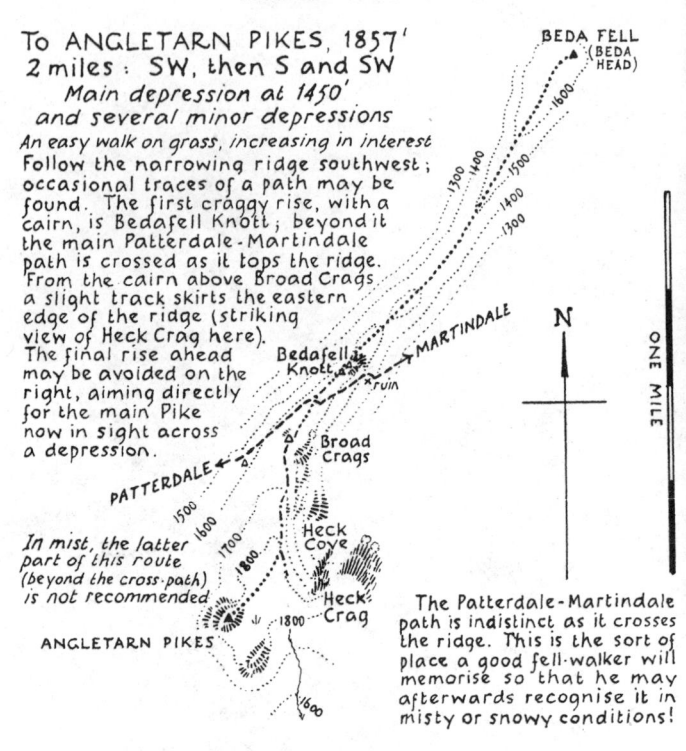

TO ANGLETARN PIKES, 1857'
2 miles : SW, then S and SW

*Main depression at 1450'
and several minor depressions*

An easy walk on grass, increasing in interest. Follow the narrowing ridge southwest; occasional traces of a path may be found. The first craggy rise, with a cairn, is Bedafell Knott; beyond it the main Patterdale-Martindale path is crossed as it tops the ridge. From the cairn above Broad Crags a slight track skirts the eastern edge of the ridge (striking view of Heck Crag here). The final rise ahead may be avoided on the right, aiming directly for the main Pike now in sight across a depression.

In mist, the latter part of this route (beyond the cross-path) is not recommended

ONE MILE

The Patterdale-Martindale path is indistinct as it crosses the ridge. This is the sort of place a good fell-walker will memorise so that he may afterwards recognise it in misty or snowy conditions!

The ridge south from the cairn above Broad Crags; on the right the main Angletarn Pike.

Beda Fell 6

*Beda Fell
from
Martindale Old Church*

Bonscale Pike 1718'

sometimes referred to as
 Swarth Fell

named Toughmoss Pike
 on Bartholomew's map

from Hallin Fell

- Pooley Bridge

▲ ARTHUR'S PIKE
▲ BONSCALE PIKE
Howtown
▲ LOADPOT HILL

MILES
0 1 2 3 4

Bonscale Pike 2

NATURAL FEATURES

Rising steeply behind the little hamlet of Howtown is a broad buttress of the High Street range, Swarth Fell, the turretted and castellated rim of which has the appearance, when seen from Ullswater far below, of the ruined battlements of a castle wall: this aspect is sufficiently arresting to earn for the rocky facade and the summit above it the separate and distinctive name of Bonscale Pike. This escarpment, however, is a sham, for it defends nothing other than a dreary plateau of grass; and indeed there is little else of interest on the fell — excepting Swarthbeck Gill, its northern boundary, which abounds in interest but is out of bounds for the walker because of its obvious dangers. Bonscale Pike presents a bold front, that overlooking the lake, but on all other sides it loses its identity in the high mass of land supporting the great dome of Loadpot Hill.

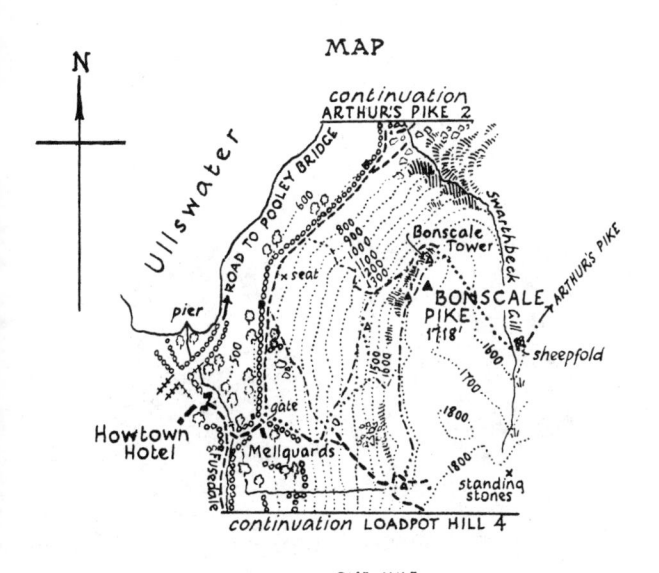

MAP

ONE MILE

Bonscale Pike 3

ASCENT FROM HOWTOWN
1200 feet of ascent : 1¼ miles

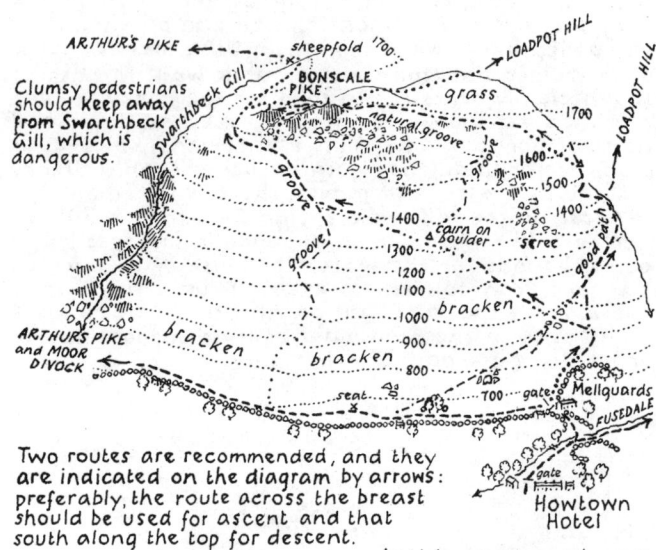

Clumsy pedestrians should keep away from Swarthbeck Gill, which is dangerous.

Two routes are recommended, and they are indicated on the diagram by arrows: preferably, the route across the breast should be used for ascent and that south along the top for descent.

looking east-south-east

The work of a craftsman
Bonscale Tower

The effort of amateurs
The higher pillar

Bonscale Pike 4

THE SUMMIT

Neither of the two stone pillars seen so prominently against the skyline from below marks the highest point, this being a grassy hummock between and behind them, with a small cairn. It is an unsatisfactory summit because higher ground rises immediately beyond on the long undulating slope to Loadpot Hill; it does, however, indicate an excellent viewpoint, and also defines the limit of interest, which is centred in the broken wall of crag immediately below. Bonscale Pike, in fact, gives a display of rock-scenery that would improve many a bigger fell.   And the men who selected the sites for the two pillars surely had a good appreciation of drama!

DESCENTS: The alternative route of ascent should be used as a way down in order to get the full benefit of the views, but in any case the length of the summit should be traversed.

In mist, a stranger may well feel cause for anxiety. The lower (in altitude), i.e. the northerly, of the two pillars should be rounded above it, by an ample margin, to reach the path below the crags, after which the slope may safely be descended anywhere if the path is lost. Note that the two pillars both stand on the brink of crags. Resist any temptation to slant down to the stream — Swarthbeck Gill is highly dangerous.

Plan of the summit

Bonscale Pike 5

THE VIEW

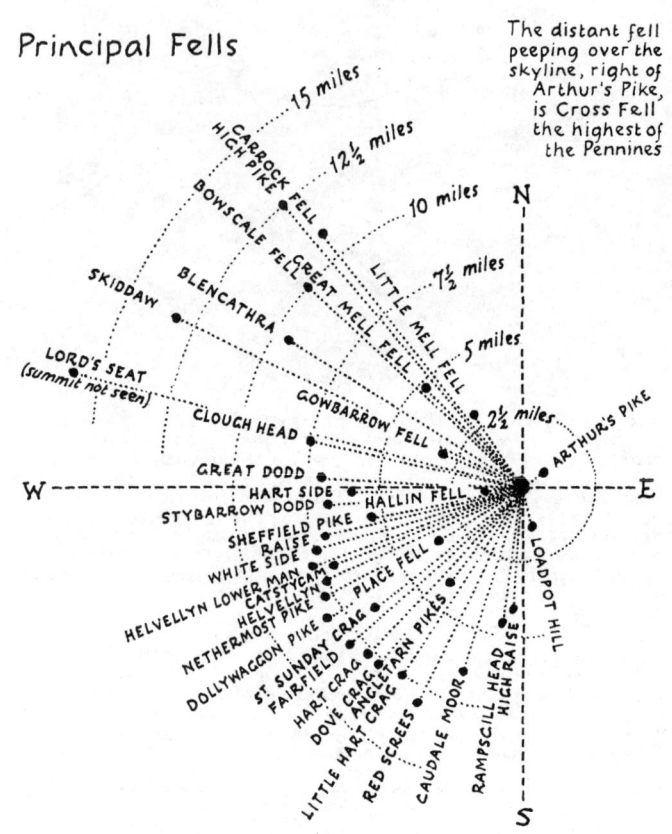

Principal Fells

The distant fell peeping over the skyline, right of Arthur's Pike, is Cross Fell the highest of the Pennines

15 miles — 12½ miles — 10 miles — 7½ miles — 5 miles — 2½ miles

CARROCK FELL
HIGH PIKE
BOWSCALE FELL
GREAT MELL FELL
LITTLE MELL FELL
SKIDDAW
BLENCATHRA
LORD'S SEAT (summit not seen)
CLOUGH HEAD
GOWBARROW FELL
ARTHUR'S PIKE
GREAT DODD
HART SIDE
HALLIN FELL
STYBARROW DODD
SHEFFIELD PIKE
RAISE
WHITE SIDE
HELVELLYN LOWER MAN
CATSTYCAM
HELVELLYN
NETHERMOST PIKE
PLACE FELL
DOLLYWAGGON PIKE
ST SUNDAY CRAG
FAIRFIELD
HART CRAG
DOVE CRAG
ANGLETARN PIKES
LITTLE HART CRAG
RED SCREES
CAUDALE MOOR
RAMPSGILL HEAD
HIGH RAISE
LOADPOT HILL

W — E
N — S

The prospect of the Helvellyn and Fairfield ranges, although crowded into a quarter-circle, is excellent, and the more distant northern fells are nicely grouped. In other directions there is little to be seen but the nearby dreary slopes falling from Loadpot Hill. The pillars are better viewpoints.

Lakes and Tarns
W to N: Ullswater (middle and lower reaches) — better seen from either of the two pillars

Bonscale Pike 6

RIDGE ROUTES

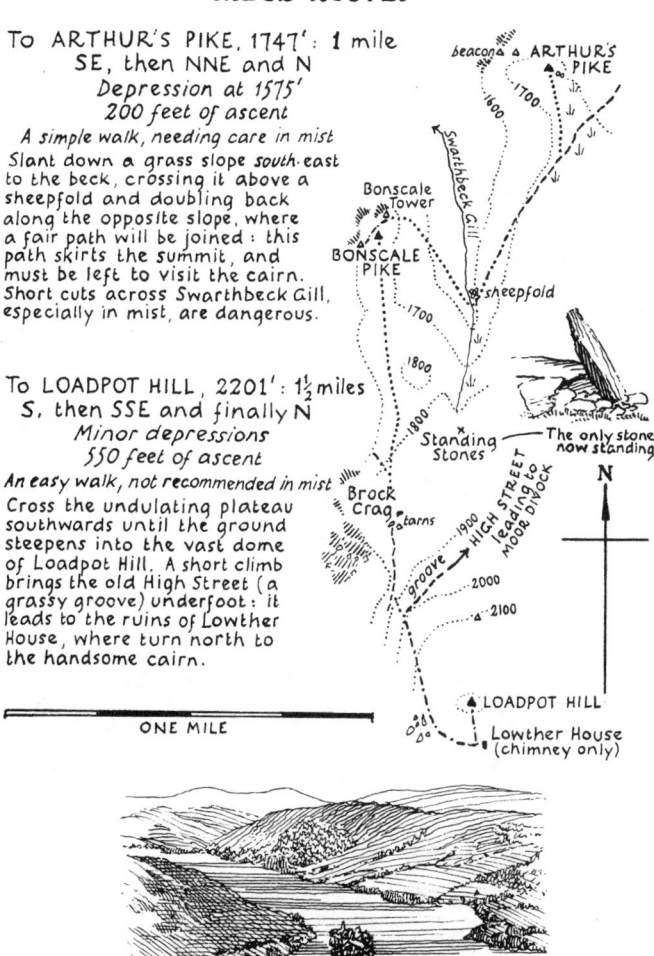

To ARTHUR'S PIKE, 1747': 1 mile
SE, then NNE and N
Depression at 1575'
200 feet of ascent

A simple walk, needing care in mist

Slant down a grass slope *south-east* to the beck, crossing it above a sheepfold and doubling back along the opposite slope, where a fair path will be joined: this path skirts the summit, and must be left to visit the cairn. Short cuts across Swarthbeck Gill, especially in mist, are dangerous.

To LOADPOT HILL, 2201': 1½ miles
S, then SSE and finally N
Minor depressions
550 feet of ascent

An easy walk, not recommended in mist

Cross the undulating plateau southwards until the ground steepens into the vast dome of Loadpot Hill. A short climb brings the old High Street (a grassy groove) underfoot: it leads to the ruins of Lowther House, where turn north to the handsome cairn.

ONE MILE

Ullswater: the middle reach

Branstree

(a corruption of Brant Street)
The summit is not named
on Ordnance Survey maps

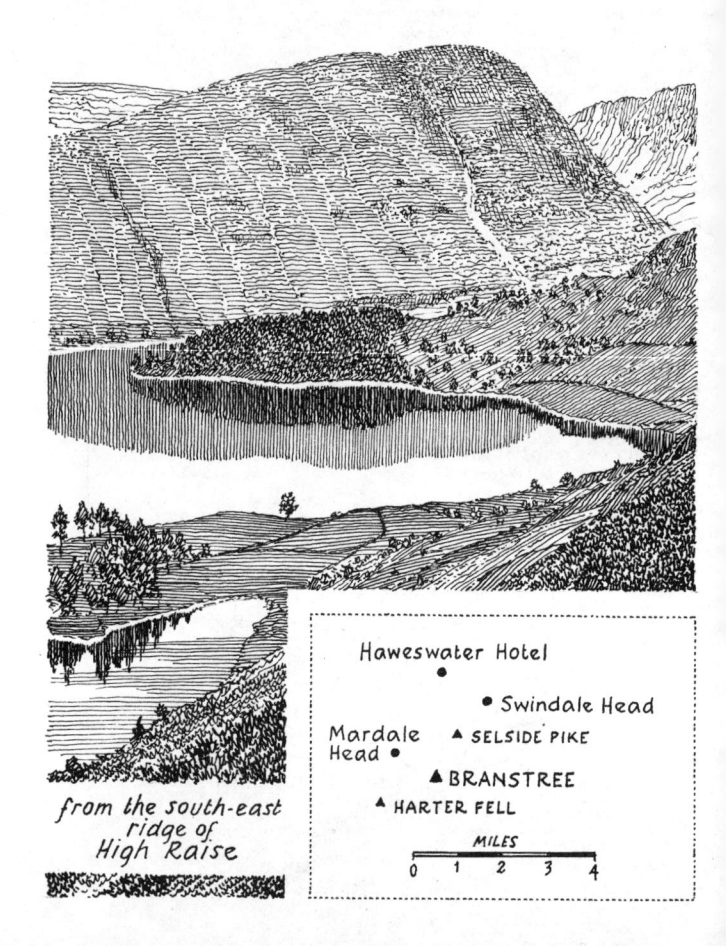

2333'

from the south-east ridge of High Raise

```
            Haweswater Hotel
                    ●
                        ● Swindale Head
    Mardale      ▲ SELSIDE PIKE
    Head ●
                 ▲ BRANSTREE
             ▲ HARTER FELL
                    MILES
             0   1   2   3   4
```

Branstree 2

NATURAL FEATURES

Branstree occupies a fine position at the head of three valleys, Mardale, Swindale and Longsleddale, and a fourth, Mosedale, runs along its southern base. This geographical attribute aside, the fell is dreary, and must disappoint all who climb it, for a good deal of perambulation is necessary across the flat and featureless top before these valleys can be brought sufficiently into view for full appreciation. All is grass, although there is a slight boulder-slope below Artlecrag Pike (extravagantly hachured as a crag on most maps), and a remarkable dry gully, the result of a landslide, cleaves the fellside on the Mardale flank from top to bottom. Eastwards there are some subsidiary summits, and a line of crags overlooking Swindale; there is an odd little hanging valley, and noble hidden waterfalls on this side. The Mosedale flank has been extensively quarried. Mosedale Beck is the principal stream: it runs into Swindale Beck, on which Manchester Corporation have covetous eyes.

High Street from the north ridge

Branstree 3

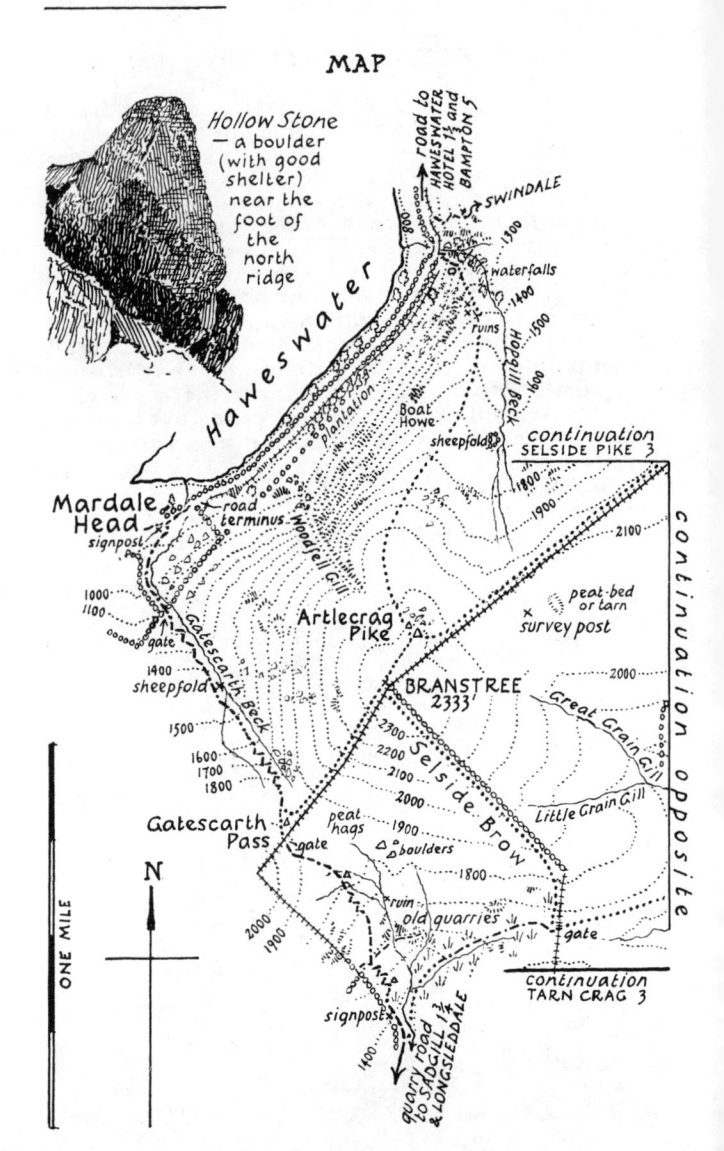

MAP

Hollow Stone — a boulder (with good shelter) near the foot of the north ridge

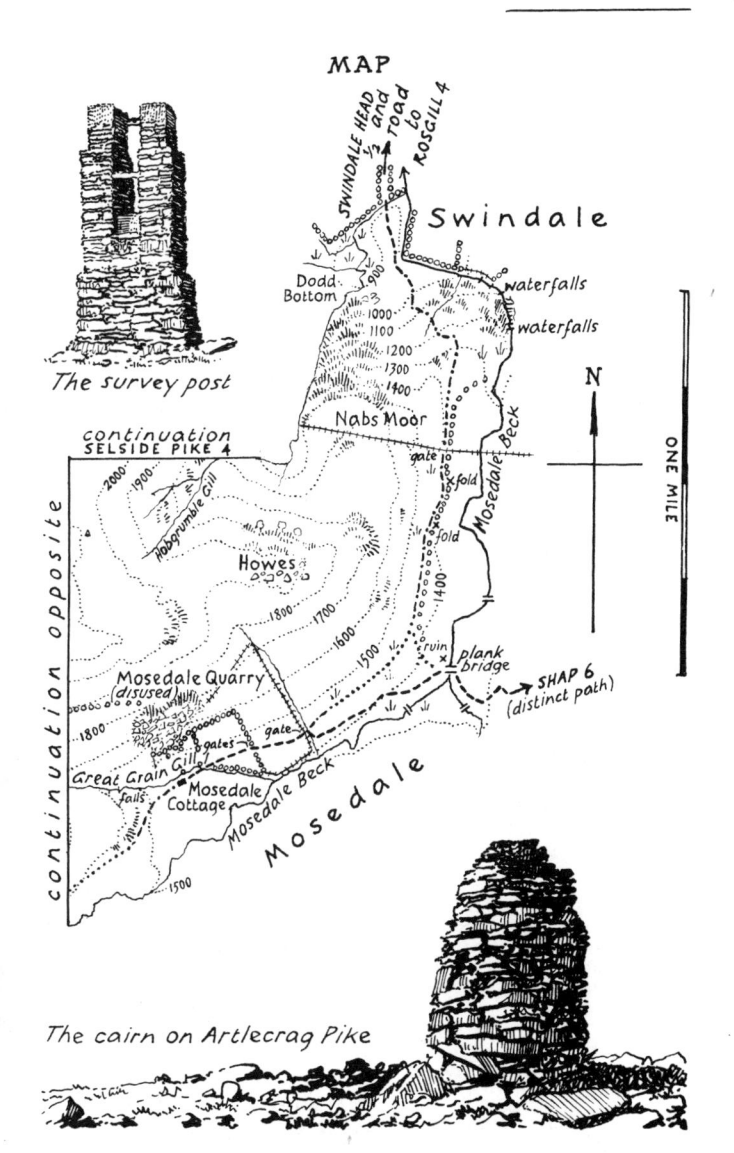

Branstree 4

The survey post

MAP

SWINDALE HEAD and road to ROSGILL 4

Swindale

Dodd Bottom

waterfalls
waterfalls

N

Nabs Moor

Mosedale Beck

continuation SELSIDE PIKE 4

Hobgrumble Gill

Howes

gate
fold
fold

ruin
plank bridge

SHAP 6 (distinct path)

Mosedale Quarry (disused)

gates gate

Great Grain Gill
falls

Mosedale Cottage

Mosedale Beck

Mosedale

continuation opposite

ONE MILE

The cairn on Artlecrag Pike

Branstree 5

ASCENT FROM MARDALE
1500 feet of ascent : 1½ miles from the road

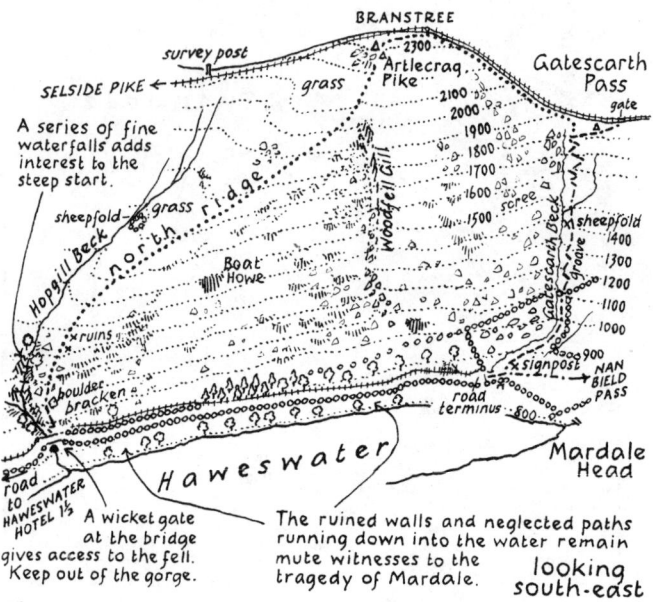

A series of fine waterfalls adds interest to the steep start

A wicket gate at the bridge gives access to the fell. Keep out of the gorge.

The ruined walls and neglected paths running down into the water remain mute witnesses to the tragedy of Mardale.

looking south-east

The merit of the ascent by the north ridge lies in its intimate views of Mardale Head and Harter Fell, the climbing itself being dull after a promising start. The Gatescarth route is better used for the return.

ASCENT FROM LONGSLEDDALE
1750 feet of ascent
3½ miles from Sadgill

Beware loose wire in the grass alongside the fence above Gatescarth Pass

By any standards, and by any route, the climbing on this flank is completely uninteresting.

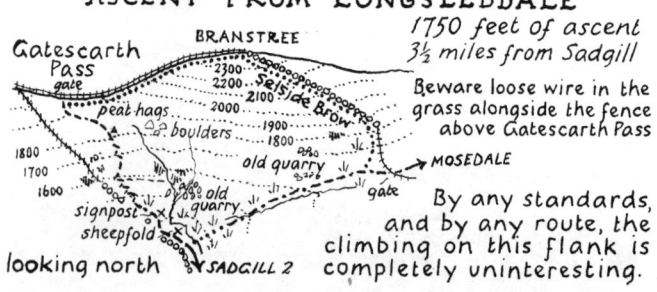

looking north

Branstree 6

THE SUMMIT

highest point

The 'official' watershed is about eighty yards north of the end of the wall; this is the highest point (2333')

The summit is grassy and flat-topped. There is no cairn on the highest point, which is situated near the junction of a well-built wall and the wire fence that traverses the fell. A better place for a halt is the fine cairn on Artlecrag Pike nearby, north-east; here also is some rock to relieve the drab surroundings.

DESCENTS: The quickest way off, and the safest in bad weather, is by the fence to Gatescarth Pass (beware loose wire in the grass, and watch for the gate that indicates the path for Longsleddale, left, and Mardale, right). The most attractive descent is that by the north ridge for Mardale, with good views of Haweswater.

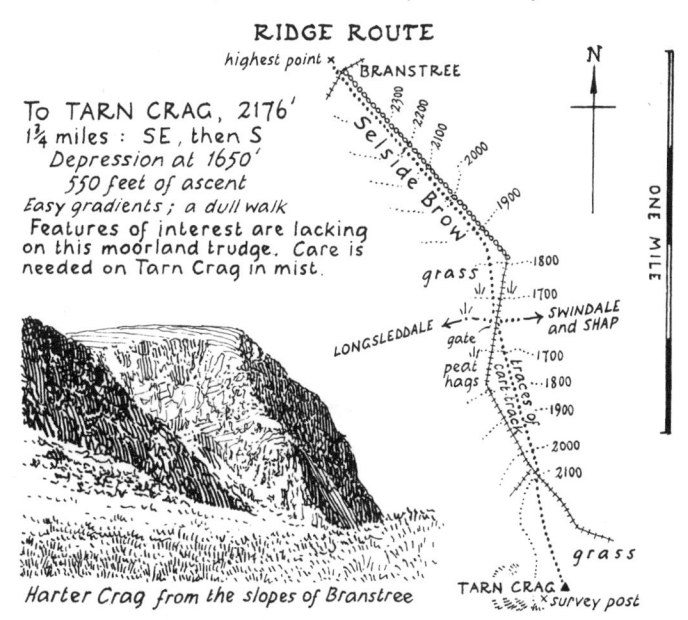

RIDGE ROUTE

To TARN CRAG, 2176'
1¾ miles : SE, then S
Depression at 1650'
550 feet of ascent
Easy gradients; a dull walk
Features of interest are lacking on this moorland trudge. Care is needed on Tarn Crag in mist.

Harter Crag from the slopes of Branstree

Branstree 7

RIDGE ROUTES

To HARTER FELL, 2539': 2 miles: SW then NW and SW
Depression at 1875'(Gatescarth Pass): 700 feet of ascent
An easy walk on grass. Safe in mist, with care

Loose wire alongside the fence going down to Gatescarth Pass is a snare for the unsuspecting walker, especially he who travels at speed. When the fence turns, continue along the line marked by the fragmentary remains of an old fence, which can be traced to the summit. In mist, this line must be followed carefully.

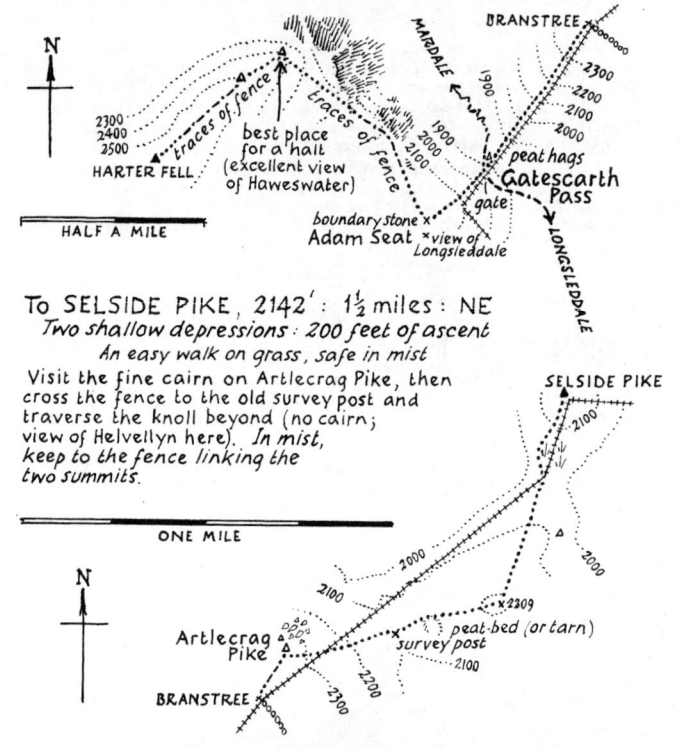

To SELSIDE PIKE, 2142': 1½ miles: NE
Two shallow depressions: 200 feet of ascent
An easy walk on grass, safe in mist

Visit the fine cairn on Artlecrag Pike, then cross the fence to the old survey post and traverse the knoll beyond (no cairn; view of Helvellyn here). *In mist, keep to the fence linking the two summits.*

The survey post was built by Manchester Corporation during the construction of the Haweswater Aqueduct. It does not stand on the crest of the depression, as might have been expected, but slightly below it; the top of the post, however, overtops the crest and the next survey post, on Tarn Crag, is visible from it (south).

Branstree 8

THE VIEW

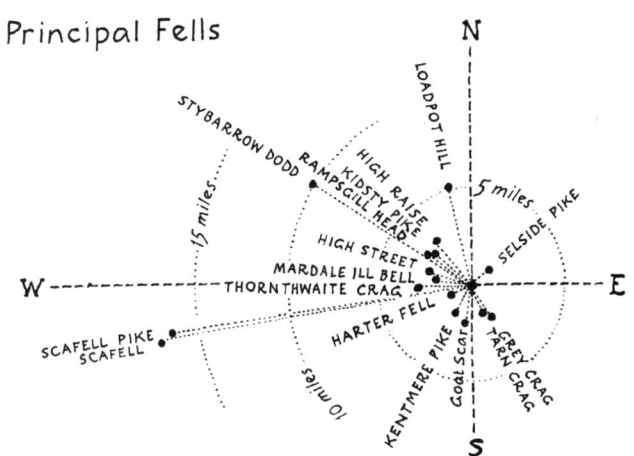

Principal Fells

Compass diagram showing fells:
- N: LOADPOT HILL
- HIGH RAISE, KIDSTY PIKE, RAMPSGILL HEAD
- STYBARROW DODD
- SELSIDE PIKE (5 miles)
- HIGH STREET
- MARDALE ILL BELL
- THORNTHWAITE CRAG
- 15 miles
- W — E
- SCAFELL PIKE, SCAFELL
- HARTER FELL
- KENTMERE PIKE, Goat Scar, GREY CRAG, TARN CRAG
- 10 miles
- S

Lakes and Tarns

Branstree is one of the very few Lakeland fells that have no view of lakes or tarns from the highest point, but Haweswater is brought into view by walking a few paces north. The long strip of water in the distance southwards is the Kent estuary.

Despite Branstree's good geographical position, little is seen of Lakeland: the lofty skyline of the Mardale heights admits only two small vistas of distant fells. Compensation is found, however, in the wide prospect of the Pennines. An interesting feature is the glimpse of the Scafells with Mickledore — note that, of this group, only the Pike is in view from the wall end.

Mosedale Cottage — occasionally occupied by shepherds

Brock Crags 1842'

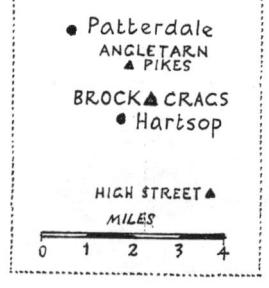

from Goldrill Beck

- Patterdale
- ANGLETARN ▲ PIKES
- BROCK ▲ CRAGS
- Hartsop
- HIGH STREET ▲

MILES
0 1 2 3 4

The unspoilt village of Low Hartsop has great charm and its environment is one of quiet loveliness, much of it contributed by the hanging woods of the steep fell that rises immediately behind. This fell, Brock Crags, is an offshoot of a ridge coming down to Ullswater from the main High Street watershed, and overlooks a meeting of many valleys: a feature in the view from the rocky top. Its slopes carry the Hayeswater aqueduct, and recent pipelaying operations there have left an ugly scar along its fair breast. Nature is a great healer: it cannot heal too swiftly here.

Brock Crags 2

MAP

ASCENT FROM HARTSOP
1300 feet of ascent : 1 mile

The exit from Hartsop is not clear. Either (a) start along a lane opposite a turning-space for cars near the end of the village, soon bearing right along a grass path between walls (ignore the road going left) and then uphill across an enclosure to the pipeline. Or (b) follow the cart-track up the valley to the filter-house, turning back along the pipeline at a higher level. Above the pipeline, find a grooved path ascending right through a gap in an old wall: it becomes indistinct at 1600', the summit then being over easy slopes to the left. Or follow the old wall straight up.

Iron gateposts are met on the grooved path at 1500'; remnants of a vanished fence.

But the great unnatural feature on this walk is the pipeline scar, which distinctly offends!

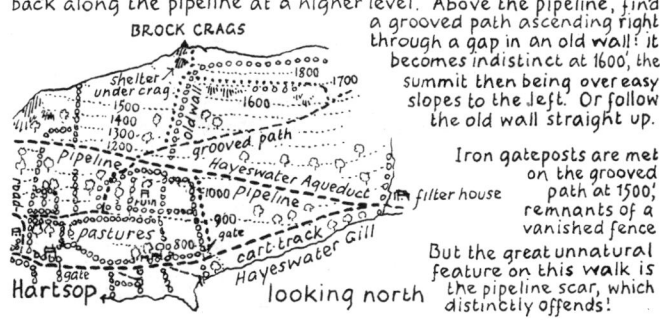

Brock Crags 3

THE SUMMIT

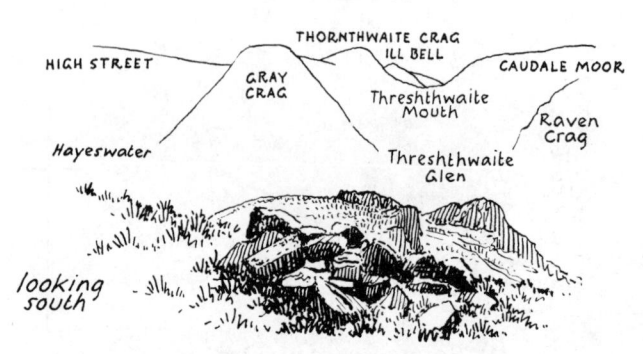

looking south

HIGH STREET — GRAY CRAG — THORNTHWAITE CRAG — ILL BELL — CAUDALE MOOR
Hayeswater — Threshthwaite Mouth — Threshthwaite Glen — Raven Crag

A series of rocky knolls, on the highest of which is a cairn, adds some interest to the rather drab surroundings. It is as a viewpoint that the summit merits most respect.
DESCENTS: A quick descent to Hartsop may be made by following downhill the old wall that crosses the fellside 150 yards south-east; descents due west encounter rough ground and should not be attempted. For Patterdale the Angle Tarn path may be joined near the Satura Crag gate by following the old wall eastwards. *In bad weather, locate the wall and follow it down to the pastures of Hartsop.*

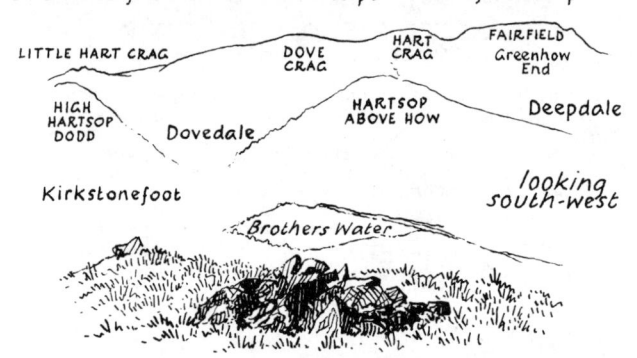

LITTLE HART CRAG — DOVE CRAG — HART CRAG — FAIRFIELD Greenhow End
HIGH HARTSOP DODD — Dovedale — HARTSOP ABOVE HOW — Deepdale
Kirkstonefoot
Brothers Water

looking south-west

RIDGE ROUTES

Brock Crags stands apart from the ridge that links Rest Dodd with Angletarn Pikes. To join the ridge, for either of these fells, follow the old wall eastwards to the gate on Satura Crag, where the connecting path will be found.

Brock Crags 4

THE VIEW

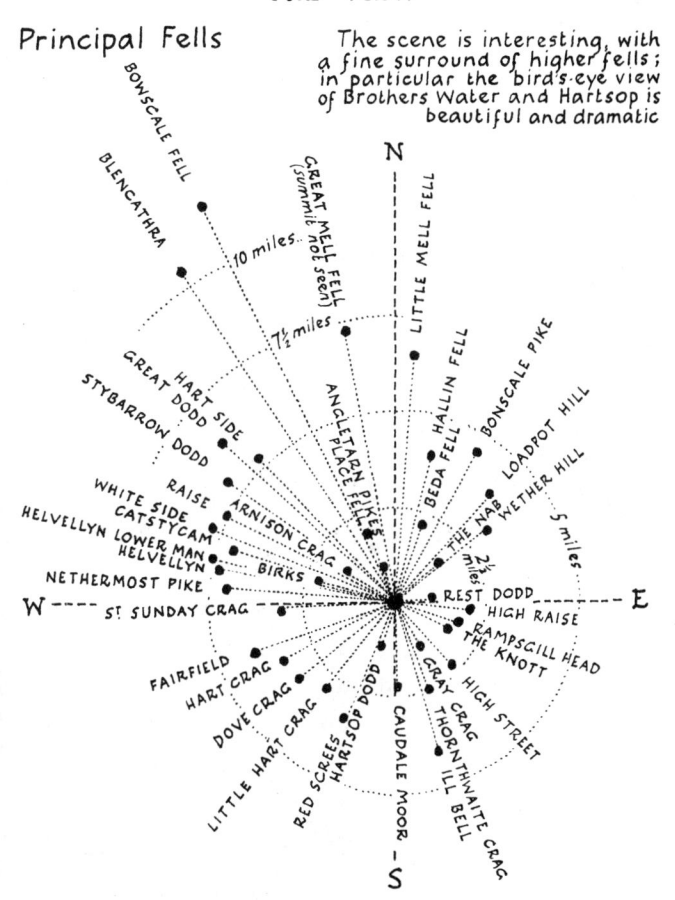

Principal Fells

The scene is interesting, with a fine surround of higher fells; in particular the bird's-eye view of Brothers Water and Hartsop is beautiful and dramatic

- BOWSCALE FELL
- BLENCATHRA
- GREAT MELL FELL (summit not seen)
- LITTLE MELL FELL
- HART SIDE
- GREAT DODD
- STYBARROW DODD
- ANGLETARN PIKES
- PLACE FELL
- BEDA FELL
- HALLIN FELL
- BONSCALE PIKE
- LOADPOT HILL
- RAISE
- WHITE SIDE
- CATSTYCAM
- ARNISON CRAG
- THE NAB
- WETHER HILL
- HELVELLYN LOWER MAN
- HELVELLYN
- BIRKS
- NETHERMOST PIKE
- ST SUNDAY CRAG
- REST DODD
- HIGH RAISE
- RAMPSGILL HEAD
- THE KNOTT
- FAIRFIELD
- HART CRAG
- DOVE CRAG
- GRAY CRAG
- HIGH STREET
- LITTLE HART CRAG
- THORNTHWAITE CRAG
- RED SCREES
- HARTSOP DODD
- ILL BELL
- CAUDALE MOOR

10 miles / 7½ miles / 5 miles / 2½ miles

Lakes and Tarns

- N: *Angle Tarn*
- SE: *Hayeswater*
- SW: *Brothers Water*
- NW: *Ullswater*

Caudale Moor 2502'

often referred to as
  John Bell's Banner
summit named
  Stony Cove Pike

from Brothers Water

Caudale Moor 2

NATURAL FEATURES

Caudale Moor deserves far more respect than it usually gets. The long featureless slope flanking the Kirkstone Pass, well known to travellers, is not at all characteristic of the fell: its other aspects, less frequently seen, are considerably more imposing. There are, in fact, no fewer than six ridges leaving the summit in other directions, four of them of distinct merit and two of these rising to subsidiary summits, Wansfell and Hartsop Dodd, on their way to valley-level. The craggy slopes bordering the upper Troutbeck valley are particularly varied and interesting: from this remote dalehead Caudale Moor looks really impressive, especially in snowy conditions. The best single feature, however, is the formidable wall of rock, Raven Crag, overlooking Pasture Beck. Of the streams draining the fell, those to the south join forces to form Trout Beck; all others go north to feed Ullswater.

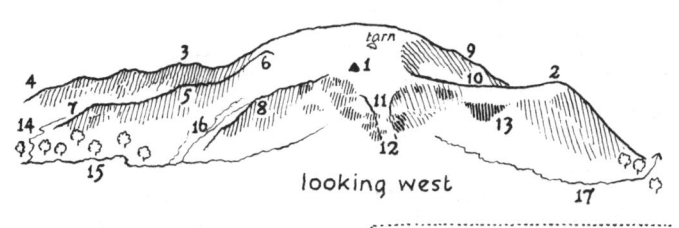

looking west

1: The summit (Stony Cove Pike)
2: Hartsop Dodd
3: St. Raven's Edge
4: Main south ridge
   continuing to Wansfell
5: Hart Crag
6: Pike How
7: Intermediate south ridge
8: South ridge (east)
9: North-west ridge
10: North ridge
11: East ridge
12: Threshthwaite Mouth
13: Raven Crag
14: Woundale Beck
15: Trout Beck
16: Sad Gill
17: Pasture Beck

The six ridges of Caudale Moor

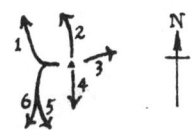

1: North-west (to Brothers Water)
2: North (to Hartsop)
3: East (to Thornthwaite Crag
   or Hartsop or Troutbeck)
4: South (east) (to Troutbeck)
5: South (intermediate)
   (to Troutbeck)
6: South (west) (to Kirkstone)

Caudale Moor 3

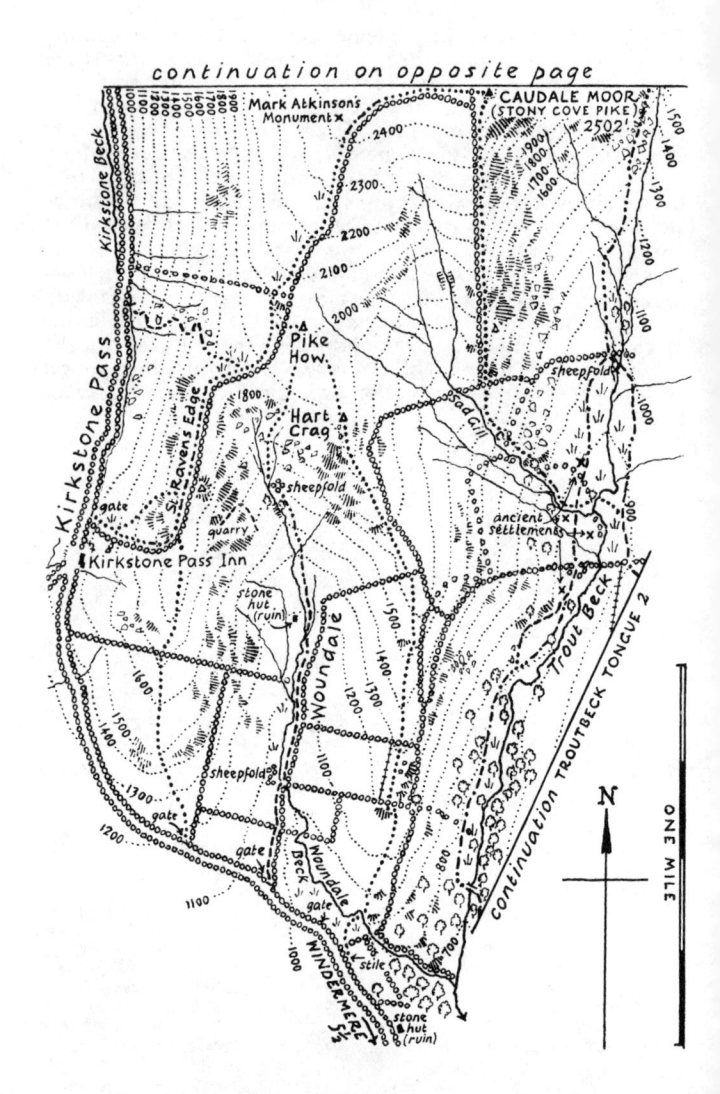

MAP

Caudale Moor 4

MAP

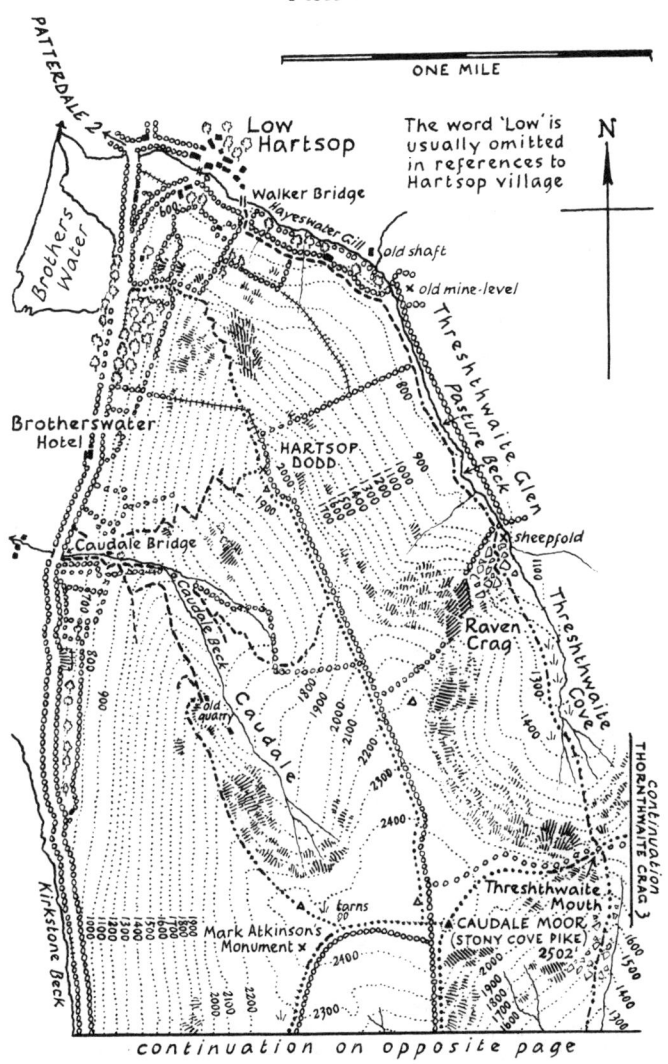

ONE MILE

The word 'Low' is usually omitted in references to Hartsop village

Caudale Moor 5

ASCENT FROM KIRKSTONE PASS
1150 feet of ascent : 2½ miles from the Inn

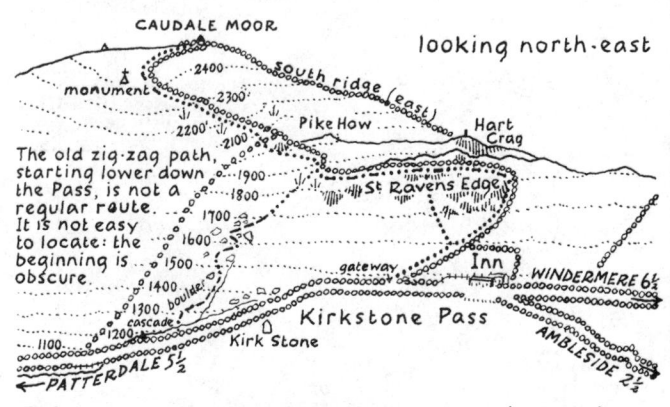

looking north-east

CAUDALE MOOR — monument — 2400 — 2300 — 2200 — south ridge (east) — Pike How — Hart Crag — 2100 — 2000 — 1900 — 1800 — St Ravens Edge — 1700 — 1600 — 1500 — gateway — Inn — WINDERMERE 6½ — 1400 — 1300 boulder — 1200 — cascade — 1100 — Kirk Stone — Kirkstone Pass — AMBLESIDE 2½ — ←PATTERDALE 5½

The old zig-zag path, starting lower down the Pass, is not a regular route. It is not easy to locate: the beginning is obscure.

This route, with the advantage of a 1500' start, is one of the easiest ways up any of the higher fells, the only steep part being the short pull on to St Ravens Edge. It is also the *dullest* way up, and does not do justice to a fine hill that has much better than this to offer.

Caudale Moor from below Scot Rake

ASCENT FROM BROTHERS WATER

2000 feet of ascent : 2½ miles from the Hotel

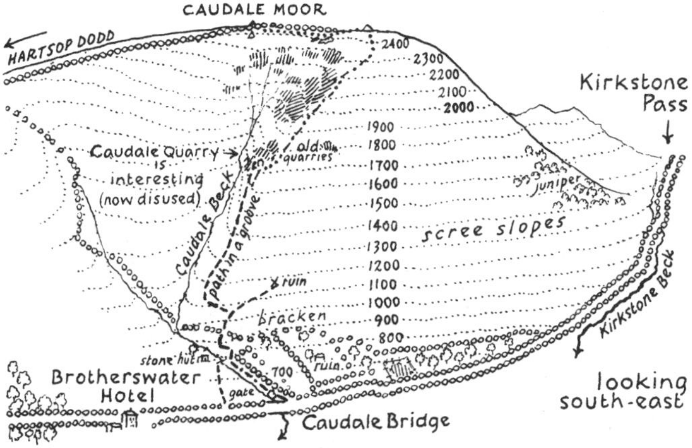
CAUDALE MOOR
HARTSOP DODD
2400
2300
2200
2100
2000
1900
1800
1700
1600
1500
1400
1300
1200
1100
1000
900
800
700
Kirkstone Pass
old quarries
Caudale Quarry is interesting (now disused)
Caudale Beck
path in a groove
juniper
scree slopes
ruin
bracken
stone hut
ruin
Brotherswater Hotel
gate
Caudale Bridge
Kirkstone Beck
looking south-east

The beautiful retrospect over Patterdale is justification for frequent halts during this continuously steep ascent. The route follows the well-defined crest of the ridge. Of the many approaches to the summit, this is by far the best.

Threshthwaite Cove from Threshthwaite Mouth

Caudale Moor 7

ASCENT FROM TROUTBECK
2200 (A) or 2350 (B) feet of ascent;
(A) 5 miles via Sad Gill; 5½ miles via Woundale (A)
(B) 6 miles via St Ravens Edge or Threshthwaite Mouth (B)

looking north

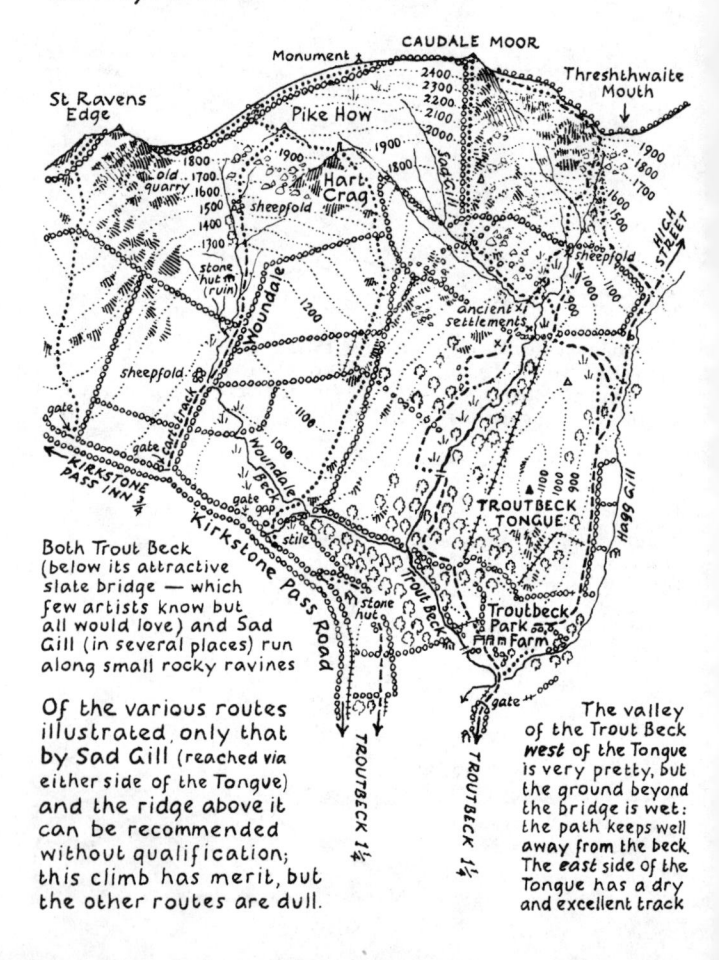

Both Trout Beck (below its attractive slate bridge — which few artists know but all would love) and Sad Gill (in several places) run along small rocky ravines

Of the various routes illustrated, only that by Sad Gill (reached via either side of the Tongue) and the ridge above it can be recommended without qualification; this climb has merit, but the other routes are dull.

The valley of the Trout Beck *west* of the Tongue is very pretty, but the ground beyond the bridge is wet: the path keeps well away from the beck. The *east* side of the Tongue has a dry and excellent track

Caudale Moor 8

THE SUMMIT

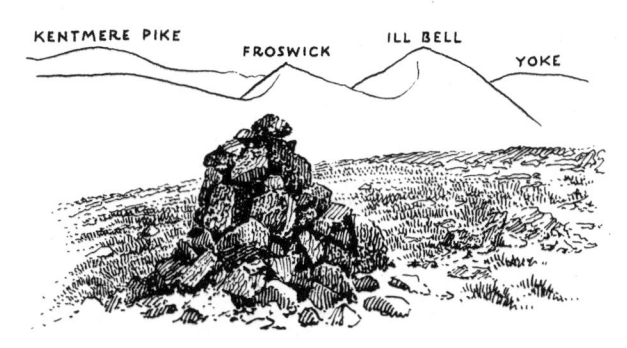

KENTMERE PIKE — FROSWICK — ILL BELL — YOKE

The summit is a dreary plateau of considerable extent, crossed by stone walls, with grey rock outcropping in the wide expanse of grass. The highest point is not easy to locate on the flat top: it is indicated by a cairn, *east* of the north-south wall, and **bears** the distinctive name of Stony Cove Pike.

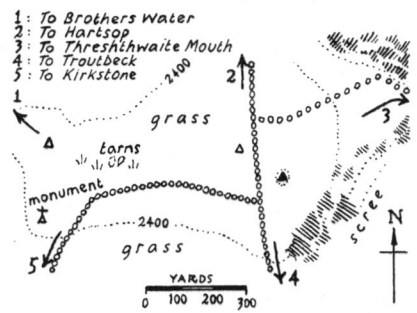

1: To Brothers Water
2: To Hartsop
3: To Threshthwaite Mouth
4: To Troutbeck
5: To Kirkstone

Mark Atkinson's Monument

Cairn above the north-west ridge

DESCENTS: All routes of ascent may be reversed in good weather. There are no paths on the top, but (excepting the north-west ridge) accompanying walls are safe guides from the summit.

In bad weather, note that the east face is everywhere craggy: it may be descended safely *only* by the broken wall going down to the Threshthwaite gap. The best way off the top in an emergency, whatever the destination, is alongside the wall running west — this continues without a break to the road near Kirkstone Pass Inn.

Caudale Moor 9

THE VIEW

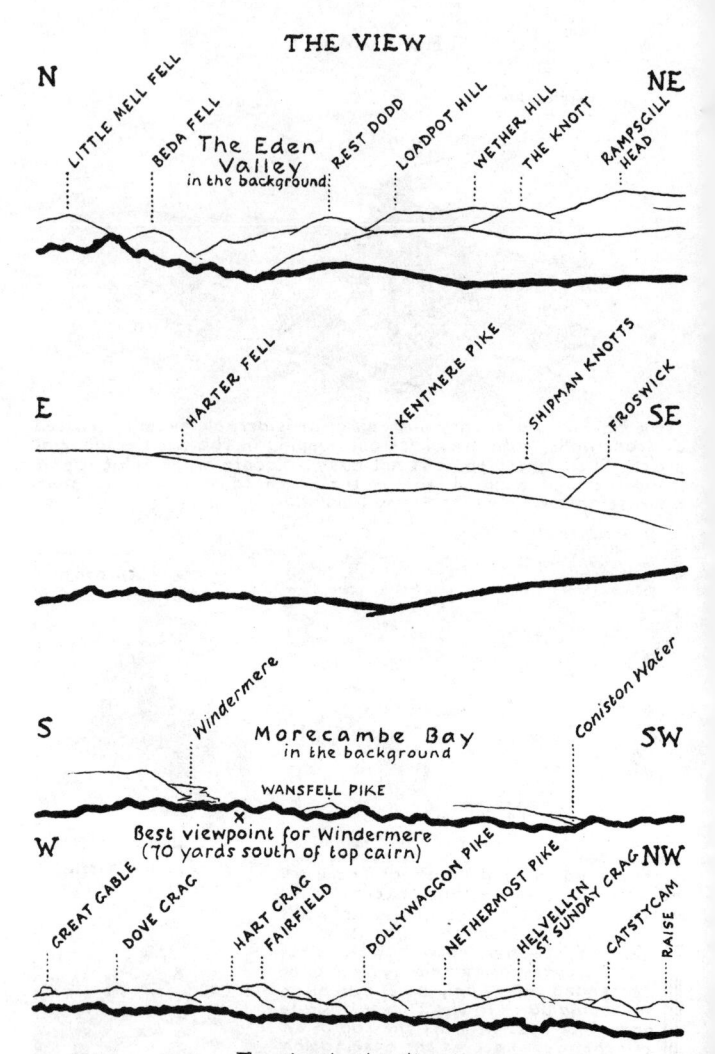

N — LITTLE MELL FELL, BEDA FELL, The Eden Valley in the background, REST DODD, LOADPOT HILL, WETHER HILL, THE KNOTT, RAMPSGILL HEAD — **NE**

E — HARTER FELL, KENTMERE PIKE, SHIPMAN KNOTTS, FROSWICK — **SE**

S — Windermere, Morecambe Bay in the background, WANSFELL PIKE, Coniston Water — **SW**

Best viewpoint for Windermere (70 yards south of top cairn)

W — GREAT GABLE, DOVE CRAG, HART CRAG, FAIRFIELD, DOLLYWAGGON PIKE, NETHERMOST PIKE, HELVELLYN, ST SUNDAY CRAG, CATSTYCAM, RAISE — **NW**

The view in this direction is much better seen from the western edge of the summit-plateau

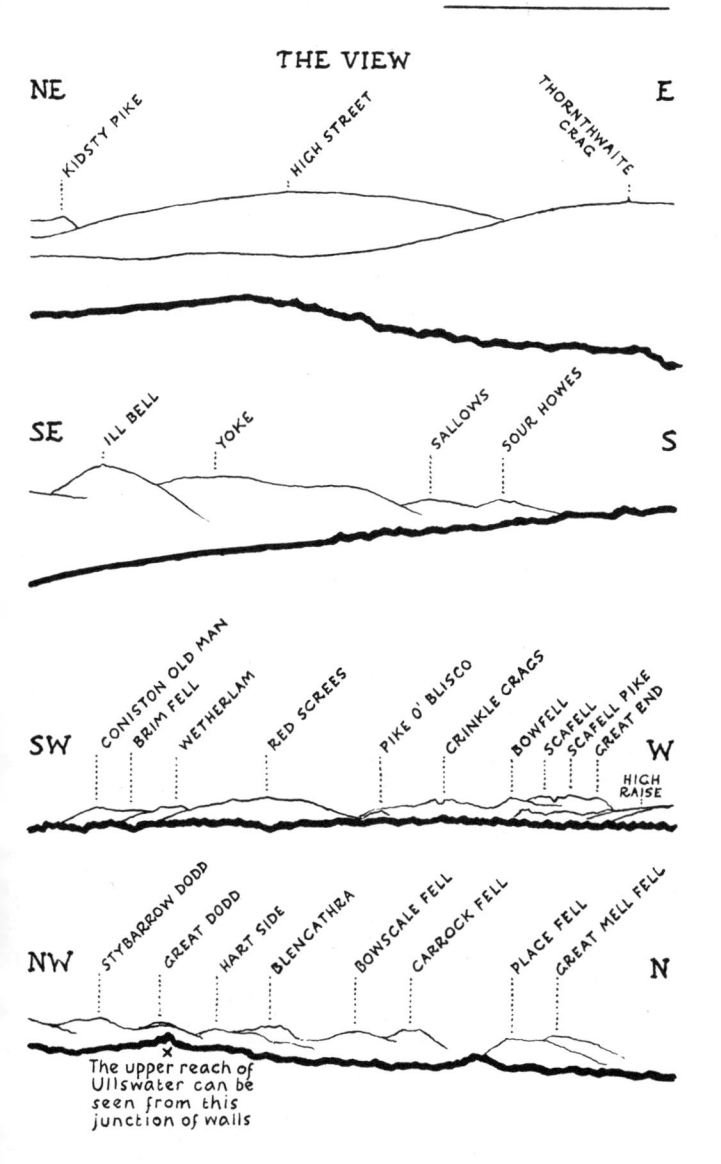

Caudale Moor 10

THE VIEW

NE — KIDSTY PIKE, HIGH STREET, THORNTHWAITE CRAG — **E**

SE — ILL BELL, YOKE, SALLOWS, SOUR HOWES — **S**

SW — CONISTON OLD MAN, BRIM FELL, WETHERLAM, RED SCREES, PIKE O' BLISCO, CRINKLE CRAGS, BOWFELL, SCAFELL, SCAFELL PIKE, GREAT END, HIGH RAISE — **W**

NW — STYBARROW DODD, GREAT DODD, HART SIDE, BLENCATHRA, BOWSCALE FELL, CARROCK FELL, PLACE FELL, GREAT MELL FELL — **N**

The upper reach of Ullswater can be seen from this junction of walls

Caudale Moor 11

RIDGE ROUTE

To WANSFELL, 1597': 4½ miles: W, then SW and S
Depression at 1100': 500 feet of ascent

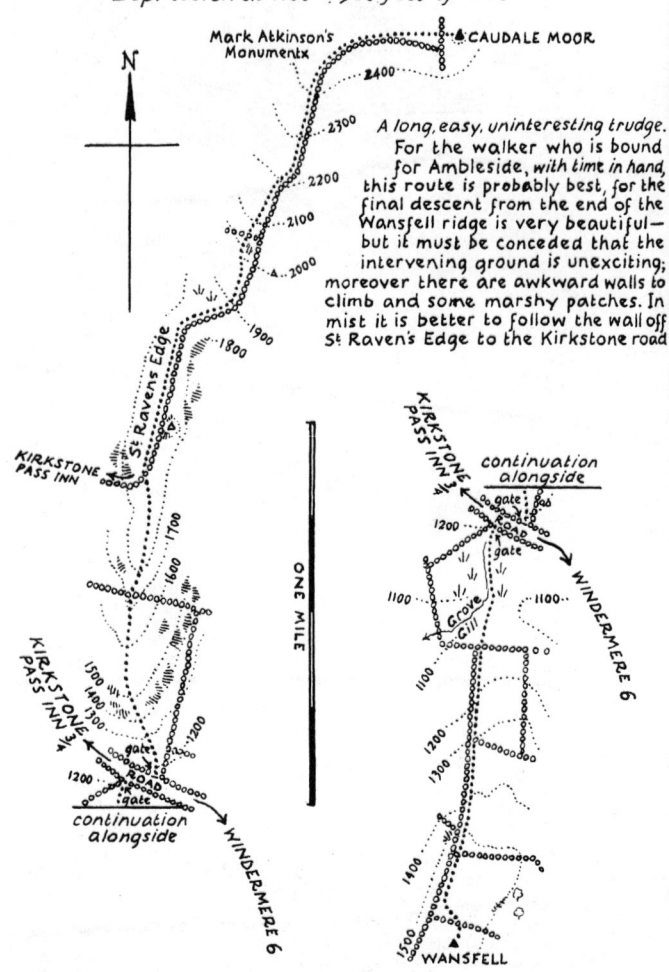

A long, easy, uninteresting trudge. For the walker who is bound for Ambleside, with time in hand, this route is probably best, for the final descent from the end of the Wansfell ridge is very beautiful— but it must be conceded that the intervening ground is unexciting; moreover there are awkward walls to climb and some marshy patches. In mist it is better to follow the wall off St Raven's Edge to the Kirkstone road

Caudale Moor 12

RIDGE ROUTES

To THORNTHWAITE CRAG, 2569': 1 mile: ENE, then E and SE
Depression at 1950': 620 feet of ascent
A rough scramble, safe in mist

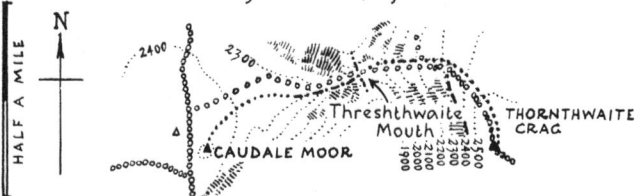

This walk is not as simple as it looks, because the deep gap or col (Threshthwaite Mouth) between the two fells is unsuspected from the top of Caudale Moor. The descent to the gap is steep (if there is snow and ice it may be dangerous) and the climb from it is stony and loose. In mist, it is important to keep alongside the crumbled wall that links the two summits.

To HARTSOP DODD, 2018': 1½ miles: N, then NNW
Depression at 1900': 120 feet of ascent
An easy, straightforward walk

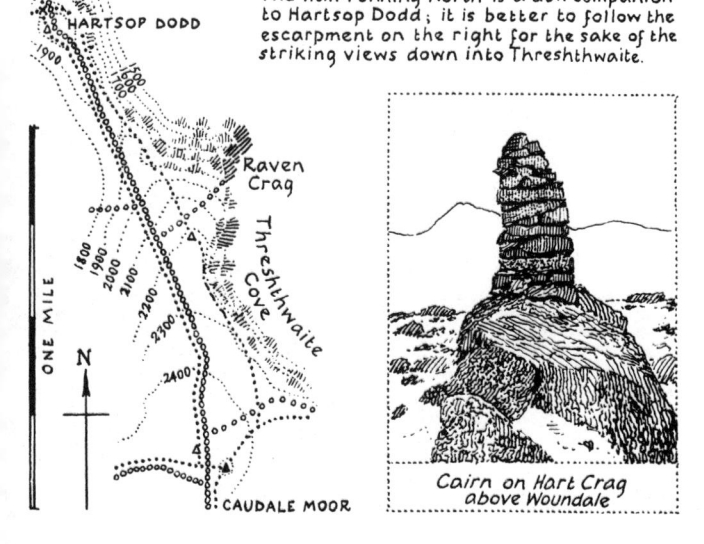

The wall running north is a dull companion to Hartsop Dodd; it is better to follow the escarpment on the right for the sake of the striking views down into Threshthwaite.

Cairn on Hart Crag above Woundale

Caudale Moor 13

Ullswater and Brothers Water from Caudale Quarry

Red Screes and Middle Dodd from the north-west ridge

Caudale Moor 14

Caudale Head

Raven Crag

Froswick   2359'

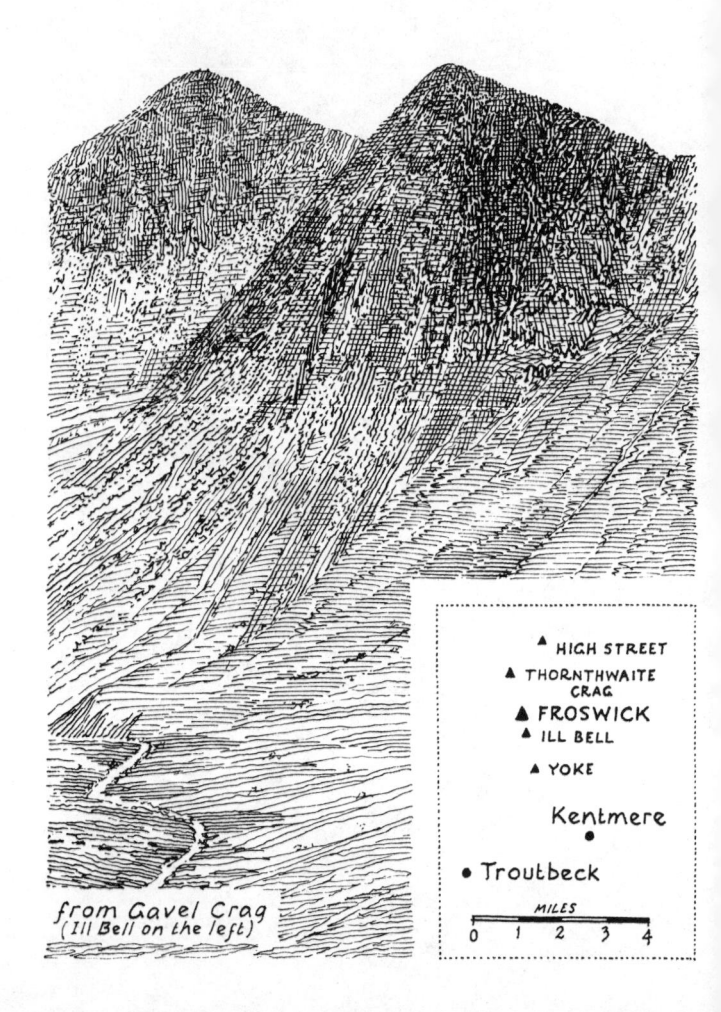

*from Gavel Crag
(Ill Bell on the left)*

▲ HIGH STREET
▲ THORNTHWAITE CRAG
▲ **FROSWICK**
▲ ILL BELL
▲ YOKE

• Kentmere
• Troutbeck

MILES
0 1 2 3 4

Froswick 2

NATURAL FEATURES

Sheltering in the shadow of Ill Bell on High Street's south ridge is the lesser height of Froswick. It takes its pattern from Ill Bell in remarkable degree, almost humorously seeming to ape its bigger neighbour. Both flanks are very steep, the Kentmere side especially being a rough tumble of scree: there are crags here facing up the valley. The grassy Troutbeck slope, west, is notable for Froswick's one touch of originality, for it is cleft by a tremendous scree gully, Blue Gill, that splits the fellside from top to bottom. Easy slopes link the summit with Thornthwaite Crag and Ill Bell; this is the finest part of the ridge.

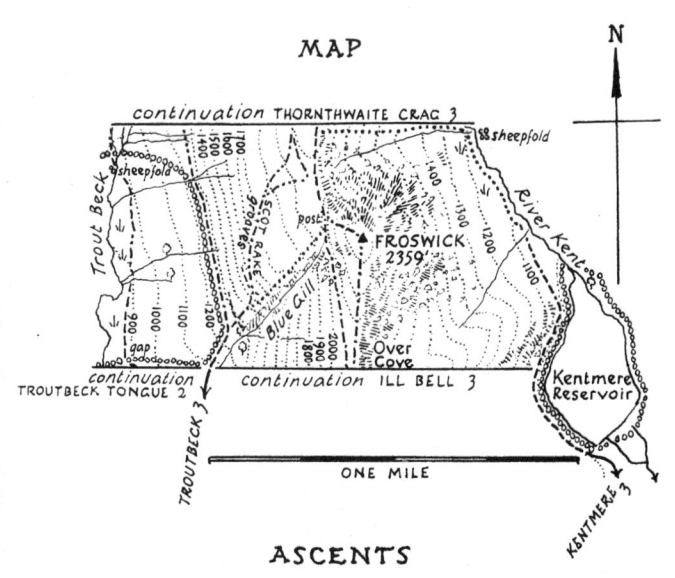

MAP

ASCENTS

Froswick is rarely climbed direct; invariably its summit is gained incidentally during the course of the Ill Bell ridge-walk, starting at Garburn Pass. From Troutbeck, however, its top may be visited on the way to High Street by Scot Rake, in which case it is quicker to climb alongside Blue Gill than to waste time trying to locate Scot Rake. A direct ascent from Kentmere is not recommended, this flank being steep, loose and unpleasant, although the ridge north of the summit may be reached up a continuous tongue of grass from the sheepfold.

Froswick 3

THE SUMMIT

THORNTHWAITE CRAG
CAUDALE MOOR
Threshthwaite Mouth

Froswick's peaked appearance from afar holds out the promise of a small pointed summit. Small it is, and neat, with a tidy cairn, but it will hardly satisfy the seeker of spires.

DESCENTS: The routes of ascent may be reversed. The western flank is safe anywhere (but keep out of Blue Gill); do not attempt the *direct* descent to Kentmere. *In mist*, reach Kentmere by way of Garburn Pass.

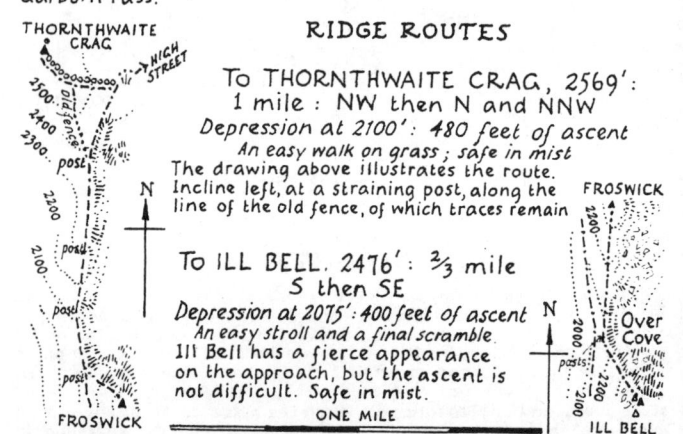

RIDGE ROUTES

To THORNTHWAITE CRAG, 2569':
1 mile : NW then N and NNW
Depression at 2100': 480 feet of ascent
An easy walk on grass; safe in mist
The drawing above illustrates the route.
Incline left, at a straining post, along the line of the old fence, of which traces remain

To ILL BELL. 2476': ⅔ mile
S then SE
Depression at 2075': 400 feet of ascent
An easy stroll and a final scramble.
Ill Bell has a fierce appearance on the approach, but the ascent is not difficult. Safe in mist.

ONE MILE

THE VIEW

Sandwiched between Thornthwaite Crag and Ill Bell, both higher, Froswick is an undistinguished viewpoint, the best feature being the serrated skyline of the Scafell and Langdale heights in the west

Principal Fells

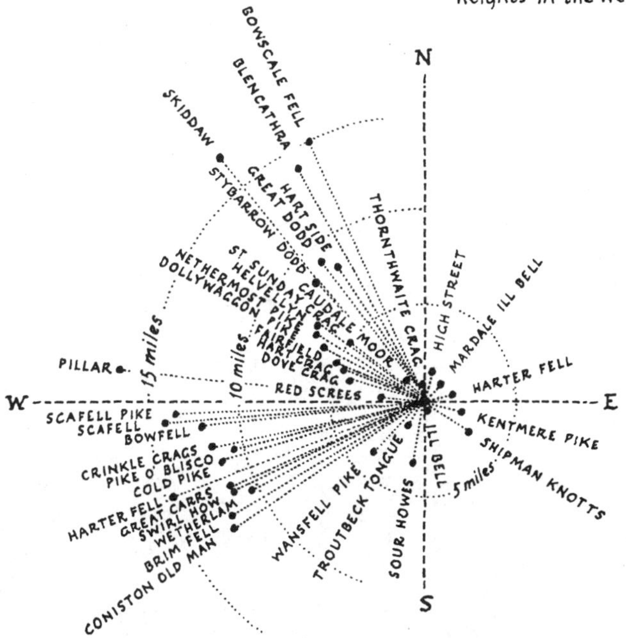
N
S
W
E
BOWSCALE FELL
BLENCATHRA
SKIDDAW
HART SIDE
GREAT DODD
STYBARROW DODD
THORNTHWAITE CRAG
HIGH STREET
MARDALE ILL BELL
HARTER FELL
KENTMERE PIKE
SHIPMAN KNOTTS
ILL BELL
ST SUNDAY CRAG
HELVELLYN
NETHERMOST PIKE
DOLLYWAGGON PIKE
CAUDALE MOOR
FAIRFIELD
HART CRAG
DOVE CRAG
RED SCREES
PILLAR
15 miles
10 miles
5 miles
SCAFELL PIKE
SCAFELL
BOWFELL
CRINKLE CRAGS
PIKE O' BLISCO
COLD PIKE
HARTER FELL
GREAT CARRS
SWIRL HOW
WETHERLAM
BRIM FELL
CONISTON OLD MAN
WANSFELL PIKE
TROUTBECK TONGUE
SOUR HOWES

Ill Bell from Froswick

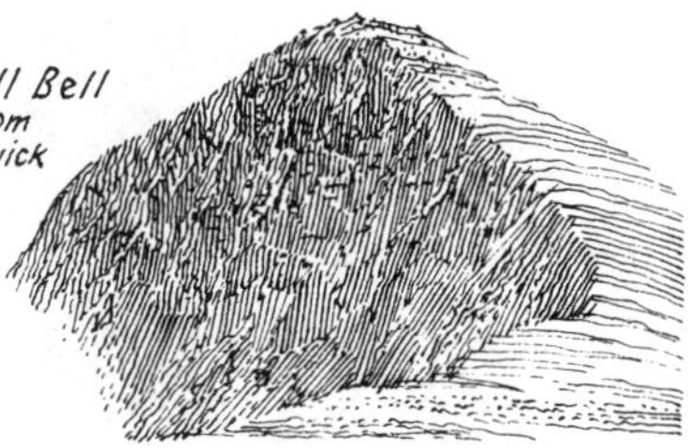

Lakes and Tarns

SE : *Kentmere Reservoir*
SSW : *Windermere*
NNW : *Ullswater*

Gray Crag 2286'

- Hartsop
  ▲ GRAY CRAG
    ▲ HIGH STREET
  ▲ THORNTHWAITE CRAG

MILES
0 1 2 3

from Hartsop

Gray Crag 2

NATURAL FEATURES

A lofty ridge, bounded by exceedingly steep flanks, extends northwards from Thornthwaite Crag with a slight curve to the west, and culminates high above Hayeswater Gill in a level platform from which, on both sides, fall precipitous crags split by deep gullies. This is Gray Crag, a prominent object in the Hartsop landscape. Hayeswater forms its eastern base, while the stream issuing therefrom defines it to the north. The western boundary, below an impressive cliff of shattered rocks, is Pasture Beck.

MAP

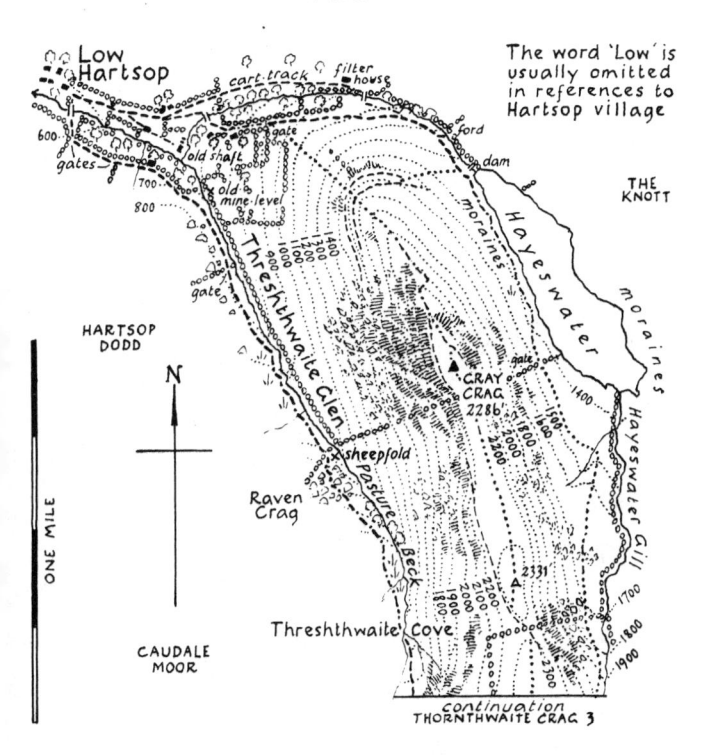

The word 'Low' is usually omitted in references to Hartsop village

Gray Crag 3

ASCENT FROM HARTSOP
1800 feet of ascent : 2 miles
(via Threshthwaite Mouth : 1950 feet of ascent : 4 miles)

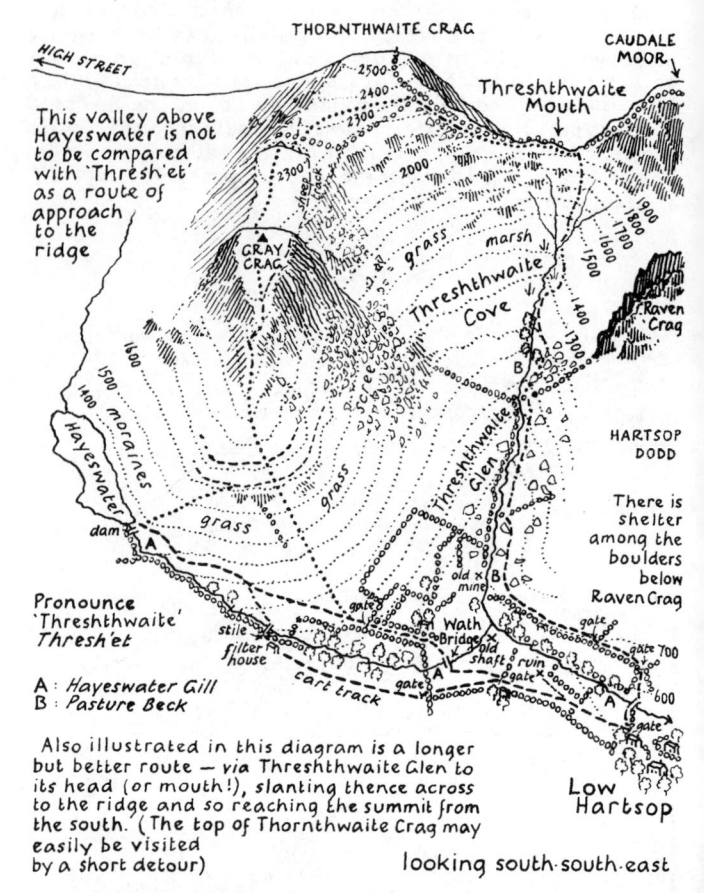

This valley above Hayeswater is not to be compared with 'Thresh'et' as a route of approach to the ridge

Pronounce 'Threshthwaite' Thresh'et

A : Hayeswater Gill
B : Pasture Beck

Also illustrated in this diagram is a longer but better route — via Threshthwaite Glen to its head (or mouth!), slanting thence across to the ridge and so reaching the summit from the south. (The top of Thornthwaite Crag may easily be visited by a short detour)

There is shelter among the boulders below Raven Crag

looking south-south-east

The direct route climbs steeply to the ridge when free of the enclosing walls above Wath Bridge, but it is easier and more interesting to continue first to Hayeswater and gain the ridge from there.

Gray Crag 4

THE SUMMUT

The summit is a pleasant level plateau of grass between steep cliffs, which should be visited for their striking downward views.
DESCENTS (to Hartsop): The *only* practicable way off is by the descending north ridge, which narrows and is very enjoyable — the bilberries here are more in evidence as plants than as fruit.
In mist, keep between the steep slopes (no rock has to be negotiated anywhere) until a plain path is reached *crossing* the fellside, and then another; beyond these, avoid a small crag and go down grass slopes to the Hayeswater path above Wath Bridge.

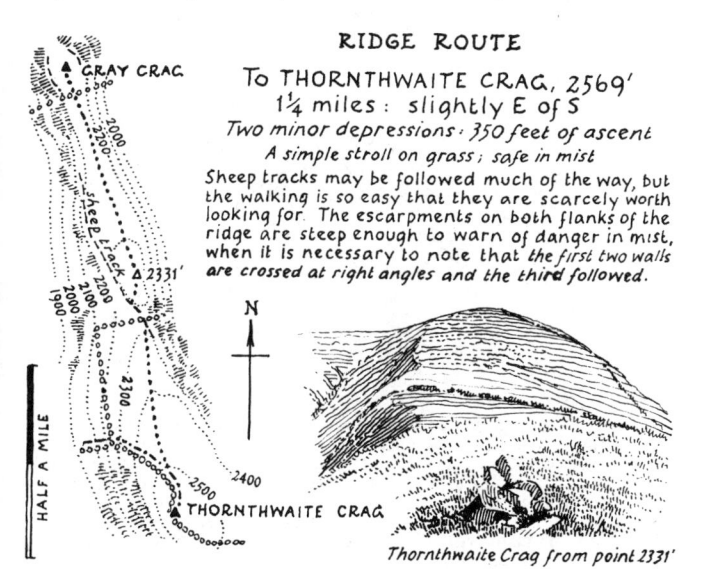

RIDGE ROUTE

To THORNTHWAITE CRAG, 2569'
1¼ miles : slightly E of S
Two minor depressions · 350 feet of ascent

A simple stroll on grass; safe in mist

Sheep tracks may be followed much of the way, but the walking is so easy that they are scarcely worth looking for. The escarpments on both flanks of the ridge are steep enough to warn of danger in mist, when it is necessary to note that *the first two walls are crossed at right angles and the third followed.*

Thornthwaite Crag from point 2331'

Gray Crag 5

THE VIEW

The edges of the escarpments are better viewpoints than the cairn, the steep declivities giving remarkable depth to the scene. While the view from the western edge of the summit is the more extensive, that from the eastern reveals the most striking picture, that of Hayeswater below.

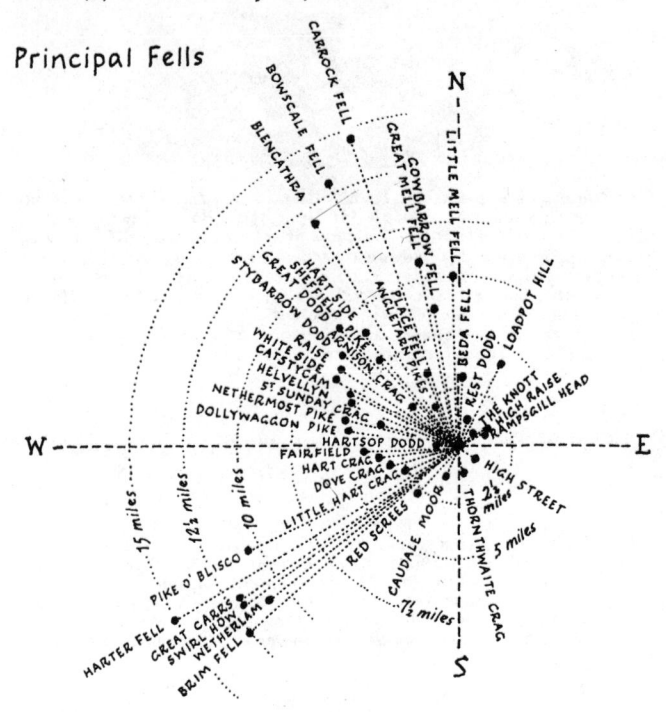

Principal Fells

Lakes and Tarns

NNW : *Ullswater* (upper reach)
S : The small sheet of water seen above Threshthwaite Mouth is *Dubbs Reservoir*, Applethwaite Common. *Windermere* can be seen in the same direction by walking 300 yards along the ridge : it is especially well seen from point 2331. *Hayeswater* is brought into view by walking 50 yards in the direction of Rampsgill Head from the cairn, *Brothers Water* by walking 80 yards in the direction of Helvellyn.

Gray Crag 6

Cascades above the filter house

Hayeswater Gill

Wath Bridge

Grey Crag 2093'

from Shipman Knotts

▲ HARTER FELL
▲ KENTMERE PIKE ▲ TARN CRAG
▲ GREY CRAG
• road summit
Longsleddale • • Hucks Bridge
• Jungle Café
Garnett Bridge • • Selside

MILES
0 1 2 3 4 5

Grey Crag 2

NATURAL FEATURES

Shap Fells are the high link between the Pennines and Lakeland. They form a broad upland area of smooth grassy slopes and plateaux, inexpressibly wild and desolate but riven by deep valleys having each its lonely sheepfarm; gradually the ground rises in undulating ridges towards a focal point above the head of Longsleddale at the 2000-feet contour. The place of convergence of the ridges is Grey Crag, where is the first evidence, in rocky outcrops and low crags, of the characteristics so peculiar to Lakeland, although the influences of the Pennines persist in the form of peat-hags and marshes. These ridges, on a map, rather resemble the spread fingers and thumb of a hand, with Grey Crag as the palm.

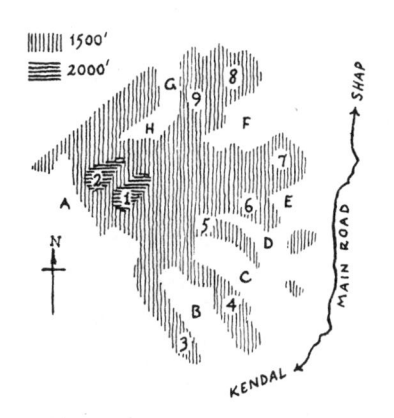

1 : Grey Crag
2 : Tarn Crag
3 : Capplebarrow
4 : White Howe
5 : Lords Seat
6 : Great Yarlside
7 : Wasdale Pike
8 : Seat Robert
9 : High Wether Howe

A : *Longsleddale*
B : *Bannisdale*
C : *Borrowdale*
D : *Crookdale*
E : *Wasdale*
F : *Wet Sleddale*
G : *Swindale*
H : *Mosedale*

There is nothing remarkable about Grey Crag, but here Lakeland may be said to start and moorland country to end — and the transition is sudden: the quiet beauty gives place to romantic beauty, placid scenery to exciting. One looks east, and the heart is soothed; west, and it is stirred. Longsleddale, at the western base of the fell, is a lovely valley and, at its head, typically Lakeland. Nearby, across a slight depression north-west, is a twin height, Tarn Crag; between them is Greycrag Tarn.

Grey Crag 3

MAP

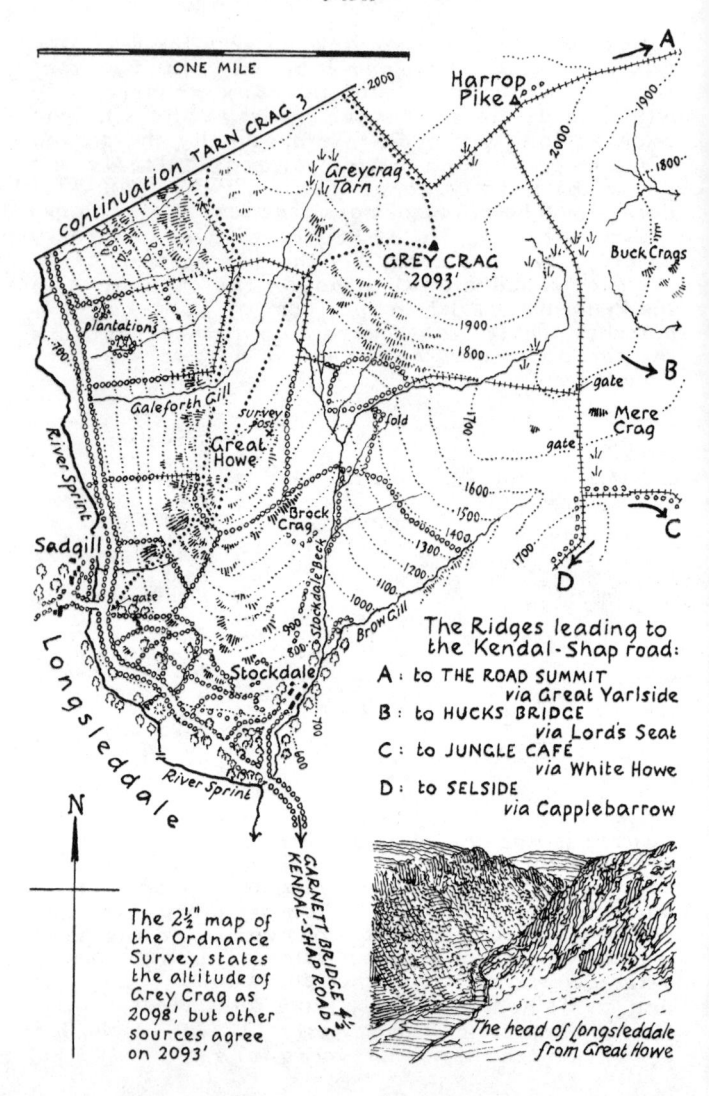

ONE MILE

continuation TARN CRAG 3

Harrop Pike

Greycrag Tarn

GREY CRAG 2093'

Buck Crags

plantations

Galeforth Gill

survey post

Great Howe

fold

gate

Mere Crag

Brock Crag

Stockdale Beck

Sadgill

gate

Brow Gill

Stockdale

River Sprint

Longsleddale

River Sprint

GARNETT BRIDGE 4½ / KENDAL-SHAP ROAD 5

N

The Ridges leading to the Kendal-Shap road:

A: to THE ROAD SUMMIT
     via Great Yarlside
B: to HUCKS BRIDGE
     via Lord's Seat
C: to JUNGLE CAFÉ
     via White Howe
D: to SELSIDE
     via Capplebarrow

The 2½" map of the Ordnance Survey states the altitude of Grey Crag as 2098', but other sources agree on 2093'

The head of Longsleddale from Great Howe

Grey Crag 4

ASCENT FROM LONGSLEDDALE
1500 feet of ascent : 1½ miles from Sadgill

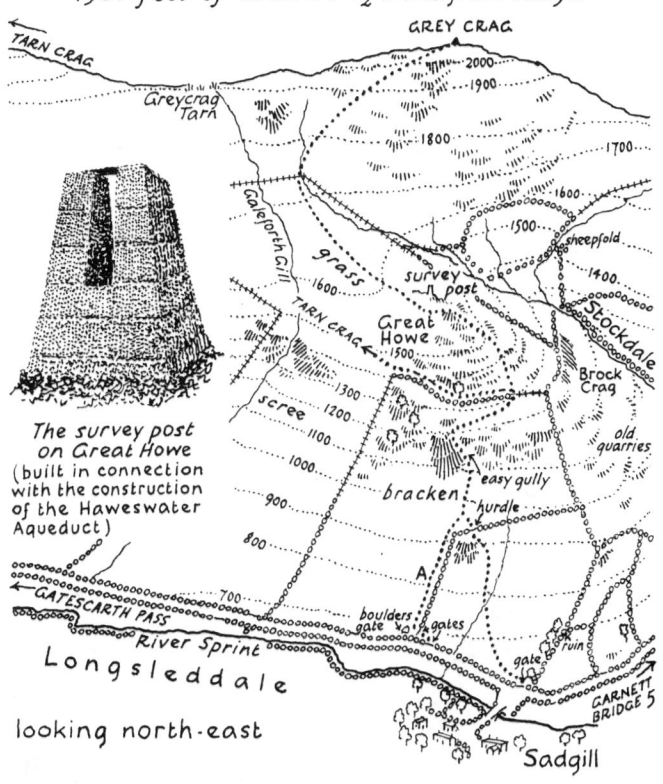

looking north-east

The survey post on Great Howe (built in connection with the construction of the Haweswater Aqueduct)

The hurdle across the gap in the wall at the top of the first enclosure is awkward to negotiate, being too frail to climb. Ladies, and gentlemen with short legs, will preserve dignity best by adopting the variation start marked A, so avoiding it.

Great Howe is an excellent viewpoint for Longsleddale.

The ascent should be commenced from Sadgill Bridge, the more direct Stockdale route being much less attractive than the climb over Great Howe. The first thousand feet is steep. In mist, the ascent has nothing to commend it. No path.

Grey Crag 5

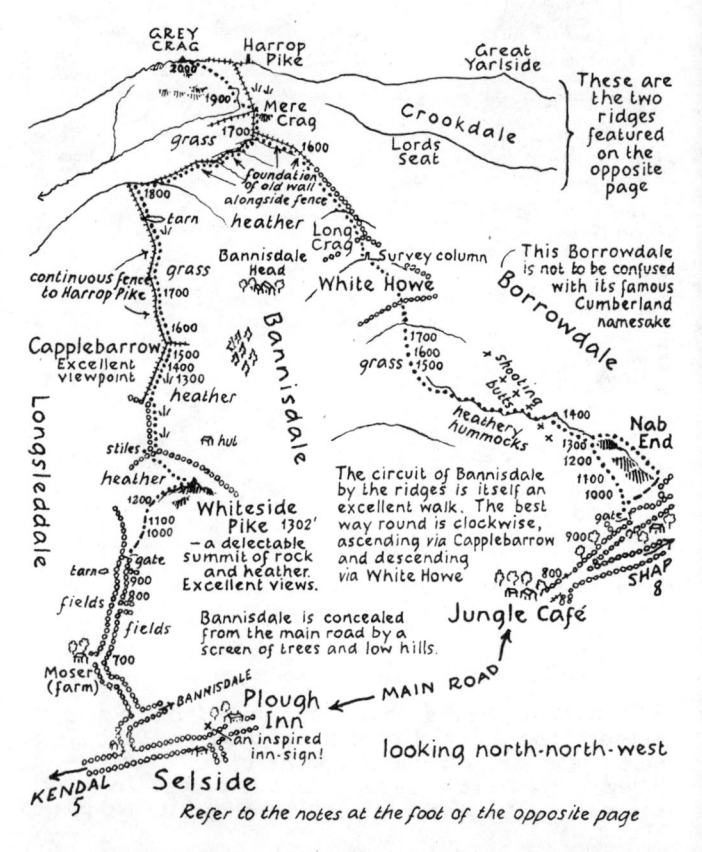

ASCENTS FROM THE KENDAL-SHAP ROAD

Grey Crag may be approached from the eastern fringe of the district along any of four clearly-defined ridges each of which has independent and distinct summits — and all of which descend to the main Kendal-Shap road. These approaches are described on this and the opposite page

1: from **SELSIDE** and **JUNGLE CAFÉ**
1700 feet of ascent   1650 feet of ascent
7 miles   6 miles

These are the two ridges featured on the opposite page

This Borrowdale is not to be confused with its famous Cumberland namesake

Cappleborrow — Excellent viewpoint

Whiteside Pike 1302' — a delectable summit of rock and heather. Excellent views.

The circuit of Bannisdale by the ridges is itself an excellent walk. The best way round is clockwise, ascending via Capplebarrow and descending via White Howe.

Bannisdale is concealed from the main road by a screen of trees and low hills.

Plough Inn — an inspired inn-sign!

← MAIN ROAD

looking north-north-west

Refer to the notes at the foot of the opposite page

Grey Crag 6

ASCENTS FROM THE KENDAL-SHAP ROAD

2 : from   HUCKS BRIDGE   and   THE ROAD SUMMIT
1700 feet of ascent   1000 feet of ascent
5 miles   5 miles

looking west-north-west

The Yarlside ridge is the easier of the two illustrated; moreover, its continuous fence makes it safe in mist.

STOP PRESS: *The proprietors of the Eagle Nest Café have recently changed its name to Fell Top Café.*

    It should be noted particularly that these routes lie across very lonely territory, in striking contrast to the pulsating life and movement of the unceasing traffic on the slender ribbon of road; there are no paths along the ridges, and visitors are infrequent. The desolation is profound. Solitary walkers who want a decent burial should bear in mind that if an accident befalls them in this wilderness their bones are likely to adorn the scene until they rot and disintegrate.
    These walks are more Pennine than Lakeland in character: there is very little rock but much tough grass and heather, and peat-hags and marshes are unwelcome features. Because of the nature of the ground, the traverse of the ridges should be undertaken only after a period of dry weather; they are best left alone on a wet day or during a rainy season or if under snow. Subject to the disabilities mentioned, it may be stated at once that the ridges offer easy and exhilarating walking in impressive surroundings, while the wide horizons and the vast skyscapes deserve the brush of a Turner.
    This is fine open country, but it is not Lakeland.

Grey Crag 7

THE SUMMIT

The top of the fell is extensive, but the highest point, indicated by a cairn, is not in doubt although it stands but little above a wide expanse of small outcrops and peat-hags.

DESCENTS: In clear weather, with ample time in hand, a way may be made to the Kendal-Shap road by any of the four ridges. If Longsleddale is the objective, the descent should be made by Great Howe in preference to a direct route via Stockdale.

‖ *In bad conditions*, the descent to the Kendal-Shap road must not be undertaken lightly. Note that only the Yarlside ridge has a continuous fence or wall all the way to the road. For Longsleddale, *in mist*, pick a way straight down into Stockdale to avoid the scarps on Great Howe.

The cairn on Harrop Pike

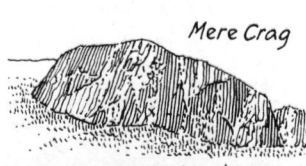

Mere Crag

— a remarkably 'clean' face of rock, showing no sign of decay; lush grass grows up to its base. Climbers will enjoy its slabs.

RIDGE ROUTE
TO TARN CRAG, 2176'
¾ mile : N then NW and SSW
Depression at 1940:
250 feet of ascent

Straightforward walking, but it is better to skirt the marshes of Greycrag Tarn by keeping along the side of the fence.

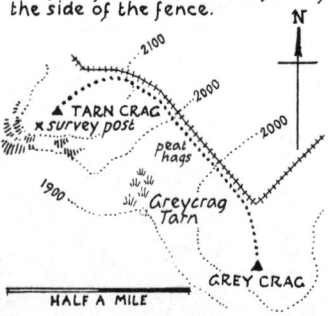

HALF A MILE

THE VIEW

Grey Crag is the most easterly of the Lakeland fells, but is not of sufficient elevation to provide the panorama across the district that might be expected from its position. Higher neighbours around the head of Longsleddale conceal most of the better-known mountains, but the Coniston group is quite prominent and there is a peep of the Scafells over the saddle between Yoke and Ill Bell.

Principal Fells

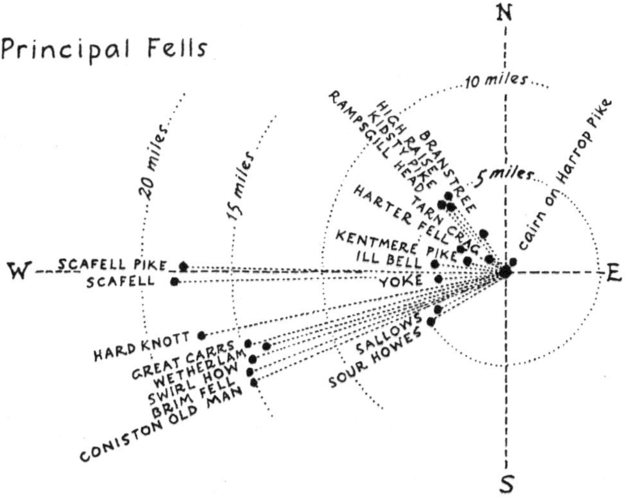
N
E
S
W
10 miles
5 miles
15 miles
20 miles
cairn on Harrop Pike
HIGH RAISE
KIDSTY PIKE
RAMPSGILL HEAD
BRANSTREE
TARN CRAG
HARTER FELL
KENTMERE PIKE
ILL BELL
YOKE
SCAFELL PIKE
SCAFELL
HARD KNOTT
GREAT CARRS
WETHERLAM
SWIRL HOW
BRIM FELL
CONISTON OLD MAN
SALLOWS
SOUR HOWES

Lakes and Tarns

SSW : *Skeggles Water*
SW : *Windermere* (two sections)

Although the view towards Lakeland is disappointingly restricted, there can be no complaint of the quality of the prospects in other directions. On a clear day the panorama is remarkably extensive and very beautiful; there is a vastness, a spaciousness, about it that is usually lacking in the views from Lakeland summits. Just to the right of the cairn on Harrop Pike, Cross Fell and the twin Dun Fells start a glorious sweep of the Pennines extending south as far as Pendle Hill, with the principal heights of Mickle Fell, the Mallerstang fells, Whernside and Ingleborough all prominent. The nearer Howgill Fells, which always look attractive, are excellently grouped. Southwards is Kendal and the Kent Valley, and, beyond, Morecambe Bay silvers the horizon round to the isolated mass of Black Combe. There can be few better views in the country—but the days on which it is fully visible are also few, unfortunately.

Hallin Fell 1271'

from above Mellguards

Hallin Fell, beautifully situated overlooking a curve of Ullswater and commanding unrivalled views of the lovely secluded hinterland of Martindale, may be regarded as the motorists' fell, for the sandals and slippers and polished shoes of the numerous car-owners who park their properties on the crest of the road above the Howtown zig-zags on Sunday afternoons have smoothed to its summit a wide track that is seldom violated by the hobnails of fellwalkers. In choosing Hallin Fell as their weekend picnic-place and playground the Penrith and Carlisle motorists show commendable discrimination, for the rich rewards its summit offers are out of all proportion to the slight effort of ascent.

```
         HALLIN FELL
           ▲
  Sandwick    Howtown

 PLACE        BEDA
 FELL ▲     ▲ FELL

  ● Patterdale
        MILES
   0    1    2    3
```

Hallin Fell 2

MAP

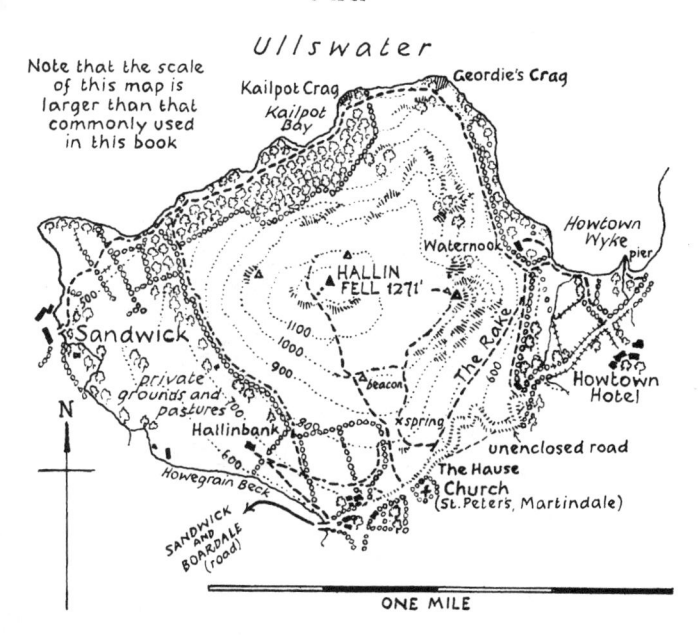

Note that the scale of this map is larger than that commonly used in this book

ONE MILE

ASCENTS

There is one royal road to the top: this is the wide grass path leaving the Hause opposite the church, and it can be ascended comfortably in bare feet; in dry weather the short smooth turf is slippery. Another track from the Hause visits the large cairn overlooking Howtown, and offers an alternative route to the top. Incidentally (although this has nothing to do with *fell-walking!*) the lakeside path *via* Kailpot Crag is entirely delightful.

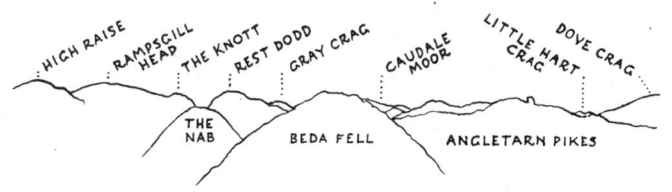

The Martindale skyline, from the top of Hallin Fell

Hallin Fell 3

THE SUMMIT

The man who built the summit-cairn of Hallin Fell did more than indicate the highest point: he erected for himself a permanent memorial. This 12-foot obelisk, a landmark for miles around, is a massive structure of squared and prepared stone.   The undulating top of the fell suffers from a rash of smaller, insignificant cairns: they occupy not merely the many vantage-points but even the bottoms of sundry hollows. The top is mainly grassy with bracken encroaching; there is a good deal of outcropping rock.

DESCENTS: The temptation to descend east directly to Howtown should be resisted for the slope above the Rake is rough and unpleasant.

The easiest way off, and the quickest, is by the path going down to the church on the Hause. In mist, no other route can safely be attempted.

The lower reach of Ullswater from the north cairn

Hallin Fell 4

THE VIEW

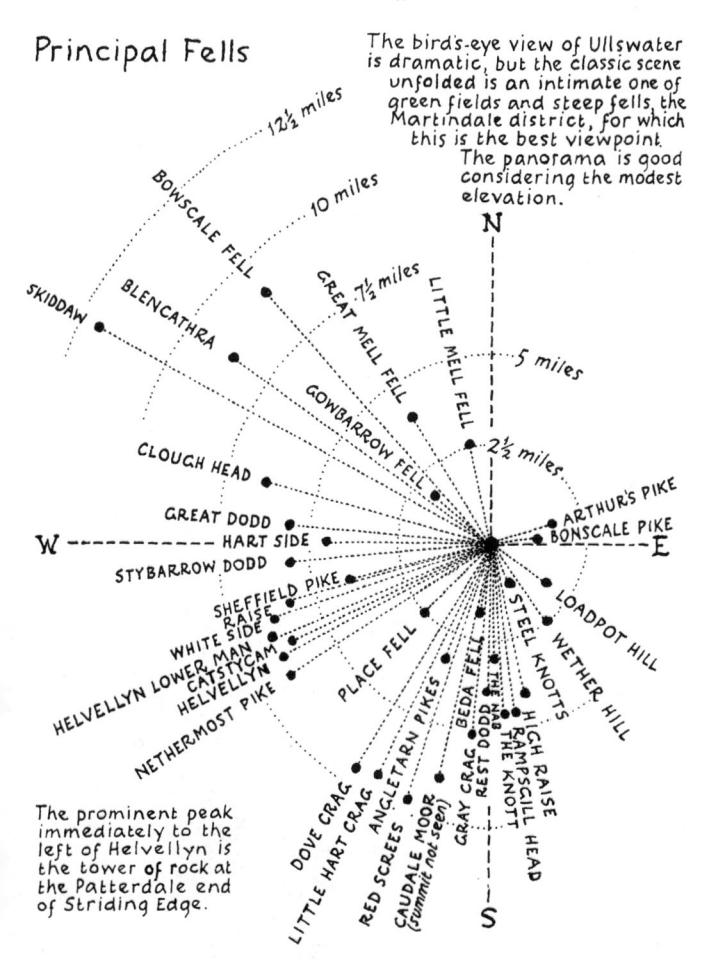

Principal Fells

The bird's-eye view of Ullswater is dramatic, but the classic scene unfolded is an intimate one of green fields and steep fells, the Martindale district, for which this is the best viewpoint. The panorama is good considering the modest elevation.

Distances shown: 12½ miles, 10 miles, 7½ miles, 5 miles, 2½ miles

Fells labelled (roughly NW clockwise to S):
- BOWSCALE FELL
- SKIDDAW
- BLENCATHRA
- GREAT MELL FELL
- LITTLE MELL FELL
- GOWBARROW FELL
- CLOUGH HEAD
- ARTHUR'S PIKE
- BONSCALE PIKE
- GREAT DODD
- HART SIDE
- STYBARROW DODD
- LOADPOT HILL
- SHEFFIELD PIKE
- RAISE
- WHITE SIDE
- WETHER HILL
- HELVELLYN LOWER MAN
- CATSTYCAM
- HELVELLYN
- PLACE FELL
- STEEL KNOTTS
- NETHERMOST PIKE
- BEDA FELL
- HIGH RAISE
- RAMPSGILL HEAD
- THE KNOT
- DOVE CRAG
- LITTLE HART CRAG
- ANGLETARN PIKES
- RED SCREES
- CAUDALE MOOR (summit not seen)
- GRAY CRAG
- REST DODD

W — E — N — S compass markers

The prominent peak immediately to the left of Helvellyn is the tower of rock at the Patterdale end of Striding Edge.

Lakes and Tarns
WSW to NE: *Ullswater*
(all of the middle and lower reaches)

Harter Fell 2539'

from The Rigg

Harter Fell 2

NATURAL FEATURES

A broad wedge of lonely upland country rises from the valley of the Kent at Burneside and continues north, narrowing, between the valleys of Kentmere and Longsleddale for nine miles; until, having very gradually attained its maximum height on Harter Fell, the ground suddenly collapses in a tremendous wall of crags, falling swiftly to the head of Mardale amongst wild and romantic surroundings — one of the noblest mountain scenes in the district. This northern face is Harter Fell's chief glory, for here, too, a shelf cradles Small Water, which is the finest of Lakeland's tarns in the opinion of many qualified to judge: seen in storm, the picture is most impressive and awe-inspiring. The other slopes have less of note although Drygrove Gill is an interesting example of landslip and Wren Gill has extensive (and dangerous) quarries. Harter Fell is one of the few fells that can claim a well-known pass on either side of its summit: Nan Bield Pass on the west and Gatescarth Pass on the east link Kentmere and Longsleddale respectively with Mardale, but since the hamlet of Mardale Head was 'drowned' by Haweswater (shame!) these passes have largely fallen from favour.

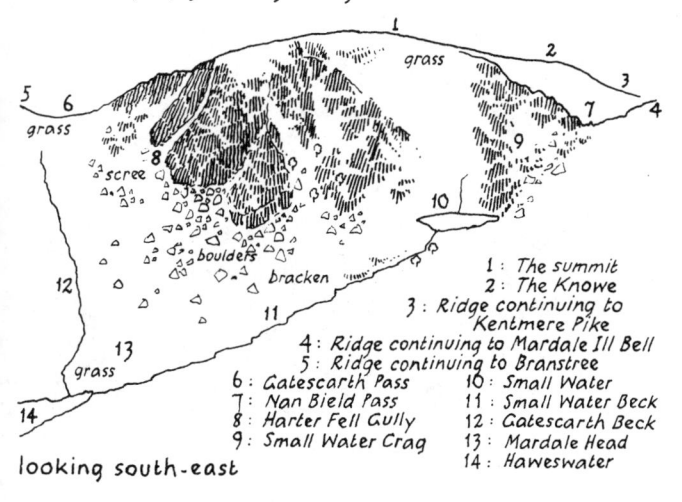

1 : The summit
2 : The Knowe
3 : Ridge continuing to Kentmere Pike
4 : Ridge continuing to Mardale Ill Bell
5 : Ridge continuing to Branstree
6 : Gatescarth Pass
7 : Nan Bield Pass
8 : Harter Fell Gully
9 : Small Water Crag
10 : Small Water
11 : Small Water Beck
12 : Gatescarth Beck
13 : Mardale Head
14 : Haweswater

looking south-east

Harter Fell 3

MAP

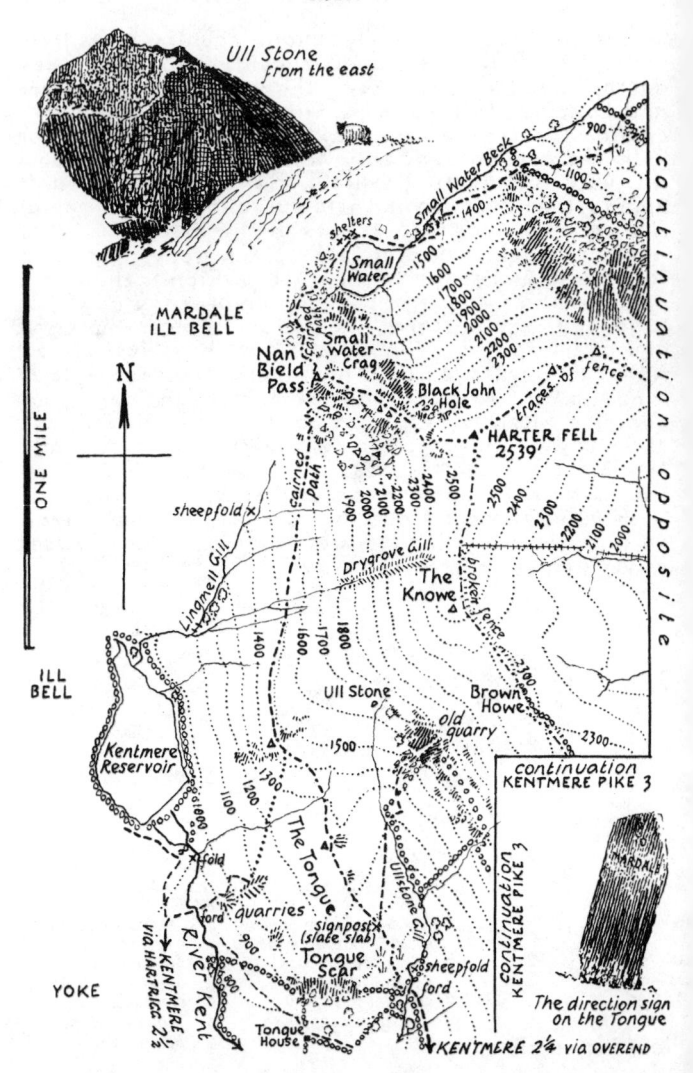

Ull Stone from the east

MARDALE ILL BELL

ONE MILE

N

ILL BELL

YOKE

Small Water Beck
shelters
Small Water
Nan Bield Pass
Small Water Crag
Black John Hole
traces of fence
HARTER FELL 2539'
cairned path
sheepfold
Lingmell Gill
Drygrove Gill
The Knowe
fence
Brown Howe
Kentmere Reservoir
Ull Stone
old quarry
The Tongue
fold
ford
quarries
Ullstone Gill
signpost (slate slab)
Tongue Scar
sheepfold
ford
Tongue House
River Kent
← KENTMERE 2¼ via HARTRIGG
KENTMERE 2¼ via OVEREND →

continuation opposite

continuation KENTMERE PIKE 3

The direction sign on the Tongue

Harter Fell 4

MAP

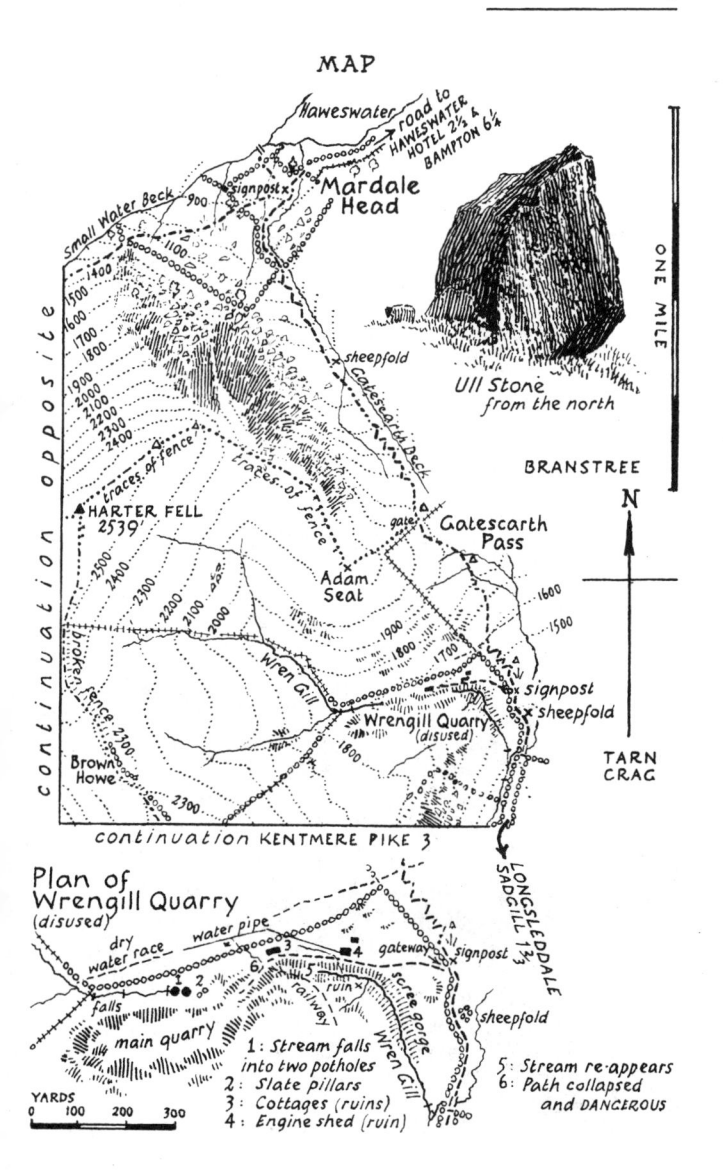

Ull Stone from the north

ONE MILE

BRANSTREE

N

TARN CRAG

Plan of Wrengill Quarry (disused)

YARDS 0 100 200 300

1: Stream falls into two potholes
2: Slate pillars
3: Cottages (ruins)
4: Engine shed (ruin)
5: Stream re-appears
6: Path collapsed and DANGEROUS

Harter Fell 5

The west face of Harter Fell from the north-east ridge of Ill Bell

Harter Fell 6

ASCENT FROM KENTMERE
2200 feet of ascent
5¼ miles via Nan Bield Pass : 4¼ miles via Kentmere Pike

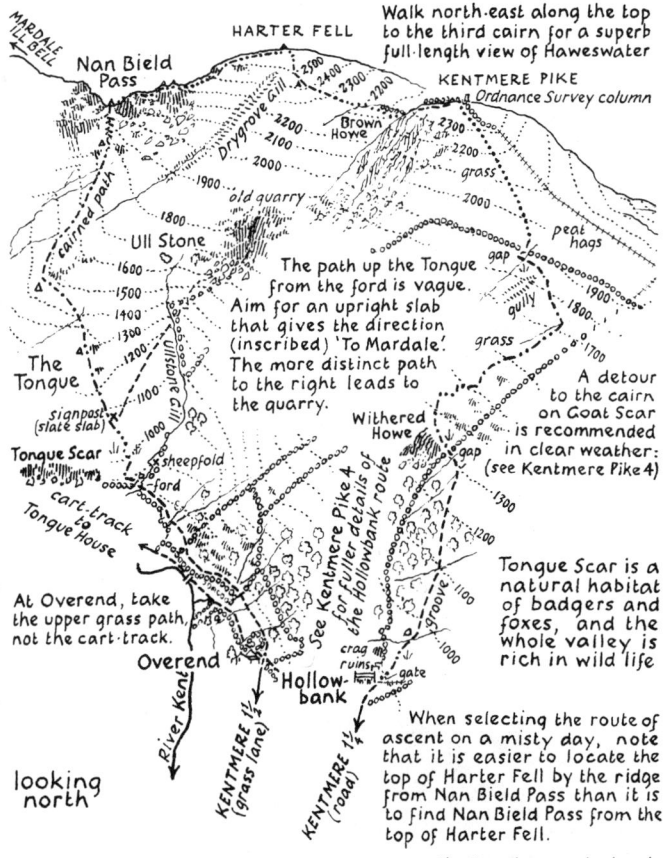

Walk north-east along the top to the third cairn for a superb full-length view of Haweswater

HARTER FELL

KENTMERE PIKE — Ordnance Survey column

MARDALE ILL BELL

Nan Bield Pass

Drygrove Gill

Brown Howe

old quarry

peat hags

Ull Stone

cairned path

The Tongue

Ullstone Gill

signpost (slate slab)

Tongue Scar

sheepfold

ford

cart-track to Tongue House

The path up the Tongue from the ford is vague. Aim for an upright slab that gives the direction (inscribed) 'To Mardale'. The more distinct path to the right leads to the quarry.

Withered Howe

gap

gully

grass

A detour to the cairn on Goat Scar is recommended in clear weather: (see Kentmere Pike 4)

See Kentmere Pike 4 for fuller details of the Hollowbank route

Tongue Scar is a natural habitat of badgers and foxes, and the whole valley is rich in wild life

At Overend, take the upper grass path, not the cart-track.

Overend

crag, ruins

Hollowbank

gate

River Kent

KENTMERE 1½ (grass lane)

KENTMERE 1¼ (road)

looking north

When selecting the route of ascent on a misty day, note that it is easier to locate the top of Harter Fell by the ridge from Nan Bield Pass than it is to find Nan Bield Pass from the top of Harter Fell.

Two routes are shown. That from Hollowbank is both easier and shorter, that from Overend much the more beautiful and interesting. The round journey serves as an excellent introduction to upper Kentmere. The sharp-crested Nan Bield is the finest of Lakeland passes.

Harter Fell 7

ASCENT FROM LONGSLEDDALE
1950 feet of ascent : 4¼ miles from Sadgill

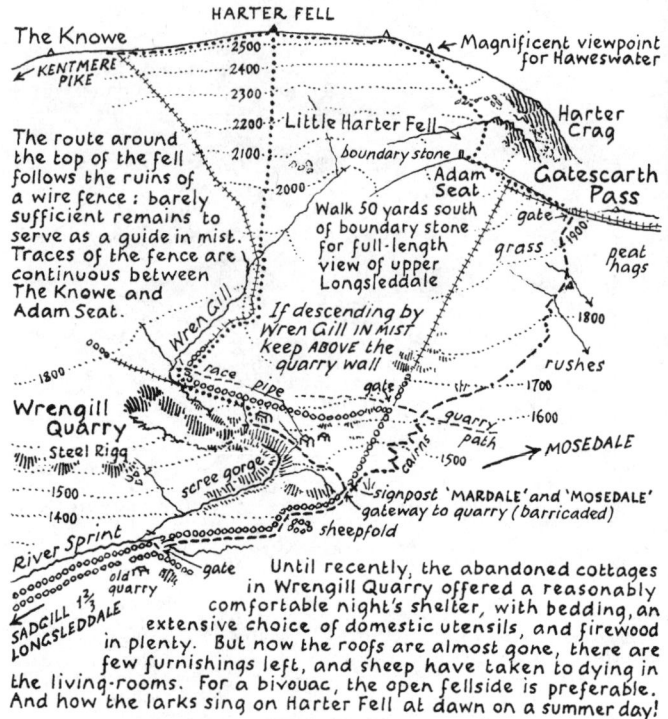

HARTER FELL

The Knowe ← Magnificent viewpoint for Haweswater

← KENTMERE PIKE

Little Harter Fell

Harter Crag

boundary stone

The route around the top of the fell follows the ruins of a wire fence: barely sufficient remains to serve as a guide in mist. Traces of the fence are continuous between The Knowe and Adam Seat.

Adam Seat

Gatescarth Pass

Walk 50 yards south of boundary stone for full-length view of upper Longsleddale

gate
grass
peat hags

Wren Gill

If descending by Wren Gill IN MIST keep ABOVE the quarry wall

rushes

race pipe

gate
quarry path → MOSEDALE
cairns

Wrengill Quarry

Steel Rigg

scree gorge

signpost 'MARDALE' and 'MOSEDALE'
gateway to quarry (barricaded)
sheepfold

River Sprint
old quarry
gate

SADGILL 1¾
LONGSLEDDALE

Until recently, the abandoned cottages in Wrengill Quarry offered a reasonably comfortable night's shelter, with bedding, an extensive choice of domestic utensils, and firewood in plenty. But now the roofs are almost gone, there are few furnishings left, and sheep have taken to dying in the living-rooms. For a bivouac, the open fellside is preferable. And how the larks sing on Harter Fell at dawn on a summer day!

looking north-west

The Gatescarth route is particularly easy: a hands-in-pockets stroll with no steep climbing, the top being reached with surprising lack of effort. Nonagenarians will find it eminently suitable.
Avoid Wren Gill in mist.

The disappearance of Wren Gill

Harter Fell 8

ASCENT FROM MARDALE
1750 feet of ascent : 2 miles from the road end

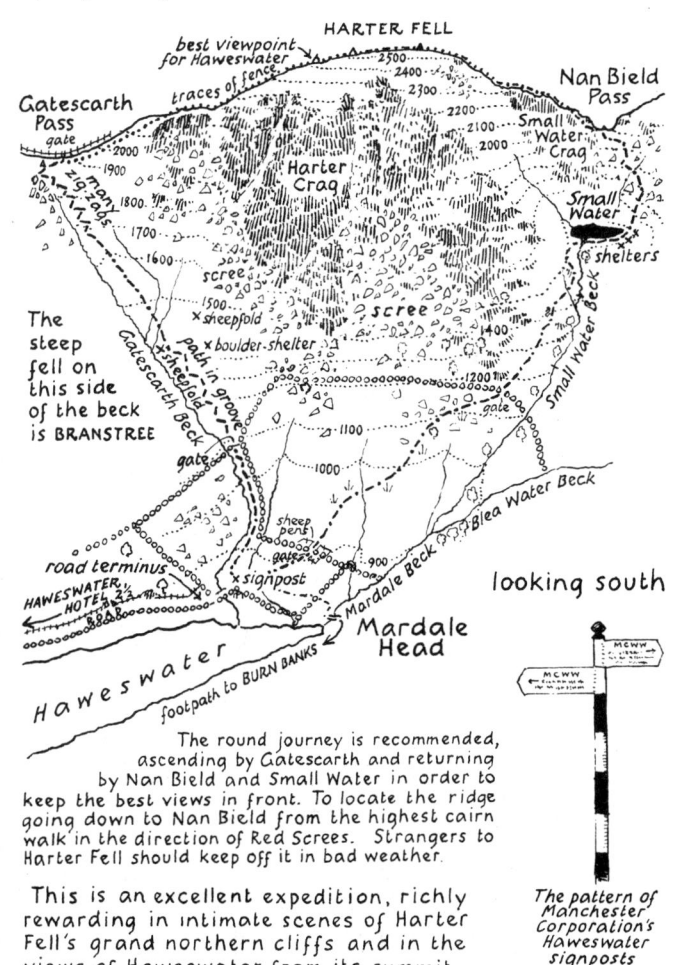

(map: looking south, showing Harter Fell, Harter Crag, Gatescarth Pass, Nan Bield Pass, Small Water, Small Water Crag, Small Water Beck, Gatescarth Beck, Mardale Beck, Blea Water Beck, Haweswater, Haweswater Hotel, road terminus, Mardale Head, footpath to BURN BANKS, signpost, sheep pens, sheepfold, boulder-shelter, shelters, scree, path in groove, gates, traces of fence, best viewpoint for Haweswater. The steep fell on this side of the beck is BRANSTREE.)

The round journey is recommended, ascending by Gatescarth and returning by Nan Bield and Small Water in order to keep the best views in front. To locate the ridge going down to Nan Bield from the highest cairn walk in the direction of Red Screes. Strangers to Harter Fell should keep off it in bad weather.

The pattern of Manchester Corporation's Haweswater signposts

This is an excellent expedition, richly rewarding in intimate scenes of Harter Fell's grand northern cliffs and in the views of Haweswater from its summit, yet short in distance and needing much less effort in execution than its formidable appearance suggests.

Harter Fell 9

THE SUMMIT

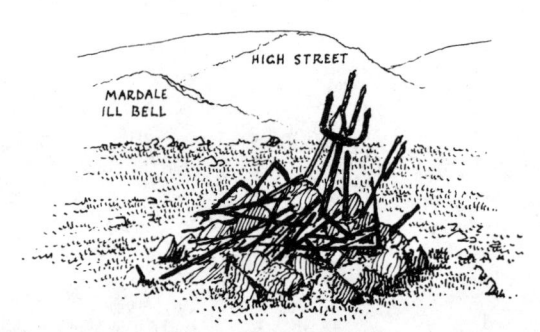

[Illustration: summit cairn with iron fence-posts, labelled MARDALE ILL BELL and HIGH STREET]

A mild shock awaits anyone reaching the top of the fell on a first visit, especially in mist, for there is a spectral weirdness about the two highest cairns. The stones support an elaborate superstructure of iron fence-posts and railings, which, having served their original mission, now act as an adornment that has a nightmarish quality.

The highest part of the fell, a graceful curve, is a long grassy sheep-walk. The fence that formerly traversed its length is now in complete ruin, but can still be traced, and is followed by the pedestrian route across the top. As so often on easy ground, no paths have been trodden out, and only occasionally does a faint track materialise.

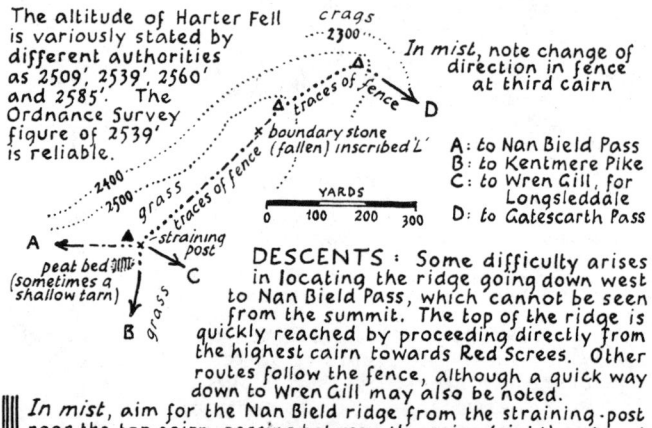

The altitude of Harter Fell is variously stated by different authorities as 2509', 2539', 2560' and 2585'. The Ordnance Survey figure of 2539' is reliable.

In mist, note change of direction in fence at third cairn

A: to Nan Bield Pass
B: to Kentmere Pike
C: to Wren Gill, for Longsleddale
D: to Gatescarth Pass

DESCENTS: Some difficulty arises in locating the ridge going down west to Nan Bield Pass, which cannot be seen from the summit. The top of the ridge is quickly reached by proceeding directly from the highest cairn towards Red Screes. Other routes follow the fence, although a quick way down to Wren Gill may also be noted.

‖ In mist, aim for the Nan Bield ridge from the straining-post near the top cairn, passing between the cairn (right) and peat bed (left). Keep to the line of the fence on other routes.

Harter Fell 10

Haweswater from the third cairn

Harter Fell 11

THE VIEW

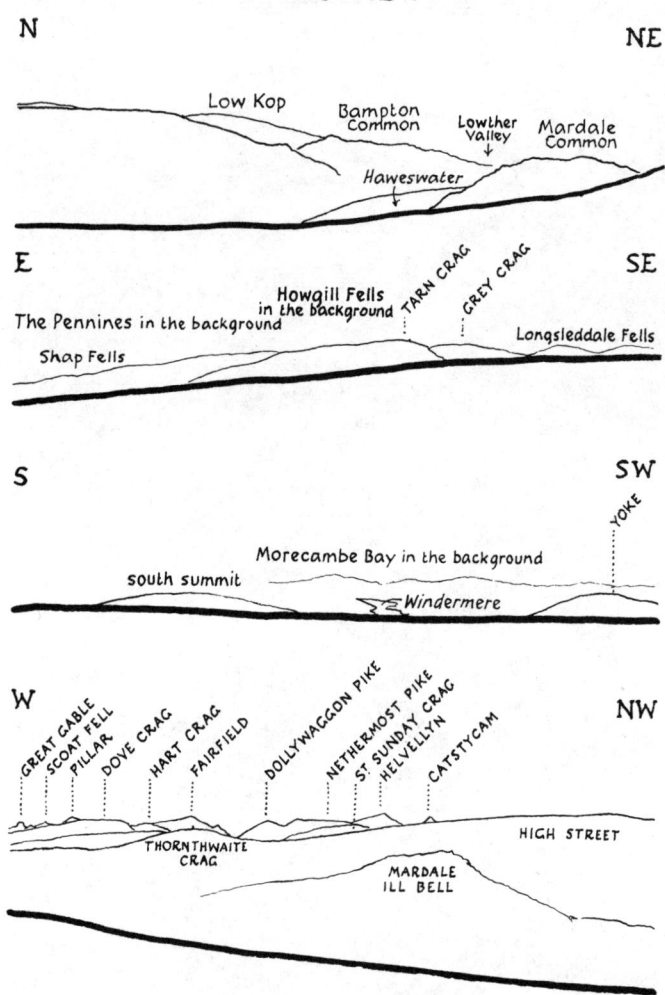

N — Low Kop, Bampton Common, Haweswater, Lowther Valley, Mardale Common — **NE**

E — The Pennines in the background, Shap Fells, Howgill Fells in the background, TARN CRAG, GREY CRAG, Longsleddale Fells — **SE**

S — south summit, Morecambe Bay in the background, Windermere, YOKE — **SW**

W — GREAT GABLE, SCOAT FELL, PILLAR, DOVE CRAG, HART CRAG, FAIRFIELD, THORNTHWAITE CRAG, DOLLYWAGGON PIKE, NETHERMOST PIKE, ST SUNDAY CRAG, HELVELLYN, CATSTYCAM, MARDALE ILL BELL, HIGH STREET — **NW**

Harter Fell 12

THE VIEW

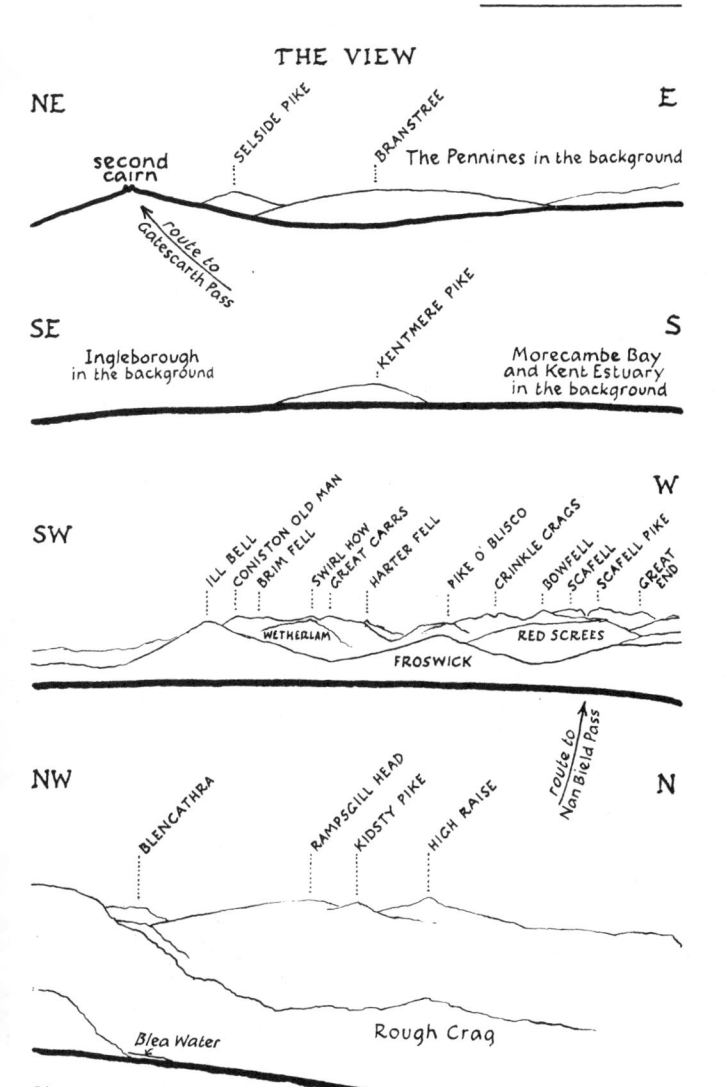

NE — second cairn / route to Gatescarth Pass / SELSIDE PIKE / BRANSTREE / The Pennines in the background — **E**

SE — Ingleborough in the background / KENTMERE PIKE / Morecambe Bay and Kent Estuary in the background — **S**

SW — ILL BELL / CONISTON OLD MAN / BRIM FELL / SWIRL HOW / GREAT CARRS / HARTER FELL / PIKE O' BLISCO / CRINKLE CRAGS / BOWFELL / SCAFELL / SCAFELL PIKE / GREAT END / WETHERLAM / RED SCREES / FROSWICK — **W**

NW — BLENCATHRA / RAMPSGILL HEAD / KIDSTY PIKE / HIGH RAISE / route to Nan Bield Pass / Blea Water / Rough Crag — **N**

Blea Water cannot be seen from the cairn, but is brought into view by walking a few yards north-west.

Harter Fell 13

RIDGE ROUTES

To BRANSTREE, 2333': 2 miles : NE then SE and NE
Depression at 1875' (Gatescarth Pass) : 465 feet of ascent
An easy walk on grass, tedious beyond Gatescarth

Follow the line of the old fence around the watershed to the good fence on Adam Seat: this runs unbroken across Gatescarth Pass and up to the top of Branstree. *In mist, it is important to note the sharp angle in the route at the third cairn : crags are ahead.*

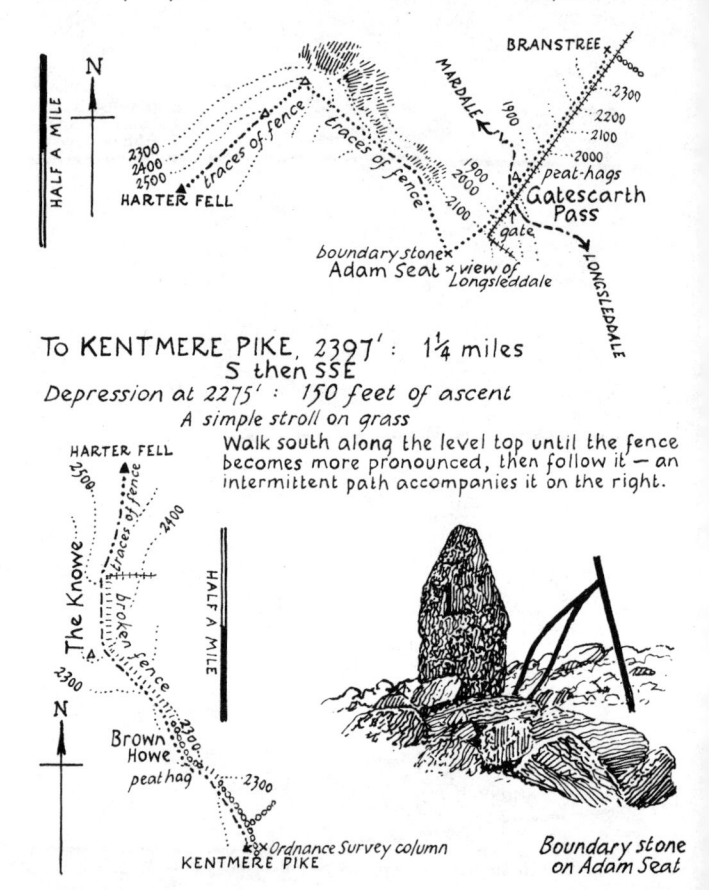

To KENTMERE PIKE, 2397': 1¼ miles
S then SSE
Depression at 2275' : 150 feet of ascent
A simple stroll on grass

Walk south along the level top until the fence becomes more pronounced, then follow it — an intermittent path accompanies it on the right.

Boundary stone on Adam Seat

Harter Fell 14

RIDGE ROUTE

To MARDALE ILL BELL, 2496': W, then WNW and NW
1 mile

Depression at 2100' (Nan Bield Pass) : 450 feet of ascent

An excellent crossing of a fine pass, with beautiful and impressive views

Aim west (in the direction of Red Screes) until the ridge going down to Nan Bield is seen below: this is a delectable descent, Small Water being a striking feature. Nan Bield is marked by a big cairn-shelter; round the outcrop beyond on the left side. Slant up to the right over rough ground when the path fades and watch for the white boulders that indicate the final rise to the summit. *In mist, Mardale Ill Bell is confusing and dangerous; there are no paths across the top.*

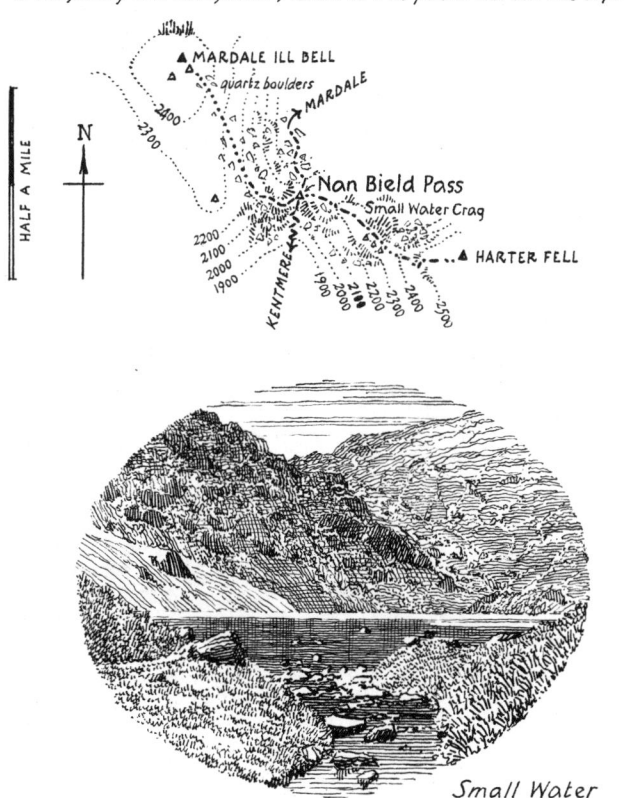

Small Water

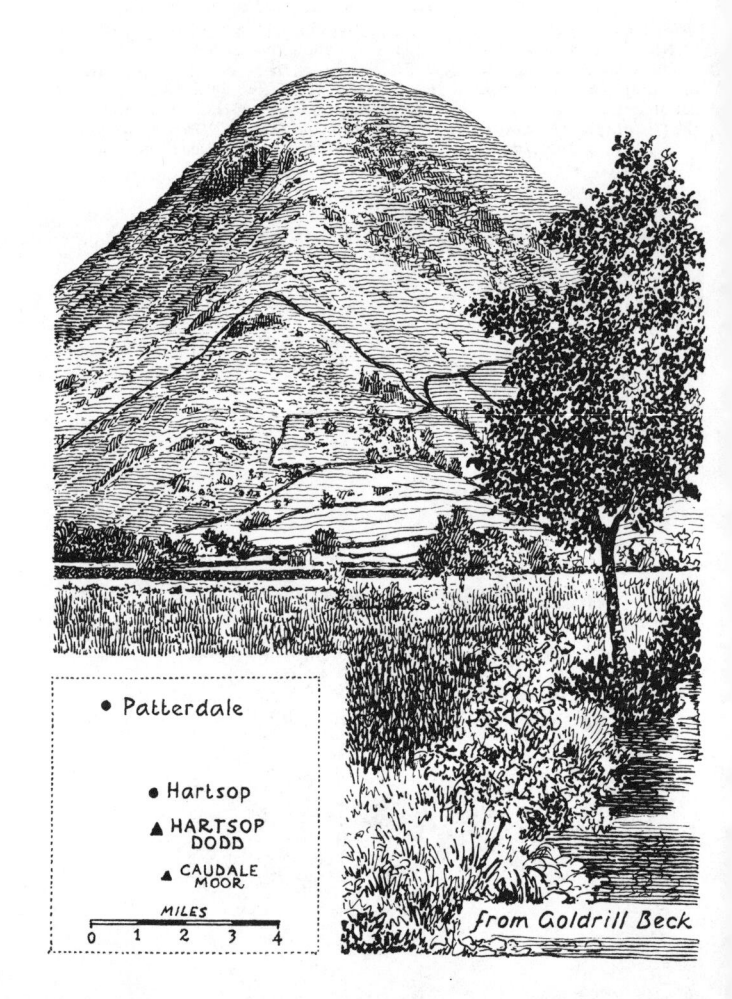

Hartsop Dodd 2018'

from Goldrill Beck

- Patterdale
- Hartsop
- ▲ HARTSOP DODD
- ▲ CAUDALE MOOR

MILES
0 1 2 3 4

Hartsop Dodd 2

NATURAL FEATURES

For a few miles along the road from Patterdale to Kirkstone, Hartsop Dodd has the form of a steepsided conical hill, rising like a giant tumulus from the flat floor of the valley; a high ridge connecting with the loftier Caudale Moor behind is unseen and unsuspected. After the fashion of many subsidiary fells in this area, the imposing front is a sham, for the Dodd is no more than the knuckled fist at the end of one of the several arms of Caudale Moor. It rises from pleasant places, pastures and woods and water, and quite rightly has been named from the delightful hamlet nestling unspoilt among trees at its foot.

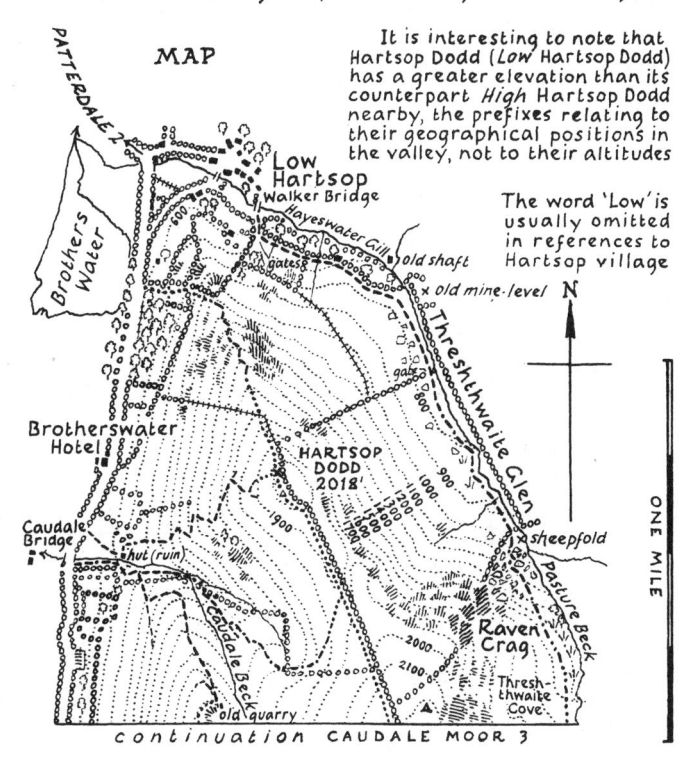

MAP

It is interesting to note that Hartsop Dodd (*Low* Hartsop Dodd) has a greater elevation than its counterpart *High* Hartsop Dodd nearby, the prefixes relating to their geographical positions in the valley, not to their altitudes

The word 'Low' is usually omitted in references to Hartsop village

continuation CAUDALE MOOR 3

Hartsop Dodd 3

ASCENTS

A feature of the paths leading up Hartsop Dodd is that, for much of their length, they run in well-engineered grooves that help considerably in defining the routes. The best way up is by the steep north ridge, a beautiful climb. The path zigzagging up the west flank is also steep, and rather dreary. The only easy route follows Caudale Beck at first and ultimately gains the ridge between the Dodd and Caudale Moor; this way is dull.

THE SUMMIT

A wall crosses the grassy top, the highest point being indicated by a wooden fence-post against the wall from which a fence formerly went down the fellside. A few stones fallen from the wall at its first bend southwards have been piled together to form a cairn of no significance.

DESCENTS: The grooves do not continue onto the summit. To find the path going down to the west, walk in the direction of Dove Crag, passing by two more fence-posts minus fence — the top of the groove is just beyond the second. To find the path down the north ridge walk towards Ullswater — the groove starts soon after the ground steepens; keep to the ridge and avoid the parallel gully on the right. The longer easy route is scarcely worth consideration.

In mist, the path on the west will be easiest to find — leave the top fence-post at right angles to the wall and look for the other two which give the key to the descent.

To CAUDALE MOOR, 2502'
1⅓ miles : SSE, then S
Depression at 1900': 620 feet of ascent

An easy climb on grass, safe in mist. The wall drearily links the two summits. In fine weather, interest may be introduced into the walk by following the edge of the escarpment on the left, the views therefrom down into Threshthwaite being very striking.

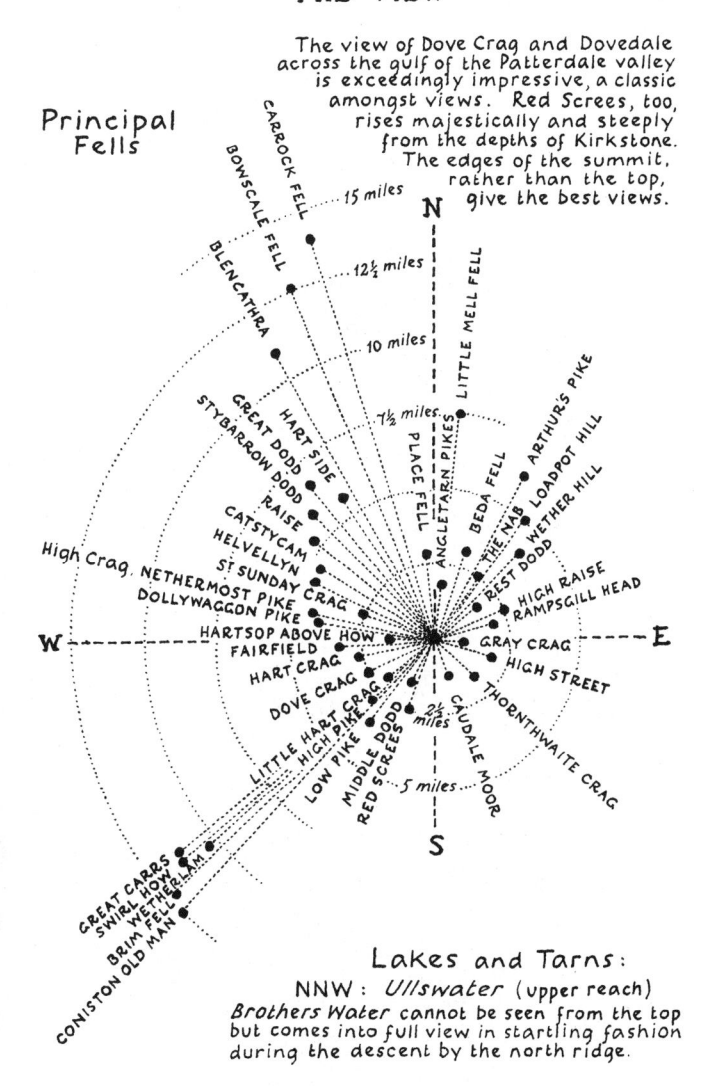

Hartsop Dodd 4

THE VIEW

The view of Dove Crag and Dovedale across the gulf of the Patterdale valley is exceedingly impressive, a classic amongst views. Red Screes, too, rises majestically and steeply from the depths of Kirkstone. The edges of the summit, rather than the top, give the best views.

Principal Fells

- CARROCK FELL
- BOWSCALE FELL
- BLENCATHRA
- 15 miles
- 12½ miles
- 10 miles
- 7½ miles
- LITTLE MELL FELL
- GREAT DODD
- HART SIDE
- STYBARROW DODD
- PLACE FELL
- RAISE
- CATSTYCAM
- HELVELLYN
- ANGLETARN PIKES
- BEDA FELL
- ARTHUR'S PIKE
- THE NAB
- LOADPOT HILL
- WETHER HILL
- REST DODD
- St SUNDAY CRAG
- NETHERMOST PIKE
- High Crag
- DOLLYWAGGON PIKE
- HIGH RAISE
- RAMPSGILL HEAD
- HARTSOP ABOVE HOW
- FAIRFIELD
- GRAY CRAG
- HART CRAG
- HIGH STREET
- DOVE CRAG
- LITTLE HART CRAG
- HIGH PIKE
- THORNTHWAITE CRAG
- LOW PIKE
- MIDDLE DODD
- CAUDALE MOOR
- RED SCREES
- 2½ miles
- 5 miles
- GREAT CARRS
- SWIRL HOW
- WETHERLAM
- BRIM FELL
- CONISTON OLD MAN

W — E
N
S

Lakes and Tarns:

NNW : *Ullswater* (upper reach)
Brothers Water cannot be seen from the top but comes into full view in startling fashion during the descent by the north ridge.

Hartsop Dodd 5

Dovedale

Hartsop Dodd 6

Patterdale

High Raise 2634'

- Howtown
- Martindale
- Bampton
- ▲ WETHER HILL
- Measand
- ▲ HIGH RAISE
- ▲ HIGH STREET
- Riggindale

MILES
0 1 2 3 4

from the col below The Knott

High Raise 2

NATURAL FEATURES

Second in altitude among the fells east of Kirkstone and Ullswater, High Raise is overtopped only by High Street itself. Topographically, it cannot be said to occupy an important position, for it commands no valleys and it is not a meeting-place of ridges; yet, nevertheless, its summit-cone rises distinctively from the lofty watershed of the main range, and it is the last fell, going north, with the characteristics of a mountain — beyond are rolling foothills. Flanking it on the west is the valley of Rampsgill, to which falls abruptly a featureless wall of grass and scree. Much more extensive, and much more interesting, are the eastern declivities, going down to Haweswater: here natural forces have scooped out a great hollow just below the subsidiary summit of Low Raise, leaving a mile-long fringe of crags between two airy ridges.

There are considerable streams on this flank, and all flow into Haweswater. Formerly these waters helped to irrigate the fertile Lowther and Eden valleys, but nowadays only the most favoured do so: the fate of the majority is captive travel along less pleasurable routes to the taps of Manchester, there to serve the needs of man in other ways.

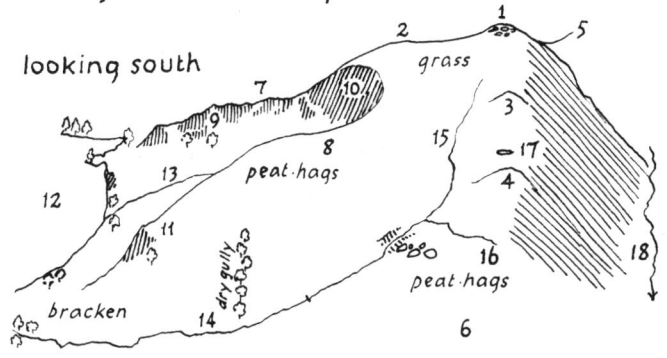

looking south

1 : The summit   2 : Low Raise   3 : Raven Howe   4 : Red Crag
5 : Ridge continuing to Rampsgill Head   6 : Ridge continuing to Wether Hill
7 : South-east ridge   8 : North-east ridge   9 : Birks Crag
10 : Whelter Crags   11 : Lad Crags   12 : Haweswater
13 : Whelter Beck   14 : Measand Beck   15 : Longgrain Beck
16 : Keasgill Head   17 : Redcrag Tarn   18 : Rampsgill Beck

High Raise 3

MAP

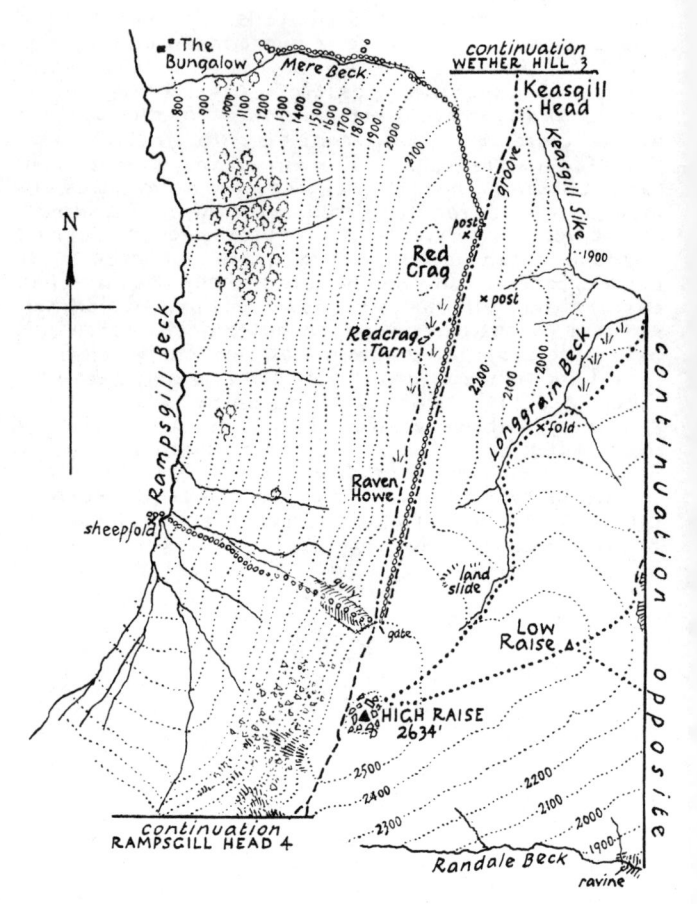

Rampsgill is within the Martindale Deer Forest.
There are no public paths in this valley.

ONE MILE

High Raise 4

MAP

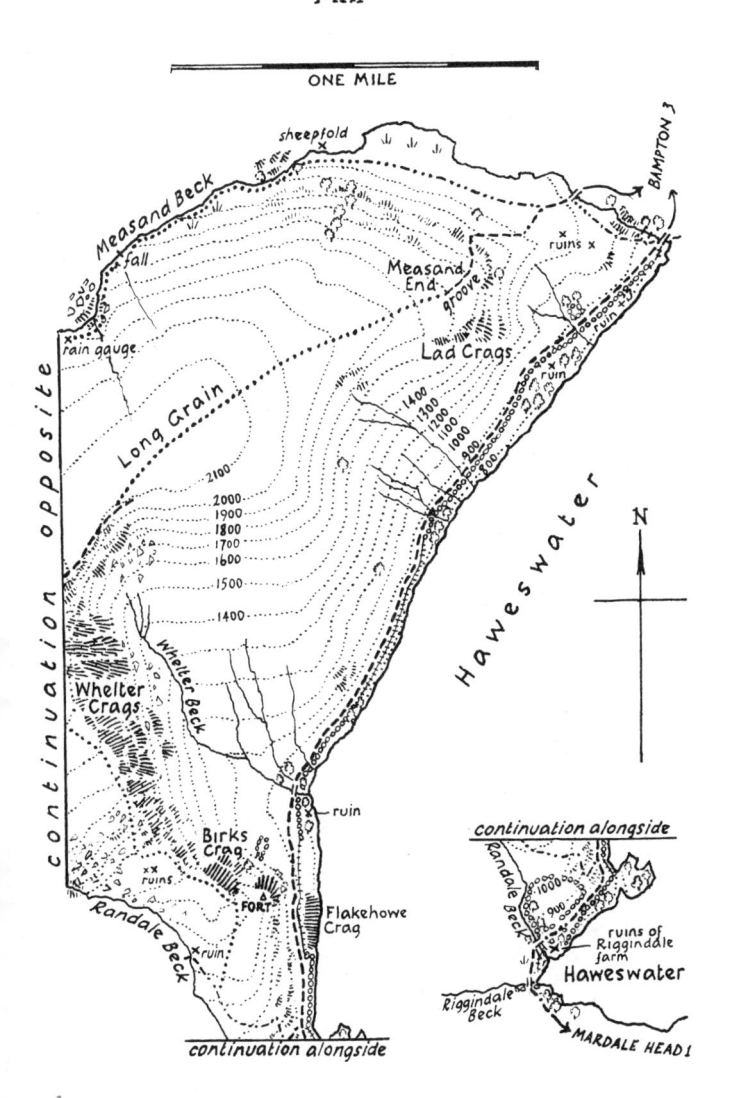

High Raise 5

ASCENTS FROM PATTERDALE AND HARTSOP
2400 feet of ascent : 5¼ miles from Patterdale
2250 feet of ascent : 3½ miles from Hartsop

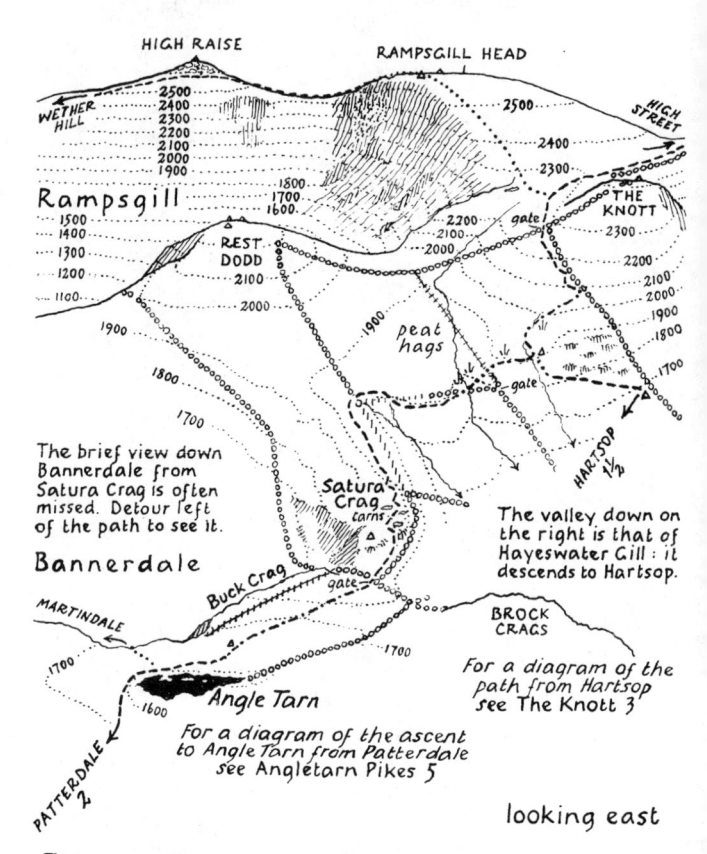

The brief view down Bannerdale from Satura Crag is often missed. Detour left of the path to see it.

The valley down on the right is that of Hayeswater Gill: it descends to Hartsop.

For a diagram of the path from Hartsop see The Knott 3

For a diagram of the ascent to Angle Tarn from Patterdale see Angletarn Pikes 5

looking east

This is a most enjoyable excursion with a succession of widely differing views, all excellent; and the route itself, never very distinct, is an interesting puzzle to unravel. In bad weather, however, there will be some difficulty, and a stranger may run into trouble on top of Rampsgill Head, where there are crags.

High Raise 6

ASCENT FROM MARTINDALE
2100 feet of ascent: 5 miles from Martindale (Old Church)

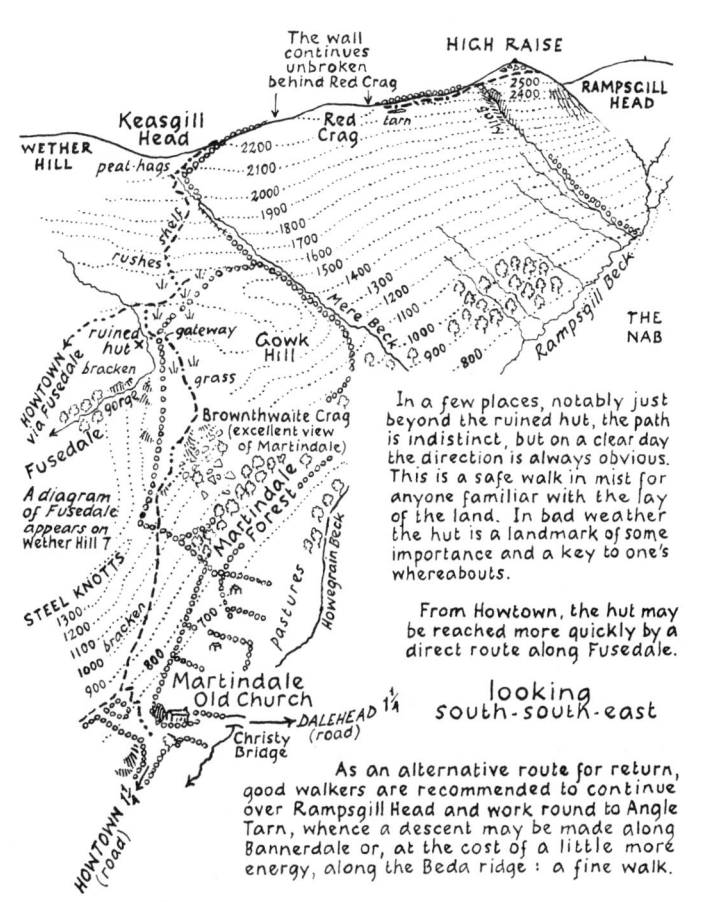

looking south-south-east

In a few places, notably just beyond the ruined hut, the path is indistinct, but on a clear day the direction is always obvious. This is a safe walk in mist for anyone familiar with the lay of the land. In bad weather the hut is a landmark of some importance and a key to one's whereabouts.

From Howtown, the hut may be reached more quickly by a direct route along Fusedale.

As an alternative route for return, good walkers are recommended to continue over Rampsgill Head and work round to Angle Tarn, whence a descent may be made along Bannerdale or, at the cost of a little more energy, along the Beda ridge: a fine walk.

This is the only full-size mountain expedition conveniently available from the neighbourhood of Martindale and Howtown. It hardly lives up to its early promise, the middle section being dull, but the views are excellent throughout.

High Raise 7

ASCENTS FROM MARDALE
1900 feet of ascent
2½ miles from Riggindale; 3½ miles from Measand

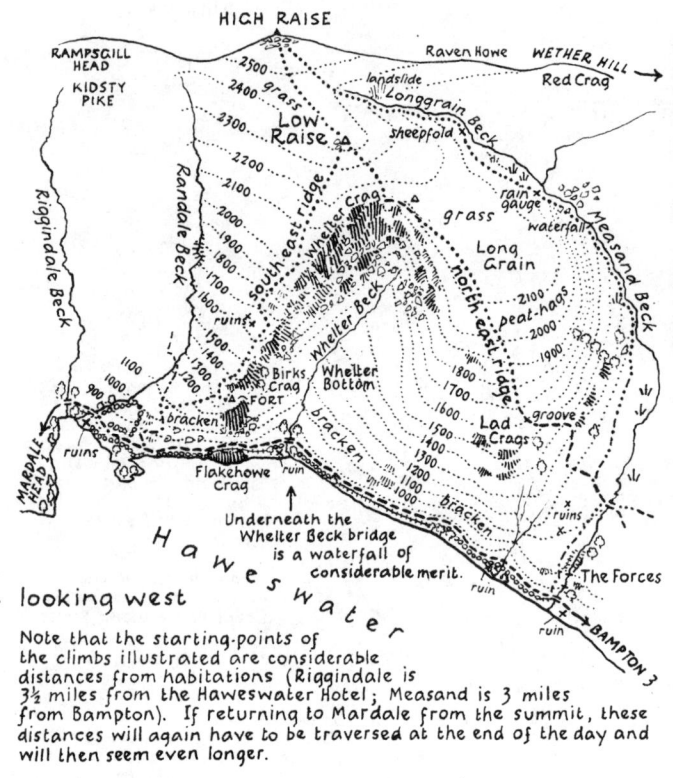

looking west

Note that the starting-points of the climbs illustrated are considerable distances from habitations (Riggindale is 3½ miles from the Haweswater Hotel; Measand is 3 miles from Bampton). If returning to Mardale from the summit, these distances will again have to be traversed at the end of the day and will then seem even longer.

The zig-zag path at the foot of the south-east ridge went out of use when the nearby buildings were submerged, and is now difficult to find and follow. All who ascend by this route are recommended to make a small detour to visit the remains of the ancient fort, which, crag-defended and double-moated, occupied a striking position, and even today its ruins are a stimulus to the imagination.

The routes depicted are unfrequented and without paths except initially. All are interesting, and the south-east ridge especially is an attractive climb.

High Raise 8

Haweswater, from Measand at the foot of the north-east ridge

The British Fort on the south-east ridge with Haweswater beyond

High Raise 9

THE SUMMIT

BRANSTREE — TARN CRAG — Gatescarth Pass — HARTER FELL — Nan Bield Pass — MARDALE ILL BELL

The true fell-walker appreciates best a summit with rocks; failing that, a summit with stones. He will, therefore, have an affectionate regard for High Raise, especially if his visit follows a tour of the neighbouring fells, for its top is crowned with stones in a quantity uncommon amongst the heights of the High Street range, which are usually grassy — they are rough, weathered and colourful stones, a pleasure to behold. Some have been used in the erection of a large cairn; others form an effective wind-shelter alongside. The old High Street, here merely a narrow track, crosses the top below the cap of stones, 100 yards west of the cairn. It is the only path.

A long half-mile away, slightly north of east, is the rounded hump of Low Raise. Here all is grass except for a remarkable oasis of bleached stones, obviously transported — a tumulus. These stones were a convenient quarry for later generations whose preference it was to build cairns rather than tumuli, and a really handsome edifice has been constructed.

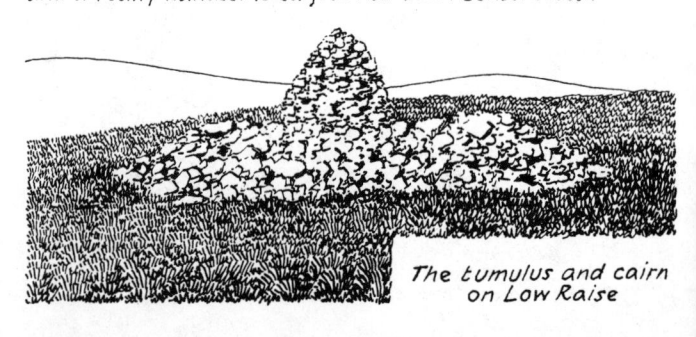

The tumulus and cairn on Low Raise

High Raise 10

DESCENTS

Since the friendly inn and farmsteads of Mardale were so cruelly sacrificed for the common good (sic), the summit of High Raise has been remote from tourist accommodation. It should be noted that the only beds in Mardale nowadays are concentrated in the new Haweswater Hotel, which, for walkers, is sited on the wrong side of the lake, and which, unlike the old Dun Bull, is much more a motorists' resort than a refuge for foot-travellers and shepherds.

Ample time should be allowed for descents, which are lengthy in all directions, and confusing in all directions except to the east, especially so in bad weather.

The natural inclination to scramble down into Rampsgill must be resisted: this valley offers sanctuary for deer, and there is neither welcome nor lodging for two-legged animals.

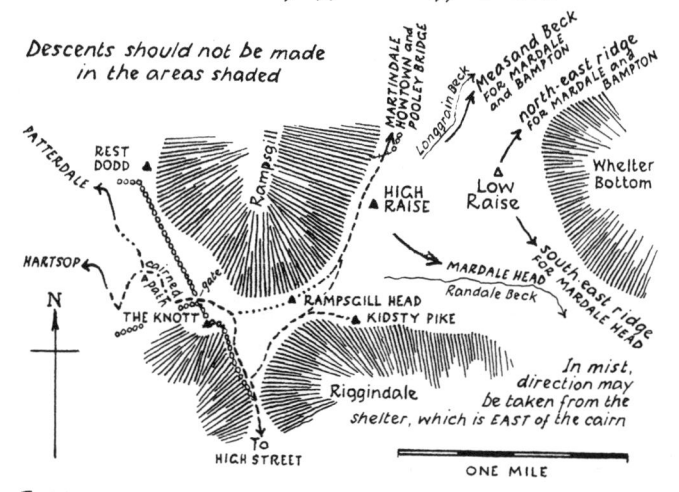

Descents should not be made in the areas shaded

TO PATTERDALE : An interesting and beautiful walk in good weather, but an anxious and complicated journey in bad. Note that Rampsgill Head must first be climbed before the descent properly commences, and that The Knott is rounded on its north side. *In bad weather, after crossing the wall between The Knott and Rest Dodd, descend directly to Hayeswater and Hartsop.*

TO MARDALE : The north-east ridge particularly is a good way down, and the best if Bampton is the objective. The south-east ridge is rougher, with excellent views, but leads only to the uninhabited head of the valley: for the Haweswater Hotel, however, it is a useful route. *In mist, the streams are safe guides to the lakeside, but care is needed along Measand Beck.*

TO MARTINDALE, HOWTOWN and POOLEY BRIDGE :   Follow the ridge north, turning down left at Keasgill Head for Martindale and Howtown — *and, in bad weather, for Pooley Bridge also. Consult the Wether Hill map.*

High Raise 11

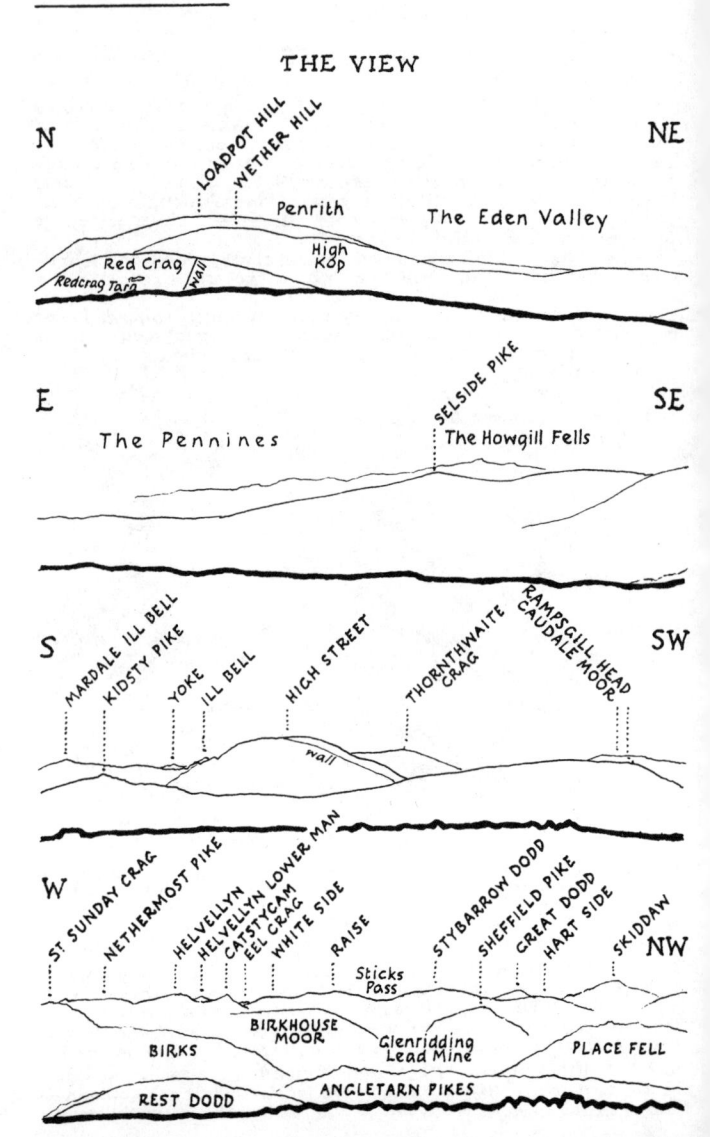

THE VIEW

High Raise 12

THE VIEW

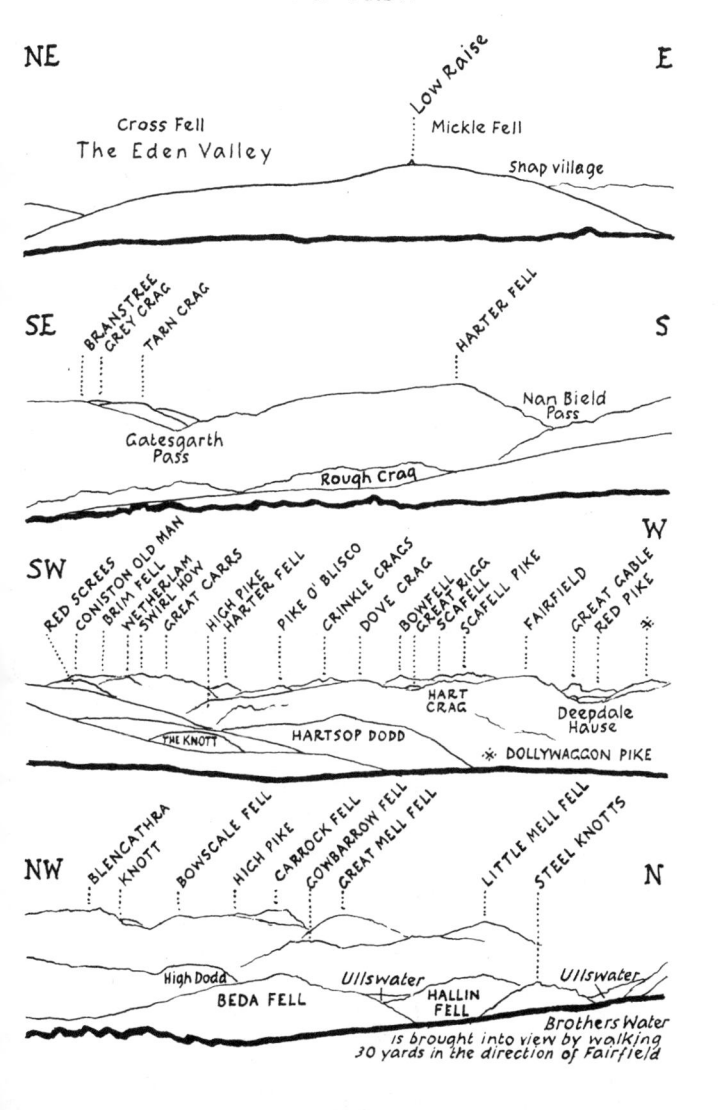

NE — Cross Fell, The Eden Valley, Low Raise, Mickle Fell, Shap village — **E**

SE — Branstree, Grey Crag, Tarn Crag, Harter Fell, Gatesgarth Pass, Nan Bield Pass, Rough Crag — **S**

SW — Red Screes, Coniston Old Man, Brim Fell, Wetherlam, Swirl How, Great Carrs, High Pike, Harter Fell, Pike o' Blisco, Crinkle Crags, Dove Crag, Bowfell, Great Rigg, Scafell, Scafell Pike, Fairfield, Great Gable, Red Pike, Hart Crag, The Knott, Hartsop Dodd, Deepdale Hause, ☀ Dollywaggon Pike — **W**

NW — Blencathra, Knott, Bowscale Fell, High Pike, Carrock Fell, Gowbarrow Fell, Great Mell Fell, Little Mell Fell, Steel Knotts, High Dodd, Beda Fell, Ullswater, Hallin Fell, Ullswater — **N**

Brothers Water is brought into view by walking 30 yards in the direction of Fairfield

High Raise 13

RIDGE ROUTES

To WETHER HILL, 2210': 2¼ miles : NNE
Depression at 2150': 100 feet of ascent
A long easy walk, safe in mist

Facing north, incline left to join the path (the old High Street), which continues, but not distinctly, to Wether Hill and beyond. It is usual to keep to the left of the wall as far as Redcrag Tarn and then cross it, but it is quicker, and in bad weather better, to follow it on the right. At the depression of Keasgill Head the path is **badly cut away** by a series of shallow ravines. Wether Hill has two tops; the cairn is on the furthest.

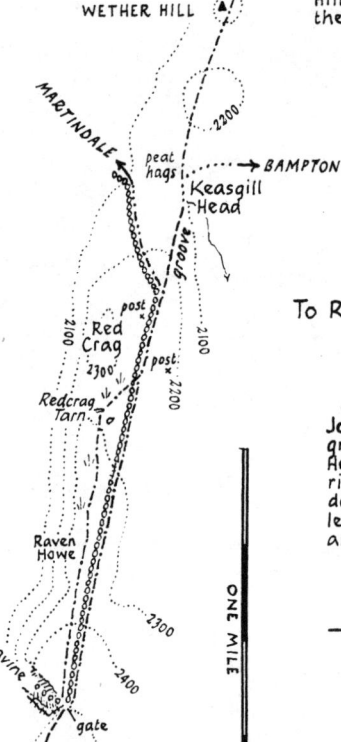

Redcrag Tarn looking to High Raise and Rampsgill Head

To RAMPSGILL HEAD, 2581'
¾ mile : SW
Depression at 2450': 140 feet of ascent
Easy, but needing care in mist

Join and follow the path to the grassy depression south-west. Here is a bifurcation: take the right fork and detour to look down the crags. In mist, keep left, on easy ground, if crags are encountered.

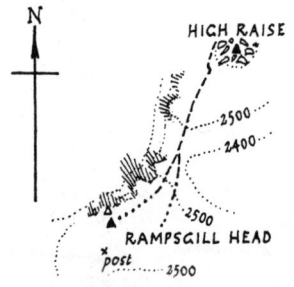

High Raise 14

Whelter Beck and Whelter Crags

High Street 2718'

from the north ridge of Branstree

High Street 2

NATURAL FEATURES

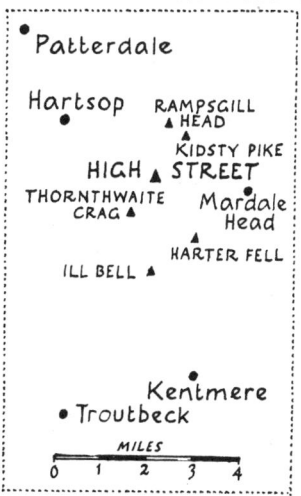

- Patterdale

Hartsop RAMPSGILL
▲ HEAD
▲ KIDSTY PIKE
HIGH ▲ STREET
THORNTHWAITE Mardale
CRAG ▲ Head
▲ HARTER FELL
ILL BELL ▲

Kentmere
• Troutbeck

MILES
0   1   2   3   4

Most of the high places in Lakeland have no mention in history books, and, until comparatively recent times, when enlightened men were inspired to climb upon them for pleasure and exercise, it was fashionable to regard them as objects of awe and terror, and their summits were rarely visited. Not so High Street, which has been known and trodden, down through the ages, by a miscellany of travellers on an odd variety of missions: by marching soldiers, marauding brigands, carousing shepherds, officials of the Governments, and now by modern hikers. Its summit has been in turn a highway and a sports arena and a racecourse, as well as, as it is today, a grazing ground for sheep.

The long whale-backed crest of High Street attains a greater altitude than any other fell east of Kirkstone. Walking is easy on the grassy top: a factor that must have influenced the Roman surveyors to throw their road along it. But High Street is much more than an elevated and featureless field, for its eastern flank, which falls precipitously from the flat top to enclose the splendid tarn of Blea Water in craggy arms, is a striking study in grandeur and wildness; on this side a straight narrow ridge running down to Mardale is particularly fine. The western face drops roughly to Hayeswater. To north and south, high ground continues to subsidiary fells along the main ridge.

Rough Crag from Long Stile

The River Kent has its birth in marshes on the south slope but most of the water draining from the fell flows northwards to Haweswater and Hayeswater.

High Street 3

NATURAL FEATURES
The main High Street range
illustrating the complexity of the valley systems

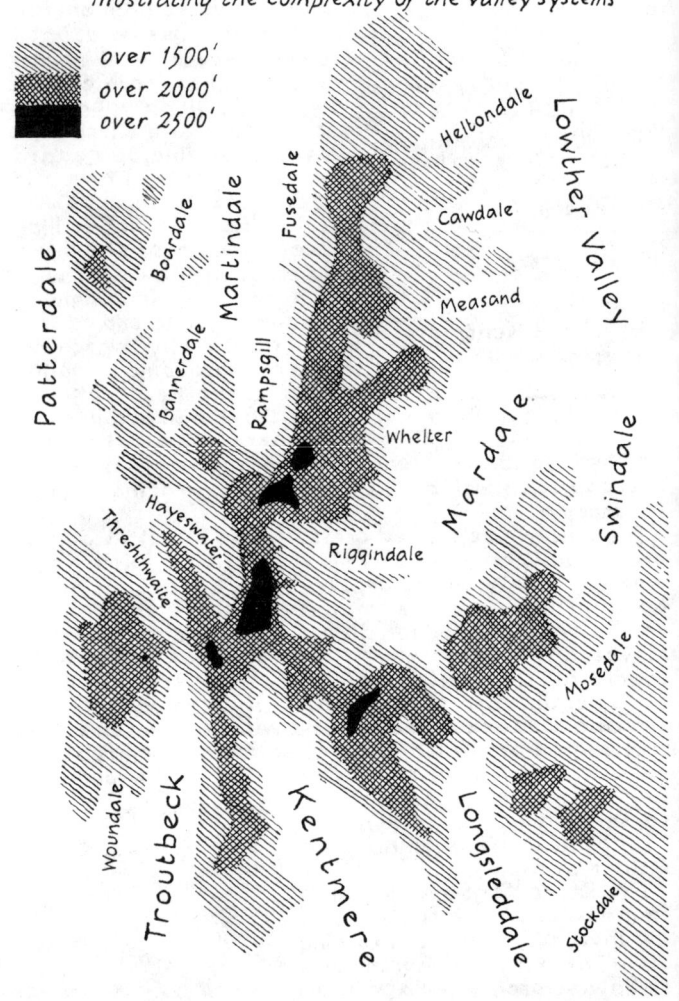

- over 1500'
- over 2000'
- over 2500'

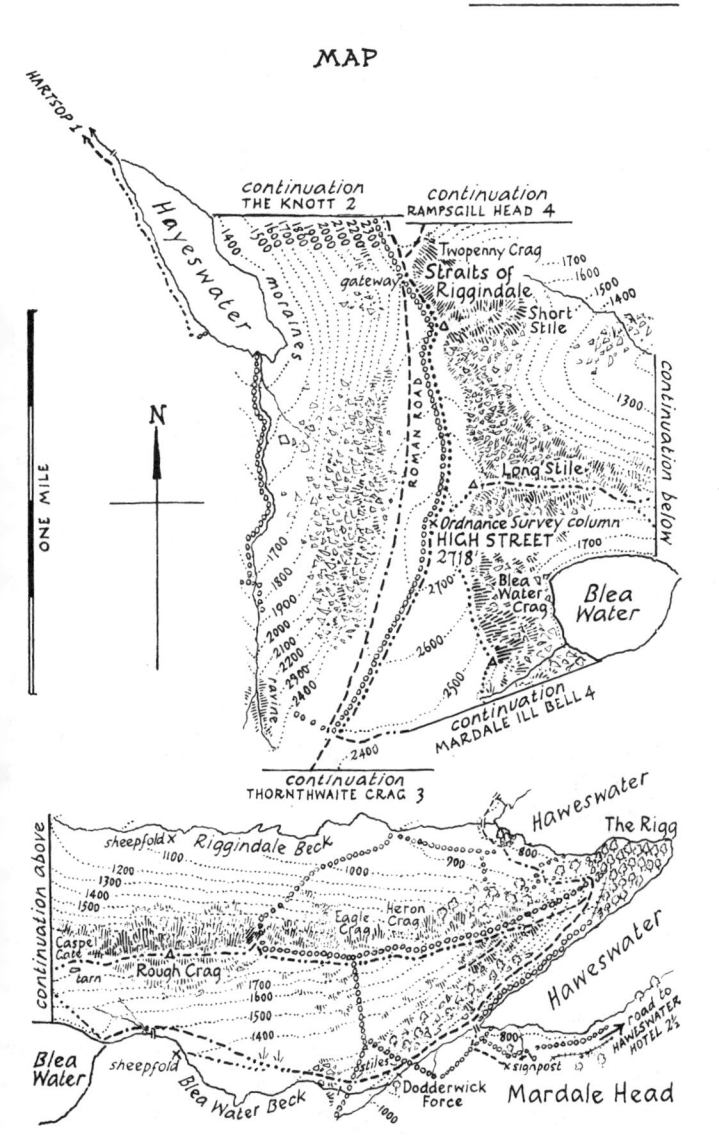

High Street 4

MAP

High Street 5

ASCENTS FROM PATTERDALE AND HARTSOP
2450 feet of ascent : 5½ miles from Patterdale
2300 feet of ascent : 3¾ miles from Hartsop

Proceed from the Straits of Riggindale to the summit not by the wall nor by the Roman Road (which are dull trudges) but by following the edge of the eastern face (which has excellent views) until the Ordnance Survey column comes into sight.

Enterprising pedestrians approaching from Hartsop may tackle High Street direct from the head of Hayeswater — but they will not enjoy the climb, which is steep, dull, and overburdened with scree.

For a diagram of the path from Hartsop to Hayeswater see The Knott 3

For a diagram of the ascent to Angle Tarn from Patterdale see Angletarn Pikes 5

looking south-east

Two good viewpoints, only a few paces from the path but often missed, are (1) the main cairn on Satura Crag (view of Bannerdale), and (2) the tarn on the col below Rampsgill Head (view of Rampsgill)

This is the least exciting approach to High Street; it is, nevertheless, a very enjoyable walk, with a series of varied and beautiful views; and the tracking of the indistinct path, which has many unexpected turns and twists, is interesting throughout.

High Street 6

ASCENT FROM MARDALE
2050 feet of ascent   3 miles from the road end

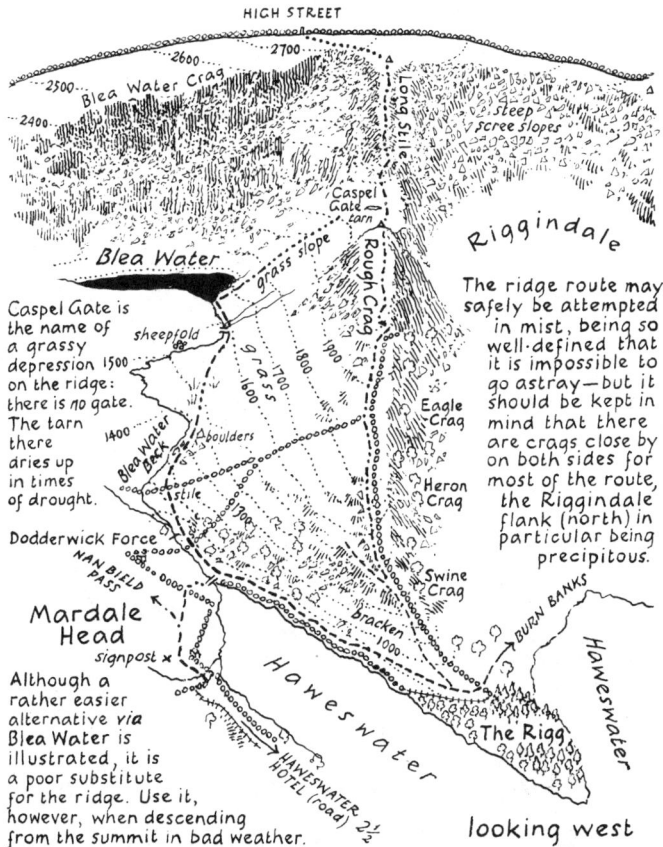

HIGH STREET

Blea Water Crag

Long Stile

steep scree slopes

Caspel Gate tarn

Blea Water

Riggindale

Caspel Gate is the name of a grassy depression on the ridge: there is no gate. The tarn there dries up in times of drought.

sheepfold

grass slope

Rough Crag

The ridge route may safely be attempted in mist, being so well-defined that it is impossible to go astray — but it should be kept in mind that there are crags close by on both sides for most of the route, the Riggindale flank (north) in particular being precipitous.

Blea Water Beck

boulders

stile

Eagle Crag

Heron Crag

Dodderwick Force

NAN BIELD PASS

Swine Crag

BURN BANKS

Mardale Head

signpost

Haweswater

Haweswater

Although a rather easier alternative via Blea Water is illustrated, it is a poor substitute for the ridge. Use it, however, when descending from the summit in bad weather.

HAWESWATER HOTEL (road) 2½

The Rigg

looking west

The ridge of Rough Crag and the rocky stairway of Long Stile together form the connoisseur's route up High Street, the only route that discloses the finer characteristics of the fell. The ascent is a classic, leading directly along the crest of a long, straight ridge that permits of no variation from the valley to the summit. The views are excellent throughout.

High Street 7

ASCENT FROM TROUTBECK
2350 feet of ascent : 6 miles

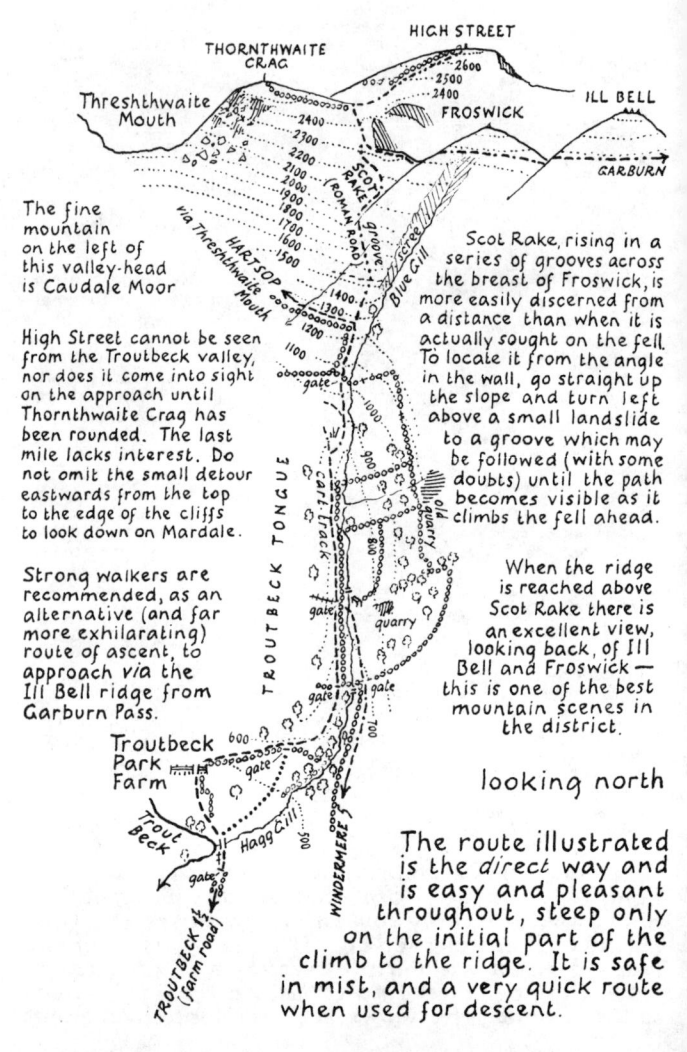

The fine mountain on the left of this valley-head is Caudale Moor.

High Street cannot be seen from the Troutbeck valley, nor does it come into sight on the approach until Thornthwaite Crag has been rounded. The last mile lacks interest. Do not omit the small detour eastwards from the top to the edge of the cliffs to look down on Mardale.

Strong walkers are recommended, as an alternative (and far more exhilarating) route of ascent, to approach via the Ill Bell ridge from Garburn Pass.

Scot Rake, rising in a series of grooves across the breast of Froswick, is more easily discerned from a distance than when it is actually sought on the fell. To locate it from the angle in the wall, go straight up the slope and turn left above a small landslide to a groove which may be followed (with some doubts) until the path becomes visible as it climbs the fell ahead.

When the ridge is reached above Scot Rake there is an excellent view, looking back, of Ill Bell and Froswick — this is one of the best mountain scenes in the district.

looking north

The route illustrated is the *direct* way and is easy and pleasant throughout, steep only on the initial part of the climb to the ridge. It is safe in mist, and a very quick route when used for descent.

High Street 8

ASCENT FROM KENTMERE
2300 feet of ascent
5½ miles via Hall Cove: 6 miles via Nan Bield Pass

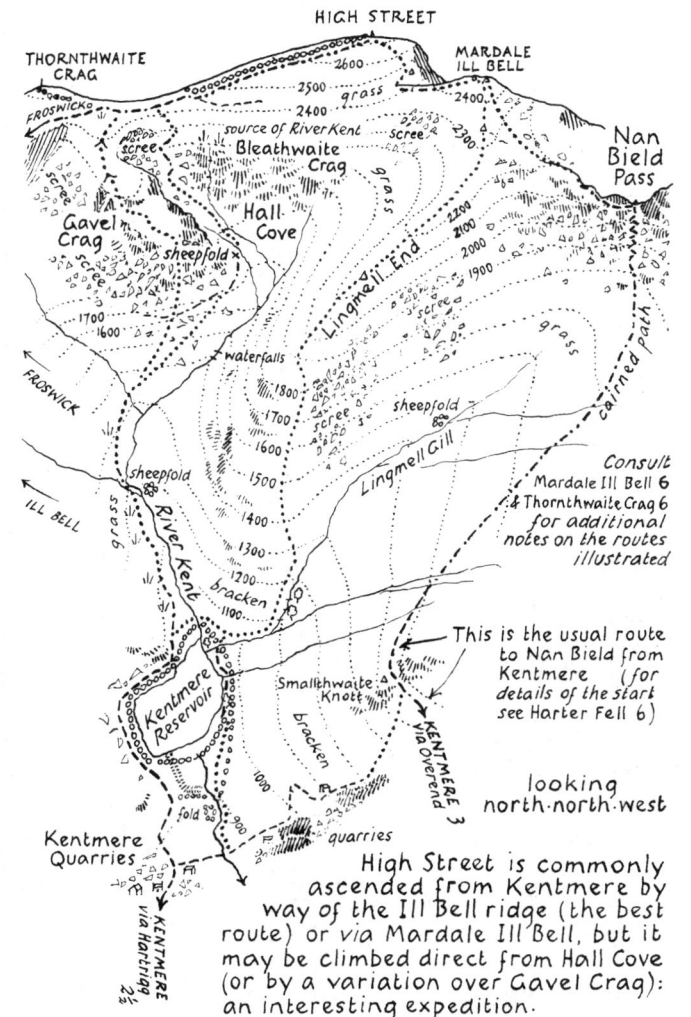

Consult Mardale Ill Bell 6 & Thornthwaite Crag 6 for additional notes on the routes illustrated

This is the usual route to Nan Bield from Kentmere (for details of the start see Harter Fell 6)

looking north-north-west

High Street is commonly ascended from Kentmere by way of the Ill Bell ridge (the best route) or via Mardale Ill Bell, but it may be climbed direct from Hall Cove (or by a variation over Gavel Crag): an interesting expedition.

High Street 9

Haweswater, from above Long Stile

Hayeswater, from the Roman Road

High Street 10

THE SUMMIT

The summit is barren of scenic interest, and only visitors of lively imagination will fully appreciate their surroundings. Any person so favoured may recline on the turf and witness, in his mind's eye, a varied pageant of history, for he has been preceded here, down the ages, by the ancient Britons who built their villages and forts in the valleys around; by the Roman cohorts marching between their garrisons at Ambleside and Brougham; by the Scots invaders who were repulsed on the Troutbeck slopes; by the shepherds, dalesmen and farmers who, centuries ago, made the summit their playground and feasting-place on the occasion of their annual meets; by racing horses (the summit is still named Racecourse Hill on the large-scale Ordnance Survey maps)..... and let us not forget Dixon of immortal legend, whose great fall over the cliff while fox-hunting is an epic in enthusiasm.

Nowadays all is quiet here and only the rising larks disturb the stillness. A pleasant place, but — to those unfortunate folk with no imagination — so dull!

DESCENTS should be made only by the regular routes. It must be emphasised that there is only one direct way to Mardale — by Long Stile, the top of which is indicated by a cairn. Direct descents into Kentmere may lead to trouble, the best plan being to aim for Nan Bield Pass, in clear weather.

In mist, consult the maps. For Mardale, stick to the crest of Long Stile, but at Caspel Gate turn down *right* to Blea Water. Kentmere is best reached by descending into Hall Cove at a point 100 yards south east of the end of the High Street wall. Avoid the Hayeswater face.

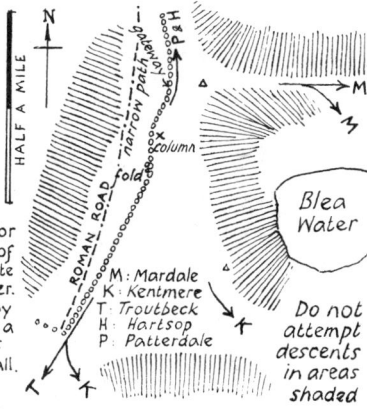

M: Mardale
K: Kentmere
T: Troutbeck
H: Hartsop
P: Patterdale

Do not attempt descents in areas shaded

High Street 11

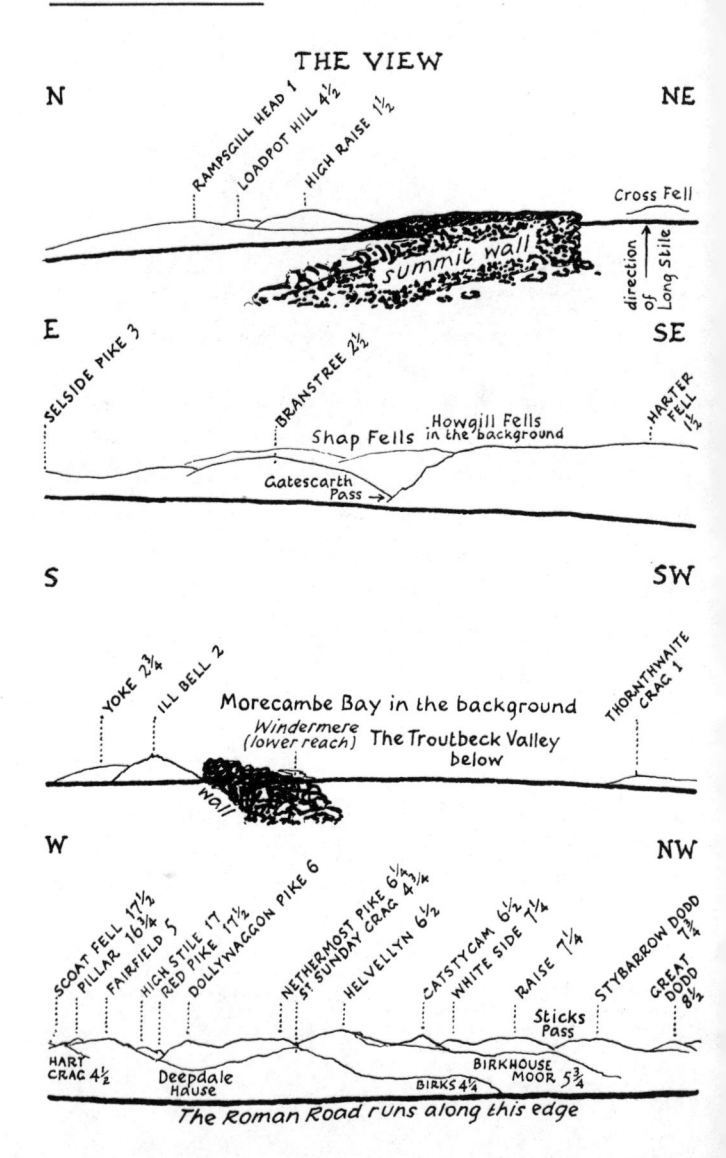

THE VIEW

N — RAMPSGILL HEAD 1, LOADPOT HILL 4½, HIGH RAISE 1½ — **NE**

Cross Fell

summit wall

direction of Long Stile

E — SELSIDE PIKE 3, BRANSTREE 2½, HARTER FELL 1½ — **SE**

Shap Fells · Howgill Fells in the background

Gatescarth Pass

S — YOKE 2¾, ILL BELL 2, THORNTHWAITE CRAG 1 — **SW**

Morecambe Bay in the background
Windermere (lower reach)
The Troutbeck Valley below

wall

W — SCOAT FELL 17½, PILLAR 16¾, FAIRFIELD 5, HIGH STILE 17½, RED PIKE 17½, DOLLYWAGGON PIKE 6, NETHERMOST PIKE 6½, ST SUNDAY CRAG 4½, HELVELLYN 6½, CATSTYCAM 6½, WHITE SIDE 7¼, RAISE 7¼, STYBARROW DODD 7¼, GREAT DODD 8½ — **NW**

HART CRAG 4½, Deepdale Hause, BIRKS 4¼, BIRKHOUSE MOOR 5¾, Sticks Pass

The Roman Road runs along this edge

THE VIEW

The figures following the names of fells indicate distances in miles

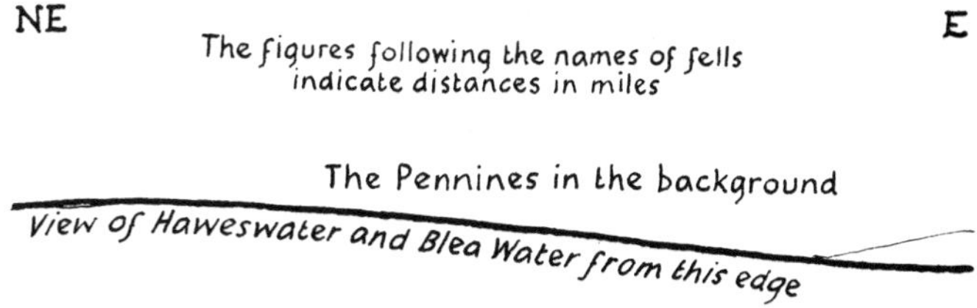
NE
E
The Pennines in the background
View of Haweswater and Blea Water from this edge

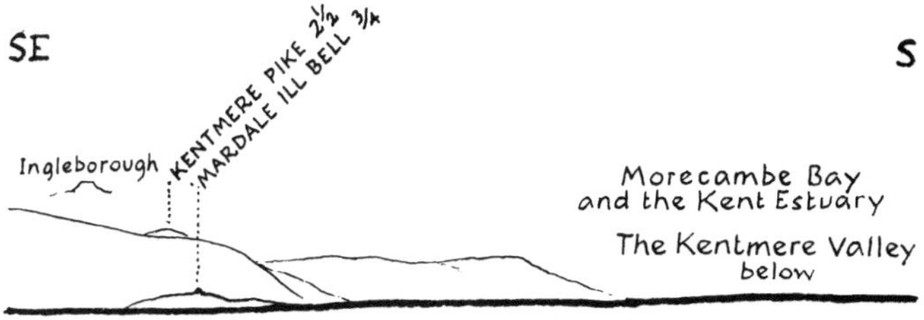
SE
S
KENTMERE PIKE 2½
MARDALE ILL BELL ¾
Ingleborough
Morecambe Bay and the Kent Estuary
The Kentmere Valley below

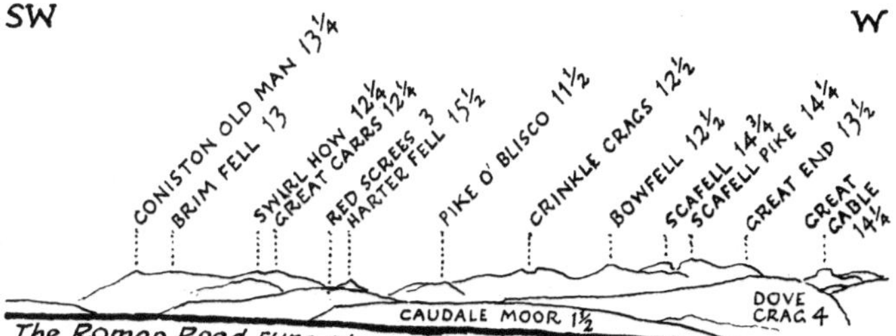
SW
W
CONISTON OLD MAN 13¼
BRIM FELL 13
SWIRL HOW 12¼
GREAT CARRS 12¼
RED SCREES 3
HARTER FELL 15½
PIKE O' BLISCO 11½
CRINKLE CRAGS 12½
BOWFELL 12½
SCAFELL 14¾
SCAFELL PIKE 14¼
GREAT END 13½
GREAT GABLE 14¼
DOVE CRAG 4
CAUDALE MOOR 1½
The Roman Road runs along this edge

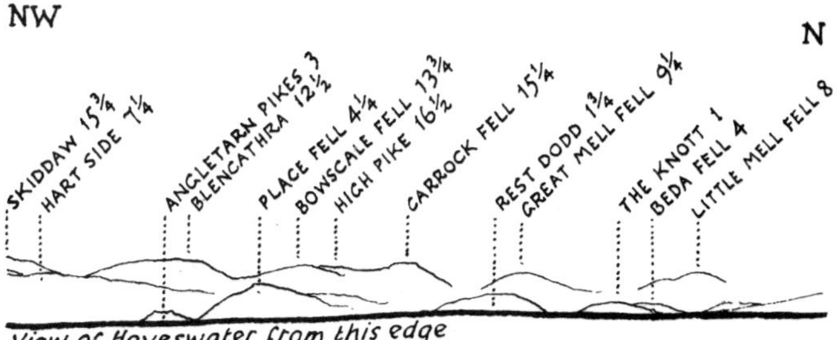
NW
N
SKIDDAW 15¾
HART SIDE 7¼
ANGLETARN PIKES 3
BLENCATHRA 12½
PLACE FELL 4¼
BOWSCALE FELL 13¾
HIGH PIKE 16½
CARROCK FELL 15¼
REST DODD 1¾
GREAT MELL FELL 9¼
THE KNOTT 1
BEDA FELL 4
LITTLE MELL FELL 8
View of Hayeswater from this edge

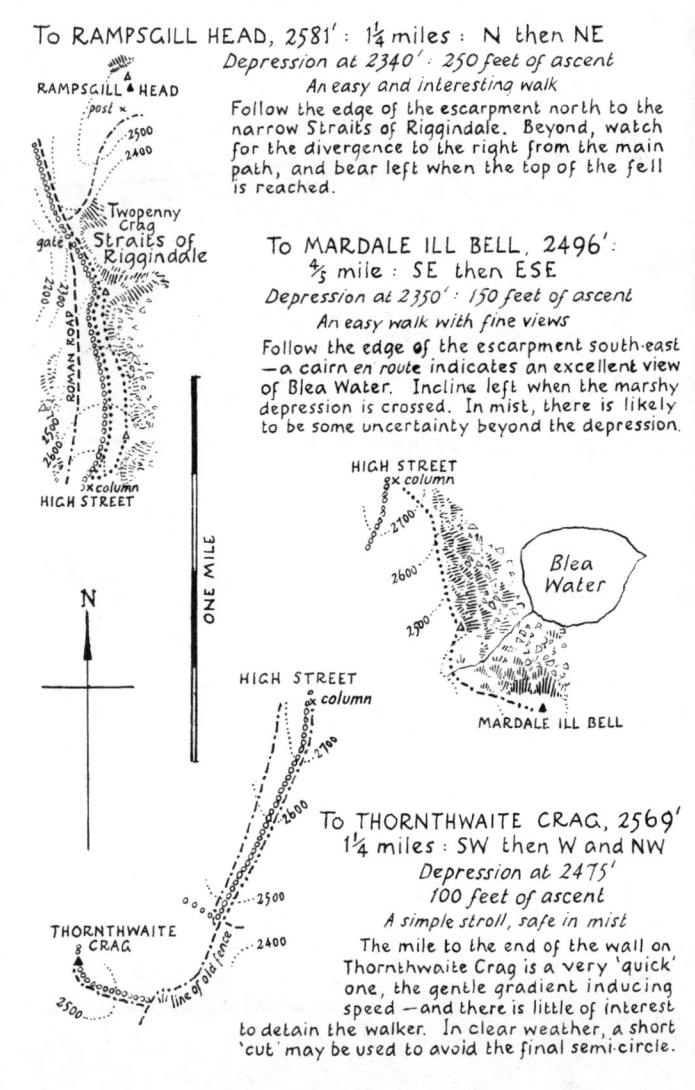

High Street 13

RIDGE ROUTES

To RAMPSGILL HEAD, 2581': 1¼ miles : N then NE
Depression at 2340': 250 feet of ascent
An easy and interesting walk

Follow the edge of the escarpment north to the narrow Straits of Riggindale. Beyond, watch for the divergence to the right from the main path, and bear left when the top of the fell is reached.

To MARDALE ILL BELL, 2496':
4/5 mile : SE then ESE
Depression at 2350': 150 feet of ascent
An easy walk with fine views

Follow the edge of the escarpment south-east — a cairn en route indicates an excellent view of Blea Water. Incline left when the marshy depression is crossed. In mist, there is likely to be some uncertainty beyond the depression.

To THORNTHWAITE CRAG, 2569'
1¼ miles : SW then W and NW
Depression at 2475'
100 feet of ascent
A simple stroll, safe in mist

The mile to the end of the wall on Thornthwaite Crag is a very 'quick' one, the gentle gradient inducing speed — and there is little of interest to detain the walker. In clear weather, a short 'cut' may be used to avoid the final semi-circle.

High Street 14

High Street from Mardale Ill Bell

Blea Water Crag

Ill Bell

2476'

named 'Hill Bell' on the
2½" Ordnance Survey map

from upper Kentmere

▲ HIGH STREET
▲ THORNTHWAITE CRAG
▲ FROSWICK
▲ ILL BELL
▲ YOKE

• Kentmere
• Troutbeck

MILES
0 1 2 3 4

Ill Bell 2

NATURAL FEATURES

The graceful cone of Ill Bell is a familiar object to most residents of south Westmorland and those visitors who approach Lakeland by way of Kendal and Windermere, although few who know it by sight can give it a name and fewer still its correct name. It is the dominating height on a steep-sided ridge, running north to High Street from the foothills of Garburn, and forms a most effective and imposing barrier between the Troutbeck and upper Kentmere valleys. It is linked by easy slopes to its neighbours, Yoke and Froswick, but both flanks are excessively steep: the Kentmere side in particular is very rough and the aspect of the fell from the upper reaches of the valley is magnificent. Crags descend northwards from the small summit. Ill Bell is distinctive and of good appearance, its peaked shape making it easily identifiable. The ridge on which it stands is probably the most popular fell-walk east of Kirkstone.

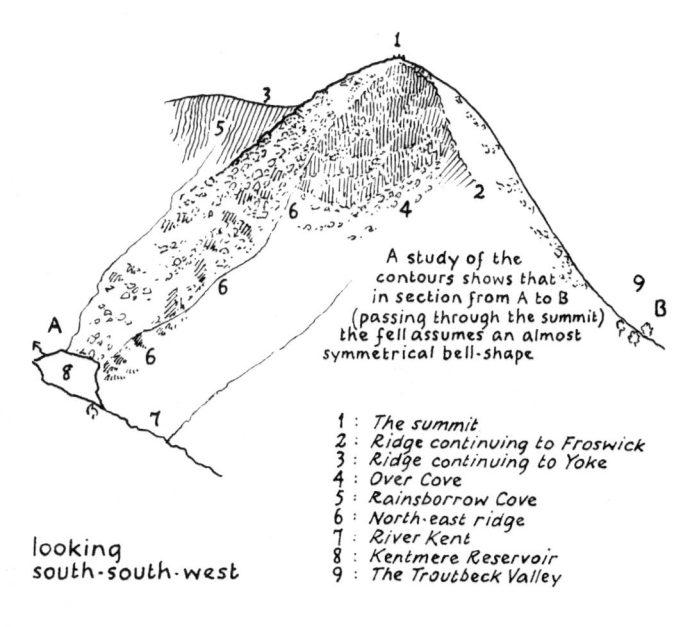

A study of the contours shows that in section from A to B (passing through the summit) the fell assumes an almost symmetrical bell-shape

1 : The summit
2 : Ridge continuing to Froswick
3 : Ridge continuing to Yoke
4 : Over Cove
5 : Rainsborrow Cove
6 : North-east ridge
7 : River Kent
8 : Kentmere Reservoir
9 : The Troutbeck Valley

looking
south-south-west

Ill Bell 3

MAP

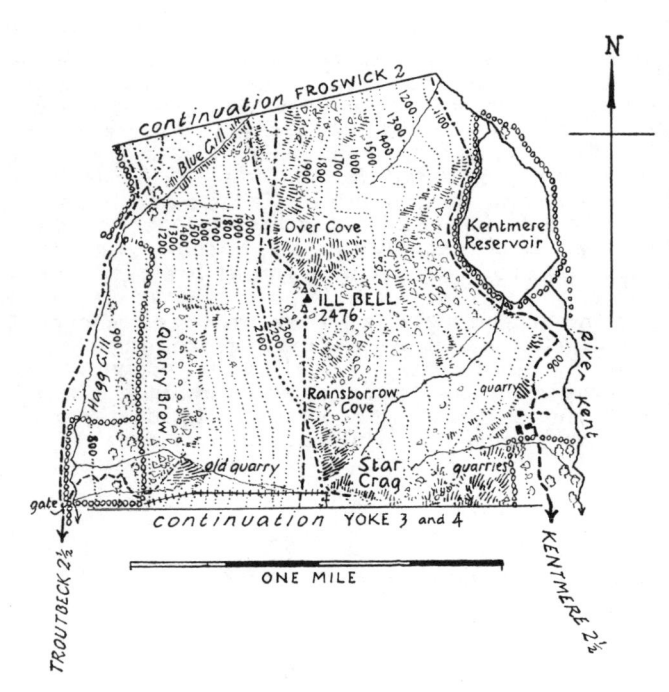

The Ill Bell ridge, from Stile End

Ill Bell 4

ASCENT FROM GARBURN PASS
1050 feet of ascent : 2½ miles

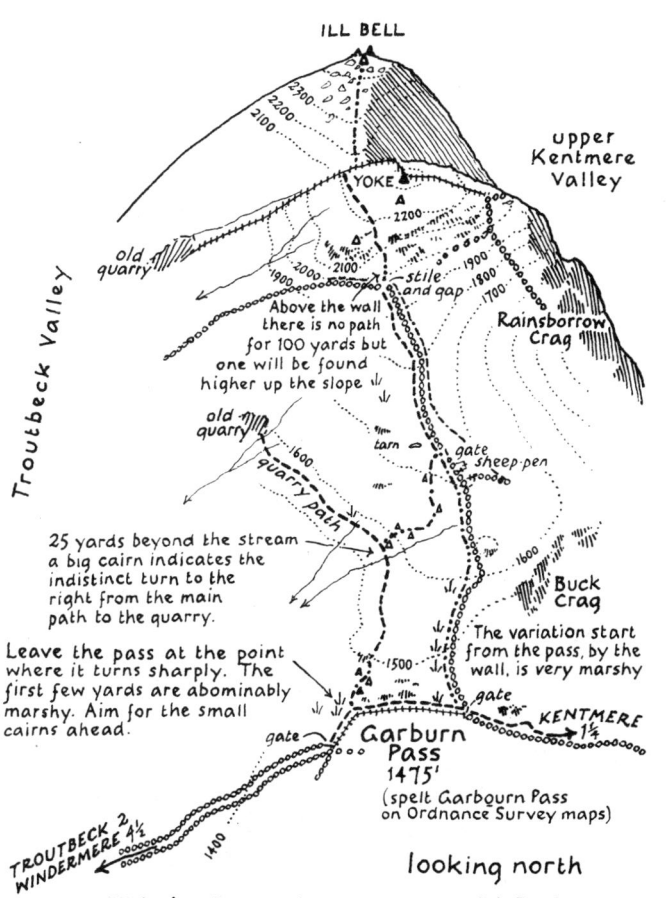

ILL BELL

upper Kentmere Valley

YOKE

old quarry

Troutbeck Valley

stile and gap

Rainsborrow Crag

Above the wall there is no path for 100 yards but one will be found higher up the slope

old quarry

tarn

gate sheep-pen

quarry path

Buck Crag

25 yards beyond the stream a big cairn indicates the indistinct turn to the right from the main path to the quarry.

The variation start from the pass, by the wall, is very marshy.

Leave the pass at the point where it turns sharply. The first few yards are abominably marshy. Aim for the small cairns ahead.

gate

Garburn Pass 1475'

gate KENTMERE 1¼

(spelt Garbourn Pass on Ordnance Survey maps)

TROUTBECK 2
WINDERMERE 4½

looking north

This is the obvious route to Ill Bell, and the only easy one. As far as Yoke it is a dull walk although the dreary foreground is relieved by the splendid views to the west. The route throughout is on grass, in places marshy to the 1800' contour.

Ill Bell 5

ASCENT FROM HAGG GILL, TROUTBECK
1700 feet of ascent

looking north-east

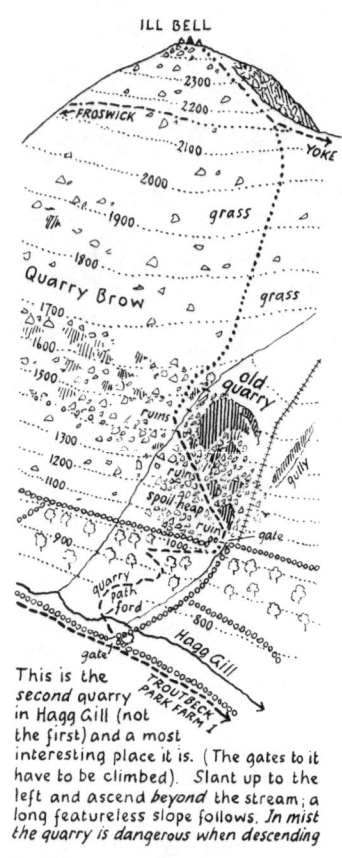

This is the *second* quarry in Hagg Gill (not the first) and a most interesting place it is. (The gates to it have to be climbed). Slant up to the left and ascend *beyond* the stream; a long featureless slope follows. *In mist the quarry is dangerous when descending*

ASCENT FROM KENTMERE RESERVOIR
1500 feet of ascent

looking south-west

Proceed to the head of the reservoir before turning up left to an obvious ridge. The rough upper slopes appear intimidating but steepness is the only difficulty. In wintry conditions this is a route for mountaineers only.

Ill Bell's continuously steep flanks are a challenge to those who prefer to reach their objective by rough scrambling, but walkers who walk for pleasure should take the easy promenade from the top of Garburn.

Ill Bell 6

THE SUMMIT

The walker who toils up to the top of Ill Bell may be pardoned for feeling that he has achieved a major climb that has played a part of some consequence in mountaineering history, for he finds himself confronted by an imposing array of fine cairns that would do credit to a Matterhorn. And in fact this is a real mountain-top, small in extent and very rough; it is one of the most distinctive summits in Lakeland. There are some traces of the wire fence that used to follow the ridge.

DESCENTS: The Troutbeck flank is steep, the Kentmere side is very steep and rough. Neither is suitable for descent, nor is there need to attempt them, for all destinations south are much more easily reached by way of the ridge to Garburn Pass.

In mist, Garburn Pass must be the objective. Join a path in the depression south of the summit and when it becomes indistinct keep on to a wall that continues to the Pass.

The main cairn

Ill Bell 7

THE VIEW

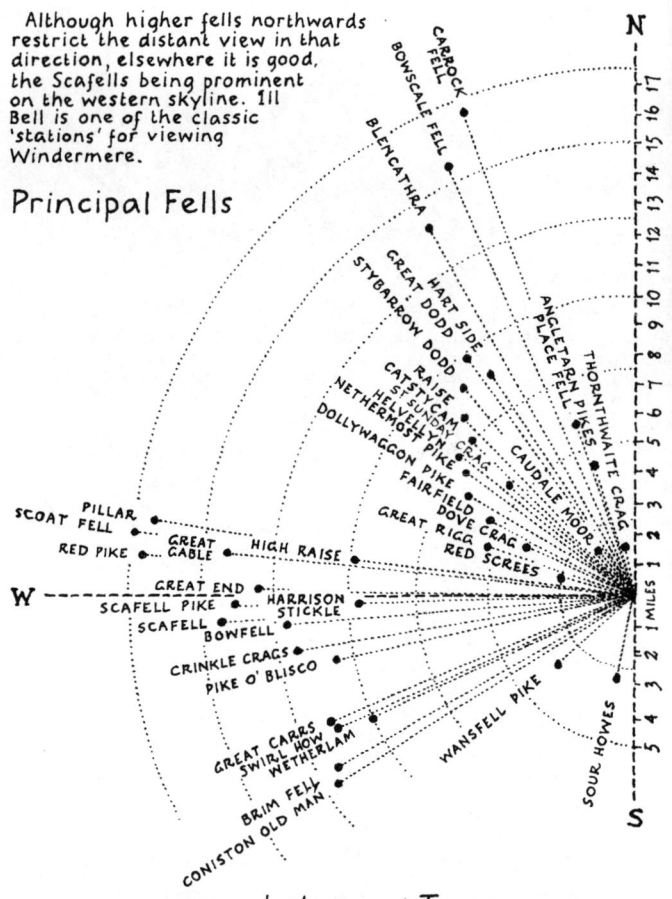

Although higher fells northwards restrict the distant view in that direction, elsewhere it is good, the Scafells being prominent on the western skyline. Ill Bell is one of the classic 'stations' for viewing Windermere.

Principal Fells

Lakes and Tarns

SSW: *Windermere*
SW: *Blelham Tarn*
NNW: A tiny strip of *Ullswater* is visible from the northern edge of the summit, 35 yards from main cairn.
E: *Kentmere Reservoir* is brought suddenly into view by walking 40 yards towards Harter Fell.

Ill Bell 8

THE VIEW

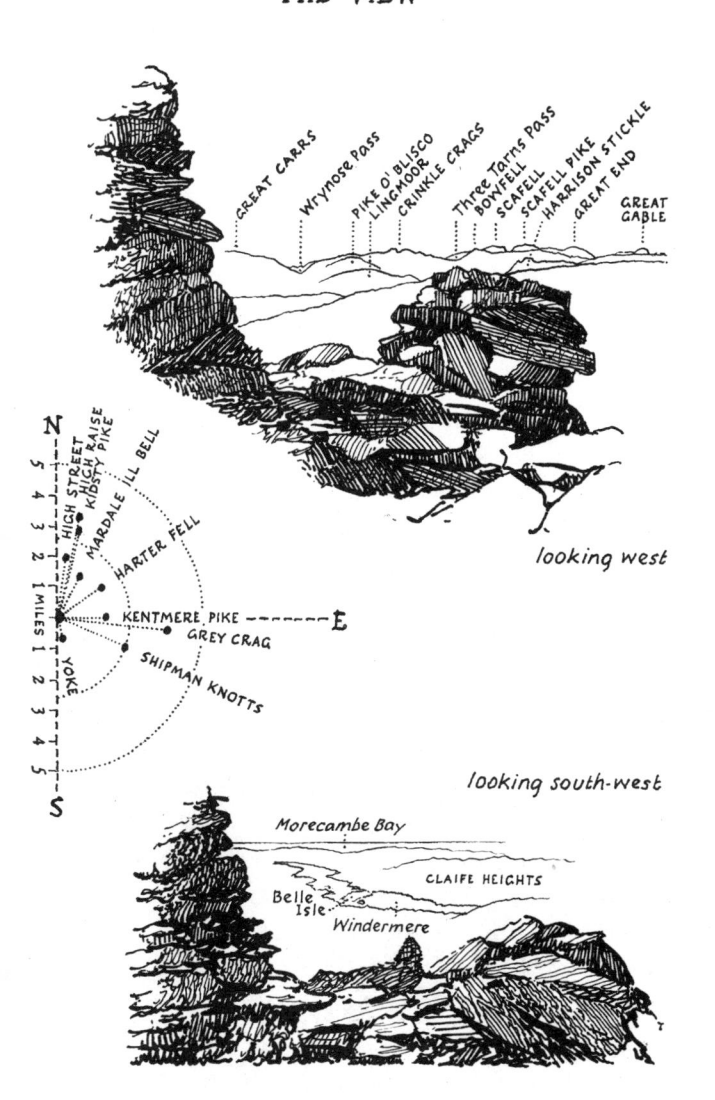

looking west

GREAT CARRS
Wrynose Pass
PIKE O' BLISCO
LINGMOOR
CRINKLE CRAGS
Three Tarns Pass
BOWFELL
SCAFELL
SCAFELL PIKE
HARRISON STICKLE
GREAT END
GREAT GABLE

HIGH STREET
KIDSTY PIKE
MARDALE ILL BELL
HARTER FELL
KENTMERE PIKE — — — E
GREY CRAG
SHIPMAN KNOTTS
YOKE

looking south-west

Morecambe Bay
CLAIFE HEIGHTS
Belle Isle
Windermere

Ill Bell 9

Thornthwaite Crag and Froswick

Two views from the summit

Rainsborrow Cove and Yoke

Ill Bell 10

RIDGE ROUTES

To FROSWICK, 2359' : ⅔ mile : NW then N
Depression at 2075' : 285 feet of ascent
Rough at first, then easy walking

Turn west by the most northerly cairn, over stones (care needed in mist), and find a path going down north-west to the depression, beyond which is an easy climb on grass.

NOTE: The 1" Ordnance Survey map shows the height of the depression as *not less than 2100'*, the 2½" map as *not more than 2050'*. 2075' has been adopted here on the principle of moderation in all things.

To YOKE, 2309' : ⅔ mile : S
Depression at 2180' : 130 feet of ascent
An easy walk, safe in mist

Descend by the southerly cairn. A faint track soon materialises and crosses the depression: at the far end, where it bifurcates, take the left branch along the edge of the escarpment. A wire fence is joined and leads over grass to the cairn. *In mist*, note that the cairn is adjacent to the *second* right-angle in the fence.

Ill Bell and the head of Kentmere

Kentmere Pike 2397'

from Ill Bell
(north-east ridge)

Kentmere Pike 2

NATURAL FEATURES

A high ridge, a counterpart to the Ill Bell range across Kentmere, rises steeply to enclose the upper part of that valley on the east. This is the south ridge of Harter Fell, which, soon after leaving the parent summit, swells into the bare, rounded top of Kentmere Pike, a fell of some importance and of more significance to the inhabitants of the valley, as its name suggests, than Harter Fell itself. The Kentmere slope, wooded at its foot and craggy above, is of little interest, but the eastern flank is altogether of sterner stuff, falling precipitously into the narrow jaws of Longsleddale: a most impressive scene. Here, abrupt cliffs riven by deep gullies tower high above the crystal waters of the winding Sprint and give to the dalehead a savageness that contrasts strikingly with the placid sweetness of the Sadgill pastures just out of their shadow.

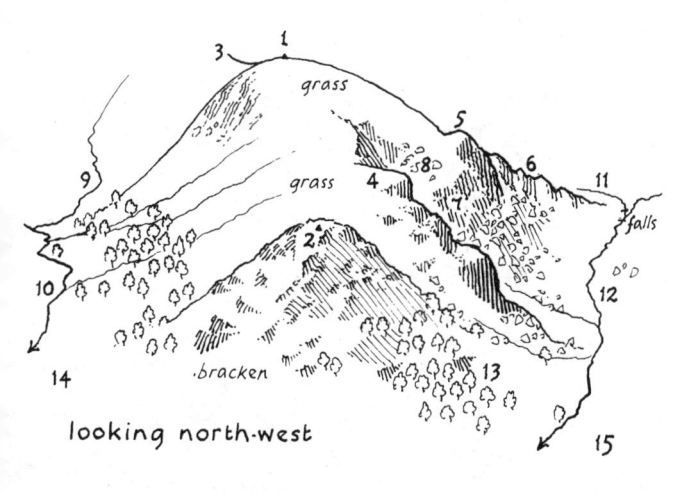

looking north-west

  1 : The summit
  2 : Shipman Knotts
  3 : Ridge continuing to Harter Fell
  4 : Goat Scar
  5 : Steel Pike
  6 : Steel Rigg
  7 : Raven Crag
  8 : Settle Earth
  9 : Ullstone Gill
 10 : River Kent
 11 : Wren Gill
 12 : River Sprint
 13 : Sadgill Woods
 14 : Kentmere
 15 : Longsleddale

Kentmere Pike 3

Steel Pike, from the quarry road

looking down a scree gully, eastern flank

Kentmere Pike 4

MAP

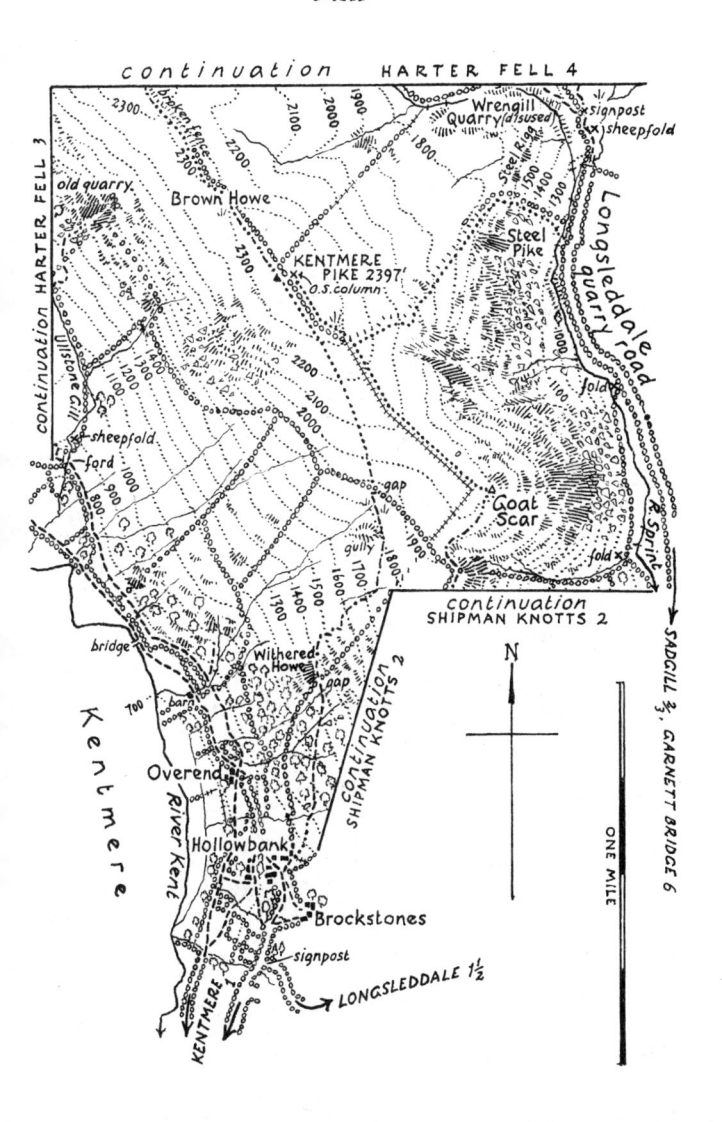

Kentmere Pike 5

ASCENT FROM KENTMERE
1900 feet of ascent : 3 miles

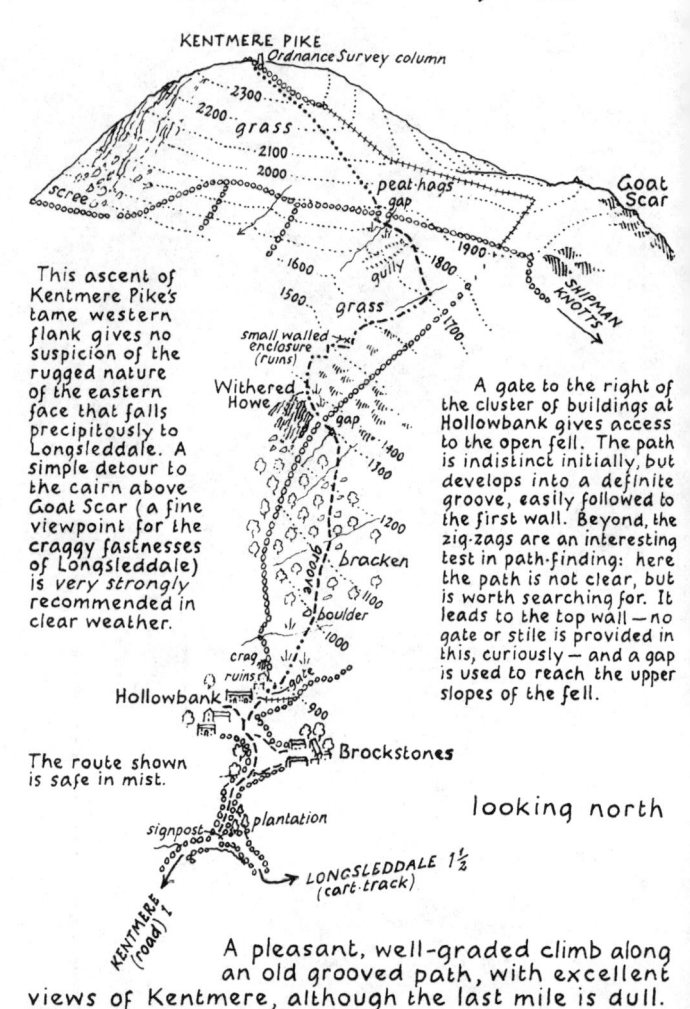

looking north

This ascent of Kentmere Pike's tame western flank gives no suspicion of the rugged nature of the eastern face that falls precipitously to Longsleddale. A simple detour to the cairn above Goat Scar (a fine viewpoint for the craggy fastnesses of Longsleddale) is very strongly recommended in clear weather.

A gate to the right of the cluster of buildings at Hollowbank gives access to the open fell. The path is indistinct initially, but develops into a definite groove, easily followed to the first wall. Beyond, the zig-zags are an interesting test in path-finding: here the path is not clear, but is worth searching for. It leads to the top wall — no gate or stile is provided in this, curiously — and a gap is used to reach the upper slopes of the fell.

The route shown is safe in mist.

A pleasant, well-graded climb along an old grooved path, with excellent views of Kentmere, although the last mile is dull. This is the easiest way onto the Harter Fell ridge.

Kentmere Pike 6

ASCENT FROM LONGSLEDDALE
1850 feet of ascent : 3 miles from Sadgill

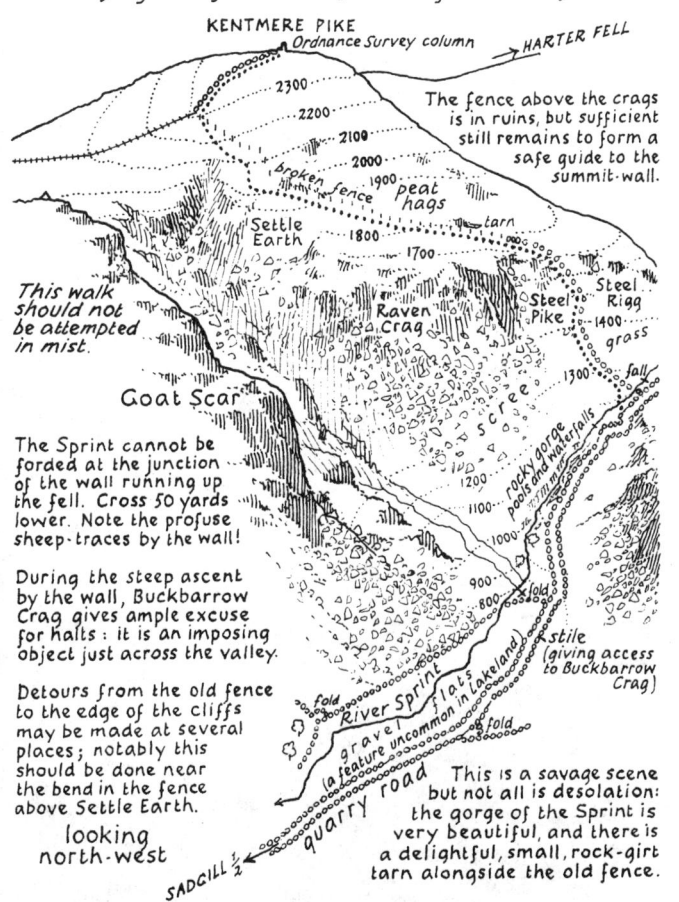

KENTMERE PIKE
Ordnance Survey column → HARTER FELL

The fence above the crags is in ruins, but sufficient still remains to form a safe guide to the summit-wall.

Settle Earth — peat hags — tarn

This walk should not be attempted in mist.

Raven Crag — Steel Pike — Steel Rigg — grass — fall

Goat Scar

The Sprint cannot be forded at the junction of the wall running up the fell. Cross 50 yards lower. Note the profuse sheep-traces by the wall!

During the steep ascent by the wall, Buckbarrow Crag gives ample excuse for halts: it is an imposing object just across the valley.

Detours from the old fence to the edge of the cliffs may be made at several places; notably this should be done near the bend in the fence above Settle Earth.

looking north-west

rocky gorge pools and waterfalls — scree — fold — stile (giving access to Buckbarrow Crag)

River Sprint — gravel flats (a feature uncommon in Lakeland) — fold — quarry road — SADGILL ½

This is a savage scene but not all is desolation: the gorge of the Sprint is very beautiful, and there is a delightful, small, rock-girt tarn alongside the old fence.

This route has been devised for walkers who have a liking for impressive rock-scenery —— it is the only practicable way up the rough eastern face, and it affords striking views of the crags, first from below then in profile and lastly from above.

Kentmere Pike 7

THE SUMMIT

The top of the fell, an unattractive and uninteresting place, is robbed of any appeal it might otherwise have had by a high wall that bisects it from end to end. A triangulation station of the Ordnance Survey in the form of a short column stands in the shelter of the east side of the wall, on a small rise, but its claim to occupy the highest point is disputed by a tiny pile of stones a few yards distant on the west side.

DESCENTS: To Kentmere: Anyone familiar with the grooved path going down to Hollowbank will have no difficulty in finding the start of it, at a break in the lower wall; strangers may not easily locate the gap and should instead continue by the ridge over Shipman Knotts to the Sadgill-Kentmere cart-track: *in mist, this route is safest.* For Longsleddale, too, it is best to make this cart-track the objective. *Much of the Longsleddale flank is craggy and dangerous*, although the route described as an ascent on page 6 is a safe way off in clear weather.

The eastern face, with Harter Fell beyond, from Goat Scar

Kentmere Pike 8

THE VIEW

The distant view of Lakeland is interrupted by the nearer heights across Kentmere; it is interesting to note that the summit-cone of Ill Bell exactly conceals Scafell Pike. More satisfactory prospects are south-east, towards the Pennines, and south-west, over Windermere to Morecambe Bay.

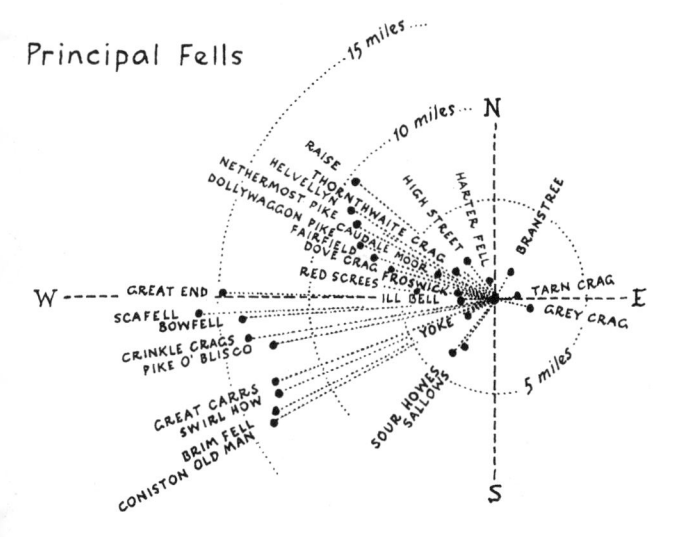

Principal Fells

(compass diagram showing fells at various bearings and distances up to 15 miles)

RAISE, HELVELLYN, THORNTHWAITE CRAG, HIGH STREET, HARTER FELL, BRANSTREE, NETHERMOST PIKE, CAUDALE MOOR, DOLLYWAGGON PIKE, FAIRFIELD, DOVE CRAG, FROSWICK, GREAT END, RED SCREES, ILL BELL, TARN CRAG, SCAFELL, BOWFELL, YOKE, GREY CRAG, CRINKLE CRAGS, PIKE O' BLISCO, GREAT CARRS, SWIRL HOW, SOUR HOWES, SALLOWS, BRIM FELL, CONISTON OLD MAN

Lakes and Tarns
SSW: *Windermere*

Kentmere Reservoir is brought into view by walking 50 yards in the direction of Ill Bell.

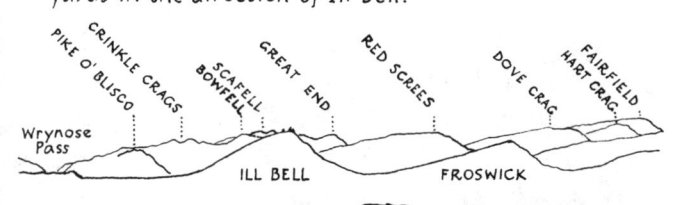

(panorama showing, left to right: Wrynose Pass, Pike O' Blisco, Crinkle Crags, Scafell, Bowfell, Great End, Ill Bell, Red Screes, Froswick, Dove Crag, Fairfield, Hart Crag)

Kentmere Pike 9

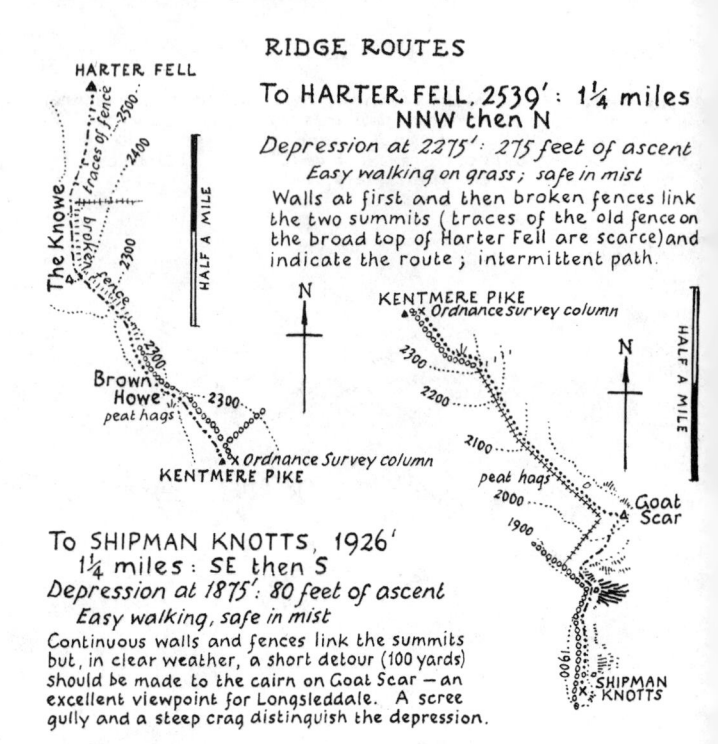

RIDGE ROUTES

TO HARTER FELL, 2539': 1¼ miles
NNW then N

Depression at 2275': 275 feet of ascent
  Easy walking on grass; safe in mist

Walls at first and then broken fences link the two summits (traces of the old fence on the broad top of Harter Fell are scarce) and indicate the route; intermittent path.

TO SHIPMAN KNOTTS, 1926'
1¼ miles: SE then S

Depression at 1875': 80 feet of ascent
  Easy walking, safe in mist

Continuous walls and fences link the summits but, in clear weather, a short detour (100 yards) should be made to the cairn on Goat Scar — an excellent viewpoint for Longsleddale. A scree gully and a steep crag distinguish the depression.

Branstree and the head of Longsleddale, from Goat Scar

Kentmere Pike 10

Goat Scar
from
Longsleddale

Kidsty Pike 2560'

from Twopenny Crag

- Patterdale

Hartsop ▲ HIGH RAISE
● RAMPSGILL HEAD
   ▲ KIDSTY PIKE
       Riggindale
       ●
       ▲ HIGH STREET

MILES
0 1 2 3 4

Kidsty Pike 2

NATURAL FEATURES

Travellers on the road and railway at Shap, looking west to the long undulating skyline of the High Street range, will find their attention focussing on the most prominent feature there, the sharp peak of Kidsty Pike. This distinctive summit, which unmistakably identifies the fell whenever it is seen in profile, is formed by the sudden breaking of the gently-rising eastern slope in a precipice of crags and scree that falls very abruptly into the depths of Riggindale. The summit is the best feature of the fell. The Riggindale face is everywhere steep, but other slopes are easy except for an extensive area of rock halfway down the long eastern shoulder.

It is interesting to note that the raising of the level of Haweswater gave Kidsty Pike a 'footing' on the shore of the lake, for the first time — previously the confining becks of Randale and Riggindale united before reaching the lake, but now each enters as a separate feeder and the small strip of shore between is the new terminus of the fell.

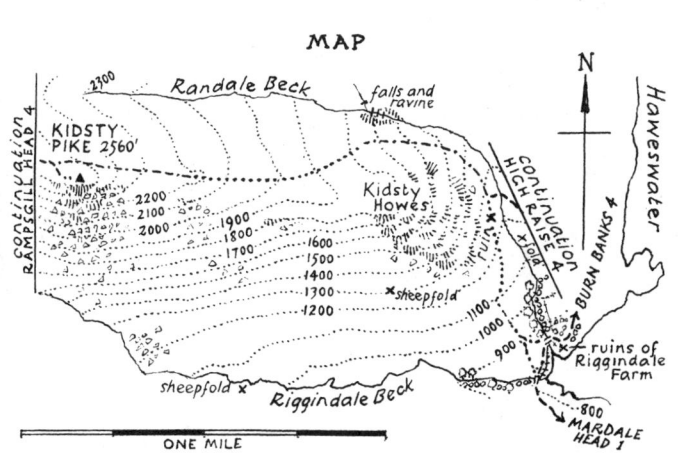

The summit crags

MAP

Kidsty Pike 3

ASCENT FROM MARDALE
1900 feet of ascent : 3 miles from the road end

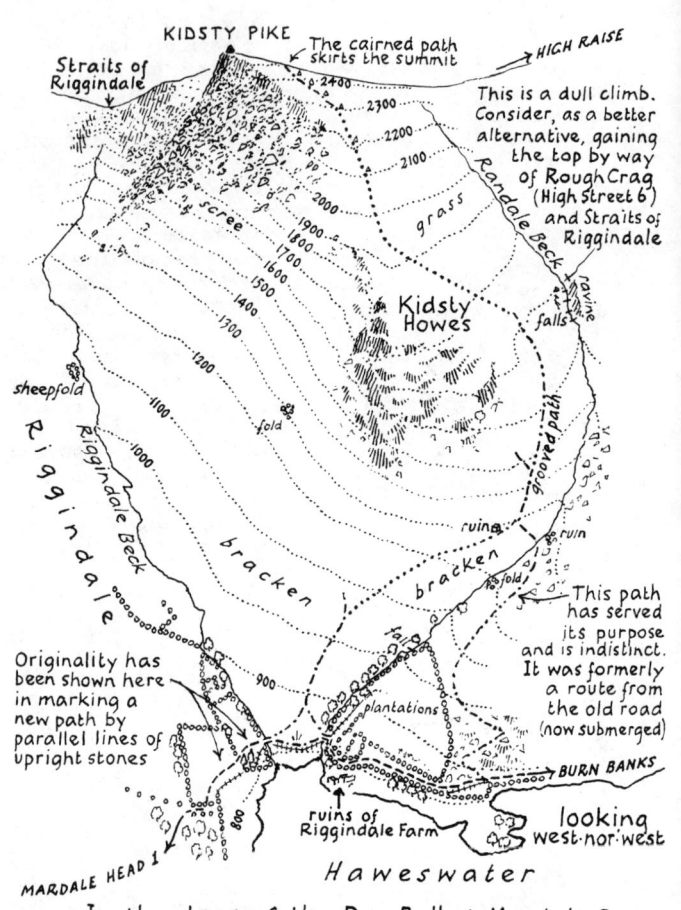

(Map annotations:)

KIDSTY PIKE — The cairned path skirts the summit — HIGH RAISE

Straits of Riggindale

This is a dull climb. Consider, as a better alternative, gaining the top by way of Rough Crag (High Street 6) and Straits of Riggindale

scree · grass · Randale Beck · ravine · falls · Kidsty Howes · grooved path

sheepfold · Riggindale Beck · Riggindale · fold · bracken · ruin · ruin · fold

This path has served its purpose and is indistinct. It was formerly a route from the old road (now submerged)

Originality has been shown here in marking a new path by parallel lines of upright stones

plantations · ruins of Riggindale Farm · BURN BANKS · looking west·nor·west

MARDALE HEAD · Haweswater

In the days of the Dun Bull at Mardale Green this was a favourite ascent. Now it is rarely used: the paths have gone to seed, and tough grass makes the climb laborious. The easiest route is that shown.

Kidsty Pike 4

THE SUMMIT

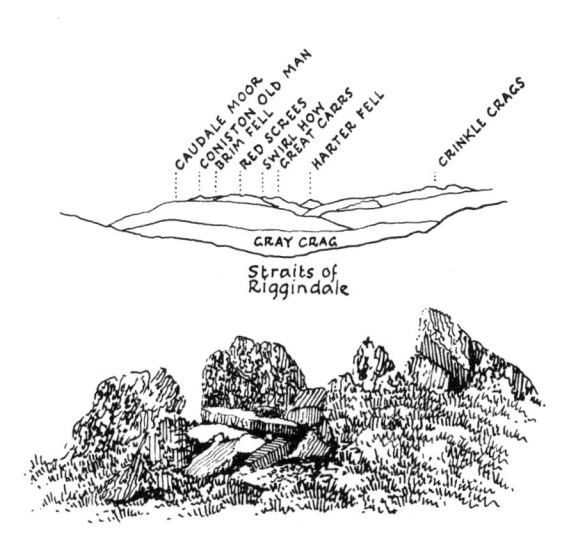

Panorama labels: CAUDALE MOOR, CONISTON OLD MAN, BRIM FELL, RED SCREES, SWIRL HOW, GREAT CARRS, HARTER FELL, CRINKLE CRAGS, GRAY CRAG

Straits of Riggindale

The summit is an eyrie perched high above Riggindale. The small cairn stands on grass amongst the boulders of the top pedestal, and crags are immediately below. The situation is dramatic. A narrow track leads to it from the north-west.

DESCENTS: For Patterdale or Hartsop, make a bee-line over Rampsgill Head, crossing it near the old signpost, and join the path below the Knott. For Mardale (if accommodation has been reserved) walk north to join a cairned track skirting the summit. Obviously there is no direct way into Riggindale. *In mist*, keep to the Straits of Riggindale track if bound for Patterdale or Hartsop, the path for which is joined near a wall. For Mardale, when the cairned track peters out bear half-left and descend with the music of Randale Beck kept a furlong away on the left hand to avoid ravines.

RIDGE ROUTE

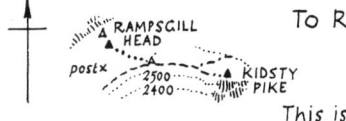

To RAMPSGILL HEAD, 2581'
⅓ mile : WNW
Depression at 2525'
60 feet of ascent

This is merely a five-minutes' stroll, but in mist it is well to remember that Rampsgill Head has crags.

Kidsty Pike 5

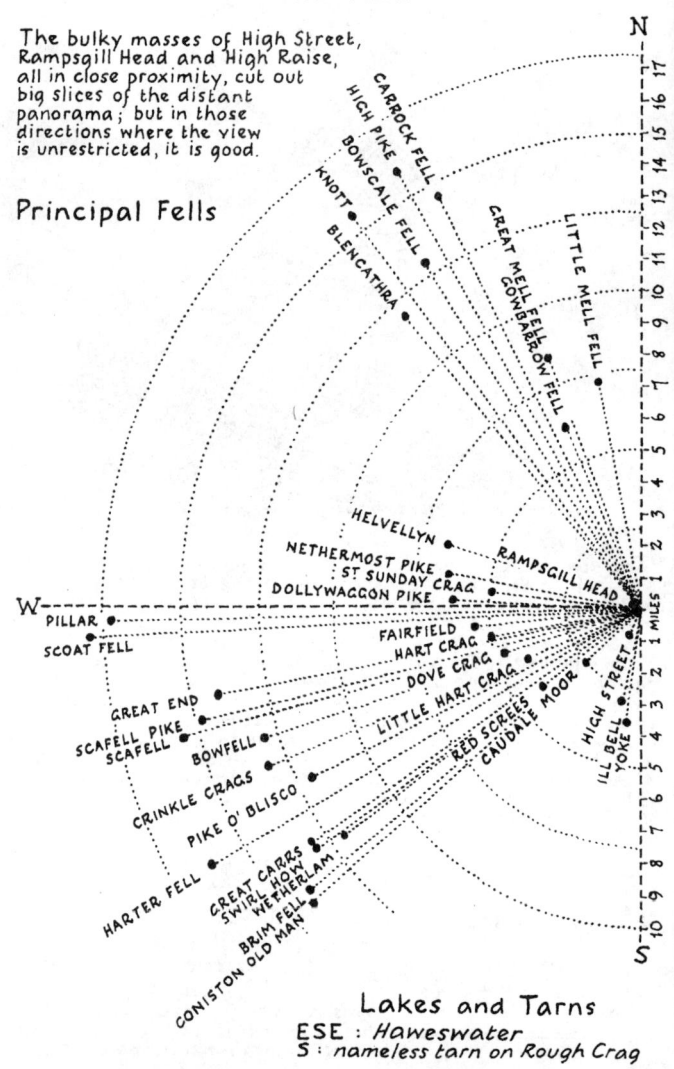

THE VIEW

The bulky masses of High Street, Rampsgill Head and High Raise, all in close proximity, cut out big slices of the distant panorama; but in those directions where the view is unrestricted, it is good.

Principal Fells

- CARROCK FELL
- HIGH PIKE
- BOWSCALE FELL
- KNOTT
- BLENCATHRA
- GREAT MELL FELL
- COWBARROW FELL
- LITTLE MELL FELL
- HELVELLYN
- NETHERMOST PIKE
- ST SUNDAY CRAG
- DOLLYWAGGON PIKE
- RAMPSGILL HEAD
- PILLAR
- SCOAT FELL
- FAIRFIELD
- HART CRAG
- DOVE CRAG
- LITTLE HART CRAG
- GREAT END
- SCAFELL PIKE
- SCAFELL
- BOWFELL
- RED SCREES
- CAUDALE MOOR
- HIGH STREET
- ILL BELL
- YOKE
- CRINKLE CRAGS
- PIKE O' BLISCO
- HARTER FELL
- GREAT CARRS
- SWIRL HOW
- WETHERLAM
- BRIM FELL
- CONISTON OLD MAN

Lakes and Tarns

ESE: *Haweswater*
S: *nameless tarn on Rough Crag*

Kidsty Pike 6

THE VIEW

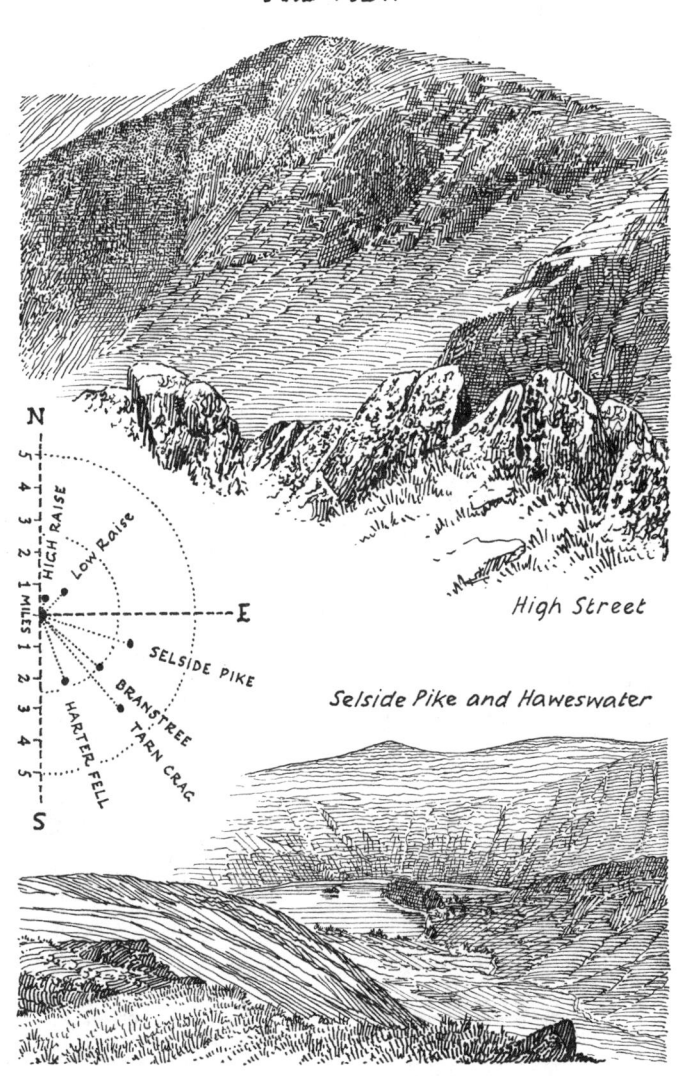

High Street

Selside Pike and Haweswater

The Knott 2423'

- Patterdale

Hartsop ▲ HIGH RAISE
● ▲▲ RAMPSGILL HEAD
THE KNOTT
▲ HIGH STREET

MILES
0 1 2 3 4

from Hayeswater Gill

The Knott 2

NATURAL FEATURES

The steep western slope descending from Rampsgill Head is arrested below the summit, just as the fall is gathering impetus, by a protuberance that takes the shape of a small conical hill. This is the Knott, a key point for walkers in this area, and although its short side rises barely a hundred feet from the main fell, its appearance is imposing when seen from other directions and especially when approached from the Hartsop valley. Fans of scree litter its western flank, which goes down steeply to Hayeswater; a tremendous scree gully here is the Knott's one interesting feature.

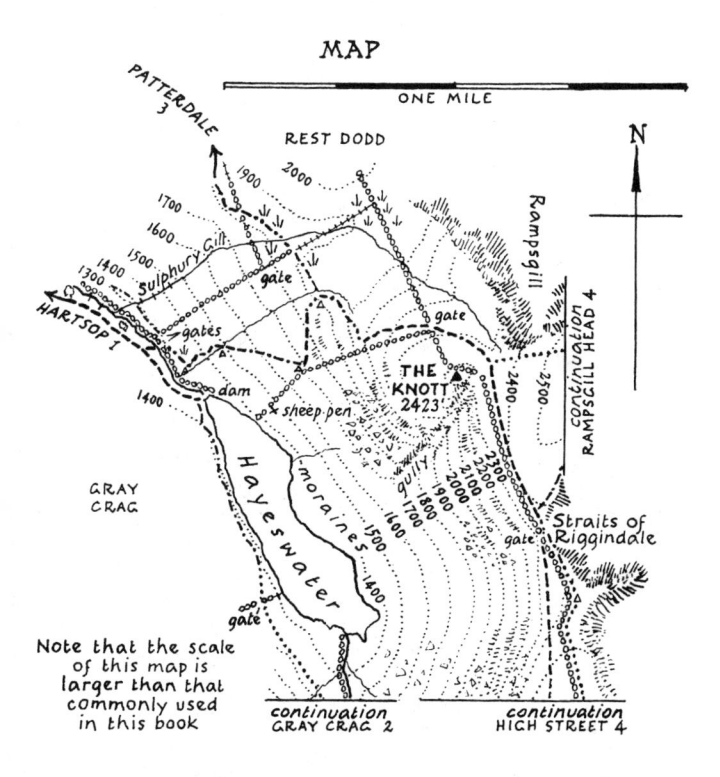

MAP

Note that the scale of this map is larger than that commonly used in this book

The Knott 3

ASCENT FROM HARTSOP
1850 feet of ascent : 2 miles

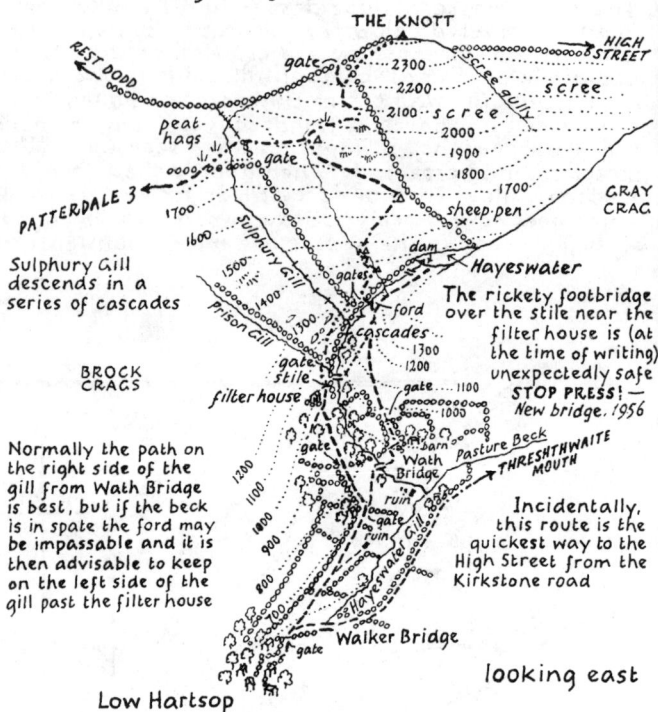

THE KNOTT
REST DODD — gate — 2300 — HIGH STREET
2200
2100 scree — scree gully
peat-hags — 2000
gate — 1900
PATTERDALE 3 — 1800
1700 — sheep pen — GRAY CRAG
1600 — dam — Hayeswater
Sulphury Gill — 1500 — gates
descends in a — 1400
series of cascades — Sulphury Gill — 1300 — ford
Prison Gill — cascades — 1300
1200
gate — stile — 1100 — gate
BROCK — filter house — 1000
CRAGS — gate — Wath Bridge — Pasture Beck — THRESHTHWAITE MOUTH

The rickety footbridge over the stile near the filter house is (at the time of writing) unexpectedly safe
STOP PRESS! — New bridge, 1956

Normally the path on the right side of the gill from Wath Bridge is best, but if the beck is in spate the ford may be impassable and it is then advisable to keep on the left side of the gill past the filter house

Incidentally, this route is the quickest way to the High Street from the Kirkstone road

1200 — gate
1100
1000 — barn
900 — gate — ruin
800 — ruin — Hayeswater Gill
700
gate — Walker Bridge

Low Hartsop

looking east

As far as Hayeswater, this is a fine approach; beyond, it deteriorates into a dull trudge.

THE SUMMIT

HIGH RAISE — RAMPSGILL HEAD

The small top of the fell is without interest except for some bouldery excavations overlooking the gully on the south which seem artificial. A wall crosses the summit, forming an angle; a few paces away is the cairn. **DESCENTS:** Follow the wall either way to join the path.

THE VIEW

Eastwards the view is severely confined to the High Street range, but in other directions it is excellent

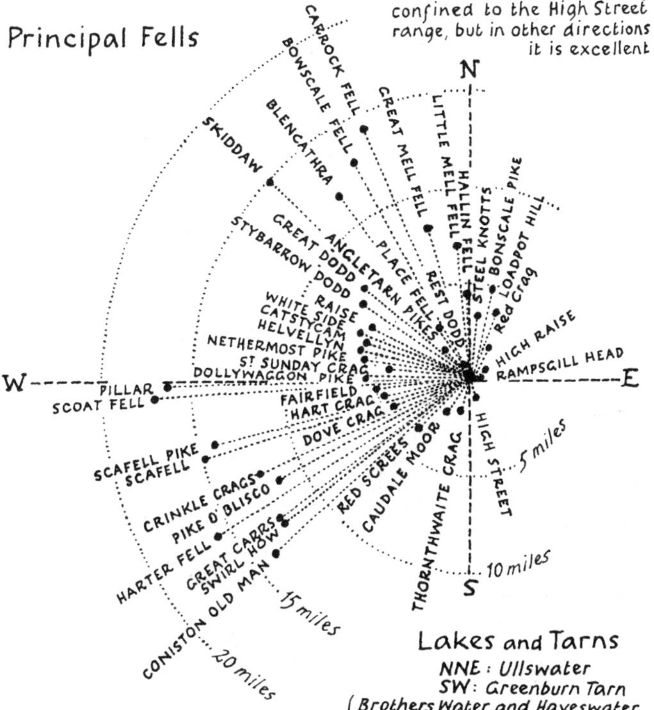
Principal Fells
N
E
S
W
CARROCK FELL
BOWSCALE FELL
GREAT MELL FELL
LITTLE MELL FELL
HALLIN FELL
STEEL KNOTTS
BONSCALE PIKE
LOADPOT HILL
Red Crag
BLENCATHRA
SKIDDAW
PLACE FELL
REST DODD
ANGLETARN PIKES
GREAT DODD
STYBARROW DODD
RAISE
WHITE SIDE
CATSTYCAM
HELVELLYN
NETHERMOST PIKE
ST SUNDAY CRAG
DOLLYWAGGON PIKE
HIGH RAISE
RAMPSGILL HEAD
PILLAR
SCOAT FELL
FAIRFIELD
HART CRAG
DOVE CRAG
HIGH STREET
5 miles
SCAFELL PIKE
SCAFELL
CRINKLE CRAGS
PIKE O' BLISCO
RED SCREES
CAUDALE MOOR
THORNTHWAITE CRAG
HARTER FELL
GREAT CARRS
SWIRL HOW
CONISTON OLD MAN
10 miles
15 miles
20 miles

Lakes and Tarns

NNE : Ullswater
SW : Greenburn Tarn
(Brothers Water and Hayeswater are both brought into view by walking 20 yards south-west)

RIDGE ROUTES

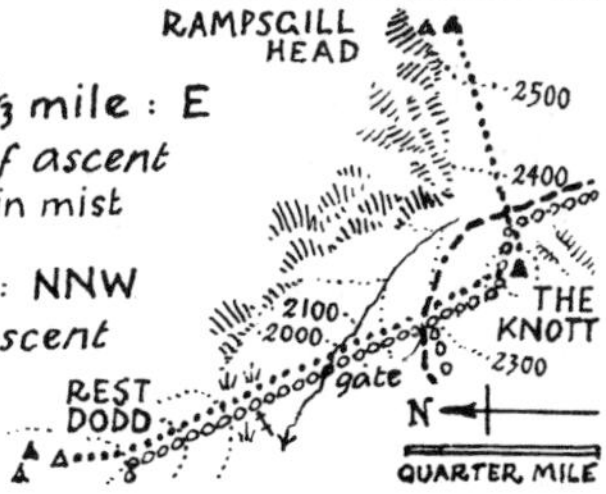
RAMPSGILL HEAD
2500
2400
THE KNOTT
2100
2000
2300
gate
REST DODD
N
QUARTER MILE

To RAMPSGILL HEAD, 2581′ : ⅓ mile : E
Depression at 2360′ : 225 feet of ascent
An easy climb. Avoid cliffs (on left) in mist

To REST DODD, 2278′ : ¾ mile : NNW
Depression at 1925′ : 360 feet of ascent
A straightforward walk, following the wall until it turns left, then directly ahead to the top

Loadpot Hill 2201'

from Sandwick

- Pooley Bridge
- Askham
- Helton
- ▲ ARTHUR'S PIKE
- Howtown
- ▲ LOADPOT HILL
- Bampton
- ▲ WETHER HILL

MILES
0 1 2 3 4

The beacon on The Pen

Loadpot Hill 2

NATURAL FEATURES

The High Street range, narrow-waisted at the impressive Straits of Riggindale, thereafter develops buxom girth as it proceeds north. Although the western flank continues steep to its extremity on Arthur's Pike, the eastern slopes descend gradually and irresolutely, halting often in wide plateaux and covering a considerable tract of moorland that is intersected by a succession of deep-cut gills, all of which join the main lateral valley of Mardale and the River Lowther. Nowhere is this characteristic manifest more than in Loadpot Hill, and because Loadpot Hill is the last of the principal eminences of the range it also has northern slopes, no less extensive, which exhibit the same reluctance to depart from the high places: hence the gradients are easy, with subsidiary hillocks arresting the decline. By Lakeland standards (which demand at least a glimpse of *rock* in every scene) territory of this type is uninteresting, for all hereabouts is tough grass and heather except for the single shattered scree-rash of Brock Crag, above Fusedale; yet there is a haunting attractiveness about these far-flung rolling expanses. There is the appearance of desolation, but no place is desolate that harbours so much life: in addition to the inevitable sheep, hardy fell ponies roam and graze at will, summer and winter alike, and the Martindale deer often cross the watershed; in springtime especially, the number and variety of birds is quite unusual for the fells. There is little to disturb these creatures. Man is not the enemy, only the fox and the buzzard. Loadpot Hill is a natural sanctuary for all wild life.

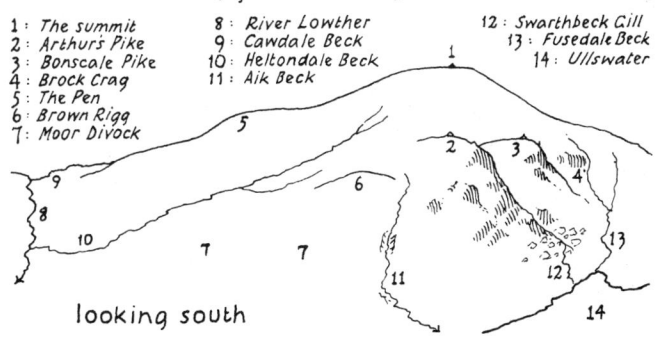

1: The summit
2: Arthur's Pike
3: Bonscale Pike
4: Brock Crag
5: The Pen
6: Brown Rigg
7: Moor Divock
8: River Lowther
9: Cawdale Beck
10: Heltondale Beck
11: Aik Beck
12: Swarthbeck Gill
13: Fusedale Beck
14: Ullswater

looking south

Loadpot Hill 3

The antiquities and oddities of Moor Divock

Cop Stone and an oddly-sited signpost

Tumuli

Man may (and does) neglect Loadpot Hill nowadays, but it was not always so. There are evidences in plenty of the esteem with which it has been regarded in the past. Even before the Romans traversed it with their High Street, its slopes were the home and meeting-place of man. There is a stone circle created by human agency near the headwaters of Swarthbeck Gill, Druidical remains and other curiosities in surprising profusion on Moor Divock on the 1050' contour, while, nearer our own time, men have laboured to erect an elaborate system of parochial boundary stones and posts along Loadpot's top and down its flanks. (It is a contrasting commentary on a modern enlightened age that the most recent erections on the Moor are shooting-hides from which the harmless and helpless grouse may be killed and crippled). And no other Lakeland fell has a domestic chimney-stack and a concrete living-room floor almost on its summit!

A boundary stone

A boundary post

Moor Divock is of very special interest to the antiquarian and archæologist, and has long been a happy hunting-ground for them. The geologist will be concerned with investigating the crater-like hollows or sinkholes (locally known as swallows), which incidentally often contain carcasses and skeletons. The humbler pedestrian, not versed in the sciences, will be impressed by the spaciousness and loneliness of the scene and the excellence of its principal path.

Stone Circles

Loadpot Hill 4

MAP

Loadpot Hill is the principal eminence of the High Street range at the northern extremity, and is extensive in area. Five pages of maps are necessary in order to show fully the main approaches to the fell from the villages at its base.

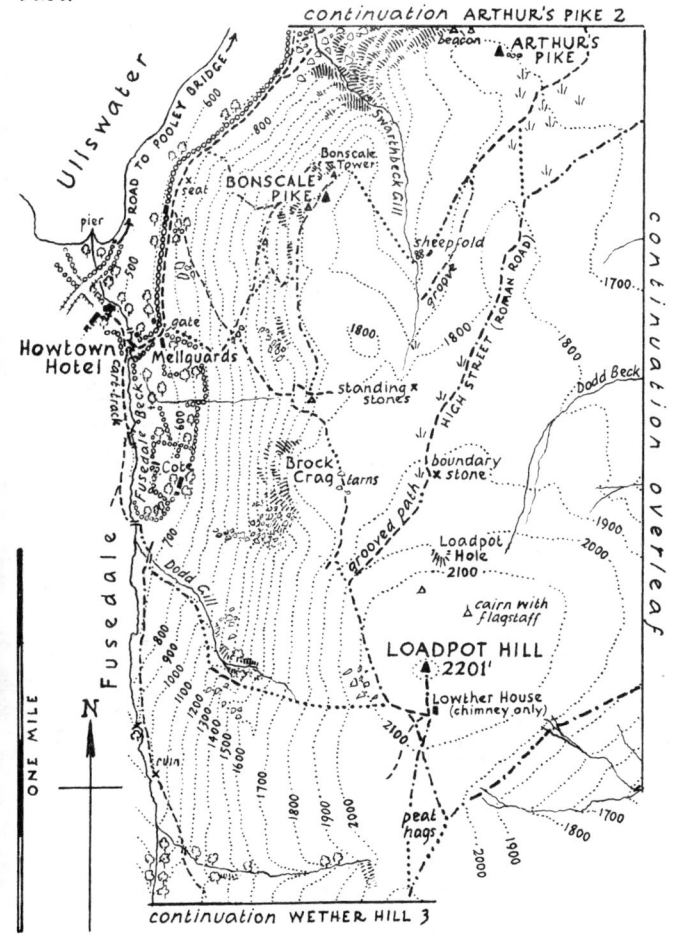

Loadpot Hill 5

MAP

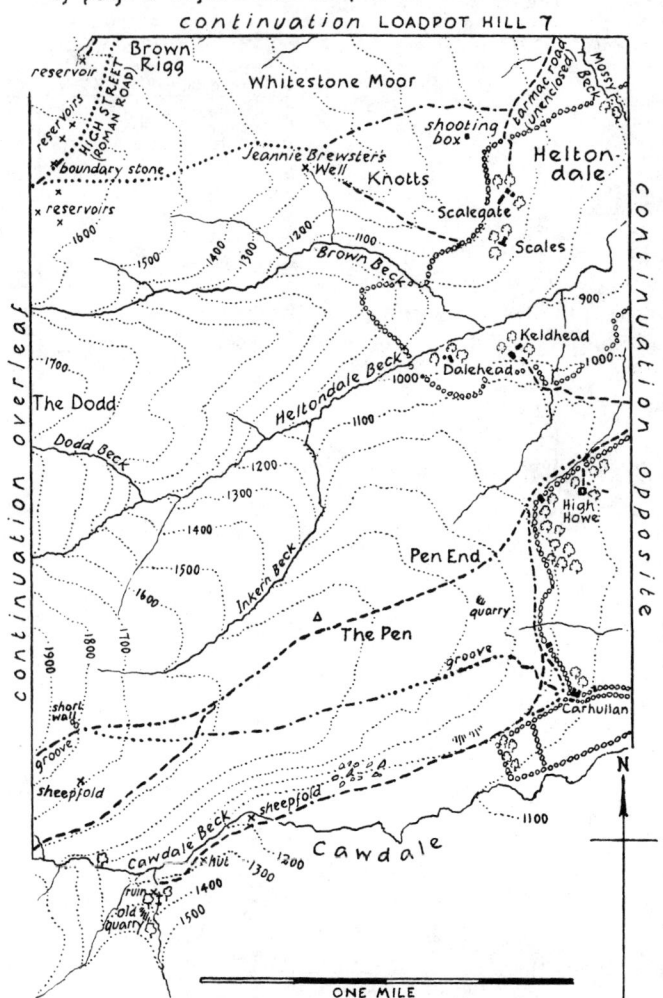

Reference should be made to the note at the top of page 8 before this map is consulted.

Loadpot Hill 6

MAP

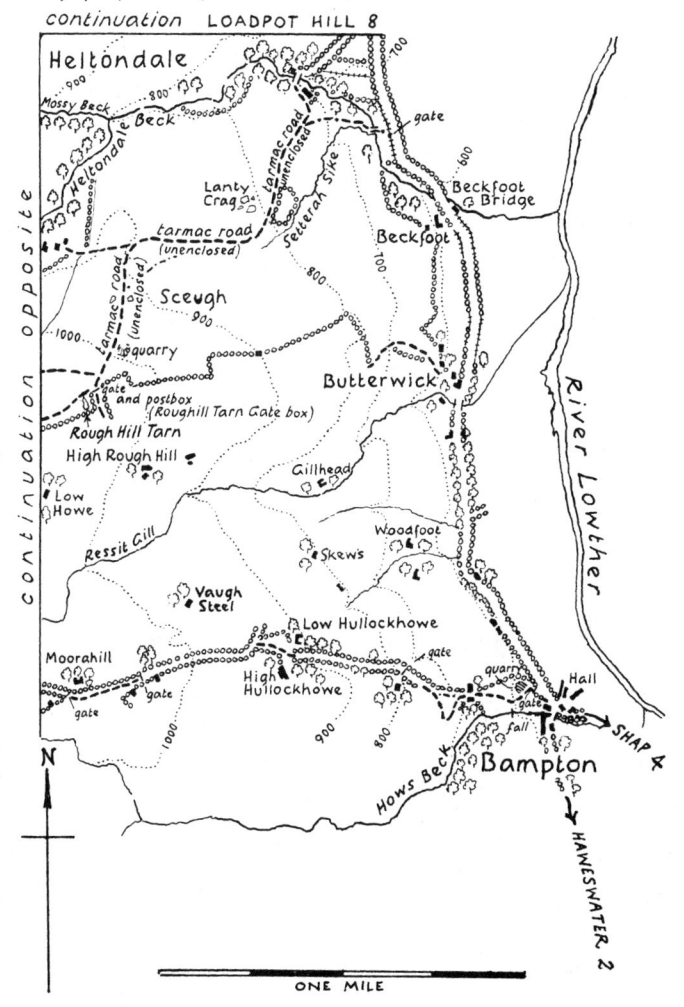

Reference should be made to the note at the top of page 8 before this map is consulted.

continuation LOADPOT HILL 8

Loadpot Hill 7

MAP

Reference should be made to the note at the top of page 8 before this map is consulted.

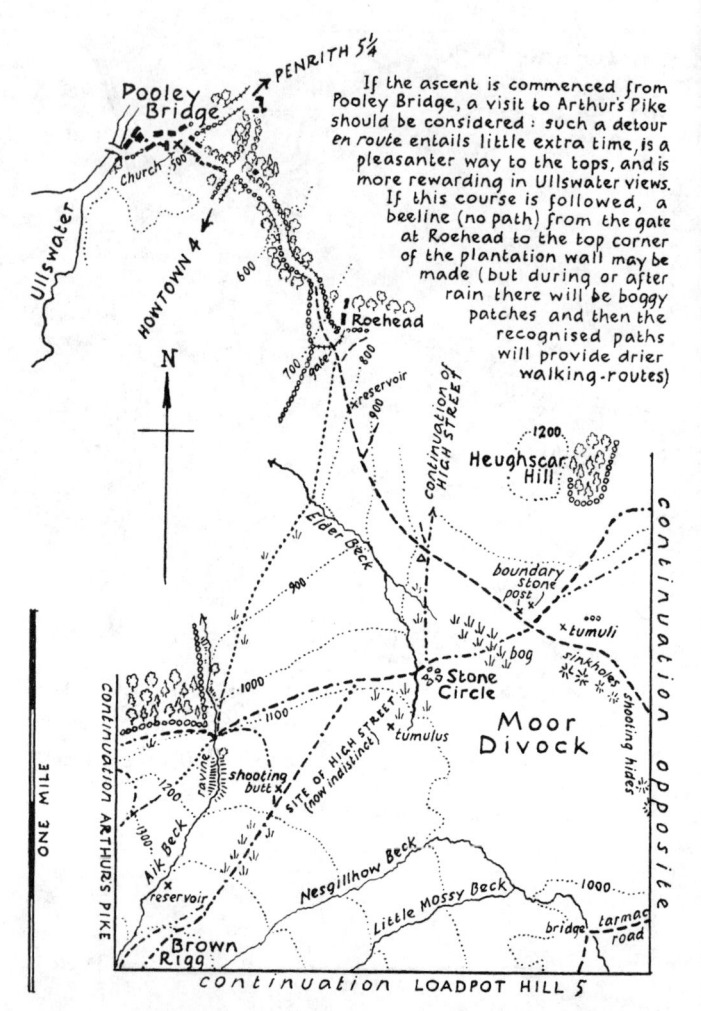

If the ascent is commenced from Pooley Bridge, a visit to Arthur's Pike should be considered: such a detour en route entails little extra time, is a pleasanter way to the tops, and is more rewarding in Ullswater views. If this course is followed, a beeline (no path) from the gate at Roehead to the top corner of the plantation wall may be made (but during or after rain there will be boggy patches and then the recognised paths will provide drier walking-routes)

Loadpot Hill 8

MAP

NOTE on the Loadpot Hill maps:

Walkers bound for the summit, especially from the north and east, may have difficulty in finding access to the fell: routes cannot be determined by observation from valley-level because of intervening tracts of cultivated farmland, which must be traversed before open ground is reached. A maze of byways and walled enclosures and farmsteads complicates the approaches. Many variations may be made, but the accompanying maps illustrate only the most direct routes, and, to depict them more clearly, *much unnecessary detail in the cultivated areas has been omitted.*

Those walkers who, like the author, do not enjoy encounters with cows and young bulls and the sundry other mammals that commonly frequent confined farmyards will be relieved to learn that the routes illustrated have been specially selected to reduce this possibility to a minimum, and only at one place (Carhullan) is it necessary to pass through a farmyard.

Loadpot Hill 9

ASCENTS FROM BAMPTON AND HELTON
1650 feet of ascent
4½ miles from Bampton; 5½ miles from Helton

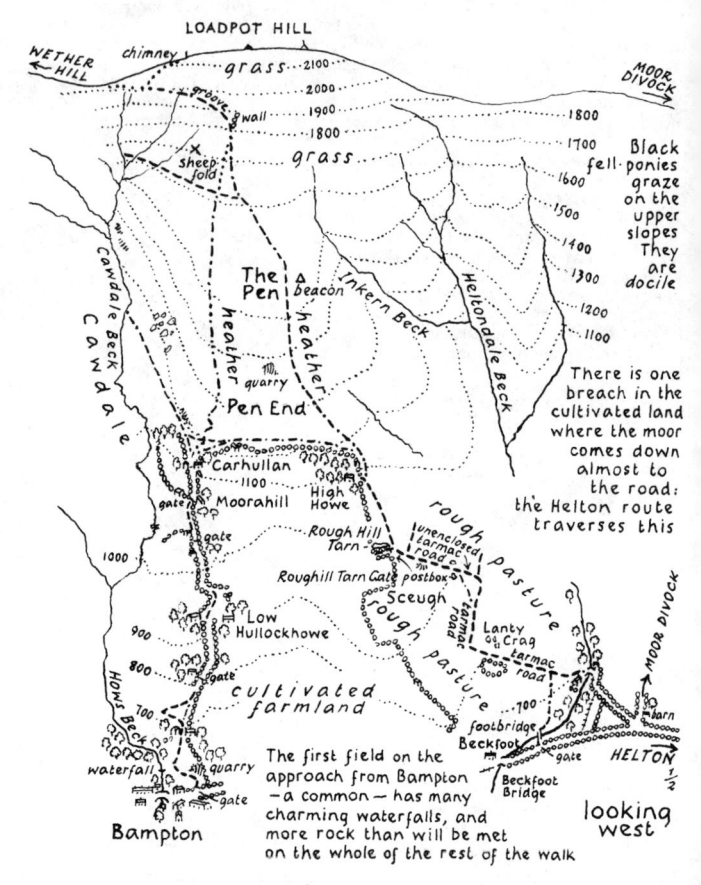

(map with labels: WETHER HILL ←, chimney, LOADPOT HILL, grass, 2100, 2000, groove, wall, 1900, 1800, 1800, 1700, → MOOR DIVOCK, sheep fold, grass, 1700, Black fell ponies graze on the upper slopes. They are docile, 1600, 1500, 1400, The Pen, beacon, Inkern Beck, Heltondale Beck, 1300, 1200, heather, heather, 1100, quarry, Pen End, Cawdale Beck, Cawdale, There is one breach in the cultivated land where the moor comes down almost to the road: the Helton route traverses this, Carhullan, 1100, Moorahill, High Howe, rough pasture, gate, Rough Hill Tarn, unenclosed tarmac road, 1000, gate, Roughhill Tarn Gate, postbox, Sceugh, tarmac road, Low Hullockhowe, rough pasture, Lanty Crag, tarmac road, 900, MOOR DIVOCK, 800, gate, Hows Beck, cultivated farmland, 700, 700, footbridge, Beckfoot, gate, barn, waterfall, quarry, gate, The first field on the approach from Bampton — a common — has many charming waterfalls, and more rock than will be met on the whole of the rest of the walk, Beckfoot Bridge, HELTON ½, Bampton, looking west)

The Helton route is rather the more interesting of the two illustrated, but both are pleasant walks in quiet, unexciting surroundings. The upper slopes are simple and very easy, but deceptively long.

Loadpot Hill 10

ASCENT FROM MOOR DIVOCK
1300 feet of ascent : 4½ miles

Full route from POOLEY BRIDGE
1800 feet of ascent : 6 miles

Full route from ASKHAM
1600 feet of ascent : 6½ miles

Fell ponies are likely to be seen on these slopes where they live all the year. When the fell is under deep snow they are fed from the farms. Many go to work in the coal-pits.

The gradients are everywhere simple. Even the most decrepit hiker will surmount them with ease.

Bridge in Heltondale

All the reservoirs shown on this diagram are covered. But not Jeannie's delectable chalice!

This is positively the worst bog on any regular Lakeland path. Avoid it!

The place to turn off the Howtown path is NOT distinct. Do this 300 yards beyond the Circle

looking south-south-west

This is not a walk for a wet or misty day, and ample time should be allowed. The High Street of the Romans is now, at best, only a line of ruts in the grass. The ascent *via* Arthur's Pike is recommended for its superior views.

Loadpot Hill 11

ASCENT FROM HOWTOWN
1750 feet of ascent : 2¼ miles

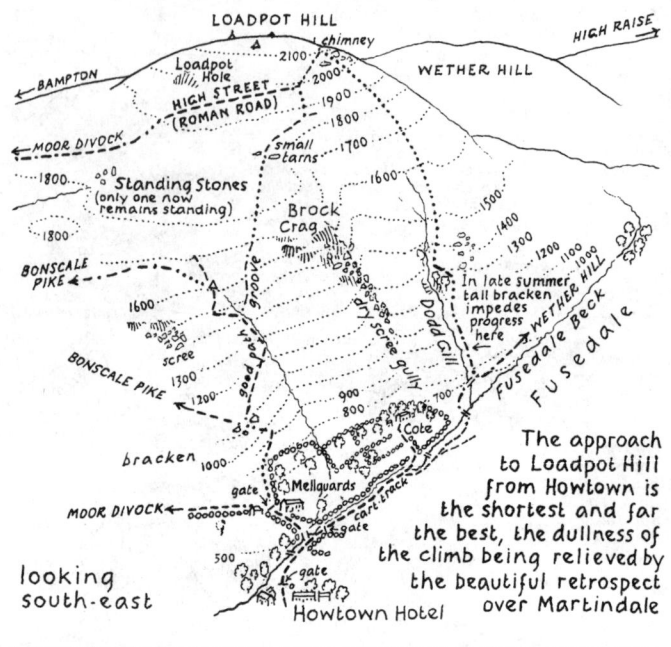

The approach to Loadpot Hill from Howtown is the shortest and far the best, the dullness of the climb being relieved by the beautiful retrospect over Martindale.

looking south-east

Fusedale and Ullswater from Dodd Gill

Brock Crag and Ullswater

Loadpot Hill 12

THE SUMMIT

Reference has already been made to the attention paid to Loadpot Hill since ancient times, and this is also manifest in the cairn on the summit — somebody, sometime, has gone to the trouble to collect, somewhere, a number of handsome stones foreign to the immediate neighbourhood, all prominently displaying a glittering quartz content, and transport them, somehow, to the highest point; these form a cairn around the base of a boundary-stone, which itself bears the inscriptions of a benchmark (⏉) and a capital letter L (probably for Lowther).

Apart from this cairn, and another adorned with a flagstaff, the summit is unremarkable. All is grass and all is flat, and more like a 30-acre field than a mountain top.

DESCENTS: Descents may be made easily and safely in any direction. (Loadpot *Hole* is not a hazard to avoid — it is not a hole one can fall into but a shallow landslip, which, because it faces north, holds the last snow on the fell every spring).

> *In mist*, the walker should not be here at all, but if he is his best plan is probably to descend westwards to the High Street (only a rut in the grass) and follow it to Moor Divock: not an easy task. *If conditions are bad* cross High Street and, still heading west, go down the steepening bracken slopes into Fusedale (for Howtown)

Just below and south of the summit is the one landmark that distinguishes this fell from all others. This is the chimney of Lowther House, a former shooting-lodge, with stables: the wooden structure has now been dismantled and taken away, but the stone stack of the chimney, now an ornament of no use, still points forlornly to the sky.

Chimney, Lowther House

Loadpot Hill 13

THE VIEW

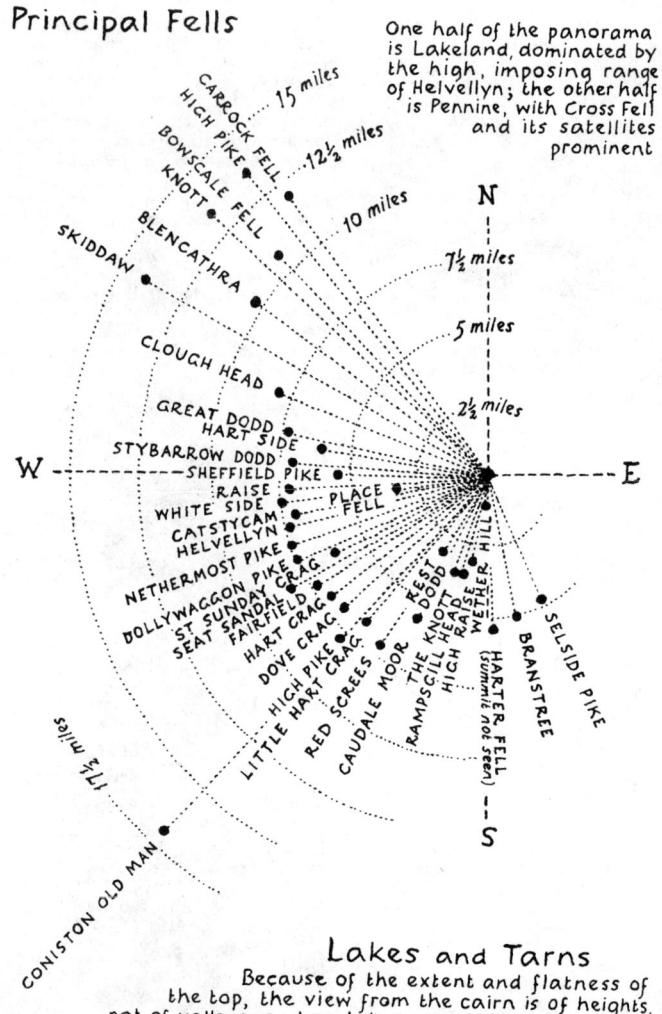

Principal Fells

One half of the panorama is Lakeland, dominated by the high, imposing range of Helvellyn; the other half is Pennine, with Cross Fell and its satellites prominent

- CARROCK FELL
- HIGH PIKE
- BOWSCALE FELL
- KNOTT
- SKIDDAW
- BLENCATHRA
- CLOUGH HEAD
- GREAT DODD
- HART SIDE
- STYBARROW DODD
- SHEFFIELD PIKE
- RAISE
- PLACE FELL
- WHITE SIDE
- CATSTYCAM
- HELVELLYN
- NETHERMOST PIKE
- DOLLYWAGGON PIKE
- ST SUNDAY CRAG
- SEAT SANDAL
- FAIRFIELD
- HART CRAG
- DOVE CRAG
- LITTLE HART CRAG
- HIGH PIKE
- RED SCREES
- CAUDALE MOOR
- RAMPSGILL HEAD
- THE KNOTT
- HIGH RAISE
- REST DODD
- WETHER HILL
- HARTER FELL (summit not seen)
- BRANSTREE
- SELSIDE PIKE
- CONISTON OLD MAN

15 miles, 12½ miles, 10 miles, 7½ miles, 5 miles, 2½ miles, 17½ miles

N, W, E, S

Lakes and Tarns

Because of the extent and flatness of the top, the view from the cairn is of heights, not of valleys, and no lakes are visible. Ullswater, however, can be seen by walking 150 yards towards the west

Loadpot Hill 14

RIDGE ROUTES

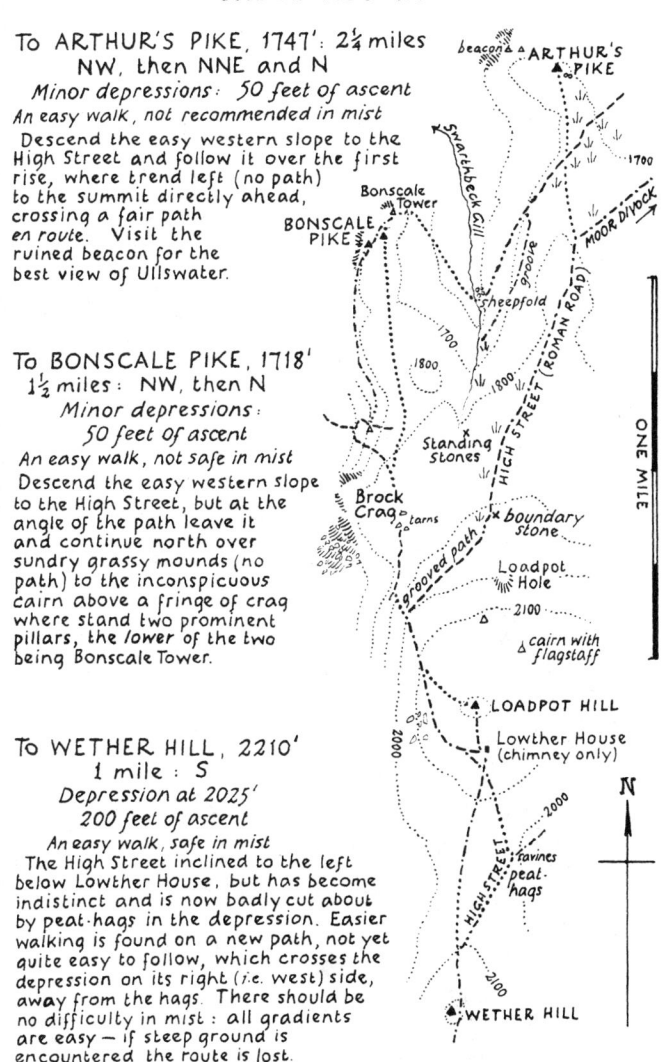

To ARTHUR'S PIKE, 1747': 2¼ miles
NW, then NNE and N
Minor depressions: 50 feet of ascent
An easy walk, not recommended in mist
Descend the easy western slope to the High Street and follow it over the first rise, where trend left (no path) to the summit directly ahead, crossing a fair path en route. Visit the ruined beacon for the best view of Ullswater.

To BONSCALE PIKE, 1718'
1½ miles: NW, then N
Minor depressions:
50 feet of ascent
An easy walk, not safe in mist
Descend the easy western slope to the High Street, but at the angle of the path leave it and continue north over sundry grassy mounds (no path) to the inconspicuous cairn above a fringe of crag where stand two prominent pillars, the *lower* of the two being Bonscale Tower.

To WETHER HILL, 2210'
1 mile: S
Depression at 2025'
200 feet of ascent
An easy walk, safe in mist
The High Street inclined to the left below Lowther House, but has become indistinct and is now badly cut about by peat-hags in the depression. Easier walking is found on a new path, not yet quite easy to follow, which crosses the depression on its right (i.e. west) side, away from the hags. There should be no difficulty in mist: all gradients are easy — if steep ground is encountered the route is lost.

Mardale Ill Bell 2496'

from the north ridge of Branstree

Mardale Ill Bell 2

NATURAL FEATURES

Mardale Ill Bell has received scant mention in Lakeland literature, and admittedly is mainly of nondescript appearance, yet one aspect of the fell is particularly good and appeals on sight to all who aspire to a little mild mountaineering. This is to the north-east, where a boulder-strewn shoulder leaves the summit and soon divides into two craggy ridges, enclosing a rocky corrie; the rugged surroundings on this side are greatly enhanced in impressiveness by the two splendid tarns of Blea Water (below High Street) and Small Water (below Harter Fell), each of them occupying a volcanic crater and deeply inurned amongst crags. These tarns, with their streams, are collectively known as Mardale Waters, and greatly contribute to the fine scenic quality of this typical Lakeland landscape.

To the west the fell merges gently and dully into High Street, with a fringe of crag throughout on the north; and south of the linking high ground is a wall of steep rock, Bleathwaite Crag, bounding the silent hollow of Hall Cove, the birthplace of the River Kent. On the south also is the most pronounced shoulder of the fell, Lingmell End, thrusting far into the valley of Kentmere, and from it descends a short spur to the top of Nan Bield Pass.

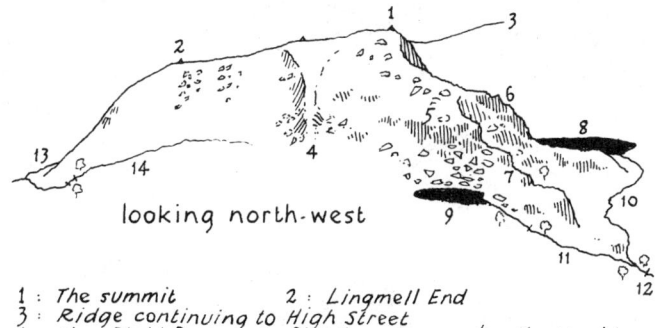

looking north-west

1 : The summit   2 : Lingmell End
3 : Ridge continuing to High Street
4 : Nan Bield Pass   5 : Piot Crag
6 : North ridge
7 : East ridge   8 : Blea Water   9 : Small Water
10 : Blea Water Beck   11 : Small Water Beck
12 : Dodderwick Force   13 : River Kent   14 : Lingmell Gill

Mardale Ill Bell 3

Waterfalls, River Kent below Hall Cove

Dodderwick Force

The north face from Blea Water

Mardale Ill Bell 4

MAP

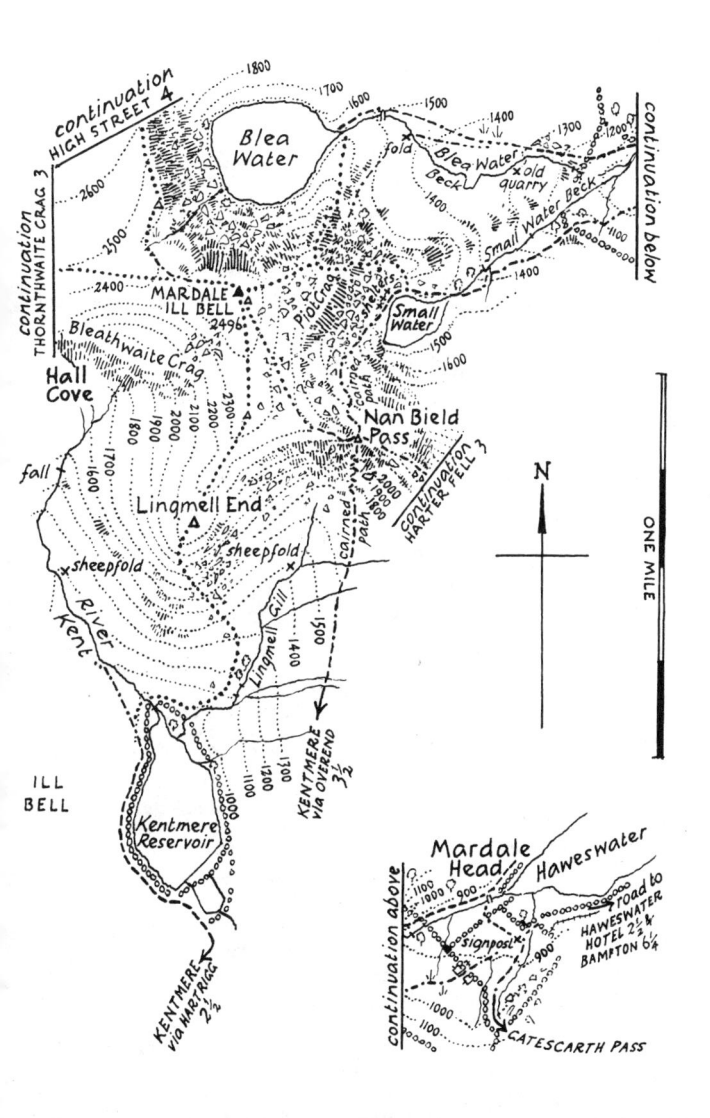

Mardale Ill Bell 5

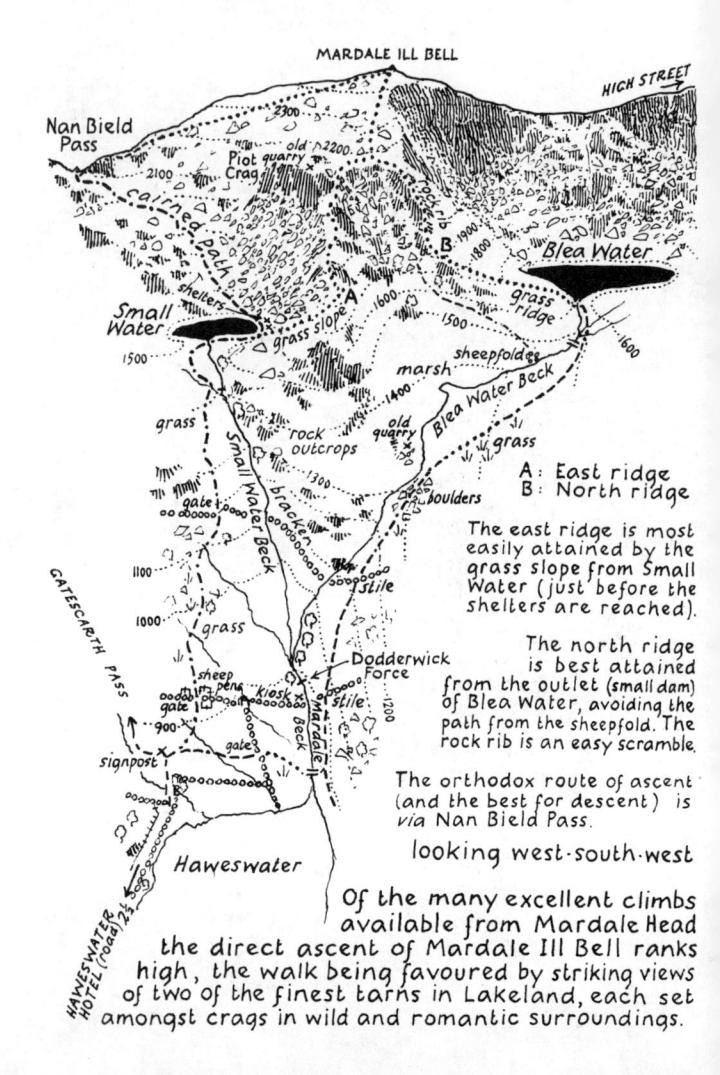

ASCENT FROM MARDALE
1700 feet of ascent : 2 miles from the road end

A: East ridge
B: North ridge

The east ridge is most easily attained by the grass slope from Small Water (just before the shelters are reached).

The north ridge is best attained from the outlet (small dam) of Blea Water, avoiding the path from the sheepfold. The rock rib is an easy scramble.

The orthodox route of ascent (and the best for descent) is via Nan Bield Pass.

looking west·south·west

Of the many excellent climbs available from Mardale Head the direct ascent of Mardale Ill Bell ranks high, the walk being favoured by striking views of two of the finest tarns in Lakeland, each set amongst crags in wild and romantic surroundings.

Mardale Ill Bell 6

ASCENT FROM KENTMERE
2100 feet of ascent : 4¾ miles

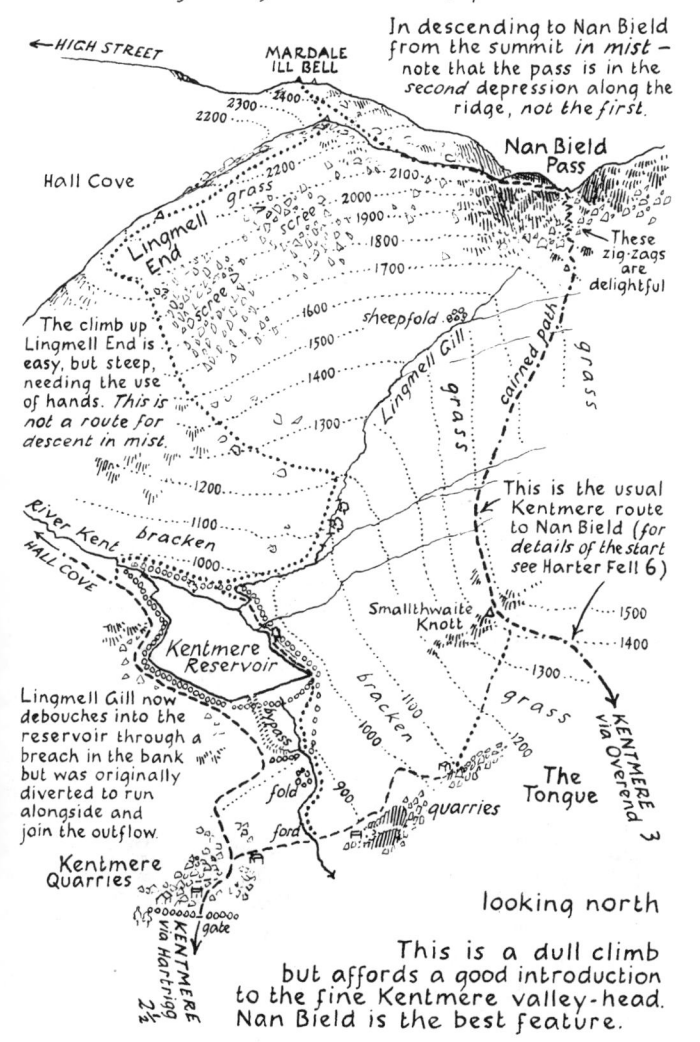

← HIGH STREET

MARDALE ILL BELL

In descending to Nan Bield from the summit *in mist* — note that the pass is in the *second depression* along the ridge, not the first.

Hall Cove

Lingmell End

Nan Bield Pass

These zig-zags are delightful

The climb up Lingmell End is easy, but steep, needing the use of hands. *This is not a route for descent in mist.*

sheepfold

Lingmell Gill

cairned path

grass

This is the usual Kentmere route to Nan Bield (for details of the start see Harter Fell 6)

River Kent

HALL COVE

bracken

Smallthwaite Knott

Kentmere Reservoir

Lingmell Gill now debouches into the reservoir through a breach in the bank but was originally diverted to run alongside and join the outflow.

bracken

grass

KENTMERE via Overend 3

The Tongue

fold ford quarries

Kentmere Quarries

KENTMERE via Hartrigg 2¼

gate

looking north

This is a dull climb but affords a good introduction to the fine Kentmere valley-head. Nan Bield is the best feature.

Mardale Ill Bell 7

THE SUMMIT

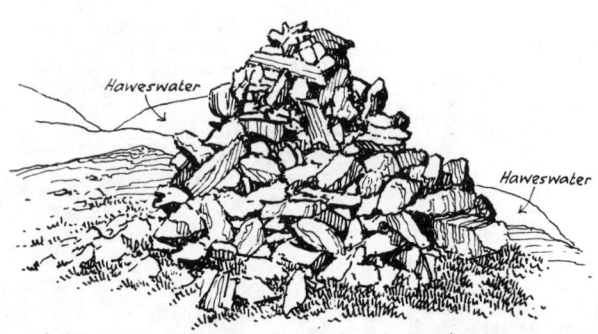

Haweswater (left)
Haweswater (right)

Two cairns, forty yards apart, crown the north-east corner of the undulating top, which is characterised by soft turf, patches of brown stones and occasional outcrops. There is nothing here to suggest the presence of fine crags close by, and a visit to them (north) adds interest to the summit.

DESCENTS: The usual way off is via Nan Bield Pass (the wall-shelter on the top of the pass is plainly visible from the summit-cairn); to reach it, keep to the right of the direct line until a cairned path materialises. Both the north and east ridges are rough and the Lingmell End route is steep.

▌*In mist, aim for Nan Bield Pass, noting that it crosses the second depression reached, not the first.*

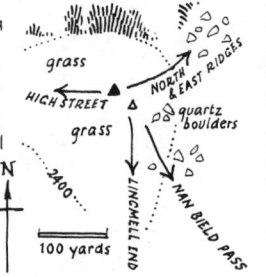

grass — NORTH & EAST RIDGES
HIGH STREET ← ▲ → quartz boulders
grass
2400 ... ↓ LINGMELL END ↘ NAN BIELD PASS
N
100 yards

The stone shelters at Small Water

Mardale Ill Bell 8

THE VIEW

Outstanding in the moderate view is the neighbouring ridge of Ill Bell, which, displaying its steep and rugged eastern face, looks magnificent from this angle. The long curve of High Street hides most of the western fells, and only the tips of the Bowfell group are visible above the rising skyline of Thornthwaite Crag.

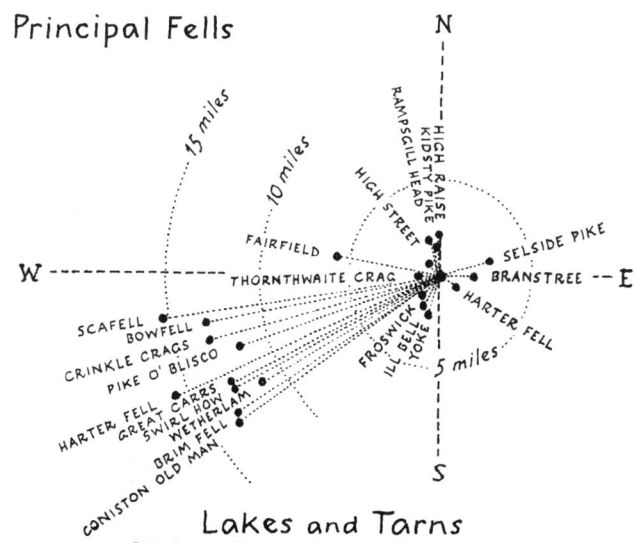

Principal Fells

Lakes and Tarns
NE and ENE: *Haweswater* (two sections)

Neither *Blea Water* nor *Small Water* can be seen from the cairn but both are worth the detour necessary to obtain bird's-eye views of them, the former from a break in the crags 100 yards north, the latter from above Piot Crag a quarter of a mile due east.

The stone shelters at Small Water (illustration opposite)

Testimony to the former importance of Nan Bield Pass as a route for travellers and trade are the three shelters alongside the track where it crosses the bouldery shore of Small Water — erected for wayfarers overtaken by bad weather or darkness. These shelters are roughly but soundly built and roofed, but they are low and can be entered only by crawling. Once the body is insinuated snugly in their spider-infested recesses, however, the weather may be defied.

Mardale Ill Bell 9

RIDGE ROUTES

To HIGH STREET, 2718': 4/5 mile : WNW then NW
Depression at 2350': 400 feet of ascent
An easy walk with interesting views

A sketchy path leaves the summit but is of little consequence; it is preferable to follow the edge of the escarpment after crossing the depression. At one point, marked by a cairn, there is a sensational downward view of Blea Water. In mist, incline west to the wall.

To THORNTHWAITE CRAG, 2569'
1⅓ miles : WNW, then WSW, W & NW
Depressions at 2350' and 2475'
250 feet of ascent

Easy walking, confusing in mist. When the short turf gives place to rough grass, keep the rising slope on the right hand and climb very slightly (do not descend to left). A track will be found as the end of the wall comes into sight.

To HARTER FELL, 2539' : 1 mile : SE, then ESE and E
Depression at 2100' (Nan Bield Pass) : 500 feet of ascent
A rough but interesting walk, with beautiful and impressive views

Aim first for the top of Nan Bield Pass (the wall-shelter there is in view from the summit) keeping to the right of the direct line until a cairned path to it is reached. Beyond the pass, an interesting ridge rises in rocky steps to the flat top of Harter Fell.   In mist, the main difficulty will be in locating the Pass

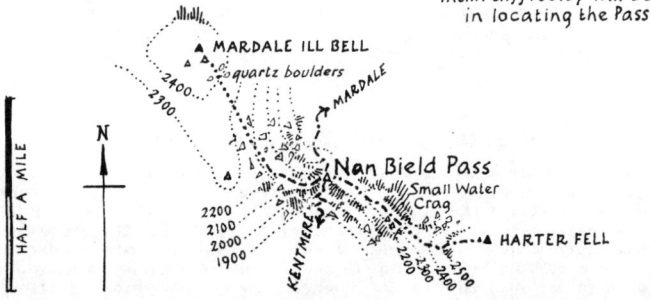

Mardale Ill Bell 10

Haweswater and Small Water from the Nan Bield ridge

The summit crags

The Nab

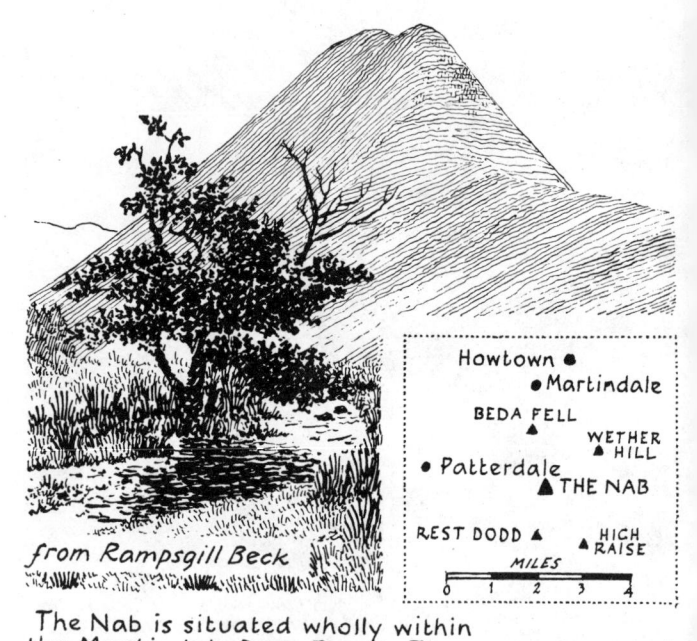

1887'

from Rampsgill Beck

Howtown •
 • Martindale
BEDA FELL
▲   WETHER
            ▲ HILL
• Patterdale
            ▲ THE NAB
REST DODD ▲   HIGH
            ▲ RAISE
MILES
0 1 2 3 4

The Nab is situated wholly within the Martindale Deer Forest. The boundaries of the Forest are principally defined by the 'Forest Wall', which encloses much of the Rampsgill and Bannerdale valleys and crosses the high ground between. This wall does not confine the deer — they roam freely beyond the boundaries — but it marks their home, their only safe refuge, their one sanctuary.

PLEASE DO NOT INTRUDE.

Red Deer Stag

The Nab 2

NATURAL FEATURES

The Nab is, in character, akin to the three Dodds around Kirkstonefoot. Very steep-sided, soaring in symmetrical lines to a slender cone, it appears from the pastures of Martindale as a lofty wedge splitting the valley into two branches, Rampsgill and Bannerdale: from this viewpoint it may well be thought to be a separate and solitary fell. But in fact, as is seen from neighbouring heights, it is merely the butt of the northern shoulder of Rest Dodd. Its lower slopes are of bracken, its higher reaches of grass, with occasional scree on both flanks and a few rocks on Nab End. In addition to its other distinctions it has, on the wide ridge behind the summit, a most unpleasant morass of peat-hags, one of the worst in the district.

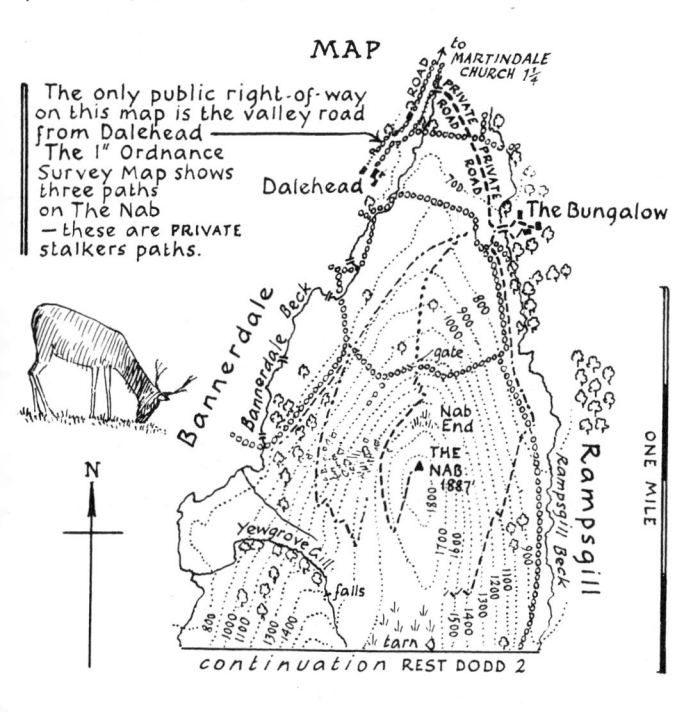

MAP

The only public right-of-way on this map is the valley road from Dalehead —
The 1" Ordnance Survey Map shows three paths on The Nab — these are PRIVATE stalkers paths.

continuation REST DODD 2

The Nab 3

ASCENTS

'Keep Out' notices, barricaded gates, and miles of barb wire must convey the impression even to the dullest-witted walker that there is no welcome here. That impression is correct. Wandering within the boundaries of the Deer Forest is not encouraged. Permission to visit the area should be sought at the keeper's Bungalow, and, justifiably, may not be granted.

The author carried out his explorations surreptitiously, and without permission (not caring to risk a refusal): he was not detected, but this may possibly have been due to his marked resemblance to an old stag, and other trespassers must not expect the same good fortune. Walkers in general should keep away. The keen 'peak-bagger' who is 'collecting' summits over 1886' must settle the matter with his conscience, and, if he decides he cannot omit The Nab, he may best approach it unobtrusively (but with permission) by way of the ridge from Rest Dodd, returning the same way. The following notes on direct ascents will therefore be of little interest to anybody but deer with a poor sense of direction.

The natural route of ascent is from Martindale. The three stalkers paths are distinct where they have been cut into the fellside, but the origins of the central and westerly paths in the lower enclosure (to which access is both barred and barbed) have largely vanished. The central route is most direct although the path becomes clear only beyond the gate in the cross-wall at 1300', and it has the advantage (which the others have not) that it continues, with one sharp angle, to within a few paces of the summit-cairn.

THE SUMMIT

The summit, a shapely dome, is completely grassy. A few stones have been carried up and make an untidy cairn.

The top of the central path is found within twenty yards on the west side of the cairn. It leads first south-west, away from its destination.

The Nab 4

THE VIEW

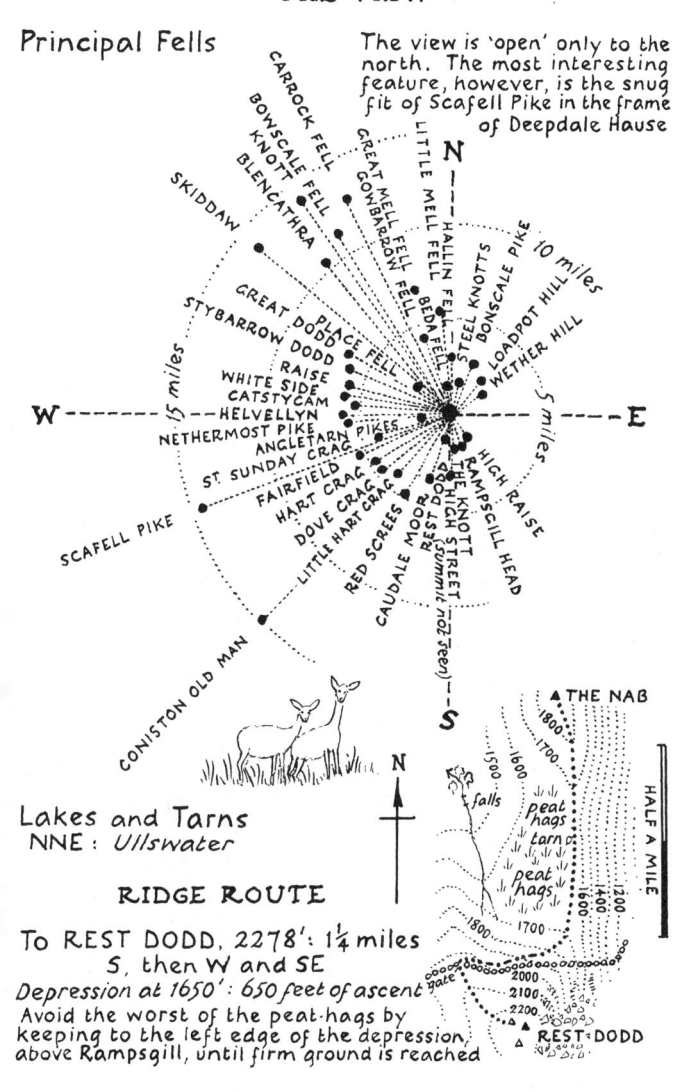

Principal Fells

The view is 'open' only to the north. The most interesting feature, however, is the snug fit of Scafell Pike in the frame of Deepdale Hause

(panorama diagram with fells labelled):
SKIDDAW, CARROCK FELL, BOWSCALE FELL, KNOTT, BLENCATHRA, GREAT MELL FELL, GOWBARROW FELL, LITTLE MELL FELL, HALLIN FELL, BEDA FELL, STEEL KNOTTS, BONSCALE PIKE, LOADPOT HILL, WETHER HILL, GREAT DODD, PLACE FELL, STYBARROW DODD, RAISE, WHITE SIDE, CATSTYCAM, HELVELLYN, NETHERMOST PIKE, ANGLETARN PIKES, ST. SUNDAY CRAG, FAIRFIELD, HART CRAG, DOVE CRAG, LITTLE HART CRAG, RED SCREES, CAUDALE MOOR, REST DODD (summit not seen), HIGH STREET, THE KNOTT, RAMPSGILL HEAD, HIGH RAISE, SCAFELL PIKE, CONISTON OLD MAN

10 miles / 5 miles / 15 miles

Lakes and Tarns
NNE: *Ullswater*

RIDGE ROUTE

To REST DODD, 2278': 1¼ miles
S, then W and SE
Depression at 1650': 650 feet of ascent
Avoid the worst of the peat-hags by keeping to the left edge of the depression above Rampsgill, until firm ground is reached

(map: THE NAB to REST DODD, HALF A MILE scale, showing falls, peat hags, tarn, peat hags, gate, contours 1200–2200)

Place Fell 2154'

from Birks

Howtown •

▲ PLACE FELL
• Patterdale

MILES
0 1 2 3

Few fells are so well favoured as Place Fell for appraising neighbouring heights. It occupies an exceptionally good position in the curve of Ullswater, in the centre of a great bowl of hills; its summit commands a very beautiful and impressive panorama. On a first visit to Patterdale, Place Fell should be an early objective, for no other viewpoint gives such an appreciation of the design of this lovely corner of Lakeland.

Place Fell 2

NATURAL FEATURES

Place Fell rises steeply from the curve formed by the upper and middle reaches of Ullswater and its bulky mass dominates the head of the lake. Of only moderate elevation, and considerably overtopped by surrounding heights, nevertheless the fell more than holds its own even in such a goodly company: it has that distinctive blend of outline and rugged solidity characteristic of the true mountain. Many discoveries await those who explore: in particular the abrupt western flank, richly clothed with juniper and bracken and heather, and plunging down to the lake in a rough tumble of crag and scree, boulders and birches, is a paradise for the scrambler, while a more adventurous walker will find a keen enjoyment in tracing the many forgotten and overgrown paths across the fellside and in following the exciting and airy sheep-tracks that so skilfully contour the steep upper slopes below the hoary crest.

The eastern face, overlooking Boardale, is riven by deepcut gullies and is everywhere steep. Northward two ridges descend more gradually to the shores of Ullswater after passing over minor summits; from a lonely hollow between them issues the main stream on the fell, Scalehow Beck, which has good waterfalls. To the south, Boardale Hause is a well-known walkers' crossroads, and beyond this depression high ground continues to climb towards the principal watershed.

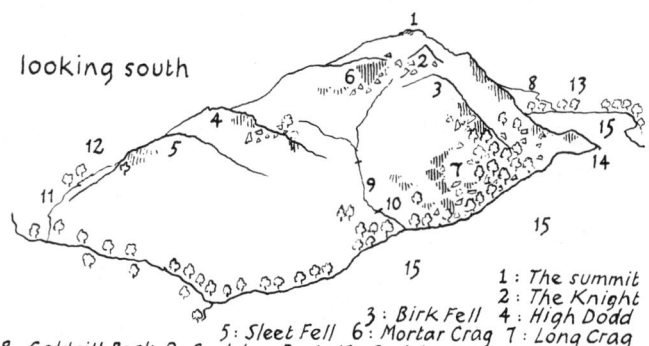

looking south

1 : The summit
2 : The Knight
3 : Birk Fell
4 : High Dodd
5 : Sleet Fell
6 : Mortar Crag
7 : Long Crag
8 : Goldrill Beck
9 : Scalehow Beck
10 : Scalehow Force
11 : Boardale Beck
12 : Boardale
13 : Patterdale
14 : Silver Point
15 : Ullswater

Place Fell 3

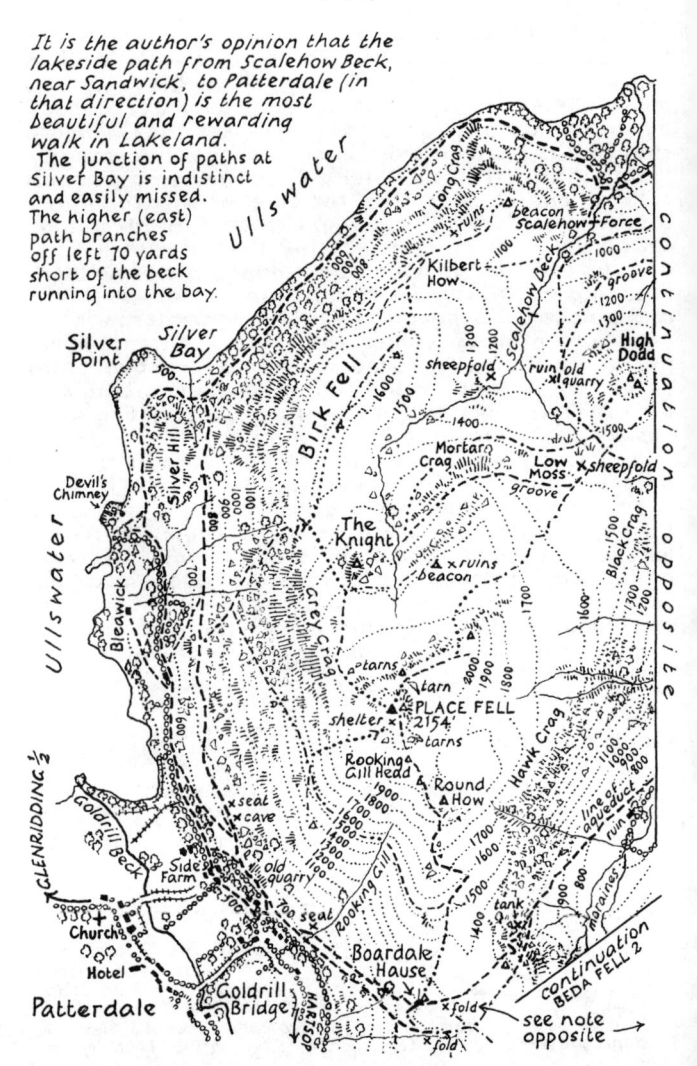

MAP

It is the author's opinion that the lakeside path from Scalehow Beck, near Sandwick, to Patterdale (in that direction) is the most beautiful and rewarding walk in Lakeland.
The junction of paths at Silver Bay is indistinct and easily missed. The higher (east) path branches off left 70 yards short of the beck running into the bay.

Place Fell 4

MAP

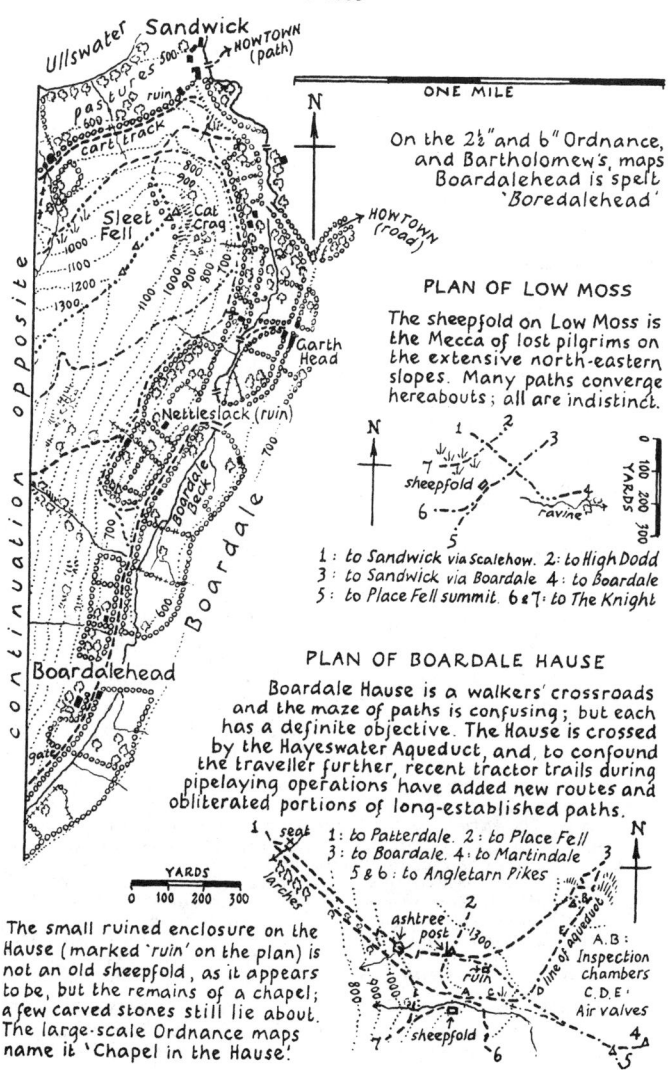

On the 2½" and 6" Ordnance, and Bartholomew's, maps Boardalehead is spelt 'Boredalehead'

PLAN OF LOW MOSS

The sheepfold on Low Moss is the Mecca of lost pilgrims on the extensive north-eastern slopes. Many paths converge hereabouts; all are indistinct.

1: to Sandwich via Scalehow. 2: to High Dodd
3: to Sandwich via Boardale 4: to Boardale
5: to Place Fell summit. 6 & 7: to The Knight

PLAN OF BOARDALE HAUSE

Boardale Hause is a walkers' crossroads and the maze of paths is confusing; but each has a definite objective. The Hause is crossed by the Hayeswater Aqueduct, and, to confound the traveller further, recent tractor trails during pipelaying operations have added new routes and obliterated portions of long-established paths.

1: to Patterdale. 2: to Place Fell
3: to Boardale. 4: to Martindale
5 & 6: to Angletarn Pikes

A, B: Inspection chambers
C, D, E: Air valves

The small ruined enclosure on the Hause (marked 'ruin' on the plan) is not an old sheepfold, as it appears to be, but the remains of a chapel; a few carved stones still lie about. The large-scale Ordnance maps name it 'Chapel in the Hause'.

Place Fell 5

ASCENT FROM PATTERDALE
1700 feet of ascent : 1¾ miles

The face of Place Fell overlooking Patterdale is unremittingly and uncompromisingly steep, and the ascent is invariably made by way of the easier gradients of Boardale Hause, there being a continuous path on this route. (From the valley there appear to be paths going straight up the fell, but these are not paths at all : they are incipient streams and runnels). As an alternative, an old neglected track that branches from the higher path to Silver Bay is recommended : this slants leftwards to the skyline depression between Birk Fell and Grey Crag, the easy remainder of the climb then following without the help of a path. This old track is difficult to locate from above and it is better not used for descent as there is rough ground in the vicinity.

The diversion of the old track from the higher path to Silver Bay is not distinct : it occurs a full half-mile beyond the quarry at a point where there is a bluff of grey rock on the left above some larches. A flat boulder marks the junction, and a few ancient cairns along the route are a help. Botanists will find much of interest here.

Note also, 200 yards up the old track, a faint path turning away on the right : this climbs high across the face below Grey Crag, is lost on scree, but can be traced beyond, on the 1500' contour, all the way to the usual route via Boardale Hause — an exhilarating high-level walk. From this path the summit may be gained without difficulty after leaving Grey Crag behind and crossing a small ravine.

On the Boardale Hause route, take the upper path at the fork near the seat. Watch for the zigzag : if this is missed the walker naturally gravitates to the lower path. The prominent ashtree is on the *upper* path.

One cannot sojourn at Patterdale without looking at Place Fell and one cannot look long at Place Fell without duly setting forth to climb it. The time is very well spent.

Place Fell 6

ASCENT FROM SANDWICK
1700 feet of ascent : 2½ miles

An ascent direct from Boardale may be made most easily by the path leaving the barn above Nettleslack.

(map showing route from Sandwick via Sleet Fell to Place Fell, with features including Boardale Hause, Nettleslack, High Dodd, Low Moss, Mortar Crag, The Knight, Birk Fell, Scalehow Force, Ullswater, and Sandwick Beck)

looking south-west

Five alternatives are shown for the initial part of the climb, the best on a clear day being the pathless route over the top of Sleet Fell (which is steep). All ways converge near the sheepfold on Low Moss, beyond which is a further choice.

THE SUMMIT
A rocky ridge overtops gently-rising slopes and has a cairn at one end and a triangulation column at the other. Many tarns adorn the top of the fell.

DESCENTS: Routes of descent are indicated in the illustration of the view; that to Boardale Hause is safest in bad weather.

Place Fell 7

THE VIEW

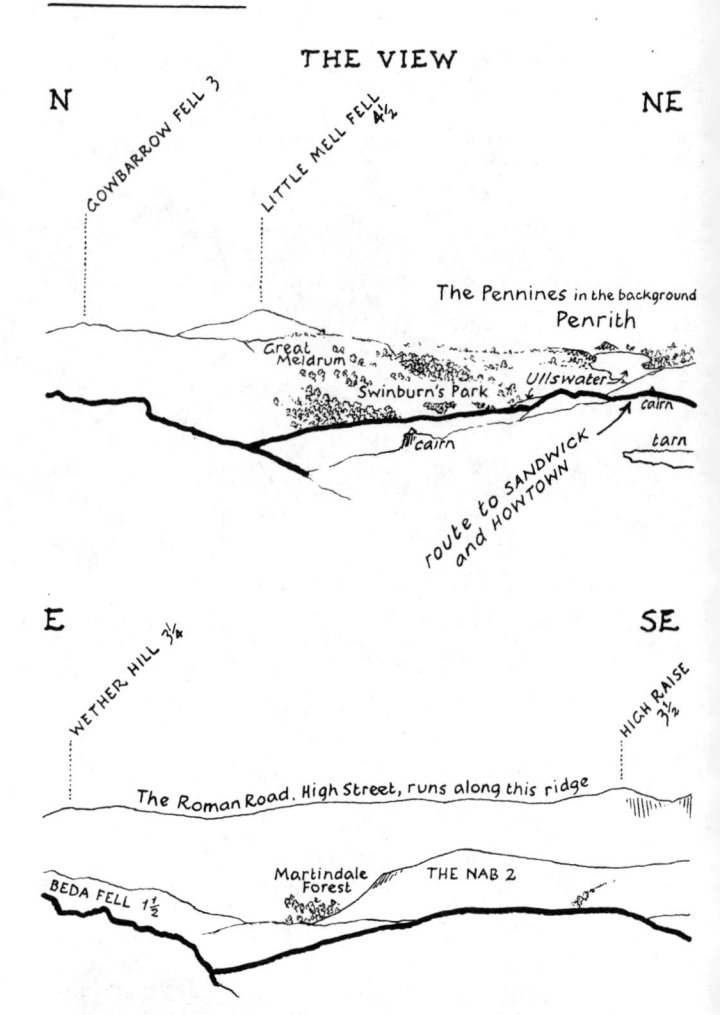

N — GOWBARROW FELL 3 — LITTLE MELL FELL 4½ — **NE**

The Pennines in the background
Penrith
Great Meldrum
Swinburn's Park
Ullswater
cairn
cairn
tarn
route to Sandwick and Howtown

E — WETHER HILL 3¾ — HIGH RAISE 3½ — **SE**

The Roman Road, High Street, runs along this ridge

BEDA FELL 1½
Martindale Forest
THE NAB 2

The thick line marks the visible boundaries of Place Fell from the summit cairn.
 The figures following the names of fells indicate distances in miles.

Place Fell 8

THE VIEW

NE — Arthur's Pike, Cross Fell (highest of the Pennines), Great Dun Fell (radar station on summit), Loadpot Hill 3¾ — **E**

The Pennines in the background
Bonscale Pike 3½
Hallin Fell 2½
Ullswater
Howtown
Winter Crag
Steel Knotts 2½
Ordnance Survey triangulation column
tarn

SE — Rampsgill Head 3½, The Knott 3¾, High Street 4¼, Gray Crag 3½, Thornthwaite Crag 4½, Ill Bell 6, Caudale Moor 4½ — **S**

Rest Dodd 2½
Threshthwaite Mouth
Raven Crag
Hartsop Dodd 3
Angletarn Pikes 1½
cairn Round How
cairn Rooking Gill Head
Path to Boardale Hause and Patterdale
tarns
tarn

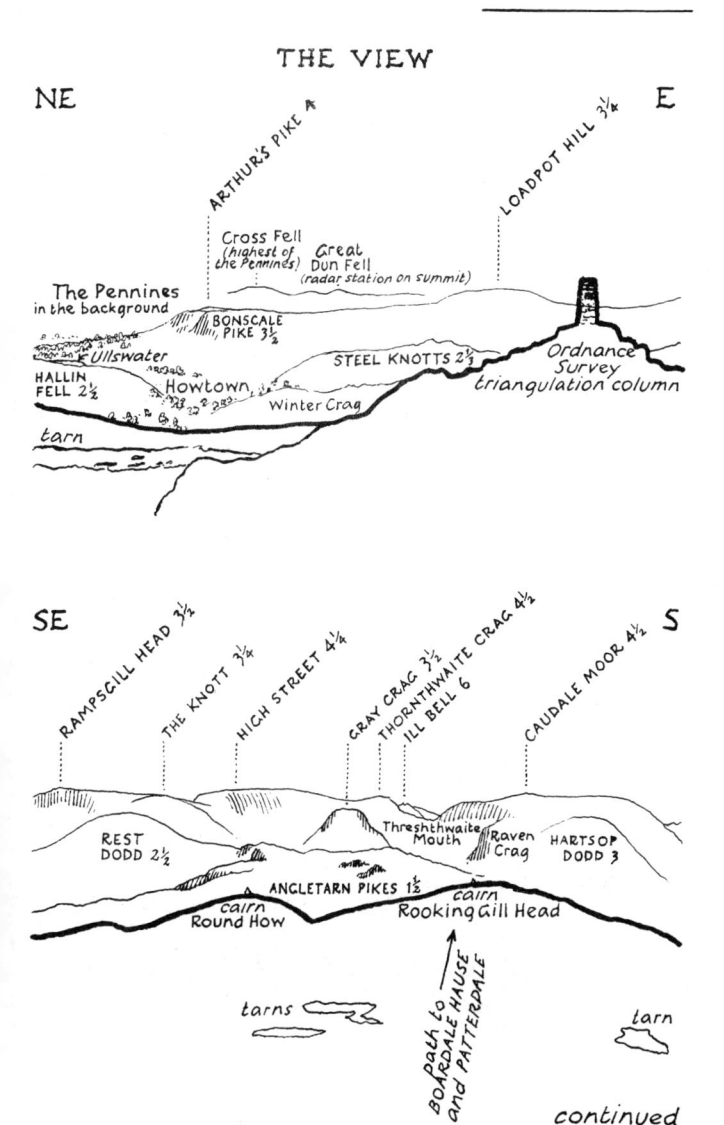

continued

Place Fell 9

THE VIEW

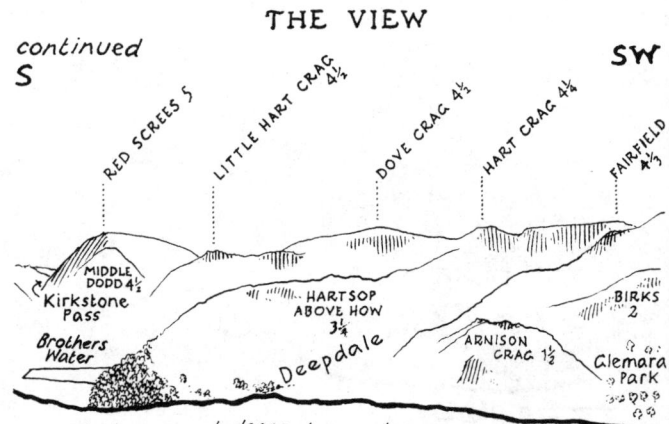

continued
S • SW

RED SCREES 5
LITTLE HART CRAG 4½
DOVE CRAG 4½
HART CRAG 4¼
FAIRFIELD 4½
MIDDLE DODD 4½
Kirkstone Pass
Brothers Water
HARTSOP ABOVE HOW 3½
Deepdale
ARNISON CRAG 1½
BIRKS 2
Glemara Park

A steep, rough descent may be made to Patterdale over this edge, but there is no path. The Boardale Hause route is to be preferred, and takes no longer

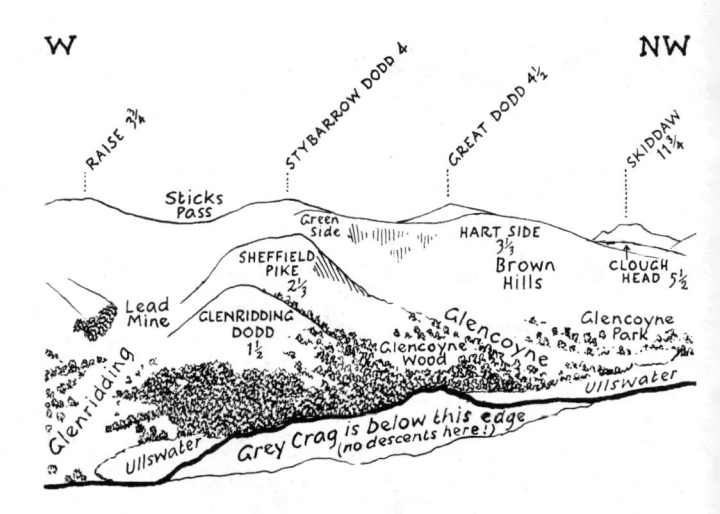

W • NW

RAISE 2¾
STYBARROW DODD 4
GREAT DODD 4½
SKIDDAW 11¾
Sticks Pass
Green Side
SHEFFIELD PIKE 2⅔
HART SIDE 3⅓
Brown Hills
CLOUGH HEAD 5½
Lead Mine
GLENRIDDING DODD 1½
Glencoyne
Glencoyne Wood
Glencoyne Park
Glenridding
Ullswater
Ullswater
Grey Crag is below this edge
(no descents here!)

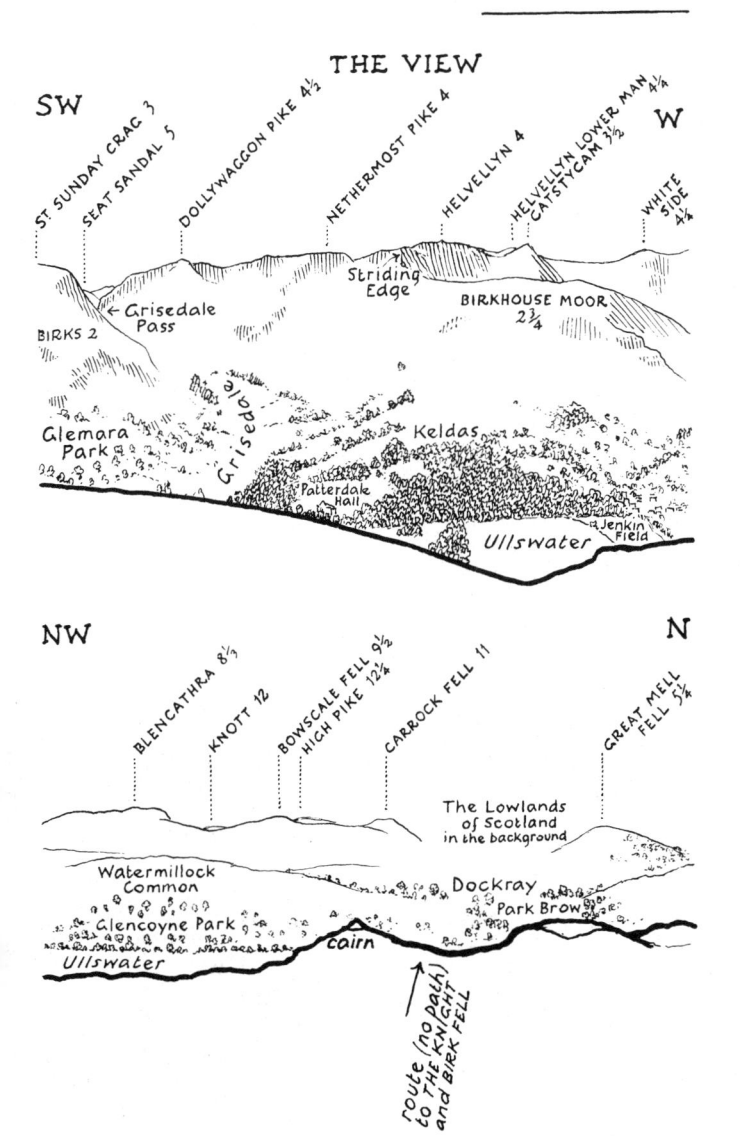

Place Fell 10

THE VIEW

SW — St Sunday Crag 3, Seat Sandal 5, Dollywaggon Pike 4½, Nethermost Pike 4, Helvellyn 4, Helvellyn Lower Man 4¼, Catstycam 3½, White Side 4¼ — **W**

Birks 2, Grisedale Pass, Striding Edge, Birkhouse Moor 2¾

Glemara Park, Grisedale, Keldas, Patterdale Hall, Jenkin Field, Ullswater

NW — Blencathra 8½, Knott 12, Bowscale Fell 12½, High Pike 12¼, Carrock Fell 11, Great Mell Fell 5¼ — **N**

The Lowlands of Scotland in the background

Watermillock Common, Glencoyne Park, Dockray, Park Brow, Ullswater, cairn

route (no path) to THE KNIGHT and BIRK FELL

Rampsgill Head 2581'

Spelt 'Ramsgill Head' on the Ordnance Survey maps. Local writers include the 'p'.

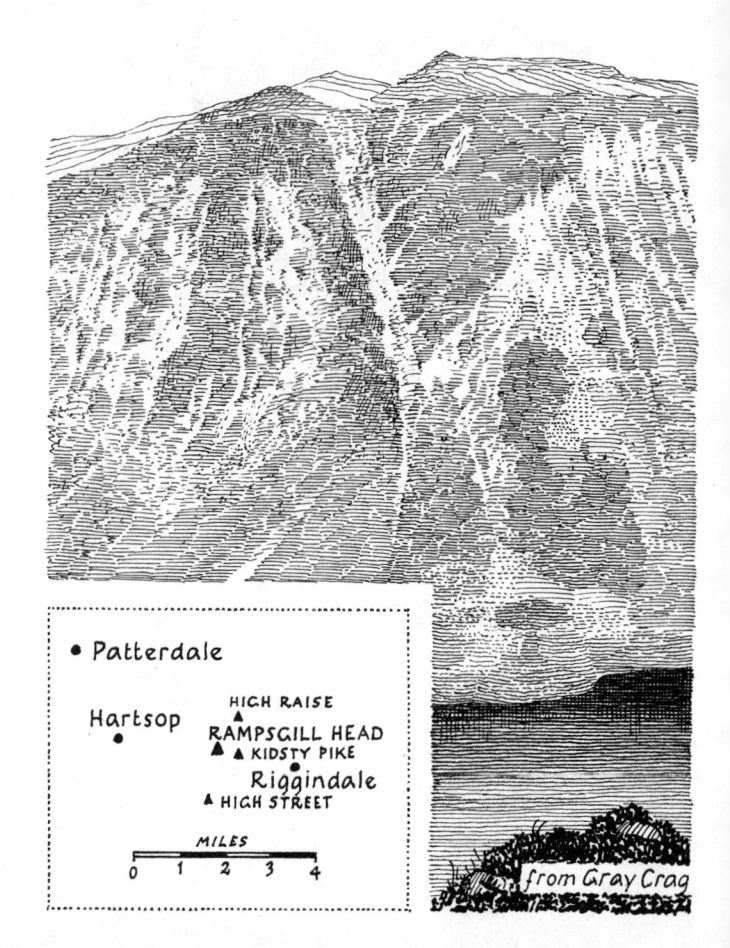

from Gray Crag

• Patterdale

Hartsop

▲ HIGH RAISE
RAMPSGILL HEAD ▲
▲ ▲ KIDSTY PIKE
Riggindale
▲ HIGH STREET

MILES
0 1 2 3 4

Rampsgill Head 2

NATURAL FEATURES

There is usually little difficulty in defining the boundaries of a mountain. If it rises in isolation there is no difficulty, and even if it is merely a high point on a ridge invariably its main slopes go down to valley-level, probably on both flanks, and the limit of its extent in other directions is, as a rule, marked by watercourses falling from the cols or depressions linking it with adjacent heights. Rampsgill Head is, geographically, a 'key' point in the High Street range, for two independent ridges of some importance leave its summit, and it is, therefore, all the more remarkable that a neat and precise definition of its natural boundaries cannot be given, largely because lower secondary summits on the side ridges are also regarded as separate fells and claim to themselves territory that would otherwise be attributed to the parent fell. It is also unusual for so prominent a height to be without an official name. Rampsgill Head is properly the name of the semicircle of high ground enclosing the rough upper reaches of the valley of Rampsgill but is now generally attached to all the fell above and beyond, although occasionally some writers have remedied the lack of a common title by referring to the whole mass hereabouts, east of the watershed, as Kidsty Pike, but this is incorrect.

The most impressive natural feature is the fringe of crags breaking abruptly at the edge of the summit facing Rampsgill, and the long slopes of boulder debris and scree below are an indication that, before the age of decay, the rock-scenery here must have been very striking. Grass predominates elsewhere but there is another steep face of rock, Twopenny Crag, falling into Riggindale. Hayeswater lies at the foot of the western slope, but the principal becks from the fell act as feeders of Ullswater and Haweswater.

Twopenny Crag

Rampsgill Head 3

This fine arête (here seen from the south) starts from a leaning pinnacle on the west face and leads directly to the top of the fell. It is littered with loose rock and is obviously in a state of decay; otherwise it would surely deserve the attention of rock-climbers

The summit crags

The eastern aspect of the arête, here illustrated, reveals a prominent vertical buttress of sound, 'clean' rock, not of great height but perhaps worth carrying a rope up from Patterdale or Hartsop

Rampsgill Head 4

MAP

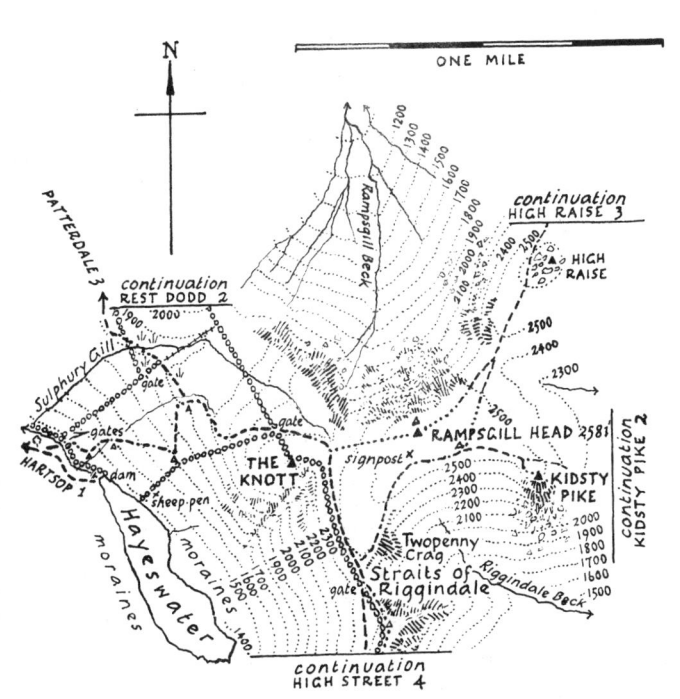

The crags above the north west face

Rampsgill Head 5

ASCENTS FROM PATTERDALE AND HARTSOP
2200 feet of ascent : 4½ miles from Patterdale
2050 feet of ascent : 2¾ miles from Hartsop

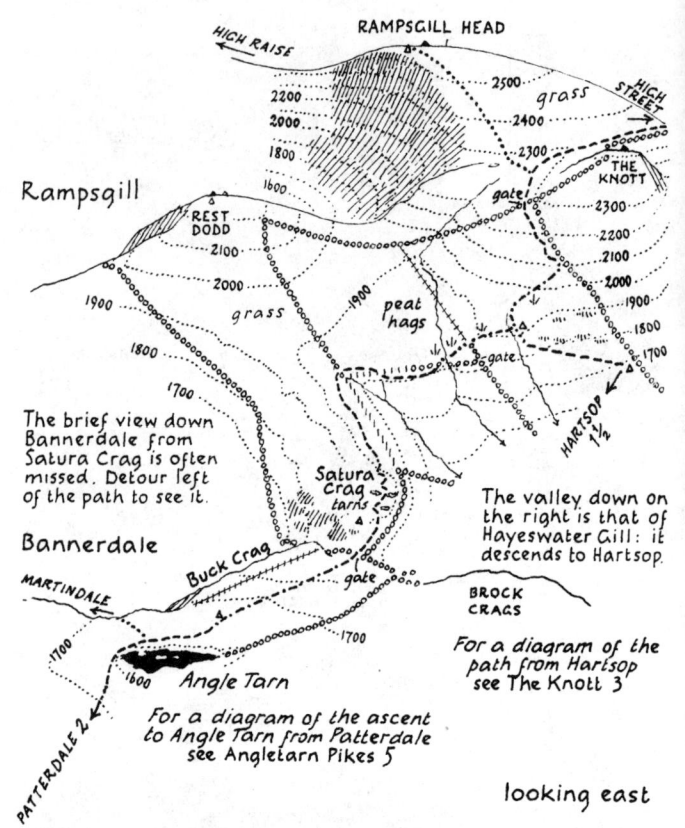

looking east

The brief view down Bannerdale from Satura Crag is often missed. Detour left of the path to see it.

The valley down on the right is that of Hayeswater Gill: it descends to Hartsop.

For a diagram of the path from Hartsop see The Knott 3

For a diagram of the ascent to Angle Tarn from Patterdale see Angletarn Pikes 5

This is a most enjoyable excursion with a succession of widely differing views, all excellent; and the route itself, never very distinct, is an interesting puzzle to unravel. In bad weather, however, there will be some difficulty, and a stranger may run into trouble on top of Rampsgill Head, where there are crags.

# Rampsgill Head 6

ASCENT FROM MARDALE
1950 feet of ascent · 3½ miles from the road end

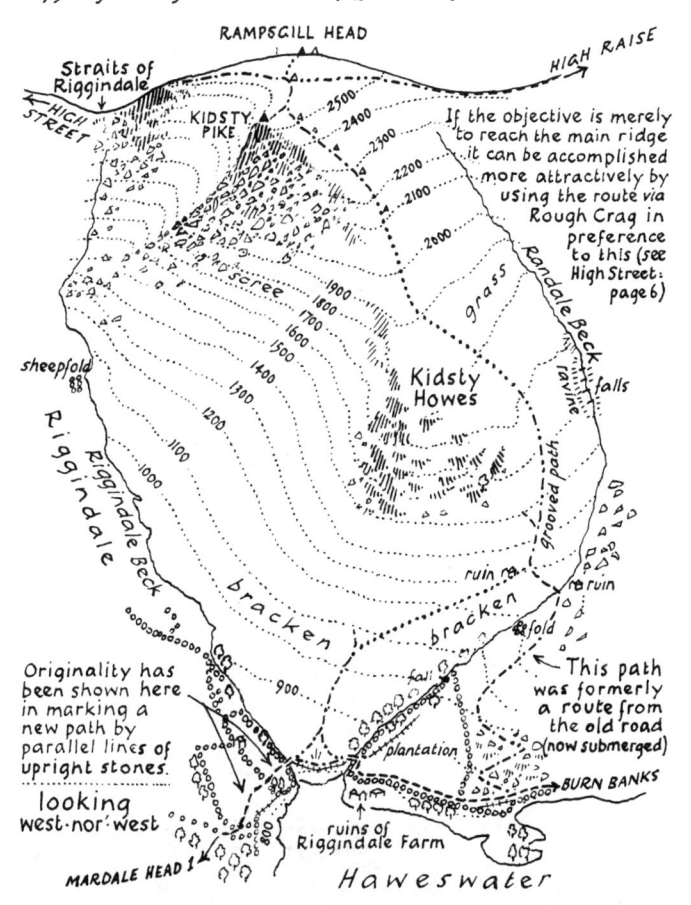

Map annotations:
- RAMPSGILL HEAD
- Straits of Riggindale
- HIGH STREET
- KIDSTY PIKE
- HIGH RAISE
- If the objective is merely to reach the main ridge it can be accomplished more attractively by using the route via Rough Crag in preference to this (see High Street page 6)
- scree
- Kidsty Howes
- Randale Beck ravine
- falls
- grass
- grooved path
- sheepfold
- Riggindale Beck
- bracken
- ruin
- ruin
- fold
- Originality has been shown here in marking a new path by parallel lines of upright stones.
- This path was formerly a route from the old road (now submerged)
- looking west-nor'west
- plantation
- BURN BANKS
- MARDALE HEAD
- ruins of Riggindale Farm
- Haweswater

This is a dull climb over neglected and fading paths that the Haweswater project committed to lingering death. Tough grass grows on the fellsides where once both dalesfolk and visitors trod. The gaunt ruins of Riggindale are symbolic of this dying route.

Rampsgill Head 7

THE SUMMIT

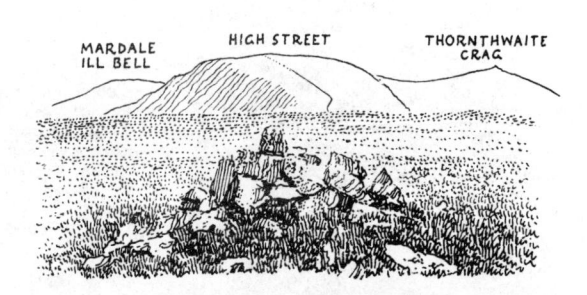

On the right sort of day, the top is a pleasant place to linger awhile. The turf is delightful, there is some outcropping rock to add interest, the rim of crags is worthy of a leisurely and detailed exploration, the views are good in all directions. A prominent, well-built cairn stands on the edge of the abrupt north-west face; thirty yards away is the highest cairn — an untidy heap of stones — and sixty yards further south-west is a spectral signpost that once directed visitors to Mardale and Patterdale but lost its arms long ago: in any case its usefulness would be largely past, for few now go to Mardale.

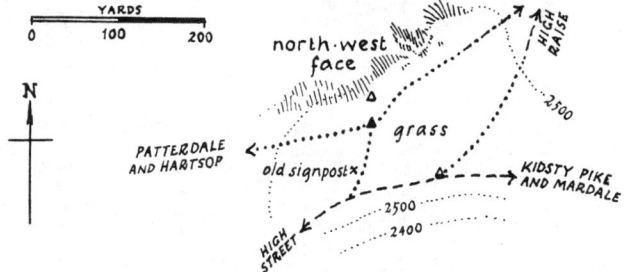

DESCENTS: For Patterdale and Hartsop, aim for The Knott to join the path there. For Mardale, use the ridge beyond Kidsty Pike — but the warning cannot be given too often until all old maps are out of circulation that Mardale Head is uninhabited, and the only beds in the valley are at the Haweswater Hotel on the far side of the lake.

In mist, the edge of the escarpment is sufficiently defined to give direction: keep it on the right hand if bound for either Patterdale or Hartsop and descend easy ground to the path. For Mardale, if the path over Kidsty Pike cannot be located, incline left and follow Randale Beck down to the valley.

Rampsgill Head 8

RIDGE ROUTES

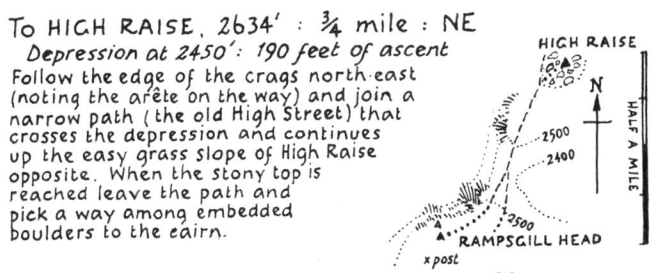

To HIGH RAISE, 2634' : ¾ mile : NE
Depression at 2450': 190 feet of ascent
Follow the edge of the crags north-east (noting the arête on the way) and join a narrow path (the old High Street) that crosses the depression and continues up the easy grass slope of High Raise opposite. When the stony top is reached leave the path and pick a way among embedded boulders to the cairn.

To THE KNOTT, 2423' : ⅓ mile : W
Depression at 2360'
65 feet of ascent
Descend the easy west slope to the wall-corner in the depression (the good path crossed here is the regular Patterdale to High Street route). He is tired indeed who cannot gain the summit of The Knott from the corner of the wall, and two minutes for the ascent is a generous time allowance.

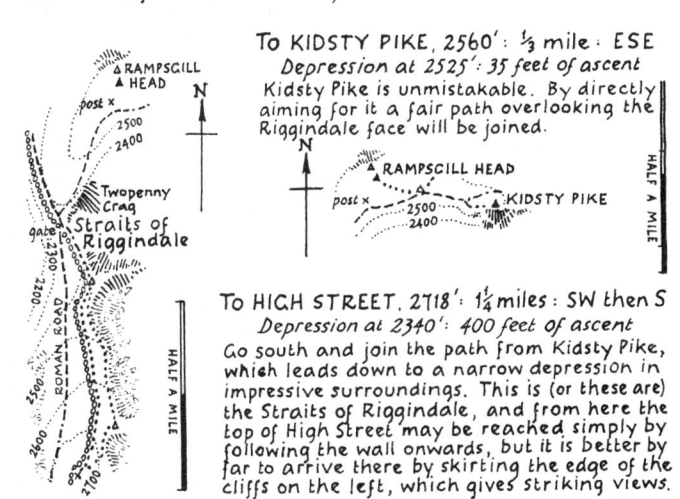

To KIDSTY PIKE, 2560' : ⅓ mile : ESE
Depression at 2525': 35 feet of ascent
Kidsty Pike is unmistakable. By directly aiming for it a fair path overlooking the Riggindale face will be joined.

To HIGH STREET, 2718' : 1¼ miles : SW then S
Depression at 2340': 400 feet of ascent
Go south and join the path from Kidsty Pike, which leads down to a narrow depression in impressive surroundings. This is (or these are) the Straits of Riggindale, and from here the top of High Street may be reached simply by following the wall onwards, but it is better by far to arrive there by skirting the edge of the cliffs on the left, which gives striking views.

All these routes are easy, and, with care, safe in mist

Rampsgill Head 9

THE VIEW

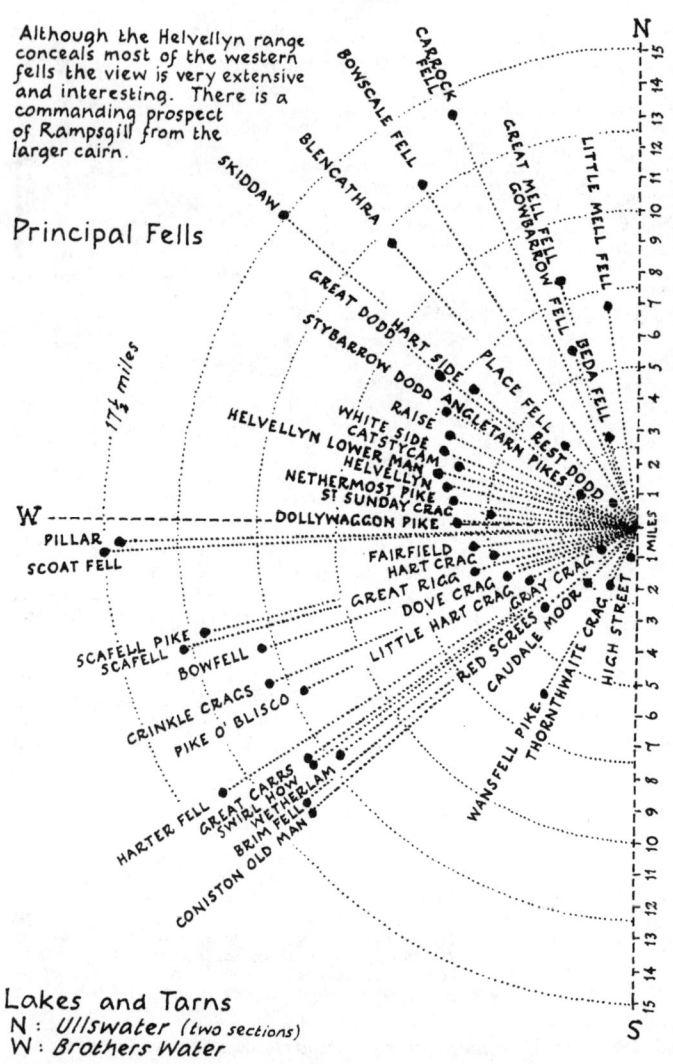

Although the Helvellyn range conceals most of the western fells the view is very extensive and interesting. There is a commanding prospect of Rampsgill from the larger cairn.

Principal Fells

17½ miles

N: Carrock Fell
Bowscale Fell
Blencathra
Skiddaw
Great Mell Fell
Gowbarrow Fell
Little Mell Fell
Beda Fell
Great Dodd
Hart Side
Stybarrow Dodd
Place Fell
Rest Dodd
Raise
Angletarn Pikes
White Side
Catstycam
Helvellyn Lower Man
Helvellyn
Nethermost Pike
St Sunday Crag
Dollywaggon Pike
Pillar
Scoat Fell
Fairfield
Hart Crag
Great Rigg
Dove Crag
Gray Crag
Scafell Pike
Scafell
Bowfell
Little Hart Crag
Red Screes
Caudale Moor
Crinkle Crags
Pike o' Blisco
Wansfell Pike
Thornthwaite Crag
High Street
Harter Fell
Great Carrs
Swirl How
Wetherlam
Brim Fell
Coniston Old Man

Lakes and Tarns
N: *Ullswater* (two sections)
W: *Brothers Water*

Rampsgill Head 10

THE VIEW

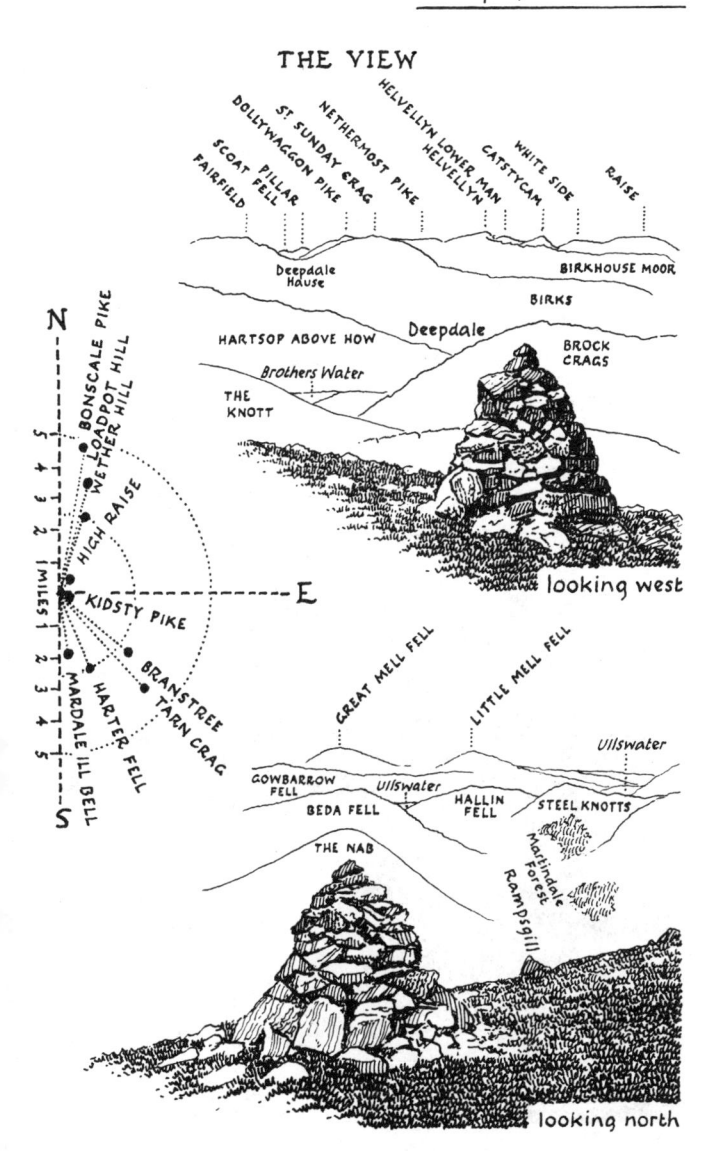

looking west

FAIRFIELD · SCOAT FELL · PILLAR · DOLLYWAGGON PIKE · ST SUNDAY CRAG · NETHERMOST PIKE · HELVELLYN LOWER MAN · HELVELLYN · CATSTYCAM · WHITE SIDE · RAISE

Deepdale Hause — BIRKHOUSE MOOR — BIRKS — Deepdale

HARTSOP ABOVE HOW — Brothers Water — THE KNOTT — BROCK CRAGS

looking north

GREAT MELL FELL · LITTLE MELL FELL · Ullswater
COWBARROW FELL · Ullswater · HALLIN FELL · STEEL KNOTTS
BEDA FELL
THE NAB — Martindale Forest — Rampsgill

N — BONSCALE PIKE · LOADPOT HILL · NETHER HILL · HIGH RAISE · KIDSTY PIKE — E
BRANSTREE · TARN CRAG · HARTER FELL · MARDALE ILL BELL — S

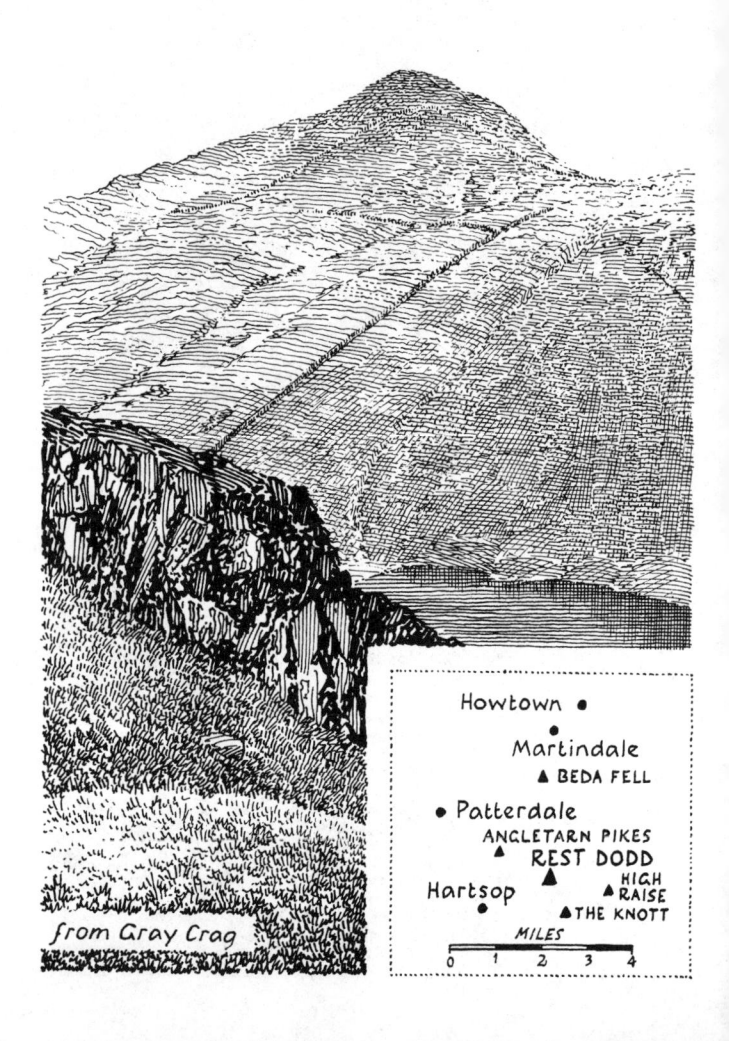

Rest Dodd

2278'

from Gray Crag

- Howtown
  - Martindale
    - ▲ BEDA FELL
- Patterdale
  - ANGLETARN PIKES
  - ▲ REST DODD
- Hartsop   ▲ HIGH RAISE
              ▲ THE KNOTT

MILES
0 1 2 3 4

Rest Dodd 2

NATURAL FEATURES

The steep-sided ridge that divides Martindale into the secluded upper valleys of Bannerdale and Rampsgill rises first to the shapely conical summit of The Nab and then more gradually to the rounded dome of Rest Dodd, which dominates both branches. It is a fell of little interest, although the east flank falls spectacularly in fans of colourful scree. Rest Dodd stands at an angle on the undulating grassy ridge coming down from the main watershed to the shores of Ullswater, and its south-west slope, which drains into Hayeswater Gill, is crossed by the track from Patterdale to High Street. Much of the fell is within the Martindale deer forest.

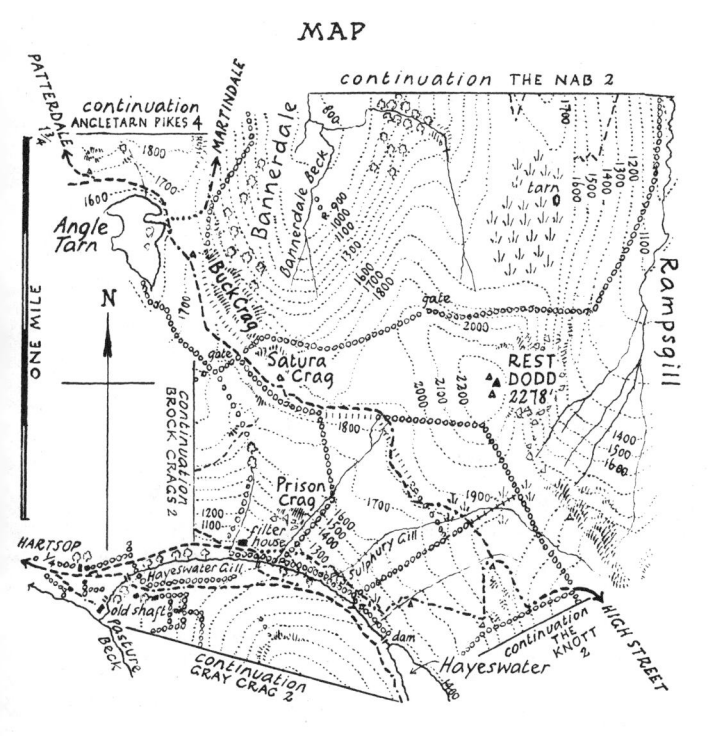

MAP

Rest Dodd 3

ASCENT FROM HARTSOP
1700 feet of ascent : 2 miles

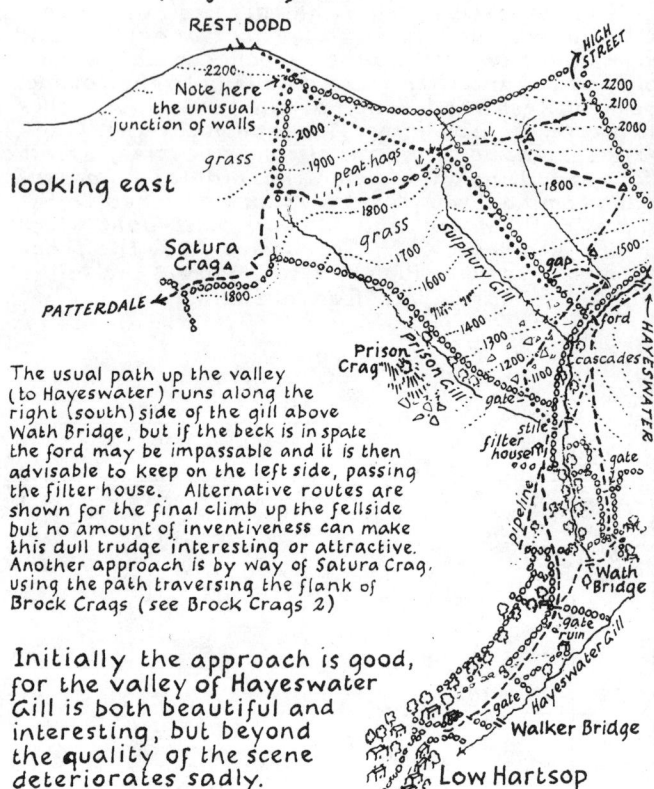

looking east

The usual path up the valley (to Hayeswater) runs along the right (south) side of the gill above Wath Bridge, but if the beck is in spate the ford may be impassable and it is then advisable to keep on the left side, passing the filter house. Alternative routes are shown for the final climb up the fellside but no amount of inventiveness can make this dull trudge interesting or attractive. Another approach is by way of Satura Crag, using the path traversing the flank of Brock Crags (see Brock Crags 2)

Initially the approach is good, for the valley of Hayeswater Gill is both beautiful and interesting, but beyond the quality of the scene deteriorates sadly.

ASCENT FROM PATTERDALE
1900 feet of ascent : 3½ miles

Take the usual route to High Street (*diagrams, Angletarn Pikes 5 and High Street 5*), which traverses the slopes of Rest Dodd, but after crossing the top of Satura Crag, continue by the wall directly ahead, bearing left at the top.

(It is an interesting fact that the Patterdale–High Street route formerly followed this wall up to its top corner and down the south slope of Rest Dodd, an extra 300 feet of climbing which the present more direct path avoids. No traces remain of a path by the wall.)

Rest Dodd 4

THE SUMMIT

A summit-cairn with a flagpole! Such is Rest Dodd's distinction, but not even this brave decoration relieves the drabness of the top of the fell. There are three cairns and a natural obstacle in the shape of an eroded peat-hag on the grassy summit.

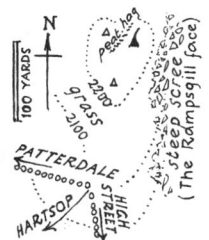

DESCENTS: Go down past the south cairn to the wall corner (or, more properly, the junction of two walls). Follow the wall west, and at its end will be found the path from High Street to Patterdale. Do not attempt any descents into Rampsgill, which is deer forest.

Buck Crag and Heck Crag from Satura Crag

Rest Dodd 5

THE VIEW

The view is neither so pleasing nor so extensive as that from The Knott nearby, although the full length of the Helvellyn range is well seen. The wild and lonely head of Rampsgill is an impressive sight. In the west, Great Gable fits snugly into the deep depression of Deepdale Hause.

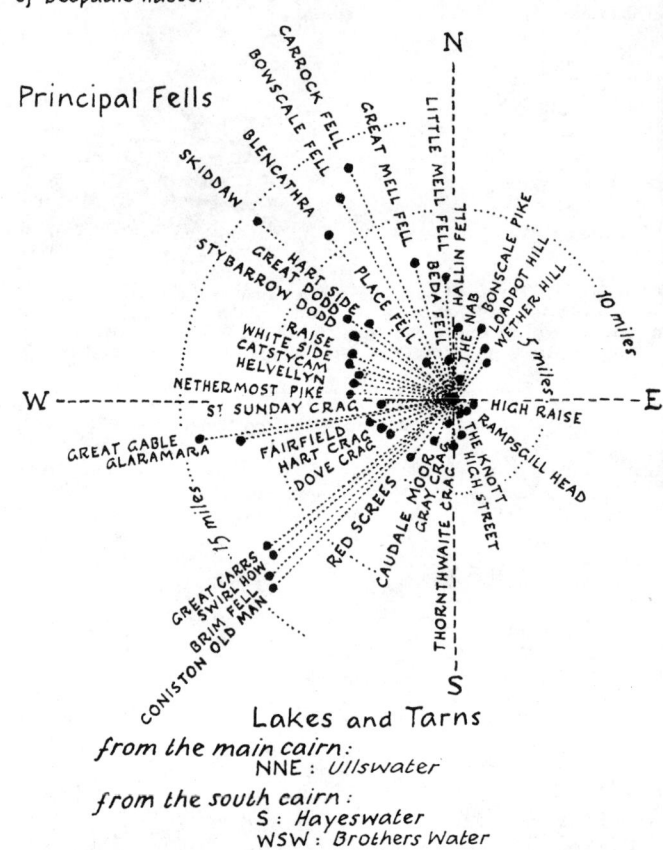

Principal Fells

- CARROCK FELL
- BOWSCALE FELL
- SKIDDAW
- BLENCATHRA
- GREAT MELL FELL
- HART SIDE
- GREAT DODD
- STYBARROW DODD
- LITTLE MELL FELL
- BEDA FELL
- PLACE FELL
- THE HALLIN FELL
- THE NAB
- BONSCALE PIKE
- LOADPOT HILL
- WETHER HILL
- RAISE
- WHITE SIDE
- CATSTYCAM
- HELVELLYN
- NETHERMOST PIKE
- ST SUNDAY CRAG
- HIGH RAISE
- GREAT GABLE
- GLARAMARA
- FAIRFIELD
- HART CRAG
- DOVE CRAG
- RAMPSGILL HEAD
- THE KNOTT
- HIGH STREET
- RED SCREES
- CAUDALE MOOR
- GRAY CRAG
- THORNTHWAITE CRAG
- GREAT CARRS
- SWIRL HOW
- BRIM FELL
- CONISTON OLD MAN

(10 miles, 5 miles, 15 miles)

Lakes and Tarns

from the main cairn:
    NNE: Ullswater

from the south cairn:
    S: Hayeswater
    WSW: Brothers Water

from the west cairn:
    NNE: Ullswater
    WSW: Brothers Water
    WNW: Angle Tarn

Rest Dodd 6

RIDGE ROUTES

To ANGLETARN PIKES, 1857': 1¾ miles: W, then NW
Depression at 1600': 300 feet of ascent

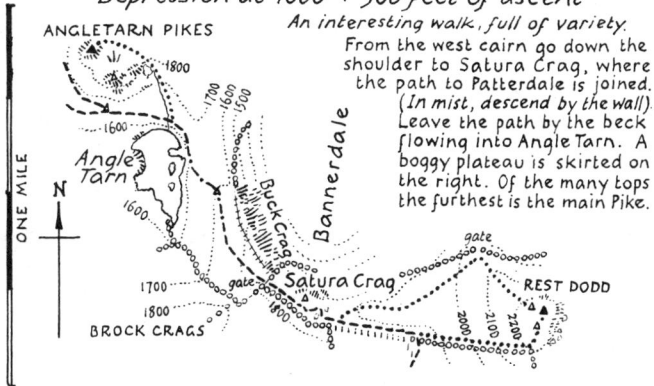

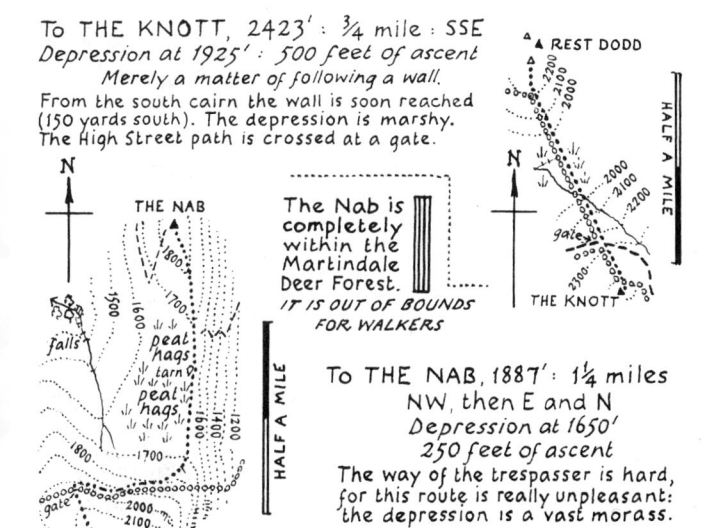

An interesting walk, full of variety.
From the west cairn go down the shoulder to Satura Crag, where the path to Patterdale is joined. *(In mist, descend by the wall).* Leave the path by the beck flowing into Angle Tarn. A boggy plateau is skirted on the right. Of the many tops the furthest is the main Pike.

To THE KNOTT, 2423': ¾ mile: SSE
Depression at 1925': 500 feet of ascent

Merely a matter of following a wall.
From the south cairn the wall is soon reached (150 yards south). The depression is marshy. The High Street path is crossed at a gate.

The Nab is completely within the Martindale Deer Forest.
IT IS OUT OF BOUNDS FOR WALKERS

To THE NAB, 1887': 1¼ miles
NW, then E and N
Depression at 1650'
250 feet of ascent

The way of the trespasser is hard, for this route is really unpleasant: the depression is a vast morass.

These notes and diagram are given only for the sake of completeness of records; no inducement to trespass is intended.

Sallows 1691'

better known locally
as Kentmere Park

from Badger Rock

▲ YOKE

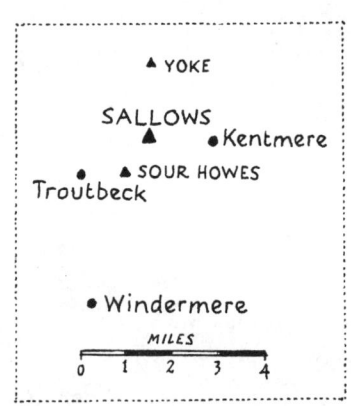

SALLOWS
▲ • Kentmere

• ▲ SOUR HOWES
Troutbeck

• Windermere

MILES
0 1 2 3 4

For most walkers, the fells proper in this region start at Garburn Pass and rise to the north, but there are two hills, twins almost, immediately to the south of the Pass, worth a mention although these are not strictly walkers' territory. The higher of the two is named Sallows (on all maps), bounding the Pass, and has much merit as a viewpoint and a scantier virtue as a grouse sanctuary. It is not worth the detour for anyone bound for Ill Bell and places north, and, in any case, there is not entirely free access to the fell and visitors may be requested to state their business

Sallows 2

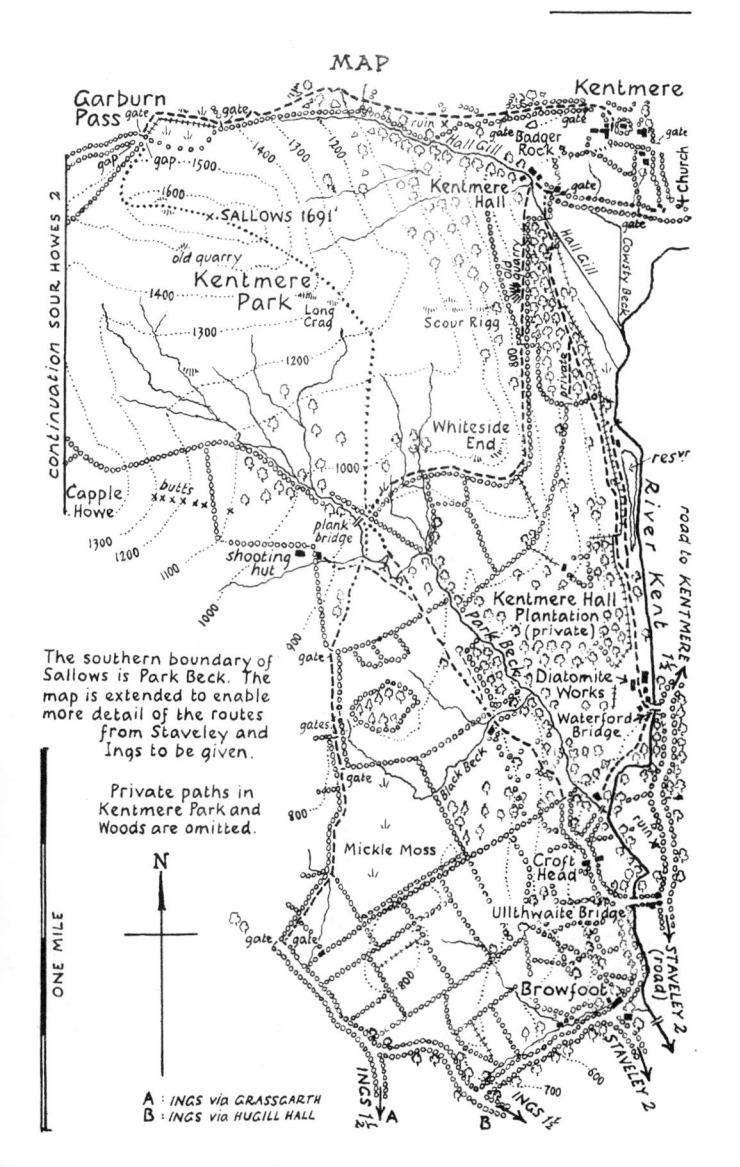

MAP

Sallows 3

ASCENTS

The summit may be most easily and quickly visited from the top of Garburn Pass, where a gateway in the wall (without a gate, but barricaded) gives access to the fell. Alternatively it can be gained by a mile-long ascent from the Ings-Kentmere Hall bridle-path: a simple gradient, but not easy walking.

Sallows is not, as it appears to be, a 'short cut' to Garburn Pass from the south. Apart from doubts as to trespass, its tough heather slopes compel slow progress, and time will be lost. Garburn is best reached by orthodox routes.

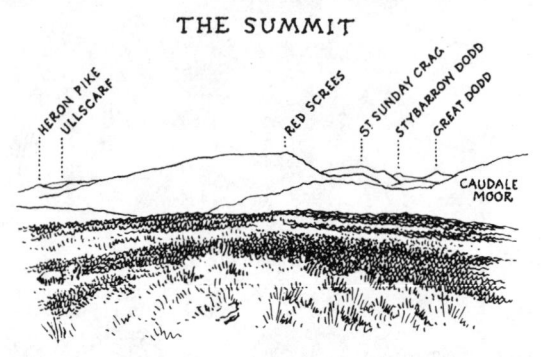

THE SUMMIT

A curious curving mound of shale and grass, thirty feet long and narrow as a parapet, marks the highest part of the fell: it seems to be man-made, but is more probably a natural formation. It has no cairn. Heather and coarse grass cover the top of the fell, but there are small outcrops of rock west of the summit.

The summit mound

Sallows 4

THE VIEW

The Lakeland scene occupies only half the panorama: it is outstandingly good to the west but unattractive northwards where Yoke fills much of the horizon. The rest of the view is exceedingly extensive, varied and interesting, covering a wide area from the Pennines across Morecambe Bay to Black Combe.

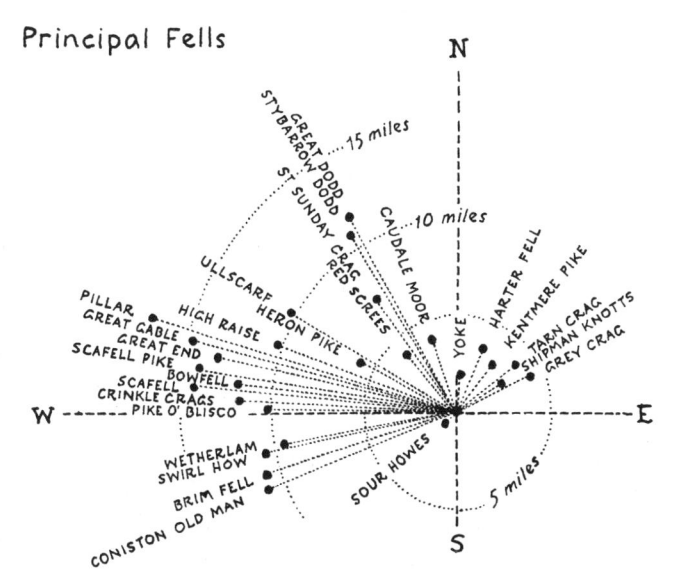

Principal Fells

- GREAT DODD
- STYBARROW DODD
- ST SUNDAY CRAG
- CAUDALE MOOR
- HARTER FELL
- KENTMERE PIKE
- ULLSCARF
- RED SCREES
- YOKE
- TARN CRAG
- HERON PIKE
- SHIPMAN KNOTTS
- GREY CRAG
- PILLAR
- GREAT GABLE
- HIGH RAISE
- GREAT END
- SCAFELL PIKE
- BOWFELL
- SCAFELL
- CRINKLE CRAGS
- PIKE O' BLISCO
- WETHERLAM
- SWIRL HOW
- SOUR HOWES
- BRIM FELL
- CONISTON OLD MAN

15 miles, 10 miles, 5 miles

Lakes and Tarns: SSW: Windermere

Sallows from Ullthwaite Bridge

Selside Pike 2142'

Haweswater Hotel
• Swindale Head
Mardale ▲ SELSIDE PIKE
Head •
▲ BRANSTREE
▲ HARTER FELL

MILES
0 1 2 3 4

from Mosedale Beck near the waterfalls

Selside Pike 2

NATURAL FEATURES

One of the lesser-known fells is Selside Pike on the eastern fringe of the district, commanding the head of the shy and beautiful little valley of Swindale. Its neglect is scarcely merited, for although the summit is a dull grass mound with little reward in views the fell has an extremely rugged eastern face that closes the valley in dramatic fashion : here are dark crags, rarely-visited waterfalls, a curious dry tarn-bed set amongst moraines and, above it, a perfect hanging valley, the two being connected by a very formidable gully.

For countless ages Selside Pike has looked down upon Swindale and seen there a picture of unspoiled charm. Now the engineers have taken over the valley — they may not spoil it, but it is more certain that they can not improve it. Swindale is almost the only remaining Lakeland valley that does not cater for the motorist. Please, Manchester, leave it as nearly as you found it!

Selside Pike from the old corpse-road

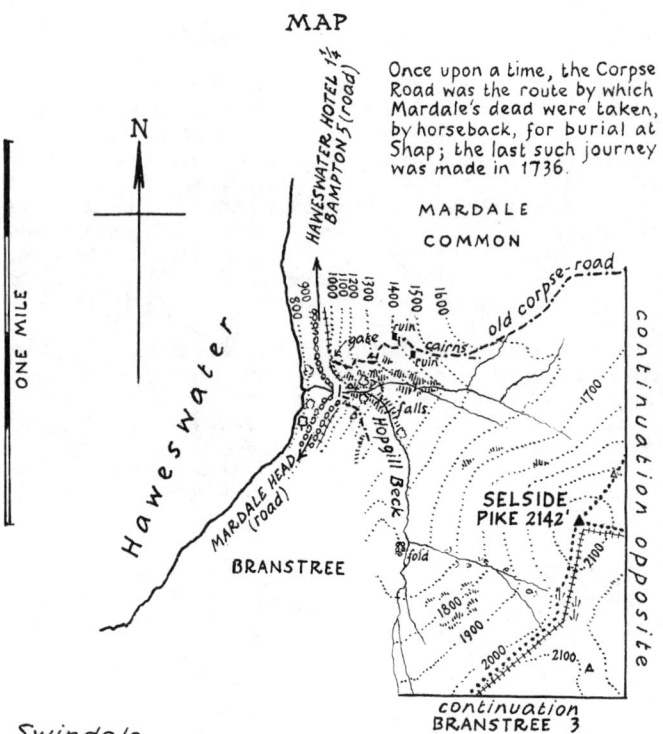

Selside Pike 3

MAP

Once upon a time, the Corpse Road was the route by which Mardale's dead were taken, by horseback, for burial at Shap; the last such journey was made in 1736.

Swindale
with Selside Pike at the head of the valley

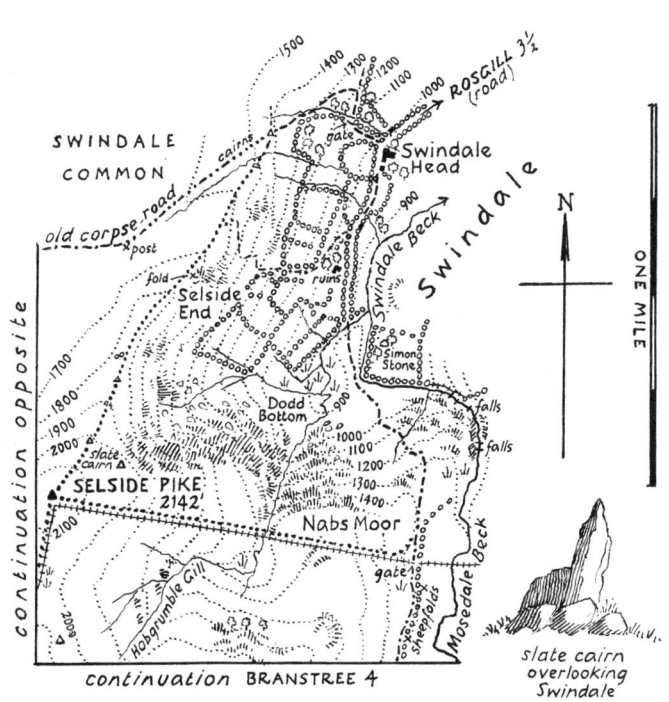

Selside Pike 4

MAP

slate cairn overlooking Swindale

Swindale Head

Selside Pike 5

ASCENT FROM SWINDALE HEAD
1200 feet of ascent : 1½ miles (via the north-east ridge)
1350 feet of ascent : 2¼ miles (via the Mosedale path)

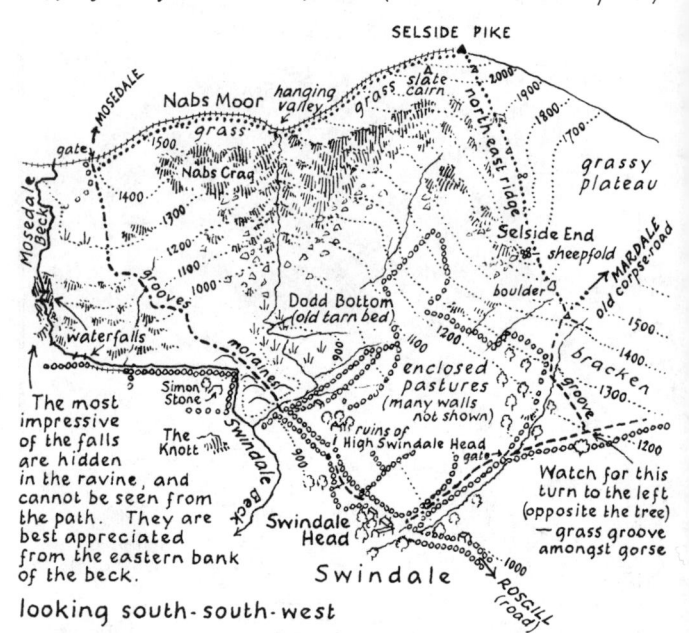

looking south-south-west

The quality of the scenery deteriorates when the tedious higher slopes are reached. If returning to Swindale, ascend by the ridge and descend by the wire fence, making a detour to see the waterfalls.

THE SUMMIT

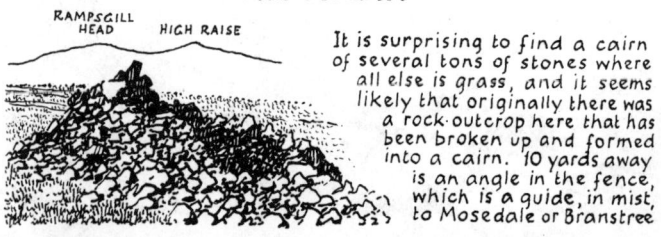

It is surprising to find a cairn of several tons of stones where all else is grass, and it seems likely that originally there was a rock outcrop here that has been broken up and formed into a cairn. 10 yards away is an angle in the fence, which is a guide, in mist, to Mosedale or Branstree

Selside Pike 6

THE VIEW

The view towards Lakeland is disappointing, being confined to the surroundings of Mardale except for a glimpse of distant fells over the Straits of Riggindale.
Eastwards, however, there is a splendid prospect of the Pennines, with Shap village prominent.

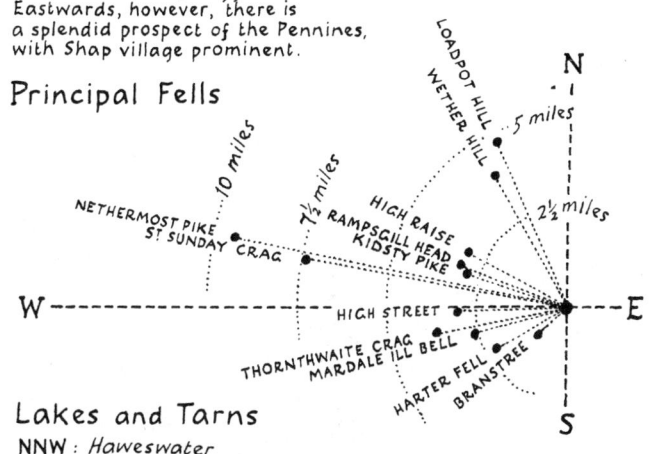

Principal Fells

Lakes and Tarns

NNW: *Haweswater*
Small Water and *Blea Water* can both be seen by walking 30 yards W in the direction of High Street.
And if *Swindale Reservoir* materialises, there will be an excellent full-length view of it from the slate cairn NE.

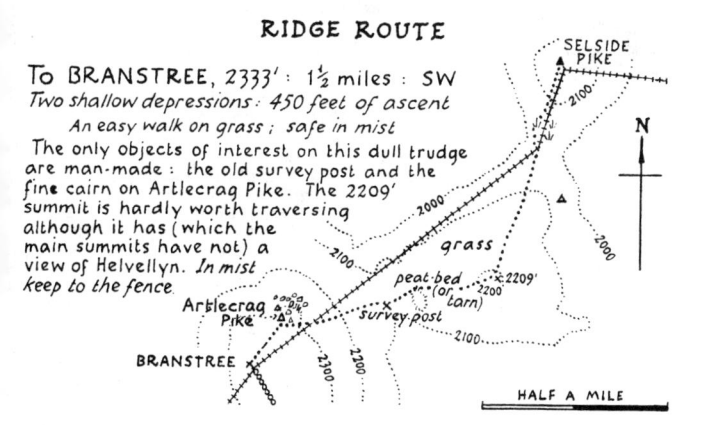

RIDGE ROUTE

To BRANSTREE, 2333′ : 1½ miles : SW
Two shallow depressions : 450 feet of ascent
  An easy walk on grass ; safe in mist
The only objects of interest on this dull trudge are man-made : the old survey post and the fine cairn on Artlecrag Pike. The 2209′ summit is hardly worth traversing although it has (which the main summits have not) a view of Helvellyn. *In mist keep to the fence.*

Shipman Knotts 1926'

from Stockdale

▲ HARTER FELL
KENTMERE　TARN
▲ PIKE　▲ CRAG
ILL BELL ▲　　　　　GREY
SHIPMAN KNOTTS ▲　CRAG

• Kentmere

Longsleddale •

0　1　2　3　4

Shipman Knotts is of moderate altitude and would have called for no more than the brief comment that it is a shoulder of Kentmere Pike had it not earned for itself a separate chapter by reason of the characteristic roughnesses of its surface. Rocky outcrops are everywhere on the steep slopes, persisting even in the woods of Sadgill, although these seldom attain the magnitude of crags. This fell is usually climbed on the way to Harter Fell from the south, and its rock should be welcomed for there is precious little beyond. The south slope carries the path from Kentmere to Longsleddale

Shipman Knotts 2

MAP

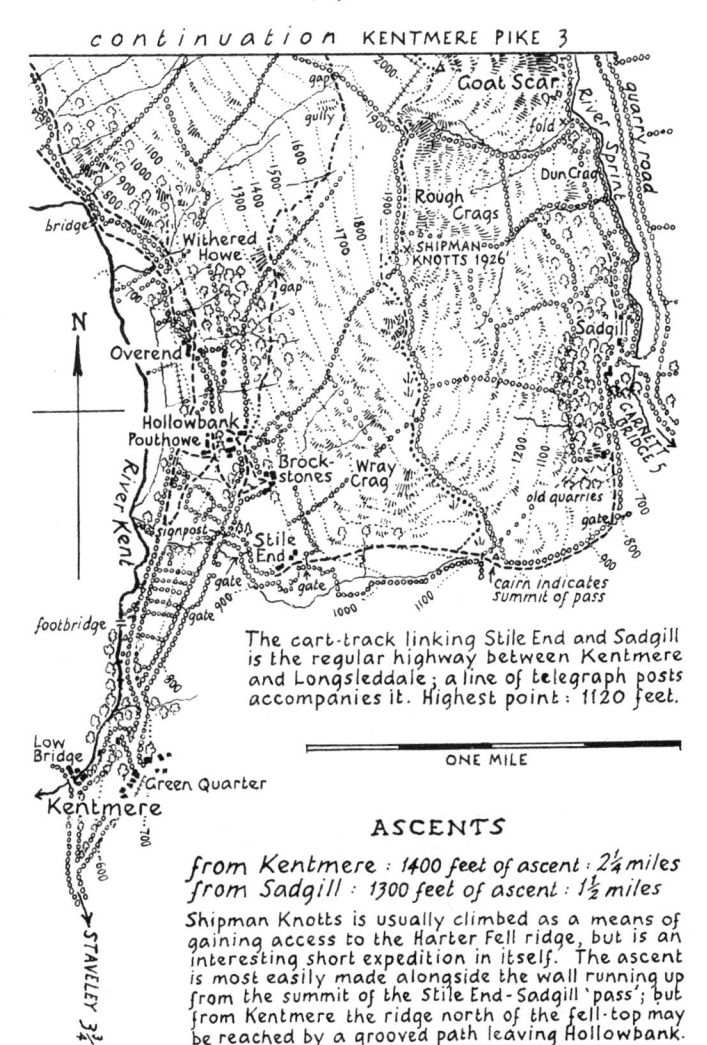

continuation KENTMERE PIKE 3

ASCENTS

from Kentmere : 1400 feet of ascent : 2¼ miles
from Sadgill : 1300 feet of ascent : 1½ miles

Shipman Knotts is usually climbed as a means of gaining access to the Harter Fell ridge, but is an interesting short expedition in itself. The ascent is most easily made alongside the wall running up from the summit of the Stile End–Sadgill 'pass'; but from Kentmere the ridge north of the fell-top may be reached by a grooved path leaving Hollowbank. *Safe in mist if the wall route is followed.*

Shipman Knotts 3

The summit from the south

THE SUMMIT

KENTMERE PIKE

Three rocky knolls, on the east side of the wall, form the summit, and of these the middle one is highest. It is without a cairn.

DESCENTS: Cross the wall and follow it south to the pass, where turn left for Longsleddale, right for Kentmere. In mist, this is a safe route

The summit-ridge from Goat Scar

Shipman Knotts 4

THE VIEW

The northern half of the panorama is restricted to nearby heights of greater elevation; the southern is open, extensive and pleasing. There is a good view of Longsleddale.

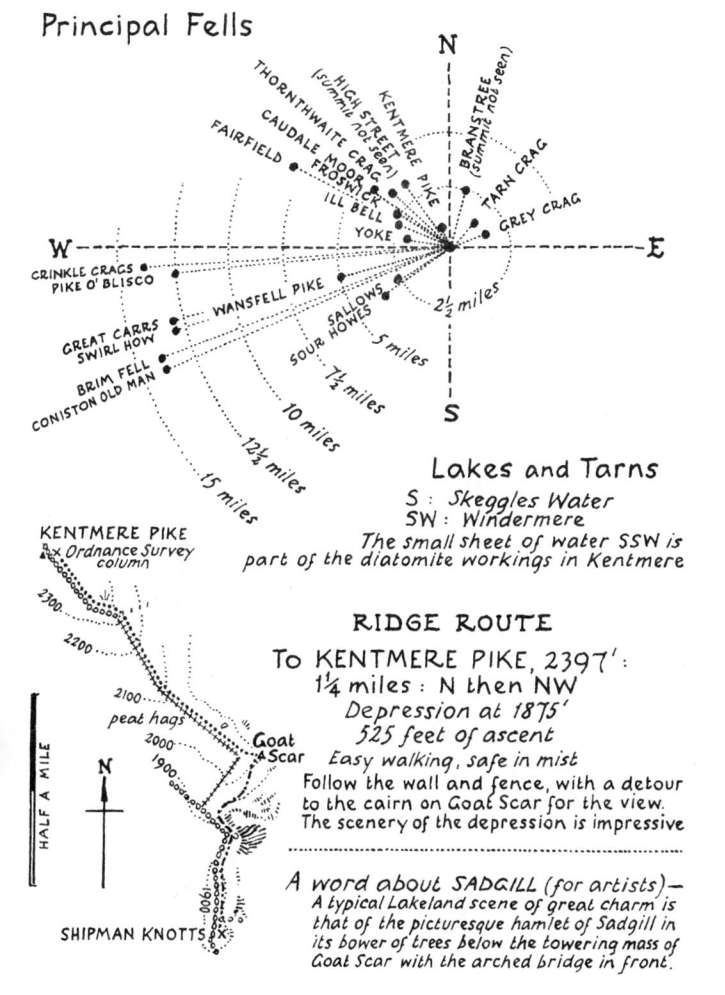

Principal Fells

Lakes and Tarns

S: Skeggles Water
SW: Windermere
The small sheet of water SSW is part of the diatomite workings in Kentmere

RIDGE ROUTE

TO KENTMERE PIKE, 2397':
1¼ miles : N then NW
Depression at 1875'
525 feet of ascent
Easy walking, safe in mist
Follow the wall and fence, with a detour to the cairn on Goat Scar for the view. The scenery of the depression is impressive

---

A word about SADGILL (for artists) —
A typical Lakeland scene of great charm is that of the picturesque hamlet of Sadgill in its bower of trees below the towering mass of Goat Scar with the arched bridge in front.

Sour Howes

1568'

better known locally as
Applethwaite Common

from Troutbeck

Although all maps agree that the summit of this fell is named Sour Howes, its broadest flank, carrying the Garburn Pass Road down to Troutbeck, is far better known as Applethwaite Common; this flank is traversed also by the pleasant Dubbs Road. There is little about the fell to attract walkers, and nothing to justify a detour from the main Ill Bell ridge to the north, for although the views are really good they are better from the main ridge. There is heather on the eastern slopes, and therefore, inevitably, grouse; and therefore, inevitably, shooting butts: one may admire the construction of these butts while deploring their purpose.

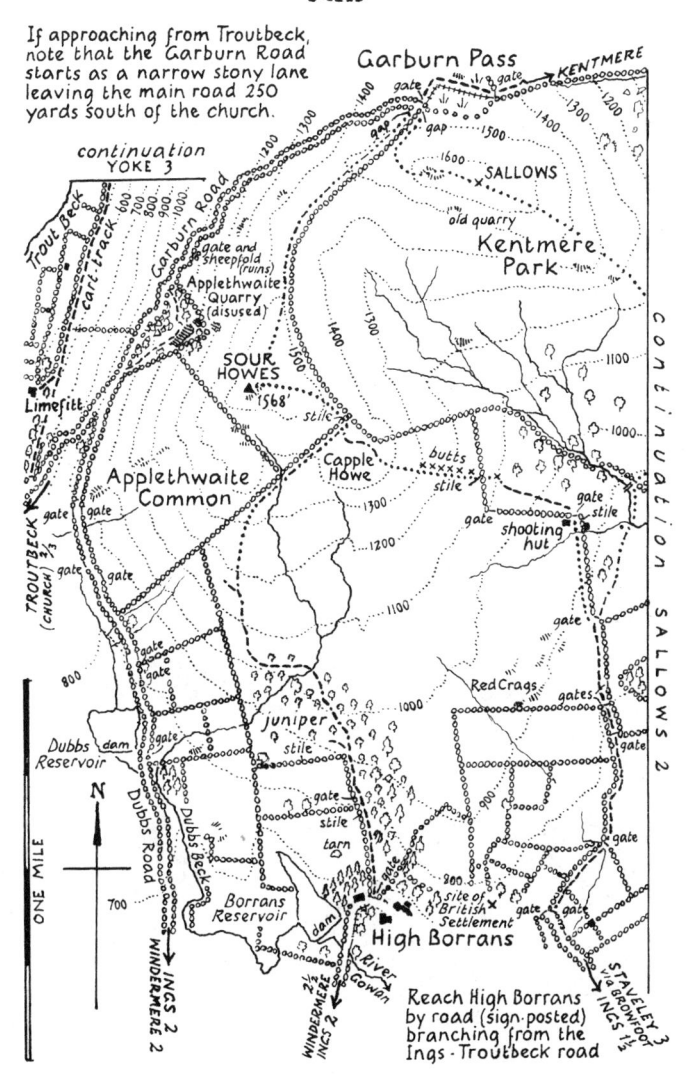

Sour Howes 2

Sour Howes 3

ASCENTS

Sour Howes is a fell with no obvious appeal to walkers, and few other than conscientious guide-book writers will visit its summit; nevertheless it makes a pleasant walk from Windermere, Ings or Staveley, especially on a clear day for the views are good.

Two lanes leave Ings (one via Grassgarth and one via Hugill Hall) and another leaves Browfoot (two miles up the Kentmere valley from Staveley): these join, and at the terminus the old bridle-path to Kentmere Hall may be followed for a mile, when it may be forsaken and a way made to the top by the shooting-butts, using the stiles to cross the walls.

An enchanting path leaves High Borrans, climbing first through juniper bushes, then bracken, then heather; when it peters out keep to the route shown on the map.

The summit is easily visited from the top of Garburn Pass: here a gap in the wall (a gateway without a gate) gives access to the enclosure containing the highest point.

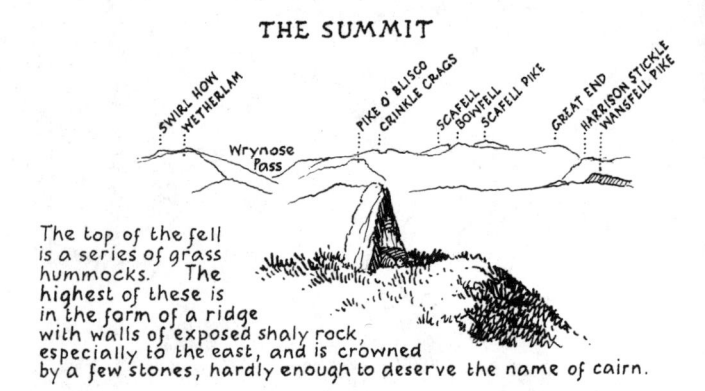

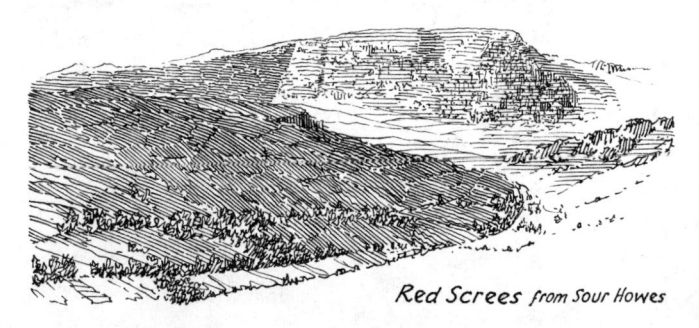

THE SUMMIT

The top of the fell is a series of grass hummocks. The highest of these is in the form of a ridge with walls of exposed shaly rock, especially to the east, and is crowned by a few stones, hardly enough to deserve the name of cairn.

Red Screes from Sour Howes

Sour Howes 4

THE VIEW

The crowded skyline in the west arrests the attention, with the vertical profile of Scafell above Mickledore prominent in the scene. Langdale Pikes are well seen between and below Great End and Great Gable. There is a very extensive and beautiful prospect southwards from the far Pennines round to Morecambe Bay and Black Combe.

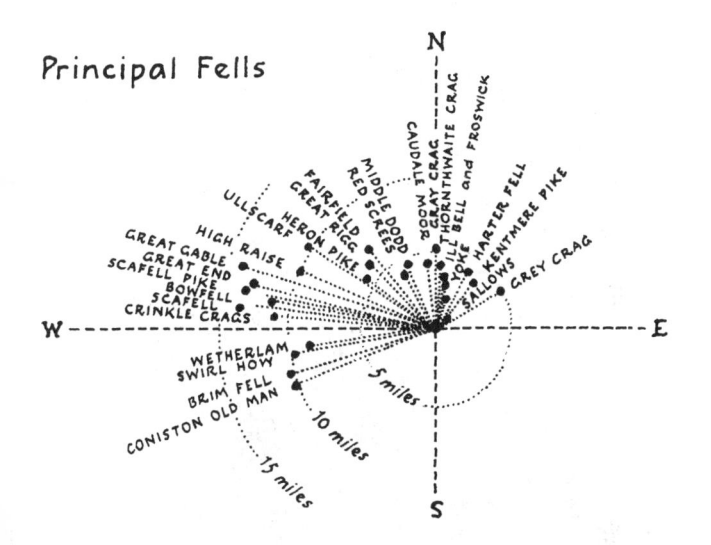

Principal Fells

N

CAUDALE
MIDDLE DODD
RED SCREES
GREAT RIGG
FAIRFIELD
HERON PIKE
ULLSCARF
HIGH RAISE
GREAT GABLE
GREAT END
SCAFELL PIKE
BOWFELL
SCAFELL
CRINKLE CRAGS
COW CRAG
ILL BELL and FROSWICK
THORNTHWAITE CRAG
YOKE
HARTER FELL
KENTMERE PIKE
SALLOWS
GREY CRAG

W — — — — — — — — — — — — — — — — — E

WETHERLAM
SWIRL HOW
BRIM FELL
CONISTON OLD MAN

5 miles
10 miles
15 miles

S

Lakes and Tarns
S: *Borrans Reservoir*
SSW: *Windermere*

Most old and disused quarries are gloomy and repellant places but Applethwaite Quarry, near the Garburn Road, is relieved from desolation by a planting of conifers and a magnificent view. An interesting feature is the old weighbridge, now overgrown. A favourite with foxes, this quarry!

Applethwaite Quarry

Steel Knotts

summit named Pikeawassa

1414'

from Howe Grain Beck

Wether Hill's western flank swells into a bulge, Gowk Hill, which itself sends out a crooked bony arm northwards to form a lofty independent ridge running parallel to the main range and enclosing with it the short hidden valley of Fusedale. On the crest of this ridge, rock is never far from the surface and it breaks through in several places, notably at the highest point, which is a craggy tor that would worthily embellish the summit of many a higher fell. This freakish gnarled ridge is Steel Knotts; the summit-tor is named, on the best of authority, (but not by many, one imagines) Pikeawassa. (O.S. 1" and 2½" maps)

Howtown
● STEEL KNOTTS
▲ ▲ LOADPOT HILL
▲ WETHER HILL

MILES
0   1   2   3

Steel Knotts 2

MAP

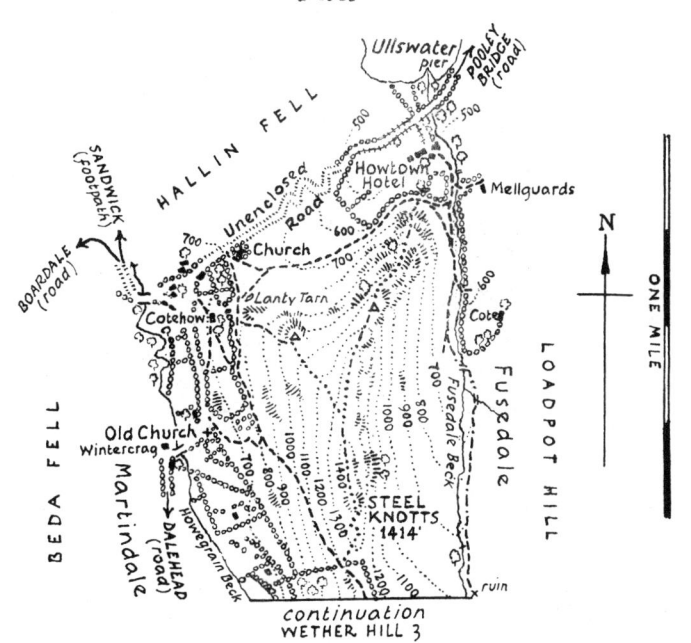

ASCENTS

FROM HOWTOWN: The natural route of ascent is by the craggy ridge above Howtown. This has an intimidating aspect but it is without perils and gives an exhilarating scramble. Leave the path at its base by a concrete waterworks notice inscribed thus: 8/AV/5 and climb upwards between the rocks; initially there is a track obscured by bracken. A cairn surmounts the steepest part of the ridge and the walking is then easy to the top of the fell.

FROM LANTY TARN: A pronounced shoulder, with two tiers of crag, descends north-west to Lanty Tarn and offers a less satisfactory route. From the tarn (a shallow pond) climb to the right (south) of the crags to a cairn above them. An easy slope then follows.

FROM MARTINDALE OLD CHURCH: This is the easiest way. Climb the fellside by the church to a good path slanting upwards (this is the Martindale path to the High Street range). Leave the path at a wall and turn up left to the ridge and again left to the top.

Although Steel Knotts is of small extent and modest elevation, it should not be climbed in mist. If caught by mist on the top, descend south to the wall and return by the path to Martindale Old Church.

Steel Knotts 3

THE SUMMIT

Steel Knotts may well claim to have the sharpest summit in Lakeland, for the rock tor (Pikeawassa) that crowns the top is so acute that only very agile walkers will be able to stand upon it, although, it will be noted, it is a popular perch for birds. There is no cairn.

RIDGE ROUTE

TO WETHER HILL, 2210'
1½ miles : S, then SSE, SE and NNE
Depression at 1200' ÷ 1100 feet of ascent
An easy walk, followed by a dull climb

Follow the ridge south, joining a fair track to a ruined hut at the foot of the final slope, which may be tackled anywhere although it is preferable to use one of the grooves. This walk is safe in mist.

Incidentally, this is the best way onto the High Street range from Martindale or Howtown, whether or not the summits of Steel Knotts and Wether Hill are visited. (The Keasgill groove is the usual one)

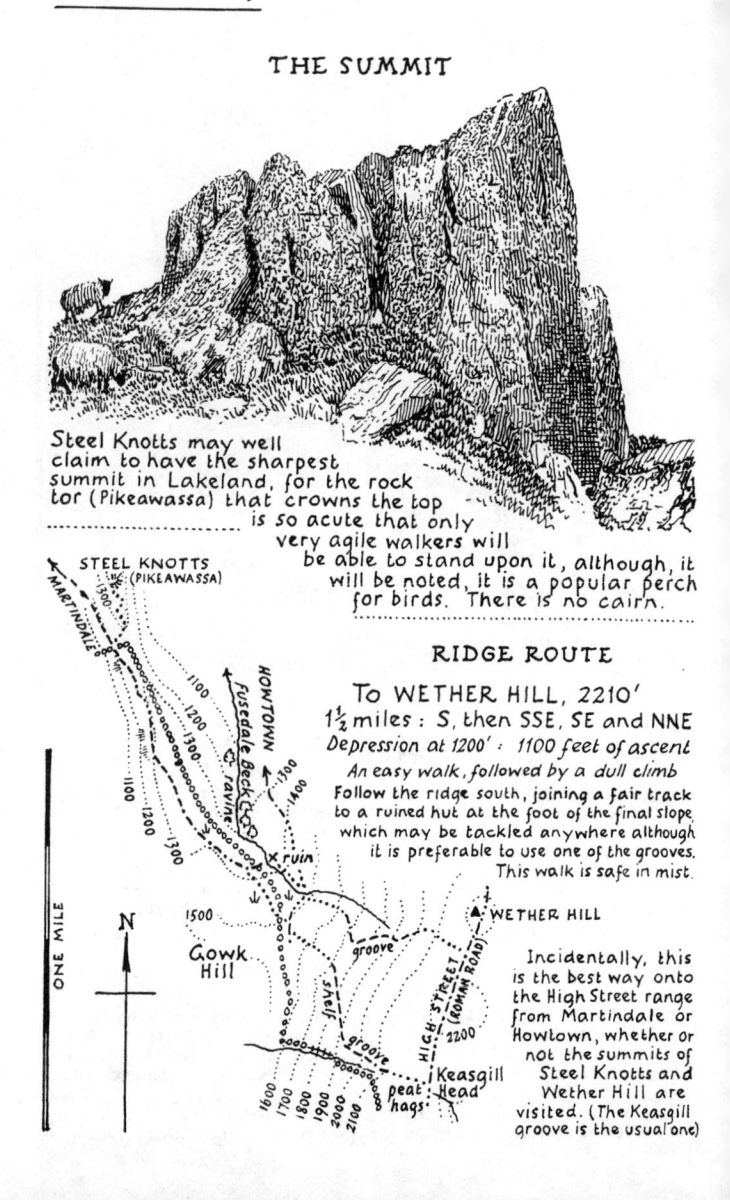

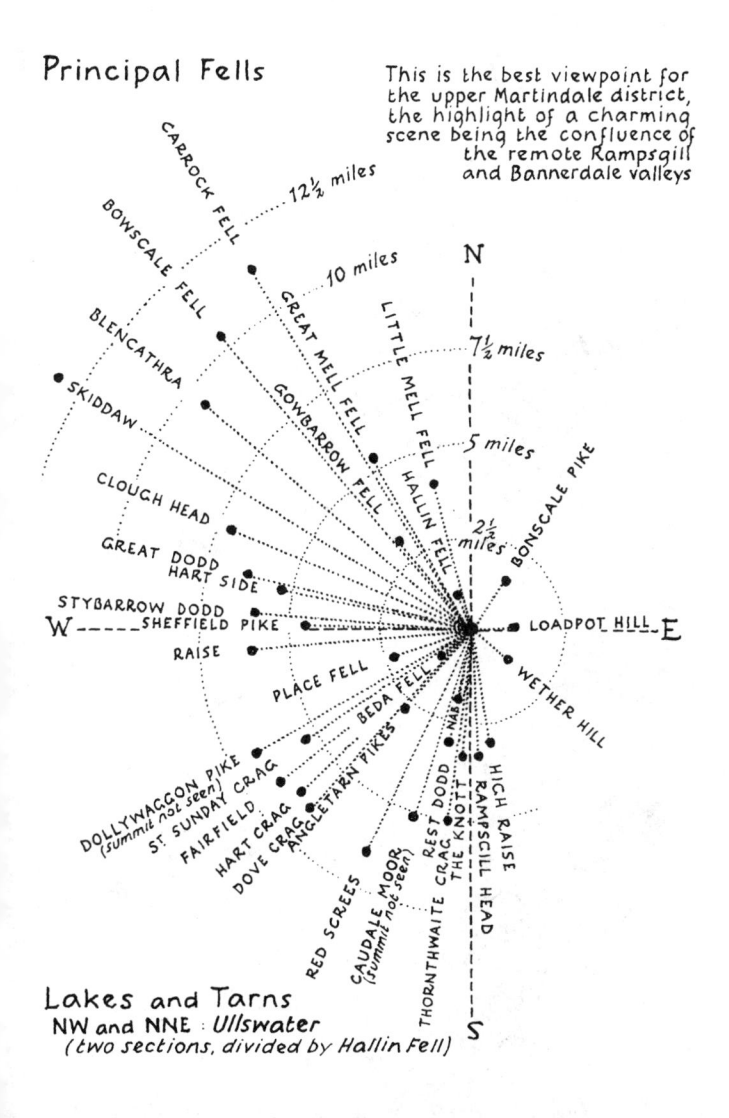

Steel Knotts 4

THE VIEW

Principal Fells

This is the best viewpoint for the upper Martindale district, the highlight of a charming scene being the confluence of the remote Rampsgill and Bannerdale valleys

CARROCK FELL — 12½ miles
BOWSCALE FELL
BLENCATHRA
SKIDDAW
GREAT MELL FELL — 10 miles
LITTLE MELL FELL — 7½ miles
GOWBARROW FELL
HALLIN FELL — 5 miles
CLOUGH HEAD
BONSCALE PIKE — 2½ miles
GREAT DODD
HART SIDE
STYBARROW DODD
SHEFFIELD PIKE
W ———— LOADPOT HILL ———— E
RAISE
PLACE FELL
BEDA FELL
WETHER HILL
DOLLYWAGGON PIKE (summit not seen)
ST. SUNDAY CRAG
FAIRFIELD
HART CRAG
DOVE CRAG
ANGLETARN PIKES
NAB
HIGH RAISE
REST DODD
RAMPSGILL HEAD
THE KNOTT
RED SCREES
CAUDALE MOOR (summit not seen)
THORNTHWAITE CRAG

N / S

Lakes and Tarns
NW and NNE: *Ullswater*
(two sections, divided by Hallin Fell)

Tarn Crag 2176'

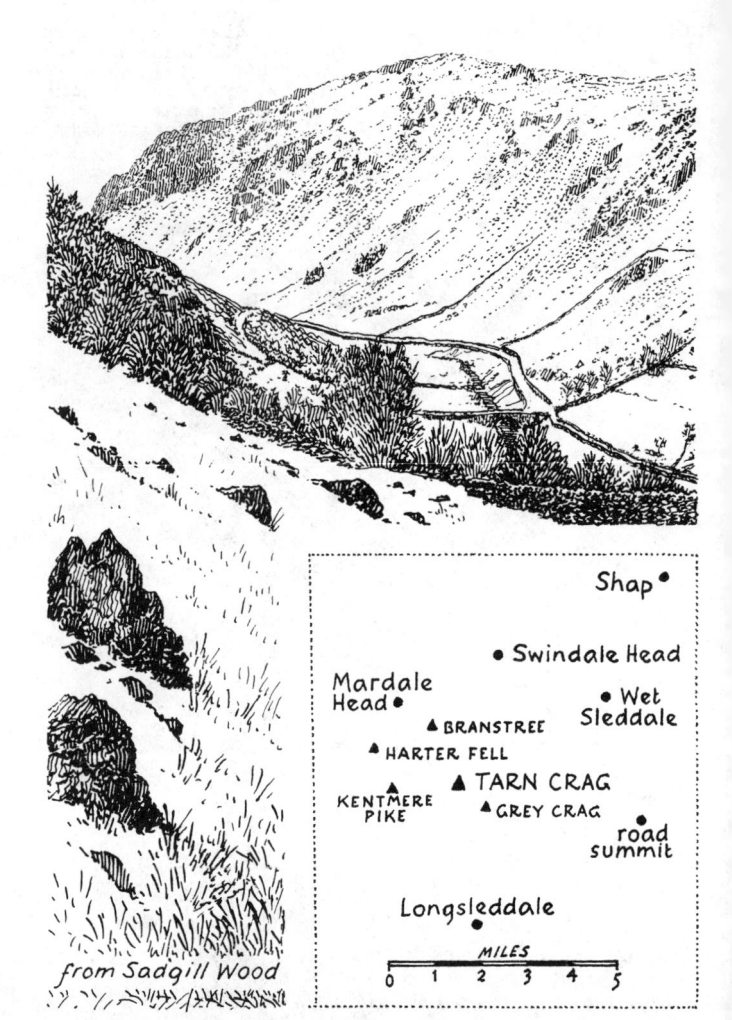

from Sadgill Wood

Shap •

• Swindale Head

Mardale Head •

• Wet Sleddale

▲ BRANSTREE

▲ HARTER FELL

▲ TARN CRAG

▲ KENTMERE PIKE

▲ GREY CRAG

• road summit

Longsleddale

MILES
0 1 2 3 4 5

Tarn Crag 2

NATURAL FEATURES

The gradually rising wall of fells bounding Longsleddale on the east reaches its greatest elevation, and its terminus, in Tarn Crag. To the valley this fell presents a bold front, with Buckbarrow Crag a conspicuous object, but on other sides it is uninteresting, especially eastwards where easy slopes merge into the desolate plateaux of Shap Fells. It is enclosed on the north by the wide, shallow depression of Mosedale, a natural pass linking Longsleddale with Swindale in wild and lonely surroundings: here a solitary shepherd's cottage merely accentuates the utter dreariness of the scene. (Yet on rare occasions of soft evening light even Mosedale can look inexpressibly beautiful!). The walker hereabouts will be in no doubt, without reference to his map, that he has passed outside the verge of Lakeland.

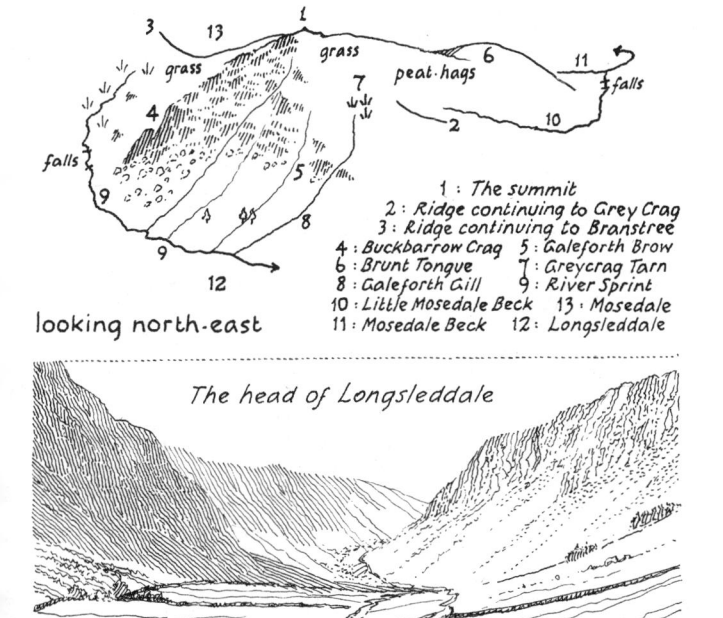

looking north-east

1 : The summit
2 : Ridge continuing to Grey Crag
3 : Ridge continuing to Branstree
4 : Buckbarrow Crag
5 : Galeforth Brow
6 : Brunt Tongue
7 : Greycrag Tarn
8 : Galeforth Gill
9 : River Sprint
10 : Little Mosedale Beck
11 : Mosedale Beck
12 : Longsleddale
13 : Mosedale

The head of Longsleddale

Tarn Crag 3

MAP

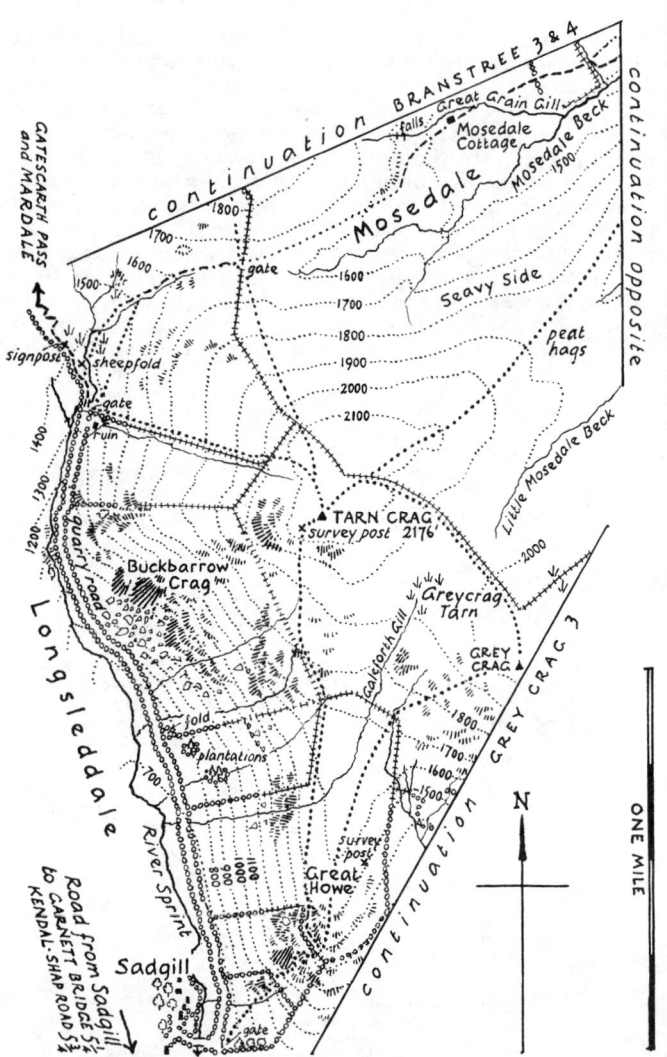

Tarn Crag 4

MAP

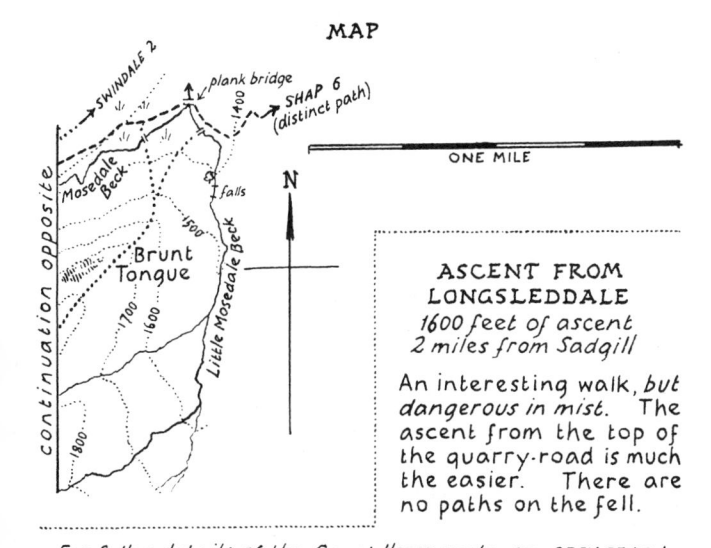

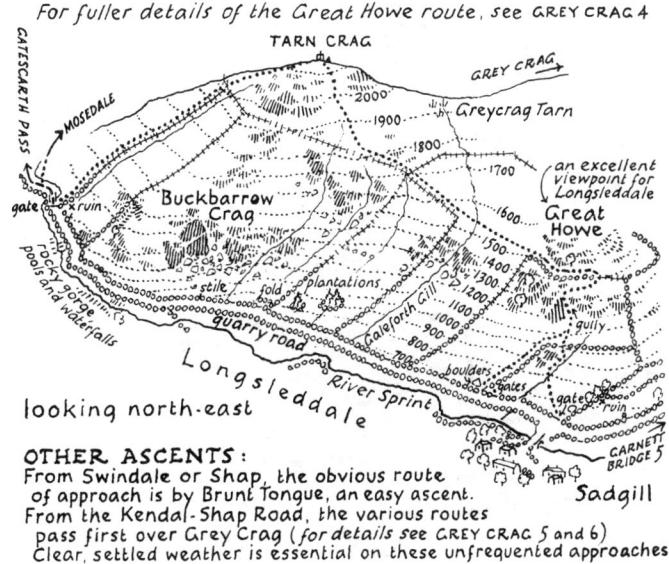

continuation opposite

SWINDALE 2
plank bridge
SHAP 6 (distinct path)
Mosedale Beck
falls
Brunt Tongue
Little Mosedale Beck

ONE MILE

ASCENT FROM LONGSLEDDALE
1600 feet of ascent
2 miles from Sadgill

An interesting walk, but dangerous in mist. The ascent from the top of the quarry-road is much the easier. There are no paths on the fell.

For fuller details of the Great Howe route, see GREY CRAG 4

TARN CRAG
GREY CRAG
MOSEDALE
Greycrag Tarn
GATESCARTH PASS
gate — ruin
Buckbarrow Crag
stile — fold — plantations
quarry road
rocky gorge pools and waterfalls
Galeforth Gill
boulders
gates
gully
gate — ruin
an excellent viewpoint for Longsleddale
Great Howe
River Sprint
Longsleddale
looking north-east
Sadgill
CARNETT BRIDGE 5

OTHER ASCENTS:
From Swindale or Shap, the obvious route of approach is by Brunt Tongue, an easy ascent.
From the Kendal-Shap Road, the various routes pass first over Grey Crag (for details see GREY CRAG 5 and 6)
Clear, settled weather is essential on these unfrequented approaches

Tarn Crag 5

THE SUMMIT

Not until Manchester Corporation's engineers climbed Tarn Crag, in the course of their duty, and departed from it for the last time, did its summit acquire distinction: the wide dreary top then found itself left with a curious structure — a high wooden platform with a core of stone and concrete, which served for a time as a survey post during the construction of the Longsleddale tunnel conveying the Haweswater Aqueduct south. Now, thirty years later, the aqueduct is in place and the scars are gone from the valley — but the hoary survey post still stands, defying the weather and puzzling the few travellers who come this way and find no clue as to its purpose.

The highest part of the fell, marked by a small undistinguished cairn, is a hundred yards away, to the east.

DESCENTS: The routes of ascent should be used for descent.
In mist, keep strictly to the fences. Crags obstruct the direct way down into Longsleddale. Eastwards, Shap Fells are a wilderness to avoid in bad weather.

Tarn Crag 6

THE VIEW

Anyone who climbs Tarn Crag for a view of Lakeland will be very disappointed, for, excepting the Coniston fells, nothing is to be seen of the distant west because of the adjacent heights across the deep trench of Longsleddale. On a clear day there is ample recompense, however, in the excellent panorama from east round to south — where, for a hundred miles, the noble skyline of the Pennines and the wide seascape of Morecambe Bay present themselves to view without obstruction.

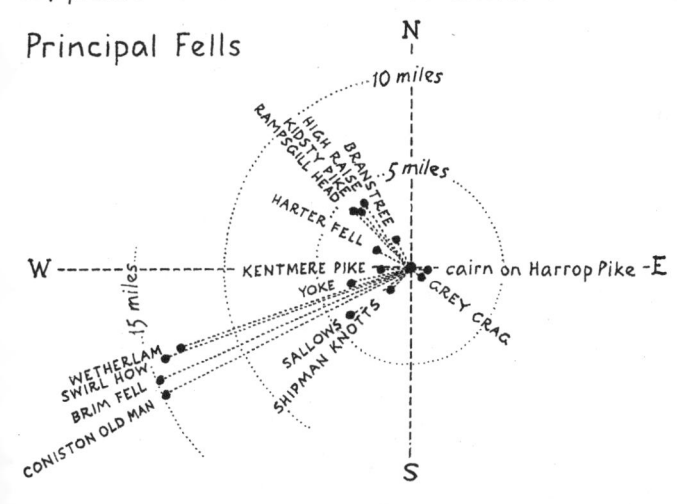

Principal Fells

- N
- 10 miles
- 5 miles
- HIGH RAISE
- KIDSTY PIKE
- BRANSTREE
- RAMPSGILL HEAD
- HARTER FELL
- KENTMERE PIKE
- cairn on Harrop Pike — E
- YOKE
- GREY CRAG
- SALLOWS
- SHIPMAN KNOTTS
- W
- 15 miles
- WETHERLAM
- SWIRL HOW
- BRIM FELL
- CONISTON OLD MAN
- S

Lakes and Tarns: SW: Windermere

Kentmere Pike across Longsleddale

Tarn Crag 7

RIDGE ROUTES

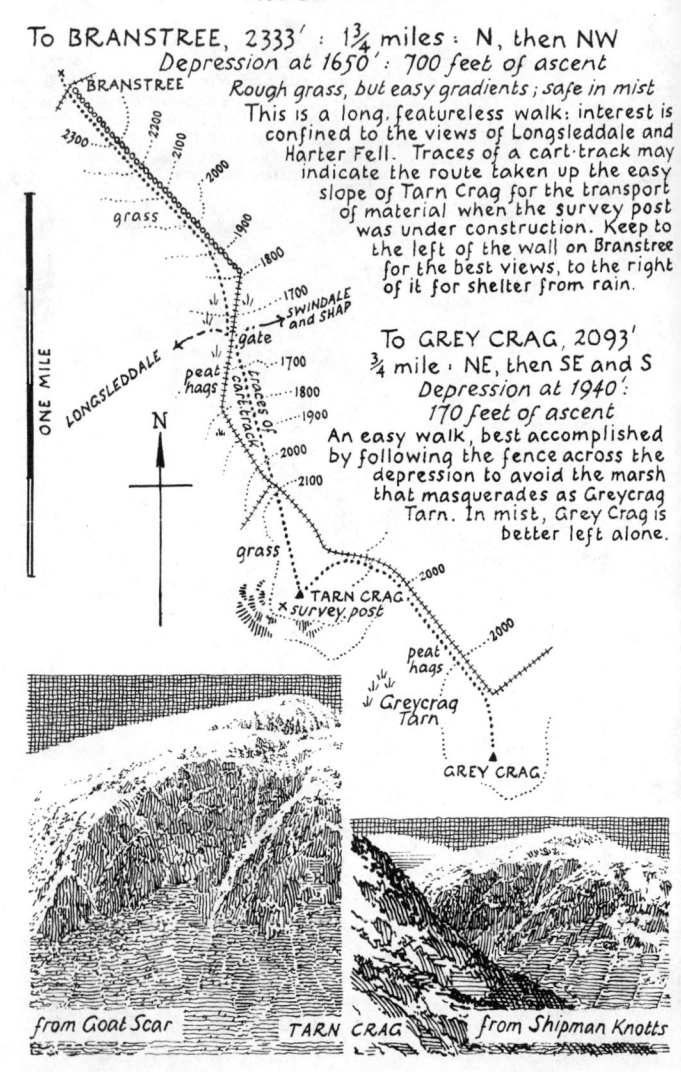

To BRANSTREE, 2333′ : 1¾ miles : N, then NW
Depression at 1650′ : 700 feet of ascent
Rough grass, but easy gradients; safe in mist

This is a long, featureless walk: interest is confined to the views of Longsleddale and Harter Fell. Traces of a cart-track may indicate the route taken up the easy slope of Tarn Crag for the transport of material when the survey post was under construction. Keep to the left of the wall on Branstree for the best views, to the right of it for shelter from rain.

To GREY CRAG, 2093′
¾ mile : NE, then SE and S
Depression at 1940′ : 170 feet of ascent

An easy walk, best accomplished by following the fence across the depression to avoid the marsh that masquerades as Greycrag Tarn. In mist, Grey Crag is better left alone.

from Goat Scar   TARN CRAG   *from Shipman Knotts*

Tarn Crag 8

Buckbarrow Crag

Thornthwaite Crag 2569'

from Caudale Moor

Thornthwaite Crag 2

NATURAL FEATURES

Occupying a commanding position overlooking four valleys, Thornthwaite Crag is one of the better-known fells east of Kirkstone, owing not a little of its fame to its tall pillar of stones, a landmark for miles around. Its name derives from the long shattered cliff facing west above the upper Troutbeck valley; there are also crags fringing the head of Hayeswater Gill and above the early meanderings of the River Kent. Apart from these roughnesses the fell is grassy, the ground to the east of the summit forming a wide plateau before rising gently to the parent height of High Street, of which Thornthwaite Crag is a subsidiary; it has, however, a ridge in its own right, this being a narrow steep-sided shoulder that ends in Gray Crag, northwards. Streams flow in three directions: north to Ullswater, south to Windermere and south-east along the Kentmere valley.

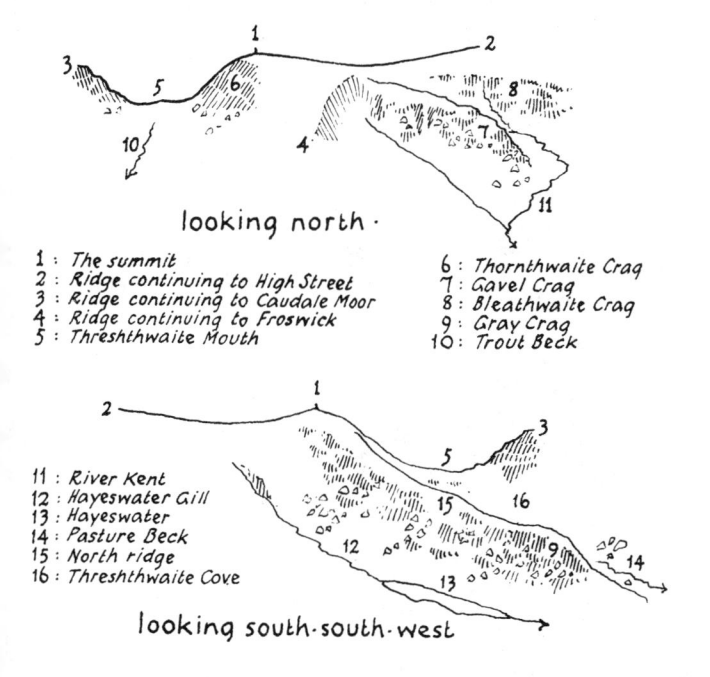

looking north

1 : The summit
2 : Ridge continuing to High Street
3 : Ridge continuing to Caudale Moor
4 : Ridge continuing to Froswick
5 : Threshthwaite Mouth
6 : Thornthwaite Crag
7 : Gavel Crag
8 : Bleathwaite Crag
9 : Gray Crag
10 : Trout Beck

11 : River Kent
12 : Hayeswater Gill
13 : Hayeswater
14 : Pasture Beck
15 : North ridge
16 : Threshthwaite Cove

looking south-south-west

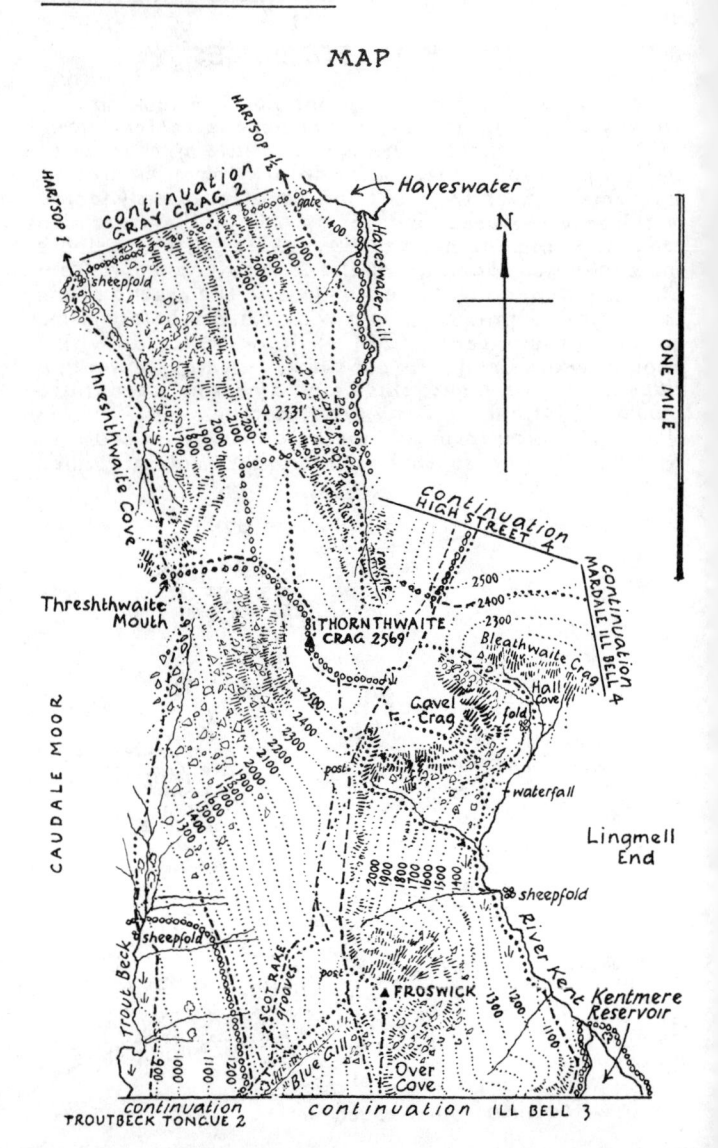

Thornthwaite Crag 3

MAP

Thornthwaite Crag 4

ASCENT FROM HARTSOP
2000 feet of ascent : 3¼ miles

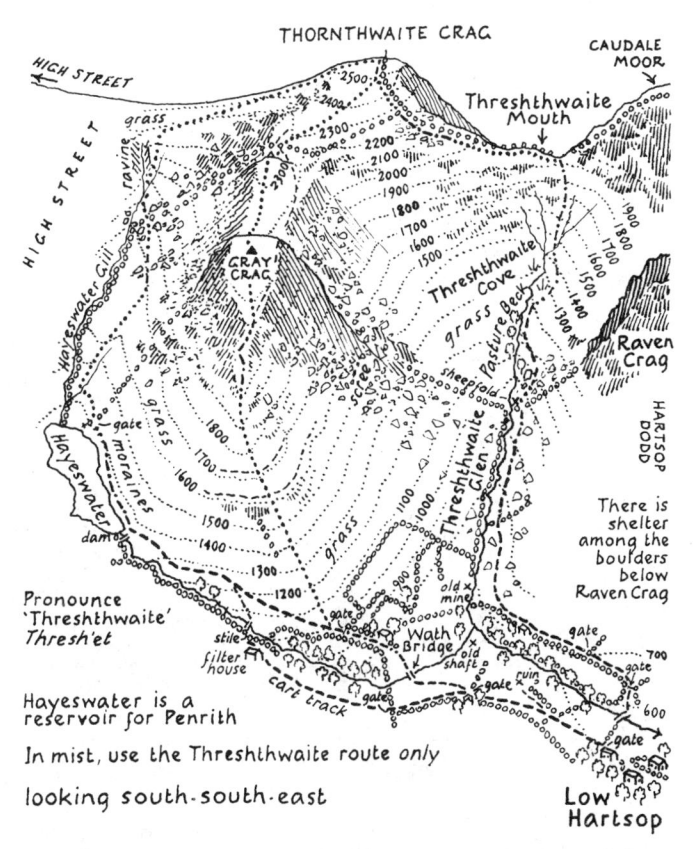

looking south-south-east

Pronounce 'Threshthwaite' Thresh'et

Hayeswater is a reservoir for Penrith

In mist, use the Threshthwaite route only

This is a very interesting and enjoyable expedition. Of the three routes illustrated, that via Hayeswater starts well but has a tame and tiring conclusion. If the return is to be made to Hartsop, Threshthwaite is the best approach, the descent being made along the north ridge over Gray Crag, which itself has an airy situation and good views.

Thornthwaite Crag 5

ASCENT FROM TROUTBECK
2200 feet of ascent
5 miles via Scot Rake; 5½ via Threshthwaite Mouth

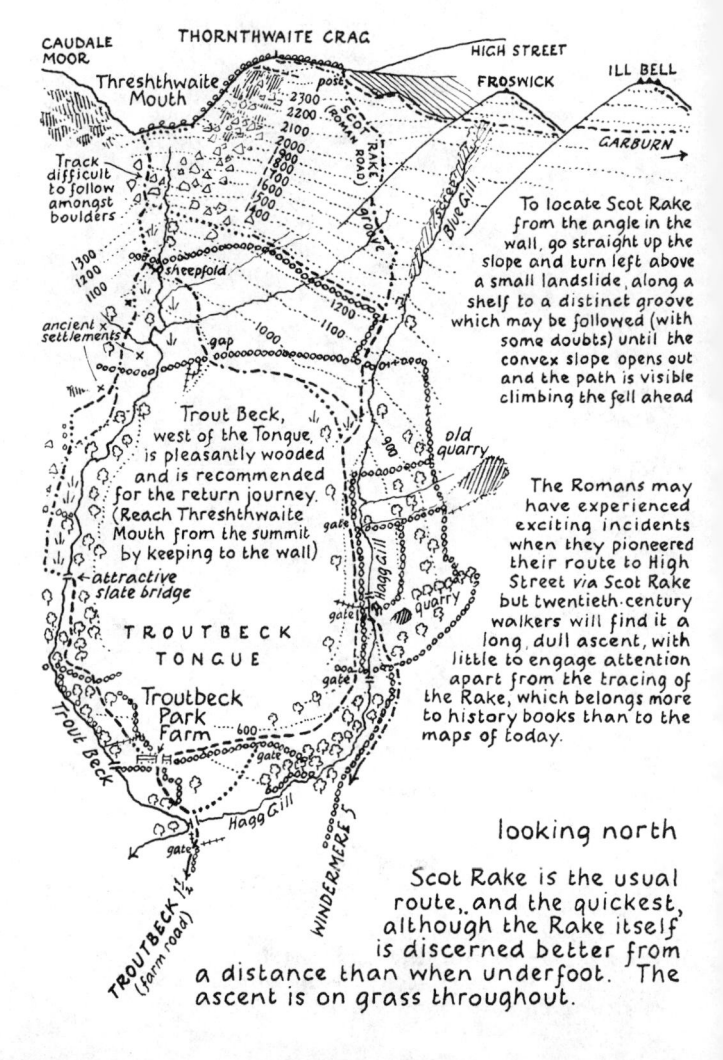

looking north

To locate Scot Rake from the angle in the wall, go straight up the slope and turn left above a small landslide, along a shelf to a distinct groove which may be followed (with some doubts) until the convex slope opens out and the path is visible climbing the fell ahead

The Romans may have experienced exciting incidents when they pioneered their route to High Street via Scot Rake but twentieth-century walkers will find it a long, dull ascent, with little to engage attention apart from the tracing of the Rake, which belongs more to history books than to the maps of today.

Trout Beck, west of the Tongue, is pleasantly wooded and is recommended for the return journey. (Reach Threshthwaite Mouth from the summit by keeping to the wall)

Track difficult to follow amongst boulders

Scot Rake is the usual route, and the quickest, although the Rake itself is discerned better from a distance than when underfoot. The ascent is on grass throughout.

Thornthwaite Crag 6

ASCENT FROM KENTMERE RESERVOIR
1650 feet of ascent : 2 miles

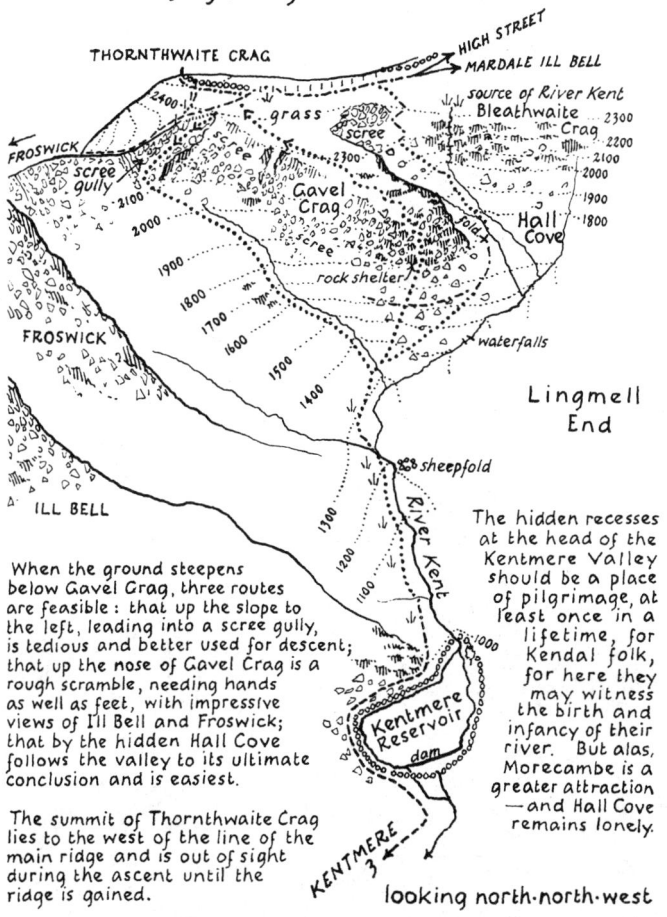

looking north-north-west

When the ground steepens below Gavel Crag, three routes are feasible: that up the slope to the left, leading into a scree gully, is tedious and better used for descent; that up the nose of Gavel Crag is a rough scramble, needing hands as well as feet, with impressive views of Ill Bell and Froswick; that by the hidden Hall Cove follows the valley to its ultimate conclusion and is easiest.

The summit of Thornthwaite Crag lies to the west of the line of the main ridge and is out of sight during the ascent until the ridge is gained.

The hidden recesses at the head of the Kentmere Valley should be a place of pilgrimage, at least once in a lifetime, for Kendal folk, for here they may witness the birth and infancy of their river. But alas, Morecambe is a greater attraction — and Hall Cove remains lonely.

This approach leads into the unfrequented dalehead of Kentmere and abounds in interest and variety all the way from the village. Rainsborrow Crag, up on the left, is a tremendous object *en route*, and Ill Bell and Froswick reveal themselves most effectively.

Thornthwaite Crag 7

THE SUMMIT

Thornthwaite Beacon

It is sometimes difficult to recall the details of familiar summits but surely all who have climbed Thornthwaite Crag will identify it in memory by its remarkable 14-feet column, one of the most distinctive cairns in Lakeland. It stands in the angle of a wall that traverses the summit. A few outcrops of flaky rock in the vicinity relieve the general grassiness of the top of the fell.

DESCENTS: In clear weather all the routes of ascent may be reversed, but that to Kentmere via Gavel Crag is not suggested nor should routes be 'invented' as there is rough ground about. *In bad conditions*, descend to Troutbeck or Hartsop via Threshthwaite Mouth — to which the wall leads when followed north-west. For Kentmere, go to the end of the wall eastwards; here turn right along a faint path for 200 yards to a scree gully on the left, which descend.

Thornthwaite Crag 8

looking north to Ullswater

Threshthwaite Mouth

looking south to Windermere

Thornthwaite Crag 9

THE VIEW

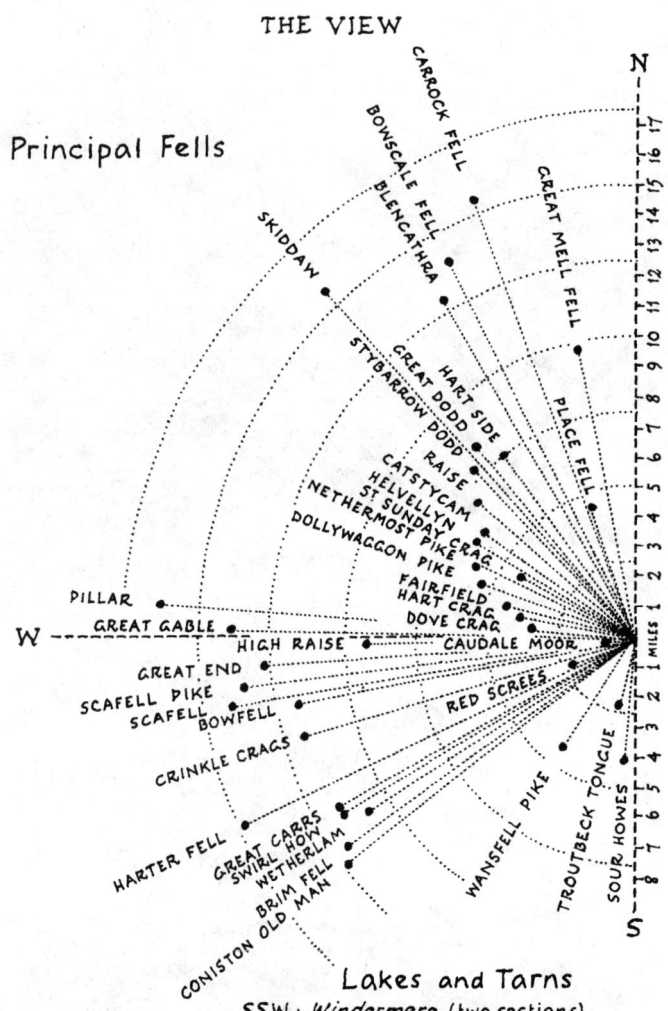

Principal Fells

(panorama diagram showing bearings and distances to surrounding fells, including: Carrock Fell, Bowscale Fell, Blencathra, Skiddaw, Great Mell Fell, Hart Side, Great Dodd, Stybarrow Dodd, Raise, Catstycam, Helvellyn, St Sunday Crag, Nethermost Pike, Dollywaggon Pike, Place Fell, Fairfield, Hart Crag, Dove Crag, Pillar, Great Gable, High Raise, Caudale Moor, Great End, Scafell Pike, Scafell, Bowfell, Red Screes, Crinkle Crags, Sour Howes, Troutbeck Tongue, Wansfell Pike, Harter Fell, Great Carrs, Swirl How, Wetherlam, Brim Fell, Coniston Old Man)

Lakes and Tarns

SSW: *Windermere* (two sections)
NNW: The upper reach of *Ullswater* may be seen by descending the west slope for 50 yards, or by following the wall north. **N:** *Hayeswater* is brought into view by a short walk (130 yards) in the direction of High Street.

Thornthwaite Crag 10

THE VIEW

The tall column, the wall, and adjacent high ground northwards between them interrupt the panorama — and various 'stations' must be visited to see all there is to see. The view is good, but not amongst the best; the northern prospect, in particular, is best surveyed from the slope going down to Threshthwaite Mouth.

The best feature in the scene is Windermere, to which the Troutbeck valley leads the eye with excellent effect.

Windermere

(A second section of the lake, Waterhead Bay, (not illustrated) appears to the right of Wansfell)

THE KNOTT
RAMPSGILL HEAD
HIGH RAISE
HIGH STREET
SELSIDE PIKE
MARDALE ILL BELL
BRANSTREE
HARTER FELL
KENTMERE PIKE
SHIPMAN KNOTTS
FROSWICK
ILL BELL
YOKE

Hayeswater

Thornthwaite Crag 11

RIDGE ROUTES

To CAUDALE MOOR, 2502': 1 mile : NW, W and WSW
Depression at 1950': 560 feet of ascent
A rough scramble, made safe in mist by walls

There is more to this walk than appears at first sight, for the gap of Threshthwaite Mouth is deep and it links slopes that are steep and rough. Keep by the wall until the broken crag of Caudale is left behind. The Caudale flank above the gap can be dangerous when the rocks are iced or under snow.

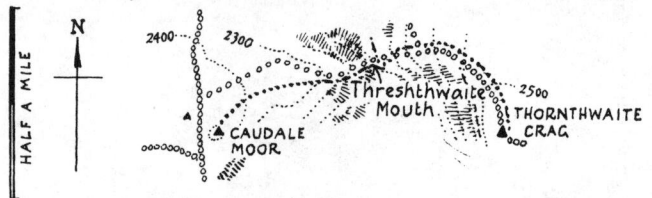

To GRAY CRAG, 2286': 1¼ miles : slightly W of N
Two minor depressions: 150 feet of ascent
An easy, interesting walk, better avoided in mist.

Straightforward walking along the descending and narrowing north ridge leads first to the nameless conical height of point 2331', then to the flat top of Gray Crag. Two broken walls are crossed *en route*. Both flanks are heavily scarped and dangerous in mist.

To FROSWICK, 2359'
1 mile
SSE then S and SE
Depression at 2100'
300 feet of ascent
A very easy walk

Follow the wall SSE, slanting along the line of the old fence to a stout straining post, where the path along the ridge may be joined. A long grassy descent leads to the final rise to the top of Froswick

Thornthwaite Crag 12

RIDGE ROUTES

To HIGH STREET, 2718': 1¼ miles : SE, then E and NE
Depression at 2475' : 250 feet of ascent
A very simple walk, safe in mist

Follow the wall to its eastern terminus, avoid the bog there, and continue along the line of an old fence to join another wall that runs directly to and beyond the top of High Street. All is grass.

To MARDALE ILL BELL, 2496'
1⅓ miles : SE, then E, ENE and ESE
Depressions at 2475' and 2350' : 200 feet of ascent
Easy walking, but a confusing area in mist

Leave the corner of the High Street wall by a plain track trending eastwards and when this becomes indistinct keep on over long grass in the same direction, descending slightly to the depression ahead. In mist, take care not to descend to the right into Hall Cove.

Thornthwaite Crag from the south ridge of Caudale Moor

Troutbeck Tongue 1191'

properly named
The Tongue, Troutbeck Park

from the Kirkstone-Windermere road

▲ CAUDALE MOOR

▲ ILL BELL

▲ TROUTBECK TONGUE

• Troutbeck

MILES
0 1 2 3

There are many Tongues in Lakeland, all of them wedges of high or rising ground between enclosing becks that join below at the tip, but none is more distinctive or aptly named than that in the middle of the Troutbeck Valley. Other Tongues usually have their roots high on a mountainside, but this one thrusts forward from the floor of the dalehead. Although of very modest altitude, it has an attraction for the gentler pedestrian as a viewpoint for the valley, and makes an admirable short excursion in pleasant scenery from Windermere or Troutbeck or, by Skelghyll Woods, from Ambleside.

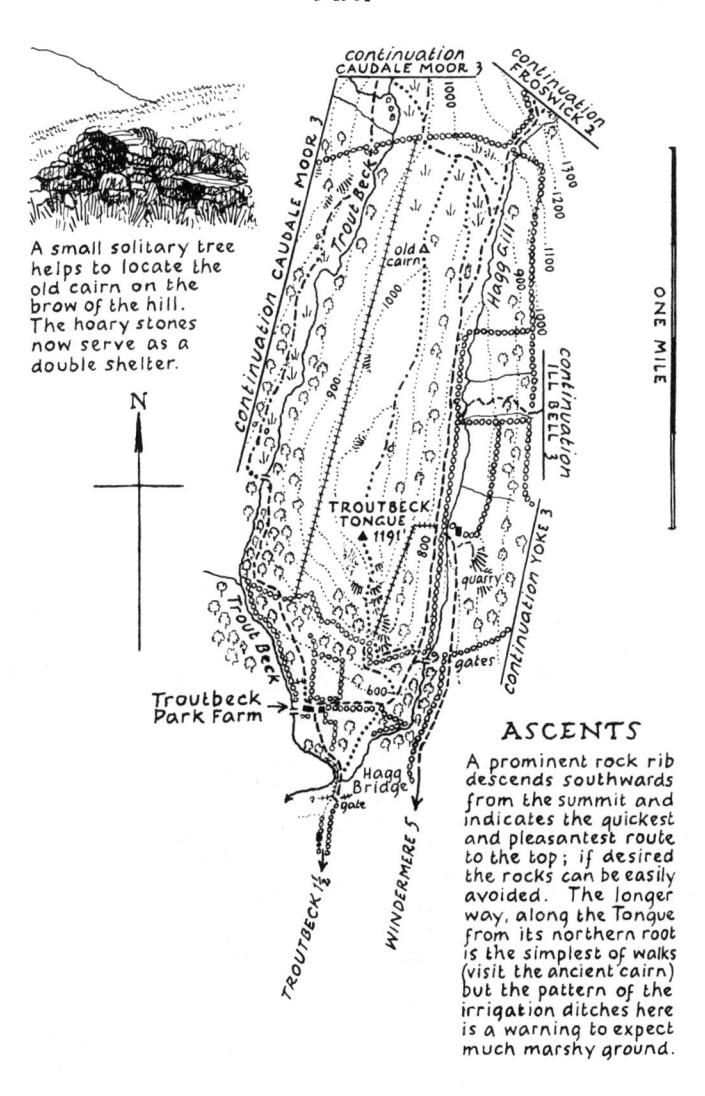

Troutbeck Tongue 2

MAP

A small solitary tree helps to locate the old cairn on the brow of the hill. The hoary stones now serve as a double shelter.

ASCENTS

A prominent rock rib descends southwards from the summit and indicates the quickest and pleasantest route to the top; if desired the rocks can be easily avoided. The longer way, along the Tongue from its northern root is the simplest of walks (visit the ancient cairn) but the pattern of the irrigation ditches here is a warning to expect much marshy ground.

Troutbeck Tongue 3

THE SUMMIT

CAUDALE MOOR — GRAY CRAG over Threshthwaite Mouth — THORNTHWAITE CRAG

The rocky scramble up the south ridge from the cart-track is entertaining enough to hold out the promise of a summit equally interesting, but the promise is not fulfilled by the reality, which is a grassy knoll a little higher than several more nearby, and graced by a small heap of stones. Apart from the view down the valley to Windermere, nothing here is worth comment.

Slate bridge, Trout Beck

Troutbeck Tongue 4

THE VIEW

Troutbeck Tongue is set deep in the bottom of a great bowl of hills, all of which overtop it and limit the scene. Only to the south is there an open view — of Windermere — but there is also a peep of distant fells to the west.

Principal Fells

N: Hart Crag (Caudale Moor), Caudale Moor, Red Screes, Gray Crag, Thornthwaite Crag, Froswick, Ill Bell, Yoke
W: Scafell Pike, Bowfell, Crinkle Crags, Pike O' Blisco
E: Sallows, Sour Howes
S: Wansfell, Dodd Hill (Wansfell)

Lakes and Tarns
SSW: *Windermere* (middle and lower reaches)

Windermere and the Troutbeck Valley

Wansfell

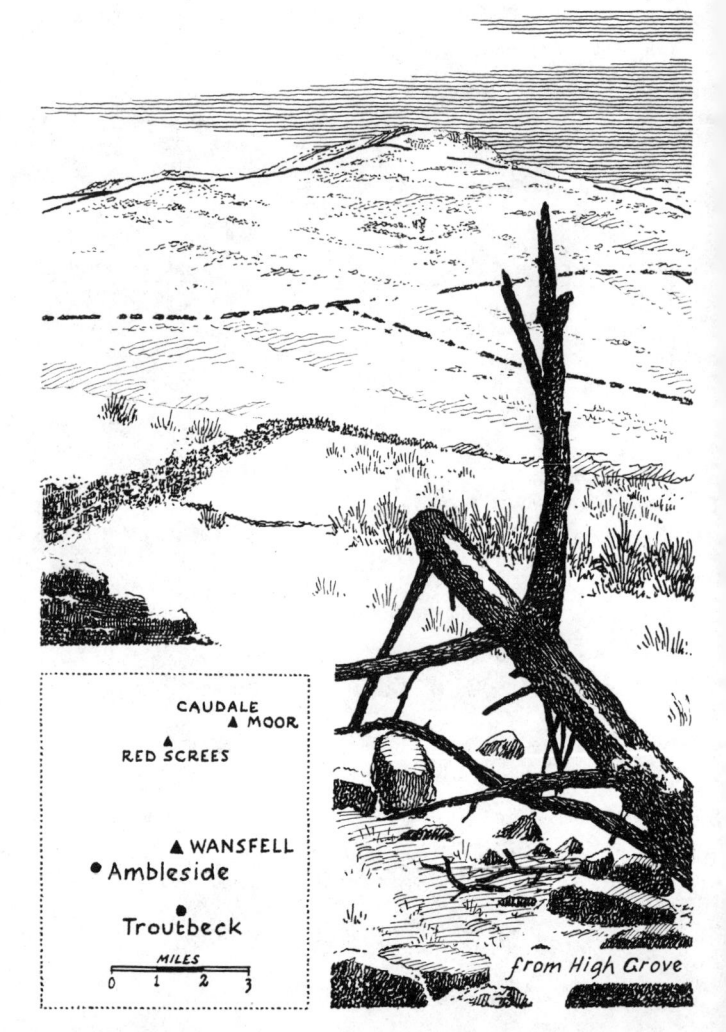

1597'

from High Grove

CAUDALE MOOR ▲
▲ RED SCREES

▲ WANSFELL
● Ambleside

● Troutbeck

MILES
0 1 2 3

Wansfell 2

NATURAL FEATURES

Caudale Moor sends out three distinct ridges to the south, and the most westerly and longest of the three descends to a wide depression (crossed by the Kirkstone road) before rising and narrowing along an undulating spur that finally falls to the shores of Windermere. This spur is Wansfell, and, although its summit-ridge is fairly narrow and well-defined, the slopes on most sides are extensive, the fell as a whole occupying a broad tract of territory between Ambleside and the Troutbeck valley. Except northwards, the lower slopes are attractively wooded; the upper reaches are mainly grassy, but at the south-west extremity of the ridge there is a rocky bluff known as Wansfell Pike, which is commonly but incorrectly regarded as the top of the fell. Other crags, masked by trees, flank the Kirkstone road at Troutbeck and Jenkins Crag in Skelghyll Woods is a very popular viewpoint. The main streams flow from marshy ground east of the ridge — this was the scene of the cloudburst in June 1953 and these the gentle becks that suddenly became raging torrents and caused so much damage in the Troutbeck district.

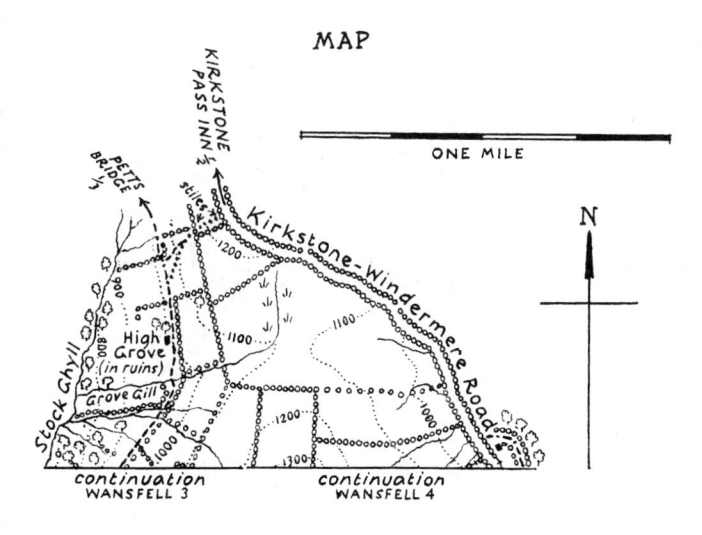

MAP

Wansfell 3

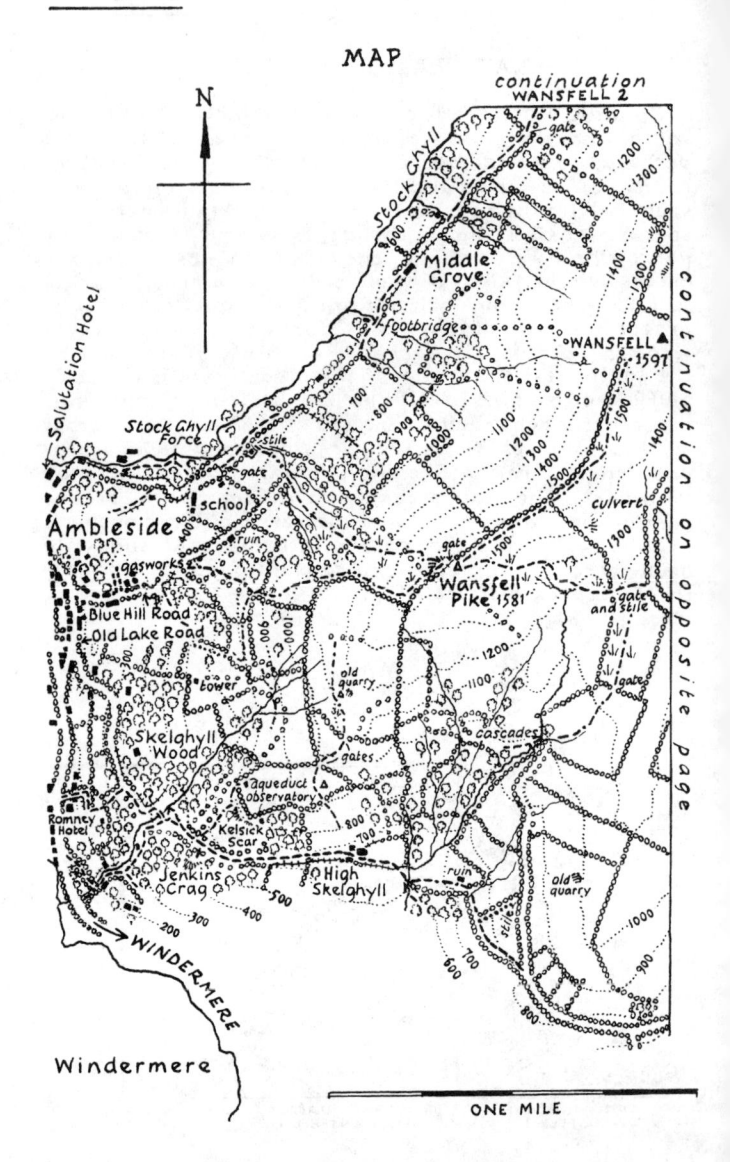

MAP

Wansfell 4

MAP

continuation WANSFELL 2

An old path (Low Kingate) enables the walker from Troutbeck to Kirkstone to avoid a mile of the hard main road — a consideration in summer.

Dodd Hill

old quarry

Kirkstone-Windermere Road

Low Kingate

WANSFELL 1597'

Raven Crag

The Troutbeck Valley

culvert

Chimney Crag

Stony Beck

ONE MILE

gate and stile

gate

Town Head

Queen's Head Hotel

Scot Bridge

Nanny Lane

Mortal Man Hotel

St Margaret's Well

WINDERMERE 3½

continuation on opposite page

Troutbeck

Institute

N

Town End

AMBLESIDE 3¾   WINDERMERE 3

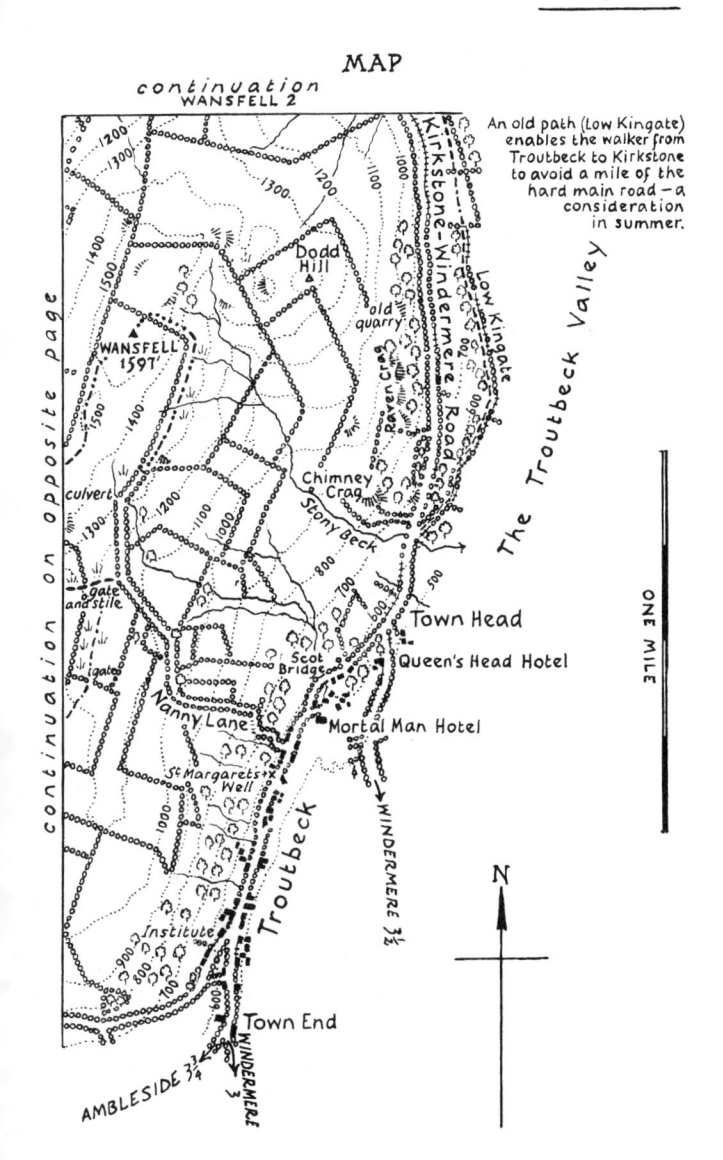

Wansfell 5

ASCENT FROM AMBLESIDE
1500 feet of ascent : 2½ miles

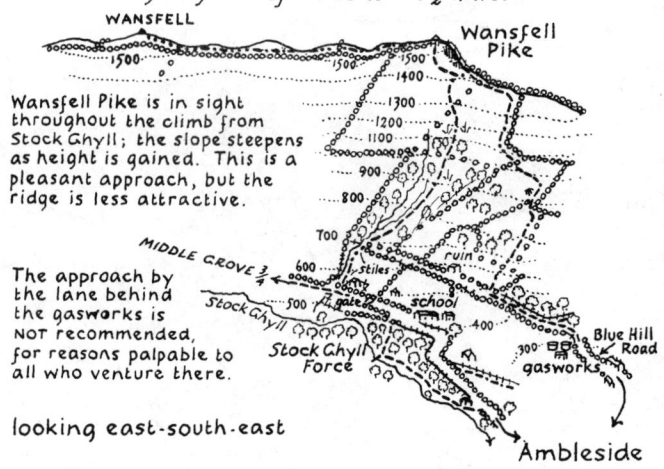

Wansfell Pike is in sight throughout the climb from Stock Ghyll; the slope steepens as height is gained. This is a pleasant approach, but the ridge is less attractive.

The approach by the lane behind the gasworks is NOT recommended, for reasons palpable to all who venture there.

looking east-south-east

ASCENT FROM TROUTBECK
1100 feet of ascent : 1¼ miles

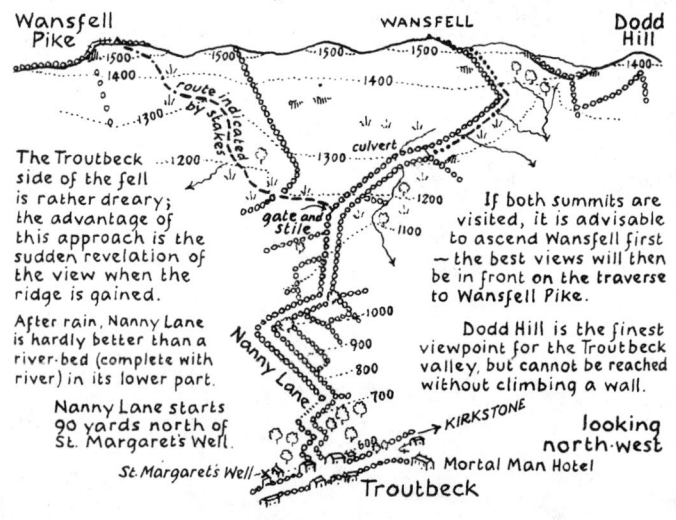

The Troutbeck side of the fell is rather dreary; the advantage of this approach is the sudden revelation of the view when the ridge is gained.

After rain, Nanny Lane is hardly better than a river-bed (complete with river) in its lower part.

Nanny Lane starts 90 yards north of St. Margaret's Well.

If both summits are visited, it is advisable to ascend Wansfell first — the best views will then be in front on the traverse to Wansfell Pike.

Dodd Hill is the finest viewpoint for the Troutbeck valley, but cannot be reached without climbing a wall.

looking north-west

Wansfell 6

THE SUMMIT

Kirkstone Pass — CAUDALE MOOR — THORNTHWAITE CRAG — Threshthwaite Mouth

A grassy hummock, a little higher than many around, is the true summit of the fell: a few small stones confirm it. It is an unattractive place, rarely visited; better is the rocky top of Wansfell Pike, which at least is mildly interesting and unique in possessing an iron gate. The higher summit lies 150 yards east of the ridge-wall, which, in mist, is a safe guide as far as Wansfell Pike, whence paths go down to Ambleside (west) and Troutbeck (east).

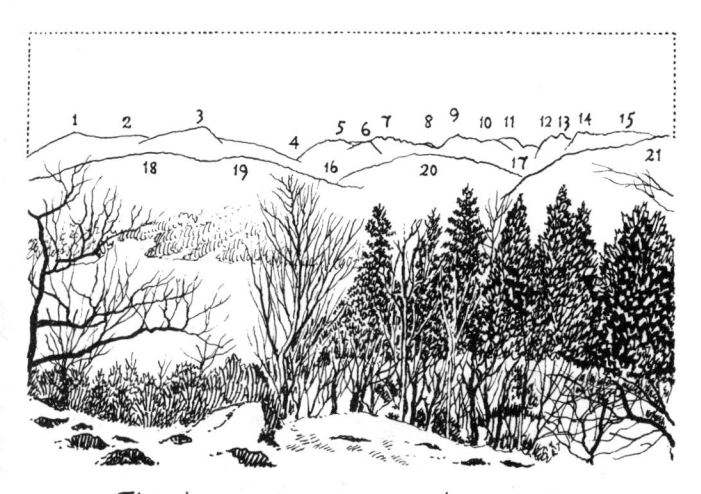

The view westwards from Jenkins Crag

1 : Coniston Old Man
2 : Brim Fell
3 : Wetherlam
4 : Wrynose Pass
5 : Cold Pike
6 : Pike o' Blisco
7 : Crinkle Crags
8 : Scafell
9 : Bowfell
10 : Esk Pike
11 : Great End
12 : Loft Crag
13 : Pike o' Stickle
14 : Harrison Stickle
15 : Pavey Ark
16 : Little Langdale
17 : Great Langdale
18 : Black Fell
19 : Park Fell
20 : Lingmoor Fell
21 : Loughrigg Fell

Wansfell 7

THE VIEW
FROM THE SUMMIT OF WANSFELL

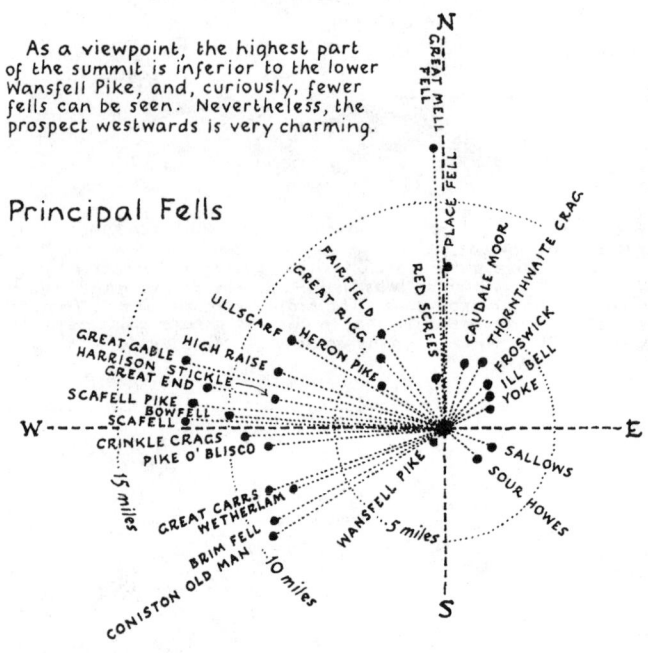

As a viewpoint, the highest part of the summit is inferior to the lower Wansfell Pike, and, curiously, fewer fells can be seen. Nevertheless, the prospect westwards is very charming.

Principal Fells

(compass diagram with fells labelled:)

N: GREAT MELL FELL
PLACE FELL
CAUDALE MOOR
RED SCREES
THORNTHWAITE CRAG
FAIRFIELD
GREAT RIGG
HERON PIKE
FROSWICK
ULLSCARF
ILL BELL
HIGH RAISE
YOKE
GREAT GABLE
HARRISON STICKLE
GREAT END
SCAFELL PIKE
BOWFELL
SCAFELL
CRINKLE CRAGS
PIKE O' BLISCO
SALLOWS
SOUR HOWES
GREAT CARRS
WETHERLAM
WANSFELL PIKE
BRIM FELL
CONISTON OLD MAN

15 miles, 10 miles, 5 miles

Lakes and Tarns

S : Windermere
WSW : Little Langdale Tarn
W : Grasmere
W : Rydal Water

Red Screes, from the summit

Wansfell 8

THE VIEW
FROM WANSFELL PIKE

Wansfell Pike excels in its view of Windermere, the graceful curve of the lake showing to great advantage. Westwards, the scene is especially beautiful.
Red Screes is a fine object in the north; the east is dull.

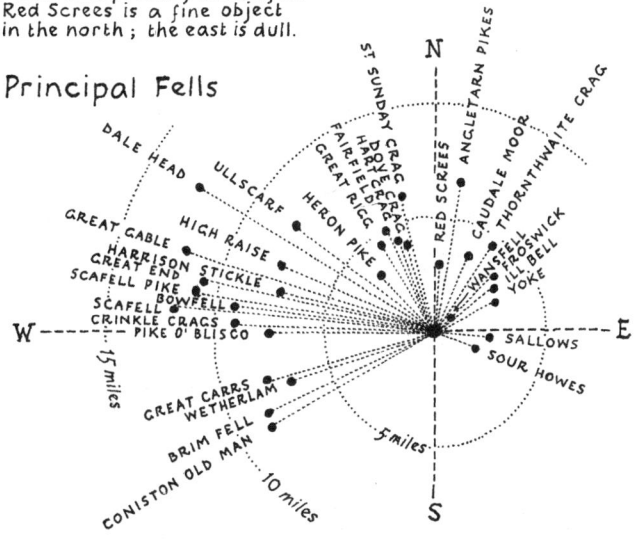

Principal Fells

(compass diagram with fells listed by direction)

- DALE HEAD
- ULLSCARF
- ST SUNDAY CRAG
- DRY CRAG
- HART CRAG
- FAIRFIELD
- GREAT RIGG
- HERON PIKE
- ANGLETARN PIKES
- RED SCREES
- THORNTHWAITE CRAG
- CAUDALE MOOR
- WANSFELL
- ILL BELL
- FROSWICK
- YOKE
- GREAT GABLE
- HIGH RAISE
- HARRISON STICKLE
- GREAT END
- SCAFELL PIKE
- BOWFELL
- SCAFELL
- CRINKLE CRAGS
- PIKE O' BLISCO
- SALLOWS
- SOUR HOWES
- GREAT CARRS
- WETHERLAM
- BRIM FELL
- CONISTON OLD MAN

15 miles / 10 miles / 5 miles

W — E, N — S

Lakes and Tarns

S : Windermere
SW : Blelham Tarn
W : Little Langdale Tarn
WNW : Grasmere
WNW : Rydal Water
The two sheets of water on the lower slopes of Sour Howes, southeast, are reservoirs.

Windermere, from Wansfell Pike

Wansfell 9

RIDGE ROUTE

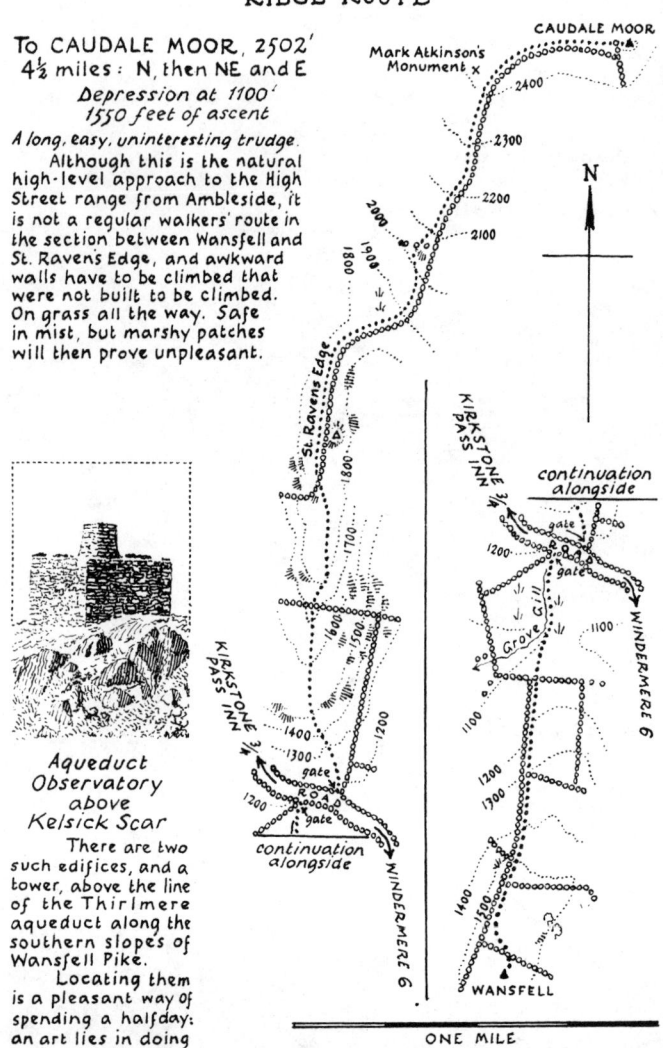

To CAUDALE MOOR, 2502'
4½ miles : N, then NE and E
Depression at 1100'
1550 feet of ascent

A long, easy, uninteresting trudge.
Although this is the natural high-level approach to the High Street range from Ambleside, it is not a regular walkers' route in the section between Wansfell and St. Raven's Edge, and awkward walls have to be climbed that were not built to be climbed. On grass all the way. Safe in mist, but marshy patches will then prove unpleasant.

Aqueduct Observatory above Kelsick Scar

There are two such edifices, and a tower, above the line of the Thirlmere aqueduct along the southern slopes of Wansfell Pike.

Locating them is a pleasant way of spending a halfday: an art lies in doing this *sans* wallscaling.

ONE MILE

Wansfell 10

Stock Ghyll Force

Wether Hill

spelt 'Weather' Hill
on Bartholomew's map

2210'
approx

from Beda Fell

- Howtown
- ▲ LOADPOT HILL
- Bampton
- ▲ WETHER HILL
- ▲ HIGH RAISE

MILES
0 1 2 3 4

Wether Hill 2

NATURAL FEATURES

The High Street range has largely lost its appeal to the walker by the time he reaches the twin grassy mounds of Wether Hill on the long tramp along its spine northwards, and there is nothing here to call for a halt. The top, scarcely higher than the general level of the ridge, is quite without interest, while the eastern slopes are little better although traversed by two good routes from Bampton; but the western flank, characteristically steeper, has the peculiarity of Gowk Hill, a subsidiary height which itself develops into a parallel ridge running north: this encloses, with the main ridge, the little hidden valley of Fusedale. The best features of Wether Hill, paradoxically, are found in its valleys: eastwards, Cawdale Beck and Measand Beck have attractions rarely visited except by the lone shepherd; westwards, Fusedale Beck is fed from two wooded ravines, and here too is lovely Martindale.

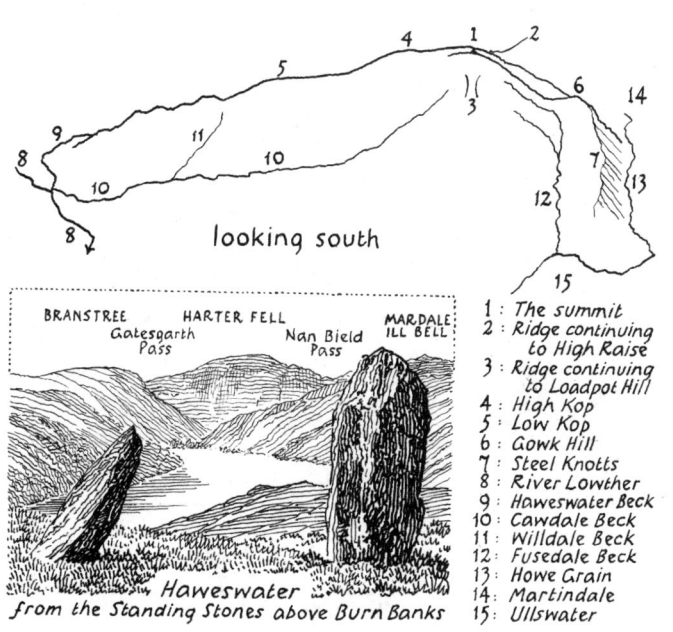

looking south

1 : The summit
2 : Ridge continuing to High Raise
3 : Ridge continuing to Loadpot Hill
4 : High Kop
5 : Low Kop
6 : Gowk Hill
7 : Steel Knotts
8 : River Lowther
9 : Haweswater Beck
10 : Cawdale Beck
11 : Willdale Beck
12 : Fusedale Beck
13 : Howe Grain
14 : Martindale
15 : Ullswater

Haweswater
from the Standing Stones above Burn Banks

Wether Hill 3

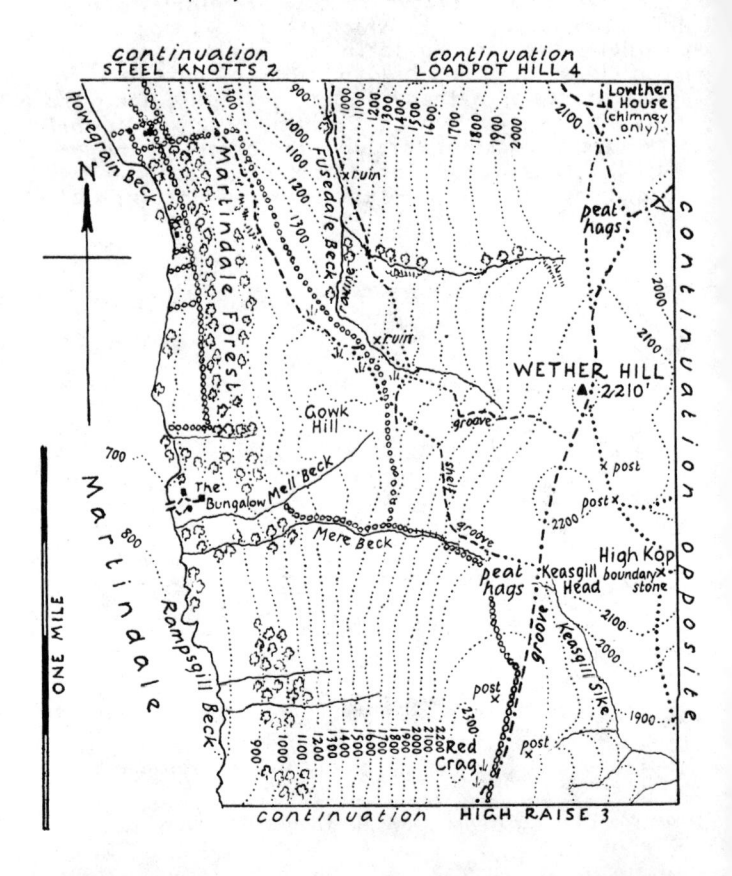

MAP

Wether Hill's slopes sprawl extensively eastwards, descending gradually in easy ridges to a wide belt of cultivated land west of the Bampton-Burn Banks road— from which the ascent will generally be commenced on this side. No details of this cultivated area are depicted on the following maps (on pages 5 and 6) other than those necessary to get the walker to the open fell as quickly as possible.

Wether Hill 4

MAP

The eastern slopes of Wether Hill are bounded on the north by Cawdale Beck and on the south by Measand Beck, but some detail of the adjacent fells is, in addition, given below because they carry routes that lead onto Wether Hill.

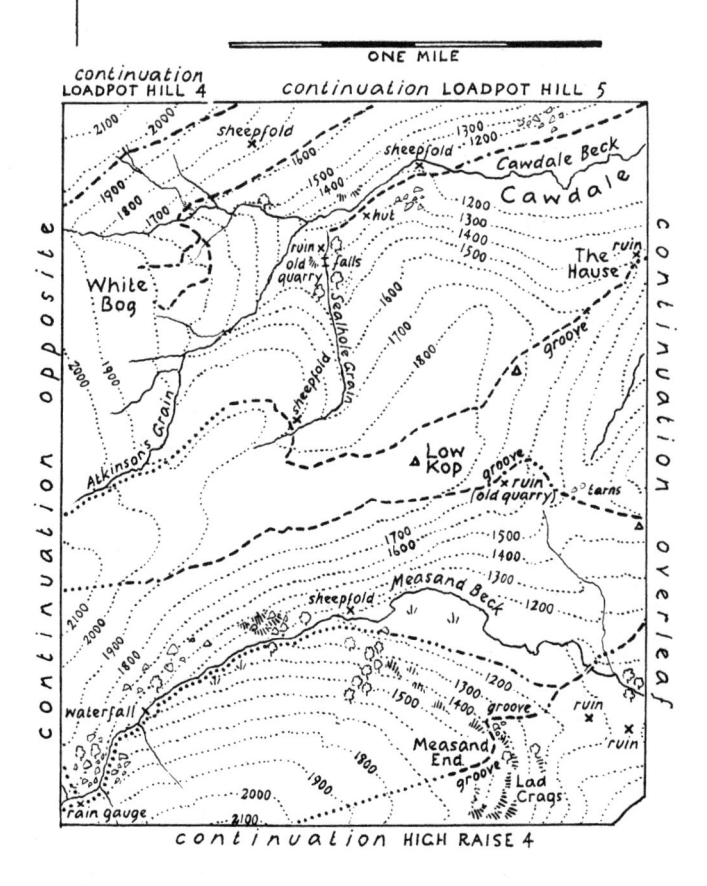

N

ONE MILE

continuation LOADPOT HILL 4
continuation LOADPOT HILL 5
continuation opposite
continuation overleaf
continuation HIGH RAISE 4

sheepfold
Cawdale Beck
Cawdale
hut
ruin, old quarry, falls
Galhole Grain
The Hause ruin
White Bog
groove
Atkinson's Grain
sheepfold
Low Kop
groove
ruin (old quarry)
tarns
Measand Beck
sheepfold
groove
ruin
waterfall
Measand End
groove
Lad Crags
rain gauge
ruin

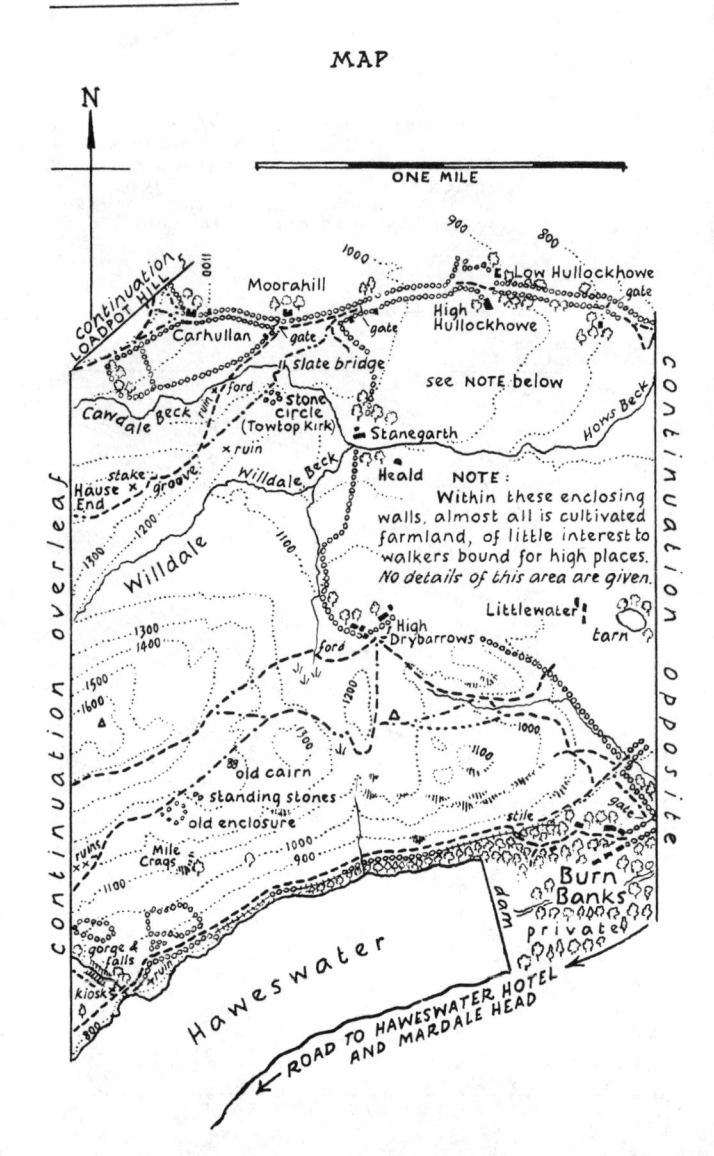

Wether Hill 5

Wether Hill 6

MAP

HELTON 2½
quarry — Bampton — gate — Hall — SHAP 4
fall
school
600
700
700
Burn Banks
HAWESWATER HOTEL AND MARDALE HEAD

continuation opposite

see NOTE on opposite page

N — ONE MILE

The stake on Hause End

Slate bridge, Cawdale Beck

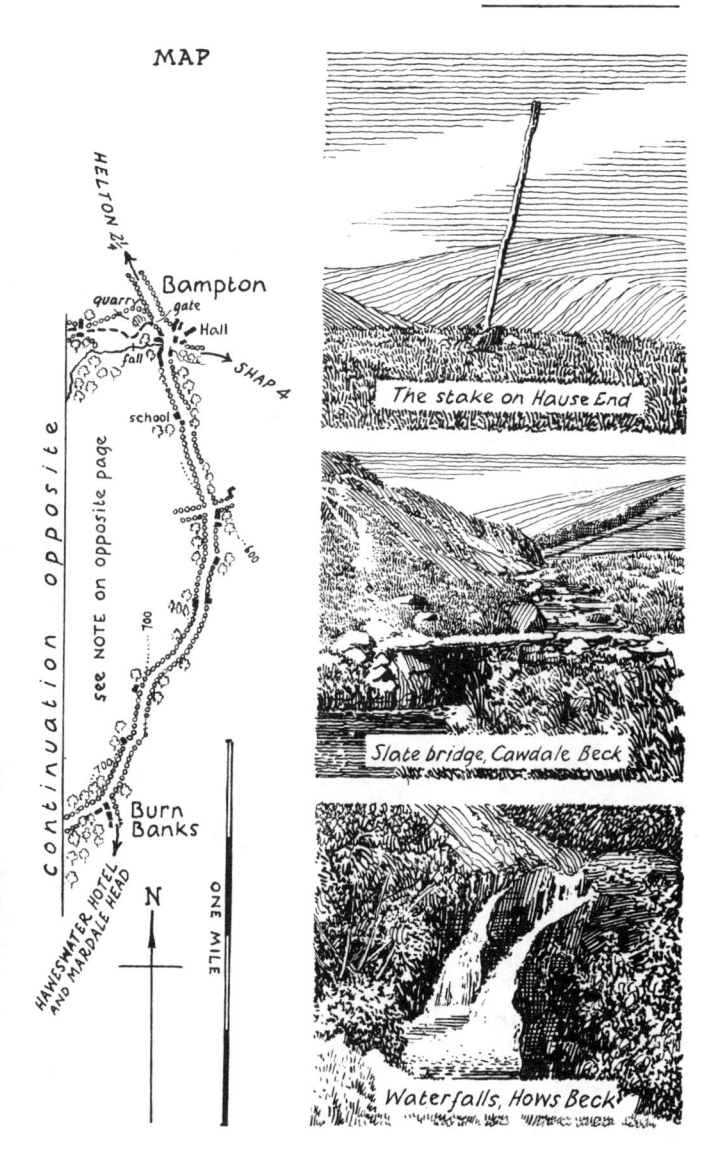

Waterfalls, Hows Beck

Wether Hill 7

ASCENTS FROM HOWTOWN AND MARTINDALE
1750 feet of ascent, 3 miles, from Howtown
1550 feet of ascent, 2½ miles, from Martindale old church

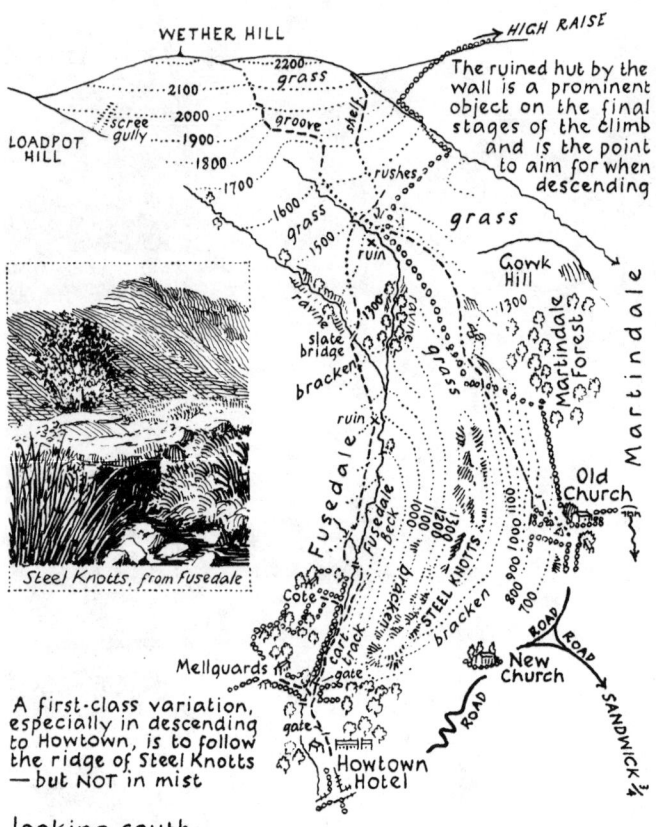

The ruined hut by the wall is a prominent object on the final stages of the climb and is the point to aim for when descending

Steel Knotts, from Fusedale

A first-class variation, especially in descending to Howtown, is to follow the ridge of Steel Knotts — but NOT in mist

looking south

There are many fells more worthy of climbing than Wether Hill, the final slope being very dull, but there are no more delightful starting-points than Howtown and Martindale, the approach from the latter being especially good — until the last slope is reached.

Wether Hill 8

ASCENTS FROM BURN BANKS AND BAMPTON
1550 feet of ascent from Burn Banks; 1750 from Bampton.
4½ miles from Burn Banks direct, 5 via Measand Beck;
5 miles from Bampton

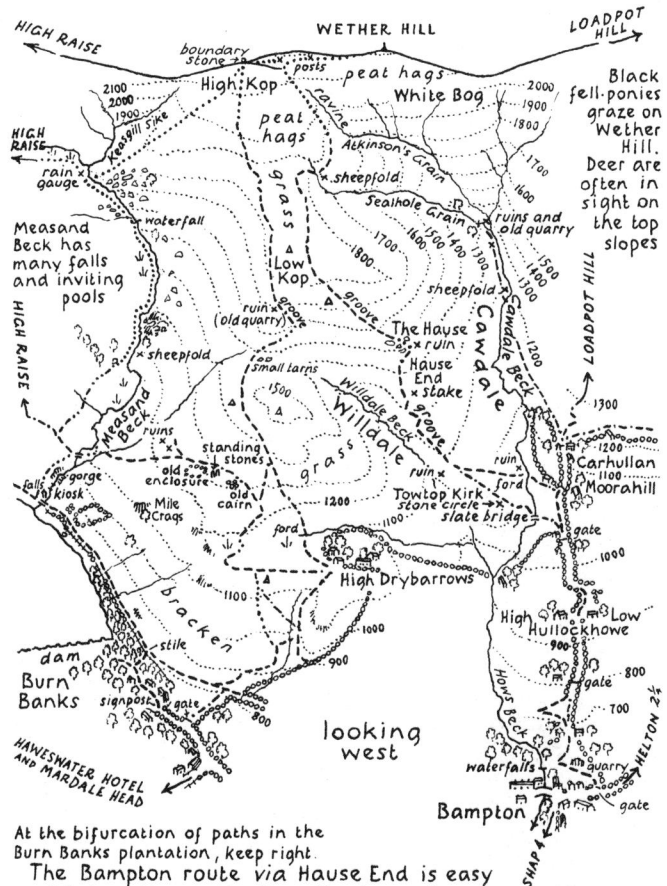

At the bifurcation of paths in the
Burn Banks plantation, keep right.

The Bampton route via Hause End is easy
and interesting; the Burn Banks route across the open
common is a little confusing in its early stages; on a hot
day the Measand route, although pathless, is attractive.

Wether Hill 9

THE SUMMIT

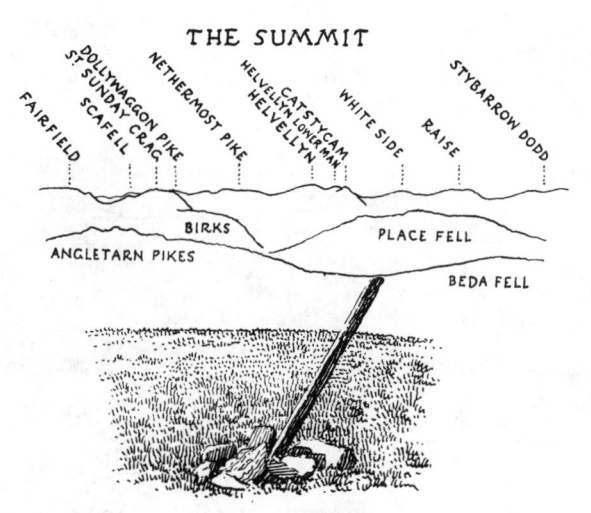

FAIRFIELD — SCAFELL — ST SUNDAY CRAG — DOLLYWAGGON PIKE — NETHERMOST PIKE — HELVELLYN LOWER MAN — HELVELLYN — CATSTYCAM — WHITE SIDE — RAISE — STYBARROW DODD

ANGLETARN PIKES — BIRKS — PLACE FELL — BEDA FELL

Two rounded grassy mounds of similar altitude, separated by a slight depression, form the summit. The more extensive of the two mounds, the southern, is quite featureless: the small northern mound is the recognised top and carries a wooden stake set in a small cairn (one stone of which is a boundary stone lying on its side). The summit is popular with grazing animals of various species, but humans will find it a dreary and uninteresting place. The High Street crosses the top, but along here is barely noticeable, being no more distinct than a sheep-trod.

DESCENTS: All slopes are easy, and it is a waste of time to look for the few paths. For Bampton, pass over High Kop to join one of two good grooves. For Martindale and Howtown descend west to the ruin by the prominent broken crosswall below: leave the ruin on the *right*, passing through the gateway in the wall, for Martindale; but for Fusedale and Howtown leave the ruin well to the *left*.

In mist, there is little danger of accident, but keep out of stream-beds which run in ravines.

The boundary stone, High Kop, with High Raise in the background

Wether Hill 10

THE VIEW

Principal Fells

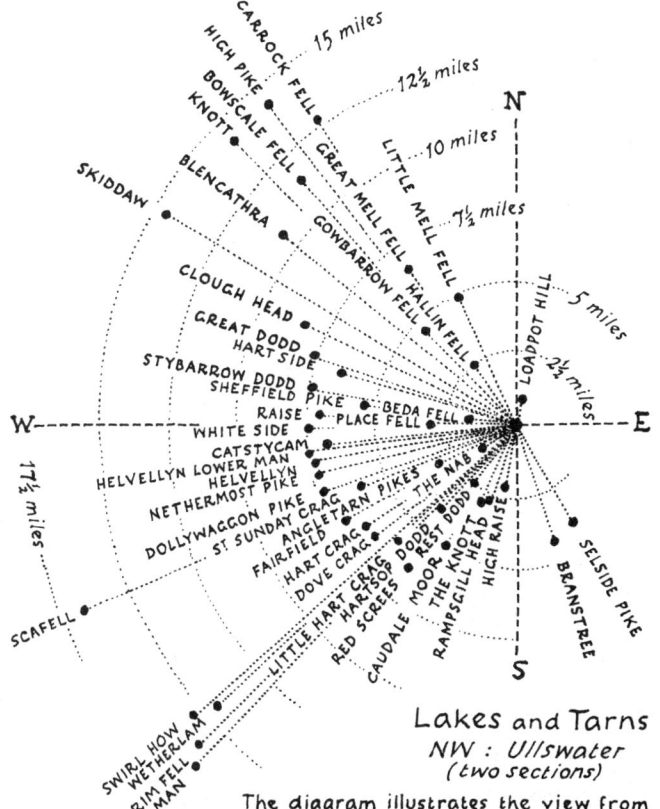

(compass diagram showing fells and distances: Carrock Fell, High Pike, Bowscale Fell, Knott, Skiddaw, Blencathra, Great Mell Fell, Little Mell Fell, Gowbarrow Fell, Clough Head, Hallin Fell, Great Dodd, Hart Side, Loadpot Hill, Stybarrow Dodd, Sheffield Pike, Beda Fell, Raise, Place Fell, White Side, Catstycam, Helvellyn Lower Man, Helvellyn, Nethermost Pike, Dollywaggon Pike, St Sunday Crag, Anglestarn Pikes, The Nab, Fairfield, Hart Crag, Harsop Dodd, Rest Dodd, High Raise, Dove Crag, Little Hart Crag, The Knott, Red Screes, Caudale Moor, Rampsgill Head, Selside Pike, Branstree, Scafell, Swirl How, Wetherlam, Brim Fell, Coniston Old Man. Distances marked: 15 miles, 12½ miles, 10 miles, 7½ miles, 5 miles, 2½ miles, 17½ miles)

Lakes and Tarns
NW : Ullswater
(two sections)

The diagram illustrates the view from the cairn on the northern summit. The view from the southern summit is the same substantially, but in addition Scafell Pike can be seen. There is a wide prospect of the Pennines, but undoubtedly the best feature is the finely-grouped Helvellyn and Fairfield fells across the rough, romantic Martindale country.

Wether Hill 11

RIDGE ROUTES

To LOADPOT HILL, 2201' : 1 mile : N
Depression at 2025' : 180 feet of ascent

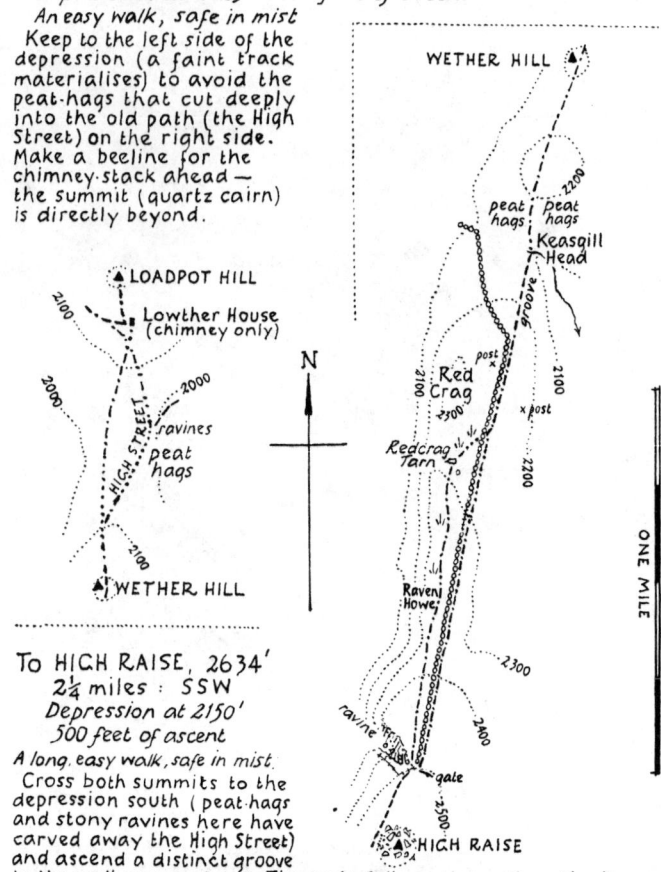

An easy walk, safe in mist

Keep to the left side of the depression (a faint track materialises) to avoid the peat-hags that cut deeply into the old path (the High Street) on the right side. Make a beeline for the chimney-stack ahead — the summit (quartz cairn) is directly beyond.

To HIGH RAISE, 2634' 2¼ miles : SSW
Depression at 2150' 500 feet of ascent

A long, easy walk, safe in mist.

Cross both summits to the depression south (peat-hags and stony ravines here have carved away the High Street) and ascend a distinct groove to the wall-corner ahead. The route follows the wall south: it may be crossed near Redcrag Tarn for the best views, but on a gusty day it offers shelter if kept immediately on the right. When the wall ends at a short fence, above a steep ravine, the path climbs across the open fell. The cairn is among stones 100 yards away to the left of the path at its highest point.

Wether Hill 12

Measand Beck

The Forces of Measand Beck, near its outlet into Haweswater, need no introduction to frequenters of this area, but the waterfalls illustrated, two miles upstream, are rarely seen.

Yoke

2309'

spelt 'Yolk' on some Ordnance Survey maps

▲ HIGH STREET

▲ ILL BELL
▲ YOKE

Kentmere
●

● Troutbeck

MILES
0 1 2 3 4

from the Kirkstone-Windermere road

Yoke 2

NATURAL FEATURES

Yoke is best known as the southern outpost of the Ill Bell ridge leading up to High Street from Garburn Pass, and is usually dismissed as a dull unattractive mound. As seen from Troutbeck, this seems a quite accurate assessment, but the Kentmere flank is very different, abounding in interest. On this side, below the summit, is the formidable thousand-foot precipice of Rainsborrow Crag (the safety of which is a subject of disagreement between rock-climbers and foxes) and, rising above Kentmere village, is a knobbly spur that looks like the knuckles of a clenched fist — a place of rocky excrescences, craggy tors and tumbled boulders, and a fine playground for the mountaineering novice. Both flanks of Yoke carry the scars of old quarrying operations.

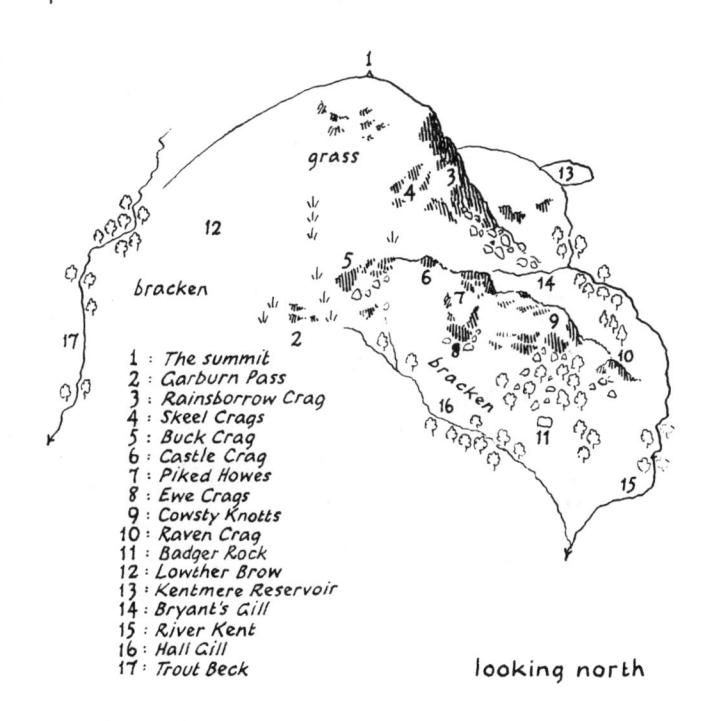

1 : The summit
2 : Garburn Pass
3 : Rainsborrow Crag
4 : Skeel Crags
5 : Buck Crag
6 : Castle Crag
7 : Piked Howes
8 : Ewe Crags
9 : Cowsty Knotts
10 : Raven Crag
11 : Badger Rock
12 : Lowther Brow
13 : Kentmere Reservoir
14 : Bryant's Gill
15 : River Kent
16 : Hall Gill
17 : Trout Beck

looking north

Yoke 3

MAP

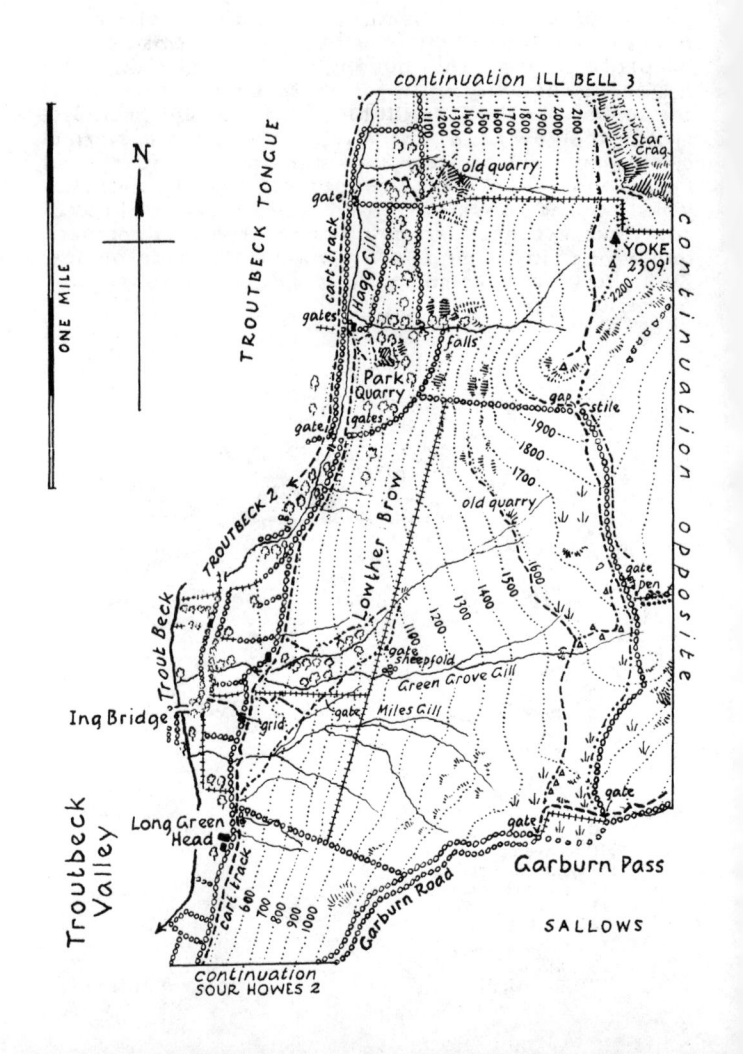

continuation ILL BELL 3

Star Crag

YOKE 2309'

continuation opposite

old quarry

gate

cart-track

TROUTBECK TONGUE

Hagg Gill

gates

falls

Park Quarry

gates

gap stile

gate

1900
1800
1700

old quarry

TROUTBECK 2

Lowther Brow

gate pen

Trout Beck

gate sheepfold
Green Grove Gill
gate Miles Gill

Ing Bridge

grid

gate

Long Green Head

cart track

Garburn Road

Garburn Pass

SALLOWS

Troutbeck Valley

ONE MILE

N

continuation SOUR HOWES 2

Yoke 4

MAP

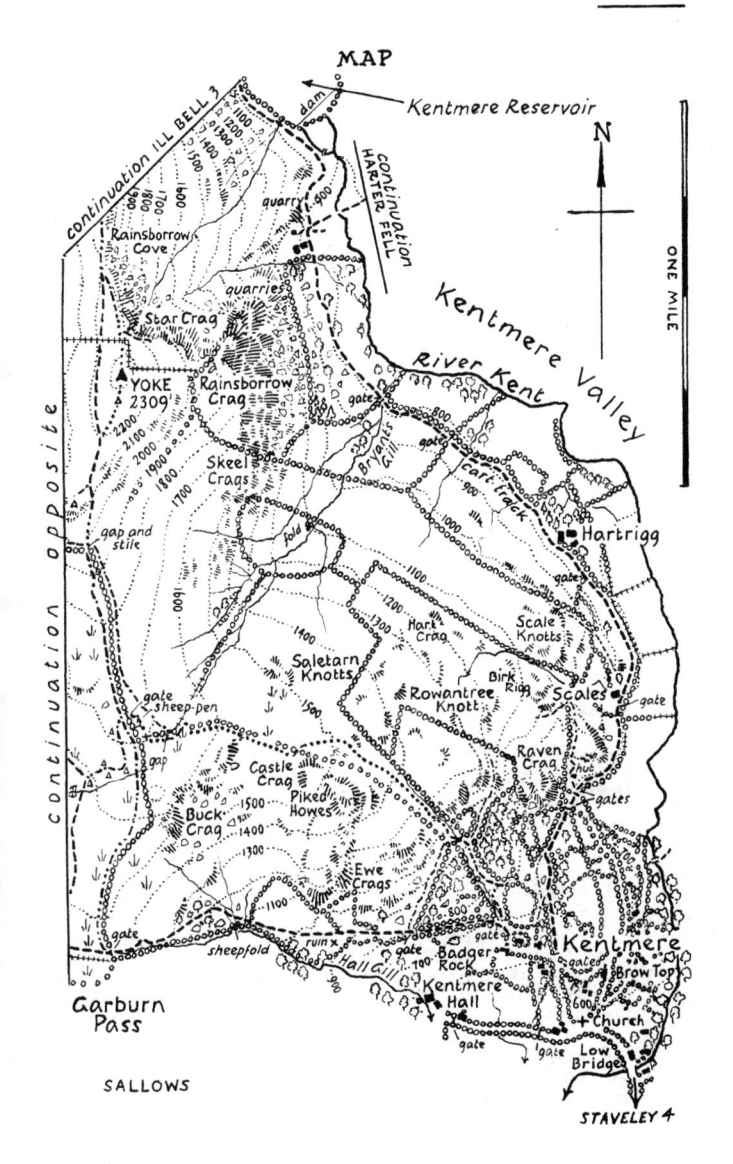

Yoke 5

ASCENT FROM GARBURN PASS
850 feet of ascent : 1¾ miles

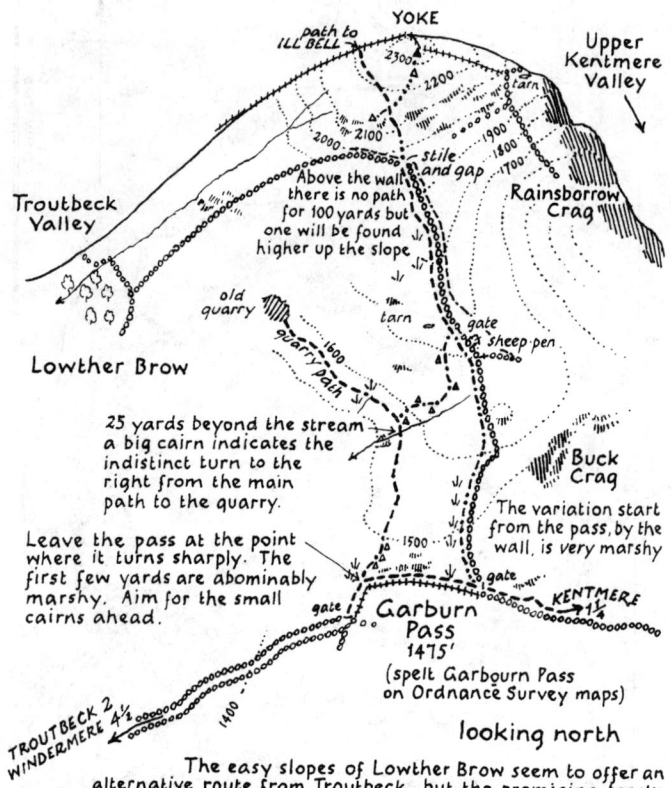

path to ILL BELL
YOKE 2300
Upper Kentmere Valley
tarn
stile and gap
Troutbeck Valley
Above the wall there is no path for 100 yards but one will be found higher up the slope
Rainsborrow Crag
old quarry
tarn
gate
sheep pen
Lowther Brow
quarry path

25 yards beyond the stream a big cairn indicates the indistinct turn to the right from the main path to the quarry.

Buck Crag

The variation start from the pass, by the wall, is very marshy.

Leave the pass at the point where it turns sharply. The first few yards are abominably marshy. Aim for the small cairns ahead.

gate
KENTMERE 2¼
Garburn Pass
1475'
(spelt Garburn Pass on Ordnance Survey maps)

TROUTBECK 2
WINDERMERE 4½

looking north

The easy slopes of Lowther Brow seem to offer an alternative route from Troutbeck, but the promising tracks climbing through the bracken from the cart-road behind Long Green Head (see map) do not continue far and the ascent becomes tiresome. The route depicted here, from Garburn Pass, is better in every way.

This is a dull, easy walk, but the dreary foreground is relieved by the splendid views to the west. There are patches of marshy ground to the 1800' contour — the route throughout is on grass.

Yoke 6

ASCENT FROM KENTMERE
1800 feet of ascent : 2½ miles (3 miles via Garburn Pass)

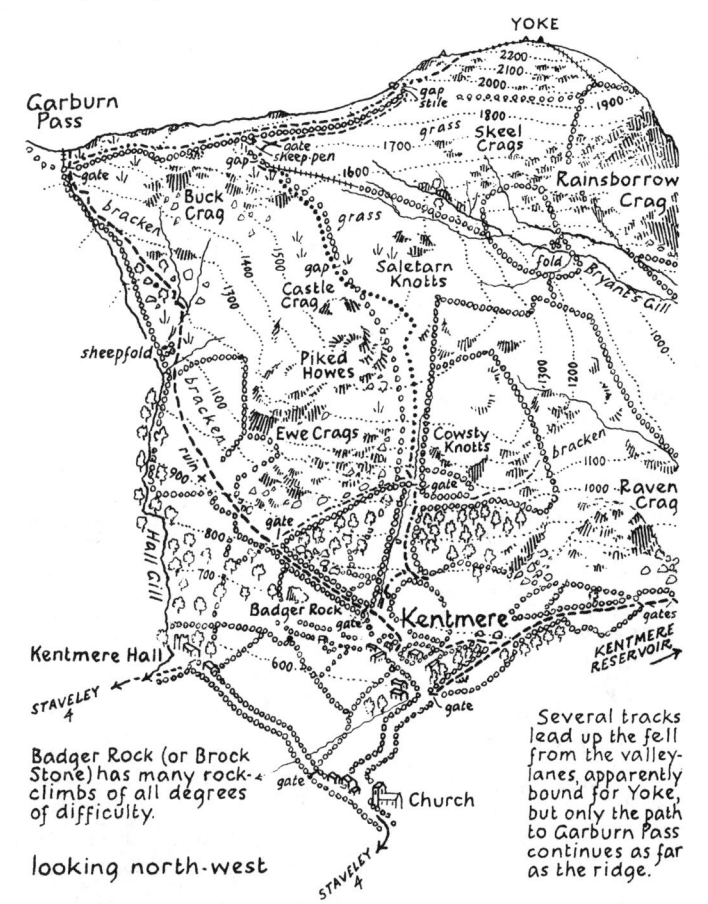

looking north-west

Badger Rock (or Brock Stone) has many rock-climbs of all degrees of difficulty.

Several tracks lead up the fell from the valley-lanes, apparently bound for Yoke, but only the path to Garburn Pass continues as far as the ridge.

Although Garburn Pass offers the easiest route, the craggy screen rising steeply behind the village will tempt the more adventurous walker: the top of the spur is a maze worth exploring, but only the route depicted guarantees to avoid unclimbable walls.

Yoke 7

THE SUMMIT

ILL BELL — HIGH STREET — MARDALE ILL BELL

The highest point on the broad grassy top is a small rock-sided platform with a cairn. A wire fence forms a right-angle nearby. Another cairn (a better viewpoint) stands 130 yards to the south.

DESCENTS: A short descent down the western slope brings into view a good track skirting the summit; this, followed to the left (south) leads to the wall that goes down to Garburn Pass.

In mist, note that the north-east and east slopes are entirely dangerous, and that the lower western flank is very rough: it features, in a walled enclosure, the bracken-concealed, fearful abyss of Park Quarry, a fall into which would definitely end the day's walk. From the top cairn, descend west (170 yards only) to the track; or, if uncertain of the compass points, follow the wire fence left, and left again at another angle — the track will be picked up as it crosses the fence at a broken stile. Turn left (south) along the track, which becomes indistinct but points the direction of the wall going down to Garburn Pass.

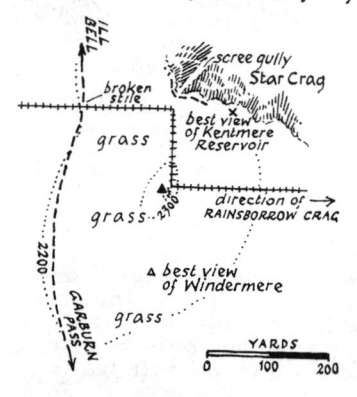

Park Quarry — in the sheltered depths of which flowers bloom and ferns flourish in December

Yoke 8

THE VIEW

This is a good viewpoint, more particularly for the wide sweep of country and sea southwards. Of the Lakeland scene, the prospect due west is especially attractive.

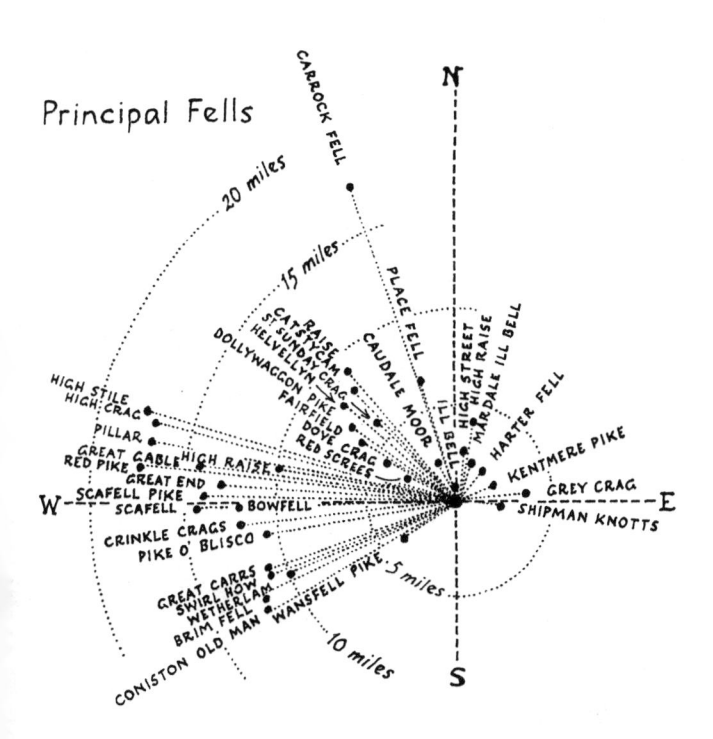

Principal Fells

- CARROCK FELL
- 20 miles
- 15 miles
- PLACE FELL
- CATSTYCAM
- RAISE
- ST SUNDAY CRAG
- HELVELLYN PIKE
- DOLLYWAGGON PIKE
- CAUDALE MOOR
- ILL BELL
- HIGH STREET
- HIGH RAISE
- MARDALE ILL BELL
- FAIRFIELD
- DOVE CRAG
- RED CRAG
- HARTER FELL
- HIGH STILE
- HIGH CRAG
- RED SCREES
- KENTMERE PIKE
- PILLAR
- HIGH RAISE
- GREAT GABLE
- RED PIKE
- GREAT END
- SCAFELL PIKE
- SCAFELL
- BOWFELL
- GREY CRAG
- SHIPMAN KNOTTS
- CRINKLE CRAGS
- PIKE O' BLISCO
- GREAT CARRS
- SWIRL HOW
- WETHERLAM
- BRIM FELL
- WANSFELL PIKE
- CONISTON OLD MAN
- 5 miles
- 10 miles

Lakes and Tarns

SSW : *Windermere* (much better seen from the south cairn : a very beautiful view)
SW : *Blelham Tarn*
———— To see Kentmere Reservoir, visit the edge of Star Crag, where the reservoir comes suddenly and dramatically into view north-east

Yoke 9

RIDGE ROUTE

To ILL BELL, 2476' : ⅔ mile : N
*Depression at 2180' : 300 feet of ascent
An easy climb, safe in mist*

Cross the fence and proceed down to and across the depression with the escarpment close by on the right. This is a simple walk in clear weather, but, although there is no difficulty in mist, it may then be not quite easy to get safely off the top of Ill Bell.

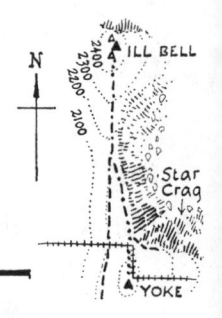

HALF A MILE

Raven Crag

Buck Crag

Badger Rock
(Brock Stone)

West face

East face

This isolated rock stands within fifty yards of the Garburn path, just beyond the last buildings of Kentmere. A well-known local landmark, it has little fame outside the valley. Although the base of the rock is now silted up, there is little doubt that it is a boulder fallen from the fellside above, a theory supported by the cavities beneath (a refuge for foxes), and it may well be the biggest boulder in Lakeland. There are rock-climbs on it of all degrees of difficulty.

Yoke 10

Rainsborrow Crag

THE FAR EASTERN FELLS
*Some Personal Notes
in conclusion*

It would be very remiss of me if I did not take this first opportunity publicly to acknowledge, with sincere gratitude, the many kind and encouraging letters that followed the publication of Book One. There have also been offers of hospitality, of transport (I have no car nor any wish for one), of company and of collaboration, and of financial help — all of which I have declined as gracefully as I could whilst feeling deeply appreciative, for I am stubbornly resolved that this must be a single-handed effort. I have set myself this task, and I am pigheaded enough to want to do it without help. So far, everything is all right. Sufficient copies of Book One were sold to pay the printer's bill, and here again I must thank all readers who recommended the book to others, for it is perfectly clear that, lacking full facilities for publicity and distribution, it could hardly have succeeded otherwise.

I have just completed the last page of Book Two, and feel like a man who has come home from a long and lonely journey. Rarely did I meet anyone on my explorations of the High Street fells. Usually I walked from morning till dusk without a sight of human beings. This is the way I like it, but what joys have been mine that other folk should share! Let me make a plea for the exhilarating hills that form the subject of this book. They should not remain neglected. To walk upon them, to tramp the ridges, to look from their tops across miles of glorious country, is constant delight. But the miles are long, and from one place of accommodation to another they are many. The Far Eastern Fells are for the strong walker and should please the solitary man of keen observation and imagination. Animal and bird life is much in evidence, and not the least of the especial charms of the area is the frequent sight of herds of ponies and deer that make these wild heights their home.

Perhaps I have been a little unkind to Manchester Corporation in referring to Mardale and Swindale in this book. If we can accept as absolutely necessary the conversion of Haweswater, then it must be conceded that Manchester have done the job as unobtrusively as possible. Mardale is still a noble valley. But man works with such clumsy hands! Gone for ever are the quiet wooded bays and shingly shores that Nature had fashioned so sweetly in the Haweswater of old; how aggressively ugly is the tidemark of the new Haweswater! A cardinal mistake has been made, from the walker's point of view, in choosing the site for the new hotel: much more convenient would have been a re-built Dun Bull at the head of the valley, or better still amongst the trees of The Rigg. For a walker who can call upon transport, however, the new road gives splendid access to the heart of the fells.

I leave this area to renew acquaintance with the more popular and frequented heights in the middle of Lakeland — the Langdale, Grasmere and Keswick triangle. This is a beautiful part of the district, and I shall enjoy it; but it is a weakness of mine to be for ever looking back, and often I shall reflect on the haunting loneliness of High Street and the supreme loveliness of Ullswater. It will please me then to think that this book may perhaps help to introduce to others the quiet delights that have been mine during the past two years.

Autumn, 1956   AW.

SIGN REFERENCES
(signs used in the maps and diagrams)

Good footpath
(sufficiently distinct to be followed in mist)

Intermittent footpath
(difficult to follow in mist)

Route recommended but no path
(if recommended one way only, arrow indicates direction)

Wall   Broken wall

Fence   Broken fence

Marshy ground   Trees

Crags   Boulders

Stream or River
(arrow indicates direction of flow)

Waterfall   Bridge

Buildings   Unenclosed road

Contours (at 100' intervals)
1900
1800
1700

Summit-cairn ▲   Other (prominent) cairns △

THE
CENTRAL
FELLS

A PICTORIAL GUIDE
TO THE
LAKELAND FELLS
50TH ANNIVERSARY EDITION

being an illustrated account
of a study and exploration
of the mountains in the
English Lake District

by

AWainwright

BOOK THREE
THE CENTRAL FELLS

Frances Lincoln Limited
4 Torriano Mews
Torriano Avenue
London NW5 2RZ
www.franceslincoln.com

Originally published by Henry Marsall, Kentmere, 1958

First published by Frances Lincoln 2003

50th Anniversary Edition with re-originated artwork
published by Frances Lincoln 2005

Copyright © The Estate of A. Wainwright 1958

All rights reserved. Without limiting the rights under
copyright reserved above, no part of this publication may
be reproduced, stored in or introduced into a retrieval
system, or transmitted, in any form or by any means
(electronic, mechanical, photocopying, or otherwise),
without either prior permission in writing from the
publisher or a licence permitting restricted copying.
In the United Kingdom such licences are issued by
the Copyright Licensing Agency, Saffron House,
6-10 Kirby Street, London EC1N 8TS.

Printed and bound in China

A CIP catalogue record for this book
is available from the British Library.

ISBN 978 0 7112 2456 8

18 17 16 15 14 13 12 11

**50TH ANNIVERSARY EDITION
PUBLISHED BY
FRANCES LINCOLN, LONDON**

THE PICTORIAL GUIDES

Book One: The Eastern Fells, 1955
Book Two: The Far Eastern Fells, 1957
Book Three: The Central Fells, 1958
Book Four: The Southern Fells, 1960
Book Five: The Northern Fells, 1962
Book Six: The North Western Fells, 1964
Book Seven: The Western Fells, 1966

PUBLISHER'S NOTE

This 50th Anniversary edition of the Pictorial Guides to the Lakeland Fells is newly reproduced from the handwritten pages created in the 1950s and 1960s by A. Wainwright. The descriptions of the walks were correct, to the best of the author's knowledge, at the time of first publication and they are reproduced here without amendment. However, footpaths, cairns and other waymarks described here are no longer all as they were fifty years ago and walkers are advised to check with an up-to-date map when planning a walk.

Fellwalking has increased dramatically since the Pictorial Guides were first published. Some popular routes have become eroded, making good footwear and great care all the more necessary for walkers. The vital points about fellwalking, as A. Wainwright himself wrote on many occasions, are to use common sense and to remember to watch where you are putting your feet.

A programme of revision of the Pictorial Guides is under way and revised editions of each of them will be published over the next few years.

BOOK THREE
is dedicated to
those eager explorers of the fells

THE DOGS OF LAKELAND

willing workers and faithful friends,
and an essential part of Lakeland life

INTRODUCTION

Classification and Definition

Any division of the Lakeland fells into geographical districts must necessarily be arbitrary, just as the location of the outer boundaries of Lakeland must always be a matter of opinion. Any attempt to define internal or external boundaries is certain to invite criticism, and he who takes it upon himself to say where Lakeland starts and finishes, or, for example, where the Central Fells merge into the Southern Fells and *which* fells are the Central Fells and which the Southern and *why* they need be so classified, must not expect his pronouncements to be generally accepted.

Yet for present purposes some plan of classification and definition must be used. County and parochial boundaries are no help, nor is the recently-defined area of the Lakeland National Park, for this book is concerned only with the high ground.

First, the external boundaries. Straight lines linking the extremities of the outlying lakes enclose all the higher fells very conveniently. There are a few fells of lesser height to the north and east, however, that are typically Lakeland in character and cannot properly be omitted: these are brought in, somewhat untidily, by extending the lines in those areas. Thus:

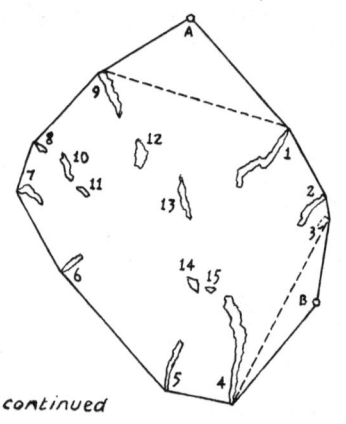

1 : *Ullswater*
2 : *Hawes Water*
3 : proposed *Swindale Resr*
4 : *Windermere*
5 : *Coniston Water*
6 : *Wast Water*
7 : *Ennerdale Water*
8 : *Loweswater*
9 : *Bassenthwaite Lake*
10 : *Crummock Water*
11 : *Buttermere*
12 : *Derwent Water*
13 : *Thirlmere*
14 : *Grasmere*
15 : *Rydal Water*
A : Caldbeck
B : Longsleddale (church)

continued

INTRODUCTION

Classification and Definition

continued   The complete Guide is planned to include all the fells in the area enclosed by the straight lines of the diagram. This is an undertaking quite beyond the compass of a single volume, and it is necessary, therefore, to divide the area into convenient sections, making the fullest use of natural boundaries (lakes, valleys and low passes) so that each district is, as far as possible, self-contained and independent of the rest.

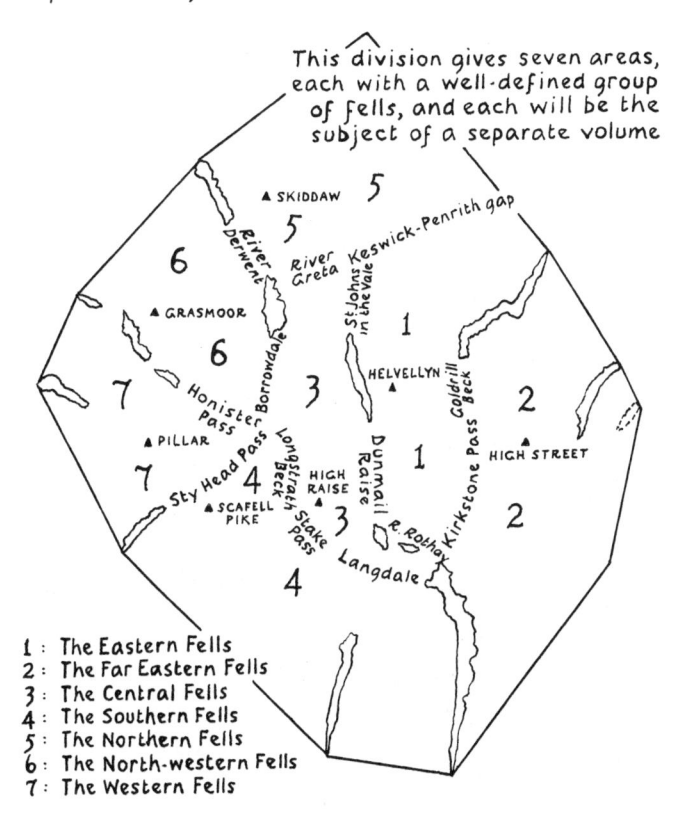

This division gives seven areas, each with a well-defined group of fells, and each will be the subject of a separate volume

1 : The Eastern Fells
2 : The Far Eastern Fells
3 : The Central Fells
4 : The Southern Fells
5 : The Northern Fells
6 : The North-western Fells
7 : The Western Fells

INTRODUCTION

Notes on the Illustrations

THE MAPS .... Many excellent books have been written about Lakeland, but the best literature of all for the walker is that published by the Director General of Ordnance Survey, the 1" map for companionship and guidance on expeditions, the 2½" map for exploration both on the fells and by the fireside. These admirable maps are remarkably accurate topographically but there is a crying need for a revision of the paths on the hills: several walkers' tracks that have come into use during the past few decades, some of them now broad highways, are not shown at all; other paths still shown on the maps have fallen into neglect and can no longer be traced on the ground.

The popular Bartholomew 1" map is a beautiful picture, fit for a frame, but this too is unreliable for paths; indeed here the defect is much more serious, for routes are indicated where no paths ever existed, nor ever could — the cartographer has preferred to take precipices in his stride rather than deflect his graceful curves over easy ground.

Hence the justification for the maps in this book: they have the one merit (of importance to walkers) of being dependable as regards delineation of *paths*. They are intended as supplements to the Ordnance Survey maps, certainly not as substitutes.

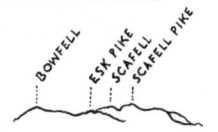

THE VIEWS .... Various devices have been used to illustrate the views from the summits of the fells. The full panorama in the form of an outline drawing is most satisfactory generally, and this method has been adopted for the main viewpoints.

THE DIAGRAMS OF ASCENTS .... The routes of ascent of the higher fells are depicted by diagrams that do not pretend to strict accuracy: they are neither plans nor elevations; in fact there is deliberate distortion in order to show detail clearly: usually they are represented as viewed from imaginary 'space-stations.' But it is hoped they will be useful and interesting.

THE DRAWINGS .... The drawings at least are honest attempts to reproduce what the eye sees: they illustrate features of interest and also serve the dual purpose of breaking up the text and balancing the layout of the pages, and of filling up awkward blank spaces, like this:

Thirlmere

THE
CENTRAL
FELLS

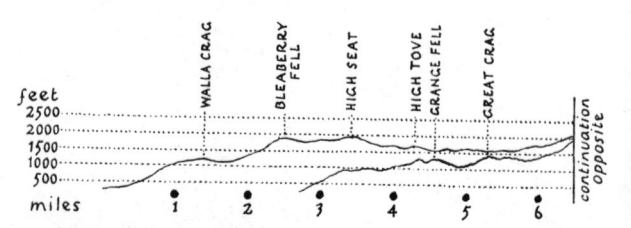

```
                                    WALLA CRAG   BLEABERRY FELL   HIGH SEAT   HIGH TOVE   GRANGE FELL   GREAT CRAG
    feet
    2500
    2000
    1500                                                                                                            continuation
    1000                                                                                                            opposite
     500
    miles           1         2         3         4         5         6
```

Similar in plan to the Eastern and the Far Eastern fells, the high ground of the central area of Lakeland is based on a north-south axis. Deep valleys isolate the mass from the surrounding fells, there being a link with other mountainous terrain only at the Stake Pass. The north-south axis in its lower extremity twists eastwards in this case, however, the area assuming the shape of a jackboot, with Ambleside at the toe, Stake Pass forming the heel's curve, and the leg extending north, between the valleys of Borrowdale and Thirlmere, to the River Greta and Keswick.

The central part of mountainous country might generally be expected to contain the highest peaks, but that is not so here, for the watershed is overtopped on all sides by summits of greater elevation, and only at one point, High Raise, is an altitude of 2500' reached. Nevertheless the central mass is not insignificant and indeed within its boundaries is one particular concentration of mountains, crowded into small space, that, for popular appeal and scenic attractiveness, ranks second to none: the Langdale Pikes.

The best part of the central area for fellwalkers is that south of the Grasmere-Borrowdale crossing via Greenup, for, in addition to the Pikes, the lesser heights declining to the rivers Rothay and Brathay are very colourful and interesting, with crags everywhere, while the views from them include a rich array of lovely lakes.

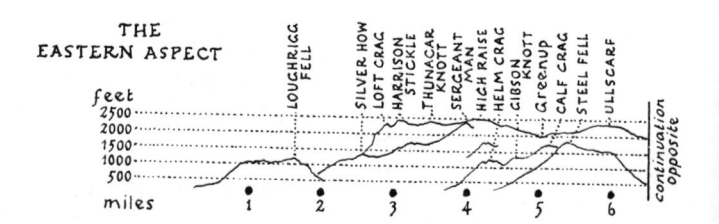

```
    THE                             LOUGHRIGG FELL   SILVER HOW   LOFT CRAG   HARRISON STICKLE   THUNACAR KNOTT   SERGEANT MAN   HIGH RAISE   HELM CRAG   GIBSON KNOTT   Greenup   CALF CRAG   STEEL FELL   ULLSCARF
    EASTERN ASPECT
    feet
    2500
    2000
    1500                                                                                                                                                                                                          continuation
    1000                                                                                                                                                                                                          opposite
     500
    miles           1         2         3         4         5         6
```

THE WESTERN ASPECT

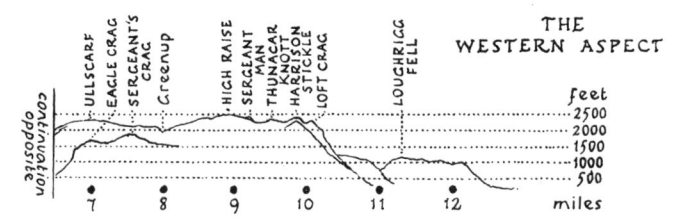

Profile labels: ULLSCARF, EAGLE CRAG, SERGEANT'S CRAG, Greenup, HIGH RAISE, SERGEANT MAN, THUNACAR KNOTT, HARRISON STICKLE, LOFT CRAG, LOUGHRIGG FELL

North of Greenup the terrain is of different character, the main watershed widening and levelling out to such an extent that the rain falling upon it can disperse but slowly; consequently there are many swamps, the worst in Lakeland, where walkers seldom venture. It is a sufficient commentary that in the course of the eight miles from Greenup to Rakefoot this ridge, although in the very heart of the district, is crossed by two footpaths only. But the shortcomings of the ridge in this section are amply compensated by the charm and beauty of the foothills, particularly overlooking Borrowdale: here the immediate surroundings and the distant views are alike supremely lovely. On the Thirlmere side, too, there is a fascination in the silent forests and gaunt crags above the dark waters of the lake.

The area south of Greenup, the fells west of Grasmere, and the Borrowdale flank are all exceedingly favoured by walkers (a circumstance that has led to the provision of much excellent accommodation in the nearby valleys) and are admirably suitable for the holiday-maker whose preference is not so much for the longer excursions and rougher walking demanded by the higher mountains but rather for easier rambles on fells of lesser altitude yet sufficiently high and distinctive to afford that feeling, so wonderfully satisfying, of 'being on the tops'.

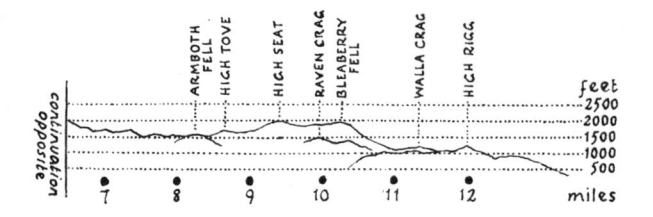

Profile labels: ARMBOTH FELL, HIGH TOVE, HIGH SEAT, RAVEN CRAG, BLEABERRY FELL, WALLA CRAG, HIGH RIGG

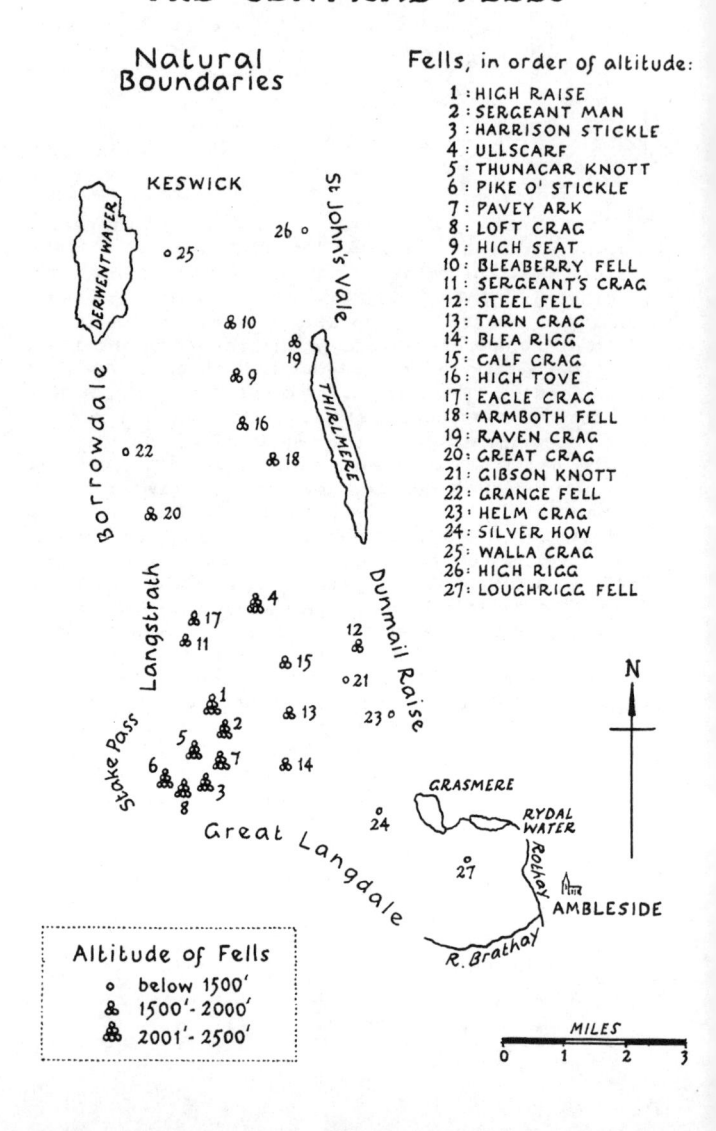

THE CENTRAL FELLS

Natural Boundaries

Fells, in order of altitude:

1: HIGH RAISE
2: SERGEANT MAN
3: HARRISON STICKLE
4: ULLSCARF
5: THUNACAR KNOTT
6: PIKE O' STICKLE
7: PAVEY ARK
8: LOFT CRAG
9: HIGH SEAT
10: BLEABERRY FELL
11: SERGEANT'S CRAG
12: STEEL FELL
13: TARN CRAG
14: BLEA RIGG
15: CALF CRAG
16: HIGH TOVE
17: EAGLE CRAG
18: ARMBOTH FELL
19: RAVEN CRAG
20: GREAT CRAG
21: GIBSON KNOTT
22: GRANGE FELL
23: HELM CRAG
24: SILVER HOW
25: WALLA CRAG
26: HIGH RIGG
27: LOUGHRIGG FELL

KESWICK
DERWENTWATER
St John's Vale
THIRLMERE
Borrowdale
Langstrath
Stake Pass
Dunmail Raise
Great Langdale
GRASMERE
RYDAL WATER
R. Rothay
R. Brathay
AMBLESIDE

N

Altitude of Fells
○ below 1500'
⛊ 1500'- 2000'
⛊ 2001'- 2500'

MILES
0 1 2 3

THE CENTRAL FELLS

Reference to map opposite

2001'–2500'
1500'–2000'
below 1500'

in the order of
their appearance
in this book

Altitude in feet

18	ARMBOTH FELL	1570
10	BLEABERRY FELL	1932
14	BLEA RIGG	1776
15	CALF CRAG	1762
17	EAGLE CRAG	1650
21	GIBSON KNOTT	1379
22	GRANGE FELL	1363
20	GREAT CRAG	1500
3	HARRISON STICKLE	2403
23	HELM CRAG	1299
1	HIGH RAISE	2500
26	HIGH RIGG	1163
9	HIGH SEAT	1995
16	HIGH TOVE	1665
8	LOFT CRAG	2270
27	LOUGHRIGG FELL	1101
7	PAVEY ARK	2288
6	PIKE O' STICKLE	2323
19	RAVEN CRAG	1520
2	SERGEANT MAN	2414
11	SERGEANT'S CRAG	1873
24	SILVER HOW	1292
12	STEEL FELL	1811
13	TARN CRAG	1801
5	THUNACAR KNOTT	2351
4	ULLSCARF	2370
25	WALLA CRAG	1234

8 12 7
―――
27

Each fell is the subject
of a separate chapter

Armboth Fell

1570'
approx.

from Fisher Crag

Armboth Fell has probably as good a claim as any to be regarded as the most centrally situated fell in Lakeland, for straight lines drawn between the northern and southern boundaries, and between the eastern and western, would bisect hereabouts. (Since these boundaries are arbitrary, however, individual opinion will differ on this point).

Peak-baggers and record-chasers may have cause to visit the summit, but other walkers may justifiably consider its ascent a waste of precious time and energy when so many more rewarding climbs are available, for the flat desolate top is little better than a quagmire, a tangle of swamp and heather and mosses, as is much of the surrounding territory. It can be said of very few fells that they are not really worth climbing; Armboth Fell is one of the few.

The fell lies to the east of the central ridge, and the rain that falls upon it either elects to stay there for ever or drains slowly away towards Thirlmere, hurrying only down the steep afforested slopes immediately flanking the reservoir. Such scenic beauty as Armboth Fell has to offer is wholly concentrated in this wooded fringe above Thirlmere, where there are splendid crags and waterfalls, of which Fisher Crag and Launchy Gill are outstanding. The dark forests conceal the dying traces of a lost civilisation, lost not so very long ago.

Armboth Fell 2

ASCENT FROM THIRLMERE

Walkers of a contrary turn of mind will summarily reject the advice to leave Armboth Fell alone and may indeed be strengthened in their determination to climb it; nor are they likely to be deterred by the many TRESPASSERS WILL BE PROSECUTED notices that Manchester Corporation have sprinkled about the landscape. They would be further outraged if, having paid 12s 6d for this book, they found it did not cater for their idiosyncrasies by offering some details of routes of ascent. Here then are four routes, all starting from the road along the west shore of Thirlmere:

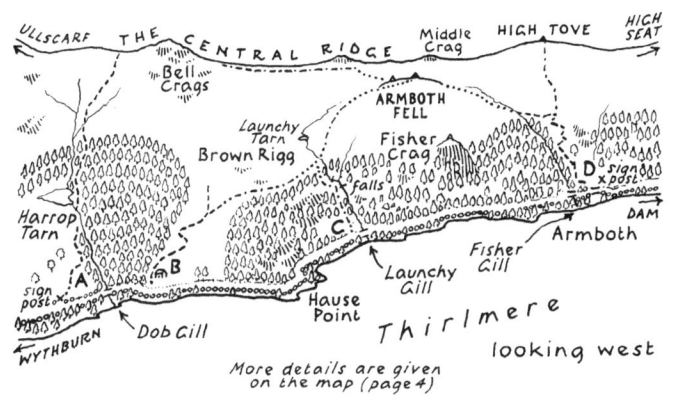

More details are given on the map (page 4)

A : Public footpath. A well-known path, going on to Watendlath. For Armboth Fell leave it at the ridge by a poor track that keeps right of the fence. This route is very wet underfoot throughout; the path in the Harrop Tarn plantations is abominably muddy and even almost impassable in places, for which state of affairs forestry operations are largely to blame.

B : North of Dobgill Bridge a wide section of fellside is unplanted, and a good dry path climbs it. For Armboth Fell leave the path at the top wall and bear right above the plantations, crossing Launchy Gill. This is not a right of way, but until the responsible authorities effect some repairs to the Harrop Tarn footpath trespass here should be forgiven.

C : An old signboard on the roadside at the foot of Launchy Gill now bears no message but in its heyday probably announced the usual threats. An intermittent track on the left (south) bank leads to a desperate struggle with massed conifers before the fell is reached. After rain, the waterfalls provide a magnificent spectacle.

D : Public footpath (to Watendlath). At the top wall bear left and cross and follow up Fisher Gill. Marshy patches.

A balanced boulder, 12 feet high, alongside the footpath from Armboth

Armboth Fell 3

MAP

Although the boundaries of Armboth Fell are strictly defined by Fisher Gill and Launchy Gill, this map includes also much indefinite country southwards to Harrop Tarn and westwards to Bleatarn Gill, some of it reaching a greater elevation than Armboth Fell but having no recognised summits.

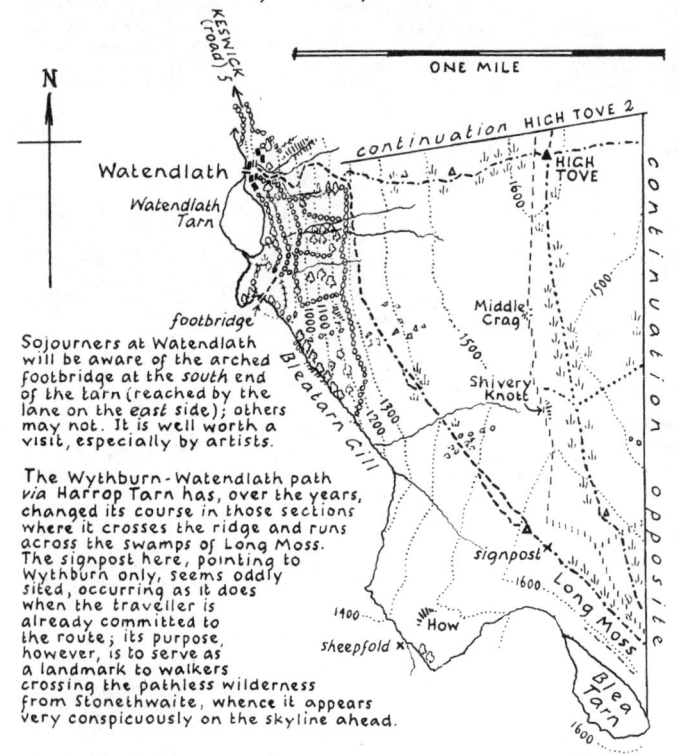

Sojourners at Watendlath will be aware of the arched footbridge at the *south* end of the tarn (reached by the lane on the *east* side); others may not. It is well worth a visit, especially by artists.

The Wythburn-Watendlath path via Harrop Tarn has, over the years, changed its course in those sections where it crosses the ridge and runs across the swamps of Long Moss. The signpost here, pointing to Wythburn only, seems oddly sited, occurring as it does when the traveller is already committed to the route; its purpose, however, is to serve as a landmark to walkers crossing the pathless wilderness from Stonethwaite, whence it appears very conspicuously on the skyline ahead.

Hidden away in the gloom of the Thirlmere plantations are many reminders of community life here before Manchester condemned the area to a slow death and an everlasting silence. Ruined farmsteads and shepherds' huts, overgrown cart-roads, and crumbling allotment and intake walls, deprived of sunlight, have become spectral ghosts, green with moss, in the depths of the forest; the cairns erected to mark the Harrop Tarn path when it traversed an open fellside still stand, heavily overshadowed by trees. The west side of Thirlmere had its illicit whisky distilleries and cockpits, too, and altogether a very interesting history. Now all is buried beneath a green shroud.

Armboth Fell 4

MAP

Armboth is still prominently featured on local signposts and on maps, but is now no more than a name — there are no habitations anywhere on the west side of Thirlmere

ONE MILE

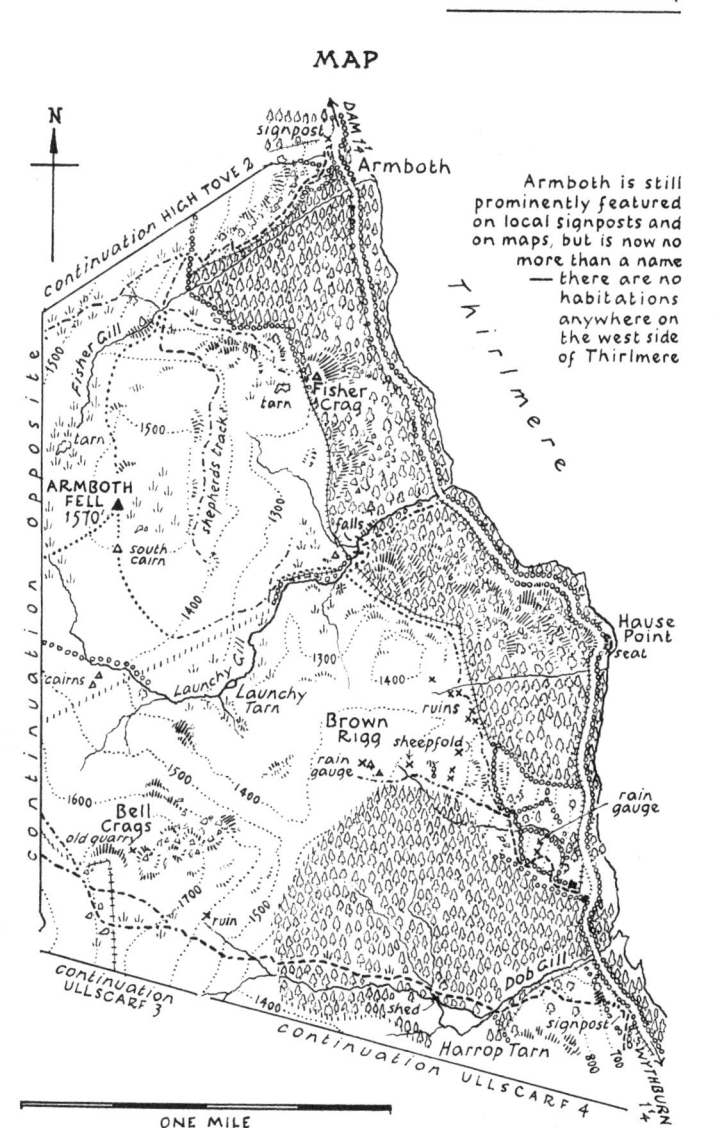

Armboth Fell 5

THE SUMMIT

A few stones heaped together on a rocky mound indicate the highest point although another prominence east of north would seem to have an equal claim to that distinction. The top of the fell is a wide plateau of heather and bog, and the cairn is not easy to locate even in clear weather, especially if approached from the east.

A furlong south of the summit-cairn, at a lower elevation, is a well-built shepherd's cairn on a rock.

THE VIEW

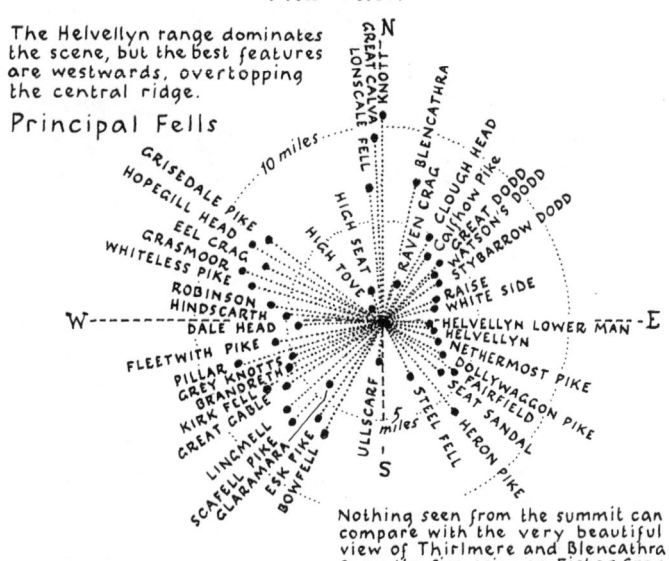

The Helvellyn range dominates the scene, but the best features are westwards, overtopping the central ridge.

Principal Fells

Nothing seen from the summit can compare with the very beautiful view of Thirlmere and Blencathra from the fine cairn on Fisher Crag

Lakes and Tarns
None, except a few nameless puddles in the vicinity.

Armboth Fell 6

RIDGE ROUTES

TO HIGH TOVE, 1665':
1 mile: W, then N
Depression at 1475'
200 feet of ascent
Dreariness and desolation
The tempting beeline cannot be done because of bog. Aim west for the ridge-path, such as it is.

TO ULLSCARF, 2370':
3 miles: SW, then S, SW and S
Sundry depressions, all marshy
950 feet of ascent
Squelch, squelch, squelch all the way.
A wet and weary trudge along the swampiest ridge in the district. A path may be joined 200 yards short of Shivery Knott (indistinct just here)

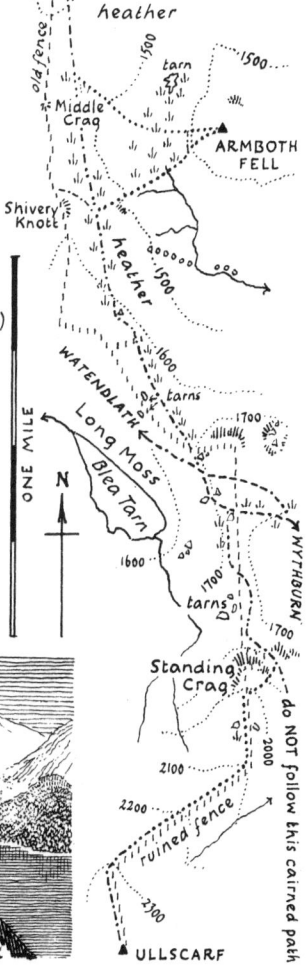

Waterfalls in Launchy Gill

View from Fisher Crag
VISITORS HERE WILL BE PROSECUTED

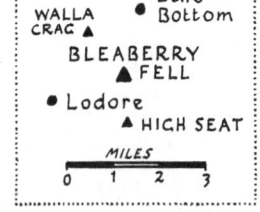

Bleaberry Fell 1932'

from Ashness Wood

- Keswick
- Dale Bottom
- WALLA CRAG ▲
- ▲ BLEABERRY FELL
- Lodore
- ▲ HIGH SEAT

MILES
0 1 2 3

The Shoulthwaite Crags

Iron Crag   Goat Crags

Bleaberry Fell 2

NATURAL FEATURES

Bleaberry Fell terminates the central ridge to the north in much the same manner as Clough Head and Loadpot Hill terminate the parallel Helvellyn and High Street ridges on the eastern side of the district, and it is similar in formation, appearing as a lofty rounded dome overlooking the Keswick to Penrith gap. Unlike the eastern ridges, however, which give good walking throughout over a series of interesting summits, the greater part of the central ridge is marshy and the summits dreary (north of Greenup): unsuitable territory for fell-walking. But Bleaberry Fell is a magnificent exception: it is a superb viewpoint, ideally situated for a long and lazy contemplation of a beautiful panorama. What is more, and here it scores heavily over other fells along the ridge, it can be climbed dryshod and the short springy heather of the top is a joy to tread.

Borrowdale on the west side, and the Naddle and Shoulthwaite valleys eastwards, are the boundaries, both flanks being buttressed by steep crags, notably Iron Crag and Goat Crags above Shoulthwaite and the better-known Falcon Crag above Derwentwater. From the summit a lower and less definite ridge continues over Dodd Crag and Pike before coming down to the pastures of Rakefoot and then sloping gently to the Vale of Keswick accompanied by the pleasant Brockle Beck, the fell's main stream.

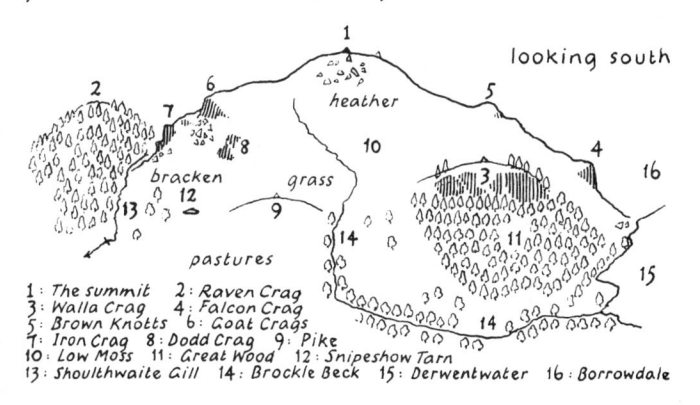

looking south

1: The summit 2: Raven Crag
3: Walla Crag 4: Falcon Crag
5: Brown Knotts 6: Goat Crags
7: Iron Crag 8: Dodd Crag 9: Pike
10: Low Moss 11: Great Wood 12: Snipeshow Tarn
13: Shoulthwaite Gill 14: Brockle Beck 15: Derwentwater 16: Borrowdale

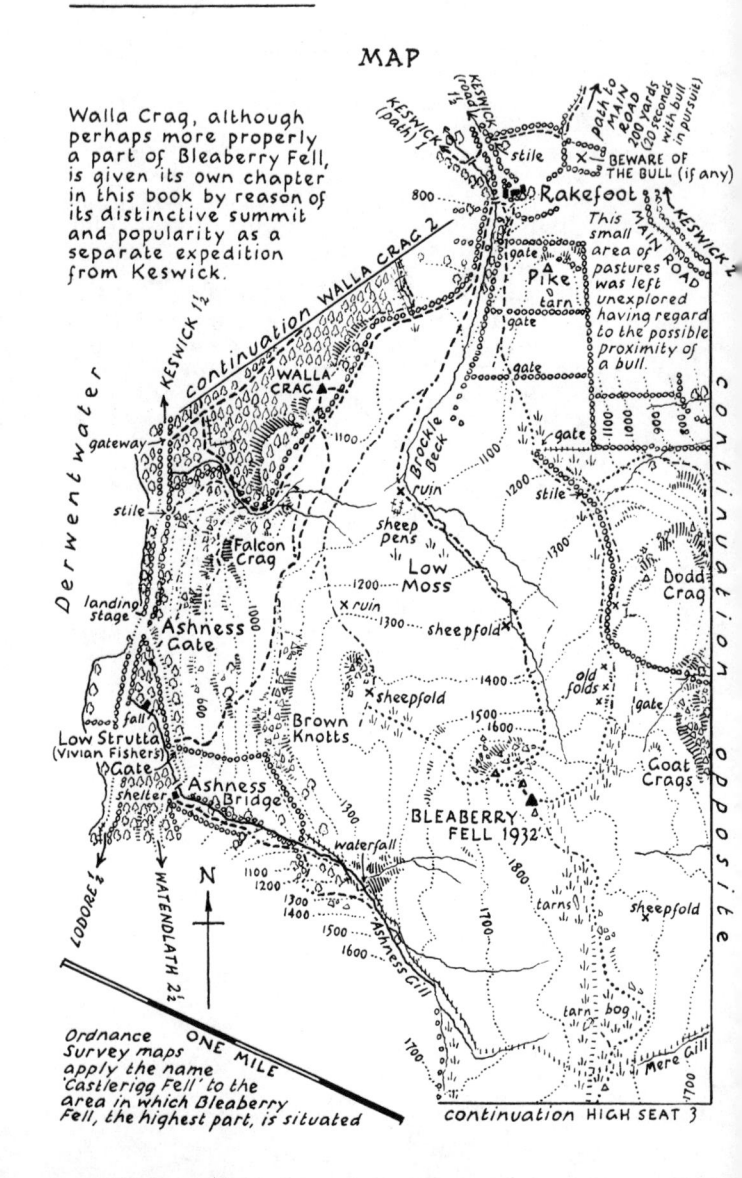

Bleaberry Fell 3

MAP

Walla Crag, although perhaps more properly a part of Bleaberry Fell, is given its own chapter in this book by reason of its distinctive summit and popularity as a separate expedition from Keswick.

Ordnance Survey maps apply the name 'Castlerigg Fell' to the area in which Bleaberry Fell, the highest part, is situated

Bleaberry Fell 4

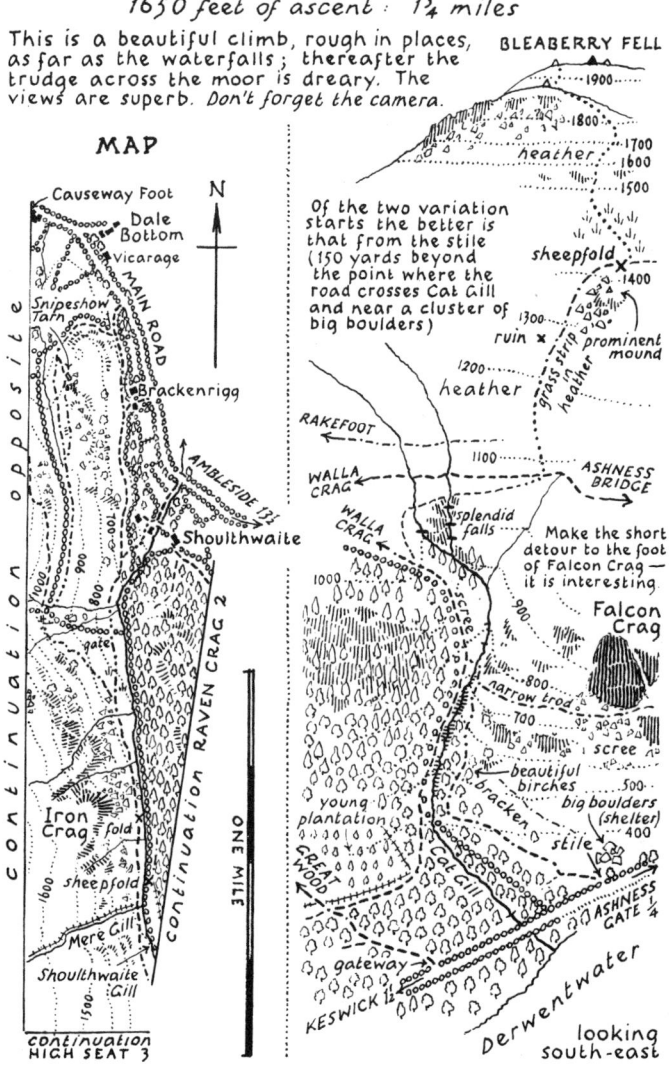

ASCENT FROM THE BORROWDALE ROAD
1650 feet of ascent : 1¼ miles

This is a beautiful climb, rough in places, as far as the waterfalls; thereafter the trudge across the moor is dreary. The views are superb. Don't forget the camera.

MAP

Of the two variation starts the better is that from the stile (150 yards beyond the point where the road crosses Cat Gill and near a cluster of big boulders)

Make the short detour to the foot of Falcon Crag — it is interesting.

looking south-east

Bleaberry Fell 5

ASCENT FROM KESWICK
1650 feet of ascent : 3½ miles

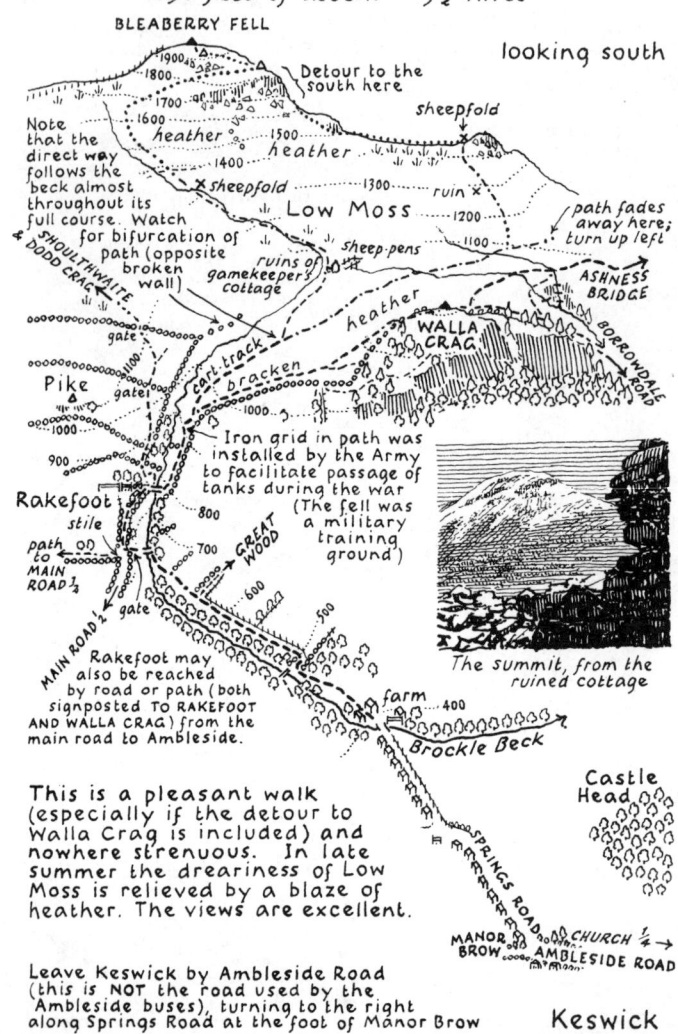

looking south

BLEABERRY FELL
1900, 1800, 1700, 1600, 1500, 1400
Detour to the south here
sheepfold
heather
Note that the direct way follows the beck almost throughout its full course. Watch for bifurcation of path (opposite broken wall)
SHOULTHWAITE & DODD CRAG
Low Moss
1300 ruin
1200
1100
path fades away here; turn up left
sheepfold
sheep pens
ruins of gamekeeper's cottage
ASHNESS BRIDGE
BORROWDALE ROAD
gate
cart-track
heather
WALLA CRAG
Pike
gate
bracken
1000
900
Iron grid in path was installed by the Army to facilitate passage of tanks during the war (The fell was a military training ground)
Rakefoot
stile
800
path on to MAIN ROAD ½
700
GREAT WOOD
600
gate
MAIN ROAD 2
500
Rakefoot may also be reached by road or path (both signposted TO RAKEFOOT AND WALLA CRAG) from the main road to Ambleside.

The summit, from the ruined cottage

farm
400
Brockle Beck

Castle Head

This is a pleasant walk (especially if the detour to Walla Crag is included) and nowhere strenuous. In late summer the dreariness of Low Moss is relieved by a blaze of heather. The views are excellent.

SPRINGS ROAD

MANOR BROW CHURCH ¼
AMBLESIDE ROAD

Leave Keswick by Ambleside Road (this is NOT the road used by the Ambleside buses), turning to the right along Springs Road at the foot of Manor Brow

Keswick

Bleaberry Fell 6

ASCENT FROM DALE BOTTOM
1600 feet of ascent · 3 miles (5½ from Keswick)

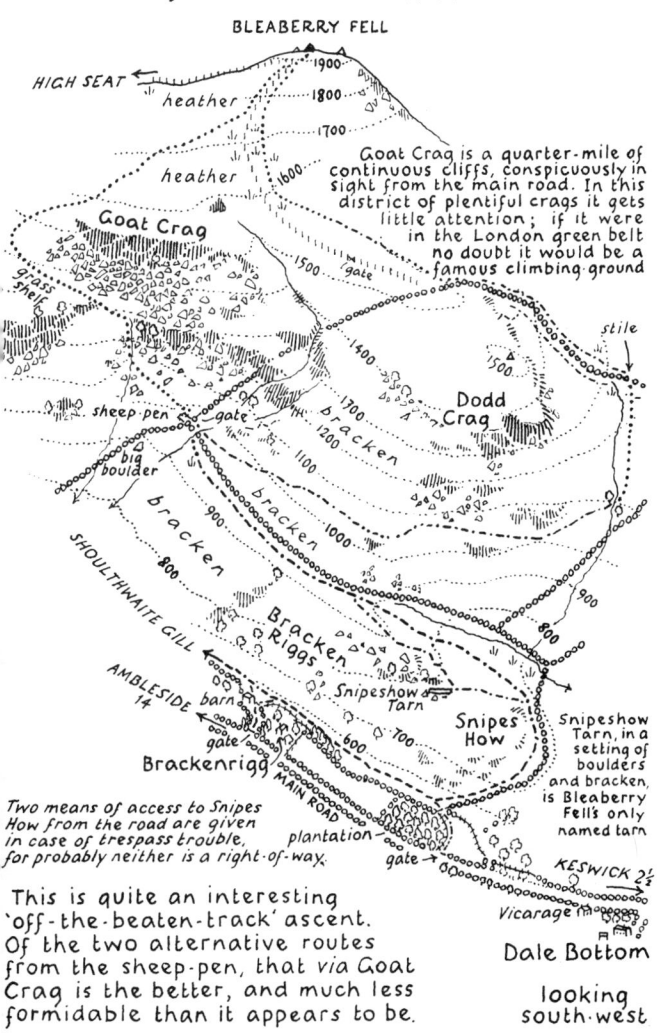

BLEABERRY FELL

HIGH SEAT ←

heather

Goat Crag is a quarter-mile of continuous cliffs, conspicuously in sight from the main road. In this district of plentiful crags it gets little attention; if it were in the London green belt no doubt it would be a famous climbing-ground

Goat Crag

grass shelf

gate

stile

Dodd Crag

sheep pen

gate

big boulder

bracken

bracken

bracken

SHOULTHWAITE GILL

Bracken Riggs

barn

AMBLESIDE 14

Snipeshow Tarn

gate

Snipes How

Snipeshow Tarn, in a setting of boulders and bracken, is Bleaberry Fell's only named tarn

Brackenrigg

MAIN ROAD

plantation

gate

KESWICK 2½ →

Vicarage

Dale Bottom

looking south-west

Two means of access to Snipes How from the road are given in case of trespass trouble, for probably neither is a right-of-way.

This is quite an interesting 'off-the-beaten-track' ascent. Of the two alternative routes from the sheep-pen, that via Goat Crag is the better, and much less formidable than it appears to be.

Bleaberry Fell 7

THE VIEW

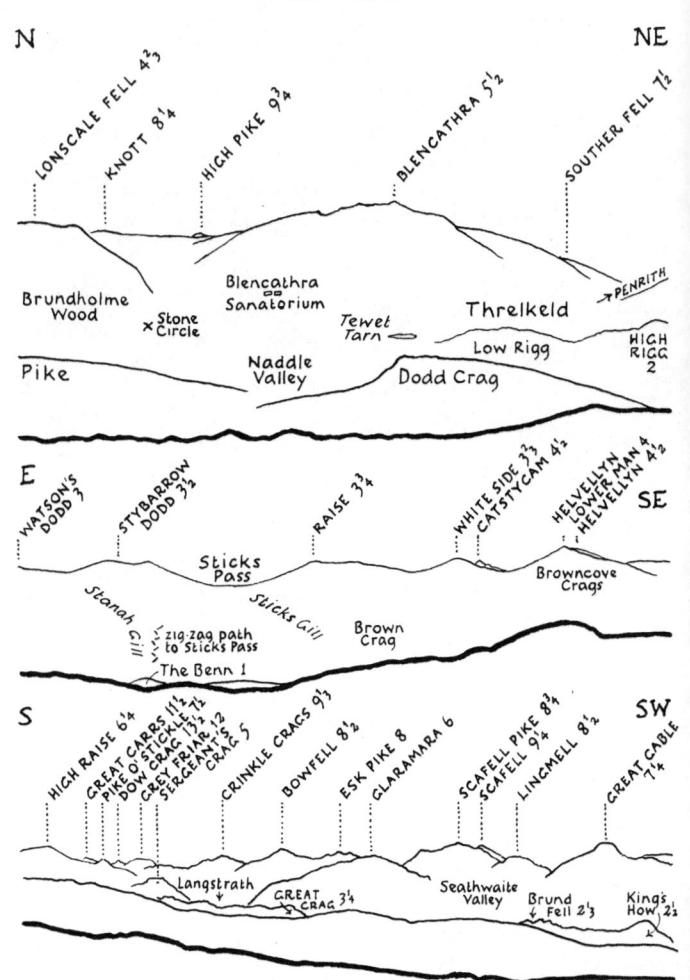

N — Lonscale Fell 4¾, Knott 8¼, High Pike 9¼, Blencathra 5½, Souther Fell 7½ — NE

Brundholme Wood, × Stone Circle, Blencathra Sanatorium, Tewet Tarn, Threlkeld, PENRITH, Pike, Naddle Valley, Dodd Crag, Low Rigg, HIGH RIGG 2

E — Watson's Dodd 3, Stybarrow Dodd 3½, Raise 3¾, White Side 3¾, Catstycam 4½, Helvellyn 4, Lower Man, Helvellyn 4½ — SE

Sticks Pass, Sticks Gill, Browncove Crags, Stanah Gill, zig-zag path to Sticks Pass, Brown Crag, The Benn 1

S — High Raise 6¼, Great Carrs 11½, Pike o' Stickle 7½, Dow Crag 13½, Grey Friar 12, Sergeant's Crag 5, Crinkle Crags 9¾, Bowfell 8½, Esk Pike 8, Claramara 6, Scafell Pike 8¾, Scafell 9¼, Lingmell 8½, Great Gable 7¼ — SW

Langstrath, GREAT CRAG 3¼, Seathwaite Valley, Brund Fell 2½, King's How 2½

The figures following the names of fells
indicate distances in miles

Bleaberry Fell 8

THE VIEW

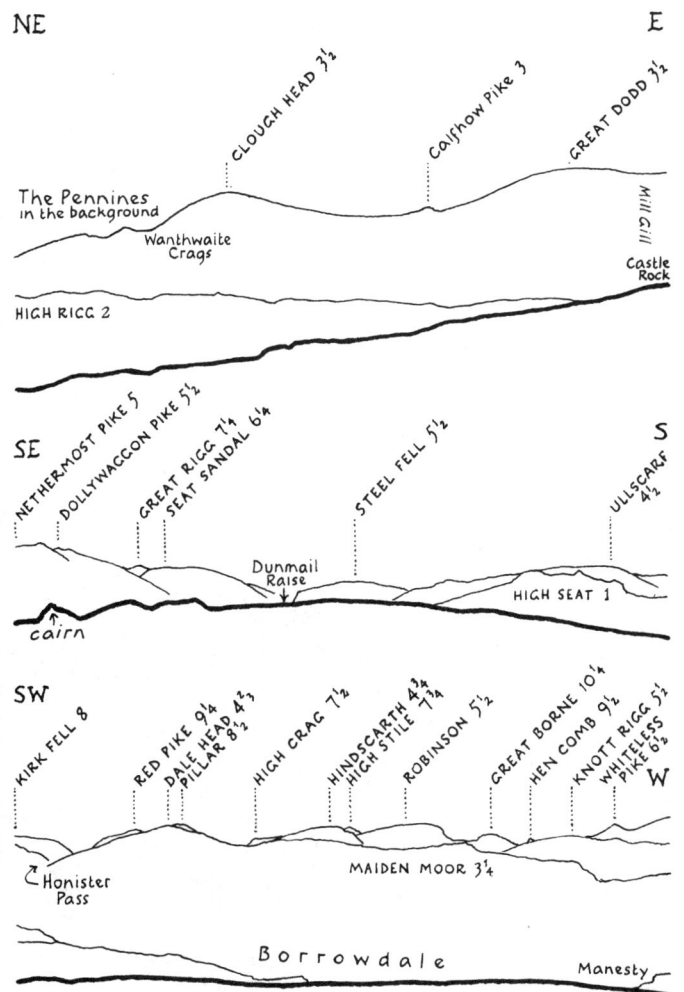

NE — **E**

The Pennines in the background
Wanthwaite Crags
CLOUGH HEAD 3½
Calfhow Pike 3
GREAT DODD 3½
Mill Gill
Castle Rock
HIGH RICC 2

SE — **S**

NETHERMOST PIKE 5
DOLLYWAGGON PIKE 5½
GREAT RIGG 7¼
SEAT SANDAL 6¼
STEEL FELL 5½
ULLSCARF 4½
Dunmail Raise
HIGH SEAT 1
cairn

SW — **W**

KIRK FELL 8
RED PIKE 9¼
DALE HEAD 4⅔
PILLAR 8½
HIGH CRAG 7½
HINDSCARTH 4¾
HIGH STILE 7¾
ROBINSON 5½
GREAT BORNE 10¼
HEN COMB 9½
KNOTT RIGG 5½
WHITELESS PIKE 6½
Honister Pass
MAIDEN MOOR 3¼

Borrowdale
Manesty

The thick line marks the visible boundaries of the summit-plateau

continued

Bleaberry Fell 9

THE VIEW

continued

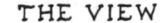

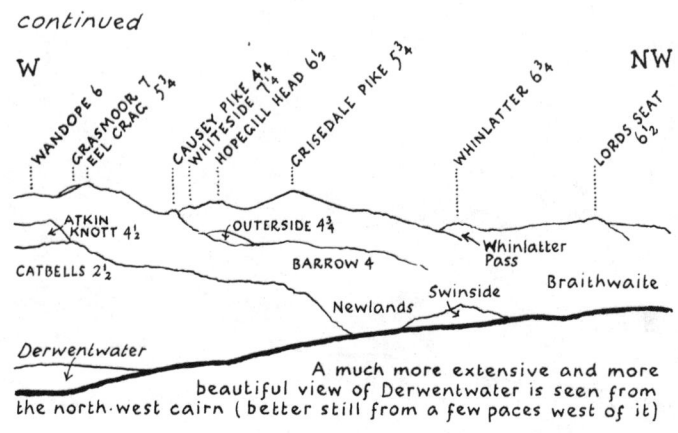

W — WANDOPE 6, GRASMOOR 7, EEL CRAG 5¾, CAUSEY PIKE 4¼, WHITESIDE 7¼, HOPEGILL HEAD 6½, GRISEDALE PIKE 5¾, WHINLATTER 6¾, LORDS SEAT 6½ — NW

ATKIN KNOTT 4½, OUTERSIDE 4¾, Whinlatter Pass
CATBELLS 2½, BARROW 4, Braithwaite
Newlands, Swinside
Derwentwater

A much more extensive and more beautiful view of Derwentwater is seen from the north-west cairn (better still from a few paces west of it)

THE SUMMIT

A carpet of short sweet heather makes the top a beautiful place, although there is nothing exciting about it other than the panorama, which is first-class. Three big cairns indicate viewpoints, while an insignificant fourth shows the way to High Seat in mist.

DESCENTS: Bearing in mind a line of low crags fringing the top to the north, there should not be any difficulty in descending to Keswick via Rakefoot, but ways down to the Borrowdale Road and Shoulthwaite need care even in clear weather. In mist, it is not advisable to try to get down to Shoulthwaite: the crags on this route are a dangerous trap.

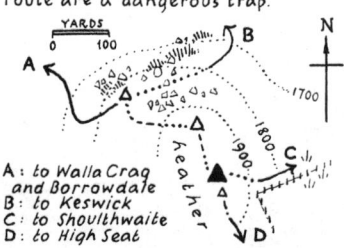

A: to Walla Crag and Borrowdale
B: to Keswick
C: to Shoulthwaite
D: to High Seat

Falcon Crag

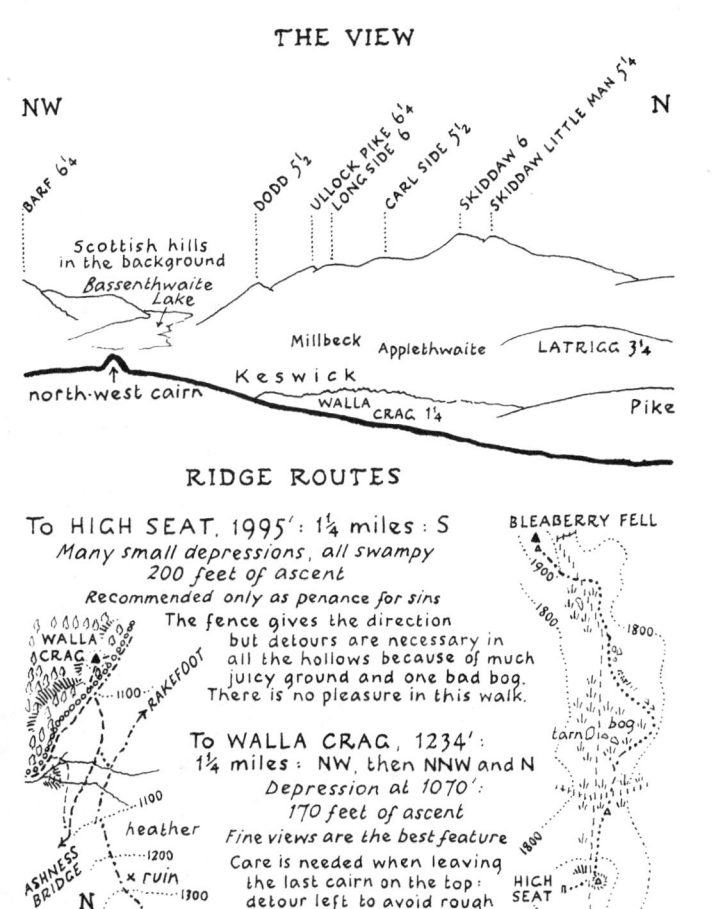

Bleaberry Fell 10

THE VIEW

NW — Barf 6¼ — Scottish hills in the background — Bassenthwaite Lake — Dodd 5½ — Ullock Pike 6¼ — Long Side 6 — Carl Side 5½ — Skiddaw 6 — Skiddaw Little Man 5¼ — N

north-west cairn — Millbeck — Applethwaite — Keswick — Latrigg 3¼ — Walla Crag 1¼ — Pike

RIDGE ROUTES

To HIGH SEAT, 1995': 1¼ miles : S
Many small depressions, all swampy
200 feet of ascent
Recommended only as penance for sins

The fence gives the direction but detours are necessary in all the hollows because of much juicy ground and one bad bog. There is no pleasure in this walk.

To WALLA CRAG, 1234':
1¼ miles : NW, then NNW and N
Depression at 1070':
170 feet of ascent
Fine views are the best feature

Care is needed when leaving the last cairn on the top: detour left to avoid rough ground directly below, then aim for the sheepfold, where a track will be found. The green path leading up to Walla Crag is clearly seen ahead: note that this is not the first path met at the depression but the second, a hundred yards on.

HALF A MILE

Blea Rigg   1776'

from Greathead Crag

Blea Rigg 2

NATURAL FEATURES

The intricate and erratic ridge or shoulder that comes down from High Raise and, after a journey of several miles, expends itself at the meeting-place of the Rothay and Brathay rivers, is broad (a mile or more in places) and undulating (its descent being interrupted by a score of separate summits — many of them nameless). Hardly anywhere can it properly be described as a ridge for its features are akin to those of an upland plateau, but at one point a mild steepening of the sides and a comparative narrowness of the crest do confer a certain boldness of character. This place is Blea Rigg, which appears as a peaked top only when seen from lower down the shoulder. A long wall of crag overlooking Easedale Tarn is the great feature here; the opposite flank, falling to Great Langdale, is less impressive although on this side too there are considerable outcrops and faces of rock, notably along the course of White Gill. The slopes of Blea Rigg come down to Stickle Tarn on the one side and Easedale Tarn on the other, and the main mass of the fell may be said to lie between, but in this chapter, for convenience, will be included also the less definite adjoining part of the shoulder south-east to the point where a link is established with Silver How.

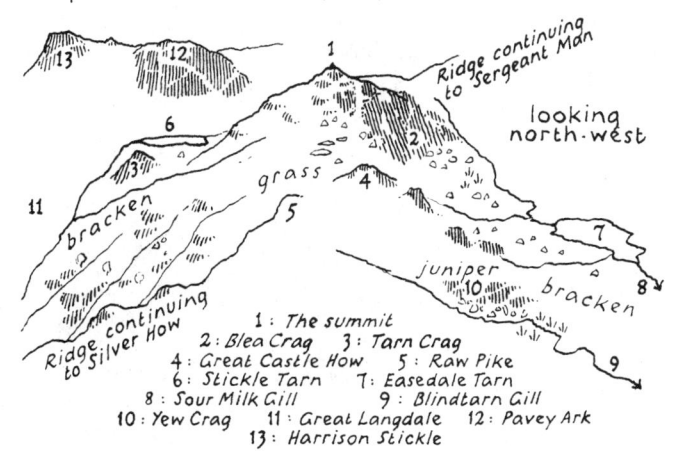

looking north-west

Ridge continuing to Sergeant Man

Ridge continuing to Silver How

1 : The summit
2 : Blea Crag   3 : Tarn Crag
4 : Great Castle How   5 : Raw Pike
6 : Stickle Tarn   7 : Easedale Tarn
8 : Sour Milk Gill   9 : Blindtarn Gill
10 : Yew Crag   11 : Great Langdale   12 : Pavey Ark
13 : Harrison Stickle

Blea Rigg 3

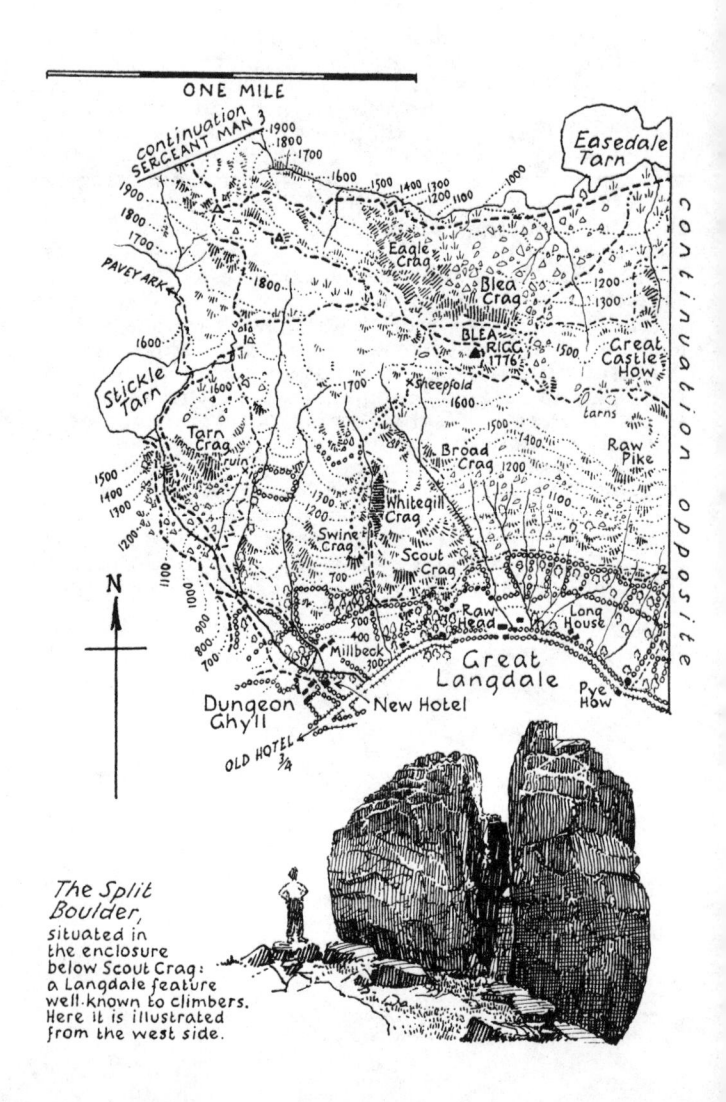

MAP

The Split Boulder, situated in the enclosure below Scout Crag: a Langdale feature well-known to climbers. Here it is illustrated from the west side.

Blea Rigg 4

MAP

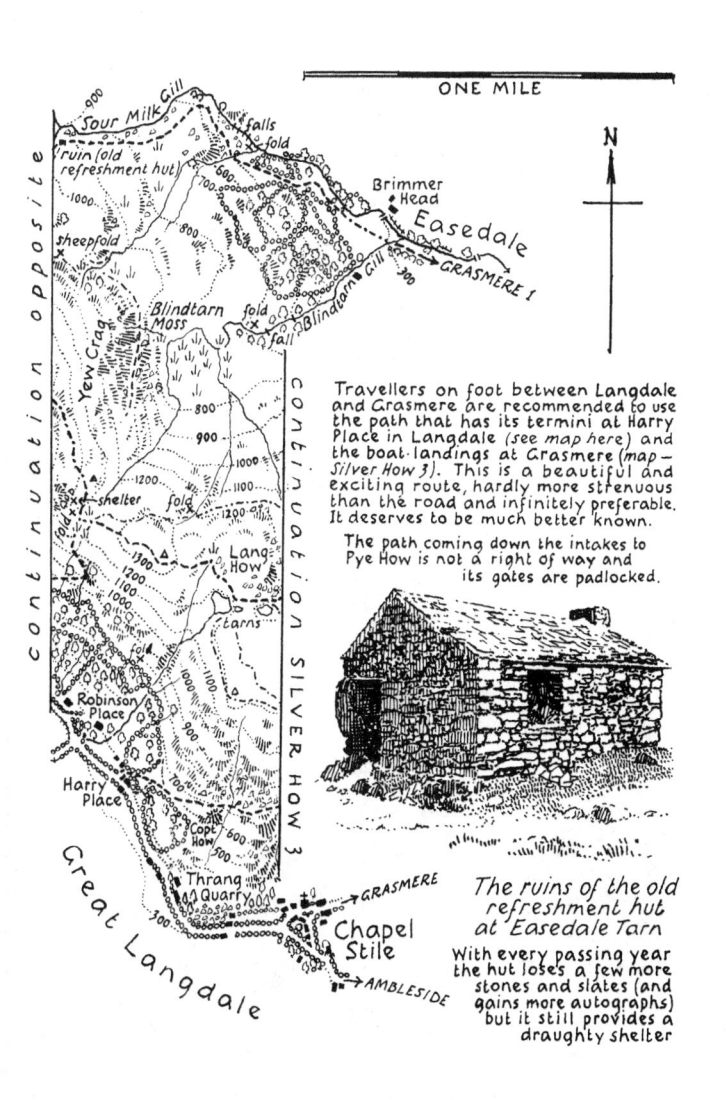

ONE MILE

N

Travellers on foot between Langdale and Grasmere are recommended to use the path that has its termini at Harry Place in Langdale (see map here) and the boat-landings at Grasmere (map – Silver How 3). This is a beautiful and exciting route, hardly more strenuous than the road and infinitely preferable. It deserves to be much better known.

The path coming down the intakes to Pye How is not a right of way and its gates are padlocked.

The ruins of the old refreshment hut at Easedale Tarn

With every passing year the hut loses a few more stones and slates (and gains more autographs) but it still provides a draughty shelter

Blea Rigg 5

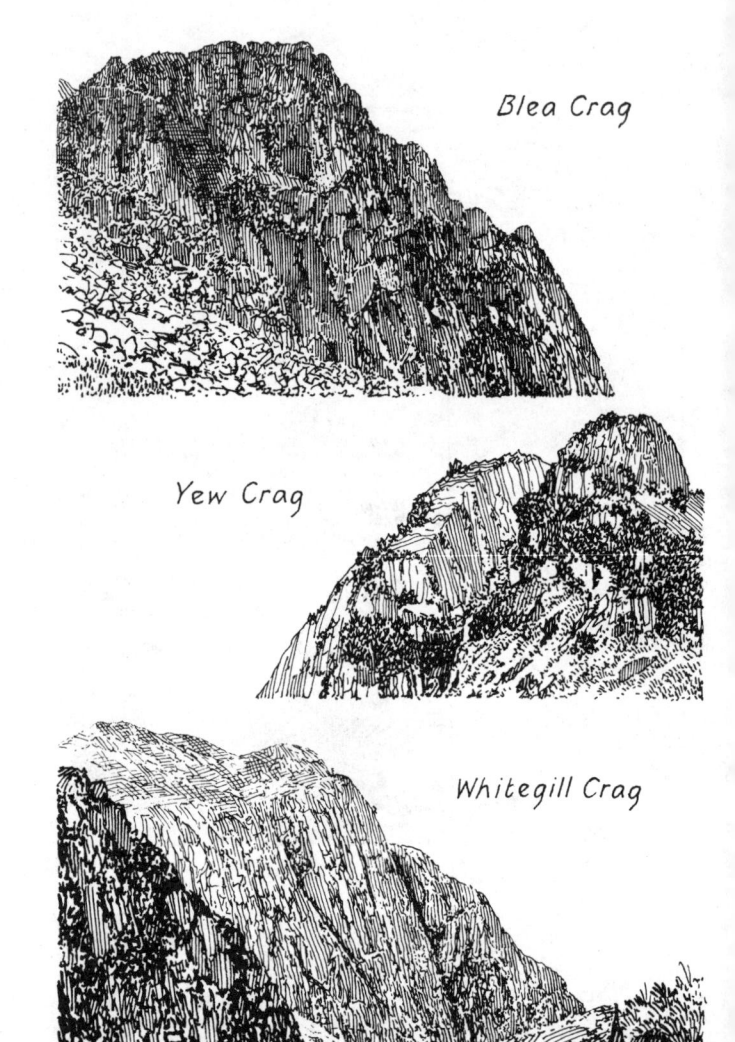

Blea Crag

Yew Crag

Whitegill Crag

Blea Rigg 6

ASCENT FROM GRASMERE
1600 feet of ascent: 3½ miles

looking south-west

Instead of following the usual boggy path alongside the tarn and its main feeder to gain the ridge beyond the summit (this is a favourite way to Dungeon Ghyll) try one of the two direct routes illustrated: the first, from behind the hut, starts promisingly and finishes well but the intermediate section is swampy and dull; the second, with an indistinct start, is the better and it has the virtue (unique hereabouts) of being reasonably dry underfoot. Incidentally, apart from being a quick way to the top of Blea Rigg, this second route provides a direct link between Easedale and Stickle Tarns; a turn left from the main path 200 yards after crossing the first beck beyond the hut soon brings the track into sight as it skirts a small hillock (moraine) on the left side.

The direct routes illustrated are alternatives to the more popular approach along the Silver How ridge: they are especially useful if it is wished to 'save' the ridge for the return to Grasmere, the better way to walk it.

Blea Rigg 7

ASCENT FROM DUNGEON GHYLL (via TARN CRAG)
1550 feet of ascent · 2 miles from the New Hotel

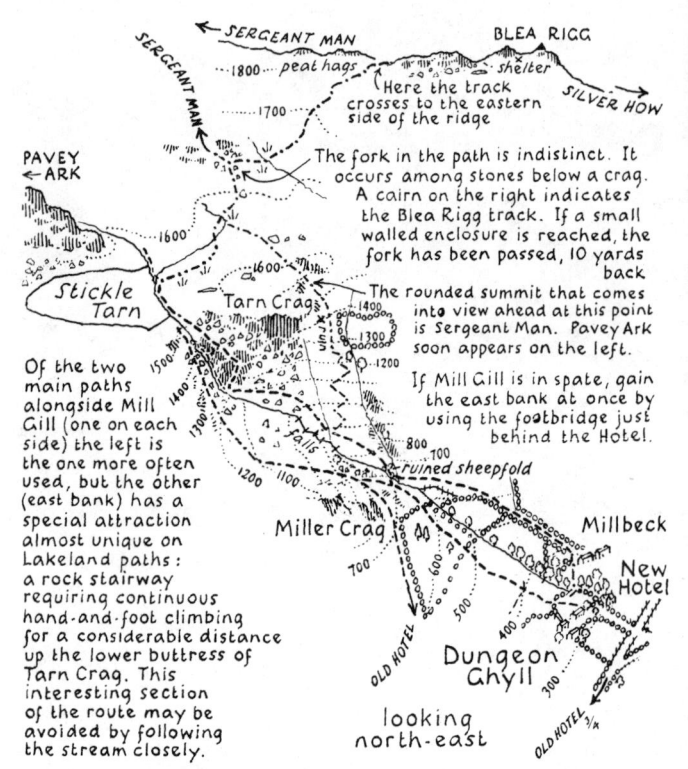

(map sketch)

- ← SERGEANT MAN
- BLEA RIGG
- shelter
- 1800 peat hags
- SILVER HOW →
- Here the track crosses to the eastern side of the ridge
- 1700
- PAVEY ← ARK
- The fork in the path is indistinct. It occurs among stones below a crag. A cairn on the right indicates the Blea Rigg track. If a small walled enclosure is reached, the fork has been passed, 10 yards back
- 1600
- Stickle Tarn
- Tarn Crag
- The rounded summit that comes into view ahead at this point is Sergeant Man. Pavey Ark soon appears on the left.
- 1400
- 1300
- 1200
- If Mill Gill is in spate, gain the east bank at once by using the footbridge just behind the Hotel.
- 1500
- 1400
- 1200 1100
- 800 700
- ruined sheepfold
- Of the two main paths alongside Mill Gill (one on each side) the left is the one more often used, but the other (east bank) has a special attraction almost unique on Lakeland paths: a rock stairway requiring continuous hand-and-foot climbing for a considerable distance up the lower buttress of Tarn Crag. This interesting section of the route may be avoided by following the stream closely.
- Miller Crag
- 700
- 600
- Millbeck
- New Hotel
- 500
- Dungeon Ghyll
- 400
- OLD HOTEL
- 300
- OLD HOTEL
- looking north-east

Try the zig-zag alternative. This is the original path, well-engineered, and its grass is a pleasant relief from the stony tracks by the gill. Its start is easily passed unnoticed, the point of divergence being at a small cairn a few yards short of the first stream after leaving the sheepfold.

The first mile is excellent, with first-class scenery all around. The route degenerates into dullness during the second mile although the final ridge of Blea Rigg is attractive and opens out new views.

Blea Rigg 8

ASCENT FROM DUNGEON GHYLL (via WHITEGILL CRAG)
1500 feet of ascent : 1½ miles from the New Hotel

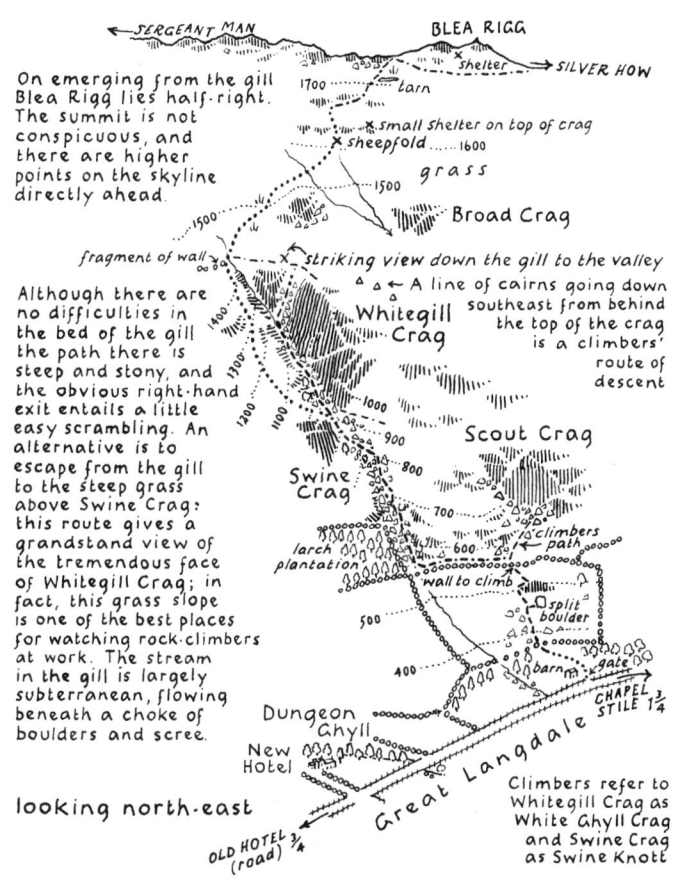

On emerging from the gill Blea Rigg lies half-right. The summit is not conspicuous, and there are higher points on the skyline directly ahead.

Although there are no difficulties in the bed of the gill the path there is steep and stony, and the obvious right-hand exit entails a little easy scrambling. An alternative is to escape from the gill to the steep grass above Swine Crag: this route gives a grandstand view of the tremendous face of Whitegill Crag; in fact, this grass slope is one of the best places for watching rock-climbers at work. The stream in the gill is largely subterranean, flowing beneath a choke of boulders and scree.

A line of cairns going down southeast from behind the top of the crag is a climbers' route of descent

looking north-east

Climbers refer to Whitegill Crag as White Ghyll Crag and Swine Crag as Swine Knott

This is a walk for those who like to see grand rock-scenery at close quarters (from positions of absolute security!). On this route, Whitegill Crag reveals itself in almost shocking intimacy. The final stages are, in contrast, deadly dull.

Blea Rigg 9

THE SUMMIT

Although Blea Rigg is traversed on the popular ridge-walk from Silver How to Sergeant Man it gets little attention and the cairn, surmounting a rocky bluff, is often passed unnoticed. The rough top, however, with its many outcrops and small tarns, is entirely attractive, and the paths hereabouts (none of them very plain) are interesting to follow. The serrated top of Blea Crag, worthy of a cautious visit, is a hundred yards north of the summit cairn. Westwards, the ridge quickly rises to higher ground.

DESCENTS: The best route for Grasmere is via the ridge-path, rounding Lang How, and the obvious way down to Great Langdale is by the Stickle Tarn path, descending thence to Dungeon Ghyll. In mist, these paths are just about good enough to trace, thanks to many cairns, and should be followed closely. For Grasmere, in really bad weather, it is better to get off the ridge at once; take the quick route down to Easedale Tarn.

A: Main path, going down to Stickle Tarn
B and C: Indistinct branches continuing ridge-walk to Sergeant Man.
   C gives a dramatic view of Blea Crag (✲); when it fades away turn up left to join B.
D: An ingenious track making use of a grassy rake immediately behind the edge of Blea Crag. (Quickest route, Stickle Tarn — Easedale Tarn)
E: Best way down to Easedale Tarn; path indistinct initially.
F: Path direct to old refreshment hut at Easedale Tarn; swampy.
G: Ridge-path to Grasmere or Silver How.   H: Junction indistinct.

Blea Rigg 10

THE VIEW

The view is good, although it contains none of the Scafell group nor the western fells. Prominent in an interesting panorama, due west, is the striking outline of Harrison Stickle and Pavey Ark: these heights are, however, better seen from several other points further along the ridge, westwards. Only a small part of Easedale Tarn is visible from the cairn; to obtain a birds-eye view of it, visit the top rocks of Blea Crag, north.

Principal Fells

BLENCATHRA
BANNERDALE CRAGS
CLOUGH HEAD
WATSONS DODD
GREAT DODD
HELVELLYN LOWER MAN
HELVELLYN
NETHERMOST PIKE
DOLLYWAGGON PIKE
ULLSCARF
TARN CRAG
STEEL FELL
HELM CRAG
SEAT SANDAL
ST SUNDAY CRAG
FAIRFIELD
HART CRAG
GREAT RIGG
DOVE CRAG
HIGH STREET
CAUDALE MOOR
SERGEANT MAN
RED SCREES
PAVEY ARK
HERON PIKE
ILL BELL
HARRISON STICKLE
YOKE
SILVER HOW
SALLOWS
CRINKLE CRAGS
LOUGHRIGG FELL
WANSFELL PIKE
LINGMOOR FELL
PIKE O' BLISCO
GREY FRIAR
GREAT CARRS
SWIRL HOW
BRIM FELL
OLD MAN
WETHERLAM
CONISTON

12½ miles
10 miles
7½ miles
2½ miles
5 miles

N, S, E, W

Lakes and Tarns

NE : Easedale Tarn
SE : Windermere (upper reach)
SE : Elterwater
SE : Wise Een Tarn
SE : Esthwaite Water
S : Lingmoor Tarn
NNW: Codale Tarn

Blea Rigg 11

RIDGE ROUTE

To SERGEANT MAN, 2414': WNW, then NW and W
1½ miles : Minor depressions only : 700 feet of ascent
A gradual climb along an interesting ridge

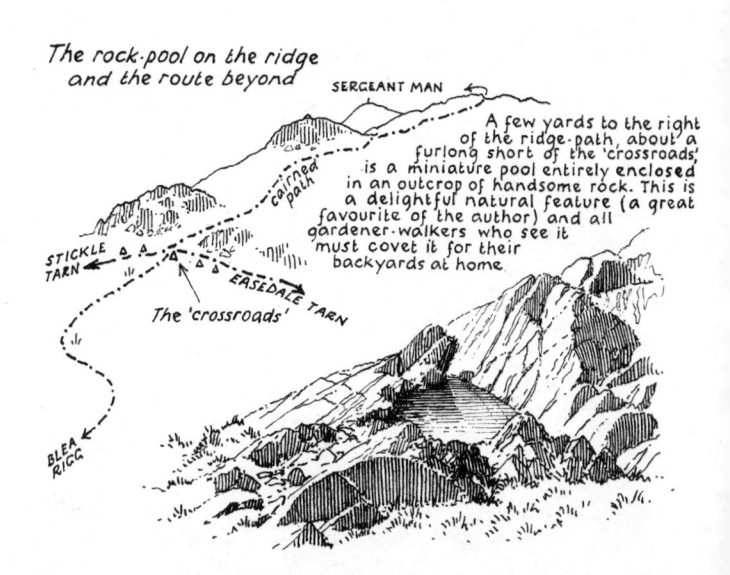

Two narrow grass trods (indistinct) leave the main path to follow the ridge, which is very wide. The route is easy and undulating to the 'crossroads' (cairns in profusion here), then climbs in an area of low crags. The path is not always clear, but is amply cairned.

The rock-pool on the ridge and the route beyond

A few yards to the right of the ridge-path, about a furlong short of the 'crossroads', is a miniature pool entirely enclosed in an outcrop of handsome rock. This is a delightful natural feature (a great favourite of the author) and all gardener-walkers who see it must covet it for their backyards at home.

Blea Rigg 12

RIDGE ROUTE

To SILVER HOW, 1292': S, then ESE and E
2 miles : Several depressions : 150 feet of ascent
An easy, undulating walk, with many fine views.

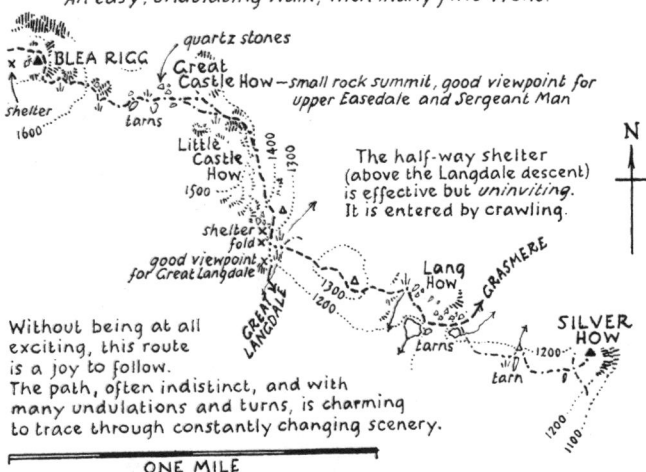

BLEA RIGG — shelter 1600 — tarns — quartz stones — Great Castle How — *small rock summit, good viewpoint for upper Easedale and Sergeant Man* — Little Castle How 1500 — 1400 — 1300 — shelter, fold — *good viewpoint for Great Langdale* — GREAT LANGDALE — 1200 — Lang How — tarns — GRASMERE — SILVER HOW — 1200 — tarn — 1100

The half-way shelter (above the Langdale descent) is effective but *uninviting*. It is entered by crawling.

N

Without being at all exciting, this route is a joy to follow. The path, often indistinct, and with many undulations and turns, is charming to trace through constantly changing scenery.

ONE MILE

The Shelter Stone on the top of Blea Rigg

This useful refuge is situated at the base of the prominent rocky tor 150 yards west of the summit-cairn. It cannot be seen from the path. The accommodation is strictly limited.

Calf Crag

1762'

from the boulders below Deer Bield Crag

Calf Crag 2

NATURAL FEATURES

The familiar pyramid of Helm Crag, rising sharply from the green fields of Grasmere, is the terminus of a ridge that curves away westwards to culminate finally in the rocky crest of a lesser-known eminence, Calf Crag. Beyond this point the characteristics of the ridge change, and sprawling slopes fall in easy gradients to the marshy flats of the Wyth Burn, the western boundary. The flanks of the fell, however, descend much more steeply and roughly in shelves of broken crag to the Greenburn valley, north, and Far Easedale, south. The county boundary traverses the broad top, coinciding with the limit of the Thirlmere catchment area, but the highest point is wholly within Westmorland.

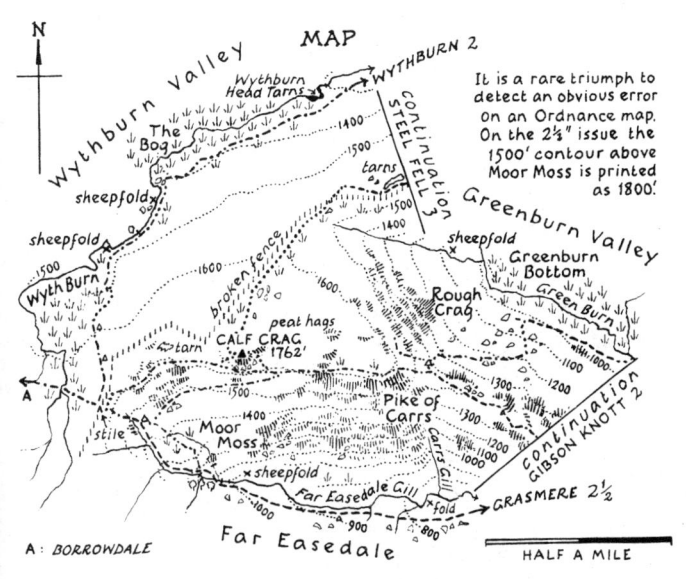

It is a rare triumph to detect an obvious error on an Ordnance map. On the 2½" issue the 1500' contour above Moor Moss is printed as 1800'.

Tourists bound for Borrowdale from Grasmere via Far Easedale should observe particularly that the Greenup crossing, between High Raise and Ullscarf, is to be found almost a mile *beyond* the stile at the head of Far Easedale and 350' higher, *in the same general direction, trending left*. The natural tendency is to turn down the valley on the right (Wythburn) under the impression that the pass has been crossed. This is a bad trap in misty weather on a first visit.

Calf Crag 3

ASCENT FROM GRASMERE (via FAR EASEDALE)
1650 feet of ascent : 4½ miles

looking west-north-west

Recent generations of walkers have blazed a new trail to the head of the valley. Formerly, the bridle-path crossed the beck by stepping-stones near the big cairn, but it cannot now be traced on the ground although still shown on some maps in current use to the exclusion of the new thoroughfare.

It is unnecessary to continue quite to the head of the valley. At the level of Moor Moss, look for a track leading away to the right below rough ground. The summit of Calf Crag is clearly in sight from here and the track runs just below it.

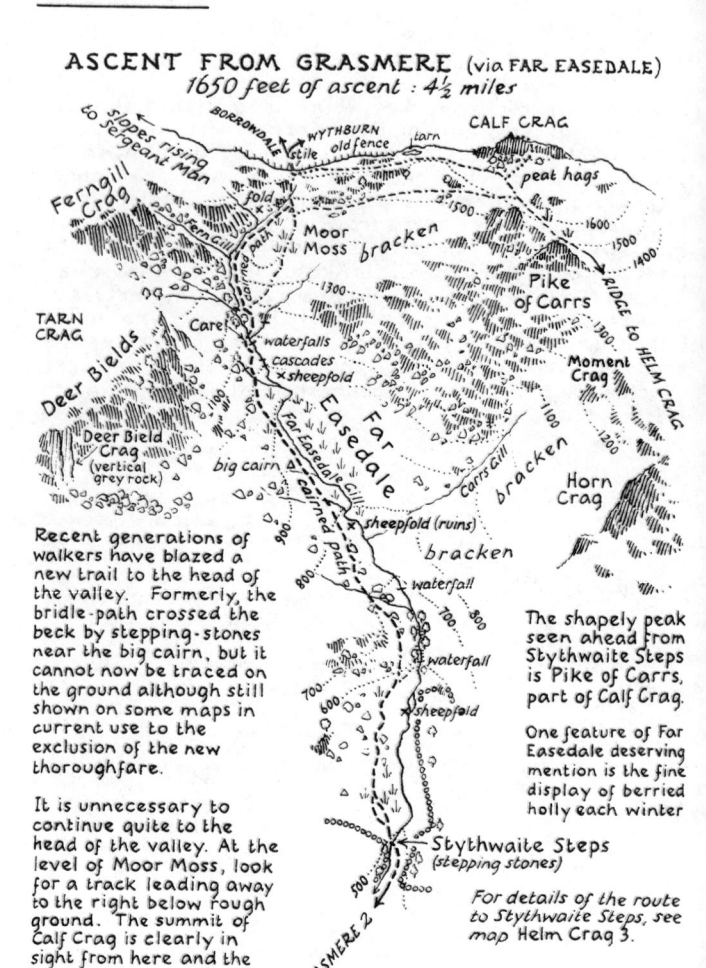

The shapely peak seen ahead from Stythwaite Steps is Pike of Carrs, part of Calf Crag.

One feature of Far Easedale deserving mention is the fine display of berried holly each winter

Stythwaite Steps (stepping stones)

For details of the route to Stythwaite Steps, see map Helm Crag 3.

Far Easedale is a beautiful and interesting valley with impressive rock scenery. The path along it is commonly used as a route to Borrowdale but can be conveniently adapted as a simple way onto Calf Crag. Far Easedale is wet underfoot in many places, always.

Calf Crag 4

ASCENT FROM GRASMERE (via GREEN BURN)
1650 feet of ascent : 4½ miles

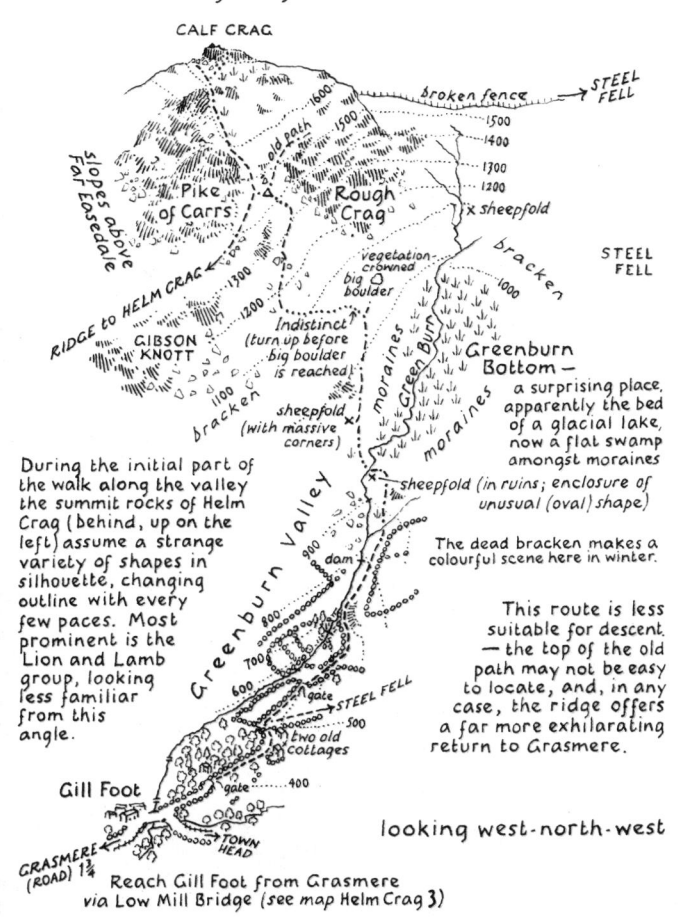

looking west-north-west

During the initial part of the walk along the valley the summit rocks of Helm Crag (behind, up on the left) assume a strange variety of shapes in silhouette, changing outline with every few paces. Most prominent is the Lion and Lamb group, looking less familiar from this angle.

Greenburn Bottom — a surprising place, apparently the bed of a glacial lake, now a flat swamp amongst moraines

sheepfold (in ruins; enclosure of unusual (oval) shape)

The dead bracken makes a colourful scene here in winter.

This route is less suitable for descent — the top of the old path may not be easy to locate, and, in any case, the ridge offers a far more exhilarating return to Grasmere.

Reach Gill Foot from Grasmere via Low Mill Bridge (see map Helm Crag 3)

This route is included mainly to introduce a valley that is unfrequented yet deserving of attention. It has also the advantage of the guidance of an old path almost to the ridge just below the summit.

Calf Crag 5

ASCENT FROM WYTHBURN
1250 feet of ascent : 4 miles from Wythburn Church

CALF CRAG

FAR EASEDALE (for GRASMERE)

slopes rising to High Raise

GREENUP EDGE (for BORROWDALE)

broken fence

STEEL FELL

Here, as elsewhere, light-coloured grass (almost white) indicates firm ground. Keep away from red grass, rushes and patches of green mosses.

peat hags

sheepfold

waterfall
boulders
sheepfold

The Bog

'The Bog' (with a capital T & B deservedly) is the official name of this morass. It may be said that here, at any rate, the foot of man has never trod (if it has, it must have made a horribly squelching sound!). The beck flows sluggishly and silently in a swamp.

The first moraine above the waterfalls stands like a sentinel at the entrance to the strange upper valley

moraines

Wythburn Head Tarns (an ambitious name for slight widenings of the beck into pools)

a particularly big boulder

Rake Crags

Black Crag

waterfall
waterfall
waterfall

brackeny

sheepfold

gate

The imposing rocky rampart overlooking the valley on the north-west is Nab Crags, a shoulder of Ullscarf

Scenically, this is the best half-mile in the valley, with the beck tumbling in a rocky bed to a wooded ravine.

Primarily this route is included to serve as an introduction to the Wythburn valley: the climbing of Calf Crag is incidental and is suggested only to provide an objective. The valley, besides being a supreme study in desolation (especially in rain and mist) has many geological and geographical features of unusual interest.
One visit will be enough for most folk, however, for the ground is abominably and unescapably WET

Wyth Burn

looking south-west

gate
gates

Steel End

GRASMERE 3½

MAIN ROAD

signpost (spells Wythburn 'Withburn')

ROAD to ARMBOTH

Thirlmere

WYTHBURN CHURCH ½

Calf Crag 6

THE SUMMIT

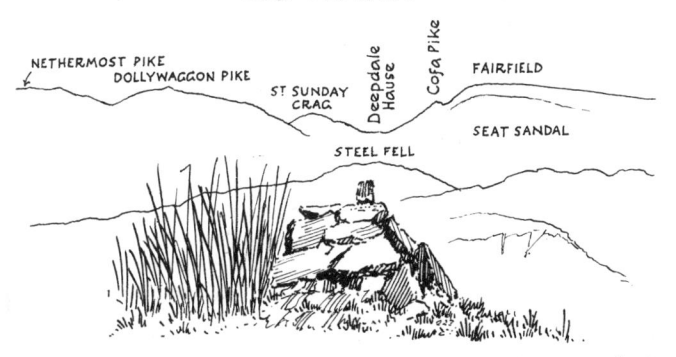

Skyline labels (left to right): NETHERMOST PIKE, DOLLYWAGGON PIKE, ST SUNDAY CRAG, Deepdale House, Cofa Pike, FAIRFIELD, SEAT SANDAL, STEEL FELL

The highest point, small and rocky, is a pleasant place for a halt and quiet contemplation of the scenery. Sheep think so, too, and wearers of new clothes should not sink into repose here without first clearing away the profuse evidences of their occupation. A feature unusual on summits is a clump of rushes, abutting on the neat cairn. Immediately below the cairn, on the south, is a wall of crag that constitutes a danger in mist.

DESCENTS: The best route of descent, full of interest, keeps to the ridge over Helm Crag and so down to Grasmere. The path going off the top into the Greenburn valley is not easy to find. *In mist and bad weather, it is advisable to retire to the shelter afforded by Far Easedale, reached by walking north of west (the rushes side of the cairn) for 200 yards and following the fence to the step-stile at the head of the valley, where turn down left.*

The summit crags
(the maximum height is about 35 feet)

Calf Crag 7

THE VIEW

The best feature in a moderate and restricted view is a beautiful vista of the Vale of Grasmere with Far Easedale curving into it from the inexpressibly wild flanks of Tarn Crag and Sergeant Man nearby: a complete contrast in landscapes in the space of two miles.

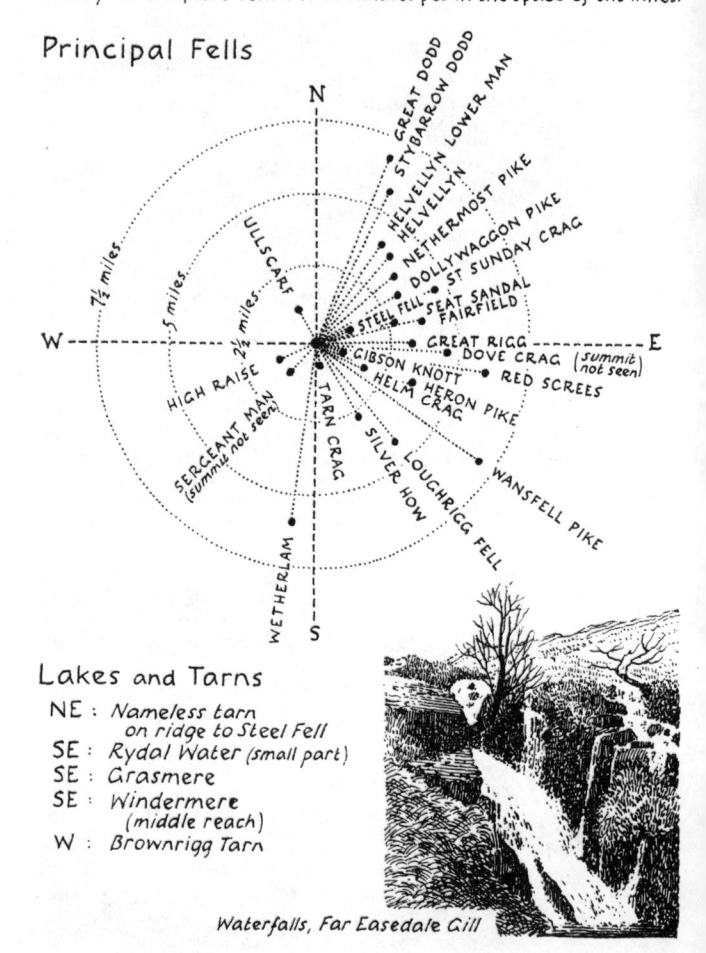

Principal Fells

- N: GREAT DODD, STYBARROW DODD
- HELVELLYN LOWER MAN, HELVELLYN, NETHERMOST PIKE, DOLLYWAGGON PIKE, ST SUNDAY CRAG, SEAT SANDAL, FAIRFIELD
- STEEL FELL
- ULLSCARF (5 miles, 7½ miles)
- E: GREAT RIGG, DOVE CRAG (summit not seen), RED SCREES
- GIBSON KNOTT, HERON PIKE, HELM CRAG
- HIGH RAISE (2½ miles)
- TARN CRAG
- SERGEANT MAN (summit not seen)
- SILVER HOW, LOUGHRIGG FELL, WANSFELL PIKE
- WETHERLAM
- S

Lakes and Tarns

- NE : Nameless tarn on ridge to Steel Fell
- SE : Rydal Water (small part)
- SE : Grasmere
- SE : Windermere (middle reach)
- W : Brownrigg Tarn

Waterfalls, Far Easedale Gill

Calf Crag 8

RIDGE ROUTES

To STEEL FELL, 1811' : 1½ miles : NE, curving E to ESE
Main depression at 1535' : 350 feet of ascent
An easy walk, with fence as guide, but very marshy initially

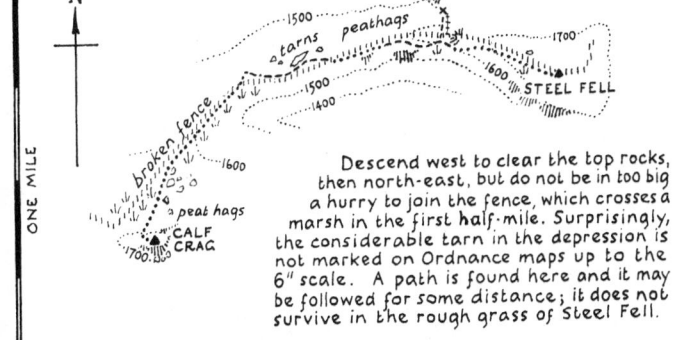

Descend west to clear the top rocks, then north-east, but do not be in too big a hurry to join the fence, which crosses a marsh in the first half-mile. Surprisingly, the considerable tarn in the depression is not marked on Ordnance maps up to the 6" scale. A path is found here and it may be followed for some distance; it does not survive in the rough grass of Steel Fell.

To GIBSON KNOTT, 1379' : 1¼ miles : E, then ESE
Several minor depressions : 100 feet of ascent
An interesting path, a beautiful walk, and splendid views

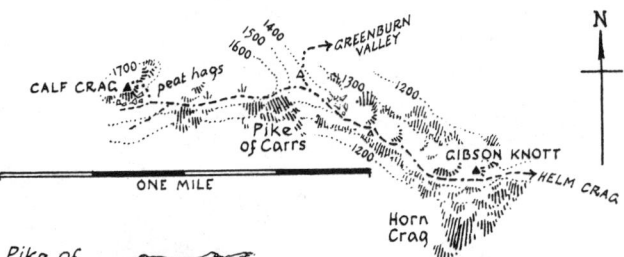

Pike of Carrs

From the summit a path can be seen running below the crags on the Easedale side: it may be joined by a wide detour and followed without difficulty, although intermittent, to Gibson Knott. The path keeps below the ridge; the crest may be followed instead but is a long succession of trivial ups and downs. If the path is adhered to too closely, however, the cairn on Gibson Knott will be missed — it stands on a rocky mound 30 yards to the left.

Eagle Crag

1650'
approx.

- Rosthwaite
- Stonethwaite
▲ ▲ ULLSCARF
EAGLE CRAG
▲ HIGH RAISE
MILES
0 1 2 3

from Stonethwaite Beck

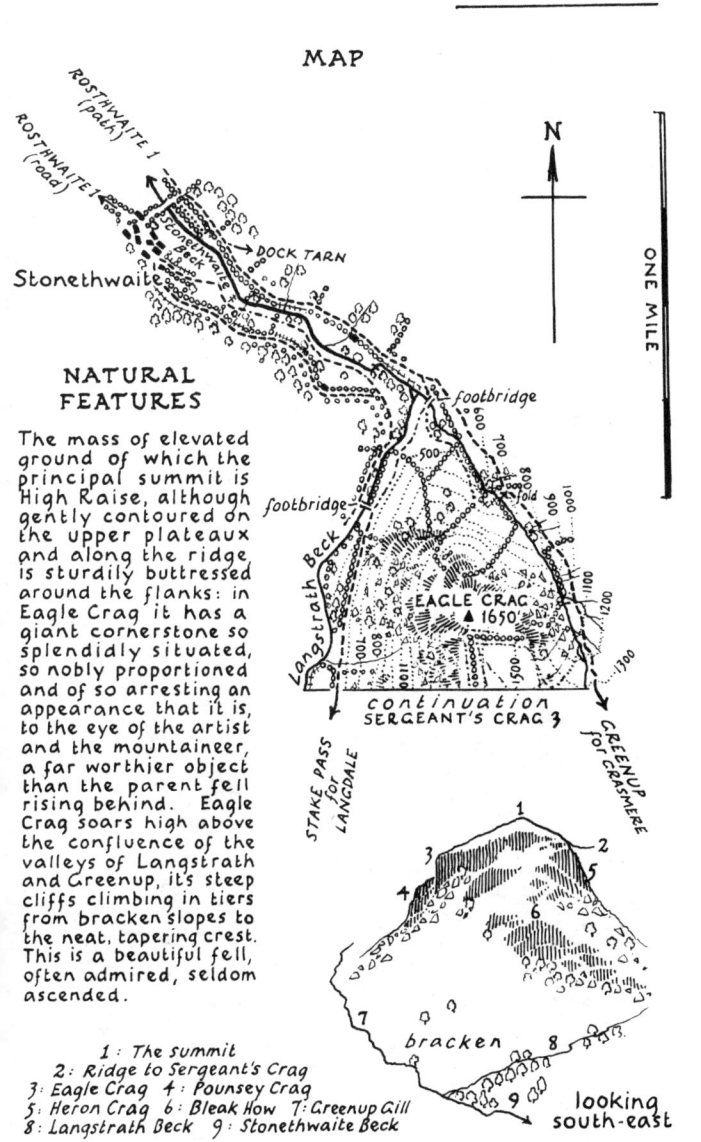

Eagle Crag 2

MAP

Stonethwaite

NATURAL FEATURES

The mass of elevated ground of which the principal summit is High Raise, although gently contoured on the upper plateaux and along the ridge is sturdily buttressed around the flanks: in Eagle Crag it has a giant cornerstone so splendidly situated, so nobly proportioned and of so arresting an appearance that it is, to the eye of the artist and the mountaineer, a far worthier object than the parent fell rising behind. Eagle Crag soars high above the confluence of the valleys of Langstrath and Greenup, its steep cliffs climbing in tiers from bracken slopes to the neat, tapering crest. This is a beautiful fell, often admired, seldom ascended.

1 : The summit
2 : Ridge to Sergeant's Crag
3 : Eagle Crag 4 : Pounsey Crag
5 : Heron Crag 6 : Bleak How 7 : Greenup Gill
8 : Langstrath Beck 9 : Stonethwaite Beck

looking south-east

Eagle Crag 3

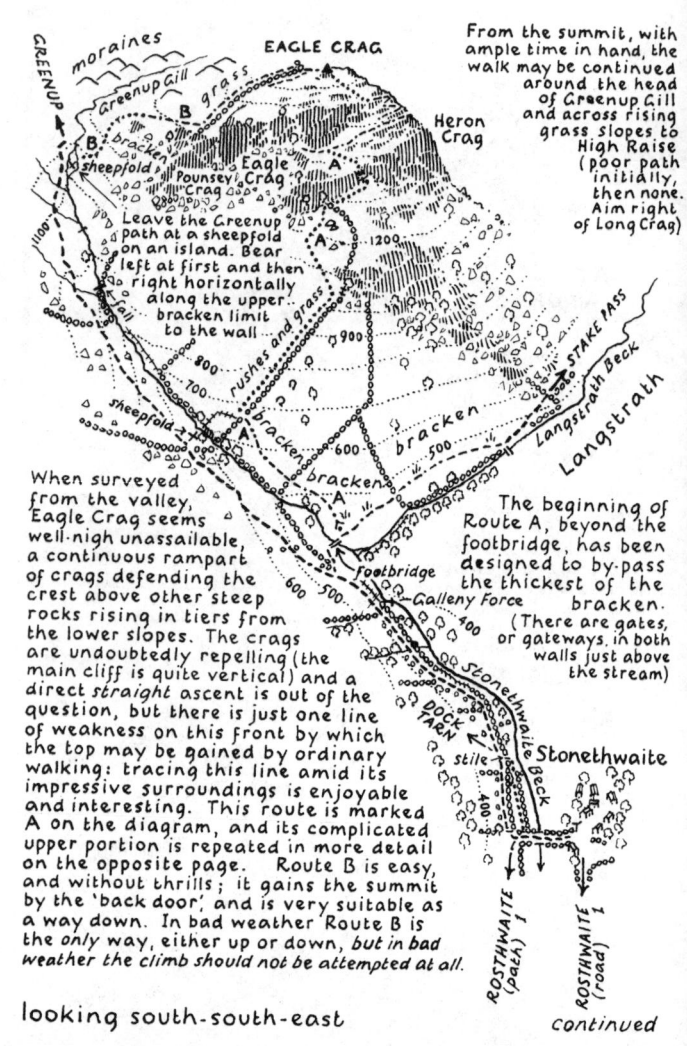

ASCENT FROM STONETHWAITE
1300 feet of ascent : 2 miles

looking south-south-east

GREENUP / moraines / EAGLE CRAG / Greenup Gill / grass / B / bracken / sheepfold / Pounsey Crag / Eagle Crag / Heron Crag

Leave the Greenup path at a sheepfold on an island. Bear left at first and then right horizontally along the upper bracken limit to the wall.

fall / rushes and grass / sheepfold / bracken / STAKE PASS / Langstrath / Langstrath Beck / bracken / bracken

footbridge / Galleny Force / Stonethwaite Beck / DOCK TARN / stile / Stonethwaite / ROSTHWAITE (path) / ROSTHWAITE (road)

From the summit, with ample time in hand, the walk may be continued around the head of Greenup Gill and across rising grass slopes to High Raise (poor path initially, then none. Aim right of Long Crag)

The beginning of Route A, beyond the footbridge, has been designed to by-pass the thickest of the bracken. (There are gates, or gateways, in both walls just above the stream)

When surveyed from the valley, Eagle Crag seems well-nigh unassailable, a continuous rampart of crags defending the crest above other steep rocks rising in tiers from the lower slopes. The crags are undoubtedly repelling (the main cliff is quite vertical) and a direct *straight* ascent is out of the question, but there is just one line of weakness on this front by which the top may be gained by ordinary walking: tracing this line amid its impressive surroundings is enjoyable and interesting. This route is marked A on the diagram, and its complicated upper portion is repeated in more detail on the opposite page. Route B is easy, and without thrills; it gains the summit by the 'back door', and is very suitable as a way down. In bad weather Route B is the *only* way, either up or down, but in bad weather the climb should not be attempted at all.

continued

Eagle Crag 4

ASCENT FROM STONETHWAITE
continued

The upper section of Route A

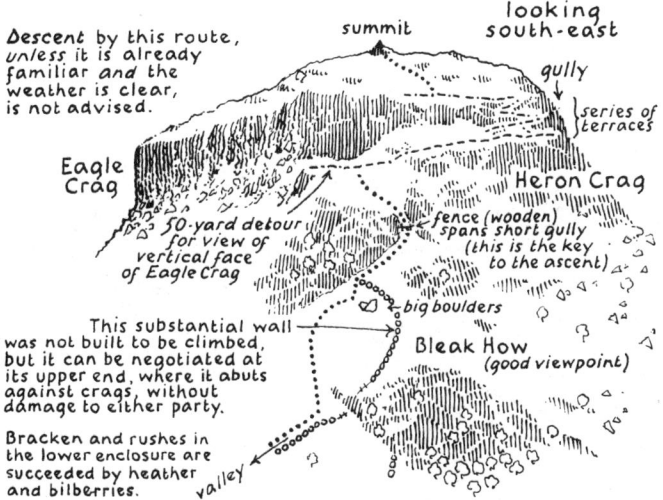

looking south-east

Descent by this route, unless it is already familiar and the weather is clear, is not advised.

Eagle Crag — summit — gully — series of terraces — Heron Crag

50-yard detour for view of vertical face of Eagle Crag

fence (wooden) spans short gully (this is the key to the ascent)

big boulders

Bleak How (good viewpoint)

This substantial wall was not built to be climbed, but it can be negotiated at its upper end, where it abuts against crags, without damage to either party.

Bracken and rushes in the lower enclosure are succeeded by heather and bilberries.

valley

Here, and in other craggy places, sheep should be disturbed as little as possible, even at inconvenience to the walker; otherwise they may become casualties. The walls are not put there for ornament: they serve a vital purpose, and if stones are displaced they should be put back, and firmly.

Eagle Crag is the most distinctive object in the Stonethwaite landscape and its ascent reveals all the beauty of the valley in a pleasant half-day's (or summer evening's) expedition.

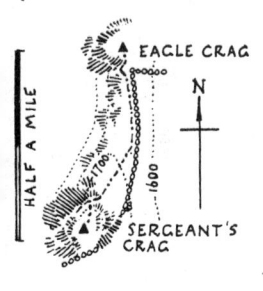

EAGLE CRAG — 1600 — SERGEANT'S CRAG
HALF A MILE — N

RIDGE ROUTE

To SERGEANT'S CRAG, 1873'
½ mile : S. then SSW
Minor depressions
250 feet of ascent
Easy, but not safe in mist

A rough little path leads down to the head of a gully at the wall-corner. Do not cross the wall, but accompany it south, finally inclining away from it.

Eagle Crag 5

THE SUMMIT

Labels on panorama: HINDSCARTH, GRASMOOR, EEL CRAG, GRISEDALE PIKE, CAUSEY PIKE, LORD'S SEAT, BARF, CATBELLS, Bassenthwaite Lake

A small cairn sits proudly on the apex of a tilted slab of rock and indicates the summit. Nothing can be seen of the crags that fall away to the valley because of an upper plateau of grass and heather, broken by many outcrops. Eastwards from the cairn there is an acre of flat marshy ground before the slopes descend from sight.

DESCENTS: There must be no thought of a quick romp straight down to the valley immediately below: *it cannot be done*. Unless the route on the Stonethwaite face (Route A) is already known, it should not be sought from above: the crags form an almost continuous barrier here. Palpitations and alarms may be avoided by following the wall down towards Greenup (away from the direction of Stonethwaite) after first crossing it at the corner, and, when rough ground appears ahead, making a wide detour to the right to join the Greenup path down easy bracken slopes. *In bad weather, or if there is deep snow, this is the only route that will ensure the due arrival of the walker at Stonethwaite in one unbroken piece.*

Eagle Crag 6

THE VIEW

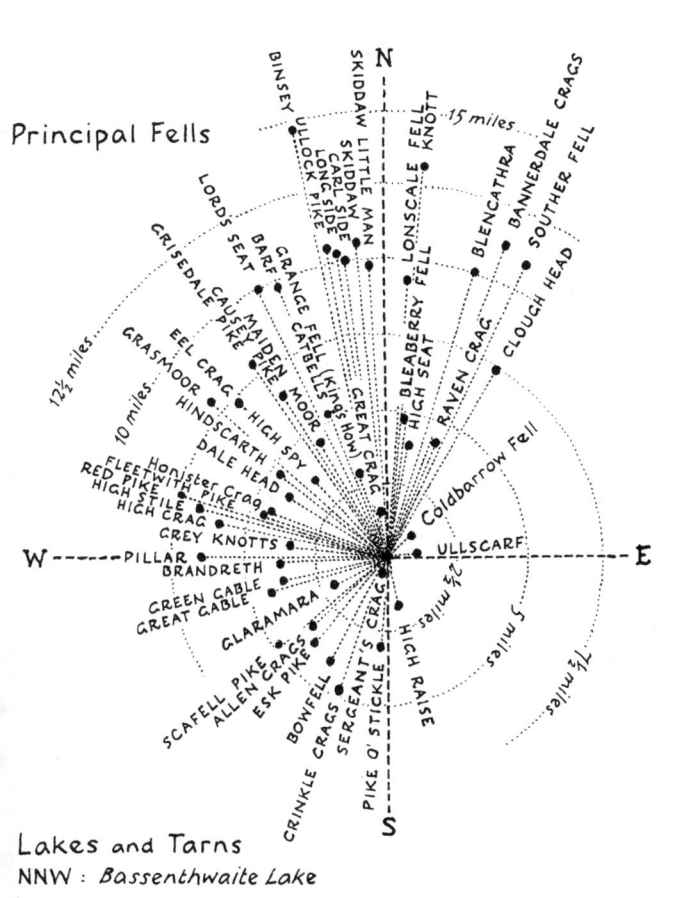

Principal Fells

(compass diagram showing bearings to fells, with 15 miles, 12½ miles, 10 miles, 7½ miles, 5 miles, 2½ miles range circles)

N: SKIDDAW LITTLE MAN, SKIDDAW, CARL SIDE, LONGSIDE
NNW: BINSEY, ULLOCK PIKE, LORD'S SEAT, BARF, GRANGE FELL, CATBELLS, MAIDEN MOOR
NW: GRISEDALE PIKE, CAUSEY PIKE, EEL CRAG, HIGH SPY, DALE HEAD, GRASMOOR, HINDSCARTH, Honister Crag, FLEETWITH PIKE, RED PIKE, HIGH STILE, HIGH CRAG, GREY KNOTTS
N/NNE: LONSCALE FELL, KNOTT, BLEABERRY FELL, HIGH SEAT, GREAT CRAG (King's How)
NE: BANNERDALE CRAGS, BLENCATHRA, SOUTHER FELL, RAVEN CRAG, CLOUGH HEAD
E: Coldbarrow Fell, ULLSCARF
W: PILLAR, BRANDRETH
SW: GREEN GABLE, GREAT GABLE, GLARAMARA, SCAFELL PIKE, ALLEN CRAGS, ESK PIKE
S: BOWFELL, CRINKLE CRAGS, SERGEANT'S CRAG, PIKE O' STICKLE, HIGH RAISE

Lakes and Tarns
NNW: Bassenthwaite Lake

The view of the Stonethwaite valley, which might be expected to be excellent, is not quite that, the summit being set rather too far back from the edge of the crags to enable all of it to be seen; a short and easy descent of the upper slope leads to better points of vantage. But generally the valley is too short to be really effective in a view, although the whole picture is very pleasing to west and north. Eastwards the scene is drab.

Gibson Knott 1379'

from Helm Crag

```
        STEEL FELL
          ▲
CALF    ▲ GIBSON
CRAG ▲    KNOTT
HELM CRAG ▲

  Grasmere ●

       MILES
  0    1    2    3
```

Gibson Knott is the most elevated of the several sundry knobs and bumps that form the crest of the mile-long ridge linking at its extremities Calf Crag and Helm Crag and dividing the valleys of Far Easedale and Greenburn. There is much rock in evidence along the serrated top and fringing steep flanks; in particular, a prominent buttress, Horn Crag, adorned with juniper, rises from the bracken of the Easedale slope. The summit is interesting, other parts less so. The fellsides are 'dry', draining without forming regular watercourses.

MAP

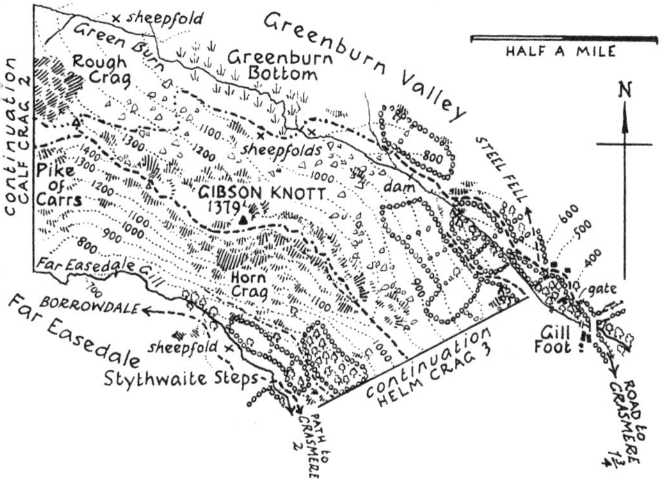
sheepfold
Green Burn
Greenburn Valley
Greenburn Bottom
Rough Crag
HALF A MILE
N
continuation CALF CRAG 2
Pike of Carrs
GIBSON KNOTT 1379'
sheepfolds
1100
1200
1300
1400
1000
900
800
700
600
500
400
dam
STEEL FELL
Far Easedale Gill
Horn Crag
BORROWDALE
gate
Gill Foot
Far Easedale
sheepfold
Stythwaite Steps
continuation HELM CRAG 3
PATH to GRASMERE 2
ROAD to GRASMERE 1¾

ASCENT FROM GRASMERE

1300 feet of ascent *4½ miles*

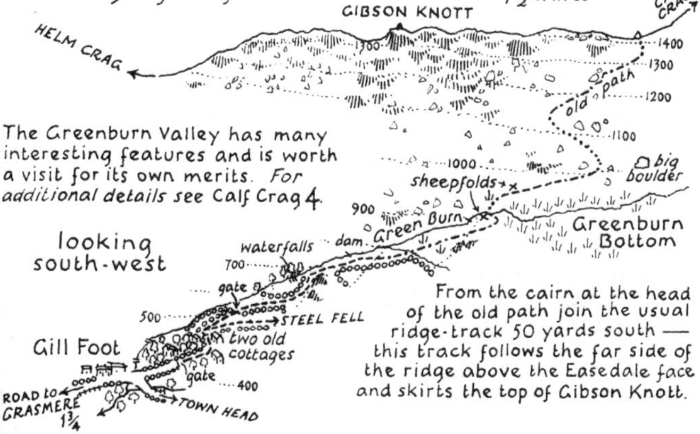
GIBSON KNOTT
CALF CRAG
HELM CRAG
1400
1300
1200
1100
1000
900
700
500
400
old path
big boulder
sheepfolds
Green Burn
Greenburn Bottom
dam
waterfalls
gate
STEEL FELL
two old cottages
gate
Gill Foot
ROAD to GRASMERE 1¾
TOWN HEAD
looking south-west

The Greenburn Valley has many interesting features and is worth a visit for its own merits. *For additional details see Calf Crag 4.*

From the cairn at the head of the old path join the usual ridge-track 50 yards south — this track follows the far side of the ridge above the Easedale face and skirts the top of Gibson Knott.

Although the usual (and best) route lies along the ridge from Helm Crag, it is suggested that this be reserved for descent and the route illustrated be used as a way up: it is full of interest and has the advantage of a path so easily graduated that the ascent is better described as a walk than a climb.

Gibson Knott 3

THE SUMMIT

It was categorically stated, two pages ago, that Gibson Knott is the highest point on the ridge. The observer on the spot will probably question this, for the next rise eastwards *seems* to be higher. Large-scale maps do not settle the doubt, and it is perhaps safer to say that Gibson Knott is the Ordnance Survey's only trigonometrical station on the ridge and that *usually* the most elevated point is selected. The summit is an abrupt rise, surmounted by a cairn above a smooth rock wall.

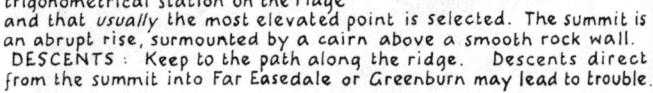

DESCENTS: Keep to the path along the ridge. Descents direct from the summit into Far Easedale or Greenburn may lead to trouble.

RIDGE ROUTES

To CALF CRAG, 1762': 1¼ miles : WNW, then W.
Several minor depressions : 450 feet of ascent
An interesting walk with good views of Far Easedale

Join the path 30 yards south of the cairn and follow it west. With a few interruptions it continues to the base of the summit crags of Calf Crag, skirting the head of the prominent Pike of Carrs: interesting throughout, it keeps on the Easedale side of the ridge and is preferable to the actual crest, which is rather tedious.

To HELM CRAG, 1299'
1 mile : E, then SE.
Depression at 1050'
320 feet of ascent
A delightful path

Join the path 30 yards south of the cairn and follow it east to the top of the next rise where it winds in and out and up and down in a charming manner before descending to the depression below Helm Crag, the curious top of which is reached by a stiff little climb.

Gibson Knott 4

THE VIEW

The cairn is not quite the best viewpoint: the ridge eastwards is more satisfying. There is strong contrast between the smooth slopes towering across the Keswick road and the rough territory and serrated skyline across Far Easedale.

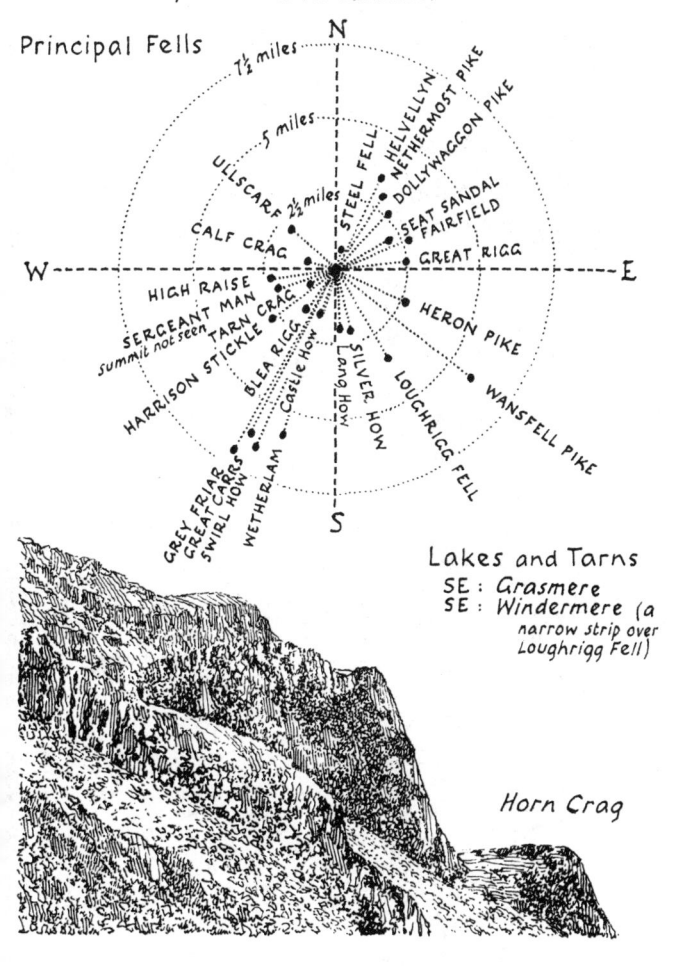

Principal Fells

- 7½ miles
- 5 miles
- 2½ miles

N
ULLSCARF
STEEL FELL
HELVELLYN
NETHERMOST PIKE
DOLLYWAGGON PIKE
CALF CRAG
SEAT SANDAL
FAIRFIELD
GREAT RIGG
W — E
HIGH RAISE
SERGEANT MAN (summit not seen)
HERON PIKE
HARRISON STICKLE
TARN CRAG
BLEA RIGG
Castle How
SILVER HOW
LOUGHRIGG FELL
WANSFELL PIKE
Lang How
GREY FRIAR
GREAT CARRS
SWIRL HOW
WETHERLAM
S

Lakes and Tarns
SE: Grasmere
SE: Windermere (a narrow strip over Loughrigg Fell)

Horn Crag

Grange Fell 1363'

King's How, from Shepherds Crag

Grange Fell is nothing on the map, everything when beneath one's feet. In small compass, here is concentrated the beauty, romance, interest and excitement of the typical Lakeland scene. Here Nature has given of her very best and produced a loveliness that is exquisite. Not strictly the territory of fellwalkers, perhaps; yet those who consistently hurry past Grange Fell to get to grips with the Scafells and Gable would do well to turn aside to it once in a while, alone, and quietly walk its sylvan glades and heathery top. The exercise will not tire the limbs, but it will do the heart and spirit and faith of the walker a power of good, and gladden his eye exceedingly.

Rising abruptly between Borrowdale and Watendlath Beck, and split by that delightful little valley of trees, Troutdale, the fell is almost encircled by a grey girdle of crags half-hidden in rich foliage; below is the wreckage of centuries in the form of masses of boulders (one of which, the Bowder Stone, is famous) overgrown by lush bracken and screened by a forest of birches. The top of the fell is an up-and-down tangled plateau, from which rise three main summits: (1) Brund Fell, the highest; (2) King's How, deservedly the best-known; and (3) Ether Knott behind a barricade of long heather.

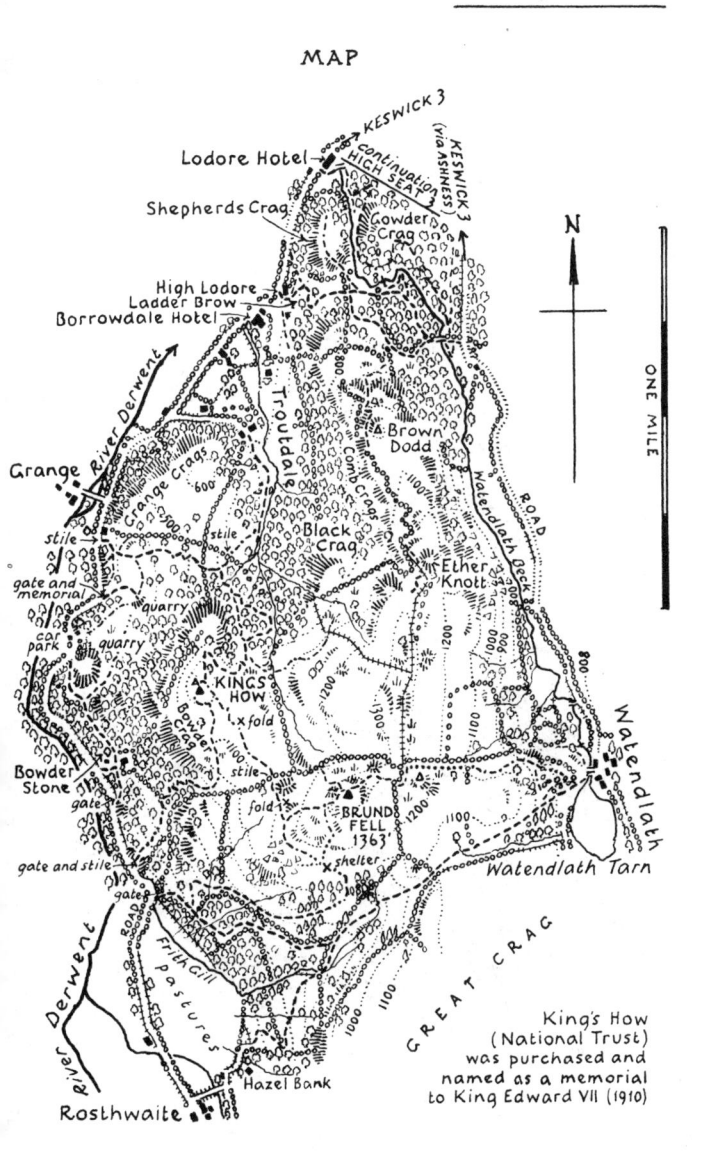

Grange Fell 2

MAP

King's How (National Trust) was purchased and named as a memorial to King Edward VII (1910)

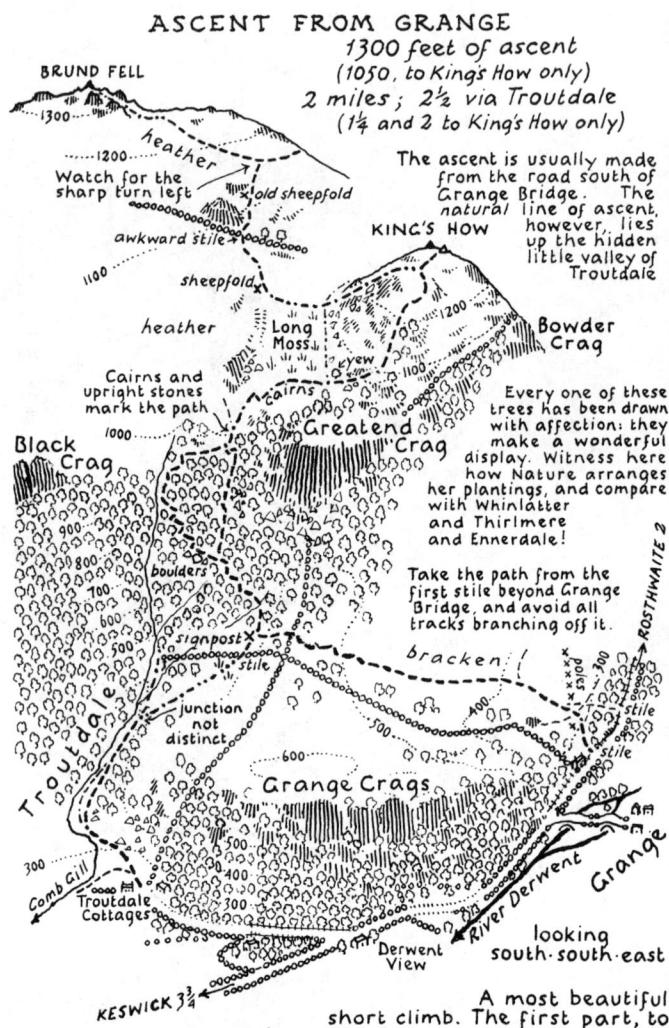

Grange Fell 3

ASCENT FROM GRANGE

*1300 feet of ascent
(1050, to King's How only)
2 miles; 2½ via Troutdale
(1¼ and 2 to King's How only)*

The ascent is usually made from the road south of Grange Bridge. The natural line of ascent, however, lies up the hidden little valley of Troutdale.

Watch for the sharp turn left

Cairns and upright stones mark the path

Every one of these trees has been drawn with affection: they make a wonderful display. Witness here how Nature arranges her plantings, and compare with Whinlatter and Thirlmere and Ennerdale!

Take the path from the first stile beyond Grange Bridge, and avoid all tracks branching off it.

looking south-south-east

A most beautiful short climb. The first part, to King's How, is exquisitely lovely (in autumn, a golden ladder to heaven) and simply must not be missed. Sacrifice any other walk, if need be, but not this!

Grange Fell 4

ASCENT FROM ROSTHWAITE
1100 feet of ascent to Brund Fell: 1½ or 2 miles
(1000 feet, 1½ miles, to King's How direct)

BRUND FELL
KING'S HOW
heather
Bowder Crag
sheepfold
stile (awkward)
Follow closely the line of cairns (especially in descent)
hut (shelter)
gap
bracken
bracken
bridle path
WATENDLATH
signpost (TO KESWICK ROAD)
KESWICK
gate and stile together
gate
gate and signpost (TO WATENDLATH)
Frith Wood
Yew Crag
Frith Gill
Note here the water-depth indicators on the side of the road, which is liable to flooding
River Derwent
Stonethwaite Beck
ROAD
Hazel Bank

Instead of using the familiar Watendlath path, try the quieter way in Frith Wood, or better still the bridle path above it, which is in some danger of neglect, undeservedly

Rosthwaite   looking north

The diagram gives separate routes for Brund Fell and King's How: if both summits are visited, as they should be, the alternative may be used for descent; the easier way round is to climb Brund Fell first.
This is an excellent little expedition, with splendid views, but is not suitable for a day of bad weather.

Grange Fell 5

ASCENT FROM WATENDLATH
550 feet of ascent · 1 mile (to Brund Fell only)

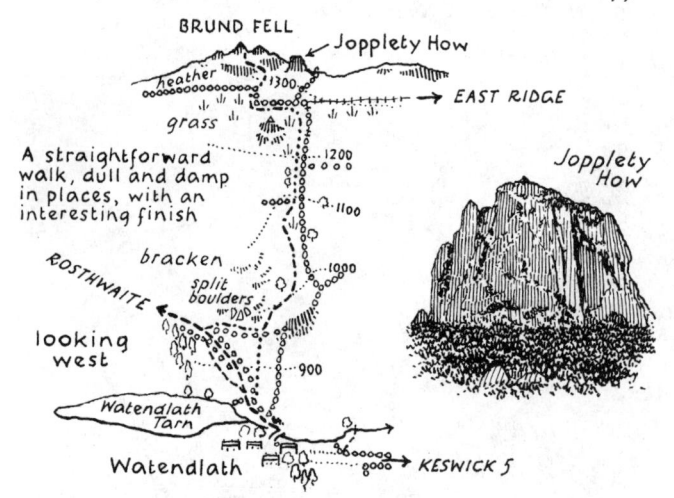

A straightforward walk, dull and damp in places, with an interesting finish

looking west

THE EAST RIDGE

The east ridge of Grange Fell is not often visited, but gives an interesting and beautiful traverse, better done from south to north. The ridge starts to take shape at Jopplety How and a fence may be followed over marshy ground (no path) to Ether Knott, the most prominent peak on the ridge, which here alters its character and becomes rough and heathery, a wall taking over the duties of the fence; the easiest walking is alongside it. Beyond, on Brown Dodd, the wall ends abruptly on the edge of crags, where a path takes shape and makes a sporting crossing of very steep ground. Escape from the escarpments hereabouts is effected down a rough gully (cairns) and, a little further, the tourist path descending Ladder Brow to High Lodore is met, but having come so far the walker should certainly complete the ridge by visiting the top of Shepherds Crag, a lovely belvedere occasionally profaned by the rich language of climbers on the cliff directly below.

Both sides of the east ridge have steep crags, continuous in the middle section. Overlooking the valley of Watendlath Beck is the gloomy wall of Caffell Side, while Comb Crags extend in an unbroken line above the trees of Troutdale.

The ridge is easily accessible from Brund Fell, but to force a way to it direct from King's How involves a laborious struggle in a tangle of thick heather. It offers a good return route to Grange or Lodore from Brund Fell (in clear weather) — but not for pedestrians who prefer simple walking on distinct paths.

Grange Fell 6

THE SUMMIT

The summit of BRUND FELL is one of exceptional interest. A number of steep-sided rock towers rise oddly from the heathery top; enthusiastic rock-scramblers will enjoy sampling them all, while less active walkers will find much fascinating detail in a perambulation of this unusual summit. A cairn identifies the highest tower.

The summit of KING'S HOW, in contrast, is a steep-sided dome, rising abruptly to a bare top with two cairns.

DESCENTS: King's How is so encircled by craggy ground that descent by the paths is imperative even in the best of weather. The lesser and lower of the two cairns marks the start of the path to Grange; the Rosthwaite path leaves in the opposite direction (south) where a line of cairns is found. Brund Fell, too, is better descended by its paths, intermittent though they are, but in bad weather a safe and quick way to the Rosthwaite-Watendlath path may be made alongside the wall running south from Jopplety How, first crossing it.

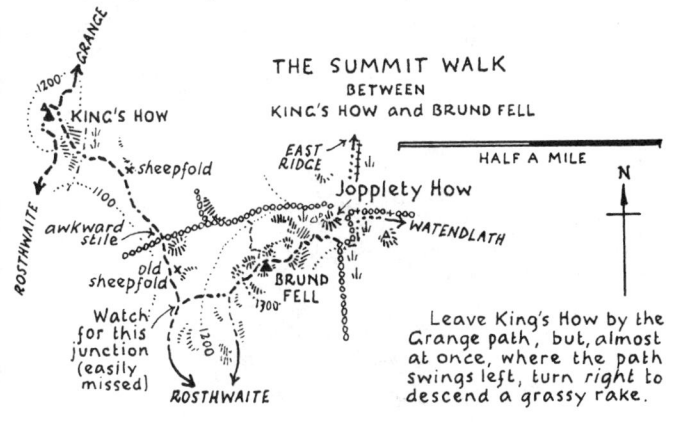

THE SUMMIT WALK
BETWEEN KING'S HOW and BRUND FELL

Leave King's How by the Grange path, but, almost at once, where the path swings left, turn *right* to descend a grassy rake.

THE VIEW

Principal Fells

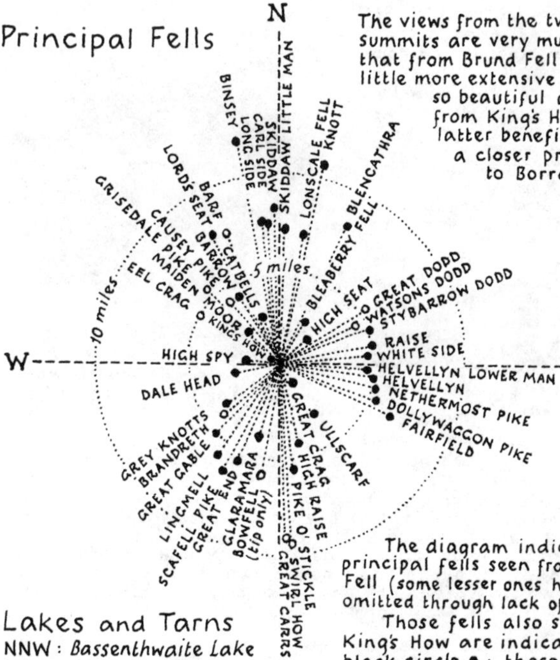
N
S
W
E
LITTLE MAN
SKIDDAW
CARL SIDE
LONG SIDE
BINSEY
LONSCALE FELL
KNOTT
BLENCATHRA
BLEABERRY FELL
LORD'S SEAT
BARF
BARROW
CATBELLS
GRISEDALE PIKE
CAUSEY PIKE
MAIDEN MOOR
EEL CRAG
KINGS HOW
5 miles
10 miles
HIGH SEAT
GREAT DODD
WATSONS DODD
STYBARROW DODD
RAISE
WHITE SIDE
HELVELLYN LOWER MAN
HELVELLYN
NETHERMOST PIKE
DOLLYWAGGON PIKE
FAIRFIELD
HIGH SPY
DALE HEAD
GREY KNOTTS
BRANDRETH
GREAT GABLE
LINGMELL
SCAFELL PIKE
GREAT END
GLARAMARA
BOWFELL (tip only)
GREAT CARRS
SWIRL HOW
PIKE O' STICKLE
HIGH RAISE
GREAT CRAG
ULLSCARF

The views from the two main summits are very much alike, that from Brund Fell being a little more extensive but not so beautiful as that from King's How, the latter benefitting by a closer proximity to Borrowdale.

The diagram indicates the principal fells seen from Brund Fell (some lesser ones have been omitted through lack of space).

Those fells also seen from King's How are indicated by a black circle ●; those not seen by a white circle o. The tip of Catstycam is additionally seen from King's How, between White Side and Helvellyn Lower Man

Lakes and Tarns

NNW : *Bassenthwaite Lake*
NNW : *Derwentwater*
(from both summits)

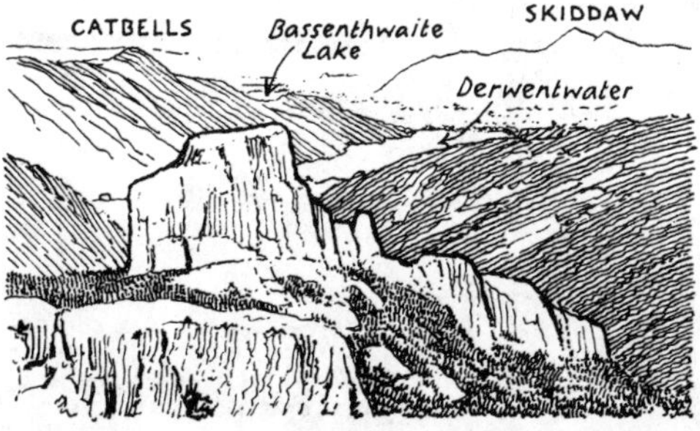
CATBELLS
Bassenthwaite Lake
SKIDDAW
Derwentwater

looking north from the top of Brund Fell

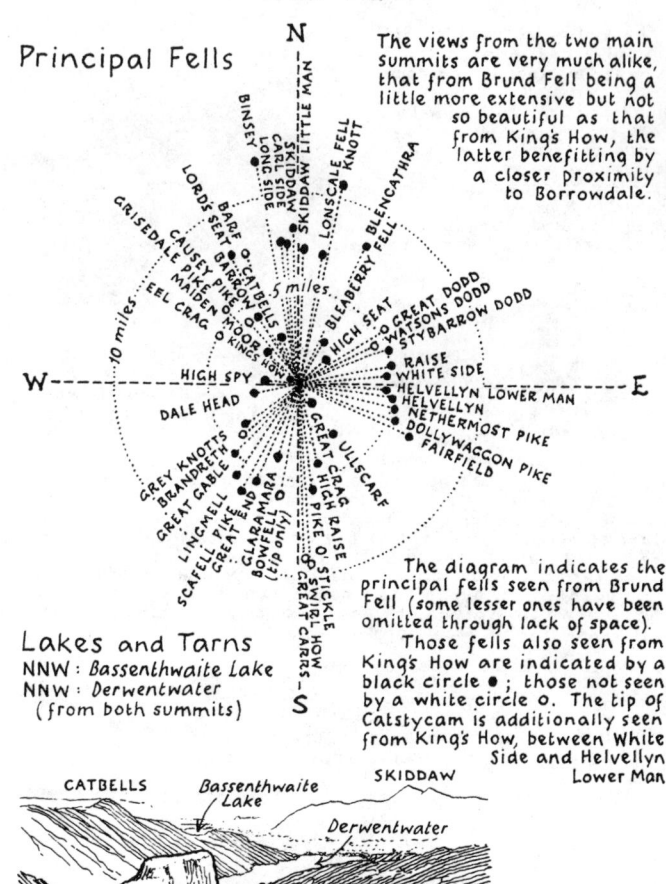

Grange Fell 8

The north ridge of King's How with Skiddaw in the background

Borrowdale, from the lower slopes of Brund Fell

Great Crag

1500'
approx.

from Watendlath

Between the deep Stonethwaite valley and the shallow depression containing Bleatarn Gill rises an indefinite and complex mass of rough undulating ground, a place of craggy and wooded slopes, of heathery tors and mossy swamps and shy little tarns — a beautiful labyrinth, a joy to the explorer but the despair of the map-maker. Nestling here is Dock Tarn, a jewel deserving a sweeter name, in a surround of rocky heights of which Great Crag is the most pronounced, and the natural summit of the fell — although perhaps not quite the highest point. Its altitude is not given on Ordnance maps, nor a 1500' contour, but the cairn can be little below this height, if at all.

- Watendlath
- Rosthwaite
▲ GREAT CRAG
- Stonethwaite
  ▲ ULLSCARF

MILES
0 1 2 3 4

Great Crag is one of those modest fells which seldom seem to invite attention, and few people know it by name, yet many are they who have trodden its lower slopes on the popular path of the pilgrims journeying to Watendlath from Rosthwaite.

Lakeland is not usually associated with heather — but here it thrives with a tropical vigour, and walking in it is arduous and difficult.

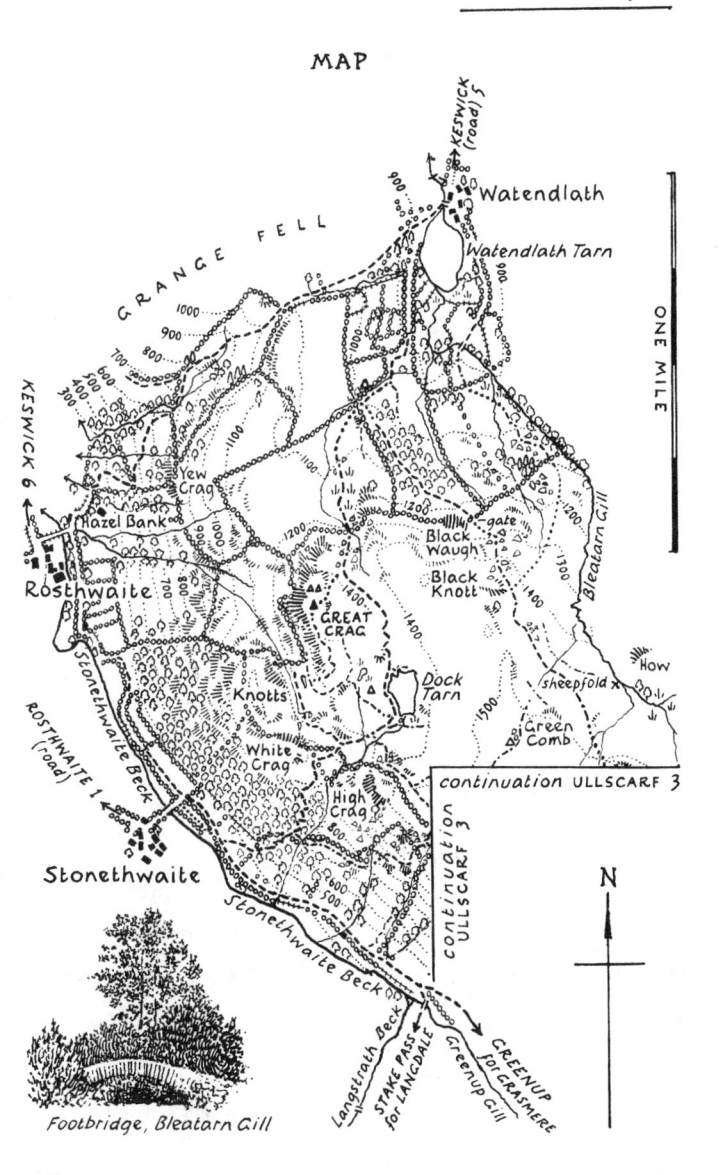

Great Crag 2

MAP

Footbridge, Bleatarn Gill

Great Crag 3

ASCENT FROM STONETHWAITE
1200 feet of ascent : 1½ miles

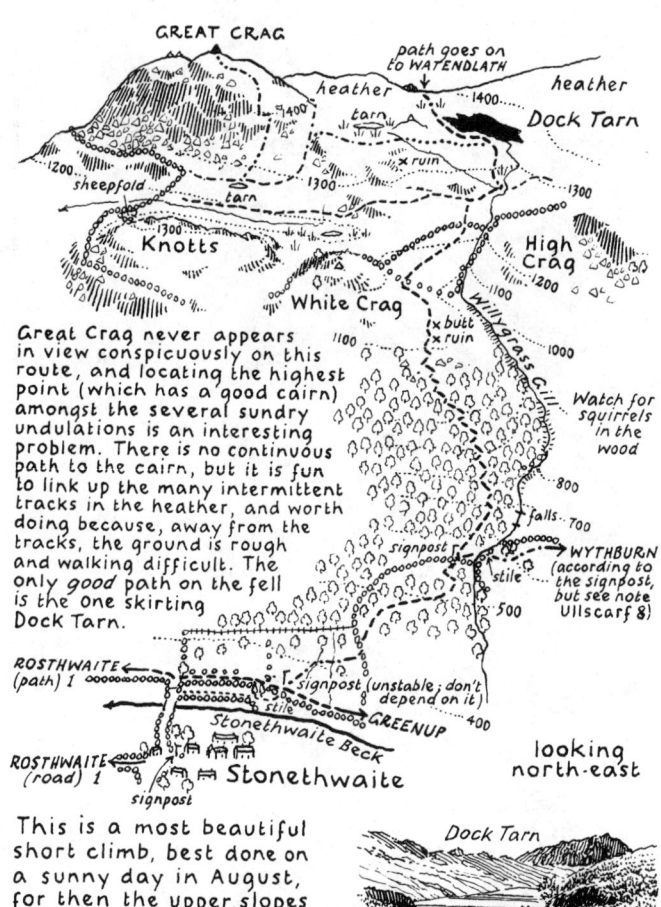

Great Crag never appears in view conspicuously on this route, and locating the highest point (which has a good cairn) amongst the several sundry undulations is an interesting problem. There is no continuous path to the cairn, but it is fun to link up the many intermittent tracks in the heather, and worth doing because, away from the tracks, the ground is rough and walking difficult. The only *good* path on the fell is the one skirting Dock Tarn.

looking north-east

This is a most beautiful short climb, best done on a sunny day in August, for then the upper slopes are ablaze with heather, Dock Tarn is a place to lie adreaming, and life seems a sweet sweet thing.

Dock Tarn

Great Crag 4

ASCENT FROM WATENDLATH
700 feet of ascent : 1½ miles

If the sun is in the sky and the heather in bloom, on no account fail to make the short detour to Dock Tarn after visiting the top.

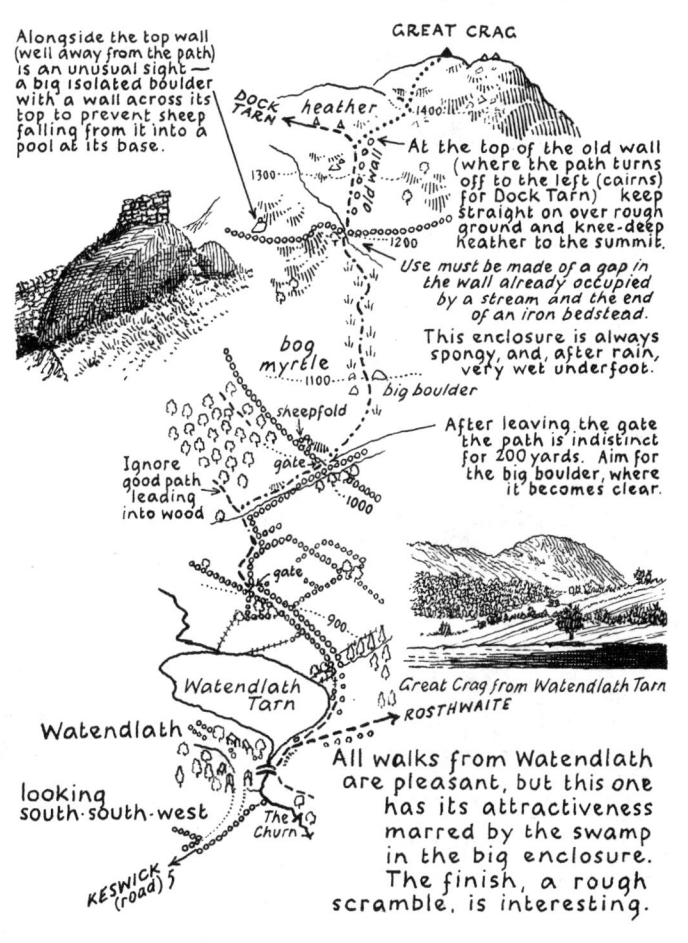

Alongside the top wall (well away from the path) is an unusual sight — a big isolated boulder with a wall across its top to prevent sheep falling from it into a pool at its base.

At the top of the old wall (where the path turns off to the left (cairns) for Dock Tarn) keep straight on over rough ground and knee-deep heather to the summit.

Use must be made of a gap in the wall already occupied by a stream and the end of an iron bedstead.

This enclosure is always spongy, and, after rain, very wet underfoot.

After leaving the gate the path is indistinct for 200 yards. Aim for the big boulder, where it becomes clear.

Ignore good path leading into wood

Great Crag from Watendlath Tarn

Watendlath
looking south-south-west

All walks from Watendlath are pleasant, but this one has its attractiveness marred by the swamp in the big enclosure. The finish, a rough scramble, is interesting.

Great Crag 5

THE SUMMIT

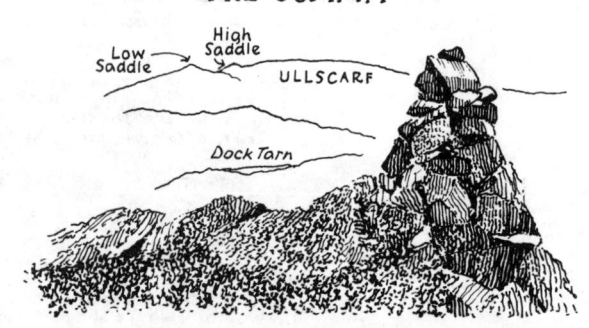

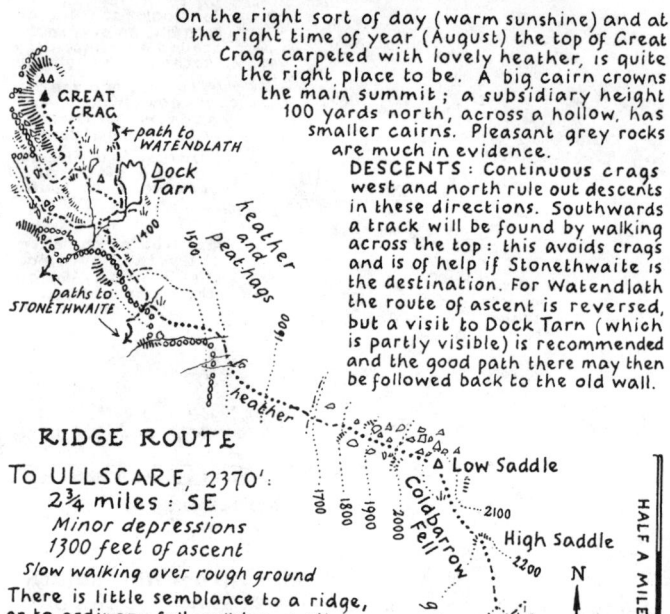

Low Saddle — High Saddle — ULLSCARF — Dock Tarn

On the right sort of day (warm sunshine) and at the right time of year (August) the top of Great Crag, carpeted with lovely heather, is quite the right place to be. A big cairn crowns the main summit; a subsidiary height 100 yards north, across a hollow, has smaller cairns. Pleasant grey rocks are much in evidence.

DESCENTS: Continuous crags west and north rule out descents in these directions. Southwards a track will be found by walking across the top: this avoids crags and is of help if Stonethwaite is the destination. For Watendlath the route of ascent is reversed, but a visit to Dock Tarn (which is partly visible) is recommended and the good path there may then be followed back to the old wall.

RIDGE ROUTE

To ULLSCARF, 2370':
2¾ miles : SE
Minor depressions
1300 feet of ascent
Slow walking over rough ground

There is little semblance to a ridge, or to ordinary fell-walking, until Coldbarrow Fell rises from the half-mile-wide plateau of heather, which is lovelier to look at than to trudge across. Use should be made of the scanty tracks available in the first mile

Great Crag 6

THE VIEW

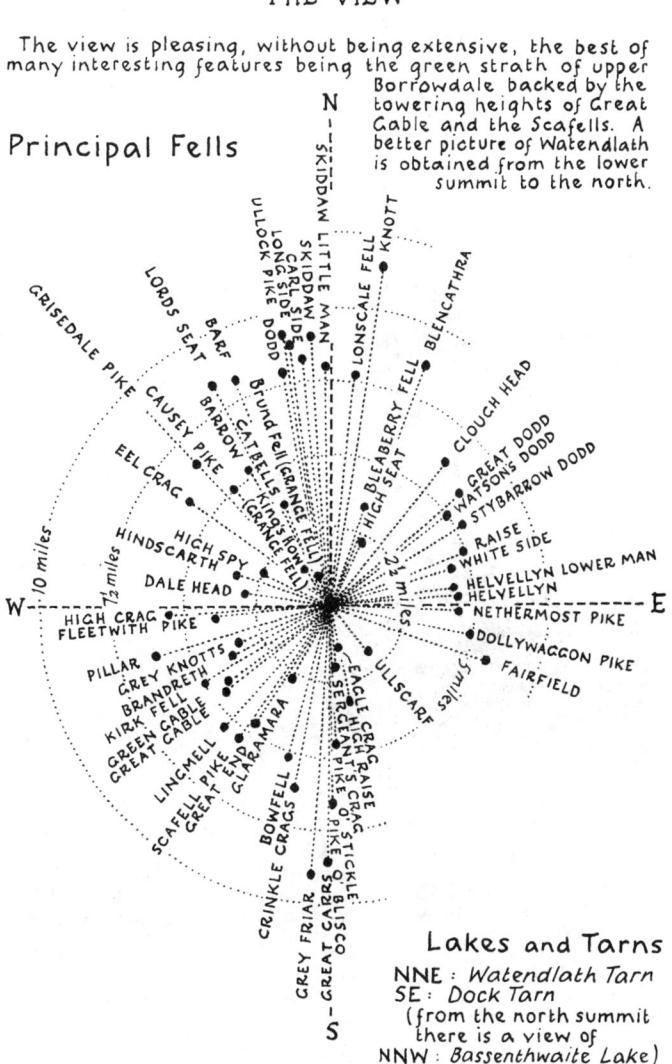

The view is pleasing, without being extensive, the best of many interesting features being the green strath of upper Borrowdale backed by the towering heights of Great Gable and the Scafells. A better picture of Watendlath is obtained from the lower summit to the north.

Principal Fells

N — SKIDDAW LITTLE MAN, SKIDDAW, CARLSIDE, LONGSIDE, ULLOCK PIKE, DODD, LONSCALE FELL, KNOTT, BLEABERRY FELL, BLENCATHRA, HIGH SEAT, CLOUGH HEAD, GREAT DODD, WATSON'S DODD, STYBARROW DODD, RAISE, WHITE SIDE, HELVELLYN LOWER MAN, HELVELLYN — E, NETHERMOST PIKE, DOLLYWAGGON PIKE, FAIRFIELD, ULLSCARF, SERGEANT'S CRAG, EAGLE CRAG, PIKE O' STICKLE, HARRISON STICKLE, PIKE O' BLISCO, GREAT CARRS, GREY FRIAR, CRINKLE CRAGS, BOWFELL, GLARAMARA, GREAT END, SCAFELL PIKE, LINGMELL, GREAT GABLE, GREEN GABLE, KIRK FELL, BRANDRETH, GREY KNOTTS, PILLAR, FLEETWITH PIKE, HIGH CRAG — W, DALE HEAD, HINDSCARTH, HIGH SPY, EEL CRAG, BARROW, CATBELLS (GRANGE FELL, KING'S HOW, GRANGE FELL), BRUND FELL (GRANGE FELL), BARF, LORDS SEAT, CAUSEY PIKE, GRISEDALE PIKE

(½ mile, 2 miles, 5 miles, 10 miles)

Lakes and Tarns

NNE: *Watendlath Tarn*
SE: *Dock Tarn*
(from the north summit there is a view of
NNW: *Bassenthwaite Lake*)

Harrison Stickle 2403'
the highest of the Langdale Pikes

HIGH RAISE ▲

PIKE O' STICKLE ▲ ▲ HARRISON STICKLE

LOFT CRAG ● New
Old Hotel ● Hotel

Dungeon Ghyll

MILES
0 1 2 3

from Great Langdale Beck

Harrison Stickle 2

NATURAL FEATURES

No mountain profile in Lakeland arrests and excites the attention more than that of the Langdale Pikes and no mountain group better illustrates the dramatic appeal of a sudden rising of the vertical from the horizontal; the full height from valley to summit is revealed at a glance in one simple abrupt upsurge to all travellers on the distant shore of Windermere and, more intimately, on the beautiful approach along Great Langdale. Nor is the appeal visual only: that steep ladder to heaven stirs the imagination, and even the emotions, and this is especially so whenever the towering peaks come into view suddenly and unexpectedly. The difference in altitude between top and base is little more than 2000 feet, yet, because it occurs in a distance laterally of only three-quarters of a mile, it is enough to convey a remarkable impression of remoteness, of inaccessibility, to the craggy summits surmounting the rugged slopes.

continued

Harrison Stickle 3

NATURAL FEATURES
continued

Of the group of peaks known collectively as Langdale Pikes, the highest is Harrison Stickle, and this is the fell that presents such a bold front to, and dominates, the middle curve of the valley. It is severed from its satellites westwards by the deep gloomy ravines of Dungeon Ghyll, which, at a lower altitude and near its famous waterfall, turns across the bottom slopes towards Mill Gill, the eastern boundary, so that the fell's actual footing in the valley is quite small, only the width of a field. The ridged summit is liberally buttressed by crags, as is a curious shoulder running down to the hanging valley occupied by Stickle Tarn, a considerable sheet of water no less attractive for being partly artificial.

The uninitiated climber who scales Harrison Stickle from Langdale expecting to find the northerly slopes descending as steeply as those he has just ascended will be surprised to see, on reaching the main cairn, that higher ground continues beyond a very shallow depression. The Pikes are, in fact, no more than the abrupt termination of a wide ridge coming down from High Raise, and on this side their aspect, in contrast, is one of almost comical insignificance. But let nothing derogatory be said of Harrison Stickle. The majesty and masculine strength of the Langdale front is itself quite enough to establish the fell as a firm favourite with all, even with those admirers who are content to stand on the road below and gape upwards, while for those who set forth to conquer, it provides a very worthy climb indeed.

1 : *The summit*
2 : *Ridge continuing to Thunacar Knott and High Raise*
3 : *Pike How*   4 : *Miller Crag*
5 : *Stickle Tarn*   6 : *Mill Gill*
7 : *Dungeon Ghyll*
8 : *Dungeon Ghyll Force*
9 : *Great Langdale Beck*

looking north-west

Harrison Stickle 4

The Ravines of Dungeon Ghyll

The upper ravine between Thorn Crag and Harrison Stickle

The middle ravine. The waterfall (on the right), which terminates this section, falls into a rock basin and escapes over a breach in the lip to form a second fall — a most charming scene, revealed only by a close visit (which entails some scrambling).

The lower ravine

Hidden amongst the trees is Dungeon Ghyll Force, a much-frequented waterfall (that does not compare, as an object of beauty, with the little-frequented one mentioned above).

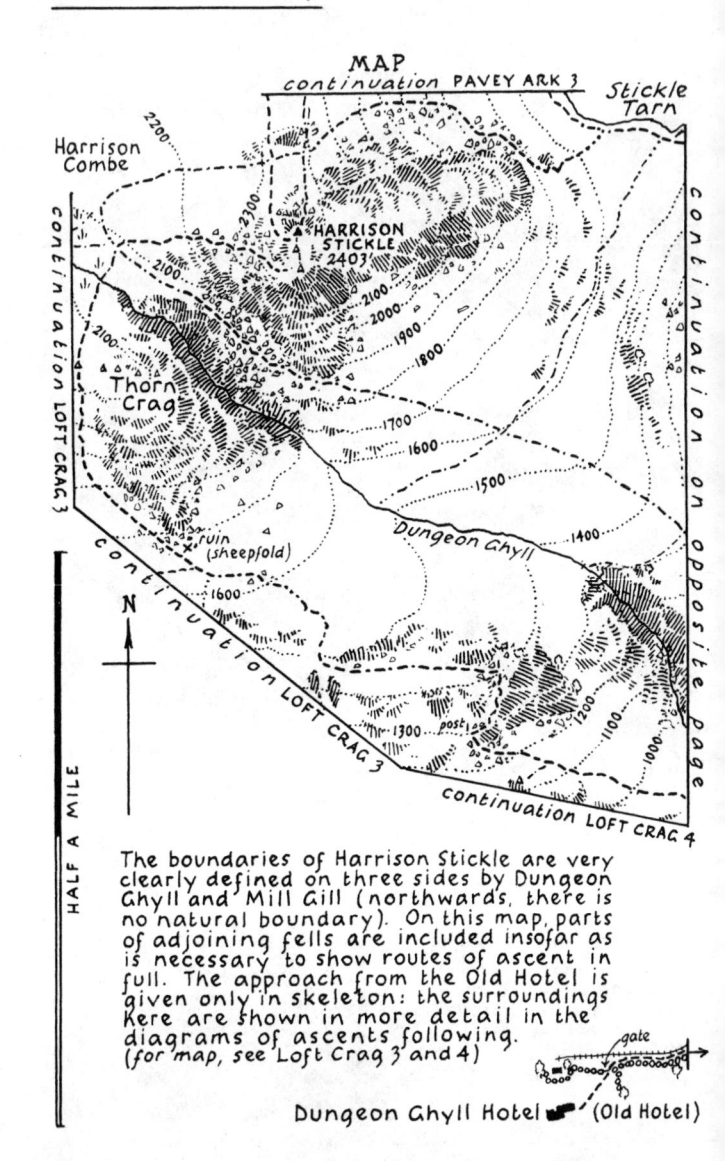

Harrison Stickle 5

MAP continuation PAVEY ARK 3

Stickle Tarn

Harrison Combe

continuation LOFT CRAG 3

HARRISON STICKLE 2403

Thorn Crag

ruin (sheepfold)

Dungeon Ghyll

N

HALF A MILE

continuation LOFT CRAG 3

continuation LOFT CRAG 4

continuation on opposite page

The boundaries of Harrison Stickle are very clearly defined on three sides by Dungeon Ghyll and Mill Gill (northwards, there is no natural boundary). On this map, parts of adjoining fells are included insofar as is necessary to show routes of ascent in full. The approach from the Old Hotel is given only in skeleton: the surroundings here are shown in more detail in the diagrams of ascents following.
(for map, see Loft Crag 3 and 4)

gate

Dungeon Ghyll Hotel (Old Hotel)

Harrison Stickle 6

MAP

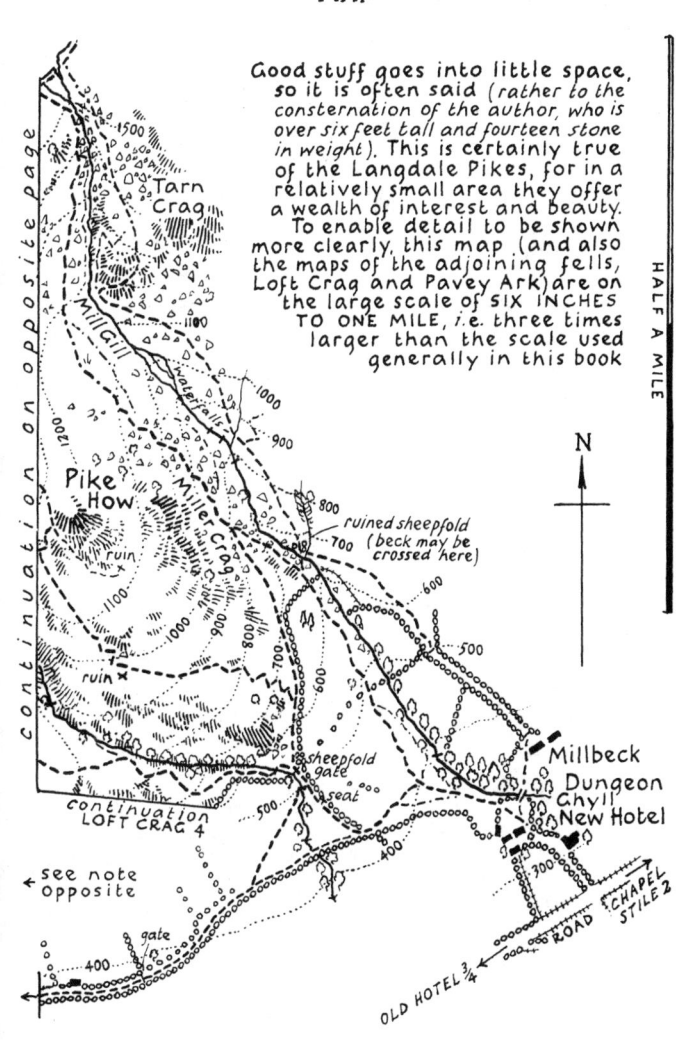

Good stuff goes into little space, so it is often said (rather to the consternation of the author, who is over six feet tall and fourteen stone in weight). This is certainly true of the Langdale Pikes, for in a relatively small area they offer a wealth of interest and beauty.

To enable detail to be shown more clearly, this map (and also the maps of the adjoining fells, Loft Crag and Pavey Ark) are on the large scale of SIX INCHES TO ONE MILE, *i.e.* three times larger than the scale used generally in this book

Harrison Stickle 7

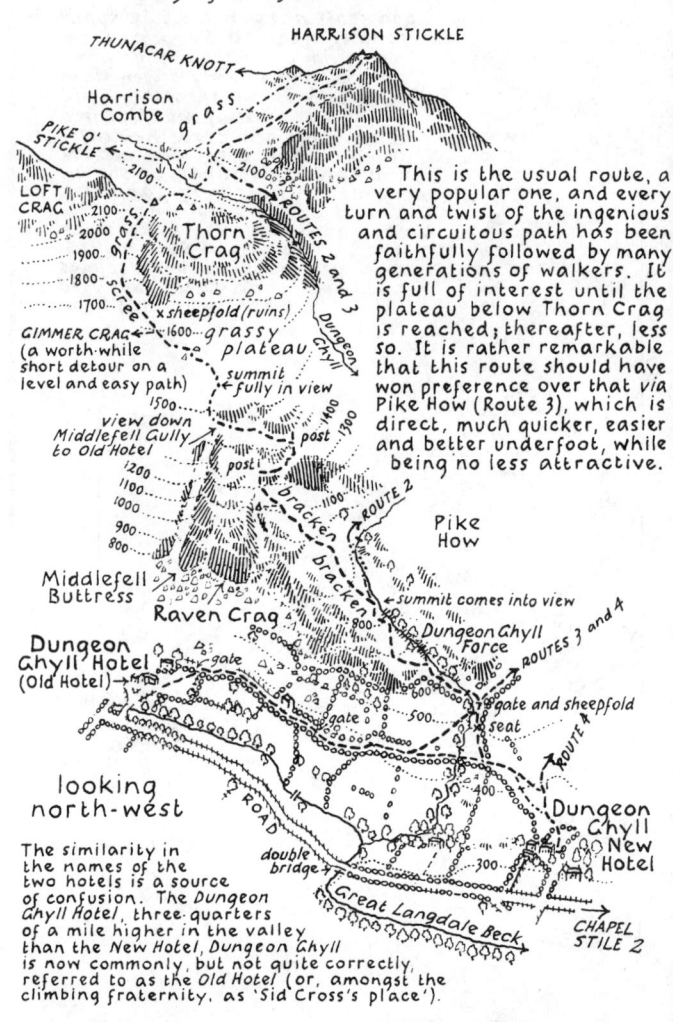

ASCENT FROM DUNGEON GHYLL
ROUTE 1 : via THORN CRAG
2150 feet of ascent : 2 miles

looking north-west

This is the usual route, a very popular one, and every turn and twist of the ingenious and circuitous path has been faithfully followed by many generations of walkers. It is full of interest until the plateau below Thorn Crag is reached; thereafter, less so. It is rather remarkable that this route should have won preference over that via Pike How (Route 3), which is direct, much quicker, easier and better underfoot, while being no less attractive.

The similarity in the names of the two hotels is a source of confusion. The *Dungeon Ghyll Hotel*, three-quarters of a mile higher in the valley than the New Hotel, *Dungeon Ghyll* is now commonly, but not quite correctly, referred to as the *Old Hotel* (or, amongst the climbing fraternity, as 'Sid Cross's place').

Harrison Stickle 8

ASCENT FROM DUNGEON GHYLL
ROUTE 2: via THE DUNGEON GHYLL RAVINES
2150 feet of ascent: 1¾ miles

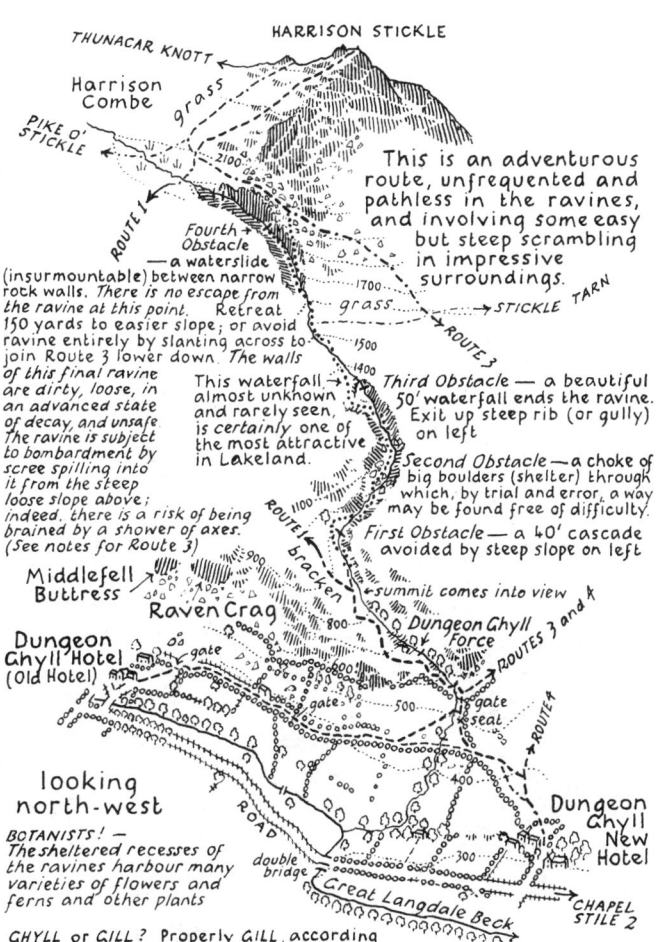

This is an adventurous route, unfrequented and pathless in the ravines, and involving some easy but steep scrambling in impressive surroundings.

Fourth Obstacle — a waterslide (insurmountable) between narrow rock walls. There is no escape from the ravine at this point. Retreat 150 yards to easier slope; or avoid ravine entirely by slanting across to join Route 3 lower down. The walls of this final ravine are dirty, loose, in an advanced state of decay, and unsafe. The ravine is subject to bombardment by scree spilling into it from the steep loose slope above; indeed, there is a risk of being brained by a shower of axes. (See notes for Route 3)

This waterfall, almost unknown and rarely seen, is certainly one of the most attractive in Lakeland.

Third Obstacle — a beautiful 50' waterfall ends the ravine. Exit up steep rib (or gully) on left

Second Obstacle — a choke of big boulders (shelter) through which, by trial and error, a way may be found free of difficulty.

First Obstacle — a 40' cascade avoided by steep slope on left

looking north-west

BOTANISTS! —
The sheltered recesses of the ravines harbour many varieties of flowers and ferns and other plants

GHYLL or GILL? Properly GILL, according to the best authorities. GHYLL is a poetical affectation: it is too well established at Dungeon Ghyll to be altered now, and is accepted in a few other cases, e.g. Stock Ghyll, Ambleside.

Harrison Stickle 9

ASCENT FROM DUNGEON GHYLL
ROUTE 3 : via PIKE HOW
2100 feet of ascent : 1½ miles

HARRISON STICKLE

THUNACAR KNOTT

Harrison Combe

PIKE O' STICKLE

ROUTE 1

This steep scree slope above the ravine is loose. Except for the path, nothing is firm. This is the recently-discovered site of a prehistoric stone-axe 'factory' and much of the scree is the debris from working the stone and not the result of the weathering of the crags above.

STICKLE TARN

Visitors to Langdale who do not know this route are urged to make its acquaintance. It is not only the quickest and easiest way to the top but has two other distinct virtues: first, it is pleasant underfoot, which is more than can be said for many Langdale paths, and, secondly, it is the 'purest' route, being a direct climb which does not encroach upon neighbouring fells.

Pike How – a splendid viewpoint

Miller Crag

Middlefell Buttress

Raven Crag

Dungeon Ghyll Hotel (Old Hotel)

Dungeon Ghyll Force

ROUTES 1 and 2

gate

gate

gate and sheepfold
seat

ROUTE 4

ROUTE

looking north-west

Dungeon Ghyll New Hotel

The rough lane along which the path runs from the Old Hotel was the main thoroughfare along the valley before the road was constructed and the hotels opened. A century ago the only place of refreshment hereabouts was Millbeck Farm, and the lane led directly to it from Mickleden. It can still be traced throughout its length but one of its enclosing walls has been allowed to crumble away.

double bridge

Great Langdale Beck

CHAPEL STILE 2

Harrison Stickle 10

ASCENT FROM DUNGEON GHYLL
ROUTE 4: via STICKLE TARN
2100 feet of ascent
1¾ miles from the New Hotel; 2¼ from the Old Hotel

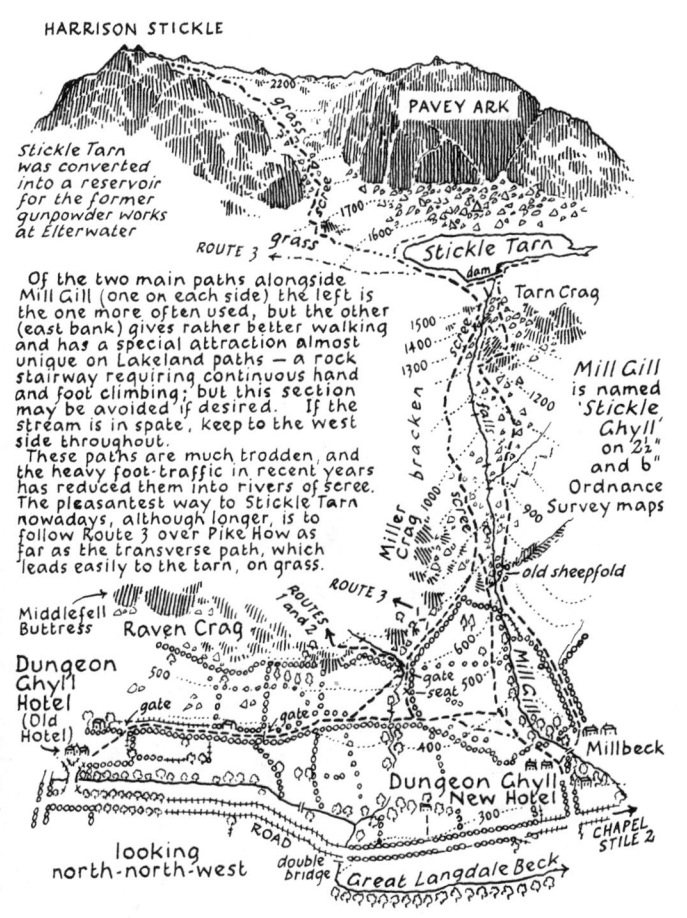

HARRISON STICKLE

PAVEY ARK

Stickle Tarn was converted into a reservoir for the former gunpowder works at Elterwater

ROUTE 3 grass — Stickle Tarn — Tarn Crag

Of the two main paths alongside Mill Gill (one on each side) the left is the one more often used, but the other (east bank) gives rather better walking and has a special attraction almost unique on Lakeland paths — a rock stairway requiring continuous hand and foot climbing; but this section may be avoided if desired. If the stream is in spate, keep to the west side throughout.
These paths are much trodden, and the heavy foot-traffic in recent years has reduced them into rivers of scree. The pleasantest way to Stickle Tarn nowadays, although longer, is to follow Route 3 over Pike How as far as the transverse path, which leads easily to the tarn, on grass.

Mill Gill is named 'Stickle Ghyll' on 2½" and 6" Ordnance Survey maps

old sheepfold

Middlefell Buttress — Raven Crag — ROUTES 1 and 2 — ROUTE 3

Dungeon Ghyll Hotel (Old Hotel) — gate — gate — gate seat — Millbeck — Mill Gill — Dungeon Ghyll New Hotel — CHAPEL STILE 2

looking north-north-west — ROAD — double bridge — Great Langdale Beck

The highlight of this route is the impressive view of Pavey Ark, one of the finest scenes in Lakeland

Harrison Stickle 11

ASCENTS FROM BORROWDALE AND GRASMERE

Harrison Stickle is remote from Borrowdale and Grasmere although not too distant to be reached, and the return made, in a day's walk.

All *natural* lines of ascent pass over intervening summits.

From BORROWDALE, either (i) first climb High Raise by the Greenup Edge path, or (ii) Pike o' Stickle by way of Langstrath and Stake Pass, in both cases then adopting the ridge routes from those summits. The alternative should be used for return.

From GRASMERE, either (i) first climb Sergeant Man, or (ii) Blea Rigg, descending from the latter to Stickle Tarn, whence the ascent may be completed.

Direct ascents *could* be worked out to avoid traversing other fells, but these would be artificial, probably no easier, and less interesting.

The fells mentioned above have separate chapters in this book, containing diagrams of ascent.

The summit from Pike How

The summit from Stickle Tarn

Harrison Stickle 12

THE SUMMIT

The summit is an elevated ridge, 70 yards long and relatively narrow, falling away very sharply in crags at both ends. The main cairn is built on a rocky platform at the northern end and there is another, slightly lower, occupying the southern extremity above the precipitous Langdale face. A scanty covering of turf barely conceals the solid rock that here is very near the surface. The loftiness of the ridge and its commanding position endow a distinction to the summit that might be expected from its noble appearance in distant views.

DESCENTS (to Dungeon Ghyll):
With such a variety of attractive routes available, it would be a pity not to use an alternative to the one adopted for ascent (but Route 2 is less satisfactory as a way down, and needs care). The Pike How route is the easiest (most grass, least scree) and much the quickest. It should be obvious that direct descents from the south cairn are impracticable, but the warning must be given. Similarly, the tempting ridge leading straight down from the top towards Stickle Tarn is defended at its base by an almost continuous wall of crags: a scree gully going down from it on the left side is often used but is unpleasantly loose. Indeed, nothing but hard labour and trouble is to be gained by attempting descents that are independent of the regular paths.

Harrison Stickle 13

THE VIEW

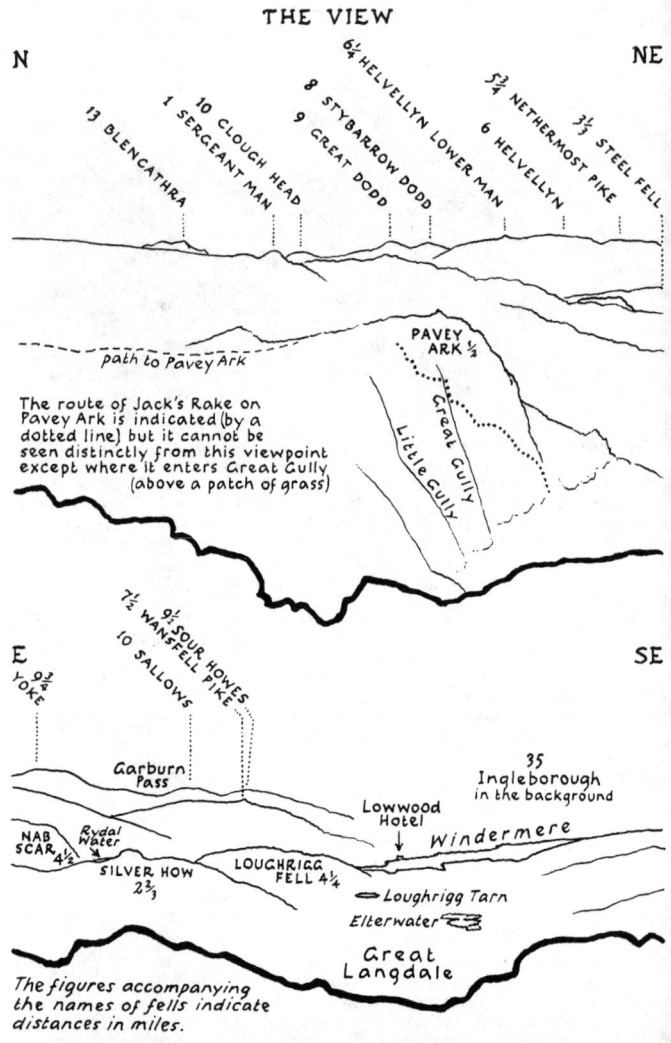

N — NE

- 13 BLENCATHRA
- 1 SERGEANT MAN
- 10 CLOUGH HEAD
- 9 GREAT DODD
- 8 STYBARROW DODD
- 6¼ HELVELLYN LOWER MAN
- 6 HELVELLYN
- 5¾ NETHERMOST PIKE
- 3½ STEEL FELL

path to Pavey Ark

PAVEY ARK ½
Great Gully
Little Gully

The route of Jack's Rake on Pavey Ark is indicated (by a dotted line) but it cannot be seen distinctly from this viewpoint except where it enters Great Gully (above a patch of grass)

E — SE

- 9¾ YOKE
- 7½ SOUR HOWES
- 9½ WANSFELL PIKE
- 10 SALLOWS

Garburn Pass

35 Ingleborough in the background

Lowwood Hotel

Windermere

NAB SCAR 4½
Rydal Water
SILVER HOW 2⅔
LOUGHRIGG FELL 4¼
← Loughrigg Tarn
Elterwater

Great Langdale

The figures accompanying the names of fells indicate distances in miles.

The thick line marks the visible boundaries of the summit from the main cairn

Harrison Stickle 14

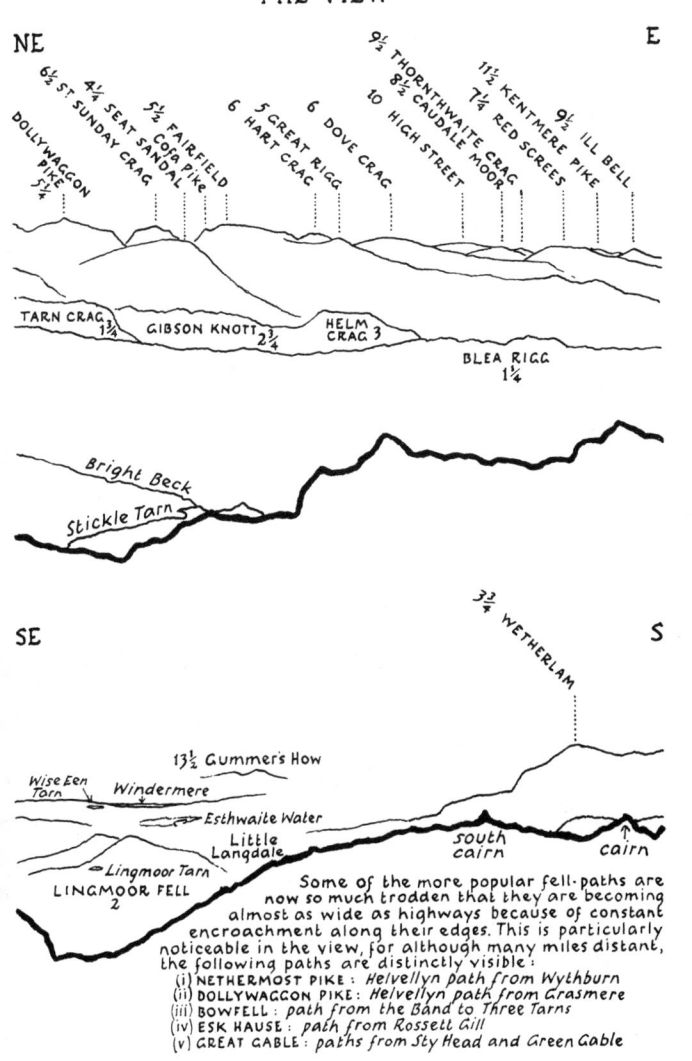

THE VIEW

NE — DOLLYWAGGON PIKE 5¼, 6½ ST SUNDAY CRAG, 4¼ SEAT SANDAL, 5½ FAIRFIELD, COFA PIKE, 6 HART CRAG, 5 GREAT RIGG, 6 DOVE CRAG, 10 HIGH STREET, 9½ THORNTHWAITE CRAG, 8½ CAUDALE MOOR, 11½ KENTMERE PIKE, 7¼ RED SCREES, 9½ ILL BELL — **E**

TARN CRAG 1¾, GIBSON KNOTT 2¾, HELM CRAG 3, BLEA RIGG 1¼

Bright Beck
Stickle Tarn

SE — 3¾ WETHERLAM — **S**

Wise Een Tarn, Windermere, 13½ Gummer's How, Esthwaite Water, Little Langdale, south cairn, cairn
Lingmoor Tarn
LINGMOOR FELL 2

Some of the more popular fell-paths are now so much trodden that they are becoming almost as wide as highways because of constant encroachment along their edges. This is particularly noticeable in the view, for although many miles distant, the following paths are distinctly visible:
(i) NETHERMOST PIKE: *Helvellyn path from Wythburn*
(ii) DOLLYWAGGON PIKE: *Helvellyn path from Grasmere*
(iii) BOWFELL: *path from the Band to Three Tarns*
(iv) ESK HAUSE: *path from Rossett Gill*
(v) GREAT GABLE: *paths from Sty Head and Green Gable*

Harrison Stickle 15

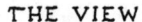

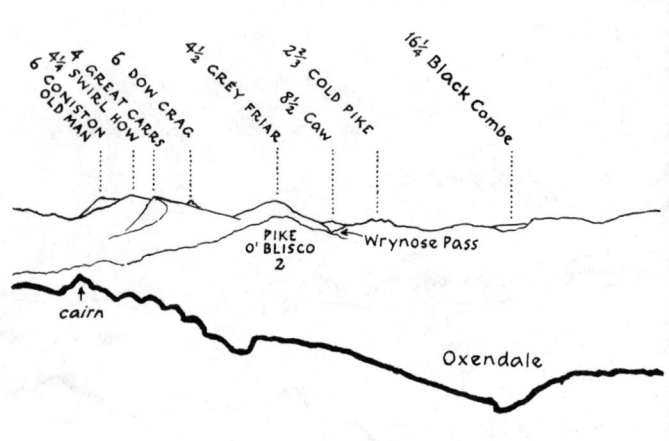

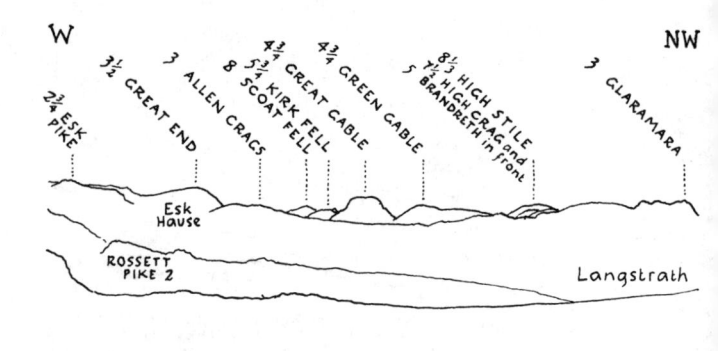

THE VIEW

S — **SW**

- 6 CONISTON OLD MAN
- 4¼ SWIRL HOW
- 4 GREAT CARRS
- 6 DOW CRAG
- 4½ GREY FRIAR
- 2¾ COLD PIKE
- 8½ Caw
- 16¼ Black Combe
- PIKE O' BLISCO 2
- Wrynose Pass
- cairn
- Oxendale

W — **NW**

- 2¾ ESK PIKE
- 3½ GREAT END
- 3 ALLEN CRAGS
- 8 SCOAT FELL
- 5¾ KIRK FELL
- 4¾ GREAT GABLE
- 4¾ GREEN GABLE
- 8½ HIGH STILE
- 7½ HIGH CRAG and BRANDRETH in front
- 5
- 3 GLARAMARA
- Esk Hause
- ROSSETT PIKE 2
- Langstrath
- Harrison Combe

Harrison Stickle 16

THE VIEW

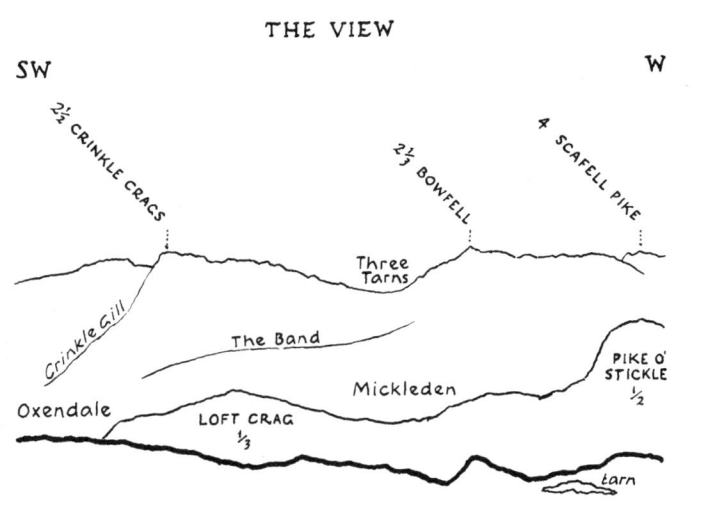

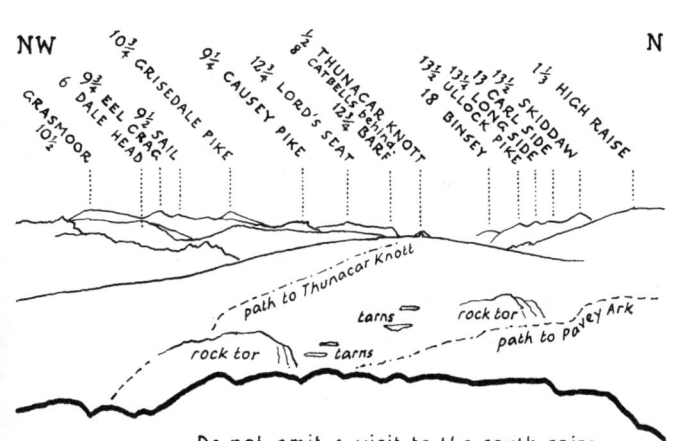

SW — 2½ CRINKLE CRAGS, Crinkle Gill, Three Tarns, 2⅔ BOWFELL, 4 SCAFELL PIKE — W

The Band, Oxendale, Mickleden, LOFT CRAG ⅓, PIKE O' STICKLE ½, tarn

NW — 6 GRASMOOR 10½, 9¾ EEL CRAG, DALE HEAD, 10¾ GRISEDALE PIKE, 9½ SAIL, 9¼ CAUSEY PIKE, ⅞ THUNACAR KNOTT, 12¾ LORD'S SEAT, 12¾ CATBELLS behind BARF, 18 BINSEY, 13¼ LONG SIDE, 13 ULLOCK PIKE, 13¼ CARL SIDE, 13½ SKIDDAW, 1⅓ HIGH RAISE — N

path to Thunacar Knott, tarns, rock tor, rock tor, tarns, path to Pavey Ark

Do not omit a visit to the south cairn, which has a striking downward view of Great Langdale. Stickle Tarn is better seen from here, and Blea Tarn comes into the picture. This is a particularly good viewpoint.

Harrison Stickle 17

RIDGE ROUTES

To PIKE O' STICKLE, 2323': ½ mile : W
Depression at 2075': 250 feet of ascent
An easy walk, ending with an enjoyable scramble

The objective is clearly in view and its distinctive outline is unmistakable. The route is direct (it 'short-cuts' the ridge) and is easily traced in clear weather, although indistinct in marshy ground near the crossing of the stream. The final scramble is steep and rocky, and permits of minor variations.

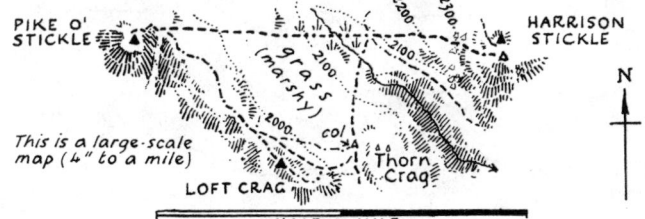

This is a large-scale map (4" to a mile)

HALF A MILE

To LOFT CRAG, 2270': ⅓ mile : W, then S and W
Depression at 2070': 200 feet of ascent
An easy walk, with a fine little summit at the finish

Loft Crag is the biggest eminence on the ridge to the left of Pike o' Stickle. Take the usual route for Langdale (Route 1), turning off right at the Thorn Crag col along a narrow track and then left up a small but prominent scree-run to the ridge.

Harrison Stickle from Loft Crag

Harrison Stickle 18

RIDGE ROUTES

To THUNACAR KNOTT, 2351': ½ mile : NNW
Depression at 2225': 140 feet of ascent
A dull trudge from the spectacular to the uninteresting.

The path starts distinctly from the main cairn but beyond the rock tor becomes obscure in a depression: here follow the line of cairns leading half-left to an improving path (another track develops from a line of cairns going straight on, but loses itself amongst the boulders ahead). The recognised top of Thunacar Knott is marked by a big cairn beyond a tarn, although higher ground is crossed on the way to it. The path keeps to the right and goes on to High Raise.

To PAVEY ARK, 2288'
½ mile : N, then NE
Depression at 2225'
100 feet of ascent
An interesting path

Although not strictly a ridge route, this is a popular walk. From the main cairn, descend the steep but easy rocks directly below to join a good path, much of it over bare rock, linking the two summits. Anyone who does not like the look of the initial descent may avoid it by taking the Thunacar Knott route at the start and slanting across to the Pavey Ark path over grass on the near side of the rock tor.

HALF A MILE

Pavey Ark from the path

top of Jack's Rake

pinnacle

Helm Crag

1299'

affectionately known as
'The Lion and The Lamb'

from Grasmere

HELM CRAG ▲

Grasmere •

MILES
0 1 2

This is the smallest (and most accurate!) map in the book

Helm Crag 2

NATURAL FEATURES

Helm Crag may well be the best-known of all Lakeland fells, and possibly even the best-known hill in the country. Generations of waggonette and motor-coach tourists have been tutored to recognise its appearance in the Grasmere landscape: it is the one feature of their Lakeland tour they hail at sight, and in unison, but the cry on their lips is not "Helm Crag!" but "The Lion and the Lamb!" — in a variety of dialects. The resemblance of the summit rocks to a lion is so striking that recognition, from several viewpoints, is instant; yet, oddly, the outline most like Leo is not the official 'Lion' at all: in fact there are two lions, each with a lamb, and each guards one end of the summit ridge as though set there by architectural design. The summit is altogether a rather weird and fantastic place, well worth not merely a visit but a detailed and leisurely exploration. Indeed the whole fell, although of small extent, is unusually interesting; its very appearance is challenging; its sides are steep, rough and craggy; its top bristles; it *looks* irascible, like a shaggy terrier in a company of sleek foxhounds, for all around are loftier and smoother fells, circling the pleasant vale of Grasmere out of which Helm Crag rises so abruptly.

The fell is not isolated, nor independent of others, for it is the termination of a long ridge enclosing Far Easedale in a graceful curve on north and east and rising, finally, to the rocky peak of Calf Crag. It drains quickly, is dry underfoot, and has no streams worthy of mention.

The virtues of Helm Crag have not been lauded enough. It gives an exhilarating little climb, a brief essay in real mountaineering, and, in a region where all is beautiful, it makes a notable contribution to the natural charms and attractions of Grasmere.

summit scene

Helm Crag 3

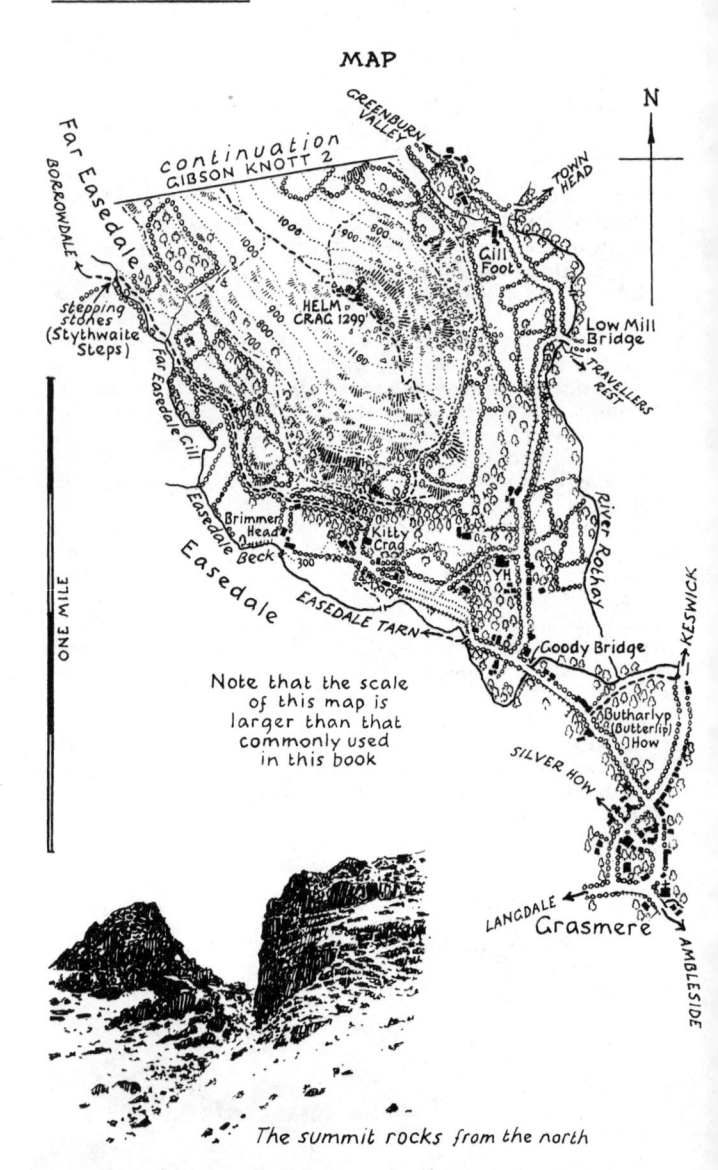

MAP

The summit rocks from the north

Helm Crag 4

ASCENT FROM GRASMERE
1100 feet of ascent : 1½ miles

HELM CRAG

When descending (especially in mist) watch for zig-zag

White Crag — Raven Crag — Jackdaw Crag — Lancrigg Crag — Kitty Crag

seat (perhaps!)

FAR EASEDALE (BORROWDALE) (footpath)

Easedale — EASEDALE TARN (footpath) — LOW MILL BRIDGE and GILL FOOT (road) — Goody Bridge — Easedale Beck — Butharlyp (Butterlip) How

studio — LANGDALE — Red Lion Hotel — KESWICK — Grasmere — Church

This is one of the few hills where ascent and descent by the same route is recommended, the popular path depicted being much the best way both up and down. An alternative route (shown on the map but not on this diagram) has nothing in its favour.

If, however, Helm Crag is to be a part only of the day's programme (e.g. the circuit of Far Easedale or the Greenburn valley) it is better reserved for descent, for then the Vale of Grasmere will be directly in view ahead; and this fair scene is at its best when the shadows of evening are lengthening, with the Langdales silhouetted in rugged outline against the sunset. Tarry long over this exquisite picture of serenity and peace, and memorise it for the long winter of exile!

looking north-west

This is a splendid little climb ; if it has a fault it is that it is too short. But for the evening of the day of arrival in Grasmere on a walking holiday it is just the thing : an epitome of Lakeland concentrated in the space of two hours — and an excellent foretaste of happy days to come.

Helm Crag 5

THE SUMMIT

Rocks at the north-west end of the summit ridge, known by various names:
(a) The 'Lion Couchant, or, more popularly, The Lion and The Lamb. (as seen from the road below Dunmail Raise)
(b) The Howitzer (as seen from Dunmail Raise)

The highest point of the rocks is the true summit of the fell

In scenic values, the summits of many high mountains are a disappointment after the long toil of ascent, yet here, on the top of little Helm Crag, a midget of a mountain, is a remarkable array of rocks, upstanding and fallen, of singular interest and fascinating appearance, that yield a quality of reward out of all proportion to the short and simple climb. The uppermost inches of Scafell and Helvellyn and Skiddaw can show nothing like Helm Crag's crown of shattered and petrified stone: indeed, its highest point, a pinnacle of rock airily thrust out above a dark abyss, is not to be attained by walking and is brought underfoot only by precarious manœuvres of the body. This is one of the very few summits in Lakeland reached only by climbing rocks, and it is certainly (but not for that reason alone) one of the very best.

continued

Helm Crag 6

THE SUMMIT

continued

The summit ridge is 250 yards in length and is adorned at each end by fangs of rock overtopping the fairly level path. Between these towers there have been others in ages past but all that remains of them now is a chaos of collapsed boulders, choking a strange depression that extends the full length of the summit on the north-east side. The depression is bounded by a secondary ridge, and this in turn descends craggily to an even more strange depression, in appearance resembling a huge ditch cleft straight as a furrow across the breast of the fell for 300 yards; or, more romantically, a deep moat defending the turreted wall of the castle above. This surprising feature, which will not be seen unless searched for, will doubtless be readily explained by geologists (or antiquaries?); to the unlearned beholder it seems likely to be the result of some ancient natural convulsion that caused the side of the fell to slip downwards a few yards before coming to rest. This ditch is also bounded on its far side by a parallel ridge or parapet (narrow, and an interesting walk) beyond which the fellside plunges down almost precipitously to the valley, falling in juniper-clad crags.

Care is necessary when exploring the boulder-strewn depressions on the summit, especially if the rocks are greasy. There are many good natural shelters here, and some dangerous clefts and fissures and holes, so well protected from the weather that summer flowers are to be found in bloom in their recesses as late as mid-winter.

The south-west side of the summit ridge consists mainly of bracken slopes and are of little interest in their upper reaches.

DESCENTS : Always use the ridge-path for descent to Grasmere. Watch for the zig-zag turning down left from the ridge, especially in mist, and ignore the misleading green path going straight on : this ends above crags.

Helm Crag 7

THE SUMMIT

Rocks at the north-west end of the summit-ridge known as The Old Woman Playing the Organ *from their appearance when seen from Tongue Gill and the vicinity of Easedale Tarn*

Rocks at the south-east end of the summit-ridge. These form the OFFICIAL Lion and The Lamb *(as seen from the Swan Hotel, Grasmere). The lion's head is the O.S. 'station' (altitude 1299') but is not quite the highest point of the fell*

Helm Crag 8

THE VIEW

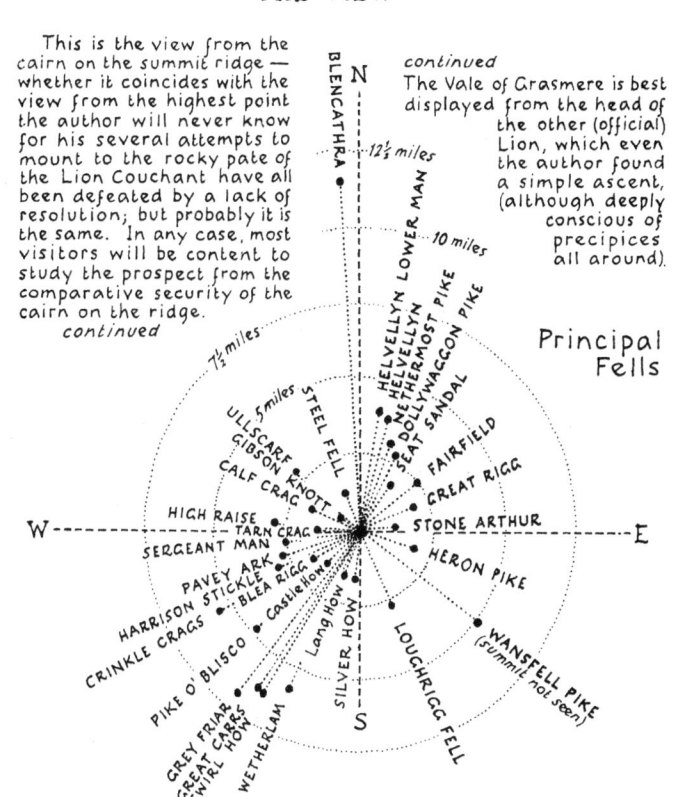

This is the view from the cairn on the summit ridge — whether it coincides with the view from the highest point the author will never know for his several attempts to mount to the rocky pate of the Lion Couchant have all been defeated by a lack of resolution; but probably it is the same. In any case, most visitors will be content to study the prospect from the comparative security of the cairn on the ridge.
continued

continued
The Vale of Grasmere is best displayed from the head of the other (official) Lion, which even the author found a simple ascent, (although deeply conscious of precipices all around).

Principal Fells

N — BLENCATHRA — 12½ miles
10 miles
7½ miles — 5 miles
HELVELLYN LOWER MAN
HELVELLYN
NETHERMOST PIKE
DOLLYWAGGON PIKE
SEAT SANDAL
FAIRFIELD
GREAT RIGG
STONE ARTHUR — E
HERON PIKE
WANSFELL PIKE (summit not seen)
LOUGHRIGG FELL
ULLSCARF
STEEL FELL
GIBSON KNOTT
CALF CRAG
HIGH RAISE
TARN CRAG
SERGEANT MAN
PAVEY ARK
HARRISON STICKLE
CRINKLE CRAGS
BLEA RIGG
Castle How
PIKE O' BLISCO
Lang How
SILVER HOW
S
GREY FRIAR
GREAT CARRS
SWIRL HOW
WETHERLAM
W

The prominent height south-south-east (to the right of Loughrigg Fell) is Gummer's How, 13 miles distant at the foot of Windermere.

Lakes and Tarns
SE : Windermere (upper reach)
SSE : Grasmere
SSE : Esthwaite Water
WSW : Easedale Tarn

This corner was reserved for an announcement that the author had succeeded in surmounting the highest point. Up to the time of going to press, however, such an announcement cannot be made.

Helm Crag 9

*Tarn Crag
across Far Easedale
from the slopes of Helm Crag*

*The north-east face
from Low Mill Bridge*

Helm Crag 10

RIDGE ROUTE

To GIBSON KNOTT, 1379'
   1 mile : NW, then W
   Depression at 1050'
   400 feet of ascent
   An interesting ridge climb

Two big cairns indicate the way off Helm Crag. A narrow path crosses the depression and continues up the opposite slope; when it starts to traverse the face leave it and keep to the ridge, where another track winds charmingly between rock outcrops. The cairned summit rises across a shallow hollow.

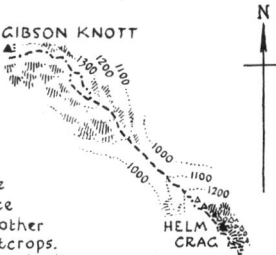

ONE MILE

Helm Crag, from the path to Gibson Knott

High Raise

2500'

summit named
High White Stones

from Great Crag,
Watendlath Fell

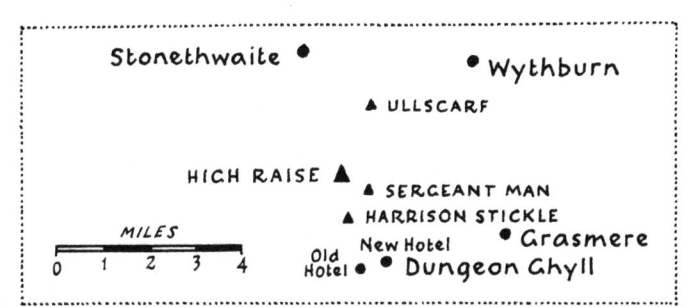

High Raise 2

```
         Stonethwaite  •              • Wythburn
                         ▲ ULLSCARF

           HIGH RAISE ▲  ▲ SERGEANT MAN
                        ▲ HARRISON STICKLE
           MILES         New Hotel    • Grasmere
        |___|___|___|___|  Old
        0   1   2   3   4  Hotel •  • Dungeon Ghyll
```

NATURAL FEATURES

It is usual to regard High Raise as Lakeland's most centrally situated fell. An area without definite boundaries cannot have a determinable centre, and the 'most central fell' must remain a matter of individual opinion. A study of the map of the district suggests that High Raise has a decided bias to the south, however, and that Ullscarf better fits the description, while, a little further north, Armboth Fell seems even more deserving of the title. The most that can be said of High Raise, with certainty, is that its summit is the maximum elevation of the central axis or watershed. Hereabouts the surround of mountainous country is complete, the western arc being occupied by a tumultuous skyline and the eastern horizon formed of lofty, smooth ranges; but, quite obviously, the viewpoint is dwarfed in altitude by many summits in this fine panorama. Nevertheless, High Raise occupies a magnificent position geographically, many valleys radiating from the wide upper slopes. The fell's attractions, except as a viewpoint and an easy promenade, are limited, distinctive natural features being absent from the rounded grassy slopes — remarkably so when one considers how full of character are the subsidiary summits of the main mass overlooking Great Langdale and Langstrath.   Drainage is provided by these two valleys, Langstrath taking away most of the water, with the assistance of Greenup Gill and Wyth Burn in the north.

High Raise 3

MAP

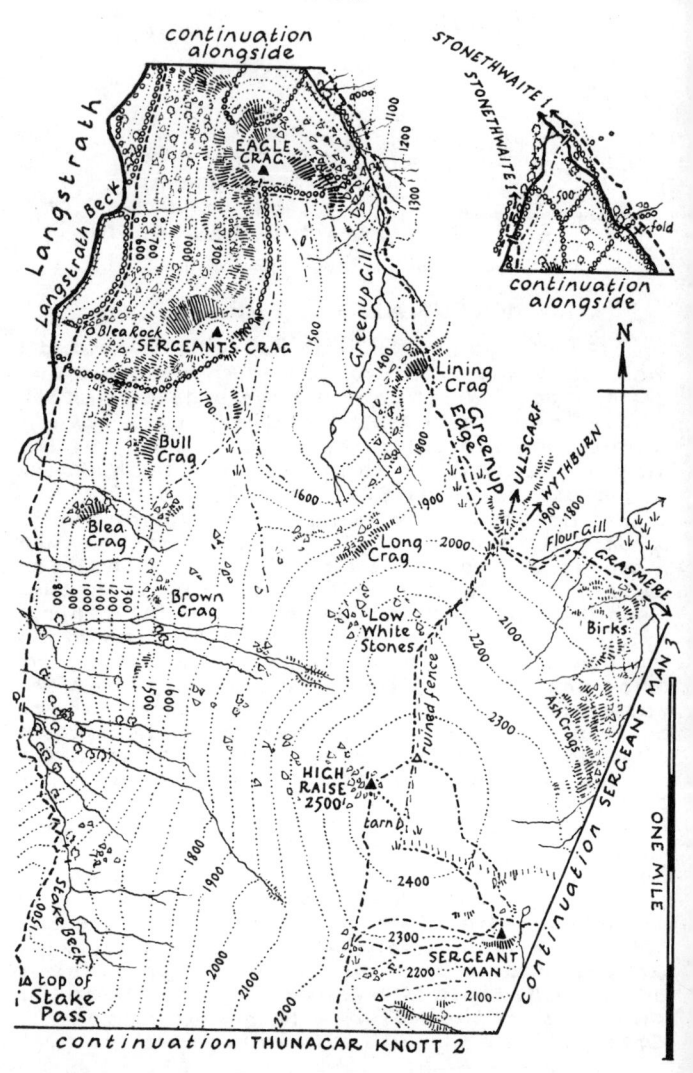

High Raise 4

ASCENT FROM DUNGEON GHYLL
2250 feet of ascent : 2½ miles from the New Hotel

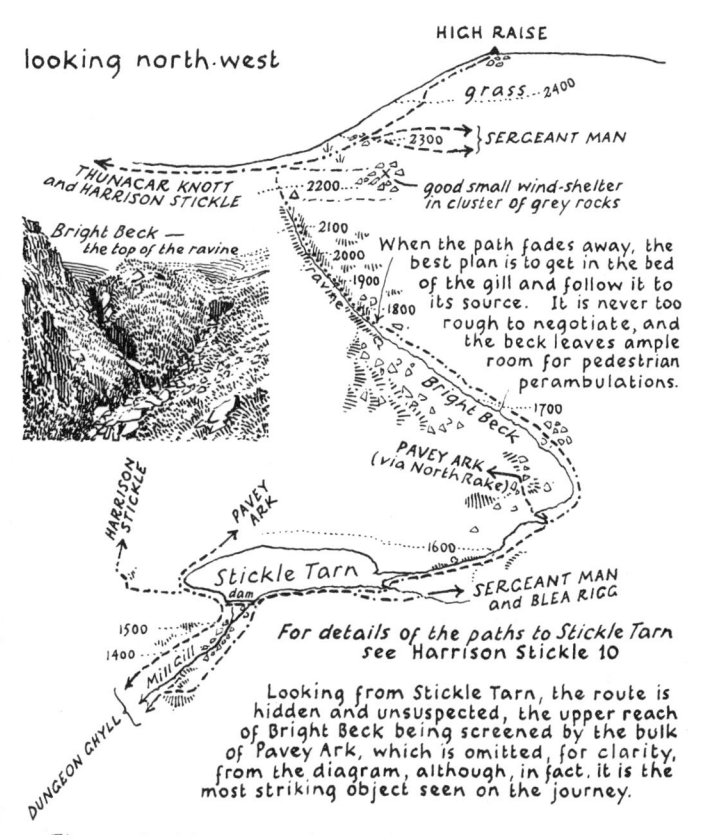

looking north-west

HIGH RAISE

grass — 2400

SERGEANT MAN — 2300

THUNACAR KNOTT and HARRISON STICKLE ← 2200

good small wind-shelter in cluster of grey rocks

Bright Beck — the top of the ravine

2100
2000
1900
1800

When the path fades away, the best plan is to get in the bed of the gill and follow it to its source. It is never too rough to negotiate, and the beck leaves ample room for pedestrian perambulations.

Bright Beck

1700

PAVEY ARK (via North Rake)

HARRISON STICKLE

PAVEY ARK

Stickle Tarn — dam

1600

SERGEANT MAN and BLEA RIGG

1500
1400

Mill Gill

DUNGEON GHYLL

For details of the paths to Stickle Tarn see Harrison Stickle 10

Looking from Stickle Tarn, the route is hidden and unsuspected, the upper reach of Bright Beck being screened by the bulk of Pavey Ark, which is omitted, for clarity, from the diagram, although, in fact, it is the most striking object seen on the journey.

The route illustrated is the only practicable direct way to High Raise from Dungeon Ghyll that does not involve the climbing of intermediate summits. It has much to commend it as a quick, easy and foolproof way to the top, for beyond Stickle Tarn the gradients are surprisingly gentle while the route is closely defined by Bright Beck, but it can hardly be described as interesting, and, if time and extra effort are of no consequence, the best way to High Raise from the south will always lie over the top of Harrison Stickle.

High Raise 5

ASCENT FROM GRASMERE
2350 feet of ascent : 5½ miles

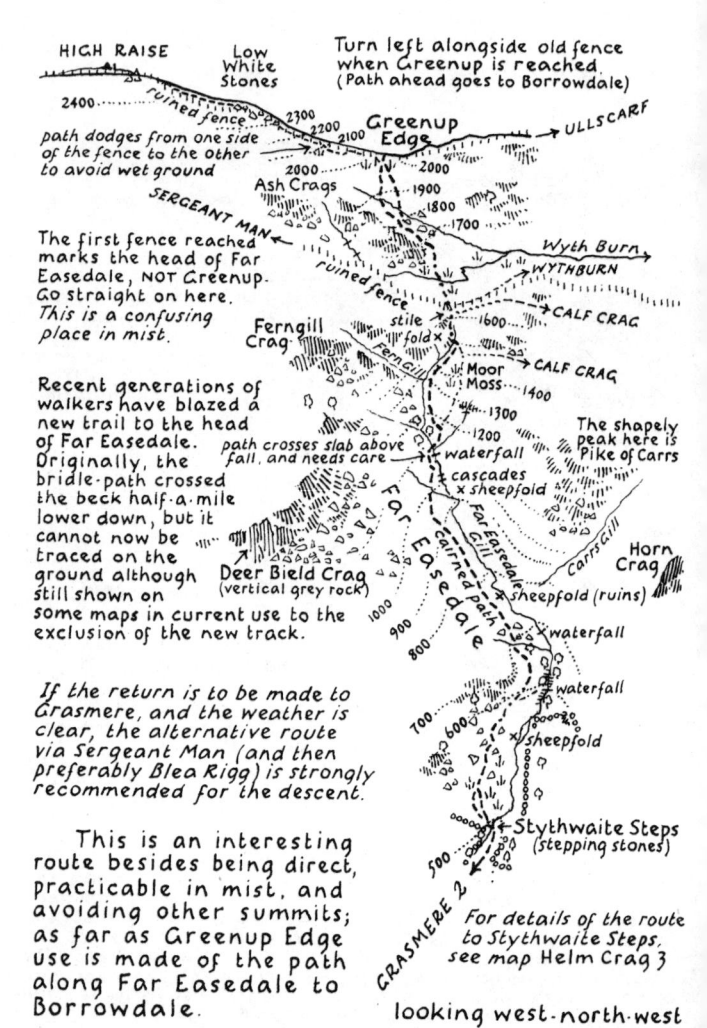

HIGH RAISE — Low White Stones — 2400 — ruined fence — 2300 — 2200 — 2100 — Greenup Edge → ULLSCARF

Turn left alongside old fence when Greenup is reached. (Path ahead goes to Borrowdale)

path dodges from one side of the fence to the other to avoid wet ground

SERGEANT MAN — Ash Crags — 2000 — 1900 — 1800 — 1700

The first fence reached marks the head of Far Easedale, NOT Greenup. Go straight on here. This is a confusing place in mist.

ruined fence — Wyth Burn → WYTHBURN — stile — fold — 1600 — CALF CRAG

Ferngill Crag — Ferngill — Moor Moss — 1400 — CALF CRAG

Recent generations of walkers have blazed a new trail to the head of Far Easedale. Originally, the bridle-path crossed the beck half-a-mile lower down, but it cannot now be traced on the ground although still shown on some maps in current use to the exclusion of the new track.

path crosses slab above fall, and needs care — 1300 — waterfall — 1200 — cascades × sheepfold

The shapely peak here is Pike of Carrs

Deer Bield Crag (vertical grey rock) — Far Easedale — cairned path — Carrs Gill — Horn Crag — sheepfold (ruins)

1000 — 900 — 800 — waterfall

If the return is to be made to Grasmere, and the weather is clear, the alternative route via Sergeant Man (and then preferably Blea Rigg) is strongly recommended for the descent.

waterfall — 700 — 600 — × sheepfold

This is an interesting route besides being direct, practicable in mist, and avoiding other summits; as far as Greenup Edge use is made of the path along Far Easedale to Borrowdale.

Stythwaite Steps (stepping stones) — 500

GRASMERE 2

For details of the route to Stythwaite Steps, see map Helm Crag 3

looking west-north-west

High Raise 6

ASCENT FROM WYTHBURN
1950 feet of ascent : 5 miles from Wythburn Church

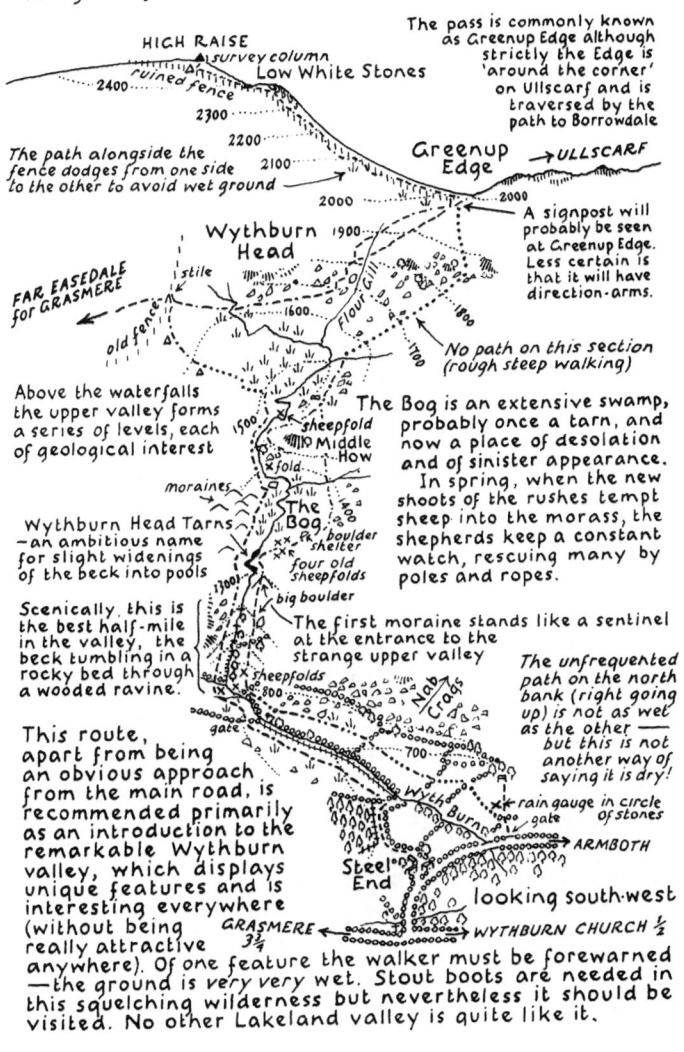

HIGH RAISE — survey column — Low White Stones

The pass is commonly known as Greenup Edge although strictly the Edge is 'around the corner' on Ullscarf and is traversed by the path to Borrowdale

ruined fence — 2400 — 2300 — 2200 — 2100 — 2000

Greenup Edge → ULLSCARF

The path alongside the fence dodges from one side to the other to avoid wet ground

A signpost will probably be seen at Greenup Edge. Less certain is that it will have direction-arms.

Wythburn Head — 1900 — Flour Gill — 1800

FAR EASEDALE for GRASMERE ← stile — old fence — 1600

No path on this section (rough steep walking)

Above the waterfalls the upper valley forms a series of levels, each of geological interest

sheepfold — Middle How — fold — moraines

The Bog is an extensive swamp, probably once a tarn, and now a place of desolation and of sinister appearance.
In spring, when the new shoots of the rushes tempt sheep into the morass, the shepherds keep a constant watch, rescuing many by poles and ropes.

Wythburn Head Tarns — an ambitious name for slight widenings of the beck into pools

The Bog — boulder shelter — four old sheepfolds — 1300 — big boulder

Scenically this is the best half-mile in the valley, the beck tumbling in a rocky bed through a wooded ravine.

The first moraine stands like a sentinel at the entrance to the strange upper valley

sheepfolds — 800 — gate — Nab Crags — 700

The unfrequented path on the north bank (right going up) is not as wet as the other — but this is not another way of saying it is dry!

Wyth Burn — rain gauge in circle of stones — gate

This route, apart from being an obvious approach from the main road, is recommended primarily as an introduction to the remarkable Wythburn valley, which displays unique features and is interesting everywhere (without being really attractive anywhere). Of one feature the walker must be forewarned — the ground is very very wet. Stout boots are needed in this squelching wilderness but nevertheless it should be visited. No other Lakeland valley is quite like it.

Steel End — ARMBOTH →

looking south-west

GRASMERE ← 3¾ — WYTHBURN CHURCH ½ →

High Raise 7

ASCENT FROM STONETHWAITE
2200 feet of ascent · 3¾ miles

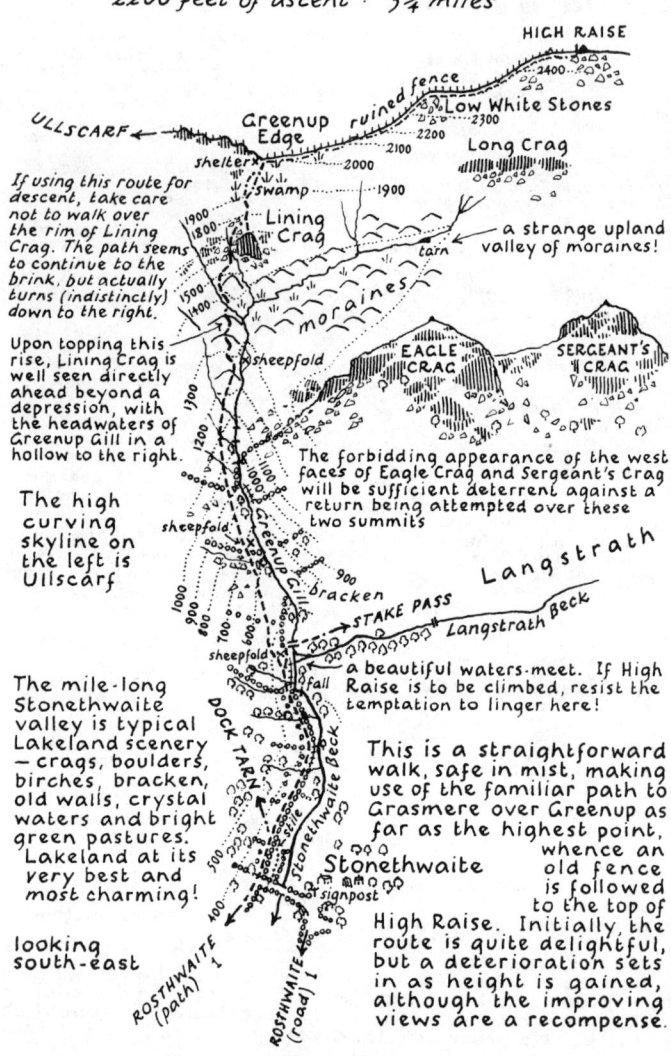

HIGH RAISE

ULLSCARF ← Greenup Edge ruined fence Low White Stones
shelter Long Crag
swamp
Lining Crag

a strange upland valley of moraines!

If using this route for descent, take care not to walk over the rim of Lining Crag. The path seems to continue to the brink, but actually turns (indistinctly) down to the right.

Upon topping this rise, Lining Crag is well seen directly ahead beyond a depression, with the headwaters of Greenup Gill in a hollow to the right.

sheepfold
moraines
tarn
EAGLE CRAG
SERGEANT'S CRAG

The high curving skyline on the left is Ullscarf

The forbidding appearance of the west faces of Eagle Crag and Sergeant's Crag will be sufficient deterrent against a return being attempted over these two summits

sheepfold
Greenup Gill
bracken
Langstrath
STAKE PASS
Langstrath Beck
sheepfold
fall

The mile-long Stonethwaite valley is typical Lakeland scenery — crags, boulders, birches, bracken, old walls, crystal waters and bright green pastures. Lakeland at its very best and most charming!

a beautiful waters-meet. If High Raise is to be climbed, resist the temptation to linger here!

DOCK TARN
Stonethwaite Beck
Stonethwaite signpost

This is a straightforward walk, safe in mist, making use of the familiar path to Grasmere over Greenup as far as the highest point, whence an old fence is followed to the top of High Raise. Initially, the route is quite delightful, but a deterioration sets in as height is gained, although the improving views are a recompense.

looking south-east

ROSTHWAITE (path) 1
ROSTHWAITE (road) 1

High Raise 8

THE SUMMIT

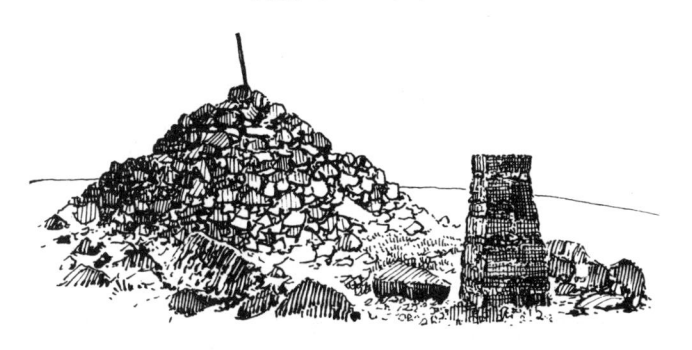

High Raise is often wrongly referred to as High White Stones. High Raise is the name of the fell, High White Stones the name of a small area of grey boulders which includes the summit. All else is grass, a vast sheepwalk in the form of a broad plateau little different from a valley pasture except that here drains and irrigation channels are absent and there is much marshy ground. The big cairn, and an adjacent survey column, stand at the top of the Langstrath slope, 150 yards west of a ruined fence: on the line of this fence, north-east, is a second cairn that features prominently in many views of the fell. Walking across the top is everywhere very easy.

DESCENTS: The path for GREAT LANGDALE leaves the main cairn, and becomes clear after crossing the stones. *In bad weather*, there is a safe escape from the ridge (which may lead to difficulties nearer to Harrison Stickle) by slanting left to Bright Beck at the first depression; this goes down to Stickle Tarn.

For GREENUP (and BORROWDALE, GRASMERE or WYTHBURN) follow the old fence northwards from the second cairn. The descent to BORROWDALE via Sergeant's Crag is pathless, takes longer than the Greenup route, and is amongst crags; *in bad weather it should not be attempted.*

STAKE PASS is in view from the main cairn and may be reached by a beeline (no path) but it is easier to take advantage at first of the Langdale path, slanting off right at the depression. It is well to remember, if time is short, that Stake Pass is far distant from habitations, and that nothing is saved by a visit thereto.

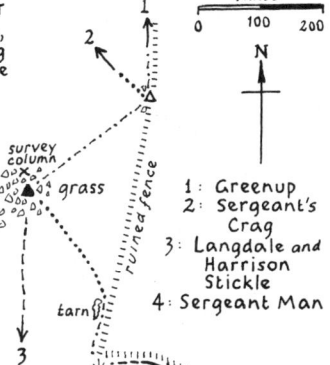

1: Greenup
2: Sergeant's Crag
3: Langdale and Harrison Stickle
4: Sergeant Man

High Raise 9

THE VIEW

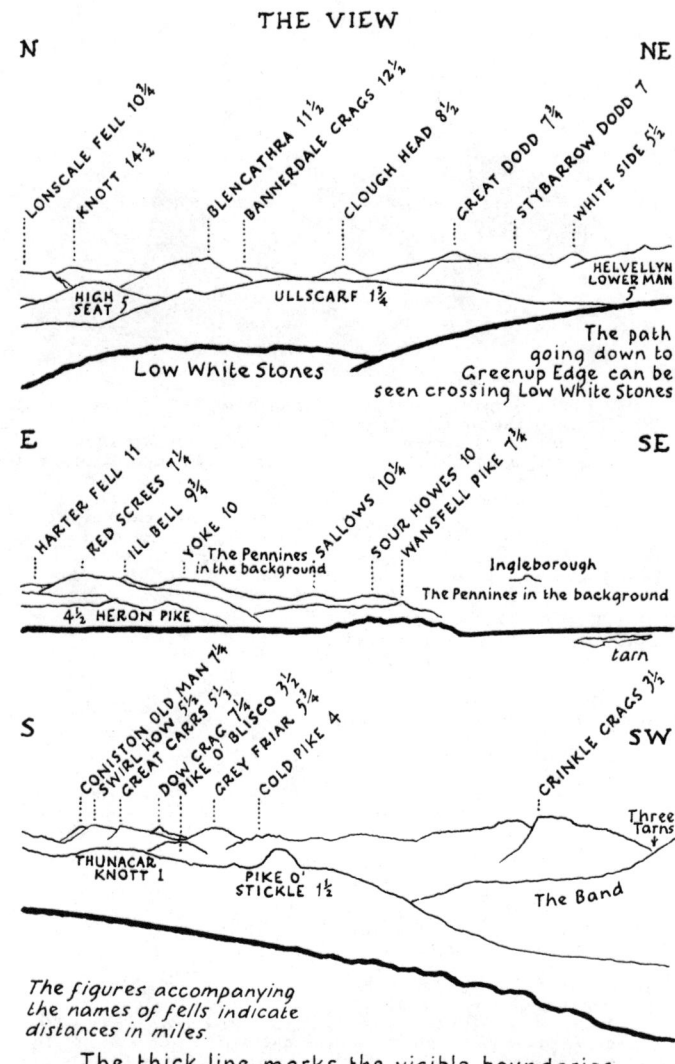

N — **NE**

- LONSCALE FELL 10¾
- KNOTT 14½
- BLENCATHRA 11½
- BANNERDALE CRAGS 12½
- CLOUGH HEAD 8½
- GREAT DODD 7¾
- STYBARROW DODD 7
- WHITE SIDE 5½
- HIGH SEAT 5
- ULLSCARF 1¼
- HELVELLYN LOWER MAN 5

Low White Stones

The path going down to Greenup Edge can be seen crossing Low White Stones

E — **SE**

- HARTER FELL 11
- RED SCREES 7¼
- ILL BELL 9¾
- YOKE 10
- SALLOWS 10¾
- SOUR HOWES 10
- WANSFELL PIKE 7¼
- The Pennines in the background
- Ingleborough
- The Pennines in the background
- 4½ HERON PIKE
- tarn

S — **SW**

- CONISTON OLD MAN 7¼
- SWIRL HOW 5½
- GREAT CARRS 5½
- DOW CRAG 7¼
- PIKE O' BLISCO 3½
- GREY FRIAR 5¾
- COLD PIKE 4
- CRINKLE CRAGS 3½
- THUNACAR KNOTT 1
- PIKE O' STICKLE 1½
- Three Tarns
- The Band

The figures accompanying the names of fells indicate distances in miles.

The thick line marks the visible boundaries of the fell from the main cairn

High Raise 10

THE VIEW

NE — HELVELLYN 5, NETHERMOST PIKE 4¾, DOLLYWAGGON PIKE 4½, ST. SUNDAY CRAG 6, WETHER HILL 11½, COFA PIKE 5, FAIRFIELD 5, HART CRAG 5½, DOVE CRAG 6, HIGH STREET 10 — **E**

SEAT SANDAL 4, GREAT RIGG 4½

↑ north-east cairn

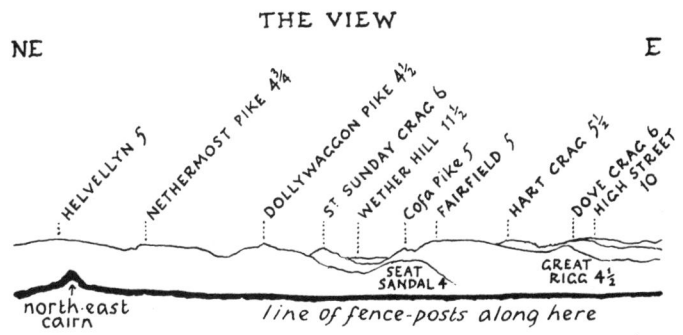

line of fence-posts along here

New features, notably the Wythburn valley and the summit of Sergeant Man, are brought into view by a visit to the north-east cairn. The conspicuous path seen climbing the breast of Nethermost Pike is the Wythburn path to Helvellyn.

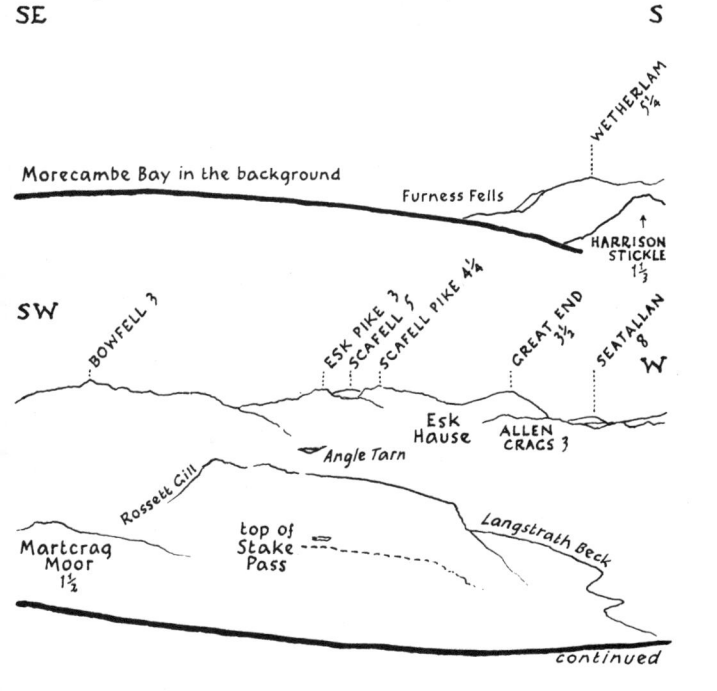

SE — **S**

WETHERLAM 5¼

Morecambe Bay in the background — Furness Fells

HARRISON STICKLE 1⅓

SW — BOWFELL 3, ESK PIKE 3, SCAFELL 5, SCAFELL PIKE 4¼, GREAT END 3½, SEATALLAN 8 — **W**

Esk Hause, ALLEN CRAGS 3

Rossett Gill, Angle Tarn

Martcrag Moor 1½, top of Stake Pass, Langstrath Beck

continued

High Raise 11

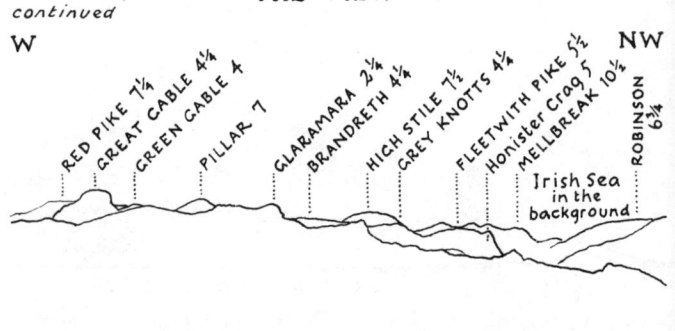

THE VIEW

continued

W — NW

RED PIKE 7¼
GREAT GABLE 4¼
GREEN GABLE 4
PILLAR 7
GLARAMARA 2¼
BRANDRETH 4½
HIGH STILE 7½
GREY KNOTTS 4¼
FLEETWITH PIKE 5½
HONISTER CRAG 5
MELLBREAK 10½
ROBINSON 6¾

Irish Sea in the background

The Langstrath Valley

RIDGE ROUTES

To THUNACAR KNOTT, 2351': 1 mile : S
Depression at 2225': 130 feet of ascent
An easy, straightforward walk

On the south side of the cairn a grassy path leaves the stones and goes easily down to cross a wide depression before climbing gently to Thunacar Knott, the summit-cairn being 60 yards west of the path. Ignore a distinct track branching left (to Pavey Ark) as the first stones of the Knott are reached.

To SERGEANT MAN, 2414': ½ mile : SE, then S
Depression at 2370': 60 feet of ascent
Merely a stroll

Sergeant Man cannot be seen from High Raise main cairn (although it is visible from the one north-east). Cross the top to the tarn and the old fence, where a path of sorts will be found.

High Raise 12

THE VIEW

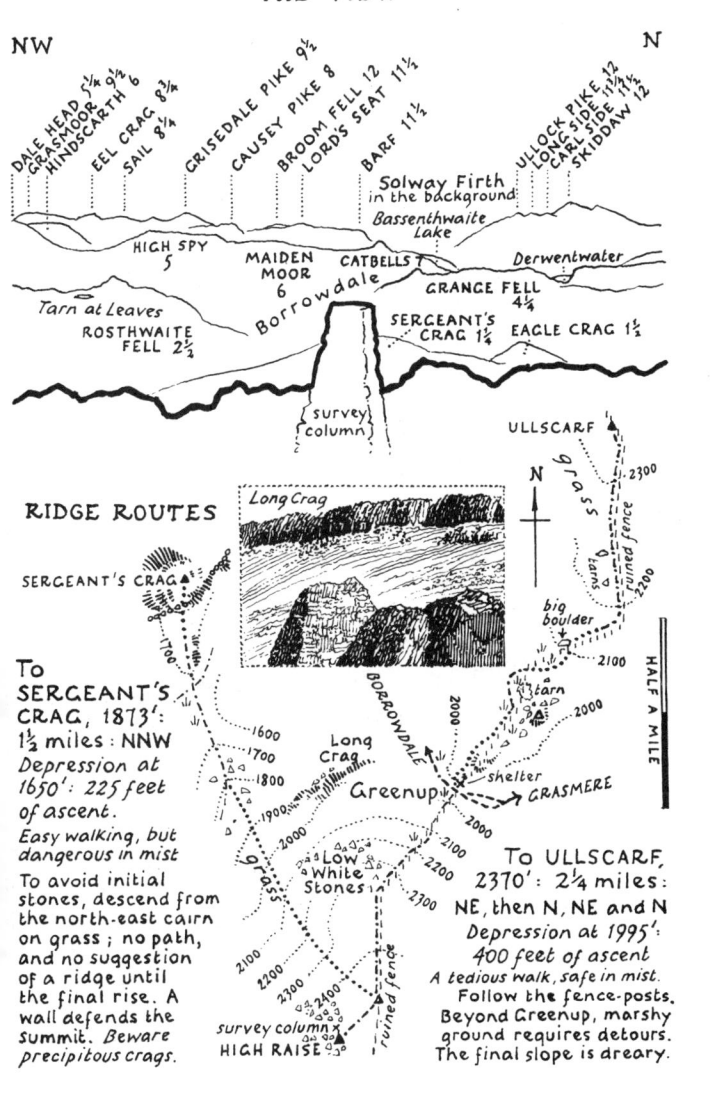

NW — DALE HEAD 7¼ 9¼ 6, GRASMOOR, HINDSCARTH, EEL CRAG 8¾, SAIL 8¼, CRISEDALE PIKE 9½, CAUSEY PIKE 8, BROOM FELL 12, LORD'S SEAT 11½, BARF 11½

N — ULLOCK PIKE 12, LONG SIDE 11½, CARL SIDE 11½, SKIDDAW 12

Solway Firth in the background
Bassenthwaite Lake
HIGH SPY, MAIDEN MOOR 6, CATBELLS, Derwentwater
Tarn at Leaves
ROSTHWAITE FELL 2½
Borrowdale
GRANGE FELL 4¼
SERGEANT'S CRAG 1½
EAGLE CRAG 1½
survey column

RIDGE ROUTES

Long Crag

SERGEANT'S CRAG

ULLSCARF

grass, ruined fence, cairns, big boulder, 2300, 2200, 2100, tarn, 2000

HALF A MILE

To SERGEANT'S CRAG, 1873': 1½ miles: NNW
Depression at 1650': 225 feet of ascent.
Easy walking, but dangerous in mist.
To avoid initial stones, descend from the north-east cairn on grass; no path, and no suggestion of a ridge until the final rise. A wall defends the summit. Beware precipitous crags.

Long Crag, BORROWDALE, Greenup, shelter, GRASMERE
Low White Stones
grass, ruined fence
survey column
HIGH RAISE 9½ 2500

To ULLSCARF, 2370': 2¼ miles: NE, then N, NE and N
Depression at 1995': 400 feet of ascent
A tedious walk, safe in mist.
Follow the fence-posts. Beyond Greenup, marshy ground requires detours. The final slope is dreary.

High Rigg 1163'

from Sosgill Bridge

The valley running north from Dunmail Raise, and containing Thirlmere, is suddenly confronted by a steep, abrupt fell just at that final stage in its course when, with the highest hills left behind, it might reasonably be expected to go on more leisurely, as is the fashion with valleys born among mountains. Escape is found in a narrow ravine to the right, which opens out into St. John's-in-the-Vale; and, because this intrusive fell stands in isolation from other high ground, a subsidiary valley, that of Naddle Beck, forms at the base of the left flank. The waters mingle only when the River Greta is joined four miles to the north. This isolated wedge is High Rigg (locally known as Naddle Fell): it is rough and craggy although of modest elevation only. Northwards the ridge falls to a pass, where there is a Church, so sited to serve both valleys equally (and an object of pilgrimage for many visitors to Keswick), beyond which rises Low Rigg, merely a rough pasture, followed by an easy slope descending to Tewet Tarn and the Keswick-Penrith road.

High Rigg 2

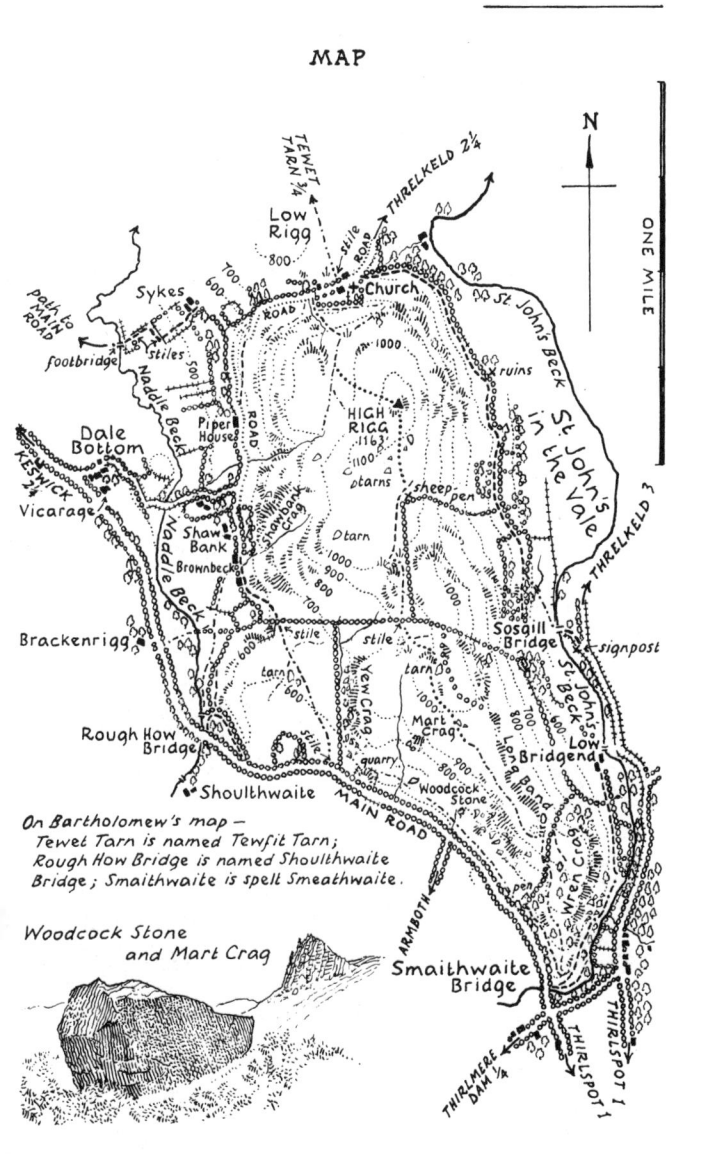

MAP

High Rigg 3

ASCENT FROM THE CHURCH OF St JOHN'S-IN-THE-VALE
450 feet of ascent : ½ mile

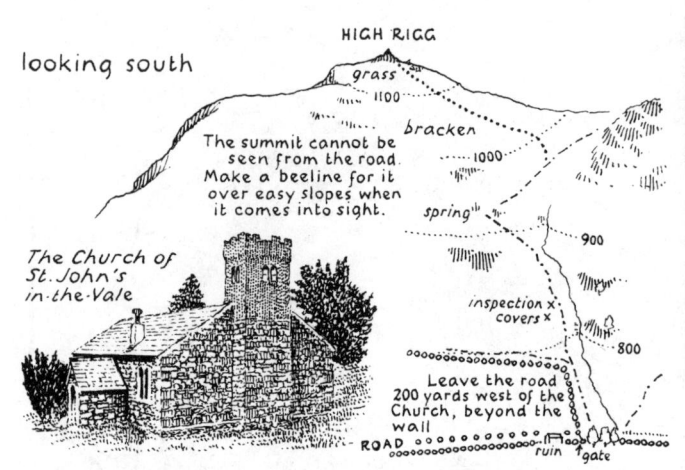

looking south

HIGH RIGG
grass
1100
bracken
1000

The summit cannot be seen from the road. Make a beeline for it over easy slopes when it comes into sight.

spring
900

The Church of St. John's-in-the-Vale

inspection covers
800

Leave the road 200 yards west of the Church, beyond the wall
ROAD
ruin gate

This short climb is as simple as the diagram suggests, although not appreciably helped by paths. Anybody full of the joy of Spring will do it in 15 minutes (author's time: 35 min.)

TRAVERSE OF THE RIDGE

The full traverse of the ridge, starting up the wooded slope from Smaithwaite Bridge and continuing over High Rigg and Low Rigg to Tewet Tarn and the Penrith road, is a splendid little expedition admirably suited to old and rickety fellwalkers long past their best. The journey should be made from south to north so that the fine view of Blencathra is in front. On a calm clear day this splendid mountain is perfectly mirrored in the waters of Tewet Tarn.

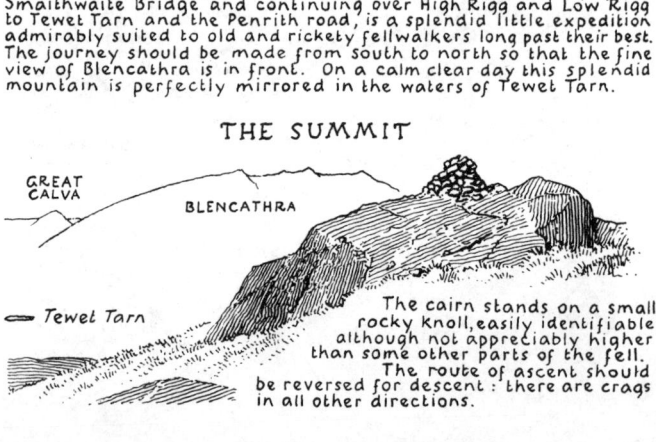

THE SUMMIT

GREAT CALVA
BLENCATHRA
← Tewet Tarn

The cairn stands on a small rocky knoll, easily identifiable although not appreciably higher than some other parts of the fell.
The route of ascent should be reversed for descent: there are crags in all other directions.

High Rigg 4

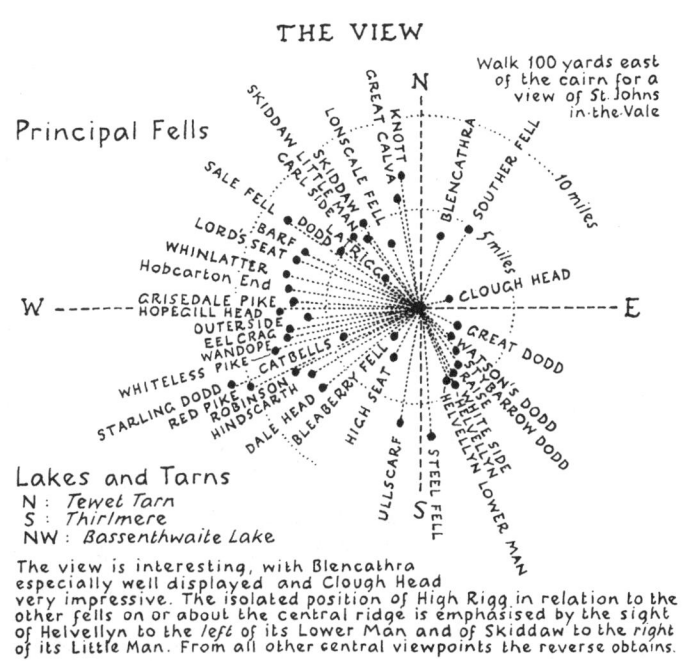

THE VIEW

Walk 100 yards east of the cairn for a view of St Johns in the Vale

Principal Fells

(compass diagram of fells, clockwise from N:)
KNOTT, GREAT CALVA, SKIDDAW, LONSCALE FELL, SKIDDAW LITTLE MAN, CARL SIDE, DODD, LATRIGG, BLENCATHRA, SOUTHER FELL, 10 miles, 5 miles, CLOUGH HEAD, GREAT DODD, WATSON'S DODD, STYBARROW DODD, RAISE, WHITE SIDE, HELVELLYN, HELVELLYN LOWER MAN, STEEL FELL, ULLSCARF, HIGH SEAT, BLEABERRY FELL, DALE HEAD, HINDSCARTH, ROBINSON, RED PIKE, STARLING DODD, CATBELLS, WHITELESS PIKE, WANDOPE, EEL CRAG, OUTERSIDE, HOPEGILL HEAD, GRISEDALE PIKE, Hobcarton End, WHINLATTER, LORD'S SEAT, BARF, SALE FELL

W — — — E

N / S

Lakes and Tarns
N : *Tewet Tarn*
S : *Thirlmere*
NW : *Bassenthwaite Lake*

The view is interesting, with Blencathra especially well displayed and Clough Head very impressive. The isolated position of High Rigg in relation to the other fells on or about the central ridge is emphasised by the sight of Helvellyn to the *left* of its Lower Man and of Skiddaw to the *right* of its Little Man. From all other central viewpoints the reverse obtains.

looking south to Helvellyn

High Seat 1995'

from Fisher Crag

- Keswick
- Dale Bottom
- BLEABERRY FELL ▲
- Lodore
- ▲ HIGH SEAT
- Armboth
- ▲ HIGH TOVE
- Watendlath
- Rosthwaite

MILES
0 1 2 3 4

Reecastle Crag

High Seat 2

NATURAL FEATURES

High Seat is the principal fell on the north section of the central ridge, overtopping all others within a radius of some miles, and is, therefore, an excellent viewpoint. Its limits are well-defined by watercourses: Ashness Gill, Watendlath Beck and Raise Gill westwards and Mere Gill and Shoulthwaite Gill on the eastern flank. As with all the fells on the Thirlmere and Borrowdale watershed the top is uninteresting, and all the charm and excitement concentrates in the steep and craggy lower slopes, especially on those to the west above Derwentwater, where the woods of Lodore and Ashness are supremely lovely, crag and coppice and cascade combining to present scenes of peerless beauty. A curiosity on the eastern side is the great rock barrier of Raven Crag, which deflects all streams north to the narrow ravine of Shoulthwaite Gill and away from Thirlmere, for which they seem, at first, to be naturally destined.

As a climb, High Seat is less meritorious than its initial approaches and fine situation suggest, due partly to the extreme dreariness of the upper plateau, that not even a rich carpet of heather can dispel, but more particularly due to the universal swampiness of the ultimate slopes.

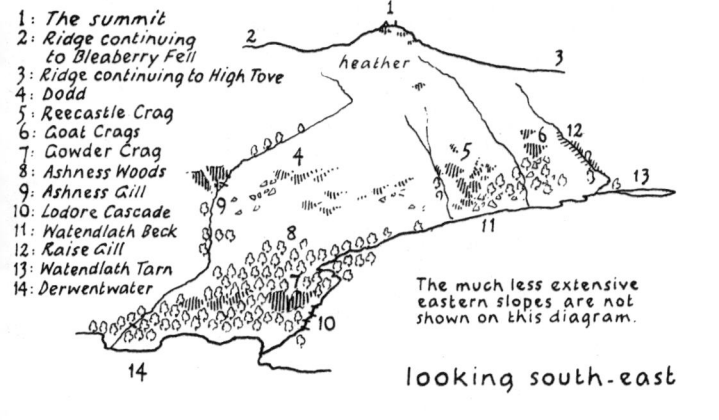

1: The summit
2: Ridge continuing to Bleaberry Fell
3: Ridge continuing to High Tove
4: Dodd
5: Reecastle Crag
6: Goat Crags
7: Gowder Crag
8: Ashness Woods
9: Ashness Gill
10: Lodore Cascade
11: Watendlath Beck
12: Raise Gill
13: Watendlath Tarn
14: Derwentwater

The much less extensive eastern slopes are not shown on this diagram.

looking south-east

High Seat 3

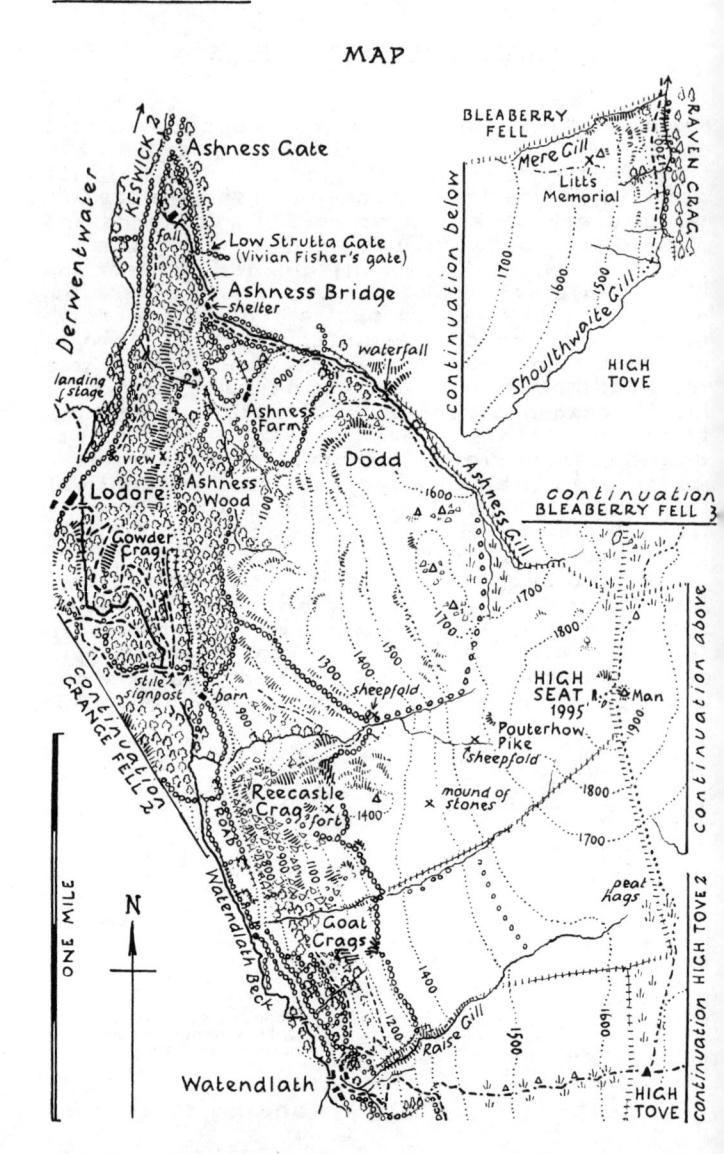

MAP

High Seat 4

ASCENT FROM ASHNESS BRIDGE
1500 feet of ascent : 2 miles (4½ from Keswick)

HIGH SEAT

BLEABERRY FELL ←

Pouterhow Pike

heather

Four cairns on rock knolls may be visited with little effort

When the fence turns away to the left a beeline may be made for the summit over undulating and marshy ground. It will be found a little drier underfoot to continue ahead to Pouterhow Pike before turning left to the top.

heather

Dodd

This is the best section. The falls will not be seen unless the beck is followed closely (and carefully)

This route avoids the roughnesses of the ravine (but misses the view of the falls) Aim for the solitary tree to find the path.

bracken

gap

looking south-east

WATENDLATH 2½

Ashness Gill is well worth a visit, the falls being spectacular, but the last half-mile to the summit of High Seat is tedious.

bracken

Ashness Gill

sheepfold

Strutta Wood

Ashness Bridge

a 'surprise' view (less well-known than the one in Ashness Wood)

KESWICK 2½

Ashness Bridge

Waterfalls in Ashness Gill

High Seat 5

ASCENT FROM WATENDLATH
1200 feet of ascent : 2 miles

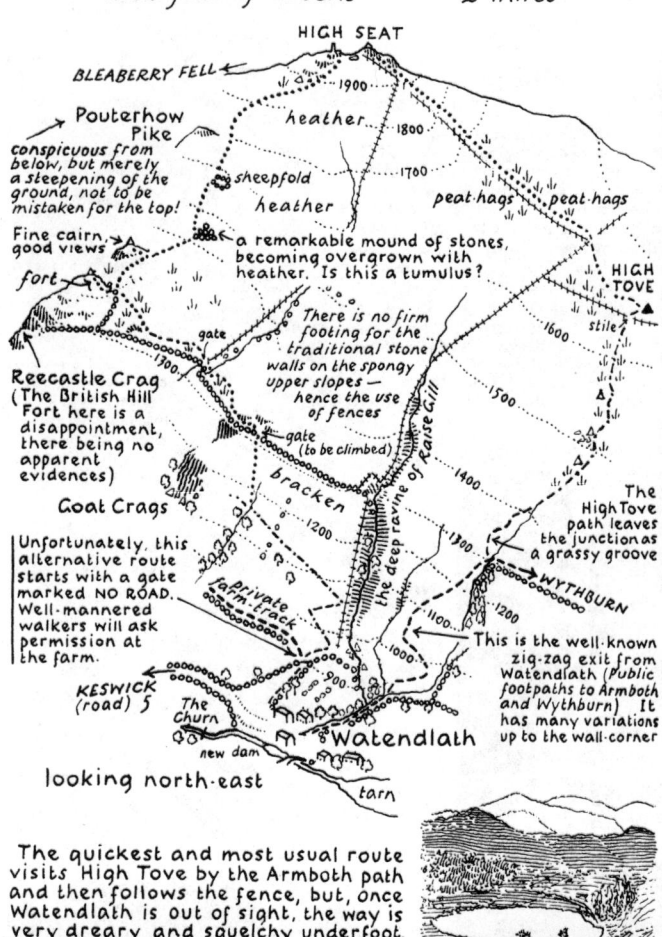

looking north-east

HIGH SEAT
BLEABERRY FELL
Pouterhow Pike — conspicuous from below, but merely a steepening of the ground, not to be mistaken for the top!
heather
sheepfold
heather
peat hags   peat hags
HIGH TOVE
stile
Fine cairn, good views
fort
a remarkable mound of stones, becoming overgrown with heather. Is this a tumulus?
There is no firm footing for the traditional stone walls on the spongy upper slopes — hence the use of fences
Reecastle Crag (The British Hill Fort here is a disappointment, there being no apparent evidences)
gate
gate (to be climbed)
the deep ravine of Raise Gill
Goat Crags
bracken
The High Tove path leaves the junction as a grassy groove
Unfortunately, this alternative route starts with a gate marked NO ROAD. Well-mannered walkers will ask permission at the farm.
Private farm-track
WYTHBURN
This is the well-known zig-zag exit from Watendlath (Public footpaths to Armboth and Wythburn) It has many variations up to the wall-corner
KESWICK (road) 5
The Churn
new dam
Watendlath
tarn

The quickest and most usual route visits High Tove by the Armboth path and then follows the fence, but, once Watendlath is out of sight, the way is very dreary and squelchy underfoot. The alternative (left) is an attempt to link together the few features of interest on this flank of High Seat, at the same time avoiding much of the worst of the wet ground.

Watendlath from Goat Crags

High Seat 6

ASCENT FROM DALE BOTTOM
1600 feet of ascent : 4 miles (6½ from Keswick)

The foot of Mere Gill may also be reached from Thirlmere Dam via the path to Castle Crag Fort (not an easy passage), or from Armboth, but Shoulthwaite Gill is much too good to be by-passed thus.

Of the many tributaries, Mere Gill can be identified exactly by its wire fence.

The steep lower part of Mere Gill may be avoided by keeping to the path upstream for a further half-mile and then doubling back at a higher level, aiming for the prominent cairn on a mound near Litt's Memorial

Pronounce
Shoulthwaite
Shoolthet

Three means of access to the path from the road are given; it is doubtful if any is a right of way. That at Brackenrigg (lane to barn between walls; two gates) is best.

Litt's Memorial
180 yards south of Mere Gill, near a prominent cairn, are two stone posts, one having a brass plate inscribed 'In memory of J. Litt who died March 9, 1880.' Can anybody decipher the message on the other? How odd to find them in this remote spot!

looking south-south-west

Shoulthwaite Gill, quite near the main road yet hidden from it, should find a place in every walker's itinerary. It forms a narrow ravine between craggy walls, afforested on one side but bare on the other, and is interesting throughout. From the upper reaches, beyond Mere Gill, High Seat is gained over very easy, but swampy slopes. The gradients from beginning to end (if the initial variation to Mere Gill is used) are so gentle that the whole walk may be done non-stop.

High Seat 7

ASCENT FROM ARMBOTH, THIRLMERE
1450 feet of ascent : 2 miles

An obvious route of ascent leaves the west Thirlmere road at Armboth, where a signposted footpath to Watendlath may be used as far as the big cairn on High Tove summit and the fence then followed to the right. There is no point in doing this in clear weather, however, for it is much shorter and at least quite as easy to make a direct course to High Seat from the upper plantation wall (half-right), and the chances are that drier walking will be found by so doing.

THE SUMMIT

The summit is a welcome dry oasis, with a few rocks to relieve the monotony of the surrounding swamps. An Ordnance Survey column marks the highest point, although there can be a difference of inches only between this and a prominent rock knoll called Man. The usually accepted height is 1995', but the 6" O.S. map shows a benchmark of 1996'. Adding to this the height of the column, it seems just possible that the triangulation plate might touch an altitude of 2000'.

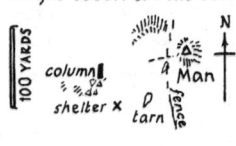

DESCENTS: Routes of ascent may be reversed, the fences being a help in mist. Remember that there are crags on both flanks below 1500'. The Ashness Gill route needs care : get on the west bank

RIDGE ROUTES

TO BLEABERRY FELL, 1932': 1¼ miles : N
Many small depressions : 150 feet of ascent
This is a walk to wish on one's worst enemy, especially after rain. There are many patches of swampy ground, necessitating wide detours.

TO HIGH TOVE, 1665': 1 mile : S
Depression at 1650': 25 feet of ascent
This is not a pleasant walk, either. The hags of rich deep peat may be wonderful stuff for growing rhododendrons but seem singularly unattractive to walkers with soaking feet.

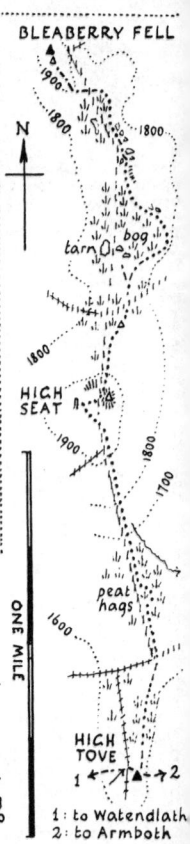

1 : to Watendlath
2 : to Armboth

High Seat 8

THE VIEW

High Seat is a first-class viewpoint, with much of interest to see in all directions. The serrated skyline from south to north-west is remarkably good and will gain most attention.

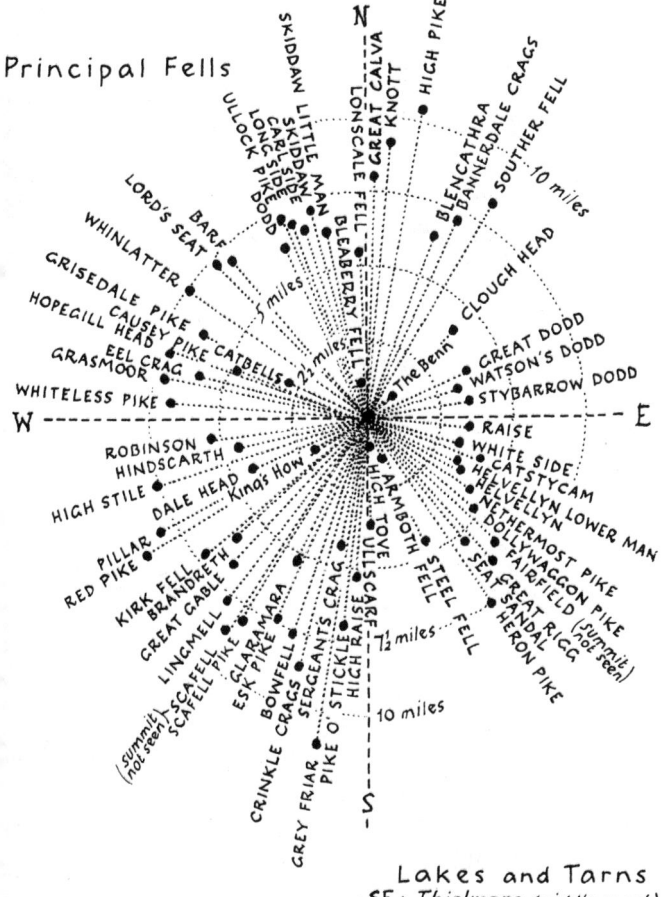

Principal Fells

(panorama diagram with fells labelled around a central point, radiating outward, with distance rings at 2½ miles, 5 miles, 7½ miles, and 10 miles; compass points N, E, S, W)

Fells labelled (clockwise from N):
LONSCALE FELL, GREAT CALVA, KNOTT, HIGH PIKE, BLENCATHRA, BANNERDALE CRAGS, SOUTHER FELL, CLOUGH HEAD, GREAT DODD, WATSON'S DODD, the Bench, STYBARROW DODD, RAISE, WHITE SIDE, CATSTYCAM, HELVELLYN LOWER MAN, HELVELLYN, DOLLYWAGGON PIKE, NETHERMOST PIKE, FAIRFIELD (summit not seen), GREAT RIGG, SEAT SANDAL, HERON PIKE, ARNBOTH FELL, HIGH TOVE, ULLSCARF, STEEL FELL, HIGH RAISE, SERGEANT'S CRAG, STICKLE PIKE, PIKE O' STICKLE, GREY FRIAR, CRINKLE CRAGS, BOWFELL, ESK PIKE, CLARAMARA, SCAFELL (summit not seen), SCAFELL PIKE, LINGMELL, GREAT GABLE, BRANDRETH, KIRK FELL, RED PIKE, PILLAR, HIGH STILE, DALE HEAD, Kings How, HINDSCARTH, ROBINSON, WHITELESS PIKE, GRASMOOR, EEL CRAG, HOPEGILL HEAD, CAUSEY PIKE, CATBELLS, GRISEDALE PIKE, WHINLATTER, LORD'S SEAT, BARF, ULLOCK PIKE, LONG SIDE, CARL SIDE, DODD, LITTLE MAN, SKIDDAW, BLEABERRY FELL

Lakes and Tarns

SE: *Thirlmere (middle reach)*
NW: *Derwentwater*
NW: *Bassenthwaite Lake*

High Tove
1665'

from Armboth Fell

It is hard to imagine that anybody feels any affection at all for High Tove, apart perhaps from the sheep whose natural heaf it is. This dark heathery mound, squatting on the ridge between Watendlath and Thirlmere, and so gently contoured that water cannot drain away from it, is everywhere shockingly wet — a condition persisting even in drought — and is without any redeeming feature except as a viewpoint. Yet it is climbed a thousand times every year, probably, and maybe more: the explanation is that High Tove is crossed by a public and fairly well used footpath that gives the shortest route across the central ridge. In fact, in this respect High Tove is unique, for where else is a summit used as a pass? This oddity arises because the depressions on either side are not only insignificant but even wetter than the way over the top.

A geographical curiosity is the twist in the indefinite north-east ridge, which, after ambling down easily towards, apparently, the obvious destination of Thirlmere, unexpectedly changes character and rises again as a high rocky rampart now heading due north in a heavy screen of trees to the abrupt, exciting top of Raven Crag

```
HIGH SEAT
  ▲      Armboth
  •    ▲ HIGH TOVE
  Watendlath
 • Rosthwaite
              Wythburn •
         ▲ ULLSCARF
         MILES
   0   1   2   3   4
```

High Tove 2

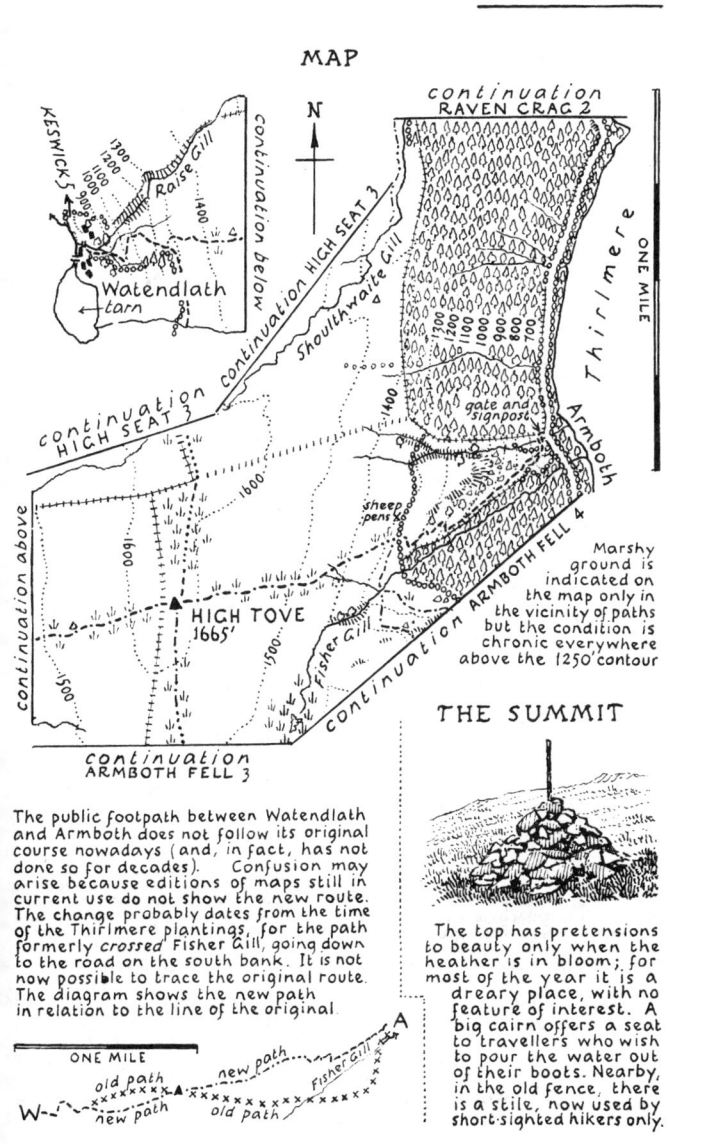

MAP

continuation RAVEN CRAG 2

continuation below HIGH SEAT 3

continuation HIGH SEAT 3

continuation above

continuation ARMBOTH FELL 3

continuation ARMBOTH FELL 4

Marshy ground is indicated on the map only in the vicinity of paths but the condition is chronic everywhere above the 1250' contour

THE SUMMIT

The top has pretensions to beauty only when the heather is in bloom; for most of the year it is a dreary place, with no feature of interest. A big cairn offers a seat to travellers who wish to pour the water out of their boots. Nearby, in the old fence, there is a stile, now used by short-sighted hikers only.

The public footpath between Watendlath and Armboth does not follow its original course nowadays (and, in fact, has not done so for decades). Confusion may arise because editions of maps still in current use do not show the new route. The change probably dates from the time of the Thirlmere plantings, for the path formerly *crossed* Fisher Gill, going down to the road on the south bank. It is not now possible to trace the original route. The diagram shows the new path in relation to the line of the original.

High Tove 3

ASCENT FROM ARMBOTH
1100 feet of ascent : 1½ miles

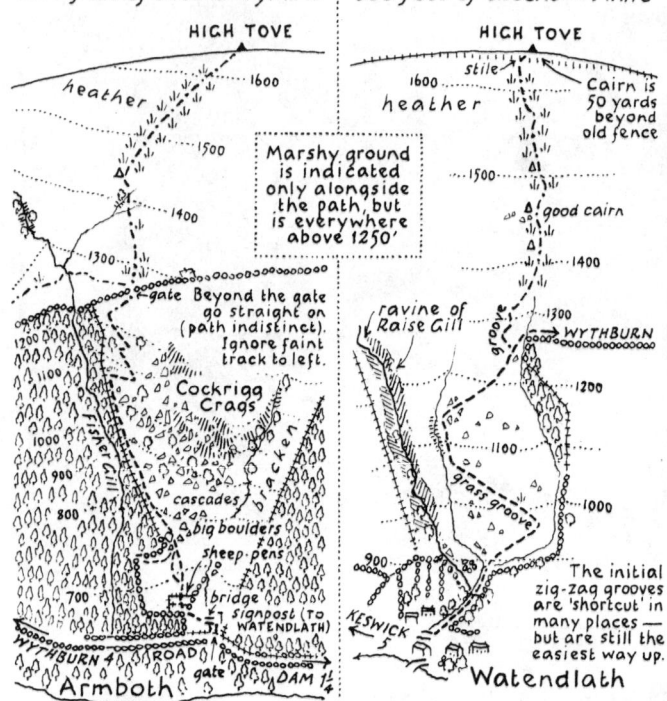

Thirlmere looking west-south-west

Armboth still features prominently on maps and signposts, but the tired traveller should not expect to find refreshment or accommodation here. Nothing is left but the name.

Marshy ground is indicated only alongside the path, but is everywhere above 1250'

ASCENT FROM WATENDLATH
800 feet of ascent : 1 mile

Cairn is 50 yards beyond old fence

The initial zig-zag grooves are 'shortcut' in many places — but are still the easiest way up.

At the wall-corner (at 1250') watch for a grass groove turning left: this is the path for High Tove (and on to Armboth), easily missed because the Wythburn path, which is stony, is the more distinct. The bifurcation is a few yards short of the wall-corner.

looking east

These two climbs have much in common —— and the greatest common factor is wetness on the ground, the last half-mile on both sides being saturated, both in rainy weather and in drought, and there is no escape from it. The two climbs are complementary, the path up one side and down the other being the public route between Armboth and Watendlath.

High Tove 4

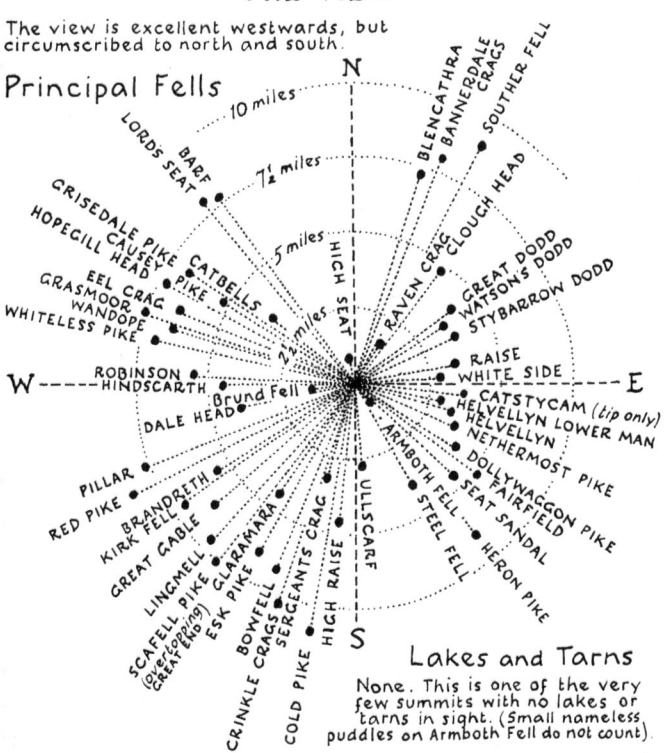

THE VIEW

The view is excellent westwards, but circumscribed to north and south.

Principal Fells

- 10 miles
- 7½ miles
- 5 miles
- 2½ miles

N — HIGH SEAT

LORDS SEAT, BARF, BLENCATHRA, BANNERDALE CRAGS, SOUTHER FELL, GRISEDALE PIKE, CAUSEY, CATBELLS, HOPEGILL HEAD, PIKE, CLOUGH HEAD, EEL CRAG, RAVEN CRAG, GREAT DODD, GRASMOOR, WATSON'S DODD, WANDOPE, STYBARROW DODD, WHITELESS PIKE, ROBINSON, RAISE, HINDSCARTH, WHITE SIDE, Brund Fell, CATSTYCAM (tip only), DALE HEAD, HELVELLYN LOWER MAN, HELVELLYN, NETHERMOST PIKE, PILLAR, DOLLYWAGGON PIKE, RED PIKE, FAIRFIELD, BRANDRETH, ARMBOTH FELL, SEAT SANDAL, KIRK FELL, STEEL FELL, GREAT GABLE, HERON PIKE, LINGMELL, SCAFELL PIKE, CLARAMARA, (overtopping) ESK PIKE, ULLSCARF, (Great End), BOWFELL, SERGEANTS CRAG, CRINKLE CRAGS, HIGH RAISE, COLD PIKE

W — — — — E

S

Lakes and Tarns

None. This is one of the very few summits with no lakes or tarns in sight. (Small nameless puddles on Armboth Fell do not count).

RIDGE ROUTES

To HIGH SEAT, 1995': 1 mile : N
Minor depressions : 300 feet of ascent
The first half-mile is all swamps and peat-hags.

To ARMBOTH FELL, 1570': 1 mile : SE
Depression at 1475': 100 feet of ascent
Not recommended. If done, avoid a bad bog in the depression.

ARMBOTH FELL
bog
heather
HIGH TOVE → ULLSCARF
peat hags
fence
← HIGH SEAT N
ONE MILE

Loft Crag

2270' approx.

the third of the
Langdale Pikes

not named on
Ordnance maps

from Pike o' Stickle

The Langdale Pikes are variously regarded as being from two to five in number. Thorn Crag and Pavey Ark, often included in the count, have not the distinctive outline of the others, and should perhaps more properly be omitted, but Loft Crag most certainly has the qualifying characteristics. It lies between Pike o' Stickle and Harrison Stickle but south of them, having a small, abrupt summit (often mistaken for Pike o' Stickle in views from the east) directly below which is the magnificent buttress of Gimmer Crag, most popular of all climbing-grounds.

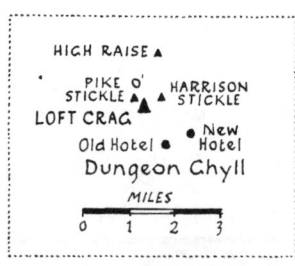

HIGH RAISE ▲

· PIKE O'   HARRISON
  STICKLE ▲ ▲ STICKLE
LOFT CRAG ▲
  Old Hotel ● ● New Hotel
  Dungeon Chyll

MILES
0   1   2   3

Beyond Thorn Crag, a subsidiary summit, the deep-cut ravines of Dungeon Chyll form the eastern boundary of the fell, but on the west side the line of demarcation is less exact, watercourses being submerged in rivers of scree. The short north slopes, after initial rocks, are soon lost in the wide depression of Harrison Combe.

Although it must rank after the two Stickles, Loft Crag is a worthy member of a fine trinity of peaks.

Loft Crag 2

Gimmer Crag
South-east face

Loft Crag 3

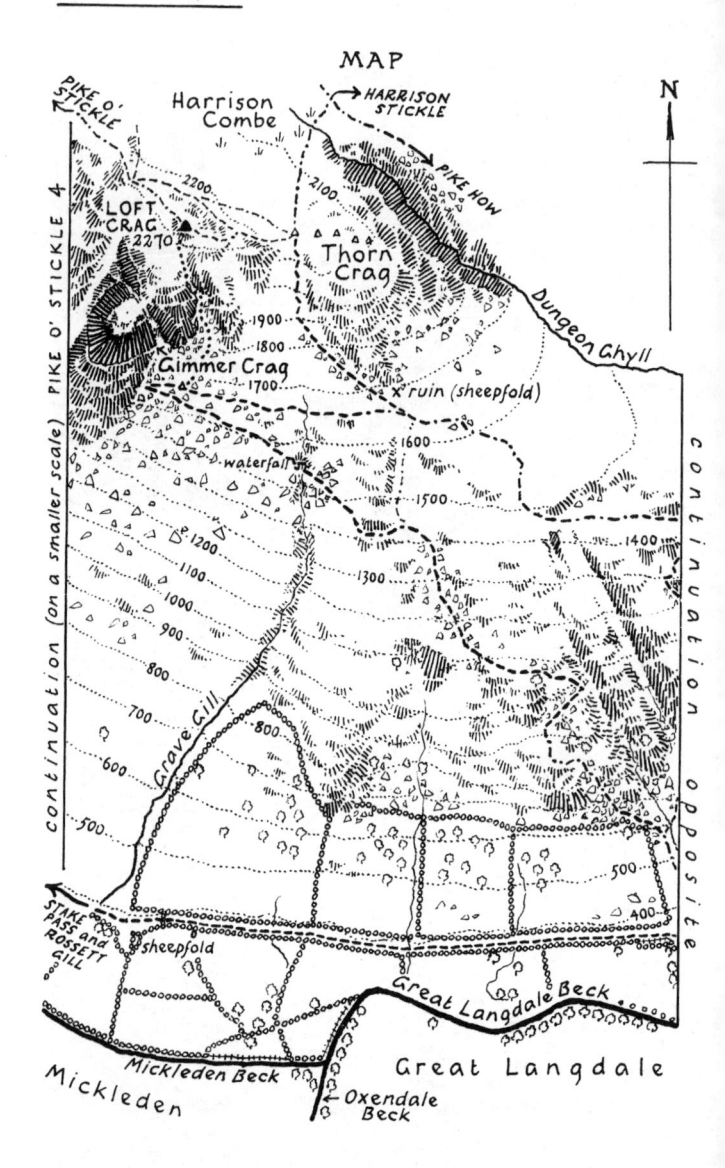

MAP

N

PIKE O' STICKLE →
Harrison Combe
→ HARRISON STICKLE
PIKE HOW

2200
LOFT CRAG 2270
2100
Thorn Crag

PIKE O' STICKLE 4 (on a smaller scale) ← continuation

Gimmer Crag
1900
1800
1700
× ruin (sheepfold)

Dungeon Ghyll

continuation opposite →

waterfall
1600
1500
1400
1200
1100
1300
1000
900
800
700
600
500

Grave Gill

800

500
400

← STAKE PASS and ROSSETT GILL

sheepfold

Great Langdale Beck

Mickleden Beck
Oxendale Beck

Mickleden

Great Langdale

Loft Crag 4

MAP

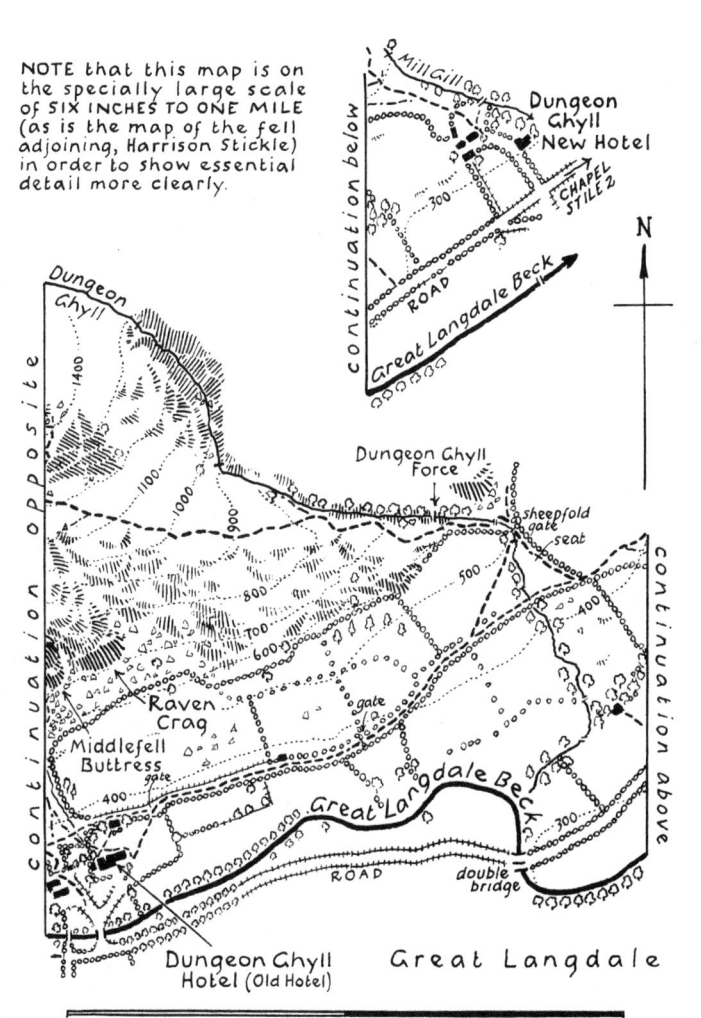

NOTE that this map is on the specially large scale of SIX INCHES TO ONE MILE (as is the map of the fell adjoining, Harrison Stickle) in order to show essential detail more clearly.

HALF A MILE

Loft Crag 5

ASCENT FROM DUNGEON GHYLL
2,000 feet of ascent:
1¼ miles from the Old Hotel (direct); 1¼ from the New Hotel

Loft Crag is reached most easily by using the popular path to Harrison Stickle as far as the Thorn Crag col, there turning left, but little is seen of Gimmer Crag on this route, and that fine rock is too grand a spectacle to miss. To see the crag, either turn off the path below Thorn Crag (cairn indicates traverse to it, left) or ascend direct from the Old Hotel. It will be palpable to the ordinary walker that progress has come to a full stop when the crag is reached, and the Thorn Crag path should then be joined for the remainder of the climb, although a possible alternative is afforded by the gully route shown, which is quite simple except for an awkward 10' chockstone pitch. Do not confuse this gully with the more obvious South-east Gully of Gimmer Crag: it is the next to the right (South-east Gully is a recognised rock-climb (graded easy). Active walkers will probably find it within their capacity, but others are advised to turn their backs on it).

looking north-west

The direct path to Gimmer Crag from the Old Hotel originated as a climbers' track, but is now in general use. Apart from the abominable scree slope just above the wall the route is interesting and easy. The steep grassy gully to the left of Middlefell Buttress is a practicable short cut from the Old Hotel to the Thorn Crag path *for scramblers only*

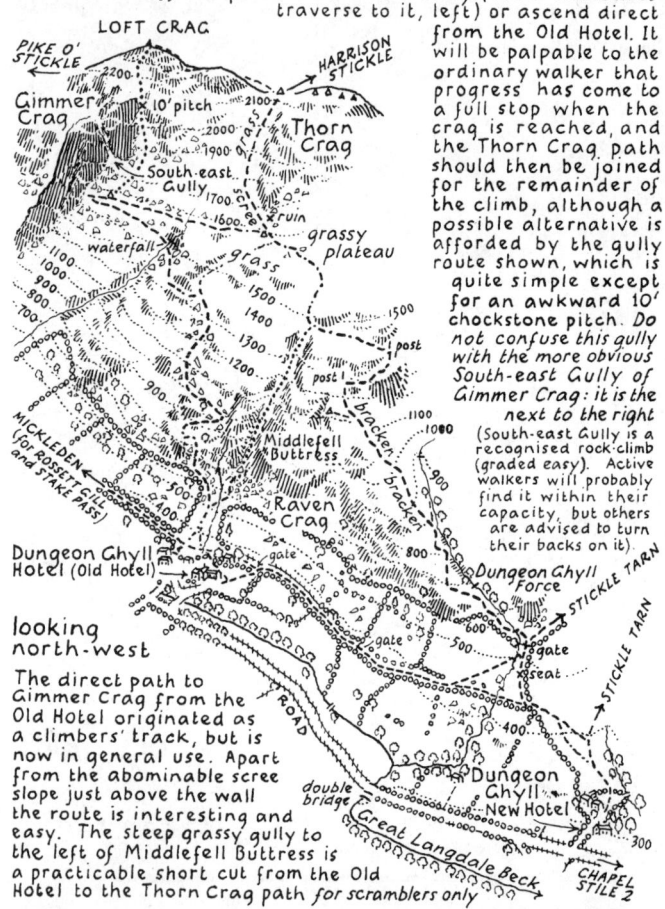

Loft Crag 6

THE SUMMIT

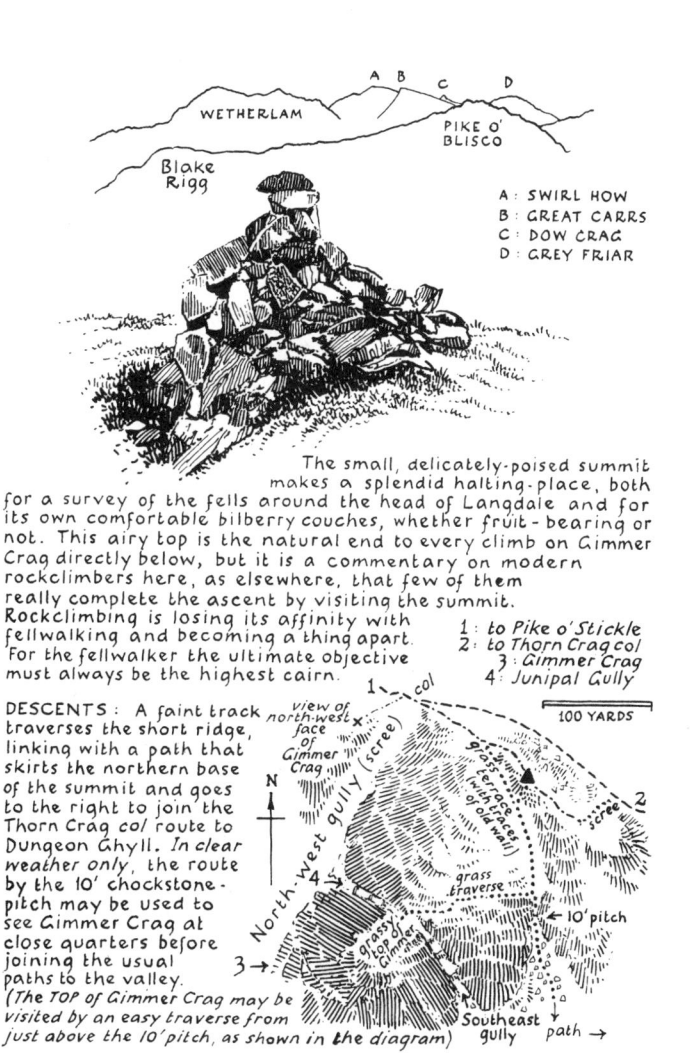

A: SWIRL HOW
B: GREAT CARRS
C: DOW CRAG
D: GREY FRIAR

The small, delicately-poised summit makes a splendid halting-place, both for a survey of the fells around the head of Langdale and for its own comfortable bilberry couches, whether fruit-bearing or not. This airy top is the natural end to every climb on Gimmer Crag directly below, but it is a commentary on modern rockclimbers here, as elsewhere, that few of them really complete the ascent by visiting the summit. Rockclimbing is losing its affinity with fellwalking and becoming a thing apart. For the fellwalker the ultimate objective must always be the highest cairn.

1: to Pike o'Stickle
2: to Thorn Crag col
3: Gimmer Crag
4: Junipal Gully

DESCENTS: A faint track traverses the short ridge, linking with a path that skirts the northern base of the summit and goes to the right to join the Thorn Crag col route to Dungeon Ghyll. In clear weather only, the route by the 10' chockstone-pitch may be used to see Gimmer Crag at close quarters before joining the usual paths to the valley.
(The TOP of Gimmer Crag may be visited by an easy traverse from just above the 10' pitch, as shown in the diagram)

Loft Crag 7

THE VIEW

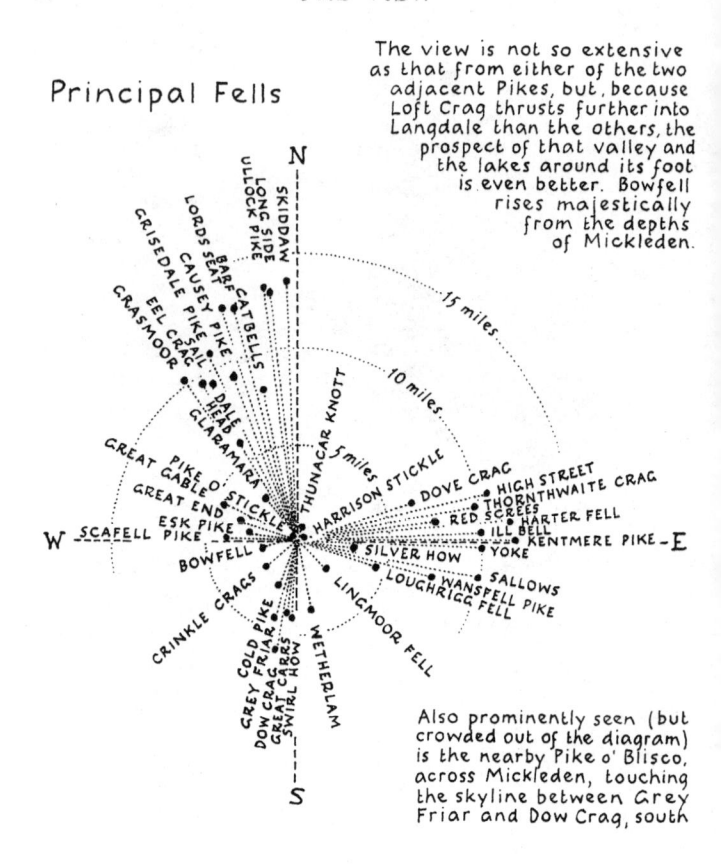

Principal Fells

The view is not so extensive as that from either of the two adjacent Pikes, but, because Loft Crag thrusts further into Langdale than the others, the prospect of that valley and the lakes around its foot is even better. Bowfell rises majestically from the depths of Mickleden.

Also prominently seen (but crowded out of the diagram) is the nearby Pike o' Blisco, across Mickleden, touching the skyline between Grey Friar and Dow Crag, south

Lakes and Tarns

E : Tarns by Lang How (Silver How)
ESE : Loughrigg Tarn
ESE : Elterwater
SE : Windermere
SE : Lingmoor Tarn
SE : Esthwaite Water
SSE : Blea Tarn
NNW : Tarn at Leaves (Rosthwaite Fell)

Loft Crag 8

RIDGE ROUTES

To HARRISON STICKLE, 2403':
½ mile : E, then N and E
Depression at 2070'
340 feet of ascent

Care is needed in getting off the east end of Loft Crag: at the first depression use a little scree-run on the left. At Thorn Crag col join the usual path from Langdale.

To PIKE O' STICKLE, 2323':
⅓ mile : NW
Two depressions at 2200'
170 feet of ascent

An interesting path follows the ridge. The final scramble is steep and rocky, and permits of minor variations

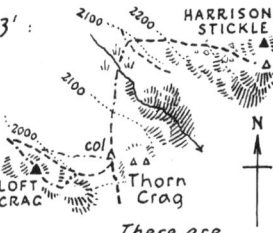

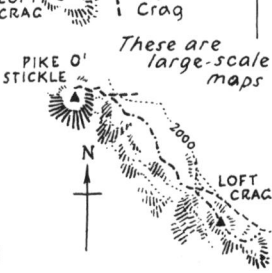

These are large-scale maps

HALF A MILE

This is the 10-foot chockstone pitch mentioned in the diagram of ascent .... (page 5) ....

Pike o' Stickle from Loft Crag

GREAT END — ALLEN CRAGS — GREAT GABLE — GLARAMARA

Loughrigg Fell 1101'

more often referred to
simply as 'Loughrigg'
(pronounced Luffrigg)

*from Mandale Bridge
(near Skelwith Bridge)*

- Grasmere
- SILVER HOW
- Rydal
- **LOUGHRIGG FELL**
- Ambleside
- Clappersgate
- Skelwith Bridge

MILES
0 1 2 3 4

Loughrigg Fell 2

NATURAL FEATURES

Of the lesser heights of Lakeland, Loughrigg Fell is pre-eminent. It has no pretensions to mountain form, being a sprawling, ill-shaped wedge of rough country rising between the park-like valleys of Brathay and Rothay, and having a bulk out of all proportion to its modest altitude; but no ascent is more repaying for the small labour involved in visiting its many cairns, for Loughrigg has delightful grassy paths, a series of pleasant surprises along the traverse of the summits, several charming vistas and magnificent views, fine contrasts of velvety turf, rich bracken and grey rock, a string of little tarns like pearls in a necklace, and a wealth of stately trees on the flanks. It is especially well endowed with lakes, with four sheets of water, all lovely, touching its lower slopes, and in addition it nurses a large tarn to which it gives its name — and this is a distinction not attained by any other fell. It has also more paths to the square mile than any other fell, great or small, and amongst them is one that far exceeds in popularity any other in the district, one that all visitors know: Loughrigg Terrace. Short crags on every flank offer excellent sport for the rock-scrambler. Woodlands surround the base of the fell and creep up the slopes; higher, juniper holly and yew straggle the fellside. Loughrigg has yet another attraction in the form of a tremendous cave, big enough to contain the entire population of Ambleside, which, although manmade and now disused, is still a remarkable place. In brief, this fell has a wealth of interests and delights, and for many people who now find pleasure in walking over the greater mountains it served as an introduction and an inspiration. Everybody likes Loughrigg.

Topographically, Loughrigg Fell is the corner-stone of the high mass of land lying south-west of the Rothay valley system, with High Raise as the loftiest point, but is almost isolated, the connecting link being a low and indefinite ridge crossed by the Red Bank road between Grasmere and Langdale. The fell, two miles long, has subsidiary summits overlooking each of the surrounding lakes.

Loughrigg Fell 3

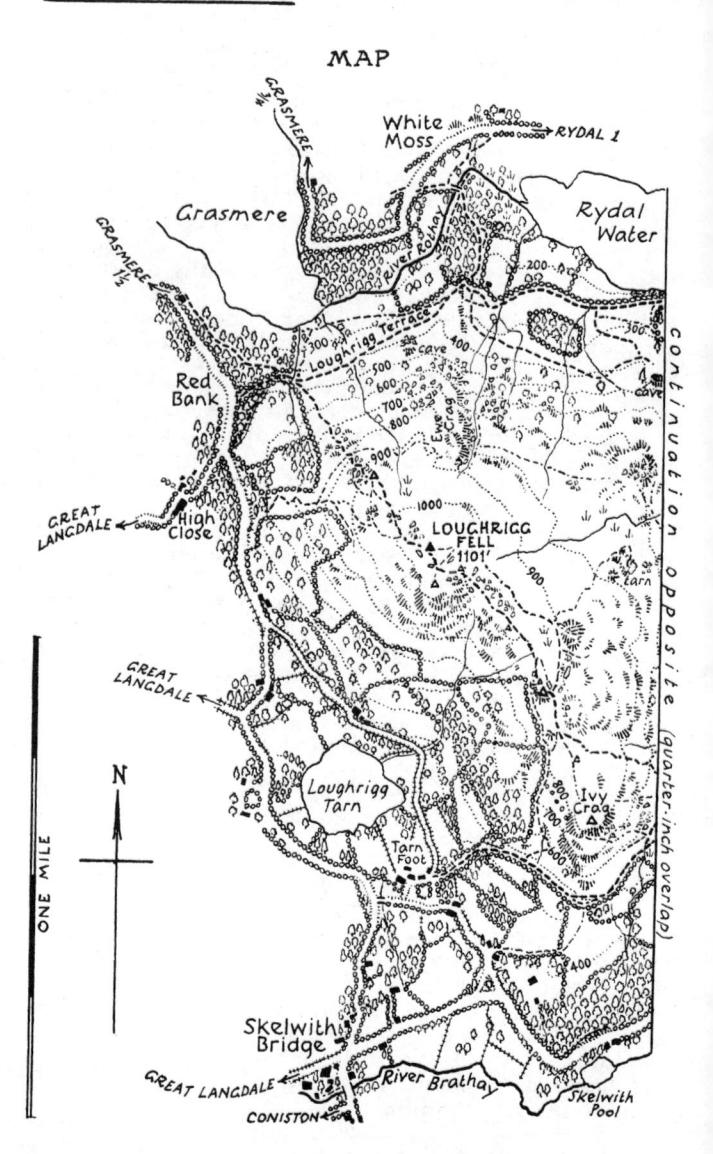

MAP

Loughrigg Fell 4

MAP

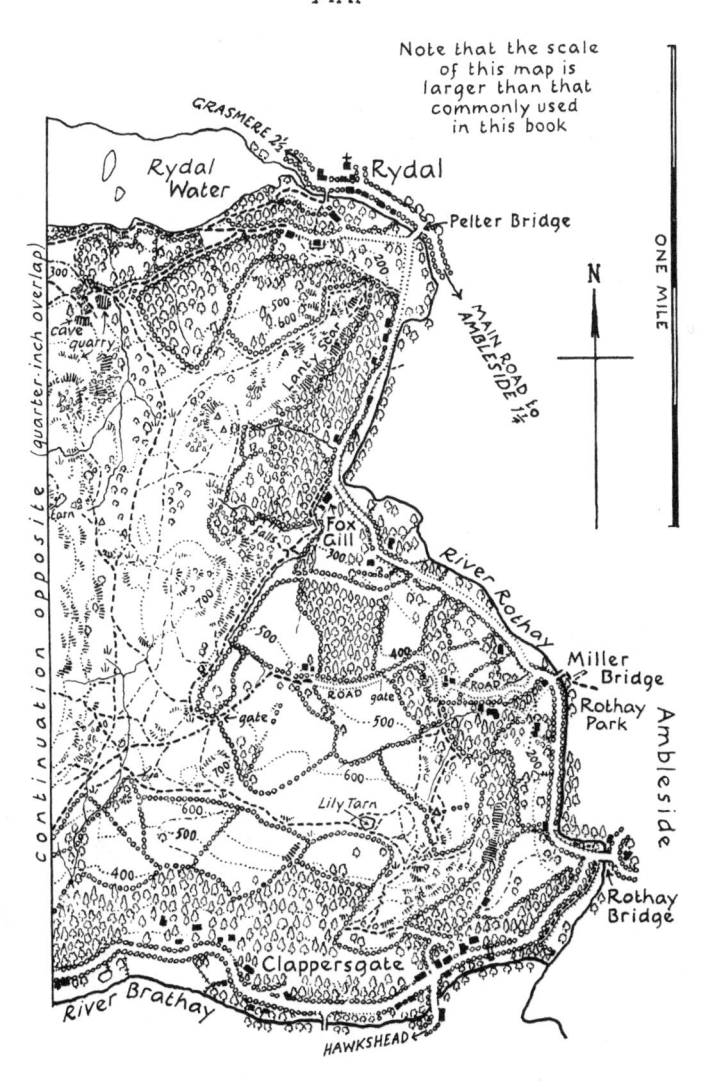

Loughrigg Fell 5

ASCENTS

When fellwalking, it is better to arrive than to travel hopefully and this is justification for the inclusion here of six pages of directions for reaching the summit of Loughrigg Fell, because, although of insignificant altitude, the fell has an extensive and confusing top, the ultimate objective remains hidden on the approach, and the maze of paths needs careful unravelling — besides, failure would be *too* humiliating! On a first visit it is not only not easy to locate the highest point amongst the score of likely-looking protuberances several of which carry likely-looking cairns, it is actually difficult not to go astray, and, in mist, positively easy to do so.

ASCENT FROM GRASMERE
920 feet of ascent : 2¼ miles

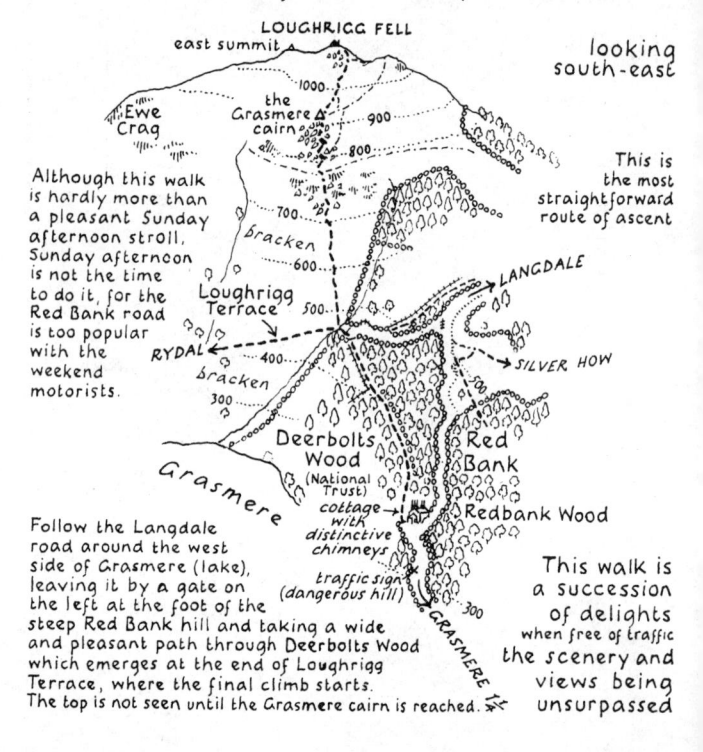

looking south-east

This is the most straightforward route of ascent

Although this walk is hardly more than a pleasant Sunday afternoon stroll, Sunday afternoon is not the time to do it, for the Red Bank road is too popular with the weekend motorists.

Follow the Langdale road around the west side of Grasmere (lake), leaving it by a gate on the left at the foot of the steep Red Bank hill and taking a wide and pleasant path through Deerbolts Wood which emerges at the end of Loughrigg Terrace, where the final climb starts.
The top is not seen until the Grasmere cairn is reached.

This walk is a succession of delights when free of traffic the scenery and views being unsurpassed

Loughrigg Fell 6

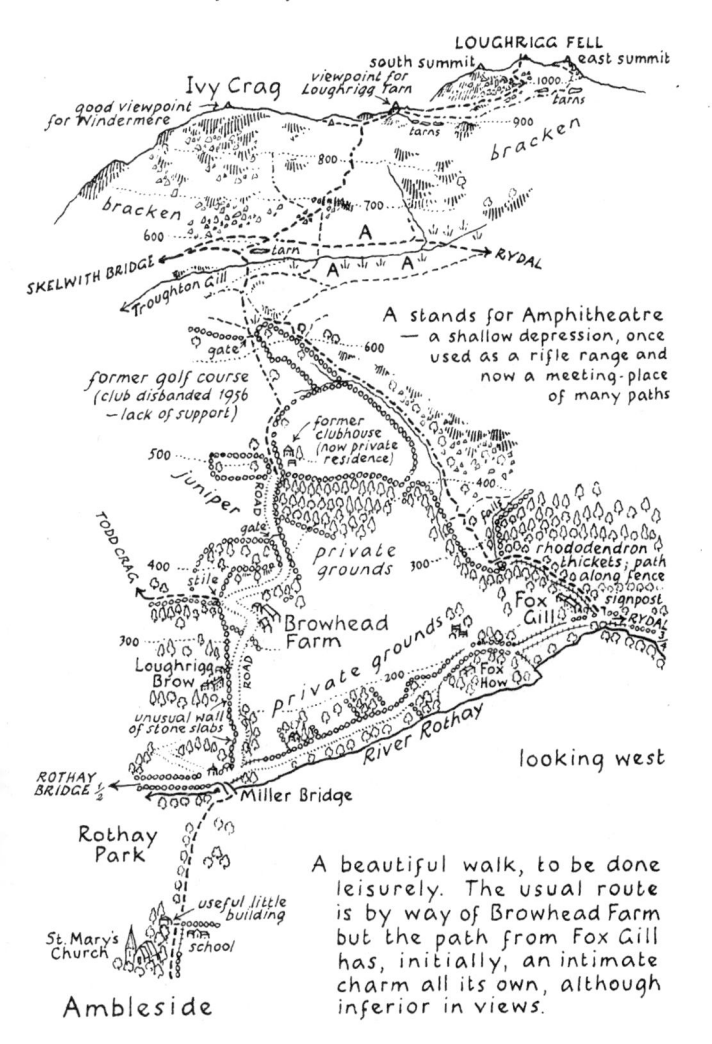

ASCENT FROM AMBLESIDE
1050 feet of ascent : 2½ miles

A stands for Amphitheatre — a shallow depression, once used as a rifle range and now a meeting-place of many paths

looking west

A beautiful walk, to be done leisurely. The usual route is by way of Browhead Farm but the path from Fox Gill has, initially, an intimate charm all its own, although inferior in views.

Loughrigg Fell 7

ASCENT FROM RYDAL
1000 feet of ascent : 2½ miles

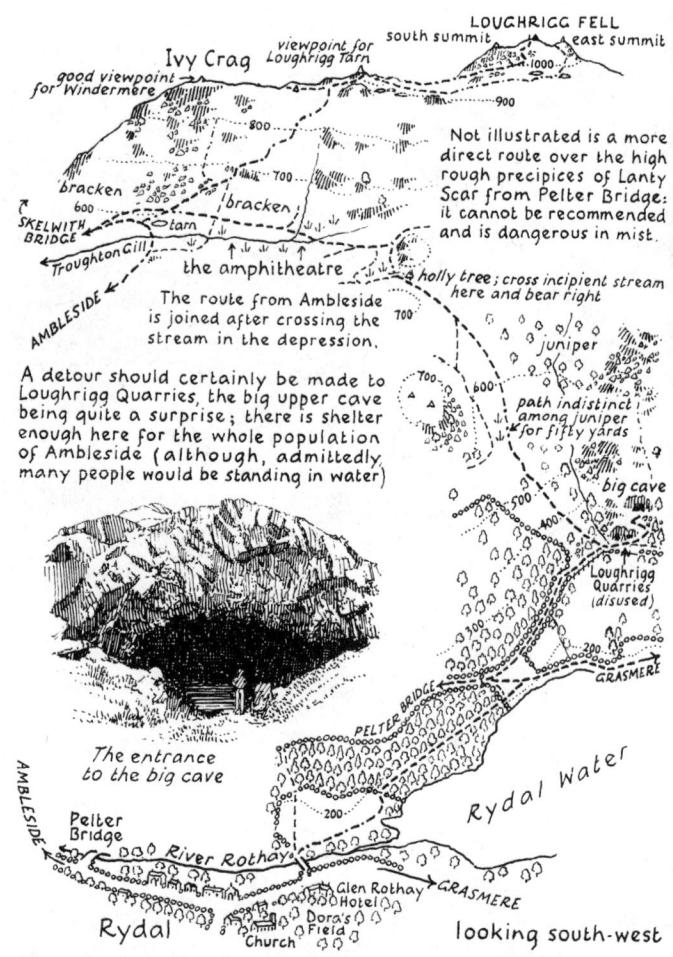

Not illustrated is a more direct route over the high rough precipices of Lanty Scar from Pelter Bridge: it cannot be recommended and is dangerous in mist.

The route from Ambleside is joined after crossing the stream in the depression.

A detour should certainly be made to Loughrigg Quarries, the big upper cave being quite a surprise; there is shelter enough here for the whole population of Ambleside (although, admittedly, many people would be standing in water)

The entrance to the big cave

looking south-west

There is no better introduction to the manifold attractions of Loughrigg Fell than this easy and delightful approach.

ASCENT FROM WHITE MOSS

925 feet of ascent : 1½ miles

LOUGHRIGG FELL
the Grasmere cairn
looking south
The route becomes identical with that from Grasmere at the far end of Loughrigg Terrace
1000
900
800
600
500
400
300
200
Ewe Crag
Red Bank
GRASMERE
Deerbolts Wood
Loughrigg Terrace
cave above quarry spoil
bracken
400
bracken
big cave
bracken
RYDAL
gate
River Rothay
Grasmere
A more direct way by the gully to the left of Ewe Crag is unattractive.
GRASMERE
GRASMERE (old road)
Rydal Water
MAIN ROAD
White Moss Common
RYDAL
old quarries

This might be described as 'the motorist's route', not because it is practicable for cars (!) but because White Moss Common is a popular parking place and the most convenient point on the road for starting the climb.

Grasmere
from Loughrigg Terrace

Loughrigg Fell 9

ASCENT FROM CLAPPERSGATE
1050 feet of ascent : 2½ miles

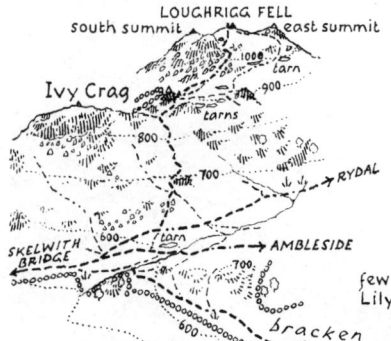

looking north-west

this is the official Todd Crag (Ordnance Survey 2½" map)

This interesting walk, combined with a descent from the summit by the Grasmere path enables a full-length traverse of the fell to be made: an easy and enjoyable excursion. Detours should be made to Todd Crag and Ivy Crag, both excellent viewpoints.

There is a tiny island, only a few feet in extent, in the middle of Lily Tarn. Some quiet humorist has erected a cairn on it.

The summit of Todd Crag, showing the 10-foot crack

Todd Crag dominates the initial part of the climb, and its summit, a small platform of naked rock, is worth a visit. It can be reached easily by a short scramble, but persons more agile than the author may prefer to attain it in more dramatic fashion by struggling up a 10 foot crack on the east side.

Similar rocky heights nearby are also interesting.

Here are the gardens of White Craggs, open to the public

Leave Clappersgate by the lane directly opposite the road junction

Loughrigg Fell 10

ASCENT FROM SKELWITH BRIDGE
1000 feet of ascent: 1¾ miles

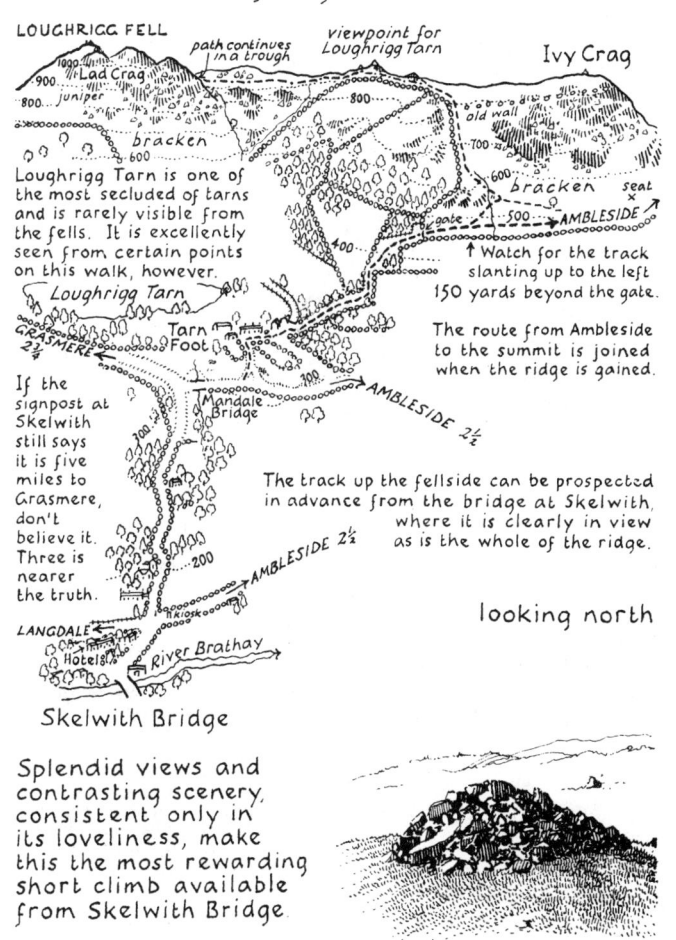

looking north

Loughrigg Tarn is one of the most secluded of tarns and is rarely visible from the fells. It is excellently seen from certain points on this walk, however.

↑ Watch for the track slanting up to the left 150 yards beyond the gate.

The route from Ambleside to the summit is joined when the ridge is gained.

If the signpost at Skelwith still says it is five miles to Grasmere, don't believe it. Three is nearer the truth.

The track up the fellside can be prospected in advance from the bridge at Skelwith, where it is clearly in view as is the whole of the ridge.

Splendid views and contrasting scenery, consistent only in its loveliness, make this the most rewarding short climb available from Skelwith Bridge.

The cairn on Ivy Crag
a good viewpoint for Windermere and Langdale, reached by a simple detour along the ridge.

Loughrigg Fell 11

THE SUMMIT

Three eminences rise close together above the undulating top of the fell, and the middle one, slightly higher than the others, bears the main cairn and an Ordnance Survey triangulation column that the surveyors who built it, after building so many, must have voted the most beautifully situated of all. The small area of the principal summit is carpeted with a velvety turf in which have been carved the initials of many visitors. There are several tarns, little more than dewponds, in the green hollows around. Bracken encroaches in patches on the higher parts of the fell and, especially in winter, makes the summit a colourful place.

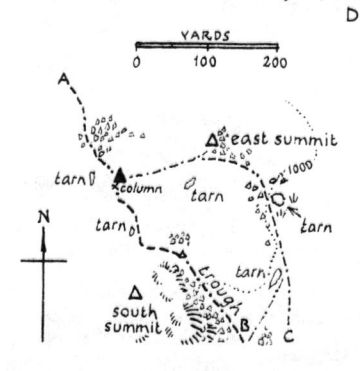

DESCENTS: There are hundreds of rocky tors and low crags scattered about the fell top and descents are most easily made by using the paths, of which there is also a great abundance. The quickest way down (and the best in mist) is by the Grasmere route to Loughrigg Terrace.

A : to Grasmere and Loughrigg Terrace
B : to Ambleside, Clappersgate, Rydal and Skelwith Bridge
C : an alternative to B (joins it in a further quarter-mile)

Loughrigg Fell 12

RIDGE ROUTE

To SILVER HOW, 1292': 2½ miles
NW, then W, WNW and N
Several depressions; main one 475'
950 feet of ascent
A sharp descent is followed by
a beautiful and easy walk

(map with labels:)
SILVER HOW
GRASMERE
BLEA RIGG
LANGDALE
Spedding Crag
WALTHWAITE
Dow Bank
At this col, climb half-right between low crags (no path)
Viewpoint for Rydal and Grasmere
GRASMERE (road)
Red Bank
Loughrigg Terrace
ELTERWATER — line of telegraph poles
ELTERWATER (road)
AMBLESIDE (road)
LOUGHRIGG FELL
HALF A MILE
N

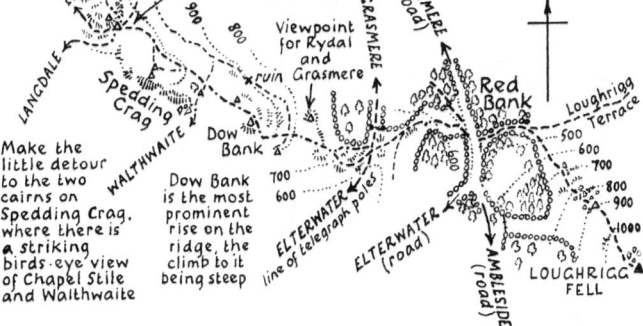

Make the little detour to the two cairns on Spedding Crag, where there is a striking bird's-eye view of Chapel Stile and Walthwaite

Dow Bank is the most prominent rise on the ridge, the climb to it being steep

This pleasant stroll is full of interest and variety: it has lake and woodland scenes, rocky outcrops, a few yards of macadam(!) and its gentle undulations are crossed by favourite paths from Grasmere to Langdale. The views are delightful on all sides. In bad weather do not proceed beyond the final col unless the ground is well known; paths on Silver How are a source of trouble in mist.

Loughrigg Tarn

Loughrigg Fell 13

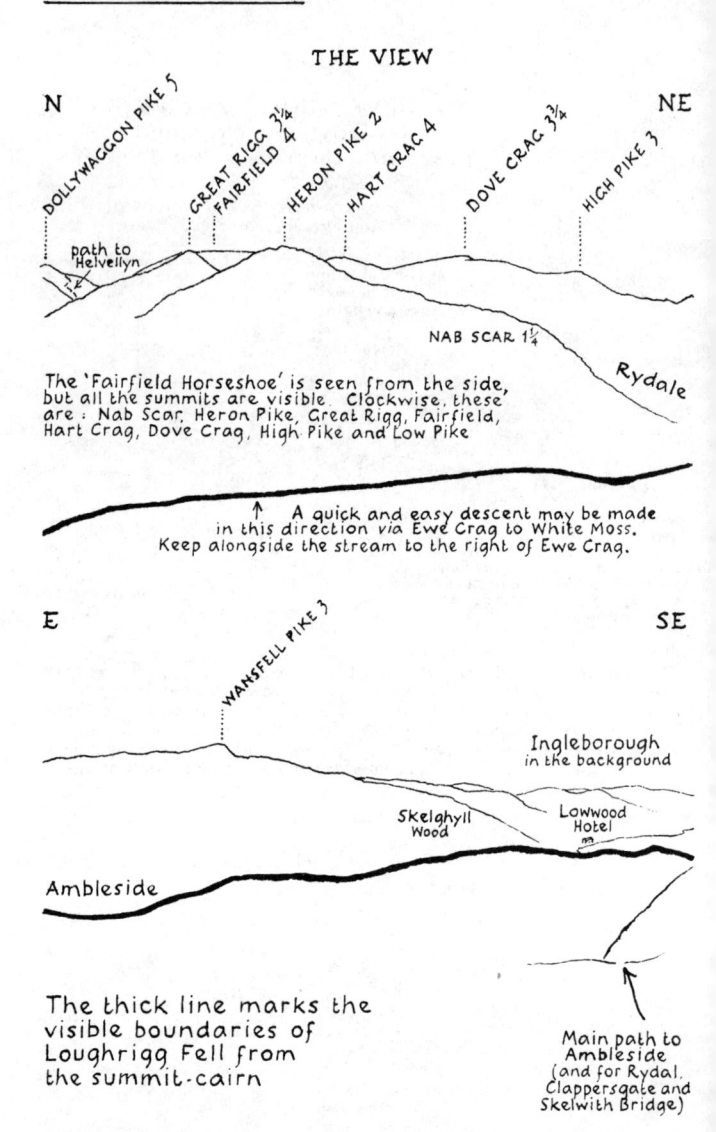

THE VIEW

N — DOLLYWAGGON PIKE 5, GREAT RIGG 3¼, FAIRFIELD 4, HERON PIKE 2, HART CRAG 4, DOVE CRAG 3¾, HIGH PIKE 3 — NE

path to Helvellyn

NAB SCAR 1¼

Rydale

The 'Fairfield Horseshoe' is seen from the side, but all the summits are visible. Clockwise, these are: Nab Scar, Heron Pike, Great Rigg, Fairfield, Hart Crag, Dove Crag, High Pike and Low Pike

↑ A quick and easy descent may be made in this direction via Ewe Crag to White Moss. Keep alongside the stream to the right of Ewe Crag.

E — WANSFELL PIKE 3 — SE

Ingleborough in the background

Skelghyll Wood

Lowwood Hotel

Ambleside

The thick line marks the visible boundaries of Loughrigg Fell from the summit-cairn

Main path to Ambleside (and for Rydal, Clappersgate and Skelwith Bridge)

Loughrigg Fell 14

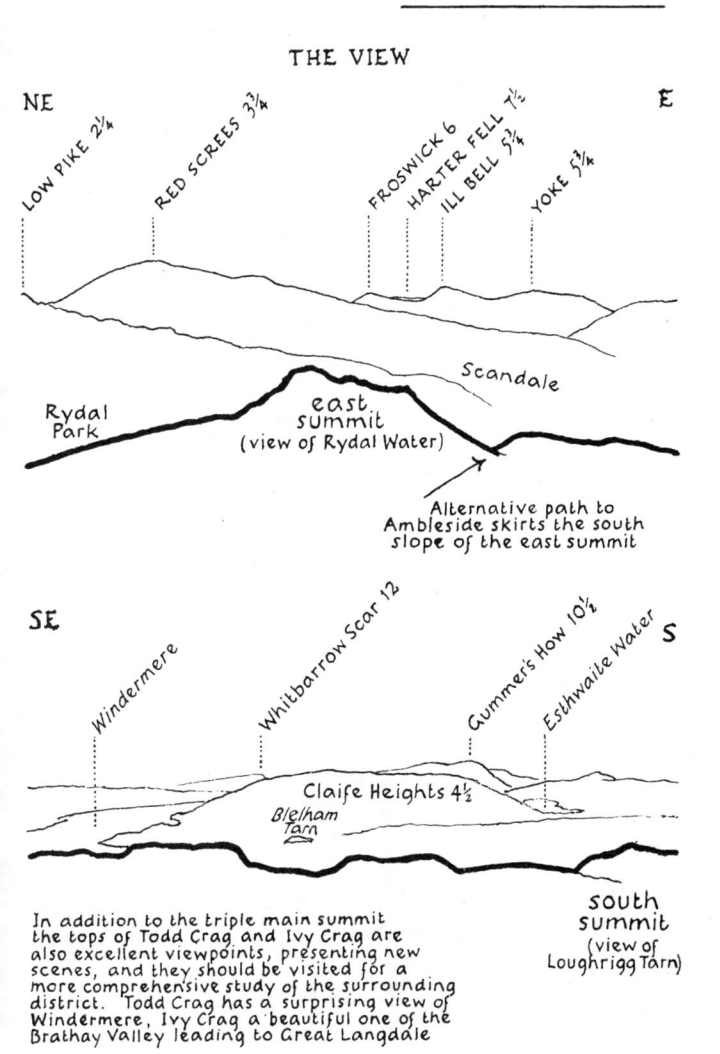

THE VIEW

NE — Low Pike 2¼, Red Screes 3¾, Froswick 6, Harter Fell 7½, Ill Bell 5¾, Yoke 5¾ — **E**

Scandale

Rydal Park

east summit (view of Rydal Water)

Alternative path to Ambleside skirts the south slope of the east summit

SE — Windermere, Whitbarrow Scar 12, Gummer's How 10½, Esthwaite Water — **S**

Claife Heights 4½

Blelham Tarn

south summit (view of Loughrigg Tarn)

In addition to the triple main summit the tops of Todd Crag and Ivy Crag are also excellent viewpoints, presenting new scenes, and they should be visited for a more comprehensive study of the surrounding district. Todd Crag has a surprising view of Windermere, Ivy Crag a beautiful one of the Brathay Valley leading to Great Langdale

The figures following the names of fells indicate distances in miles

Loughrigg Fell 15

THE VIEW

Anybody spending a first holiday in Ambleside cannot do better than make an early visit to the top of Loughrigg Fell. From this elevation he will get an excellent idea of the topography of the neighbourhood, all the fells and valleys within easy reach being attractively displayed. He will see around him a land very rich in promise — and find it even richer in fulfilment. The following fellwalks suggest themselves for a week's stay: 1 - THE FAIRFIELD HORSESHOE; 2 - THE CONISTON FELLS (ridgewalk, Wetherlam to Old Man) 3 - BOWFELL and CRINKLE CRAGS; 4 - HARRISON STICKLE, SERGEANT MAN and the SILVER HOW ridge; 5 - THE EASEDALE FELLS (circuit of Far Easedale) 6 - DOLLYWAGGON PIKE and HELVELLYN. Of course the separate ascents of RED SCREES and WANSFELL PIKE cannot possibly be omitted — if time is short, these two climbs should be done before breakfast (best part of the day for fellwalking) on the day of departure. A better plan, however, is to stay on for another week, for the suggested itinerary by no means exhausts the area's attractions.

SW

S

Black Fell 2¼
Road to Coniston →
Skelwith Bridge   The Brathay Valley   Colwith   River Brathay
Loughrigg Fold

W — SCAFELL 8⅔ — BOWFELL 6⅔ — ESK PIKE 7 — GREAT END 7⅔ — LOFT CRAG 4½ — PIKE O' STICKLE 4⅓ — HARRISON STICKLE 4¼ — PAVEY ARK 4 — BLEA RIGG 2¼ — SERGEANT MAN 4⅓ — NW

TARN CRAG 3¾ i

Langdale Pikes
SILVER HOW 1⅔
Dow Bank

Great Langdale
Chapel Stile
Hammerscar Plantation
High Close
Wyke Plantation

Over this edge will be found an intermittent path that goes down (between walls) to the road near the grounds of High Close.

Loughrigg Fell 16

THE VIEW

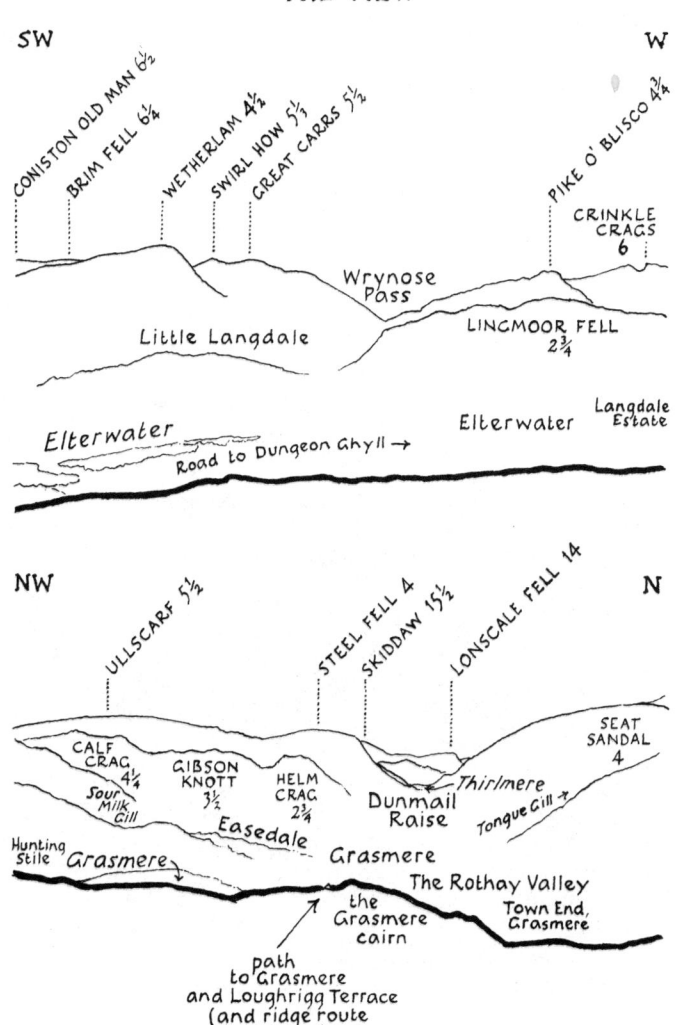

SW — W

- CONISTON OLD MAN 6½
- BRIM FELL 6¼
- WETHERLAM 4½
- SWIRL HOW 5⅓
- GREAT CARRS 5½
- PIKE O' BLISCO 4¾
- CRINKLE CRAGS 6
- Wrynose Pass
- Little Langdale
- LINGMOOR FELL 2¾
- Elterwater
- Road to Dungeon Ghyll →
- Elterwater
- Langdale Estate

NW — N

- ULLSCARF 5½
- STEEL FELL 4
- SKIDDAW 15½
- LONSCALE FELL 14
- CALF CRAG 4¼
- GIBSON KNOTT 3½
- HELM CRAG 2¼
- SEAT SANDAL 4
- Sour Milk Gill
- Easedale
- Dunmail Raise
- Thirlmere
- Tongue Gill →
- Hunting Stile
- Grasmere
- Grasmere
- The Rothay Valley
- Town End, Grasmere
- the Grasmere cairn
- path to Grasmere and Loughrigg Terrace (and ridge route to Silver How)

Pavey Ark 2288'

HIGH RAISE ▲
SERGEANT MAN ▲
THUNACAR ▲ ▲ PAVEY
KNOTT   ARK
HARRISON STICKLE ●
Dungeon Ghyll

0 1 2 3
  MILES

from the western slopes of Blea Rigg

Pavey Ark 2

NATURAL FEATURES

Pavey Ark is Langdale's biggest cliff. In an area where crags and precipices abound, here is the giant of them all, and, scenically, it is the best. The view of the Ark across the waters of Stickle Tarn, at its foot, is superior to all others of this type in Lakeland, having an advantage over the principal rival team of Dow Crag - Goats Water in that the scene, being invariably reached by the steep climb from Dungeon Ghyll, bursts upon the eye with dramatic effect. The crag itself has been superseded in the esteem of climbers by Gimmer Crag and other rock-faces nearer the valley, but is still a great favourite, and Stickle Tarn has many visitors.

It is usual to think of Pavey Ark as a crag, not as a fell. In a strict geographical sense the crag is the eastern boundary of Thunacar Knott, to which the ground above the crag gradually rises. But the Ark has its own proud little summit, an exhilarating place of grey rock, small tarns and soft vegetation that, in interest and charm, quite puts to shame the dreary top of the main fell. At the risk of offending Thunacar Knott, Pavey Ark must have a chapter to itself. The area to be covered is no more than a square half-mile but it is full of good things.

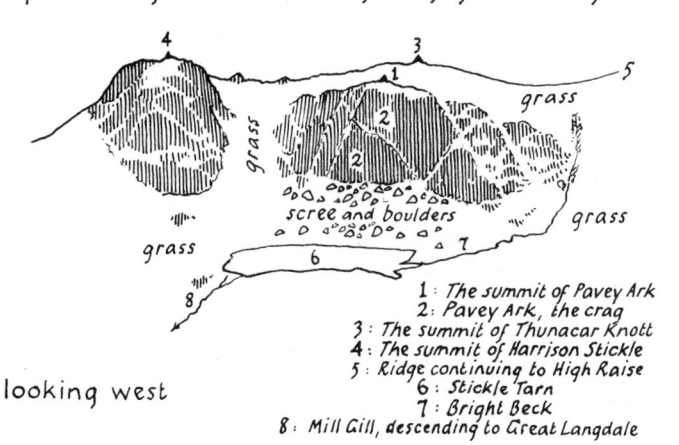

1 : The summit of Pavey Ark
2 : Pavey Ark, the crag
3 : The summit of Thunacar Knott
4 : The summit of Harrison Stickle
5 : Ridge continuing to High Raise
6 : Stickle Tarn
7 : Bright Beck
8 : Mill Gill, descending to Great Langdale

looking west

Pavey Ark 3

MAP

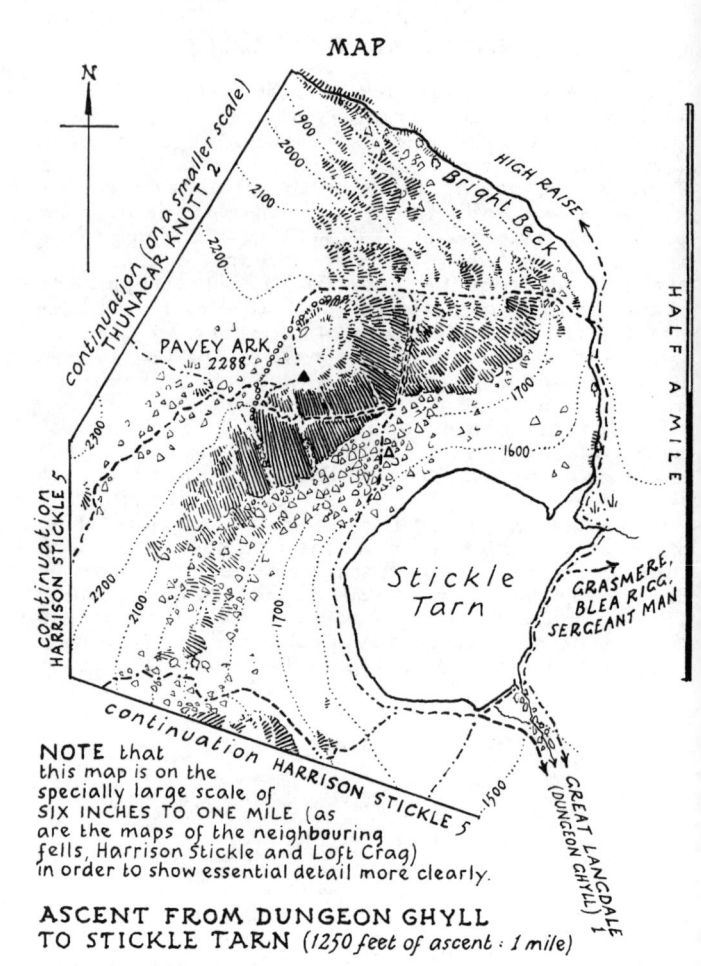

NOTE that this map is on the specially large scale of SIX INCHES TO ONE MILE (as are the maps of the neighbouring fells, Harrison Stickle and Loft Crag) in order to show essential detail more clearly.

ASCENT FROM DUNGEON GHYLL TO STICKLE TARN (1250 feet of ascent : 1 mile)

Pavey Ark overlooks Great Langdale and the natural (and only direct) route of ascent is from that valley. Stickle Tarn is a place of popular resort, and on most summer days it is only necessary to follow the crowds, but if a diagram and details are required, refer to Harrison Stickle 10. From Stickle Tarn onwards, consult the following pages in this chapter.

Pavey Ark 4

ASCENTS FROM STICKLE TARN

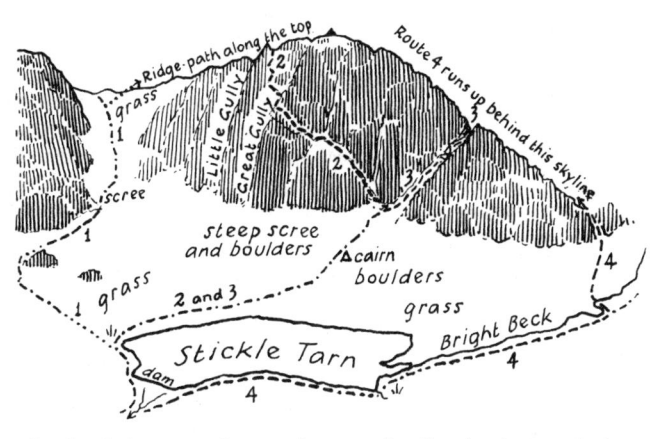

Pedestrian routes only are indicated, but the inclusion of Jack's Rake as such is subject to the qualification that the pedestrian must be agile and have flexible limbs and joints.

1 : An easy but tedious route that avoids the crag altogether, and is therefore something of a cheat. This is the usual path to Harrison Stickle from the tarn, but it may be used for Pavey Ark by working to the right when the skyline is reached and so joining the good ridge-path that leads to the summit-cairn.

2 : *Jack's Rake*, about which a wealth of gruesome detail is to be found on the next two pages. This is a rock-climb rather than a walk. The rock scenery is very impressive.

3 : *Easy Gully*, an interesting route, without difficulty except at one point where a long stride upwards may prove too much for short-legged individuals. The gully runs into the North Rake at two-thirds the height of the latter. There are intimate views of the East Buttress. A diagram appears on page 7.

4 : *North Rake*, a surprising and remarkable grassy breach in the crags, cleaving them from top to bottom on their north side, and affording a simple route of ascent. It is not visible from Stickle Tarn and its presence is not suspected. (It is well seen from high on the slopes of Blea Rigg opposite). This route is recommended to persons who do not like handling rocks and to the short-legged individuals who have suffered defeat in Easy Gully, but is too remote from the main face of the Ark to yield good views. A fair path is developing along the Rake.
Officially, this route has no name, but it deserves one. *North Rake* seems as appropriate as any. There is a diagram on page 7.

Pavey Ark 5

ASCENT via JACK'S RAKE

Jack's Rake is classified as a ROCK CLIMB. Its grading is *easy* — it is the easiest of the recognised climbs in the Langdale area.

Nonetheless, as a WALK it is both *difficult* and *awkward*: in fact, for much of the way the body is propelled forwards by a series of convulsions unrelated to normal walking, the knees and elbows contributing as much to progress as hands and feet. Walkers who can still put their toes in their mouths and bring their knees up to their chins may embark upon the ascent confidently; others, unable to perform these tests, will find the route arduous.

The most awkward scrambling occurs in the initial section, to the third ashtree. Once fairly started, it is easier to go on than to retreat. The upper parts are enjoyable. The humble walker is rarely afforded such an opportunity to enter the realm of the climber, and the rock scenery is magnificent throughout.

Although the Rake climbs high across the face of a fearful precipice, there is curiously little sense of exposure, for a comforting parapet of rock accompanies all the steeper parts of the ascent. The character of the climbing changes when Great Gully is reached.

Care should be taken to avoid falling down the precipice or sending stones over the edge. Falling bodies, human or mineral, may constitute a danger to unseen climbers on the rocks or the scree below, or to grazing sheep.

looking back to the platform below Gwynnes Chimney, from the easy terrace

looking up the Rake to the groove leading to Great Gully, from the easy terrace

It should be noted that the grooves of the Rake form a natural drainage channel for water from the rocks above, and will therefore be wet after rain, thus adding further to the discomforts of the journey. Mist or high winds need not deter an ascent, but snow or ice put the Rake out of bounds decisively.

(Significantly, both sketches are from the easy terrace, the only section where the author's mind was not fully occupied with a primitive desire for survival)

Jack's Rake is just about the limit that the ordinary common garden or fell walker reasonably may be expected to attempt.

continued

Pavey Ark 6

ASCENT via JACK'S RAKE

continued

This diagram will make more sense if it is read from the bottom upwards

From the top exit of Jack's Rake, the summit cairn is 100 yards to the right. Elated by their achievement, most pedestrians tackle the fine rocks on the right and so gain the cairn without crossing the summit-wall

15 YARDS: easy walk from depression to summit-wall

40 YARDS: Horizontal path to the left leads from Great Gully to an open area of big rock steps, where there is a choice of routes. Easy climbing. Aim for the depression to the *right* of the pinnacle

15 YARDS: path turns right and ascends gully

Great Gully is reached. Pinnacle comes into view

25 YARDS: easier rock groove becoming a channel

15 YARDS: easy terrace

10 YARDS: steep groove (awkward start)

8 YARDS: slight descent *(above steep grass slope — care!)*

25 YARDS: easier climbing on more open slope *(the steepest part of the precipice is directly below)*

Several rock-climbs from the base of the crag finish up the steep grass below Gwynne's Chimney

platform *(foot of Gwynne's Chimney)*

path turns slightly right

40 YARDS: steep rock groove *(the worst section)*

5 YARDS: easy platform *(foot of Rake End Chimney)*

15 YARDS: steep rock groove

20 YARDS: easy path on grass

Start from the base of the East Buttress (foot of Easy Gully)

All distances are approximate

JWS 1900

big cairn, with built-in tablet

STICKLE TARN OUTLET

Total length of Rake: 225 yards.
400 feet of ascent at average angle of 30°
(but 50° in steepest sections)

Pavey Ark 7

ASCENTS via EASY GULLY and NORTH RAKE

View from top of Easy Gully

The Coniston Fells
1: Wetherlam
2: Coniston Old Man
3: Swirl How
4: Great Carrs

Stickle Tarn

looking west

Path continues to summit-cairn over grassy top of fell

Easy Gully is mainly a steep walk on grass and sliding scree, but near the top the gully is completely blocked by huge boulders (good shelter here), and for 50 feet the route lies over them, with one awkward obstacle

NORTH RAKE

boulders

East Buttress

Jacks Rake

Easy Gully levels out at the top and joins the North Rake by a grass path

EASY GULLY

big cairn

HIGH RAISE

To locate North Rake from below, follow the course of the main feeder of Stickle Tarn (Bright Beck) for 300 yards by an improving path on the east bank. Here the path crosses the beck and slants up rightwards to the foot of the Rake

If ascending by North Rake make the short detour to the top of Easy Gully for the view

Stickle Tarn

Bright Beck

STICKLE TARN OUTLET → SERGEANT MAN and BLEA RIGG

The North Rake

Easy Gully joins here

North Rake starts with a little scree gully, then, after a short turn to the left, is a perfectly straight grassy uphill trudge, confined between crags. At the top, turn left to reach the cairn in 200 yards, crossing a broken wall midway. This is a surprisingly easy way to the summit, without difficulties of any sort. It deserves to be far better known. Try it sometime!

Pavey Ark 8

THE SUMMIT

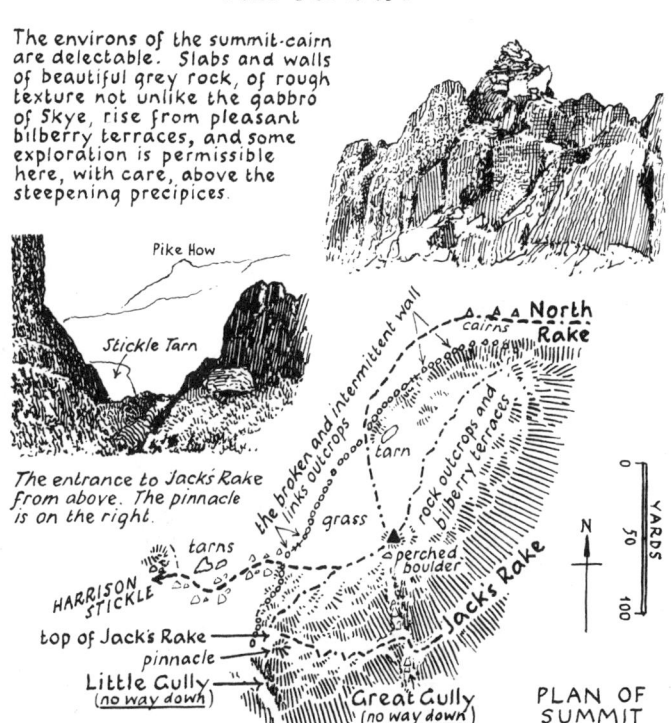

The environs of the summit-cairn are delectable. Slabs and walls of beautiful grey rock, of rough texture not unlike the gabbro of Skye, rise from pleasant bilberry terraces, and some exploration is permissible here, with care, above the steepening precipices.

The entrance to Jack's Rake from above. The pinnacle is on the right.

PLAN OF SUMMIT

DESCENTS (TO STICKLE TARN): The North Rake is the best for descent and is virtually fool-proof, even in mist. (Easy Gully, leading from it, is NOT a time-saver.) If, alternatively, the Harrison Stickle-Stickle Tarn path is used, it should be joined high up over easy ground. Jack's Rake should be used as a way down only by walkers who have previously (and recently) ascended by this route and are aware of the difficulties. The place where the Rake leaves the top cannot be seen from the summit-cairn. It MUST be identified EXACTLY (see plan and illustration above). Keep strictly to the path (in places no more than nail-scratches on rocks) and assume that deviations will end fatally.

The omission of RIDGE ROUTES from this chapter is not due to an oversight, but to the fact that Pavey Ark is not a point on a ridge. (See Thunacar Knott 4).

Pavey Ark 9

THE VIEW

Seated comfortably with his back against the cairn, one leg pointing to Loughrigg Fell and the other to Lingmoor Fell, the walker finds reward for his toil, for between his feet is a gem of a view: that of Great Langdale's graceful curves continued by the long sylvan upper reach of Windermere, a view greatly enhanced by the steep plunge of the ground immediately beyond his boots. In other directions the view is marred by a dull middle distance.

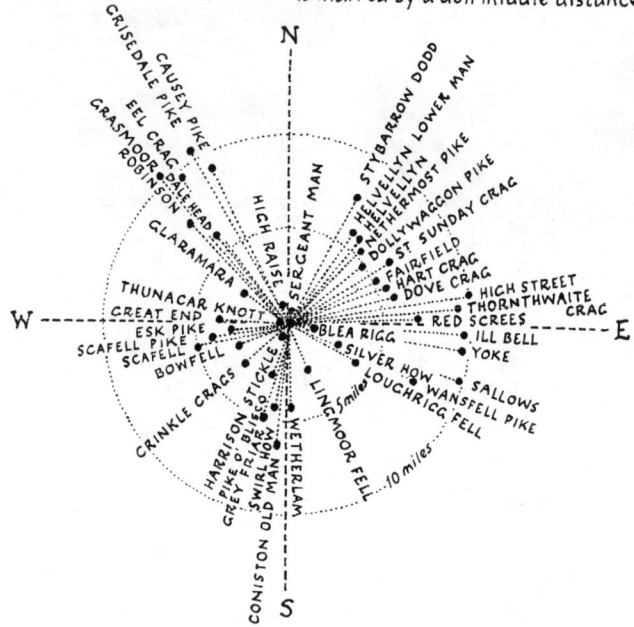

Principal Fells

[compass diagram showing surrounding fells:]

CAUSEY PIKE, CRISEDALE PIKE, EEL CRAG, GRASMOOR, DALEHEAD, ROBINSON, CLARAMARA, THUNACAR KNOTT, GREAT END, ESK PIKE, SCAFELL PIKE, SCAFELL, BOWFELL, CRINKLE CRAGS, HARRISON STICKLE, PIKE OF BLISCO, GREY FRIAR, SWIRL HOW, OLD MAN, CONISTON OLD MAN, WETHERLAM, LINGMOOR FELL, LOUGHRIGG FELL, Smiler, SILVER HOW, BLEA RIGG, SERGENT MAN, HIGH RAISE, STYBARROW DODD, HELVELLYN LOWER MAN, HELVELLYN, NETHERMOST PIKE, DOLLYWAGGON PIKE, ST SUNDAY CRAG, FAIRFIELD, HART CRAG, DOVE CRAG, HIGH STREET, THORNTHWAITE CRAG, RED SCREES, ILL BELL, YOKE, SALLOWS, WANSFELL PIKE

10 miles

Lakes and Tarns

ESE: *Rydal Water*
SE: *Windermere (two sections)*
SE: *Loughrigg Tarn*
SE: *Elterwater*
SE: *Wise Een Tarn*
SE: *Esthwaite Water*
SSE: *Lingmoor Tarn*
SSE: *Stickle Tarn*
S: *Blea Tarn*

Pavey Ark 10

Pavey Ark

Pike o' Stickle 2323'

the second of the
Langdale Pikes

Pike OF Stickle,
to be correct

from Gimmer Crag

HIGH RAISE ▲
PIKE O' ▲ ▲ HARRISON
STICKLE   STICKLE
LOFT CRAG ▲
Old Hotel ● ● New Hotel
Dungeon Ghyll

MILES
0   1   2   3

Pike o' Stickle 2

NATURAL FEATURES

Simple lines are often the most effective, and the smoothly-soaring pyramid of Pike o' Stickle, rising to a tapering thimble of rock without interruption or halt between valley and summit, is an imposing and impressive feature that contributes much to the grandeur of the head of Great Langdale. The unbroken sweep of Stickle Breast above Mickleden is one of the most continuously steep slopes in the district, rising nearly 2,000 feet over a lateral distance of half a mile. Dry scree gullies sever the craggy upper storey from the neighbouring fellsides, but a lofty ridge connects it with the castellated skyline overlooking Dungeon Ghyll and Langdale. A strong contrast to this battlemented facade is that provided by the dreary upland hollow lying beyond (Harrison Combe) from which easy slopes fall away to Stake Pass, northwest, pausing in their descent to form the broad plateau of Martcrag Moor.

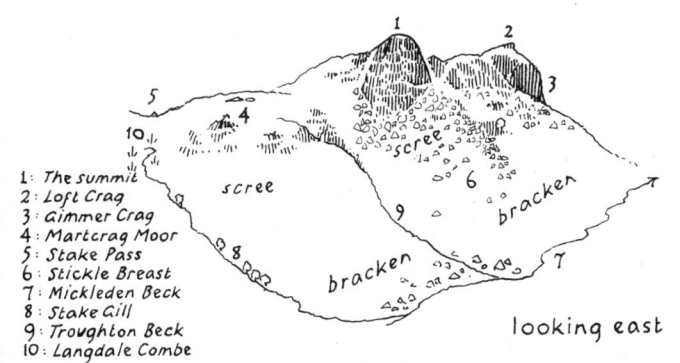

1: The summit
2: Loft Crag
3: Gimmer Crag
4: Martcrag Moor
5: Stake Pass
6: Stickle Breast
7: Mickleden Beck
8: Stake Gill
9: Troughton Beck
10: Langdale Combe

looking east

Thousands of years ago, before the dawn of history, Pike o' Stickle was the scene of an industry the evidences of which have only recently been discovered, and the fell is now established as the country's most important site of stone-axe manufacture by neolithic man. As such it is attracting increasing attention by archaeologists and geologists, but walkers with no expert knowledge of the subject will also find an absorbing interest in a study of the related literature, as yet incomplete, and they may care to combine with their expeditions in this area a search into the dim but fascinating secrets of the past.

Pike o' Stickle 3

The Stone Axe Factory

The south scree, from Mickleden

The intrusion of a narrow vein of a very hard stone in the volcanic rocks of Great Langdale, emerging on the surface along a high-level contour around the head of the valley, provided the material from which the prehistoric natives of the district fashioned their axes. Working sites have been located from Martcrag Moor to Harrison Stickle, but the screes of Pike o' Stickle have yielded the most prolific discoveries, and especially the 'south scree' where hundreds of specimens, originally rejected because of imperfections, have been collected in recent years. The really remarkable feature is not so much the presence of this particular variety of stone, nor the making of implements from it so long ago; the facts that most tax the imagination are, first, that the primitive inhabitants of Lakeland should have located such an insignificant geological fault and recognised its value, and secondly, that the plentiful evidences of their industry should have remained undisturbed and unnoticed throughout the ages until modern times.

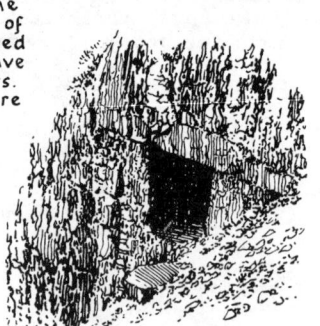

In the rock wall of the south scree is this well-made artificial cave. Its connection with stone-axe manufacture hereabouts has not yet been accepted authoritatively, although the coincidence seems too great to be denied.

A few feet square, it provides excellent shelter for several persons.

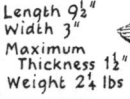

Length 9½"
Width 3"
Maximum Thickness 1½"
Weight 2¼ lbs

Stone axe found on Pike o' Stickle — a particularly good specimen in the collection of Mr. R.G. Plint, of Kendal

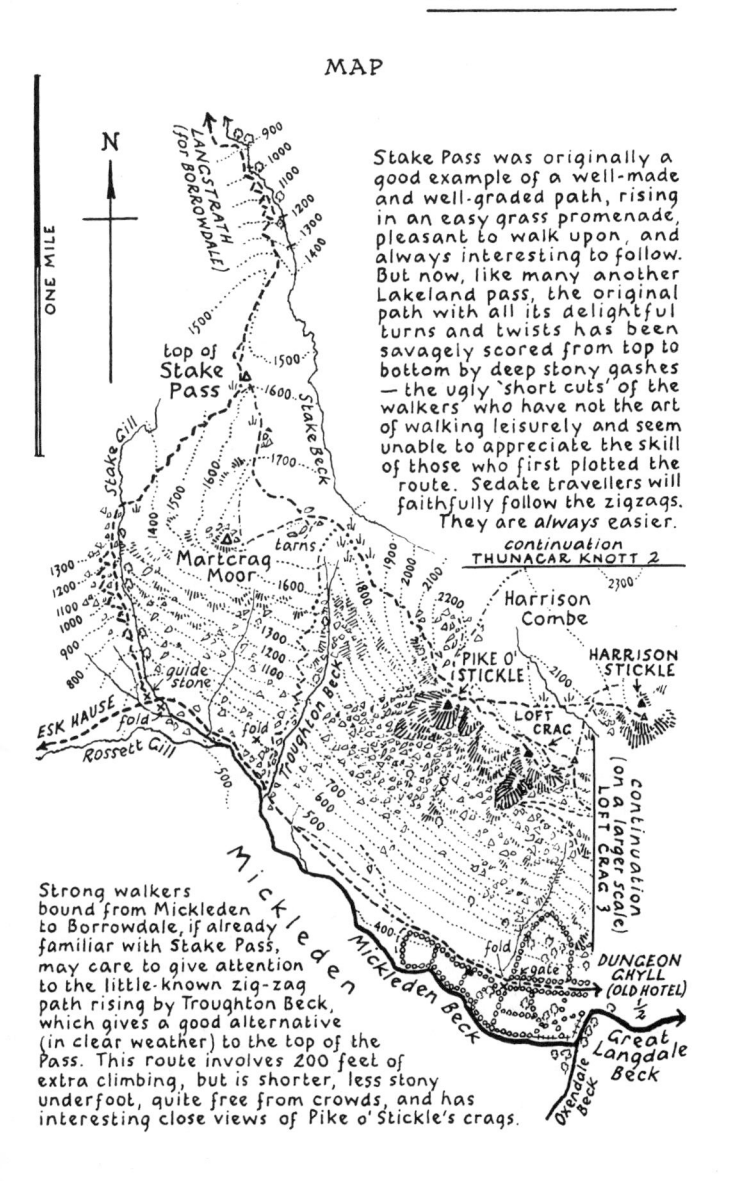

Pike o' Stickle 4

MAP

ONE MILE

N

LANGSTRATH (for BORROWDALE)

top of Stake Pass

Stake Gill

Stake Beck

Martcrag Moor

tarns

guide stone

ESK HAUSE

Fold

Rossett Gill

Troughton Beck

fold

Mickleden

Mickleden Beck

fold

gate

Oxendale Beck

Great Langdale Beck

Harrison Combe

PIKE O' STICKLE

HARRISON STICKLE

LOFT CRAG

continuation (on a larger scale) LOFT CRAG 3

DUNGEON GHYLL (OLD HOTEL)

continuation THUNACAR KNOTT 2

Stake Pass was originally a good example of a well-made and well-graded path, rising in an easy grass promenade, pleasant to walk upon, and always interesting to follow. But now, like many another Lakeland pass, the original path with all its delightful turns and twists has been savagely scored from top to bottom by deep stony gashes — the ugly 'short cuts' of the walkers who have not the art of walking leisurely and seem unable to appreciate the skill of those who first plotted the route. Sedate travellers will faithfully follow the zigzags. They are always easier.

Strong walkers bound from Mickleden to Borrowdale, if already familiar with Stake Pass, may care to give attention to the little-known zig-zag path rising by Troughton Beck, which gives a good alternative (in clear weather) to the top of the Pass. This route involves 200 feet of extra climbing, but is shorter, less stony underfoot, quite free from crowds, and has interesting close views of Pike o' Stickle's crags.

Pike o' Stickle 5

ASCENT FROM MICKLEDEN
2000 feet of ascent

3¼ miles via Troughton Beck,
1¾ miles direct (from the
Dungeon Ghyll Old Hotel)

PIKE O' STICKLE

TOP OF STAKE PASS

Martcrag Moor

cave

Initially there is no path by the beck, but one materialises as the ground steepens. It is indistinct on top of the fell.

In the final gully the best footing is on the east side.

sheepfold

Troughton Beck

STAKE PASS and ESK HAUSE

bracken — grass — scree-run — bracken

shallow dry gully

This path in the strip of bracken between scree-runs has obviously been made by travellers descending at speed; it is not 'stepped' and is of little help in ascent.

patch of rushes

big boulder

bracken

looking north-north-west

Mickleden Beck

Mickleden

ruin

gate

sheepfold

DUNGEON GHYLL (OLD HOTEL)

Pike o' Stickle is almost invariably reached from the valley by turning left off the usual Harrison Stickle path at the Thorn Crag col, but illustrated here are two other possibilities —
first, via the unfrequented zig-zags climbing the west bank of Troughton Beck, by which the path coming up from the top of Stake Pass may be joined for the summit of the Pike;
second, direct up the south scree, a continuously steep and unpleasant scramble in prickly, unstable scree, and of interest only to searchers after stone axes; the route is dry and dusty but bilberries will be found in season higher up and will seem, by the time they are reached, a greater prize than stone axes to the untrained eye and unlearned mind, which will already have selected and discarded hundreds of likely axes in the splintery stones and debris heaps that litter this desperate climb. In a buttoned-up plastic mac, the ascent is purgatory.

Pike o' Stickle 6

ASCENT FROM THE TOP OF STAKE PASS
800 feet of ascent : 1⅓ miles

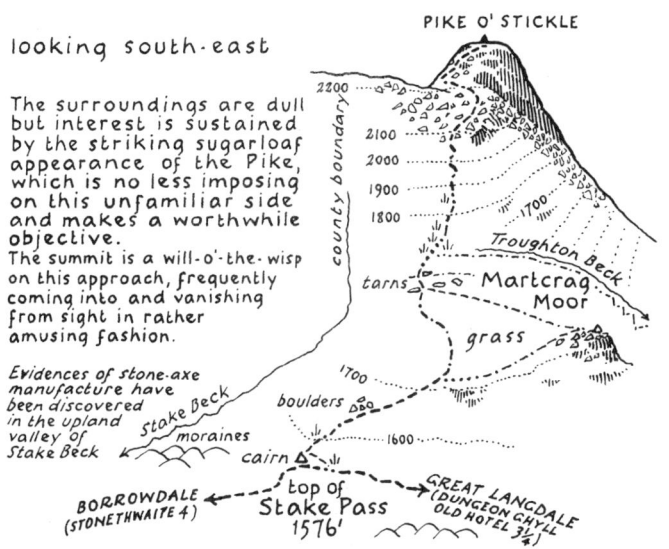

looking south-east

The surroundings are dull but interest is sustained by the striking sugarloaf appearance of the Pike, which is no less imposing on this unfamiliar side and makes a worthwhile objective.
The summit is a will-o'-the-wisp on this approach, frequently coming into and vanishing from sight in rather amusing fashion.

Evidences of stone-axe manufacture have been discovered in the upland valley of Stake Beck

By a short detour the cairn on Martcrag Moor may be visited. This rocky little top is a commanding viewpoint for the head of Mickleden and it is wonderfully satisfying to lie here in the sunshine and watch parties struggling up Rossett Gill and Stake Pass from the sheepfold far below. Here, too, is one of the most impressive views of Bowfell.

The summit of Pike o' Stickle from the north-west

The cairn on Martcrag Moor

Pike o' Stickle 7

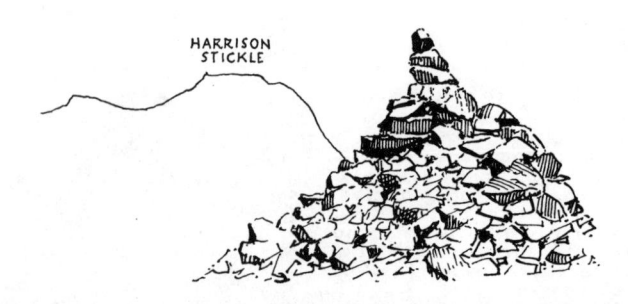

THE SUMMIT

The summit is the perfect dome suggested by its appearance from a distance, being circular in plan and bell-shaped, with almost precipitous slopes rising up to it on all sides before finally tapering away gently to the highest point. The top is a pleasant green sward of ample proportions, but exploration is severely restricted by the surrounding crags. Access to the cairn is gained by an easy scramble on the more broken northern slope, this being the only side 'open' to walkers.

DESCENTS:

To Great Langdale: Expert scree-runners will come down the open gully immediately east of the summit-dome and reach the valley-bottom in Mickleden in a matter of minutes, but ordinary mortals will find this route very trying to the temper, although it is probably the safest way in mist and the most sheltered in bad weather. The more usual procedure normally is to join a good path (from Harrison Stickle) at the Thorn Crag col. The route via Troughton Beck has no merits in descent.

1: top of Stake Pass
ignore these paths, which go nowhere in particular.
2: Harrison Stickle
3: Loft Crag; Thorn Crag
4: Mickleden (direct)

To Borrowdale: The path to the top of Stake Pass presents no difficulties in clear weather and must be attempted in mist because there is no other; take care to start on the right track

RIDGE ROUTE

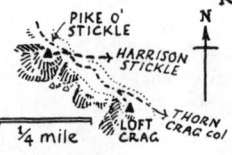

TO LOFT CRAG, 2270'
⅓ mile : E, then SE
100 feet of ascent

At the first depression, follow the less distinct track branching up right: this keeps an interesting course along the ridge

Pike o' Stickle 8

THE VIEW

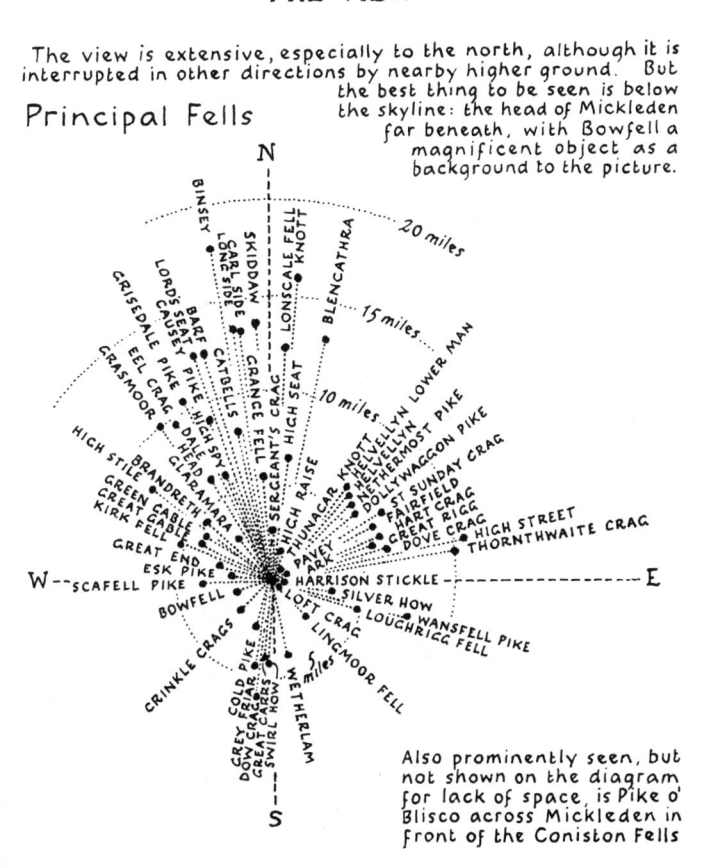

The view is extensive, especially to the north, although it is interrupted in other directions by nearby higher ground. But the best thing to be seen is below the skyline: the head of Mickleden far beneath, with Bowfell a magnificent object as a background to the picture.

Principal Fells

(diagram of fells radiating from centre, with compass points N, E, S, W and distance rings at 10 miles, 15 miles, 20 miles)

Fells labelled (clockwise from N): BINSEY, SKIDDAW, CARLSIDE, LONGSIDE, BAKESTALL, LORD'S SEAT, CAUSEY PIKE, CRISEDALE PIKE, EEL CRAG, GRASMOOR, HIGH STILE, BRANDRETH, GREEN GABLE, GREAT GABLE, KIRK FELL, CLARAMARA, DALE HEAD, HIGH SPY, CATBELLS, GRANGE FELL, SERGEANT'S CRAG, HIGH SEAT, HIGH RAISE, LONSCALE FELL, KNOTT, BLENCATHRA, THUNACAR KNOTT, HELVELLYN LOWER MAN, HELVELLYN, NETHERMOST PIKE, DOLLYWAGGON PIKE, ST SUNDAY CRAG, FAIRFIELD, HART CRAG, PAVEY ARK, GREAT RIGG, DOVE CRAG, HIGH STREET, THORNTHWAITE CRAG, HARRISON STICKLE, SILVER HOW, WANSFELL PIKE, LOUGHRIGG FELL, LOFT CRAG, LINGMOOR FELL, WETHERLAM, SWIRL HOW, GREAT CARRS, COLD PIKE, GREY FRIAR, DOW CRAG, CRINKLE CRAGS, ESK PIKE, GREAT END, SCAFELL PIKE, BOWFELL

W — SCAFELL PIKE .... HARRISON STICKLE .... E

Also prominently seen, but not shown on the diagram for lack of space, is Pike o' Blisco across Mickleden in front of the Coniston Fells

Lakes and Tarns

ESE : *Loughrigg Tarn*
ESE : *Elterwater*
SE : *Windermere (upper reach and strip of middle)*
SE : *Lingmoor Tarn*
SE : *Esthwaite Water*
SSE : *Blea Tarn*
WNW : *Nameless tarns on Martcrag Moor*
NNW : *Tarn at Leaves (on Rosthwaite Fell)*

Raven Crag

1520' approx.

from the Thirlmere dam

Dale Bottom

BLEABERRY FELL ▲   Smeathwaite ● Bridge

▲ RAVEN CRAG

HIGH ▲ SEAT   ● Armboth

MILES
0 1 2 3 4

Raven Crag 2

NATURAL FEATURES

Of the many dozens of Raven Crags in Lakeland, best known of all, and the subject of this chapter, is the mighty buttress of grey rock towering above the Thirlmere dam. The vertical face of the crag, now receiving the attention of expert rock-climbers, is a truly formidable object, standing out starkly from a dense surround of plantations.

Raven Crag, which is properly a ridge of High Tove, must have caused problems (left unsolved) for the reservoir engineers because this tremendous barrier of rock turns many streams descending from the central ridge northwards into the Naddle Valley and away from Thirlmere. Oddly, a similar but smaller formation occurs on the opposite side of the dam, where the wooded height of Great How also originally diverted many streams of the Helvellyn mass northwards into St. John's-in-the-Vale — here, however, the engineers captured them by a water-race and turned them into Thirlmere.

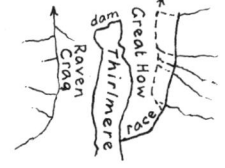

North from Raven Crag the ridge is terminated by The Benn, dropping to valley level at Shoulthwaite.

MAP

Shoulthwaite is pronounced 'Shoolthet' and Smaithwaite 'Smethet'

Raven Crag 3

ASCENT FROM THIRLMERE DAM
950 feet of ascent : 1 mile

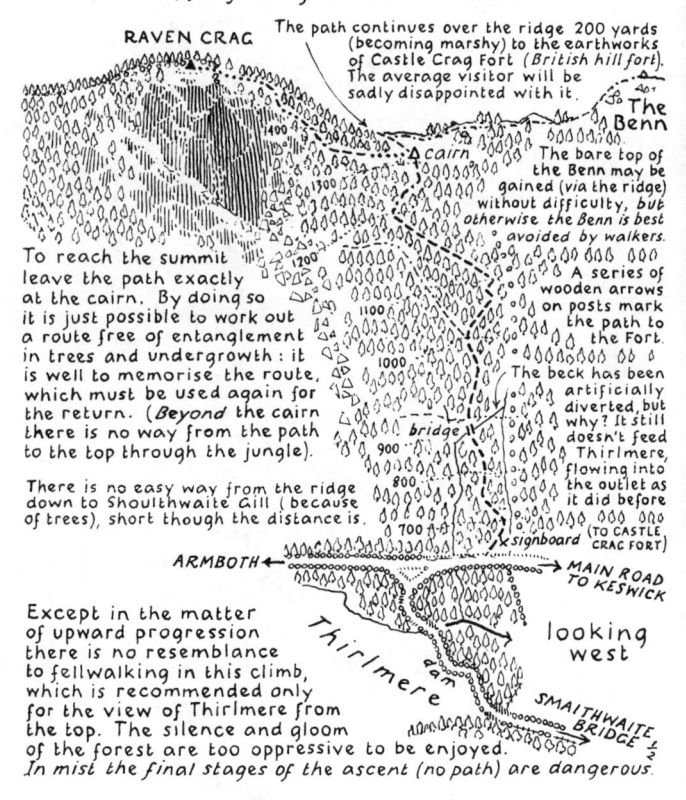

The path continues over the ridge 200 yards (becoming marshy) to the earthworks of Castle Crag Fort *(British hill fort)*. The average visitor will be sadly disappointed with it.

The bare top of the Benn may be gained (via the ridge) without difficulty, but otherwise the Benn is best avoided by walkers.

A series of wooden arrows on posts mark the path to the Fort.

To reach the summit leave the path exactly at the cairn. By doing so it is just possible to work out a route free of entanglement in trees and undergrowth: it is well to memorise the route, which must be used again for the return. *(Beyond the cairn there is no way from the path to the top through the jungle).*

The beck has been artificially diverted, but why? It still doesn't feed Thirlmere, flowing into the outlet as it did before.

There is no easy way from the ridge down to Shoulthwaite Gill (because of trees), short though the distance is.

ARMBOTH ←   → MAIN ROAD TO KESWICK

looking west

SMAITHWAITE BRIDGE ½

Except in the matter of upward progression there is no resemblance to fellwalking in this climb, which is recommended only for the view of Thirlmere from the top. The silence and gloom of the forest are too oppressive to be enjoyed.
In mist the final stages of the ascent (no path) are dangerous.

THE SUMMIT

The summit, of tough heather, is unusual because of its screen of trees. The highest point is a small outcrop of rock, bearing a few stones built into a meagre cairn. A ruined wall crosses the top, a relic of days when sheep lived here — before the growing plantations drove them to other pastures. The summit breaks away suddenly into the most fearful precipice and exploration here is severely restricted. *The only way down is the route used for ascent, not easily located as far as the cairn unless memorised on the way up.*

Raven Crag 4

THE VIEW

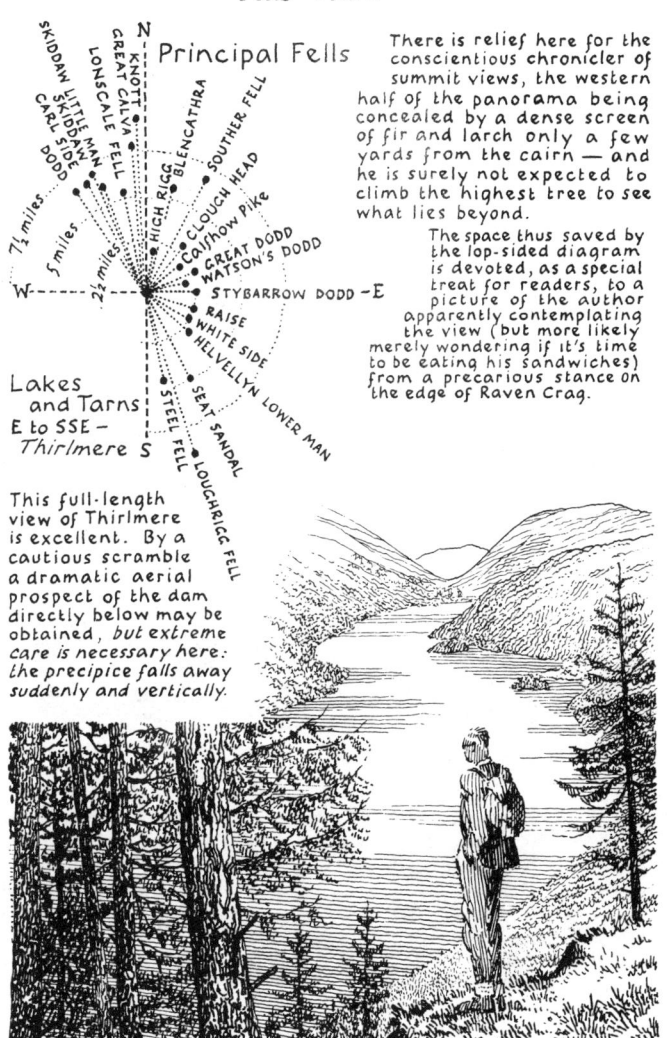

Principal Fells (compass diagram):
N — KNOTT, GREAT CALVA, LONSCALE FELL, SKIDDAW, LITTLE MAN SKIDDAW, CARL SIDE, DODD (7¼ miles, 5 miles, 2½ miles)
BLENCATHRA, SOUTHER FELL, HIGH RIGG, CLOUGH HEAD, Calfhow Pike, GREAT DODD, WATSON'S DODD
E — STYBARROW DODD
RAISE, WHITE SIDE, HELVELLYN LOWER MAN, SEAT SANDAL, STEEL FELL, LOUGHRIGG FELL

Lakes and Tarns
E to SSE –
Thirlmere S

There is relief here for the conscientious chronicler of summit views, the western half of the panorama being concealed by a dense screen of fir and larch only a few yards from the cairn — and he is surely not expected to climb the highest tree to see what lies beyond.

The space thus saved by the lop-sided diagram is devoted, as a special treat for readers, to a picture of the author apparently contemplating the view (but more likely merely wondering if it's time to be eating his sandwiches) from a precarious stance on the edge of Raven Crag.

This full-length view of Thirlmere is excellent. By a cautious scramble a dramatic aerial prospect of the dam directly below may be obtained, *but extreme care is necessary here: the precipice falls away suddenly and vertically.*

Sergeant Man 2414'

from Great Castle How

HIGH RAISE ▲ ▲ TARN CRAG
SERGEANT MAN
HARRISON ▲   • Grasmere
STICKLE
• Dungeon Ghyll
MILES
0 1 2 3 4

Sergeant Man 2

NATURAL FEATURES

Sergeant Man is merely a rocky excrescence at the edge of the broad expanse forming the top of High Raise, but is so prominent an object and offers so compelling a challenge (in these respects being far superior to the summit of High Raise itself) that it is often given preference over the main fell as the target of a day's outing, and for that reason it is deserving of a separate chapter. Behind the abrupt peak, which rises steeply from the basin containing Stickle Tarn, is a hinterland of craggy outcrops and ravines that are rarely visited although yielding, in fact, more interest than the environs of the summit; in particular the area of Fern Gill and Broadstone Head, descending with the county boundary to the valley heads of Wythburn and Far Easedale is fruitful ground for the explorer.

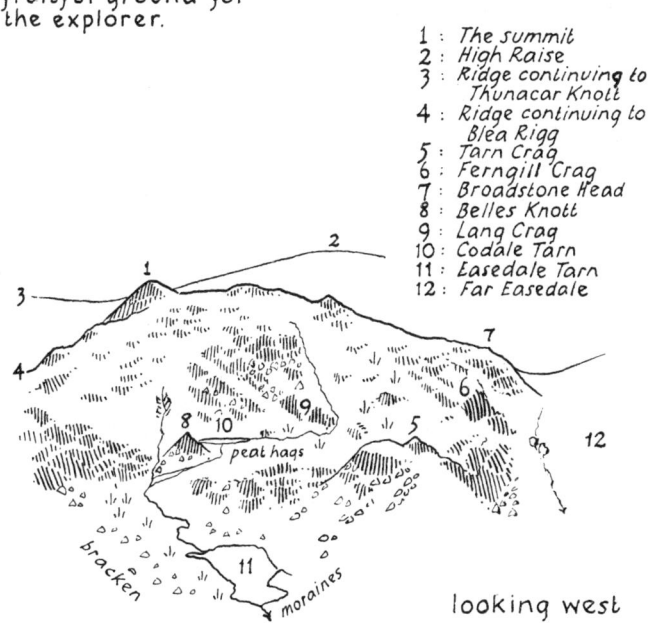

1 : The summit
2 : High Raise
3 : Ridge continuing to Thunacar Knott
4 : Ridge continuing to Blea Rigg
5 : Tarn Crag
6 : Ferngill Crag
7 : Broadstone Head
8 : Belles Knott
9 : Lang Crag
10 : Codale Tarn
11 : Easedale Tarn
12 : Far Easedale

looking west

Sergeant Man 3

MAP

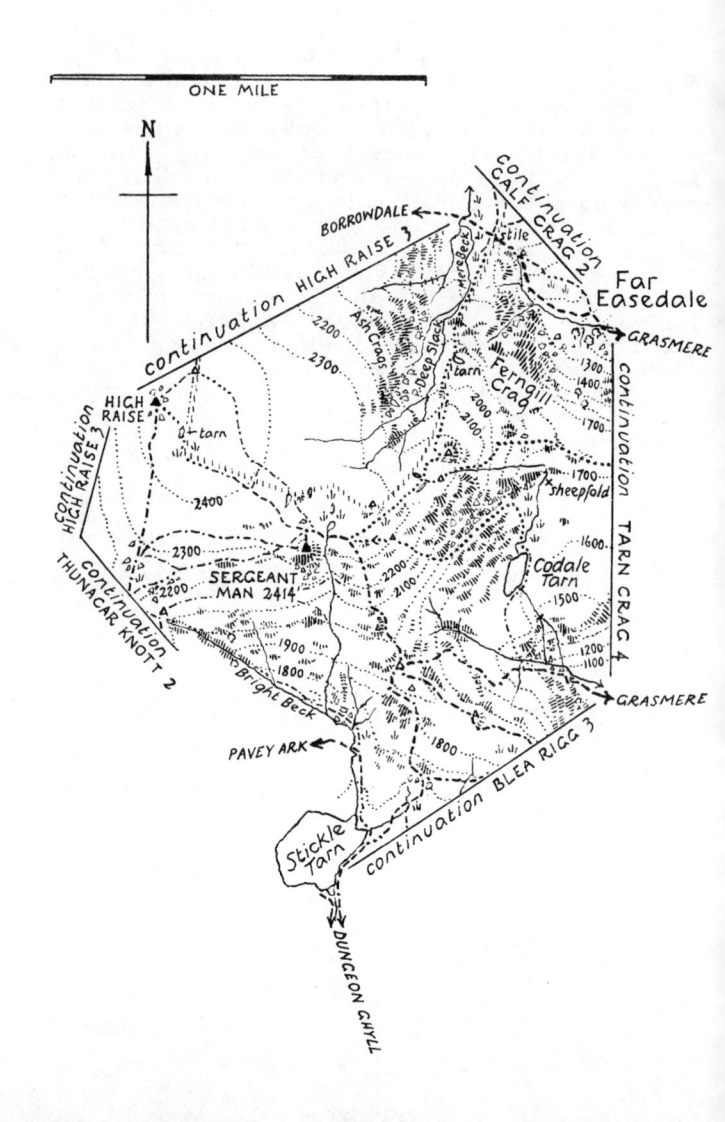

Sergeant Man 4

ASCENT FROM DUNGEON GHYLL
2¼ miles : 2200 feet of ascent from the New Hotel

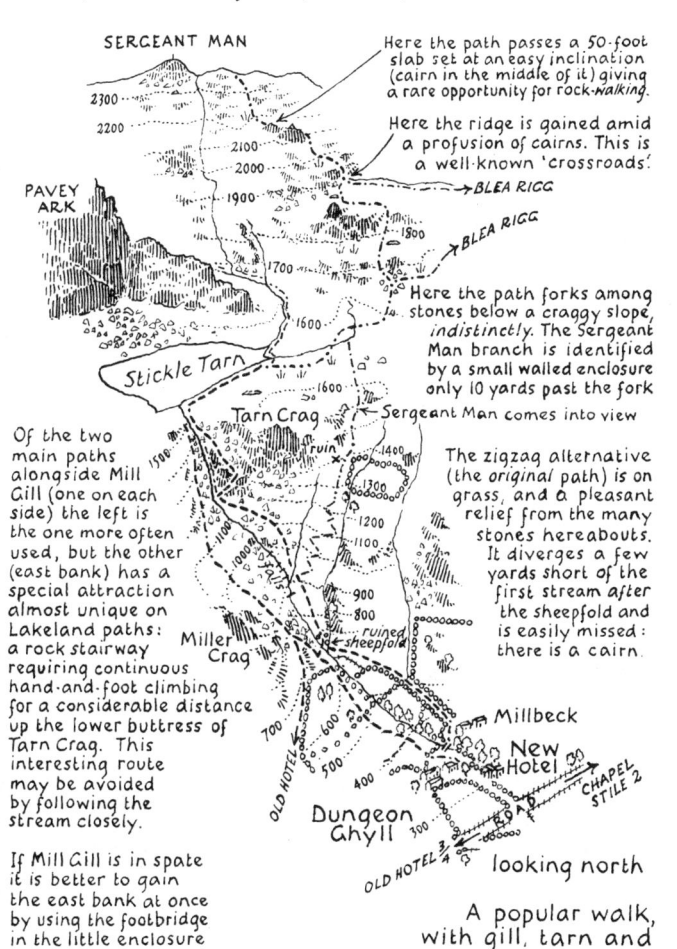

Here the path passes a 50-foot slab set at an easy inclination (cairn in the middle of it) giving a rare opportunity for rock-*walking*.

Here the ridge is gained amid a profusion of cairns. This is a well-known 'crossroads'.
→ BLEA RIGG
→ BLEA RIGG

Here the path forks among stones below a craggy slope, *indistinctly*. The Sergeant Man branch is identified by a small walled enclosure only 10 yards past the fork

Sergeant Man comes into view

The zigzag alternative (the *original* path) is on grass, and a pleasant relief from the many stones hereabouts. It diverges a few yards short of the first stream *after* the sheepfold and is easily missed: there is a cairn.

Of the two main paths alongside Mill Gill (one on each side) the left is the one more often used, but the other (east bank) has a special attraction almost unique on Lakeland paths: a rock stairway requiring continuous hand-and-foot climbing for a considerable distance up the lower buttress of Tarn Crag. This interesting route may be avoided by following the stream closely.

If Mill Gill is in spate it is better to gain the east bank at once by using the footbridge in the little enclosure behind the hotel and following the path from Millbeck Farm

looking north

A popular walk, with gill, tarn and rock scenery of the highest order and good views all the way.

Sergeant Man 5

ASCENT FROM GRASMERE
2200 feet of ascent : 4 miles

SERGEANT MAN

Here the path passes a 50-foot rock slab with a cairn oddly set in the middle. Its easy gradient makes it climbable by walking.

Here the ridge is gained amid a profusion of cairns. This is a well-known 'crossroads'. Routes from Dungeon Ghyll and Blea Rigg to Sergeant Man join in at this point.

The path becomes a scramble on easy rock as it skirts the edge of the crags above point marked A.

'A' indicates the start of the variation by Codale Tarn, illustrated opposite.

Black slime is experienced at its blackest and slimiest at frequent intervals on the path alongside Easedale Tarn and beyond, but conditions underfoot improve as soon as the old tarn is passed.

The summit of Sergeant Man cannot be seen from the hut and does not come into sight until the final stages of the climb.

Blea Crag and Eagle Crag form an imposing precipice on the left but the dominating feature on the march up the valley is the peak of Belles Knott, which assumes a striking appearance from the path as it is approached.

looking west

This is the most direct and the quickest route. From Easedale Tarn the path follows the main feeder almost to its source before slanting up to the ridge. The route is too deeply enclosed to be attractive, although there are several interesting features. If returning to Grasmere, the more exhilarating Blea Rigg ridge is a better route of descent than the one illustrated above.

Sergeant Man 6

ASCENT FROM GRASMERE
(VARIATION BY CODALE TARN)
2200 feet of ascent : 4¼ miles

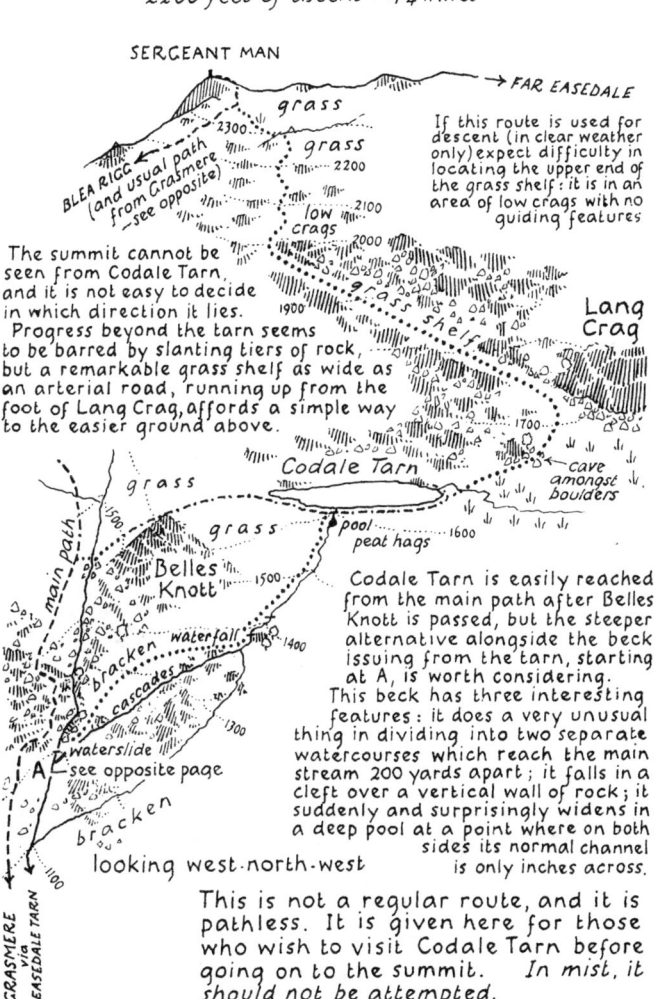

SERGEANT MAN → FAR EASEDALE

BLEA RIGG (and usual path from Grasmere — see opposite)

grass 2300
grass 2200
low crags 2100
2000
grass shelf 1900

Lang Crag

If this route is used for descent (in clear weather only) expect difficulty in locating the upper end of the grass shelf: it is in an area of low crags with no guiding features

The summit cannot be seen from Codale Tarn, and it is not easy to decide in which direction it lies.
Progress beyond the tarn seems to be barred by slanting tiers of rock, but a remarkable grass shelf as wide as an arterial road, running up from the foot of Lang Crag, affords a simple way to the easier ground above.

1700

cave amongst boulders

Codale Tarn

grass
main path
grass 1500
pool
peat hags 1600

Belles Knott
1500
bracken
waterfall
cascades 1400

A — see opposite page
waterslide
1300
bracken
1100

GRASMERE via EASEDALE TARN

looking west-north-west

Codale Tarn is easily reached from the main path after Belles Knott is passed, but the steeper alternative alongside the beck issuing from the tarn, starting at A, is worth considering.
This beck has three interesting features: it does a very unusual thing in dividing into two separate watercourses which reach the main stream 200 yards apart; it falls in a cleft over a vertical wall of rock; it suddenly and surprisingly widens in a deep pool at a point where on both sides its normal channel is only inches across.

This is not a regular route, and it is pathless. It is given here for those who wish to visit Codale Tarn before going on to the summit.   In mist, it should not be attempted.

Sergeant Man 7

ASCENT FROM THE HEAD OF FAR EASEDALE
(reached from GRASMERE or WYTHBURN)
from Grasmere: 2200 feet of ascent : 5½ miles
from Wythburn: 1850 feet of ascent : 5 miles

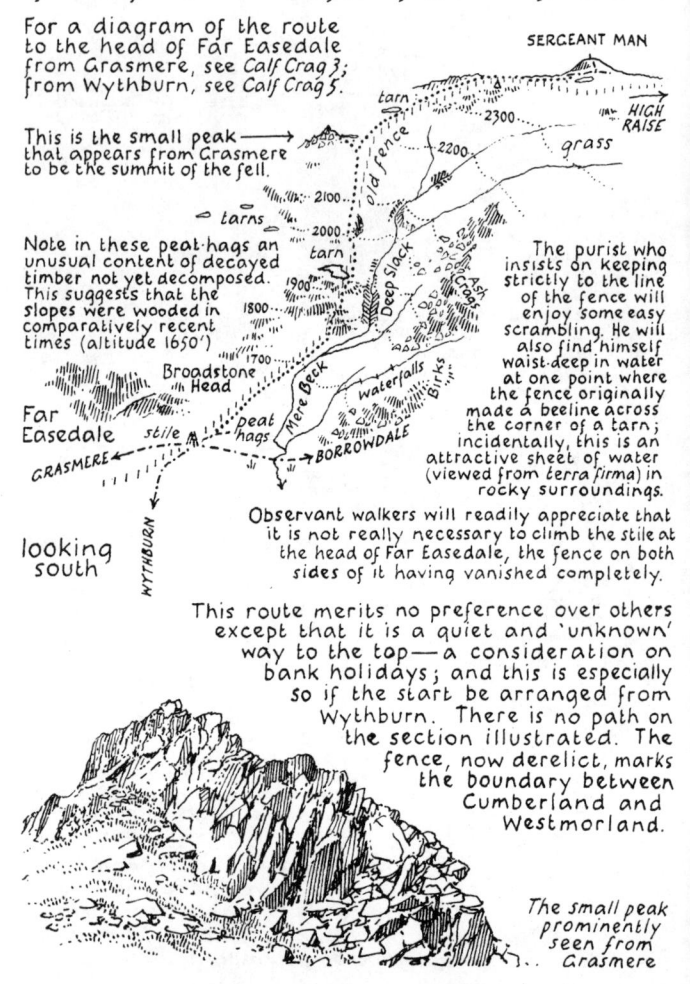

For a diagram of the route to the head of Far Easedale from Grasmere, see *Calf Crag 3*; from Wythburn, see *Calf Crag 5*.

SERGEANT MAN

This is the small peak that appears from Grasmere to be the summit of the fell.

HIGH RAISE

grass

Note in these peat hags an unusual content of decayed timber not yet decomposed. This suggests that the slopes were wooded in comparatively recent times (altitude 1650')

The purist who insists on keeping strictly to the line of the fence will enjoy some easy scrambling. He will also find himself waist-deep in water at one point where the fence originally made a beeline across the corner of a tarn; incidentally, this is an attractive sheet of water (viewed from *terra firma*) in rocky surroundings.

Far Easedale

looking south

Observant walkers will readily appreciate that it is not really necessary to climb the stile at the head of Far Easedale, the fence on both sides of it having vanished completely.

This route merits no preference over others except that it is a quiet and 'unknown' way to the top — a consideration on bank holidays; and this is especially so if the start be arranged from Wythburn. There is no path on the section illustrated. The fence, now derelict, marks the boundary between Cumberland and Westmorland.

The small peak prominently seen from Grasmere

Sergeant Man 8

THE SUMMIT

The stones around the cairn have been scratched white by the nailed boots of visitors, testifying to the popularity of this summit. Southwards the ground falls away steeply and roughly, and it is usual to leave the cairn northwards, where a spiny little ridge descends easily to a network of paths. There is swampy ground on the top of the fell, and many small tarns. Sergeant Man is distinctive in having a stream within a furlong of the cairn, a point for specialists in mountain bivouacs to note. The well-built cairn is a prominent landmark.

DESCENTS: The usual way off the top is by the Blea Rigg path. In mist, the Blea Rigg path is best, being well-cairned although indistinct in places, if Grasmere or Langdale is the destination. For Borrowdale or Wythburn, strike north to the old fence (250 yards) and follow it left over High Raise to Greenup Edge.

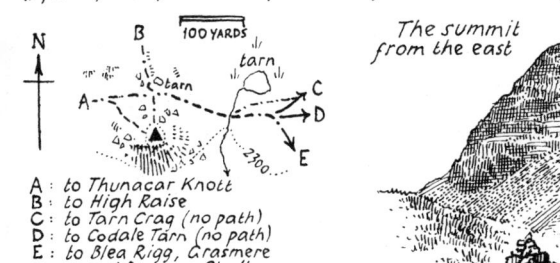

A: to Thunacar Knott
B: to High Raise
C: to Tarn Crag (no path)
D: to Codale Tarn (no path)
E: to Blea Rigg, Grasmere and Dungeon Ghyll.

The summit from the east

Sergeant Man 9

THE VIEW

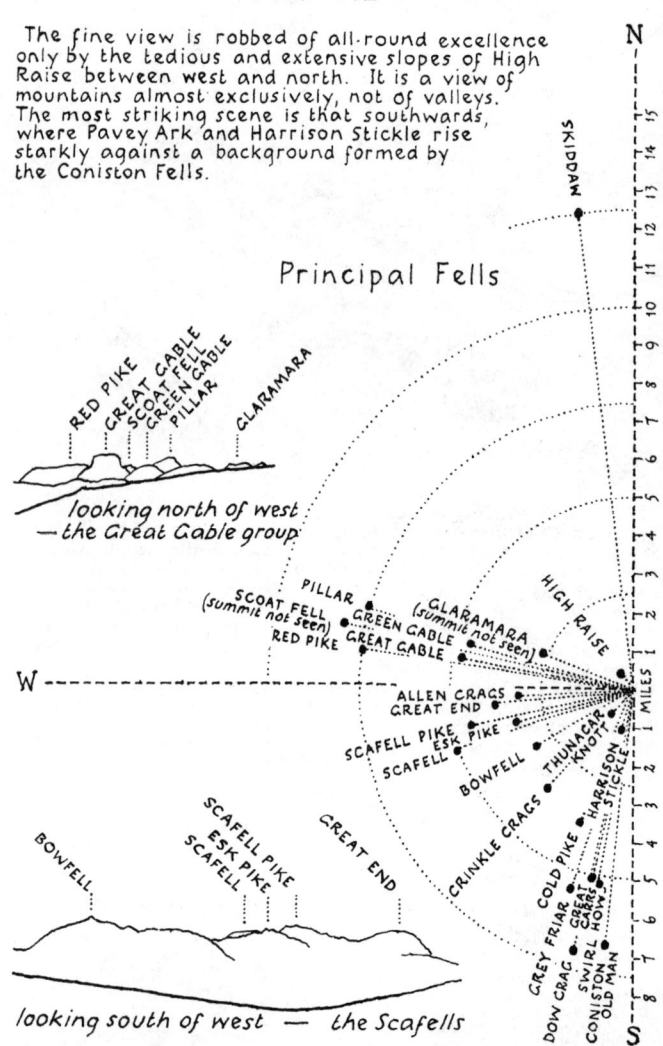

The fine view is robbed of all-round excellence only by the tedious and extensive slopes of High Raise between west and north. It is a view of mountains almost exclusively, not of valleys. The most striking scene is that southwards, where Pavey Ark and Harrison Stickle rise starkly against a background formed by the Coniston Fells.

Principal Fells

looking north of west — the Great Gable group

Labels: RED PIKE, GREAT GABLE, SCOAT FELL, GREEN GABLE, PILLAR, GLARAMARA

looking south of west — the Scafells

Labels: BOWFELL, SCAFELL PIKE, ESK PIKE, SCAFELL, GREAT END

Compass bearings (clockwise from N):
- SKIDDAW
- HIGH RAISE
- GLARAMARA (summit not seen)
- PILLAR
- GREEN GABLE
- SCOAT FELL (summit not seen)
- GREAT GABLE
- RED PIKE
- ALLEN CRAGS
- GREAT END
- SCAFELL PIKE
- ESK PIKE
- SCAFELL
- BOWFELL
- CRINKLE CRAGS
- THUNACAR KNOTT
- HARRISON STICKLE
- COLD PIKE
- GREAT HOW
- GREY FRIAR
- DOW CRAG
- SWIRL HOW
- CONISTON OLD MAN

W — — — MILES — — — (scale 1–15)

Sergeant Man 10

THE VIEW

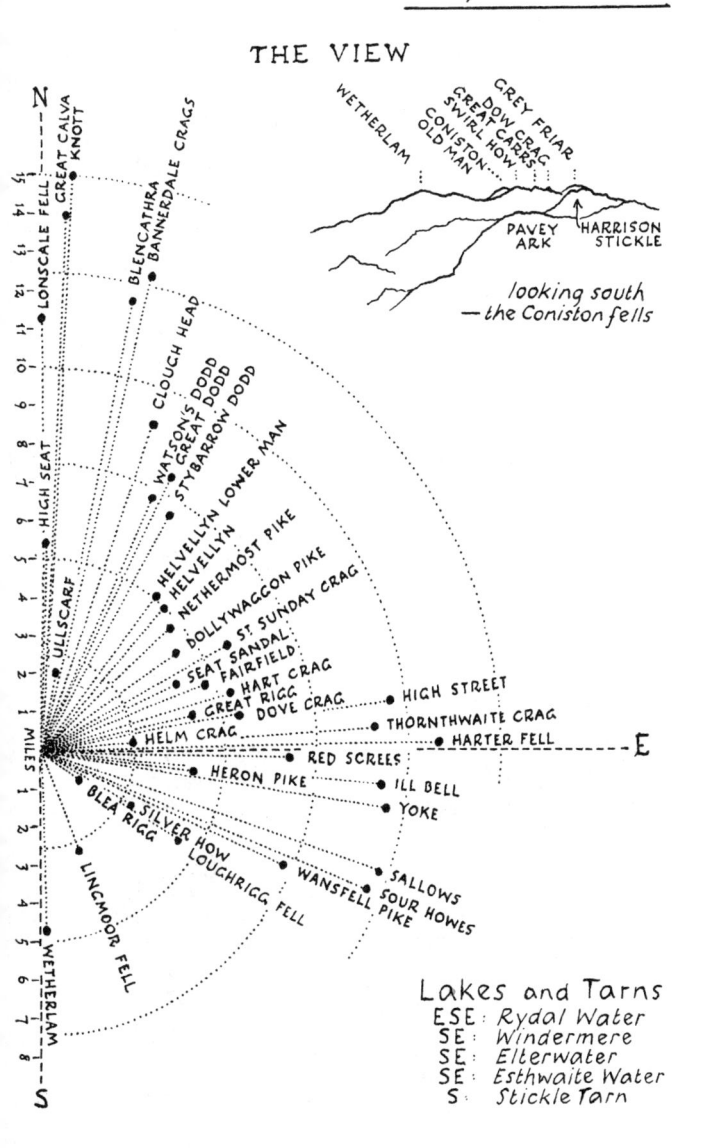

looking south — the Coniston fells

Peaks on horizon (left to right): WETHERLAM, GREY FRIAR, DOW CRAG, GREAT CARRS, SWIRL HOW, CONISTON OLD MAN, PAVEY ARK, HARRISON STICKLE

Radial view (N to S):
- LONSCALE FELL
- GREAT CALVA
- KNOTT
- BLENCATHRA
- BANNERDALE CRAGS
- CLOUGH HEAD
- HIGH SEAT
- WATSON'S DODD
- GREAT DODD
- STYBARROW DODD
- HELVELLYN LOWER MAN
- HELVELLYN
- NETHERMOST PIKE
- ULLSCARF
- DOLLYWAGGON PIKE
- ST. SUNDAY CRAG
- SEAT SANDAL
- FAIRFIELD
- HART CRAG
- GREAT RIGG
- DOVE CRAG
- HIGH STREET
- HELM CRAG
- THORNTHWAITE CRAG
- RED SCREES
- HARTER FELL — E
- HERON PIKE
- ILL BELL
- BLEA RIGG
- SILVER HOW
- YOKE
- LOUGHRIGG FELL
- WANSFELL PIKE
- SALLOWS
- SOUR HOWES
- LINGMOOR FELL
- WETHERLAM
- S

Lakes and Tarns
- ESE: *Rydal Water*
- SE: *Windermere*
- SE: *Elterwater*
- SE: *Esthwaite Water*
- S: *Stickle Tarn*

Sergeant Man 11

RIDGE ROUTES

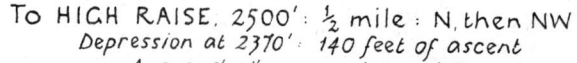

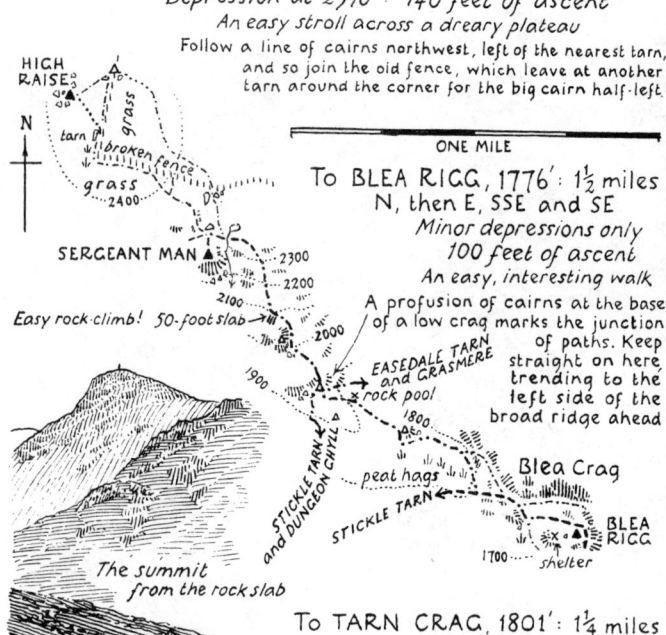

To HIGH RAISE, 2500': ½ mile: N, then NW
Depression at 2370': 140 feet of ascent
An easy stroll across a dreary plateau
Follow a line of cairns northwest, left of the nearest tarn, and so join the old fence, which leave at another tarn around the corner for the big cairn half-left.

ONE MILE

To BLEA RIGG, 1776': 1½ miles
N, then E, SSE and SE
Minor depressions only
100 feet of ascent
An easy, interesting walk
A profusion of cairns at the base of a low crag marks the junction of paths. Keep straight on here trending to the left side of the broad ridge ahead

The summit from the rock slab

To TARN CRAG, 1801': 1¼ miles
NE, then E
Slight depressions: 100 feet of ascent
An interesting test in route-finding

There is no path. The difficulty is to find the line of cairns leading away from the fence. The point occurs near two tarns *before* the prominent rocky peak is reached and the route descends alongside a runnel in the grass at first. The cairns are continuous to the end of the wide ridge, where the summit of Tarn Crag is near on the left.

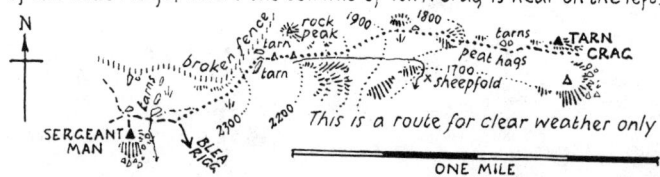

This is a route for clear weather only

ONE MILE

Sergeant Man 12

Belles Knott, the 'Matterhorn' of Easedale

This sharp peak is a prominent feature in the early stages of the walk by the path from Easedale Tarn to Dungeon Ghyll. Its shapeliness diminishes as the path is ascended, however, and the summit is finally seen to be approachable from behind by a simple grass promenade at a very easy gradient. Codale Tarn is nearby.

Sergeant's Crag 1873'

- Rosthwaite
- Stonethwaite
- ▲ EAGLE CRAG
- **SERGEANT'S CRAG**
- ▲ HIGH RAISE

MILES
0 1 2 3

from Eagle Crag

Sergeant's Crag 2

NATURAL FEATURES

The extensive north-western slopes of High Raise descend gradually and uneventfully at first, with nothing of interest to show; and then, after some hesitation, rise sharply to the walled summit of Sergeant's Crag before plunging precipitously, without further delay, to Langstrath far below. The change is sudden and the contrast complete, for High Raise is smooth and grassy for the most part, Sergeant's Crag is all rock and rough fell. The main crag, overlooking the valley, is a sheer wall of rock split by two gullies of which the more prominent is, or was before fashions changed, a favourite resort of climbers. The Langstrath slopes are very steep everywhere, and a tumble of fallen blocks obstructs easy passage of the popular path to Stake Pass along the base — one huge boulder in particular, Blea Rock, crowning a little rise, is a conspicuous landmark here.

Blackmoss Pot (or Blackmer Pot) Here Langstrath Beck forms a deep, silent pool in a rocky gorge, a picturesque scene, and one that should be visited by all who pass along the valley. The Pot cannot be seen from the path although quite near. It is located where the wall comes down the fellside to the beck and crosses it.

Blea Rock (also known as Gash Rock)

Sergeant's Crag 3

MAP

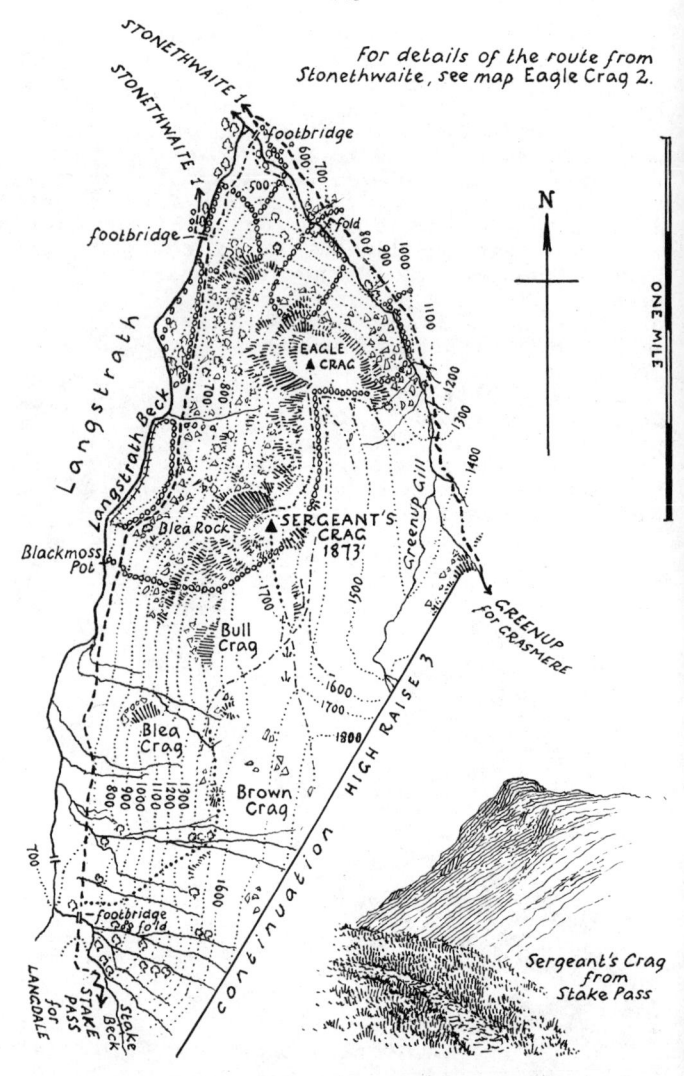

for details of the route from Stonethwaite, see map Eagle Crag 2.

ONE MILE

Sergeant's Crag from Stake Pass

Sergeant's Crag 4

ASCENT FROM STONETHWAITE
1600 feet of ascent
4½ miles by the route illustrated

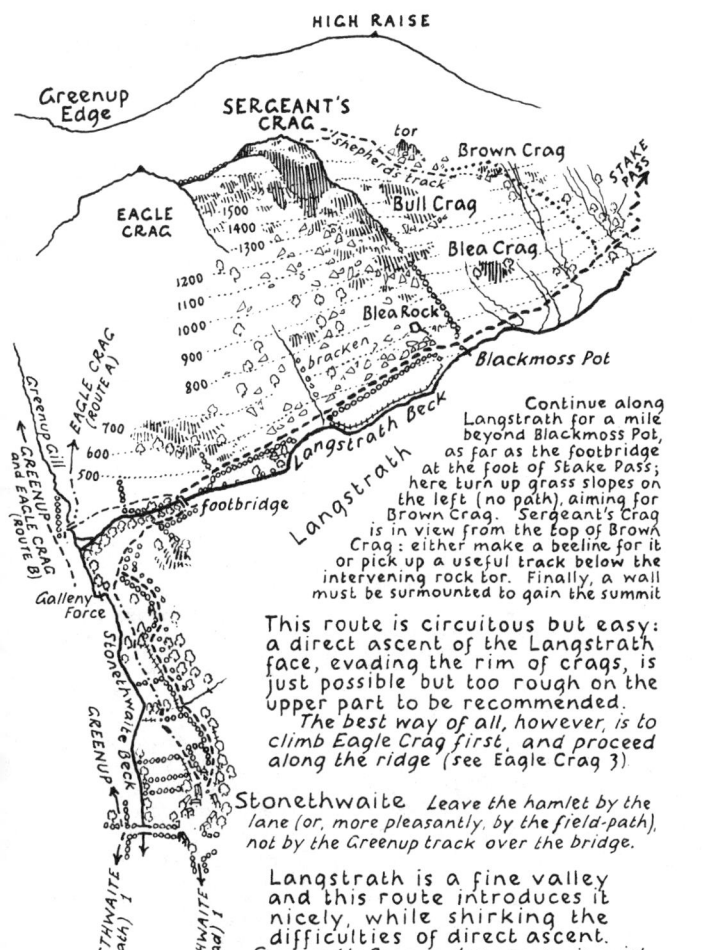

looking south-east

Continue along Langstrath for a mile beyond Blackmoss Pot, as far as the footbridge at the foot of Stake Pass; here turn up grass slopes on the left (no path), aiming for Brown Crag. Sergeant's Crag is in view from the top of Brown Crag: either make a beeline for it or pick up a useful track below the intervening rock tor. Finally, a wall must be surmounted to gain the summit

This route is circuitous but easy: a direct ascent of the Langstrath face, evading the rim of crags, is just possible but too rough on the upper part to be recommended.

The best way of all, however, is to climb Eagle Crag first, and proceed along the ridge (see Eagle Crag 3)

Stonethwaite *Leave the hamlet by the lane (or, more pleasantly, by the field-path), not by the Greenup track over the bridge.*

Langstrath is a fine valley and this route introduces it nicely, while shirking the difficulties of direct ascent. Sergeant's Crag is dangerous in mist.

Sergeant's Crag 5

THE SUMMIT

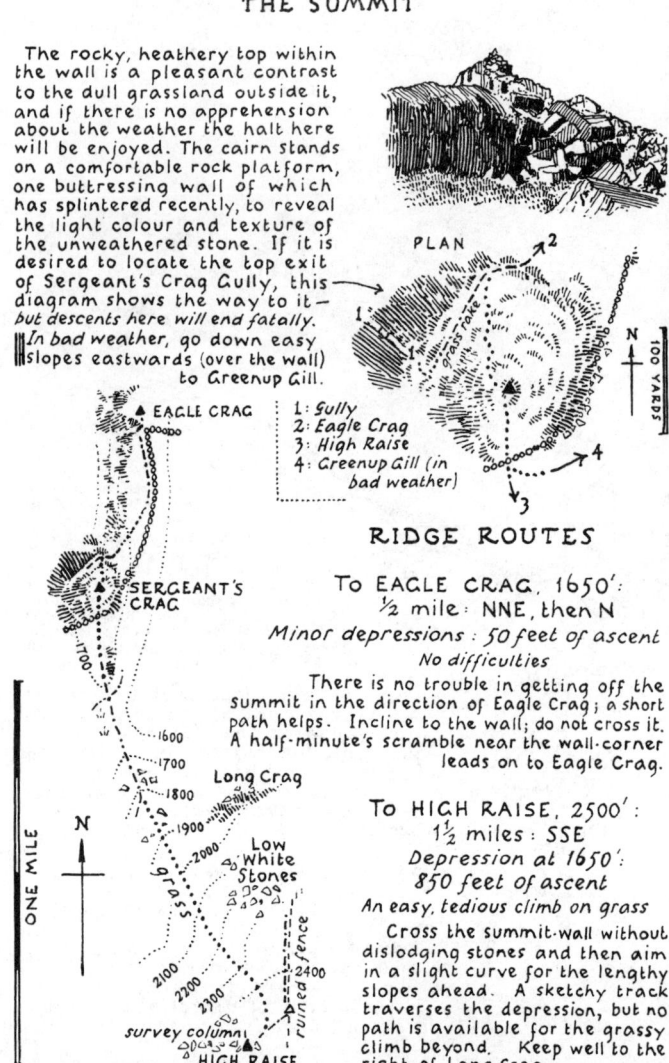

The rocky, heathery top within the wall is a pleasant contrast to the dull grassland outside it, and if there is no apprehension about the weather the halt here will be enjoyed. The cairn stands on a comfortable rock platform, one buttressing wall of which has splintered recently, to reveal the light colour and texture of the unweathered stone. If it is desired to locate the top exit of Sergeant's Crag Gully, this diagram shows the way to it — but descents here will end fatally. In bad weather, go down easy slopes eastwards (over the wall) to Greenup Gill.

PLAN

1: Gully
2: Eagle Crag
3: High Raise
4: Greenup Gill (in bad weather)

RIDGE ROUTES

To EAGLE CRAG, 1650':
½ mile : NNE, then N
Minor depressions : 50 feet of ascent
No difficulties

There is no trouble in getting off the summit in the direction of Eagle Crag; a short path helps. Incline to the wall; do not cross it. A half-minute's scramble near the wall-corner leads on to Eagle Crag.

To HIGH RAISE, 2500':
1½ miles : SSE
Depression at 1650':
850 feet of ascent
An easy, tedious climb on grass

Cross the summit-wall without dislodging stones and then aim in a slight curve for the lengthy slopes ahead. A sketchy track traverses the depression, but no path is available for the grassy climb beyond. Keep well to the right of Long Crag.

Sergeant's Crag 6

THE VIEW

There is a splendid prospect up Langstrath to Bowfell and Esk Pike. Nearer, High Raise and Ullscarf form a vast, high screen eastwards, displaying little of interest, but elsewhere the view is fairly good, with many familiar 'tops' peeping over Glaramara.

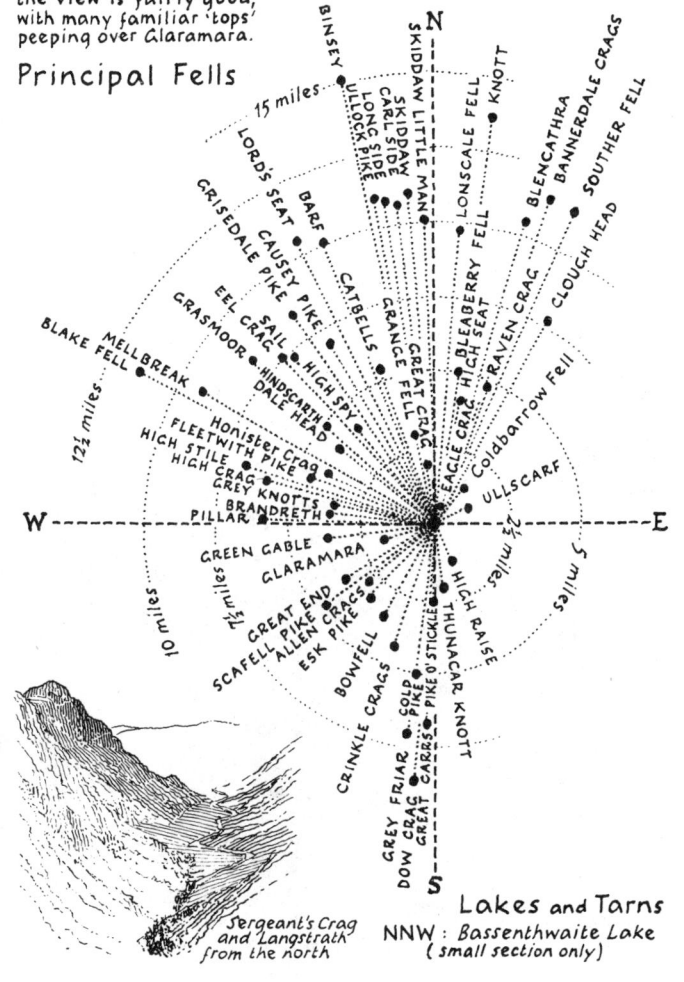

Principal Fells

(panoramic compass diagram showing fells around all points; 15 miles, 12½ miles, 10 miles, 7½ miles, 5 miles, 2½ miles range rings)

Fells labelled (clockwise from N):
BINSEY · SKIDDAW LITTLE MAN · SKIDDAW · CARL SIDE · LONG SIDE · ULLOCK PIKE · KNOTT · LONSCALE FELL · BLENCATHRA · BANNERDALE CRAGS · SOUTHER FELL · BLEABERRY FELL · HIGH SEAT · RAVEN CRAG · CLOUGH HEAD · EAGLE CRAG · COLDBARROW FELL · GREAT CRAG · GRANGE FELL · CATBELLS · HIGH SPY · DALE HEAD · HINDSCARTH · CAUSEY PIKE · EEL CRAG · SAIL · GRASMOOR · BARF · LORD'S SEAT · GRISEDALE PIKE · MELLBREAK · BLAKE FELL · HONISTER CRAG · FLEETWITH PIKE · HIGH STILE · HIGH CRAG · GREY KNOTTS · BRANDRETH · PILLAR · GREEN GABLE · GLARAMARA · ULLSCARF · HIGH RAISE · THUNACAR KNOTT · PIKE O'STICKLE · GREAT END · SCAFELL PIKE · ALLEN CRAGS · ESK PIKE · BOWFELL · CRINKLE CRAGS · GOLD PIKE · GREY FRIAR · DOW CRAG · GREAT CARRS

Sergeant's Crag and Langstrath from the north

Lakes and Tarns

NNW : Bassenthwaite Lake (small section only)

Silver How 1292'

'Silver Howe' on
Ordnance Survey maps

from Loughrigg Terrace

Grasmere •
SILVER HOW ▲
Chapel •   LOUGHRIGG
Stile   ▲ FELL
   Elterwater •

MILES
0   1   2   3   4

Silver How 2

NATURAL FEATURES

A lovely name for a lovely fell: Silver How is delightful. Not because the summit is remarkable, except for the view; the grassy top is, indeed, the least of its attractions. It is the rough slopes that delight the eye, especially on the Grasmere side, for the intermingling of crag and conifer, juniper and bracken, is landscape artistry at its best. A wealth of timber adorns the lower slopes and trees persist into the zone of crags fringing the summit. Fine waterfalls are another characteristic, though none is well known: Blindtarn Gill, Wray Gill, and Meg's Gill, the latter the best, all have spectacular cataracts.

Silver How is a prominent height on the wide and broken ridge that may be said to start with Loughrigg Fell and continue, dividing Langdale and Easedale, to High Raise, the highest point.

looking north-west

1: The summit
2: Ridge continuing to Loughrigg Fell
3: Red Bank
4: Spedding Crag
5: Raven Crag
6: Megs Gill
7: Wray Gill
8: Blindtarn Gill
9: Easedale
10: Great Langdale
11: Grasmere
12: River Rothay

Passes between Grasmere and Great Langdale:
A: via Megs Gill
B: via Hunting Stile
C: via Red Bank

Silver How 3

MAP

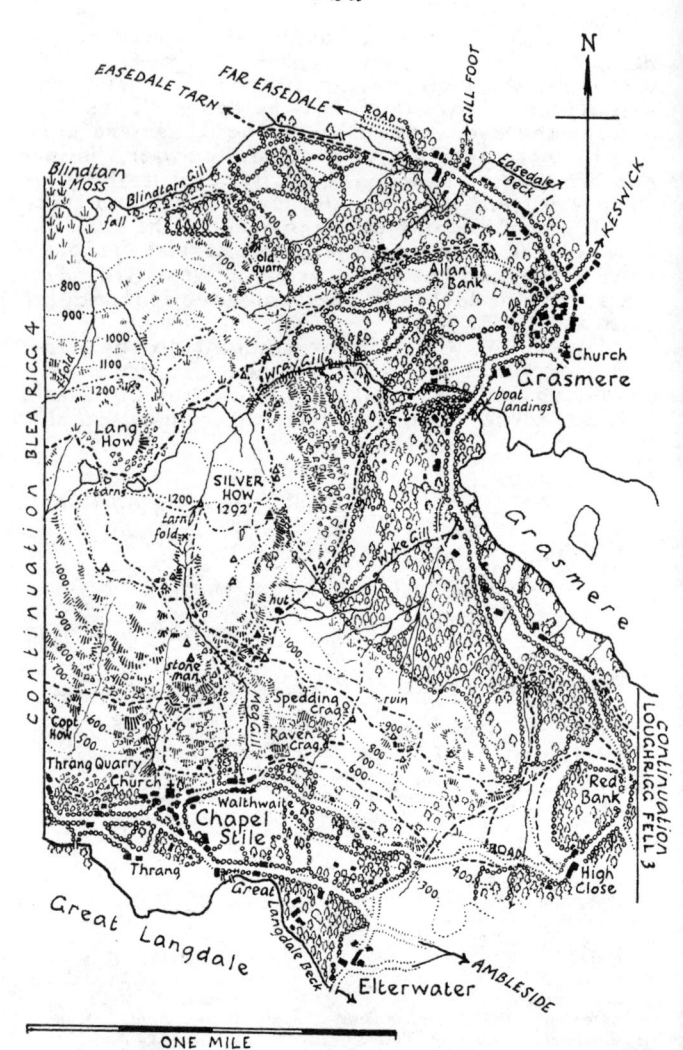

Silver How 4

ASCENT FROM GRASMERE
1100 feet of ascent : 1½ miles

Two routes are given, both supremely beautiful walks, with a rough variation by Wray Gill if desired. The views are charming. Alternatively, the summit may be reached from any of the ridge-passes to Langdale.

Silver How 5

ASCENT FROM ELTERWATER
1200 feet of ascent : 2¼ miles

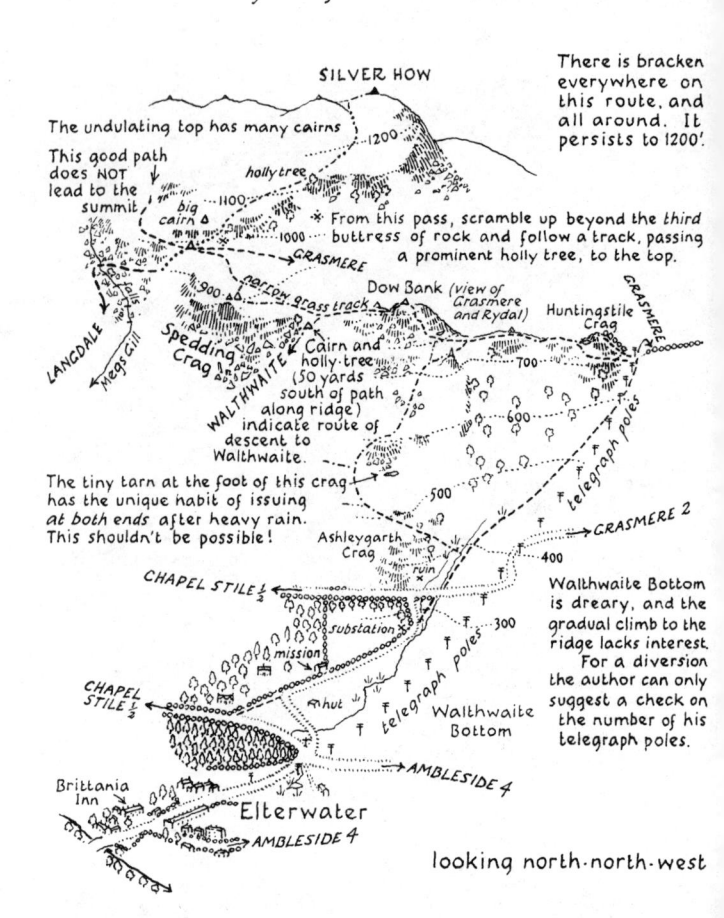

There is bracken everywhere on this route, and all around. It persists to 1200'.

SILVER HOW

The undulating top has many cairns — 1200

This good path does NOT lead to the summit

holly tree
big cairn
1100
1000
GRASMERE

From this pass, scramble up beyond the *third* buttress of rock and follow a track, passing a prominent holly tree, to the top.

narrow grass track

900
LANGDALE
Megs Gill

Dow Bank (view of Grasmere and Rydal)

Spedding Crag
WALTHWAITE
Cairn and holly tree (50 yards south of path along ridge) indicate route of descent to Walthwaite.

Huntingstile Crag
GRASMERE
700
600

The tiny tarn at the foot of this crag has the unique habit of issuing *at both ends* after heavy rain. This shouldn't be possible!

Ashleygarth Crag
ruin
500
telegraph poles
GRASMERE 2
400

CHAPEL STILE ½
substation
mission
300
telegraph poles

CHAPEL STILE ½
hut
Walthwaite Bottom

Walthwaite Bottom is dreary, and the gradual climb to the ridge lacks interest.
For a diversion the author can only suggest a check on the number of his telegraph poles.

Brittania Inn
Elterwater
AMBLESIDE 4
AMBLESIDE 4

looking north-north-west

After a dull start, interest quickens when the ridge is reached (at either of the points indicated) and the view opens out over Grasmere; thereafter the walk increases in beauty. Winter colourings are very good.

Silver How 6

ASCENT FROM CHAPEL STILE
1050 feet of ascent : 1¼ miles

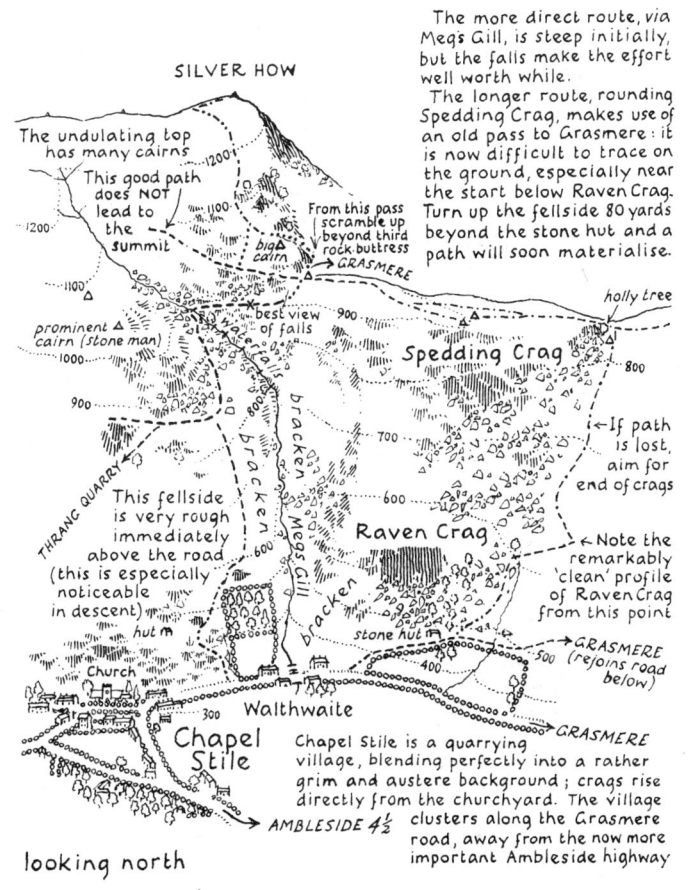

looking north

The more direct route, via Meg's Gill, is steep initially, but the falls make the effort well worth while.

The longer route, rounding Spedding Crag, makes use of an old pass to Grasmere: it is now difficult to trace on the ground, especially near the start below Raven Crag. Turn up the fellside 80 yards beyond the stone hut and a path will soon materialise.

Chapel Stile is a quarrying village, blending perfectly into a rather grim and austere background; crags rise directly from the churchyard. The village clusters along the Grasmere road, away from the now more important Ambleside highway.

Silver How displays its finest features to Grasmere and turns a comparatively dowdy back to Langdale; nevertheless the short climb is attractive and the views when the ridge is reached are very charming.

Silver How 7

THE SUMMIT

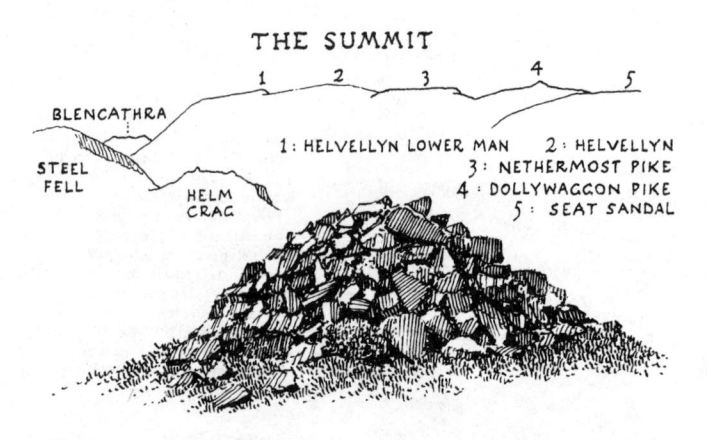

1: HELVELLYN LOWER MAN 2: HELVELLYN
3: NETHERMOST PIKE 4: DOLLYWAGGON PIKE
5: SEAT SANDAL

BLENCATHRA
STEEL FELL
HELM CRAG

The top of the fell is extensive and forms several rounded elevations, most of them cairned, but the actual summit is conspicuously situated above the steep Grasmere face. The paths across the top are little better than narrow sheep-tracks in the grass.

DESCENTS: Commence all descents from the small depression 100 yards west-south-west, turning right for Grasmere and left for Langdale via Meg's Gill. Do not attempt descents *directly* to Grasmere: a wall of crags lies below the summit on this side. *In mist the paths will not be easy to follow; if they are lost in the early stages keep on in the same direction and they will re-appear.*

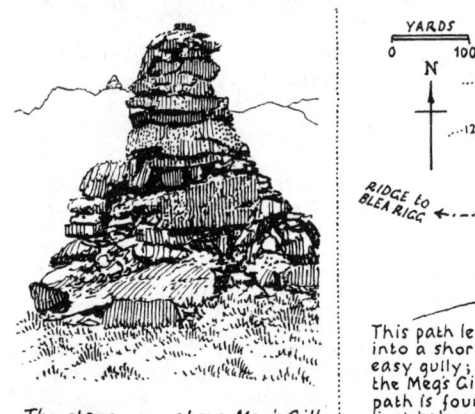

The stone man above Meg's Gill

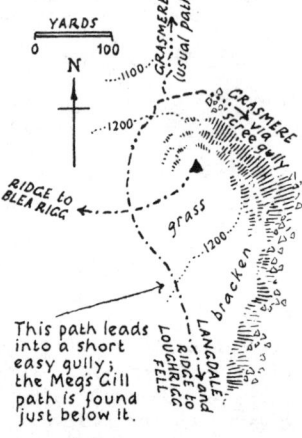

This path leads into a short easy gully; the Meg's Gill path is found just below it.

GRASMERE (usual path)
GRASMERE via the gully
RIDGE to BLEA RIGG
grass
bracken
LANGDALE
RIDGE to LOUGHRIGG FELL

Silver How 8

THE VIEW

The vale and village of Grasmere, seen in great detail, take pride of place in a very pleasing view, rich in lake scenery. There is good contrast between the sylvan beauty of the valleys of the Rothay and Brathay and the stark outline of the Coniston and Langdale fells.

This is probably as good a place as any for a newcomer to the district to appreciate its variety and unique charm.

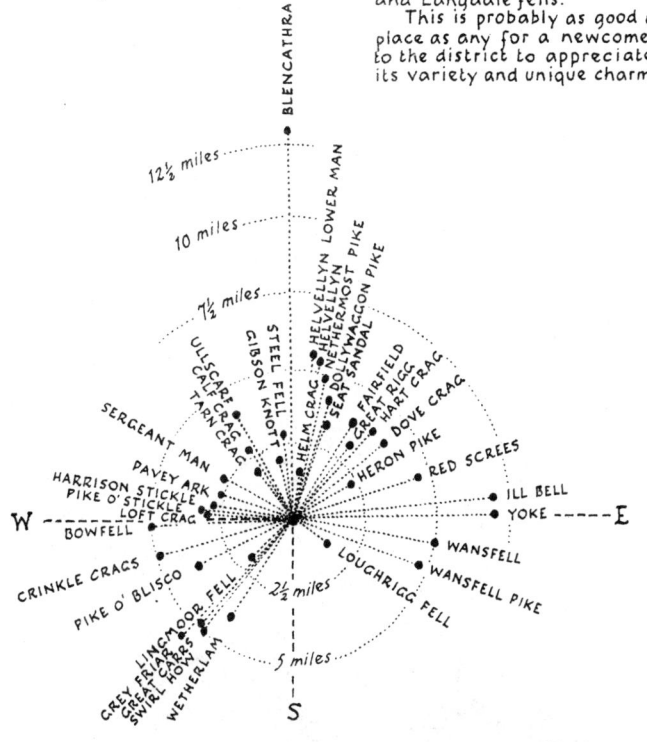

Principal Fells

N
- BLENCATHRA

12½ miles
10 miles
7½ miles

- HELVELLYN LOWER MAN
- HELVELLYN
- NETHERMOST PIKE
- DOLLYWAGGON PIKE
- SEAT SANDAL
- HELM CRAG
- STEEL FELL
- GIBSON KNOTT
- FAIRFIELD
- GREAT RIGG
- HART CRAG
- ULLSCARF
- CALF CRAG
- TARN CRAG
- DOVE CRAG
- SERGEANT MAN
- HERON PIKE
- PAVEY ARK
- RED SCREES
- HARRISON STICKLE
- PIKE O' STICKLE
- LOFT CRAG
- ILL BELL
- BOWFELL — YOKE — E
W —
- WANSFELL
- CRINKLE CRAGS
- WANSFELL PIKE
- PIKE O' BLISCO
- LOUGHRIGG FELL
- 2½ miles
- LINGMOOR FELL
- GREY FRIAR
- GREAT CARRS
- SWIRL HOW
- WETHERLAM
- 5 miles

S

Lakes and Tarns
- E : *Grasmere*
- E : *Rydal Water*
- SE : *Loughrigg Tarn*
- SE : *Windermere* (upper reach)
- S : *Coniston Water* (small part)

Walk 50 yards south of the cairn for a view of *Elterwater* (SSE)

Silver How 9

RIDGE ROUTE

To LOUGHRIGG FELL, 1101': 2½ miles
S, then ESE, E and SE
Several depressions; main one 475'
850 feet of ascent
A very beautiful and easy walk,
finishing with a steep climb

A branch path detours to two cairns on Spedding Crag, where there is a striking birds-eye view of Chapel Stile and Walthwaite

Dow Bank is the most prominent rise on the ridge

On merit, this should be a well-blazed route, for there are few more beautiful and interesting, but in fact for much of the way a narrow grass trod is the only guide. The views are delightful. Three passes between Grasmere and Langdale are crossed, the first the Meg's Gill route, the second the Hunting Stile route, and the well-known Red Bank road is the third. There should be no difficulty in mist.

Meg's Gill

Cairn on the ridge overlooking Elterwater

Silver How 10

RIDGE ROUTE

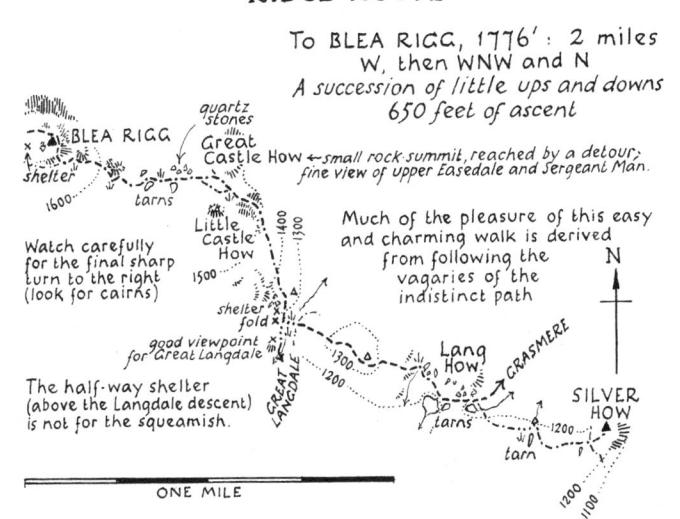

To BLEA RIGG, 1776': 2 miles
W, then WNW and N
A succession of little ups and downs
650 feet of ascent

BLEA RIGG
shelter
1600
tarns
quartz stones
Great Castle How ← *small rock summit, reached by a detour; fine view of upper Easedale and Sergeant Man.*
Little Castle How
1500
1400
1300
shelter
fold
good viewpoint for Great Langdale
GREAT LANGDALE
1200
1300
tarns
Lang How
GRASMERE
tarn
SILVER HOW
1200
1200
1100

Watch carefully for the final sharp turn to the right (look for cairns)

Much of the pleasure of this easy and charming walk is derived from following the vagaries of the indistinct path

N

The half-way shelter (above the Langdale descent) is not for the squeamish.

ONE MILE

Langdale Pikes from the tarns below Lang How

Steel Fell

1811'

from Helm Crag

Steel Fell 2

NATURAL FEATURES

Travellers north on the main road over Dunmail Raise are accompanied on the west side soon after leaving Town Head, Grasmere, by a rising ridge of high ground that culminates in a formidable wall of rough fell overlooking the pass itself and then falls abruptly to valley-level before Thirlmere is reached. This familiar height is Steel Fell. It stands on a triangular base, being bounded on the other two sides by the deep troughs of Greenburn and Wythburn,* which are separated by a ridge that forms Steel Fell's only high link with other fells. There is much craggy ground on all flanks. Moraines are in evidence on the easier southern slopes below Dunmail Raise and in the secluded valley of Greenburn, which has other interesting geographical features, also.

* The Scottish influence in the naming of *becks* as *burns* hereabouts is interesting. It occurs again on the west side of Ullswater in the naming of *dales* as *glens*, but rarely elsewhere in the district.

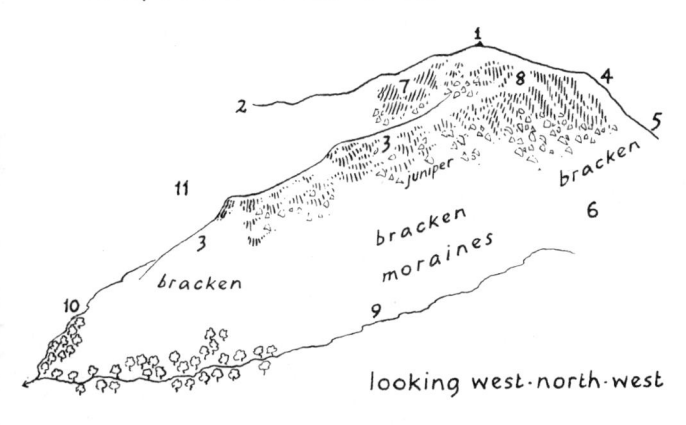

looking west·north·west

1 : The summit   2 : Ridge continuing to Calf Crag
3 : South-east ridge   4 : North ridge
5 : Steel End   6 : Dunmail Raise
7 : Blakerigg Crag   8 : Ash Crags
9 : Raise Beck   10 : Green Burn
            11 : The Greenburn Valley

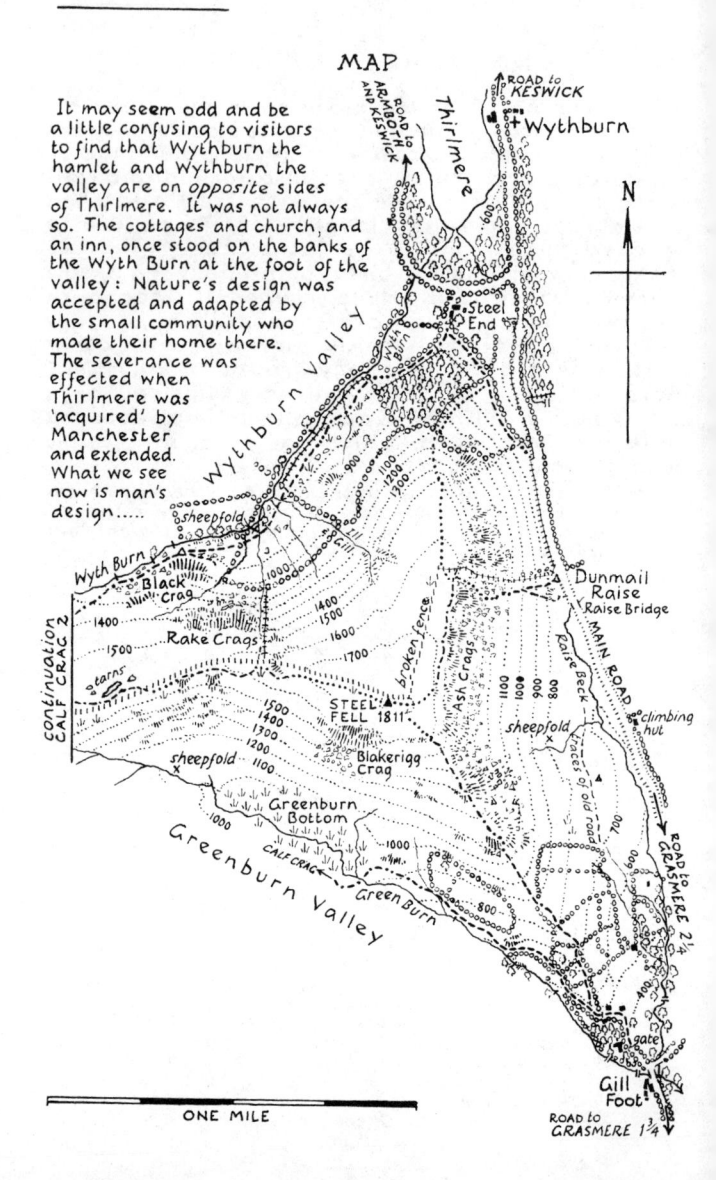

Steel Fell 3

MAP

It may seem odd and be a little confusing to visitors to find that Wythburn the hamlet and Wythburn the valley are on *opposite* sides of Thirlmere. It was not always so. The cottages and church, and an inn, once stood on the banks of the Wyth Burn at the foot of the valley: Nature's design was accepted and adapted by the small community who made their home there. The severance was effected when Thirlmere was 'acquired' by Manchester and extended. What we see now is man's design.....

ONE MILE

Steel Fell 4

ASCENT FROM GRASMERE
1650 feet of ascent : 3¼ miles from Grasmere Church

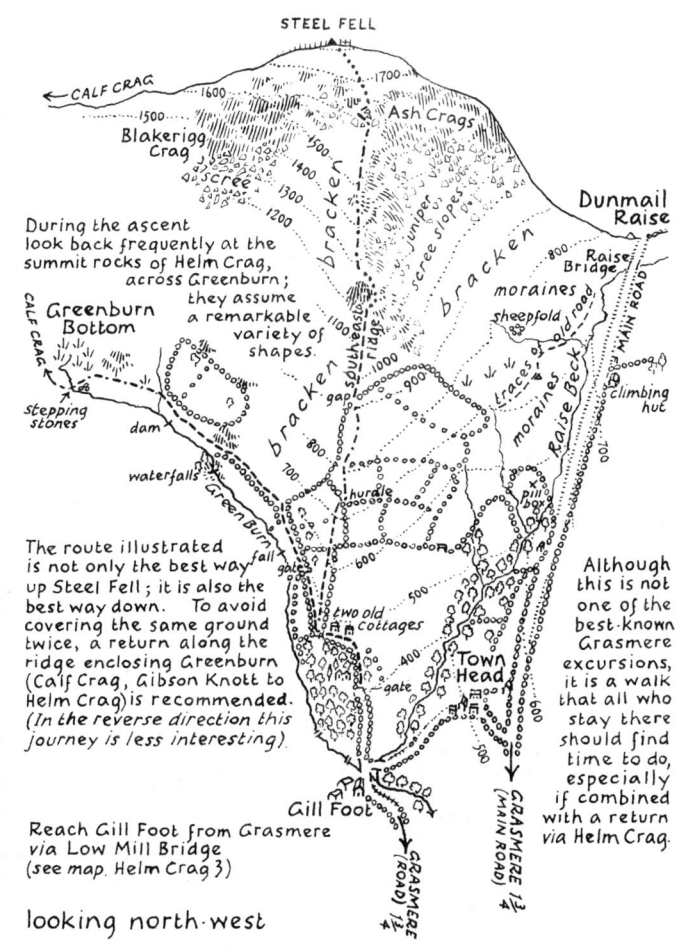

STEEL FELL

← CALF CRAG

Ash Crags

Blakerigg Crag

Dunmail Raise

Raise Bridge

During the ascent look back frequently at the summit rocks of Helm Crag, across Greenburn; they assume a remarkable variety of shapes.

Greenburn Bottom

CALF CRAG

stepping stones

dam

waterfalls

sheepfold

old road

Raise Beck

climbing hut

MAIN ROAD

The route illustrated is not only the best way up Steel Fell; it is also the best way down. To avoid covering the same ground twice, a return along the ridge enclosing Greenburn (Calf Crag, Gibson Knott to Helm Crag) is recommended. (In the reverse direction this journey is less interesting).

Reach Gill Foot from Grasmere via Low Mill Bridge (see map, Helm Crag 3)

hurdle

two old cottages

gate

Gill Foot

Town Head

Although this is not one of the best-known Grasmere excursions, it is a walk that all who stay there should find time to do, especially if combined with a return via Helm Crag.

GRASMERE (ROAD)

GRASMERE 1¼ (MAIN ROAD)

looking north-west

The approach is pleasant and the climbing along the mile of ascending ridge is very enjoyable, the slope being well-graded and of good dry turf.

Steel Fell 5

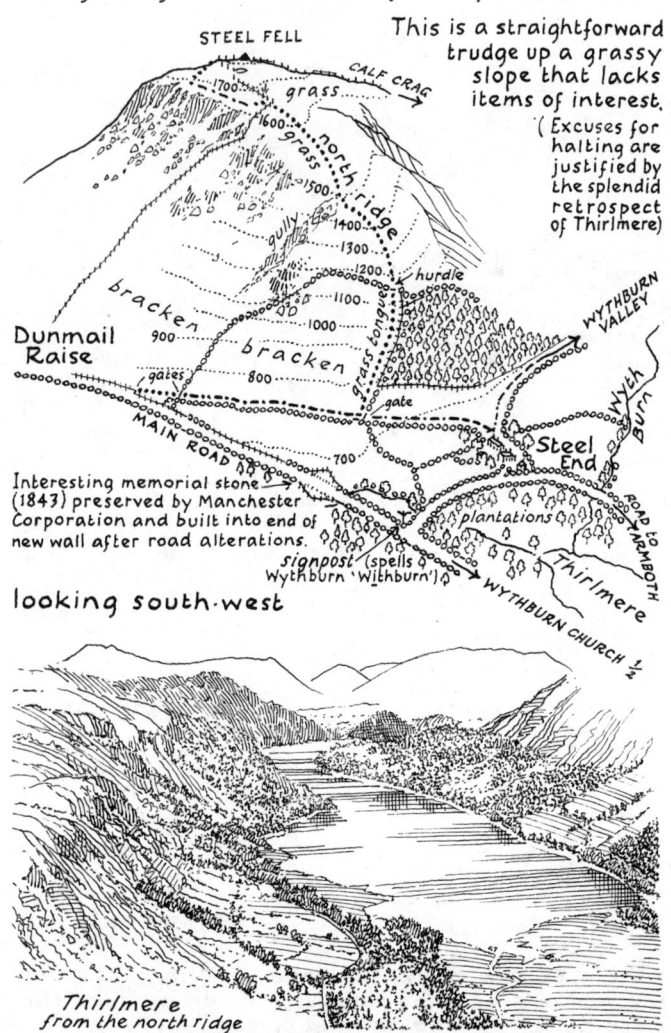

ASCENT FROM WYTHBURN
1250 feet of ascent : 2 miles from Wythburn Church

This is a straightforward trudge up a grassy slope that lacks items of interest.

(Excuses for halting are justified by the splendid retrospect of Thirlmere)

Interesting memorial stone (1843) preserved by Manchester Corporation and built into end of new wall after road alterations.

signpost (spells Wythburn 'Withburn')

looking south-west

Thirlmere from the north ridge

Steel Fell 6

ASCENT FROM DUNMAIL RAISE
1050 feet of ascent : 1 mile

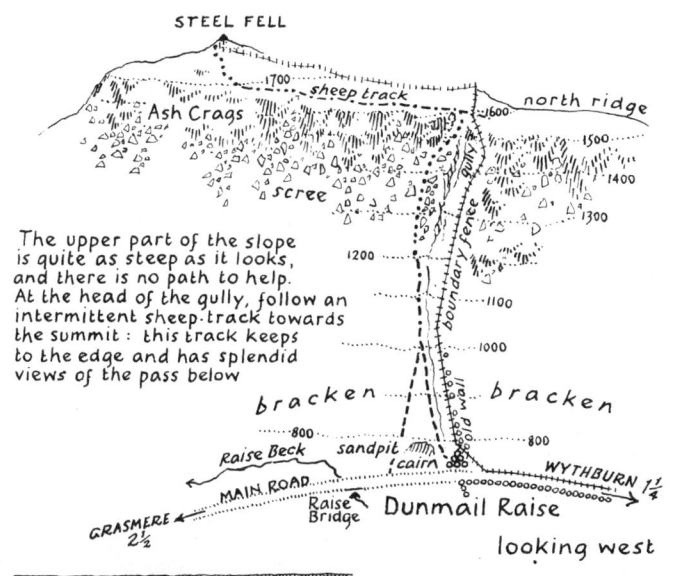

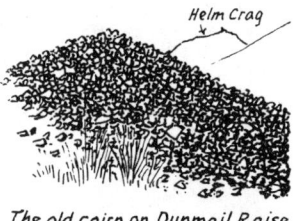

STEEL FELL
sheep track
1700
Ash Crags
1600 north ridge
1500
scree
1400
1300

The upper part of the slope
is quite as steep as it looks,
and there is no path to help.
At the head of the gully, follow an
intermittent sheep-track towards
the summit: this track keeps
to the edge and has splendid
views of the pass below

1200
boundary fence gully
1100
1000
bracken   bracken
800   800
Raise Beck   sandpit
cairn   WYTHBURN 1¼
MAIN ROAD
GRASMERE 2½   Raise Bridge   Dunmail Raise

looking west

The old cairn on Dunmail Raise
— reputed to mark the site
of burial of Dunmail, the last
king of Cumberland, 945 A.D.

Helm Crag

looking along Raise Beck to
Fairfield from the top of the
gully above Dunmail Raise.

Steel Fell 7

THE SUMMIT

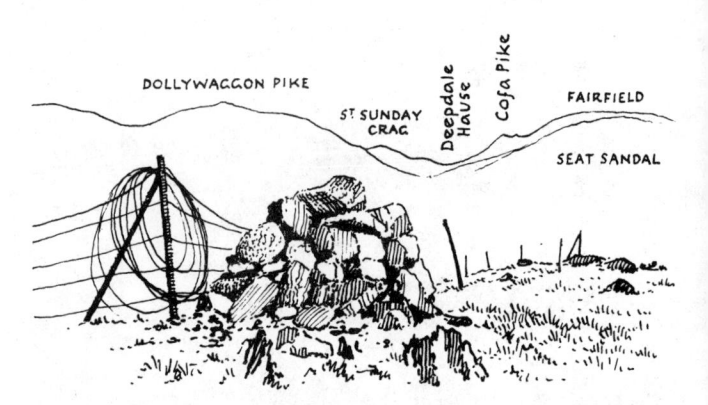

Panorama labels: DOLLYWAGGON PIKE, ST SUNDAY CRAG, Deepdale House, Cofa Pike, FAIRFIELD, SEAT SANDAL

A heap of heavy red stones forms a colourful cairn on the highest part of the fell alongside the County boundary fence, which is now in disrepair. Several small tarns lie around, like an untidy and unattractive necklace, in the depressions of the undulating top.

DESCENTS: For Grasmere direct, proceed in the direction of Heron Pike, south-east, until, from the brink of a steep edge, the south ridge is seen below; gain this by an old zig-zag path. For Wythburn, follow the fence, east turning north, for about half a mile, where it forms a right angle and goes down steeply to Dunmail Raise; a pleasanter way down is afforded by the grassy ridge *beyond* the right angle, descending to Steel End.

‖ *In mist*, it is well to bear in mind that the summit is ringed by crags, and that the fence is an infallible guide to the road at Dunmail Raise, where the only hazards are borne on wheels.

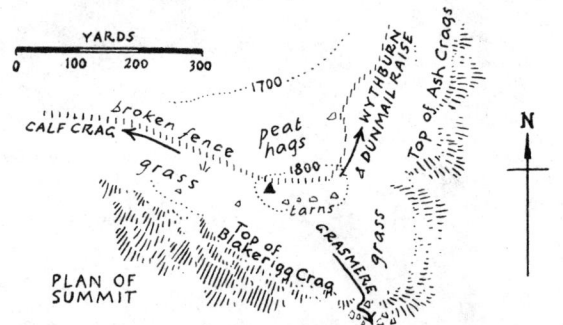

PLAN OF SUMMIT — labels: broken fence, CALF CRAG, 1700, peat hags, WYTHBURN & DUNMAIL RAISE, Top of Ask Crags, grass, 1800, tarns, Top of Blakerigg Crag, GRASMERE, grass. Scale: YARDS 0 100 200 300. N.

Steel Fell 8

THE VIEW

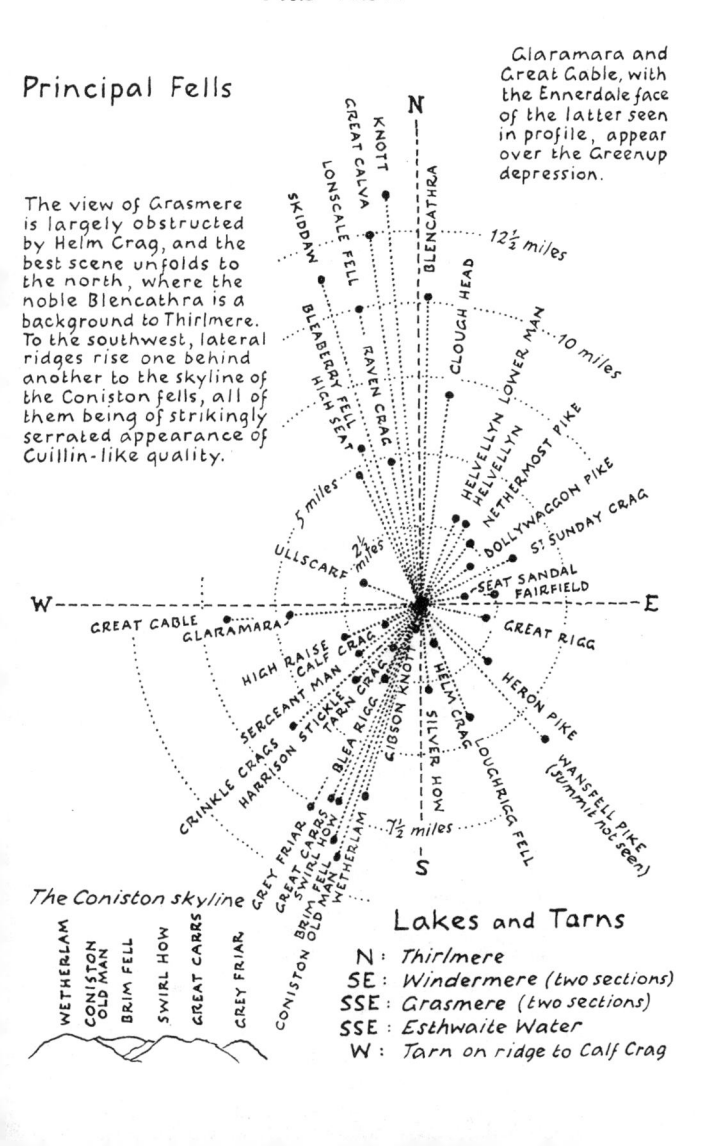

Principal Fells

The view of Grasmere is largely obstructed by Helm Crag, and the best scene unfolds to the north, where the noble Blencathra is a background to Thirlmere. To the southwest, lateral ridges rise one behind another to the skyline of the Coniston fells, all of them being of strikingly serrated appearance of Cuillin-like quality.

Glaramara and Great Gable, with the Ennerdale face of the latter seen in profile, appear over the Greenup depression.

Fells labelled on the panorama (clockwise from N): BLENCATHRA, KNOTT, GREAT CALVA, LONSCALE FELL, SKIDDAW, BLEABERRY FELL, RAVEN CRAG, HIGH SEAT, CLOUGH HEAD, HELVELLYN LOWER MAN, HELVELLYN, NETHERMOST PIKE, DOLLYWAGGON PIKE, ST SUNDAY CRAG, SEAT SANDAL, FAIRFIELD, GREAT RIGG, HERON PIKE, WANSFELL PIKE (summit not seen), LOUGHRIGG FELL, SILVER HOW, HELM CRAG, GIBSON KNOTT, TARN CRAG, BLEA RIGG, HARRISON STICKLE, SERGEANT MAN, CALF CRAG, HIGH RAISE, GLARAMARA, GREAT GABLE, ULLSCARF, CRINKLE CRAGS, GREY FRIAR, GREAT CARRS, SWIRL HOW, BRIM FELL, CONISTON OLD MAN, WETHERLAM.

Distance rings: 2½ miles, 5 miles, 7½ miles, 10 miles, 12½ miles.

The Coniston skyline

WETHERLAM — CONISTON OLD MAN — BRIM FELL — SWIRL HOW — GREAT CARRS — GREY FRIAR

Lakes and Tarns

N : Thirlmere
SE : Windermere (two sections)
SSE : Grasmere (two sections)
SSE : Esthwaite Water
W : Tarn on ridge to Calf Crag

Steel Fell 9

RIDGE ROUTE

To CALF CRAG, 1762': 1½ miles : WNW, then W curving S.
Main depression at 1535' : 300 feet of ascent
An easy walk, with fence as guide, but very marshy in places

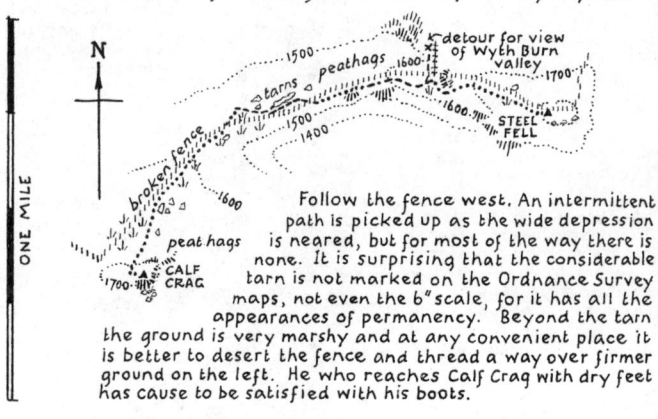

Follow the fence west. An intermittent path is picked up as the wide depression is neared, but for most of the way there is none. It is surprising that the considerable tarn is not marked on the Ordnance Survey maps, not even the 6" scale, for it has all the appearances of permanency. Beyond the tarn the ground is very marshy and at any convenient place it is better to desert the fence and thread a way over firmer ground on the left. He who reaches Calf Crag with dry feet has cause to be satisfied with his boots.

Nab Crags and the Wyth Burn valley
(from the viewpoint indicated on the map above)

Steel Fell 10

Waterfall in the Greenburn valley

The upper part of the south-east ridge

Tarn Crag

1801'

from Easedale Tarn

Tarn Crag 2

NATURAL FEATURES

Ever since it first became fashionable to make excursions to behold the scenic wonders of the English Lake District Easedale Tarn has been a popular venue for visitors: a romantic setting, inurned in bracken-clad moraines with a background of craggy fells, and easy accessibility from Grasmere, have combined to make this a favourite place of resort. The dominant feature in the rugged skyline around the head of the tarn is the arching curve of Tarn Crag, above a wild rocky slope that plunges very steeply to the dark waters at its base. But rough though this slope is, it at least has the benefit of sunlight to colour and illuminate the grimness, whereas the opposite flanks, facing north into Far Easedale, form a scene of unrelieved gloom, with the black forbidding precipices of Deer Bields and Fern Gill seeming to cast a permanent shadow across the valley: one vertical and fissured crag here has quite a reputation amongst rock-climbers.

Easedale Tarn is not the only jewel in Tarn Crag's lap. A smaller sheet of water, Codale Tarn, occupies a hollow on a higher shelf; beyond, indefinite slopes climb to the top of the parent fell, High Raise.

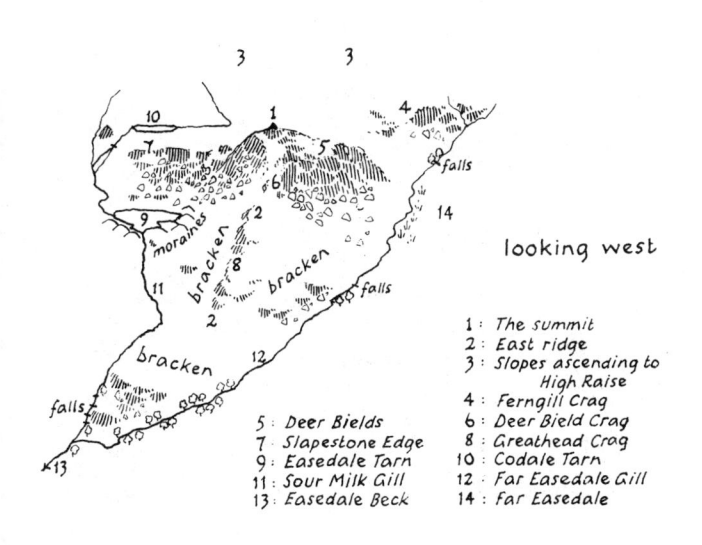

looking west

1 : The summit
2 : East ridge
3 : Slopes ascending to High Raise
4 : Ferngill Crag
5 : Deer Bields
6 : Deer Bield Crag
7 : Slapestone Edge
8 : Greathead Crag
9 : Easedale Tarn
10 : Codale Tarn
11 : Sour Milk Gill
12 : Far Easedale Gill
13 : Easedale Beck
14 : Far Easedale

Tarn Crag 3

Deer Bield Crag

Tarn Crag 4

MAP

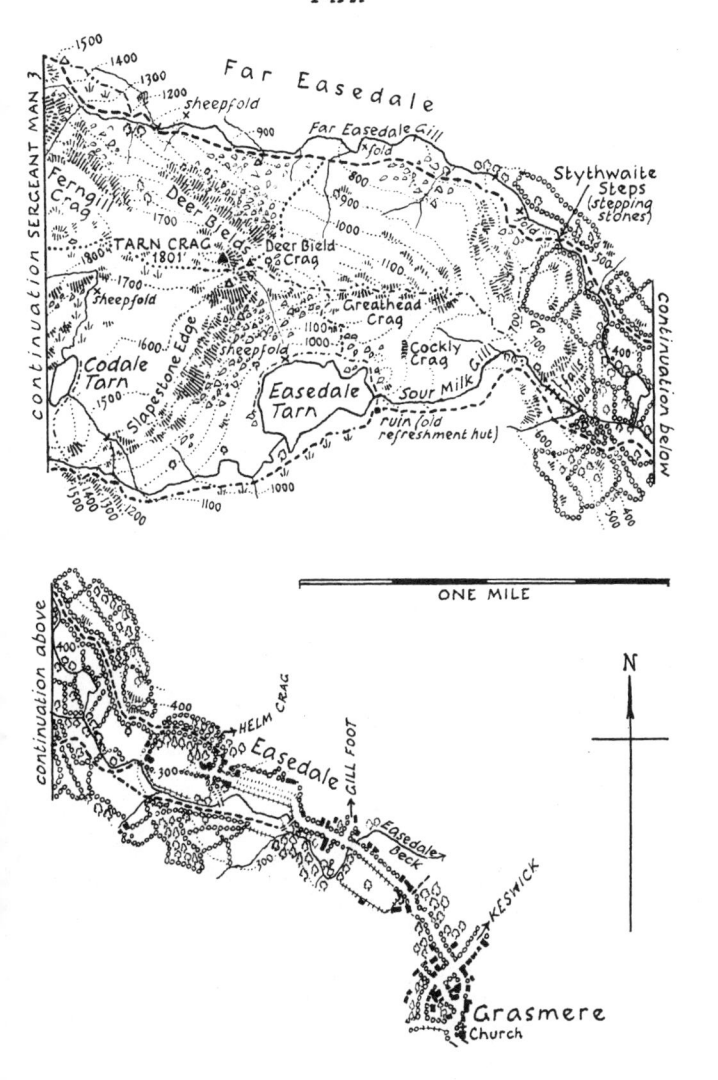

Tarn Crag 5

ASCENT FROM GRASMERE
via SOUR MILK GILL
1600 feet of ascent : 3 miles

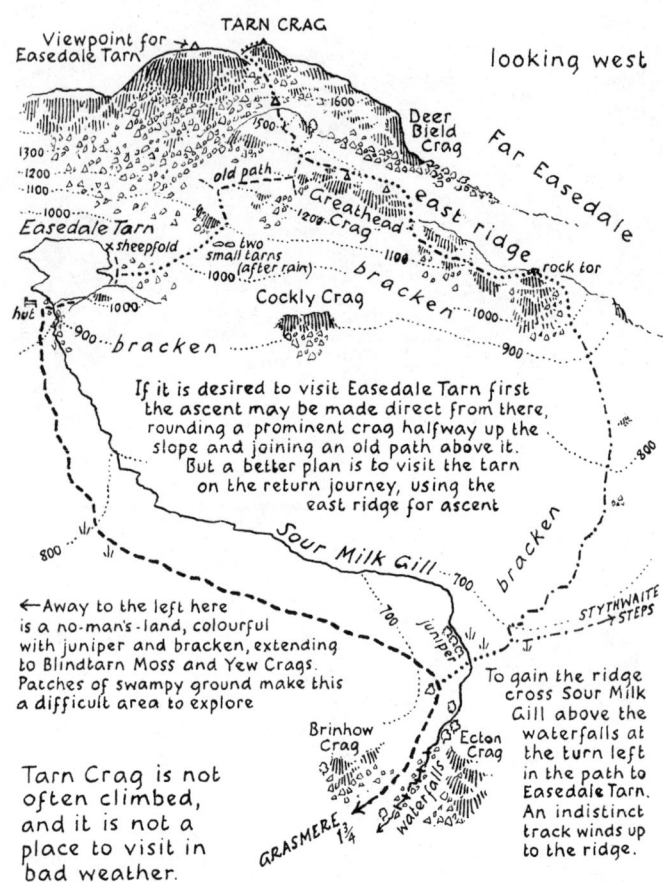

looking west

Labels on diagram: Viewpoint for Easedale Tarn, TARN CRAG, Deer Bield Crag, Far Easedale, east ridge, old path, Greathead Crag, Easedale Tarn, sheepfold, two small tarns (after rain), Cockly Crag, rock tor, bracken, hut, bracken, Sour Milk Gill, juniper, STYTHWAITE STEPS, Brinhow Crag, Ecton Crag, waterfalls, GRASMERE 1¾

If it is desired to visit Easedale Tarn first the ascent may be made direct from there, rounding a prominent crag halfway up the slope and joining an old path above it. But a better plan is to visit the tarn on the return journey, using the east ridge for ascent

←Away to the left here is a no-man's-land, colourful with juniper and bracken, extending to Blindtarn Moss and Yew Crags. Patches of swampy ground make this a difficult area to explore

To gain the ridge cross Sour Milk Gill above the waterfalls at the turn left in the path to Easedale Tarn. An indistinct track winds up to the ridge.

Tarn Crag is not often climbed, and it is not a place to visit in bad weather.
It is not blessed with paths, but an intermittent track follows the natural line of ascent, the east ridge. As the summit is approached it assumes a formidable appearance but is easily reached by a grassy rake.

Tarn Crag 6

ASCENT FROM GRASMERE
via STYTHWAITE STEPS
1650 feet of ascent : 3½ miles

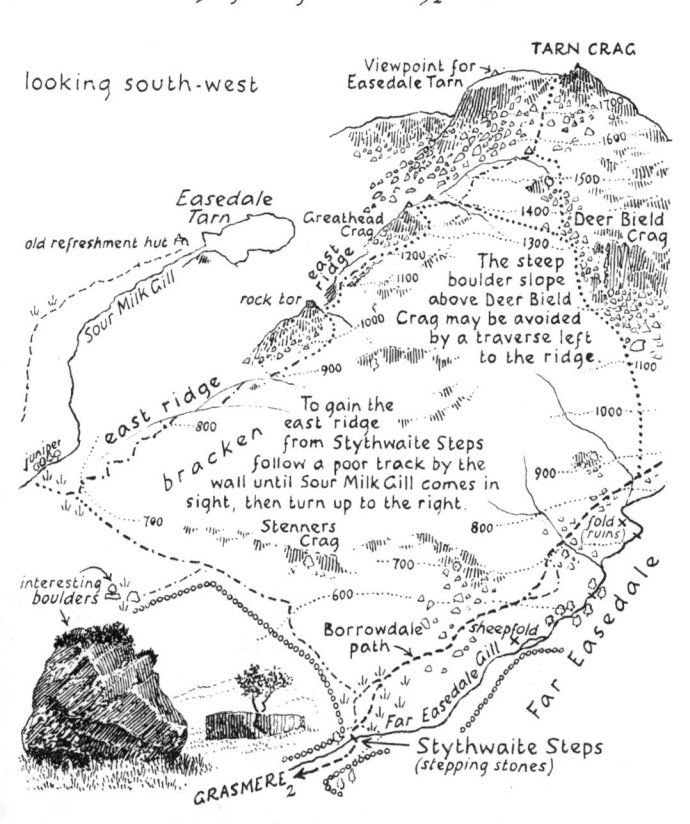

looking south-west

TARN CRAG
Viewpoint for Easedale Tarn
Easedale Tarn
old refreshment hut
Sour Milk Gill
Greathead Crag
east ridge
rock tor
Deer Bield Crag
The steep boulder slope above Deer Bield Crag may be avoided by a traverse left to the ridge.
juniper
east ridge
bracken
To gain the east ridge from Stythwaite Steps follow a poor track by the wall until Sour Milk Gill comes in sight, then turn up to the right.
Stenners Crag
fold (ruins)
interesting boulders
Borrowdale path
sheepfold
Far Easedale Gill
Far Easedale
Stythwaite Steps (stepping stones)
GRASMERE 2

This approach to the east ridge is rather less attractive than that via Sour Milk Gill, but thereafter the route is the same. Walkers who want to see Deer Bield Crag at close quarters should continue along Far Easedale for nearly a mile beyond the stepping stones; the base of the Crag is reached from here by an easy slope.

Tarn Crag 7

THE SUMMIT

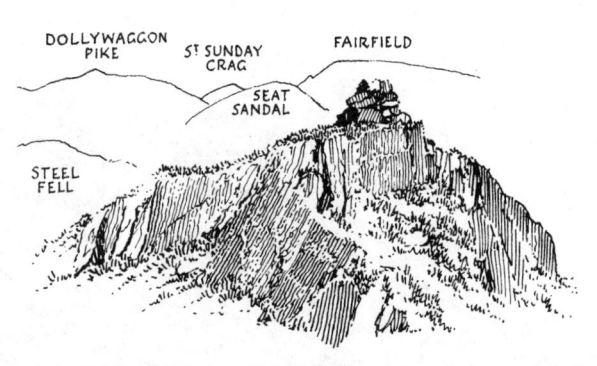

DOLLYWAGGON PIKE St SUNDAY CRAG FAIRFIELD
SEAT SANDAL
STEEL FELL

This is a beautiful little top, the highest point, a sharp peak, being just big enough to accommodate the neat cairn. Crags fall away steeply to east and south, but there are comfortable ledges from which the charming view of Grasmere may be surveyed in between searches for bilberries on the before-mentioned ledges which will probably prove fruitless. The broad summit of the fell is much broken by rocky outcrops and small tarns. The Ordnance Survey map is too generous with its 1800' contour, giving it a circumference of several hundred yards instead of a few feet, which is the maximum possible if in fact the highest point is 1801'.

DESCENTS: The only path on the fell (marked by cairns) traverses a grassy hollow 30 yards south of the cairn, and is the only way off. It goes down to the east ridge, for Grasmere. If it is desired to visit Easedale Tarn turn down to the right NOT at the foot of the first slope but 300 yards beyond at a grassy depression. From this depression Deer Bield Crag may be safely visited by turning left. Or it can be seen in profile merely by walking left 20 yards.

....

The summit crags
The cairn is reached, on grass, by rounding the pinnacle on the left

Tarn Crag 8

THE VIEW

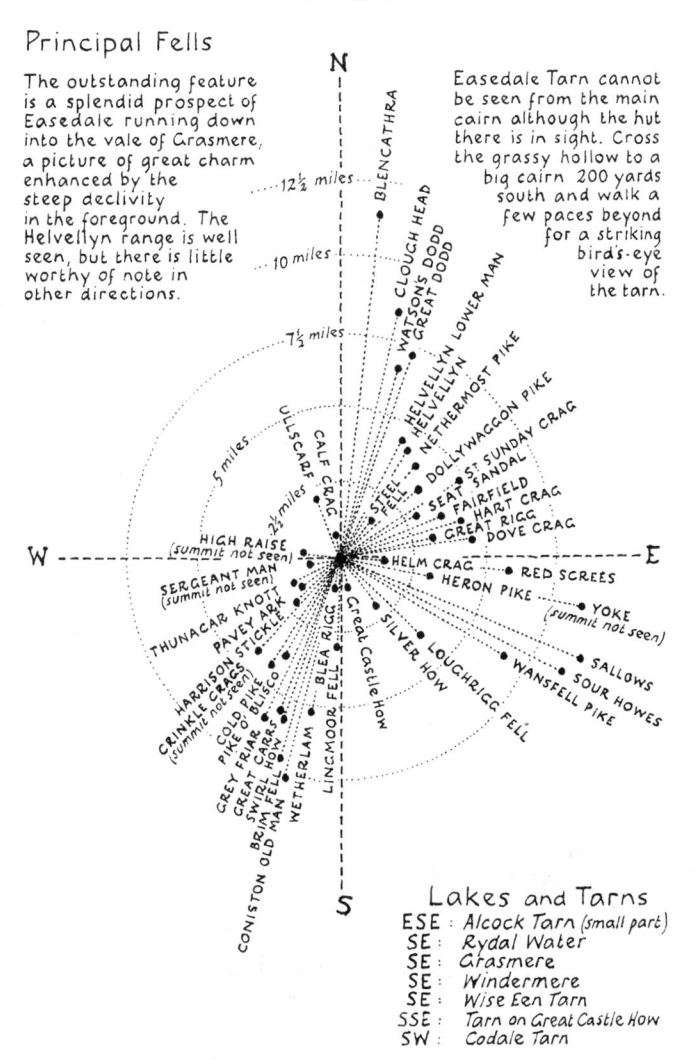

Principal Fells

The outstanding feature is a splendid prospect of Easedale running down into the vale of Grasmere, a picture of great charm enhanced by the steep declivity in the foreground. The Helvellyn range is well seen, but there is little worthy of note in other directions.

Easedale Tarn cannot be seen from the main cairn although the hut there is in sight. Cross the grassy hollow to a big cairn 200 yards south and walk a few paces beyond for a striking bird's-eye view of the tarn.

Lakes and Tarns

ESE : Alcock Tarn (small part)
SE : Rydal Water
SE : Grasmere
SE : Windermere
SE : Wise Een Tarn
SSE : Tarn on Great Castle How
SW : Codale Tarn

Tarn Crag 9

RIDGE ROUTE

To SERGEANT MAN, 2414': 1¼ miles: W, then SW.
Slight depressions only : 700 feet of ascent
An interesting test in route-finding

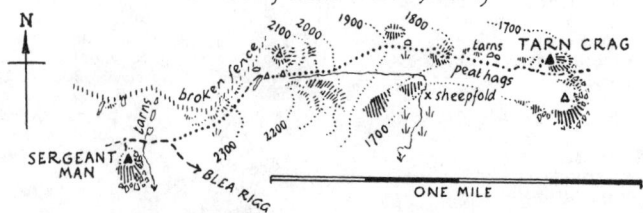

There is no path. A continuous line of small cairns traces out an easy route across rough country, and is interesting to follow. A grassy watercourse (distinctly seen from Tarn Crag) leads up to the boundary fence, but it is easier to turn left 100 yards short of the fence (after crossing a narrow tarn by stepping stones) and proceed south-west; the abrupt peak of Sergeant Man soon comes in view for the first time during the walk. Although there is nothing exciting about this route (there is little semblance of a ridge) the colourful slopes of heather, bilberry and mosses, intermingled with grey rocks, make it pleasant. *This walk is not recommended in mist: the cairns are too widely spaced to follow in poor visibility, and there are crags on all sides.*

Tarn Crag and its east ridge from Easedale

Tarn Crag 10

Sour Milk Gill

Thunacar Knott 2351'

from Harrison Stickle

From north and south and east and west, Thunacar Knott is completely unphotogenic, and the best that any illustration can produce is a slight roughness of the slowly-swelling curve that forms its broad summit. This uninspiring characteristic extends to the whole fell, which is quite deficient in interest (if, as has already been decided for the purposes of this book, Pavey Ark is not regarded as a part of it, although it really is). Grey stones on the summit and spilling in patches down the easy slopes to Langstrath, do little to relieve the drab monotony of spacious sheep-walks. When fixing the county boundaries between Cumberland and Westmorland the surveyors decided that the demarcation should make a sharp angle on the top — which is probably the most exciting thing that ever happened to Thunacar Knott.

The upper valley of Stake Beck, draining the western slopes in a dreary landscape of moraines, may yet bring a belated fame to the fell, for preliminary searches here suggest it as a likely area of activity by neolithic man.

HIGH RAISE
▲
THUNACAR ▲ KNOTT
HARRISON ▲ STICKLE

Old Hotel ●   ● New Hotel
Dungeon Ghyll

MILES
0 1 2 3

Thunacar Knott 2

MAP

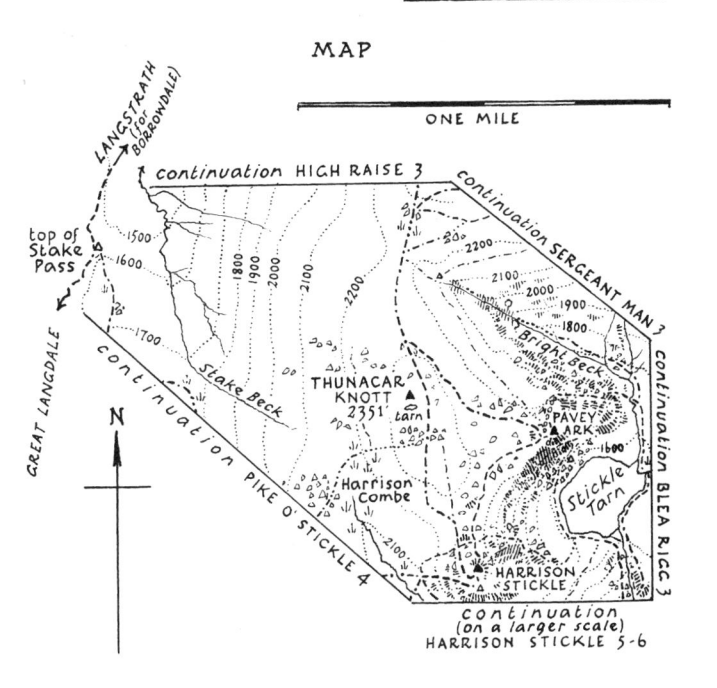

ASCENT FROM DUNGEON GHYLL

Thunacar Knott is not popularly known by name, and is the one unattractive summit in a distinguished Langdale company. It is inconceivable, therefore, that anyone should set forth with the sole object of scaling this particular fell and no others *en route*, but such an eccentric person may exist, and must be provided with directions, although little space can be spared for notes that are not likely to be read. The direct ascent, if made at all, will be made from Dungeon Ghyll.

Refer to the diagrams of ascent for Harrison Stickle, and use Routes 1, 2 or 3, but beyond Thorn Crag and after starting the final rise to the top, watch for a line of small cairns rising to the left: these lead to a depression on the ridge north of the rock tor and here the ridge-path is met and may be traced, with a little difficulty at first, to Thunacar Knott

Thunacar Knott 3

THE SUMMIT

The fell has two tops, with a tarn occupying the slight depression between. The recognised summit, surmounted by a well-made cairn, is a mound north of the tarn (which has interesting amphibious plant growth); the benchmark height is 2351'. A furlong south, however, the ground gradually rises to 2362' in an area of attractive grey stones. The ridge path crosses the higher top and passes 60 yards east of the main cairn.

DESCENTS: For Great Langdale, if it is not desired to visit the summit of Harrison Stickle en route, turn off the path thereto, following a line of cairns leading to the right from the depression between the two fells: this by-passes the Stickle, avoiding further climbing, and soon joins the regular path going down to Dungeon Ghyll. For Langstrath, the easy western slopes may be descended anywhere, with safety, in any sort of weather; aim north of west, crossing Stake Beck to join the Stake Pass path.

*The main summit from point 2362'
with High Raise beyond*

Thunacar Knott 4

RIDGE ROUTES

To HIGH RAISE, 2500': 1 mile: N
Depression at 2225': 275 feet of ascent

An easy walk, interesting only for the view
The path will be found 60 yards east of the cairn. It is not quite continuous, being lost for a short distance in marshy ground across the depression; otherwise it is distinct and direct, and mainly on grass. In mist, ignore branches turning off to the right.

To SERGEANT MAN, 2414':
1 mile: N, then E
Depression at 2225'
200 feet of ascent

An easy walk, with a good finish
Take the High Raise path, leaving it NOT at the first track going off to the right at the depression (this goes only to a cluster of grey rocks, amongst which is a good wind-shelter) but, further, at a scatter of boulders, where alternative tracks branch off to the right, both being continuous to the dome-shaped top of Sergeant Man. This is strictly not a ridge-walk but a skirting of the valley containing Bright Beck.

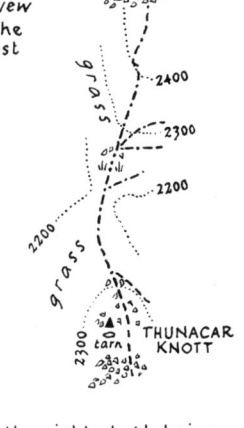

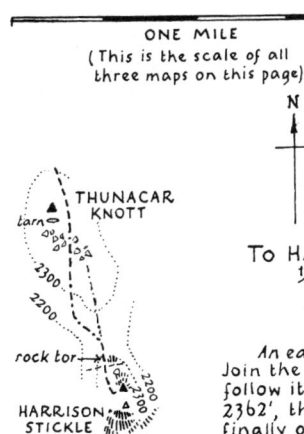

ONE MILE
(This is the scale of all three maps on this page)

To HARRISON STICKLE, 2403':
½ mile: S, then SSE
Depression at 2225'
150 feet of ascent

An easy walk, in improving scenery
Join the path 60 yards east of the cairn and follow it south, ascending slightly over point 2362', then down a grass slope before rising finally over rougher terrain to the top.

Thunacar Knott 5

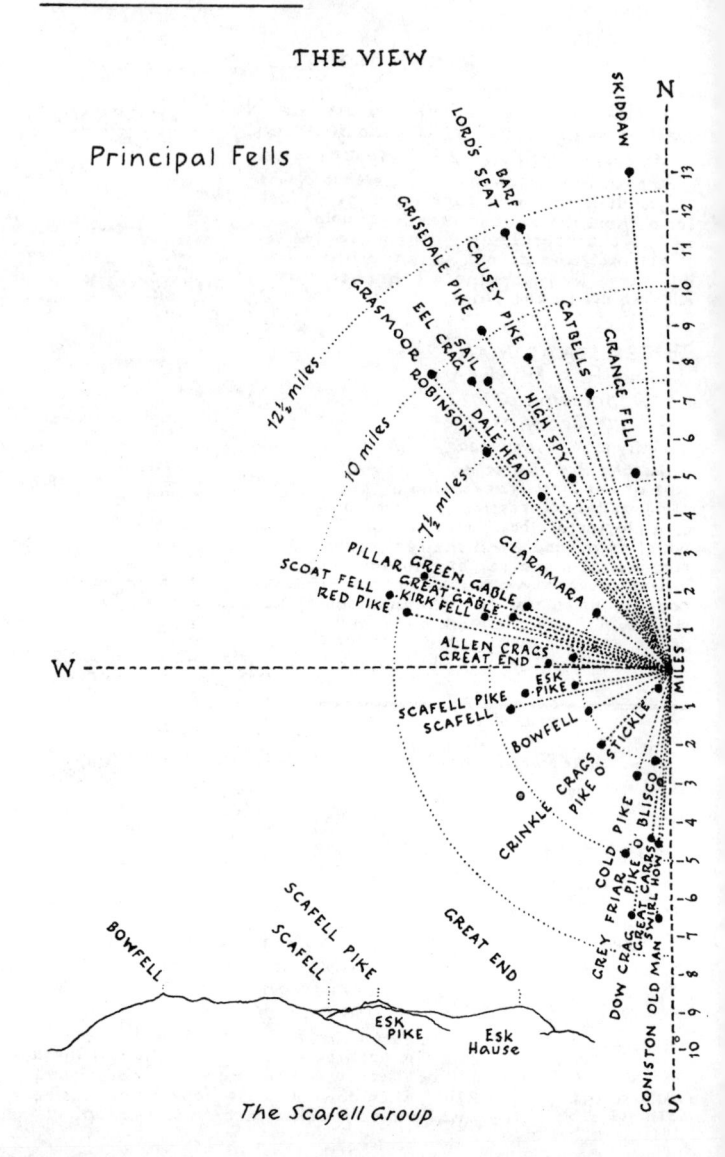

THE VIEW

Principal Fells

The Scafell Group

Thunacar Knott 6

THE VIEW

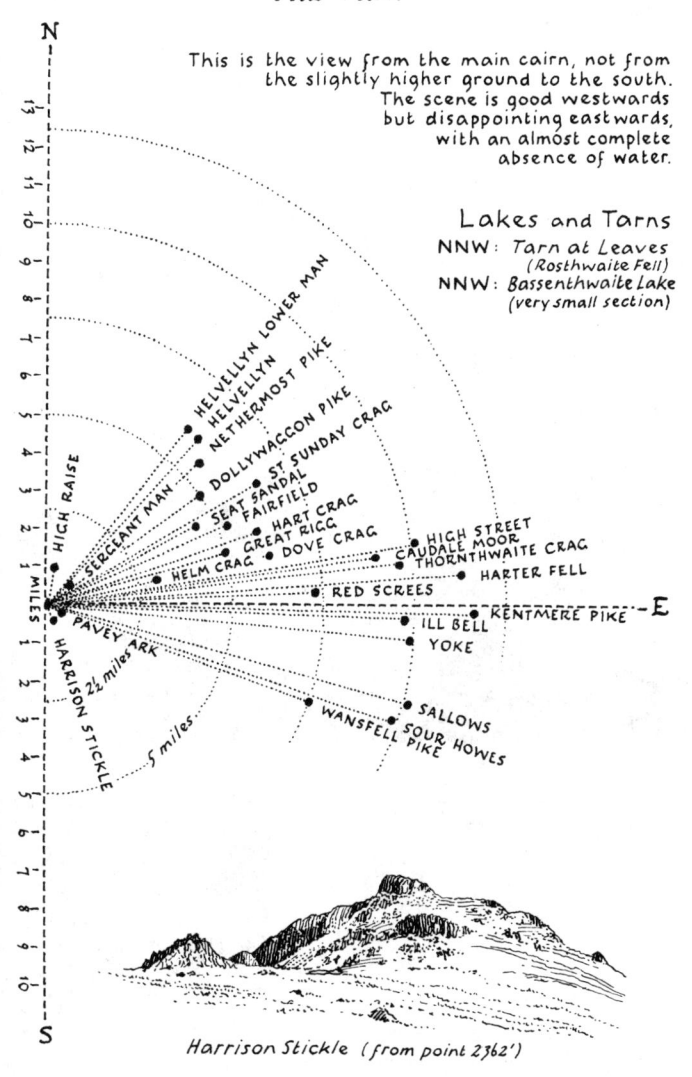

This is the view from the main cairn, not from the slightly higher ground to the south. The scene is good westwards but disappointing eastwards, with an almost complete absence of water.

Lakes and Tarns
NNW: Tarn at Leaves (Rosthwaite Fell)
NNW: Bassenthwaite Lake (very small section)

Helvellyn Lower Man
Helvellyn
Nethermost Pike
Dollywaggon Pike
St Sunday Crag
Seat Sandal
Fairfield
Hart Crag
Great Rigg
Helm Crag
Dove Crag
High Street
Caudale Moor
Thornthwaite Crag
Harter Fell
High Raise
Sergeant Man
Red Screes
Kentmere Pike
Pavey Ark
Ill Bell
Yoke
Harrison Stickle
Sallows
Sour Howes
Wansfell Pike

2½ miles
5 miles

Harrison Stickle (from point 2362')

Ullscarf 2370'

*from Great Crag
Watendlath Fell*

*Binka Stone
near Dobgill Bridge*

Ullscarf 2

NATURAL FEATURES

Ullscarf rises from the surrounding valleys so steeply and with such a display of fierce crags that, up to 2,000 feet, it has all the makings of a great mountain. These crags defend the fell on most flanks, and there are few breaches in its seven-mile circumference of which walkers may take advantage to gain the summit without becoming involved in desperate scrambling. But unfortunately the higher slopes do not live up to the promise of the lower, being, in fact, quite featureless and inexpressibly dreary, with grass pastures swelling in easy gradients to the cairn marking the highest part of the summit plateau. Were it not for an old fence that crosses the top this would be a very bad place in mist for there are no natural landmarks to serve as guides and the wide and indefinite ridge changes direction repeatedly.

The crags are most in evidence above Thirlmere where they extend along the Wythburn valley and round into the wooded basin of Harrop Tarn, while others decorate the edge overlooking Greenup Gill. On the north side above Bleatarn Gill and near the Greenup pass they are absent and access is simple.

The main streams, Wyth Burn, Ullscarf Gill and Dob Gill, feed Thirlmere; Bleatarn Gill sets a course for Derwentwater, which it enters at Lodore; and a number of tributaries of Greenup Gill have carved ravines in the western face.

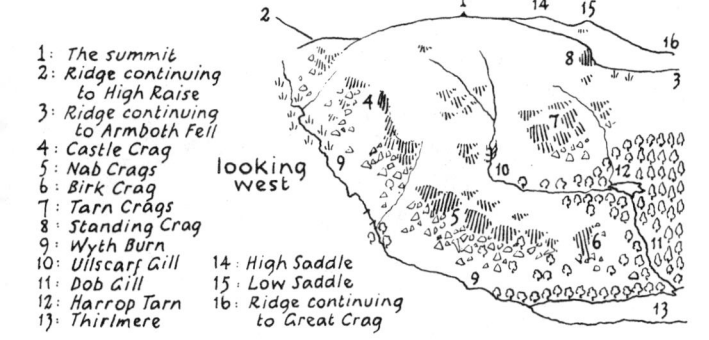

looking west

1: The summit
2: Ridge continuing to High Raise
3: Ridge continuing to Armboth Fell
4: Castle Crag
5: Nab Crags
6: Birk Crag
7: Tarn Crags
8: Standing Crag
9: Wyth Burn
10: Ullscarf Gill
11: Dob Gill
12: Harrop Tarn
13: Thirlmere
14: High Saddle
15: Low Saddle
16: Ridge continuing to Great Crag

Ullscarf 3

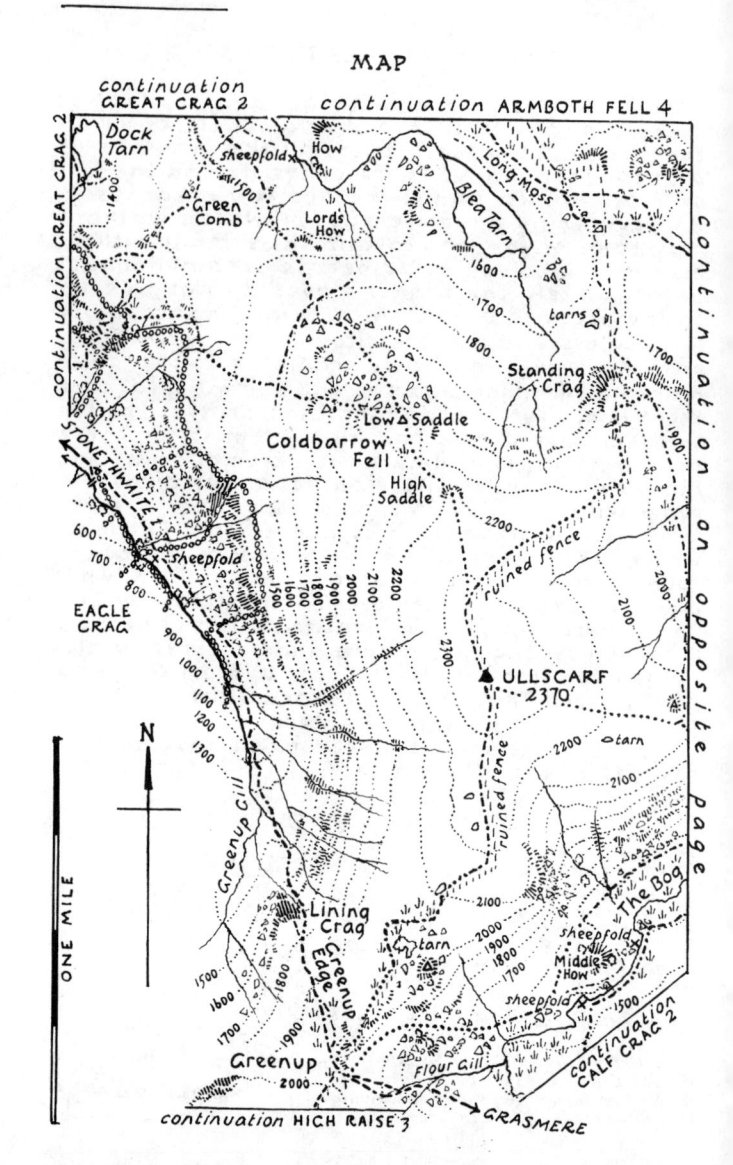

MAP

… Ullscarf 4

MAP

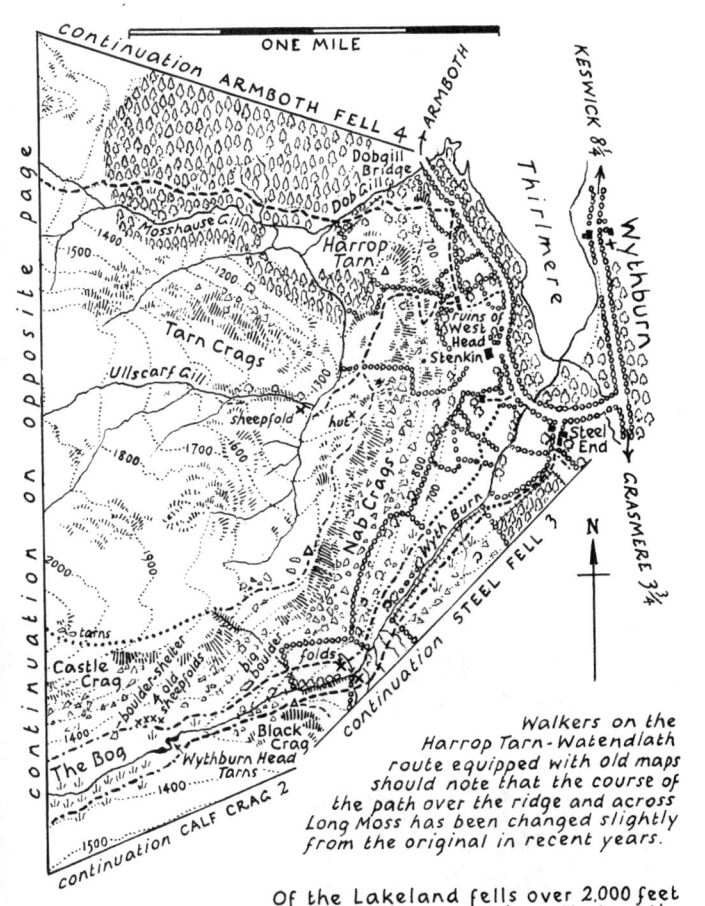

Walkers on the Harrop Tarn-Watendlath route equipped with old maps should note that the course of the path over the ridge and across Long Moss has been changed slightly from the original in recent years.

Of the Lakeland fells over 2,000 feet Ullscarf will generally be adjudged the most central, and it is a pity that Nature has not endowed it with a distinctive superstructure worthy of the honour. If only the crags extended a thousand feet higher, and if only the summit took the shape of a Matterhorn!   Instead of which, the top of the fell is the dullest imaginable. The most central, perhaps, but not, alas, a very distinguished pivot!

Ullscarf 5

The Wythburn Valley

a study in desolation

top
The Bog

middle
Wythburn Head Tarns

bottom
the highest waterfall

Ullscarf 6

ASCENT FROM WYTHBURN
1800 feet of ascent: 3½ miles (via West Head)

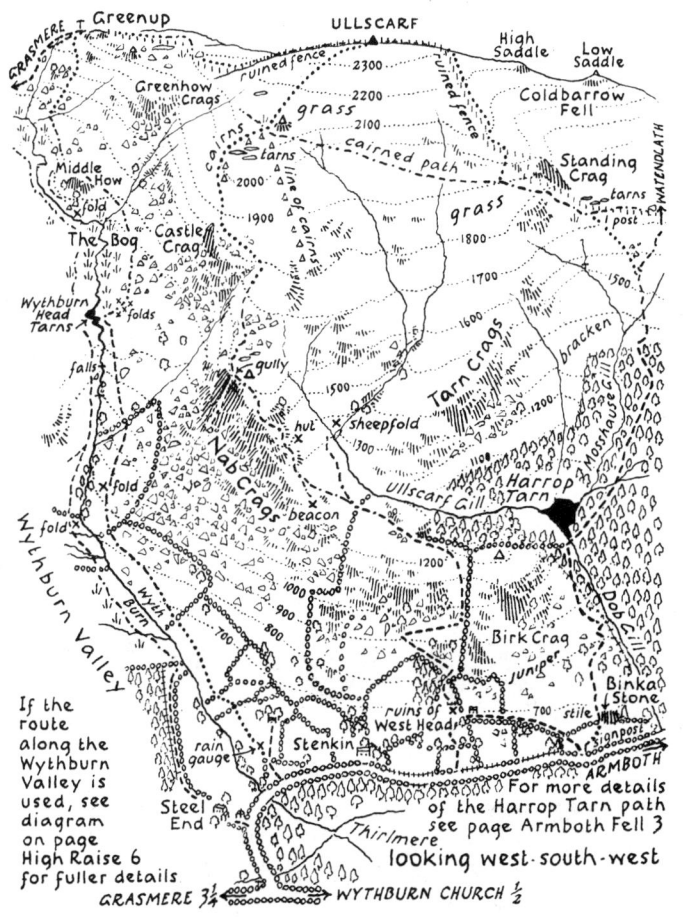

The middle route, from West Head Farm (demolished) and along the ridge overlooking the Wythburn valley, is the best in clear weather, but the ascent, although free from difficulty, should not be under-estimated: the upper slopes are pathless, unfrequented and vast, and route-selection is not too easy.

Ullscarf 7

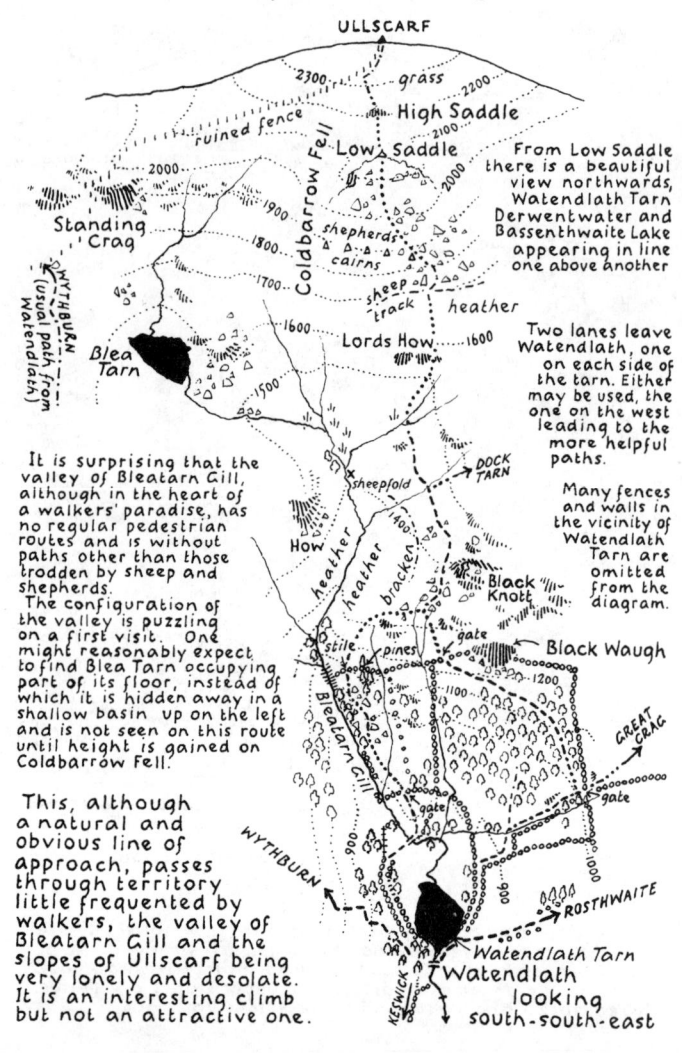

ASCENT FROM WATENDLATH
1600 feet of ascent : 3½ miles

ULLSCARF

High Saddle

Low Saddle

Coldbarrow Fell

ruined fence

Standing Crag

WYTHBURN (usual path from Watendlath)

Blea Tarn

shepherds cairns

sheep track

heather

Lords How

From Low Saddle there is a beautiful view northwards, Watendlath Tarn, Derwentwater and Bassenthwaite Lake appearing in line one above another.

Two lanes leave Watendlath, one on each side of the tarn. Either may be used, the one on the west leading to the more helpful paths.

Many fences and walls in the vicinity of Watendlath Tarn are omitted from the diagram.

sheepfold

DOCK TARN

How

heather

heather

bracken

Black Knott

stile

pines

gate

Black Waugh

Bleatarn Gill

GREAT CRAG

gate

gate

WYTHBURN

ROSTHWAITE

KESWICK

Watendlath Tarn
Watendlath
looking south-south-east

It is surprising that the valley of Bleatarn Gill, although in the heart of a walkers' paradise, has no regular pedestrian routes and is without paths other than those trodden by sheep and shepherds.
The configuration of the valley is puzzling on a first visit. One might reasonably expect to find Blea Tarn occupying part of its floor, instead of which it is hidden away in a shallow basin up on the left and is not seen on this route until height is gained on Coldbarrow Fell.

This, although a natural and obvious line of approach, passes through territory little frequented by walkers, the valley of Bleatarn Gill and the slopes of Ullscarf being very lonely and desolate. It is an interesting climb but not an attractive one.

Ullscarf 8

ASCENT FROM STONETHWAITE
2100 feet of ascent : 3¾ miles

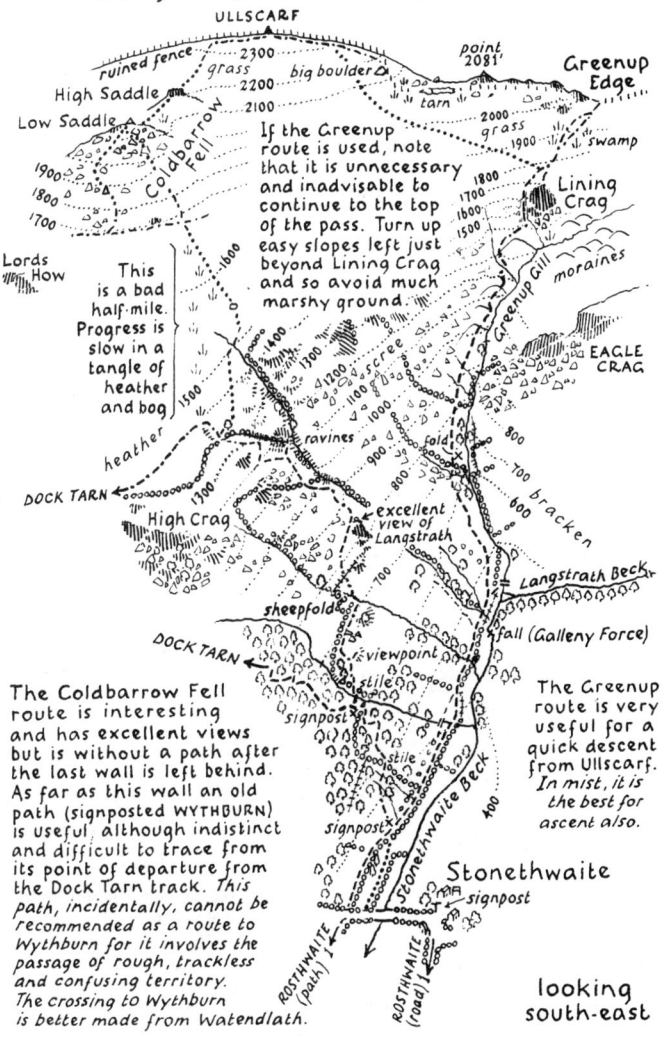

looking south-east

If the Greenup route is used, note that it is unnecessary and inadvisable to continue to the top of the pass. Turn up easy slopes left just beyond Lining Crag and so avoid much marshy ground.

This is a bad half-mile. Progress is slow in a tangle of heather and bog.

The Coldbarrow Fell route is interesting and has excellent views but is without a path after the last wall is left behind. As far as this wall an old path (signposted WYTHBURN) is useful, although indistinct and difficult to trace from its point of departure from the Dock Tarn track. This path, incidentally, cannot be recommended as a route to Wythburn for it involves the passage of rough, trackless and confusing territory. The crossing to Wythburn is better made from Watendlath.

The Greenup route is very useful for a quick descent from Ullscarf. In mist, it is the best for ascent also.

Ullscarf 9

Lining Crag, Greenup

The Beacon, Nab Crags

But for the stupid conduct of a party of schoolboys, there would have been an illustration here of a fine beacon that stood on Nab Crags for half a century: it was a conspicuous landmark, a reliable guide for shepherds on the fells in bad weather, and it kept alive locally a memory of the Wythburn man who built it.

The boys (on holiday a few years ago from a school outside the district) wilfully destroyed the beacon and rolled the stones down the fellside. *Two masters were with the party during this senseless act of vandalism: two brainless idiots, a disgrace to their profession.* Lakeland can do without visitors of this type.

Malicious damage is beyond pardon, and a source of endless trouble to farmers and shepherds. Rolling or throwing stones down the fellsides is CRIMINAL — sheep have been killed and crippled by such reprehensible folly.

Respectable walkers (readers of this book, for example) should please stop mischief of this sort whenever they witness it — and punish the offenders to the best of their ability.

Standing Crag

Ullscarf 10

THE SUMMIT

The top of Ullscarf is a cheerless place, even in sunshine; in storm there is no vestige of shelter. All is grass on this vast summit, and the only adornments are a cairn and a line of forlorn fence posts running both ways to the horizon; the posts are now useless for the purpose they originally served, but for the lost wanderer they have a real value in fixing his direction, and they lead unerringly to the highest point, which, without them, would be in some doubt.

DESCENTS: Although the upper slopes are gently inclined, and free from roughnesses, crags appear on all flanks when the ground steepens and the absence of paths makes this a particularly bad fell to get off in mist unless the safety of the fence is preferred.
TO STONETHWAITE: Follow the fence south at first, but avoid the marshy flats around point 2081' by bearing to the right, well away from the fence and joining the Greenup path above Lining Crag.
TO GRASMERE: Follow the fence south to Greenup Edge where the path from Borrowdale will be joined.
TO WATENDLATH: There will be no difficulty in reversing the route of ascent in clear weather, but in mist it is advisable to follow the fence north beyond Standing Crag and join the cairned path from Wythburn. Look for it near a big boulder on the left of the fence.
TO WYTHBURN (DIRECT): This interesting way down calls for special directions. There is no path until the sheepfold alongside Ullscarf Gill is reached. From the summit proceed in the direction of Fairfield for half a mile to a prominent rock for with a cairn on top. Immediately beyond is a maze of cairns which resolve into three distinct routes. (These cairns, some of them very old, were erected by shepherds). A fair path accompanies one line of cairns going left (this traverses the fellside to the fence at Standing Crag, and is of no help in the descent). The other two lines of cairns are pathless and indicate only the direction of safe descents. One leads down directly towards Wythburn: when the cairns end continue ahead and join Ullscarf Gill as far as a big sheepfold at a meeting of becks, where a path to West Head will be found on the right bank. The other swings to the right past some small tarns and goes down to the grassy neck behind Castle Crag where the ridge may be followed to the West Head path, or, alternatively, a straight descent is possible to Wythburn Head Tarns from this point, leaving the ridge with the crag on the left.

Shepherds' routes on east slope

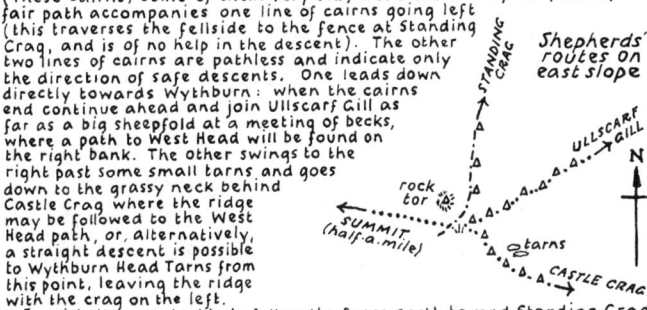

In mist, it is advisable to follow the fence north beyond Standing Crag and join the path from Watendlath to Wythburn. The alternative, of following the fence south to Greenup, thence descending the Wythburn valley, takes much longer, while the valley itself is a bad place to be in if the mist persists down at this level.

Ullscarf 11

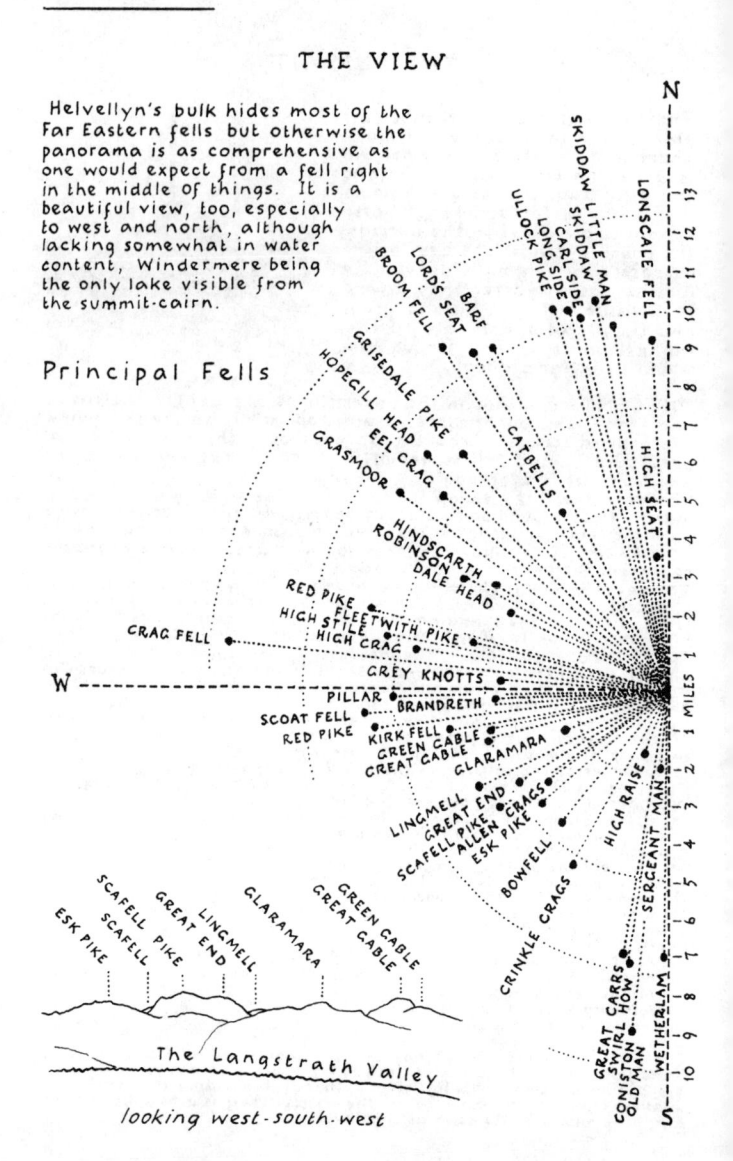

THE VIEW

Helvellyn's bulk hides most of the Far Eastern fells but otherwise the panorama is as comprehensive as one would expect from a fell right in the middle of things. It is a beautiful view, too, especially to west and north, although lacking somewhat in water content, Windermere being the only lake visible from the summit-cairn.

Principal Fells

looking west-south-west

The Langstrath Valley

Ullscarf 12

THE VIEW

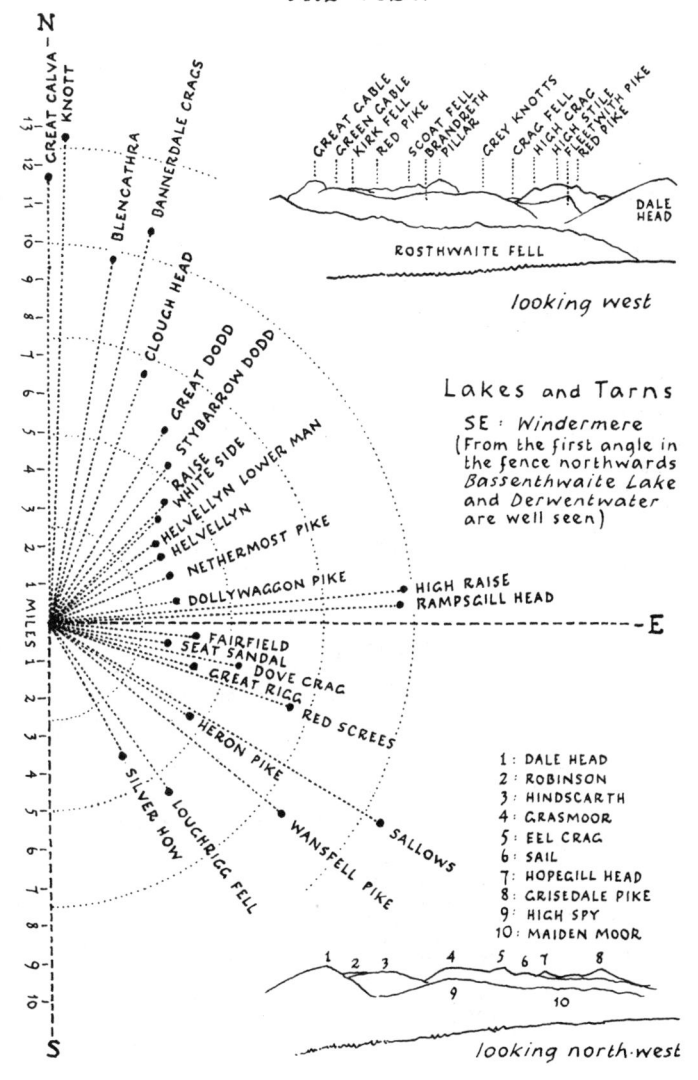

looking west

Lakes and Tarns

SE: *Windermere*
(From the first angle in the fence northwards *Bassenthwaite Lake* and *Derwentwater* are well seen)

Labels on compass diagram (N clockwise to S):
- GREAT CALVA
- KNOTT
- BLENCATHRA
- DANNERDALE CRAGS
- CLOUGH HEAD
- GREAT DODD
- STYBARROW DODD
- RAISE
- WHITE SIDE
- HELVELLYN LOWER MAN
- HELVELLYN
- NETHERMOST PIKE
- DOLLYWAGGON PIKE
- HIGH RAISE
- RAMPSGILL HEAD
- FAIRFIELD
- SEAT SANDAL
- DOVE CRAG
- GREAT RIGG
- RED SCREES
- HERON PIKE
- SALLOWS
- WANSFELL PIKE
- LOUGHRIGG FELL
- SILVER HOW

Labels on western panorama:
- GREAT GABLE
- GREEN GABLE
- KIRK FELL
- RED PIKE
- SCOAT FELL
- BRANDRETH
- PILLAR
- GREY KNOTTS
- CRAG FELL
- HIGH CRAG
- HIGH STILE
- RED PIKE
- DALE HEAD
- ROSTHWAITE FELL

1: DALE HEAD
2: ROBINSON
3: HINDSCARTH
4: GRASMOOR
5: EEL CRAG
6: SAIL
7: HOPEGILL HEAD
8: GRISEDALE PIKE
9: HIGH SPY
10: MAIDEN MOOR

looking north-west

Ullscarf 13

RIDGE ROUTES

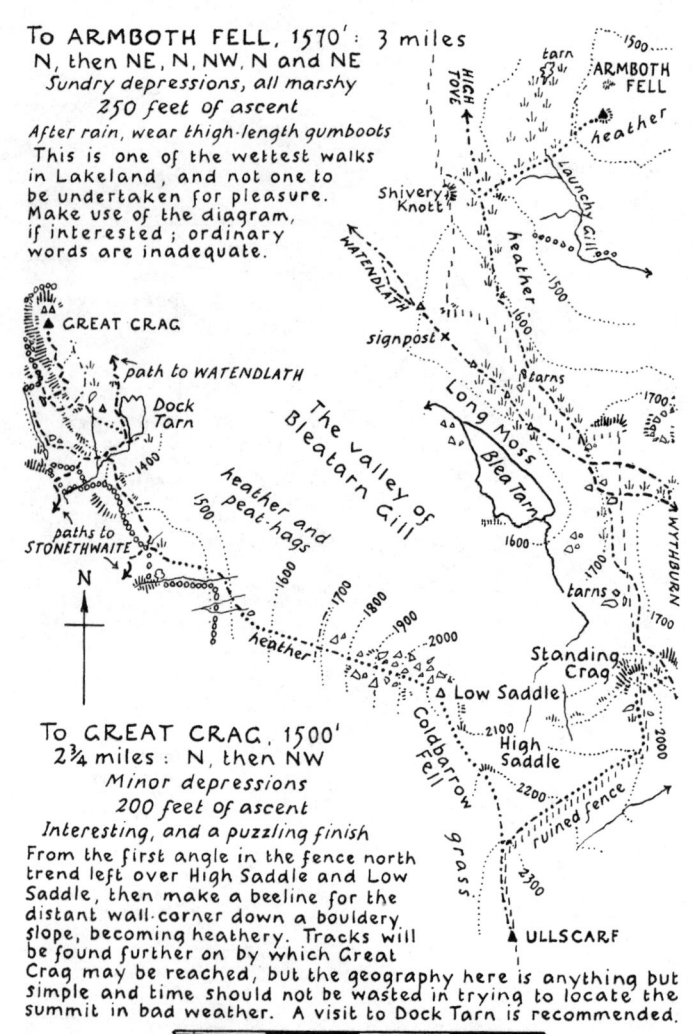

To ARMBOTH FELL, 1570': 3 miles
N, then NE, N, NW, N and NE
Sundry depressions, all marshy
250 feet of ascent
After rain, wear thigh-length gumboots
This is one of the wettest walks in Lakeland, and not one to be undertaken for pleasure. Make use of the diagram, if interested; ordinary words are inadequate.

To GREAT CRAG, 1500'
2¾ miles: N, then NW
Minor depressions
200 feet of ascent
Interesting, and a puzzling finish

From the first angle in the fence north trend left over High Saddle and Low Saddle, then make a beeline for the distant wall-corner down a bouldery slope, becoming heathery. Tracks will be found further on by which Great Crag may be reached, but the geography here is anything but simple and time should not be wasted in trying to locate the summit in bad weather. A visit to Dock Tarn is recommended.

ONE MILE

Ullscarf 14

RIDGE ROUTE

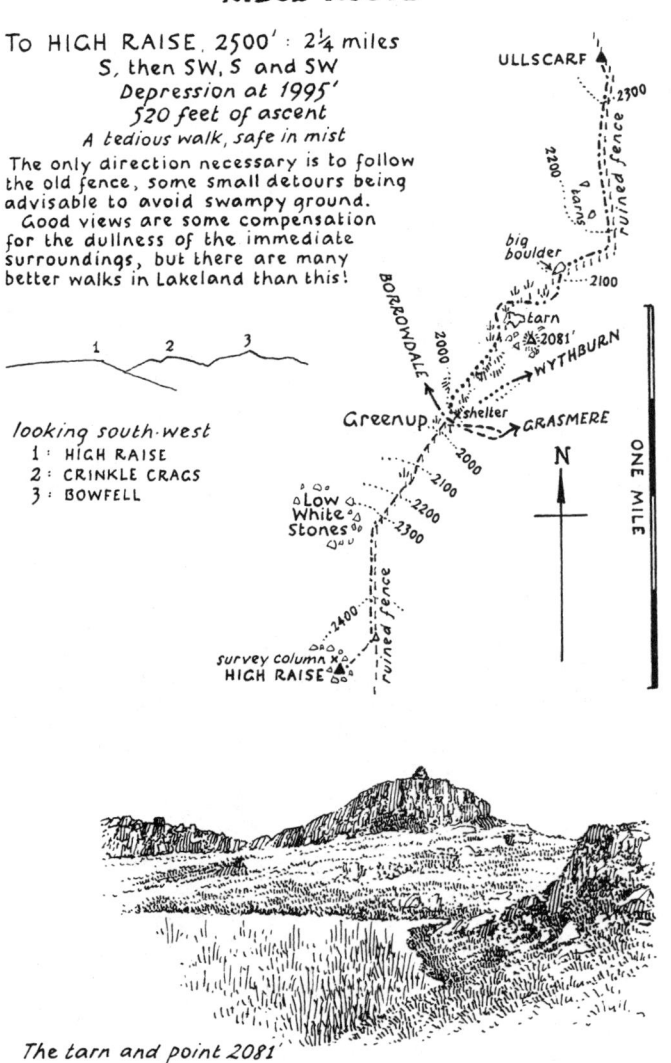

To HIGH RAISE, 2500': 2¼ miles
S, then SW, S and SW
Depression at 1995'
520 feet of ascent
A tedious walk, safe in mist

The only direction necessary is to follow the old fence, some small detours being advisable to avoid swampy ground.
 Good views are some compensation for the dullness of the immediate surroundings, but there are many better walks in Lakeland than this!

looking south-west
1: HIGH RAISE
2: CRINKLE CRAGS
3: BOWFELL

ONE MILE

The tarn and point 2081'

Walla Crag 1234'

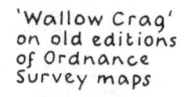

'Wallow Crag' on old editions of Ordnance Survey maps

Some walkers have difficulty in remembering the altitudes of the fells. There is no excuse here for anybody who can count up to four.

from Falcon Crag

- Keswick
  - Rakefoot
  - ▲ WALLA CRAG
  BLEABERRY
  ▲ FELL
- Lodore

MILES
0 1 2 3

from near Rakefoot

Walla Crag 2

NATURAL FEATURES

The pleasant Vale of Keswick, surely one of earth's sweetest landscapes, is surrounded by mountains of noble proportions with an inner circle of lesser fells which deserve more than the name of foothills, each having strong individual characteristics, a definite and distinctive appearance, and a natural beauty all its own. Among these is Walla Crag, an eminence of intermingled rocks and trees overlooking the east shore of lovely Derwentwater: of moderate elevation yet steep, romantic, challenging. Seen from the lake the hoary top seems unattainable, yet it may be gained by the gentlest of ascents for the slopes beyond the upper fringe of crag descend easily, accompanied by Brockle Beck, almost to the streets of Keswick.

MAP

Private and forestry paths in the plantations are not shown. The public path in Great Wood is an excellent short cut between Borrowdale and the main road to Ambleside

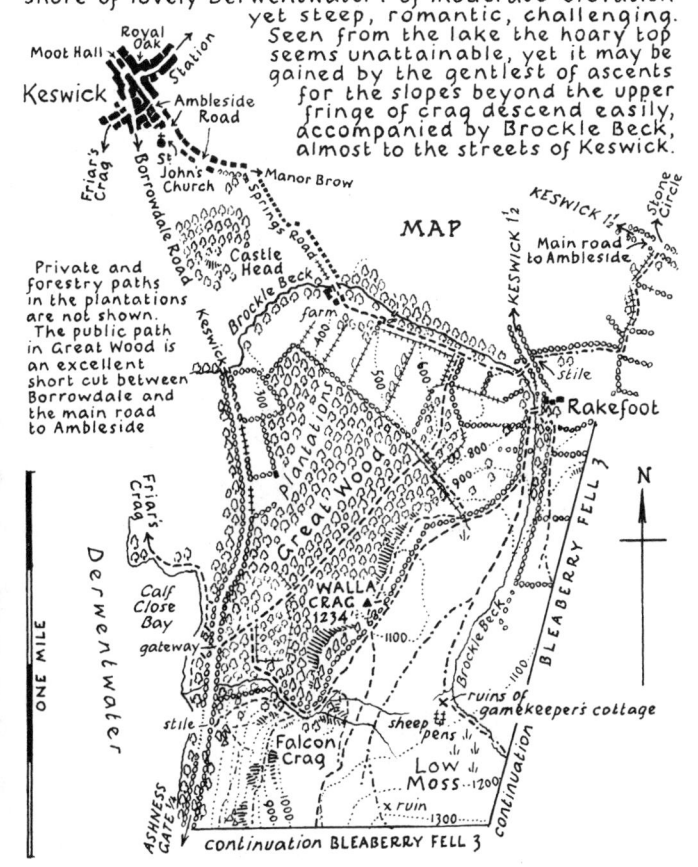

Walla Crag 3

ASCENT FROM KESWICK
1000 feet of ascent : 2½ miles

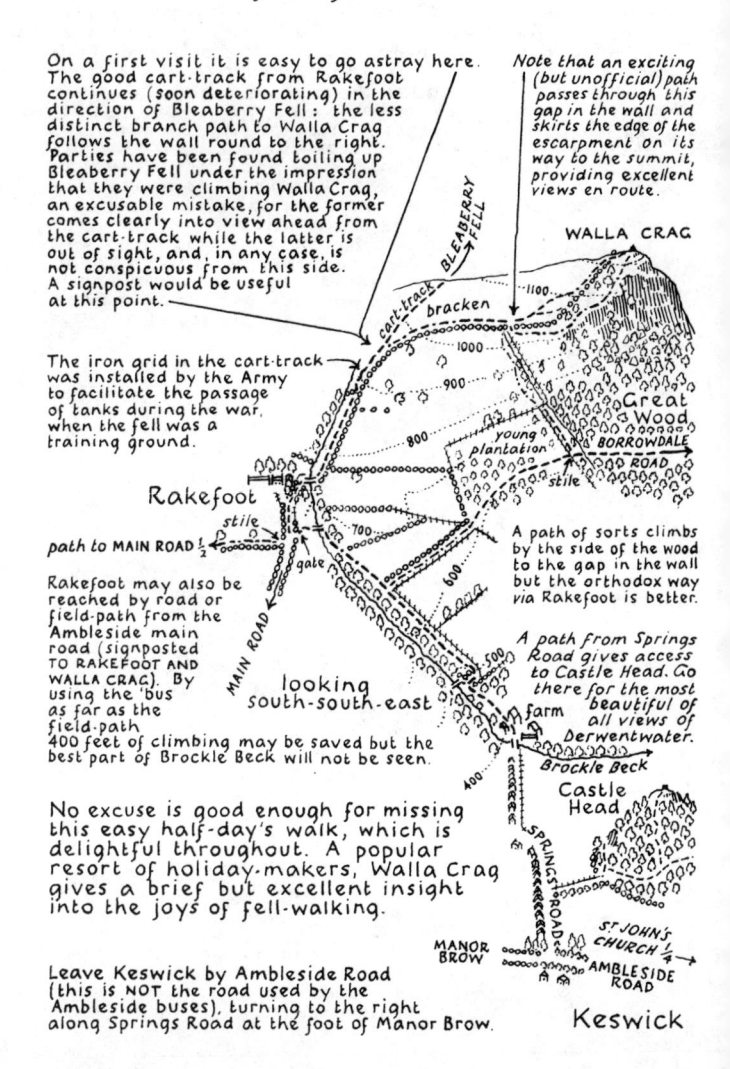

On a first visit it is easy to go astray here. The good cart-track from Rakefoot continues (soon deteriorating) in the direction of Bleaberry Fell: the less distinct branch path to Walla Crag follows the wall round to the right. Parties have been found toiling up Bleaberry Fell under the impression that they were climbing Walla Crag, an excusable mistake, for the former comes clearly into view ahead from the cart-track while the latter is out of sight, and, in any case, is not conspicuous from this side. A signpost would be useful at this point.

The iron grid in the cart-track was installed by the Army to facilitate the passage of tanks during the war, when the fell was a training ground.

Note that an exciting (but unofficial) path passes through this gap in the wall and skirts the edge of the escarpment on its way to the summit, providing excellent views en route.

path to MAIN ROAD ½

Rakefoot may also be reached by road or field-path from the Ambleside main road (signposted TO RAKEFOOT AND WALLA CRAG). By using the 'bus as far as the field-path 400 feet of climbing may be saved but the best part of Brockle Beck will not be seen.

looking south-south-east

A path of sorts climbs by the side of the wood to the gap in the wall but the orthodox way via Rakefoot is better.

A path from Springs Road gives access to Castle Head. Go there for the most beautiful of all views of Derwentwater.

No excuse is good enough for missing this easy half-day's walk, which is delightful throughout. A popular resort of holiday-makers, Walla Crag gives a brief but excellent insight into the joys of fell-walking.

Leave Keswick by Ambleside Road (this is NOT the road used by the Ambleside buses), turning to the right along Springs Road at the foot of Manor Brow.

Walla Crag 4

ASCENT FROM THE BORROWDALE ROAD
950 feet of ascent : 1 mile (2½ from Keswick)

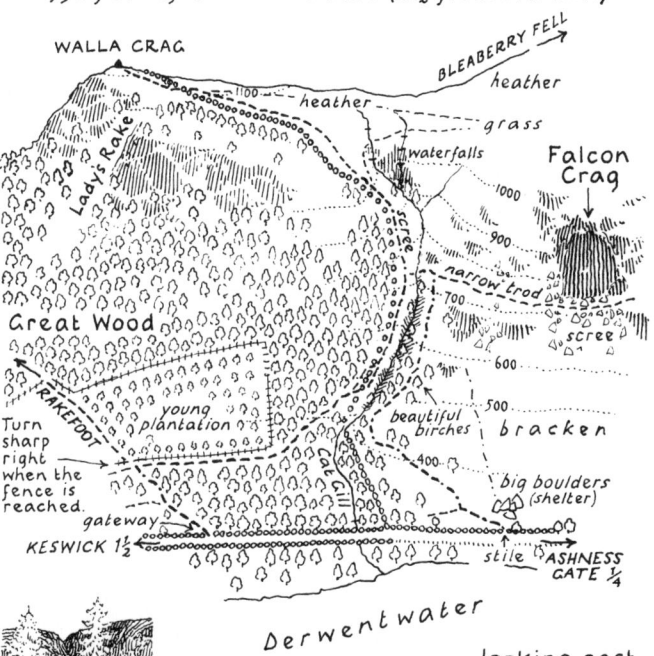

looking east

Waterfalls in Cat Gill

Alternative starts are given. The 'purest' route is that from the gateway, which keeps throughout to the Walla Crag side of Cat Gill, but trees shut out views that are too good to be missed. This defect is remedied by starting from the stile 150 yards beyond the point where the road crosses Cat Gill, a route with excellent views but calling for a little care higher up, just before joining the other path on the north bank of the gill. (A narrow trod here, on the south bank, leads excitingly to the base of Falcon Crag, which is worth seeing at close quarters, especially so from the small rise beyond).

A beautiful short climb up steep colourful slopes overlooking Derwentwater. If the starting point on the road is reached via Friar's Crag and Calf Close Bay, and if the return is made via Rakefoot and Brockle Beck, this becomes the best walk easily attainable in a half-day from Keswick.

Walla Crag 5

THE SUMMIT

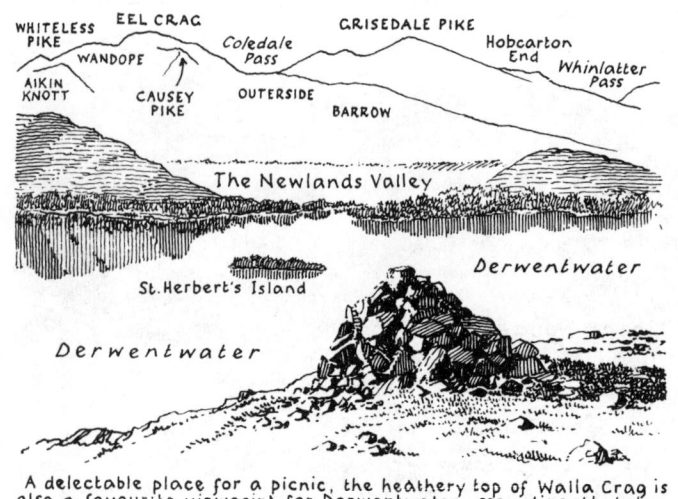

illustration: panorama showing Whiteless Pike, Eel Crag, Coledale Pass, Grisedale Pike, Hobcarton End, Whinlatter Pass, Wandope, Aikin Knott, Causey Pike, Outerside, Barrow, above The Newlands Valley; St. Herbert's Island in Derwentwater; summit cairn

A delectable place for a picnic, the heathery top of Walla Crag is also a favourite viewpoint for Derwentwater, seen directly below the long steep escarpment. A profusion of decayed tree-stumps indicates that the summit, now bare, was at one time thickly wooded; many trees survive nearby, all west of the wall crossing the top of the fell, as is the cairn, 60 yards distant.

DESCENTS: Keep to the paths: the dangers of straying from them should be obvious. An inviting opening in the cliff (Lady's Rake) 150 yards south of the cairn is a trap to be avoided. In mist, note that the wall links Rakefoot and the Borrowdale road, and that the paths follow it. The descent to Rakefoot is easy; the other route is rough but more interesting.

RIDGE ROUTE

TO BLEABERRY FELL, 1932'
1¼ miles : S, then SSE curving SE
Depression at 1070'
900 feet of ascent
A dull climb relieved by fine views

Start along the Ashness Bridge path, crossing to a higher track when a stream is reached and then aiming for the left side of the prominent mound. Detour right to join the first cairn.

THE VIEW

This well-known view has earned its popularity not by its extensiveness but by the variety and charm of many nearby features, with Borrowdale an outstanding study of mountain grouping and the exciting downward prospect of Derwentwater of more general appeal. An interesting emphasis is placed on the relatively low elevation of much of the central part of Lakeland by the distant view of Grey Friar in the Coniston fells — hardly to be expected from Walla Crag's modest height so far to the north.

Principal Fells

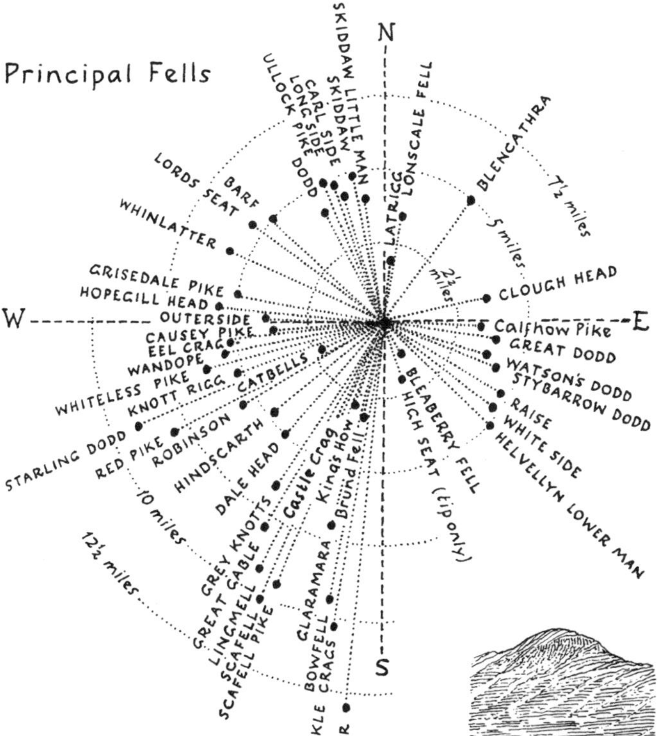
N
E
S
W
2½ miles
5 miles
7½ miles
10 miles
12½ miles
SKIDDAW LITTLE MAN
SKIDDAW
CARL SIDE
LONG SIDE
ULLOCK PIKE
DODD
LONSCALE FELL
LATRIGG
BLENCATHRA
CLOUGH HEAD
Calfhow Pike
GREAT DODD
WATSON'S DODD
STYBARROW DODD
RAISE
WHITE SIDE
HELVELLYN LOWER MAN
BLEABERRY FELL
HIGH SEAT (tip only)
Brund Fell
Kings How
Castle Crag
DALE HEAD
HINDSCARTH
ROBINSON
RED PIKE
STARLING DODD
KNOTT RIGG
WHITELESS PIKE
WANDOPE
EEL CRAG
CAUSEY PIKE
OUTERSIDE
HOPEGILL HEAD
GRISEDALE PIKE
WHINLATTER
LORDS SEAT
BARF
CATBELLS
GREY KNOTTS
GREAT GABLE
LINGMELL
SCAFELL
SCAFELL PIKE
GLARAMARA
BOWFELL
CRINKLE CRAGS
GREY FRIAR

Lakes and Tarns

NE : *Tewet Tarn*
W : *Derwentwater*
NW : *Bassenthwaite Lake*

Bleaberry Fell

THE CENTRAL FELLS
Some Personal notes in conclusion

If I were thirty years younger I should already be looking forward to the time when, with the seventh and last book in this series finished (round about 1965) I could start to go over all the ground once again with a view to making such revisions as may be found to be necessary. I fear, however, that by that time age will have shackled my limbs to such an extent that the joyful task may be beyond me.

Guidebooks that are inaccurate and unreliable are worse than none at all, and I am aware that in a few small respects Books One and Two are already out of date. It is most exasperating, for instance, to learn of fences appearing on land where I have shown none, or of the erection of new buildings, or that signposts or cairns have been destroyed or established — all in the short interval since the books were originally published. Even as I write, there is a proposal afoot to demolish the dam at Stickle Tarn, which would shrink considerably the size of the tarn, and alter its shape — and this news comes to me only a few days after sending to the printer several pages which feature the tarn and on which its present proportions are most carefully delineated. There is no stopping these changes — but I do wish people would leave things alone! Substantially, of course, the books will be useful for many years to come, especially in the detail and description of the fell tops, while the views will remain unaltered for ever, assuming that falling satellites and other fancy gadgets of man's invention don't blow God's far worthier creations to bits. But, this dire possibility apart, the books must inevitably show more and more inaccuracies as the years go by. Therefore, because it is unlikely that there will ever be revised editions, and because I should just hate to see my name on anything that could not be relied on, the probability is that the books will progressively be withdrawn from publication after a currency of a few years.

All this is leading to a suggestion that readers who are really enthusiastic about fellwalking and have several more seasons of happy wandering to look forward to, should start to use these volumes as basic notebooks for their own personal records, making such amendments (neatly, I hope!) as they find necessary during their walks and adapting the page-margins for dates and details of their own ascents and other notes of special interest.

I had intended (under pressure from publisher, printer and booksellers alike) to demonstrate in these final pages that an increase in the price of the books had become urgently necessary to cover rising costs of production — but I haven't left myself enough space to do it; besides, I have no stomach for such unpalatable discourse. So for the time being the price will continue uniform at 12s 6d — let's say for the sake of tidiness.

Away with such trivial matters! It is better by far that my last few lines should tell of the Central Fells, even though this area will already be well known to most readers and in places is much frequented; indeed the presence of other walkers was often rather an embarrassment to me, although my mission was never suspected. The popular heights above Derwentwater I left until the holiday crowds (and Vivian Fisher, <u>and</u> his gate!) had all departed from the scene. Alone, what a celestial beauty I found there in the quiet of late autumn and early winter! What rich warm colours! I walked on golden carpets between golden tapestries, marvelling anew at the supreme craftsmanship that had created so great a loveliness, and at my own good fortune to be in its midst, enjoying a heaven I had done nothing to deserve. One cannot find the words to describe it: only an inexpressible humility fills the heart....

12s 6d, 15s, 17s 6d — what does it matter? I must hasten now to the Scafells, noblest of Lakeland's cathedrals, while good health and appreciation of beauty and simple reverence and gratitude remain with me, for when I have lost these blessings I shall have little left. This one lesson, above all others, the hills have taught me.

new year 1958

A.W.

SIGN REFERENCES
(signs used in the maps and diagrams)

Good footpath ‑ ‑ ‑ ‑ ‑ ‑ ‑ ‑ ‑
(sufficiently distinct to be followed in mist)

Intermittent footpath ‑ ‑ ‑ ‑ ‑ ‑
(difficult to follow in mist)

Route recommended but no path ······>······>·····
(if recommended one way only, arrow indicates direction)

Wall ∞∞∞∞∞∞ **Broken wall** ○○○○○○○○○○○

Fence ++++++++ **Broken fence** ıııııııııııııı

Marshy ground ⅍⅍⅍⅍ **Trees** 🌳🌳🌳

Crags 🪨🪨🪨 **Boulders** ▫▫▫▫

Stream or River ～～～→
(arrow indicates direction of flow)

Waterfall ⌒⌒ **Bridge** ～✕～

Buildings ▪▪ **Unenclosed road** ····················

Contours (at 100' intervals) ······
1900
1800
1700

Summit-cairn ▲ **Other (prominent) cairns** △

THE
NORTH WESTERN
FELLS

A PICTORIAL GUIDE
TO THE
LAKELAND FELLS
50TH ANNIVERSARY EDITION

being an illustrated account
of a study and exploration
of the mountains in the
English Lake District

by

A Wainwright

BOOK SIX
THE NORTH WESTERN FELLS

Frances Lincoln Limited
4 Torriano Mews
Torriano Avenue
London NW5 2RZ
www.franceslincoln.com

Originally published by
Westmorland Gazette, Kendal, 1964

First published by Frances Lincoln 2003

50th Anniversary Edition with re-originated artwork
published by Frances Lincoln 2005

Copyright © The Estate of A. Wainwright 1964

All rights reserved. Without limiting the rights under copyright reserved above, no part of this publication may be reproduced, stored in or introduced into a retrieval system, or transmitted, in any form or by any means (electronic, mechanical, photocopying, or otherwise), without either prior permission in writing from the publisher or a licence permitting restricted copying. In the United Kingdom such licences are issued by the Copyright Licensing Agency, Saffron House, 6-10 Kirby Street, London EC1N 8TS.

Printed and bound in China

A CIP catalogue record for this book
is available from the British Library.

ISBN 978 0 7112 2459 9

18 17 16 15 14 13 12 11

50TH ANNIVERSARY EDITION
PUBLISHED BY
FRANCES LINCOLN, LONDON

THE PICTORIAL GUIDES

Book One: The Eastern Fells, 1955
Book Two: The Far Eastern Fells, 1957
Book Three: The Central Fells, 1958
Book Four: The Southern Fells, 1960
Book Five: The Northern Fells, 1962
Book Six: The North Western Fells, 1964
Book Seven: The Western Fells, 1966

PUBLISHER'S NOTE

This 50th Anniversary edition of the Pictorial Guides to the Lakeland Fells is newly reproduced from the handwritten pages created in the 1950s and 1960s by A. Wainwright. The descriptions of the walks were correct, to the best of the author's knowledge, at the time of first publication and they are reproduced here without amendment. However, footpaths, cairns and other waymarks described here are no longer all as they were fifty years ago and walkers are advised to check with an up-to-date map when planning a walk.

Fellwalking has increased dramatically since the Pictorial Guides were first published. Some popular routes have become eroded, making good footwear and great care all the more necessary for walkers. The vital points about fellwalking, as A. Wainwright himself wrote on many occasions, are to use common sense and to remember to watch where you are putting your feet.

A programme of revision of the Pictorial Guides is under way and revised editions of each of them will be published over the next few years.

BOOK SIX

is dedicated to
those unlovely twins

MY RIGHT LEG and MY LEFT LEG

staunch supporters
that have carried me about
for over half a century,
endured much without complaint
and never once let me down

Nevertheless, they are unsuitable subjects for illustration

INTRODUCTION

Classification and Definition

Any division of the Lakeland fells into geographical districts must necessarily be arbitrary, just as the location of the outer boundaries of Lakeland must always be a matter of opinion. Any attempt to define internal or external boundaries is certain to invite criticism, and he who takes it upon himself to say where Lakeland starts and finishes, or, for example, where the Central Fells merge into the Southern Fells and *which* fells are the Central Fells and which the Southern and *why* they need be so classified, must not expect his pronouncements to be generally accepted.

Yet for present purposes some plan of classification and definition must be used. County and parochial boundaries are no help, nor is the recently-defined area of the Lakeland National Park, for this book is concerned only with the high ground.

First, the external boundaries. Straight lines linking the extremities of the outlying lakes enclose all the higher fells very conveniently. There are a few fells of lesser height to the north and east, however, that are typically Lakeland in character and cannot properly be omitted: these are brought in, somewhat untidily, by extending the lines in those areas. Thus:

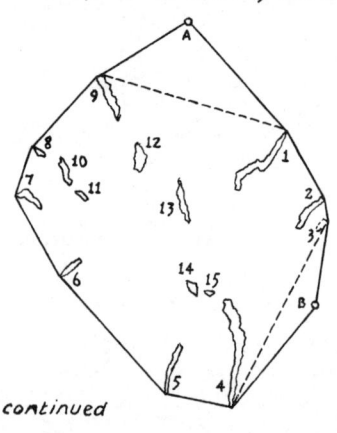

1 : *Ullswater*
2 : *Hawes Water*
3 : proposed *Swindale Resr*
4 : *Windermere*
5 : *Coniston Water*
6 : *Wast Water*
7 : *Ennerdale Water*
8 : *Loweswater*
9 : *Bassenthwaite Lake*
10 : *Crummock Water*
11 : *Buttermere*
12 : *Derwent Water*
13 : *Thirlmere*
14 : *Grasmere*
15 : *Rydal Water*
A : Caldbeck
B : Longsleddale (church)

continued

INTRODUCTION

Classification and Definition
continued

The complete Guide is planned to include all the fells in the area enclosed by the straight lines of the diagram. This is an undertaking quite beyond the compass of a single volume, and it is necessary, therefore, to divide the area into convenient sections, making the fullest use of natural boundaries (lakes, valleys and low passes) so that each district is, as far as possible, self-contained and independent of the rest.

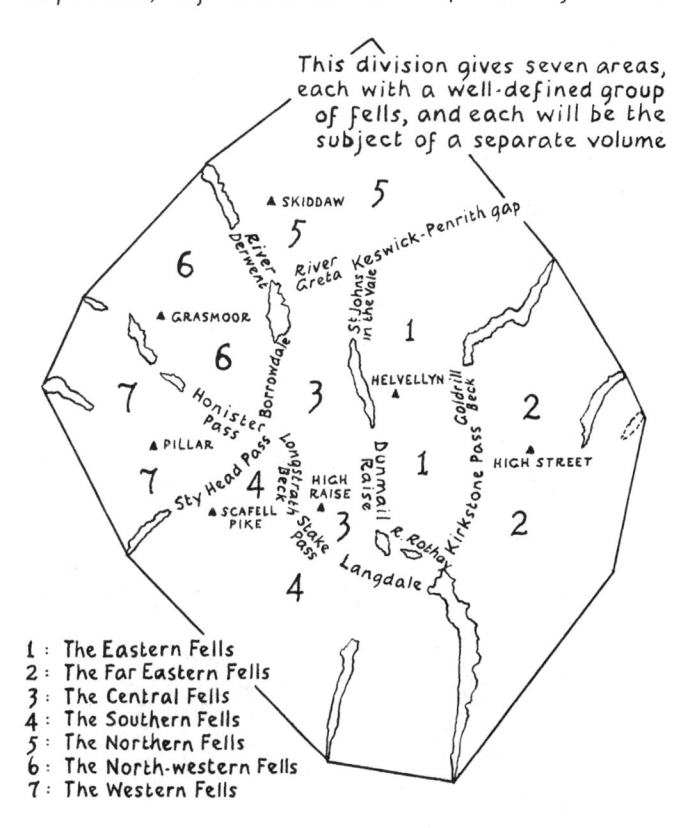

This division gives seven areas, each with a well-defined group of fells, and each will be the subject of a separate volume

1 : The Eastern Fells
2 : The Far Eastern Fells
3 : The Central Fells
4 : The Southern Fells
5 : The Northern Fells
6 : The North-western Fells
7 : The Western Fells

INTRODUCTION

Notes on the Illustrations

THE MAPS.................Many excellent books have been written about Lakeland, but the best literature of all for the walker is that published by the Director General of Ordnance Survey, the 1" map for companionship and guidance on expeditions, the 2½" map for exploration both on the fells and by the fireside. These admirable maps are remarkably accurate topographically but there is a crying need for a revision of the paths on the hills: several walkers' tracks that have come into use during the past few decades, some of them now broad highways, are not shown at all; other paths still shown on the maps have fallen into neglect and can no longer be traced on the ground.

The popular Bartholomew 1" map is a beautiful picture, fit for a frame, but this too is unreliable for paths; indeed here the defect is much more serious, for routes are indicated where no paths ever existed, nor ever could — the cartographer has preferred to take precipices in his stride rather than deflect his graceful curves over easy ground.

Hence the justification for the maps in this book: they have the one merit (of importance to walkers) of being dependable as regards delineation of *paths*. They are intended as supplements to the Ordnance Survey maps, certainly not as substitutes.

THE VIEWS...............Various devices have been used to illustrate the views from the summits of the fells. The full panorama in the form of an outline drawing is most satisfactory generally, and this method has been adopted for the main viewpoints.

THE DIAGRAMS OF ASCENTS....................The routes of ascent of the higher fells are depicted by diagrams that do not pretend to strict accuracy: they are neither plans nor elevations; in fact there is deliberate distortion in order to show detail clearly: usually they are represented as viewed from imaginary 'space-stations.' But it is hoped they will be useful and interesting.

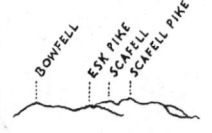

THE DRAWINGS.......The drawings at least are honest attempts to reproduce what the eye sees: they illustrate features of interest and also serve the dual purpose of breaking up the text and balancing the layout of the pages, and of filling up awkward blank spaces, like this:

Thirlmere

THE
NORTH WESTERN
FELLS

The North Western Fells occupy a compact area, elliptical in plan, with clearly defined boundaries formed by the Rivers Derwent and Cocker. Only at one point, Honister Pass, is there a link with other high country, but even here, quite obviously, one mountain system ends and another begins. In all other places around the perimeter of the area deep valleys sever the North Western Fells from the neighbouring heights.

The Cocker is a tributary of the Derwent, and it follows, therefore, that the North Western Fells are wholly within the catchment of a single river — which further illustrates the geographical unity and separate identity of the group. Elsewhere, no combination of fells of similar extent is so neatly defined.

In size, the area is not very extensive on the map of Lakeland, but because its slopes rise immediately and steeply from the deep surrounding valleys, nothing is wasted: all is mountain country, first-class fellwalking territory. The hills tend to crowd together in the confined space available, but not in confusion and disarray, for connecting links bridge the tops in a pattern of high crests and scarped aretes that are a joy to explore. Indeed, here is to be found some of the finest ridge-walking in the district, smooth going for the most part, none of it difficult, none of it dangerous with ordinary care, all of it very pleasant and providing views of unsurpassed beauty.

THE THREE SECTORS

Northern

Central

SouthEastern

Bassenthwaite Lake
River Cocker
Crummock Water
Buttermere
WHINLATTER PASS
NEWLANDS HAUSE
Derwentwater
River Derwent
HONISTER PASS

Two motor roads cross the area, attaining their highest points at Whinlatter Pass and Newlands Hause and conveniently making three sectors.

The northern sector may be classed under the general title of Thornthwaite Forest. Slate is the underlying rock of the low rounded foothills comprising the region, but is not much in evidence, being well covered with vegetation and timber. A large part is occupied by the Forestry Commission, and here are being developed the most extensive plantations in the district. Perhaps because of this activity, the sector is less favoured by walkers than used to be the case, but it still offers many routes of unusual interest and charm.

The central sector contains the highest fells, all of them steep-sided and shapely, making arresting and exciting skylines. These, too, are of slate, and in the vicinity of Grasmoor particularly the steep slopes are excessively eroded and exhibit the most extensive wastes of scree in the district. These stony inclines are rarely climbed, but the summits and ridges above are very much frequented by walkers. The western flanks, rich in flora, are a happy hunting-ground for botanists. This sector is bisected by a foot-pass at Coledale Hause.

The south-eastern sector, too, is a place of fine ridges and shapely summits, and a great favourite of discerning walkers. The slate persists, but towards Borrowdale gives place to coarser, rougher volcanic ash.

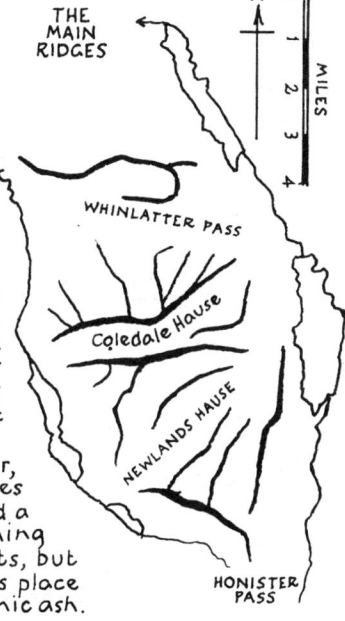

1

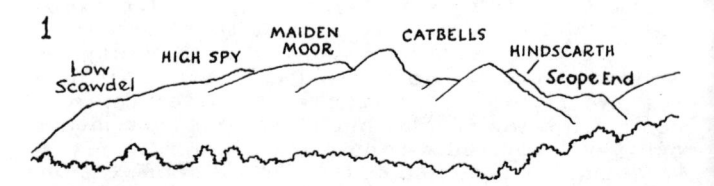

Low Scawdel — HIGH SPY — MAIDEN MOOR — CATBELLS — HINDSCARTH — Scope End

The North Western Fells, as seen from The Heads, Keswick

This geological change is noticeable on the ground and manifests itself in the only tarns amongst the North Western Fells. Rock-climbers appreciate the change and here find their only major interests in the area.

Accommodation is available at several places around the perimeter, being in plentiful supply in Borrowdale, where it is a local industry, but less easy to find at Buttermere and Lorton in summer. Braithwaite is a good jumping-off place, but the finest centre for a fellwalking holiday is Newlands, the only populated valley *within* the area. All the fells in this book may, however, be visited, with the help of the local bus services, from Keswick. It is worth noting that the best approaches to the area are from the north-east, the gradients being easier and the ascending ridges longer in this direction.

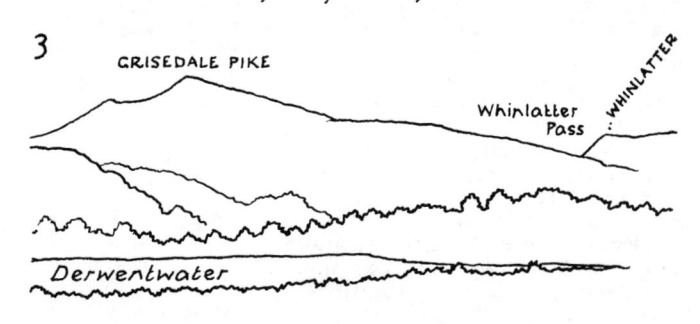

3

GRISEDALE PIKE — Whinlatter Pass — WHINLATTER

Derwentwater

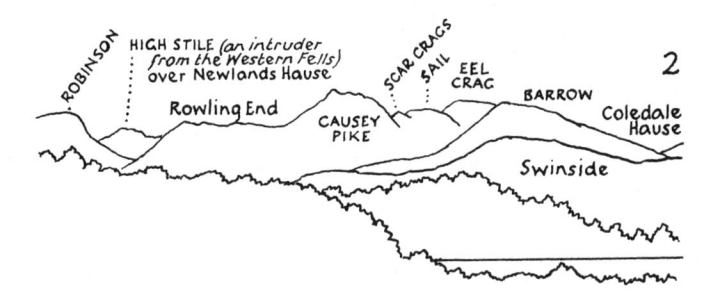

panorama labels: ROBINSON, HIGH STILE (an intruder from the Western Fells) over Newlands Hause, Rowling End, CAUSEY PIKE, SCAR CRAGS, SAIL, EEL CRAG, BARROW, Coledale Hause, Swinside

2

The main watershed lies close above the Cocker, and ascents from the southwest, in consequence, are short, abrupt and steep.

The North Western Fells, with riparian rights in four beautiful lakes, and sharing the proprietorship of the two lovely valleys of Borrowdale and Buttermere, can not be described as characteristic of Lakeland, the underlying slate tending to a smoothness of outline and an absence of tarns, but for walkers who prefer rather easier progression than is to be found amongst the more rugged volcanic fells, even at some sacrifice of romantic scenery, there are none better than these.

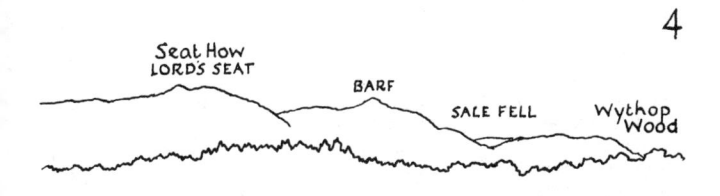

map: THE WATERSHED south of Whinlatter Pass — Cocker, Derwent, N

panorama labels: Seat How, LORD'S SEAT, BARF, SALE FELL, Wythop Wood

4

The North Western Fells, as seen from The Heads, Keswick

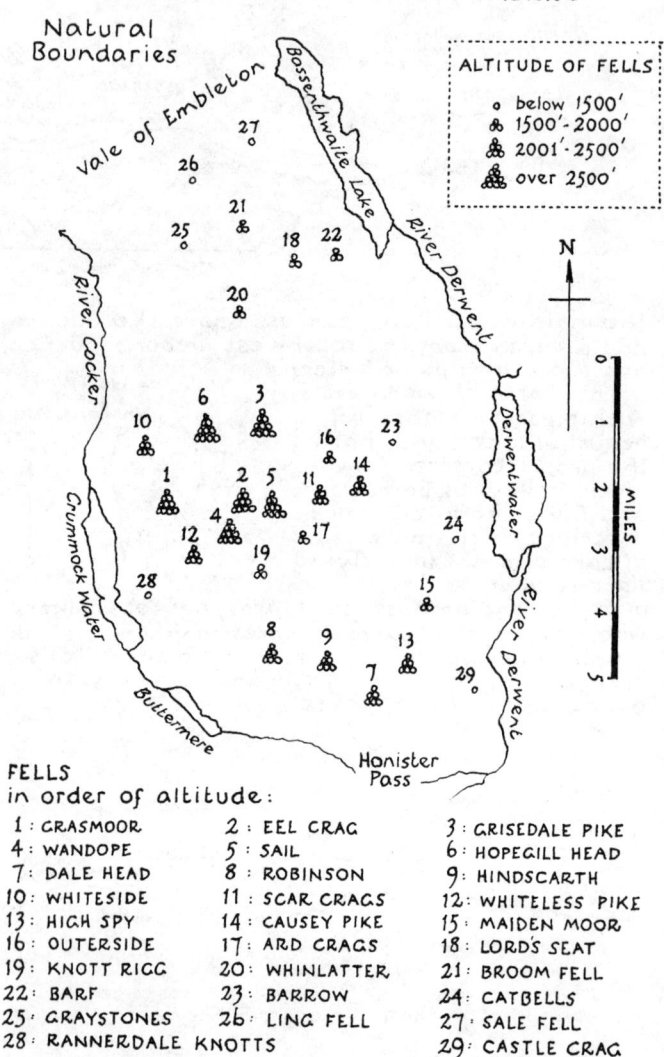

THE NORTH WESTERN FELLS

Natural Boundaries

ALTITUDE OF FELLS
- below 1500'
- 1500'–2000'
- 2001'–2500'
- over 2500'

FELLS
in order of altitude:

1: GRASMOOR	2: EEL CRAG	3: GRISEDALE PIKE
4: WANDOPE	5: SAIL	6: HOPEGILL HEAD
7: DALE HEAD	8: ROBINSON	9: HINDSCARTH
10: WHITESIDE	11: SCAR CRAGS	12: WHITELESS PIKE
13: HIGH SPY	14: CAUSEY PIKE	15: MAIDEN MOOR
16: OUTERSIDE	17: ARD CRAGS	18: LORD'S SEAT
19: KNOTT RIGG	20: WHINLATTER	21: BROOM FELL
22: BARF	23: BARROW	24: CATBELLS
25: GRAYSTONES	26: LING FELL	27: SALE FELL
28: RANNERDALE KNOTTS		29: CASTLE CRAG

THE NORTH WESTERN FELLS

Reference to map opposite

over 2500' / *2001'-2500'* / *1500'-2000'* / *below 1500'*

in the order of their appearance in this book

			Altitude in feet
17	..	ARD CRAGS ..	1860
22	..	BARF ..	1536
23	..	BARROW ..	1494
21	..	BROOM FELL ..	1670
29	..	CASTLE CRAG ..	985
24	..	CATBELLS ..	1481
14	..	CAUSEY PIKE ..	2035
7	..	DALE HEAD ..	2473
2	..	EEL CRAG ..	2749
1	..	GRASMOOR ..	2791
25	..	GRAYSTONES ..	1476
3	..	GRISEDALE PIKE ..	2593
13	..	HIGH SPY ..	2143
9	..	HINDSCARTH ..	2385
6	..	HOPEGILL HEAD ..	2525
19	..	KNOTT RIGG ..	1790
26	..	LING FELL ..	1224
18	..	LORD'S SEAT ..	1811
15	..	MAIDEN MOOR ..	1887
16	..	OUTERSIDE ..	1863
28	..	RANNERDALE KNOTTS ..	1160
8	..	ROBINSON ..	2417
5	..	SAIL ..	2530
27	..	SALE FELL ..	1170
11	..	SCAR CRAGS ..	2205
4	..	WANDOPE ..	2533
20	..	WHINLATTER ..	1696
12	..	WHITELESS PIKE ..	2159
10	..	WHITESIDE ..	2317

6 8 8 7
29

Each fell is the subject of a separate chapter

Ard Crags

1860' approx.

from Rigg Beck

There is one point on the path alongside Rigg Beck where the defile ahead is occupied by the shapely pyramid of Ard Crags, its appearance suggesting a complete isolation from other fells. At the top of Rigg Beck, however, a high pass forms a bridge with the greater mass of the Eel Crag range; nevertheless, a clear identity is maintained by the ridge of Ard Crags as it runs southwest over Knott Rigg to Newlands Hause.

Both flanks are rough and exceedingly steep. Erosion on the south side — facing Newlands — has been halted by a plantation to protect the road and farmstead of Keskadale at its foot.

EEL CRAG ▲   Rigg Beck ●
              ▲ ARD CRAGS
KNOTT RIGG ▲ ● Keskadale

⤢ Newlands Hause

● Buttermere

MILES
0   1   2   3

Ard Crags 2

MAP

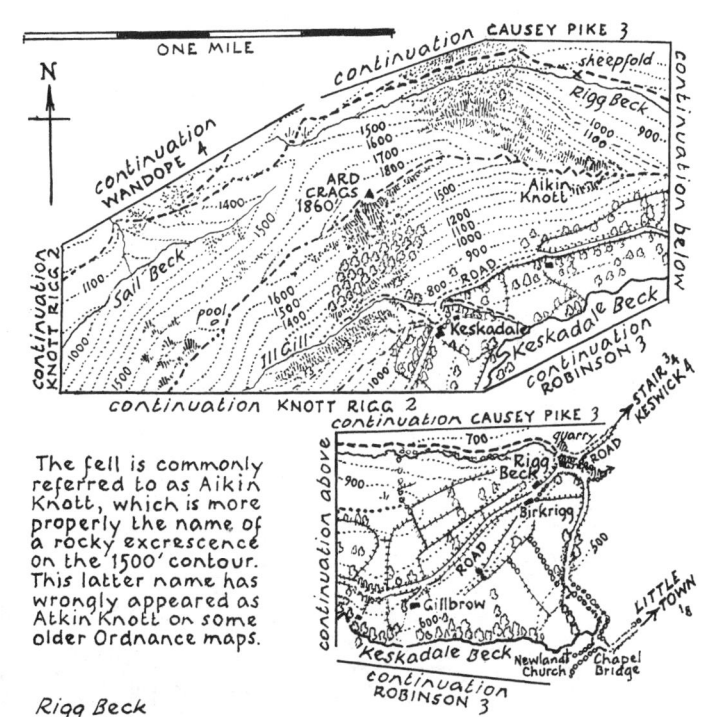

The fell is commonly referred to as Aikin Knott, which is more properly the name of a rocky excrescence on the 1500' contour. This latter name has wrongly appeared as Atkin Knott on some older Ordnance maps.

Rigg Beck

The sharp bend carrying the road over Rigg Beck is comparatively new. Formerly the road crossed at a ford lower down (still to be seen). Nearby, but now vanished, was a place of call, the Mill Dam Inn.
  Higher up the road, at a wooded bend west of Gillbrow, the ruins of Bawd Hall can be seen, and, a little further, Aikin House, now a barn.
  Keskadale is the only inhabited dwelling on the four miles of road between Gillbrow and Buttermere, and there is no place of rest and refreshment for travellers.

Ard Crags 3

ASCENT FROM RIGG BECK
1350 feet of ascent : 1½ miles

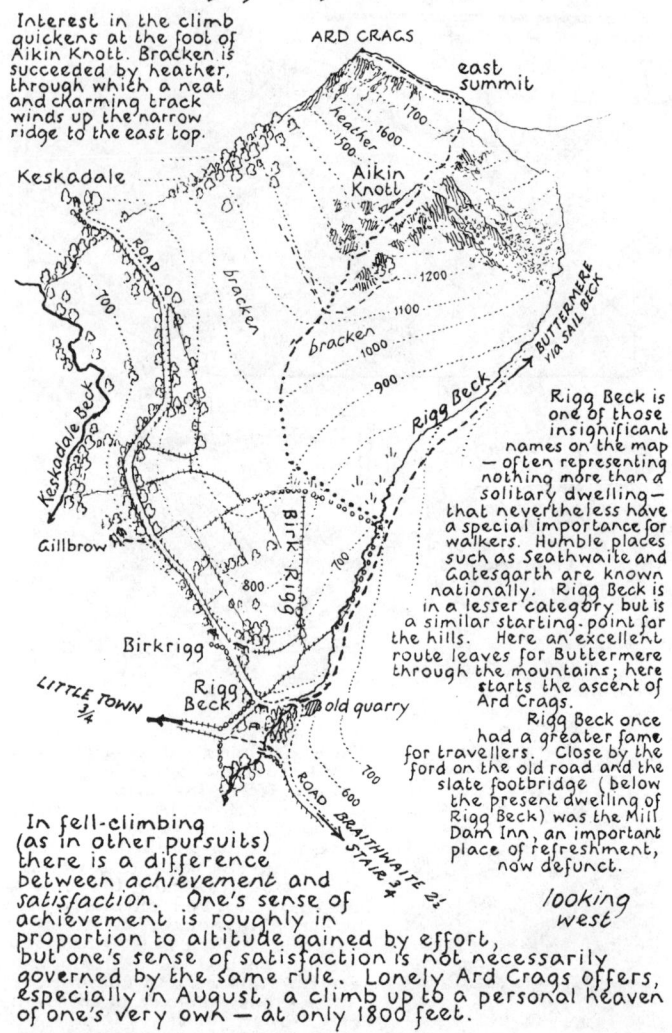

Interest in the climb quickens at the foot of Aikin Knott. Bracken is succeeded by heather, through which a neat and charming track winds up the narrow ridge to the east top.

looking west

Rigg Beck is one of those insignificant names on the map — often representing nothing more than a solitary dwelling — that nevertheless have a special importance for walkers. Humble places such as Seathwaite and Gatesgarth are known nationally. Rigg Beck is in a lesser category but is a similar starting-point for the hills. Here an excellent route leaves for Buttermere through the mountains; here starts the ascent of Ard Crags.

Rigg Beck once had a greater fame for travellers. Close by the ford on the old road and the slate footbridge (below the present dwelling of Rigg Beck) was the Mill Dam Inn, an important place of refreshment, now defunct.

In fell-climbing (as in other pursuits) there is a difference between *achievement* and *satisfaction*. One's sense of achievement is roughly in proportion to altitude gained by effort, but one's sense of satisfaction is not necessarily governed by the same rule. Lonely Ard Crags offers, especially in August, a climb up to a personal heaven of one's very own — at only 1800 feet.

THE SUMMIT

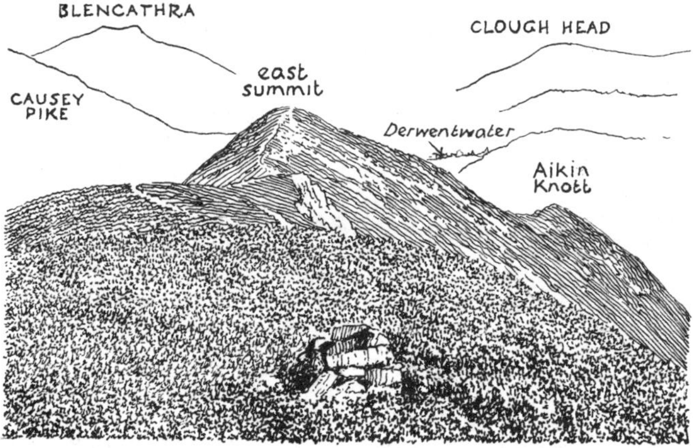
BLENCATHRA
CLOUGH HEAD
east summit
CAUSEY PIKE
Derwentwater
Aikin Knott

Save a visit here for a warm still day in August, and envy not the crowds heading for Great Gable. This is easier, more rewarding, and *solitary*. The narrow crest is a dense carpet of short springy heather, delightful to walk upon and even better as a couch for rest and meditation. But slumber is a hazard, for crags fall away sharply below one's boots to Keskadale. The highest point, marked by a cairn, has no official altitude, the surveyors having preferred to adopt the eastern end of the summit, at 1821', for their use.

DESCENTS: *For Newlands*, follow the ridge over the east summit and Aikin Knott. *For Buttermere*, traverse Knott Rigg and aim for Newlands Hause. *The flanks of the fell are too rough for descent.*

The summit crags

looking down to Keskadale from the summit

Ard Crags 5

THE VIEW

The highlight of the view is the beautiful detail of Newlands, a picture of bright pastures intermingled with heathery ridges, backed by the Helvellyn range, which is seen end to end in the distance. In other directions, nearby higher fells seriously curtail the view, and this is especially so between west and north, where the massive wall of the Eel Crag range towers above, impressively close. Eel Crag itself impends on the scene overpoweringly. Also of interest is the regular pattern of aretes descending from the long summit of Scar Crags just across the deep valley of Rigg Beck.

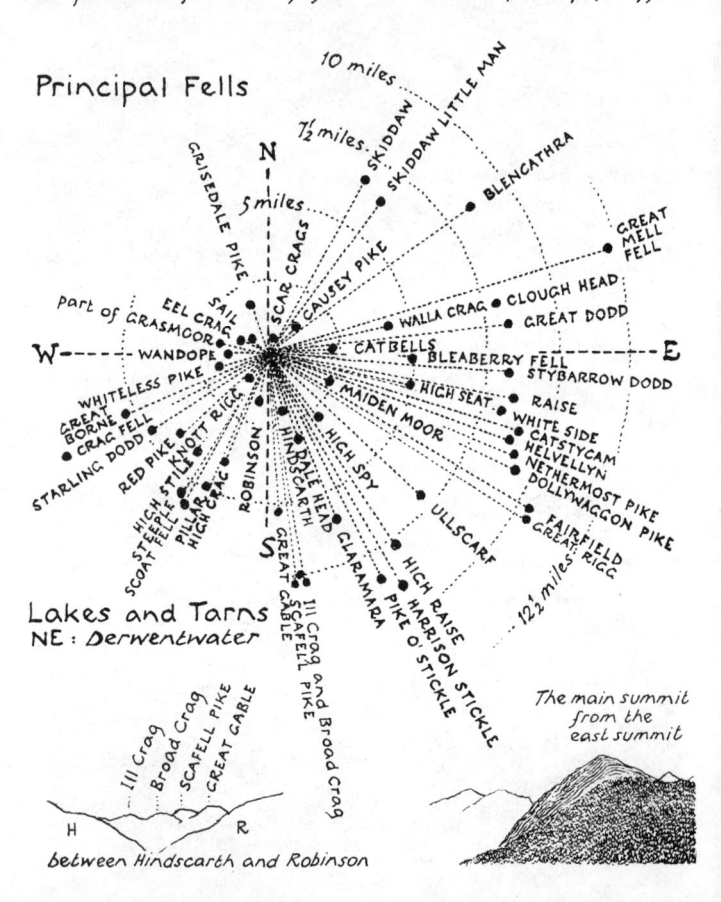

Principal Fells

Lakes and Tarns
NE: Derwentwater

between Hindscarth and Robinson

The main summit from the east summit

Ard Crags 6

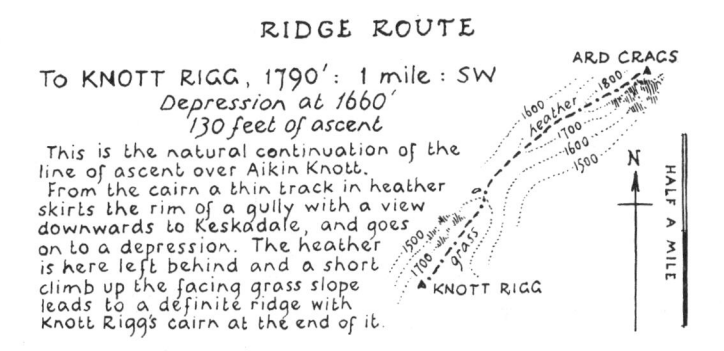

RIDGE ROUTE

To KNOTT RIGG, 1790': 1 mile : SW
Depression at 1660'
130 feet of ascent

This is the natural continuation of the line of ascent over Aikin Knott.

From the cairn a thin track in heather skirts the rim of a gully with a view downwards to Keskadale, and goes on to a depression. The heather is here left behind and a short climb up the facing grass slope leads to a definite ridge with Knott Rigg's cairn at the end of it.

looking southwest along the ridge to Knott Rigg

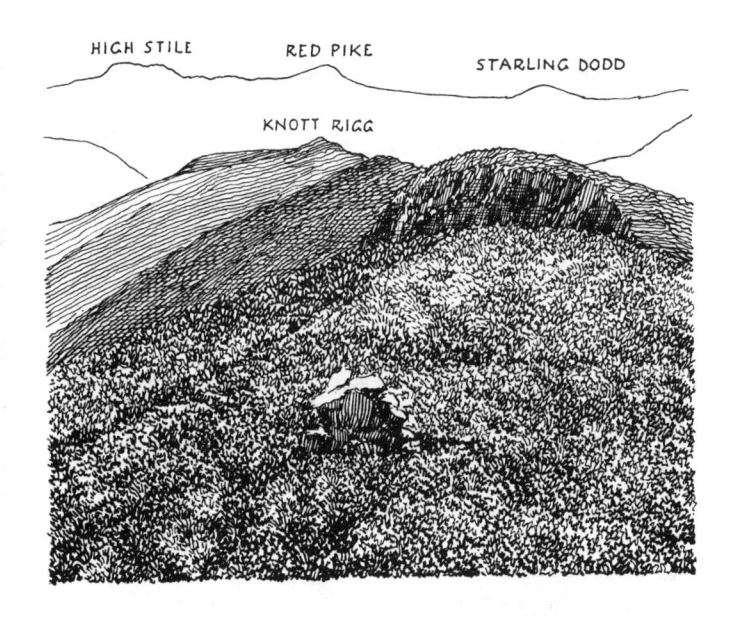

HIGH STILE   RED PIKE   STARLING DODD

KNOTT RIGG

Barf

1536'

from the main road near Beckstones

Barf 2

NATURAL FEATURES

Insignificant in height and of no greater extent than half a mile square, the rugged pyramid of Barf near the head of Bassenthwaite Lake yet contrives to arrest and retain the attention of travellers along the road at its base. Its outline is striking, its slopes seemingly impossibly steep; the direct ascent from its foot appears to be barred by an uncompromising cliff. There are few fells, large or small, of such hostile and aggressive character, for unrelenting steepness is allied to unstable runs of scree and outcrops. The rough ground is masked by bracken and heather, both enemies of smooth walking and rhythmical progression.... Passers-by look up at Barf with no thought of climbing it.

Barf is really a shoulder of Lord's Seat, which rises beyond but is unseen from the road. The neighbouring fells on both sides are densely planted with trees, but not so Barf. Crags and steep slopes do not normally deter the forestry workers but significantly they have not acquired any rights on Barf. This little rogue mountain cannot be tamed.

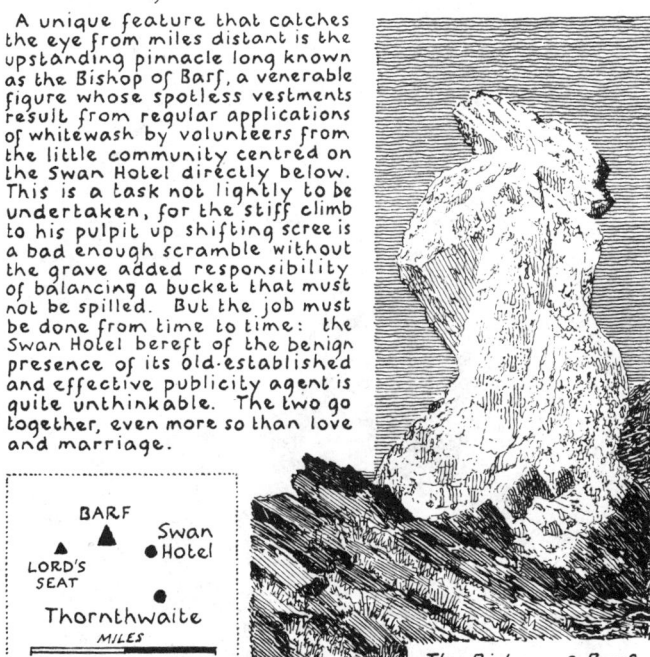

A unique feature that catches the eye from miles distant is the upstanding pinnacle long known as the Bishop of Barf, a venerable figure whose spotless vestments result from regular applications of whitewash by volunteers from the little community centred on the Swan Hotel directly below. This is a task not lightly to be undertaken, for the stiff climb to his pulpit up shifting scree is a bad enough scramble without the grave added responsibility of balancing a bucket that must not be spilled. But the job must be done from time to time: the Swan Hotel bereft of the benign presence of its old-established and effective publicity agent is quite unthinkable. The two go together, even more so than love and marriage.

The Bishop of Barf

Barf 3

MAP

The scale of this map is larger than that commonly used in the book

N ↑

COCKERMOUTH 8

Wythop Wood

Woodend

BARF 1536

Slape Crag

Falls

The Bishop

Beckstones Gill

The Clerk

Swan Hotel

Beckstones

MAIN ROAD

Seat Howe

old shaft

Beckstones Plantation

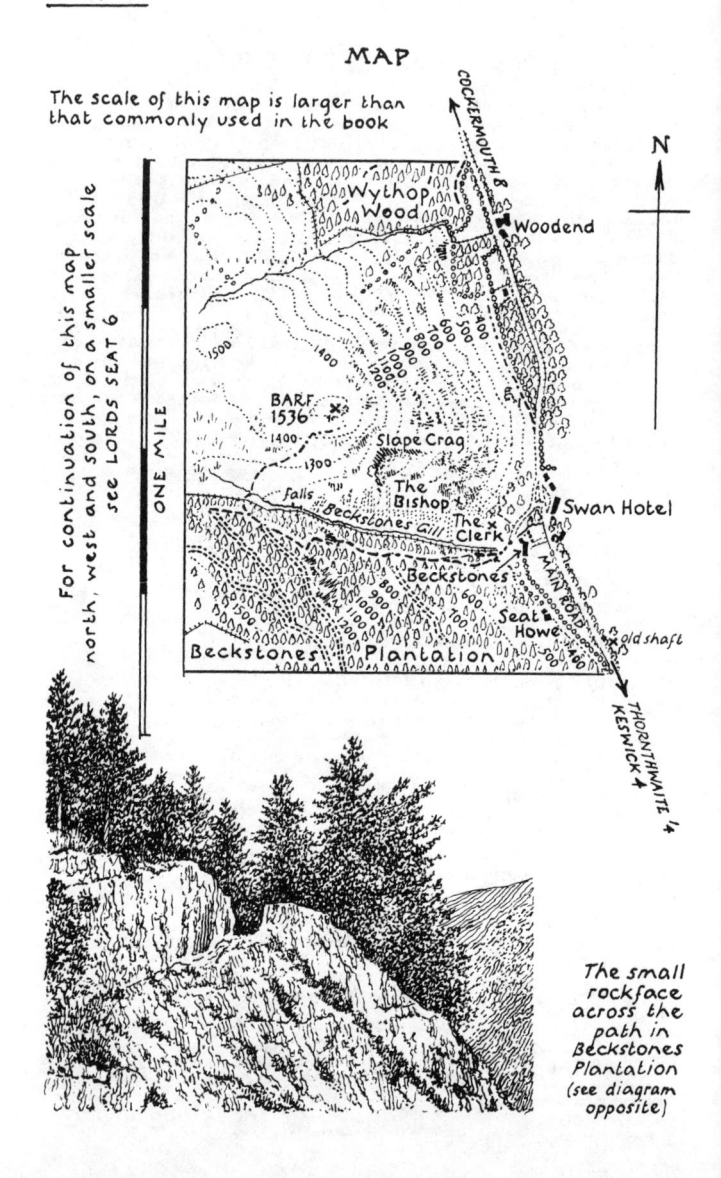

THORNTHWAITE ¼
KESWICK 4

For continuation of this map north, west and south, on a smaller scale see LORDS SEAT 6

ONE MILE

The small rockface across the path in Beckstones Plantation (see diagram opposite)

Barf 4

ASCENT FROM THORNTHWAITE
1220 feet of ascent : 1 mile (from the Swan Hotel)

Above the tree-line, easier slopes lead up to Lord's Seat

USUAL ROUTE

The path loses itself below the top. The highest point is above a white (quartz) rock

BARF

Blasted out of crags, this road is a considerable engineering achievement

new forest road

50 yards beyond the terminus of the forest road turn off the path continuing distinctly up through the wood, branching to the right and scaling the fence with the help of a few stones piled there for the purpose.

Beckstones Plantation

The route is in doubt at a small rockface. Climb this by a ledge running right and then left to a clear continuation of the path above.

old forest road

The lower (and older) plantings are mainly *larch*; higher, *spruce*.

✓ The Bishop

old path in groove — new track alongside

Beckstones Gill

The Bishop is conspicuous from the road, appearing as a detached pinnacle only for a short distance 55-60 yards north of the bus stop.

Take the path rising through the wood

bracken

Beckstones

MAIN ROAD — PHEASANT INN ¾
COCKERMOUTH 8½

looking west

THORNTHWAITE 2
KESWICK 4¼

bus stop

Swan Hotel

Bus route 34 (Keswick-Whitehaven) or 37 (Keswick-Thornthwaite terminus)

Once a popular ascent, this route has fallen from favour, and the path has been disturbed by forestry operations. Nevertheless, it remains one of the very best of the shorter Lakeland climbs.

Barf 5

The Clerk

In comparison with the commanding figure of the Bishop, the Clerk is a poor drooping individual who attracts little attention to himself. He stands amidst bracken at the foot of the slope. Once he too wore white vestments (which are sadly in need of renewal, a few ragged traces only remaining).

A visit to the Bishop discloses that, behind the spotless raiment he displays to the road below, his rear quarters are shamefully and indecently naked. Nor is he as tall as may be imagined: seven feet on the shortest side. Nevertheless it is to his credit that he has maintained his stately presence, for all around is the debris of shattered and eroded slate; the Bishop is slate, too, although obviously cast in a sterner mould. The time will come, however, when a collapsing pulpit will topple him down the screes.

The Bishop — rear view, looking down to the Swan Hotel

Barf 6

ASCENT FROM THORNTHWAITE
1200 feet of ascent : ¾ mile (from the Swan Hotel)

DIRECT ROUTE

Notes arranged from the bottom upwards

BARF
1500
looking west-north-west
second false summit: true summit in view
grass
first false summit: sudden, dramatic view of Bassenthwaite Lake below
heather
1400

Easier slopes now; difficulties over. sheep track
upper escarpment. Ignore track going up to it from end of traverse.

Round the escarpment on the left, at base of pinnacle.
pinnacle
steep heather 1200
traverse

The traverse revives lurid memories of Jack's Rake on Pavey Ark, but is short and easy.

Slape Crag — This obstacle can be safely negotiated at one point only. Bear left at its base, across scree, to a rock traverse above an oak and a rowan together.

Oak tree (a surprise!) and a rowan growing together on crags.
steep heather 1000

At last, a few yards of level walking

Slape Crag is now in view
solitary rowan tree
heather
900

By the time the rowan tree is reached the feeling that one is pioneering a new ascent, treading where no man has trodden before, is very strong, and consequently it is mortifying to find the slender trunk of the tree elaborately carved with the initials of countless earlier visitors.

Escape left over loose rock to a small arête, then go up an easier heather slope above
800
700

The Bishop

Scramble up to the Bishop and pass behind him to a scree gully beyond
gorse
600
scree

The scree gully is unpleasant. Its walls of rotten rock cannot be trusted for handholds and fall apart at a touch. The 'tiles' here pull out like drawers.

The Bishop stands on a remarkable pulpit built up of small flat tiles (of slate) lying horizontally.

Look out for the Clerk, an insignificant figure almost hidden amongst bracken in a clearing at the foot of the slope
500
400

This wide scree slope, although not dangerous, is arduous to ascend, the feet often slipping down two steps for every step up — from which it should not be supposed that better progress will be made by going up backwards. Keep to the scanty vegetation (gorse and bracken) where it exists.
In June, foxgloves make a colourful display here.

The Clerk
Beckstones
MAIN ROAD → PHEASANT INN 3¼
COCKERMOUTH 8½

Bus routes 34 or 37

Swan Hotel
bus stop

THORNTHWAITE 2
KESWICK 4¼

Not a walk.
A very stiff scramble, suitable only for people overflowing with animal strength and vigour.

Barf 7

THE SUMMIT

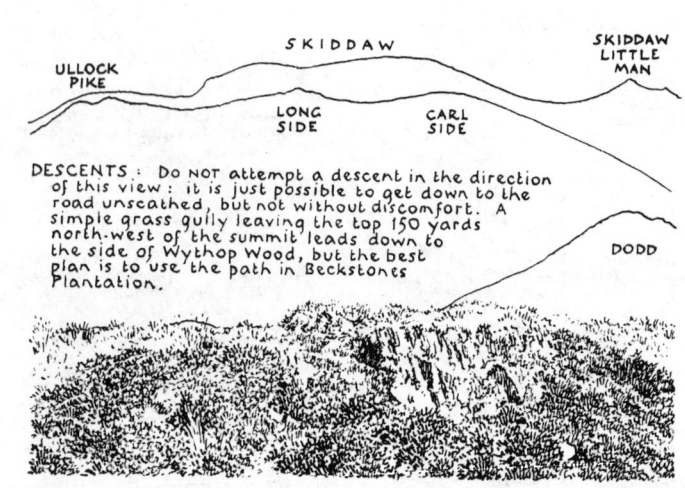

```
        SKIDDAW                    SKIDDAW
ULLOCK                             LITTLE
PIKE                                MAN
              LONG      CARL
              SIDE      SIDE
                                           DODD
```

DESCENTS: Do not attempt a descent in the direction of this view: it is just possible to get down to the road unscathed, but not without discomfort. A simple grass gully leaving the top 150 yards north-west of the summit leads down to the side of Wythop Wood, but the best plan is to use the path in Beckstones Plantation.

Heather encroaches almost to the bare top, a small platform with grass growing thinly on underlying rock, which, in places, shows through to form a pavement. There is no cairn, nor facilities for making one. The summit breaks away in an unseen crag on the side facing Skiddaw, a fact to bear well in mind if there are children in the party.

The top of Barf

Barf 8

THE VIEW

The summit of Barf is the one place above all others for appreciating the massive build-up of Skiddaw, here seen, at mid-height, piling up from the shore of Bassenthwaite Lake in three great leaps to the summit 1500 feet above the viewpoint. The lake, too, is exceptionally well displayed directly below — a sensational surprise for those who reach the top from 'behind'. There is a pleasing view of the Vale of Keswick and Derwentwater and an extensive prospect seawards.

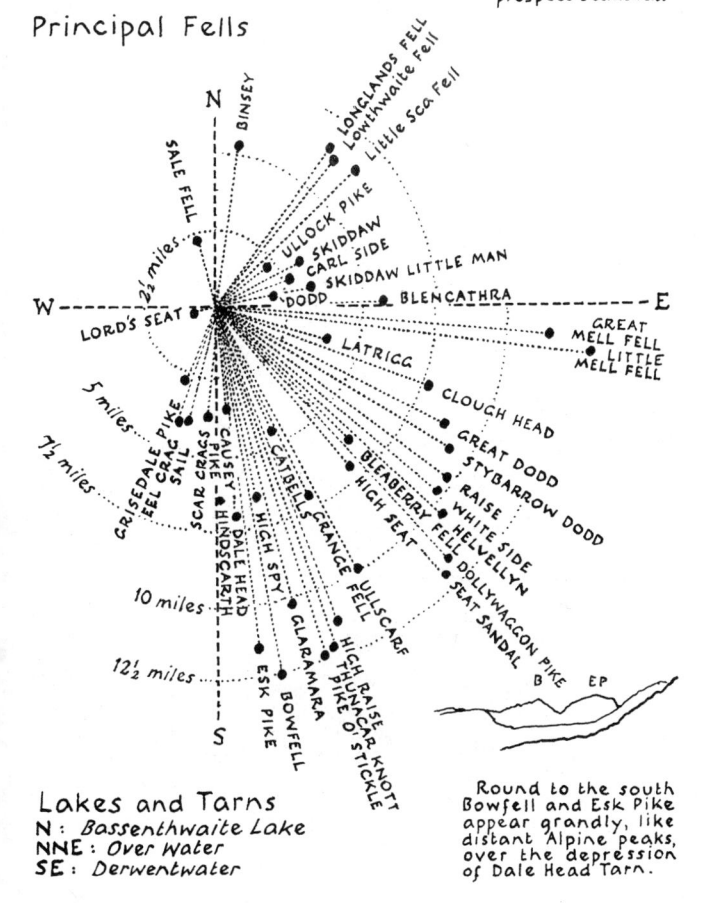

Principal Fells

BINSEY
LONGLANDS FELL
Lowthwaite Fell
Little Sca Fell
SALE FELL
ULLOCK PIKE
SKIDDAW
CARL SIDE
SKIDDAW LITTLE MAN
DODD
BLENCATHRA
LORD'S SEAT
2½ miles
W — — — — — — — — E
GREAT MELL FELL
LITTLE MELL FELL
LATRIGG
CLOUGH HEAD
GREAT DODD
5 miles
GRISEDALE PIKE
EEL CRAG
SAIL
STYBARROW DODD
7½ miles
SCAR CRAGS
CAUSEY PIKE
RAISE
WHITE SIDE
HELVELLYN
DALE HEAD
HINDSCARTH
CATBELLS
GRANGE FELL
BLEABERRY FELL
HIGH SEAT
DOLLYWAGGON PIKE
10 miles
HIGH SPY
ULLSCARF
SEAT SANDAL
12½ miles
GLARAMARA
HIGH RAISE
THUNACAR KNOTT
PIKE O' STICKLE
ESK PIKE
BOWFELL
S

B   EP

Lakes and Tarns
N: Bassenthwaite Lake
NNE: Over Water
SE: Derwentwater

Round to the south Bowfell and Esk Pike appear grandly, like distant Alpine peaks, over the depression of Dale Head Tarn.

Barf 9

RIDGE ROUTE

TO LORD'S SEAT, 1811' : ¾ mile : W
Depression at 1400' : 420 feet of ascent

The objective is clear enough, but the route is a matter of choice. Intermittent tracks are a help. It is generally better to prefer the bracken to the wide tracts of thick heather, where walking is rough. In mist, it is advisable to go down to the fence and, without crossing it, follow it up, skirting some swampy patches in the hollow.

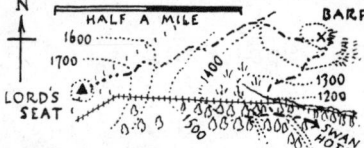

Lord's Seat from Barf

Barf 10

Barf, south side, from a forest road in Beckstones Plantation

Barf, north side, from a dead forest above Wythop Wood

Barrow 1494'

from Outerside
Stile End in the middle distance; Stonycroft Gill mine road down on the right

```
                Braithwaite
GRISEDALE          •
  ▲ PIKE
OUTERSIDE    ▲ BARROW
    ▲           • Stair
CAUSEY PIKE
         MILES
  ┠───┼───┼───┨
  0   1   2   3
```

from Newlands Beck

Barrow 2

NATURAL FEATURES

Barrow occupies an enviable position overlooking a scene as fair as any in the kingdom. In shape a long narrow ridge, rooted in Braithwaite, it rises to present a broad flank to the valley of Newlands before curving west, bounded by Stonycroft Gill, to join the mass of Outerside across the gap of Barrow Door. A great scar on the Newlands face marks the site of the once-famous Barrow Mine; on the opposite flank facing Coledale is another great scar, this one a natural formation, at a point where Barrow Gill, after an uneventful meandering from Barrow Door, is suddenly engulfed in a remarkable ravine, a gorge of amazing proportions for so slender a stream and deeper even than Piers Gill, which continues down, becoming wooded, to the cottages of Braithwaite. Bracken clothes the lower slopes of Barrow, but a dark cap of heather covers the higher reaches.

At Stonycroft Bridge an old water-cut (now dry) can be traced up, first carved in the rock and then following the contour of the fellside, with the gorge steeply below. The old level illustrated, half-hidden by gorse, is alongside the cut in its top part. This is the setting of the old Stonycroft Mine

Under Stonycroft Bridge. The beck enters the picture from the left. The dry watercut comes down on the right.

Barrow is 'the shivering mountain' of Lakeland. The great fan of spoil from the old mines on the Newlands face sweeps down to the road near Uzzicar and is prevented from burying it in debris only by a retaining parapet with a cleared space behind to accommodate major falls. The spoil is a sandy gravel constantly in slight motion, and the rustle of movement on the slope (no more than a whisper) can be heard on the road below. Note also an air shaft in the small field south of Uzzicar.

Barrow 3

Barrow Gill

looking up
the gill to
Barrow Door
and
Causey Pike

looking down
the gill to
Braithwaite

Barrow 4

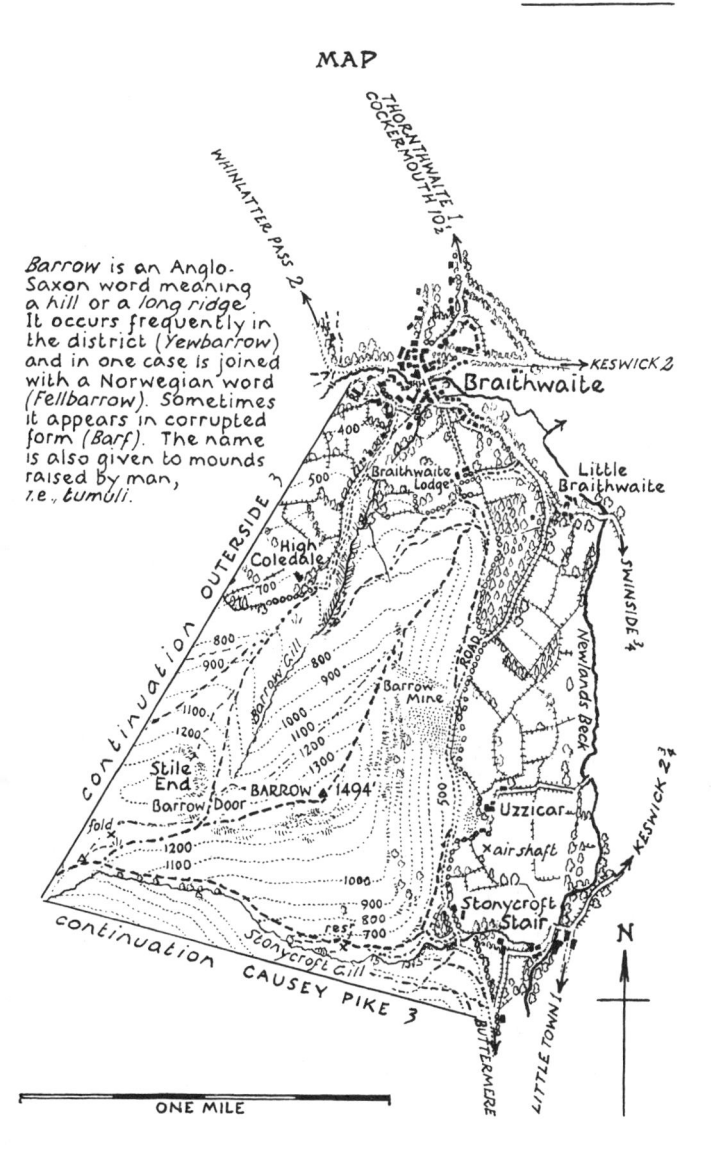

MAP

Barrow is an Anglo-Saxon word meaning a *hill* or a *long ridge*. It occurs frequently in the district (*Yewbarrow*) and in one case is joined with a Norwegian word (*Fellbarrow*). Sometimes it appears in corrupted form (*Barf*). The name is also given to mounds raised by man, i.e., *tumuli*.

ONE MILE

Barrow 5

ASCENT FROM BRAITHWAITE
1250 feet of ascent : 1½ miles

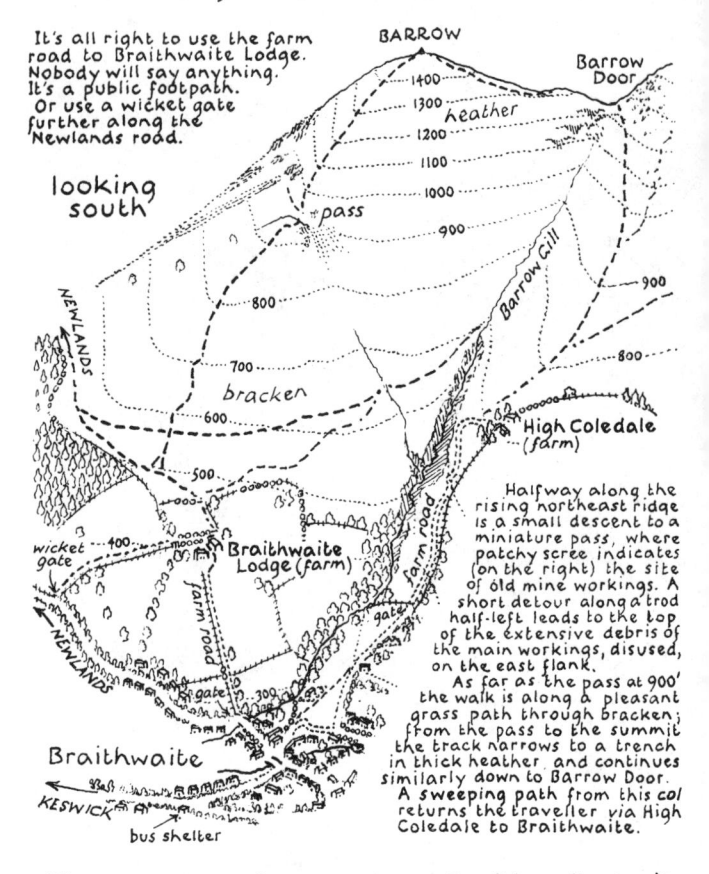

It's all right to use the farm road to Braithwaite Lodge. Nobody will say anything. It's a public footpath. Or use a wicket gate further along the Newlands road.

looking south

BARROW
Barrow Door
heather
pass
Barrow Gill
bracken
High Coledale (farm)
NEWLANDS
wicket gate
Braithwaite Lodge (farm)
farm road
gate
gate
Braithwaite
NEWLANDS
KESWICK
bus shelter

Halfway along the rising northeast ridge is a small descent to a miniature pass, where patchy scree indicates (on the right) the site of old mine workings. A short detour along a trod half-left leads to the top of the extensive debris of the main workings, disused, on the east flank.

As far as the pass at 900' the walk is along a pleasant grass path through bracken; from the pass to the summit the track narrows to a trench in thick heather and continues similarly down to Barrow Door. A sweeping path from this col returns the traveller via High Coledale to Braithwaite.

The ascent of Barrow from Braithwaite by its facing ridge is a favourite Sunday afternoon ramble, in the category of Latrigg and Catbells and Loughrigg Fell, and every step of the way is a joy. The walk can be extended, as indicated, to make a round journey of about two hours.

Barrow 6

ASCENT FROM STAIR
1200 feet of ascent : 2¼ miles

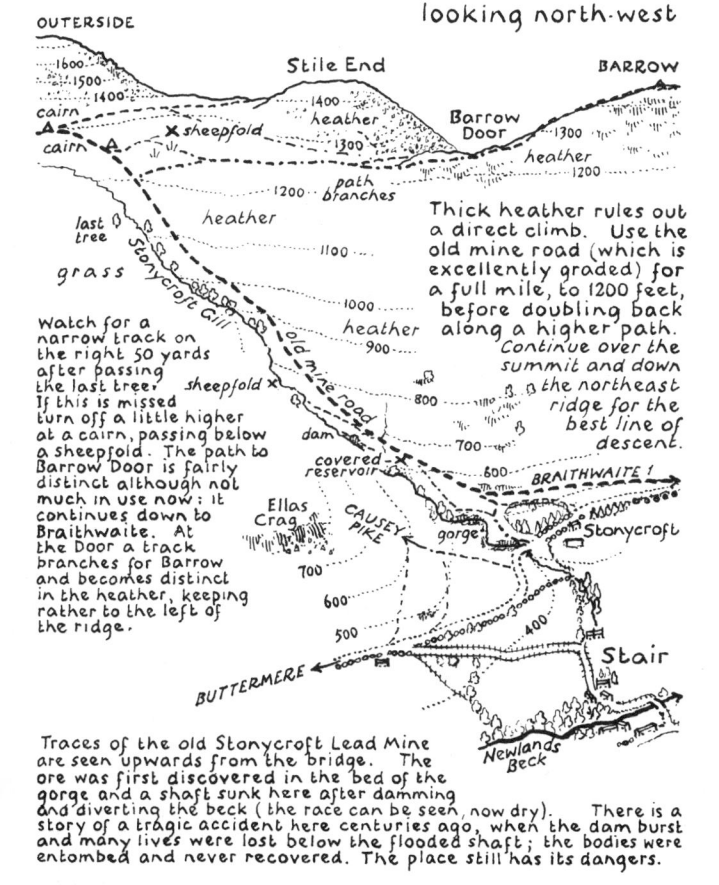

looking north-west

OUTERSIDE — Stile End — BARROW — Barrow Door — heather — cairn — sheepfold — path branches — heather — last tree — grass — Stonycroft Gill — old mine road — heather — sheepfold — dam — covered reservoir — Ellas Crag — CAUSEY PIKE — gorge — Stonycroft — BRAITHWAITE — Stair — Newlands Beck — BUTTERMERE

Thick heather rules out a direct climb. Use the old mine road (which is excellently graded) for a full mile, to 1200 feet, before doubling back along a higher path. Continue over the summit and down the northeast ridge for the best line of descent.

Watch for a narrow track on the right 50 yards after passing the last tree. If this is missed turn off a little higher at a cairn, passing below a sheepfold. The path to Barrow Door is fairly distinct although not much in use now: it continues down to Braithwaite. At the Door a track branches for Barrow and becomes distinct in the heather, keeping rather to the left of the ridge.

Traces of the old Stonycroft Lead Mine are seen upwards from the bridge. The ore was first discovered in the bed of the gorge and a shaft sunk here after damming and diverting the beck (the race can be seen, now dry). There is a story of a tragic accident here centuries ago, when the dam burst and many lives were lost below the flooded shaft; the bodies were entombed and never recovered. The place still has its dangers.

The old mine road has become a first-class walkers' way into the hills, progress being fast and easy, and it lends itself well, coupled with a linking path from Braithwaite, to an ascent of Barrow, while giving an introduction to the quiet upper reaches of Stonycroft Gill. Causey Pike on the left of the valley dominates the walk throughout.

Barrow 7

THE SUMMIT

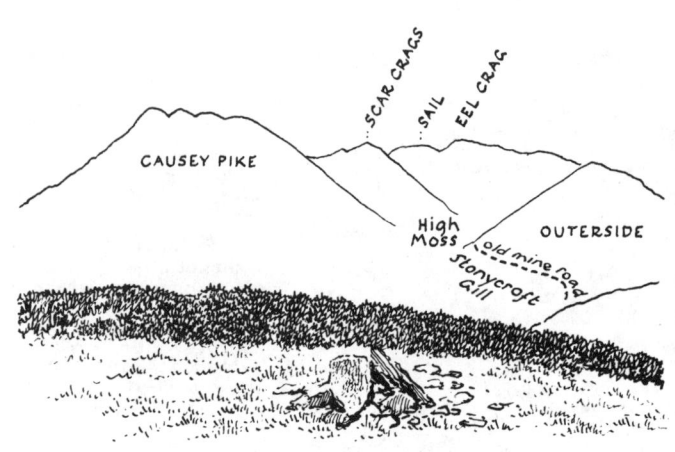

A small cairn occupies a patch of grass on the highest point with heather all around. On the right sort of day this is a grand place for settling down and getting the old pipe out for an hour's quiet meditation.
DESCENTS: Use only the track along the ridge, either way. In particular do not attempt a direct route for Newlands.

RIDGE ROUTE

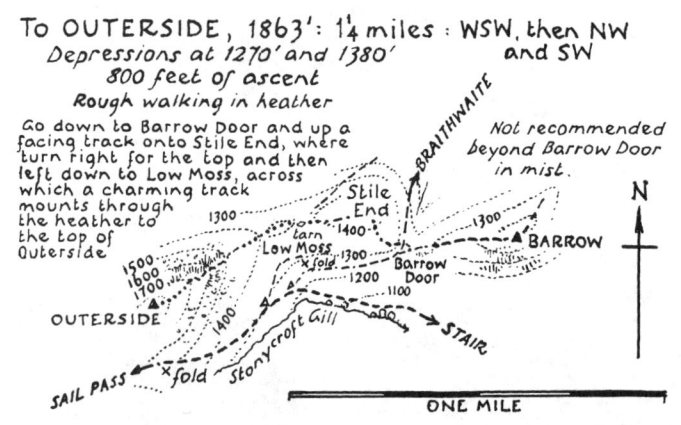

To OUTERSIDE, 1863': 1¼ miles: WSW, then NW and SW
Depressions at 1270' and 1380'
800 feet of ascent
Rough walking in heather

Go down to Barrow Door and up a facing track onto Stile End, where turn right for the top and then left down to Low Moss, across which a charming track mounts through the heather to the top of Outerside.

Not recommended beyond Barrow Door in mist.

ONE MILE

Barrow 8

THE VIEW

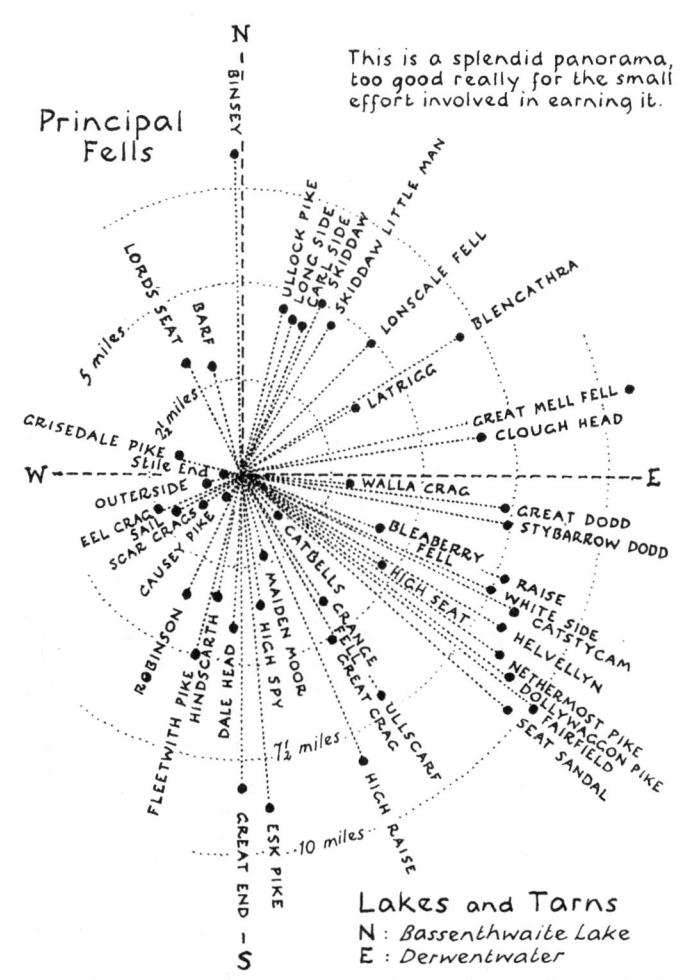

This is a splendid panorama, too good really for the small effort involved in earning it.

Principal Fells

N — BINSEY
ULLOCK PIKE
LONG SIDE
CARL SIDE
SKIDDAW
SKIDDAW LITTLE MAN
LONSCALE FELL
BLENCATHRA
LORDS SEAT
BARF
5 miles
2½ miles
LATRIGG
GREAT MELL FELL
CLOUGH HEAD
GRISEDALE PIKE
Stile End
W — — — — — E
OUTERSIDE
WALLA CRAG
GREAT DODD
EEL CRAG
STYBARROW DODD
SAIL
BLEABERRY FELL
SCAR CRAGS
RAISE
CAUSEY PIKE
HIGH SEAT
WHITE SIDE
CATSTYCAM
CATBELLS
HELVELLYN
MAIDEN MOOR
GRANGE FELL
NETHERMOST PIKE
ROBINSON
HIGH SPY
GREAT CRAG
DOLLYWAGGON PIKE
FLEETWITH PIKE
FAIRFIELD
HINDSCARTH
DALE HEAD
ULLSCARF
SEAT SANDAL
7½ miles
GREAT END
ESK PIKE
HIGH RAISE
10 miles
S

Lakes and Tarns
N: Bassenthwaite Lake
E: Derwentwater

There is a remarkable contrast between the smiling Vale of Keswick, where Derwentwater is excellently displayed, and the sombre ring of fells crowded nearby in the west. Away over the head of Newlands is Esk Hause with Esk Pike soaring magnificently to the left of it and looking every inch a mountain

Broom Fell 1670'

from Aiken Plantation

Cockermouth
Wythop Mill
LING FELL ▲ ▲ SALE FELL
GRAYSTONES   ▲ BROOM FELL
Low Lorton   ▲ LORDS SEAT
• High Lorton
Whinlatter Pass

MILES
0 1 2 3 4

Broom Fell 2

NATURAL FEATURES

Broom Fell is the geographical centre of the upland mass rising between Bassenthwaite Lake in the north and Whinlatter Pass in the south, but acknowledges the superiority of a near and higher neighbour, Lord's Seat, to which it is connected by a high ridge. There is little of interest on this rounded grassy hill, and nothing to justify a special visit to the summit; its flanking valleys, however, are sharply contrasted, each having distinguishing features worthy of note. North is the open valley of Wythop, a place of farms and green pastures, but before the descending slopes reach cultivable levels they are halted at a morass, the remarkable mile-wide Wythop Moss — a hopeless, lifeless swamp that can be traversed conveniently only at the one place where a causeway of firmer ground has been laid out and ditched to facilitate a crossing. South is the narrow side valley of Aiken Beck, with the rare distinction of being enclosed on all four sides: a hidden valley, uninhabited, and frequented only for purposes of forestry, most of it being under timber.

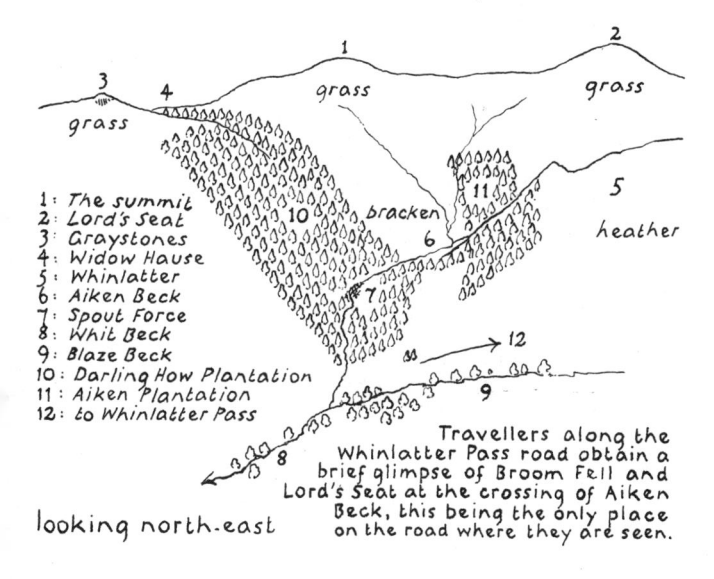

1: The summit
2: Lord's Seat
3: Graystones
4: Widow Hause
5: Whinlatter
6: Aiken Beck
7: Spout Force
8: Whit Beck
9: Blaze Beck
10: Darling How Plantation
11: Aiken Plantation
12: to Whinlatter Pass

looking north-east

Travellers along the Whinlatter Pass road obtain a brief glimpse of Broom Fell and Lord's Seat at the crossing of Aiken Beck, this being the only place on the road where they are seen.

Broom Fell 3

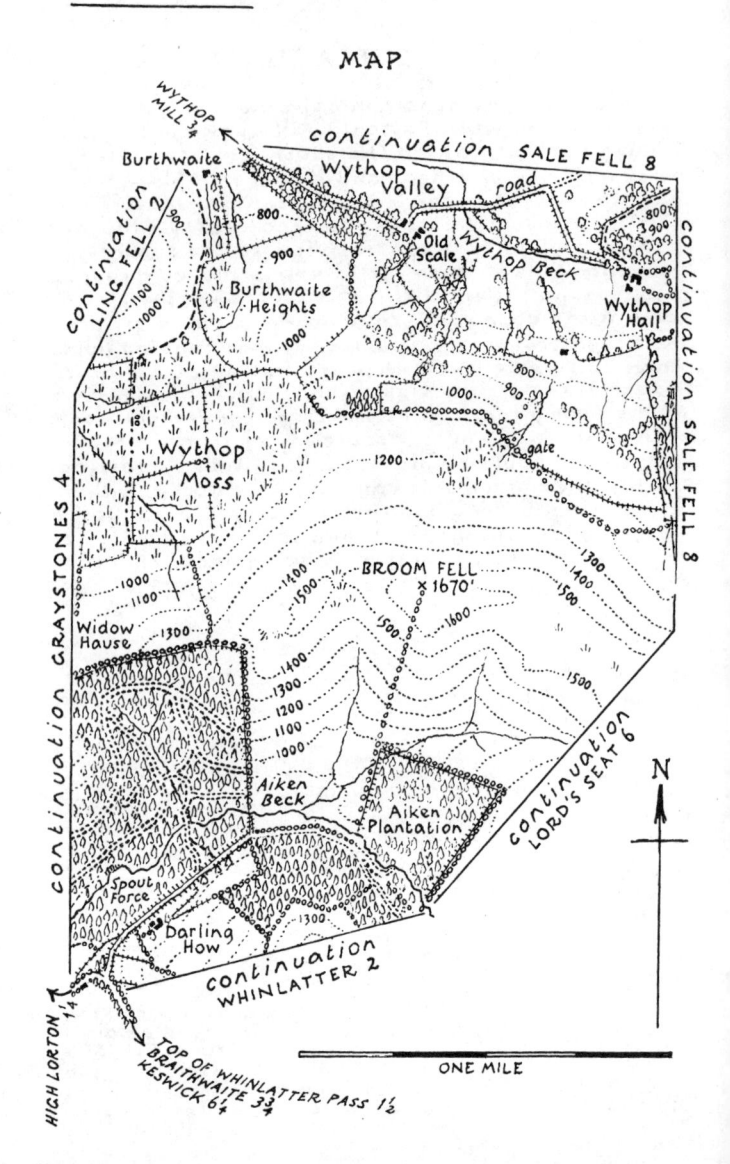

MAP

Broom Fell 4

ASCENT FROM WYTHOP MILL
1450 feet of ascent : 4 miles

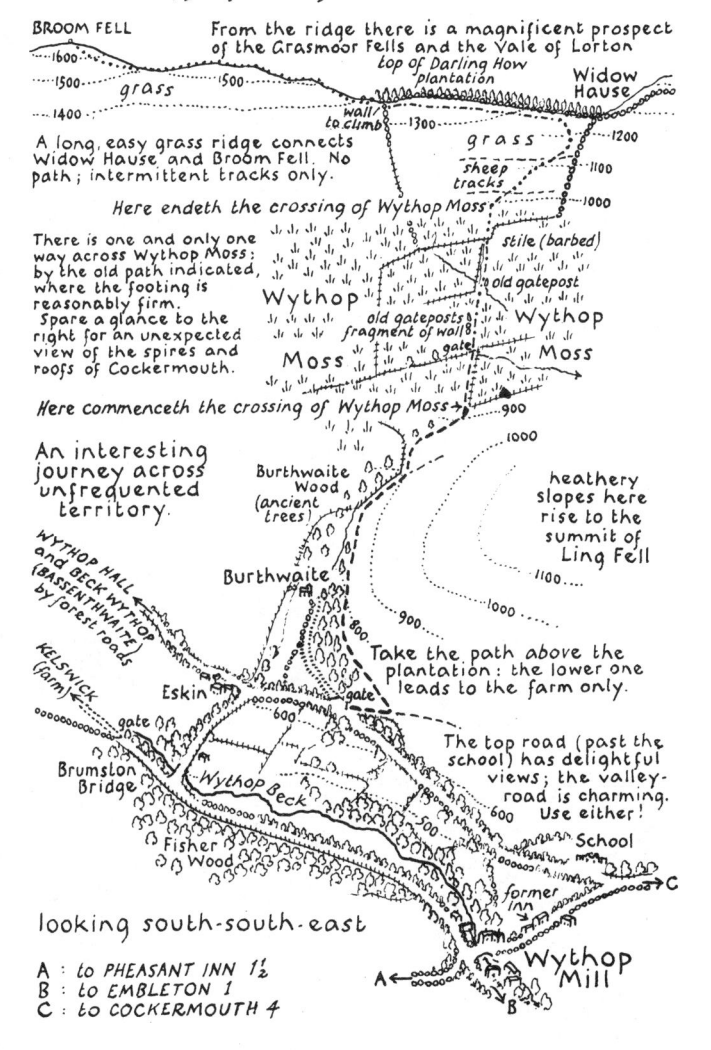

BROOM FELL — From the ridge there is a magnificent prospect of the Grasmoor Fells and the Vale of Lorton

top of Darling How plantation

Widow Hause

grass

wall to climb

A long, easy grass ridge connects Widow Hause and Broom Fell. No path; intermittent tracks only.

grass

sheep tracks

Here endeth the crossing of Wythop Moss

stile (barbed)

There is one and only one way across Wythop Moss: by the old path indicated, where the footing is reasonably firm.
Spare a glance to the right for an unexpected view of the spires and roofs of Cockermouth.

Wythop Moss

old gatepost

old gateposts fragment of wall

Wythop Moss

gate

Here commenceth the crossing of Wythop Moss →

An interesting journey across unfrequented territory.

Burthwaite Wood (ancient trees)

heathery slopes here rise to the summit of Ling Fell

Burthwaite

WYTHOP HALL and BECK WYTHOP (BASSENTHWAITE) by forest roads

KELSWICK (farm)

Take the path above the plantation: the lower one leads to the farm only.

Eskin

gate

gate

Brumston Bridge

Wythop Beck

The top road (past the school) has delightful views; the valley road is charming. Use either!

Fisher Wood

School

former inn

looking south-south-east

Wythop Mill

A : to PHEASANT INN 1½
B : to EMBLETON 1
C : to COCKERMOUTH 4

Broom Fell 5

ASCENT FROM HIGH LORTON
1400 feet of ascent : 3 miles

looking east-north-east

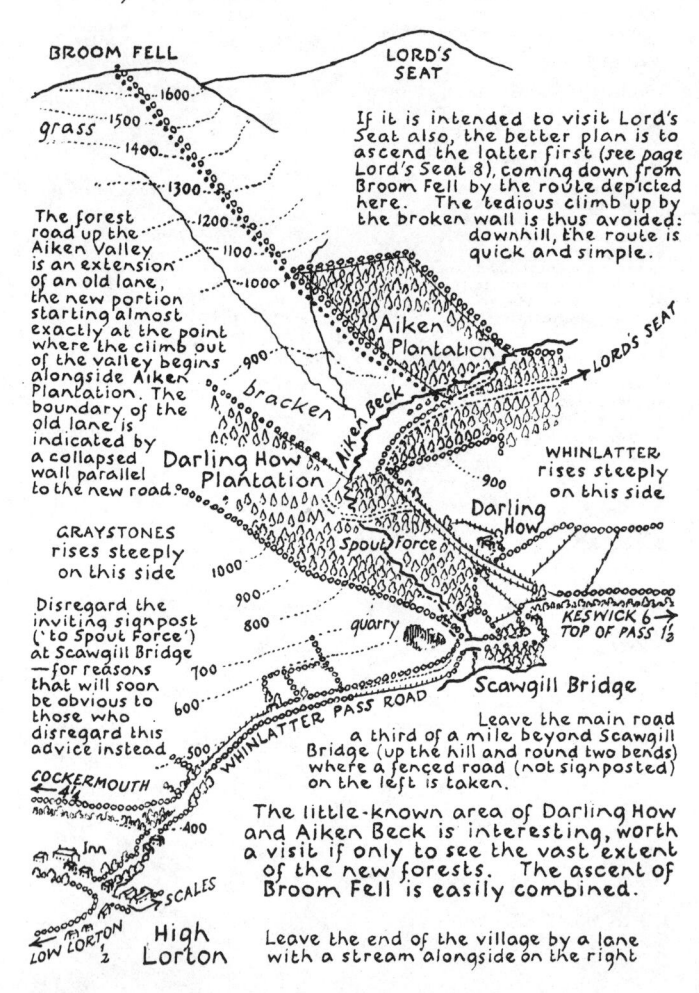

BROOM FELL — LORD'S SEAT

grass — 1600, 1500, 1400, 1300, 1200, 1100, 1000

If it is intended to visit Lord's Seat also, the better plan is to ascend the latter first (see page Lord's Seat 8), coming down from Broom Fell by the route depicted here. The tedious climb up by the broken wall is thus avoided: downhill, the route is quick and simple.

The forest road up the Aiken Valley is an extension of an old lane, the new portion starting almost exactly at the point where the climb out of the valley begins alongside Aiken Plantation. The boundary of the old lane is indicated by a collapsed wall parallel to the new road.

Aiken Plantation

bracken

Aiken Beck

← LORD'S SEAT

Darling How Plantation

WHINLATTER rises steeply on this side

Darling How

Spout Force

GRAYSTONES rises steeply on this side

KESWICK 6 →
TOP OF PASS 1½

quarry

Scawgill Bridge

Disregard the inviting signpost ('to Spout Force') at Scawgill Bridge — for reasons that will soon be obvious to those who disregard this advice instead

WHINLATTER PASS ROAD

← COCKERMOUTH 4

Inn

→ SCALES

← LOW LORTON ½

High Lorton

Leave the main road a third of a mile beyond Scawgill Bridge (up the hill and round two bends) where a fenced road (not signposted) on the left is taken.

The little-known area of Darling How and Aiken Beck is interesting, worth a visit if only to see the vast extent of the new forests. The ascent of Broom Fell is easily combined.

Leave the end of the village by a lane with a stream alongside on the right

Broom Fell 6

THE SUMMIT
looking southeast

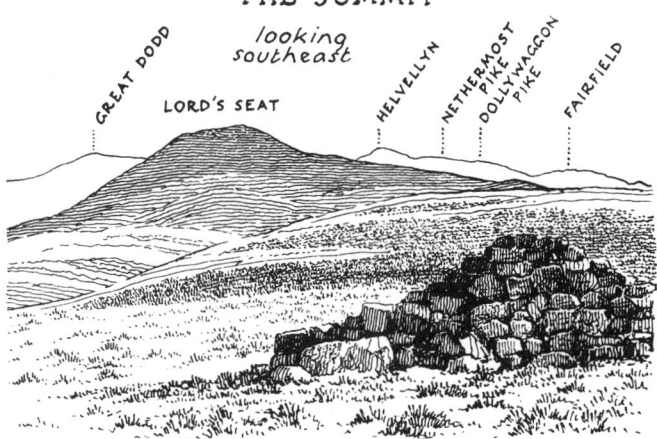

GREAT DODD — LORD'S SEAT — HELVELLYN — NETHERMOST PIKE — DOLLYWAGGON PIKE — FAIRFIELD

The grassy top of the fell is featureless except for an oddity in the shape of a wall that comes up the fellside from Aiken Beck to end precisely at the highest point — the odd thing being that it is a perfectly straight wall throughout its length, enclosing nothing, defending nothing, sheltering nothing, marking nothing and obviously of little value because it has fallen into disrepair.

DESCENTS: All slopes are easy, the western going down to Wythop Moss, where the old path must be used to cross the morass. In mist, let the wall serve as a guide downhill for Lorton.

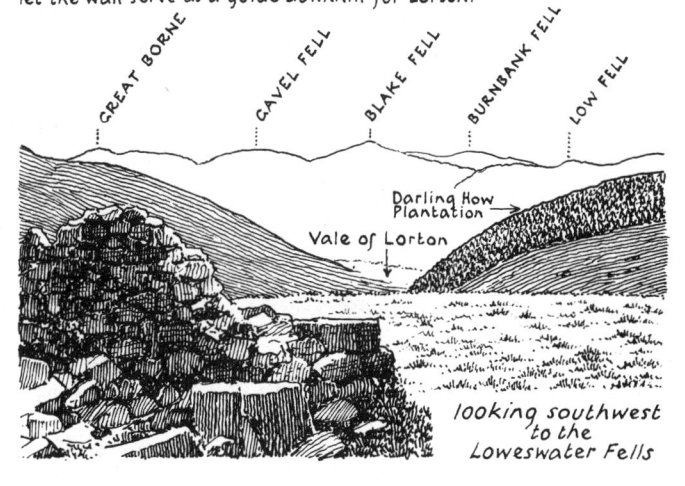

GREAT BORNE — GAVEL FELL — BLAKE FELL — BURNBANK FELL — LOW FELL

Darling How Plantation

Vale of Lorton

looking southwest to the Loweswater Fells

Broom Fell 7

THE VIEW

The gem of the view is the Vale of Lorton backed by the fells around Loweswater — a lovely scene. The Grasmoor group is massed impressively across the gulf of Whinlatter Pass. Beyond Bassenthwaite Lake Skiddaw rises grandly.
Northwest is a wide sweep of the
Solway Firth and the
Scottish hills, with
Criffell prominent.

Principal Fells

(compass diagram showing bearings and distances to surrounding fells)

N: BINSEY, SALE FELL, LONGLANDS FELL, Lowthwaite Fell, Little Sca Fell, GREAT SCA FELL, KNOTT
LING FELL
ULLOCK PIKE, SKIDDAW, CARL SIDE, SKIDDAW LITTLE MAN, BLENCATHRA
DODD
LITTLE MELL FELL
LORD'S SEAT
CLOUGH HEAD
GREAT DODD
GRAYSTONES
FELLBARROW
LOW FELL
BURNBANK FELL, BLAKE FELL
WHITESIDE, GRASMOOR, HOPEGILL HEAD, EEL CRAG, GRISEDALE PIKE, SCAR CRAGS, CAUSEY PIKE, HIGH SPY
HELVELLYN, NETHERMOST PIKE, DOLLYWAGGON PIKE, FAIRFIELD
GAVEL FELL
GREAT BORNE
ULLSCARF
HIGH RAISE, THUNACAR KNOTT
CLARAMARA

Distances: 2½ miles, 5 miles, 7½ miles, 10 miles, 12½ miles

Lakes and Tarns:
NE: Over Water
NE: Bassenthwaite Lake (two sections)

The skyline to the south: GRISEDALE PIKE — EEL CRAG — Sand Hill — HOPEGILL HEAD — GRASMOOR — WHITESIDE

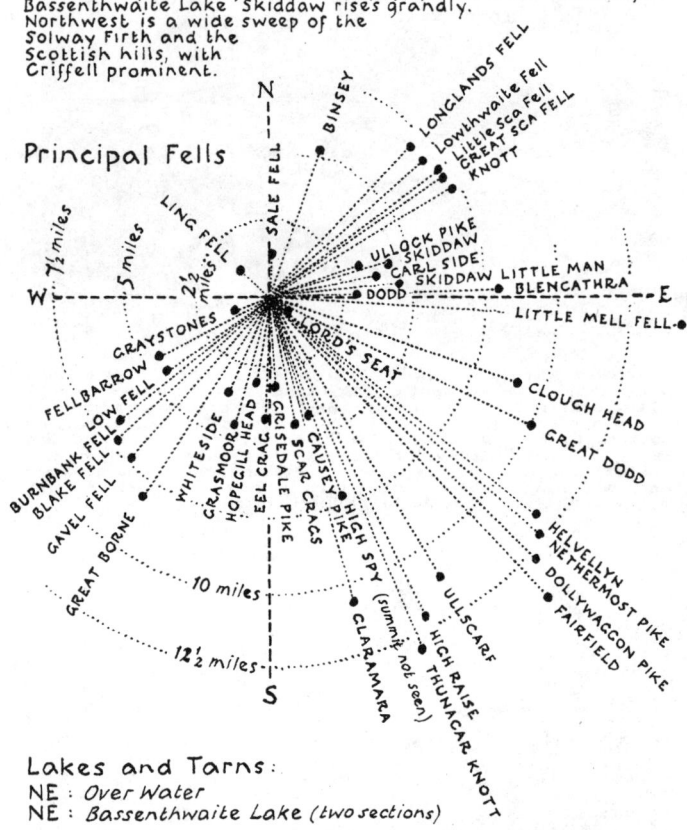

Broom Fell 8

RIDGE ROUTES

To LORD'S SEAT, 1811' : 7/8 mile : SE
Depression at 1586' : 260 feet of ascent
An easy ridge, with nothing of special interest.

The ridge is wide, marshy in places, and carries no path; it has many small undulations, and the actual lowest point, at 1586', just before the ground steepens into the final rise of Lord's Seat, cannot be identified with certainty; not that it matters. This is the slope of Lord's Seat on which the 'seat' is supposed to be found, but its exact location is also in doubt. This doesn't matter either, the author having personally installed himself in every rock recess hereabouts (anxious as always for the comfort of his readers) and found the process merely painful.

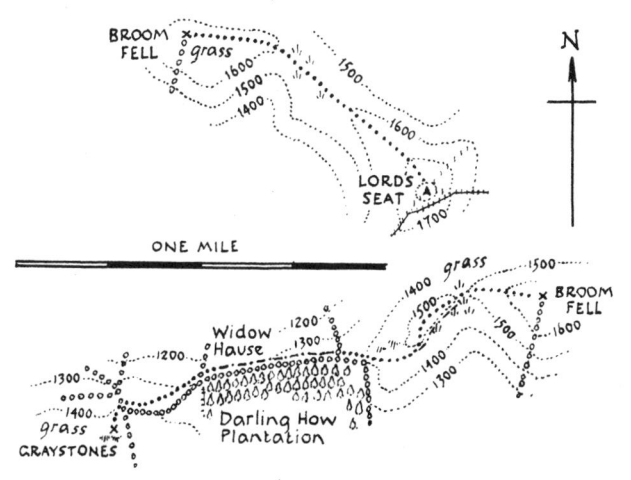

To GRAYSTONES, 1476' : 1¼ miles : WSW
Depression at 1240' (Widow Hause) : 260 feet of ascent
Interest is sustained on this easy walk by the variety of scenery

Starting due west, follow the height of land across a moist depression to firmer ground beyond, which trends south to the corner of Darling How Plantation. (Or use a narrow track that keeps just left of the 1500' contour) Here the crumbling wall that formerly ran solitary along the descending ridge to Widow Hause is now accompanied by a tight forest fence, the plantings here having been carried the full height of the fellside from the valley of Aiken Beck below. The fence continues on to Graystones, enclosing an area not yet planted, and the crossing of three walls is involved in keeping outside it. When it finally turns south the summit of Graystones is only two minutes away.

Castle Crag

**985'
approx.**

Grange
CASTLE ▲ CRAG
Rosthwaite
ONE MILE

from the south

Castle Crag 2

NATURAL FEATURES

Perhaps, to be strictly correct, Castle Crag should be regarded not as a separate fell but as a protuberance on the rough breast of Low Scawdel, occurring almost at the foot of the slope and remote from the ultimate summit of High Spy far above and out of sight. Castle Crag has no major geographical function — it is not a watershed, does not persuade the streams of Scawdel from their predestined purpose of joining the Derwent and interrupts only slightly the natural fall of the fell to Borrowdale: on the general scale of the surrounding heights it is of little significance.

Yet Castle Crag is so magnificently independent, so ruggedly individual, so aggressively unashamed of its lack of inches, that less than justice would be done by relegating it to a paragraph in the High Spy chapter. If its top is below 1000 feet, which is doubtful (no 'official' height having been determined), it is the only fell below 1000 feet in this series of books that is awarded the 'full treatment', a distinction well earned.

Castle Crag conforms to no pattern. It is an obstruction in the throat of Borrowdale, confining passage therein to the width of a river and a road, hiding what lies beyond, defying cultivation. Its abrupt pyramid, richly wooded from base almost to summit but bare at the top, is a wild tangle of rough steep ground, a place of crags and scree and tumbled boulders, of quarry holes and spoil dumps, of confusion and disorder. But such is the artistry of nature, such is the mellowing influence of the passing years, that the scars of disarray and decay have been transformed in a romantic harmony, cloaked by a canopy of trees and a carpet of leaves. There are lovely copses of silver birch by the crystal-clear river, magnificent specimens of Scots pine higher up. Naked of trees, Castle Crag would be ugly; with them, it has a sylvan beauty unsurpassed, unique.

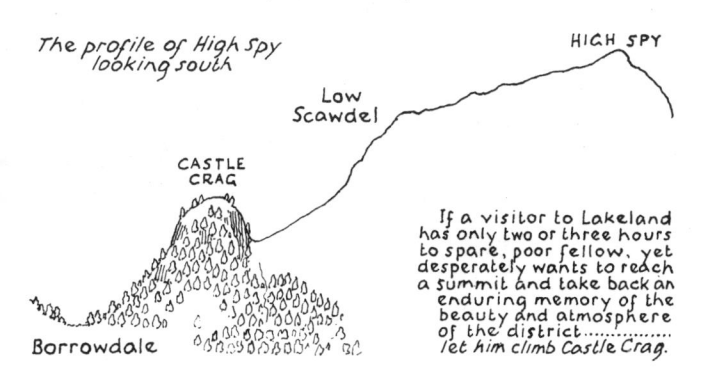

The profile of High Spy looking south

HIGH SPY

Low Scawdel

CASTLE CRAG

Borrowdale

If a visitor to Lakeland has only two or three hours to spare, poor fellow, yet desperately wants to reach a summit and take back an enduring memory of the beauty and atmosphere of the district............ let him climb Castle Crag.

Castle Crag 3

The summit-quarry

The pedestrian path to the top goes up the grass on the right

summit

Quarries and caves of Castle Crag

In addition to the summit-quarry, which is open to the sky and obvious to all who climb the fell, the steep flank above the Derwent is pitted with cuttings and caverns and levels, every hole having its tell-tale spoilheap, but the scars of this former industrial activity are largely concealed by a screen of trees and not generally noticed. Much of this flank is precipitous, the ground everywhere is very rough, and the vertically-hewn walls of naked stone are dangerous traps for novice explorers.

Of these quarries the best known is High Hows, the debris of which is passed on the riverside walk from Grange to Rosthwaite. A detour up the quarry road leads to a series of caverns, which for older walkers have a nostalgic interest: here in one of them Millican Dalton, a mountaineering adventurer and a familiar character in the district between the wars (died 1947, aged 80) furnished a home for his summer residence, using an adjacent cave at a higher level (the 'Attic') as sleeping quarters. Note here his lettering cut in the rock at the entrance —
'Don't!! Waste words, jump to conclusions'

The Attic

Millican's Cave

Castle Crag 4

MAP

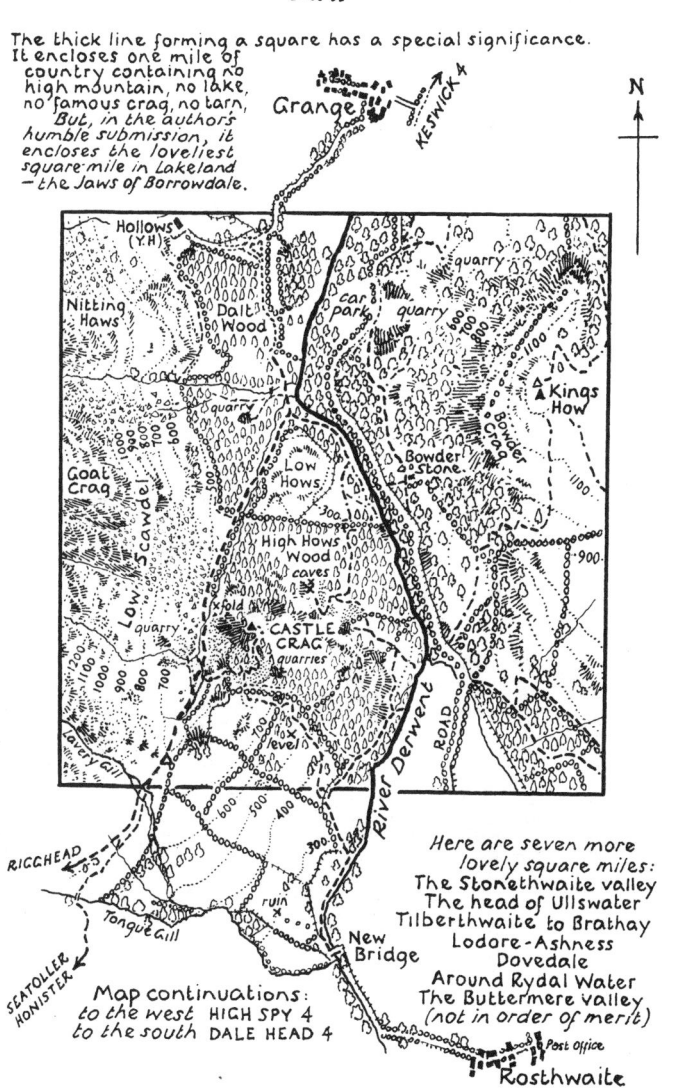

The thick line forming a square has a special significance. It encloses one mile of country containing no high mountain, no lake, no famous crag, no tarn. But, in the author's humble submission, it encloses the loveliest square mile in Lakeland — the Jaws of Borrowdale.

Here are seven more lovely square miles:
The Stonethwaite valley
The head of Ullswater
Tilberthwaite to Brathay
Lodore-Ashness
Dovedale
Around Rydal Water
The Buttermere valley
(not in order of merit)

Map continuations:
to the west HIGH SPY 4
to the south DALE HEAD 4

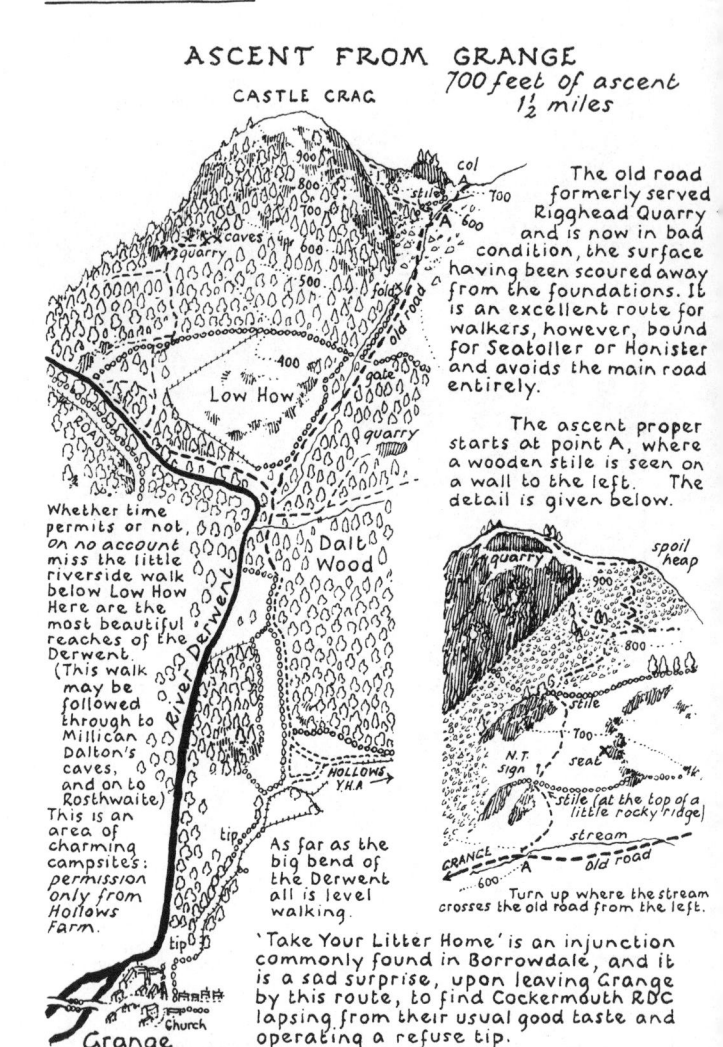

Castle Crag 5

ASCENT FROM GRANGE
CASTLE CRAG
700 feet of ascent
1½ miles

The old road formerly served Rigghead Quarry and is now in bad condition, the surface having been scoured away from the foundations. It is an excellent route for walkers, however, bound for Seatoller or Honister and avoids the main road entirely.

The ascent proper starts at point A, where a wooden stile is seen on a wall to the left. The detail is given below.

Whether time permits or not, on no account miss the little riverside walk below Low How. Here are the most beautiful reaches of the Derwent. (This walk may be followed through to Millican Dalton's caves, and on to Rosthwaite.) This is an area of charming campsites: permission only from Hollows Farm.

As far as the big bend of the Derwent all is level walking.

Turn up where the stream crosses the old road from the left.

'Take Your Litter Home' is an injunction commonly found in Borrowdale, and it is a sad surprise, upon leaving Grange by this route, to find Cockermouth RDC lapsing from their usual good taste and operating a refuse tip.

Grange
looking south

Leave Grange by a lane (YHA sign) almost opposite the Church

Castle Crag 6

ASCENT FROM ROSTHWAITE
700 feet of ascent
1½ miles

looking north-west

From the ridge, the old Rigghead-Grange 'road' can be seen ahead and below in a wild setting.

There are magnificent Scots pines near the wall at the top of the wood.

A quarry path ascends the big enclosure (A). A detour of 50 yards to the old level and stone shelter, which are typical evidences of former quarrying operations, is recommended. Near the top corner of the enclosure the original path crossed the wall (step-stile, not obvious) and proceeded on the far side to the ridge. This route is not now used, and it is more usual to pass through the gap in the cross-wall to enclosure B (note another level here in the corner) and, upon reaching the ridge, climb the wall to join the original route: a stile is needed here. Now the spoil-heap ahead is climbed by a zig-zag path carved in the naked stones, after which the way to the summit is clear.

Leave Rosthwaite by the lane opposite the post office, bearing right at the farm buildings.

Old quarry workings, Castle Crag

A typical stone store or shelter hut (only 3 to 4 feet high)

An old level

Castle Crag 7

THE SUMMIT

The summit is circular in plan, about 60 yards in diameter, and a perfect natural stronghold. Even today, one man in possession, armed with a stick, could prevent its occupation by others whatever their number, there being one strategic point (the place of access to the top) where passage upward is restricted to single-file traffic. Authorities agree that there was once a fort here, probably early British, but it needs a trained eye to trace any earthworks — which, in any case, must have been severely disturbed by an old quarry that has cut a big slice out of the summit and, be it noted, constitutes an unprotected danger. Photographers (who have a habit of taking backward steps when composing their pictures) should take care lest they suddenly vanish.

The highest point is a boss of rock, and this is crowned by a professionally-made round flat-topped cairn, below which, set in the rock, is a commemorative tablet: a war memorial to the men of Borrowdale, effective and imaginative. A stunted larch grows alongside, clinging for dear life to the rim of a crag, and better specimens surround the perimeter.

DESCENTS: For the ordinary walker there is only one way on and off, and this is on the south side, by a clump of larch, where a clear track descends between the edge of the quarry (right) and a cutting (left) to the flat top of the spoil-heap, at the end of which a ramp on the right inclines in zigzags to the grass below. Here, if bound for Rosthwaite, climb the wall on the left; for Grange the way continues down, crossing two walls by stiles, to the old Rigghead road.

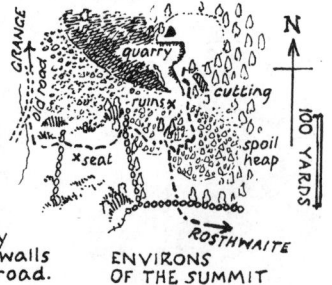

ENVIRONS OF THE SUMMIT

Castle Crag 8

THE SUMMIT

The altitude of the summit has not been determined by the men of the Ordnance Survey. It is often quoted as 900 feet, but is in excess of this figure.

From High Doat (927'; 1 mile south) the summit appears to be above the horizontal plane of Latrigg (1203'; 6½ miles), giving a height of not less than 970', and probably 980' or 990'.

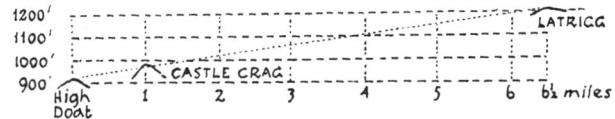

Look at High Doat from Castle Crag: it is obviously lower.

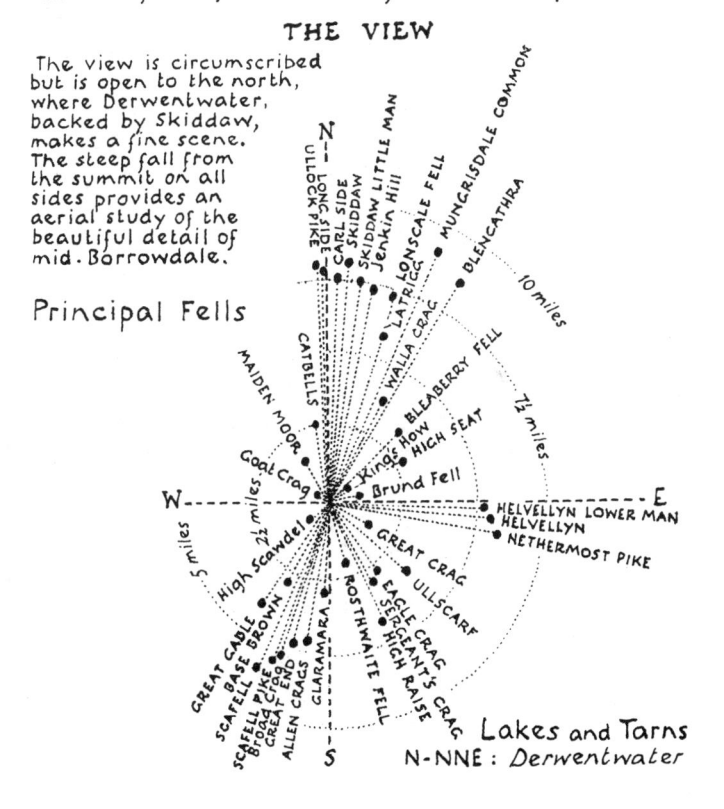

THE VIEW

The view is circumscribed but is open to the north, where Derwentwater, backed by Skiddaw, makes a fine scene. The steep fall from the summit on all sides provides an aerial study of the beautiful detail of mid-Borrowdale.

Principal Fells

Lakes and Tarns
N-NNE: Derwentwater

Catbells

1481'

Cat Bells
(two words)
on Ordnance maps

from Derwentwater

- Portinscale
- Keswick
- Stair
- ▲ CATBELLS
- Little Town
- ▲ MAIDEN MOOR
- Grange

MILES
0 1 2 3 4

from the Portinscale path

Catbells 2

NATURAL FEATURES

Catbells is one of the great favourites, a family fell where grandmothers and infants can climb the heights together, a place beloved. Its popularity is well deserved: its shapely topknot attracts the eye, offering a steep but obviously simple scramble to the small summit; its slopes are smooth, sunny and sleek; its position overlooking Derwentwater is superb. Moreover, for stronger walkers it is the first step on a glorious ridge that bounds Borrowdale on the west throughout its length with Newlands down on the other side. There is beauty everywhere — and nothing but beauty. Its ascent from Keswick may conveniently, in the holiday season, be coupled with a sail on the lake, making the expedition rewarding out of all proportion to the small effort needed. Even the name has a magic challenge.

Yet this fell is not quite so innocuous as is usually thought, and grandmothers and infants should have a care as they romp around. There are some natural hazards in the form of a line of crags that starts at the summit and slants down to Newlands, and steep outcrops elsewhere. More dangerous are the levels and open shafts that pierce the fell on both flanks: the once-prosperous Yewthwaite Mine despoils a wide area in the combe above Little Town in Newlands, to the east the debris of the ill-starred Brandley Mine is lapped by the water of the lake, and the workings of the Old Brandley Mine, high on the side of the fell at Skelgill Bank, are in view on the ascent of the ridge from the north. A tragic death in one of the open Yewthwaite shafts in 1962 serves as a warning.

Words cannot adequately describe the rare charm of Catbells, nor its ravishing view. But no publicity is necessary: its mere presence in the Derwentwater scene is enough. It has a bold 'come hither' look that compels one's steps, and no suitor ever returns disappointed, but only looking back often. It has only to be seen from Friar's Crag — and a spell is cast. No Keswick holiday is consummated without a visit to Catbells.

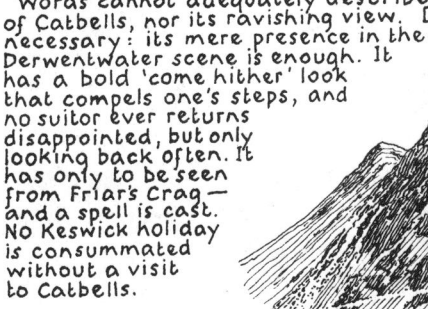

from Yewthwaite Combe

Catbells 3

Crags and Caverns of Catbells

left: The crags of Mart Bield, below the summit on the Newlands side of the fell

right: A dangerous hole at Yewthwaite Mine. At the end of a rock cutting the adit suggests a level (horizontal tunnel) but in fact is the opening of a vertical shaft.

below: Workings at the Old Brandley Mine. A shaft with twin entrances, overhung by a tree, *left*, and a nearby level, *right*.

Catbells 4

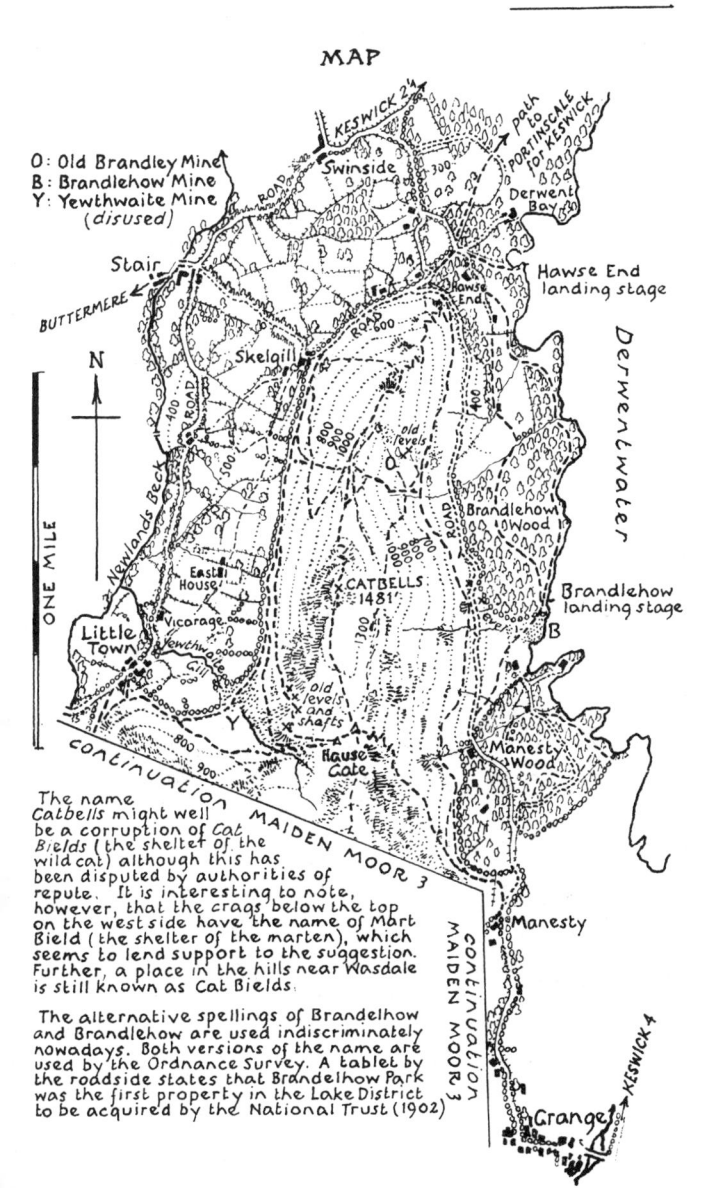

MAP

O: Old Brandley Mine
B: Brandlehow Mine
Y: Yewthwaite Mine
(disused)

The name Catbells might well be a corruption of *Cat Bields* (the shelter of the wild cat) although this has been disputed by authorities of repute. It is interesting to note, however, that the crags below the top on the west side have the name of Mart Bield (the shelter of the marten), which seems to lend support to the suggestion. Further, a place in the hills near Wasdale is still known as Cat Bields.

The alternative spellings of Brandelhow and Brandlehow are used indiscriminately nowadays. Both versions of the name are used by the Ordnance Survey. A tablet by the roadside states that Brandelhow Park was the first property in the Lake District to be acquired by the National Trust (1902)

Catbells 5

ASCENT FROM HAWSE END
1250 feet of ascent : 1½ miles

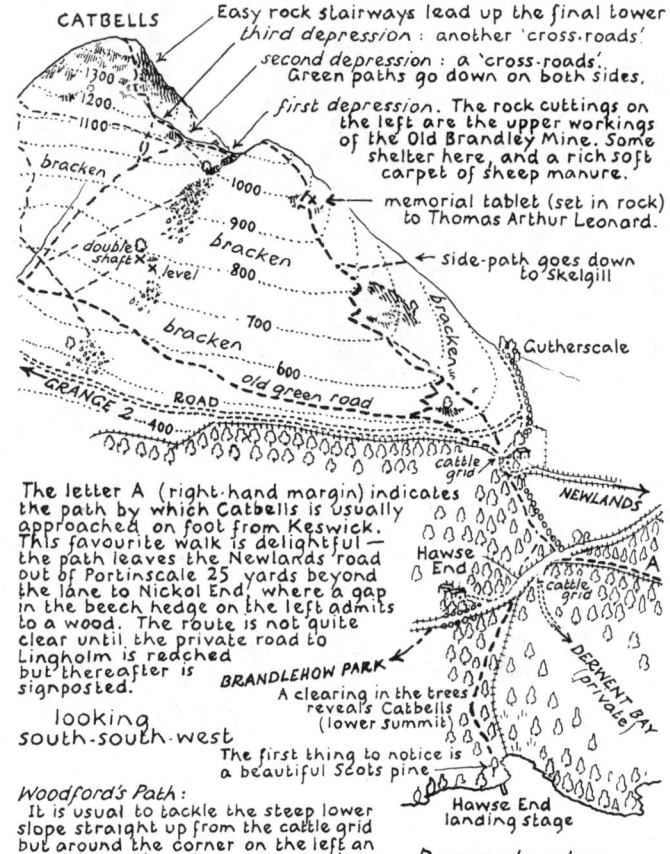

CATBELLS

Easy rock stairways lead up the final tower
third depression : another 'cross-roads'

second depression : a 'cross-roads'.
Green paths go down on both sides.

first depression. The rock cuttings on the left are the upper workings of the Old Brandley Mine. Some shelter here, and a rich soft carpet of sheep manure.

memorial tablet (set in rock) to Thomas Arthur Leonard.

← side-path goes down to Skelgill

Gutherscale

NEWLANDS

Hawse End

DERWENT BAY (private)

BRANDLEHOW PARK
A clearing in the trees reveals Catbells (lower summit)

looking south-south-west

The first thing to notice is a beautiful Scots pine

Hawse End landing stage

The letter A (right-hand margin) indicates the path by which Catbells is usually approached on foot from Keswick. This favourite walk is delightful— the path leaves the Newlands road out of Portinscale 25 yards beyond the lane to Nickol End, where a gap in the beech hedge on the left admits to a wood. The route is not quite clear until the private road to Lingholm is reached but thereafter is signposted.

Woodford's Path:
It is usual to tackle the steep lower slope straight up from the cattle grid but around the corner on the left an exquisite series of zigzags provides a more enjoyable start to the ascent. These zigzags leave the old green road 80 yards along it : watch for the first. The direct route joins in at the top of the series ; another series is then soon reached. *This path was engineered by a Sir John Woodford, who lived near, and his name deserves to be remembered by those who use his enchanting stairway.*

Derwentwater

Hawse End is served by motor-launch from Keswick (summer only)

One of the very best of the shorter climbs. A truly lovely walk.

Catbells 6

ASCENT FROM GRANGE
1250 feet of ascent : 2 miles

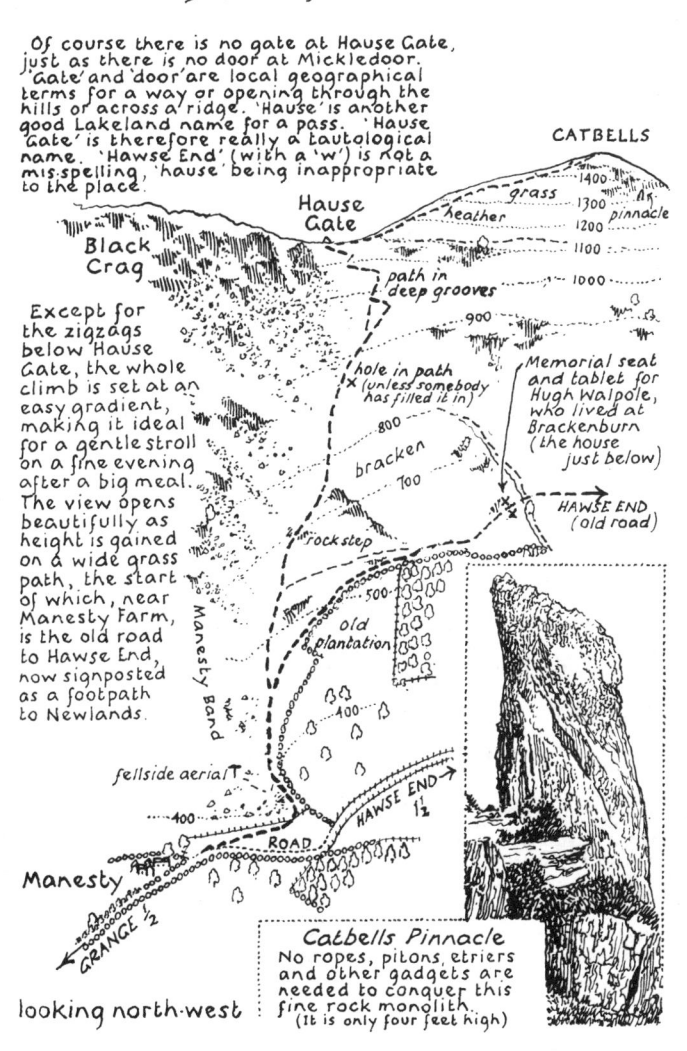

Of course there is no gate at Hause Gate, just as there is no door at Mickledoor. 'Gate' and 'door' are local geographical terms for a way or opening through the hills or across a ridge. 'Hause' is another good Lakeland name for a pass. 'Hause Gate' is therefore really a tautological name. 'Hawse End' (with a 'w') is not a mis-spelling, 'hause' being inappropriate to the place.

CATBELLS

Hause Gate

Black Crag

path in deep grooves

hole in path (unless somebody has filled it in)

Memorial seat and tablet for Hugh Walpole, who lived at Brackenburn (the house just below)

Except for the zigzags below Hause Gate, the whole climb is set at an easy gradient, making it ideal for a gentle stroll on a fine evening after a big meal. The view opens beautifully as height is gained on a wide grass path, the start of which, near Manesty Farm, is the old road to Hawse End, now signposted as a footpath to Newlands.

bracken

HAWSE END (old road)

rock step

old plantation

Manesty Band

fellside aerial

HAWSE END 1½

ROAD

Manesty

GRANGE ½

looking north-west

Catbells Pinnacle
No ropes, pitons, etriers and other gadgets are needed to conquer this fine rock monolith.
(It is only four feet high)

Catbells 7

ASCENT FROM NEWLANDS

via SKELGILL
1200 feet of ascent : 1½ miles
from Stair

via LITTLE TOWN
950 feet of ascent : 1¼ miles
from Little Town

The open fell is reached at Skelgill. The big zigzag was originally a miners' route — walkers have added the inevitable short cut.

A signpost in Stair village points to Skelgill along a side-road that looks private but is public; it goes through Skelgill farmyard to Hawse End, joining the Grange road.

looking south-east

Little Town is the littlest town of all — no shop, no inn, no post office, some lodging.

The steep lower flank of Maiden Moor rises on this side

Leave the road by a gate just before the last cottage.

looking east

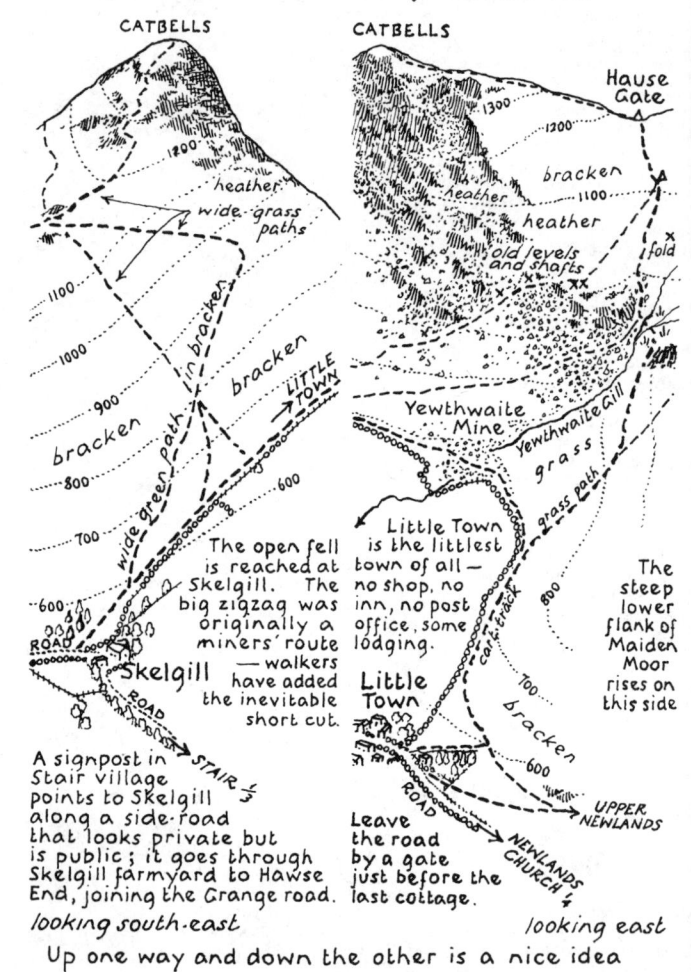

Up one way and down the other is a nice idea

THE SUMMIT

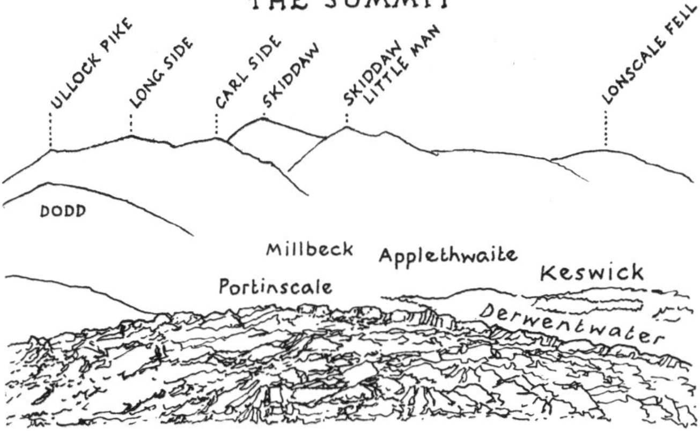
ULLOCK PIKE
LONG SIDE
CARL SIDE
SKIDDAW
SKIDDAW LITTLE MAN
LONSCALE FELL
DODD
Millbeck
Applethwaite
Keswick
Portinscale
Derwentwater

The summit, which has no cairn, is a small platform of naked rock, light brown in colour and seamed and pitted with many tiny hollows and crevices that collect and hold rainwater — so that, long after the skies have cleared, glittering diamonds adorn the crown. Almost all the native vegetation has been scoured away by the varied footgear of countless visitors; so popular is this fine viewpoint that often it is difficult to find a vacant perch. In summer this is not a place to seek quietness.

DESCENTS: Leave the top only by the ridge; lower down there is a wealth of choice. Keep clear of the craggy Newlands face.

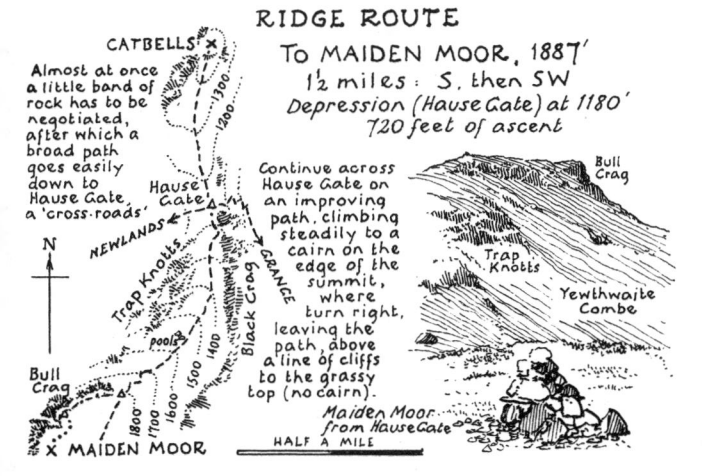

RIDGE ROUTE

TO MAIDEN MOOR, 1887'

1½ miles: S. then SW

Depression (Hause Gate) at 1180'

720 feet of ascent

Almost at once a little band of rock has to be negotiated, after which a broad path goes easily down to Hause Gate, a 'cross-roads'

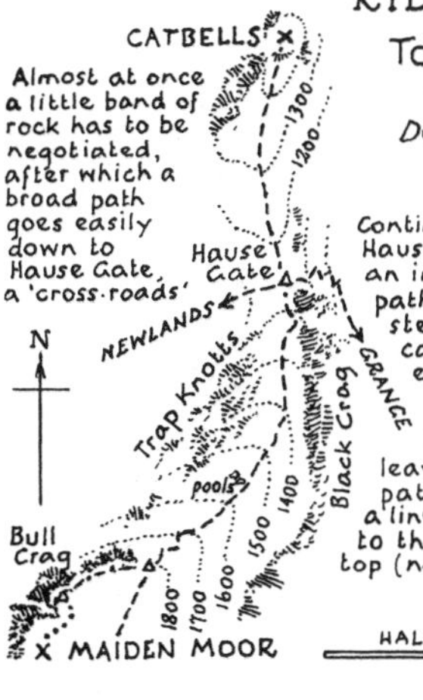
CATBELLS
1300
1200
Hause Gate
NEWLANDS
GRANGE
N
Trap Knotts
Black Crag
pools
1400
1500
1600
1700
1800
Bull Crag
MAIDEN MOOR
HALF A MILE

Continue across Hause Gate on an improving path, climbing steadily to a cairn on the edge of the summit, where turn right, leaving the path, above a line of cliffs to the grassy top (no cairn).

Bull Crag
Trap Knotts
Yewthwaite Combe

Maiden Moor from Hause Gate

Catbells 9

THE VIEW

Scenes of great beauty unfold on all sides, and they are scenes in depth to a degree not usual, the narrow summit permitting downward views of Borrowdale and Newlands within a few paces. Nearby valley and lake attract the eye more than the distant mountain surround, although Hindscarth and Robinson are particularly prominent at the head of Newlands and Causey Pike towers up almost grotesquely directly opposite. On this side the hamlet of Little Town is well seen down below, a charming picture, but it is to Derwentwater and mid-Borrowdale that the captivated gaze returns again and again.

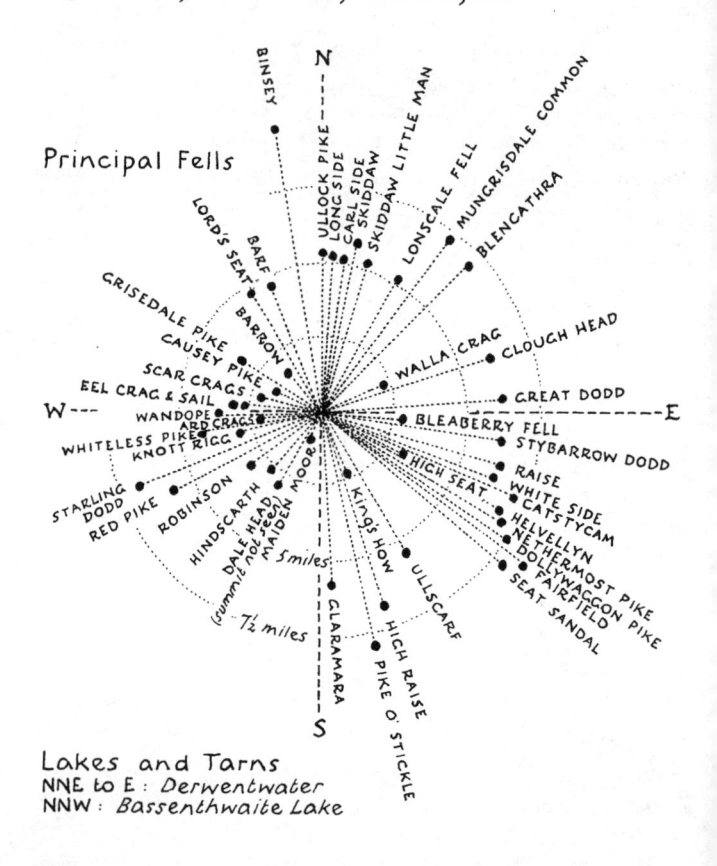

Principal Fells

Lakes and Tarns
NNE to E: *Derwentwater*
NNW: *Bassenthwaite Lake*

Catbells 10

Hindscarth and Robinson from Catbells

Causey Pike

2035'
approx

from Swinside

Causey Pike 2

NATURAL FEATURES

Most fells conform to a general pattern, but some have an unorthodoxy of shape, a peculiarity of outline, that identifies them on sight from wherever they may be seen. These not only help to fix a bearing in moments of doubt but serve also as pointers to neighbouring fells not favoured with distinctive features.

A landmark of this kind is Causey Pike, dominant in the Newlands and Derwentwater scene. The knob of the summit would itself be enough for identification in most views; repeated four times in lesser undulations as it is, like the legendary sea-serpent, the top is quite unmistakable. Even when the lesser ups and downs are concealed from sight, as when the fell is seen end on, the pyramid of the main summit is no less impressive because then it gains in slimness and elegance.

Causey Pike rises very sharply from Newlands but the steepness abates on Rowling End at 1400', whence a half-mile ridge continues easily to Sleet Hause, just below the final tower, where the steepness recurs on a narrowing crest. Rock is in evidence here, and must be handled to attain the summit. Thereafter the top of the fell is a succession of gentle undulations leading on to Scar Crags and the fine ridge that climbs up to Eel Crag and descends beyond to Crummock Water.

Bracken clothes the lower slopes and heather the higher. The confining streams are Stonycroft Beck and Rigg Beck, both feeders of Newlands Beck.

from Whiteless Breast

from Little Town

looking up the valley of
Sail Beck, with Eel Crag
and Sail on the left and
Ard Crags on the right

Causey Pike belongs wholly and exclusively to Newlands but peeps over the watershed of the Cocker, southwest, at several points.

Causey Pike 3

MAP

The map is extended to the west, beyond the boundaries of Causey Pike, to illustrate how the summit may be reached from the 'back' by way of Sail Pass (at the same altitude), gaining the pass by using either the Stonycroft mine road or the Rigg Beck path.   The Stonycroft route is excellently graded and a very quick way of getting up to 2000' from Newlands; using this route, if Causey Pike is the sole objective, the 'road' can be left on High Moss and a beeline made for the depression between Scar Crags and the Pike. The Rigg Beck route is less satisfactory.

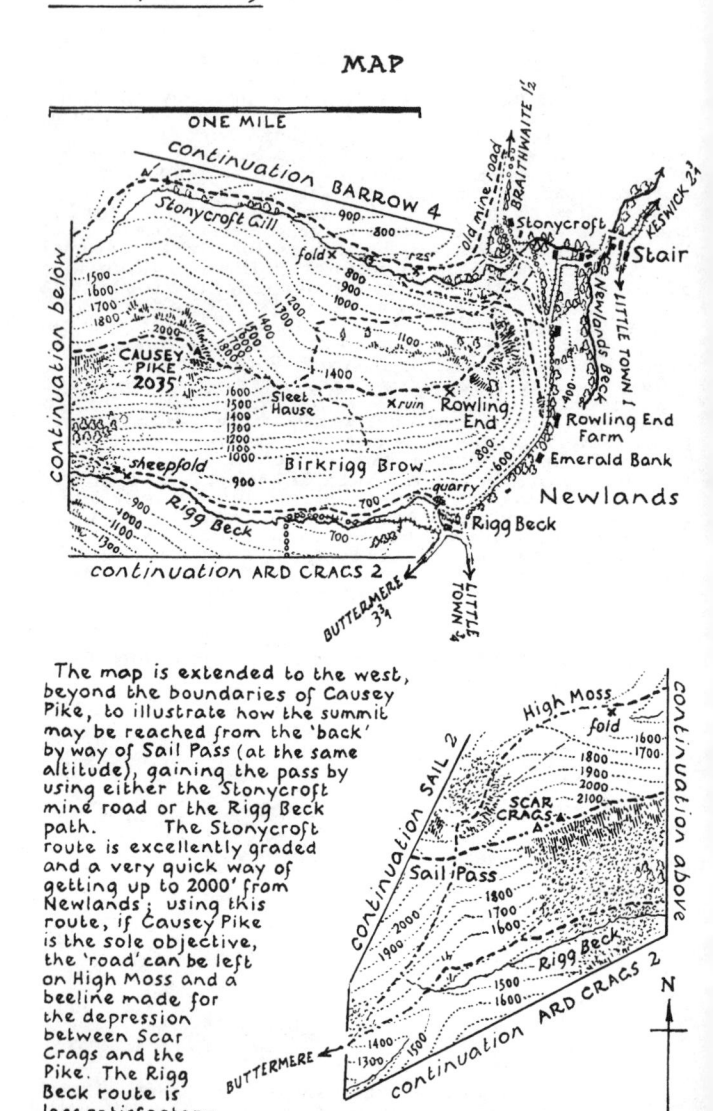

Causey Pike 4

ASCENT FROM STAIR
1750 feet of ascent : 1½ miles

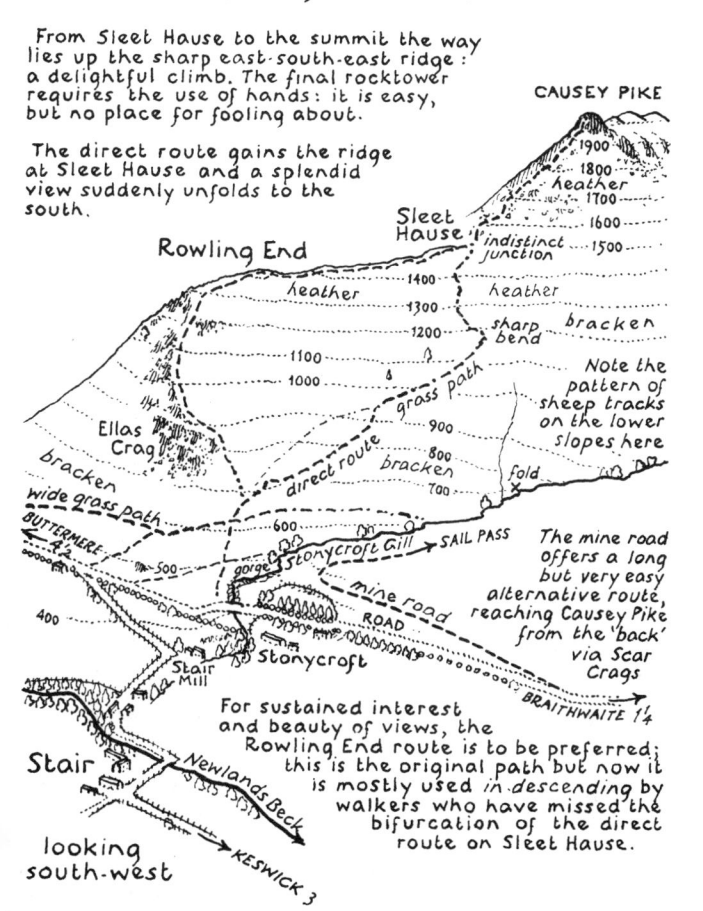

From Sleet Hause to the summit the way lies up the sharp east-south-east ridge: a delightful climb. The final rocktower requires the use of hands: it is easy, but no place for fooling about.

The direct route gains the ridge at Sleet Hause and a splendid view suddenly unfolds to the south.

looking south-west

Note the pattern of sheep tracks on the lower slopes here

The mine road offers a long but very easy alternative route, reaching Causey Pike from the 'back' via Scar Crags

For sustained interest and beauty of views, the Rowling End route is to be preferred; this is the original path but now it is mostly used in descending by walkers who have missed the bifurcation of the direct route on Sleet Hause.

Deservedly this is a popular climb, with a heavy summer traffic, the route being quite charming, the views superlative, the finish a bit of real mountaineering, and the summit a place of distinctive character.

ASCENT FROM BRAITHWAITE

2150 feet of ascent : 4½ miles (via Sail Pass)

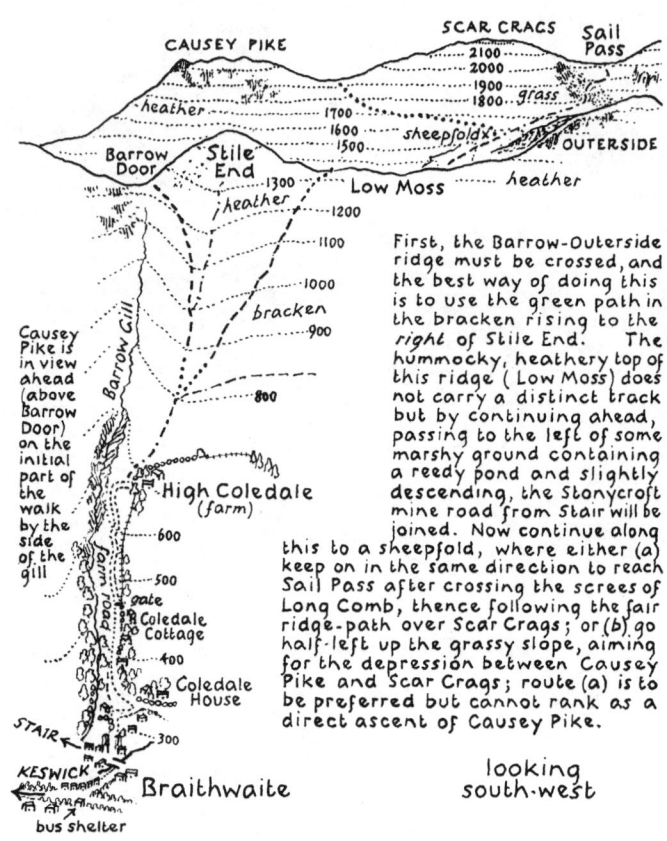

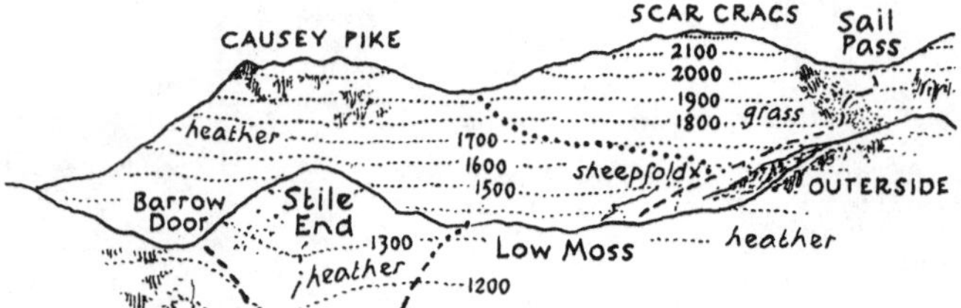
SCAR CRAGS
Sail Pass
CAUSEY PIKE
2100
2000
1900
1800
grass
heather
1700
1600
1500
sheepfold
OUTERSIDE
Barrow Door
Stile End
1300
Low Moss
heather
heather

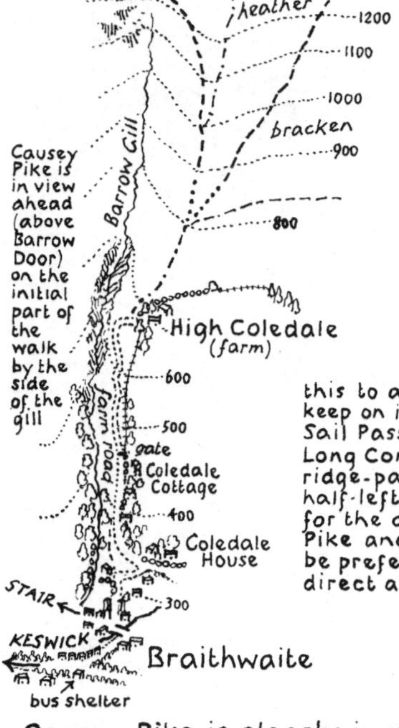
1200
1100
1000
bracken
900
800
Barrow Gill
Causey Pike is in view ahead (above Barrow Door) on the initial part of the walk by the side of the gill
High Coledale (farm)
600
500
farm road
gate
Coledale Cottage
400
Coledale House
300
STAIR
KESWICK
Braithwaite
bus shelter

First, the Barrow-Outerside ridge must be crossed, and the best way of doing this is to use the green path in the bracken rising to the *right* of Stile End. The hummocky, heathery top of this ridge (Low Moss) does not carry a distinct track but by continuing ahead, passing to the left of some marshy ground containing a reedy pond and slightly descending, the Stonycroft mine road from Stair will be joined. Now continue along this to a sheepfold, where either (a) keep on in the same direction to reach Sail Pass after crossing the screes of Long Comb, thence following the fair ridge-path over Scar Crags; or (b) go half-left up the grassy slope, aiming for the depression between Causey Pike and Scar Crags; route (a) is to be preferred but cannot rank as a direct ascent of Causey Pike.

looking south-west

Causey Pike is clearly in view from Braithwaite, and its quaint and challenging outline makes it an obvious objective for a day's walk. The route, however, is somewhat 'artificial', as an intervening ridge must first be crossed, and a better plan is to ascend direct from Stair, using the above route for the return journey.

Causey Pike 6

THE SUMMIT

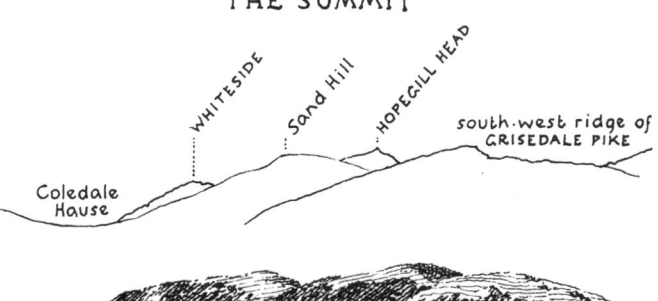

Coledale Hause — WHITESIDE — Sand Hill — HOPEGILL HEAD — south-west ridge of GRISEDALE PIKE

This delightful 'top' is quite unlike any other, its narrow crest undulating over five distinct bumps (meticulous visitors will count seven), the most prominent being the one terminating so abruptly the eastern end of the crest: this is the rocky knob that identifies Causey Pike unmistakably in distant views of the fell. There is no official height, which is surprising because the summit of this prominent knob seems a ready-made survey station — generally it is quoted as 2000', an approximation, but the 2½" Ordnance maps show three contour rings at 2025'. The eastern knob appears to have a slight advantage in altitude, a matter of a few feet or even inches only, over the third bump — the second bump is clearly lower yet bears the one respectable cairn. Heather covers the sides of the crest, but pedestrians are catered for by a well-worn strip of grass along the top.

DESCENTS: Leave the top by the path down the east-south-east ridge from the eastern knob; this is rocky at first, needing care in bad conditions, and is not pleasant to descend.   At the foot of the steep section, on Sleet Hause, the direct route to Stair goes off to the left at once and the original path over Rowling End continues ahead, the bifurcation (on grass) being indistinct. It is advisable to use the direct route: the way off Rowling End is on a plain but abominably rough path with no alternative possible. A little-used track also goes off to the right from Sleet Hause for Rigg Beck but after clearly threading a way through thick heather it unaccountably comes to a sudden end halfway down the slope.

Causey Pike 7

THE VIEW

In all directions the scenery is of the highest order. Predominantly the view is of mountains, but the severity and starkness of their outlines is softened by the verdant loveliness of the Vales of Keswick and Newlands. Nothing is better than the challenging ridge continuing to Eel Crag. The head of Newlands, displaying the great humps of Dale Head, Hindscarth and Robinson — a magnificent grouping — is exceptionally well seen. The several Pikes of Scafell appear from this viewpoint as separate mountains.

Principal Fells

N
- BINSEY
- ULLOCK PIKE
- LONG SIDE
- SKIDDAW LITTLE MAN
- LORD'S SEAT
- BROOM FELL
- WHINLATTER
- BARF
- BARROW
- SKIDDAW
- LONSCALE FELL
- BOWSCALE FELL
- BLENCATHRA — 10 miles
- 12½ miles
- CRISEDALE PIKE
- OUTERSIDE
- HOPEGILL HEAD
- Sand Hill
- WHITE SIDE
- Stile End
- LATRIGG — 7½ miles
- GREAT MELL FELL
- CLOUGH HEAD
- WALLA CRAG
- GREAT DODD
- SCAR CRAGS
- EEL CRAG
- CATBELLS
- BLEABERRY FELL
- STYBARROW DODD
- WANDOPE and SAIL
- WHITELESS PIKE
- ARD CRAGS
- HIGH SEAT
- RAISE
- WHITE SIDE
- CATSTYCAM
- STARLING DODD
- MAIDEN MOOR
- Kings How
- HELVELLYN
- RED PIKE
- ROBINSON
- HINDSCARTH
- HIGH SPY
- DALE HEAD
- NETHERMOST PIKE
- DOLLYWAGGON PIKE
- HIGH STILE
- ULLSCAR
- SEAT SANDAL
- FAIRFIELD
- SCOAT FELL
- KIRK FELL
- FLEETWITH PIKE
- GLARAMARA
- GREAT RIGG
- STEEPLE
- PILLAR
- GREAT GABLE
- HERON PIKE
- BOWFELL
- HIGH RAISE
- SCAFELL PIKE
- ESK PIKE
- HARRISON STICKLE
- GREAT END
- Ill Crag and Broad Crag
- PIKE O' STICKLE
- WETHERLAM
- S

W ← → E

Just to fill up this corner, it might be mentioned that the two Lakeland Cats, —bells and —stycam, appear directly in a straight line from this viewpoint only.

Lakes & Tarns
E: Derwentwater
SE: Blea Tarn
S: Dalehead Tarn
SW: Bleaberry Tarn
N: Bassenthwaite Lake

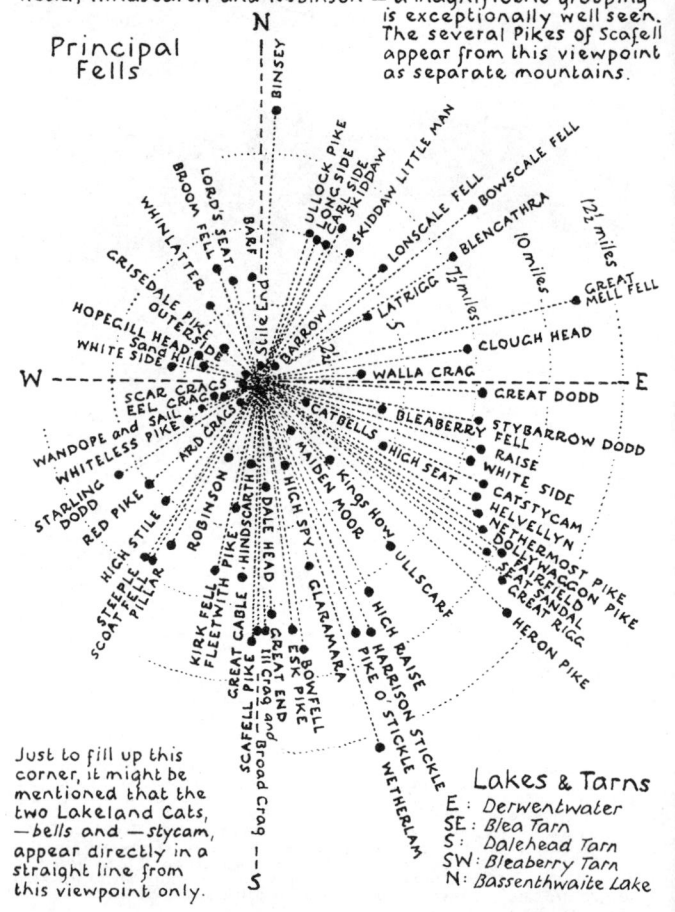

Causey Pike 8

RIDGE ROUTE

To SCAR CRAGS, 2205' : ¾ mile : WNW, then W.
Depression at 1915' : 320 feet of ascent

Traverse all the bumps and descend a wide grass path to the depression beyond. The ragged edge of Scar Crags now rears imposingly ahead, but the rising track alongside has no difficulties and the flat top is reached after a simple climb, during which striking downward views are available on the left.

looking back to Causey Pike from the depression

looking south

Causey Pike 9

The valley of Rigg Beck, from Causey Pike

Causey Pike 10

The ridge west from Causey Pike

Key to drawings

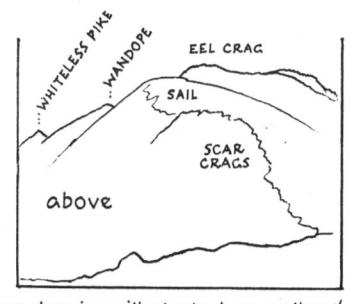

left: HIGH STILE, RED PIKE, STARLING DODD, WHITELESS PIKE, KNOTT RIGG, ARD CRAGS, Rigg Beck, path to Buttermere

above: WHITELESS PIKE, WANDOPE, EEL CRAG, SAIL, SCAR CRAGS

These drawings illustrate two walkers' ways from Newlands to Buttermere. That via Rigg Beck is suitable for a wet day, but the route *par excellence* in clear weather is the ridge from Causey Pike to Whiteless Pike — a magnificent walk.

Dale Head 2473'

from Castle Nook

Little Town
HINDSCARTH
DALE HEAD ▲ HIGH SPY
Gatesgarth   Rosthwaite
Honister Pass Seatoller

MILES
0 1 2 3 4

Dale Head 2

NATURAL FEATURES

Dale Head has much in common with Eel Crag in the Grasmoor group. Their summits are focal points of high country, the meeting-place of ascending ridges. Both have craggy northern fronts, darkly shadowed, and easy southern approaches. Both enjoy extensive views of great merit, particularly northwards to Skiddaw. Taking everything into account, these two may be considered the most satisfying summits in the north western area.

Dale Head was named from Newlands, of which valley it commands a remarkable full-length view, and it is in this direction that the best, but not the best-known, items of interest are to be found. There are no walkers' tracks on the rocky northern breast of the fell, but a zigzag path to its copper veins was engineered by miners five or six centuries ago and can still be traced, while recently its steep buttresses have become a climbing-ground. The miners have long departed, but on the opposite flank of the fell, overlooking Honister Pass, quarrymen are still winning a beautiful stone from the Yew Crag workings.

For the walker, the finest attraction is the north-west ridge leading to Hindscarth, which is excellent. The easy southern slope, rising from the top of Honister Pass, lacks interest. The sharp descent to the east from the summit is soon halted by the extensive plateau of High Scawdel before continuing roughly down to the lovely foothills and woods of Borrowdale.

Dale Head has interest for the geologist, for beneath the carpet of grass there is a fusion of the Skiddaw slates and the volcanic rock of central Lakeland, some evidences of the joint being seen on the actual summit. But perhaps Dale Head's greatest triumph over its north western fellows is that it holds in its lap the only tarns of any size between Bassenthwaite and Honister, a further manifestation of the change in the underlying rock. Streams flow to all directions except west, yet it is in the west their ultimate destiny lies, the fell being wholly within the catchment of the Derwent.

Dalehead Tarn from High Scawdel

Dale Head 3

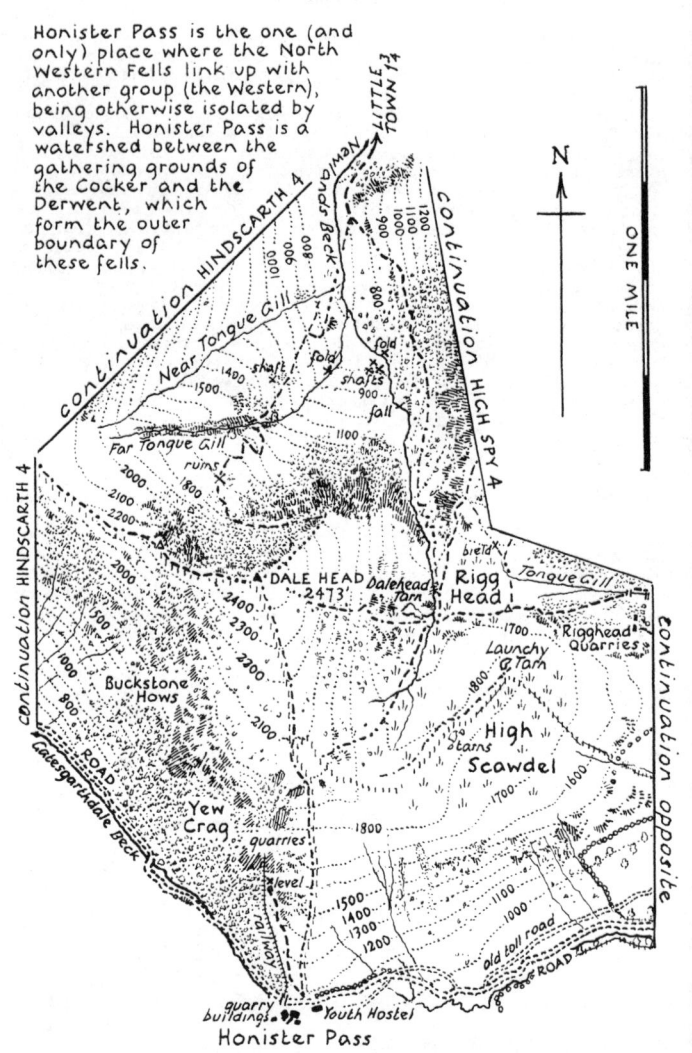

MAP

Honister Pass is the one (and only) place where the North Western Fells link up with another group (the Western), being otherwise isolated by valleys. Honister Pass is a watershed between the gathering grounds of the Cocker and the Derwent, which form the outer boundary of these fells.

ONE MILE

Dale Head 4

MAP

Honister Pass can only be reached on foot from Gatesgarthdale by walking along the motor road, but from Seatoller a good alternative is provided by the former toll road, which, being unfit for vehicles, has become a first-class walkers' way, in fact, a pedestrian by-pass. The surface is rough and rutted, but no fellwalker will object to this. It is the smooth hard surfaces of modern roads that tire the legs and feet, the monotony of repeating ad nauseum the same stride exactly. On rough ground no two movements are quite the same.

A good fellwalker never tramps a road that has a bus service.

A level, Rigghead Quarry

Launchy Tarn

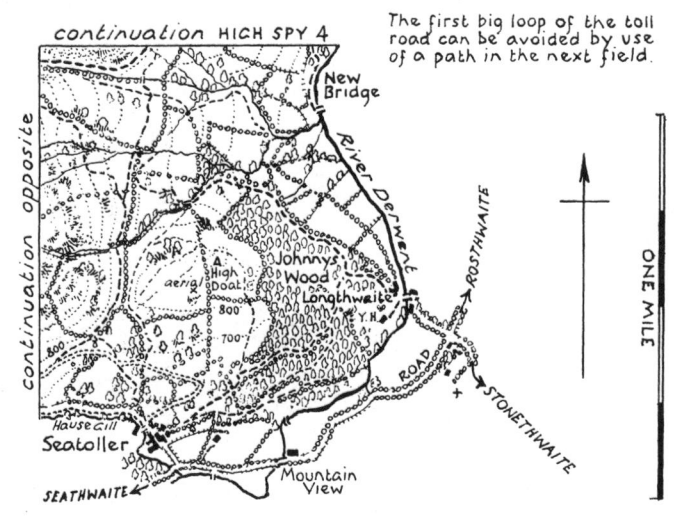

The first big loop of the toll road can be avoided by use of a path in the next field.

Dale Head 5

below: Mine cuttings near the foot of Far Tongue Gill adopted for use with a sheepfold.

Copper Mines and Crags of Dale Head

left: Two mine cuttings near the sheepfold on Newlands Beck at 800'; the lower one is flooded, forming a rocky-sided pool.

below: Dale Head Pillar, Gable Crag, from the ruined mine buildings.

Dale Head 6

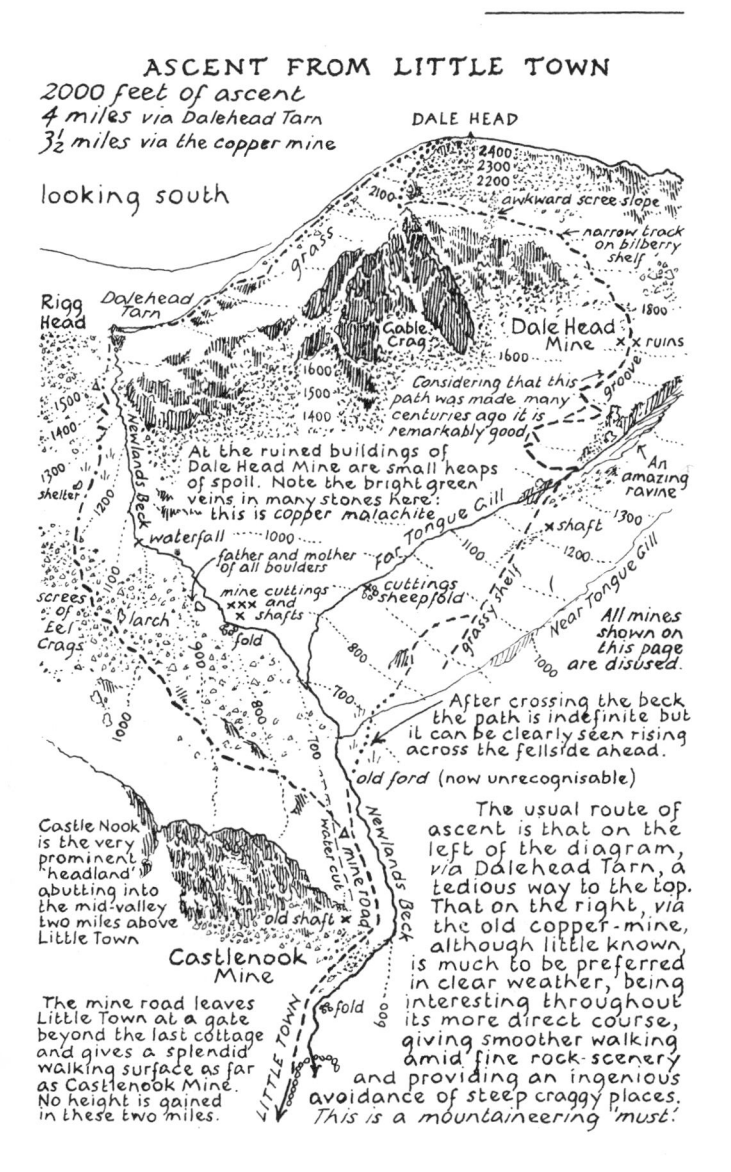

ASCENT FROM LITTLE TOWN

2000 feet of ascent
4 miles via Dalehead Tarn
3½ miles via the copper mine

looking south

DALE HEAD
2400
2300
2200
awkward scree slope
narrow track on bilberry shelf
2100
grass
Rigg Head
Dalehead Tarn
Gable Crag
1800
Dale Head Mine ×× ruins
1600
1600
1500
Considering that this path was made many centuries ago it is remarkably good.
groove
1400
1500
1400
An amazing ravine
1300
Newlands Beck
1200
shelter
At the ruined buildings of Dale Head Mine are small heaps of spoil. Note the bright green veins in many stones here: this is copper malachite
1300
× shaft
1200
waterfall — 1000 —
for Tongue Gill
1100
father and mother of all boulders
cuttings sheepfold
grassy shelf
Near Tongue Gill
screes of Eel Crags
larch
mine cuttings ××× and × shafts
800
All mines shown on this page are disused.
fold
700
After crossing the beck the path is indefinite but it can be clearly seen rising across the fellside ahead.
old ford (now unrecognisable)

Castle Nook is the very prominent 'headland' abutting into the mid-valley two miles above Little Town

The usual route of ascent is that on the left of the diagram, via Dalehead Tarn, a tedious way to the top. That on the right, via the old copper-mine, although little known, is much to be preferred in clear weather, being interesting throughout its more direct course, giving smoother walking amid fine rock-scenery and providing an ingenious avoidance of steep craggy places. This is a mountaineering 'must'.

water cut
old shaft

Castlenook Mine

The mine road leaves Little Town at a gate beyond the last cottage and gives a splendid walking surface as far as Castlenook Mine. No height is gained in these two miles.

fold
Newlands Beck
LITTLE TOWN

Dale Head 7

ASCENT FROM HONISTER PASS
1300 feet of ascent : 1¼ miles

The first lesson that every fellwalker learns, and learns afresh every time he goes on the hills, is that summits are almost invariably more distant, a good deal higher, and require greater effort, than expected. Fellwalking and wishful thinking have nothing in common.

Here is an exception. This ascent may well be longer than expected, but the climbing is so very simple and the gradients so very easy that the top cairn is reached, unbelievably, before one has started to feel that enough has been done to earn it.

Apparently for no reason at all the path switches from one side of the fence-posts to the other. A likely explanation is that there would be a gate at this point when the fence was in its heyday.

← This line of fence-posts leads to High Scawdel and Launchy Tarn

looking north-north-east

At this point a quarry hole encroaches almost to the fence. Its dangers are obvious when ascending, but could be realised too late in a running descent in mist.

The fence wires have gone completely but the iron posts are still in place (with a few exceptions) and make a perfect guide-line to the top.

SEATOLLER 1½
BUTTERMERE 4 ROAD
Youth Hostel
cutting sheds
Honister Pass 1190'

Old level, indicated on diagram. The hut nearby provides shelter.

No other summit of like altitude is reached so quickly and easily from a motor road. Indeed, if a car be used to the top of the pass, a man of conscience must feel he is cheating the mountain.

Dale Head 8

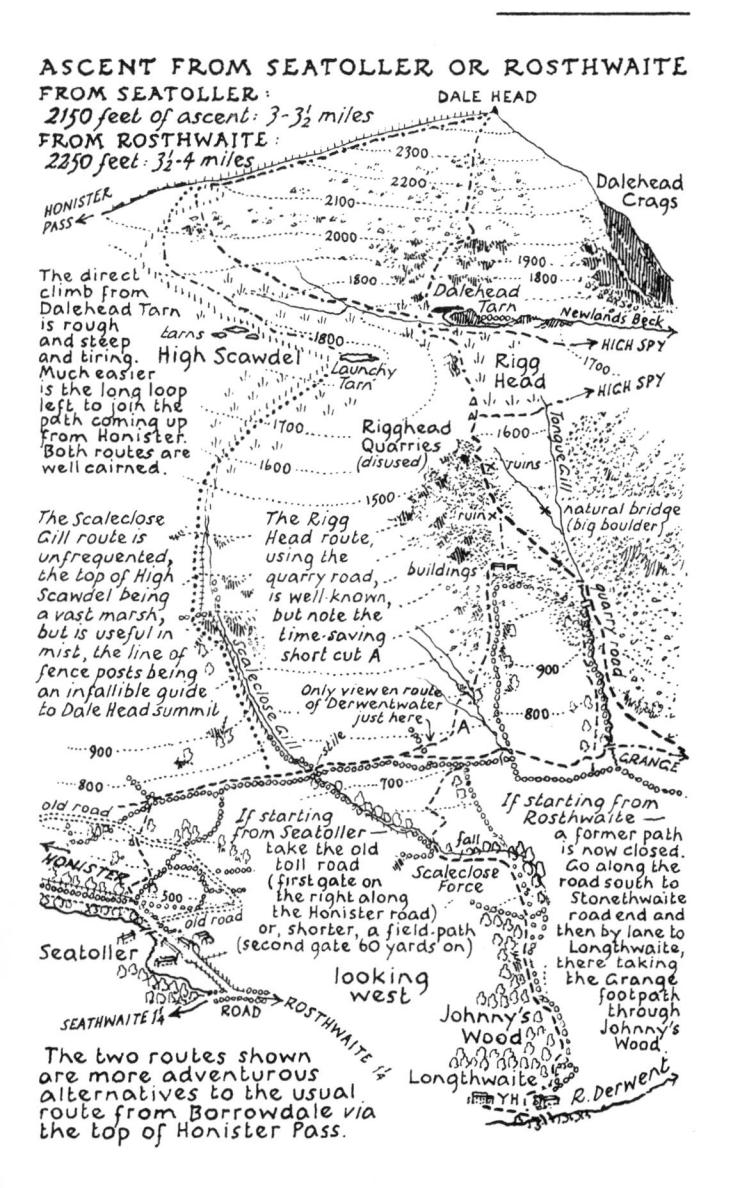

ASCENT FROM SEATOLLER OR ROSTHWAITE

FROM SEATOLLER:
2150 feet of ascent: 3-3½ miles
FROM ROSTHWAITE:
2250 feet: 3½-4 miles

DALE HEAD

HONISTER PASS

Dalehead Crags

The direct climb from Dalehead Tarn is rough and steep and tiring. Much easier is the long loop left to join the path coming up from Honister. Both routes are well cairned.

tarns — High Scawdel — Launchy Tarn

Dalehead Tarn — Newlands Beck — HIGH SPY

Rigg Head — HIGH SPY

Rigghead Quarries (disused)

Tongue Gill — ruins

The Scaleclose Gill route is unfrequented, the top of High Scawdel being a vast marsh, but is useful in mist, the line of fence posts being an infallible guide to Dale Head summit

The Rigg Head route, using the quarry road, is well-known, but note the time-saving short cut A

ruin — natural bridge (big boulder)

buildings — quarry road

Only view en route of Derwentwater just here

GRANGE

old road — HONISTER — old road

Seatoller

SEATHWAITE 1¼ — ROAD — ROSTHWAITE 1¼

If starting from Seatoller — take the old toll road (first gate on the right along the Honister road) or, shorter, a field path (second gate 60 yards on)

Scaleclose Force — fall

looking west

Johnny's Wood

Longthwaite — YH — R. Derwent

If starting from Rosthwaite — a former path is now closed. Go along the road south to Stonethwaite road end and then by lane to Longthwaite, there taking the Grange footpath through Johnny's Wood

The two routes shown are more adventurous alternatives to the usual route from Borrowdale via the top of Honister Pass.

Dale Head 9

THE SUMMIT

SKIDDAW

Newlands

There are hundreds of unnecessary cairns on the fells, and no great loss would be suffered if they were scattered, but those on the summits of the mountains have a special significance: they are old friends and should be left inviolate in their lonely stations to greet their visitors. This was how it used to be, and they were treated with respect. Fellwalkers knew them well.
But not now. Lunatics are loose on the hills; not many, just a few idiots whose limit of bravery is to destroy what others have created. The fine columns on Pike o'Blisco and Lingmell have both been wrecked in recent years (and rebuilt by walkers who felt bereaved by their absence, and to whom thanks are due). Dale Head's original cairn has fallen to the destroyers, too; but here has arisen an even nobler edifice. An expert working party has been on the job, and the stones appear to have come from Yew Crag quarry. This new cairn is unusual in shape being wider at mid-height than at the base, but it is a very solid and sound effort. Long may it reign over Dale Head.
Its situation is dramatic, immediately on the brink of the great northern downfall, but there is an easy parade on both sides. It is along here that the Skiddaw slates and the Borrowdale volcanic rocks converge, but a knowledge of geology is needed to find evidence of this.

DESCENTS: The way down to Honister Pass, with fenceposts as infallible guides, is foolproof, fast and easy. Do not stray from the fence in mist (quarry holes).
For Dalehead Tarn and Borrowdale or Newlands, aim east and find a line of cairns and then a track.
For Newlands direct, via the copper mine, clear weather is essential unless the way is already known. The place to leave the north-east ridge is a pale outcrop with steep ground obviously beyond: here turn very sharp left to find a thin track to easy ground.

Dale Head 10

RIDGE ROUTES

TO HINDSCARTH, 2385': 1¼ miles: WNW, then NNE
Depression at 2156': 250 feet of ascent
An easy walk, with excellent views.

Starting along the top westwards (no path at first), with intermittent fenceposts on the left, a gradual descent soon leads to the finest part of the ridge, which here narrows above a steep gully. A good path now appears and winds round a rocky rise; Buttermere is now in view. Beyond, a big cairn is reached on an outcrop (bit rough) and then the way is clear across a depression to the ridge ahead, where a right-angled turn, leaving the fence, leads easily over the gravelly top of Hindscarth for half a mile to the summit.

Two white cairns on the Newlands side of the depression indicate the line of a pathless short cut that saves a few minutes by avoiding the sharp bend on the normal route.

The first rocky rise on the Hindscarth ridge, looking west

TO HIGH SPY, 2143': 1½ miles: ESE, NNE
Depression at 1600': 550 feet of ascent
An interesting journey from one ridge to another

Starting eastwards, the first cairn met indicates the place to turn away from the curving north-east ridge, and others follow in succession down the slope, becoming accompanied by a track as the ground steepens. Aim for the south side of the tarn, now in sight below. Across the beck a sketchy path climbs the long slope of High Spy with thrilling views down the crags on the left.

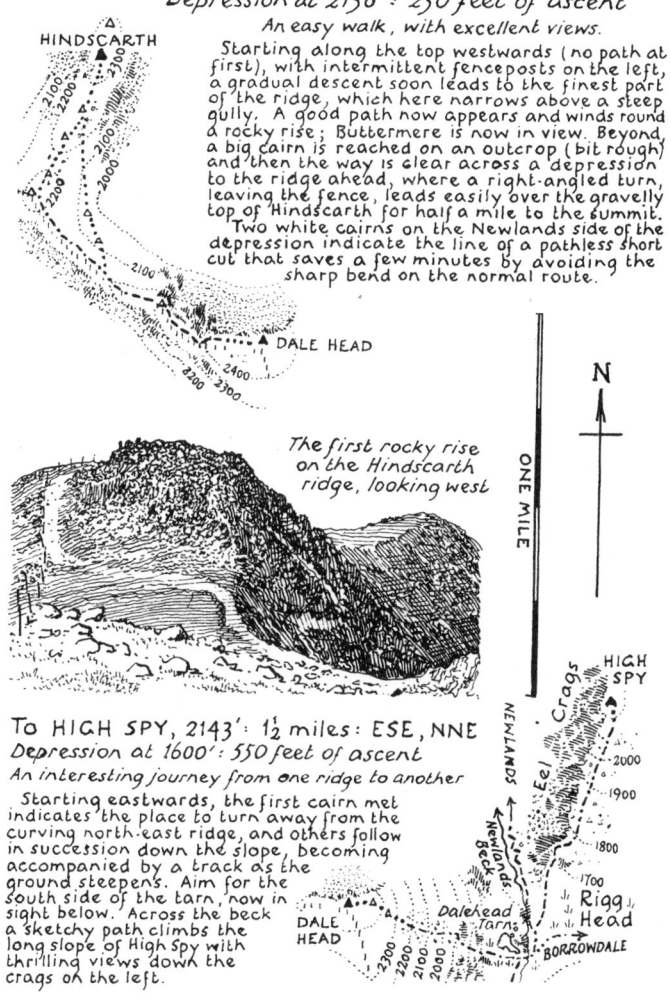

Dale Head 11

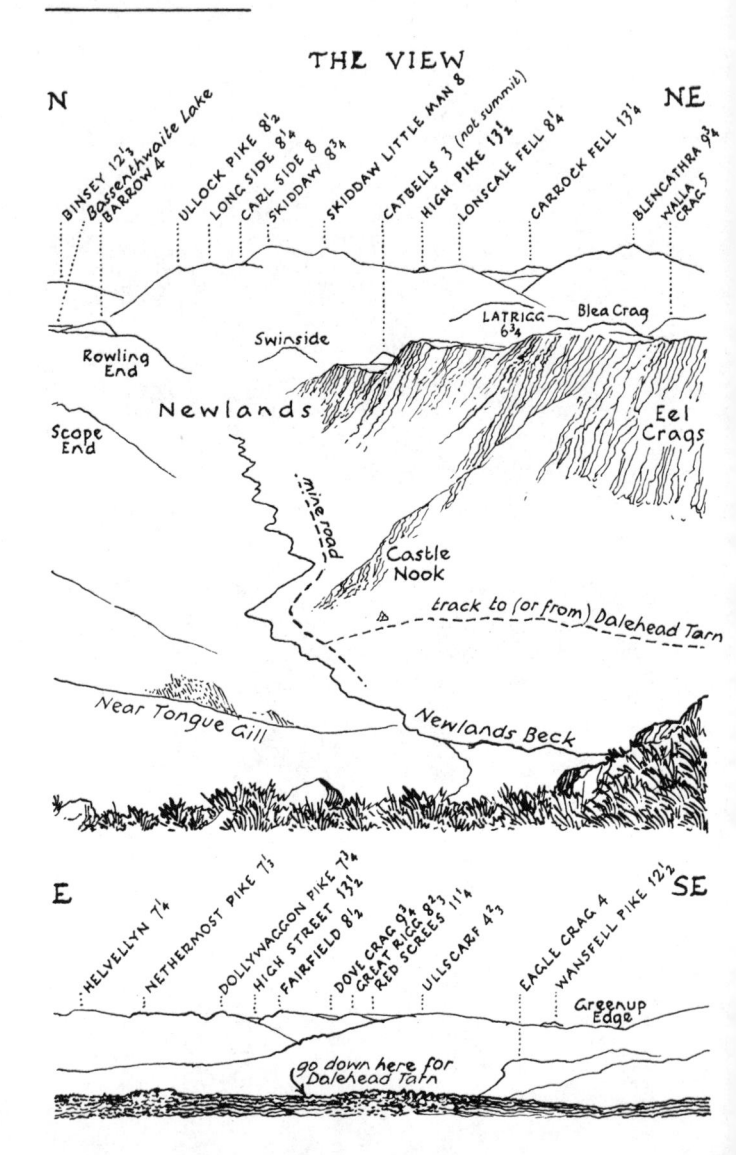

THE VIEW

N — BINSEY 12½ · Bassenthwaite Lake · BARROW 4 · ULLOCK PIKE 8½ · LONG SIDE 8¼ · CARL SIDE 8 · SKIDDAW 8¾ · SKIDDAW LITTLE MAN 8 · CATBELLS 3 (not summit) · HIGH PIKE 13½ · LONSCALE FELL 8¼ · CARROCK FELL 13¾ · BLENCATHRA 9¾ · WALLA CRAG 5 — NE

Rowling End · Swinside · LATRIGG 6¾ · Blea Crag

Scope End · Newlands · Eel Crags

mine road · Castle Nook · track to (or from) Dalehead Tarn

Near Tongue Gill · Newlands Beck

E — HELVELLYN 7¼ · NETHERMOST PIKE 7½ · DOLLYWAGGON PIKE 7¼ · HIGH STREET 13½ · FAIRFIELD 8½ · DOVE CRAG 9¾ · GREAT RIGG 8¾ · RED SCREES 11¼ · ULLSCARF 4¾ · EAGLE CRAG 4 · WANSFELL PIKE 12½ — SE

go down here for Dalehead Tarn · Greenup Edge

Dale Head 12

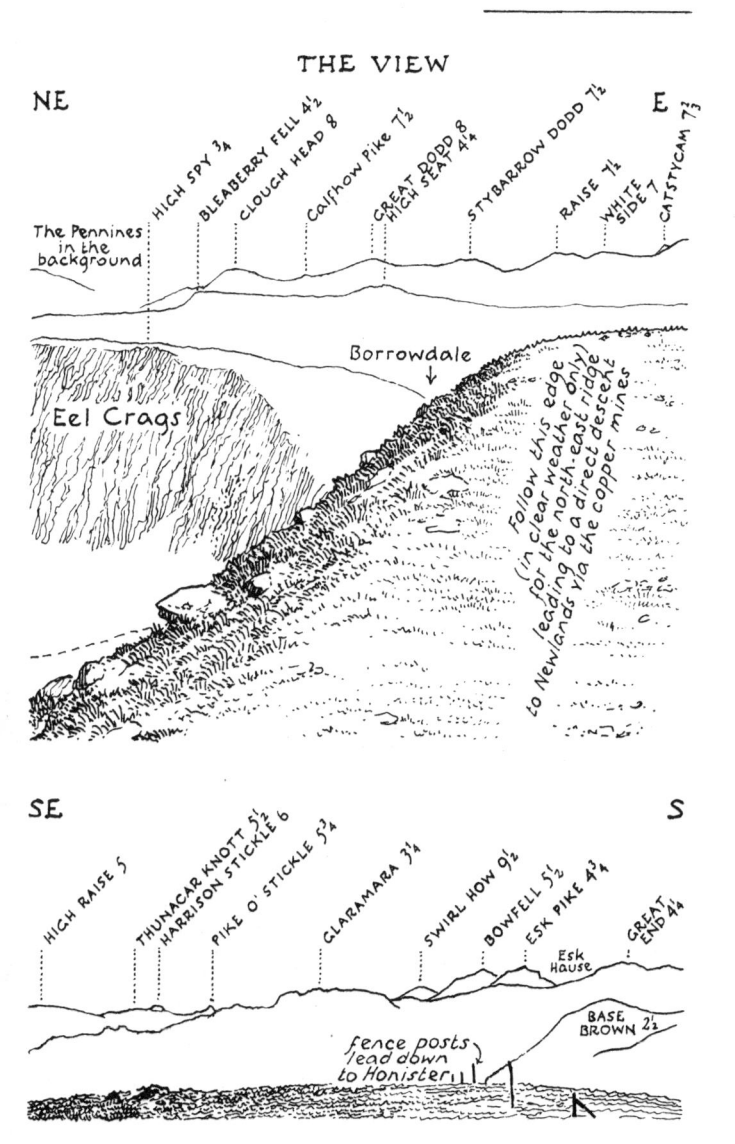

THE VIEW

NE — HIGH SPY 3¾, BLEABERRY FELL 4½, CLOUGH HEAD 8, CALFHOW PIKE 7½, GREAT DODD 8, HIGH SEAT 4¼, STYBARROW DODD 7½, RAISE 7½, WHITE SIDE 7, CATSTYCAM 7¾ — **E**

The Pennines in the background

Eel Crags

Borrowdale

Follow this edge (in clear weather only) for the north-east ridge leading to a direct descent to Newlands via the copper mines

SE — HIGH RAISE 5, THUNACAR KNOTT 5½, HARRISON STICKLE 6, PIKE O' STICKLE 5¾, GLARAMARA 3¼, SWIRL HOW 9½, BOWFELL 5½, ESK PIKE 4¾, GREAT END 4¼ — **S**

Esk Hause

BASE BROWN 2½

fence posts lead down to Honister

Dale Head 13

THE VIEW

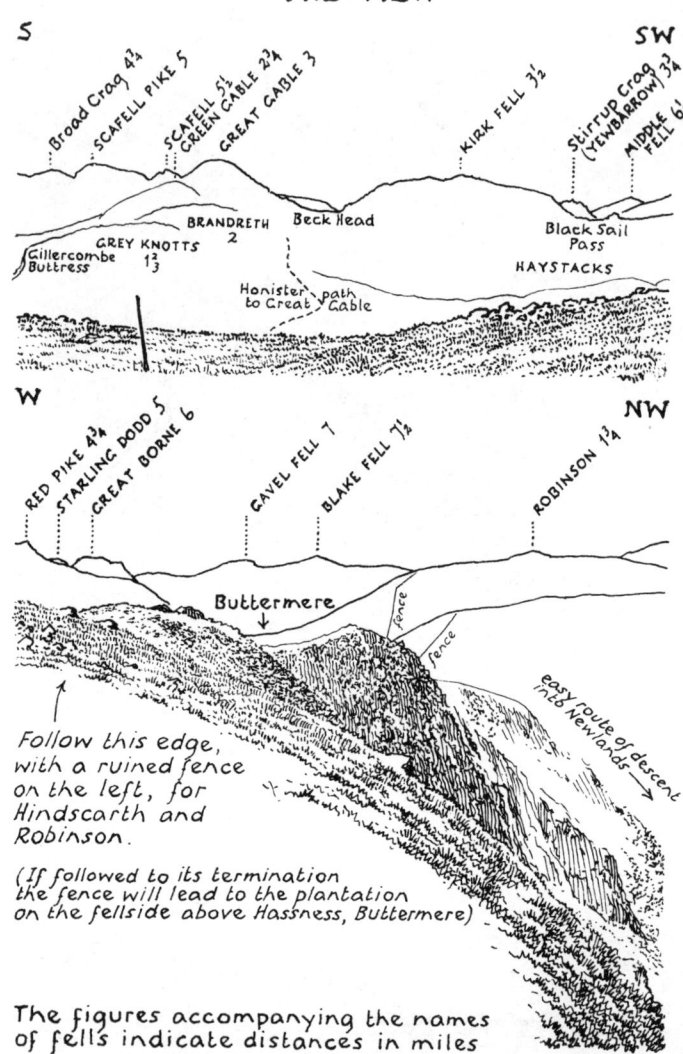

S — Broad Crag 4¾, SCAFELL PIKE 5, SCAFELL 5½, GREEN GABLE 2¾, GREAT GABLE 3, BRANDRETH 2, Beck Head, Gillercombe Buttress, GREY KNOTTS 1¾, Honister, path to Great Gable

SW — KIRK FELL 3½, Stirrup Crag (YEWBARROW) 7¾, MIDDLE FELL 6½, Black Sail Pass, HAYSTACKS

W — RED PIKE 4¾, STARLING DODD 5, GREAT BORNE 6, GAVEL FELL 7, BLAKE FELL 7½, Buttermere

NW — ROBINSON 1¾, fence, easy route of descent into Newlands

Follow this edge, with a ruined fence on the left, for Hindscarth and Robinson.

(If followed to its termination the fence will lead to the plantation on the fellside above Hassness, Buttermere)

The figures accompanying the names of fells indicate distances in miles

Dale Head 14

THE VIEW

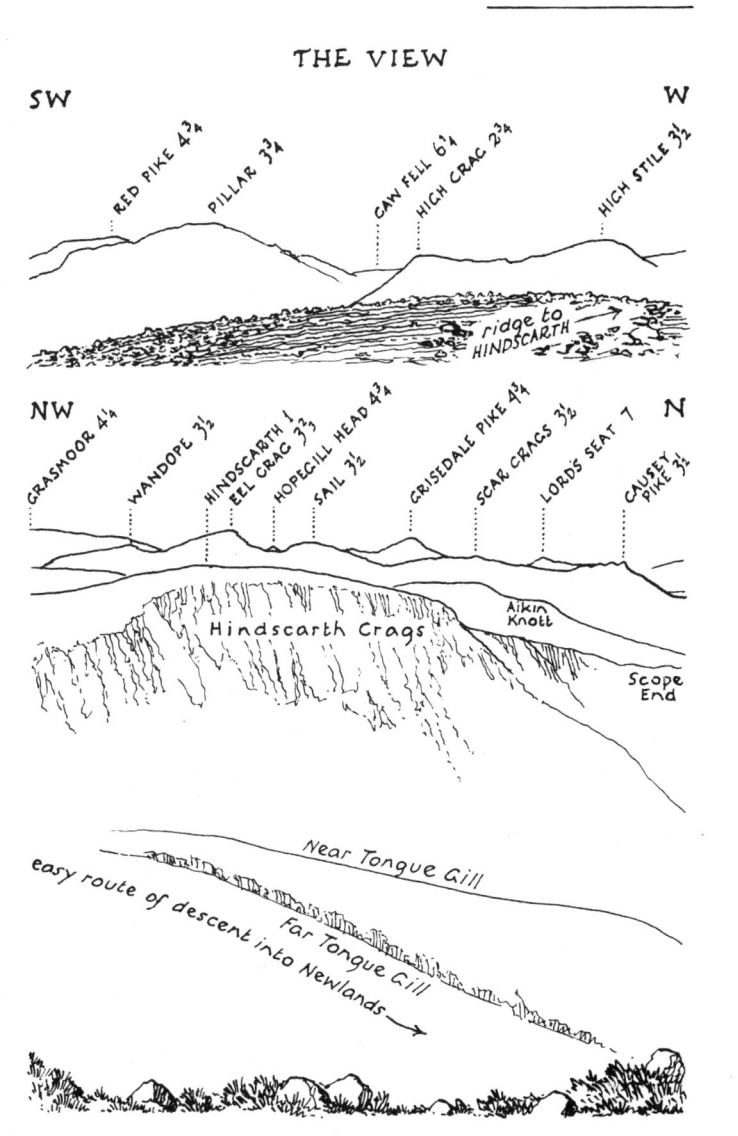

SW — RED PIKE 4¾, PILLAR 3¾, CAW FELL 6¼, HIGH CRAG 2¾, HIGH STILE 3½ — **W**

ridge to HINDSCARTH →

NW — GRASMOOR 4¼, WANDOPE 3½, HINDSCARTH 1, EEL CRAG 3¾, HOPEGILL HEAD 4¼, SAIL 3½, GRISEDALE PIKE 4¼, SCAR CRAGS 3½, LORD'S SEAT 7, CAUSEY PIKE 3½ — **N**

Hindscarth Crags

Aikin Knott

Scope End

Near Tongue Gill

Far Tongue Gill

easy route of descent into Newlands →

Eel Crag 2749'

Crag Hill
on Ordnance
Survey maps

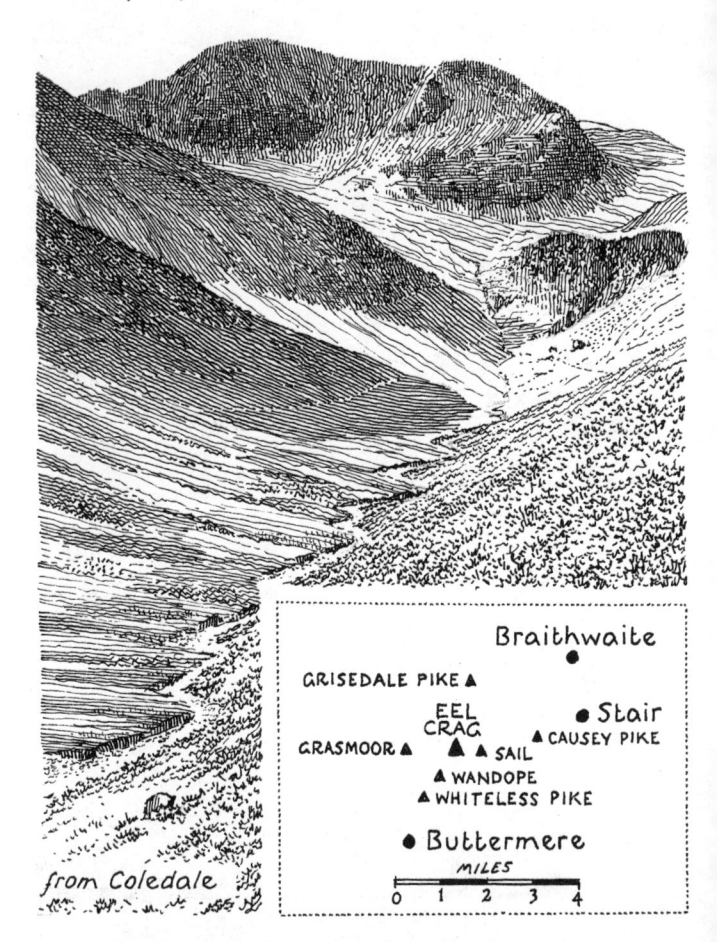

from Coledale

```
                                    Braithwaite
                                       •
        GRISEDALE PIKE ▲
                         EEL
                         CRAG              • Stair
GRASMOOR ▲               ▲  ▲ SAIL    ▲ CAUSEY PIKE
                         ▲ WANDOPE
                         ▲ WHITELESS PIKE

                         • Buttermere
                                MILES
                         0  1  2  3  4
```

Eel Crag 2

NATURAL FEATURES

Although of rather lower elevation than the neighbouring Grasmoor, Eel Crag is more truly the focal point of the concentration of fells rising between the valleys of Newlands and Lorton.   Unlike Grasmoor, Eel Crag is supported by ridges.   Unlike Grasmoor, it stands in the midst of a group of satellites. Unlike Grasmoor, it commands an excellent all-round view.   It is in the centre of things. It is an obvious objective.   Tracks lead up to its stony top naturally and inevitably.   It is a traffic junction, while Grasmoor is a cul-de-sac.

The shadowed north-east face of the fell, towering high above the head of Coledale, is a fine sight.   Even steeper, but less familiar, is the craggy southern slope, seamed with gullies, overlooking Sail Beck: this is a no-man's-land. Walkers prefer the exciting ridges, of which a narrowing crest coming up from the east gives the best approach; another, shorter, traverses the summit from Coledale Hause, and a third curves south-west to a grassy depression from which three spurs lead separately to Wandope, Whiteless Pike and the great bulk of Grasmoor. Streams from the fell flow to two main rivers, from Grasmoor to one, and this is the great test of superiority. Eel Crag is a watershed but Grasmoor is not.

The east ridge — EEL CRAG, SAIL, Sail Pass, SCAR CRAGS, CAUSEY PIKE, Rowling End, Newlands (2500', 2000', 1500', 1000', 500')

The name of the fell is unfortunate and inaccurate. Eel Crag is properly the rocky buttress above Coledale Hause, but for a century or more the whole fell has been popularly known by this name.   The Ordnance maps, in all series, use *Crag Hill*, and, if adopted generally, this name would avoid the confusion that has arisen due to the recent development of Eel Crags in nearby Newlands as a climbing ground. But walkers are conservative folk: they do not like change in old favourites, and Eel Crag it will remain.

Eel Crag 3

The north-east face, from the lower slopes of Sand Hill

The south face, with Sail beyond, from Wandope

Eel Crag 4

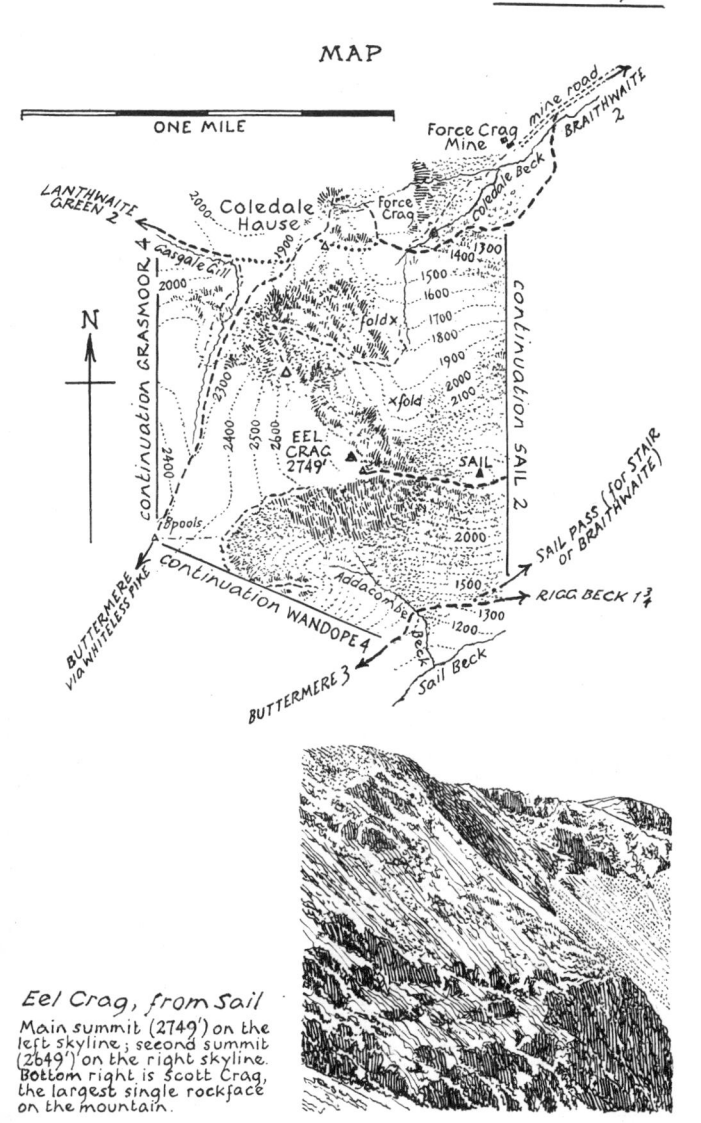

MAP

ONE MILE

- Force Crag Mine
- mine road → BRAITHWAITE 2
- LANTHWAITE GREEN 2
- Coledale Hause
- Force Crag
- Coledale Beck
- Gasgale Gill
- continuation GRASMOOR 4
- fold
- fold
- continuation SAIL 2
- EEL CRAG 2749'
- SAIL
- SAIL PASS (for STAIR or BRAITHWAITE)
- 18 pools
- BUTTERMERE VIA WHITELESS PIKE
- continuation WANDOPE 4
- Addacomb beck
- → RIGG BECK 1¾
- → BUTTERMERE 3
- Sail Beck

N

Eel Crag, from Sail

Main summit (2749') on the left skyline; second summit (2649') on the right skyline. Bottom right is Scott Crag, the largest single rockface on the mountain.

Eel Crag 5

ASCENT FROM RANNERDALE
2400 feet of ascent : 2½ miles

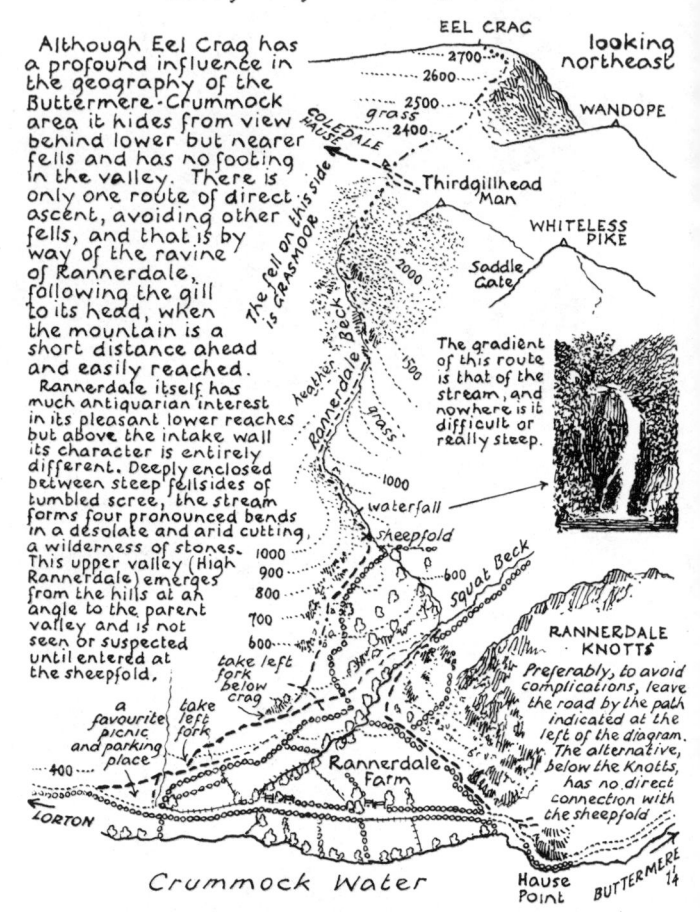

looking northeast

Although Eel Crag has a profound influence in the geography of the Buttermere-Crummock area it hides from view behind lower but nearer fells and has no footing in the valley. There is only one route of direct ascent, avoiding other fells, and that is by way of the ravine of Rannerdale, following the gill to its head, when the mountain is a short distance ahead and easily reached.

Rannerdale itself has much antiquarian interest in its pleasant lower reaches but above the intake wall its character is entirely different. Deeply enclosed between steep fellsides of tumbled scree, the stream forms four pronounced bends in a desolate and arid cutting, a wilderness of stones. This upper valley (High Rannerdale) emerges from the hills at an angle to the parent valley and is not seen or suspected until entered at the sheepfold.

a favourite picnic and parking place

take left fork
take left fork below crag

The fell on this side is GRASMOOR

The gradient of this route is that of the stream, and nowhere is it difficult or really steep.

RANNERDALE KNOTTS
Preferably, to avoid complications, leave the road by the path indicated at the left of the diagram. The alternative, below the Knotts, has no direct connection with the sheepfold.

LORTON — Rannerdale Farm — Crummock Water — House Point — BUTTERMERE

Every direct route has something to commend it, if only its directness. Rannerdale additionally is sheltered, has water at hand, and is absolutely unloseable in mist. BUT its charms are few, and, in the upper reaches, the view is limited to the immediate unattractive surroundings.

Eel Crag 6

ASCENT FROM STAIR
2,700 feet of ascent
3½ miles

If it becomes necessary to get off the ridge because of bad weather do not attempt to do so on the left (except at Sail Pass, if aiming for Buttermere). The quickest route of evacuation is provided by the mine road.

It is generally more satisfying to climb a mountain from base to top than to hop onto the summit by a connecting ridge from another fell, and certainly by so doing a more detailed knowledge of its structure is gained. But the finest walking on the fells (as distinct from wandering and exploration), which give greater interest, is obtained by following linking ridges, even though the visits to the various summits en route are brief and superficial: one keeps high above the world, the views are extensive and ever changing, and distances are quickly covered.

Illustrated here is a grand ridge walk leading to Eel Crag over three intermediate tops, and this is the best line of ascent. The first two may be avoided (but shouldn't be), and time saved, by joining the ridge at Sail Pass, using the mine road alongside Stonycroft Gill (or the pass may be reached less easily from the valley of Rigg Beck on the left).

looking west

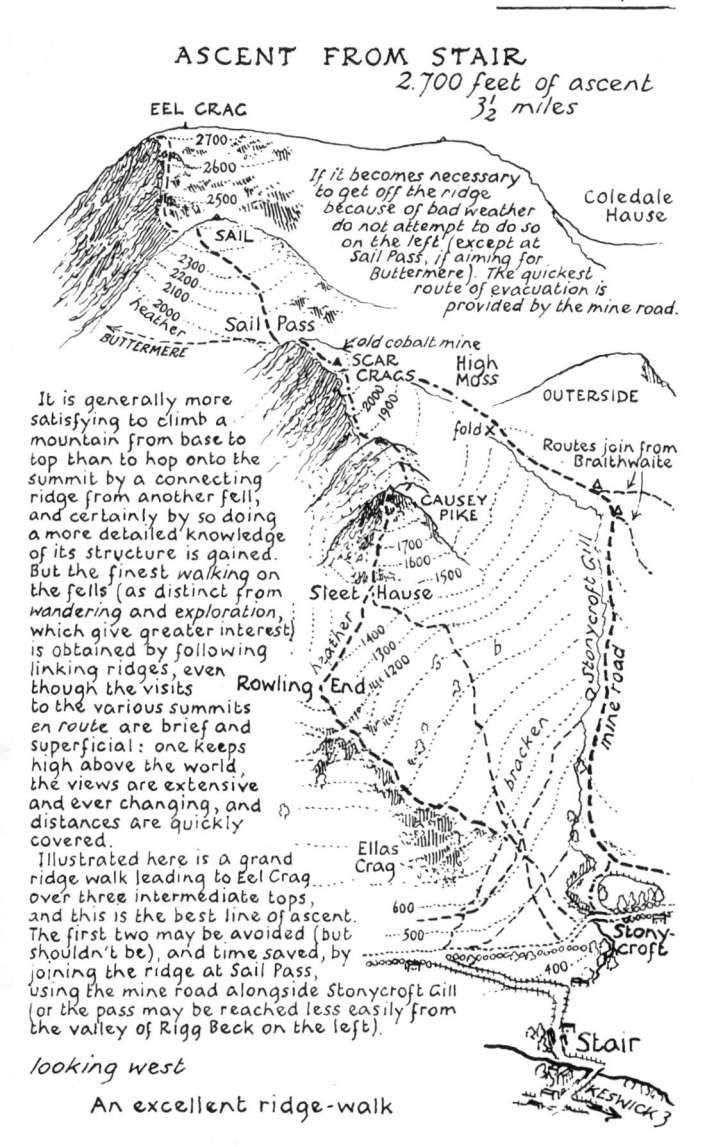

An excellent ridge-walk

Eel Crag 7

ASCENT FROM BRAITHWAITE
(DIRECT) 2500 feet of ascent
3¾ miles (A); 4 miles (B).

looking south-west

EEL CRAG

Turn up the ridge, joining the route from the Hause

Eel Crag
Coledale Hause

Scott Crag

field
bog
grass

× sheepfold

grass
× sheepfold
mosses
causeway
mine road
COLEDALE HAUSE

A : TOWER RIDGE
B : SHELF ROUTE

In this cairn is buried much broken glass, interred by the author after finding it scattered in the grass nearby. Broken glass is the worst sort of litter. Leaving it on ground where animals graze is wickedness.

landslip

Force Crag

HIGH MOSS SAIL PASS

mine road

grass

hut
× fold

grass

Coledale Beck

spoil heaps

Force Crag Mine

mine road

ford

← BRAITHWAITE 2½

← The ford is usually unfordable, easier crossings being made upstream.

It is usual to ascend by way of Coledale Hause, a frequented but tedious route. Here are given two quiet alternatives for discerning walkers, one up and one across the stony breast of the mountain — in the absence of official names for them they are described in this book as Tower Ridge and Shelf Route. Both are plainly in view on the walk up Coledale from Braithwaite.

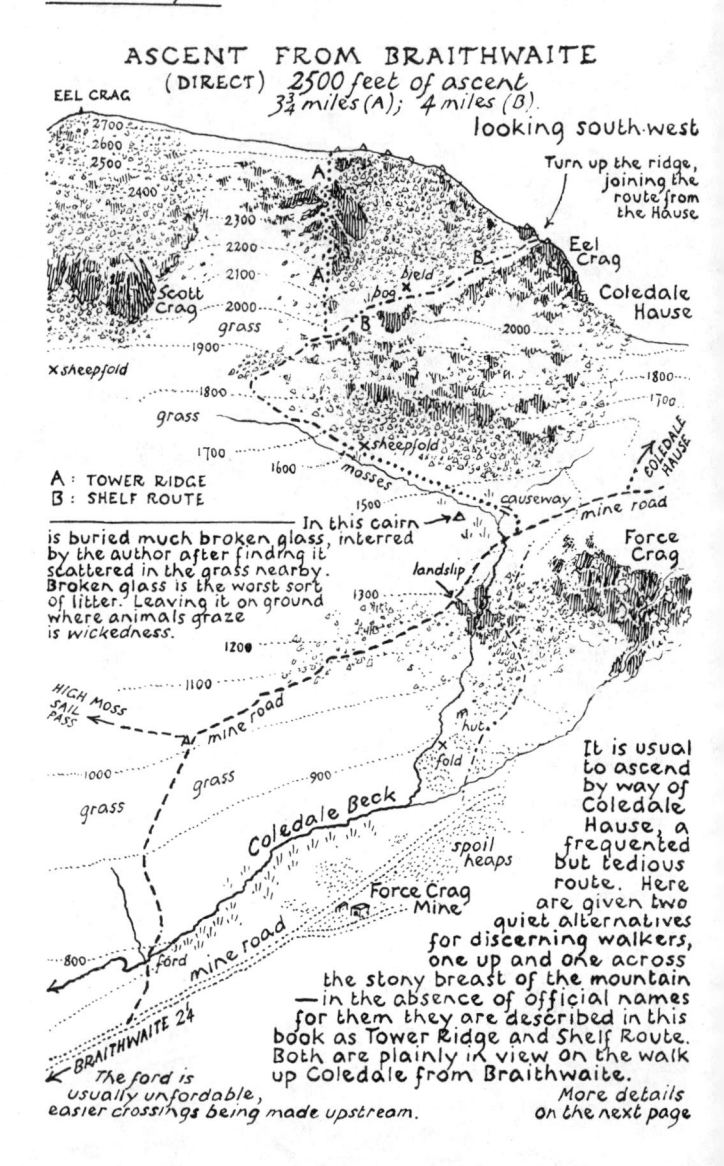

More details on the next page

Eel Crag 8

The Shelf Route and Tower Ridge

On the ordinary route from Braithwaite, via Coledale Hause, it is usual to tackle the slope of scree 'around the corner' from the Hause (although this can be avoided by continuing forward to the headwaters of Gasgale Gill). This scree is extensive; it is tiresome to ascend and unpleasant to descend.

A way of cutting out this abomination is provided by the Shelf Route, which, rarely used, adds a little thrill of exploration and more interest to the climb. The Shelf, once reached, is obvious ahead: a rising green strip of bilberry and mosses between the screes from the summit-rim and the broken line of crags facing the head of Coledale. It joins the usual route on the ridge at a point just above the steeper rocks overlooking the Hause.

The approach from Braithwaite.

In spring and autumn the Shelf and Tower Ridge are the last two places on the face to be illumined by morning sunlight, the rest then being in dark shadow.

A very thin track runs along the shelf. Cairns are absent, but a few small ones would be a help in navigation. A guide-cairn never needs to consist of more than two or three stones, placed one on top of another. Siting is more important. From one cairn the next should be visible, preferably on a skyline.

The end of the shelf
Turn up the ridge behind the rocks on the left

Tower Ridge:

Just before reaching the start of the shelf (at a green bog behind a prominent rocky tor) walkers who like a scramble may make their way up the bouldery ridge on the left, which is broad but soon narrows to a well-defined rocky tower, with a secondary buttress alongside on the right. The steeper rises on the ridge can be avoided on the left until the final pyramid, of short vertical steps, is reached. A ledge of scree rising 20 yards to the right is now followed and then a grass terrace rising to the left for the same distance, a high stride in a corner here gaining the easy ground at the top of the tower. A simple grassy neck then connects with the summit of the mountain just south of the big cairn on the lower top at 2649'. This variation is direct and cuts out the scree slope altogether. It is necessary in a few places to handle rocks but there is nothing to cause fear or panic, although ladies in ankle-length skirts may find odd places a little troublesome.

Tower Ridge from the end of the shelf

Eel Crag 9

ASCENT FROM COLEDALE HAUSE
850 feet of ascent : 1 mile

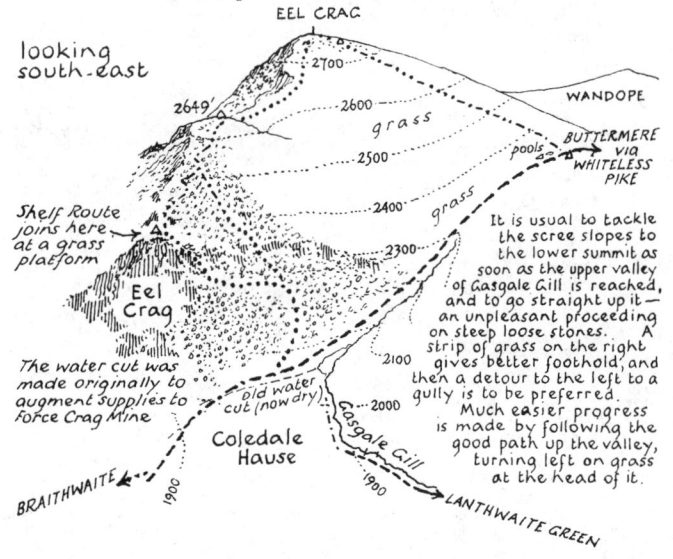

looking south-east

EEL CRAG — 2700 — 2600 — *grass* — 2500 — pools — WANDOPE — BUTTERMERE VIA WHITELESS PIKE

2649' — 2400 — *grass* — 2300

Shelf Route joins here at a grass platform

Eel Crag

The water cut was made originally to augment supplies to Force Crag Mine

It is usual to tackle the scree slopes to the lower summit as soon as the upper valley of Gasgale Gill is reached, and to go straight up it — an unpleasant proceeding on steep loose stones. A strip of grass on the right gives better foothold, and then a detour to the left to a gully is to be preferred.
Much easier progress is made by following the good path up the valley, turning left on grass at the head of it.

Old water cut (now dry) — 2100 — 2000

Coledale Hause — Gasgale Gill

BRAITHWAITE ← 1900 — 1900 → LANTHWAITE GREEN

THE SUMMIT

The top is flat and stony, being littered with slate fragments easy to walk upon, so that no paths have been formed in the vicinity of the survey column marking the highest point (S.5993)

DESCENTS:
All routes of ascent may be reversed, but the bad scree above Coledale Hause ought to be avoided in favour of a direct descent on grass, west, to the headwaters of Gasgale Gill. This is the best line off the top in mist for Braithwaite (path right), Buttermere (path left) or Lanthwaite Green (follow stream).

The route to Stair over Causey Pike (or turning off left at Sail Pass) is picked up at the corner of the summit formed by the north-east and south slopes of the fell, 100 yards south-east of the column; in mist it is quite safe, but under snow or ice care is needed on the rocksteps.

Eel Crag 10

RIDGE ROUTES

To SAIL, 2530': ⅖ mile : E
Depression at 2430'
100 feet of ascent
The best way off Eel Crag

No definite path leaves the survey column, but one starts at a cairn in the 'corner' of the summit 100 yds south-east and is thereafter clear, there being no possibility of going astray on the narrow falling ridge. Timid walkers will be aware of their disability at two places where rock must be descended, but may safely venture. Across the depression (not to be mistaken for Sail Pass) a good path climbs up to Sail summit, the small cairn here being half-hidden by vegetation some 25 yards to the left of the path and often passed unnoticed.

looking to Sail from the top of the east ridge.

To GRASMOOR, 2791': 1¼ miles : generally W.
Depression at 2350': 450 feet of ascent
A long moorland tramp, not recommended in mist

Go down the easy slope west to cross the Coledale Hause-Whiteless Pike path near two small pools. Beyond, follow a rising line of cairns up the grassy breast to the vast, gently rising top of Grasmoor, the main cairn of which is still a further half-mile distant.

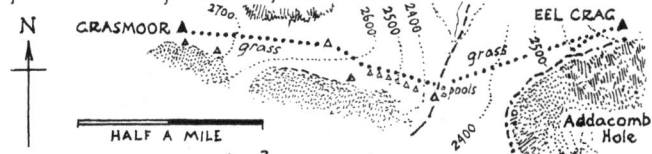

To WANDOPE, 2533': ¾ mile : SW, then S
Depression at 2420': 120 feet of ascent
A bird's-eye view of Addacomb Hole

A beeline may be made, soon joining a track skirting the edge of the steep south face overlooking the hanging valley of Addacomb Hole. A simple final slope, all grass, curves round to the top of Wandope.

Eel Crag 11

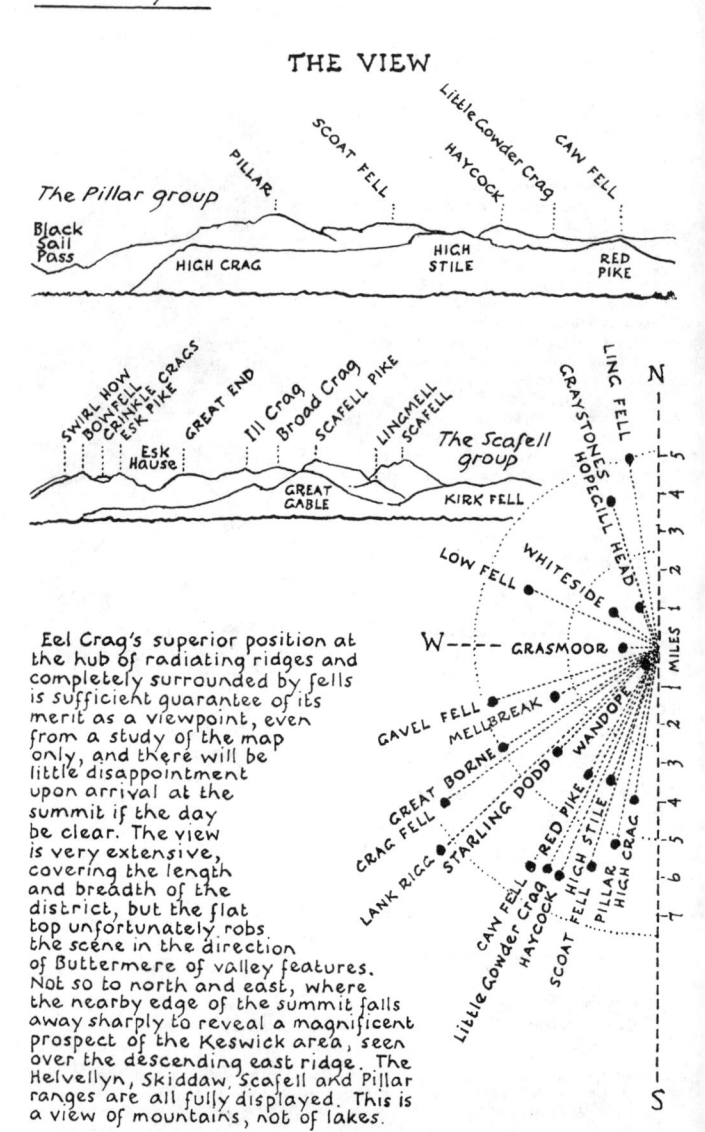

THE VIEW

The Pillar group

Black Sail Pass — PILLAR — SCOAT FELL — Little Gowder Crag — HAYCOCK — CAW FELL — HIGH CRAG — HIGH STILE — RED PIKE

The Scafell group

SWIRL HOW — BOWFELL — CRINKLE CRAGS — ESK PIKE — Esk Hause — GREAT END — Ill Crag — Broad Crag — SCAFELL PIKE — LINGMELL — SCAFELL — GREAT GABLE — KIRK FELL

Eel Crag's superior position at the hub of radiating ridges and completely surrounded by fells is sufficient guarantee of its merit as a viewpoint, even from a study of the map only, and there will be little disappointment upon arrival at the summit if the day be clear. The view is very extensive, covering the length and breadth of the district, but the flat top unfortunately robs the scene in the direction of Buttermere of valley features. Not so to north and east, where the nearby edge of the summit falls away sharply to reveal a magnificent prospect of the Keswick area, seen over the descending east ridge. The Helvellyn, Skiddaw, Scafell and Pillar ranges are all fully displayed. This is a view of mountains, not of lakes.

Compass diagram (MILES, N–S, W):
LING FELL, GRAYSTONES, HOPEGILL HEAD, WHITESIDE, LOW FELL, GRASMOOR, GAVEL FELL, MELLBREAK, GREAT BORNE, WANDOPE, CRAG FELL, STARLING DODD, RED PIKE, HIGH STILE, LANK RIGG, CAW FELL, HIGH CRAG, LITTLE GOWDER CRAG, HAYCOCK, SCOAT FELL, PILLAR

Eel Crag 12

THE VIEW

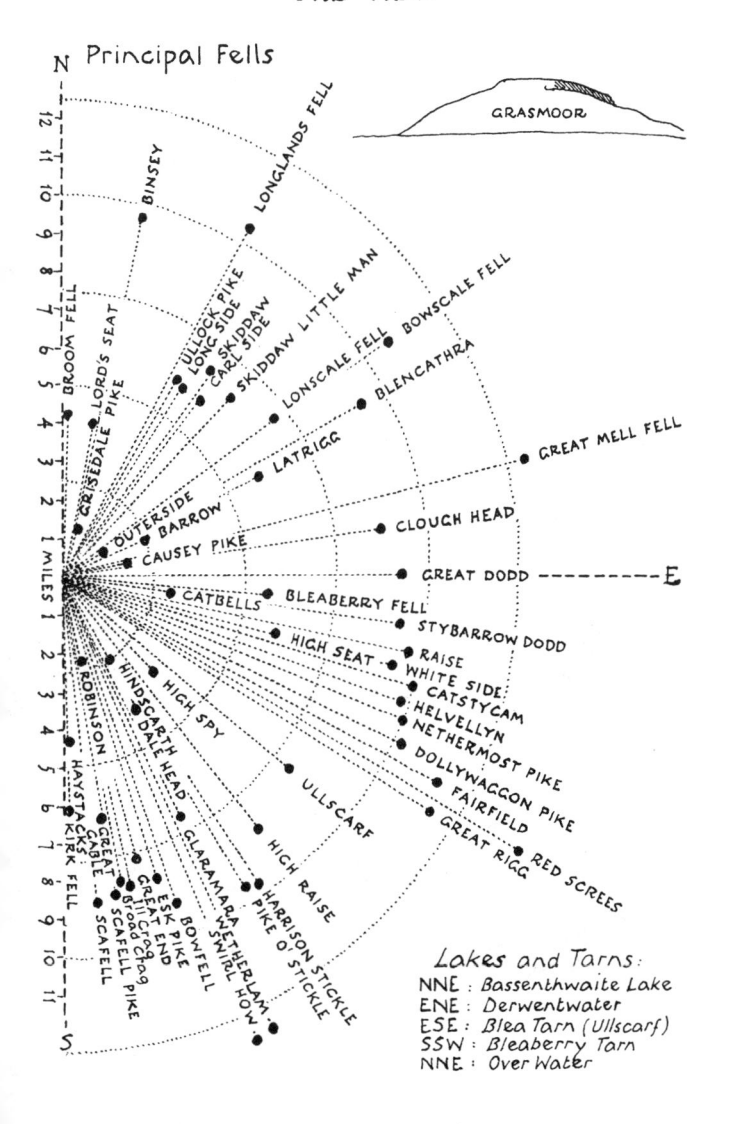

Principal Fells

GRASMOOR

N
BINSEY
LONGLANDS FELL
BROOM FELL
LORD'S SEAT
CRISEDALE PIKE
ULLOCK PIKE
LONG SIDE
SKIDDAW
CARL SIDE
SKIDDAW LITTLE MAN
LONSCALE FELL
BOWSCALE FELL
BLENCATHRA
OUTSIDE
BARROW
LATRIGG
GREAT MELL FELL
CAUSEY PIKE
CLOUGH HEAD
GREAT DODD — — — — — E
CATBELLS
BLEABERRY FELL
STYBARROW DODD
HIGH SEAT
RAISE
WHITE SIDE
CATSTYCAM
HIGH SPY
HELVELLYN
NETHERMOST PIKE
ROBINSON
HINDSCARTH
DOLLYWAGGON PIKE
FAIRFIELD
HIGH RAISE
ULLSCARF
GREAT RIGG
RED SCREES
HAYSTACKS
DALE HEAD
KIRK FELL
GREAT GABLE
GLARAMARA
HARRISON STICKLE
GREEN GABLE
WETHERLAM
ESK PIKE
BOWFELL
PIKE O'STICKLE
GREAT END
BROAD CRAG
SCAFELL PIKE
SWIRL HOW
SCAFELL
S

Lakes and Tarns:
NNE : Bassenthwaite Lake
ENE : Derwentwater
ESE : Blea Tarn (Ullscarf)
SSW : Bleaberry Tarn
NNE : Over Water

Grasmoor 2791'

from Lanthwaite Hill

Grasmoor 2

NATURAL FEATURES

The culminating point of the North Western Fells occurs overlooking Crummock Water, where the massive bulk of Grasmoor towers above the threshold of the Buttermere valley, showing its full height to great advantage from the shores of the lake.   As Nature has arranged matters this particular aspect of the fell, facing west, is also the finest: a steep pyramid of rocky ribs and broken crags suspended far above the road along its base, the road that carries travellers to Buttermere — and few go this way who do not look upwards rather fearfully to the cliffs poised overhead, seeming to threaten safe passage. Yet familiarity with this monstrous monolith dispels fear and the brackeny hollows below, adjoining the unfenced road, harbour summer migrants in the shape of campers, motorists and caravanners: it is a favourite picnic and recreation ground for discerning West Cumbrians.   Apart from the two dark clefts on this face, there are no continuous courses to attract rockclimbers; the only crags of any size circle an upland combe on the north flank and rim the edge of the summit. On the south side are the most extensive scree-slopes in the district: a colourful but arid desert of stones.   Eastwards there is a high link with Eel Crag and a fine ridge descending into Newlands.   But probably most visitors to Grasmoor will remember the fell for a summit-plateau remarkable both for its extent and its luxurious carpet of mossy turf, close-cropped by the resident sheep who range these broad acres. In structure the fell assumes a simple form, the only unorthodoxy being a ramp down the middle of the south slope curving round into the heathery spur of Lad House, now known as Lad Hows. The streams bounding Grasmoor occupy the stony side-valleys of Gasgale Gill and Rannerdale Beck. It has no tarns.

```
                    Braithwaite ●
         ● Scale Hill Road End
                  ▲ WHITESIDE
   ● Loweswater
   GRASMOOR ▲    ▲ EEL CRAG
         WANDOPE ▲
              ▲
         WHITELESS PIKE
                   ● Buttermere
                MILES
         0    1    2    3    4
```

The name of the fell is commonly mis-spelt as Grassmoor, even in print, by writers who would never dream of mis-spelling Grasmere Grassmere. There is only one 's'. The gras derives from grise — wild boar — as in so many Lakeland names e.g. Grisedale.

Grasmoor 3

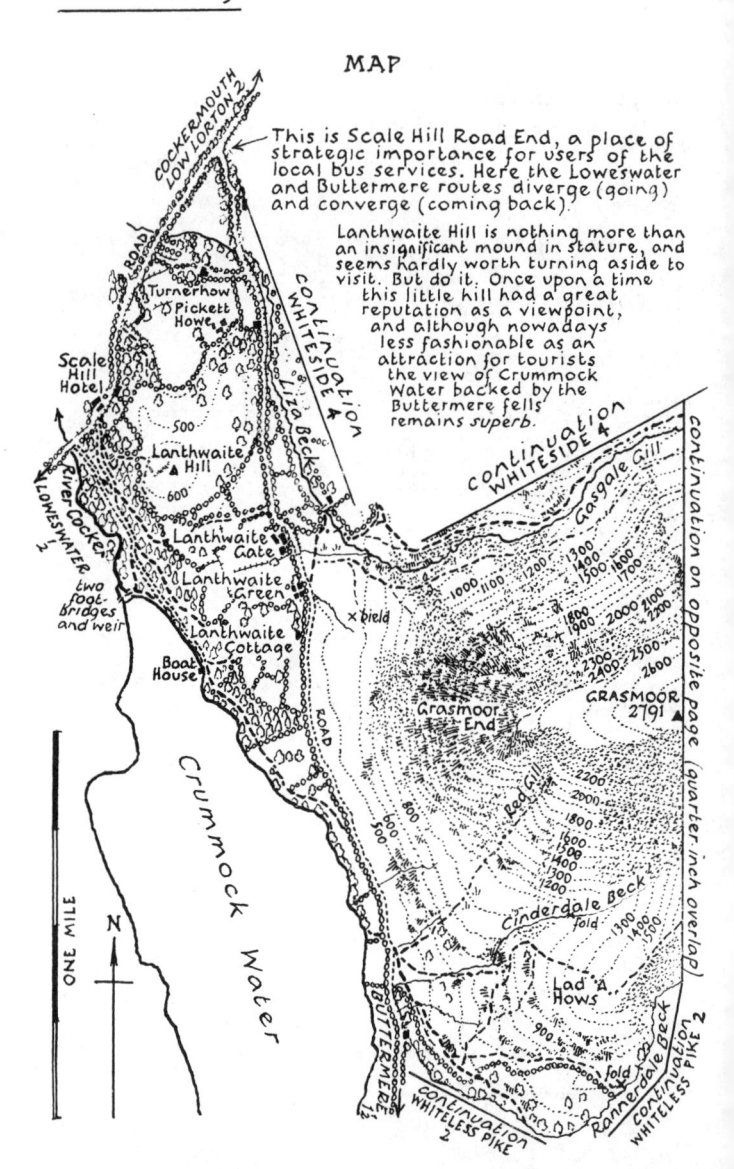

MAP

This is Scale Hill Road End, a place of strategic importance for users of the local bus services. Here the Loweswater and Buttermere routes diverge (going) and converge (coming back).

Lanthwaite Hill is nothing more than an insignificant mound in stature, and seems hardly worth turning aside to visit. But do it. Once upon a time this little hill had a great reputation as a viewpoint, and although nowadays less fashionable as an attraction for tourists the view of Crummock Water backed by the Buttermere fells remains *superb*.

Grasmoor 4

MAP

The natural boundaries of mountains tend to be obscured by man's lines of communications. It is not the valley roads that define the limits of a mountain but the main watercourses. Here is a case in point (opposite page). The road along the bases of Whiteside and Grasmoor appears to terminate their slopes, but these fells are divided by Liza Beck (Gasgale Gill higher up), which, instead of completing the severance neatly by a direct cut into Crummock Water, turns north to join the River Cocker beyond the outflow of the lake and thereby claims for Grasmoor a wedge of low country that, to a casual observer, would seem to belong to Whiteside. Thus Lanthwaite Hill is Grasmoor's cub although it sits at the feet of Whiteside.

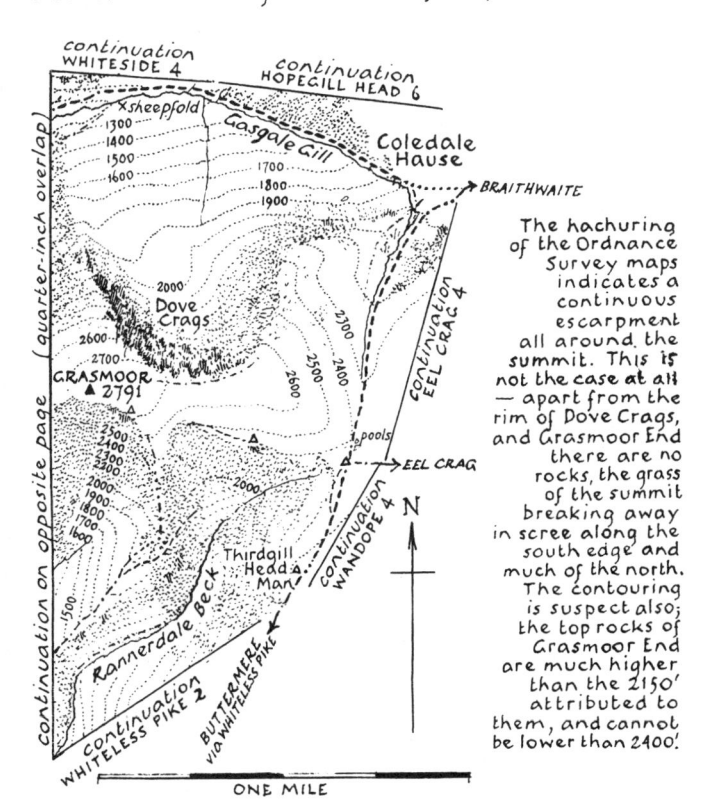

The hachuring of the Ordnance Survey maps indicates a continuous escarpment all around the summit. This is not the case at all — apart from the rim of Dove Crags, and Grasmoor End there are no rocks, the grass of the summit breaking away in scree along the south edge and much of the north. The contouring is suspect also; the top rocks of Grasmoor End are much higher than the 2150' attributed to them, and cannot be lower than 2400'.

ONE MILE

Grasmoor 5

ASCENT FROM LANTHWAITE GREEN
VIA DOVE CRAGS
2300 feet of ascent : 2 miles

GRASMOOR

Dove Crags

Grasmoor End

One of the natural wonders of Grasmoor is the profound hollow scooped out of its north flank and encircled by Dove Crags. The floor of this amphitheatre is a grassy basin, surrounded on all sides by higher ground. It seems an obvious site for a tarn, yet is dry, although clearly all the drainage from the crags must be received there. Because of the raised edge of the hollow there is no issuing stream, nor indeed are there any watercourses within it. All this is very odd. What happens to all the water falling within the area of the combe? The explanation can only be that the screes below the crags act as soak-aways and absorb all moisture from above as it falls, releasing it to the basin so slowly that evaporation and not accumulation takes place.

Many sheep tracks are crossed during the early stages of the climb from the valley. One of these (at about 1500') is a particularly clear trail (it is used by shepherds also): it traverses the fellside and links with the terrace on the direct route.

Gasgale Gill

usual path to Coledale Hause

This old walkers' path on the Grasmoor side of the gill now serves only for sheep. It is rough, but still fairly clear.

Gasgale Gill is a narrow V-shaped cutting, no wider than the bed of the stream. On the north side Whiteside rises even more steeply than Grasmoor on the south side.

Nature never uses straight lines in her designs, but has come remarkably close to doing so in fashioning this arete and the approach to it from the gill along the edge of the scree. A plumb-line dropped from the summit to the valley would lie over the route almost exactly. This is very noticeable from the top of Whiteside.

There are no difficulties in this ascent. The rock slab is set at an easy gradient but is greasy and needs care. The views down the crags from the arete are tremendous.

The route can be identified from the road. Looking up the valley of Gasgale Gill, it is the skyline ridge rising smoothly to the right, the one roughness on it being the rock slab.

Lanthwaite Green
Lanthwaite Gate
LORTON 3

looking south-south-east

Grasmoor 6

ASCENT FROM LANTHWAITE GREEN DIRECT
2300 feet of ascent
1½ miles

GRASMOOR
grass and mosses
2500
Grasmoor End 2400'
2300
2200
2100
Pinnacle 2000'
arete
Fat Man's Agony
terrace (1600')
rake (1500'-1600')

Upon reaching the Pinnacle (a fine vantage point) jaws drop with dismay at the sight of Grasmoor End, still distant and considerably higher. The ground between is very rough, but a curving ridge (not at first obvious) leads up to it.

The Pinnacle dominates this section of the route, forming a fine rock pyramid high above the terrace. Take to a rocky arête on the left from the terrace by way of a splintered crag (a Fat Man's Agony) and gain height by scrambling over or around a series of little cliffs.

Immediately above the rock gateway turn up a green rake on the right (this reminds one of Lord's Rake — on a smaller and gentler scale). The rake leads to a terrace carrying (unexpectedly) a clear track, but this runs horizontally both ways and is no help in the ascent.

rock gateway 1500'
rock gateway now seen directly ahead
a detached block below the first crag
1300
Take direction from this conspicuous tongue of light-coloured scree (it is plainly in view from the road).
1200
1100
Go straight up (a rough, steep pull up heather and stones)

The tortuous crawl up the 40° slope provides opportunity for observing the flora at very close range. There are various berried shrublets, and, on the higher rocks, excellent specimens of prostrate juniper.

heather
800
falls
bracken
A fair path through the bracken comes to an end when the first stones are reached
700

Grasmoor is a very formidable object above Lanthwaite, its tiered crags seeming almost impregnable. The direct climb, up the angle between the north and west faces, is a continuously steep and rough scramble and a severe test in route selection.

On the whole, however, the climb is probably less difficult than the North Wall of the Eiger.

climbers' track to Grasmoor gullies
x bield
600
Liza Beck
water cut
weir
Pick up a thin track on the south side of the water cut (a line of rushes)
500
B.S.
grass
cattle grid
BUTTERMERE
Lanthwaite Green
ROAD
LORTON 3½
Lanthwaite Gate

looking southeast

Grasmoor 7

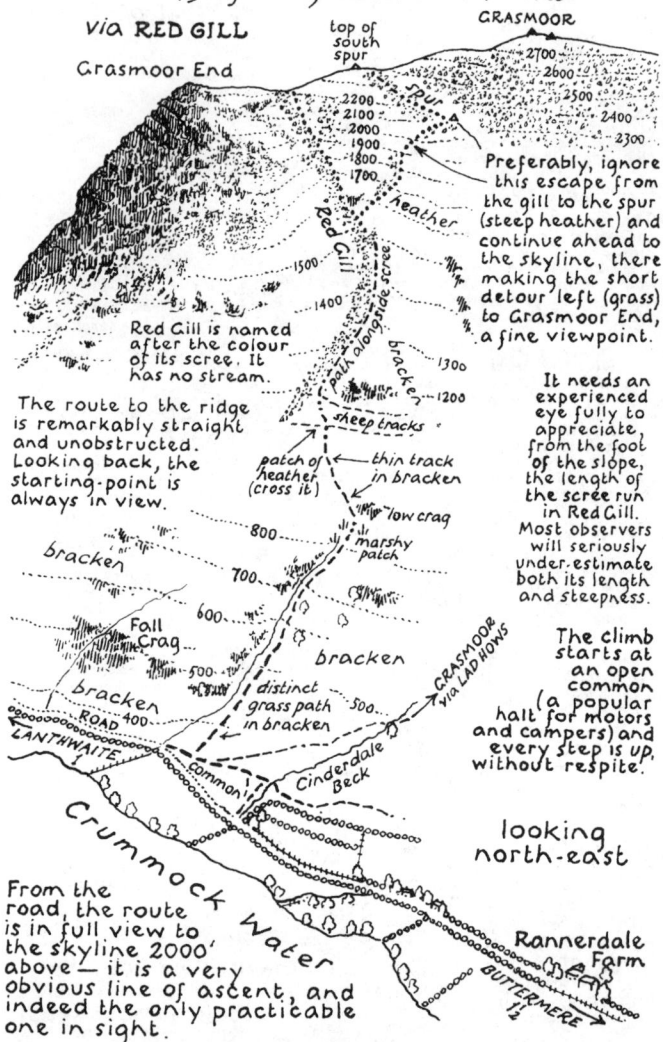

ASCENT FROM RANNERDALE
2430 feet of ascent : 1¼ miles

via RED GILL

Grasmoor End — top of south spur — GRASMOOR

2700, 2600, 2500, 2400, 2300
2200, 2100, 2000, 1900, 1800, 1700

Preferably, ignore this escape from the gill to the spur (steep heather) and continue ahead to the skyline, there making the short detour left (grass) to Grasmoor End, a fine viewpoint.

Red Gill — path alongside scree — heather — 1500, 1400, 1300, 1200 — bracken

Red Gill is named after the colour of its scree. It has no stream.

The route to the ridge is remarkably straight and unobstructed. Looking back, the starting-point is always in view.

sheep tracks — patch of heather (cross it) — thin track in bracken — low crag — marshy patch

800, 700, 600, 500, 400

bracken — Fall Crag — bracken — distinct grass path in bracken — ROAD — LANTHWAITE — Common — Cinderdale Beck — GRASMOOR via LAD HOWS

It needs an experienced eye fully to appreciate, from the foot of the slope, the length of the scree run in Red Gill. Most observers will seriously under-estimate both its length and steepness.

The climb starts at an open common (a popular halt for motors and campers) and every step is up, without respite.

looking north-east

Crummock Water

From the road, the route is in full view to the skyline 2000' above — it is a very obvious line of ascent, and indeed the only practicable one in sight.

Rannerdale Farm — BUTTERMERE

Grasmoor 8

ASCENT FROM RANNERDALE
2450 feet of ascent : 1¾ miles
VIA LAD HOWS

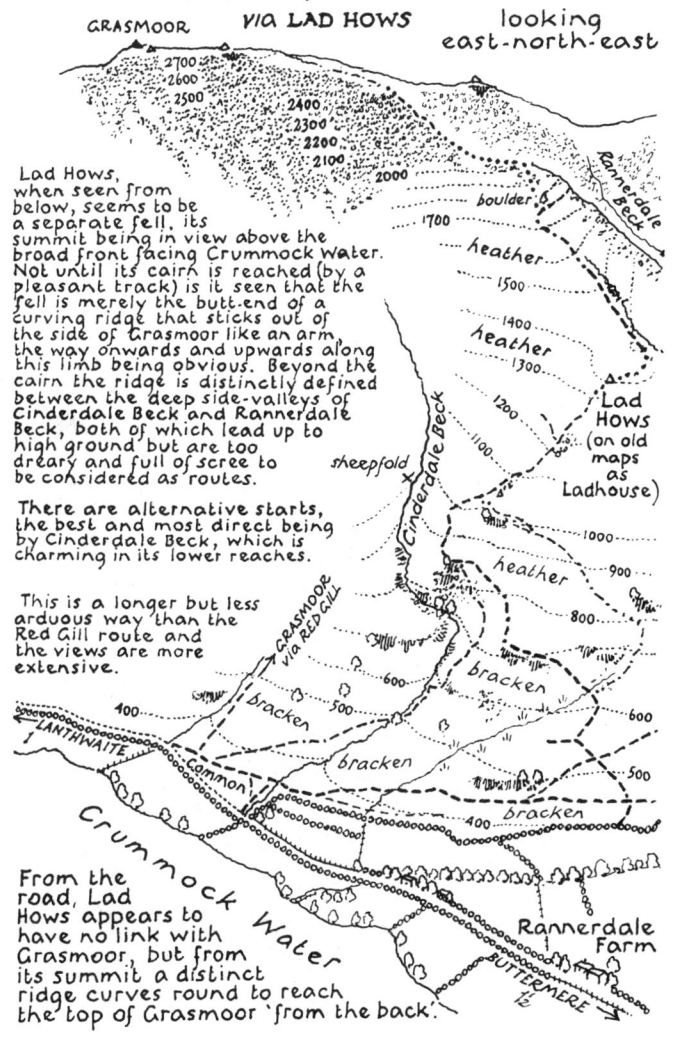

looking east-north-east

Lad Hows, when seen from below, seems to be a separate fell, its summit being in view above the broad front facing Crummock Water. Not until its cairn is reached (by a pleasant track) is it seen that the fell is merely the butt-end of a curving ridge that sticks out of the side of Grasmoor like an arm, the way onwards and upwards along this limb being obvious. Beyond the cairn the ridge is distinctly defined between the deep side-valleys of Cinderdale Beck and Rannerdale Beck, both of which lead up to high ground but are too dreary and full of scree to be considered as routes.

There are alternative starts, the best and most direct being by Cinderdale Beck, which is charming in its lower reaches.

This is a longer but less arduous way than the Red Gill route and the views are more extensive.

From the road, Lad Hows appears to have no link with Grasmoor, but from its summit a distinct ridge curves round to reach the top of Grasmoor 'from the back'.

Grasmoor 9

The Scafell group

Grasmoor 10

from Grasmoor

Grasmoor 11

ASCENT FROM COLEDALE HAUSE
850 feet of ascent
1¼ miles

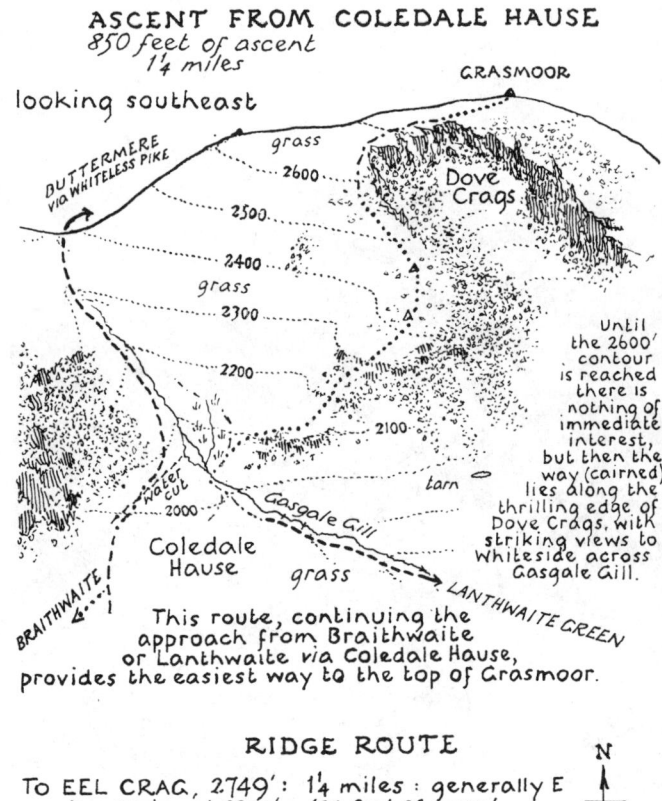

looking southeast

Until the 2600' contour is reached there is nothing of immediate interest, but then the way (cairned) lies along the thrilling edge of Dove Crags, with striking views to Whiteside across Gasgale Gill.

This route, continuing the approach from Braithwaite or Lanthwaite via Coledale Hause, provides the easiest way to the top of Grasmoor.

RIDGE ROUTE

To EEL CRAG, 2749' : 1¼ miles : generally E
Depression at 2350' : 400 feet of ascent
A long moorland tramp, excellent underfoot

The first half-mile is the easiest walking to be found anywhere; keep left for a sight of Dove Crags. After crossing the depression, bear right for a look down into Addacomb Hole. These are the only excitements.

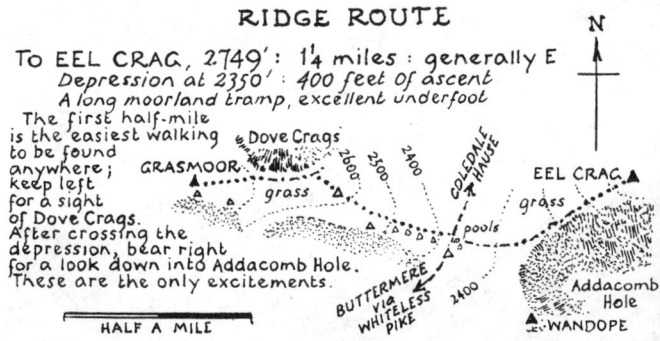

HALF A MILE

Grasmoor 12

THE SUMMIT

There are many cairns at various stations on the broad top, but no mistaking the highest of all, which is a huge heap of stones divided into shelter compartments, open to the sky, designed to give protection from wind (but not wet) coming from any direction. Some skill and much labour has gone into its construction (where did the stones come from?) and visitors should feel a sense of responsibility for keeping it in repair. It stands a score of yards only from the edge of the south face, and a smaller wind-shelter perched here on the brink marks a better viewpoint. The summit has a covering of shale hereabouts, but elsewhere a soft mossy turf is a pleasure to walk upon.

The top of the fell is a long plateau coming up from the east and is generally broad but midway it narrows to a waist a hundred yards wide, the north side of this section being rimmed by the top rocks of Dove Crags. This scene, and the exciting scaffold of Grasmoor End (which should be visited if time permits) are the finest topographical features of an otherwise rather dull summit.

DESCENTS: Generally, ways off lie along the plateau eastwards whatever the destination, but Red Gill is a quick and safe way down to Crummock Water for Buttermere, and the left edge of Dove Crags is a practicable route down to Gasgale for Lanthwaite and Loweswater. Grasmoor End leads only to trouble. *In mist, go east for half a mile, descending very little, to the good path through the grassy hollow between Grasmoor and Eel Crag, and here turn left for Coledale Hause, right for Buttermere.*

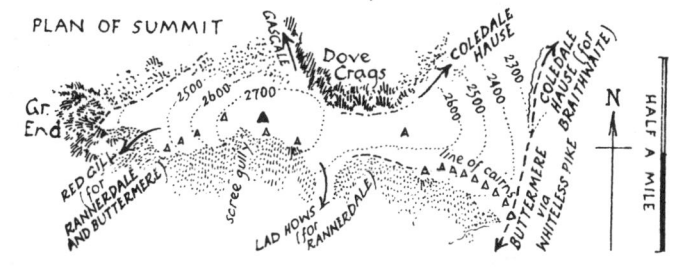

PLAN OF SUMMIT

Grasmoor 13

THE VIEW

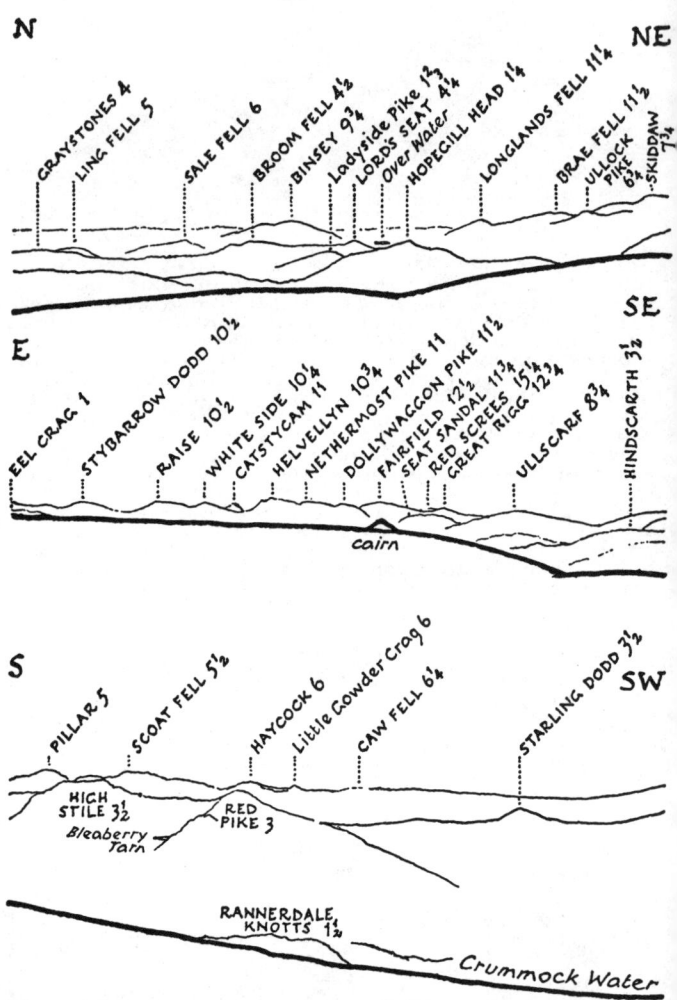

N — Craystones 4, Ling Fell 5, Sale Fell 6, Broom Fell 4½, Binsey 9¾, Ladyside Pike 1¾, Lord's Seat 4¼, Over Water, Hopegill Head 1¼, Longlands Fell 11¼, Brae Fell 11½, Ullock Pike 6¾, Skiddaw 7¼ — **NE**

E — Eel Crag 1, Stybarrow Dodd 10½, Raise 10½, White Side 10¼, Catstycam 11, Helvellyn 10¾, Nethermost Pike 11, Dollywaggon Pike 11½, Fairfield 12½, Seat Sandal 11¾, Red Screes 15¼, Great Rigg 12¾, Ullscarf 8¾, Hindscarth 3½ — **SE**

cairn

S — Pillar 5, Scoat Fell 5½, High Stile 3½, Bleaberry Tarn, Red Pike 3, Haycock 6, Little Gowder Crag 6, Caw Fell 6¼, Starling Dodd 3½ — **SW**

Rannerdale Knotts 1½

Crummock Water

The thick line marks the visible boundaries of the summit from the cairn

Grasmoor 14

THE VIEW

NE — **E**

- GRISEDALE PIKE 2
- SKIDDAW LITTLE MAN 7¾
- BOWSCALE FELL 11¾
- LONSCALE FELL 8¾
- BLENCATHRA 10¼
- CLOUGH HEAD 10
- GREAT DODD 10¾
- EEL CRAG 1

SE — **S**

- HIGH RAISE 9¼
- DALE HEAD 4¼
- HARRISON STICKLE 10¼
- PIKE O' STICKLE 10
- GLARAMARA 7½
- WETHERLAM 13¾
- BOWFELL 9½
- ESK PIKE 8¼
- GREAT END 8
- Ill Crag 8¼
- Broad Crag 8¼
- SCAFELL PIKE 8¾
- LINGMELL 7½
- SCAFELL 8¾
- KIRK FELL 6
- GREEN CRAG 13½
- HIGH CRAG 4
- ROBINSON 2¾
- FLEETWITH PIKE 4¼
- GREAT GABLE 6½
- Scarth Gap
- wall shelter

SW — **W**

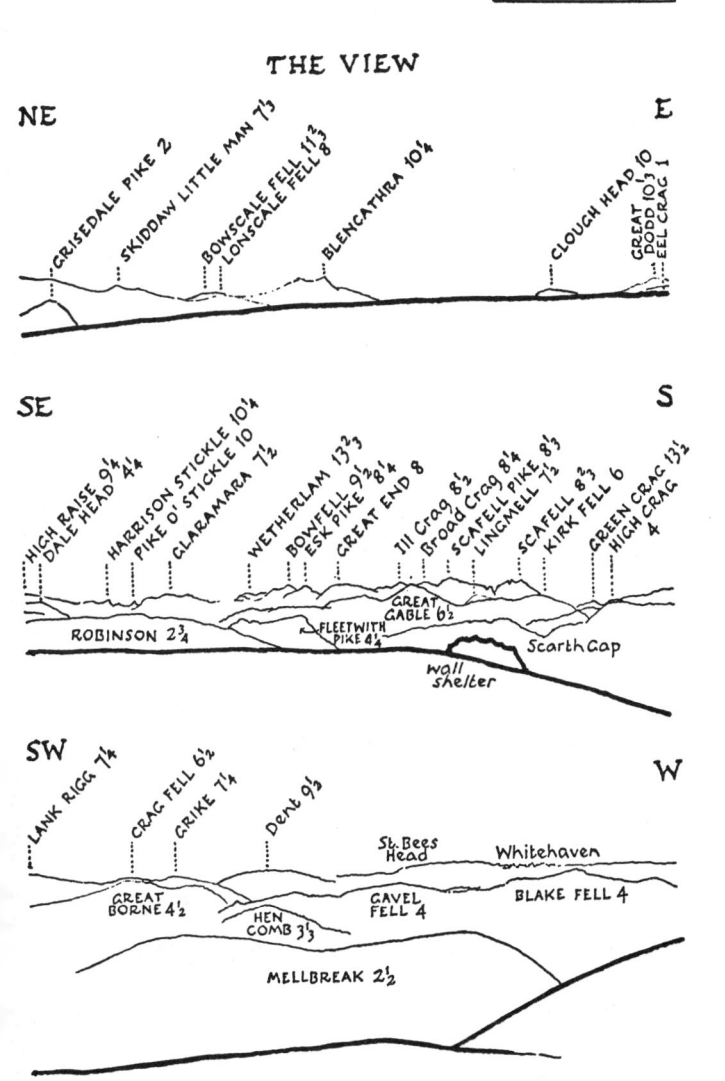

- LANK RIGG 7¼
- CRAG FELL 6½
- GRIKE 7¼
- Dent 9½
- St. Bees Head
- Whitehaven
- GREAT BORNE 4½
- HEN COMB 3⅓
- GAVEL FELL 4
- BLAKE FELL 4
- MELLBREAK 2½

The figures accompanying the names of fells indicate distances in miles

continued

Grasmoor 15

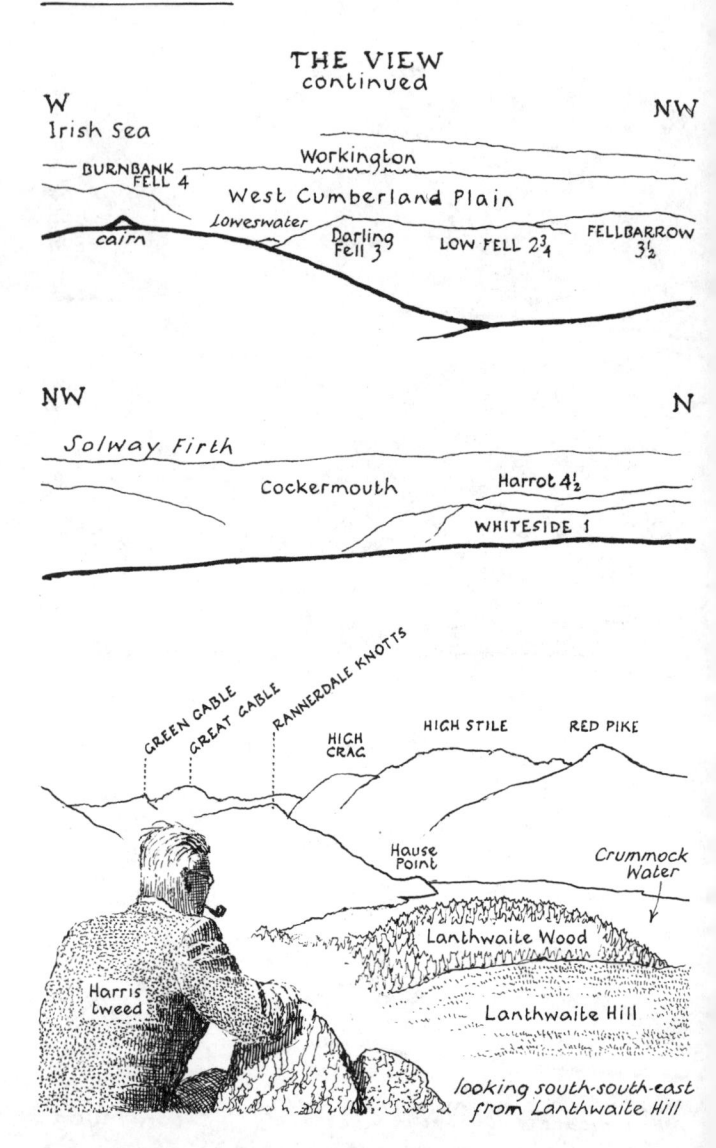

THE VIEW
continued

W — Irish Sea — BURNBANK FELL 4 — Workington — West Cumberland Plain — cairn — Loweswater — Darling Fell 3 9 — LOW FELL 2¾ — FELLBARROW 3½ — NW

NW — Solway Firth — Cockermouth — Harrot 4½ — WHITESIDE 1 — N

GREEN GABLE — GREAT GABLE — RANNERDALE KNOTTS — HIGH CRAG — HIGH STILE — RED PIKE — Hause Point — Crummock Water — Lanthwaite Wood — Harris tweed — Lanthwaite Hill

looking south-south-east from Lanthwaite Hill

Grasmoor 16

Cinderdale Beck: a favourite stream, well known (but not by name) to the many motorists and campers who enjoy the freedom of the open fell alongside the road to Buttermere at the base of Grasmoor.

Dove Crags

Grasmoor End
from Crummock Water

Graystones 1476'

from Aiken Plantation

Cockermouth
• Wythop Mill
LING FELL ▲
GRAYSTONES ▲ BROOM FELL
Low ▲ LORD'S SEAT
Lorton • • High
Lorton
Whinlatter Pass

MILES
0 1 2 3 4

Graystones 2

NATURAL FEATURES

Graystones is the name of a summit only. The fell of which it is the highest point is Kirk Fell, rising above the western end of the motor road through the pass of Whinlatter at the head of the Vale of Lorton. This aspect of the fell is its most impressive, the declivity here being rough and steep, but northwards, facing Wythop, the slopes fall away more easily to merge in upland and undulating pastures before declining finally to the wide Embleton valley.   The western flanks too descend in simple stages to the flat land of the River Cocker, although interrupted, midway, by the small eminence of Harrot, which has a lovely view to the south. These smooth upper expanses are of grass, but the sharper eastern slope, overlooking the side valley of Aiken Beck where the long climb to Whinlatter Pass starts in earnest, is now almost completely patterned by the young evergreens and forest roads of Darling How Plantation.   At the foot of this slope, hidden in a jungle of new conifers, is a fine waterfall, Spout Force, where Aiken Beck plunges into a deep chasm before joining Whit Beck, a principal tributary of the Cocker.

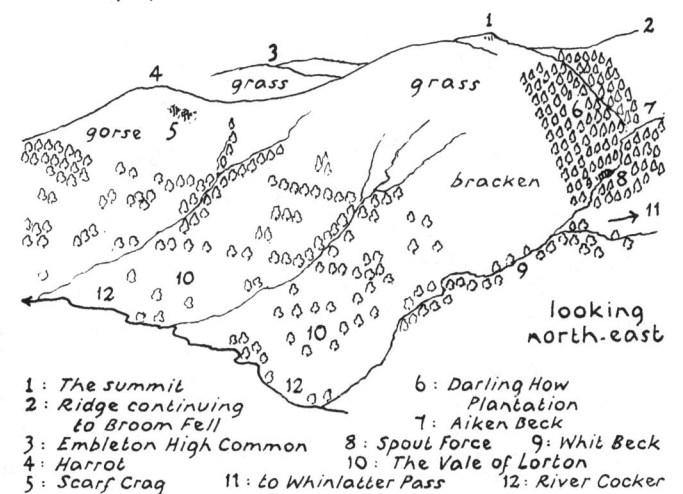

looking north-east

1 : The summit
2 : Ridge continuing to Broom Fell
3 : Embleton High Common
4 : Harrot
5 : Scarf Crag
6 : Darling How Plantation
7 : Aiken Beck
8 : Spout Force
9 : Whit Beck
10 : The Vale of Lorton
11 : to Whinlatter Pass
12 : River Cocker

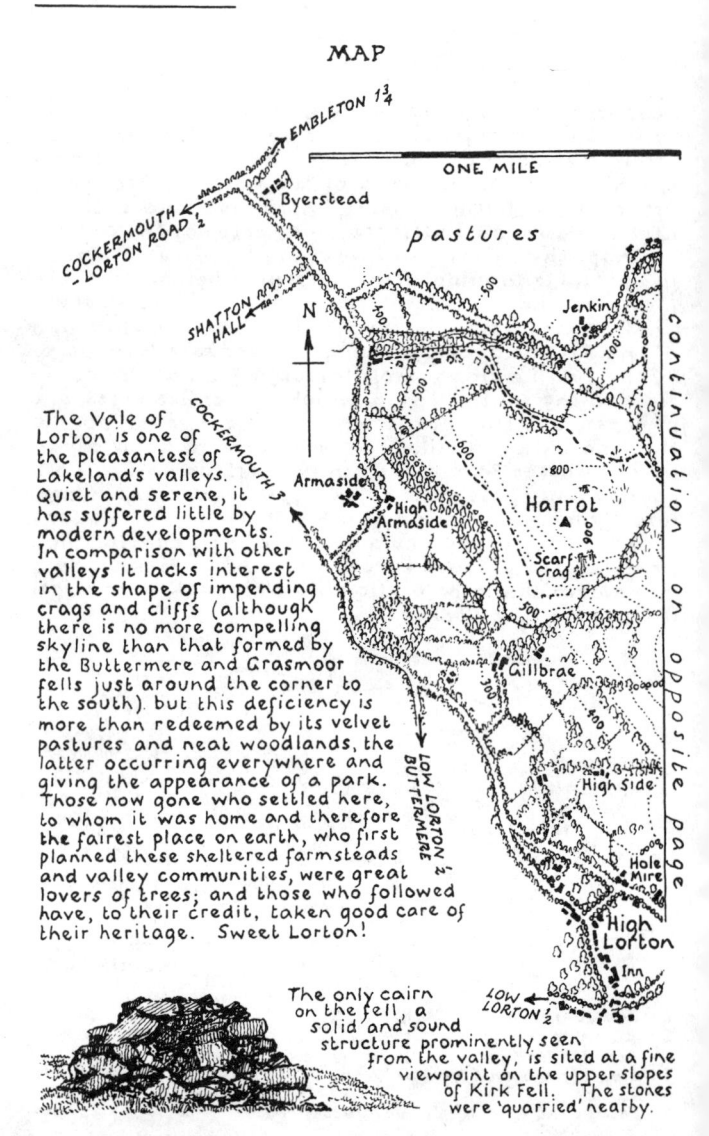

Graystones 3

MAP

ONE MILE

EMBLETON 1¾
COCKERMOUTH - LORTON ROAD ½
Byerstead
SHATTON HALL
pastures
N
Jenkin
COCKERMOUTH 3
Armaside
High Armaside
Harrot
Scarf Crag
Gillbrae
LOW LORTON 2 / BUTTERMERE
High Side
Hole Mire
High Lorton
Inn
LOW LORTON ½

continuation on opposite page

The Vale of Lorton is one of the pleasantest of Lakeland's valleys. Quiet and serene, it has suffered little by modern developments. In comparison with other valleys it lacks interest in the shape of impending crags and cliffs (although there is no more compelling skyline than that formed by the Buttermere and Grasmoor fells just around the corner to the south), but this deficiency is more than redeemed by its velvet pastures and neat woodlands, the latter occurring everywhere and giving the appearance of a park. Those now gone who settled here, to whom it was home and therefore the fairest place on earth, who first planned these sheltered farmsteads and valley communities, were great lovers of trees; and those who followed have, to their credit, taken good care of their heritage. Sweet Lorton!

The only cairn on the fell, a solid and sound structure prominently seen from the valley, is sited at a fine viewpoint on the upper slopes of Kirk Fell. The stones were 'quarried' nearby.

Graystones 4

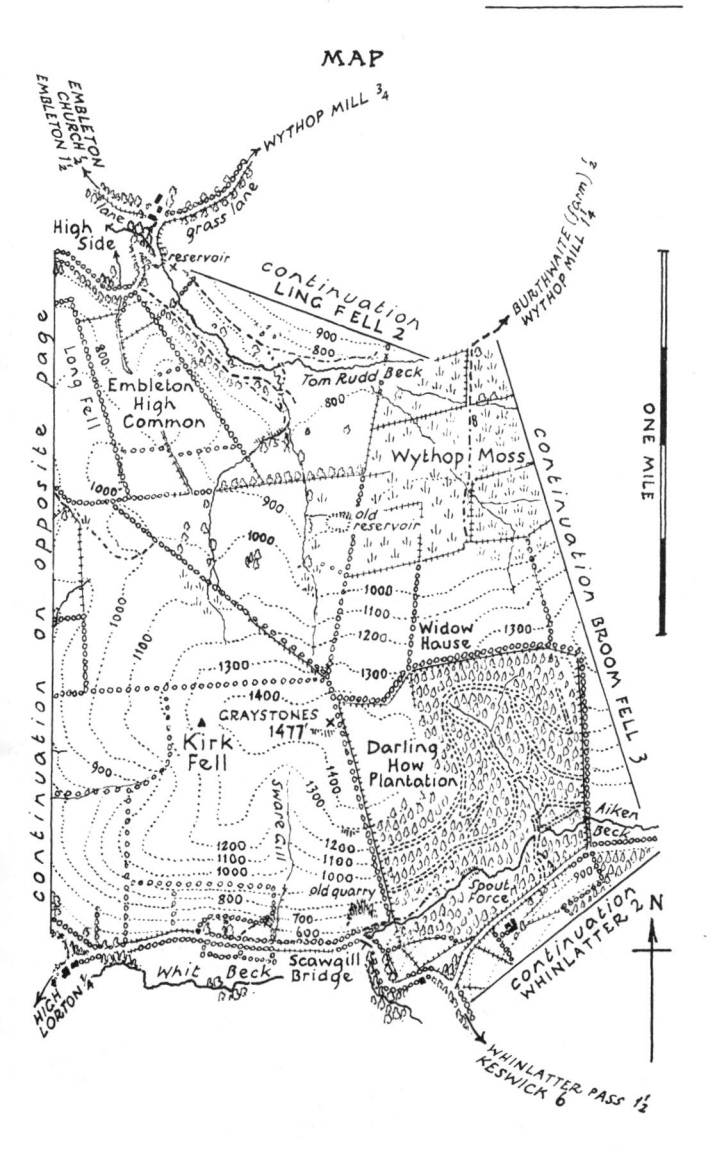

MAP

Graystones 5

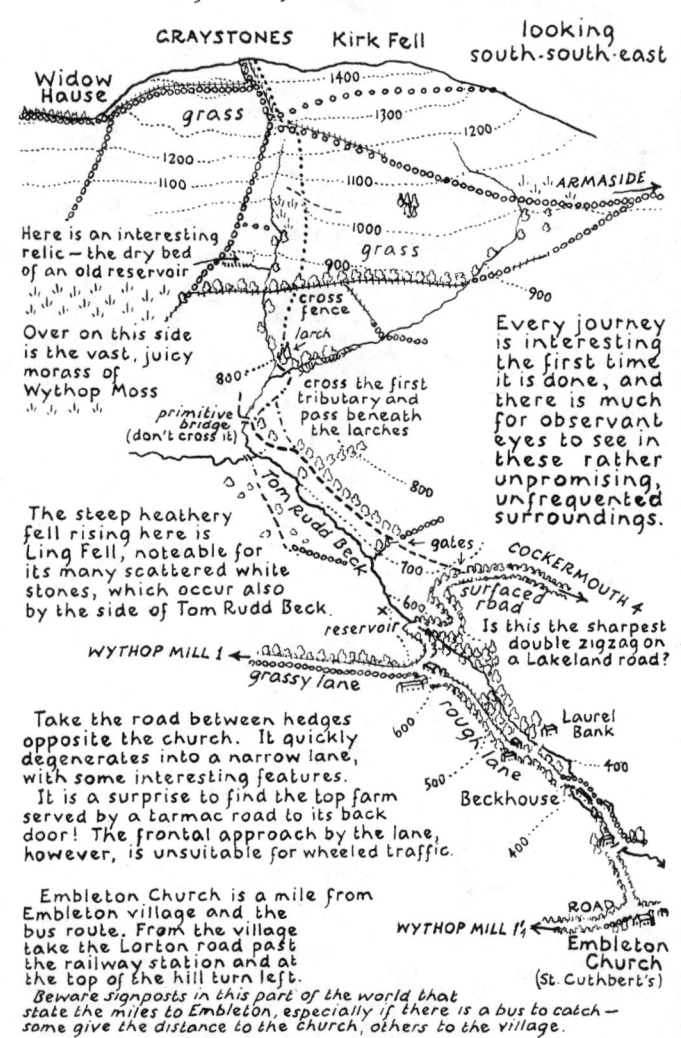

ASCENT FROM EMBLETON CHURCH
1200 feet of ascent : 2½ miles

GRAYSTONES — Kirk Fell — looking south-south-east

Widow Hause

grass

ARMASIDE →

Here is an interesting relic — the dry bed of an old reservoir

Over on this side is the vast, juicy morass of Wythop Moss

cross fence
larch
cross the first tributary and pass beneath the larches

primitive bridge (don't cross it)

Tom Rudd Beck

The steep heathery fell rising here is Ling Fell, noteable for its many scattered white stones, which occur also by the side of Tom Rudd Beck.

gates
COCKERMOUTH ←
surfaced road

Is this the sharpest double zigzag on a Lakeland road?

← WYTHOP MILL 1
reservoir
grassy lane

Every journey is interesting the first time it is done, and there is much for observant eyes to see in these rather unpromising, unfrequented surroundings.

Laurel Bank
rough lane
Beckhouse

Take the road between hedges opposite the church. It quickly degenerates into a narrow lane, with some interesting features.
It is a surprise to find the top farm served by a tarmac road to its back door! The frontal approach by the lane, however, is unsuitable for wheeled traffic.

Embleton Church is a mile from Embleton village and the bus route. From the village take the Lorton road past the railway station and at the top of the hill turn left.

ROAD
WYTHOP MILL 1¼ ←
Embleton Church (St. Cuthbert's)

Beware signposts in this part of the world that state the miles to Embleton, especially if there is a bus to catch — some give the distance to the church, others to the village.

Graystones 6

ASCENT FROM ARMASIDE
1200 feet of ascent : 2¾ miles

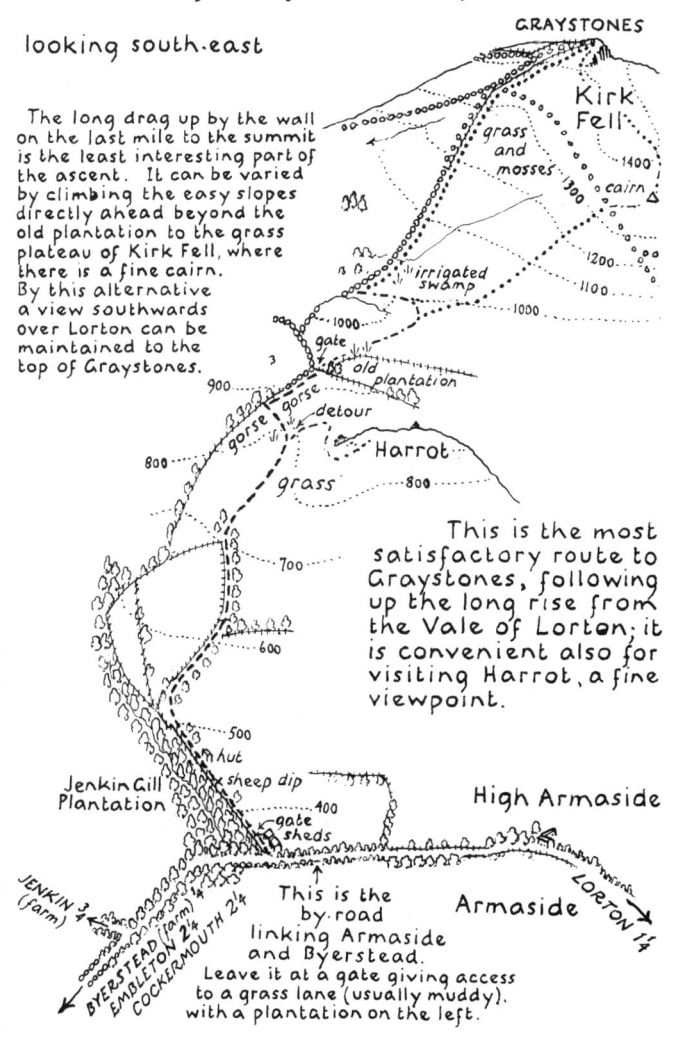

looking south-east

The long drag up by the wall on the last mile to the summit is the least interesting part of the ascent. It can be varied by climbing the easy slopes directly ahead beyond the old plantation to the grass plateau of Kirk Fell, where there is a fine cairn. By this alternative a view southwards over Lorton can be maintained to the top of Graystones.

This is the most satisfactory route to Graystones, following up the long rise from the Vale of Lorton; it is convenient also for visiting Harrot, a fine viewpoint.

This is the by-road linking Armaside and Byerstead. Leave it at a gate giving access to a grass lane (usually muddy), with a plantation on the left.

Graystones 7

ASCENT FROM SCAWGILL BRIDGE
900 feet of ascent : ¾ mile

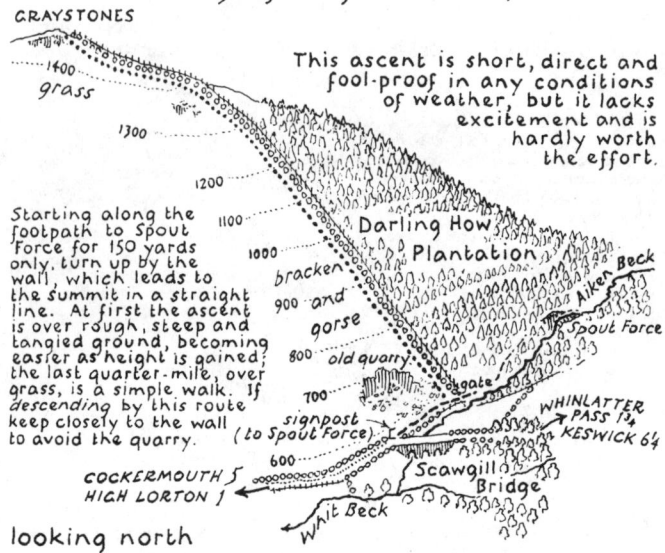

GRAYSTONES

This ascent is short, direct and fool-proof in any conditions of weather, but it lacks excitement and is hardly worth the effort.

Starting along the footpath to Spout Force for 150 yards only, turn up by the wall, which leads to the summit in a straight line. At first the ascent is over rough, steep and tangled ground, becoming easier as height is gained; the last quarter-mile, over grass, is a simple walk. If descending by this route keep closely to the wall to avoid the quarry.

looking north

A big bridge and a little one......
Scawgill Bridge on the Whinlatter road

Graystones 8

Spout Force

A signpost at Scawgill Bridge, inviting passers-by to use a footpath "to Spout Force only", must tempt many people upstream in search of it. Only a few, grimly determined, will ever see it.

The signpost, due to the effluxion of time and in particular to the habit of young spruce to add a foot a year to their height, has become a bad joke. Originally it was provided by the Forestry Commission as a concession to the public, the waterfall in its rocky gorge being well worth seeing. Notwithstanding their signpost, the Commission then proceeded to plant the route with prickly young trees, which, with the passing years, have encroached upon the path and obliterated it.

There are evidences of violent struggles, man versus vegetation, and signs that some hardy individuals have forced a way into the jungle, emerging on an extremely dangerous slope above the gorge, but the nearest approach is gained by following the stream strictly almost to the portals of the gorge, where a water-barrier stops further progress. In neither case does one get a glimpse of the waterfall. A few yards above the stream, after more painful gymnastics, a forlorn noticeboard is found in the forest and this announces the end of the path (joke no.2). At this point an abnormally tall person could just see the upper part of the fall up to 1963, but from 1964 onwards the growing trees will have concealed it completely.

Unless and until it occurs to the Commission to clear the path, the only place for viewing Spout Force is the old Scale Hill road, south of Scawgill Bridge, half a mile distant.

right: The gorge

below: The force (top left corner, as seen in 1962)

Graystones 9

THE SUMMIT

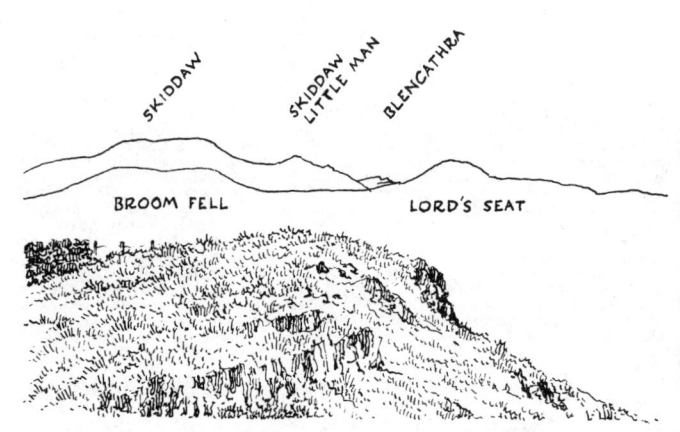

There is no cairn, but the highest point, on grass above a slight upthrust of rocky ground, is not in doubt; it occurs within a few yards of the broken wall and fence crossing the top of the fell.

DESCENTS: The most direct way off follows the wall straight down to Scawgill Bridge on the Whinlatter Pass road; simple at first, the ground steepens and becomes very rough near the bottom, but keep closely to the wall to avoid a gaping quarry at the foot of the slope. The other routes of ascent provide pleasant walking in reverse and should give no trouble even in mist, using as guides the walls indicated on the map.

RIDGE ROUTE

TO BROOM FELL, 1670' : 1½ miles : N, then ENE.
 Depression at 1240' (Widow Hause) · 450 feet of ascent
 A pleasant walk on grass, interest being added by the plantation.

Keep outside the forest fence by starting north, then east down to Widow Hause and so along above the plantation, crossing three walls en route. Bear left when the open fell is reached.

Graystones 10

THE VIEW

A dreary foreground detracts from the view, which reveals a fine sweep of the Scottish coast with Criffell prominent, the Skiddaw group, a good section of the Helvellyn skyline and the towering Grasmoor mass across Whinlatter Pass as its best features. The Vale of Lorton, backed by the Loweswater Fells, is well seen.

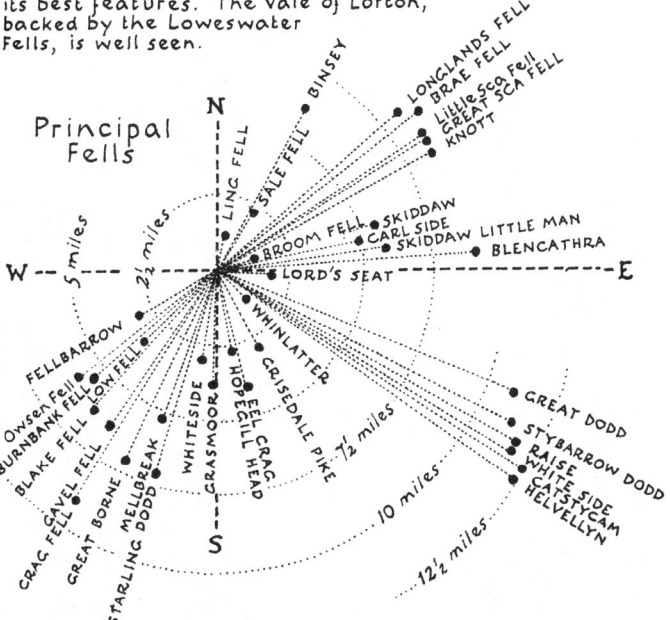

Principal Fells

- N
- BINSEY
- LING FELL
- SALE FELL
- LONGLANDS FELL
- BRAE FELL
- Little Sca Fell
- GREAT SCA FELL
- KNOTT
- BROOM FELL
- SKIDDAW
- CARL SIDE
- SKIDDAW LITTLE MAN
- BLENCATHRA
- LORD'S SEAT
- W — 5 miles — 2½ miles
- E
- FELLBARROW
- Owsen Fell
- BURNBANK FELL
- LOW FELL
- BLAKE FELL
- CRAG FELL
- GAVEL FELL
- GREAT BORNE
- MELLBREAK
- STARLING DODD
- WHITESIDE
- GRASMOOR
- WHINLATTER
- EEL CRAG
- HOPEGILL HEAD
- GRISEDALE PIKE
- 7½ miles
- GREAT DODD
- STYBARROW DODD
- RAISE
- WHITE SIDE
- CATSTYCAM
- HELVELLYN
- 10 miles
- 12½ miles
- S

Lakes and Tarns

No lakes or tarns can be seen, but Crummock Water is brought into view by walking west to the next prominence and more of it by continuing to the subsidiary summit of Harrot, where too the Vale of Lorton appears at its best.

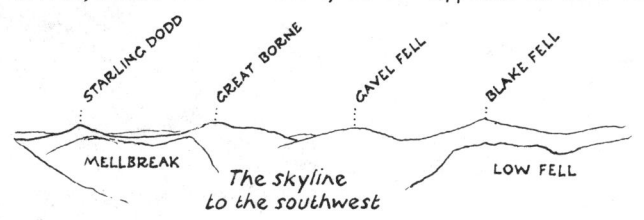

The skyline to the southwest

STARLING DODD — GREAT BORNE — GAVEL FELL — BLAKE FELL
MELLBREAK — LOW FELL

Grisedale Pike 2593'

from High Moss

Grisedale Pike 2

NATURAL FEATURES

All visitors to Lakeland who come to walk on the hills turn their footsteps in due course to Grisedale Pike. It is seldom a prime objective, being a little out of the way, but the graceful peak piercing the western sky is a nagger of conscience and cannot long be ignored. Nor should it be. Conspicuously in view from the environs of Keswick, it is one of those fells that compels attention by reason of shapeliness and height.

The Pike, although of slender proportions on and towards the top, is quite broadly based, occupying the west side of Coledale through the three-mile length of the valley, from which the slopes of the fell rise steeply and unbroken for 2000 feet to a narrow crest. On this face heather and scree below the summit-rocks offer nothing to the climber but hard labour, a fact so obvious that it is virtually a no-man's-land; and the lines of approach lie along four ridges— a short one joined from Coledale Hause, and, at divergent points between north and east, three others rise from the plantations of Whinlatter, the most easterly carrying the popular route from Braithwaite. These three ridges enclose two deep valleys, partly afforested, pathless, and unfrequented, while the sombre depths of Hobcarton mark the boundary of the fell and an impressive neighbour, Hopegill Head, which are linked also at a high level, above a rim of crags, by the short ridge referred to.

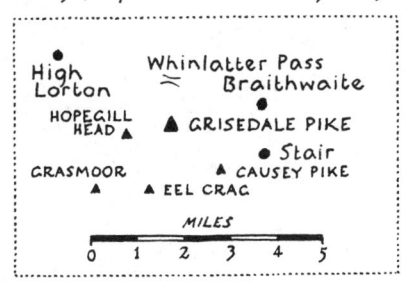

```
• High         Whinlatter Pass
  Lorton     ≈   Braithwaite
 HOPEGILL    ▲ GRISEDALE PIKE
  HEAD ▲
                      • Stair
 GRASMOOR         ▲ CAUSEY PIKE
     ▲    ▲ EEL CRAG
              MILES
    0    1    2    3    4    5
```

Why *Grisedale* Pike? Why not *Coledale* Pike after the valley below? Generally a mountain takes its name from a valley only if it stands at the head, and the rule is followed here — one of the two short valleys running north-east is named Grisedale (a fact little known), the summit of the fell being centred exactly at the head.

Grisedale Pike 3

Force Crag

Coledale is straight and narrow, and without incident until, two miles up, a high barrier of rock extends across the valley like a huge dam. This is Force Crag. Over its lip pours a long cascade (Low Force) and at its foot are the buildings and the spoil-heaps of Force Crag Mine. The scene, backed by the towering skyline of Eel Crag, is magnificently wild.

Escape for the walker bound for Coledale Hause is provided by a wide path that crosses the beck and climbs round to the left of the crag. Ahead, grass slopes lead to Coledale Hause. But follow the path: it passes through a portal on the right into an amphitheatre above Force Crag, where, amazingly, the scene below is repeated. In front again now is another high wall of rock, and again a long cascade (High Force) pours over the lip. Here, too, are mine-buildings and spoil-heaps. The stream (Pudding Beck) is the same; between its two excitements it meanders quietly through this hanging valley. Force Crag is a natural formation not repeated in any other Lakeland dale and to find its unusual arrangement occurring twice, in close proximity, is remarkable.

The mine, always a rich one but not continuously worked, is again operating, after a lengthy closure, for the extraction of barytes.

High Force

Grisedale Pike 4

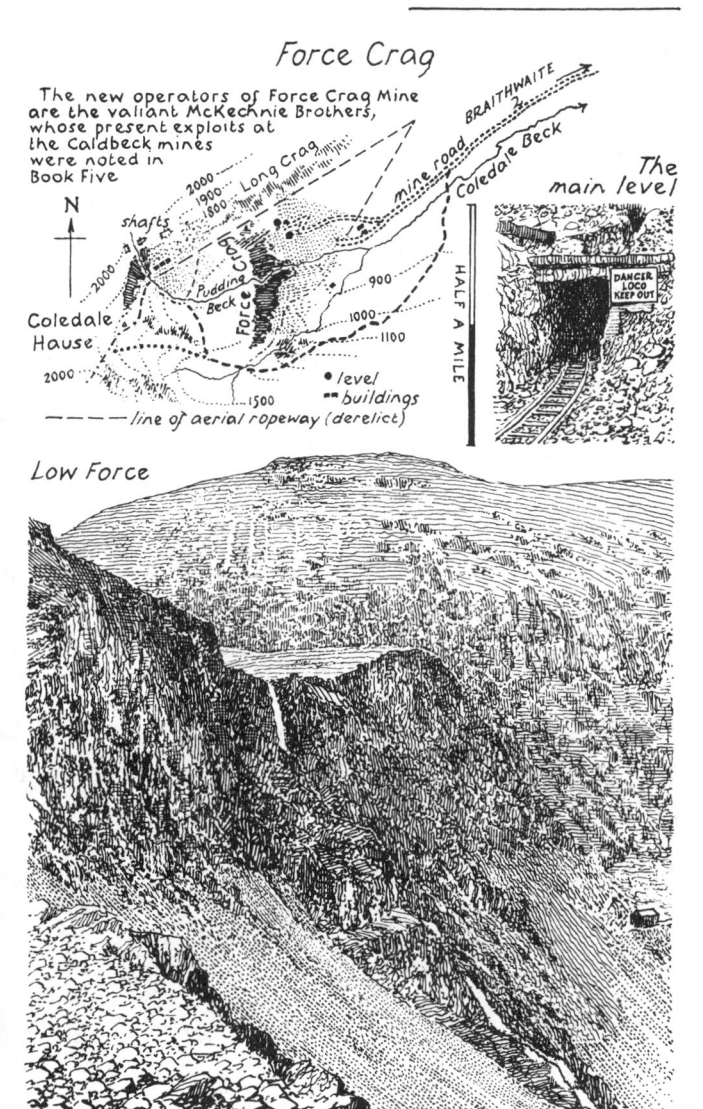

Force Crag

The new operators of Force Crag Mine are the valiant McKechnie Brothers, whose present exploits at the Caldbeck mines were noted in Book Five

- level
- - buildings
- – – – line of aerial ropeway (derelict)

HALF A MILE

The main level

Low Force

Grisedale Pike 5

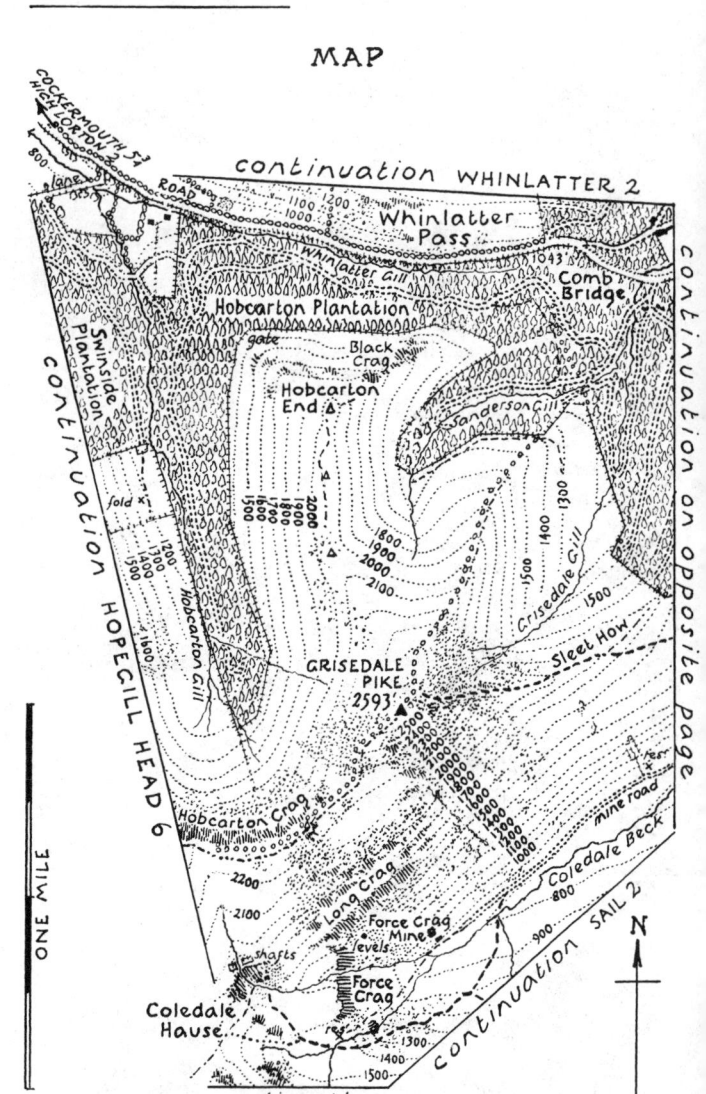

MAP

Grisedale Pike 6

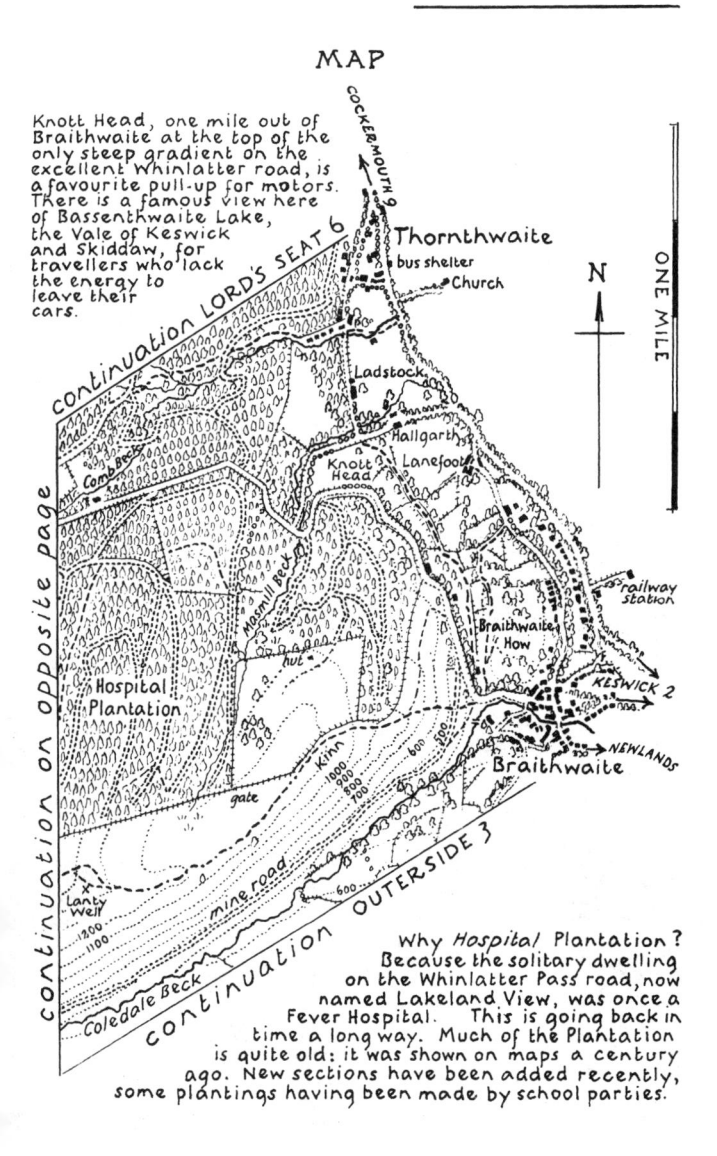

MAP

Knott Head, one mile out of Braithwaite at the top of the only steep gradient on the excellent Whinlatter road, is a favourite pull-up for motors. There is a famous view here of Bassenthwaite Lake, the Vale of Keswick and Skiddaw, for travellers who lack the energy to leave their cars.

Why *Hospital* Plantation? Because the solitary dwelling on the Whinlatter Pass road, now named Lakeland View, was once a Fever Hospital. This is going back in time a long way. Much of the Plantation is quite old: it was shown on maps a century ago. New sections have been added recently, some plantings having been made by school parties.

Grisedale Pike 7

Three Ridges

the east ridge — *the final section, from Sleet How*

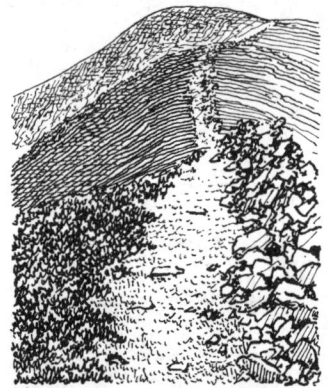

the north-east ridge — *the path by the broken wall*

the north ridge — *looking from Hobcarton End*

Grisedale Pike 8

ASCENT FROM BRAITHWAITE
2400 feet of ascent : 3 miles

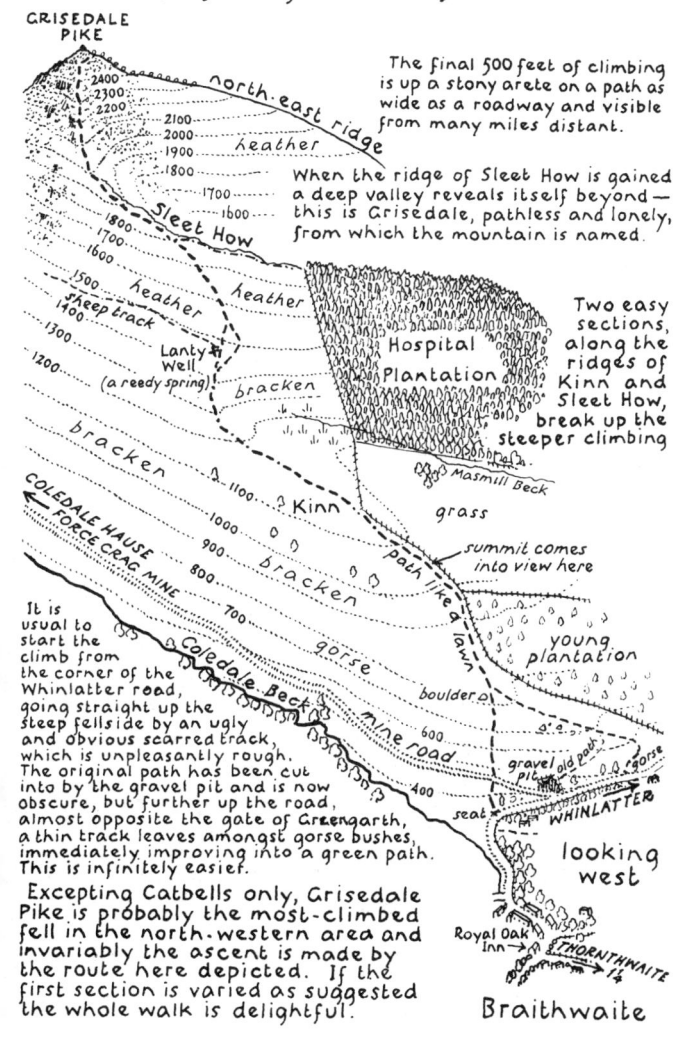

The final 500 feet of climbing is up a stony arete on a path as wide as a roadway and visible from many miles distant.

When the ridge of Sleet How is gained a deep valley reveals itself beyond — this is Grisedale, pathless and lonely, from which the mountain is named.

Two easy sections, along the ridges of Kinn and Sleet How, break up the steeper climbing

summit comes into view here

It is usual to start the climb from the corner of the Whinlatter road, going straight up the steep fellside by an ugly and obvious scarred track, which is unpleasantly rough. The original path has been cut into by the gravel pit and is now obscure, but further up the road, almost opposite the gate of Greengarth, a thin track leaves amongst gorse bushes, immediately improving into a green path. This is infinitely easier.

Excepting Catbells only, Grisedale Pike is probably the most-climbed fell in the north-western area and invariably the ascent is made by the route here depicted. If the first section is varied as suggested the whole walk is delightful.

looking west

Braithwaite

Grisedale Pike 9

ASCENT FROM THORNTHWAITE
2350 feet of ascent : 3¼ miles
via the north-east ridge
2400 feet of ascent : 3¾ miles
via the north ridge

GRISEDALE PIKE

east ridge
BRAITHWAITE (usual route)

north ridge — Hobcarton End

north-east ridge

Grisedale Gill

heather

Black Crag

heather

bracken

young plantation

Sanderson Gill

Emerge from the plantations at A for the north east ridge and at B for Hobcarton End. In each case a wire fence must be crossed (no stiles) — an easy task for long-legged walkers but others will be in some danger of bisecting themselves

tree break

30 yards beyond fork of forest roads

Enter the plantations by forest road (public notice) near Comb Bridge

Whinlatter Pass summit

forestry huts

Comb Bridge

Right-of-way notice

Hospital Plantation

young plantation

forestry cottage

Comb Plantation

BRAITHWAITE 1½

ROAD

Lakeland View

Comb Beck

Comb Bridge may be reached with equal facility from Braithwaite by using the Whinlatter road for two miles

Completely hidden from the busy main road at Thornthwaite, a charming glen comes down through the plantations; it carries a public footpath, which climbs to the Whinlatter road but is cut by forest roads and often obstructed by fallen trees. Follow the arrows.

LADSTOCK

KESWICK 3¼
bus shelter
→ COCKERMOUTH 9¼

Thornthwaite

Ascents by two little-known ridges are illustrated here, coupled with an unusual line of approach calling for interesting route-finding. A splendid expedition of charm and variety.

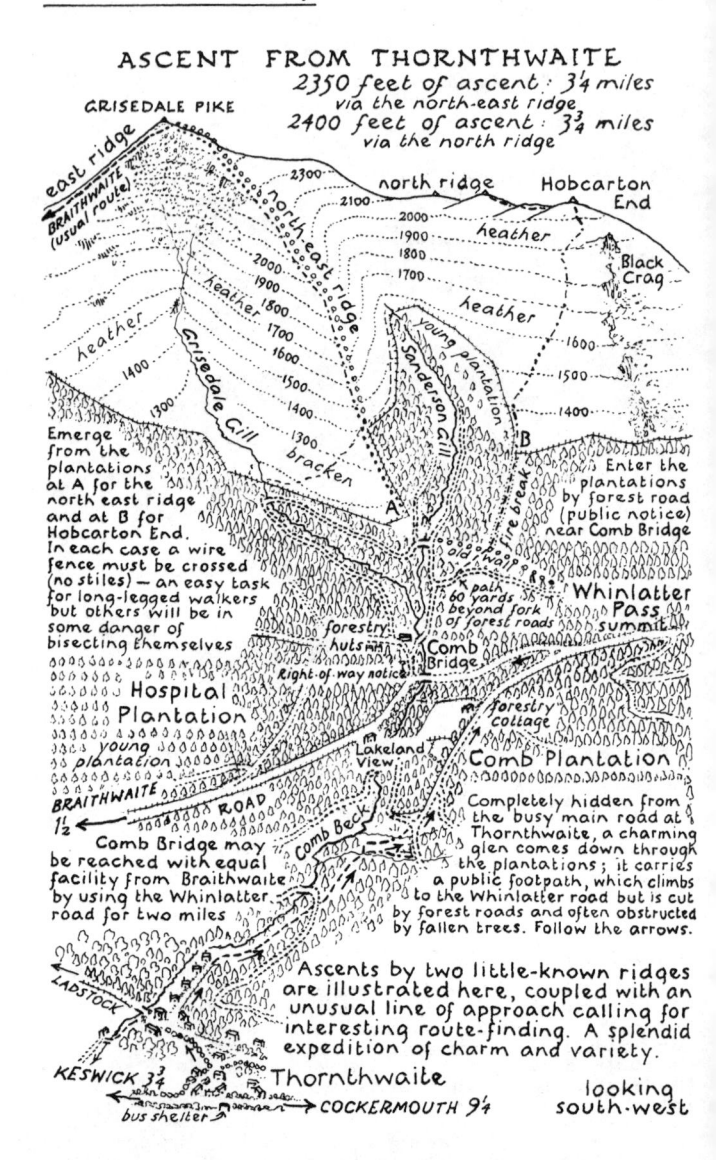

looking south-west

Grisedale Pike 10

ASCENT FROM WHINLATTER PASS
1600 feet of ascent : 2¼ miles from the road

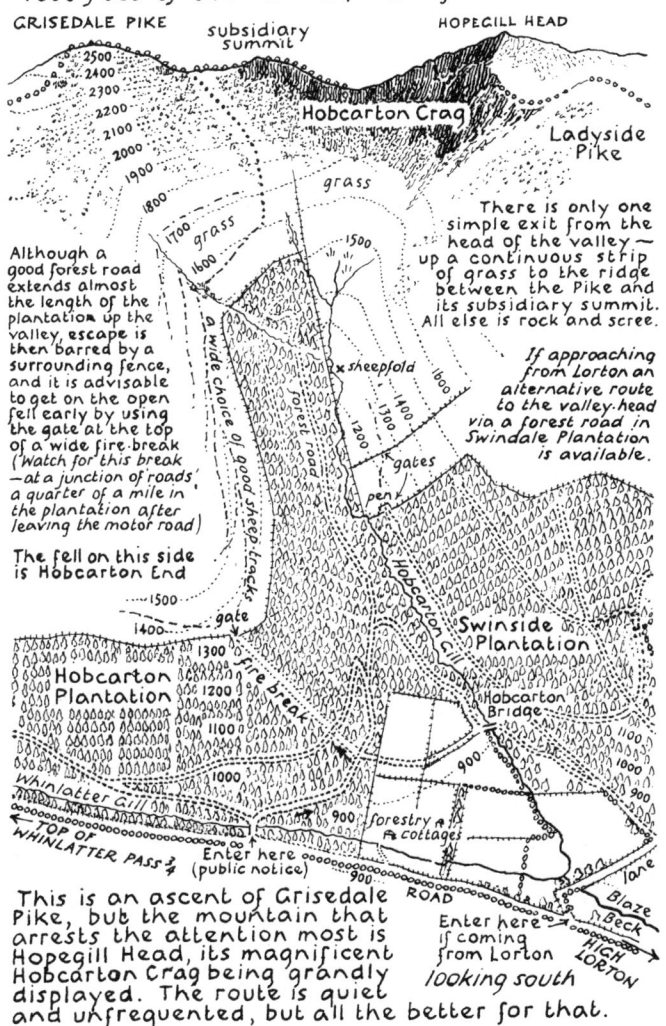

GRISEDALE PIKE — subsidiary summit — HOPEGILL HEAD
Hobcarton Crag
Ladyside Pike

Although a good forest road extends almost the length of the plantation up the valley, escape is then barred by a surrounding fence, and it is advisable to get on the open fell early by using the gate at the top of a wide fire-break ('Watch for this break — at a junction of roads a quarter of a mile in the plantation after leaving the motor road)

The fell on this side is Hobcarton End

There is only one simple exit from the head of the valley — up a continuous strip of grass to the ridge between the Pike and its subsidiary summit. All else is rock and scree.

If approaching from Lorton an alternative route to the valley-head via a forest road in Swindale Plantation is available.

grass
grass
×sheepfold
forest road
gates
pen
a wide choice of good sheep tracks

Hobcarton Beck

gate
fire break
Hobcarton Plantation
Swinside Plantation
Hobcarton Bridge

Whinlatter Gill
TOP OF WHINLATTER PASS
Enter here (public notice)
forestry cottages
ROAD
Enter here if coming from Lorton
lane
Blaze Beck
HIGH LORTON

looking south

This is an ascent of Grisedale Pike, but the mountain that arrests the attention most is Hopegill Head, its magnificent Hobcarton Crag being grandly displayed. The route is quiet and unfrequented, but all the better for that.

Grisedale Pike 11

ASCENT FROM COLEDALE HAUSE
700 feet of ascent : 1¼ miles

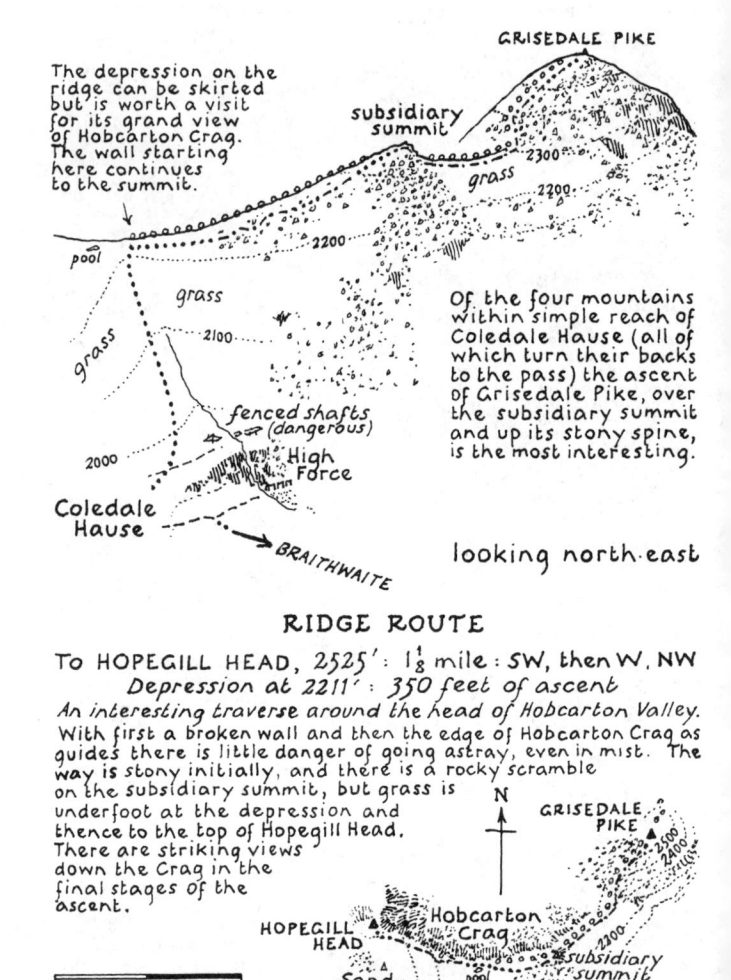

The depression on the ridge can be skirted but is worth a visit for its grand view of Hobcarton Crag. The wall starting here continues to the summit.

Of the four mountains within simple reach of Coledale Hause (all of which turn their backs to the pass) the ascent of Grisedale Pike, over the subsidiary summit and up its stony spine, is the most interesting.

looking north-east

RIDGE ROUTE

TO HOPEGILL HEAD, 2525′ : 1⅛ mile : SW, then W, NW
Depression at 2211′ : 350 feet of ascent

An interesting traverse around the head of Hobcarton Valley. With first a broken wall and then the edge of Hobcarton Crag as guides there is little danger of going astray, even in mist. The way is stony initially, and there is a rocky scramble on the subsidiary summit, but grass is underfoot at the depression and thence to the top of Hopegill Head. There are striking views down the Crag in the final stages of the ascent.

HALF A MILE

Grisedale Pike 12

THE SUMMIT

BLENCATHRA

The cairn sits upon a plinth of slate, fragments of which litter the summit thickly and add a musical tinkling to the march of boots. Much of this debris originated as a wall, now unrecognisable as such. The ridge is narrow at this point, only a few paces wide, and provides little shelter against the strong winds to which it is exposed.

DESCENTS: There may be initial difficulty in locating the start of the path down to Braithwaite, which is over-run by scree, but it soon becomes obvious, taking a line down the distinct ridge from the eastern corner of the summit; in mist, turn right where the wall turns left. A smoother alternative is provided by the north-east ridge, keeping alongside the wall down to the plantations. For Coledale Hause follow the wall west to its sudden end over and beyond the subsidiary top and then turn left, bearing right when fenced shafts appear ahead.

PLAN OF SUMMIT

The main summit (left) from the subsidiary summit (right)

The subsidiary summit has no name. It is often wrongly referred to as Sand Hill (due probably to a bad placing of this name on Bart's maps). Sand Hill is on Hopegill Head.

Grisedale Pike 13

THE VIEW

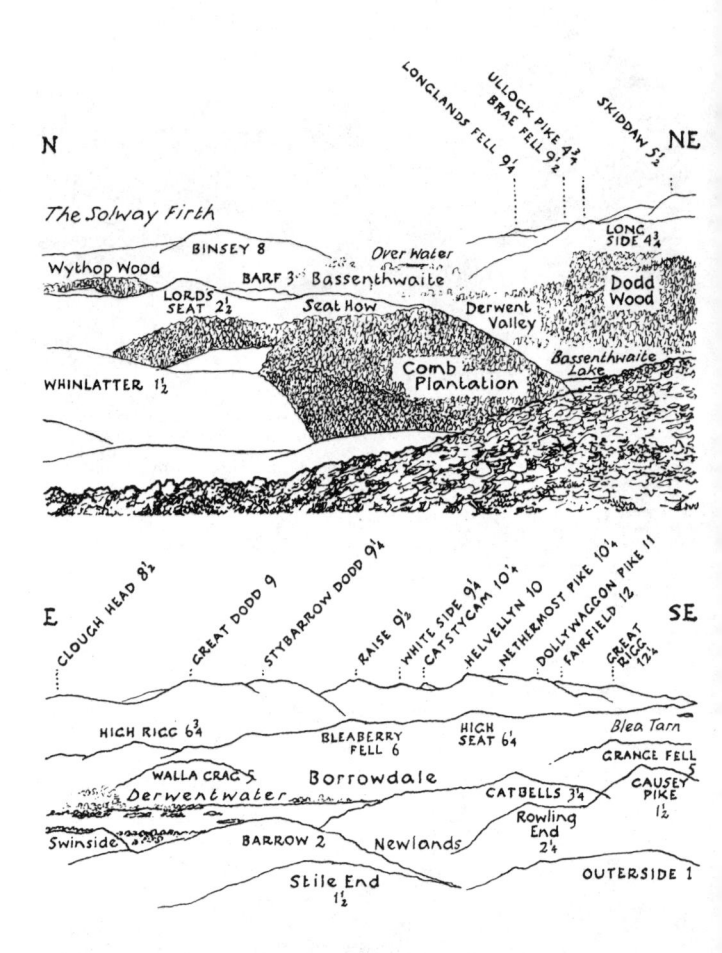

From E to S, Coledale occupies the bottom of the view

Grisedale Pike 14

THE VIEW

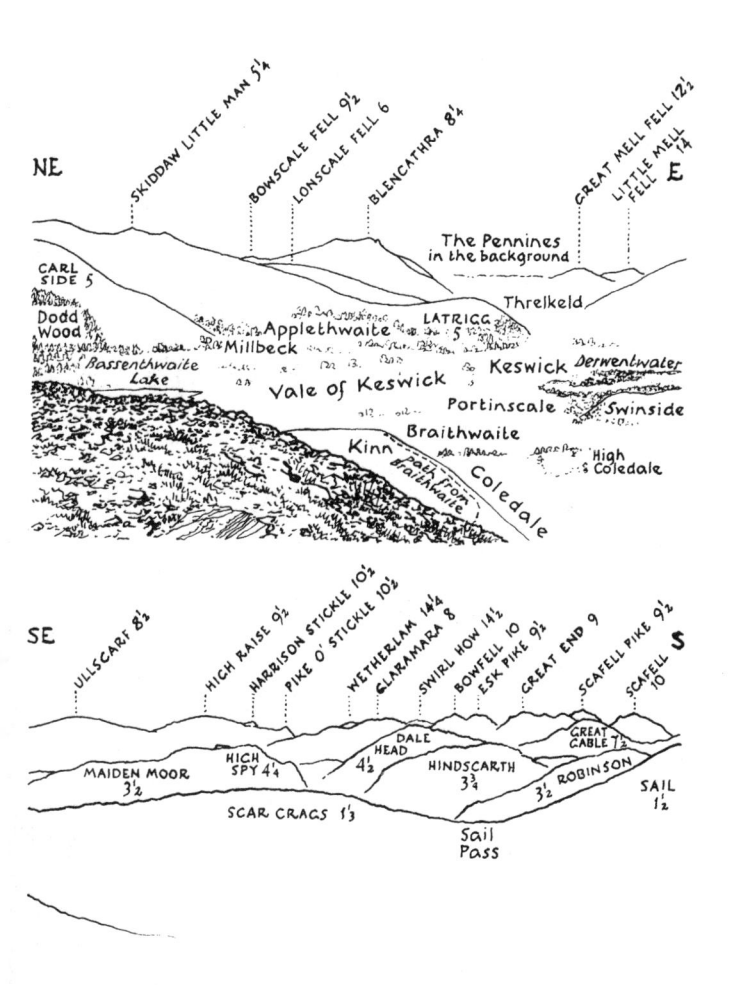

NE

SKIDDAW LITTLE MAN 5½
BOWSCALE FELL 9½
LONSCALE FELL 6
BLENCATHRA 8¼
GREAT MELL FELL 12½
LITTLE MELL FELL 14
E

The Pennines in the background

CARL SIDE 5
Dodd Wood
Bassenthwaite Lake
Applethwaite
Millbeck
LATRIGG 5
Threlkeld
Keswick   Derwentwater
Vale of Keswick
Portinscale   Swinside
Braithwaite
Kinn
Coledale
path from Braithwaite
High Coledale

SE
ULLSCARF 8½
HIGH RAISE 9½
HARRISON STICKLE 10½
PIKE O' STICKLE 10½
WETHERLAM 14¼
GLARAMARA 8
SWIRL HOW 10
BOWFELL 14½
ESK PIKE 9½
GREAT END 9
SCAFELL PIKE 9½
SCAFELL 10
S

MAIDEN MOOR 3½
HIGH SPY 4¼
DALE HEAD 4½
HINDSCARTH 3¾
GREAT GABLE 7½
ROBINSON 3½
SAIL 1½
SCAR CRAGS 1⅓
Sail Pass

The figures accompanying the names of fells indicate distances in miles

continued

Grisedale Pike 15

THE VIEW

S — KIRK FELL 7¼ — SAIL 1½ — EEL CRAG 1½ — Scott Crag — Eel Crag — RED PIKE 5 — Coledale Hause — GRASMOOR 2 — subsidiary summit — SW

wall

Coledale Head

Do NOT attempt a direct descent southwards. The ONLY safe route to Coledale Hause, Coledale Head or Force Crag Mine lies over the subsidiary summit, then left at the col.

Force Crag Mine (below)

W — Workington — West Cumberland coast — Maryport — NW

FELLBARROW 4¼

Ladyside Pike ¾

Swinside 2

Vale of Lorton

Swinside Plantation

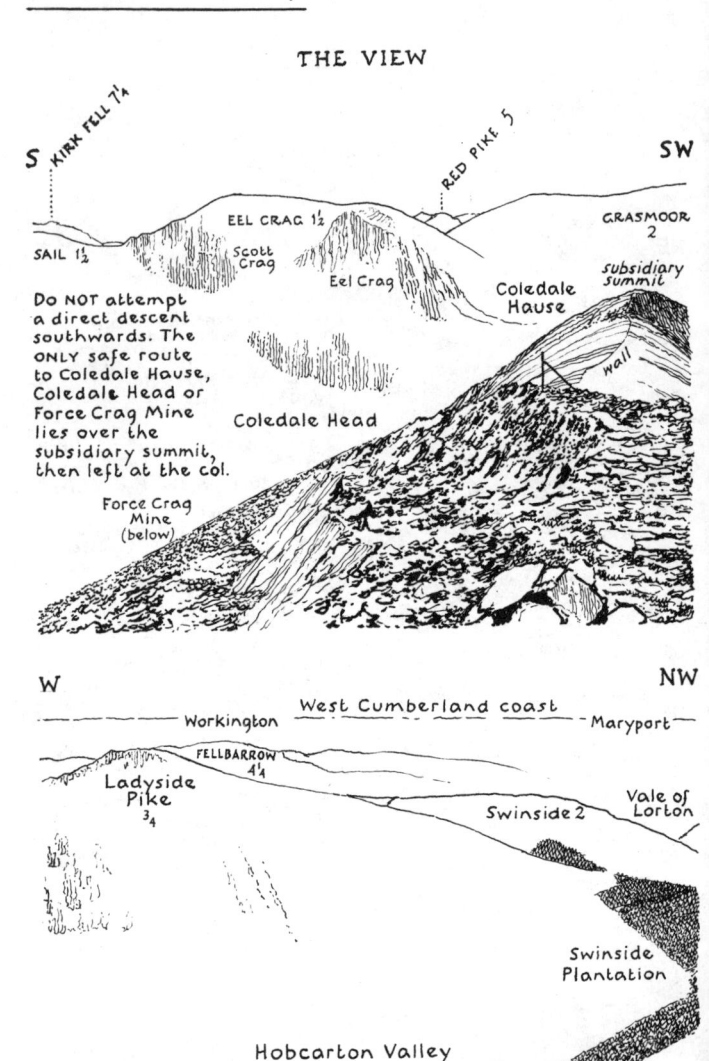

Hobcarton Valley

Grisedale Pike 16

THE VIEW

SW — W

GRASMOOR 2
GAVEL FELL 5½
Sand Hill ¾
col
HOPEGILL HEAD ¾
WHITESIDE 1¾
LOW FELL 3¾
Hobcarton Crag
Hobcarton Valley

NW — N

West Cumberland coast
Cockermouth
Harrot 4
Aspatria
Bothel
CRAYSTONES 3
LING FELL 4
BROOM FELL 3
Kirk Fell 3
Darling How Plantation
WHINLATTER 1½
Swinside Plantation
Whinlatter Pass road
Hobcarton End ¾
Hobcarton Plantation

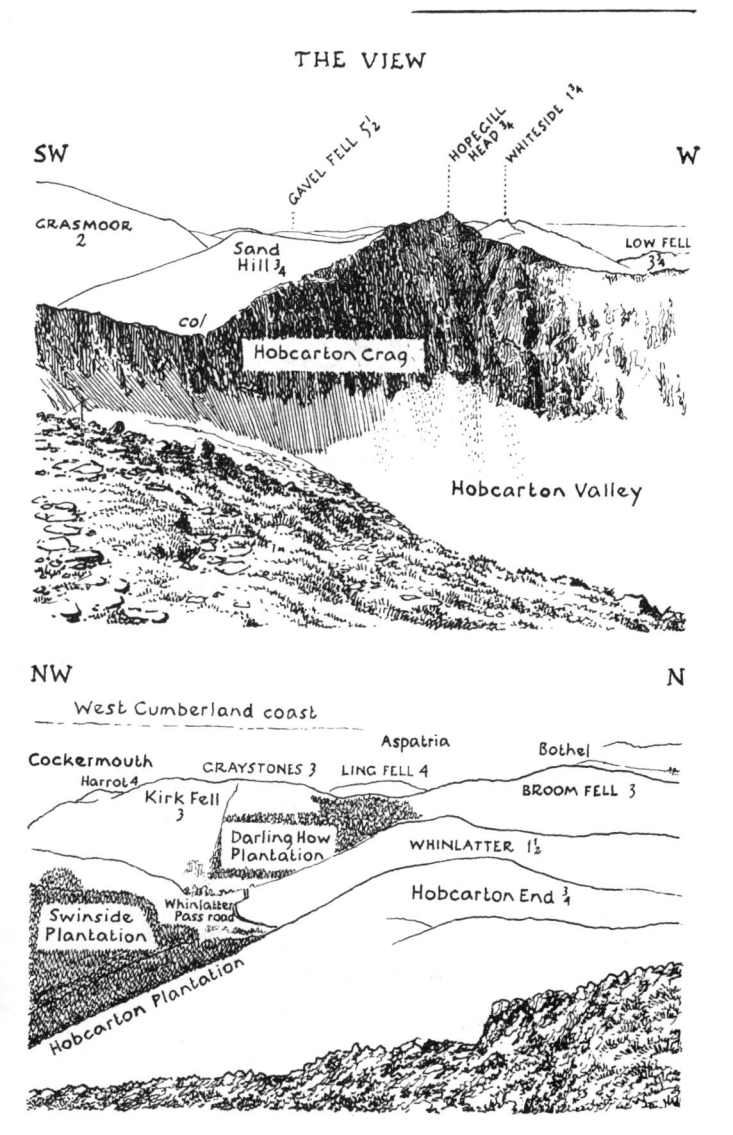

High Spy 2143'

*also variously known as
Eel Crags, Lobstone Band
and Scawdel Fell*

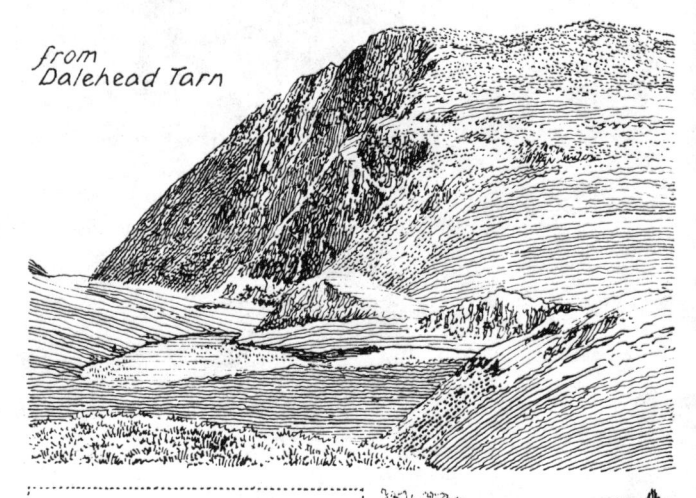

*from
Dalehead Tarn*

Little Town
● MAIDEN
▲ MOOR
Grange ●
▲ HIGH SPY
DALE
HEAD ▲   Rosthwaite ●
Honister
Pass ≍   Seatoller ●

MILES
0   1   2   3

Hollows Farm

High Spy 2

NATURAL FEATURES

The middle reaches of Borrowdale are bounded on the west by high fellsides, colourful and attractive side-curtains that contribute much to the beauty of the valley, yet which have never really been fully accepted by visitors as part of the lovely setting of the natural stage they come to admire. This lack of popular appeal, which is relative only to the quite unsurpassed scenery all around, is mainly because, when viewed from the valley, the rough slopes offer no obvious routes for walkers and the flat skyline promises no interesting summits above. In fact, between Catbells and Honister there is only a single breach in the four-mile wall carrying a beaten path (and *that* was beaten by quarrymen, not fellwalkers) and consequently the scenic beauties of Borrowdale are more often sought on the eastern slopes, where good paths abound.

High country can rarely be appraised properly from valley-level, however. The long skyline visible from below is not the ridge of the fell, as it appears to be, but the edge of a wide plateau where the steep rise of the slopes eases to a gentler gradient, the true spine lying well back, and it is here, along a crest, that one really enters upon fellwalkers' territory, a splendid elevated track traversing the whole length of the fell. Interest is sustained by the succession of cliffs and aretes falling away abruptly from the crest to the desolate upper Newlands valley, for on this western flank there is no wide plateau, but, in contrast, the appalling mile-long precipice known to the rock-climbing fraternity as Eel Crags. This, and the great bastion of Goat Crag above Borrowdale, are distinctive features.

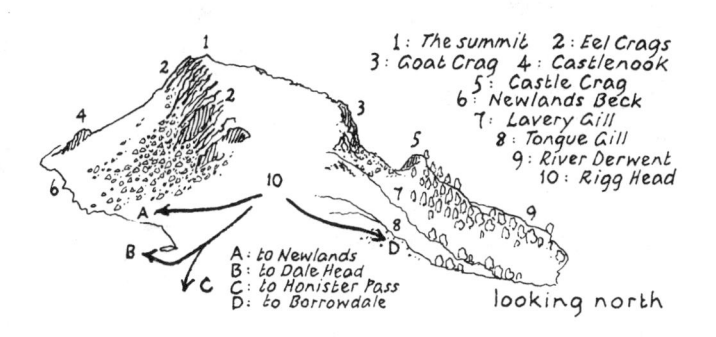

The culminating point on a top of fairly uniform height is High Spy. To the south there is an easy decline to the marshy depression of Rigg Head, where many routes converge; north, the long crest descends to the level summit of Maiden Moor and continues to Catbells.

1: The summit 2: Eel Crags
3: Goat Crag 4: Castlenook
5: Castle Crag
6: Newlands Beck
7: Lavery Gill
8: Tongue Gill
9: River Derwent
10: Rigg Head

A: to Newlands
B: to Dale Head
C: to Honister Pass
D: to Borrowdale

looking north

High Spy 3

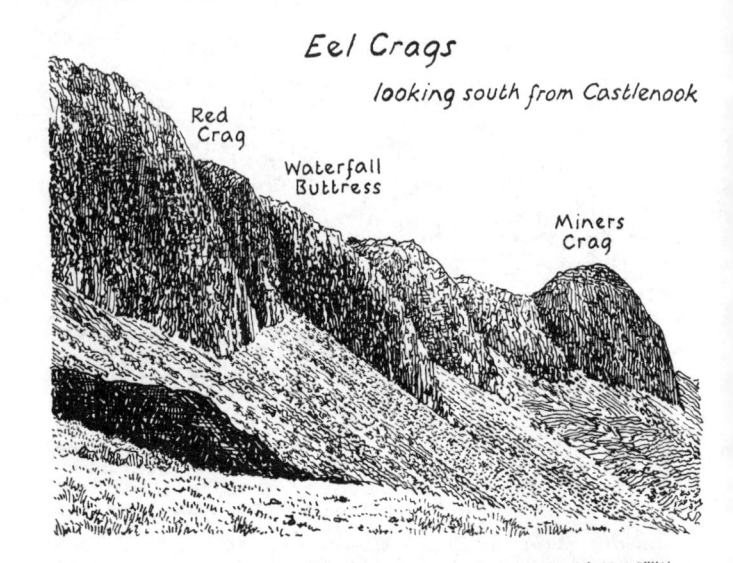

Eel Crags

looking south from Castlenook

- Red Crag
- Waterfall Buttress
- Miners Crag

looking north from the foot of Miners Crag

High Spy 4

MAP

ONE MILE

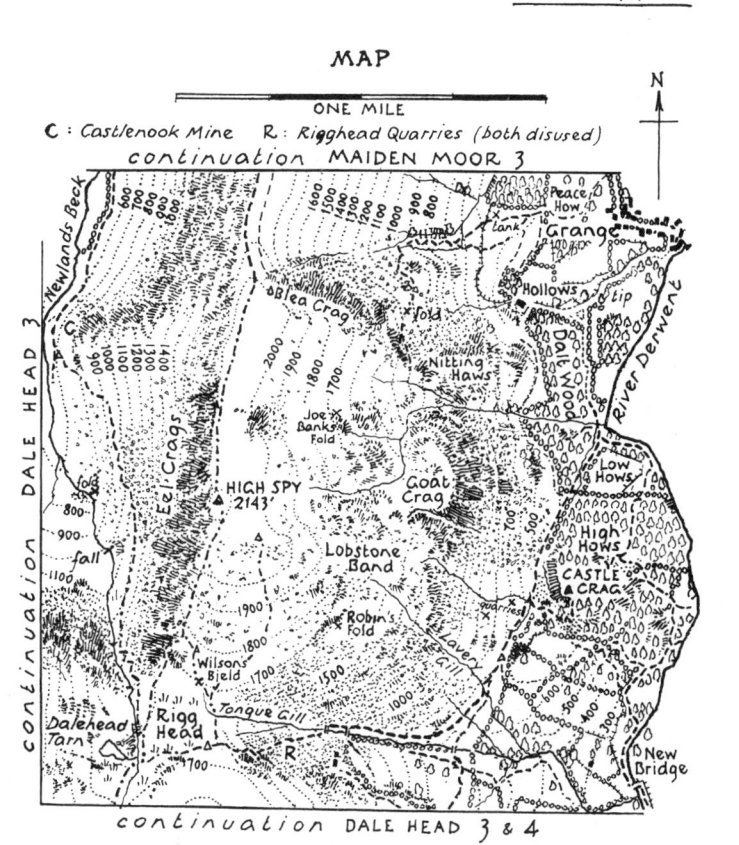

C : Castlenook Mine   R : Rigghead Quarries (both disused)

continuation MAIDEN MOOR 3

continuation DALE HEAD 3 & 4

For the place-names on their maps, the Ordnance Survey rely on the information gathered over the years in their files, supplied or verified by church records, title deeds, estate books and other written sources, and often on the statements of local residents. On the Lakeland map, much reliance has been placed on spoken information volunteered locally (and in a few instances it would seem that the dialect has not been interpreted quite correctly). The Ordnance map of the High Spy area is interesting because of the naming of the sheepfolds. This occurs elsewhere in the district, but infrequently. All sheepfolds, of course, have identifying names known to farmers and shepherds, but not normally made public. It would appear, however, that the tenant of the grazing on Scawdel has been unusually communicative. Thus the Ordnance map names Joe Bank's (? Banks') Fold, Robin's Fold and Wilson's Bield on 2½" and 6" editions, yet these are unremarkable structures bettered by many others elsewhere not distinguished by 'official' names.

High Spy 5

The hinterland of Goat Crag

Joe Banks' Fold

The only frequented walkers' route on the higher parts of the fell runs along the crest of the ridge; the wide upland east of the summit, ending in a two-mile escarpment above Borrowdale, is rarely visited. This escarpment is almost continuous from Blea Crag to and beyond Goat Crag, being breached only by High White Rake and Low White Rake, both very steep passages. The upland, however, although broken by many outcrops, is good grazing ground. Getting the sheep down through the escarpment to the valley, as is necessary on occasion, is a problem that has been solved by slanting a drove-way between the top of Low White Rake and the foot of High White Rake, and this is the only route by which sheep may safely be brought down from the tops.

Immediately behind the rocky turrets of Nitting Haws and Goat Crag there is a spacious hollow, an amphitheatre, before the slope resumes its climb over the upland to the summit of High Spy, and in this hollow, where the sheep are gathered, a meandering stream finds a way down a stony ravine to the valley.

This hollow is a surprising place: it is unsuspected from the valley and is unseen from the summit-ridge. Although poised close above the busy holiday traffic of Borrowdale, it lies lonely and silent in a circle of craggy outcrops. Vegetation is lush: bracken, heather and mosses form a rich carpet of colourful pattern. Here the staghorn moss occurs profusely, covering large areas in dense mats resembling crowded nests of little green snakes, which writhe and squirm realistically under the tread of a boot.

Staghorn moss (Common Club-moss)

A: Amphitheatre
H: High White Rake
L: Low White Rake

QUARTER MILE

High Spy 6

ASCENT FROM GRANGE
1950 feet of ascent : 2 miles via High White Rake
2½ miles via Narrow Moor

HIGH SPY
Minum Crag
Blea Crag
cairn (viewpoint)
Narrow Moor
Behind Nitting Haws is an amphitheatre of heather, bracken and mosses set amongst rocks
High White Rake
Nitting Haws
sheep track
heather — dense and floriferous and vastly more extensive than it appears from below
drove road
Low White Rake
fold
bracken
From the sheepfold the drove road may be used instead; this avoids the steepness
boulders
Cockley How
Greenup
bracken
bracken
During the early stages of the walk there is a growing appreciation of the ruggedness of the great rampart of rock ahead to the left. This is a formidable barrier with only two breaches available to the walker — Low White Rake is too steep and unpromising to be considered; High White Rake becomes more obvious as it is approached and, although rough, is a practicable route to the plateau above. Alternatively, avoiding the crags altogether, the slope may be followed up to the skyline of Narrow Moor, and the ridge-path there joined — a tedious ascent.
waterfalls — a fine spectacle (few yards detour)
water pipes
weir
gate
Ellers Beck
bracken
sluice valve
Swanesty How
gate
water tank
bracken
Ellers
HOLLOWS

looking west

Leave Grange by the Manesty road, turning off at a gate (signposted 'To Peace How') almost opposite the Borrowdale Gates Hotel.

school
gate
× stone seat
Peace How
ROAD
gate
Hotel
Grange

High Spy 7

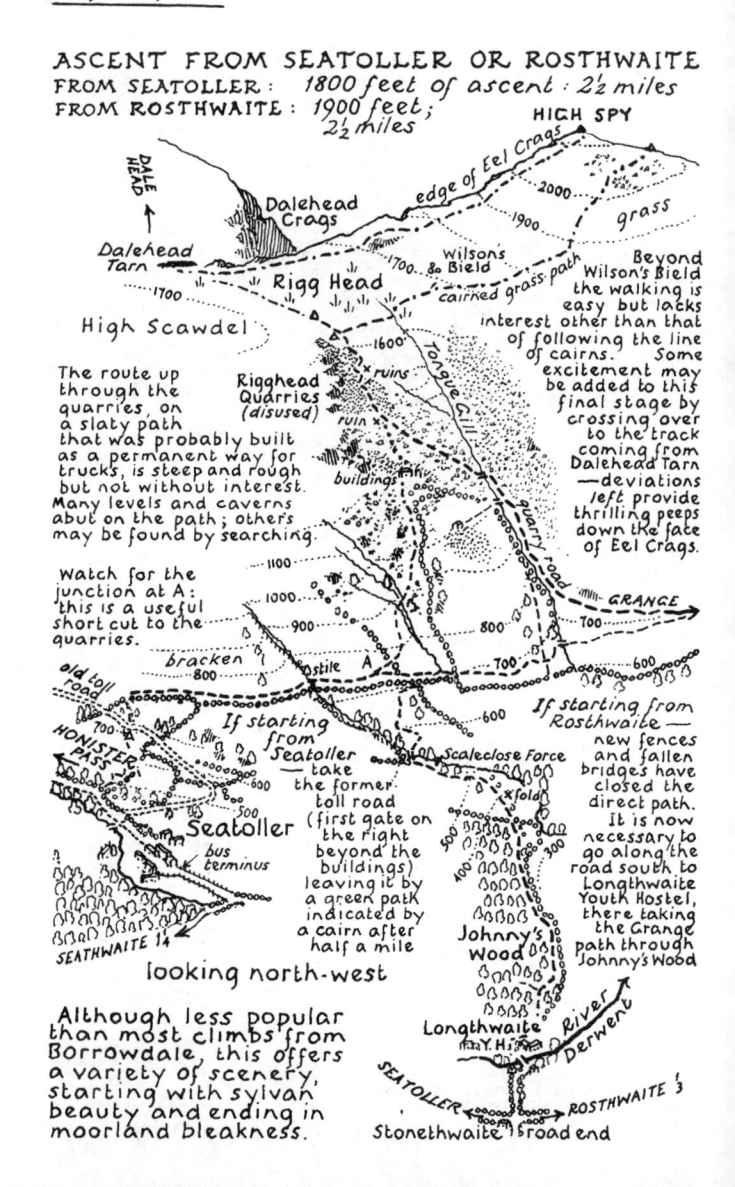

ASCENT FROM SEATOLLER OR ROSTHWAITE
FROM SEATOLLER: 1800 feet of ascent; 2½ miles
FROM ROSTHWAITE: 1900 feet; 2½ miles

looking north-west

Beyond Wilson's Bield the walking is easy but lacks interest other than that of following the line of cairns. Some excitement may be added to this final stage by crossing over to the track coming from Dalehead Tarn — deviations left provide thrilling peeps down the face of Eel Crags.

The route up through the quarries, on a slaty path that was probably built as a permanent way for trucks, is steep and rough but not without interest. Many levels and caverns abut on the path; others may be found by searching.

Watch for the junction at A: this is a useful short cut to the quarries.

If starting from Seatoller — take the former toll road (first gate on the right beyond the buildings) leaving it by a green path indicated by a cairn after half a mile.

If starting from Rosthwaite — new fences and fallen bridges have closed the direct path. It is now necessary to go along the road south to Longthwaite Youth Hostel, there taking the Grange path through Johnny's Wood.

Although less popular than most climbs from Borrowdale, this offers a variety of scenery, starting with sylvan beauty and ending in moorland bleakness.

High Spy 8

ASCENT FROM LITTLE TOWN
1650 feet of ascent : 4 miles

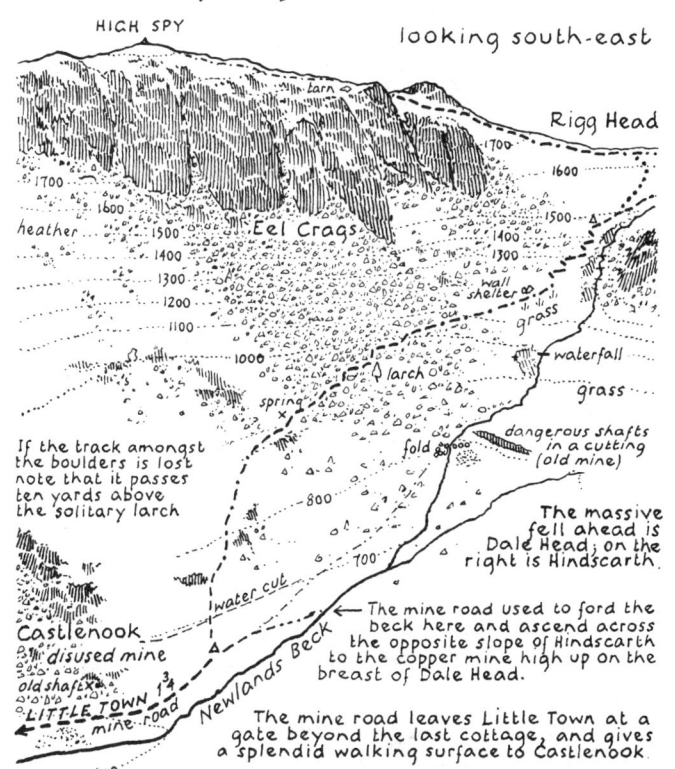

looking south-east

HIGH SPY — tarn — Rigg Head — 1700 — 1600 — heather — 1700 — 1600 — Eel Crags — 1500 — 1400 — 1300 — wall shelter — grass — 1200 — 1100 — waterfall — grass — 1000 — larch — spring — dangerous shafts in a cutting (old mine) — fold

If the track amongst the boulders is lost note that it passes ten yards above the solitary larch

800 — The massive fell ahead is Dale Head; on the right is Hindscarth.

700 — water cut

Castlenook — disused mine — old shafts — LITTLE TOWN 1¼ — mine road — Newlands Beck

← The mine road used to ford the beck here and ascend across the opposite slope of Hindscarth to the copper mine high up on the breast of Dale Head.

The mine road leaves Little Town at a gate beyond the last cottage, and gives a splendid walking surface to Castlenook.

600

The first thing to note about this route (which may also be used for crossing from Newlands to Borrowdale or Honister) is that the path as delineated on Ordnance and other maps, closely following the side of the beck, has largely gone to seed. Instead, a popular track now turns off the mine road just around the corner from the old workings at Castlenook, a cairn marking the junction, and at once starts climbing to swing round across the screes of Eel Crags, finally joining the original zig-zags.

The upper reaches of the Newlands valley are wild and secluded, with many evidences of man's searches for its precious minerals, and this route gives an excellent opportunity of seeing its features at close quarters.

High Spy 9

THE SUMMIT

Bassenthwaite Lake — SKIDDAW — SKIDDAW LITTLE MAN

The top of the fell undulates without much variation in height over a considerable distance, and although the ultimate point is not in doubt the rough ground above Blea Crag, half a mile from the summit-cairn, is little inferior in elevation. Between the two is a simple promenade, easy walking among many small outcrops, but sustained excitement may be added to the journey by keeping to the fringe of the precipice of Eel Crags, which extends unbroken along the Newlands edge in a bewildering array of aretes, gullies and cliffs. The summit cairn is a solid, well-built structure, the result of diligent toil: a memorial to its unknown builders.

DESCENTS: Leave the fell by the ridge, either south to Rigg Head or north to Hause Gate before turning off. The easy slope down towards Borrowdale is tempting, but ends in crags; and a direct descent unscathed into Newlands is palpably impossible.

The summit, looking south — GREAT END — SCAFELL PIKE — SCAFELL — GREAT GABLE — DALE HEAD — *Dalehead Tarn*

THE VIEW

The view is extensive and generally good, the main interest being centred in the south, where the Scafell group captures attention and Great Gable is especially prominent. The long ten-mile wall of the Helvellyn range forms the limit of view eastwards, and Skiddaw and Blencathra stand up well in the north. As a viewpoint, the cairn is a little too far from the edge of the precipice to add drama to the scene, but there are several places nearby where profound glimpses down into the wild recesses of upper Newlands may be obtained.

Principal Fells

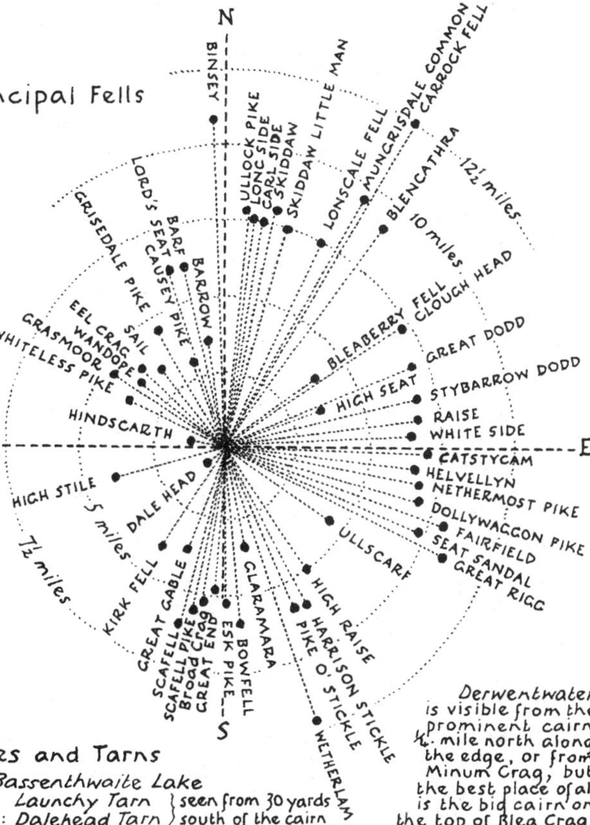
N
S
E
W
BINSEY
ULLOCK PIKE
LONG SIDE
CARL SIDE
SKIDDAW
SKIDDAW LITTLE MAN
LONSCALE FELL
MUNGRISDALE COMMON
CARROCK FELL
BLENCATHRA
12½ miles
10 miles
CLOUGH HEAD
BLEABERRY FELL
GREAT DODD
HIGH SEAT
STYBARROW DODD
RAISE
WHITE SIDE
CATSTYCAM
HELVELLYN
NETHERMOST PIKE
DOLLYWAGGON PIKE
FAIRFIELD
SEAT SANDAL
GREAT RIGG
ULLSCARF
HIGH RAISE
HARRISON STICKLE
PIKE O' STICKLE
WETHERLAM
CLARAMARA
BOWFELL
ESK PIKE
GREAT END
Broad Crag
SCAFELL PIKE
SCAFELL
GREAT GABLE
KIRK FELL
DALE HEAD
5 miles
7½ miles
HIGH STILE
HINDSCARTH
WHITELESS PIKE
GRASMOOR
WANDOPE
EEL CRAG
SAIL
GRISEDALE PIKE
LORD'S SEAT
BARF
CAUSEY PIKE
BARROW

Lakes and Tarns

N : *Bassenthwaite Lake*
S : *Launchy Tarn* } seen from 30 yards
SSW : *Dalehead Tarn* } south of the cairn

Derwentwater is visible from the prominent cairn ¼ mile north along the edge, or from Minum Crag, but the best place of all is the big cairn on the top of Blea Crag.

High Spy 11

RIDGE ROUTES

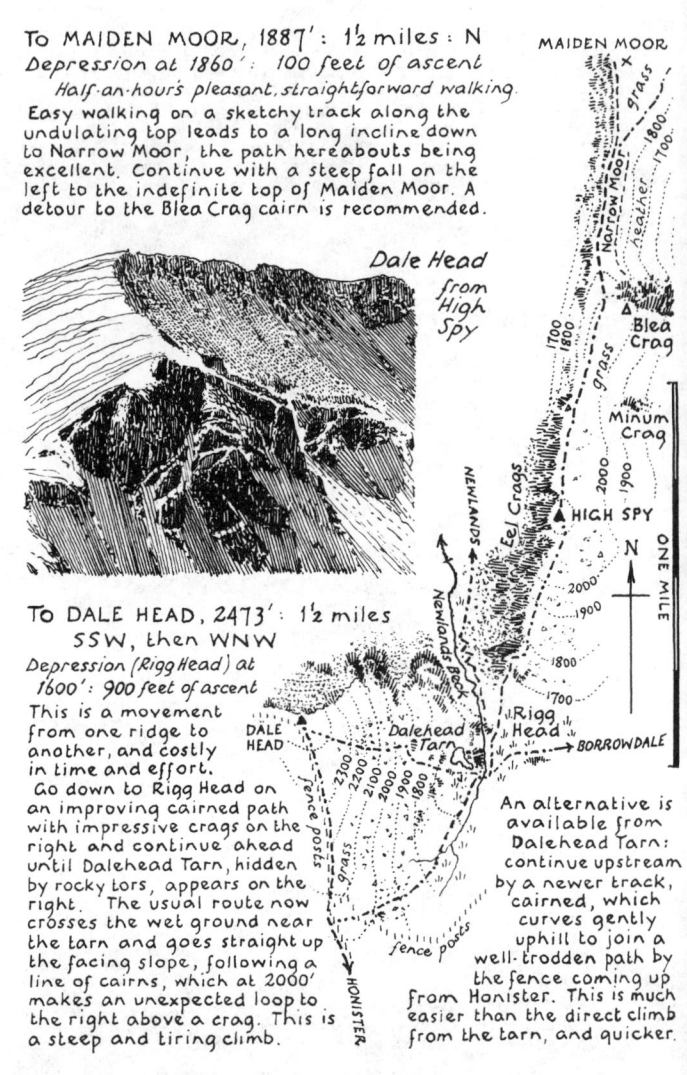

TO MAIDEN MOOR, 1887': 1½ miles : N
Depression at 1860': 100 feet of ascent
Half-an-hour's pleasant, straightforward walking.

Easy walking on a sketchy track along the undulating top leads to a long incline down to Narrow Moor, the path hereabouts being excellent. Continue with a steep fall on the left to the indefinite top of Maiden Moor. A detour to the Blea Crag cairn is recommended.

Dale Head from High Spy

TO DALE HEAD, 2473': 1½ miles
SSW, then WNW
Depression (Rigg Head) at 1600': 900 feet of ascent

This is a movement from one ridge to another, and costly in time and effort.
Go down to Rigg Head on an improving cairned path with impressive crags on the right and continue ahead until Dalehead Tarn, hidden by rocky tors, appears on the right. The usual route now crosses the wet ground near the tarn and goes straight up the facing slope, following a line of cairns, which at 2000' makes an unexpected loop to the right above a crag. This is a steep and tiring climb.

An alternative is available from Dalehead Tarn: continue upstream by a newer track, cairned, which curves gently uphill to join a well-trodden path by the fence coming up from Honister. This is much easier than the direct climb from the tarn, and quicker.

High Spy 12

Goat (or Gate) Crag from Castle Crag

Hindscarth 2385'

from High Snab Bank

Little Town ●
⤺ Newlands Hause
ROBINSON
● ▲ ▲ HINDSCARTH
Buttermere
DALE HEAD ▲
Seatoller ●
Honister Pass ⤺
MILES
0 1 2 3 4

Hindscarth 2

NATURAL FEATURES

Only a minority of the walkers who traverse the fine ridge between Dale Head and Robinson turn aside for a visit to the intermediate summit of Hindscarth, this lying half a mile off the direct course across a simple but uninteresting plateau. Comparatively few, too, climb the fell for its own sake; those who do invariably ascend from Newlands along the only natural line of approach, the ridge of Scope End. Steep-sided and narrow-crested, and richly carpeted in heather, this ridge is a beauty.

Hindscarth is a twin to Robinson. Both were created in the same upheaval and sculptured in the same mould. They turn broad backs to the Buttermere valley and go hand-in-hand together down to Newlands, their ridges reaching the valley at the beautiful watersmeet near the little church. Between them is the upland hollow of Little Dale, much of it a bog, but having an interesting feature in a rocky gorge where waterfalls leap to lower levels beneath the near-vertical acclivity of Scope End; further down an old reservoir has served its purpose and become a charming pool. Mining operations have left a few scars on Scope End, and some open shafts, levels and fractures that invite attention. Gold has been won here, giving Hindscarth its greatest distinction — but walkers who halt in their travels to search the spoilheaps for discarded nuggets will be wasting their time, the area having already been thoroughly combed by the author — also without success. Those who carry their search into the long-abandoned workings are unlikely to return.

The eastern flank of Hindscarth falls very roughly and steeply into the upper Newlands valley, draining to the fell's main watercourse, Newlands Beck, which goes on to join the Derwent. A few feeble streams flow south to Gatesgarthdale and unexpectedly become subterranean at the 500' contour.

1 : The summit
2 : Ridge continuing to Robinson
3 : High Crags
4 : Scope End
5 : Little Dale
6 : Scope Beck
7 : Newlands Beck
8 : Step Gill

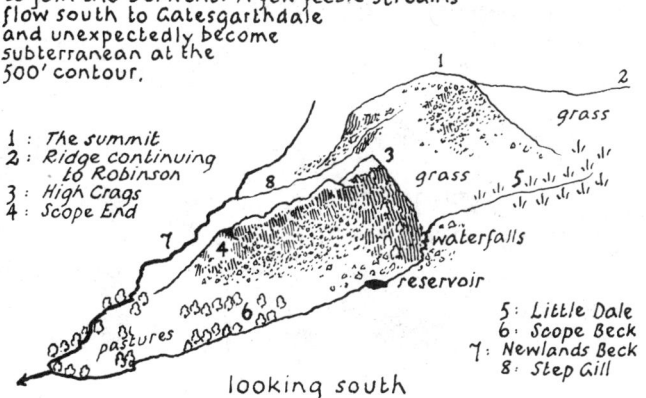

looking south

Hindscarth 3

Newlands is exceptionally well-favoured by its circle of exciting mountain peaks and wide choice of ascents, and is an ideal centre for fellwalking. Among many striking outlines, Scope End in particular arrests one's attention, assuming, when seen from Little Town, the shape of a narrow-crested ridge with three turrets — an aspect illustrated above. In this view Hindscarth (on the left) appears to be quite detached from Scope End, but they are connected by a simple rising ridge.

Newlands Church

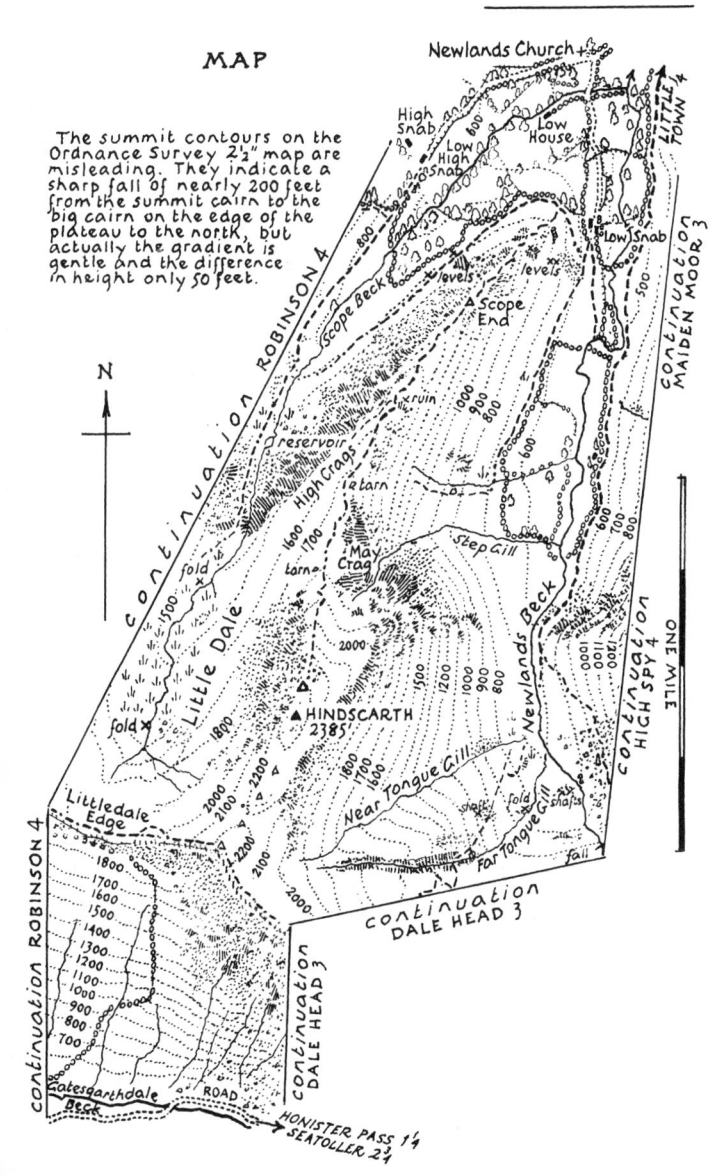

Hindscarth 4

MAP

The summit contours on the Ordnance Survey 2½" map are misleading. They indicate a sharp fall of nearly 200 feet from the summit cairn to the big cairn on the edge of the plateau to the north, but actually the gradient is gentle and the difference in height only 50 feet.

Hindscarth 5

Goldscope Mine

Goldscope Mine was abandoned a hundred years ago after intermittent operation over a period of six centuries. One of the oldest mines in the district, it was also the most important in output, having rich veins of lead and copper. Silver and gold, too, have been extracted. Its early development, on a large scale, was undertaken by Germans, and its long history has been marked by many adventures and much litigation.

Upper Pan Holes

External evidence of the mine is indicated mainly by spoil-heaps on the Newlands Beck side of Scope End: immediately above is the main adit of Lower Pan Holes (from which a stream issues) with a second opening a few yards higher, under a tree. Further up the fellside is a curious slanting gash in a rockface — the Upper Pan Holes. On the other (Scope Beck) flank of the ridge are several levels.

Scope End is therefore pierced from both sides and the main level runs into the fell for such a considerable distance (over 300 yards) before becoming impassable, due to roof-falls, that it is reasonable to suppose that in the later years of operation it would be possible to walk right through the heart of it. In the darkness of these inner workings is a great shaft, which was sunk to such a depth ultimately that the pumping of water from it became too costly — this, not exhaustion of the minerals, was the reason for closure.

Lower Pan Holes

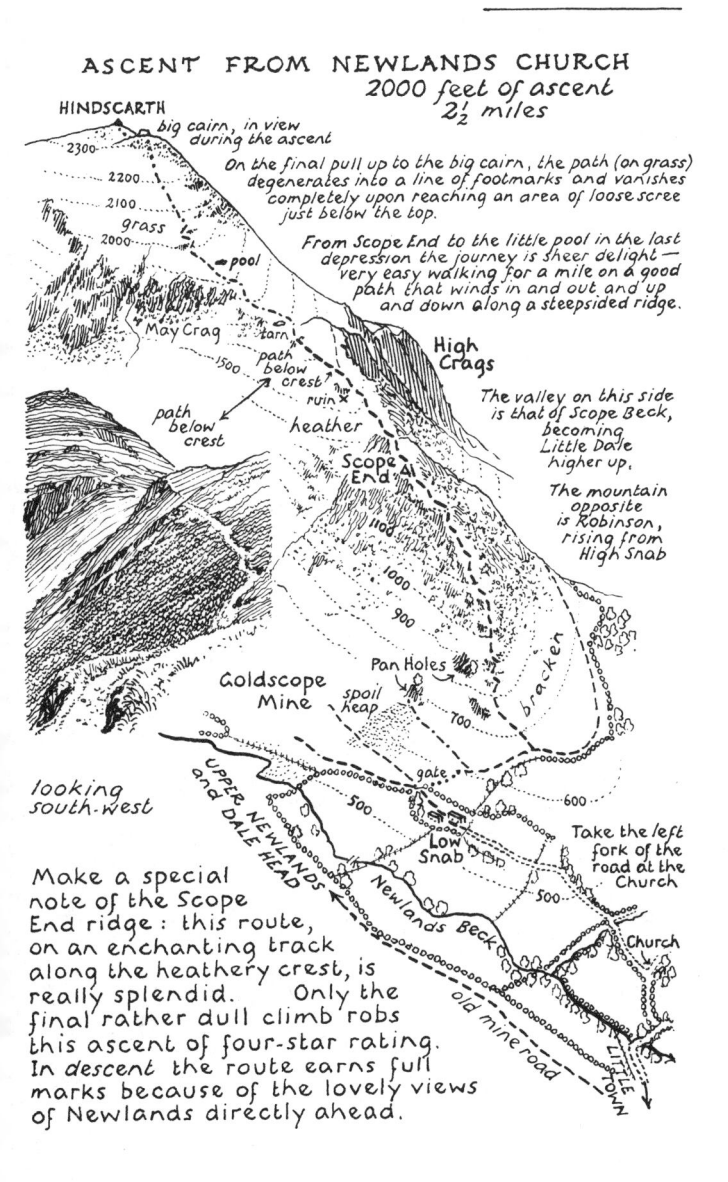

Hindscarth 6

ASCENT FROM NEWLANDS CHURCH
2000 feet of ascent
2½ miles

HINDSCARTH — big cairn, in view during the ascent

On the final pull up to the big cairn, the path (on grass) degenerates into a line of footmarks and vanishes completely upon reaching an area of loose scree just below the top.

From Scope End to the little pool in the last depression the journey is sheer delight — very easy walking for a mile on a good path that winds in and out and up and down along a steepsided ridge.

May Crag — tarn — path below crest — ruin — heather — Scope End — High Crags

The valley on this side is that of Scope Beck, becoming Little Dale higher up.

The mountain opposite is Robinson, rising from High Snab.

path below crest

Pan Holes — Goldscope Mine — spoil heap — bracken

looking south-west

UPPER NEWLANDS AND DALE HEAD — gate — Low Snab — Newlands Beck — old mine road — Church — LITTLE TOWN

Take the left fork of the road at the Church

Make a special note of the Scope End ridge: this route, on an enchanting track along the heathery crest, is really splendid. Only the final rather dull climb robs this ascent of four-star rating. In descent the route earns full marks because of the lovely views of Newlands directly ahead.

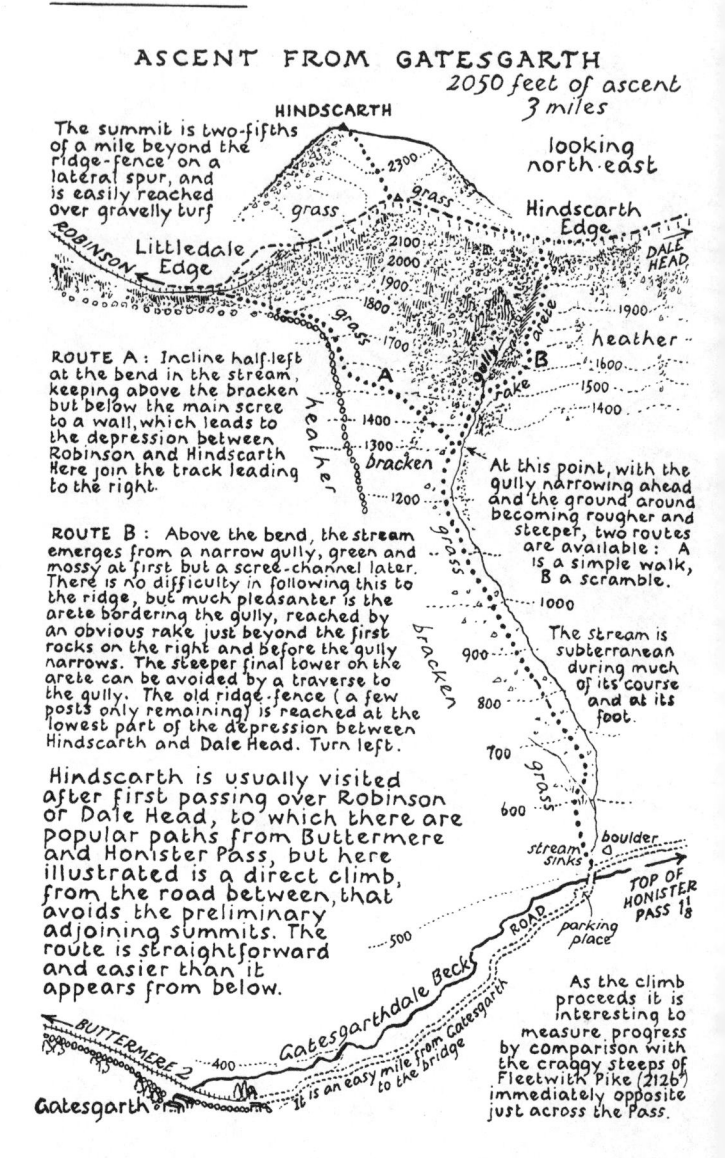

Hindscarth 7

ASCENT FROM GATESGARTH
2050 feet of ascent
3 miles

looking north-east

HINDSCARTH

Hindscarth Edge

Littledale Edge

ROBINSON

DALE HEAD

The summit is two-fifths of a mile beyond the ridge-fence on a lateral spur, and is easily reached over gravelly turf.

ROUTE A: Incline half-left at the bend in the stream, keeping above the bracken but below the main scree to a wall, which leads to the depression between Robinson and Hindscarth. Here join the track leading to the right.

ROUTE B: Above the bend, the stream emerges from a narrow gully, green and mossy at first but a scree-channel later. There is no difficulty in following this to the ridge, but much pleasanter is the arête bordering the gully, reached by an obvious rake just beyond the first rocks on the right and before the gully narrows. The steeper final tower on the arête can be avoided by a traverse to the gully. The old ridge-fence (a few posts only remaining) is reached at the lowest part of the depression between Hindscarth and Dale Head. Turn left.

Hindscarth is usually visited after first passing over Robinson or Dale Head, to which there are popular paths from Buttermere and Honister Pass, but here illustrated is a direct climb, from the road between, that avoids the preliminary adjoining summits. The route is straightforward and easier than it appears from below.

At this point, with the gully narrowing ahead and the ground around becoming rougher and steeper, two routes are available: A is a simple walk, B a scramble.

The stream is subterranean during much of its course and at its foot.

stream sinks

boulder

TOP OF HONISTER PASS 1⅛

parking place

ROAD

Gatesgarthdale Beck

BUTTERMERE 2

Gatesgarth

it is an easy mile from Gatesgarth to the bridge

As the climb proceeds it is interesting to measure progress by comparison with the craggy steeps of Fleetwith Pike (2126') immediately opposite just across the Pass.

Hindscarth 8

THE SUMMIT

1: BOWFELL
2: ESK PIKE
3: GREAT END
4: Ill Crag
5: Broad Crag
6: SCAFELL PIKE
7: GREAT GABLE
8: GREEN GABLE
9: BRANDRETH
10: GREY KNOTTS

The top of Hindscarth is a full half-mile in length, the contours gently building up to the highest point, near the north-east end, where a large and untidy pile of stones stands amongst embedded rocks. Elsewhere the summit is grassy, with patches of gravel.

Continuing the line of the ridge and 200 paces away, on the edge of the north-east declivity, there is a big circular cairn of some antiquity, the Ordnance Survey maps giving it distinction by the use of the lettering reserved for objects of historic interest. This is the cairn prominently seen from Newlands, and it commands the finest view from the mountain. The interior is hollowed out to provide a wind-shelter — a function performed with increasing inefficiency as the cavity slowly fills with stones fallen from the parapet.

DESCENTS: The summit is pathless, but simple in design and uncomplicated in structure. Ways off are along the axis, which runs NNE and SSW. Both flanks are scarped.

For Newlands, go down by the big cairn, keeping the long ridge of Scope End in front and descending to it. A fair track materialises below the initial scree. *In mist, it is important (but not easy) to find it.*

Go SSW to the fence, for Buttermere or Honister. Leftwards the fence climbs over Dale Head (which can NOT be by-passed) before going down to Honister Pass. Rightwards, from the first depression a safe descent may be made down an easy slope to Gatesgarthdale.

"A..... cairn of some antiquity"

Hindscarth 9

THE VIEW

There is a good all-round panorama, especially pleasing over Newlands to the Vale of Keswick and Skiddaw — the big north cairn is a better place for photographs in this direction — with, in contrast, a rugged skyline forming the southern horizon. The familiar shape of Scafell is missing from the scene, hidden behind Great Gable.

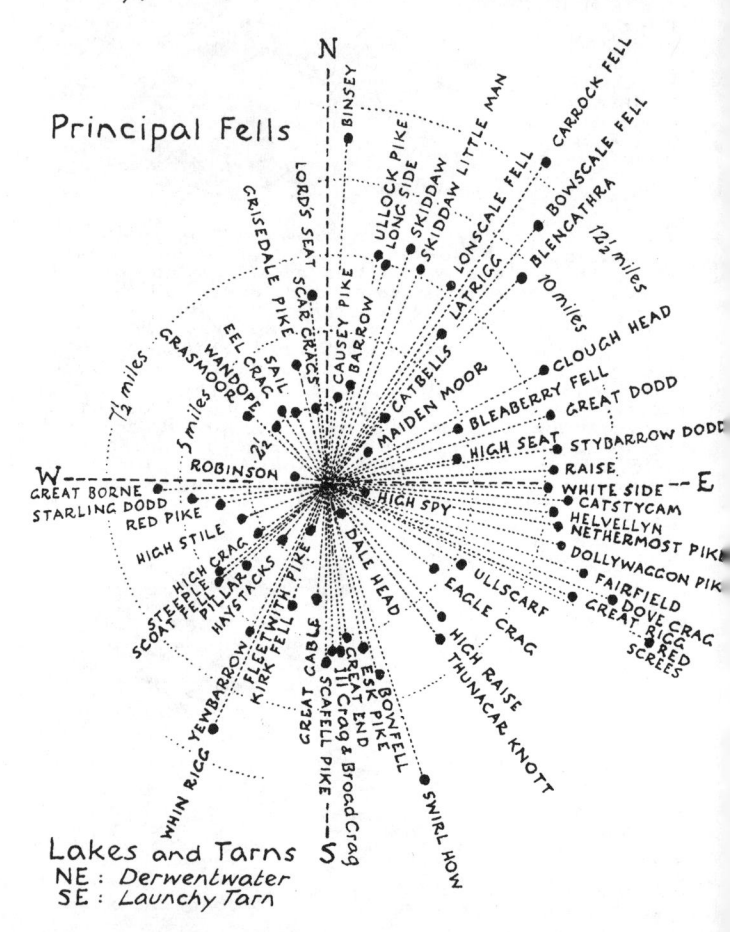

Principal Fells

N — BINSEY, LORD'S SEAT, GRISEDALE PIKE, SCAR CRAGS, EEL CRAG, SAIL, GRASMOOR, WANDOPE, CAUSEY PIKE, BARROW, ULLOCK PIKE, LONG SIDE, SKIDDAW, SKIDDAW LITTLE MAN, LONSCALE FELL, LATRIGG, CARROCK FELL, BOWSCALE FELL, BLENCATHRA

12½ miles, 10 miles, 7½ miles, 5 miles

CATBELLS, MAIDEN MOOR, CLOUGH HEAD, BLEABERRY FELL, GREAT DODD, HIGH SEAT, STYBARROW DODD, RAISE, WHITE SIDE — E, CATSTYCAM, HELVELLYN, NETHERMOST PIKE, DOLLYWAGGON PIKE, FAIRFIELD, DOVE CRAG, GREAT RIGG, RED SCREES

W — GREAT BORNE, STARLING DODD, RED PIKE, HIGH STILE, HIGH CRAG, STEEPLE, SCOAT FELL, PILLAR, HAYSTACKS, KIRK FELL, FLEETWITH PIKE, YEWBARROW, WHIN RIGG, GREAT GABLE, DALE HEAD, HIGH SPY, ROBINSON

SCAFELL PIKE, ILL CRAG & BROAD CRAG, ESK PIKE, ESK END, BOWFELL, ULLSCARF, EAGLE CRAG, HIGH RAISE, THUNACAR KNOTT, SWIRL HOW

S

Lakes and Tarns
NE: Derwentwater
SE: Launchy Tarn

Hindscarth 10

RIDGE ROUTES

TO ROBINSON, 2417': 1½ miles: SSW, WNW and N.
Depression at 1880': 550 feet of ascent
A simple circuit around the head of Little Dale

Hindscarth and Robinson are lateral spurs springing from the main fenced ridge of the north wall of Gatesgarthdale. A beeline between the two summits is out of the question and the ridge must be used to pass from one to the other. The depression midway is considerable. An interest can be added to the climb therefrom by a short detour over the fence to look at the strange formation known as Hackney Holes.

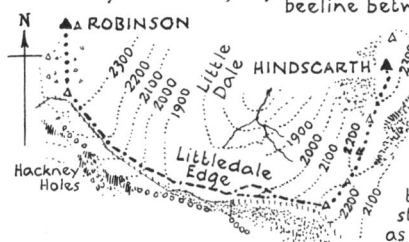

TO DALE HEAD, 2473': 1¼ miles: SSW, then ESE
Depression at 2156': 330 feet of ascent
Increasing interest and excellent views

The intervening depression is slight, and, in clear weather, a short cut to it is feasible. (In mist, continue SSW to join the fence). The main ridge from here onwards is very good, although not as exciting as it promises to be. Buttermere is in view temporarily when the ridge narrows. In mist, keep the line of fence-posts in sight.

Briefly and inadequately glimpsed from the ridge to Dale Head, down on the left, is the strange ravine of Far Tongue Gill. For half a mile this huge cut in the side of Hindscarth, a remarkable chasm out of all proportion to the stream it accommodates, is walled by great pale slabs of slate. Remote from usual walkers tracks, the best view of it from a distance is seen along the ridge of High Spy.

The ravine of Far Tongue Gill

Hopegill Head 2525'

also known as Hobcarton Pike

from Scar Crags

Hopegill Head 2

NATURAL FEATURES

A high mountain ridge leaps like a rainbow from the woods and fields of Brackenthwaite and arcs through the sky for five miles to the east, where the descending curve comes down to the village of Braithwaite. This ridge has three main summits, of which the central one (and the finest, but not the highest) is known locally as Hobcarton Pike and to mapmakers as Hopegill Head. The supporting fell stretches far to the north, having roots in Whinlatter and the Vale of Lorton, whence the heathery flanks of Swinside rise to form the main ridge to the top peak, passing over the subsidiary Ladyside Pike (formerly Lady's Seat). Scarped edges join the two neighbouring fells of Grisedale Pike, east, and Whiteside, west, while a short slope, halted by the rounded hump of Sand Hill, falls easily to Coledale Hause southwards. But it is the aspect to the north that invests the mountain with its special character. Here, Swinside is bounded, on both sides, by deep valleys: sterile Hope Gill and afforested Hobcarton. The latter, now a coniferous jungle, leads up to a great semicircle of cliffs around the valley-head: this is a nature stronghold, Hobcarton Crag. The valley of Hope Gill is rarely visited and has little of interest; it seems rather surprising that this valley, and not the other, has given its name to the fell — until one stands on the shapely summit and sees Hope Gill winding away directly below, while the valley of Hobcarton is obscured by the north ridge. Then the choice of name of the cartographers cannot be questioned. 'Hopegill Head' is right.

1: The summit
2: Ridge continuing to Grisedale Pike
3: Ridge continuing to Whiteside
4: Ladyside Pike
5: Swinside
6: Hobcarton Crag
7: Swinside Plantation
8: Hobcarton Plantation
9: Hobcarton Gill
10: Hope Gill

looking south

Hopegill Head 3

Hobcarton Crag

Hobcarton Crag is the property of the National Trust, and no ordinary cliff. Its size is impressive — 500 feet in height above the scree along a half-mile curve — but the rocks are broken and interspersed with lush bilberry meadows, so that the appeal of the crag is not related to climbing: indeed, the rock is unsuitable for exploration.

This is Skiddaw slate, fracturing and splintering easily, yet it has a special attraction nevertheless, obvious to all who observe as they walk: where natural weathering has taken place and erosion is absent there is a very high degree of contortion and striation, evidence of the severe pressures to which it was subjected during formation.

A greater fame, although also within a specialist field of study, is attributable to the rare species of flora in the two main gullies; in particular, here is the only known habitat in England of the red alpine catchfly (*Viscaria alpina*). The National Trust were largely influenced in their acquisition of the Crag by its great botanical interest (and partly by a desire to limit the afforestation of the valley-head below).

The Crag is a haven of quiet solitude, within sight but out of reach of a popular walking route. In summer sunlight there is pleasant colour, the bilberry — greenest of greens — making a luxuriant velvety patchwork among the grey and silver rocks. In shadow, the scene is sombre and forbidding. The silence is interrupted only by the croaking of the resident ravens and the occasional thud of a falling botanist.

This is a place to look at and leave alone.

Hopegill Head 4

A feature of the northern rim of Hobcarton Crag is a curious break in the curtain of rocks forming the sharp arête below the summit: here, a steep scree gully falls from a square cleft in the vertical wall of crag. A name is needed for this strange place and The Notch fits it well.

The lower picture shows the arête rising above the Notch to the summit. An arrow at the side indicates the direction of a groove or fault in the slabs, and this is advised for ascent or descent if the rocks are icy or greasy. In the foreground is a platform of rock — a perfect spot for a sunbathe but not for slumber, the unprotected edge here falling away sheer.

The Notch, Hobcarton Crag

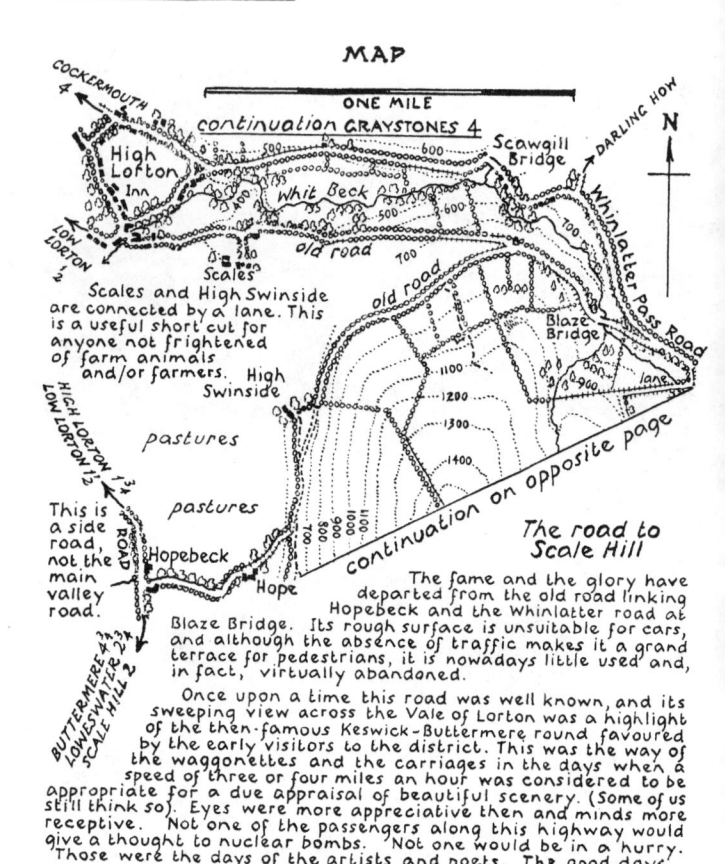

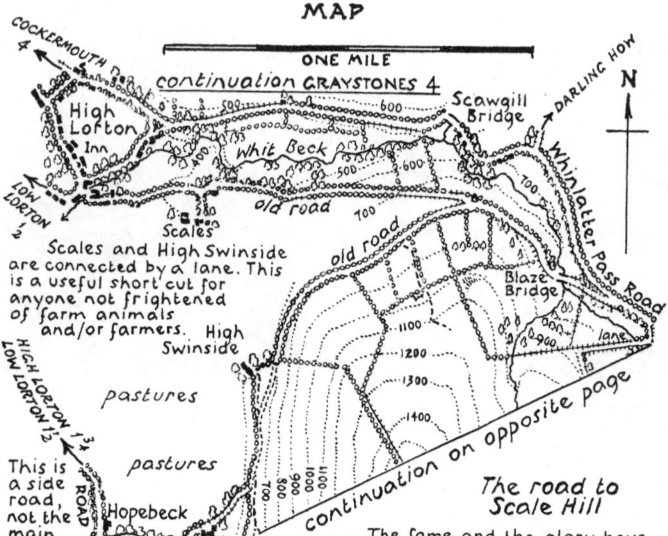
MAP
ONE MILE
continuation GRAYSTONES 4
COCKERMOUTH 4
DARLING HOW
N
High Lorton
Inn
Scawgill Bridge
Whit Beck
500
600
400
700
old road
Scales
LOW LORTON 1/2
Whinlatter Pass Road
Blaze Bridge
lane
900
1100
1200
1300
1400
Scales and High Swinside are connected by a lane. This is a useful short cut for anyone not frightened of farm animals and/or farmers.
High Swinside
pastures
pastures
HIGH LORTON 1 3/4
LOW LORTON 1 1/2
This is a side road, not the main valley road.
ROAD
Hopebeck
Hope
continuation on opposite page
BUTTERMERE 4 3/4
LOWESWATER 2 3/4
SCALE HILL 2

The road to Scale Hill

The fame and the glory have departed from the old road linking Hopebeck and the Whinlatter road at Blaze Bridge. Its rough surface is unsuitable for cars, and although the absence of traffic makes it a grand terrace for pedestrians, it is nowadays little used and, in fact, virtually abandoned.

Once upon a time this road was well known, and its sweeping view across the Vale of Lorton was a highlight of the then-famous Keswick-Buttermere round favoured by the early visitors to the district. This was the way of the waggonettes and the carriages in the days when a speed of three or four miles an hour was considered to be appropriate for a due appraisal of beautiful scenery. (Some of us still think so). Eyes were more appreciative then and minds more receptive. Not one of the passengers along this highway would give a thought to nuclear bombs. Not one would be in a hurry. Those were the days of the artists and poets. The good days.

The coaching-house in the valley was the Scale Hill Inn, a hostelry of renown and good reputation, the accepted centre for visitors to western Lakeland. Today the Scale Hill Inn (now Hotel) is as charming as ever, and no less favourably situated in one of the most delectable corners of a lovely landscape, but its former significance in the itinerary of tourists has gone. Langdale and Borrowdale are in current fashion. Most visitors have never heard of Scale Hill, and anyway would consider the place too remote, too quiet, off today's beaten tracks.

In these changed circumstances it gives an old-timer a certain nostalgic pleasure to note that the old signpost at the junction with the Whinlatter road still points to 'Scale Hill', a name that thrilled Victorian and Edwardian hearts but now means nothing to the neurotic Elizabethan lunatics who rattle past at 60 m.p.h. This old signpost is a last link with the days of sanity. But few choose to follow its direction.

Hopegill Head 6

MAP

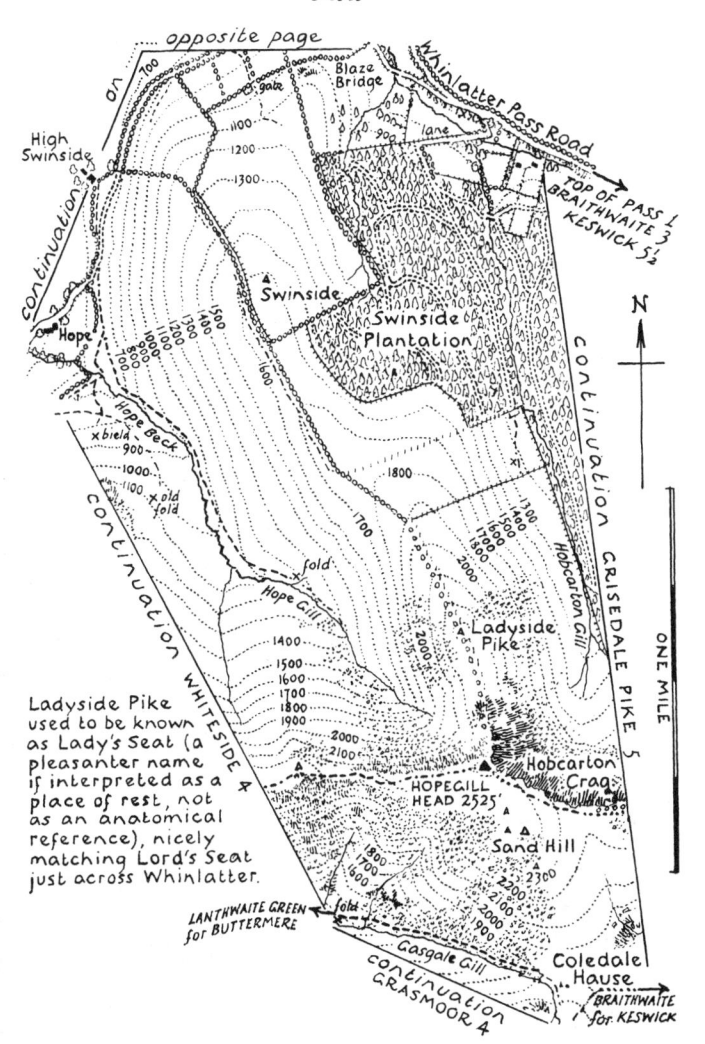

Ladyside Pike used to be known as Lady's Seat (a pleasanter name if interpreted as a place of rest, not as an anatomical reference), nicely matching Lord's Seat just across Whinlatter.

Hopegill Head 7

Hobcarton

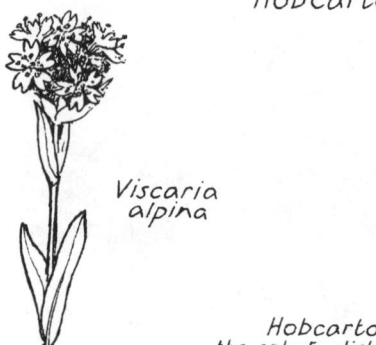

Viscaria alpina

Hobcarton Valley and Crag —
the only English home of *Viscaria alpina*

Hopegill Head 8

ASCENT FROM COLEDALE HAUSE
600 feet of ascent : ¾ mile

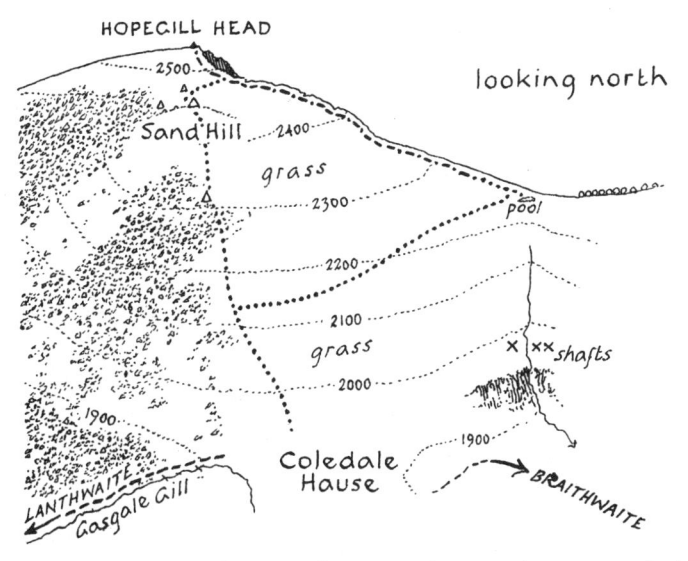

looking north

There is no path, and the summit remains concealed until the cairn on Sand Hill is reached. Go anywhere up the easy slope, keeping rather to the Gasgale side for a view to relieve the monotony of the ascent; or, more interesting, contour round to the depression on the right and then go up the edge of Hobcarton Crag.

The summit of Hopegill Head, from the cairn on Sand Hill

Hopegill Head 9

ASCENT FROM WHINLATTER PASS
1850 feet of ascent : 2½ miles from the road

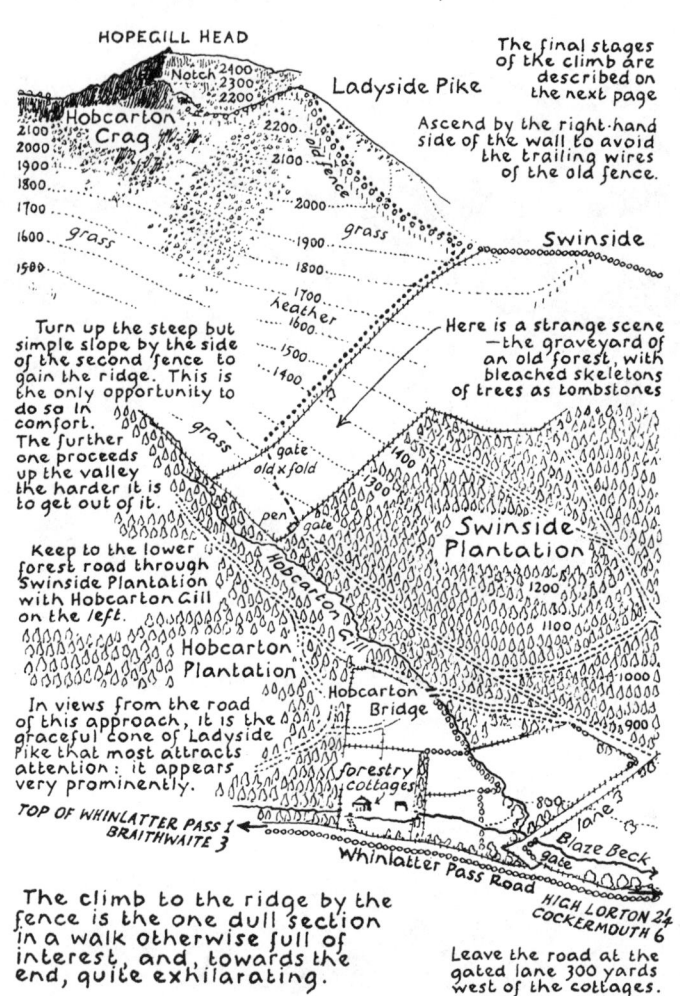

HOPEGILL HEAD

The final stages of the climb are described on the next page

Ascend by the right-hand side of the wall to avoid the trailing wires of the old fence.

Hobcarton Crag

Ladyside Pike

Swinside

Turn up the steep but simple slope by the side of the second fence to gain the ridge. This is the only opportunity to do so in comfort. The further one proceeds up the valley the harder it is to get out of it.

Here is a strange scene — the graveyard of an old forest, with bleached skeletons of trees as tombstones

Keep to the lower forest road through Swinside Plantation with Hobcarton Gill on the *left*.

Swinside Plantation

Hobcarton Plantation

Hobcarton Gill

In views from the road of this approach, it is the graceful cone of Ladyside Pike that most attracts attention: it appears very prominently.

Hobcarton Bridge

forestry cottages

TOP OF WHINLATTER PASS 1
BRAITHWAITE 3 ←

Whinlatter Pass Road

Blaze Beck

HIGH LORTON 2½
COCKERMOUTH 6

The climb to the ridge by the fence is the one dull section in a walk otherwise full of interest, and, towards the end, quite exhilarating.

Leave the road at the gated lane 300 yards west of the cottages.

looking south

Hopegill Head 10

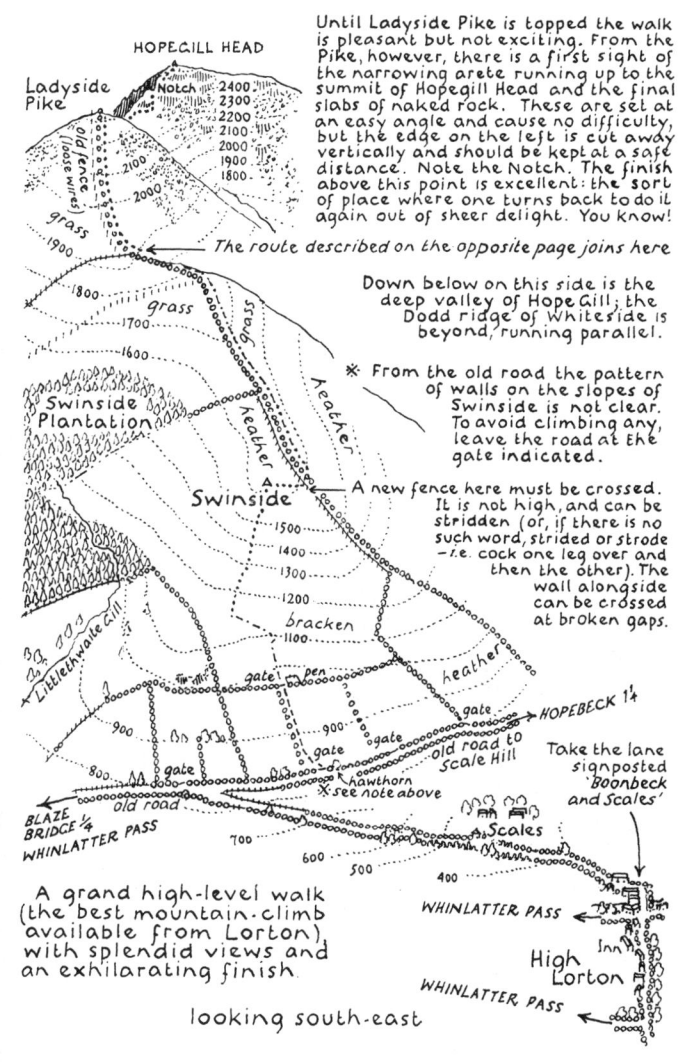

ASCENT FROM HIGH LORTON
2450 feet of ascent : 3¼ miles

Until Ladyside Pike is topped the walk is pleasant but not exciting. From the Pike, however, there is a first sight of the narrowing arête running up to the summit of Hopegill Head and the final slabs of naked rock. These are set at an easy angle and cause no difficulty, but the edge on the left is cut away vertically and should be kept at a safe distance. Note the Notch. The finish above this point is excellent: the sort of place where one turns back to do it again out of sheer delight. You know!

The route described on the opposite page joins here

Down below on this side is the deep valley of Hope Gill; the Dodd ridge of Whiteside is beyond, running parallel.

✱ From the old road the pattern of walls on the slopes of Swinside is not clear. To avoid climbing any, leave the road at the gate indicated.

A new fence here must be crossed. It is not high, and can be stridden (or, if there is no such word, strided or strode — i.e. cock one leg over and then the other). The wall alongside can be crossed at broken gaps.

A grand high-level walk (the best mountain-climb available from Lorton) with splendid views and an exhilarating finish.

looking south-east

Hopegill Head 11

ASCENT FROM HOPEBECK
2150 feet of ascent : 2½ miles

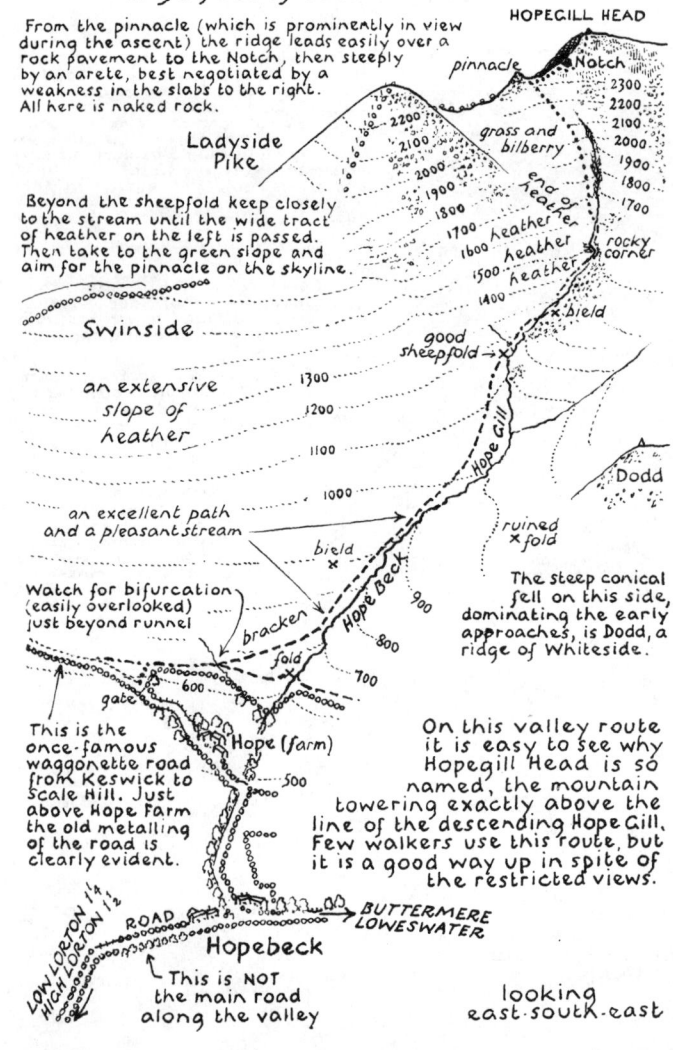

From the pinnacle (which is prominently in view during the ascent) the ridge leads easily over a rock pavement to the Notch, then steeply by an arete, best negotiated by a weakness in the slabs to the right. All here is naked rock.

Beyond the sheepfold keep closely to the stream until the wide tract of heather on the left is passed. Then take to the green slope and aim for the pinnacle on the skyline.

Watch for bifurcation (easily overlooked) just beyond runnel

This is the once-famous waggonette road from Keswick to Scale Hill. Just above Hope Farm the old metalling of the road is clearly evident.

This is NOT the main road along the valley

The steep conical fell on this side, dominating the early approaches, is Dodd, a ridge of Whiteside.

On this valley route it is easy to see why Hopegill Head is so named, the mountain towering exactly above the line of the descending Hope Gill. Few walkers use this route, but it is a good way up in spite of the restricted views.

looking east-south-east

Hopegill Head 12

THE SUMMIT

The culmination of the rising lines of the fell occurs where the slender ridge coming up from Whiteside quite suddenly collapses in the contorted rocks of Hobcarton Crag, exactly at the point of junction of routes ascending the two flanks of the precipice to its apex. Thus, in the space of a few feet, is formed a small, neat summit, a true peak poised above a profound abyss, its delicate proportions uncharacteristic of the general expansiveness of the fell. It is a delightful top, fashioned for the accommodation of solitary walkers: large parties here are an intrusion. Slate debris litters the ground and visitors occasionally scrape a little together to make an insignificant cairn.

The summit is a favourite haunt of birds, which have quick selective eyes for good vantage points. The Hobcarton ravens make a fine sight as they soar and spiral above the gullies and rock battlements, often alighting on the narrow top to survey the domain of which they are undisputed overlords; and particular mention must be made of the regular summer visitations of swifts, which have a liking for steep cliffs and airy summits, and here dart and swoop through the air in an ecstatic and erratic highspeed flight, their whirring wings creating a commotion of vibrating sound.

This summit is a generous reward for the effort of reaching it.

BOWSCALE FELL — BLENCATHRA — GRISEDALE PIKE — GREAT MELL FELL — CLOUGH HEAD

DESCENTS: For High Lorton, Hopebeck or Whinlatter Pass, reverse the routes of ascent: they have a common start down the north slabs. Use a fault or groove away from the edge for safer foothold. *In mist*, this initial section looks intimidating, but step bravely into the void and go cautiously. Anybody who finds himself falling through space will have missed the route.

PLAN OF SUMMIT

Coledale Hause is quickly reached by following the natural slope down from the protuberance of Sand Hill, taking patches of scree in the stride. *In mist*, be on guard against two hazards, dangerous because unexpected: the fenced mine-shafts and the crag-edge of High Force; keep well to the right if these appear out of the gloom.

Hopegill Head 13

THE VIEW

The view is less comprehensive than the diagram suggests, the best part of the Lakeland skyline, to the south, being concealed by Grasmoor and Eel Crag, but in other directions, particularly west (across the Solway Firth) and east (to the Helvellyn range) the panorama is unrestricted. There is a satisfactory grouping of the Scafells just left of Wandope, however, and a quaint glimpse of Pike o' Stickle — a remarkable outline — between Sail and Eel Crag.

Principal Fells

N

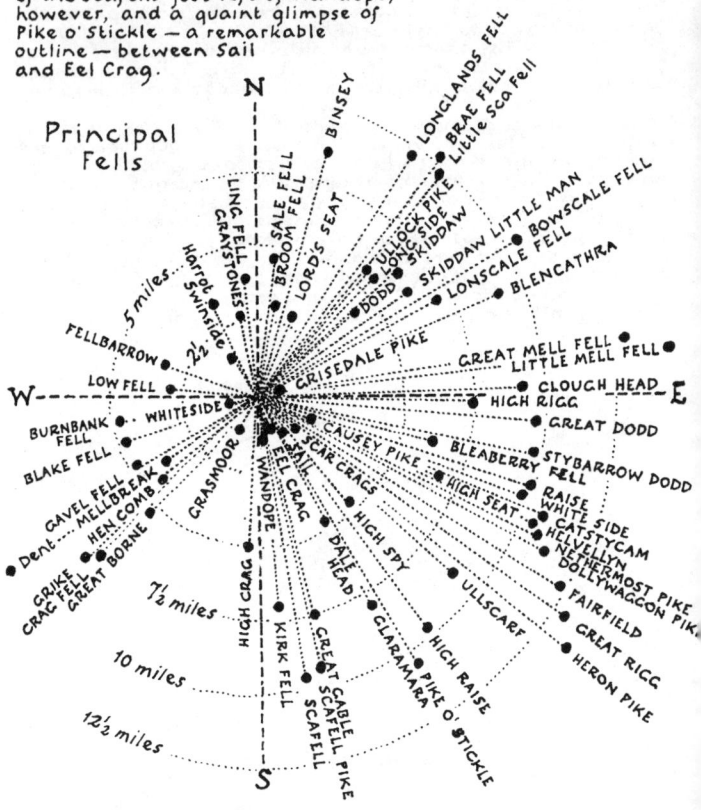

BINSEY
LONGLANDS FELL
BRAE FELL
Little Sca Fell
LING FELL
BROOM FELL
SALE FELL
LORD'S SEAT
ULLOCK PIKE
LONG SIDE
SKIDDAW LITTLE MAN
BOWSCALE FELL
GRAYSTONES
Horrok
DODD
SKIDDAW
LONSCALE FELL
BLENCATHRA
Swinside
5 miles
FELLBARROW
2½
CRISEDALE PIKE
GREAT MELL FELL
LITTLE MELL FELL

W — LOW FELL — — — CLOUGH HEAD — E
HIGH RIGG
BURNBANK FELL
WHITESIDE
GREAT DODD
BLAKE FELL
CAUSEY PIKE
BLEABERRY FELL
STYBARROW DODD
GRASMOOR
SAIL
SCAR CRAGS
HIGH SEAT
RAISE
GAVEL FELL
MELBREAK
EEL CRAG
WHITE SIDE
Dent
HEN COMB
WANDOPE
HIGH SPY
CATSTYCAM
HELVELLYN
GRIKE
NETHERMOST PIKE
CRAG FELL
GREAT BORNE
DOLLYWAGGON PIKE
HIGH CRAG
BASE
FAIRFIELD
7½ miles
BROWN
GREAT RIGG
KIRK FELL
GREAT GABLE
HERON PIKE
10 miles
SCAFELL PIKE
GLARAMARA
HIGH RAISE
12½ miles
SCAFELL
PIKE O' STICKLE
ULLSCARF

S

Lakes and Tarns
NNE: *Over Water*
SE: *Blea Tarn (Ullscarf)*
WSW: *Crummock Water*

Hopegill Head 14

RIDGE ROUTES

To GRISEDALE PIKE, 2593′ : 1⅛ mile : SE, then E, NE
Depression at 2211′ : 400 feet of ascent

An interesting traverse around the head of Hobcarton Valley.
With the precipice close on the left hand, but not too close, go down to the grassy depression south-eastwards, where a broken wall is joined and followed upwards, first over a minor summit and then on to the main top. The well-defined rim of crags on the left throughout, plus the wall, makes the crossing safe in mist.

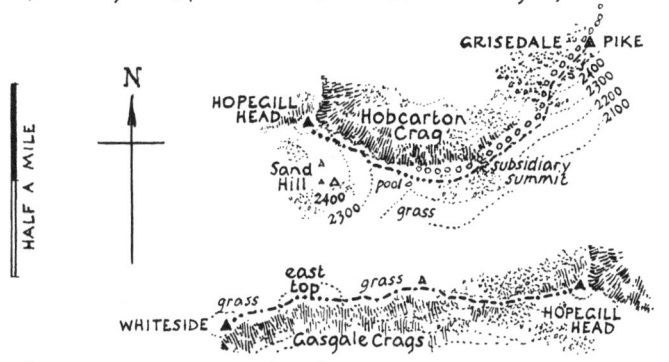

To WHITESIDE, 2317′ : 1⅛ mile : Generally W, then SW
Main depression at 2200′ : 150 feet of ascent

A splendid high-level walk with striking views of Gasgale Gill.
The way leads down the straight and narrow grassy west ridge, becoming rough and rocky as it descends to a pronounced hollow bridged by a heathery crest: this is the best section of the journey. Beyond, easy rocks are climbed, or skirted on the right, and the ridge widens although continuing sharply defined along the left edge. In mist, the east top may be mistakened for the main top.

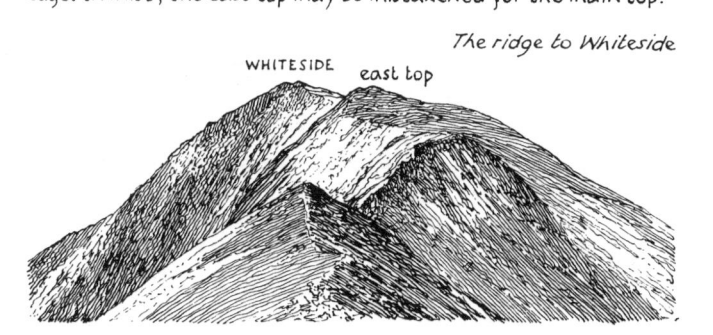

The ridge to Whiteside

Knott Rigg

1790'
approx.

from Buttermere

Keskadale is the long arm of Newlands extending southwest and providing the only outlet for vehicles from the head of the valley. The road is accommodated for two long miles along the side of a narrow and steepsided ridge of moderate height before climbing over a pass, Newlands Hause, formed by the gentle termination of the ridge; lovely Buttermere is beyond. This ridge has two distinct summits: the higher, overlooking Newlands, is Ard Crags; the lower, overlooking Buttermere, is Knott Rigg.

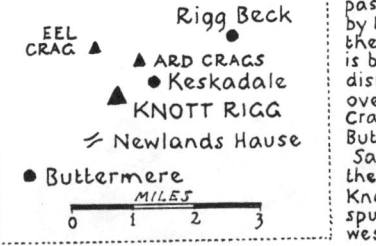

Sail Beck, coming down from the Eel Crag massif, of which Knott Rigg is an offshooting spur, very sharply marks the western boundary of the fell.

Knott Rigg 2

MAP

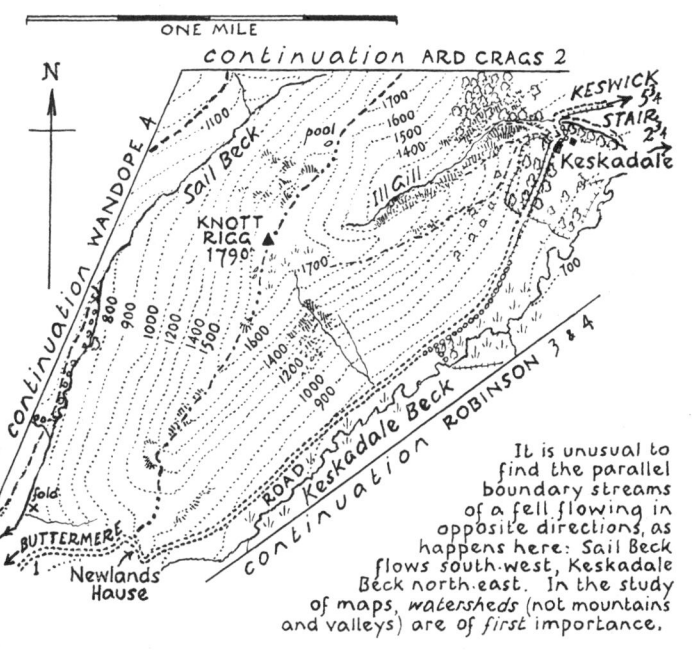

It is unusual to find the parallel boundary streams of a fell flowing in opposite directions, as happens here: Sail Beck flows south-west, Keskadale Beck north-east. In the study of maps, watersheds (not mountains and valleys) are of first importance.

looking down to the Buttermere valley from the south end of the ridge, with High Stile and Red Pike in the background and the Newlands road descending across the side of Robinson in the middle distance

Knott Rigg 3

ASCENT FROM NEWLANDS HAUSE
720 feet of ascent : 1 mile

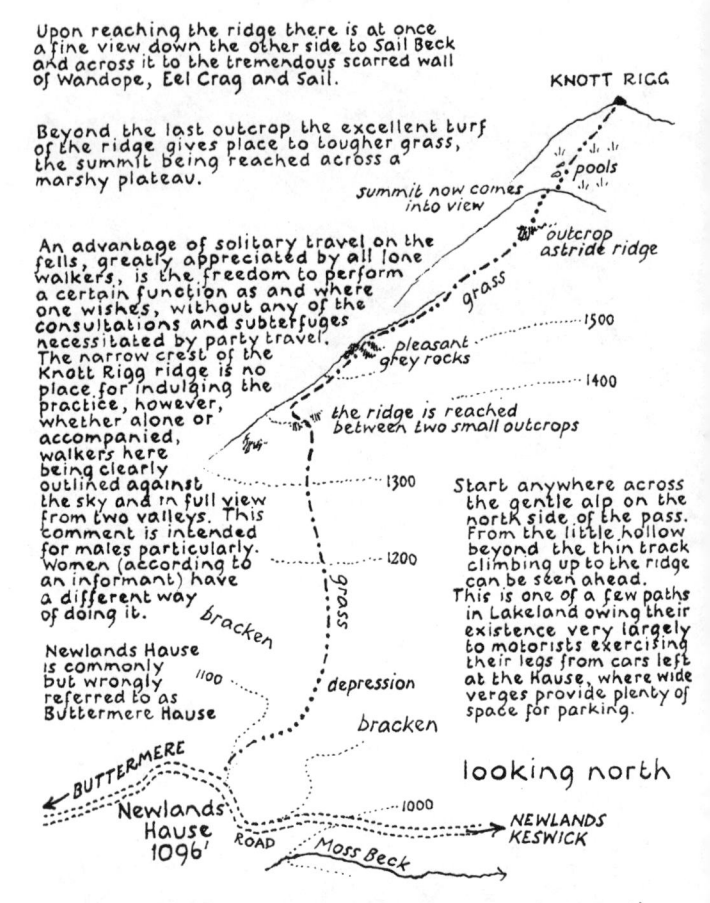

Upon reaching the ridge there is at once a fine view down the other side to Sail Beck and across it to the tremendous scarred wall of Wandope, Eel Crag and Sail.

Beyond the last outcrop the excellent turf of the ridge gives place to tougher grass, the summit being reached across a marshy plateau.

An advantage of solitary travel on the fells, greatly appreciated by all lone walkers, is the freedom to perform a certain function as and where one wishes, without any of the consultations and subterfuges necessitated by party travel. The narrow crest of the Knott Rigg ridge is no place for indulging the practice, however, whether alone or accompanied, walkers here being clearly outlined against the sky and in full view from two valleys. This comment is intended for males particularly. Women (according to an informant) have a different way of doing it.

Newlands Hause is commonly but wrongly referred to as Buttermere Hause

KNOTT RIGG

pools

summit now comes into view

outcrop astride ridge

grass

1500

pleasant grey rocks

1400

the ridge is reached between two small outcrops

1300

Start anywhere across the gentle alp on the north side of the pass. From the little hollow beyond the thin track climbing up to the ridge can be seen ahead.
This is one of a few paths in Lakeland owing their existence very largely to motorists exercising their legs from cars left at the Hause, where wide verges provide plenty of space for parking.

1200

grass

bracken

1100

depression

bracken

looking north

← BUTTERMERE

Newlands Hause 1096'

ROAD

1000

Moss Beck

NEWLANDS KESWICK →

This is a simple and straightforward climb on the sunny side of the Hause, requiring an absence of one hour only from a car parked there. It affords a pleasant exercise, very suitable for persons up to 7 years of age or over 70.

Knott Rigg 4

ASCENT FROM KESKADALE
1000 feet of ascent : 1¼ miles

Upland *marshes* occur on almost all fells: on flat summits and plateaux, in hollows and on grassy shelves. They act as reservoirs for the streams, draining very slowly and holding back moisture to ensure continuous supplies independent of present prevailing weather. It is because of the marshes that the streams seldom lack water. They are safe to walk upon and cause little discomfort.
Bogs are not functional. They are infrequent in Lakeland; there are no places bad enough to trap walkers, but some are a danger to sheep.

looking west

The two bogholes indicated are fenced to keep sheep out of trouble.

The drove road (A) is a splendid green path in the bracken, the start above the fence being indefinite. When the zone of heather is reached it degenerates into a narrow track but can still be followed without difficulty to its end in a marsh just short of the summit.

Ill Gill is closely confined in its lower reaches, progress being assisted by a sketchy shepherd's track. It is the source of a private water supply. In places the ravine scenery and the surroundings are rather reminiscent of Miterdale.

Keskadale is the last house on the Buttermere road out of Newlands, and is identifiable by a sharp 'hairpin' at this point.

The ridge (Route B) is distinctive enough to deserve a name — *Keskadale Edge* is suggested.

Three routes are shown. They lie closely parallel, but are quite different in character. Route A uses a drove road rising across the side of the fell, and is easy; Route B is a ridge climb, and is steep initially; Route C ascends the unfrequented side-valley of Ill Gill, and is rough.
If returning to Keskadale, save Route B for descent so as to enjoy an uninterrupted view over Newlands directly ahead.

Knott Rigg 5

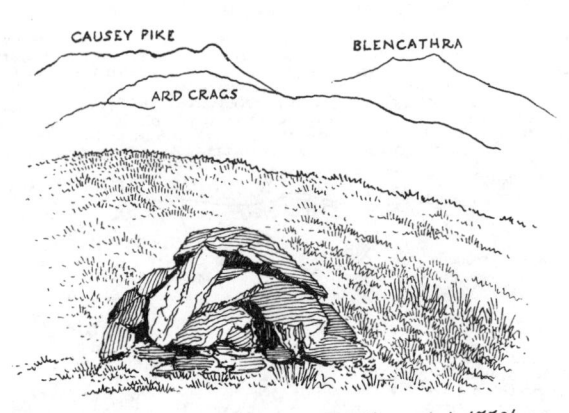

THE SUMMET

The summit, a grassy mound, is not the point 1772' as maps appear to suggest. It lies 400 yards beyond, across a marsh, and overlooking the valley of Sail Beck.

DESCENTS:
The simplest way off the fell is south to Newlands Hause, and the finest is via Keskadale Edge, but between these routes (assuming they cannot be located in mist) there should not be any trouble in going straight down to the road at the base of the fell. Sail Beck is rougher to approach and saves nothing.

Considering that it is clearly in view to travellers along the Buttermere road and conveniently near, the side valley of Ill Gill is rarely entered. It has many charming features beyond its rather hostile portals and is worth a visit as far as a waterslide a quarter-mile in.

Keskadale Edge and Ill Gill

Knott Rigg 6

THE VIEW

Knott Rigg is so tightly sandwiched between the impending masses of Robinson and the Eel Crag range that an extensive view is not to be expected. The distant scene is not completely restricted, however, and eastwards there is a glorious outlook across the valley of Newlands to the lofty skyline of Helvellyn and the Dodds.

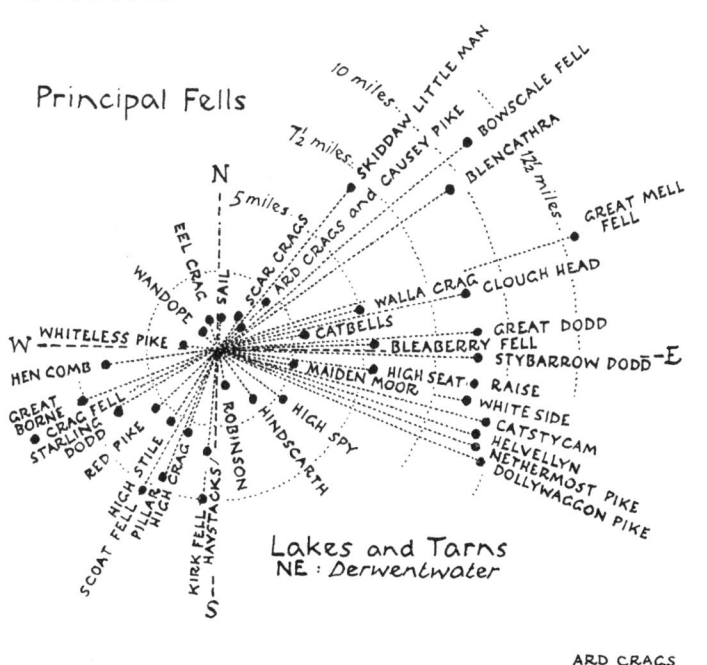

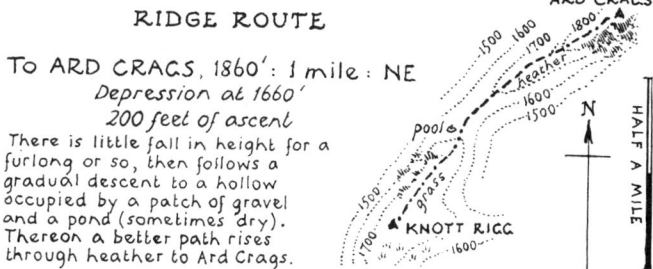

Principal Fells

(panorama diagram, clockwise from N)

- 10 miles: SKIDDAW LITTLE MAN
- 7½ miles: SKIDDAW and CAUSEY PIKE
- BOWSCALE FELL
- 3RD CRAGS
- BLENCATHRA
- 12½ miles: GREAT MELL FELL
- 5 miles: SCAR CRAGS
- N
- SAIL
- EEL CRAG
- WANDOPE
- WALLA CRAG
- CLOUGH HEAD
- CATBELLS
- GREAT DODD
- W — WHITELESS PIKE — BLEABERRY FELL — STYBARROW DODD — E
- HEN COMB
- MAIDEN MOOR
- HIGH SEAT
- RAISE
- GREAT BORNE
- WHITE SIDE
- CRAG FELL
- STARLING DODD
- CATSTYCAM
- RED PIKE
- HELVELLYN
- HIGH SPY
- NETHERMOST PIKE
- HIGH STILE
- ROBINSON
- DOLLYWAGGON PIKE
- HIGH CRAG
- HINDSCARTH
- PILLAR
- KIRK FELL
- SCOAT FELL
- HAYSTACKS
- S

Lakes and Tarns
NE: Derwentwater

RIDGE ROUTE

To ARD CRAGS, 1860′ : 1 mile : NE
Depression at 1660′
200 feet of ascent

There is little fall in height for a furlong or so, then follows a gradual descent to a hollow occupied by a patch of gravel and a pond (sometimes dry). Thereon a better path rises through heather to Ard Crags.

Ling Fell

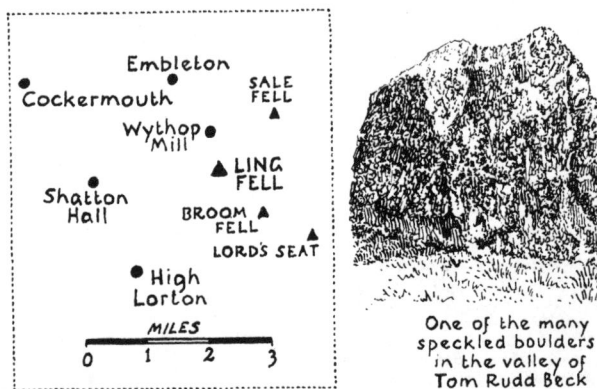

1224'

from Sale Fell

One of the many speckled boulders in the valley of Tom Rudd Beck

Ling Fell 2

NATURAL FEATURES

Ling Fell is an isolated rounded hill on the northwest perimeter of Lakeland, its unattractive appearance on all sides being accentuated by a dark covering of heather that makes it look gloomy and sulky even on the sunniest of days. Its lack of visual appeal, however, is somewhat misleading and belies its nature, for the easy slopes and commodious top are extremely pleasant to wander upon, heather, bracken, incipient gorse and grass alternating underfoot in colourful patches but never so densely as to impede progress.

The fell is one of the portals of the quiet Wythop dale, which lies alongside and behind, hidden and unsuspected, but is overshadowed by the higher western ridge of Kirk Fell coming down from Lord's Seat. In spite of its inferior height the Ordnance Survey have recognised its worth as a triangulation station and erected a stone column on the summit. This is almost the only feature of note, although the attention of geologists may be directed to a scattering of handsome white stones on the steeper southwest flank overlooking the little valley of Tom Rudd Beck, which has the function of draining the morass of Wythop Moss, a job it performs ineffectively. An insignificant spring on this side rejoices in the name of Bladder Keld — which is more than it deserves.

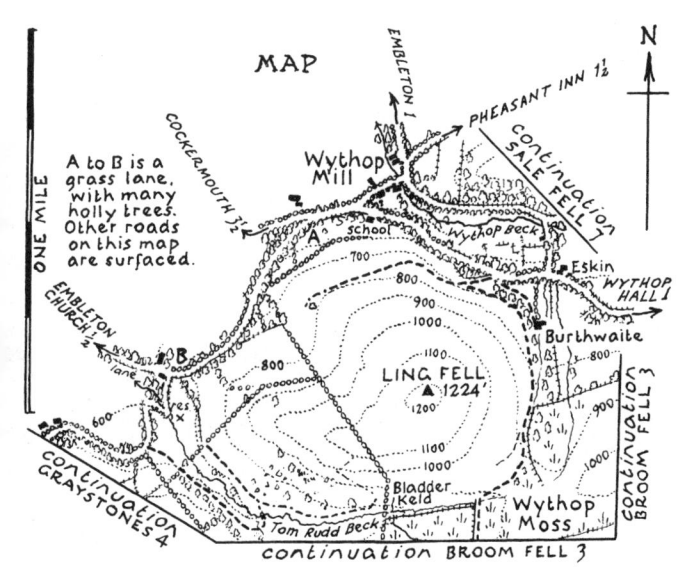

Ling Fell 3

ASCENT FROM WYTHOP MILL
850 feet of ascent : 1½ miles

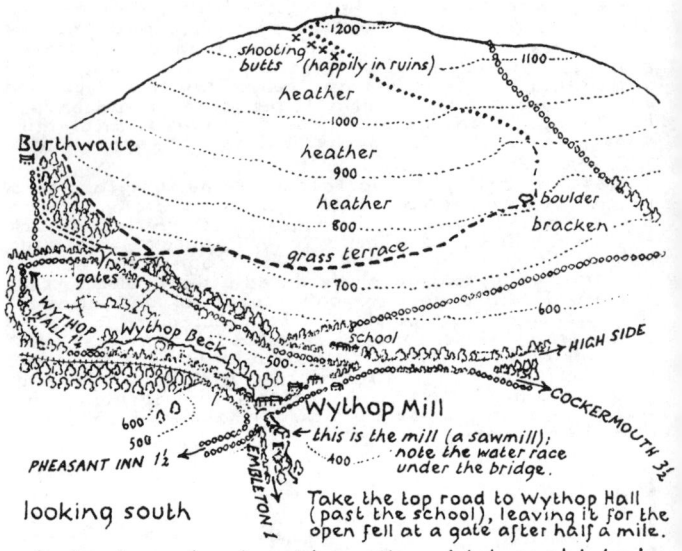

looking south

shooting butts (happily in ruins)
heather
heather
heather
boulder
bracken
grass terrace
Burthwaite
gates
Wythop Beck
WYTHOP MILL
school
HIGH SIDE
COCKERMOUTH 3½
PHEASANT INN 1½
EMBLETON 1
Wythop Mill — this is the mill (a sawmill); note the water race under the bridge.

Take the top road to Wythop Hall (past the school), leaving it for the open fell at a gate after half a mile.

A simple and enjoyable walk, which ought to be, but isn't, a popular ramble for Cockermouth folk.

THE SUMMIT

SKIDDAW SKIDDAW LITTLE MAN
ULLOCK PIKE LONG SIDE CARL SIDE
DODD

Cockermouth folk haven't even marked their infrequent visits to the summit by building a cairn; but the Ordnance surveyors obviously have a greater regard for the highest point in this sea of heather and have selected it as a trigonometrical station.

Ling Fell 4

THE VIEW

Broom Fell, rising just across Wythop Moss, severely circumscribes the view inland, but the Skiddaw group is impressive and the skyline of the Grasmoor fells is good — otherwise this is not a favourable station for viewing the hills of Lakeland and the main interest is found by looking away from it, to Criffell and the Galloway hills.

Ling Fell, however, is the best Lakeland height for seeing the town of Cockermouth.

Principal Fells

(compass diagram showing fells at various bearings and distances: BINSEY, LONGLANDS FELL, BRAE FELL, Little Sca Fell, GREAT SCA FELL, KNOTT, SALE FELL, SKIDDAW, ULLOCK PIKE, LONG SIDE, CARL SIDE, SKIDDAW LITTLE MAN, DODD, CLOUGH HEAD, LORD'S SEAT (tip only), BROOM FELL, GRISEDALE PIKE, EEL CRAG, HOPEGILL HEAD, WHITESIDE, GRAYSTONES, GRASMOOR, LOW FELL, FELLBARROW, BURNBANK FELL, BLAKE FELL, GAVEL FELL; distances marked 5 miles, 22 miles, 7½ miles, 10 miles)

Lakes and Tarns
NE: *Bassenthwaite Lake (foot of)*

RIDGE ROUTES

Ling Fell is dome-shaped, like the top of a Christmas pudding. A Christmas pudding, in its pristine state, has no ridges. Neither has Ling Fell.

looking southeast — LORD'S SEAT, BROOM FELL

Lord's Seat 1811'

from a forest road in Comb Plantation

Lord's Seat 2

NATURAL FEATURES

Some mountains have better names than they deserve and some deserve better names than they have. Lord's Seat is a fine title for any ultimate peak amongst the clouds, and while the modest Lakeland fell of this name hardly aspires to the nobility it suggests it is a pleasing recognition of the commanding position and superior height of this central point in the distinctive group of hills comprising Thornthwaite Forest, between Bassenthwaite Lake and Whinlatter Pass. It is the pivot of this upland area, having four ridges radiating from the summit that enclose streams flowing north, south, east and west — all of which join later in the Derwent. Within the last forty years the fell has been given a dark overcoat of timber by the Forestry Commission, an operation that has detracted from its native appearance, but added to its interest. Once a fashionable climb, Lord's Seat is now out of favour — yet the heathery top is a pleasant lunching-place no less than of yore, retaining the indefinable charm of Lakeland in spite of the advancing march of the Norwegian and American spruces in all directions.

Two elevations on the descending ridges, Barf and Seat How, overlook the Vale of Keswick and are excellent viewpoints.

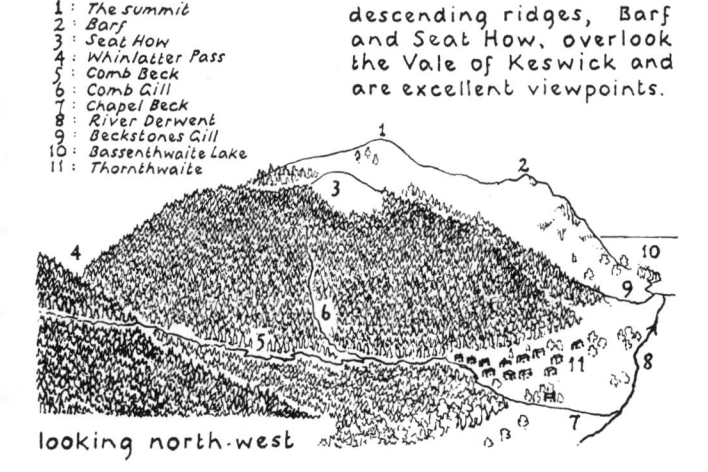

1 : The summit
2 : Barf
3 : Seat How
4 : Whinlatter Pass
5 : Comb Beck
6 : Comb Gill
7 : Chapel Beck
8 : River Derwent
9 : Beckstones Gill
10 : Bassenthwaite Lake
11 : Thornthwaite

looking north-west

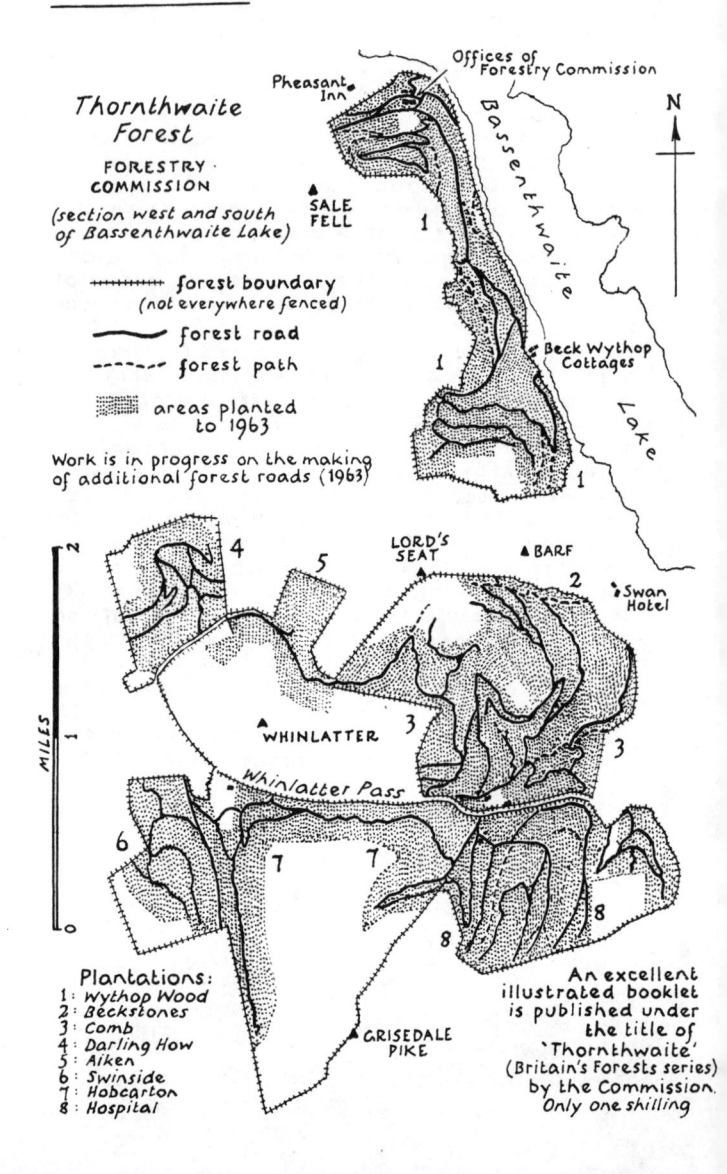

Lord's Seat 3

Thornthwaite Forest
FORESTRY COMMISSION
(section west and south of Bassenthwaite Lake)

++++++++ forest boundary
(not everywhere fenced)

──── forest road

------ forest path

▓▓▓▓ areas planted to 1963

Work is in progress on the making of additional forest roads (1963)

Pheasant Inn
Offices of Forestry Commission
▲ SALE FELL
Bassenthwaite Lake
Beck Wythop Cottages

1: Wythop Wood

▲ LORD'S SEAT
▲ BARF
Swan Hotel
▲ WHINLATTER
Whinlatter Pass
▲ GRISEDALE PIKE

Plantations:
1: Wythop Wood
2: Beckstones
3: Comb
4: Darling How
5: Aiken
6: Swinside
7: Hobcarton
8: Hospital

An excellent illustrated booklet is published under the title of 'Thornthwaite' (Britain's Forests series) by the Commission. Only one shilling

Lord's Seat 4

Thornthwaite Forest

Lord's Seat cannot be ascended from any direction without an increasing awareness of the vast areas of this and neighbouring fells now under timber as a result of the operations of the Forestry Commission. Lord's Seat is the geographical centre of their activities south of Bassenthwaite Lake; on all sides there are plantations. Except for the slopes of Barf the full length of this side of the lake is now afforested, the old-established Wythop Wood being adopted and extended to a new forest fence along the top of the declivity, and further south the Beckstones and Comb Plantations cover the flanks of Lord's Seat, while round to the west the new Darling How and Aiken Plantations are creeping up to the skyline. Over Whinlatter Pass the Hobcarton and Hospital Plantations are firmly entrenched on the northern slopes of Grisedale Pike, and Swinside Plantation clothes the foothills of Hopegill Head. It is interesting to note that the tops of both Lord's Seat and Grisedale Pike are reached by the forest boundary, but not yet planted. All this wealth of timber is, for administrative purposes, known as Thornthwaite Forest, the name including also Dodd Wood across Bassenthwaite Lake and plantations nearer Cockermouth.

The newer plantings are coniferous, spruce predominating, and dense on the ground to promote upright growth. Approach to all parts of the forest, and removal of the timber harvest, is facilitated by a well-planned network of forest roads. The roads generally have a good dry surface and are excellent to walk upon, but one's sense of direction is soon at fault in these dark cuttings, which 'hairpin' and spiral considerably to gain height. This maze has largely come into being since the last revision of the Ordnance maps, but the author's map on the opposite page, compiled after a score of expeditions in the forest (without meeting a soul) corrects this deficiency and is complete to the end of 1961. Road extensions and new links are made from time to time as required.

A forest road — Comb Plantation

There is no objection to the public use of the forest roads (on foot) but (a) the gloom of the plantations, (b) the silence, (c) lack of views, and (d) the close confinement between evergreens, are more than many people can stand. The roads are occasionally, but rarely, useful in ascents of the fells, but, however, the forest has the advantage of being cool on hot days and sheltered on cold days and may then provide good walking when conditions on the open fells may not be tolerable. The forest should be avoided, especially the older parts, in high winds, when the veterans creak and sway alarmingly, and in gales, when dozens come toppling to earth — a circumstance in which the danger lies not in being knocked down and squashed by a trunk but in being pinned to the ground by a tangle of branches. Another *don't* is to wander off the roads, into the forest, where ghastly privations in dense jungle can be suffered before emerging (if at all) in rags. And *don't don't for heavens' sake start fires*, or there'll be hell to pay.

Lord's Seat 5

MAP

Thornthwaite Mine

An area of some acres of sterile, spoil-covered ground between the road and the railway north of the village of Thornthwaite is almost all that remains to be seen of the once-valuable and extensive Thornthwaite Mine. The head of the engine-shaft, which went down about 500 feet, well below sea-level, and served several long galleries at different depths, is amongst trees by the roadside further north. Other shafts and adits at higher points on the side of the fell have been engulfed by the Beckstones and Comb Plantations. The workings were far-reaching, following the line of mineral veins up to Seat How and beyond, and they were in use, with few interruptions, for hundreds of years until the early decades of the present century. A variety of ores was extracted but the mine was usually referred to as a lead mine.

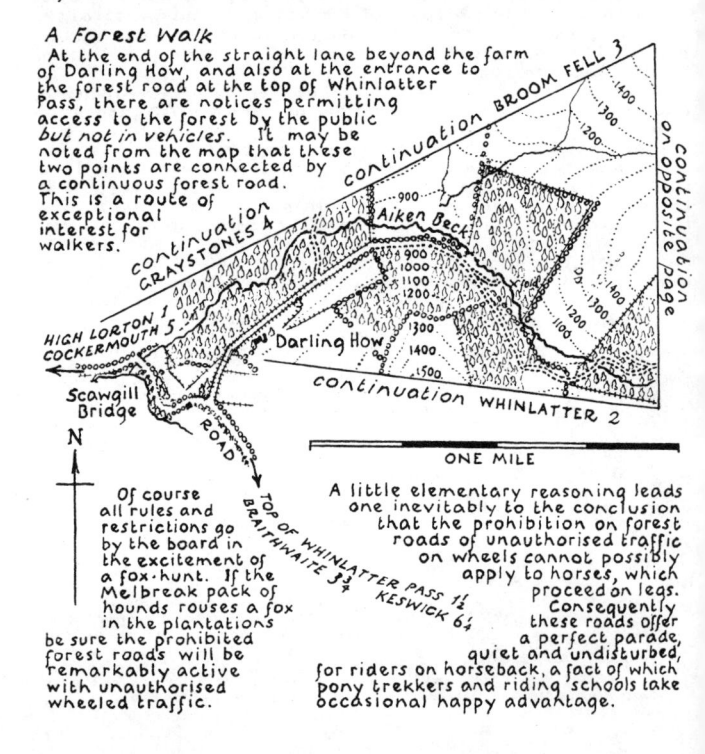

A Forest Walk

At the end of the straight lane beyond the farm of Darling How, and also at the entrance to the forest road at the top of Whinlatter Pass, there are notices permitting access to the forest by the public *but not in vehicles*. It may be noted from the map that these two points are connected by a continuous forest road. This is a route of exceptional interest for walkers.

Of course all rules and restrictions go by the board in the excitement of a fox-hunt. If the Melbreak pack of hounds rouses a fox in the plantations be sure the prohibited forest roads will be remarkably active with unauthorised wheeled traffic.

A little elementary reasoning leads one inevitably to the conclusion that the prohibition on forest roads of unauthorised traffic on wheels cannot possibly apply to horses, which proceed on legs. Consequently these roads offer a perfect parade, quiet and undisturbed, for riders on horseback, a fact of which pony trekkers and riding schools take occasional happy advantage.

Lord's Seat 6

MAP

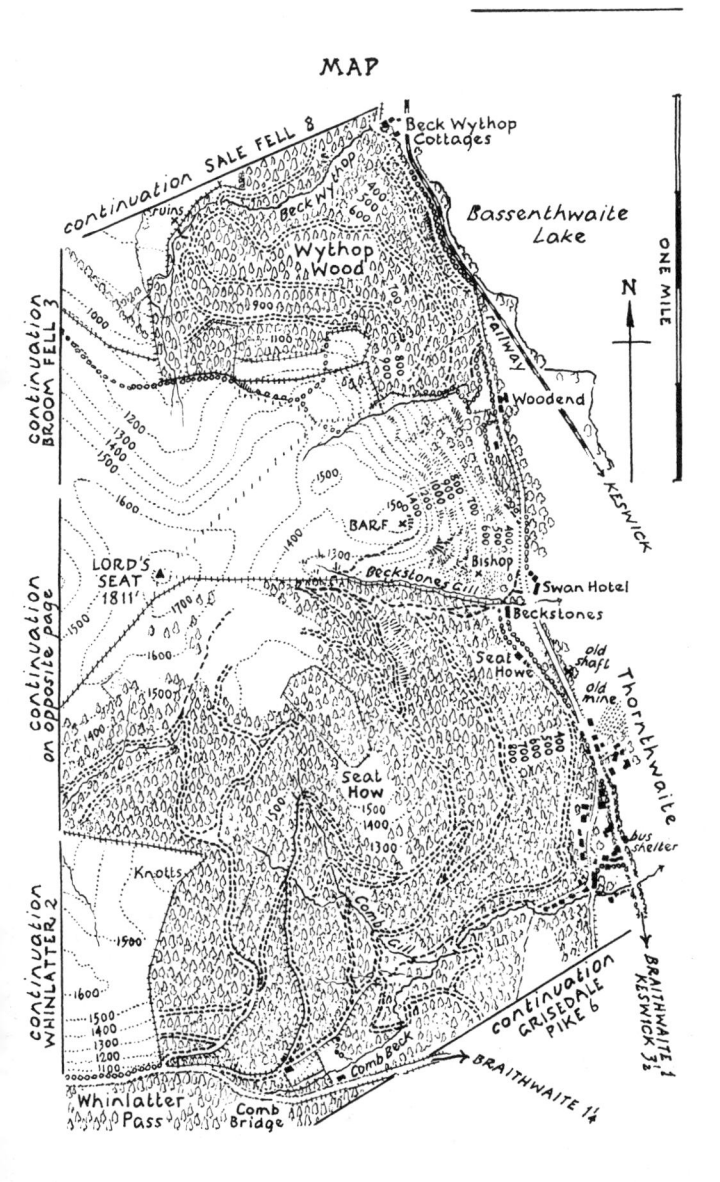

Lord's Seat 7

ASCENT FROM THORNTHWAITE
1550 feet of ascent : 2½ miles

The public footpath climbing through Beckstones Plantation is of long standing, though not now used as much as in years gone by, when the combined ascent of Lord's Seat and Barf was one of the fashionable tours. The path can still be followed, and is no less pleasant, but it has suffered some disturbance by the cutting of forest roads, two of which now terminate exactly on the line of the path. Although the fence indicates a possible route in the later (pathless) section of the climb, trees and thick heather on one side and a swamp on the other make it desirable to use one or other of the forest roads (it doesn't matter which) to gain another that doubles back at a higher level above the trees with the summit of Lord's Seat directly ahead across a rising slope of heather (rough going).

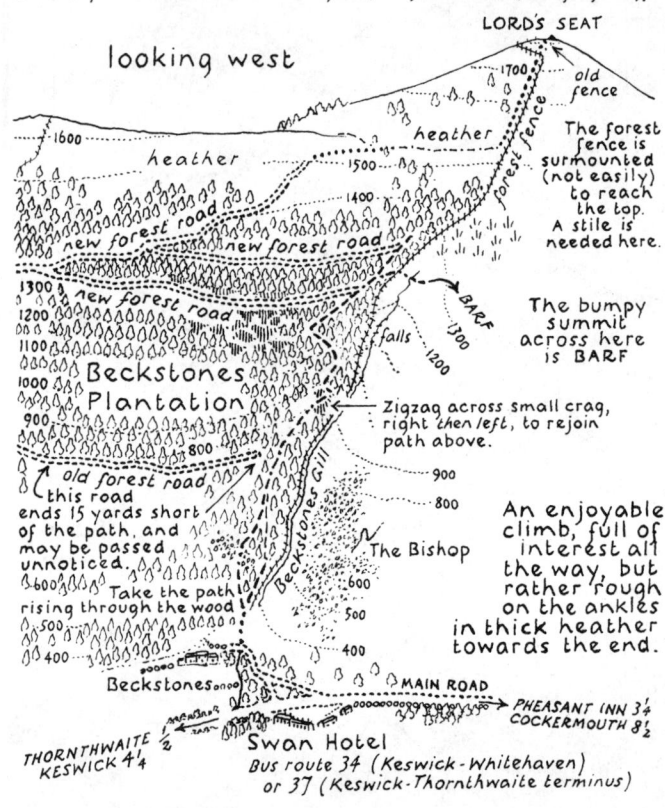

looking west

LORD'S SEAT

old fence

heather

heather

forest fence

The forest fence is surmounted (not easily) to reach the top. A stile is needed here.

new forest road

new forest road

BARF

falls

new forest road

The bumpy summit across here is BARF

Beckstones Plantation

Zigzag across small crag, right *then* left, to rejoin path above.

old forest road
this road ends 15 yards short of the path, and may be passed unnoticed.

Beckstones Gill

The Bishop

An enjoyable climb, full of interest all the way, but rather rough on the ankles in thick heather towards the end.

Take the path rising through the wood!

Beckstones — MAIN ROAD → PHEASANT INN 3¼
COCKERMOUTH 8½

THORNTHWAITE ½
KESWICK 4¼

Swan Hotel
Bus route 34 (Keswick-Whitehaven)
or 37 (Keswick-Thornthwaite terminus)

Lord's Seat 8

ASCENT FROM HIGH LORTON
1550 feet of ascent : 4 miles

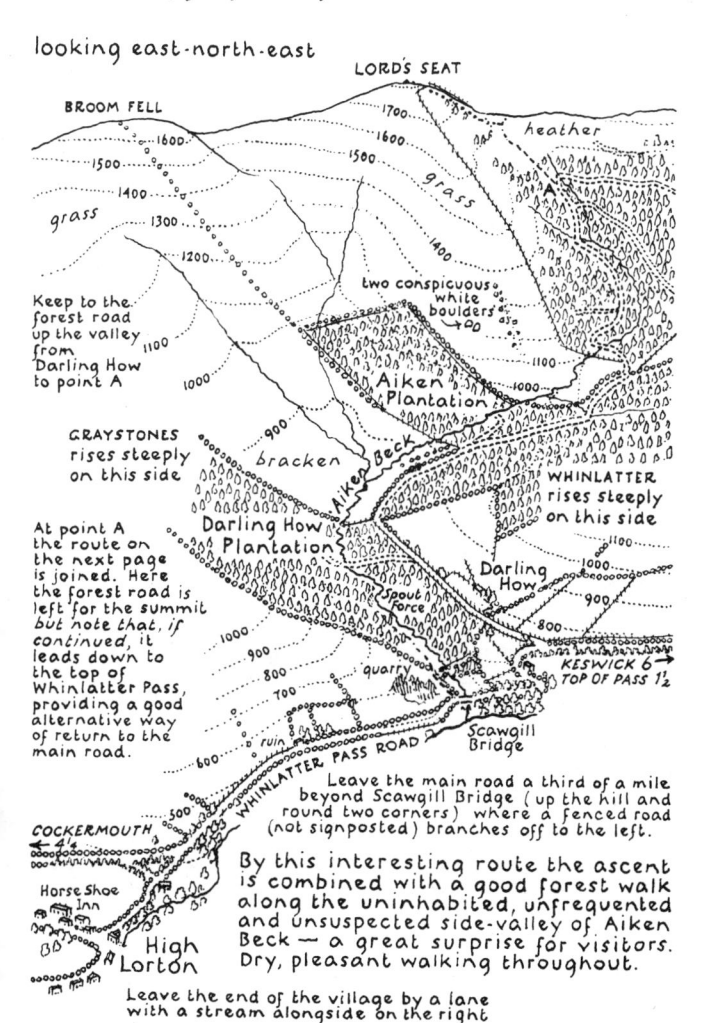

looking east-north-east

LORD'S SEAT
BROOM FELL
heather
grass
two conspicuous white boulders
Aiken Plantation
Keep to the forest road up the valley from Darling How to point A

GRAYSTONES rises steeply on this side

bracken
Aiken Beck
WHINLATTER rises steeply on this side

Darling How Plantation
Darling How

At point A the route on the next page is joined. Here the forest road is left for the summit but note that, if continued, it leads down to the top of Whinlatter Pass, providing a good alternative way of return to the main road.

Spout Force
quarry
KESWICK 6
TOP OF PASS 1½

ruin
WHINLATTER PASS ROAD
Scawgill Bridge

COCKERMOUTH 4¼

Horse Shoe Inn

High Lorton

Leave the main road a third of a mile beyond Scawgill Bridge (up the hill and round two corners) where a fenced road (not signposted) branches off to the left.

By this interesting route the ascent is combined with a good forest walk along the uninhabited, unfrequented and unsuspected side-valley of Aiken Beck — a great surprise for visitors. Dry, pleasant walking throughout.

Leave the end of the village by a lane with a stream alongside on the right

Lord's Seat 9

ASCENT FROM WHINLATTER PASS
800 feet of ascent : 2 miles

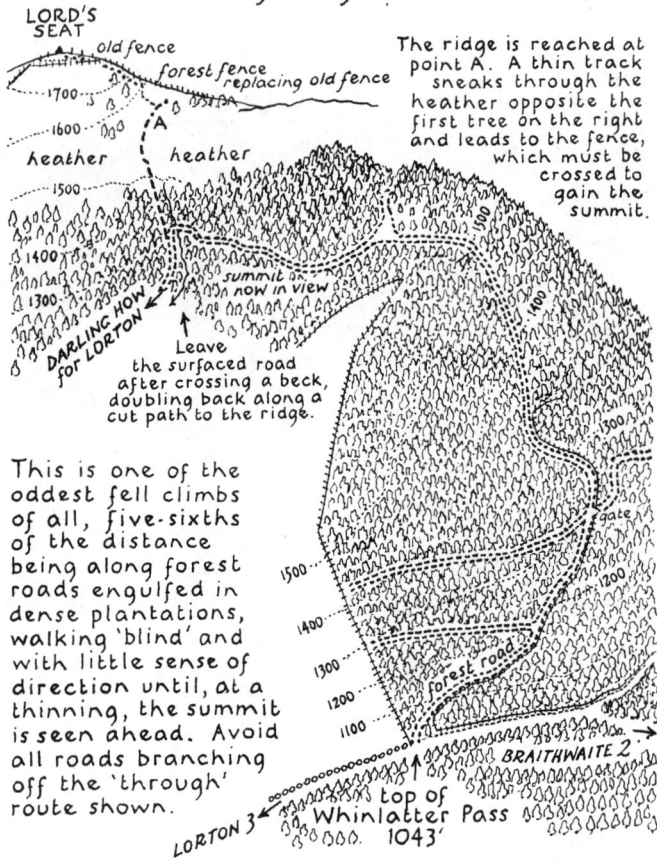

LORD'S SEAT — old fence — forest fence replacing old fence — 1700 — 1600 — A — heather — heather — 1500

The ridge is reached at point A. A thin track sneaks through the heather opposite the first tree on the right and leads to the fence, which must be crossed to gain the summit.

1400 — 1300 — DARLING HOW for LORTON — summit now in view — 1500 — 1400 — 1300 — 1200 — 1100 — gate — forest road — LORTON 3 — top of Whinlatter Pass 1043' — BRAITHWAITE 2

Leave the surfaced road after crossing a beck, doubling back along a cut path to the ridge.

This is one of the oddest fell climbs of all, five-sixths of the distance being along forest roads engulfed in dense plantations, walking 'blind' and with little sense of direction until, at a thinning, the summit is seen ahead. Avoid all roads branching off the 'through' route shown.

A delightfully easy ascent — but silent gloomy forests aren't everybody's cup of tea!

looking nor'nor'east

Two forest roads (both with notice boards) leave the level top of the Pass. Be sure to start along the right one (i.e. the *left* on the diagram), just where the fence between the plantation and the open fell comes down to the main road.

… Lord's Seat 10

THE SUMMIT

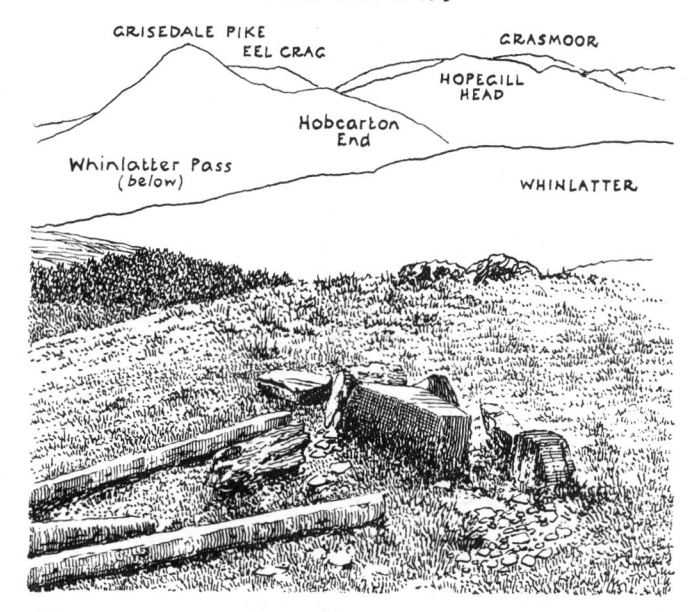

GRISEDALE PIKE
EEL CRAG
GRASMOOR
HOPEGILL HEAD
Hobcarton End
Whinlatter Pass (below)
WHINLATTER

The summit is bare and open to the sky, refreshingly so if the ascent has been made through the plantations.   There are a few stones and the scattered remains of three fences that formerly met on the highest point but which have been superseded by a new forest fence, which, out of deference for the freedom of the summit, crosses the top of the fell a hundred yards distant.

It is said that the name of the fell derives from a natural rock seat just below the top on the north-west side — but anyone who spends time trying to identify the place will question the legend, for not even the commonest commoner could instal himself in any of the few rocky recesses hereabouts with the standard of comfort his lordship would surely have demanded.

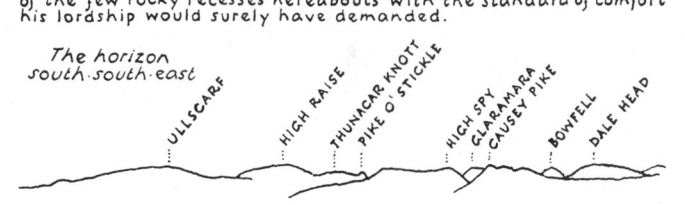

The horizon south-south-east

ULLSCARF
HIGH RAISE
THUNACAR KNOTT
PIKE O' STICKLE
HIGH SPY
GLARAMARA
CAUSEY PIKE
BOWFELL
DALE HEAD

Lord's Seat 11

THE VIEW

The pleasantest scene is eastward, where there is a view down to the Vale of Keswick and beyond, in the distance, the far Pennines, with Cross Fell appearing on the skyline between Blencathra and Great Mell Fell. Southeast is the long line of the Helvellyn range; the little green oasis and white farmhouse seen in this direction is Askness Farm. But note especially the nearby Wythop valley, north-west, rising as a green shelf and then plunging suddenly down a wooded declivity to Bassenthwaite Lake: an unusual geographical arrangement; above and beyond is an excellent view of the Solway Firth and Criffell. The Grasmoor fells conceal many of the central heights, which are revealed only in unfamiliar fragments above the skyline of Scar Crags.

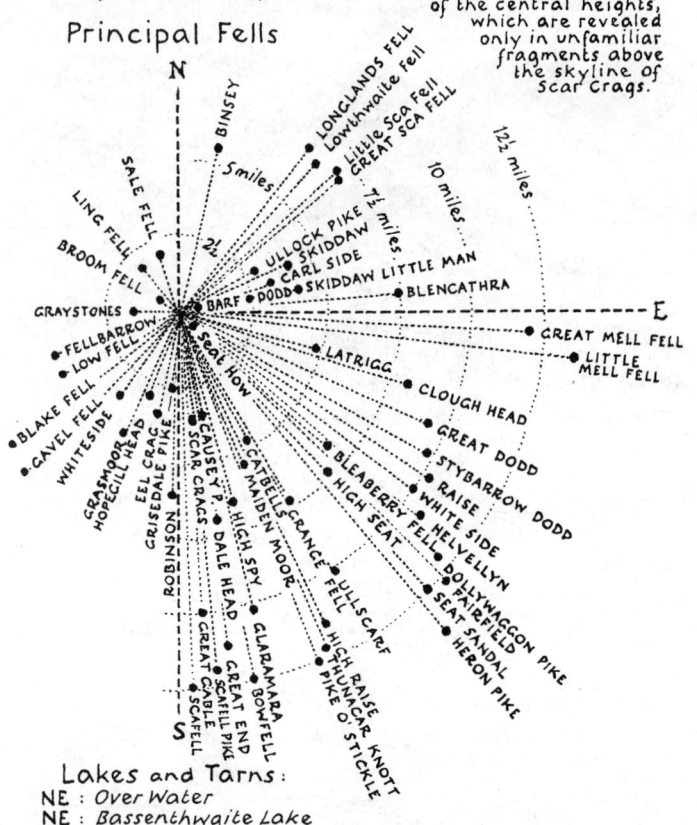

Principal Fells

[compass diagram of fells omitted]

Lakes and Tarns:
NE : Over Water
NE : Bassenthwaite Lake
Derwentwater is in view SE from 100 yards down the north-east ridge

Lord's Seat 12

RIDGE ROUTES

To BROOM FELL, 1670': 7/8 mile : NW
Depression at 1586': 120 feet of ascent
Easy, uninteresting walking on a wide ridge

There is no path. Go down north-west from Lord's Seat to the obvious connecting ridge, which is marshy in patches, wide, and gently undulating for half a mile, without any definite col, before rising to the flat top of Broom Fell, where a wall identifies the highest point. *In mist*, there may be indecision as to route but there is no danger in straying from the course.

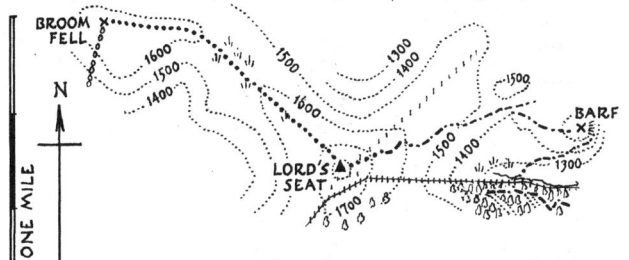

To BARF, 1536': 3/4 mile : ENE, then E
Depression at 1400': 150 feet of ascent
Rough walking; best left alone in mist

Patches of thick heather impede progress, but sections of an intermittent track may be found by following the line indicated. Note that the far side of Barf's summit is craggy, and leave it by a path on the south flank.

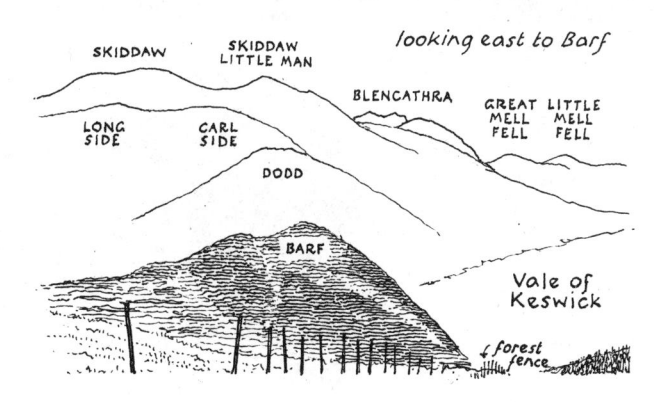

looking east to Barf

Maiden Moor 1887'

from Rigg Beck

- Stair
- ▲ CATBELLS
- Little Town
- ▲ MAIDEN MOOR
- Grange
- ▲ HIGH SPY
- Rosthwaite

MILES
0 1 2 3

from Scope End

Maiden Moor 2

NATURAL FEATURES

From mid-Newlands, Maiden Moor is seen to rise in three tiers: the lowest, rock-crowned, behind the hamlet of Little Town; the second, also craggy, above but some distance back; and finally the summit, set at the edge of a steep fall to the upper reaches of the valley. To the left of these successive steps is the wide hollow of Yewthwaite Combe, formerly a scene of mining activity but now a quiet sheep-pasture, below the slow decline of the summit-slope eastwards across a tilted plateau.

On the opposite side of the fell is the parallel valley of Borrowdale, to which Maiden Moor presents a steep slope of undistinguished appearance and a high level skyline, this being not the ridge but the plateau edge, the summit itself being out of sight.

Maiden Moor is the middle section of a very popular fellwalk, starting with Catbells and ending at Honister, along the spine of the ridge forming the Newlands and Borrowdale watershed. Both flanks are scarped — that facing Newlands almost continuously — so that, while the walk along the top is simple and pleasant, on grass, direct access from either valley is possible only in a few places without encountering rock.

The streams are small and insignificant; they drain into the River Derwent to the east and Newlands Beck to the west, joining, however, in the flat country before Bassenthwaite Lake.

1: The summit
2: High Crags
3: Knott End
4: Yewthwaite Combe
5: Yewthwaite Mine
6: Newlands Beck
7: Yewthwaite Gill
8: High Spy
9: Slope of Catbells

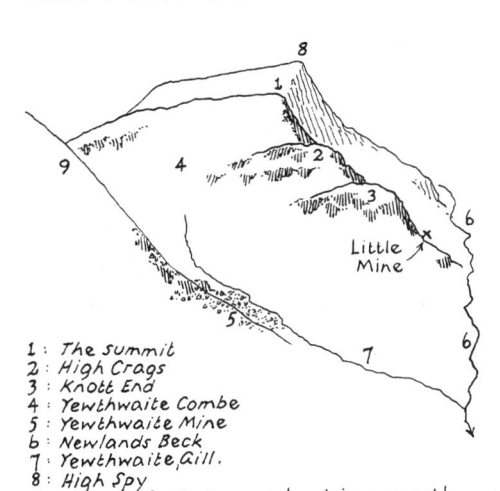

looking south

The entrance to Little Mine — one of two small mines opened on the lower slopes above Newlands, in view from the old road leading up the valley.

Maiden Moor 3

MAP

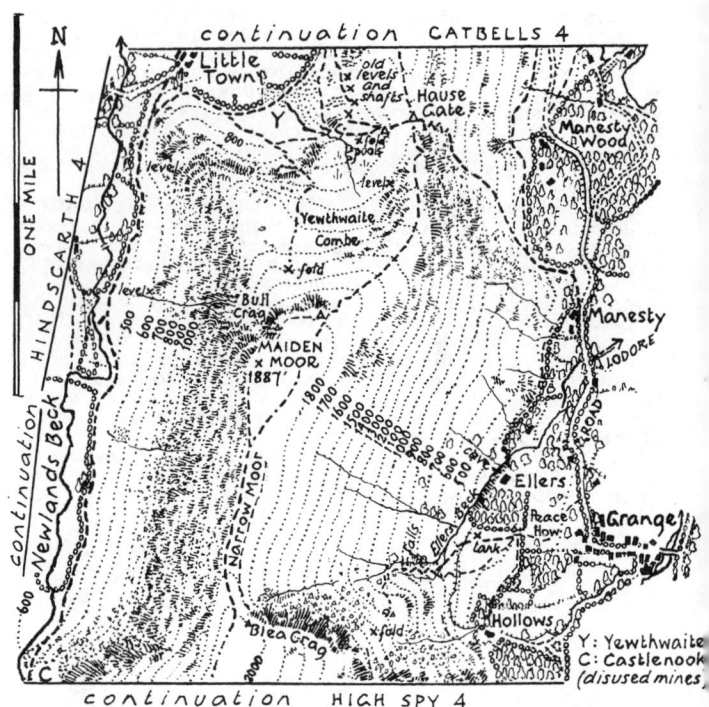

continuation CATBELLS 4

N ← ONE MILE →

continuation HINDSCARTH 4

Little Town
old levels and shafts
House Gate
Manesty Wood
Yewthwaite Combe
x fold
Bull Crag
MAIDEN x MOOR 1887
Manesty
LODORE
Narrow Moor
Ellers
Peace How
tank
Grange
Blea Crag
x fold
Hollows

Y: Yewthwaite
C: Castlenook
(disused mines)

continuation Newlands Beck

continuation HIGH SPY 4

In the vicinity of Ellers.......

Peace How

Ellers Beck flows alongside the grounds of Ellers, a natural boundary being provided by a long wall of rock bordering the stream. In this rockface is an attractive cave, directly behind the house of Ellers — evidence of old mining activity, as is a cutting in the nearby fellside

Bedecked with rhododendrons and watered by a sweet stream, this is Lakeland's most exotic cave.

Maiden Moor 4

ASCENTS FROM GRANGE
via MANESTY
1600 feet of ascent
2½ miles

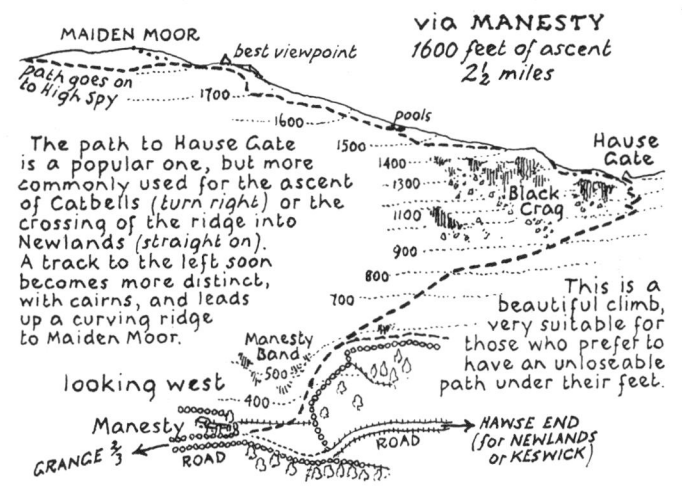

MAIDEN MOOR — best viewpoint
path goes on to High Spy
1700, 1600, pools, 1500, 1400, 1300, 1100, 900, 800, 700
Hause Gate
Black Crag

The path to Hause Gate is a popular one, but more commonly used for the ascent of Catbells (turn right) or the crossing of the ridge into Newlands (straight on). A track to the left soon becomes more distinct, with cairns, and leads up a curving ridge to Maiden Moor.

Manesty Band 500, 400

This is a beautiful climb, very suitable for those who prefer to have an unloseable path under their feet.

looking west

Manesty
GRANGE ⅔ ← ROAD — ROAD → HAWSE END (for NEWLANDS or KESWICK)

---

via PEACE HOW : 1600 feet of ascent : 2 miles

HIGH SPY — Narrow Moor — MAIDEN MOOR
Blea Crag — grass — 1800
sheep track
1600
heather
1300
Greenup
900
bracken
waterfalls
700, 600
weir 500
Ellers Beck
400 cave

There is no path above the falls. The final heathery slope is very much longer than it appears to be from below

For further details of this route see High Spy 6

As far as the waterfalls this walk is delightful, but then follows a tiring trudge up a steepening, uninteresting slope.

water tank × Ellers
Swanesty How
× seat Peace How
Grange school MANESTY
ROAD Hotel

looking west

Waterfalls above Ellers Beck

Maiden Moor 5

ASCENT FROM LITTLE TOWN
1250 feet of ascent: 1½ or 2 miles

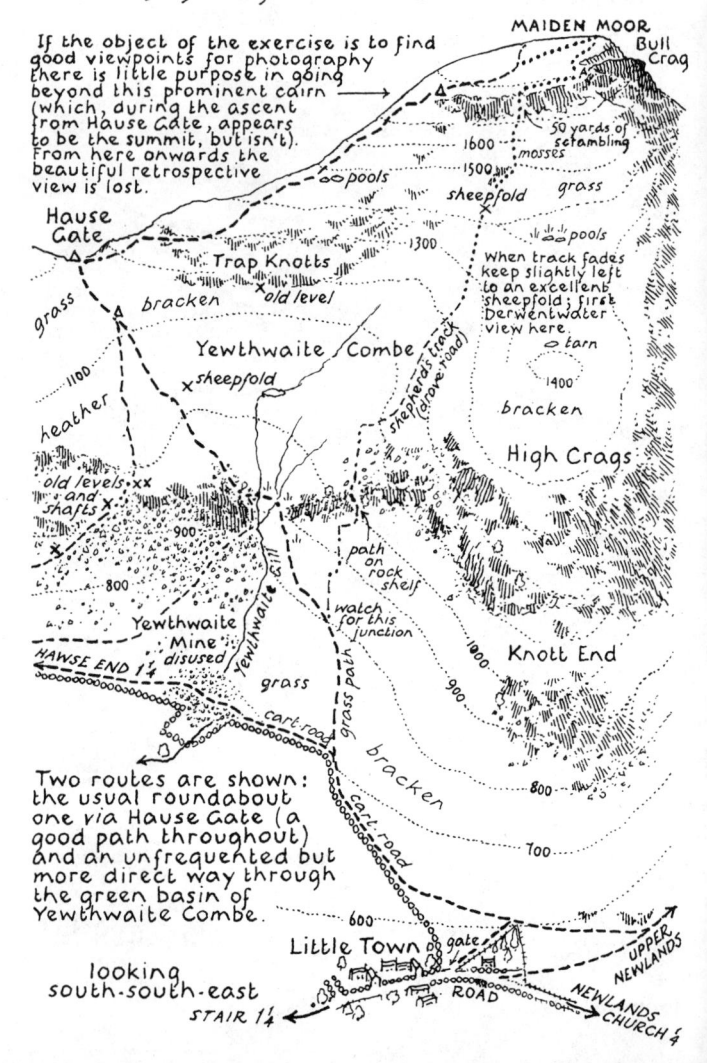

If the object of the exercise is to find good viewpoints for photography there is little purpose in going beyond this prominent cairn ⟶ (which, during the ascent from Hause Gate, appears to be the summit, but isn't). From here onwards the beautiful retrospective view is lost.

MAIDEN MOOR
Bull Crag
50 yards of scrambling mosses
grass
sheepfold

When track fades keep slightly left to an excellent sheepfold: first Derwentwater view here.

Hause Gate
Trap Knotts
old level
Yewthwaite Combe
sheepfold
shepherds track (drove road)
High Crags
tarn
bracken
heather
old levels and shafts
path on rock shelf
watch for this junction
Yewthwaite Mine disused
Yewthwaite Gill
HAWSE END 1¼
grass
cart road
grass path
bracken
Knott End
cart road

Two routes are shown: the usual roundabout one via Hause Gate (a good path throughout) and an unfrequented but more direct way through the green basin of Yewthwaite Combe.

Little Town — gate
looking south-south-east
STAIR ¼ ← ROAD → NEWLANDS CHURCH ¼
UPPER NEWLANDS

Maiden Moor 6

THE SUMMIT

Short of lying down with eyes at ground level and taking a few elementary perspectives, there is no way by which a layman can determine the highest point of the fell — and although the Ordnance Survey have been on the spot with instruments and arrived at their own expert conclusions they have left no sign of their visit, and there is no cairn. The actual top could be anywhere within a twenty-yard radius. All is grassy and uninteresting here, without as much as a stone to sit on or an outcrop to recline against, but those who feel the ascent has merited a rest can take their reward on the edge of the steep drop into Newlands, just west of whatever is decided as the summit. A track follows this edge, but the main path across the moor runs some 200 yards to the east.

DESCENTS: Join the path referred to (in mist, watch for it closely: in places it is little more than a flattened trail in the grass) and follow it *left* down to Hause Gate for Newlands, *left*, or Borrowdale, *right*.

Bull Crag is bull-nosed, i.e. in profile it appears as a rounded overhang

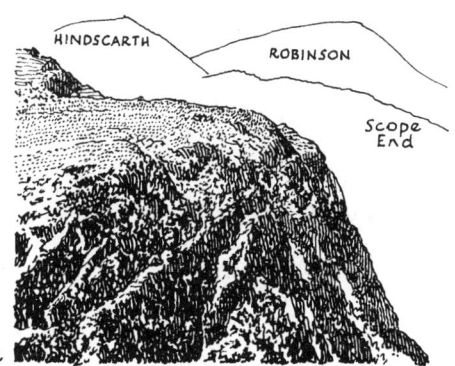

The Newlands edge from the top of Bull Crag, looking south-west

Maiden Moor 7

THE VIEW

A dreary foreground detracts from the view and unfortunately hides Derwentwater and Borrowdale. In other respects the scene is satisfactory, and especially good looking north. A cairn on the edge of the plateau where the descent to Hause Gate commences commands a much more beautiful though less extensive view.

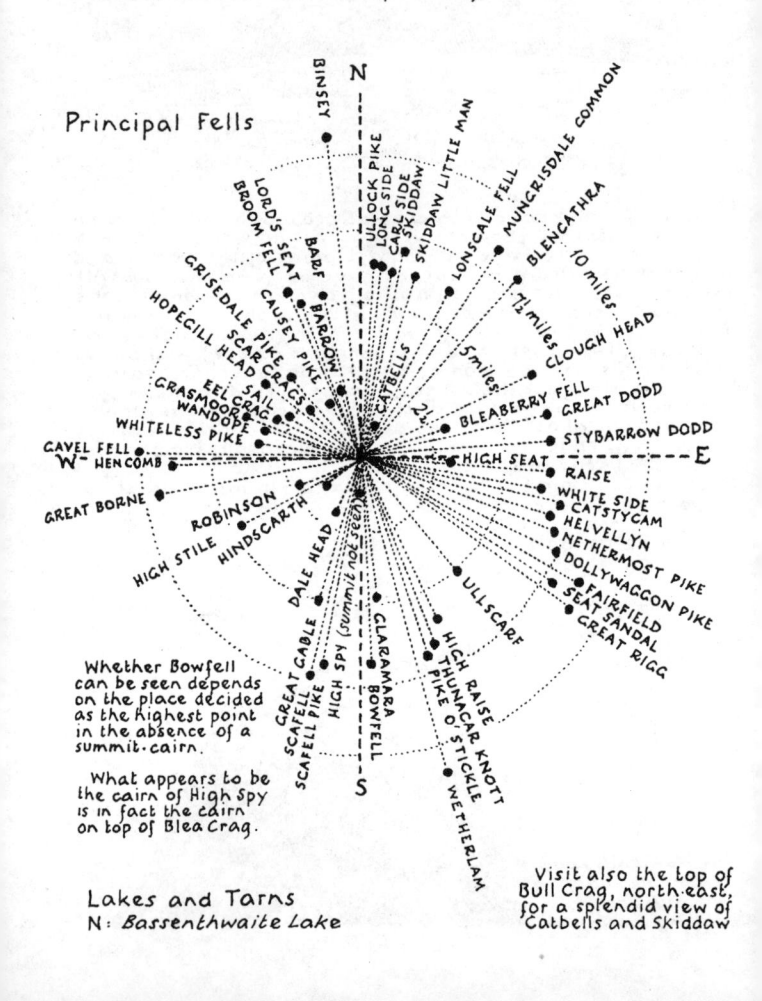

Principal Fells

(compass diagram of surrounding fells, with labels including:)

BINSEY, ULLOCK PIKE, LONG SIDE, CARL SIDE, SKIDDAW, SKIDDAW LITTLE MAN, LONSCALE FELL, MUNGRISDALE COMMON, BLENCATHRA, CLOUGH HEAD, GREAT DODD, STYBARROW DODD, BLEABERRY FELL, HIGH SEAT, RAISE, WHITE SIDE, CATSTYCAM, HELVELLYN, NETHERMOST PIKE, DOLLYWAGGON PIKE, FAIRFIELD, SEAT SANDAL, GREAT RIGG, WETHERLAM, ULLSCARF, HIGH RAISE, THUNACAR KNOTT, PIKE O' STICKLE, BOWFELL, GLARAMARA, HIGH SPY (summit not seen), SCAFELL PIKE, SCAFELL, GREAT GABLE, DALE HEAD, HINDSCARTH, HIGH STILE, ROBINSON, GREAT BORNE, CAVEL FELL, W^m HEN COMB, WHITELESS PIKE, WANDOPE, GRASMOORE, EEL CRAG, HOPEGILL HEAD, CAUSEY PIKE, SCAR CRAGS, GRISEDALE PIKE, BARROW, BARF, LORD'S SEAT, BROOM FELL, CATBELLS

(with distance rings: 2½, 5 miles, 7½ miles, 10 miles)

N — W — E — S

Whether Bowfell can be seen depends on the place decided as the highest point in the absence of a summit cairn.

What appears to be the cairn of High Spy is in fact the cairn on top of Blea Crag.

Lakes and Tarns
N: *Bassenthwaite Lake*

Visit also the top of Bull Crag, north-east, for a splendid view of Catbells and Skiddaw

Maiden Moor 8

RIDGE ROUTES

To CATBELLS, 1481': 1½ miles : N.E, then N.
Depression (Hause Gate) at 1180': 310 feet of ascent
It must be something like this in Heaven

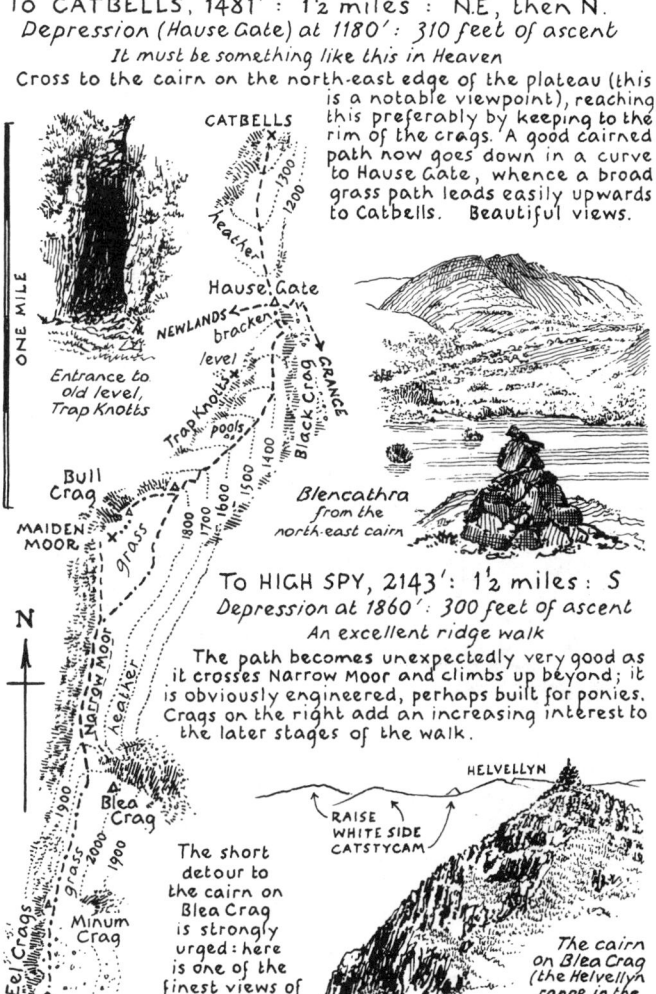

Cross to the cairn on the north-east edge of the plateau (this is a notable viewpoint), reaching this preferably by keeping to the rim of the crags. A good cairned path now goes down in a curve to Hause Gate, whence a broad grass path leads easily upwards to Catbells. Beautiful views.

Blencathra from the north-east cairn

To HIGH SPY, 2143': 1½ miles : S
Depression at 1860': 300 feet of ascent
An excellent ridge walk

The path becomes unexpectedly very good as it crosses Narrow Moor and climbs up beyond; it is obviously engineered, perhaps built for ponies. Crags on the right add an increasing interest to the later stages of the walk.

The short detour to the cairn on Blea Crag is strongly urged: here is one of the finest views of Derwentwater

The cairn on Blea Crag (the Helvellyn range in the background)

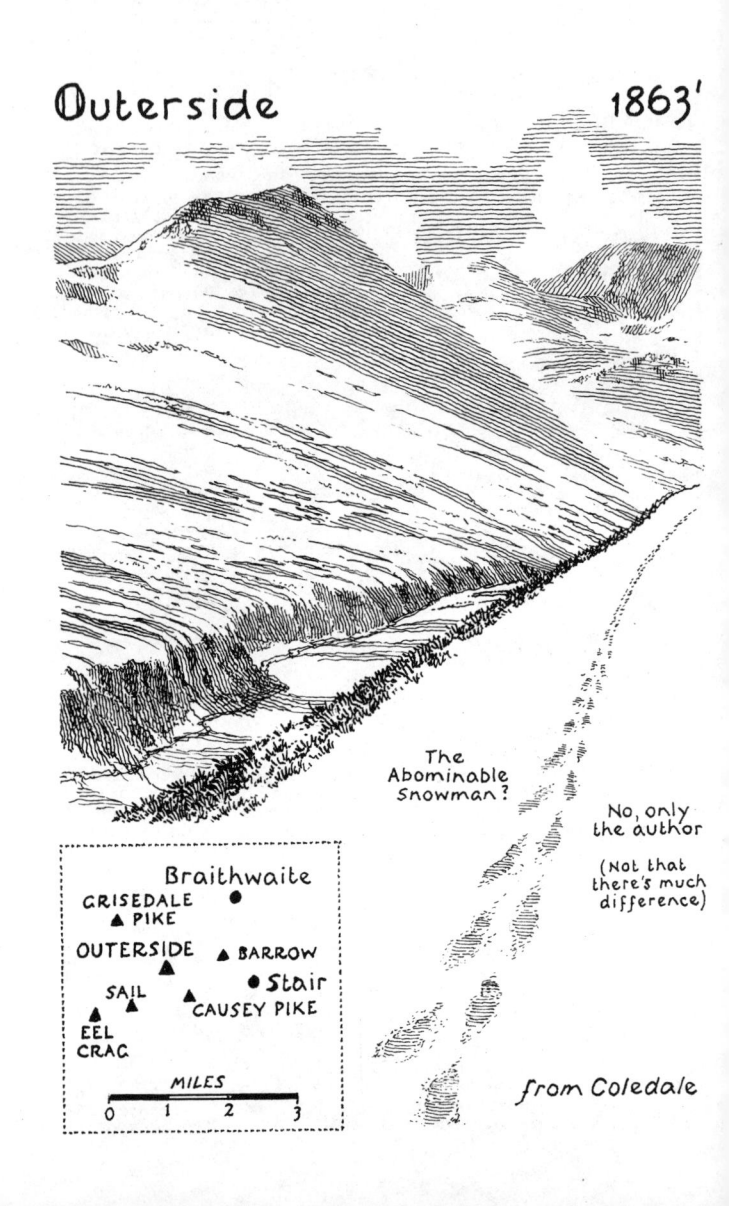

Outerside 1863'

The Abominable Snowman?

No, only the author

(Not that there's much difference)

Braithwaite
GRISEDALE PIKE
OUTERSIDE — BARROW
SAIL — Stair
EEL CRAG — CAUSEY PIKE

MILES
0 1 2 3

from Coledale

Outerside 2

NATURAL FEATURES

The valley of Coledale, coming down straight as an arrow to Braithwaite, is deeply enclosed by a continuous horseshoe rim of high summits, from Causey Pike round to Grisedale Pike, but while the latter descends uncompromisingly in a very steep and unbroken slope, the opposite ridge of Causey Pike is accompanied by a lower and parallel ridge like an inner balcony, the fall to the valley being thereby interrupted. The main eminence on this subsidiary ridge is the abrupt summit of Outerside, and its position is such that it looks *down* into the vast pit of the head of Coledale and *up* to the exciting skyline of the surrounding ring of peaks. This secondary ridge ends in Barrow, overlooking Newlands, and above a thousand feet has a rich heather cover, which gives to the upper expanses a gloomy and forbidding appearance that is belied by a close acquaintance. Between Outerside and Barrow, but out of alignment like a dog's back leg, rises the lesser height of Stile End, which, seen from the Braithwaite approach, forms a noble pyramid.

Outerside springs quite steeply from the abyss of Coledale, and in a less distinctive company it would attract much attention. As it is, visitors rarely tread its pleasant summit.

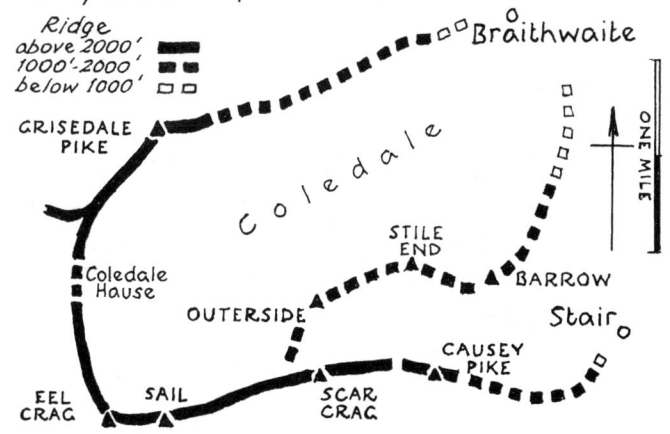

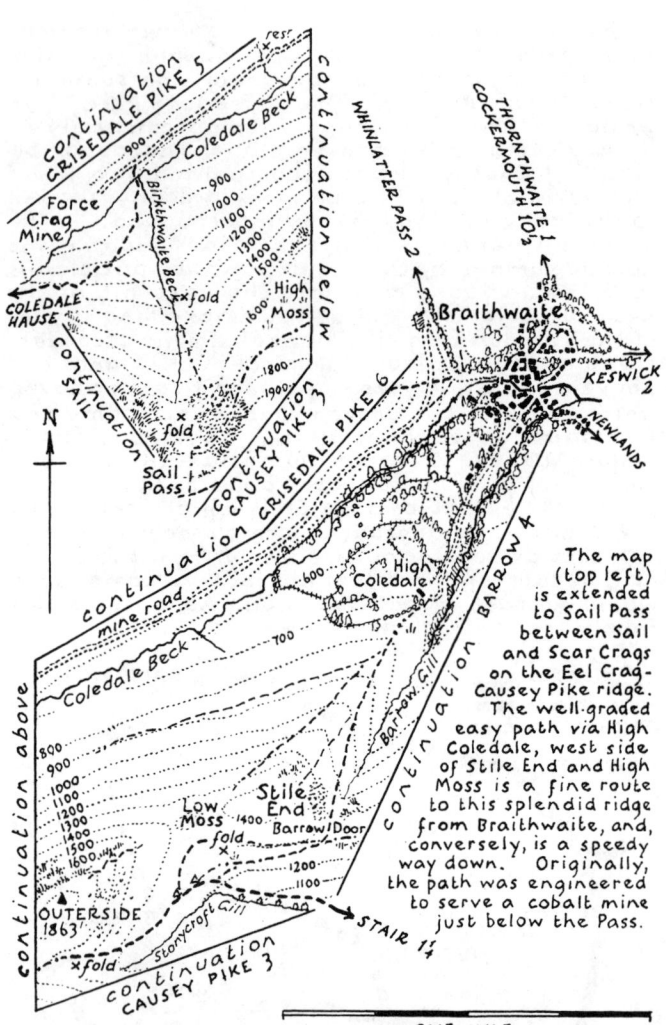

Outerside 3

MAP

The map (top left) is extended to Sail Pass between Sail and Scar Crags on the Eel Crag-Causey Pike ridge. The well-graded easy path via High Coledale, west side of Stile End and High Moss is a fine route to this splendid ridge from Braithwaite, and, conversely, is a speedy way down. Originally, the path was engineered to serve a cobalt mine just below the Pass.

ONE MILE

Outerside 4

ASCENT FROM STAIR
1550 feet of ascent : 2¼ miles

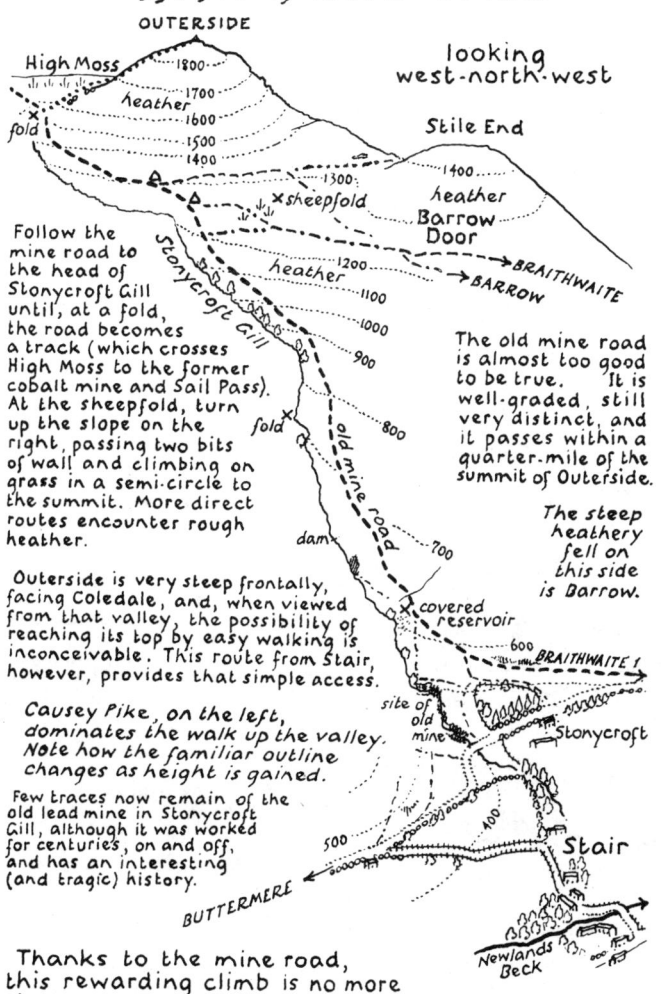

OUTERSIDE

looking west-north-west

Stile End

Barrow Door

Follow the mine road to the head of Stonycroft Gill until, at a fold, the road becomes a track (which crosses High Moss to the former cobalt mine and Sail Pass). At the sheepfold, turn up the slope on the right, passing two bits of wall and climbing on grass in a semi-circle to the summit. More direct routes encounter rough heather.

The old mine road is almost too good to be true. It is well-graded, still very distinct, and it passes within a quarter-mile of the summit of Outerside.

The steep heathery fell on this side is Barrow.

Outerside is very steep frontally, facing Coledale, and, when viewed from that valley, the possibility of reaching its top by easy walking is inconceivable. This route from Stair, however, provides that simple access.

Causey Pike, on the left, dominates the walk up the valley. Note how the familiar outline changes as height is gained.

Few traces now remain of the old lead mine in Stonycroft Gill, although it was worked for centuries, on and off, and has an interesting (and tragic) history.

Stonycroft

Stair

Newlands Beck

Thanks to the mine road, this rewarding climb is no more than a simple uphill walk for nine-tenths of the way.

Outerside 5

ASCENT FROM BRAITHWAITE
1650 feet of ascent : 2½ miles

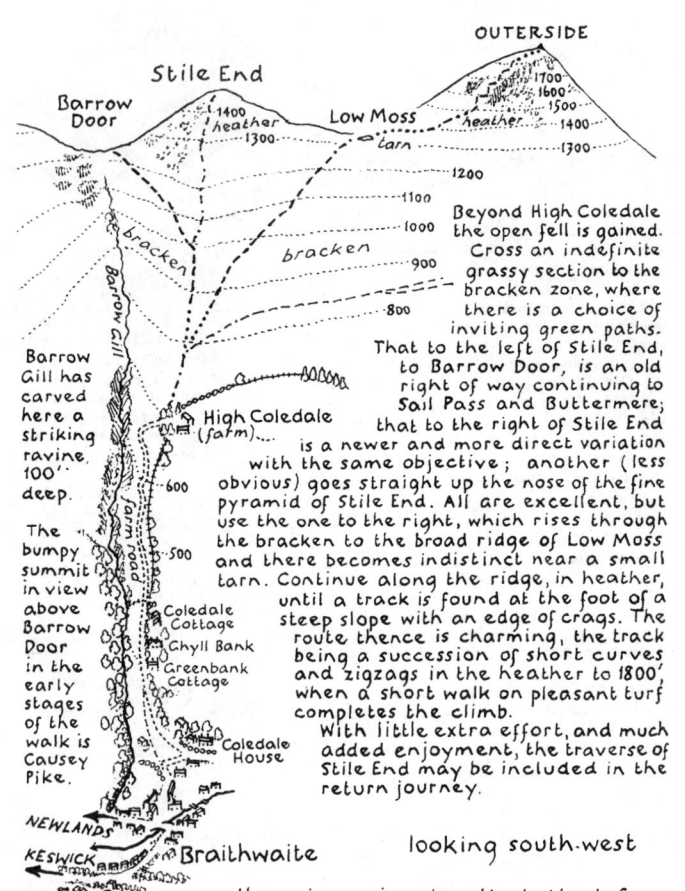

looking south-west

Beyond High Coledale the open fell is gained. Cross an indefinite grassy section to the bracken zone, where there is a choice of inviting green paths. That to the left of Stile End, to Barrow Door, is an old right of way continuing to Sail Pass and Buttermere; that to the right of Stile End is a newer and more direct variation with the same objective; another (less obvious) goes straight up the nose of the fine pyramid of Stile End. All are excellent, but use the one to the right, which rises through the bracken to the broad ridge of Low Moss and there becomes indistinct near a small tarn. Continue along the ridge, in heather, until a track is found at the foot of a steep slope with an edge of crags. The route thence is charming, the track being a succession of short curves and zigzags in the heather to 1800', when a short walk on pleasant turf completes the climb.

With little extra effort, and much added enjoyment, the traverse of Stile End may be included in the return journey.

Barrow Gill has carved here a striking ravine, 100' deep.

The bumpy summit in view above Barrow Door in the early stages of the walk is Causey Pike.

Here is a simple climb that few walkers ever bother to do; and by this omission they deny themselves a lot of pleasure and a rewarding introduction to the grand circle of hills around Coledale.

Outerside 6

THE SUMMIT

From the east the highest point is reached at the end of a gradual incline; from the west it appears abruptly at the top of a rising pavement of embedded rocks: here a few loose stones form a small cairn. The Coledale edge is close by, falling away sharply in an escarpment, and in mist this edge may be followed as a guide to a track down the eastern ridge, the only path off the top.

DESCENTS: The escarpment can be negotiated, with care, on initially steep ground if a direct way down into Coledale is desired, but there is little point in this since Coledale leads only to Braithwaite, which is more quickly and attractively reached by the eastern ridge (watch for a track in the heather) and then by a good path slanting down to the left below the rise to Stile End. For Stair, too, the eastern ridge is best, turning down to the right at the depression to join the Stonycroft mine road.

*Sail Pass (left), Sail and Eel Crag
 from Outerside*

Outerside 7

THE VIEW

Outerside is severely circumscribed by the mountains around Coledale, which maintain a consistently higher skyline, and only between north and south-east is there an open prospect. The view lacks charm, but its intimate detail of the tremendous declivities amongst which the head of Coledale is so deeply inurned — a fine mountain scene — is very impressive. Who dare tackle Grisedale Pike direct from the beck after seeing its 2000 feet of near-verticality from this viewpoint? Only the brave!

Principal Fells

N — BINSEY
LORD'S SEAT
ULLOCK PIKE
LONG SIDE
SKIDDAW
SKIDDAW LITTLE MAN
LONSCALE FELL
BLENCATHRA
LATRIGG
GREAT MELL FELL
GRISEDALE PIKE
CLOUGH HEAD
Sand Hill
HIGH RIGG
BARROW
W — WALLA CRAG — E
GREAT DODD
EEL CRAG
SAIL
SCAR CRAGS
CAUSEY PIKE
CATBELLS
BLEABERRY FELL
STYBARROW DODD
2½ miles
HIGH SEAT
RAISE
WHITE SIDE
CATSTYCAM
5 miles
HELVELLYN
NETHERMOST PIKE
7½ miles
DOLLYWAGGON PIKE
10 miles
S

Lakes and Tarns
N: Bassenthwaite Lake
E: Derwentwater

Stile End, as seen on the approach from Braithwaite, with Barrow Door on the left and Causey Pike beyond

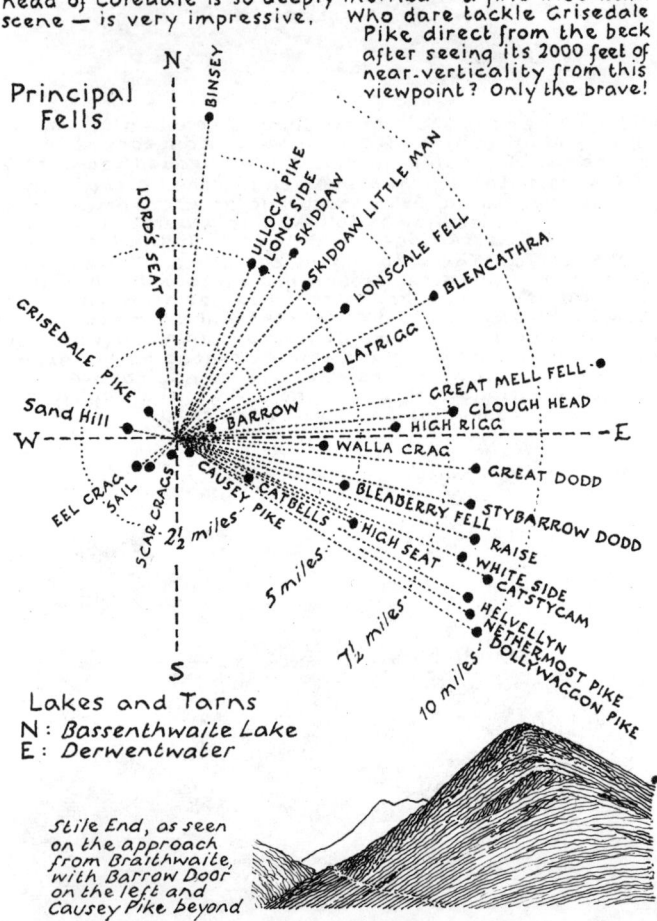

Outerside 8

RIDGE ROUTE

To BARROW, 1494': 1¼ miles : ENE, then SE and ENE
Depressions at 1380' and 1270'
400 feet of ascent
Rough walking in heather. Avoid Stile End in mist.

If the ridge is to be followed conscientiously, the traverse of Stile End must be included in this walk, although this middle height can more easily be bypassed between Low Moss and Barrow Door. Starting down the eastern ridge, keep always to the highest ground ahead; on Stile End this means a sharp turn to the right.

Outerside from Stile End

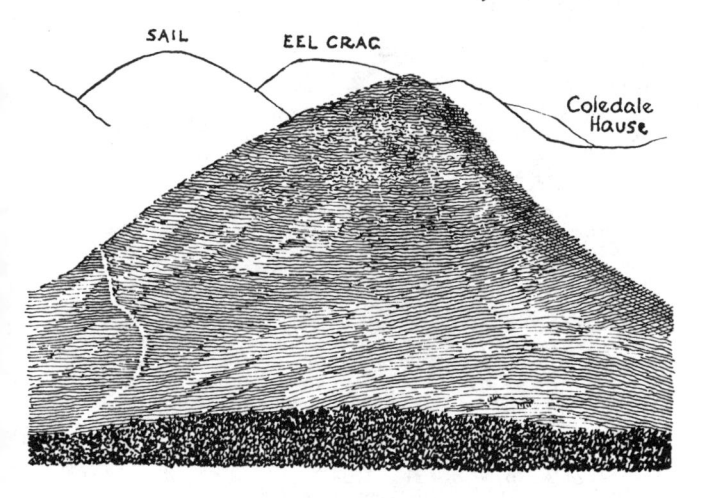

SAIL   EEL CRAG   Coledale Hause

Rannerdale Knotts 1160'

from High Rannerdale

Rannerdale is seen by most visitors to Buttermere — but only as a farm and a cottage and a patchwork of fields on the shore of Crummock Water: a pleasant green oasis in the lap of shaggy fells, but unremarkable. Passers-by sometimes tarry in the limpid coves of Crummock, or stroll along convenient paths in the bracken, but most hurry past, to or from Buttermere, unsuspecting that these few acres, now peaceful pastures, were once a scene of violent strife. Rannerdale has a lasting place in history as the setting of a fierce battle in which the Norman invaders were ambushed and routed by the English in the years after the Conquest.

Alongside the fields, and thrusting as a headland into the lake, is the abrupt and rugged end of a low fell that extends south-east for a mile, gradually declining to Sail Beck. All the excitement is concentrated in the dark tower of rock above the lake. Behind, a quiet valley isolates the fell from the greater heights in the rear.

This is Rannerdale Knotts, a mountain in miniature, and a proud one. Not even Gable has witnessed a real battle! And, what's more, our side won!!

Rannerdale Knotts 2

MAP

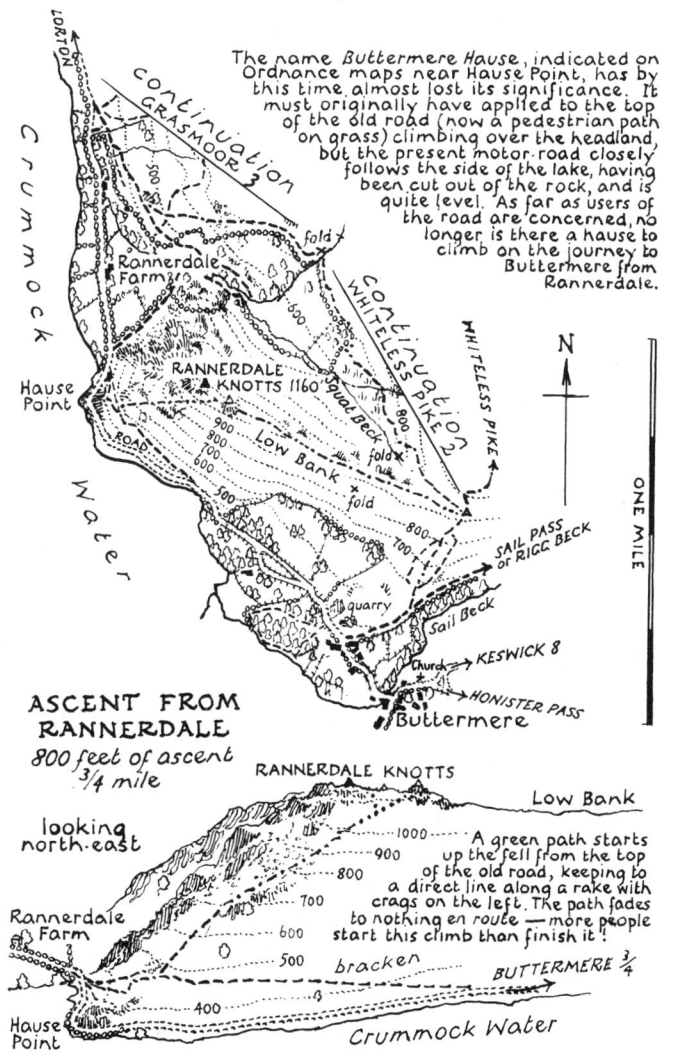

The name *Buttermere Hause*, indicated on Ordnance maps near Hause Point, has by this time almost lost its significance. It must originally have applied to the top of the old road (now a pedestrian path on grass) climbing over the headland, but the present motor-road closely follows the side of the lake, having been cut out of the rock, and is quite level. As far as users of the road are concerned, no longer is there a hause to climb on the journey to Buttermere from Rannerdale.

ASCENT FROM RANNERDALE
800 feet of ascent
¾ mile

looking north-east

A green path starts up the fell from the top of the old road, keeping to a direct line along a rake with crags on the left. The path fades to nothing en route — more people start this climb than finish it!

BUTTERMERE ¾ →

Rannerdale Knotts 3

ASCENT FROM BUTTERMERE
850 feet of ascent : 1½ miles

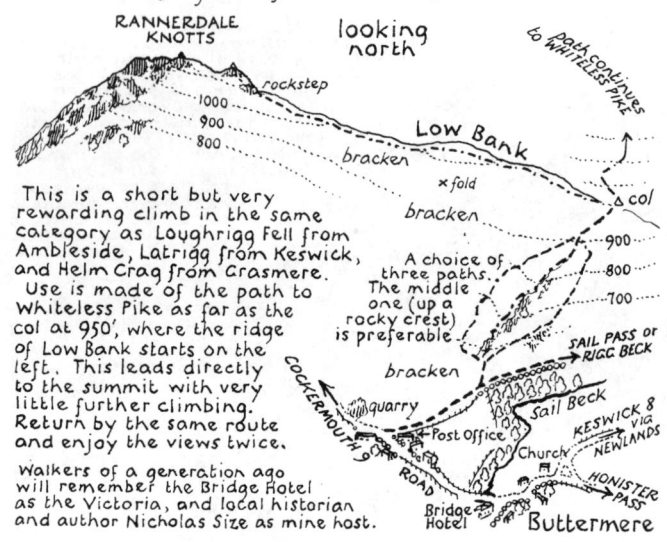

looking north

This is a short but very rewarding climb in the same category as Loughrigg Fell from Ambleside, Latrigg from Keswick, and Helm Crag from Grasmere.
Use is made of the path to Whiteless Pike as far as the col at 950', where the ridge of Low Bank starts on the left. This leads directly to the summit with very little further climbing. Return by the same route and enjoy the views twice.

Walkers of a generation ago will remember the Bridge Hotel as the Victoria, and local historian and author Nicholas Size as mine host.

THE SUMMIT

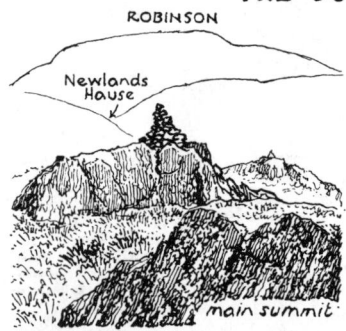

A succession of rocky tors athwart the narrow crest gives a fine distinction to this modest fell. Glorious views in addition make this a place for leisurely exploration. Rock formations and striations are interesting.

DESCENTS: The best way off is along the ridge of the fell, Low Bank, to Buttermere, and, after an initial rockstep just beyond the second summit, is a very easy stroll indeed. In mist, the road may be safely reached by a straight descent to Crummock Water from the depression between the two summits, but not elsewhere.

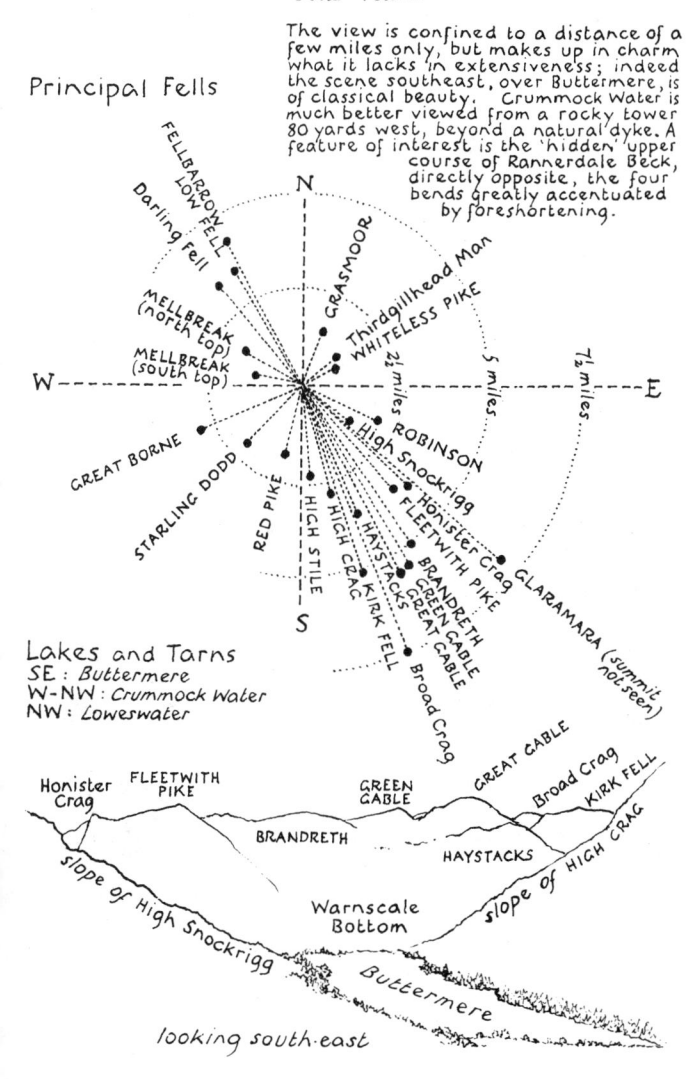

Rannerdale Knotts 4

THE VIEW

The view is confined to a distance of a few miles only, but makes up in charm what it lacks in extensiveness; indeed the scene southeast, over Buttermere, is of classical beauty. Crummock Water is much better viewed from a rocky tower 80 yards west, beyond a natural dyke. A feature of interest is the 'hidden' upper course of Rannerdale Beck, directly opposite, the four bends greatly accentuated by foreshortening.

Principal Fells

FELLBARROW
LOW FELL
Darling Fell
MELLBREAK (north top)
MELLBREAK (south top)
GREAT BORNE
STARLING DODD
RED PIKE
HIGH STILE
HIGH CRAG
KIRK FELL
Broad Crag
GREAT GABLE
GREEN GABLE
BRANDRETH
FLEETWITH PIKE
HAYSTACKS
Honister Crag
High Snockrigg
ROBINSON
GRASMOOR
Thirdgillhead Man
WHITELESS PIKE
GLARAMARA (summit not seen)

2½ miles
5 miles
7½ miles

Lakes and Tarns
SE: *Buttermere*
W-NW: *Crummock Water*
NW: *Loweswater*

looking south-east

Robinson 2417'

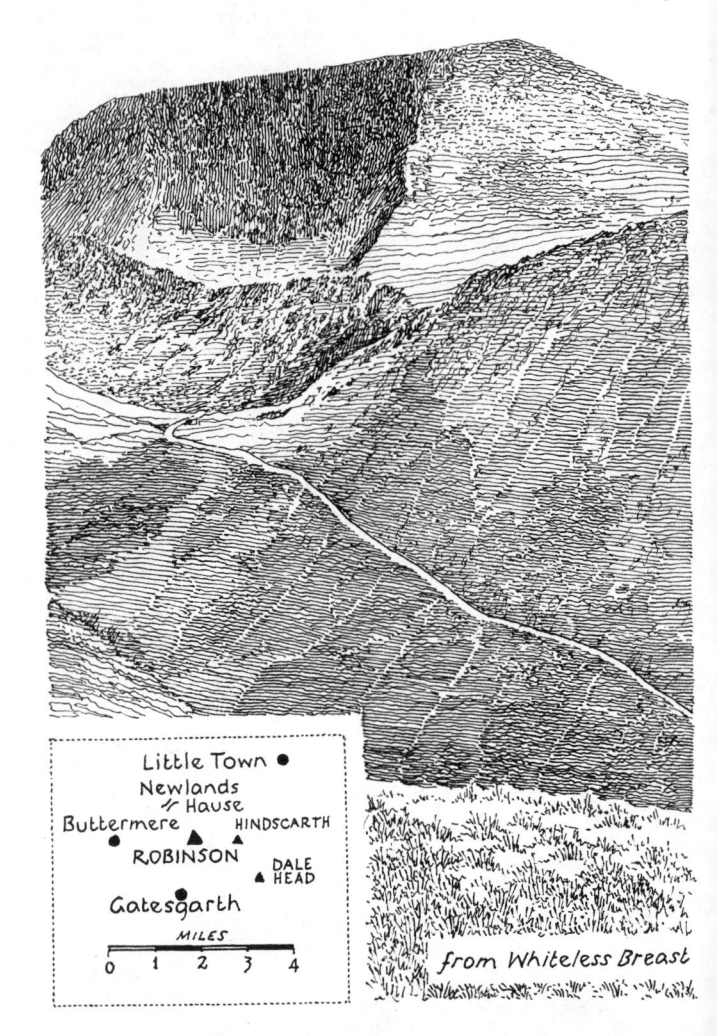

from Whiteless Breast

Little Town
Newlands Hause
Buttermere   HINDSCARTH
ROBINSON
DALE HEAD
Gatesgarth

MILES
0 1 2 3 4

Robinson 2

NATURAL FEATURES

This fell with the prosaic name is, to look at, the least attractive of the group around Buttermere, a defect largely due to its position on the sunny side of the valley. Lack of shadow always reduces the visual appeal of mountain scenery, and on Robinson the steep slopes rise blandly to the sky with nothing in particular to attract the eye, nothing to exercise curiosity and imagination — in complete contrast to the darkly mysterious and more challenging heights across the lake. Robinson's summit lies back, out of sight, beyond a wide shelf at mid-height that serves as an effective gathering ground for Keskadale Beck: this wet expanse is Buttermere Moss, a bad place for walkers. Except for the neat apex of a lower summit, High Snockrigg, and a rough cleft above the woods of Hassness, Robinson contributes little to the scenic value of the Buttermere picture, and one must see it from Newlands to appreciate its distinctive skyline and the long ridge that characterises this aspect, its finest; while from Newlands Hause, too, where passing motorists are excited by a close view of Moss Force, it is strongly in evidence, here fringed by the half-mile precipice of Robinson Crags.

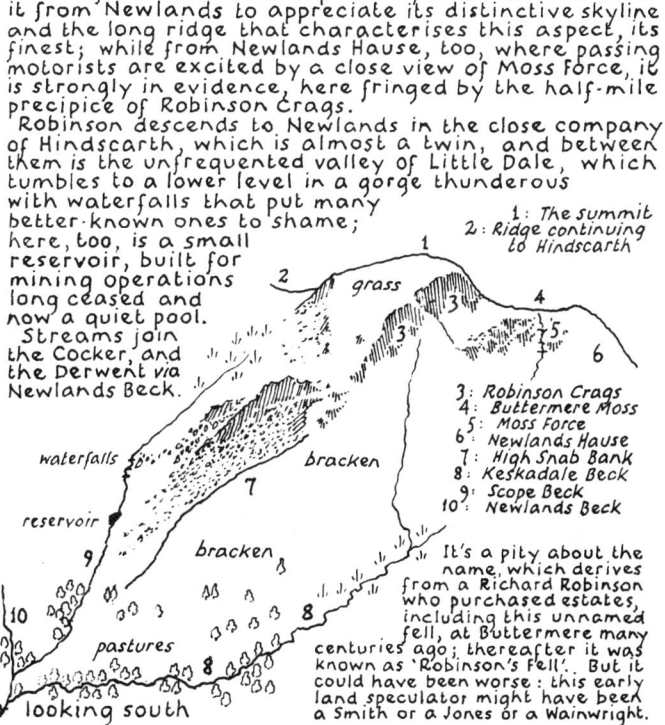

Robinson descends to Newlands in the close company of Hindscarth, which is almost a twin, and between them is the unfrequented valley of Little Dale, which tumbles to a lower level in a gorge thunderous with waterfalls that put many better-known ones to shame; here, too, is a small reservoir, built for mining operations long ceased and now a quiet pool.

Streams join the Cocker, and the Derwent via Newlands Beck.

1: The summit
2: Ridge continuing to Hindscarth
3: Robinson Crags
4: Buttermere Moss
5: Moss Force
6: Newlands Hause
7: High Snab Bank
8: Keskadale Beck
9: Scope Beck
10: Newlands Beck

looking south

It's a pity about the name, which derives from a Richard Robinson who purchased estates, including this unnamed fell, at Buttermere many centuries ago; thereafter it was known as 'Robinson's Fell'. But it could have been worse: this early land speculator might have been a Smith or a Jones or a Wainwright.

Robinson 3

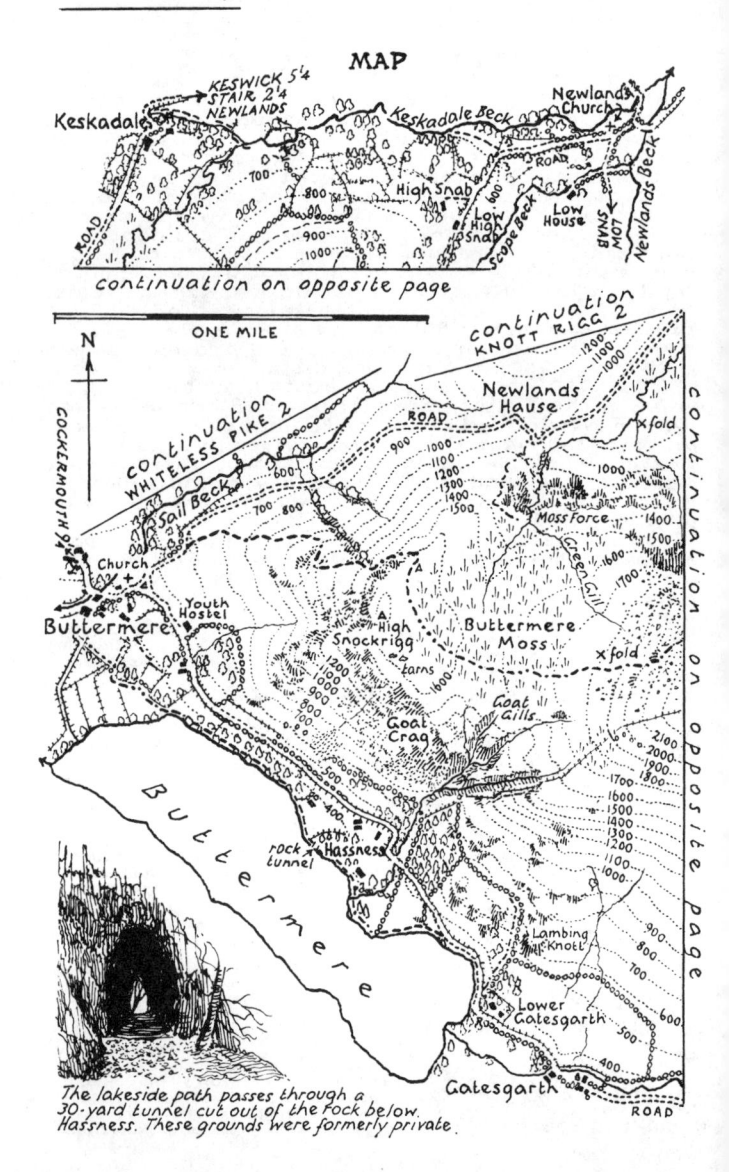

MAP

The lakeside path passes through a 30-yard tunnel cut out of the rock below Hassness. These grounds were formerly private.

Robinson 4

MAP

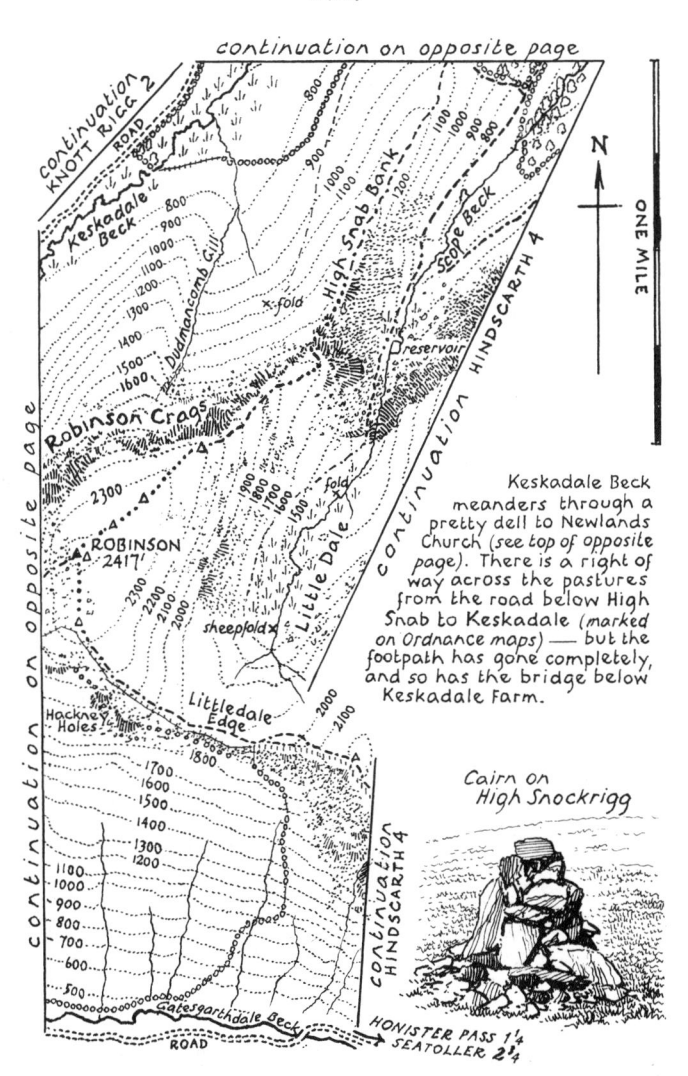

Keskadale Beck meanders through a pretty dell to Newlands Church (see top of opposite page). There is a right of way across the pastures from the road below High Snab to Keskadale (marked on Ordnance maps) — but the footpath has gone completely, and so has the bridge below Keskadale Farm.

Cairn on High Snockrigg

Robinson 5

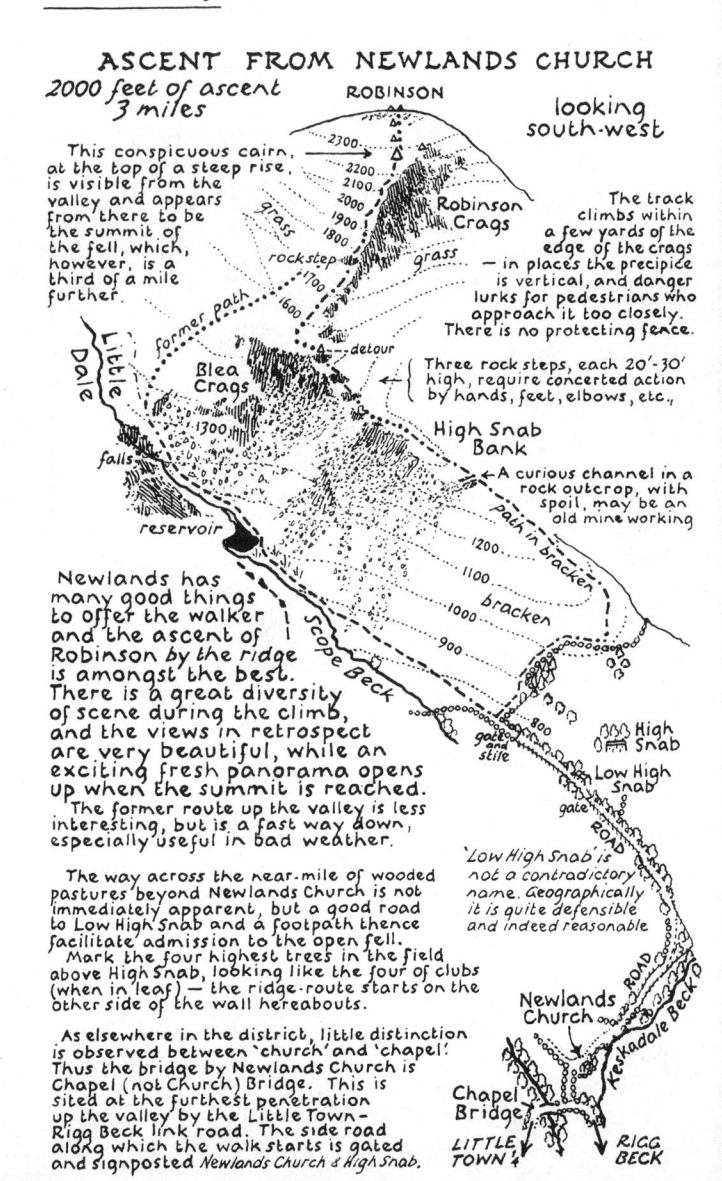

ASCENT FROM NEWLANDS CHURCH
*2000 feet of ascent
3 miles*

looking south-west

ROBINSON

This conspicuous cairn, at the top of a steep rise, is visible from the valley and appears from there to be the summit of the fell, which, however, is a third of a mile further.

Robinson Crags

The track climbs within a few yards of the edge of the crags — in places the precipice is vertical, and danger lurks for pedestrians who approach it too closely. There is no protecting fence.

Little Dale

former path

detour

Blea Crags

Three rock steps, each 20'-30' high, require concerted action by hands, feet, elbows, etc.,

High Snab Bank

falls

A curious channel in a rock outcrop, with spoil, may be an old mine working

reservoir

path in bracken

bracken

Scope Beck

Newlands has many good things to offer the walker and the ascent of Robinson by the ridge is amongst the best. There is a great diversity of scene during the climb, and the views in retrospect are very beautiful, while an exciting fresh panorama opens up when the summit is reached.

The former route up the valley is less interesting, but is a fast way down, especially useful in bad weather.

gate and stile

High Snab

Low High Snab

gate

'Low High Snab' is not a contradictory name. Geographically it is quite defensible and indeed reasonable

The way across the near-mile of wooded pastures beyond Newlands Church is not immediately apparent, but a good road to Low High Snab and a footpath thence facilitate admission to the open fell.

Mark the four highest trees in the field above High Snab, looking like the four of clubs (when in leaf) — the ridge-route starts on the other side of the wall hereabouts.

ROAD

Newlands Church

Keskadale Beck

As elsewhere in the district, little distinction is observed between 'church' and 'chapel'. Thus the bridge by Newlands Church is Chapel (not Church) Bridge. This is sited at the furthest penetration up the valley by the Little Town–Rigg Beck link road. The side road along which the walk starts is gated and signposted *Newlands Church & High Snab*.

Chapel Bridge

LITTLE TOWN ↙   ↘ RIGG BECK

Robinson 6

ASCENT FROM NEWLANDS HAUSE
1400 feet of ascent : 1¼ miles

Except for two short sections, the full length of the route is clearly in view from the Hause. The wife, left in the car, will be watching every move!

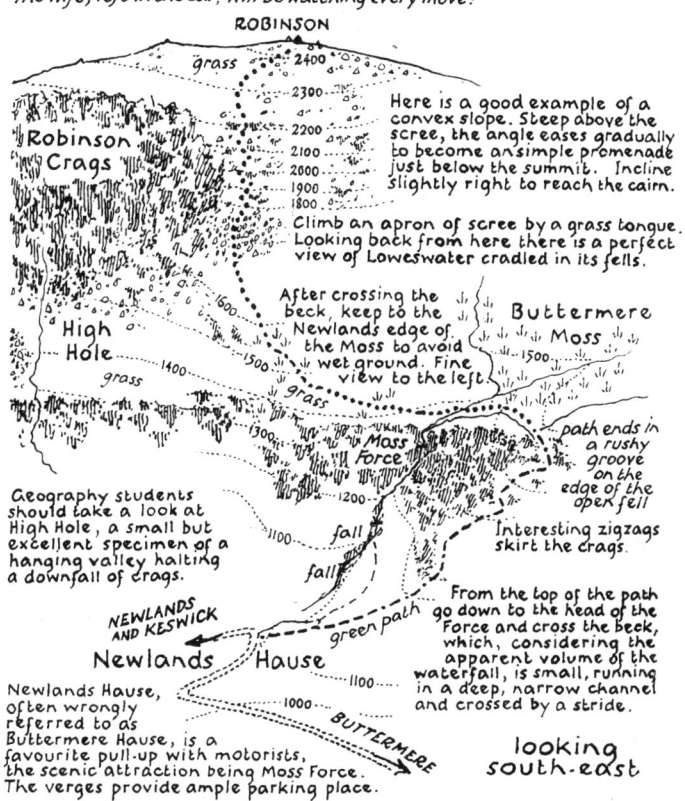

ROBINSON 2400

grass 2300, 2200, 2100, 2000, 1900, 1800

Robinson Crags

Here is a good example of a convex slope. Steep above the scree, the angle eases gradually to become an simple promenade just below the summit. Incline slightly right to reach the cairn.

Climb an apron of scree by a grass tongue. Looking back from here there is a perfect view of Loweswater cradled in its fells.

After crossing the beck, keep to the Newlands edge of the Moss to avoid wet ground. Fine view to the left.

High Hole — 1400 grass — 1500 grass

Buttermere Moss — 1500

1300 — Moss Force — path ends in a rushy groove on the edge of the open fell

Geography students should take a look at High Hole, a small but excellent specimen of a hanging valley halting a downfall of crags.

1200 — fall — fall

Interesting zigzags skirt the crags.

NEWLANDS AND KESWICK

green path — From the top of the path go down to the head of the Force and cross the beck, which, considering the apparent volume of the waterfall, is small, running in a deep, narrow channel and crossed by a stride.

Newlands Hause — 1100

Newlands Hause, often wrongly referred to as Buttermere Hause, is a favourite pull-up with motorists, the scenic attraction being Moss Force. The verges provide ample parking place.

1000 — BUTTERMERE →

looking south-east

Motorists, having less energy than walkers, may be attracted by this opportunity of starting 1100 feet up and so shortening the climb. The ascent does not live up to its early promise, however, becoming very dreary at the level of the Moss. Wet ground cannot be avoided entirely, but the walk is generally better in this respect than the direct route from Buttermere across the Moss. Try to do it in one hour.

Robinson 7

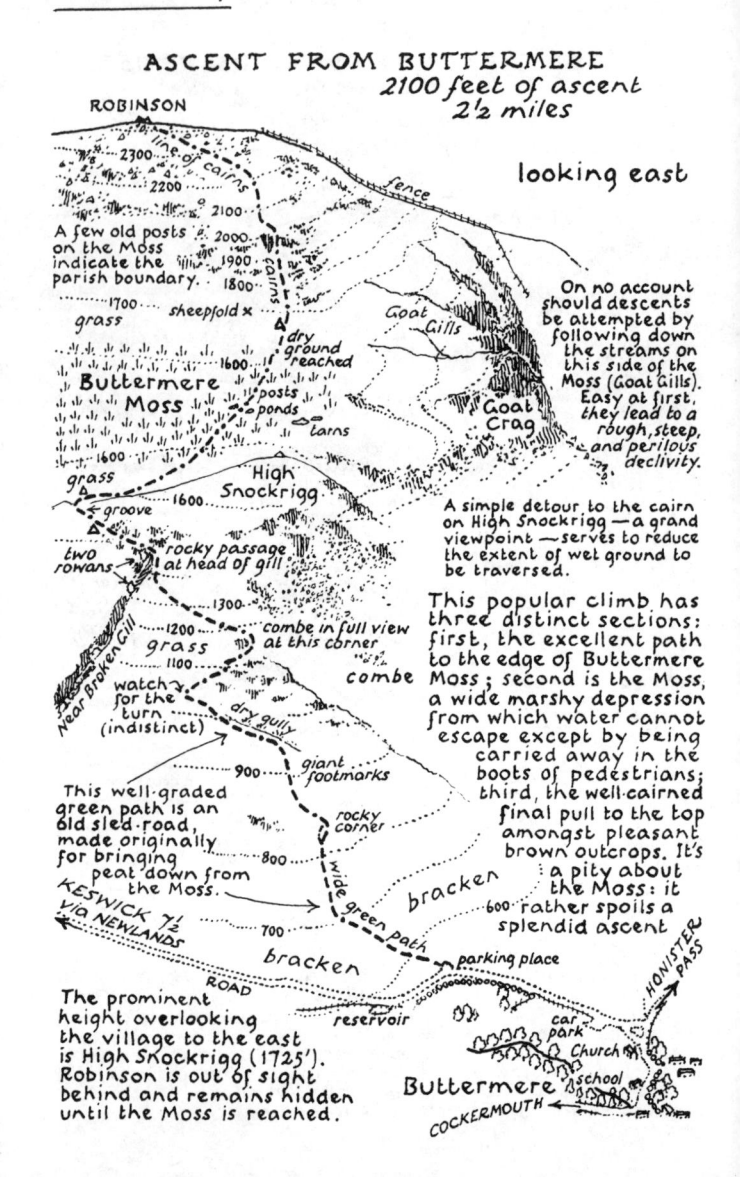

ASCENT FROM BUTTERMERE
2100 feet of ascent
2½ miles

looking east

ROBINSON

A few old posts on the Moss indicate the parish boundary.

Buttermere Moss

High Snockrigg

two rowans — rocky passage at head of gill

Near Broken Gill

watch for the turn (indistinct)

This well-graded green path is an old sled-road, made originally for bringing peat down from the Moss.

KESWICK 7½ VIA NEWLANDS

The prominent height overlooking the village to the east is High Snockrigg (1725'). Robinson is out of sight behind and remains hidden until the Moss is reached.

sheepfold × — dry ground reached — posts — ponds — tarns — groove — combe in full view at this corner — grass — combe — dry gully — giant footmarks — rocky corner — wide green path — bracken — parking place — reservoir — car park — Church — school

Goat Gills — Goat Crag

On no account should descents be attempted by following down the streams on this side of the Moss (Goat Gills). Easy at first, they lead to a rough, steep, and perilous declivity.

A simple detour to the cairn on High Snockrigg — a grand viewpoint — serves to reduce the extent of wet ground to be traversed.

This popular climb has three distinct sections: first, the excellent path to the edge of Buttermere Moss; second is the Moss, a wide marshy depression from which water cannot escape except by being carried away in the boots of pedestrians; third, the well-cairned final pull to the top amongst pleasant brown outcrops. It's a pity about the Moss: it rather spoils a splendid ascent.

HONISTER PASS

Buttermere

COCKERMOUTH

ROAD

Robinson 8

ASCENT FROM HASSNESS
1900 feet of ascent : 1½ miles

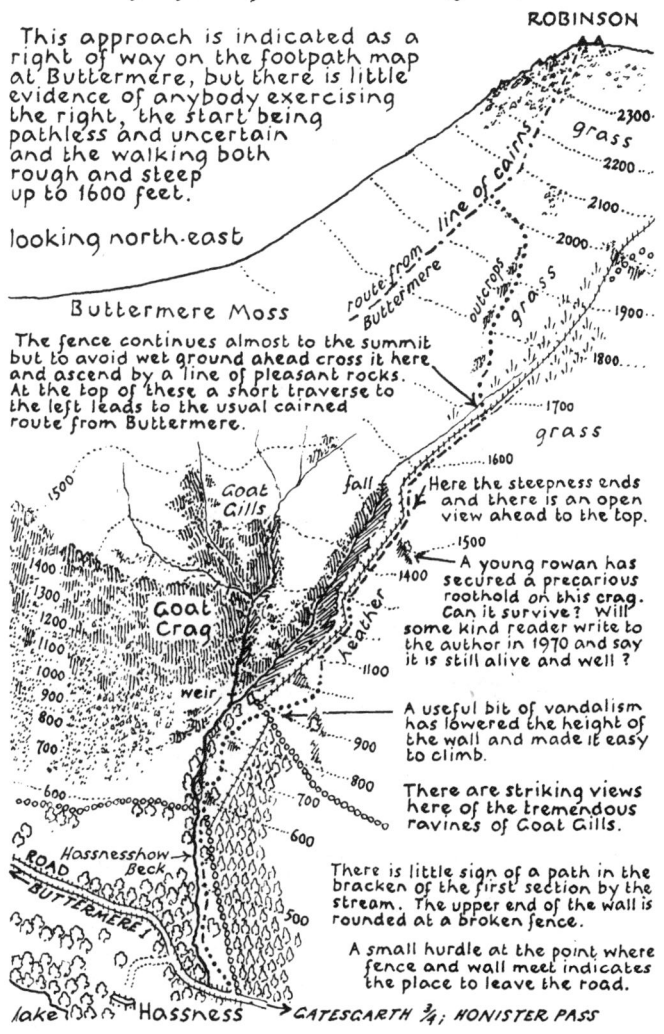

ROBINSON

This approach is indicated as a right of way on the footpath map at Buttermere, but there is little evidence of anybody exercising the right, the start being pathless and uncertain and the walking both rough and steep up to 1600 feet.

looking north-east

Buttermere Moss

The fence continues almost to the summit but to avoid wet ground ahead cross it here and ascend by a line of pleasant rocks. At the top of these a short traverse to the left leads to the usual cairned route from Buttermere.

Here the steepness ends and there is an open view ahead to the top.

A young rowan has secured a precarious roothold on this crag. Can it survive? Will some kind reader write to the author in 1970 and say it is still alive and well?

A useful bit of vandalism has lowered the height of the wall and made it easy to climb.

There are striking views here of the tremendous ravines of Goat Gills.

There is little sign of a path in the bracken of the first section by the stream. The upper end of the wall is rounded at a broken fence.

A small hurdle at the point where fence and wall meet indicates the place to leave the road.

lake Hassness ← GATESGARTH ¾; HONISTER PASS

Robinson 9

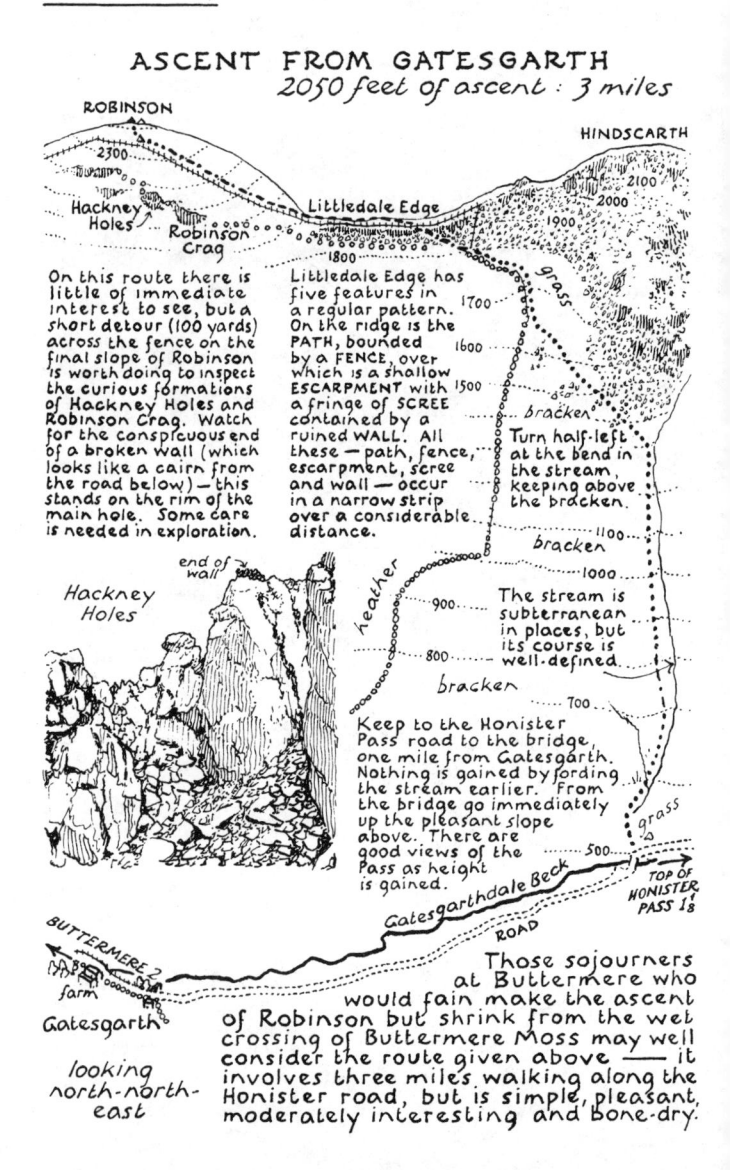

ASCENT FROM GATESGARTH
2050 feet of ascent : 3 miles

ROBINSON — HINDSCARTH
Hackney Holes — Robinson Crag — Littledale Edge

On this route there is little of immediate interest to see, but a short detour (100 yards) across the fence on the final slope of Robinson is worth doing to inspect the curious formations of Hackney Holes and Robinson Crag. Watch for the conspicuous end of a broken wall (which looks like a cairn from the road below) — this stands on the rim of the main hole. Some care is needed in exploration.

Littledale Edge has five features in a regular pattern. On the ridge is the PATH, bounded by a FENCE, over which is a shallow ESCARPMENT with a fringe of SCREE contained by a ruined WALL. All these — path, fence, escarpment, scree and wall — occur in a narrow strip over a considerable distance.

Turn half-left at the bend in the stream, keeping above the bracken.

The stream is subterranean in places, but its course is well-defined.

Hackney Holes — end of wall

Keep to the Honister Pass road to the bridge, one mile from Gatesgarth. Nothing is gained by fording the stream earlier. From the bridge go immediately up the pleasant slope above. There are good views of the Pass as height is gained.

Gatesgarthdale Beck — ROAD — TOP OF HONISTER PASS 1¼

BUTTERMERE 2 — farm — Gatesgarth

looking north-north-east

Those sojourners at Buttermere who would fain make the ascent of Robinson but shrink from the wet crossing of Buttermere Moss may well consider the route given above —— it involves three miles walking along the Honister road, but is simple, pleasant, moderately interesting and bone-dry.

Robinson 10

THE SUMMIT

Two long low outcrops of rock run parallel across the summit, the width of a road apart, almost like natural kerbstones or parapets — the westerly is slightly the higher and has the main cairn. The 'road' between is surfaced with loose stones. The top of the fell is a broad plateau with nothing of interest and no hazards.

DESCENTS: A line of cairns heads northeast for the Newlands descent: there is no path until the ground steepens suddenly beyond a superior cairn after a third of a mile. The Buttermere (direct) route goes off southwest: cairns and a track are soon found.

In mist, the top is confusing and bad conditions may make it advisable to find the ridge-fence as a preliminary to descent. For Newlands, go left alongside the fence to the first depression, where turn down left into Little Dale. For Buttermere, if the usual track cannot be located, the fence is a good guide to the intake wall above Hassness, the last part being very steep and slippery, and having dangerous ground immediately to the right.

Moss Force,
Newlands Hause

Goat Gills, Hassness

Robinson 11

THE VIEW

The broad, nearly-flat summit detracts from the quality of the view, but although the valleys are hidden the surround of fells is excellent. Honister Pass, with the motor road snaking over it, is an interesting feature. It is odd to find Scafell Pike's towering summit for once missing from a view, especially as all its satellites are there in force: the Pike is exactly covered by the top of Great Gable, but its south-west slope going down to the gap of Mickledore is clearly visible. Robinson is one of the few fells that has the shy Floutern Tarn in its sights.

Principal Fells

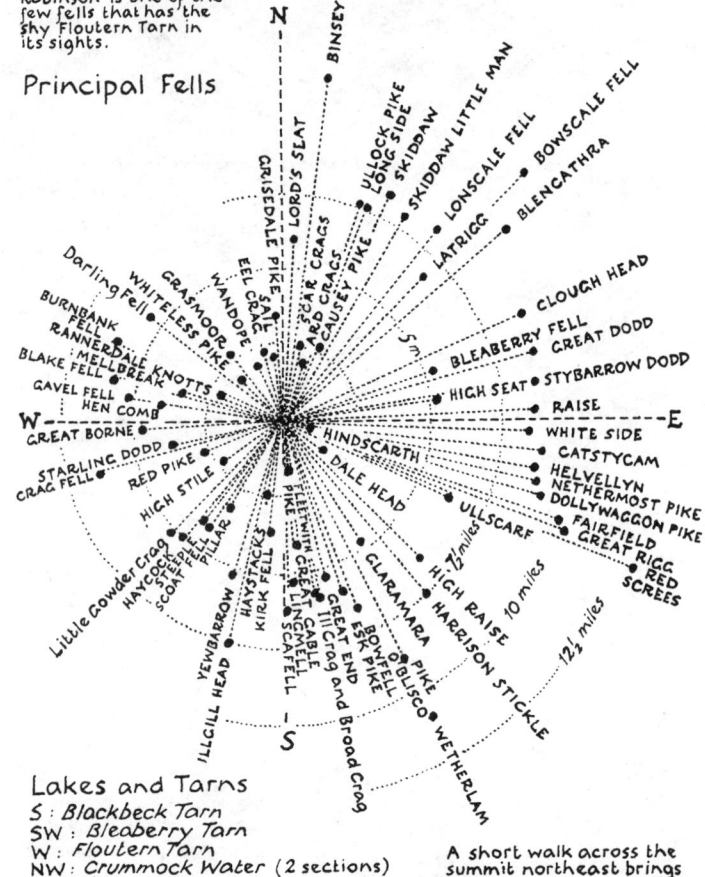

[Radial panorama diagram showing fells in all directions from the summit, with distance rings at 5 miles, 7½ miles, 10 miles, and 12½ miles. Directions marked N, E, S, W.]

N: Binsey, Lord's Seat, Grisedale Pike, Ullock Pike, Long Side, Skiddaw, Skiddaw Little Man, Eel Crag, Ard Crags, Causey Pike, Lonscale Fell, Bowscale Fell, Latrigg, Blencathra

E: Grasmoor, Whiteless Pike, Wandope, Clough Head, Bleaberry Fell, Great Dodd, Stybarrow Dodd, High Seat, Raise, White Side, Catstycam, Hindscarth, Helvellyn, Nethermost Pike, Dale Head, Dollywaggon Pike, Ullscarf, Fairfield, Great Rigg, Red Screes

S: Darling Fell, Burnbank Fell, Rannerdale Knolls, Mellbreak, Blake Fell, Gavel Fell, Hen Comb, Great Borne, Starling Dodd, Crag Fell, Red Pike, High Stile, Little Gowder Crag, Haycock, Scoat Fell, Pillar, Yewbarrow, Haystacks, Kirk Fell, Fleetwith Pike, Great Gable, Green Gable, Lingmell, Scafell, Ill Gill Head, Till Crag and Broad Crag, Great End, Esk Pike, Glaramara, Bowfell, Pike o' Blisco, High Raise, Harrison Stickle, Wetherlam

Lakes and Tarns

S : Blackbeck Tarn
SW : Bleaberry Tarn
W : Floutern Tarn
NW : Crummock Water (2 sections)
NW : Loweswater

A short walk across the summit northeast brings Derwentwater into sight NE.

Robinson 12

RIDGE ROUTE

To HINDSCARTH, 2385′ : 1½ miles : S, ESE and NNE
Depression at 1880′ : 520 feet of ascent
A linking of two lateral spurs

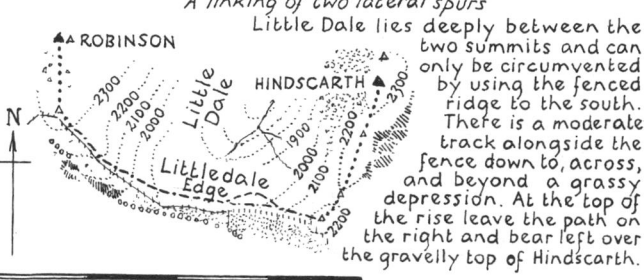

Little Dale lies deeply between the two summits and can only be circumvented by using the fenced ridge to the south. There is a moderate track alongside the fence down to, across, and beyond a grassy depression. At the top of the rise leave the path on the right and bear left over the gravelly top of Hindscarth.

ONE MILE

The north-east ridge of Robinson, from Scope End

Sail 2530'

from Sail Beck

- Braithwaite
- CRISEDALE ▲ PIKE
- Stair
- GRASMOOR ▲ SAIL ▲
- EEL CRAG ▲ ▲ CAUSEY PIKE
- ARD CRAGS ▲
- Buttermere

MILES
0 1 2 3 4

Sail 2

NATURAL FEATURES

Sail is the least obtrusive of the 2500-footers, being completely dominated by its vaster and more rugged neighbour, Eel Crag, and an absence of attractive or interesting features adds to its inferiority complex.

Sail is, however, an unavoidable obstacle on the way to or from the bigger fell by the fine east ridge rooted in Newlands, and the well-trodden path to its summit is invariably used for this purpose and not with Sail as the main object of the walk; indeed, the path does not even trouble to visit the cairn. The flanks of the fell are steep, excessively so to the south, above Sail Beck, with much scree and heather; northwards they fall more gently to Coledale, where, low down, they are traversed by the rising path from Force Crag Mine.

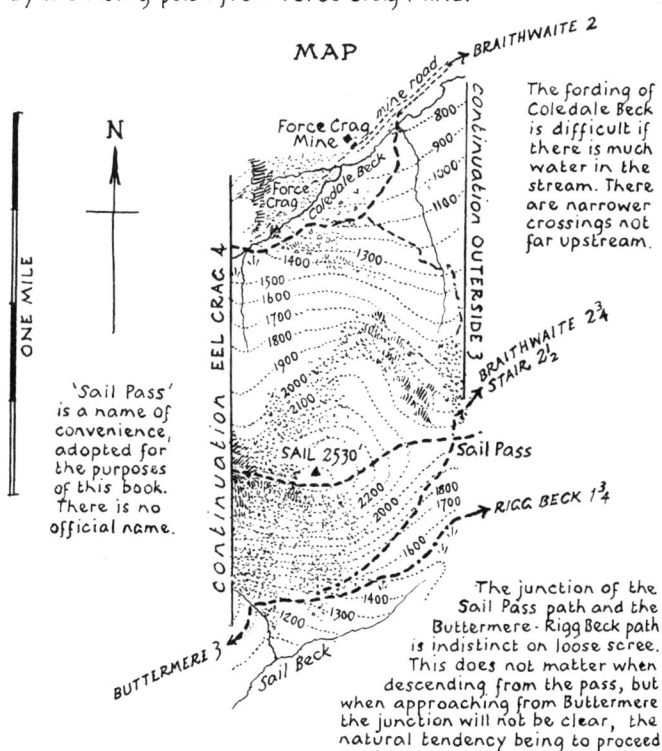

MAP

ONE MILE

BRAITHWAITE 2
continuation OUTERSIDE 3
BRAITHWAITE 2¾
STAIR 2½
RIGG BECK 1¼
BUTTERMERE 3
continuation EEL CRAG 4

Force Crag Mine
Force Crag
Coledale Beck
SAIL 2530'
Sail Pass
Sail Beck

The fording of Coledale Beck is difficult if there is much water in the stream. There are narrower crossings not far upstream.

'Sail Pass' is a name of convenience, adopted for the purposes of this book. There is no official name.

The junction of the Sail Pass path and the Buttermere-Rigg Beck path is indistinct on loose scree. This does not matter when descending from the pass, but when approaching from Buttermere the junction will not be clear, the natural tendency being to proceed too far along the Rigg Beck path.

Sail 3

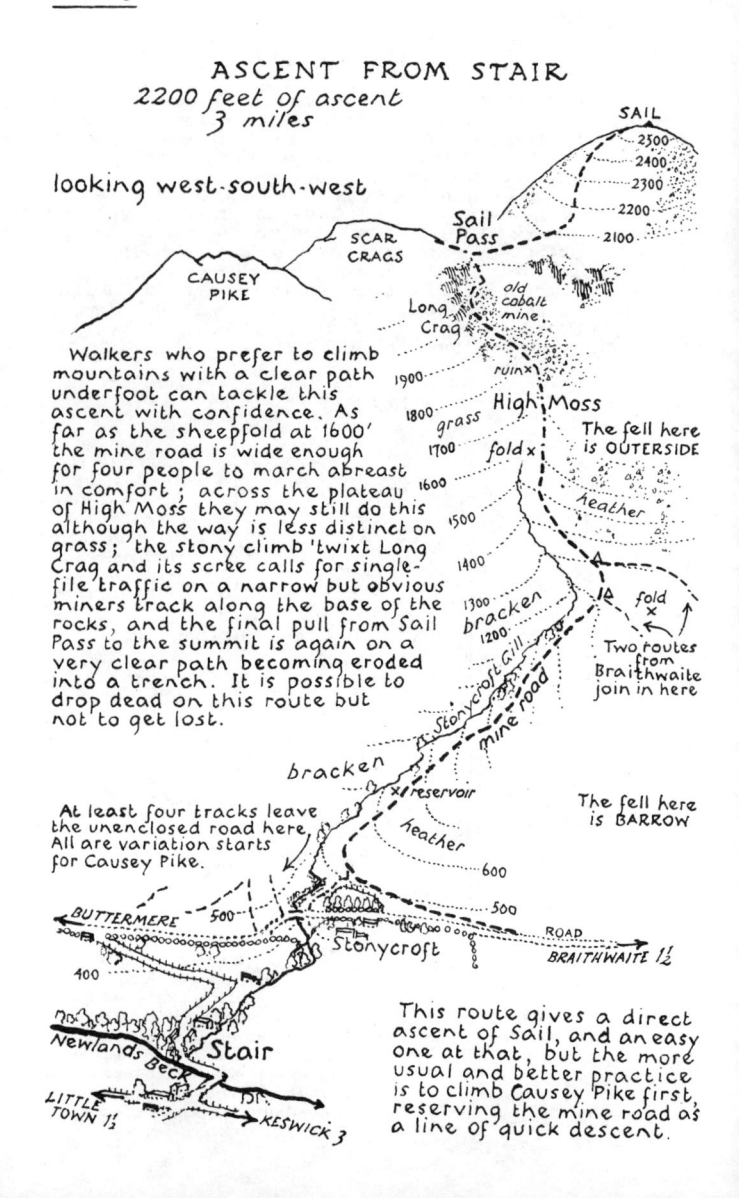

ASCENT FROM STAIR
2200 feet of ascent
3 miles

looking west-south-west

Walkers who prefer to climb mountains with a clear path underfoot can tackle this ascent with confidence. As far as the sheepfold at 1600' the mine road is wide enough for four people to march abreast in comfort; across the plateau of High Moss they may still do this although the way is less distinct on grass; the stony climb 'twixt Long Crag and its scree calls for single-file traffic on a narrow but obvious miners track along the base of the rocks, and the final pull from Sail Pass to the summit is again on a very clear path becoming eroded into a trench. It is possible to drop dead on this route but not to get lost.

At least four tracks leave the unenclosed road here. All are variation starts for Causey Pike.

The fell here is OUTERSIDE

Two routes from Braithwaite join in here

The fell here is BARROW

This route gives a direct ascent of Sail, and an easy one at that, but the more usual and better practice is to climb Causey Pike first, reserving the mine road as a line of quick descent.

Sail 4

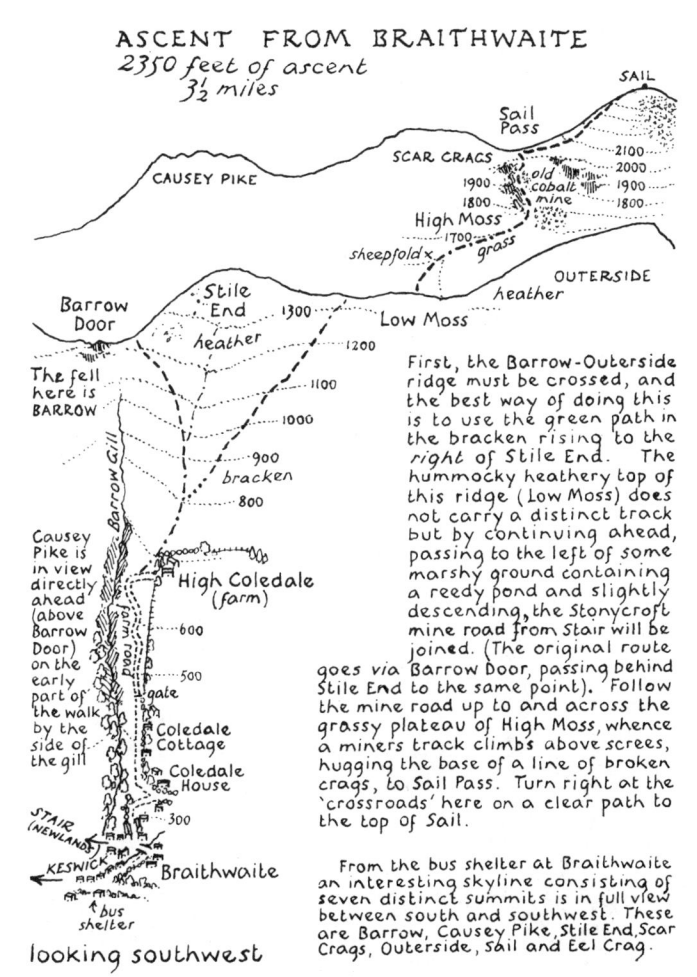

ASCENT FROM BRAITHWAITE
2350 feet of ascent
3½ miles

Map labels:
- SAIL
- Sail Pass
- SCAR CRAGS
- CAUSEY PIKE
- old cobalt mine — 2100, 2000, 1900, 1800
- High Moss — 1900, 1800, 1700
- sheepfold × grass
- OUTERSIDE heather
- Barrow Door
- Stile End heather — 1300
- Low Moss — 1200
- The fell here is BARROW
- Barrow Gill
- 1100, 1000, 900, bracken, 800
- Causey Pike is in view directly ahead (above Barrow Door) on the early part of the walk by the side of the gill
- High Coledale (farm)
- 600
- gate 500
- Coledale Cottage
- Coledale House
- 300
- STAIR (NEWLANDS)
- KESWICK
- Braithwaite
- bus shelter

looking southwest

First, the Barrow-Outerside ridge must be crossed, and the best way of doing this is to use the green path in the bracken rising to the *right* of Stile End. The hummocky heathery top of this ridge (Low Moss) does not carry a distinct track but by continuing ahead, passing to the left of some marshy ground containing a reedy pond and slightly descending, the Stonycroft mine road from Stair will be joined. (The original route goes via Barrow Door, passing behind Stile End to the same point). Follow the mine road up to and across the grassy plateau of High Moss, whence a miners' track climbs above screes, hugging the base of a line of broken crags, to Sail Pass. Turn right at the 'crossroads' here on a clear path to the top of Sail.

From the bus shelter at Braithwaite an interesting skyline consisting of seven distinct summits is in full view between south and southwest. These are Barrow, Causey Pike, Stile End, Scar Crags, Outerside, Sail and Eel Crag.

This route coincides with that from Stair beyond a subsidiary ridge linking Barrow and Outerside, but is more attractive initially, being easier to the feet and having wider views. All gradients are moderate and this is the simplest way of getting a high footing on the Coledale 'horse-shoe' from Braithwaite.

Sail 5

THE SUMMIT

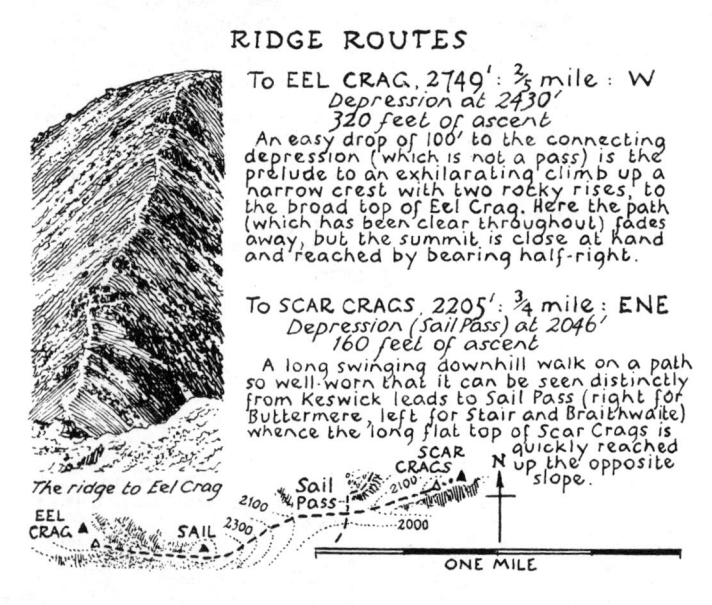

Panorama labels: SWIRL HOW, BOWFELL, ESK PIKE, GREAT END, Ill Crag, Broad Crag, SCAFELL PIKE, SCAFELL, Esk Hause, GREAT GABLE, ROBINSON, Robinson Crags

The summit, a rounded dome of heather and mosses, has nothing of immediate interest, and the much-trodden path across the top does not even trouble to visit the small cairn 25 yards distant.

DESCENTS: Join the path and go down to Sail Pass, where either continue over Scar Crags and on to Causey Pike, or turn left along the mine road, for Stair, Newlands.

RIDGE ROUTES

TO EEL CRAG, 2749': ⅗ mile : W
Depression at 2430'
320 feet of ascent

An easy drop of 100' to the connecting depression (which is not a pass) is the prelude to an exhilarating climb up a narrow crest with two rocky rises, to the broad top of Eel Crag. Here the path (which has been clear throughout) fades away, but the summit is close at hand and reached by bearing half-right.

TO SCAR CRAGS, 2205': ¾ mile : ENE
Depression (Sail Pass) at 2046'
160 feet of ascent

A long swinging downhill walk on a path so well-worn that it can be seen distinctly from Keswick leads to Sail Pass (right for Buttermere, left for Stair and Braithwaite) whence the long flat top of Scar Crags is quickly reached up the opposite slope.

The ridge to Eel Crag

Map: EEL CRAG — SAIL — Sail Pass — SCAR CRAGS; ONE MILE

Sail 6

THE VIEW

Few walkers will hesitate long over this panorama, with the better viewpoint of Eel Crag so near (or just visited), but those who cannot go a step further without a rest may settle down to enjoy what is really a very fine prospect, although unbalanced by the disproportionate bulk of Eel Crag filling the western sky.

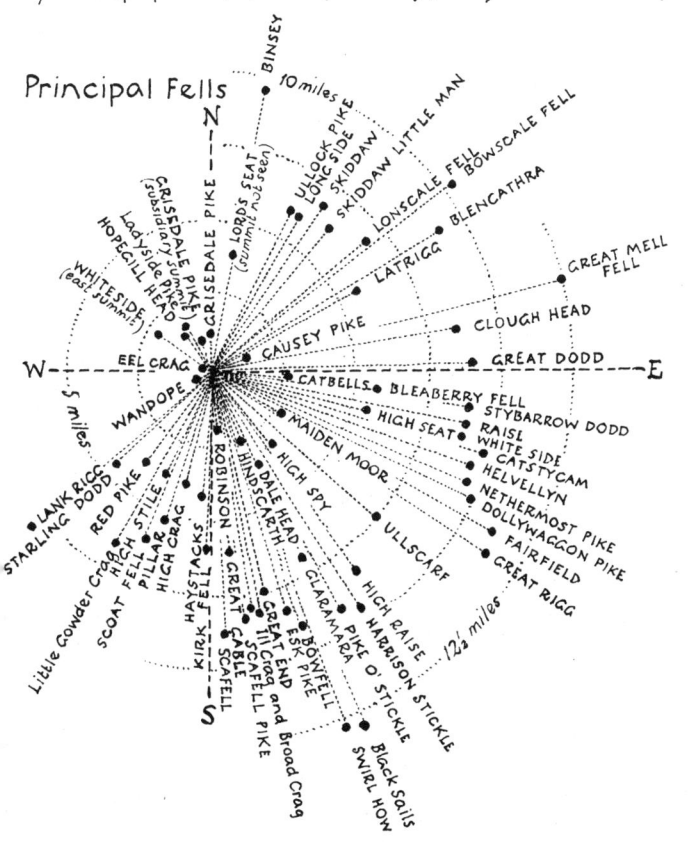

Principal Fells

- N: BINSEY (10 miles), ULLOCK PIKE, LONG SIDE, SKIDDAW, SKIDDAW LITTLE MAN
- LORDS SEAT (summit not seen)
- LONSCALE FELL, BOWSCALE FELL
- CRISEDALE PIKE (subsidiary summit)
- LADYSIDE PIKE
- HOPEGILL HEAD
- WHITESIDE (east summit)
- GRISEDALE PIKE
- LATRIGG, BLENCATHRA, GREAT MELL FELL
- CAUSEY PIKE, CLOUGH HEAD
- W: EEL CRAG (5 miles) — GREAT DODD : E
- WANDOPE
- CATBELLS, BLEABERRY FELL, STYBARROW DODD
- HIGH SEAT, RAISL
- MAIDEN MOOR, WHITE SIDE, CATSTYCAM
- HELVELLYN
- LANK RIGG, ROBINSON, HIGH SPY, NETHERMOST PIKE
- STARLING DODD, DALE HEAD, DOLLYWAGGON PIKE
- RED PIKE, HINDSCARTH, FAIRFIELD
- SCOAT FELL, PILLAR, HIGH STILE, HIGH CRAG, ULLSCARF, GREAT RIGG (12½ miles)
- Little Gowder Crag, HAYSTACKS, KIRK FELL, GREAT GABLE, GREAT END, ESK PIKE, BOWFELL, GLARAMARA, HIGH RAISE, PIKE O' STICKLE, HARRISON STICKLE
- TH Crag, SCAFELL PIKE and Broad Crag, SCAFELL
- S
- Black Sails, SWIRL HOW

Lakes and Tarns

NNE: *Bassenthwaite Lake* and *Over Water*
ENE: *Derwentwater* } in view 10 yards from the cairn.
SSW: *Buttermere*
SSW: *Bleaberry Tarn*   SE: *Blea Tarn (Ullscarf)*

Sale Fell 1170'

from the Wythop valley

Sale Fell 2

NATURAL FEATURES

Sale Fell is the extreme corner-stone of the North Western Fells, with an outlook ranging far across the Cumberland plain to the Scottish coast. It is a familiar sight on the busy Keswick-Workington road, of which it has an oversight for several miles; going west along this road, Sale Fell marks the end of Lakeland.

It is a pleasant eminence of low altitude, not remarkable in itself (although of some interest to geologists) and its main attraction to walkers will be as an easy promenade providing an aerial survey of the hidden Wythop valley. The fell is grassy, with bracken, but the eastern slopes, going down sharply to Bassenthwaite Lake, are within the boundary of Thornthwaite Forest, and thickly planted. This is an old part of the forest, long known as Wythop Wood, and there is a welcome blend of its natural growth of deciduous trees with the more-favoured evergreens introduced commercially in recent decades.

There is a significance in the name of the olde hostelry, the Pheasant Inn, at the foot of the fell. At one time this neighbourhood was actively engaged in the rearing of game birds. There were pheasantries at Lothwaite Side and in the Wood itself, within easy memory.

One very delightful feature of Wythop Wood is the presence of the lovely little roe deer, shyest of creatures. The new plantations are fenced off against them, but they have freedom to roam in the older woodlands, and the men of the Forestry Commission deserve a very good mark for tolerating and harbouring these gentle animals in their preserves.

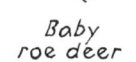

Baby roe deer

born to be free? or to be hunted and snared and shot by brave sportsmen?

Roe buck

Sale Fell 3

The Wythop Valley

The name is pronounced With-up locally. This quiet valley, almost unknown to Lakeland's visitors, is unique, not moulded at all to the usual pattern, a geographical freak.

The opening into it at Wythop Mill, between Sale Fell and Ling Fell, is so narrow and so embowered in trees that it might well pass without notice but for a signpost indicating a byway to Wythop Hall. Following this through a richly-wooded dell, the view up the valley opens suddenly beyond the farm of Eskin to reveal a lofty mountain directly ahead a few miles distant — a sight to stop explorers in their tracks. Of course all valleys run up into hills..... but what can this towering height be?.... Hearts quicken.... have we discovered an unknown 3000' peak? Wainwright's map on page 8 indicates no mountain ahead.... Get out a *decent* map, the Ordnance Survey one-inch — and the truth slowly dawns..... why, of course....it's dear old Skiddaw, of course, not immediately recognisable from this angle...... But how odd! What an illusion! The valley certainly *appears* to lead directly to the mountain, *but*, completely out of sight and unsuspected from this viewpoint, the wide trench containing Bassenthwaite Lake profoundly interrupts the rising contours in the line of vision. The fact is that the Wythop valley, like all others, has hills along both sides, but instead of the normal steepening of ground at its head there occurs a sharp declivity to another (and major) valley system, the Derwent, occupied here by the unseen lake with Skiddaw rising from its far shore. The Wythop valley, elevated 600 feet above that of the Derwent, drains *away* from it, and the unobtrusive watershed (a meeting of green pastures and dark forest) may therefore be likened to a pass. The whole arrangement is unusual and remarkable.

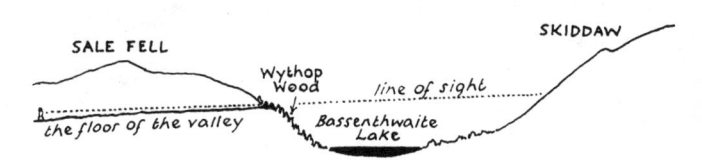

SALE FELL — Wythop Wood — line of sight — SKIDDAW
the floor of the valley — Bassenthwaite Lake

Having described the valley as a freak, it is important to say also, and emphasise, that its scenery is in no way freakish. Here is a charming and secluded natural sanctuary in an idyllic setting, a place of calm, where a peaceful farming community husband the good earth now as for centuries past. Every rod, pole and perch of it is delightful and unspoilt. Motorcars can penetrate as far as Wythop Hall but happily are unaware of this. The valley is undisturbed and quiet; men still travel on horseback. There are five scattered farmsteads and, at the head, Wythop Hall, rich in story and legend. In days gone by the valley maintained a larger population and a church.

Sale Fell 4

The Wythop Valley

The Great Illusion
(see opposite page)

Looking up the Wythop Valley to Skiddaw, from the slopes of Ling Fell. The furthest line of trees marks the end of the valley and Skiddaw rises beyond the unseen Bass Lake.

In this view from Lord's Seat, the Wythop Valley is seen sloping up gently from the left to the plantations of Wythop Wood, which fall steeply to Bass Lake. The distant hill on the right is Binsey.

Sale Fell 5

In Wythop Wood

Ladies Table

Ladies Table is a little peak at the head of the Wythop Valley above the declivity to Bassenthwaite Lake and within the forest boundary. Now wooded to the top, at 950', it has lost its former reputation as a viewpoint. A flat boulder, probably used by Victorian picnickers, may have given the place its name, but more likely it is a gentle parody on Lord's Seat nearby.

Much tree-felling of late has cluttered up and partly concealed the paths in the vicinity, and a visit is not recommended. Former paths giving access to the Table from private woods adjoining are now fenced off. The place is forgotten and only the name remains.

The Walton Memorial

Perched on the edge of a crag in the heart of the forest, with a splendid vista of Skiddaw, is a memorial seat in native green stone, with a tablet inscribed "Thornthwaite Forest. In memory of WILFRED WALTON, Head Forester 1948-1959. In appreciation."

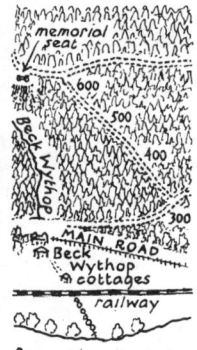

Bassenthwaite Lake looking southwest

Putting out pipes and cigarettes, follow the forest roads from the cottages as indicated, watching for the first turn left in 250 yards. Don't let the children go on ahead: DANGER!

Sale Fell 6

Looking across the Wythop Valley to Lord's Seat, from Lothwaite

Lothwaite is the eastern shoulder of Sale Fell. A grassy alp, it is a pleasant sheep pasture and in summer is a floral garden. Apart from a solitary boulder and two strange circular heaps of stones like small tumuli — not cairns, and possibly (but incredibly) collected to keep the grass tidy — it is featureless. The suffix 'thwaite' is unusual for an open upland.

Sale Fell 7

MAP

At the side of a public footpath beyond Kelswick is the crumbled masonry of a small building that would be passed without notice but for a tablet inscribed 'SITE OF WYTHOP OLD CHURCH' against the inner wall. (On Ordnance maps it is indicated by 'Chapel — Remains of')

This old church has been replaced by a new one — St. Margarets — on the road between Wythop Mill and Routenbeck, but once a year a public service (necessarily open-air) is held in the ruins.

St. Margarets

ONE MILE

Wythop Beck and Beck Wythop
— a clever distinction in names.

These are separate streams following widely different courses. The map has been extended in the south (next page) to illustrate how they come down from Lord's Seat together, side by side and almost arm in arm, until an insignificant watershed causes them to part company. Thereupon *Wythop Beck* proceeds to act as main drain for the Wythop Valley, escaping through a narrow gap at Wythop Mill to enter the broad strath of Embleton, and here it meanders, contrary to expectations, 'backwards' to Bassenthwaite Lake, joining it just north of the railway station (that's it at the top of the map, next page) after a circular tour around the base of Sale Fell. *Beck Wythop* has a much briefer passage, falling rapidly in its wooded gorge to join Bass Lake at Beck Wythop cottages.

Failure of an Enterprise

There is a story behind the ruins on the edge of the wood (south of Wythop Hall, map next page). Here are substantial foundations of buildings, and it is a great surprise to find them in so remote a place and in such rural surroundings. In the 1930's modern plant was installed here for the manufacture of silica bricks, a mineral railway laid, the road to Wythop Hall improved and re-routed and scores of workmen engaged. The product was not of sufficiently good quality. The buildings and plant were dismantled and taken away, the men dismissed and the site vacated. Today only the road-extension to Wythop Hall remains in use.

Sale Fell 8

MAP

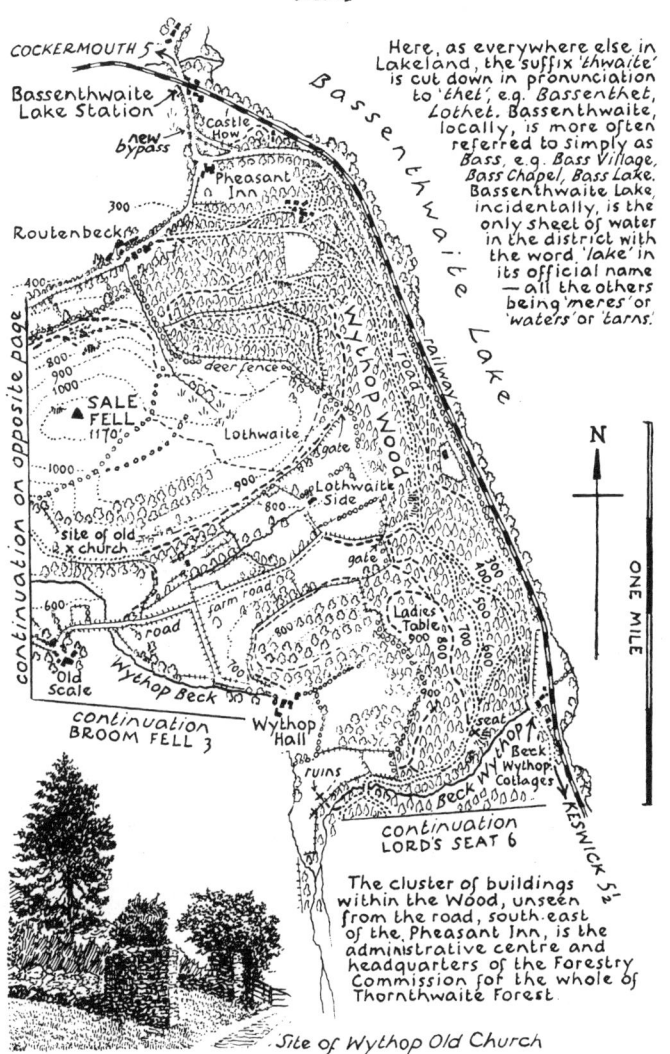

Here, as everywhere else in Lakeland, the suffix 'thwaite' is cut down in pronunciation to 'thet', e.g. Bassenthet, Lothet. Bassenthwaite, locally, is more often referred to simply as Bass, e.g. Bass Village, Bass Chapel, Bass Lake. Bassenthwaite Lake, incidentally, is the only sheet of water in the district with the word 'lake' in its official name — all the others being 'meres' or 'waters' or 'tarns'.

The cluster of buildings within the Wood, unseen from the road, south-east of the Pheasant Inn, is the administrative centre and headquarters of the Forestry Commission for the whole of Thornthwaite Forest.

Site of Wythop Old Church

Sale Fell 9

ASCENT FROM BASSENTHWAITE LAKE STATION
930 feet of ascent : 2 miles

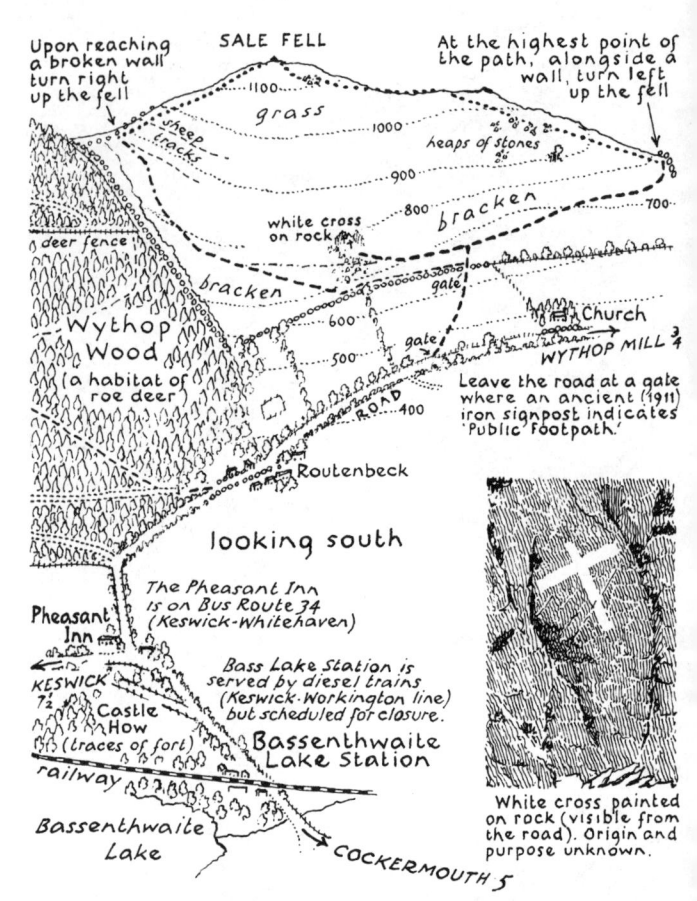

Upon reaching a broken wall turn right up the fell

SALE FELL

At the highest point of the path, alongside a wall, turn left up the fell

grass
sheep tracks
heaps of stones
bracken
white cross on rock
bracken
deer fence
gate
Wythop Wood (a habitat of roe deer)
gate
Church
WYTHOP MILL ¾

Leave the road at a gate where an ancient (1911) iron signpost indicates 'Public Footpath'.

ROAD
Routenbeck

looking south

The Pheasant Inn is on Bus Route 34 (Keswick-Whitehaven)

Pheasant Inn
KESWICK 7½
Castle How (traces of fort)

Bass Lake Station is served by diesel trains (Keswick-Workington line) but scheduled for closure.

Bassenthwaite Lake Station
railway
Bassenthwaite Lake
COCKERMOUTH 5

White cross painted on rock (visible from the road). Origin and purpose unknown.

A pleasant little climb. Make a traverse of the fell by using both routes; preferably that on the left for ascent, that on the right as a way down. The round journey can be done in an hour from the gate at the roadside. Good views.

Sale Fell 10

ASCENT FROM WYTHOP MILL
750 feet of ascent : 1½ miles

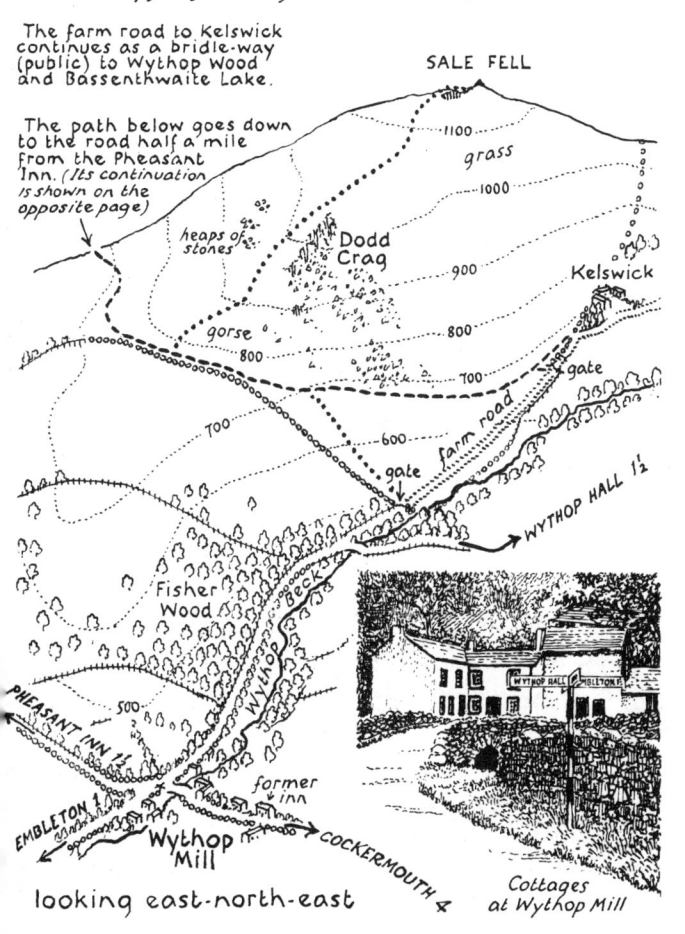

The farm road to Kelswick continues as a bridle-way (public) to Wythop Wood and Bassenthwaite Lake.

The path below goes down to the road half a mile from the Pheasant Inn. (Its continuation is shown on the opposite page)

SALE FELL

grass

Dodd Crag

heaps of stones

Kelswick

gorse

gate

farm road

WYTHOP HALL 1½

gate

Fisher Wood

Wythop Beck

PHEASANT INN 1½

former inn

EMBLETON 1

Wythop Mill

COCKERMOUTH 4

looking east-north-east

Cottages at Wythop Mill

A sylvan approach gives added pleasure to this simple climb. As an introduction to the Wythop Valley (an introduction warmly to be commended) this route is excellent and instructive.

Sale Fell 11

THE SUMMIT

SKIDDAW — ULLOCK PIKE — LONG SIDE — SKIDDAW LITTLE MAN — CARL SIDE — DODD

Lothwaite (subsidiary ridge)

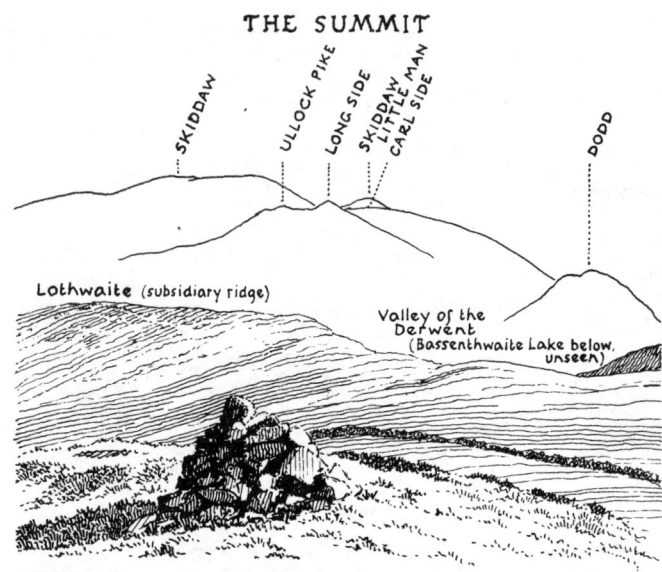

Valley of the Derwent (Bassenthwaite Lake below, unseen)

The top is a pleasant grassy pasture populated by sheep but unfrequented by man — which makes it a desirable objective on a summer's day for anyone who would like to visit a summit for quiet meditation without, however, incurring the expenditure of much energy on the ascent.

For ordinary mortals there is nothing of interest in the vicinity of the cairn, but visitors with geological knowledge might add to it by doing a little exploring. John Postlethwaite's excellent *Mines and Mining in the Lake District* contains this impressive paragraph:—

"Near the summit of Sale Fell, there is a small mass of very beautiful rock. It consists of a pink crystalline felspathic base, in which there are numerous crystals of dark-green mica. The base is chiefly composed of orthoclase, but some triclinic, probably oligoclase, is also present. There is no quartz visible to the naked eye, but small crystals may be detected under the microscope. There is also a little hornblende present. The rock is very hard and tough, and in lithological character is unlike any other rock in the Lake Country." *(with acknowledgments)*

All this is Greek to the poor layman, and he would be no wiser after an inspection of three possible sites: (1) a rockface in view from the cairn, (2) a collection of upstanding boulders, and (3) a scattering of 'white' stones, although he might notice that some of the latter appear to have been chipped by hammers. There is no other rock in sight, and one of these must be Mr. P's 'small mass', but, in spite of his liberal detail, *which?* What is 'orthoclase'? Or, worse still, 'oligoclase'? Resuming his meditations at the cairn after this abortive tour, let him now reflect on the poverty of his education. How much there is to learn about this fair earth and how little we know! How much beauty is never seen!

stones — boulders — grass — rockface

N — 100 YARDS

Sale Fell 12

THE VIEW

The Skiddaw group is the best thing in the view, the top being displayed, not as the usual pyramid but as a long, level skyline. The Helvellyn range is also well seen as a tremendous wall running across the district, but elsewhere the prospect towards Lakeland is disappointing, the higher Lord's Seat nearby concealing the mountains of the interior. The Wythop valley below is very pleasant, a restful hollow of woodlands and green fields. Criffell is conspicuous on a Scottish horizon extending west to the hills of Galloway.

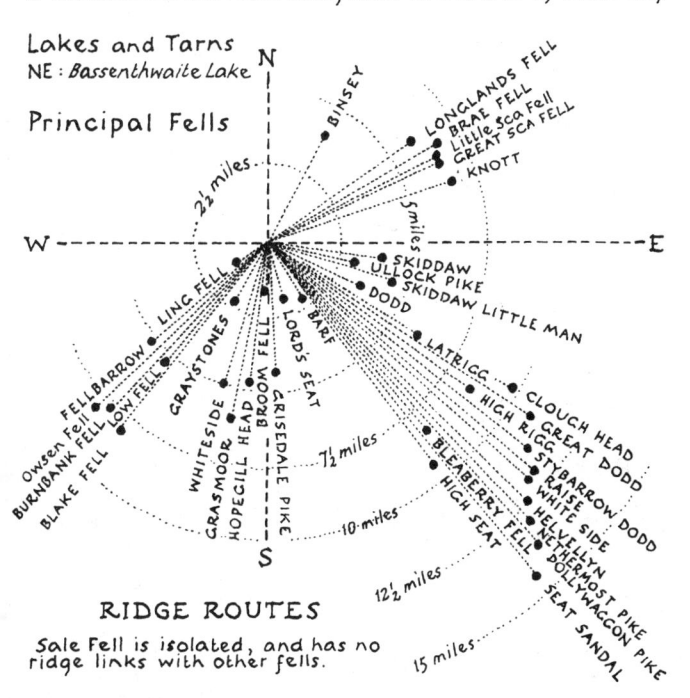

Lakes and Tarns
NE: Bassenthwaite Lake

Principal Fells

RIDGE ROUTES

Sale Fell is isolated, and has no ridge links with other fells.

A note for sheep fanciers:

The oldest strain of sheep in Lakeland is the Herdwick, a small, ragged but very hardy breed, tough enough to winter on the tops, and producer of the best mutton. Latterly, the Swaledale and the Rough Fell varieties, bigger animals with a heavier crop of wool but needing the shelter of the valleys in winter, have been increasingly introduced. The sheep on Sale Fell are a cross between Herdwick and Swaledale and so combine the best qualities of each — but only in half-measure.

Scar Crags 2205'

the eastern ridge

Scar Crags is the big brother of Causey Pike, topping the latter by 170 feet, but it is the lesser height that captures the fancy, that provides the challenge, that steals the picture and is the better known by far. Scar Crags continues the line of the ridge towards Eel Crag, and does so in rather striking fashion, having a ragged edge of broken heathery crag throughout its length, and, below, an excessively rough slope falls steeply to Rigg Beck. There is a regular and recurring pattern of arete and gully on this southern face, as though the fellside had been scraped by a giant comb: an effect best seen from Ard Crags directly opposite. The north flank has nothing of interest; once however it was the scene of unusual industrial activity, Lakeland's only cobalt mine being situated here in the stony amphitheatre of Long Crag.

West of the summit, the fell drops gently to Sail Pass, a useful crossing between Braithwaite and Buttermere for travellers on foot.

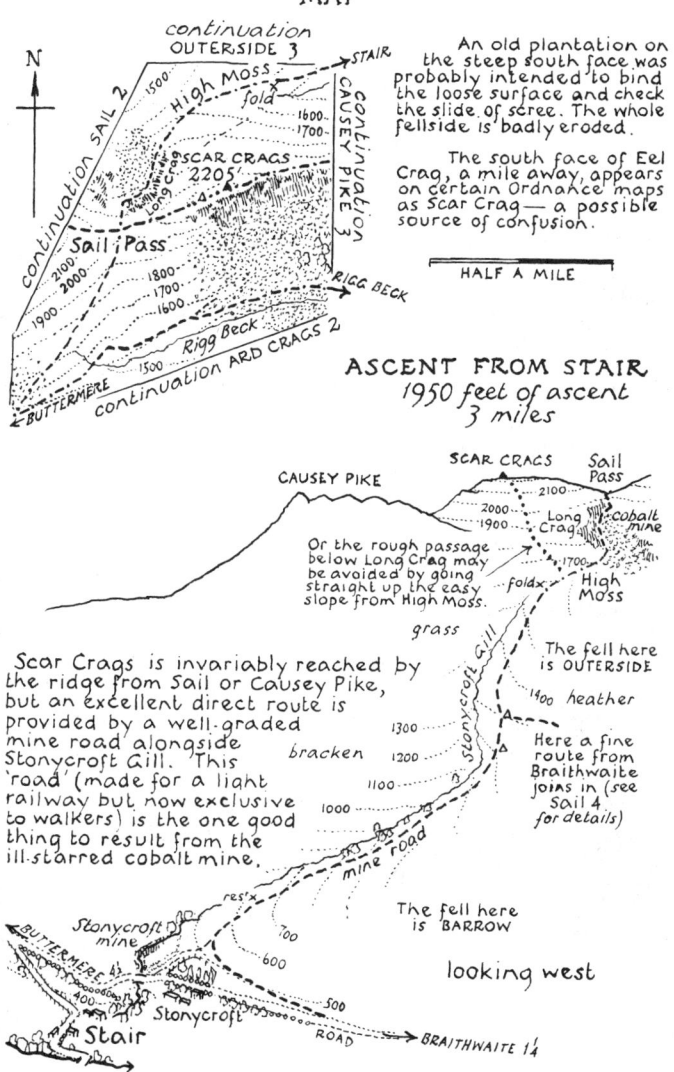

Scar Crags 2

MAP

An old plantation on the steep south face was probably intended to bind the loose surface and check the slide of scree. The whole fellside is badly eroded.

The south face of Eel Crag, a mile away, appears on certain Ordnance maps as Scar Crag — a possible source of confusion.

HALF A MILE

continuation OUTERSIDE 3
continuation SAIL 2
continuation CAUSEY PIKE 3
continuation ARD CRAGS 2

High Moss fold
SCAR CRAGS 2205'
Sail Pass
RIGG BECK
Rigg Beck
BUTTERMERE
STAIR

ASCENT FROM STAIR
1950 feet of ascent
3 miles

CAUSEY PIKE — SCAR CRAGS — Sail Pass
Long Crag — cobalt mine
High Moss
Or the rough passage below Long Crag may be avoided by going straight up the easy slope from High Moss.

The fell here is OUTERSIDE — heather

Stonycroft Gill — grass — bracken

Here a fine route from Braithwaite joins in (see Sail 4 for details)

Scar Crags is invariably reached by the ridge from Sail or Causey Pike, but an excellent direct route is provided by a well-graded mine road alongside Stonycroft Gill. This 'road' (made for a light railway but now exclusive to walkers) is the one good thing to result from the ill-starred cobalt mine.

mine road — rest

Stonycroft mine
BUTTERMERE
Stonycroft
Stair
ROAD → BRAITHWAITE 1¼

The fell here is BARROW

looking west

Scar Crags 3

THE SUMMIT

looking down to Causey Pike

Unexpectedly the top is flat, and there is no obvious sign of the double breaking wave formed by the summit-outline as seen from the Keswick area, although this can be identified after a study of the ground. The largest cairn is not on the highest point, which overlooks Causey Pike (as illustrated). The top is grassy.
DESCENTS: It is usual to descend by the ridge, via Causey Pike, but simpler and quicker to go down the north slope (no path) to join the Stonycroft mine road. The south slope is impossible.

RIDGE ROUTES

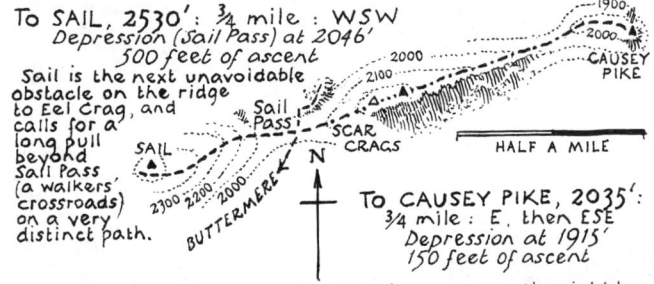

To SAIL, 2530': ¾ mile: WSW
Depression (Sail Pass) at 2046'
500 feet of ascent
Sail is the next unavoidable obstacle on the ridge to Eel Crag, and calls for a long pull beyond Sail Pass (a walkers' crossroads) on a very distinct path.

To CAUSEY PIKE, 2035':
¾ mile: E, then ESE
Depression at 1915'
150 feet of ascent
Keeping the steep edge on the right hand, a pleasant track leads down to a depression, beyond which is a short climb and a switchback journey over the several bumps of Causey Pike to the last one.

Scar Crags 4

THE VIEW

The view is good, but its detail is not so well composed as in the panorama from the neighbouring Causey Pike, while the advantage in altitude contributes little extra to the scene; in particular the valley and lake scenery between north and east is less satisfactory. The mountain picture is inspiring, however, especially to the south, and close by in the west the head of Coledale is very well displayed. The more intimate peep downwards to Rigg Beck from the edge of the crags near at hand should not be omitted.

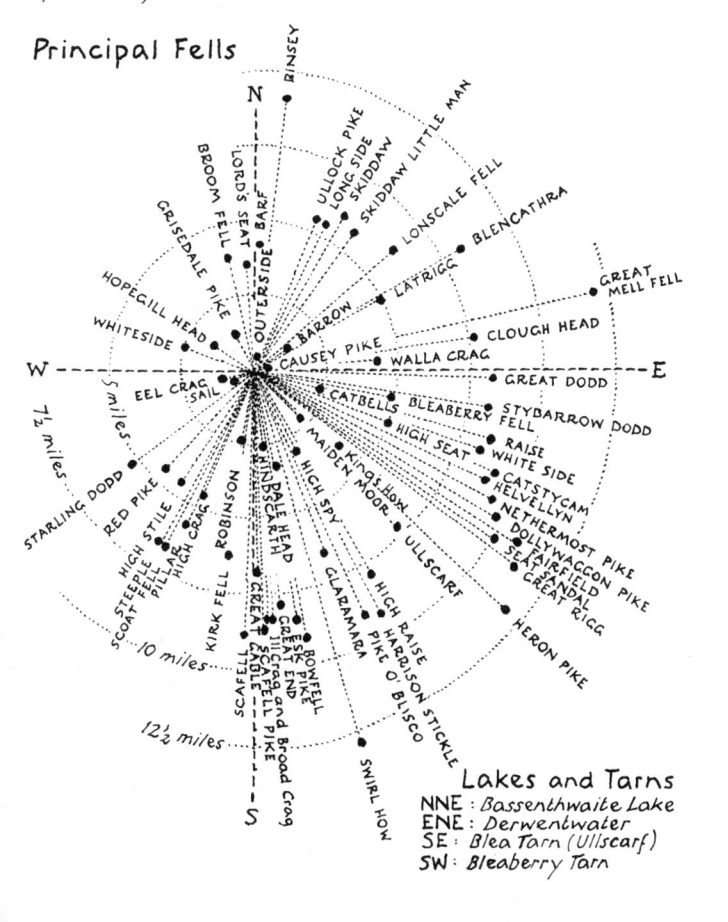

Principal Fells

Lakes and Tarns
NNE: Bassenthwaite Lake
ENE: Derwentwater
SE: Blea Tarn (Ullscarf)
SW: Bleaberry Tarn

Wandope 2533'

'Wanlope' on recent issues
of Ordnance Survey maps

from Ard Crags

GRASMOOR ▲ EEL CRAG
WANDOPE ▲ ▲ WHITELESS PIKE
● Rannerdale
● Buttermere

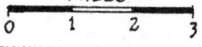

MILES 0 1 2 3

Wandope 2

NATURAL FEATURES

There is no mountain not worth climbing, and any summit above the magic figure of 2,500 feet might be expected to attract fellwalkers and peakbaggers in large numbers. To some extent, Wandope does this, but only because the top almost gets in the way of a popular triangular tour based on Buttermere — Whiteless Pike, Eel Crag, Grasmoor — and the cairn is visited almost as a matter of course (if indeed it is noticed at all) and by the simplest of detours. The other three, too, feature more prominently in the landscape and are often climbed individually as sole objectives — but rarely Wandope, which is sandwiched between neighbours and too hidden to attract separate attention. In fact, Wandope is only well seen from the uninhabited valley of Sail Beck, from which it rises in a mile-long wall rimmed a thousand feet above by a line of shattered crags. The hinterland of the summit is an upland prairie dominated by Grasmoor and Eel Crag, and it is along here that most walkers pass, often without realising that the insignificant swell of grass on the eastern fringe is distinguished both by a name and an altitude above the 2500' contour.

Wandope might be expected to stand out more conspicuously from the greater mass behind, for it is partly severed by two gills which drain from the plateau and immediately form, on either side, deeply carved rifts, one a scree-choked ravine, the other a profound hollow. These are Third Gill, south, and Addacomb Gill, north, and both go down to Sail Beck. The first is a place to avoid, the second a place to visit or at least look at from the rim of its crater: the profound cwm is Addacomb Hole, a perfect example of a hanging valley, quite the finest in Lakeland, and a remarkable specimen of natural sculpturing. The issuing stream has high waterfalls and the whole scene is a complete geography lesson without words. Wandope is also a feeder of Rannerdale Beck.

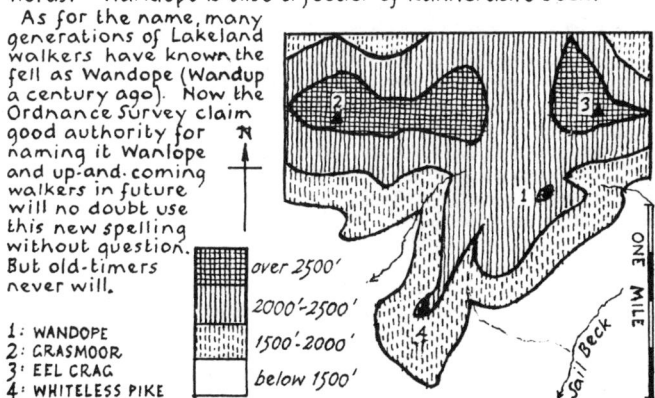

As for the name, many generations of Lakeland walkers have known the fell as Wandope (Wandup a century ago). Now the Ordnance Survey claim good authority for naming it Wanlope and up-and-coming walkers in future will no doubt use this new spelling without question. But old-timers never will.

over 2500'
2000'-2500'
1500'-2000'
below 1500'

1: WANDOPE
2: GRASMOOR
3: EEL CRAG
4: WHITELESS PIKE

ONE MILE

Sail Beck

Wandope 3

The Addacomb Ridge, from Sail Beck

The Thirdgill Ridge, from Whiteless Breast

Wandope 4

MAP

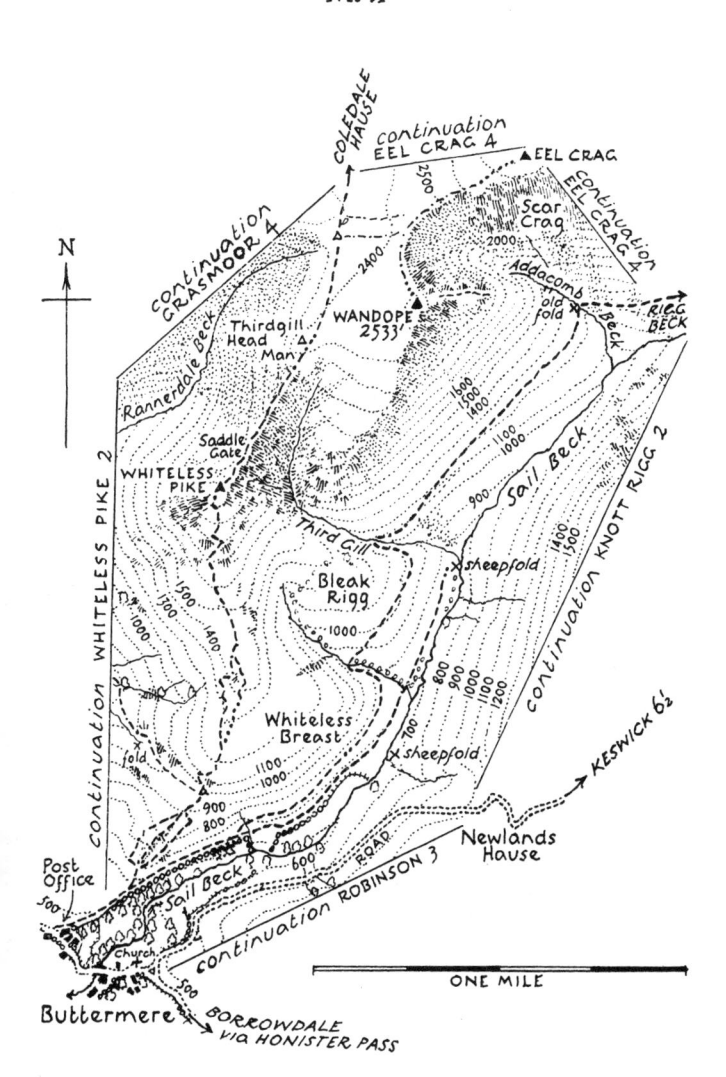

Wandope 5

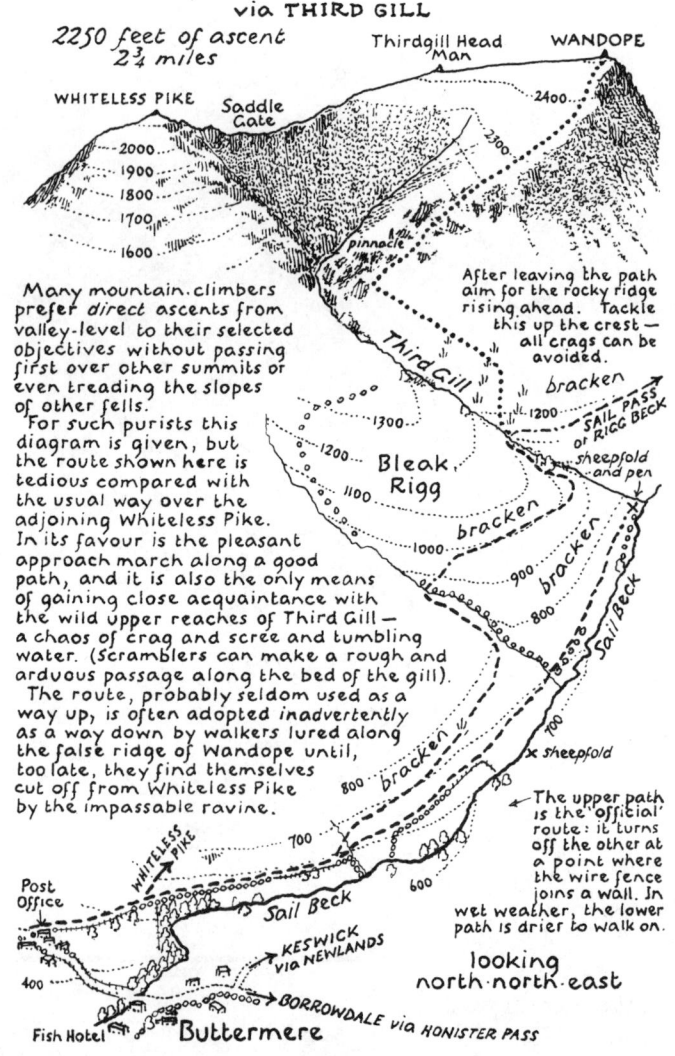

ASCENT FROM BUTTERMERE
via THIRD GILL

2250 feet of ascent
2¾ miles

looking north-north-east

Many mountain climbers prefer *direct* ascents from valley-level to their selected objectives without passing first over other summits or even treading the slopes of other fells.

For such purists this diagram is given, but the route shown here is tedious compared with the usual way over the adjoining Whiteless Pike. In its favour is the pleasant approach march along a good path, and it is also the only means of gaining close acquaintance with the wild upper reaches of Third Gill — a chaos of crag and scree and tumbling water. (Scramblers can make a rough and arduous passage along the bed of the gill).

The route, probably seldom used as a way up, is often adopted inadvertently as a way down by walkers lured along the false ridge of Wandope until, too late, they find themselves cut off from Whiteless Pike by the impassable ravine.

After leaving the path aim for the rocky ridge rising ahead. Tackle this up the crest — all crags can be avoided.

The upper path is the 'official' route: it turns off the other at a point where the wire fence joins a wall. In wet weather, the lower path is drier to walk on.

Wandope 6

ASCENT FROM BUTTERMERE
via THE ADDACOMB RIDGE
2250 feet of ascent
3½ miles

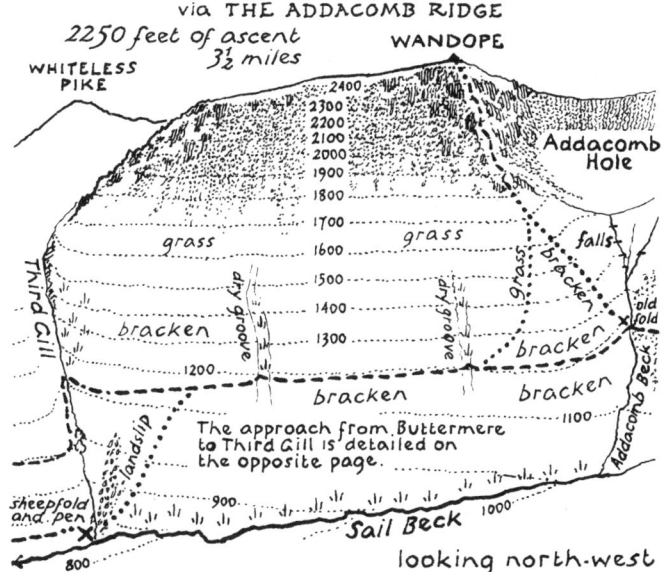

looking north-west

The path across the breast is part of the through-route from Buttermere to Rigg Beck, Newlands — a grand walkers' way among the hills, avoiding the motor road. A branch goes over Sail Pass to link with Braithwaite.

From the sheepfold at the crossing of Addacomb Beck go left straight up the ridge (here ill-defined), or, to avoid overmuch bracken, cut the corner from the second of two rushy grooves. When the first rocks are reached the ridge becomes narrower and a thin track climbs up through heather and bilberry and sundry Alpine flora, with Addacomb Hole sinking ever lower on the right. This section of the ridge is excellent and the route continues first-class to the top, which is reached exactly at the summit-cairn.

If using this route in reverse (or travelling to Buttermere from Newlands by the path) pedestrians hurrying to catch a bus, or desperate for a pint, can save ten minutes by dropping down to the sheepfold at Third Gill and using the lower (straighter) path.

The great feature of this route, apart from the ridge itself (the upper half of which is delightful) is Addacomb Hole — a perfect hanging valley.
Only by the gradual gaining of height along the ridge can the proportions of this remarkable half-crater be fully appreciated.

Wandope 7

ASCENT FROM BUTTERMERE
2300 feet of ascent : 2½ miles

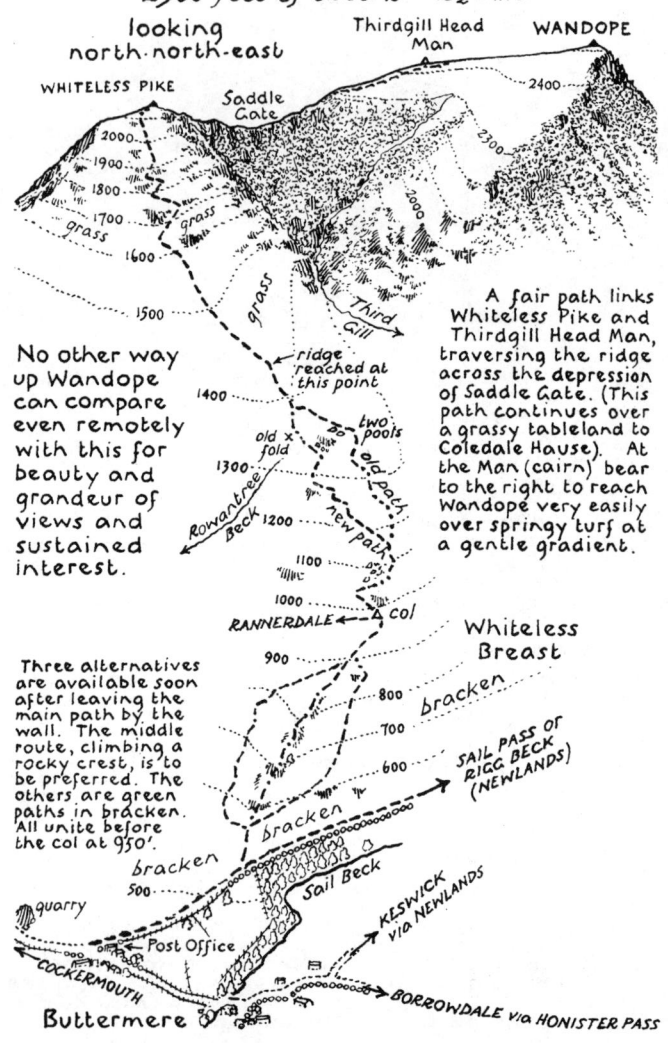

looking north-north-east

WHITELESS PIKE — Saddle Gate — Thirdgill Head Man — WANDOPE

A fair path links Whiteless Pike and Thirdgill Head Man, traversing the ridge across the depression of Saddle Gate. (This path continues over a grassy tableland to Coledale House). At the Man (cairn) bear to the right to reach Wandope very easily over springy turf at a gentle gradient.

No other way up Wandope can compare even remotely with this for beauty and grandeur of views and sustained interest.

ridge reached at this point
old x fold — two pools
Rowantree Beck — old path / new path

RANNERDALE ← col
Whiteless Breast
bracken
SAIL PASS OR RIGG BECK (NEWLANDS)

Three alternatives are available soon after leaving the main path by the wall. The middle route, climbing a rocky crest, is to be preferred. The others are green paths in bracken. All unite before the col at 950'.

bracken
quarry
Post Office
Sail Beck
COCKERMOUTH
Buttermere
KESWICK via NEWLANDS
BORROWDALE via HONISTER PASS

Wandope 8

THE SUMMIT

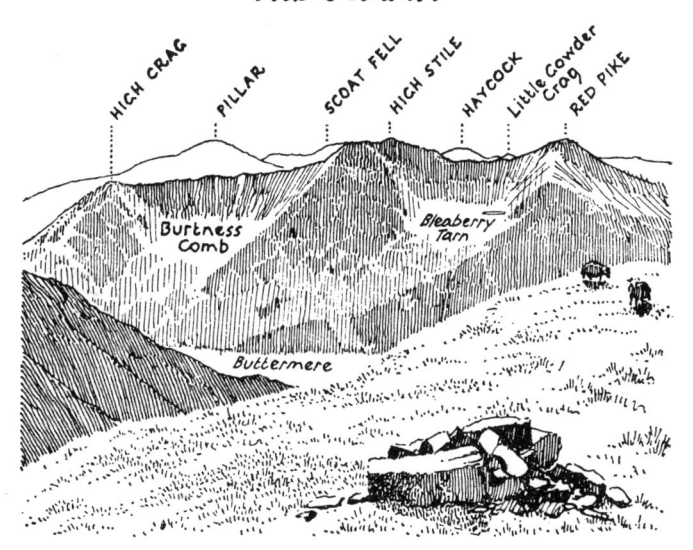

Apart from the view, the summit is unremarkable, being a smooth grassy parade kept neat and trim by grazing sheep. The stones of the cairn, which stands near the brink of the great downfall to Sail Beck, were obviously not provided by the summit itself, and some anonymous enthusiast must, in days gone by, have laboured mightily in bringing them up from the escarpment.

DESCENTS : The quickest way down (for Buttermere) is by the steepening southern slope, keeping the edge of the craggy east face close on the left until the ground falls more abruptly to Third Gill. There are crags below, which can be avoided, but it is best to break out of them to the left to a grassy slope, which can be followed down to join the Sail Beck path for Buttermere. If time permits, the Addacomb ridge should be preferred — this is useful also for Newlands — or the valley may be reached by a detour over Whiteless Pike, this being the usual course. In mist the Addacomb ridge is least likely to lead to trouble.

For destinations north, there is a very fast descent via Coledale Hause to Braithwaite in 1½ hours.

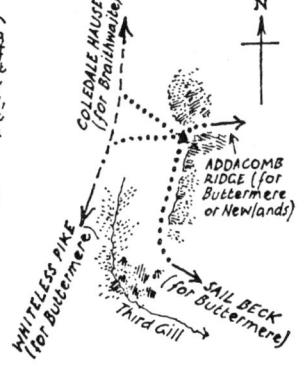

Wandope 9

THE VIEW

Pride of place in the view must be conceded to the Scafells, from here looking magnificent, but scarcely less impressive is the scene eastwards, where range after range of tall fells cross the line of vision to culminate finally in the long Helvellyn skyline. The head of Sail Beck is a striking feature far below. Grasmoor and Eel Crag occupy much of the horizon, appearing dreary and shapeless at such close quarters, and Hopegill Head fits neatly into the gap between. Ingleborough, Cross Fell, and the Isle of Man are all visible on a clear day.

Principal Fells

(radial diagram showing fells at various distances — 2½ miles, 5 miles, 7½ miles, 10 miles, 12½ miles — with compass directions N, W, E, S)

N: HOPEGILL HEAD
10 miles: BOWSCALE FELL
7½ miles: BLENCATHRA
GRASMOOR, EEL CRAG, SAIL, CAUSEY PIKE, GREAT MELL FELL, CLOUGH HEAD, GREAT DODD
BURNBANK FELL, BLAKE FELL, ARD CRAGS, BLEABERRY FELL, STYBARROW DODD
W — BLAKE FELL ... BLEABERRY FELL — E
GAVEL FELL, MELLBREAK, HIGH SEAT, RAISE
HEN COMB, MAIDEN MOOR, WHITE SIDE, CATSTYCAM, HELVELLYN
GREAT BORNE, KNOTT RIGG, HIGH SPY, NETHERMOST PIKE
CRAG FELL, ROBINSON, HINDSCARTH, DOLLYWAGGON PIKE
LANK RIGG, STARLING DODD, FLEETWITH PIKE, DALE HEAD, FAIRFIELD
RED PIKE, HAYSTACKS, ULLSCARF, RED SCREES
CAW FELL, HIGH STILE, KIRK FELL, GREAT RIGG
Little Gowder Crag, HAYCOCK, PILLAR, GREAT GABLE, GLARAMARA, HIGH RAISE
SCOAT FELL, HIGH CRAG, GREAT END, BOWFELL, ESK PIKE, HARRISON STICKLE
SCAFELL PIKE, LINGMELL, SCAFELL
12½ miles
S: WETHERLAM

The Scafell group

B EP G.E.   G.G. SP   S   KF
                      L
      FP   H

Lakes and Tarns
E: Derwentwater
S: Buttermere
SSW: Bleaberry Tarn

Wandope 10

RIDGE ROUTES

To GRASMOOR, 2791': 1¼ miles: NW, then W.
Depression at 2375': 430 feet of ascent
An uninteresting journey over wide plateaux

Aim north-west to reach the Coledale-Whiteless Pike path where it skirts the head of Rannerdale. There is a cairn here on a little patch of gravel. Turning towards Coledale, watch for a series of cairns ascending the fellside on the left and do likewise. Along the wide top of Grasmoor, at the head of the slope, the track is more imaginary than real, but the walking, on mossy turf, could not be better; there is a half-mile of it before the top is reached.

To EEL CRAG, 2749': ¾ mile: N, then NE.
Depression at 2420': 340 feet of ascent
A cliff-edge circuit of Addacomb Hole

The only instruction necessary is to follow the semi-circular rim of the crater immediately to the north. There is no path at first, but a thin one is soon picked up and this becomes more distinct on rougher ground as height is gained.

To WHITELESS PIKE, 2159': ⅞ mile: W, then SW.
Depression at 2050': 110 feet of ascent
A good finish along an excellent ridge

Many walkers must have been beguiled by the southern ridge of Wandope into the false assumption that, if they follow it down, it will lead them to Whiteless Pike. Every step along here, however, puts Whiteless Pike further out of reach while bringing it nearer, because of the rough ravine forming between. The southern ridge is, in fact, a snare and a delusion. To gain the true one, aim west from the summit and make for the cairn of Thirdgill Head Man: it comes into view after a few paces. Here a path will be met; turn left along it and go down a narrowing crest to Saddle Gate for the climb to the Pike, now directly ahead.

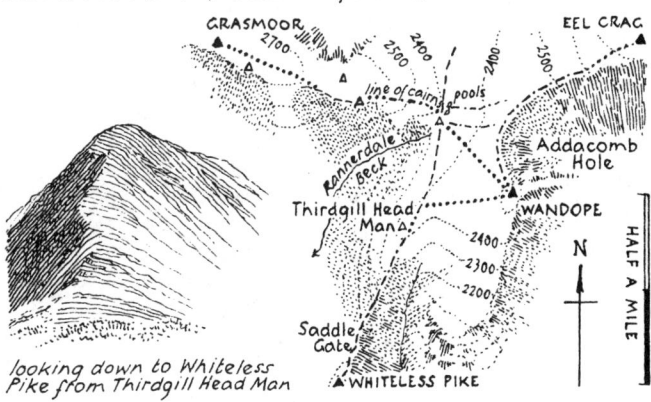

looking down to Whiteless Pike from Thirdgill Head Man

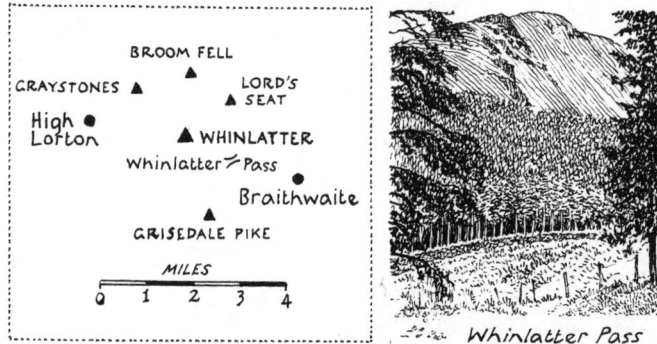

Whinlatter 1696'

from High Lorton

Whinlatter Pass

Whinlatter 2

NATURAL FEATURES

Whinlatter the Pass, an excellent motor road, is known to many; Whinlatter the Fell, a lonely sheep pasture, is known to few. The abrupt heathery slopes, streaked with long tongues of scree, form an effective northern wall to the pass, and there is little in this rough and forbidding declivity to suggest the pleasant heights above, where an undulating plateau trends downwards to the quiet valley of Aiken Beck. This stream defines the boundaries to west and north; the eastern termination of the fell, among the Thornthwaite plantations, is less distinct. From the top the extent of the afforestation of the surrounding area is appreciated fully: plantations almost encircle the fell, and indeed its own western and northern flanks are under timber. The rough face above the pass, significantly, has not been acquired for forestry, and the solitary sheep-farm of Darling How has retained much of its open range.

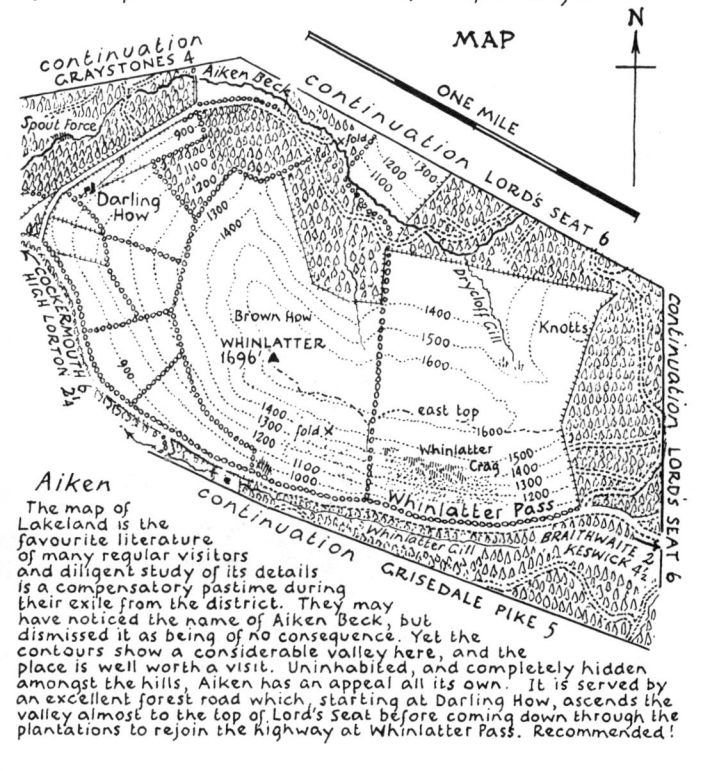

MAP

Aiken

The map of Lakeland is the favourite literature of many regular visitors and diligent study of its details is a compensatory pastime during their exile from the district. They may have noticed the name of Aiken Beck, but dismissed it as being of no consequence. Yet the contours show a considerable valley here, and the place is well worth a visit. Uninhabited, and completely hidden amongst the hills, Aiken has an appeal all its own. It is served by an excellent forest road which, starting at Darling How, ascends the valley almost to the top of Lord's Seat before coming down through the plantations to rejoin the highway at Whinlatter Pass. Recommended!

Whinlatter 3

Grisedale Pike, from the east ridge of Whinlatter

Whinlatter 4

ASCENT FROM WHINLATTER PASS
750 feet of ascent : 1¼ miles

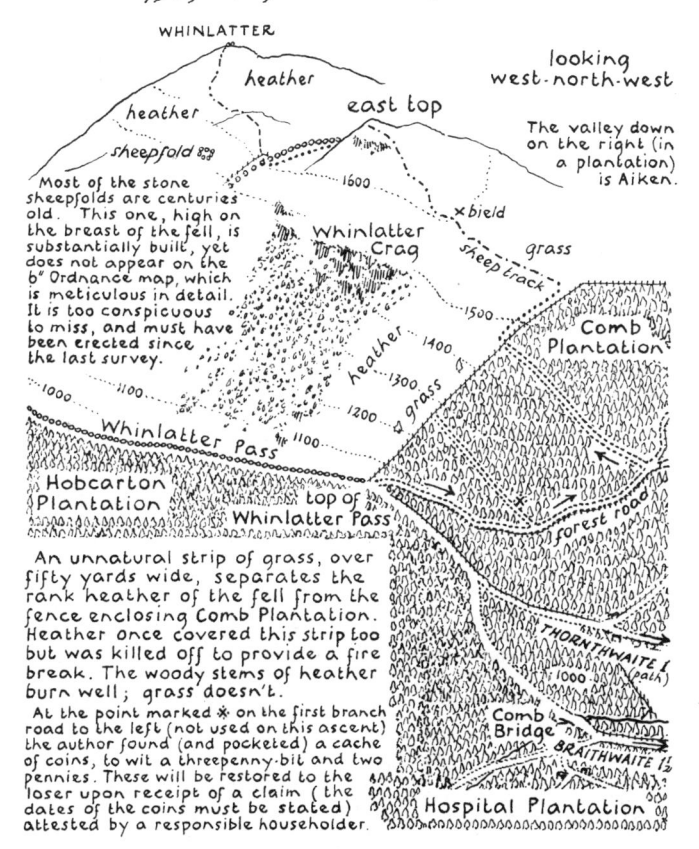

WHINLATTER

heather

heather — east top

looking west-north-west

The valley down on the right (in a plantation) is Aiken.

sheepfold

Most of the stone sheepfolds are centuries old. This one, high on the breast of the fell, is substantially built, yet does not appear on the 6" Ordnance map, which is meticulous in detail. It is too conspicuous to miss, and must have been erected since the last survey.

Whinlatter Crag

× bield

sheep track

grass

1600 — 1500 — 1400 — 1300 — 1200 — heather — grass

Comb Plantation

1000 — 1100

Whinlatter Pass

1100

Hobcarton Plantation

top of Whinlatter Pass

forest road

An unnatural strip of grass, over fifty yards wide, separates the rank heather of the fell from the fence enclosing Comb Plantation. Heather once covered this strip too but was killed off to provide a fire break. The woody stems of heather burn well; grass doesn't.

At the point marked ✲ on the first branch road to the left (not used on this ascent) the author found (and pocketed) a cache of coins, to wit a threepenny-bit and two pennies. These will be restored to the loser upon receipt of a claim (the dates of the coins must be stated) attested by a responsible householder.

THORNTHWAITE

1000 (path)

Comb Bridge

BRAITHWAITE

Hospital Plantation

Whinlatter tempts few walkers, the steep slopes of heather and scree above the Pass being too rough to contemplate, but the crest of the fell is entirely different — a delightfully undulating ridge, a joy to walk upon. It can be attained, moreover, by the simplest of gradients if the direct climb alongside the fence is disregarded in favour of the helpful forest roads depicted in the diagram, the whole of the walk then being no more than an hour's ramble.

Whinlatter 5

THE SUMMIT

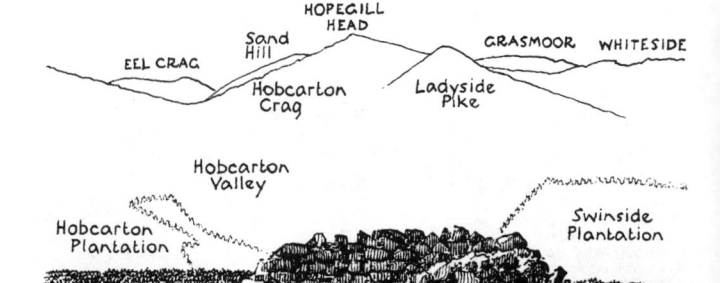

(panorama labels: EEL CRAG — Sand Hill — HOPEGILL HEAD — Hobcarton Crag — Ladyside Pike — GRASMOOR — WHITESIDE)

Hobcarton Valley — Hobcarton Plantation — Swinside Plantation

The part of the fell recognised as the summit is the small heathery dome of Brown How at the westerly end of its long undulating top. Here, still in a good state of preservation, is a wall in the form of a crescent, which, if intended as a wind-shelter, seems an extravagance in a place so seldom visited; more probably, considering the ocean of heather all around, it was built to serve as a shooting-hide.

The Ordnance Surveyors had no doubts that this was the highest point of the fell, at 1696', for only here is a 25' contour shown (on their 2½" map) above 1650', yet the eastern top appears from here to be at least equally high. This may be an illusion of the sort familiar to all who frequent mountain-tops, for subsidiary summits often have a trick of appearing higher than the true summit when viewed from the latter, the eye having no horizontal level to assist in hilly terrain. In this case, however, the illusion is strengthened by the distant background to the eastern top, formed by Stybarrow Dodd (2770') with Sticks Pass (2420') to its right — for the line of vision from the main top to the eastern top strikes the background only a few hundred feet lower than the Pass, say at 2000', and is therefore rising, from which it follows that any intermediate points on that line (including the eastern top) must be at a greater elevation than the viewpoint. Without instruments allowances must be made for defective vision and mental weakness, while refraction of light and curvature of the earth may be factors necessary to correct the judgment of the eye. The most that one dare bet is that the eastern top should be credited with at least a 1675' contour — an investment worthy of anybody's bottom dollar.

STYBARROW DODD 2770' — Sticks Pass 2420' — eastern top

looking from the summit

DESCENTS: Routes down to Aiken Beck are easy if the plantation is avoided, down to Whinlatter Pass are exceedingly rough other than by the line suggested as a route of ascent (see page 4).

Whinlatter 6

THE VIEW

The view generally is inferior to those from neighbouring heights, but in one direction it excels, this being to the south, where the supporting buttresses of the lofty Grisedale Pike - Hopegill Head ridge build up magnificently across the depths of Whinlatter Pass and reveal various lines of ascent that have tended to become overlooked as afforestation of the lower slopes has taken place.

The Vale of Lorton also features well, but here is viewed from the side and is less effective than when seen end-on along its full length.

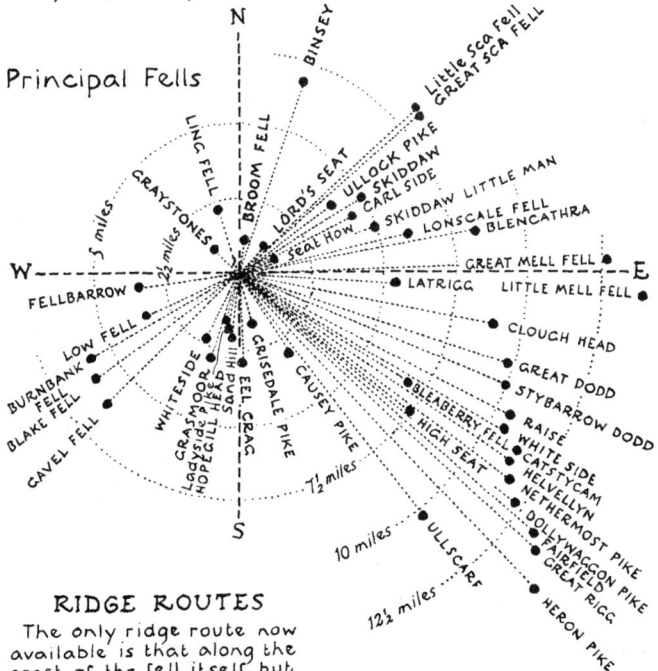

Principal Fells

RIDGE ROUTES

The only ridge route now available is that along the crest of the fell itself, but at one time it was possible to make a high-level way round to Lord's Seat and Broom Fell, keeping above 1500' throughout — a fine circuit of the Aiken valley. Afforestation and fences have put an end to this.

Lakes and Tarns

The Solway Firth is the only sheet of water in sight, but from the eastern top of the fell Derwentwater makes a charming picture above the intervening plantations.

Whiteless Pike 2159'

from Rannerdale Farm

The popular concept of a true mountain shape is a pyramid, with steep uniform sides on all flanks and a sharp peak. For a short distance along the road near Rannerdale Farm, on the shores of Crummock Water, it seems that Whiteless Pike has the qualifying attributes. But it falls to present an outline of similar shapeliness and beauty to other angles of view, and so cannot rank for stardom. Yet, seen from Rannerdale, surely it is the Weisshorn of Buttermere.

Whiteless Pike 2

MAP

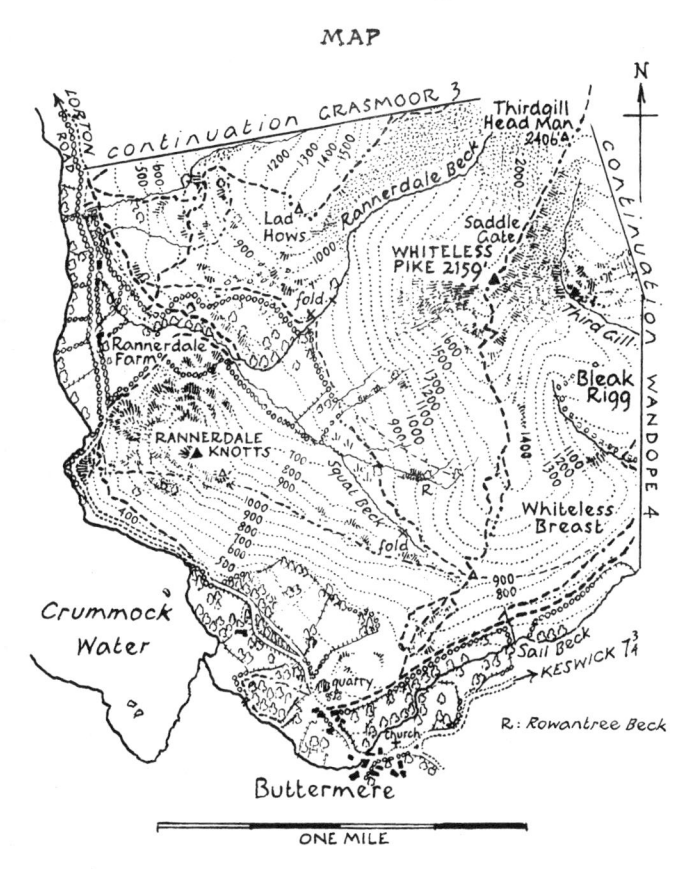

A peculiarity of the streams flowing down to join Squat Beck is that they become subterranean, sinking in their beds at the 700' contour. The largest of these, Rowantree Beck, is crossed by the path on dry stones although there is surface water just above and below.

The face of Whiteless Pike overlooking Rannerdale is too steep to be climbed direct in comfort, but the path of ascent from Buttermere may be joined very pleasantly by following the valley of Squat Beck to its head. (Parts of a former path through the enclosures have gone but the walking is easy). Or, if a drove road slanting across the side of the fell to an old sheepfold near the head of Rowantree Beck is seen, this may be taken instead to cut off a big corner. It may be remarked here that Squat Beck does not occupy the main valley of Rannerdale as it appears to do: note the course of Rannerdale Beck.

Whiteless Pike 3

ASCENT FROM BUTTERMERE
1800 feet of ascent : 1¼ miles

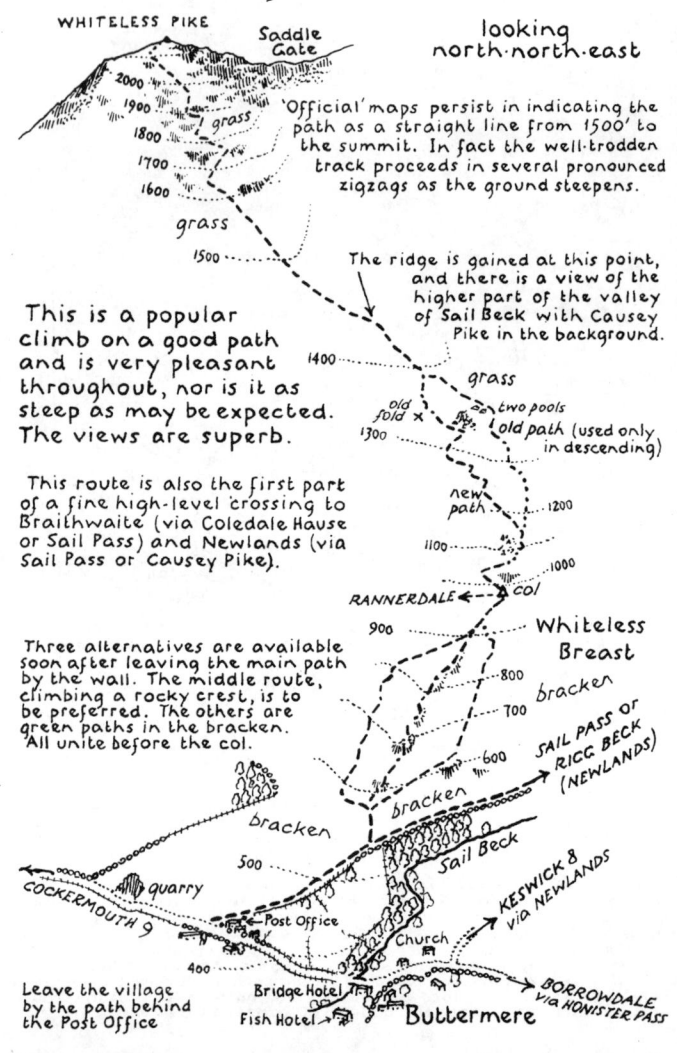

WHITELESS PIKE — Saddle Gate

looking north·north·east

'Official' maps persist in indicating the path as a straight line from 1500' to the summit. In fact the well-trodden track proceeds in several pronounced zigzags as the ground steepens.

grass

The ridge is gained at this point, and there is a view of the higher part of the valley of Sail Beck with Causey Pike in the background.

old fold × — two pools
old path (used only in descending)

new path

RANNERDALE ← COL
Whiteless Breast

This is a popular climb on a good path and is very pleasant throughout, nor is it as steep as may be expected. The views are superb.

This route is also the first part of a fine high-level crossing to Braithwaite (via Coledale Hause or Sail Pass) and Newlands (via Sail Pass or Causey Pike).

Three alternatives are available soon after leaving the main path by the wall. The middle route, climbing a rocky crest, is to be preferred. The others are green paths in the bracken. All unite before the col.

bracken

SAIL PASS or RIGG BECK (NEWLANDS)

Sail Beck

quarry

COCKERMOUTH 9

Post Office

KESWICK 8 via NEWLANDS

Church

Leave the village by the path behind the Post Office

Bridge Hotel
Fish Hotel

Buttermere

BORROWDALE via HONISTER PASS

Whiteless Pike 4

THE SUMMIT

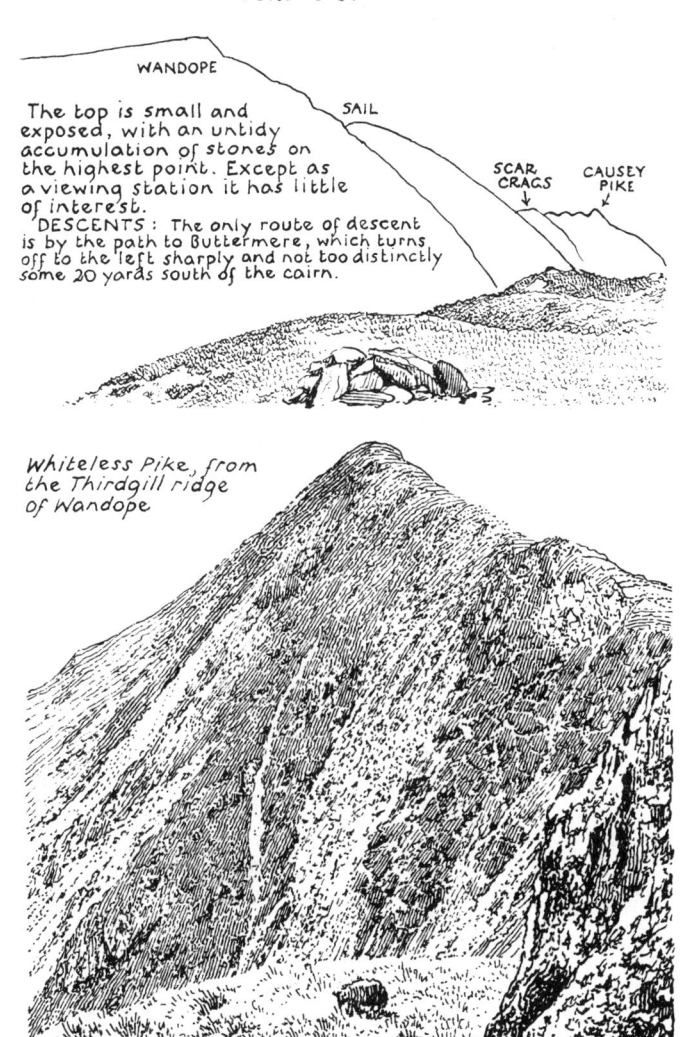

The top is small and exposed, with an untidy accumulation of stones on the highest point. Except as a viewing station it has little of interest.

DESCENTS: The only route of descent is by the path to Buttermere, which turns off to the left sharply and not too distinctly some 20 yards south of the cairn.

Whiteless Pike, from the Thirdgill ridge of Wandope

Whiteless Pike 5

THE VIEW

Like Causey Pike, its counterpart at the other extreme of the Eel Crag ridge, Whiteless Pike has a great advantage as a viewpoint, by reason of the small uplifted summit and the abrupt downfall therefrom, which together permit a prospect both wide and deep, a view of valleys as well as of mountains. The Scafell mass is most excellently displayed, and is nowhere better seen than from this northern side of Buttermere, the valley scene below the distant lofty skyline being very beautiful; indeed the whole rich picture in this direction is crowded with lovely detail. Less rugged but not less charming is the appearance of Crummock Water and Loweswater to the west. In contrast, nearby Grasmoor and Wandope fill up the northern horizon unattractively.

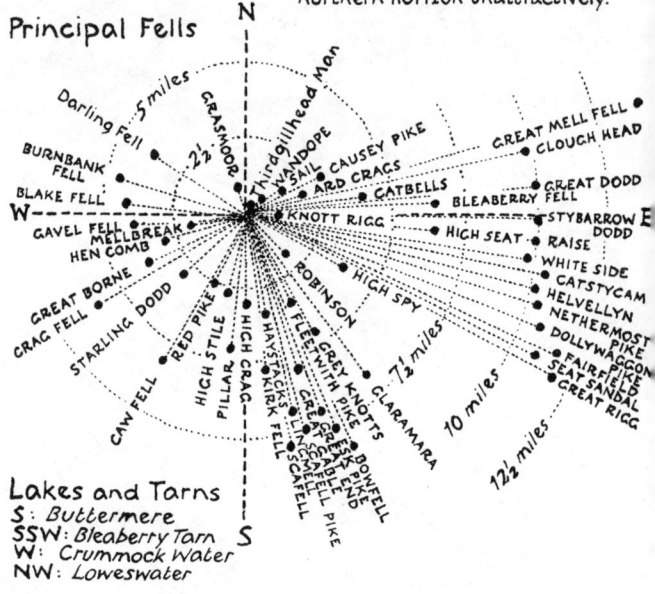

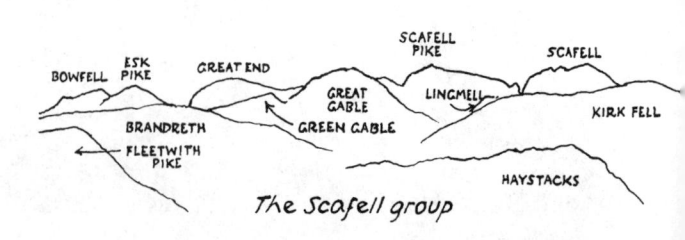

Principal Fells

Lakes and Tarns
S: Buttermere
SSW: Bleaberry Tarn
W: Crummock Water
NW: Loweswater

The Scafell group

Whiteless Pike 6

RIDGE ROUTE

To WANDOPE, 2533': ⅞ mile: NE, then E.
Depression at 2050': 500 feet of ascent

A winding path leads down to, and traverses, the depression of Saddle Gate before climbing up to the cairn of Thirdgill Head Man (which, in mist, should not be mistaken for Wandope). Here desert the path and cross the meadow on the right to its culminating point.

The illustration below shows the ridge rising to Thirdgill Head Man (left skyline). Wandope's summit is on the right.

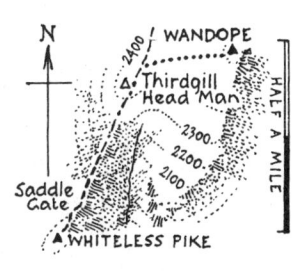

Whiteside 2317'

from the road to Scale Hill

- High Lorton
- Hopebeck
- WHITESIDE ▲   HOPEGILL ▲ HEAD
- Loweswater
- Lanthwaite   ▲ GRASMOOR

MILES
0 1 2 3

Whiteside 2

NATURAL FEATURES

As travellers make their way up the Vale of Lorton, eager for sight of the thrilling Buttermere skyline just around the corner, their enthusiasm is kept in check by the successive buttresses of Whiteside, which descend steeply into the valley on the left and conceal the desired view of lake and mountain ahead. There are three buttresses on this western flank of Whiteside — Dodd, Penn and Whiteside End — and together they form a cornerstone in triplicate to the high fells in the rear, for it is here that Lakeland really leaps into the sky from the flatlands of West Cumberland. These steep acclivities are rough and stony, and bulky rather than graceful — but many a beautiful picture is seen in an unattractive frame, and so it is here, the gaunt, massive portal enhancing the delicate, exciting scene ahead. The three buttresses rise in convex slopes to a sharply-cut summit ridge, and in a matter of yards the immediate dreariness of the grassy top is succeeded by a dramatic view down the other side of the mountain to Gasgale Gill in its ravine below. This south-eastern side presents an entirely different aspect: here are no sturdy buttresses but a vast scoop hollowed out of the fell, the debris of powerful forces of erosion, a place of shattered aretes, a natural quarry. This is Gasgale Crags, which a rich growth of heather is doing its best to make attractive by softening its naked harshness. From the ridge above, or the stream below, the natural architecture of the face cannot be appreciated, and one needs to visit Grasmoor, directly opposite, to observe the remarkable repeated pattern of aretes and scree-runs. This scene is unique. A splendid ridge from the summit eastwards leads on to Hopegill Head and Grisedale Pike. All waters drain into the River Cocker.

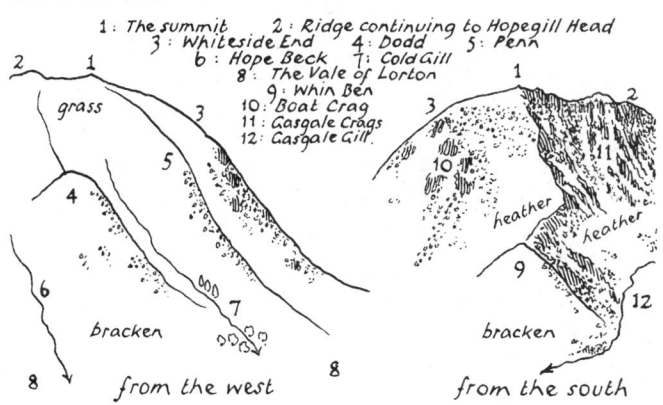

1 : The summit   2 : Ridge continuing to Hopegill Head
3 : Whiteside End   4 : Dodd   5 : Penn
6 : Hope Beck   7 : Cold Gill
8 : The Vale of Lorton
9 : Whin Ben
10 : Boat Crag
11 : Gasgale Crags
12 : Gasgale Gill

from the west

from the south

Whiteside 3

Gasgale Gill

Between Lorton and Buttermere the only route through the mountains is provided by a rough path along the side of Gasgale Gill, starting from Lanthwaite and leading up to Coledale Hause, at 1900', for Braithwaite. This is an excellent way for walkers in a hurry, Crummock Water and Keswick thereby being linked in a half-day's march. In Gasgale Gill the path runs along the base of Whiteside.

The rockstep

Waterfalls near the head of the gill

Proceeding eastwards, just after rounding the corner of Whin Ben, it is necessary to negotiate an awkward rocky obstacle at a place where a recent landslip has carried away the path. The illustration is of the scene looking back. Shuffling bottoms provide sufficient security here. There is no need for pitons.

The lower section

The middle section

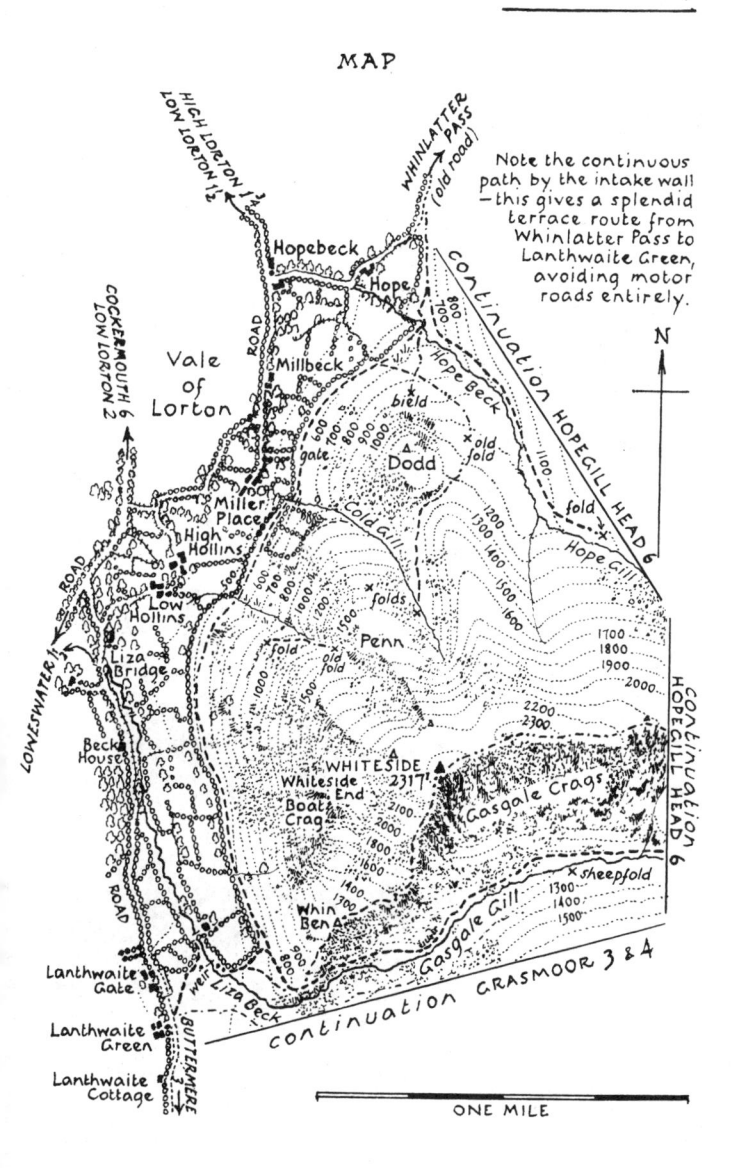

Whiteside 4

MAP

Note the continuous path by the intake wall — this gives a splendid terrace route from Whinlatter Pass to Lanthwaite Green, avoiding motor roads entirely.

N

Whiteside 5

Dodd Pass

A pronounced indentation in the ridge of Dodd serves as a pass between Hope Gill and Cold Gill, and is much used by sheep. One side of the pass is a tumble of scree, and it is clear that the rocks still standing here are the remains of what must at one time have been a continuous rampart. A counterpart to this curious gap is to be found at Trusmadoor in the Northern Fells.

Cold Gill

Just above the intake wall, Cold Gill is crossed by a stone bridge carrying a path to a walled enclosure alongside. This is possibly the smallest stonebuilt bridge in Lakeland. Or is it only a culvert?

Whiteside 6

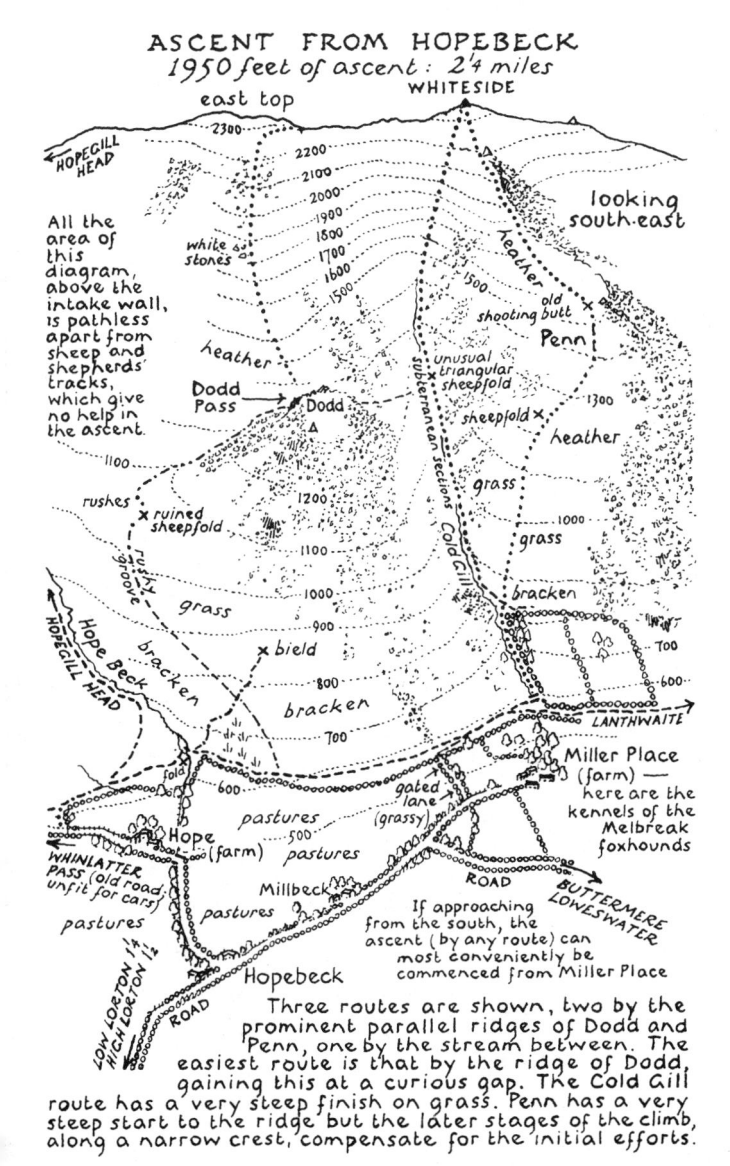

ASCENT FROM HOPEBECK
1950 feet of ascent: 2¼ miles

looking south-east

All the area of this diagram, above the intake wall, is pathless apart from sheep and shepherds tracks, which give no help in the ascent.

If approaching from the south, the ascent (by any route) can most conveniently be commenced from Miller Place

Miller Place (farm) — here are the kennels of the Melbreak foxhounds

Three routes are shown, two by the prominent parallel ridges of Dodd and Penn, one by the stream between. The easiest route is that by the ridge of Dodd, gaining this at a curious gap. The Cold Gill route has a very steep finish on grass. Penn has a very steep start to the ridge but the later stages of the climb, along a narrow crest, compensate for the initial efforts.

Whiteside 7

ASCENT FROM BECK HOUSE
1950 feet of ascent : 1¼ miles

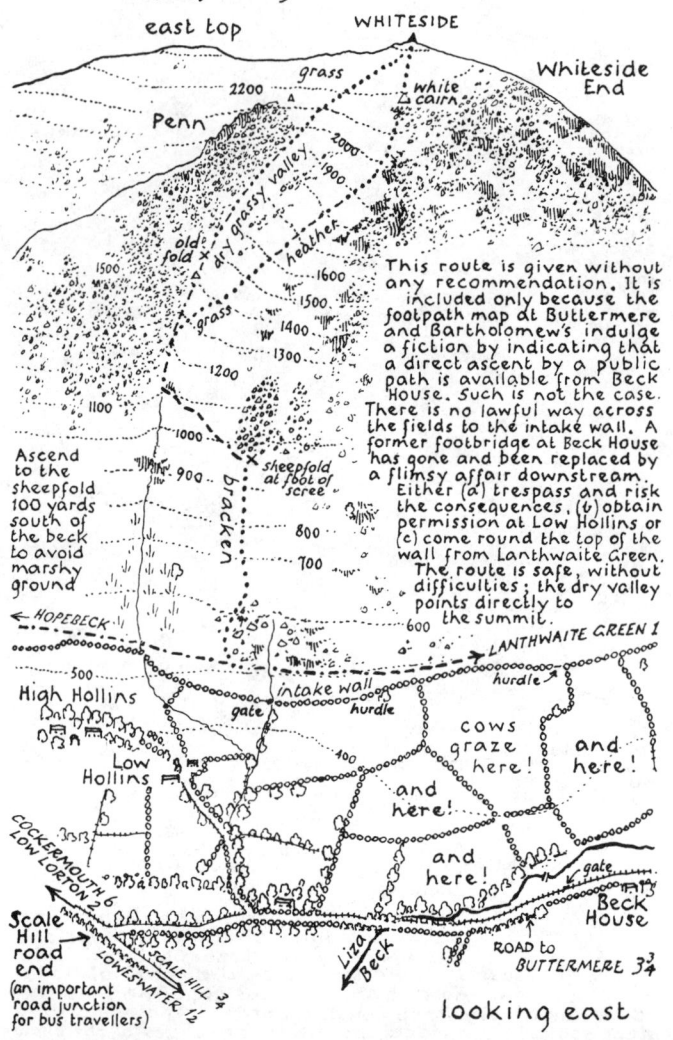

This route is given without any recommendation. It is included only because the footpath map at Buttermere and Bartholomew's indulge a fiction by indicating that a direct ascent by a public path is available from Beck House. Such is not the case. There is no lawful way across the fields to the intake wall. A former footbridge at Beck House has gone and been replaced by a flimsy affair downstream. Either (a) trespass and risk the consequences, (b) obtain permission at Low Hollins or (c) come round the top of the wall from Lanthwaite Green.

The route is safe, without difficulties; the dry valley points directly to the summit.

Ascend to the sheepfold 100 yards south of the beck to avoid marshy ground

Scale Hill road end (an important road junction for bus travellers)

looking east

Whiteside 8

ASCENT FROM LANTHWAITE GREEN
1850 feet of ascent : 1½ miles

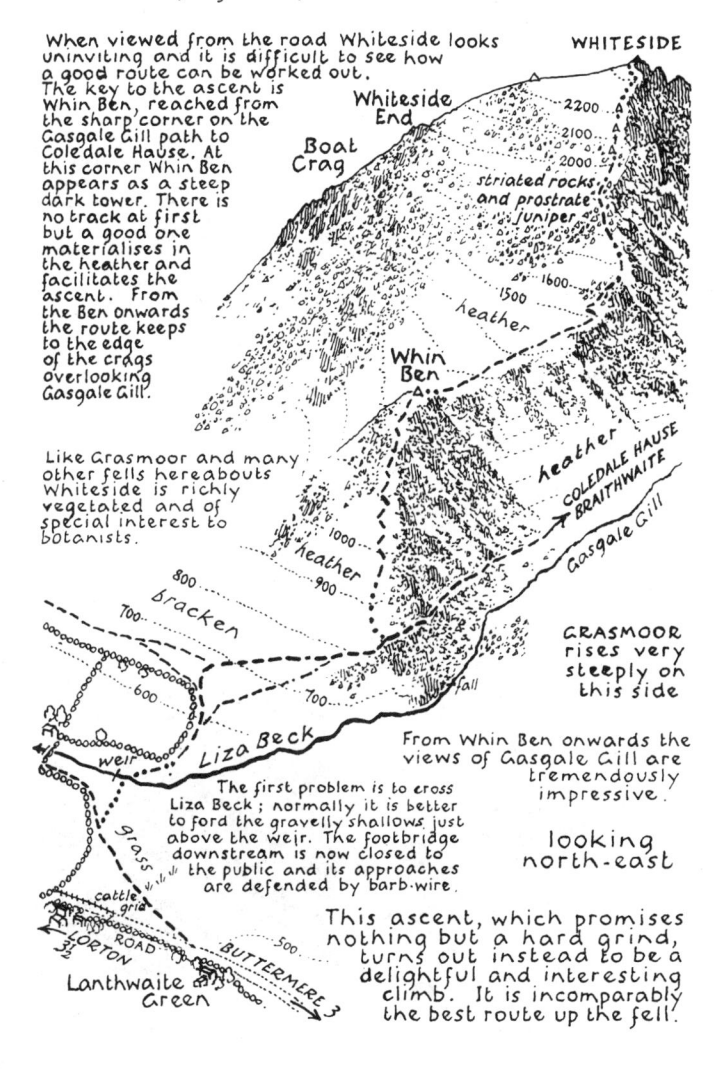

WHITESIDE

Whiteside End

Boat Crag

striated rocks and prostrate juniper

2200
2100
2000
1600
1500

heather

Whin Ben

When viewed from the road Whiteside looks uninviting and it is difficult to see how a good route can be worked out. The key to the ascent is Whin Ben, reached from the sharp corner on the Gasgale Gill path to Coledale Hause. At this corner Whin Ben appears as a steep dark tower. There is no track at first but a good one materialises in the heather and facilitates the ascent. From the Ben onwards the route keeps to the edge of the crags overlooking Gasgale Gill.

Like Grasmoor and many other fells hereabouts Whiteside is richly vegetated and of special interest to botanists.

heather
COLEDALE HAUSE
BRAITHWAITE →
Gasgale Gill

1000
heather
900
800
bracken
700
600
700
fall

Liza Beck
weir

GRASMOOR rises very steeply on this side

From Whin Ben onwards the views of Gasgale Gill are tremendously impressive.

looking north-east

The first problem is to cross Liza Beck; normally it is better to ford the gravelly shallows just above the weir. The footbridge downstream is now closed to the public and its approaches are defended by barb-wire.

grass
cattle grid
LORTON 3½
ROAD
BUTTERMERE 3
500
Lanthwaite Green

This ascent, which promises nothing but a hard grind, turns out instead to be a delightful and interesting climb. It is incomparably the best route up the fell.

Whiteside 9

THE SUMMIT

east top — GRISEDALE PIKE — HOPEGILL HEAD — Sand Hill

The cairn is well sited at the end of the ridge, just above the steepening drop to Crummock Water, and on the edge of an abrupt downfall of crags. But there is little doubt that this is not the highest point of the fell: the first pronounced rise on the ridge eastwards certainly seems to have an advantage in altitude — looking back from here the official summit fits into the same horizontal plane as Blake Fell, 1878', four miles in the background, and therefore the view of it is downward.
The top is grassy, away from the rim of crags. The only other cairn is prominently seen 300 yards in a westerly direction.
DESCENTS: The best way down is to Lanthwaite Green via Whin Ben, keeping the steep edge on the left throughout; a fair track soon materialises. *In mist, a complete stranger to the mountain would be better advised to aim northwest and descend the grassy valley there found: it has no difficulties, and leads down to the intake wall.* This route is also to be preferred to the Dodd and Penn ridges in bad weather.

The summit rocks
from the south *from the east*

Whiteside 10

THE VIEW

Whiteside is the finest viewpoint for the coastal plain of West Cumberland, the Solway Firth, and the hills of Scotland beyond: a magnificent uninterrupted panorama crammed with detail; it is surprising to find the intervening Fellbarrow range sunk into complete insignificance from this elevation.

In other directions the view is patchy. The Skiddaw and Helvellyn ranges are well seen but the best skyline in Lakeland (south to the Scafells) is completely hidden by Grasmoor.

More intimately, the glimpses down the aretes of Gasgale Crags to the gill far below are very striking.

Principal Fells

[compass diagram showing fells in all directions: Harrot, Swinside, Graystones, Ling Fell, Sale Fell, Broom Fell, Whinlatter, Lords Seat, Binsey, Longlands Fell, Brae Fell, Ullock Pike, Little Sca Fell, Great Sca Fell, Skiddaw, Skiddaw Little Man, Fellbarrow, Low Fell, Grisedale Pike, Hopegill Head, Sand Hill, Causey Pike, Sail, Scar Crags, Eel Crag, Bleaberry Fell, Stybarrow Dodd, Raise, White Side, Catstycam, Helvellyn, Nethermost Pike, Burnbank Fell, Carling Knott, Blake Fell, Gavel Fell, Grasmoor, Grike, Hen Comb, Great Borne, Mellbreak, Starling Dodd, Lank Rigg, Caw Fell, Haycock, Little Gowder Crag; distance rings at 2½ miles, 5 miles, 7½ miles, 10 miles, 12½ miles]

Crummock Water (SW) cannot be seen from the summit-cairn; a stroll of 30 yards in the direction of the Whin Ben descent brings it into sight.

The cairn 300 yards west across the grassy top is worth a visit — from this point Loweswater and Crummock Water are both seen in a comprehensive valley view.

Lakes and Tarns
NNE: Over Water
    (a faint trace only)
W: Loweswater

Whiteside 11

RIDGE ROUTE

To HOPEGILL HEAD, 2525′ : 1⅛ mile : ENE, then E.
  Main depression at 2200′ : 360 feet of ascent

An exhilarating high-level traverse with a grand finish. The path is sketchy, but the sharp rim of the great downfall to Gasgale Gill is an infallible guide. The best part of the walk is the final depression, where a narrow heathery crest with a distinct track leads across to the pyramid of Hopegill Head. Approach this depression down the grass to the left of the rocks of the ridge.

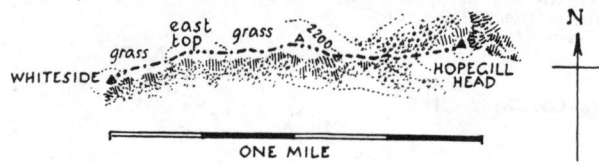

Whiteside, with Whin Ben (right) from Lanthwaite Green

Whiteside 12

Gasgale Crags, Whiteside from Dove Crags, Grasmoor

looking east along the ridge to Hopegill Head and Sand Hill

THE NORTH WESTERN FELLS
Some Personal notes in conclusion

When concluding Book Five I expressed the opinion that the North Western Fells were the most delectable of all, and, after two years in their charming company, I hold to that view. In other areas I have sometimes tired a little of repeatedly tramping the same tracks, but not here. Times without number I came off the hills faced with a long trudge down Whinlatter, or along the Coledale mine road or Newlands, until every stone and every tree became familiar, but never, rain or shine, did I do so wearily, but only regretting that another day was done, that another week must pass before I could return. Always I was lingering, always looking back.

All this territory is wonderful walking country. Much of it, south of the Grisedale Pike ridge, is well known and needs no introduction (although I have just completed nearly 300 pages doing that!). Even so, there are many corners rarely visited, many excellent routes rarely trodden, many interesting features rarely seen. Several of the lines of ascent described in this book are as good as anything else in Lakeland, which is saying a lot, yet the majority of walkers are unaware of them. Searchers after traces of ancient history, or old industrial activity will find much of interest. Geologists and botanists are well catered for here. Photographers cannot fail to produce beautiful pictures.

On the whole, the walking is quite excellent. The hills are easier to climb than their abrupt appearance suggests: the secret is to get on the ridges early, because it is the ridges, not the fellsides, that provide the best travelling underfoot and the finest views, and give the area its special appeal.

Newlands is a privileged valley, not only extraordinarily pleasant in itself but ringed by grand fells; for a quiet fellwalking holiday there is no better centre. Borrowdale we all know and love, but this valley is not so well placed for the area, and is nowadays so busy with cars that its joys are best experienced in winter. Buttermere is beautiful, but a better base for the western

Fells than the North Western. I ought to put in a good word for Thornthwaite Forest, to the north of Whinlatter, which, in spite of much afforestation, is a fascinating place to explore. I never saw a soul here in eight months' weekend wandering, except once when I found myself mixed up in a foxhunt. Nothing in this region pleased me more than the shy Wythop Valley, so easy to walk, so charming and unspoiled, a little tranquil world apart.

Several times I came down to Buttermere, and it was hard to deny myself an occasional excursion to the magnificent mountains on the far side, but now the time has come when I am free to do this, and Book Seven will tell of High Stile and of Great Gable and Pillar and others that yet remain unrecorded. If I say that I start upon the last book in the series with mixed feelings, many of you will know what I mean.

AW

Autumn, 1963.

SIGN REFERENCES
(signs used in the maps and diagrams)

Good footpath ------
(sufficiently distinct to be followed in mist)

Intermittent footpath -·-·-·-
(difficult to follow in mist)

Route recommended but no path ··>·······>····
(if recommended one way only, arrow indicates direction)

Wall ∞∞∞∞∞∞   **Broken wall** ∘∘∘∘∘∘∘∘∘

Fence ++++++++   **Broken fence** ''''''''''''

Marshy ground ↯↯↯↯   **Trees** 🌳🌳🌳

Crags   **Boulders**

Stream or River
(arrow indicates direction of flow) →

Waterfall   **Bridge**

Buildings ▪▪▪   **Unenclosed road** ''''''''''''

Contours (at 100' intervals)
······1900······
······1800······
······1700······

Summit-cairn ▲   **Other** (prominent) **cairns** △

THE
SOUTHERN
FELLS

A PICTORIAL GUIDE
TO THE
LAKELAND FELLS
50TH ANNIVERSARY EDITION

being an illustrated account
of a study and exploration
of the mountains in the
English Lake District

by

A Wainwright

BOOK FOUR
THE SOUTHERN FELLS

Frances Lincoln Limited
4 Torriano Mews
Torriano Avenue
London NW5 2RZ
www.franceslincoln.com

Originally published by Henry Marshall, Kentmere, 1960

First published by Frances Lincoln 2003

50th Anniversary Edition with re-originated artwork
published by Frances Lincoln 2005

Copyright © The Estate of A. Wainwright 1960

All rights reserved. Without limiting the rights under
copyright reserved above, no part of this publication may
be reproduced, stored in or introduced into a retrieval
system, or transmitted, in any form or by any means
(electronic, mechanical, photocopying, or otherwise),
without either prior permission in writing from the
publisher or a licence permitting restricted copying.
In the United Kingdom such licences are issued by
the Copyright Licensing Agency, Saffron House,
6-10 Kirby Street, London EC1N 8TS.

Printed and bound in China

A CIP catalogue record for this book
is available from the British Library.

ISBN 978 0 7112 2457 5

18 17 16 15 14 13 12 11

50TH ANNIVERSARY EDITION
PUBLISHED BY
FRANCES LINCOLN, LONDON

Gladstone's Finger,
Gladstone Knott,
Crinkle Crags

THE PICTORIAL GUIDES

Book One: The Eastern Fells, 1955
Book Two: The Far Eastern Fells, 1957
Book Three: The Central Fells, 1958
Book Four: The Southern Fells, 1960
Book Five: The Northern Fells, 1962
Book Six: The North Western Fells, 1964
Book Seven: The Western Fells, 1966

PUBLISHER'S NOTE

This 50th Anniversary edition of the Pictorial Guides to the Lakeland Fells is newly reproduced from the handwritten pages created in the 1950s and 1960s by A. Wainwright. The descriptions of the walks were correct, to the best of the author's knowledge, at the time of first publication and they are reproduced here without amendment. However, footpaths, cairns and other waymarks described here are no longer all as they were fifty years ago and walkers are advised to check with an up-to-date map when planning a walk.

Fellwalking has increased dramatically since the Pictorial Guides were first published. Some popular routes have become eroded, making good footwear and great care all the more necessary for walkers. The vital points about fellwalking, as A. Wainwright himself wrote on many occasions, are to use common sense and to remember to watch where you are putting your feet.

A programme of revision of the Pictorial Guides is under way and revised editions of each of them will be published over the next few years.

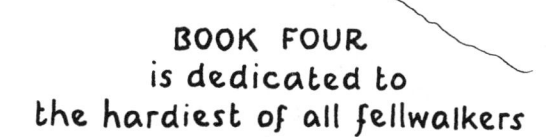

BOOK FOUR
is dedicated to
the hardiest of all fellwalkers

THE SHEEP OF LAKELAND

the truest lovers of the mountains,
their natural homes
and providers of their food and shelter

INTRODUCTION

Classification and Definition

Any division of the Lakeland fells into geographical districts must necessarily be arbitrary, just as the location of the outer boundaries of Lakeland must always be a matter of opinion. Any attempt to define internal or external boundaries is certain to invite criticism, and he who takes it upon himself to say where Lakeland starts and finishes, or, for example, where the Central Fells merge into the Southern Fells and *which* fells are the Central Fells and which the Southern and *why* they need be so classified, must not expect his pronouncements to be generally accepted.

Yet for present purposes some plan of classification and definition must be used. County and parochial boundaries are no help, nor is the recently-defined area of the Lakeland National Park, for this book is concerned only with the high ground.

First, the external boundaries. Straight lines linking the extremities of the outlying lakes enclose all the higher fells very conveniently. There are a few fells of lesser height to the north and east, however, that are typically Lakeland in character and cannot properly be omitted: these are brought in, somewhat untidily, by extending the lines in those areas. Thus:

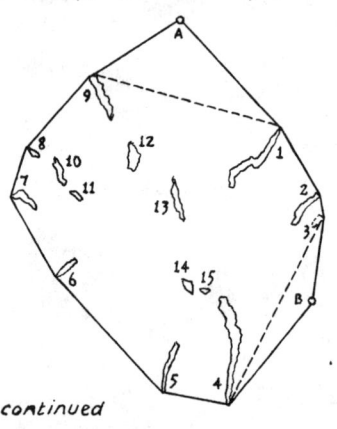

1 : *Ullswater*
2 : *Hawes Water*
3 : proposed *Swindale Resr*
4 : *Windermere*
5 : *Coniston Water*
6 : *Wast Water*
7 : *Ennerdale Water*
8 : *Loweswater*
9 : *Bassenthwaite Lake*
10 : *Crummock Water*
11 : *Buttermere*
12 : *Derwent Water*
13 : *Thirlmere*
14 : *Grasmere*
15 : *Rydal Water*
A : *Caldbeck*
B : *Longsleddale* (church)

continued

INTRODUCTION

Classification and Definition
continued

The complete Guide is planned to include all the fells in the area enclosed by the straight lines of the diagram. This is an undertaking quite beyond the compass of a single volume, and it is necessary, therefore, to divide the area into convenient sections, making the fullest use of natural boundaries (lakes, valleys and low passes) so that each district is, as far as possible, self-contained and independent of the rest.

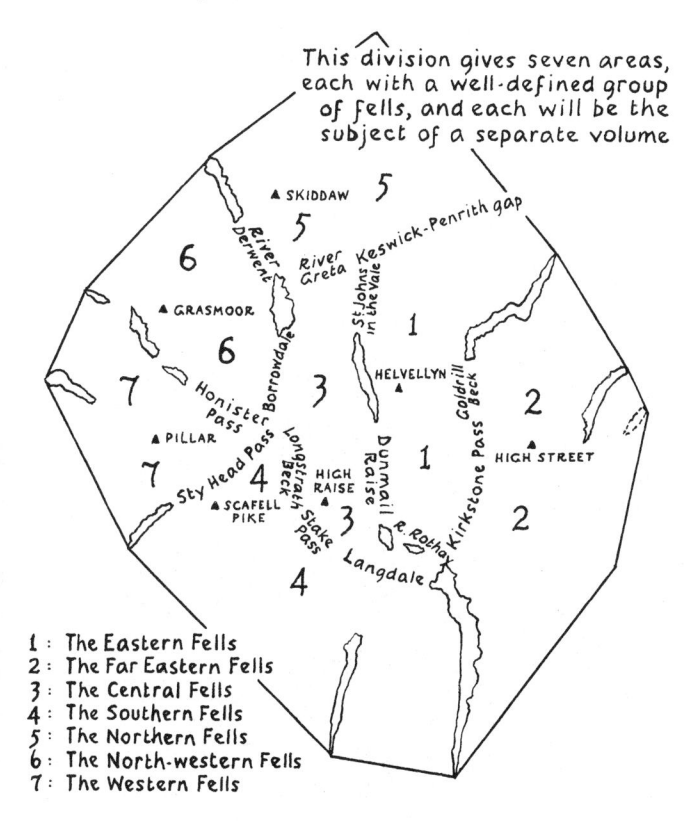

This division gives seven areas, each with a well-defined group of fells, and each will be the subject of a separate volume

1 : The Eastern Fells
2 : The Far Eastern Fells
3 : The Central Fells
4 : The Southern Fells
5 : The Northern Fells
6 : The North-western Fells
7 : The Western Fells

INTRODUCTION

Notes on the Illustrations

THE MAPS............... Many excellent books have been written about Lakeland, but the best literature of all for the walker is that published by the Director General of Ordnance Survey, the 1" map for companionship and guidance on expeditions, the 2½" map for exploration both on the fells and by the fireside. These admirable maps are remarkably accurate topographically but there is a crying need for a revision of the paths on the hills: several walkers' tracks that have come into use during the past few decades, some of them now broad highways, are not shown at all; other paths still shown on the maps have fallen into neglect and can no longer be traced on the ground.

The popular Bartholomew 1" map is a beautiful picture, fit for a frame, but this too is unreliable for paths; indeed here the defect is much more serious, for routes are indicated where no paths ever existed, nor ever could — the cartographer has preferred to take precipices in his stride rather than deflect his graceful curves over easy ground.

Hence the justification for the maps in this book: they have the one merit (of importance to walkers) of being dependable as regards delineation of *paths*. They are intended as supplements to the Ordnance Survey maps, certainly not as substitutes.

THE VIEWS............... Various devices have been used to illustrate the views from the summits of the fells. The full panorama in the form of an outline drawing is most satisfactory generally, and this method has been adopted for the main viewpoints.

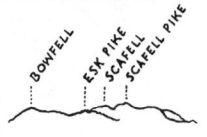

THE DIAGRAMS OF ASCENTS................ The routes of ascent of the higher fells are depicted by diagrams that do not pretend to strict accuracy: they are neither plans nor elevations; in fact there is deliberate distortion in order to show detail clearly: usually they are represented as viewed from imaginary 'space-stations.' But it is hoped they will be useful and interesting.

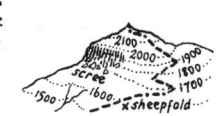

THE DRAWINGS....... The drawings at least are honest attempts to reproduce what the eye sees: they illustrate features of interest and also serve the dual purpose of breaking up the text and balancing the layout of the pages, and of filling up awkward blank spaces, like this:

Thirlmere

THE
SOUTHERN
FELLS

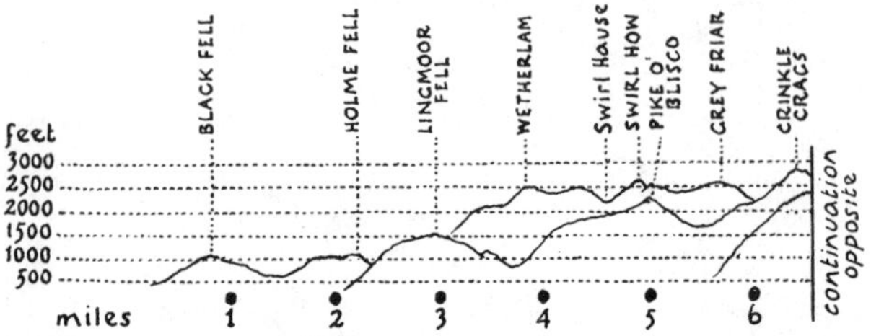
BLACK FELL
HOLME FELL
LINGMOOR FELL
WETHERLAM
Swirl Hause
SWIRL HOW
PIKE O' BLISCO
GREY FRIAR
CRINKLE CRAGS
feet
3000
2500
2000
1500
1000
500
miles
1
2
3
4
5
6
continuation opposite

The Southern Fells comprise two well-defined mountain systems.

The larger is the Scafell-Bowfell massif, which forms a great arc around the head of Eskdale; it is bounded by Wasdale in the west, and eastwards by the headwaters of the Duddon and the Brathay, while to the north the high ground descends into Borrowdale and Great Langdale. Within this area the fells are the highest, the roughest and the grandest in Lakeland: they are of volcanic origin and the naked rock is much in evidence in the form of towering crags and wildernesses of boulders and scree. Progress on foot across these arid wastes is slow and often laborious, but there is an exhilarating feeling of freedom and sense of achievement on the airy ridges poised high above deep valleys. This is magnificent territory for the fellwalker. There is nothing better than this.

The smaller group, the Coniston fells, rises east of the Duddon and west of Yewdale; the Brathay is the northern boundary. Compact, distinctive, with several summits of uniform height just above 2500' the slaty Coniston fells bear many industrial scars which detract little from the general excellence of the scenery and, indeed, provide an added interest. The dry turfy ridges are a joy to tread.

THE SOUTHERN ASPECT

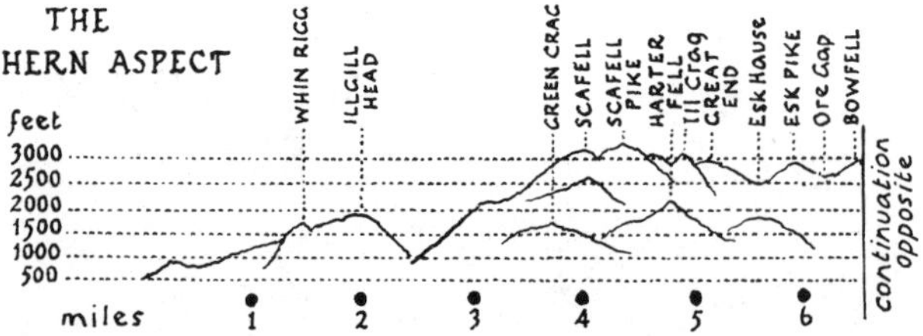
WHIN RIGG
ILLGILL HEAD
GREEN CRAG
SCAFELL
SCAFELL PIKE
HARTER FELL
Ill Crag
GREAT END
Esk Hause
ESK PIKE
Ore Gap
BOWFELL
feet
3000
2500
2000
1500
1000
500
miles
1
2
3
4
5
6
continuation opposite

THE NORTHERN ASPECT

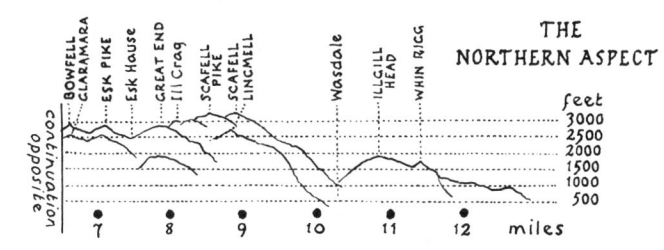

The rugged heights of the Southern Fells are set off to perfection by the lovely valleys leading into them, and much of the pleasure of mountain days spent in this region is contributed by the delightful approaches. The valleys have strongly individual characteristics —— Great Langdale has glorious curves and a simple grandeur; Wasdale is primitive and unspoiled, an emerald amongst sombre hills; Borrowdale has enchanting recesses and side-valleys; the Duddon is newly afforested — yet all are alike in their sparkling radiance, in their verdant freshness. But precedence must be granted to Eskdale, the one valley that gives full allegiance to the Southern Fells and in some ways the most delectable of all. This is a valley where walkers really come into their own, a sanctuary of peace and solitude, a very special preserve for those who travel on foot.

The provision of accommodation is a major industry in Borrowdale and Great Langdale, and at Coniston, but is strictly limited in the remote, less accessible and sparsely populated southern valleys. In summertime, in all the valleys serving the area, the available accommodation is fully taxed, and seekers after beds and breakfasts are advised to arrange each night's lodging in advance.

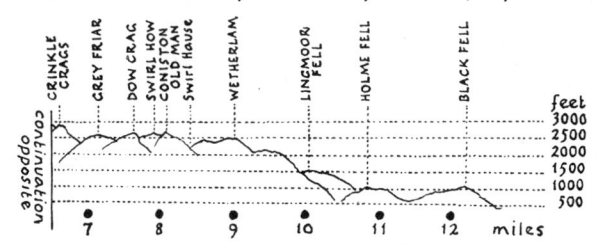

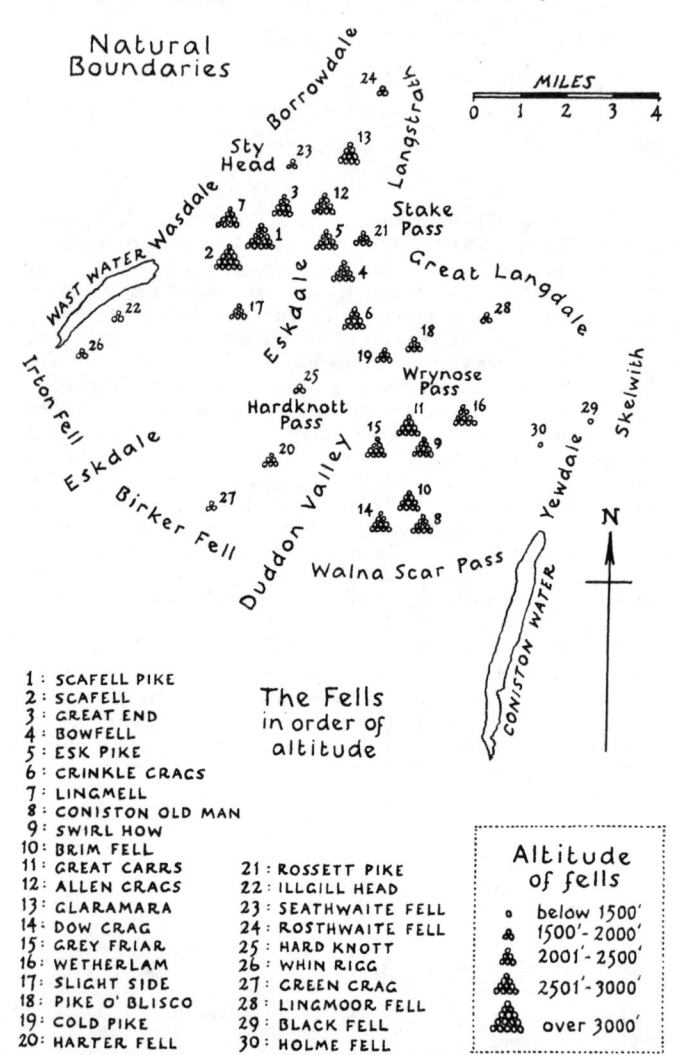

THE SOUTHERN FELLS

Natural Boundaries

Map labels:
- Borrowdale
- Sty Head
- Langstrath
- Wasdale
- Wast Water
- Stake Pass
- Eskdale
- Great Langdale
- Irton Fell
- Eskdale
- Hardknott Pass
- Wrynose Pass
- Skelwith
- Birker Fell
- Duddon Valley
- Yewdale
- Walna Scar Pass
- Coniston Water

MILES 0 1 2 3 4

N

The Fells in order of altitude

1 : SCAFELL PIKE
2 : SCAFELL
3 : GREAT END
4 : BOWFELL
5 : ESK PIKE
6 : CRINKLE CRAGS
7 : LINGMELL
8 : CONISTON OLD MAN
9 : SWIRL HOW
10 : BRIM FELL
11 : GREAT CARRS
12 : ALLEN CRAGS
13 : GLARAMARA
14 : DOW CRAG
15 : GREY FRIAR
16 : WETHERLAM
17 : SLIGHT SIDE
18 : PIKE O' BLISCO
19 : COLD PIKE
20 : HARTER FELL
21 : ROSSETT PIKE
22 : ILLGILL HEAD
23 : SEATHWAITE FELL
24 : ROSTHWAITE FELL
25 : HARD KNOTT
26 : WHIN RIGG
27 : GREEN CRAG
28 : LINGMOOR FELL
29 : BLACK FELL
30 : HOLME FELL

Altitude of fells

- below 1500'
- 1500' - 2000'
- 2001' - 2500'
- 2501' - 3000'
- over 3000'

THE SOUTHERN FELLS

in the order of their appearance in this book

Reference to map opposite:
over 3000' / 2501'-3000' / 2001'-2500' / 1500'-2000' / below 1500'

Ref	Fell	Altitude in feet
12	ALLEN CRAGS	2572
29	BLACK FELL	1056
4	BOWFELL	2960
10	BRIM FELL	2611
19	COLD PIKE	2300
8	CONISTON OLD MAN	2633
6	CRINKLE CRAGS	2816
14	DOW CRAG	2555
5	ESK PIKE	2903
13	GLARAMARA	2569
11	GREAT CARRS	2575
3	GREAT END	2984
27	GREEN CRAG	1602
15	GREY FRIAR	2536
25	HARD KNOTT	1803
20	HARTER FELL	2140
30	HOLME FELL	1040
22	ILLGILL HEAD	1983
7	LINGMELL	2649
28	LINGMOOR FELL	1539
18	PIKE O' BLISCO	2313
21	ROSSETT PIKE	2106
24	ROSTHWAITE FELL	1807
2	SCAFELL	3162
1	SCAFELL PIKE	3210
23	SEATHWAITE FELL	1970
17	SLIGHT SIDE	2499
9	SWIRL HOW	2630
16	WETHERLAM	2502
26	WHIN RIGG	1755

2 14 5 7 2
30

Each fell is the subject of a separate chapter

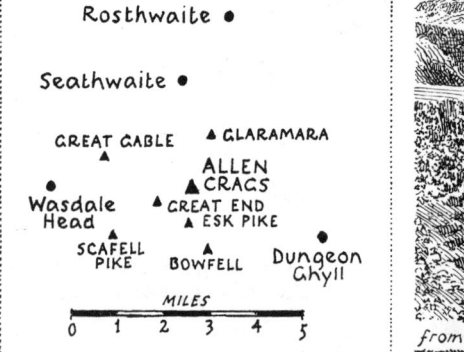

Allen Crags 2572'

from Sprinkling Tarn

from Ruddy Gill

Allen Crags 2

NATURAL FEATURES

Some fells there are, of respectable height, of distinct merit as viewpoints, and often in fine situations, which never seem to attract or challenge walkers and have no place in fireside memories of Lakeland: they are 'left for another day', habitually passed by, and rarely find mention in print or conversation. Such a one is Allen Crags, grandly positioned overlooking Esk Hause; it is really in the heart of things and on intimate terms with Bowfell, the Scafells and Great Gable — old favourites, glorious objectives for a day's walk and climbed many thousands of times every year. But did anyone, apart from an odd guide-book writer or other eccentric, ever set forth from Wasdale or Borrowdale or Langdale with the sole unswerving purpose of climbing Allen Crags?

It is true that the summit is frequently traversed, but only because it lies athwart the fine ridge between Esk Hause and Glaramara and so cannot well be avoided on this journey. The ridge must properly be regarded as the most northerly extremity of the Scafell structure for the Esk Hause-Sty Head path, which is often thought to mark its furthest extension, merely runs along a high shelf, geographically insignificant, across the gradual fall to valley-level. The Scafell *massif* has its northern roots in Borrowdale.

The two principal summits on the ridge are Allen Crags and Glaramara. The former is slightly the higher, but Glaramara has the greater appeal and is a popular ascent. A low depression between them, occupied by a cluster of miniature tarns, is a convenient common boundary. On the crest of Allen Crags walking is simple, but rocky outcrops occur everywhere. To east and west the fell is clearly defined, with a rough declivity to Allencrags Gill on the east flank and an easier slope, characterised by grey slabs, descending to Grains Gill westwards.

The position of Allen Crags in the Scafell ridge system

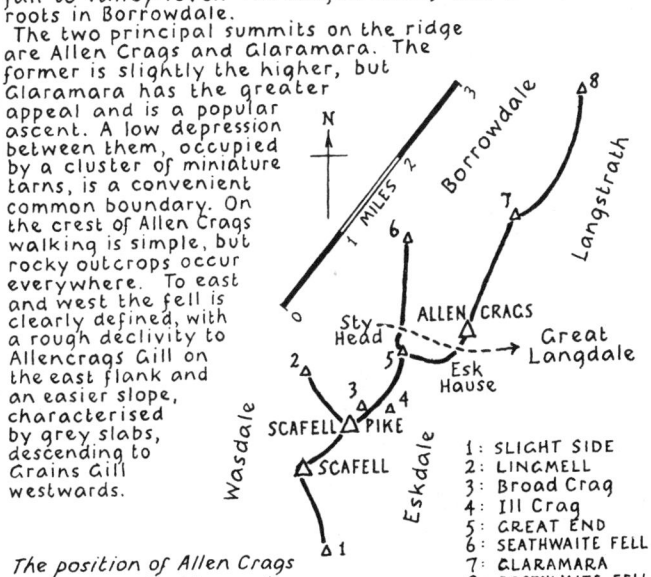

1: SLIGHT SIDE
2: LINGMELL
3: Broad Crag
4: Ill Crag
5: GREAT END
6: SEATHWAITE FELL
7: GLARAMARA
8: ROSTHWAITE FELL

Allen Crags 3

MAP

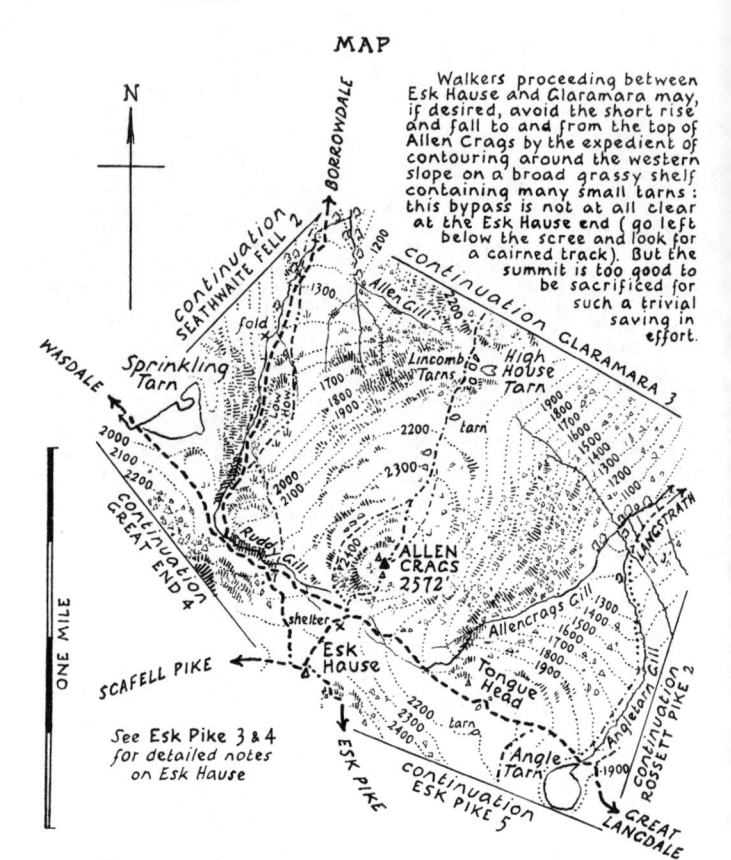

Walkers proceeding between Esk Hause and Glaramara may, if desired, avoid the short rise and fall to and from the top of Allen Crags by the expedient of contouring around the western slope on a broad grassy shelf containing many small tarns: this bypass is not at all clear at the Esk Hause end (go left below the scree and look for a cairned track). But the summit is too good to be sacrificed for such a trivial saving in effort.

See Esk Pike 3 & 4 for detailed notes on Esk Hause

Attention is drawn to a new variation path recently brought into use to cut off the sharp corner of Ruddy Gill. Particularly in ascending from Borrowdale the variation is not easily located although its course will be obvious from the old bridle path above Low How: it starts across marshy ground from the old path, then climbs steeply up a grass bank, with frequent cairns, to easy ground above, Ruddy Gill being met and crossed just at the point where the ravine commences. In descending from Esk Hause it is more likely to be noticed, as a narrow grassy trod.
This variation will probably become popular as the usual well-beaten path alongside Ruddy Gill, already unpleasantly stony, deteriorates still further, and, when its roughnesses are smoothed out by foot-traffic, will save a few minutes for anyone journeying between Borrowdale and Esk Hause. Its scenery and views, however, do not compare favourably with those of Ruddy Gill.

Allen Crags 4

ASCENT FROM BORROWDALE
2250 feet of ascent : 4½ miles from Seatoller
(4 miles via Allen Gill)

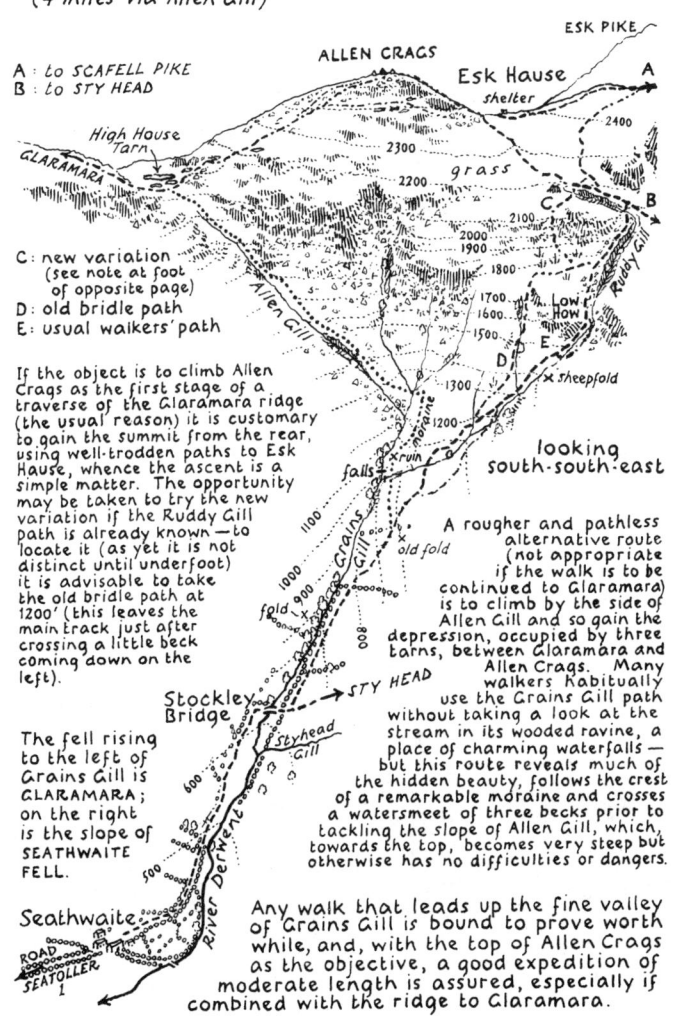

A : to SCAFELL PIKE
B : to STY HEAD

C : new variation
 (see note at foot
 of opposite page)
D : old bridle path
E : usual walkers' path

If the object is to climb Allen
Crags as the first stage of a
traverse of the Glaramara ridge
(the usual reason) it is customary
to gain the summit from the rear,
using well-trodden paths to Esk
Hause, whence the ascent is a
simple matter. The opportunity
may be taken to try the new
variation if the Ruddy Gill
path is already known — to
locate it (as yet it is not
distinct until underfoot)
it is advisable to take
the old bridle path at
1200' (this leaves the
main track just after
crossing a little beck
coming down on the
left).

looking
south-south-east

A rougher and pathless
alternative route
(not appropriate
if the walk is to be
continued to Glaramara)
is to climb by the side of
Allen Gill and so gain the
depression, occupied by three
tarns, between Glaramara and
Allen Crags. Many
walkers habitually
use the Grains Gill path
without taking a look at the
stream in its wooded ravine, a
place of charming waterfalls —
but this route reveals much of
the hidden beauty, follows the crest
of a remarkable moraine and crosses
a watersmeet of three becks prior to
tackling the slope of Allen Gill, which,
towards the top, becomes very steep but
otherwise has no difficulties or dangers.

The fell rising
to the left of
Grains Gill is
GLARAMARA;
on the right
is the slope of
SEATHWAITE
FELL.

Any walk that leads up the fine valley
of Grains Gill is bound to prove worth
while, and, with the top of Allen Crags
as the objective, a good expedition of
moderate length is assured, especially if
combined with the ridge to Glaramara.

Allen Crags 5

THE SUMMIT

GLARAMARA (main summit)

This quiet, attractive top is a pleasant refuge from the busy thoroughfares converging on Esk Hause, only five minutes away. Unexpectedly there are three good cairns on the twenty yards of level summit, that in the middle, set on a rock, being slightly the highest. Patches of stones and low outcrops add an interest to the top of the fell but the distant views will appeal more.

DESCENTS: The quickest and easiest way to anywhere is to go down the short south slope to the Esk Hause shelter and make use of the good paths there found, which bring Great Langdale, Wasdale or Borrowdale within an hour and a half's march. *In mist*, the smallest of the three cairns serves a useful function, as an indicator of the direction of Esk Hause. A small crag to the right of the route makes it desirable to keep to the sketchy path if possible, or, if not, to proceed warily.

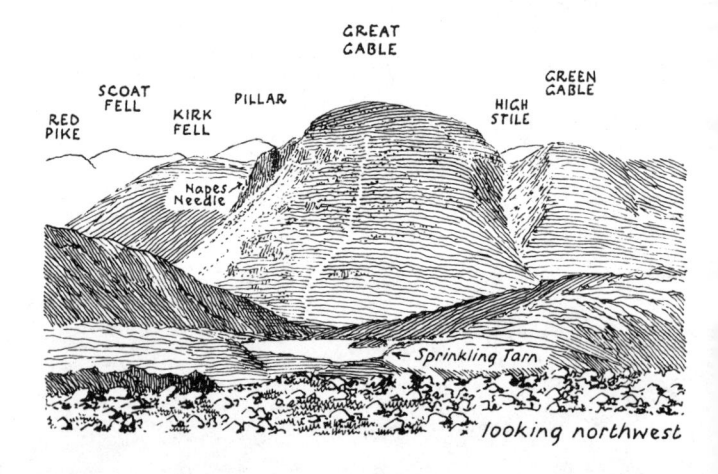

GREAT GABLE

RED PIKE — SCOAT FELL — KIRK FELL — PILLAR — Napes Needle — HIGH STILE — GREEN GABLE

← Sprinkling Tarn

looking northwest

Allen Crags 6

THE VIEW

The high shadowed walls of the Bowfell and Scafell groups effectively close the southern horizon at close quarters (although there is a distant view to Black Combe over Esk Hause) and from this viewpoint appear sombre, gloomy and unattractive.

Interest lies mainly in the northern arc, where there is a wealth of detail, all of it pleasant to behold, Borrowdale and its environs making a beautiful picture. It may be noted that from this summit (and no other) the two High Raises are seen, one beyond the other, in a direct line, but this is hardly worth writing home about.

The furrowed precipice of Great End holds the attention, but the finest mountain scene is provided by Great Gable, and keen eyes may detect the black silhouette of Napes Needle on its steep southern slope.

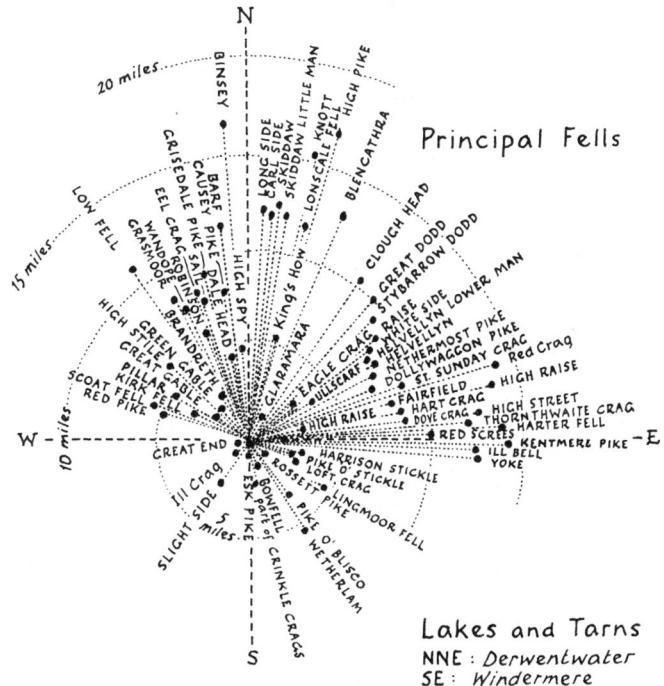

Principal Fells

Lakes and Tarns

NNE: Derwentwater
SE: Windermere
SE: Wise Een Tarn

NW to NE: tarns on Allen Crags
NW: Sprinkling Tarn and other tarns on Seathwaite Fell

Allen Crags 7

RIDGE ROUTE

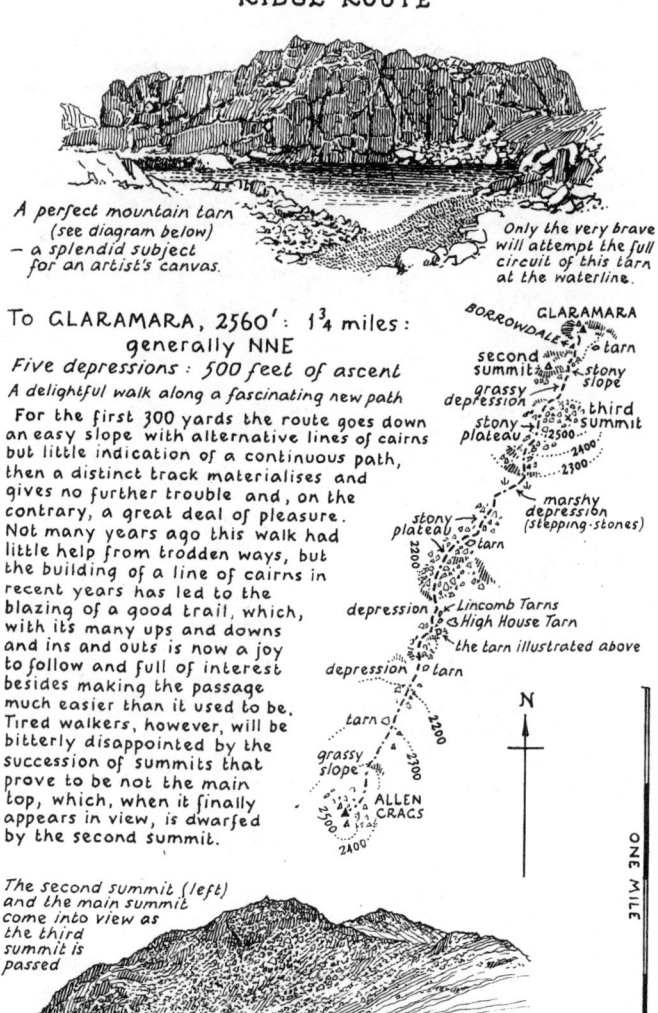

A perfect mountain tarn (see diagram below) — a splendid subject for an artist's canvas.

Only the very brave will attempt the full circuit of this tarn at the waterline.

To GLARAMARA, 2560': 1¾ miles: generally NNE
Five depressions: 500 feet of ascent
A delightful walk along a fascinating new path

For the first 300 yards the route goes down an easy slope with alternative lines of cairns but little indication of a continuous path, then a distinct track materialises and gives no further trouble and, on the contrary, a great deal of pleasure. Not many years ago this walk had little help from trodden ways, but the building of a line of cairns in recent years has led to the blazing of a good trail, which, with its many ups and downs and ins and outs is now a joy to follow and full of interest besides making the passage much easier than it used to be. Tired walkers, however, will be bitterly disappointed by the succession of summits that prove to be not the main top, which, when it finally appears in view, is dwarfed by the second summit.

The second summit (left) and the main summit come into view as the third summit is passed

ONE MILE

Allen Crags 8

Great End from Allen Crags

Allen Crags from Grains Gill

Black Fell

1056'

Ambleside •
Skelwith • Bridge
▲
BLACK FELL

Hawkshead
• Coniston

MILES
0 1 2 3 4

from Tarn Hows

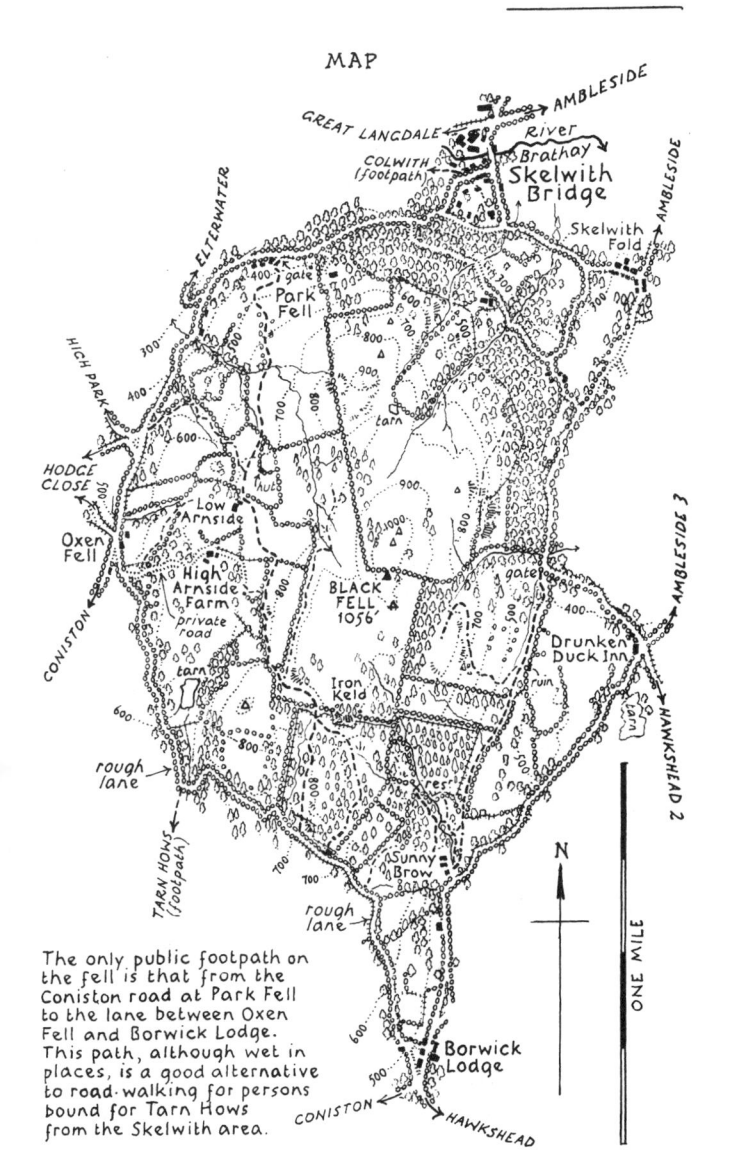

Black Fell 2

MAP

The only public footpath on the fell is that from the Coniston road at Park Fell to the lane between Oxen Fell and Borwick Lodge. This path, although wet in places, is a good alternative to road walking for persons bound for Tarn Hows from the Skelwith area.

Black Fell 3

NATURAL FEATURES

Everybody knows Tarn Hows, but few the summit of the fell rising behind, above immature plantations and slopes richly clothed in bracken, to the north-east. This is Black Fell, springing rather steeply in dense woodlands from the Brathay at Skelwith and occupying a considerable area between the Ambleside-Coniston road on the west and the fields of Outgate to the east. It is thus isolated from other high ground, and because it is the first substantial elevation west of the head of Windermere the view in that direction is particularly good.

ASCENTS

None of the paths on the fell is continuous to the summit; a simple walk across grass from the main bridleway west of Iron Keld, however, soon brings it underfoot, and this is the easiest route to the top. Starts up the east flank may quickly lead to desperate manoeuvres in thick plantations.*

THE SUMMIT

The highest point is a small outcrop with the ambitious name of Black Crag, and is given further distinction by the erection thereon of a triangulation column of the standard pattern to which has been affixed the extra adornment of the familiar metal symbol of the National Trust (this has been defaced by the scratched initials of visitors of the type who seem to see in this practice a chance of immortality. It must be readily conceded that, for people of such mentality, probably it is their only chance). South-east, and lower, is a big well-built cairn with a plinth-seat: still a noble edifice but falling into disrepair. A nearby wall is continuous from one end of the fell to the other. Decayed treestumps on the upper heights indicate that once the woods extended almost to the top.

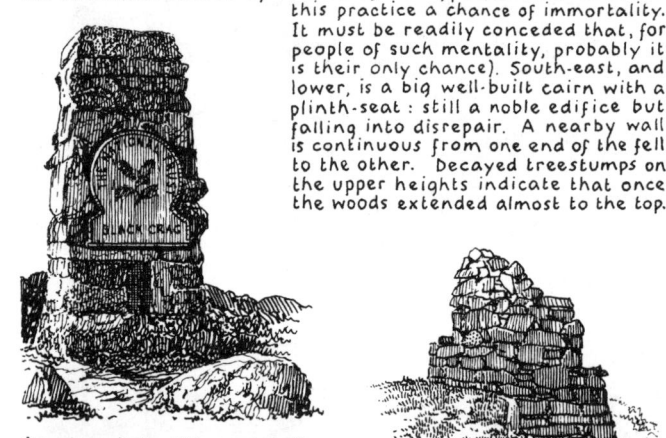

*perhaps it should be made quite clear that this latter note is also intended for the guidance of walkers, not of courting couples.

The south-east cairn

Black Fell 4

THE VIEW

The lovely countryside around the head of Windermere is delightfully pictured, this being the best viewpoint for the sylvan charms of the area between Ambleside, Wray Castle and Hawkshead. Southwards, Coniston Water is seen above the indented and wooded shores of Tarn Hows, which appears as beautiful as ever but a trifle foreign to the district. The mountain scene, although restricted, is good, the Langdale Pikes being especially well displayed. There is a peep of Scafell Pike, just overtopping the north ridge of the Crinkles. North, the various tops of the Helvellyn range are not seen distinctively, the mass appearing as a single mountain.

Lakes and Tarns

E: Windermere
ESE: Blelham Tarn
ESE: Barngates Tarn
SE: Various tarns on Claife Heights
SSE: Priest Pot
SSE: Esthwaite Water
SSW: Tarn Hows
SSW: Coniston Water

Principal Fells

BLENCATHRA (summit not seen)
HELVELLYN LOWER MAN
HELVELLYN
NETHERMOST PIKE
DOLLYWAGGON PIKE
FAIRFIELD
GREAT RIGG
HART CRAG
DOVE CRAG
HIGH PIKE
LITTLE HART CRAG
RED SCREES
CAUDALE MOOR
THORNTHWAITE CRAG
MARDALE ILL BELL
FROSWICK
ILL BELL
YOKE
SALLOWS
SOUR HOWES
WANSFELL PIKE
ULLSCARF
STEEL FELL
SILVER HOW
SERGEANT MAN
HIGH RAISE
HARRISON STICKLE
PAVEY ARK
LOUGHRIGG
PIKE HOW
THUNACAR KNOTT
LINGMOOR FELL
GLARAMARA
ALLEN CRAGS (summit not seen)
GREAT END
SCAFELL PIKE
BOWFELL
PIKE O' BLISCO
CRINKLE CRAGS
COLD PIKE
Little Carrs
WETHERLAM
BRIM FELL
CONISTON OLD MAN

15 miles
10 miles
2½ miles
5 miles

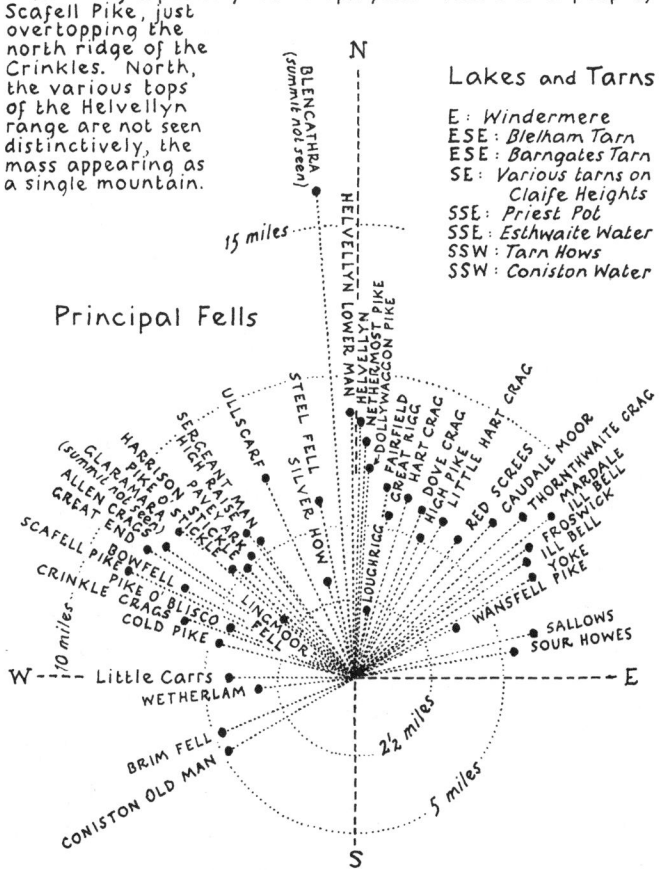

W — E
N
S

Bowfell 2960'

'Bow Fell' (two words)
on Ordnance Survey maps

from Lingmoor Fell

Bowfell 2

NATURAL FEATURES

A favourite of all fellwalkers, Bowfell is a mountain that commands attention whenever it appears in a view. And more than attention, respect and admiration, too; for it has the rare characteristic of displaying a graceful outline and a sturdy shapeliness on all sides. The fell occupies a splendid position at the hub of three well-known valleys, Great Langdale, Langstrath and Eskdale, rising as a massive pyramid at the head of each, and it is along these valleys that its waters drain, soon assuming the size of rivers. The higher the slopes rise the rougher they become, finally rearing up steeply as a broken rim of rock around the peaked summit and stony top. These crags are of diverse and unusual form, natural curiosities that add an exceptional interest and help to identify Bowfell in the memory. Under the terraced northern precipices, in a dark hollow, is Angle Tarn.

As much as any other mountain, the noble Bowfell may be regarded as affording an entirely typical Lakeland climb, with easy walking over grass giving place to rough scrambling on scree, and a summit deserving of detailed exploration and rewarding visitors with very beautiful views.

Rank Bowfell among the best half-dozen! ✲

✲ The author is not prepared to say, at this stage, which he considers to be the other five. This opinion will be given in the last pages of Book Seven.

• Stonethwaite

▲ GLARAMARA

Wasdale •
Head

▲ ESK PIKE
SCAFELL PIKE ▲ ▲ BOWFELL
• Dungeon Ghyll
CRINKLE CRAGS ▲

Boot •

MILES
0 1 2 3 4 5

Bowfell 3

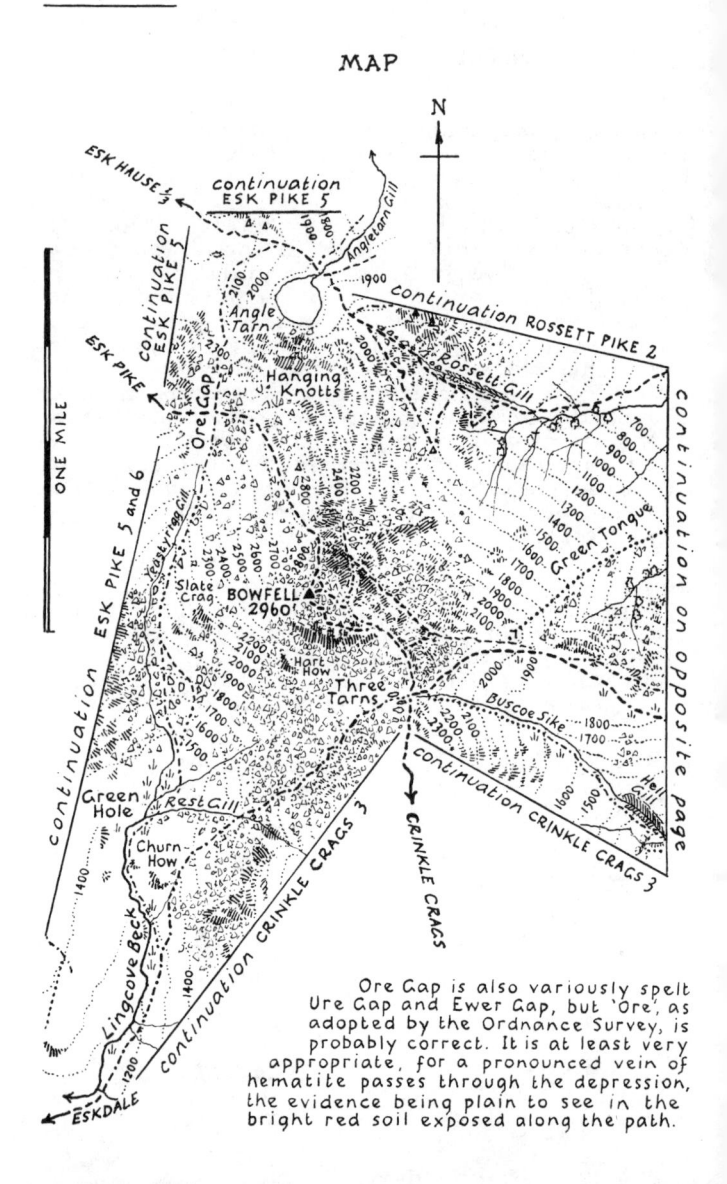

MAP

Ore Gap is also variously spelt Ure Gap and Ewer Gap, but 'Ore', as adopted by the Ordnance Survey, is probably correct. It is at least very appropriate, for a pronounced vein of hematite passes through the depression, the evidence being plain to see in the bright red soil exposed along the path.

Bowfell 4

MAP

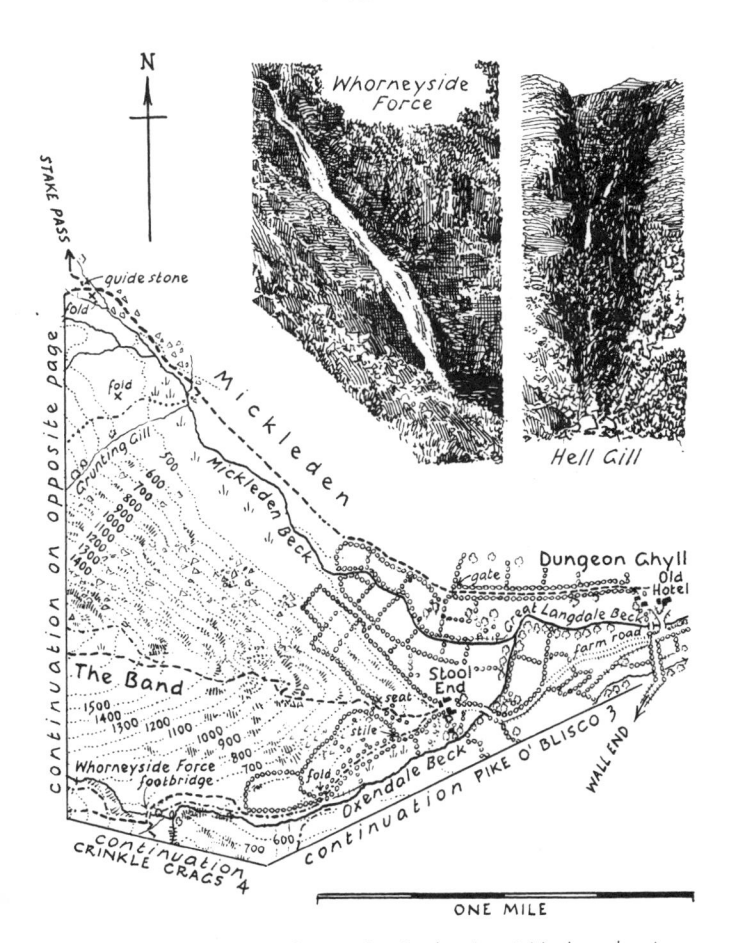

Whorneyside Force

Hell Gill

The county boundary between Cumberland and Westmorland passes over the top of Bowfell, coming up from Wrynose Pass via Crinkle Crags and Three Tarns. From the summit it follows the height of land to Hanging Knotts, where the main ridge is left in favour of the lesser watershed of Rossett Pass, whence it continues the circuit of Mickleden. Thus, Great Langdale and all the waters thereof are wholly within Westmorland.

Bowfell 5

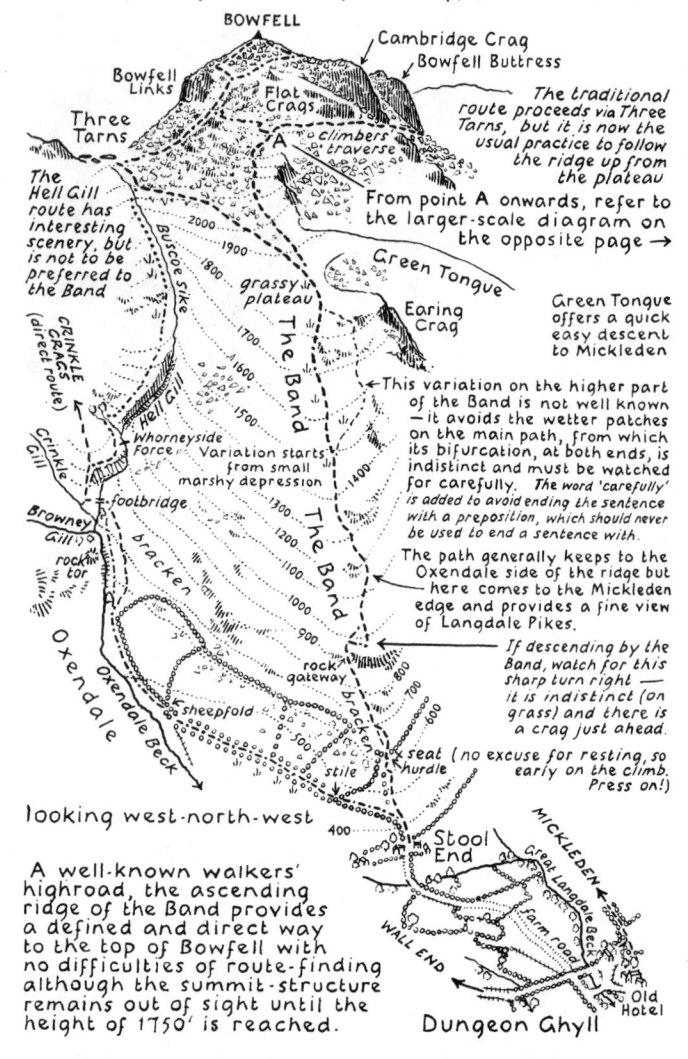

ASCENT FROM DUNGEON GHYLL
2700 feet of ascent : 3 miles (3¼ via Three Tarns)

BOWFELL
Cambridge Crag
Bowfell Buttress
Bowfell Links
Flat Crags
Three Tarns
climbers' traverse
A

The traditional route proceeds via Three Tarns, but it is now the usual practice to follow the ridge up from the plateau

From point A onwards, refer to the larger-scale diagram on the opposite page →

The Hell Gill route has interesting scenery, but is not to be preferred to the Band.

Buscoe Sike
2000
1900
1800
grassy plateau
Green Tongue
Earing Crag

Green Tongue offers a quick easy descent to Mickleden

1700
The Band
1600
1500
Hell Gill
Whorneyside Force
1400
Variation starts from small marshy depression
The Band

CRINKLE CRAGS (direct route)
Crinkle Gill
Browney Gill
footbridge
rock tor

This variation on the higher part of the Band is not well known — it avoids the wetter patches on the main path, from which its bifurcation, at both ends, is indistinct and must be watched for carefully. *The word 'carefully' is added to avoid ending the sentence with a preposition, which should never be used to end a sentence with.*

1300
1200
1100
1000
900
bracken
The Band

The path generally keeps to the Oxendale side of the ridge but here comes to the Mickleden edge and provides a fine view of Langdale Pikes.

Oxendale
Oxendale Beck
sheepfold
rock gateway
bracken
800
700
600
500
stile
400
seat
hurdle

If descending by the Band, watch for this sharp turn right — it is indistinct (on grass) and there is a crag just ahead.

seat (no excuse for resting, so early on the climb. Press on!)

looking west·north·west

A well-known walkers' highroad, the ascending ridge of the Band provides a defined and direct way to the top of Bowfell with no difficulties of route-finding although the summit-structure remains out of sight until the height of 1750' is reached.

Stool End
MICKLEDEN
Great Langdale Beck
farm road
WALL END
Old Hotel
Dungeon Ghyll

Bowfell 6

ASCENT FROM DUNGEON GHYLL

The upper section, looking west

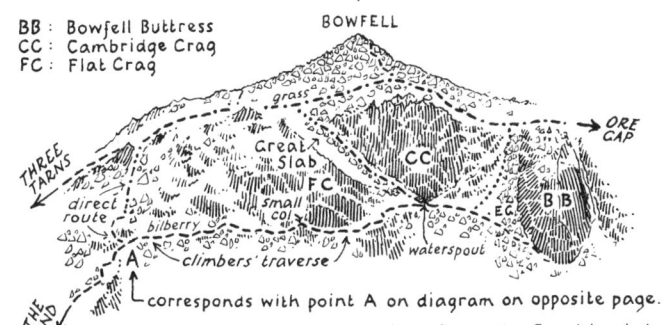

BB: Bowfell Buttress
CC: Cambridge Crag
FC: Flat Crag

[Diagram showing Bowfell summit with Three Tarns, The Band, direct route, climbers' traverse, bilberry, small col, Great Slab, FC, CC, BB, waterspout, and Ore Gap labelled. Point A marked on climbers' traverse.]

— corresponds with point A on diagram on opposite page.

The stony path coming up the ridge from the Band leads to, and is continued as, the climbers' traverse. Ten yards below the point where the horizontal traverse commences the direct route wiggles away up to the left and may be passed unnoticed.

The climbers' traverse is a very enjoyable high-level route leading to excellent rock-scenery. Two recent minor rockfalls have slightly disturbed the path but it is quite distinct and perfectly easy, with a very little very mild scrambling, hardly worth mentioning. The traverse is a series of little ups and downs, but generally keeps to a horizontal course. Except at the small col the ground falls away steeply on the valley side of the path.

The best way off the traverse to the summit lies up the fringe of a 'river' of boulders along the south side of Cambridge Crag, or, more tediously, the wide scree gully between Cambridge Crag and Bowfell Buttress may be ascended. (Cambridge Crag is identifiable, beyond all doubt, by the waterspout gushing from the base of the cliff — and nothing better ever came out of a barrel or a bottle).

The striations of Flat Crags are of particular interest, even to non-geologists. Note how the angle of tilt is repeated in the slope of the Great Slab.

The climbers' traverse

ASCENT FROM WASDALE

Although Bowfell is well hidden from Wasdale Head it is not too distant to be climbed from there in comfortable time, but the walk has the disadvantage (for those who object to re-tracing footsteps) that very little variation of route is possible on the return journey to Wasdale Head. Esk Pike stands in the way and must be climbed first (and traversed later).

For a diagram of the ascent of Esk Pike from Wasdale Head see Esk Pike 8

Bowfell 7

ASCENT FROM MICKLEDEN
2500 feet of ascent : 1¼ miles from the sheepfold

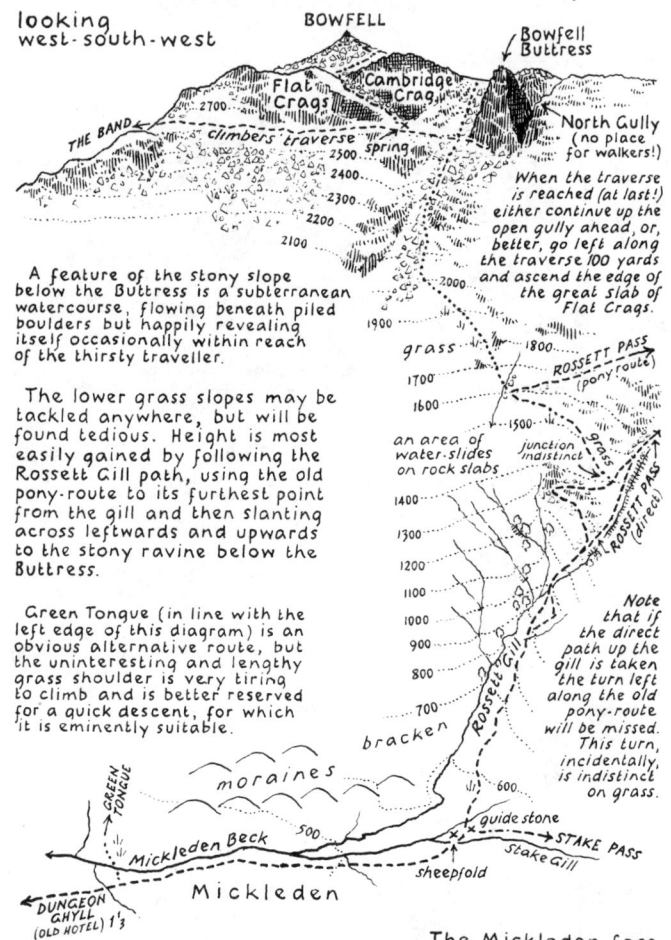

looking west-south-west

BOWFELL

Bowfell Buttress

Flat Crags   Cambridge Crag

THE BAND

2700

Climbers' traverse — spring

2500
2400
2300
2200
2100

North Gully (no place for walkers!)

When the traverse is reached (at last!) either continue up the open gully ahead, or, better, go left along the traverse 100 yards and ascend the edge of the great slab of Flat Crags.

A feature of the stony slope below the Buttress is a subterranean watercourse, flowing beneath piled boulders but happily revealing itself occasionally within reach of the thirsty traveller.

The lower grass slopes may be tackled anywhere, but will be found tedious. Height is most easily gained by following the Rossett Gill path, using the old pony-route to its furthest point from the gill and then slanting across leftwards and upwards to the stony ravine below the Buttress.

Green Tongue (in line with the left edge of this diagram) is an obvious alternative route, but the uninteresting and lengthy grass shoulder is very tiring to climb and is better reserved for a quick descent, for which it is eminently suitable.

2000
1900
grass
1800   ROSSETT PASS (pony route)
1700
1600
1500   junction indistinct
an area of water-slides on rock slabs
1400
1300   ROSSETT PASS (direct)
1200
1100
1000
900
800
Rossett Gill
700
bracken

Note that if the direct path up the gill is taken the turn left along the old pony-route will be missed. This turn, incidentally, is indistinct on grass.

moraines

GREEN TONGUE

Mickleden Beck   500

600   guide stone   STAKE PASS
sheepfold   Stake Gill

Mickleden

← DUNGEON GHYLL (OLD HOTEL) 1'3

The Mickleden face, 2500 feet of continuous ascent, is a route for scramblers rather than walkers. The rock-scenery becomes imposing as height is gained, Bowfell Buttress in particular being an impressive object when seen at close quarters.

Bowfell 8

ASCENT FROM ESKDALE
2900 feet of ascent : 7½ miles from Boot

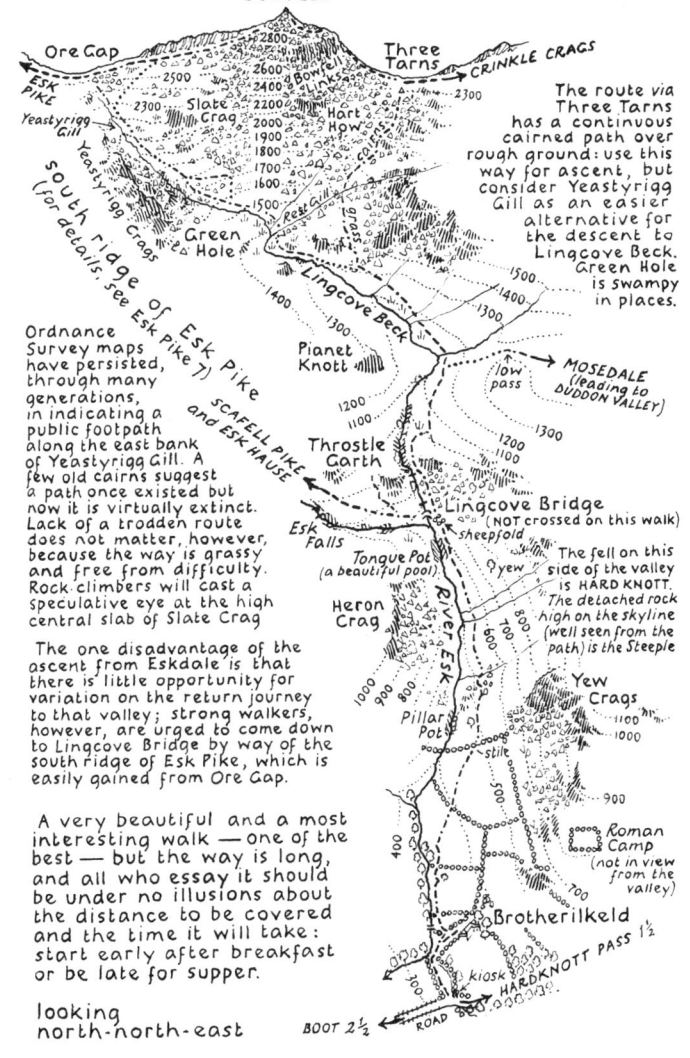

The route via Three Tarns has a continuous cairned path over rough ground: use this way for ascent, but consider Yeastyrigg Gill as an easier alternative for the descent to Lingcove Beck. Green Hole is swampy in places.

Ordnance Survey maps have persisted, through many generations, in indicating a public footpath along the east bank of Yeastyrigg Gill. A few old cairns suggest a path once existed but now it is virtually extinct. Lack of a trodden route does not matter, however, because the way is grassy and free from difficulty. Rock-climbers will cast a speculative eye at the high central slab of Slate Crag.

The one disadvantage of the ascent from Eskdale is that there is little opportunity for variation on the return journey to that valley; strong walkers, however, are urged to come down to Lingcove Bridge by way of the south ridge of Esk Pike, which is easily gained from Ore Gap.

A very beautiful and a most interesting walk — one of the best — but the way is long, and all who essay it should be under no illusions about the distance to be covered and the time it will take: start early after breakfast or be late for supper.

looking north-north-east

Bowfell 9

ASCENT FROM STONETHWAITE
2650 feet of ascent : 6½ miles

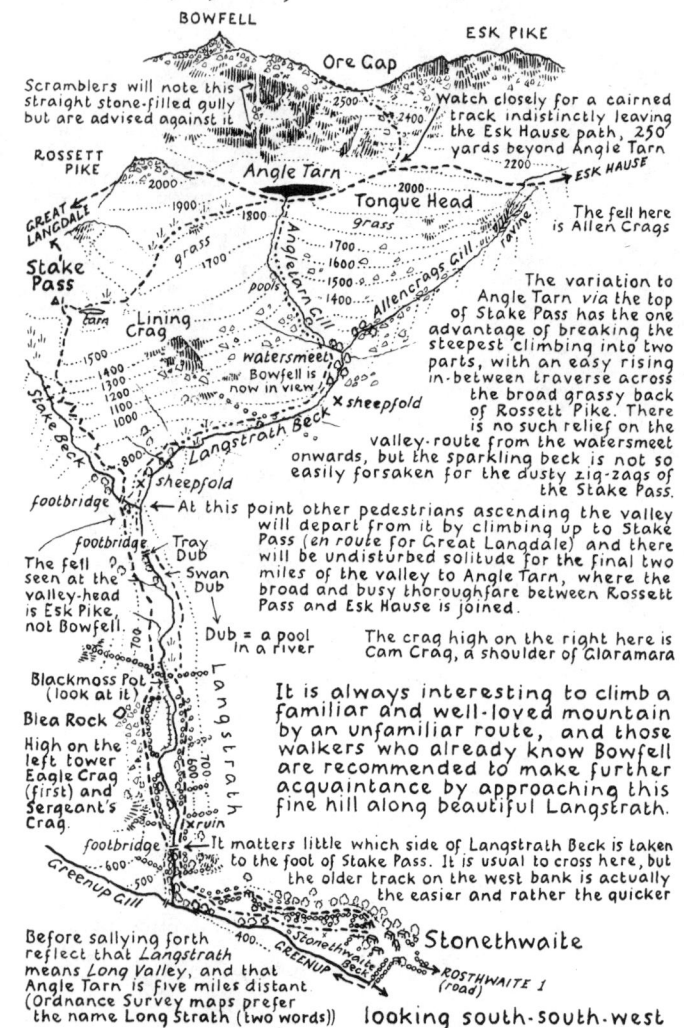

BOWFELL — ESK PIKE — Ore Gap

Scramblers will note this straight stone-filled gully but are advised against it

Watch closely for a cairned track indistinctly leaving the Esk Hause path, 250 yards beyond Angle Tarn

ROSSETT PIKE — Angle Tarn — Tongue Head — ESK HAUSE

The fell here is Allen Crags

GREAT LANGDALE — Stake Pass — Lining Crag — watersmeet — Angletarn Gill — Allencrags Gill

Bowfell is now in view

The variation to Angle Tarn via the top of Stake Pass (en route for Great Langdale) has the one advantage of breaking the steepest climbing into two parts, with an easy rising in-between traverse across the broad grassy back of Rossett Pike. There is no such relief on the valley-route from the watersmeet onwards, but the sparkling beck is not so easily forsaken for the dusty zig-zags of the Stake Pass.

× sheepfold — Langstrath Beck — × sheepfold — footbridge

At this point other pedestrians ascending the valley will depart from it by climbing up to Stake Pass (en route for Great Langdale) and there will be undisturbed solitude for the final two miles of the valley to Angle Tarn, where the broad and busy thoroughfare between Rossett Pass and Esk Hause is joined.

footbridge — Tray Dub — Swan Dub — Dub = a pool in a river

The fell seen at the valley-head is Esk Pike, not Bowfell

The crag high on the right here is Cam Crag, a shoulder of Glaramara

Blackmoss Pot (look at it) — Blea Rock

High on the left tower Eagle Crag (first) and Sergeant's Crag

It is always interesting to climb a familiar and well-loved mountain by an unfamiliar route, and those walkers who already know Bowfell are recommended to make further acquaintance by approaching this fine hill along beautiful Langstrath.

footbridge — ruin — Langstrath

It matters little which side of Langstrath Beck is taken to the foot of Stake Pass. It is usual to cross here, but the older track on the west bank is actually the easier and rather the quicker

Greenup Gill — Stonethwaite Beck — Stonethwaite → ROSTHWAITE 1 (road)

Before sallying forth reflect that *Langstrath* means *Long Valley*, and that Angle Tarn is five miles distant (Ordnance Survey maps prefer the name *Long Strath* (two words))

looking south-south-west

Bowfell 10

Cambridge Crag and Bowfell Buttress from the top of the Great Slab

Bowfell 11

THE SUMMIT

Bowfell's top is a shattered pyramid, a great heap of stones and boulders and naked rock, a giant cairn in itself.

The rugged summit provides poor picking for the Bowfell sheep, who draw the line at mosses and lichens and look elsewhere for their mountain greenery, and reserves its best rewards for the walkers who climb the natural rocky stairway to its upper limit for here, spread before them for their delectation, is a glorious panorama, which, moreover, may be surveyed and appreciated from positions of repose on the comfortable flat seats of stone (comfortable in the sense that everybody arriving here says how nice it is to sit down) with which the summit is liberally equipped. The leisurely contemplation of the scene will not be assailed by doubts as to whether the highest point has in fact been gained for rough slopes tumble away steeply on all sides.

The top pyramid stands on a sloping plinth which, to the east, extends beyond the base of the pyramid and forms a shelf or terrace where stones are less in evidence. It is from this shelf that Bowfell's main crags fall away, and from which, with care, they may be viewed; care is necessary because the boulders to be negotiated in carrying out this inspection are in a state of balance, in places, and liable to heel over and trap a leg.

It is possible, and does happen, that walkers ascend Bowfell and traverse its top quite unaware of the imposing line of crags overlooking Mickleden: from the summit and the shelf-track there is little to indicate the presence of steep cliffs.   But to miss seeing the crags is to miss seeing half the glory of Bowfell.

Bowfell 12

THE SUMMIT

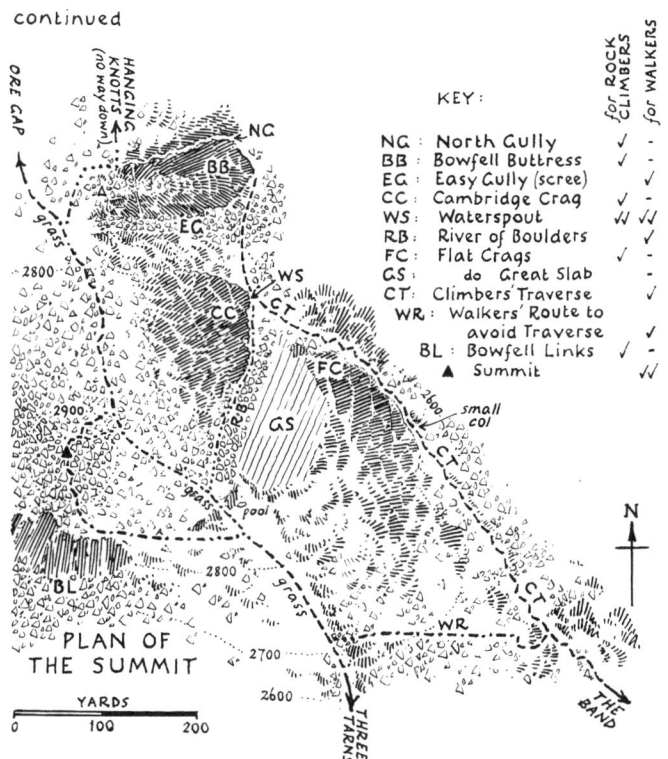

continued

PLAN OF THE SUMMIT

KEY:

		for ROCK CLIMBERS	for WALKERS
NG:	North Gully	✓	–
BB:	Bowfell Buttress	✓	–
EG:	Easy Gully (scree)	✓	✓
CC:	Cambridge Crag	✓	–
WS:	Waterspout	✓✓	✓✓
RB:	River of Boulders	✓	–
FC:	Flat Crags	✓	–
GS:	do Great Slab	✓	–
CT:	Climbers' Traverse	✓	–
WR:	Walkers' Route to avoid Traverse		✓
BL:	Bowfell Links	✓	–
▲	Summit		✓✓

DESCENTS: The sloping grass shelf, east of the actual summit, carries the only path across the top: it links Ore Gap with Three Tarns. Two well-scratched tracks go down from the cairn and join this path: one, on the south, descends first in line with Three Tarns but is turned leftwards by the uncompromising rim of Bowfell Links; the other, shorter, goes down north inclining north-east with many simple variations among the boulders. For Langdale the steep lower section of the Three Tarns path may be avoided by using a terrace on the left at a gap in the wall of rocks (WR on the plan above). Direct descents to Eskdale over the steepening boulder slopes are not feasible.

┃┃┃ In mist, the only safe objectives are Ore Gap (for Wasdale, Borrowdale or Eskdale) and Three Tarns (for Langdale via the Band, or Eskdale) avoiding Bowfell Links on the way thereto.

Bowfell 13

Bowfell 14

The Great Slab of Flat Crags

Bowfell 15

RIDGE ROUTES

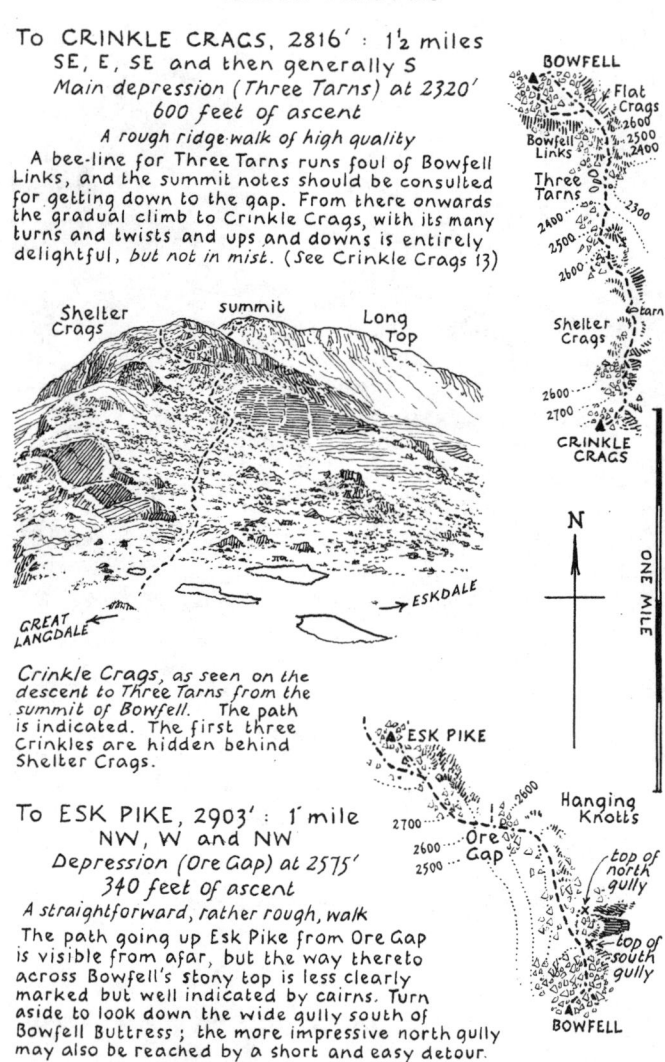

To CRINKLE CRAGS, 2816′ : 1½ miles
SE, E, SE and then generally S
Main depression (Three Tarns) at 2320′
600 feet of ascent
A rough ridge walk of high quality

A bee-line for Three Tarns runs foul of Bowfell Links, and the summit notes should be consulted for getting down to the gap. From there onwards the gradual climb to Crinkle Crags, with its many turns and twists and ups and downs is entirely delightful, but not in mist. (See Crinkle Crags 13)

Crinkle Crags, as seen on the descent to Three Tarns from the summit of Bowfell. The path is indicated. The first three Crinkles are hidden behind Shelter Crags.

To ESK PIKE, 2903′ : 1 mile
NW, W and NW
Depression (Ore Gap) at 2575′
340 feet of ascent
A straightforward, rather rough, walk

The path going up Esk Pike from Ore Gap is visible from afar, but the way thereto across Bowfell's stony top is less clearly marked but well indicated by cairns. Turn aside to look down the wide gully south of Bowfell Buttress; the more impressive north gully may also be reached by a short and easy detour.

Bowfell 16

Three views from the Band

Right:
 Browney Gill and Cold Pike

Bottom Right:
 Pike o' Blisco

Below:
 Pike o' Stickle

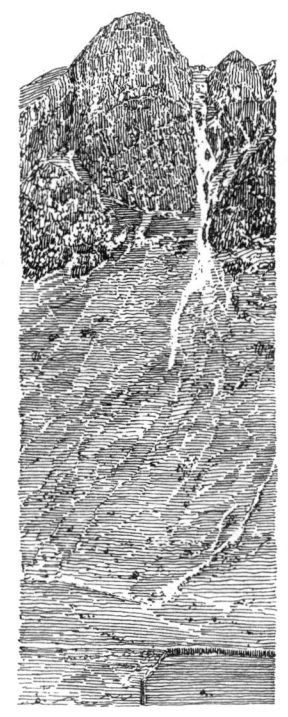

Bowfell 17

THE VIEW

N — NE

- ULLOCK PIKE 13¾
- LONG SIDE 13½
- CARL SIDE 13½
- SKIDDAW 14
- SKIDDAW LITTLE MAN 13¼
- LONSCALE FELL 13
- KNOTT 16¼
- WALLA CRAG 9½
- HIGH PIKE 18¼
- BLEABERRY FELL 8½
- BLENCATHRA 14
- HIGH SEAT 7¾
- RAVEN CRAG 8½
- SOUTHER FELL 16
- CLOUGH HEAD 11½
- GREAT DODD 10½
- STYBARROW DODD 9¾
- RAISE 9

GLARAMARA 2½
Keswick
Dock Tarn
SERGEANT'S CRAG 3½
ULLSCARF 4½

position of Bowfell Buttress
Langstrath
Path to ORE GAP

E — SE

- YOKE 12
- SALLOWS 12
- WANSFELL PIKE 9⅔
- SOUR HOWES 11½
- PIKE O' BLISCO 2

The Pennines in the background

LOUGHRIGG FELL 6½
Windermere
Esthwaite Water
LINGMOOR FELL 3¾
Great Langdale
Side Pike
road to Blea Tarn
Kettle Crag

Flat Crags
path to THREE TARNS
edge of Bowfell Links

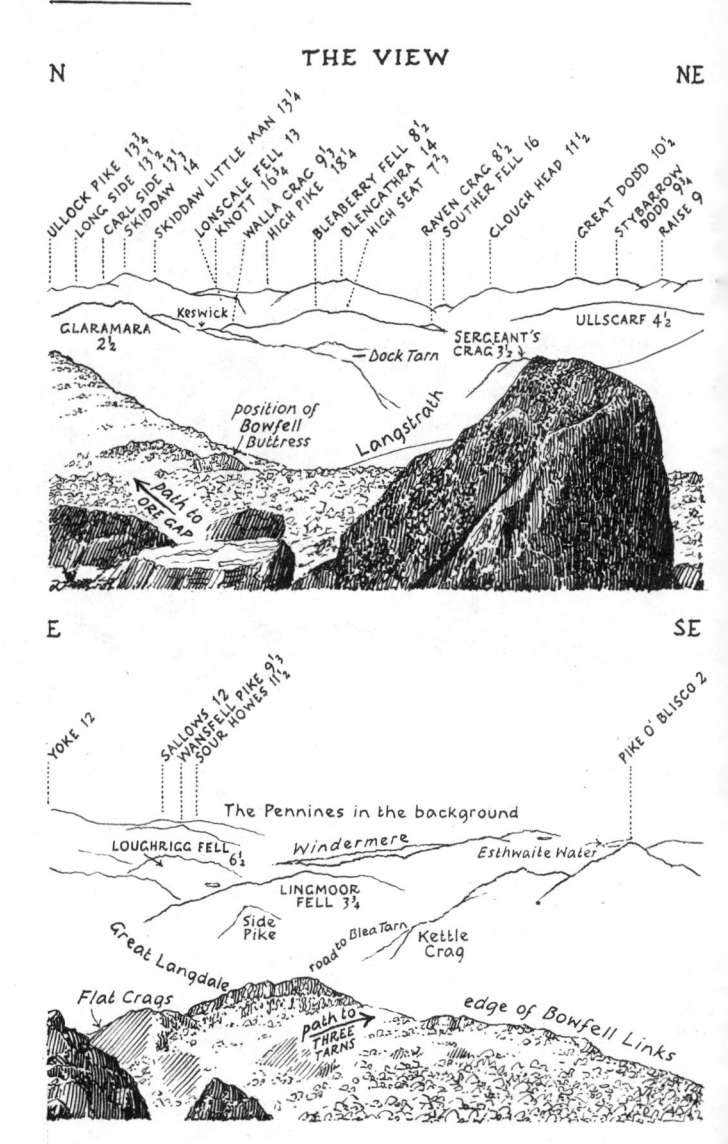

Bowfell 18

THE VIEW

NE — HELVELLYN LOWER MAN 8, HELVELLYN 8, NETHERMOST PIKE 7¾, DOLLYWAGGON PIKE 7½, ST. SUNDAY CRAG 8¾, LOADPOT HILL 15, FAIRFIELD 7¾, HART CRAG 8¼, HIGH RAISE 13¼, RAMPSGILL HEAD 13, KIDSTY PIKE 13, HIGH STREET 12½, THORNTHWAITE CRAG 11¾, RED SCREES 9½, HARTER FELL 13½, FROSWICK 12, ILL BELL 12, KENTMERE PIKE 13¼ — **E**

HIGH RAISE 3, SERGEANT MAN 3, SEAT SANDAL 7, HARRISON STICKLE 2½, PIKE O' STICKLE 2, Gimmer Crag, SILVER HOW 5

Martcrag Moor

edge of Cambridge Crag

On a clear day, Cross-Fell (the highest of the Pennines) is seen, with Little Dun Fell, to the left of St. Sunday Crag; Great Dun Fell (radar station) is just to the right.

SE — WETHERLAM 4½, Black Sails 4¼, COLD PIKE 2, SWIRL HOW 4, CONISTON OLD MAN 5½, GREY FRIAR 3¾, DOW CRAG 5½ — **S**

Red Tarn, Great Knott, CRINKLE CRAGS 1, Long Top

path to Crinkle Crags

The view is magnificent in all directions, being enhanced by the sharp fall of the bouldery slopes from the summit-cairn, which adds depth as well as distance to every prospect.

Three Tarns

edge of Bowfell Links

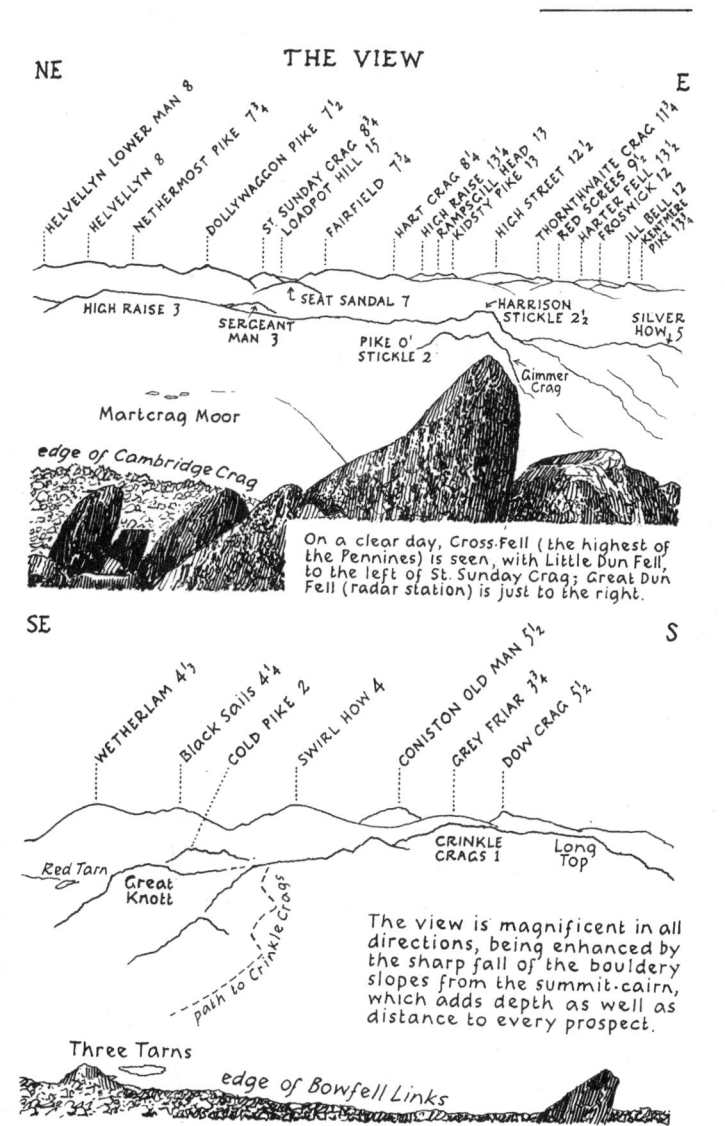

Bowfell 19

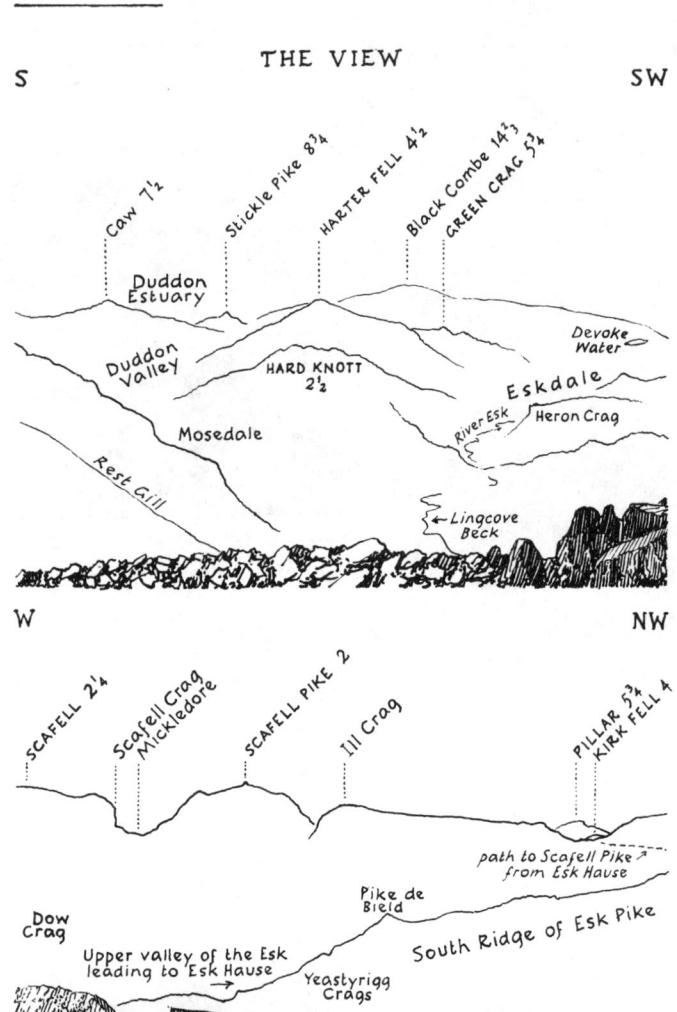

THE VIEW

S • SW

Caw 7½ · Duddon Estuary · Slickle Pike 8¾ · HARTER FELL 4½ · Black Combe 14¾ · GREEN CRAG 5¾

Duddon Valley · HARD KNOTT 2½ · Devoke Water · Eskdale · River Esk · Heron Crag

Mosedale

Rest Gill

Lingcove Beck

W • NW

SCAFELL 2¼ · Scafell Crag Mickledore · SCAFELL PIKE 2 · Ill Crag · PILLAR 5¾ · KIRK FELL 4

path to Scafell Pike from Esk Hause

Dow Crag · Upper valley of the Esk leading to Esk Hause · Pike de Bield · Yeastyrigg Crags · South Ridge of Esk Pike

Bowfell 20

THE VIEW

SW W

SLIGHT SIDE 24

Estuary of the Esk
Eskdale

Esk Gorge
Cam Spout Crag
Cam Spout
River Esk

NW N

GREAT END 1¾
GREAT GABLE 3¼
ESK PIKE 3¾
GREEN GABLE 3¼
WHITELESS PIKE 8¾
GRASMOOR 9¾
WANDOPE 9
ROBINSON 7
EEL CRAG 9¼
SAIL 9
GRISEDALE PIKE 10
DALE HEAD 5¾
LORDS SEAT 12¾
CAUSEY PIKE 9
BARF 12¾
BINSEY 18

Solway Firth
BRANDRETH 3¾
ALLEN CRAGS 1¾
Solway Firth
path to Esk Pike and Esk Hause
Ore Gap
path to Esk Hause from Angle Tarn
top of Hanging Knotts

Yeastyrigg Gill

Brim Fell 2611'

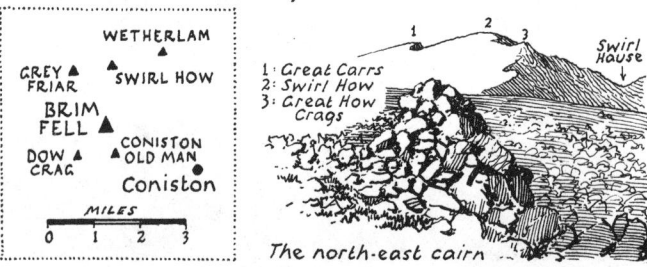

from Little How Crags

WETHERLAM
GREY FRIAR ▲ ▲ SWIRL HOW
BRIM FELL ▲
DOW CRAG ▲ ▲ CONISTON OLD MAN
● Coniston

MILES
0   1   2   3

1: Great Carrs
2: Swirl How
3: Great How Crags

Swirl House →

The north-east cairn

Brim Fell 2

NATURAL FEATURES

Brim Fell is the mile-long whalebacked ridge linking Coniston Old Man with Swirl How, the latter fell being joined at the narrow depression of Levers Hause, a high pass across the main watershed. Throughout its length the ridge is furnished with a most excellent turf, firm and dry and a pleasure to tread, but the featureless top, where a few stones intrude, is without interest. The western slope going steeply and roughly down amongst crags to Seathwaite Tarn is likewise dull, but the east face, craggy everywhere and narrowing quickly to the confluence of Low Water Beck and Levers Water Beck, is full of interesting detail, the best feature being the prominent buttress of Raven Tor thrusting out between the two attractive tarns of Low Water and Levers Water and the most fearsome a group of dangerous coppermine shafts in the vicinity of the sinister gash of Simon's Nick.

MAP

The approaches from Coniston are illustrated in the diagram on the next page following →

Brim Fell 3

ASCENT FROM CONISTON
2450 feet of ascent : 3 miles (3½ via Gill Cove)

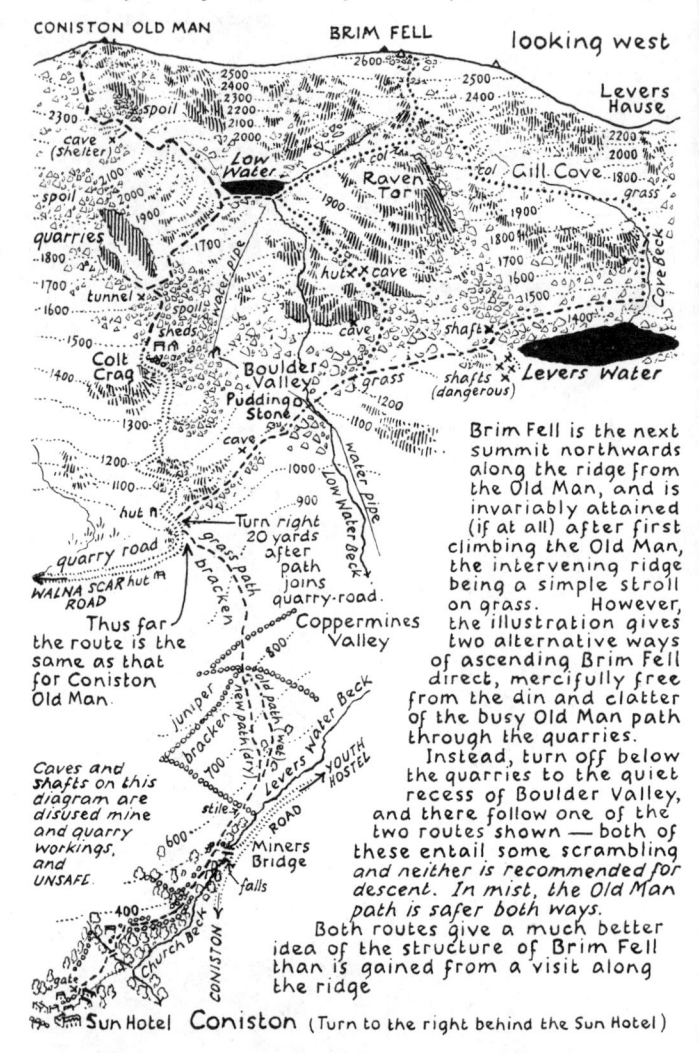

looking west

Brim Fell is the next summit northwards along the ridge from the Old Man, and is invariably attained (if at all) after first climbing the Old Man, the intervening ridge being a simple stroll on grass. However, the illustration gives two alternative ways of ascending Brim Fell direct, mercifully free from the din and clatter of the busy Old Man path through the quarries.

Instead, turn off below the quarries to the quiet recess of Boulder Valley, and there follow one of the two routes shown — both of these entail some scrambling and neither is recommended for descent. In mist, the Old Man path is safer both ways.

Both routes give a much better idea of the structure of Brim Fell than is gained from a visit along the ridge

Thus far the route is the same as that for Coniston Old Man.

Caves and shafts on this diagram are disused mine and quarry workings, and UNSAFE.

Sun Hotel Coniston (Turn to the right behind the Sun Hotel)

Brim Fell 4

THE SUMMIT

(panorama labels: HAYCOCK, SLIGHT SIDE, SCOAT FELL, SCAFELL, SCAFELL PIKE, Broad Crag, Ill Crag, GREAT END, ESK PIKE, CRINKLE CRAGS, BOWFELL, GREY FRIAR)

A big cairn, originally well built but becoming shattered, marks the highest part of the broad grassy plateau on top of the fell. 100 yards north-east is a second big cairn in an eruption of grey stones. There is nothing else to mention.

DESCENTS: The summit is usually left along the ridge, but it is useful to know that the north-east cairn stands at the head of a simple direct descent for Coniston (the only easy breach in the eastern escarpment): on this route aim for the col linking Raven Tor to the fell and here turn right down a grass slope to Low Water. But *in mist* go first to the Old Man and descend from there.

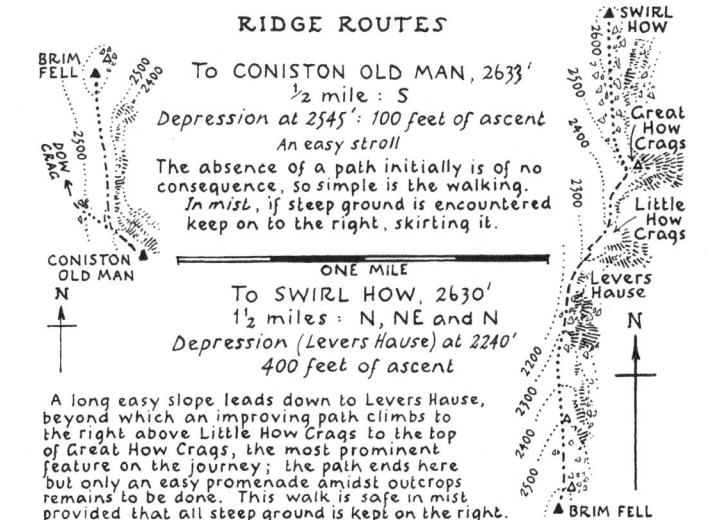

RIDGE ROUTES

To CONISTON OLD MAN, 2633'
½ mile : S
Depression at 2545': 100 feet of ascent
An easy stroll

The absence of a path initially is of no consequence, so simple is the walking.
In mist, if steep ground is encountered keep on to the right, skirting it.

───── ONE MILE ─────

To SWIRL HOW, 2630'
1½ miles : N, NE and N
Depression (Levers Hause) at 2240'
400 feet of ascent

A long easy slope leads down to Levers Hause, beyond which an improving path climbs to the right above Little How Crags to the top of Great How Crags, the most prominent feature on the journey; the path ends here but only an easy promenade amidst outcrops remains to be done. This walk is safe in mist provided that all steep ground is kept on the right.

Brim Fell 5

THE VIEW

The view, although extensive, suffers in comparison with that from the adjacent Old Man because of the broadness of the summit, there being no single vantage point that brings the surrounding tarns into the picture. The scene therefore depends for attractiveness on the far skyline of fells in the northern arc, with the other Coniston hills looming rather too largely to present a balanced view. A quite unexpected glimpse of Little Mell Fell is seen above Grisedale Hause; it is interesting also to see the atomic power plants on the coast neatly bisected by the peak of the Eskdale Harter Fell.

Principal Fells

The distant fell seen over Dow Crag is Black Combe.

Lakes and Tarns:
ENE: *Tarn Hows*
E: *Windermere (2 sections)*
W: *Devoke Water*

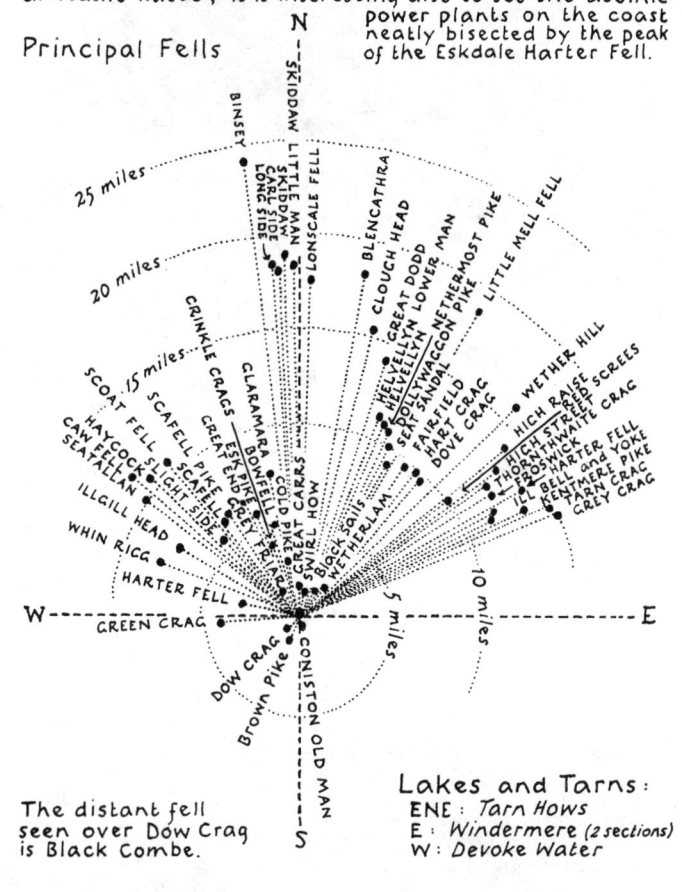

Brim Fell 6

Simon's Nick (top left) and the upper valley of Levers Water Beck from one of the old levels, Paddy End Copper Works.

Raven Tor, the east buttress of Brim Fell, from the dam at Levers Water

Cold Pike 2259'

from Pike o' Blisco

The true south ridge of Crinkle Crags follows the compass bearing to end in a long steep descent to Cockley Beck, but a spur running off south-east is more usually considered to continue the main spine of the mountain. This spur rises to the three rocky summits of Cold Pike before dropping down Wrynose Breast to the pass below; a concave eastern slope descends to the desolate upland hollow containing Red Tarn, so named from the rich colour of the shaly subsoil.

Although not of great significance, Cold Pike is prominent when seen from the north and east, and it has lovely views in those directions. All around, nearby, are higher fells, and they may be studied profitably from the triple peaks of this lowly one in their midst. Cold Pike is a Crinkle Crags in miniature.

Cold Pike 2

MAP

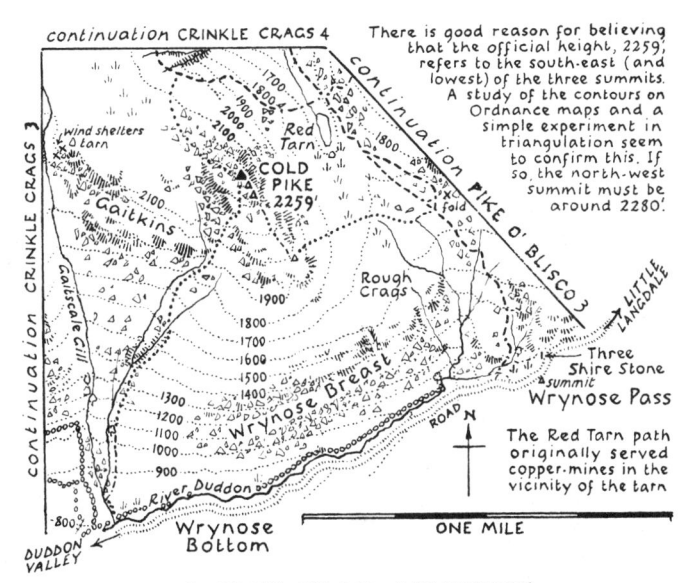

continuation CRINKLE CRAGS 4

There is good reason for believing that the official height, 2259, refers to the south-east (and lowest) of the three summits. A study of the contours on Ordnance maps and a simple experiment in triangulation seem to confirm this. If so, the north-west summit must be around 2280'.

COLD PIKE 2259

wind shelters & tarn

Gaitkins

Red Tarn

Rough Crags

Wrynose Breast

continuation CRINKLE CRAGS 3

continuation PIKE O' BLISCO 3

Gaissale Gill

River Duddon

Wrynose Bottom

DUDDON VALLEY

Three Shire Stone ▲ summit
Wrynose Pass

LITTLE LANGDALE

ROAD

N

The Red Tarn path originally served copper-mines in the vicinity of the tarn

ONE MILE

ASCENT FROM WRYNOSE

Below the crag west of the summit are many mammoth boulders and one grotesque 12-foot fanged splinter

An appropriate name for it would be Cold Pike Tooth. Try to locate it!

COLD PIKE

Gaitkins

RED TARN moraines

grass

solitary larch

scree

Wrynose Breast

bracken

River Duddon

Wrynose Bottom

DUDDON VALLEY

▲ summit
Wrynose Pass

1500 feet of ascent (from Wrynose Bottom)
1000 feet of ascent (from Wrynose Pass)
1¼ miles

Two simple routes on grass.

An initial problem on the Wrynose Bottom route is to get across the river (no bridge, no ford)

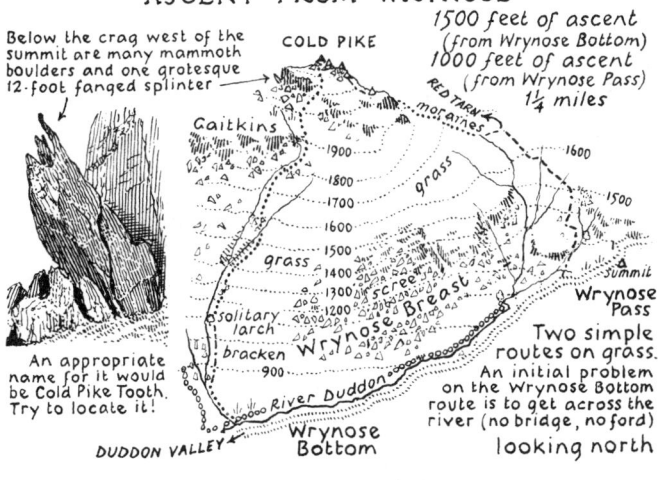

looking north

Cold Pike 3

THE SUMMIT

CRINKLE CRAGS   BOWFELL

The summit is the best part of the fell. It consists of three rocky humps, each with a cairn and sprinkled with boulders, descending in altitude from north-west to south-east, and strongly reminiscent, on a small scale, of Crinkle Crags, of which they are strictly a continuation. The principal cairn stands on a pleasant rock platform.

DESCENTS: The top of the fell is without paths, but in clear weather there is no difficulty in finding an easy way off through the outcrops. In mist, it is well to note that the summit ridge is buttressed by crags along its eastern fringe, and more distantly on the west, while Wrynose Breast is much too rough and steep to be considered as a route. The safest places to aim for are Red Tarn (for Oxendale) and Wrynose Pass, either of which may be reached by following the ridge south-east (in line with the three humps) as far as a cairn and a small tarn together, with rising ground beyond: here go down grass to the left and continue eastwards to join the path linking Red Tarn and Wrynose Pass.

RIDGE ROUTES

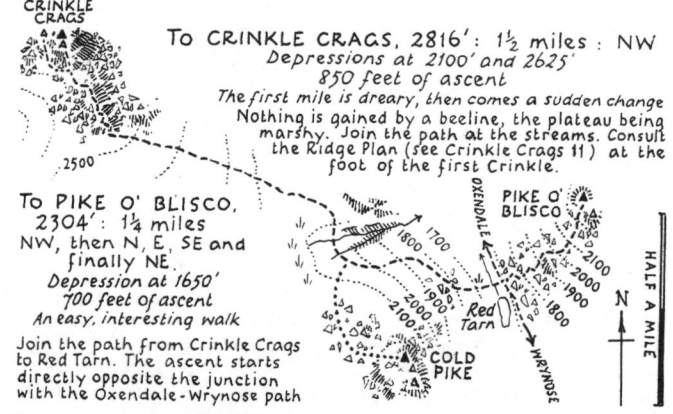

TO CRINKLE CRAGS, 2816': 1½ miles : NW
Depressions at 2100' and 2625'
850 feet of ascent

The first mile is dreary, then comes a sudden change. Nothing is gained by a beeline, the plateau being marshy. Join the path at the streams. Consult the Ridge Plan (see Crinkle Crags 11) at the foot of the first Crinkle.

TO PIKE O' BLISCO, 2304': 1¼ miles
NW, then N, E, SE and finally NE.
Depression at 1650'
700 feet of ascent
An easy, interesting walk

Join the path from Crinkle Crags to Red Tarn. The ascent starts directly opposite the junction with the Oxendale-Wrynose path

Cold Pike 4

THE VIEW

The view between north and east is very extensive, but on the west side is severely restricted by the lofty south ridge coming down from Crinkle Crags. Perhaps the best features are the two splendid lowland prospects (1) over Little Langdale to Windermere and the distant Pennines, and (2) down the Duddon Valley to the estuary and the sea beyond.

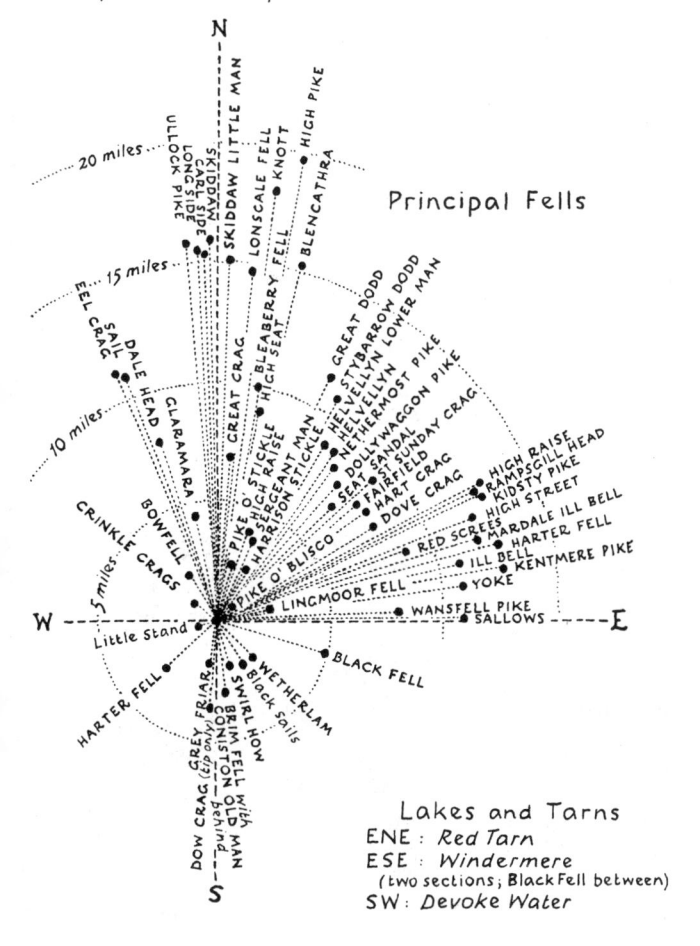

Principal Fells

Lakes and Tarns
ENE: Red Tarn
ESE: Windermere
(two sections; Black Fell between)
SW: Devoke Water

Coniston Old Man   2633'
properly
The Old Man of Coniston

from Red Dell Head

Coniston Old Man 2

NATURAL FEATURES

The Coniston fells form a separate geographical unit. They are almost entirely severed from the adjacent mountainous parts of Lakeland by the Duddon and Brathay valleys, with the watershed between the two, Wrynose Pass, 1270', providing the only link with other fells. The whole of the Coniston group lies within Lancashire, the two valleys mentioned containing the boundaries of Cumberland (Duddon) and Westmorland (Brathay).

Whilst the characteristics of the Coniston fells are predominantly Lakeland, with lofty ridges, steep and craggy declivities, lovely waterfalls and lonely tarns and the general scenic charm so typical of the district, there has been a great deal of industrial exploitation here, principally in copper mining (now abandoned) and quarrying (still active), resulting in much disfigurement. So strongly sculptured are these fine hills, however, and so pronounced is their appeal that the scars detract but little from the attractiveness of the picture: many people, indeed, will find that the decayed skeletons of the mine-workings add an unusual, and if explored an absorbing, interest to their walks.

The western slopes are comparatively dull, and the appeal of these hills lies in their aspect to the east, where the village of Coniston, in an Alpine setting, is the natural base for explorations. The ridge-walking, on soft turf, is excellent, but all slopes are very rough down to valley-level. As viewpoints, the summits have the advantage of isolation between the main mass of Lakeland and the fine indented coastline of Morecambe Bay, the prospects in all directions being of a high quality.

Waterfalls
Church Beck

continued

Coniston Old Man 3

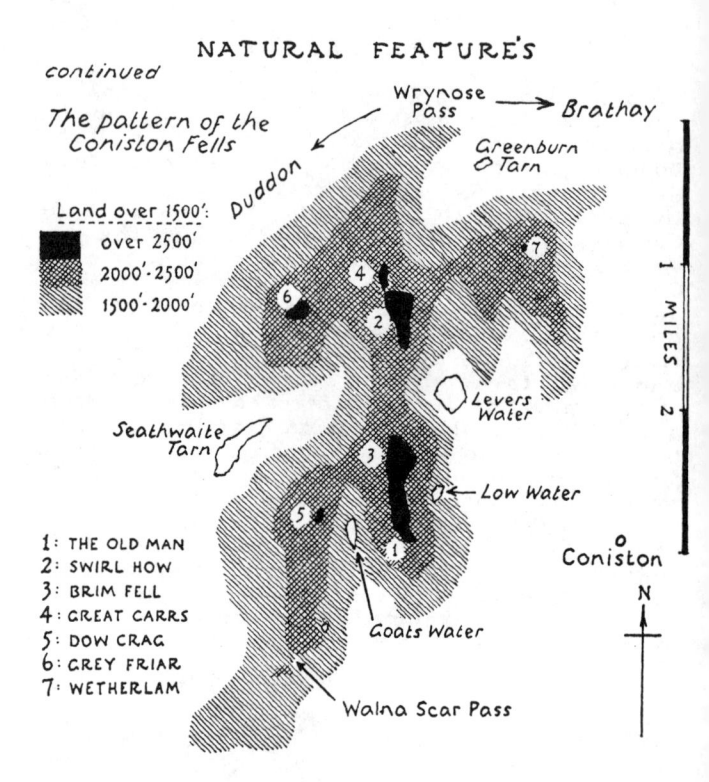

NATURAL FEATURES
continued

The pattern of the Coniston Fells

Land over 1500':
- over 2500'
- 2000'-2500'
- 1500'-2000'

Wrynose Pass → Brathay
Duddon
Greenburn Tarn
Levers Water
Seathwaite Tarn
Low Water
Coniston
Goats Water
Walna Scar Pass

N

0 — 1 — 2 MILES

1: THE OLD MAN
2: SWIRL HOW
3: BRIM FELL
4: GREAT CARRS
5: DOW CRAG
6: GREY FRIAR
7: WETHERLAM

The northern Coniston Fells from Little Langdale

Wrynose Pass

Coniston Old Man 4

NATURAL FEATURES

The highest (by a few feet) and best-known of the Coniston fells is the Old Man, a benevolent giant revered by generations of walkers and of particular esteem in the eyes of the inhabitants of the village he shelters, for he has contributed much to their prosperity. The Old Man is no Matterhorn, nor is Coniston a Zermatt, but an affinity is there in the same close links between mountain and village, and the history of the one is the history of the other. Coniston without its Old Man is unthinkable.

Yet the Old Man has little significance in the geographical arrangements hereabouts, the true hub of this group of hills being Swirl How, a summit of slightly lower elevation northwards. The Old Man is merely the termination of Swirl How's main ridge and ends high Lakeland in the south: the last outpost, looking far over the sea.

Although cruelly scarred and mutilated by quarries the Old Man has retained a dignified bearing, and still raises his proud and venerable head to the sky. His tears are shed quietly, into Low Water and Goats Water, two splendid tarns, whence, in due course, and after further service to the community in the matter of supplies of electricity and water, they ultimately find their way into Coniston's lake, and there bathe his ancient feet.

The Old Man from Low Water

Yet even during these peaceful ablutions the Old Man continues to be harassed. On the day this page was prepared (November 10th. 1958) the world's water speed record was broken on Coniston Water. Thus, from tip to toe, the mountain serves man.

POSTSCRIPT: The speed record was later broken again here (May 1959)

Coniston Old Man 5

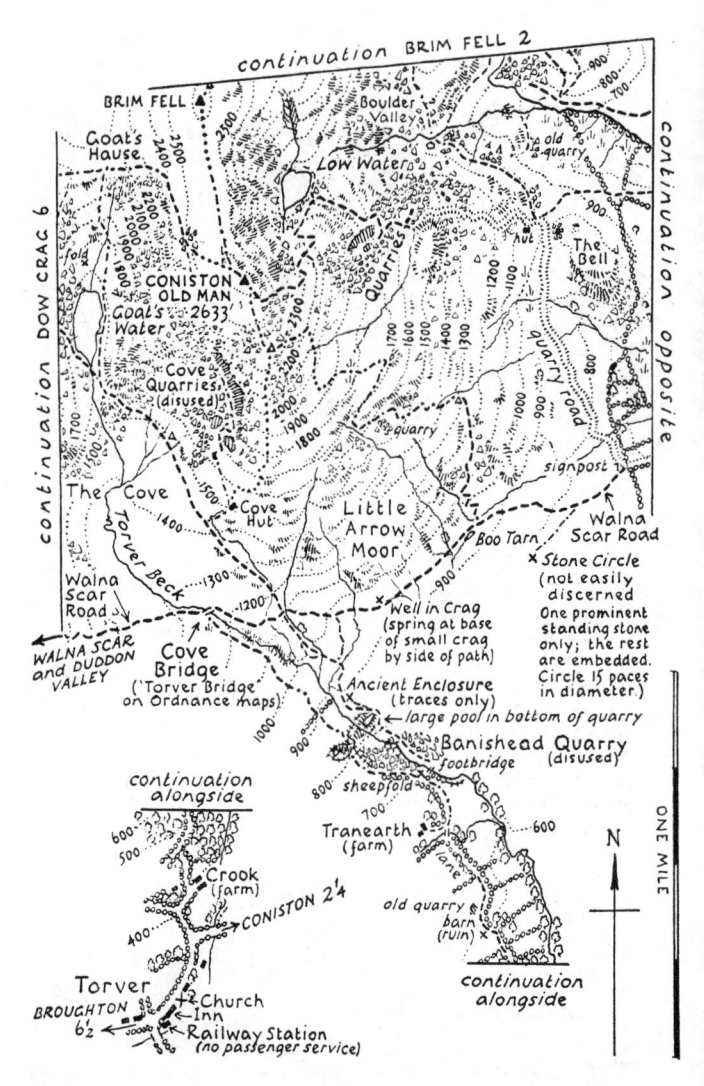

MAP

Coniston Old Man 6

MAP

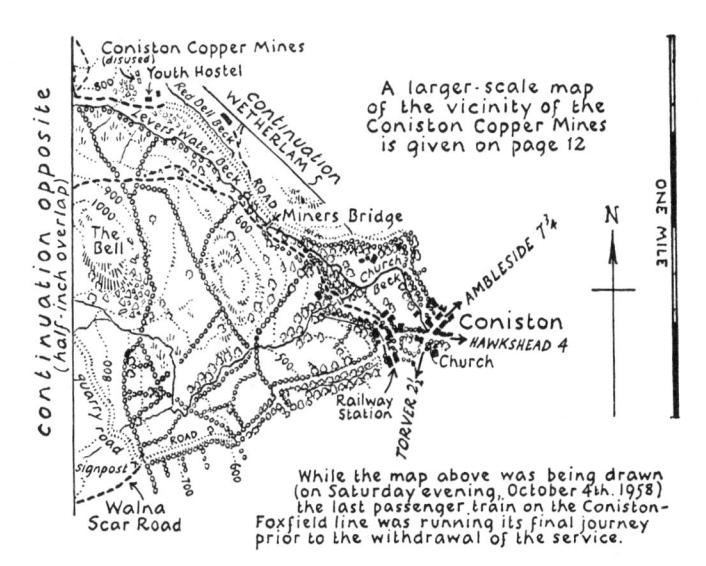

A larger-scale map of the vicinity of the Coniston Copper Mines is given on page 12

ONE MILE

While the map above was being drawn (on Saturday evening, October 4th, 1958) the last passenger train on the Coniston-Foxfield line was running its final journey prior to the withdrawal of the service.

Detail is not given of the territory south of the Walna Scar Road except in the vicinity of the approach from Torver. Here is little to tempt the fellwalker, for a broad and dreary moor declines to the cultivated shores of Coniston Water, but this rather desolate expanse nevertheless is fruitful ground for the antiquary, there being many evidences of a civilisation long past. Ancient cairns, walled enclosures and stone circles are all revealed to the eager and learned searcher amongst the bracken, and excavators have unearthed a Bronze Age cemetery. How odd that the scene of these mouldering relics should be also the place where an ultra-modern flying saucer was first photographed!

Somewhere in the area covered by the map on the opposite page, *but not indicated*, is a small upright memorial stone roughly inscribed 'CHARMER 1911'. Charmer was a foxhound killed in a fall on Dow Crag, and it is rather nice to know that the memory of a faithful dog was revered in this way. But some visitors have seen nothing sacred in the stone and it has been uprooted and cast aside on occasion. For this reason it has been thought best not to disclose its exact location. Rest in peace, Charmer. They were happy days.........

Charmer's Grave

ASCENT FROM CONISTON (via BOO TARN)

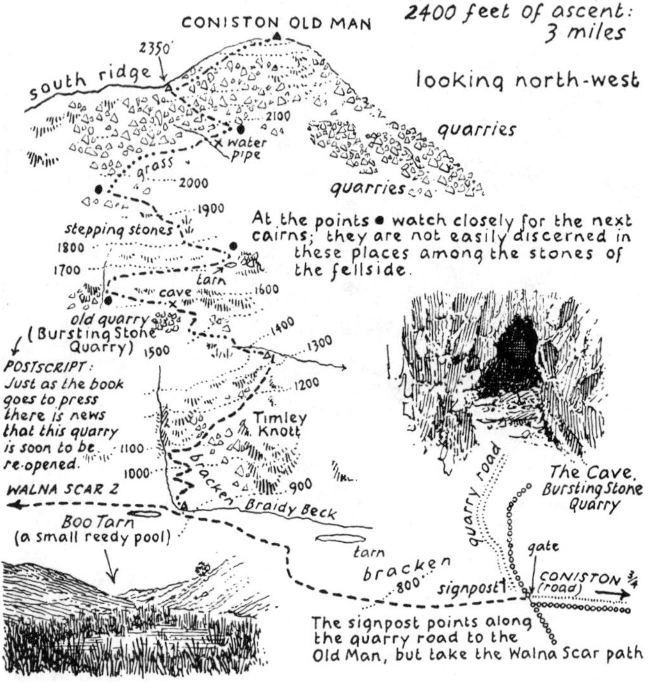
2400 feet of ascent: 3 miles
looking north-west
CONISTON OLD MAN
2350'
south ridge
2100
water pipe
quarries
grass
2000
quarries
1900
stepping stones
At the points ● watch closely for the next cairns; they are not easily discerned in these places among the stones of the fellside.
1800
1700
tarn
cave
1600
old quarry (Bursting Stone Quarry)
1500
1400
1300
POSTSCRIPT: Just as the book goes to press there is news that this quarry is soon to be re-opened.
1200
Timley Knott
1100
1000
900
bracken
WALNA SCAR 2
Braidy Beck
Boo Tarn (a small reedy pool)
The Cave, Bursting Stone Quarry
quarry road
tarn
bracken
gate
800
signpost
CONISTON 3/4 (road)
The signpost points along the quarry road to the Old Man, but take the Walna Scar path

For every hundred ascents of the Old Man by the signposted route through the labyrinth of big quarries on the east flank, perhaps one is made by the little-known alternative detailed above — and even this modest estimate may be too high. But here is a climb for which the discerning walker will cherish a strong preference over the usual quarries path, for the latter is not only unpleasantly stony but passes through a region of downright ugliness — hence its relegation to the next page.→ The way up from Boo Tarn is a succession of fascinating and unexpected zig-zags, making use of grassy terraces scented with thyme and tiny alpines on the south-east side of the fell. The path is mainly good as far as the old quarry (only a little one), beyond which dependence must be placed on a series of cairns, going first one way and then another and often seeming to be leading away from the objective, but, if trusted, in due course the walker will be unerringly led to the south ridge at a grassy saddle just below the summit. The man who worked out this delightful, well-graded and ingenious route clearly hated the sight of the big quarries. He deserved a medal.

Coniston Old Man 8

ASCENT FROM CONISTON (DIRECT)
2450 feet of ascent : 3 miles (2½ via Church Beck)

CONISTON OLD MAN

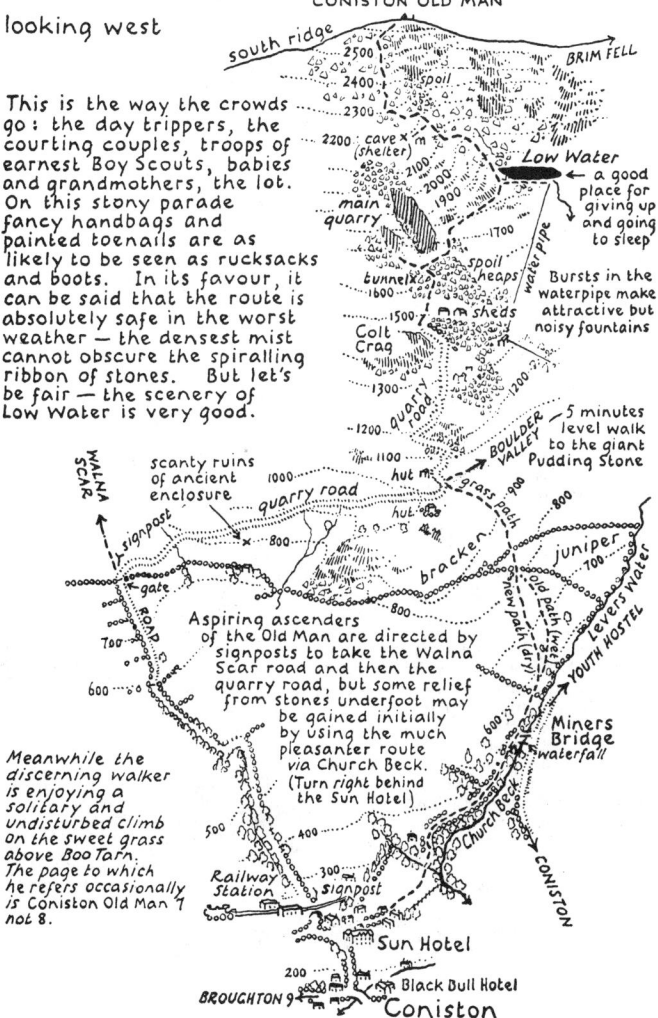

looking west

This is the way the crowds go: the day trippers, the courting couples, troops of earnest Boy Scouts, babies and grandmothers, the lot. On this stony parade fancy handbags and painted toenails are as likely to be seen as rucksacks and boots. In its favour, it can be said that the route is absolutely safe in the worst weather — the densest mist cannot obscure the spiralling ribbon of stones. But let's be fair — the scenery of Low Water is very good.

Low Water — a good place for giving up and going to sleep

Bursts in the waterpipe make attractive but noisy fountains

5 minutes level walk to the giant Pudding Stone

Aspiring ascenders of the Old Man are directed by signposts to take the Walna Scar road and then the quarry road, but some relief from stones underfoot may be gained initially by using the much pleasanter route via Church Beck. (Turn right behind the Sun Hotel)

Meanwhile the discerning walker is enjoying a solitary and undisturbed climb on the sweet grass above Boo Tarn. The page to which he refers occasionally is Coniston Old Man 7 not 8.

Railway Station

Sun Hotel
Black Bull Hotel
BROUGHTON 9
Coniston

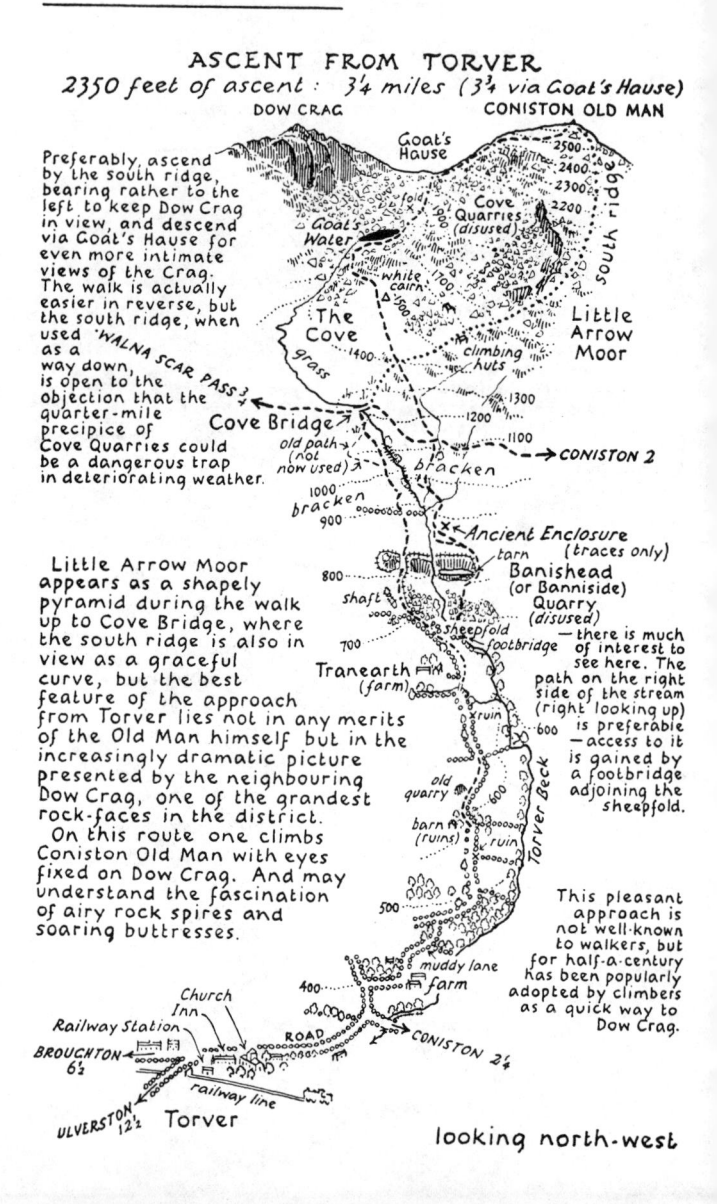

Coniston Old Man 9

ASCENT FROM TORVER
2350 feet of ascent : 3¼ miles (3¾ via Goat's Hause)

DOW CRAG — CONISTON OLD MAN

Preferably, ascend by the south ridge, bearing rather to the left to keep Dow Crag in view, and descend via Goat's Hause for even more intimate views of the Crag. The walk is actually easier in reverse, but the south ridge, when used as a way down, is open to the objection that the quarter-mile precipice of Cove Quarries could be a dangerous trap in deteriorating weather.

Little Arrow Moor appears as a shapely pyramid during the walk up to Cove Bridge, where the south ridge is also in view as a graceful curve, but the best feature of the approach from Torver lies not in any merits of the Old Man himself but in the increasingly dramatic picture presented by the neighbouring Dow Crag, one of the grandest rock-faces in the district. On this route one climbs Coniston Old Man with eyes fixed on Dow Crag. And may understand the fascination of airy rock spires and soaring buttresses.

— there is much of interest to see here. The path on the right side of the stream (right looking up) is preferable — access to it is gained by a footbridge adjoining the sheepfold.

This pleasant approach is not well-known to walkers, but for half-a-century has been popularly adopted by climbers as a quick way to Dow Crag.

looking north-west

Coniston Old Man 10

Boulder Valley

Low Water Beck falls in steep cascades from its tarn to a level shelf 600 feet below and there meanders uncertainly before resuming its hurried journey to join Levers Water Beck. This shelf is littered with boulders tumbled from the craggy slopes above, a scene common enough among the mountains, but in this particular instance several of the boulders are of quite uncommon size, big enough indeed to provide some entertainment and practice for rock-climbers, who name the area Boulder Valley.

The most massive and most prominent of the boulders is the Pudding Stone, 25 feet high and as big as a house, which has a dozen climbing routes, one of them being considered easy, but not by everybody, and the others, by walkers' standards, ranging between various grades of impossibility. The Pudding Stone may not have the overall dimensions of the Bowder Stone in Borrowdale, but certainly gives the impression of a greater bulk and weight.

The Pudding Stone
(the easy side)

It is perhaps unnecessary to add that the figure up aloft is not the author

Coniston Old Man 11

Coppermines Valley

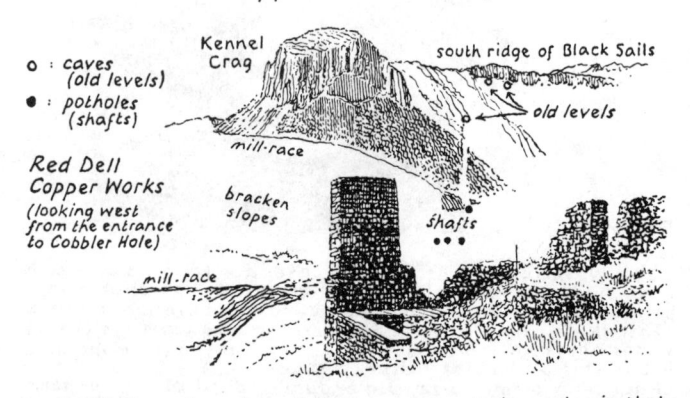

Red Dell Copper Works (looking west from the entrance to Cobbler Hole)

○ : caves (old levels)
● : potholes (shafts)

Kennel Crag — south ridge of Black Sails — old levels — mill-race — bracken slopes — shafts — mill-race

Fellwalkers based on Coniston need not sit moping in their lodgings if a wet day puts the high tops out of bounds for it is possible to occupy the mind and keep the body reasonably dry by dodging from one to another of the many caves, levels and tunnels of the Coppermines Valley, one mile distant.

This hollow among the hills presents a surprising scene of squalid desolation, typical of the dreary outskirts of many coalmining towns but utterly foreign to the Lake District, and it says much for the quality of the encircling mountains that they can triumph over the serious disfigurement of ugly spoil heaps and gaping wounds, and still look majestic. Here, in this strange amphitheatre, where flowers once grew, one sees the hopeless debris of the ruins of industries long abandoned, where flowers will never grow again, and, as always in the presence of death, is saddened — but a raising of the eyes discloses a surround of noble heights, and then the heart is uplifted too.

There is good fun and absorbing interest in locating all the tunnels and shafts of the old quarries and mines; *exploration must be carried no further than the entrances.* These workings, untouched for half a century or more, are in a state of decay and many are flooded. The shafts of the mines in particular, hideous potholes falling sheer into black depths, and without protecting fences, should be approached with great caution: we can't afford to lose any readers here, not with a further three volumes in this series still to be sold. Curious, too, are the mill-races, still coursing horizontally across steep slopes although their function has long since ended, and, in places where time has breached them, often squirting unnatural streams down fellsides not fashioned to accommodate them.

The accompanying map indicates the various holes of one sort and another in the Coppermines Valley area. There are others elsewhere on the Coniston fells, notably on Wetherlam.

continuing *Coppermines Valley*

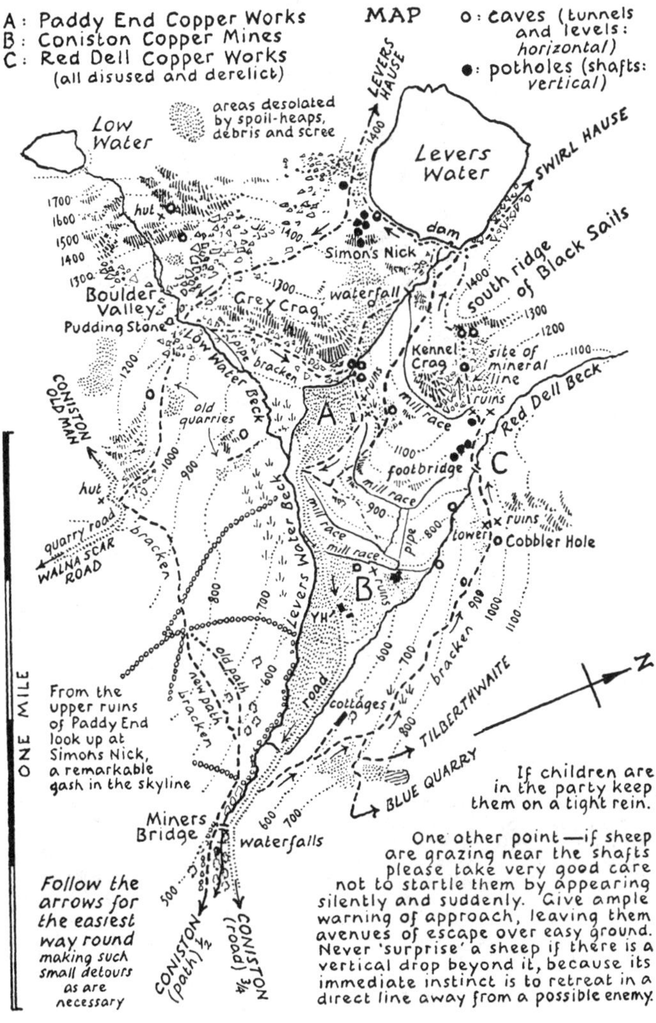

From the upper ruins of Paddy End look up at Simons Nick, a remarkable gash in the skyline

Follow the arrows for the easiest way round making such small detours as are necessary

If children are in the party keep them on a tight rein.

One other point — if sheep are grazing near the shafts please take very good care not to startle them by appearing silently and suddenly. Give ample warning of approach, leaving them avenues of escape over easy ground. Never 'surprise' a sheep if there is a vertical drop beyond it, because its immediate instinct is to retreat in a direct line away from a possible enemy.

Coniston Old Man 13

THE SUMMIT

Tourists looking for Blackpool Tower
Boy Scouts
Typical summit scene
Solitary fellwalker, bless him, looking north to the hills

There may be a cairn on the summit, or there may not.......
Sometimes there is, sometimes there isn't .... The frequent
visitor gains the impression that a feud rages here between
cairn-builders and cairn-destroyers, with the contestants
evenly matched, so that one week there will be a cairn, the
next week not, and so on. Indestructible, however, is a big
solidly-constructed slate platform on which the cairn, when
there is one, stands, and which has no counterpart on other
fells; into it a recess has been provided and this serves as a
shallow wind-shelter on occasions when it is not cluttered up
with the debris of shattered cairns, the latter circumstance
depending on which of the rival factions is, at the moment,
enjoying a temporary and fleeting triumph. One hesitates
to join in, if this is a private fight, but may suggest
that if the word 'man' means 'a summit cairn', as authorities
seem to be agreed, then, of all fells, the Old Man should be
allowed to have one and that it should be left alone to grow
hoary and ancient. But it never could. Not with those crowds.
An Ordnance Survey column stands on the north side of the
platform. Recent editions of Survey maps are unanimous in
accrediting 2635 feet to the fell, but an older generation
of walkers was brought up to believe it was 2633.

The summit is directly above
the very rough eastern slope,
which falls precipitously to
the black pool of Low Water;
in other directions gradients
are easy, predominantly with
a surface of grass but having
an occasional rash of stones.
In places where the native
rock crops out, weathering
has reduced it to vertical
flakes occurring in series.

Typical rock formations on the summit

Coniston Old Man 14

THE SUMMIT

DESCENTS:

TO CONISTON:

Although the start of the usual quarries path is indistinct for a few yards as it leaves the summit there should be no difficulty in finding and following it, even in the thickest mist: the path is one of the safest and surest (and stoniest) in the district.

The Boo Tarn route leaves the south ridge after 400 yards, at the first grassy depression: look for a cairn on the left marking the head of the path. Remember that this route has many acute turns and that the track disappears in places. This is a better way up than down, and is confusing in mist. Keep looking ahead for the next cairn.

TO TORVER:

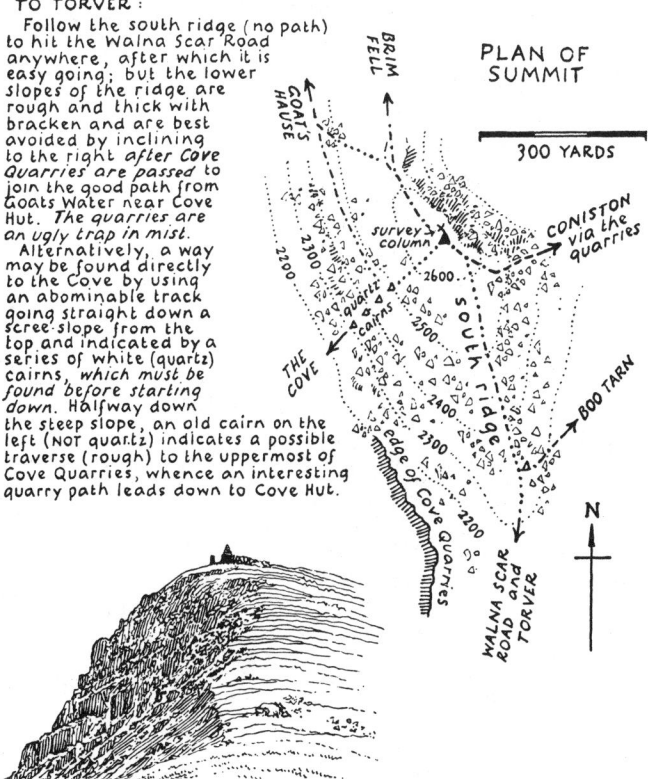

Follow the south ridge (no path) to hit the Walna Scar Road anywhere, after which it is easy going; but the lower slopes of the ridge are rough and thick with bracken and are best avoided by inclining to the right *after Cove Quarries are passed* to join the good path from Goats Water near Cove Hut. *The quarries are an ugly trap in mist.*

Alternatively, a way may be found directly to the Cove by using an abominable track going straight down a scree slope from the top and indicated by a series of white (quartz) cairns, *which must be found before starting down*. Halfway down the steep slope, an old cairn on the left (NOT quartz) indicates a possible traverse (rough) to the uppermost of Cove Quarries, whence an interesting quarry path leads down to Cove Hut.

PLAN OF SUMMIT

300 YARDS

The summit from the north

Coniston Old Man 15

The Coniston Fells: looking north along the ridge from the Old Man

A note on the names of fells:

Newcomers to Lakeland may wonder why many names of fells are prominently inscribed on Ordnance Survey maps yet rarely find mention in guidebooks and other literature descriptive of the district. This neglect of official names can be explained by reference to the Coniston area as an example. Thus the compact group of hills known to walkers as the Coniston Fells is, according to the Ordnance Survey, more properly described as a part of the Furness Fells, and this latter title appears in widely-spaced capital letters on their maps. So far all right, but then this general name of the whole has several sub-titles in smaller but quite prominent letters for particular (but ill-defined) sections — Cockley Beck Fell, Seathwaite Fells, Tilberthwaite Fells, Troutal Fell, Coniston Fells (an area east of the principal ridge), Above Beck Fells, and so on. These names mean little to the walker, who soon trains his eye, when looking at the map, to ignore them. His interest is in the names of the separate hills and summits.

Of course the Ordnance Survey is correct in using the local names of fells, which indicate not hills but indefinite areas of uncultivated high ground and other rough pastures: in general, sheep-grazing areas. Walkers are quite wrong in applying the name of a summit to the whole fell as they do. Wetherlam, for instance, is the name of the top of a fell only, the fell itself being named variously according to its different sections, e.g. Tilberthwaite High Fell, Low Fell, Above Beck Fells. These local distinctions are of no use to walkers, who want one name per hill, although, on occasion, in the absence of a name for a summit, one of them may be adopted, e.g. Brim Fell.

The ideal map for fellwalkers would omit detail of purely local interest (and parish and other boundaries), and name all summits distinctively. *Do one for us, O.S., please.*

Coniston Old Man 16

RIDGE ROUTES

To BRIM FELL, 2611': ½ mile : N
Depression at 2545': 80 feet of ascent
  A ten minutes' stroll on excellent turf
Brim Fell is the rounded top next on the
ridge northwards. As is often the case on
easy ground, where the feet are free to
wander without impediment, no path
has been formed on the grassy incline
beyond the slight depression.

To DOW CRAG, 2555': 1 mile :
  NW, W, SW and S
Depression (Goat's Hause) at 2130'
  425 feet of ascent
  A walk of increasing interest

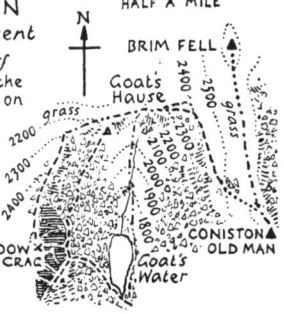

An expert rockclimber who is also a good swimmer might attempt a straight course between the two summits, but ordinary mortals are forced to make a considerable detour via Goat's Hause. There is no path at first from the top of the Old Man, but a good one is picked up at a patch of boulders. Note that, after crossing the Hause, a simple but 98% stony horizontal traverse (the start of which, at a cairn not seen from the ridge-path, must be looked for) may be made to the base of the great crag for a close view of the rock buttresses.

*Dow Crag
from the Old Man*

Coniston Old Man 17

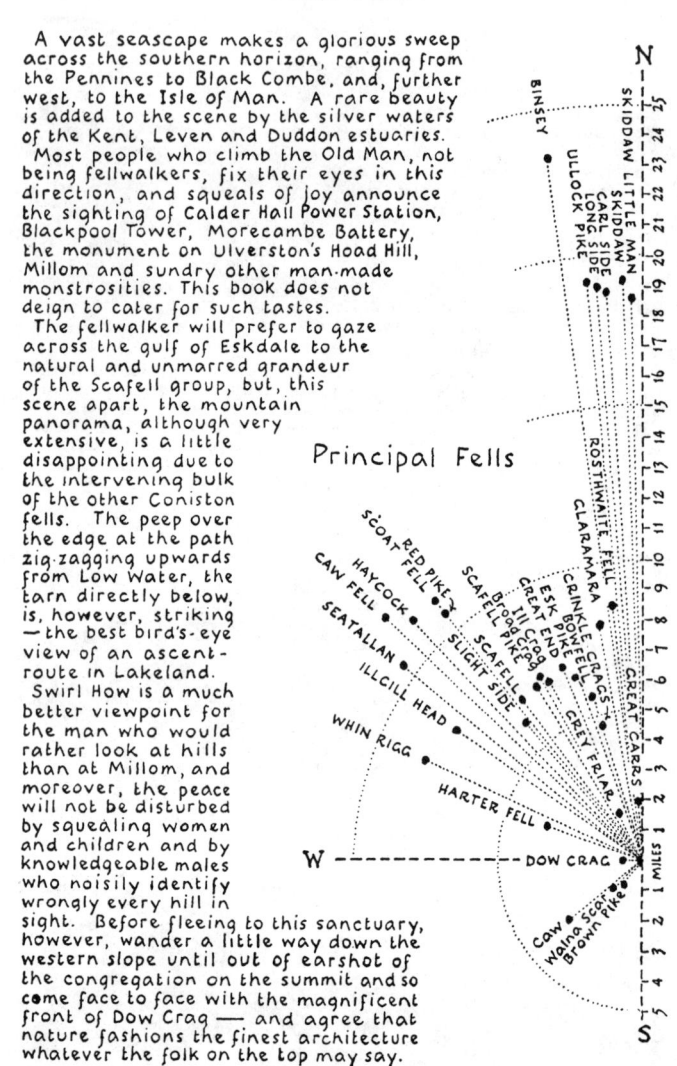

THE VIEW

A vast seascape makes a glorious sweep across the southern horizon, ranging from the Pennines to Black Combe, and, further west, to the Isle of Man. A rare beauty is added to the scene by the silver waters of the Kent, Leven and Duddon estuaries.

Most people who climb the Old Man, not being fellwalkers, fix their eyes in this direction, and squeals of joy announce the sighting of Calder Hall Power Station, Blackpool Tower, Morecambe Battery, the monument on Ulverston's Hoad Hill, Millom and sundry other man-made monstrosities. This book does not deign to cater for such tastes.

The fellwalker will prefer to gaze across the gulf of Eskdale to the natural and unmarred grandeur of the Scafell group, but, this scene apart, the mountain panorama, although very extensive, is a little disappointing due to the intervening bulk of the other Coniston fells. The peep over the edge at the path zig-zagging upwards from Low Water, the tarn directly below, is, however, striking — the best bird's-eye view of an ascent-route in Lakeland.

Swirl How is a much better viewpoint for the man who would rather look at hills than at Millom, and moreover, the peace will not be disturbed by squealing women and children and by knowledgeable males who noisily identify wrongly every hill in sight. Before fleeing to this sanctuary, however, wander a little way down the western slope until out of earshot of the congregation on the summit and so come face to face with the magnificent front of Dow Crag — and agree that nature fashions the finest architecture whatever the folk on the top may say.

Principal Fells

Coniston Old Man 18

THE VIEW

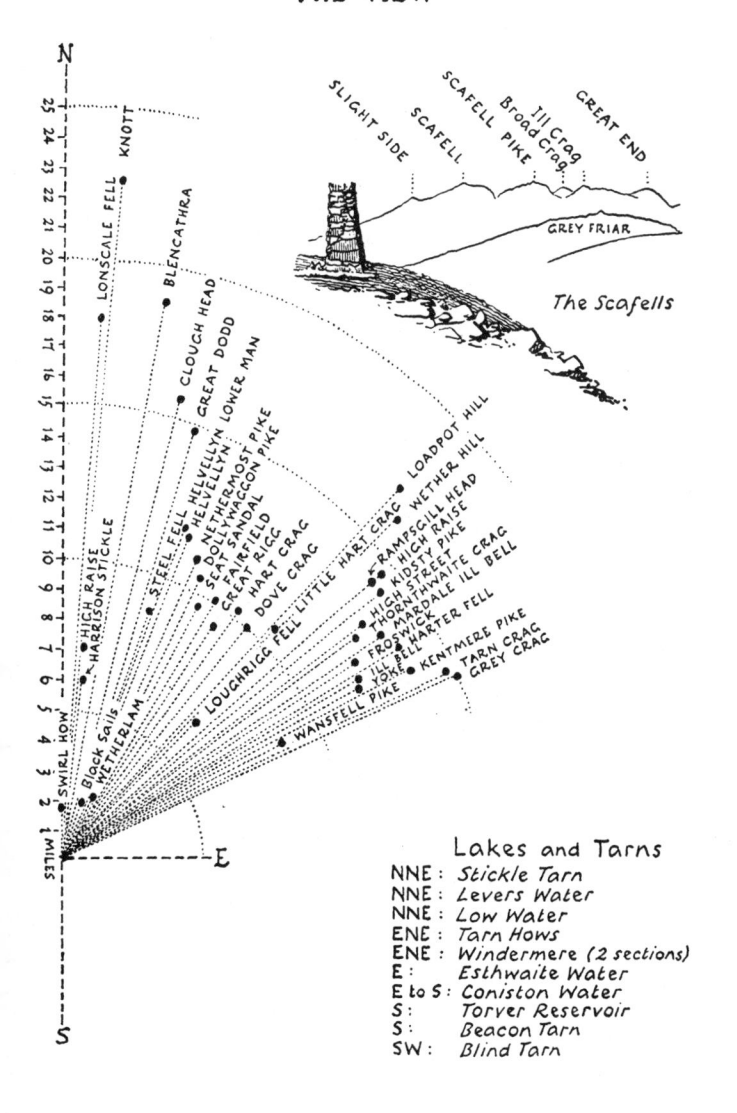

The Scafells: SLIGHT SIDE, SCAFELL, SCAFELL PIKE, Broad Crag, Ill Crag, GREAT END, GREY FRIAR

Peaks (N to E):
- KNOTT
- LONSCALE FELL
- BLENCATHRA
- CLOUGH HEAD
- GREAT DODD
- HELVELLYN LOWER MAN
- HELVELLYN
- NETHERMOST PIKE
- DOLLYWAGGON PIKE
- SEAT SANDAL
- FAIRFIELD
- GREAT RIGG
- HART CRAG
- DOVE CRAG
- HIGH RAISE
- HARRISON STICKLE
- STEEL FELL
- LOUGHRIGG FELL
- LITTLE HART CRAG
- RAMPSGILL HEAD
- WETHER HILL
- LOADPOT HILL
- HIGH RAISE
- KIDSTY PIKE
- HIGH STREET
- THORNTHWAITE CRAG
- MARDALE ILL BELL
- FROSWICK
- ILL BELL
- YOKE
- HARTER FELL
- KENTMERE PIKE
- TARN CRAG
- GREY CRAG
- WANSFELL PIKE
- SWIRL HOW
- BLACK SAILS
- WETHERLAM

Lakes and Tarns
- NNE: *Stickle Tarn*
- NNE: *Levers Water*
- NNE: *Low Water*
- ENE: *Tarn Hows*
- ENE: *Windermere (2 sections)*
- E: *Esthwaite Water*
- E to S: *Coniston Water*
- S: *Torver Reservoir*
- S: *Beacon Tarn*
- SW: *Blind Tarn*

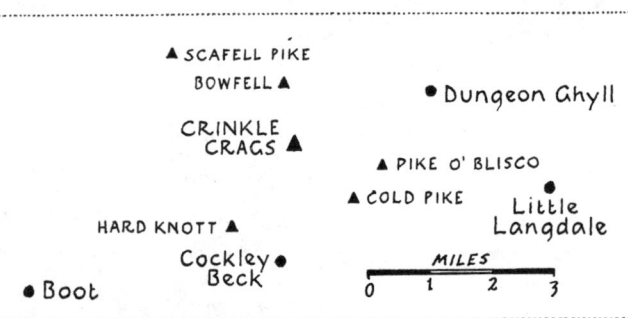

Crinkle Crags 2816'

from Pike o' Blisco

▲ SCAFELL PIKE
BOWFELL ▲
● Dungeon Ghyll
CRINKLE CRAGS ▲
▲ PIKE O' BLISCO
▲ COLD PIKE
● Little Langdale
HARD KNOTT ▲
Cockley ● Beck
● Boot

MILES
0 1 2 3

Crinkle Crags 2

NATURAL FEATURES

Some mountains are obviously named by reference to their physical characteristics. Crinkle Crags is one of these, and it was probably first so called by the dalesfolk of the valleys to the east and around the head of Windermere, whence its lofty serrated ridge, a succession of knobs and depressions, is aptly described by the name. These undulations, seeming trivial from a distance, are revealed at close range as steep buttresses and gullies above wild declivities, a scene of desolation and rugged grandeur equalled by few others in the district. Nor is the Eskdale flank any gentler, for here too are gaunt shattered crags rising from incredibly rough slopes. The high pass of Three Tarns links the ridge with Bowfell to the north while southwards Wrynose Bottom is the boundary.

Crinkle Crags is much too good to be missed. For the mountaineer who prefers his mountains rough, who likes to see steep craggy slopes towering before him into the sky, who enjoys an up-and-down ridge walk full of interesting nooks and corners, who has an appreciative eye for magnificent views, this is a climb deserving of high priority. But it is not a place to visit in bad weather for the top is confusing, with ins and outs as well as ups and downs and a sketchy path that cannot be relied on. Crinkle Crags merits respect, and should be treated with respect; then it will yield the climber a mountain walk long to be remembered with pleasure.

Is it 'Crinkle Crags IS ...' or 'Crinkle Crags ARE ...' ?
Is it 'Three Tarns IS ....' or 'Three Tarns ARE ...' ?
                                    IS sounds right but looks wrong!

The outline of Crinkle Crags from Great Langdale

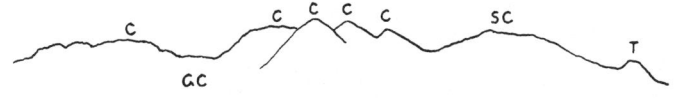

C : The five Crinkles   GC : Great Cove
T : Rock tower near Three Tarns   SC : Shelter Crags

The highest Crinkle (2816') is second from the left on the diagram. When seen from the valley it does not appear to be the highest, as it is set back a little from the line of the others.

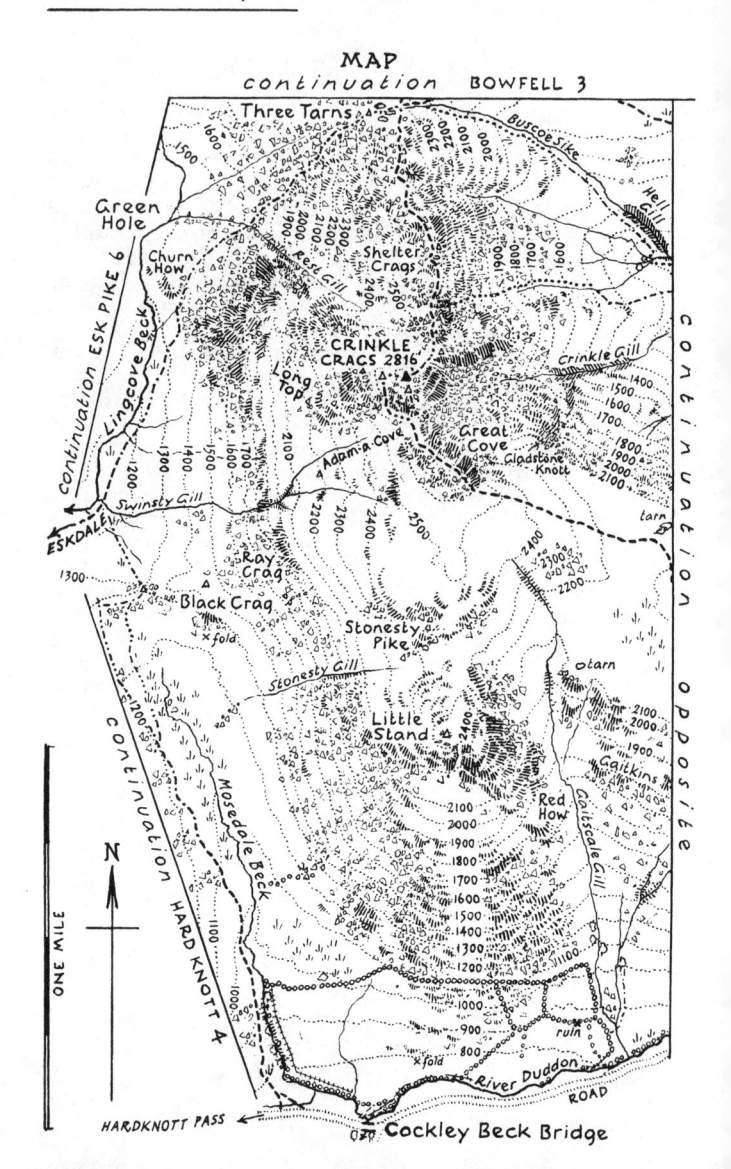

Crinkle Crags 3

Crinkle Crags 4

MAP

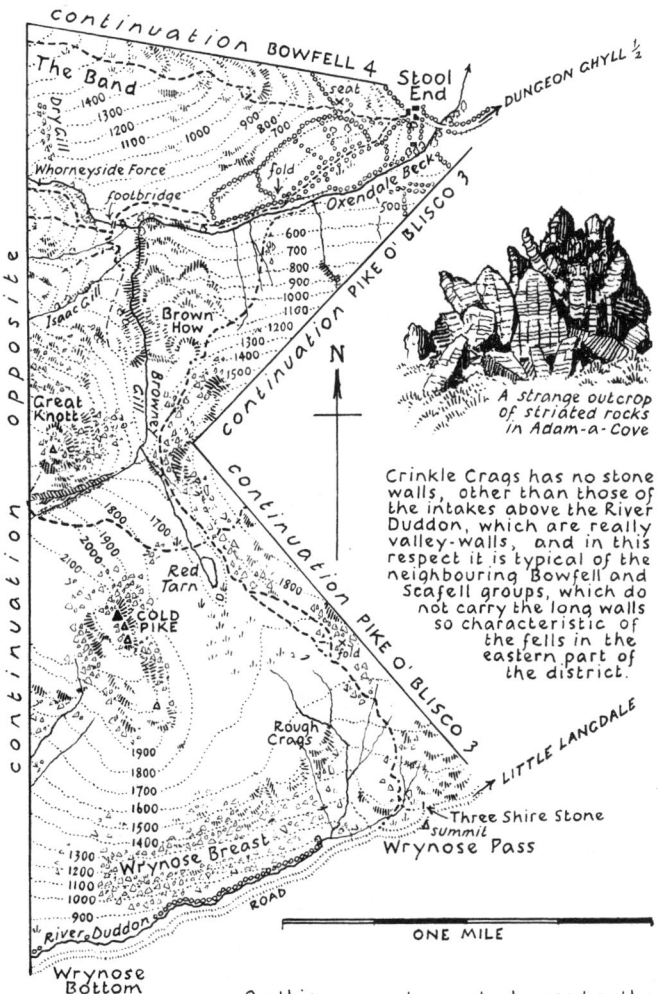

A strange outcrop of striated rocks in Adam-a-Cove

Crinkle Crags has no stone walls, other than those of the intakes above the River Duddon, which are really valley-walls, and in this respect it is typical of the neighbouring Bowfell and Scafell groups, which do not carry the long walls so characteristic of the fells in the eastern part of the district.

ONE MILE

On this map, only regularly-used paths are shown. Other routes are suggested, with qualifications, on the diagrams of ascents.

Crinkle Crags 5

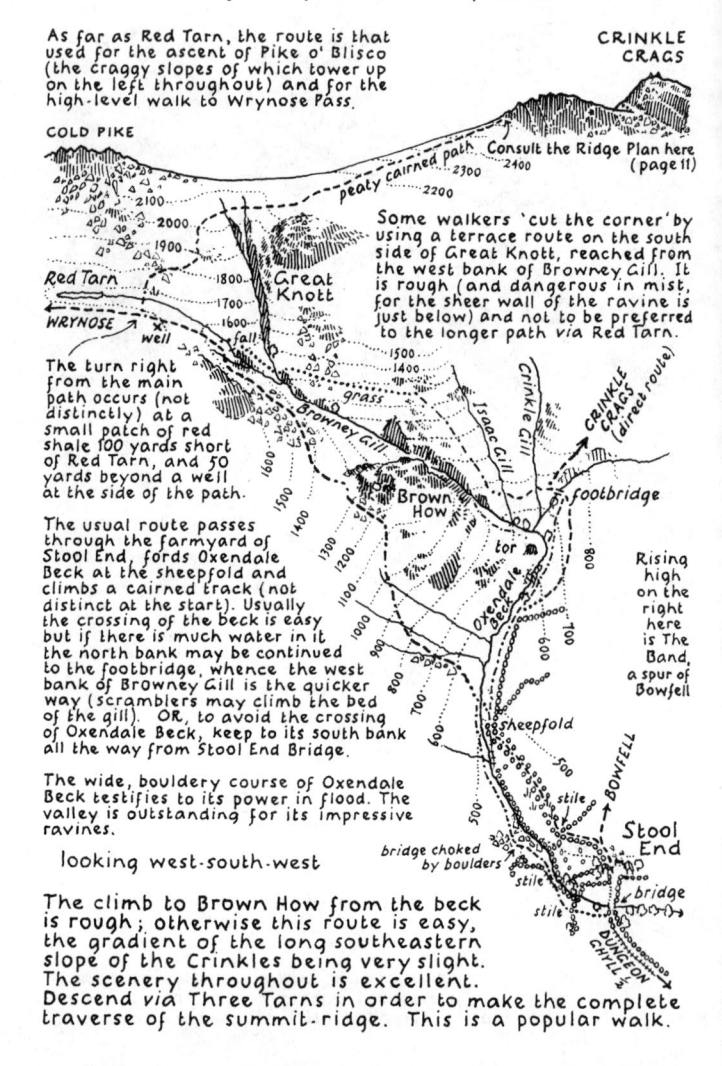

ASCENT FROM DUNGEON GHYLL (via RED TARN)
2600 feet of ascent : 4 miles

As far as Red Tarn, the route is that used for the ascent of Pike o' Blisco (the craggy slopes of which tower up on the left throughout) and for the high-level walk to Wrynose Pass.

CRINKLE CRAGS

COLD PIKE

Consult the Ridge Plan here (page 11)

Some walkers 'cut the corner' by using a terrace route on the south side of Great Knott, reached from the west bank of Browney Gill. It is rough (and dangerous in mist, for the sheer wall of the ravine is just below) and not to be preferred to the longer path via Red Tarn.

The turn right from the main path occurs (not distinctly) at a small patch of red shale 100 yards short of Red Tarn, and 50 yards beyond a well at the side of the path.

The usual route passes through the farmyard of Stool End, fords Oxendale Beck at the sheepfold and climbs a cairned track (not distinct at the start). Usually the crossing of the beck is easy but if there is much water in it the north bank may be continued to the footbridge, whence the west bank of Browney Gill is the quicker way (scramblers may climb the bed of the gill). OR, to avoid the crossing of Oxendale Beck, keep to its south bank all the way from Stool End Bridge.

The wide, bouldery course of Oxendale Beck testifies to its power in flood. The valley is outstanding for its impressive ravines.

Rising high on the right here is The Band, a spur of Bowfell

looking west-south-west

The climb to Brown How from the beck is rough; otherwise this route is easy, the gradient of the long southeastern slope of the Crinkles being very slight. The scenery throughout is excellent. Descend via Three Tarns in order to make the complete traverse of the summit-ridge. This is a popular walk.

Crinkle Crags 6

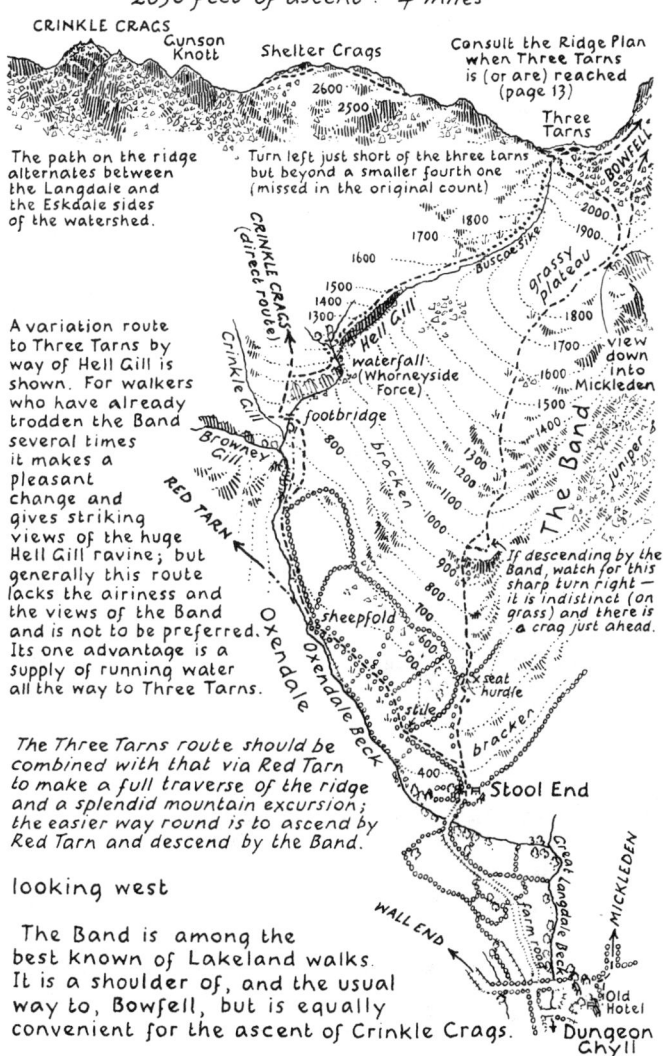

ASCENT FROM DUNGEON GHYLL (via THREE TARNS)
2650 feet of ascent : 4 miles

CRINKLE CRAGS
Gunson Knott
Shelter Crags
Three Tarns

Consult the Ridge Plan when Three Tarns is (or are) reached (page 13)

BOWFELL

The path on the ridge alternates between the Langdale and the Eskdale sides of the watershed.

Turn left just short of the three tarns but beyond a smaller fourth one (missed in the original count)

CRINKLE CRAGS (direct route)

Buscoe Pike

grassy plateau

view down into Mickleden

Hell Gill

waterfall (Whorneyside Force)

A variation route to Three Tarns by way of Hell Gill is shown. For walkers who have already trodden the Band several times it makes a pleasant change and gives striking views of the huge Hell Gill ravine; but generally this route lacks the airiness and the views of the Band and is not to be preferred. Its one advantage is a supply of running water all the way to Three Tarns.

footbridge

Browney Gill

Crinkle Gill

RED TARN

bracken

The Band

juniper

If descending by the Band, watch for this sharp turn right — it is indistinct (on grass) and there is a crag just ahead.

Oxendale
Oxendale Beck

sheepfold

stile

seat hurdle

bracken

The Three Tarns route should be combined with that via Red Tarn to make a full traverse of the ridge and a splendid mountain excursion; the easier way round is to ascend by Red Tarn and descend by the Band.

Stool End

looking west

The Band is among the best known of Lakeland walks. It is a shoulder of, and the usual way to, Bowfell, but is equally convenient for the ascent of Crinkle Crags.

WALL END

Great Langdale Beck

Mickleden farm road

MICKLEDEN

Old Hotel

Dungeon Ghyll

Crinkle Crags 7

ASCENT FROM DUNGEON GHYLL
(DIRECT CLIMB FROM OXENDALE)
2550 feet of ascent : 3½ miles

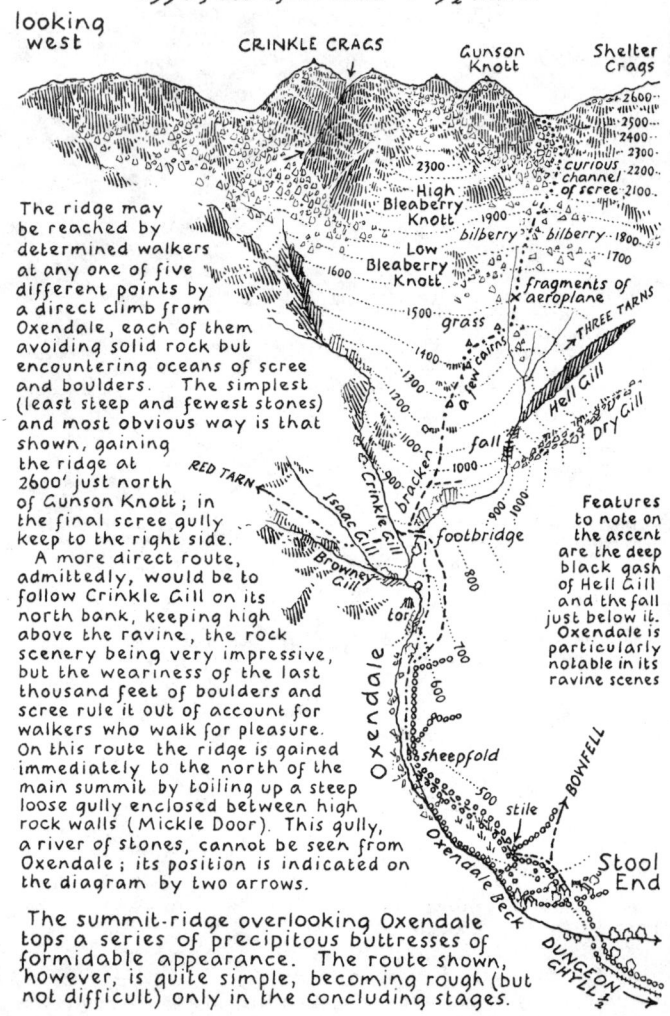

looking west

CRINKLE CRAGS — Gunson Knott — Shelter Crags

High Bleaberry Knott
Low Bleaberry Knott
bilberry
fragments of aeroplane
curious channel of scree
grass
few cairns
THREE TARNS
Hell Gill
Dry Gill
fall
bracken
RED TARN
Crinkle Gill
Isaac Gill
Browney Gill
footbridge
tor
Oxendale
sheepfold
stile
BOWFELL
Oxendale Beck
Stool End
DUNGEON GHYLL

The ridge may be reached by determined walkers at any one of five different points by a direct climb from Oxendale, each of them avoiding solid rock but encountering oceans of scree and boulders. The simplest (least steep and fewest stones) and most obvious way is that shown, gaining the ridge at 2600' just north of Gunson Knott; in the final scree gully keep to the right side.

A more direct route, admittedly, would be to follow Crinkle Gill on its north bank, keeping high above the ravine, the rock scenery being very impressive, but the weariness of the last thousand feet of boulders and scree rule it out of account for walkers who walk for pleasure. On this route the ridge is gained immediately to the north of the main summit by toiling up a steep loose gully enclosed between high rock walls (Mickle Door). This gully, a river of stones, cannot be seen from Oxendale; its position is indicated on the diagram by two arrows.

Features to note on the ascent are the deep black gash of Hell Gill and the fall just below it. Oxendale is particularly notable in its ravine scenes

The summit-ridge overlooking Oxendale tops a series of precipitous buttresses of formidable appearance. The route shown, however, is quite simple, becoming rough (but not difficult) only in the concluding stages.

Crinkle Crags 8

ASCENT FROM ESKDALE
2650 feet of ascent : 7½ miles from Boot
(8 miles via Three Tarns)

Rest Gill is identifiable by its very bouldery bed.

In Adam-a-Cove an uncharacteristic outcrop of striated rocks is marked by two cairns.

MOSEDALE (for the DUDDON VALLEY)

Lingcove Bridge (which is NOT crossed on this walk)

The fell on this side of the valley is HARD KNOTT. The detached rock high on the skyline is the Steeple.

- A study of the map suggests Long Top, the western shoulder of the highest Crinkle, as an obvious approach to the summit from Eskdale, but the wild appearance of its lower crags makes it a less inviting proposition when seen 'in the flesh'. Nevertheless the cliff can be by-passed by a bouldery scramble up the bilberry slope alongside Rest Gill, and a series of stony rises then leads to the top; this is a rough but interesting route, suitable only in fine weather.

- The usual route proceeds to Three Tarns and then follows the ridge, so taking the fullest advantage of paths. The section between Rest Gill and Three Tarns is rough, but most ingeniously and delightfully cairned.

- The easiest route follows Swinsty Gill up into Adam-a-Cove. This is everywhere grassy — a surprising weakness in the armour of the Crinkles — and it is just possible to come within a few feet of the summit cairn without handling rock or treading on stones.

looking north-east

Crinkle Crags 9

ASCENT FROM COCKLEY BECK BRIDGE
2350 feet of ascent : 3 miles

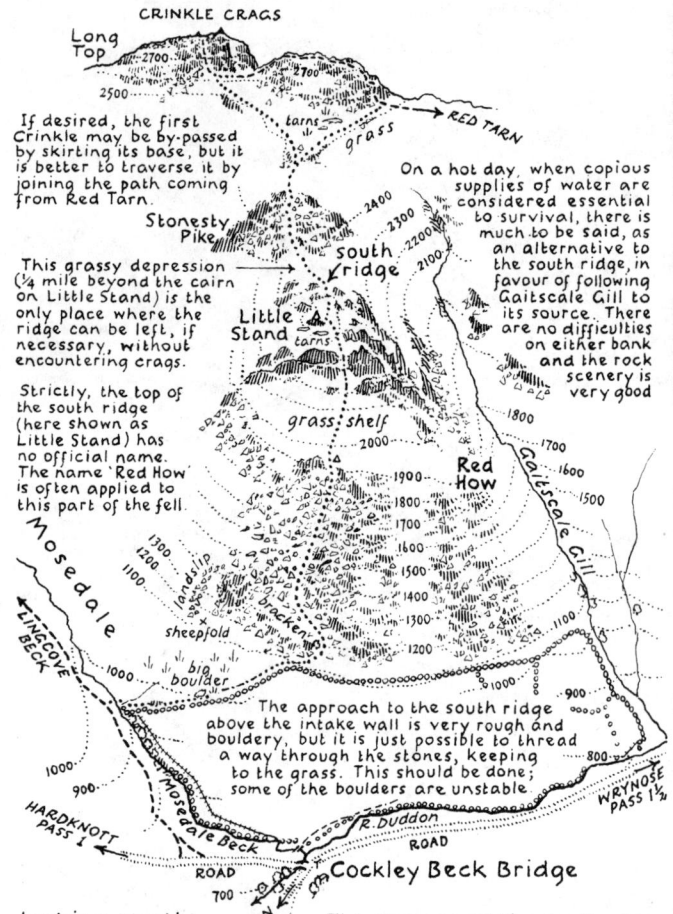

CRINKLE CRAGS
Long Top
RED TARN

If desired, the first Crinkle may be by-passed by skirting its base, but it is better to traverse it by joining the path coming from Red Tarn.

Stonesty Pike

This grassy depression (¼ mile beyond the cairn on Little Stand) is the only place where the ridge can be left, if necessary, without encountering crags.

south ridge

Little Stand

On a hot day, when copious supplies of water are considered essential to survival, there is much to be said, as an alternative to the south ridge, in favour of following Gaitscale Gill to its source. There are no difficulties on either bank and the rock scenery is very good.

Strictly, the top of the south ridge (here shown as Little Stand) has no official name. The name 'Red How' is often applied to this part of the fell.

grass shelf

Red How

Gaitscale Gill

Mosedale
LINGCOVE BECK

landslip
bracken
sheepfold
big boulder

The approach to the south ridge above the intake wall is very rough and bouldery, but it is just possible to thread a way through the stones, keeping to the grass. This should be done; some of the boulders are unstable.

WRYNOSE PASS 1½

HARDKNOTT PASS 1
Mosedale Beck
ROAD
R. Duddon
ROAD
Cockley Beck Bridge

looking north

DUDDON VALLEY

The scenery of the south ridge is good, with crags and outcrops in abundance, but the approach is fatiguing. This route should not be attempted in bad weather: there is no path to, or on, the ridge, which has escarpments on both flanks.

Crinkle Crags 10

ASCENT FROM WRYNOSE PASS
1650 feet of ascent : 2¾ miles

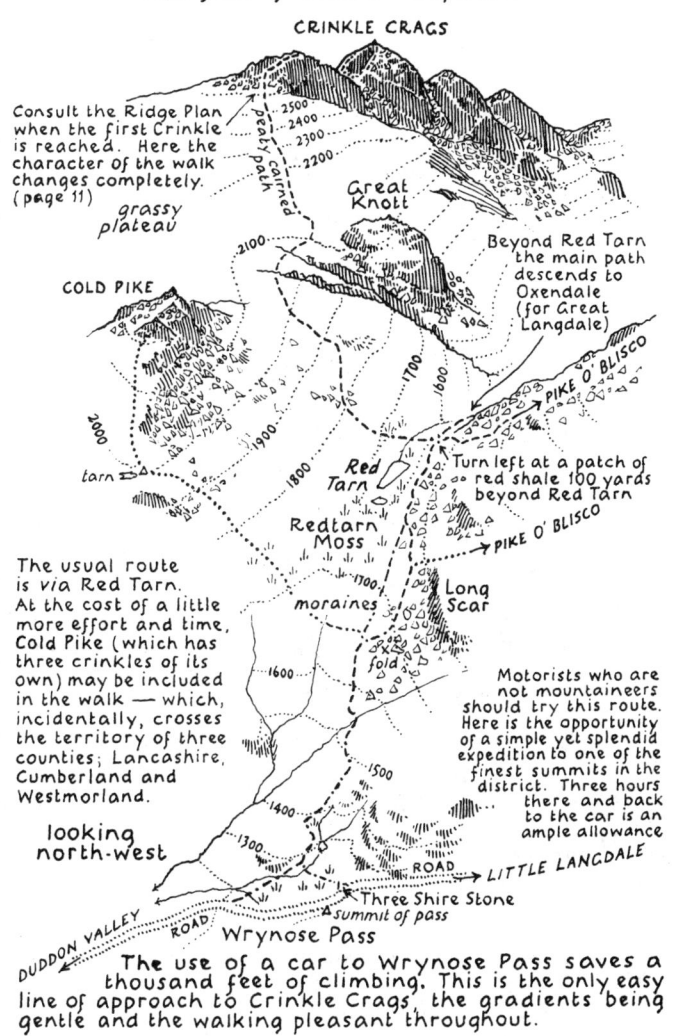

CRINKLE CRAGS

Consult the Ridge Plan when the first Crinkle is reached. Here the character of the walk changes completely. (page 11)

grassy plateau

peaty cairned path

Great Knott

COLD PIKE

Beyond Red Tarn the main path descends to Oxendale (for Great Langdale)

PIKE O' BLISCO

tarn

Red Tarn

Turn left at a patch of red shale 100 yards beyond Red Tarn

Redtarn Moss

→ PIKE O' BLISCO

The usual route is via Red Tarn. At the cost of a little more effort and time, Cold Pike (which has three crinkles of its own) may be included in the walk — which, incidentally, crosses the territory of three counties; Lancashire, Cumberland and Westmorland.

moraines

Long Scar

fold

Motorists who are not mountaineers should try this route. Here is the opportunity of a simple yet splendid expedition to one of the finest summits in the district. Three hours there and back to the car is an ample allowance

looking north-west

ROAD → LITTLE LANGDALE

Three Shire Stone
▲ summit of pass

DUDDON VALLEY ROAD   Wrynose Pass

The use of a car to Wrynose Pass saves a thousand feet of climbing. This is the only easy line of approach to Crinkle Crags, the gradients being gentle and the walking pleasant throughout.

Crinkle Crags 11

RIDGE PLAN
for use when traversing the ridge from SOUTH to NORTH

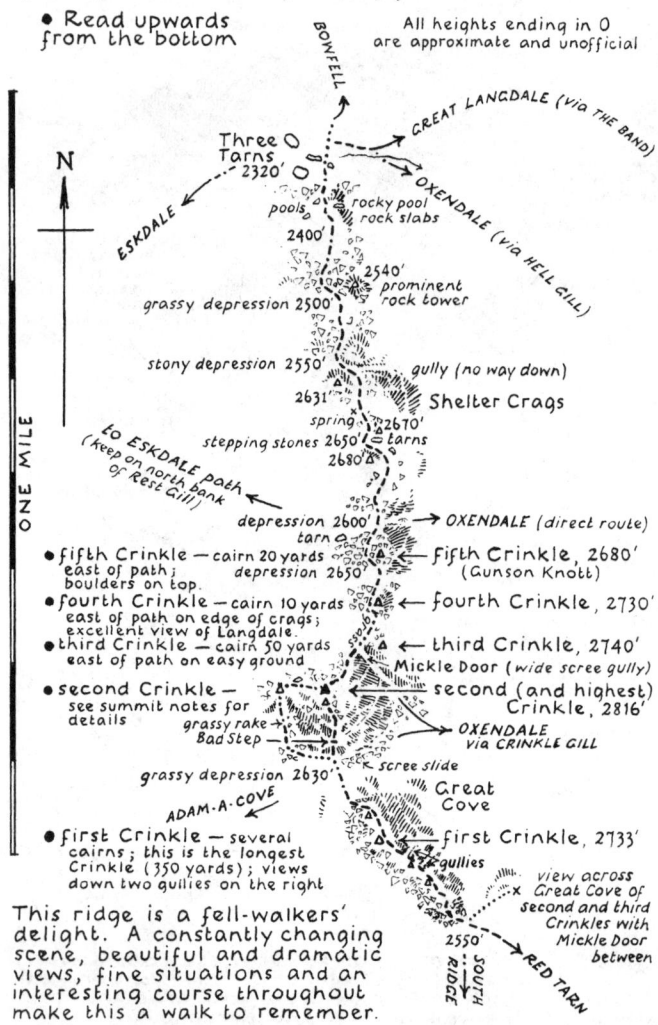

● Read upwards from the bottom

All heights ending in 0 are approximate and unofficial

ONE MILE

BOWFELL

GREAT LANGDALE (via THE BAND)

Three Tarns 2320'

ESKDALE

OXENDALE (via HELL GILL)

pools 2400'

rocky pool rock slabs

2540' prominent rock tower

grassy depression 2500'

stony depression 2550'

gully (no way down)

2631' Shelter Crags

spring 2670'

stepping stones 2650' tarns 2680'

to ESKDALE path (keep on north bank of Rest Gill)

depression 2600'

OXENDALE (direct route)

tarn depression 2650'

● fifth Crinkle — cairn 20 yards east of path; boulders on top.

Fifth Crinkle, 2680' (Gunson Knott)

● fourth Crinkle — cairn 10 yards east of path on edge of crags; excellent view of Langdale.

fourth Crinkle, 2730'

● third Crinkle — cairn 50 yards east of path on easy ground

third Crinkle, 2740' Mickle Door (wide scree gully)

● second Crinkle — see summit notes for details

second (and highest) Crinkle, 2816'

grassy rake

Bad Step

OXENDALE via CRINKLE GILL

scree slide

grassy depression 2630'

Great Cove

ADAM-A-COVE

● first Crinkle — several cairns; this is the longest Crinkle (350 yards); views down two gullies on the right

first Crinkle, 2733'

gullies

view across Great Cove of second and third Crinkles with Mickle Door between

2550'

SOUTH RIDGE

RED TARN

This ridge is a fell-walkers' delight. A constantly changing scene, beautiful and dramatic views, fine situations and an interesting course throughout make this a walk to remember.

Crinkle Crags 12

Looking NORTH along the ridge ....

The second (and highest) Crinkle, Mickle Door, and the third Crinkle, seen across Great Cove

The fourth and fifth Crinkles (Shelter Crags and Bowfell behind), seen from the third Crinkle

Crinkle Crags 13

RIDGE PLAN
for use when traversing the ridge from NORTH to SOUTH

• **Read upwards from the bottom**

This is, of course, the same plan as that already given for the south-to-north traverse but reversed for easier reference. Reading upwards, left and right on the plan will agree with left and right as they appear to the walker.

All heights ending in 0 are approximate and unofficial.

RED TARN

SOUTH RIDGE 2550'

viewpoint × (fourth and third Crinkles, with Mickle Door between)

gullies

Great Cove

• **fifth Crinkle, 2733'** — the longest Crinkle; several cairns along its top

grassy depression: 2630' — ADAM-A-COVE

Bad Step — grassy rake

OXENDALE via CRINKLE GILL

• **fourth Crinkle** — see summit notes for details

fourth (and highest) Crinkle 2816'

Mickle Door (wide scree gully)

third Crinkle, 2740' → • **third Crinkle** — cairn 50 yards east of path on easy ground

second Crinkle, 2730' → • **second Crinkle** — cairn on edge of crags 10 yards east of path; excellent view of Langdale

2650'

first Crinkle, 2680' (Gunson Knott) — tarn — • **first Crinkle** — cairn 20 yards east of path; boulders (shelter) on top

OXENDALE (direct route) ← 2600'

first four Crinkles came into sight × 2680'

easy route to ESKDALE path (keep on north bank of Rest Gill)

tarns — stepping stones
2670' — 2650'

Shelter Crags — × spring
▲ 2631'
gully — 2550' stony depression

2500' grassy depression

prominent rock tower
2540' — 2400'

rock slabs — rocky pool — pools

OXENDALE (via HELL GILL) ⋯ ⋯ ⋯ ESKDALE →

○ ○ Three Tarns 2320'

GREAT LANGDALE (via THE BAND) ↙   ↘ BOWFELL

HALF A MILE

↓
N

Note that the arrow is upside-down, too

Some writers have greatly exaggerated the dangers of the ridge. Nowhere is it anything but a pleasantly rough walk — except for the Bad Step, which can be avoided. (Bowfell and Scafell Pike are rougher)

Introducing Lakeland's best ridge-mile!

Crinkle Crags 14

Looking SOUTH along the ridge.........

Four Crinkles come suddenly into view from the path as it rounds a corner of Shelter Crags

The fifth Crinkle as seen from the main Crinkle on the descent to the Bad Step

Crinkle Crags 15

THE SUMMIT

←BOWFELL

There are five Crinkles (not counting Shelter Crags) and therefore five summits, each with its own summit-cairn. The highest is, however, so obviously the highest that the true top of the fell is not in doubt in clear visibility, and this is the Crinkle (the fourth from the north and second from the south) with which these notes are concerned. It is not the stoniest of the five, nor the greatest in girth, but, unlike the others, it extends a considerable distance as a lateral ridge (Long Top) descending westwards. On the actual summit are two principal cairns separated by 40 yards of easy ground; that to the north, standing on a rock platform, is slightly the more elevated. The eastern face descends in precipices from the easy grass terraces above it; there are crags running down steeply from the south cairn also, but in other directions the top terrain is not difficult although everywhere rough.

1: grassy rake (easy way)
2: direct route (steep scree)
3: the Bad Step (see next page)
4: detour to avoid the Bad Step

The highest Crinkle, from the south   continued

Crinkle Crags 16

THE SUMMIT
continued

DESCENTS

- **to GREAT LANGDALE**: The orthodox routes are (1) via Red Tarn and Brown How, and (2) via Three Tarns and the Band, both excellent walks, and in normal circumstances no other ways should be considered. If time is very short, however, or if it is necessary to escape quickly from stormy conditions on the ridge, quick and sheltered routes are provided by (3) the scree gully of Mickle Door or (4) the Gunson Knott gully, which is easier: both are very rough initially but lead to open slopes above Oxendale.
- **to ESKDALE**: Much the easiest way, and much the quickest, is to descend from Adam-a-Cove (no path), keeping *left* of Swinsty Gill where it enters a ravine. Long Top is a temptation to be resisted, for it leads only to trouble.
- **to COCKLEY BECK BRIDGE**: The south ridge is interesting (no path and not safe in mist), but tired limbs had better take advantage of the easy way down from Adam-a-Cove, inclining left below Ray Crag into Mosedale
- **to WRYNOSE PASS**: Reverse the route of ascent. Cold Pike may be traversed with little extra cost in energy.

> In mist, take good care to keep to the ridge-path, which, in many places, is no more than nail-scratches on rocks and boulders but is generally simple to follow. Go nowhere unless there is evidence that many others have passed that way before. (The exception to this golden rule is Adam-a-Cove, which is perfectly safe *if it is remembered to keep to the left bank of the stream*).

The Bad Step

Caution is needed on the descent southwards from the summit. A walker crossing the top from the north will naturally gravitate to the south cairn and start his descent here. A steep path goes down rock ledges to a slope of loose scree, which spills over the lip of a chockstone (two, really) bridging and blocking a little gully. Anyone descending at speed here is asking for a nasty fall. The impasse is usually avoided and the gully regained below the chockstone by an awkward descent of the rock wall to the left, which deserves the name 'The Bad Step', for it is 10 feet high and as near vertical as makes no difference. This is the sort of place that everybody would get down in a flash if a £5 note was waiting to be picked up on the scree below, but, without such an inducement, there is much wavering on the brink. Chicken-hearted walkers, muttering something about discretion being the better part of valour, will sneak away and circumvent the difficulty by following the author's footsteps around the left flank of the buttress forming the retaining wall of the gully, where grassy ledges enable the foot of the gully to be reached without trouble; here they may sit and watch, with ill-concealed grins, the discomfiture of other tourists who may come along.

The Bad Step is the most difficult obstacle met on any of the regular walkers' paths in Lakeland.

The Bad Step from below

continued

Crinkle Crags 17

THE SUMMIT
continued

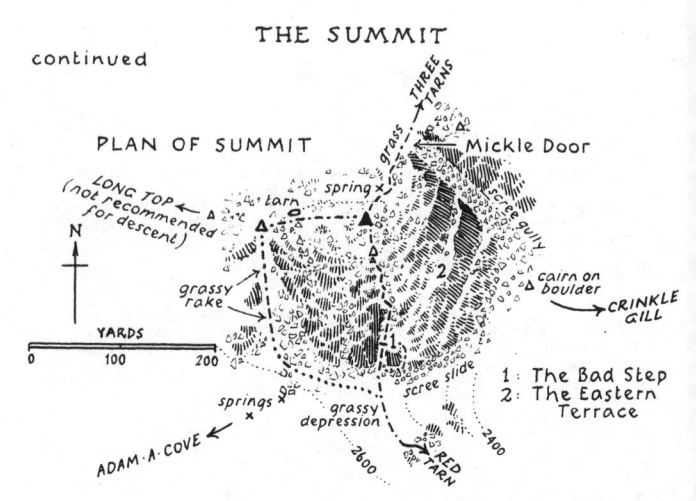

PLAN OF SUMMIT

(map with labels: THREE TARNS, Mickle Door, spring, tarn, LONG TOP (not recommended for descent), grassy rake, scree gully, cairn on boulder, CRINKLE GILL, scree slide, grassy depression, RED TARN, springs, ADAM-A-COVE, 2400, 2600; 1: The Bad Step, 2: The Eastern Terrace)

Note that the steep direct descent from the south cairn may be by-passed altogether (it was formerly customary to do so) by proceeding west from the main cairn for 140 yards to another on grass in a slight depression, whence a grassy rake on the left goes down, skirting completely the rocks of the Crinkle, to join the direct route at its base.

The welcome spring on the summit (usually reliable after recent rain) is remarkable for its proximity to the top cairn (30 yards north-east, in the bend of the path); it is only 20 feet lower than the cairn, and has a very limited gathering-ground. Find it by listening for it — it emerges as a tiny waterfall from beneath a boulder. This is not the highest spring in the district but it is the nearest to a high summit.

The Eastern Terrace

A conspicuous grass terrace slants at an angle of 30° across the eastern cliffs of the main Crinkle, rising from the screes of the Mickle Door gully to the direct ridge-route just above the Bad Step. It is not seen from the ridge but appears in views of the east face clearly, being the middle of three such terraces and most prominent. It is of little use to walkers, except those who (in defiance of advice already given) are approaching the summit from Crinkle Gill: for them it offers

The Eastern Face — 1: the Bad Step, 2: the Eastern Terrace, 3: Mickle Door, 4: scree slide, cairn on boulder

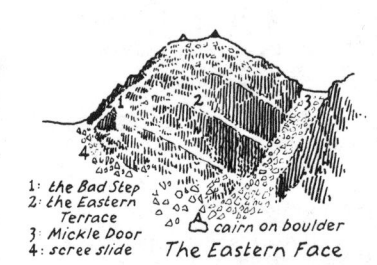

a way of escape from the final screes. The terrace (identified by a little wall at the side of the gully) is wide and without difficulties but is no place for loitering, being subject to bombardments of stones by bloody fools, if any, on the summit above. It is well to remember, too, that the terrace is bounded by a precipice. At the upper end the terrace becomes more broken near the Bad Step and is not quite easy to locate when approached from this direction.

Crinkle Crags 18

RIDGE ROUTES

To BOWFELL, 2960' : 1½ miles : Generally N, then WNW
Five depressions; final one (Three Tarns) at 2320': 850 feet of ascent
Positively one of the finest ridge-walks in Lakeland.

The rough stony ground makes progress slow, but this walk is, in any case, deserving of a leisurely appreciation; it is much too good to be done in a hurry. Every turn of the fairly distinct track is interesting, and in places even exciting, although no difficulty is met except for an occasional awkward stride on rock. In mist, the walker will probably have to descend to Three Tarns anyway, but should give Bowfell a miss, especially if the route is unfamiliar.

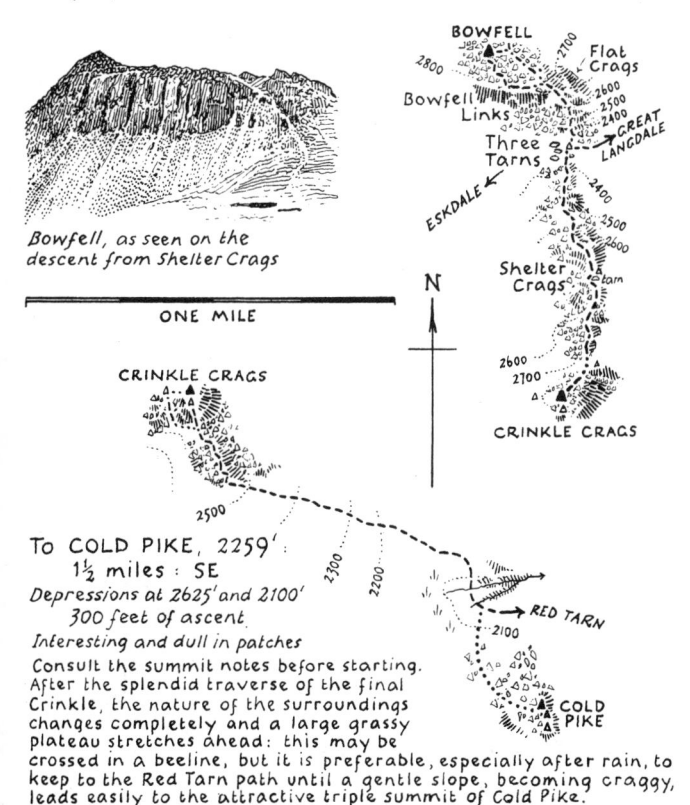

Bowfell, as seen on the descent from Shelter Crags

ONE MILE

To COLD PIKE, 2259' : 1½ miles : SE
Depressions at 2625' and 2100'
300 feet of ascent
Interesting and dull in patches

Consult the summit notes before starting. After the splendid traverse of the final Crinkle, the nature of the surroundings changes completely and a large grassy plateau stretches ahead: this may be crossed in a beeline, but it is preferable, especially after rain, to keep to the Red Tarn path until a gentle slope, becoming craggy, leads easily to the attractive triple summit of Cold Pike.

Crinkle Crags 19

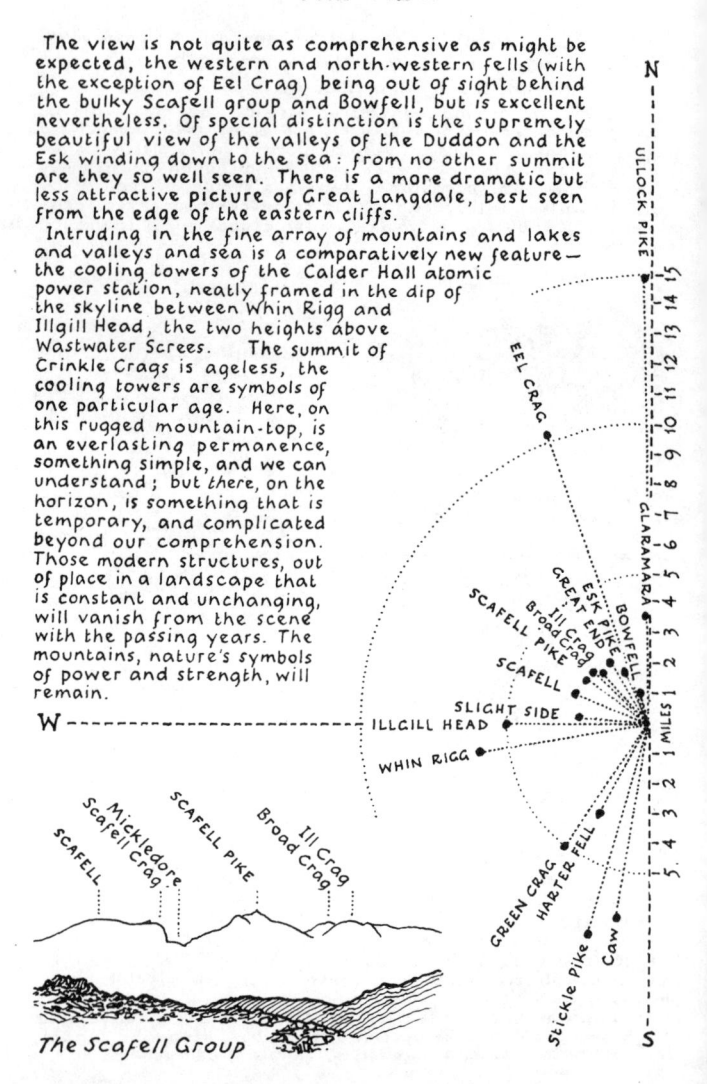

THE VIEW

The view is not quite as comprehensive as might be expected, the western and north-western fells (with the exception of Eel Crag) being out of sight behind the bulky Scafell group and Bowfell, but is excellent nevertheless. Of special distinction is the supremely beautiful view of the valleys of the Duddon and the Esk winding down to the sea: from no other summit are they so well seen. There is a more dramatic but less attractive picture of Great Langdale, best seen from the edge of the eastern cliffs.

Intruding in the fine array of mountains and lakes and valleys and sea is a comparatively new feature — the cooling towers of the Calder Hall atomic power station, neatly framed in the dip of the skyline between Whin Rigg and Illgill Head, the two heights above Wastwater Screes. The summit of Crinkle Crags is ageless, the cooling towers are symbols of one particular age. Here, on this rugged mountain-top, is an everlasting permanence, something simple, and we can understand; but *there*, on the horizon, is something that is temporary, and complicated beyond our comprehension. Those modern structures, out of place in a landscape that is constant and unchanging, will vanish from the scene with the passing years. The mountains, nature's symbols of power and strength, will remain.

The Scafell Group

Crinkle Crags 20

THE VIEW

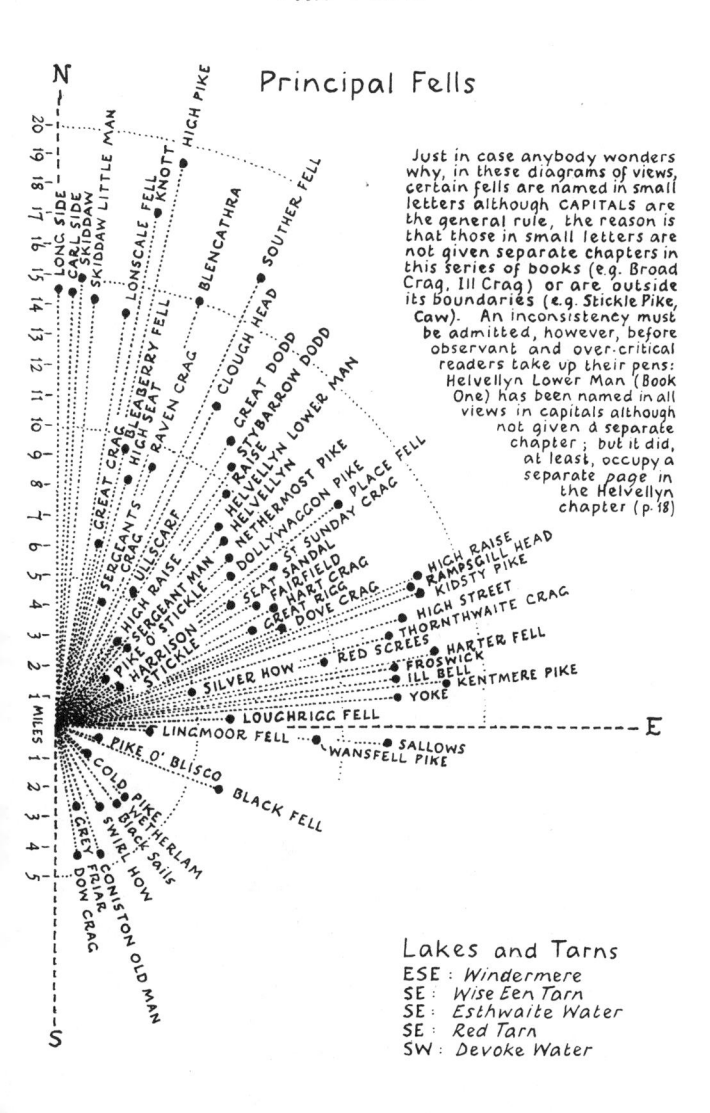

Principal Fells

Just in case anybody wonders why, in these diagrams of views, certain fells are named in small letters although CAPITALS are the general rule, the reason is that those in small letters are not given separate chapters in this series of books (e.g. Broad Crag, Ill Crag) or are outside its boundaries (e.g. Stickle Pike, Caw). An inconsistency must be admitted, however, before observant and over-critical readers take up their pens: Helvellyn Lower Man (Book One) has been named in all views in capitals although not given a separate chapter; but it did, at least, occupy a separate page in the Helvellyn chapter (p.18)

Lakes and Tarns
ESE: Windermere
SE: Wise Een Tarn
SE: Esthwaite Water
SE: Red Tarn
SW: Devoke Water

Dow Crag 2555'

from the Cove

GREY FRIAR ▲   SWIRL HOW ▲

Troutal ●   CONISTON OLD MAN ▲

DOW CRAG ▲   Coniston ●

● Seathwaite

MILES 0 1 2 3

Dow Crag 2

NATURAL FEATURES

Second only to Scafell Crag in the magnificence of its rock architecture is the imposing precipice towering above the stony hollow of Goat's Water, a favourite climbing ground hallowed by memories of the earliest and greatest of Lakeland cragsmen and so obviously the supreme natural attraction hereabouts that its name is given to the whole of the fell of which it is a part. Controversy raged at one time on the spelling of the name, DOW or DOE, but the former is now generally accepted.

The fell is extensive, and in marked contrast to the near-vertical eastern face is the smooth and gentle contour of the western slope descending to the little valley of Tarn Beck. The northern flank is easy too, except for a fringe of crag overlooking Seathwaite Tarn. South of the top, on a well-defined ridge, are the subsidiary summits of Buck Pike and Brown Pike, and beyond the latter is the lofty pass of Walna Scar, not now a traffic route since the closing of nearby quarries but remaining a most excellent walkers' highway.

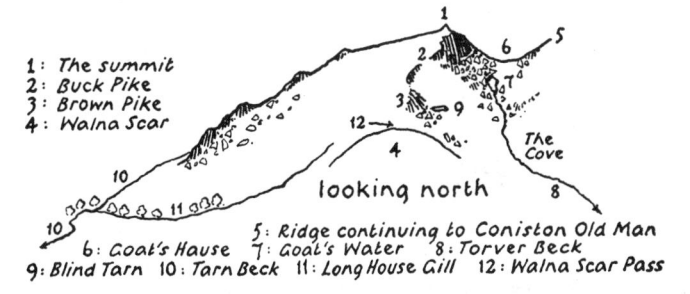

1: The summit
2: Buck Pike
3: Brown Pike
4: Walna Scar
5: Ridge continuing to Coniston Old Man
6: Goat's Hause   7: Goat's Water   8: Torver Beck
9: Blind Tarn 10: Tarn Beck 11: Long House Gill 12: Walna Scar Pass

Although really beyond the boundaries of fellwalking country, and therefore outside the area covered by this book, the ridge continuing south-west from the Walna Scar Pass deserves some attention. The 2000' contour occurs twice on Walna Scar itself and then across a wide depression rises the splendid little peak of Caw (1735') followed by a switchback ridge over the miniature Matterhorn of Stickle Pike (1231') and so ultimately, in a wealth of bracken, down to Duddon Bridge at the head of the estuary.

For seven miles this ridge forms the eastern watershed of the Duddon Valley and offers to strong walkers starting from Duddon Bridge a natural high-level approach to Dow Crag. Anyone doing this walk — a day's march in itself — will have fully merited his feeling of achievement when the top rocks are finally reached.

Dow Crag 3

NATURAL FEATURES

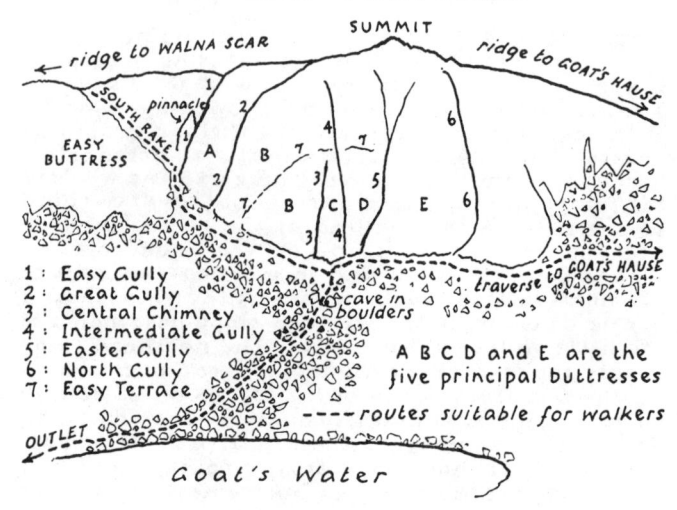

THE PATTERN OF DOW CRAG
as seen from the slopes of Coniston Old Man

1: Easy Gully
2: Great Gully
3: Central Chimney
4: Intermediate Gully
5: Easter Gully
6: North Gully
7: Easy Terrace

A B C D and E are the five principal buttresses

---- routes suitable for walkers

The Crag is the preserve of rock-climbers, but walkers may visit the base of the great cliff by taking the climbers' path from the outlet of Goat's Water. A simple traverse to the right across a scree slope then leads to the ridge just above Goat's Hause. This route, although involving boulder-hopping, is much more interesting than the usual way to the Hause on the eastern shore of the tarn.

Easy Buttress, *Easy* Gully and *Easy* Terrace are easy by rock-climbing, not walking, standards. Rock-climbers don't seem to know the meaning of easy. True, most walkers would manage to get up these places if a mad bull was in pursuit, but, if there is no such compelling circumstance, better they should reflect soberly.... and turn away.

There is, however, a coward's way to the top of the crag. From the lowest point of the cliff turn up left past the striking entrance to Great Gully and then more roughly up to the foot of Easy Gully, which is choked with stones. Here, unexpectedly, (it is not seen until reached) a straight ribbon of scree in a shallow gully goes up to the left (at a right-angled tangent to Easy Gully) — this route, although steep and loose, leads directly to the ridge above all difficulties. Climbers often use this as a quick way down, and it is comfortably within the capacity of most walkers. Lacking a name, but deserving one, SOUTH RAKE is suggested:

The entrance to Great Gully

Dow Crag 4

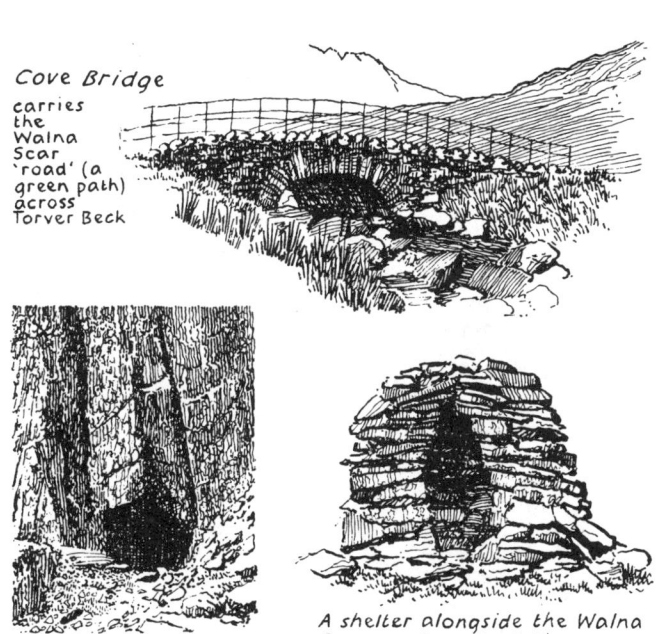

Cove Bridge carries the Walna Scar 'road' (a green path) across Torver Beck

The big cave, Blind Tarn Quarry

A shelter alongside the Walna Scar road, east of the pass, just big enough for one person or a honeymoon couple

Brown Pike and Blind Tarn from Buck Pike
Brown Pike has a fine cairn. Blind Tarn is one of the few tarns without an outlet — hence its name.

Dow Crag 5

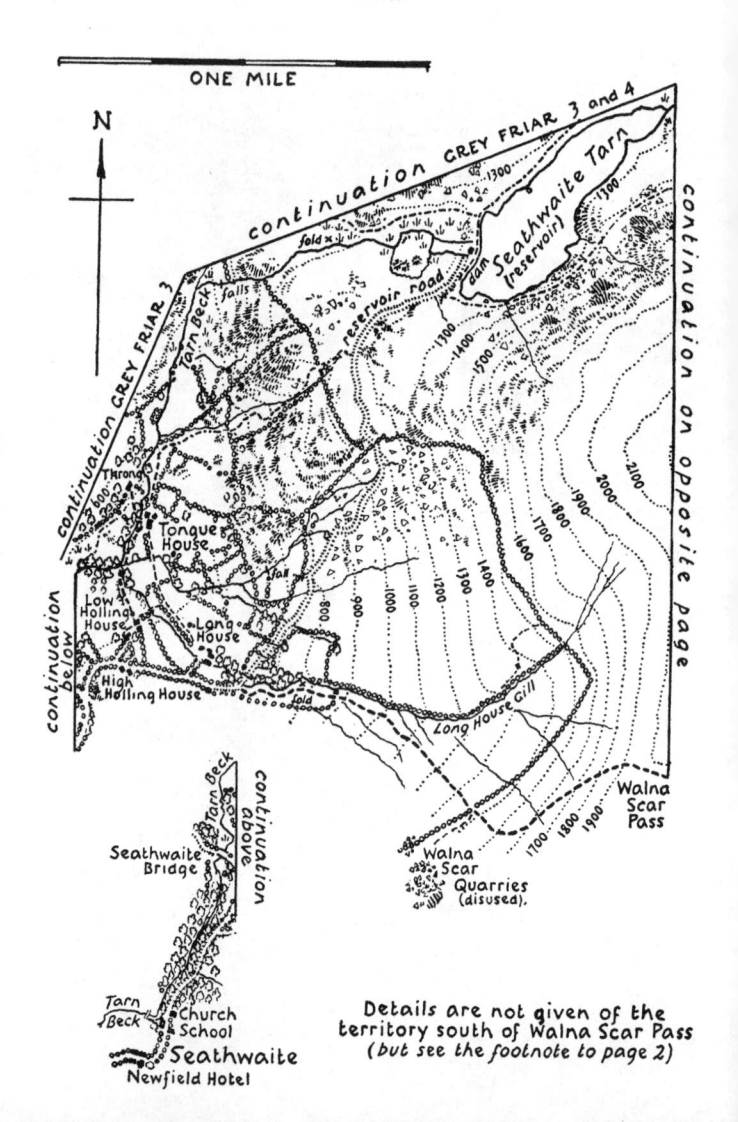

MAP

Dow Crag 6

MAP

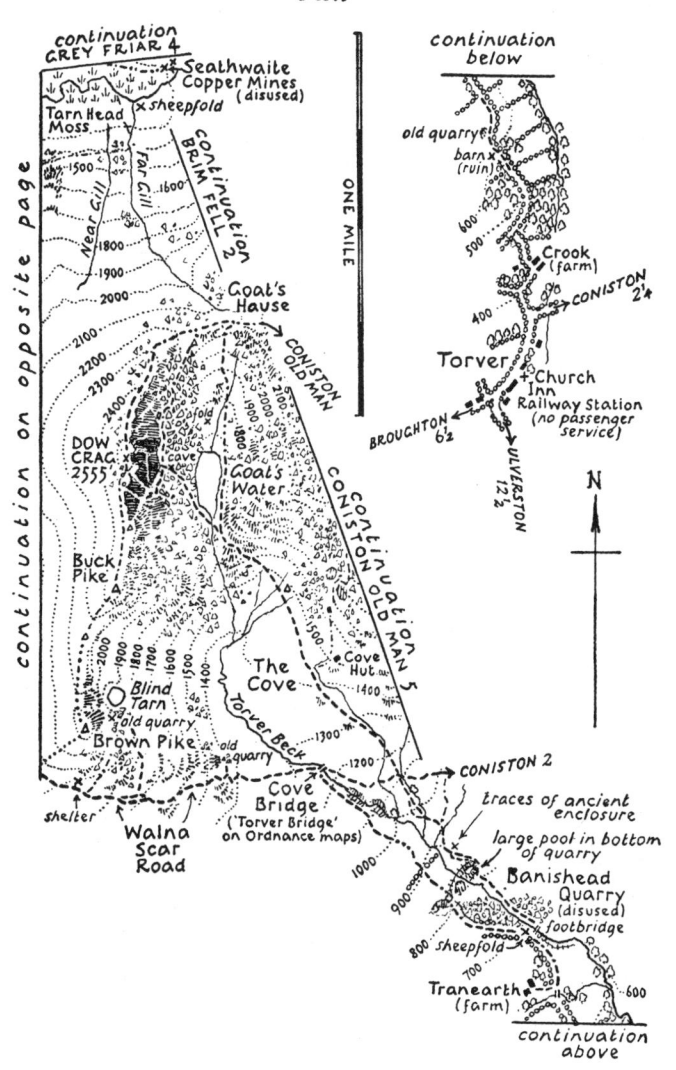

Dow Crag 7

ASCENT FROM TORVER
2250 feet of ascent: 3¾ miles

Some altitudes:
Summit 2555'
Buck Pike 2430'
Brown Pike 2237'
Goat's Water 1646'
Goat's Hause 2130'
Walna Scar Pass 1995'

From Cove Bridge, either go forward into the Cove, joining the white-cairn path, or go left to the top of Walna Scar Pass and thence follow the ridge over Brown Pike. The latter is the easier route, with pleasant walking, and is particularly good for descent.
If the Cove is entered, then from the outlet of Goat's Water either continue to Goat's Hause, there turning left to the summit (simple walking), or take the climbers' track to the base of the crags (some boulder-hopping) and traverse to the right below them, across scree, to join the other route on the skyline. There is an alternative way from the base of the crags *for scramblers* (South Rake — see page 3) not shown on this diagram.

This is the natural line of approach, following upstream the beck issuing from Goat's Water; it is also the most attractive, for when the pleasant woods of Torver are left behind the view forwards to the great buttresses of Dow Crag grows more dramatic with every step.

Banishead (or Baniside) Quarry (disused) — there is much of interest to see here

Many walkers will not be familiar with this approach but it has long been popular with rock-climbers — a favourite way to a favourite crag!

looking north-west

Dow Crag 8

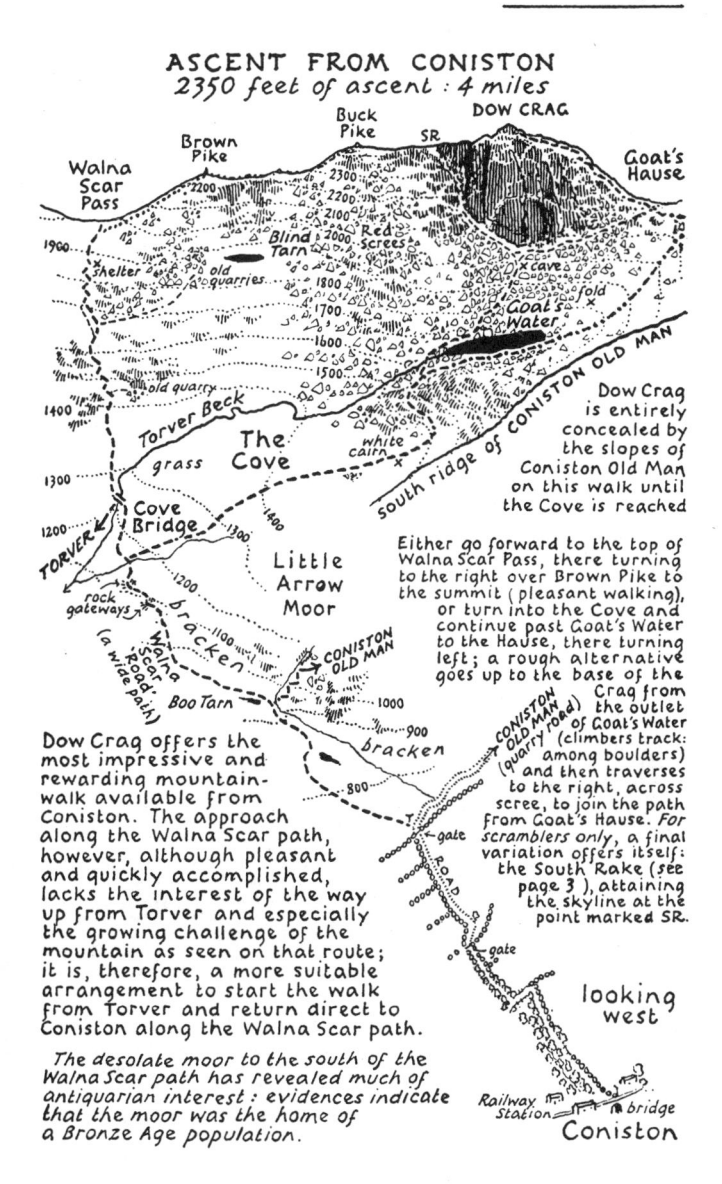

ASCENT FROM CONISTON
2350 feet of ascent : 4 miles

Dow Crag is entirely concealed by the slopes of Coniston Old Man on this walk until the Cove is reached

Either go forward to the top of Walna Scar Pass, there turning to the right over Brown Pike to the summit (pleasant walking), or turn into the Cove and continue past Goat's Water to the Hause, there turning left; a rough alternative goes up to the base of the Crag from the outlet of Goat's Water (climbers track: among boulders) and then traverses to the right, across scree, to join the path from Goat's Hause. For scramblers only, a final variation offers itself: the South Rake (see page 3), attaining the skyline at the point marked SR.

Dow Crag offers the most impressive and rewarding mountain-walk available from Coniston. The approach along the Walna Scar path, however, although pleasant and quickly accomplished, lacks the interest of the way up from Torver and especially the growing challenge of the mountain as seen on that route; it is, therefore, a more suitable arrangement to start the walk from Torver and return direct to Coniston along the Walna Scar path.

The desolate moor to the south of the Walna Scar path has revealed much of antiquarian interest: evidences indicate that the moor was the home of a Bronze Age population.

looking west

Dow Crag 9

ASCENT FROM THE DUDDON VALLEY
2300 feet of ascent : 3¾ miles from Seathwaite

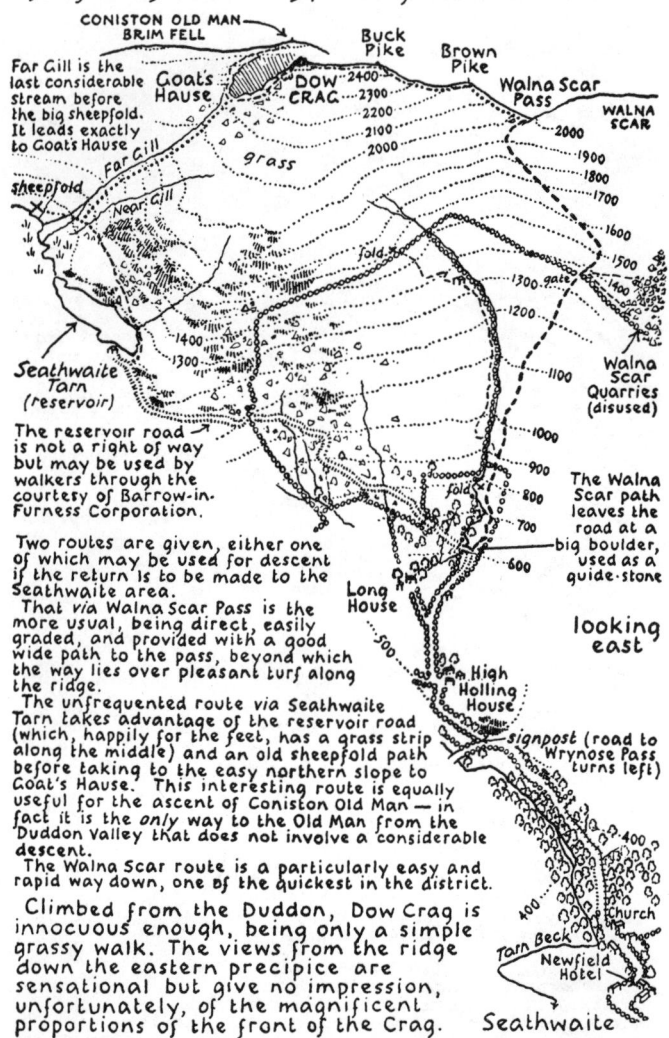

Far Gill is the last considerable stream before the big sheepfold. It leads exactly to Goat's House.

The reservoir road is not a right of way but may be used by walkers through the courtesy of Barrow-in-Furness Corporation.

The Walna Scar path leaves the road at a big boulder, used as a guide-stone.

looking east

Two routes are given, either one of which may be used for descent if the return is to be made to the Seathwaite area.

That via Walna Scar Pass is the more usual, being direct, easily graded, and provided with a good wide path to the pass, beyond which the way lies over pleasant turf along the ridge.

The unfrequented route via Seathwaite Tarn takes advantage of the reservoir road (which, happily for the feet, has a grass strip along the middle) and an old sheepfold path before taking to the easy northern slope to Goat's House. This interesting route is equally useful for the ascent of Coniston Old Man — in fact it is the *only* way to the Old Man from the Duddon Valley that does not involve a considerable descent.

The Walna Scar route is a particularly easy and rapid way down, one of the quickest in the district.

Climbed from the Duddon, Dow Crag is innocuous enough, being only a simple grassy walk. The views from the ridge down the eastern precipice are sensational but give no impression, unfortunately, of the magnificent proportions of the front of the Crag.

Dow Crag 10

THE SUMMIT

Count this amongst the most delectable and exhilarating of Lakeland summits, for the sublime architecture of the great crag directly below is manifest in the topmost rocks also, forming an airy perch on a fang of naked stone elevated high above the tremendous precipice: a scene that cannot fail to exalt the minds of those who have lifted their bodies to it. An easy scramble gives access to the highest point: there is no room for a cairn. For peeps down the vertical rifts of Great Gully and Easy Gully follow a crumbled wall south along the ridge for 200 yards.

DESCENTS: Use the two ridges only: north curving east to Goat's Hause (fair path) for Coniston Old Man or Seathwaite Tarn, keeping steep ground on the right hand; or south over Buck Pike and Brown Pike to Walna Scar Pass (intermittent path ceases on Brown Pike) for Coniston or the Duddon, keeping steep ground on the left hand. Both routes are easy.

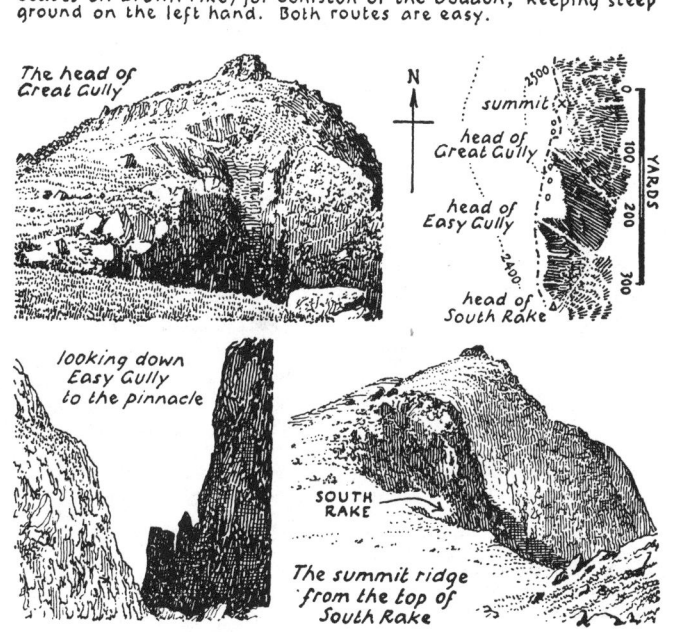

The head of Great Gully

looking down Easy Gully to the pinnacle

SOUTH RAKE

The summit ridge from the top of South Rake

Dow Crag 11

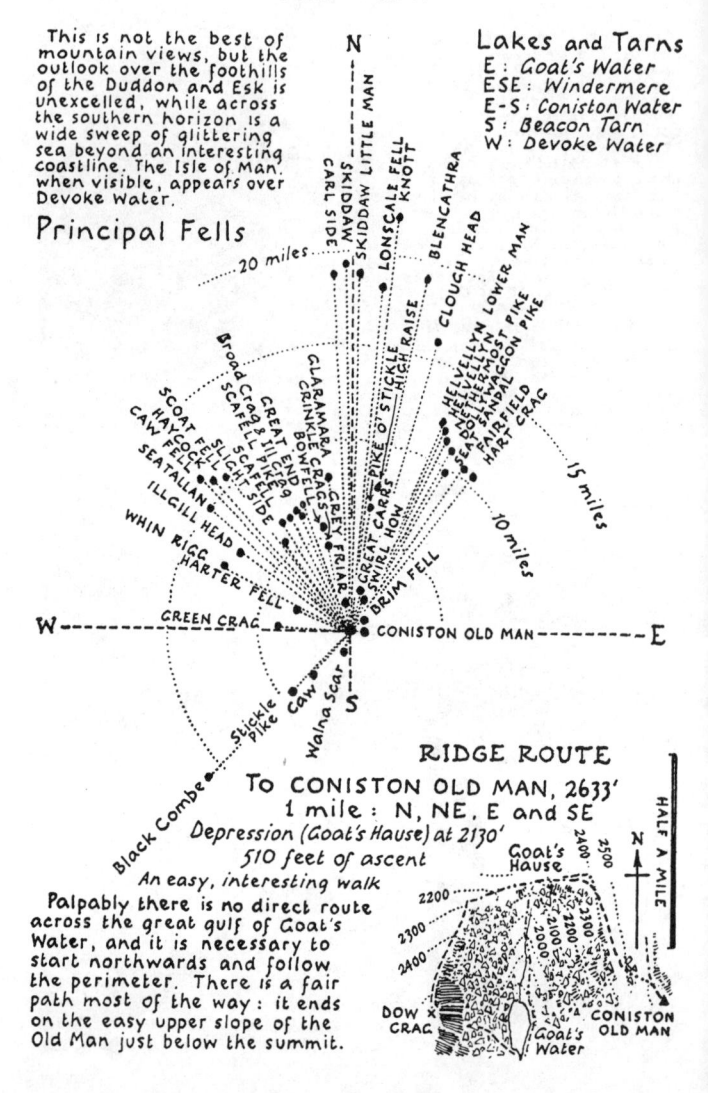

THE VIEW

This is not the best of mountain views, but the outlook over the foothills of the Duddon and Esk is unexcelled, while across the southern horizon is a wide sweep of glittering sea beyond an interesting coastline. The Isle of Man, when visible, appears over Devoke Water.

Lakes and Tarns
E: Goat's Water
ESE: Windermere
E–S: Coniston Water
S: Beacon Tarn
W: Devoke Water

Principal Fells

... 20 miles
15 miles
10 miles

SKIDDAW LITTLE MAN, SKIDDAW, CARL SIDE, LONSCALE FELL, KNOTT, BLENCATHRA, CLOUGH HEAD, HELVELLYN LOWER MAN, HELVELLYN, DOLLYWAGGON PIKE, SEAT SANDAL, NETHERMOST PIKE, FAIRFIELD, RANDAL CRAG, HART CRAG

BROAD CRAG, GREAT END, SCAFELL PIKE, CRINKLE CRAGS, BOWFELL, GLARAMARA, GREY FRIAR, GREAT CARRS, PIKE O'STICKLE, HIGH RAISE

SCOAT FELL, HAYCOCK, CAW FELL, SCAFELL, SLIGHT SIDE, SEATALLAN, ILLGILL HEAD, SWIRL HOW, DOW CRAG, GRIT FELL

WHIN RIGG, HARTER FELL

W – – – GREEN CRAG – – – – – – – – – – – – – – CONISTON OLD MAN – – – – – E

Black Combe, Stickle Pike, Caw, Walna Scar

S

RIDGE ROUTE
TO CONISTON OLD MAN, 2633'
1 mile : N, NE, E and SE
Depression (Goat's Hause) at 2130'
510 feet of ascent
An easy, interesting walk

Palpably there is no direct route across the great gulf of Goat's Water, and it is necessary to start northwards and follow the perimeter. There is a fair path most of the way: it ends on the easy upper slope of the Old Man just below the summit.

HALF A MILE

Dow Crag 12

Dow Crag from Goat's Water

Esk Pike

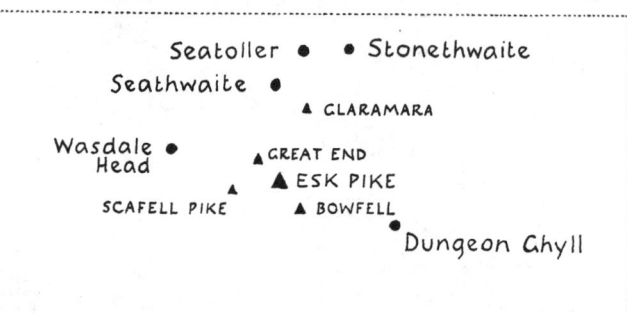

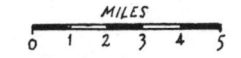

2903'

not named on maps of
the Ordnance Survey

*from Rest Gill,
Crinkle Crags*

- Seatoller
- Stonethwaite
- Seathwaite
- ▲ CLARAMARA
- Wasdale Head
- ▲ GREAT END
- ▲ ESK PIKE
- ▲ SCAFELL PIKE
- ▲ BOWFELL
- Dungeon Ghyll
- Boot

MILES
0 1 2 3 4 5

Esk Pike 2

NATURAL FEATURES

The central height in the semi-circle of fine peaks around the lonely head of upper Eskdale, nameless on Ordnance Survey maps, has long been known to walkers as Esk Pike. In the splendid panorama of the Eskdale skyline the fell is the least prominent, not because it competes for attention with popular favourites such as the Scafells and Bowfell and the Crinkles but rather because its top is the furthest removed from the valley and appears dwarfed in relation to the others. Yet this is, in fact, a most attractive summit, deserving a separate ascent but invariably combined with a greater objective, Bowfell. Did it but stand alone, away from such enticing neighbours, Esk Pike would rank highly among the really worth-while mountain climbs.

The outstanding feature is a lengthy south ridge, bounded by the River Esk westwards, and to the east by Yeastyrigg Gill and Lingcove Beck: a ridge with many abrupt crags. Northwards a short steep tongue of land goes down into Langstrath, enclosed between Allencrags Gill and Angletarn Gill. Lofty ridges, crossed by the passes of Esk Hause and Ore Gap, connect with Great End and Bowfell.

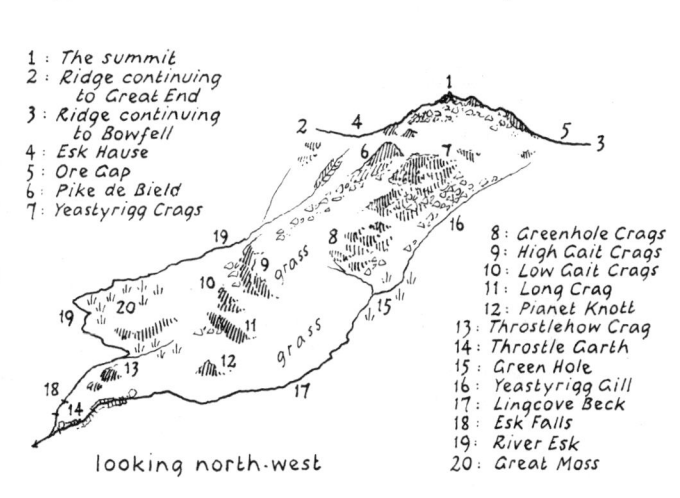

1 : The summit
2 : Ridge continuing to Great End
3 : Ridge continuing to Bowfell
4 : Esk Hause
5 : Ore Gap
6 : Pike de Bield
7 : Yeastyrigg Crags
8 : Greenhole Crags
9 : High Gait Crags
10 : Low Gait Crags
11 : Long Crag
12 : Planet Knott
13 : Throstlehow Crag
14 : Throstle Garth
15 : Green Hole
16 : Yeastyrigg Gill
17 : Lingcove Beck
18 : Esk Falls
19 : River Esk
20 : Great Moss

looking north-west

Esk Pike 3

Esk Hause

Sooner or later every fellwalker finds himself for the first time at Esk Hause, the highest, best-known and most important of Lakeland foot-passes, and he will probably have read, or been told, that this is a place where it is easy to go astray. There should be no danger of this, however, even in bad conditions. Nevertheless the lie of the land is curious (but not confusing). Esk Hause is a tilted grass plateau, high among the mountains. The unusual thing about it is that *two* passes have their summits on the plateau, two passes carrying entirely different routes; in fact, in general direction they are at right angles. If these routes crossed at the highest point of the plateau there would be a simple 'crossroads', but they do not: one is a hundred feet higher than the other and 300 yards distant.

The name Esk Hause is commonly but incorrectly applied to the lower of the passes, a much-trodden route, but properly belongs to the higher and less-favoured pass. What is almost always referred to as Esk Hause is not Esk Hause at all; the true Esk Hause is rarely so named except by the cartographers. The true Esk Hause (2490') is the head of Eskdale, a shallow depression between Esk Pike and Great End, and is an infrequently-used pass between Eskdale and Borrowdale; the general direction is south-west to north-east. The false Esk Hause (2386', with a wall shelter in the form of a cross) is a shallow depression in the high skyline between the true Esk Hause and Allen Crags, and is a much used pass between Great Langdale and Wasdale, general direction being south-east to north-west.

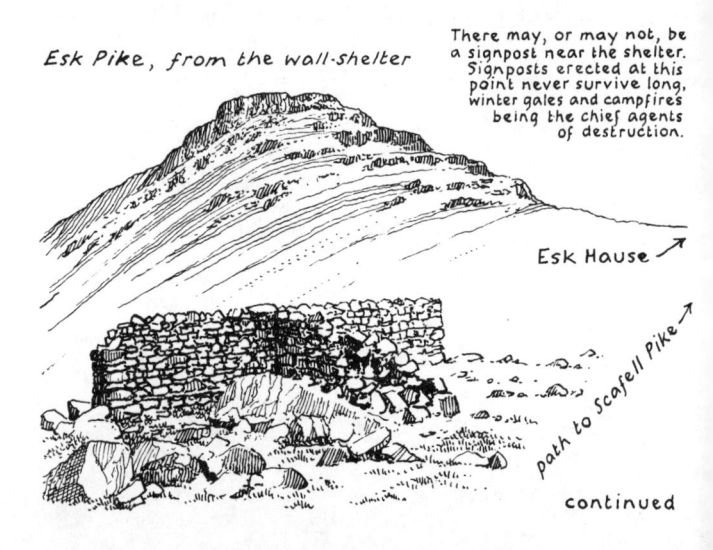

Esk Pike, from the wall-shelter

There may, or may not, be a signpost near the shelter. Signposts erected at this point never survive long, winter gales and campfires being the chief agents of destruction.

Esk Hause ↗

path to Scafell Pike ↗

continued

Esk Pike 4

Esk Hause

continued

The likeliest mistake in bad weather is that a walker approaching from Langdale and bound for Wasdale may continue along the plain path beyond the shelter and so unwittingly be ascending Scafell Pike when he should be going down to Wasdale. (The path to Scafell Pike from the shelter, incidentally, first goes up to the *true* Esk Hause and there swings away to the right; fortunately there is no track leading down into Eskdale from the Hause, otherwise it might be thought that the valley below is Wasdale — which would be a still worse mistake). The correct continuation to Wasdale is indistinct on the grass for 30 yards beyond the shelter before becoming clear. Here is an example of a bifurcation (to Scafell Pike) having become better marked on the ground than the original path (to Wasdale). It is well to remember that the shelter is the *highest* point attained on the Langdale-Wasdale route.

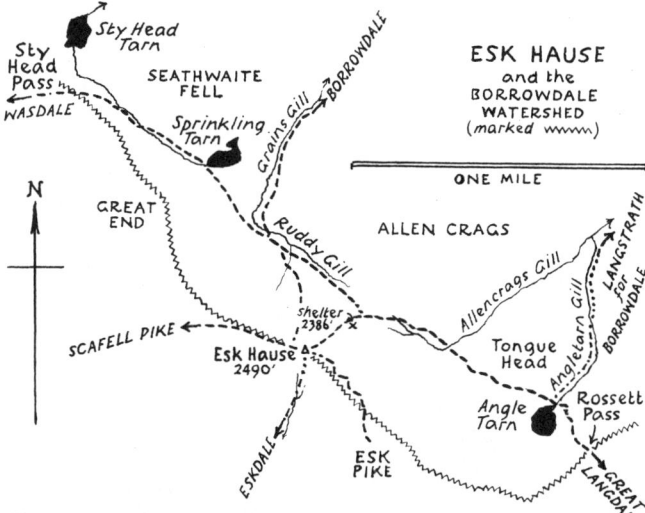

ESK HAUSE and the BORROWDALE WATERSHED (marked wwww)

ONE MILE

The greater importance of the higher pass as a watershed is well seen from a study of the map. All streams crossed on the Langdale-Wasdale route within the area between Rossett Pass and Sty Head Pass find their way into Borrowdale, although the latter valley is largely screened by Allen Crags. No water from this wide area flows into Langdale or Wasdale, and the lower pass therefore has little geographical significance: it is merely an intrusion in the vast system of the Eskdale-Borrowdale gathering grounds. The one function of the spurious Esk Hause is to deflect the plateau's waters into Borrowdale either by way of Langstrath or Grains Gill.

Esk Pike 5

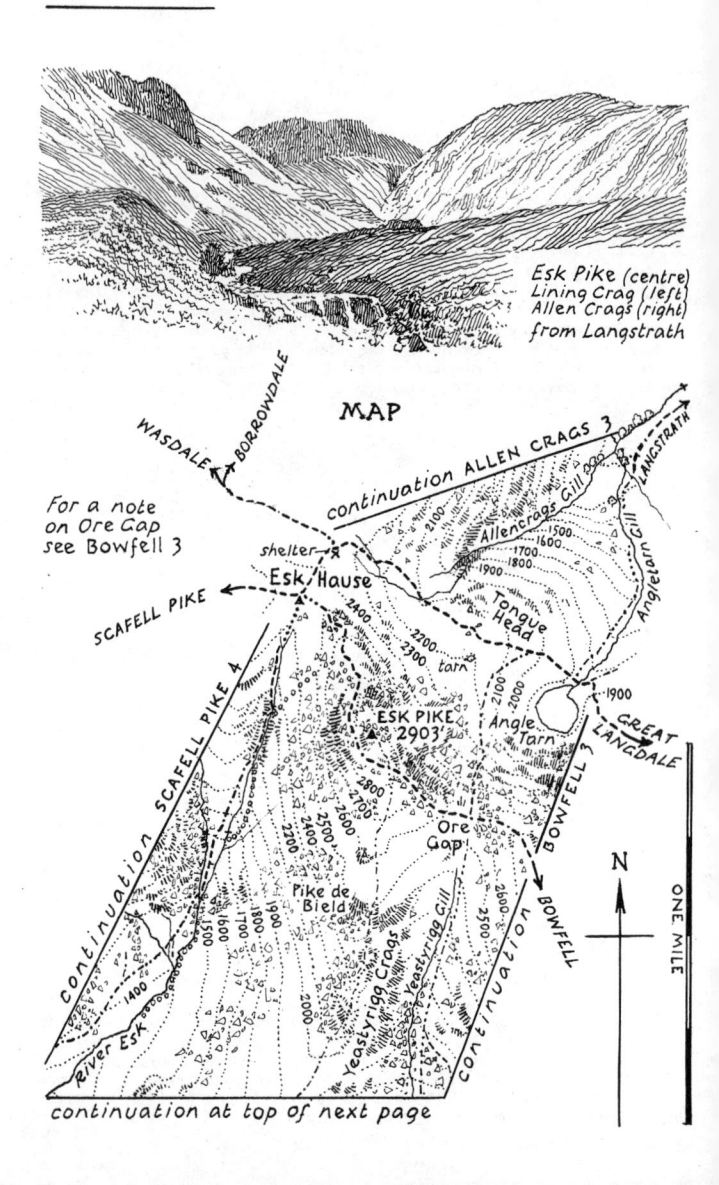

Esk Pike (centre)
Lining Crag (left)
Allen Crags (right)
from Langstrath

MAP

For a note on Ore Gap see Bowfell 3

WASDALE / BORROWDALE

continuation ALLEN CRAGS 3 — LANGSTRATH

Allencrags Gill
Angletarn Gill

shelter
Esk Hause
SCAFELL PIKE
Tongue Head
tarn
ESK PIKE 2903'
Angle Tarn
GREAT LANGDALE

continuation SCAFELL PIKE 4
Ore Gap
continuation BOWFELL 3 — BOWFELL

Pike de Bield
Yeastyrigg Crags
Yeastyrigg Gill

River Esk

N
ONE MILE

continuation at top of next page

Esk Pike 6

MAP

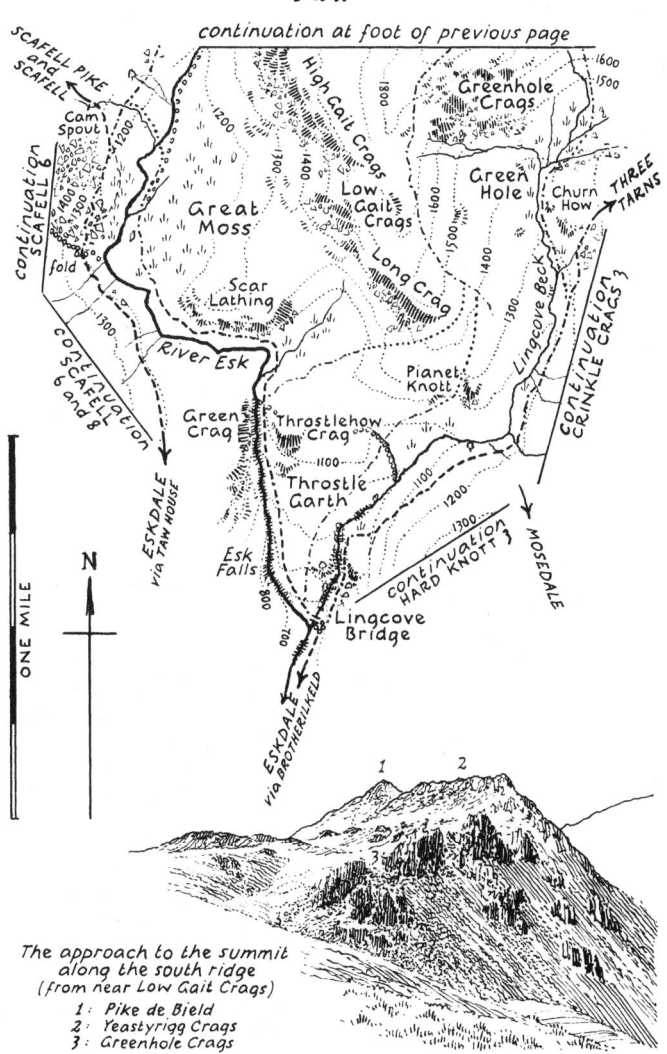

continuation at foot of previous page

The approach to the summit along the south ridge (from near Low Gait Crags)
1: Pike de Bield
2: Yeastyrigg Crags
3: Greenhole Crags

Esk Pike 7

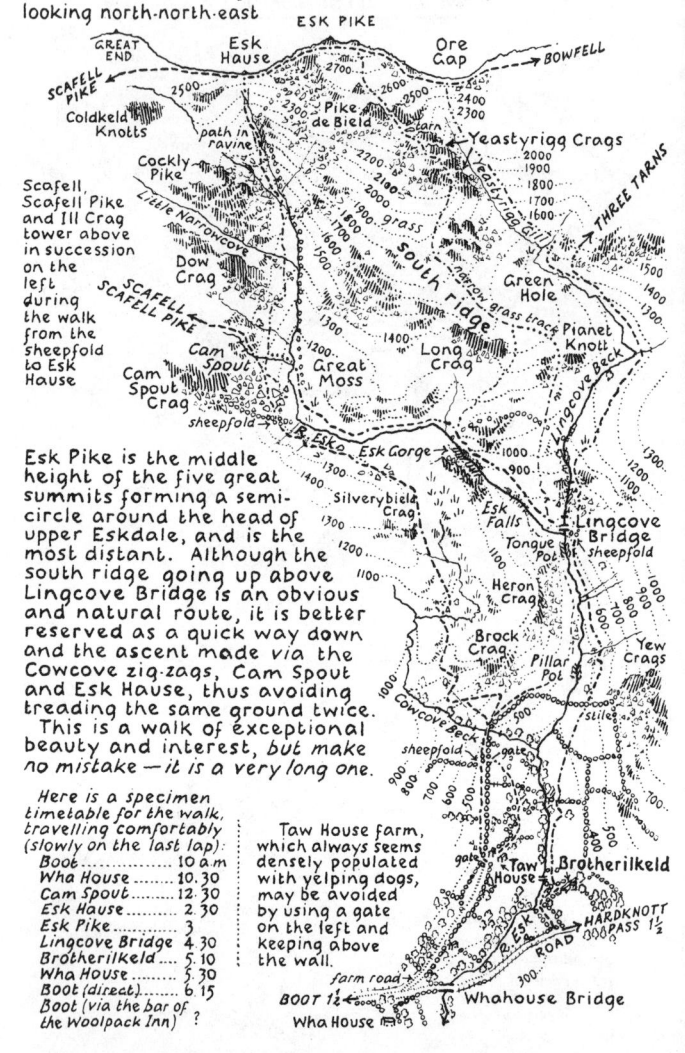

ASCENT FROM ESKDALE
2800 feet of ascent : 8½ miles from Boot
looking north-north-east

Scafell, Scafell Pike and Ill Crag tower above in succession on the left during the walk from the sheepfold to Esk Hause.

Esk Pike is the middle height of the five great summits forming a semi-circle around the head of upper Eskdale, and is the most distant. Although the south ridge going up above Lingcove Bridge is an obvious and natural route, it is better reserved as a quick way down and the ascent made via the Cowcove zig-zags, Cam Spout and Esk Hause, thus avoiding treading the same ground twice.

This is a walk of exceptional beauty and interest, *but make no mistake — it is a very long one.*

Here is a specimen timetable for the walk, travelling comfortably (slowly on the last lap):
- Boot .... 10 a.m
- Wha House 10.30
- Cam Spout 12.30
- Esk Hause 2.30
- Esk Pike 3
- Lingcove Bridge . 4.30
- Brotherilkeld ... 5.10
- Wha House 5.30
- Boot (direct) ... 6.15
- Boot (via the bar of the Woolpack Inn) ?

Taw House farm, which always seems densely populated with yelping dogs, may be avoided by using a gate on the left and keeping above the wall.

Esk Pike 8

ASCENT FROM WASDALE HEAD
2700 feet of ascent : 4¼ miles

This is also the route of ascent to Bowfell from Wasdale Head — it is reached by going on along the ridge from the top of Esk Pike south-east, crossing the depression of Ore Gap.

Esk Pike remains concealed by Great End almost until Esk Hause is reached

While nothing should be said that might be thought to detract from this excellent climb there will be no doubt in the mind of anybody who does it that the finest scenes are met in the vicinity of Sprinkling Tarn and the towering cliffs of Great End and that, in comparison with these awesome surroundings, the way beyond deteriorates in quality — which is rather a pity, for those climbs are best that grow in interest throughout, the climax coming only as the final steps are taken

Looking back and upwards to the Napes from this point, the Needle can just be discerned. The prominent rock like a sitting cat on the skyline is the Sphinx.

Towering high into the sky on the left here is GREAT GABLE. The crags are the Napes Ridges.

Strongly recommended as an alternative to the busy path to Sty Head rising across the screes of Great Gable is the old now-neglected valley track, a route of delightful grassy zig-zags. (For a description and eulogy of this forgotten path see Great End 7)

looking east

Wasdale Head

Esk Pike 9

ASCENT FROM BORROWDALE
2550 feet of ascent : 4¾ miles from Seatoller

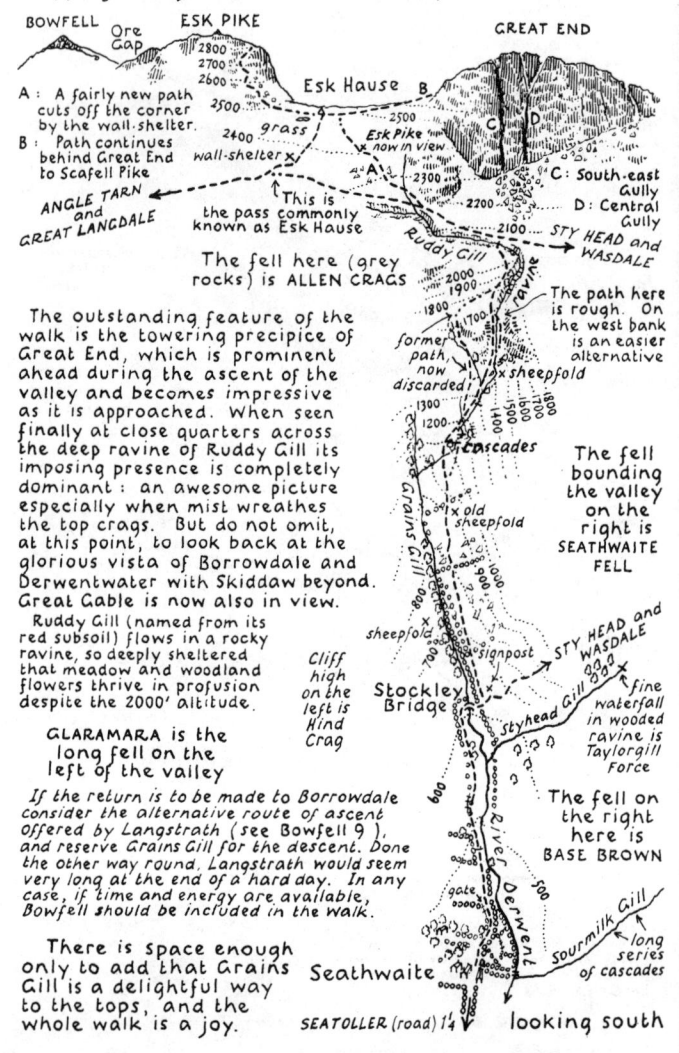

BOWFELL — Ore Gap — ESK PIKE — GREAT END

2800, 2700, 2600, 2500, 2400, 2300, 2200, 2100

Esk Hause

A: A fairly new path cuts off the corner by the wall-shelter.
B: Path continues behind Great End to Scafell Pike

grass — Esk Pike now in view
wall-shelter x
ANGLE TARN and GREAT LANGDALE
↑ This is the pass commonly known as Esk Hause

C: South-east Gully
D: Central Gully
STY HEAD and WASDALE

The fell here (grey rocks) is ALLEN CRAGS

Ruddy Gill — ravine
2000, 1900, 1800, 1700

The path here is rough. On the west bank is an easier alternative

former path, now discarded
x sheepfold
1300, 1200, 1400, 1500, 1600, 1700, 1800

cascades

The outstanding feature of the walk is the towering precipice of Great End, which is prominent ahead during the ascent of the valley and becomes impressive as it is approached. When seen finally at close quarters across the deep ravine of Ruddy Gill its imposing presence is completely dominant: an awesome picture especially when mist wreathes the top crags. But do not omit, at this point, to look back at the glorious vista of Borrowdale and Derwentwater with Skiddaw beyond. Great Gable is now also in view.

Ruddy Gill (named from its red subsoil) flows in a rocky ravine, so deeply sheltered that meadow and woodland flowers thrive in profusion despite the 2000' altitude.

The fell bounding the valley on the right is SEATHWAITE FELL

Grains Gill
x old sheepfold
1100, 1000, 900, 800, 700

GLARAMARA is the long fell on the left of the valley

sheepfold
Cliff high on the left is Kind Crag

signpost
Stockley Bridge
STY HEAD and WASDALE
Styhead Gill
fine waterfall in wooded ravine is Taylorgill Force

If the return is to be made to Borrowdale consider the alternative route of ascent offered by Langstrath (see Bowfell 9), and reserve Grains Gill for the descent. Done the other way round, Langstrath would seem very long at the end of a hard day. In any case, if time and energy are available, Bowfell should be included in the walk.

The fell on the right here is BASE BROWN

600

River Derwent
500
gate

Sourmilk Gill ← long series of cascades

There is space enough only to add that Grains Gill is a delightful way to the tops, and the whole walk is a joy.

Seathwaite

SEATOLLER (road) 1¼ ↓   looking south

Esk Pike 10

ASCENT FROM GREAT LANGDALE
2800 feet of ascent : 4·4 miles (from Dungeon Ghyll Old Hotel)

ESK PIKE

A : to SCAFELL PIKE
B : to WASDALE HEAD

Ore Gap — BOWFELL

Esk Hause → A

shelter → B

The climb to Ore Gap from the Esk Hause path is unexpectedly easy; the track is cairned after an indistinct start (watch for narrow trod trending left 250 yards beyond the Angle Tarn outlet) and is being increasingly used.

Angle Tarn

Tongue Head

Allencrags Gill

Rossett Pass → ROSSETT PIKE

pony route
water!
grass
indistinct
Rossett Gill
bracken
Rossett Gill

The alternative path to the summit, from Esk Hause (the more usual way) is good and interesting, passing across shelves of rock higher up.

The walker in Lakeland is apt to weigh very very carefully, in advance, the merits of any mountain climb if it involves an ascent of Rossett Gill. Bowfell and Scafell Pike are generally considered worth the toil of the Gill, but is the less popular Esk Pike? A census of opinion may say not, yet Esk Pike really is a most attractive peak and its summit-paths are thoroughly interesting. It is too good to be omitted because of Rossett Gill!

Let every man make his own choice, but the author always prefers to go up Rossett Gill by the two zig-zags. (The second starts indistinctly and is not nowadays generally known)

For further details of Rossett Gill see Rossett Pike 3 and 4

guide stone
STAKE PASS
Stake Gill
sheepfold
moraines
Mickleden
← DUNGEON GHYLL (OLD HOTEL) 1½

looking west

Esk Pike is useful as an easier objective if an attempt on Scafell Pike is frustrated by lack of time or flagging limbs or doubtful weather when in the vicinity of Esk Hause. A good route of return, at the cost of little extra effort, is to traverse Bowfell, reaching Great Langdale via the Band.

Esk Pike 11

THE SUMMIT

The summit is characterised by its colourful rocks, which, unlike those of the other tops in this area of 'Borrowdale volcanics', are sharp and splintery, in predominantly brown or coppery hues with generous splashes of white and heavily stained with vivid patches of green lichen. These stones are profusely scattered and it is from a debris of flakes and fragments that the highest point, a craggy outcrop, emerges. In the lee of this small crag, which is cut away vertically to the north, is the most effective of all summit shelters, formed by two short but substantial walls: a good refuge in storm. The path across the top of the fell does not visit the outcrop, its obvious purpose being to link Esk Hause and Bowfell and not to lead its passengers to the summit of Esk Pike. Most walkers adhere to the path and by-pass the highest rocks; they miss also the short and easy detour on grass to the pleasant tops of the buttresses forming the abrupt northern edge of the summit.

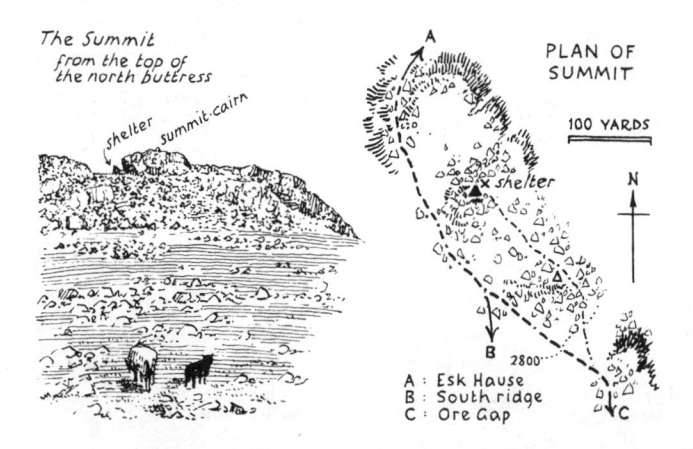

The Summit from the top of the north buttress

PLAN OF SUMMIT

100 YARDS

2800

A : Esk Hause
B : South ridge
C : Ore Gap

Esk Pike 12

RIDGE ROUTES

To BOWFELL, 2960': 1 mile
SE, E and SE
Depression (Ore Gap) at 2575'
400 feet of ascent
Rough in places but path generally good.

A faint track skirts the north side of the next prominent outcrop along the top and then goes down to join the ridge-path, when the walk across Ore Gap (note red soil here, due to presence of hematite) and onwards is straightforward. If the day is clear and time permits, a good alternative from Ore Gap is to bear left and over the top of Hanging Knotts to get views of Angle Tarn and Rossett Pass, which will otherwise not be seen during the walk.

To GREAT END, 2984':
1¼ miles: N, NNW, W and N
Depression (Esk Hause) at 2490'
525 feet of ascent
A pleasant high-level walk

An interesting path goes down to Esk Hause (the *true* Esk Hause) where the well-trodden route to Scafell Pike is joined: this may be followed into and out of Calf Cove, when turn right up an easy ridge to the stony top of Great End. A more direct finish, avoiding Calf Cove, will encounter rougher ground.

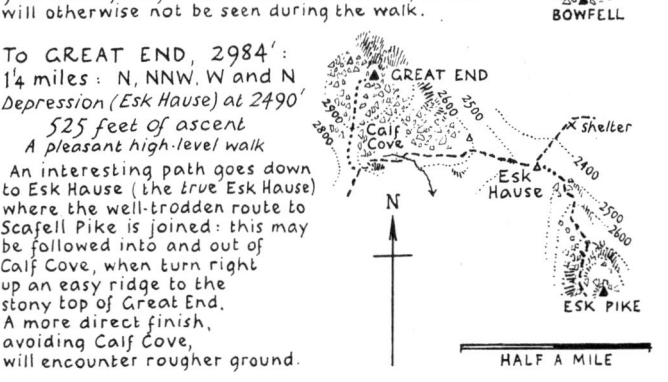

HALF A MILE

looking north-west to Great End

GREAT END — GREAT GABLE — GREEN GABLE

Calf Cove
path to Scafell Pike
top of north buttress of Esk Pike (concealing Esk Hause)
path to Esk Hause

Esk Pike 13

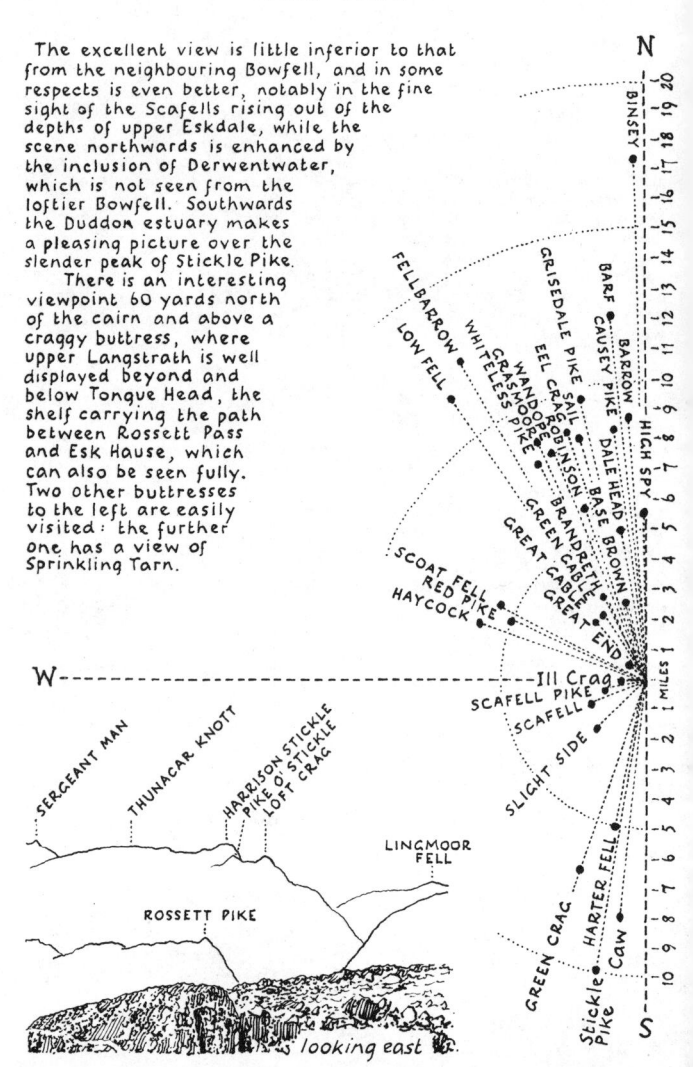

THE VIEW

The excellent view is little inferior to that from the neighbouring Bowfell, and in some respects is even better, notably in the fine sight of the Scafells rising out of the depths of upper Eskdale, while the scene northwards is enhanced by the inclusion of Derwentwater, which is not seen from the loftier Bowfell. Southwards the Duddon estuary makes a pleasing picture over the slender peak of Stickle Pike.

There is an interesting viewpoint 60 yards north of the cairn and above a craggy buttress, where upper Langstrath is well displayed beyond and below Tongue Head, the shelf carrying the path between Rossett Pass and Esk Hause, which can also be seen fully. Two other buttresses to the left are easily visited: the further one has a view of Sprinkling Tarn.

looking east

THE VIEW

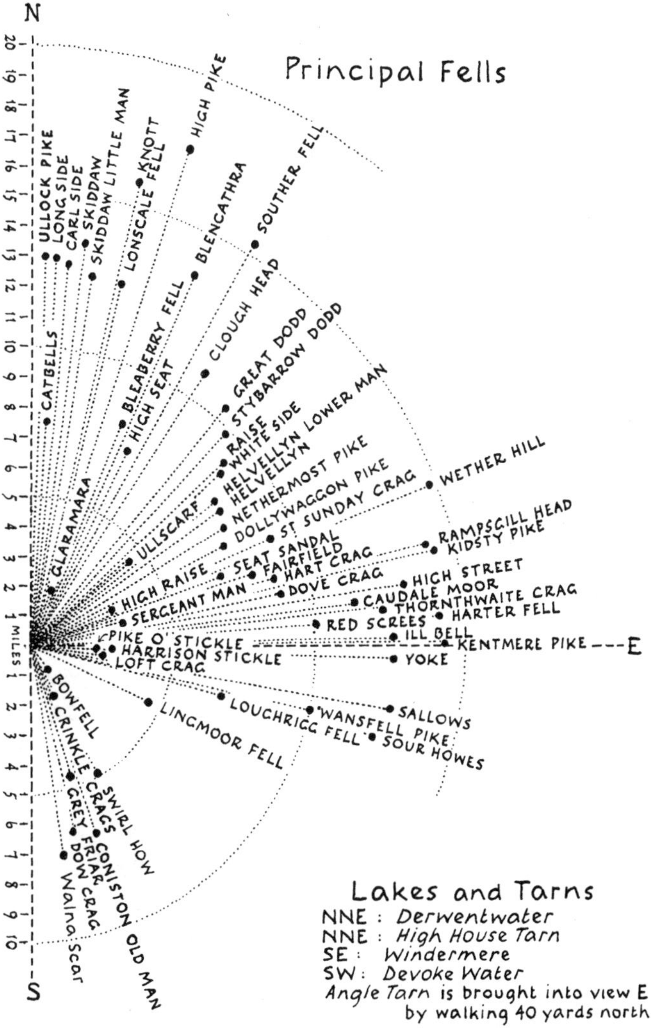
N
S
E
MILES
20
19
18
17
16
15
14
13
12
11
10
9
8
7
6
5
4
3
2
1
1
2
3
4
5
6
7
8
9
10
Principal Fells
ULLOCK PIKE
LONG SIDE
CARL SIDE
SKIDDAW
SKIDDAW LITTLE MAN
KNOTT
LONSCALE FELL
HIGH PIKE
BLENCATHRA
SOUTHER FELL
CATBELLS
BLEABERRY FELL
HIGH SEAT
CLOUGH HEAD
GREAT DODD
STYBARROW DODD
RAISE
WHITE SIDE
HELVELLYN LOWER MAN
HELVELLYN
NETHERMOST PIKE
DOLLYWAGGON PIKE
ST SUNDAY CRAG
WETHER HILL
GLARAMARA
ULLSCARF
HIGH RAISE
SEAT SANDAL
FAIRFIELD
HART CRAG
RAMPSGILL HEAD
KIDSTY PIKE
SERGEANT MAN
DOVE CRAG
HIGH STREET
CAUDALE MOOR
THORNTHWAITE CRAG
HARTER FELL
RED SCREES
ILL BELL
PIKE O' STICKLE
HARRISON STICKLE
LOFT CRAG
KENTMERE PIKE
YOKE
BOWFELL
CRINKLE CRAGS
LINGMOOR FELL
LOUGHRIGG FELL
WANSFELL PIKE
SALLOWS
SOUR HOWES
SWIRL HOW
GREY FRIAR
CONISTON OLD MAN
DOW CRAG
Walna Scar

Lakes and Tarns

NNE : *Derwentwater*
NNE : *High House Tarn*
SE : *Windermere*
SW : *Devoke Water*
Angle Tarn is brought into view E by walking 40 yards north

Glaramara　　　2560'

from Grange Fell

Glaramara 2

NATURAL FEATURES

Prominent in the mid-Borrowdale scene is the bulky fell of Glaramara, which, with an ally in Rosthwaite Fell, seems, on the approach from the north, to throw a great barrier across the valley; although in fact the level strath turns away to the right to persist as far as Seathwaite, two miles further, while a shorter branch goes left to Stonethwaite. Seen from the north the most notable feature is a gigantic hollow scooped out of the craggy mountain wall — this is Comb Gill, a splendid example of a hanging valley caused by glacial erosion and containing in its recesses the biggest cave of natural origin in the district. Considering the short distance from the road, the charmingly-wooded climb to its portals, and the impressive surround of crags, the Gill is surprisingly little visited.

Comb Gill apart, Glaramara exhibits sterile slopes of scree and rock on both east and west sides, where deep valleys, Langstrath and Grains Gill, effectively sever it from other high ground, but southwards a broad grass ridge continues with many undulations but with little general change in altitude over Allen Crags to join, at Esk Hause, a high link with the Scafell mass, of which, geographically, Glaramara and Rosthwaite Fell form the northern extremity.

The ancient and beautiful name really applies only to the grey turret of rock at the summit but happily has been commonly adopted for the fell as a whole, and it is pleasing to record that no attempt has been made to rob it of this heritage of the past, as in the case of Blencathra.

Much of Lakeland's appeal derives from the very lovely names of its mountains and valleys and lakes and rivers, which fit the scenery so well. These names were given by the earliest settlers, rough men, invaders and robbers: they were here long before Wordsworth — but they, too, surely had poetry in their hearts?

Comb Head and Raven Crag

Glaramara 3

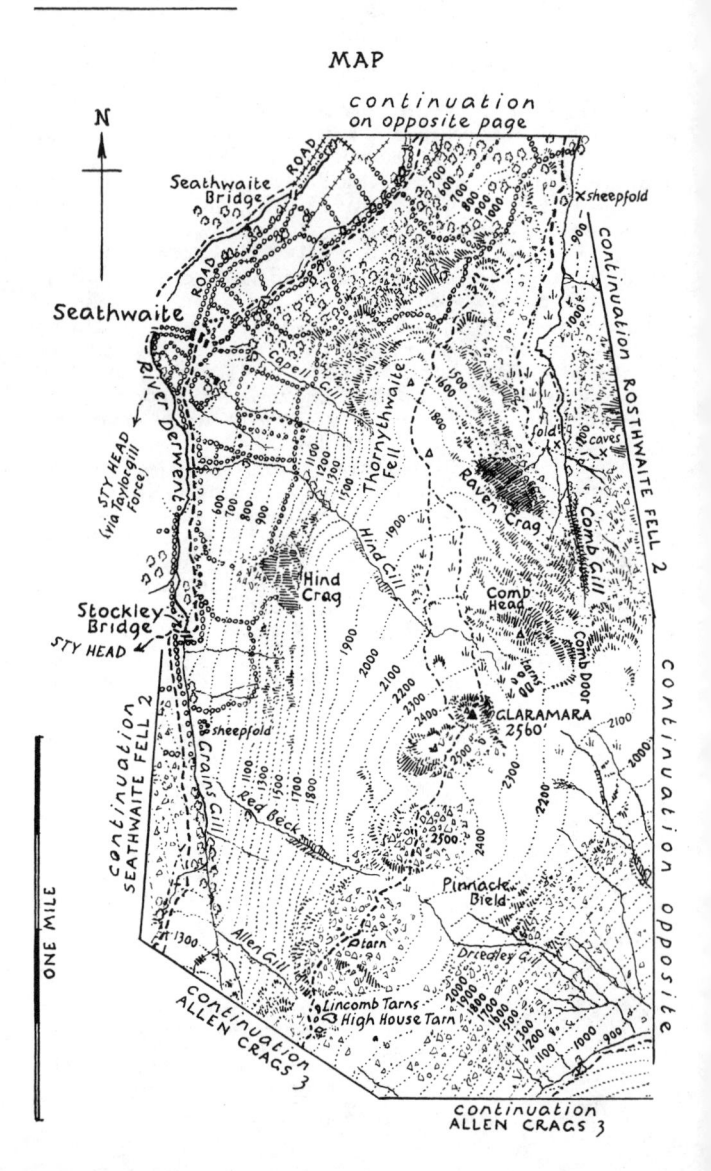

MAP

Glaramara 4

MAP

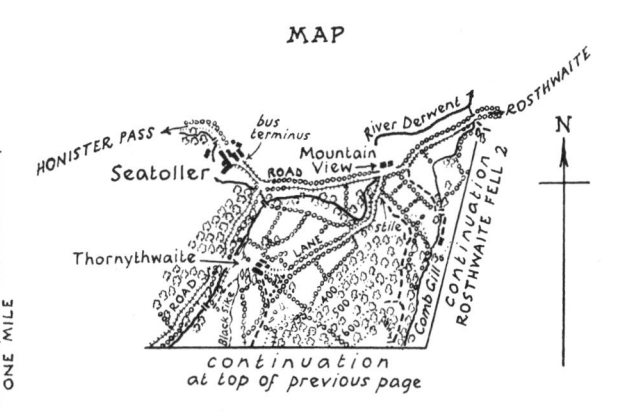

A new generation seems to have sprung up that knows not the pleasant path from Mountain View to Seathwaite, at first along the lane almost to Thornythwaite and then on through the fields; indeed it is unusual nowadays to see anyone using it, even though the hard road to Seathwaite yearly becomes busier and busier with pedestrian and motor traffic and, in the season, is a trial to walk upon. The field-path is an excellent start to a day's walk on the hills; returning, when one no longer has strength left even to climb stiles and ambition has narrowed to the sole objective of reaching the bus terminus before collapse is complete, the road will be rather the easier.

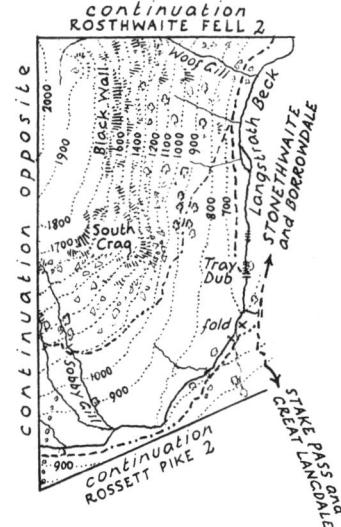

Tray Dub

ASCENT FROM BORROWDALE

2300 feet of ascent : 3¾ miles (from Rosthwaite)

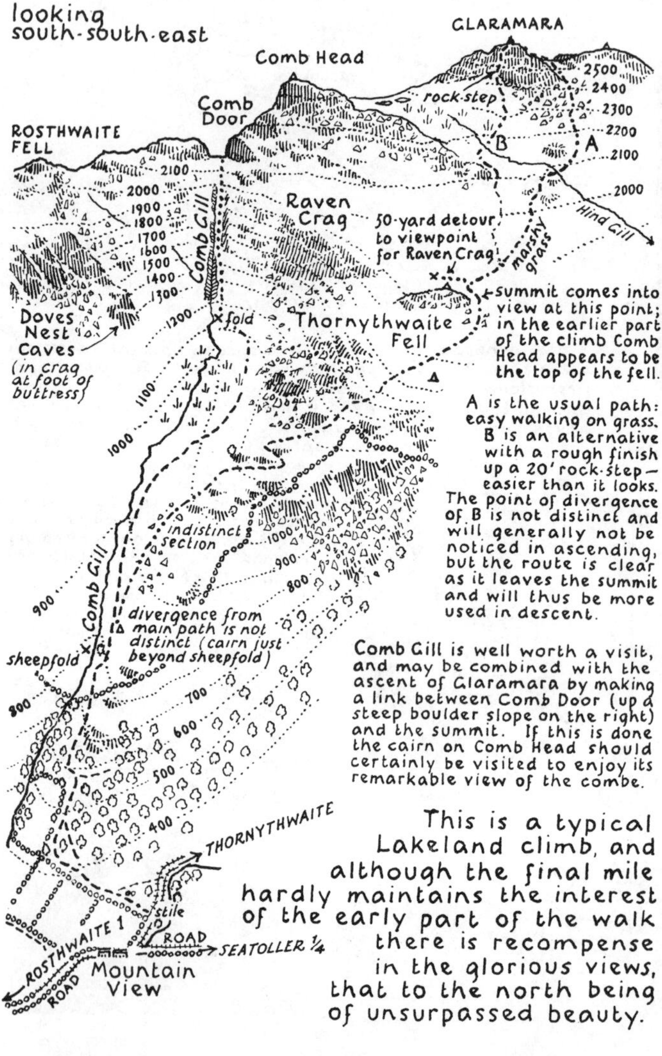
looking south-south-east
GLARAMARA
Comb Head
Comb Door
ROSTHWAITE FELL
rock-step
2500
2400
2300
2200
2100
2000
B
A
Hind Gill
Raven Crag
50-yard detour to viewpoint for Raven Crag
marshy grass
2100
2000
1900
1800
1700
1600
1500
1400
1300
1200
1100
1000
Comb Gill
Doves Nest Caves (in crag at foot of buttress)
fold
Thornythwaite Fell
summit comes into view at this point; in the earlier part of the climb Comb Head appears to be the top of the fell.
indistinct section
1000
900
800
900
Comb Gill
divergence from main path is not distinct (cairn just beyond sheepfold)
sheepfold
800
700
600
500
400
THORNYTHWAITE
stile
ROAD
SEATOLLER ¼
ROSTHWAITE 1
ROAD
Mountain View

A is the usual path: easy walking on grass. B is an alternative with a rough finish up a 20' rock-step — easier than it looks. The point of divergence of B is not distinct and will generally not be noticed in ascending, but the route is clear as it leaves the summit and will thus be more used in descent.

Comb Gill is well worth a visit, and may be combined with the ascent of Glaramara by making a link between Comb Door (up a steep boulder slope on the right) and the summit. If this is done the cairn on Comb Head should certainly be visited to enjoy its remarkable view of the combe.

This is a typical Lakeland climb, and although the final mile hardly maintains the interest of the early part of the walk there is recompense in the glorious views, that to the north being of unsurpassed beauty.

Glaramara 6

ASCENT FROM LANGSTRATH
2300 feet of ascent : 4½ miles (from Stonethwaite)

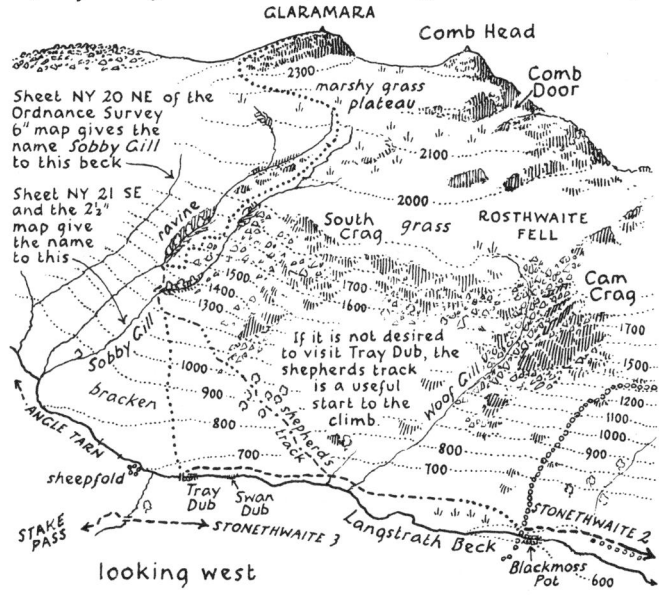

GLARAMARA — Comb Head — Comb Door

Sheet NY 20 NE of the Ordnance Survey 6" map gives the name *Sobby Gill* to this beck

Sheet NY 21 SE and the 2½" map give the name to this —

marshy grass plateau

South Crag — grass — ROSTHWAITE FELL — Cam Crag

Sobby Gill — bracken

If it is not desired to visit Tray Dub, the shepherds track is a useful start to the climb.

Woof Gill

ANGLE TARN ← sheepfold — Tray Dub — Swan Dub
STAKE PASS ← ← STONETHWAITE 3 — Langstrath Beck — STONETHWAITE 2 →
Blackmoss Pot

looking west

This route is submitted without recommendation that it should be tried: it lacks interest above Tray Dub and does not favourably compare with the usual approach over Thornythwaite Fell. One purpose it serves, and serves well, is to introduce Langstrath but otherwise the climb from the valley-floor is dull, although the route will satisfy purists who like to traverse their mountains. Sobby Gill marks the first real break in the long escarpment above Langstrath and the climbing here, pathless on grass, is straightforward, simple and trouble-free: in fact the only easy route on this flank. (Woof Gill looks inviting, but is all stones).

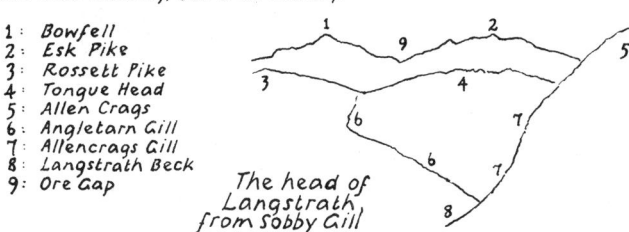

1: Bowfell
2: Esk Pike
3: Rossett Pike
4: Tongue Head
5: Allen Crags
6: Angletarn Gill
7: Allencrags Gill
8: Langstrath Beck
9: Ore Gap

The head of Langstrath from Sobby Gill

Glaramara 7

THE SUMMIT

Twin summits of rock rise from a surrounding ocean of grass, each within its own circle of crags. They are much alike, and of similar elevation, but indisputably the finer is that to the north-east, the top of which is a rocky platform bearing two cairns: this is Glaramara proper, a pleasant halting-place on the right sort of day. The other summit, strictly, is nameless.

DESCENTS: All descents must lead to Borrowdale because all the flanking valleys flow thereto. The usual route starts indistinctly (cairn) down a little ravine from the slight hollow between the two summits. The alternative route, initially rough, goes sharply down north-east from the main cairn and breaches the escarpment at a 20' rock-step, which is easier than it looks. (Ladies wearing skirts, in mixed parties, can best preserve their decorum at this point by insisting on going down first and rejecting offers of male assistance. Conversely, when *ascending* here, they must send the men up first)

The alternative crosses much marshy ground, aided by stepping stones provided by various public benefactors, and joins the usual route 150 yards short of the cairn on Thornythwaite Fell. Comb Gill is too rough and bumpy to give a good way down, and takes an hour longer.

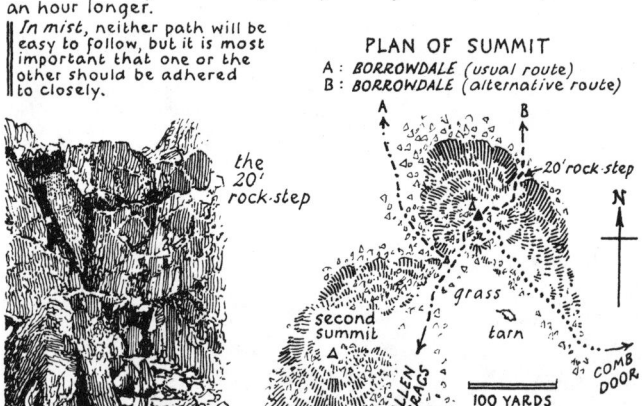

In mist, neither path will be easy to follow, but it is most important that one or the other should be adhered to closely.

the 20' rock-step

PLAN OF SUMMIT
A: *BOROWDALE* (usual route)
B: *BOROWDALE* (alternative route)

Glaramara 8

RIDGE ROUTES

To ALLEN CRAGS, 2572': 1¾ miles : generally SSW
Five depressions : 500 feet of ascent
A delightful walk along a fascinating new path

The time when this ridge-walk was a rough and disagreeable scramble will be within the memory of many walkers, but in recent years a well-cairned and continuous path has come into being, skilfully planned so that the easy passages are linked together, resulting in a simple walk throughout; time formerly spent in hunting the route can now be employed in admiring the excellent views. The track, with many turns and twists and undulations, is fairly distinct (more so, for instance, than that up Glaramara from the valley) and can be followed in any weather. Look out for a perfect mountain tarn in a rocky setting.

Which comes first, the line of cairns or the path? Usually, as here, the cairns, the path materialising gradually as walkers aim from one to the next. Paths often become, in due course, so distinct that the cairns lose their function except in deep snow.

To ROSTHWAITE FELL (BESSYBOOT), 1807': 1¼ miles
ESE, then NE and N
Not as good as it looks on the map
200 feet of ascent

Confusing, marshy, pathless terrain makes this a disappointing walk. (Wanted: a line of cairns!). If the idea is to find an alternative way down to Borrowdale, it should be discarded. The easiest way lies on the Langstrath side. Definitely not a walk to attempt in mist.

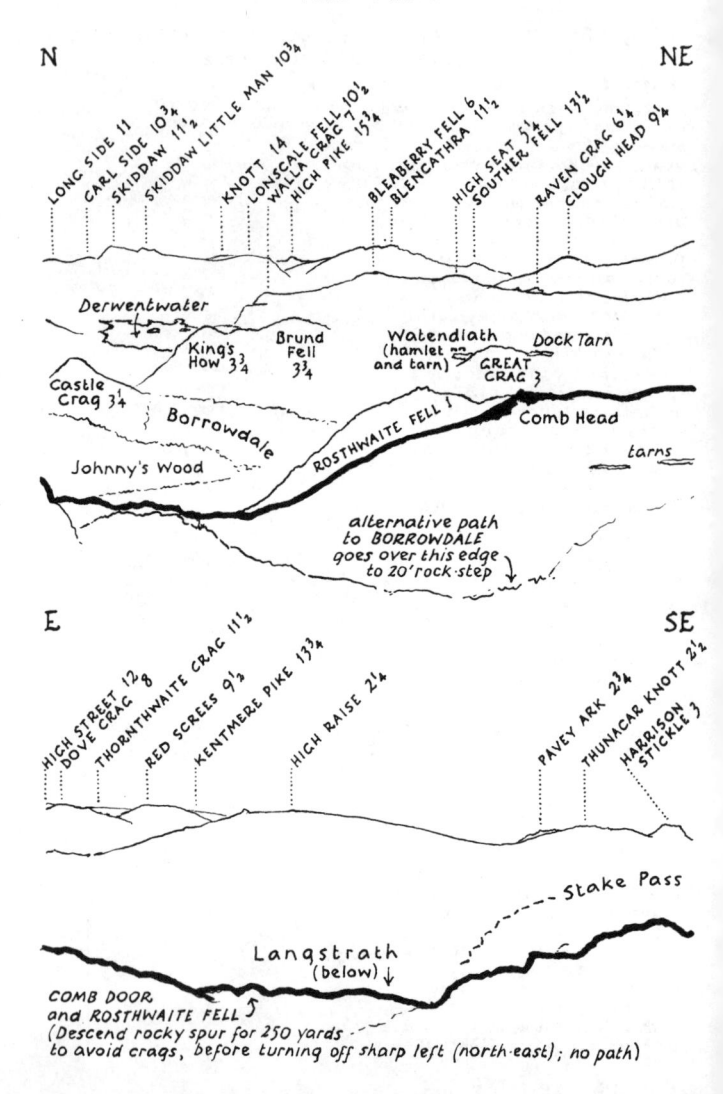

Glaramara 9

THE VIEW

N — LONG SIDE 11, CARL SIDE 10¾, SKIDDAW 11½, SKIDDAW LITTLE MAN 10¾, KNOTT 14, LONSCALE FELL 10½, WALLA CRAG 7, HIGH PIKE 13¾, BLEABERRY FELL 6, BLENCATHRA 11½, HIGH SEAT 5½, SOUTHER FELL 13½, RAVEN CRAG 6¾, CLOUGH HEAD 9¼ — NE

Derwentwater

King's How 3¾, Brund Fell 3¾, Watendlath (hamlet and tarn), Dock Tarn, GREAT CRAG 3

Castle Crag 3¼

Borrowdale

ROSTHWAITE FELL 1 — Comb Head

Johnny's Wood

tarns

alternative path to BORROWDALE goes over this edge to 20' rock step

E — HIGH STREET 12, DOVE CRAG 8, THORNTHWAITE CRAG 11½, RED SCREES 9½, KENTMERE PIKE 13¾, HIGH RAISE 2¼, PAVEY ARK 2¾, THUNACAR KNOTT 2½, HARRISON STICKLE 3 — SE

Stake Pass

Langstrath (below) ↓

COMB DOOR and ROSTHWAITE FELL
(Descend rocky spur for 250 yards to avoid crags, before turning off sharp left (north-east); no path)

Glaramara 10

THE VIEW

NE — Great Dodd 8½, Stybarrow Dodd 8, Raise 7½, White Side 6¾, Helvellyn Lower Man 6½, Helvellyn 6½, Nethermost Pike 6½, Dollywaggon Pike 6½, Rest Dodd 11¾, High Raise 12¾, Fairfield 7, Hart Crag 7½ — E

Ullscarf 3

Eagle Crag 2, Sergeant's Crag 1¾

tarn

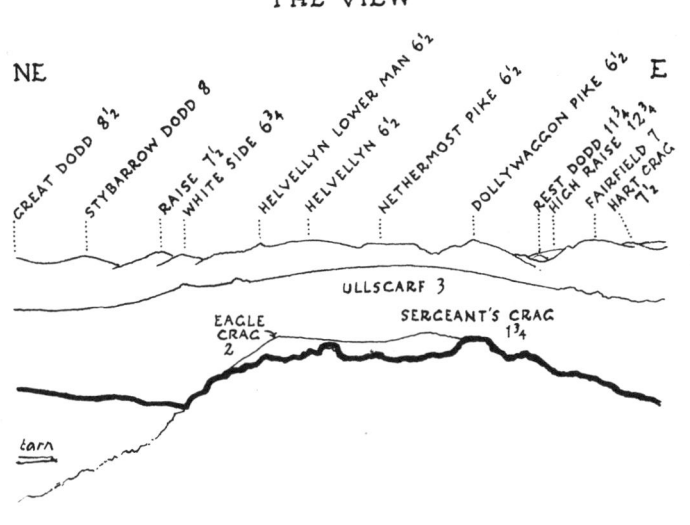

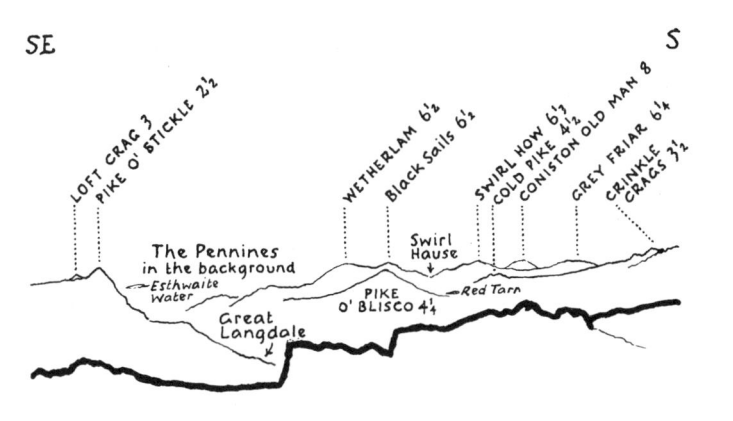

SE — Loft Crag 3, Pike o' Stickle 2½, Wetherlam 6½, Black Sails 6½, Swirl How 6⅓, Cold Pike 4½, Coniston Old Man 8, Grey Friar 6¼, Crinkle Crags 3½ — S

The Pennines in the background
Esthwaite Water
Swirl Hause
Red Tarn
Pike o' Blisco 4¼
Great Langdale

The thick line marks the visible boundaries of the fell from the main cairn

Glaramara 11

THE VIEW

S — SW

Bowfell 2½, Ore Gap, Esk Pike 2, Allen Crags 1½, Esk Hause, Ill Crag 2½, Great End 2

third summit
(a stony plateau with a crown of rocks)
From Rossett Pass this seems to be the highest point of the fell, the true summit being concealed by it.

ridge path to ALLEN CRAGS

W — NW

Red Pike 5, Green Gable 2, Scoat Fell 5½, Pillar 4¾, West Cumberland Coast, Brandreth 2¼, High Crag 4½, High Stile 5½, Blake Fell 10, Grey Knotts 2, Carling Knott 10, Mellbreak 8, Fleetwith Pike 3½

BASE BROWN 1½

Gillercombe Buttress, Honister Crag

← Sty Head

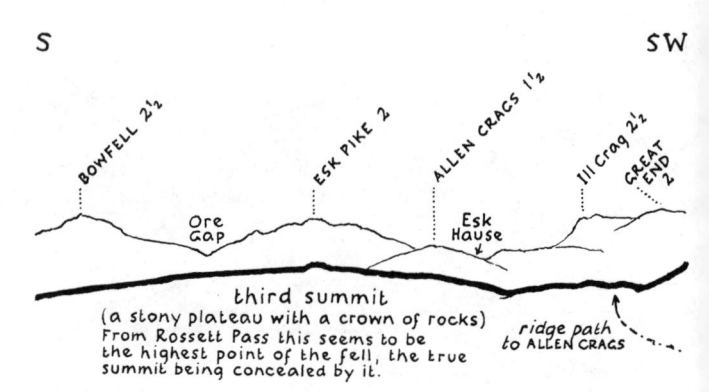

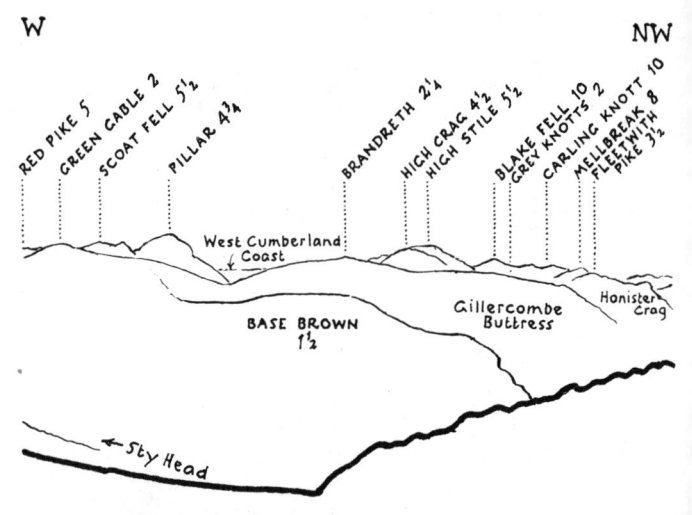

The figures accompanying the names of fells indicate distances in miles

Glaramara 12

THE VIEW

SW — panorama labels: LINGMELL 2¾, MIDDLE FELL 6½, SEATALLAN 6¾, GREAT GABLE 2¼, Irish Sea, YEWBARROW 4¾, ← Sty Head, Aaron Slack, SEATHWAITE FELL 1

second summit (this appears to be higher than the main summit, but there can be little difference for the upper 100 feet of Lingmell (2649') is seen overtopping it.

ridge path to ALLEN CRAGS

BORROWDALE (usual path) **W**

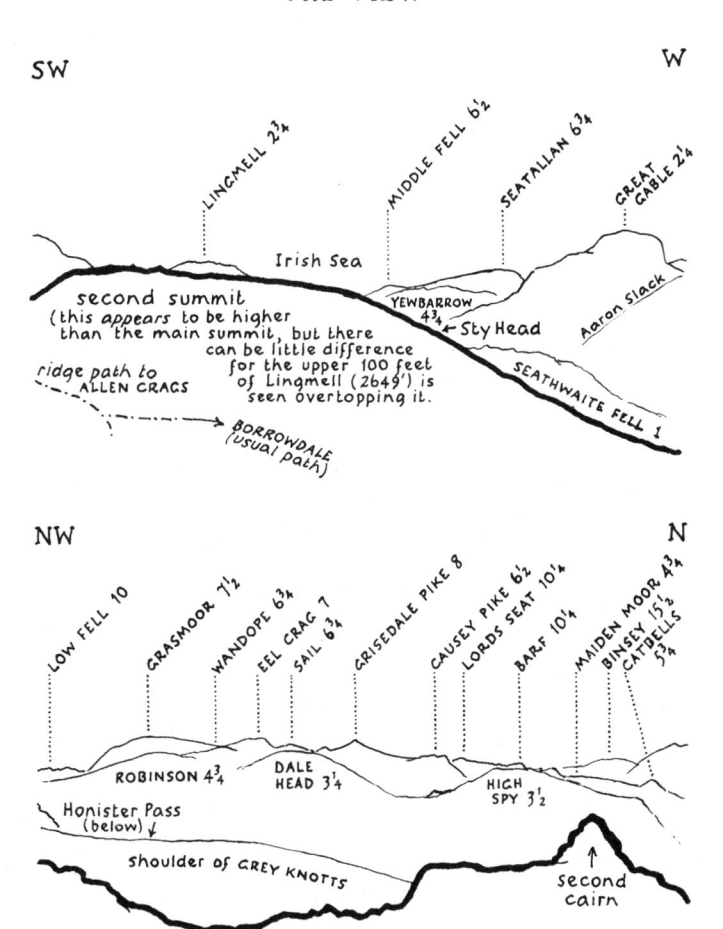

NW — panorama labels: LOW FELL 10, GRASMOOR 7½, WANDOPE 6¾, EEL CRAG 7, SAIL 6¾, GRISEDALE PIKE 8, CAUSEY PIKE 6½, LORDS SEAT 10¼, BARF 10¼, MAIDEN MOOR 4¾, BINSEY 15½, CATBELLS 5¾

ROBINSON 4¾, DALE HEAD 3¾, HIGH SPY 3½

Honister Pass (below) ↓

shoulder of GREY KNOTTS

second cairn **N**

Glaramara's unique situation, in the heart of the district yet isolated by deep valleys, is emphasised by the splendid view. Overtopped by many fells but overshadowed by none, the summit provides a spacious and interesting panorama. But the best scene of all is that of the curve of Borrowdale with Derwentwater and Skiddaw beyond: a superb picture.

Great Carrs 2575'

from Greenburn Beck

Great Carrs 2

NATURAL FEATURES

Curved like a scythe, the shapely ridge springing from the fields of Little Langdale to the crest of Rough Crags and climbing gradually thence along the grassy rim of Wet Side Edge to a lofty altitude between deep valleys, has little to arouse interest until the mild excitement of a bouldery stairway skirting the edge of crags promises better things ahead. The airy summit of Great Carrs follows at once, a splendid perch on the edge of the profound abyss of Greenburn. A short distance beyond, the ridge terminates in the peak of Swirl How.

Apart from its eastern precipice Great Carrs has few features out of the ordinary and the western slopes going down to the valley of the Duddon are generally dull: on this flank the cliffs of Hell Gill Pike, below the subsidiary summit of Little Carrs, are more worthy of note.

The ridge, which bounds Wrynose Pass on the south, separates the waters of the Brathay from those of Greenburn, but they mingle finally in Little Langdale Tarn. Westwards, Hell Gill, in a steep ravine, is the most prominent of the early feeders of the Duddon.

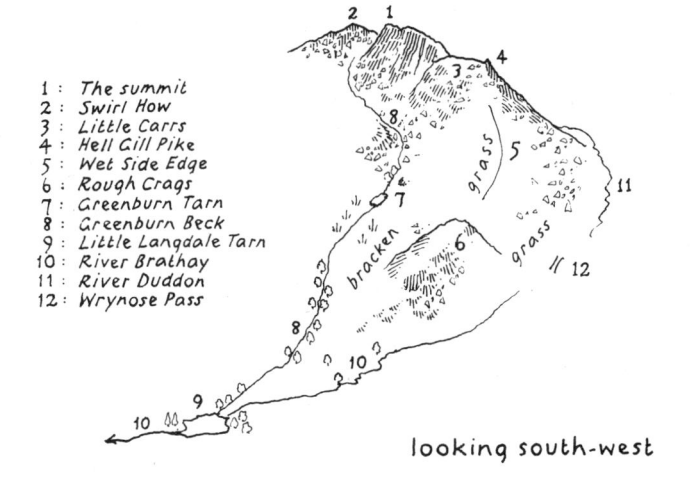

1 : The summit
2 : Swirl How
3 : Little Carrs
4 : Hell Gill Pike
5 : Wet Side Edge
6 : Rough Crags
7 : Greenburn Tarn
8 : Greenburn Beck
9 : Little Langdale Tarn
10 : River Brathay
11 : River Duddon
12 : Wrynose Pass

looking south-west

Great Carrs 3

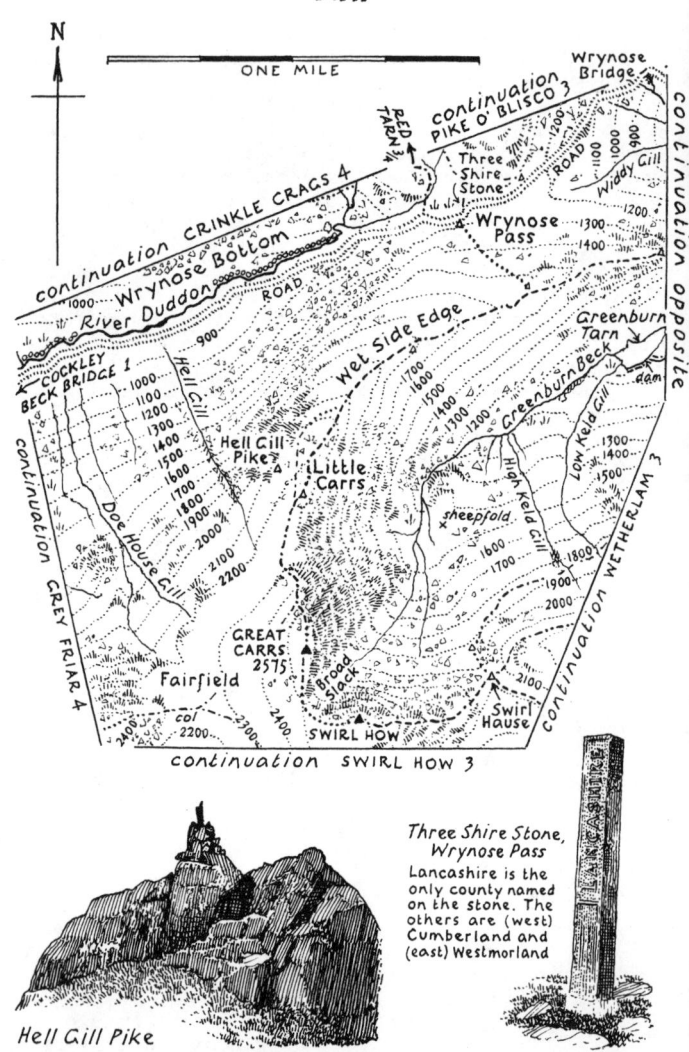

MAP

Three Shire Stone, Wrynose Pass

Lancashire is the only county named on the stone. The others are (west) Cumberland and (east) Westmorland

Hell Gill Pike

Great Carrs 4

MAP

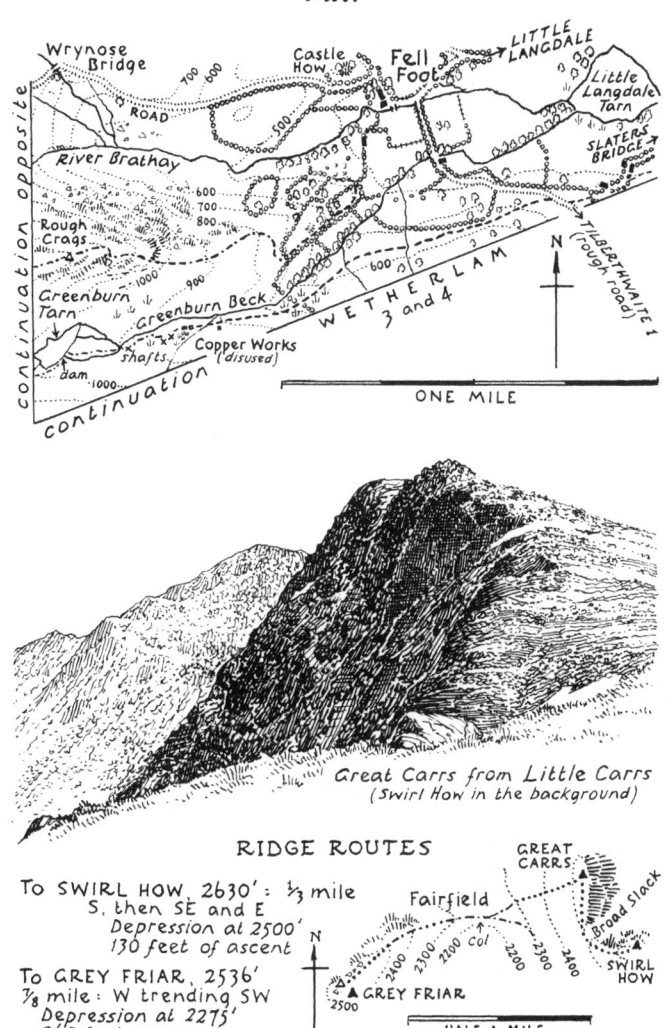

Great Carrs from Little Carrs
(Swirl How in the background)

RIDGE ROUTES

To SWIRL HOW, 2630': ⅓ mile
S, then SE and E
Depression at 2500'
130 feet of ascent

To GREY FRIAR, 2536'
⅞ mile: W trending SW
Depression at 2275'
265 feet of ascent

Both easy walks, but Grey Friar is not a place to visit in mist.

Great Carrs 5

ASCENT FROM LITTLE LANGDALE
2350 feet of ascent
4 miles (from the village)

looking west-south-west

Wet Side Edge is very easy. Ignore tracks contouring to the right from the ridge. (When descending by this route a variation path going left from the top cairn on Little Carrs is a trap. Keep to the ridge)

If there is a strong wind, listen to the music of the stones of this big cairn

The natural line of ascent of a ridge starts from its foot, but be it noted that the tempting ridge running up to Great Carrs from Fell Foot has no right of way in the walled intakes at its base, nor are the gates openable (whether Copper Works there *is* such a word or not!). The route shown on the diagram should not be used without permission from the farm. Better, gain the ridge from Greenburn Tarn. (If descending by the ridge the natural tendency is to follow the fair path over Rough Crags (instead of going down to Wrynose) in which case the same difficulties will be met in reverse and one should seek not permission but forgiveness — if observed!)

SWIRL HOW — GREAT CARRS — Broad Slack — wreckage of aeroplane — Little Carrs — Wet Side Edge — Rough Crags — DUDDON VALLEY — Wrynose Pass — Three Shire Stone — sheepfold — bracken — route to ridge avoiding intakes — Greenburn Tarn (reservoir) — shafts — Greenburn Copper Works (disused) — Greenburn Beck — hurdle — fold — hurdle — gate — barn — Wrynose Bridge — ROAD — DUNGEON GHYLL — Bridge End — Castle How — Fell Foot — BLEA TARN & DUNGEON GHYLL — River Brathay — TILBERTHWAITE — rough ROAD — Little Langdale Tarn — Little Langdale — LITTLE LANGDALE village — Black Hole Quarry (disused) — tunnel — Low Hall Garth — Slaters Bridge — LITTLE LANGDALE village

The ascent via Wrynose is quick and easy; via Greenburn it ends in a steep but not difficult scramble (Broad Slack). There is no public path direct from Fell Foot

Great Carrs 6

THE SUMMIT

1 : slope of Swirl How
2 : Coniston Old Man
3 : Brim Fell
4 : Dow Crag

south summit

The easily-graded upper western slope of Great Carrs breaks very abruptly into a long eastern precipice, the highest point of the fell therefore being on the rim, and here, on a small outcrop, is the cairn, airily perched in a splendid position high above the great hollow formed by the deep-set Greenburn valley in its circle of peaks. A short tour along the ridge, which is grassy on either side of the cairn, reveals striking gullies falling very steeply in the direction of Greenburn Tarn.

An unnatural and unwelcome adornment to the top is provided by the wreckage of an aeroplane, 150 yards south of the cairn. It is easy to reconstruct the accident. The aeroplane, travelling from west to east, failed to clear the ridge by a few feet only; at the place of impact the undercarriage was ripped off (and still lies there in a rough grave of stones) but the crippled machine went on over the edge to crash far down the precipice: the remains can be discerned from the top of Broad Slack.

DESCENTS : Go along the declining ridge, over Little Carrs, to Wet Side Edge, where incline *left* for Wrynose Pass, *right* for Greenburn Tarn — an easy descent, safe in mist.

The summit ridge, looking north

Great Carrs 7

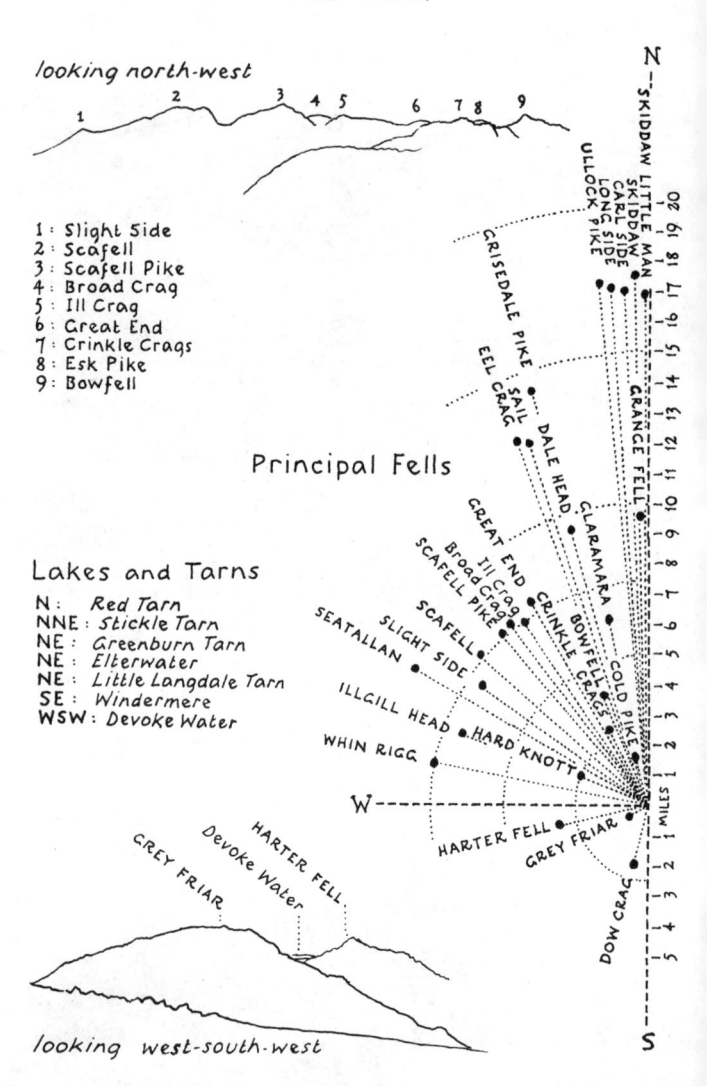

THE VIEW

looking north-west

1 : Slight Side
2 : Scafell
3 : Scafell Pike
4 : Broad Crag
5 : Ill Crag
6 : Great End
7 : Crinkle Crags
8 : Esk Pike
9 : Bowfell

Principal Fells

SKIDDAW LITTLE MAN
SKIDDAW
CARL SIDE
LONG SIDE
ULLOCK PIKE
GRISEDALE PIKE
SAIL
EEL CRAG
DALE HEAD
GRANGE FELL
GREAT END
ILL CRAG
BROAD CRAG
SCAFELL PIKE
GLARAMARA
CRINKLE CRAGS
BOWFELL
COLD PIKE
SCAFELL
SLIGHT SIDE
SEATALLAN
ILLGILL HEAD
HARD KNOTT
WHIN RIGG
HARTER FELL
GREY FRIAR
DOW CRAG

Lakes and Tarns

N : *Red Tarn*
NNE : *Stickle Tarn*
NE : *Greenburn Tarn*
NE : *Elterwater*
NE : *Little Langdale Tarn*
SE : *Windermere*
WSW : *Devoke Water*

GREY FRIAR
Devoke Water
HARTER FELL

looking west-south-west

Great Carrs 8

THE VIEW

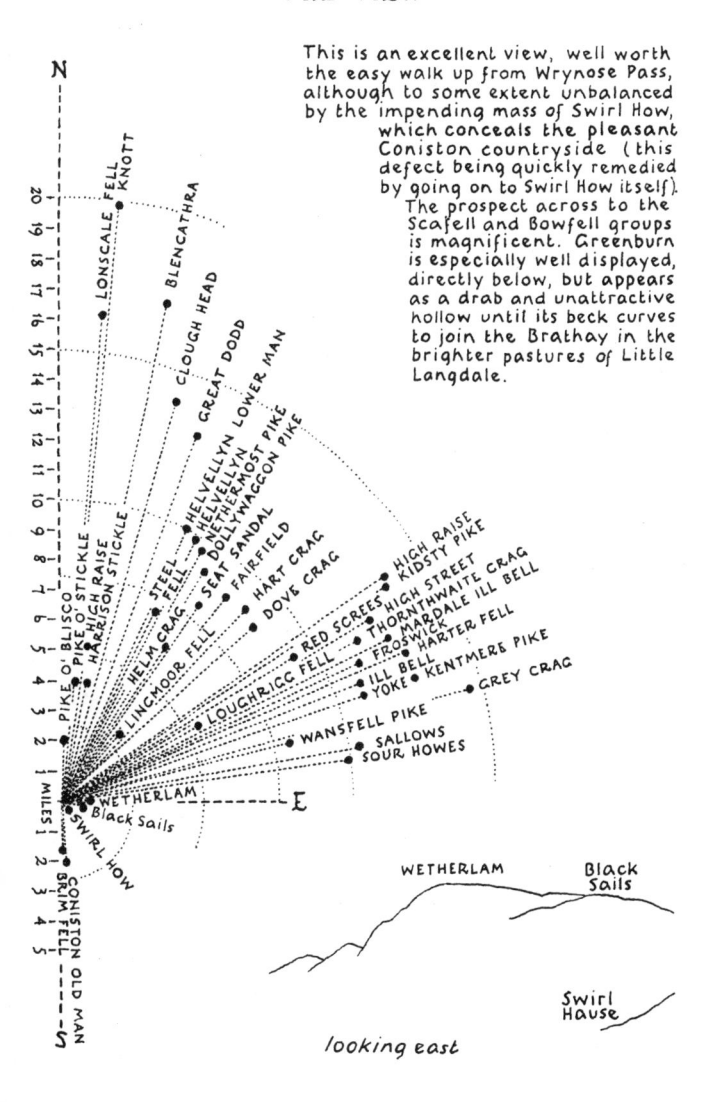

This is an excellent view, well worth the easy walk up from Wrynose Pass, although to some extent unbalanced by the impending mass of Swirl How, which conceals the pleasant Coniston countryside (this defect being quickly remedied by going on to Swirl How itself). The prospect across to the Scafell and Bowfell groups is magnificent. Greenburn is especially well displayed, directly below, but appears as a drab and unattractive hollow until its beck curves to join the Brathay in the brighter pastures of Little Langdale.

looking east

Great End 2984'

Rosthwaite •

Seathwaite •

GREAT GABLE ▲   ▲ GLARAMARA

•
Wasdale   ▲ GREAT
Head   END   Dungeon
  ▲   ▲   Ghyll •
SCAFELL BOWFELL
PIKE

MILES
0 1 2 3 4 5

from Sty Head

Great End 2

NATURAL FEATURES

Nobody who is familiar with the topography of the Scafell area will have any doubts why Great End was so named: there could not have been a more descriptive choice for the tremendous northern buttress of the mass. Great it is, and the end of the highest plateau in the country.

Without losing much altitude, the lofty spine of Scafell Pike extends north-eastwards a mile to the domed summit of Great End, which, when approached in this direction, has little to show other than a bouldery waste, a stony wilderness. But the vast northern fall of the mountain is one of the finest scenes in the district, awe-inspiring in its massive strength and all the more imposing for being eternally in shadow. The summit breaks immediately in a long cliff seamed by dark gullies, below which a broad shelf holds Sprinkling Tarn and continues as Seathwaite Fell, but a shoulder (the Band) also fiercely scarped and severed from the main fell by the deep ravine of Skew Gill, runs down to Sty Head.

When mist wreathes the summit and clings like smoke in the gullies, when ravens soar above the lonely crags, when snow lies deep and curtains of ice bejewel the gaunt cliffs, then Great End is indeed an impressive sight. Sunshine never mellows this grim scene but only adds harshness.

This is the true Lakeland of the fellwalker, the sort of terrain that calls him back time after time, the sort of memory that haunts his long winter exile.

It is not the pretty places — the flowery lanes of Grasmere or Derwentwater's wooded bays — that keep him restless in his bed; it is the magnificent ones.

Places like Great End.....

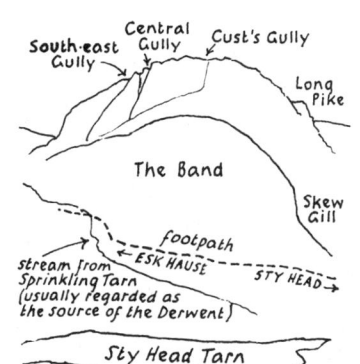

Key to drawing opposite.

Great End 3

*Borrowdale
from the top of
Central Gully*

Great End 4

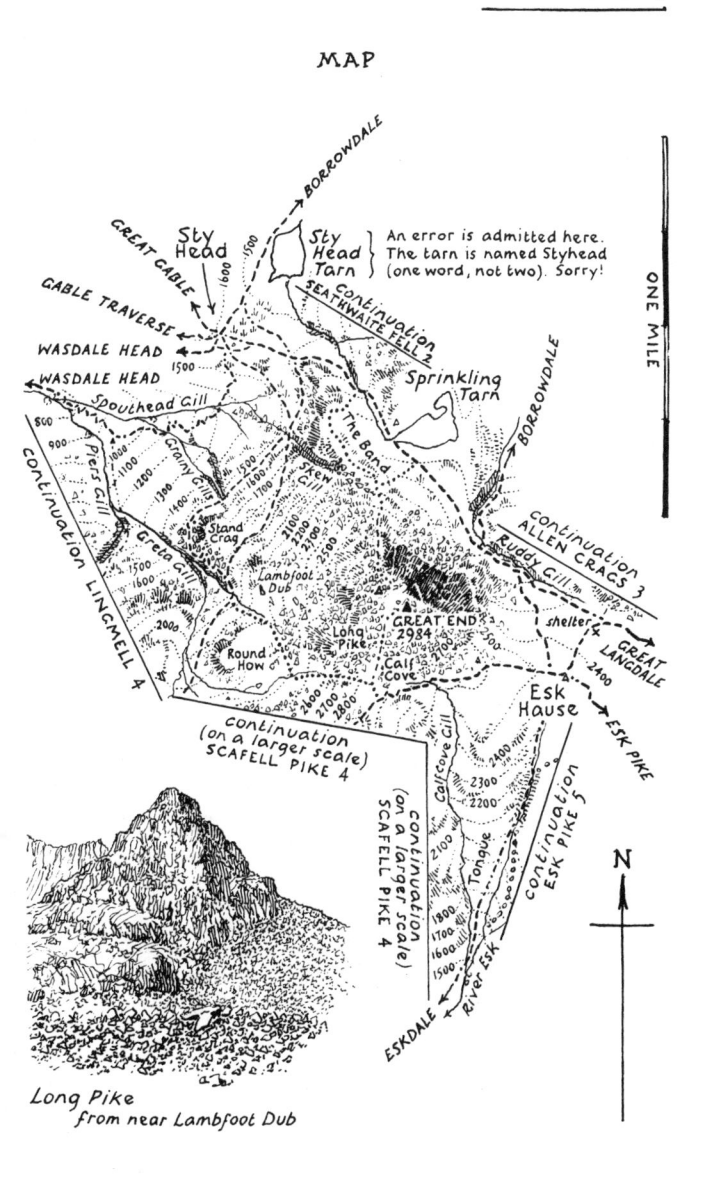

MAP

Long Pike from near Lambfoot Dub

Great End 5

Sty Head

Once upon a time Sty Head was a simple pass between Wasdale and Borrowdale, providing also a link with Great Langdale: the two routes served the dalesmen sufficiently and no others were needed in the vicinity to carry them about their business.

Then, a century ago, came the first walkers, in occasional twos and threes, hesitant to venture into this wild place; and later, in greater numbers, with growing confidence and much more often — for Sty Head became known as a convenient springboard for excursions into the surrounding mountains.

At the present time, it is doubtful whether Sty Head is without a visitor on any day of any year; and on most days scores, and, in high summer, hundreds of walkers pass this way — some, as the early dalesmen, seeking only an easy crossing from one valley to another, but the majority starting from this point to ascend the hills and win for themselves one more memorable experience. The needs of these happy wanderers could only be met by additional paths, and their boots have brought into existence a network of well-trodden tracks.

It is important to know these various tracks and the purpose and objective of each.

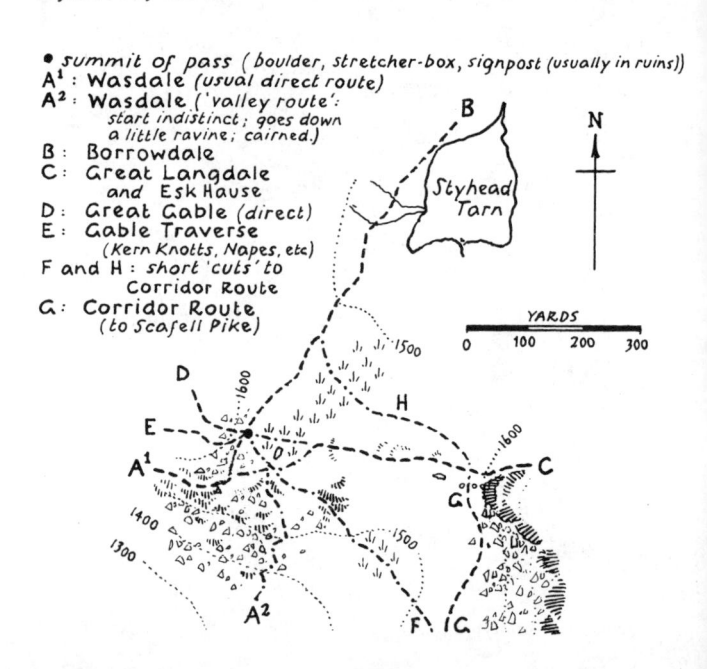

- • *summit of pass (boulder, stretcher-box, signpost (usually in ruins))*
- A^1: **Wasdale** *(usual direct route)*
- A^2: **Wasdale** *('valley route':*
    start indistinct; goes down
    a little ravine; cairned.)
- B: **Borrowdale**
- C: **Great Langdale**
    and **Esk Hause**
- D: **Great Gable** *(direct)*
- E: **Gable Traverse**
    (Kern Knotts, Napes, etc)
- F and H: *short 'cuts' to*
    Corridor Route
- G: **Corridor Route**
    (to Scafell Pike)

Great End 6

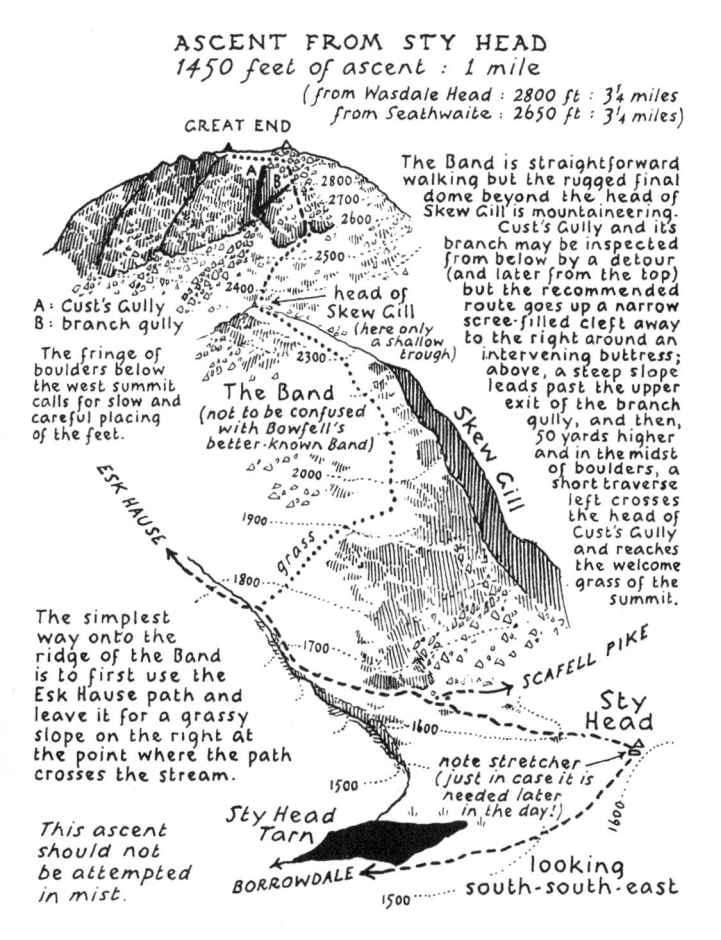

ASCENT FROM STY HEAD
1450 feet of ascent : 1 mile
(from Wasdale Head: 2800 ft : 3¼ miles
from Seathwaite: 2650 ft : 3¼ miles)

GREAT END

A: Cust's Gully
B: branch gully

The fringe of boulders below the west summit calls for slow and careful placing of the feet.

head of Skew Gill (here only a shallow trough)

The Band (not to be confused with Bowfell's better-known Band)

Skew Gill

ESK HAUSE

grass

SCAFELL PIKE

Sty Head

note stretcher (just in case it is needed later in the day!)

Sty Head Tarn

BORROWDALE

looking south-south-east

The Band is straightforward walking but the rugged final dome beyond the head of Skew Gill is mountaineering. Cust's Gully and its branch may be inspected from below by a detour (and later from the top) but the recommended route goes up a narrow scree-filled cleft away to the right around an intervening buttress; above, a steep slope leads past the upper exit of the branch gully, and then, 50 yards higher and in the midst of boulders, a short traverse left crosses the head of Cust's Gully and reaches the welcome grass of the summit.

The simplest way onto the ridge of the Band is to first use the Esk Hause path and leave it for a grassy slope on the right at the point where the path crosses the stream.

This ascent should not be attempted in mist.

Subject to the qualification that the last section is a very rough climb, this is an excellent ascent, giving a satisfying sense of achievement. The route depicted is within the capacity of energetic walkers; experienced scramblers may vary it by ascending Skew Gill (instead of the Band) and by finishing up the branch gully, both of which entail some handling of easy rocks.

Great End 7

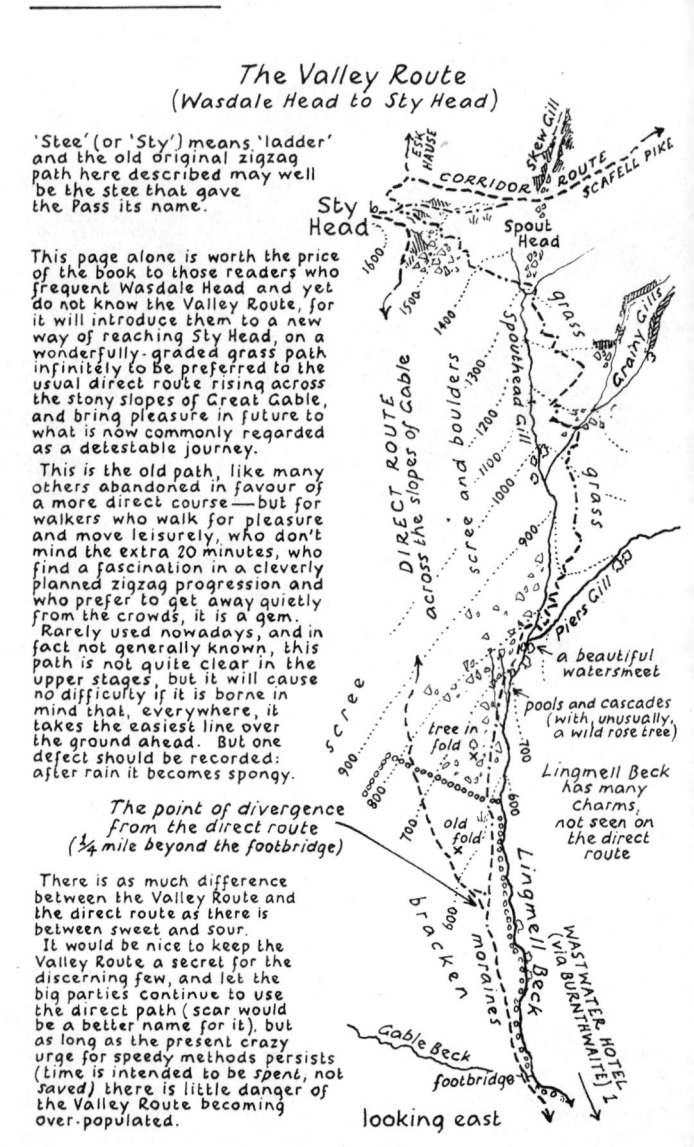

The Valley Route
(Wasdale Head to Sty Head)

'Stee' (or 'Sty') means 'ladder' and the old original zigzag path here described may well be the stee that gave the Pass its name.

This page alone is worth the price of the book to those readers who frequent Wasdale Head and yet do not know the Valley Route, for it will introduce them to a new way of reaching Sty Head, on a wonderfully-graded grass path infinitely to be preferred to the usual direct route rising across the stony slopes of Great Gable, and bring pleasure in future to what is now commonly regarded as a detestable journey.

This is the old path, like many others abandoned in favour of a more direct course — but for walkers who walk for pleasure and move leisurely, who don't mind the extra 20 minutes, who find a fascination in a cleverly planned zigzag progression and who prefer to get away quietly from the crowds, it is a gem. Rarely used nowadays, and in fact not generally known, this path is not quite clear in the upper stages, but it will cause no difficulty if it is borne in mind that, everywhere, it takes the easiest line over the ground ahead. But one defect should be recorded: after rain it becomes spongy.

The point of divergence from the direct route (¼ mile beyond the footbridge)

There is as much difference between the Valley Route and the direct route as there is between sweet and sour.

It would be nice to keep the Valley Route a secret for the discerning few, and let the big parties continue to use the direct path (scar would be a better name for it), but as long as the present crazy urge for speedy methods persists (time is intended to be spent, not saved) there is little danger of the Valley Route becoming over-populated.

a beautiful watersmeet

pools and cascades (with, unusually, a wild rose tree)

Lingmell Beck has many charms, not seen on the direct route

looking east

Great End 8

ASCENT FROM WASDALE HEAD
2750 feet of ascent: 4 miles

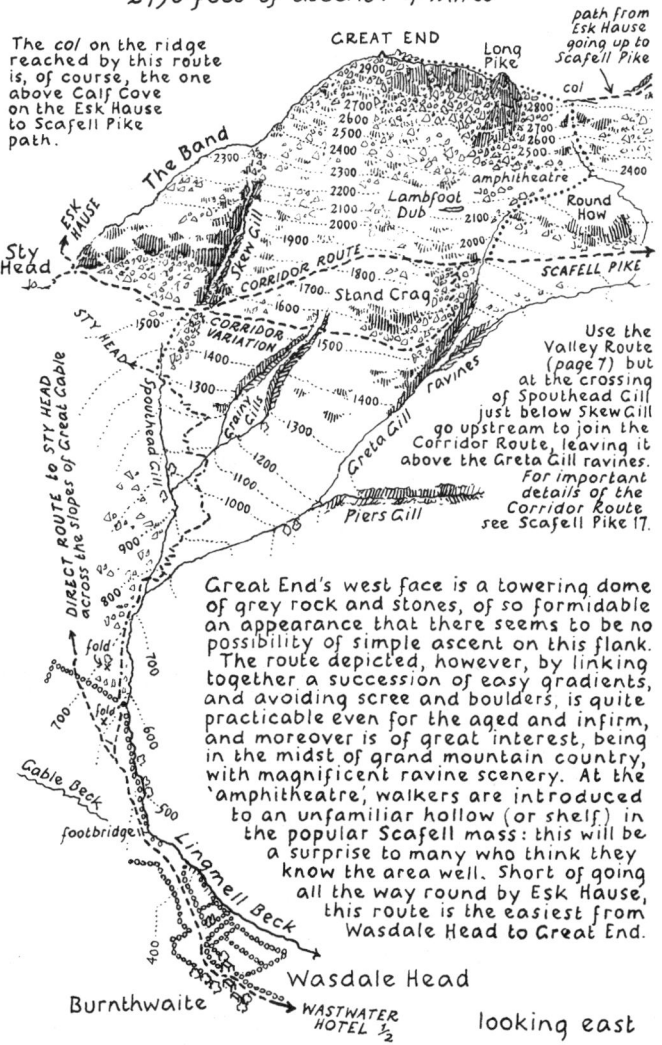

The col on the ridge reached by this route is, of course, the one above Calf Cove on the Esk Hause to Scafell Pike path.

path from Esk Hause going up to Scafell Pike

Use the Valley Route (page 7) but at the crossing of Spouthead Gill just below Skew Gill go upstream to join the Corridor Route, leaving it above the Greta Gill ravines. For important details of the Corridor Route see Scafell Pike 17.

Great End's west face is a towering dome of grey rock and stones, of so formidable an appearance that there seems to be no possibility of simple ascent on this flank. The route depicted, however, by linking together a succession of easy gradients, and avoiding scree and boulders, is quite practicable even for the aged and infirm, and moreover is of great interest, being in the midst of grand mountain country, with magnificent ravine scenery. At the 'amphitheatre', walkers are introduced to an unfamiliar hollow (or shelf) in the popular Scafell mass: this will be a surprise to many who think they know the area well. Short of going all the way round by Esk Hause, this route is the easiest from Wasdale Head to Great End.

looking east

Great End 9

ASCENT FROM BORROWDALE
2650 feet of ascent : 5 miles from Seatoller

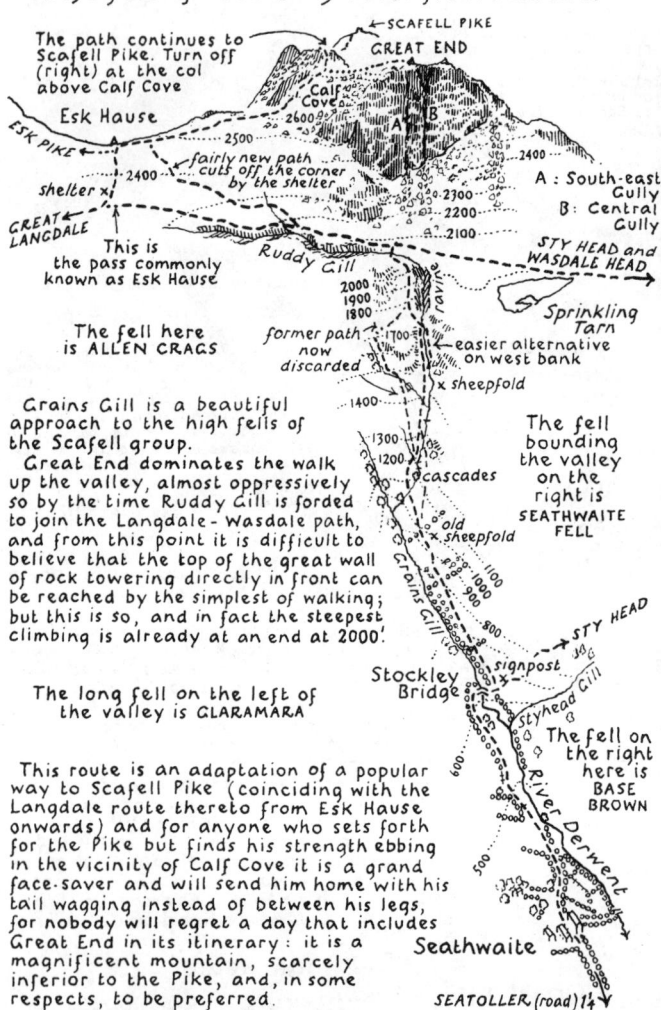

The path continues to Scafell Pike. Turn off (right) at the col above Calf Cove

← SCAFELL PIKE
GREAT END
Calf Cove

ESK PIKE
Esk Hause
2600
2500
fairly new path cuts off the corner by the shelter
shelter ×
2400
2300
2200
2100
2400

A: South-east Gully
B: Central Gully

GREAT LANGDALE
This is the pass commonly known as Esk Hause

Ruddy Gill

STY HEAD and WASDALE HEAD

2000
1900
1800

The fell here is ALLEN CRAGS

former path now discarded
1700
easier alternative on west bank

Sprinkling Tarn

× sheepfold
1400

Grains Gill is a beautiful approach to the high fells of the Scafell group.
  Great End dominates the walk up the valley, almost oppressively so by the time Ruddy Gill is forded to join the Langdale-Wasdale path, and from this point it is difficult to believe that the top of the great wall of rock towering directly in front can be reached by the simplest of walking; but this is so, and in fact the steepest climbing is already at an end at 2000!

1300
1200
cascades
old sheepfold
1000
900
800

The fell bounding the valley on the right is SEATHWAITE FELL

STY HEAD
signpost

Stockley Bridge

Styhead Gill

The long fell on the left of the valley is GLARAMARA

The fell on the right here is BASE BROWN

This route is an adaptation of a popular way to Scafell Pike (coinciding with the Langdale route thereto from Esk Hause onwards) and for anyone who sets forth for the Pike but finds his strength ebbing in the vicinity of Calf Cove it is a grand face-saver and will send him home with his tail wagging instead of between his legs, for nobody will regret a day that includes Great End in its itinerary: it is a magnificent mountain, scarcely inferior to the Pike, and, in some respects, to be preferred.

600
500
River Derwent

Seathwaite

SEATOLLER (road) 1½

looking south-south-west

Great End 10

ASCENT FROM GREAT LANGDALE
2900 feet of ascent : 5 miles (from Dungeon Ghyll Old Hotel)

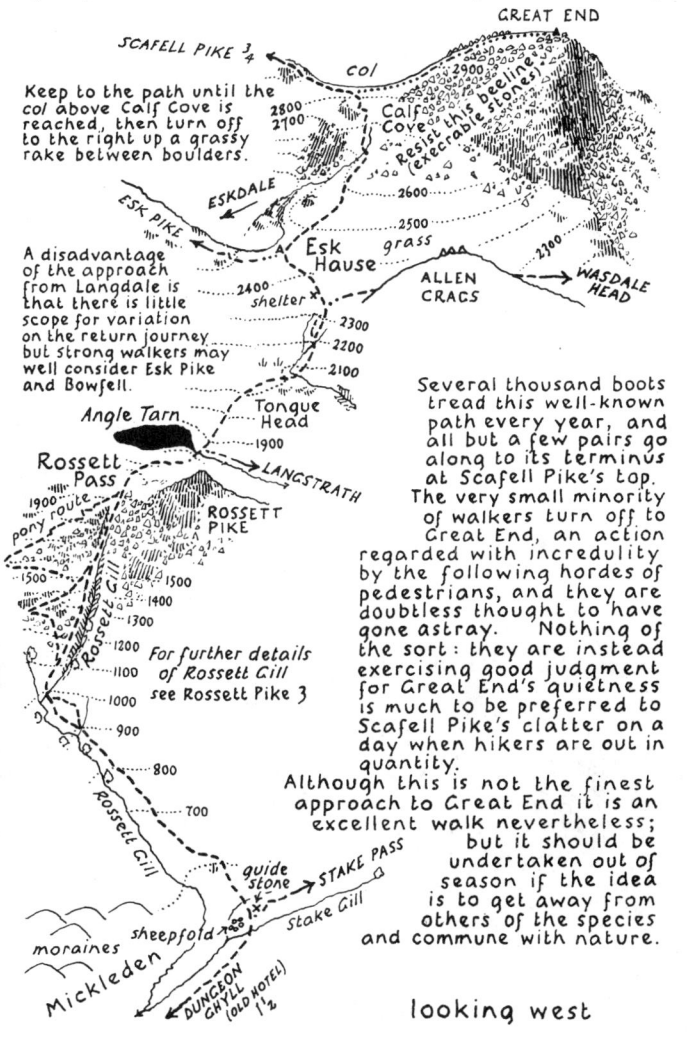

Keep to the path until the col above Calf Cove is reached, then turn off to the right up a grassy rake between boulders.

A disadvantage of the approach from Langdale is that there is little scope for variation on the return journey but strong walkers may well consider Esk Pike and Bowfell.

For further details of Rossett Gill see Rossett Pike 3

Several thousand boots tread this well-known path every year, and all but a few pairs go along to its terminus at Scafell Pike's top. The very small minority of walkers turn off to Great End, an action regarded with incredulity by the following hordes of pedestrians, and they are doubtless thought to have gone astray. Nothing of the sort: they are instead exercising good judgment for Great End's quietness is much to be preferred to Scafell Pike's clatter on a day when hikers are out in quantity.

Although this is not the finest approach to Great End it is an excellent walk nevertheless; but it should be undertaken out of season if the idea is to get away from others of the species and commune with nature.

looking west

Great End 11

Cust's Gully

Sooner or later, every Lakeland walker hears mention of Cust's Gully, but written references to it are confined to rock-climbing literature, which dismiss the place as of little consequence although grudgingly conceding that there is one small and insignificant pitch.

Looking up from the path near Sprinkling Tarn, Cust's Gully is situated high to the western end of the Great End cliffs, a clue to its position being given by the long conspicuous tongue of light-coloured stones debouching from it. On this approach the gully is concealed until its foot is reached, when it is revealed suddenly and impressively as a straight rising channel of scree between vertical walls that wedge a great boulder high above the bed of the gully and thereby provide a sure means of identification. There is no mistaking Cust's Gully.

Progress up the stony bed of the gully is easy but very rough for 50 yards to the pitch, where a chockstone blocks the way. Sloping shelves of rock, one on each side, lead up beyond the obstruction, that on the left requiring an awkward final movement, that on the right steepening for a few critical feet. The walls of the gully are here quite vertical, and directly above is poised the wedged boulder.

This pitch is the one difficulty: above there is nothing but simple scrambling to the top of the gully. The pitch may therefore be visited from either exit and the splendid rock-scenes certainly justify an inspection.

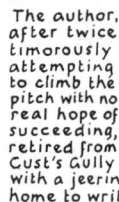

the pitch

The author, after twice timorously attempting to climb the pitch with no real hope of succeeding, retired from Cust's Gully with a jeering conscience and went home to write, in capital letters, on page 11 of his Great End chapter:
NO WAY FOR WALKERS

from above

from below

Note that the wedged boulder itself supports a number of smaller stones which can only be at *temporary* rest. Heaven help anybody in Cust's Gully when they fall off. It won't be the author, anyway: he's not going again.

Great End 12

The branch gully

On the direct climb from the path below Cust's Gully slants away to the left, but an ill-defined branch gully continues the line of ascent, its course after 20 yards being interrupted by a chockstone pitch, mossy and of formidable appearance. This can be avoided, but not easily and only by handling rocks, over broken ground (steep) immediately to the right; beyond is scree to the open fellside.

The branch gully cannot be described as a walkers route, either.

The pitch, branch gully

The pedestrian route

Frustrated and humbled by defeats in Cust's and the branch gully, the dispirited pedestrian, his ego in shreds, can still find a way to the top of the fell without losing more than 100 feet in height, by sneaking round the toe of the buttress to the right (west) of both gullies and ascending the first obvious breach in the crags, a short scree-filled ravine, which will be found easy after what has just been endured and which gives access to a steep, simple slope above, where an incipient track will be found. Halfway up this slope the top exit of the branch gully is passed and higher a fringe of boulders is reached; by stumbling upwards over these wretched stones for 50 further yards and then traversing left the open top of Cust's Gully will be skirted and the grassy summit of the fell reached, with sighs of relief, immediately beyond.

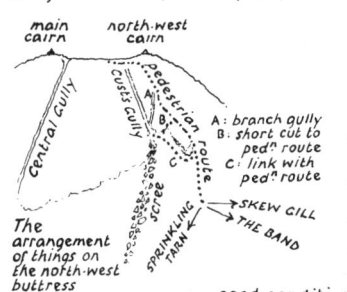

A: branch gully
B: short cut to pedⁿ route
C: link with pedⁿ route

The arrangement of things on the north-west buttress

Skew Gill

Skew Gill is a tremendous gash in the Wasdale side of Great End with proportions little inferior to those of Piers Gill. The floor of the ravine is littered with stones of all shapes and sizes which can be negotiated by agile walkers, but in the upper reaches the bed of the gill is composed of naked rock at an easy angle, calling for care; the final climb out, round a corner, is rather steeper. The sides of the ravine are loose; it is important to keep throughout in the company of the stream. In good conditions this may be regarded as a way for experienced scramblers. The author managed to ascend the gill (on the end of the publisher's rope) so there seems to be no good reason why everybody shouldn't, but his sufferings were such that he can NOT recommend it as a route for decent walkers.

in Skew Gill

the lower entrance, Skew Gill

Great End 13

THE SUMMIT

There are two cairns, each centred in a rash of stones, linked by a grassy saddle of slightly lower altitude. The main cairn (trigonometrical station) is that to the south-east, although the difference in elevation between the two can be a matter of inches only. There is little interest on the actual top of the fell but it would be almost a sin to go away without searching for the various upper exits of the gullies. Only the gaping main exit of Central Gully is likely to be noticed on a walk across the summit; the others have to be hunted and each in turn provides an excitement with its startling downward plunge and fine rock scenery.

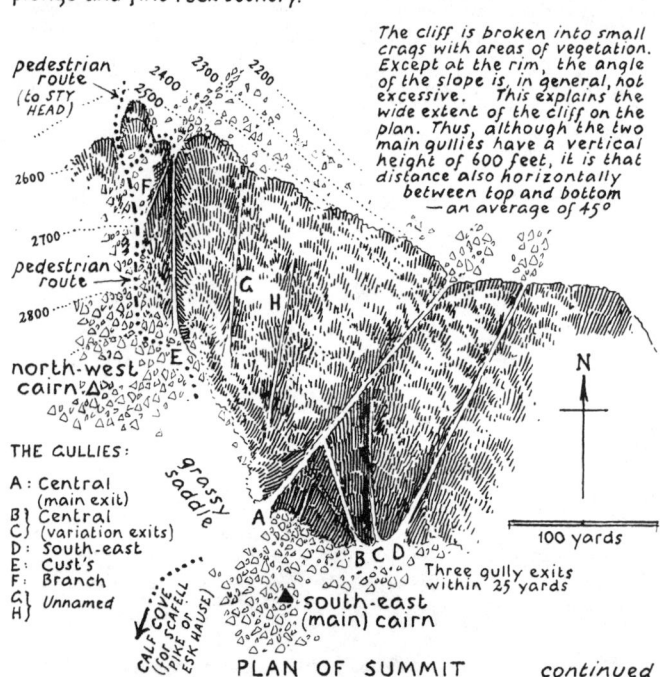

north-west cairn   GREAT GABLE

The cliff is broken into small crags with areas of vegetation. Except at the rim, the angle of the slope is, in general, not excessive. This explains the wide extent of the cliff on the plan. Thus, although the two main gullies have a vertical height of 600 feet, it is that distance also horizontally between top and bottom — an average of 45°

pedestrian route (to STY HEAD)

2200, 2300, 2400, 2500

2600

2700

pedestrian route

2800

north-west cairn

grassy saddle

N

100 yards

THE GULLIES:

A: Central (main exit)
B) Central
C) (variation exits)
D: South-east
E: Cust's
F: Branch
G) Unnamed
H)

Three gully exits within 25 yards

CALF COVE (for SCAFELL PIKE or ESK HAUSE)

south-east (main) cairn

PLAN OF SUMMIT   *continued*

Great End 14

THE SUMMIT
continued

DESCENTS: There is only one simple way off Great End, and that is to proceed south-south-west, keeping to a grass strip between acres of stones, to the Calf Cove depression, where the path from Scafell Pike may be followed to Esk Hause for whatever destination is required. Although this way is roundabout and long, it is possible to work up a spanking pace on the easy gradient to Esk Hause.

The pedestrian route below the north-west cairn is not quite easy to determine from above, the stony ground is very rough, and progress is painfully slow. This route goes down parallel to and 30 yards west of Cust's Gully.

In mist, do be careful and sensible. Go round by Calf Cove to Esk Hause. The inviting openings in the edge of the cliff are all traps and will quickly lead to serious trouble. The pedestrian route is out of the question unless its location is already well known and its course has been followed recently.

RIDGE ROUTES

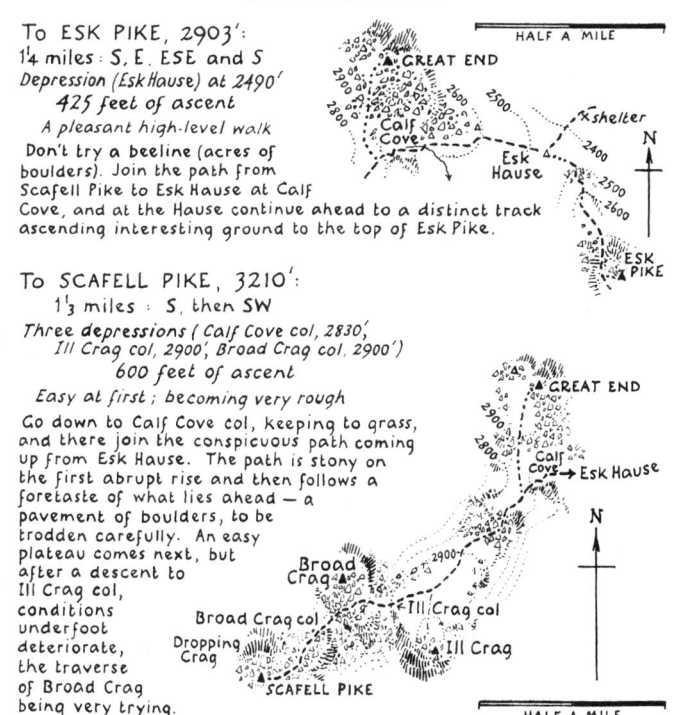

To ESK PIKE, 2903':
1¼ miles : S, E, ESE and S
Depression (Esk Hause) at 2490'
425 feet of ascent
A pleasant high-level walk

Don't try a beeline (acres of boulders). Join the path from Scafell Pike to Esk Hause at Calf Cove, and at the Hause continue ahead to a distinct track ascending interesting ground to the top of Esk Pike.

To SCAFELL PIKE, 3210':
1⅓ miles : S, then SW
Three depressions (Calf Cove col, 2830', Ill Crag col, 2900', Broad Crag col, 2900')
600 feet of ascent
Easy at first; becoming very rough

Go down to Calf Cove col, keeping to grass, and there join the conspicuous path coming up from Esk Hause. The path is stony on the first abrupt rise and then follows a foretaste of what lies ahead — a pavement of boulders, to be trodden carefully. An easy plateau comes next, but after a descent to Ill Crag col, conditions underfoot deteriorate, the traverse of Broad Crag being very trying.

Great End 15

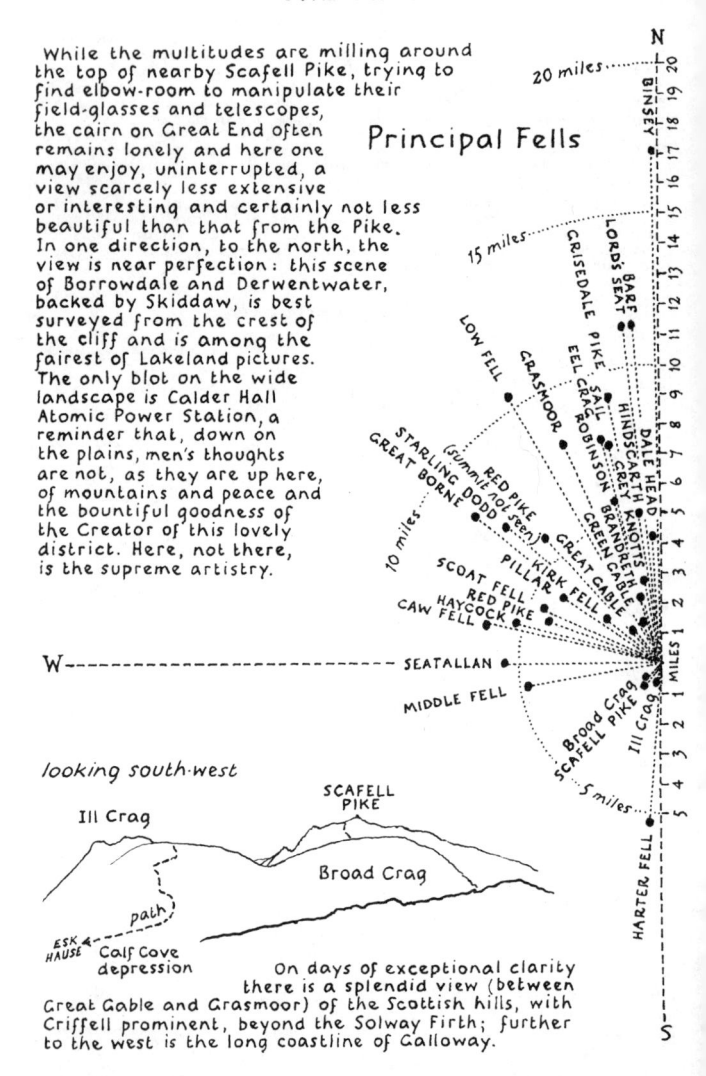

THE VIEW

While the multitudes are milling around the top of nearby Scafell Pike, trying to find elbow-room to manipulate their field-glasses and telescopes, the cairn on Great End often remains lonely and here one may enjoy, uninterrupted, a view scarcely less extensive or interesting and certainly not less beautiful than that from the Pike. In one direction, to the north, the view is near perfection: this scene of Borrowdale and Derwentwater, backed by Skiddaw, is best surveyed from the crest of the cliff and is among the fairest of Lakeland pictures. The only blot on the wide landscape is Calder Hall Atomic Power Station, a reminder that, down on the plains, men's thoughts are not, as they are up here, of mountains and peace and the bountiful goodness of the Creator of this lovely district. Here, not there, is the supreme artistry.

Principal Fells

looking south-west

On days of exceptional clarity there is a splendid view (between Great Gable and Grasmoor) of the Scottish hills, with Criffell prominent, beyond the Solway Firth; further to the west is the long coastline of Galloway.

Great End 16

THE VIEW

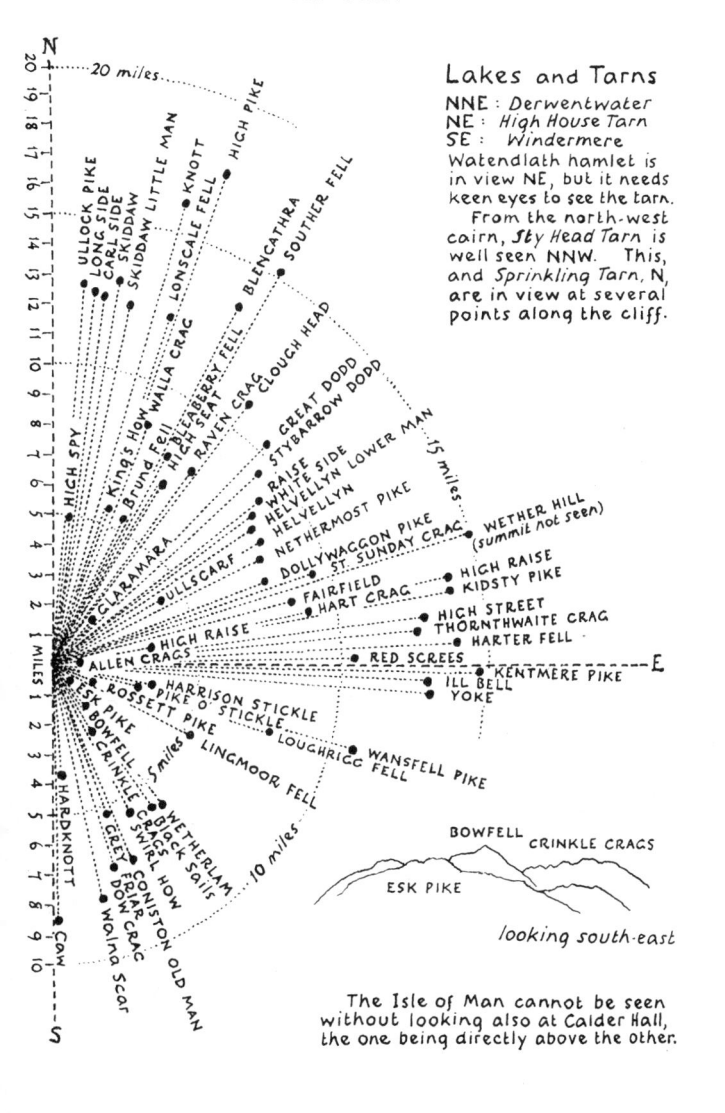

Lakes and Tarns
NNE: *Derwentwater*
NE: *High House Tarn*
SE: *Windermere*
Watendlath hamlet is in view NE, but it needs keen eyes to see the tarn.

From the north-west cairn, *Sty Head Tarn* is well seen NNW. This, and *Sprinkling Tarn*, N, are in view at several points along the cliff.

Compass bearings with peaks visible:

- N / 20 miles
- ULLOCK PIKE
- LONG SIDE
- CARL SIDE
- SKIDDAW LITTLE MAN
- SKIDDAW
- LONSCALE FELL
- KNOTT
- HIGH PIKE
- BLENCATHRA
- SOUTHER FELL
- HIGH SPY
- KING'S HOW
- BRUND FELL
- WALLA CRAG
- HIGH SEAT
- BLEABERRY FELL
- RAVEN CRAG
- CLOUGH HEAD
- GREAT DODD
- STYBARROW DODD
- RAISE
- WHITE SIDE
- HELVELLYN LOWER MAN
- HELVELLYN
- NETHERMOST PIKE
- DOLLYWAGGON PIKE
- ST. SUNDAY CRAG
- ULLSCARF
- WETHER HILL (summit not seen)
- FAIRFIELD
- HART CRAG
- HIGH RAISE
- KIDSTY PIKE
- HIGH STREET
- THORNTHWAITE CRAG
- HARTER FELL
- GLARAMARA
- HIGH RAISE
- ALLEN CRAGS
- RED SCREES
- KENTMERE PIKE — E
- ILL BELL
- YOKE
- HARRISON STICKLE
- PIKE O' STICKLE
- ROSSETT PIKE
- LOUGHRIGG FELL
- WANSFELL PIKE
- ESK PIKE
- BOWFELL
- LINGMOOR FELL
- CRINKLE CRAGS
- HARDKNOTT
- WETHERLAM
- BLACK SAILS
- SWIRL HOW
- GREY FRIAR
- CONISTON OLD MAN
- DOW CRAG
- WALNA SCAR
- COW
- S

15 miles / 10 miles / 5 miles / 1 MILE

looking south-east

BOWFELL   CRINKLE CRAGS
ESK PIKE

The Isle of Man cannot be seen without looking also at Calder Hall, the one being directly above the other.

Green Crag 1602'

from Birker Fell

from Boot

On the crest of the moorland between the Duddon Valley and Eskdale there rises from the heather a series of serrated peaks, not of any great height but together forming a dark and jagged outline against the sky that, seen from certain directions, arrest the eye as do the Black Coolin of Skye. The highest of these peaks is Green Crag, a single summit, and its principal associate is Crook Crag, with many separate tops. Together they provide an excellent objective for exploration, or as viewpoints, and, if the climb is made from Eskdale, as it should be for full enjoyment, the whole walk is a delight, best saved for a sunny afternoon in August.

- Boot
- Eskdale Green
- HARTER FELL ▲
- GREEN CRAG ▲
- Seathwaite •

MILES
0 1 2 3 4

on the approach from Eskdale

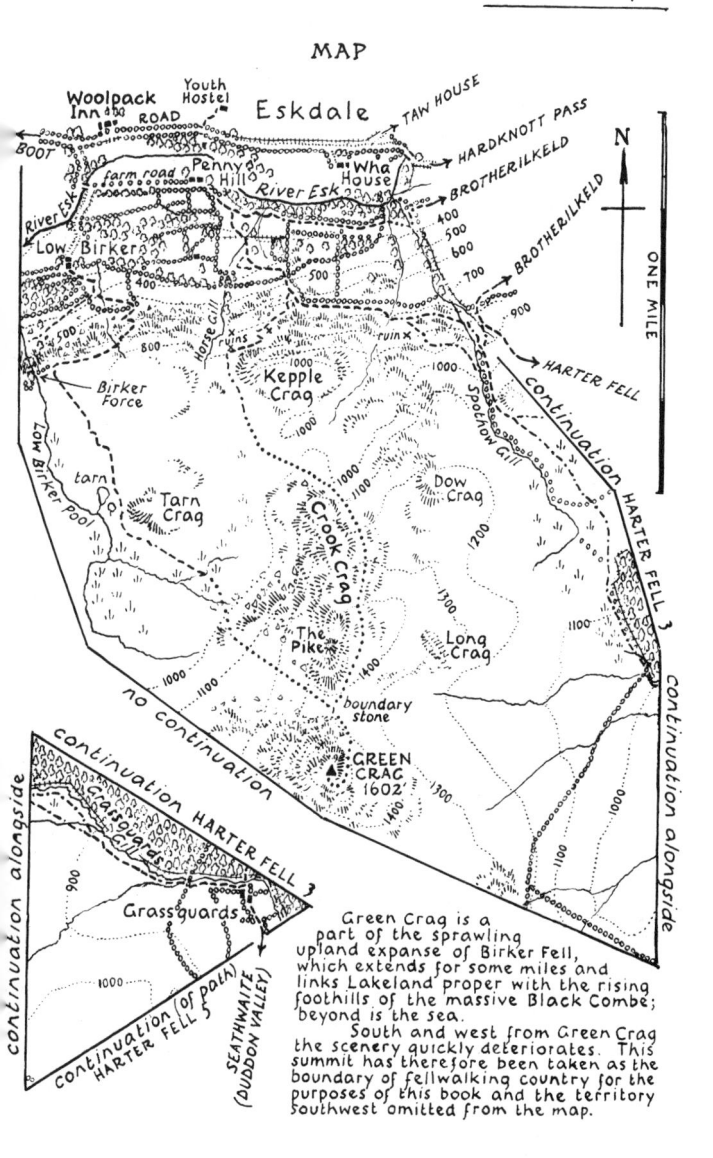

Green Crag 2

MAP

Green Crag is a part of the sprawling upland expanse of Birker Fell, which extends for some miles and links Lakeland proper with the rising foothills of the massive Black Combe; beyond is the sea.

South and west from Green Crag the scenery quickly deteriorates. This summit has therefore been taken as the boundary of fellwalking country for the purposes of this book and the territory southwest omitted from the map.

Green Crag 3

ASCENT FROM ESKDALE
1450 feet of ascent : 2½ miles from the Woolpack Inn

[Map illustration labelled with: GREEN CRAG; The rocky top is most easily gained from the rear; A standing stone in the depression marks the parish boundary; Crook Crag is a cockscomb ridge, interesting to follow, but it may be avoided on the east if desired; many perched boulders in this area; Crook Crag; bracken; bog myrtle; Low Birker Pool; Low Birker Tarn; Tarn Crag; plateau; fold; heathery swamps; old fold; the Low Birker peat-hut; Kepple Crag; peat road; stone hut (ruin); HARTER FELL ruins; In descent, the top of the Penny Hill peat road is not easy to locate. Keep left of the last bulky rise on the plateau (Kepple Crag); stone hut; peat road; heather; Birker Force; Detour to foot of Birker Force (not a public path); hurdles; juniper; gate; path to DALEGARTH; Crag Coppice; enclosure of rough bouldery ground (glacier debris?); Low Birker; farm road; footpath to CHURCH; footpath to BROTHERILKELD; sheepfold; Penny Hill; farm road; Doctor Bridge; River Esk; UPPER ESKDALE; Woolpack Inn; BOOT; looking south-south-east]

A wet morning in Eskdale need not necessarily mean a day's fellwalking lost, for if the sky clears by the early afternoon here is a short expedition well worth trying. The two old peat roads are excellent ways to the lip of the plateau; beyond is a heathery wilderness from which rise several rocky tors, the furthermost (and loftiest) being Green Crag. Preferably, ascend by Low Birker and return by Penny Hill: the walk is easier and less confusing done so.

An interesting feature of this walk is the acquaintance made with the old peat roads so characteristic of Eskdale. From most of the valley farms a wide, well-graded 'road' (usually a grassy path) zig-zags up the fellside to the peaty heights above, and there ends; the stone huts used for storing a supply of peat are still to be seen, now in ruins or decay, on or just below the skyline. Time has marched fast in Eskdale: at the foot of the valley is the world's first atomic power station, and peat is out of fashion. Alas!

Green Crag 4

OTHER ASCENTS

FROM THE DUDDON VALLEY: Reach Grassguards by one of the three routes mentioned on page Harter Fell 5, continuing onwards by the Eskdale path until the open fell is gained beyond the last wall, and there turning due west up a grassy, often wet, and very easy slope.

FROM THE BIRKER FELL ROAD: An obvious starting-point is the top of the unenclosed road between Ulpha and Eskdale Green, whence simple and straightforward walking leads to the summit. To avoid swamps keep to the heights over Great Worm Crag.

THE SUMMIT

A ring of crags gives the appearance of impregnability to the summit, but an easy scramble reveals the highest point, a fine place of vantage, as a small grassy sward, with an old and hoary cairn occupying the place of honour and looking as though it has stood there since the beginning of time.

THE VIEW

DESCENTS in mist: Get down, with care, to the grassy depression between Green Crag and Crook Crag (a standing stone may be noted here) and walk east, down a gentle gradient, to join the path connecting the Duddon Valley (right) and Eskdale (left).

Principal Fells

The view is better than will generally be expected, and in some respects even surpasses that from Harter Fell, the high Mosedale Fells being seen to advantage over the wide depression of Burnmoor Tarn, while the Scafell-Bowfell groups losing nothing in majesty at this greater distance. Seawards there is a fine prospect interrupted only by the bulky Black Combe.

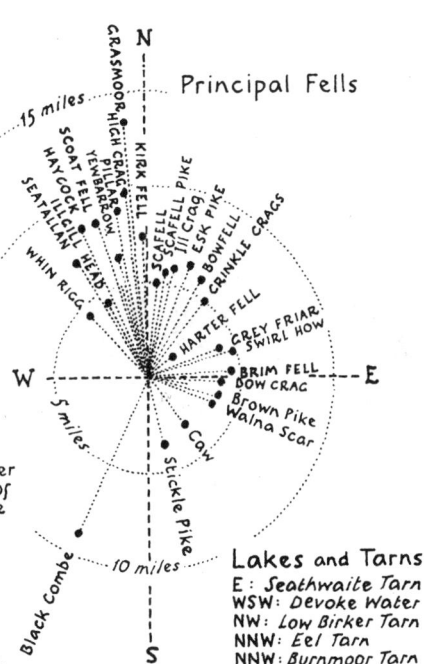

Lakes and Tarns
E: *Seathwaite Tarn*
WSW: *Devoke Water*
NW: *Low Birker Tarn*
NNW: *Eel Tarn*
NNW: *Burnmoor Tarn*

Grey Friar 2536'

from Hell Gill Pike

Cockley Beck •   Little Langdale •
GREY FRIAR ▲   ▲ SWIRL HOW
Troutal •   CONISTON OLD MAN ▲
DOW CRAG ▲
Coniston
Seathwaite •

MILES 0 1 2 3 4

Grey Friar 2

NATURAL FEATURES

Grey Friar, like Dow Crag, stands aloof from the main spine of the Coniston Fells, but, unlike Dow Crag, has no great single natural feature to attract attention and is consequently the least-frequented of the group. Yet it is a fine mountain of considerable bulk, and forms the eastern wall of the Duddon Valley for several miles, rising high above the foothill series of knobbly tors and hanging crags that so greatly contribute to the unique beauty of that valley. In topographical fact, Grey Friar belongs exclusively to the Duddon, to which all its waters drain, and not to Coniston. Great Blake Rigg and Little Blake Rigg are extensive rock-faces in the neighbourhood of Seathwaite Tarn, and there are others, but generally the higher reaches are grassy and the summit assumes the shape of a rounded dome, which is of no particular interest except as a viewpoint, the scene westwards to the Scafells being magnificent.

Grey Buttress, Great Blake Rigg

1: The summit
2: Wet Side Edge
3: Great Blake Rigg
4: Little Blake Rigg
5: Troutal Tongue
6: High Tongue
7: Holling House Tongue
8: Hinning House Plantation (Hardknott National Park)
9: Seathwaite Tarn
10: Tarn Beck
11: The valley of Tarn Beck
12: Cockley Beck
13: River Duddon
14: Wallowbarrow Gorge

looking east-south-east

Grey Friar 3

MAP

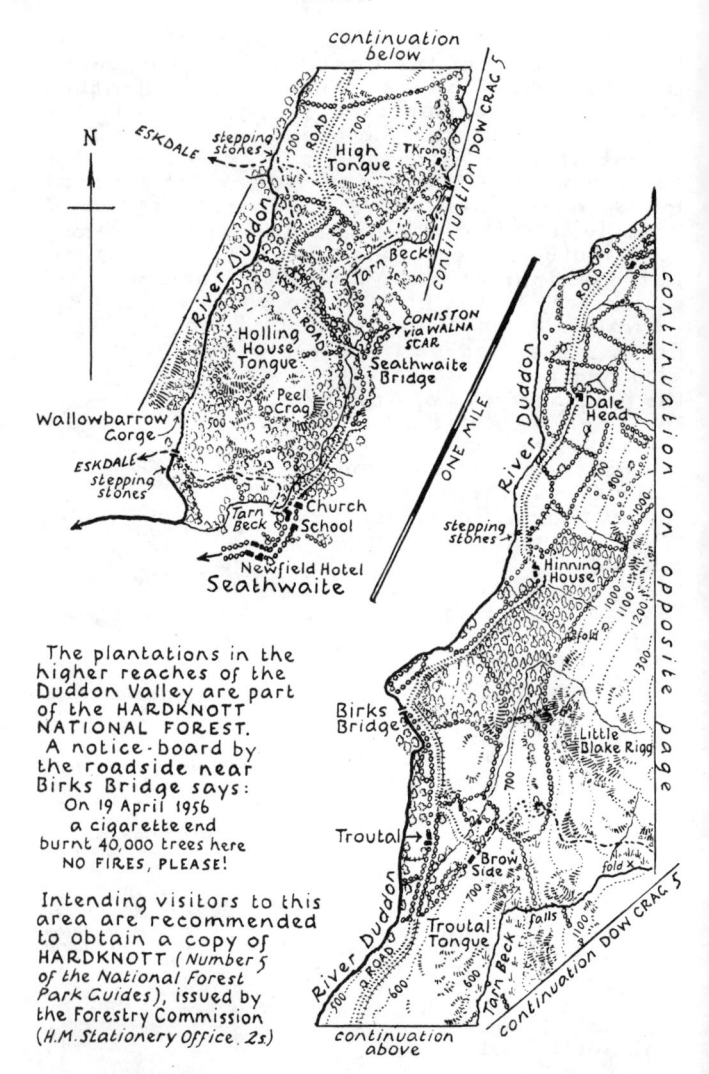

The plantations in the higher reaches of the Duddon Valley are part of the HARDKNOTT NATIONAL FOREST. A notice-board by the roadside near Birks Bridge says:
  On 19 April 1956
  a cigarette end
  burnt 40,000 trees here
  NO FIRES, PLEASE!

Intending visitors to this area are recommended to obtain a copy of HARDKNOTT (Number 5 of the National Forest Park Guides), issued by the Forestry Commission (H.M. Stationery Office. 2s)

Grey Friar 4

MAP

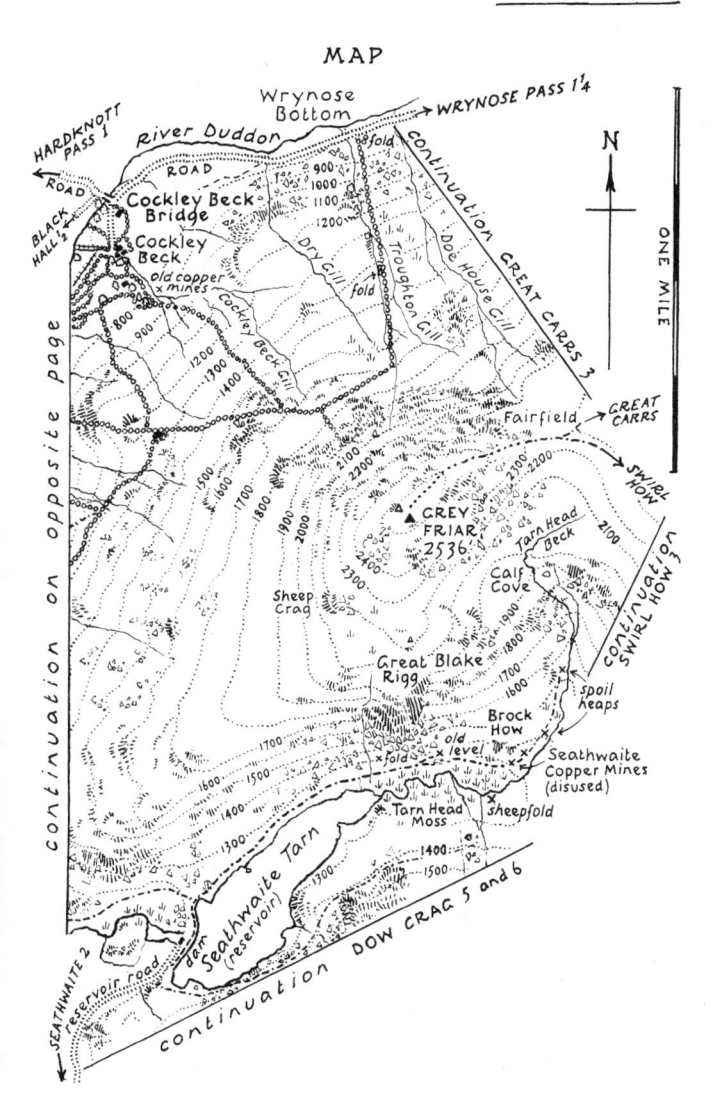

Grey Friar 5

The Valley of Tarn Beck

The geography of the Duddon Valley above Seathwaite is confusing, and calls for a close study of the map. The tributary Tarn Beck is the cause of the perplexity: this considerable stream issues from Seathwaite Tarn and at first heads directly for the River Duddon in accordance with the natural instinct of all water to go downhill by the shortest route and has almost finished the journey when it runs up against the low rocky barrier of Troutal Tongue, which turns it south, parallel to the Duddon. A continuation of the Tongue then persists in keeping Tarn Beck away from its objective until gentler pastures are reached below Seathwaite, where the waters are finally united. Tarn Beck, after thousands of years of constant frustration, has carved out its own beautiful valley, so that for two miles the dale has twin parallel troughs running closely side by side.

Confusion is worse confounded because the road along the valley switches from one to the other, unobtrusively. Thus the river bordering the road north of the village of Seathwaite is Tarn Beck, not the Duddon as is commonly supposed, while higher, after the road has crossed again to the Duddon, the valley of Tarn Beck widens into a neat cultivated strath with a small farming community, but the main river hereabouts remains hidden in its wooded gorge.

Ancient footbridge over Long House Gill in the valley of Tarn Beck

Man rarely beautifies nature, but the exception most certainly occurs in the cultivated valleys of Lakeland. Every walker on the hills must often have been stopped in his tracks by some entrancing glimpse of beautiful green pastures and stately trees in a valley below, a perfect picture of charm and tranquillity in utter contrast to his own rugged surroundings. So delightfully fresh and sparkling, those lovely fields and meadows, that they seem to be in sunshine even in rain; so trim and well-kept that they might be the lawns of some great parkland. But they were not always so. Before man settled here these same valleys were dreary marshes.

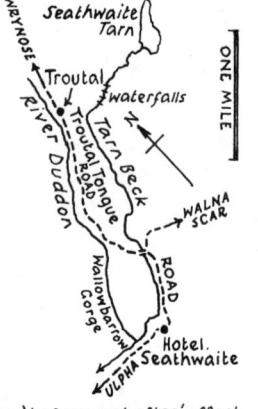

The little valley of Tarn Beck illustrates the 'before and after' effect very well. Beyond and around the walled boundaries of the cultivated area — a patchwork of level pastures — there is at once a morass of bracken and coarse growth littered with stones, with much standing water that cannot escape the choke of vegetation. Once all the dale was like this. So was Borrowdale, and Langdale, and other valleys that today enchant the eye. Hard work and long perseverance have brought fertility from sterility. Rough hands have won a very rare beauty from the wilderness.... Man here has improved on nature.

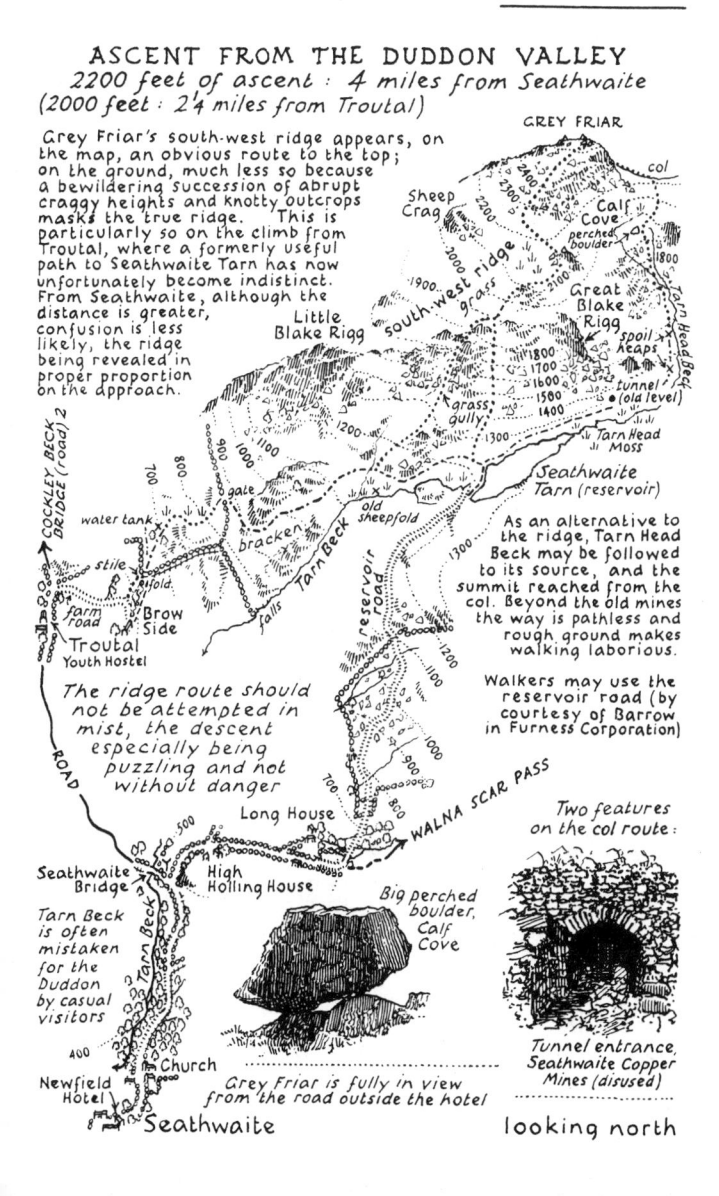

Grey Friar 6

ASCENT FROM THE DUDDON VALLEY
2200 feet of ascent : 4 miles from Seathwaite
(2000 feet : 2¼ miles from Troutal)

Grey Friar's south-west ridge appears, on the map, an obvious route to the top; on the ground, much less so because a bewildering succession of abrupt craggy heights and knotty outcrops masks the true ridge. This is particularly so on the climb from Troutal, where a formerly useful path to Seathwaite Tarn has now unfortunately become indistinct. From Seathwaite, although the distance is greater, confusion is less likely, the ridge being revealed in proper proportion on the approach.

As an alternative to the ridge, Tarn Head Beck may be followed to its source, and the summit reached from the col. Beyond the old mines the way is pathless and rough ground makes walking laborious.

Walkers may use the reservoir road (by courtesy of Barrow in Furness Corporation)

The ridge route should not be attempted in mist, the descent especially being puzzling and not without danger

Tarn Beck is often mistaken for the Duddon by casual visitors

Two features on the col route:

Big perched boulder, Calf Cove

Tunnel entrance, Seathwaite Copper Mines (disused)

Grey Friar is fully in view from the road outside the hotel

looking north

Grey Friar 7

ASCENT FROM WRYNOSE PASS
1350 feet of ascent : 2¼ miles

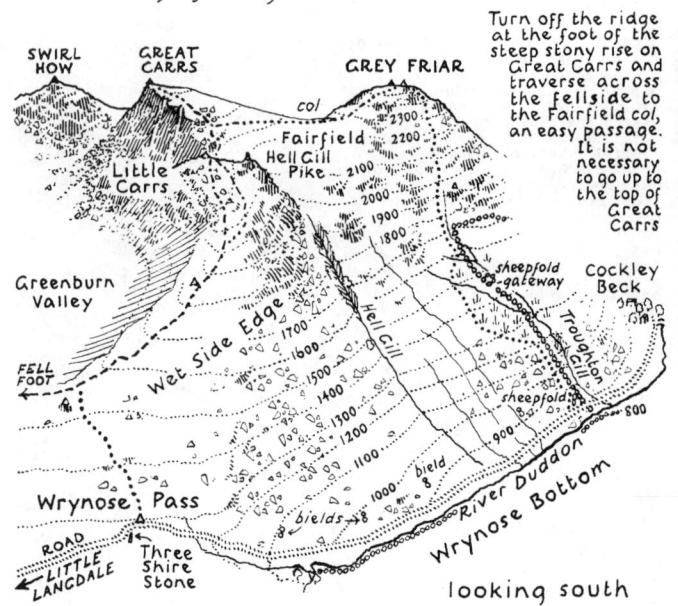

Turn off the ridge at the foot of the steep stony rise on Great Carrs and traverse across the fellside to the Fairfield col, an easy passage. It is not necessary to go up to the top of Great Carrs

looking south

Once the ridge is gained from the Pass (a matter of 15 minutes simple climbing over rough grass and mosses) the remainder of this walk, with views improving the whole way, is merely a stroll. Wet Side Edge is one of the easiest ridges in the district, and, in spite of its name, quite dry underfoot. In mist, keep to the edge and be content with Great Carrs instead.

The alternative route depicted (a direct climb from the road in Wrynose Bottom) is less interesting and rather spoiled by much wet ground alongside the wall (which, usefully, points straight to the unseen summit). When the wall turns away to the right, keep on ahead, first up a grassy rake between crags and then selecting a route between the several outcrops below the top.

Fairfield, well named, is a wide gently-contoured grassy expanse, and a favourite sheep-walk, sloping to a shallow *col* between Grey Friar and the main ridge.

Travellers along Wrynose Bottom may have their curiosity aroused by the short stone walls, only a few yards in length, built at intervals at right angles to the road and not far distant from it. These walls are BIELDS, shelters for sheep from strong winds and drifting snow.

Grey Friar 8

THE SUMMIT

Labels on illustration: SLIGHT SIDE, SCAFELL, SCAFELL PIKE, Broad Crag, Ill Crag, GREAT END, north-west cairn

On the usual approach to the summit, from the Fairfield col, a long level promenade of excellent turf precedes a stonier area where two rock outcrops 40 yards apart, each bearing a cairn, are slightly elevated above the plateau: the one to the south-east is the true summit, having an advantage of a few feet in altitude, but the one north-west (which may be reached by a simple 20' rock climb, if desired) commands the better view. Other outcrops carry smaller cairns, a source of confusion in mist.

DESCENTS: In clear weather there should be no difficulty in getting down by any of the routes given for ascent, but the south-west ridge may involve some trial and error in finding an easy passage at its extremity. *In mist*, it is advisable to go down first to the Fairfield col, whatever the ultimate aim, and take bearings there. The track to the col is so sketchy as to be virtually non-existent, and a few more cairns would be useful here: incline slightly right rather than left where the descent from the summit plateau commences.

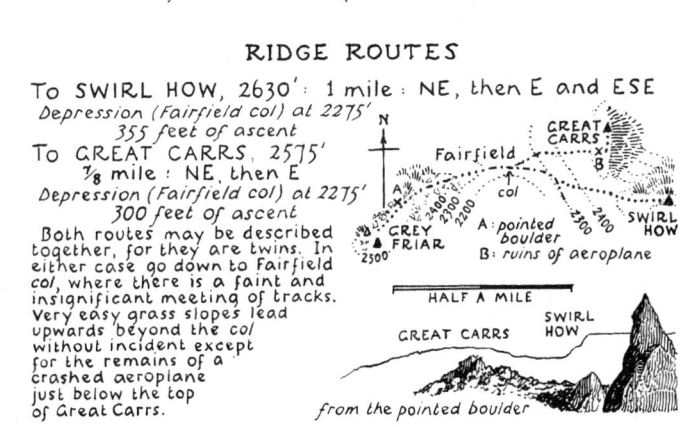

RIDGE ROUTES

To SWIRL HOW, 2630': 1 mile: NE, then E and ESE
  Depression (Fairfield col) at 2275'
    355 feet of ascent
To GREAT CARRS, 2575'
  ⅞ mile: NE, then E
  Depression (Fairfield col) at 2275'
    300 feet of ascent

Both routes may be described together, for they are twins. In either case go down to Fairfield col, where there is a faint and insignificant meeting of tracks. Very easy grass slopes lead upwards beyond the col without incident except for the remains of a crashed aeroplane just below the top of Great Carrs.

Map labels: GREY FRIAR, Fairfield, col, GREAT CARRS, SWIRL HOW, A: pointed boulder, B: ruins of aeroplane

Lower sketch: GREAT CARRS, SWIRL HOW — *from the pointed boulder*

Grey Friar 9

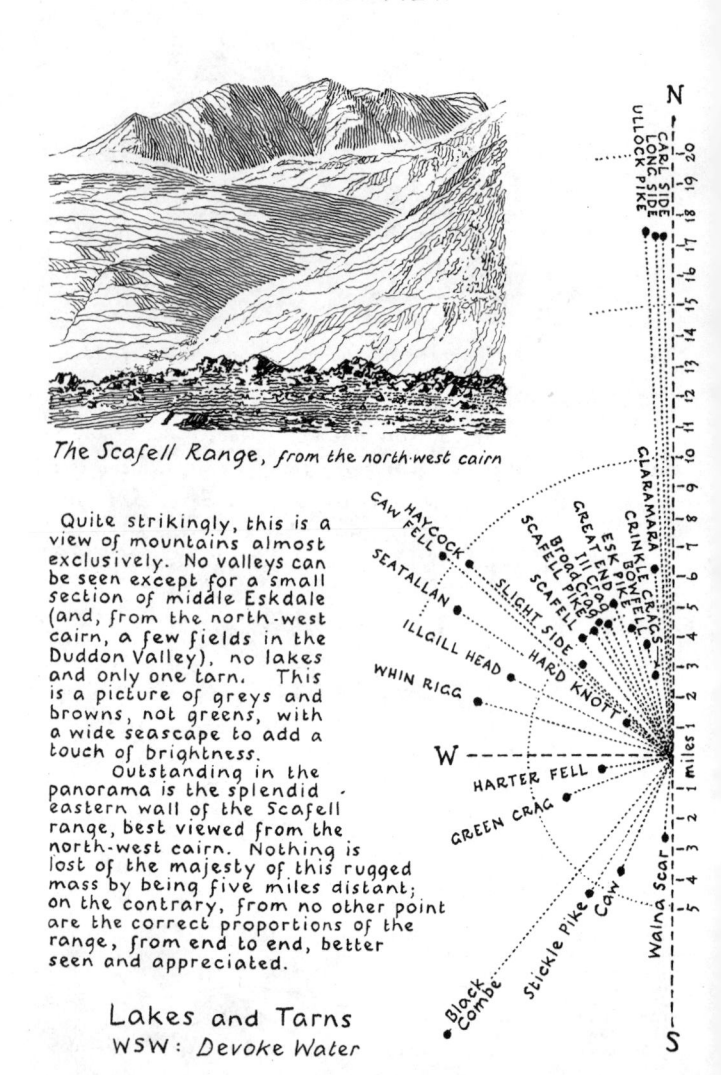

THE VIEW

The Scafell Range, from the north-west cairn

Quite strikingly, this is a view of mountains almost exclusively. No valleys can be seen except for a small section of middle Eskdale (and, from the north-west cairn, a few fields in the Duddon Valley), no lakes and only one tarn. This is a picture of greys and browns, not greens, with a wide seascape to add a touch of brightness.

Outstanding in the panorama is the splendid eastern wall of the Scafell range, best viewed from the north-west cairn. Nothing is lost of the majesty of this rugged mass by being five miles distant; on the contrary, from no other point are the correct proportions of the range, from end to end, better seen and appreciated.

Lakes and Tarns
WSW: Devoke Water

Grey Friar 10

THE VIEW

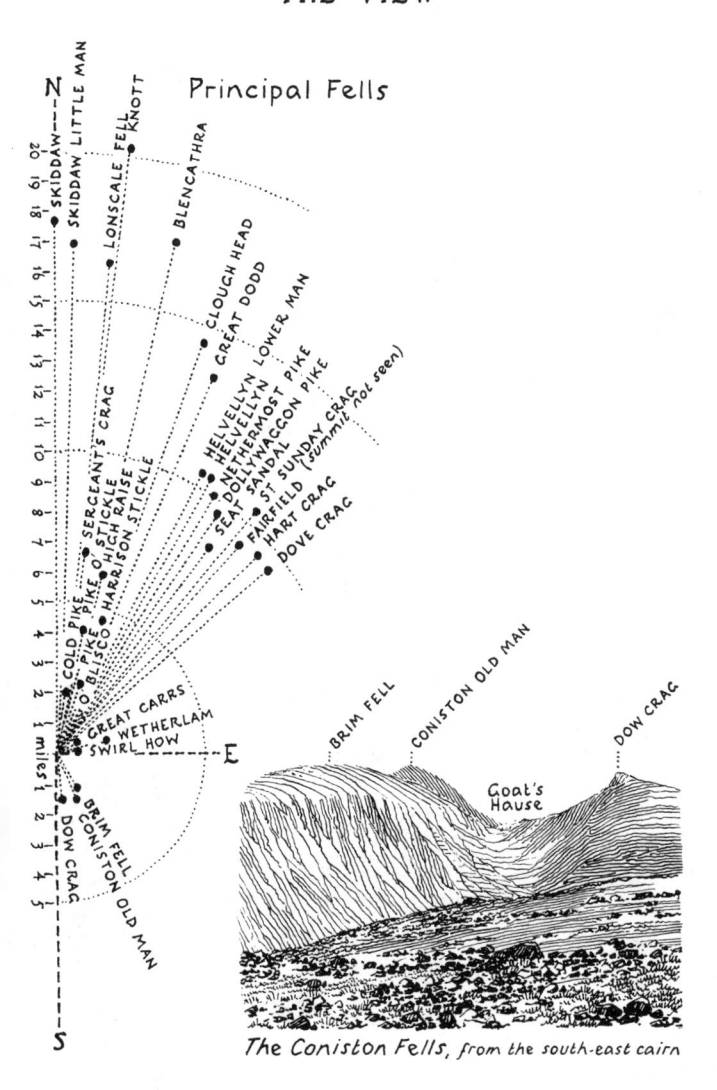

Principal Fells

The Coniston Fells, from the south-east cairn

Hard Knott

1803'

from Whahouse Bridge

Hard Knott is well known for three features: the pass of the same name, a Roman camp, and the view of the Scafells from its summit. The fell itself is not especially remarkable, and is best described as a wedge of high ground dividing Eskdale and Mosedale, the latter running down into the Duddon Valley

Geographically, Hard Knott is a continuation of the north-eastern ridge of Harter Fell, with the pass occupying a depression thereon.

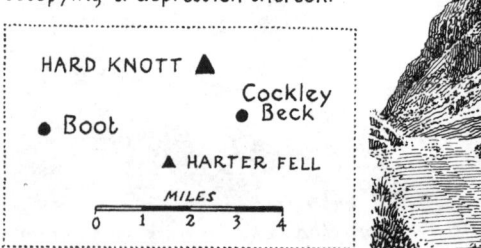

Hardknott Pass

Hard Knott 2

The Roman Fort

On the south-western slope of Hard Knott the rocky cliffs of Border End fall steeply to an inclined grassy shelf, which extends for half a mile and then breaks abruptly in a line of crags overlooking the Esk. This shelf, a splendid place of vantage commanding a view of the valley from the hills down to the sea, was selected by the Romans towards the end of the first century A.D. as a site for the establishment of a garrison to reinforce their military occupation of the district. Here they built a fort, MEDIOBOGDVM, which today is more usually, and certainly more easily, referred to as HARDKNOTT CASTLE. The main structure and outbuildings have survived the passing years sufficiently to provide a valuable source of information and study for the expert and an object of considerable interest for the layman. At present the walls of the fort are being rebuilt by the Ministry of Works, a slate course indicating the original wall below and the restored portion above. There is divided opinion as to whether this physical reconstruction is desirable: would not the mouldering ruins, left to their natural decay, have had a greater appeal to the imagination?

A : Commandant's House
B : Headquarters
C : Granaries
D : Bath-houses

One wonders what were the thoughts of the sentries as they kept watch over this lonely outpost amongst the mountains, nearly two thousand years ago? Did they admire the massive architecture of the Scafell group as they looked north, the curve of the valley from source to sea as their eyes turned west? Or did they feel themselves to be unwanted strangers in a harsh and hostile land? Did their hearts ache for the sunshine of their native country, for their families, for their homes?

There is an informative article on the Roman fort in the publication of the Forestry Commission "HARDKNOTT: Number Five of the National Forest Park Guides" (H.M. Stationery Office, 2s.). This is an excellent book, dealing with the history, geology, wild life, botany, and so on, of Eskdale and the Duddon Valley. It isn't as good as "The Southern Fells," though, in its detail of the walking routes in the area, not by a long chalk.

Hard Knott 3

MAP

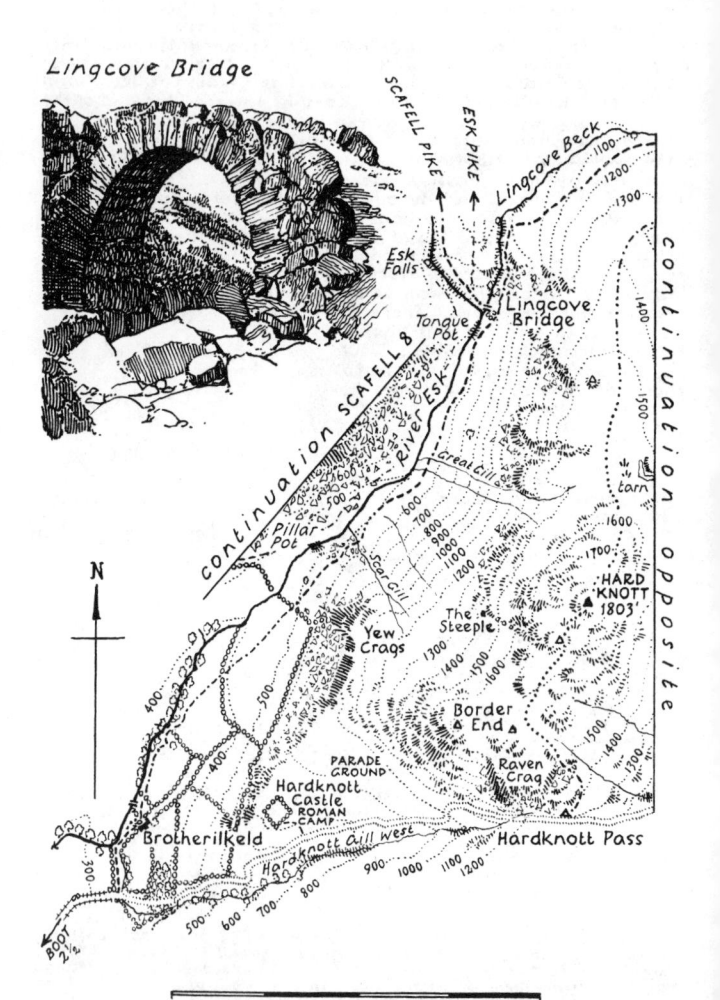

Hard Knott 4

MAP

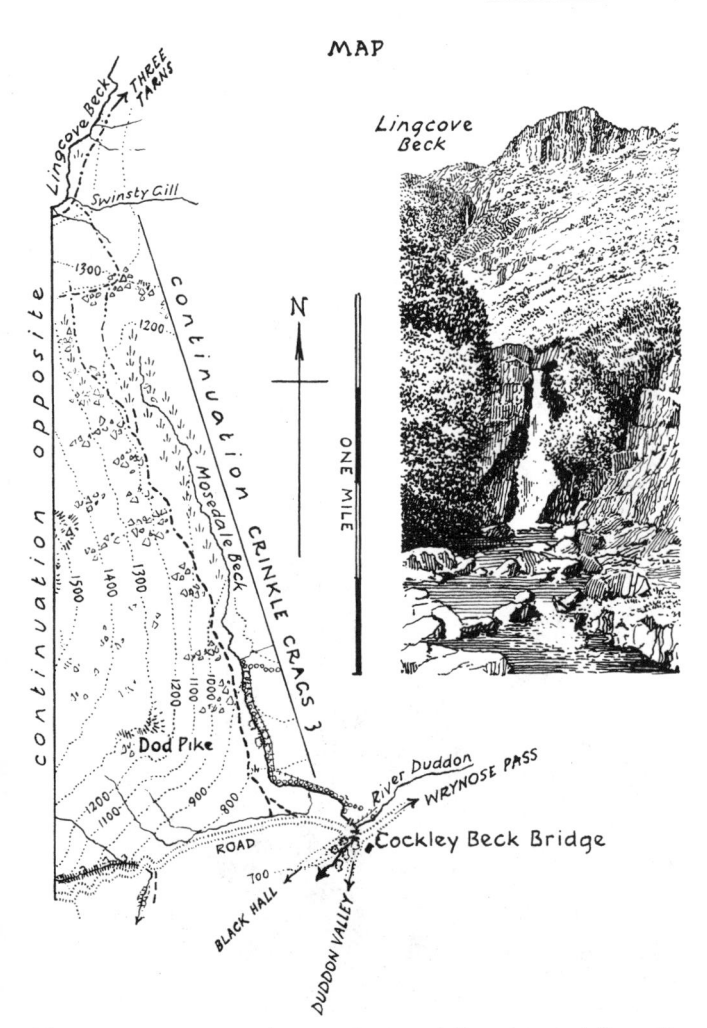

The present motor road across Hardknott Pass does not lie on the line of the Roman road. The latter generally lay to the north of the present road on the Eskdale side of the Pass (and, of course, went up to the fort), and on the Duddon side made a wide detour to the south, coming down to the valley where Black Hall now stands.

Hard Knott 5

ASCENT FROM HARDKNOTT PASS
550 feet of ascent : ¾ mile

This short climb hardly calls for a diagram.   Leave the road exactly at the cairn on the highest point of the Pass — not from the rocky defile to the west, where crags bar the way. From the cairn a grass track slants up to the right, then left to a run of scree, above which easier ground is reached, amongst outcrops, and followed to the summit along an indefinite ridge. (There is a view of the Steeple, down on the left, at one place on the ridge).   Memorise the position of the scree-run, if returning to the road : it is elusive when sought from above.   While on the top it is worth while making the short detour to Border End for a glorious prospect of Eskdale.

The Steeple,
also known as
Eskdale Needle
(about 50' high
on its longest side,
facing the valley)

Hard Knott 6

THE SUMMIT

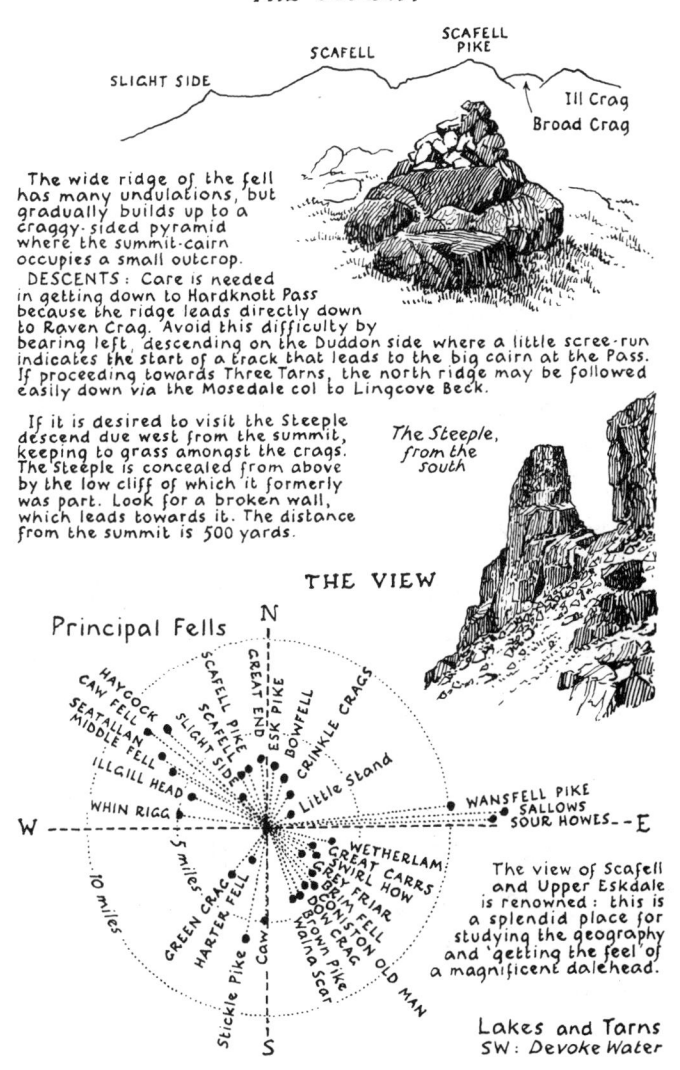

SLIGHT SIDE — SCAFELL — SCAFELL PIKE — Ill Crag — Broad Crag

The wide ridge of the fell has many undulations, but gradually builds up to a craggy-sided pyramid where the summit-cairn occupies a small outcrop.

DESCENTS: Care is needed in getting down to Hardknott Pass because the ridge leads directly down to Raven Crag. Avoid this difficulty by bearing left, descending on the Duddon side where a little scree-run indicates the start of a track that leads to the big cairn at the Pass. If proceeding towards Three Tarns, the north ridge may be followed easily down via the Mosedale col to Lingcove Beck.

If it is desired to visit the Steeple descend due west from the summit, keeping to grass amongst the crags. The Steeple is concealed from above by the low cliff of which it formerly was part. Look for a broken wall, which leads towards it. The distance from the summit is 500 yards.

The Steeple, from the south

THE VIEW

Principal Fells

N — GREAT END, SCAFELL PIKE, SCAFELL, SLIGHT SIDE, HAYCOCK, CAW FELL, SEATALLAN, MIDDLE FELL, ILLGILL HEAD, BOWFELL, CRINKLE CRAGS, Little Stand

W — WHIN RIGG

E — WANSFELL PIKE, SALLOWS, SOUR HOWES

WETHERLAM, GREAT CARRS, SWIRL HOW, GREY FRIAR, DOW CRAG, BROWN PIKE, CONISTON OLD MAN, DOW CRAG, BROWN PIKE, Walna Scar, GREEN CRAG, HARTER FELL, Stickle Pike, Caw

S

5 miles / 10 miles

The view of Scafell and Upper Eskdale is renowned: this is a splendid place for studying the geography and 'getting the feel of' a magnificent dalehead.

Lakes and Tarns
SW: Devoke Water

Harter Fell

2140'

from Penny Hill

Birks Bridge

HARD KNOTT ▲

• Boot   Cockley
          • Beck

▲ HARTER FELL

▲ GREEN CRAG

• Seathwaite

MILES
0 1 2 3 4

Harter Fell 2

NATURAL FEATURES

Not many fells can be described as *beautiful*, but the word fits Harter Fell, especially so when viewed from Eskdale. The lower slopes on this flank climb steeply from the tree-lined curves of the River Esk in a luxurious covering of bracken, higher is a wide belt of heather, and finally spring grey turrets and ramparts of rock to a neat and shapely pyramid. The Duddon slopes are now extensively planted, and here too, thanks to the good taste of the Forestry Commission in this area, deciduous trees and evergreens amongst the crags will, in due course, make a colourful picture.

The fell is not only good to look at, but good to climb, interest being well sustained throughout and reaching a climax in the last few feet, an upthrust of naked rock where the walker must turn cragsman if he is to enjoy the magnificent panorama from the uttermost point.

Harter Fell rises between the mid-valleys of the Esk and the Duddon, not at the head, and is therefore not the source of either river although it feeds both.

The head of Eskdale, from the summit of Harter Fell

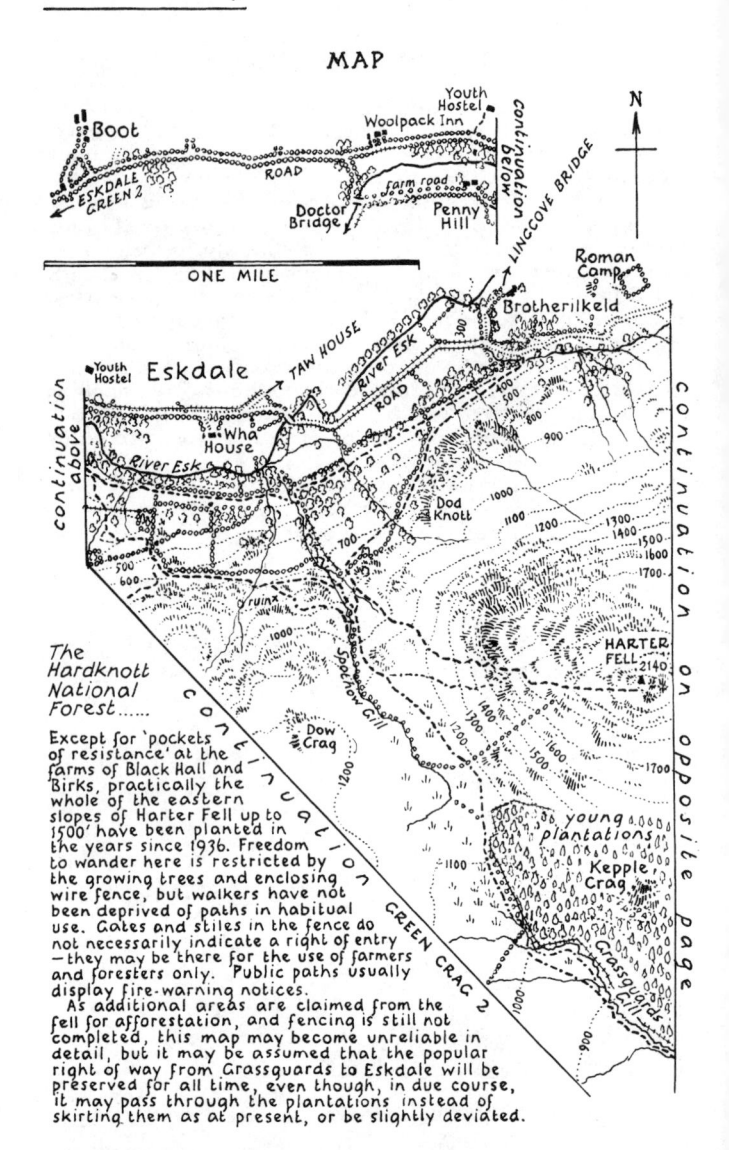

Harter Fell 3

MAP

The Hardknott National Forest.....

Except for 'pockets of resistance' at the farms of Black Hall and Birks, practically the whole of the eastern slopes of Harter Fell up to 1500' have been planted in the years since 1936. Freedom to wander here is restricted by the growing trees and enclosing wire fence, but walkers have not been deprived of paths in habitual use. Gates and stiles in the fence do not necessarily indicate a right of entry — they may be there for the use of farmers and foresters only. Public paths usually display fire-warning notices.

As additional areas are claimed from the fell for afforestation, and fencing is still not completed, this map may become unreliable in detail, but it may be assumed that the popular right of way from Grassguards to Eskdale will be preserved for all time, even though, in due course, it may pass through the plantations instead of skirting them as at present, or be slightly deviated.

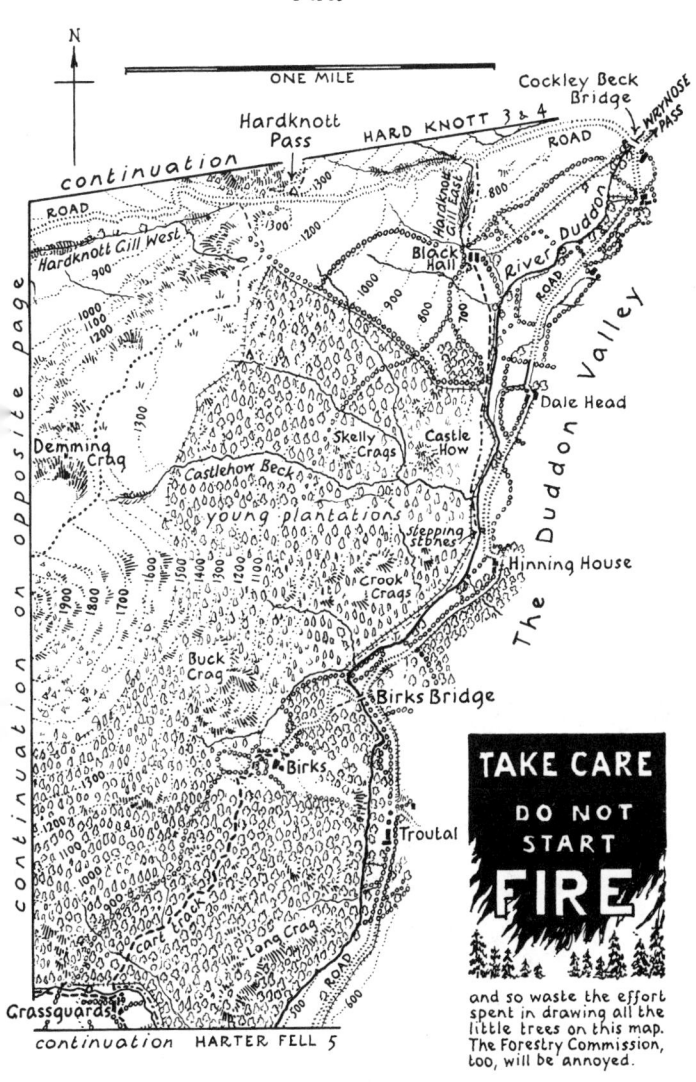

Harter Fell 4

MAP

and so waste the effort spent in drawing all the little trees on this map. The Forestry Commission, too, will be annoyed.

TAKE CARE DO NOT START FIRE

Harter Fell 5

MAP

There are three ways of reaching Grassguards from the Duddon Valley, and all are beautiful.

Best known is the good path from Seathwaite via High Wallowbarrow, which has pleasant views; then there is the chancier route from Fickle Steps (which may not be practicable if the river is high) ascending the north bank of Grassguards Gill, where there is a good waterfall; third is a cart track from Birks (the only access for vehicles), which winds through the plantations.

Grassguards is a farm with many dogs, not particularly friendly, and no advice is offered as to whether it is safer to stand still when sighted by them or to run like fury. Some of us are past running, anyway.

Fickle Steps (Ordnance Survey spelling) are also known locally as Fiddle Steps

ONE MILE

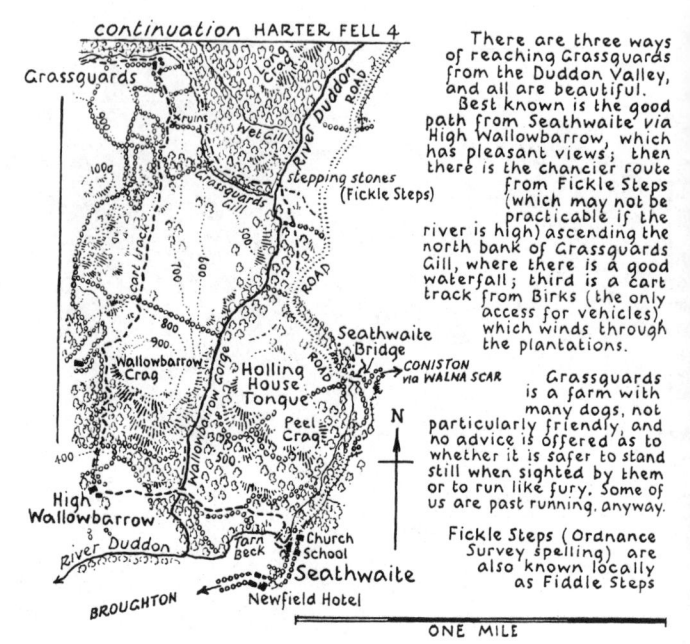

Grassguards Gill forms the southern boundary of Harter Fell, but the map has been extended in that direction to include the approaches from Seathwaite.

Harter Fell
from the Walna Scar path

Harter Fell 6

ASCENT FROM ESKDALE
2000 feet of ascent : 3½ miles from Boot

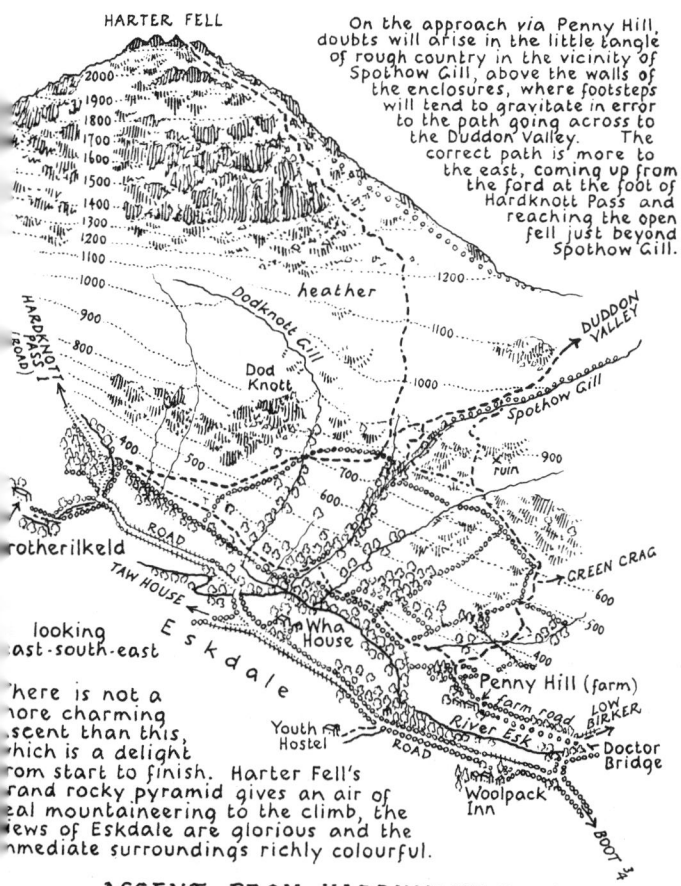

On the approach via Penny Hill, doubts will arise in the little tangle of rough country in the vicinity of Spothow Gill, above the walls of the enclosures, where footsteps will tend to gravitate in error to the path going across to the Duddon Valley. The correct path is more to the east, coming up from the ford at the foot of Hardknott Pass and reaching the open fell just beyond Spothow Gill.

looking east-south-east

There is not a more charming ascent than this, which is a delight from start to finish. Harter Fell's grand rocky pyramid gives an air of real mountaineering to the climb, the views of Eskdale are glorious and the immediate surroundings richly colourful.

ASCENT FROM HARDKNOTT PASS
900 feet of ascent : 1½ miles

Little can be said in favour of the obvious route along the swampy ridge from the top of Hardknott Pass, which is pathless and lacking in interest. Keep left of the conspicuous Demming Crag and gain the final rocks by a grassy shelf slanting up to the right (north) of the summit.

Harter Fell 7

ASCENT FROM THE DUDDON VALLEY

There is no longer free and open access to the fellside from the Duddon because of the plantations, and the approach is almost exclusively restricted to the time-honoured route to Eskdale from Grassguards, and even here there have been slight deviations, with possibly further deflections to come if planting is extended. Reach Grassguards by any of the three public paths shown on the map, and here (the farm-dogs permitting) go on across the swampy moor until the wide top of the pass is gained beyond the plantation. A broken wall running up Harter Fell may now be followed; or by continuing towards Eskdale for a quarter-mile further a narrow track turning off to the right may be used: in either case the distinct path to the summit from Eskdale will be joined.

THE SUMMIT

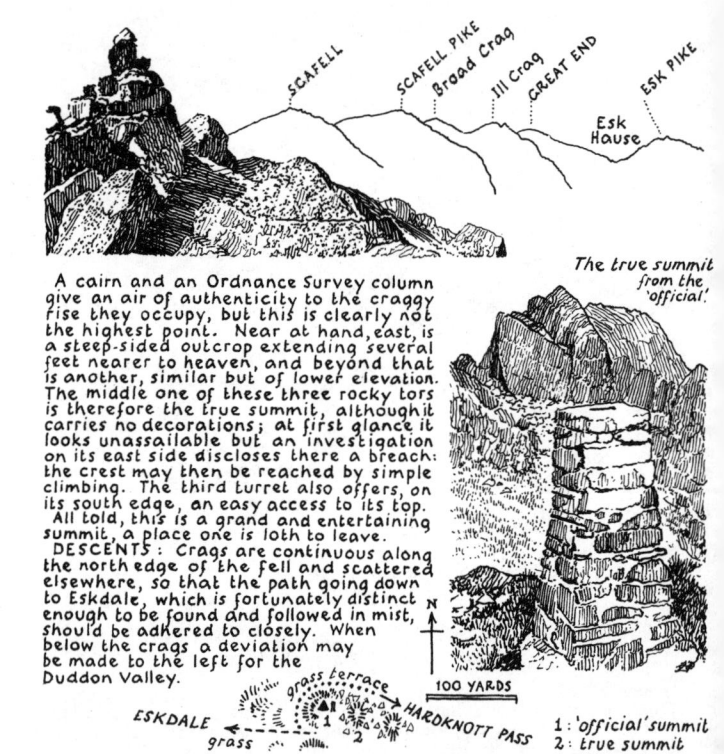

SCAFELL — SCAFELL PIKE — Broad Crag — Ill Crag — GREAT END — Esk Hause — ESK PIKE

The true summit from the 'official'

A cairn and an Ordnance Survey column give an air of authenticity to the craggy rise they occupy, but this is clearly not the highest point. Near at hand, east, is a steep-sided outcrop extending several feet nearer to heaven, and beyond that is another, similar but of lower elevation. The middle one of these three rocky tors is therefore the true summit, although it carries no decorations; at first glance it looks unassailable but an investigation on its east side discloses there a breach: the crest may then be reached by simple climbing. The third turret also offers, on its south edge, an easy access to its top.
All told, this is a grand and entertaining summit, a place one is loth to leave.

DESCENTS: Crags are continuous along the north edge of the fell and scattered elsewhere, so that the path going down to Eskdale, which is fortunately distinct enough to be found and followed in mist, should be adhered to closely. When below the crags a deviation may be made to the left for the Duddon Valley.

ESKDALE ← grass terrace → HARDKNOTT PASS
grass
100 YARDS

1: 'official' summit
2: true summit

Harter Fell 8

THE VIEW

Having exercised himself by scrambling up and down the three summits, the visitor can settle himself on the sharp arete of the highest and enjoy a most excellent view. The Scafell group and Upper Eskdale dominate the scene, appearing not quite in such detail as when surveyed from Hard Knott but in better balance — added distance often adds quality to a picture. Over Wrynose Pass there is an array of faraway fells in the Kirkstone area, which will not surprise walkers familiar with that district, where Harter Fell often pops into the views therefrom. Near at hand, east, the Coniston fells bulk largely but unattractively. Lower Eskdale and the Duddon Valley lead the eye to golden sands and glittering sea.

Principal Fells

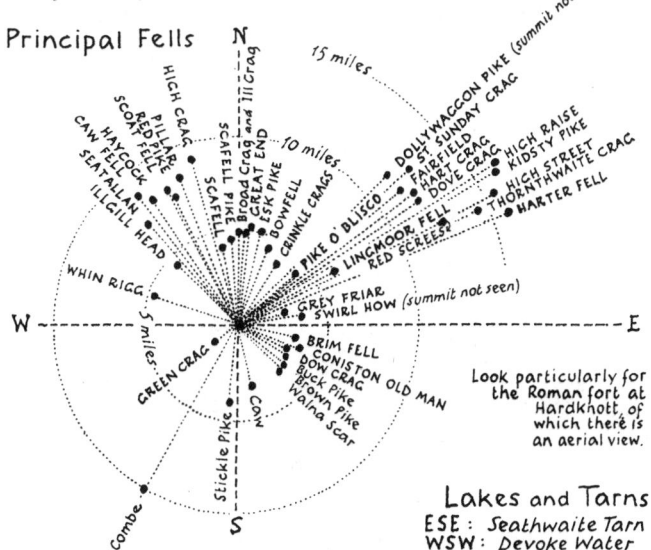

(diagram of principal fells as viewed from Harter Fell, showing compass directions N, S, E, W with distance rings at 5, 10, and 15 miles)

Fells shown include: HIGH CRAG, PILLAR, RED PIKE, SCOAT FELL, HAYCOCK, CAW FELL, SEATALLAN, ILLGILL HEAD, SCAFELL, SCAFELL PIKE, Broad Crag and Ill Crag, GREAT END, ESK PIKE, BOWFELL, CRINKLE CRAGS, PIKE O' BLISCO, DOLLYWAGGON PIKE (summit not seen), ST. SUNDAY CRAG, FAIRFIELD, HART CRAG, DOVE CRAG, HIGH RAISE, KIDSTY PIKE, HIGH STREET, THORNTHWAITE CRAG, HARTER FELL, LINGMOOR FELL, RED SCREES, WHIN RIGG, GREY FRIAR, SWIRL HOW (summit not seen), GREEN CRAG, BRIM FELL, CONISTON OLD MAN, DOW CRAG, BUCK PIKE, BROWN PIKE, WALNA SCAR, STICKLE PIKE, CAW, Black Combe.

Look particularly for the Roman fort at Hardknott, of which there is an aerial view.

Lakes and Tarns

ESE : Seathwaite Tarn
WSW : Devoke Water
WNW : Blea Tarn
NW : Eel Tarn
NNW : Burnmoor Tarn

RIDGE ROUTES

There is no defined ridge seawards, although it is possible to keep to the height of land for a dozen miles without (except at one point) descending below 1000'! Northeast, a high ridge continues to Hard Knott and at its lowest depression is crossed by a motor road (Hardknott Pass), from whence the route onwards has been described as a separate ascent (see page Hard Knott 5).

Holme Fell

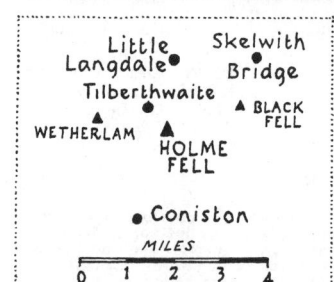

1040' approx

from Tunnel Quarry Low Fell

from the north ridge (Ivy Crag on the left)

the big cairn of Ivy Crag (there are two smaller cairns nearby at a slightly higher elevation)

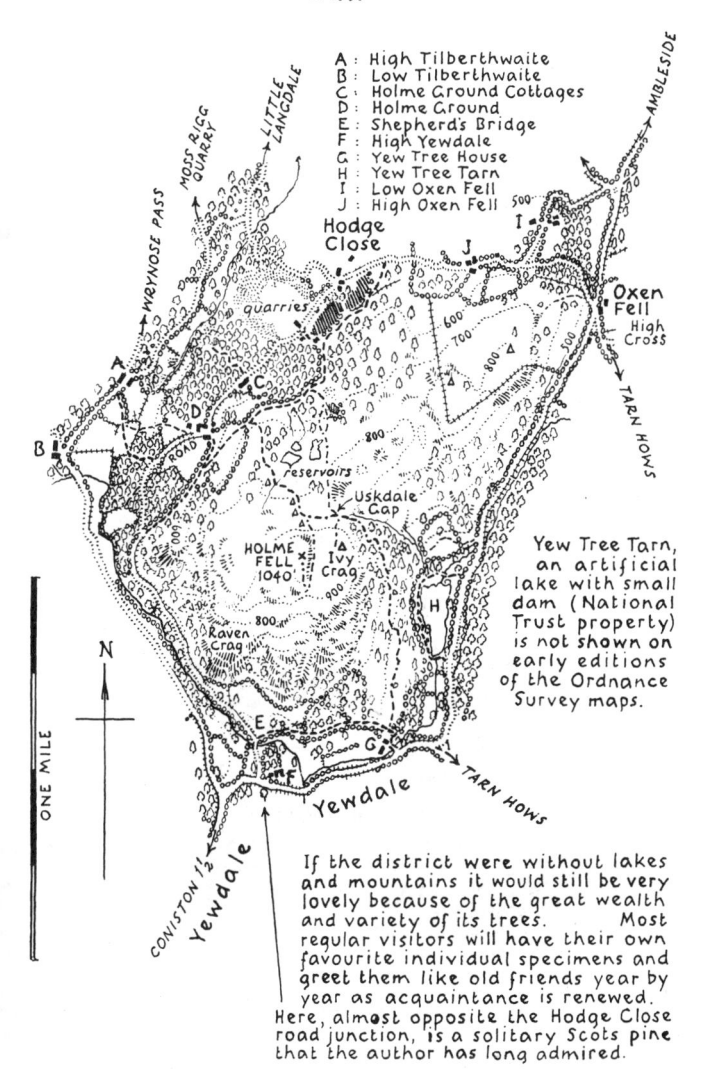

Holme Fell 2

MAP

A : High Tilberthwaite
B : Low Tilberthwaite
C : Holme Ground Cottages
D : Holme Ground
E : Shepherd's Bridge
F : High Yewdale
G : Yew Tree House
H : Yew Tree Tarn
I : Low Oxen Fell
J : High Oxen Fell

Yew Tree Tarn, an artificial lake with small dam (National Trust property) is not shown on early editions of the Ordnance Survey maps.

If the district were without lakes and mountains it would still be very lovely because of the great wealth and variety of its trees. Most regular visitors will have their own favourite individual specimens and greet them like old friends year by year as acquaintance is renewed. Here, almost opposite the Hodge Close road junction, is a solitary Scots pine that the author has long admired.

Holme Fell 3

NATURAL FEATURES

It is a characteristic of many of Lakeland's lesser heights that what they lack in elevation they make up in ruggedness. Slopes a thousand feet high can be just as steep and rough as those three times as long, while crags occur at all levels and are by no means the preserve of the highest peaks, so that the climbing of a small hill, what there is of it, can call for as much effort, over a shorter time, as a big one; moreover, the lower tops have the further defence of a tangle of tough vegetation, usually heather and bracken, through which progress is a far more laborious task than on the grassy slopes of higher zones. Such a one is Holme Fell, at the head of Yewdale, isolated by valleys yet very much under the dominance of Wetherlam. A craggy southern front, a switchback ridge, a cluster of small but very beautiful tree-girt tarns (old reservoirs), and a great quarry that reveals the core of colourful slate lying beneath the glorious jungle of juniper and birch, heather and bracken, make this one of the most attractive of Lakeland's fells.

ASCENTS

The worst roughnesses may be avoided, fortunately, by using a charming path that crosses the fell north of the summit. From the east, the path starts at Yew Tree Farm and slants upwards, mostly amongst trees, to Uskdale Gap on the ridge, where the cairn on Ivy Crag is in sight and quickly reached. From the west, the path may be joined above Holme Ground (see map), in which case it is not necessary to continue quite as far as the Gap, the main summit being gained by a scramble on the right.

THE SUMMIT

The highest point is a platform of naked rock, set at the top of slabs and curiously weathered into pockets of small pebbles, in the middle of a summit-ridge with a continuous escarpment on the east side. 200 yards away, across a heathery plateau, is the subsidiary summit of Ivy Crag, identified by a big cairn.

DESCENTS : Uskdale Gap is the key to easy descent. Avoid the steep southern declivities, which are much too rough for comfort.

Holme Fell 4

THE VIEW

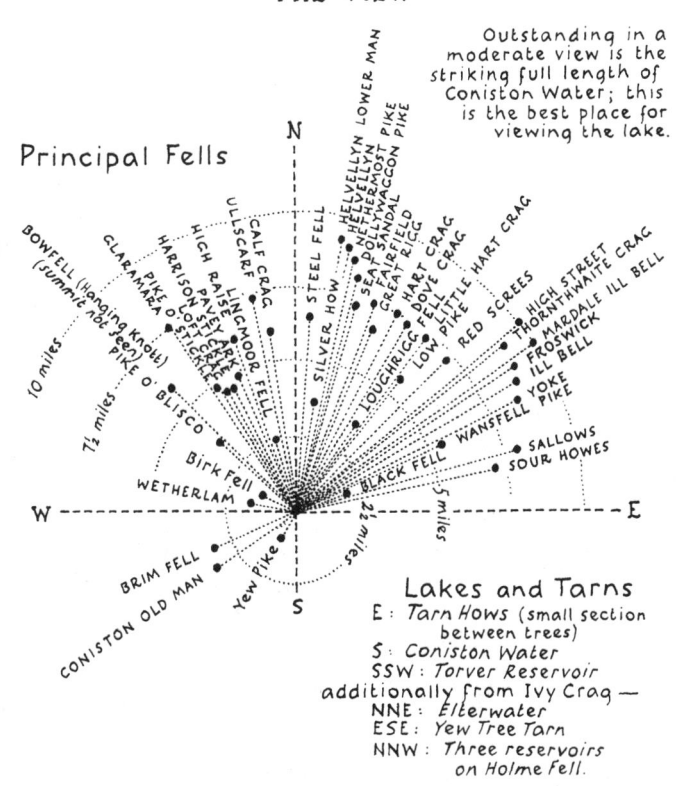

Outstanding in a moderate view is the striking full length of Coniston Water; this is the best place for viewing the lake.

Principal Fells

- BOWFELL (Hanging Knott) (summit not seen) — 10 miles
- PIKE O'STICKLE
- HARRISON STICKLE
- GLARAMARA
- PAVEY ARK
- LOFT CRAG
- HIGH RAISE
- ULLSCARF
- CALF CRAG
- LINGMOOR FELL
- PIKE O'BLISCO
- STEEL FELL
- SILVER HOW
- HELVELLYN LOWER MAN
- HELVELLYN
- DOLLYWAGGON PIKE
- NETHERMOST PIKE
- SEAT SANDAL
- FAIRFIELD
- GREAT RIGG
- HART CRAG
- DOVE CRAG
- LOUGHRIGG
- LOW PIKE
- LITTLE HART CRAG
- RED SCREES
- HIGH STREET
- THORNTHWAITE CRAG
- FROSWICK
- MARDALE ILL BELL
- ILL BELL
- YOKE
- Birk Fell
- WETHERLAM
- BLACK FELL
- WANSFELL PIKE
- SALLOWS
- SOUR HOWES
- BRIM FELL
- Yew Pike
- CONISTON OLD MAN

(7½ miles, 2½ miles, 5 miles marked)

Lakes and Tarns

- E: Tarn Hows (small section between trees)
- S: Coniston Water
- SSW: Torver Reservoir

additionally from Ivy Crag —
- NNE: Elterwater
- ESE: Yew Tree Tarn
- NNW: Three reservoirs on Holme Fell.

The Hodge Close quarries have many features of interest — a travelling crane, an aqueduct, a mineral railway, tunnels and a great arch, an emerald lake — while the two tremendous holes are extremely impressive. The disused northern quarry may be entered by a steep path at the northern end and its stony floor crossed to the arch connecting with the second quarry and the green lake.

The arch

Illgill Head

1983'

often referred to as Wastwater Screes

from Green How

Wasdale Head •

SCAFELL ▲

ILLGILL HEAD ▲
• Strands
▲ WHIN RIGG

• Santon Bridge
• Boot

MILES
0 1 2 3 4

from Miterdale

Illgill Head 2

NATURAL FEATURES

Illgill Head is known to most visitors to Lakeland as Wastwater Screes, although this latter title is strictly appropriate only to the stone-strewn flank that falls so spectacularly into the depths of Wast Water. Much of this north-western slope, however, is bracken-covered and grassy, the screes descending only from the actual summit and its southerly continuation to Whin Rigg. It is here that the fellside from top to bottom, down even to the floor of the lake 250' below the surface, is piled deep with stones lying at their maximum angle of rest, 35°-40°, through a vertical height of almost 2000'. The top of the fell is a smooth sheepwalk; these many acres of loose and shifting debris must therefore have resulted from the disintegration of crags that, ages ago, rimmed the top of the fell: some rocks remain still in a state of dangerous decay. The screes, when seen in the light of an evening sun, make a picture of remarkable colour and brilliance: a scene unique in this country.

The opposite flank, descending to Burnmoor and the shy little valley of Miterdale in patches of heather and bracken, has, in contrast, nothing of interest to show.

Wastwater Screes

Illgill Head 3

MAP

The Lakeside Path

From Wasdale Head Hall the lakeside path starts innocuously as a broad avenue in the bracken, and although it soon climbs a little and narrows to a track the way continues quite easy, even when the first screes are reached and for a mile beyond, during which section the path returns almost to the lakeside, crossing successive bands of stony debris which cause no trouble.   Then just as the walker who has been forewarned of the difficulties of the route is beginning to wonder what all the fuss is about, and with the end almost in sight, there comes a vicious quarter-mile compared with which the top of Scafell Pike is like a bowling green — here the screes take the form of big awkward boulders, loosely piled at a steep angle and avoidable only by a swim in the lake; it has been impossible to tread out a path here despite a brave effort by somebody to cairn a route. This section is really trying and progress is slow, laborious and just a little dangerous unless the feet are placed carefully; ladies wearing stiletto heels will be gravely inconvenienced and indeed many a gentle pedestrian must have suffered nightmares in this dreadful place and looked with hopelessness and envy at people striding along the smooth road on the opposite shore.   The boulders end abruptly at a little copse of trees, and here, in between giving thanks for deliverance, the tremendous cliffs and gullies high above may be studied in comfort. A distinct path now leads easily to the foot of the lake.

To get to the Screes from the road, use the field-gate opposite Woodhow (closing it afterwards), go down to the River Irt, cross Lund Bridge and follow the south bank of the river to the outlet of the lake.

continuation WHIN RIGG 4

Illgill Head 4

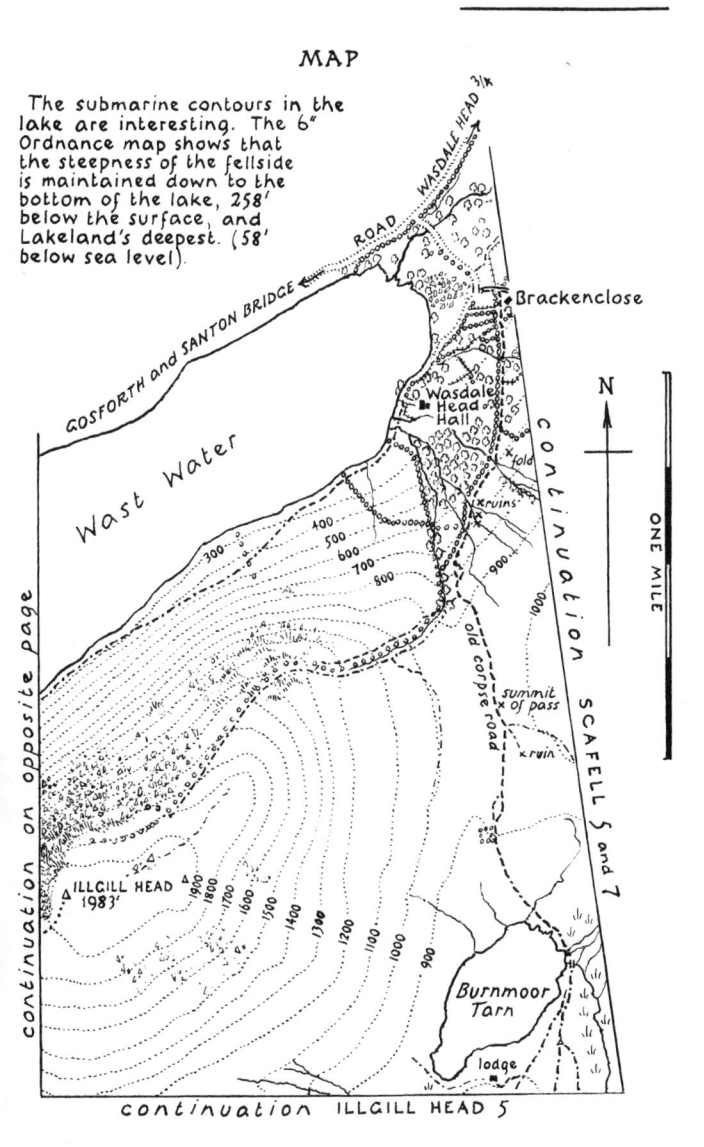

MAP

The submarine contours in the lake are interesting. The 6" Ordnance map shows that the steepness of the fellside is maintained down to the bottom of the lake, 258' below the surface, and Lakeland's deepest. (58' below sea level).

Illgill Head 5

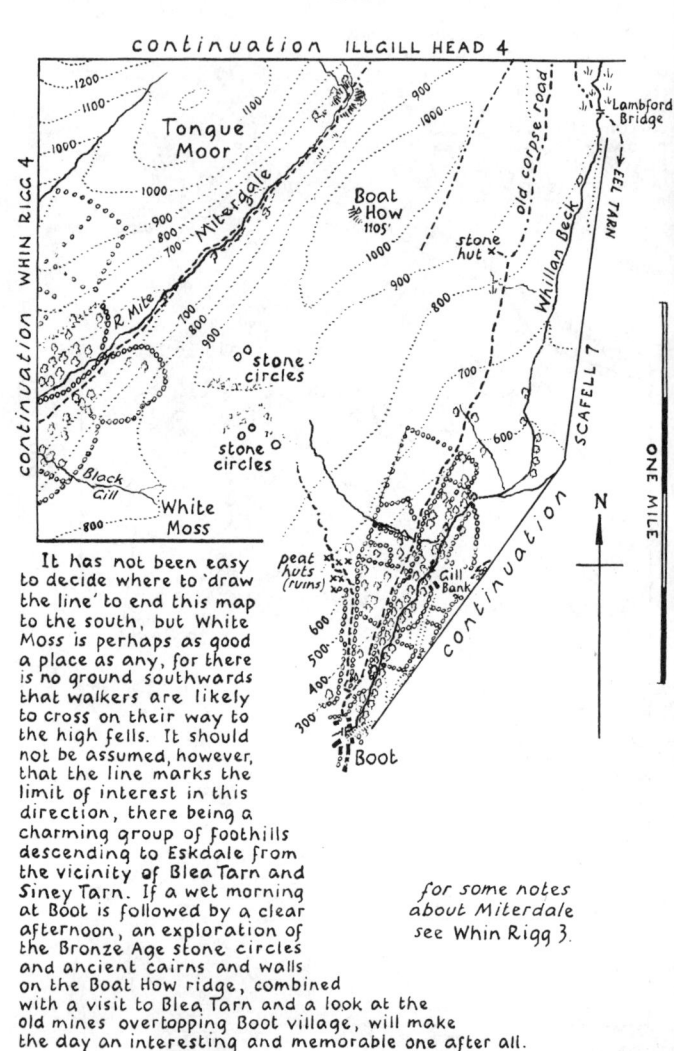

MAP

It has not been easy to decide where to 'draw the line' to end this map to the south, but White Moss is perhaps as good a place as any, for there is no ground southwards that walkers are likely to cross on their way to the high fells. It should not be assumed, however, that the line marks the limit of interest in this direction, there being a charming group of foothills descending to Eskdale from the vicinity of Blea Tarn and Siney Tarn. If a wet morning at Boot is followed by a clear afternoon, an exploration of the Bronze Age stone circles and ancient cairns and walls on the Boat How ridge, combined with a visit to Blea Tarn and a look at the old mines overtopping Boot village, will make the day an interesting and memorable one after all.

for some notes about Miterdale see Whin Rigg 3.

Illgill Head 6

ASCENT FROM WASDALE HEAD
1750 feet of ascent : 4 miles (from Wastwater Hotel)

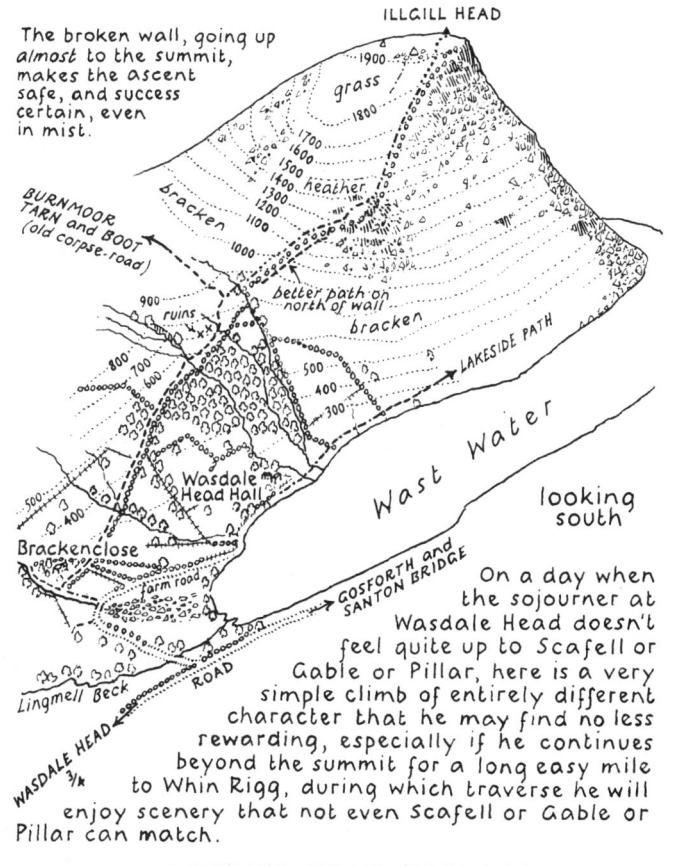

The broken wall, going up almost to the summit, makes the ascent safe, and success certain, even in mist.

(map labels: ILLGILL HEAD, grass, heather, bracken, BURNMOOR TARN and BOOT (old corpse-road), ruins, better path on north of wall, LAKESIDE PATH, Wast Water, looking south, Wasdale Head Hall, Brackenclose, GOSFORTH and SANTON BRIDGE, Lingmell Beck, ROAD, WASDALE HEAD 3/4)

On a day when the sojourner at Wasdale Head doesn't feel quite up to Scafell or Gable or Pillar, here is a very simple climb of entirely different character that he may find no less rewarding, especially if he continues beyond the summit for a long easy mile to Whin Rigg, during which traverse he will enjoy scenery that not even Scafell or Gable or Pillar can match.

ASCENTS FROM ESKDALE

The climb may be made with equal facility from Boot by using the old corpse-road to and beyond Burnmoor Tarn until it begins a gentle descent to Wasdale Head, when the route by the broken wall may be joined. Or a shorter but more tedious ascent direct from the Tarn may be made. But, from Eskdale, a more rewarding plan is to climb Whin Rigg first, then go on to Illgill Head and return via the broken wall and Burnmoor Tarn : a splendid round.

Illgill Head 7

THE SUMMIT

There is nothing at all about the actual summit to give a hint of its dramatic situation almost on the lip of the tremendous plunge to Wast Water. All is grass — dry springy turf that, on a hot day, cries aloud for a siesta; but heavy sleepers should not so position themselves that they can slide down the gradual decline to the rim of the cliffs, 35 yards from the cairn. This remarkable point of vantage, high above the lake, should be visited nevertheless: if it is omitted the whole ascent becomes purposeless. There is a lower cairn in a rash of stones nearer to Wasdale Head: this may be mistaken in mist for the true summit on the northeast approach.

RIDGE ROUTE

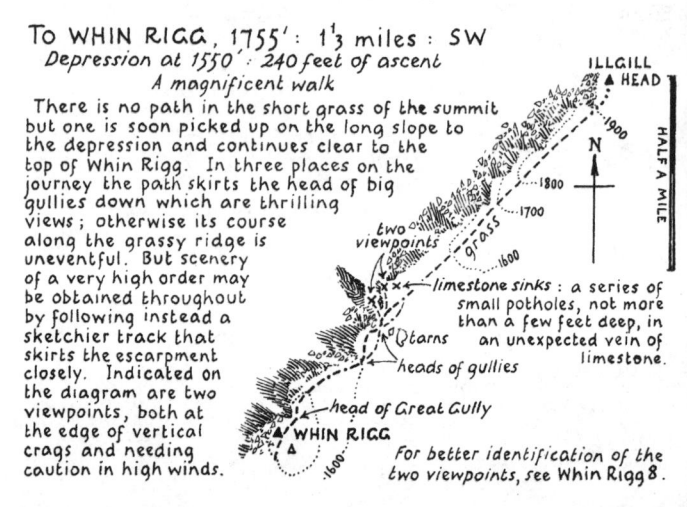

TO WHIN RIGG, 1755': 1⅓ miles : SW
Depression at 1550': 240 feet of ascent
A magnificent walk

There is no path in the short grass of the summit but one is soon picked up on the long slope to the depression and continues clear to the top of Whin Rigg. In three places on the journey the path skirts the head of big gullies down which are thrilling views; otherwise its course along the grassy ridge is uneventful. But scenery of a very high order may be obtained throughout by following instead a sketchier track that skirts the escarpment closely. Indicated on the diagram are two viewpoints, both at the edge of vertical crags and needing caution in high winds.

limestone sinks: a series of small potholes, not more than a few feet deep, in an unexpected vein of limestone.

For better identification of the two viewpoints, see Whin Rigg 8.

Illgill Head 8

THE VIEW

This summit is the only really satisfactory viewpoint for Wasdale Head — a finely proportioned scene, with gaunt mountains soaring up suddenly from the level strath of this grandest of all daleheads. (It is better seen from the lower cairn). Scafell is disappointing: a vast and featureless mass, showing its dullest side. Visitors will, *of course*, walk across to the rim of the escarpment for the view down the screes into Wast Water far below; an impressive scene indeed.

Principal Fells

- 15 miles — LONG SIDE, SKIDDAW
- ROBINSON
- SCOAT FELL
- RED PIKE
- PILLAR
- KIRK FELL
- YEWBARROW
- GT. GABLE
- BRANDRETH
- HAYCOCK
- MIDDLE FELL
- SEATALLAN
- LINGMELL
- BUCKBARROW
- SCAFELL
- SLIGHT SIDE
- CRINKLE CRAGS
- WHIN RIGG
- 5 miles
- WETHERLAM
- GREAT CARRS
- SWIRL HOW
- GREY FRIAR
- BRIM FELL
- CONISTON OLD MAN
- DOW CRAG
- BROWN PIKE
- HARTER FELL
- GREEN CRAG
- CAW
- STICKLE PIKE
- 10 miles — Black Combe

looking down on Wast Water from the summit

Lakes and Tarns

The summit-cairn is not the best place for viewing lakes and tarns, the only sheets of water clearly seen (apart from the sea) being those in the depression southwest below Whin Rigg, and an easterly perambulation of the top will be necessary if it is desired to view the Eskdale tarns. But the *piece de resistance*, is Wast Water, which comes amazingly into the picture after a walk of only 35 yards west.

Lingmell

2649'

Seathwaite •

▲ GREAT GABLE
• Wasdale Head
▲ LINGMELL
▲ SCAFELL PIKE
▲ SCAFELL

MILES
0　1　2　3

from the Corridor route, Great End

Lingmell 2

NATURAL FEATURES

Following the general pattern of the fells, Lingmell has a smooth outline to the south and west but exhibits crags and steep rough slopes to the north and east. The distinction is very marked, the ground falling away precipitously from the gentle western rise to the watershed as though severed by a great knife and laying naked a decaying confusion of crags and aretes, screes and boulders. On this flank is the huge cleft of Piers Gill, a natural chute for the stones that pour down the thousand-foot declivity, and the finest ravine in the district. Eastwards, a high saddle connects the fell with Scafell Pike, but on other sides steep slopes descend abruptly from the wide top. Lingmell Beck and Lingmell Gill are its streams, both flowing into Wast Water in wide channels and boulder-choked courses, testimony to the fury of the storms and cloudbursts that have riven the fellsides in past years; there is, indeed, a vast area of denudation (Lingmell Scars) on the slope overlooking Brown Tongue, and the devastated lakeside fields below Brackenclose add their witness to the power of the floods that have carried the debris down to the valley.

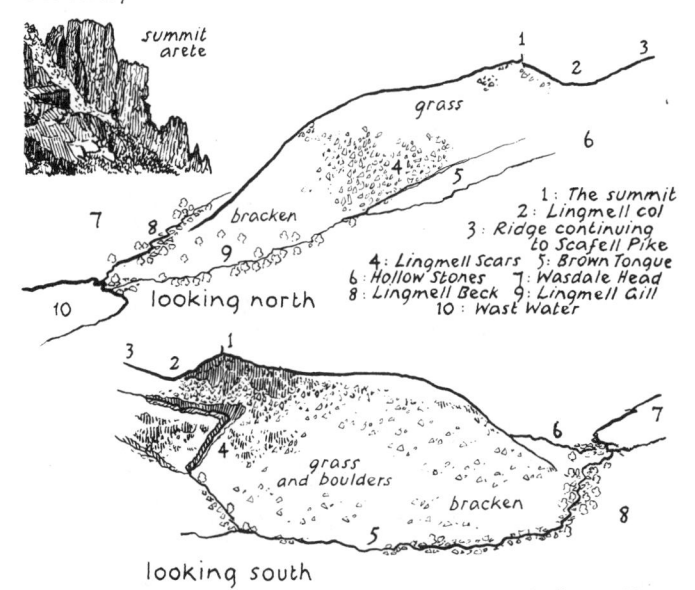

looking north

1: The summit
2: Lingmell col
3: Ridge continuing to Scafell Pike
4: Lingmell Scars   5: Brown Tongue
6: Hollow Stones   7: Wasdale Head
8: Lingmell Beck   9: Lingmell Gill
10: Wast Water

looking south

1: The summit   2: Lingmell col   3: Ridge continuing to Scafell Pike
4: Piers Gill   5: Lingmell Beck   6: Lingmell Gill   7: Wast Water
8: Wasdale Head

Lingmell 3

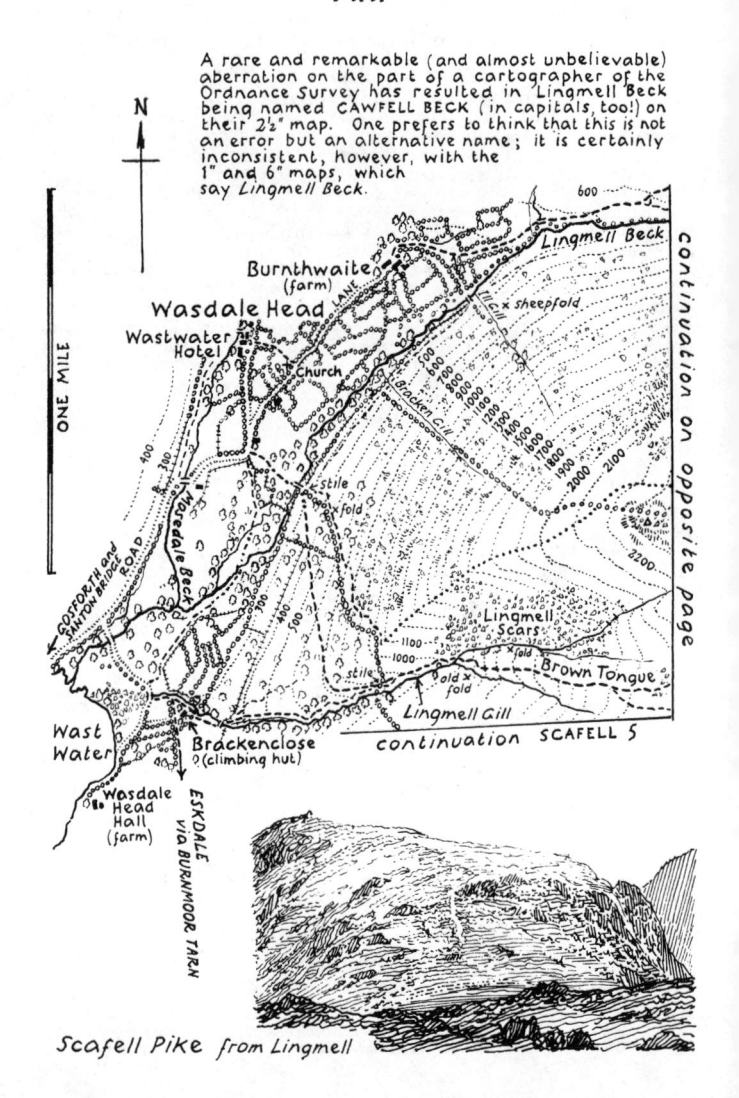

MAP

A rare and remarkable (and almost unbelievable) aberration on the part of a cartographer of the Ordnance Survey has resulted in Lingmell Beck being named CAWFELL BECK (in capitals, too!) on their 2½" map. One prefers to think that this is not an error but an alternative name; it is certainly inconsistent, however, with the 1" and 6" maps, which say Lingmell Beck.

Scafell Pike from Lingmell

Lingmell 4

MAP

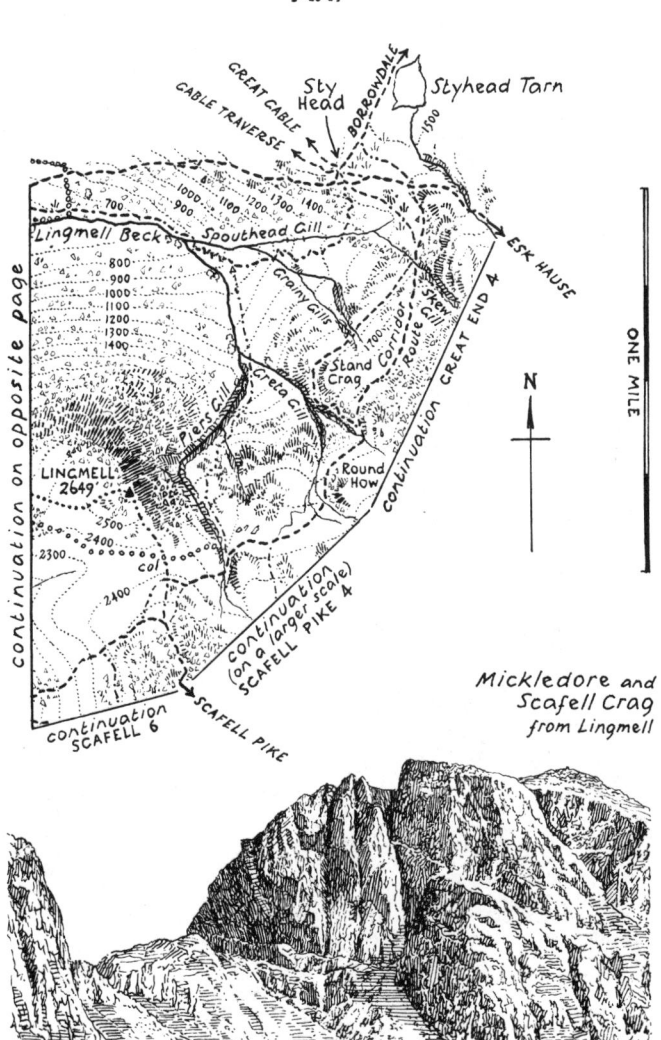

Mickledore and Scafell Crag from Lingmell

Lingmell 5

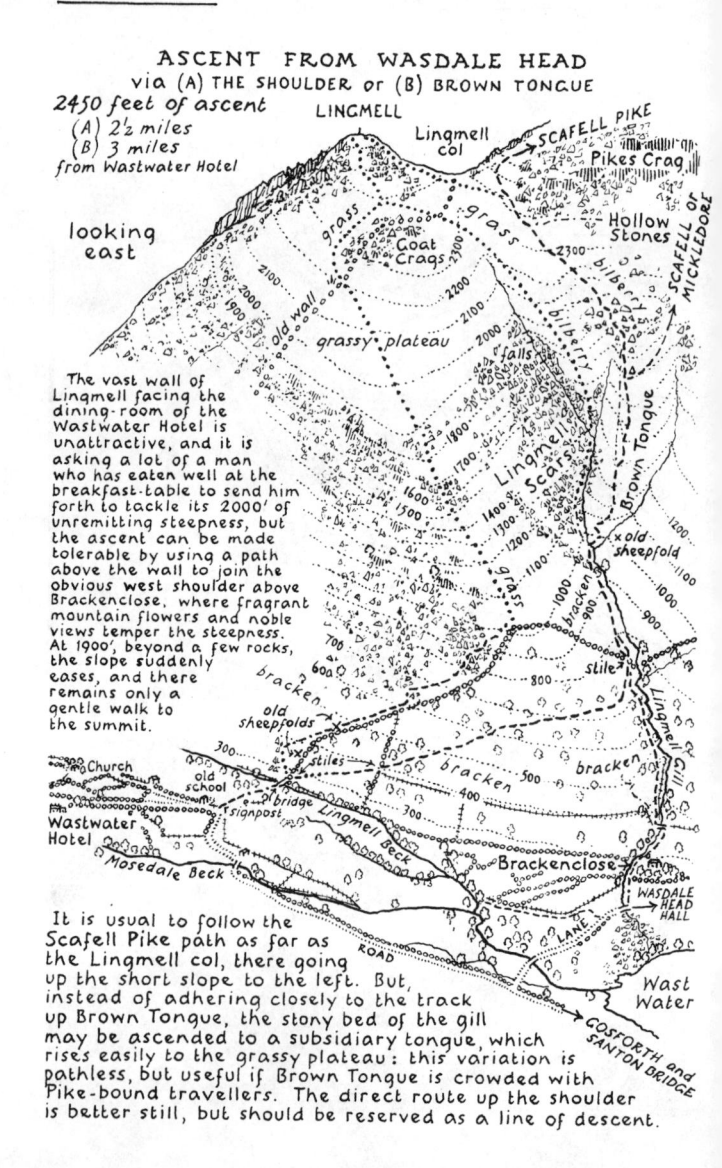

ASCENT FROM WASDALE HEAD
via (A) THE SHOULDER or (B) BROWN TONGUE

2450 feet of ascent
(A) 2½ miles
(B) 3 miles
from Wastwater Hotel

looking east

The vast wall of Lingmell facing the dining-room of the Wastwater Hotel is unattractive, and it is asking a lot of a man who has eaten well at the breakfast-table to send him forth to tackle its 2000' of unremitting steepness, but the ascent can be made tolerable by using a path above the wall to join the obvious west shoulder above Brackenclose, where fragrant mountain flowers and noble views temper the steepness. At 1900', beyond a few rocks, the slope suddenly eases, and there remains only a gentle walk to the summit.

It is usual to follow the Scafell Pike path as far as the Lingmell col, there going up the short slope to the left. But, instead of adhering closely to the track up Brown Tongue, the stony bed of the gill may be ascended to a subsidiary tongue, which rises easily to the grassy plateau: this variation is pathless, but useful if Brown Tongue is crowded with Pike-bound travellers. The direct route up the shoulder is better still, but should be reserved as a line of descent.

Lingmell 6

ASCENT FROM WASDALE HEAD
via PIERS GILL
2450 feet of ascent : 3½ miles (from Wastwater Hotel)

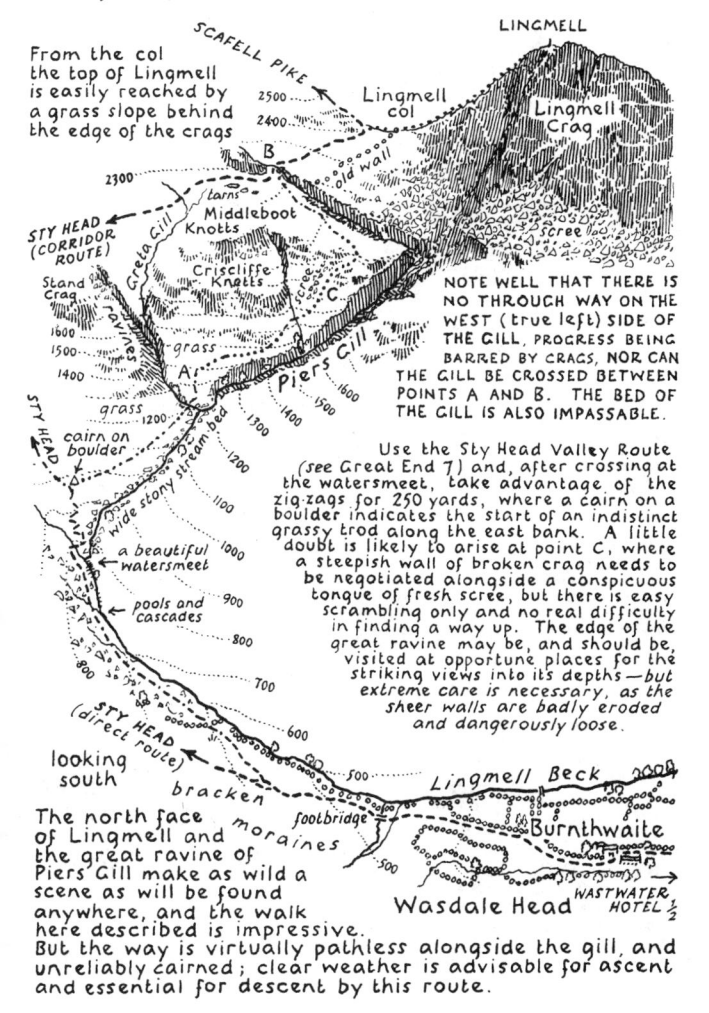

From the col the top of Lingmell is easily reached by a grass slope behind the edge of the crags

NOTE WELL THAT THERE IS NO THROUGH WAY ON THE WEST (true left) SIDE OF THE GILL, PROGRESS BEING BARRED BY CRAGS, NOR CAN THE GILL BE CROSSED BETWEEN POINTS A AND B. THE BED OF THE GILL IS ALSO IMPASSABLE.

Use the Sty Head Valley Route (see Great End 7) and, after crossing at the watersmeet, take advantage of the zig-zags for 250 yards, where a cairn on a boulder indicates the start of an indistinct grassy trod along the east bank. A little doubt is likely to arise at point C, where a steepish wall of broken crag needs to be negotiated alongside a conspicuous tongue of fresh scree, but there is easy scrambling only and no real difficulty in finding a way up. The edge of the great ravine may be, and should be, visited at opportune places for the striking views into its depths — but extreme care is necessary, as the sheer walls are badly eroded and dangerously loose.

The north face of Lingmell and the great ravine of Piers Gill make as wild a scene as will be found anywhere, and the walk here described is impressive. But the way is virtually pathless alongside the gill, and unreliably cairned; clear weather is advisable for ascent and essential for descent by this route.

Lingmell 7

THE SUMMIT

Summit-cairns are welcome sights, but they are seldom objects of beauty or admiration. Here, however, on the highest point of Lingmell, is one of singular elegance, a graceful ten-foot spire that quite puts to shame the squat and inartistic edifice crowning the neighbouring very superior Scafell Pike. Long may it escape the attentions of the new gallants, the cairn-wreckers.

Its position, on the rim of the tremendous downfall of Lingmell Crag, commanding the length of the Corridor Route, is superb.

The summit area is stony, but not too stony to hamper progress unduly, and a short exploration along the top of the cliff northwards earns a reward of magnificent views.

DESCENTS:
TO WASDALE HEAD: The shoulder route is a quick and easy way down, with excellent views right left and centre, and much better than the longer alternative via Lingmell col and the Brown Tongue path. *In mist* the latter is to be preferred, as the pathless shoulder at first is too broad to give direction naturally.
TO BORROWDALE: Join the Corridor Route just beyond Lingmell col.

RIDGE ROUTE

To SCAFELL PIKE, 3210':
⅛ mile : SSE
Depression (Lingmell col) at 2370'
850 feet of ascent
A tedious half-hour

With steep ground on the left hand descend the grass slope (not much of a track) to Lingmell col, where cross the broken wall and join the cairned path coming up from Brown Tongue; this is distinct over stones and boulders to the summit.

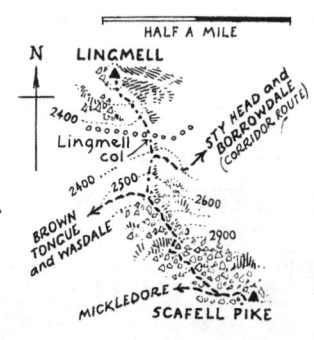

Lingmell 8

THE VIEW

Scafell Pike dominates the scene, but from this side is the dullest of mountains; Scafell is better, but the grouping of the western fells around Mosedale is best of all. The views of Borrowdale and down Wast Water to the coastal plain and the sea are also good.

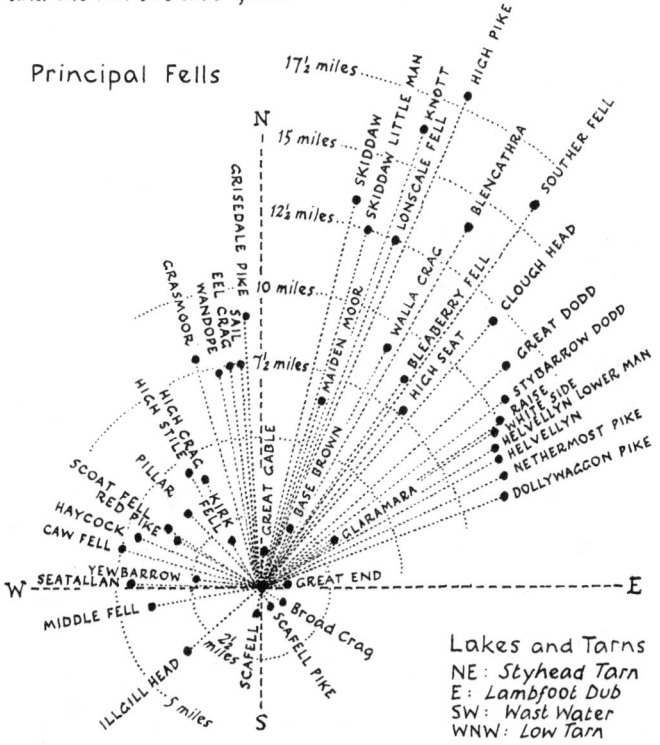

Principal Fells

(diagram of bearings from summit, showing distances 17½ miles, 15 miles, 12½ miles, 10 miles, 7½ miles, 5 miles, 2½ miles, with fells listed around the compass:)

HIGH PIKE, KNOTT, LITTLE MAN, SKIDDAW LITTLE MAN, SKIDDAW, SOUTHER FELL, LONSCALE FELL, BLENCATHRA, WALLA CRAG, MAIDEN MOOR, BLEABERRY FELL, CLOUGH HEAD, HIGH SEAT, GREAT DODD, STYBARROW DODD, RAISE, WHITE SIDE, HELVELLYN LOWER MAN, HELVELLYN, NETHERMOST PIKE, DOLLYWAGGON PIKE, GRISEDALE PIKE, GRASMOOR, EEL CRAG, SAIL, WANDOPE, HIGH CRAG, HIGH STILE, SCOAT FELL, RED PIKE, PILLAR, KIRK FELL, HAYCOCK, CAW FELL, YEWBARROW, SEATALLAN, MIDDLE FELL, ILLGILL HEAD, GREAT GABLE, BASE BROWN, GREAT END, BROAD CRAG, SCAFELL, SCAFELL PIKE, GLARAMARA

W — E, N, S

Lakes and Tarns
NE: Styhead Tarn
E: Lambfoot Dub
SW: Wast Water
WNW: Low Tarn

Two features of the view deserve special mention. The first is the surprising aspect of Great Gable across the deep gulf of Lingmell Beck (seen more fully from the summit-ridge north of the main cairn), the eye being deceived into seeing its half-mile of height as quite perpendicular: a remarkable picture. The other is the astonishing downward view into the stony depths of Piers Gill, a thousand-foot drop which again is not nearly so vertical as it appears at first sight to the startled beholder.

Lingmell 9

Piers Gill

above
 the upper section (looking down from the Corridor Route)

right
 the lower section (looking up)

top right
 pinnacles and spires in the gill

Lingmell 10

Great Gable from Lingmell

Lingmoor Fell 1530'

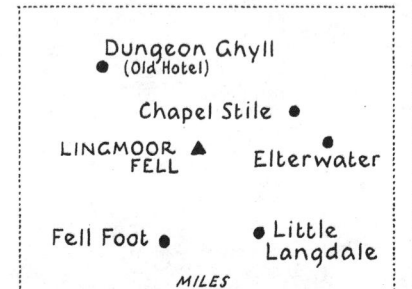

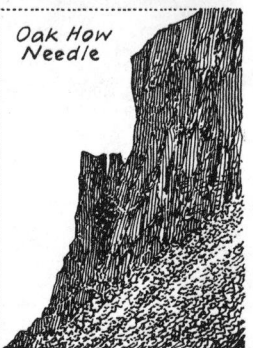

from Elterwater

Dungeon Ghyll
● (Old Hotel)

Chapel Stile ●

LINGMOOR ▲   ● Elterwater
   FELL

Fell Foot ●   ● Little
                 Langdale

MILES
0   1   2

Oak How Needle

Lingmoor Fell 2

NATURAL FEATURES

A crescent-shaped ridge of high ground rises to the west from Elterwater's pleasant pastures, climbs to a well-defined summit, a fine vantage point, and then curves northwards as it descends to valley-level near Dungeon Ghyll. Within the crescent lies Great Langdale, the longer outside curve sloping down into Little Langdale and the Blea Tarn depression. The mass is Lingmoor Fell, so named because of the extensive zone of heather clothing the northern flanks below the summit. The fell has contributed generously to the prosperity of the surrounding valleys, for not only has it nurtured the sheep but it has also been quarried extensively for many generations, yielding a very beautiful and durable green stone. Bracken and heather, some ragged patches of juniper and well-timbered estate woods, many crags and a delectable little tarn, all combine to make this fell a colourful addition to the varied attractions of the Langdale area.

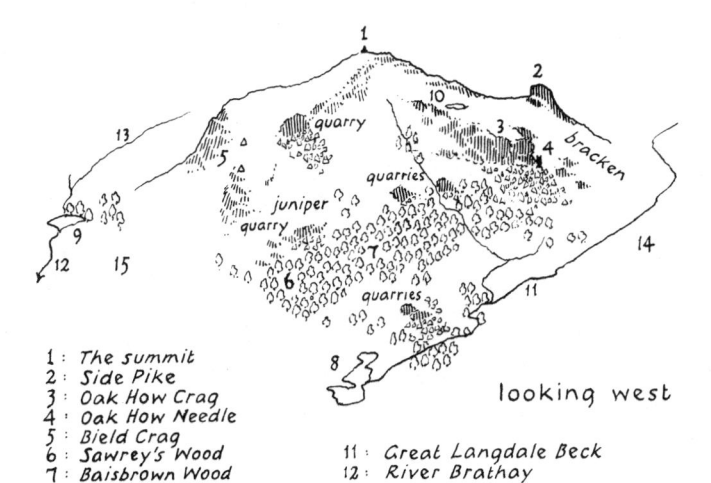

looking west

1: The summit
2: Side Pike
3: Oak How Crag
4: Oak How Needle
5: Bield Crag
6: Sawrey's Wood
7: Baisbrown Wood
8: Elterwater
9: Little Langdale Tarn
10: Lingmoor Tarn
11: Great Langdale Beck
12: River Brathay
13: Bleamoss Beck
14: Great Langdale
15: Little Langdale

Lingmoor Fell 3

MAP

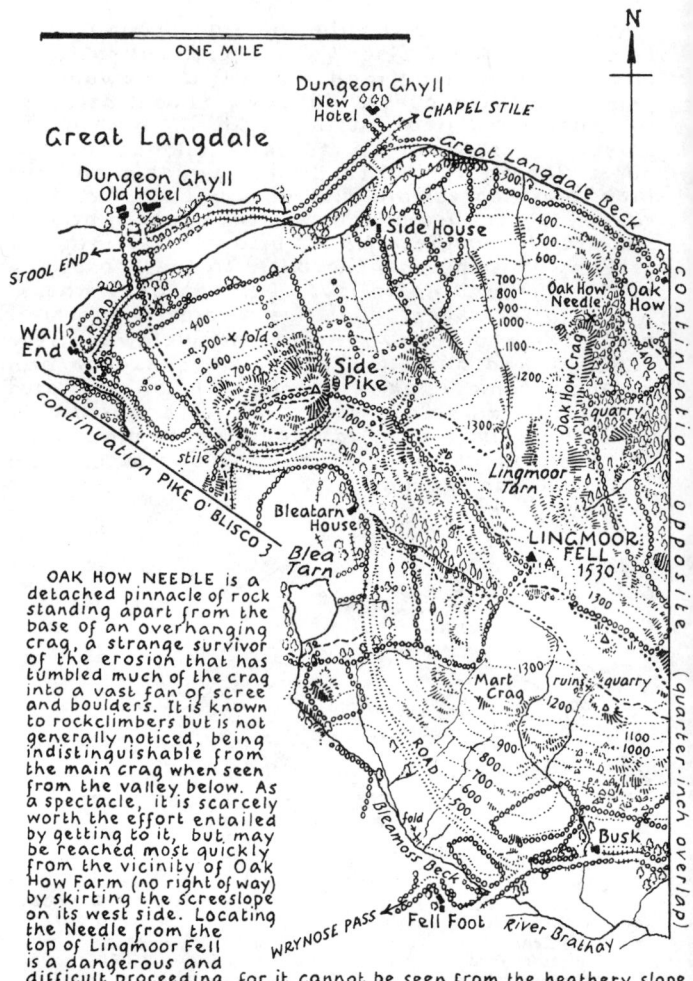

OAK HOW NEEDLE is a detached pinnacle of rock standing apart from the base of an overhanging crag, a strange survivor of the erosion that has tumbled much of the crag into a vast fan of scree and boulders. It is known to rockclimbers but is not generally noticed, being indistinguishable from the main crag when seen from the valley below. As a spectacle, it is scarcely worth the effort entailed by getting to it, but may be reached most quickly from the vicinity of Oak How Farm (no right of way) by skirting the screeslope on its west side. Locating the Needle from the top of Lingmoor Fell is a dangerous and difficult proceeding, for it cannot be seen from the heathery slope above the crag, which breaks away suddenly in a vertical cliff: the safest course is to descend the east bank of the beck issuing from Lingmoor Tarn until a big area of juniper is seen on the right, whence by walking eastwards above it, a small bracken *col* is reached — and there, directly in front and quite close, is Oak How Needle.

Lingmoor Fell 4

MAP

Great Langdale is probably the most-frequented valley in the district, with a heavy inflow of visitors summer and winter alike, most of them bound for Dungeon Ghyll. It is all the more strange, therefore, that the whole of the traffic, both on foot and awheel, is confined to the one road in the valley, on the north side, while the south side along the base of Lingmoor Fell, although scenically more attractive, seldom sees a soul. Obviously there should be a public footpath linking Baisbrown, Oak How, Side House and Wall End — and how much pleasanter than the busy road this would be! — but there isn't. Almost every other inhabited valley in Lakeland has popular rights of way along *both* sides of the main stream.

But not Great Langdale.

Alternative spellings of Baisbrown:
Baysbrown (Ordnance maps)
Bayes Brown (the tenant, if reported correctly).

Lingmoor Tarn

ONE MILE

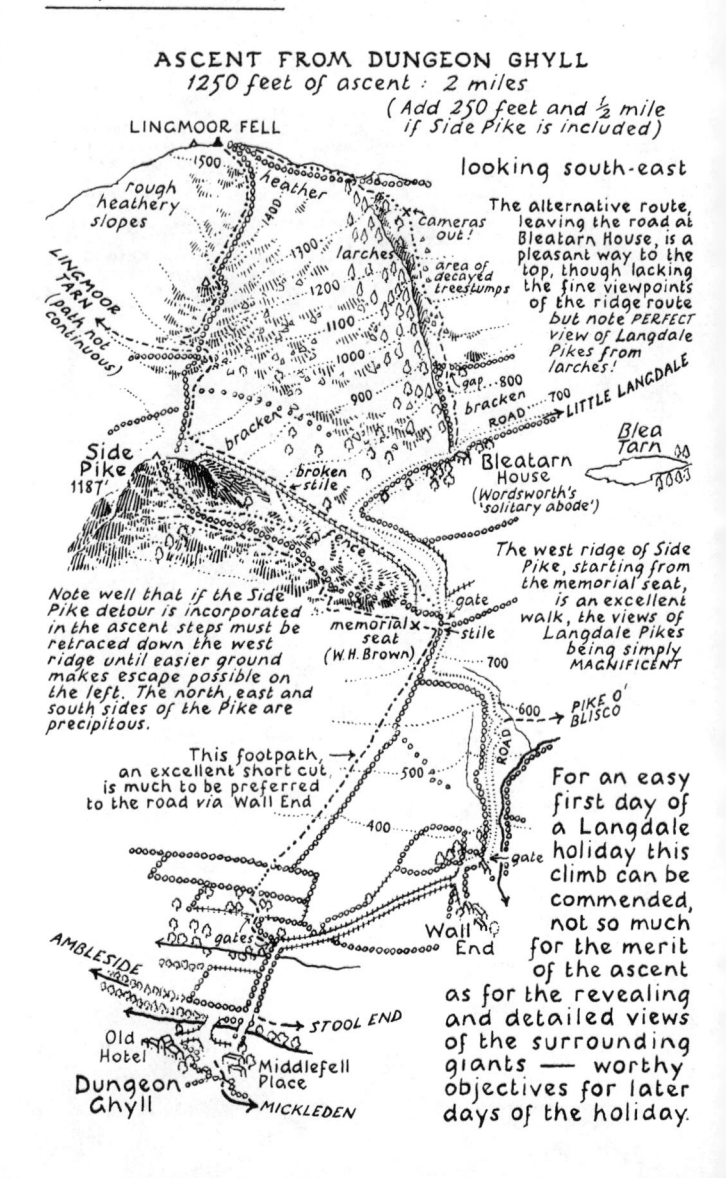

Lingmoor Fell 5

ASCENT FROM DUNGEON GHYLL
1250 feet of ascent : 2 miles
(Add 250 feet and ½ mile if Side Pike is included)

looking south-east

LINGMOOR FELL 1500

rough heathery slopes

heather

1400

cameras out!

larches

1300

area of decayed treestumps

1200

1100

LINGMOOR TARN (path not continuous)

1000

900

gap...800

bracken

700

ROAD — LITTLE LANGDALE

bracken

Blea Tarn

Side Pike 1187'

broken stile

Bleatarn House (Wordsworth's 'solitary abode')

The alternative route, leaving the road at Bleatarn House, is a pleasant way to the top, though lacking the fine viewpoints of the ridge route but note PERFECT view of Langdale Pikes from larches!

fence

gate

memorial × stile
seat
(W.H. Brown)

700

The west ridge of Side Pike, starting from the memorial seat, is an excellent walk, the views of Langdale Pikes being simply MAGNIFICENT

Note well that if the Side Pike detour is incorporated in the ascent steps must be retraced down the west ridge until easier ground makes escape possible on the left. The north east and south sides of the Pike are precipitous.

600 → PIKE O' BLISCO

ROAD

This footpath, an excellent short cut is much to be preferred to the road via Wall End

500

400

gate

gates

AMBLESIDE

Wall End

→ STOOL END

Old Hotel

Dungeon Ghyll

Middlefell Place

MICKLEDEN

For an easy first day of a Langdale holiday this climb can be commended, not so much for the merit of the ascent as for the revealing and detailed views of the surrounding giants — worthy objectives for later days of the holiday.

Lingmoor Fell 6

Side Pike
from the ridge running up to Lingmoor Fell

Side Pike is accessible to the walker by its west ridge only, and there is no other safe way off. When descending from the cairn do not be tempted by a track going down eastwards: this ends suddenly above a vertical drop, with easy ground tantalisingly close, but out of reach. On the drawing above, this dangerous trap is seen directly below the X.

Langdale Pikes from Side Pike
1: Pike o' Stickle
2: Loft Crag
3: Thorn Crag
4: Harrison Stickle
5: Pavey Ark

Lingmoor Fell 7

ASCENTS FROM ELTERWATER AND CHAPEL STILE
1350 feet of ascent : 2½ miles

When the ridge-wall is reached, cross it at the hurdle and follow it to the right. The wall is not continuous to the summit. The edge of the top quarry is unprotected and dangerous.

LINGMOOR FELL

quarries

hurdle

prominent yew — Watch for sharp turn left when opposite to it

If the route from the gate on the road is taken, watch for the indistinct bifurcation left, passing through a gap in the wall

juniper

bracken

quarries

From this section of the path, Oak How Needle is clearly in view (to the right) standing apart from the base of a crag.

cave

LITTLE LANGDALE ½

gate

Baisbrown Wood

From Elterwater it is a simpler plan to by-pass the lower quarries by using one of the two routes leaving the upper Little Langdale road

Sawrey's Wood

BAISBROWN ½

Baisbrown Estate

store ground spoil heaps

Great Langdale Beck

DUNGEON GHYLL 2

quarries

CONISTON

steps

Chapel Stile

Youth Hostel

GRASMERE 3

Langdale Estate

Britannia Inn

looking west-south-west

AMBLESIDE 4

Elterwater

AMBLESIDE 4

The lower quarries are a labyrinth of paths and cart-tracks, confusing on a first visit. The extensive spoil-heaps are not pretty, the many trees being an ineffective screen; nevertheless, this is an interesting and attractive approach to the ridge.

Lingmoor Fell 8

ASCENT FROM LITTLE LANGDALE
1100 feet of ascent :
1½ miles (from Dale End)

The quarry track may be followed (easy walking) to its terminus at some ruins, disused workings, whence the same direction may be continued along a shallow trough to join the Bleatarn House route at a wall. Or the track may be left when it turns towards the ridge-wall beyond the big cairn above Bield Crag, and the ridge then followed to the top. Watch for the junction or it will be missed.

The edge of this quarry is unprotected and dangerous.

A grassy quarry track serves excellently to point the way and ease the journey. On this route the best views remain hidden until the moment of arrival at the summit.

looking west

THE SUMMIT

The highest point, adjacent to an angle in the summit wall, is a stony mound superimposed on a dome dark with heather (Brown How), and owns a large cairn. 150 yards east, along the line of a badly broken fence, is a second cairn, a good viewpoint.

DESCENTS: Routes of ascent may be reversed, with the wall as guide initially. In mist, when descending the south-east ridge, care should be taken to skirt the quarry and not fall into it — many people have had a shock here.

The Coniston Fells
WETHERLAM — SWIRL HOW — GREAT CARRS

RIDGE ROUTES : Lingmoor Fell is isolated from other fells and therefore has no connecting ridges. Its nearest neighbour is Pike o' Blisco, but the considerable descent to the Bleatarn road makes a climb therefrom virtually a complete ascent.

Lingmoor Fell 9

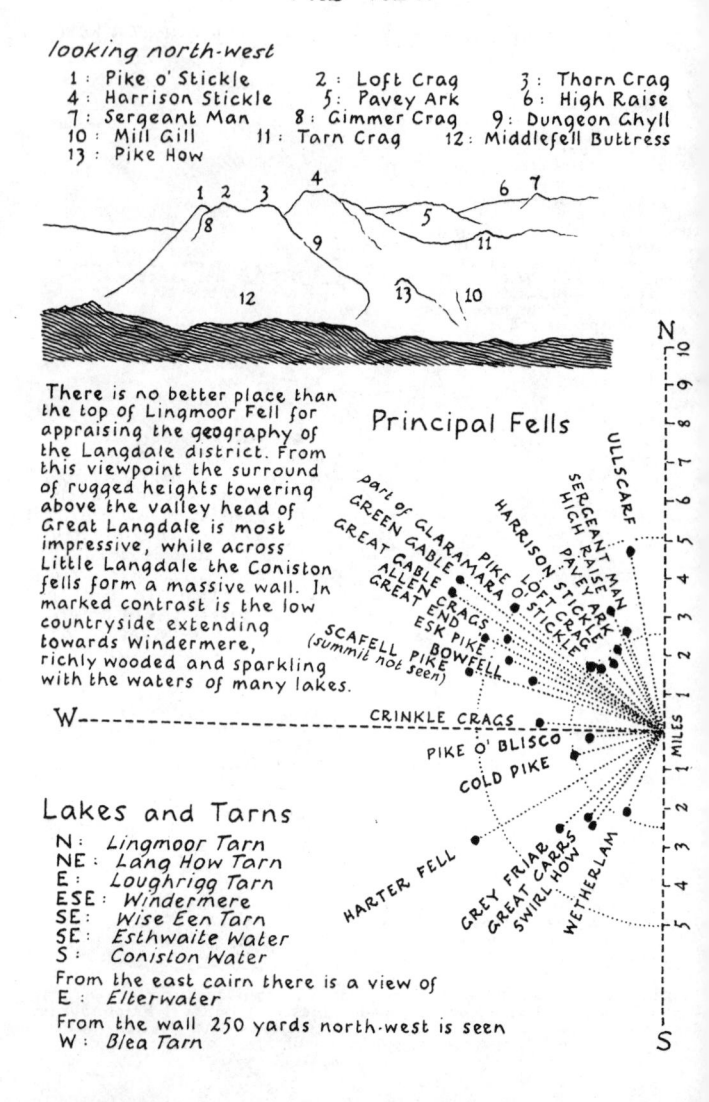

THE VIEW

looking north-west

1: Pike o' Stickle
2: Loft Crag
3: Thorn Crag
4: Harrison Stickle
5: Pavey Ark
6: High Raise
7: Sergeant Man
8: Gimmer Crag
9: Dungeon Ghyll
10: Mill Gill
11: Tarn Crag
12: Middlefell Buttress
13: Pike How

There is no better place than the top of Lingmoor Fell for appraising the geography of the Langdale district. From this viewpoint the surround of rugged heights towering above the valley head of Great Langdale is most impressive, while across Little Langdale the Coniston fells form a massive wall. In marked contrast is the low countryside extending towards Windermere, richly wooded and sparkling with the waters of many lakes.

Principal Fells

part of CLARAMARA
GREEN GABLE
PIKE O' STICKLE
GREAT GABLE
LOFT CRAG
HARRISON STICKLE
PAVEY ARK
HIGH RAISE
SERGEANT MAN
ULLSCARF
ALLEN CRAGS
ESK PIKE
SCAFELL PIKE (summit not seen)
BOWFELL
CRINKLE CRAGS
PIKE O' BLISCO
COLD PIKE
HARTER FELL
GREY FRIAR
GREAT CARRS
SWIRL HOW
WETHERLAM

Lakes and Tarns

N: Lingmoor Tarn
NE: Lang How Tarn
E: Loughrigg Tarn
ESE: Windermere
SE: Wise Een Tarn
SE: Esthwaite Water
S: Coniston Water

From the east cairn there is a view of
E: Elterwater

From the wall 250 yards north-west is seen
W: Blea Tarn

Lingmoor Fell 10

THE VIEW

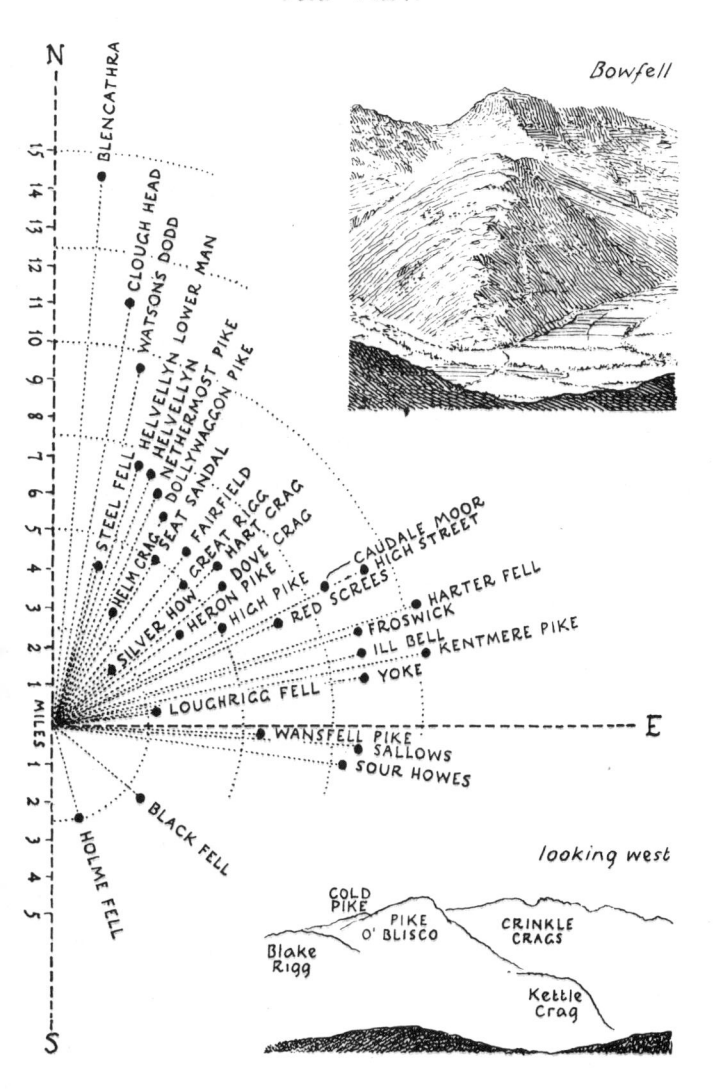

Bowfell

looking west

Blake Rigg — COLD PIKE — PIKE O' BLISCO — CRINKLE CRAGS — Kettle Crag

Compass/panorama labels (N to S, clockwise):
- BLENCATHRA
- CLOUGH HEAD
- WATSONS DODD
- HELVELLYN LOWER MAN
- HELVELLYN
- NETHERMOST PIKE
- DOLLYWAGGON PIKE
- STEEL FELL
- SEAT SANDAL
- HELM CRAG
- FAIRFIELD
- GREAT RIGG
- SILVER HOW
- HART CRAG
- HERON PIKE
- DOVE CRAG
- HIGH PIKE
- CAUDALE MOOR
- HIGH STREET
- RED SCREES
- FROSWICK
- HARTER FELL
- ILL BELL
- KENTMERE PIKE
- LOUGHRIGG FELL
- YOKE
- WANSFELL PIKE
- SALLOWS
- SOUR HOWES
- BLACK FELL
- HOLME FELL

Pike o' Blisco

Sunday name: Pike OF Blisco

2304'

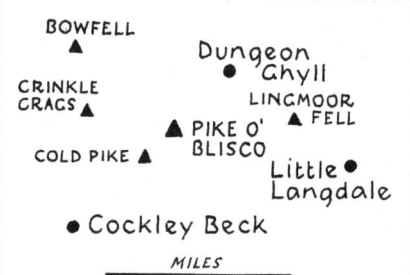

BOWFELL ▲

Dungeon
● Ghyll

CRINKLE
CRAGS ▲

LINGMOOR
▲ FELL

▲ PIKE O'
BLISCO

COLD PIKE ▲

Little ●
Langdale

● Cockley Beck

MILES
0 1 2 3

from Side Pike

Pike o' Blisco 2

NATURAL FEATURES

A mountain has added merit if its highest point can be seen from the valley below, instead of being hidden beyond receding upper slopes as is often the case, for then the objective is clear to the climber, there is no deception about height or steepness, and the full stature from base to summit can readily be comprehended. Such a mountain is Pike o' Blisco, with a tall columnar cairn plainly in view from the floor of Great Langdale and perched high above the steep and rugged flank that forms a massive south wall to the side valley of Oxendale. This peak has great character, for shapeliness and a sturdy strength combine well in its appearance, and that splendid cairn etched against the sky is at once an invitation and a challenge — while the man has no blood in his veins who does not respond eagerly to its fine-sounding swashbuckling name, savouring so much of buccaneers and the Spanish Main. There are higher summits all around, some of far greater altitude; but height alone counts for nothing, and Pike o' Blisco would hold its own in any company.

Easy routes to the top can be worked out between the crags, which are in abundance. Kettle Crag above Wall End, and Blake Rigg towering over Blea Tarn, are notable. Except for minor runnels near the top of Wrynose Pass, all streams from the fell join ultimately in the River Brathay.

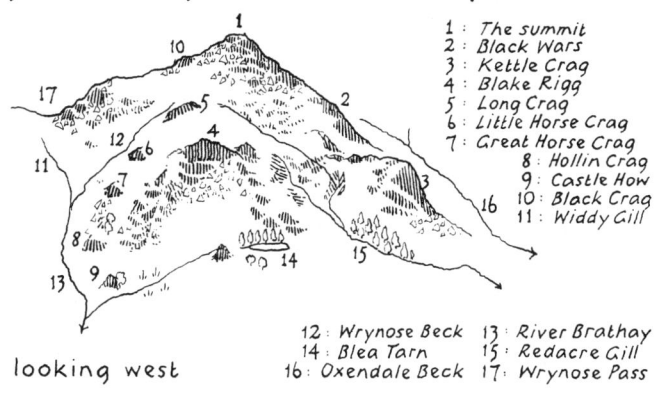

1 : The summit
2 : Black Wars
3 : Kettle Crag
4 : Blake Rigg
5 : Long Crag
6 : Little Horse Crag
7 : Great Horse Crag
8 : Hollin Crag
9 : Castle How
10 : Black Crag
11 : Widdy Gill
12 : Wrynose Beck
13 : River Brathay
14 : Blea Tarn
15 : Redacre Gill
16 : Oxendale Beck
17 : Wrynose Pass

looking west

Pike o' Blisco 3

MAP

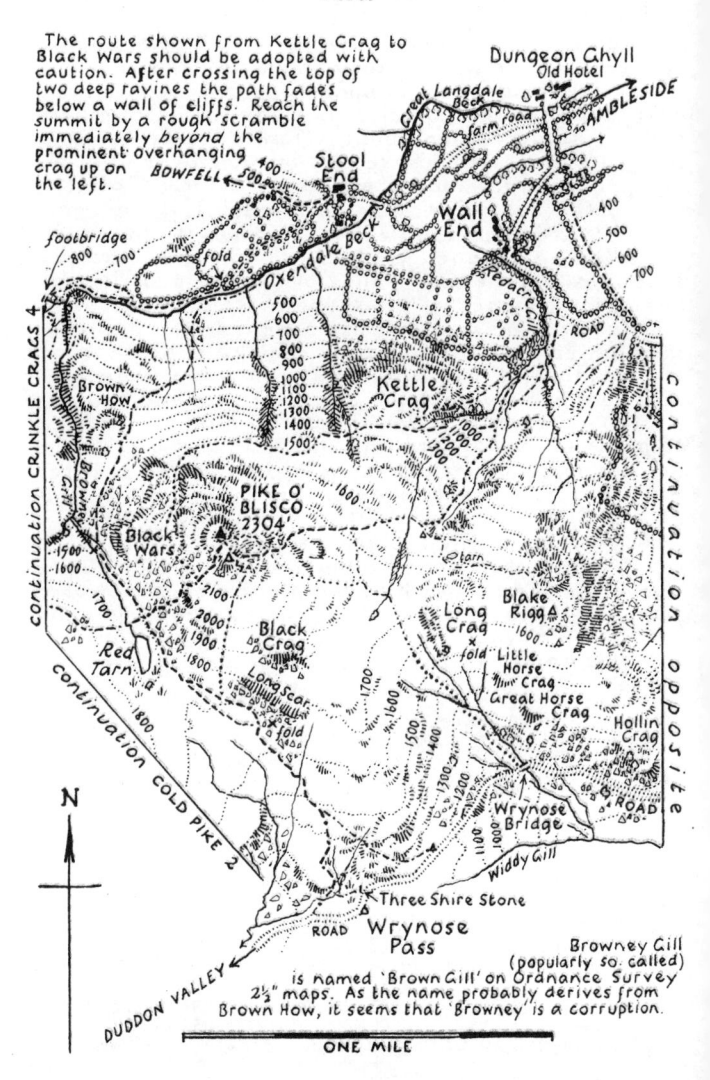

The route shown from Kettle Crag to Black Wars should be adopted with caution. After crossing the top of two deep ravines the path fades below a wall of cliffs. Reach the summit by a rough scramble immediately *beyond* the prominent overhanging crag up on the left.

Browney Gill (popularly so called) is named 'Brown Gill' on Ordnance Survey 2½" maps. As the name probably derives from Brown How, it seems that 'Browney' is a corruption.

ONE MILE

Pike o' Blisco 4

Blea Tarn's once well-wooded western shore is now denuded of many of its trees, although a fringe has been left by the water's edge (including the pines that have graced many a thousand photographs).
Rhododendron thickets, spreading unchecked in the vicinity, are choking paths and the whole place bears the appearance of a garden that has long been neglected

MAP

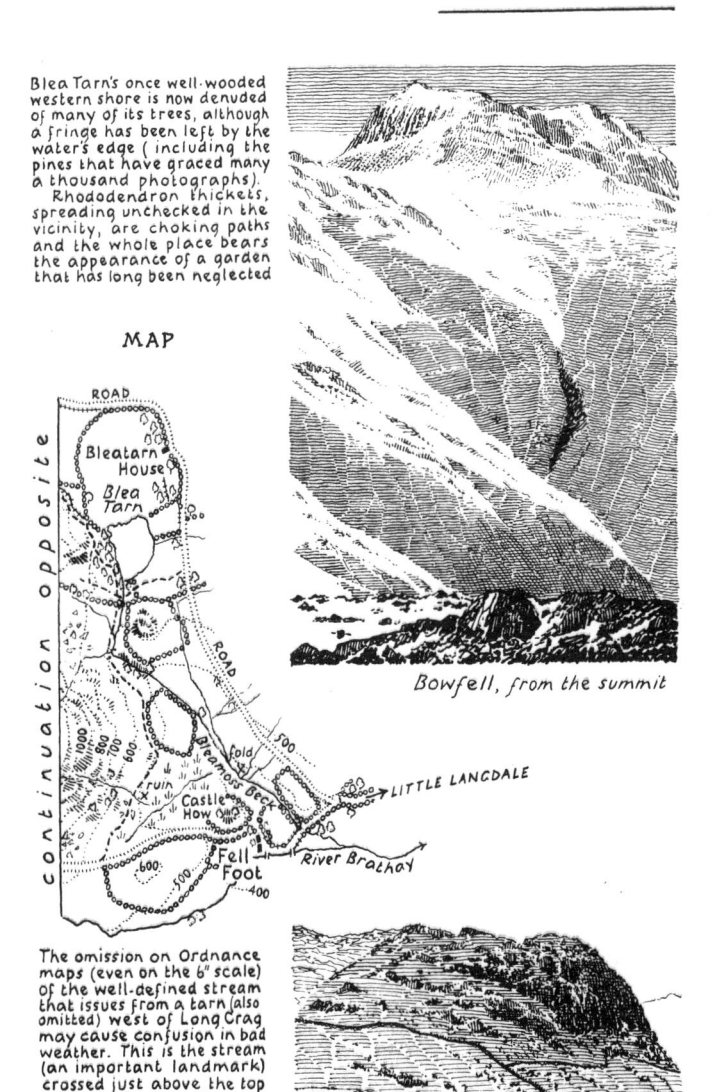

continuation opposite

Bowfell, from the summit

The omission on Ordnance maps (even on the 6" scale) of the well-defined stream that issues from a tarn (also omitted) west of Long Crag may cause confusion in bad weather. This is the stream (an important landmark) crossed just above the top of Redacre Gill on the Wall End route.

Kettle Crag

Pike o' Blisco 5

ASCENT FROM DUNGEON GHYLL (via WALL END)
2100 feet of ascent : 2¼ miles

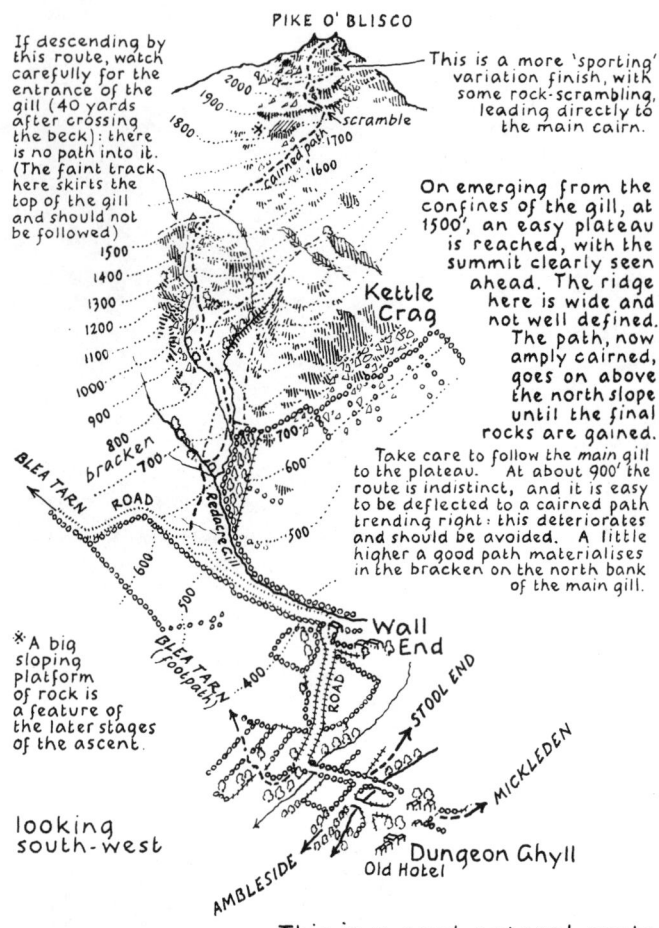

PIKE O' BLISCO

If descending by this route, watch carefully for the entrance of the gill (40 yards after crossing the beck): there is no path into it. (The faint track here skirts the top of the gill and should not be followed)

This is a more 'sporting' variation finish, with some rock-scrambling, leading directly to the main cairn.

On emerging from the confines of the gill, at 1500', an easy plateau is reached, with the summit clearly seen ahead. The ridge here is wide and not well defined. The path, now amply cairned, goes on above the north slope until the final rocks are gained.

Take care to follow the *main* gill to the plateau. At about 900' the route is indistinct, and it is easy to be deflected to a cairned path trending right: this deteriorates and should be avoided. A little higher a good path materialises in the bracken on the north bank of the main gill.

* A big sloping platform of rock is a feature of the later stages of the ascent.

looking south-west

This is a good natural route, much easier than is suggested by the formidable appearance of the objective. The path, although occasionally intermittent, is generally good.

Pike o' Blisco 6

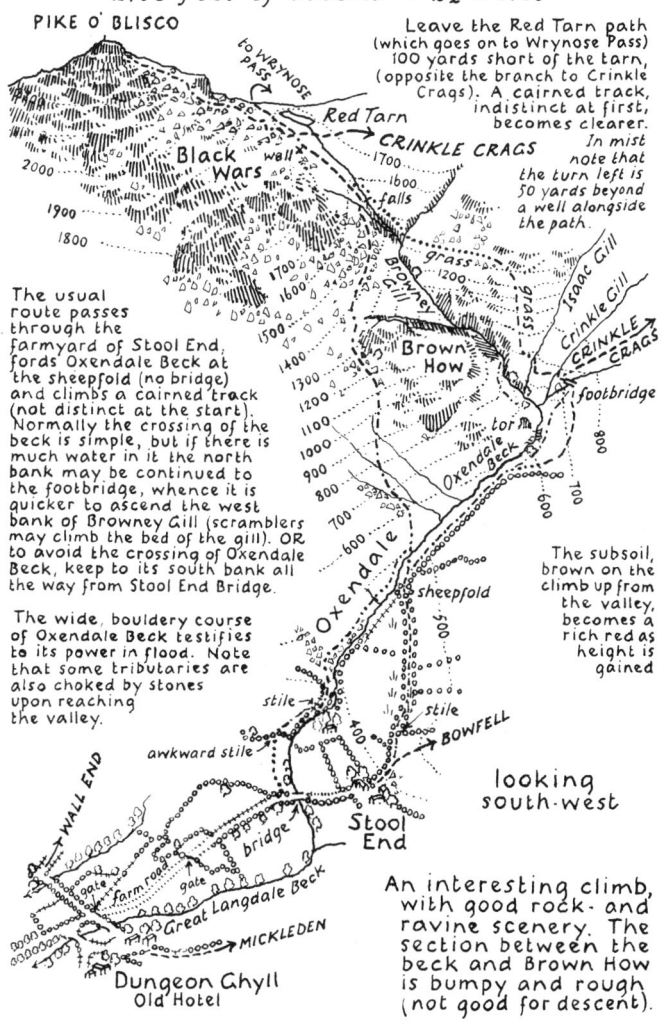

ASCENT FROM DUNGEON GHYLL (via STOOL END)
2100 feet of ascent : 2½ miles

Leave the Red Tarn path (which goes on to Wrynose Pass) 100 yards short of the tarn, (opposite the branch to Crinkle Crags). A cairned track, indistinct at first, becomes clearer.

In mist note that the turn left is 50 yards beyond a well alongside the path.

The usual route passes through the farmyard of Stool End, fords Oxendale Beck at the sheepfold (no bridge) and climbs a cairned track (not distinct at the start). Normally the crossing of the beck is simple, but if there is much water in it the north bank may be continued to the footbridge, whence it is quicker to ascend the west bank of Browney Gill (scramblers may climb the bed of the gill). OR to avoid the crossing of Oxendale Beck, keep to its south bank all the way from Stool End Bridge.

The wide, bouldery course of Oxendale Beck testifies to its power in flood. Note that some tributaries are also choked by stones upon reaching the valley.

The subsoil, brown on the climb up from the valley, becomes a rich red as height is gained

looking south-west

An interesting climb, with good rock- and ravine scenery. The section between the beck and Brown How is bumpy and rough (not good for descent).

Pike o' Blisco 7

ASCENT FROM LITTLE LANGDALE
1800 feet of ascent · 2½ miles from Fell Foot

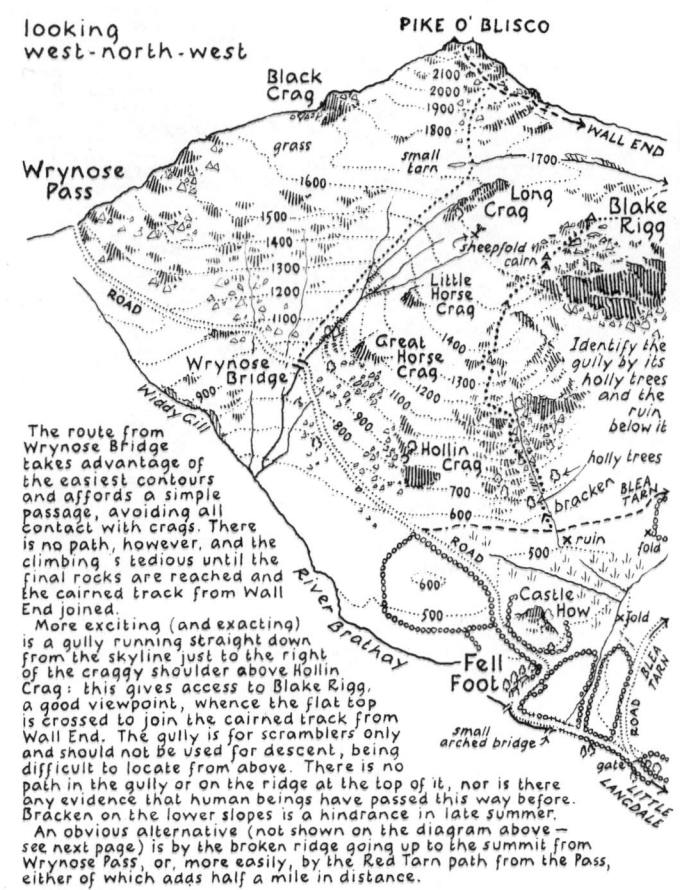

looking west-north-west

(map with labels: PIKE O' BLISCO, Black Crag, Wrynose Pass, WALL END, Long Crag, Blake Rigg, small tarn, grass, ROAD, Widdy Gill, Wrynose Bridge, sheepfold, cairn, Little Horse Crag, Great Horse Crag, Hollin Crag, River Brathay, Identify the gully by its holly trees and the ruin below it, holly trees, bracken, BLEA TARN, ruin, fold, Castle How, Fell Foot, small arched bridge, gate, LITTLE LANGDALE)

Identify the gully by its holly trees and the ruin below it

The route from Wrynose Bridge takes advantage of the easiest contours and affords a simple passage, avoiding all contact with crags. There is no path, however, and the climbing is tedious until the final rocks are reached and the cairned track from Wall End joined.

More exciting (and exacting) is a gully running straight down from the skyline just to the right of the craggy shoulder above Hollin Crag: this gives access to Blake Rigg, a good viewpoint, whence the flat top is crossed to join the cairned track from Wall End. The gully is for scramblers only and should not be used for descent, being difficult to locate from above. There is no path in the gully or on the ridge at the top of it, nor is there any evidence that human beings have passed this way before. Bracken on the lower slopes is a hindrance in late summer.

An obvious alternative (not shown on the diagram above — see next page) is by the broken ridge going up to the summit from Wrynose Pass, or, more easily, by the Red Tarn path from the Pass, either of which adds half a mile in distance.

Pike o' Blisco is well worth climbing from any direction, and, indeed, from all directions. The approach from Little Langdale by the usual way leaving Wrynose Bridge, however, is rather dull in comparison with those from Great Langdale.

Pike o' Blisco 8

ASCENT FROM WRYNOSE PASS
1100 feet of ascent : 1¼ miles

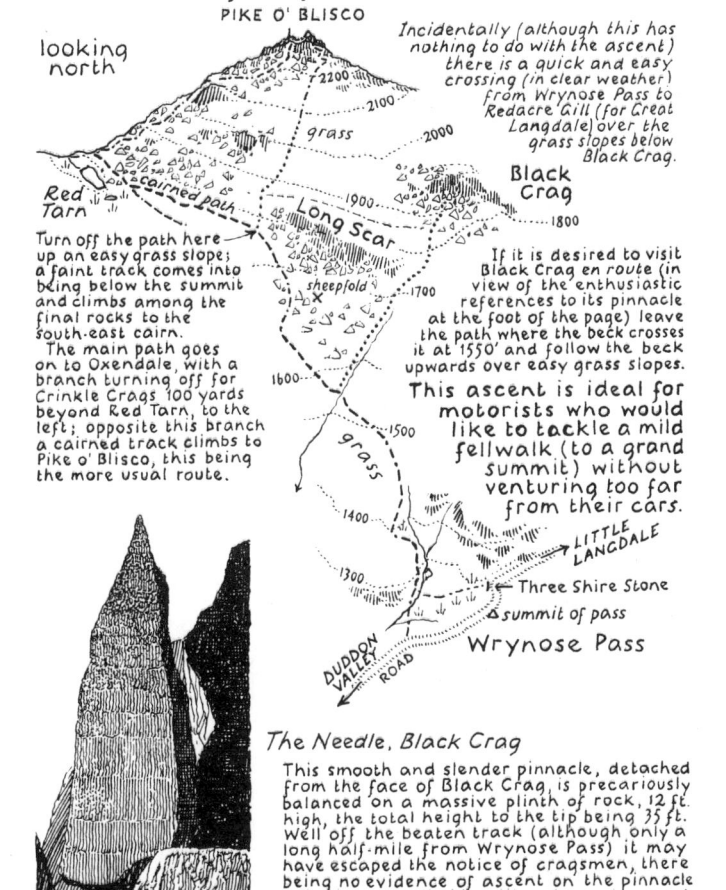

PIKE O' BLISCO

looking north

Red Tarn

Incidentally (although this has nothing to do with the ascent) there is a quick and easy crossing (in clear weather) from Wrynose Pass to Redacre Gill (for Great Langdale) over the grass slopes below Black Crag.

Black Crag

Long Scar

sheepfold

Turn off the path here up an easy grass slope; a faint track comes into being below the summit and climbs among the final rocks to the south-east cairn.

The main path goes on to Oxendale, with a branch turning off for Crinkle Crags 100 yards beyond Red Tarn, to the left; opposite this branch a cairned track climbs to Pike o' Blisco, this being the more usual route.

If it is desired to visit Black Crag en route (in view of the enthusiastic references to its pinnacle at the foot of the page) leave the path where the beck crosses it at 1550' and follow the beck upwards over easy grass slopes.

This ascent is ideal for motorists who would like to tackle a mild fellwalk (to a grand summit) without venturing too far from their cars.

LITTLE LANGDALE
Three Shire Stone
summit of pass
Wrynose Pass
DUDDON VALLEY ROAD

The Needle, Black Crag

This smooth and slender pinnacle, detached from the face of Black Crag, is precariously balanced on a massive plinth of rock, 12 ft. high, the total height to the tip being 35 ft. Well off the beaten track (although only a long half-mile from Wrynose Pass) it may have escaped the notice of cragsmen, there being no evidence of ascent on the pinnacle or in the rock-climbing literature at present available for the area. It seems (to a novice who hasn't tried) that the tip may be gained by 'bridging' the gap with the main crag. He will be a good man who can stand erect on the point of the needle.

The author feels rather proud of this 'discovery' and hopes people will not write to claim (i) a knowledge of the pinnacle (since they were children), (ii) that they have climbed it (blindfolded), and (iii) stood for hours on its point (on their heads).

Pike o' Blisco 9

THE SUMMIT

see "Some Personal Notes in conclusion"

This is a beautiful 'top', and a colourful one, with pinky-grey rocks outcropping everywhere from dark heather and green mosses. The main cairn is a shapely edifice, gloriously situated on a platform of naked rock at the north-western terminus of a summit-ridge 100 yards long. At the south-east extremity is another cairn, less imposing; this too crowns a craggy pyramid.

BOWFELL

PLAN OF SUMMIT

GREAT LANGDALE (follow cairns)
WRYNOSE BRIDGE (bear right below top rocks)
RED TARN (cairned path)
WRYNOSE PASS (path fades; keep to grass)

DESCENTS:
Use the paths when leaving the summit, in fair weather or foul. The north face is terraced with crags, making a direct descent to Oxendale impracticable, nor should streams be followed, many of them plunging into rough and deep ravines.

RIDGE ROUTE

PIKE O' BLISCO
Red Tarn
COLD PIKE
HALF A MILE

To COLD PIKE, 2259': 1¼ miles
SW, then W, NW, W, S and SE
Depression at 1650'
650 feet of ascent
An easy, interesting walk

Follow the line of cairns down to Red Tarn and then make use of the path to Crinkle Crags, turning left at the first stream on the plateau and crossing the bouldery slope to the prominent cairn of Cold Pike.

THE VIEW

As the diagram suggests, most of the detail in the panorama is concentrated between north and east, and here the distant views, from Skiddaw round to the Kentmere fells, are certainly good. At close quarters, however, are Bowfell and Crinkle Crags, displaying their features to such effect that they will win most attention. Wander a few paces (not too many!) from the cairn, in the direction of Great Langdale, for a splendid prospect of that valley.

Principal Fells

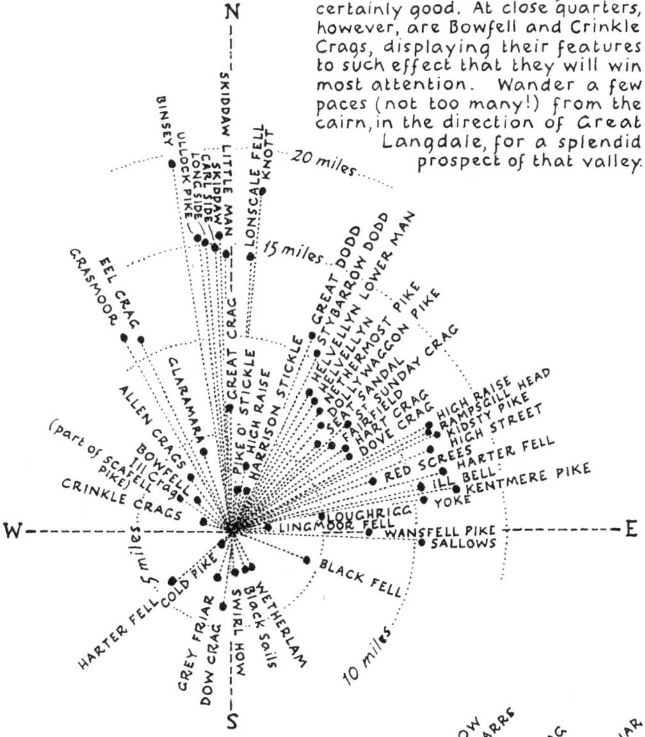
N
E
S
W
20 miles
15 miles
10 miles
5 miles
BINSEY
ULLOCK PIKE
LONG SIDE
CARL SIDE
SKIDDAW
SKIDDAW LITTLE MAN
LONSCALE FELL
KNOTT
GREAT DODD
STYBARROW DODD
LOWER MAN
HELVELLYN
NETHERMOST PIKE
DOLLYWAGGON PIKE
SEAT SANDAL
ST SUNDAY CRAG
FAIRFIELD
HART CRAG
DOVE CRAG
HIGH RAISE
RAMPSGILL HEAD
KIDSTY PIKE
HIGH STREET
RED SCREES
HARTER FELL
ILL BELL
KENTMERE PIKE
YOKE
LOUGHRIGG
LINGMOOR FELL
WANSFELL PIKE
SALLOWS
BLACK FELL
WETHERLAM
Black Sails
SWIRL HOW
DOW CRAG
GREY FRIAR
COLD PIKE
HARTER FELL
CRINKLE CRAGS
(part of SCAFELL PIKE)
Ill Crag
BOWFELL
ALLEN CRAGS
GLARAMARA
GREAT CRAG
PIKE O' STICKLE
HIGH RAISE
HARRISON STICKLE
EEL CRAG
GRASMOOR

Lakes and Tarns

NNE : *Stickle Tarn*
ENE : *Rydal Water*
ESE : *Windermere (3 sections)*
SE : *Wise Een Tarn*
SE : *Esthwaite Water*
SW : *Red Tarn*

SWIRL HOW
GREAT CARRS
DOW CRAG
GREY FRIAR

looking south

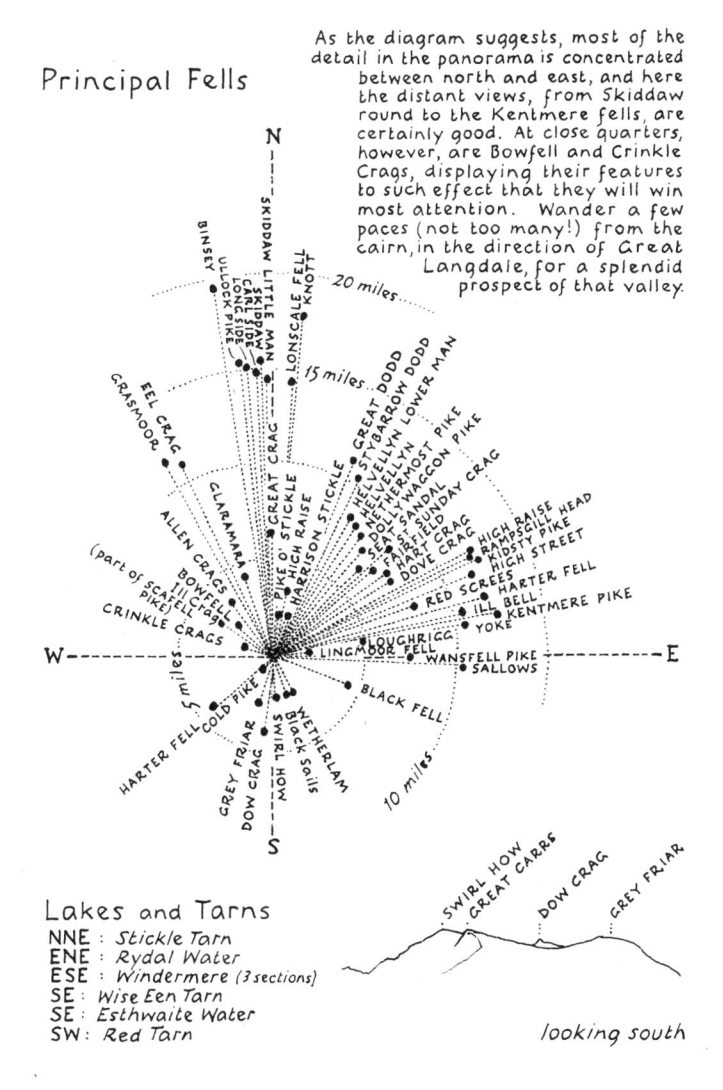

Rossett Pike 2106'

from Mickleden

from the top of Rossett Pass

Stonethwaite
▲ GLARAMARA
ROSSETT ▲ PIKE
▲ BOWFELL
● Dungeon Ghyll

MILES
0 1 2 3

Rossett Pike 2

NATURAL FEATURES

Perhaps, to be strictly correct, Rossett Pike and the fell of which it is part should be regarded as the north-east shoulder of Bowfell continuing from Hanging Knotts to Langstrath, but the sharp rise across the high saddle of Rossett Pass is so pronounced that, for present purposes, Bowfell may be considered to terminate at the Pass. It is especially convenient to regard Rossett Pike as having a separate identity because of its splendid strategical position (independent of and different in function from Bowfell's own and even more splendid position) dominating the deep glacial hollow of Mickleden and rising steeply between the two passes that provide the only routes of exit from that valley. Rossett Pass (south-west) and Stake Pass (north-east), both well-known and much-trodden walkers' routes, define the fell exactly. The east face, between the two diverging passes (which start from the same point at its foot), is excessively rough, but the western slopes are grassy and slope easily to Langstrath with the solitary rocky exception of Lining Crag. The crest of the fell, which carries the county boundary of Cumberland and Westmorland, is undulating and interesting.

Rossett Pike 3

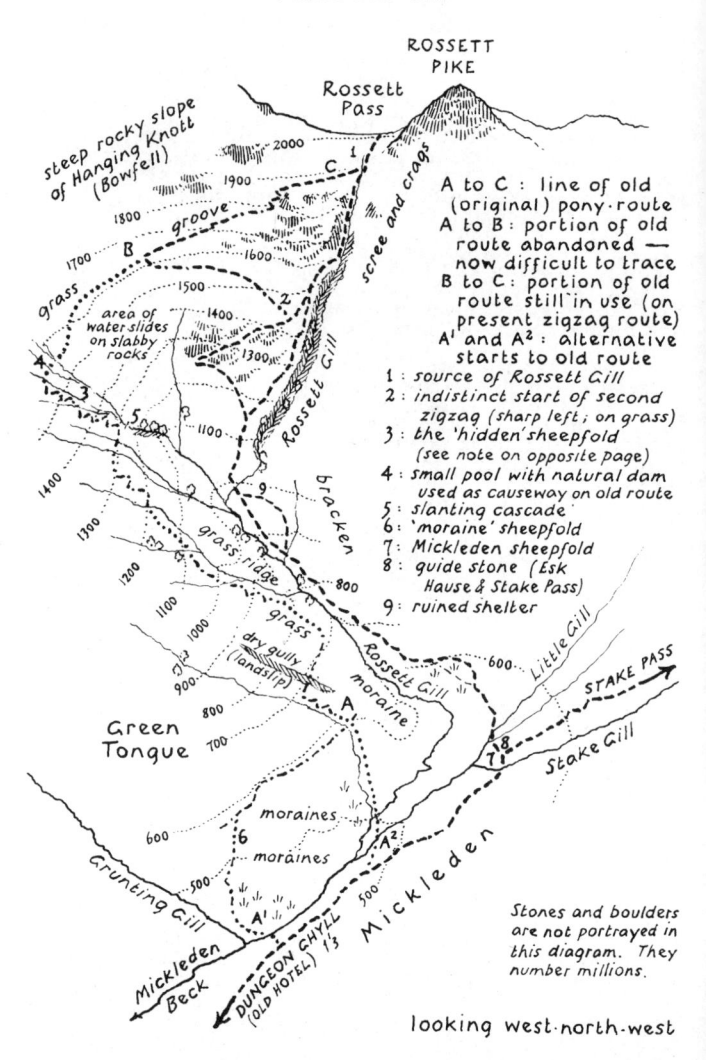

Rossett Gill

looking west-north-west

A to C: line of old (original) pony route
A to B: portion of old route abandoned — now difficult to trace
B to C: portion of old route still in use (on present zigzag route)
A¹ and A²: alternative starts to old route

1 : source of Rossett Gill
2 : indistinct start of second zigzag (sharp left; on grass)
3 : the 'hidden' sheepfold (see note on opposite page)
4 : small pool with natural dam used as causeway on old route
5 : slanting cascade
6 : 'moraine' sheepfold
7 : Mickleden sheepfold
8 : guide stone (Esk Hause & Stake Pass)
9 : ruined shelter

Stones and boulders are not portrayed in this diagram. They number millions.

Rossett Pike 4

Rossett Gill

Rossett Gill is probably the best-known of Lakeland foot-passes, which is not to say that it is the most popular; indeed it is almost certainly the least-liked, due not so much to its steepness (which is more apparent than real, the gradient being nowhere in excess of 30°) but to its stoniness (a condition worsening year by year as swarming legions of booted pedestrians grind away the scanty vestiges of grass and soil). The two zigzags are an aid to easier progress, but the time has come for discriminating fellwalkers to revive the use of the old pony-route, which makes a leisurely way around the base of Green Tongue and, keeping entirely to the slopes of Bowfell, avoids the gill altogether; its final stage is the 'zag' of the second zigzag. The point where the old route left Mickleden is now obscure, but the streams there may easily be forded almost anywhere in normal weather: the route itself is also obscure for most of the way, although a few ancient cairns remain; curiously it is better discerned from a distance (eg. the Stake Pass path, or Rossett Pike) than when underfoot. The old route is especially useful in descent (keep straight on from the bend in the big zigzag), providing a carpet of soft grass for the feet and a solitude that contrast well with the execrable stones and clatter of boots and tongues on the usual direct route.

Rossett Gill has a history, and a few evidences remain, although now almost forgotten or unknown. A knowledge of them will add some interest to the tedious climb.

The old pony route: From the traces still existing it is obvious that this was originally a skilfully-graded and well-engineered path. It is believed to have been used for the secret transporting of goods smuggled into Ravenglass. Much of the former route seems to have been later abandoned in favour of the present double zigzag, but they coincide in the upper stages.

The hidden sheepfold: Cleverly screened from the sight of people passing along Mickleden and Rossett Gill, and situated within the big curve of the old route, is an old sheepfold, still in good condition, used to hide sheep in the far-off days when raiders often looted the valleys.

The packwoman's grave: Neglected and forgotten, yet within very easy reach of the gill, is the grave of a woman who used to call at Langdale farms carrying a pack of articles for sale — and whose mortal remains were found and buried here 170 years ago. A simple cross of stones laid on the ground, pointing southeast, indicates the grave; it has suffered little disturbance down the years, but because so many folk nowadays seem unable to leave things alone its precise location is not divulged here.

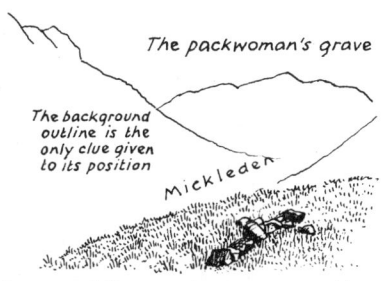

The packwoman's grave

The background outline is the only clue given to its position

Mickleden

(Historical notes on this page kindly supplied by MR. H. MOUNSEY, Skelwith)

Rossett Pike 5

Rossett Pike and Rossett Gill from the old pony-route

From this viewpoint it would appear that the Pike can be reached from the top of the pass only by a steep climb. But in fact the top of the pass is further back than the illustration suggests, and a gentle grass slope there leads up to the rear of the Pike

Rossett Pike 6

ASCENT FROM MICKLEDEN
1600 feet of ascent : 1½ miles from the sheepfold

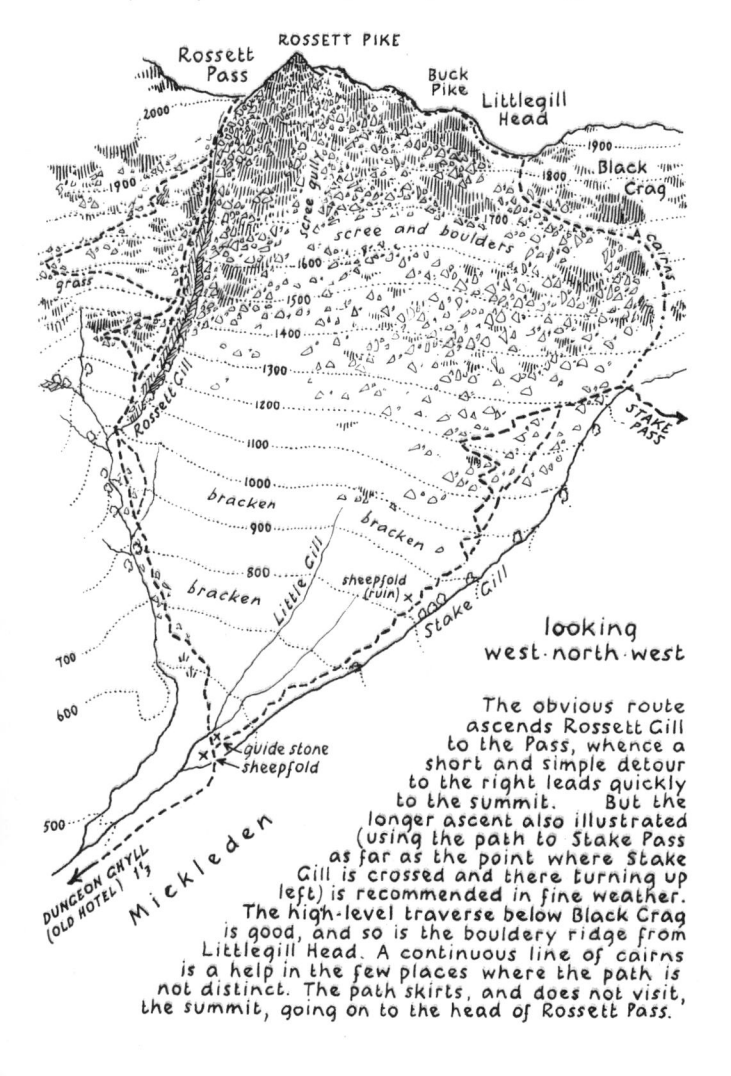

looking west·north·west

The obvious route ascends Rossett Gill to the Pass, whence a short and simple detour to the right leads quickly to the summit. But the longer ascent also illustrated (using the path to Stake Pass as far as the point where Stake Gill is crossed and there turning up left) is recommended in fine weather. The high-level traverse below Black Crag is good, and so is the bouldery ridge from Littlegill Head. A continuous line of cairns is a help in the few places where the path is not distinct. The path skirts, and does not visit, the summit, going on to the head of Rossett Pass.

Rossett Pike 7

THE SUMMIT

1: Harrison Stickle
2: Pike o' Stickle
3: Loft Crag
4: Gimmer Crag

LANGDALE PIKES

Mickleden cairn

The Mickleden cairn

The summit is in the form of a stony ridge running parallel to Rossett Gill, about 120 yards in length and gently inclined down to the sudden plunge of the Mickleden face; here is the principal cairn. The west end of the ridge is higher; a small cairn here is actually overtopped by outcropping rocks nearby. A continuous escarpment fringes the ridge on the Rossett Gill side, but the west and north slopes below the top are easy.

Mickleden

Rossett Pike 8

THE VIEW

The view is naturally inferior to those from the greater fells close by, but it excels in an impressive aerial scene of Mickleden and in the intimate detail of Bowfell's northern cliffs, the great sloping slab of Flat Crags, unique in the district, appearing as a striking feature.

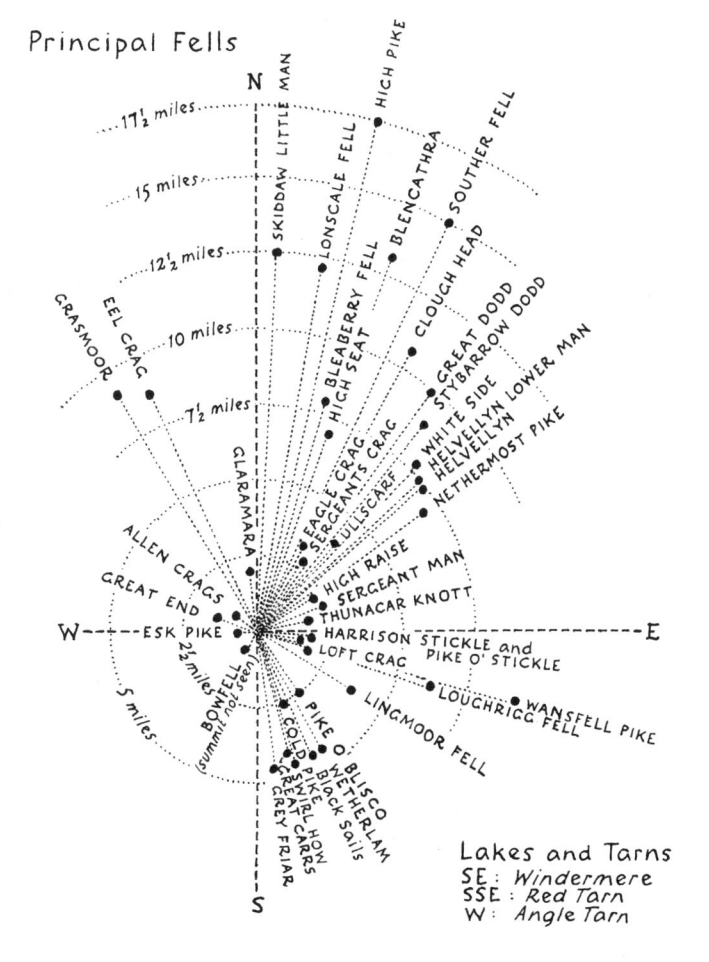

Principal Fells

Lakes and Tarns
SE: Windermere
SSE: Red Tarn
W: Angle Tarn

Rosthwaite Fell

1807'

from Stonethwaite road end

Rosthwaite Fell, shadowing the level strath of the Stonethwaite valley, is really the northern extremity of the Scafells (although seldom recognised as such) and a strong walker may start from the green pastures here and make a fine high-level walk over the fell and the adjacent Glaramara to the summit of Scafell Pike. Few do this, preferring the more orthodox approaches, and Rosthwaite Fell's pathless and undulating top is rarely visited, understandably so for the rough stony sides yield no easy and attractive routes of ascent and the summit is rather a dreary place when compared with more worth-while objectives all around.

- Rosthwaite
- Stonethwaite
- ▲ ROSTHWAITE FELL
- Seathwaite
- ▲ GLARAMARA

MILES
0 1 2 3

Rosthwaite Fell is flanked by the Langstrath and Seathwaite extensions of Borrowdale, to both of which, and to Stonethwaite, it presents a rim of crags. The top has two sections, distinctly divided by the hollow of Tarn at Leaves; the highest point of the northern half is Bessyboot (treated in this chapter as the summit of the fell), the southern rising in greater steps until, at Comb Door, it merges into Glaramara. Of special interest are Comb Gill, the rock summit of Rosthwaite Cam, and Doves Nest Caves. Tarn at Leaves has a lovely name but no other appeal.

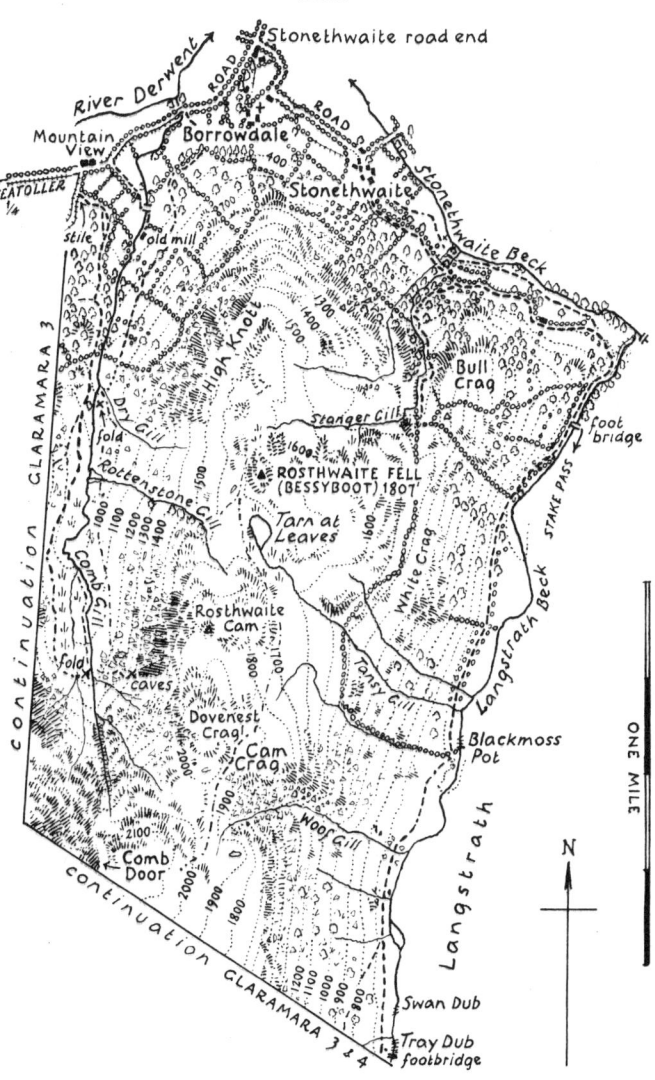

Rosthwaite Fell 2

MAP

Rosthwaite Fell 3

Doves Nest Caves

At some time in the distant past, as the result of a natural convulsion, Doves Nest Crag in Comb Gill gave a great shudder, part of the rockface breaking away and slipping downwards for a few feet before again coming to rest and thus creating a cavity which today gives unusual sport: a subterranean rock climb in darkness.

The interior is out of bounds for walkers, but the place is worth a visit and a gentle exploration. A path leads up scree to the bouldery entrance of South Cave.

To locate the Crag, first find the sheepfold at the head of the Comb: the Crag is plainly in view here — up on the left — and is reached by a stiff climb of ten minutes.

A good idea for a wet day!

South Chimney and Cave

1 : South Chimney and Cave (usual entrance)
2 : Attic Cave (the place of emergence)
3 : North Cave
4 : The Pinnacle
5 : Central Chimney
6 : North Chimney
7 : North Gully

Caves in Lakeland

Some readers have written to ask whether there are caves in the Lake District. If they have in mind natural caves eroded by water, as in the Craven underworld of Yorkshire, the answer is NO; for the rocks of Lakeland are hard volcanic ash, granite and slate, resistant to the action of water. The softer limestone occurs in the neighbouring fringes only, chiefly to the south-east.

The natural Lakeland caves, hardly worth the name, are formed by the wedging of fallen rocks (chockstones) in gullies and clefts, or by the piling-up of boulders below crags, or, infrequently, by a slip of a rock-face, as at Doves Nest. The first variety are beloved of climbers, the second of foxes, but neither will appeal to cavers.

Artificial man-made caves are plentiful, particularly in areas of copper and lead-mining operations, where tunnels, adits, levels and shafts are all to be found; more generally distributed are similar engineering devices to facilitate the shifting of stone in quarries on steep fellsides. Many of them are objects of great interest, and, if it is remembered that they were constructed manually long before the age of modern machines, of admiration too; but the strongest warning must be given to intending explorers that, except in a few cases, the mines and quarries have been unworked and abandoned for many years and their subterranean passages are derelict, often blocked by roof-falls, often flooded, and supporting timbers may be rotted and ready to collapse at a whisper. In other words, these ugly black holes and pits are not merely dangerous but damned dangerous. Sons should think of their mothers, and turn away. Husbands should think of their wives, after which gloomy contemplation many no doubt will march cheerfully in to a possible doom.

No, there is nothing in Lakeland for speleologists and cavers, unless they care to try fellwalking, i.e. crawling about on the surface.

Rosthwaite Fell 4

ASCENT FROM STONETHWAITE
1500 feet of ascent : 1½ miles

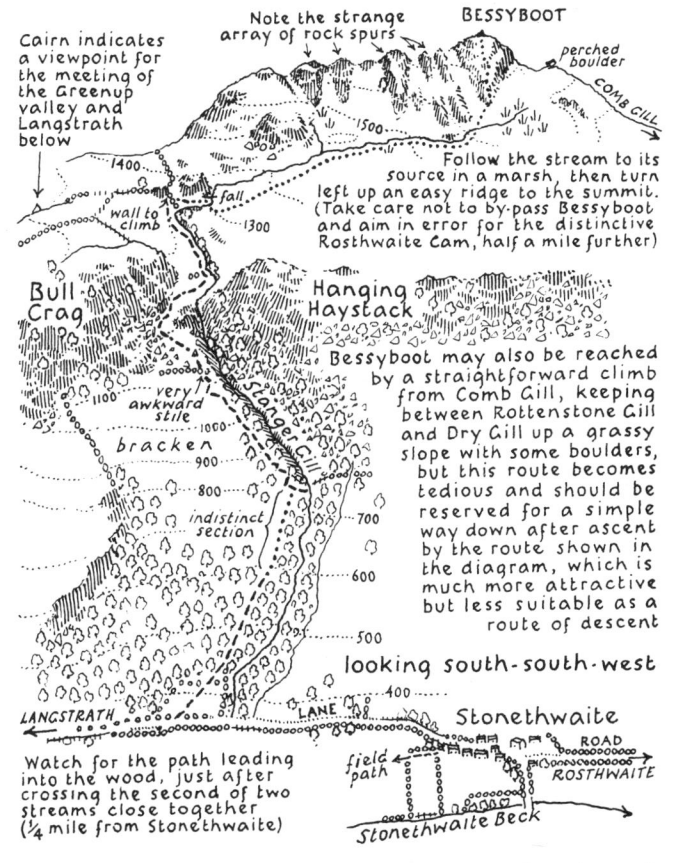

Cairn indicates a viewpoint for the meeting of the Greenup valley and Langstrath below

Note the strange array of rock spurs

BESSYBOOT

perched boulder

COMB GILL

Follow the stream to its source in a marsh, then turn left up an easy ridge to the summit. (Take care not to by-pass Bessyboot and aim in error for the distinctive Rosthwaite Cam, half a mile further)

Bull Crag

Hanging Haystack

very awkward stile

bracken

indistinct section

wall to climb

fall

Bessyboot may also be reached by a straightforward climb from Comb Gill, keeping between Rottenstone Gill and Dry Gill up a grassy slope with some boulders, but this route becomes tedious and should be reserved for a simple way down after ascent by the route shown in the diagram, which is much more attractive but less suitable as a route of descent

looking south-south-west

LANGSTRATH

LANE

Stonethwaite

field path

ROAD
ROSTHWAITE

Stonethwaite Beck

Watch for the path leading into the wood, just after crossing the second of two streams close together (¼ mile from Stonethwaite)

This route takes advantage of the one obvious breach in the rim of cliffs overlooking Stonethwaite, where a great notch in the skyline is formed by the deep cleft of Stanger Gill. The steep climb up the gill, amongst trees, is charming, with lovely views of Borrowdale in retrospect, and the ravine itself is scenically good: a fair path here is a help over rough ground

Rosthwaite Fell 5

THE SUMMIT

Bessyboot is the most distinctive height in the northern half of the fell, and its small, neat top, easily reached through breaches in a surround of low crags, is pleasant enough, but somewhat disappointing in the matter of views.

Rosthwaite Cam (from the south)

The southern half of the fell, of greater general elevation, rises towards Glaramara; the finest of many summits in this section (although not the highest) is Rosthwaite Cam, and a really good one it is, all rock, and unassailable except for one weakness by which an agile walker may climb to touch the cairn. The summit resembles a lion (without a lamb) when seen from the approach to Comb Gill.

Arrow indicates start of easy way up.

RIDGE ROUTE

To GLARAMARA, 2560': 1¾ miles
S, then SW and finally WNW
1000 feet of ascent
A path would improve matters

Much marshy, trackless and confusing ground detracts from this unfrequented walk; nevertheless it is better done in this direction than in the reverse. Keep generally to the Langstrath side of the ridge, where there is a little help from occasional traces of a path. Interest may be added to the walk, if time is available, by visits to Rosthwaite Cam, Comb Door and Comb Head. *This is dangerous country in mist.*

Rosthwaite Fell 6

THE VIEW

This is the view from the summit of Bessyboot. It will disappoint people who expect to look down on the villages of Borrowdale or on Stonethwaite or Langstrath, these valleys being concealed by the wide slopes around the top. The best views are obtained from mid-height during the ascent.

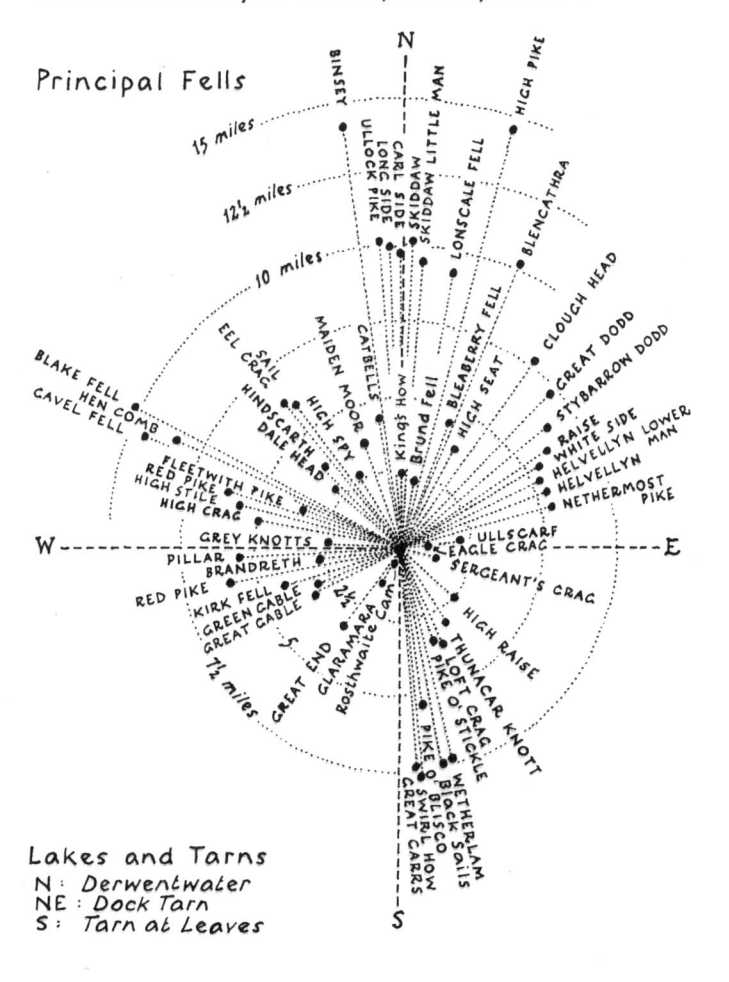

Principal Fells

Lakes and Tarns
N: Derwentwater
NE: Dock Tarn
S: Tarn at Leaves

Scafell

3162'

formerly Scawfell or Scaw Fell
(pronounced Scawfle)

from Cam Spout

- Wasdale Head
- SCAFELL PIKE ▲
- BOWFELL ▲
- SCAFELL ▲
- ILLGILL HEAD ▲
- SLIGHT SIDE ▲
- Boot

MILES
0 1 2 3 4

Scafell 2

NATURAL FEATURES

When men first named the mountains, the whole of the high mass south of Sty Head was known as Scaw Fell; later, as the work of the dalesfolk took them more and more onto the heights and closer identification became necessary, they applied the name to the mountain that seemed to them the greatest, the other summits in the range, to them individually inferior, being referred to collectively as the Pikes of Scaw Fell. Many folk today, even with the added knowledge that the main Pike is not only higher but actually the highest land in the country, share the old opinion that Scaw Fell (now Scafell) is the superior mountain of the group.

This respect is inspired not by the huge western flank going down to Wasdale nor by the broad southern slopes ending in the Eskdale foothills but rather by the towering rampart of shadowed crags facing north and east below the summit, the greatest display of natural grandeur in the district, a spectacle of massive strength and savage wildness but without beauty, an awesome and a humbling scene. A man may stand on the lofty ridge of Mickledore, or in the green hollow beneath the precipice amongst the littered debris and boulders fallen from it, and witness the sublime architecture of buttresses and pinnacles soaring into the sky, silhouetted against racing clouds or, often, tormented by writhing mists, and, as in a great cathedral, lose all his conceit. It does a man good to realise his own insignificance in the general scheme of things, and that is his experience here.

Fuller notes on the topography are contained in the Scafell Pike chapter

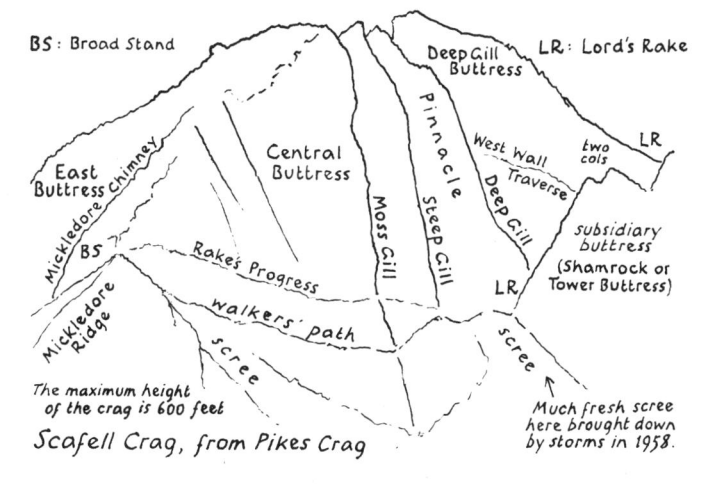

BS: Broad Stand   LR: Lord's Rake

Deep Gill Buttress
East Buttress
Mickledore Chimney
Central Buttress
Pinnacle
Moss Gill
Steep Gill
Deep Gill
West Wall Traverse
two cols
LR
subsidiary buttress (Shamrock or Tower Buttress)
BS
Rake's Progress
Mickledore Ridge
Walkers' Path
scree
LR
scree

The maximum height of the crag is 600 feet

Much fresh scree here brought down by storms in 1958.

Scafell Crag, from Pikes Crag

Scafell 3

Broad Stand

entrance

Broad Stand and Mickledore

The greatest single obstacle confronting ridge-walkers on the hills of Lakeland is the notorious Broad Stand, with which every traveller from Scafell Pike to Scafell comes face to face at the far end of the Mickledore traverse. Obstacles met on other ridges can be overcome or easily by-passed; not so Broad Stand. It is an infuriating place, making a man angry with himself for his inability to climb the thirty feet of rock that bar his way to the simple rising slope beyond. From a distance it looks nothing; close at hand it still looks not much to worry about; but with the first platform underfoot, while still not seeming impossible, the next awkward movement to the left plus an uneasy fear of worse hazards above and as yet unseen, influences sensible walkers to retreat from the scene and gain access to Scafell's top by using one or the other of the two orthodox pedestrian routes (via Lord's Rake or Foxes Tarn), each of which entails a long detour and, unfortunately, a considerable descent.

Nevertheless, Broad Stand has a long history and a lot of stories to its name, and it should at least be visited. Where the Mickledore ridge abuts against the broken crags of Scafell turn down the scree on the Eskdale side (east) and in no more than a dozen yards a deep vertical cleft, paved with stones, can be entered and passed through to a small platform. This cleft is a tight squeeze, well named as "Fat Man's Agony," and ladies, too, whose statistics are too vital, will have an uncomfortable time in it. The platform is shut in by smooth walls, the route of exit (for experts only) being up the scratched corner on the left. But for mere pedestrians the platform is the limit of their exploration and they should return through the cleft, resolving, as is customary, to do the climb next time. The author first made this resolve in 1930 and has repeated it a score of times since then; his continuing disappointment is amply compensated by the pleasure of going on living.

YOU HAVE BEEN WARNED!

Scafell 4

Lord's Rake

Lord's Rake is a classic route, uncomfortable underfoot but magnificent all around. It is used on the ascent of Scafell from Wasdale Head via Brown Tongue and on the traverse of the main ridge. The Rake is unique, and one's fellwalking education is not complete until its peculiar delights and horrors have been experienced.

Strangers to Scafell may have some difficulty in locating the Rake, small-scale maps being unable to supply the details, but users of this book will have no such worries, of course.

The Rake starts (in ascent) as a steep, wide scree-gully or channel rising not into the mountain but obliquely across it and between the main crag and a subsidiary buttress, the top edge of which forms a parapet to the Rake. This first section is almost 100 yards in length, and ends at a perfect little col, so narrow that it can be straddled. A descent of 10 feet and a rise of 20 feet leads in 20 yards to another col, equally sweet, and the end of the Rake is now in sight 100 yards ahead and at the same elevation, although a steep descent to a stony amphitheatre is necessary before the exit can be reached. Here, now, is the open fell, and a rough track (left) leads to the top of Scafell.

The great thing to remember (important in mist) is that Lord's Rake has 3 ups and 2 downs, and maintains a dead-straight course throughout.

The first section calls for strenuous effort, as the assortment of buttons, boot soles, dentures, broken pipes and other domestic articles scattered en route testifies. The best footing higher up is at the right side. In a place like this, where boots cannot gain a purchase on the sliding stones and polished rocks, other methods of locomotion may usefully be adopted, especially when descending. It is no disgrace even for stalwart men to come down here on their bottoms, while ladies may certainly use their feminine equivalents without any feeling of shame. The yellow flower growing in crevices of the rock walls is the starry saxifrage.

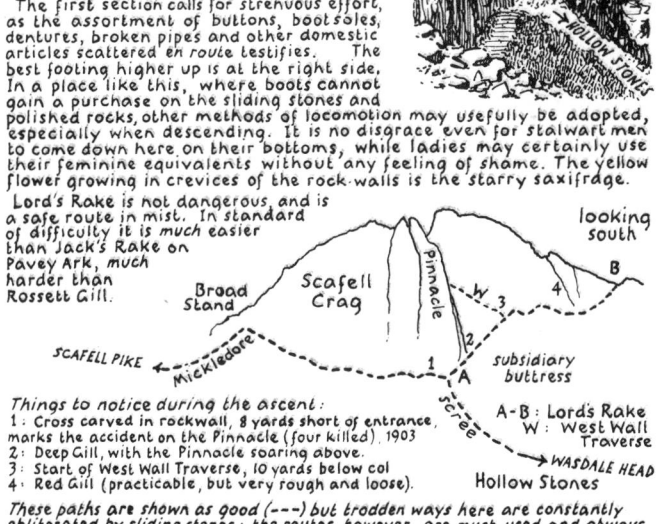

Lord's Rake is not dangerous, and is a safe route in mist. In standard of difficulty it is *much easier* than Jack's Rake on Pavey Ark, much harder than Rossett Gill.

Things to notice during the ascent:
1: Cross carved in rockwall, 8 yards short of entrance, marks the accident on the Pinnacle (four killed), 1903
2: Deep Gill, with the Pinnacle soaring above.
3: Start of West Wall Traverse, 10 yards below col
4: Red Gill (practicable, but very rough and loose).

A-B : Lord's Rake
W : West Wall Traverse

These paths are shown as good (---) but trodden ways here are constantly obliterated by sliding stones: the routes, however, are much used and obvious.

Scafell 5

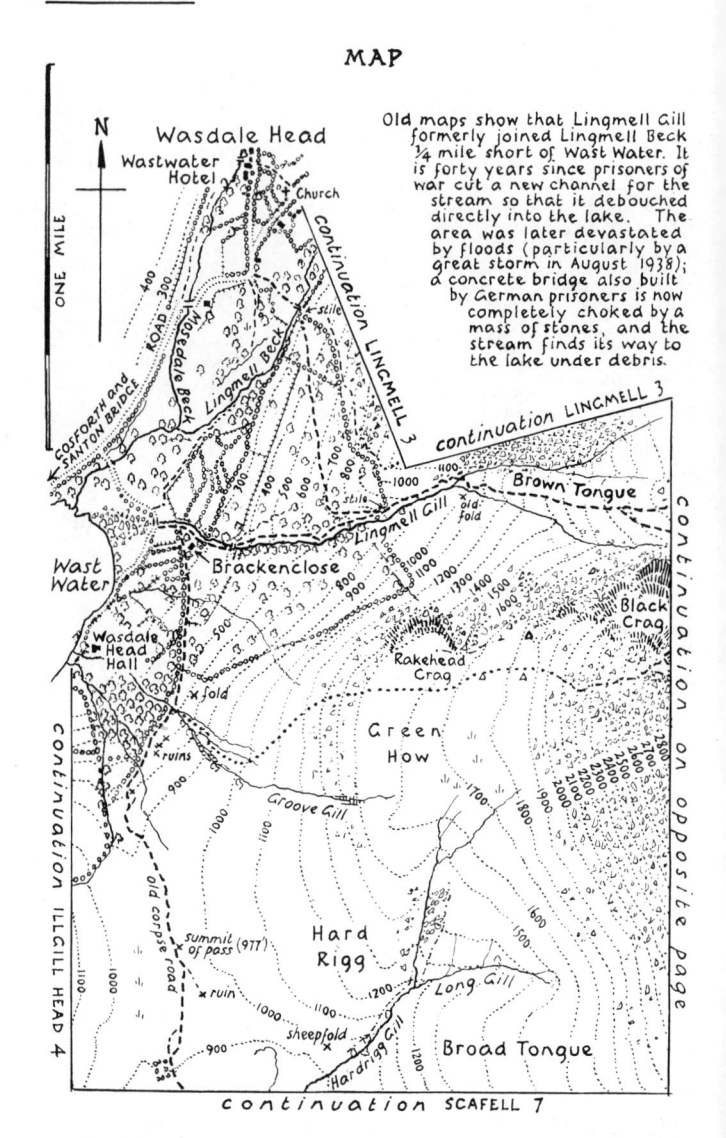

MAP

Old maps show that Lingmell Gill formerly joined Lingmell Beck ¼ mile short of Wast Water. It is forty years since prisoners of war cut a new channel for the stream so that it debouched directly into the lake. The area was later devastated by floods (particularly by a great storm in August 1938); a concrete bridge also built by German prisoners is now completely choked by a mass of stones, and the stream finds its way to the lake under debris.

Scafell 6

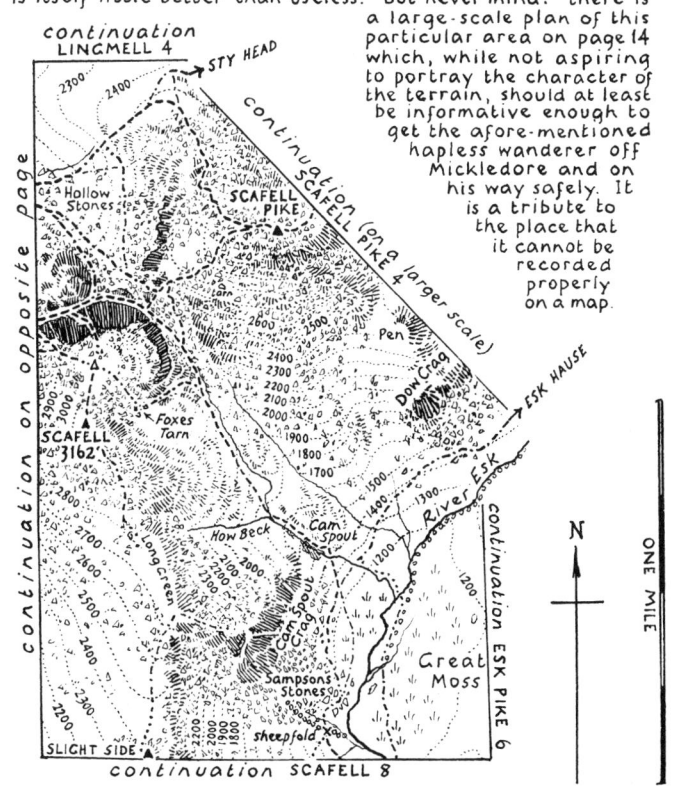

MAP

The inadequacy of maps to serve as a guide over rough and complicated ground, more especially where there are vertical elevations, is nowhere better illustrated than in the small area between Scafell and Scafell Pike. A lost and hapless wanderer standing on Mickledore ridge, trying to fit the tremendous scene around him into a half-inch space on his map, is deserving of every sympathy. So is the map-maker, furnished with many details and festooned with merging contours — and nowhere to put them; but this does not really excuse the rather nonchalant hachuring of crags on both the Ordnance Survey and Bartholomews maps, nor the omission of important paths. The map on this page is itself little better than useless. But never mind: there is a large-scale plan of this particular area on page 14 which, while not aspiring to portray the character of the terrain, should at least be informative enough to get the afore-mentioned hapless wanderer off Mickledore and on his way safely. It is a tribute to the place that it cannot be recorded properly on a map.

Scafell 7

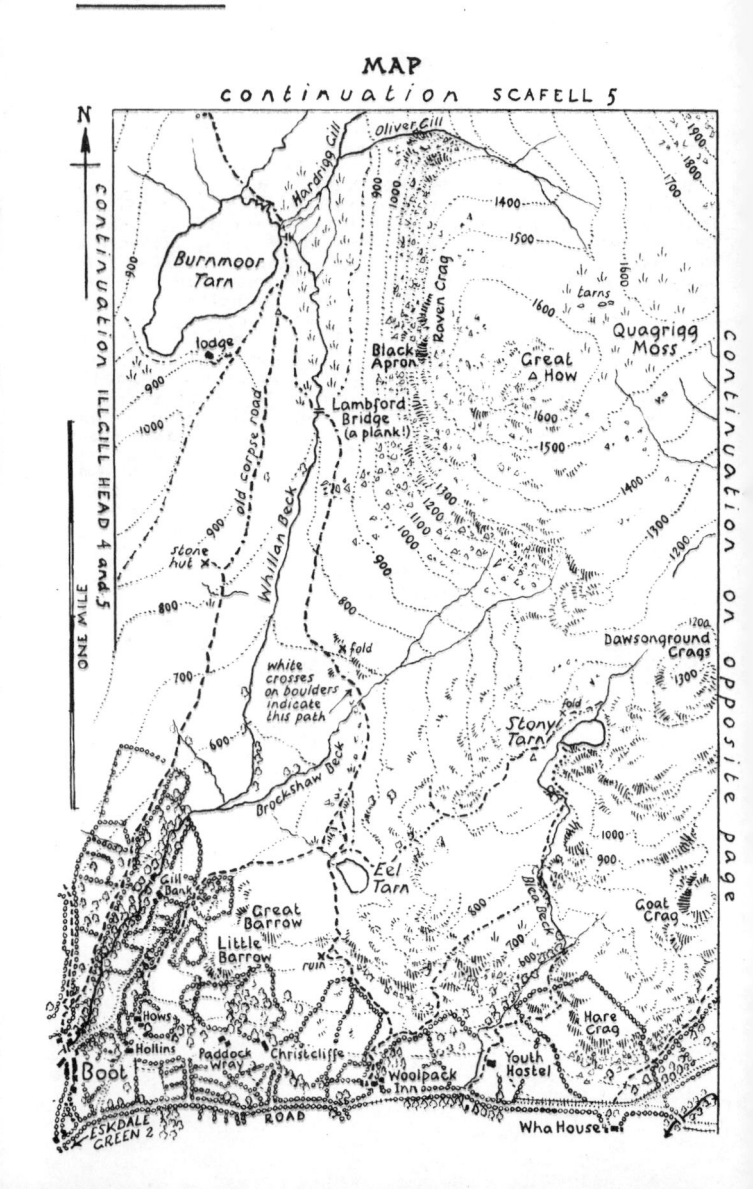

Scafell 8

MAP

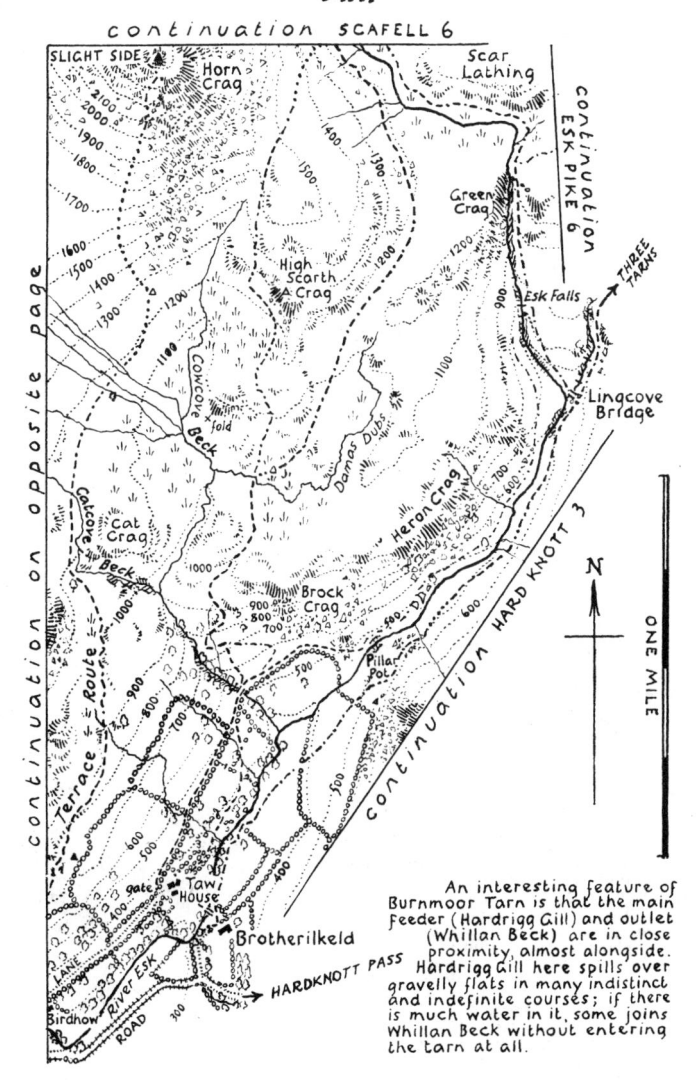

An interesting feature of Burnmoor Tarn is that the main feeder (Hardrigg Gill) and outlet (Whillan Beck) are in close proximity, almost alongside. Hardrigg Gill here spills over gravelly flats in many indistinct and indefinite courses; if there is much water in it, some joins Whillan Beck without entering the tarn at all.

Scafell 9

The head of Deep Gill (the top of the descent to the West Wall Traverse) with the Pinnacle (left-centre) and the Oracle (bottom right)

The West Wall Traverse

The massive crags of Scafell are split asunder by the tremendous chasm of Deep Gill, which has two vertical pitches in its lower part that put the through route out of bounds for walkers. The upper half, however, although excessively stony, can be used by all and sundry without difficulty, and is linked with Lord's Rake by a simple path across a grassy shelf. This is the West Wall Traverse. The rock scenery is awe-inspiring.

ASCENT: Go up the first section of Lord's Rake. On the left, 10 yards short of the col, a distinct path goes up to the grassy shelf, along which it rises to enter Deep Gill, the two pitches now being below. Steep scree then follows to the open fell at the top of the Gill. The exit used to be a desperate scramble up a loose and earthy wall, but clutching hands over the years have torn down the cornice and escape is now easy, especially on the left.

DESCENT: Go down into Deep Gill (easier on the right), a descent not as bad as may be thought from its appearance, but made unpleasant by sliding stones. Watch for the path turning left out of the Gill 80 yards down, where the crag on this side eases off: this path slants easily across a shelf into Lord's Rake. It is vital that this path be taken; the Gill itself, further down, drops vertically over chockstones and is entirely impracticable for walkers.

SCAFELL PIKE — col

The start of Lord's Rake (in descent)

Scafell 10

ASCENT FROM WASDALE HEAD
via BROWN TONGUE: 3,000 feet of ascent: 3 miles
via GREEN HOW:
2,950 feet; 3¼ miles
(from Wastwater Hotel)

The Brown Tongue – Lord's Rake route is becoming increasingly popular, although very rough above 2000', and is much the finest way to the summit. The Green How route is as much out of fashion as the Victorians who favoured it.

Upon arrival at the scree-slope debouching from Lord's Rake refer to page 4 for greater detail of the remainder of the climb.

Whatever the demerits of the Green How route as an ascent (and admittedly it is a dull and tiring climb) there is no denying that as a quick way down it is first-class.

looking south-east

Scafell 11

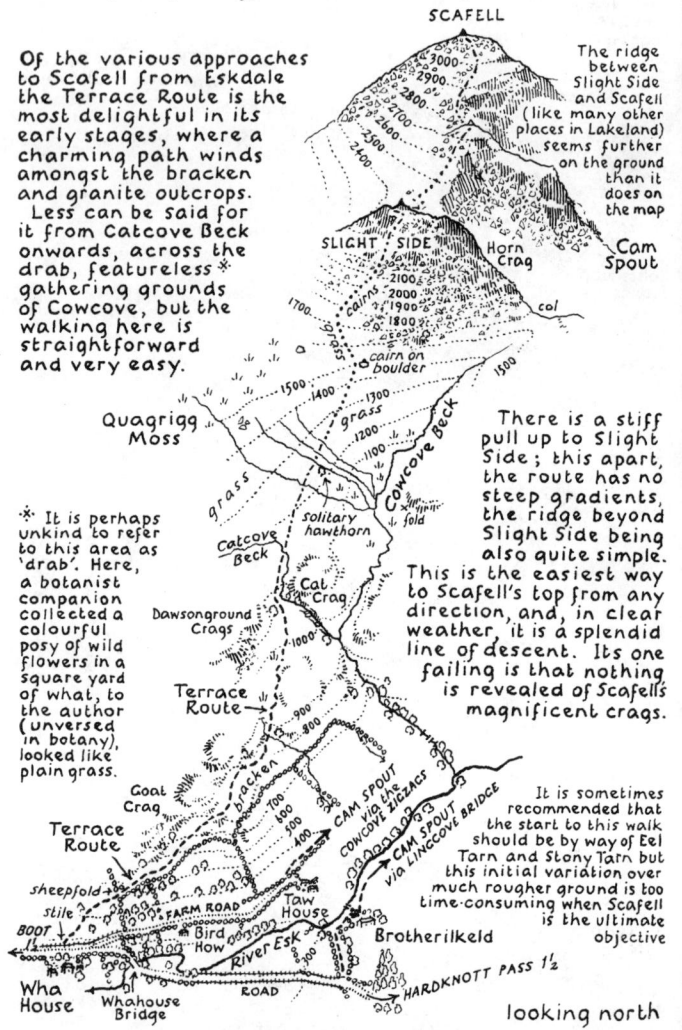

ASCENT FROM ESKDALE
3100 feet of ascent : 6 miles from Boot

Of the various approaches to Scafell from Eskdale the Terrace Route is the most delightful in its early stages, where a charming path winds amongst the bracken and granite outcrops.

Less can be said for it from Catcove Beck onwards, across the drab, featureless ✻ gathering grounds of Cowcove, but the walking here is straightforward and very easy.

✻ It is perhaps unkind to refer to this area as 'drab'. Here, a botanist companion collected a colourful posy of wild flowers in a square yard of what, to the author (unversed in botany), looked like plain grass.

The ridge between Slight Side and Scafell (like many other places in Lakeland) seems further on the ground than it does on the map.

There is a stiff pull up to Slight Side; this apart, the route has no steep gradients, the ridge beyond Slight Side being also quite simple. This is the easiest way to Scafell's top from any direction, and, in clear weather, it is a splendid line of descent. Its one failing is that nothing is revealed of Scafell's magnificent crags.

It is sometimes recommended that the start to this walk should be by way of Eel Tarn and Stony Tarn but this initial variation over much rougher ground is too time-consuming when Scafell is the ultimate objective

looking north

Scafell 12

ASCENT FROM ESKDALE
via CAM SPOUT
3050 feet of ascent : 7¼ miles from Boot

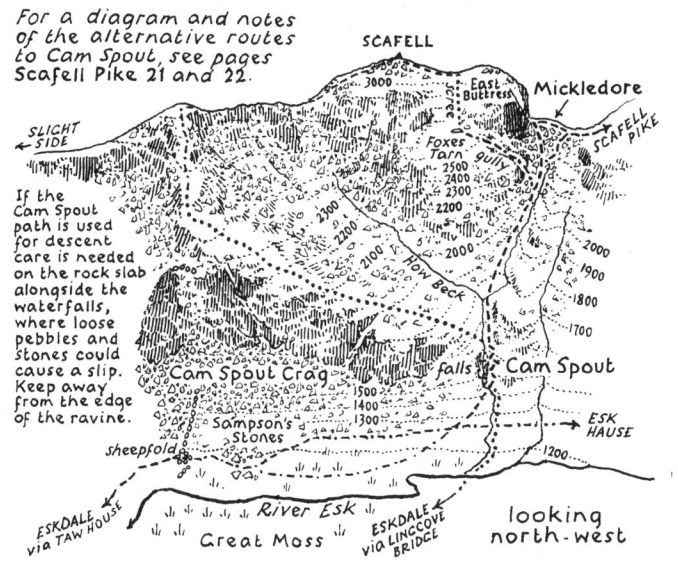

For a diagram and notes of the alternative routes to Cam Spout, see pages Scafell Pike 21 and 22.

If the Cam Spout path is used for descent care is needed on the rock slab alongside the waterfalls, where loose pebbles and stones could cause a slip. Keep away from the edge of the ravine.

looking north-west

Take the scrambling route alongside the waterfalls, above which a good path goes up towards Mickledore, but before reaching the level of East Buttress and 100 yards below its nearest crags enter a stony gully going up squarely to the left; a small stream emerges from it. The gully, rough but not difficult, leads directly to Foxes Tarn (which is no more than a tiny pond with a large boulder in it), whence a long scree-slope is climbed to the saddle above, the top then being 250 easy yards distant. This is the quickest route to the summit from Cam Spout, and avoids the worst sections of the Mickledore screes.

Gluttons for punishment may, instead, continue up loose scree to the Mickledore ridge, descend the other side, and finish the climb by way of Lord's Rake, taking half an hour longer and making personal acquaintance with a few thousand more stones, but being rewarded by the finest scenery Scafell has to offer.

The pathless route along the curving ridge of Cam Spout Crag is very roundabout and the ridge itself is too broad to be exciting, although it narrows and becomes quite attractive near the end. The one advantage of this route, of importance to people with bunions, is that it is possible to walk on grass throughout, and in fact it is the only way to the main ridge of Scafell from Cam Spout that avoids scree entirely.

Scafell 13

THE SUMMIT

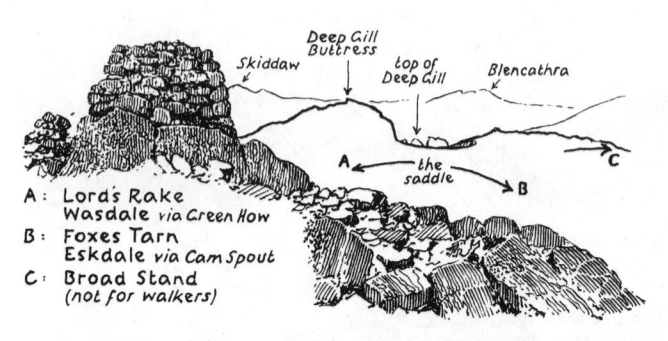

Labels on sketch: Skiddaw, Deep Gill Buttress, top of Deep Gill, Blencathra, the saddle, A, B, C

- A: Lord's Rake
  Wasdale *via Green How*
- B: Foxes Tarn
  Eskdale *via Cam Spout*
- C: Broad Stand
  (not for walkers)

The face of Scafell Crag is the grandest sight in the district, and if only the highest point of the fell were situated on the top of Deep Gill Buttress, perched above the tremendous precipices of stone, it would be the best summit of all. As nature has arranged things, however, it lies back, away and remote from the excitement, the cairn being on a simple rise where there is little of interest at close quarters although the view southwards is enough to transfix the visitor's attention for some minutes. On the south side of the cairn is a ruinous shelter, not now more serviceable as a protection against wind and rain than the cairn itself. The top is everywhere stony.

DESCENTS:

More than ordinary care is needed in choosing a route of descent. The western slope is stony, the eastern craggy, the northern precipitous. Except for Eskdale via Slight Side, recommended routes leave the saddle: turn left for Wasdale, right for Eskdale; go straight ahead for Deep Gill and the West Wall Traverse if Borrowdale is the objective *but only if the Traverse is already known*; otherwise use Lords Rake.

In mist, the Slight Side route may be tried, but if lost turn right down to Hardrigg Gill and the Burnmoor path. For other destinations aim for the saddle (big cairn) to which the path is clear but there is indistinct, and follow, cautiously, the fine-weather routes; see also map, page 14.

RIDGE ROUTE

To SLIGHT SIDE, 2499' : 1¼ miles : S
Depression at 2400'
100 feet of ascent

An easy walk, becoming pathless on grass. In clear weather there is no difficulty. In mist, when the path fades, remember to keep the escarpment on the left hand throughout.

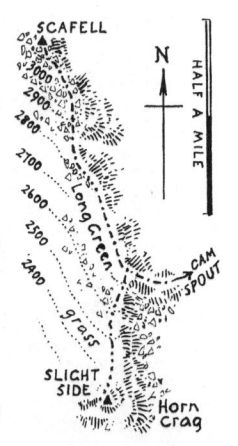

Scafell 14

RIDGE ROUTE

To SCAFELL PIKE, 3210': 1¼ miles : compass useless.
750' of ascent via Lord's Rake, 900' via Foxes Tarn.
Loins should be girded up for an hour's hard labour.

There is no bigger trap for the unwary and uninformed walker than this. Scafell Pike is clearly in view but the intervening crags cannot be seen. The natural inclination will be to make a beeline for the Pike and to be deflected by the edge of the precipice down the easy slope to the right, encouraged by a good path that now appears. But this is the climbers' way to Broad Stand, which walkers cannot safely attempt. A desperate situation now arises. Just beyond the drop of Broad Stand, and tantalisingly near, is Mickledore Ridge, the easy connecting link between Scafell and the Pike. The choice is to risk a serious accident or toil all the way back and start again : not an easy decision for a walker already tired and pressed for time. The advice is to go back and start again.

From the grassy saddle (cairn) three routes are available:

1 : via LORD'S RAKE : This is the usual way, and it is arduous. Turn *left* down a slope that steepens and becomes all stones. The start of the Rake is further down the fellside than will generally be expected, and it should be identified exactly *(see illustration, page 9).* Avoid the gaping entrance to Red Gill midway. For details of the Rake, see page 4, where it is described in ascent — it will occur to the mentally alert that if there are 3 ups and 2 downs in the ascent there must be 3 downs and 2 ups in the descent. From the foot of the Rake continue ahead below the crags and scramble up to Mickledore Ridge, where turn *left* along a good path to the Pike.

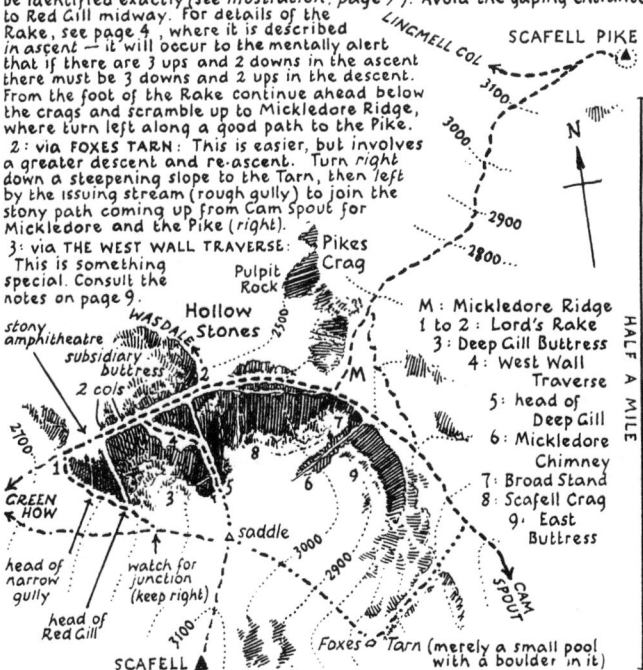

2 : via FOXES TARN : This is easier, but involves a greater descent and re-ascent. Turn *right* down a steepening slope to the Tarn, then *left* by the issuing stream (rough gully) to join the stony path coming up from Cam Spout for Mickledore and the Pike (*right*).

3 : via THE WEST WALL TRAVERSE : This is something special. Consult the notes on page 9.

M : Mickledore Ridge
1 to 2 : Lord's Rake
3 : Deep Gill Buttress
4 : West Wall Traverse
5 : head of Deep Gill
6 : Mickledore Chimney
7 : Broad Stand
8 : Scafell Crag
9 : East Buttress

Note that this map is on the scale of six inches to one mile. To assist clarity, areas of stones and boulders are omitted, but nobody should assume there aren't any : they occur all over the place.

Scafell 15

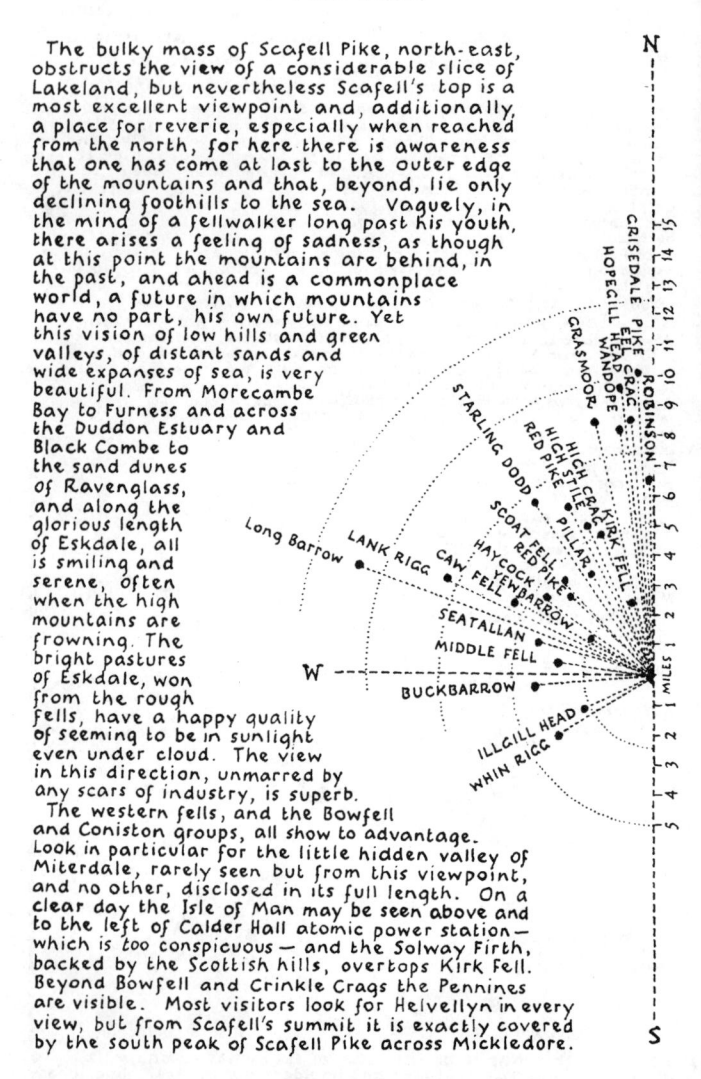

THE VIEW

The bulky mass of Scafell Pike, north-east, obstructs the view of a considerable slice of Lakeland, but nevertheless Scafell's top is a most excellent viewpoint and, additionally, a place for reverie, especially when reached from the north, for here there is awareness that one has come at last to the outer edge of the mountains and that, beyond, lie only declining foothills to the sea. Vaguely, in the mind of a fellwalker long past his youth, there arises a feeling of sadness, as though at this point the mountains are behind, in the past, and ahead is a commonplace world, a future in which mountains have no part, his own future. Yet this vision of low hills and green valleys, of distant sands and wide expanses of sea, is very beautiful. From Morecambe Bay to Furness and across the Duddon Estuary and Black Combe to the sand dunes of Ravenglass, and along the glorious length of Eskdale, all is smiling and serene, often when the high mountains are frowning. The bright pastures of Eskdale, won from the rough fells, have a happy quality of seeming to be in sunlight even under cloud. The view in this direction, unmarred by any scars of industry, is superb.

The western fells, and the Bowfell and Coniston groups, all show to advantage. Look in particular for the little hidden valley of Miterdale, rarely seen but from this viewpoint, and no other, disclosed in its full length. On a clear day the Isle of Man may be seen above and to the left of Calder Hall atomic power station — which is too conspicuous — and the Solway Firth, backed by the Scottish hills, overtops Kirk Fell. Beyond Bowfell and Crinkle Crags the Pennines are visible. Most visitors look for Helvellyn in every view, but from Scafell's summit it is exactly covered by the south peak of Scafell Pike across Mickledore.

THE VIEW

Principal Fells

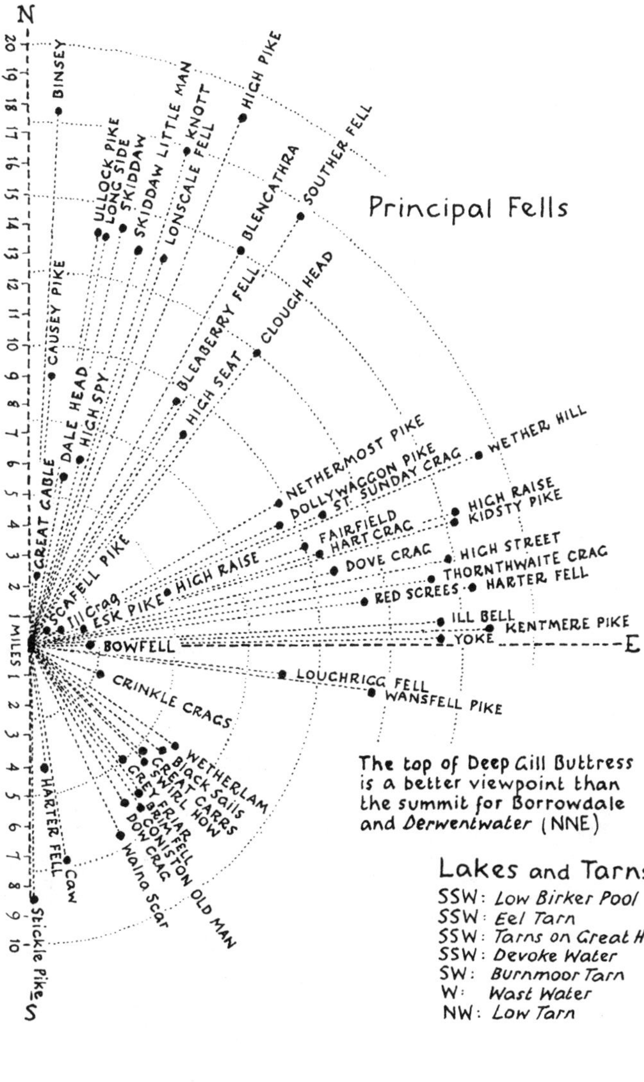
N
S
E
MILES
BINSEY
ULLOCK PIKE
LONG SIDE
SKIDDAW
SKIDDAW LITTLE MAN
KNOTT
LONSCALE FELL
HIGH PIKE
BLENCATHRA
SOUTHER FELL
CAUSEY PIKE
BLEABERRY FELL
CLOUGH HEAD
DALE HEAD
HIGH SPY
HIGH SEAT
GREAT GABLE
NETHERMOST PIKE
DOLLYWAGGON PIKE
ST. SUNDAY CRAG
WETHER HILL
HIGH RAISE
KIDSTY PIKE
FAIRFIELD
HART CRAG
SCAFELL PIKE
HIGH RAISE
DOVE CRAG
HIGH STREET
THORNTHWAITE CRAG
HARTER FELL
Ill Crag
ESK PIKE
RED SCREES
ILL BELL
KENTMERE PIKE
YOKE
BOWFELL
LOUGHRIGG FELL
WANSFELL PIKE
CRINKLE CRAGS
WETHERLAM
Black Sails
GREAT CARRS
SWIRL HOW
GREY FRIAR
BRIM FELL
CONISTON OLD MAN
DOW CRAG
Walna Scar
HARTER FELL
Caw
Stickle Pike

The top of Deep Gill Buttress is a better viewpoint than the summit for Borrowdale and *Derwentwater* (NNE)

Lakes and Tarns

SSW: *Low Birker Pool*
SSW: *Eel Tarn*
SSW: *Tarns on Great How*
SSW: *Devoke Water*
SW: *Burnmoor Tarn*
W: *Wast Water*
NW: *Low Tarn*

Scafell Pike 3210'

the highest mountain in England

formerly 'The Pikes' or 'The Pikes of Scawfell';
'Scafell Pikes' on Ordnance Survey maps.

from Great Moss,
Upper Eskdale

Scafell Pike 2

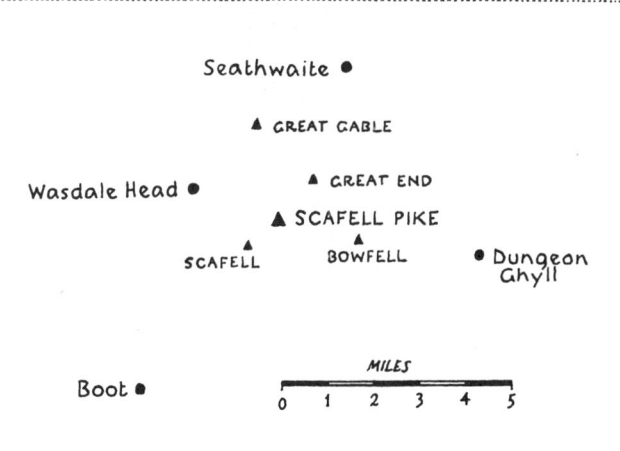

Scafell Pike Ill Crag

from the gorge of the Esk

Seathwaite •

▲ GREAT GABLE

Wasdale Head •   ▲ GREAT END
              ▲ SCAFELL PIKE
         SCAFELL   ▲
                BOWFELL   • Dungeon Ghyll

Boot •

MILES
0 1 2 3 4 5

Scafell Pike 3

The Scafell Range

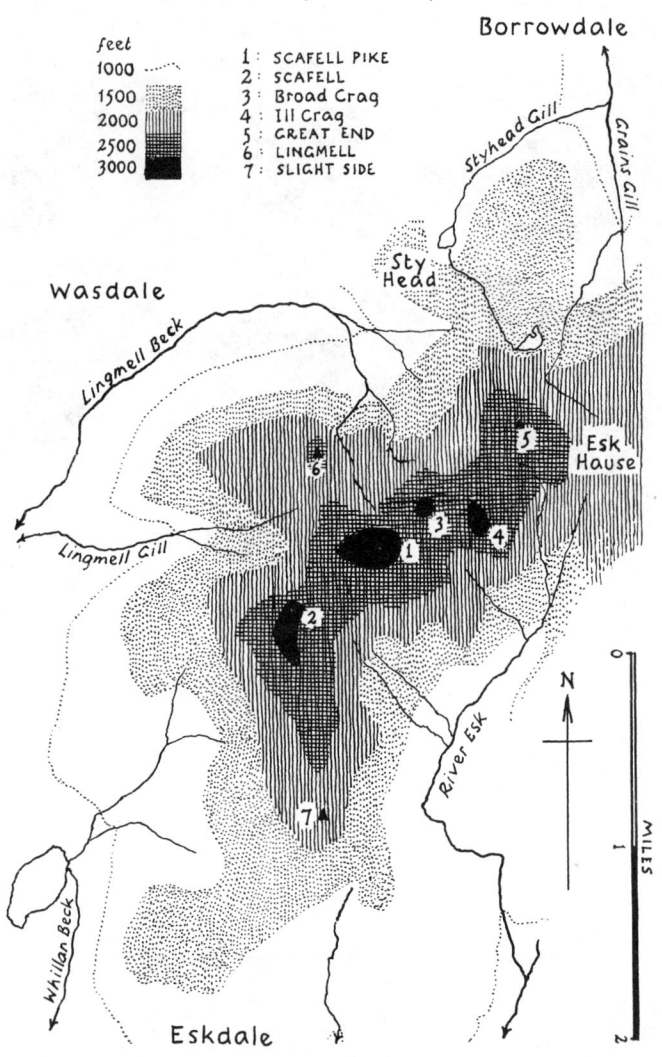

feet	
1000	····
1500	
2000	
2500	
3000	■

1 : SCAFELL PIKE
2 : SCAFELL
3 : Broad Crag
4 : Ill Crag
5 : GREAT END
6 : LINGMELL
7 : SLIGHT SIDE

Borrowdale

Styhead Gill

Grains Gill

Sty Head

Wasdale

Lingmell Beck

Lingmell Gill

Esk House

River Esk

N

0 — 1 — 2 MILES

Whillan Beck

Eskdale

Scafell Pike 4

Scafell Pike's grandest crag:
Dow Crag

Known to climbers as Esk Buttress, this 400-foot near-vertical crag rises from the fellside low down on the mountain's east flank, overlooking the River Esk.

Scafell Pike's best-known crag:
Pulpit Rock

This fine pinnacle (seen here from Mickledore) is the best feature of Pikes Crag, above Hollow Stones. Its top (easily reached from the summit-to-Mickledore path) is the best of all viewpoints for Scafell Crag.

Scafell Pike 5

NATURAL FEATURES

The difference between a hill and a mountain depends on *appearance*, not on *altitude* (whatever learned authorities may say to the contrary), and is thus arbitrary and a matter of personal opinion. Grass predominates on a hill, rock on a mountain. A hill is smooth, a mountain rough. In the case of Scafell Pike, opinions must agree that here is a mountain without doubt, and a mountain that is, moreover, every inch a mountain. Roughness and ruggedness are the necessary attributes, and the Pike has these in greater measure than other high ground in the country —— which is just as it should be, for there is no higher ground than this.

Strictly, the name 'Scafell Pike' should be in the plural, there being three principal summits above 3000 feet, the two lesser having the distinguishing titles of Broad Crag and Ill Crag. The main Pike is, however, pre-eminent, towering over the others seemingly to a greater extent than the mere 160 feet or so by which it has superiority in altitude, and in general being a bulkier mass altogether.

The three summits rise from the main spine of an elevated ridge which keeps above 2800 feet to its abrupt termination in the cliffs of Great End, facing north to Borrowdale; lower spurs then run down to that valley. In the opposite direction, southwest, across the deep gulf of Mickledore, is the tremendous rock-wall of the neighbouring and separate mountain of Scafell, which also exceeds 3000 feet: this is the parent mountain in the one sense that its name has been passed on to the Pikes. Scafell's summit-ridge runs south and broadens into foothills, descending ultimately to mid-Eskdale.

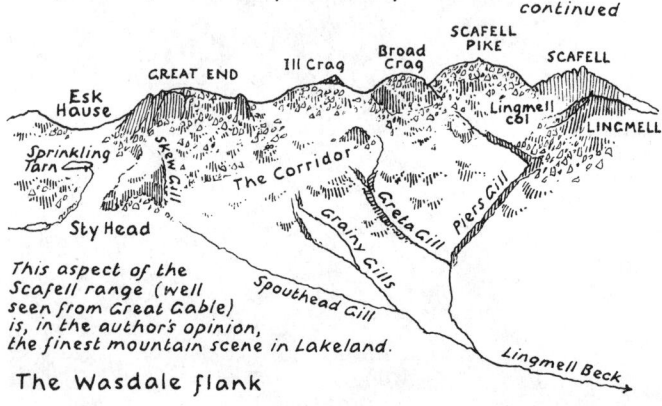

continued

This aspect of the Scafell range (well seen from Great Gable) is, in the author's opinion, the finest mountain scene in Lakeland.

The Wasdale flank

Scafell Pike 6

NATURAL FEATURES

The flanks of the range are bounded on the west by Wasdale, and by the upper reaches of Eskdale, east. All the waters from the Pikes (and from Scafell) flow into one or other of these two valleys, ultimately to merge in the Ravenglass estuary. Thus it will be seen that Scafell Pike, despite a commanding presence, has not the same importance, geographically, as many other fells in the district. It does not stand at the head of any valley, but between valleys: it is not the hub of a wheel from which watercourses radiate; it is one of the spokes. It is inferior, in this respect, to Great Gable or Bowfell nearby, or even its own Great End.

Another interesting feature of Scafell Pike is that although it towers so mightily above Wasdale it can claim no footing in that valley, its territory tapering quickly to Brown Tongue, at the base of which it is nipped off by the widening lower slopes of Lingmell and Scafell.

Tarns are noticeably absent on the arid, stony surface of the mountain, but there is one sheet of water below the summit to the south, Broadcrag Tarn, which is small and unattractive, but, at 2725 feet, can at least boast the highest standing water in Lakeland.

Crags are in evidence on all sides, and big areas of the upper slopes lie devastated by a covering of piled-up boulders, a result not of disintegration but of the volcanic upheavals that laid waste to the mountain during its formation. The landscape is harsh, even savage, and has attracted to itself nothing of romance or historical legend. There is no sentiment about Scafell Pike.

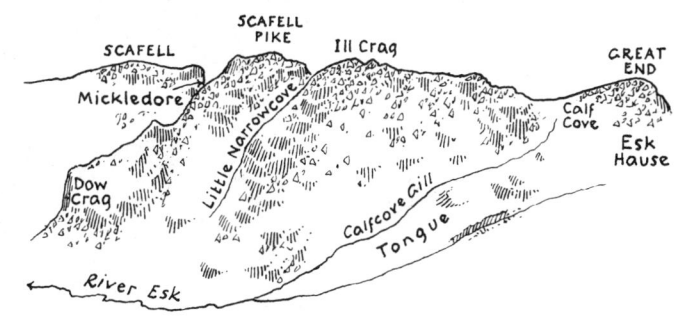

This view is as seen from the south ridge of Esk Pike

The Eskdale flank

Scafell Pike 7

MAP

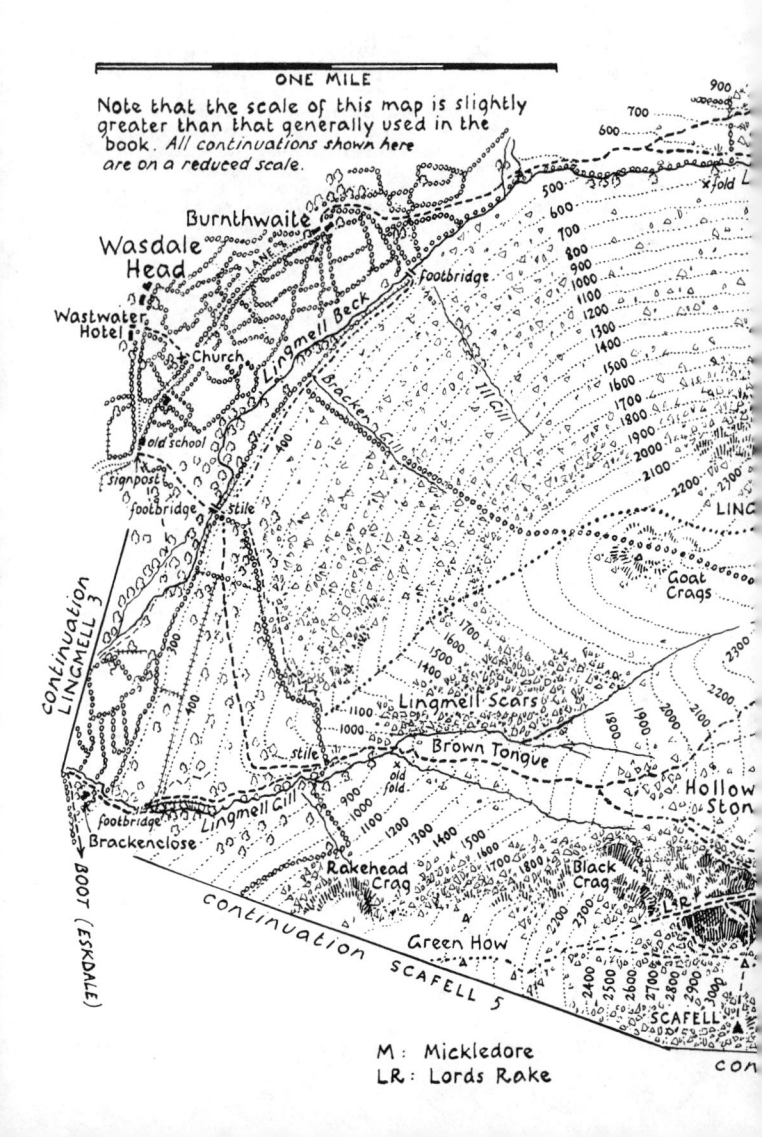

ONE MILE

Note that the scale of this map is slightly greater than that generally used in the book. All continuations shown here are on a reduced scale.

M : Mickledore
LR : Lords Rake

Scafell Pike 8

MAP

A: to BORROWDALE
B: to GREAT LANGDALE
C: to ESKDALE (via CAM SPOUT)

Scafell Pike 9

Broad Crag, 3054'

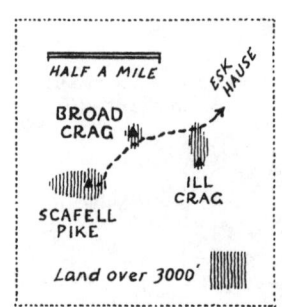

HALF A MILE
BROAD CRAG
ESK HAUSE
ILL CRAG
SCAFELL PIKE
Land over 3000'

Broad Crag is the second of the Scafell Pikes, and a worthy mountain in itself — but it has little fame, is not commonly regarded as a separate fell, and its summit is rarely visited. This latter circumstance appears strange, because the blazed highway between Esk Hause and the main Pike not only climbs over the shoulder of Broad Crag but actually passes within a hundred yards of its summit, which is not greatly elevated above the path. Yet not one person in a thousand passing along here (and thousands do!) turns aside to visit the cairn. The reason for this neglect is more obvious when on the site than it is from a mere study of the map, for the whole of the top is littered deep with piled boulders across which it is quite impossible to walk with any semblance of dignity, the detour involving a desperate and inelegant scramble and the risk of breaking a leg at every stride. Most walkers using the path encounter enough trouble underfoot without seeking more in the virgin jungle of tumbled rock all around. Broad Crag is, in fact, the roughest summit in Lakeland.

The eastern slope descends into Little Narrowcove, and is of small consequence, but the western flank is imposing. On this side the top breaks away in a semi-circle of crags, below which is a shelf traversed by the Corridor Route and bounded lower down a steepening declivity by the great gash of Piers Gill.

Only the proximity of the main Scafell Pike, overtopping the scene, robs Broad Crag of its rightful place as one of the finest of fells.

Broad Crag, and Broad Crag col (right) from the Corridor Route

Scafell Pike 10

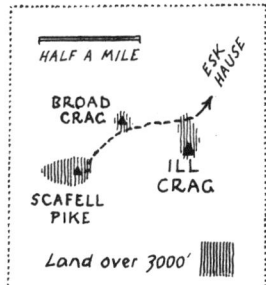

Ill Crag, 3040'

Map: Half a mile. Broad Crag, Esk Hause, Ill Crag, Scafell Pike. Land over 3000'

Ill Crag is the third of the Scafell Pikes, and the most shapely, appearing as a graceful peak when viewed from upper Eskdale, which it dominates. Like Broad Crag, the summit lies off the path from Esk Hause to the main Pike but is more distant, although in this case too the shoulder of the fell is crossed at a height exceeding 3000', so that the summit is raised but little above it. The detour to the top is simple, only the final short rise being really rougher than the boulder-crossings on the path itself. Ill Crag is prominently seen from the vicinity of Esk Hause, and many wishful (and subsequently disappointed) walkers hereabouts, engaged on their first ascent of Scafell Pike will wrongly assume it to be their objective.

The western slope goes down uneventfully between Broad Crag and Great End to the Corridor Route, and the glory of the fell is its excessively steep and rough fall directly from the cairn eastwards into the wilderness of upper Eskdale: a chaotic and desolate scene set at a precipitous gradient, a frozen avalanche of crags and stones, much of it unexplored and uncharted, wild in the extreme, and offering a safe refuge for escaped convicts or an ideal depository for murdered corpses. Someday, when the regular paths become overcrowded, it may be feasible to track out an exciting and alternative route of ascent for scramblers here, but the author prefers to leave the job to someone with more energy and a lesser love of life.

Ill Crag, from the path above Esk Hause

Scafell Pike 11

Pikes Crag — Pulpit Rock — Mickledore Buttress — Mickledore — Scafell Crag

from Hollow Stones

Once in a while every keen fellwalker should have a *pre-arranged* night out amongst the mountains. Time drags and the hours of darkness can be bitterly cold, but to be on the tops at dawn is a wonderful experience and much more than recompense for the temporary discomfort.

Hollow Stones is an excellent place for a bivouac, with a wide choice of overhanging boulders for shelter, many of which have been walled-up and made draught-proof by previous occupants. Watch the rising sun flush Scafell Crag and change a black silhouette into a rosy-pink castle! (This doesn't always happen. Sometimes it never stops raining).

Not many readers, not even those who are frequent visitors to Scafell Pike, could give a caption to this picture. It is, in fact, a scene in the unfrequented hollow of Little Narrowcove, looking up towards the summit of the Pike (the top cairn is out of sight). The crags, unsuspected on the usual routes, are a great surprise. Little Narrowcove (reached from Broad Crag col) is a grassy basin sheltered or encircled by cliffs: a good site for a mountain camp.

Scafell Pike 12

ASCENTS

The ascent of Scafell Pike is the toughest proposition the 'collector' of summits is called upon to attempt, and it is the one above all others that, as a patriot, he cannot omit. The difficulties are due more to roughness of the ground than to altitude, and to the remoteness of the summit from frequented valleys. From all bases except Wasdale Head the climb is long and arduous, and progress is slow: this is a full-day expedition, and the appropriate preparations should be made. Paths are good, but only in the sense that they are distinct; they are abominably stony, even bouldery — which is no great impediment when ascending but mitigates against quick descent. Ample time should be allowed for getting off the mountain.

In winter especially, when conditions can be Arctic, it is important to select a fine clear day, to start early, and keep moving; reserve three hours of daylight for the return journey. If under deep snow the mountain is better left alone altogether, for progress would then be laborious, and even dangerous across the concealed boulders, with a greater chance of death from exposure than of early rescue if an accident were to occur.

Scafell Pike may be ascended most easily from Wasdale Head, less conveniently from Borrowdale or Great Langdale or Eskdale. But all routes are alike in grandeur of scenery.

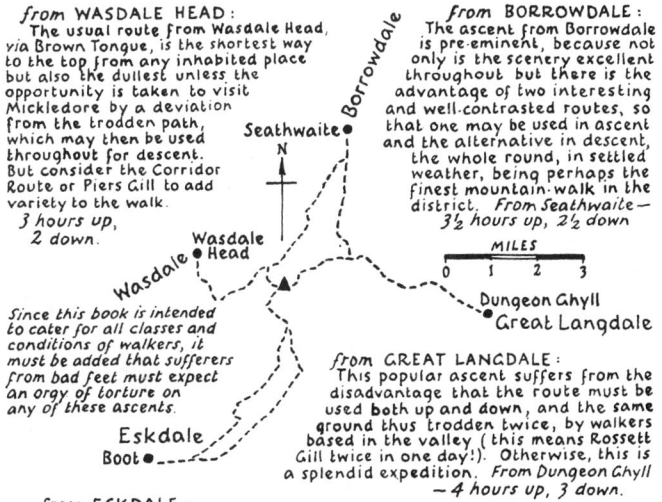

from WASDALE HEAD:
The usual route from Wasdale Head, via Brown Tongue, is the shortest way to the top from any inhabited place but also the dullest unless the opportunity is taken to visit Mickledore by a deviation from the trodden path, which may then be used throughout for descent. But consider the Corridor Route or Piers Gill to add variety to the walk.
3 hours up,
2 down.

from BORROWDALE:
The ascent from Borrowdale is pre-eminent, because not only is the scenery excellent throughout but there is the advantage of two interesting and well-contrasted routes, so that one may be used in ascent and the alternative in descent, the whole round, in settled weather, being perhaps the finest mountain-walk in the district. *From Seathwaite —*
3½ hours up, 2½ down

Since this book is intended to cater for all classes and conditions of walkers, it must be added that sufferers from bad feet must expect an orgy of torture on any of these ascents.

from GREAT LANGDALE:
This popular ascent suffers from the disadvantage that the route must be used both up and down, and the same ground thus trodden twice, by walkers based in the valley (this means Rossett Gill twice in one day!). Otherwise, this is a splendid expedition. *From Dungeon Ghyll* — 4 hours up, 3 down.

from ESKDALE:
This is the best line of approach to the mountain: from the south its grandest and most rugged aspect is seen. Variations of route may be adopted, but time is a great enemy: the walk is lengthy (a feature most noticed when returning). *From Boot* — 4½ hours up, 3½ down.

Scafell Pike 13

ASCENT FROM WASDALE HEAD
via BROWN TONGUE

3,000 feet of ascent
3½ miles
(from Wastwater Hotel)

The tourist route goes round by Lingmell col and is a tiring and uninteresting grind, designed to preserve its users from fears and falterings. The path is good, well-cairned, and practicable in mist.

More enterprising walkers will deviate from the track up Brown Tongue into Hollow Stones and reach the summit by way of Mickledore, a journey as magnificent as the other is dull, although calling for rather more effort: the surround of crags is tremendously impressive, with Scafell Crag impending sensationally overhead. The ridge of Mickledore, gained by a steep scree gully, is the best place in Lakeland for viewing the vertical from the comfort and safety of the horizontal.

Either way, the last half-mile lies across stones.

If bound for Mickledore, look for the deviation on Brown Tongue (cairn on right) when almost at the level of Black Crag.

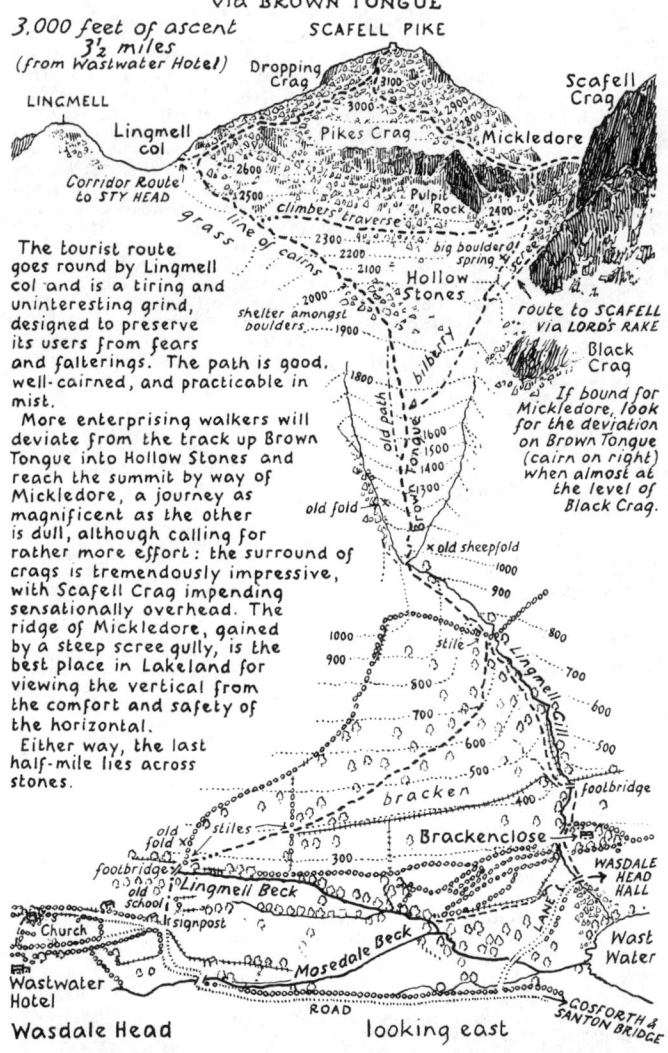

looking east

Scafell Pike 14

ASCENT FROM WASDALE HEAD
via PIERS GILL

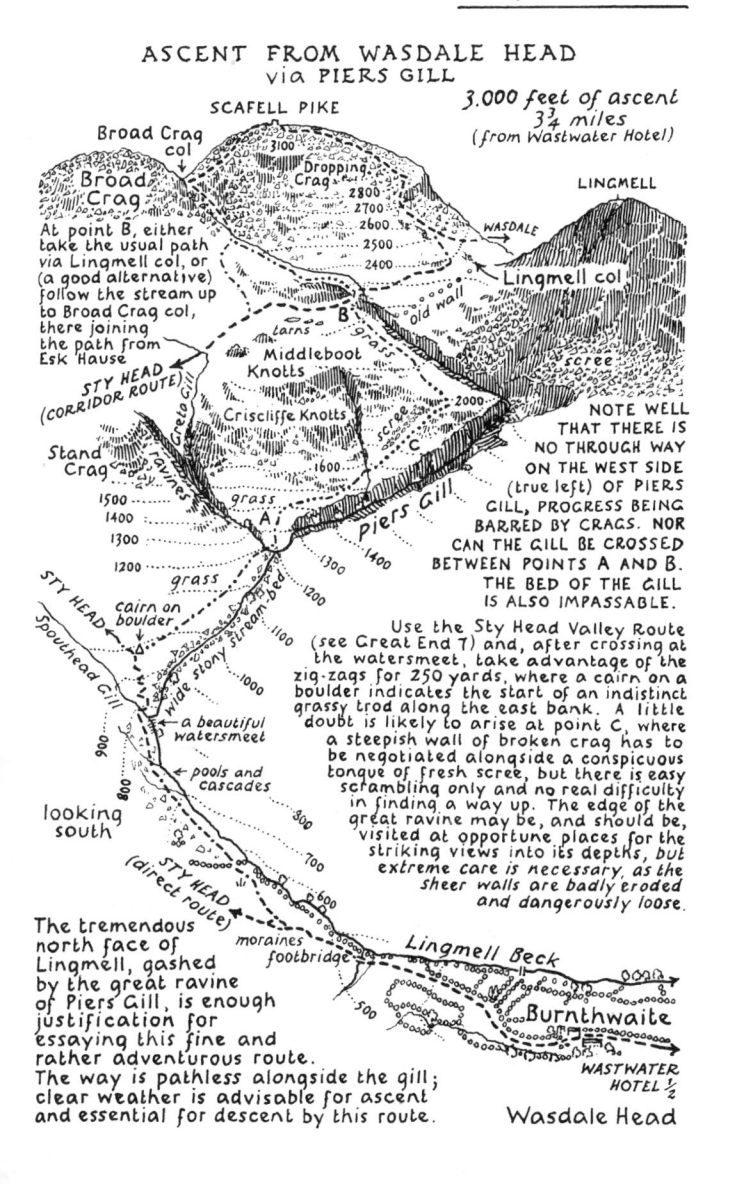

3,000 feet of ascent
3¾ miles
(from Wastwater Hotel)

SCAFELL PIKE — 3100
Broad Crag col
Broad Crag
Dropping Crag — 2800, 2700, 2600, 2500, 2400
LINGMELL
WASDALE →
Lingmell col
scree
old wall
grass
tarns
Middleboot Knotts
STY HEAD (CORRIDOR ROUTE)
Greta Gill
Criscliffe Knotts
scree
2000
B
C

At point B, either take the usual path via Lingmell col, or (a good alternative) follow the stream up to Broad Crag col, there joining the path from Esk Hause.

Stand Crag
ravines
1500, 1400, 1300, 1200
A
grass
Piers Gill
1300, 1400

NOTE WELL THAT THERE IS NO THROUGH WAY ON THE WEST SIDE (true left) OF PIERS GILL, PROGRESS BEING BARRED BY CRAGS. NOR CAN THE GILL BE CROSSED BETWEEN POINTS A AND B. THE BED OF THE GILL IS ALSO IMPASSABLE.

STY HEAD
Spouthead Gill
cairn on boulder
grass
wide stony stream-bed
1200, 1100, 1000
— a beautiful watersmeet
900
800
pools and cascades
looking south
STY HEAD (direct route)
700
600
moraines
footbridge
500
Lingmell Beck
Burnthwaite
WASTWATER HOTEL ½
Wasdale Head

Use the Sty Head Valley Route (see Great End 7) and, after crossing at the watersmeet, take advantage of the zig-zags for 250 yards, where a cairn on a boulder indicates the start of an indistinct grassy trod along the east bank. A little doubt is likely to arise at point C, where a steepish wall of broken crag has to be negotiated alongside a conspicuous tongue of fresh scree, but there is easy scrambling only and no real difficulty in finding a way up. The edge of the great ravine may be, and should be, visited at opportune places for the striking views into its depths, but extreme care is necessary, as the sheer walls are badly eroded and dangerously loose.

The tremendous north face of Lingmell, gashed by the great ravine of Piers Gill, is enough justification for essaying this fine and rather adventurous route. The way is pathless alongside the gill; clear weather is advisable for ascent and essential for descent by this route.

Scafell Pike 15

ASCENT FROM BORROWDALE
via STY HEAD
3,000 feet of ascent
6 miles from Seatoller

Sty Head

Having duly arrived at Styhead Tarn (so proving the reliability of the diagram thus far) refer now (with confidence) to the foot of the next page for the continuation of the route.

Styhead Tarn

boulder

Patterson's Fold (sheepfold)

By keeping to the left of the many variations, a section of the original grooved and paved path will be found, and how superior it is to the modern 'short-cuts'!

Don't panic if unable to ford the stream here (normally easy); keep on along the west bank

The footbridge was originally sited 150 yards downstream, where the buttresses of the former bridge can still be seen.

cascades

ESK HAUSE

Taylorgill Force

The steep fell here is BASE BROWN

Stockley Bridge

Styhead Gill — old folds

The crag high on the left is Hind Crag

River Derwent

GREAT GABLE via GREEN GABLE

gates

Seathwaite Slabs

Sourmilk Gill

Seathwaite — one of the friendliest of farms. No need to fear the dogs or other animals here: visitors merely bore them. The lane to the footbridge here passes under the arch of the farm buildings.

LANE

sheepfold

disused plumbago mines

The Borrowdale Yews ('the fraternal four')

Taylorgill Force

Seathwaite Bridge

gate

Few readers will need to refer to this page, as the walk to Sty Head is amongst the best-known in the district, this being evidenced by the severe wear and tear of the path.

ROAD

River Derwent

It is remarkable that the splendid variation route passing up through the gorge of Taylorgill Force has never found popular favour and is ignored by map-makers although it has been used by discerning walkers for many decades. This, compared with the usual Stockley Bridge path, is often rather wet in the lower intakes, a small disadvantage to set against its merits of quietness, quickness, sustained interest and waterfall and ravine scenery of high quality. A certain amount of delectable clambering on rocky sections of the path is likely to prohibit its use generally by all and sundry (including the many Sunday afternoon picnic parties), which is a good thing for the genuine fellwalker.

ROSTHWAITE 1¼

Seatoller

bus terminus → HONISTER PASS

looking south-south-west

Scafell Pike 16

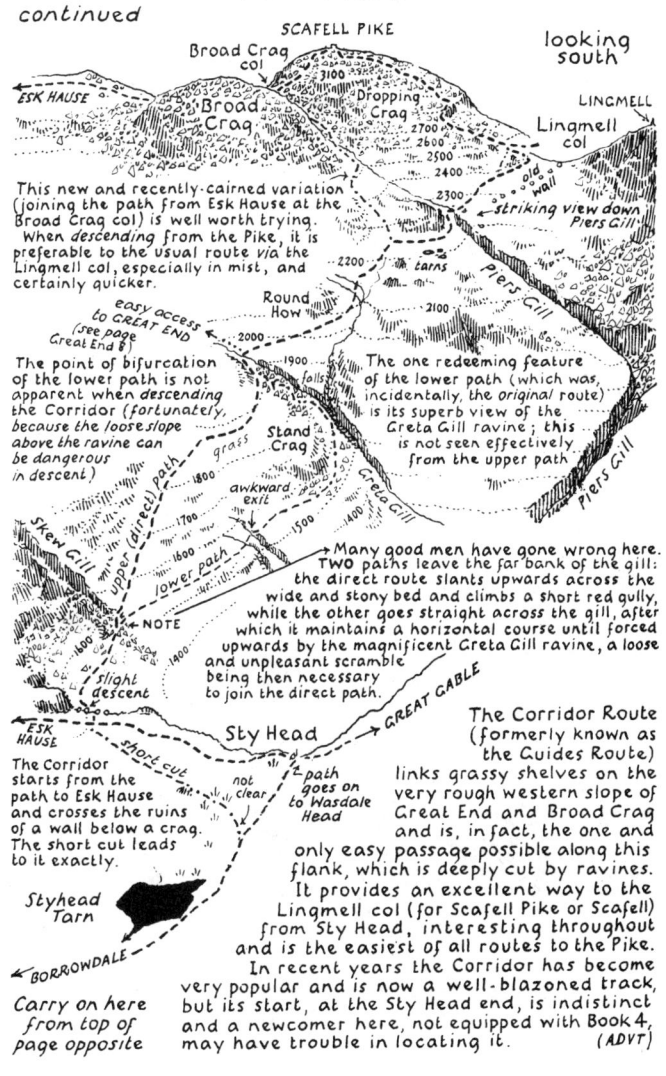

ASCENT FROM BORROWDALE
via STY HEAD

continued

looking south

SCAFELL PIKE — Broad Crag col — Broad Crag — Dropping Crag — LINGMELL — Lingmell col
ESK HAUSE

old wall
striking view down Piers Gill

This new and recently-cairned variation (joining the path from Esk Hause at the Broad Crag col) is well worth trying.
When *descending* from the Pike, it is preferable to the usual route *via* the Lingmell col, especially in mist, and certainly quicker.

tarns — Piers Gill
Round How
easy access to GREAT END (see page Great End 8)

The point of bifurcation of the lower path is not apparent when descending the Corridor (fortunately, because the loose slope above the ravine can be dangerous in descent)

falls

The one redeeming feature of the lower path (which was, incidentally, the *original* route) is its superb view of the Greta Gill ravine; this is not seen effectively from the upper path

Stand Crag
grass
awkward exit
Greta Gill
Skew Gill
upper (direct) path
lower path
NOTE
slight descent

→ Many good men have gone wrong here. TWO paths leave the far bank of the gill: the direct route slants upwards across the wide and stony bed and climbs a short red gully, while the other goes straight across the gill, after which it maintains a horizontal course until forced upwards by the magnificent Greta Gill ravine, a loose and unpleasant scramble being then necessary to join the direct path.

ESK HAUSE ← *short cut* — Sty Head ← GREAT GABLE

The Corridor starts from the path to Esk Hause and crosses the ruins of a wall below a crag. The short cut leads to it exactly.

not clear
path goes on to Wasdale Head

Styhead Tarn

← BORROWDALE

Carry on here from top of page opposite

The Corridor Route (formerly known as the Guides' Route) links grassy shelves on the very rough western slope of Great End and Broad Crag and is, in fact, the one and only easy passage possible along this flank, which is deeply cut by ravines. It provides an excellent way to the Lingmell col (for Scafell Pike or Scafell) from Sty Head, interesting throughout and is the easiest of all routes to the Pike. In recent years the Corridor has become very popular and is now a well-blazoned track, but its start, at the Sty Head end, is indistinct and a newcomer here, not equipped with Book 4, may have trouble in locating it.   (ADVT)

Scafell Pike 17

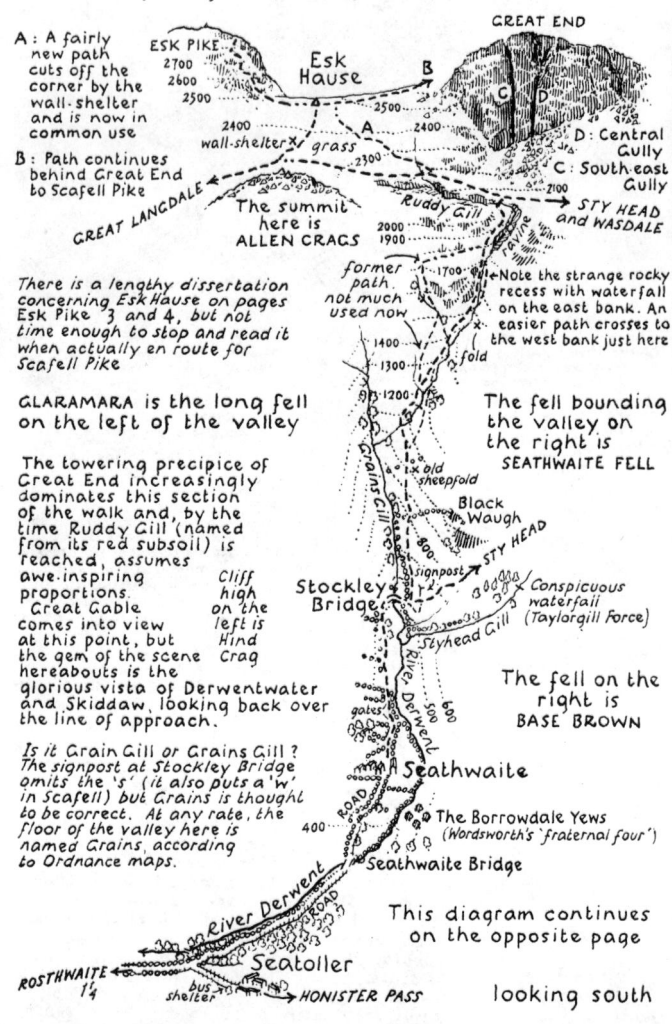

ASCENT FROM BORROWDALE
via ESK HAUSE
3,200 feet of ascent : 5½ miles from Seatoller

A: A fairly new path cuts off the corner by the wall-shelter and is now in common use

B: Path continues behind Great End to Scafell Pike

GREAT END
ESK PIKE 2700, 2600, 2500
Esk Hause
2400 wall-shelter × grass
2300
D: Central Gully
C: South-east Gully
STY HEAD and WASDALE

GREAT LANGDALE
The summit here is ALLEN CRAGS
Ruddy Gill
2000, 1900
1700
former path, not much used now
1400
1300
1200
fold

Note the strange rocky recess with waterfall on the east bank. An easier path crosses to the west bank just here

There is a lengthy dissertation concerning Esk Hause on pages Esk Pike 3 and 4, but not time enough to stop and read it when actually en route for Scafell Pike

GLARAMARA is the long fell on the left of the valley

The fell bounding the valley on the right is SEATHWAITE FELL

The towering precipice of Great End increasingly dominates this section of the walk and, by the time Ruddy Gill (named from its red subsoil) is reached, assumes awe-inspiring proportions.
Great Gable comes into view at this point, but the gem of the scene hereabouts is the glorious vista of Derwentwater and Skiddaw, looking back over the line of approach.

Cliff high on the left is Hind Crag

× old sheepfold
Black Waugh
STY HEAD
signpost
Stockley Bridge
Styhead Gill

Conspicuous waterfall (Taylorgill Force)

The fell on the right is BASE BROWN

Is it Grain Gill or Grains Gill? The signpost at Stockley Bridge omits the 's' (it also puts a 'w' in Scafell) but Grains is thought to be correct. At any rate, the floor of the valley here is named Grains, according to Ordnance maps.

gates
River Derwent
Seathwaite
ROAD
The Borrowdale Yews (Wordsworth's 'fraternal four')
400
Seathwaite Bridge

This diagram continues on the opposite page

River Derwent
ROSTHWAITE 1¼
Seatoller
bus shelter → HONISTER PASS

looking south

Scafell Pike 18

ASCENT FROM BORROWDALE
via ESK HAUSE

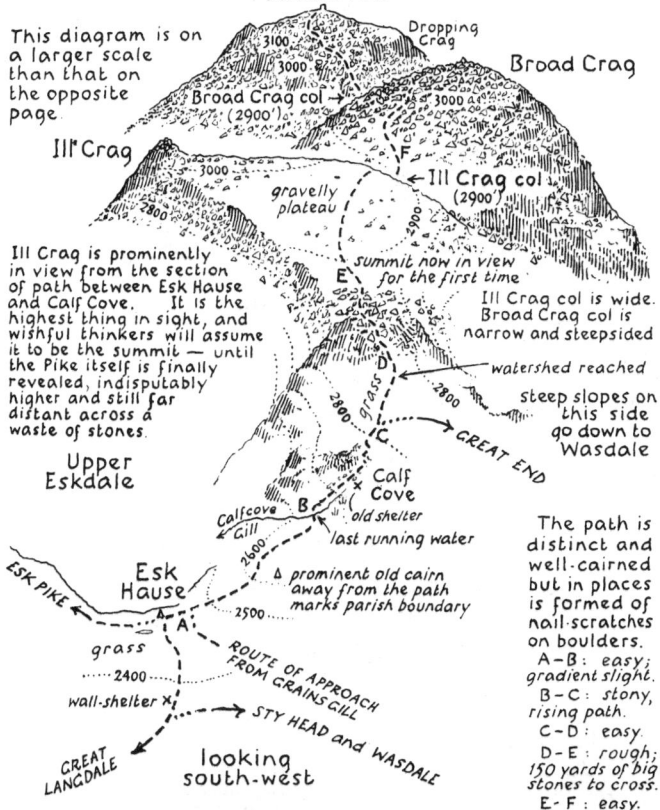

continued

This diagram is on a larger scale than that on the opposite page.

SCAFELL PIKE 3100, 3000
Dropping Crag
Broad Crag 3000
Broad Crag col (2900)
Ill Crag 3000
2800
F
gravelly plateau
← Ill Crag col (2900)
summit now in view for the first time
E

Ill Crag is prominently in view from the section of path between Esk Hause and Calf Cove. It is the highest thing in sight, and wishful thinkers will assume it to be the summit — until the Pike itself is finally revealed, indisputably higher and still far distant across a waste of stones.

Ill Crag col is wide. Broad Crag col is narrow and steepsided

D
watershed reached
C 2800
steep slopes on this side go down to Wasdale
GREAT END →

Upper Eskdale

Calfcove Gill
B Calf Cove
old shelter
last running water

Esk Hause
A
△ prominent old cairn away from the path marks parish boundary
2600

ESK PIKE ←
grass
....2400....
wall-shelter ×
ROUTE OF APPROACH FROM GRAINS GILL
→ STY HEAD and WASDALE

GREAT LANGDALE

looking south-west

The path is distinct and well-cairned but in places is formed of nail-scratches on boulders.
A–B: easy; gradient slight.
B–C: stony, rising path.
C–D: easy.
D–E: rough; 150 yards of big stones to cross.
E–F: easy.
F onwards: excessively rough — inescapable boulders, stones and scree.

Of the many routes of approach to Scafell Pike, this, from Borrowdale via Esk Hause, is the finest. The transition from the quiet beauty of the valley pastures and woods to the rugged wildness of the mountain-top is complete, but comes gradually as height is gained and after passing through varied scenery, both nearby and distant, that sustains interest throughout the long march.

Scafell Pike 19

ASCENT FROM GREAT LANGDALE
3,400 feet of ascent: 5½ miles (from Dungeon Ghyll, Old Hotel)

From Esk Hause onwards the route coincides with that from Borrowdale. Please see the previous page for a description.

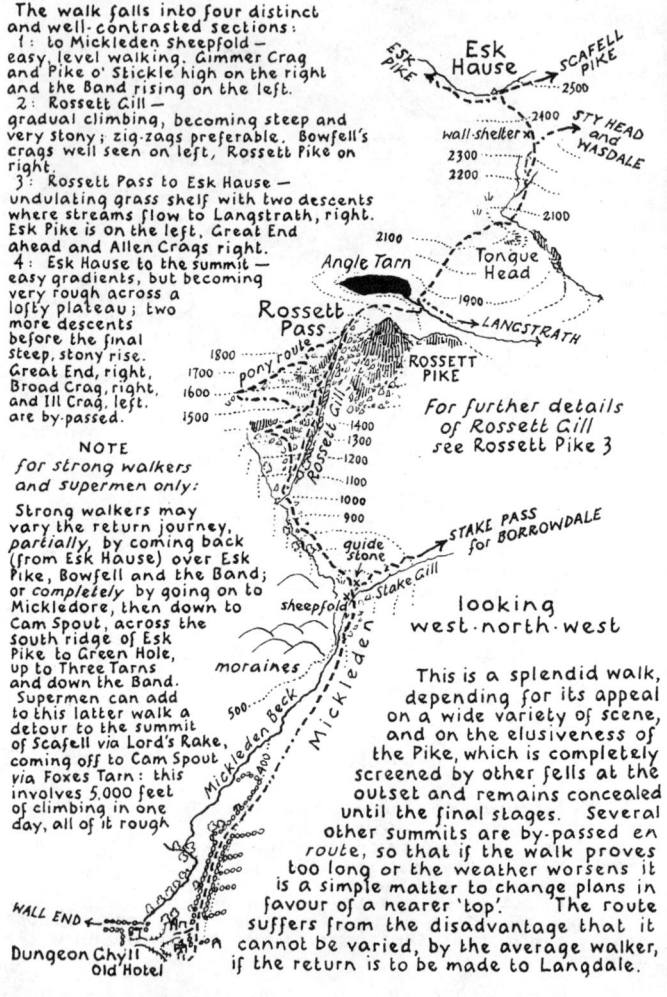

The walk falls into four distinct and well-contrasted sections:

1: to Mickleden sheepfold — easy, level walking. Gimmer Crag and Pike o' Stickle high on the right and the Band rising on the left.

2: Rossett Gill — gradual climbing, becoming steep and very stony; zig-zags preferable. Bowfell's crags well seen on left, Rossett Pike on right.

3: Rossett Pass to Esk Hause — undulating grass shelf with two descents where streams flow to Langstrath, right. Esk Pike is on the left, Great End ahead and Allen Crags right.

4: Esk Hause to the summit — easy gradients, but becoming very rough across a lofty plateau; two more descents before the final steep, stony rise. Great End, right, Broad Crag, right, and Ill Crag, left, are by-passed.

For further details of Rossett Gill see Rossett Pike 3

NOTE
for strong walkers and supermen only:

Strong walkers may vary the return journey, partially, by coming back (from Esk Hause) over Esk Pike, Bowfell and the Band; or completely by going on to Mickledore, then down to Cam Spout, across the south ridge of Esk Pike to Green Hole, up to Three Tarns and down the Band. Supermen can add to this latter walk a detour to the summit of Scafell via Lord's Rake, coming off to Cam Spout via Foxes Tarn: this involves 5,000 feet of climbing in one day, all of it rough.

looking west-north-west

This is a splendid walk, depending for its appeal on a wide variety of scene, and on the elusiveness of the Pike, which is completely screened by other fells at the outset and remains concealed until the final stages. Several other summits are by-passed en route, so that if the walk proves too long or the weather worsens it is a simple matter to change plans in favour of a nearer 'top'. The route suffers from the disadvantage that it cannot be varied, by the average walker, if the return is to be made to Langdale.

Scafell Pike 20

Two views on the walk from Esk Hause to the summit

Many hearts have sunk into many boots as this scene unfolds. Here, on the shoulder of Ill Crag, the summit comes into sight, at last; not almost within reach as confidently expected by walkers who feel they have already done quite enough to deserve success, but still a rough half-mile distant, with two considerable descents (Ill Crag col and Broad Crag col) and much climbing yet to be faced before the goal is reached.

Bowfell — Crinkle Crags

Looking down into Little Narrowcove and Eskdale, with Ill Crag on the left, from Broad Crag col

Scafell Pike 21

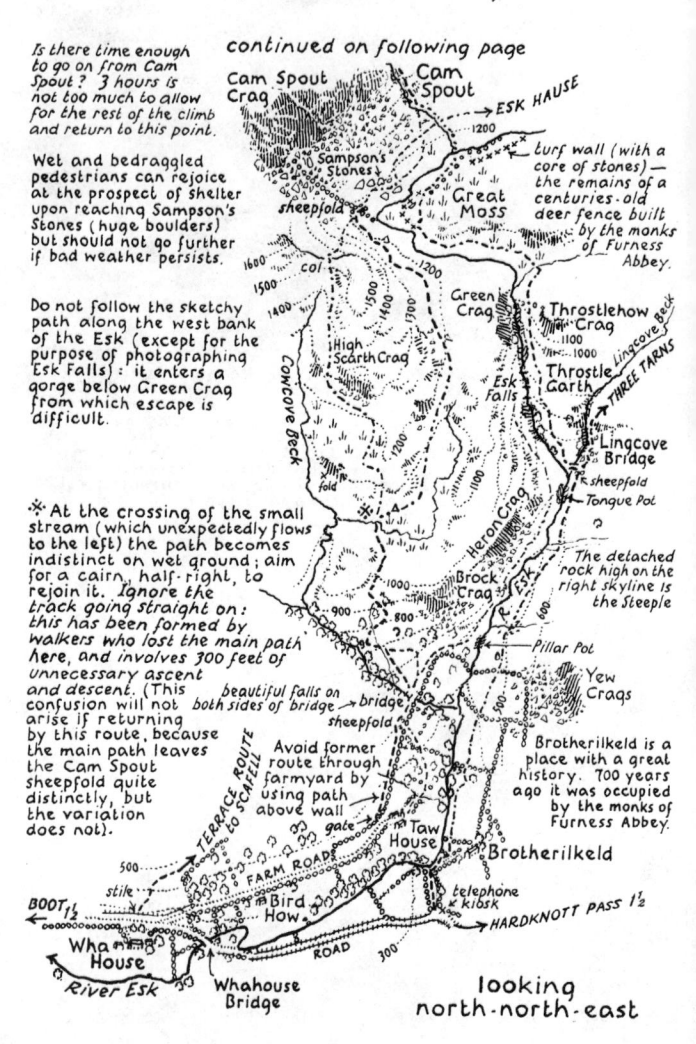

ASCENT FROM ESKDALE
3100 feet of ascent : 7½ miles from Boot

continued on following page

Is there time enough to go on from Cam Spout? 3 hours is not too much to allow for the rest of the climb and return to this point.

Wet and bedraggled pedestrians can rejoice at the prospect of shelter upon reaching Sampson's Stones (huge boulders) but should not go further if bad weather persists.

Do not follow the sketchy path along the west bank of the Esk (except for the purpose of photographing Esk Falls): it enters a gorge below Green Crag from which escape is difficult.

✳ At the crossing of the small stream (which unexpectedly flows to the left) the path becomes indistinct on wet ground; aim for a cairn, half-right, to rejoin it. Ignore the track going straight on: this has been formed by walkers who lost the main path here, and involves 300 feet of unnecessary ascent and descent. (This confusion will not arise if returning by this route, because the main path leaves the Cam Spout sheepfold quite distinctly, but the variation does not).

Turf wall (with a core of stones) — the remains of a centuries-old deer fence built by the monks of Furness Abbey.

The detached rock high on the right skyline is the Steeple.

Brotherilkeld is a place with a great history. 700 years ago it was occupied by the monks of Furness Abbey.

Avoid former route through farmyard by using path above wall

looking north-north-east

Scafell Pike 22

ASCENT FROM ESKDALE

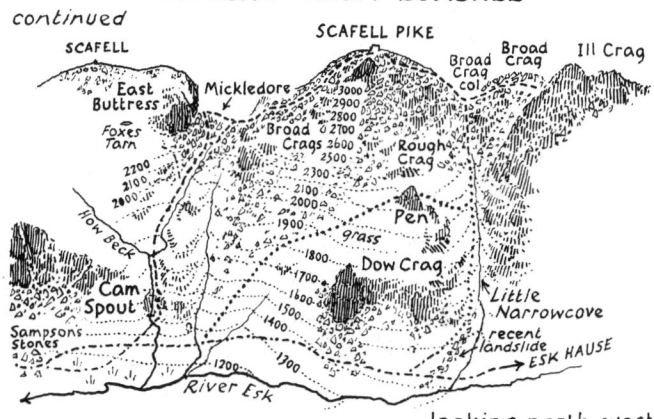

looking north-west

TO CAM SPOUT:

There is no time for dawdling when bound for Scafell Pike, and the fine high-level approach by way of Taw House and the Cowcove zigzags (avoiding the new variation via High Scarth Crag) is recommended as the quickest route to Cam Spout. The path from Brotherilkeld via Lingcove Bridge has too many distractions and temptations to halt and provides a final problem in crossing Great Moss dryshod.

FROM CAM SPOUT ONWARDS:

The usual route from Cam Spout goes up steeply by the waterfalls and proceeds thereafter on a good path, becoming a river of stones, to the ridge of Mickledore, where a well-blazed track climbs across boulders to the summit. The rock-scenery on the last stages of the struggle to Mickledore is good, Scafell East Buttress being extremely impressive, but conditions underfoot are abominable. The variation just below Mickledore that cuts off a corner and gains the ridge at its lowest point is rather easier. This route can be done in mist.

A secluded but circuitous and no less rough alternative is offered by Little Narrowcove, reached by passing below the imposing buttress of Dow Crag and completely dominated by the tremendous cliff of Ill Crag. Note the dotted line on the diagram indicating a shorter way that skirts the left edge of Dow Crag, crosses a col near the rocky peak of Pen and enters Little Narrowcove at mid-height; by careful observation it is possible, on this variation, to keep to grass all the way across the breast of the Pike. Clear weather is needed here.

It seems remarkable that England's highest mountain has no direct path to its summit on this, its finest side. It is not merely steepness that has kept walkers away from it, but rather the unavoidable, inescapable shawl of boulders covering the final 500 feet, where progress is not only painfully slow but carries a risk of displacing stones that have never before been trodden and may be balanced precariously and easily disturbed. There is no fun in pioneering routes over such rough terrain, which is safest left in virgin state.

Scafell Pike 23

THE SUMMIT

This is it: the Mecca of all weary pilgrims in Lakeland; the place of many ceremonies and celebrations, of bonfires and birthday parties; the ultimate; the supreme; the one objective above all others; the highest ground in England; the top of Scafell Pike.

It is a magnet, not because of its beauty for this is not a place of beauty, not because of the exhilaration of the climb for there is no exhilaration in toiling upwards over endless stones, not because of its view for although this is good there are others better. It is a magnet simply because it is the highest ground in England.

There is a huge cairn that from afar looks like a hotel: a well-built circular edifice now crumbling on its east side, with steps leading up to its flat top. Set into the vertical nine-foot north wall of the cairn is a tablet commemorating the gift of the summit to the nation. A few yards distant, west, is a triangulation column of the Ordnance Survey; a visitor in doubt and seeking confirmation of his whereabouts should consult the number on the front plate of the column: if it is anything other than S.1537 he has good cause for doubt — heaven knows where his erring steps have led him, but it is certainly not to the summit of Scafell Pike.

The surrounding area is barren, a tumbled wilderness of stones of all shapes and sizes, but it is not true, as has oft been written and may be thought, that the top is entirely devoid of vegetation: there is, indeed, a patch of grass on the south side of the cairn sufficient to provide a couch for a few hundredweights of exhausted flesh.

Yet this rough and desolate summit is, after all, just as it should be, and none of us would really want it different. A smooth green promenade here would be wrong. This is the summit of England, and it is fitting that it should be sturdy and rugged and strong.

Scafell Pike 24

THE SUMMIT

DESCENTS: It is an exaggeration to describe walkers' routes across the top of Scafell Pike as *paths*, because they make an uneasy pavement of angular boulders that are too unyielding ever to be trodden into subjection; nevertheless the routes are quite distinct, the particular boulders selected for their feet by the pioneers having, in the past century or so, become so extensively scratched by bootnails that they now appear as white ribbons across the grey waste of stones. Thus there is no difficulty in following them, even in mist.

The only place in descent where a walker might go astray is in going down by the Wasdale Head path to join the Corridor Route for Sty Head, the bifurcation above Lingmell col being surprisingly vague: in mist a walker might find himself well down Brown Tongue before discovering his error. It is actually safer for a stranger seeking the Corridor Route, particularly in mist, to use the Esk Hause path as far as the first col, at this point turning off *left* down into a hollow; a stream rises here and is a certain guide to the Corridor, which is reached exactly and unmistakably at the head of Piers Gill.

PLAN OF SUMMIT

Soliloquy.........

In summertime the cairn often becomes over-run with tourists, and a seeker after solitary contemplation may then be recommended to go across to the south peak, where, after enjoying the splendid view of Eskdale, he can observe the visitors to the summit from this distance. He may find himself wondering what impulse had driven these good folk to leave the comforts of the valley and make the weary ascent to this inhospitable place.

Why *does* a man climb mountains? Why has he forced his tired and sweating body up here when he might instead have been sitting at his ease in a deckchair at the seaside, looking at girls in bikinis, or fast asleep, or sucking ice-cream, according to his fancy. On the face of it the thing doesn't make sense.

Yet more and more people are turning to the hills; they find something in these wild places that can be found nowhere else. It may be solace for some, satisfaction for others: the joy of exercising muscles that modern ways of living have cramped, perhaps; or a balm for jangled nerves in the solitude and silence of the peaks; or escape from the clamour and tumult of everyday existence. It may have something to do with a man's subconscious search for beauty, growing keener as so much in the world grows uglier. It may be a need to re-adjust his sights, to get out of his own narrow groove and climb above it to see wider horizons and truer perspectives. In a few cases, it may even be a curiosity inspired by awainwright's Pictorial Guides. Or it may be, and for most walkers it *will* be, quite simply, a deep love of the hills, a love that has grown over the years, whatever motive first took them there: a feeling that these hills are friends, tried and trusted friends, always there when needed.

It is a question every man must answer for himself.

Scafell Pike 25

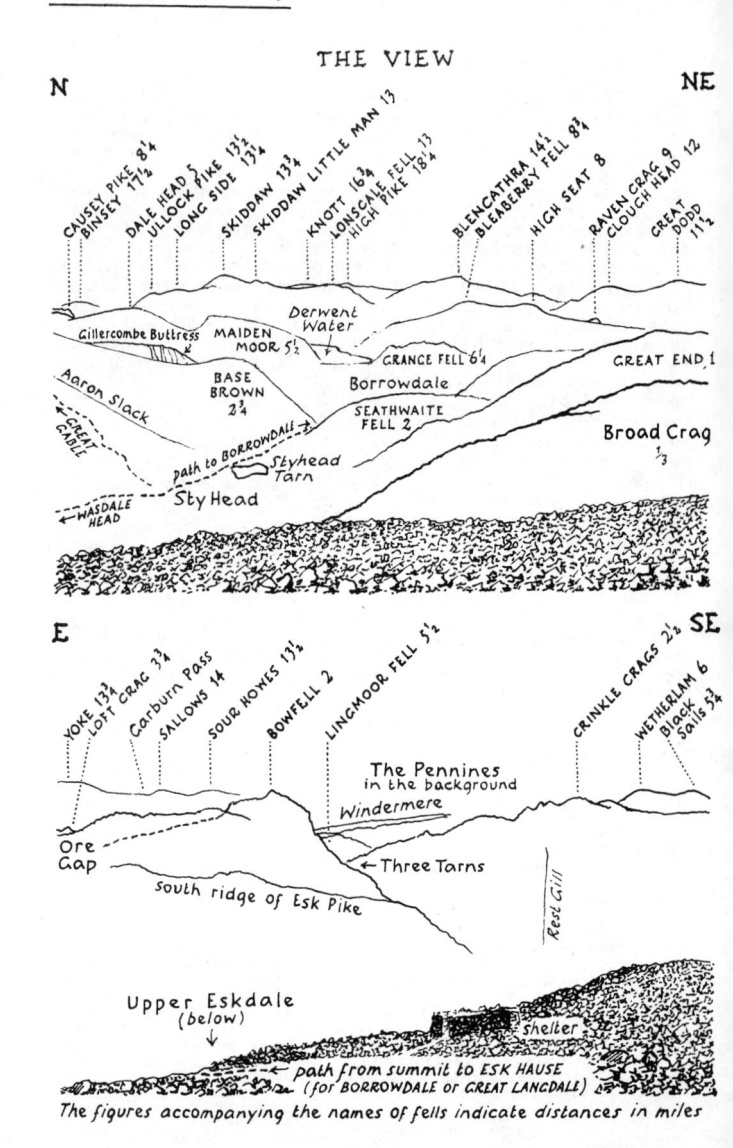

THE VIEW

N — NE

CAUSEY PIKE 8¼
BINSEY 17½
DALE HEAD 5
ULLOCK PIKE 13½
LONG SIDE 13¾
SKIDDAW 13¾
SKIDDAW LITTLE MAN 13
KNOTT 16¾
LONSCALE FELL 13
HIGH PIKE 18¼
BLENCATHRA 14½
BLEABERRY FELL 8¾
HIGH SEAT 8
RAVEN CRAG 9
CLOUGH HEAD 12
GREAT DODD 11½

Gillercombe Buttress
MAIDEN MOOR 5½
Derwent Water
BASE BROWN 2¾
GRANGE FELL 6¼
Borrowdale
SEATHWAITE FELL 2
GREAT END 1

Aaron Slack
GREAT GABLE
path to BORROWDALE →
Styhead Tarn
Sty Head
WASDALE HEAD ←
Broad Crag ⅓

E — SE

YOKE 13¼
LOFT CRAG 3¾
Garburn Pass
SALLOWS 14
SOUR HOWES 13½
BOWFELL 2
LINGMOOR FELL 5½
CRINKLE CRAGS 2½
WETHERLAM 6
Black Sails 5¾

The Pennines in the background
Windermere
Ore Gap
← Three Tarns
south ridge of Esk Pike
Rest Gill

Upper Eskdale (below) ↓
shelter
← path from summit to ESK HAUSE (for BORROWDALE or GREAT LANGDALE)

The figures accompanying the names of fells indicate distances in miles

THE VIEW

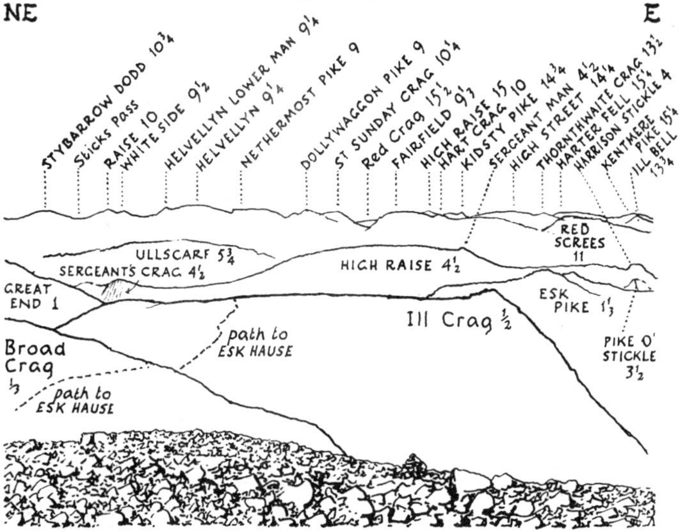
NE
E
STYBARROW DODD 10¾
Sticks Pass
RAISE 10
WHITESIDE 9½
HELVELLYN LOWER MAN 9¼
HELVELLYN 9¼
NETHERMOST PIKE 9
DOLLYWAGGON PIKE 9
St SUNDAY CRAG 10¼
Red Crag 15½
FAIRFIELD 9⅓
HIGH RAISE 15
HART CRAG 10
KIDSTY PIKE 14¾
SERGEANT MAN 4½
HIGH STREET 14¼
THORNTHWAITE CRAG 13½
HARTER FELL 15¼
HARRISON STICKLE 4
KENTMERE PIKE 15¼
ILL BELL 13¾
RED SCREES 11
ULLSCARF 5¾
SERGEANT'S CRAG 4½
HIGH RAISE 4½
GREAT END 1
ESK PIKE 1⅓
Ill Crag ½
Broad Crag ⅓
path to ESK HAUSE
path to ESK HAUSE
PIKE O' STICKLE 3½

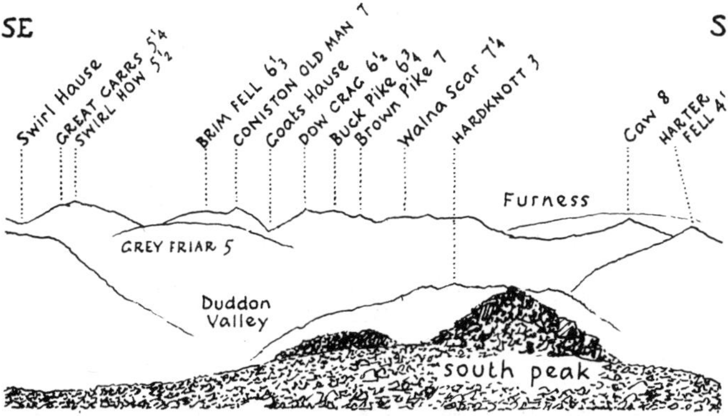
SE
S
Swirl Hause
GREAT CARRS 5¼
SWIRL HOW 5½
BRIM FELL 6⅓
CONISTON OLD MAN 7
Goats Hause
DOW CRAG 6½
Buck Pike 6¾
Brown Pike 7
Walna Scar 7¼
HARDKNOTT 3
Caw 8
HARTER FELL 4½
Furness
GREY FRIAR 5
Duddon Valley
south peak

This being the highest ground in England the view is the most extensive, although not appreciably more so than those seen from many nearby fells. There is much interesting detail in every direction, and no denying the superiority of altitude, for all else is below eye-level, with old favourites like Great Gable and Bowfell seeming, if not humbled, less proud than they usually do (Scafell, across Mickledore, often *looks* of equal or greater height). Despite the wide variety of landscape, however, this is not the most pleasing of summit views, none of the valleys or lakes in view being seen really well.

Scafell Pike 27

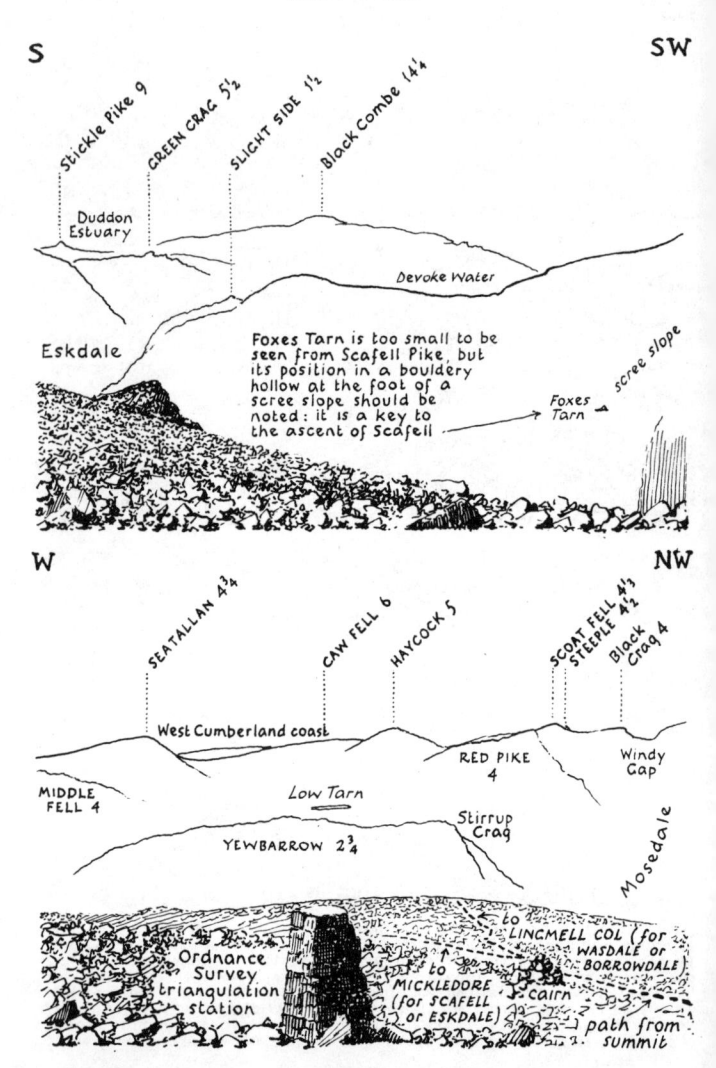

THE VIEW

S — **SW**

- Stickle Pike 9
- GREEN CRAG 5½
- SLIGHT SIDE 1½
- Black Combe 14¼

Duddon Estuary

Devoke Water

Eskdale

Foxes Tarn is too small to be seen from Scafell Pike, but its position in a bouldery hollow at the foot of a scree slope should be noted: it is a key to the ascent of Scafell

→ Foxes Tarn

scree slope

W — **NW**

- SEA TALLAN 4¾
- CAW FELL 6
- HAYCOCK 5
- SCOAT FELL 4⅓
- STEEPLE 4½
- Black Crag 4

West Cumberland coast

RED PIKE 4

Windy Gap

MIDDLE FELL 4

Low Tarn

Stirrup Crag

YEWBARROW 2¾

Mosedale

Ordnance Survey triangulation station

to LINGMELL COL (for WASDALE or BORROWDALE)

to MICKLEDORE (for SCAFELL or ESKDALE)

cairn

path from summit

Scafell Pike 28

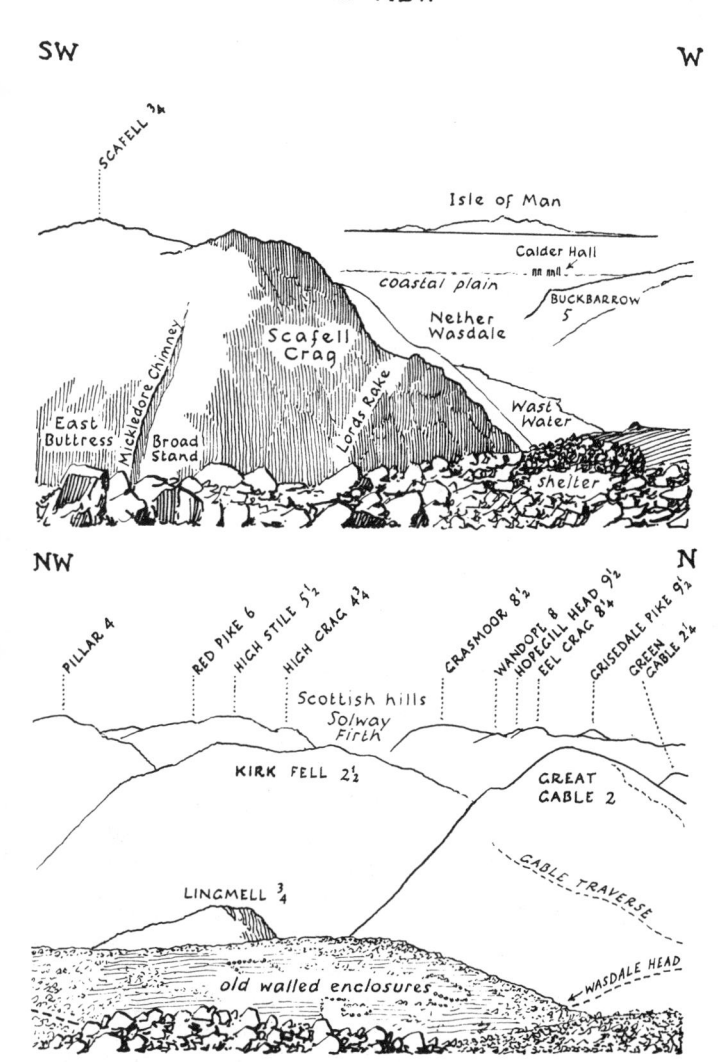

THE VIEW

SW / W

- SCAFELL ¾
- Isle of Man
- Calder Hall
- coastal plain
- BUCKBARROW S
- Scafell Crag
- Nether Wasdale
- East Buttress
- Mickledore Chimney
- Broad Stand
- Lords Rake
- Wast Water
- shelter

NW / N

- PILLAR 4
- RED PIKE 6
- HIGH STILE 5½
- HIGH CRAG 4¾
- GRASMOOR 8½
- WANDOPE & HOPEGILL HEAD 9½
- EEL CRAG 8¼
- GRISEDALE PIKE 9½
- GREEN GABLE 2¼
- Scottish hills
- Solway Firth
- KIRK FELL 2½
- GREAT GABLE 2
- GABLE TRAVERSE
- LINGMELL ¾
- old walled enclosures
- WASDALE HEAD

Scafell Pike 29

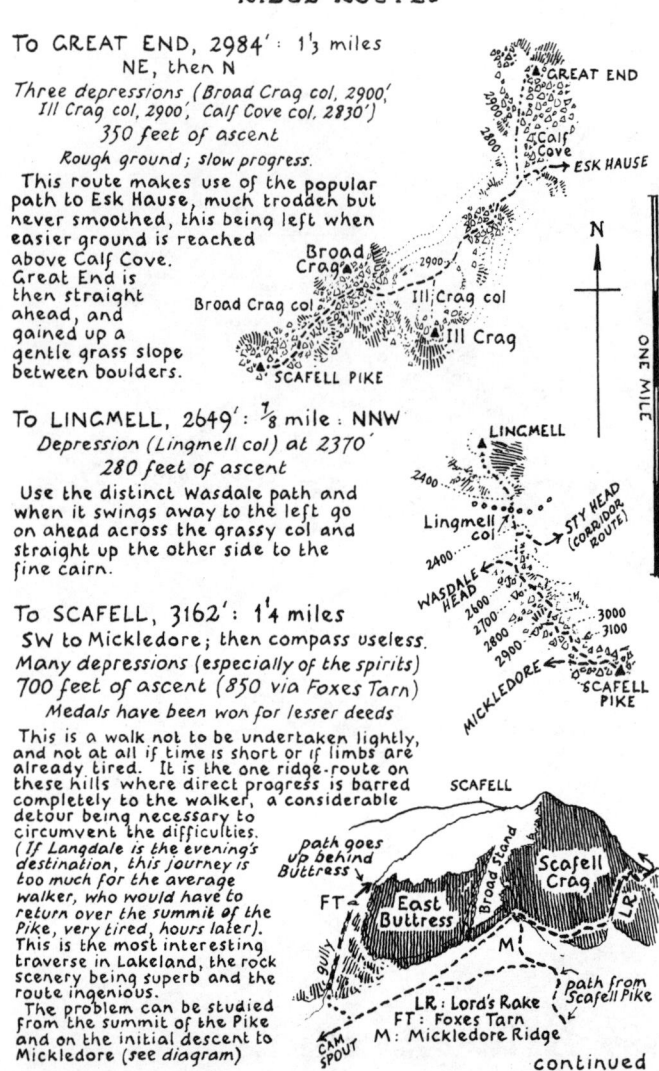

RIDGE ROUTES

To GREAT END, 2984': 1⅓ miles
NE, then N
Three depressions (Broad Crag col, 2900', Ill Crag col, 2900', Calf Cove col, 2830')
350 feet of ascent
Rough ground; slow progress.

This route makes use of the popular path to Esk Hause, much trodden but never smoothed, this being left when easier ground is reached above Calf Cove. Great End is then straight ahead, and gained up a gentle grass slope between boulders.

To LINGMELL, 2649': ⅞ mile: NNW
Depression (Lingmell col) at 2370'
280 feet of ascent

Use the distinct Wasdale path and when it swings away to the left go on ahead across the grassy col and straight up the other side to the fine cairn.

To SCAFELL, 3162': 1¼ miles
SW to Mickledore; then compass useless.
Many depressions (especially of the spirits)
700 feet of ascent (850 via Foxes Tarn)
Medals have been won for lesser deeds

This is a walk not to be undertaken lightly, and not at all if time is short or if limbs are already tired. It is the one ridge-route on these hills where direct progress is barred completely to the walker, a considerable detour being necessary to circumvent the difficulties. (If Langdale is the evening's destination, this journey is too much for the average walker, who would have to return over the summit of the Pike, very tired, hours later). This is the most interesting traverse in Lakeland, the rock scenery being superb and the route ingenious.

The problem can be studied from the Pike and on the initial descent to Mickledore (see diagram)

LR: Lord's Rake
FT: Foxes Tarn
M: Mickledore Ridge

continued

Scafell Pike 30

RIDGE ROUTES

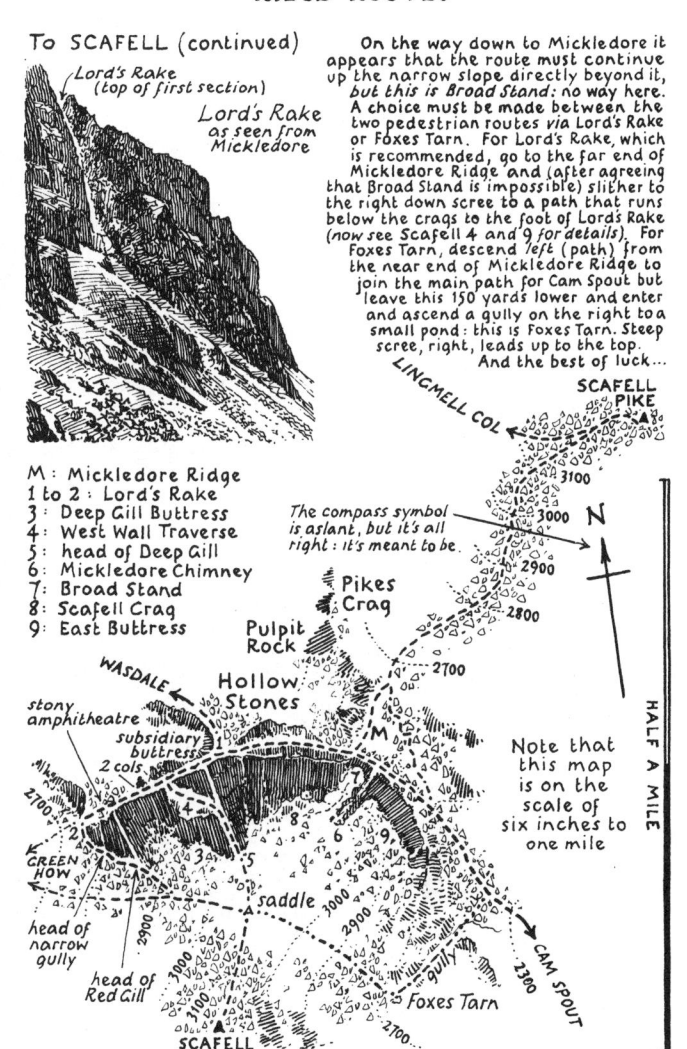

To SCAFELL (continued)

Lord's Rake (top of first section)

Lord's Rake as seen from Mickledore

On the way down to Mickledore it appears that the route must continue up the narrow slope directly beyond it, *but this is Broad Stand*: no way here. A choice must be made between the two pedestrian routes *via* Lord's Rake or Foxes Tarn. For Lord's Rake, which is recommended, go to the far end of Mickledore Ridge and (after agreeing that Broad Stand is impossible) slither to the right down scree to a path that runs below the crags to the foot of Lord's Rake (now see Scafell 4 and 9 for details). For Foxes Tarn, descend *left* (path) from the near end of Mickledore Ridge to join the main path for Cam Spout but leave this 150 yards lower and enter and ascend a gully on the right to a small pond: this is Foxes Tarn. Steep scree, right, leads up to the top.

And the best of luck...

M : Mickledore Ridge
1 to 2 : Lord's Rake
3 : Deep Gill Buttress
4 : West Wall Traverse
5 : head of Deep Gill
6 : Mickledore Chimney
7 : Broad Stand
8 : Scafell Crag
9 : East Buttress

The compass symbol is aslant, but it's all right: it's meant to be.

Note that this map is on the scale of six inches to one mile

HALF A MILE

Seathwaite Fell   1970'

from Seathwaite

Seathwaite Fell, after the fashion of Rossett Pike, rises from, and causes, the bifurcation of two well-known mountain paths, Grains Gill and Sty Head, but additionally is crossed at the neck joining it to the parent fell of Great End by a third, the popular Esk Hause track. Thus it is completely surrounded by much-used pedestrian highways, but the fell itself, with few attractions to compare with those of the greater mountains around, is rarely visited — except, of course, by the custodian of the infamous rain-gauges which record, to its shame, that the fell and its vicinity has much the heaviest rainfall in the country.

Steep, rough slopes and a rim of crags on three sides offer no encouragement to stray from the beaten paths, but the top is easily gained from Sprinkling Tarn, which, with lesser sheets of water, provide the interest of a wide, undulating plateau. Sprinkling Tarn is commonly accredited as the source of the River Derwent.

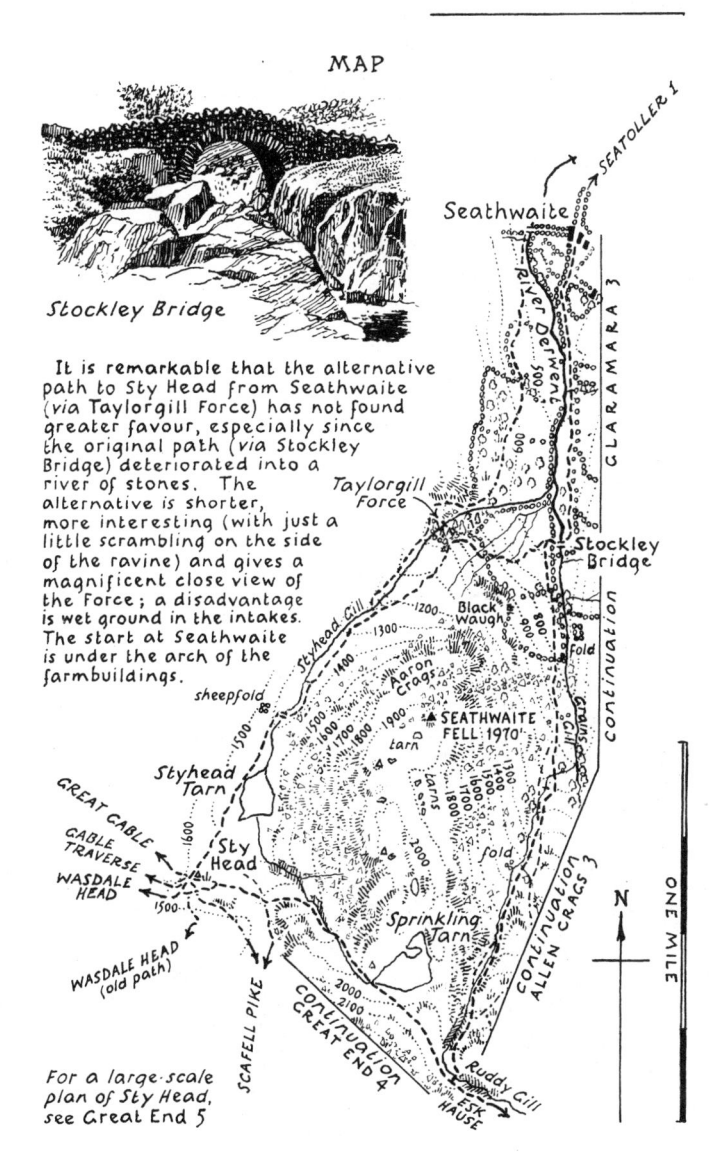

Seathwaite Fell 2

MAP

Stockley Bridge

It is remarkable that the alternative path to Sty Head from Seathwaite (via Taylorgill Force) has not found greater favour, especially since the original path (via Stockley Bridge) deteriorated into a river of stones. The alternative is shorter, more interesting (with just a little scrambling on the side of the ravine) and gives a magnificent close view of the Force; a disadvantage is wet ground in the intakes. The start at Seathwaite is under the arch of the farmbuildings.

For a large-scale plan of Sty Head, see Great End 5

Seathwaite Fell 3

ASCENT FROM BORROWDALE
1550 feet of ascent : 1¼ miles from Seathwaite

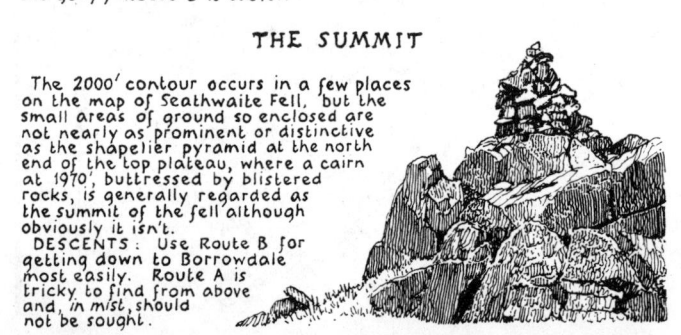

looking south-west

The open scree gully on the east, above Grains Gill, is not advised.

The position of the raingauges is not indicated on this diagram or the map (so as not to invite damage). One will be seen on Route A.

There are no paths to the summit. The best plan is to gain height by using the Sty Head path from Stockley Bridge, leaving it either immediately above the intake wall (Route A) or half-a-mile further where a streamlet crosses the path 150 yards short of the point at which the path comes alongside Styhead Gill (Route B). In each case aim for a grassy gully ahead. The top of the rock tower on the left of Route A affords a startling view of Grains Gill. Route A becomes very steep in the gully; Route B is easier.

THE SUMMIT

The 2000' contour occurs in a few places on the map of Seathwaite Fell, but the small areas of ground so enclosed are not nearly as prominent or distinctive as the shapelier pyramid at the north end of the top plateau, where a cairn at 1970', buttressed by blistered rocks, is generally regarded as the summit of the fell although obviously it isn't.

DESCENTS: Use Route B for getting down to Borrowdale most easily. Route A is tricky to find from above and, in mist, should not be sought.

Seathwaite Fell 4

THE VIEW

The diagram indicates the view from the distinctive summit at 1970', the usually-accepted 'top' but not quite the highest point of the fell. Northwards the scene is excellent: there is no better place for viewing the Seathwaite valley. Less beautiful, but more impressive, is the close surround of much higher mountains. Seathwaite Fell is such a lowly member of this group that it is a surprise to see a considerable mileage of the ridge of the Helvellyn Dodds occupying the skyline.

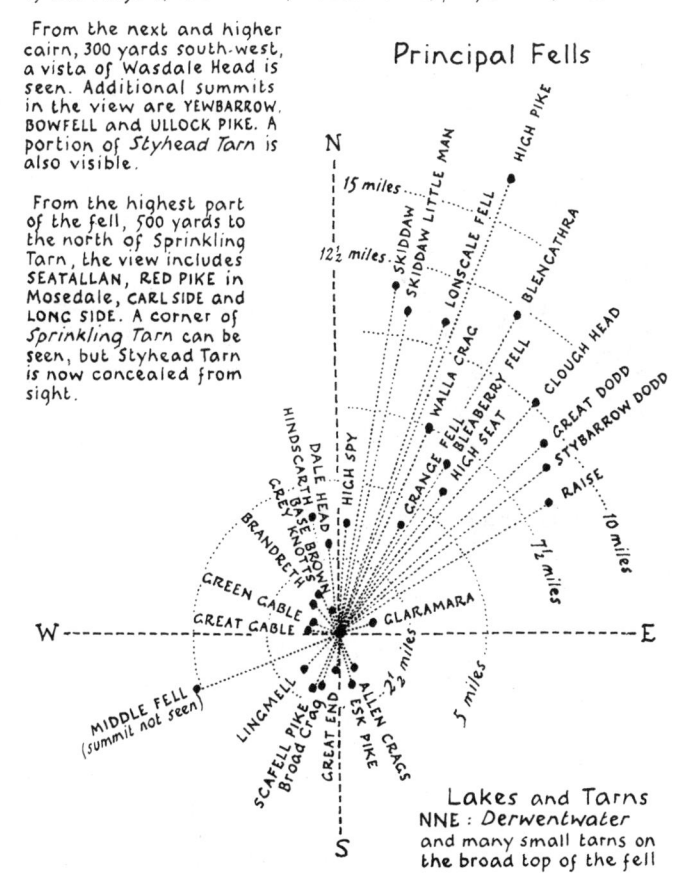

From the next and higher cairn, 300 yards south-west, a vista of Wasdale Head is seen. Additional summits in the view are YEWBARROW, BOWFELL and ULLOCK PIKE. A portion of *Styhead Tarn* is also visible.

From the highest part of the fell, 500 yards to the north of Sprinkling Tarn, the view includes SEATALLAN, RED PIKE in Mosedale, CARL SIDE and LONG SIDE. A corner of *Sprinkling Tarn* can be seen, but Styhead Tarn is now concealed from sight.

Principal Fells

- HIGH PIKE
- SKIDDAW LITTLE MAN
- SKIDDAW
- LONSCALE FELL
- BLENCATHRA
- WALLA CRAG
- BLEABERRY FELL
- GRANGE FELL
- HIGH SEAT
- CLOUGH HEAD
- GREAT DODD
- STYBARROW DODD
- HIGH SPY
- DALE HEAD
- HINDSCARTH
- BASE BROWN
- GREY KNOTTS
- BRANDRETH
- RAISE
- GREEN GABLE
- GREAT GABLE
- GLARAMARA
- MIDDLE FELL (summit not seen)
- LINGMELL
- SCAFELL PIKE
- Broad Crag
- GREAT END
- ESK PIKE
- ALLEN CRAGS

15 miles, 12½ miles, 10 miles, 7½ miles, 5 miles, 2½ miles

Lakes and Tarns
NNE : *Derwentwater*
and many small tarns on the broad top of the fell

Slight Side 2499'

from Catcove Beck

- Wasdale Head
  - SCAFELL PIKE
- SCAFELL ▲   ▲ BOWFELL
- ▲ ILLGILL HEAD   ▲ SLIGHT SIDE
- Boot

MILES 0 1 2 3 4

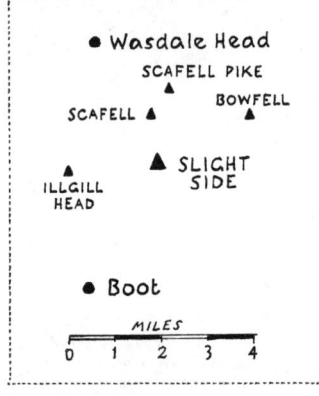

The mile-long south ridge of Scafell descends loftily to an abrupt terminus at a barrier of rock, which rises to a neat peak, Slight Side, and, to the east, falls sharply to Eskdale from the steep cliff of Horn Crag (a name sometimes given to the fell itself). The southern slope widens into a strange plateau, Quagrigg Moss, beyond which is a charming tangle of foothills, where pink granite, ling and bracken colour the environs of Stony Tarn and Eel Tarn.

The official altitude of Slight Side is a tribute to the meticulous care of the Ordnance Survey. But if Nelson had been in charge of the surveying party, and been a mountaineer too, surely he would have recorded 2500!

Slight Side 2

MAP

At this late stage in the book's preparation, space is becoming terribly short and cannot be spared for repetition of information already given. As the map of Scafell includes the whole area of Slight Side, would readers mind referring to pages Scafell 5-8?

ASCENT FROM ESKDALE
2350 feet of ascent : 4¾ miles from Boot

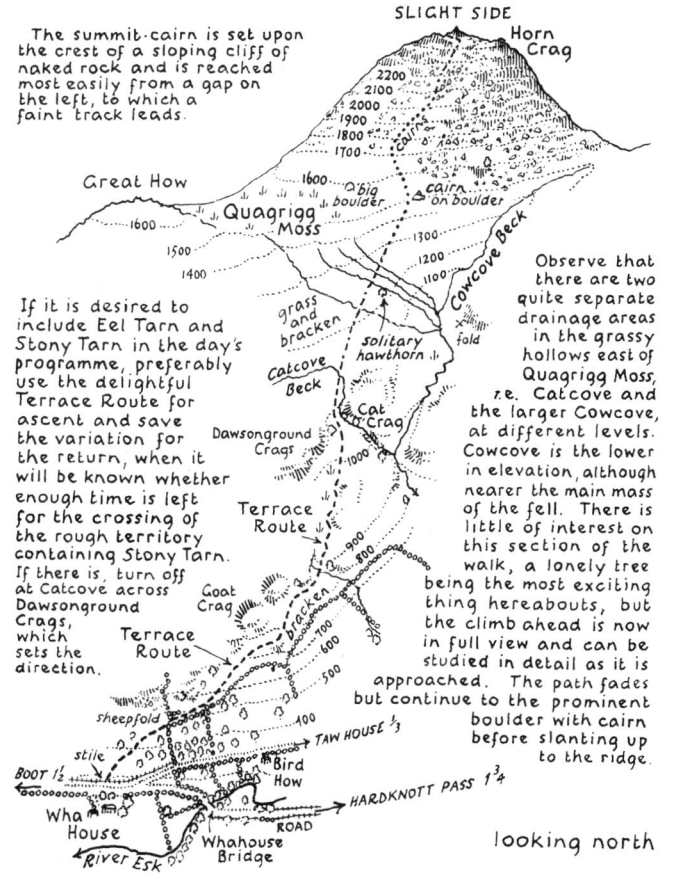

The summit-cairn is set upon the crest of a sloping cliff of naked rock and is reached most easily from a gap on the left, to which a faint track leads.

Observe that there are two quite separate drainage areas in the grassy hollows east of Quagrigg Moss, i.e. Catcove and the larger Cowcove, at different levels. Cowcove is the lower in elevation, although nearer the main mass of the fell. There is little of interest on this section of the walk, a lonely tree being the most exciting thing hereabouts, but the climb ahead is now in full view and can be studied in detail as it is approached. The path fades but continue to the prominent boulder with cairn before slanting up to the ridge.

If it is desired to include Eel Tarn and Stony Tarn in the day's programme, preferably use the delightful Terrace Route for ascent and save the variation for the return, when it will be known whether enough time is left for the crossing of the rough territory containing Stony Tarn. If there is, turn off at Catcove across Dawsonground Crags, which sets the direction.

looking north

Slight Side 3

THE SUMMIT

Fellwalkers, having climbed their mountain, prefer to find that the summit is rocky, shapely and well-defined; and if, in addition, it can be attained only by a rough final scramble, so much the better. Slight Side has all these qualifications, and the further merit of an excellent view. A defect in its architecture is that the lofty ridge continuing to Scafell behind it is but little lower than the summit itself, so that when seen from this direction it has less significance. Still, this is a grand airy perch, the cairn being poised on the crest of a sweep of slabs of good clean rock, and many must be the walkers who have set out from Eskdale to climb Scafell and given up here.

Considered only as a summit, and not as a fell, Slight Side is the neatest and best of the Scafell group's many tops.

DESCENTS:

TO ESKDALE: The usual route of ascent should be reversed, and no other way from the top is worth considering. In mist find the sketchy track among the upper crags.

TO WASDALE: From the plateau north of the summit turn left (west) down a grassy slope, Broad Tongue, to Hardrigg Gill and the Burnmoor path.

RIDGE ROUTE

To SCAFELL, 3162': 1¼ miles : N
Depression at 2400'
750 feet of ascent
An easy climb with little of interest

There is no path worthy of the name until the scree of the final slopes is reached, beyond Long Green. Keep to the edge of the continuous escarpment on the right for good views to relieve the dull ascent.

THE VIEW

Slight Side's unique situation, at the point where the high mountains of the Scafell range sweep majestically down in foothills to green valleys and the silver sea, gives it a rare distinction as a viewpoint for the coastal area of Lakeland. The prospect seawards is in fact even better than it is from the parent Scafell although much inferior in other directions — but it must be stated in Slight Side's favour that the unlovely cooling towers of Calder Hall are concealed by Illgill Head. As a geography lesson in mountain structure, on the formation and flow of rivers and valleys and the winning of land by man from nature, the picture here simply presented is excellent. There is historical significance in the scene, too, for this is the land the Romans knew, and, before them, the primitive Britons of the Bronze Age.

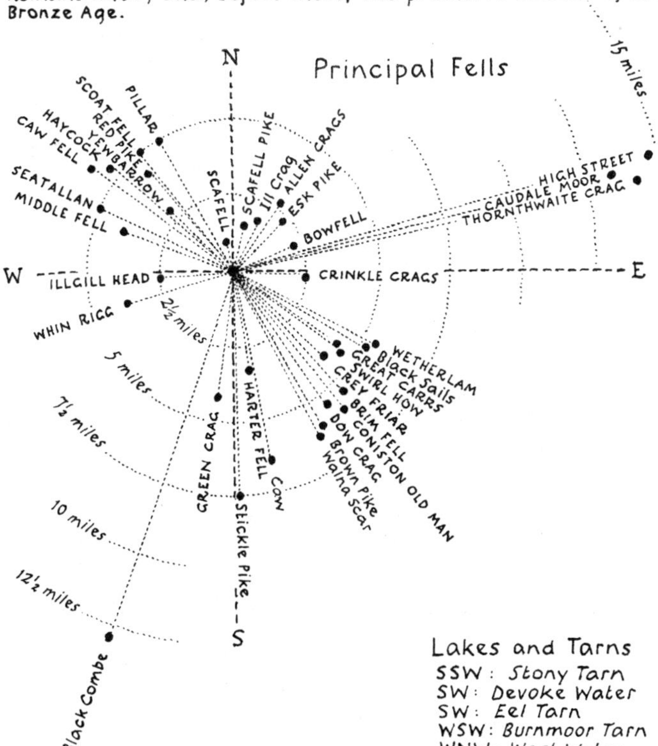
Principal Fells
N
S
E
W
2½ miles
5 miles
7½ miles
10 miles
12½ miles
15 miles
PILLAR
SCOAT FELL
RED PIKE
YEWBARROW
HAYCOCK
CAW FELL
SEATALLAN
MIDDLE FELL
SCAFELL
SCAFELL PIKE
Ill Crag
ALLEN CRAGS
ESK PIKE
BOWFELL
HIGH STREET
CAUDALE MOOR
THORNTHWAITE CRAG
CRINKLE CRAGS
ILLGILL HEAD
WHIN RIGG
WETHERLAM
Black Sails
GREAT CARRS
SWIRL HOW
GREY FRIAR
BRIM FELL
CONISTON OLD MAN
DOW CRAG
Brown Pike
Walna Scar
HARTER FELL
Caw
GREEN CRAG
Stickle Pike
Black Combe

Lakes and Tarns

SSW: *Stony Tarn*
SW: *Devoke Water*
SW: *Eel Tarn*
WSW: *Burnmoor Tarn*
WNW: *Wast Water*

Swirl How 2630'

*from Rough Crags
(Great Carrs on the right)*

- Dungeon Ghyll
- ▲ PIKE O'BLISCO
- Cockley Beck
- GREAT CARRS
- Little Langdale
- ▲ WETHERLAM
- GREY FRIAR ▲
- ▲ SWIRL HOW
- ▲ BRIM FELL
- CONISTON OLD MAN ▲
- Coniston
- Seathwaite

MILES
0 1 2 3 4

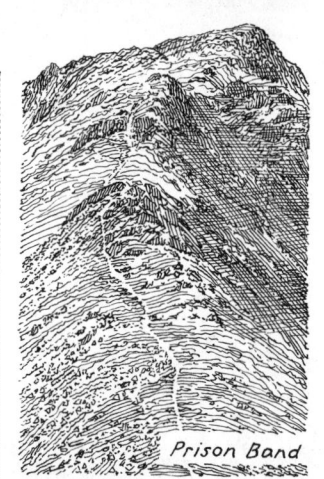

Prison Band

Swirl How 2

NATURAL FEATURES

Swirl How, although not quite the highest of the Coniston Fells, is the geographical centre of the group, radiating splendid ridges from a peaked summit to the four points of the compass. It is never seen really conspicuously in distant views, being crowded by surrounding fells; nevertheless its appearance is good, especially in profile, for the long southern plateau breaks sharply at the actual summit into a steep and craggy declivity. The area of Swirl How is not extensive, the ridges quickly merging into other fells on all four sides, but worthy of mention is the subsidiary height of Great How Crags on the southern plateau, a pillar of rock rising from the deep hollow of Levers Water and seeming from some viewpoints to be a separate summit.

The geographical supremacy of Swirl How is well illustrated by the direction of flow of its streams, which join the Duddon and the Brathay and Coniston Water (a distinction not shared by any other fell in the group) whereas those of the Old Man, which is slightly higher and popularly but wrongly regarded as the principal fell in the area, feed Coniston Water only. If only Swirl How asserted itself a little more and overtopped its satellites by a few hundred feet it would rank with the noblest fells in Lakeland, its "build-up" being topographically excellent.

Q.E.D. In fact the Old Man and Grey Friar are the only fells with a single drainage system

1: SWIRL HOW 2: GREY FRIAR
3: GREAT CARRS 4: Little Carrs
5: Black Sails 6: WETHERLAM
7: Great How Crags
8: BRIM FELL 9: DOW CRAG
10: CONISTON OLD MAN

The main ridges, and direction of flow of waters

Swirl How 3

MAP

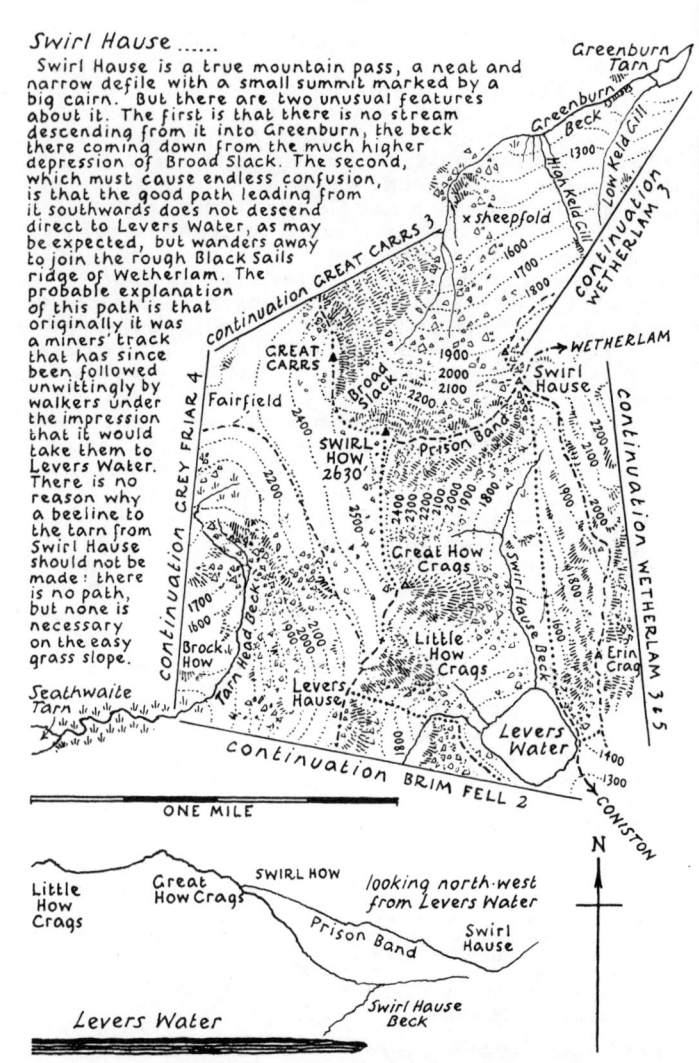

Swirl Hause......

Swirl Hause is a true mountain pass, a neat and narrow defile with a small summit marked by a big cairn. But there are two unusual features about it. The first is that there is no stream descending from it into Greenburn, the beck there coming down from the much higher depression of Broad Slack. The second, which must cause endless confusion, is that the good path leading from it southwards does not descend direct to Levers Water, as may be expected, but wanders away to join the rough Black Sails ridge of Wetherlam. The probable explanation of this path is that originally it was a miners' track that has since been followed unwittingly by walkers under the impression that it would take them to Levers Water. There is no reason why a beeline to the tarn from Swirl Hause should not be made: there is no path, but none is necessary on the easy grass slope.

ONE MILE

looking north-west from Levers Water

Swirl How 4

ASCENT FROM CONISTON
2450 feet of ascent : 3½ miles

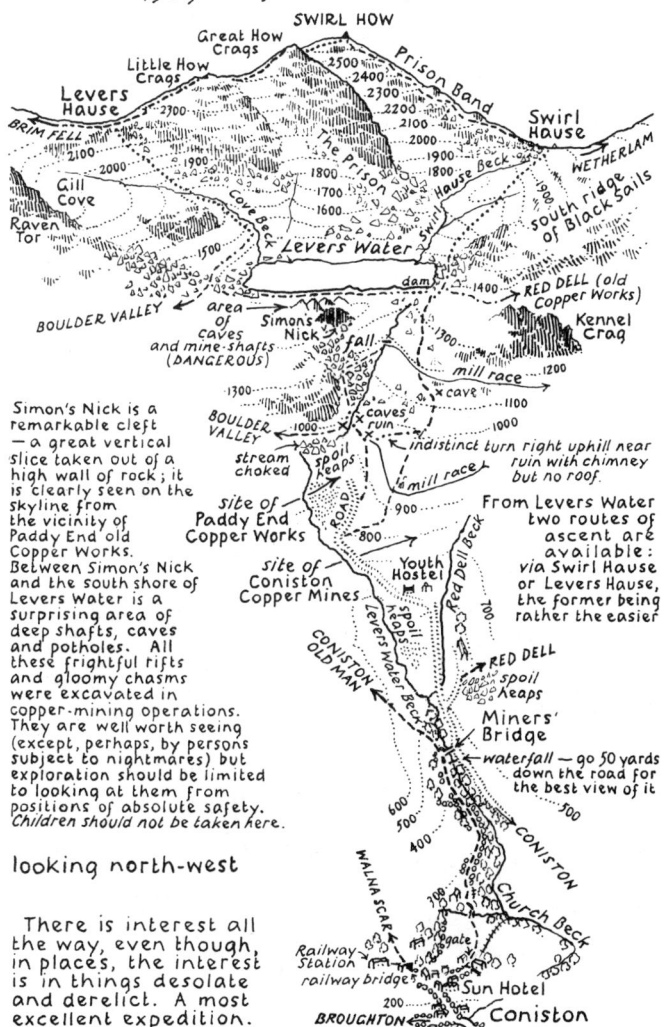

Simon's Nick is a remarkable cleft — a great vertical slice taken out of a high wall of rock; it is clearly seen on the skyline from the vicinity of Paddy End old Copper Works. Between Simon's Nick and the south shore of Levers Water is a surprising area of deep shafts, caves and potholes. All these frightful rifts and gloomy chasms were excavated in copper-mining operations. They are well worth seeing (except, perhaps, by persons subject to nightmares) but exploration should be limited to looking at them from positions of absolute safety. Children should not be taken here.

From Levers Water two routes of ascent are available: via Swirl Hause or Levers Hause, the former being rather the easier.

looking north-west

There is interest all the way, even though, in places, the interest is in things desolate and derelict. A most excellent expedition.

Swirl How 5

ASCENT FROM LITTLE LANGDALE
2400 feet of ascent : 4 miles

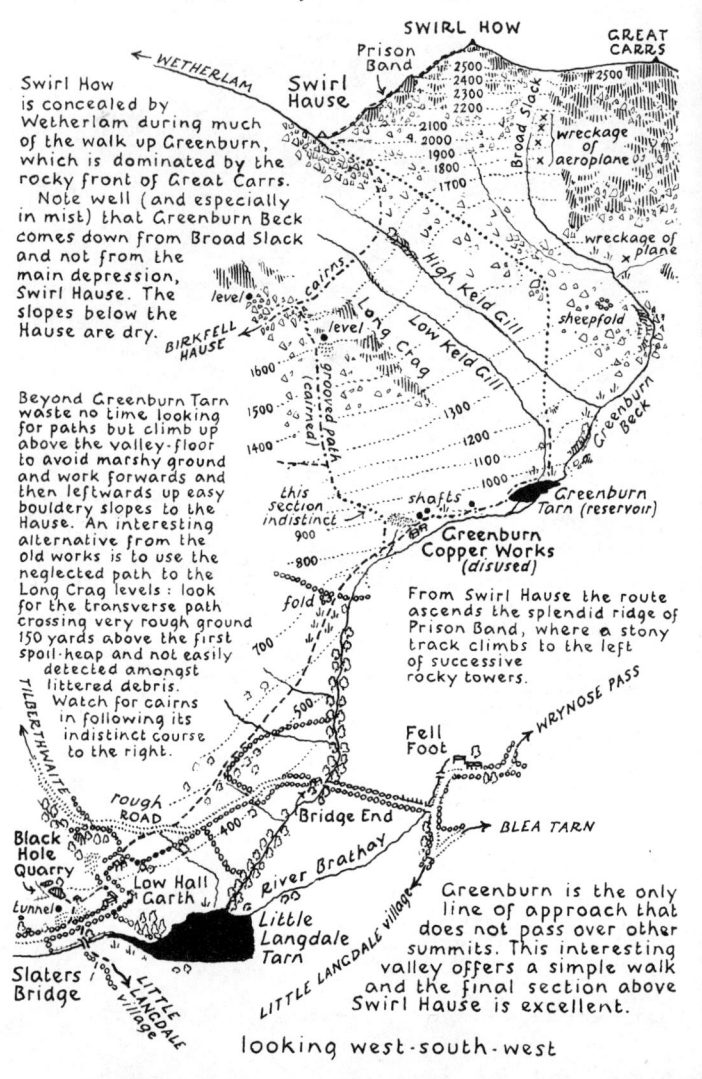

Swirl How is concealed by Wetherlam during much of the walk up Greenburn, which is dominated by the rocky front of Great Carrs.

Note well (and especially in mist) that Greenburn Beck comes down from Broad Slack and not from the main depression, Swirl Hause. The slopes below the Hause are dry.

Beyond Greenburn Tarn waste no time looking for paths but climb up above the valley-floor to avoid marshy ground and work forwards and then leftwards up easy bouldery slopes to the Hause. An interesting alternative from the old works is to use the neglected path to the Long Crag levels: look for the transverse path crossing very rough ground 150 yards above the first spoil-heap and not easily detected amongst littered debris. Watch for cairns in following its indistinct course to the right.

From Swirl Hause the route ascends the splendid ridge of Prison Band, where a stony track climbs to the left of successive rocky towers.

Greenburn is the only line of approach that does not pass over other summits. This interesting valley offers a simple walk and the final section above Swirl Hause is excellent.

looking west-south-west

Swirl How 6

THE SUMMIT

The cairn is splendidly sited at the extreme end of the long and level summit-plateau, just at the point where the northern slope falls away abruptly; perhaps it is not quite on the highest ground, which appears to be a few yards west. The turf on the top is interspersed with many small outcrops of grey rock.

DESCENTS: TO CONISTON: Swirl Hause is a better way off the fell than Levers Hause, but, especially in mist, go straight down to Levers Water from the Hause, ignoring the good path bearing away to the left. TO LITTLE LANGDALE: The finest route of descent lies over Great Carrs and Wet Side Edge, but if Greenburn is preferred descend thereto by the easy slope from Swirl Hause, not via Broad Slack. No trouble need be expected on either route in mist.

RIDGE ROUTES

To BRIM FELL, 2611': 1½ miles: S, SW and S
Depression (Levers Hause) at 2240'
380 feet of ascent

Aim south across the plateau, joining a path at Great How Crags that goes down to Levers Hause; beyond, it fades on the easy slopes of Brim Fell. In mist, keep to the right of the escarpment.

To WETHERLAM, 2502': 1¼ miles
ENE, NE, ENE and E
Depression (Swirl Hause) at 2020'
500 feet of ascent

Go down Prison Band by the track, cross the Hause, and bear left up the opposite slope. A sketchy path on the Greenburn edge loses itself short of Red Dell Head but sets the direction for the top. The first summit on the right is Black Sails, not to be mistaken for Wetherlam.

To GREAT CARRS, 2575': ⅓ mile: W, NW and N
Depression at 2500' 75 feet of ascent
A simple seven-minute stroll

To GREY FRIAR, 2536'
1 mile: WNW, W and SW.
Depression at 2275'
270 feet of ascent
Steeper climbing follows an easy descent. Not recommended in mist.

Swirl How 7

THE VIEW

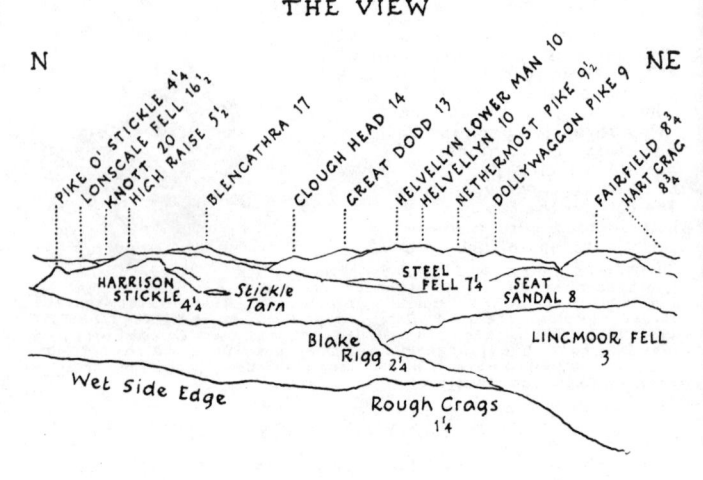

N — NE

- PIKE O' STICKLE 4¼
- LONSCALE FELL 16½
- KNOTT 20
- HIGH RAISE 5½
- BLENCATHRA 17
- CLOUGH HEAD 14
- GREAT DODD 13
- HELVELLYN LOWER MAN 10
- HELVELLYN 10
- NETHERMOST PIKE 9½
- DOLLYWAGGON PIKE 9
- FAIRFIELD 8¾
- HART CRAG 8¾

HARRISON STICKLE 4¼ — Stickle Tarn

STEEL FELL 7¼   SEAT SANDAL 8

Blake Rigg 2¼

LINGMOOR FELL 3

Wet Side Edge   Rough Crags 1¼

Greenburn Valley   Greenburn Tarn

E — SE

The Pennines in the background

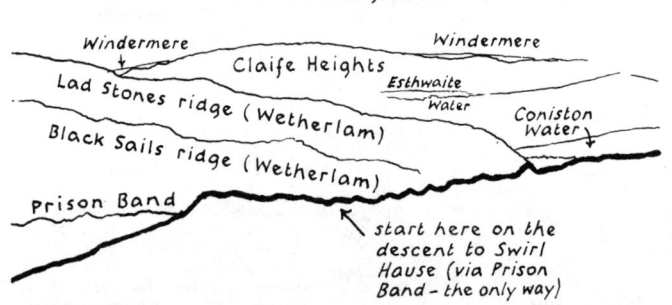

Windermere   Windermere
Claife Heights   Esthwaite Water
Lad Stones ridge (Wetherlam)
Black Sails ridge (Wetherlam)   Coniston Water
Prison Band

← start here on the descent to Swirl Hause (via Prison Band - the only way)

Swirl How 8

THE VIEW

NE — **E**

- DOVE CRAG 8¾
- REST DODD 13
- HIGH RAISE 13½
- KIDSTY PIKE 13
- RED SCREES 9¼
- HIGH STREET 12¼
- FROSWICK 11¼
- HARTER FELL 12¼
- ILL BELL 11
- KENTMERE PIKE 12¾
- GREY CRAG 14½

The Pennines in the background

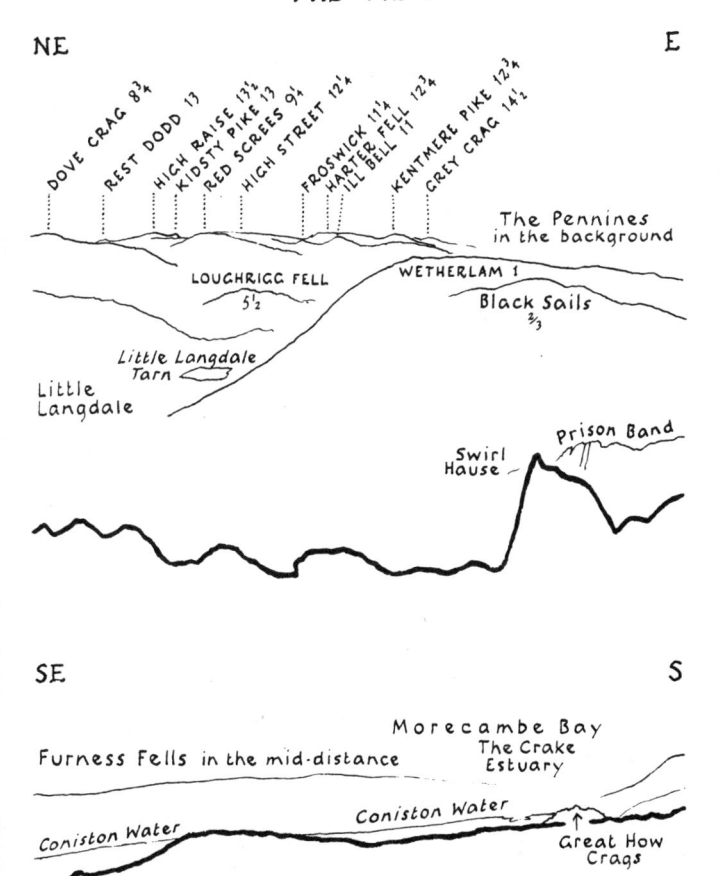

LOUGHRIGG FELL 5½

WETHERLAM 1

Black Sails ⅔

Little Langdale Tarn

Little Langdale

Swirl Hause

Prison Band

SE — **S**

Furness Fells in the mid-distance

Morecambe Bay
The Crake Estuary

Coniston Water

Coniston Water

Great How Crags

The figures accompanying the names of fells indicate distances in miles

The thick line marks the visible boundaries of the summit from the cairn

Swirl How 9

THE VIEW

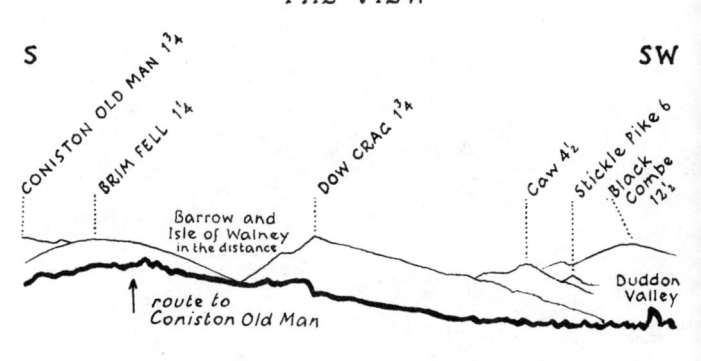

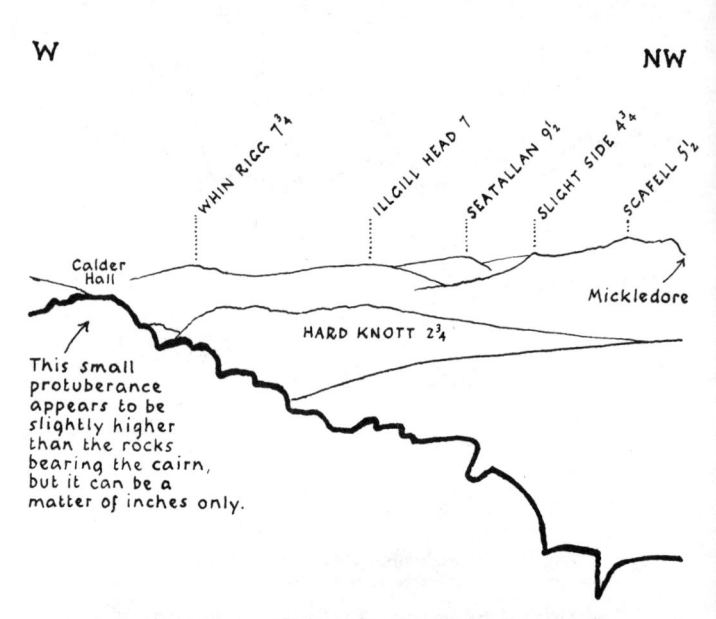

S — **SW**

- CONISTON OLD MAN 1¾
- BRIM FELL 1¼
- DOW CRAG 1¾
- CAW 4½
- Stickle Pike 6
- Black Combe 12½

Barrow and Isle of Walney in the distance

route to Coniston Old Man

Duddon Valley

W — **NW**

- WHIN RIGG 7¾
- ILLGILL HEAD 7
- SEATALLAN 9½
- SLIGHT SIDE 4¾
- SCAFELL 5½

Calder Hall

HARD KNOTT 2¾

Mickledore

This small protuberance appears to be slightly higher than the rocks bearing the cairn, but it can be a matter of inches only.

These rocks are above the steep and rough Greenburn face. Descents here should be eschewed *(Eschewed means don't do it!)*

Swirl How 10

THE VIEW

SW / W

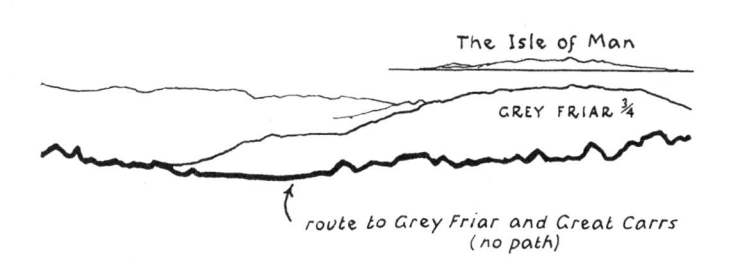

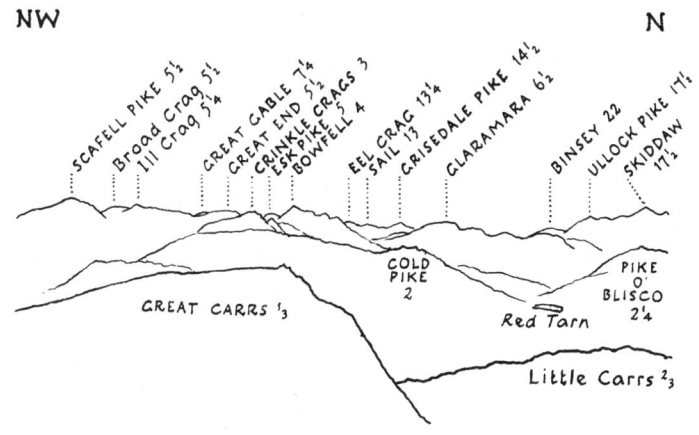

The Isle of Man

GREY FRIAR ¾

← route to Grey Friar and Great Carrs (no path)

NW / N

SCAFELL PIKE 5½
Broad Crag 5½
Ill Crag 5¼
GREAT GABLE 7¼
GREAT END 5½
CRINKLE CRAGS 3
ESK PIKE 5
BOWFELL 4
EEL CRAG 13¼
SAIL 13
CRISEDALE PIKE 14½
GLARAMARA 6½
BINSEY 22
ULLOCK PIKE 17½
SKIDDAW 17½

COLD PIKE 2
PIKE O' BLISCO 2¼
Red Tarn
GREAT CARRS 1⅓
Little Carrs 2⅓

Some walkers seem to experience a fierce joy in the sight of the Isle of Man in a view; others find greater pleasure in the sight of a first primrose in springtime. For the benefit of the former, the Isle of Man is shown in this diagram: it is visible from many Lakeland tops in good conditions, but from Swirl How its location can be determined particularly quickly for it appears exactly above the long flat top of Grey Friar nearby. The odds against seeing it on any given day are 50 to 1. At dusk or during night-bivouacs on the tops its position can be fixed in clear weather by the regular beams of its shore lighthouses. But oh! the delights of that first primrose..........

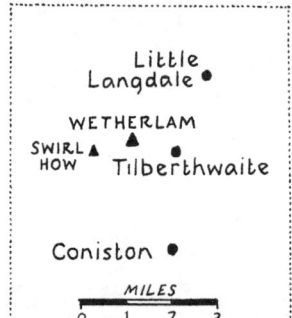

Wetherlam

2502'

from Little Langdale

from Great Carrs

Wetherlam 2

NATURAL FEATURES

Wetherlam features prominently in Brathay views like a giant whale surfacing above waves of lesser hills: the long rising line of the back springs from the fields of Coniston to a maximum height at the tip of the head, from which the blunt nose curves steeply down into Little Langdale. The outline is simple, but deceptive, for the rising ridge coming up from the south is one only (and not the best) of three parallel ridges that give this fell a strong individuality. Quite apart from an unusual shape of structure, however, and in addition to its merit both as a climb and as a viewpoint, Wetherlam has one great claim deserving of close attention.

Ingleborough, which is in view thirty miles away, is often and with much justification considered to be the most interesting mountain in England because of its potentialities to the explorer on, in and under the ground. But Wetherlam, too, is pierced and pitted with holes — caves, tunnels, shafts and excavations — in not less profusion, although, unlike Ingleborough's, all are man-made. These are the levels and shafts and workings of a dead industry — copper-mining — and of a living industry — quarrying — that between them, over the centuries, have made Wetherlam the most-industrialised of Lakeland mountains. This fine hill, however, is too vast and sturdy to be disfigured and weakened by man's feeble scratchings of its surface, and remains today, as of old, a compelling presence to which walkers in Brathay will oft turn their eager steps.

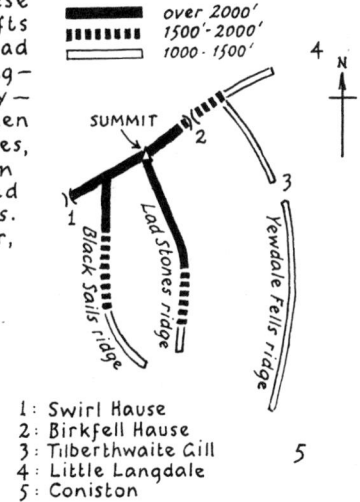

▬▬▬ over 2000'
▦▦▦ 1500'-2000'
☐☐☐ 1000-1500'

1: Swirl Hause
2: Birkfell Hause
3: Tilberthwaite Gill
4: Little Langdale
5: Coniston

The Plan of the Main Ridges

Wetherlam 3

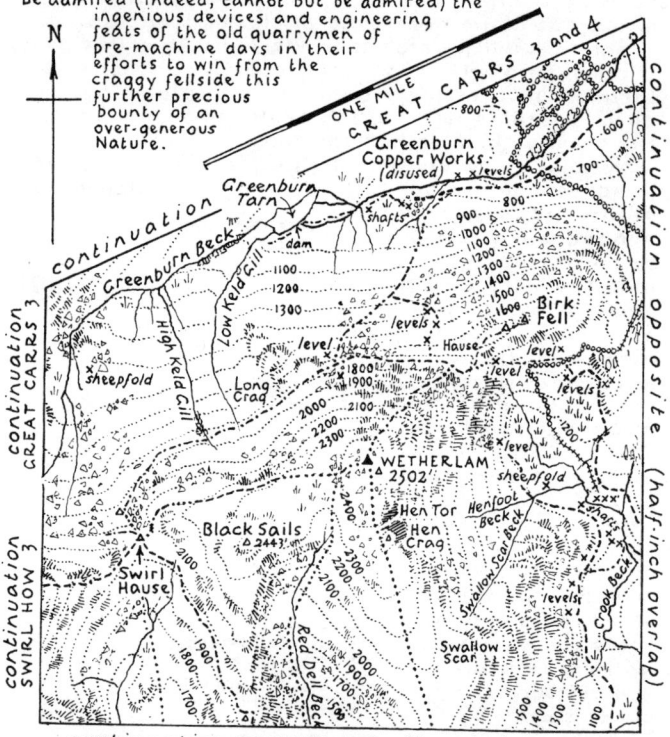

MAP

On this and the next three pages, levels and shafts of old mine and quarry workings are indicated only in locations where they may be noticed on usual walking routes, in order to relieve the maps of overmuch detail. A simplified diagram on page 7 gives the positions of the various workings.

The square mile of territory between Tilberthwaite Gill and the Brathay (see map on opposite page) is scenically one of the loveliest in Lakeland (in spite of the quarries) and surely one of the most interesting (because of the quarries). The valley-road is a favourite of visitors, but they generally have little knowledge of the many fascinating places concealed by the screen of trees. Here, in the quarries, it can be seen that Lakeland's beauty is not merely skin deep, that it goes down below the surface in veins of rich and colourful stone. Here, too, can be admired (indeed, cannot but be admired) the ingenious devices and engineering feats of the old quarrymen of pre-machine days in their efforts to win from the craggy fellside this further precious bounty of an over-generous Nature.

Wetherlam 4

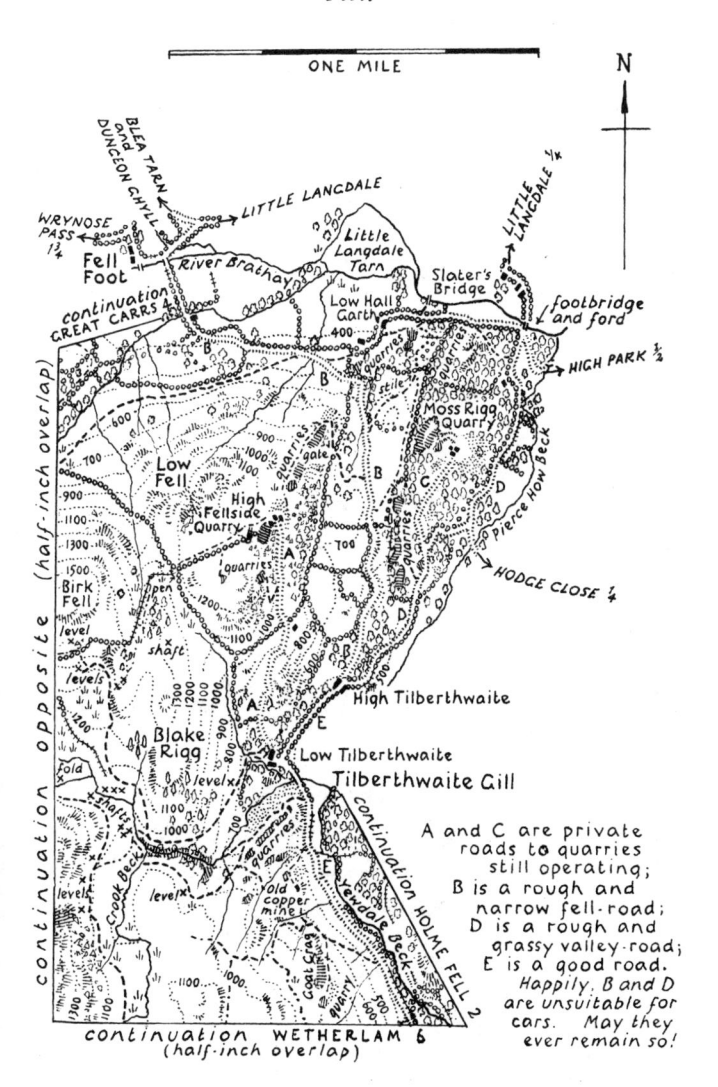

MAP

Wetherlam 5

MAP

ONE MILE

continuation WETHERLAM 3 (half-inch overlap)

A: Paddy End Copper Works
B: Coniston Copper Mines
C: Red Dell Copper Works
(all disused and derelict)

Kennel Crag (O.S. spelling) is Kernel Crag locally. (The Survey may be in error here for their same map (6") names Kernel Level just below the Crag)

Wetherlam from the lower slopes of Coniston Old Man

Wetherlam 6

MAP

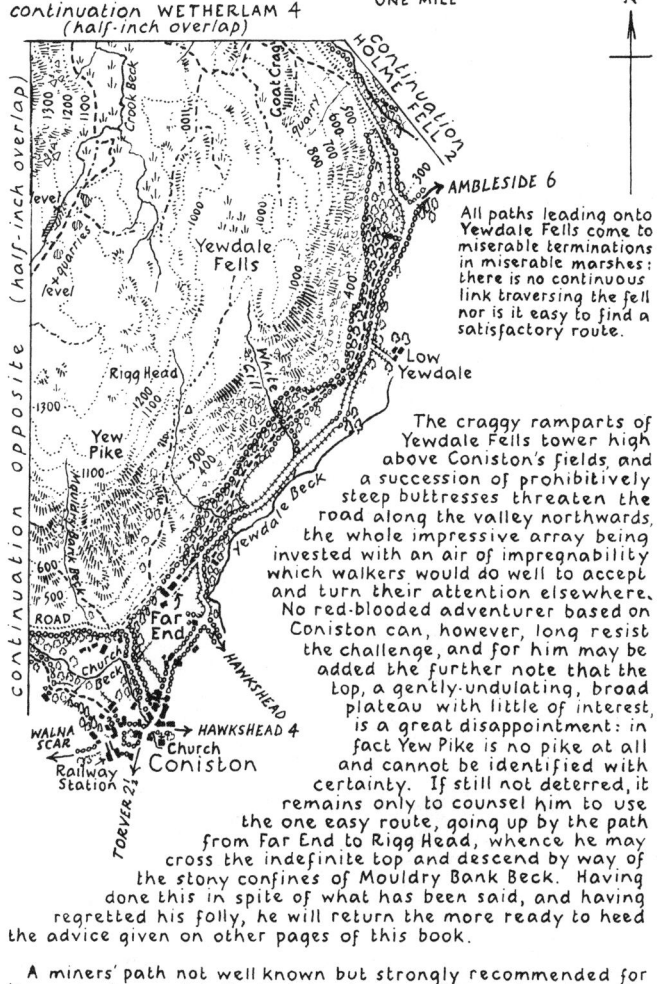

All paths leading onto Yewdale Fells come to miserable terminations in miserable marshes: there is no continuous link traversing the fell nor is it easy to find a satisfactory route.

The craggy ramparts of Yewdale Fells tower high above Coniston's fields, and a succession of prohibitively steep buttresses threaten the road along the valley northwards, the whole impressive array being invested with an air of impregnability which walkers would do well to accept and turn their attention elsewhere. No red-blooded adventurer based on Coniston can, however, long resist the challenge, and for him who may be added the further note that the top, a gently-undulating, broad plateau with little of interest, is a great disappointment: in fact Yew Pike is no pike at all and cannot be identified with certainty. If still not deterred, it remains only to counsel him to use the one easy route, going up by the path from Far End to Rigg Head, whence he may cross the indefinite top and descend by way of the stony confines of Mouldry Bank Beck. Having done this in spite of what has been said, and having regretted his folly, he will return the more ready to heed the advice given on other pages of this book.

A miners' path not well known but strongly recommended for its unusual appeal is that rising by the old quarries above the cottages in Coppermines Valley and continuing to the head of Tilberthwaite Gill; a good alternative to the usual walk by road.

Wetherlam 7

Wetherlam's Hundred Holes —

The sole object of this map is to indicate the locations of the various caves, shafts and quarries, and detail has been omitted other than that helpful in the fascinating pastime of finding them.

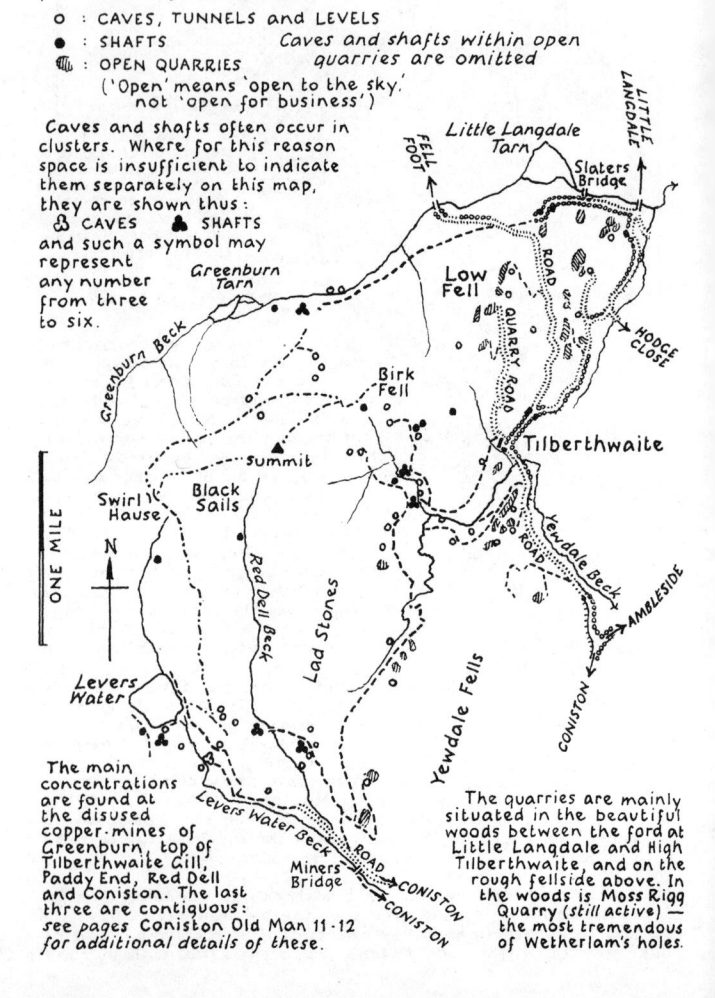

- ○ : CAVES, TUNNELS and LEVELS
- ● : SHAFTS
- 🕮 : OPEN QUARRIES

Caves and shafts within open quarries are omitted

('Open' means 'open to the sky,' not 'open for business')

Caves and shafts often occur in clusters. Where for this reason space is insufficient to indicate them separately on this map, they are shown thus:

₿ CAVES   ♣ SHAFTS

and such a symbol may represent any number from three to six.

The main concentrations are found at the disused copper-mines of Greenburn, top of Tilberthwaite Gill, Paddy End, Red Dell and Coniston. The last three are contiguous: see pages Coniston Old Man 11·12 for additional details of these.

The quarries are mainly situated in the beautiful woods between the ford at Little Langdale and High Tilberthwaite, and on the rough fellside above. In the woods is Moss Rigg Quarry (still active) — the most tremendous of Wetherlam's holes.

Wetherlam 8

Typical copper-mine shafts

A quarry cave

A copper level

Be content to find the openings, and do not be tempted to enter them. Roof-falls, flooded passages and rotted timber supports make them DANGEROUS. The unprotected, unfenced shafts are particularly so. Keep children away, and do not frighten sheep in the vicinity. It really is a matter for surprise that these fearful death-traps are not half-choked with the mingled remains of too-intrepid explorers, sheep, foxes, dogs, and women whose husbands have tired of them.

The Great Arch, Black Hole Quarry
This disused quarry near Slaters Bridge has features common to many hereabouts: the arch, the ravine entrance, the deep shaft from which a tunnel connects with the open fellside.

Wetherlam 9

ASCENT FROM LITTLE LANGDALE
2250 feet of ascent : 3 miles

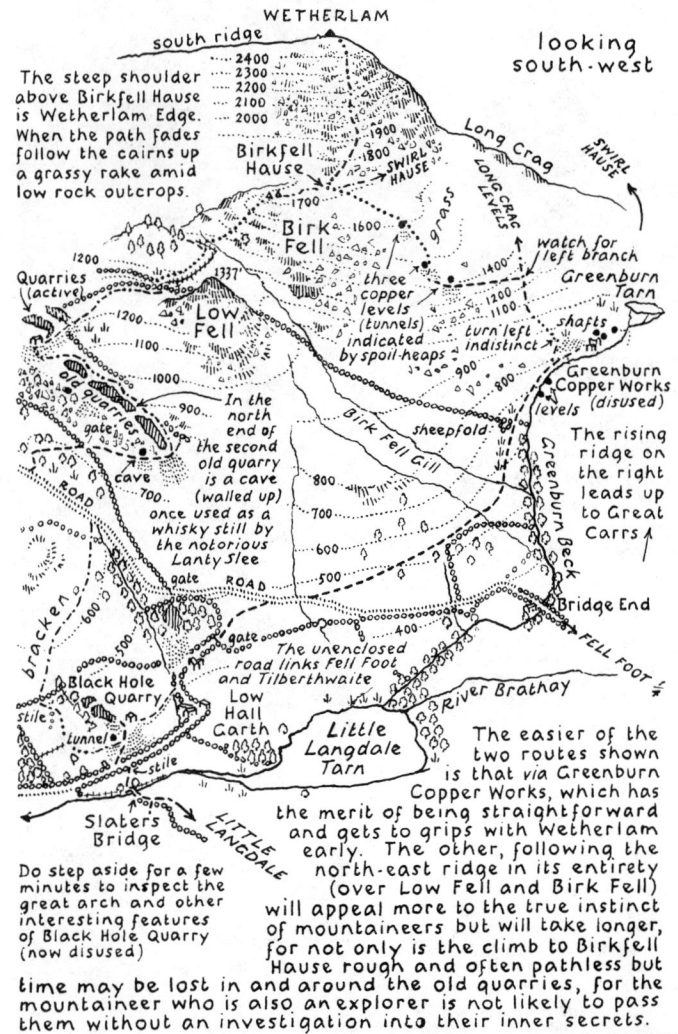

looking south-west

WETHERLAM

south ridge

The steep shoulder above Birkfell Hause is Wetherlam Edge. When the path fades follow the cairns up a grassy rake amid low rock outcrops.

Birkfell Hause

Long Crag

SWIRL HAUSE

Birk Fell

Quarries (active)

Low Fell 1337

three copper levels (tunnels) indicated by spoil-heaps

watch for left branch

Greenburn Tarn

turn left indistinct

shafts

Greenburn Copper Works levels (disused)

In the north end of the second old quarry is a cave (walled up) once used as a whisky still by the notorious Lanty Slee

old quarries

cave

gate

ROAD

sheepfold

Birk Fell Gill

The rising ridge on the right leads up to Great Carrs ↑

Greenburn Beck

gate

ROAD

bracken

Bridge End

FELL FOOT

Black Hole Quarry

stile

tunnel

gate

Low Hall Garth

The unenclosed road links Fell Foot and Tilberthwaite

River Brathay

Little Langdale Tarn

stile

SLATERS BRIDGE

LITTLE LANGDALE

Do step aside for a few minutes to inspect the great arch and other interesting features of Black Hole Quarry (now disused)

The easier of the two routes shown is that via Greenburn Copper Works, which has the merit of being straightforward and gets to grips with Wetherlam early. The other, following the north-east ridge in its entirety (over Low Fell and Birk Fell) will appeal more to the true instinct of mountaineers but will take longer, for not only is the climb to Birkfell Hause rough and often pathless but time may be lost in and around the old quarries, for the mountaineer who is also an explorer is not likely to pass them without an investigation into their inner secrets.

Wetherlam 10

ASCENT FROM TILBERTHWAITE
2100 feet of ascent : 2 miles

levels: horizontal underground passages with cave entrances. Many are flooded.

shafts: vertical rifts, usually with narrow slit openings. Deep. Frightful places!

This is the easiest way up Wetherlam. Gradients are easy to the Hause (very easy to Hawk Rigg). On the steeper Edge watch for cairns when the path fades.

Tilberthwaite Gill is usually ascended on the south bank but the well-engineered path on the north bank should be used on this occasion to its terminus at the old copper mines at Hawk Rigg.

Don't come this way down in the dark!

looking north-west

This splendid climb in attractive and contrasting scenery is given added interest by short detours of inspection to the many old copper workings, which, however, should be approached with caution, the shafts being unfenced and dangerous.

Wetherlam 11

ASCENT FROM CONISTON
2350 feet of ascent : 3½ miles

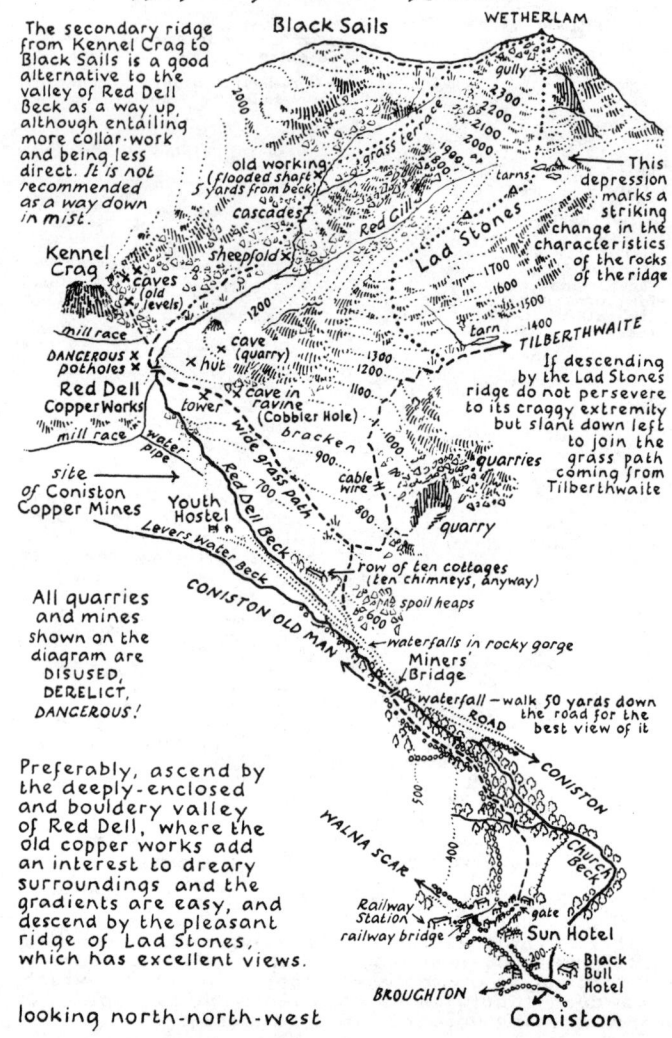

The secondary ridge from Kennel Crag to Black Sails is a good alternative to the valley of Red Dell Beck as a way up, although entailing more collar-work and being less direct. It is not recommended as a way down in mist.

This depression marks a striking change in the characteristics of the rocks of the ridge

If descending by the Lad Stones ridge do not persevere to its craggy extremity but slant down left to join the grass path coming from Tilberthwaite

All quarries and mines shown on the diagram are DISUSED, DERELICT, DANGEROUS!

Preferably, ascend by the deeply-enclosed and bouldery valley of Red Dell, where the old copper works add an interest to dreary surroundings and the gradients are easy, and descend by the pleasant ridge of Lad Stones, which has excellent views.

looking north-north-west

Wetherlam 12

THE SUMMIT

The summit is gently domed on three sides, with steepening curves to north and east, the fourth (south) being a level ridge. There is much rock about, weathered to an ashen-grey colour but, when broken, revealing the tinges of brown characteristic of the spoil-heaps of the copper mines on the lower slopes. The highest point is occupied by a large cairn. Although the summit is much trodden it bears little imprint of paths.

DESCENTS : Considering the popularity of the fell as a climb it is remarkable that there are not good paths linking summit and valley, but there are not, and in fact the selection of a way across the foothills, especially to Little Langdale, is not simple.

TO LITTLE LANGDALE : Go down Wetherlam Edge, keeping slightly to the left at first, on grass, and looking for the insufficient cairns. A stony track materialises and descends roughly to Birkfell Hause; a turn down the pathless slope to the left here (into Greenburn) is the simplest and quickest route to take. The direct ridge-route beyond the Hause goes on over Birk Fell and Low Fell, and is interesting (if there is ample time for trial and error), but is unsuitable in mist.

TO TILBERTHWAITE : From Birkfell Hause slant down to the right, immediately passing an old copper mine, from which a track goes on to the wall ahead, crosses it (not distinctly) and joins the wide grassy mines-path seen in front : this descends easily to the valley.

TO CONISTON : Go along the gradual south ridge for a full mile until easier ground on the left permits a descent to a path going down to the Coppermines Valley. The south ridge, if persisted in too far, will lead to difficulties above Red Dell Copper Works.

In mist, the absence of paths make the top confusing. If quite unable to take bearings, it is useful to know that the smaller cairn 20 yards away is *south-east* of the main cairn, and a tiny rocky pool (which dries in drought) a few paces distant is to the *west*. The start of the route down the convex slope to Birkfell Hause is not easy to locate : hunt around for cairns (they are insufficient at first but become profuse). The only difficulty of the south ridge is to decide when to leave it, on the left. The ridge running south from Black Sails is best left alone.

Wetherlam 13

THE VIEW

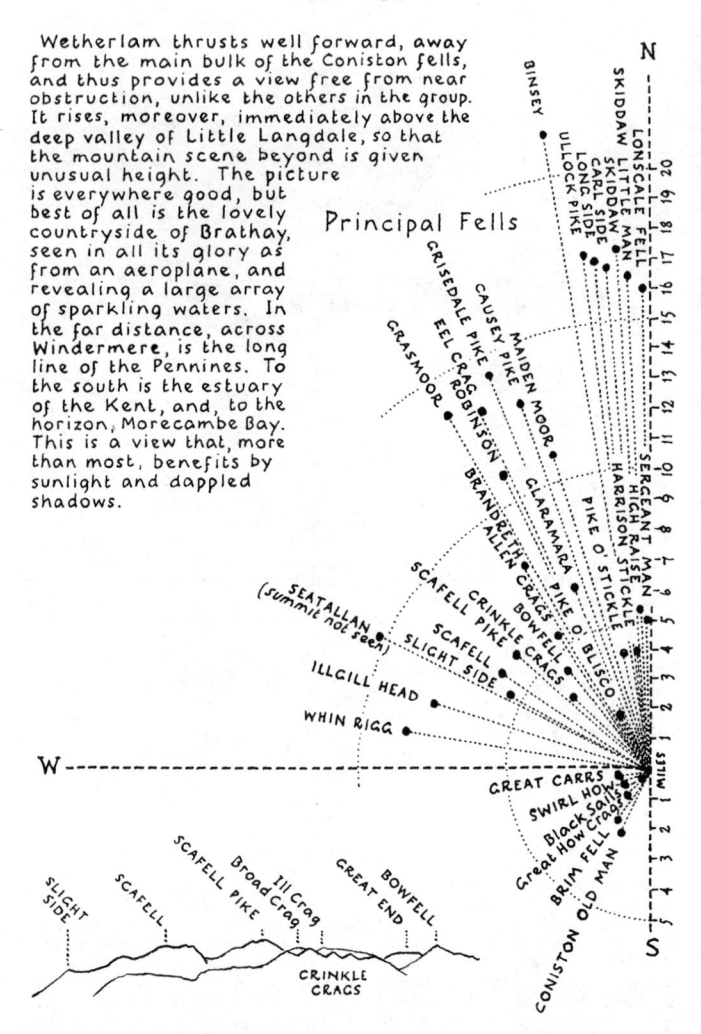

Wetherlam thrusts well forward, away from the main bulk of the Coniston fells, and thus provides a view free from near obstruction, unlike the others in the group. It rises, moreover, immediately above the deep valley of Little Langdale, so that the mountain scene beyond is given unusual height. The picture is everywhere good, but best of all is the lovely countryside of Brathay, seen in all its glory as from an aeroplane, and revealing a large array of sparkling waters. In the far distance, across Windermere, is the long line of the Pennines. To the south is the estuary of the Kent, and, to the horizon, Morecambe Bay. This is a view that, more than most, benefits by sunlight and dappled shadows.

Principal Fells

N

BINSEY
LONSCALE FELL
SKIDDAW LITTLE MAN
SKIDDAW
CARL SIDE
LONG SIDE
ULLOCK PIKE
SERGEANT MAN
HIGH RAISE
HARRISON STICKLE
PIKE O' STICKLE
CAUSEY PIKE
MAIDEN MOOR
EEL CRAG
GRISEDALE PIKE
ROBINSON
GRASMOOR
CLARAMARA
PIKE O' BLISCO
BRANDRETH
ALLEN CRAGS
SCAFELL PIKE
CRINKLE CRAGS
BOWFELL
SCAFELL
SLIGHT SIDE
SEATALLAN (summit not seen)
ILLGILL HEAD
WHIN RIGG

W - - - - - - - - - -

GREAT CARRS
SWIRL HOW
Black Sails
Great How Crags
BRIM FELL
CONISTON OLD MAN

S

SLIGHT SIDE | SCAFELL | SCAFELL PIKE | Broad Crag | Ill Crag | GREAT END | BOWFELL
CRINKLE CRAGS

looking north-west

Wetherlam 14

THE VIEW

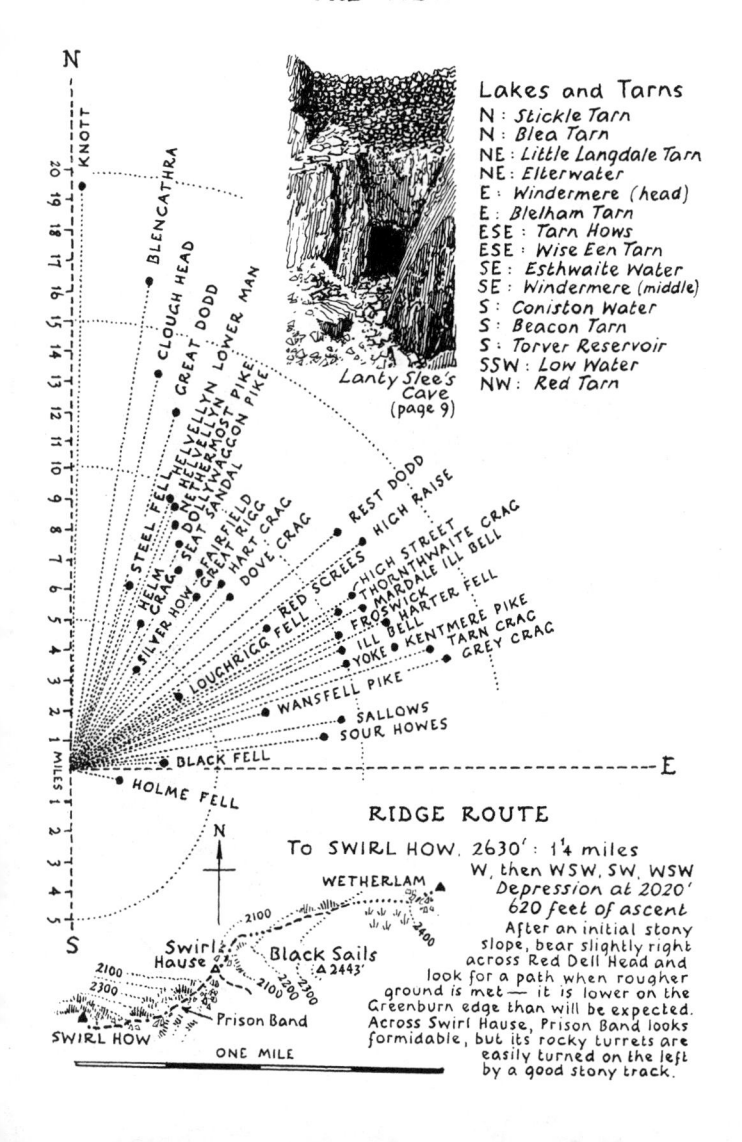

Lakes and Tarns
N: Stickle Tarn
N: Blea Tarn
NE: Little Langdale Tarn
NE: Elterwater
E: Windermere (head)
E: Blelham Tarn
ESE: Tarn Hows
ESE: Wise Een Tarn
SE: Esthwaite Water
SE: Windermere (middle)
S: Coniston Water
S: Beacon Tarn
S: Torver Reservoir
SSW: Low Water
NW: Red Tarn

Lanty Slee's Cave
(page 9)

Points on the panorama (clockwise from N):
KNOTT, BLENCATHRA, CLOUGH HEAD, GREAT DODD, HELVELLYN LOWER MAN, DOLLYWAGGON PIKE, ONE HELVELLYN, NETHERMOST PIKE, STEEL FELL, HELM CRAG, SILVER HOW, SEAT SANDAL, FAIRFIELD, GREAT RIGG, HART CRAG, DOVE CRAG, LOUGHRIGG FELL, RED SCREES, REST DODD, HIGH RAISE, HIGH STREET, THORNTHWAITE CRAG, FROSWICK, MARDALE ILL BELL, ILL BELL, HARTER FELL, YOKE, KENTMERE PIKE, TARN CRAG, GREY CRAG, WANSFELL PIKE, SALLOWS, SOUR HOWES, BLACK FELL, HOLME FELL

RIDGE ROUTE

To SWIRL HOW, 2630': 1¼ miles
W, then WSW, SW, WSW
Depression at 2020'
620 feet of ascent

After an initial stony slope, bear slightly right across Red Dell Head and look for a path when rougher ground is met — it is lower on the Greenburn edge than will be expected. Across Swirl Hause, Prison Band looks formidable, but its rocky turrets are easily turned on the left by a good stony track.

(Map: WETHERLAM, Black Sails 2443', Swirl Hause, SWIRL HOW, Prison Band; contours 2100, 2200, 2300; scale ONE MILE)

Whin Rigg 1755'

from Strands

Wasdale Head •

SCAFELL ▲

ILLGILL HEAD ▲
• Strands
▲ WHIN RIGG

• Santon Bridge
• Eskdale Green

MILES
0 1 2 3 4

*from the north-east
(on the approach from Illgill Head)*

Whin Rigg 2

NATURAL FEATURES

No mountain in Lakeland, not even Great Gable nor Blencathra nor the Langdale Pikes, can show a grander front than Whin Rigg, modest in elevation though the latter is, and so little known that most visitors to the district will not have heard the name.   Wastwater Screes, of course, is a place familiar to many; Whin Rigg is the southern terminus of the shattered ridge above Wast Water, beyond the screes, where the great grey cliffs have resisted erosion and rise in gigantic towers over the foot of the lake to culminate finally in a small shapely summit, a proud eyrie indeed. This savage scene is tempered and given a rare beauty by the blending of dark waters and rich woodlands that form the base of every view of the soaring buttresses — but there is no denying the steepness and severity of its precipices and chasms. This is one fellside that walkers can write off at a glance as having no access for them.

The opposite flank, to the east, is, in a contrast absolute, gently graded and everywhere grassy; it descends dully to the narrow branch-valley of Miterdale, a lovely and almost secret fold of the hills, unspoiled, serene.

The southern ridge of the fell declines to the long grassy shoulder of Irton Fell and the rocky Irton Pike, now largely under timber; beyond is a pleasant countryside watered by the Esk and the Irt, both of them fed by Whin Rigg, and then, to the far horizon, is the sea.

It is along this ridge that walkers may find a simple way to the summit and so look down on the lake from the cairn, and, by going a little further, between the vertical walls of the tremendous gullies. This is dramatic scenery, quite unique, and with an abiding impression of grandeur that makes the ascent of Whin Rigg a walk to be remembered and thought about often.

Whin Rigg 3

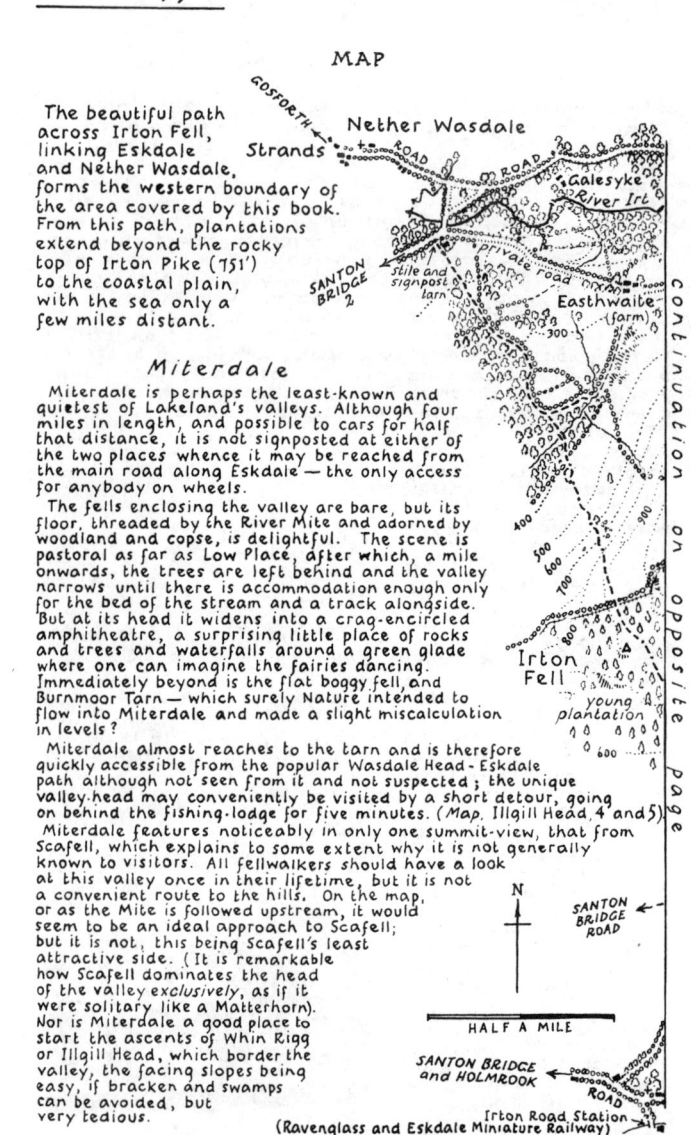

MAP

The beautiful path across Irton Fell, linking Eskdale and Nether Wasdale, forms the western boundary of the area covered by this book. From this path, plantations extend beyond the rocky top of Irton Pike (751') to the coastal plain, with the sea only a few miles distant.

continuation on opposite page

Miterdale

Miterdale is perhaps the least-known and quietest of Lakeland's valleys. Although four miles in length, and possible to cars for half that distance, it is not signposted at either of the two places whence it may be reached from the main road along Eskdale — the only access for anybody on wheels.

The fells enclosing the valley are bare, but its floor, threaded by the River Mite and adorned by woodland and copse, is delightful. The scene is pastoral as far as Low Place, after which, a mile onwards, the trees are left behind and the valley narrows until there is accommodation enough only for the bed of the stream and a track alongside. But at its head it widens into a crag-encircled amphitheatre, a surprising little place of rocks and trees and waterfalls around a green glade where one can imagine the fairies dancing. Immediately beyond is the flat boggy fell, and Burnmoor Tarn — which surely Nature intended to flow into Miterdale and made a slight miscalculation in levels?

Miterdale almost reaches to the tarn and is therefore quickly accessible from the popular Wasdale Head - Eskdale path although not seen from it and not suspected; the unique valley head may conveniently be visited by a short detour, going on behind the fishing-lodge for five minutes. (Map, Illgill Head, 4 and 5).

Miterdale features noticeably in only one summit-view, that from Scafell, which explains to some extent why it is not generally known to visitors. All fellwalkers should have a look at this valley once in their lifetime, but it is not a convenient route to the hills. On the map, or as the Mite is followed upstream, it would seem to be an ideal approach to Scafell; but it is not, this being Scafell's least attractive side. (It is remarkable how Scafell dominates the head of the valley exclusively, as if it were solitary like a Matterhorn). Nor is Miterdale a good place to start the ascents of Whin Rigg or Illgill Head, which border the valley, the facing slopes being easy, if bracken and swamps can be avoided, but very tedious.

HALF A MILE

SANTON BRIDGE and HOLMROOK

Irton Road Station
(Ravenglass and Eskdale Miniature Railway)

Whin Rigg 4

MAP

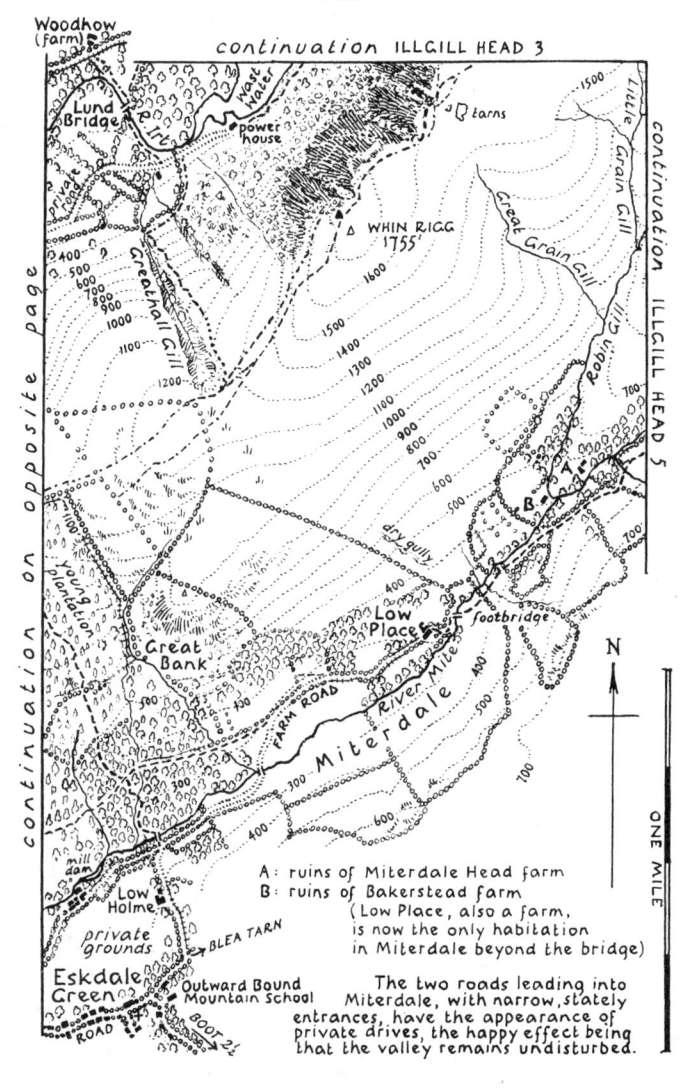

A: ruins of Miterdale Head farm
B: ruins of Bakerstead farm
(Low Place, also a farm, is now the only habitation in Miterdale beyond the bridge)

The two roads leading into Miterdale, with narrow, stately entrances, have the appearance of private drives, the happy effect being that the valley remains undisturbed.

Whin Rigg 5

ASCENT FROM NETHER WASDALE
1600 feet of ascent : 2 miles from Woodhow farm

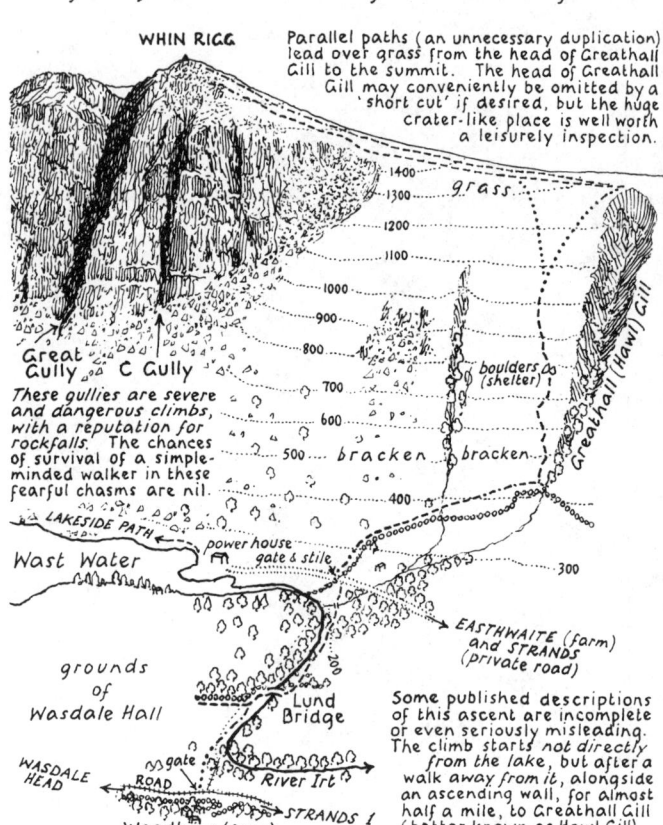

WHIN RIGG

Parallel paths (an unnecessary duplication) lead over grass from the head of Greathall Gill to the summit. The head of Greathall Gill may conveniently be omitted by a 'short cut' if desired, but the huge crater-like place is well worth a leisurely inspection.

Great Gully C Gully

These gullies are severe and dangerous climbs, with a reputation for rockfalls. The chances of survival of a simple-minded walker in these fearful chasms are nil.

boulders (shelter)

bracken   bracken

Greathall (Hawl) Gill

LAKESIDE PATH

Wast Water

power house gate & stile

EASTHWAITE (farm) and STRANDS (private road)

grounds of Wasdale Hall

Lund Bridge

WASDALE HEAD ← gate ROAD

River Irt

STRANDS ↓

Woodhow (farm)

There is no difficulty in identifying Woodhow: it is the only farm on the roadside between Wasdale Hall and Strands.

The new power-house at the foot of the lake, expelling hot air from its grills, is a useful drying-out place for wet walkers.

Some published descriptions of this ascent are incomplete or even seriously misleading. The climb starts *not directly from the lake*, but after a walk *away from it*, alongside an ascending wall, for almost half a mile, to Greathall Gill (better known as Hawl Gill). The Gill, a tremendous slice cut out of the fellside, is a favourite hunting-ground of geologists. A path zigzags upwards here but ceases at the upper limit of bracken.

looking east

The reward for this climb comes not from the doing of it but from the unique, beautiful and inspiring situation to which it leads: the top of the towering crags and gullies of the Screes, a scene without a counterpart elsewhere.

Whin Rigg 6

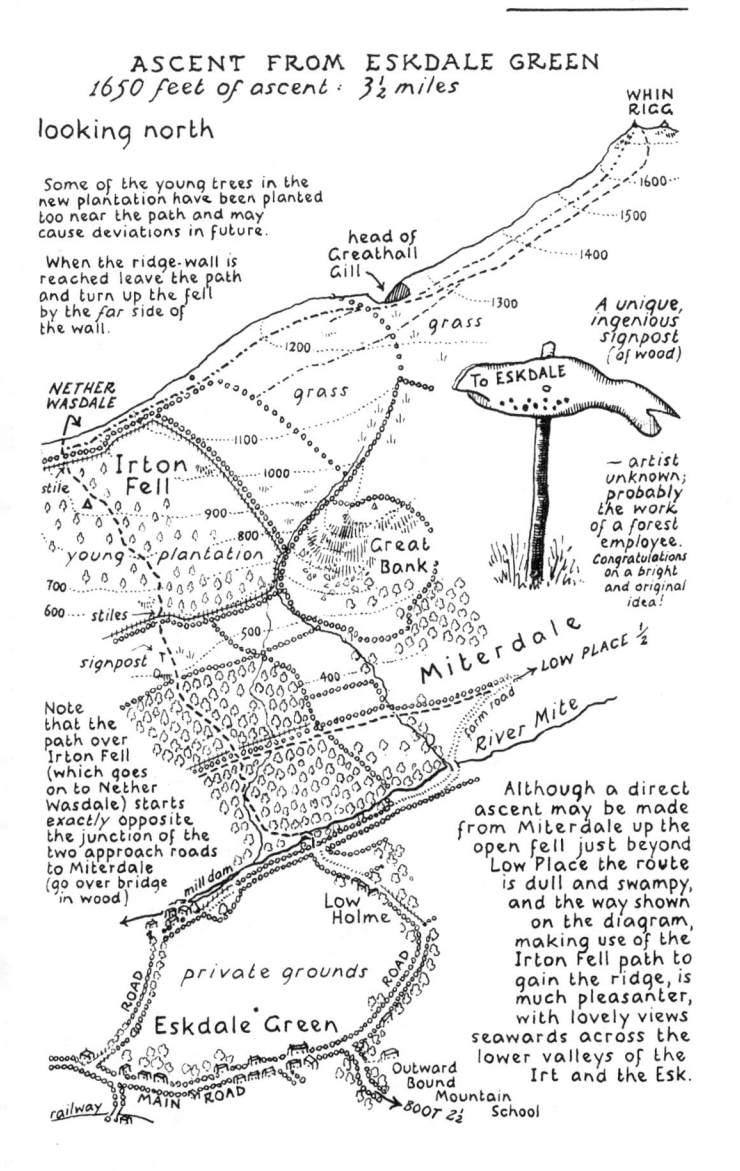

ASCENT FROM ESKDALE GREEN
1650 feet of ascent · 3½ miles

looking north

Some of the young trees in the new plantation have been planted too near the path and may cause deviations in future.

When the ridge-wall is reached leave the path and turn up the fell by the *far* side of the wall.

head of Greathall Gill

WHIN RIGG

grass

A unique, ingenious signpost (of wood)

To ESKDALE

— artist unknown; probably the work of a forest employee. Congratulations on a bright and original idea!

NETHER WASDALE

stile

Irton Fell

young plantation

Great Bank

stiles

signpost

Miterdale

LOW PLACE ½

form road

River Mite

Note that the path over Irton Fell (which goes on to Nether Wasdale) starts *exactly* opposite the junction of the two approach roads to Miterdale (go over bridge in wood)

Although a direct ascent may be made from Miterdale up the open fell just beyond Low Place the route is dull and swampy, and the way shown on the diagram, making use of the Irton Fell path to gain the ridge, is much pleasanter, with lovely views seawards across the lower valleys of the Irt and the Esk.

mill dam

Low Holme

private grounds

Eskdale Green

ROAD

ROAD

railway

MAIN ROAD

Outward Bound Mountain School

BOOT 2½

Whin Rigg 7

THE SUMMIT

The cairn is so delicately poised above the cliffs that a single stride from one side to the other is sufficient to bring Wast Water into view, and a dramatic moment this is, a highlight indeed. In other directions the summit is simple; there is a second cairn on the Eskdale edge. The ridge path, grassy, passes within a few feet of the main cairn.

ILLGILL HEAD

DESCENTS: Descend only by the routes of ascent, which are safe in mist. There is positively no way straight down to the lake. Don't be tempted into the wide opening of Great Gully: this fearful chasm has seventeen near-vertical pitches (as well as the remains of an aeroplane).

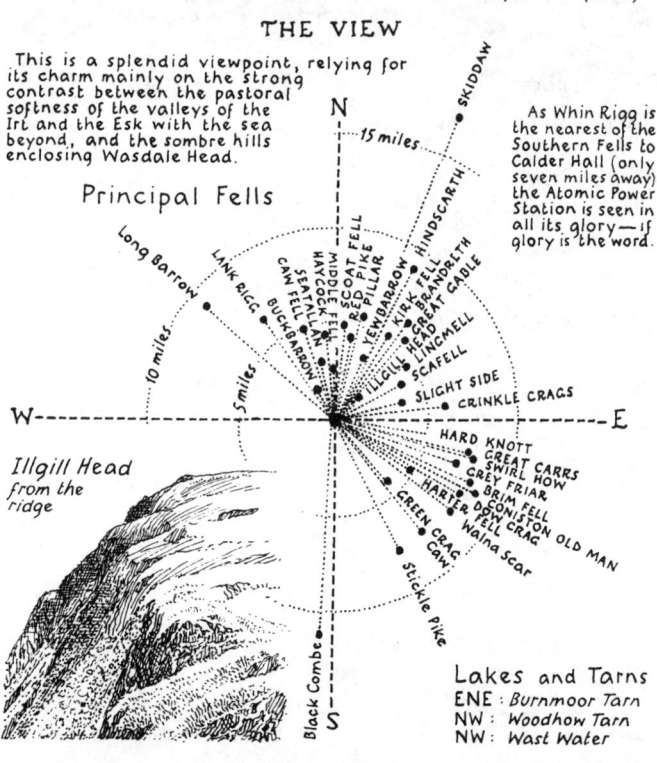

THE VIEW

This is a splendid viewpoint, relying for its charm mainly on the strong contrast between the pastoral softness of the valleys of the Irt and the Esk with the sea beyond, and the sombre hills enclosing Wasdale Head.

As Whin Rigg is the nearest of the Southern Fells to Calder Hall (only seven miles away) the Atomic Power Station is seen in all its glory — if glory is the word.

Principal Fells

- SKIDDAW
- HINDSCARTH
- SCOAT FELL
- RED PIKE
- MIDDLE FELL
- HAYCOCK
- PILLAR
- SEATALLAN
- CAW FELL
- LEWDBARROW
- KIRK FELL
- BUCKBARROW
- GREAT GABLE
- BRANDELTH
- ILLGILL HEAD
- LINGMELL
- SCAFELL
- SLIGHT SIDE
- CRINKLE CRAGS
- HARD KNOTT
- GREAT CARRS
- SWIRL HOW
- GREY FRIAR
- BRIM FELL
- CONISTON OLD MAN
- DOW CRAG
- HARTER FELL
- Walna Scar
- GREEN CRAG
- CAW
- Stickle Pike
- Black Combe
- Lank Rigg
- Long Barrow

Illgill Head from the ridge

Lakes and Tarns
ENE: *Burnmoor Tarn*
NW: *Woodhow Tarn*
NW: *Wast Water*

Whin Rigg 8

RIDGE ROUTE

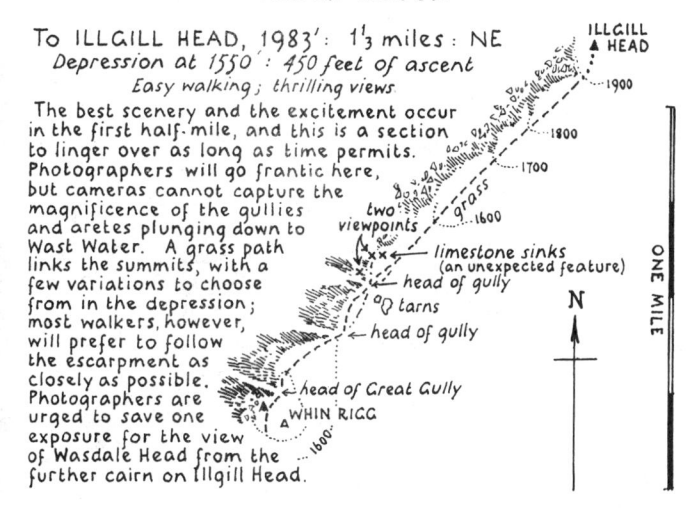

To ILLGILL HEAD, 1983': 1⅓ miles: NE
Depression at 1550': 450 feet of ascent
Easy walking; thrilling views.

The best scenery and the excitement occur in the first half-mile, and this is a section to linger over as long as time permits. Photographers will go frantic here, but cameras cannot capture the magnificence of the gullies and aretes plunging down to Wast Water. A grass path links the summits, with a few variations to choose from in the depression; most walkers, however, will prefer to follow the escarpment as closely as possible. Photographers are urged to save one exposure for the view of Wasdale Head from the further cairn on Illgill Head.

The two viewpoints
indicated on the diagram
(as seen from the north-east,
i.e. the Illgill Head side)

That on the left forms a small peak on the brink of the escarpment, and is a prominent object on the ridge-walk. The other is a narrow arete (Broken Rib) going down from the ridge. Both places are easily visited.

Whin Rigg 9

Wastwater Screes and Gullies

Here is the fines
example of the natur
ravages of weather, the whole fellside being in a state of decay. T
disintegration of the crags has produced many grotesque formations, fi

Whin Rigg 10

sections of rock remaining like fangs amidst the crumbled debris. (Note the dark tower isolated in scree, 2" from the left edge of the drawing).
 Climbing on these freak pinnacles and spires is unsafe.
 Whin Rigg is the summit on the extreme right.

THE SOUTHERN FELLS

Some Personal Notes in conclusion

I have said my farewells to Mickledore and Esk Hause and Bowfell and all the other grand places described in this book, with the same 'hollow' feeling one has when taking leave of friends knowing that it may be for the last time. For the next few years I shall be engaged elsewhere, to the north and west, and although I shall be straining my eyes to see these old favourites from afar, I shall not be visiting them during this period; and perhaps never again.

There has been a clamour for Book Four ever since the first in the series appeared, and there is no doubt at all that the region of the Southern Fells has priority in the minds of most lovers of the Lake District, and especially those whose joy it is to walk upon the mountains. I agree, without saying a word to detract from the merits of other areas. All Lakeland is exquisitely beautiful; the Southern Fells just happen to be a bit of heaven fallen upon the earth.

The past two years, spent preparing the book, have been a grand experience — in spite of countless ascents of Rossett Gill (which, incidentally, seems to get easier if you keep on doing it). Fortune smiled on me hugely during the months I had set aside for the Scafells — day after day of magnificent weather, with visibility so amazingly good that one simply got used to seeing the Scottish hills and the Isle of Man permanently on the horizon. I had feared delays on the Scafells by unsuitable conditions or even normal weather, but this never happened. Many glorious mountain days, followed by happy evenings in Wasdale and Eskdale — that was the pattern for the summer of 1959.

It has taken me over 300 pages to describe the fells in this area, and I need say no more about them; but I must emphasise the supreme beauty of the approaches along the valleys — every yard of the way to the tops, and every minute of every day, is utter joy. But a special word for Eskdale: this is walkers' territory par excellence, and as traffic in other valleys increases, it is likely to become the last stronghold

for travellers on foot. This lovely valley
is quiet and unfrequented. I rarely met
anybody when climbing out of Eskdale
but, on reaching the watershed, found
the ridges alive with folk who had come
up from Borrowdale and Langdale.

 Great Langdale is a growing problem.
This used to be a walkers' valley too, and
one of the best. Nowadays walkers are
beginning to feel out of place. Coaches,
cars, caravans, motor-bikes and tents
throng the valley. One cannot complain
about people who want to see the scenery
but some of the characters infesting the
place at weekends have eyes only for
mischief. These slovenly layabouts, of
both sexes, cause endless damage and
trouble, and it behoves all respectable
visitors (still in the majority) to help
the police and farmers to preserve order.
Poor Langdale! How green was my valley!

 I finished the Langdale tops in 1958
but had occasion to return in the spring
of 1959. Glancing up from the valley to
the cairn on Pike o' Blisco (as I always
do) I was dismayed to notice that it
had been mutilated. I went up to see
and found that the tall column of stones
had been beheaded, the top part having

been demolished, apparently by human agency. Are the wreckers getting up on the tops, too?..... If all readers who visit this summit will replace one stone firmly, please, the cairn may in time again look as it does in the Pike o' Blisco chapter.

I ought to mention that I am aware that the Duddon Valley is also properly known as Dunnerdale, a name I haven't used in the book, preferring the former; just as I never refer to Blencathra by its better-known modern name of Saddleback. It's a matter of personal choice. I like the Duddon Valley and Blencathra. I don't like Dunnerdale and Saddleback.

Several letters, and even petitions, from Great Gable enthusiasts have been sent in asking me to do Book Seven next after Book Four, and Book Five last. What a frightfully untidy suggestion! It springs from a generally accepted view, of course, that there is nothing "back o' Skidda" worth exploring. I want to go and find out. There is a big tract of lonely fells here, wild and desolate; but this is immortal ground, the John Peel country, and I rely further on a centuries-old saying that "Caldbeck Fells are worth all England else". A land rich with promise, surely!

On this occasion I intend to make an excuse for defects in penmanship. I am going to lay the blame fairly and squarely on the head of Cindy, a Sealyham puppy with roving eyes, introduced to the household some time ago. Cindy has shown absolutely no sympathy whatever with my efforts to write a classic — a fearful waste of time when I might otherwise be tickling her tummy or throwing her ball or having a tug-of-war with an old stocking. Her persistent pokings and tuggings at critical moments of concentration must have resulted in inferior work, for which I am sorry. But it's Cindy's fault, not mine.

AW

Christmas 1959.

SIGN REFERENCES
(signs used in the maps and diagrams)

Good footpath
(sufficiently distinct to be followed in mist)

Intermittent footpath
(difficult to follow in mist)

Route recommended but no path
(if recommended one way only, arrow indicates direction)

Wall   **Broken wall**

Fence   **Broken fence**

Marshy ground   **Trees**

Crags   **Boulders**

Stream or River
(arrow indicates direction of flow)

Waterfall   **Bridge**

Buildings   **Unenclosed road**

Contours (at 100' intervals)   1900   1800   1700

Summit-cairn ▲   **Other** (prominent) **cairns** △

THE
NORTHERN
FELLS

A PICTORIAL GUIDE
TO THE
LAKELAND FELLS
50TH ANNIVERSARY EDITION

being an illustrated account
of a study and exploration
of the mountains in the
English Lake District

by

A Wainwright

BOOK FIVE
THE NORTHERN FELLS

Frances Lincoln Limited
4 Torriano Mews
Torriano Avenue
London NW5 2RZ
www.franceslincoln.com

Originally published by Henry Marshall, Kentmere, 1962

First published by Frances Lincoln 2003

50th Anniversary Edition with re-originated artwork
published by Frances Lincoln 2005

Copyright © The Estate of A. Wainwright 1962

All rights reserved. Without limiting the rights under
copyright reserved above, no part of this publication may
be reproduced, stored in or introduced into a retrieval
system, or transmitted, in any form or by any means
(electronic, mechanical, photocopying, or otherwise),
without either prior permission in writing from the
publisher or a licence permitting restricted copying.
In the United Kingdom such licences are issued by
the Copyright Licensing Agency, Saffron House,
6-10 Kirby Street, London EC1N 8TS.

Printed and bound in China

A CIP catalogue record for this book
is available from the British Library.

ISBN 978 0 7112 2458 2

18 17 16 15 14 13 12 11

50TH ANNIVERSARY EDITION
PUBLISHED BY
FRANCES LINCOLN, LONDON

THE PICTORIAL GUIDES

Book One: The Eastern Fells, 1955
Book Two: The Far Eastern Fells, 1957
Book Three: The Central Fells, 1958
Book Four: The Southern Fells, 1960
Book Five: The Northern Fells, 1962
Book Six: The North Western Fells, 1964
Book Seven: The Western Fells, 1966

PUBLISHER'S NOTE

This 50th Anniversary edition of the Pictorial Guides to the Lakeland Fells is newly reproduced from the handwritten pages created in the 1950s and 1960s by A. Wainwright. The descriptions of the walks were correct, to the best of the author's knowledge, at the time of first publication, and they are reproduced here without amendment. However, footpaths, cairns and other waymarks described here are no longer all as they were fifty years ago and walkers are advised to check with an up-to-date map when planning a walk.

Fellwalking has increased dramatically since the Pictorial Guides were first published. Some popular routes have become eroded, making good footwear and great care all the more necessary for walkers. The vital points about fellwalking, as A. Wainwright himself wrote on many occasions, are to use common sense and to remember to watch where you are putting your feet.

A programme of revision of the Pictorial Guides is under way and revised editions of each of them will be published over the next few years.

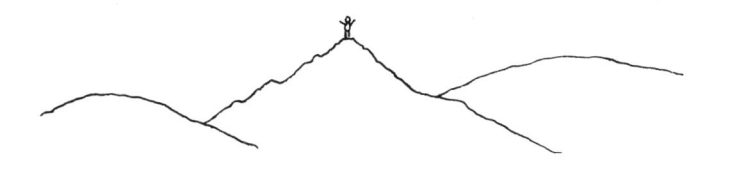

BOOK FIVE
is dedicated to
those who travel alone

THE SOLITARY WANDERERS
ON THE FELLS
who find contentment
in the companionship of the mountains
and of the creatures of the mountains

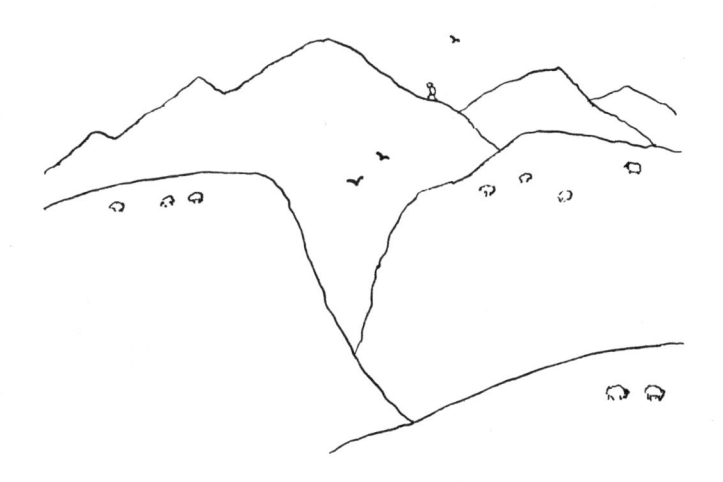

INTRODUCTION

Classification and Definition

Any division of the Lakeland fells into geographical districts must necessarily be arbitrary, just as the location of the outer boundaries of Lakeland must always be a matter of opinion. Any attempt to define internal or external boundaries is certain to invite criticism, and he who takes it upon himself to say where Lakeland starts and finishes, or, for example, where the Central Fells merge into the Southern Fells and *which* fells *are* the Central Fells and which the Southern and *why* they need be so classified, must not expect his pronouncements to be generally accepted.

Yet for present purposes some plan of classification and definition must be used. County and parochial boundaries are no help, nor is the recently-defined area of the Lakeland National Park, for this book is concerned only with the high ground.

First, the external boundaries. Straight lines linking the extremities of the outlying lakes enclose all the higher fells very conveniently. There are a few fells of lesser height to the north and east, however, that are typically Lakeland in character and cannot properly be omitted: these are brought in, somewhat untidily, by extending the lines in those areas. Thus:

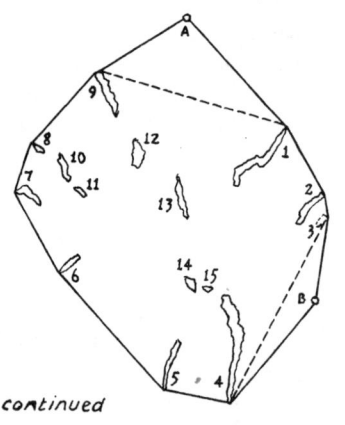

1 : *Ullswater*
2 : *Hawes Water*
3 : proposed *Swindale Resr*
4 : *Windermere*
5 : *Coniston Water*
6 : *Wast Water*
7 : *Ennerdale Water*
8 : *Loweswater*
9 : *Bassenthwaite Lake*
10 : *Crummock Water*
11 : *Buttermere*
12 : *Derwent Water*
13 : *Thirlmere*
14 : *Grasmere*
15 : *Rydal Water*
A : *Caldbeck*
B : *Longsleddale* (church)

continued

INTRODUCTION

Classification and Definition
continued

The complete Guide is planned to include all the fells in the area enclosed by the straight lines of the diagram. This is an undertaking quite beyond the compass of a single volume, and it is necessary, therefore, to divide the area into convenient sections, making the fullest use of natural boundaries (lakes, valleys and low passes) so that each district is, as far as possible, self-contained and independent of the rest.

This division gives seven areas, each with a well-defined group of fells, and each will be the subject of a separate volume

1 : The Eastern Fells
2 : The Far Eastern Fells
3 : The Central Fells
4 : The Southern Fells
5 : The Northern Fells
6 : The North-western Fells
7 : The Western Fells

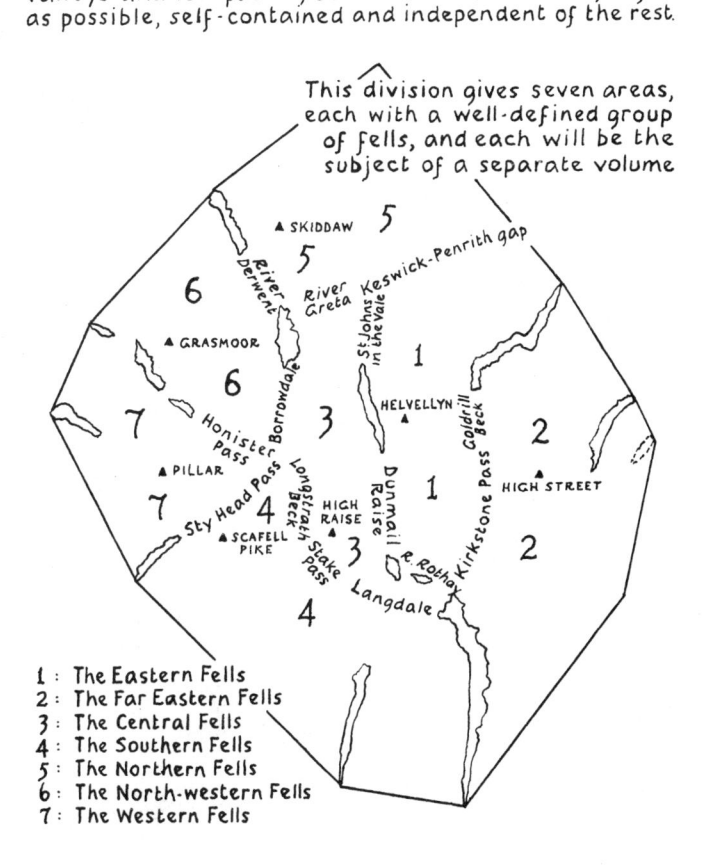

INTRODUCTION

Notes on the Illustrations

THE MAPS.................. Many excellent books have been written about Lakeland, but the best literature of all for the walker is that published by the Director General of Ordnance Survey, the 1" map for companionship and guidance on expeditions, the 2½" map for exploration both on the fells and by the fireside. These admirable maps are remarkably accurate topographically but there is a crying need for a revision of the paths on the hills: several walkers' tracks that have come into use during the past few decades, some of them now broad highways, are not shown at all; other paths still shown on the maps have fallen into neglect and can no longer be traced on the ground.

The popular Bartholomew 1" map is a beautiful picture, fit for a frame, but this too is unreliable for paths; indeed here the defect is much more serious, for routes are indicated where no paths ever existed, nor ever could — the cartographer has preferred to take precipices in his stride rather than deflect his graceful curves over easy ground.

Hence the justification for the maps in this book: they have the one merit (of importance to walkers) of being dependable as regards delineation of *paths*. They are intended as supplements to the Ordnance Survey maps, certainly not as substitutes.

THE VIEWS.............. Various devices have been used to illustrate the views from the summits of the fells. The full panorama in the form of an outline drawing is most satisfactory generally, and this method has been adopted for the main viewpoints.

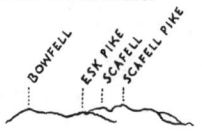

THE DIAGRAMS OF ASCENTS.................. The routes of ascent of the higher fells are depicted by diagrams that do not pretend to strict accuracy: they are neither plans nor elevations; in fact there is deliberate distortion in order to show detail clearly: usually they are represented as viewed from imaginary 'space-stations.' But it is hoped they will be useful and interesting.

THE DRAWINGS....... The drawings at least are honest attempts to reproduce what the eye sees: they illustrate features of interest and also serve the dual purpose of breaking up the text and balancing the layout of the pages, and of filling up awkward blank spaces, like this:

THE
NORTHERN
FELLS

Circular in plan, the area of the Northern Fells is completely severed from all other mountainous parts of the Lake District by Bassenthwaite Lake, the Vale of Keswick and the low country of the Glenderamackin River, which extend like a wide moat around the southern base of the group. West and north these fells are bounded by the coastal plain of Cumberland and east by the valley of the Eden. Thus they rise in isolation as an independent and separate geographical unit.

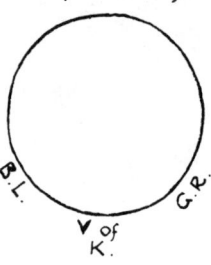

This circle of high ground is divided naturally into three almost equal segments by the main valleys draining the area, the headwaters of which spring from the vast upland basin of Skiddaw Forest. The south-western sector is occupied by the mass of Skiddaw, the south-eastern by Blencathra and its satellites, and the northern, which is of lower elevation and consequently hidden in views from the south by the other two, is a tract of rolling hills comprising the Caldbeck and Uldale Fells.

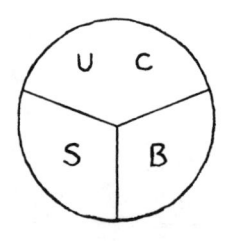

Journeys around the perimeter and into the silent interior along the three valleys forming the segments (the Dash, Caldew and Glenderaterra) give an excellent idea of the composition and character of these fells and are recommended as a preliminary to the exploration of the group.

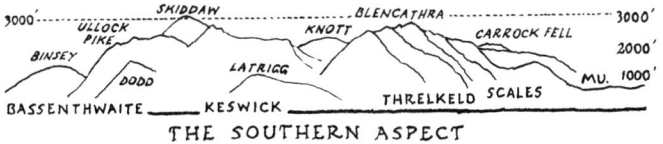

```
3000'·······SKIDDAW············BLENCATHRA··············· 3000'
      ULLOCK                KNOTT
      PIKE                              CARROCK FELL   2000'
BINSEY        LATRIGG
         DODD                                    MU. 1000'
                                  THRELKELD  SCALES
BASSENTHWAITE    KESWICK
              THE SOUTHERN ASPECT
```

←---------------- 10 miles ----------------→

The vertical scale in these diagrams is exaggerated.
(The hills don't *really* look as good as this!)

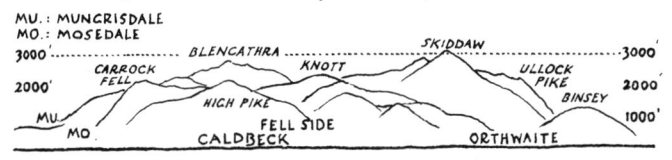

MU.: MUNGRISDALE
MO.: MOSEDALE

```
3000'·········BLENCATHRA············SKIDDAW··············· 3000'
      CARROCK            KNOTT           ULLOCK
2000'  FELL                              PIKE          2000'
               HIGH PIKE                    BINSEY
  MU.              FELL SIDE                            1000'
    MO         CALDBECK           ORTHWAITE
              THE NORTHERN ASPECT
```

The southern aspects of Skiddaw and Blencathra are familiar to frequenters of the Lake District, and the usual approaches on this side are well known. Their northern slopes, falling to the unseen and undefiled hollow of Skiddaw Forest, are less in favour and rarely visited.

Skiddaw Forest is a remarkable place, unique in Lakeland. Common geographical concepts are upset here: the Forest occupies a central position amongst the Northern Fells, but instead of being a concentration of lofty ground from which descending ridges radiate it is actually an upland depression rimmed by summits. The Forest is uncultivated, a desert of heather, trees being entirely absent save for a windbreak at the one solitary dwelling.

The Caldbeck and Uldale Fells are more appropriately classed as hills than as rough mountains, having smooth rounded slopes, an absence of rock and few defined ridges. The whole of these uplands is a vast sheep pasture, without the obstruction of walls and fences and free from natural hazards. (Carrock Fell wishes to be disassociated from this general description). Although relatively unexciting in scenic quality, however, these hills afford excellent tramping and an exhilarating freedom to wander at will, with added interest provided by the evidences, now decaying, of centuries of mining activity. The Caldbeck and Uldale Fells, remote, quieter and lonelier now than they have ever been since men first made their homes nearby, have never received much attention from visitors. Guide books have ignored them completely. It is true that for excitement of outline and challenging situations and beauty of scenery they fall far short of the mountains to the south, yet there is a strong appeal about them not found in (or lost to) the more popular areas of Lakeland — they are unspoilt, serene and restful, a perfect sanctuary for birds and animals and fellwalkers who prefer to be away from crowds, even though this means also being away from ice-cream and pop and crisps. Oh, and juke-boxes.

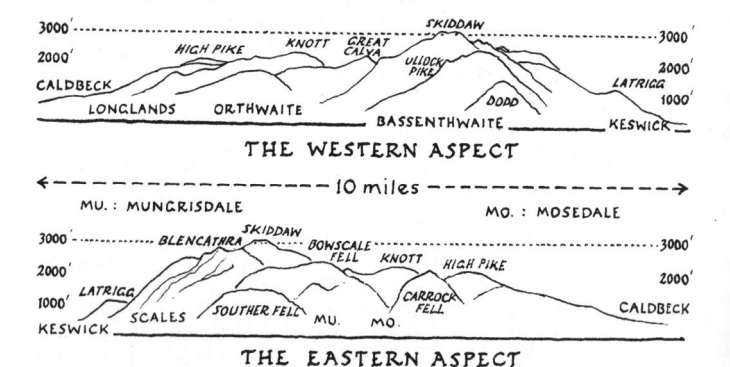

THE WESTERN ASPECT

<- - - - - - - - - - - 10 miles - - - - - - - - - - - ->

MU.: MUNGRISDALE   MO.: MOSEDALE

THE EASTERN ASPECT

Roads of one sort or another completely encircle the Northern Fells, ringing their bases but touching 1000' in the north, and these have been adopted in this book as defining the limits of the territory to be described. Outside, all around, is a richly wooded, fertile countryside, everywhere occupied by little communities who are busily engaged in farming their land, not in providing caravan sites, refreshment and lodging for holiday makers. Back o'Skidda' especially is another world, a place that hasn't changed.

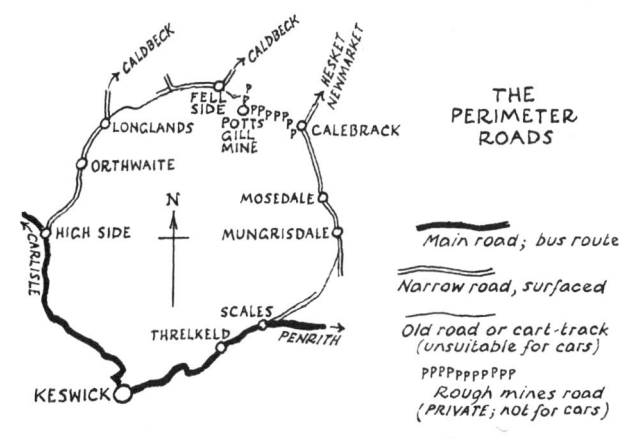

THE PERIMETER ROADS

Main road; bus route

Narrow road, surfaced

Old road or cart-track (unsuitable for cars)

PPPPPPPPPPP
Rough mines road (PRIVATE; not for cars)

Keswick is, with the help of buses, the best single base of operations, and there is no lack of accommodation elsewhere around the southern arc of these fells, from the foot of Bassenthwaite to Scales. Around the northern arc, however, there is very little — and even this little is not adequately brought to the notice of those who are seeking a refuge, the reason being that so few are. There are no hotels, no guest houses. It should therefore be mentioned that *limited* accommodation may be found on the perimeter *by enquiry* at Orthwaite, Fell Side, Mosedale and Mungrisdale, and, just outside, at Ireby, Caldbeck and in the vicinity of Hesket Newmarket, *but make sure in advance.*

THE NORTHERN FELLS
Natural Boundaries

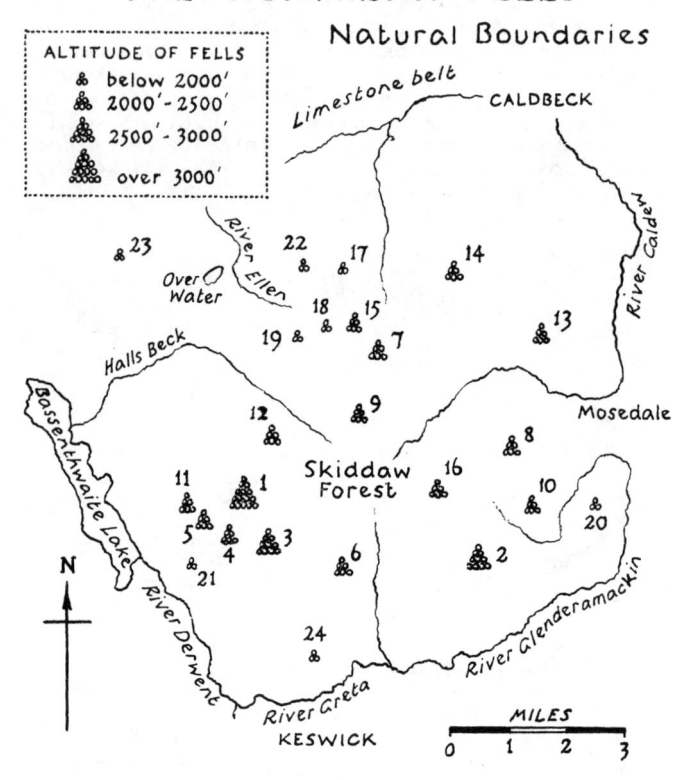

ALTITUDE OF FELLS
- 🔺 below 2000'
- 🔺 2000' - 2500'
- 🔺 2500' - 3000'
- 🔺 over 3000'

1 : SKIDDAW
2 : BLENCATHRA
3 : SKIDDAW LITTLE MAN
4 : CARL SIDE
5 : LONG SIDE
6 : LONSCALE FELL
7 : KNOTT
8 : BOWSCALE FELL
9 : GREAT CALVA
10 : BANNERDALE CRAGS
11 : ULLOCK PIKE
12 : BAKESTALL
13 : CARROCK FELL
14 : HIGH PIKE
15 : GREAT SCA FELL
16 : MUNGRISDALE COMMON
17 : BRAE FELL
18 : MEAL FELL
19 : GREAT COCKUP
20 : SOUTHER FELL
21 : DODD
22 : LONGLANDS FELL
23 : BINSEY
24 : LATRIGG

THE NORTHERN FELLS

in the order of their appearance in this book

Reference to map opposite

over 3000'
2500-3000'
2000-2500'
below 2000'

Altitude in feet

			12	..	BAKESTALL	..	2189
		10		..	BANNERDALE CRAGS	..	2230
			23	..	BINSEY	..	1466
	2			..	BLENCATHRA	..	2847
		8		..	BOWSCALE FELL	..	2306
			17	..	BRAE FELL	..	1920
	4			..	CARL SIDE	..	2420
		13		..	CARROCK FELL	..	2174
			21	..	DODD	..	1612
		9		..	GREAT CALVA	..	2265
			19	..	GREAT COCKUP	..	1720
		15		..	GREAT SCA FELL	..	2131
		14		..	HIGH PIKE	..	2157
		7		..	KNOTT	..	2329
			24	..	LATRIGG	..	1203
			22	..	LONGLANDS FELL	..	1580
	5			..	LONG SIDE	..	2405
	6			..	LONSCALE FELL	..	2344
			18	..	MEAL FELL	..	1770
		16		..	MUNGRISDALE COMMON		2068
1				..	SKIDDAW	..	3053
	3			..	SKIDDAW LITTLE MAN		2837
			20	..	SOUTHER FELL	..	1680
			11	..	ULLOCK PIKE	..	2230

1 2 13 8
———
24

Each fell is the subject of a separate chapter

Bakestall

2189'

not named on
1" Ordnance
Survey maps

from Brockle Crag

- Orthwaite
- Bassenthwaite
- High Side
- ▲ GREAT CALVA
- ▲ BAKESTALL
- SKIDDAW ▲
- Skiddaw House

MILES
0 1 2 3 4

Bakestall 2

NATURAL FEATURES

Even the most diligent student of maps of Lakeland is not likely to have noticed the name of Bakestall and few walkers will have heard of it. Bakestall (the name of a summit rather than of a fell) is a rough raised platform on the sprawling north flank of Skiddaw, merely a halt in the easy slopes and barely qualifying for recognition as a separate top. It would pass almost without comment but for its command of a scene of extra-ordinary interest: a unique combination of natural features that arrests the attention all the more because it is unexpected, startling and seemingly out of place amongst the smooth heathery uplands all around. The summit is perched high above a steepening slope from which has been scooped an enormous hollow, as though a giant hand had clawed at and ripped away the fellside, leaving a rim of crags along the line of cleavage. This escarpment, a rising horseshoe of cliffs half-a-mile in length, is Dead Crags, a dark yet colourful rampart of buttresses and jutting aretes patched a vivid green with bilberry and brown and purple with ling. But grander even than this strange and silent crater are the magnificent waterfalls in the precipitous wooded ravine at its base, where Dash Beck, issuing from the vast waste of Skiddaw Forest, leaps exultantly at its first glimpse of gentle pastures and plunges over the lip in a series of falls, one following another in a mighty torrent of roaring and thrashing waters — the finest spectacle of its kind in the district. This is Whitewater Dash, also known as Dash Falls, a tremendous sight in spate, when the thunder of its great cataracts can be heard miles away down the valley. The brave little road to Skiddaw House, climbing sinuously in and out of the hollow to disappear over the skyline, is the one evidence of man, but instead of intruding, as roads so often do, this desolate track merely adds to the loneliness of the scene. On the west, Bakestall is clearly defined by Dead Beck, which flows down a rough and rocky gutter to join Dash Beck en route for Bassenthwaite Lake.

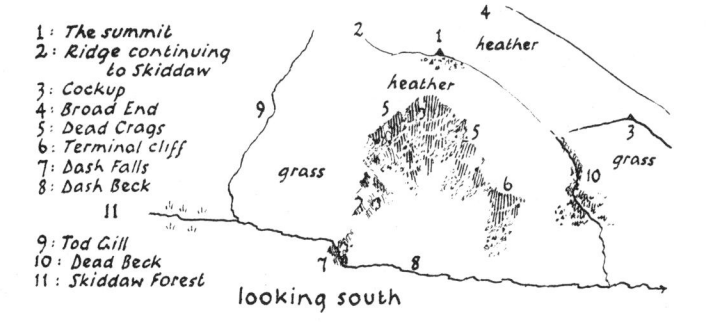

1: The summit
2: Ridge continuing to Skiddaw
3: Cockup
4: Broad End
5: Dead Crags
6: Terminal cliff
7: Dash Falls
8: Dash Beck
9: Tod Gill
10: Dead Beck
11: Skiddaw Forest

looking south

Bakestall 3

MAP

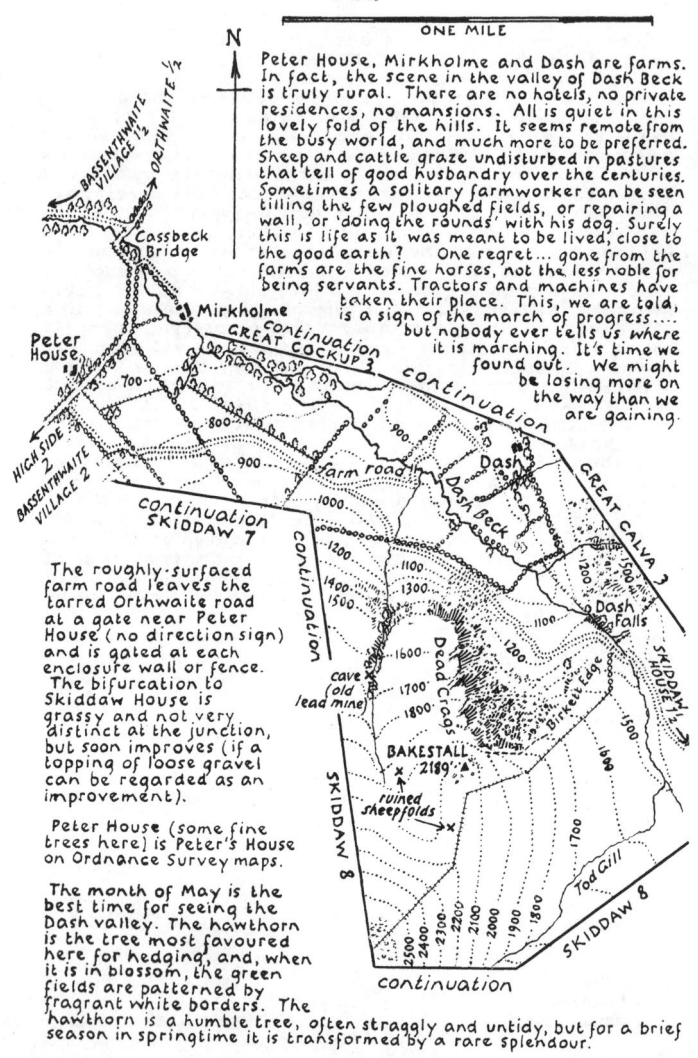

ONE MILE

Peter House, Mirkholme and Dash are farms. In fact, the scene in the valley of Dash Beck is truly rural. There are no hotels, no private residences, no mansions. All is quiet in this lovely fold of the hills. It seems remote from the busy world, and much more to be preferred. Sheep and cattle graze undisturbed in pastures that tell of good husbandry over the centuries. Sometimes a solitary farmworker can be seen tilling the few ploughed fields, or repairing a wall, or 'doing the rounds' with his dog. Surely this is life as it was meant to be lived, close to the good earth? One regret... gone from the farms are the fine horses, not the less noble for being servants. Tractors and machines have taken their place. This, we are told, is a sign of the march of progress.... but nobody ever tells us where it is marching. It's time we found out. We might be losing more on the way than we are gaining.

The roughly-surfaced farm road leaves the tarred Orthwaite road at a gate near Peter House (no direction sign) and is gated at each enclosure wall or fence. The bifurcation to Skiddaw House is grassy and not very distinct at the junction, but soon improves (if a topping of loose gravel can be regarded as an improvement).

Peter House (some fine trees here) is Peter's House on Ordnance Survey maps.

The month of May is the best time for seeing the Dash valley. The hawthorn is the tree most favoured here for hedging, and, when it is in blossom, the green fields are patterned by fragrant white borders. The hawthorn is a humble tree, often straggly and untidy, but for a brief season in springtime it is transformed by a rare splendour.

Bakestall 4

ASCENT FROM THE ROAD TO SKIDDAW HOUSE
900 feet of ascent : 2/3 mile from Dash Falls
(1750 feet, 4⅔ miles from High Side or Bassenthwaite Village)

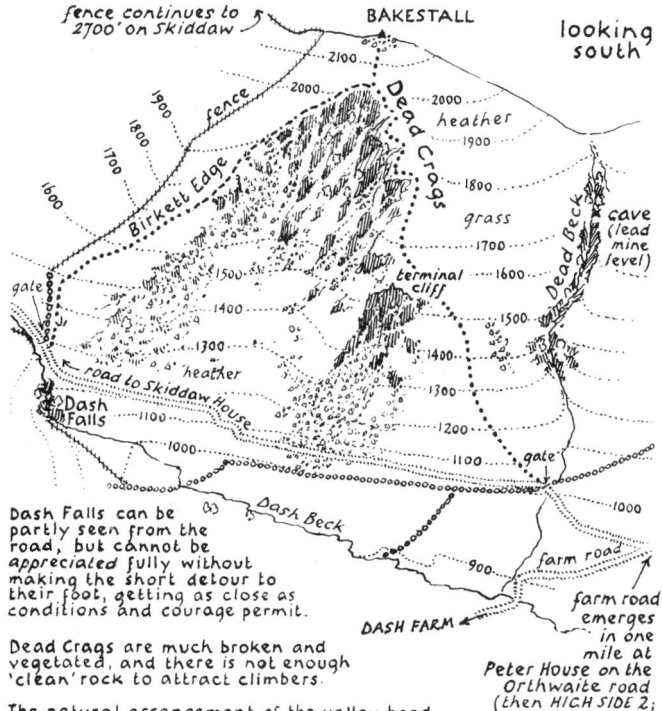

looking south

Dash Falls can be partly seen from the road, but cannot be appreciated fully without making the short detour to their foot, getting as close as conditions and courage permit.

Dead Crags are much broken and vegetated, and there is not enough 'clean' rock to attract climbers.

The natural arrangement of the valley-head, although on no great scale, offers an excellent composition for an artist (stationed near Dash farm) and a perfect object-lesson for a geography class.

farm road emerges in one mile at Peter House on the Orthwaite road (then HIGH SIDE 2; BASSENTHWAITE VILLAGE 2)

Two routes are given, that by Birkett Edge being the better for views of Dead Crags and convenient for an easy visit to Dash Falls. (This is also, incidentally, the best way to Skiddaw from any point on the rough Skiddaw House road). The more direct route, going up steeply between the terminal cliff and Dash Beck from the gate in the intake wall, is less interesting; note that this route should not be used for descent in mist, when only sheer good luck could prevent one from running foul of crags.

Bakestall 5

THE SUMMIT

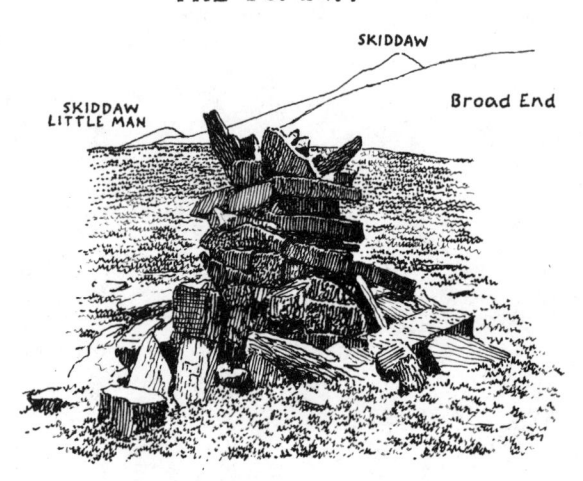

SKIDDAW LITTLE MAN *SKIDDAW* *Broad End*

The summits of the Northern Fells are not, as a rule, distinguished by handsome and imposing cairns, due more to a lack of suitable building material in the vicinity, no doubt, than to a lack of industry on the part of visitors, and the uncharacteristic summit of Bakestall, where good rough rock outcropping amongst the heather has served to provide a solid and substantial column, is nostalgically refreshing to a walker whose preference is for rugged tops. This cairn does not occupy the highest point of the summit (which occurs at the angle of the fence) but is 100 yards to the north at a better place of vantage overlooking a very pleasant pastoral scene: the Dash valley.

DESCENTS: All descents must of necessity be to the road to Skiddaw House skirting the base of the fell, and this is quickly reached by following first the fence down Birkett Edge (detour to the left to see the combe of Dead Crags) and then a short wall. In mist, there is no safe alternative, but in clear weather the steep slope may be descended directly to the rim of Dead Crags (taking care not to panic the sheep grazing there) where a rough track will be found slanting down on the right to Birkett Edge.

If it is desired to locate the old mine level in the Dead Beck ravine on the way down to the road descend the easy slope of heather northwest to the beck. The 'cave' is in the far bank, 50 yards below the first rowan trees and a few feet above the stream-bed.

A: Dead Crags
B: Birkett Edge
C: Dead Beck
D: to Skiddaw

The ravine becomes too rough to follow in comfort lower down but the road may be reached by a detour on the steep grass of either bank. It should be noted that on this route nothing will be seen of Dead Crags or Dash Falls, the cave and ravine, although interesting, being poor compensation.

Bakestall 6

THE VIEW

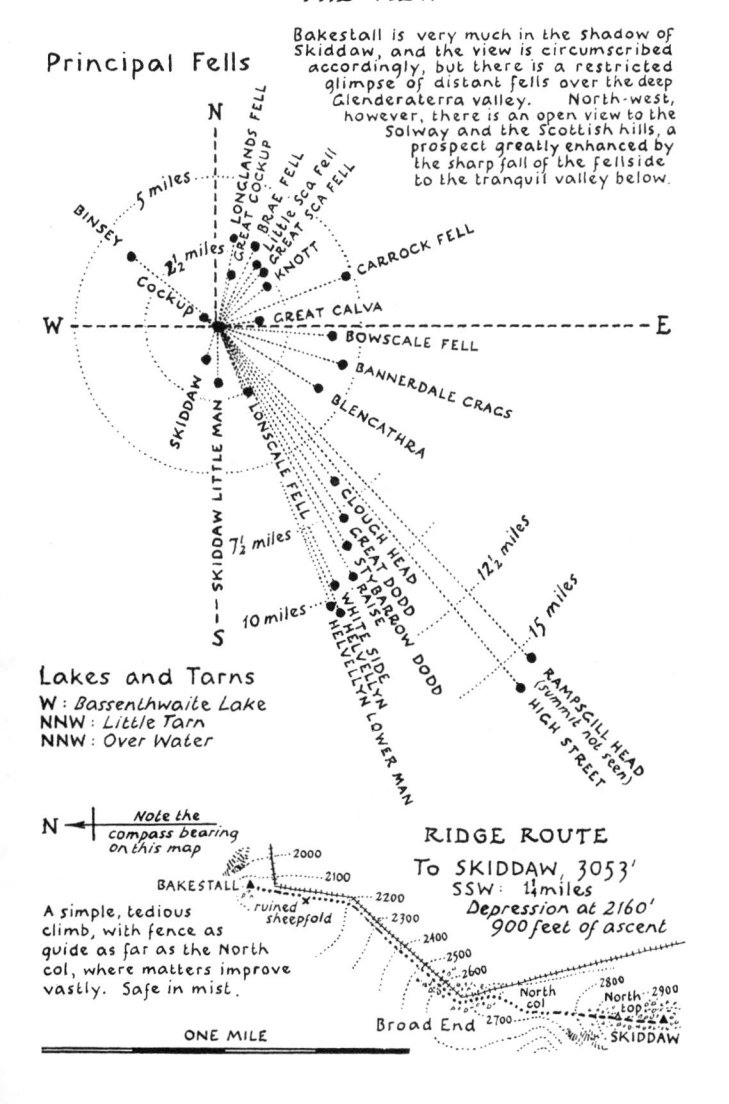

Bakestall is very much in the shadow of Skiddaw, and the view is circumscribed accordingly, but there is a restricted glimpse of distant fells over the deep Glenderaterra valley. North-west, however, there is an open view to the Solway and the Scottish hills, a prospect greatly enhanced by the sharp fall of the fellside to the tranquil valley below.

Principal Fells

- BINSEY
- GREAT COCKUP
- LONGLANDS FELL
- BRAE FELL
- LITTLE SCA FELL
- GREAT SCA FELL
- COCKUP
- KNOTT
- CARROCK FELL
- GREAT CALVA
- BOWSCALE FELL
- BANNERDALE CRAGS
- BLENCATHRA
- SKIDDAW
- SKIDDAW LITTLE MAN
- LONSCALE FELL
- CLOUGH HEAD
- GREAT DODD
- STYBARROW DODD
- WATSON'S DODD
- RAISE
- WHITE SIDE
- HELVELLYN
- HELVELLYN LOWER MAN
- RAMPSGILL HEAD (summit not seen)
- HIGH STREET

(2½ miles, 5 miles, 7½ miles, 10 miles, 12½ miles, 15 miles)

Lakes and Tarns
W : Bassenthwaite Lake
NNW : Little Tarn
NNW : Over Water

RIDGE ROUTE

To SKIDDAW, 3053'
SSW : 1¼ miles
Depression at 2160'
900 feet of ascent

A simple, tedious climb, with fence as guide as far as the North col, where matters improve vastly. Safe in mist.

N ← Note the compass bearing on this map

BAKESTALL ▲ — ruined sheepfold — Broad End — North col — North top — SKIDDAW ▲

ONE MILE

Bakestall 7

a Bakestall portfolio

Dead Crags, from Birkett Edge

Bakestall 8

as seen on the approach along the Skiddaw House road

The head of the Dash valley

as seen from the top of Dead Crags

Bakestall 9

The Terminal Cliffs of Dead Crags from Birkett Edge; Binsey in the background

Blencathra from the summit of Bakestall

Bakestall 10

The old mine level in the ravine of Dead Beck (Cave entrance 5' x 3', but flooded)

Dash Falls
(Whitewater Dash on Ordnance maps)

There are many finer *individual* waterfalls in Lakeland, but for a grand *succession* of falls the first place must undoubtedly be given to Dash Falls.

Little more than half the total height is shown in the illustration.

Bannerdale Crags

2230' approx.

east ridge

BOWSCALE FELL ▲
Mungrisdale ●
▲ BANNERDALE CRAGS
▲ BLENCATHRA
● Scales
● Threlkeld

MILES
0 1 2 3 4

from the ridge leading to Bowscale Fell

Bannerdale Crags 2

NATURAL FEATURES

Bannerdale Crags, to be appreciated fully, should be approached from the pleasant village of Mungrisdale, for only in this direction, eastwards, is revealed the mile-long rim of cliffs that gives the fell a name and is its one great scenic attraction. This escarpment is interrupted by a pronounced spur, the east ridge, but otherwise falls very steeply to the little side-valley of Bannerdale, which is uninhabited, uncultivated and — since the closing of the Lead Mine — unfrequented, much of it being a swamp. Few traces now remain of the old mine at the foot of the crags, nature having cloaked the ravages of man with her own processes.

Westwards and southwards mainly grassy slopes, with one extensive fan of scree, fall steeply from the plateau to the headwaters of the River Glenderamackin; beyond is the towering mass of Blencathra. The river pursues an erratic course and bounds the fell on three sides, but to the north high land continues to Bowscale Fell.

Few visitors to Lakeland will have seen the crags, which turn their back on the district and are quite concealed from all places and viewpoints of popular resort. They are worth a visit, as is delightful Mungrisdale, an alpine old-world village that has so far escaped the invasions of tourists. But one must choose between stout boots and wet feet on the lonely march to Bannerdale.

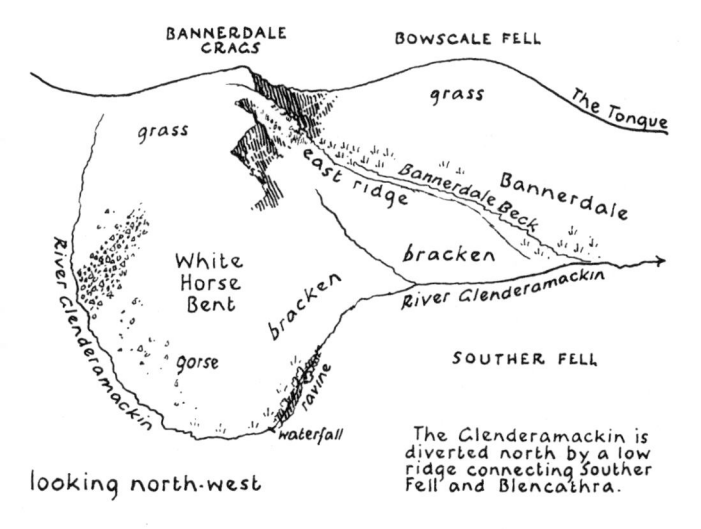

looking north-west

The Glenderamackin is diverted north by a low ridge connecting Souther Fell and Blencathra.

Bannerdale Crags 3

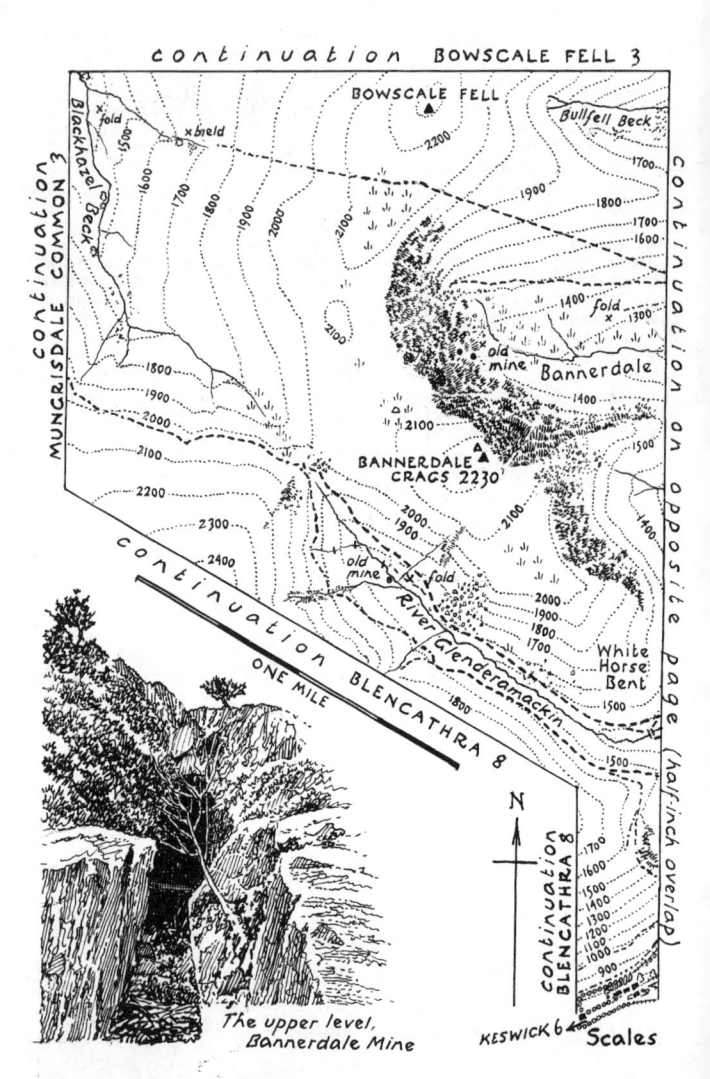

MAP

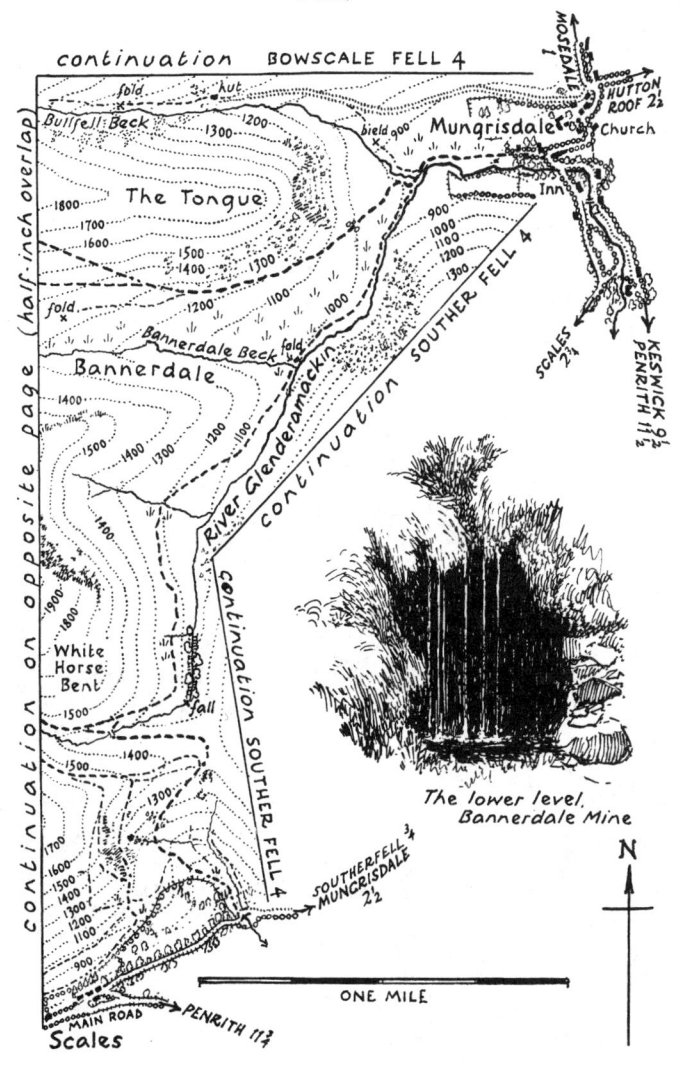

Bannerdale Crags 4

MAP

The lower level, Bannerdale Mine

Bannerdale Crags 5

Bannerdale Crags from Mungrisdale

right:
The east ridge, with the summit to the right

below:
The summit from the final tower of the east ridge

Between the east ridge and the main mass of the summit is a long, steep and rough scree-gully, to which the attention of experienced scramblers is directed. It looks interesting.

Bannerdale Crags 6

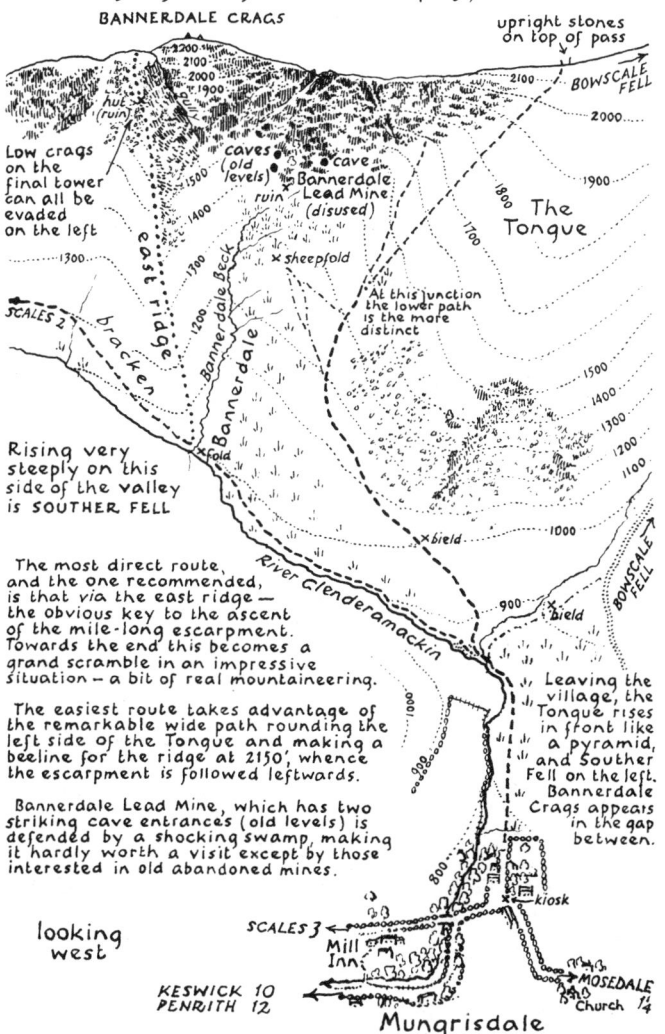

ASCENT FROM MUNGRISDALE
1500 feet of ascent : 2 (or 3) miles

BANNERDALE CRAGS

upright stones on top of pass

BOWSCALE FELL

Low crags on the final tower can all be evaded on the left

hut (ruin)

caves (old levels)

cave

Bannerdale Lead Mine (disused)

ruin

The Tongue

east ridge

SCALES 2

bracken

Bannerdale Beck

Bannerdale

× sheepfold

"At this junction the lower path is the more distinct"

Rising very steeply on this side of the valley is SOUTHER FELL

× fold

× bield

River Glenderamackin

× bield

BOWSCALE FELL

The most direct route, and the one recommended, is that via the east ridge — the obvious key to the ascent of the mile-long escarpment. Towards the end this becomes a grand scramble in an impressive situation — a bit of real mountaineering.

The easiest route takes advantage of the remarkable wide path rounding the left side of the Tongue and making a beeline for the ridge at 2150', whence the escarpment is followed leftwards.

Bannerdale Lead Mine, which has two striking cave entrances (old levels) is defended by a shocking swamp, making it hardly worth a visit except by those interested in old abandoned mines.

Leaving the village, the Tongue rises in front like a pyramid, and Souther Fell on the left. Bannerdale Crags appears in the gap between.

looking west

SCALES 3

Mill Inn

× kiosk

MOSEDALE Church

KESWICK 10
PENRITH 12

Mungrisdale

Bannerdale Crags 7

ASCENT FROM SCALES
1550 feet of ascent : 2½ miles

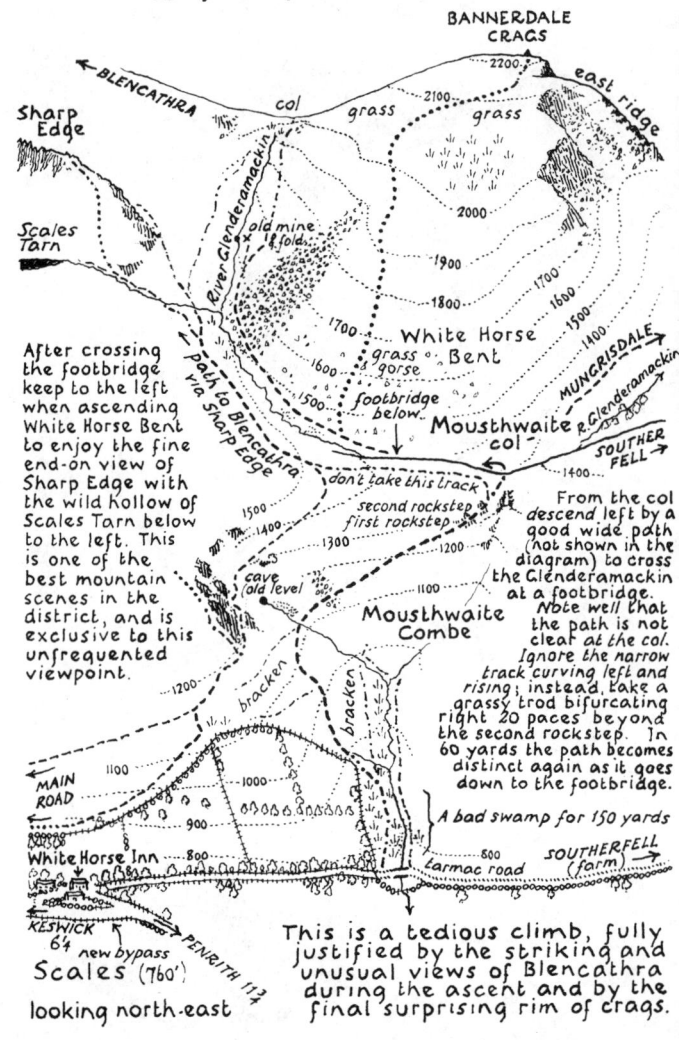

After crossing the footbridge keep to the left when ascending White Horse Bent to enjoy the fine end-on view of Sharp Edge with the wild hollow of Scales Tarn below to the left. This is one of the best mountain scenes in the district, and is exclusive to this unfrequented viewpoint.

From the col descend left by a good wide path (not shown in the diagram) to cross the Glenderamackin at a footbridge. Note well that the path is not clear at the col. Ignore the narrow track curving left and rising; instead, take a grassy trod bifurcating right 20 paces beyond the second rockstep. In 60 yards the path becomes distinct again as it goes down to the footbridge.

A bad swamp for 150 yards

Scales (760')
looking north-east

This is a tedious climb, fully justified by the striking and unusual views of Blencathra during the ascent and by the final surprising rim of crags.

Bannerdale Crags 8

THE SUMMIT

BOWSCALE FELL

This summit is distinguished by the Ordnance Survey's rare use of the word *Curricks* (on their large-scale maps), but the patient enquirer who, having searched his dictionary and drawn a blank, has toiled up here to find out what exactly a currick is will discover only two quite ordinary cairns. After a search for something unusual as barren of results as his dictionary he might be forgiven for pointing out to the Ordnance Survey peevishly that the 25-foot contours (on their 2½" maps) seem to be too narrowly drawn on the wide top of the fell; in fact, the highest point is 100 yards west of the accepted summit and is uncairned. Currick or no currick, however, the main cairn is excellently sited near the edge of the great downfall into Bannerdale, and the crater-like rim in view to the north is magnificent.

DESCENTS: Good paths can be reached *north* below the rise to Bowscale Fell (turn right for Mungrisdale); or *west* at the Glenderamackin col (turn left for Scales): the top itself is pathless. The broad south slope is everywhere easy, and a quick way off. Descent by the east ridge is also practicable, and safe in mist if the top of it can be located, but the ridge can be dangerous when under snow or ice.

PLAN OF SUMMIT

Bannerdale Crags 9

THE VIEW

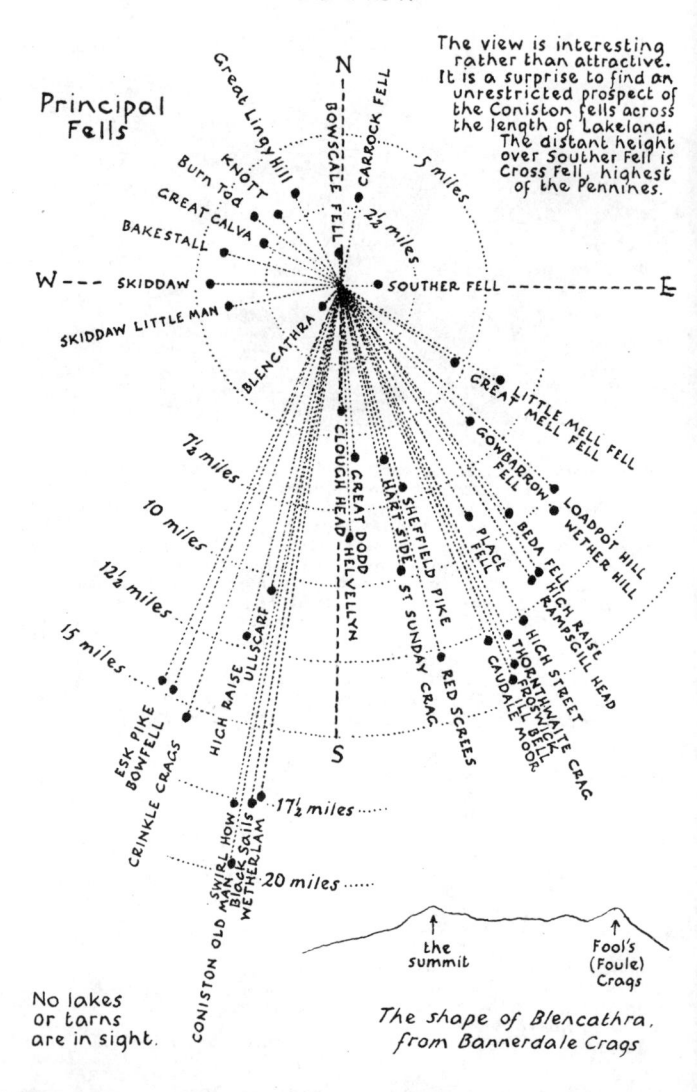

The view is interesting rather than attractive. It is a surprise to find an unrestricted prospect of the Coniston fells across the length of Lakeland. The distant height over Souther Fell is Cross Fell, highest of the Pennines.

Principal Fells

N — Bowscale Fell
Great Lingy Hill
Knott
Carrock Fell
Burn Tod
Great Calva
Bakestall
5 miles
2½ miles
W — Skiddaw — Souther Fell — E
Skiddaw Little Man
Blencathra
Great Little Mell Fell
Mell Fell
Gowbarron Fell
Loadpot Hill
Wether Hill
7½ miles
Clough Head
Great Dodd
Sheffield Pike
Beda Fell
Place
High Raise
Rampsgill Head
10 miles
Helvellyn
Hart Side
St Sunday Crag
Thornthwaite Crag
High Street
Froswick
12½ miles
Ullscarf
Red Screes
Caudale Moor
15 miles
S
Esk Pike
Bowfell
High Raise
Crinkle Crags
17½ miles
Swirl How
Black Sails
Wetherlam
20 miles
Coniston Old Man

No lakes or tarns are in sight.

The shape of Blencathra, from Bannerdale Crags

the summit — Fool's (Foule) Crags

Bannerdale Crags 10

RIDGE ROUTES

To BOWSCALE FELL, 2306':
1¼ miles : NW, then NNE
Depression at 2060'
250 feet of ascent

An easy stroll, calling for some skill in negotiating swampy ground. Keep to the edge of the escarpment, which is drier and has striking views.

To BLENCATHRA, 2847'
1½ miles : W, then SW and S
Depression at 2010'
850 feet of ascent

A direct line is not practicable. Aim for the Glenderamackin col and ascend the grassy ridge rising directly opposite: this has an interesting 'back' view of Sharp Edge, but the great feature of the route is Foule Crag, which is skirted to the right, the saddle above being reached by a stiff pull.

below:
A mature tree grows out of the chimney-breast of the ruined hut.

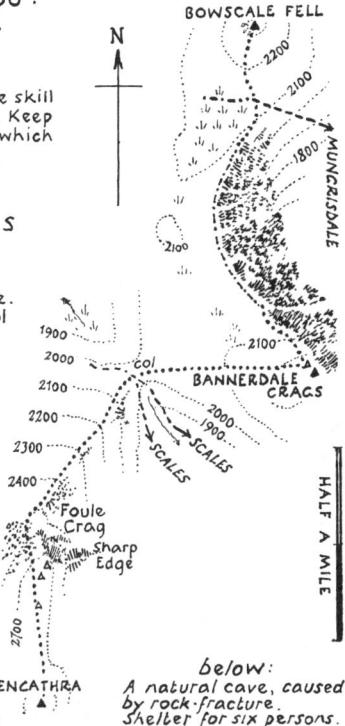

below:
A natural cave, caused by rock-fracture. Shelter for six persons.

Odd features at Bannerdale Mine

Binsey 1466'

from Robin Hood, near Bassenthwaite

Private path in Binsey Plantation

- Ireby
- High Ireby
- Uldale
- ▲ BINSEY
- Bewaldeth
- Bassenthwaite

MILES
0 1 2 3

Binsey 2

NATURAL FEATURES

Binsey is the odd man out. This gentle hill rises beyond the circular perimeter of the Northern Fells, detached and solitary, like a dunce set apart from the class. It is of no great height, is well within the category of Sunday afternoon strolls, has an easy slope just right for exercising the dog or the children, is without precipices and pitfalls, never killed or injured anybody, breeds hares instead of foxes, and is generally of benign appearance. Yet it is much too good to be omitted from these pages.

For one thing it is a most excellent station for appraising the Northern Fells as a preliminary to their exploration. For another, it is a viewpoint of outstanding merit. For another, it possesses a grand little summit with a once-important but now-forgotten history. For another, its rocks are volcanic, not slate as are those of all neighbour fells.

Binsey occupies the extreme north-west corner of the Lake District. Beyond is the coastal plain, then the sea, then Scotland; nothing intervenes to interrupt this sweeping panorama. What a domain, and what a throne to view it from!

the summit ridge, looking east

West Crag

Binsey 3

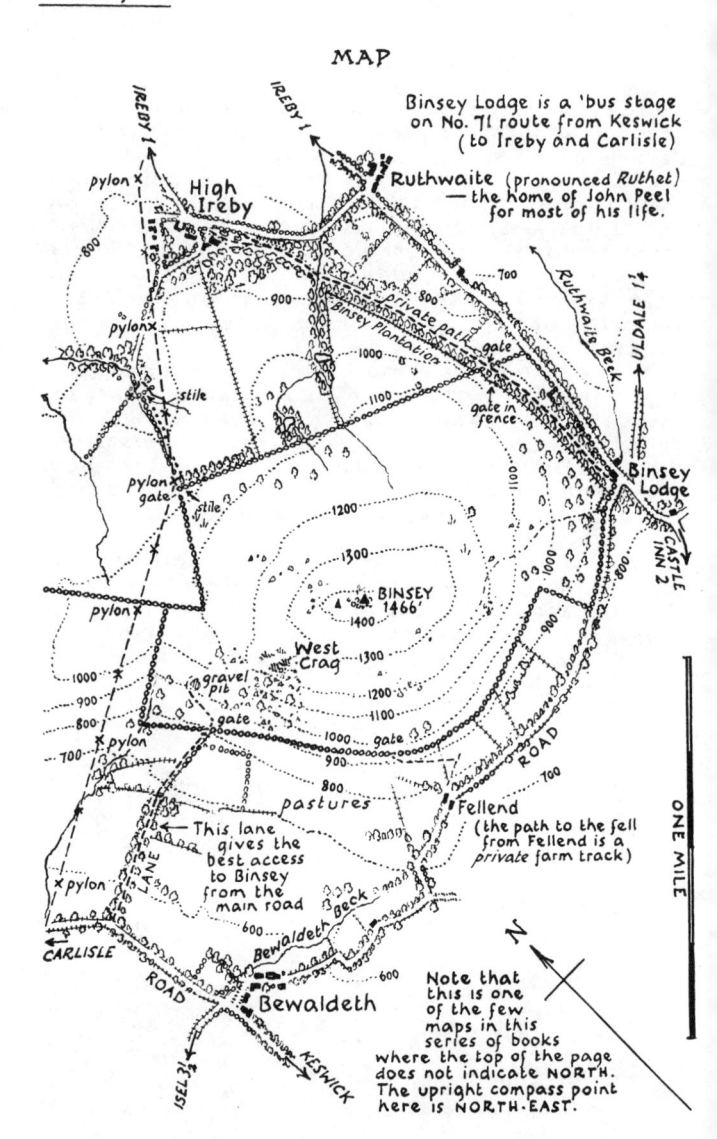

Binsey 4

ASCENT FROM BEWALDETH
950 feet of ascent : 1¼ miles

The summit of Binsey is remarkable for the ancient tumulus crowning the highest point: this is now surmounted by a modern cairn. An Ordnance Survey column stands alongside, and there is a neat wind-shelter amongst the stones on the north side.

West Crag — BINSEY — heather — gravel pit — gate

The lane is a green avenue between trees, much cut up by tractors.

Binsey's outline is too smooth and gently graded to attract much attention, and its ascent from most directions is an easy trudge lacking in excitement. The route here shown is the best that can be contrived, bringing the few features of interest into view, notably the small cliffs and boulder slopes of West Crag. The rock here is a colourful volcanic, the whole fell being just outside the area of the Skiddaw slates, of which most of north-west Lakeland is formed.

CARLISLE ← MAIN ROAD → KESWICK — Bewaldeth — ISEL

This lane, a third of a mile north of Bewaldeth, is the best (and the only direct) access to the fell from the main Keswick-Carlisle road.

looking north-east

This is a pleasant little climb at any season of the year, but on a warm clear day in August the purple heather and glorious panoramic view together make Binsey one of the best places for spending an hour of undisturbed peace and enjoyment. Or take the family.

Binsey 5

ASCENT FROM BINSEY LODGE
620 feet of ascent : 1 mile

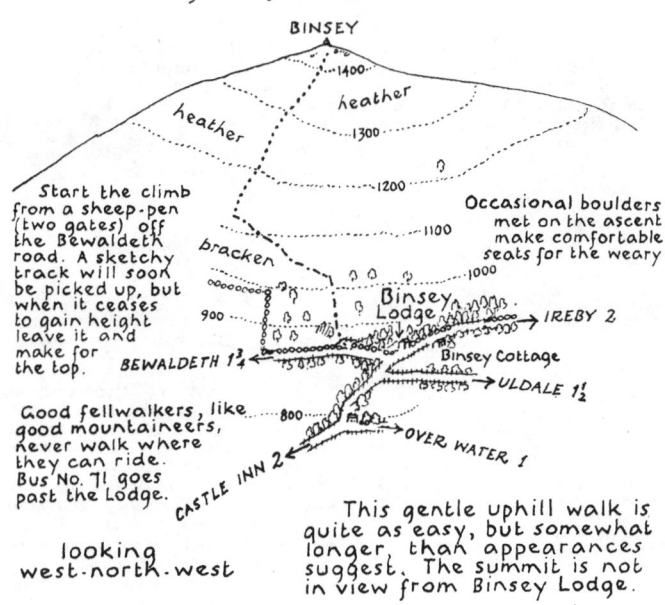

BINSEY

heather — heather

Start the climb from a sheep-pen (two gates) off the Bewaldeth road. A sketchy track will soon be picked up, but when it ceases to gain height leave it and make for the top.

bracken

Binsey Lodge

Occasional boulders met on the ascent make comfortable seats for the weary

BEWALDETH 1¼ ← → IREBY 2

Binsey Cottage → ULDALE 1½

CASTLE INN 2 ← → OVER WATER 1

Good fellwalkers, like good mountaineers, never walk where they can ride. Bus No. 71 goes past the Lodge.

looking west-north-west

This gentle uphill walk is quite as easy, but somewhat longer, than appearances suggest. The summit is not in view from Binsey Lodge.

Binsey Lodge

Binsey 6

ASCENT FROM HIGH IREBY
700 feet of ascent: 1½ miles

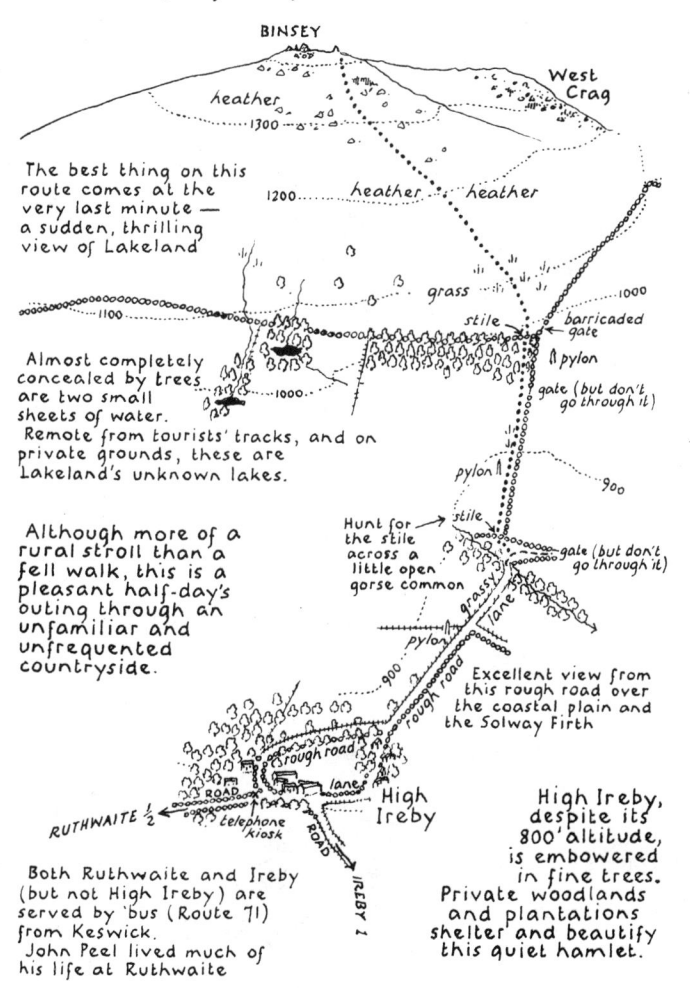

BINSEY

West Crag

heather

1300

heather   heather

1200

The best thing on this route comes at the very last minute — a sudden, thrilling view of Lakeland

grass

1100

1000

stile

barricaded gate

pylon

gate (but don't go through it)

Almost completely concealed by trees are two small sheets of water. Remote from tourists' tracks, and on private grounds, these are Lakeland's unknown lakes.

pylon

900

stile

Hunt for the stile across a little open gorse common

gate (but don't go through it)

Although more of a rural stroll than a fell walk, this is a pleasant half-day's outing through an unfamiliar and unfrequented countryside.

grassy lane

pylon

900

rough road

Excellent view from this rough road over the coastal plain and the Solway Firth

RUTHWAITE ½

ROAD

rough road

lane

telephone kiosk

High Ireby

ROAD

IREBY 1

High Ireby, despite its 800' altitude, is embowered in fine trees. Private woodlands and plantations shelter and beautify this quiet hamlet.

Both Ruthwaite and Ireby (but not High Ireby) are served by 'bus (Route 71) from Keswick.
John Peel lived much of his life at Ruthwaite

looking south-south-west

Binsey 7

THE SUMMIT

The summit is the best part of the fell, taking the form of a small ridge surmounted by a great heap of stones (in fact a tumulus) with an Ordnance Survey column alongside and a well-built wall shelter at the foot of the tumble of stones on the north side. There is a lower cairn to the north-west. With the added attraction of an excellent view, this summit is worthy of a greater mountain than Binsey.

DESCENTS: All routes of descent are simple. At West Crag there is a little roughness. *In mist, bearings can be taken at the summit: the Survey column is east of the tumulus, and the shelter north.*

Binsey Lodge (which is not in sight) is reached by aiming for Over Water (which is).

On the top of Binsey.........

...... Prehistoric Tumulus and Ancient Briton

Binsey 8

THE VIEW

The Lakeland segment is only a third of the whole, but is full of interest, especially to the south, where again the surprising fact is demonstrated, by the unobstructed view of the faraway Coniston fells, that the central part of the district is generally of lower altitude than the perimeter.

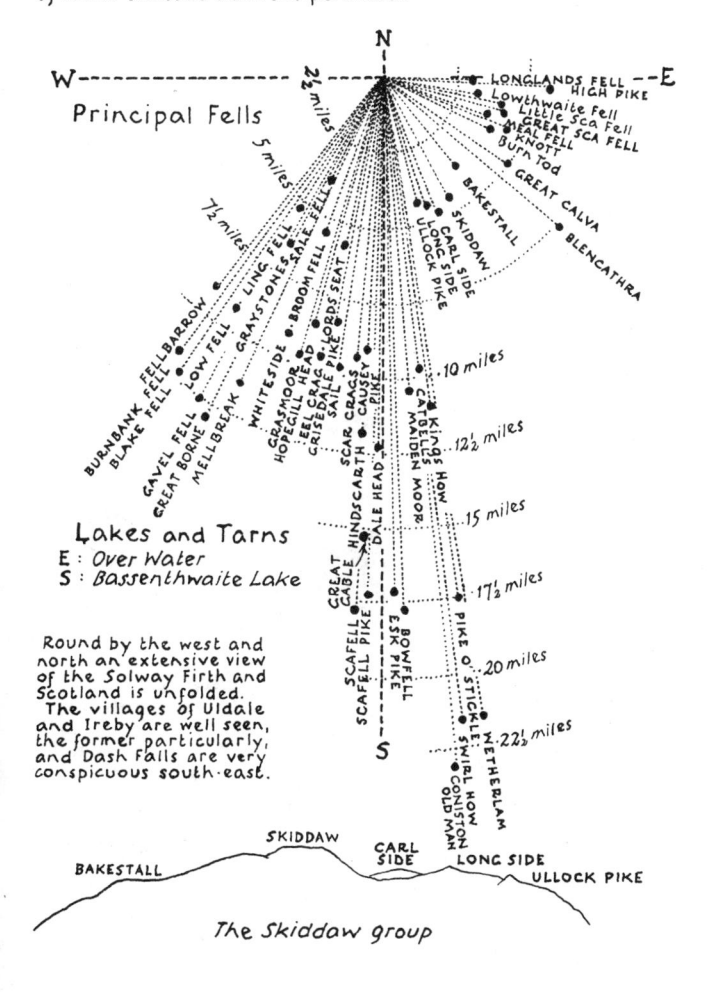

Principal Fells

W — — — — — — — — — — N — — — — — — — — — — E

- LONGLANDS FELL
- HIGH PIKE
- Lowthwaite Fell
- Little Sca Fell
- GREAT SCA FELL
- MEAL FELL
- KNOTT
- Burn Tod
- GREAT CALVA
- BAKESTALL
- SKIDDAW
- CARL SIDE
- LONG SIDE
- ULLOCK PIKE
- BLENCATHRA
- FELLBARROW
- BURNBANK FELL
- BLAKE FELL
- LOW FELL
- LING FELL
- GAVEL FELL
- GREAT BORNE
- GRAYSTONES FELL
- BROOM FELL
- MELLBREAK
- WHITESIDE
- GRASMOOR
- HOPEGILL HEAD
- EEL CRAGS
- LORDS SEAT
- GRISEDALE PIKE
- SAIL
- SCAR CRAGS
- CAUSEY PIKE
- HINDSCARTH
- DALE HEAD
- CATBELLS
- MAIDEN MOOR
- KINGS HOW
- GREAT GABLE
- SCAFELL
- SCAFELL PIKE
- BOWFELL
- ESK PIKE
- PIKE O'STICKLE
- SWIRL HOW
- WETHERLAM
- CONISTON OLD MAN

2½ miles, 5 miles, 7½ miles, 10 miles, 12½ miles, 15 miles, 17½ miles, 20 miles, 22½ miles

S

Lakes and Tarns
E : Over Water
S : Bassenthwaite Lake

Round by the west and north an extensive view of the Solway Firth and Scotland is unfolded.
The villages of Uldale and Ireby are well seen, the former particularly, and Dash Falls are very conspicuous south-east.

BAKESTALL — SKIDDAW — CARL SIDE — LONG SIDE — ULLOCK PIKE

The Skiddaw group

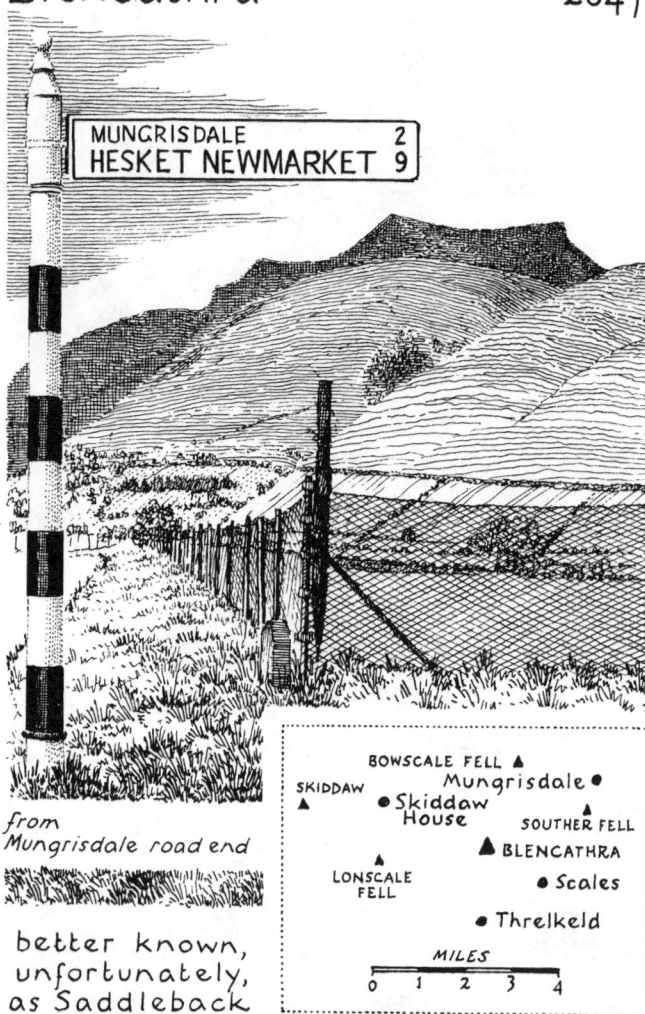

Blencathra 2847'

from Mungrisdale road end

better known, unfortunately, as Saddleback

MUNGRISDALE 2
HESKET NEWMARKET 9

BOWSCALE FELL ▲
SKIDDAW ▲   ● Mungrisdale
   ● Skiddaw House   SOUTHER FELL
▲ LONSCALE FELL   ▲ BLENCATHRA
   ● Scales
● Threlkeld

MILES
0 1 2 3 4

Blencathra 2

NATURAL FEATURES

Blencathra is one of the grandest objects in Lakeland. And one of the best known. Seen from the south-west, the popular aspect, the mountain rises steeply and in isolation above the broad green fields of Threlkeld, a feature being the great sweeping curve leaping out of the depths to a lofty summit-ridge, where the skyline then proceeds in a succession of waves to a sharp peak before descending, again in a graceful curve, to the valley pastures far to the east.

This is a mountain that compels attention, even from those dull people whose eyes are not habitually lifted to the hills. To artists and photographers it is an obvious subject for their craft; to sightseers passing along the road or railway at its base, between Keswick and Penrith, its influence is magnetic; to the dalesfolk it is the eternal background to their lives, there at birth, there at death. But most of all it is a mountaineers' mountain.

continued

from Castlerigg Stone Circle

Blencathra 3

NATURAL FEATURES
continued

The supreme feature of Blencathra, the one that invests the mountain with special grandeur, is the imposing southern front, a remarkable example of the effect of elemental natural forces. It forms a tremendous facade above the valley, and makes a dark, towering backcloth to a stage of farmsteads and cottages, of emerald pastures and meadows and woodlands along its base. There is nothing inviting in these shattered cliffs and petrified rivers of stone that seem to hold a perpetual threat over the little community below: the scene arrests attention, but intimidates and repels. Few who gaze upon these desolate walls are likely to feel any inclination and inspiration to scramble up through their arid, stony wildernesses to the contorted skyline so high above. Consequently the area has remained a no-man's-land for walkers, even though closely within sight of road and railway travellers. Blencathra is ascended thousands of times a year but rarely by ways up the southern front. This is a pity. Here is the greatness of the mountain. Its detail is a fascinating study.

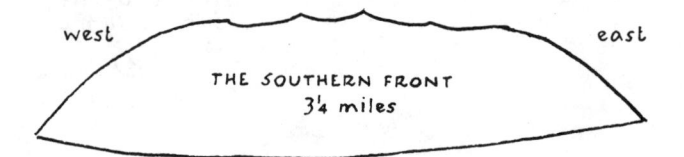

west   east

THE SOUTHERN FRONT
3¼ miles

The outer slopes, rising on the west and east flanks from valley level to the uppermost escarpment below the summit ridge, are smoothly curved, massive and yet so symmetrical that they might well have been designed by a master architect to supply a perfect balance to the structure. These two outlyers are Blease Fell and Scales Fell.

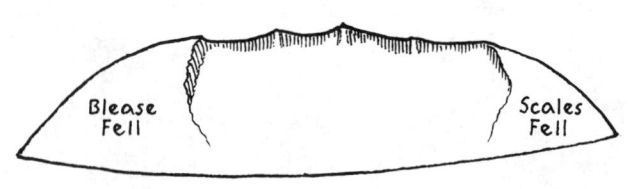

Blease Fell   Scales Fell

continued

Blencathra 4

NATURAL FEATURES
continued

From their extremities the slopes of Bleas Fell and Scales Fell extend uneventfully towards each other across the front until, suddenly and dramatically, they are halted at the edge of a scene of devastation, the wreckage of what appears to have been, in ages past, a tremendous convulsion that tore the heart out of the mountain and left the ruins seemingly in a state of tottering collapse. The picture is chaotic: a great upheaval of ridges and pinnacles rising out of dead wastes of scree and penetrated by choked gullies and ravines, the whole crazily tilted through 2000' of altitude. Even in this area of confusion and disorder, however, Nature has sculptured a distinct pattern.

Four watercourses emerge from surrounding debris to escape to the valley:

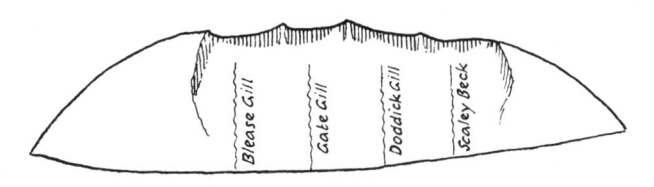

Blease Gill — Gate Gill — Doddick Gill — Scaley Beck

Between the four ravines, three lofty spurs, alike in main characteristics, thrust far out; narrow and frail where they leave the solid mass of the mountain, they widen into substantial buttresses as they descend to the valley. It is as though a giant hand had clawed at the mountain, each finger scooping out a deep hollow, with narrow strips of ground left undisturbed between.

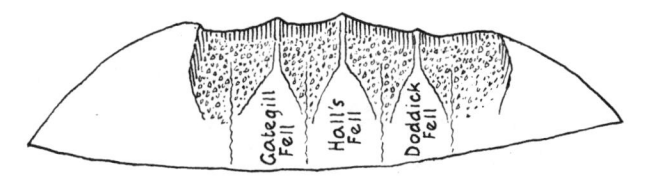

Gategill Fell — Hall's Fell — Doddick Fell

There are thus five buttresses on the southern front, each named as a separate fell. The two outer are grassy, with flat tops; the three in the middle are heathery and rise to distinct peaks, the central one being Blencathra's summit. Such is the pattern of the southern front.

continued

Blencathra 5

NATURAL FEATURES
continued

The other flanks of the mountain are mainly smooth and rounded, although on the east side Scales Fell breaks its curve to form the hollow of Mousthwaite Combe. But, from the summit, high ground continues north across a slight depression (the Saddle) to the prominent top of Foule Crag, this being the outline from which the alternative name, Saddleback, derives. A distinct ridge curves away to the Glenderamackin col from Foule Crag, while a rocky spur goes off to the east, this latter being the well-known Sharp Edge, second in fame to Striding Edge on Helvellyn as a test for walkers. Deepset in the hollow between Sharp Edge and the main ridge is one of the most characteristic mountain tarns in the district, Scales Tarn.

It is interesting to note that although Blencathra lies well to the east of the axis of Lakeland, approximately 99% of its drainage joins the Derwent in the west, only a few drops being gathered by the Eden catchment.

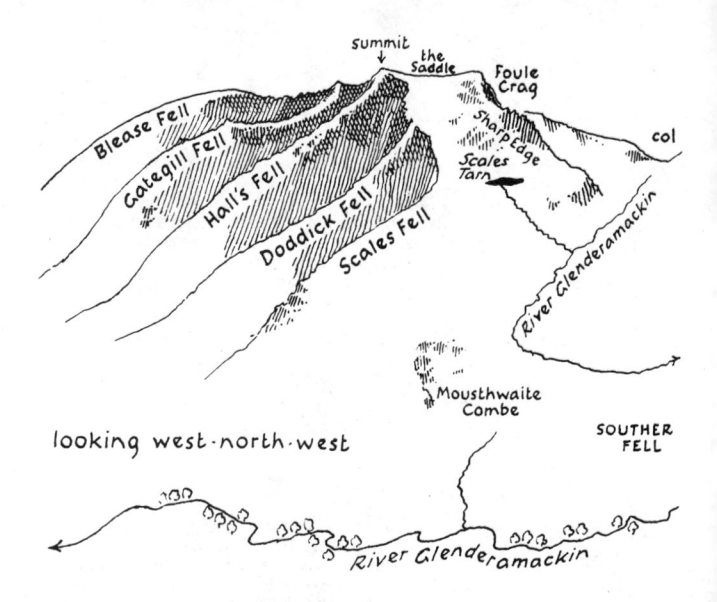

looking west-north-west

Blencathra joins Bowfell in the author's best half-dozen.

Blencathra 6

The summit escarpment

looking west

from Scales Fell to the summit

from the summit to Gategill Fell Top

from Gategill Fell Top to Blease Fell

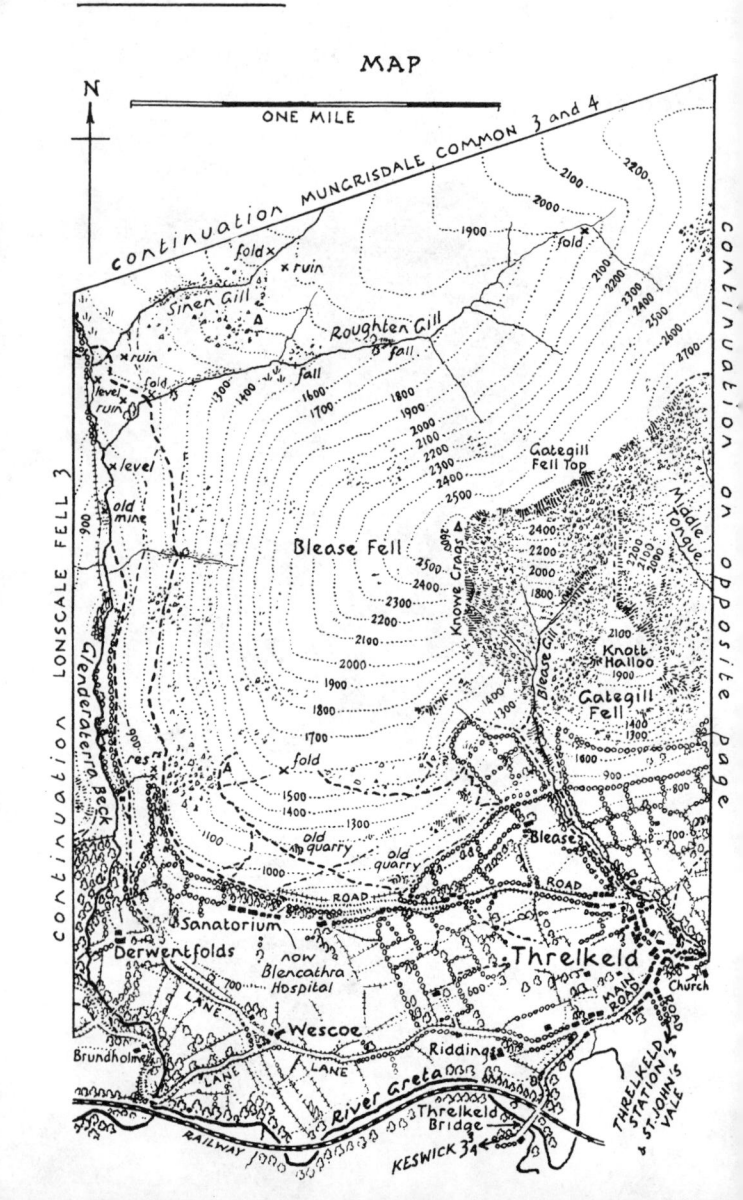

Blencathra 7

MAP

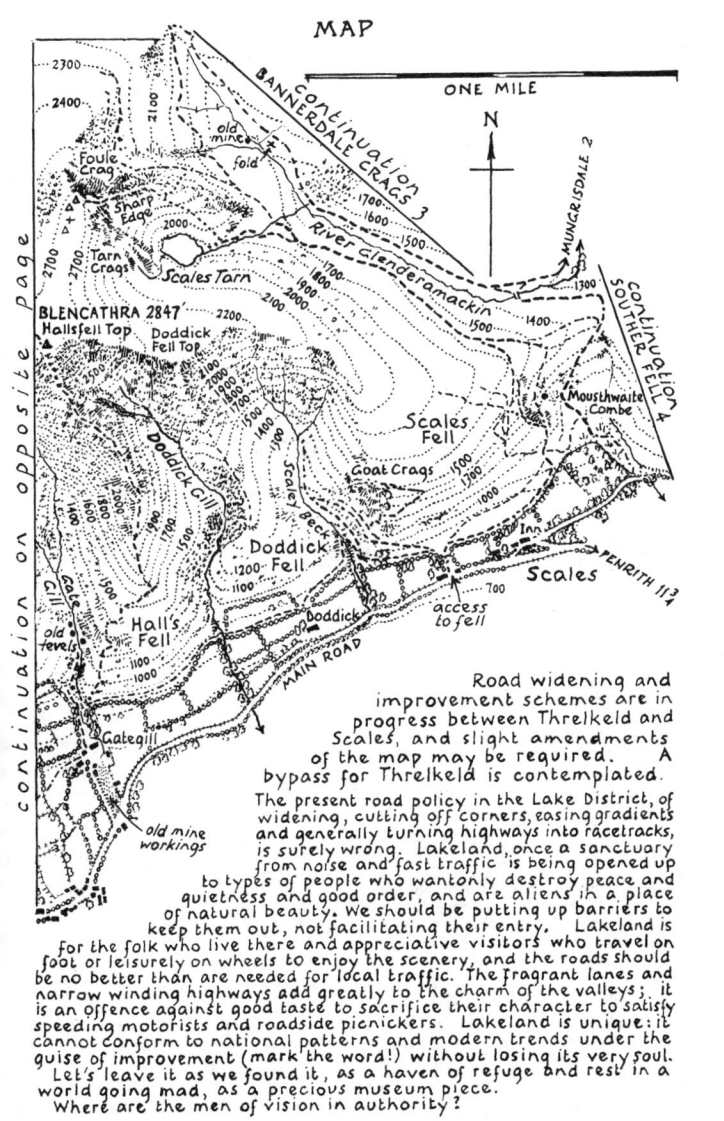

Blencathra 8

MAP

Road widening and improvement schemes are in progress between Threlkeld and Scales, and slight amendments of the map may be required. A bypass for Threlkeld is contemplated.

The present road policy in the Lake District, of widening, cutting off corners, easing gradients and generally turning highways into racetracks, is surely wrong. Lakeland, once a sanctuary from noise and fast traffic, is being opened up to types of people who wantonly destroy peace and quietness and good order, and are aliens in a place of natural beauty. We should be putting up barriers to keep them out, not facilitating their entry. Lakeland is for the folk who live there and appreciative visitors who travel on foot or leisurely on wheels to enjoy the scenery, and the roads should be no better than are needed for local traffic. The fragrant lanes and narrow winding highways add greatly to the charm of the valleys; it is an offence against good taste to sacrifice their character to satisfy speeding motorists and roadside picnickers. Lakeland is unique: it cannot conform to national patterns and modern trends under the guise of improvement (mark the word!) without losing its very soul.

Let's leave it as we found it, as a haven of refuge and rest in a world going mad, as a precious museum piece.

Where are the men of vision in authority?

Blencathra 9

ASCENT FROM THRELKELD
via ROUGHTEN GILL
2400 feet of ascent : 5 miles

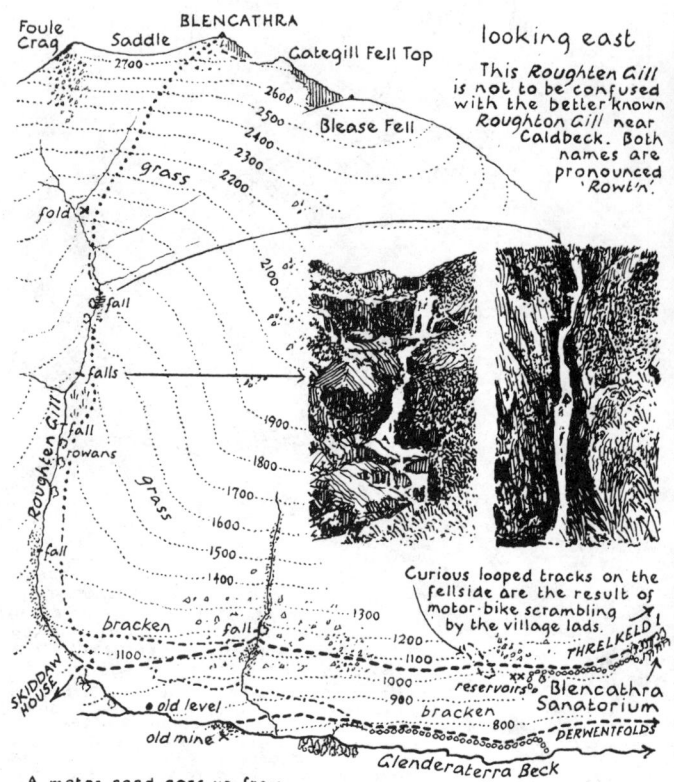

looking east

This *Roughten Gill* is not to be confused with the better known *Roughton Gill* near Caldbeck. Both names are pronounced 'Rowt'n'.

Curious looped tracks on the fellside are the result of motor-bike scrambling by the village lads.

A motor-road goes up from Threlkeld to the Sanatorium and ends there. Its direction is continued by a wide grass path (gate in fence) along the side of the Sanatorium wall. Use this.

For walkers who panic at the proximity of precipices and cannot face steep slopes, the roundabout route by Roughten Gill, which holds no terrors at all, is a good way to the top, but most people will find it unexciting and dreary. The best thing about it is delayed until the very end: the sudden thrilling view of Lakeland, which has been hidden during the climb.

Blencathra 10

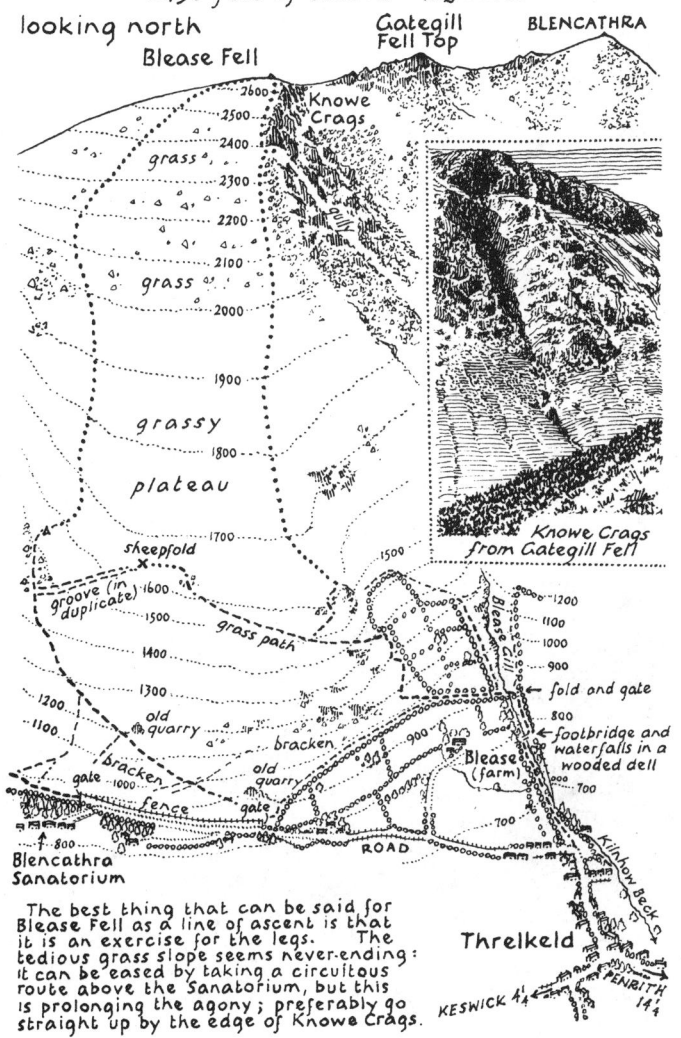

ASCENT FROM THRELKELD
via BLEASE FELL
2450 feet of ascent : 2½ miles

looking north — Blease Fell — Gategill Fell Top — BLENCATHRA

Knowe Crags

grass

grassy plateau

sheepfold
groove (in duplicate)
grass path
old quarry
bracken
old quarry
gate
fence
gate
Blencathra Sanatorium

Knowe Crags from Gategill Fell

Blease Gill
fold and gate
footbridge and waterfalls in a wooded dell
Blease (farm)

ROAD

Kilnhow Beck

Threlkeld

KESWICK 4¼   PENRITH 14¼

The best thing that can be said for Blease Fell as a line of ascent is that it is an exercise for the legs. The tedious grass slope seems never-ending: it can be eased by taking a circuitous route above the Sanatorium, but this is prolonging the agony; preferably go straight up by the edge of Knowe Crags.

Blencathra 11

Blease Gill

Blencathra 12

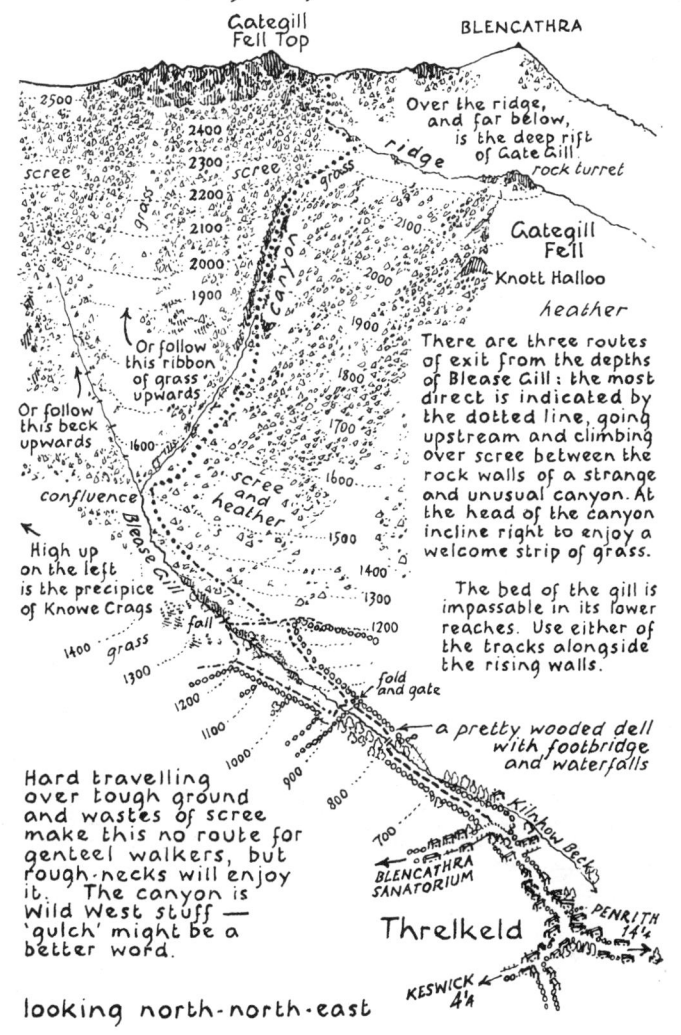

ASCENT FROM THRELKELD
via BLEASE GILL
2400 feet of ascent : 2 miles

looking north-north-east

Over the ridge, and far below, is the deep rift of Gate Gill

Gategill Fell Top — BLENCATHRA — rock turret — Gategill Fell — Knott Halloo — heather

There are three routes of exit from the depths of Blease Gill: the most direct is indicated by the dotted line, going upstream and climbing over scree between the rock walls of a strange and unusual canyon. At the head of the canyon incline right to enjoy a welcome strip of grass.

The bed of the gill is impassable in its lower reaches. Use either of the tracks alongside the rising walls.

Or follow this ribbon of grass upwards

Or follow this beck upwards

confluence — Blease Gill — fall

High up on the left is the precipice of Knowe Crags

canyon — scree and heather — grass

fold and gate — a pretty wooded dell with footbridge and waterfalls — Kilnhow Beck

BLENCATHRA SANATORIUM

Threlkeld — KESWICK 4¼ — PENRITH 14¼

Hard travelling over tough ground and wastes of scree make this no route for genteel walkers, but rough-necks will enjoy it. The canyon is Wild West stuff — 'gulch' might be a better word.

Blencathra 13

ASCENT FROM THRELKELD
via GATEGILL FELL
2450 feet of ascent : 2 miles

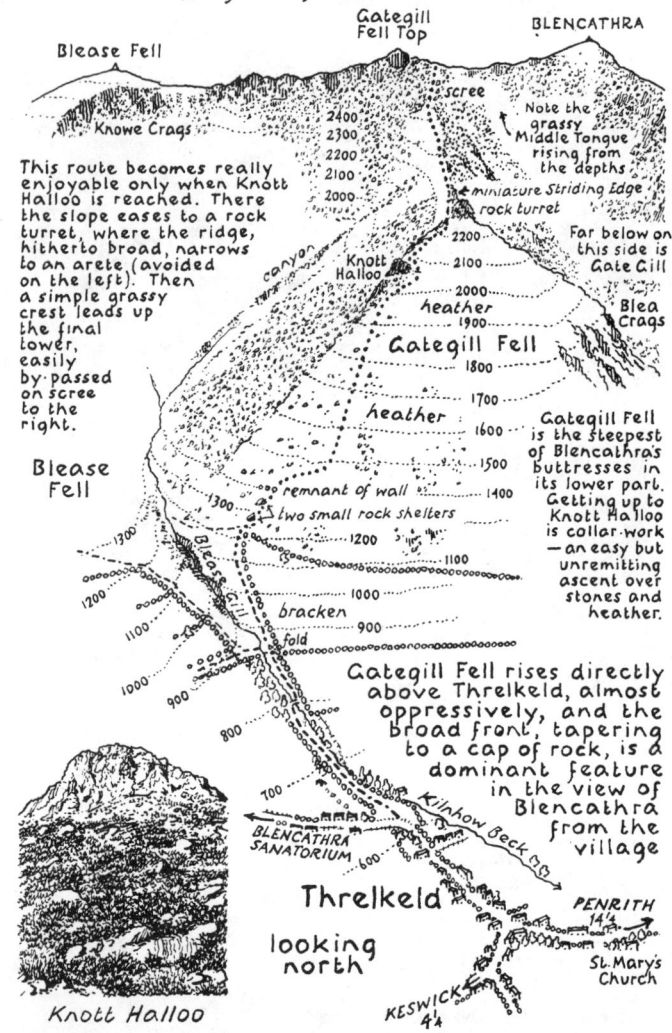

Blease Fell — Knowe Crags — Gategill Fell Top — BLENCATHRA

Note the grassy Middle Tongue rising from the depths

miniature Striding Edge rock turret

Far below on this side is Gate Gill

Knott Halloo — canyon

heather — Gategill Fell — Blea Crags

heather

remnant of wall
two small rock shelters

Blease Fell

Blease Gill

bracken
fold

This route becomes really enjoyable only when Knott Halloo is reached. There the slope eases to a rock turret, where the ridge, hitherto broad, narrows to an arete (avoided on the left). Then a simple grassy crest leads up the final tower, easily by-passed on scree to the right.

Gategill Fell is the steepest of Blencathra's buttresses in its lower part. Getting up to Knott Halloo is collar-work — an easy but unremitting ascent over stones and heather.

Gategill Fell rises directly above Threlkeld, almost oppressively, and the broad front, tapering to a cap of rock, is a dominant feature in the view of Blencathra from the village

BLENCATHRA SANATORIUM

Kilnhow Beck

Threlkeld
looking north

PENRITH 14¼
St. Mary's Church
KESWICK 4¼

Knott Halloo

Blencathra 14

looking up to Gategill Fell Top from just above Knott Halloo, with the rock turret on the right

Gategill Fell

looking up the ridge from the rock turret

looking down the ridge from Gategill Fell Top

The rock turret is at the far end of the shadow; to the right is Knott Halloo, the furthest point in view.

Blencathra 15

Gate Gill

Blencathra's summit is directly ahead. Gategill Fell rises on the left, and Hall's Fell on the right.

Blencathra 16

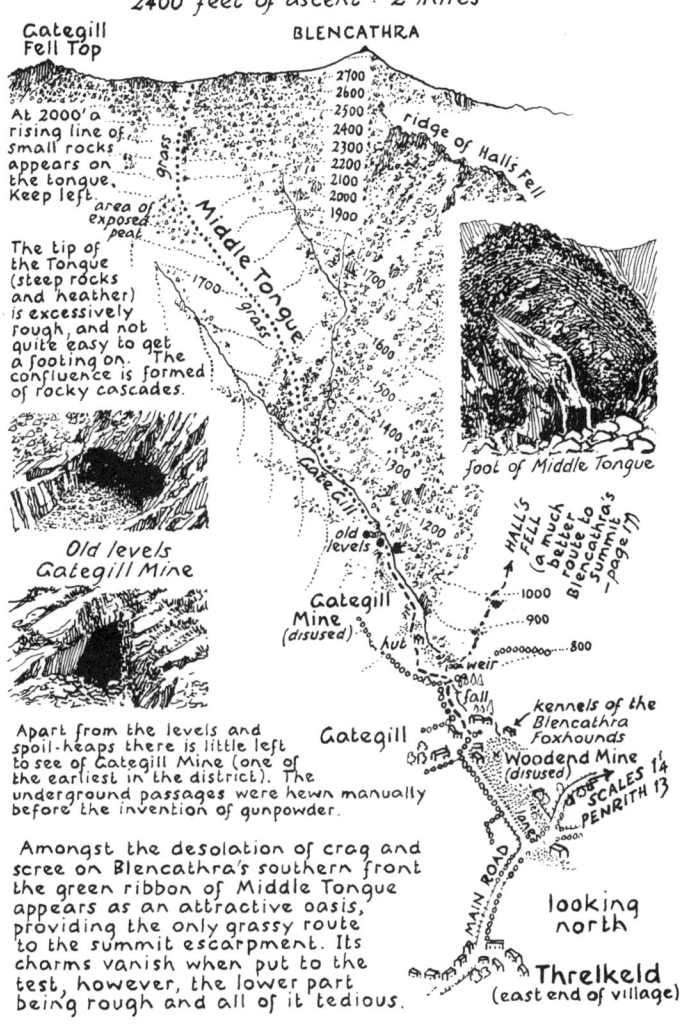

ASCENT FROM THRELKELD
via MIDDLE TONGUE
2400 feet of ascent : 2 miles

Gategill Fell Top

BLENCATHRA

ridge of Halls Fell

At 2000' a rising line of small rocks appears on the tongue. Keep left.

area of exposed peat

Middle Tongue

The tip of the Tongue (steep rocks and heather) is excessively rough, and not quite easy to get a footing on. The confluence is formed of rocky cascades.

foot of Middle Tongue

Old levels Gategill Mine

Gate Gill

old levels

Gategill Mine (disused)

HALLS FELL (a much better route to Blencathra's summit — page 17)

hut
weir
fall

Gategill

kennels of the Blencathra Foxhounds

Woodend Mine (disused)

SCALES 1¼
PENRITH 13

Apart from the levels and spoil-heaps there is little left to see of Gategill Mine (one of the earliest in the district). The underground passages were hewn manually before the invention of gunpowder.

Amongst the desolation of crag and scree on Blencathra's southern front the green ribbon of Middle Tongue appears as an attractive oasis, providing the only grassy route to the summit escarpment. Its charms vanish when put to the test, however, the lower part being rough and all of it tedious.

MAIN ROAD

looking north

Threlkeld
(east end of village)

Blencathra 17

ASCENT FROM THRELKELD
via HALL'S FELL
2400 feet of ascent : 2 miles

Gategill Fell Top

BLENCATHRA (Hallsfell Top)

Doddick Fell Top

The last half mile of the ridge, from 2000', is entirely delightful. This section, known as Narrow Edge with good reason, is a succession of low crags, with steps and gateways and towers of rock. A distinct track on grass is available for walkers — at first this keeps mostly on the Doddick side and later prefers the other, occasionally being forced along the crest. Care is needed in places but there are no difficulties. Scramblers will enjoy following the crest throughout.

care needed in traversing rockface by horizontal crack

From the ridge there are tremendous views down to Doddick and Gate Gills

Under ice and snow the ridge is for experts only

Doddick Fell and Scales Fell come into view

An enchanting track climbs the broad base of the fell. Unseen from below, this track reveals itself in the heather a few yards at a time, beckoning irresistibly upwards to the exciting ridge above.

Gategill Mine (disused)

Gategill — kennels (the home of the Blencathra Foxhounds)
Woodend Mine (disused)
spoil heaps → SCALES 1¼ PENRITH 13

THRELKELD HALL (from which Hall's Fell is named)

For active walkers and scramblers, this route is positively the finest way to any mountain-top in the district. It is direct, exhilarating, has glorious views, and (especially satisfying) scores a bulls-eye by leading unerringly to the summit-cairn.

looking north

Threlkeld (east end of village)

Blencathra 18

looking down the ridge from the summit

Hall's Fell

the middle section

the curve in the ridge

looking up the ridge to the summit

Blencathra 19

Doddick Gill — from 1350' on Doddick Fell. On the left is Hall's Fell, rising to Hall's Fell Top (the summit of Blencathra).

Blencathra 20

ASCENT FROM THRELKELD
via DODDICK GILL
2150 feet of ascent : 2¾ miles

From the confluence there is a simple escape to the ridge of Doddick Fell by contouring the slope on the right. This is the only easy exit from the gill.

On the map Doddick Gill appears to be an obvious and direct route — hence its inclusion in this book — but the truth is different. This is the roughest way of all. There is no comfort in it. Almost every step has to be planned. In the easy lower section, some dodging from one side to the other is necessary; around the big bend the east bank is followed, using heather as handholds, until a crag stops this tortuous progress, whereupon continue along the slabby bed of the stream. At the confluence an intimidating 1000-foot facade of chaotic crags and scree appears ahead. Go up the ravine to the left but get out of it before the walls narrow. Climb the bilberry slope alongside, returning to the gully in its grassy upper section. A little chimney leads up to the ridge of Hall's Fell exactly at the pinnacle. Thence the route goes up the arête to the summit.

looking north

- Hard scrambling throughout.
- For tough guys only.
- Not for solitary walkers.
- Not to be used for descent
- A route to commend heartily to one's worst enemy.

Blencathra 21

ASCENT FROM SCALES
via DODDICK FELL
2150 feet of ascent : 1¾ miles

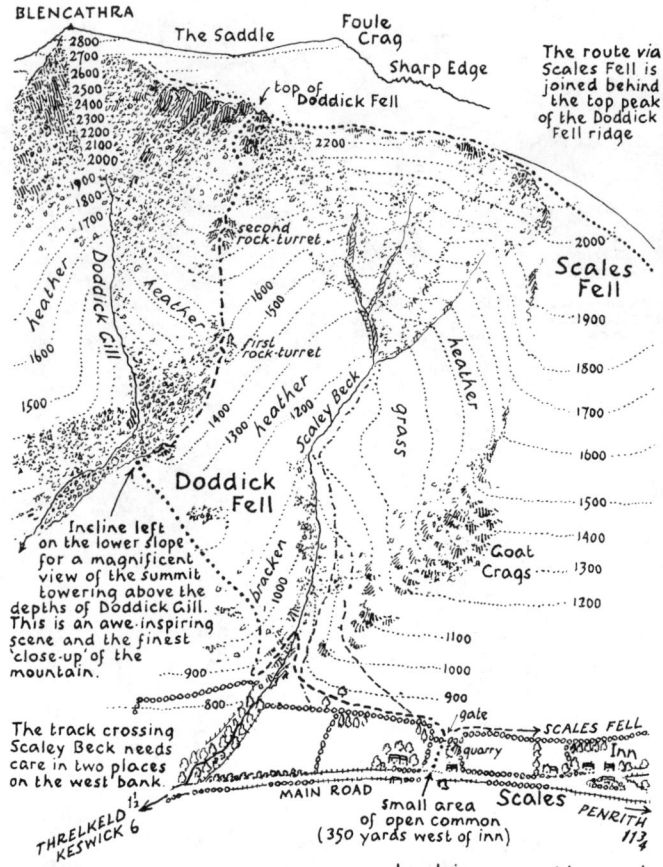

The route via Scales Fell is joined behind the top peak of the Doddick Fell ridge

Incline left on the lower slope for a magnificent view of the summit towering above the depths of Doddick Gill. This is an awe-inspiring scene and the finest 'close-up' of the mountain.

The track crossing Scaley Beck needs care in two places on the west bank.

small area of open common (350 yards west of inn)

THRELKELD 1½
KESWICK 6

PENRITH 11¾

looking north-west

It is usual, from Scales, to ascend by way of Scales Fell, a very popular route, but better by far is the more direct ridge of Doddick Fell, a grand climb, quite easy, with striking views of the objective. This is a splendid way to the top of Blencathra.

Blencathra 22

looking up to Doddick Fell Top from 1450'

Doddick Fell

looking down the ridge from Doddick Fell Top

Blencathra 23

Scaley Beck

Doddick Fell is on the left, rising to the peak of Doddick Fell Top. Blencathra's summit is seen in the top left corner.

Blencathra 24

ASCENT FROM SCALES
via SCALEY BECK
2150 feet of ascent : 2 miles

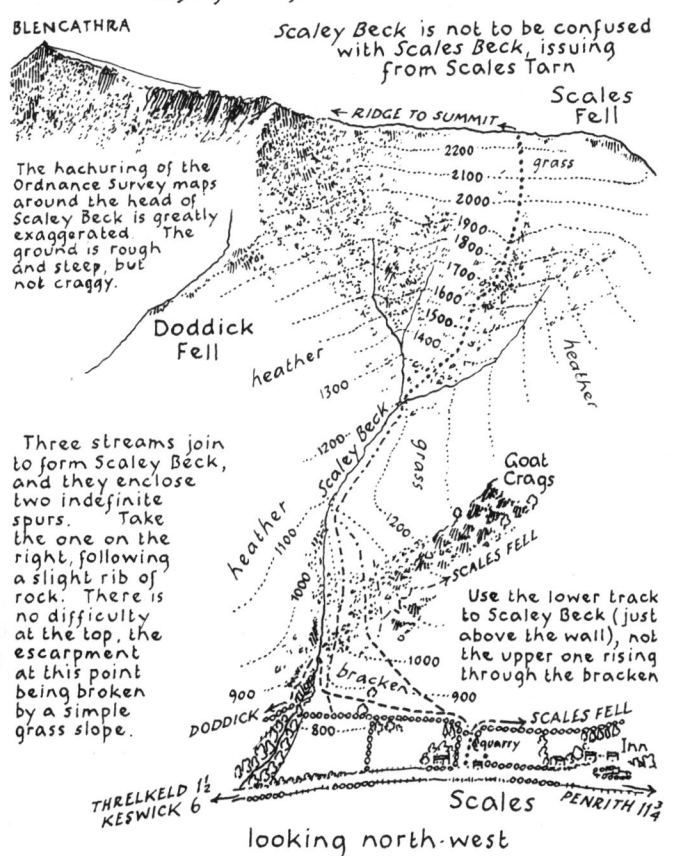

BLENCATHRA

Scaley Beck is not to be confused with Scales Beck, issuing from Scales Tarn

← RIDGE TO SUMMIT →

Scales Fell

grass

The hachuring of the Ordnance Survey maps around the head of Scaley Beck is greatly exaggerated. The ground is rough and steep, but not craggy.

Doddick Fell

heather

heather

Three streams join to form Scaley Beck, and they enclose two indefinite spurs. Take the one on the right, following a slight rib of rock. There is no difficulty at the top, the escarpment at this point being broken by a simple grass slope.

heather

Scaley Beck

grass

Goat Crags

SCALES FELL

Use the lower track to Scaley Beck (just above the wall), not the upper one rising through the bracken

bracken

DODDICK

SCALES FELL

quarry

Inn

THRELKELD 1½
KESWICK 6

Scales

PENRITH 11¾

looking north-west

Of the various watercourses on the south front Scaley Beck is the most practicable as a route of ascent, being nowhere too rough to stop progress; the exit, too, is easy. There is little of interest, however, and the route falls far short of that via the adjacent ridge of Doddick Fell.

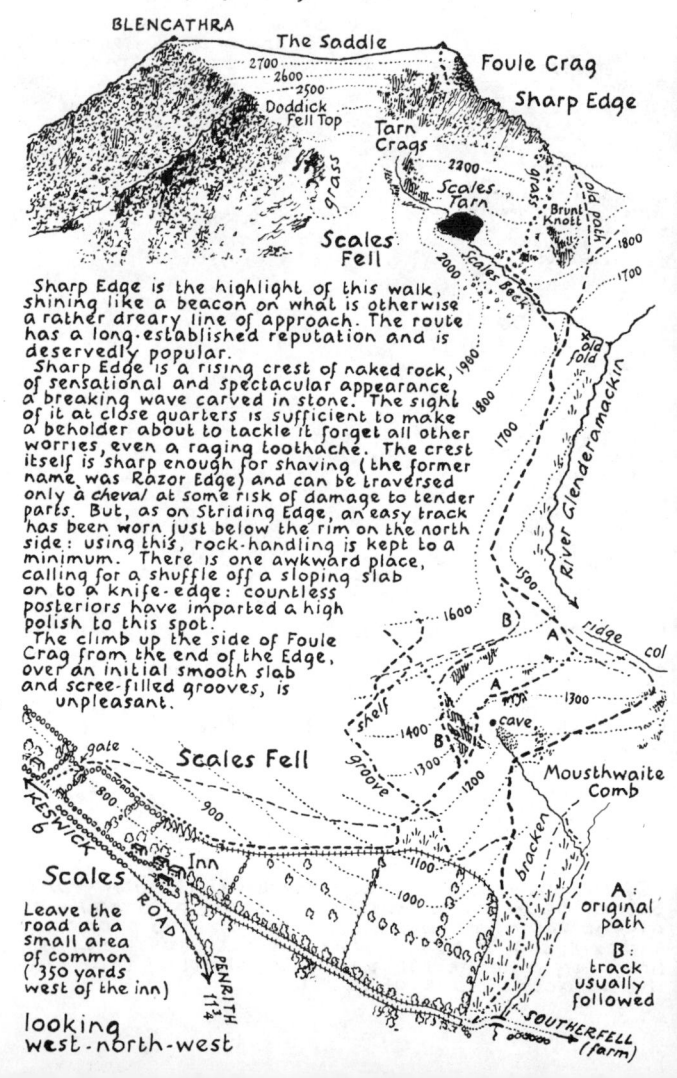

Blencathra 25

ASCENT FROM SCALES
via SHARP EDGE
2250 feet of ascent : 2¾ miles

Sharp Edge is the highlight of this walk, shining like a beacon on what is otherwise a rather dreary line of approach. The route has a long-established reputation and is deservedly popular.

Sharp Edge is a rising crest of naked rock, of sensational and spectacular appearance, a breaking wave carved in stone. The sight of it at close quarters is sufficient to make a beholder about to tackle it forget all other worries, even a raging toothache. The crest itself is sharp enough for shaving (the former name was Razor Edge) and can be traversed only *a cheval* at some risk of damage to tender parts. But, as on Striding Edge, an easy track has been worn just below the rim on the north side: using this, rock-handling is kept to a minimum. There is one awkward place, calling for a shuffle off a sloping slab on to a knife-edge: countless posteriors have imparted a high polish to this spot.

The climb up the side of Foule Crag from the end of the Edge, over an initial smooth slab and scree-filled grooves, is unpleasant.

Leave the road at a small area of common (350 yards west of the inn)

looking west-north-west

A: original path
B: track usually followed

Blencathra 26

looking down from Foule Crag

looking east along the Edge (the 'awkward place' in the foreground)

Sharp Edge

the approach from Scales Tarn

from Scales Tarn

Foule Crag
Sharp Edge
Brunt Knott

the path from Scales

Blencathra 27

ASCENT FROM SCALES
via SCALES FELL
2150 feet of ascent : 2¼ miles

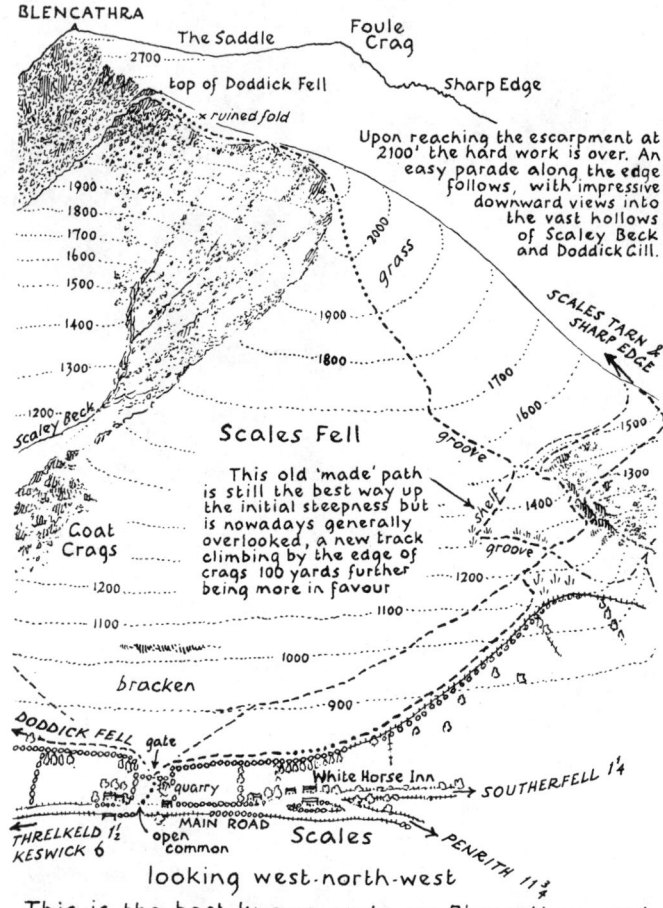

BLENCATHRA — The Saddle — Foule Crag
2700
top of Doddick Fell — Sharp Edge
× ruined fold

Upon reaching the escarpment at 2100' the hard work is over. An easy parade along the edge follows, with impressive downward views into the vast hollows of Scaley Beck and Doddick Gill.

SCALES TARN & SHARP EDGE

Scaley Beck

Scales Fell

This old 'made' path is still the best way up the initial steepness but is nowadays generally overlooked, a new track climbing by the edge of crags 100 yards further being more in favour

shelf
groove

Coat Crags

bracken

DODDICK FELL — gate
quarry — White Horse Inn → SOUTHERFELL 1¼
THRELKELD 1½   open   MAIN ROAD   Scales   → PENRITH 11¾
KESWICK 6   common

looking west·north·west

This is the best-known route up Blencathra, and has been in common use for over a century. Even so, the tough grass of Scales Fell has resisted the formation of a continuous track. The climb, tedious up to 2000', becomes excellent in its later stages.

Blencathra 28

ASCENT FROM MUNGRISDALE
2250 feet of ascent : 4 miles

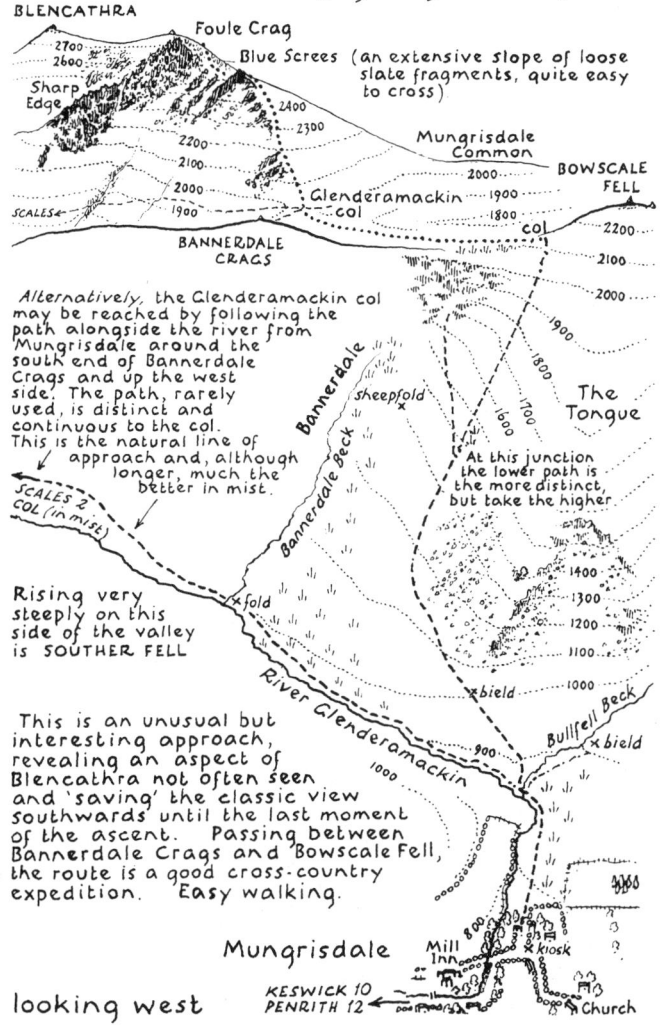

BLENCATHRA Foule Crag
Blue Screes (an extensive slope of loose slate fragments, quite easy to cross)
Sharp Edge
Mungrisdale Common
BOWSCALE FELL
Glenderamackin col
SCALES
BANNERDALE CRAGS
col

Alternatively, the Glenderamackin col may be reached by following the path alongside the river from Mungrisdale around the south end of Bannerdale Crags and up the west side. The path, rarely used, is distinct and continuous to the col. This is the natural line of approach and, although longer, much the better in mist.

Bannerdale
sheepfold
The Tongue

At this junction the lower path is the more distinct, but take the higher

SCALES 2
COL (in mist)

Bannerdale Beck

Rising very steeply on this side of the valley is SOUTHER FELL

×fold

×bield

River Glenderamackin

Bullfell Beck
×bield

This is an unusual but interesting approach, revealing an aspect of Blencathra not often seen and 'saving' the classic view southwards until the last moment of the ascent. Passing between Bannerdale Crags and Bowscale Fell, the route is a good cross-country expedition. Easy walking.

Mungrisdale
Mill Inn
×kiosk
KESWICK 10
PENRITH 12
Church

looking west

Blencathra 29

THE VIEW

N — NE

CARROCK FELL 3¾
BOWSCALE FELL 2

top of Foule Crag
white cross
The Saddle
SCALES VIA SHARP EDGE
east ridge of Bowscale Fell
SCALES VIA SCALES FELL
BANNERDALE CRAGS 1¼

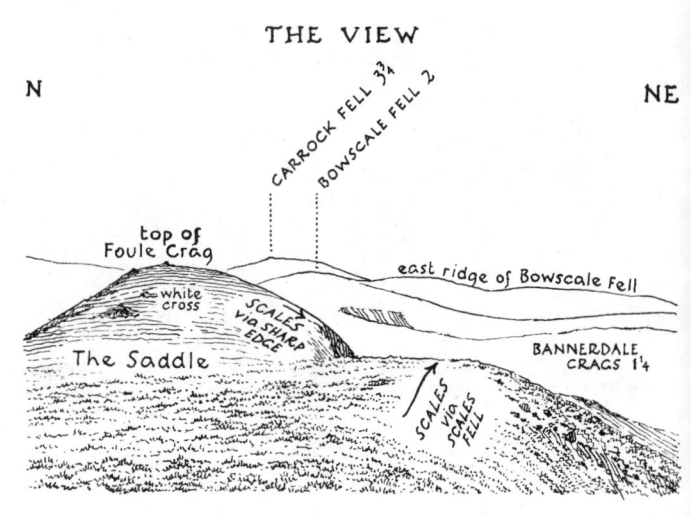

THE SUMMIT

The summit is effectively poised above the abyss, precisely at the point where the ridge of Hall's Fell comes up out of the depths to a jutting headland. The summit is, in fact, known as Hallsfell Top. Much slaty stone is lying exposed here, but it is small stuff unsuitable for building imposing cairns, and nothing marks the highest point but a poor untidy heap of rubble; on occasion attempts are made to give the thing some shape and dignity but until somebody carries up a few decent-sized blocks the cairn will continue to disappoint by its insignificance.

The summit is windswept and shelterless and lacks a natural seat, but a few yards down Hall's Fell on the left the lee-side of a small outcrop usually cuts off the prevailing wind.

The excellent turf along the top deserves special mention.

continued

Blencathra 30

THE VIEW

NE E

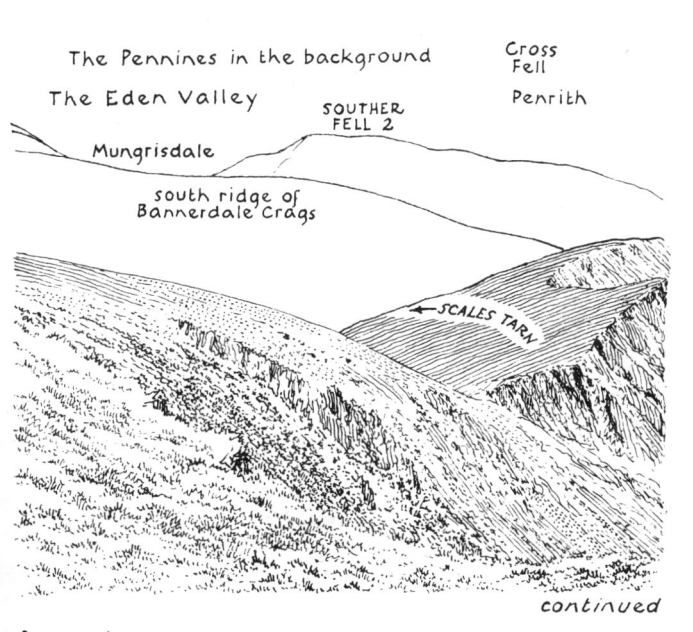

The Pennines in the background — Cross Fell
The Eden Valley — Penrith
Mungrisdale — SOUTHER FELL 2
south ridge of Bannerdale Crags
← SCALES TARN

continued

Descents:

The best *ascents* are by the narrow ridges —— Hall's Fell, Sharp Edge, Doddick Fell and Gategill Fell, *in that order* —— but the best routes of *descent* are those tedious in ascent: Blease Fell, Scales Fell, Glenderamackin col and Roughten Gill, *in that order*. The latter two are roundabout and not suitable in mist, but Blease Fell and Scales Fell, lying at opposite ends of the well-defined summit escarpment, are simple ways off in any weather. The narrow ridges will be found bumpy going down, although Hall's Fell and Doddick Fell are quite practicable and enjoyable, but all may become dangerous under ice and snow.   The gills and ravines on the southern front are much too rough to be considered for descent no matter how good the weather.

Blencathra 31

THE VIEW

continued
E

(panorama labels: GREAT MELL FELL 4½, LITTLE MELL FELL 6½, GOWBARROW FELL 6½, LOADPOT HILL 10¼, WETHER HILL 10½)

SE

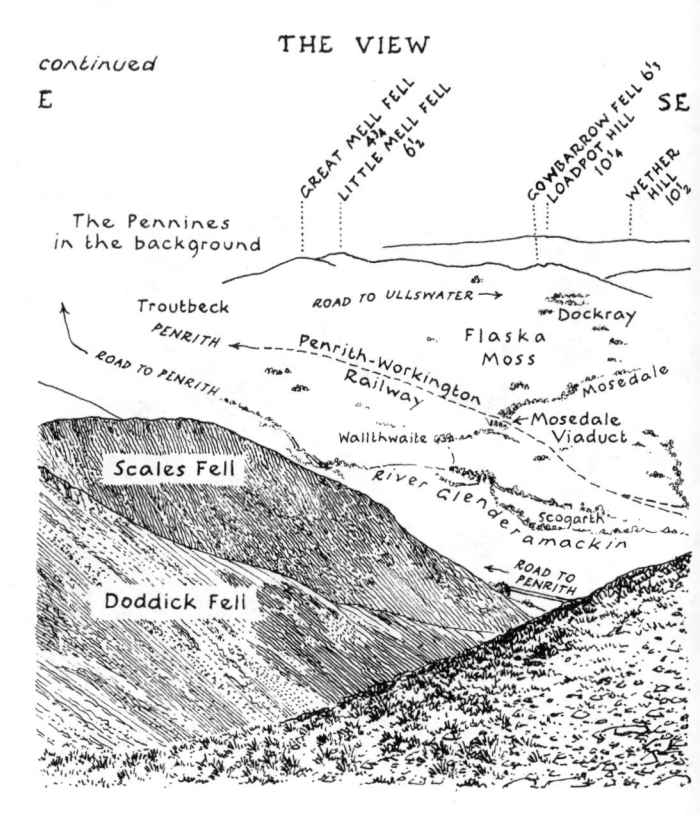

The Pennines in the background

Troutbeck · ROAD TO ULLSWATER → · Dockray
PENRITH ← Penrith-Workington Railway · Flaska Moss
ROAD TO PENRITH · Mosedale
Wallthwaite · Mosedale Viaduct
Scales Fell · River Glenderamackin
Doddick Fell · Scoggarth
ROAD TO PENRITH

Mosedale....

The Mosedale appearing in the view above is not the Mosedale mentioned elsewhere in this book and situated at the foot of Carrock Fell. There are, in fact, six valleys of this name (signifying *desolation, dreariness*) in Lakeland and a pastime that might be adopted to fill in a few minutes while waiting for the rain to stop is to find them all on the 1" Ordnance Survey map of the district (one of them is spelt *Moasdale*). If, having done this, it still looks like raining for ever, make a list of all the different names on the map in which "thwaite" (*a clearing*) appears: this occupation will fill in the rest of the day until bedtime. On the 1" Tourist Map there are 81 *different*, many of them recurring. Enthusiastic thwaite-spotters will find several others on larger-scale maps.

Blencathra 32

THE VIEW

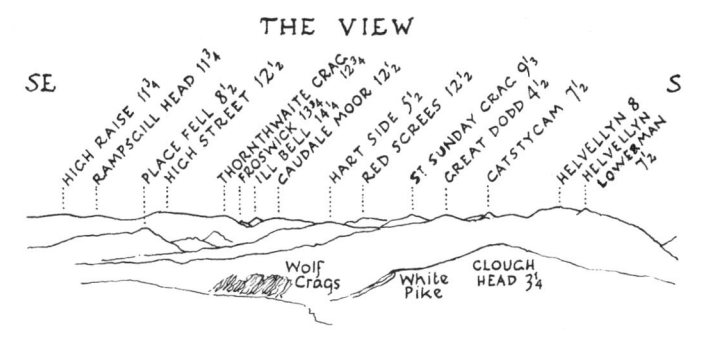

SE — HIGH RAISE 11¾, RAMPSGILL HEAD 11¾, PLACE FELL 8½, HIGH STREET 12½, THORNTHWAITE CRAG 12¾, FROSWICK 13¾, ILL BELL 14¼, CAUDALE MOOR 12½, HART SIDE 5½, RED SCREES 12½, ST. SUNDAY CRAG 9⅓, GREAT DODD 4½, CATSTYCAM 7½, HELVELLYN 8, HELVELLYN LOWER MAN 7½ — S

Wolf Crags — White Pike — CLOUGH HEAD 3¼

Threlkeld Common

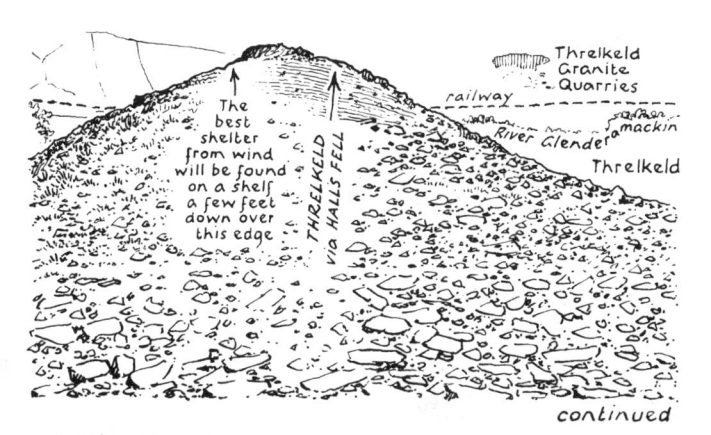

Threlkeld Granite Quarries
railway
River Glenderamackin
Threlkeld

The best shelter from wind will be found on a shelf a few feet down over this edge

THRELKELD VIA HALLS FELL

continued

at Threlkeld....

- Look over both parapets of Threlkeld Bridge. Two streams, the River Glenderamackin and St. John's Beck, at this point unite, passing under the bridge individually but emerging as one: the River Greta. The bridge is built over the confluence.
- Walk up the lane signposted Wescoe for 200 yards to the entrance to Riddings, where excellent effigies of a fox and a hound surmount the gateposts. The Blencathra pack was formerly kennelled at Riddings, but is now at Gategill.
- Visit the little glen of Kilnhow Beck. A pleasant path starts near the Horse and Farrier and proceeds upstream to the open fell at Blease Gill with the help of footbridges. This sylvan dell is not publicised and is a charming surprise.

Blencathra 33

THE VIEW

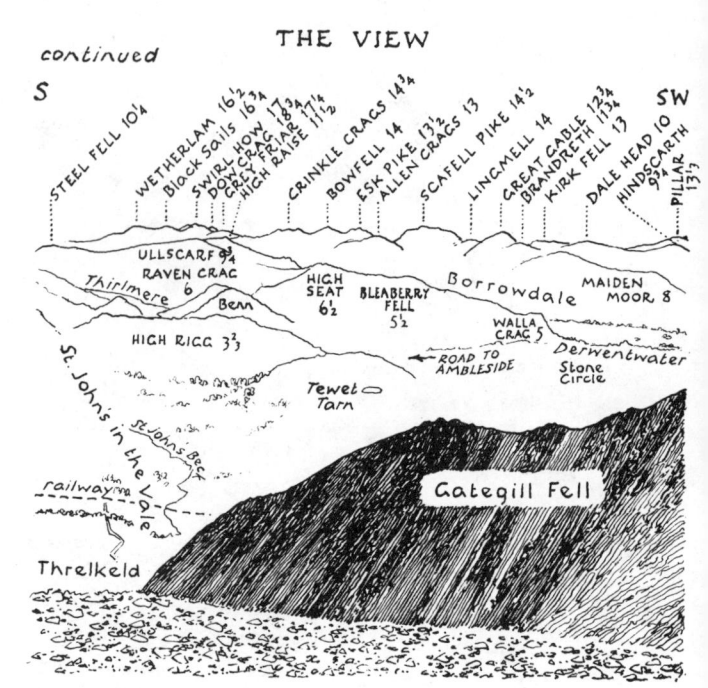

continued

S — STEEL FELL 10¼, WETHERLAM 16½, Block Sails 16¼, SWIRL HOW 17, DOW CRAG 18¾, GREY FRIAR 11¼, HIGH RAISE 11½, CRINKLE CRAGS 14¾, BOWFELL 14, ESK PIKE 13½, ALLEN CRAGS 13, SCAFELL PIKE 14½, LINGMELL 14, GREAT GABLE 12¾, BRANDRETH 11¾, KIRK FELL 13, DALE HEAD 10, HINDSCARTH 9¾, PILLAR 13⅓ — SW

ULLSCARF 9¾, RAVEN CRAG 6, Thirlmere, Bern, HIGH SEAT 6½, BLEABERRY FELL 5½, Borrowdale, MAIDEN MOOR 8, HIGH RIGG 3⅔, WALLA CRAG 5, Derwentwater, ROAD TO AMBLESIDE, Tewet Tarn, Stone Circle

St. John's in the Vale, railway, Threlkeld, Gategill Fell

The White Cross

In view from the summit is a landmark that has aroused the curiosity of visitors for a great many years: a collection of white crystallised stones of high quartz content, laid on the grass in the form of a cross on the easy rise to the top of Foule Crag, north of the Saddle.

This cross owes its existence to the industry of Harold Robinson of Threlkeld. Formerly there was a very small cross of stones here (locally ascribed as a memorial to a walker who lost his life on a rough slope adjacent) and Mr. Robinson, an enthusiastic lone hill-wanderer who has climbed his favourite Blencathra hundreds of times, collected more stones (veins of quartzite occur in the native slate nearby) and extended the cross to its present size of 16' by 10' during a succession of visits from 1945 onwards.

A much smaller but similar white cross on the southern slope of the Saddle is more recent, and the work of persons unknown.

Blencathra 34

THE VIEW

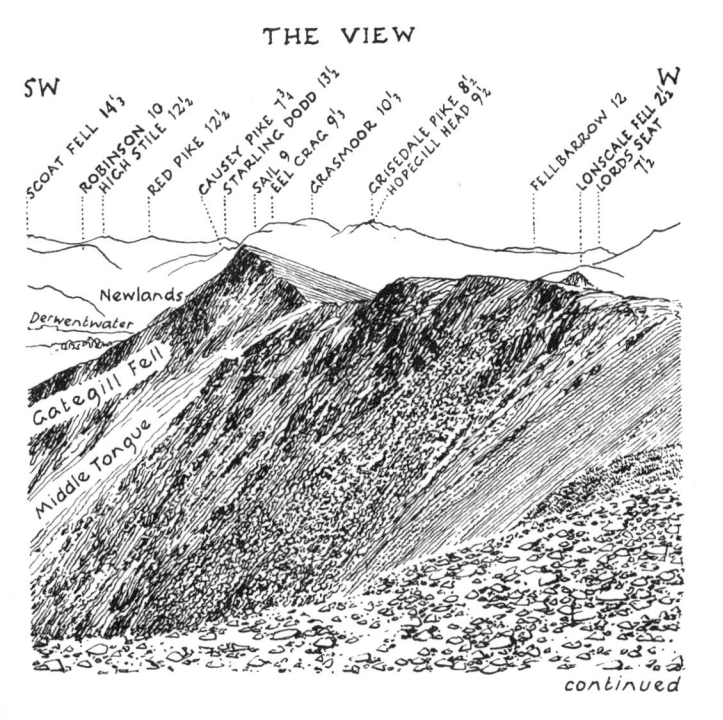

SW — SCOAT FELL 14½, ROBINSON 10, HIGH STILE 12½, RED PIKE 12½, CAUSEY PIKE 7¼, STARLING DODD 13½, SAIL 9, EEL CRAG 9½, GRASMOOR 10½, GRISEDALE PIKE 8½, HOPEGILL HEAD 9½, FELLBARROW 12, LONSCALE FELL 2½, LORDS SEAT 7½ — W

Newlands
Derwentwater
Gategill Fell
Middle Tongue

continued

Blencathra's old mines

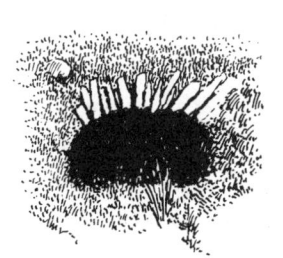

Blencathra has been mined fairly extensively and a variety of ores extracted from workings in the valleys of the Glenderaterra and Glenderamackin and from the adjacent and interlinked Gategill and Woodend mines, the debris of which is still very conspicuous in the Threlkeld landscape. All the mines are now closed, but within living memory were in production and prospering, and finding work for a labour force of 100.

Illustrated is an old level (a little beauty) at the northern workings of the Glenderaterra Mine, leading to a copper vein. The warning must be repeated that disused mine levels are unsafe because of flooding and collapse and often open into vertical pits.

Blencathra 35

THE VIEW

continued

W — SKIDDAW LITTLE MAN 3½ — SKIDDAW 4 — BAKESTALL 4 — BINSEY 7½ — NW

path to Skiddaw from Keswick

Skiddaw Forest

Skiddaw House

Little Calva

THRELKELD via BLEASE FELL

RIDGE ROUTE

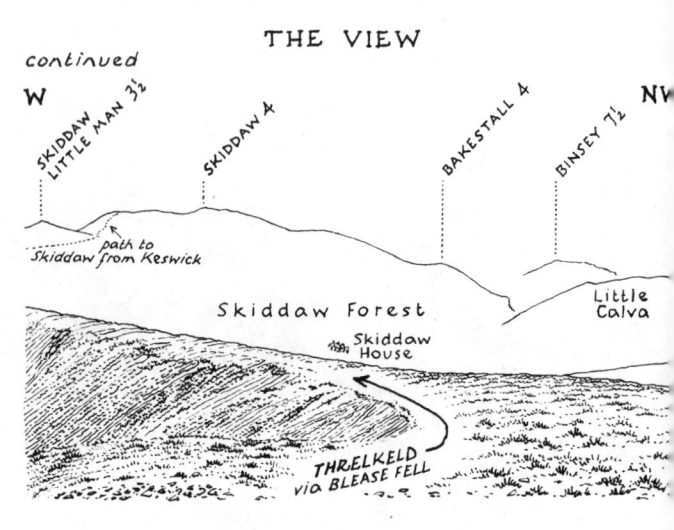

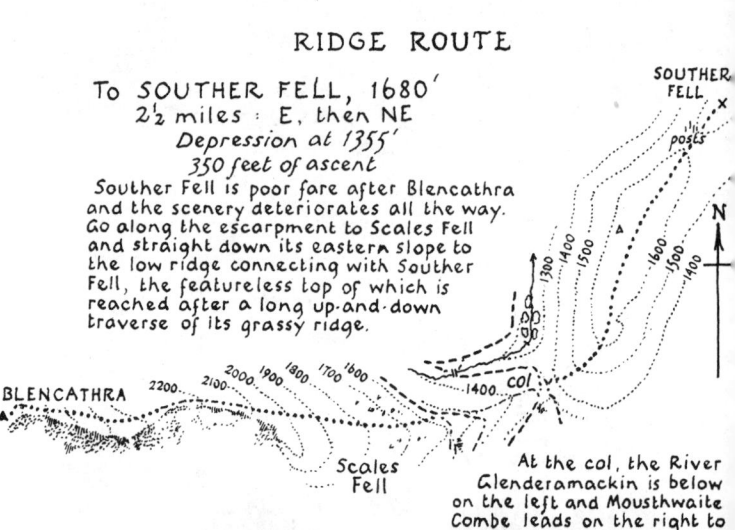

To SOUTHER FELL, 1680'
2½ miles : E, then NE
Depression at 1355'
350 feet of ascent

Souther Fell is poor fare after Blencathra and the scenery deteriorates all the way. Go along the escarpment to Scales Fell and straight down its eastern slope to the low ridge connecting with Souther Fell, the featureless top of which is reached after a long up-and-down traverse of its grassy ridge.

SOUTHER FELL
posts
N

BLENCATHRA
2200, 2100, 2000, 1900, 1800, 1700, 1600
1400 col
Scales Fell

HALF A MILE

At the col, the River Glenderamackin is below on the left and Mousthwaite Combe leads on the right to the fields of Scales. There are many tracks hereabouts.

Blencathra 36

THE VIEW

NW — GREAT CALVA 3 — MUNGRISDALE COMMON 1¾ — KNOTT 3¾ — Great Lingy Hill 4 — Hare Stones 4¼ — HIGH PIKE 4½ — N

The Scottish hills and Solway Firth in the background

Snab — Coomb Height

The Valley of the Caldew

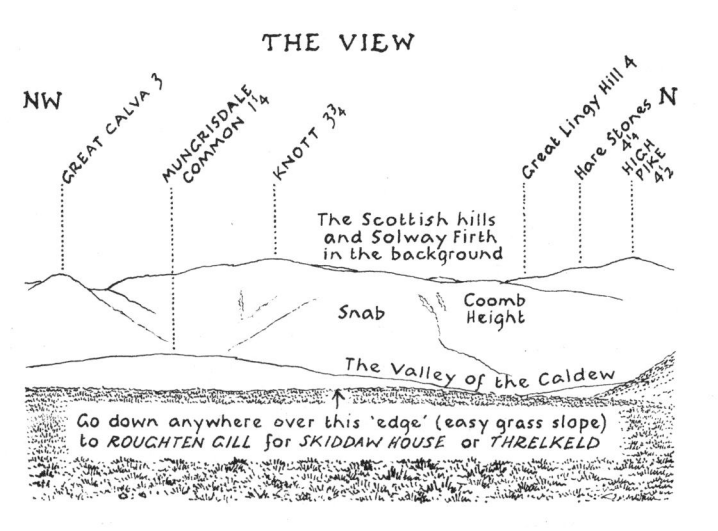

Go down anywhere over this 'edge' (easy grass slope) to *ROUGHTEN GILL* for *SKIDDAW HOUSE* or *THRELKELD*

RIDGE ROUTE

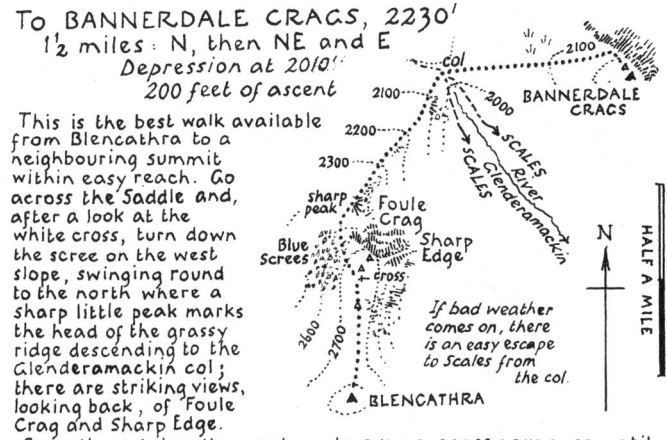

To BANNERDALE CRAGS, 2230'
1½ miles: N, then NE and E
Depression at 2010'
200 feet of ascent

This is the best walk available from Blencathra to a neighbouring summit within easy reach. Go across the Saddle and, after a look at the white cross, turn down the scree on the west slope, swinging round to the north where a sharp little peak marks the head of the grassy ridge descending to the Glenderamackin col; there are striking views, looking back, of Foule Crag and Sharp Edge.

If bad weather comes on, there is an easy escape to Scales from the col.

HALF A MILE

Cross the col, heading eastwards over a grassy expanse until halted by the edge of Bannerdale Crags, then turn to the right to reach the summit.

Bowscale Fell 2306'

from the shooting-box on Great Lingy Hill

CARROCK FELL
▲

Mosedale ●
Bowscale ●
▲ BOWSCALE FELL
●
Mungrisdale
▲ BANNERDALE
   CRAGS
▲ BLENCATHRA

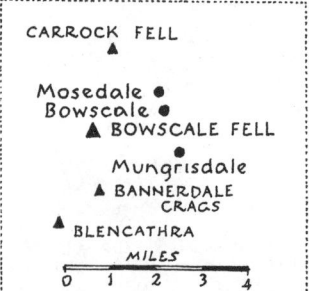

MILES
0 1 2 3 4

Point 1876' on the east ridge

Bowscale Fell 2

NATURAL FEATURES

The Caldew is the greatest watercourse among the northern fells, and for three miles before the river escapes to open country it is bounded and deflected considerably to the north by broad grassy buttresses descending from the domed summit of Bowscale Fell, a fine eminence on the eastern perimeter of the group. Southwards a high link connects with Blencathra and Bannerdale Crags, and an undistinguished moorland sprawls away to Skiddaw Forest in the west. It is only from the valley pastures to the east that Bowscale Fell really exhibits the proportions of a mountain, this view revealing two lofty ridges that rise steeply above the white cottages of Mungrisdale. The finest feature of the fell, however, is the craggy combe and tarn on the north flank, overlooking the Caldew: a scene of utter solitude that can be seen today just as the glacier left it in ages past.

A topographical curiosity may be noted: it is more apparent from a study of the map than from a study of the ground. The Eden-Derwent watershed passes over the summit; the odd thing about it is that the *western* slopes feed the Eden, which is to the east, and the *eastern* effluent finds its way into the Derwent, a river far beyond the mountain barrier to the west.

A glacial combe.....

    tiered crags carved by ice; silent waters embanked by moraines; scattered rocks in the wake of the departed glacier........

       ..... *Bowscale Tarn from the north*

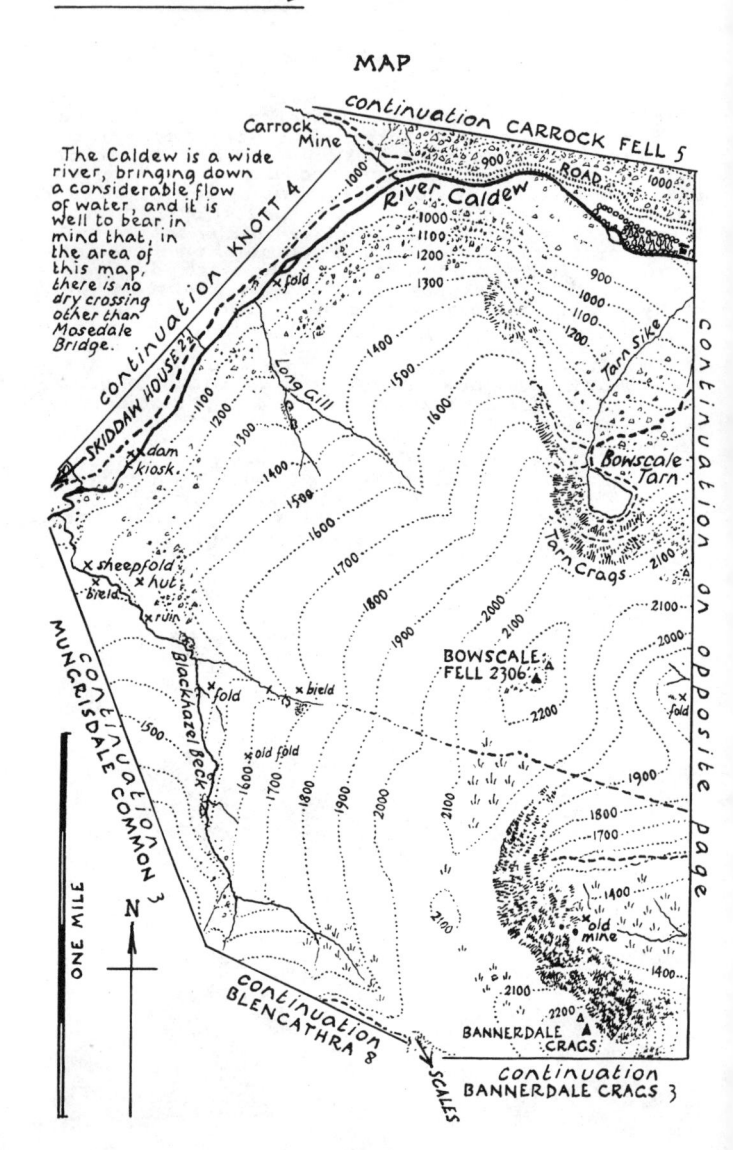

Bowscale Fell 3

MAP

The Caldew is a wide river, bringing down a considerable flow of water, and it is well to bear in mind that, in the area of this map, there is no dry crossing other than Mosedale Bridge.

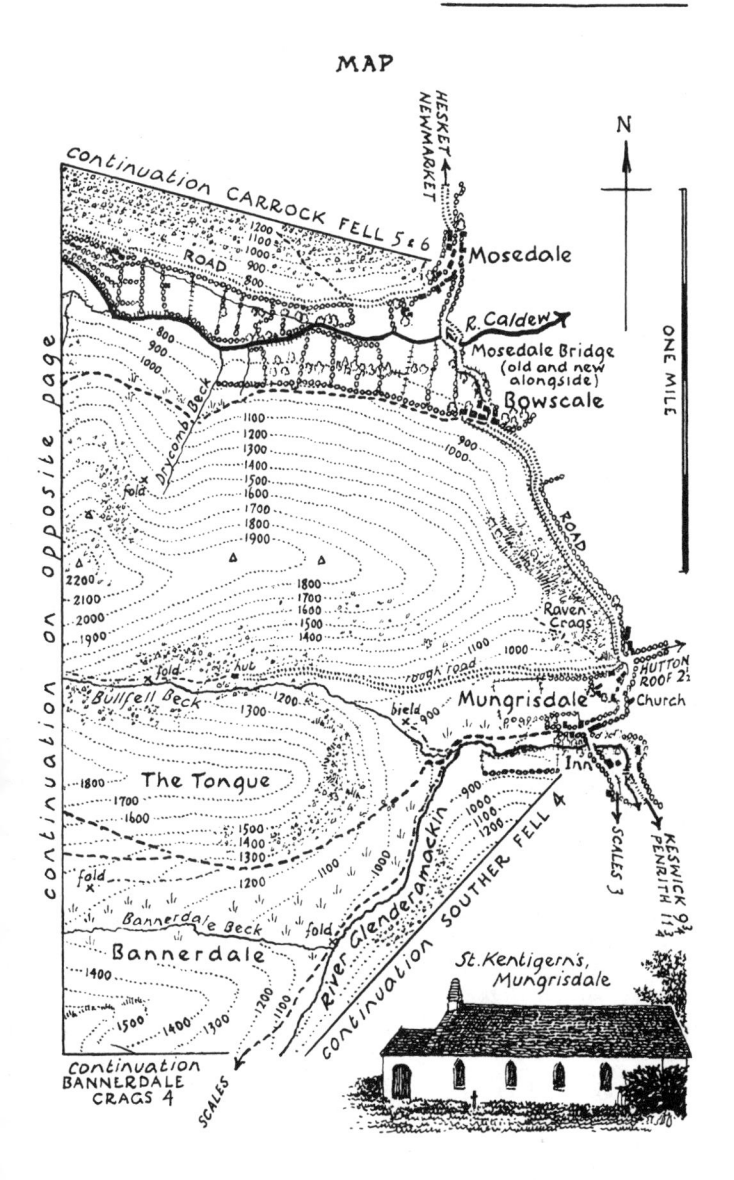

Bowscale Fell 4

MAP

Bowscale Fell 5

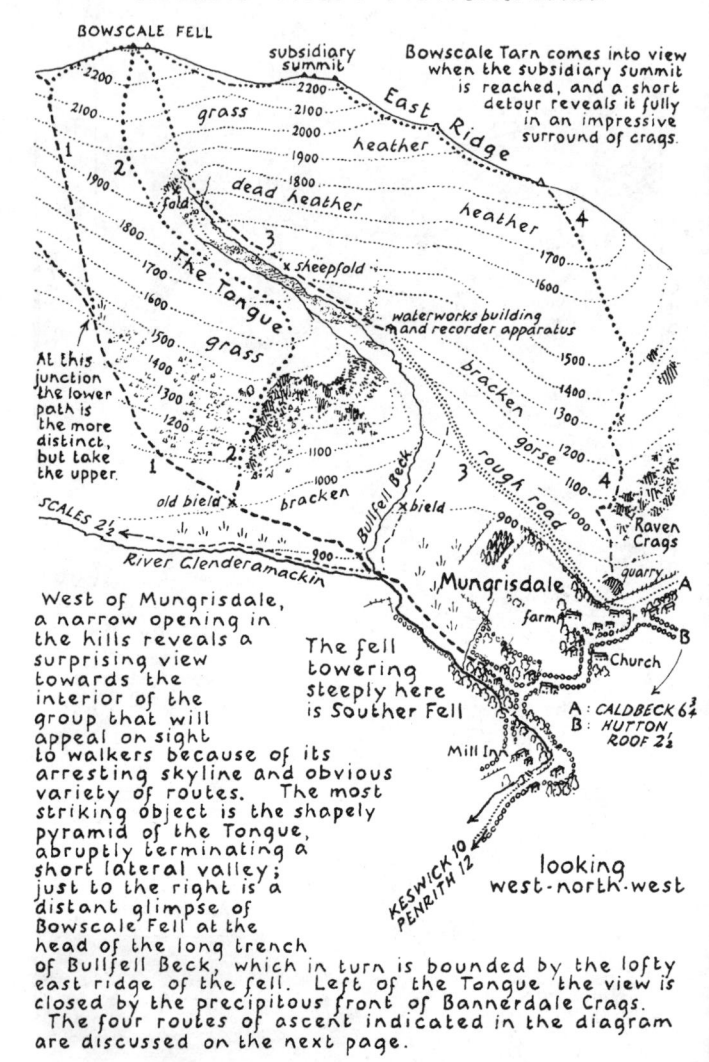

ASCENT FROM MUNGRISDALE

BOWSCALE FELL
subsidiary summit
East Ridge

Bowscale Tarn comes into view when the subsidiary summit is reached, and a short detour reveals it fully in an impressive surround of crags.

grass
heather
dead heather
fold
sheepfold
heather
The Tongue grass
waterworks building and recorder apparatus
bracken
rough road
gorse

At this junction the lower path is the more distinct, but take the upper.

old bield
bracken
Bullfell Beck
bield
Raven Crags
quarry

SCALES 2½
River Glenderamackin
Mungrisdale
farm
Church

A: CALDBECK 6¾
B: HUTTON ROOF 2½

West of Mungrisdale, a narrow opening in the hills reveals a surprising view towards the interior of the group that will appeal on sight to walkers because of its arresting skyline and obvious variety of routes. The most striking object is the shapely pyramid of the Tongue, abruptly terminating a short lateral valley; just to the right is a distant glimpse of Bowscale Fell at the head of the long trench of Bullfell Beck, which in turn is bounded by the lofty east ridge of the fell. Left of the Tongue the view is closed by the precipitous front of Bannerdale Crags.

The four routes of ascent indicated in the diagram are discussed on the next page.

The fell towering steeply here is Souther Fell

Mill In

KESWICK 10
PENRITH 12

looking west-north-west

Bowscale Fell 6

ASCENT FROM MUNGRISDALE

← *Diagram on opposite page*

ROUTE 1 : This is the least obvious (it seems to be aiming for Bannerdale Crags) but the easiest route; in fact, the easiest route to any summit over 2000' in Lakeland. It makes use of an old bridle-path skirting the south flank of the Tongue and rising to the skyline of Bowscale Fell only a simple five-minutes' walk from the top. *1450': 2¼ miles*

ROUTE 2 : Leave Route 1 at a ruined bield in the bracken and scramble steeply alongside the rising escarpment of the Tongue. Once above this a level ridge continues to the easy final slope of Bowscale Fell. *1470': 2¼ miles.*

ROUTE 3 : Bullfell Beck offers a direct route, but is deeply enclosed and uninteresting. Its one merit is the shelter it provides in stormy or windy weather. *1450': 2¼ miles.*

ROUTE 4 : Best of all is the east ridge. Climbing starts at once over a pleasant alp of gorse and bracken and grey rock, after which there is a gentle rise to the heathery ridge, a grouse moor, and two further undulations before the top of the fell is reached. The second of these undulations is big enough and high enough (over 2200') to be regarded as a subsidiary summit. From its slopes Bowscale Tarn is in view below. This is the only route on which the tarn is seen. A prominent cairn on a spur north of this subsidiary summit gives a fine view of Mosedale and the Caldew Valley. *1550': 2½ miles*

Routes 1 and 2 leave Mungrisdale along a short lane with a telephone kiosk at the corner. Routes 3 and 4 start along a rough lane (gated) at a signposted road-junction at the north end of the village.

For the best 'round tour' ascend by Route 4 and descend by Route 1. Route 4 follows the Eden-Derwent watershed exactly.

*Bowscale Tarn and moraine
from the slopes of the subsidiary summit*

Bowscale Fell 7

ASCENT FROM BOWSCALE
1550 feet of ascent : 2½ miles

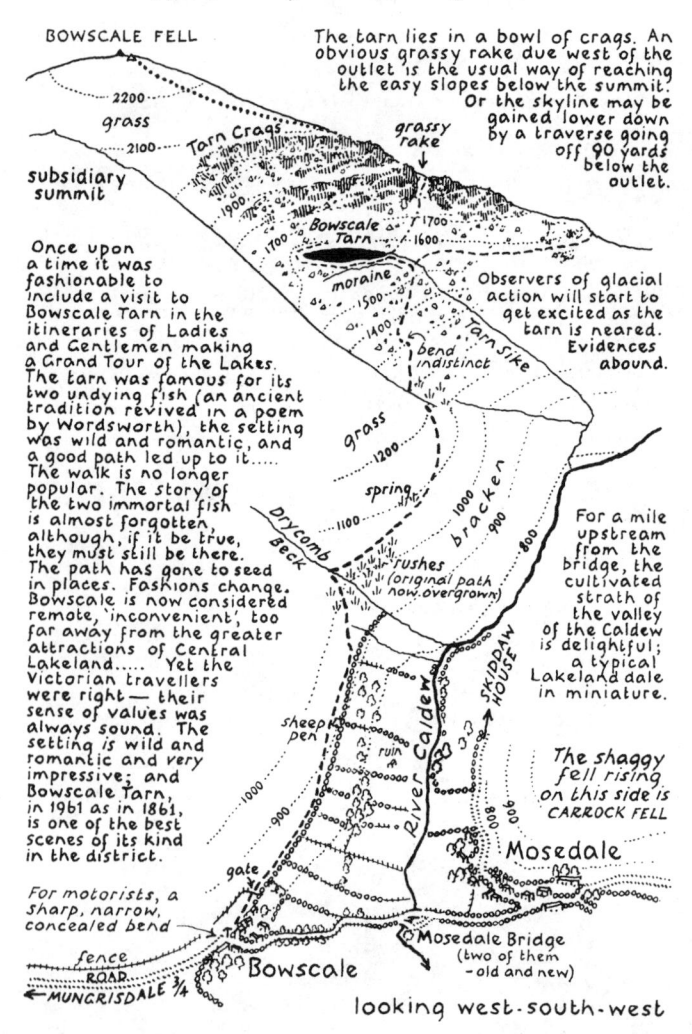

BOWSCALE FELL

The tarn lies in a bowl of crags. An obvious grassy rake due west of the outlet is the usual way of reaching the easy slopes below the summit. Or the skyline may be gained lower down by a traverse going off 90 yards below the outlet.

subsidiary summit

Once upon a time it was fashionable to include a visit to Bowscale Tarn in the itineraries of Ladies and Gentlemen making a Grand Tour of the Lakes. The tarn was famous for its two undying fish (an ancient tradition revived in a poem by Wordsworth), the setting was wild and romantic, and a good path led up to it..... The walk is no longer popular. The story of the two immortal fish is almost forgotten, although, if it be true, they must still be there. The path has gone to seed in places. Fashions change. Bowscale is now considered remote, 'inconvenient', too far away from the greater attractions of Central Lakeland..... Yet the Victorian travellers were right — their sense of values was always sound. The setting is wild and romantic and very impressive; and Bowscale Tarn, in 1961 as in 1861, is one of the best scenes of its kind in the district.

Observers of glacial action will start to get excited as the tarn is neared. Evidences abound.

For a mile upstream from the bridge, the cultivated strath of the valley of the Caldew is delightful; a typical Lakeland dale in miniature.

The shaggy fell rising on this side is CARROCK FELL

For motorists, a sharp, narrow, concealed bend

← MUNGRISDALE ¾

Bowscale

Mosedale

Mosedale Bridge (two of them – old and new)

looking west-south-west

Bowscale Fell 8

THE SUMMIT

What appears from a distance to be a big square cairn turns out on closer enquiry to be a roughly-built shelter. A truer cairn stands 100 yards north-east, at a slightly lower level, and points the way to Bowscale Tarn (which is out of sight) and the east ridge. The top of the fell is grassy except for a liberal scattering of small stones on the highest part.

DESCENTS: There are no paths on the top but all routes off are easy. If Bowscale Tarn is to be visited, keep the descending rim of Tarn Crags on the right until a grassy strip can be seen going down to the tarn's outlet — use this.

In bad weather, Mungrisdale is the best place to make for; it can be reached comfortably in an hour. Aim south from the summit to join the path across the col: this may not be distinct at the point reached — keep a lookout for upright stones.

The subsidiary summit

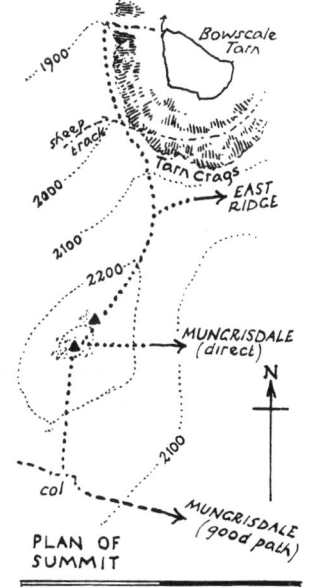

PLAN OF SUMMIT

HALF A MILE

Bowscale Fell 9

RIDGE ROUTE

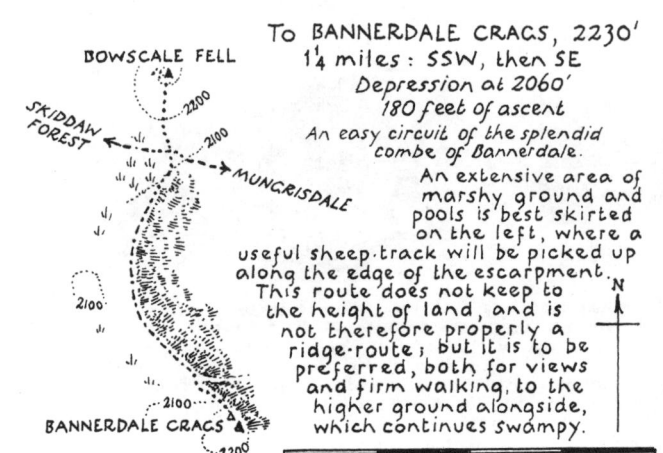

To BANNERDALE CRAGS, 2230'
1¼ miles: SSW, then SE
Depression at 2060'
180 feet of ascent
An easy circuit of the splendid combe of Bannerdale.

An extensive area of marshy ground and pools is best skirted on the left, where a useful sheep-track will be picked up along the edge of the escarpment. This route does not keep to the height of land, and is not therefore properly a ridge-route; but it is to be preferred, both for views and firm walking, to the higher ground alongside, which continues swampy.

ONE MILE

looking west to Skiddaw
Skiddaw Little Man (left) Great Calva (right)

Bowscale Fell 10

THE VIEW

Bowscale Fell and its near neighbour, Bannerdale Crags, are usually visited during the same walk, and it is especially interesting to note how the distant view southwest changes in the short mile between the two summits, due to the impending mass of Blencathra. From Bowscale Fell the distant skyline appears to the *right* of Blencathra and features the Buttermere fells; from Bannerdale Crags the view is seen to the *left* of Blencathra and is of the Langdale and Coniston fells.

Blencathra is a striking object from Bowscale Fell, appearing as a black tower, and there is a good prospect of the upper Caldew valley.

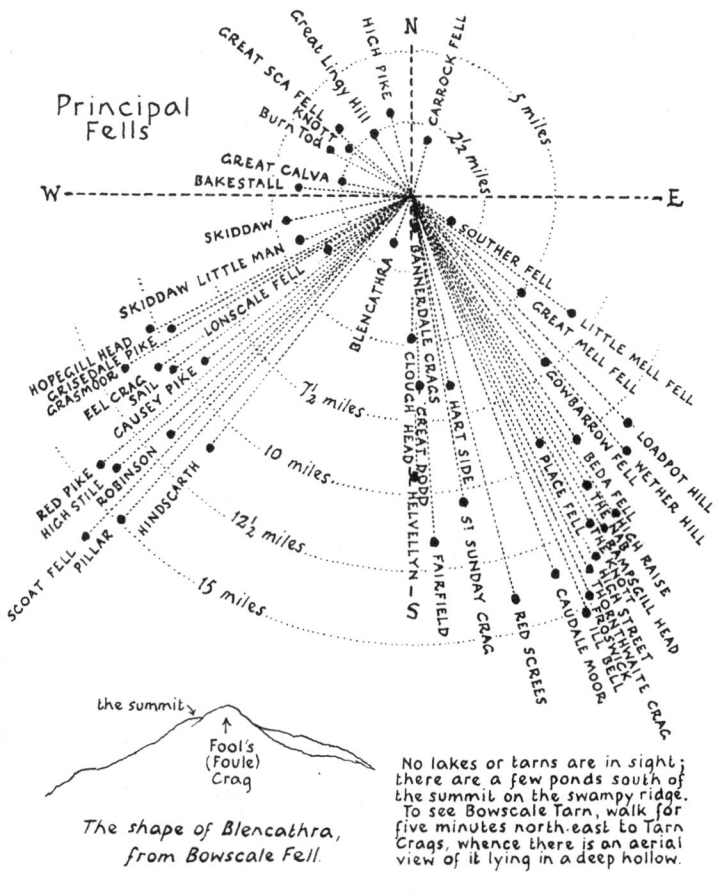

Principal Fells

The shape of Blencathra, from Bowscale Fell.

No lakes or tarns are in sight; there are a few ponds south of the summit on the swampy ridge. To see Bowscale Tarn, walk for five minutes north-east to Tarn Crags, whence there is an aerial view of it lying in a deep hollow.

Brae Fell 1920'

from Fell Side

from Birk Moss

Caldbeck •
• Fell Side
• Uldale • Greenhead
• Longlands
LONGLANDS ▲ ▲ HIGH PIKE
FELL ▲ BRAE FELL
Orthwaite ▲ GREAT SCA FELL

MILES
0 1 2 3 4

Brae Fell 2

NATURAL FEATURES

Brae Fell, with a name that seems a marriage of Scottish and Cumbrian influences, is a last outpost of Lakeland in the north and already the typical characteristics of the district are left behind: the outlook is towards the Border — and the name is therefore perhaps not inappropriate. It is a bare grassy fell of moderate altitude only, though prominent in many views because of its position. A fine cairn crowns the summit, which is a good viewpoint, but there is little else of appeal: if all hills were like Brae Fell there would be far fewer fellwalkers. On the east side, however, there is a series of ravines going down to Dale Beck, and drift-mining operations have further scarred the flank with artificial gullies and spoil-heaps. Red Gill at one time was mined extensively, producing a rich yield of ores, but the traces are now almost lost in the bracken.

Geographically, Brae Fell is really a buttress of the double-headed Sca Fell, to which it is joined by a high saddle; on other flanks watercourses define its boundaries clearly.

Charleton Gill, bounding Brae Fell on the west, is an ordinary mountain stream in spite of its rather 'posh' name, but at one place a peculiar formation may be noted on its eastern bank. Here the flank of Brae Fell descends uneventfully, but, almost at valley level, takes the shape of a curved ridge that forces the stream into a sharp detour at its base. This ridge, all grass, has a narrow crest (a favourite sheep-walk); it is probably a glacial moraine of more elegance than is usual: in fact the scene is charming. Few walkers will ever have seen the place, which is not in view from the little-used bridleroad nearby, but it is known to the shepherds and the mapmakers, whose name for it is Saddleback.
In this case there can be no quarrel with the name.

Saddleback, Charleton Gill

Brae Fell 3

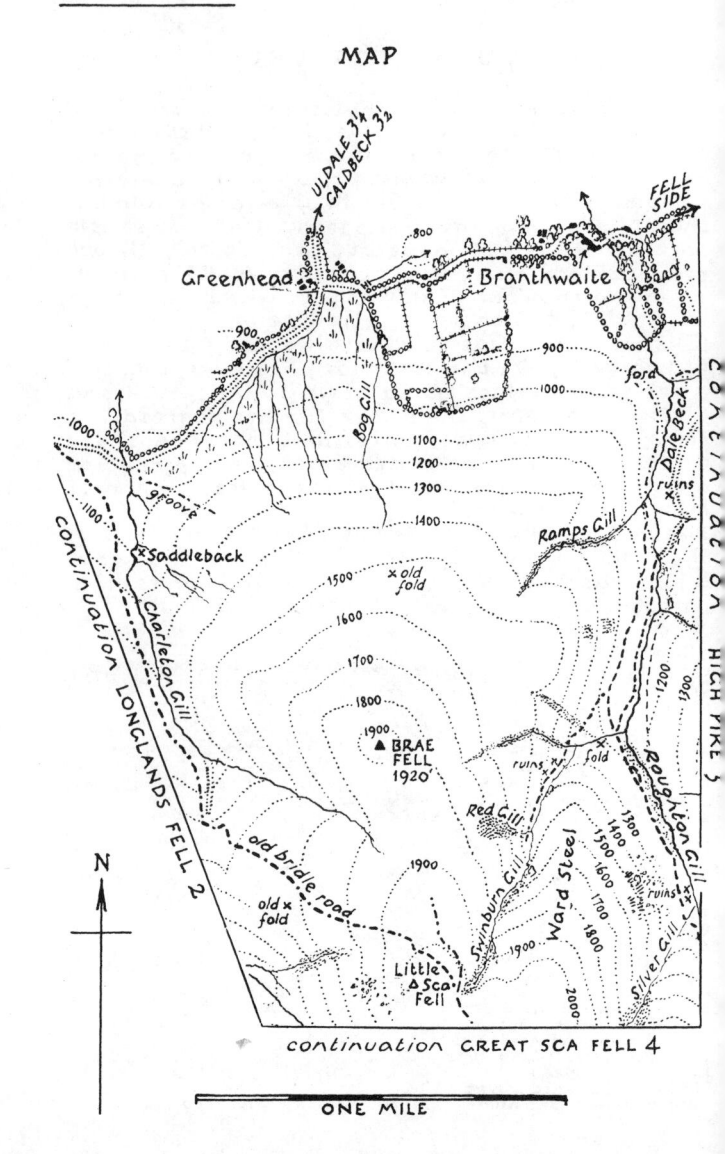

MAP

Brae Fell 4

ASCENT FROM GREENHEAD
1100 feet of ascent
2 miles

looking south

The base of the fell is unfenced and the climb may therefore be started anywhere, but an initial tract of flat marshy ground makes it worth while to use the old Longlands road to a ford (cars may be taken this far) at the crossing of Charleton Gill, where the fellside is scored by grooves which may be followed up. Ordnance Survey maps of 2½" and 6" scale show a footpath up to 1350 feet, but this is now largely a fiction.

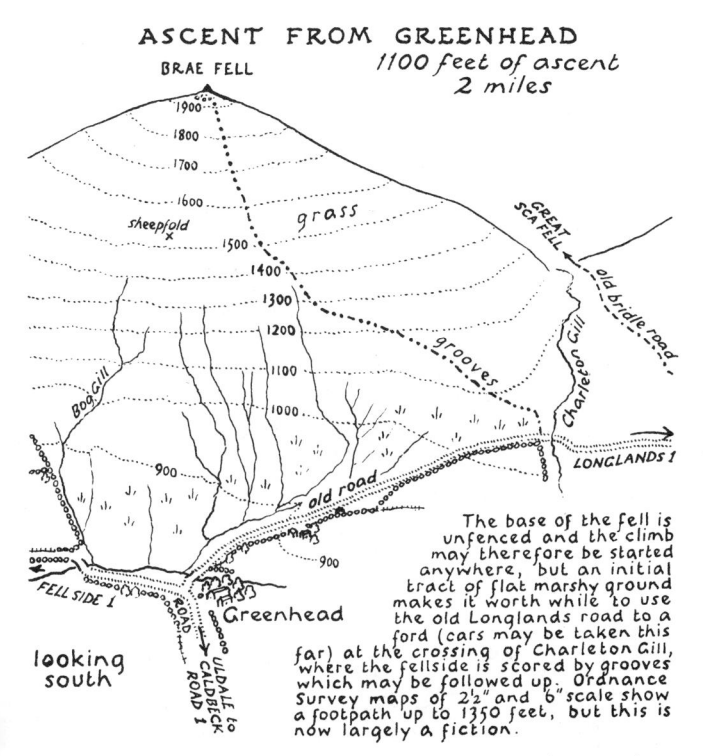

One wearies of the search for anything interesting during this overlong and featureless grassy trudge.

ASCENT FROM FELL SIDE
1150 feet of ascent : 2½ miles

The ascent, anywhere up the grass of the north-east slope, is straightforward, and needs no diagram. This is the aspect seen in the title drawing, the prominent ravine there shown being Ramps Gill.

There may be difficulty in crossing Dale Beck, the old ford and stepping stones having become unserviceable; in which case it may be necessary to go upstream half a mile before a dry crossing can be made. It is, in fact, better to do this, and go up by the south side of Ramps Gill to give the eyes something to look at during the ascent other than interminable grass slopes.

Brae Fell 5

THE SUMMIT

Nature left a scattering of stones on the highest part of Brae Fell and Man has tidied up the litter by piling it into a splendid cairn, a landmark for several miles. Apart from this feature the summit is undistinguished. There is very little fall on the south side, and from this direction the fell is seen to be no more than a shoulder of the Sca Fell mass.

DESCENTS: The long easy north slope is the best way off, inclining left for Longlands or right for Fell Side to avoid a wide tract of marshy ground at the central base of the fell.

RIDGE ROUTE

To GREAT SCA FELL, 2131':
1 mile : S
Depression at 1865'

Proceed across the slight depression to the south, aiming to the left of Little Sca Fell, across the upper slopes of which the old bridle road can be seen rising. A rutted track will be joined: this joins the bridle road above a dry ravine, but instead of following the bridle road, which soon fades away, strike straight up the facing slope to the flat top of Great Sca Fell. It calls for little more effort, alternatively, to visit the top of Little Sca Fell en route.

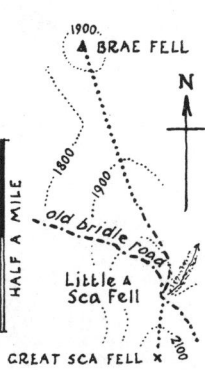

Brae Fell 6

THE VIEW

The weariness of the climb to the cairn is dispelled by the beauty of the view, which extends without interruption from the Cumberland coast near Workington around the northern arc formed by the Solway Firth, the Scottish lowlands and the Border Country, to the Pennines across the Eden Valley in the east. This is a magnificent view, second only in extensiveness, among the northern fells, to that from High Pike.

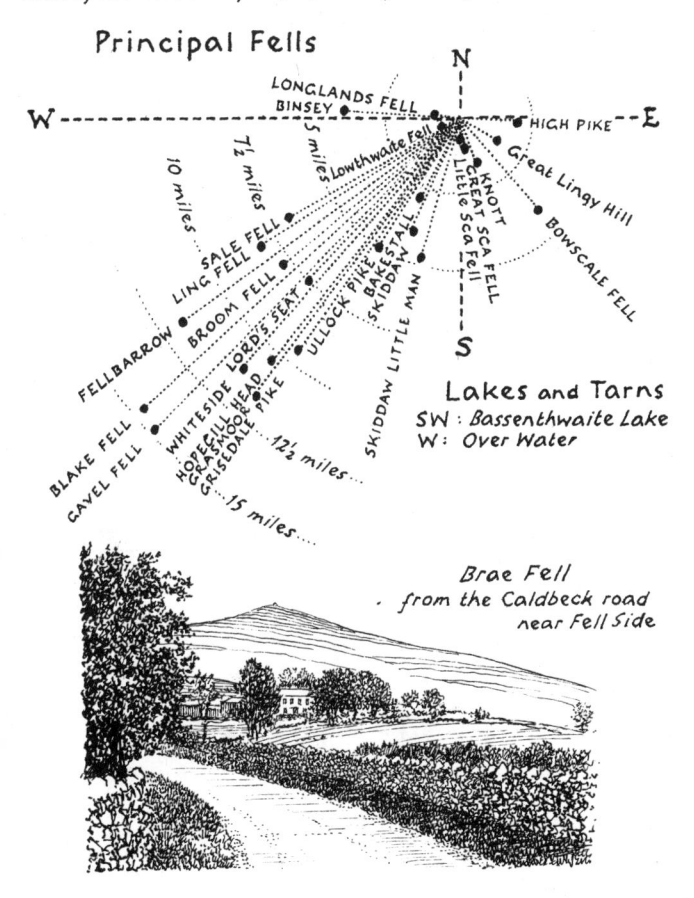

Principal Fells

W — — — N — — — E

LONGLANDS FELL
BINSEY
HIGH PIKE
Lowthwaite Fell
Great Lingy Hill
KNOTT
GREAT SCA FELL
Little Sca Fell
BOWSCALE FELL
5 miles
7½ miles
SALE FELL
LING FELL
10 miles
FELLBARROW
BROOM FELL
LORD'S SEAT
ULLOCK PIKE
BAKESTALL
SKIDDAW
SKIDDAW LITTLE MAN
BLAKE FELL
GAVEL FELL
WHITESIDE
HOPEGILL HEAD
GRASMOOR
GRISEDALE PIKE
12½ miles
15 miles

S

Lakes and Tarns
SW: Bassenthwaite Lake
W: Over Water

Brae Fell from the Caldbeck road near Fell Side

Carl Side

2420'
approx.

from the main road near Millbeck

- Bassenthwaite
- High Side

ULLOCK PIKE ▲ ▲ SKIDDAW
　　　　▲ LONG SIDE
　● 　▲ CARL　▲ SKIDDAW
　↑　SIDE　　LITTLE MAN
DODD　● Millbeck

Little
Crosthwaite

Keswick ●

MILES
0 1 2 3

Carl Side 2

NATURAL FEATURES

Where the steep and stony upper western slope of Skiddaw curves round to the equally steep and stony southern slope there is formed a massive rounded shoulder, which is halted in its descent at 2300' by a grassy saddle, and immediately beyond the dip is the domed summit of Carl Side, a well-defined green plateau. After this interruption, a narrowing ridge resumes the descent southwards to the foothills and fields of Millbeck, this being the natural line of fall of Skiddaw. But also from the summit of Carl Side a sharp ridge, Longside Edge, turns back north-west and finally north, thus circling and concealing Skiddaw's lower western flank: the deep 'moat' thus created is the upland valley of Southerndale, three miles long but so well hidden from popular approaches that walkers in general neither know it nor have even heard the name. This is an unusual geographical arrangement, giving Skiddaw a second wall of defence.

The south ridge, Carl Side proper, is unremarkable except for a distinctive rash of white stones at 1600' extending over several acres, unique in Lakeland and identifying the fell exactly in many distant views. A spur runs off the south ridge to the east and is densely carpeted with heather: this spur, when viewed from the valley, forms the beautiful, symmetrical, dark pyramid of Carsleddam, flanked on the east by the deep trough of Mill Beck, which cleanly severs Carl Side from its towering grey neighbour, Skiddaw Little Man. All streams from the fell go into Bassenthwaite Lake either direct or by way of the main feeder, the River Derwent.

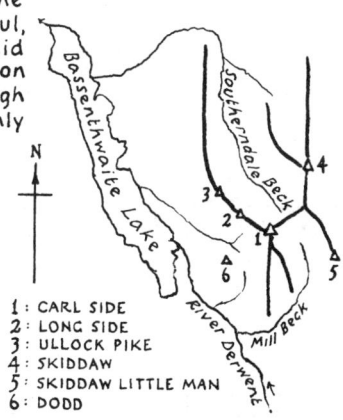

1: CARL SIDE
2: LONG SIDE
3: ULLOCK PIKE
4: SKIDDAW
5: SKIDDAW LITTLE MAN
6: DODD

The Ridges and Watercourses of Carl Side

Carl Side 3

MAP

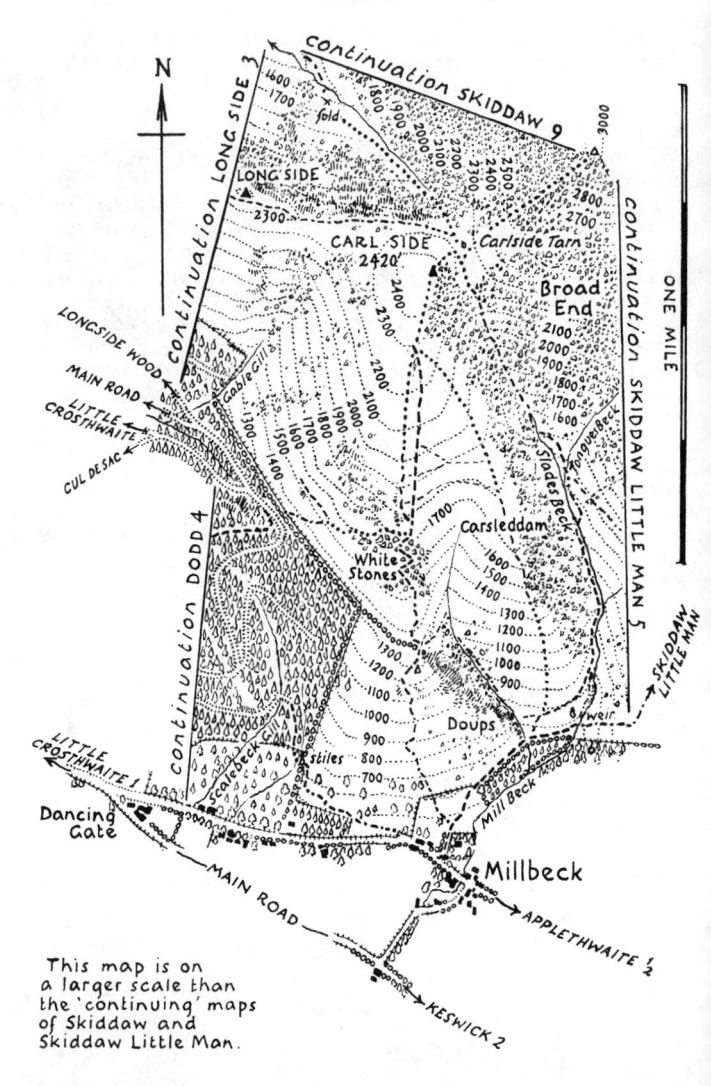

This map is on a larger scale than the 'continuing' maps of Skiddaw and Skiddaw Little Man.

Carl Side 4

ASCENT FROM LITTLE CROSTHWAITE
2070 feet of ascent : 2¼ miles

CARL SIDE

looking east

White Stones

The section between the col and White Stones is rough. Bear right from the stiles, climbing gradually in thick heather: a narrow trod of flattened heather-stalks is helpful if it can be found. *From White Stones onwards consult the diagram on page 5.*

short arête of striated rocks.

col

stiles

Long Doors

This ascent falls into two contrasting parts — the first section, to the col, lies through the heart of a forest (on an excellent surface), the second across bare slopes.

A and B are the two public entrances to the forest (signposted DODD WOOD) — happily, cars are not permitted. The road from A is the more direct; that from B winds round the lower slopes of Dodd before getting fairly under way, but they converge just below the col.

If the plantations arouse interest, consult the chapter on Dodd for details.

This route is an excellent variant to the ascent from Millbeck, unusually interesting, and is easier, the climb to the col being merely a simple walk on a metalled surface. At White Stones the direct ascent from Millbeck by the south ridge is joined.

hut

A — CASTLE INN 3

milestone

B — KESWICK 3½

Little Crosthwaite

Carl Side 5

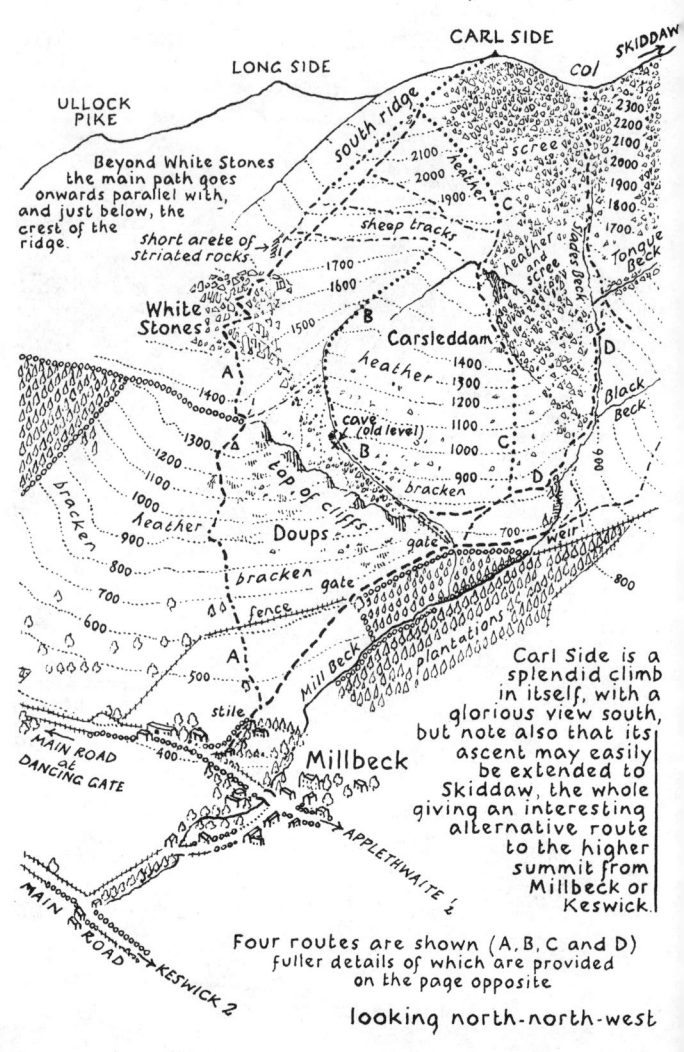

ASCENT FROM MILLBECK
2100 feet of ascent : 1¾ miles (all routes)

Map labels (looking north-north-west):

SKIDDAW — CARL SIDE col — LONG SIDE — ULLOCK PIKE

Beyond White Stones the main path goes onwards parallel with, and just below, the crest of the ridge.

south ridge — scree — Slades Beck — Tongue Beck — heather and scree — sheep tracks — short arete of striated rocks — White Stones — Carsleddam — heather — cave (old level) — bracken — Black Beck — top of cliffs — Doups — heather — bracken — fence — gate — gate — weir — Mill Beck — plantations — stile — Millbeck — MAIN ROAD at DANCING GATE — APPLETHWAITE ½ — MAIN ROAD KESWICK 2

Carl Side is a splendid climb in itself, with a glorious view south, but note also that its ascent may easily be extended to Skiddaw, the whole giving an interesting alternative route to the higher summit from Millbeck or Keswick.

Four routes are shown (A, B, C and D) fuller details of which are provided on the page opposite

looking north-north-west

Carl Side 6

ASCENT FROM MILLBECK

continued

A : This is the natural route of ascent, and the best in spite of the tedious initial climb straight up from Millbeck: there is recompense on this section in the glorious view southwards.
  Turn off the wide path to the weir almost at once after leaving civilisation, by a little embankment (this used to support a fence) and, avoiding rabbit-holes, go directly up the brow of the fell, crossing a fence, by a track not too easy to follow in places. A wall is reached, and rounded at its end by the edge of the cliff of Doups (which comes as a surprise). Ahead, a rising zig-zag path goes up through the low crags of White Stones — another surprising place. Some beautiful cairns could be erected here from the plentiful supplies of sparkling quartz, and one or two would be useful. Above White Stones a remarkably straight track rises ahead through the heather, keeping just below the ridge proper until it slants easily to the crest with the summit 300 yards further over a declining grass slope.

B : This route is more sheltered than A or C, and passes along the foot of the unexpected line of cliffs of Doups, which are quite impressive at such close quarters; otherwise the route lacks views and has little to commend it.

C : Carsleddam is a most attractive peak when seen from a distance but becomes less shapely as it is approached; nevertheless, the final stages of the climb and its narrow summit are exhilarating, and the view south is superb.
  Leave Route D at the terrace and slant up the slope rather to the right where, after a struggle with long heather, a faint track will be found climbing the steep edge of the shoulder. Beyond a conspicuous outcrop the gradient eases and an improving but still narrow path winds up over the tiny, delectable, cairnless summit of Carsleddam and, descending slightly, continues forward on a good ridge. It ends where a track traverses left to the south ridge and this may be used, although a curving course across the rising expanse of heather ahead (here of short and springy growth) is a pleasanter link with Route A.

The summit of Carsleddam, looking north

D : This route is so obvious and well-defined that it is impossible to stray from it, but two things should be noted. First that the Ordnance Survey maps insist that a public footpath ascends the east bank of the stream above the weir, but recent generations of walkers have preferred to keep to the west bank until higher up the valley and worn a better path in so doing. The second point to notice is that, after the second gate (where Route B turns off), a green path climbs to join a terrace route 100 feet higher: use this instead of continuing along the wide path to the weir. This terrace is the start of the new route. The stream is crossed half-a-mile further, near a lonely tree, and then the way climbs directly to the col far ahead: a long long drag. At the col turn left up a short stony slope to the summit.

Carl Side 7

ASCENT FROM HIGH SIDE
2050 feet of ascent : 3 miles

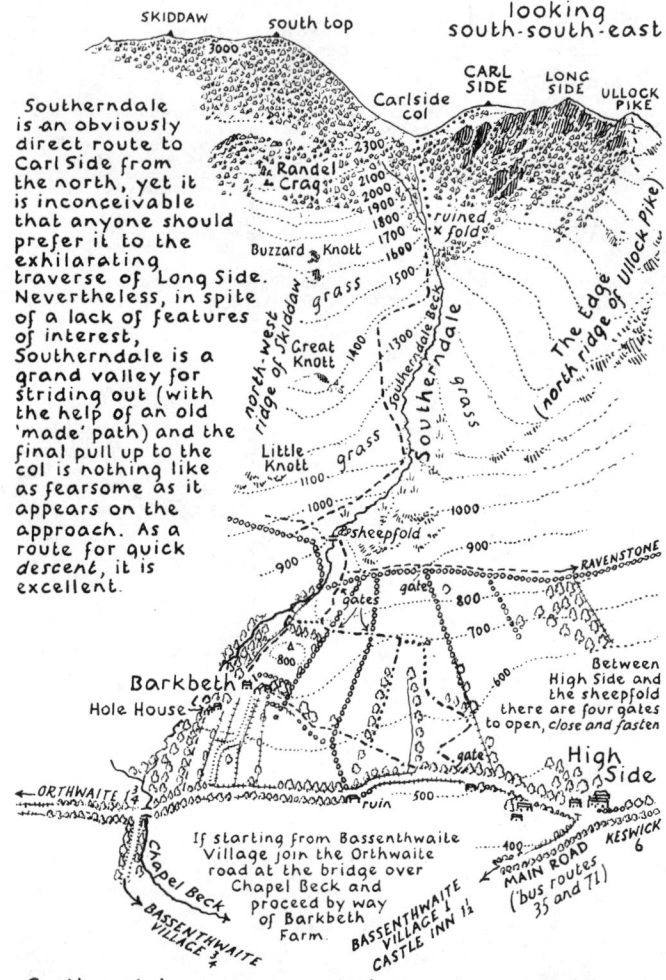

looking south-south-east

Southerndale is an obviously direct route to Carl Side from the north, yet it is inconceivable that anyone should prefer it to the exhilarating traverse of Long Side. Nevertheless, in spite of a lack of features of interest, Southerndale is a grand valley for striding out (with the help of an old 'made' path) and the final pull up to the col is nothing like as fearsome as it appears on the approach. As a route for quick descent, it is excellent.

Between High Side and the sheepfold there are four gates to open, *close and fasten*

If starting from Bassenthwaite Village join the Orthwaite road at the bridge over Chapel Beck and proceed by way of Barkbeth Farm.

Southerndale, an unsuspected valley concealed from the popular haunts of tourists, leads naturally to Carl Side and provides an easy route of approach.

Carl Side 8

THE SUMMIT

The summit is a wide, undistinguished grassy plateau, sloping easily away on three sides but exhibiting a shattered remnant of cliff at the top of the steep, stony and loose east face.

DESCENTS: To MILLBECK (for KESWICK) — In clear weather, descend in a line with Derwentwater's west shore. A path starts after 300 yards on the east side of a circular patch of scree and is more or less continuous to Millbeck. Or, on a wild or misty day, the shelter of the valley opening up from Carlside Tarn in a southerly direction is to be preferred. To HIGH SIDE (for BASSENTHWAITE) — From Carlside Tarn, go down Southerndale (the valley north-west); the initial scree soon gives place to grass.

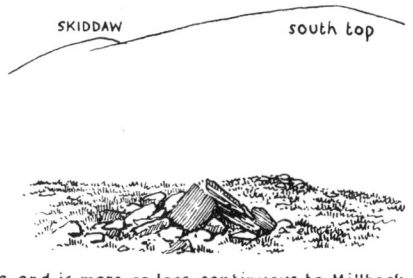

RIDGE ROUTES

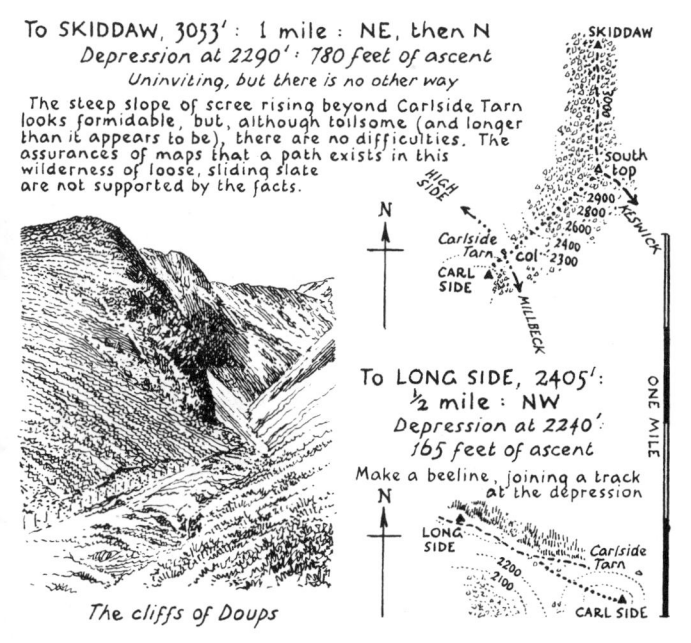

To SKIDDAW, 3053': 1 mile : NE, then N
Depression at 2290': 780 feet of ascent
Uninviting, but there is no other way

The steep slope of scree rising beyond Carlside Tarn looks formidable, but, although toilsome (and longer than it appears to be), there are no difficulties. The assurances of maps that a path exists in this wilderness of loose, sliding slate are not supported by the facts.

To LONG SIDE, 2405': ½ mile : NW
Depression at 2240'
165 feet of ascent

Make a beeline, joining a track at the depression

The cliffs of Doups

Carl Side 9

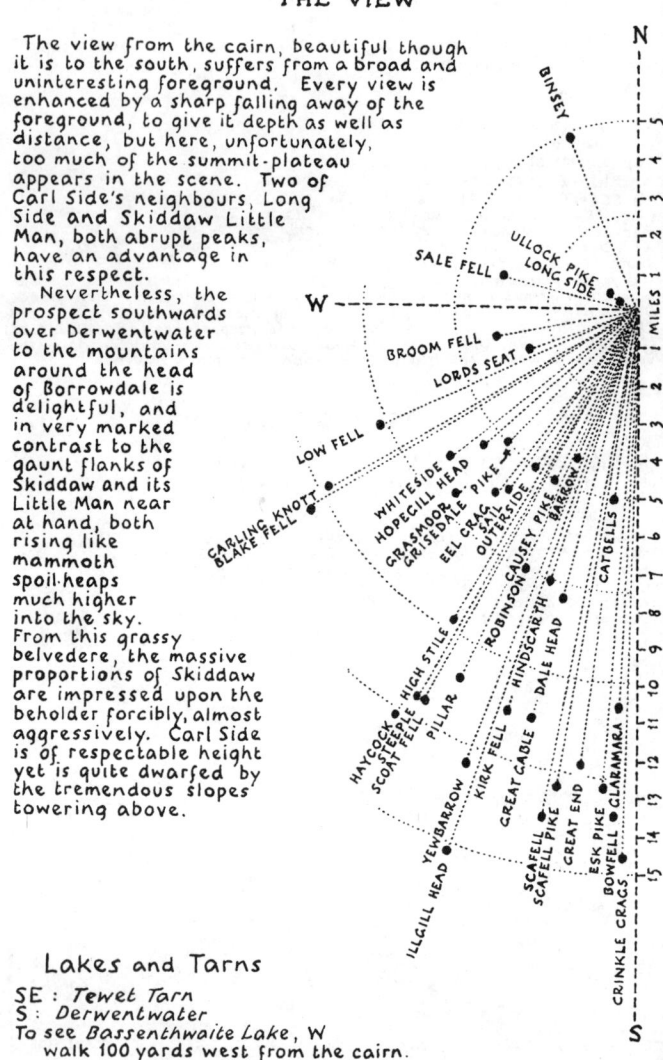

THE VIEW

The view from the cairn, beautiful though it is to the south, suffers from a broad and uninteresting foreground. Every view is enhanced by a sharp falling away of the foreground, to give it depth as well as distance, but here, unfortunately, too much of the summit-plateau appears in the scene. Two of Carl Side's neighbours, Long Side and Skiddaw Little Man, both abrupt peaks, have an advantage in this respect.

Nevertheless, the prospect southwards over Derwentwater to the mountains around the head of Borrowdale is delightful, and in very marked contrast to the gaunt flanks of Skiddaw and its Little Man near at hand, both rising like mammoth spoil-heaps much higher into the sky. From this grassy belvedere, the massive proportions of Skiddaw are impressed upon the beholder forcibly, almost aggressively. Carl Side is of respectable height yet is quite dwarfed by the tremendous slopes towering above.

Lakes and Tarns

SE : *Tewet Tarn*
S : *Derwentwater*
To see *Bassenthwaite Lake*, W
  walk 100 yards west from the cairn.

Carl Side 10

THE VIEW

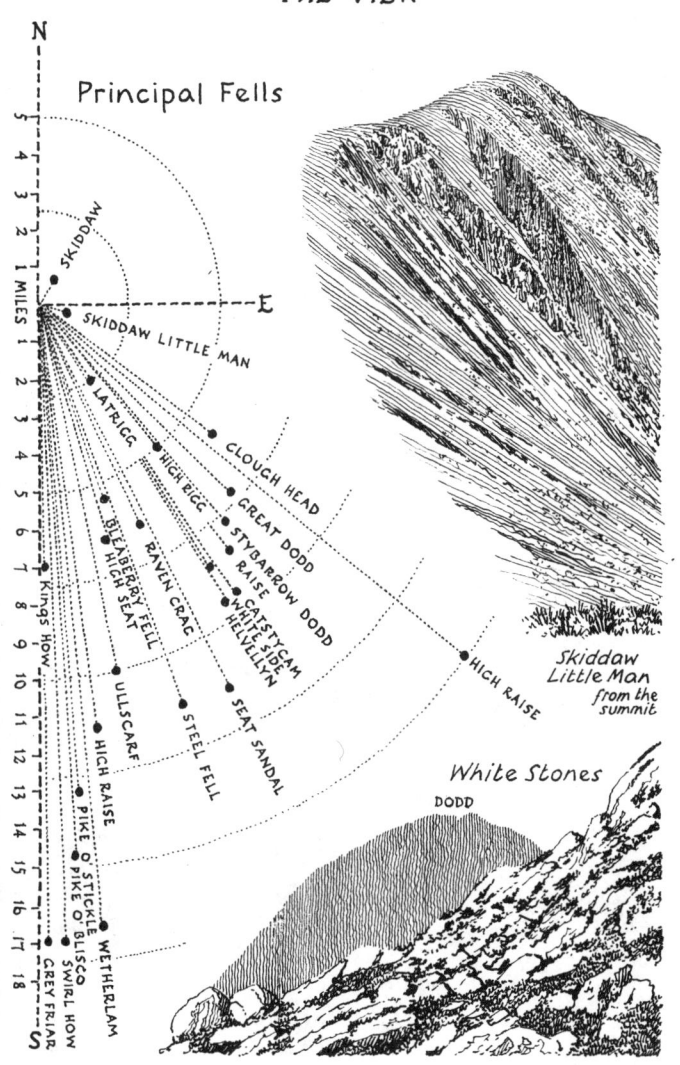

Principal Fells

N
- Skiddaw
- Skiddaw Little Man
- Latrigg
- High Rigg
- Bleaberry Fell
- Raven Crag
- High Seat
- Kings How
- Ullscarf
- High Raise
- Pike o' Stickle
- Pike o' Blisco
- Clough Head
- Great Dodd
- Stybarrow Dodd
- Raise
- Catstycam
- White Side
- Helvellyn
- Seat Sandal
- Steel Fell
- High Raise
- Wetherlam
- Swirl How
- Grey Friar

Skiddaw Little Man from the summit

White Stones

DODD

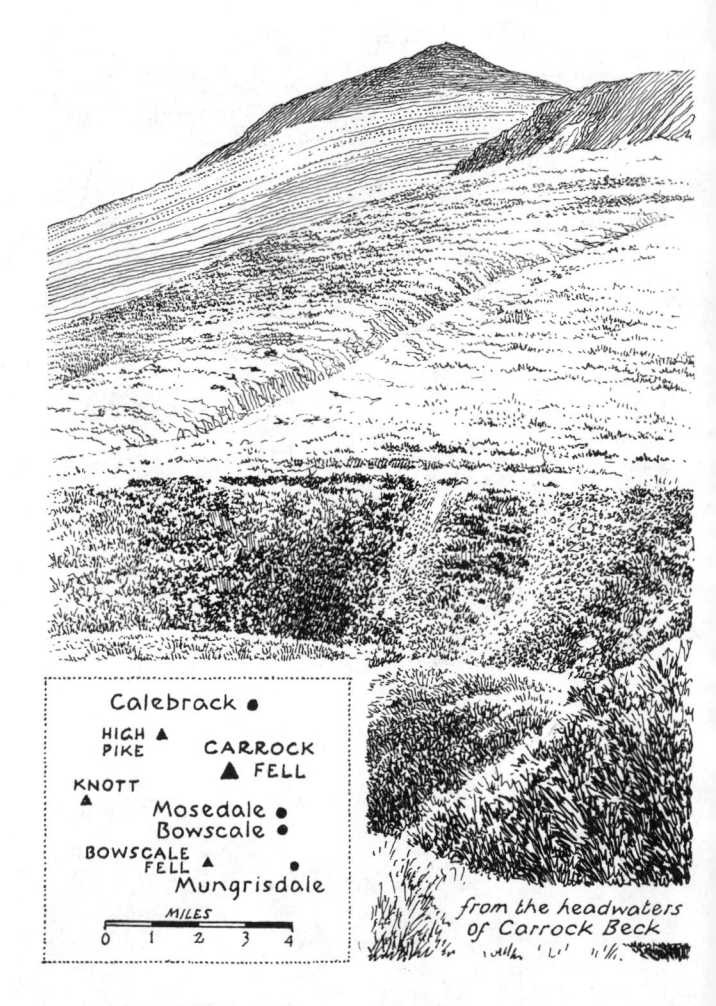

Carrock Fell 2174'

Calebrack •
HIGH ▲
PIKE   CARROCK
            ▲ FELL
KNOTT ▲
        Mosedale •
        Bowscale •
BOWSCALE ▲
FELL   Mungrisdale •

MILES
0 1 2 3 4

from the headwaters of Carrock Beck

Carrock Fell 2

NATURAL FEATURES

Carrock Fell caters for a wide variety of interests. More than any other fell in the district it attracts people who are not regular walkers or climbers — people, indeed, to whom walking for its own sake has little appeal and is here, on Carrock, only a means to an end and not an end in itself.
This rough little height is, first and foremost, a very rich geological field, for here the extensive area of Skiddaw slates and shales, the basic foundation of practically the whole of the Northern Fells, abruptly terminates against a rugged upthrust of igneous or volcanic rocks of different series dovetailed in such a way as to provide an absorbing study for the geologist, while the bed of the Caldew at the western base is notable as one of the few places where the underlying creamy-pink Skiddaw granite is exposed.   One need have no special knowledge to see at a glance that Carrock Fell is different from its neighbours: appearance alone is enough, the bouldery slopes contrasting sharply with those of smooth grass all around.   Carrock Fell is something of a rebel, a nonconformist, the odd man out — it would look more at home at the head of Borrowdale or Langdale amongst others of like kind.

In the field of mining Carrock is a famous name, having a series of veins that have yielded a variety of rich and rare metals and other minerals. Carrock Mine is especially well known for its supplies of wolfram. Although not now being worked the area is often visited by mineralogists.

Other fells have interesting rocks and minerals also — but Carrock has more than natural attractions on display. Its summit is unique, being ringed by the collapsed walls of an ancient hill-fort of unknown age and origin, thought to be early British, which must, in its time, have been a remarkable stronghold. This in itself is enough to excite the many archaeologists and antiquaries who, individually and in groups, make pilgrimages to the place, but the east base of the fell, too, has scores of artificial mounds that might upon investigation reveal something of the story of Carrock B.C.

continued

Carrock Fell, from the shooting-box on Great Lingy Hill

Carrock Fell 3

NATURAL FEATURES
continued

Amongst the igneous rocks of which the fell is formed is gabbro — the stuff the Black Coolin of Skye are made of but a rarity in Lakeland. It is in evidence in the crags of the eastern escarpment and on the boulder-strewn slopes below. Gabbro is an ideal rock for climbing, and here is the one and only climbing-ground in the Northern Fells — very handily situated just above an unenclosed road (the one going *north* out of Mosedale) where cars may be parked. The eastern face of the fell, in fact, everywhere presents attractive scenery.

The heaps of piled boulders on the fell, both on the south and east fronts, provide several safe borrans for foxes in their crevices, these refuges being well-known to followers of the Blencathra pack. When a fox is run to earth on Carrock the hunt is often called off and the frustrated pursuers retire brushless. Cheers for Carrock, therefore, on humane grounds also.

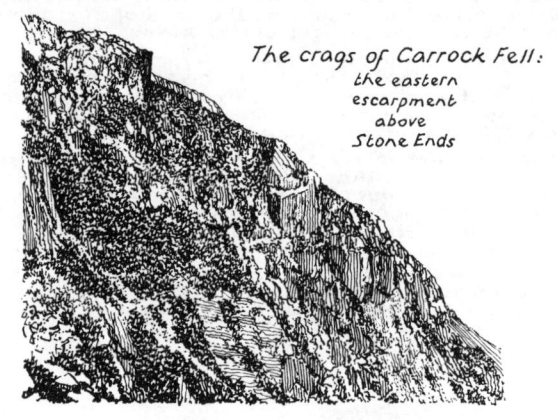

The crags of Carrock Fell:
the eastern
escarpment
above
Stone Ends

Geologists, mineralogists, archaeologists, rock-climbers and foxes : all these are provided for. What is there for the ordinary walker, who simply ascends hills because he likes doing it ? Well, Carrock is a delightful climb, as rough as one cares to make it. In the northern area of Lakeland it ranks next to Blencathra for interest and excitement and beauty of surroundings; in season it has its own special reward for bilberry addicts: there are acres to graze upon. Let others tap rocks with hammers, and dig holes, and prospect with pans, and scale precipices if they wish; heaven for the walker with no special scholarship is at hand in the lush green pastures around the summit. But visit the cairn, of course, for yet another of Carrock's manifold attractions is its glorious view.

Carrock Fell 4

Carrock Mine

Carrock Mine is situated at the confluence of Grainsgill Beck and Brandy Gill, in a side-valley of the Caldew. It has been a productive source of mineral wealth in variety, but is best known for its output of the heavy metal *tungsten* (*wolfram*), a rare mineral not found elsewhere in Lakeland. The mine closed a few decades ago, not due to exhaustion of supplies but because of a fall in world prices — therefore its re-opening is a future possibility, although clearly any speculator will be faced with a big capital expenditure, the buildings having decayed beyond repair.

Mineral veins occur in fractures of the rock, commonly following straight courses of varying depth, with branches, and it is usual to find veins running parallel to each other. Carrock Mine offers a good illustration of this. Standing at the head of the artificial 'cut' on the eastern shoulder of Coomb Height one can look directly down its length to Grainsgill Beck and see the line continuing up the opposite slope in a series of levels and shafts — a perfectly straight line over a distance of half a mile. Similarly, on the east side of Brandy Gill another vein is noticeable parallel to the first. The spoil-heaps of mica-quartz are almost white and very conspicuous.

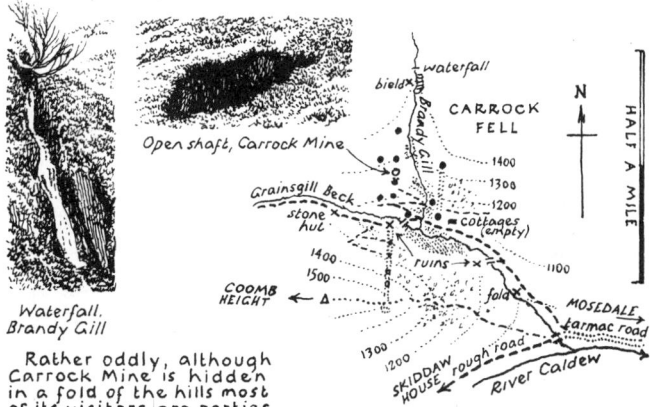

Waterfall, Brandy Gill

Open shaft, Carrock Mine

Rather oddly, although Carrock Mine is hidden in a fold of the hills most of its visitors are parties of motorists, their presence being due to the proximity of the mine to the terminus of the surfaced road along the Caldew valley, which is becoming increasingly popular as a Sunday afternoon picnic-place. These visitors are not shod for scrambling over rough ground and often have children and dogs with them: the warning must be repeated that *disused mine-workings are dangerous*, Carrock Mine in fact having some unfenced open shafts. Inspection at a distance is safe; exploration is hazardous.

A source of valuable information on the geology and mineralogy of Lakeland is provided by a book now out of print but still obtainable through public libraries: MINES AND MINING IN THE LAKE DISTRICT *by John Postlethwaite (published 1877; second edition 1889; third 1913).*

Carrock Fell 5

MAP

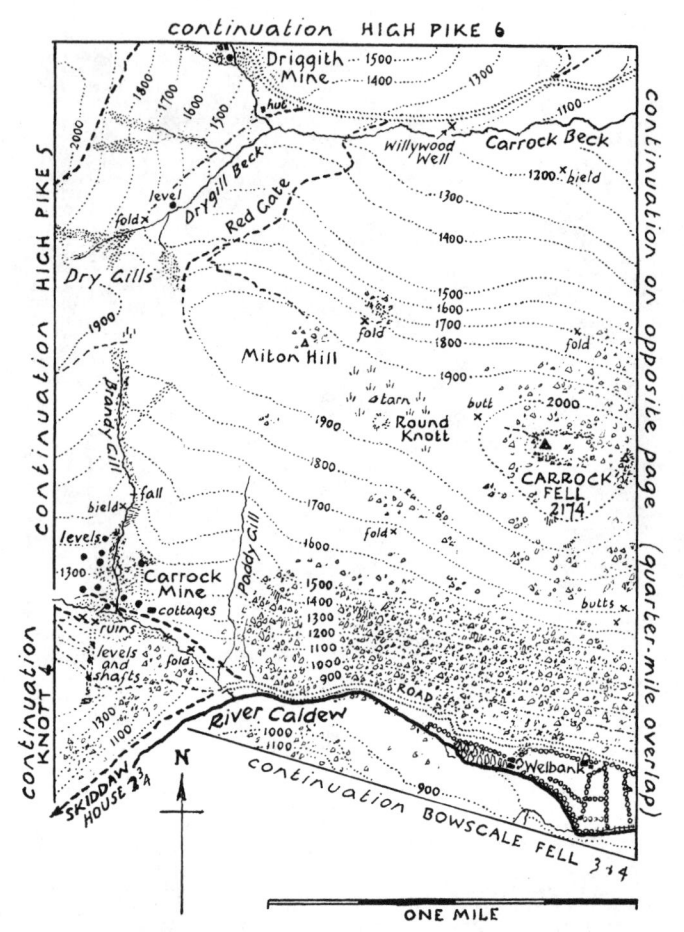

Mosedale means dreary valley, but the name is inappropriate to the mile of emerald pastures watered by the Caldew between the hamlet and Welbank — a charming example of the result of many centuries of patient husbandry, and a typical Lakeland scene.

Carrock Fell 6

MAP

Carrock Fell from the Caldew Valley

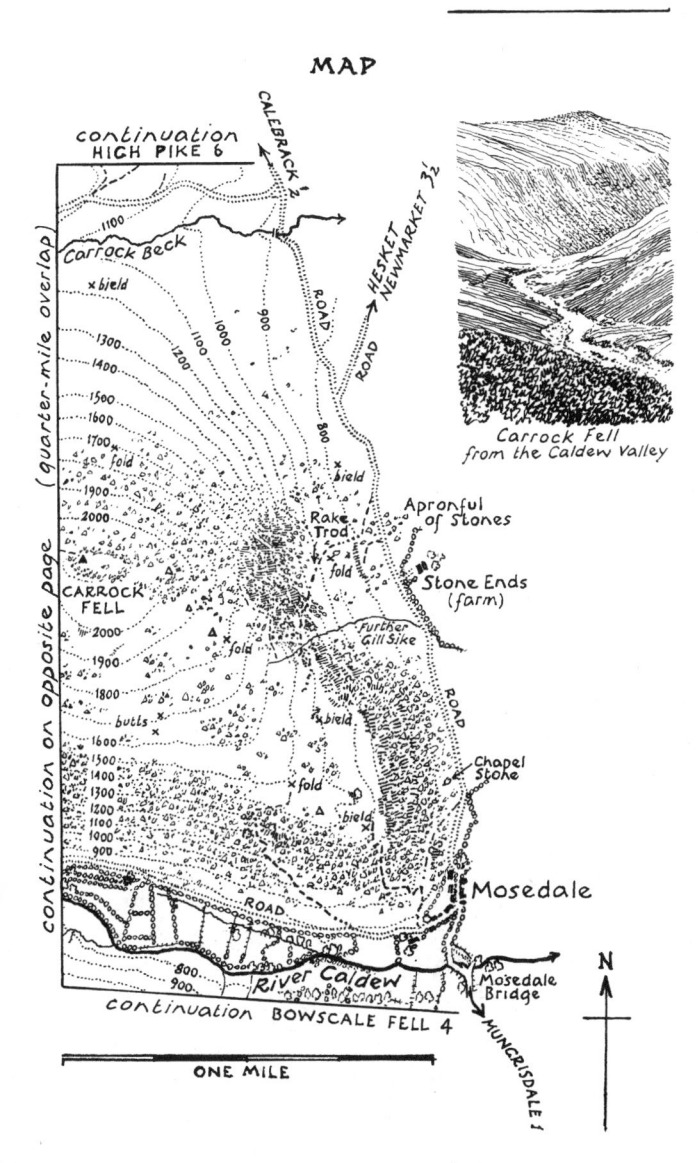

Carrock Fell 7

ASCENT FROM MOSEDALE
1450 feet of ascent : 2 miles

- Carrock Fell should not be climbed in mist

A necklace of stones — the fallen ramparts of an ancient Hill Fort

CARROCK FELL tumulus east peak

The descent of the fell to Mosedale will be found troublesome if neither route can be located. Memorise the details on the way up!

two short walls (bields)

plateau — a strange landscape of scattered blocks and boulders in heather

no beaten track but a natural path suggests itself

good sheepfold against crag

edge of plateau

conspicuous tree (a useful landmark for finding the path when descending)

scree rake

path obliterated by scree

bield

gorse and scree

crag

green path on shelf

STONE ENDS 3

Leave road at corner of wall (no path at first)

sheep tracks

bracken

gorse

ROAD

← CARROCK MINE 2

Mosedale looking north-west

Mosedale Bridge (old and new)

Two paths are shown, and the help of one or the other is necessary to negotiate safely the barrier of boulders on the steep initial slope. The paths, neither of them cairned nor continuously distinct, come to an end when the broad heathery plateau is reached — progress is then easy and gradients gentle.

River Caldew

MUNGRISDALE 1

Carrock Fell has quite exceptional interest for the geologist, the mineralogist and the antiquary, and even the unlearned fellwalker will find the ascent out of the ordinary.

Carrock Fell 8

ASCENT FROM STONE ENDS
1400 feet of ascent : 1¼ miles

looking west

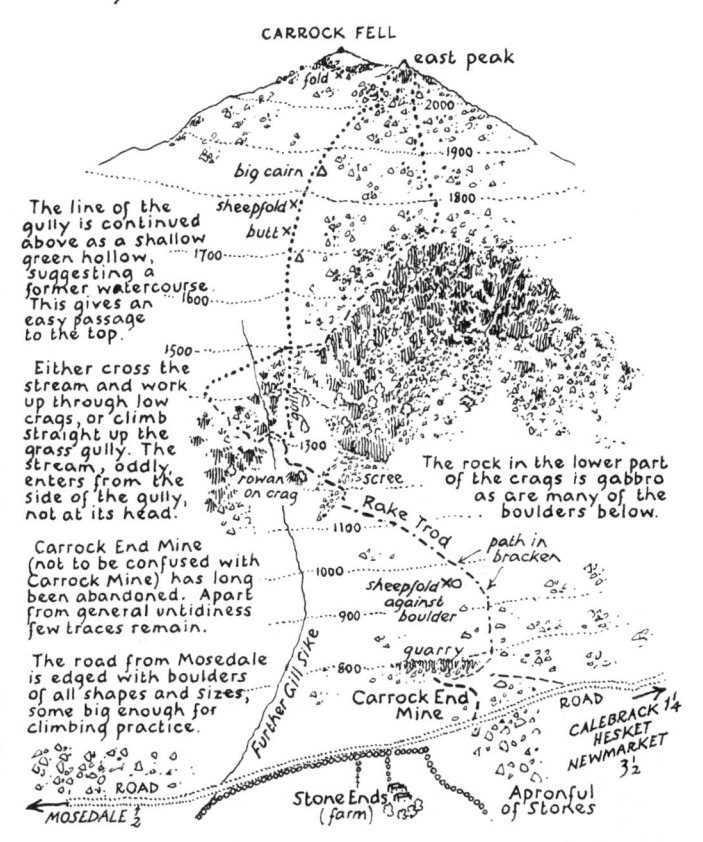

CARROCK FELL — east peak — fold — 2000 — 1900 — big cairn — 1800 — sheepfold — butt — 1700 — 1600 — 1500 — 1300 — rowan on crag — scree — Rake Trod — 1100 — path in bracken — 1000 — sheepfold against boulder — 900 — quarry — 800 — Carrock End Mine — ROAD — CALEBRACK 1¼ HESKET NEWMARKET 3½ — Further Gill Sike — MOSEDALE ½ — ROAD — Stone Ends (farm) — Apronful of Stones

The line of the gully is continued above as a shallow green hollow, suggesting a former watercourse. This gives an easy passage to the top.

Either cross the stream and work up through low crags, or climb straight up the grass gully. The stream, oddly, enters from the side of the gully, not at its head.

Carrock End Mine (not to be confused with Carrock Mine) has long been abandoned. Apart from general untidiness few traces remain.

The road from Mosedale is edged with boulders of all shapes and sizes, some big enough for climbing practice.

The rock in the lower part of the crags is gabbro as are many of the boulders below.

This is the shortest way to the top from a motor road, and the most straightforward. It affords intimate views of the crags, passing through them by a simple grass gully. This route, 'Rake Trod', is the one used and recommended by local people.

Carrock Fell 9

ASCENT FROM CALEBRACK
1300 feet of ascent : 3½ miles

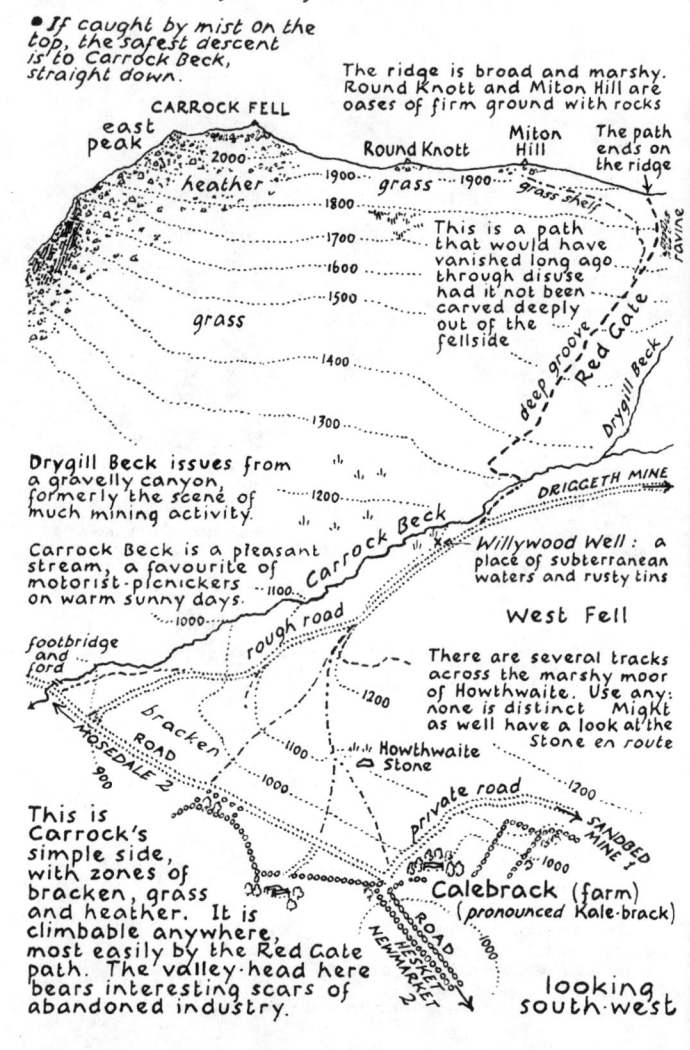

• If caught by mist on the top, the safest descent is to Carrock Beck, straight down.

The ridge is broad and marshy. Round Knott and Miton Hill are oases of firm ground with rocks

CARROCK FELL — east peak — 2000 — heather

Round Knott 1900 — grass — Miton Hill 1900 — grass shelf — The path ends on the ridge

scree ravine

grass

This is a path that would have vanished long ago through disuse had it not been carved deeply out of the fellside

deep groove — Red Gate — Drygill Beck

Drygill Beck issues from a gravelly canyon, formerly the scene of much mining activity.

Carrock Beck — DRIGGETH MINE

Willywood Well: a place of subterranean waters and rusty tins

Carrock Beck is a pleasant stream, a favourite of motorist-picnickers on warm sunny days.

rough road

West Fell

footbridge and ford

bracken

There are several tracks across the marshy moor of Howthwaite. Use any: none is distinct. Might as well have a look at the Stone en route

ROAD MOSEDALE 2

Howthwaite Stone

private road — SANDBED MINE

This is Carrock's simple side, with zones of bracken, grass and heather. It is climbable anywhere, most easily by the Red Gate path. The valley-head here bears interesting scars of abandoned industry.

Calebrack (farm)
(pronounced Kale-brack)

ROAD HESKET NEWMARKET 2

looking south-west

Carrock Fell 10

THE SUMMIT

The top of the fell is elliptical in plan, with a cairn on low rocks at each extremity. Draped like a necklace around the western top (the higher) is a broad band of stones, the ruined wall of the ancient fort: a continuous link except for four breaches corresponding to the main points of the compass and serving as gateways. Within this wall is a heap of stones, possibly a tumulus, now hollowed out as a shelter. There is no obvious trace of buildings, and visitors should not be deceived by an enclosure on the south side, this being only a sheepfold built from the stones of the wall. New bilberry shoots impart a bright sheen to the top in early summer.

best fragment of original masonry

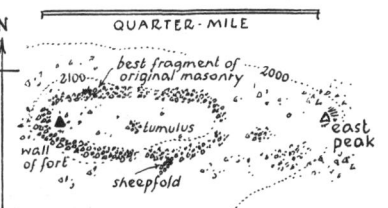

PLAN OF SUMMIT

The collapsed walls of the fort, at the south gateway

continued

Carrock Fell 11

THE SUMMIT
continued

DESCENTS. Descent on the east and south flanks is tricky, the few breaches in the impassable slope of crags and boulders at the edge of the plateau being difficult to locate, even in clear weather. The simplest plan is to follow the natural fall of land to the dry gully into which Further Gill Sike enters on the right and go down to Stone Ends by way of Rake Trod. A route to Mosedale direct may be attempted if it has been used observantly for the ascent.

In mist, the safest plan is to go down the easy north slope to Carrock Beck and follow the stream to the road.

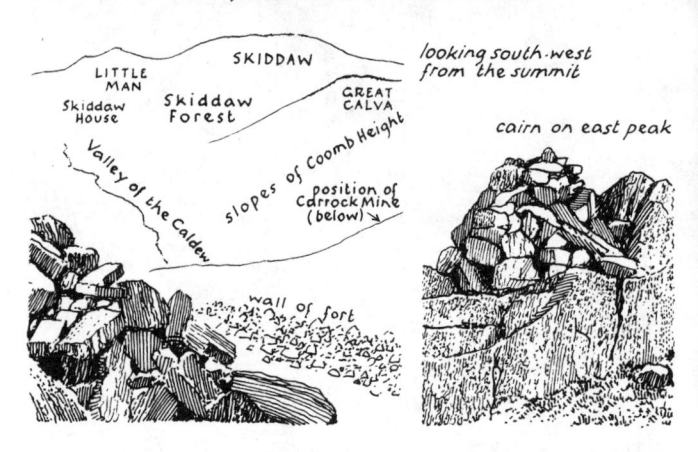

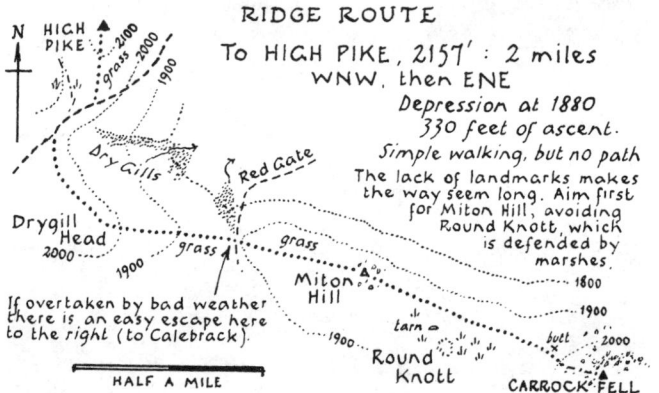

looking south-west from the summit

LITTLE MAN — SKIDDAW — GREAT CALVA
Skiddaw House — Skiddaw Forest
Valley of the Caldew
slopes of Coomb Height
position of Carrock Mine (below)
wall of fort

cairn on east peak

RIDGE ROUTE

TO HIGH PIKE, 2157′ : 2 miles
WNW, then ENE
Depression at 1880
330 feet of ascent.
Simple walking, but no path

The lack of landmarks makes the way seem long. Aim first for Miton Hill, avoiding Round Knott, which is defended by marshes.

HIGH PIKE 2100, grass 2000, 1900
Dry Gills — Red Gate
Drygill Head 2000 — 1900 — grass — grass — Miton Hill — 1800 — 1900
If overtaken by bad weather there is an easy escape here to the right (to Calebrack).
tarn — Round Knott — 1900 — butt 2000 — CARROCK FELL

HALF A MILE

Carrock Fell 12

THE VIEW

The best section of the view is eastwards, not towards Lakeland but away from it, across the wide and fertile valley of the Eden to the Pennines beyond: an extensive yet detailed scene better observed from the east peak.
 The neighbouring heights do not show to advantage, but there is a good prospect of the fells around Ullswater, and Great Gable, Pillar & Co. fill in the notch of the Glenderaterra valley quite neatly. The upper Caldew valley features well.
 The Solway Firth appears in the north-west, with Criffell prominent just to the right of the summit of High Pike.

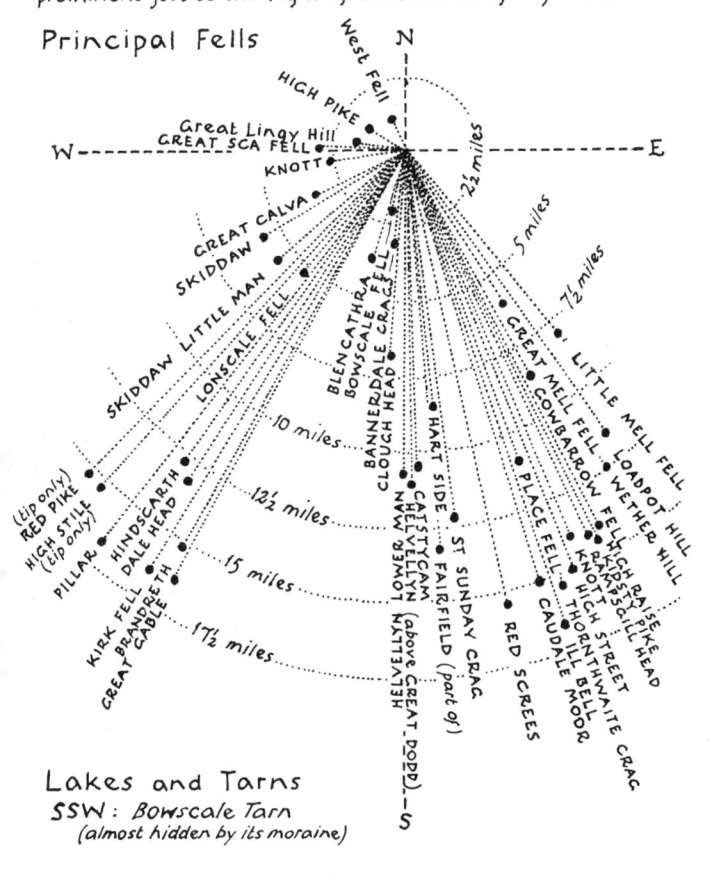

Principal Fells

Lakes and Tarns
SSW: Bowscale Tarn
(almost hidden by its moraine)

Dodd

1612'

also variously known
as Skiddaw Dodd
and Little Dodd
and named Dodd Fell
on Bartholomews maps

from Longside Wood

from Millbeck road end

- Bassenthwaite
- ▲ SKIDDAW
- ▲ CARL SIDE
- ▲ DODD
- Dancing Gate
- Millbeck
- Little Crosthwaite
- Keswick

MILES
0 1 2 3

Dodd 2

NATURAL FEATURES

Dodd, like Latrigg, can be described as a whelp of Skiddaw crouched at the feet of his parent. But Dodd has latterly shown nothing of the family characteristics and the old man must today regard his offspring with surprise and growing doubt, and feel like denying his paternity and disowning the little wretch.

Skiddaw is a high, bare, rangy mountain, open to the winds of heaven; Dodd is stunted, and in the course of recent years has become clothed from tip to toe and on all sides in a growth of trees so luxurious that scarcely any part of the original appearance of the fell remains in view. Skiddaw is Lakeland through and through, one of the respected dignitaries of the district, absolutely true blue; Dodd would seem more in place in the dense and steaming jungles of the Amazon.

But Dodd is really an innocent party in this matter, the great change being none of his seeking but having been thrust upon him. In years gone by Dodd sported a few small woodlands, like a young man his first moustaches, with such success and evidence of fertility as to attract the attention of the Forestry Commission, then developing the Thornthwaite Forest just across Bassenthwaite Lake. Since 1920 the Commission have been rampant here, and, except for a single field at Little Crosthwaite, they have covered the fell thickly with growing timber.

The work has been tackled with imagination, and with due regard to amenity. Nobody is likely to complain much about the results of this enterprise. There might be a little regret that the regimentation and segregation of species is still persisted in, giving an unnatural patchwork effect, but, in general, Dodd has come through the transformation fairly well. The older deciduous trees fringing the base of the fell have been retained as a screen, and, where they occur elsewhere, have been left to develop; many of the matured pines and firs in the early plantations, growing singly, are excellent specimens, and there has been a fair mixing of species in the new plantations, with larch, spruce, pine and fir in variety. Admirable roads have been made, to give access to all parts of the forest, and it requires only a walk along them to appreciate the extent of the work involved in the maintenance of a great industry of this sort, and the skill and resource of those responsible for the enterprise. Dodd has not been spoiled, but given a new look; and it is a more

continued

Scots pine

Larch

Dodd 3

NATURAL FEATURES
continued

interesting, and certainly a more fascinating, place than ever it was in the past. Skiddaw's frown betrays an old prejudice; true, Skiddaw has long had his own Forest but *that* is fine rolling upland country not desecrated by fancy trees..... *foreign* trees, moreover! If there *must* be trees on Dodd, aren't Lakeland trees good enough? Bah! says Skiddaw.

As far as walkers are concerned, they may walk along the forest roads — but not as of right, and the courtesy thus extended is one that ought to be fully respected, please.

Only if it is desired to visit the summit of the fell is it necessary to leave the roads, and that objective can be reached, carefully, without causing damage to trees. There is no excuse at all for barging through the plantations and crippling young trees; none, either, for defying the fire-warning notices.

Douglas fir

Sitka spruce

The Forestry Commission refer to their plantations in this area by the title of Dodd Wood, and, because the fell is now completely covered, Dodd and Dodd Wood are often used as synonymous names; not always correctly, for the adjoining plantations on Long Side and north to Ravenstone are also part of the official Dodd Wood.

Geographically, Dodd is the first of the three great steps of Skiddaw rising from the head of Bassenthwaite Lake. The second step, Carl Side, is joined at mid-height: the link is a distinctive col from which flow the boundary streams, Skill Beck and Scale Beck. A feature is the pronounced northwest ridge; a less conspicuous ridge descends southeast from the summit. These ridges are followed closely by a wide fire-break amongst the dense plantations, resembling, from a distance, a centre parting in a head of hair. In any view in which it can be seen, Dodd is readily identifiable by the dark covering of conifers and black cap of mountain pines.

The Forestry Commission publish many excellent booklets of general interest, obtainable from H.M. Stationery Office. Their NATIONAL FOREST PARK GUIDES and BRITAIN'S FORESTS series make a splendid little library for walkers and other country-lovers at low cost. (*Free list from the Commission, 25 Savile Row, London, W.1*)

A visit to Dodd will be enjoyed all the more by a pre-reading of "THORNTHWAITE" (one shilling), which describes the geology and geography, history, botany and other aspects of the district around Bassenthwaite and makes reference to Dodd Wood.

Dodd 4

MAP

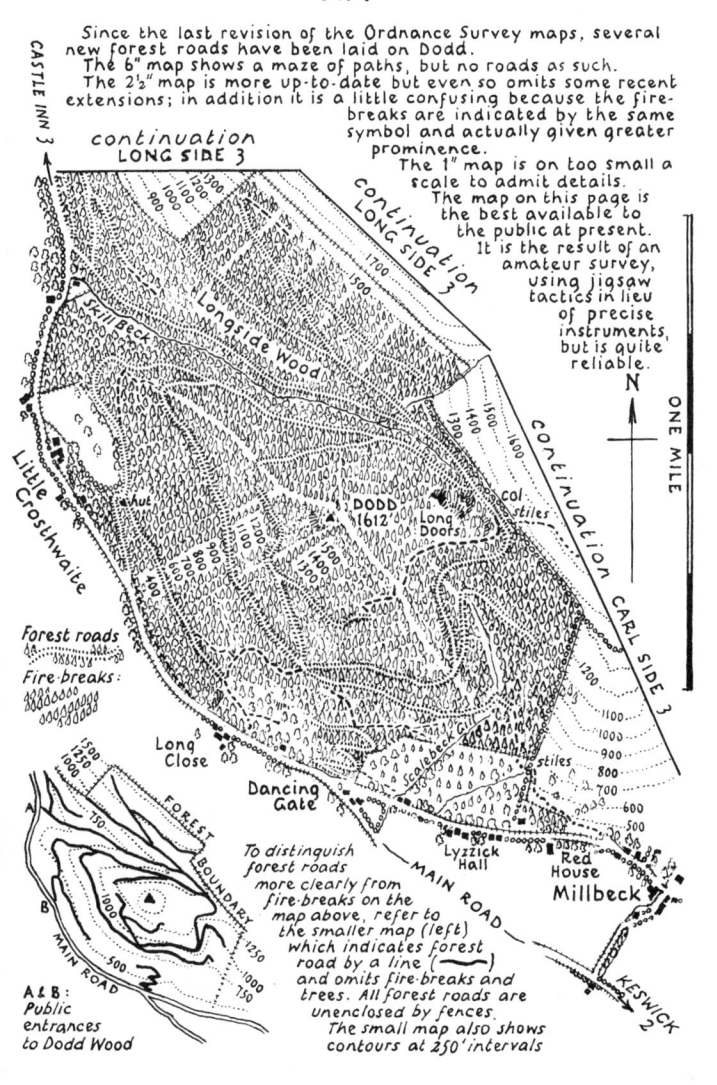

Since the last revision of the Ordnance Survey maps, several new forest roads have been laid on Dodd.

The 6" map shows a maze of paths, but no roads as such.

The 2½" map is more up-to-date but even so omits some recent extensions; in addition it is a little confusing because the fire-breaks are indicated by the same symbol and actually given greater prominence.

The 1" map is on too small a scale to admit details.

The map on this page is the best available to the public at present. It is the result of an amateur survey, using jigsaw tactics in lieu of precise instruments, but is quite reliable.

To distinguish forest roads more clearly from fire-breaks on the map above, refer to the smaller map (left) which indicates forest road by a line (———) and omits fire-breaks and trees. All forest roads are unenclosed by fences.

The small map also shows contours at 250' intervals

A & B: Public entrances to Dodd Wood

Dodd 5

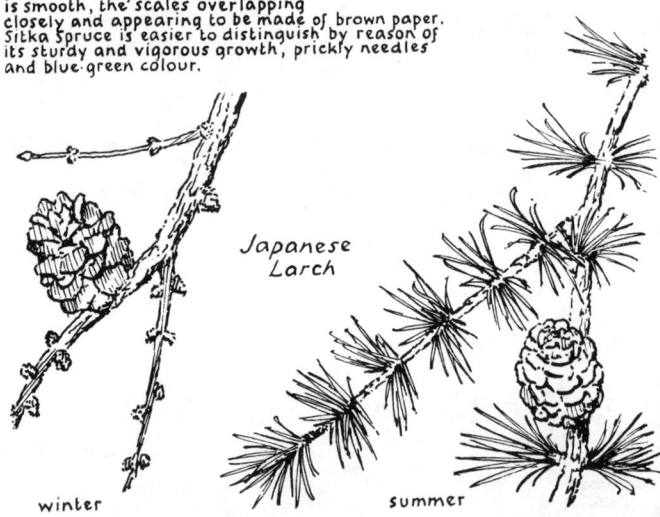

Dodd Wood

The wide variety of tree species in Dodd Wood, unusual in coniferous plantations, adds an interest for observant visitors. The deciduous trees are old favourites, generally well-known; but there is difficulty to the untrained eye in identifying the softwood timber trees, which are of the same habit of growth and similar in appearance. All are evergreen, except the larch, and grow straight and tall from a main stem.

Of the species planted most extensively, the pines and the larches are distinctive enough to be recognised at sight, but there is much doubt about the firs and the spruces.

Douglas Fir and Norway Spruce (the latter being the 'Christmas Tree') look very much alike, but can be identified with certainty by their cones, which litter the ground beneath the older trees. The cone of the Douglas Fir (next page) has peculiar three-pronged bracts issuing between the scales, but the cone of the Norway Spruce is smooth, the scales overlapping closely and appearing to be made of brown paper. Sitka Spruce is easier to distinguish by reason of its sturdy and vigorous growth, prickly needles and blue-green colour.

Scots Pine

Japanese Larch

winter

summer

Dodd 6

Dodd Wood

The Forestry Commission's publication "Thornthwaite" mentions the following species as in cultivation on Dodd (apart from deciduous trees):

- Scots pine
- Lodgepole pine
- Mountain pine
- Norway spruce
- Sitka spruce
- Japanese larch
- European larch
- Douglas fir
- Noble fir
- Western hemlock
- Lawson's cypress
- Western red cedar

The four last-named are not much in evidence. Douglas Fir is extensive up to 1000'; larch occurs in big 'stands' at middle height, 800'-1200'; the spruces thrive, Sitka especially, up to 1500', and the pines at all elevations and on the summit itself.

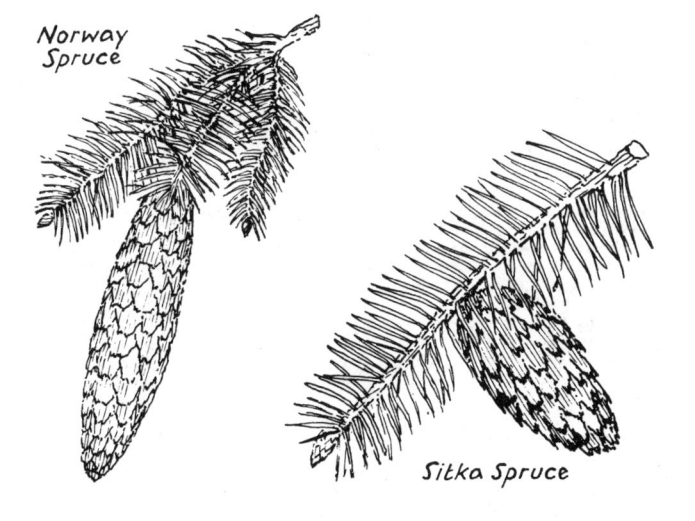

Douglas Fir

Norway Spruce

Sitka Spruce

Dodd 7

ASCENTS

The climbing of Dodd is not to be achieved merely by repeating the process of putting one foot before and higher than the other, as in the case of most ascents. On Dodd the Forestry Commission and a million or so allies in a massed formation — spruces, firs and larch (to say nothing of *Pinus mugo*) — must be outwitted, and some crafty manoeuvring is required to reach the summit. Forcing a way ever upwards through the trees is not playing the game, and is out of the question anyway because the depths of the forest are quite impassable. Recourse must therefore be had to (a) the forest roads, (b) the forest paths, and (c) the fire-breaks.

THE FOREST ROADS:

The forest workers know not only how to grow trees but how to plan roads too, and they have made a really excellent job of laying passages for their vehicles. Considering the steepness of the fell the roads are wonderfully well graded, reaching to all parts of the forest without ever exceeding the gentlest of slopes, and they are well culverted, providing dry surfaces for walking even on the wettest days. Roughly metalled, they are not hard to the feet but are generally shaly, rather loose and soft. In long spirals and zigzags the roads climb as high as 1350 feet; some other means of access must be used, therefore, in later stages of the ascent to the summit, 250' higher.

Dodd is a small fell, yet there are already nearly five miles of 10' roads hidden amongst the plantations. In the contiguous Longside Wood (under the same management) are several more miles of forest roads, similarly concealed from the sight of travellers on the busy Keswick-Carlisle highway running along the base of the plantations.

Forest road

At two places, forest roads effect junctions with the main road. Here are signboards which, after quoting the *Rights of Way Act, 1932*, go on to say '*This road is not dedicated to public use as a highway, but the public are permitted to use it (during such times as it is not closed) except with vehicles.*' A rather negative and unenthusiastic invitation, perhaps; but it is one that walkers should accept, for the forest roads are not only pleasant avenues to parade but afford an insight of the enterprise and achievements of the Commission.

ASCENTS

continued

THE FOREST PATHS:

Before the forest roads were cut the workers in the new plantations made use of a network of footpaths between the growing trees. Many of these paths have gone out of commission or been superceded by the roads; others can still be traced although now heavily overshadowed; a few remain in regular use. Where the paths can be followed they are quite fascinating, but, oftener than not, they are now overgrown or choked with brushwood. This latter circumstance is galling to the conscientious walker who is keeping his pipe and matches in his pocket, having heeded the warning fire notices, for this dry and highly inflammable rubbish lying in profusion beneath the trees, ready to start and spread a conflagration, should surely be cleared as a first precaution?

Forest path

THE FOREST RIDES (FIRE-BREAKS):

The fire-breaks, like many mountain tracks, are better seen from a mile away than when in their vicinity. Viewed from a distance they seem to offer obvious bee-lines to the crest of the fell, but actually they are easily passed unnoticed; even when discovered they turn out to be not at all the easy grass stairways expected. Remember that they have not been levelled or smoothed in any way, but are simply unplanted strips of rough fellside in its natural state and often very steep and craggy in places. They have become rank and untidy due to the absence of sheep and are occasionally barred by cut logs, branches or brushwood. In short, they do not provide comfortable walking — some call for desperate struggles, some have dangerous traps. One must be used in the final stage of the ascent of Dodd, however, and that reaching almost to the summit from the southeast is easy in its higher section and is therefore recommended. The others are not.

Fire-break (north-west ridge)

It will be realised that the forest roads serve as breaks also. There are no streams wide enough to halt a fire.

Dodd 9

ASCENT FROM LITTLE CROSTHWAITE
1300 feet of ascent : 2½ miles

Continuation of route from the col:
Watch for a wide grassy path leaving the road on the right, almost as the col is reached: this leads through pleasant woodland to a fire-break, which follow upwards to the top of the fell. The actual summit is then nearby on the left, but is concealed by trees. The cairn will be found immediately beyond an intersection of fire-breaks.

This forest road continues around the fell to arrive at the col from the opposite side. It is thus possible to encircle the fell entirely on a good walking surface — an interesting little tour.

Skill Beck forms a more pronounced valley than the diagram suggests, while the roads ascending on either side are much less steep than they appear here. (Actually, all the forest roads are gently graded, as, of course, they must be to permit the passage of loaded timber vehicles).

looking south-east

A and B are the two points where forest roads come down to the public highway. Both roads lead directly to the Long Doors col: in fact, they converge below it. The col is an interesting place, with unexpected cliffs.
The route from the col onwards lies on the far side of the fell and is not shown in the diagram (see note at top of page).   A shorter alternative, not visiting the col, turns along a branch road to the depot indicated, when the fire-break there found can be ascended to the top of the fell, *but the final section is steeply tilted, recently planted, and unpleasantly rough : this route is not recommended.*

Dodd 10

ASCENT FROM DANCING GATE
1320 feet of ascent : 1½ miles

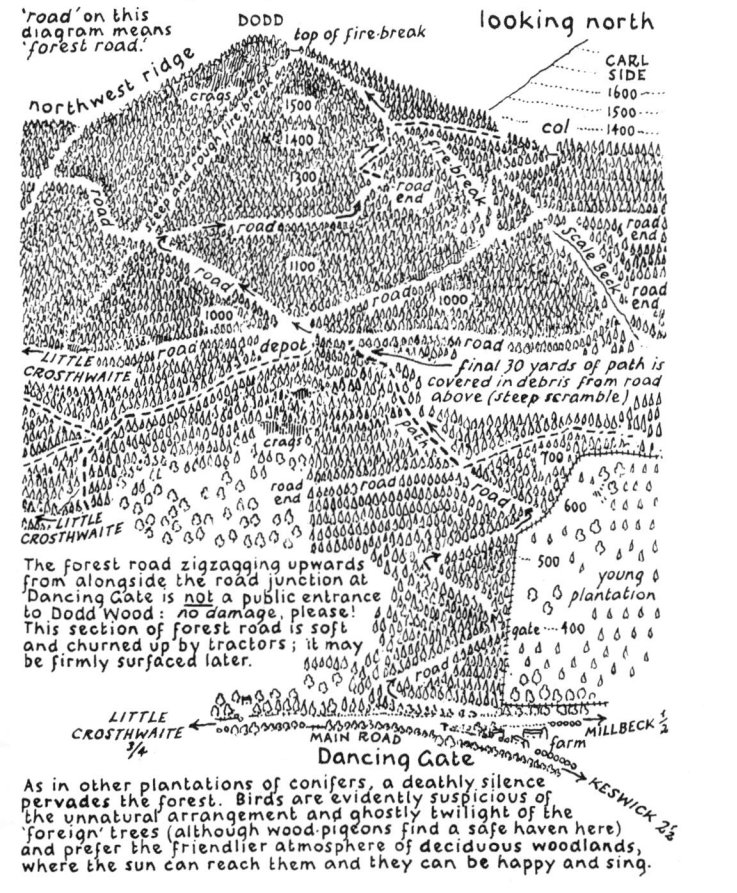

'road' on this diagram means 'forest road'.

DODD — top of fire-break

looking north

northwest ridge — crags — 1500 — 1400 — 1300 — fire-break — 'road' end

CARL SIDE 1600 — 1500 — col — 1400

steep and rough fire-break

road — 1100 — 1000 — road end — Scale Beck — road end

LITTLE CROSTHWAITE — road — depot — road — 1000 — road

final 30 yards of path is covered in debris from road above (steep scramble)

LITTLE CROSTHWAITE — crags — road end — road end — road

700 — 600 — 500 — young plantation — gate — 400

The forest road zigzagging upwards from alongside the road junction at Dancing Gate is **not** a public entrance to Dodd Wood: *no damage, please!* This section of forest road is soft and churned up by tractors; it may be firmly surfaced later.

LITTLE CROSTHWAITE ¼ ← MAIN ROAD — **Dancing Gate** — farm — MILLBECK ½ / KESWICK 2½

As in other plantations of conifers, a deathly silence pervades the forest. Birds are evidently suspicious of the unnatural arrangement and ghostly twilight of the 'foreign' trees (although wood-pigeons find a safe haven here) and prefer the friendlier atmosphere of deciduous woodlands, where the sun can reach them and they can be happy and sing.

This is more a game than a walk. Snakes-and-ladders enthusiasts will find the route absorbing. The whole of Dodd is a labyrinth of forest roads and paths and breaks and these are all the more confusing because the dense screen of trees everywhere makes it impossible to view the way ahead or to take bearings. Follow the arrows.

Dodd 11

ASCENT FROM MILLBECK
1250 feet of ascent : 1½ miles

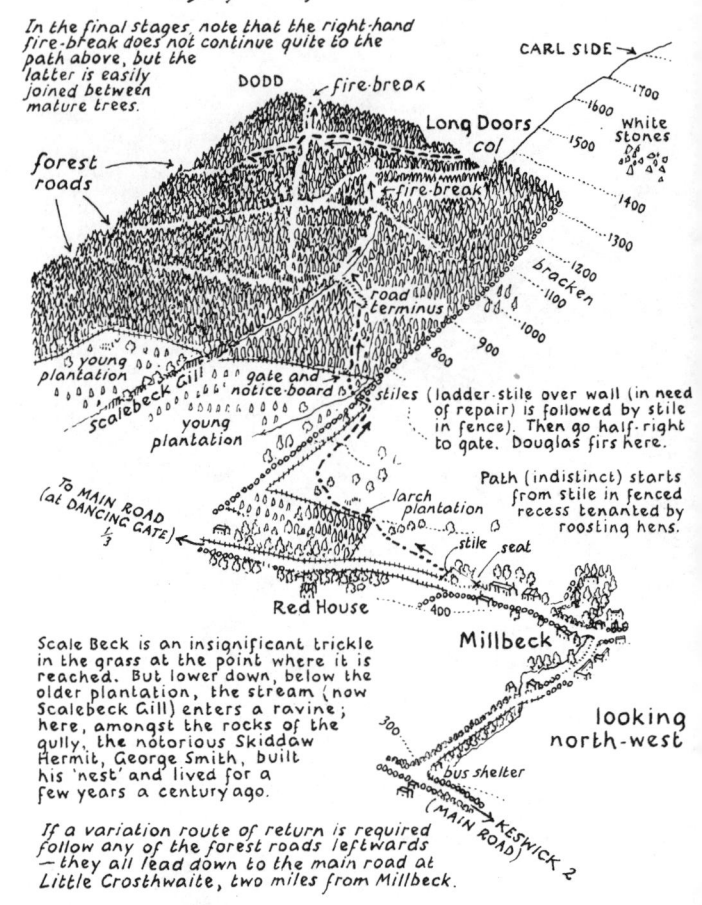

In the final stages, note that the right-hand fire-break does not continue quite to the path above, but the latter is easily joined between mature trees.

[Illustration labels:]
CARL SIDE
DODD — fire-break
Long Doors col
fire-break
forest roads
White Stones
1700, 1600, 1500, 1400, 1300, 1200, 1100, 1000, 900, 800
bracken
road terminus
young plantation
Scalebeck Gill
gate and notice-board
young plantation
stiles (ladder-stile over wall (in need of repair) is followed by stile in fence). Then go half-right to gate. Douglas firs here.
TO MAIN ROAD (AT DANCING GATE) ⅓
larch plantation
Path (indistinct) starts from stile in fenced recess tenanted by roosting hens.
stile seat
Red House
Millbeck
400
looking north-west
300
bus shelter
(MAIN ROAD) KESWICK 2

Scale Beck is an insignificant trickle in the grass at the point where it is reached. But lower down, below the older plantation, the stream (now Scalebeck Gill) enters a ravine; here, amongst the rocks of the gully, the notorious Skiddaw Hermit, George Smith, built his 'nest' and lived for a few years a century ago.

If a variation route of return is required follow any of the forest roads leftwards — they all lead down to the main road at Little Crosthwaite, two miles from Millbeck.

Millbeck is conveniently placed for an ascent of Dodd, yet this is not a popular climb, and nobody will be encountered on 360 days in the year. The path across the lower slopes of Carl Side has gone to seed and the forest itself is a maze, but follow the arrows and the top will be reached in due course.

Dodd 12
===

THE SUMMIT

This is the weirdest of all summits, a place to visit — and flee from. The old cairn is there, as it was when the hilltop was grass pasture but in the course of the years it has been insidiously overshadowed by a new and taller growth: a few hundred specimens of *Pinus mugo*, the mountain pine. This unsightly tree, of a strange and ghostly appearance, now covers the top completely, though a tiny clearing has been left in deference to the cairn. It is obviously not a natural adornment of Dodd, because nature does not grow her trees at regularly-spaced intervals, as these are; but it would seem to a layman that the planting has not been successful. Few of the trees are flourishing: the majority look unhealthy and even diseased and dying. The grass, due to banishment of sheep from the fell, is now coarse and tussocky.

The cairn is difficult to find. Because of the screen of vegetation, it is not seen until almost underfoot.

──────── *fire-break*
- - - - - *path leading to forest road*

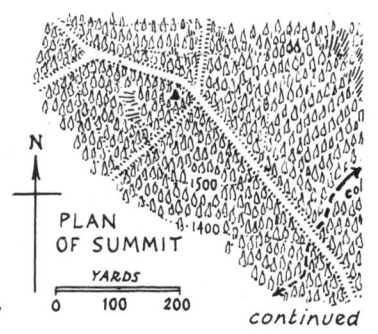

PLAN OF SUMMIT

YARDS
0   100   200

continued

Dodd 13

THE SUMMIT

continued

DESCENTS: Attempts to get down from the cairn by any route other than directly back into the main fire-break are likely to be regretted: apart from the probability of causing some damage and the certainty of suffering much discomfort the trespasser in the forest faces the hazard of crags concealed by trees growing on their very brink and may find himself falling through space before being aware of them. So get back into the fire-break 20 yards away and follow this south-east, gradually descending; after 330 yards, and in a small hollow, look for paths leading off both sides of the break: either path links with safe forest roads, that to the left going to the col and generally being the better.
Do not follow the fire-break *north-west* from the summit: the top section is rough heather, steeply tilted, and has new plantings. The two narrower fire-breaks leaving the top north and southwest are steep and treacherous, and should be left severely alone.

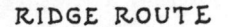

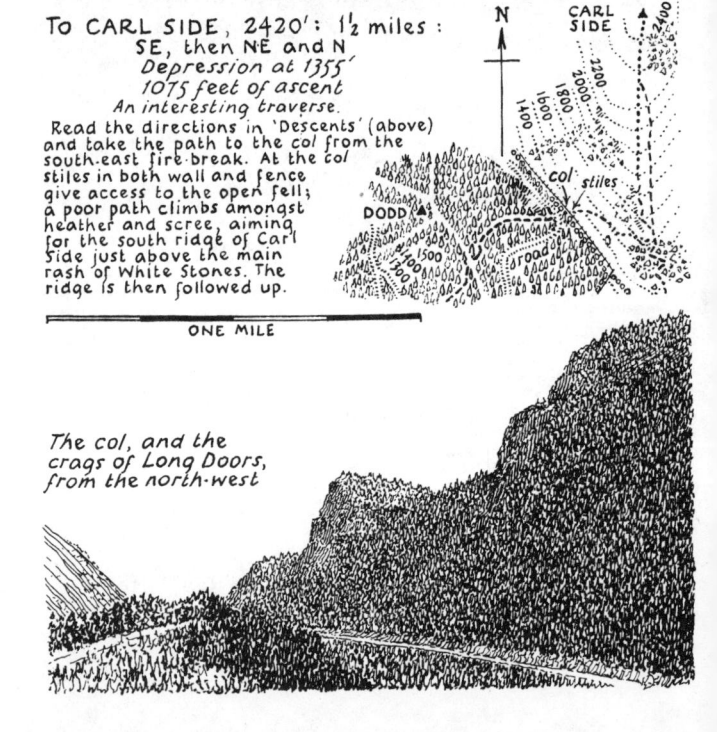

RIDGE ROUTE

To CARL SIDE, 2420': 1½ miles:
SE, then NE and N
Depression at 1355'
1075 feet of ascent
An interesting traverse.

Read the directions in 'Descents' (above) and take the path to the col from the south-east fire-break. At the col stiles in both wall and fence give access to the open fell; a poor path climbs amongst heather and scree, aiming for the south ridge of Carl Side just above the main rash of White Stones. The ridge is then followed up.

ONE MILE

The col, and the crags of Long Doors, from the north-west

Dodd 14

THE VIEW

By standing on tiptoes, craning the neck, leaping in the air and miscellaneous gyrations of the body not normally indulged in by people in their right senses it is just possible, on a clear day, to see all the fells indicated on the diagram. The obstruction is caused by *Pinus mugo*, the gaunt bare branches of which form an unbroken screen up to ten feet high all round the cairn. This is unfortunate, because enough can be seen, with difficulty, to suggest that the view south, if uninterrupted, would be simply glorious.

Principal Fells

N

ULLOCK PIKE
LONG SIDE
SKIDDAW
CARL SIDE
SKIDDAW LITTLE MAN

SALE FELL — 2½ miles

W ———————————————————— E

BROOM FELL
LORD'S SEAT
WHINLATTER

LATRIGG
HIGH RIGG — 5 miles
CLOUGH HEAD — 7½ miles
GREAT DODD
STYBARROW DODD
RAISE
CATSTYCAM
WHITE SIDE
HELVELLYN

GRISEDALE PIKE
EEL CRAG
SAIL
OUTERSIDE
SCAR CRAGS
CAUSEY PIKE
BARROW
CATBELLS
BLEABERRY FELL
RAVEN CRAG
HIGH SEAT

HINDSCARTH
DALE HEAD
MAIDEN MOOR
KINGS HOW
GRANGE FELL

10 miles

GREAT RIGG
SEAT SANDAL

12½ miles
GABLE
GREAT END
ESK PIKE
GLARAMARA
BOWFELL
PIKE O' STICKLE
PIKE O' BLISCO
SWIRL HOW

SCAFELL
GREAT PIKE

ULLSCARF
HIGH RAISE

15 miles

S

Lakes and Tarns
SSE: Derwentwater
NW: Bassenthwaite Lake

Once upon a time, the summit of Dodd was renowned for its view of Bassenthwaite Lake, and Derwentwater too was well displayed. Now, both are greatly obscured by the aforementioned *Pinus mugo*.

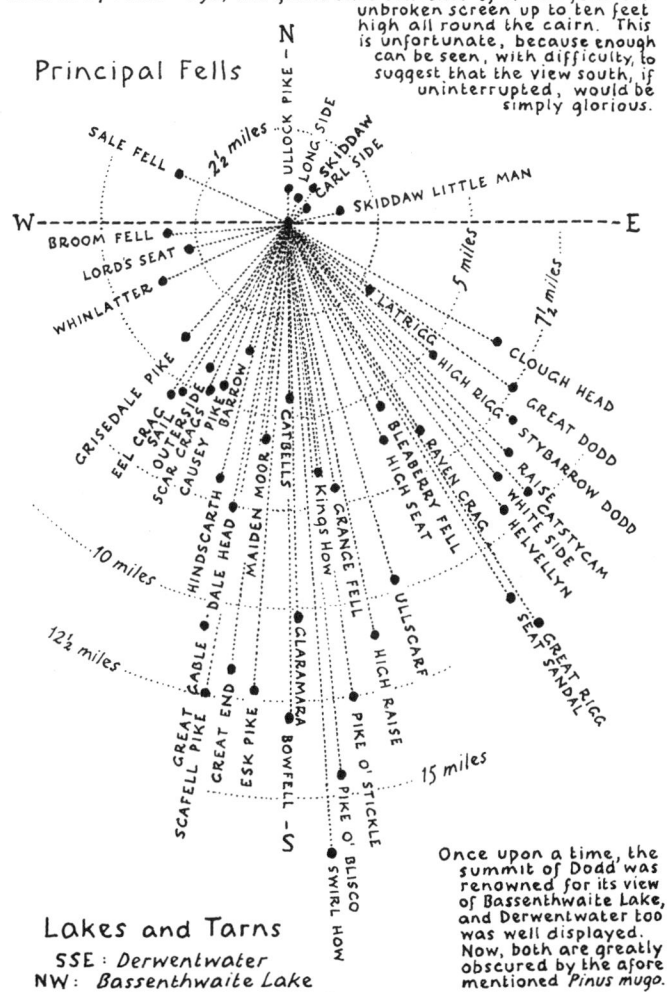

Great Calva 2265'

from the path to Skiddaw House

from Burn Tod

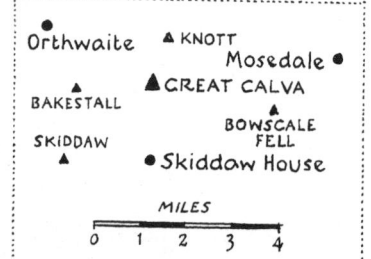

Great Calva 2

NATURAL FEATURES

Most regular visitors to Lakeland will be familiar with the outline of Great Calva even though they may never in their wanderings have been within miles of it, because its symmetrical pyramid neatly fills in the head of the valley opening south between the Skiddaw and Blencathra massifs and is conspicuously seen from many points on the busy road approaching Keswick from Grasmere.

It occupies a splendid position overlooking the broad depression of Skiddaw Forest, with which it seems to be inseparably associated, more so even than Skiddaw itself. Calva dominates the Forest, rising from it in a strange patchwork of colours indicative of areas of heather, its principal covering, that have been burnt off, are newly shooting up or are long established, giving odd contrasts in appearance.

The actual top, which is stony, is a fine belvedere, but behind is an extensive plateau without an irrigation system and so forming a morass across which one can step gingerly to the solid ground of Little Calva, a place of little interest; and, beyond, the fell drops away steeply in a series of spiky aretes to the magnificent Dash Falls. This is Calva's best aspect; nevertheless the fell's appeal is more likely to depend upon its unique function as the watchtower of Skiddaw Forest.

Bridge on the road to Skiddaw House, above Dash Falls

Great Calva 3

MAP

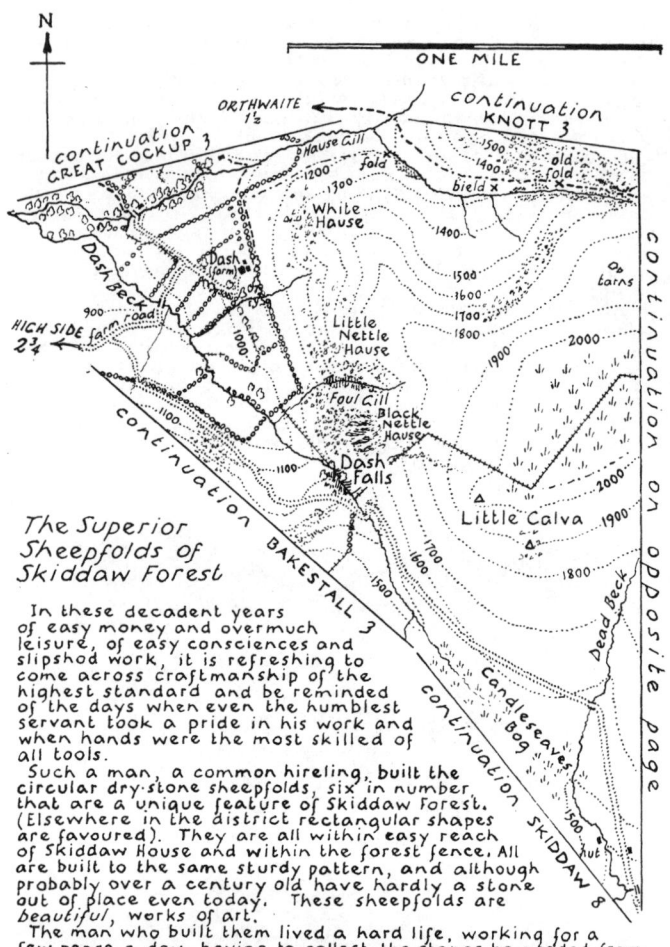

The Superior Sheepfolds of Skiddaw Forest

In these decadent years of easy money and overmuch leisure, of easy consciences and slipshod work, it is refreshing to come across craftmanship of the highest standard and be reminded of the days when even the humblest servant took a pride in his work and when hands were the most skilled of all tools.

Such a man, a common hireling, built the circular dry-stone sheepfolds, six in number, that are a unique feature of Skiddaw Forest. (Elsewhere in the district rectangular shapes are favoured). They are all within easy reach of Skiddaw House and within the forest fence. All are built to the same sturdy pattern, and although probably over a century old have hardly a stone out of place even today. These sheepfolds are *beautiful*, works of art.

The man who built them lived a hard life, working for a few pence a day, having to collect the stones he needed from the fellside and often sleeping rough on the job at nights. He did the task he was hired to do, and did it well. When, in due course, he passed away from this life he left no name behind him. Only his work remains. Just an unknown labourer......... but how many of us today, with far greater opportunities and education, will be remembered by our work hundreds of years after we are gone? Few indeed! Idleness builds no monuments.

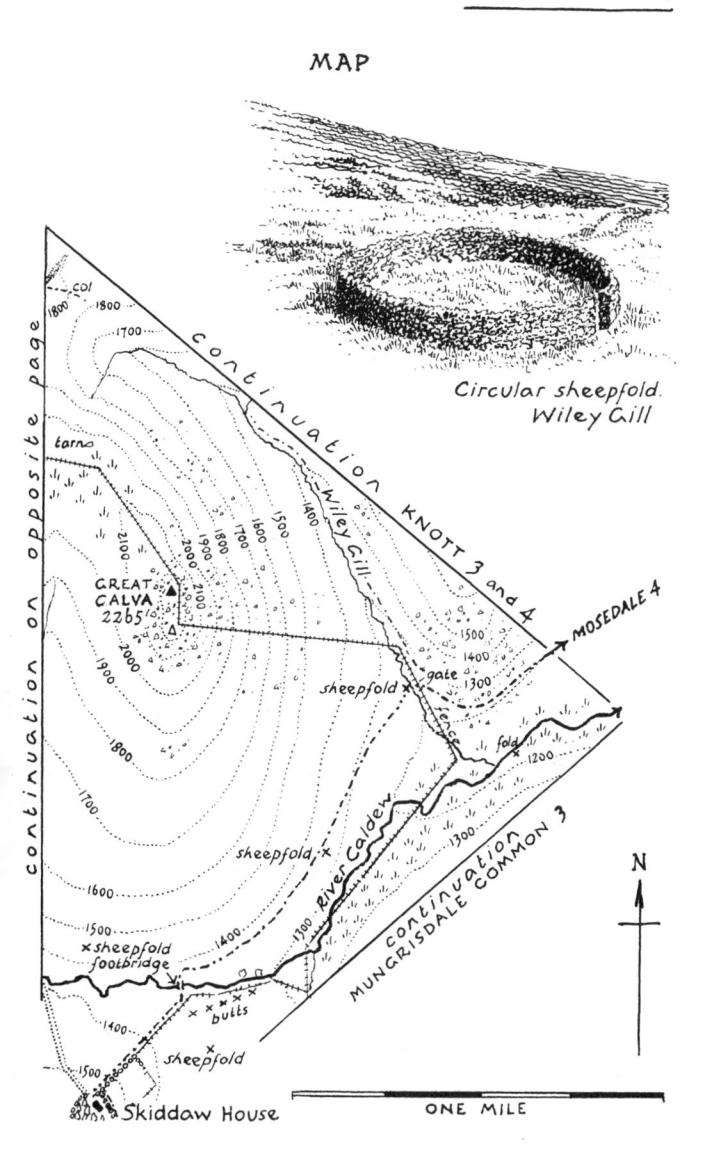

Great Calva 4

MAP

Circular sheepfold, Wiley Gill

Great Calva 5

ASCENT FROM ORTHWAITE
1500 feet of ascent : 3¾ miles

GREAT CALVA

The col is grassy, but, unlike most green hollows between two hills, is narrow and well defined. Turn sharp right here to reach the fence, which goes directly to the top (left).

The summit comes into view at the col for the first time during the walk.

heather

Little Calva

col — two tarns — cotton grass — fence

KNOTT

Burn Tod
heather and stones

The upper reaches of Hause Gill are very wild and stony. Keep to the bed of the stream, emerging where the ravine bends left. There are many skulls and bones in the ravine: none appear to be human, however.

sheepfold (ruin)
landslip
bracken
grass
× bield
× sheepfold

Hause Gill

Note the difference between a sheepfold and a bield. A fold is an enclosure of stone walls to contain sheep; a bield is an open shelter of stone walls to protect sheep from bad weather. Thus a fold acts as a bield also, but a bield never serves as a fold.

The fell rising on the left throughout the walk thus far is GREAT COCKUP

boulder

Path A is an old bridle-way, now rarely used and not easy to discern when the bracken is high. Path B, keeping just above the wall, is more distinct. Path A has superior views; the feature of Path B is Brockle Crag, remarkable for its many pure white (quartz) stones.

posts
Brockle Crag

DASH FARM

An easy walk in interesting territory above the pleasant Dash valley, but the last mile (beyond the col) is tedious.

Brocklecrag (farm)

bracken
Hall
Cottage — gate — sandpit
Farm
Orthwaite
Horsemoor Hills (farm)

Mirkholme (farm)

pastures

Cassbeck Bridge

HIGH SIDE 2

looking south-east

ROAD

BASSENTHWAITE VILLAGE 1½

There is good but limited accommodation at Orthwaite Cottage. This is the only place offering refuge and refreshment for miles around.

Great Calva 6

ASCENT FROM SKIDDAW HOUSE
900 feet of ascent : 2 miles

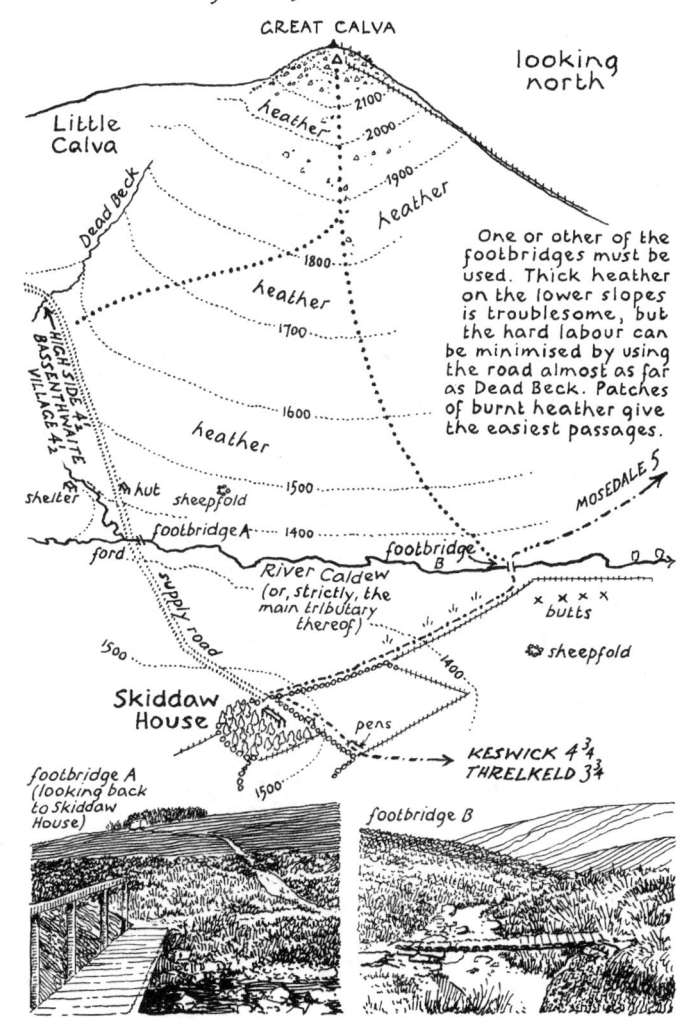

looking north

One or other of the footbridges must be used. Thick heather on the lower slopes is troublesome, but the hard labour can be minimised by using the road almost as far as Dead Beck. Patches of burnt heather give the easiest passages.

footbridge A (looking back to Skiddaw House)

footbridge B

Great Calva 7

THE SUMMIT

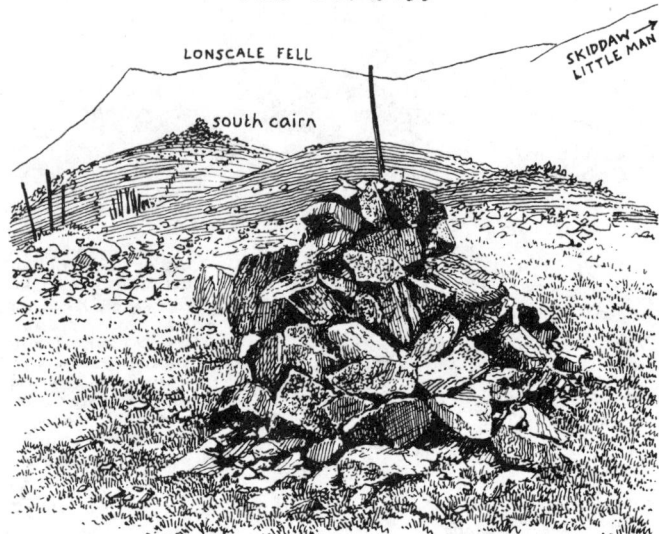

What appears to be the obvious top of the symmetrical pyramid of Great Calva, as seen on the climb up from Skiddaw Forest, is found on investigation to be not the true summit at all, and the prominent cairn overlooking this approach is succeeded by one at a greater elevation 130 yards further along a gentle incline. The top of the fell is made interesting by a scattering of stones, and is given added distinction by a wire fence, which is in disrepair but more intact than is usual with hill-fences. *In mist, note that the right-angle in the fence occurs at the lower (south) cairn.*

DESCENTS: The fence is a guide to the Caldew Valley, descending east from the south cairn; and, starting north-west from the top cairn, it leads safely down, after many changes of direction and a traverse of Little Calva, to the Skiddaw House road just above Dash Falls. For Threlkeld or Keswick, via Skiddaw House, go straight down the south slope but incline to the right when the steepness and stoniness have subsided, gaining the Skiddaw House road at the footbridge. (A beeline might be halted by the beck, which although here only a mere infant and not yet even christened Caldew, is already lusty).

The south cairn

Great Calva 8

THE SUMMIT
continued

There is no need to sit shivering in the lee of the cairn. A few yards down the east slope, across the fence, is a splendidly-constructed windproof shelter.

summit shelter

RIDGE ROUTE

To KNOTT, 2329' : 1½ miles : NW, then NE
Depression at 1810'
550 feet of ascent
Walkers whose boots let water in will soon be cognisant of the fact.

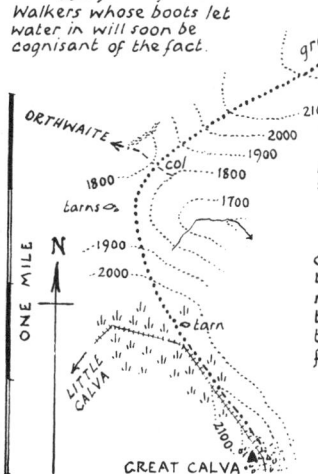

It matters not which side of the fence is taken; it is slightly easier to avoid the bogs on the east side. Proceed to the accompaniment of loud squelches as far as the angle of the fence, where swing down to the col, which is neat and narrow. The pull up on to Knott is steep initially, becoming easy.

To SKIDDAW
there is no convenient ridge, a descent to the Skiddaw House road being necessary whichever route is taken. The best plan is to go up to Skiddaw House and ascend from there (see Skiddaw page 21). (As a point of interest, it may be mentioned that the fence, if followed closely and starting *northwest*, will lead almost to the top of Skiddaw, after many changes of direction).

Great Calva 9

THE VIEW

An observation of particular interest is mentioned on the next page following.

From the lower cairn there is the best of all prospects of Skiddaw Forest — a strange, silent wilderness irrigated by the infant Caldew. The neighbouring fells are not well presented, but there is a distant view of the Solway Firth bisected by the Sandale television mast, which isn't a very inspiring sight either.

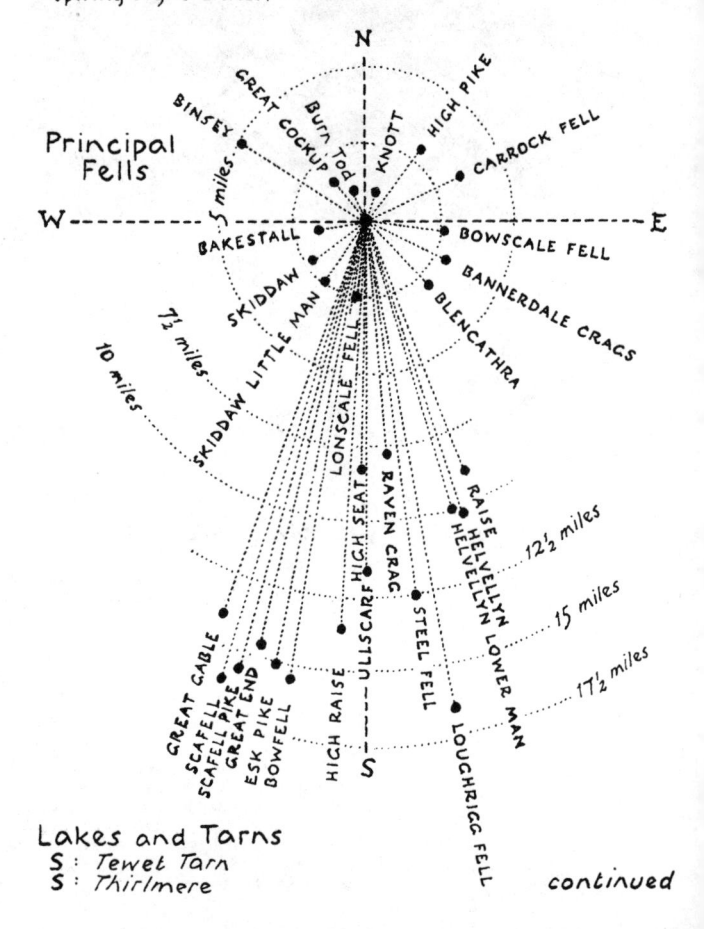

Principal Fells

N — BINSEY, GREAT COCKUP, Burn Tod, KNOTT, HIGH PIKE, CARROCK FELL, BAKESTALL, BOWSCALE FELL, SKIDDAW, BANNERDALE CRAGS, SKIDDAW LITTLE MAN, BLENCATHRA, LONSCALE FELL, HIGH SEAT, RAVEN CRAG, RAISE, HELVELLYN, HELVELLYN LOWER MAN, GREAT GABLE, SCAFELL, SCAFELL PIKE, GREAT END, ESK PIKE, BOWFELL, HIGH RAISE, ULLSCARF, STEEL FELL, LOUGHRIGG FELL

5 miles, 7½ miles, 10 miles, 12½ miles, 15 miles, 17½ miles

W ———— E
S

Lakes and Tarns
S: Tewet Tarn
S: Thirlmere

continued

Great Calva 10

THE VIEW

continued

Lakeland is severed by a great geological fault: a deep trough running north and south across the district. The lakes of Windermere, Rydal Water, Grasmere and Thirlmere lie in this trough and the main road north of Ambleside takes advantage of the simple passage it affords, Dunmail Raise at 782' being the highest point. The rift continues through the Vale of St. Johns and the Glenderaterra valley to Skiddaw Forest, where, situated exactly at its head, there rises the graceful cone of Great Calva. The trough is steeply bounded by high hills on both sides, notably the Helvellyn range. Great Calva's unique position provides it with a view along the direct line of the fault, so that, despite the mountains crowding into the scene, there is a remarkable vista, like looking along the sights of a gun, through the heart of the district to the low Windermere fells in the extreme south.

THE GREAT CENTRAL FAULT

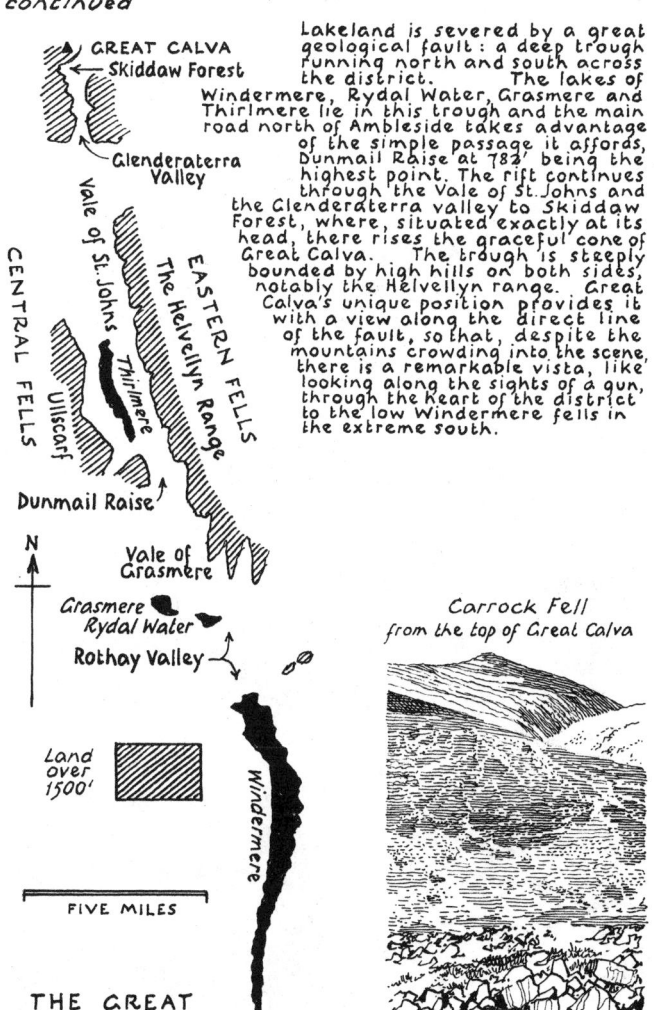

Carrock Fell from the top of Great Calva

Great Cockup

1720'
approx

from Longlands

- Uldale
- Longlands
- Orthwaite
- GREAT SCA FELL ▲
- GREAT COCKUP ▲
- MEAL FELL ▲
- KNOTT ▲
- Bassenthwaite Village

MILES
0 1 2 3 4

Orthwaite Hall

Great Cockup 2

NATURAL FEATURES

Viewed from a distance, Great Cockup appears as a modest but extensive eminence with no obvious summit and nothing calling for closer inspection. First impressions are confirmed by a tour of exploration, the fell underfoot proving no more attractive than the fell at a distance. Bracken is rampant on the lower slopes, much burning of heather has resulted in a dark and patchy appearance higher up, and the skyline never bestirs itself from placid curves to produce even the slightest excitement. Although not ornamental, however, Great Cockup is strongly functional, which perhaps matters more: its long spine, rising steeply from Orthwaite, divides the waters of the River Ellen from those of tributaries of the Derwent. The fell terminates abruptly in the deep cut of Trusmadoor; beyond, a ridge continues the height of land over Meal Fell to the major summit of the Uldale group, Great Sca Fell.

A feature of the south flank of Great Cockup and always conspicuous on a bright day is the white-streaked *Brockle Crag*. This is disappointing on close inspection, being no more than an untidy fall of quartzite rocks.

Brockle Crag

The Boulder
(Burn Tod behind)

The Boulder. On the Ordnance map of scale 6"= 1 mile there is inscribed the word 'Boulder' at a point alongside the old bridleway crossing the south flank of Great Cockup — a distinction so rare that a walker of an enquiring turn of mind must needs go in search of this natural wonder. Finding it is easy — it stands in isolation — but its dimensions are rather a disappointment, none exceeding a few feet. There are thousands of bigger specimens within a mile of Sty Head. This recording of an ordinary stone illustrates the dearth of features on the fell.
The boulder may be the debris of a now-vanished crag but its situation suggests that it is more probably an erratic left by a retreating glacier.

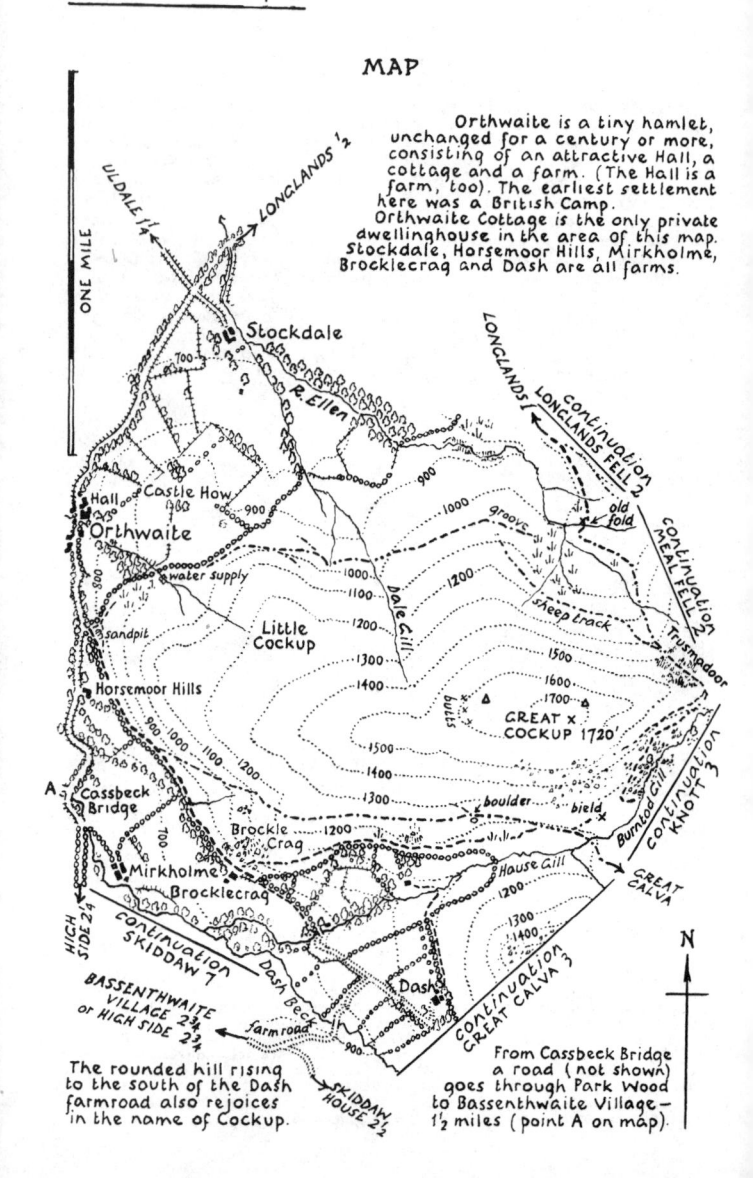

Great Cockup 3

MAP

Orthwaite is a tiny hamlet, unchanged for a century or more, consisting of an attractive Hall, a cottage and a farm. (The Hall is a farm, too). The earliest settlement here was a British Camp.
Orthwaite Cottage is the only private dwellinghouse in the area of this map. Stockdale, Horsemoor Hills, Mirkholme, Brocklecrag and Dash are all farms.

The rounded hill rising to the south of the Dash farmroad also rejoices in the name of Cockup.

From Cassbeck Bridge a road (not shown) goes through Park Wood to Bassenthwaite Village — 1½ miles (point A on map).

Great Cockup 4

ASCENT FROM ORTHWAITE
950 feet of ascent : 2 miles

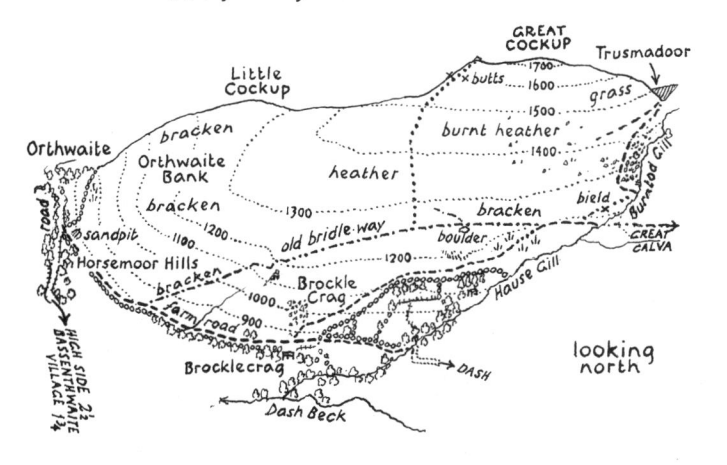

The summit is easily reached from the highest part of the old bridle-way, up a simple slope of grass and heather, the true summit being 300 yards beyond the cairned top first gained, just above the shooting butts. This route is better than a direct climb up Orthwaite Bank, where the bracken is dense and extensive. For a different route of return, go down the far slope to Trusmadoor and then use sheep-tracks alongside Burntod Gill; a further variation, crossing marshy ground, passes below Brockle Crag and joins the farm-road.

The Dash Valley

Great Cockup 5

THE SUMMIT

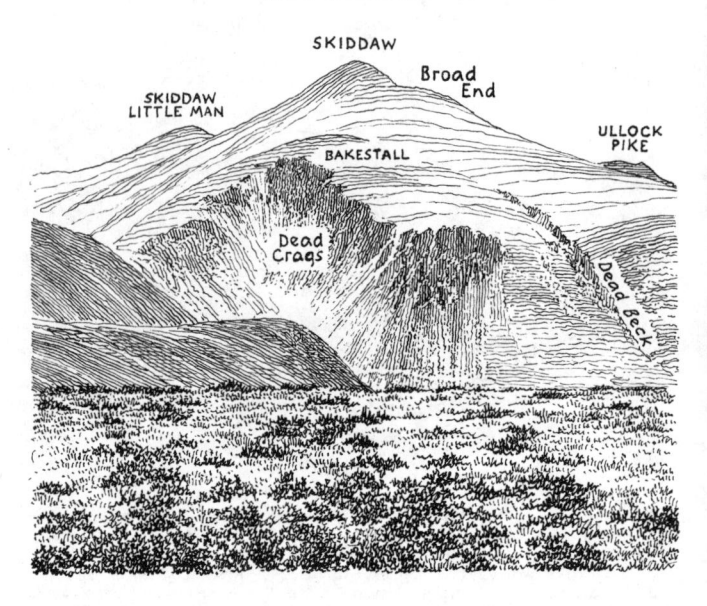

A visitor here must do his own surveying to determine the highest point, there being no cairn on it, but, subject to a difference of opinion of a few yards, all will agree it is in the midst of an expanse of scanty, anaemic-looking heather on the crest of a gentle dome. 300 yards west is a more definite top with a few stones, but this is quite obviously lower. Nearer, north-east, there is also a cairn on a rise: this, too, is lower.

On the 6" Ordnance map three surface-levels are given — 1690, 1673 and 1701. The heights of 1690 and 1701 would seem to apply to the two tops with cairns. The highest point must be in the middle of the wide 1700' contour on the 2½" map; there is no 1725' contour and the true altitude of the fell may reasonably be taken to be around 1720'.

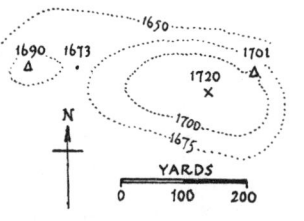

DESCENTS may safely be made in any direction, a little care being necessary in bad weather in the neighbourhood of Trusmadoor, where there are small cliffs.

Great Cockup 6

THE VIEW

Great Cockup is the most westerly of the Uldale Fells and thus has an unrestricted view across to the Solway Firth and Scotland, which deserves more attention than the rather unattractive mountain scene. Nevertheless the undisputed monarch in this picture is Skiddaw, rising magnificently nearby in the south.

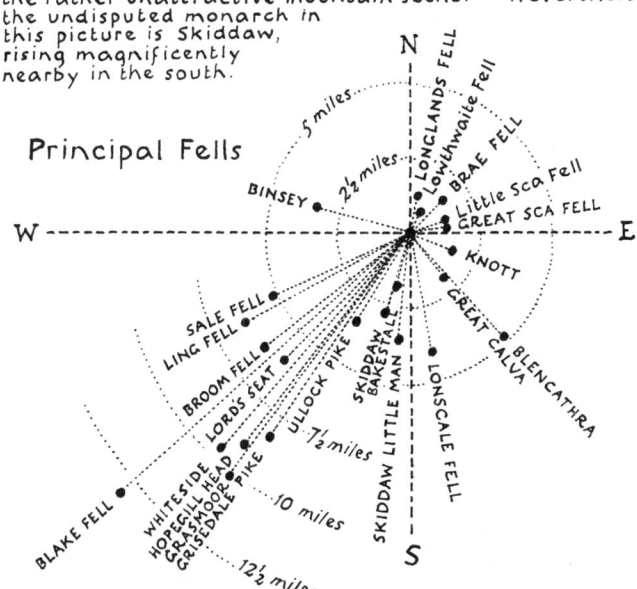

Principal Fells

(N) LONGLANDS FELL, LOWTHWAITE FELL, BRAE FELL, Little Sca Fell, GREAT SCA FELL, KNOTT, GREAT CALVA, BLENCATHRA, LONSCALE FELL, SKIDDAW LITTLE MAN, SKIDDAW, BAKESTALL, ULLOCK PIKE, LORD'S SEAT, BROOM FELL, LING FELL, SALE FELL, BINSEY, WHITESIDE, HOPEGILL HEAD, GRASMOOR, GRISEDALE PIKE, BLAKE FELL

Distances: 2½ miles, 5 miles, 7½ miles, 10 miles, 12½ miles

Lakes and Tarns

WSW: Bassenthwaite Lake
Over Water (NW) cannot be seen from the highest point, but is in view from the two cairned tops.

RIDGE ROUTE

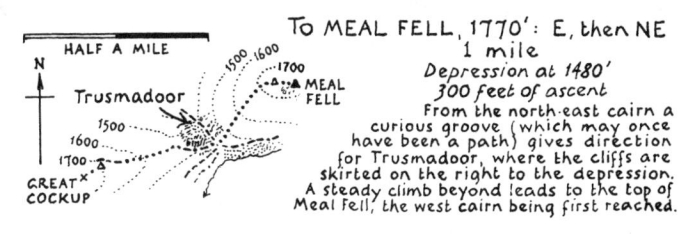

TO MEAL FELL, 1770': E, then NE
1 mile
Depression at 1480'
300 feet of ascent

From the north-east cairn a curious groove (which may once have been a path) gives direction for Trusmadoor, where the cliffs are skirted on the right to the depression. A steady climb beyond leads to the top of Meal Fell, the west cairn being first reached.

HALF A MILE

Trusmadoor, GREAT COCKUP, MEAL FELL (1500, 1600, 1700)

Great Sca Fell 2131'

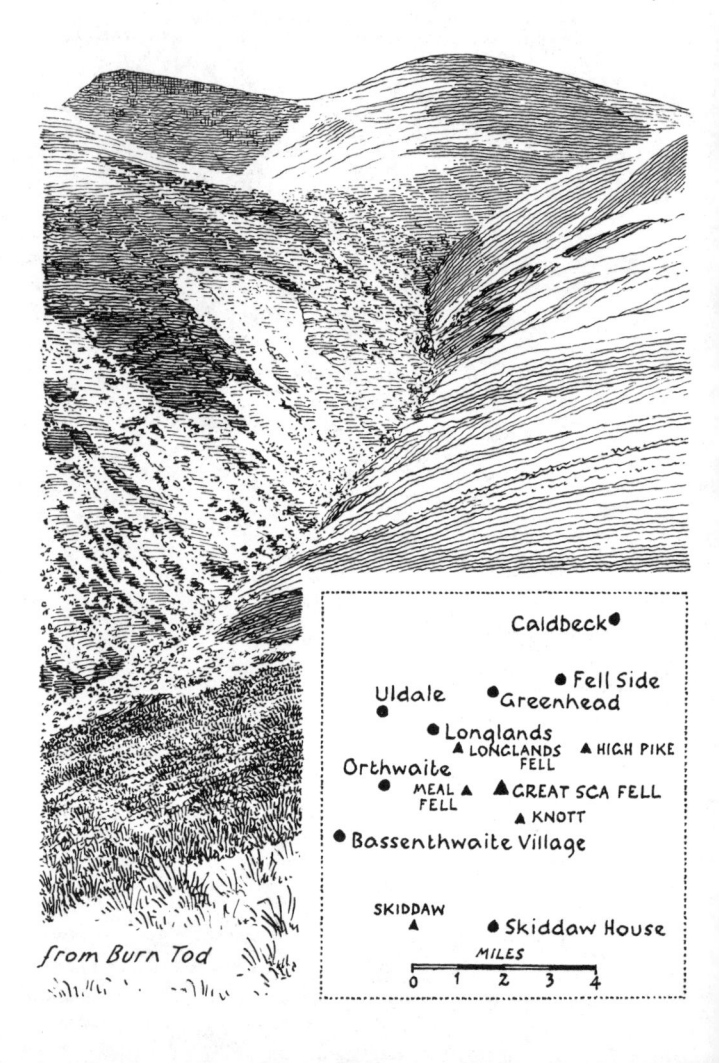

from Burn Tod

- Caldbeck
- Fell Side
- Uldale
- Greenhead
- Longlands
- ▲ LONGLANDS FELL
- ▲ HIGH PIKE
- Orthwaite
- ▲ MEAL FELL
- ▲ GREAT SCA FELL
- ▲ KNOTT
- Bassenthwaite Village
- SKIDDAW ▲
- Skiddaw House

MILES
0 1 2 3 4

Great Sca Fell 2

NATURAL FEATURES

The Uldale Fells rise in three ridges between west and north to merge in one common meeting-ground at the place of greatest altitude, this focal point being a smooth double-headed uplift of grassy fell, known to cartographers by the names of the twin summits, Great and Little Sca Fell, but to farmers and shepherds merely as Scafell. (No resemblance to any other Scafell is intended, nor does it exist). All these ridges are gently-contoured and grassy, with bracken below 1500' and some patches of heather. They are excellent sheep-pastures, and it may be remarked that flocks can be watched with much greater facility on these smooth slopes than in rockier parts of the district: from any suitable vantage-point the movements of sheep can be observed over great distances. The watercourses, characteristic of the northern fells, are deeply cut and so steep-sided that vegetational matter ekes a precarious existence between regular scourings by landslips.

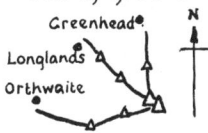

Much the same pattern applies to the eastern side of the fell, which is intimately linked with Knott, the highest fell north of Skiddaw Forest, grass slopes and stony ravines predominating: here, however, the stony debris has been augmented by accumulations of waste from the extensive mining operations of past centuries. Nowadays Great Sca Fell is as it was before the miners came, a peaceful and undisturbed sheep pasture — and a quiet sanctuary in a world becoming discordant and noisy, where natural sanctuaries are shrinking fast yet were never in greater need.

Little Sca Fell (left) and Great Sca Fell, from the Longlands valley

Great Sca Fell 3

MAP

Fellwalking is the healthiest and most satisfying of all outdoor exercises. Climbing the hills and tramping over rough country makes a man strong and keeps him fit (it cleans his mind and does his soul good, too). But many enthusiasts, the author one of them, are nevertheless quite happy to reach the tops with a minimum expenditure of effort, short of being carried upwards on the backs of their wives or other companions, which is simply not in the best traditions of fellwalking. Easy paths are more to their liking than steep scrambles.

These seekers after simple routes should note with gratification the particular attractions of the maps of the Uldale and Caldbeck fells. The starting-points on the roads are considerably elevated, especially in the north, where climbing proper commences with a big advantage of close on 1000' already accounted for; the main summits lie well back at little more than 2000'; easy gradients are the rule. Walkers do not drop in their tracks here: they just go on and on.......

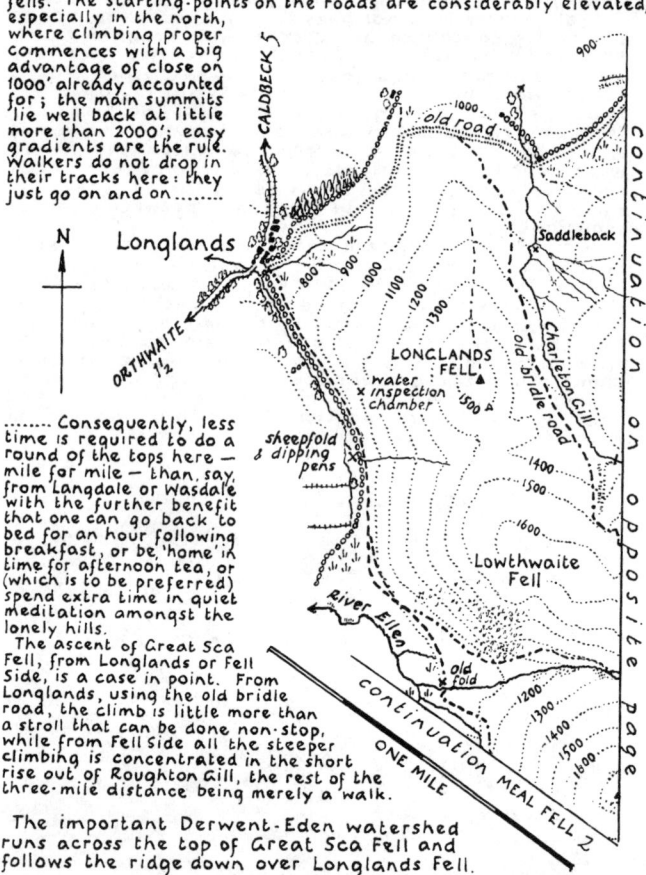

.... Consequently, less time is required to do a round of the tops here — mile for mile — than, say, from Langdale or Wasdale with the further benefit that one can go back to bed for an hour following breakfast, or be 'home' in time for afternoon tea, or (which is to be preferred) spend extra time in quiet meditation amongst the lonely hills.

The ascent of Great Sca Fell, from Longlands or Fell Side, is a case in point. From Longlands, using the old bridle road, the climb is little more than a stroll that can be done non-stop, while from Fell Side all the steeper climbing is concentrated in the short rise out of Roughton Gill, the rest of the three-mile distance being merely a walk.

The important Derwent-Eden watershed runs across the top of Great Sca Fell and follows the ridge down over Longlands Fell.

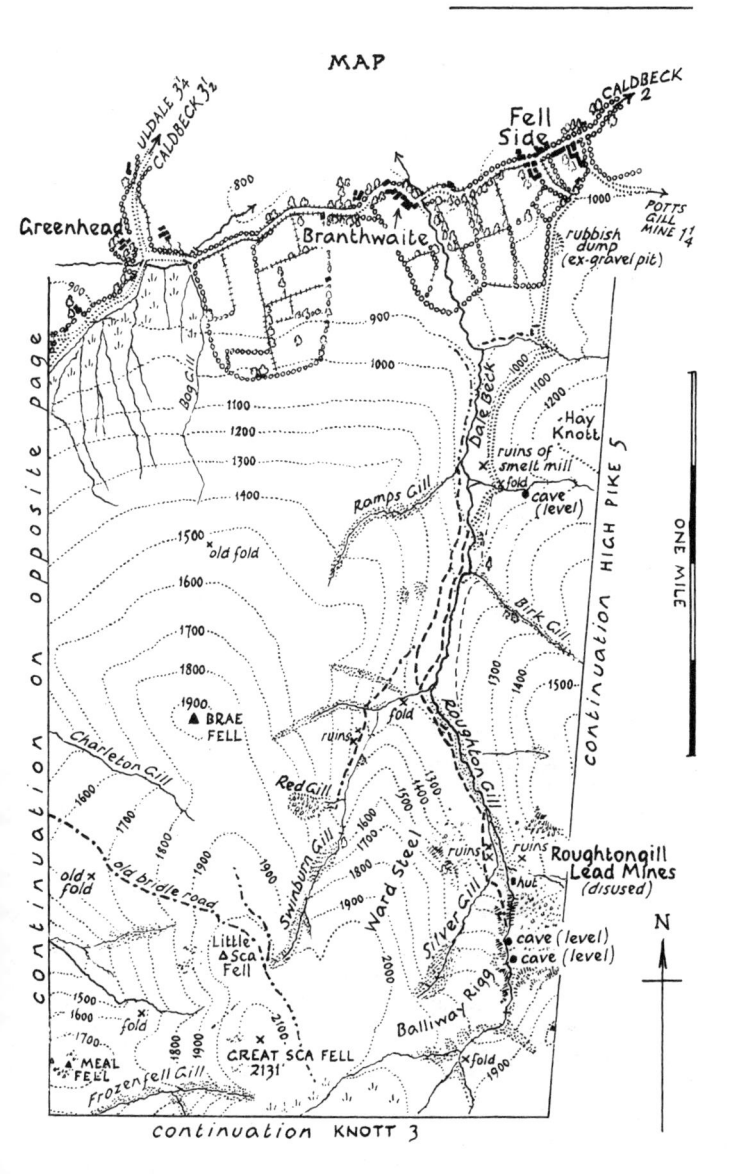

Great Sca Fell 4

MAP

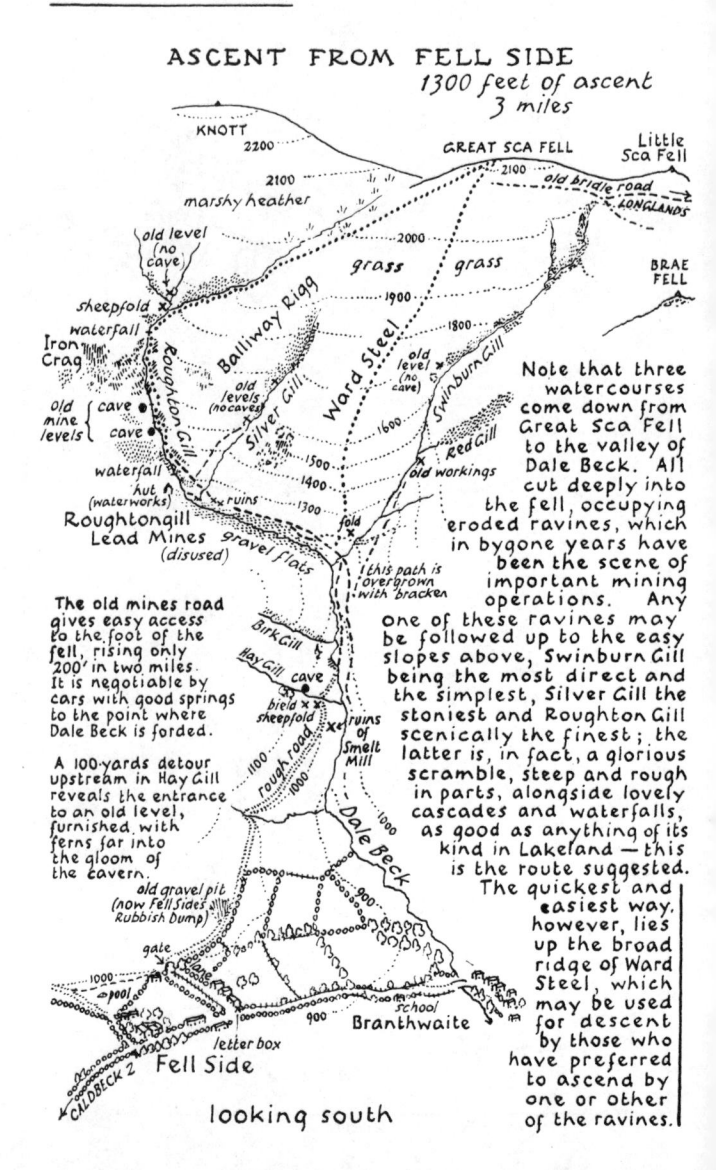

Great Sca Fell 5

ASCENT FROM FELL SIDE
1300 feet of ascent
3 miles

looking south

Note that three watercourses come down from Great Sca Fell to the valley of Dale Beck. All cut deeply into the fell, occupying eroded ravines, which in bygone years have been the scene of important mining operations. Any one of these ravines may be followed up to the easy slopes above, Swinburn Gill being the most direct and the simplest, Silver Gill the stoniest and Roughton Gill scenically the finest; the latter is, in fact, a glorious scramble, steep and rough in parts, alongside lovely cascades and waterfalls, as good as anything of its kind in Lakeland — this is the route suggested. The quickest and easiest way, however, lies up the broad ridge of Ward Steel, which may be used for descent by those who have preferred to ascend by one or other of the ravines.

The old mines road gives easy access to the foot of the fell, rising only 200' in two miles. It is negotiable by cars with good springs to the point where Dale Beck is forded.

A 100-yards detour upstream in Hay Gill reveals the entrance to an old level, furnished with ferns far into the gloom of the cavern.

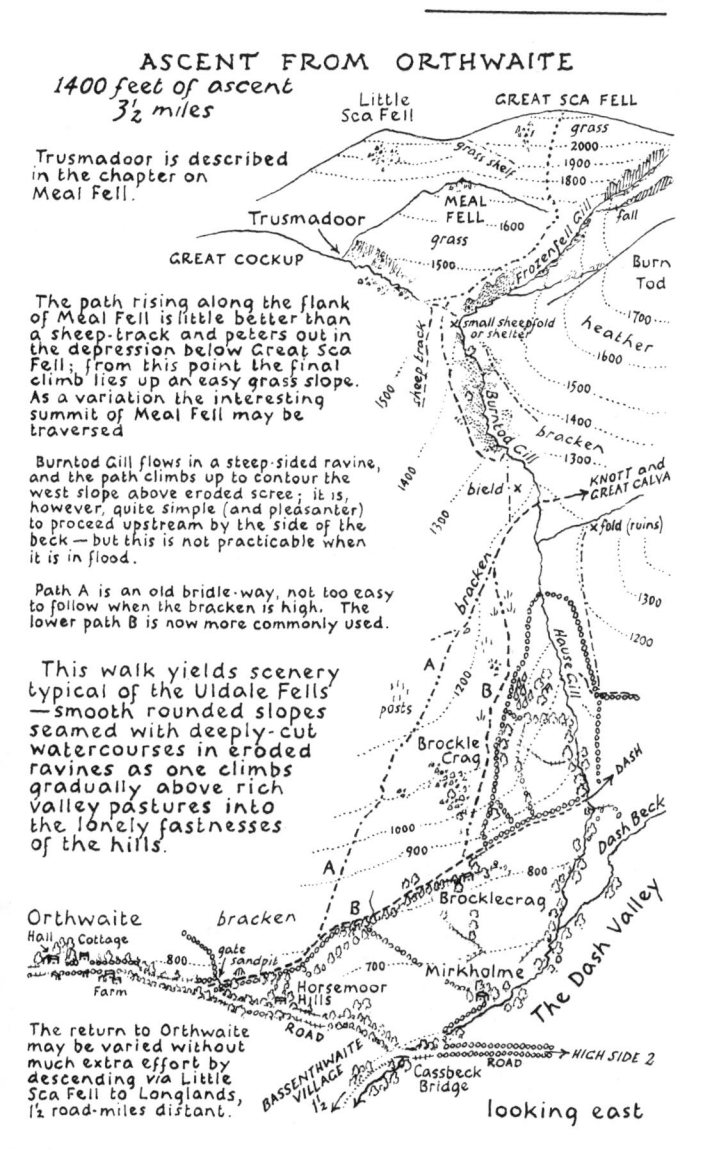

Great Sca Fell 6

ASCENT FROM ORTHWAITE
1400 feet of ascent
3½ miles

Trusmadoor is described in the chapter on Meal Fell.

The path rising along the flank of Meal Fell is little better than a sheep-track and peters out in the depression below Great Sca Fell; from this point the final climb lies up an easy grass slope. As a variation the interesting summit of Meal Fell may be traversed

Burntod Gill flows in a steep-sided ravine, and the path climbs up to contour the west slope above eroded scree; it is, however, quite simple (and pleasanter) to proceed upstream by the side of the beck — but this is not practicable when it is in flood.

Path A is an old bridle-way, not too easy to follow when the bracken is high. The lower path B is now more commonly used.

This walk yields scenery typical of the Uldale Fells — smooth rounded slopes seamed with deeply-cut watercourses in eroded ravines as one climbs gradually above rich valley pastures into the lonely fastnesses of the hills.

Orthwaite

The return to Orthwaite may be varied without much extra effort by descending via Little Sca Fell to Longlands, 1½ road-miles distant.

looking east

Great Sca Fell 7

ASCENT FROM LONGLANDS
1550 feet of ascent : 2½ miles (3 via the bridle road)

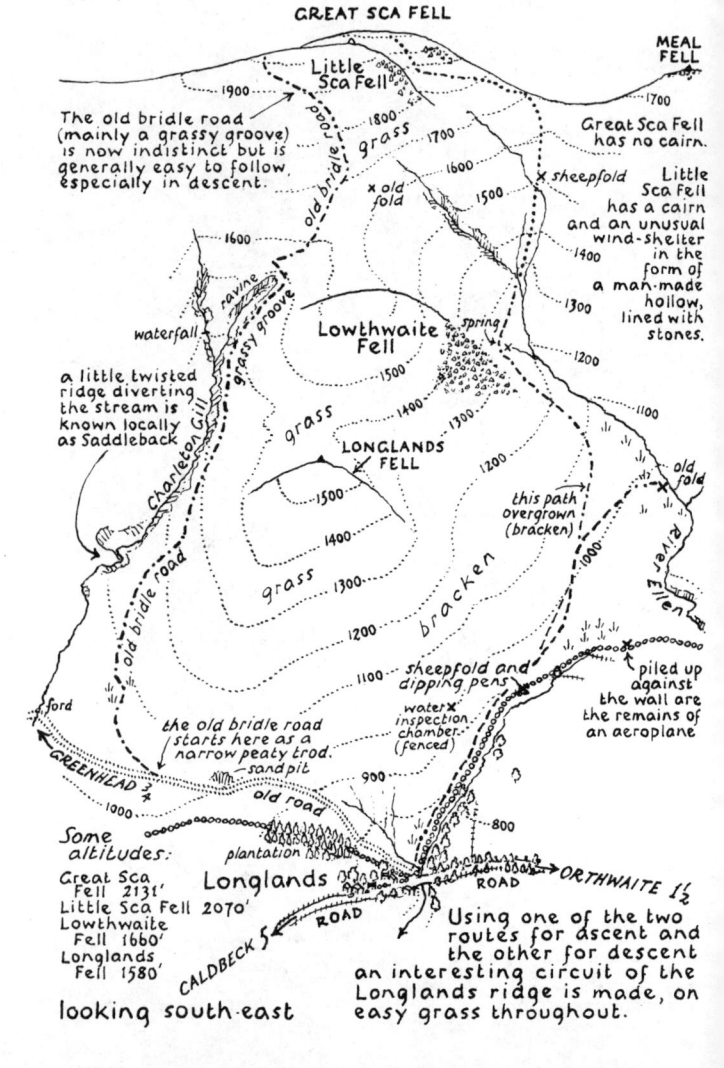

GREAT SCA FELL — MEAL FELL — Little Sca Fell

The old bridle road (mainly a grassy groove) is now indistinct but is generally easy to follow, especially in descent.

Great Sca Fell has no cairn.

Little Sca Fell has a cairn and an unusual wind-shelter in the form of a man-made hollow, lined with stones.

x old fold — sheepfold — spring

Lowthwaite Fell

waterfall — ravine — grassy groove

a little twisted ridge diverting the stream is known locally as Saddleback

Charleton Gill

LONGLANDS FELL

grass

this path overgrown (bracken)

old fold

River Ellen

old bridle road

bracken

ford

sheepfold and dipping pens — water inspection chamber (fenced)

piled up against the wall are the remains of an aeroplane

the old bridle road starts here as a narrow peaty trod — sandpit

GREENHEAD

old road — plantation — Longlands

ROAD — ORTHWAITE 1½

CALDBECK 5 — ROAD

Some altitudes:
Great Sca Fell 2131'
Little Sca Fell 2070'
Lowthwaite Fell 1660'
Longlands Fell 1580'

Using one of the two routes for ascent and the other for descent an interesting circuit of the Longlands ridge is made, on easy grass throughout.

looking south-east

Great Sca Fell 8

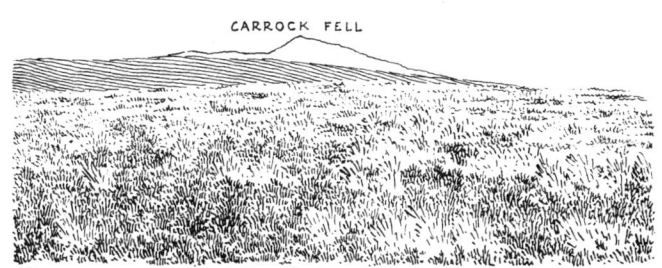

THE SUMMIT

The summit of Great Sca Fell (CARROCK FELL)

The top of the fell is as flat as a crown bowling green and several acres in extent. There is no summit-cairn on the wide expanse of windswept grass, and, without such a guide, a margin of error of 30 yards must be allowed in deciding the highest point. The survey height of 2131' appears to be plotted off the watershed and some distance north of the true top, which may therefore be a few feet greater in altitude.

The lower summit, Little Sca Fell, is more distinguished, having a cairn and a peculiar depression around which a low wall has been built (stones being available nearby) to make it of service as a wind-shelter.

DESCENTS: The old bridle road is most easily picked up as it slants across the north side of Little Sca Fell. For Fell Side the ridge of Ward Steel is best: persevere to its extremity to join the mines path. Generally, whatever the destination, the grassy slopes are preferable to the ravines.

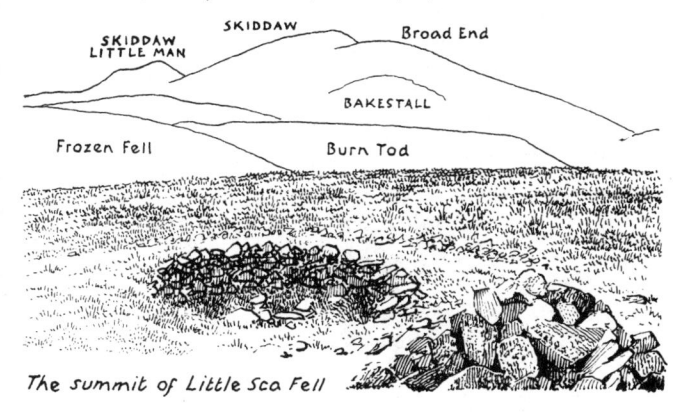

The summit of Little Sca Fell (SKIDDAW LITTLE MAN, SKIDDAW, Broad End, BAKESTALL, Frozen Fell, Burn Tod)

Great Sca Fell 9

THE VIEW

The scene is barren indeed, a sea of smooth unexciting hills, but fellwalkers who have deserted their favourite mountain haunts in Langdale or Borrowdale to come here on the recommendations of this book, and are regretting it, will note with nostalgic tears in their eyes an unexpected and faraway vista of the Bowfell group, today quite out of their reach. They must admit, however, albeit bitterly, that the view over the Cumberland plain to and beyond the Solway Firth is one that not even Bowfell can surpass.

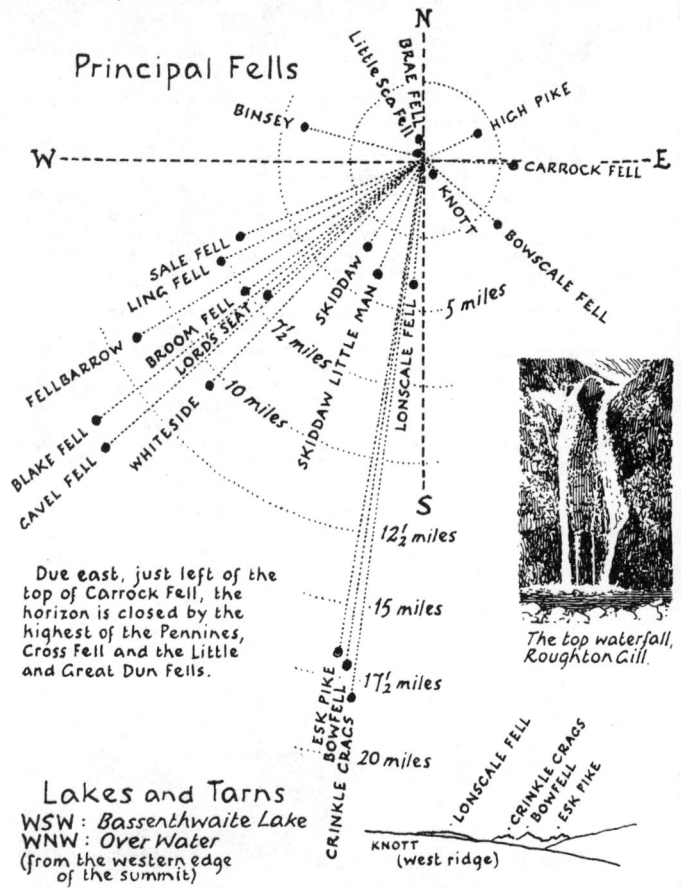

Principal Fells

(compass diagram with fells labelled:)
N — BRAE FELL, Little Sca Fell
HIGH PIKE
W — E — CARROCK FELL
BINSEY
KNOTT
BOWSCALE FELL
SALE FELL
LING FELL
BROOM FELL
LORDS SEAT
SKIDDAW
SKIDDAW LITTLE MAN
LONSCALE FELL
FELLBARROW
BLAKE FELL
GAVEL FELL
WHITESIDE
5 miles
7½ miles
10 miles
S
12½ miles
15 miles
17½ miles — ESK PIKE, BOWFELL
20 miles — CRINKLE CRAGS

Due east, just left of the top of Carrock Fell, the horizon is closed by the highest of the Pennines, Cross Fell and the Little and Great Dun Fells.

The top waterfall, Roughton Gill.

Lakes and Tarns
WSW : *Bassenthwaite Lake*
WNW : *Over Water*
(from the western edge of the summit)

(skyline sketch:) LONSCALE FELL, CRINKLE CRAGS, BOWFELL, ESK PIKE
KNOTT (west ridge)

Great Sca Fell 10

RIDGE ROUTES

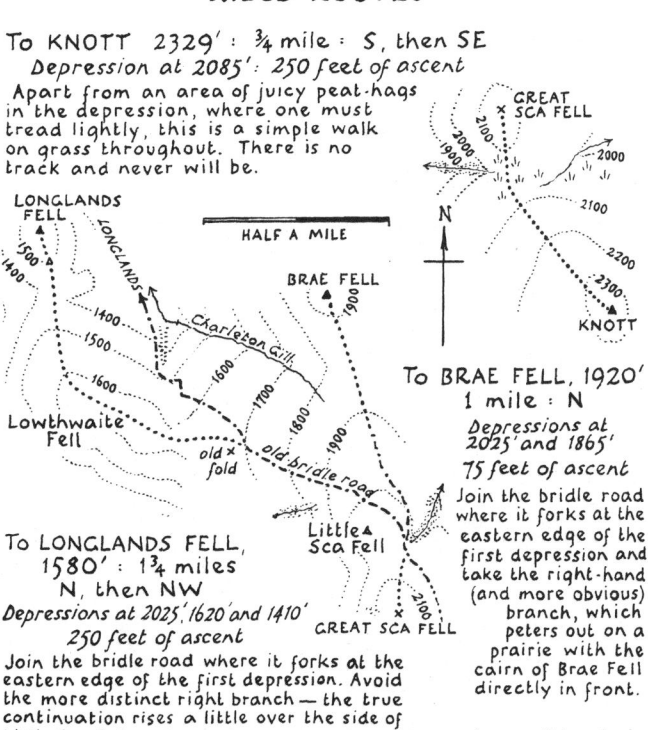

To KNOTT 2329' : ¾ mile : S, then SE
Depression at 2085' : 250 feet of ascent

Apart from an area of juicy peat-hags in the depression, where one must tread lightly, this is a simple walk on grass throughout. There is no track and never will be.

To BRAE FELL, 1920', 1 mile : N
Depressions at 2025' and 1865'
75 feet of ascent

Join the bridle road where it forks at the eastern edge of the first depression and take the right-hand (and more obvious) branch, which peters out on a prairie with the cairn of Brae Fell directly in front.

To LONGLANDS FELL, 1580' : 1¾ miles N, then NW
Depressions at 2025', 1620' and 1410'
250 feet of ascent

Join the bridle road where it forks at the eastern edge of the first depression. Avoid the more distinct right branch — the true continuation rises a little over the side of Little Sca Fell and soon becomes a clear groove. Leave this where it starts to slant down to Charleton Gill and keep on ahead over the grassy hump of Lowthwaite Fell. This is all easy going, and a grand way down from the tops on a summer's evening.

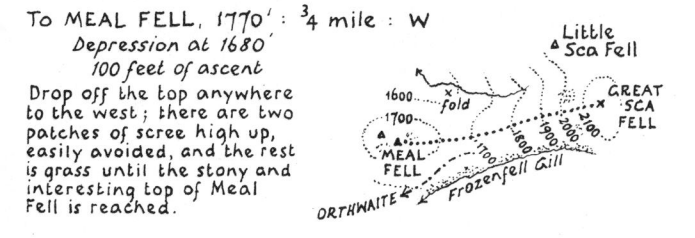

To MEAL FELL, 1770' : ¾ mile : W
Depression at 1680'
100 feet of ascent

Drop off the top anywhere to the west; there are two patches of scree high up, easily avoided, and the rest is grass until the stony and interesting top of Meal Fell is reached.

High Pike 2157'

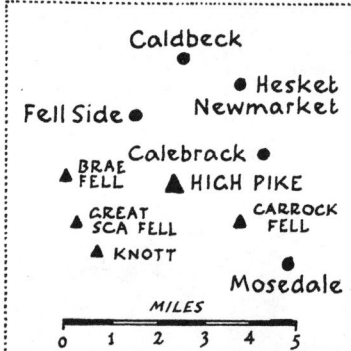

from the west gate, Carrock Hill Fort

Caldbeck
● Hesket Newmarket
Fell Side ●
▲ BRAE FELL Calebrack ● ▲ HIGH PIKE
▲ GREAT SCA FELL ▲ CARROCK FELL
▲ KNOTT
● Mosedale

MILES
0 1 2 3 4 5

from Bowscale Fell

High Pike 2

NATURAL FEATURES

All natives of Caldbeck and district have a deep-rooted respect for High Pike: it is a natural background to their lives, its name is a household word. This, not because the fell dominates the neighbourhood by a commanding presence — it is too flat and sprawling to catch the eye — but simply because it happens to be there, just over the treetops, and always has been there, playing a part in the development of the community.

In bygone days its rich mines provided a livelihood for the men, producing such a prolific variety of minerals that it used to be said, with much truth, *"Caldbeck Fells are worth all England else."* Most of this former industry has gone (and so have five of the six public-houses in Caldbeck at the turn of the century!) and the only mineral now being won is barytes. But High Pike is still, as ever, a grand sheep range and a fine territory for walking and leisurely pursuits, while the view from the summit, as an outlyer of Lakeland, is superb. Big events in history are celebrated here by the building and firing of a beacon. Carlisle knows when Caldbeck rejoices.

The fell is massive, occupying the north-east corner of the high country "back o' Skidda'," where it overlooks the Border and the valley of the Eden. There is volcanic rock underlying the higher parts but this is not greatly in evidence, the slopes being uniformly smooth and grassy except where broken by the eroded ravines that contain watercourses and are such a feature of the area. Beyond the summit is a hinterland of heathery moors, rarely visited and in a fair way to becoming a natural reserve for birds and animals.

High Pike from Knott

High Pike 3

The Caldbeck Fell mines

All the mines in the Caldbeck Fells are located on the slopes of High Pike, along its boundaries or in proximity; and all are within the narrow belt of volcanic rock bounding the area of the Skiddaw slates.

The older mines are now disused, most of them having been worked from a very early date (sixteenth century or before) and been productive of a great variety of valuable minerals. The oldest and richest mine, Roughtongill, is reputed to have yielded 23 different ores and other minerals.

Caldbeck •

Fell Side •   Nether Row •

1   5   6

2   HIGH PIKE ▲   7

3   8
4

9
10

1: Hay Gill
2: Red Gill
3: Silver Gill
4: Roughton Gill
5: Potts Gill
6: Sandbed
7: Driggeth
8: Dry Gill
9: Brandy Gill
10: Carrock

Old level, Hay Gill

These places, for so long scenes of great activity, have today the sad desolation of death about them, but Nature is a great healer, given time, and traces of many former workings have disappeared except for the adits to the old levels. The tunnels and shafts penetrated to great distances and depths in the fellside, forming a labyrinth of subterranean passages along the mineral veins, and when it is remembered that they were hewn with primitive tools and wedges long before gunpowder was known, imagination cannot start to comprehend the skill and industry of the miners of those days, and one is left merely wondering why the fortunate workers of today are prepared to debase their vocations and professions for greater personal rewards. The Caldbeck miners had little schooling yet had nothing to learn about the dignity of labour or of loyalty in service.

Old level, Potts Gill

Two mines opened in more recent times are still operating. Sandbed is the main source of supply, Potts Gill the processing and despatching station, and the mineral now being won is *barytes* (pronounced brytees, locally brytas) a crystallised heavy stone with many commercial uses principally in the manufacture of glass and paint. The present operators are McKechnie Brothers Limited.

Iron Crag
above Roughton Gill

High Pike 4

Roughton Gill
pronounced 'Rowt'n Gill'

The lowest waterfall

Old mine-level (left) and cascades

High Pike 5

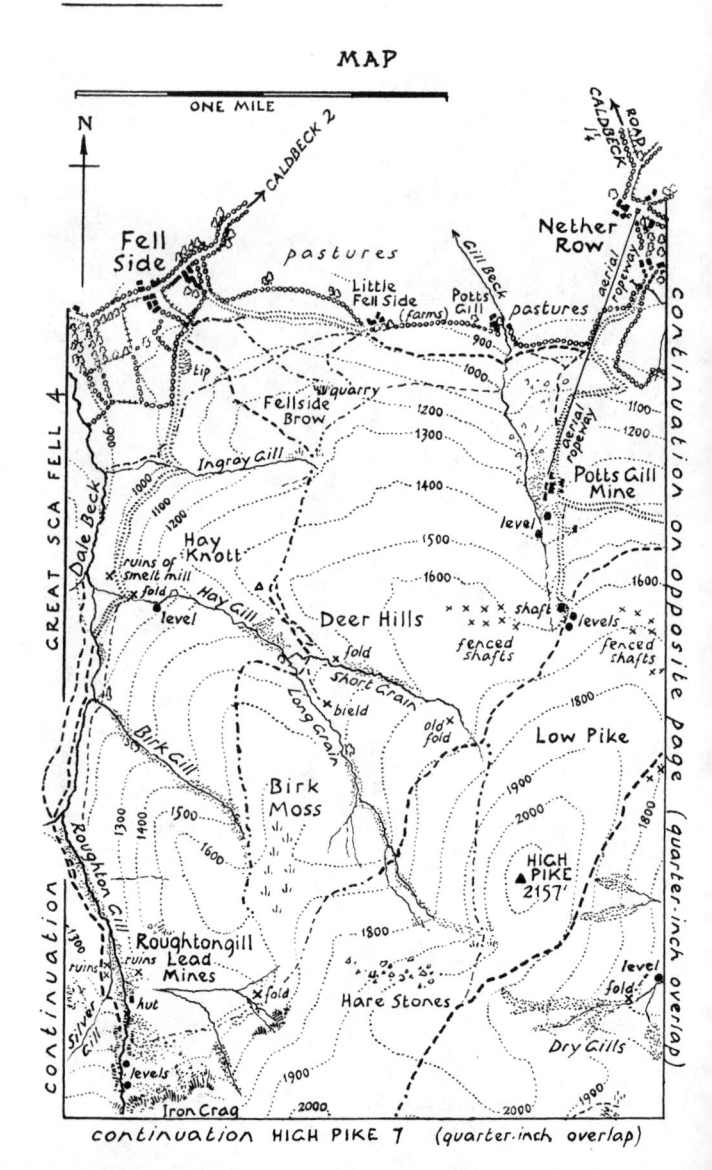

High Pike 6

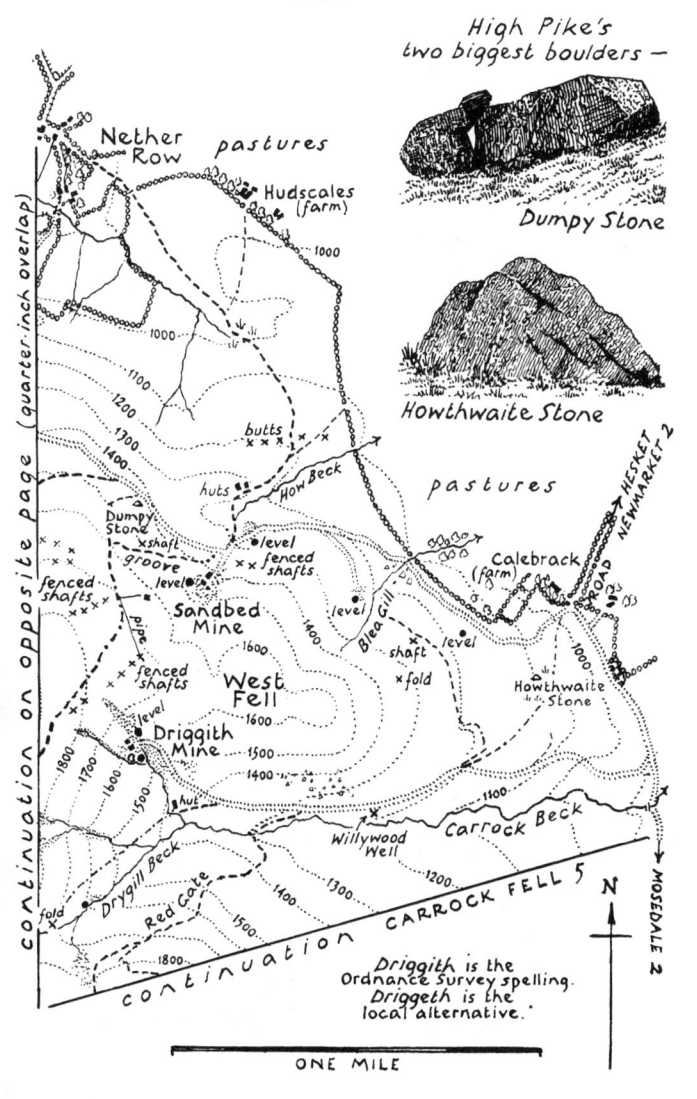

MAP

High Pike 7

MAP

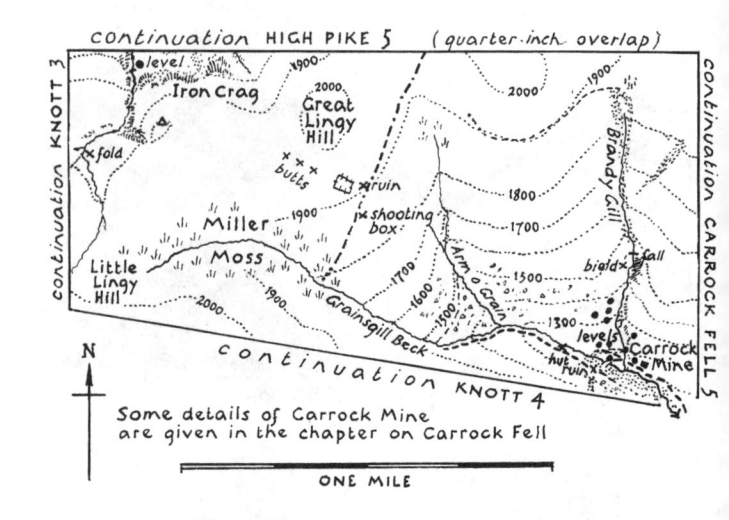

Some details of Carrock Mine are given in the chapter on Carrock Fell

ONE MILE

Death of an Industry
Ruins, spoil-heaps and a scarred landscape mark the grave of the once-renowned Roughtongill Mine

High Pike 8

ASCENT FROM FELL SIDE
1350 feet of ascent : 2½ miles

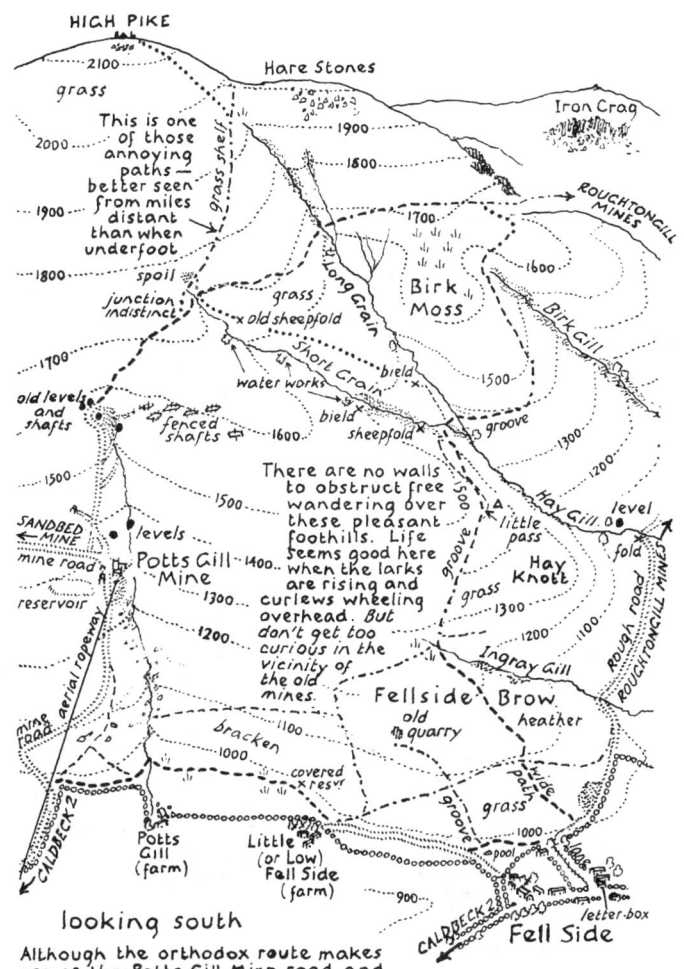

looking south

Although the orthodox route makes use of the Potts Gill Mine road and the path beyond, a more enjoyable plan in clear weather is to follow the drove road (a grassy rutted path or groove) going over Fellside Brow to Birk Moss, leaving this to turn up the tongue between Short Grain and Long Grain.

ASCENT FROM NETHER ROW
1300 feet of ascent : 2½ miles

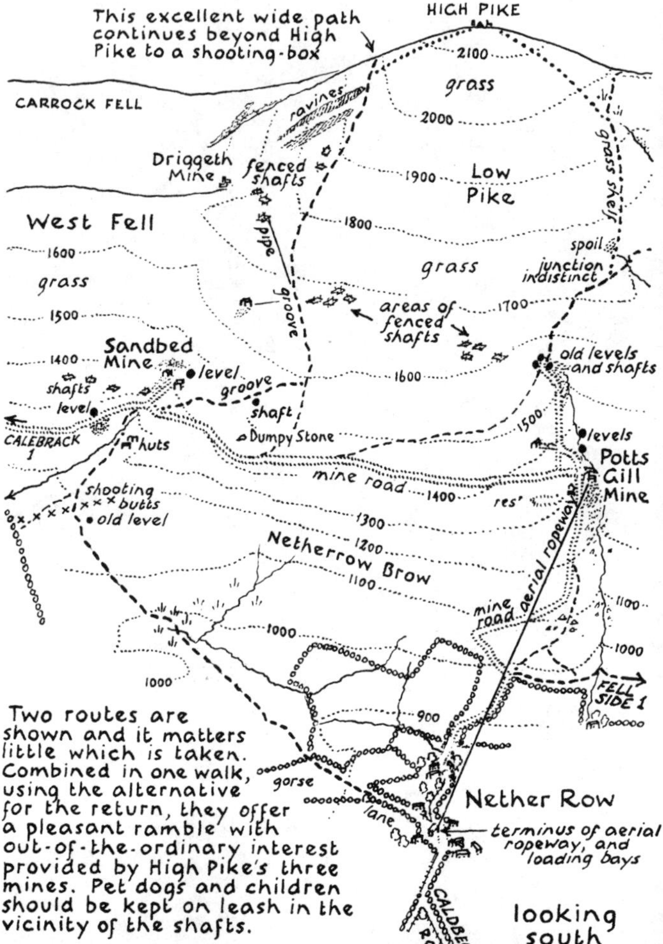
This excellent wide path continues beyond High Pike to a shooting-box
HIGH PIKE
2100
grass
CARROCK FELL
ravines
2000
Driggeth Mine
fenced shafts
1900
Low Pike
West Fell
pipe
1800
1600
grass
grass
spoil
junction indistinct
grass shelf
groove
areas of fenced shafts
1700
1500
Sandbed Mine
1400
old levels and shafts
shafts
level
groove
1600
level
shaft
CALEBRACK 1
huts
Dumpy Stone
1500
levels
Potts Gill Mine
mine road
1400
res'
shooting butts
old level
1300
aerial ropeway
Netherrow Brow
1200
1100
1100
mine road
1000
1000
1000
FELL SIDE 1
900
gorse
Nether Row
lane
terminus of aerial ropeway, and loading bays
CALDBECK 1¼
ROAD
looking south

Two routes are shown and it matters little which is taken. Combined in one walk, using the alternative for the return, they offer a pleasant ramble with out-of-the-ordinary interest provided by High Pike's three mines. Pet dogs and children should be kept on leash in the vicinity of the shafts.

This is the most convenient fell-walk available from Caldbeck.

High Pike 10

ASCENT FROM CALEBRACK
1300 feet of ascent · 2¾ miles

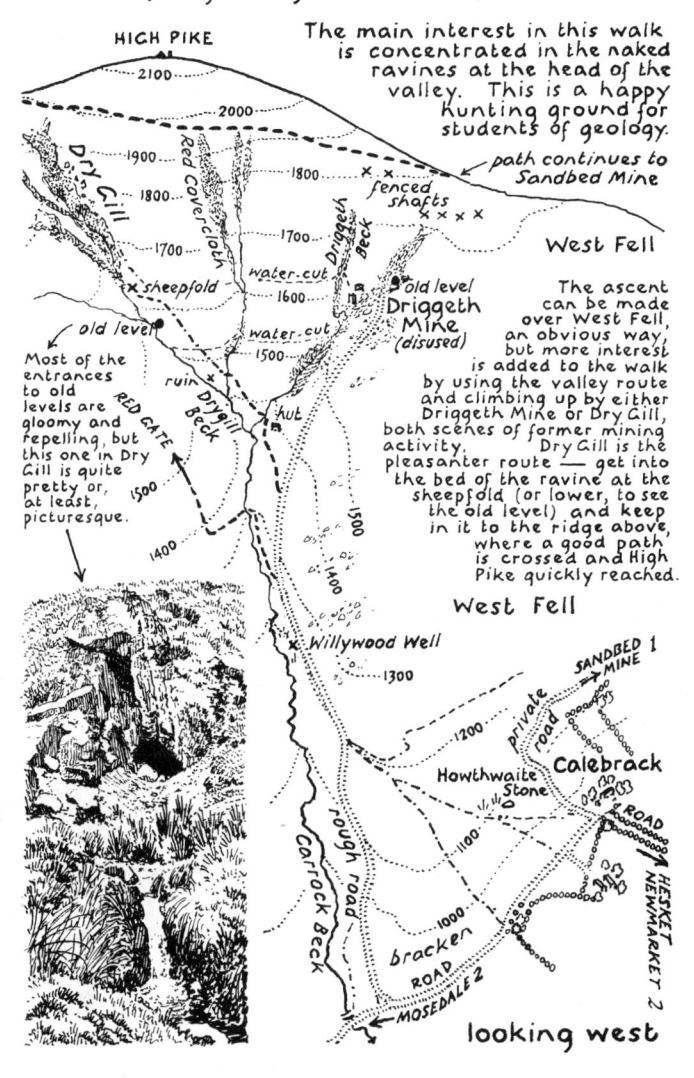

The main interest in this walk is concentrated in the naked ravines at the head of the valley. This is a happy hunting ground for students of geology.

path continues to Sandbed Mine

West Fell

The ascent can be made over West Fell, an obvious way, but more interest is added to the walk by using the valley route and climbing up by either Driggeth Mine or Dry Gill, both scenes of former mining activity. Dry Gill is the pleasanter route — get into the bed of the ravine at the sheepfold (or lower, to see the old level) and keep in it to the ridge above, where a good path is crossed and High Pike quickly reached.

West Fell

Most of the entrances to old levels are gloomy and repelling, but this one in Dry Gill is quite pretty or, at least, picturesque.

looking west

High Pike 11

THE SUMMIT

1960 looking south

Apart from the mines on the lower slopes, High Pike is so deprived of landmarks and other distinguishing features that a visitor is likely to approach the summit expecting only a plain grassy top, perhaps even without a cairn since stones are at a premium in the vegetatious prairies all around. It is a surprise, therefore, to find a positive array of objects of interest set out for inspection.
- The cairn is there all right, although the great sprawl of heaped stones hardly deserves the name (a separate small pile better qualifies). Obviously at some time in the past a good deal of hard labour has gone into the collection of these stones and their conveyance to the highest point of the fell. Hollowed out on the east side, away from the prevailing wind, this 'tumulus' is better described as a shelter.

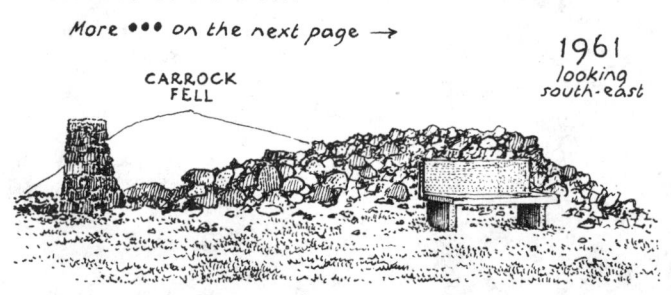

More ••• on the next page →

1961 looking south-east

High Pike 12

THE SUMMIT

continued

- Some of the stones have been appropriated by the Ordnance Surveyors to provide material for a triangulation column nearby.
- North of the column the turf is interrupted by a circular patch of stones and gravel: this is the site of the beacon, reserved for very special occasions.
- A few paces still further north is a commodious ruin. Amazingly, this was originally a shepherd's cottage and has been occupied as such within living memory. A house with a view, indeed! Not even the most ardent fellwalker's ambition can have aspired to a residence on a mountain top.

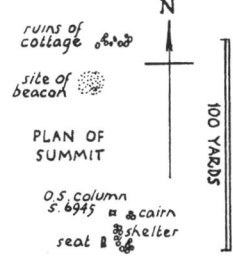

PLAN OF SUMMIT

O.S. column
5.6945

- But, up to the end of 1960, the biggest surprise of all was a wrought-iron garden seat, a contraption of elaborate embellishments into the voluptuous curves of which tired limbs surrendered gratefully: no other fell-top provided such luxurious comfort. Its very ornamentation proved its undoing, however, and it was removed and replaced late in 1960 by another seat — a structure of slate slabs, severely simple in design — after sheep had been found held captive by it, their horns entangled in the ironwork. Both seats, old and new, were placed there as memorials to Mick Lewis, a youth of Nether Row, "who loved all these fells". Which is a nice thing to say of anybody.

DESCENTS: If it were not for the mine shafts, High Pike could be descended blindfold, so easy are its gradients. In clear weather, a way off may be found in any direction, but *in mist* preferably make for the shooting-box path 300 yards south-east and follow it *left* to gain the Potts Gill - Sandbed mine road near Dumpy Stone.

Two subsidiary summits:

Nameless top above Iron Crag
(looking to Knott)

Great Lingy Hill
(looking to Blencathra)
Acres of dense fragrant heather (hence the name) make this the most delectable top in Lakeland for a summer day's siesta.

High Pike 13

THE VIEW

Southwards, the high skyline of the Skiddaw-Blencathra mass permits only narrow vistas of distant Lakeland. As a viewpoint for looking out *from* Lakeland, and not *into* it, however, High Pike takes full advantage of its position on the perimeter and commands a magnificent prospect, all of it fair to look upon, ranging from the West Cumbrian coast and Solway Firth northwards to the Scottish hills and then, from the Border round to the east, the lofty Pennines rise beyond the wide Eden Valley.

Principal Fells

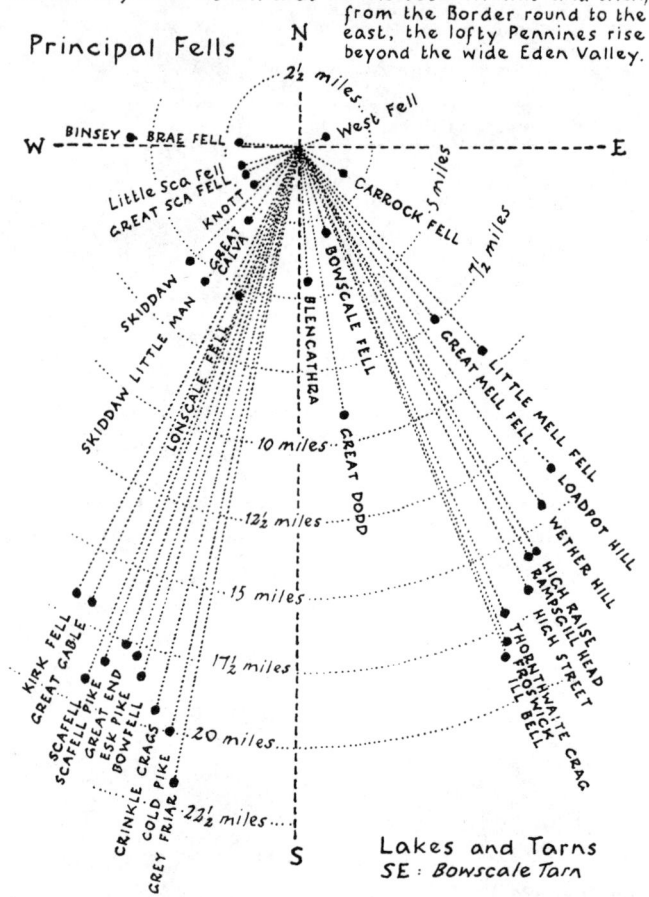

Lakes and Tarns
SE: Bowscale Tarn

High Pike 14

RIDGE ROUTES

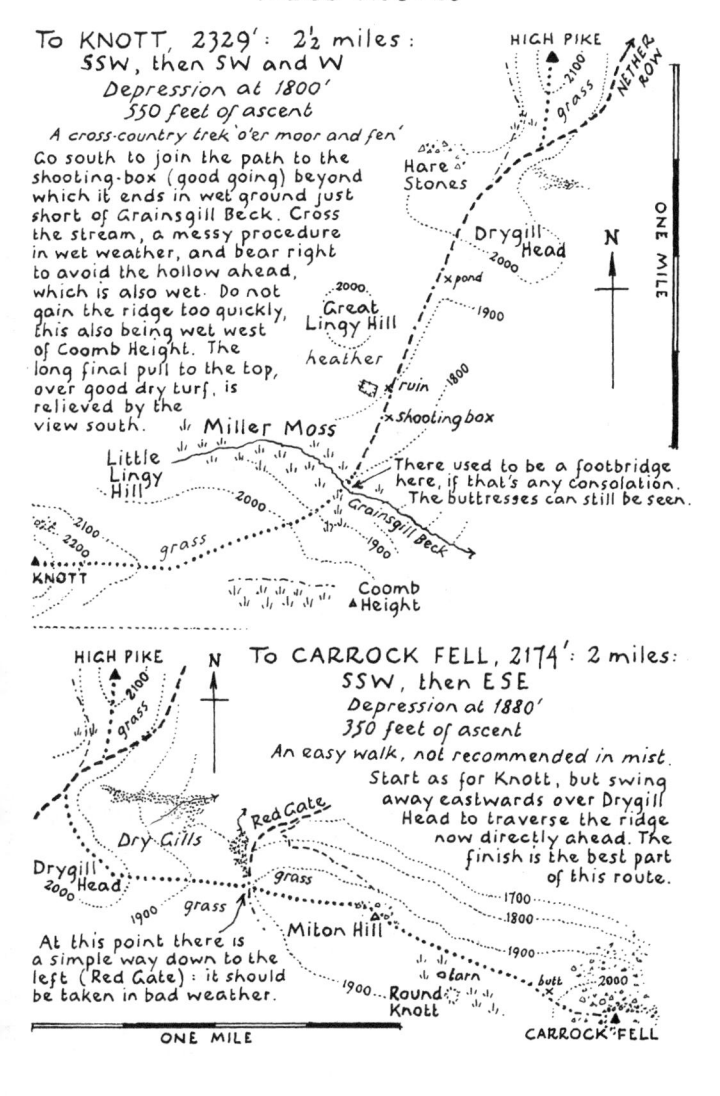

To KNOTT, 2329': 2½ miles:
SSW, then SW and W
Depression at 1800'
550 feet of ascent

A cross-country trek 'o'er moor and fen'

Go south to join the path to the shooting-box (good going) beyond which it ends in wet ground just short of Grainsgill Beck. Cross the stream, a messy procedure in wet weather, and bear right to avoid the hollow ahead, which is also wet. Do not gain the ridge too quickly, this also being wet west of Coomb Height. The long final pull to the top, over good dry turf, is relieved by the view south.

There used to be a footbridge here, if that's any consolation. The buttresses can still be seen.

To CARROCK FELL, 2174': 2 miles:
SSW, then ESE
Depression at 1880'
350 feet of ascent

An easy walk, not recommended in mist.

Start as for Knott, but swing away eastwards over Drygill Head to traverse the ridge now directly ahead. The finish is the best part of this route.

At this point there is a simple way down to the left (Red Gate): it should be taken in bad weather.

Knott 2329'

from Bowscale Fell

- Fell Side
- Greenhead
- Uldale
- Longlands
- Orthwaite
- ▲ HIGH PIKE
- ▲ GREAT SCA FELL
- ▲ KNOTT
- ▲ CARROCK FELL
- Bassenthwaite Village
- Mosedale
- ▲ GREAT CALVA
- ▲ BOWSCALE FELL
- SKIDDAW ▲
- Skiddaw House

MILES
0 1 2 3 4 5

Knott 2

NATURAL FEATURES

Knott occupies a commanding position across the middle of the group of fells north of Skiddaw Forest, of which it is the highest.   Long and narrow, it is nearly four miles from end to end, the extremities being rough but the in-between a vast smooth sheep pasture — grand tramping country in spite of a lack of paths, landmarks and features of interest. Side spurs run down from the main ridge to the Caldew, which takes away most of the fell's water. Other streams go west ultimately to join the Derwent at the foot of Bassenthwaite Lake; northwards, Roughton Gill is the sole agent of drainage. Like all the fells in this area, the watercourses have carved deep ravines, the sides of which are stripped of vegetation, leaving exposed a gravelly subsoil, often of such garish colour that the rifts are conspicuous from afar as bright yellow and red curtains draping the green slopes.

On the whole this is an easy, accommodating fell with no natural hazards, but it is the very absence of identifiable objects that makes the top especially confusing in mist, and in such conditions it is well to bear in mind that these innocuous pastures contain, near the extremity of the eastern shoulder, a very dangerous trap for walkers not familiar with the lie of the land.

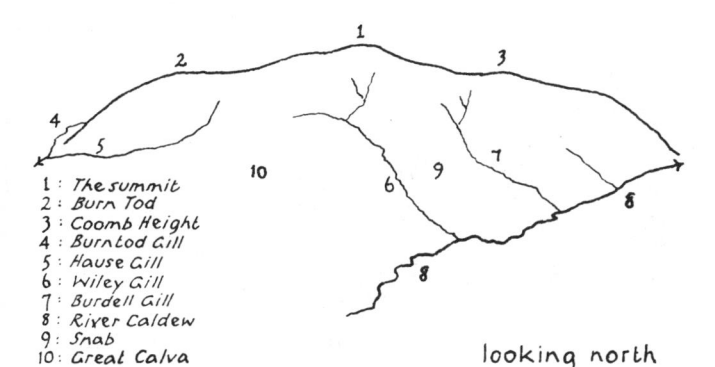

1 : The summit
2 : Burn Tod
3 : Coomb Height
4 : Burntod Gill
5 : Hause Gill
6 : Wiley Gill
7 : Burdell Gill
8 : River Caldew
9 : Snab
10 : Great Calva

looking north

Knott 3

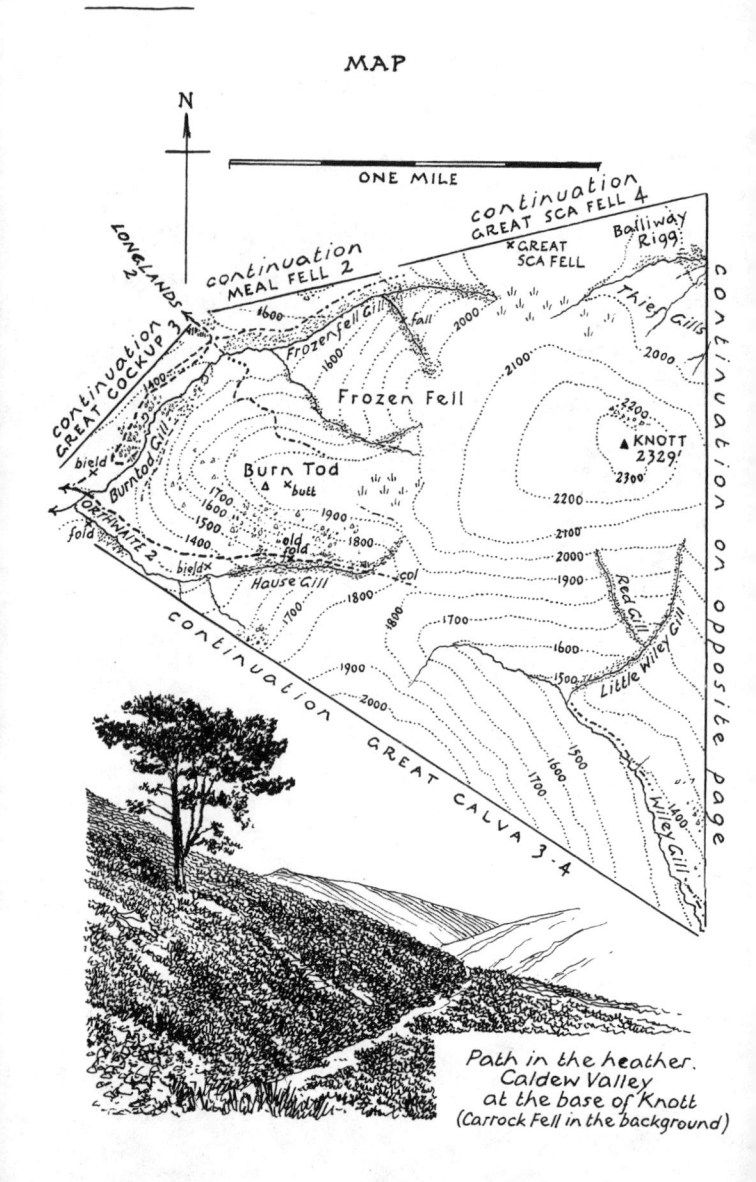

MAP

One mile

continuation LONGLANDS 2
continuation MEAL FELL 2
continuation GREAT SCA FELL 4
continuation GREAT COCKUP 3
continuation ORTHWAITE 2
continuation GREAT CALVA 3-4
continuation on opposite page

× GREAT SCA FELL
Balliway Rigg
Thief Gills
Frozenfell Gill
fall
Frozen Fell
Burntod Gill
bield
Burn Tod △ × butt
old
old
Hause Gill
col
fold
bield ×
▲ KNOTT 2329'
Red Gill
Little Wiley Gill
Wiley Gill

Path in the heather.
Caldew Valley
at the base of Knott
(Carrock Fell in the background)

Knott 4

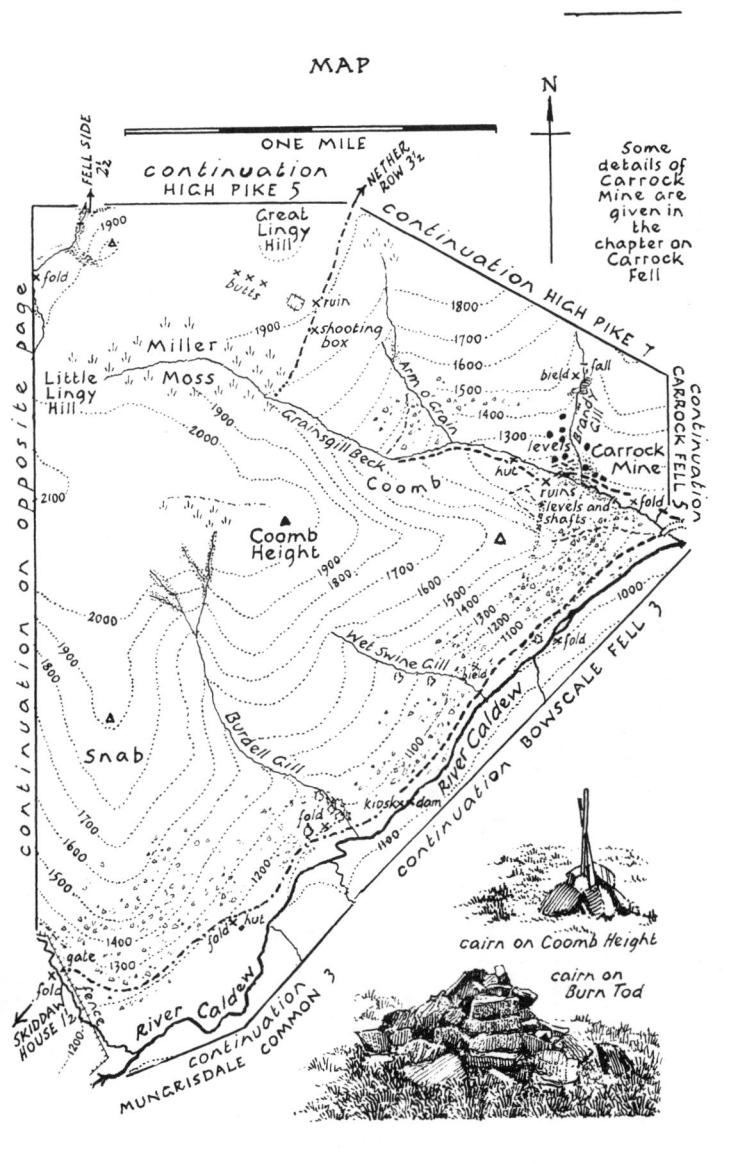

MAP

Knott 5

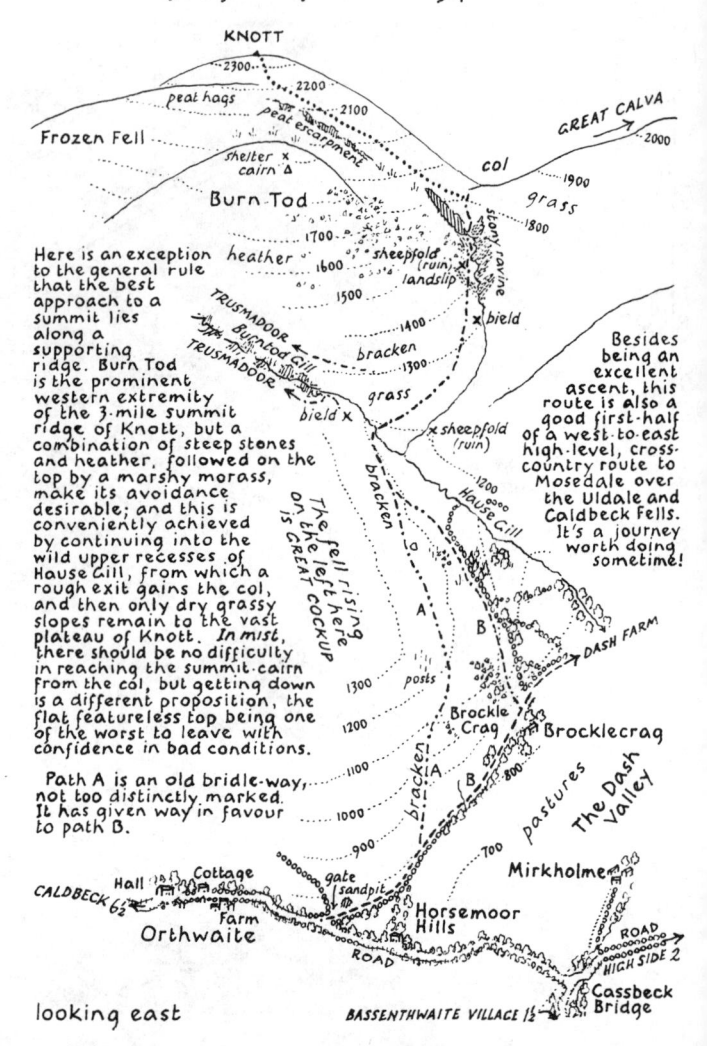

ASCENT FROM ORTHWAITE
1500 feet of ascent : 3¾ miles

Here is an exception to the general rule that the best approach to a summit lies along a supporting ridge. Burn Tod is the prominent western extremity of the 3-mile summit ridge of Knott, but a combination of steep stones and heather, followed on the top by a marshy morass, make its avoidance desirable; and this is conveniently achieved by continuing into the wild upper recesses of Hause Gill, from which a rough exit gains the col, and then only dry grassy slopes remain to the vast plateau of Knott. In mist, there should be no difficulty in reaching the summit-cairn from the col, but getting down is a different proposition, the flat featureless top being one of the worst to leave with confidence in bad conditions.

Path A is an old bridle-way, not too distinctly marked. It has given way in favour to path B.

Besides being an excellent ascent, this route is also a good first-half of a west-to-east high-level, cross-country route to Mosedale over the Uldale and Caldbeck Fells. It's a journey worth doing sometime!

looking east

Knott 6

ASCENT FROM LONGLANDS
1700 feet of ascent : 3½ miles

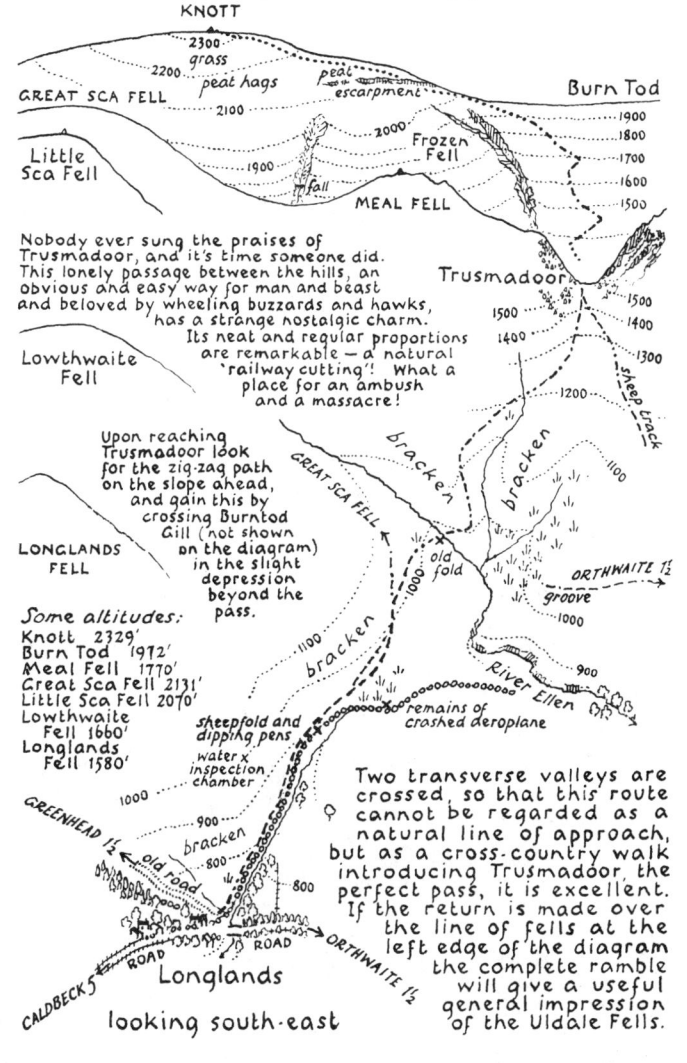

KNOTT

GREAT SCA FELL — grass — peat hags — peat escarpment — Burn Tod

Little Sca Fell — Frozen Fell — fall — MEAL FELL

Nobody ever sung the praises of Trusmadoor, and it's time someone did. This lonely passage between the hills, an obvious and easy way for man and beast and beloved by wheeling buzzards and hawks, has a strange nostalgic charm.
Its neat and regular proportions are remarkable — a natural 'railway cutting'! What a place for an ambush and a massacre!

Trusmadoor

sheep track

Lowthwaite Fell

Upon reaching Trusmadoor look for the zig-zag path on the slope ahead, and gain this by crossing Burntod Gill (not shown on the diagram) in the slight depression beyond the pass.

GREAT SCA FELL

bracken

old fold

groove

ORTHWAITE 1½

LONGLANDS FELL

River Ellen

Some altitudes:
Knott 2329'
Burn Tod 1972'
Meal Fell 1770'
Great Sca Fell 2131'
Little Sca Fell 2070'
Lowthwaite Fell 1660'
Longlands Fell 1580'

bracken

sheepfold and dipping pens
water × inspection chamber

remains of crashed aeroplane

GREENHEAD 1½ — old road — bracken

Two transverse valleys are crossed, so that this route cannot be regarded as a natural line of approach, but as a cross-country walk introducing Trusmadoor, the perfect pass, it is excellent. If the return is made over the line of fells at the left edge of the diagram the complete ramble will give a useful general impression of the Uldale Fells.

CALDBECK 5 — ROAD — Longlands — ROAD — ORTHWAITE 1½

looking south-east

Knott 7

ASCENT FROM FELL SIDE
1500 feet of ascent
3½ miles

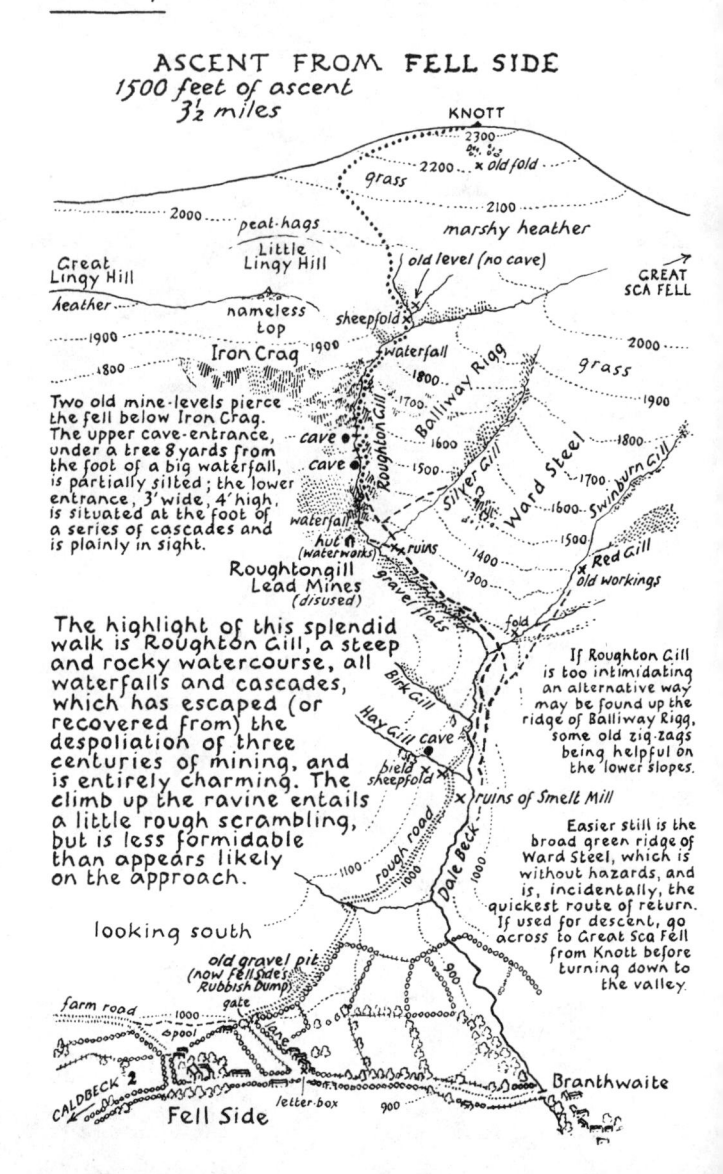

KNOTT 2300
× old fold
2200
grass
2100
2000 peat-hags
Little Lingy Hill
marshy heather
old level (no cave)
Great Lingy Hill
heather
nameless top
sheepfold
GREAT SCA FELL
1900
Iron Crag
1900
waterfall
2000 grass
1800
Balliway Rigg
1800
1700
1900

Two old mine-levels pierce the fell below Iron Crag. The upper cave-entrance, under a tree 8 yards from the foot of a big waterfall, is partially silted; the lower entrance, 3' wide, 4' high, is situated at the foot of a series of cascades and is plainly in sight.

cave
cave
1600
Silver Gill
Ward Steel
1700
Swinburn Gill
1600
1500
waterfall
hut (waterworks)
ruins
Red Gill
× old workings
1400
Roughtongill Lead Mines (disused)
1300
gravel flats

The highlight of this splendid walk is Roughton Gill, a steep and rocky watercourse, all waterfalls and cascades, which has escaped (or recovered from) the despoliation of three centuries of mining, and is entirely charming. The climb up the ravine entails a little rough scrambling, but is less formidable than appears likely on the approach.

fold

If Roughton Gill is too intimidating an alternative way may be found up the ridge of Balliway Rigg, some old zig-zags being helpful on the lower slopes.

Birk Gill
Hay Gill cave
field sheepfold
× ruins of Smelt Mill

Easier still is the broad green ridge of Ward Steel, which is without hazards, and is, incidentally, the quickest route of return. If used for descent, go across to Great Sca Fell from Knott before turning down to the valley.

Dale Beck
1100 rough road
1000

looking south

old gravel pit (now Fellside's Rubbish Dump)
farm road
1000
gate
pool
CALDBECK 2
letter-box
Branthwaite
900
Fell Side

Knott 8

*The valley of Dale Beck, leading to Roughton Gill
In the foreground are the ruins of the smelt mill*

Knott 9

ASCENT FROM MOSEDALE
1650 feet of ascent : 4½ miles

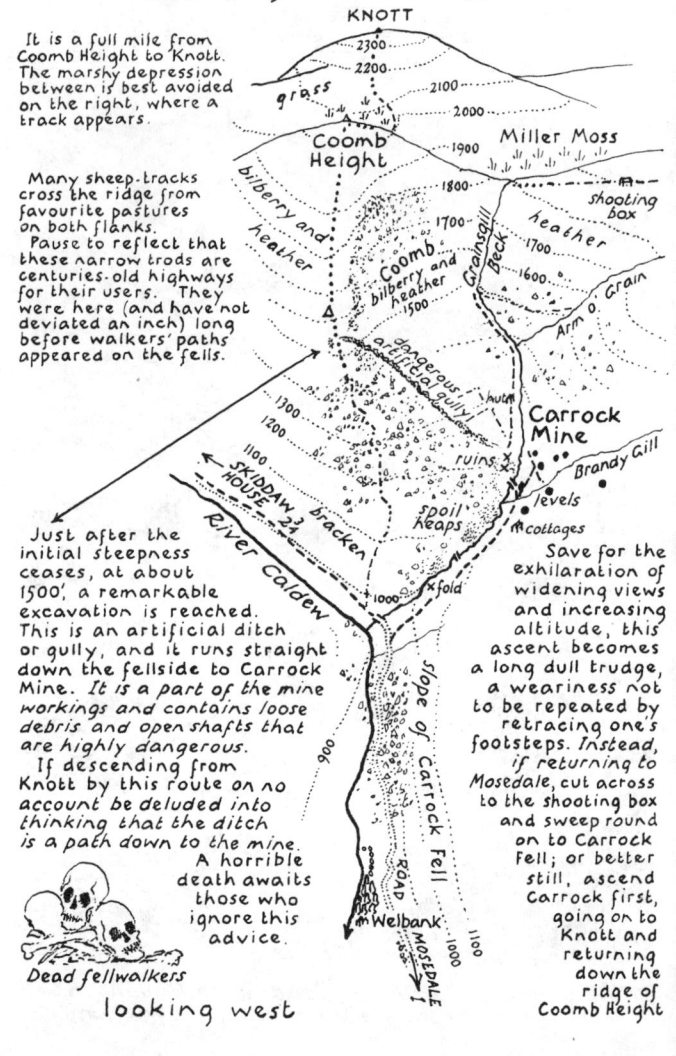

KNOTT

It is a full mile from Coomb Height to Knott. The marshy depression between is best avoided on the right, where a track appears.

Many sheep-tracks cross the ridge from favourite pastures on both flanks.
Pause to reflect that these narrow trods are centuries-old highways for their users. They were here (and have not deviated an inch) long before walkers' paths appeared on the fells.

Coomb Height
Miller Moss
grass
bilberry and heather
Coomb bilberry and heather
Grainsgill Beck
shooting box
heather
Grain o' Grain Arm
dangerous artificial gully
hut
Carrock Mine
ruins
Brandy Gill
levels
spoil heaps
cottages
SKIDDAW HOUSE 3¼
River Caldew
bracken
× fold
slope of Carrock Fell
ROAD
Welbank
MOSEDALE 1

Just after the initial steepness ceases, at about 1500', a remarkable excavation is reached. This is an artificial ditch or gully, and it runs straight down the fellside to Carrock Mine. It is a part of the mine workings and contains loose debris and open shafts that are highly dangerous.
If descending from Knott by this route on no account be deluded into thinking that the ditch is a path down to the mine.
A horrible death awaits those who ignore this advice.

Dead fellwalkers

Save for the exhilaration of widening views and increasing altitude, this ascent becomes a long dull trudge, a weariness not to be repeated by retracing one's footsteps. Instead, if returning to Mosedale, cut across to the shooting box and sweep round on to Carrock Fell; or better still, ascend Carrock first, going on to Knott and returning down the ridge of Coomb Height

looking west

Knott 10

THE SUMMIT

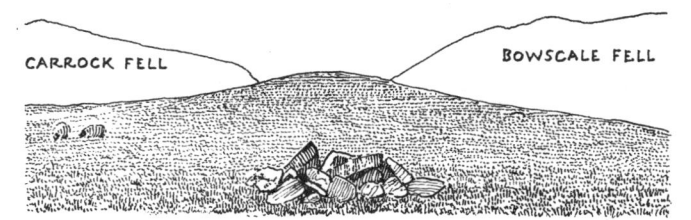

CARROCK FELL

BOWSCALE FELL

On a recent visit the cairn was found built up into a neat column

looking east to the gap of Mosedale

If the party consists of more than one person, and if, further, a bat, ball and wickets can be found in the depths of somebody's rucksack, a cricket match can be played on turf that many a county ground might covet. Apart from this, no suggestions can be made for whiling away the time (unless the party be a mixed one), the smooth top being completely without anything worth investigating. The solitary walker, unable to indulge in communal games or pastimes, will find himself wondering who carried up the stones to make the cairn, and whence they came: must have been another lonely soul with nobody to play with!

DESCENTS: Routes of ascent may be reversed (Roughton Gill requires care). The territory is confusing in mist, due to the absence of landmarks. The most obvious route is east to Mosedale: if this way off is used *keep strictly to the ridge down to the road, avoiding an artificial 'ditch' cutting across the crest: this is part of the Carrock Mine workings, NOT A PATH.*

above
Mosedale from the eastern shoulder

In the foreground is an abandoned 'dig' (mine workings). It is near to the end of the 'ditch' or gully that goes steeply and dangerously (shafts) down to Carrock Mine

left
The eastern shoulder from Mosedale

Knott 11

THE VIEW

This view hardly comes up to expectations: the highest of the Caldbeck Fells is rather disappointing in this respect. The scene is extensive enough in the northern arc, ranging across the Solway Firth to the Scottish hills and round to the Pennines in the east, there being nothing higher to obstruct, but this panorama is more pleasing from the neighbouring High Pike. To the south there is a restricted glimpse of the central peaks of Lakeland between the masses of Blencathra and Skiddaw.

The broad top of the fell permits no depth to the picture in any direction and its worth as a viewpoint suffers accordingly.

Principal Fells

Don't waste time trying to sort out this untidy mess; instead, use the illustration given below

Lakes and Tarns

S : Thirlmere
WSW : Bassenthwaite Lake

looking south

Knott 12

RIDGE ROUTES

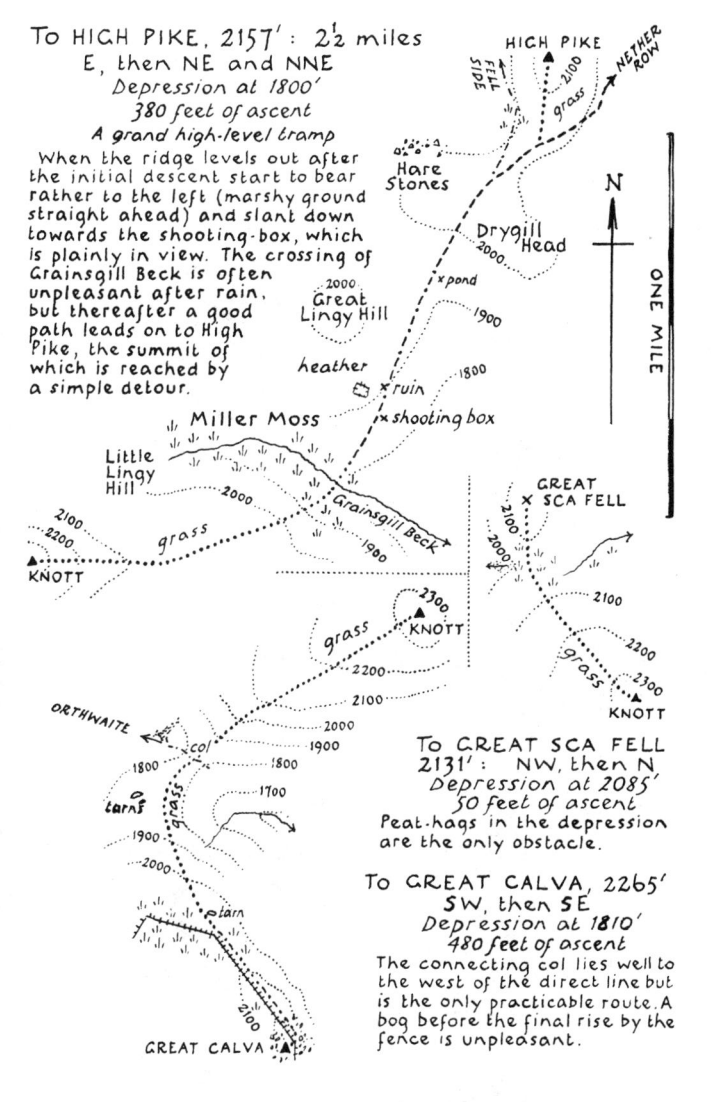

TO HIGH PIKE, 2157': 2½ miles
E, then NE and NNE
Depression at 1800'
380 feet of ascent
A grand high-level tramp

When the ridge levels out after the initial descent start to bear rather to the left (marshy ground straight ahead) and slant down towards the shooting-box, which is plainly in view. The crossing of Grainsgill Beck is often unpleasant after rain, but thereafter a good path leads on to High Pike, the summit of which is reached by a simple detour.

TO GREAT SCA FELL 2131': NW, then N
Depression at 2085'
50 feet of ascent
Peat-hags in the depression are the only obstacle.

TO GREAT CALVA, 2265'
SW, then SE
Depression at 1810'
480 feet of ascent
The connecting col lies well to the west of the direct line but is the only practicable route. A bog before the final rise by the fence is unpleasant.

Latrigg 1203'

This is the Latrigg near Keswick
— there is another,
less well-known,
near Over Water.

from Blencathra Sanatorium
(showing the east ridge going down to Brundholme Woods)

▲ SKIDDAW
   ▲ LITTLE MAN
      ▲ LONSCALE FELL
● Millbeck
   Threlkeld ●
   ▲ LATRIGG
● Keswick

MILES
0 1 2 3 4

from the Orthwaite road

Latrigg 2

NATURAL FEATURES

Latrigg is to Keswick what Loughrigg is to Ambleside and Helm Crag to Grasmere: a small hill, an excellent viewpoint, a great favourite of local folk and visitors. Latrigg is pastoral and parkland in character, not rough fell, and the summit is the easiest of promenades, so that this is not a climb calling for old clothes and heavy boots: 'Sunday best' is quite appropriate dress. New plantations and de-forestation have changed the appearance of the fell often during the past century, and not always for the better; at present the top is polled and thick fringes of trees at mid-height suggest an experimental coiffure by a mad barber. The woods harbour courting couples and other wild life and are not safe for solo explorers.

Latrigg has been well described as 'the cub of Skiddaw.' It crouches at the foot of the broad southern slopes of the parent, too small to be significant in the geography of the mass, although a long east ridge is responsible for the formation of the short side-valley of Lonscale. The River Greta flows along the southern base, occupying a wooded gorge of outstanding scenic beauty, appreciated best on a railway journey between Keswick and Threlkeld.

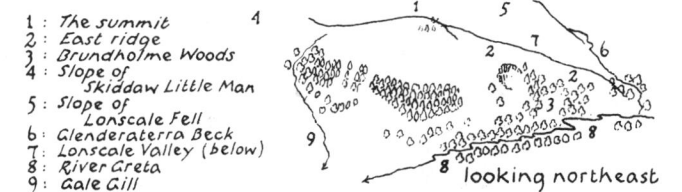

1 : The summit
2 : East ridge
3 : Brundholme Woods
4 : Slope of Skiddaw Little Man
5 : Slope of Lonscale Fell
6 : Glenderaterra Beck
7 : Lonscale Valley (below)
8 : River Greta
9 : Gale Gill

looking northeast

Latrigg's top is a smooth grassy pasture innocent of rock except for a few yards of outcrop at the summit where the native stone breaks through the turf. This is seen to be slate. The wall across the top to the east is built of slate.

Not very long ago, in fact since the turn of the century, Latrigg's top was described as having a scattering of boulders of volcanic rock deposited there by a retreating glacier. These boulders were identified as having their origin in the crags of Clough Head and it is therefore simple to reconstruct (but difficult to imagine) the scene here at the end of the Ice Age: the glacier tore from its moorings in the narrows of St. John's Vale, and, taking the route of the present St. John's Beck and River Greta and being joined by tributaries of ice from the Glenderamackin, the Glenderaterra and the Naddle Valleys, slowly withdrew from the hills, scouring the side of Lonscale Fell and Skiddaw and depositing the rubble collected on its journey as it disintegrated. The presence of Clough Head rocks on the top of Latrigg indicates that the surface of the glacier must have been higher than the present elevation of the fell.

These boulders have now gone, possibly removed with the trees to make a smooth sheepwalk. Just a few 'erratics' can still be found by diligent search, but the evidence of the movement of the glacier is more abundant lower down the fellside and about the bed of the Greta, where, to a trained eye, there are several manifestations of glacial action, much of it unearthed during the construction of the railway.

Latrigg 3

MAP

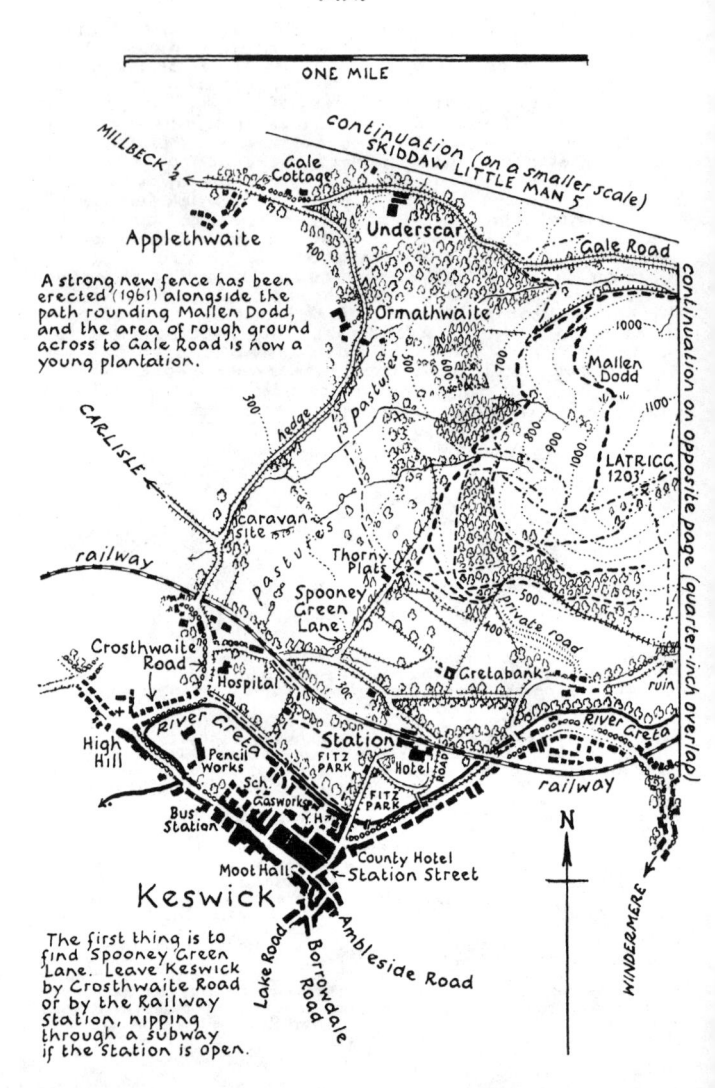

ONE MILE

continuation (on a smaller scale) SKIDDAW LITTLE MAN 5

MILLBECK ½
Gale Cottage
Applethwaite
Underscar
Gale Road
Ormathwaite

A strong new fence has been erected (1961) alongside the path rounding Mallen Dodd, and the area of rough ground across to Gale Road is now a young plantation.

Mallen Dodd
LATRIGG 1203'

CARLISLE
hedge
pastures
caravan site
railway
Thorny Plats
Spooney Green Lane
Crosthwaite Road
Hospital
Gretabank
private road
ruin

continuation on opposite page (quarter-inch overlap)

High Hill
River Greta
Pencil Works
Sch
Gasworks
Bus Station
Y.H.
FITZ PARK
Station
Hotel
FITZ PARK
River Greta
railway

N
WINDERMERE

Moot Hall
County Hotel
Station Street

Keswick

The first thing is to find Spooney Green Lane. Leave Keswick by Crosthwaite Road or by the Railway Station, nipping through a subway if the station is open.

Lake Road
Borrowdale Road
Ambleside Road

Latrigg 4

MAP

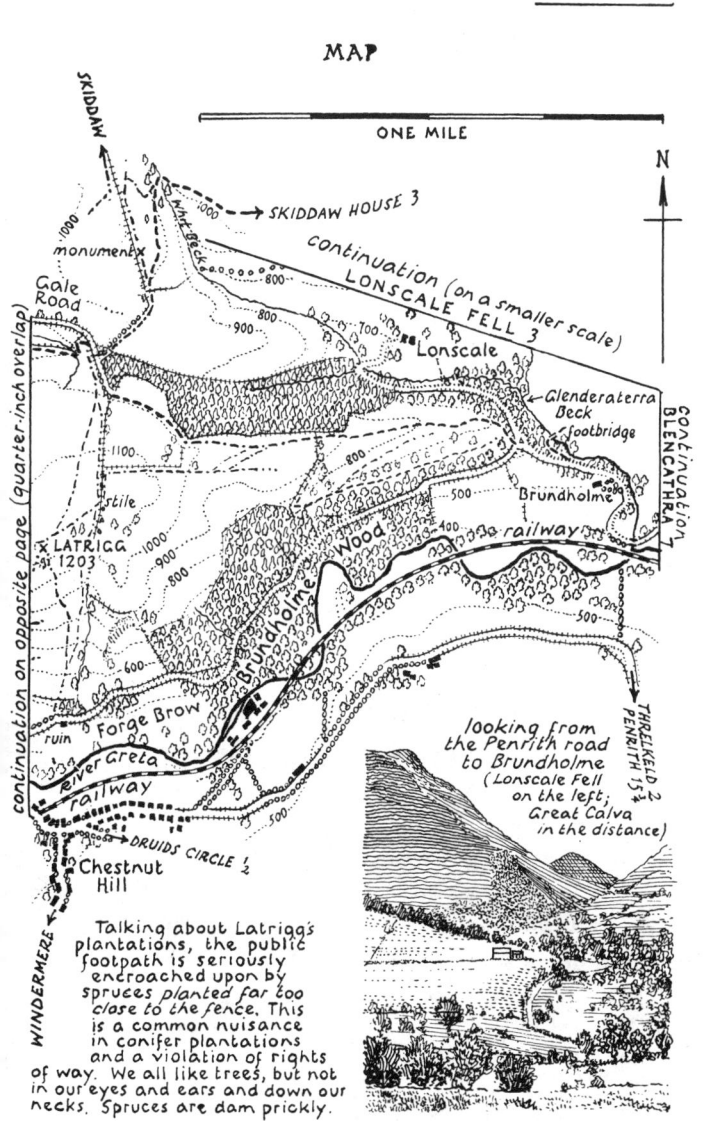

ONE MILE

N

SKIDDAW
monument ×
Gale Road
SKIDDAW HOUSE 3
continuation (on a smaller scale) LONSCALE FELL 3
Lonscale
Glenderaterra Beck footbridge
continuation BLENCATHRA
Brundholme
railway
stile
× LATRIGG 1203
Brundholme Wood
continuation on opposite page (quarter-inch overlap)
Forge Brow
ruin
river Greta
railway
DRUIDS CIRCLE ½
Chestnut Hill
WINDERMERE
THRELKELD 2 PENRITH 15

looking from the Penrith road to Brundholme (Lonscale Fell on the left; Great Calva in the distance)

Talking about Latrigg's plantations, the public footpath is seriously encroached upon by spruces *planted far too close to the fence*. This is a common nuisance in conifer plantations and a violation of rights of way. We all like trees, but not in our eyes and ears and down our necks. Spruces are dam prickly.

Latrigg 5

ASCENT FROM KESWICK
950 feet of ascent: 2½ miles

Latrigg's appearance has changed considerably in recent decades, and old-timers who have not climbed it since the inter-war years would nowadays hardly recognise the way up via Spooney Green Lane, the traditional route. Gone is the golf course, gone is the signpost at the start (this should be replaced), gone are the tight fences and dense woodlands formerly enclosing the path, gone are the trees that decorated the fell almost to its very summit and gone is the fence that ran along the top. This new freedom to wander at will has led to the creation of many tracks and short-cuts, but the original path, rounding Mallen Dodd, is still the easiest route to the top (watch for the zigzag, which may be passed unnoticed).

Happily, the superb view from the summit is available also to non-climbers, and the old and infirm, with the assistance of a car, can enjoy it by a simple stroll from the road end.

Road end
Cars may be taken to this point (via Underscar) and parked here

looking east

Just above Thorny Plats the lane has become overgrown and wet, and the path takes to grass alongside

The fields here were formerly a golf course

There is a bewildering choice of paths, that by Mallen Dodd being best.
The descent by the east ridge and return to Keswick by Brundholme Woods completes a very beautiful short walk.

Latrigg 6

ASCENT FROM THRELKELD
900 feet of ascent : 3 miles

This simple climb by the east ridge can be made with equal facility from Keswick. Take the road behind the railway station signposted "Windebrowe & Brundholme" — this degenerates into a lane but improves in scenery as it enters and passes through the woods: a delightful walk with interesting glimpses of the River Greta below.

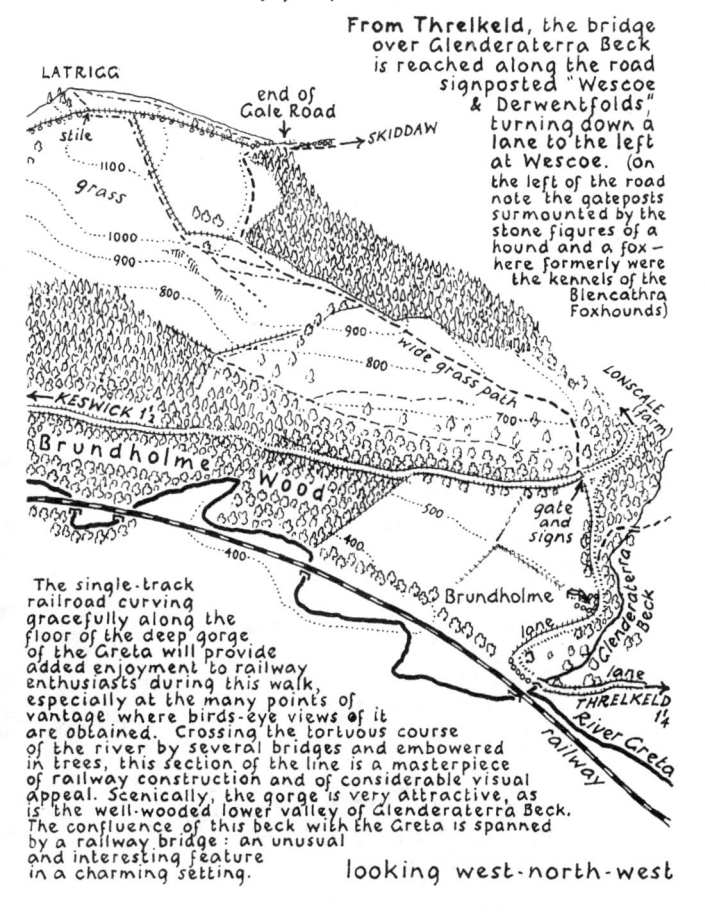

From Threlkeld, the bridge over Glenderaterra Beck is reached along the road signposted "Wescoe & Derwentfolds", turning down a lane to the left at Wescoe. (On the left of the road note the gateposts surmounted by the stone figures of a hound and a fox — here formerly were the kennels of the Blencathra Foxhounds)

The single-track railroad curving gracefully along the floor of the deep gorge of the Greta will provide added enjoyment to railway enthusiasts during this walk, especially at the many points of vantage where birds-eye views of it are obtained. Crossing the tortuous course of the river by several bridges and embowered in trees, this section of the line is a masterpiece of railway construction and of considerable visual appeal. Scenically, the gorge is very attractive, as is the well-wooded lower valley of Glenderaterra Beck. The confluence of this beck with the Greta is spanned by a railway bridge: an unusual and interesting feature in a charming setting.

looking west-north-west

Latrigg 7

Underskiddaw, looking to Bassenthwaite Lake

.... **Two views from Latrigg** ....

Blease Fell, Blencathra, from the east ridge

Latrigg 8

THE SUMMIT

Although the top of Latrigg is a green sward, it is pitted with the decayed stumps of trees long since felled, and a few solitary straining posts survive to tell of the time when this popular walk was contained by a fence. A ditch and parapet running over the crest might quicken the interest of those who look for evidences of bygone civilisations, but here was no ancient fort or defence wall: the ditch merely provided the earth for the parapet, which originally formed the base of the now-vanished wire fence. A thin line of untidy and unhappy trees has been preserved nearby — why? They are no ornament to the fell and from the streets of Keswick simply give the impression of a badly-shaven chin —— or, more appropriately, the last few feeble sprouts on a bald head.

This is a grand place, all the same, especially for fellwalkers on the retired list: here they can recline for hours, recalling joyful days when they had energy enough to climb to the tops of all the mountains in view. Strange how all the best days of memory are to do with summit-cairns..... Will there be mountains like these in heaven ..... or is *this* heaven, before death, and will there never again be hills to climb? Is Latrigg the last of all? But no, it needn't be — there's still Orrest Head, even easier..... Funny, *that's* where we came in .....

CAUSEY PIKE   BARROW   SCAR CRAGS   SAIL   EEL CRAG / OUTERSIDE   GRASMOOR   Coledale Hause   GRISEDALE PIKE

The Grasmoor group, from Gale Road

Latrigg 9

THE VIEW

There is complete contrast between the northern and southern halves of the view. The northern, consisting of featureless slopes sweeping up to a high skyline, will hardly get a second glance unless the ling is in bloom, but to the south is a panorama of crowded detail, all of it of great beauty: indeed, this scene is one of the gems of the district. The roofs of Keswick are below, Derwentwater is set out just beyond, in its lovely entirety, and in the distance Borrowdale and the Newlands Valley are seen winding deeply amongst the sombre mountains. The far horizon is a jumbled upheaval of peaks, with many dear old friends standing up proudly: Helvellyn, Bowfell, the Scafells, Great Gable, Pillar, the Buttermere fells, and, much nearer, the striking outline of the Grasmoor group. There is enough of interest in this charming picture to engage the attention for many hours, and Latrigg is a place to visit time and time again, for the scene is never quite the same but always fresh and exciting. The view is so much the best reason for climbing Latrigg that it is almost a pity to make the ascent on a day of poor visibility.

Principal Fells

- SKIDDAW LITTLE MAN
- SKIDDAW (summit not seen)
- CARL SIDE
- DODD
- BARF
- LORD'S SEAT
- WHINLATTER
- GRISEDALE PIKE
- GRASMOOR
- OUTERSIDE
- EEL CRAG
- SAIL
- BARROW
- CAUSEY PIKE
- RED PIKE
- HIGH STILE
- ROBINSON
- HINDSCARTH
- CATBELLS
- DALE HEAD
- KING'S HOW
- WALLA CRAG
- PILLAR
- GRANGE FELL
- GREAT CRAG
- GREAT GABLE
- LINGMELL
- SCAFELL
- BASE BROWN
- SCAFELL PIKE
- GREAT END
- ESK PIKE
- BOWFELL
- GLARAMARA
- CRINKLE CRAGS
- COLD PIKE
- GREY FRIAR
- DOW CRAG

Lakes and Tarns
ESE: Tewet Tarn
SSW: Derwentwater
NW: Bassenthwaite Lake

Latrigg 10

THE VIEW

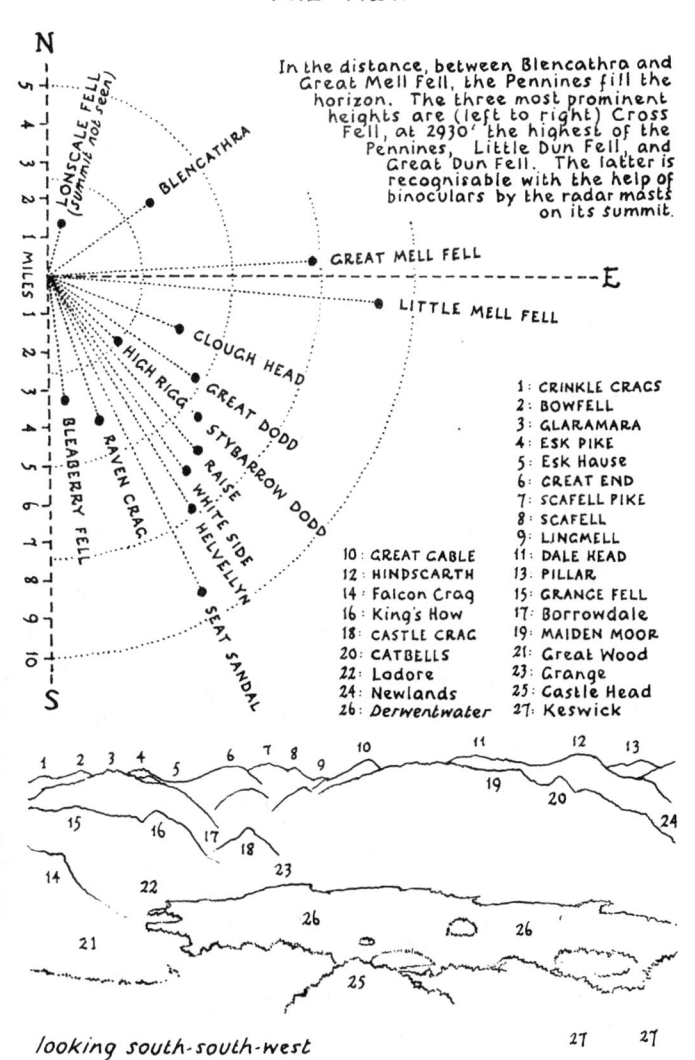

In the distance, between Blencathra and Great Mell Fell, the Pennines fill the horizon. The three most prominent heights are (left to right) Cross Fell, at 2930' the highest of the Pennines, Little Dun Fell, and Great Dun Fell. The latter is recognisable with the help of binoculars by the radar masts on its summit.

- LONSCALE FELL (summit not seen)
- BLENCATHRA
- GREAT MELL FELL
- LITTLE MELL FELL
- CLOUGH HEAD
- HIGH RIGG
- GREAT DODD
- STYBARROW DODD
- RAISE
- WHITE SIDE
- HELVELLYN
- SEAT SANDAL
- BLEABERRY FELL
- RAVEN CRAG

1: CRINKLE CRAGS
2: BOWFELL
3: GLARAMARA
4: ESK PIKE
5: Esk Hause
6: GREAT END
7: SCAFELL PIKE
8: SCAFELL
9: LINGMELL
10: GREAT GABLE
11: DALE HEAD
12: HINDSCARTH
13: PILLAR
14: Falcon Crag
15: GRANGE FELL
16: King's How
17: Borrowdale
18: CASTLE CRAG
19: MAIDEN MOOR
20: CATBELLS
21: Great Wood
22: Lodore
23: Grange
24: Newlands
25: Castle Head
26: *Derwentwater*
27: Keswick

looking south-south-west

Longlands Fell 1580'

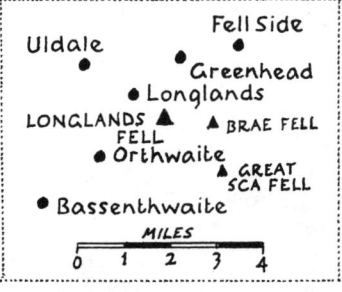

from the north-west

```
Uldale        Fell Side
                •
        •        Greenhead
              • Longlands
LONGLANDS ▲    ▲ BRAE FELL
   FELL
       • Orthwaite
                   ▲ GREAT
                   SCA FELL
  • Bassenthwaite
           MILES
    0   1   2   3   4
```

The simple, uncomplicated pyramid of Longlands Fell terminates the northwest ridge of Great Sca Fell. It marks the end of Lakeland in this direction: beyond is a pleasant countryside extending to the Solway Firth. It is a neat little hill, conspicuous in many views although overtopped by bulkier masses behind. The waters of the Ellen and the Eden catchments divide along its crest.

Longlands Fell 2

MAP

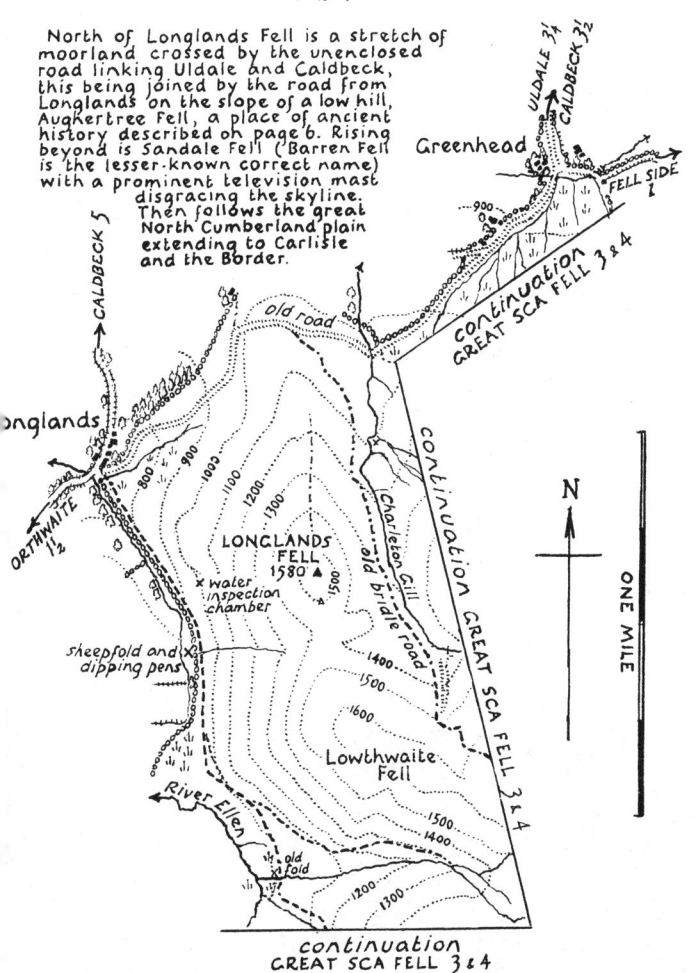

North of Longlands Fell is a stretch of moorland crossed by the unenclosed road linking Uldale and Caldbeck, this being joined by the road from Longlands on the slope of a low hill, Aughertree Fell, a place of ancient history described on page 6. Rising beyond is Sandale Fell ('Barren Fell' is the lesser-known correct name) with a prominent television mast disgracing the skyline. Then follows the great North Cumberland plain extending to Carlisle and the Border.

The ridge of Longlands Fell is the watershed between the River Ellen (west) and the Eden catchment (east). This is worthy of comment, the fell being the lowest and smallest of three ridges jutting northwards from a central mass; the others are Brae Fell and High Pike.

Longlands Fell 3

ASCENT FROM LONGLANDS
900 feet of ascent : 1¼ miles

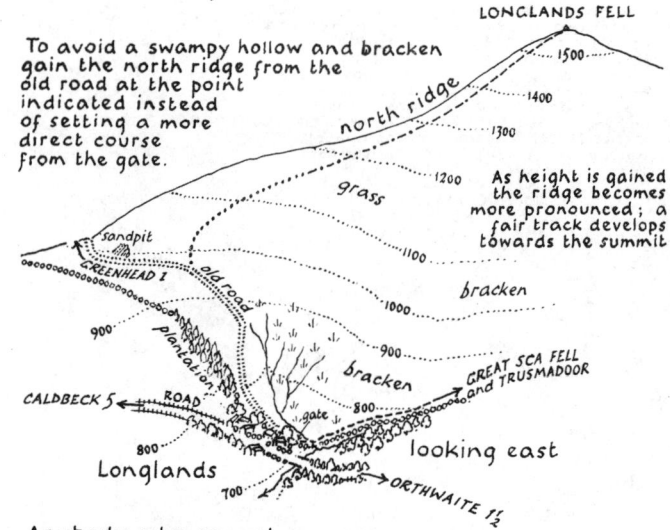

To avoid a swampy hollow and bracken gain the north ridge from the old road at the point indicated instead of setting a more direct course from the gate.

As height is gained the ridge becomes more pronounced; a fair track develops towards the summit

looking east

Anybody who cannot manage this short and simple climb is advised to give up the idea of becoming a fellwalker.

Longlands

Longlands Fell 4

THE SUMMIT

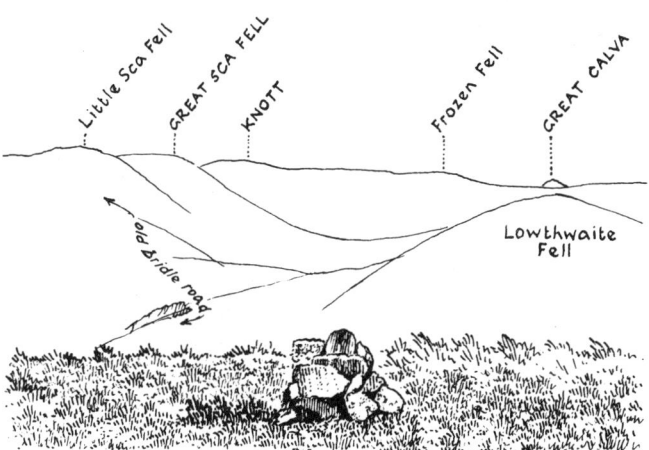

The grassy top of the fell is small and neat, and crowned by a small and neat cairn. It has merit both as a viewpoint and a place for a siesta, but no features of interest.

DESCENTS: A fair track leaves the summit, aiming north for the highest point of the old road between Longlands and Greenhead, and this route is usually followed. Some swampy ground would be met by taking a more direct line for Longlands. But the grassy slopes may be descended with ease anywhere —— indeed, if nobody is watching, rapid progression by roly-poly may be indulged in by the young in heart; but *mind that swamp!*

RIDGE ROUTE: For a diagram, see Great Sca Fell 10.

Longlands Fell, from Over Water

Longlands Fell 5

THE VIEW

As befits its position as the northern outpost of Lakeland Longlands Fell commands an excellent view over declining foothills to the Solway Firth and Scotland, the prospect in this direction being in fact more satisfactory than that to the south, where higher fells obstruct the distant scene; but the Grasmoor fells display an exciting skyline to the west of Skiddaw.

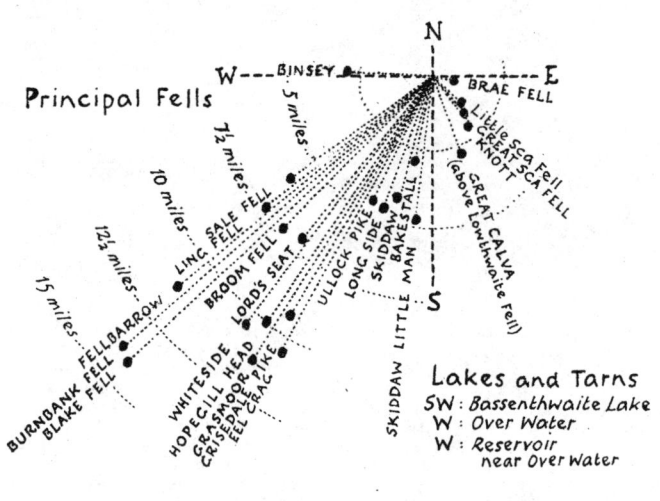

Principal Fells

N — BINSEY
E — BRAE FELL
Little Sca Fell
GREAT SCA FELL
KNOTT
GREAT CALVA (above Lowthwaite Fell)
ULLOCK PIKE
LONG SIDE
SKIDDAW
BAKESTALL
SKIDDAW LITTLE MAN
5 miles — LING FELL
7½ miles — SALE FELL
10 miles — BROOM FELL, LORDS SEAT
12½ miles — FELLBARROW, WHITESIDE, HOPEGILL HEAD, GRASMOOR, GRISEDALE PIKE, EEL CRAG
15 miles — BURNBANK FELL, BLAKE FELL

Lakes and Tarns
SW : Bassenthwaite Lake
W : Over Water
W : Reservoir near Over Water

1 : LITTLE MAN
2 : SKIDDAW
3 : LONG SIDE
4 : ULLOCK PIKE
5 : BAKESTALL

Skiddaw
(over Great Cockup)

Longlands Fell 6

Aughertree Fell

Let's get the name right first. It is pronounced *Affertree*. This low hill, a continuation of the moorland running from Longlands Fell in a north-westerly direction, is really outside the area covered by this book, but is worthy of mention.

There is not enough of it to occupy more than a half-hour's walking, but it has a special interest for the student of past civilisations. On the gentle northern slope are traces of three ancient enclosures and tumuli. The enclosures are circular, about 70 yards in diameter, and although now overgrown the parapets and ditches are still plain to see. There is no good point of vantage for surveying the encampment as a whole (an aerial view would reveal the arrangement better) and in fact some searching of the wide breast of the fell is necessary to locate the various earthworks. The site has been excavated on several occasions and yielded many of its secrets.

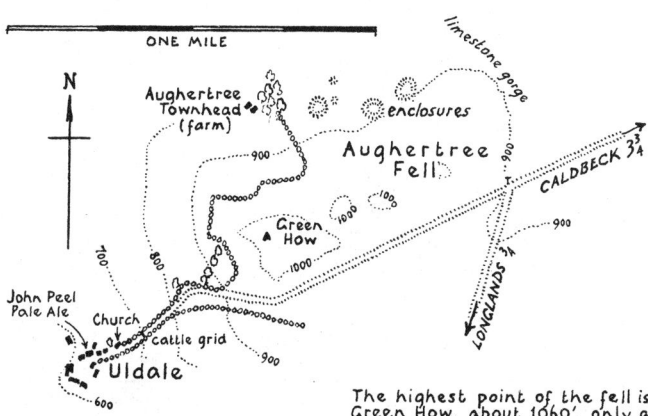

The highest point of the fell is Green How, about 1060', only a few minutes' easy climbing from the unenclosed motor road above Uldale, which gives convenient access, the whole fell being an open sheep pasture. The northern slope descends to a dry gorge, where limestone is in evidence: the fell lies within the continuous strata of limestone (very narrow just here) that extends from Egremont to Shap along the western and northern perimeter of Lakeland. There are good formations at Caldbeck. A line of pylons lower down the slope and a horrible object on the nearby skyline (Sandale Television Mast) contrast oddly with the ancient earthworks of Aughertree Fell.

Long Side 2405'

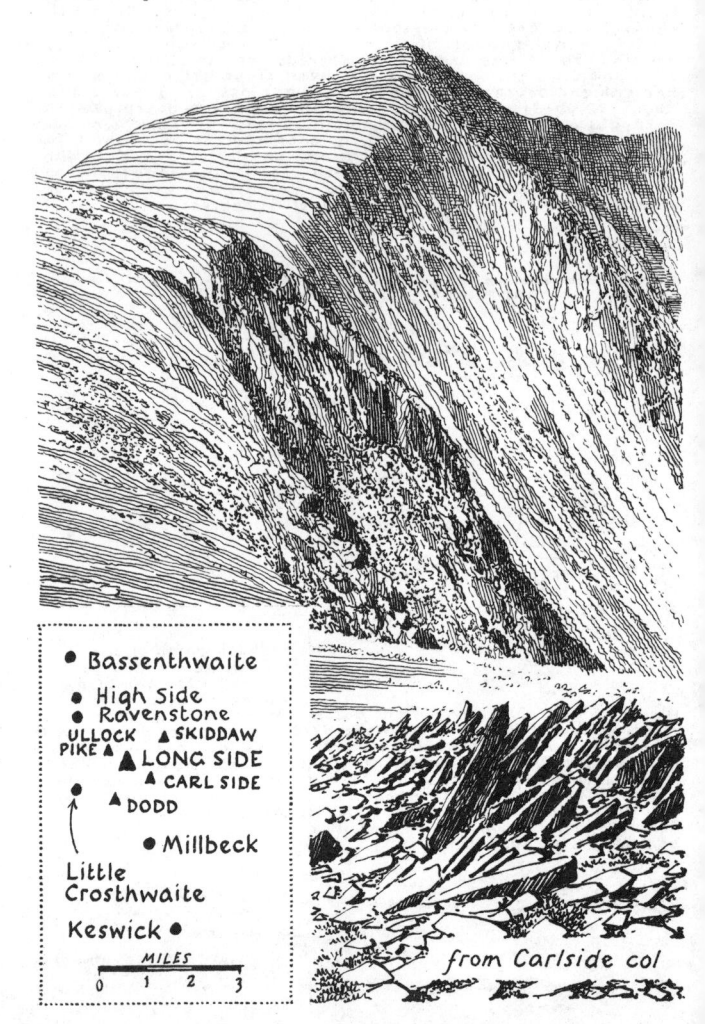

from Carlside col

- Bassenthwaite
- High Side
- Ravenstone
- ULLOCK PIKE ▲ ▲ SKIDDAW
- ▲ LONG SIDE
- ▲ CARL SIDE
- ▲ DODD
- Millbeck
- Little Crosthwaite
- Keswick

MILES
0 1 2 3

Long Side 2

NATURAL FEATURES

The highest point on the lofty, steep-sided ridge rising between Bassenthwaite Lake and the 'hidden' valley of Southerndale is a small and shapely pyramid delicately poised above a rough, shadowed declivity facing into the massive breast of Skiddaw. The ridge leading up over Ullock Pike from the north, Longside Edge, is neat and interesting — a splendid high-level way for walkers — but beyond the highest point soon loses itself in the wide plateau of Carl Side.

The summit is strictly nameless, Long Side proper being the broad heathery flank overlooking Bassenthwaite Lake. Below 1500' this slope is planted with massed regiments of conifers and forms a part of the Forestry Commission's Dodd Wood.

Longside Edge, looking from Ullock Pike

Long Side 3

MAP

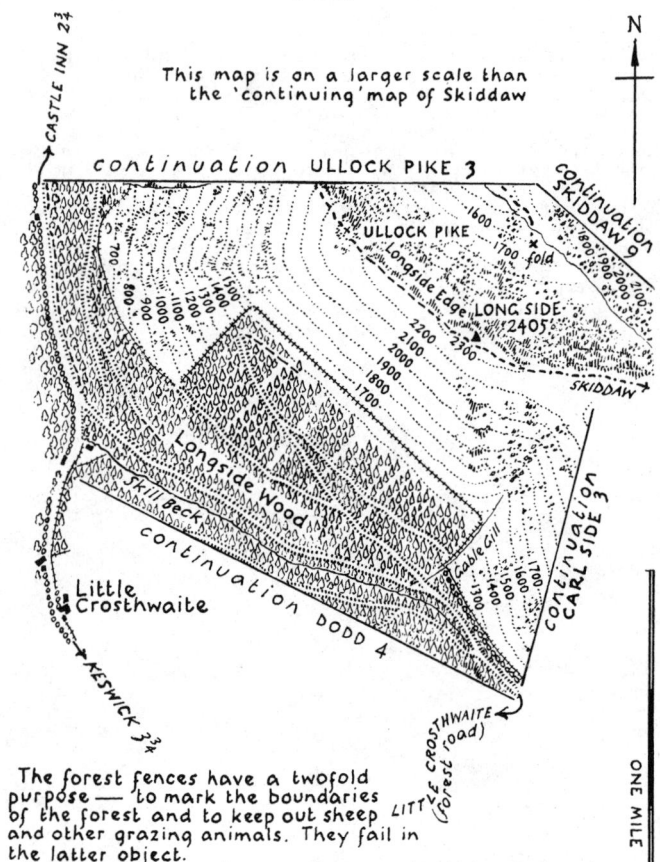

This map is on a larger scale than the 'continuing' map of Skiddaw

N

CASTLE INN 2¾

continuation ULLOCK PIKE 3

continuation SKIDDAW 9

ULLOCK PIKE
Longside Edge
LONG SIDE 2405

SKIDDAW

Longside Wood

Skill Beck

continuation DODD 4

Gable Gill

continuation CARL SIDE 3

Little Crosthwaite

KESWICK 3¼

LITTLE CROSTHWAITE (forest road)

ONE MILE

The forest fences have a twofold purpose — to mark the boundaries of the forest and to keep out sheep and other grazing animals. They fail in the latter object.

Nothing on this or the opposite page should be construed as implying that walkers have a right to surmount such fences at places other than where stiles are provided, or as encouraging them to commit trespass. The ascent to the uppermost limits of the forest meets the obstacle of a fence at 1600' (no stile, few weaknesses, very awkward to cross direct but easier at the side). To avoid this trap, and keep on the right side of the law, leave the forest at its corner where Gable Gill comes in from the open fell and follow this watercourse up to the ridge, a stony scramble.

Long Side 4

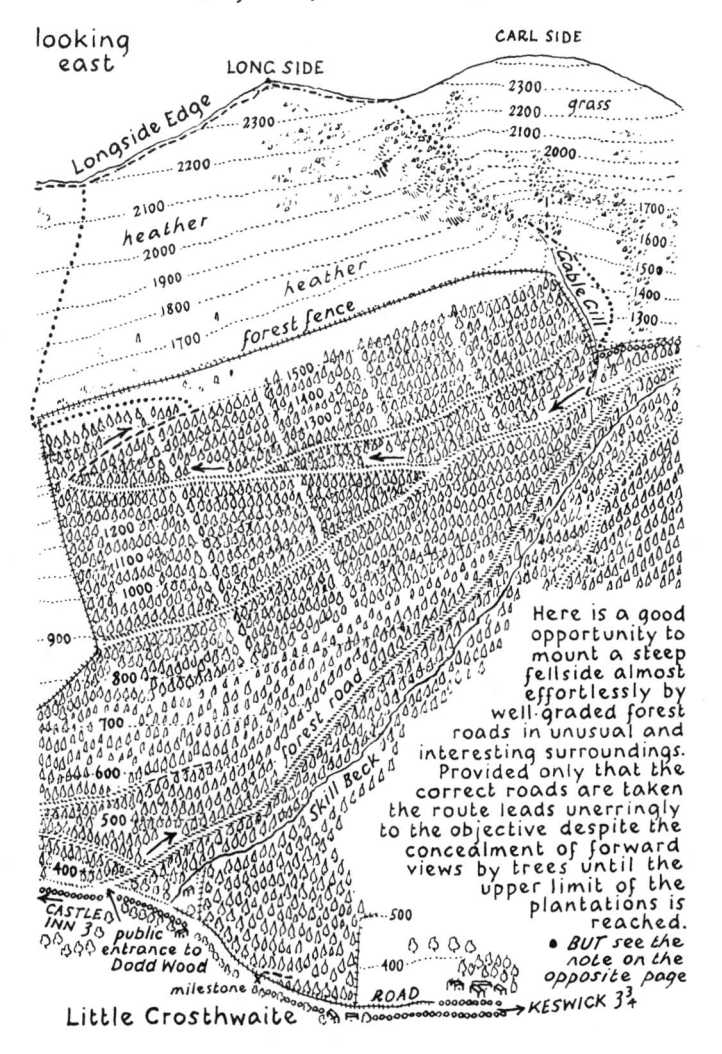

ASCENT FROM LITTLE CROSTHWAITE
2050 feet of ascent : 2½ miles

looking east

LONG SIDE — CARL SIDE

Longside Edge — heather — forest fence — Gable Gill

Here is a good opportunity to mount a steep fellside almost effortlessly by well-graded forest roads in unusual and interesting surroundings. Provided only that the correct roads are taken the route leads unerringly to the objective despite the concealment of forward views by trees until the upper limit of the plantations is reached.

• *BUT see the note on the opposite page*

CASTLE INN — public entrance to Dodd Wood — milestone — Skill Beck — forest road — ROAD → KESWICK 3¾

Little Crosthwaite

Long Side 5

ASCENT FROM RAVENSTONE
2150 feet of ascent : 2¼ miles

Neither The Edge nor Longside Edge can be compared with Striding Edge on Helvellyn or Sharp Edge on Blencathra, for there is no rock to handle and nothing steep enough to carry a risk of accident; nevertheless they provide fine walking on a ridge narrow enough in places to give startling glimpses downwards and heathery enough to supply springy couches for better enjoyment of the delectable views. This is a good route and it should be noted as a line of approach to Skiddaw more interesting than others preferred by the crowds

SKIDDAW
CARL SIDE   LONG SIDE   Longside Edge
ULLOCK PIKE
2400
2300   Carlside col
2100
2000
1900 heather
1800
1700

On gaining the ridge, Skiddaw is massively in sight across the valley of Southerndale — an aspect of Skiddaw not generally known.

fold x

1600   The track on The Edge is very sketchy lower down, but improves as the final pyramid of Ullock Pike — a glorious object — is neared. On Longside Edge it is quite distinct.

Southerndale
Southerndale Beck
grass   The Edge
1500
1400 Kiln Pots
1300
1200   Raven Crag

← BARKBETH
1100
1000

Start up the steep path, between fences, from a gate on the roadside at the end of the grounds of the hotel.

900   Watch for green path inclining right at junction of fence and wall
800
700   stile
young plantation   forest road

This delightful climb deserves a high, even urgent, priority from fellwalkers who know it not. The undulating Edge, of firm dry turf, is an inspiring ladder to the eminently desirable Ullock Pike, the ridge beyond is fine and the views are excellent.

600
500   Ravenstone Hotel
400   KESWICK →
signpost (DODD WOOD)
← HIGH SIDE ¾   Main road
CASTLE INN 2½   (Buses No. 35 and 71)

looking south-east

Long Side 6

THE SUMMIT

The hills of Galloway — Criffel
Solway Firth — West Cumberland plain
Bassenthwaite Lake — ULLOCK PIKE

Its furnishings of fragrant vegetation — small soft carpets of dry mosses, bilberry and short heather; its quietness, airy elevation and glorious views make this one of the choicest of summits. It is a place fashioned by heaven for the repose and recuperation of tired limbs — or designed by the devil for the abandonment of all further effort. Before composing oneself to slumber, however, it is well to reflect that the edge of a profound abyss is only a short roll distant.

DESCENTS: Best way off is provided by the Edge, but if aiming for the Keswick area the south ridge of Carl Side is more convenient. In m..t, Gable Gill is a safe but rough route to Dodd Wood and the road.

RIDGE ROUTES

To ULLOCK PIKE, 2230': ⅓ mile : NW
Depression at 2185'
50 feet of ascent
A pity it isn't much longer!
A distinct and delightful track in the heather skirts the rim of Longside Edge and links the two summits.

To CARL SIDE, 2420': ½ mile: SE
Depression at 2240': 180 feet of ascent
A narrow trod goes down to the depression and continues to Carlside Tarn (for Skiddaw). Carl Side's top is reached by a beeline on grass.

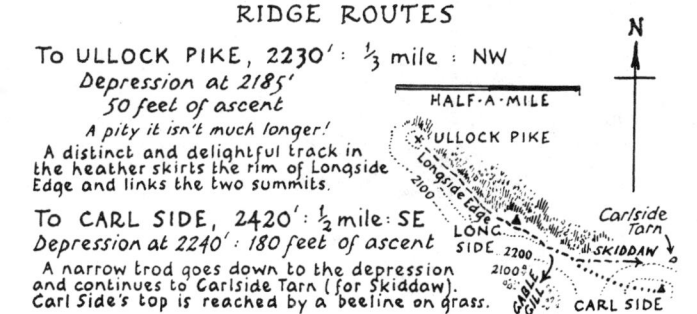

Long Side 7

THE VIEW

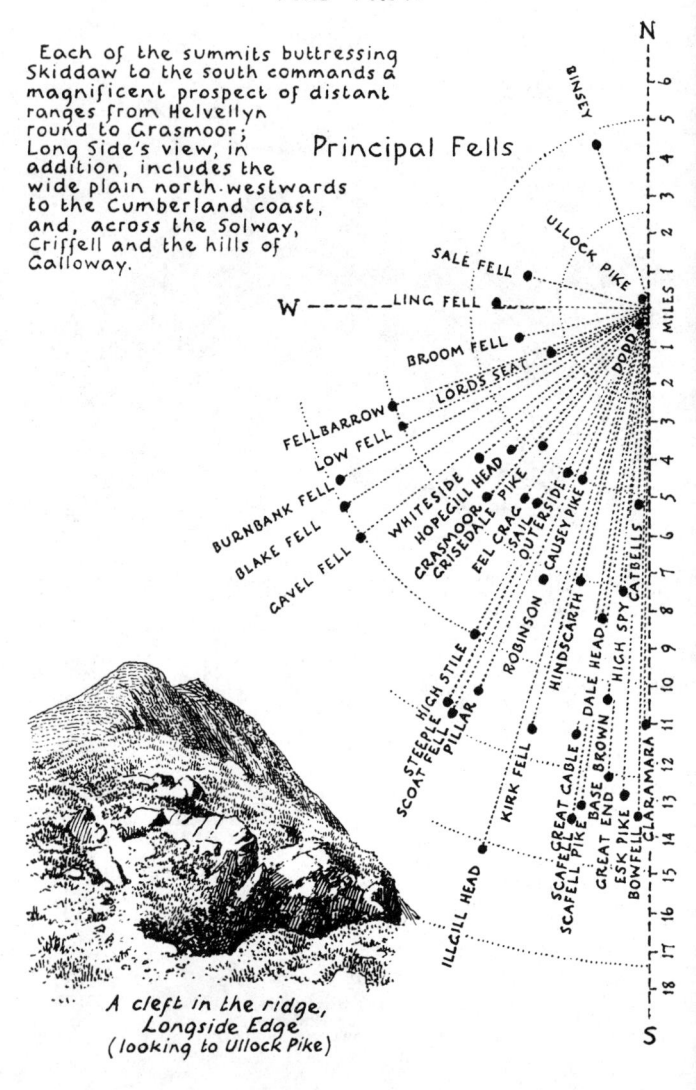

Each of the summits buttressing Skiddaw to the south commands a magnificent prospect of distant ranges from Helvellyn round to Grasmoor; Long Side's view, in addition, includes the wide plain north-westwards to the Cumberland coast, and, across the Solway, Criffell and the hills of Galloway.

Principal Fells

A cleft in the ridge, Longside Edge (looking to Ullock Pike)

Long Side 8

THE VIEW

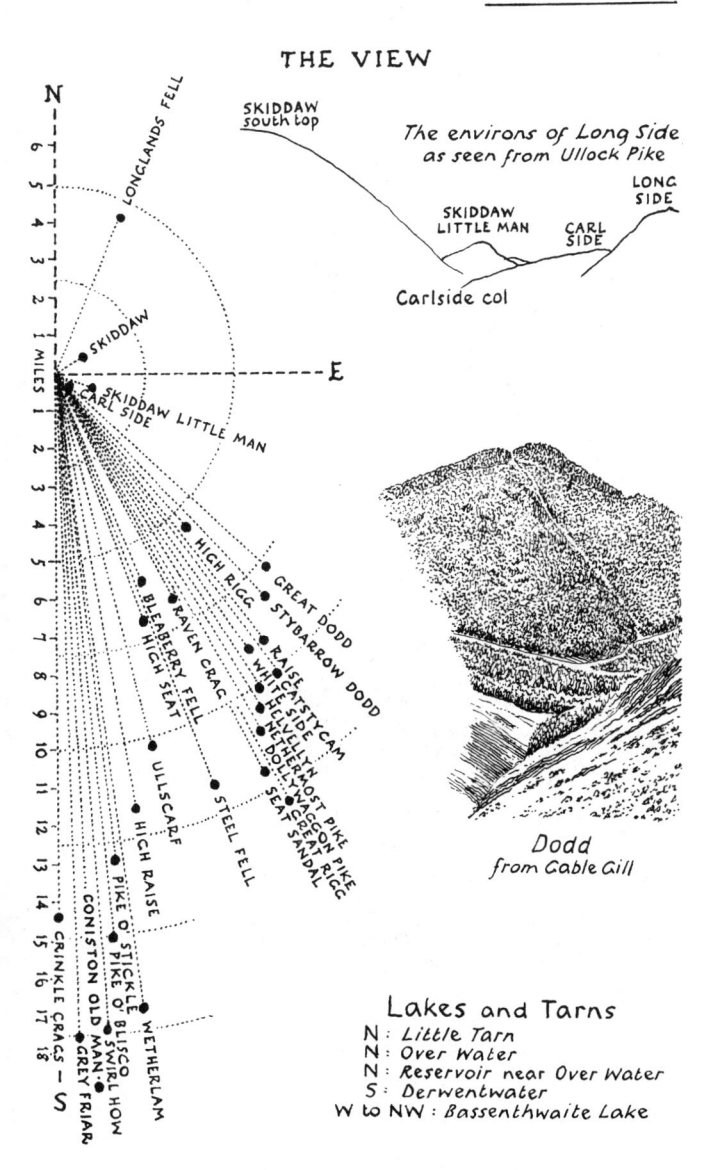

The environs of Long Side as seen from Ullock Pike

SKIDDAW south top
SKIDDAW LITTLE MAN
CARL SIDE
LONG SIDE
Carlside col

LONGLANDS FELL
SKIDDAW
SKIDDAW LITTLE MAN
CARL SIDE
HIGH RIGG
GREAT DODD
STYBARROW DODD
BLEABERRY FELL
RAVEN CRAG
RAISE
WHITESIDE
HIGH SEAT
CATSTYCAM
HELVELLYN LOWER MAN
HELVELLYN
NETHERMOST PIKE
DOLLYWAGGON PIKE
GREAT RIGG
SEAT SANDAL
ULLSCARF
HIGH RAISE
STEEL FELL
PIKE O' STICKLE
PIKE O' BLISCO
SWIRL HOW
CONISTON OLD MAN
WETHERLAM
CRINKLE CRAGS
GREY FRIAR

Dodd from Gable Gill

Lakes and Tarns

N : *Little Tarn*
N : *Over Water*
N : *Reservoir near Over Water*
S : *Derwentwater*
W to NW : *Bassenthwaite Lake*

Lonscale Fell 2344'

from Roughten Gill

Lonscale Fell 2

NATURAL FEATURES

From the summit-ridge of Skiddaw the main watershed eastwards switchbacks over Little Man and Jenkin Hill to Lonscale Fell, this being the familiar outline so conspicuously in view on the southern approaches to Keswick. Lonscale Fell, a graceful and gentle curve against the sky, ends very abruptly in a sharp peak (which also features prominently in most views of the range) whence the ground falls away steeply to the deep narrow valley of Glenderaterra Beck; beyond rises Blencathra.

It is interesting to note that the watershed, between Derwent (south) and Caldew (north), does not persist along the highest ground of Lonscale Fell and the function is taken over by a low ridge that runs away north-east just short of the summit and continues as a wide marshy upland separating the headwaters of the Glenderaterra from the basin of the upper Caldew.

All the interest of Lonscale Fell lies in its east face, a mile-long rough declivity out of character with the general structure of the fell and unusual in an area where smooth grass slopes predominate.

Nowadays exclusively used for sheep-rearing, there was a time when minerals were won from the fell and the old mine-workings are still in evidence on the floor of the Glenderaterra valley.

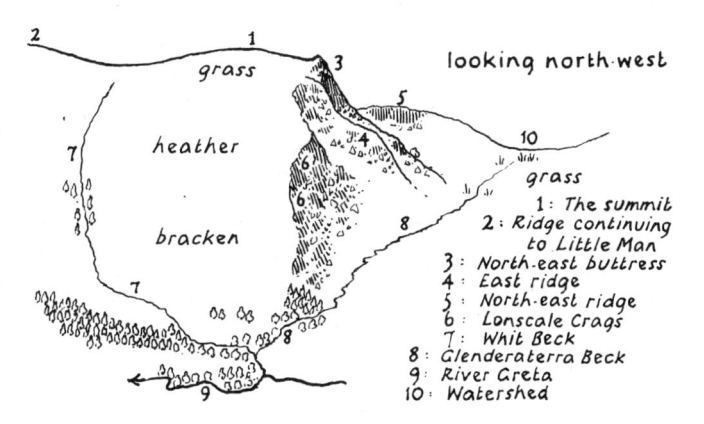

looking north-west

1: The summit
2: Ridge continuing to Little Man
3: North-east buttress
4: East ridge
5: North-east ridge
6: Lonscale Crags
7: Whit Beck
8: Glenderaterra Beck
9: River Greta
10: Watershed

Lonscale Fell 3

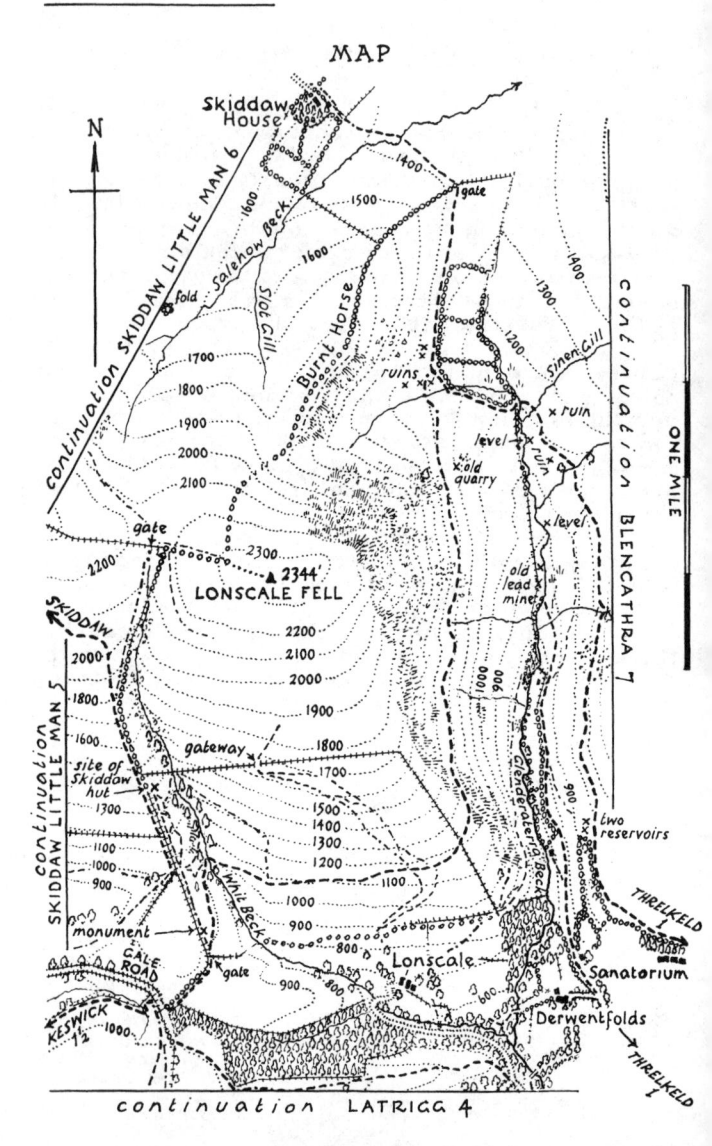

MAP

Lonscale Fell 4

ASCENT FROM KESWICK
2150 feet of ascent : 3¾ - 4¼ miles

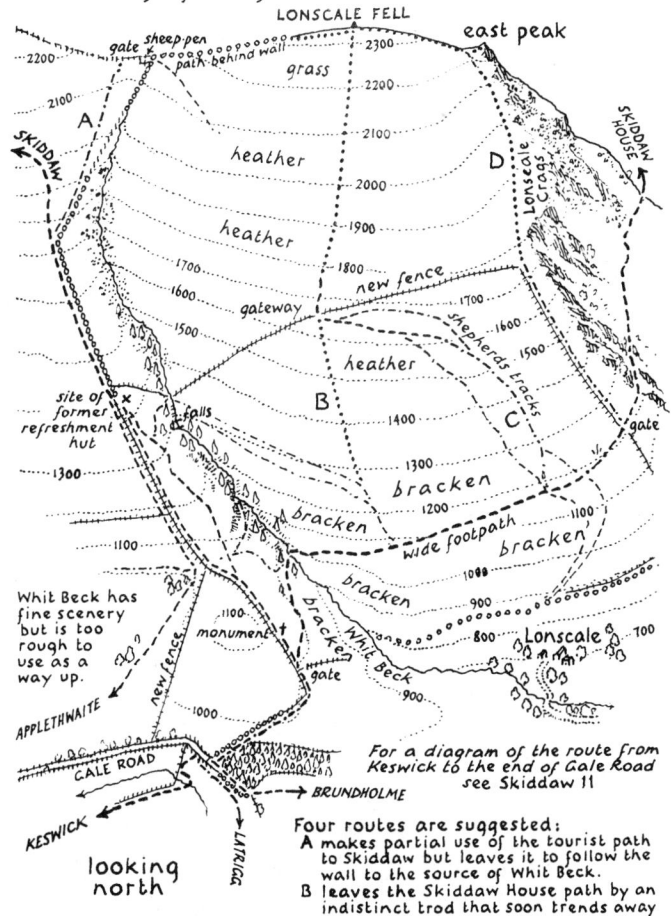

looking north

Whit Beck has fine scenery but is too rough to use as a way up.

For a diagram of the route from Keswick to the end of Gale Road see Skiddaw 11

Four routes are suggested:
A makes partial use of the tourist path to Skiddaw but leaves it to follow the wall to the source of Whit Beck.
B leaves the Skiddaw House path by an indistinct trod that soon trends away to the left. Go straight ahead to a gateway in the fence above.
C is a continuous track (with variations) to the gateway.
B and C will be passed unnoticed unless watched for, not that this would matter much because the broad front of the fell may be climbed almost anywhere, but they are useful when the bracken is high. B and C unite at the gateway. There is no path in the short heather beyond.
D has an interest the other routes lack: it climbs along the rising rim of Lonscale Crags with splendid views down into the Glenderaterra Valley.

Lonscale Fell 5

ASCENT FROM THE GLENDERATERRA VALLEY
(DIRECT to the EAST PEAK)

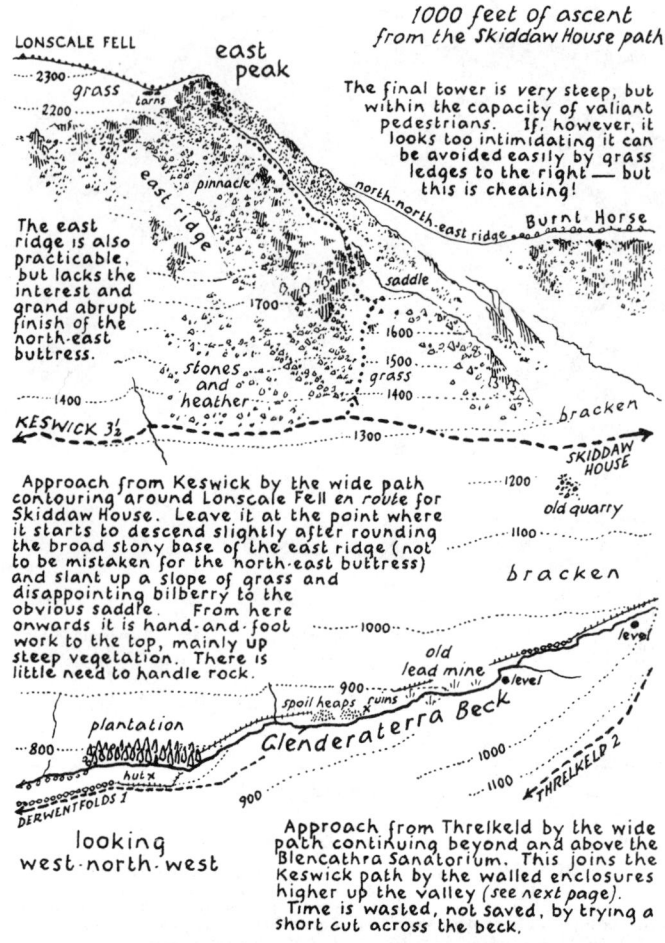

1000 feet of ascent from the Skiddaw House path

The final tower is very steep, but within the capacity of valiant pedestrians. If, however, it looks too intimidating it can be avoided easily by grass ledges to the right — but this is cheating!

The east ridge is also practicable, but lacks the interest and grand abrupt finish of the north-east buttress.

Approach from Keswick by the wide path contouring around Lonscale Fell en route for Skiddaw House. Leave it at the point where it starts to descend slightly after rounding the broad stony base of the east ridge (not to be mistaken for the north-east buttress) and slant up a slope of grass and disappointing bilberry to the obvious saddle. From here onwards it is hand-and-foot work to the top, mainly up steep vegetation. There is little need to handle rock.

looking west-north-west

Approach from Threlkeld by the wide path continuing beyond and above the Blencathra Sanatorium. This joins the Keswick path by the walled enclosures higher up the valley (see next page).
Time is wasted, not saved, by trying a short cut across the beck.

For scramblers only. From some viewpoints the north-east buttress looks excessively steep, almost precipitous, but it is much easier than appearances suggest. *Nevertheless this is not a route for descent.*

Lonscale Fell 6

ASCENT FROM THE GLENDERATERRA VALLEY
(via the BURNT HORSE RIDGE)
1000 feet of ascent from the watershed.

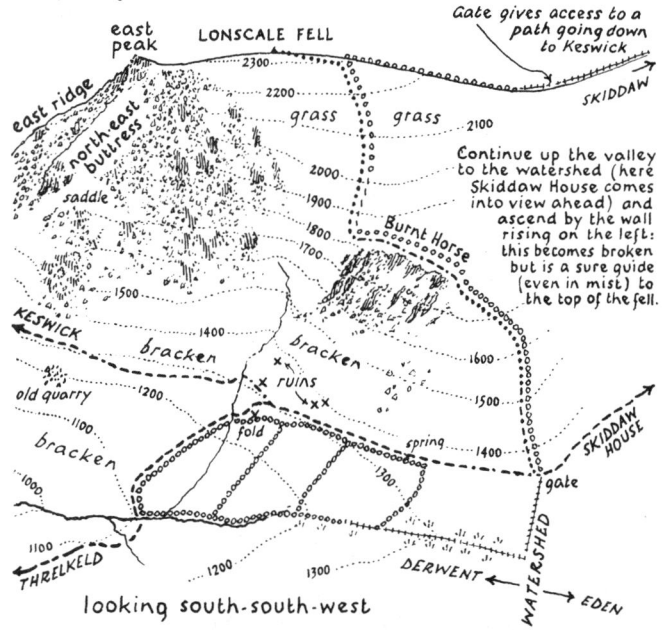

looking south-south-west

Continue up the valley to the watershed (here Skiddaw House comes into view ahead) and ascend by the wall rising on the left: this becomes broken but is a sure guide (even in mist) to the top of the fell.

Gate gives access to a path going down to Keswick

This is an interesting 'face-saver' for people who have set forth to climb the north-east buttress — and wish they hadn't when they see it. The route is simple, and quite good above the Burnt Horse crags, the dominating feature being the east peak, which soars up grandly (but somewhat reproachfully) ahead.

The Burnt Horse ridge, looking north

Lonscale Fell 7

RIDGE ROUTE

To SKIDDAW LITTLE MAN, 2837': 1½ miles: WNW
Depression at 2180': 675 feet of ascent.
Easy, straightforward walking

This route, a bee-line, is without a path but on grass throughout, following a wall and a fence most of the way. On Jenkin Hill the much-frequented tourist path to Skiddaw is crossed.

Lonscale Crags, from the path to Skiddaw House

At the point illustrated, the path from Keswick swings sharply to the north, being here roughly hewn out of the living rock, and contours at 1250' along the side of Glenderaterra Valley.

Lonscale Fell 8

THE SUMMIT

(illustration labelled: LITTLE MAN, SKIDDAW, Jenkin Hill, old wall)

The cairn owes its existence to the enviable energy of some person or persons unknown, who have carried stones from the old wall to make it. There is no other decoration on the featureless top. Do not omit the short walk to the East Peak — a magnificent belvedere.

The summit tower, East Peak

Lonscale Fell 9

THE VIEW

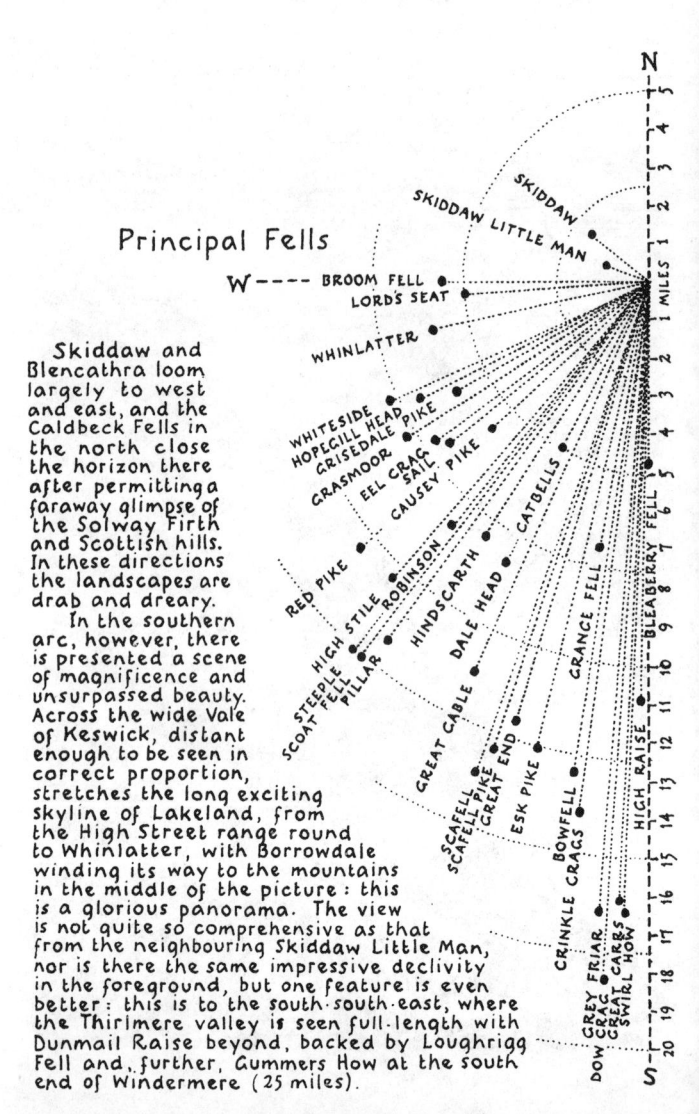

Principal Fells

Skiddaw and Blencathra loom largely to west and east, and the Caldbeck Fells in the north close the horizon there after permitting a faraway glimpse of the Solway Firth and Scottish hills. In these directions the landscapes are drab and dreary.

In the southern arc, however, there is presented a scene of magnificence and unsurpassed beauty. Across the wide Vale of Keswick, distant enough to be seen in correct proportion, stretches the long exciting skyline of Lakeland, from the High Street range round to Whinlatter, with Borrowdale winding its way to the mountains in the middle of the picture: this is a glorious panorama. The view is not quite so comprehensive as that from the neighbouring Skiddaw Little Man, nor is there the same impressive declivity in the foreground, but one feature is even better: this is to the south·south·east, where the Thirlmere valley is seen full-length with Dunmail Raise beyond, backed by Loughrigg Fell and, further, Gummers How at the south end of Windermere (25 miles).

Lonscale Fell 10

THE VIEW

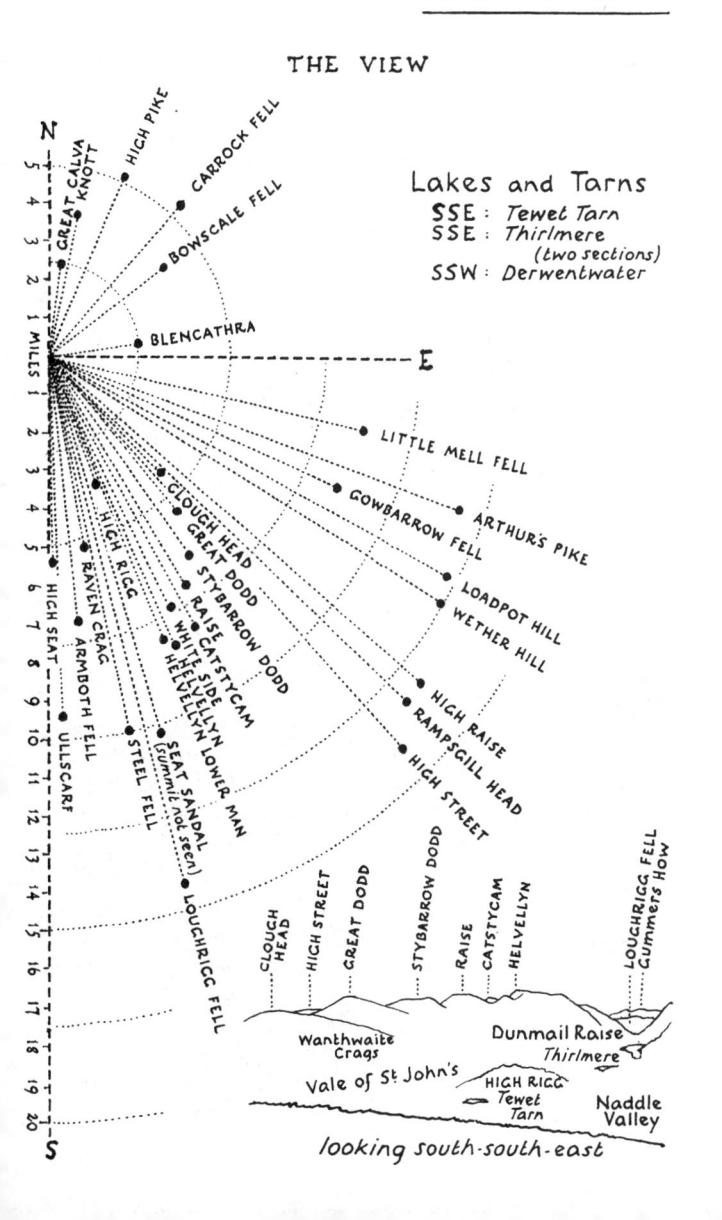

Lakes and Tarns
SSE: *Tewet Tarn*
SSE: *Thirlmere*
  (two sections)
SSW: *Derwentwater*

looking south-south-east

Meal Fell

not named on
1" Ordnance maps

1770'
approx.

from Burntod Gill

- Uldale
- Longlands
- Orthwaite
- ▲ MEAL FELL
- ▲ GREAT SCA FELL
- ▲ KNOTT
- Bassenthwaite Village

MILES
0 1 2 3 4

Meal Fell 2

NATURAL FEATURES

Thrusting out from the smooth western declivity of Great Sca Fell is a long ridge that swells into two subsidiary fells before coming down sharply to the little hamlet of Orthwaite. The first of these, that nearer Great Sca Fell, takes the form of a pyramid, its summit appearing from certain viewpoints as a shapely peak. Although of small and slender proportions, this fell is distinctive and its summit is unusual, yet the usual maps do not give it a name, the information being vouchsafed only in the Ordnance sheets of 2½" scale and upwards, as Meal Fell. The smooth grassy slopes, badly eroded where they drop steeply into the bounding ravines, have little of interest, the one remarkable feature being the great cleft of Trusmadoor, which conclusively marks the boundary between the fell and the second elevation on the ridge, Great Cockup.

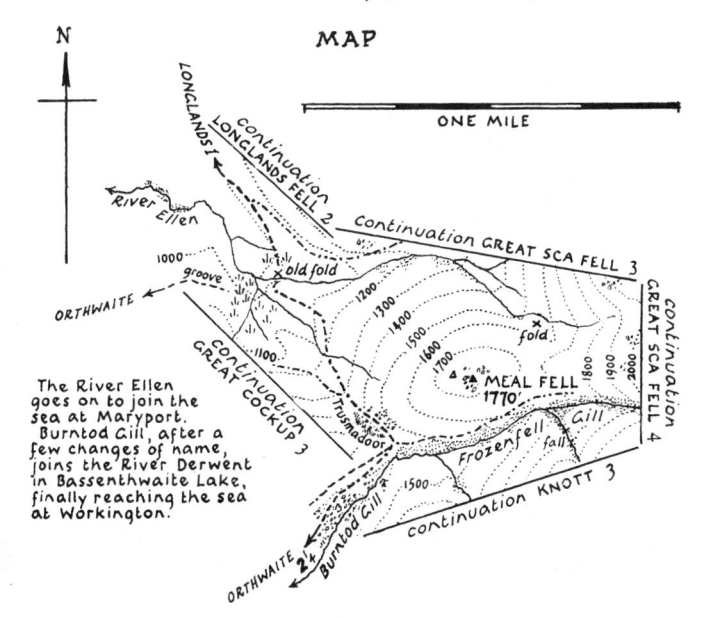

MAP

The River Ellen goes on to join the sea at Maryport.
Burntod Gill, after a few changes of name, joins the River Derwent in Bassenthwaite Lake, finally reaching the sea at Workington.

Strictly speaking, a *path* is a *made* way, a *track* is a *trodden* way. The only *path* on this map is the one between the old sheepfold and Longlands; the others are *tracks*, the ways used by sheep over the centuries, narrow trods that never deviate. Many of these are quite distinct and well-trodden — but examine the footprints of those who have passed along: they usually reveal only the hooves of sheep and the hobnails of shepherds. Walkers rarely visit these lonely valleys among the Uldale Fells.

Meal Fell 3

ASCENT FROM ORTHWAITE
1050 feet of ascent : 3 miles

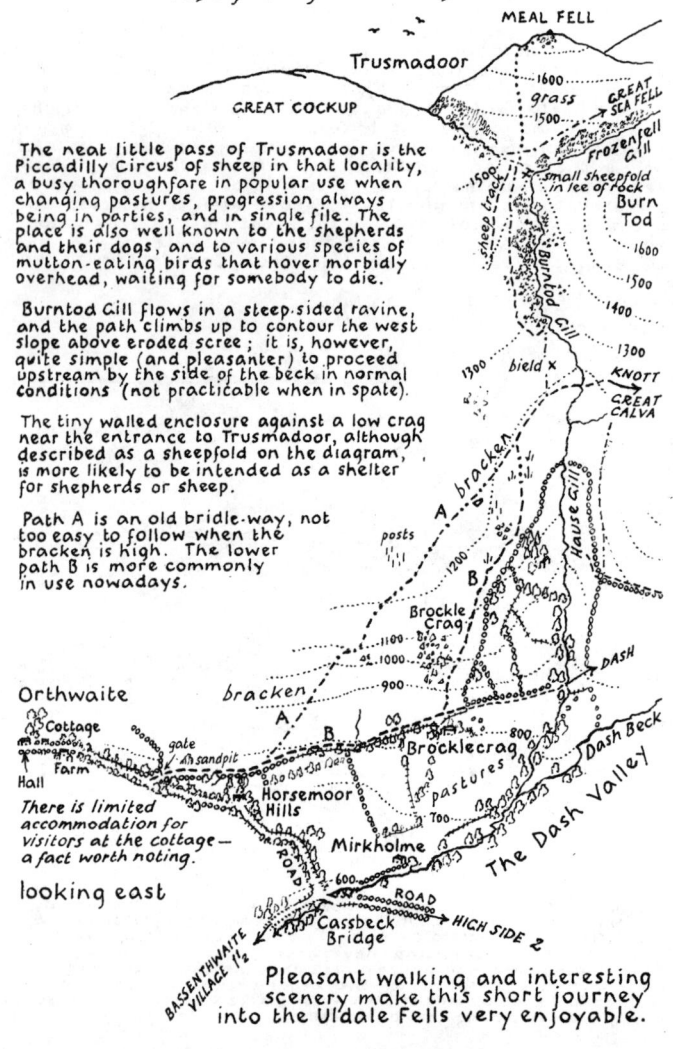

The neat little pass of Trusmadoor is the Piccadilly Circus of sheep in that locality, a busy thoroughfare in popular use when changing pastures, progression always being in parties, and in single file. The place is also well known to the shepherds and their dogs, and to various species of mutton-eating birds that hover morbidly overhead, waiting for somebody to die.

Burntod Gill flows in a steep-sided ravine, and the path climbs up to contour the west slope above eroded scree; it is, however, quite simple (and pleasanter) to proceed upstream by the side of the beck in normal conditions (not practicable when in spate).

The tiny walled enclosure against a low crag near the entrance to Trusmadoor, although described as a sheepfold on the diagram, is more likely to be intended as a shelter for shepherds or sheep.

Path A is an old bride-way, not too easy to follow when the bracken is high. The lower path B is more commonly in use nowadays.

There is limited accommodation for visitors at the cottage — a fact worth noting.

looking east

Pleasant walking and interesting scenery make this short journey into the Uldale Fells very enjoyable.

Meal Fell 4

ASCENT FROM LONGLANDS
1100 feet of ascent : 2¼ miles

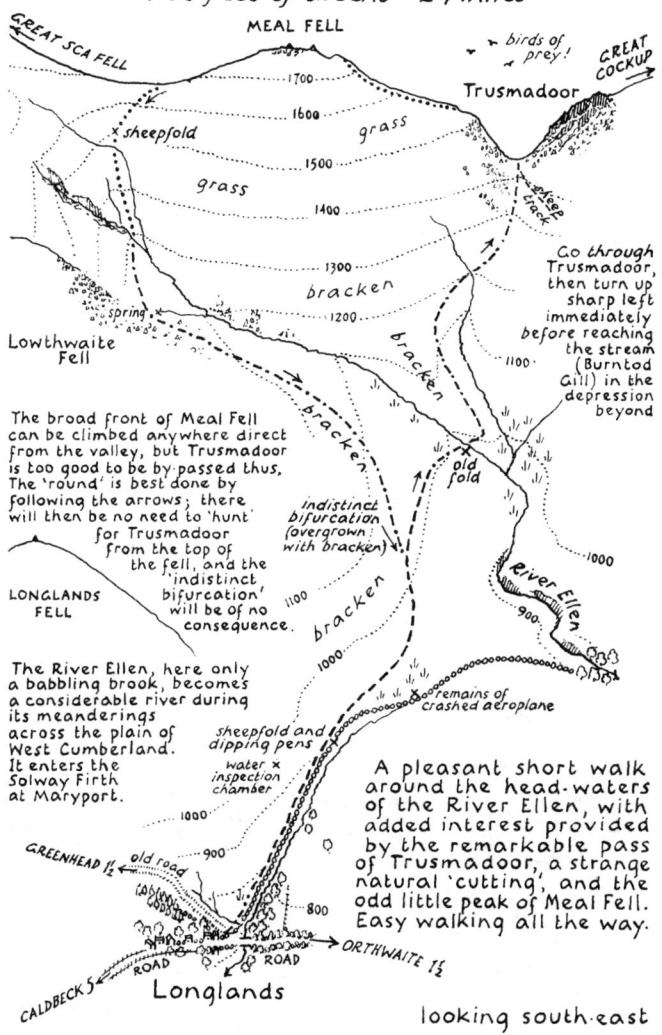

looking south-east

Go through Trusmadoor, then turn up sharp left immediately before reaching the stream (Burntod Gill) in the depression beyond

The broad front of Meal Fell can be climbed anywhere direct from the valley, but Trusmadoor is too good to be by-passed thus. The 'round' is best done by following the arrows; there will then be no need to 'hunt' for Trusmadoor from the top of the fell, and the 'indistinct bifurcation' will be of no consequence.

The River Ellen, here only a babbling brook, becomes a considerable river during its meanderings across the plain of West Cumberland. It enters the Solway Firth at Maryport.

A pleasant short walk around the head-waters of the River Ellen, with added interest provided by the remarkable pass of Trusmadoor, a strange natural 'cutting', and the odd little peak of Meal Fell. Easy walking all the way.

Meal Fell 5

THE SUMMIT

SKIDDAW

A surprise awaits the visitor, for the summit-cairn turns out to be not a cairn at all but a circular wall-shelter, like a shooting-butt, a ring of loose stones having been superimposed on outcropping rocks at the highest point. The top of the fell is a plateau, with a cairn on the western edge and ponds in a slight depression. Some rashes of scree make this the one stony top in the Uldale Fells. Descents are simple, on grass, in any direction.

from the west

Trusmadoor from Burntod Gill

Meal Fell 6

THE VIEW

As from all the Uldale Fells the prospect seawards will appeal more than the view inland, which, from Meal Fell, consists only of the featureless grass slopes of higher fells close at hand.

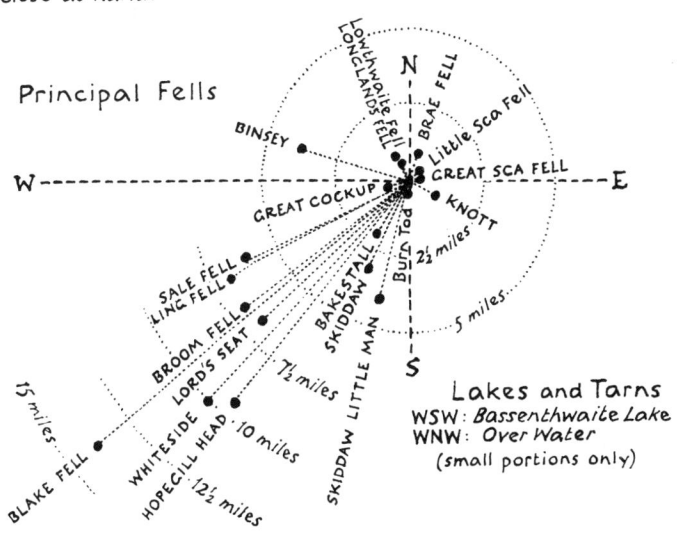

Principal Fells

(compass diagram showing: Lowthwaite Fell, Longlands Fell, Brae Fell, Little Sca Fell, Great Sca Fell, Knott, Burn Tod, Binsey, Great Cockup, Bakestall, Skiddaw, Skiddaw Little Man, Sale Fell, Ling Fell, Broom Fell, Lord's Seat, Whiteside, Hopegill Head, Blake Fell; distance rings at 2½ miles, 5 miles, 7½ miles, 10 miles, 12½ miles, 15 miles)

Lakes and Tarns
WSW: Bassenthwaite Lake
WNW: Over Water
(small portions only)

RIDGE ROUTES

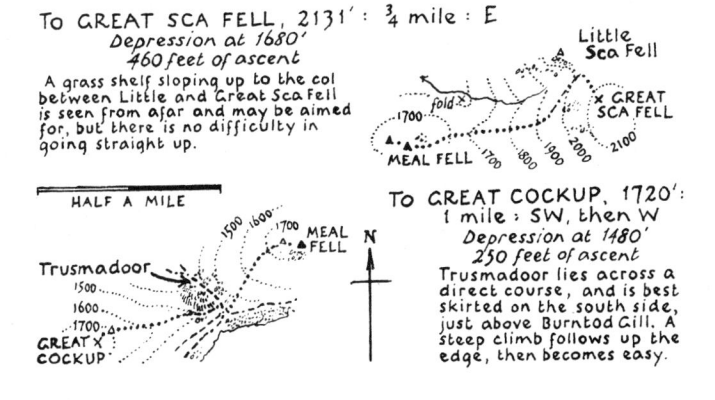

TO GREAT SCA FELL, 2131': ¾ mile: E
Depression at 1680'
460 feet of ascent

A grass shelf sloping up to the col between Little and Great Sca Fell is seen from afar and may be aimed for, but there is no difficulty in going straight up.

TO GREAT COCKUP, 1720': 1 mile: SW, then W
Depression at 1480'
250 feet of ascent

Trusmadoor lies across a direct course, and is best skirted on the south side, just above Burntod Gill. A steep climb follows up the edge, then becomes easy.

Mungrisdale Common 2068'

Mungrisdale is pronounced
Mun-grize-dl, with the
emphasis on *grize*

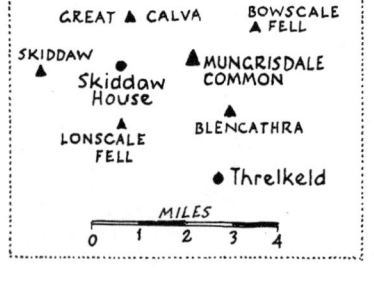

from Skiddaw

GREAT ▲ CALVA   BOWSCALE ▲ FELL
SKIDDAW ▲   ▲ MUNGRISDALE COMMON
   Skiddaw House
LONSCALE ▲   BLENCATHRA
FELL
         ● Threlkeld

MILES
0 1 2 3 4

To add to its other failings, Mungrisdale Common does not lend itself to illustration. Most fells have at least one good aspect, but the Common, from whatever side it is seen, has no more pretension to elegance than a pudding that has been sat on.

In the drawing above, the skyline is formed by Bowscale Fell and Blencathra. Below, appearing as a flat-topped dome, is the Common, rising beyond Skiddaw Forest.

Mungrisdale Common 2

NATURAL FEATURES

Mungrisdale Common's natural attractions are of a type that appeals only to sheep: it is more an upland prairie than a hill. There is little on these extensive grass slopes to provide even a passing interest for an ordinary walker, and nothing at all to encourage a visit. Sinen Gill, however, has long been known to geologists, the shy Skiddaw granite here, in the heart of slate country, revealing itself as a surface rock.

The Common, which is actually across the watershed from Mungrisdale and therefore rather oddly named, is bounded on three sides by the Caldew and its tributaries, and rises to Blencathra gently in the south, with Roughten Gill providing a useful line of demarcation. In point of fact the Common is properly the further northern slope of Blencathra, a dreary appendage to a fine mountain.

The Eden-Derwent catchment boundary traverses the height of land from the Stake, but is not well defined.

Waterfall, Sinen Gill

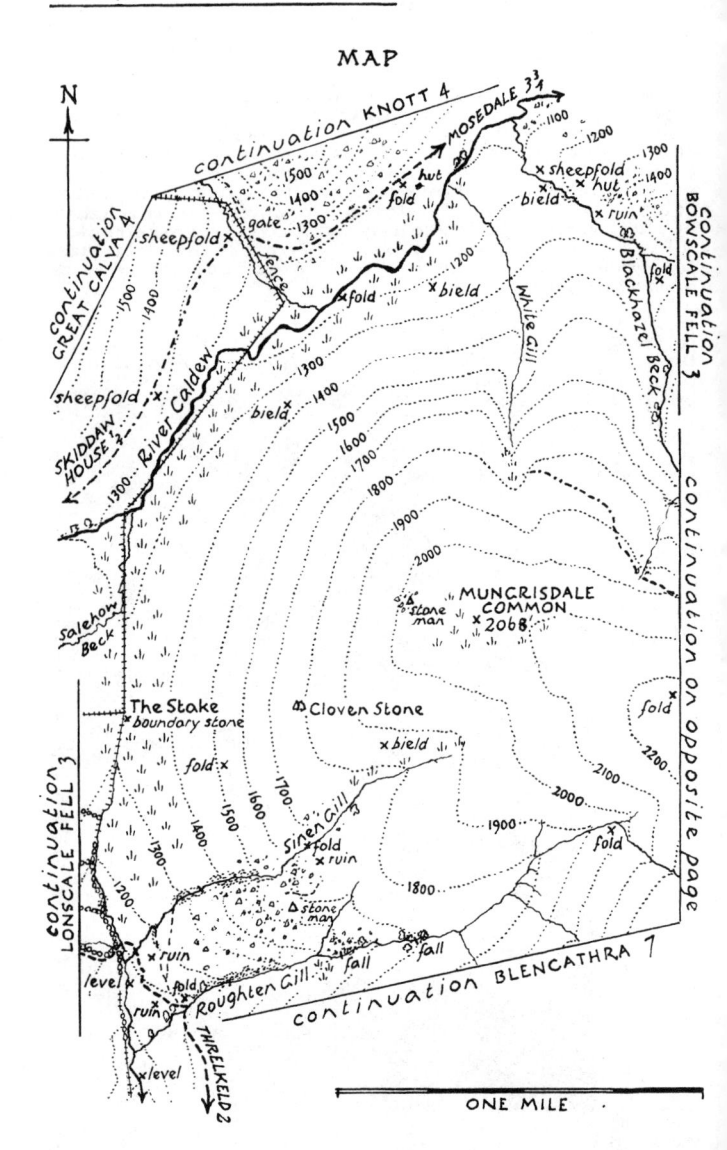

Mungrisdale Common 3

MAP

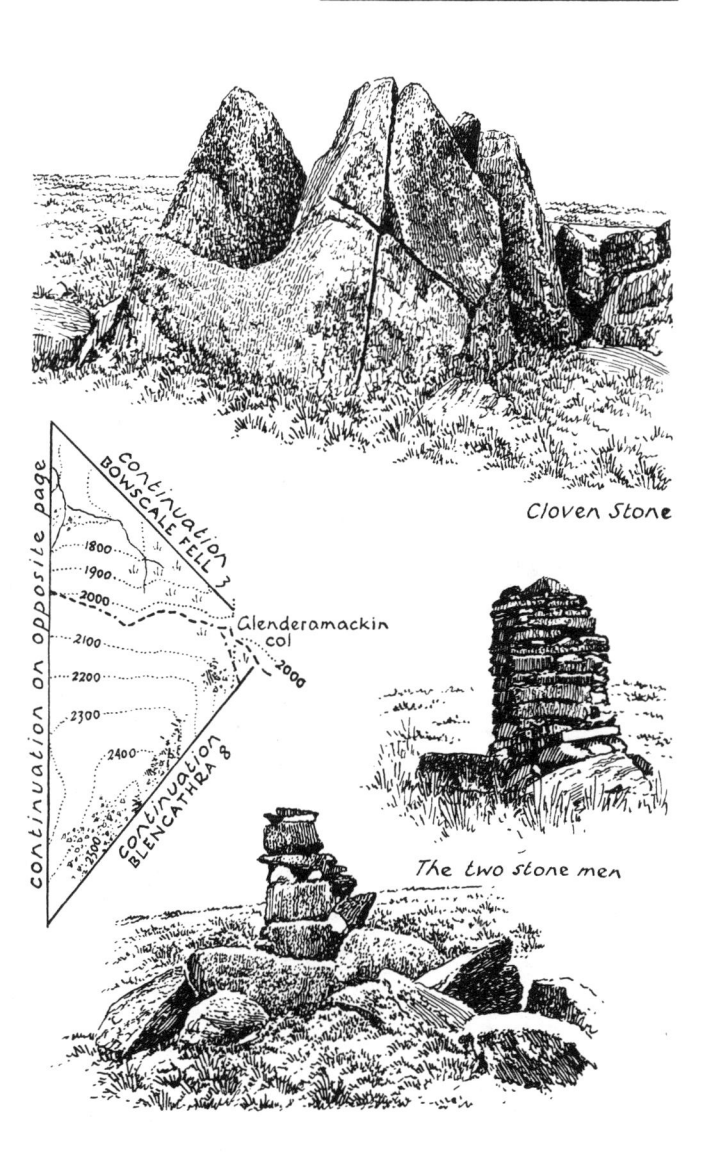

Mungrisdale Common 4

Cloven Stone

The two stone men

Mungrisdale Common 5

ASCENTS

There is little point in providing diagrams of ascent that will never be used. Only shepherds are likely to wander across the top of the Common, and they know the way to it well enough already. It is a place best left to them and the sheep. Precious holiday hours should not be wasted here.

The ascent (for people who won't be told) is accomplished with ease either from the Glenderamackin col (a dull walk) or from the Glenderaterra valley (which, combined with an inspection of Sinen Gill and having a good view in the rear, has rather more purpose to it). Purists who prefer to follow watersheds must start from The Stake, passing Cloven Stone. But, if the top is to be visited at all, it can most conveniently be done, and with least sacrifice of time, as an unorthodox route of descent from Blencathra, sweeping in a wide arc round to the Glenderaterra for Threlkeld: all easy going.

Granite slabs in the bed of the Caldew   *The Stake*

THE SUMMIT

Any one of a thousand tufts of tough bent and cotton-grass might lay claim to crowning the highest point of the plateau forming the summit, a point that cannot be determined exactly by observation and probably not by instruments either; nor is there a cairn to settle the matter.   A thousand tufts, yet not one can be comfortably reclined upon, this being a summit that holds indefinitely all the water that falls upon it.

Strictly this is not a top that could be accepted by standards of mountaineering as a separate summit: it forfeits this proud qualification because on one side (that linking with Blencathra) the loss of altitude to the connecting depression (peat-hags and ponds here) is barely perceptible — perhaps 15 feet at most.

Descents are simple in all directions, but it is as well to note that the Caldew, along the northern base, cannot be forded.

Mungrisdale Common 6

THE VIEW

The view is redeemed from mediocrity only by a striking grouping southwest, above the valley of the Glenderaterra. In other directions, apart from a distant glimpse of the Solway, there is little of interest.

Principal Fells

(Compass diagram showing fells: GREAT CALVA, KNOTT, HIGH PIKE, CARROCK FELL, BAKESTALL, BOWSCALE FELL, SKIDDAW, BANNERDALE CRAGS, SKIDDAW LITTLE MAN, BLENCATHRA, LONSCALE FELL, ROBINSON, PILLAR, HINDSCARTH, DALE HEAD, GREAT GABLE, LINGMELL, SCAFELL PIKE, ESK PIKE, BOWFELL, CRINKLE CRAGS. Distance rings at 5 miles, 10 miles, 15 miles.)

Lakes and Tarns

SW: Derwentwater (not quite in view from the highest point, but quickly brought into sight by walking 100 yards across the top)

(Panorama looking south-west showing: CRINKLE CRAGS, BOWFELL, ESK PIKE, ESK HAUSE, SCAFELL PIKE, LINGMELL, GREAT GABLE, KIRK FELL, DALE HEAD, HINDSCARTH, PILLAR, ROBINSON; foreground: Blease Fell (BLENCATHRA), Borrowdale, WALLA CRAG, Derwentwater (below), MAIDEN MOOR, LONSCALE FELL)

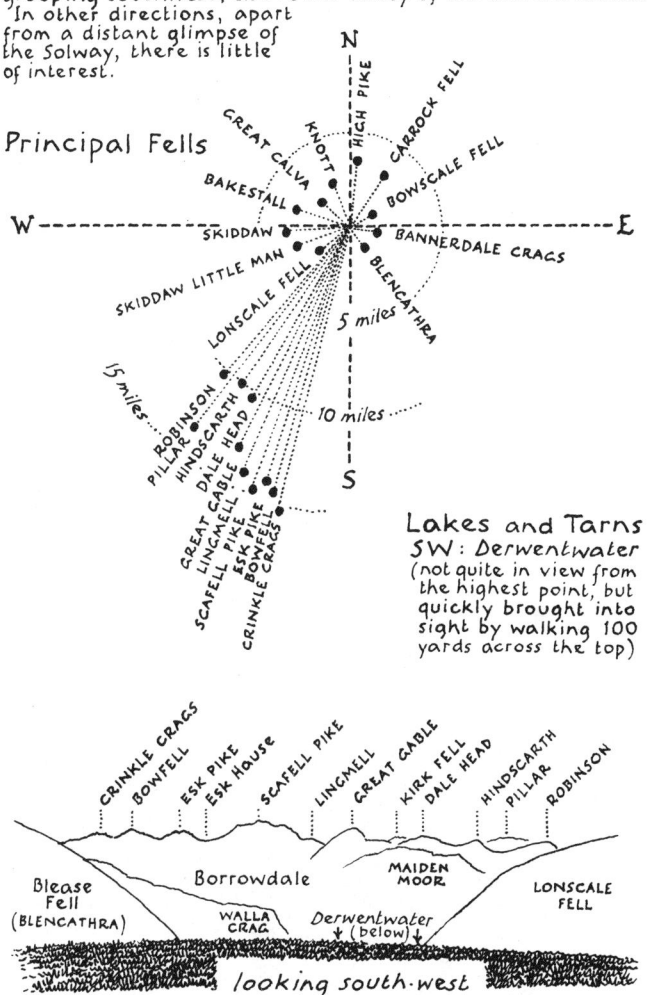

looking south-west

Skiddaw 3053'

from Burntod Gill

Skiddaw 2

NATURAL FEATURES

Make no mistake about Skiddaw.

Heed not the disparaging criticisms that have been written from time to time, often by learned men who ought to have known better, about this grand old mountain. It is an easy climb, yes; its slopes are smooth and grassy, yes; it has no frightful precipices, no rugged outcrops, agreed; it offers nothing of interest or entertainment to rock-gymnasts, agreed. If these are failings, they must be conceded. But are they not quite minor failings? Are they failings at all?

Skiddaw is the fourth highest peak in Lakeland and but little lower than the highest, Scafell Pike. It is the oldest mountain in the district, according to the evidence of its rocks, definitely not the most impressive in appearance but certainly one of the noblest. The summit is buttressed magnificently by a circle of lesser heights, all of them members of the proud Skiddaw family, the whole forming a splendid and complete example of the structure of mountains, especially well seen from all directions because of its isolation. Its lines are smooth, its curves graceful; but because the slopes are steep everywhere, the quick build-up of the *massif* from valley levels to central summit is appreciated at a glance — and it should be an appreciative glance, for such massive strength and such beauty of outline rarely go together....... Here, on Skiddaw, they do.

- Orthwaite

Bassenthwaite
-
  - Dash
  - ▲ BAKESTALL

High Side
  SKIDDAW
  ▲
ULLOCK PIKE ▲   • Skiddaw
LONG SIDE ▲   House
  CARL SIDE ▲   ▲ SKIDDAW LITTLE MAN
Little • Crosthwaite   ▲ LONSCALE
     ▲ DODD   FELL
        • Millbeck
          • Applethwaite
       LATRIGG ▲ Threlkeld

MILES
0   1   2   3
              • Keswick

continued

Skiddaw 3

NATURAL FEATURES
continued

Geographically, too, the mountain is of great importance, its main ridge forming the watershed between the Derwent and the Eden. This feature emphasises Skiddaw's supremacy over the rest of the northern fells, for, although situated in the south-west corner of the group, the waters from its eastern slopes cut through the middle of this outlying barrier to augment the drainage from the Pennines — and not even the neighbouring Blencathra, much more handily placed to the east, has been able to accomplish this feat. Engineers have noted this enterprise on the part of Skiddaw and are planning to impound its eastern flow in a reservoir at Caldew Head.

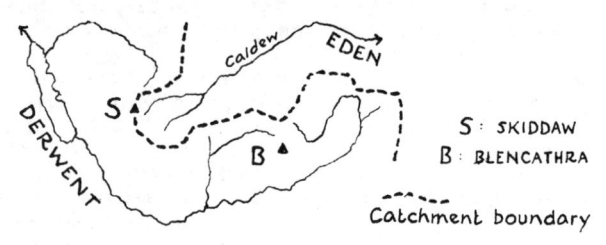

S: SKIDDAW
B: BLENCATHRA

--- Catchment boundary

Skiddaw has special interests for geologists. It is apparent, even to unobservant walkers, that the stones covering the summit and exposed in eroded gullies and valleys are very different in character from those seen in the central parts of the district: the latter are of volcanic origin, those on Skiddaw are marine deposits and consist in the main of soft shale or slate which splits readily into thin wafers and soon decays and crumbles when exposed to the atmosphere; hence it has no commercial value.

Skiddaw was formed long before the volcanos of central Lakeland became active; later it overlooked a vast glacier system, a world of ice. Some volcanic boulders are found along the lower southern slopes of the Skiddaw group: these rocks have been identified with those of the cliffs enclosing St. John's-in-the-Vale, having been carried along and deposited here when the glaciers retreated and scoured the flanks of Skiddaw on their passage to the frozen sea.

continued

Skiddaw 4

NATURAL FEATURES
continued

Skiddaw displays a quite different appearance to each of the four points of the compass. The southern aspect is a very familiar sight to visitors, being in unrestricted view from Derwentwater, the Borrowdale fells and most of the higher summits of Lakeland. There is a classical quality about this view from the south. Skiddaw and its outliers rise magnificently across the wide Vale of Keswick in a beautifully-symmetrical arrangement, as if posed for a family photograph. The old man himself is the central figure at the back of the group, with his five older children in a line before him (the favourite son, Little Man, being placed nearest) and the two younger children at the front. (Finicky readers who dispute this analogy because no mother to the brood is included in the picture (this is admitted, all the characters being masculine except sweet little Latrigg) are proferred the explanation that Skiddaw is a widower, the old lady having perished in the Ice Age — she couldn't stand the cold).

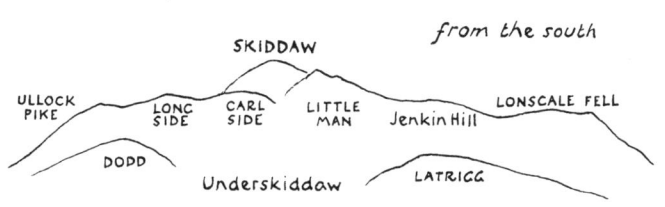

from the south

SKIDDAW

ULLOCK PIKE — LONG SIDE — CARL SIDE — LITTLE MAN — Jenkin Hill — LONSCALE FELL

DODD

Underskiddaw — LATRIGG

The western aspect is best known to Bassenthwaite folk, who enjoy a secret delight few others have discovered — the glorious sunset colourings of the mountain, winter and summer alike: a beauty that brings people to their doors in rapt admiration. There is little beauty of outline, though, Skiddaw here appearing at its most massive, a great arc high in the sky, and the only shapeliness in the scene from the west is provided by the graceful cone of Ullock Pike and the curving ridge beyond. Two deep valleys, long shadowy recesses in the mountain, are conspicuous features.

from the west

SKIDDAW
Broad End — CARL SIDE — LITTLE MAN
BAKESTALL
Cockup — LONG SIDE
ULLOCK PIKE
DODD — LATRIGG

Bassenthwaite

continued

Skiddaw 5

NATURAL FEATURES

continued

Skiddaw, northwards, faces the unfrequented Uldale Fells, and not many regular visitors to Lakeland would recognise it in an uncaptioned photograph taken from this side. The northern aspect is truly impressive nonetheless; not quite so overpowering as when viewed from Bassenthwaite to the west but having now a greater majesty and dignity. The summit-ridge is seen end-on and appears as a neat pyramid overtopping the sprawling mass of Broad End, below which is the remarkable combe of Dead Crags. All waters coming down this side of Skiddaw, as those on the south and west, in due course reach the Derwent.

from the north

LONSCALE FELL — LITTLE MAN — SKIDDAW — LONG SIDE — ULLOCK PIKE
Skiddaw Forest — BAKESTALL — Broad End — Dead Crags — Cockup

The east slopes of the mountain, collectively known as Skiddaw Forest, dominate the vast upland basin of Caldew Head, a scene more suggestive of a Scottish glen than of Lakeland, a place incredibly wild and desolate and bare, its loneliness accentuated by the solitary dwellings of Skiddaw House, yet strongly appealing and, in certain lights, often strangely beautiful. In this great hollow the waters unite to form the River Caldew, an important feeder of the Eden. Skiddaw is least impressive from the east because there is much less fall on this side. The scene is in view, although not intimately, from Blencathra.

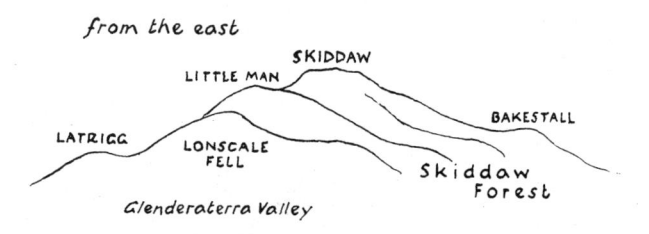

from the east

LATRIGG — LITTLE MAN — SKIDDAW — BAKESTALL
LONSCALE FELL — Skiddaw Forest
Glenderaterra Valley

continued

Skiddaw 6

NATURAL FEATURES

continued

This, then, is Skiddaw, a giant in stature. But an affable and friendly giant.

And a benevolent one. Keswick people have an inborn affection for Skiddaw, and it is well earned. The mountain makes a great contribution to the scenic beauty of this most attractively-situated town, shelters it from northerly gales, supplies it with pure water, feeds its sheep, and provides a recreation ground for its visitors. Throughout the centuries Skiddaw's beacon has warned of the town's troubles and alarms — "the red glare on Skiddaw roused the burghers of Carlisle" — and today shares in its rejoicings.

Skiddaw's critics have passed on, or will soon pass on. Their span of life is short. Skiddaw has stood there in supreme majesty, the sole witness to the creation of Lakeland, for millions of years and will be there to the end of time, continuing to give service and pleasure to insignificant and unimportant mortals.

Let us at least be grateful.

At the back o' beyond.....   Skiddaw House

Skiddaw 7

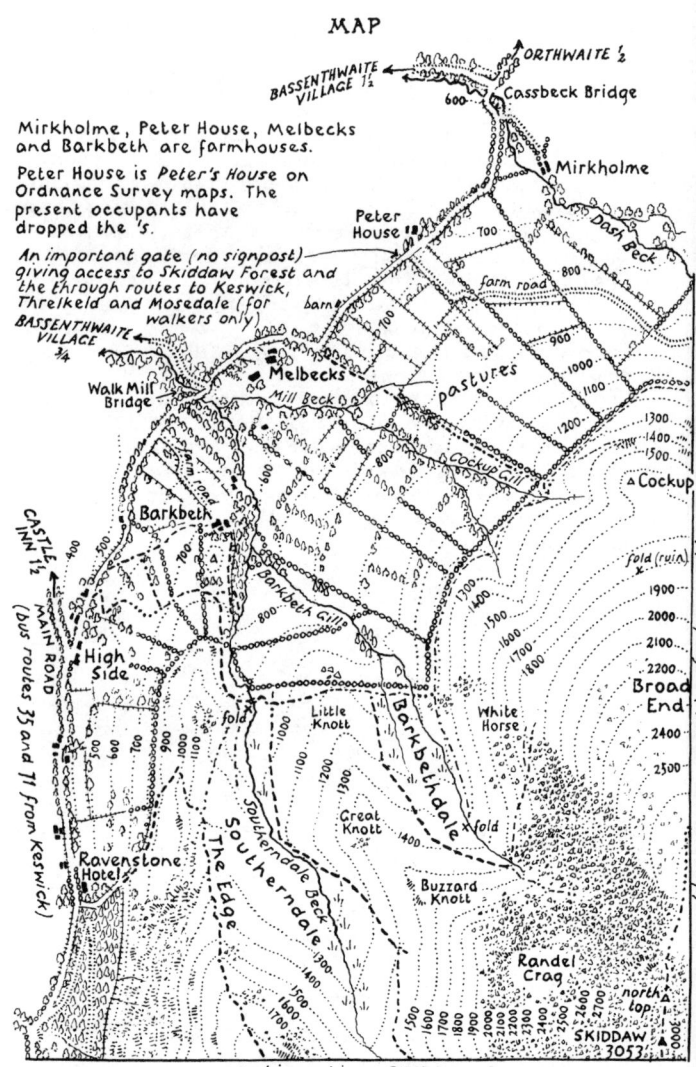

MAP

Skiddaw 8

MAP

For ease of reference, the map of Skiddaw on this and the accompanying pages includes the whole *massif*, although the outlying summits (shown in CAPITALS) have separate chapters in the book.

The supply road to Skiddaw House is narrow and unenclosed, with a loose and gravelly surface. It is not good enough for cars (cheers) but is a very convenient means of access to the great wilderness of Skiddaw Forest for travellers on foot.

Skiddaw Forest is the general name of the vast heathery amphitheatre at the base of the eastern slopes of Skiddaw. It is a forest entirely without trees (except for a planted windbreak at Skiddaw House).

Skiddaw House is not a single residence, but a row of cottages in partial occupation by shepherds. The present shepherd in residence here (five days a week, with only his dogs for company) is Pearson Dalton of Fell Side.

The shelter indicated on this page is a substantial open-fronted, well-roofed structure, furnished with seats. (Weary novices should note that it's no use waiting here for a bus). The presence of butts in the vicinity suggests that it was provided originally for shooting parties.

ONE MILE

continuation SKIDDAW 10
(two-thirds inch overlap)

Skiddaw 9

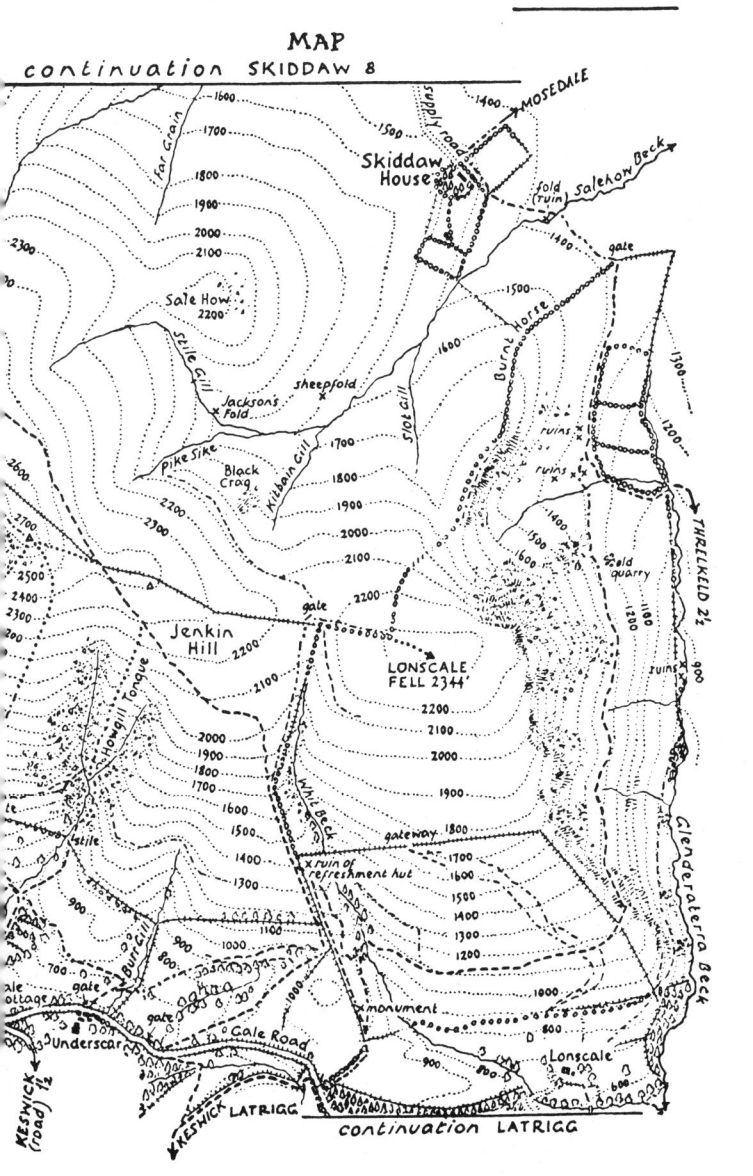

Skiddaw 10

MAP

continuation SKIDDAW 8

- Far Grain
- MOSEDALE
- Skiddaw House
- supply road
- fold (ruin)
- Salehow Beck
- gate
- Sale How 2200
- Stile Gill
- sheepfold
- Jackson's Fold
- Burnt Horse
- Slot Gill
- Pike Sike
- Kitbain Gill
- Black Crag
- ruins
- ruins
- THRELKELD 2½
- old quarry
- ruins
- gate
- Jenkin Hill 2200
- LONSCALE FELL 2344'
- Howgill Tongue
- Whit Beck
- stile
- gateway
- × ruin of refreshment hut
- Glenderaterra Beck
- gate
- gate
- Underscar
- Gale Road
- monument
- Lonscale
- KESWICK (road) 1½
- KESWICK LATRIGG
- *continuation LATRIGG*

Skiddaw 11

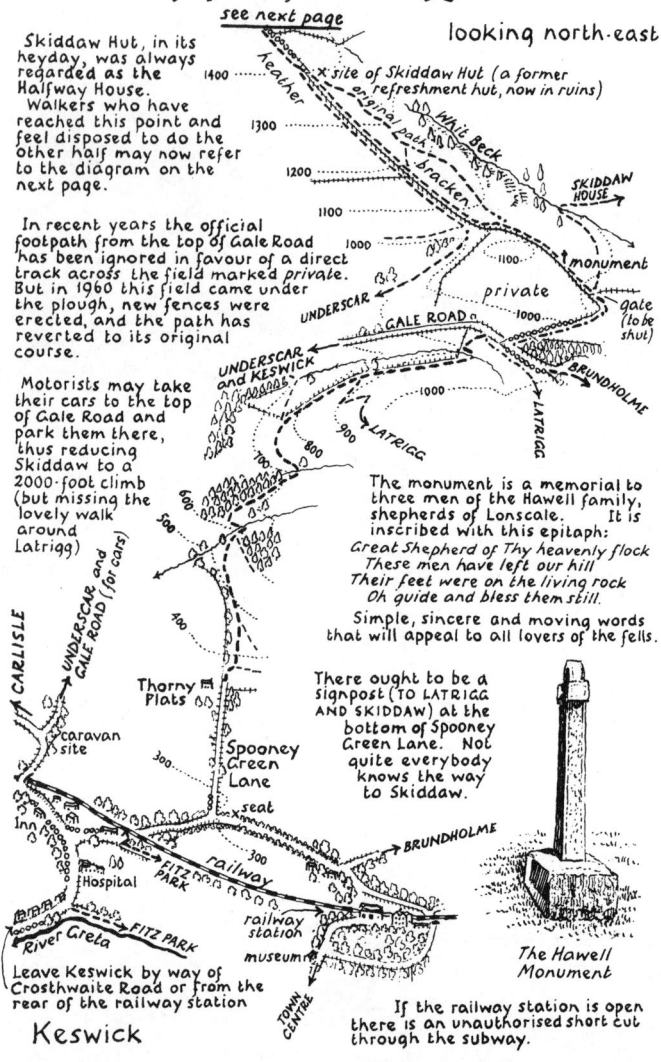

ASCENT FROM KESWICK
2850 feet of ascent : 5½ miles

see next page

looking north-east

Skiddaw Hut, in its heyday, was always regarded as the Halfway House.
Walkers who have reached this point and feel disposed to do the other half may now refer to the diagram on the next page.

In recent years the official footpath from the top of Gale Road has been ignored in favour of a direct track across the field marked *private*. But in 1960 this field came under the plough, new fences were erected, and the path has reverted to its original course.

Motorists may take their cars to the top of Gale Road and park them there, thus reducing Skiddaw to a 2000-foot climb (but missing the lovely walk around Latrigg)

× site of Skiddaw Hut (a former refreshment hut, now in ruins)

SKIDDAW HOUSE

monument

private

gate (to be shut)

UNDERSCAR GALE ROAD

UNDERSCAR and KESWICK

BRUNDHOLME

LATRIGG

The monument is a memorial to three men of the Hawell family, shepherds of Lonscale. It is inscribed with this epitaph:

*Great Shepherd of Thy heavenly flock
These men have left our hill
Their feet were on the living rock
Oh guide and bless them still.*

Simple, sincere and moving words that will appeal to all lovers of the fells.

CARLISLE

UNDERSCAR and GALE ROAD (for cars)

caravan site

Thorny Plats

Spooney Green Lane

Inn

seat

Hospital

FITZ PARK

railway

BRUNDHOLME

River Greta   FITZ PARK

railway station

museum

TOWN CENTRE

Leave Keswick by way of Crosthwaite Road or from the rear of the railway station

Keswick

There ought to be a signpost (TO LATRIGG AND SKIDDAW) at the bottom of Spooney Green Lane. Not quite everybody knows the way to Skiddaw.

The Hawell Monument

If the railway station is open there is an unauthorised short cut through the subway.

Skiddaw 12

ASCENT FROM KESWICK

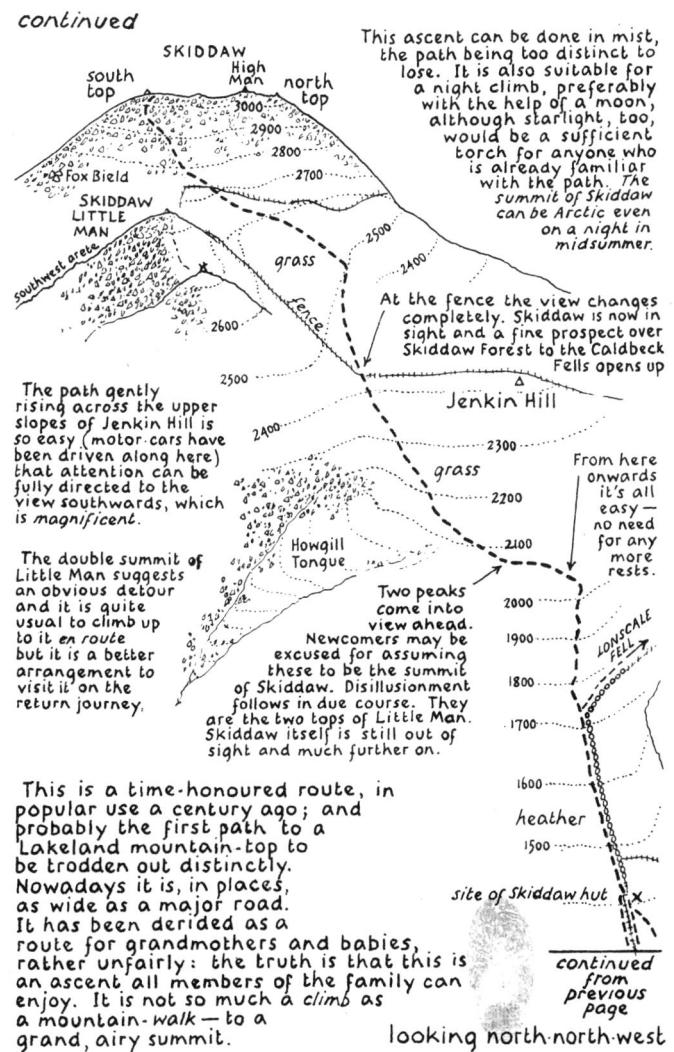

continued

This ascent can be done in mist, the path being too distinct to lose. It is also suitable for a night climb, preferably with the help of a moon, although starlight, too, would be a sufficient torch for anyone who is already familiar with the path. The summit of Skiddaw can be Arctic even on a night in midsummer.

At the fence the view changes completely. Skiddaw is now in sight and a fine prospect over Skiddaw Forest to the Caldbeck Fells opens up

The path gently rising across the upper slopes of Jenkin Hill is so easy (motor-cars have been driven along here) that attention can be fully directed to the view southwards, which is *magnificent*.

From here onwards it's all easy — no need for any more rests.

The double summit of Little Man suggests an obvious detour and it is quite usual to climb up to it *en route* but it is a better arrangement to visit it on the return journey.

Two peaks come into view ahead. Newcomers may be excused for assuming these to be the summit of Skiddaw. Disillusionment follows in due course. They are the two tops of Little Man. Skiddaw itself is still out of sight and much further on.

This is a time-honoured route, in popular use a century ago; and probably the first path to a Lakeland mountain-top to be trodden out distinctly. Nowadays it is, in places, as wide as a major road. It has been derided as a route for grandmothers and babies, rather unfairly: the truth is that this is an ascent all members of the family can enjoy. It is not so much *a climb* as *a mountain-walk* — to a grand, airy summit.

site of Skiddaw hut

continued from previous page

looking north-north-west

Skiddaw 13

ASCENT FROM MILLBECK
2750 feet of ascent : 2¾ miles

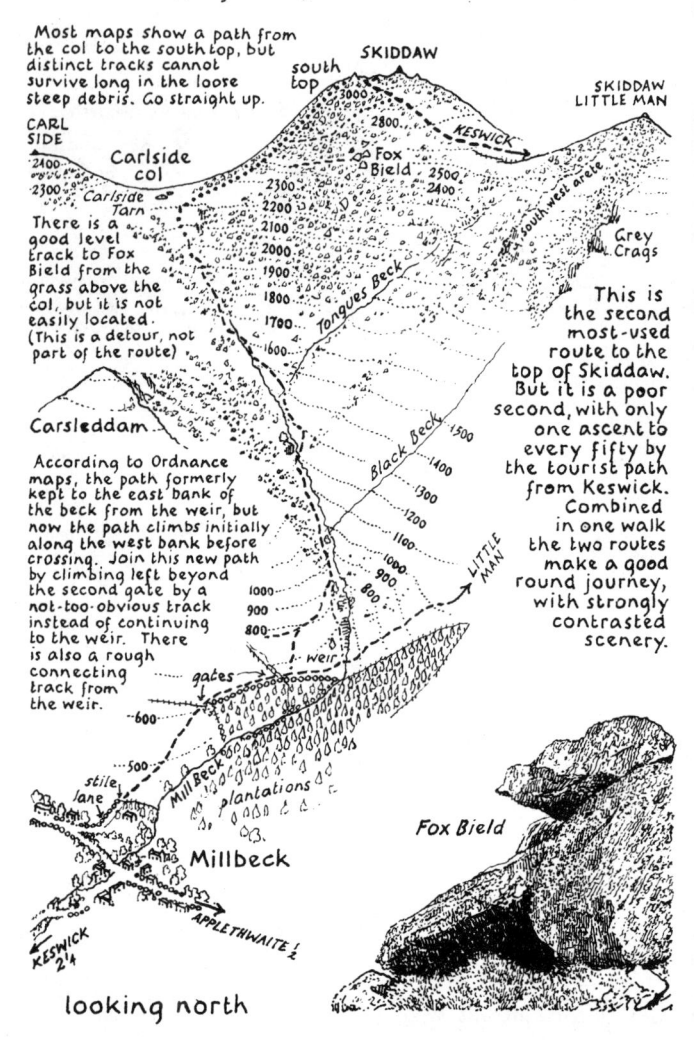

looking north

Most maps show a path from the col to the south top, but distinct tracks cannot survive long in the loose steep debris. Go straight up.

SKIDDAW
south top
SKIDDAW LITTLE MAN
KESWICK
CARL SIDE
Carlside col
Carlside Tarn
Fox Bield
Grey Crags
south-west arête
Tongues Beck
Black Beck
LITTLE MAN
weir
gates
Millbeck
plantations
stile, lane
Millbeck
KESWICK 2¼
APPLETHWAITE 1
Carsleddam

There is a good level track to Fox Bield from the grass above the col, but it is not easily located. (This is a detour, not part of the route)

According to Ordnance maps, the path formerly kept to the east bank of the beck from the weir, but now the path climbs initially along the west bank before crossing. Join this new path by climbing left beyond the second gate by a not-too-obvious track instead of continuing to the weir. There is also a rough connecting track from the weir.

This is the second most-used route to the top of Skiddaw. But it is a poor second, with only one ascent to every fifty by the tourist path from Keswick. Combined in one walk the two routes make a good round journey, with strongly contrasted scenery.

Fox Bield

Skiddaw 14

ASCENT FROM APPLETHWAITE
2700 feet of ascent : 3 miles

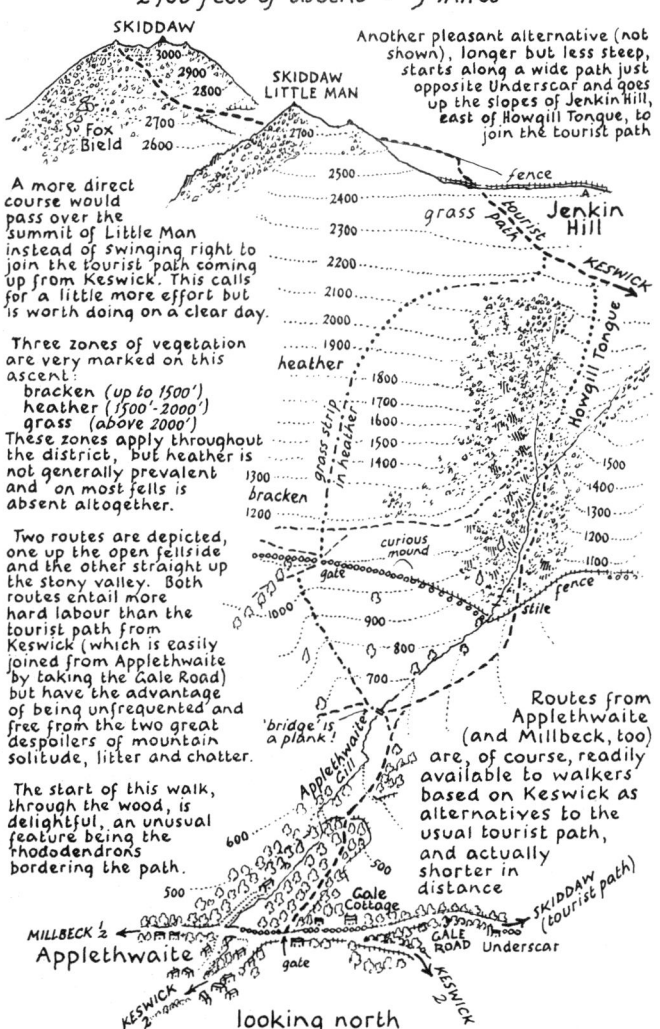

Another pleasant alternative (not shown), longer but less steep, starts along a wide path just opposite Underscar and goes up the slopes of Jenkin Hill, east of Howgill Tongue, to join the tourist path

A more direct course would pass over the summit of Little Man instead of swinging right to join the tourist path coming up from Keswick. This calls for a little more effort but is worth doing on a clear day.

Three zones of vegetation are very marked on this ascent:
  bracken (up to 1500')
  heather (1500'-2000')
  grass (above 2000')
These zones apply throughout the district, but heather is not generally prevalent and on most fells is absent altogether.

Two routes are depicted, one up the open fellside and the other straight up the stony valley. Both routes entail more hard labour than the tourist path from Keswick (which is easily joined from Applethwaite by taking the Gale Road) but have the advantage of being unfrequented and free from the two great despoilers of mountain solitude, litter and chatter.

The start of this walk, through the wood, is delightful, an unusual feature being the rhododendrons bordering the path.

Routes from Applethwaite (and Millbeck, too) are, of course, readily available to walkers based on Keswick as alternatives to the usual tourist path, and actually shorter in distance

looking north

Skiddaw 15

ASCENTS FROM BASSENTHWAITE VILLAGE AND HIGH SIDE

2800 feet of ascent : 4 - 4½ miles (from Bassenthwaite Village)

2700 feet 3¾ - 3¾ miles (from High Side)

SKIDDAW — north top, south top

North col — Gibraltar Crag — Carlside col

plateau — Randel Crag — ruined fold

Buzzard Knott

Barkbethdale — north-west — sledgate — Southerndale — Southerndale beck — ULLOCK PIKE

Great Knott — Little Knott — The Edge

boulders (a little Stonehenge) — fold

RAVENSTONE → intake wall

Barkbeth — farm road — boulder

gorse — High Side

← ORTHWAITE — ruin

Chapel Beck — Burthwaite

MAIN ROAD — KESWICK 6
BASSENTHWAITE VILLAGE ½ — CASTLE INN 1½

Bassenthwaite Village

looking south-east

Lakeland is far removed from world events and it is unusual to find a 'foreign' name in use here. Gibraltar Crag must owe its title to an enthusiastic local patriot.

Gibraltar Crag and Randel Crag are merely steep loose roughnesses. Neither would earn the name of crag in the Scafell area.

The sledgates are wide grassy paths originally made for the passage of sledges (here probably bringing down stones for the walls). Nowadays their only use is as "drove roads" when sheep are being gathered.

More details of the routes are given on the opposite page

Skiddaw 16

ASCENTS FROM BASSENTHWAITE VILLAGE AND HIGH SIDE
continued

THE NORTH-WEST RIDGE: Ask a Barkbeth sheep what the north-west ridge of Skiddaw is like and it will reply without hesitation "C'est magnifique" (if it is French, which is unlikely) — which just shows how tastes differ, for most walkers, less easily satisfied, will consider it disappointing. Its one attribute is its peace and quietness. There is no path along it, no line of cairns, no litter, nothing to show that others may have passed this way. It is a low, gentle hump, entirely grassy (hence the enthusiastic rejoinder quoted above), rising between Southerndale and Barkbethdale and not too well-defined until the ground steepens into Randel Crag; a few easy rocks here may be scrambled up or circumvented to give access to a grassy shelf, where the ridge proper ends. A tiny tarn here is shaped like a W. Rising ahead is the scree-slope falling from Skiddaw's top: this is vaster than it appears to be and much longer, but not unpleasant to ascend, the scree being a soft, yielding shale. The only interest here derives from an attempt to score a bull's-eye by 'hitting' the summit-cairn direct (it is out of sight until the last minute).

SOUTHERNDALE, too, is quiet and unfrequented although a clear-cut valley and useful for quick and easy progress, the final climb up to Carlside col giving less trouble than the approach to it suggests. A sledgate 'road' is a good help; when it ceases (close by an old and scattered cairn) a narrow trod continues to the sheepfold. At the col turn half-left up a scree-slope to the south top. Southerndale is dominated more by Long Side and Ullock Pike than by Skiddaw.

Neither of these routes, nor that via Barkbethdale, is to be compared as a way up Skiddaw from the north-west, in interest, views or grandeur, with the fine high-level traverse of Ullock Pike and Long Side; they are direct routes, however, and as such have a certain appeal.

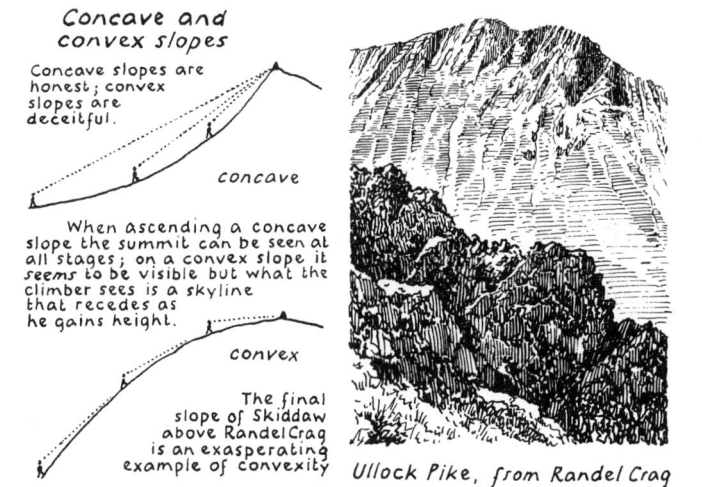

Concave and convex slopes

Concave slopes are honest; convex slopes are deceitful.

concave

When ascending a concave slope the summit can be seen at all stages; on a convex slope it seems to be visible but what the climber sees is a skyline that recedes as he gains height.

convex

The final slope of Skiddaw above Randel Crag is an exasperating example of convexity

Ullock Pike, from Randel Crag

Skiddaw 17

ASCENTS FROM BASSENTHWAITE VILLAGE AND HIGH SIDE

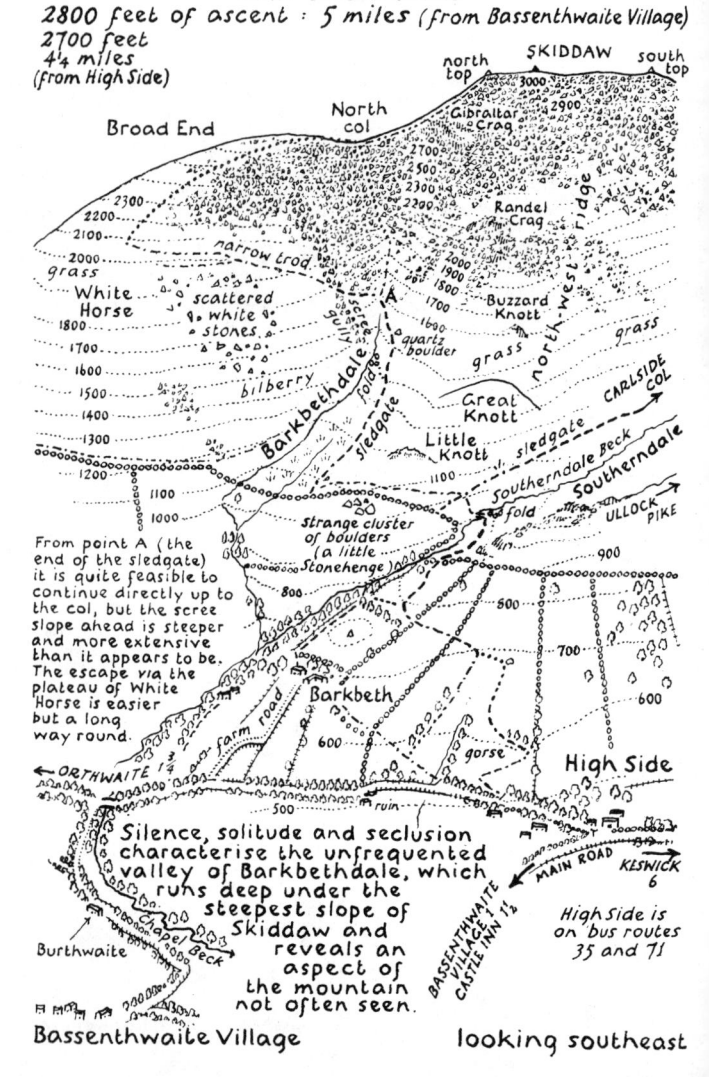

2800 feet of ascent : 5 miles (from Bassenthwaite Village)
2700 feet
4¼ miles
(from High Side)

looking southeast

From point A (the end of the sledgate) it is quite feasible to continue directly up to the col, but the scree slope ahead is steeper and more extensive than it appears to be. The escape via the plateau of White Horse is easier but a long way round.

Silence, solitude and seclusion characterise the unfrequented valley of Barkbethdale, which runs deep under the steepest slope of Skiddaw and reveals an aspect of the mountain not often seen.

High Side is on bus routes 35 and 71

Skiddaw 18

Southerndale from the gate in the intake wall above Barkbeth. Carlside col, Long Side and Ullock Pike on skyline.

Barkbethdale from Little Knott on the north-west ridge. Looking to Skiddaw; Randel Crag below on right.

Skiddaw 19

ASCENT FROM MELBECKS
2500 feet of ascent : 3 miles

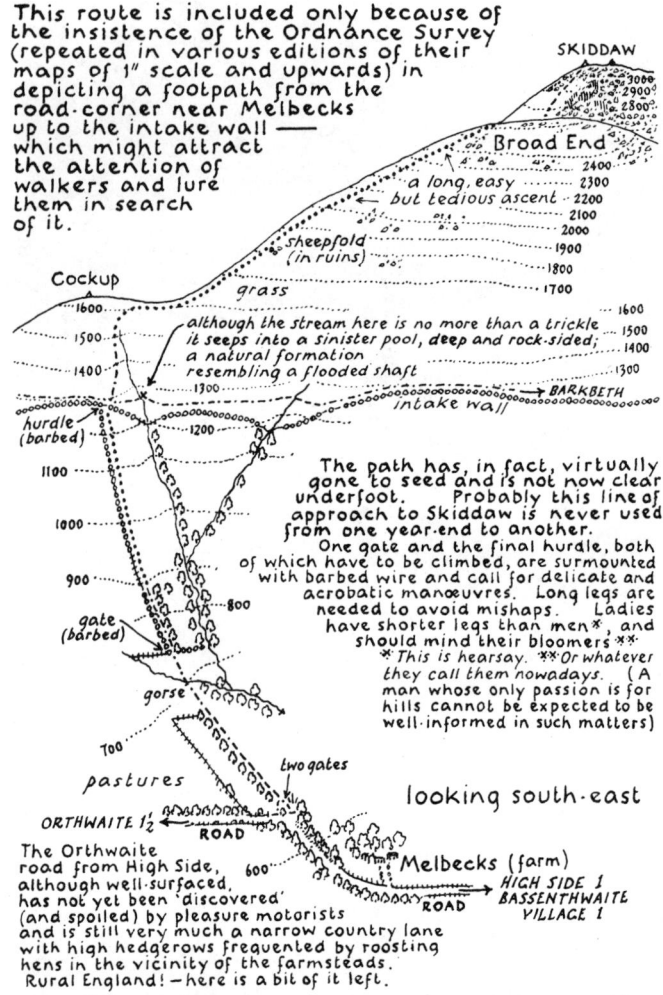

This route is included only because of the insistence of the Ordnance Survey (repeated in various editions of their maps of 1" scale and upwards) in depicting a footpath from the road-corner near Melbecks up to the intake wall — which might attract the attention of walkers and lure them in search of it.

SKIDDAW — 3000, 2900, 2800

Broad End

a long, easy — 2400, 2300
but tedious ascent — 2200, 2100, 2000

sheepfold (in ruins) — 1900, 1800, 1700

Cockup — 1600

grass

although the stream here is no more than a trickle it seeps into a sinister pool, deep and rock-sided; a natural formation resembling a flooded shaft — 1500, 1400, 1300

→ BARKBETH

intake wall

hurdle (barbed) — 1200

The path has, in fact, virtually gone to seed and is not now clear underfoot. Probably this line of approach to Skiddaw is never used from one year-end to another.

One gate and the final hurdle, both of which have to be climbed, are surmounted with barbed wire and call for delicate and acrobatic manœuvres. Long legs are needed to avoid mishaps. Ladies have shorter legs than men*, and should mind their bloomers**

* This is hearsay. ** Or whatever they call them nowadays. (A man whose only passion is for hills cannot be expected to be well-informed in such matters)

gate (barbed) — 900, 800

gorse — 700

pastures

two gates

looking south-east

ORTHWAITE 1½ ← ROAD

Melbecks (farm)

HIGH SIDE 1
BASSENTHWAITE VILLAGE 1

ROAD

The Orthwaite road from High Side, although well-surfaced, has not yet been 'discovered' (and spoiled) by pleasure motorists and is still very much a narrow country lane with high hedgerows frequented by roosting hens in the vicinity of the farmsteads. Rural England! — here is a bit of it left.

Of all ways up Skiddaw this is the least interesting.

Skiddaw 20

ASCENT FROM THE ROAD TO SKIDDAW HOUSE
1800 feet of ascent : 2 miles from Dash Falls
2750 feet : 6 miles from High Side or Bassenthwaite Village

looking south

SKIDDAW LITTLE MAN — SKIDDAW 2900, 2800, 2700 — North col — Broad End

tourist path from Keswick — 2600 — fence — 2600, 2500, 2400

If the purpose of the fence was originally to contain sheep, it is no longer functional, but it still serves as a sure guide to the top of the mountain. With its help this route, although pathless, is practicable in mist. The section between Bakestall and the North col is tedious, in any weather, but made tolerable by a soft carpet of heather, dry mosses and bilberry.

fence — 2300, 2200, 2100 — x ruined sheepfold — △ BAKESTALL 2189'

The great combe of Dead Crags and the magnificent waterfalls at the head of the pleasant little valley of Dash are a grand natural attraction, typically Lakeland in character and atmosphere, yet quite unlike any other scene in the district.

Long may this charming, lonely and impressive sanctuary remain unspoilt (that is to say, undiscovered by and inaccessible to picnicking sightseers on wheels). Long may the road to Skiddaw House remain rough, gated and unsignposted, and long may the farmer of Dash be given strength to play merry hell with inquisitive motorists who venture on it. The place should remain as a reward for the physical effort of reaching it on foot.

SKIDDAW HOUSE 2 — 1500, 1400, 1300 — gate — Dead Crags — 1900, 1800, 1700, 1600, 1500, 1400, 1300, 1200 — Dead Beck

Dash Falls — 1100 — gate — 1000

Dash (farm) — farm road — Dash Beck

Dash Falls are named Whitewater Dash on large-scale Ordnance maps

The 'road' to Skiddaw House turns off indistinctly (over grass) but soon becomes well defined.

They know Skiddaw not who have climbed it only from Keswick! The little-known Dash Falls and Dead Crags, blushing unseen, make an exciting start from the north.

High Side (6 miles from Keswick) is on 'bus routes 35 and 71

ORTHWAITE 1 — ROAD — gates — gate — HIGH SIDE 2 or BASSENTHWAITE VILLAGE 2 — Peter House (farm)

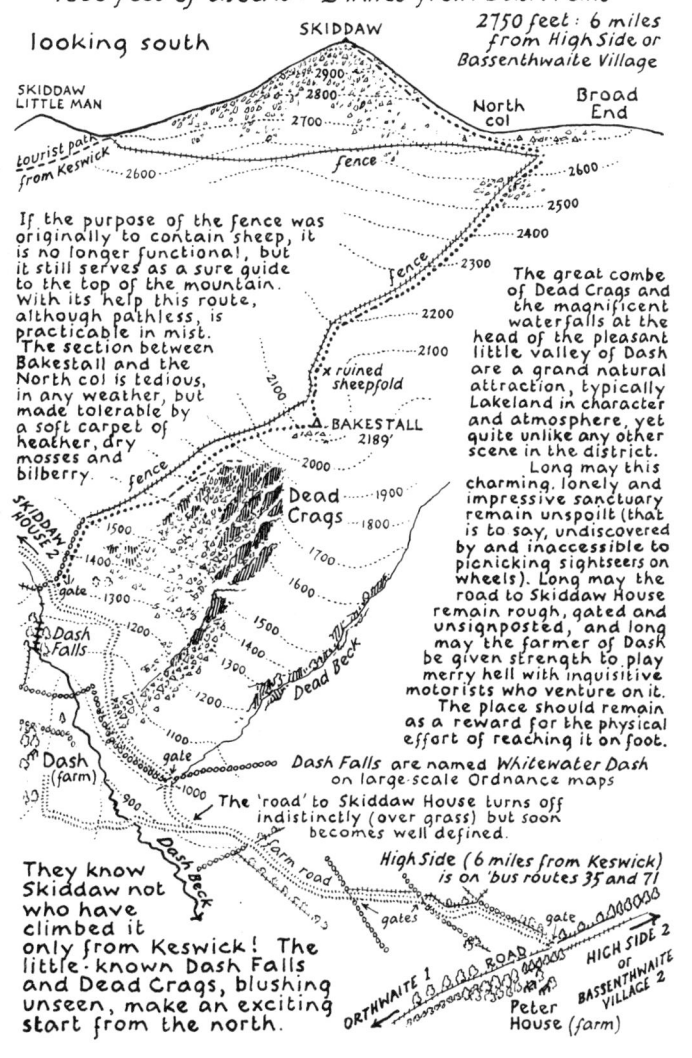

Skiddaw 21

ASCENT FROM SKIDDAW HOUSE
1600 feet of ascent: 2½ miles (via Sale How); 1700 feet, 3 miles (via Hare Crag)

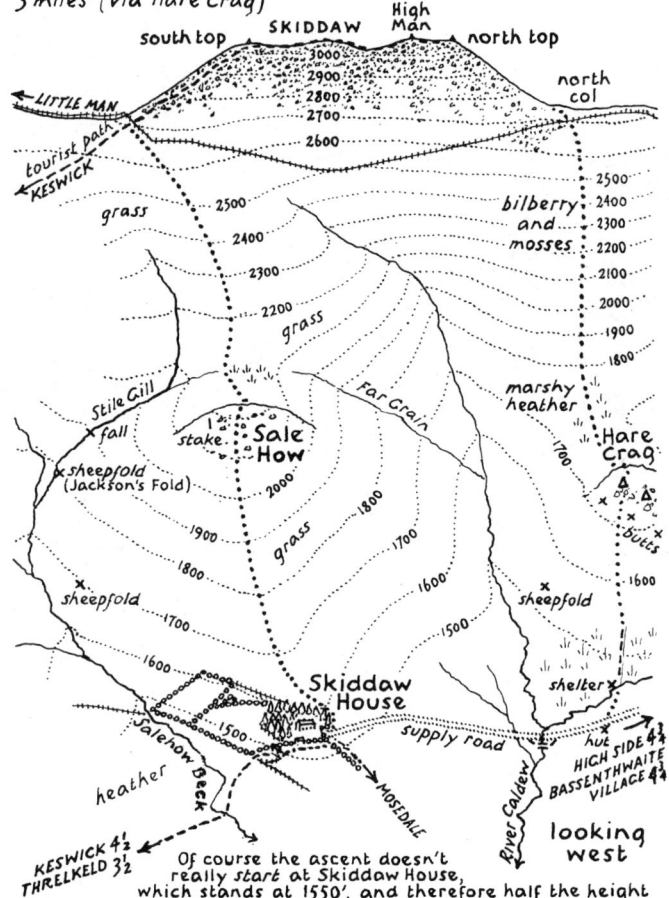

Of course the ascent doesn't really *start* at Skiddaw House, which stands at 1550', and therefore half the height of the mountain has been climbed by the time it is reached.

The eastern slopes of Skiddaw are gently inclined, and progress is smooth and simple. Two routes are given, alike in having an intermediate height; the more direct, by Sale How, is on dry grass; that by Hare Crag is rather more interesting but wet initially. The Hare Crag route follows the important Derwent-Eden watershed.

Skiddaw 22

THE SUMMIT

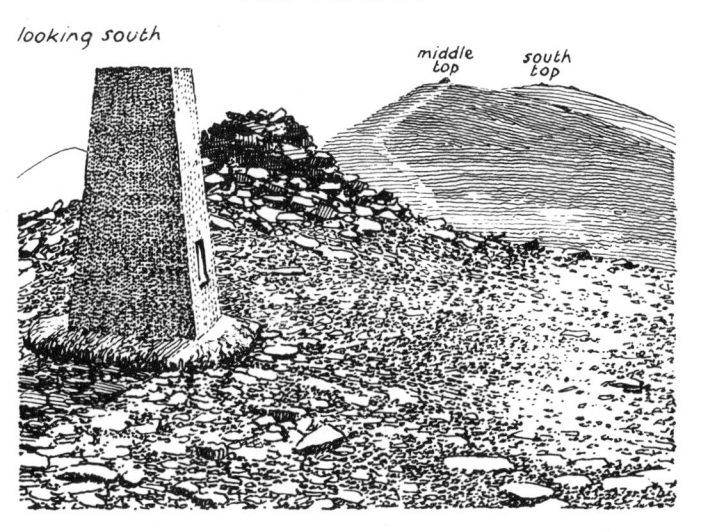

looking south

middle top
south top

Some walkers, but not many, will be disappointed by the ease with which the summit of Skiddaw can be gained and the lack of exciting terrain during the ascent, especially if they have used the tourist path from Keswick, but the top itself is rough enough and airy enough to suit all tastes. It takes the form of a stony, undulating ridge exceeding 3000' throughout its length of almost half a mile and provides a glorious promenade high in the sky where one can enjoy a rare feeling of freedom and escape from a world far below, and, for a time, forgotten.

There is a south top and a north top, a middle top and a main top, all in line and connected by a pavement of slaty stones. In mist it is not uncommon to assume the middle top to be the highest point, there being a descent immediately following (when approached from the south, as is usual) but a final halt should not be made until the Ordnance Survey's triangulation column (S 1543) is reached: this is the true, the indisputable, summit.

A feature of the ridge is a series of roughly-erected wind shelters of stones, crescent-shaped to make them snug (they fail lamentably in this object) — these are only partially effective against cruel gales and useless as a protection in rain. The summit is completely exposed to the north and its weather can be fierce.

Skiddaw is often described as 'merely a grassy hill'. But its summit is the summit of a mountain.

continued

Skiddaw 23

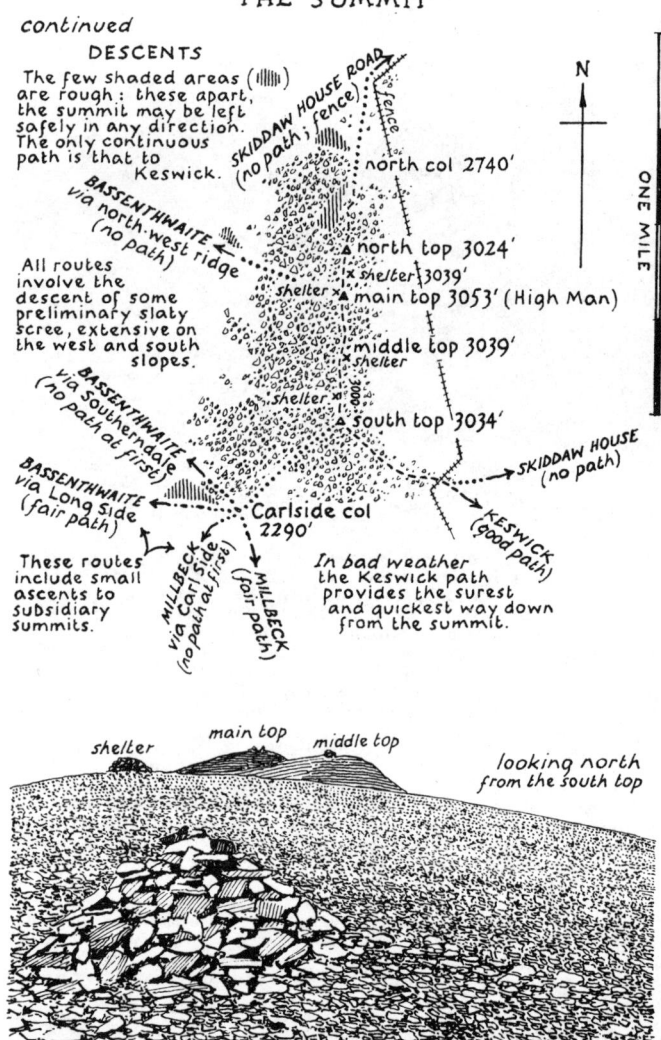

THE SUMMIT
continued
DESCENTS

The few shaded areas (▦) are rough: these apart, the summit may be left safely in any direction. The only continuous path is that to Keswick.

All routes involve the descent of some preliminary slaty scree, extensive on the west and south slopes.

These routes include small ascents to subsidiary summits.

In bad weather the Keswick path provides the surest and quickest way down from the summit.

N ↑

ONE MILE

SKIDDAW HOUSE ROAD (no path; fence)

north col 2740'
△ north top 3024'
× shelter 3039'
shelter × ▲ main top 3053' (High Man)
middle top 3039'
shelter
shelter
south top 3034'

BASSENTHWAITE via north-west ridge (no path)
BASSENTHWAITE via Southerndale (no path at first)
BASSENTHWAITE via Long Side (fair path)

Carlside col 2290'

MILLBECK via Carlside (no path at first)
MILLBECK (fair path)

→ SKIDDAW HOUSE (no path)
→ KESWICK (good path)

shelter — main top — middle top

looking north from the south top

Skiddaw 24

RIDGE ROUTES

To SKIDDAW LITTLE MAN, 2837': 1 mile : S, then SSE
Depression at 2680'
190 feet of ascent

A good detour on the way down to Keswick.
Use the Keswick path to the first fence, which follow to the right across a grassy furrowed depression to the stony cone now directly ahead.

To CARL SIDE, 2420': 1 mile : S, then SW
Depression at 2290'
160 feet of ascent

One unavoidably rough section
From the south top go bravely down the steepening slope of loose scree south-west, wasting no time looking for a path. Aim for the depression soon in view below, escaping to grass at the foot of the scree. The flat plateau of Carl Side rises directly beyond the two small tarns. This route is often used, every passage causing a fresh disturbance of the scree on the big slope and obliterating the incipient paths that would otherwise develop. If used less often, a path would survive!

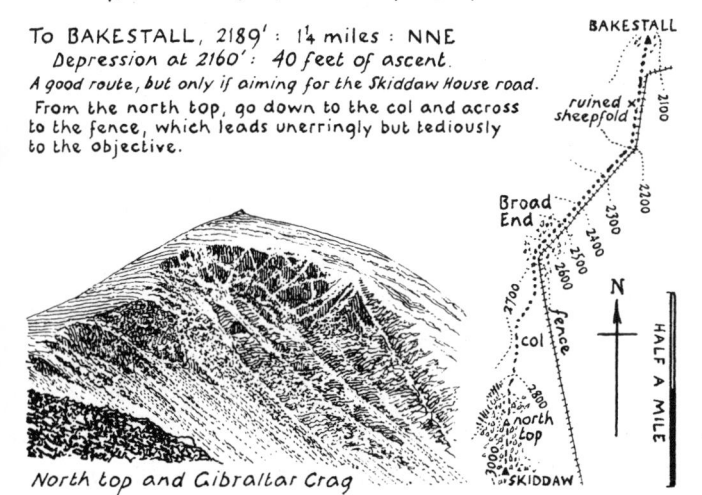

To BAKESTALL, 2189': 1¼ miles : NNE
Depression at 2160': 40 feet of ascent.

A good route, but only if aiming for the Skiddaw House road.
From the north top, go down to the col and across to the fence, which leads unerringly but tediously to the objective.

North top and Gibraltar Crag

Skiddaw 25

THE VIEW

N — LONGLANDS FELL 4 — BRAE FELL 4 — GREAT SCA FELL 3½ — HIGH PIKE 5, KNOTT 3¼ — NE

Solway Firth

Carlisle

north top
(view north of Over Water and Little Tarn (and a nearby reservoir) — Lakeland's most northerly and least known sheets of water)

Burn Tod

Little Calva

If, for some strange reason, it is desired to see the Sandale Television Transmitter, the north top is the best place to indulge the wish, but unless the mast is glinting in the sun it is not easy to distinguish: it stands almost due north, 6½ miles distant, on a low hill above two small but conspicuous plantations.

The figures accompanying the names of fells indicate distances in miles

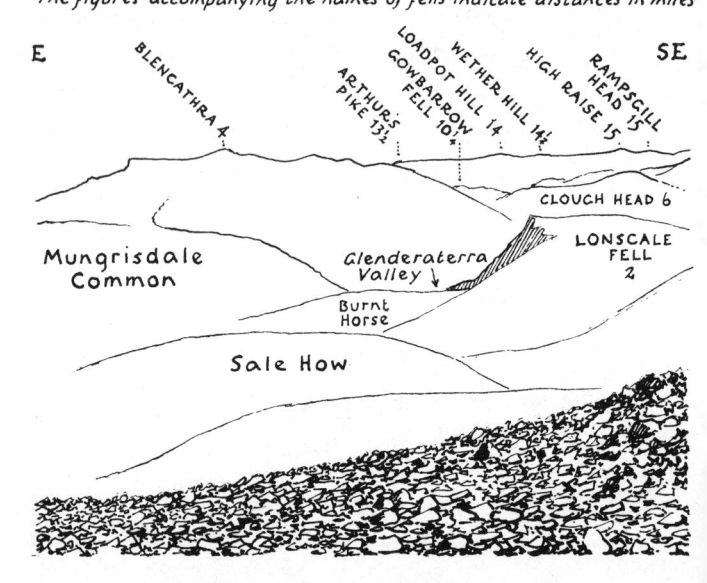

E — BLENCATHRA 4 — ARTHUR'S PIKE 13½, LOADPOT HILL 14, GOWBARROW FELL 10* — WETHER HILL 14½, HIGH RAISE 15 — RAMPSGILL HEAD 15 — SE

CLOUGH HEAD 6

LONSCALE FELL 2

Mungrisdale Common

Glenderaterra Valley

Burnt Horse

Sale How

Skiddaw 26

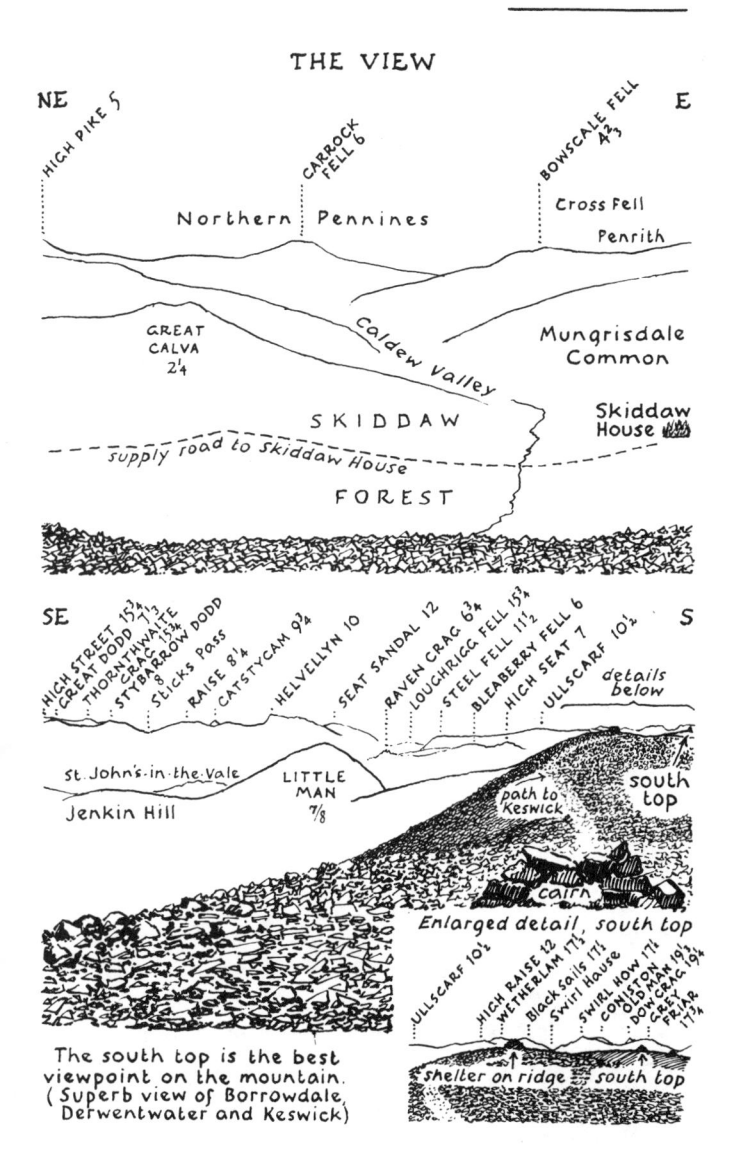

THE VIEW

NE — HIGH PIKE 5, CARROCK FELL 6, Northern Pennines, BOWSCALE FELL 4½, Cross Fell, Penrith — **E**

GREAT CALVA 2¼, Caldew Valley, Mungrisdale Common, Skiddaw House

SKIDDAW FOREST

supply road to Skiddaw House

SE — HIGH STREET 15¾, GREAT DODD 7⅓, THORNTHWAITE CRAG 15¼, STYBARROW DODD 8, Sticks Pass, RAISE 8¼, CATSTYCAM 9¼, HELVELLYN 10, SEAT SANDAL 12, RAVEN CRAG 6¾, LOUGHRIGG FELL 15¾, STEEL FELL 11½, BLEABERRY FELL 6, HIGH SEAT 7, ULLSCARF 10½ — **S**

details below

St. John's-in-the-Vale, LITTLE MAN 7/8, Jenkin Hill

path to Keswick, south top, cairn

Enlarged detail, south top

ULLSCARF 10½, HIGH RAISE 12, WETHERLAM 17½, Black Sails 17½, Swirl How 17½, CONISTON 17½, OLD MAN 19½, DOW CRAG 19¼, GREY FRIAR 17¾

shelter on ridge ↑ south top

The south top is the best viewpoint on the mountain. (Superb view of Borrowdale, Derwentwater and Keswick)

Skiddaw 27

THE VIEW

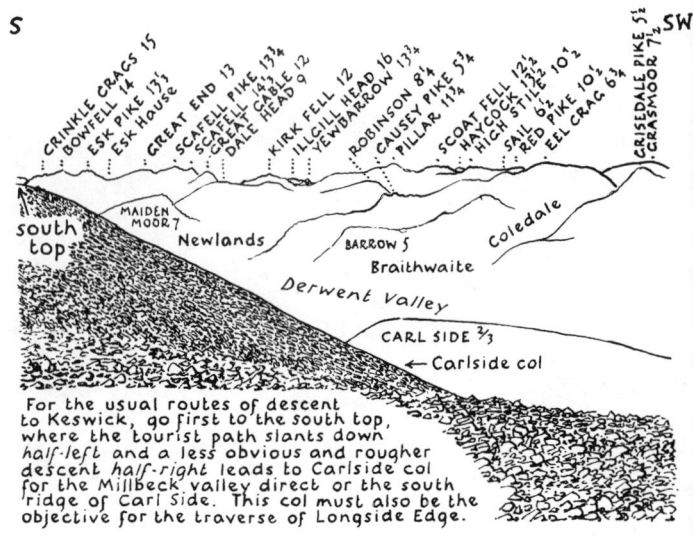

S — SW

CRINKLE CRAGS 15
BOWFELL 14
ESK PIKE 13½
ESK House
GREAT END 13
SCAFELL PIKE 13½
SCAFELL 14½
GREAT GABLE 12
DALE HEAD 9
KIRK FELL 12
ILLGILL HEAD 16
YEWBARROW 13½
ROBINSON 8½
CAUSEY PIKE 5¾
PILLAR 11¼
SCOAT FELL 12½
HAYCOCK 13½
HIGH STILE 10½
SAIL 6½
RED PIKE 10½
EEL CRAG 6¾
GRISEDALE PIKE 5½
GRASMOOR 7½

south top
MAIDEN MOOR 7
Newlands
BARROW 5
Coledale
Braithwaite
Derwent Valley
CARL SIDE ⅔
← Carlside col

For the usual routes of descent to Keswick, go first to the south top, where the tourist path slants down half-left and a less obvious and rougher descent half-right leads to Carlside col for the Millbeck valley direct or the south ridge of Carl Side. This col must also be the objective for the traverse of Longside Edge.

W — NW

Solway Firth   Hills of Galloway

Cumberland coastal plain

SALE FELL 4
plantations
Bassenthwaite Lake

shelter

Skiddaw 28

THE VIEW

SW — W

- HOPEGILL HEAD 6½
- WHITESIDE 7¼
- GAVEL FELL 11
- BLAKE FELL 11
- Isle of Man
- FELLBARROW 8½
- Irish Sea
- West Cumberland coast
- Whinlatter Pass
- BARF 3¼
- LORD'S SEAT 3¾
- BROOM FELL 4½
- LING FELL 5
- Thornthwaite Forest
- Longside Edge
- plantations
- LONG SIDE 7/8
- ULLOCK PIKE 1

NW — N

- Criffell 27½
- Scottish Lowlands
- Solway Firth
- Four white towers are the cooling towers of a generating station near Annan, Scotland
- Bothel
- Solway Marshes
- Ireby
- BINSEY 4½
- Bassenthwaite Village
- Routes of descent northwards (to the Skiddaw House road) pass over the north top

For a quick descent to Bassenthwaite Village or High Side (via Randel Crag and Southerndale) go down the steepening scree slope here (no path) aiming for the foot of Bassenthwaite Lake.

Skiddaw Little Man 2837'

'Little Man' on Ordnance Survey maps
'Low Man' on Bartholomews maps

from the weir, Mill Beck

SKIDDAW ▲   ● Skiddaw House
CARL SIDE ▲   ▲ SKIDDAW LITTLE MAN
● Millbeck
● Applethwaite
● Keswick

MILES
0 1 2 3 4

Skiddaw Little Man 2

NATURAL FEATURES

Skiddaw's Little Man is situated fully one mile from its High Man and forms a distinctive peaked summit with independent routes of ascent, commanding the most magnificent panoramic view of the heart and soul of Lakeland and controlling a major watershed — and on these grounds is treated here as a separate fell and deservedly given a separate chapter.

The Little Man is so fine a mountain that it is less than justice that its name must forever acknowledge subservience to the parent Skiddaw.   And 'Little' indeed! — the top soars half-a-mile above the valley. From the base of the steep and shattered western face three scree-covered buttresses rise out of the general angle of slope to appear as distinct peaks so far above that the walker here whose mind is saturated with Himalayan literature will irresistably be reminded of Kangchenjunga.   From Carsleddam opposite, at 1700', the whole face is displayed in truer perspective, and the buttresses are seen to lose their identity below a single towering summit, the likeness now being more that of K2. (It is taken for granted that Himalayan enthusiasts are blessed with a little imagination). The west face is quite tremendous.

In complete contrast all other slopes of the fell, the stony rift of How Gill excepted, are smooth and grassy or heathery, rarely exhibiting rock although everywhere steep. The Little Man has a second and lower summit, a 'Lesser Man', prominently in view and often mistaken for the Little Man or even Skiddaw itself on the usual line of climb from Keswick via the back of Latrigg.

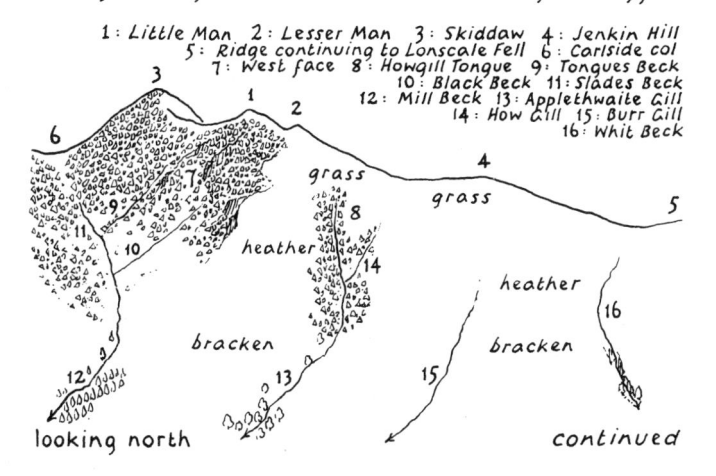

1: Little Man 2: Lesser Man 3: Skiddaw 4: Jenkin Hill
5: Ridge continuing to Lonscale Fell 6: Carlside col
7: West face 8: Howgill Tongue 9: Tongues Beck
10: Black Beck 11: Slades Beck
12: Mill Beck 13: Applethwaite Gill
14: How Gill 15: Burr Gill
16: Whit Beck

looking north   continued

Skiddaw Little Man 3

NATURAL FEATURES
continued

The lofty ridge from which the summit rises is of geographical importance, forming the watershed between the Eden and the Derwent catchment areas — and it is interesting to note that the common boundary is more clearly defined on the elegant lines of the Little Man than on the broader slopes of Skiddaw.

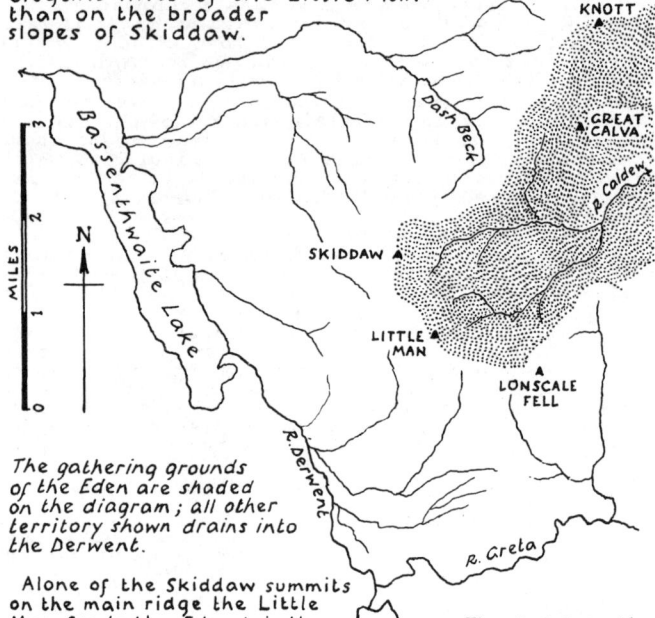

The gathering grounds of the Eden are shaded on the diagram; all other territory shown drains into the Derwent.

Alone of the Skiddaw summits on the main ridge the Little Man feeds the Eden (via the Caldew) exclusively on its eastern flank; the eastern waters of Skiddaw High Man partly, and of Lonscale Fell wholly, feed the Derwent.

The deep intrusion of the Eden system into Skiddaw Forest strongly emphasises the superior altitude of the Skiddaw massif, which is the hub of the Northern Fells — geographically, that is, not geometrically.

The fall from the summit of Little Man to the valley is so unremitting on all sides that in no place do the slopes halt sufficiently to contain a tarn, or even patches of wet ground. Walking on the fell is dry and pleasant even after much rain.

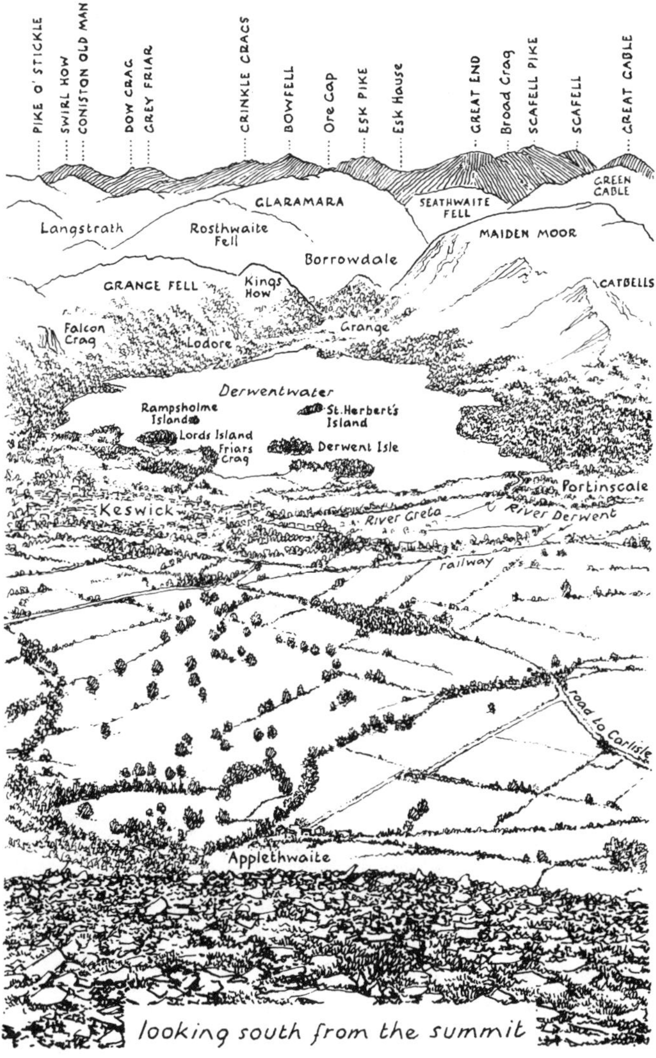

looking south from the summit

Skiddaw Little Man 5

MAP

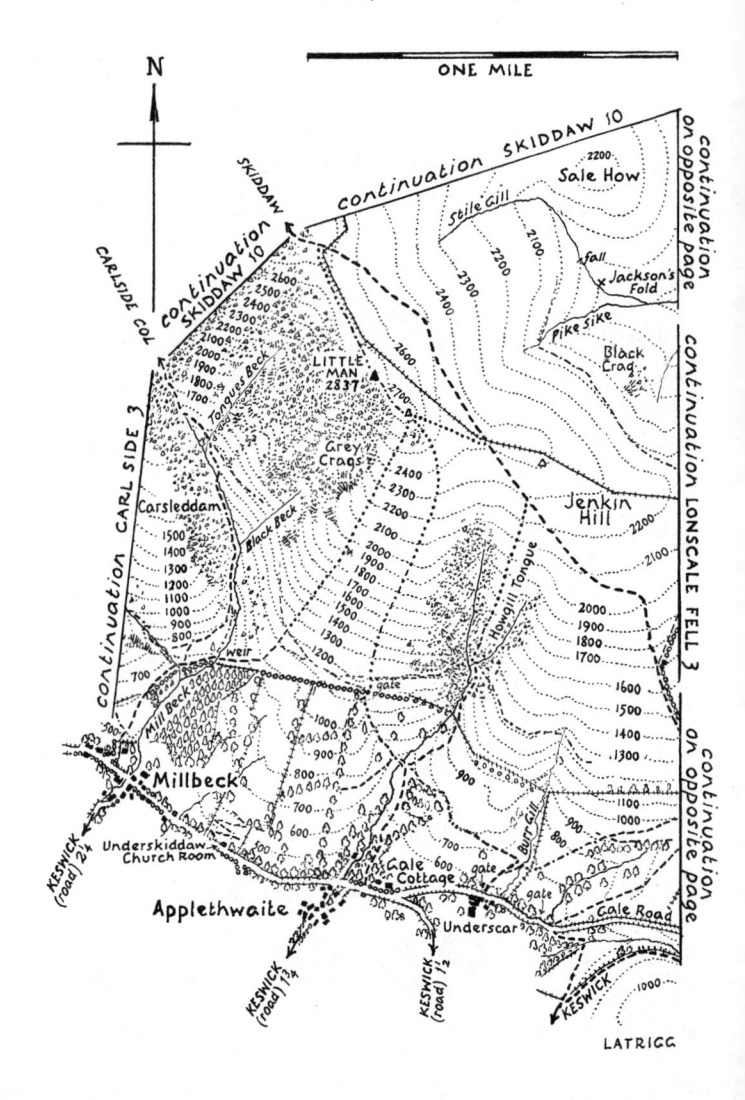

Skiddaw Little Man 6

MAP

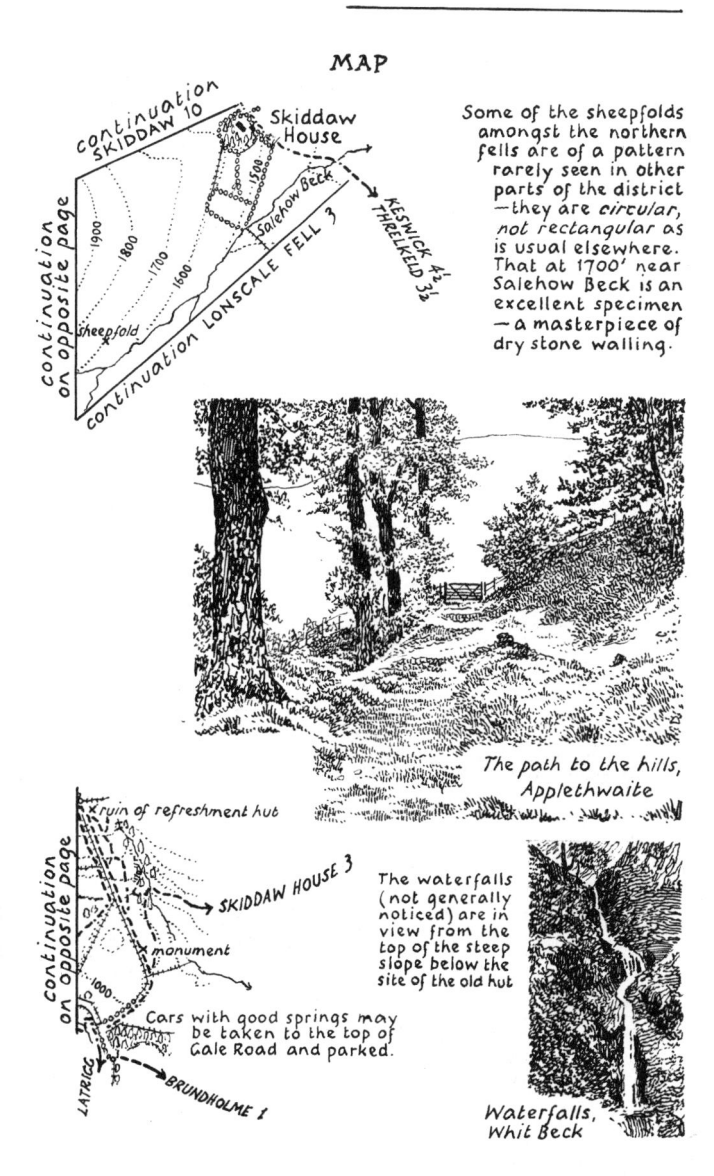

Some of the sheepfolds amongst the northern fells are of a pattern rarely seen in other parts of the district — they are *circular, not rectangular* as is usual elsewhere. That at 1700' near Salehow Beck is an excellent specimen — a masterpiece of dry stone walling.

The path to the hills, Applethwaite

The waterfalls (not generally noticed) are in view from the top of the steep slope below the site of the old hut

Cars with good springs may be taken to the top of Gale Road and parked.

Waterfalls, Whit Beck

Skiddaw Little Man 7

ASCENT FROM MILLBECK
2500 feet of ascent : 1¾ miles

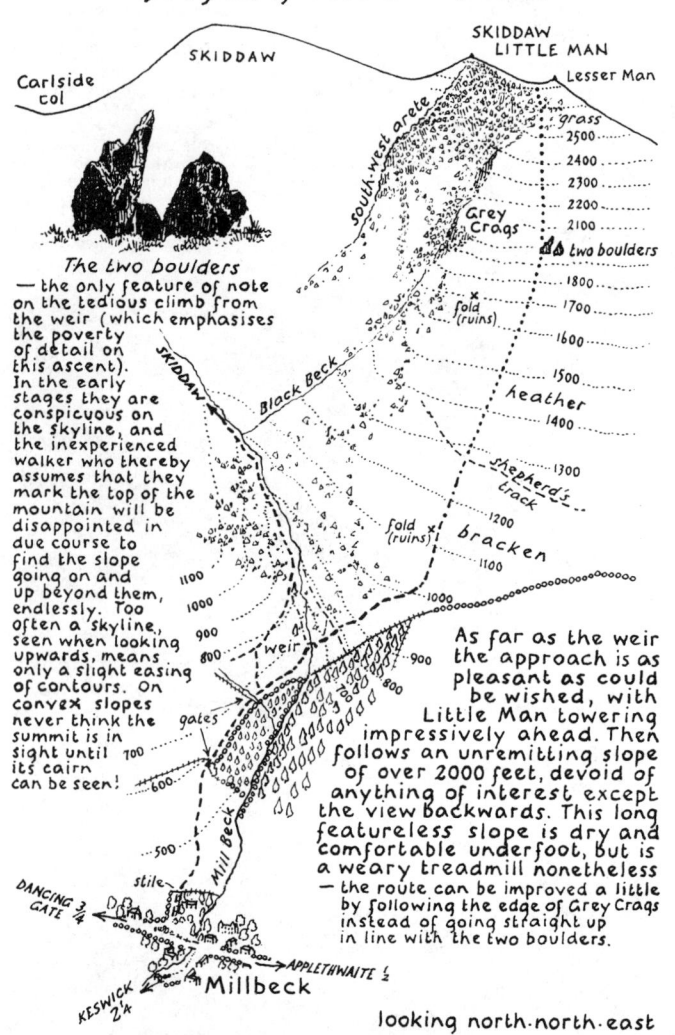

The two boulders
— the only feature of note on the tedious climb from the weir (which emphasises the poverty of detail on this ascent). In the early stages they are conspicuous on the skyline, and the inexperienced walker who thereby assumes that they mark the top of the mountain will be disappointed in due course to find the slope going on and up beyond them, endlessly. Too often a skyline, seen when looking upwards, means only a slight easing of contours. On convex slopes never think the summit is in sight until its cairn can be seen!

As far as the weir the approach is as pleasant as could be wished, with Little Man towering impressively ahead. Then follows an unremitting slope of over 2000 feet, devoid of anything of interest except the view backwards. This long featureless slope is dry and comfortable underfoot, but is a weary treadmill nonetheless — the route can be improved a little by following the edge of Grey Crags instead of going straight up in line with the two boulders.

looking north-north-east

Skiddaw Little Man 8

ASCENT FROM MILLBECK (VIA THE SOUTH-WEST ARETE)
2500 feet of ascent : 1¼ miles

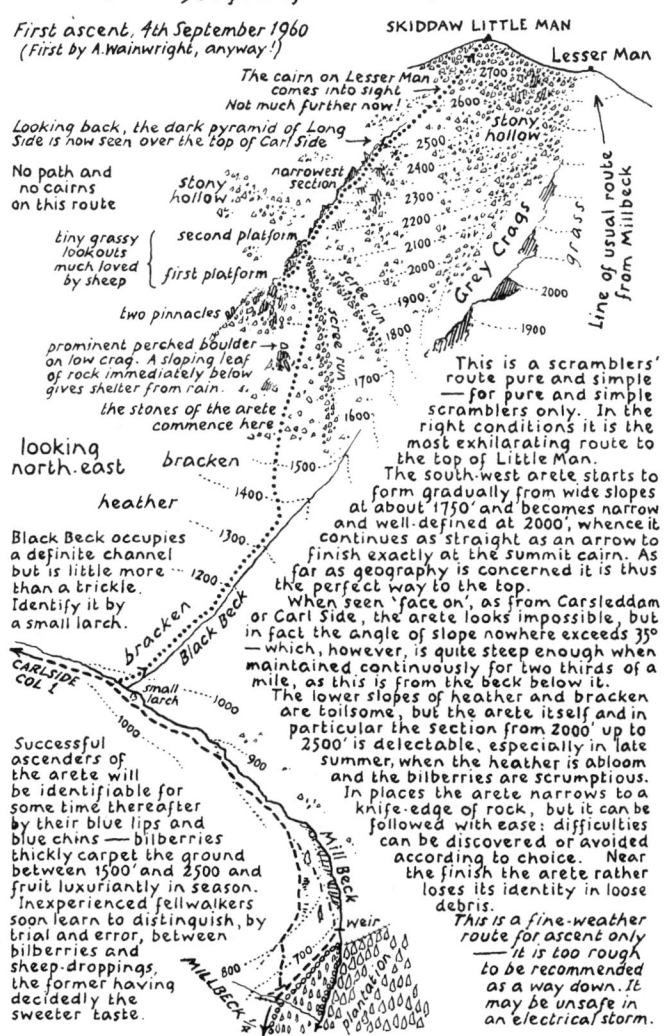

First ascent, 4th September 1960
(First by A. Wainwright, anyway!)

SKIDDAW LITTLE MAN
Lesser Man

The cairn on Lesser Man comes into sight. Not much further now!

Looking back, the dark pyramid of Long Side is now seen over the top of Carl Side

No path and no cairns on this route

stony hollow

narrowest section

tiny grassy lookouts much loved by sheep

second platform
first platform

two pinnacles

prominent perched boulder on low crag. A sloping leaf of rock immediately below gives shelter from rain.

the stones of the arete commence here

looking north-east

bracken
heather

Black Beck occupies a definite channel but is little more than a trickle. Identify it by a small larch.

bracken
Black Beck

CARLSIDE COL
small larch

Successful ascenders of the arete will be identifiable for some time thereafter by their blue lips and blue chins — bilberries thickly carpet the ground between 1500 and 2500 and fruit luxuriantly in season. Inexperienced fellwalkers soon learn to distinguish, by trial and error, between bilberries and sheep-droppings, the former having decidedly the sweeter taste.

Grey Crags
grass
Line of usual route from Millbeck

Mill Beck
weir
MILLBECK
plantation

This is a scramblers' route pure and simple — for pure and simple scramblers only. In the right conditions it is the most exhilarating route to the top of Little Man.
The south-west arete starts to form gradually from wide slopes at about 1750' and becomes narrow and well-defined at 2000', whence it continues as straight as an arrow to finish exactly at the summit cairn. As far as geography is concerned it is thus the perfect way to the top.
When seen 'face on', as from Carsleddam or Carl Side, the arete looks impossible, but in fact the angle of slope nowhere exceeds 35° — which, however, is quite steep enough when maintained continuously for two thirds of a mile, as this is from the beck below it.
The lower slopes of heather and bracken are toilsome, but the arete itself and in particular the section from 2000' up to 2500' is delectable, especially in late summer, when the heather is abloom and the bilberries are scrumptious.
In places the arete narrows to a knife-edge of rock, but it can be followed with ease: difficulties can be discovered or avoided according to choice. Near the finish the arete rather loses its identity in loose debris.
This is a fine-weather route for ascent only — it is too rough to be recommended as a way down. It may be unsafe in an electrical storm.

Skiddaw Little Man 9

ASCENT FROM APPLETHWAITE
2450 feet of ascent : 1¾ miles
(2 miles via Howgill Tongue)

On Bartholomews maps the name 'Howgill Tongue' is placed, wrongly, on the wide southern shoulder (to the left). Their cartographers do not seem to have comprehended that a *tongue* (commonly used in Lakeland to indicate a narrowing strip of raised ground) must have a tip. The tip is invariably formed by the confluence of two streams. Howgill Tongue is a perfect example. It *looks* like a tongue. No other word would suit as well.

The 'curious mound' is circular and grassy, with a shallow crater a few yards wide. Obviously made by man, but why?

This is a twin to the ascent from Millbeck. The start is even pleasanter (amongst rhododendrons!) — but the long climb from the 'bridge', over 2000 feet without halt, is very tedious and lacking in interest. The alternative via Howgill Tongue is a little more exciting but rougher. The view southwards, on both routes, is a redeeming feature.

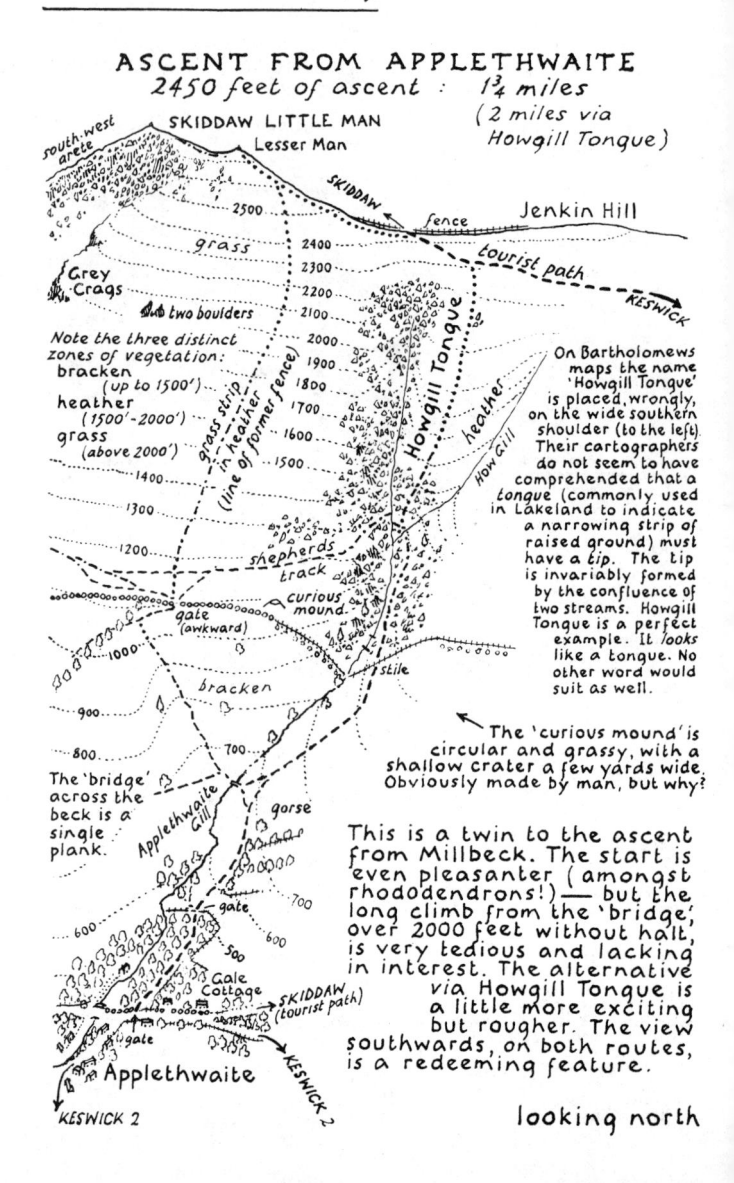

looking north

Skiddaw Little Man 10

ASCENT FROM SKIDDAW HOUSE
1350 feet of ascent : 2¼ miles

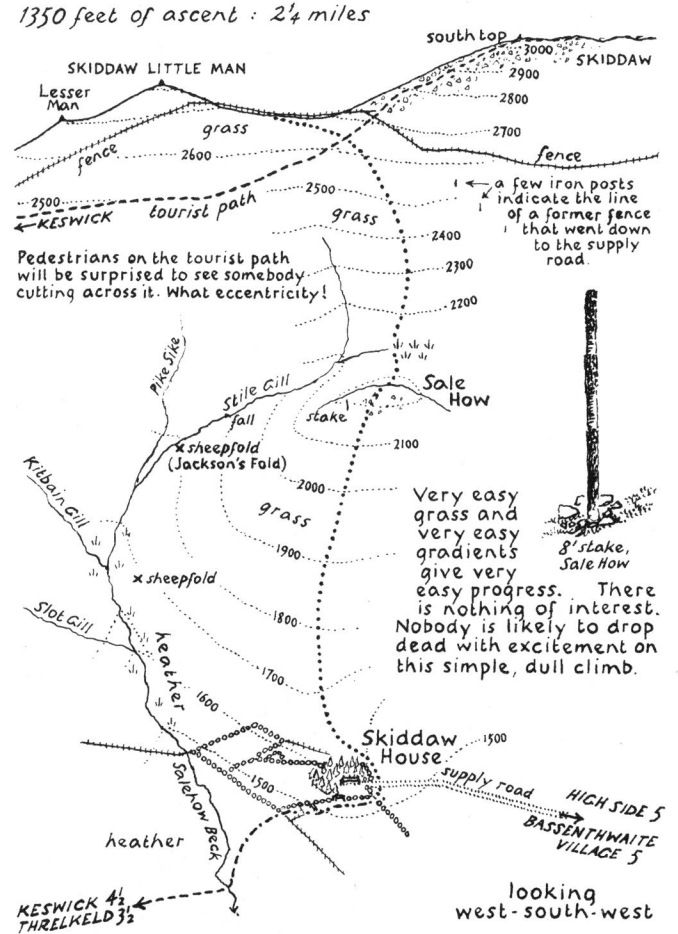

Pedestrians on the tourist path will be surprised to see somebody cutting across it. What eccentricity!

a few iron posts indicate the line of a former fence that went down to the supply road.

8' stake, Sale How

Very easy grass and very easy gradients give very easy progress. There is nothing of interest. Nobody is likely to drop dead with excitement on this simple, dull climb.

looking west-south-west

ASCENT FROM KESWICK

Little Man may, of course, be very conveniently ascended by a short deviation from the tourist path to Skiddaw, and it is quite usual to visit its summit either en route to Skiddaw or on the way down, the latter being the easier and better arrangement. For a diagram see Skiddaw 11 and 12.

Skiddaw Little Man 11

THE SUMMIT

The cairn on Little Man

The summit is small and shapely, but its elegance is rather spoiled by an untidy cairn. The top is mainly grassy and has no features of interest near at hand but its deficiencies are more than made good by the superb view. There is space enough around the cairn for perambulation, but it is obvious that the slopes west and south fall away very steeply, curving over out of sight almost at once. The cairn on the lower summit ('Lesser Man') is adorned by an elaborate arrangement of fence-posts.

DESCENTS: By passing over the summit of Lesser Man and going down the rougher ground beyond the broad highway from Skiddaw is joined at a fence. But consider as a quiet alternative gaining the valley at Applethwaite or Millbeck by way of the wide shoulder descending west of south. Avoid a false start on this latter route by first going over Lesser Man and then immediately swing downhill to the right. Do not attempt to descend directly from Little Man's cairn: steep screes bar the way here (from Lesser Man nothing worse than grass, a belt of heather and an expanse of bracken is met).

The cairn on Lesser Man

Bear right for Millbeck and left for Applethwaite on approaching the cross-wall at 1200'.

Skiddaw Little Man 12

RIDGE ROUTES

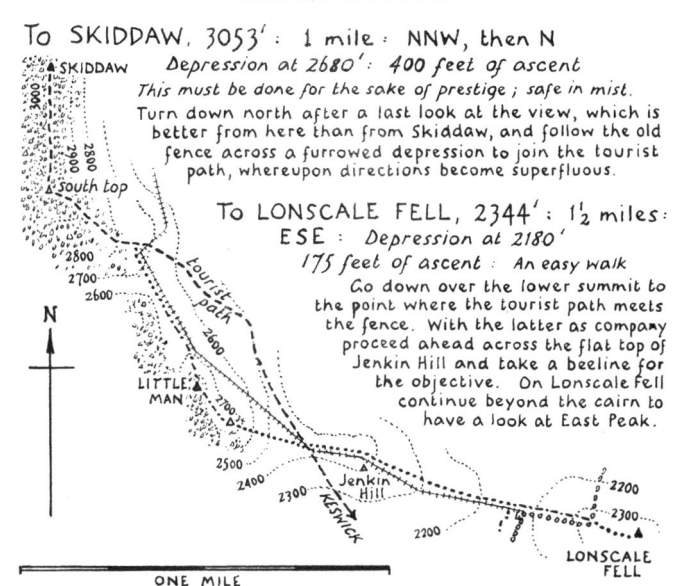

To SKIDDAW, 3053': 1 mile : NNW, then N
Depression at 2680' : 400 feet of ascent
This must be done for the sake of prestige; safe in mist.

Turn down north after a last look at the view, which is better from here than from Skiddaw, and follow the old fence across a furrowed depression to join the tourist path, whereupon directions become superfluous.

To LONSCALE FELL, 2344' : 1½ miles :
ESE : Depression at 2180'
175 feet of ascent : *An easy walk*

Go down over the lower summit to the point where the tourist path meets the fence. With the latter as company proceed ahead across the flat top of Jenkin Hill and take a beeline for the objective. On Lonscale Fell continue beyond the cairn to have a look at East Peak.

looking down the south-west arete to Millbeck

Skiddaw Little Man 13

THE VIEW

There will never be general agreement on the answer to the question: which is the finest view in Lakeland?

Some views depend for their appeal on beauty of foreground, Tarn Hows for example; some on their intimate detail of a particular and pleasing feature, such as Castle Head's view of Derwentwater; some on colour and interesting arrangement, such as those from Ashness Bridge and Loughrigg Terrace. Other scenes have drama as their theme, Scafell Crag from Mickledore for example; popular, too, are the unforgettable birds-eye views from such heights as Great Gable and Great End, while many folk favour the most extensive prospects, as seen from Scafell Pike, Bowfell and Helvellyn. Opinions differ according to individual preference.

But for a classic view of the heart of Lakeland from a position on its perimeter Skiddaw Little Man must have majority support as the one place above all others. This viewpoint is detached and distant, and situated high above the wide Vale of Keswick, so that the mountain skyline beyond is seen across a great gulf, as if being approached by aeroplane, and sufficiently removed to admit correct perspectives and relationships. From this viewpoint, as the onlooker turns his gaze through the southern arc, the picture unfolds like the canvas of a master. This is Cinemascope in excelsis, on a scale never envisaged by Hollywood, a vast scene on a screen as wide as the heavens. And all of it is beautiful, nature's quiet artistry. Men are clever enough to make atomic bombs, and strut about like lords of creation, yet they can't even make a blade of grass or a sprig of heather, let alone build up a landscape like this. Which is as well.

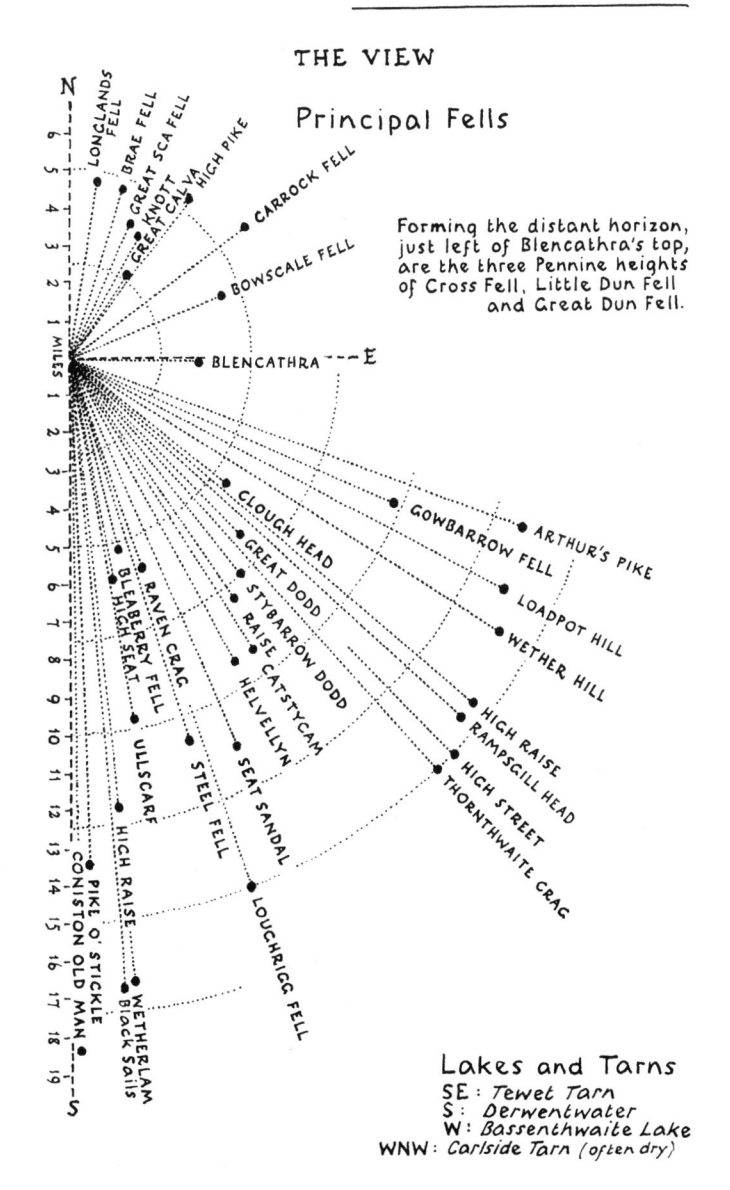

Skiddaw Little Man 14

THE VIEW

Principal Fells

Forming the distant horizon, just left of Blencathra's top, are the three Pennine heights of Cross Fell, Little Dun Fell and Great Dun Fell.

Lakes and Tarns
SE: *Tewet Tarn*
S: *Derwentwater*
W: *Bassenthwaite Lake*
WNW: *Carlside Tarn (often dry)*

Souther Fell 1680'

from Mungrisdale, obviously

(Telegraph poles removed from this view without permission of the P.O. Engineers)

Souther is pronounced *Souter*

Mungrisdale is pronounced *Mun-grize-dl* with the emphasis on *grize*

Mungrisdale
BANNERDALE CRAGS ▲
BLENCATHRA ▲
SOUTHER FELL
● Scales

MILES
0 1 2 3 4

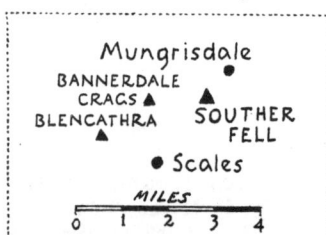

from Scales Fell

Souther Fell 2

NATURAL FEATURES

Souther Fell, taking the form of a long ridge, extends Blencathra to the east and curves northwards to its extremity, where there is an abrupt fall of altitude to the fields of Mungrisdale — and no more high ground thereafter until, far beyond the broad valley of the Eden, the dark wall of the Pennines closes the horizon. Thus Souther Fell, although of little merit as a climb and of unattractive appearance, occupies an important position as a cornerstone of the Northern Fells, having an extensive view out of proportion to its modest height.

An unusual geographical feature is revealed by a study of the map. Although the fell has slopes facing all points of the compass the whole of its drainage is conducted by a single stream, the Glenderamackin, which encircles its base almost completely like a great moat, with the narrow Mousthwaite col serving as drawbridge.

Blencathra, over the south ridge of Bannerdale Crags, from a cairn on Souther Fell

Souther Fell 3

The River Glenderamackin

The course of the Glenderamackin is remarkable. Starting as a trickle from a marsh below the col linking Bannerdale Crags and Blencathra, it soon gathers strength and aims purposefully for a gap in the hills to the south, eager to be away from its desolate place of birth and join other waters in a tranquil and pleasant passage through Lakeland — for are not the streams of Lakeland the most beautiful of all? But, alas, it cannot find a way across the gap: a low barrier of land, Mousthwaite Col, defeats this object and turns the young river east, and then — a greater disappointment — Souther Fell thrusts across the route. Now there is no alternative but to go due north, and indications suggest that the Eden Valley, and not Lakeland, is destined to receive its waters. But, almost by a freak, it is prevented by a slight and otherwise insignificant eminence at Mungrisdale from entering the Eden catchment area, and here it is again turned to the south. Hope revives. Perhaps, after all, it may be permitted by friendly contours at least to join some tributary of Ullswater? But no, better still: after almost encircling Souther Fell a sudden glorious view of Lakeland opens up to the west, the way thereto at last being clear, and lying through sylvan meadows and rocky gorges and woodlands and great lakes. Now the Glenderamackin is no longer a neglected beck. It has become a river and men to cross it must build bridges. It has acquired a stately loveliness, a leisurely flow — it is a Lakeland river and therefore is beautiful. Artists will paint its picture, and cows stand in its waters.

An ambition has been realised, but it so nearly wasn't!

Souther Fell 4

MAP

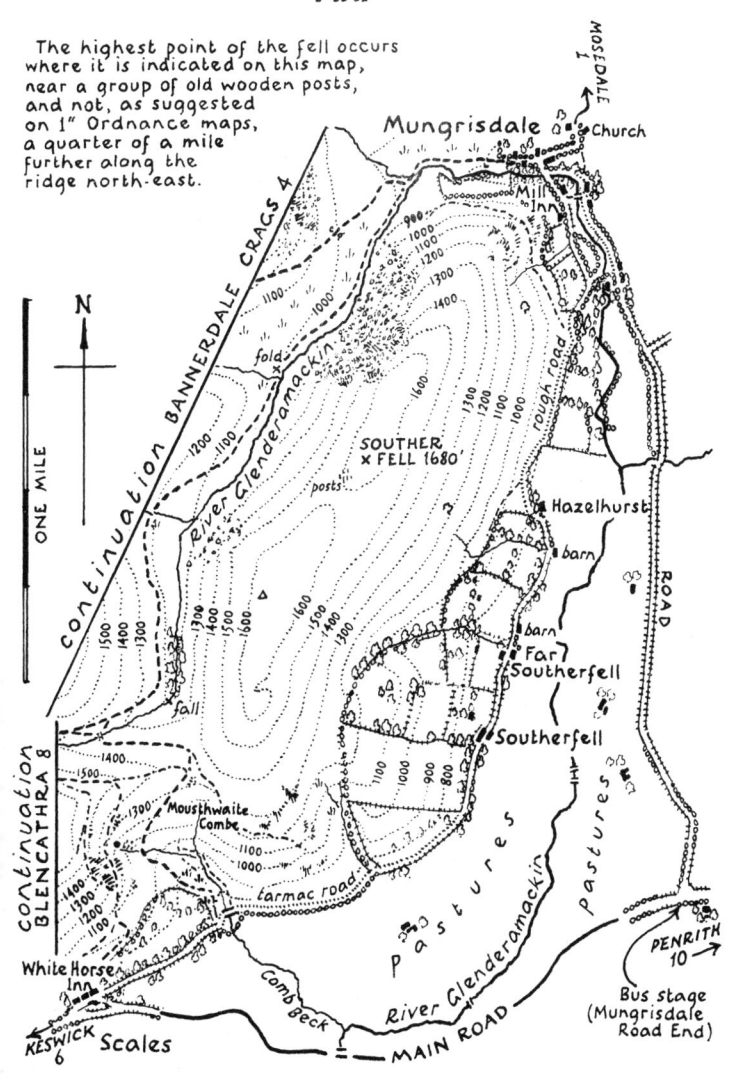

The highest point of the fell occurs where it is indicated on this map, near a group of old wooden posts, and not, as suggested on 1" Ordnance maps, a quarter of a mile further along the ridge north-east.

Souther Fell 5

ASCENT FROM MUNGRISDALE
950 feet of ascent : 1¼ miles

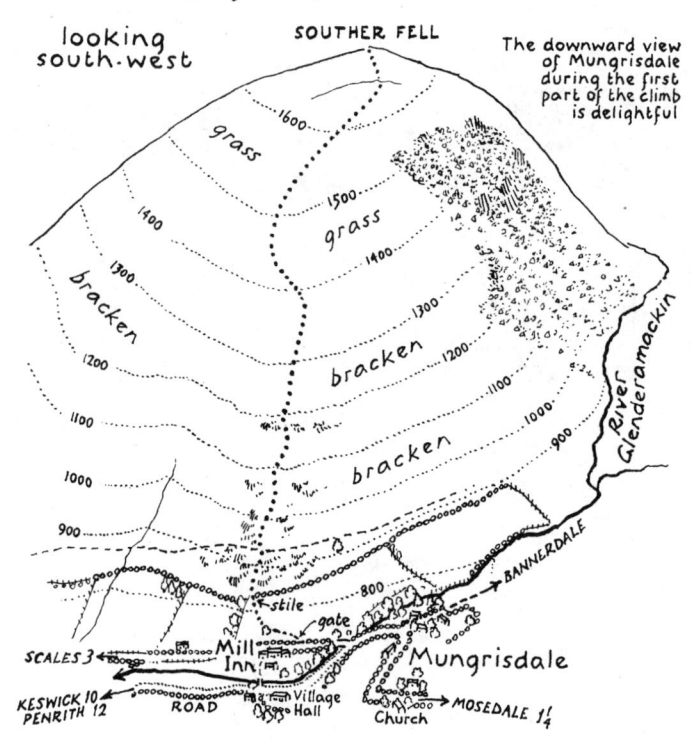

looking south-west

SOUTHER FELL

The downward view of Mungrisdale during the first part of the climb is delightful

This pleasant little climb (no path) is simple and straightforward, although rougher just above the wall than will be expected, rocks in the bracken here making progress none too easy.

RIDGE ROUTE

A study of the Ordnance map shows that Souther Fell is really a ridge of Blencathra, a continuation of Scales Fell across the depression of Mousthwaite Col, and there is thus an obvious link with that mountain. To reach it, go along the ridge to the col (which lies well to the left of the direct line) and there join one of the alternative routes of ascent coming up from Scales (see Blencathra 25). A separate diagram of the ridge-route is hardly necessary. There isn't space for one, anyway: the page is full *now*.

Souther Fell 6

ASCENT FROM SCALES
1000 feet of ascent : 2 miles

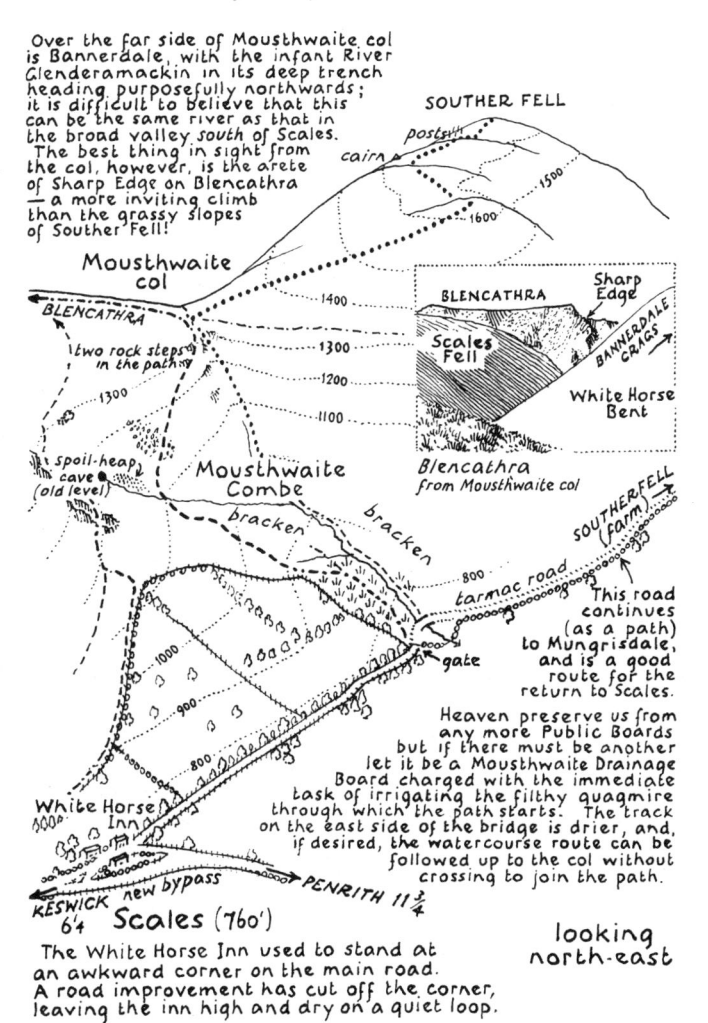

Over the far side of Mousthwaite col is Bannerdale, with the infant River Glenderamackin in its deep trench heading purposefully northwards; it is difficult to believe that this can be the same river as that in the broad valley south of Scales. The best thing in sight from the col, however, is the arête of Sharp Edge on Blencathra — a more inviting climb than the grassy slopes of Souther Fell!

Blencathra from Mousthwaite col

Heaven preserve us from any more Public Boards but if there must be another let it be a Mousthwaite Drainage Board charged with the immediate task of irrigating the filthy quagmire through which the path starts. The track on the east side of the bridge is drier, and, if desired, the watercourse route can be followed up to the col without crossing to join the path.

This road continues (as a path) to Mungrisdale, and is a good route for the return to Scales.

The White Horse Inn used to stand at an awkward corner on the main road. A road improvement has cut off the corner, leaving the inn high and dry on a quiet loop.

looking north-east

Souther Fell 7

THE SUMMIT

The top of the fell is an undulating grass ridge at around 1600 feet for half a mile. The highest point can only be decided after careful observation, there being no cairn. The actual summit is one of several grassy hillocks, identified by an embedded stone and having a few wooden posts nearby. Ordnance maps indicate a trigonometrical station at a height of 1680' but a mistake is evident: the trig. station is at 1650' (according to the contours on the 2½" map), but the actual summit, to which the altitude of 1680' seems appropriate, lies a quarter of a mile south-west. This allegation against the veracity of the Ordnance surveyors having been confirmed, there is nothing else for the walker to do and see on the pathless and featureless top of Souther Fell.

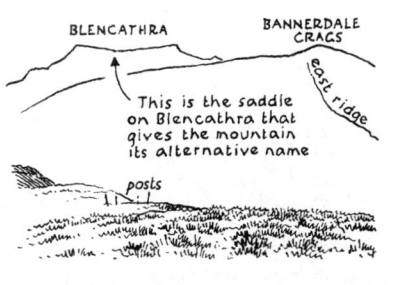

DESCENTS, both to Scales and Mungrisdale, are best made along the ridge (no easy matter in mist). The Bannerdale slope is rough and steep, and the Glenderamackin at its base cannot be forded. The eastern slope is gentler but obstructed by dense bracken.

The Spectral Army of Soutra Fell

This is no legend.

This is the solemn truth, as attested on oath before a magistrate by 26 sober and respected witnesses. These good people assembled on the evening before Midsummer Day 1745 at a place of vantage in the valley to the east to test incredulous reports that soldiers and horsemen had been seen marching across the top of Souter Fell (*Soutra Fell* was probably its name in those days). They saw them all right: an unbroken line of quickly-moving troops, horses and carriages extending over the full length of the top of Souter, continuously appearing at one end and vanishing at the other — and passing unhesitatingly over steep places that horses and carriages could not possibly negotiate, as the bewildered observers well knew. The procession went on until darkness concealed the marching army. Next morning the skyline was deserted, and a visit to the summit was made by a party of local worthies, fearful that the expected invasion from over the border had started (this was the year of the '45 Rebellion). There was not a trace of the previous night's visitors. Not a footprint, not a hoofmark, not a wheel rut in the grass. Nothing.

There was no doubting the evidence of so many witnesses, and yet it was equally certain that the marching figures had no substance. Scientists and students of the supernatural had no solution to offer. The only explanation ever given was that some kind of a mirage had been seen, probably a vapourous reflection of Prince Charlie's rebels, who (it was discovered on enquiry) had that very evening been exercising on the west coast of Scotland... This beats radar!

Souther Fell 8

THE VIEW

Souther Fell is the most easterly of the northern group and enjoys an uninterrupted prospect across the valley of the Eden to the Pennines. The Lakeland scene is confined to an interesting view of the Patterdale country east of Helvellyn, and a delightful vista southwest in a frame of neighbouring fells. Blencathra dominates the picture.

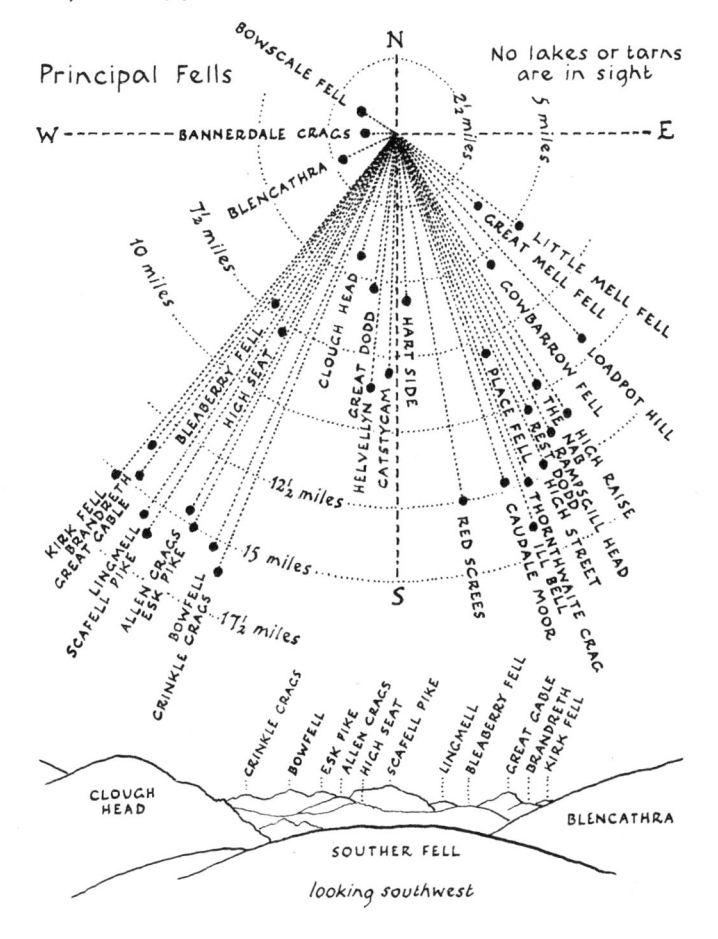

Principal Fells

No lakes or tarns are in sight

Ullock Pike 2230'

from Southerndale

- Bassenthwaite
- High Side
- Ravenstone
- ▲ SKIDDAW
- ▲ ULLOCK PIKE
- ▲ LONG SIDE
- ▲ CARL SIDE
- ▲ DODD
- Little Crosthwaite
- Keswick

MILES
0 1 2 3

Ullock Pike 2

NATURAL FEATURES

South-east of Bassenthwaite village, pleasant pastures rise to form, at the top intake wall, a wide shoulder of rough fell, and this in turn runs south and climbs as a narrowing ridge to a dark and symmetrical peak. The ridge, curved like a bow, is known as the Edge, and the dark peak is Ullock Pike. As seen on the approach from Bassenthwaite this slender pyramid is one of the simplest yet finest mountain forms in Lakeland, but its outline commands little attention from other directions, whence it is seen to be no more than a hump at the end of a greater and elevated ridge springing out of the stony bosom of Skiddaw. The western flank falls roughly to Bassenthwaite Lake, the lower slopes here being afforested, and this aspect of the fell is familiar to frequenters of the district; the less well known eastern flank, concealed from the gaze of tourists, drops even more steeply to the upland hollow of Southerndale. Streams are few, the fell drying quickly like the ridged roof of a building, which it resembles.

Watches

Astride the lower level section of the Edge, not far above the intake wall and directly overlooking the footbridge in Southerndale, is a strange and interesting congregation of upstanding rocks, huddled together as though assembled in conference, and suggesting, at first sight, a Druids' Circle. The formation is natural, however, but unusual and (being in the midst of grass) unexpected. Large-scale Ordnance maps give the equally-intriguing name of WATCHES to this place.

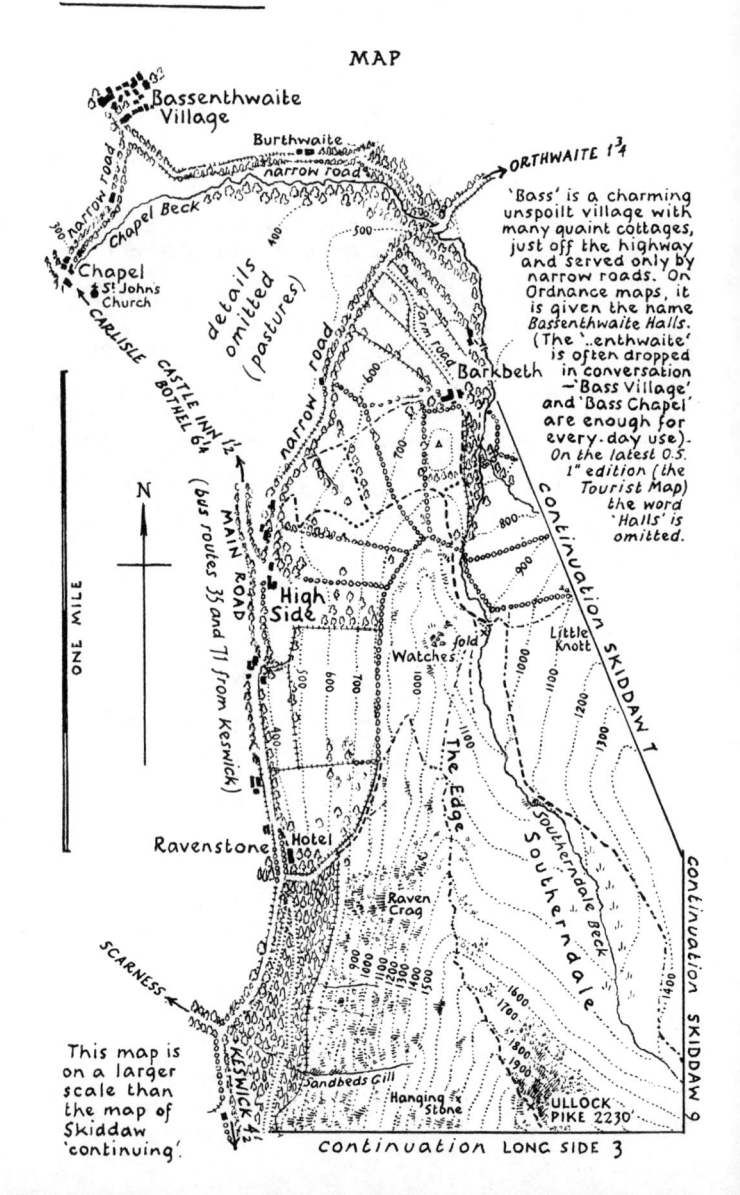

Ullock Pike 3

MAP

'Bass' is a charming unspoilt village with many quaint cottages, just off the highway and served only by narrow roads. On Ordnance maps, it is given the name Bassenthwaite Halls. (The '..enthwaite' is often dropped in conversation — 'Bass Village' and 'Bass Chapel' are enough for every-day use). On the latest O.S. 1" edition (the Tourist Map) the word 'Halls' is omitted.

This map is on a larger scale than the map of Skiddaw 'continuing'.

Ullock Pike 4

Ullock Pike from Chapel

Access to Ullock Pike : the Drove Roads

The lower slopes of Ullock Pike, skirting the public roads from which the ascent must be made, consist of a continuous belt of fenced pastures and plantations, and it is not easy in the absence of walkers' paths and signposts to determine a line of access to the prominent ridge (the Edge) rising to the Pike. The one hopeful breach is provided by the farm-road leading up to Barkbeth (name on gate).

It is unnecessary, however, to disturb the little community of Barkbeth (including the farmyard livestock). Most walkers will find it convenient to approach from the little hamlet ('bus-stop) of High Side, using the Orthwaite road, which there leaves the main road: at the top of the first straight rise (300 yards) is a gate in a recess of the hedge on the right and this opens on to a green zig-zag which ultimately swings away to the left, passing through three more gates to the open fell beyond the intake wall at the narrow entrance to Southerndale, the Edge then rising on the right. (A second gate, also recessed on the Orthwaite road, and 150 yards further, can alternatively be used as a start: join the first path by following a line of thorn trees up to the right). On this route of approach, by either start, the walker is out of sight and earshot of Barkbeth and the farmyard livestock: a small hillock (Barkbeth Hill) intervenes and ensures privacy.

This grass path, obviously engineered although vague in places, is a drove road, used for bringing sheep down from Southerndale. (It is easier to trace in descent, when it is better seen to curve downwards with the natural slope. Note how it avoids Barkbeth, the explanation being that it serves Southerndale flocks owned by other farms). The pleasant pastures through which it passes up to the intake wall are often occupied by sheep. On the rough fells sheep are at home, need no fences, and do not stray, but in the lower pastures they are less at ease and will stray given the opportunity. Therefore it is important that all gates should be fastened securely. A habitually-solitary walker always closes gates, instinctively; a party is often careless, leaving the duty to each other instead of delegating it to one member.

Another green 'road' comes down to Ravenstone, and may also be used as a means of access (see page 6) but is less attractive.

If starting the walk from Bassenthwaite Village, Barkbeth then straddles the direct route (path beyond the farm buildings, left of Barkbeth Hill).

Ullock Pike 5

ASCENTS FROM BASSENTHWAITE VILLAGE AND HIGH SIDE
2000 feet of ascent : 3¼ miles (from Bassenthwaite Village)
1900 feet : 2½ miles (from High Side)

"..... by heather tracks wi' heaven in their wilds"
The last quarter-mile

Above the intake wall the Edge may be gained easily at any point.

The top appears so clean-cut and well-defined on the ascent that, on reaching it, a second and higher top just beyond comes as a surprise.

The rising ground above the Orthwaite road leads naturally to the Edge, the long north ridge of Ullock Pike, a splendid line of approach along a narrowing and elevated stairway: a short, enjoyable climb, with superb views from the small peaked summit.

Bassenthwaite Village

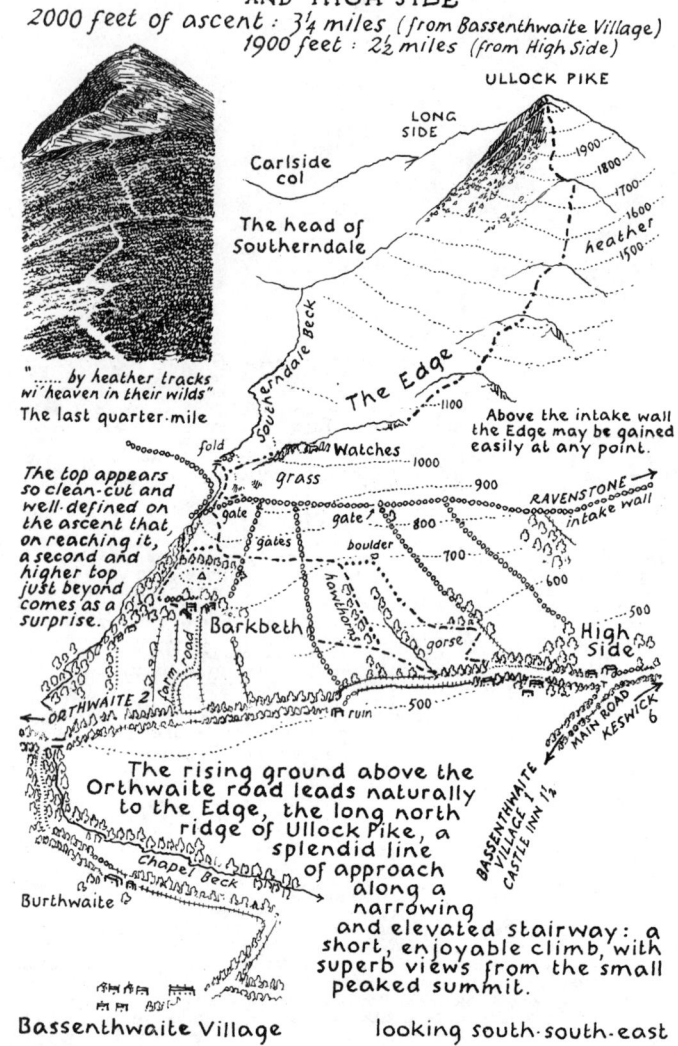

looking south-south-east

Ullock Pike 6

ASCENT FROM RAVENSTONE
1850 feet of ascent : 1¾ miles

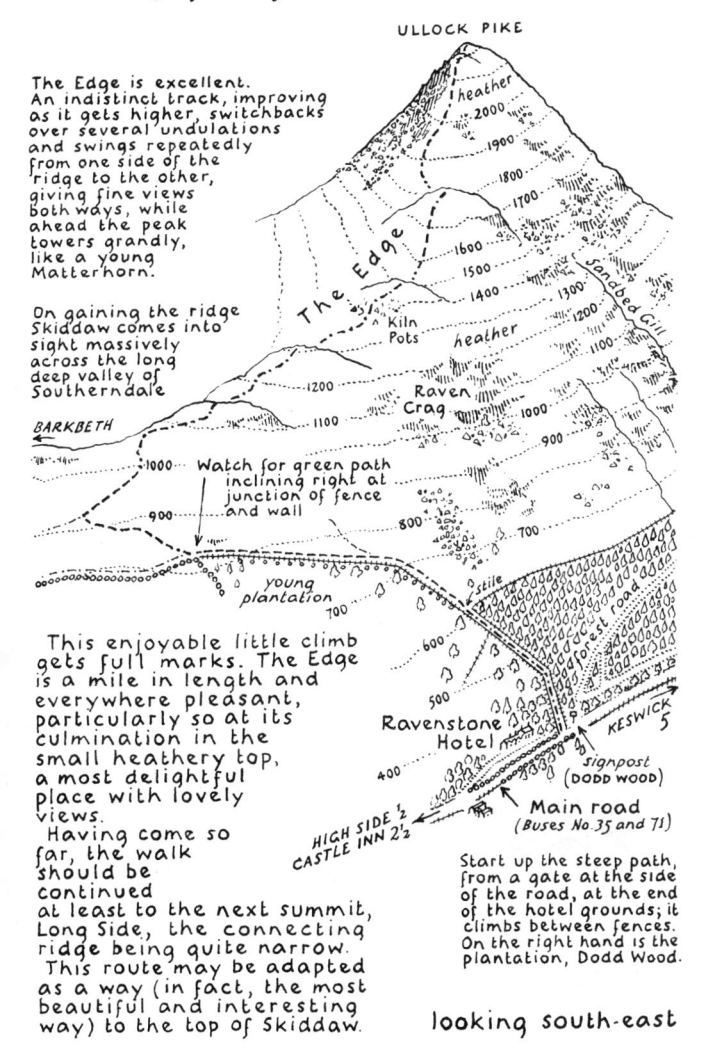

ULLOCK PIKE

The Edge is excellent. An indistinct track, improving as it gets higher, switchbacks over several undulations and swings repeatedly from one side of the ridge to the other, giving fine views both ways, while ahead the peak towers grandly, like a young Matterhorn.

On gaining the ridge Skiddaw comes into sight massively across the long deep valley of Southerndale

BARKBETH

Watch for green path inclining right at junction of fence and wall

young plantation

Raven Crag

Kiln Pots

heather

Sandbed Gill

The Edge

stile

forest road

Ravenstone Hotel

KESWICK 5

signpost (DODD WOOD)

HIGH SIDE ½
CASTLE INN 2½

Main road (Buses No. 35 and 71)

This enjoyable little climb gets full marks. The Edge is a mile in length and everywhere pleasant, particularly so at its culmination in the small heathery top, a most delightful place with lovely views.
Having come so far, the walk should be continued at least to the next summit, Long Side, the connecting ridge being quite narrow.
This route may be adapted as a way (in fact, the most beautiful and interesting way) to the top of Skiddaw.

Start up the steep path, from a gate at the side of the road, at the end of the hotel grounds; it climbs between fences. On the right hand is the plantation, Dodd Wood.

looking south-east

Ullock Pike 7

THE SUMMIT

The neat domed summit, upholstered in heather and crossed by a narrow track, is just the sort of place to make one wish it could be parcelled up and taken home for the back garden. There is no cairn. Just below the top, north, the ridge halts at a false summit, which is nothing more than a little platform but from below appears to be the highest point of the fell.

The highest point

DESCENTS: Both flanks of the fell are very rough, that dropping into Southerndale being initially craggy and the Bassenthwaite side steepening lower down. The best way off is down the Edge, a splendid line of descent, there being a track good enough to follow in mist until the highest rocks are left behind.

RIDGE ROUTE

To LONG SIDE, 2405'
⅓ mile : SE
Depression at 2185'
230 feet of ascent
An enjoyable ten minutes

The route follows the rim of Longside Edge, where a distinct but narrow track has been worn in the heather. The walking is quite easy, but there is one spot where anyone striding along with eyes on the distant view might step over the brink of a rocky cleft.

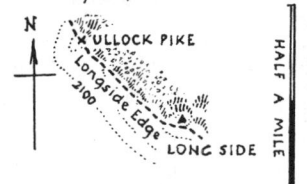

The true summit from the false one

Hanging Stone

The 2½" and 6" Ordnance maps give prominence to a 'Hanging Stone' on Ullock Pike 400 yards west of the summit, but it is hardly worth searching for, being merely an unremarkable block anchored to the lip of a small crag. It attracts attention only when seen from below.

Ullock Pike 8

THE VIEW

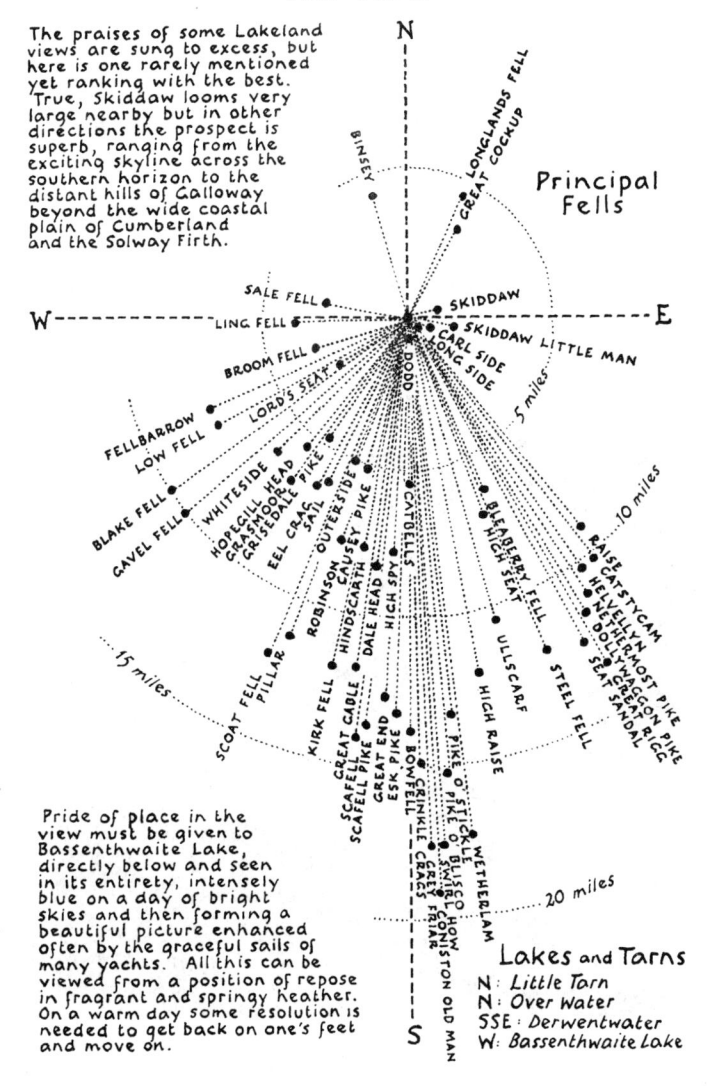

The praises of some Lakeland views are sung to excess, but here is one rarely mentioned yet ranking with the best. True, Skiddaw looms very large nearby but in other directions the prospect is superb, ranging from the exciting skyline across the southern horizon to the distant hills of Galloway beyond the wide coastal plain of Cumberland and the Solway Firth.

Principal Fells

N — Binsey, Great Cockup, Great Longlands Fell
W — Sale Fell, Ling Fell
E — Skiddaw, Skiddaw Little Man, Carl Side, Long Side, Dodd
Broom Fell, Fellbarrow, Low Fell, Lord's Seat, Blake Fell, Gavel Fell, Whiteside, Hopegill Head, Grasmoor Pike, Grisedale Pike, Eel Crag, Sail, Robinson, Outerside, Hindscarth, Causey Pike, Dale Head, High Spy, Catbells, Bleaberry Fell, High Seat, Raise, Catstycam, Helvellyn Lowest Pike, Helvellyn, Dollywaggon Pike, Great Rigg, Seat Sandal, Steel Fell, Scoat Fell, Pillar, Kirk Fell, Great Gable, Scafell, Scafell Pike, Great End, Esk Pike, Bowfell, Pike o' Stickle, Pike o' Blisco, Swirl How, Crinkle Crags, Coniston Old Man, High Raise, Ullscarf, Wetherlam

5 miles, 10 miles, 15 miles, 20 miles

Pride of place in the view must be given to Bassenthwaite Lake, directly below and seen in its entirety, intensely blue on a day of bright skies and then forming a beautiful picture enhanced often by the graceful sails of many yachts. All this can be viewed from a position of repose in fragrant and springy heather. On a warm day some resolution is needed to get back on one's feet and move on.

Lakes and Tarns

N: *Little Tarn*
N: *Over Water*
SSE: *Derwentwater*
W: *Bassenthwaite Lake*

Ullock Pike 9

Bassenthwaite, from Ullock Pike

Some Personal notes in conclusion

Well, that's another finished.

Up to two years ago I hadn't known the northern Fells intimately, and the remoter parts I had known merely as names on the map. Imaginative and romantic names, many of them: Arm o' Grain, Red Covercloth, Frozen Fell, Ward Steel, Balliway Rigg, Thief Gills, Trusmadoor, Whitewater Dash, Brandy Gill, Black Nettle House, Candleseaves Bog, and others. Significantly, these names, foreign-sounding in Lakeland, are all of wild places in the hills, and it would seem that many of them can be attributed to the mining prospectors who first explored these uplands some five or six centuries ago, giving identity to the various landmarks. Down in the surrounding valleys, though, the dalesfolk adopted traditional Lakeland names for their farms and local features — 'thwaite', 'dale' and 'beck' occurring everywhere.

The era of mining activity has largely passed, barytes being the only mineral now being won, and the hills are quiet again. The creatures of the high places are undisturbed. Even in summer, few walkers visit the tops. In winter the Blencathra pack roam the fellsides occasionally. Both summer and winter, Pearson Dalton crosses the hills with his dogs, twice a week making the journey between his home at Fell Side and the lonely Skiddaw House, where he is shepherd. The only sounds are the call of the birds, the cries of sheep, the murmur of streams, the wind rustling the coarse bents and heather. There are no false notes in this peaceful symphony, no discords, no harshness. This is a land of solitude and silence.

On the southern fringe of the group Skiddaw and Blencathra are, however, old favourites. Skiddaw is climbed by the popular path from Keswick every day of the year, often by scores and sometimes by hundreds of people. And Blencathra is deservedly a much-visited peak. These two apart, the only other fell on which I saw another person in the whole of my walks, and then at a distance, was Carrock Fell, and this happened on three different occasions. As for the rest — nobody, not a soul, not once. I felt I was preparing a book that would have no readers at all, a script that would have no players and no public. Nevertheless, these were glorious days for me — days of absolute freedom, days of feeling like the only man on earth. No crowds to dodge, no noisy chatter, no litter. Just me, and the sheep, and singing larks overhead. All of us well content.

I must not eulogise the northern Fells too much. These lonely hills do not compare at all for grand scenery and situations with those of Wasdale and Langdale and Borrowdale. (But Blencathra and Carrock Fell and the Ullock Pike ridge of Skiddaw are very definite exceptions that would rank high in any company). Generally, they are not in the same class. From a walkers point of view, Caldbeck Fells are NOT 'worth all England else'. But they have one great attraction the others are fast losing — for the walker who prefers solitude, for the naturalist, they offer undisturbed enjoyment at all seasons of the year. They are a perfect Bank Holiday refuge. They are just right, too, for the aged hiker who can no longer force his jaded legs up Rossett Gill or around Mickledore — here, on gentler gradients, is a new lease of life for him.

Skiddaw Forest, magnificent walking country very reminiscent of Scotland, is under a threat. Engineers have their eyes on this vast gathering ground, and possibly an impounding reservoir will occupy the floor of this basin, or the Caldew valley, before long. If it does, this book will badly need revision. Why can't these high and mighty public bodies be content with surplus water only (goodness knows, there's plenty!), piping it to reservoirs built in their own areas?

I must mention the grand people of the little communities around the base of these fells, especially in the remote north. Holiday-makers have made very little impact here. Sturdily independent, here are folk, unspoiled by 'tourism', whose roots go deep in their own soil. Ever alert for sights and sounds on the fellsides or in the valley fields, their work is their life.   It is a pleasure to be in their company, an honour to be in their confidence. John Peel was not the only worthy character raised in these parts.

All my walks during the past few years have ended at Keswick Bus Station, where there is a splendid open view of the mountains between Borrowdale and Bassenthwaite, a tremendously exciting array of sharp peaks and lofty ridges. Sometimes, in winter, I have seen them as a black silhouette, or silvered by moonlight, against the fading colours of the western sky; and, in summer, purpling in the dusk of evening with a skyline edged in gold. These are the North-western Fells, which I have long considered the most delectable of all. Envy me my next two years, for this is the area next on my programme. Ready Easter 1964, old Kruscher willing.

I thank those readers who helped to restore the cairn on Pike O'Blisco. A correspondent now tells me that the fine column on Lingmell has been wantonly thrown down. I hardly like to mention it, but.......... do you mind? Next time you're passing?

Autumn, 1961   AW.